MW01618669

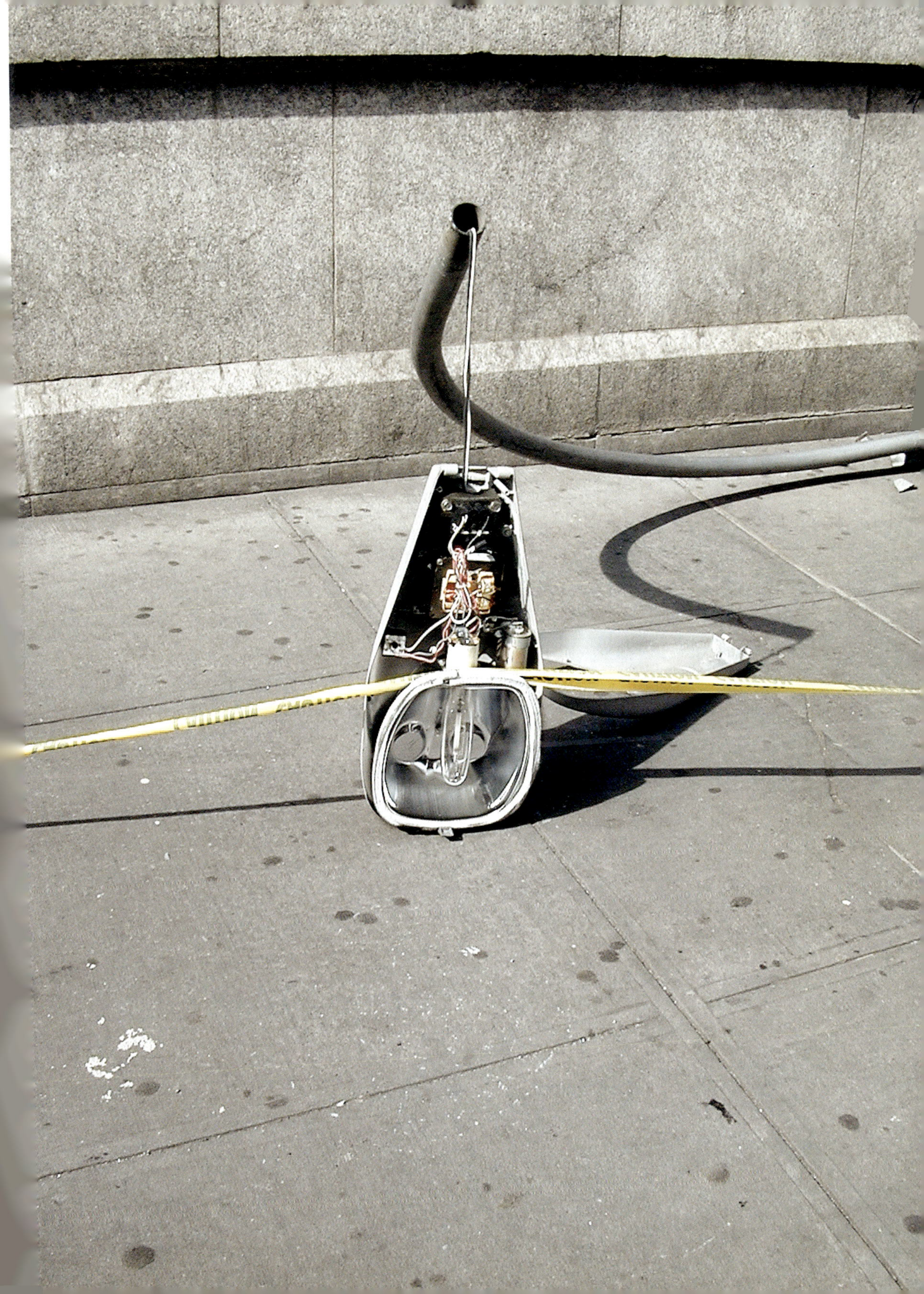

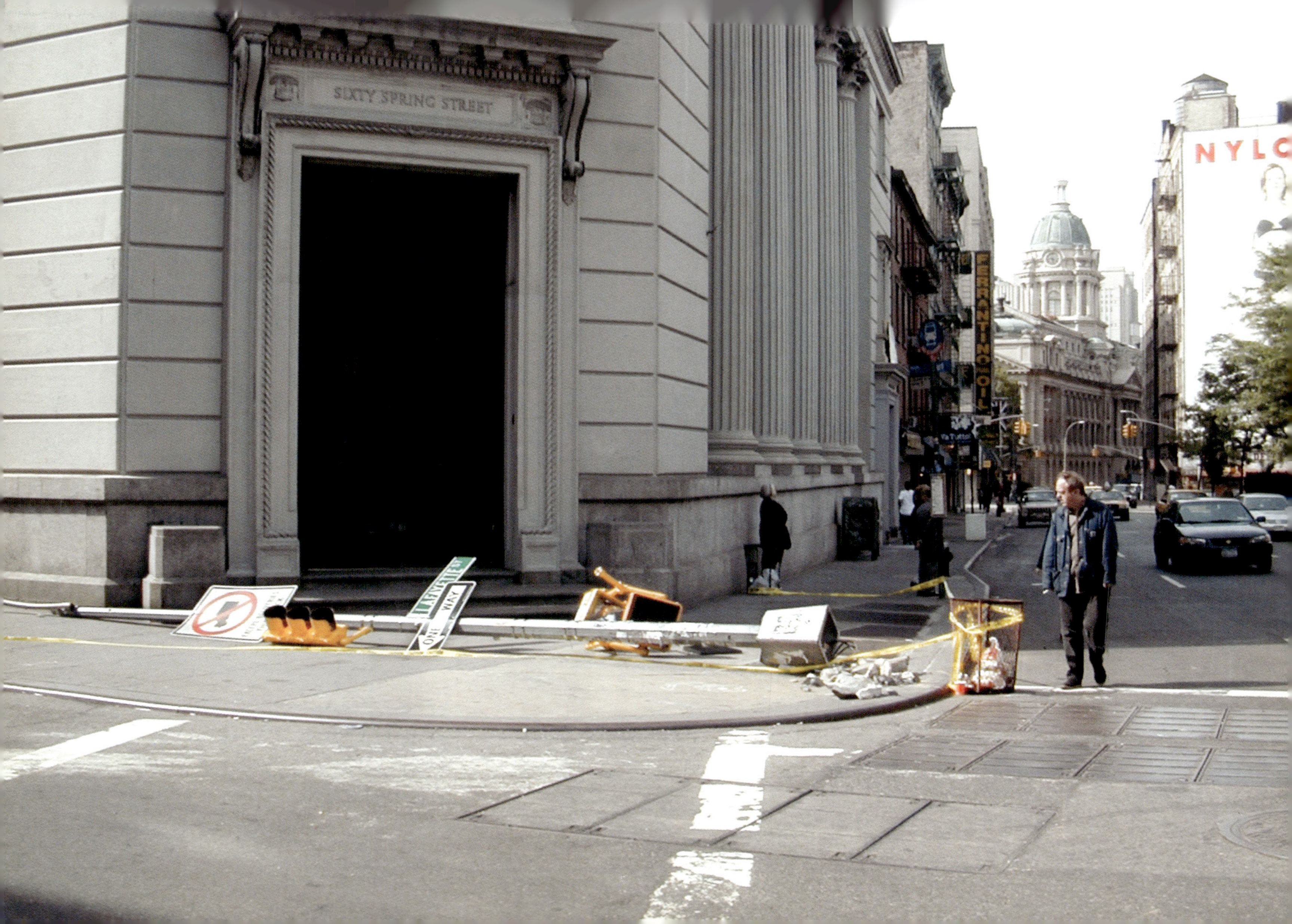
SIXTY SPRING STREET
LAFAYETTE ST
ONE WAY

ENDCOMMERCIAL®

A case study by SBA / Scheppe Böhm Associates

HAVE A GOOD TRIP!

PEACE

2005

Reading the City

FLORIAN BÖHM

LUCA PIZZARONI

WOLFGANG SCHEPPE

ENDCOMMERCIAL®

Reading the City

hatje cantz publishers

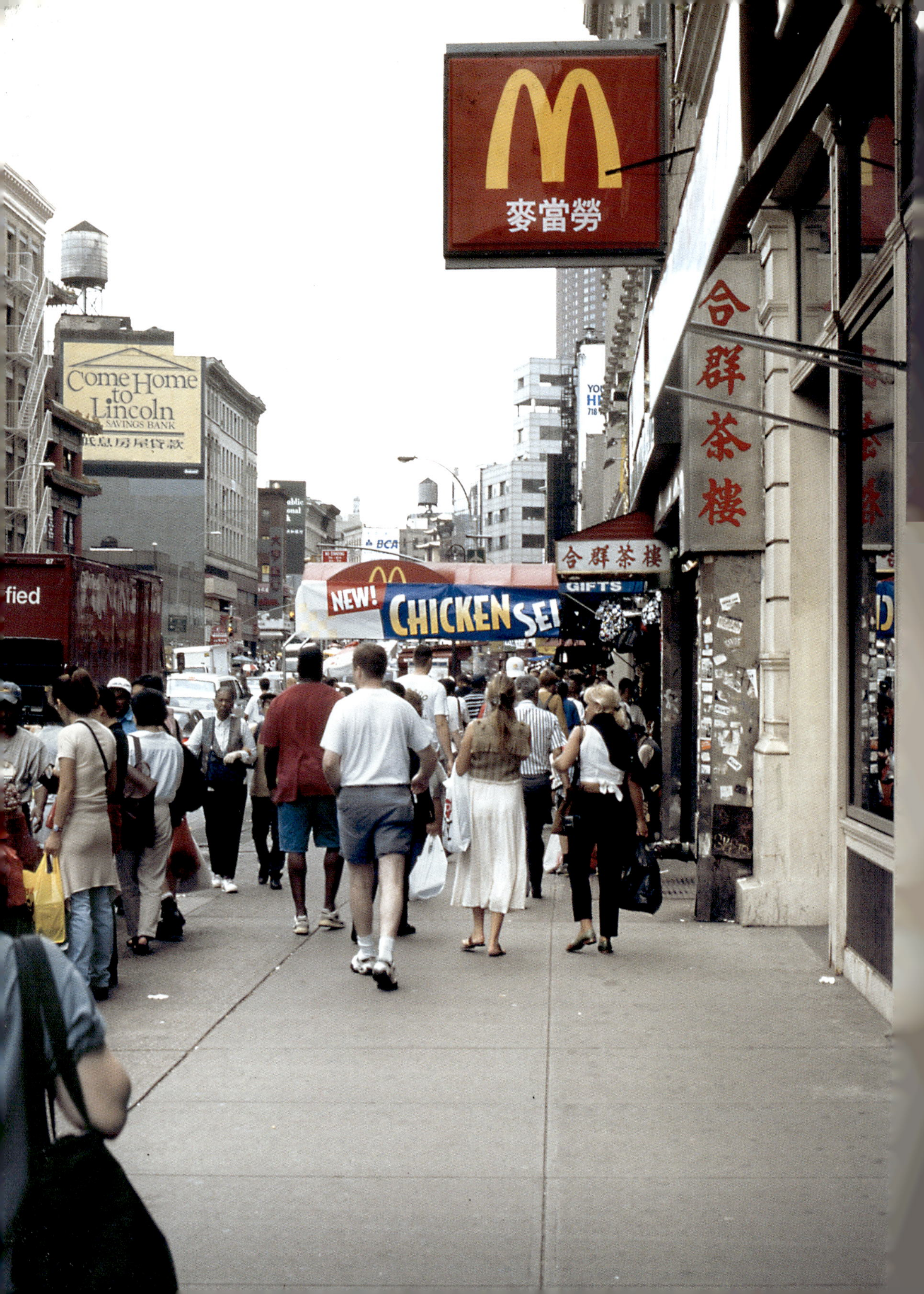

麥當勞
Come Home to Lincoln
SAVINGS BANK
NEW!
CHICKEN
合群茶樓
GIFTS
合群茶樓

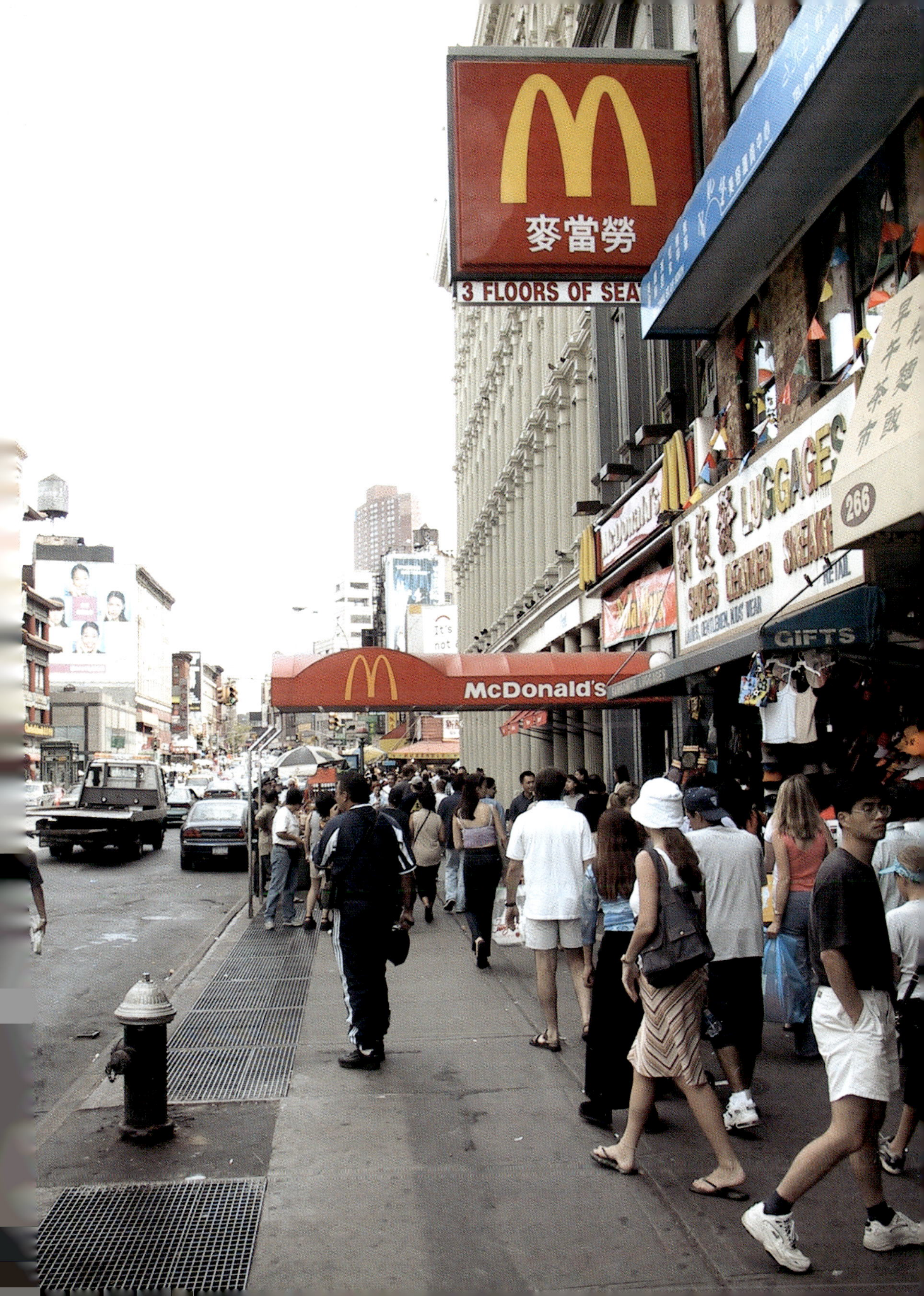
麥當勞
3 FLOORS OF SEA
McDonald's
LUGGAGES
SHOES LEATHER
GIFTS
266

System

Property Phenomenon

Dysfunctional Speech Act

Commerce

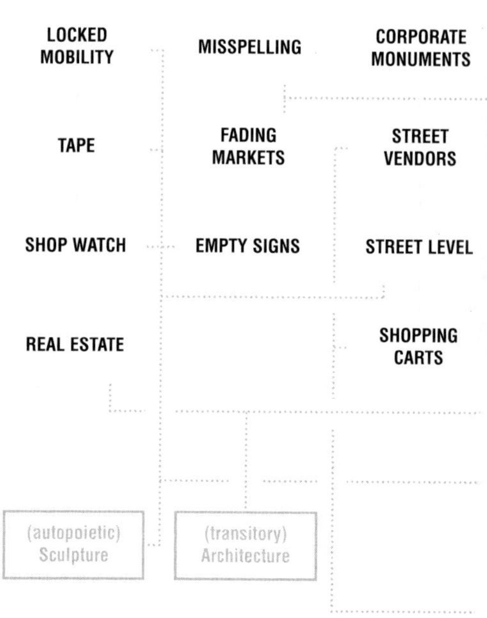

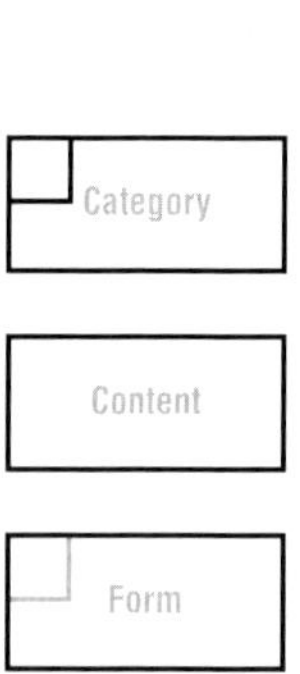

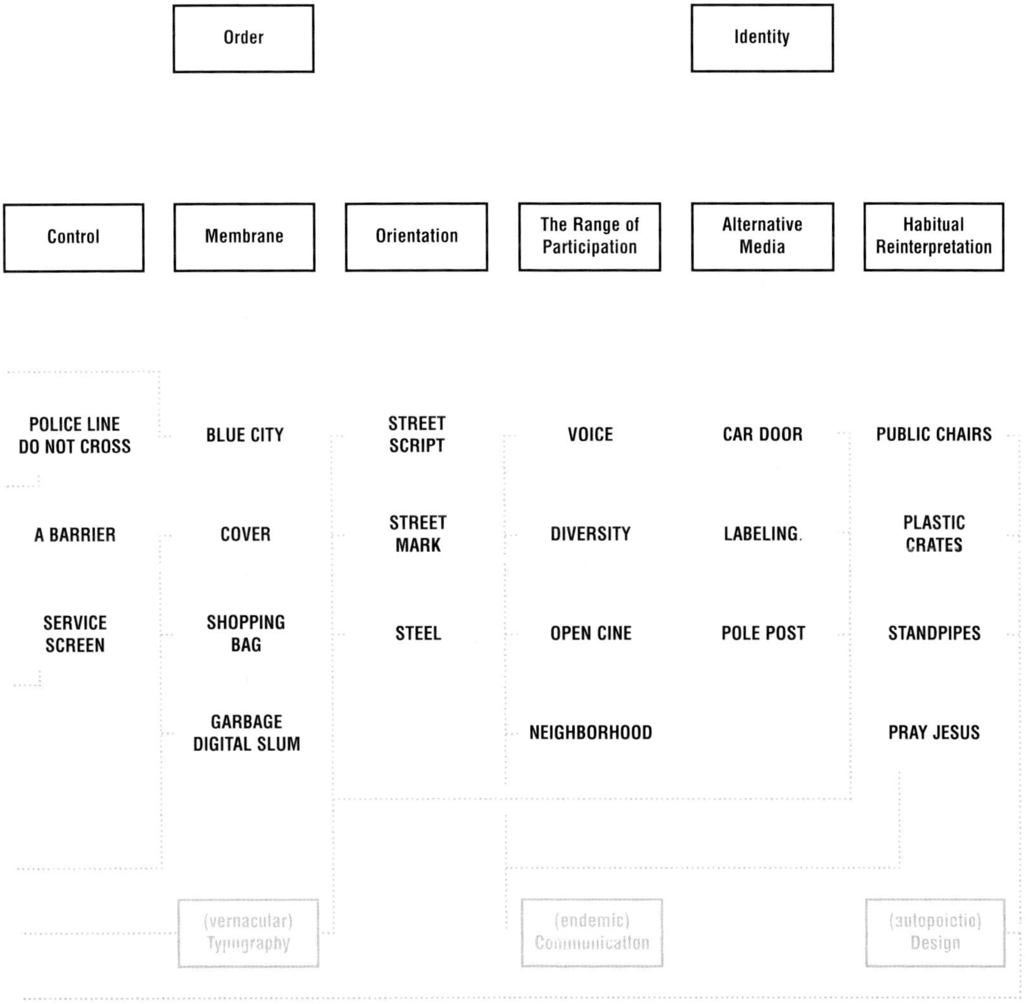

Order

Identity

Control

Membrane

Orientation

The Range of Participation

Alternative Media

Habitual Reinterpretation

POLICE LINE DO NOT CROSS

A BARRIER

SERVICE SCREEN

BLUE CITY

COVER

SHOPPING BAG

GARBAGE DIGITAL SLUM

STREET SCRIPT

STREET MARK

STEEL

VOICE

DIVERSITY

OPEN CINE

NEIGHBORHOOD

CAR DOOR

LABELING.

POLE POST

PUBLIC CHAIRS

PLASTIC CRATES

STANDPIPES

PRAY JESUS

(vernacular) Typography

(endemic) Communication

(autopoietic) Design

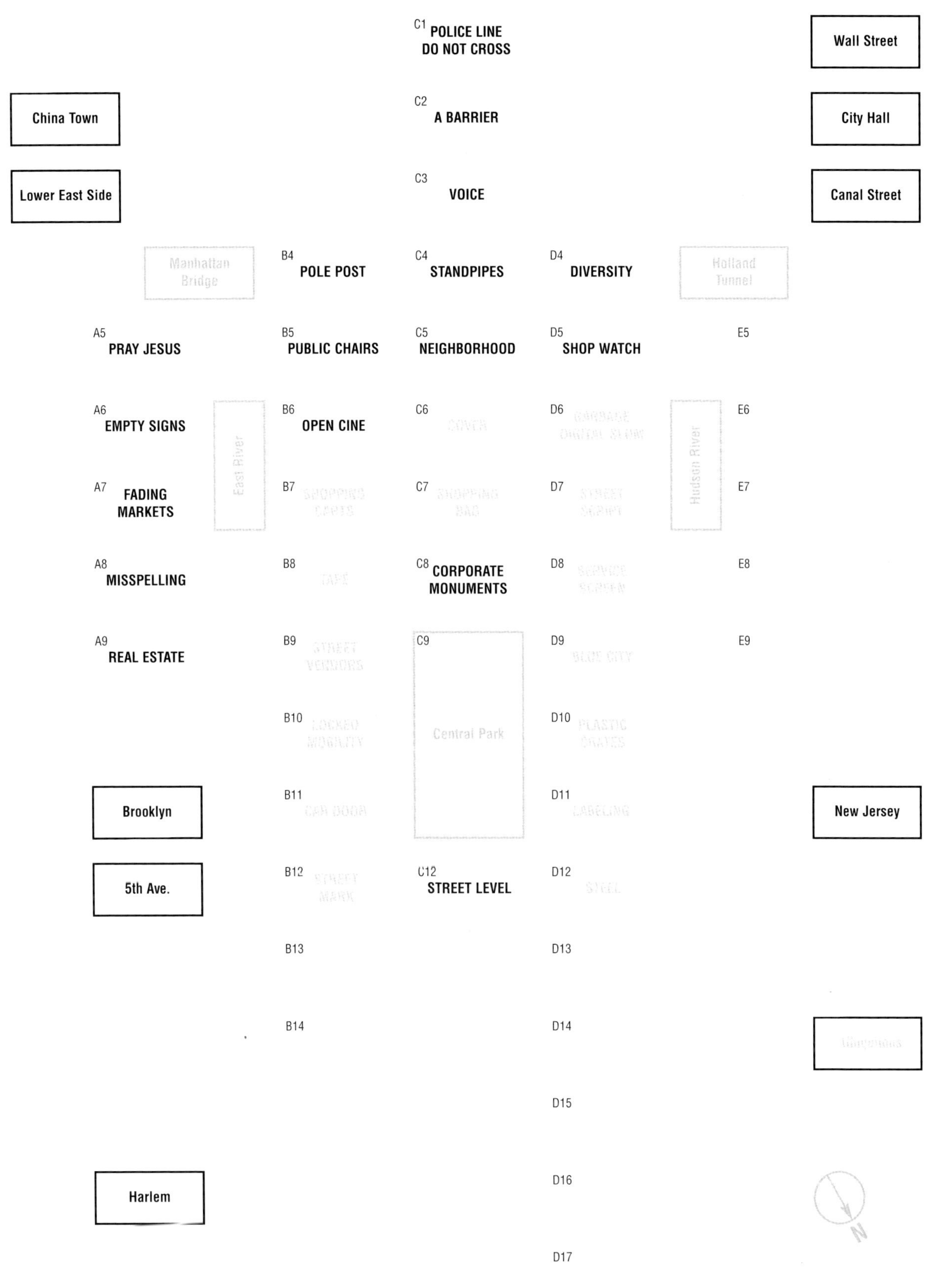

C1 POLICE LINE DO NOT CROSS
Wall Street
China Town
C2 A BARRIER
City Hall
Lower East Side
C3 VOICE
Canal Street
Manhattan Bridge
B4 POLE POST
C4 STANDPIPES
D4 DIVERSITY
Holland Tunnel
A5 PRAY JESUS
B5 PUBLIC CHAIRS
C5 NEIGHBORHOOD
D5 SHOP WATCH
E5
A6 EMPTY SIGNS
East River
B6 OPEN CINE
C6 COVER
D6
Hudson River
E6
A7 FADING MARKETS
B7 SHOPPING CARTS
C7 SHOPPING BAG
D7 STREET SCRIPT
E7
A8 MISSPELLING
B8 TAPE
C8 CORPORATE MONUMENTS
D8 SERVICE SCREEN
E8
A9 REAL ESTATE
B9 STREET VENDORS
C9
Central Park
D9 BLUE CITY
E9
B10 LOCKED MOBILITY
D10 PLASTIC CRATES
Brooklyn
B11 CAR DOOR
D11 LABELING
New Jersey
5th Ave.
B12 STREET MARK
C12 STREET LEVEL
D12 STEEL
B13
D13
B14
D14
D15
Harlem
D16
N
D17

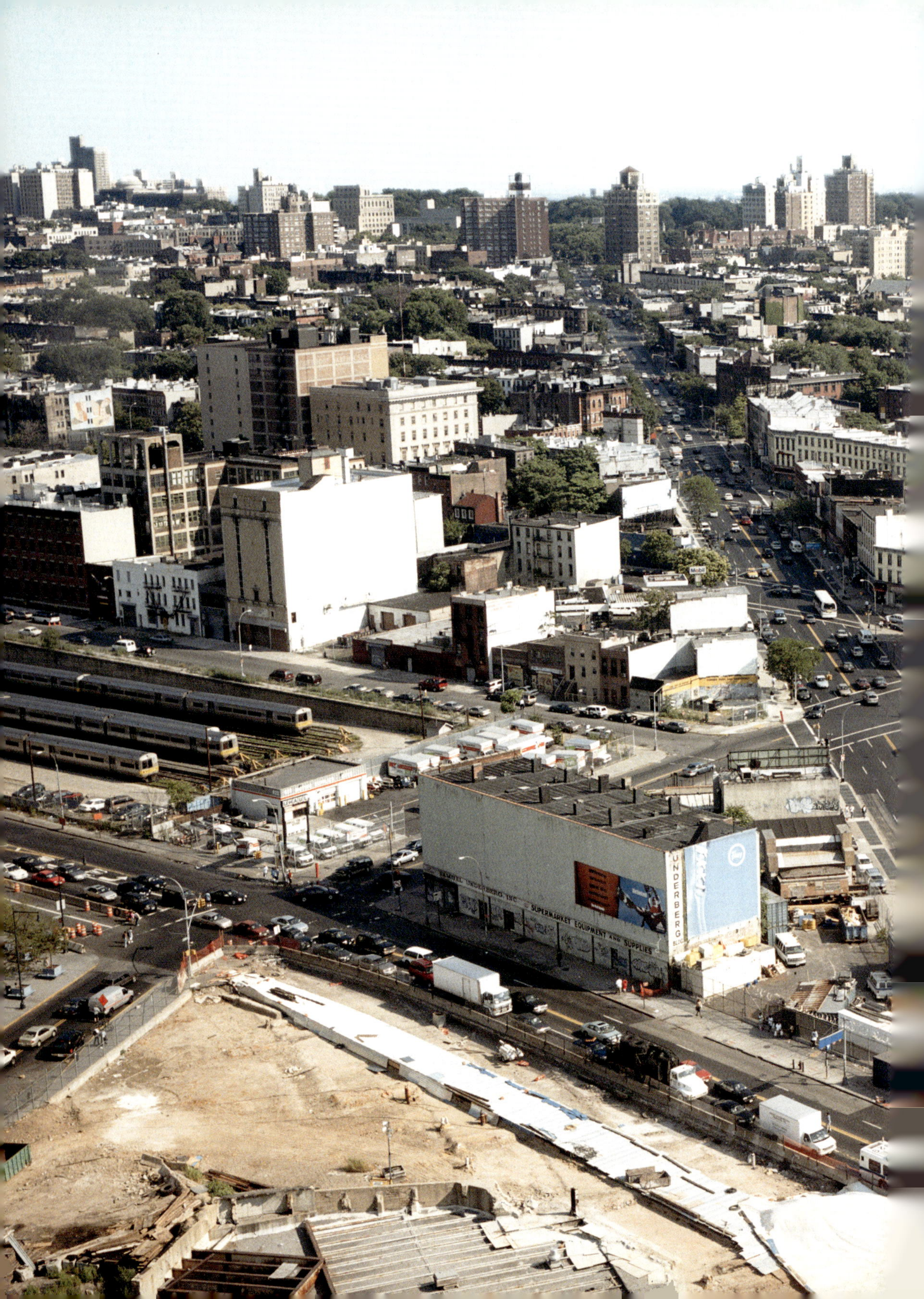
SAMUEL UNDERBERG INC
SUPERMARKET EQUIPMENT AND SUPPLIES
UNDERBERG BLDG.
Mobil

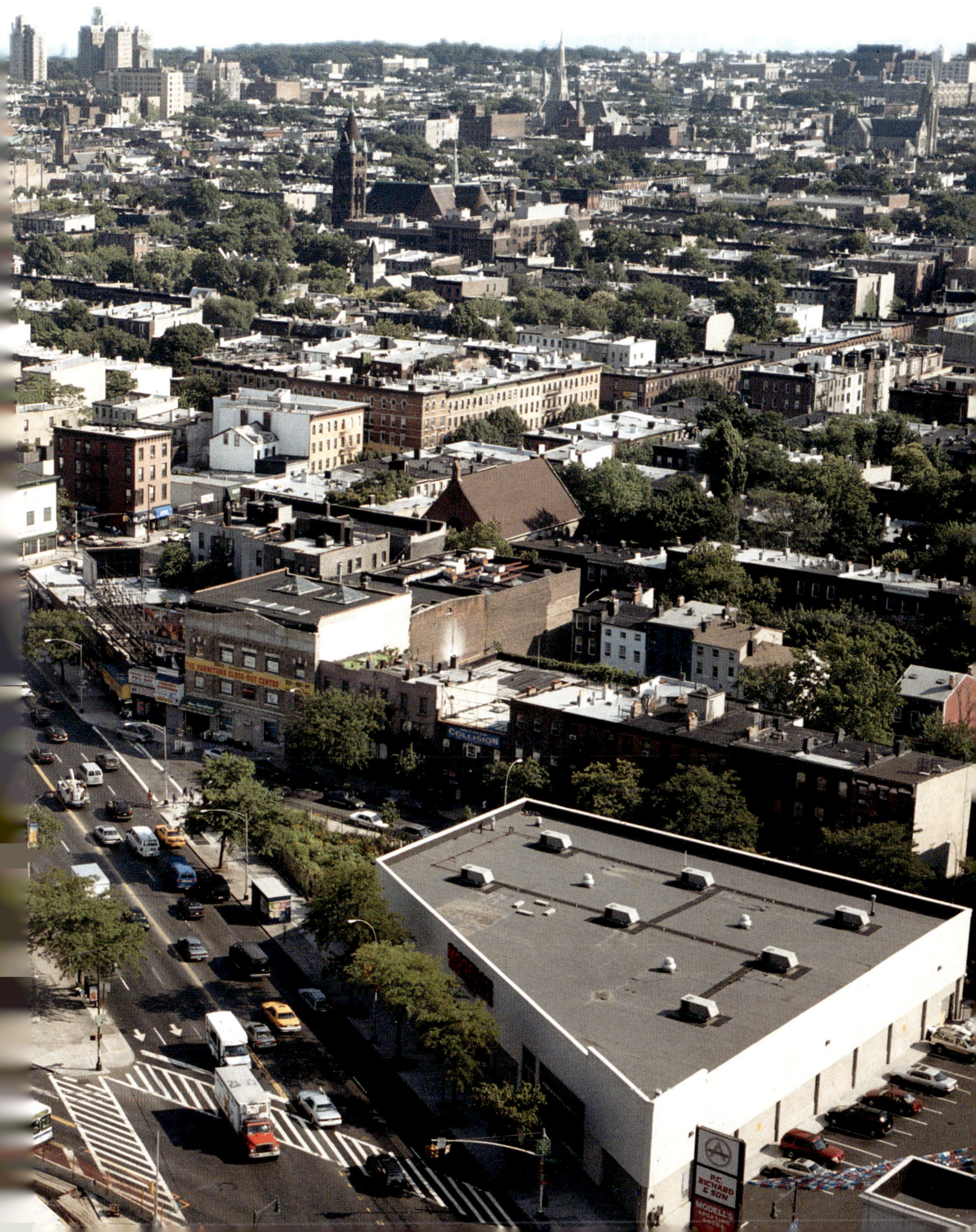
COLLISION
P.C. RICHARD & SON

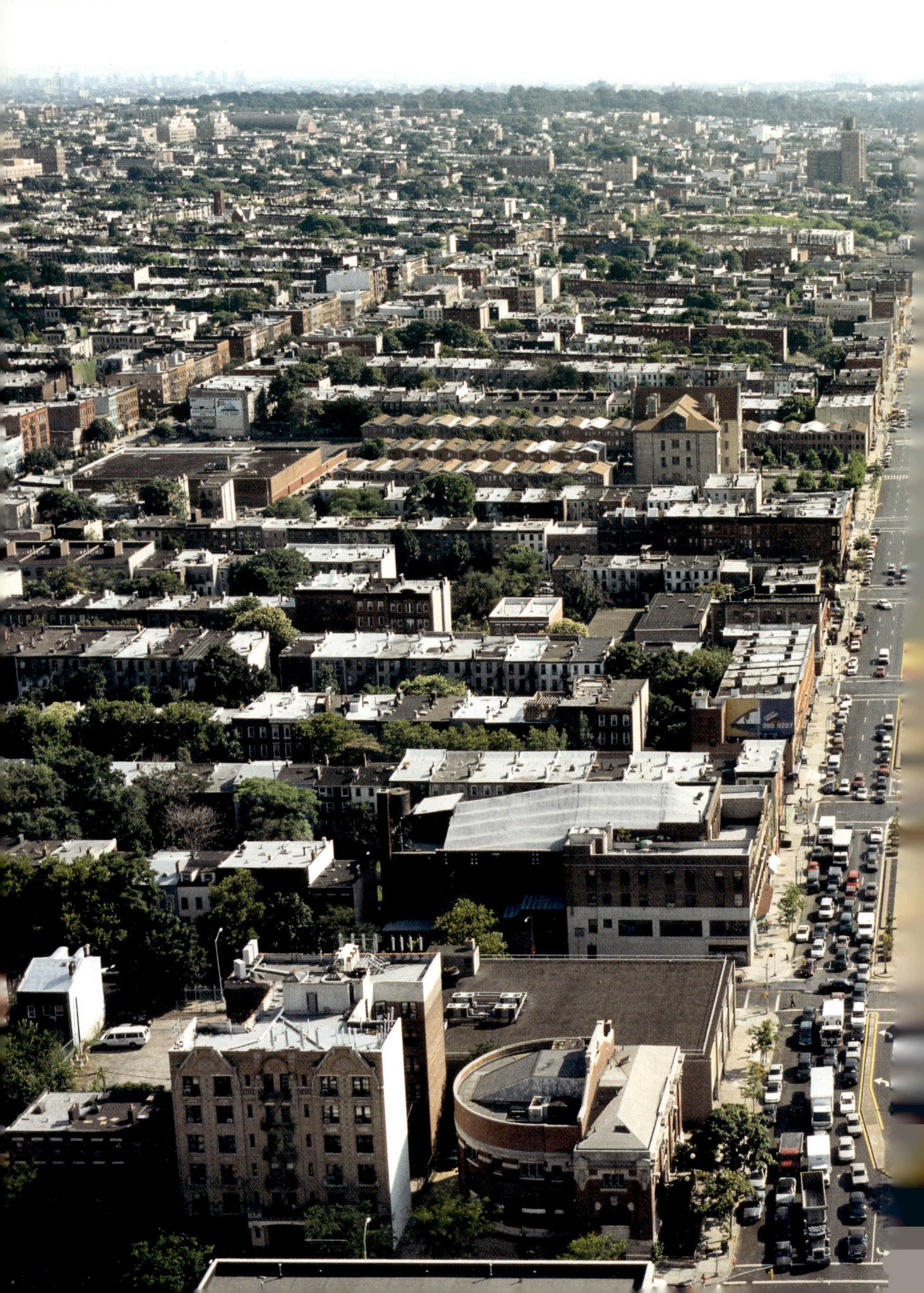

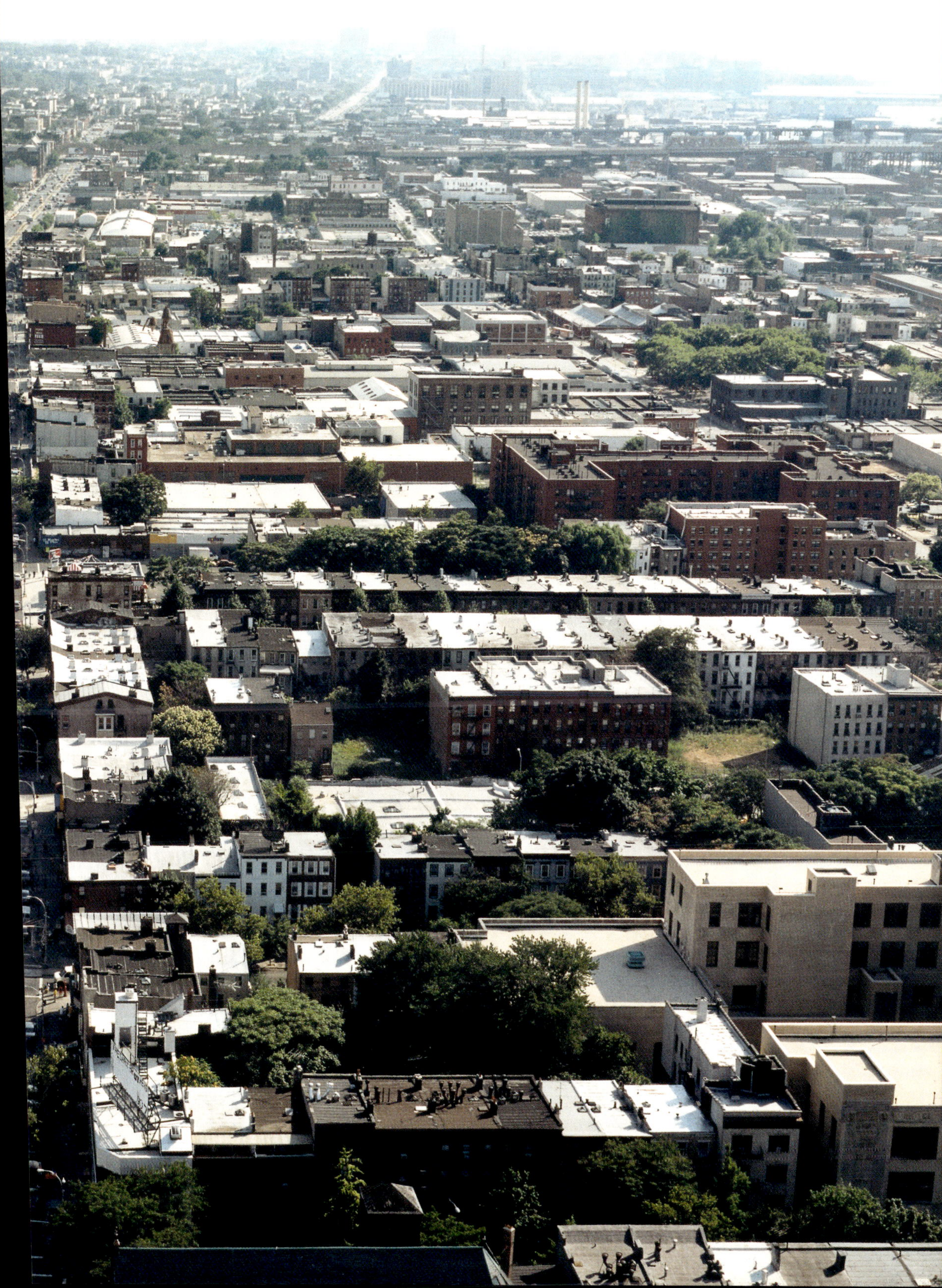

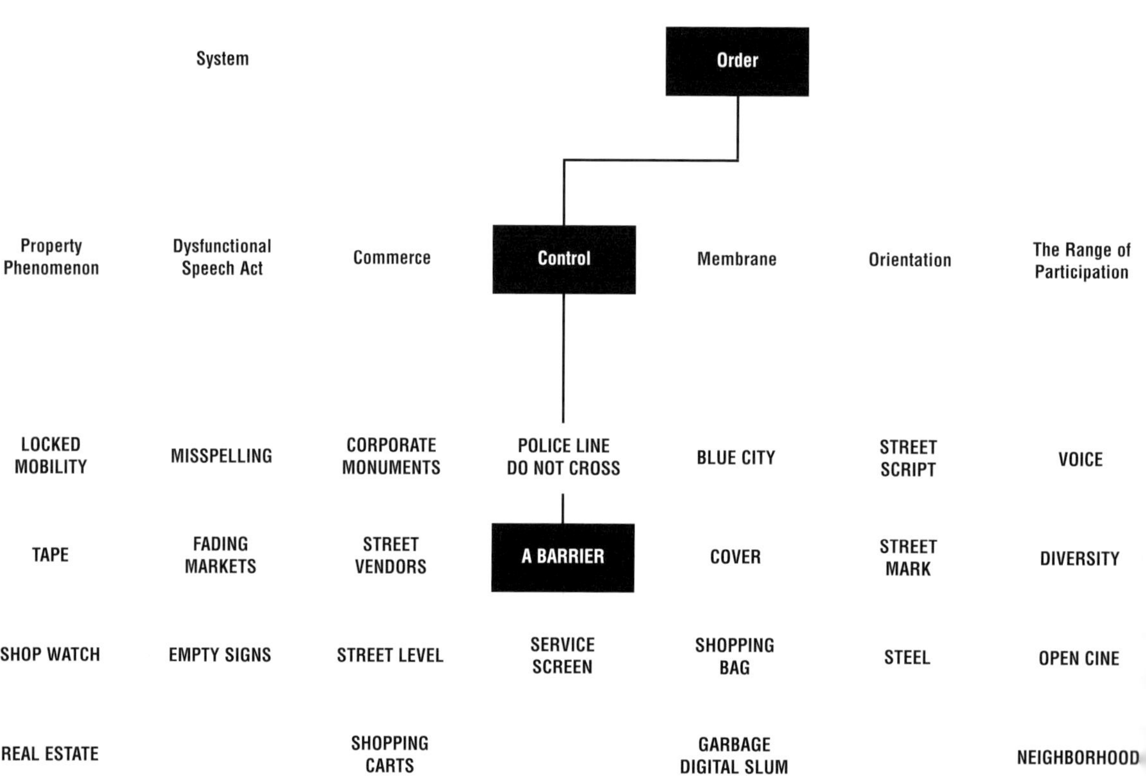

System
Order
Property Phenomenon
Dysfunctional Speech Act
Commerce
Control
Membrane
Orientation
The Range of Participation
LOCKED MOBILITY
MISSPELLING
CORPORATE MONUMENTS
POLICE LINE DO NOT CROSS
BLUE CITY
STREET SCRIPT
VOICE
TAPE
FADING MARKETS
STREET VENDORS
A BARRIER
COVER
STREET MARK
DIVERSITY
SHOP WATCH
EMPTY SIGNS
STREET LEVEL
SERVICE SCREEN
SHOPPING BAG
STEEL
OPEN CINE
REAL ESTATE
SHOPPING CARTS
GARBAGE DIGITAL SLUM
NEIGHBORHOOD

Identity

Alternative Media

Habitual Reinterpretation

A BARRIER

A is for Barricade

CAR DOOR

PUBLIC CHAIRS

LABELING.

PLASTIC CRATES

POLE POST

STANDPIPES

PRAY JESUS

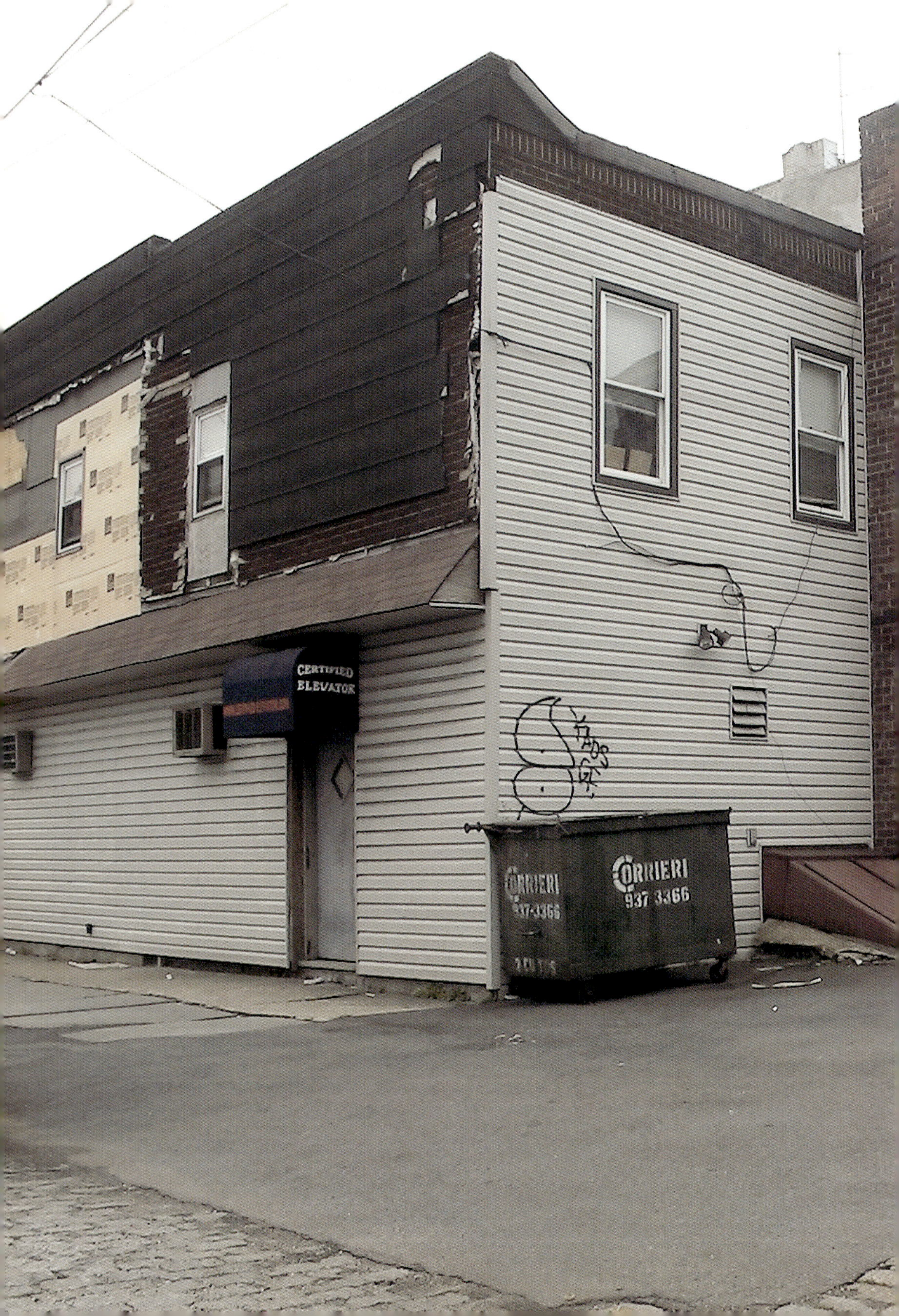
CERTIFIED
ELEVATOR
CORRIERI
937-3366
CORRIERI
937 3366

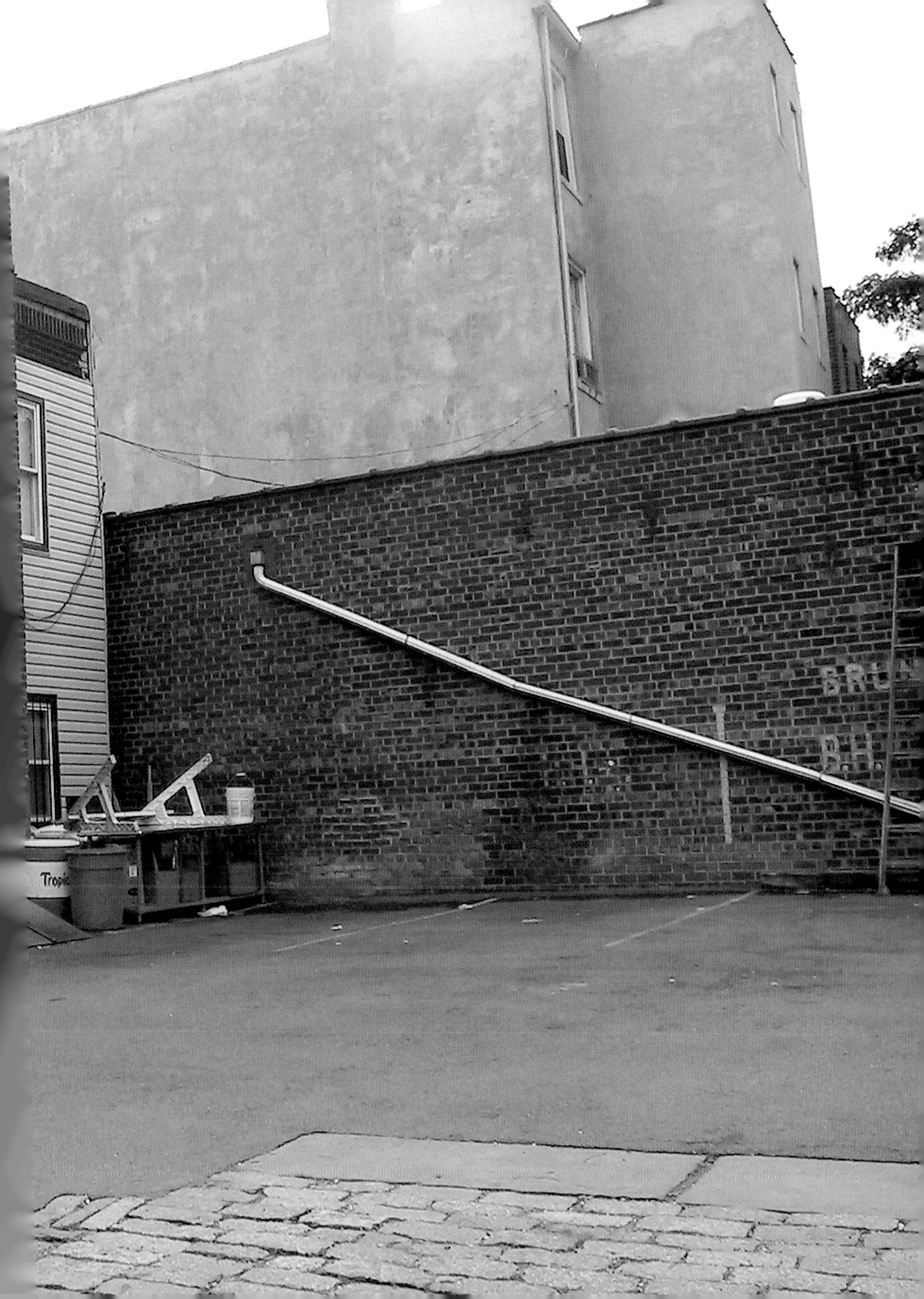
Tropic

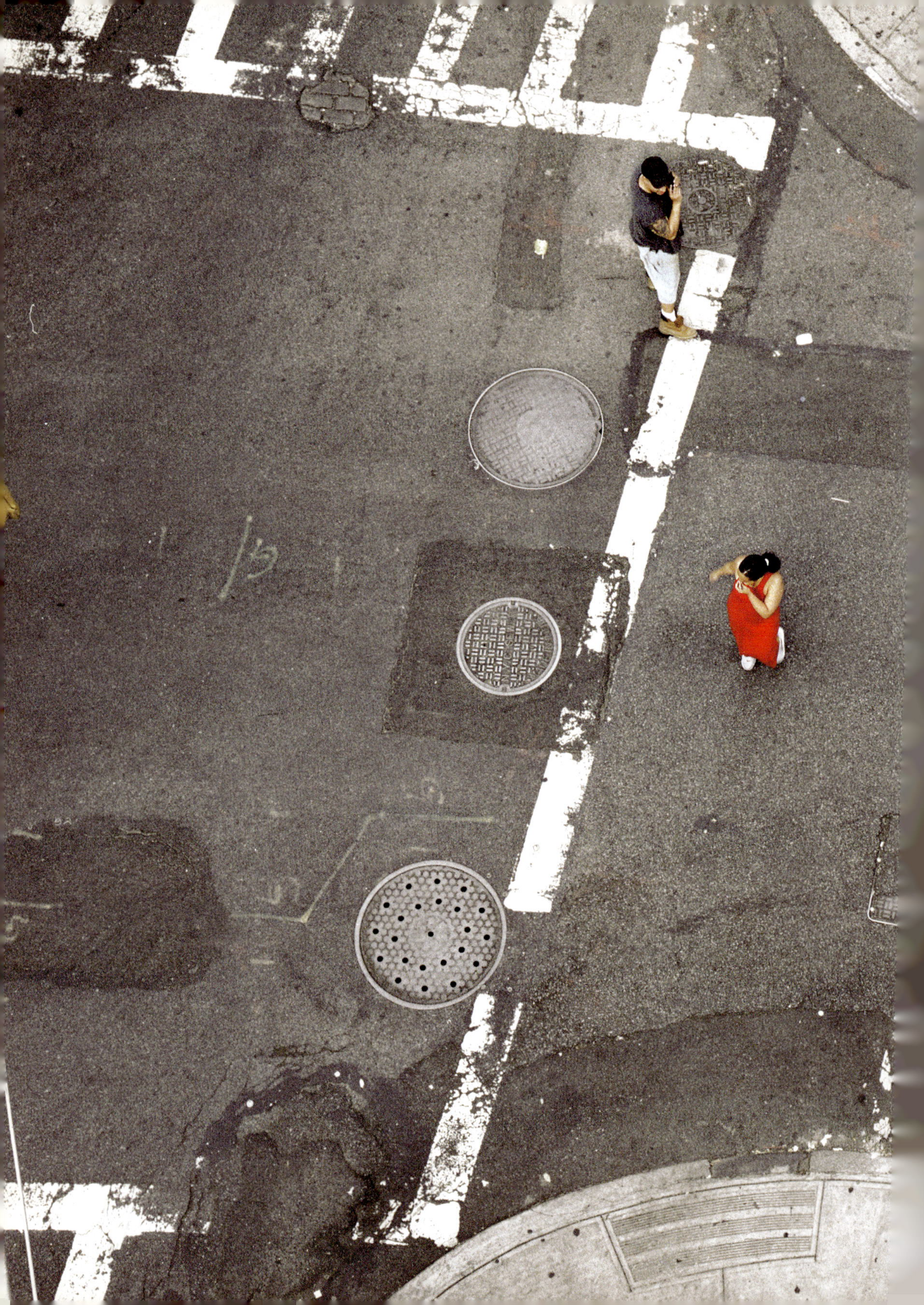

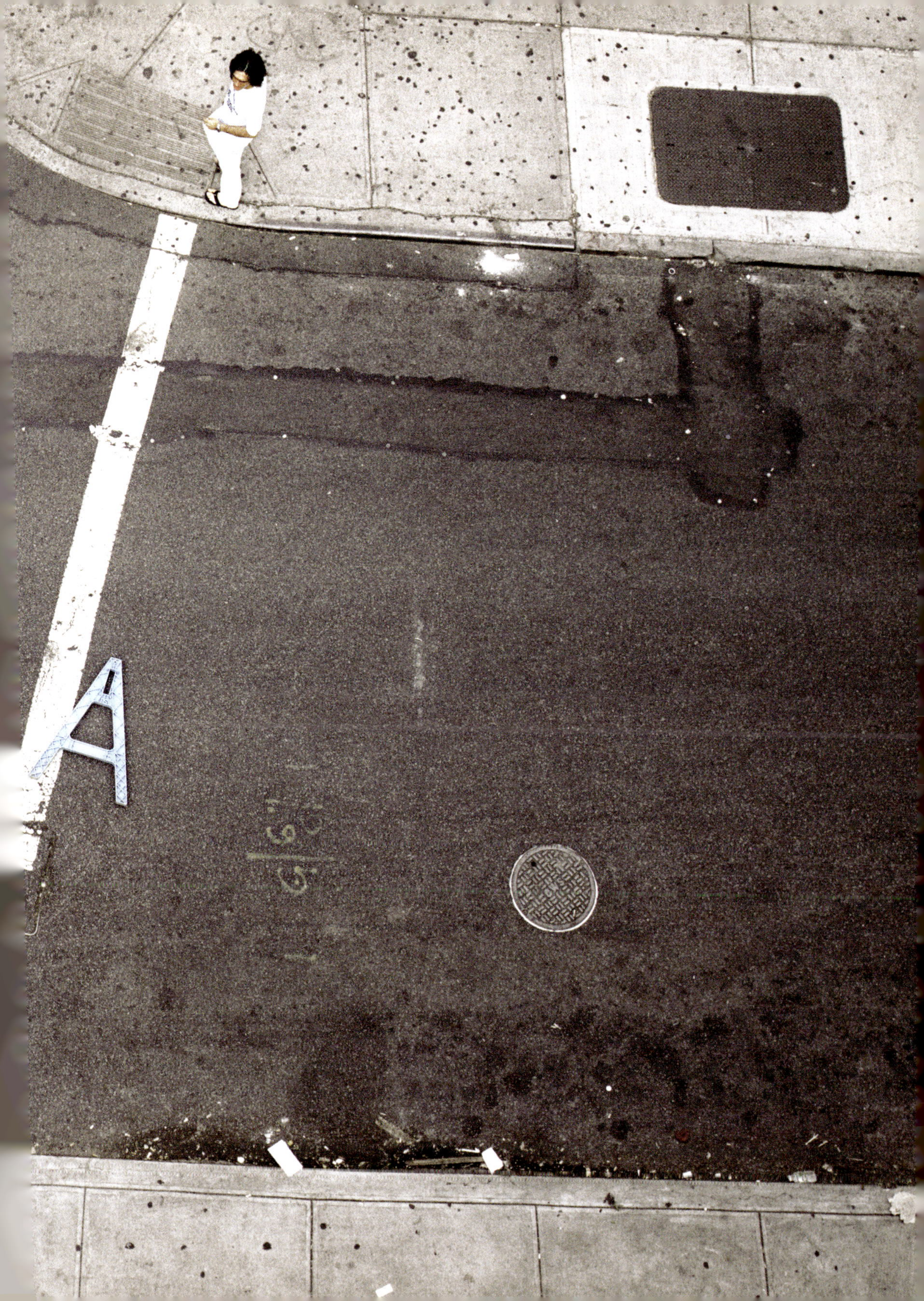

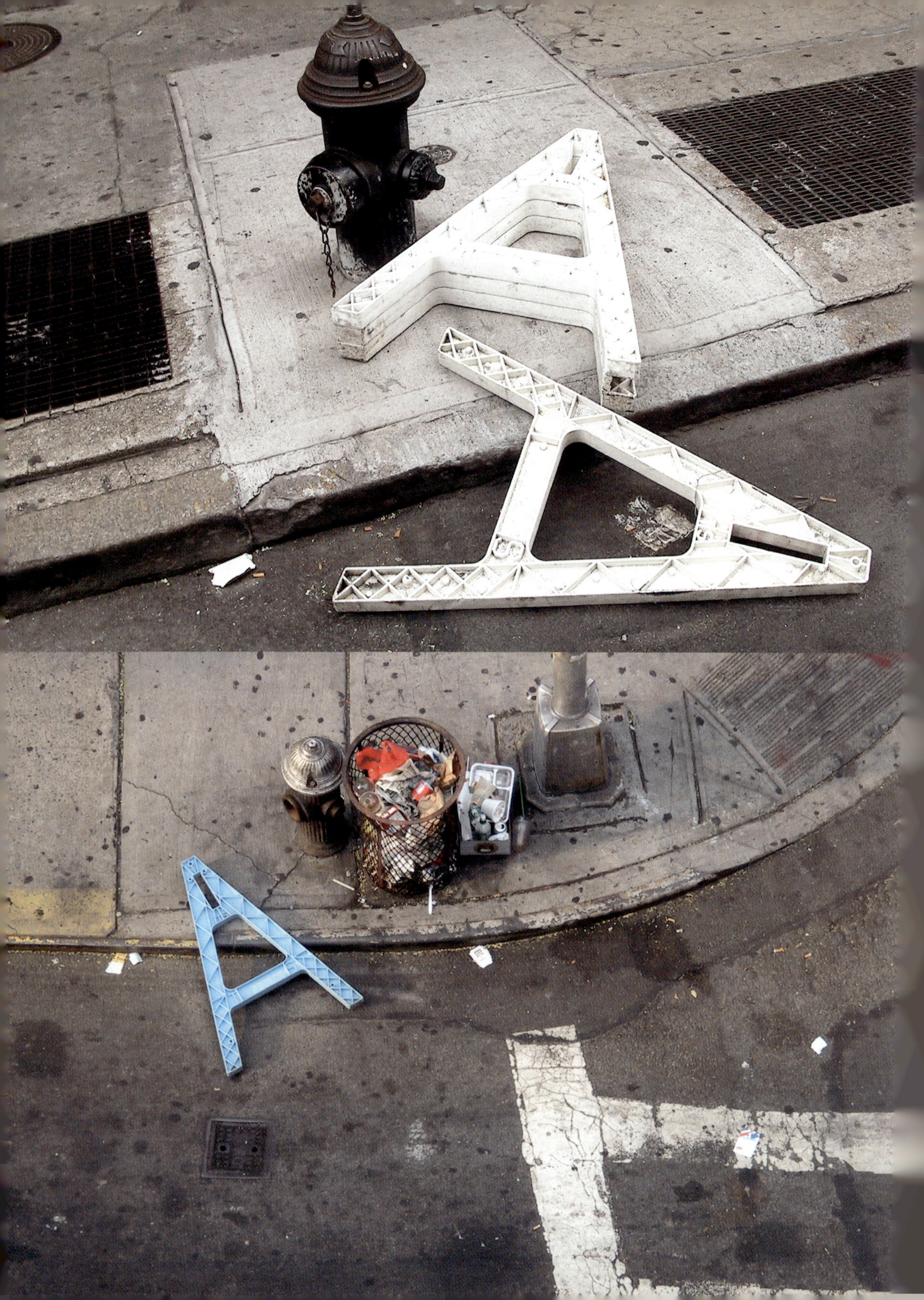

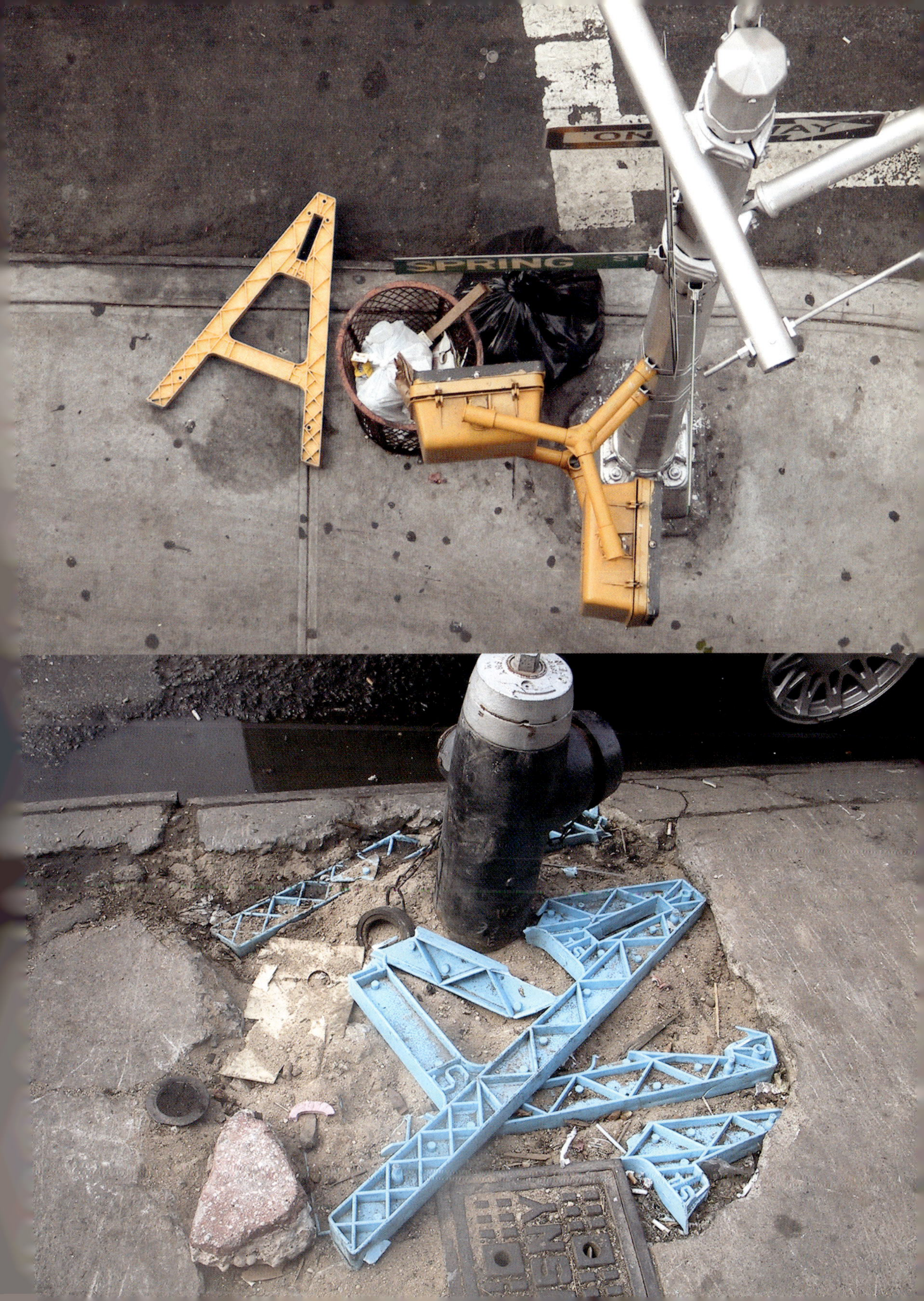
SPRING ST

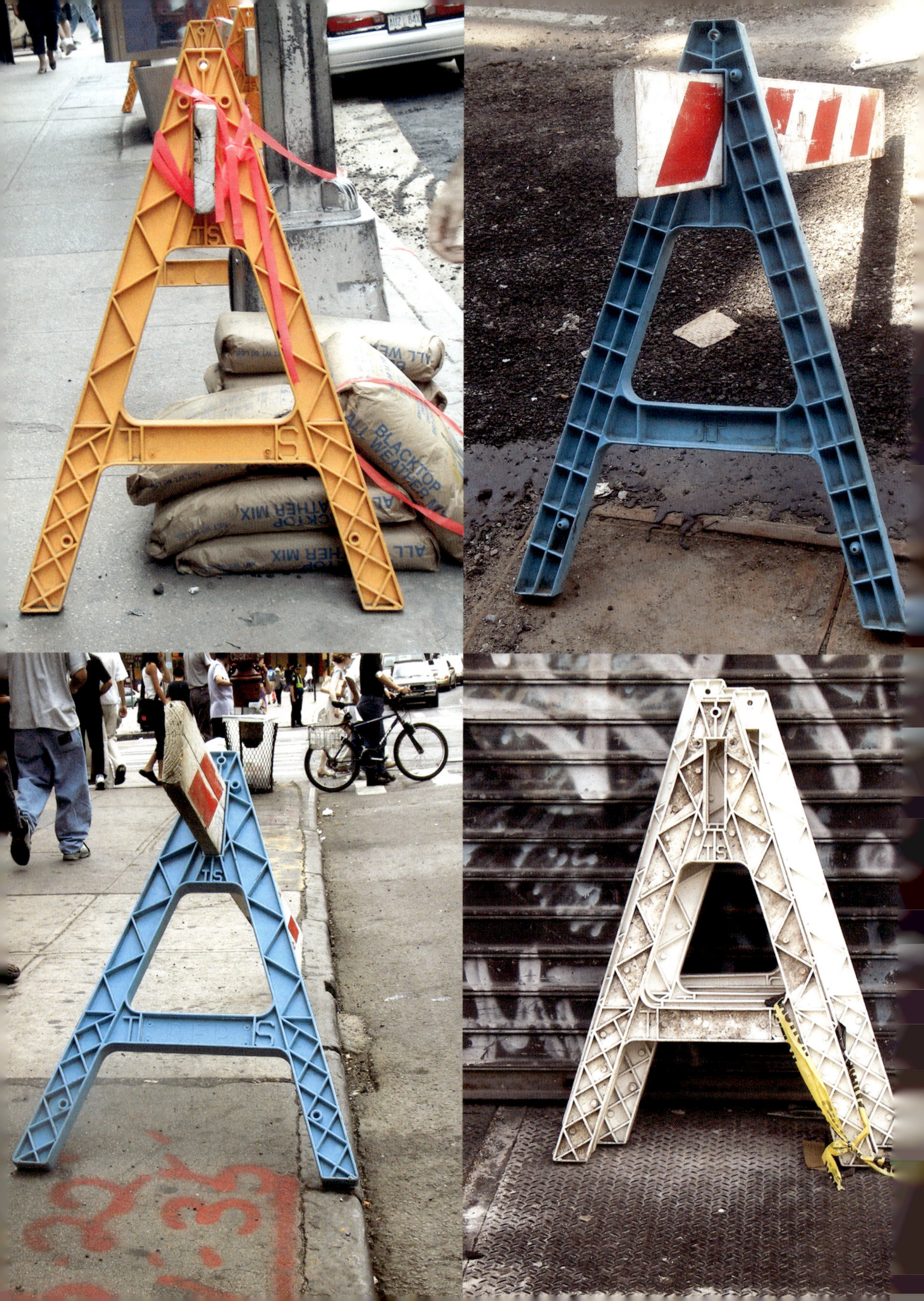
BLACKTOP
ALL WEATHER

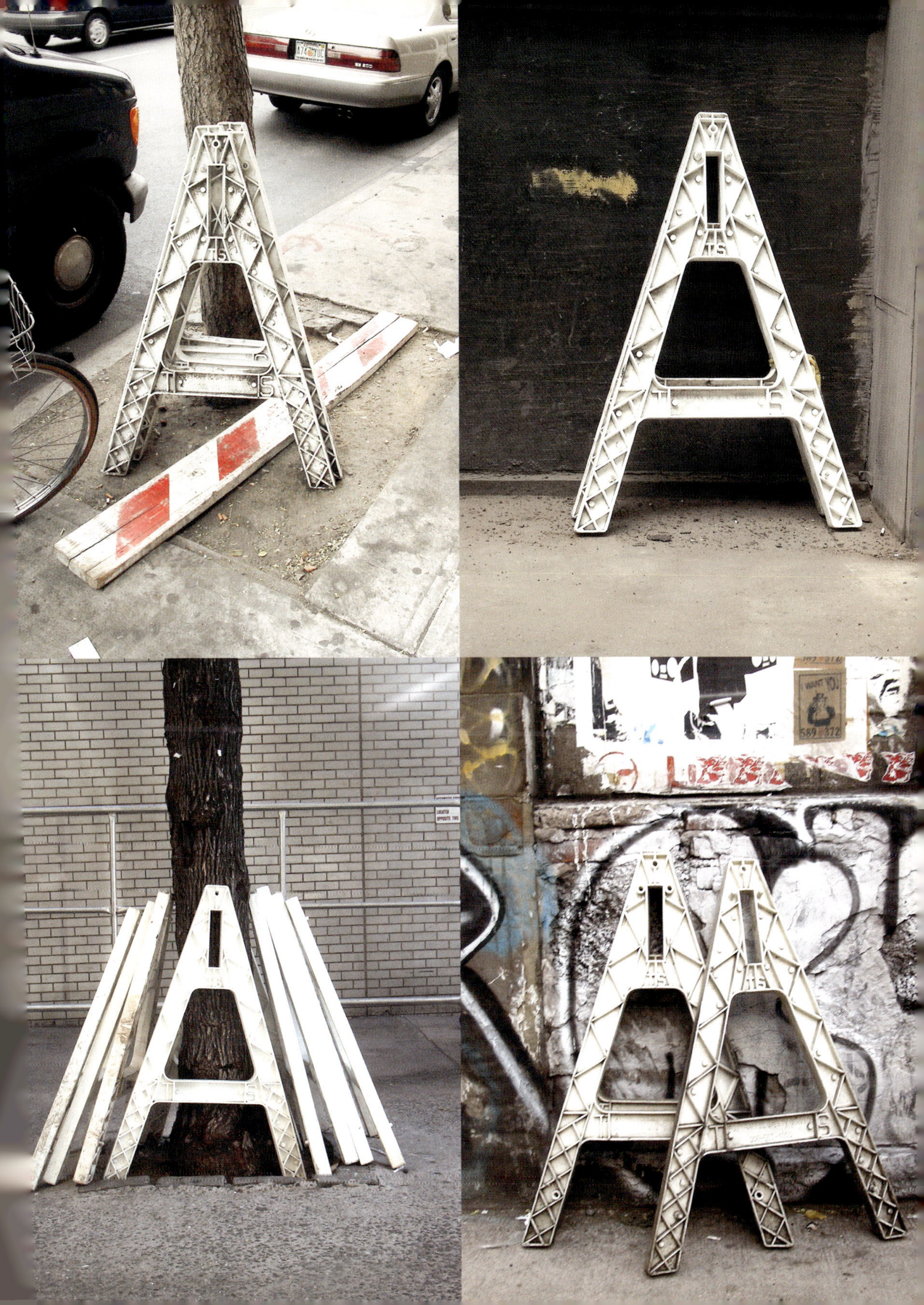
I WANT YOU

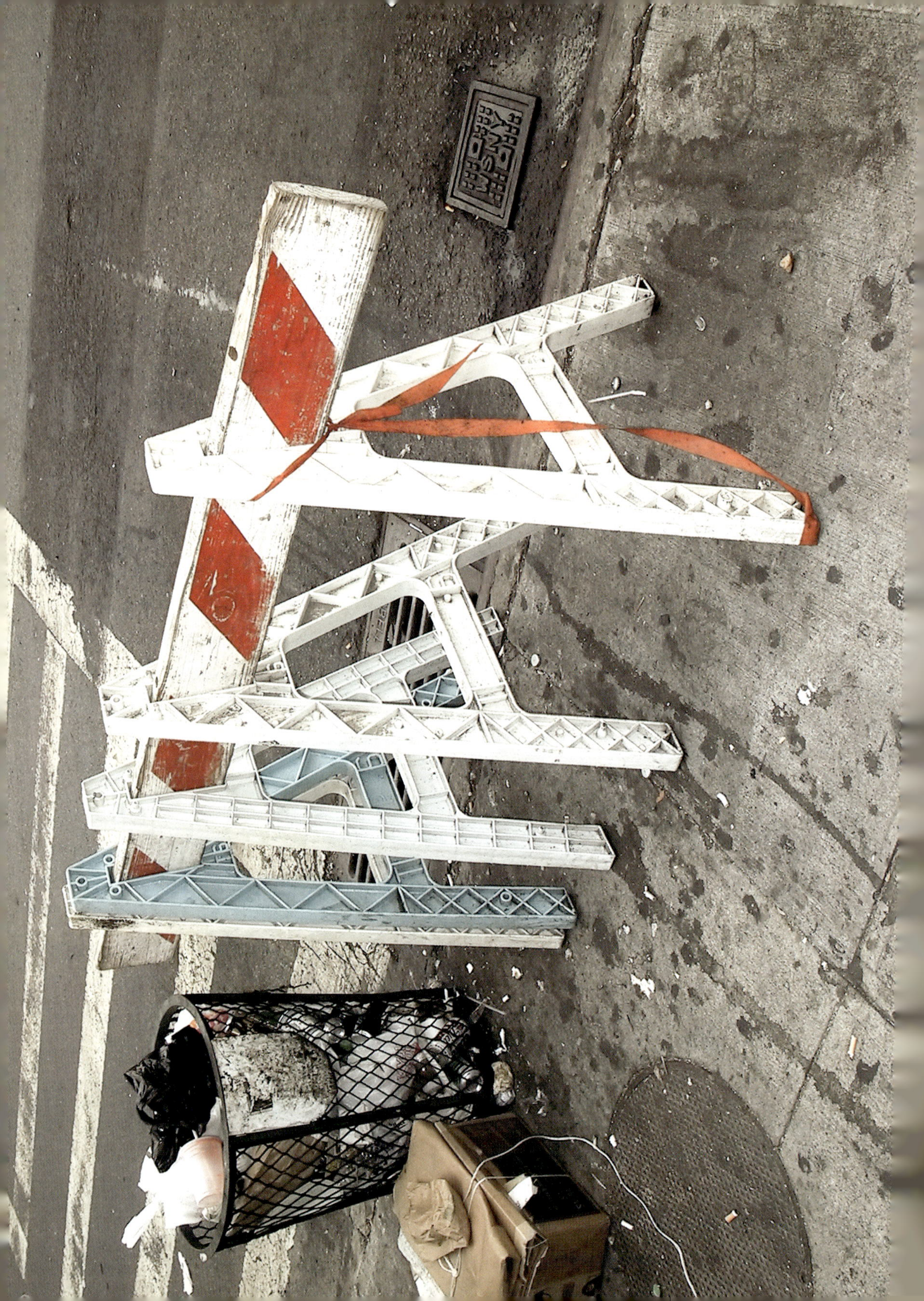

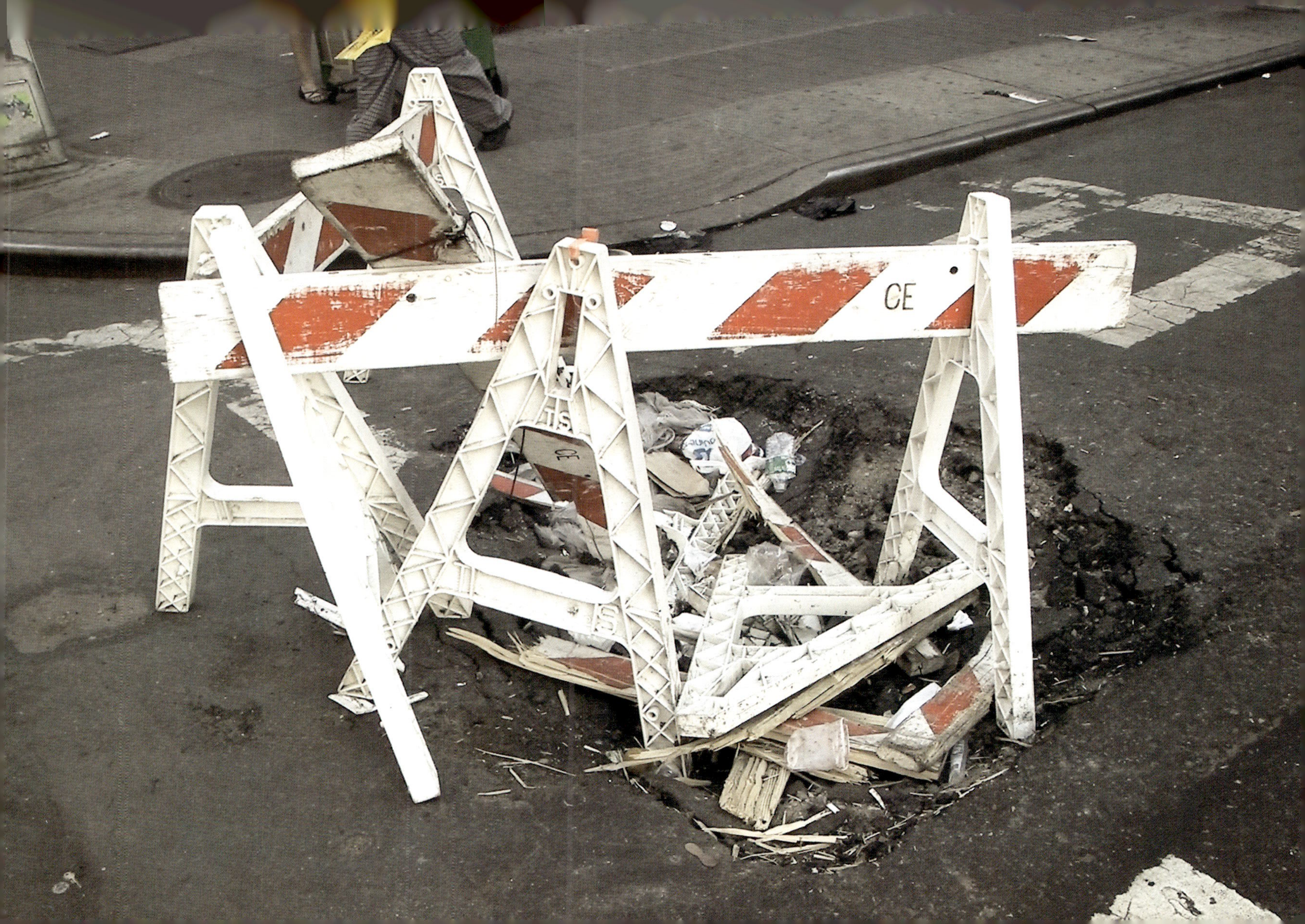
CE

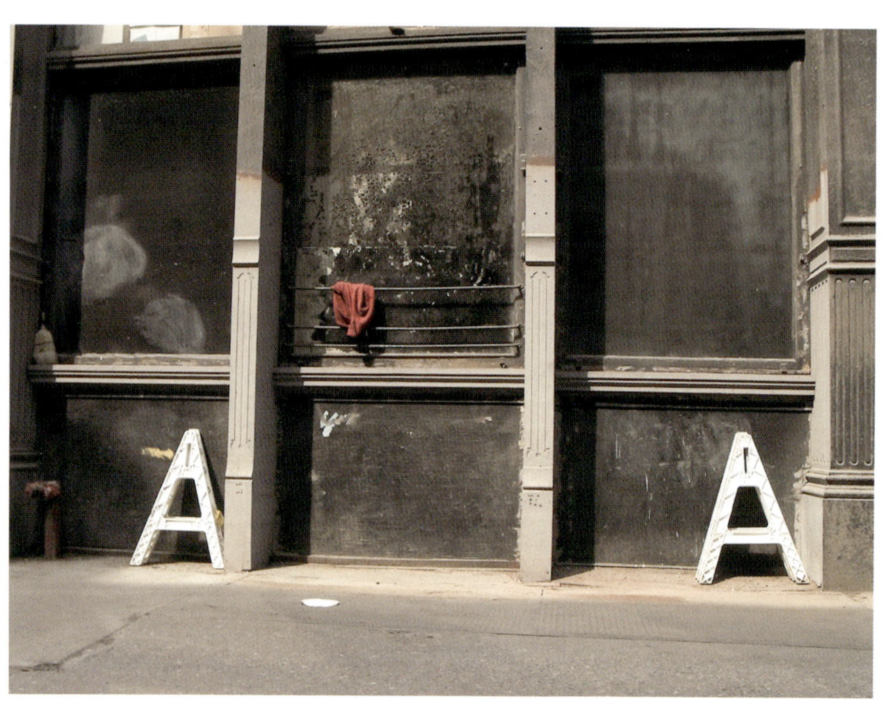

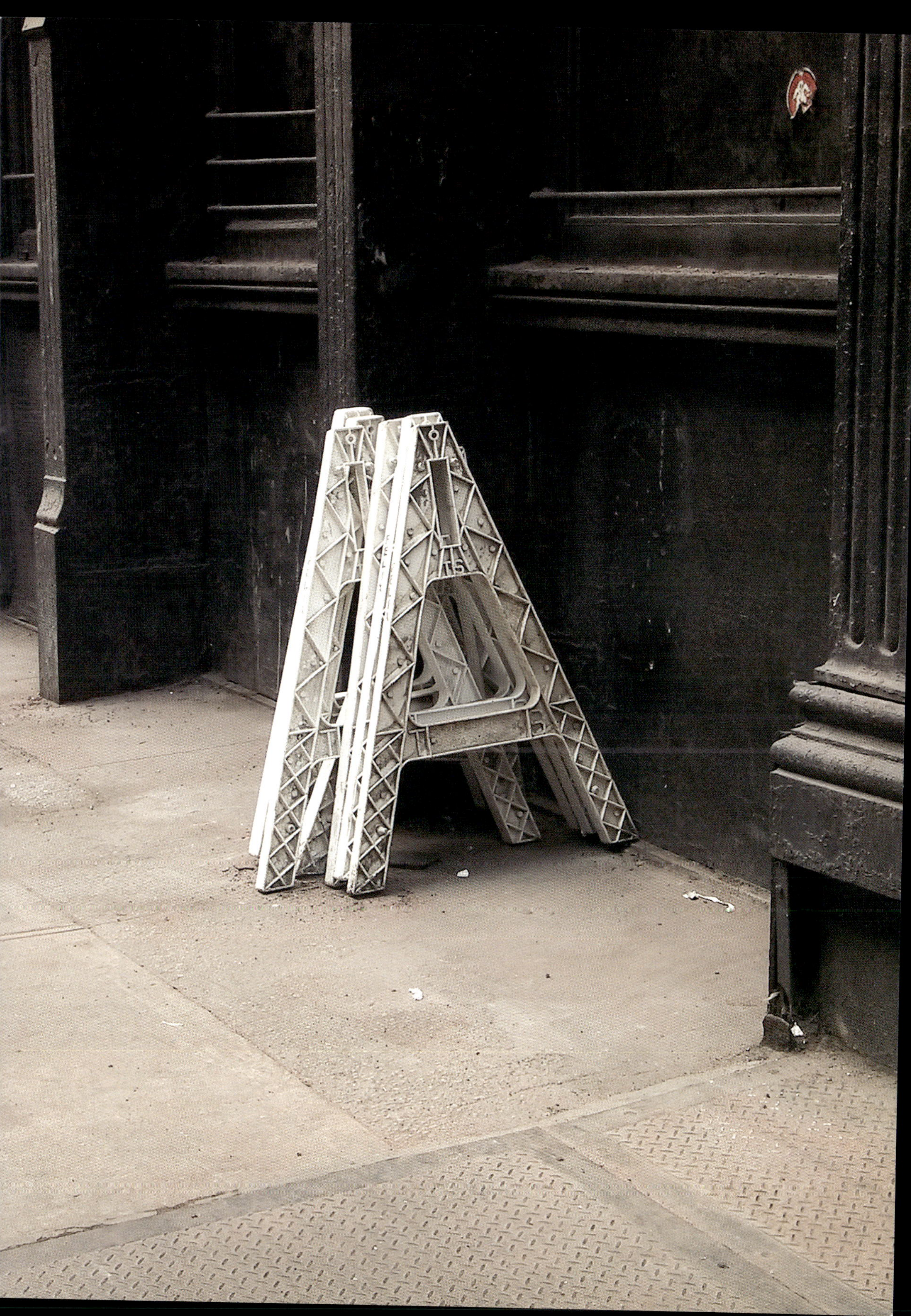
TS

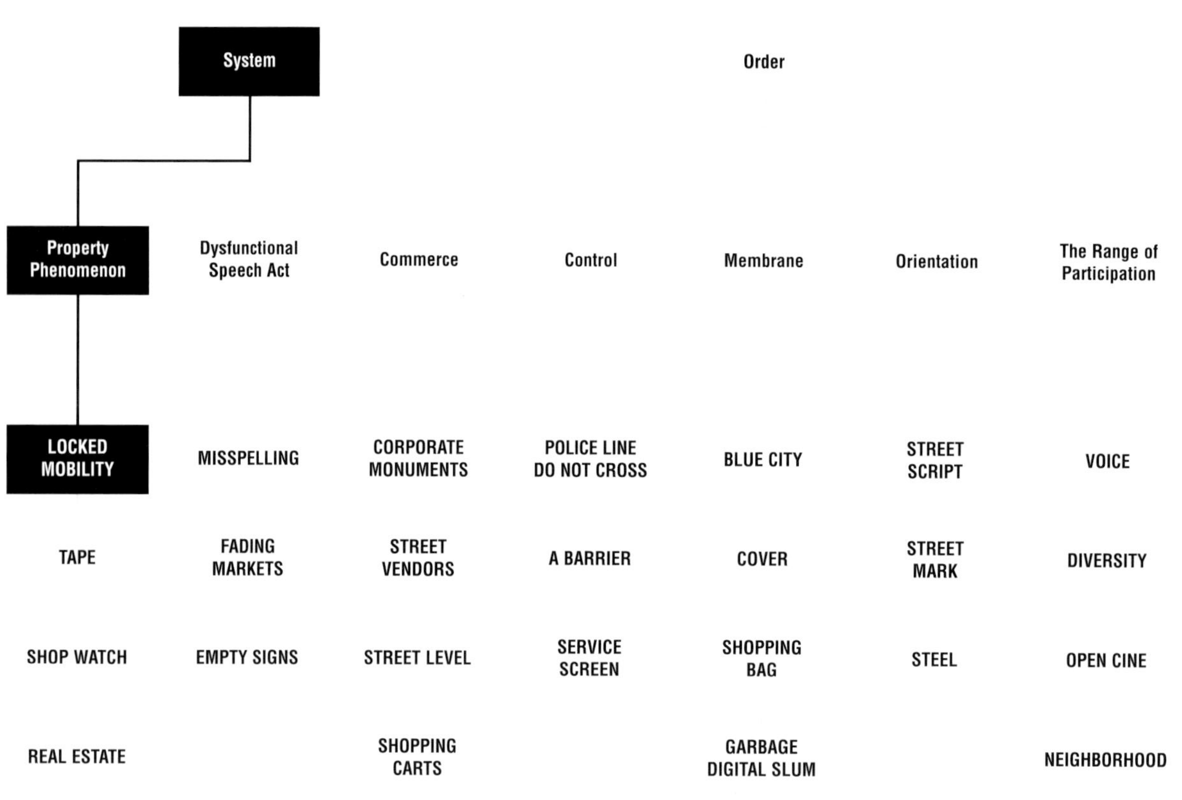
System
Order
Property Phenomenon
Dysfunctional Speech Act
Commerce
Control
Membrane
Orientation
The Range of Participation
LOCKED MOBILITY
MISSPELLING
CORPORATE MONUMENTS
POLICE LINE DO NOT CROSS
BLUE CITY
STREET SCRIPT
VOICE
TAPE
FADING MARKETS
STREET VENDORS
A BARRIER
COVER
STREET MARK
DIVERSITY
SHOP WATCH
EMPTY SIGNS
STREET LEVEL
SERVICE SCREEN
SHOPPING BAG
STEEL
OPEN CINE
REAL ESTATE
SHOPPING CARTS
GARBAGE DIGITAL SLUM
NEIGHBORHOOD

Identity

Alternative Media

Habitual Reinterpretation

LOCKED MOBILITY

Unattended Possessions / Survival of Decay

CAR DOOR

PUBLIC CHAIRS

LABELING.

PLASTIC CRATES

POLE POST

STANDPIPES

PRAY JESUS

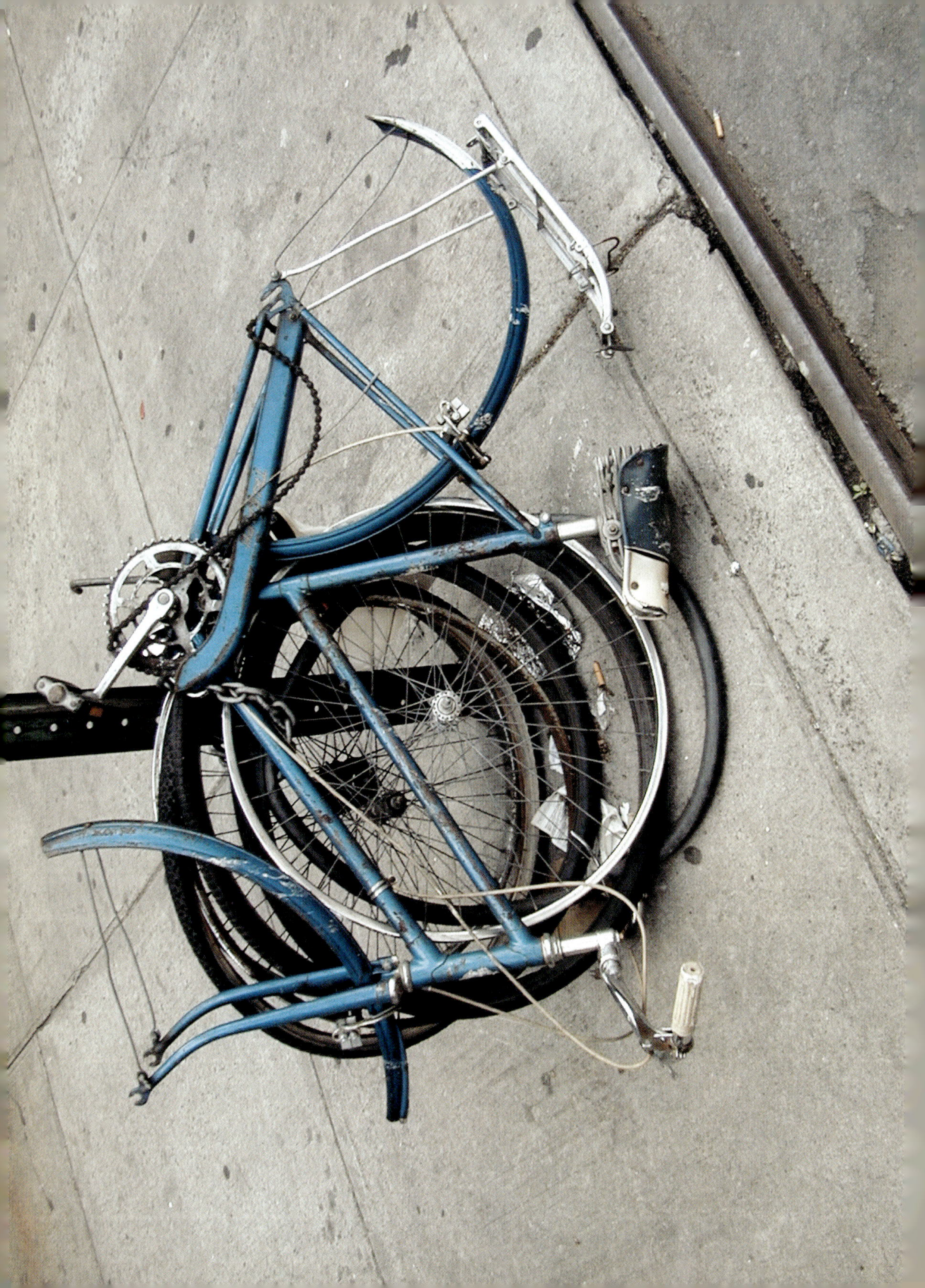

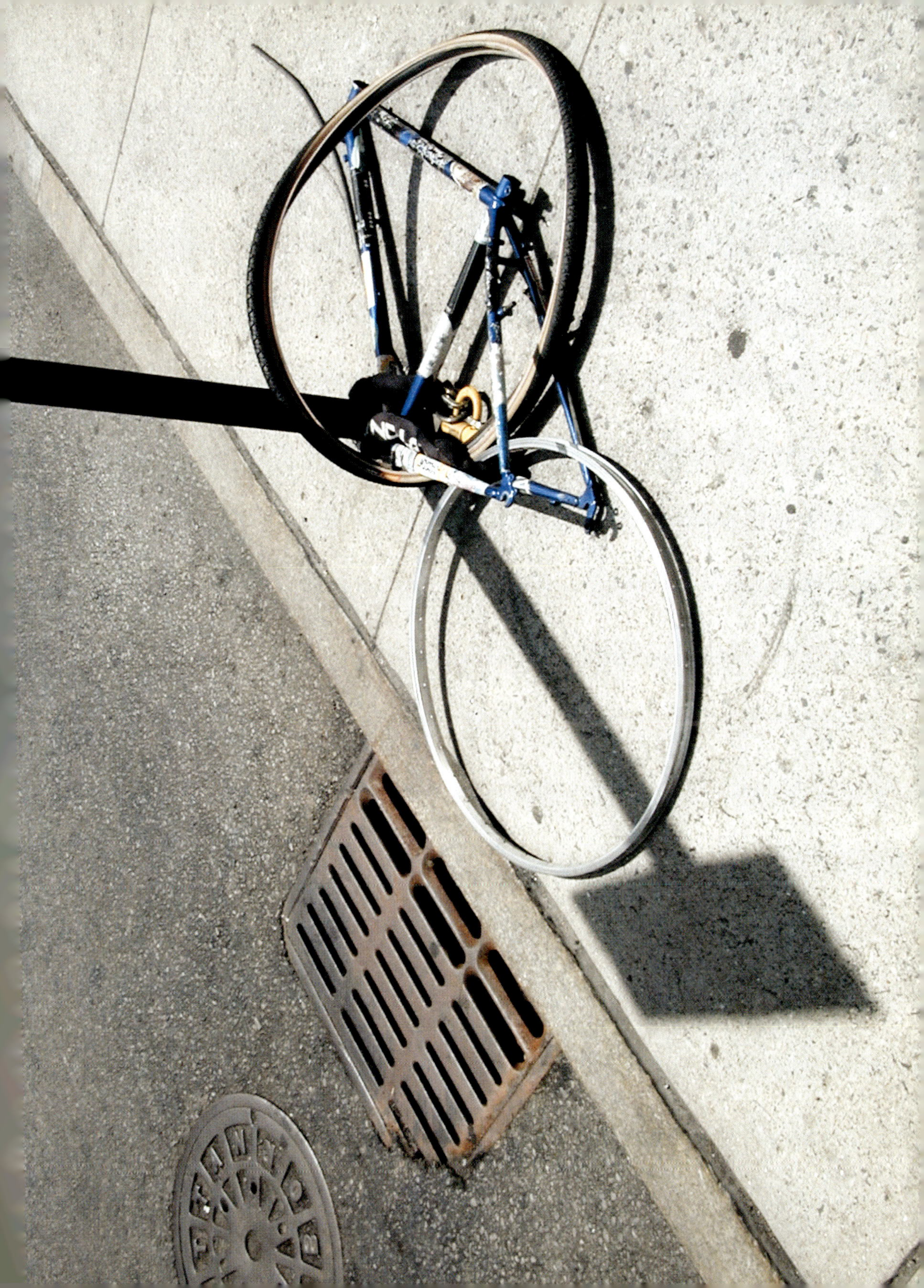

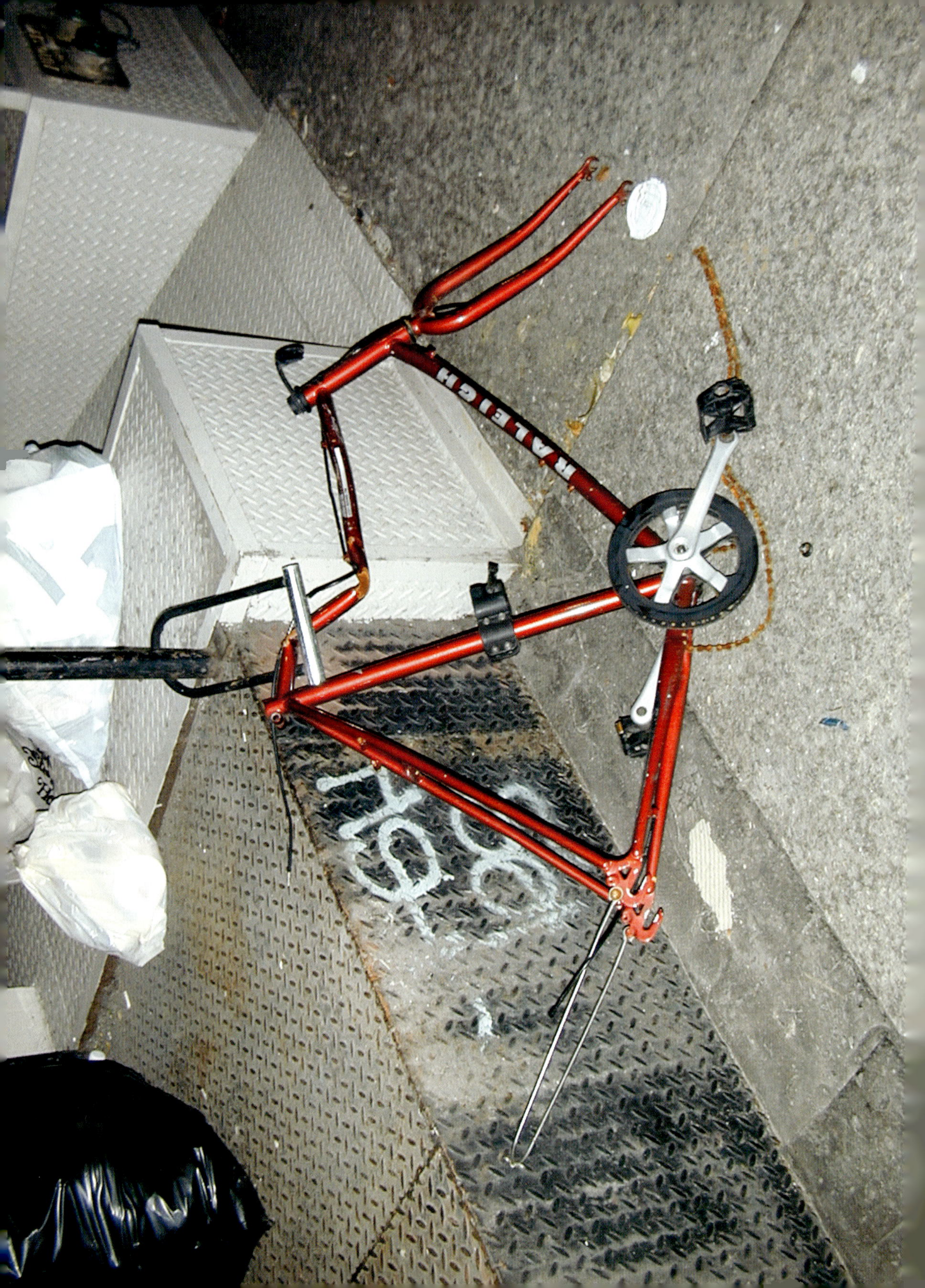
RALEIGH

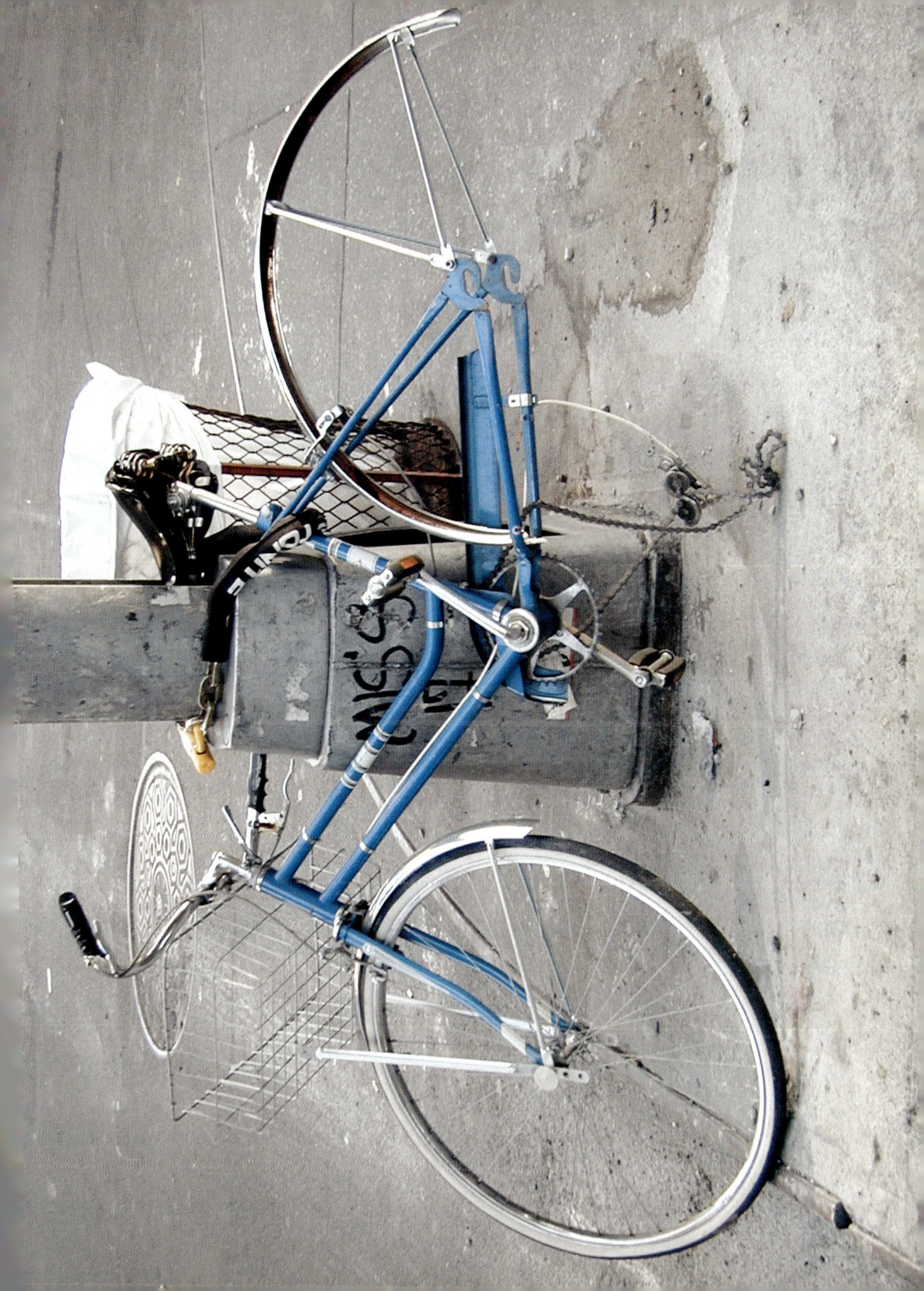

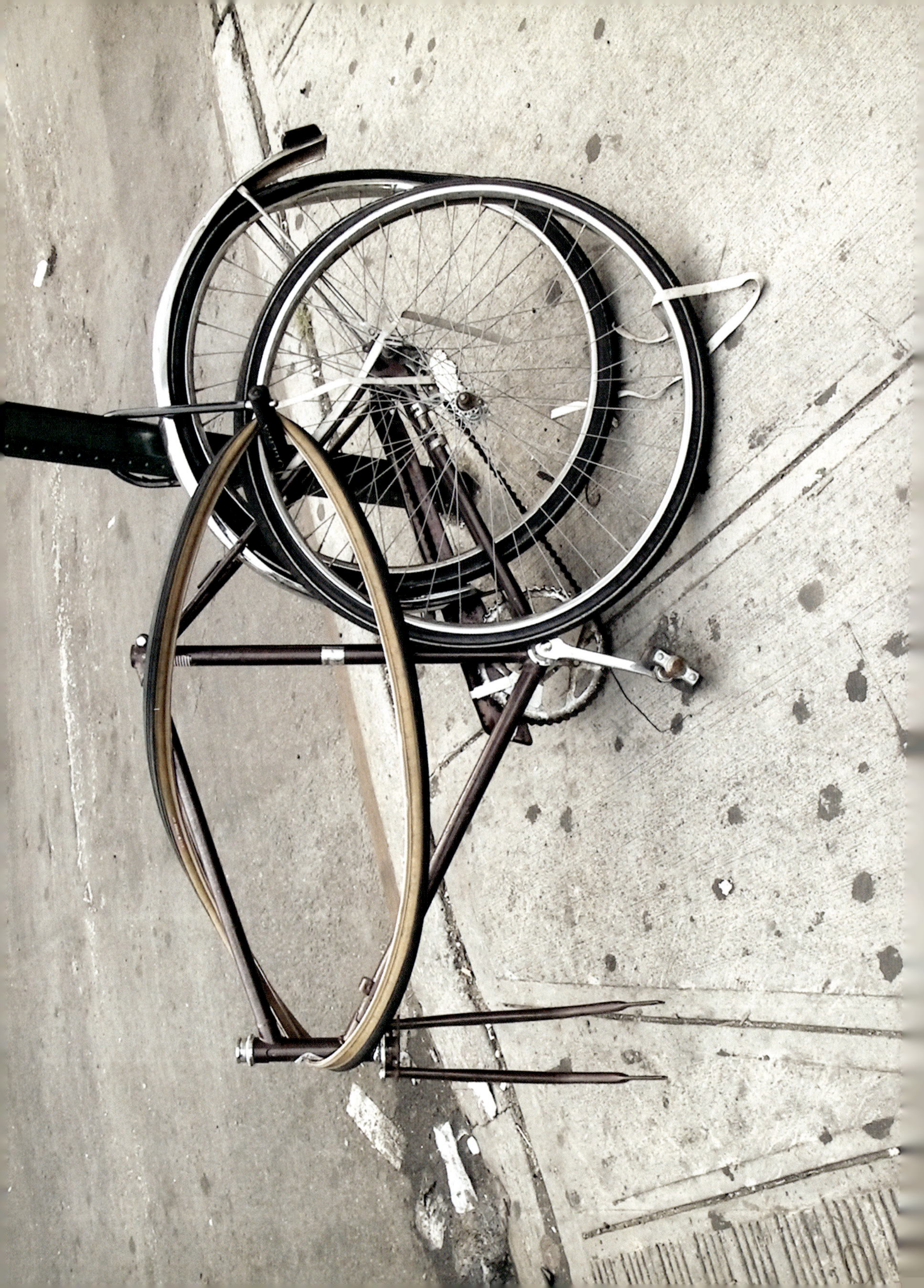

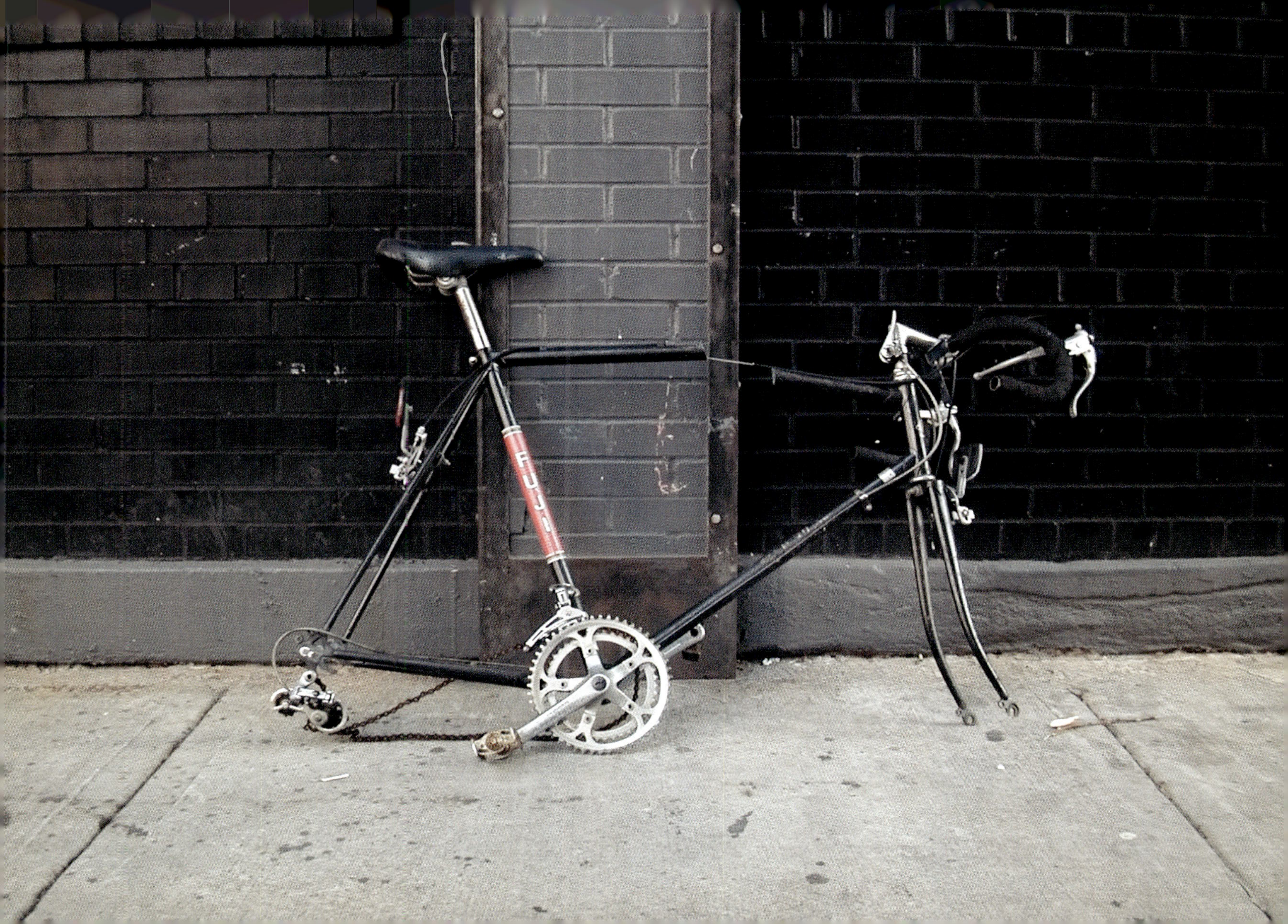
FUJI

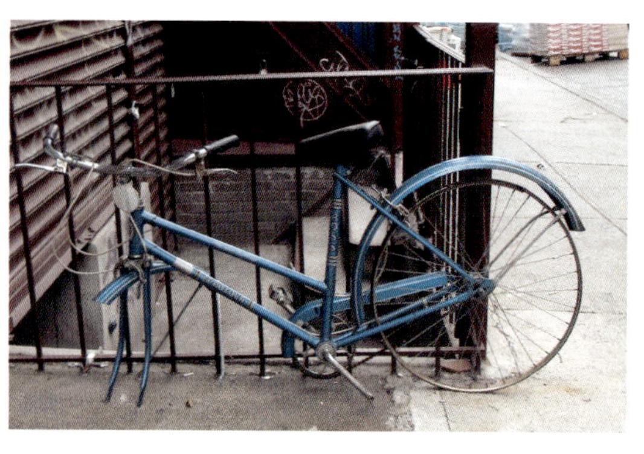
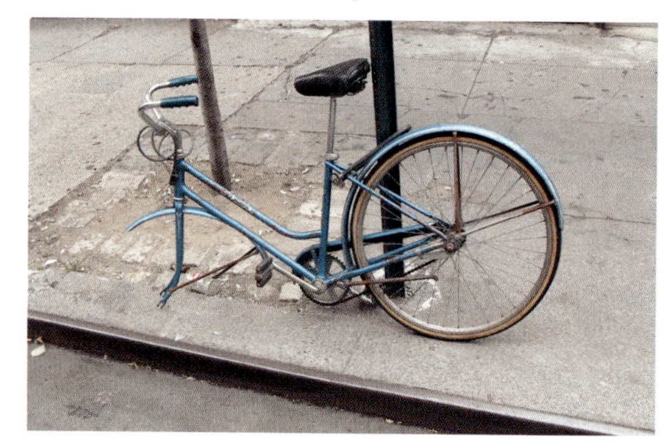
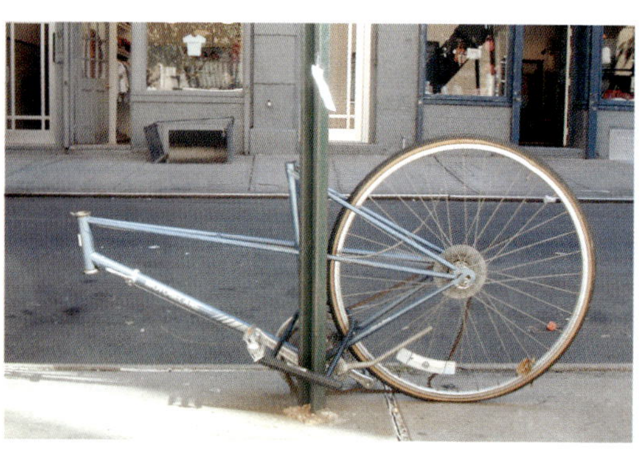
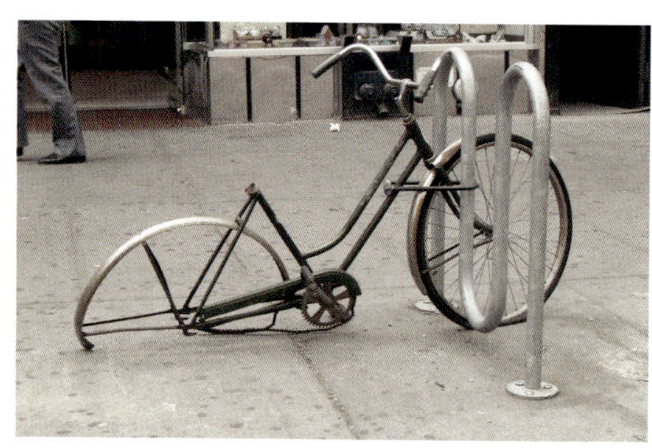
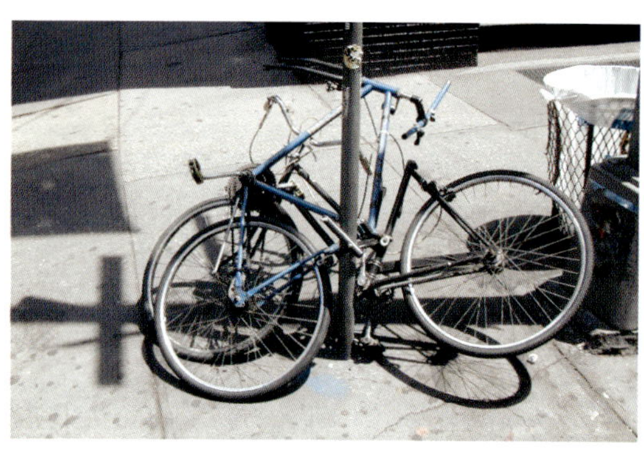
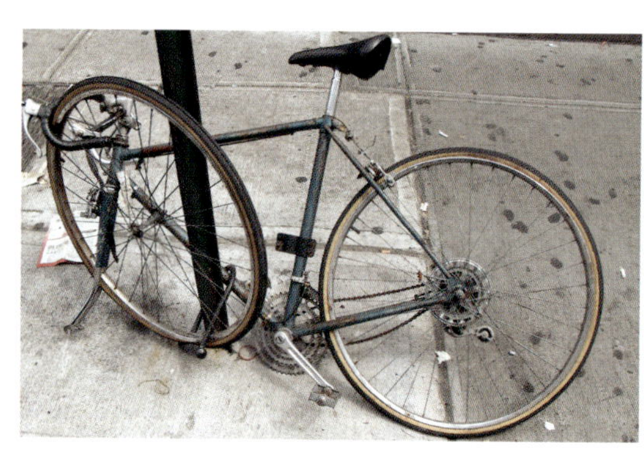
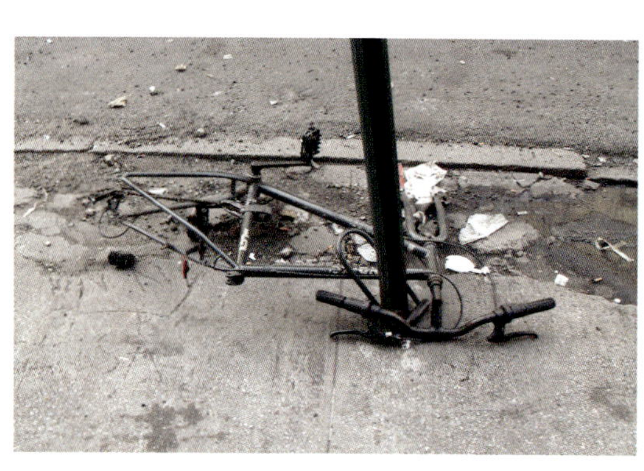
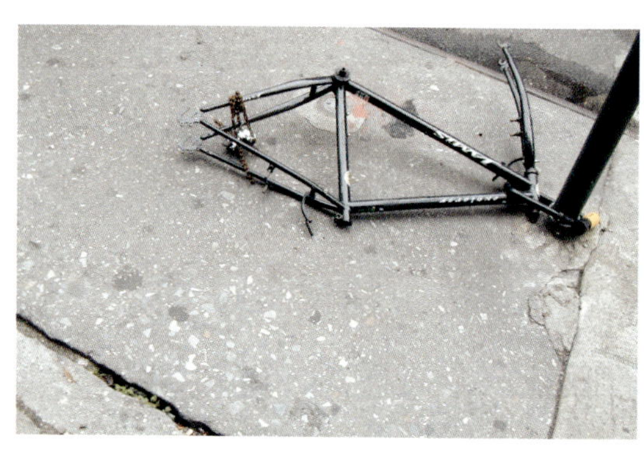

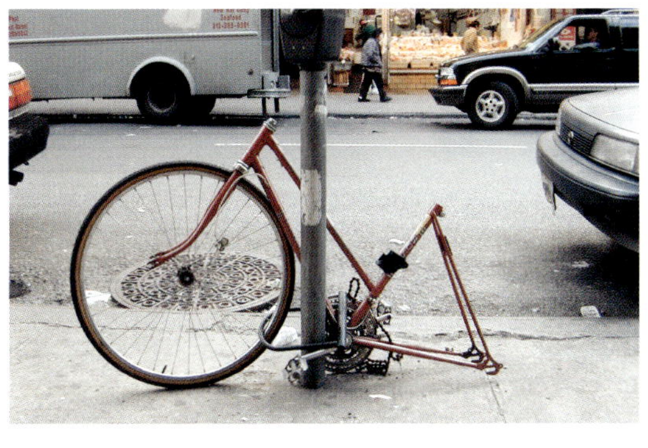

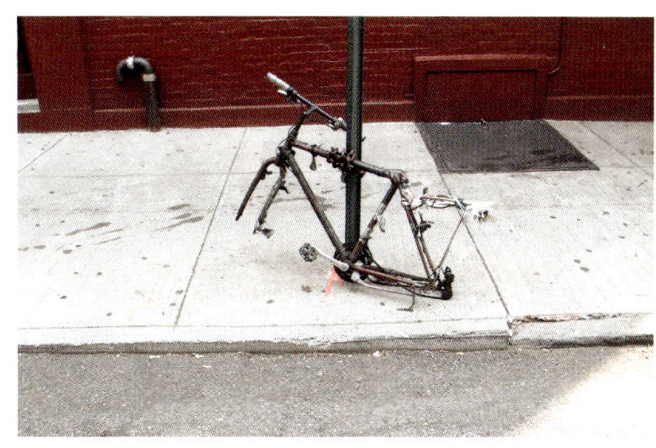

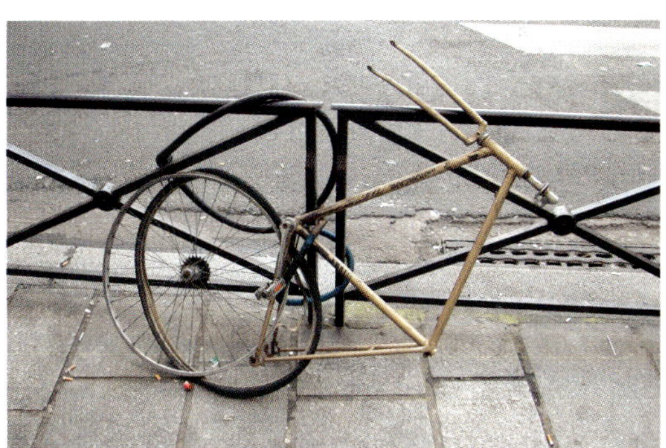

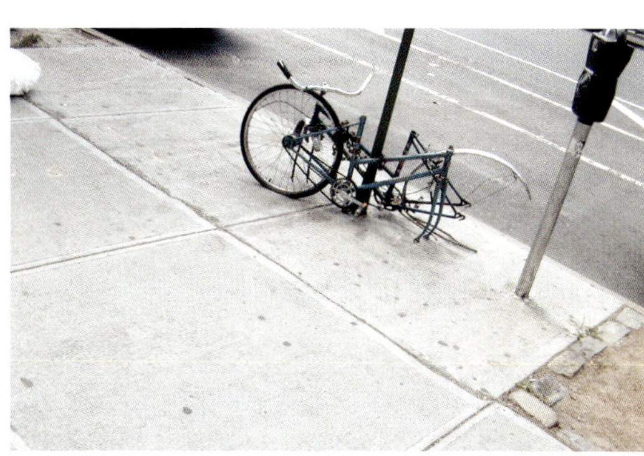

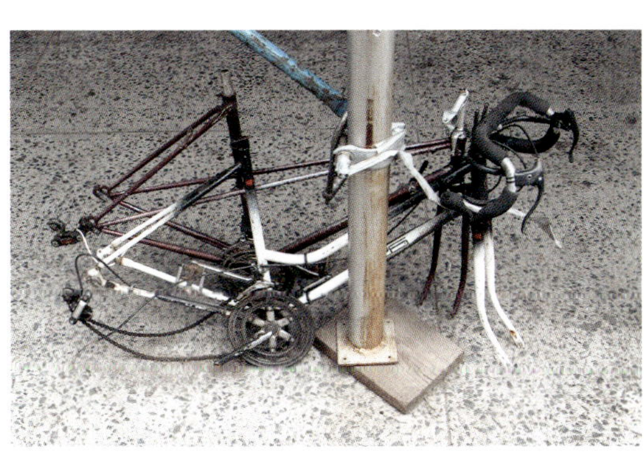

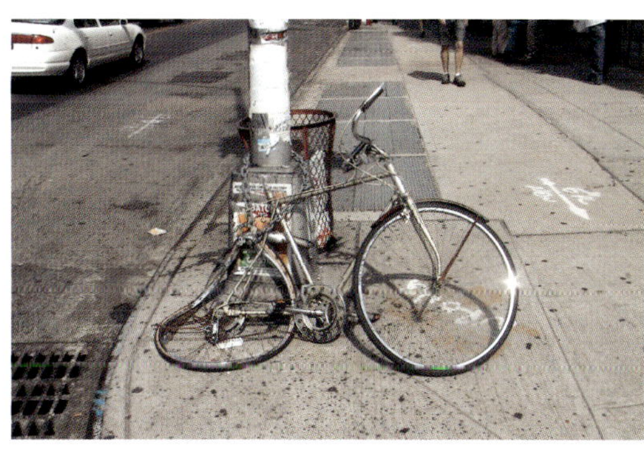

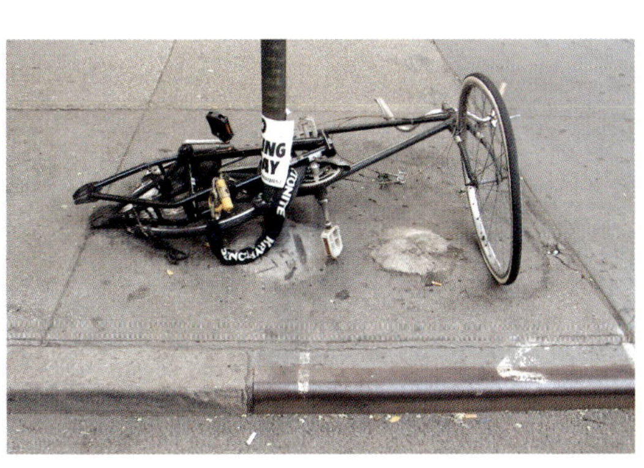

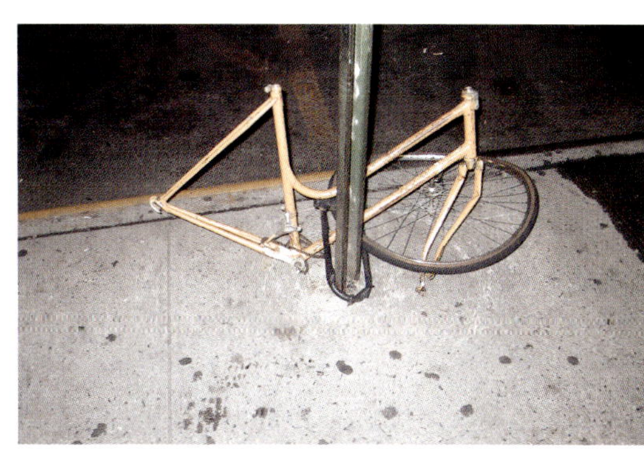

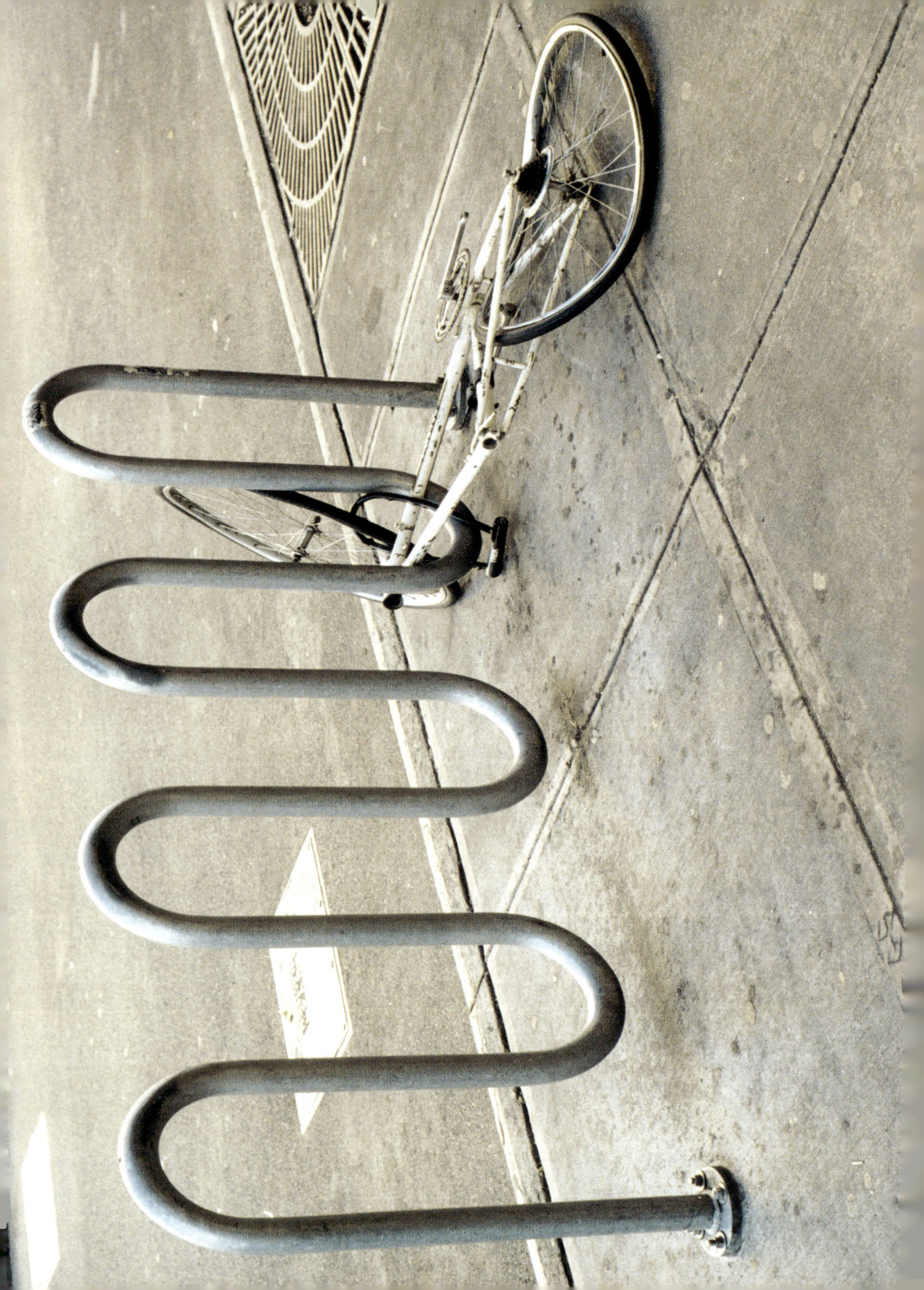

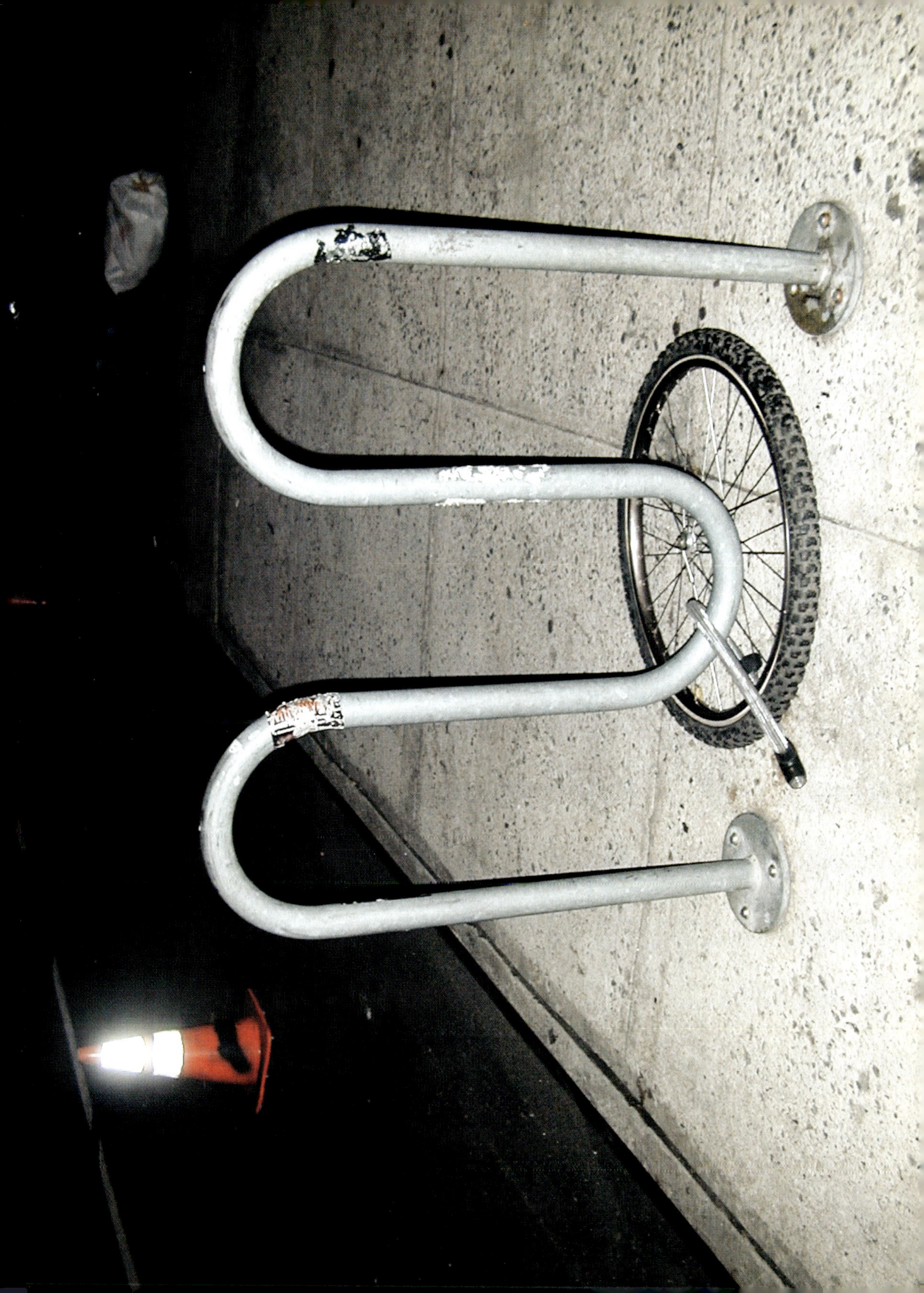

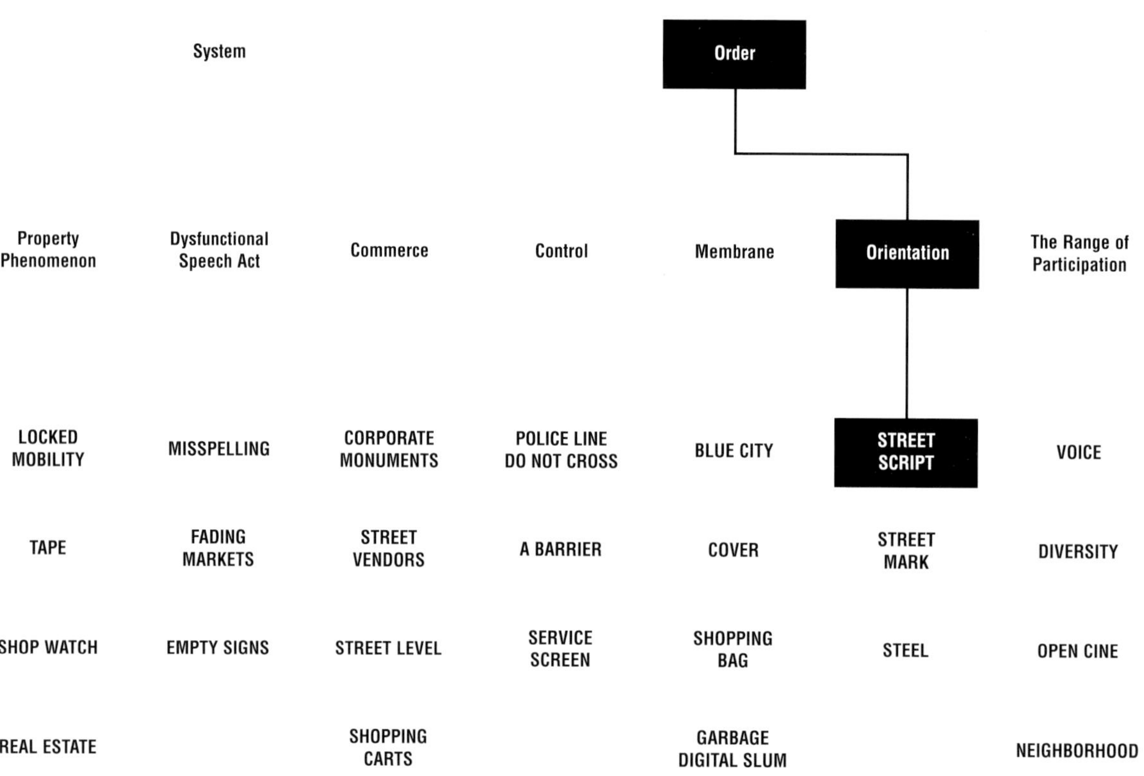
System
Order
Property Phenomenon
Dysfunctional Speech Act
Commerce
Control
Membrane
Orientation
The Range of Participation
LOCKED MOBILITY
MISSPELLING
CORPORATE MONUMENTS
POLICE LINE DO NOT CROSS
BLUE CITY
STREET SCRIPT
VOICE
TAPE
FADING MARKETS
STREET VENDORS
A BARRIER
COVER
STREET MARK
DIVERSITY
SHOP WATCH
EMPTY SIGNS
STREET LEVEL
SERVICE SCREEN
SHOPPING BAG
STEEL
OPEN CINE
REAL ESTATE
SHOPPING CARTS
GARBAGE DIGITAL SLUM
NEIGHBORHOOD

Identity

Alternative Media

Habitual Reinterpretation

STREET SCRIPT

Public Codes denoting the Depth

CAR DOOR

PUBLIC CHAIRS

LABELING.

PLASTIC CRATES

POLE POST

STANDPIPES

PRAY JESUS

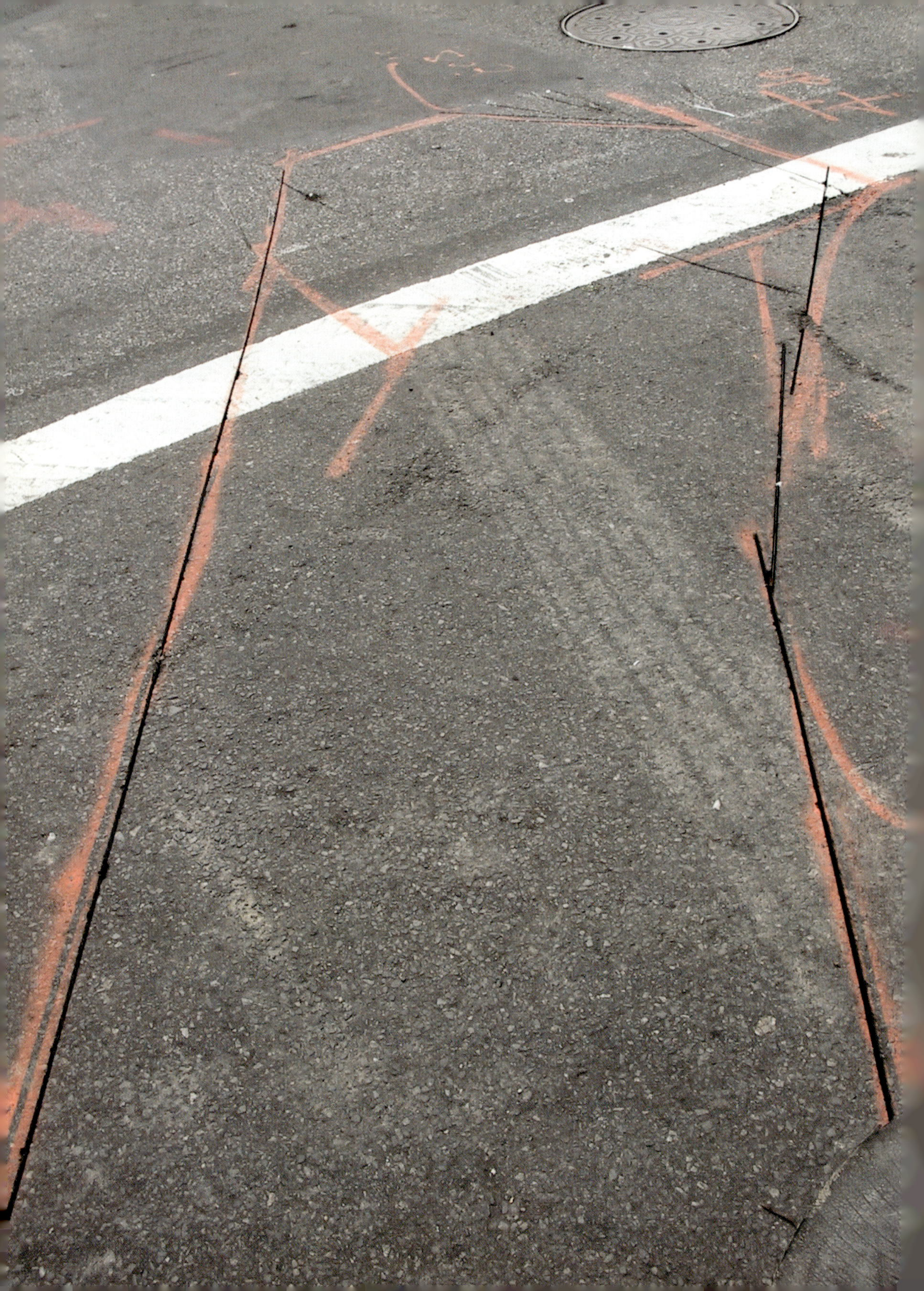

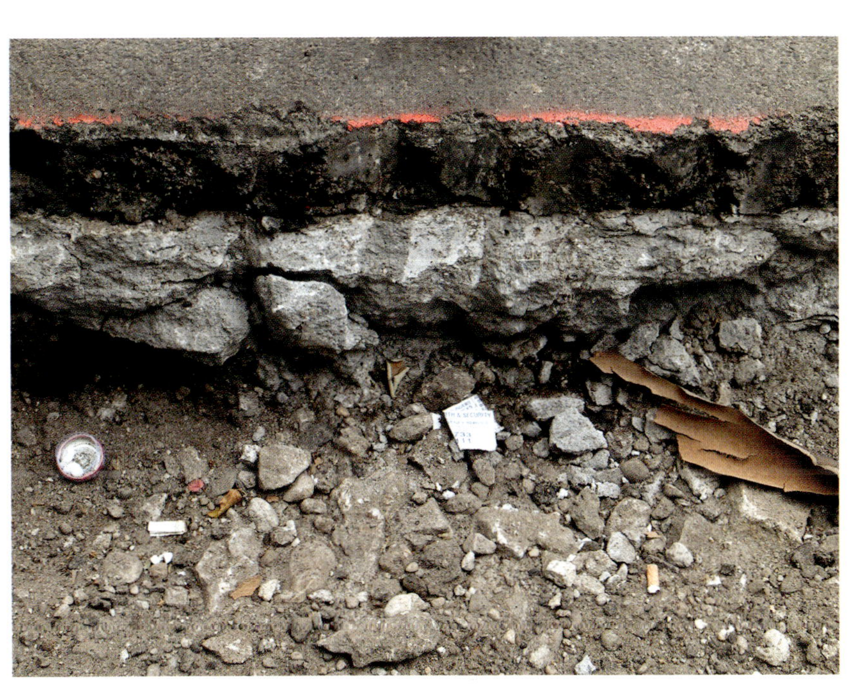

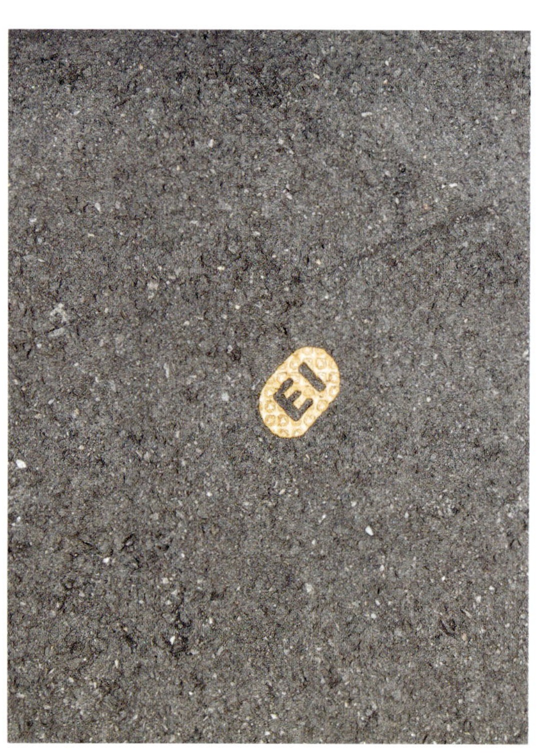
EI

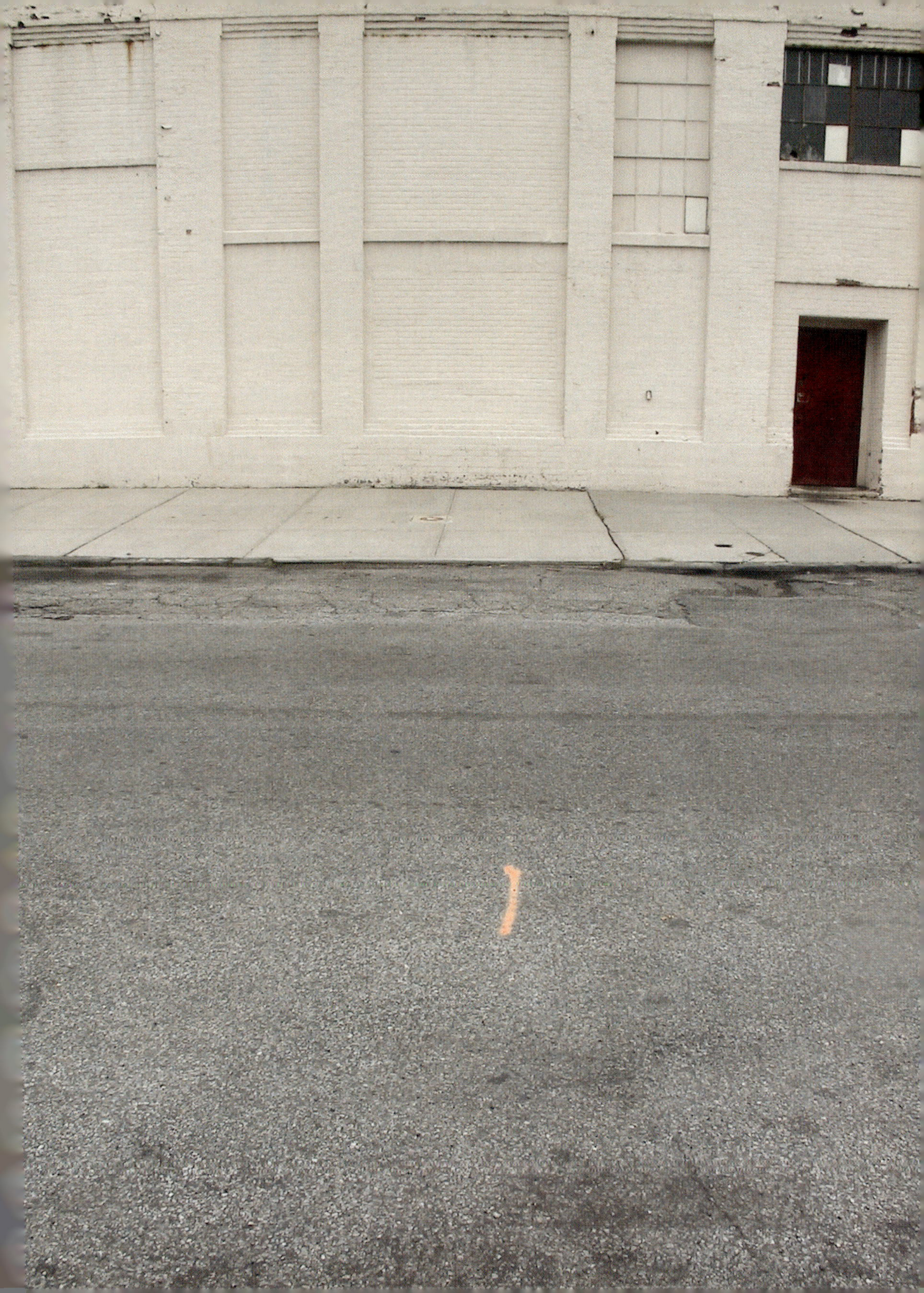

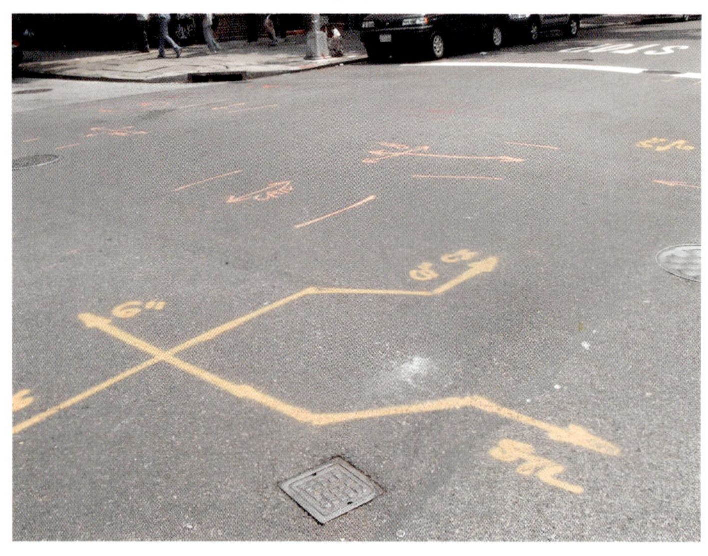
6"

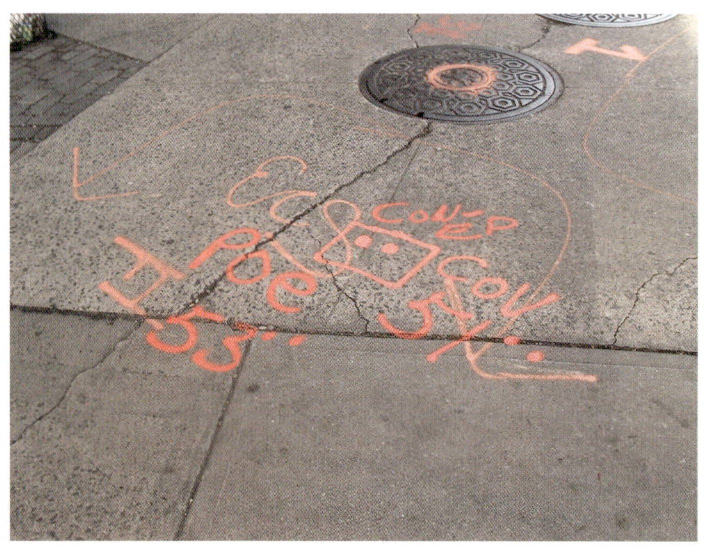

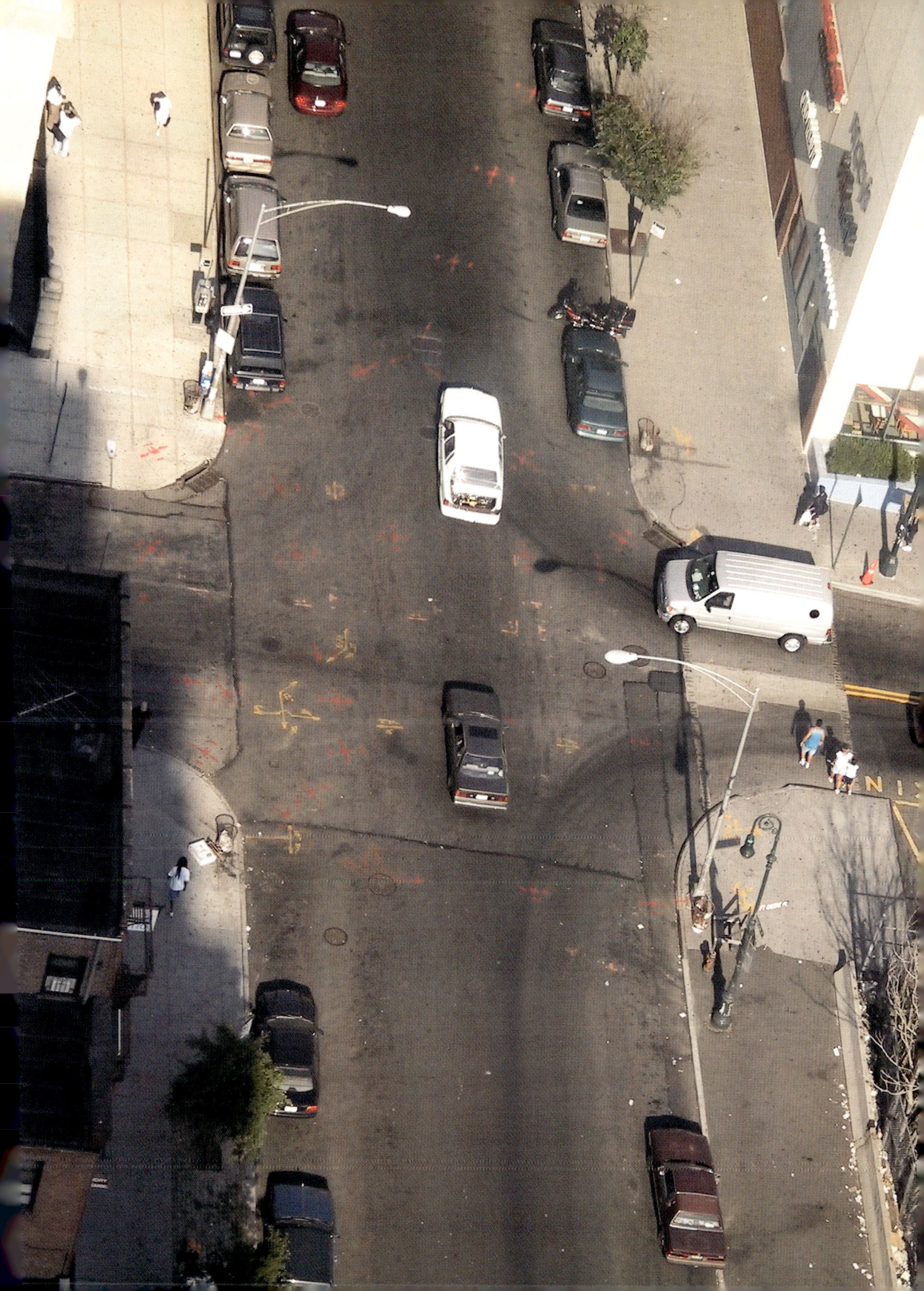

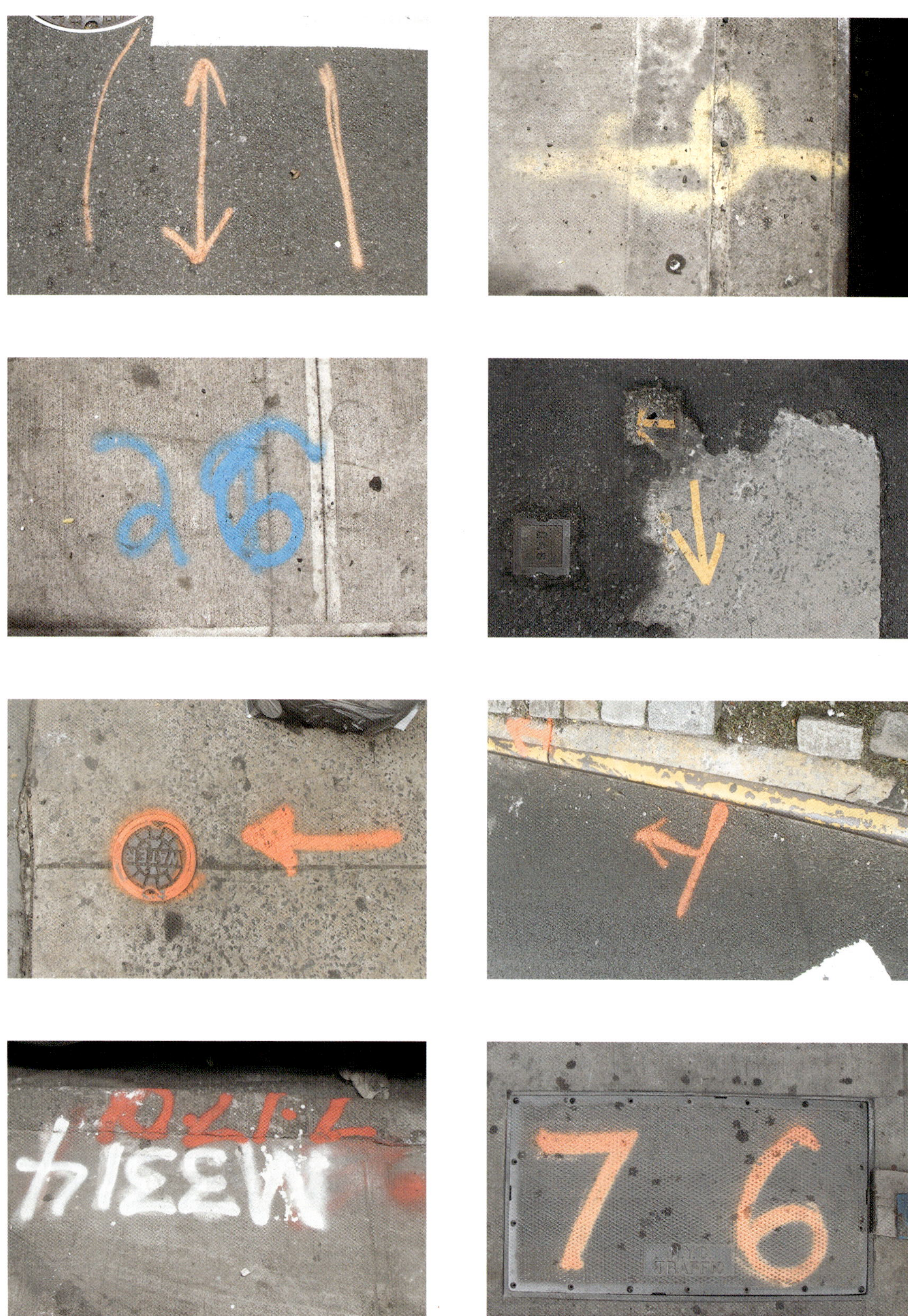
7 6
NYC
TRAFFIC

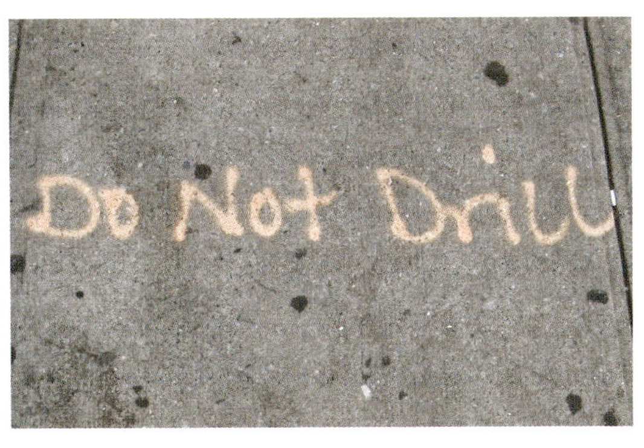
Do Not Drill

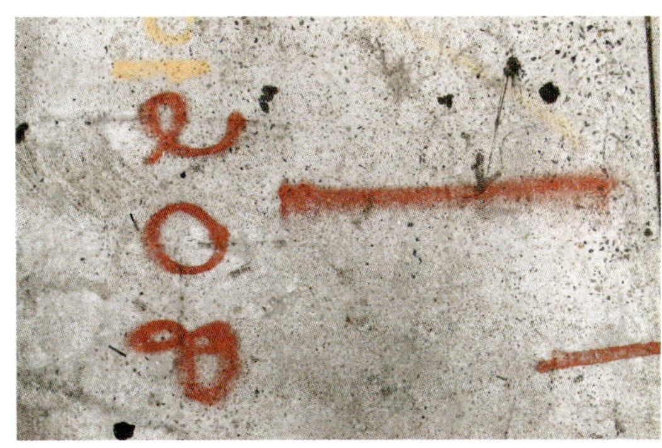

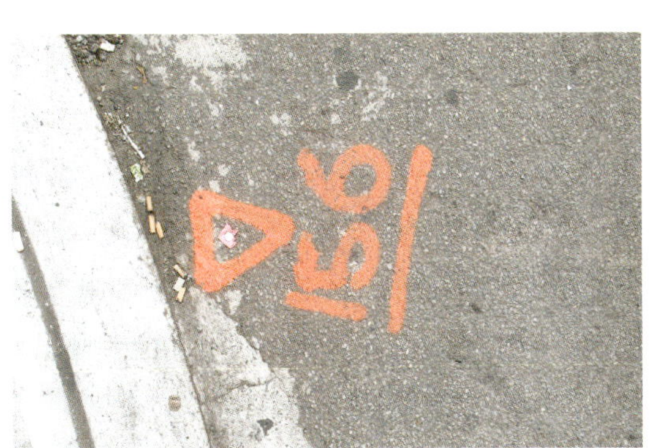

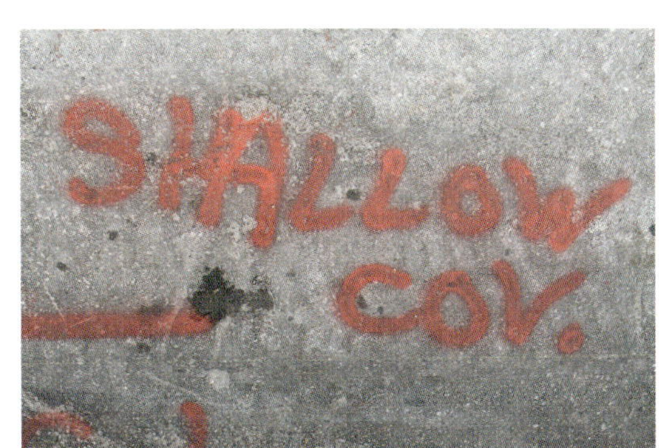
SHALLOW
COV.

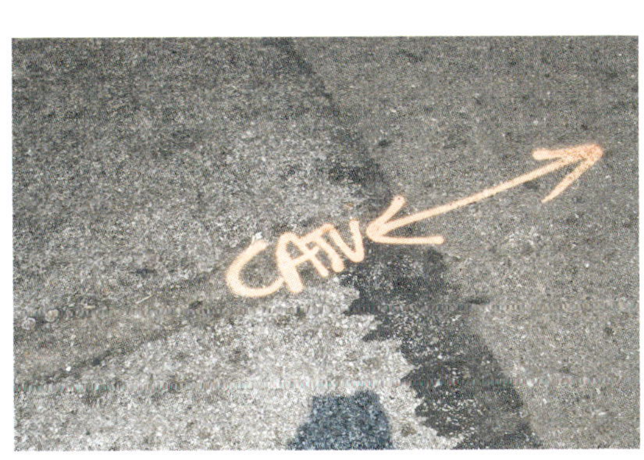
CATV

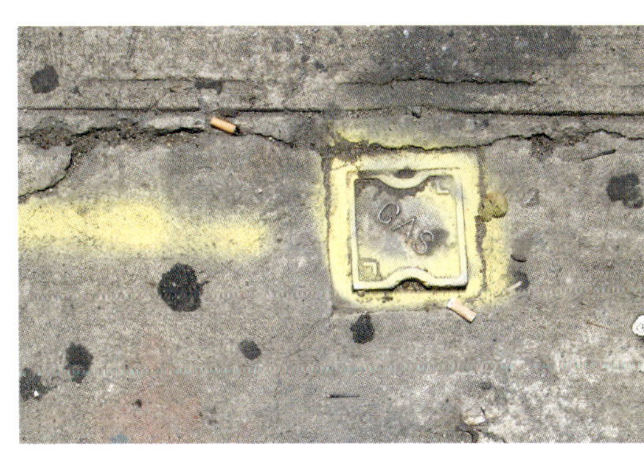

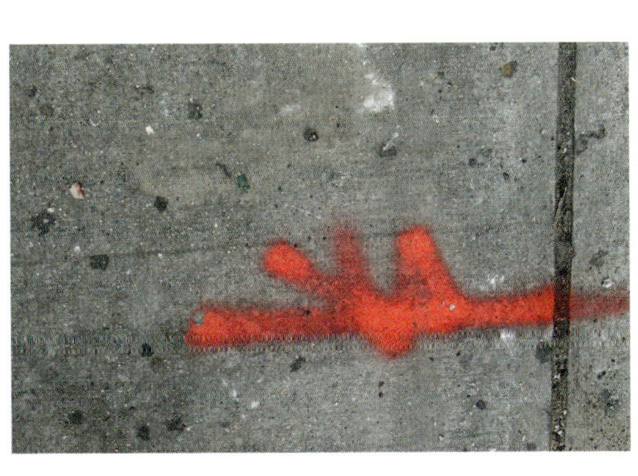

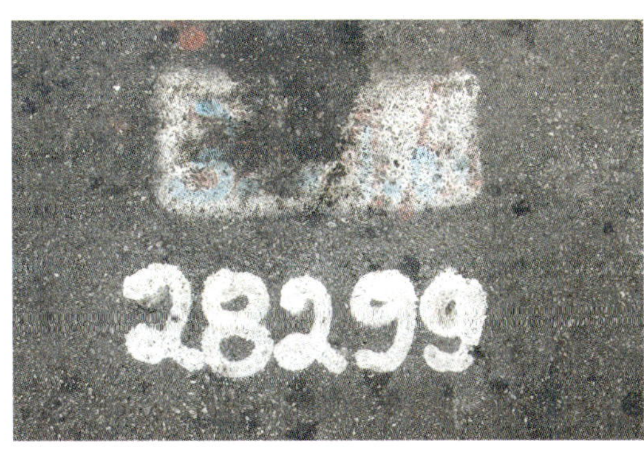
28299

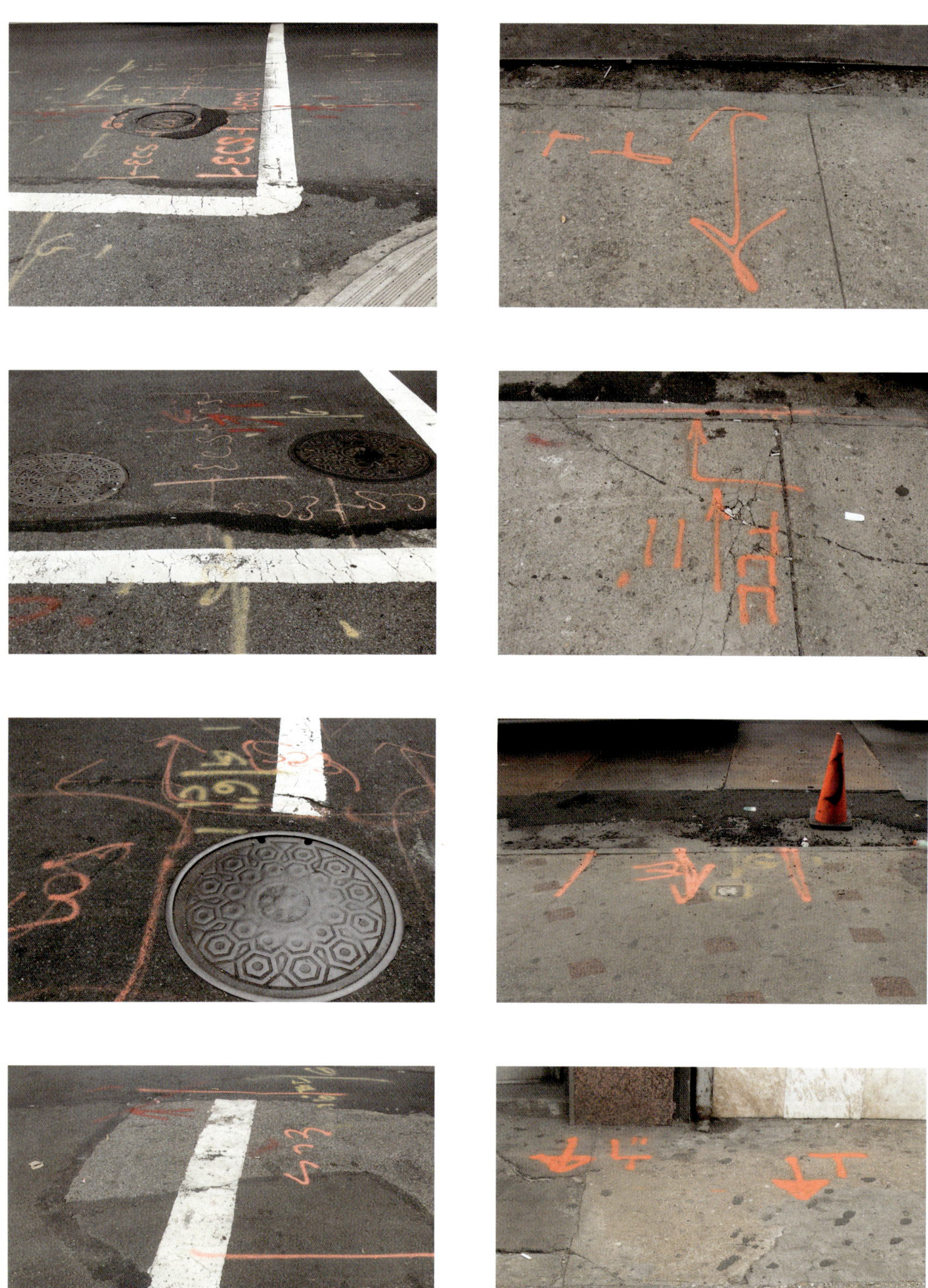

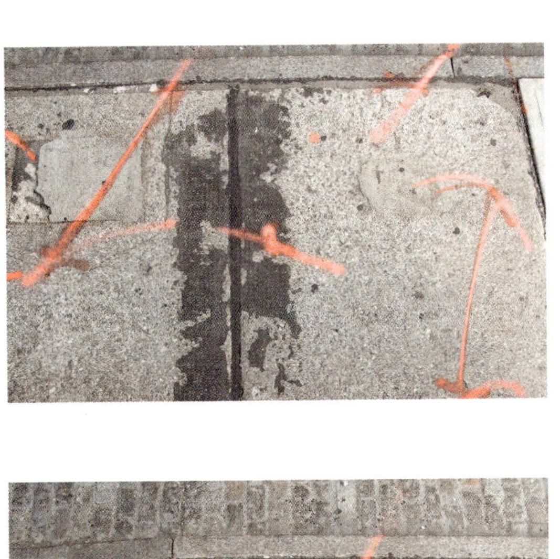
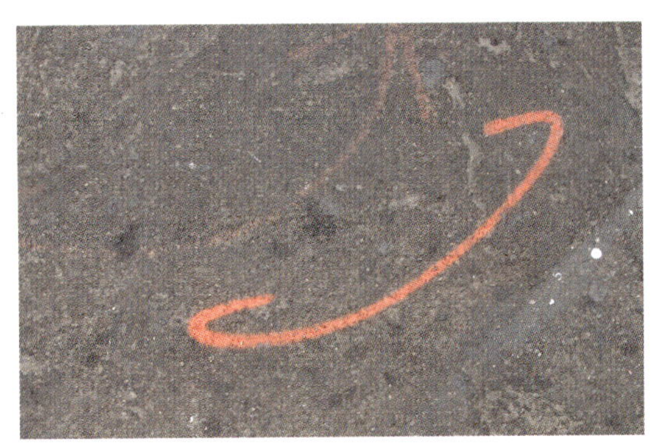
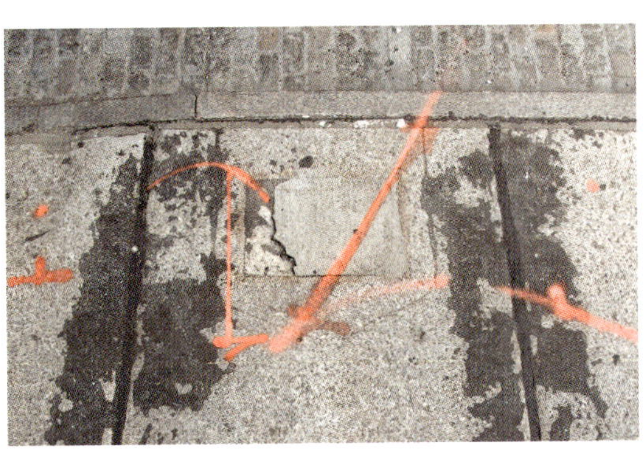
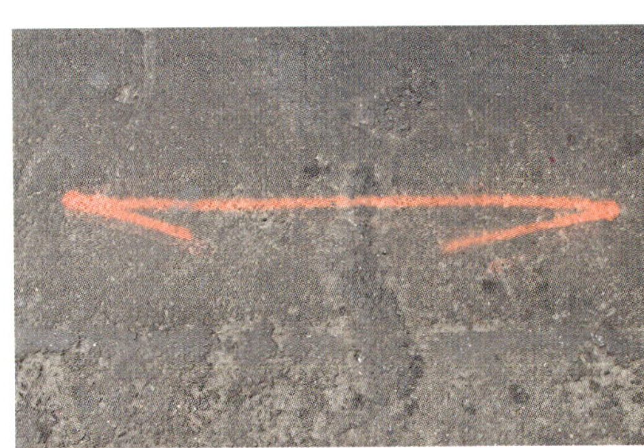
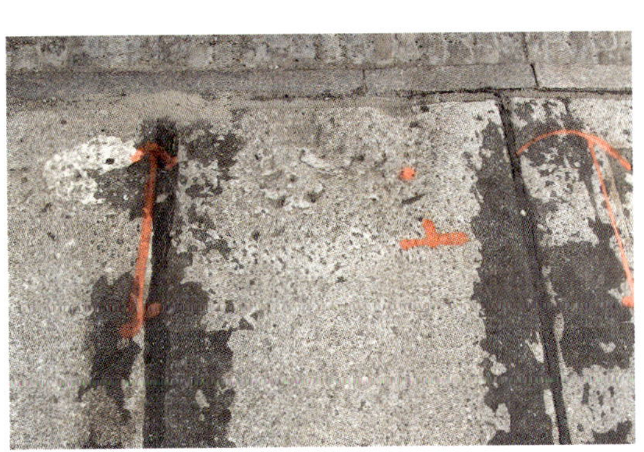
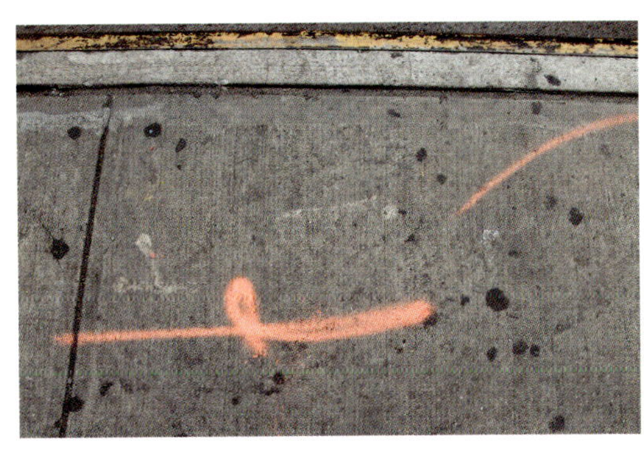
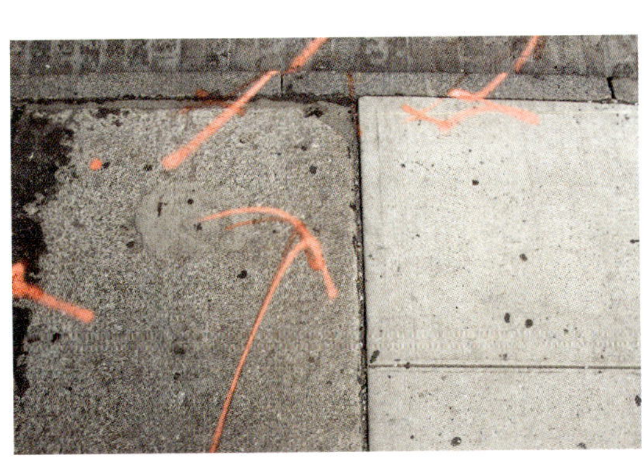
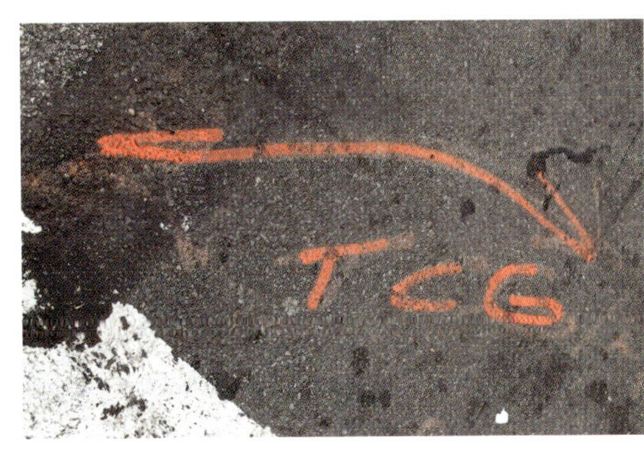
TCG

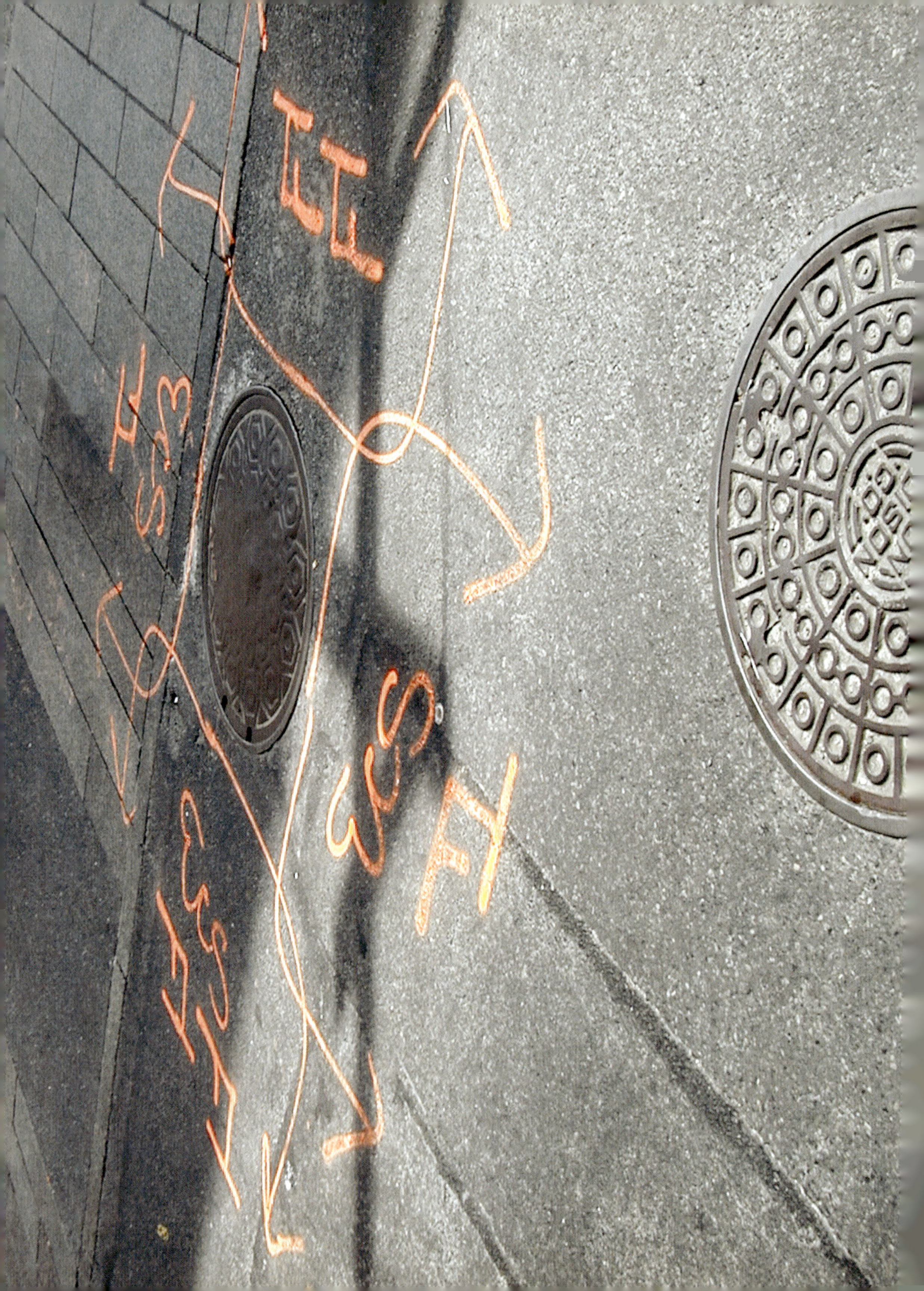

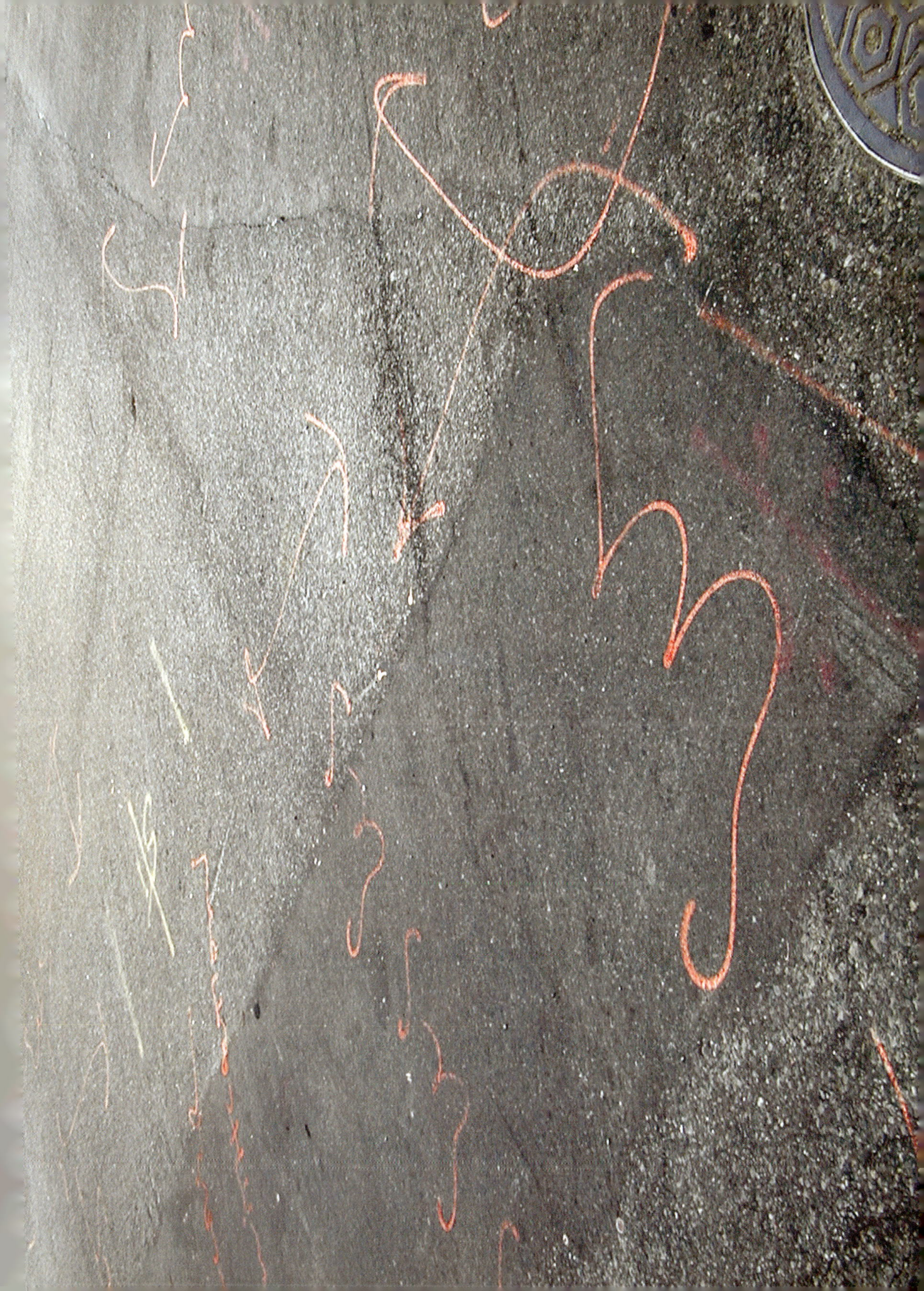

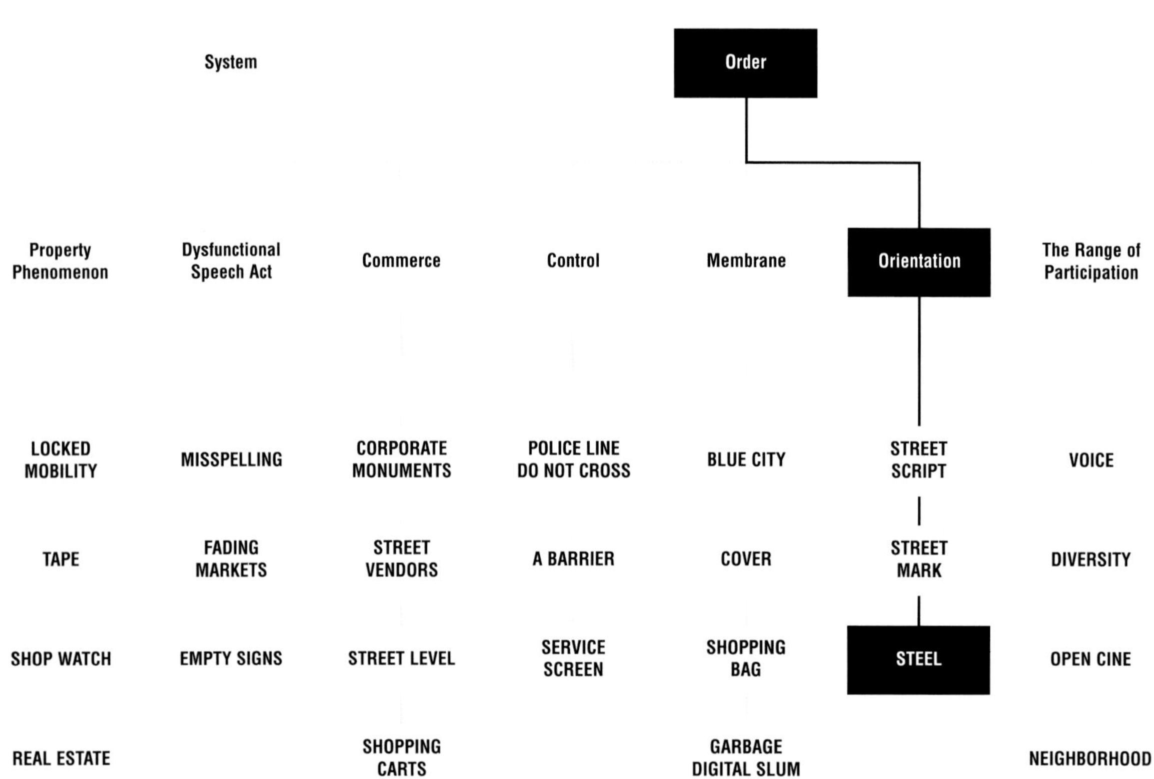

System
Order
Property Phenomenon
Dysfunctional Speech Act
Commerce
Control
Membrane
Orientation
The Range of Participation
LOCKED MOBILITY
MISSPELLING
CORPORATE MONUMENTS
POLICE LINE DO NOT CROSS
BLUE CITY
STREET SCRIPT
VOICE
TAPE
FADING MARKETS
STREET VENDORS
A BARRIER
COVER
STREET MARK
DIVERSITY
SHOP WATCH
EMPTY SIGNS
STREET LEVEL
SERVICE SCREEN
SHOPPING BAG
STEEL
OPEN CINE
REAL ESTATE
SHOPPING CARTS
GARBAGE DIGITAL SLUM
NEIGHBORHOOD

Identity

Alternative Media

Habitual Reinterpretation

STEEL

Signature is a Scar

CAR DOOR

PUBLIC CHAIRS

LABELING.

PLASTIC CRATES

POLE POST

STANDPIPES

PRAY JESUS

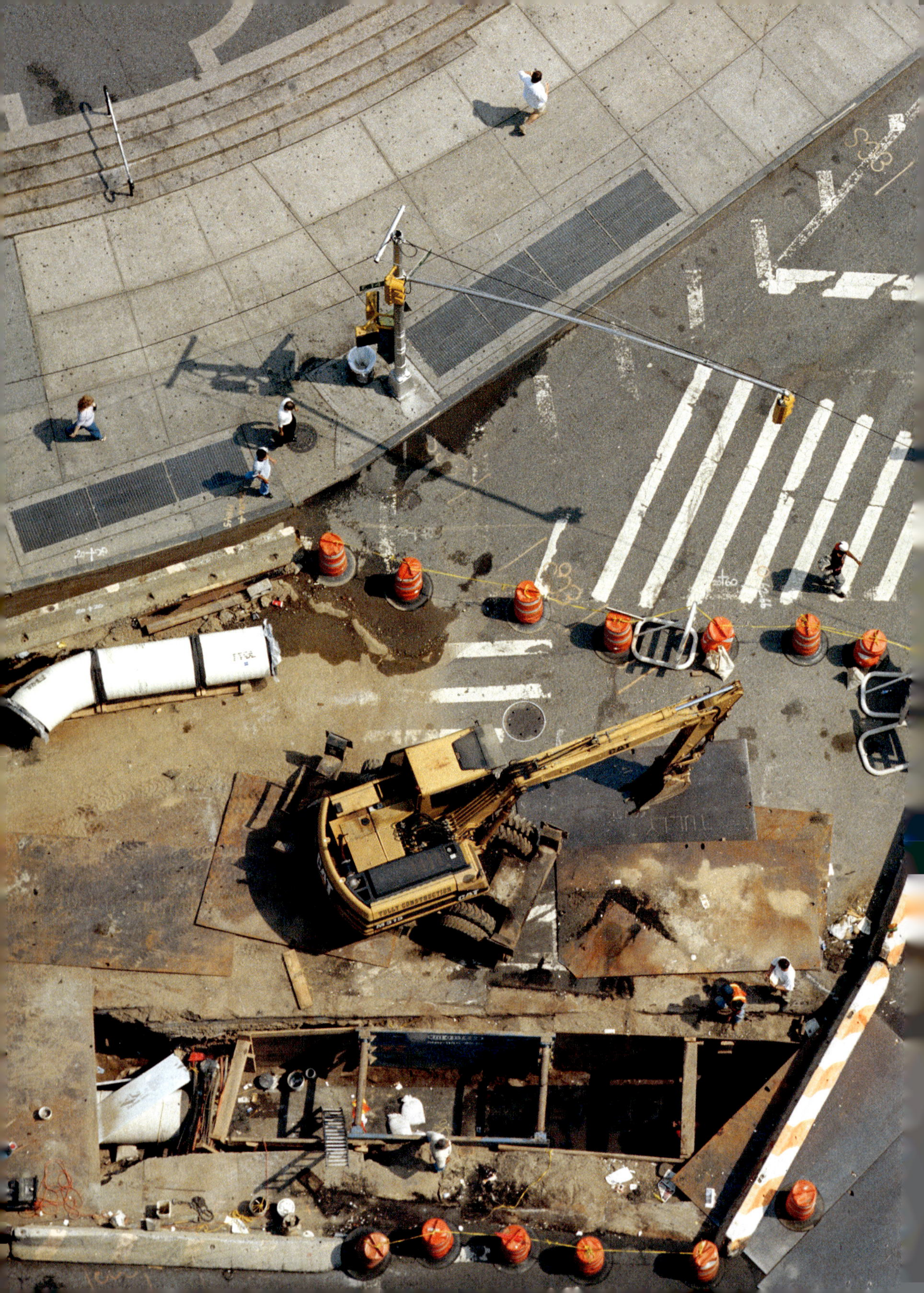

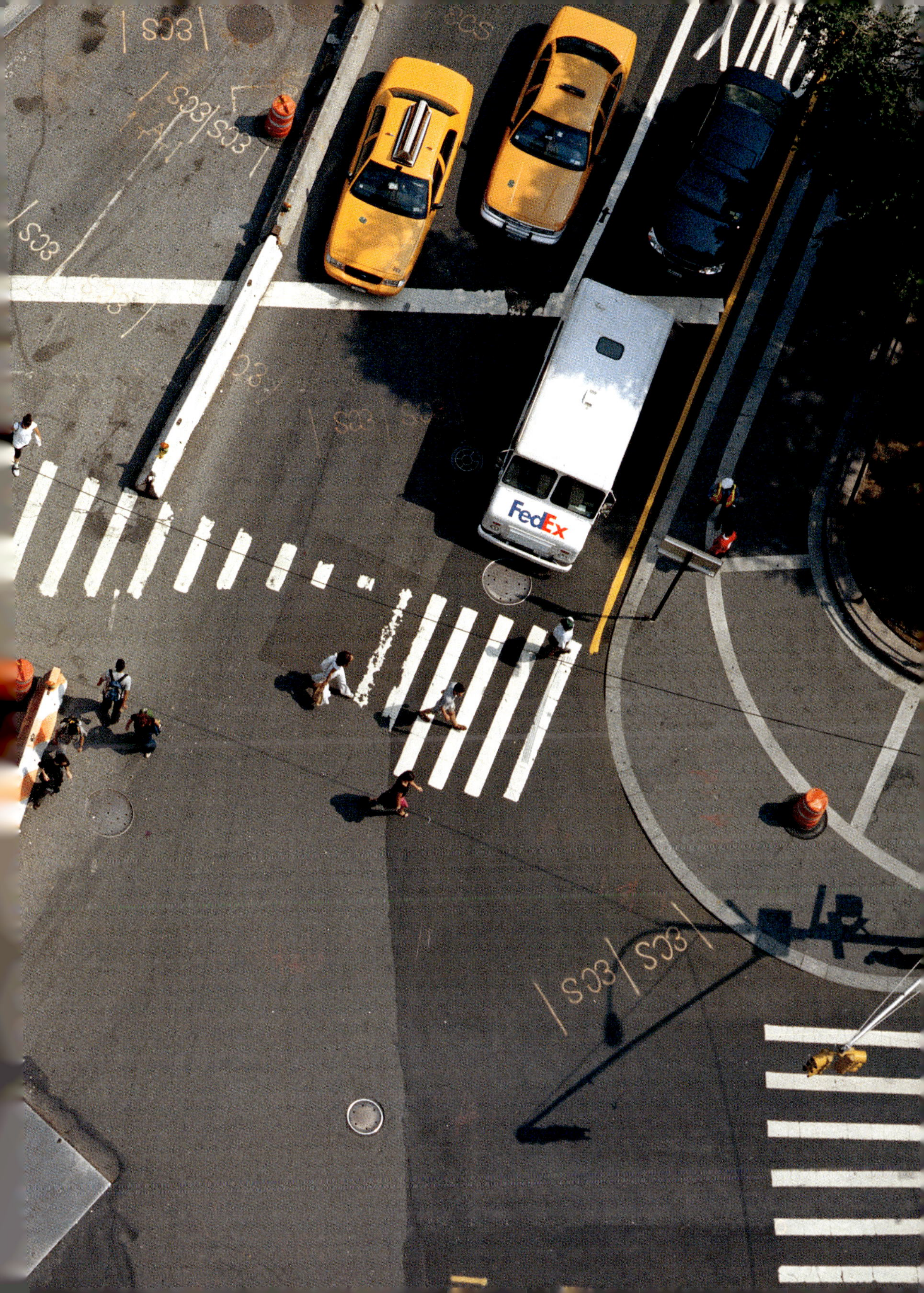
FedEx

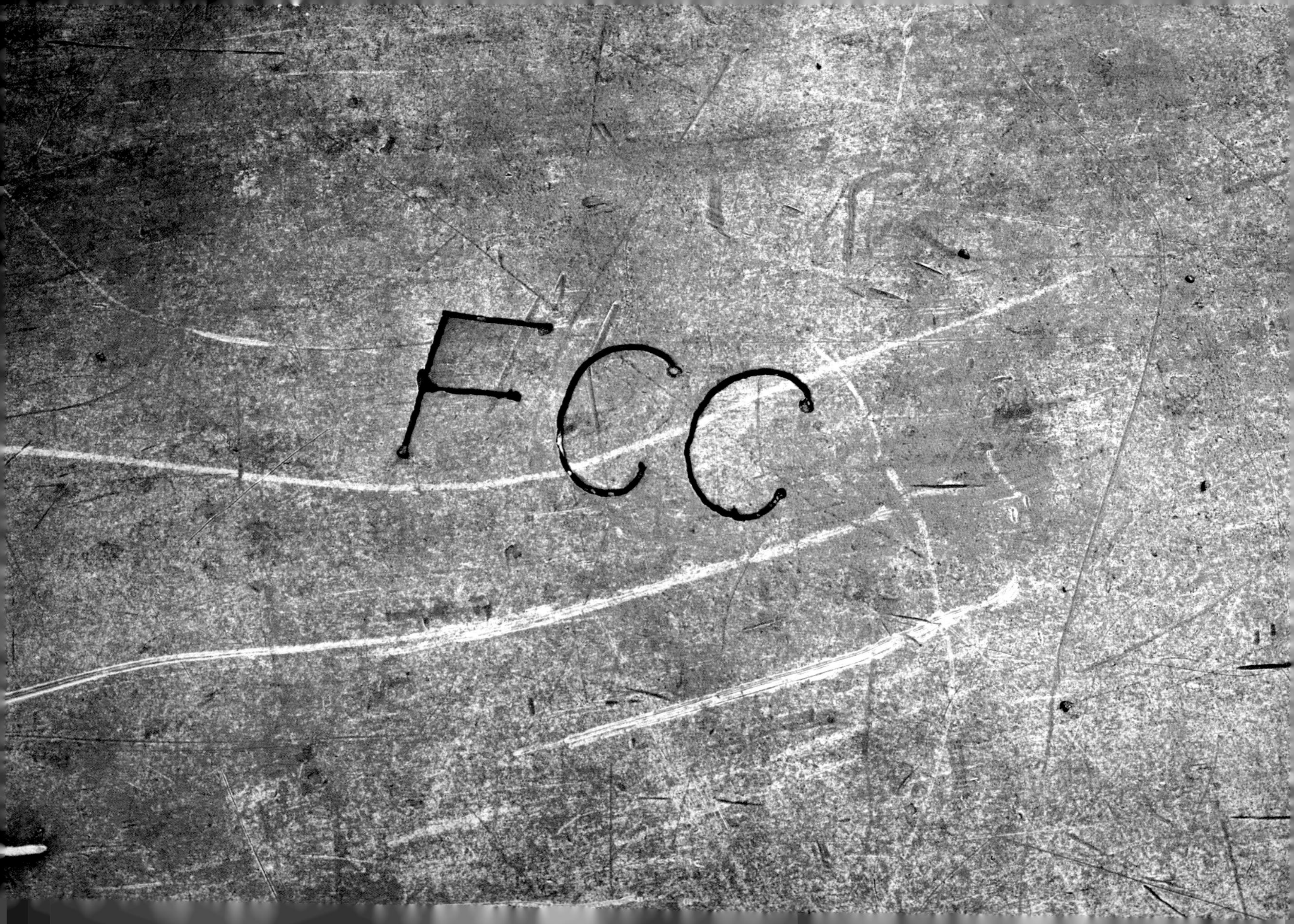
FCC

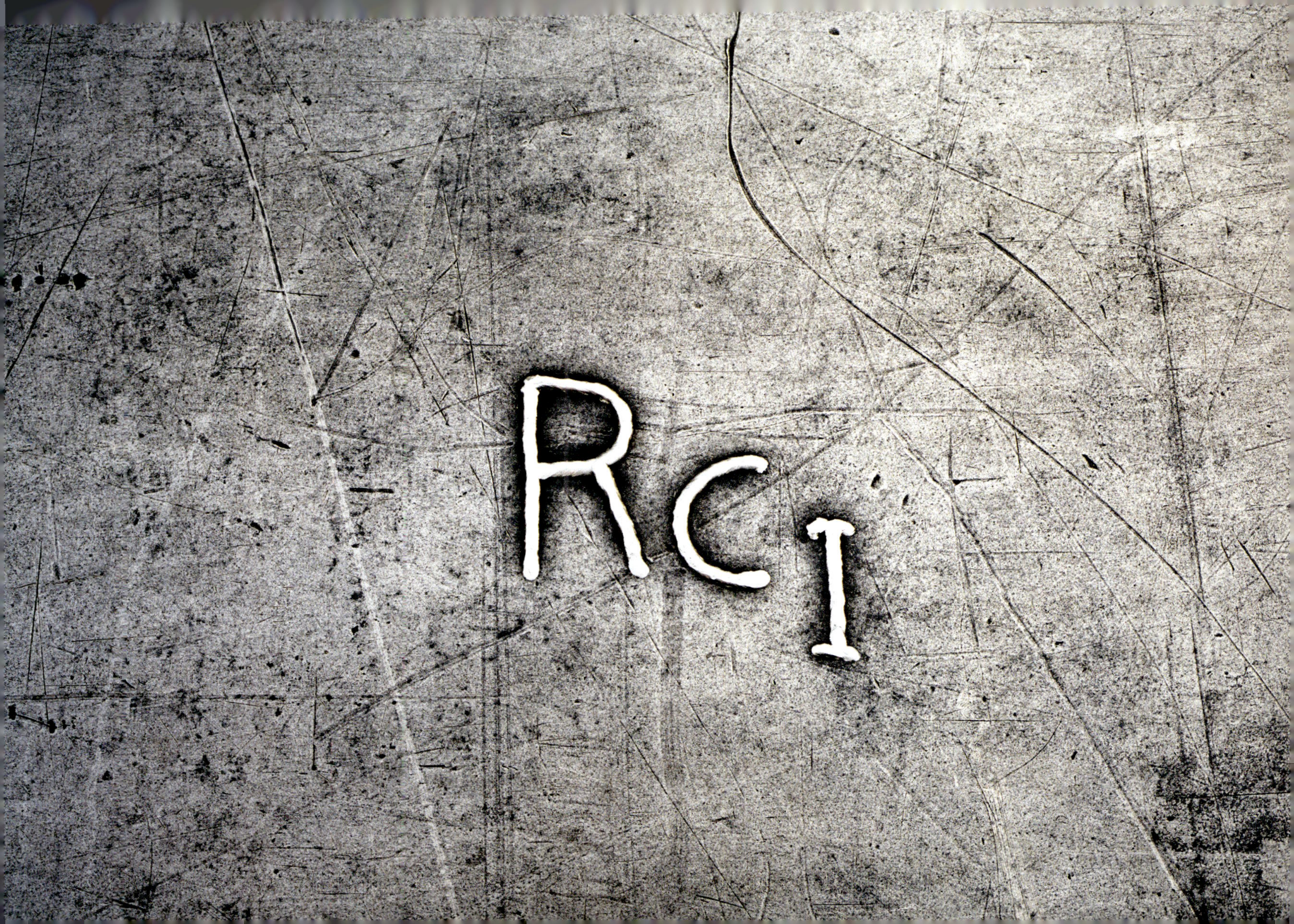
RC1

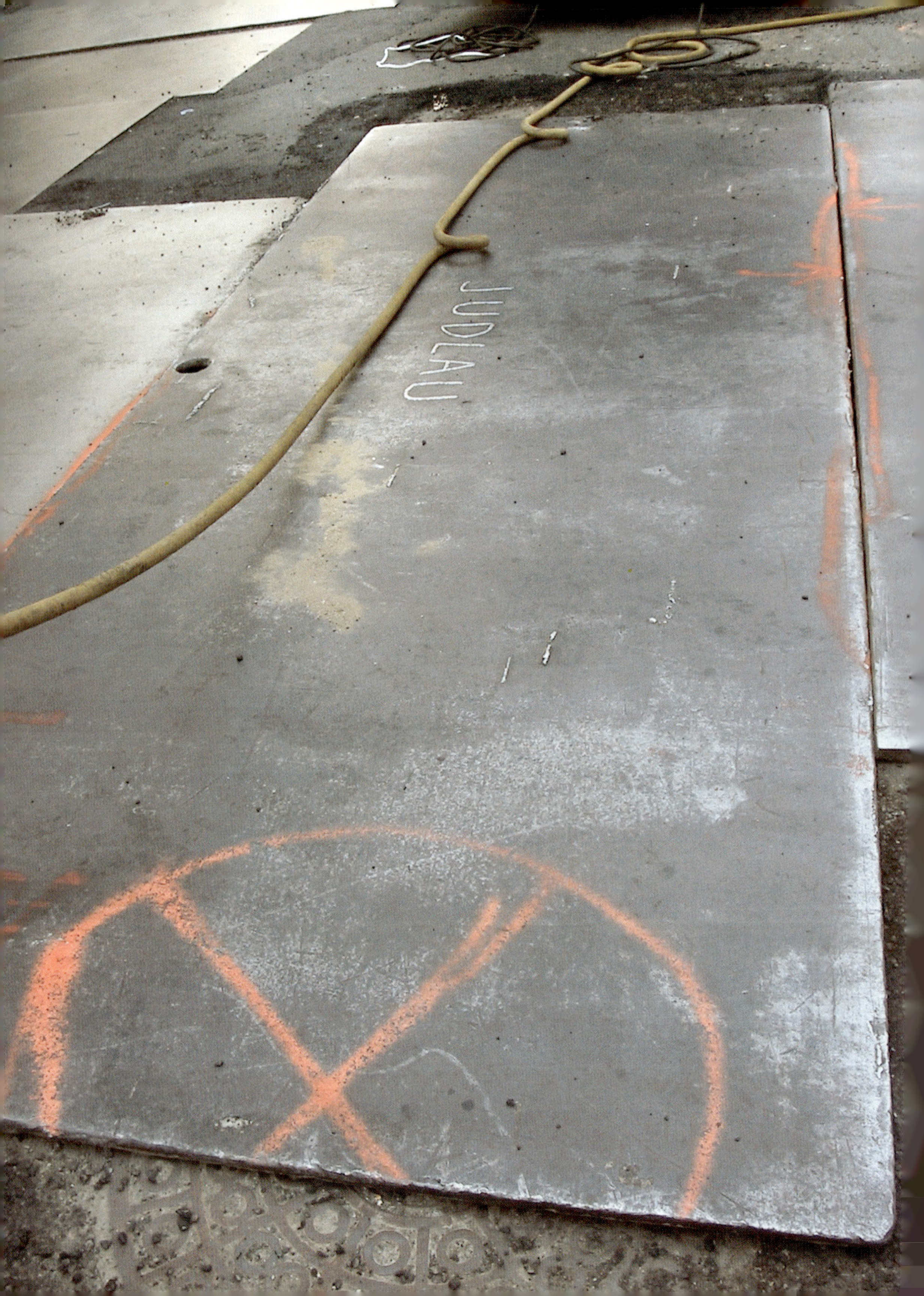
JUDLAU

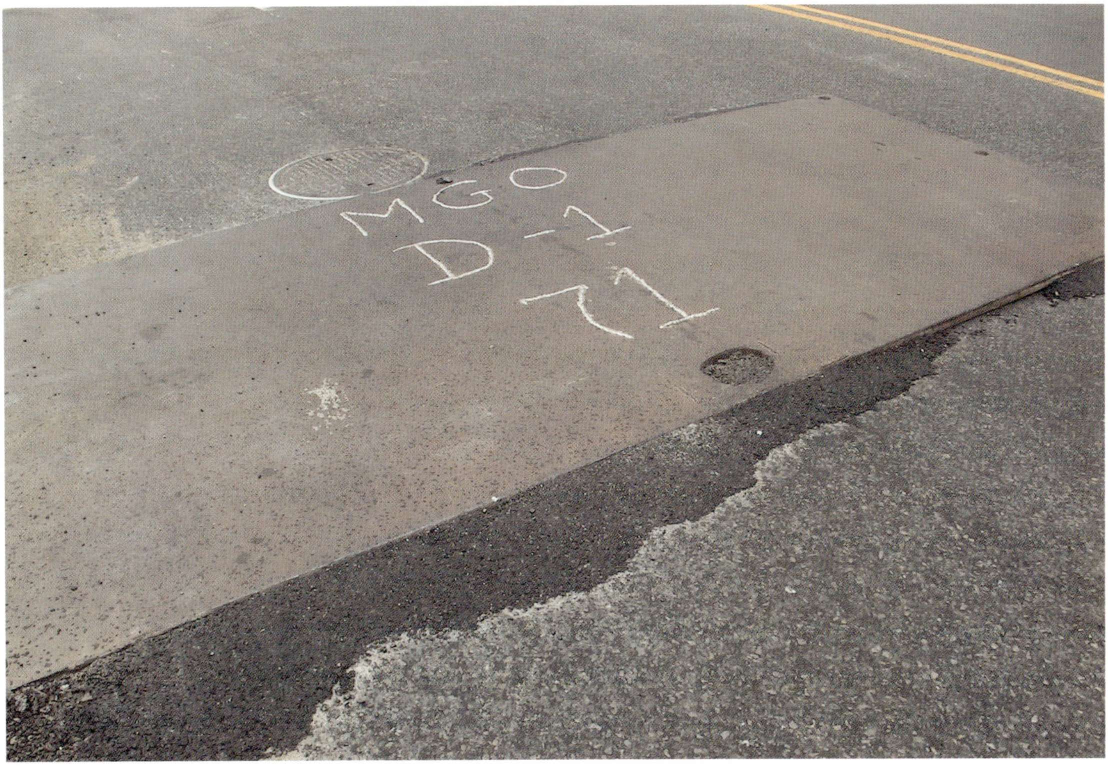

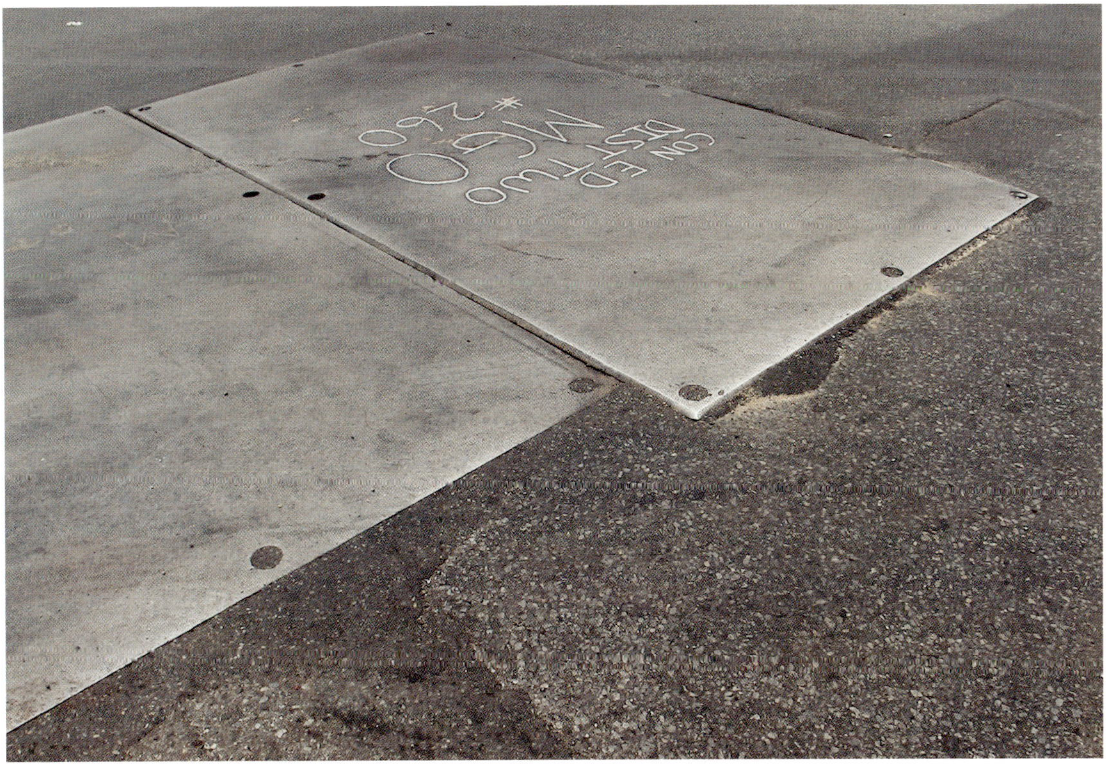

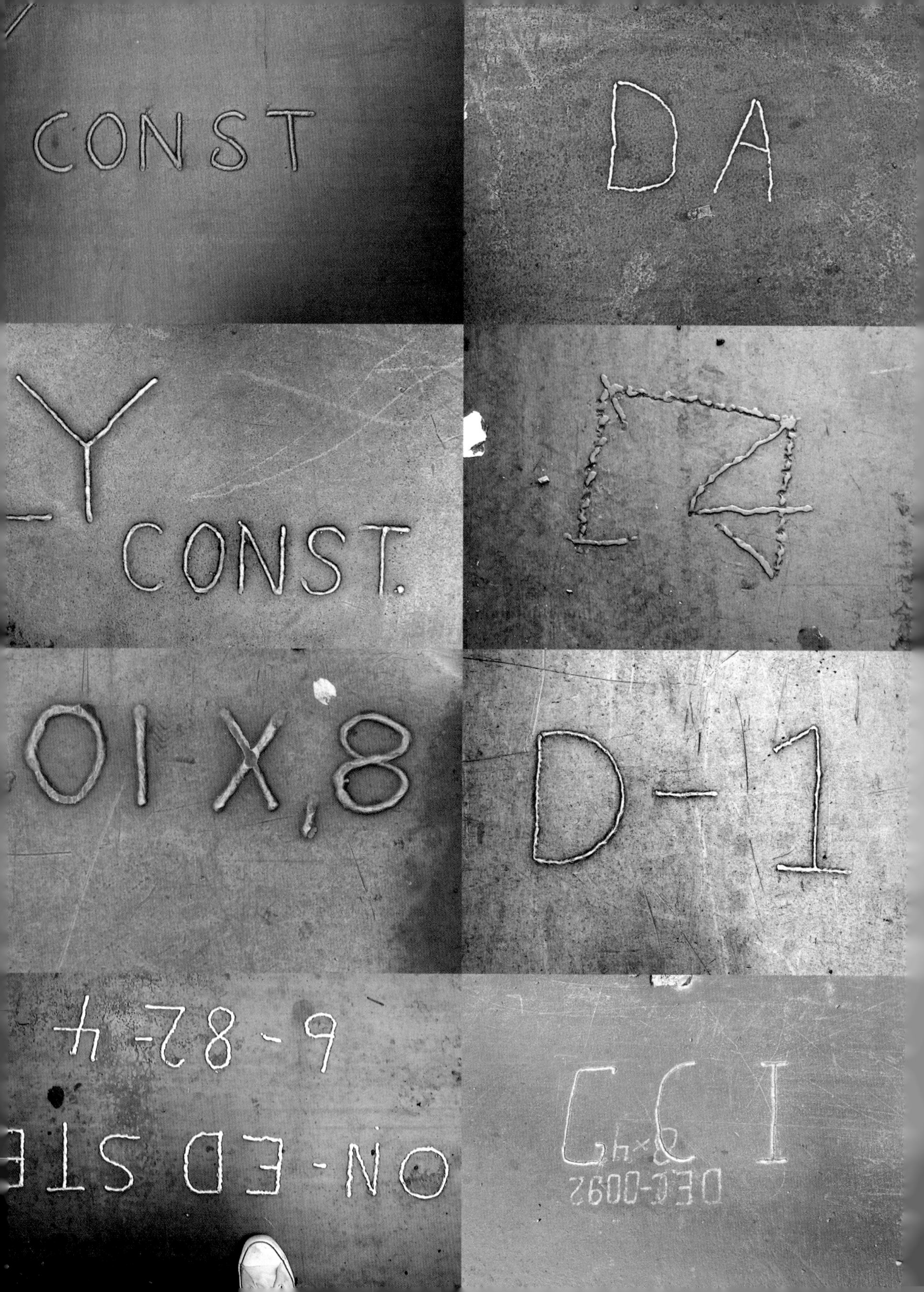

CONST

DA

Y
CONST.

01 X,8

D-1

6-82-4

ON-ED STE

G G I

8×49

DEC-0092

F.I.
74

MGO
238

CON ED
DIST TWO
MGO
#260

AF

MGO
D 1

STEAM

T & D

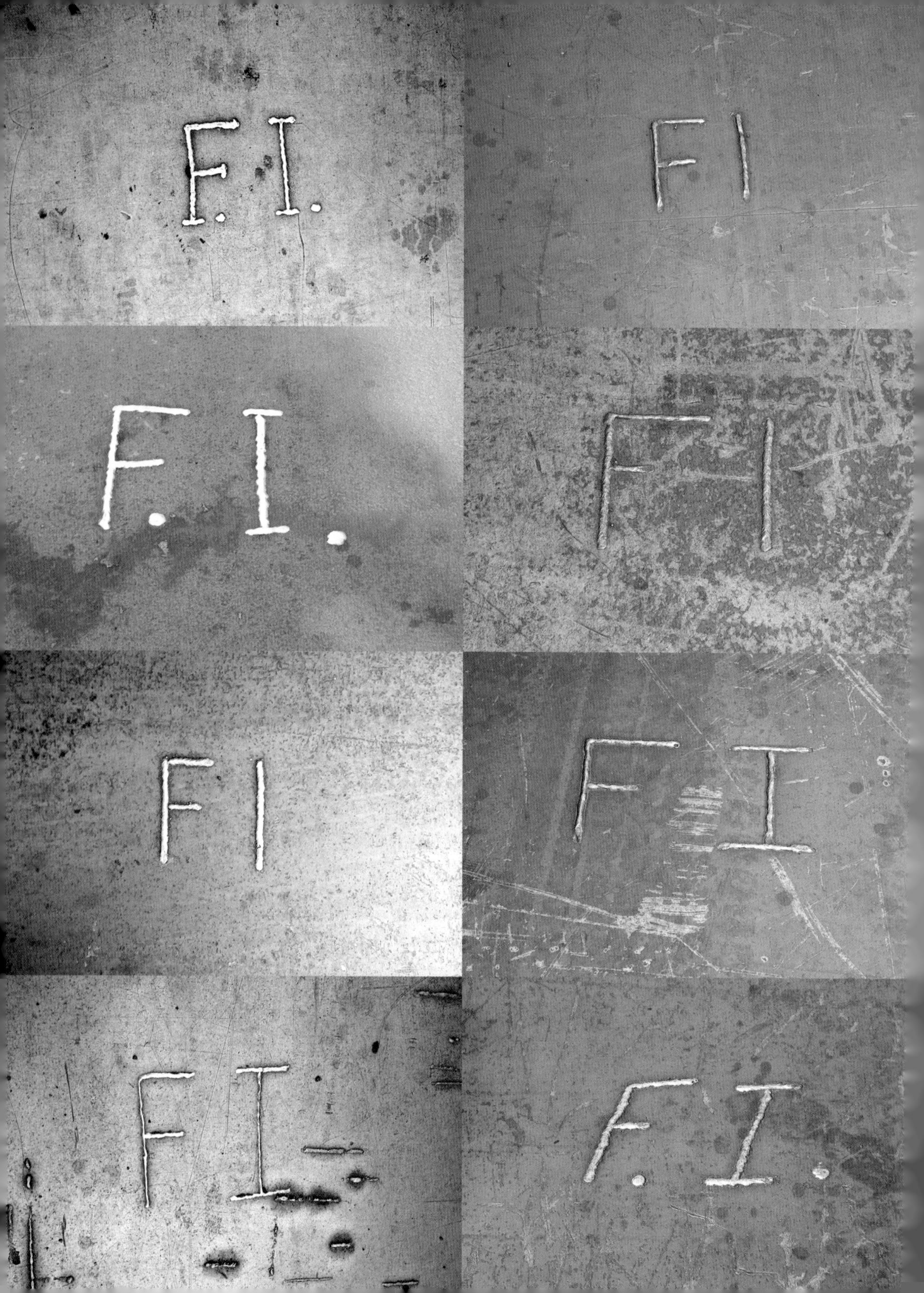
F.I.
FI
F.I.
FI
FI
FI
FI
F.I.

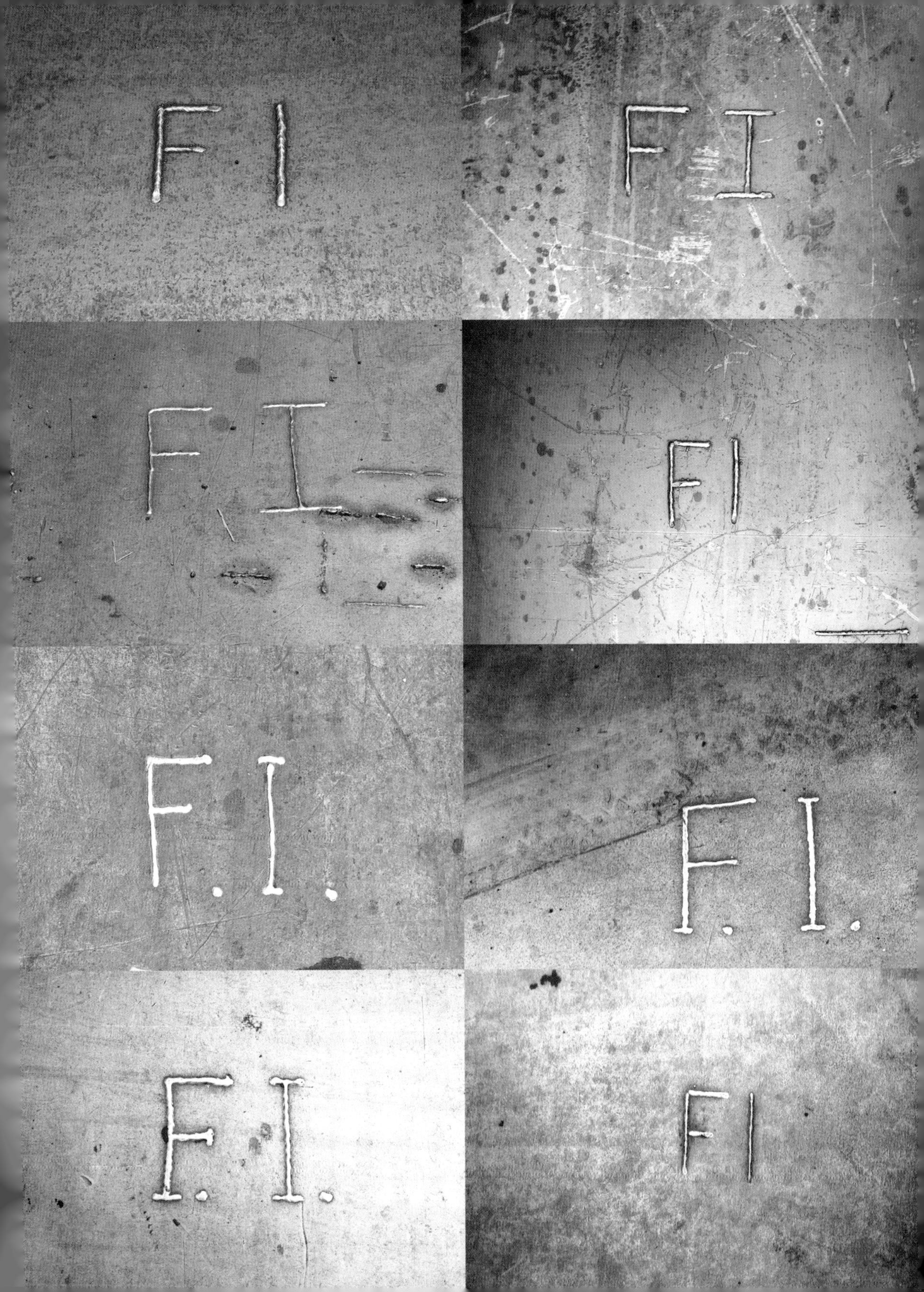
F I
F I
F I
F I
F. I.
F. I.
F. I.
F I

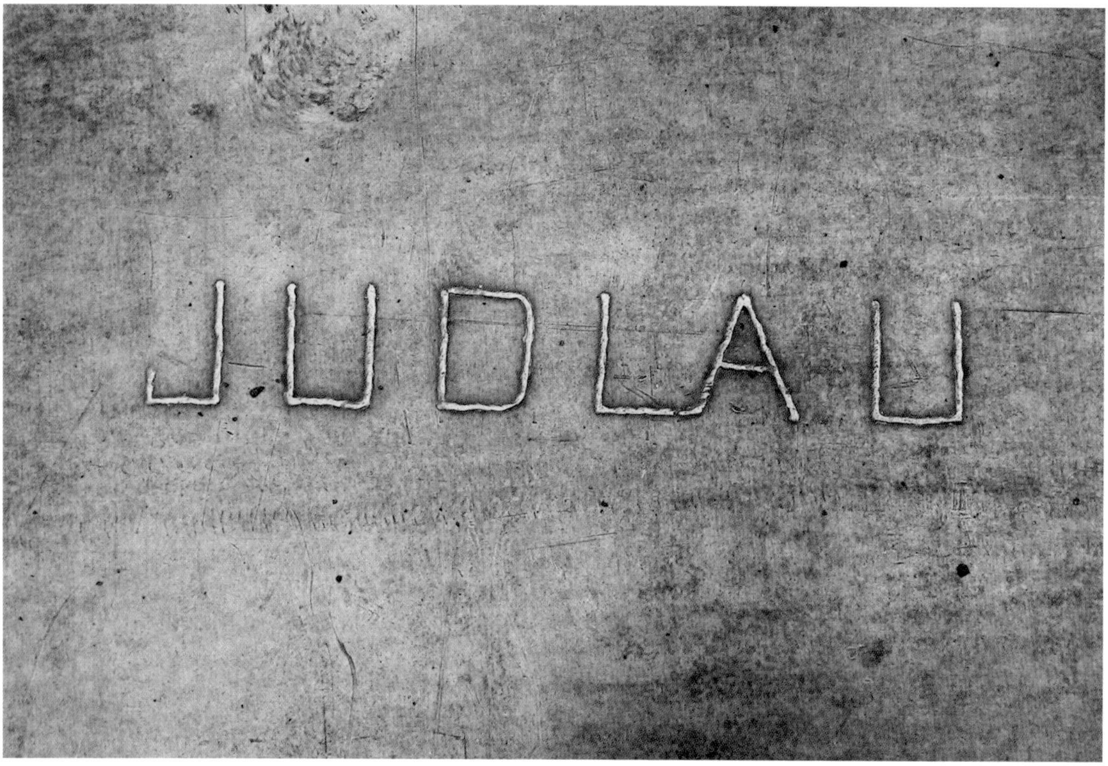

JUDLAU

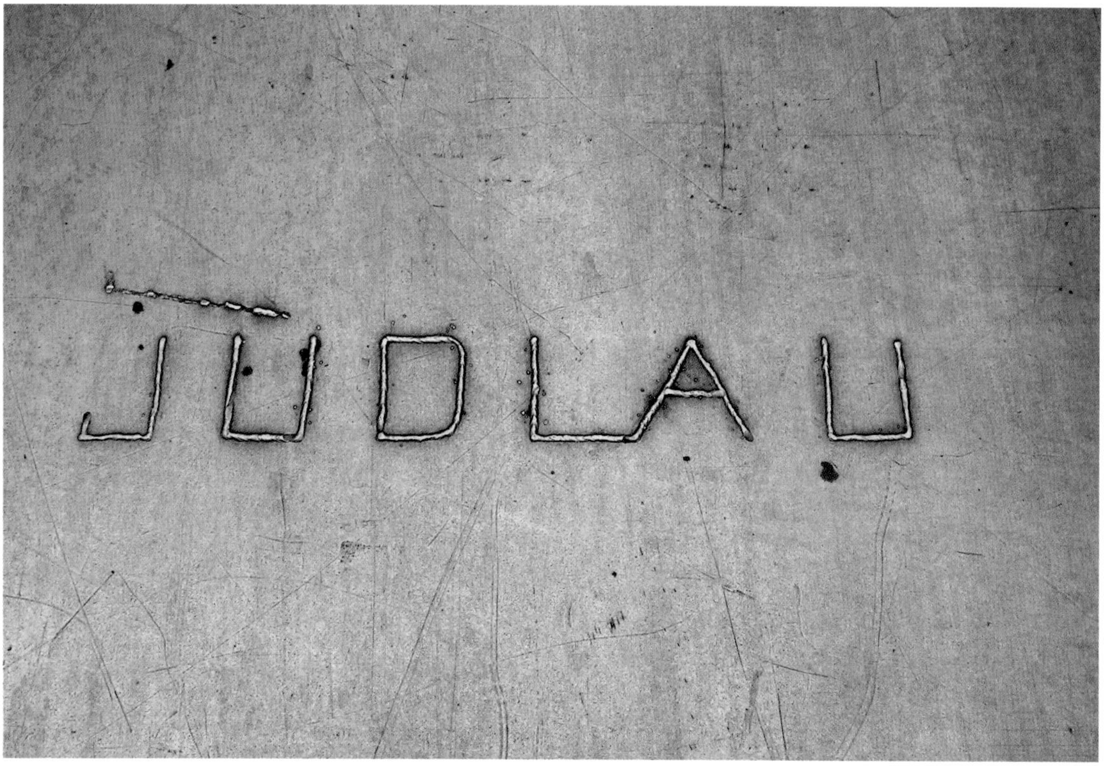

JUDLAU

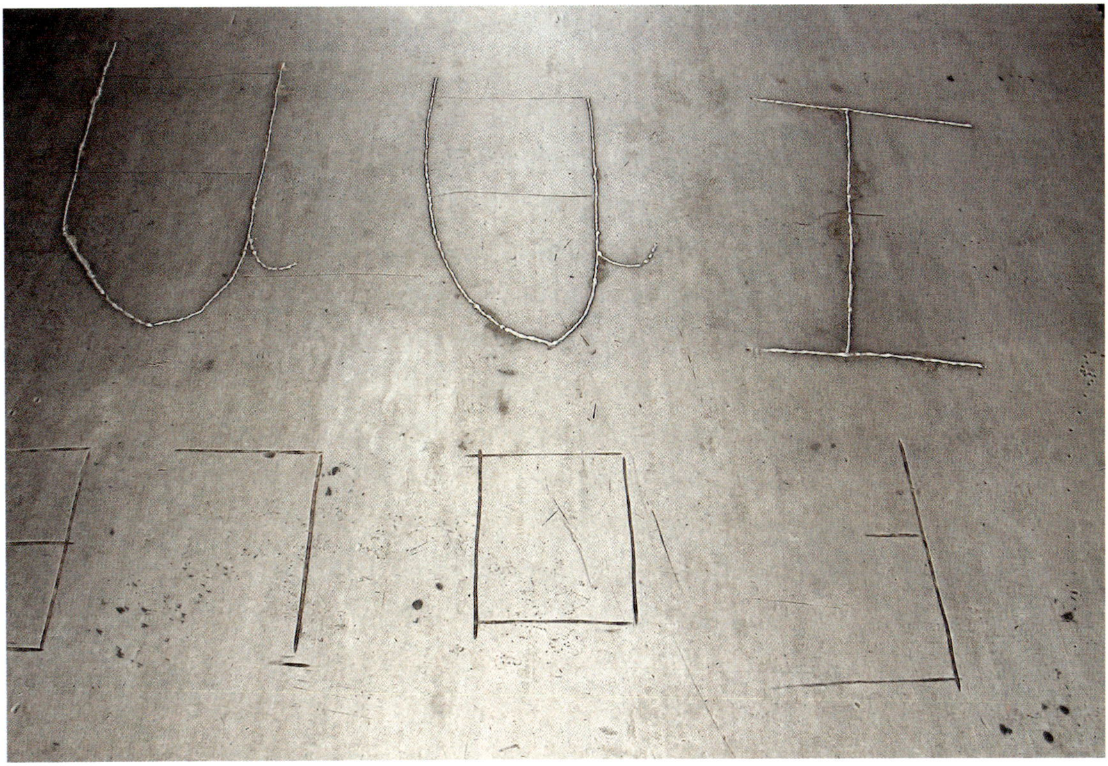

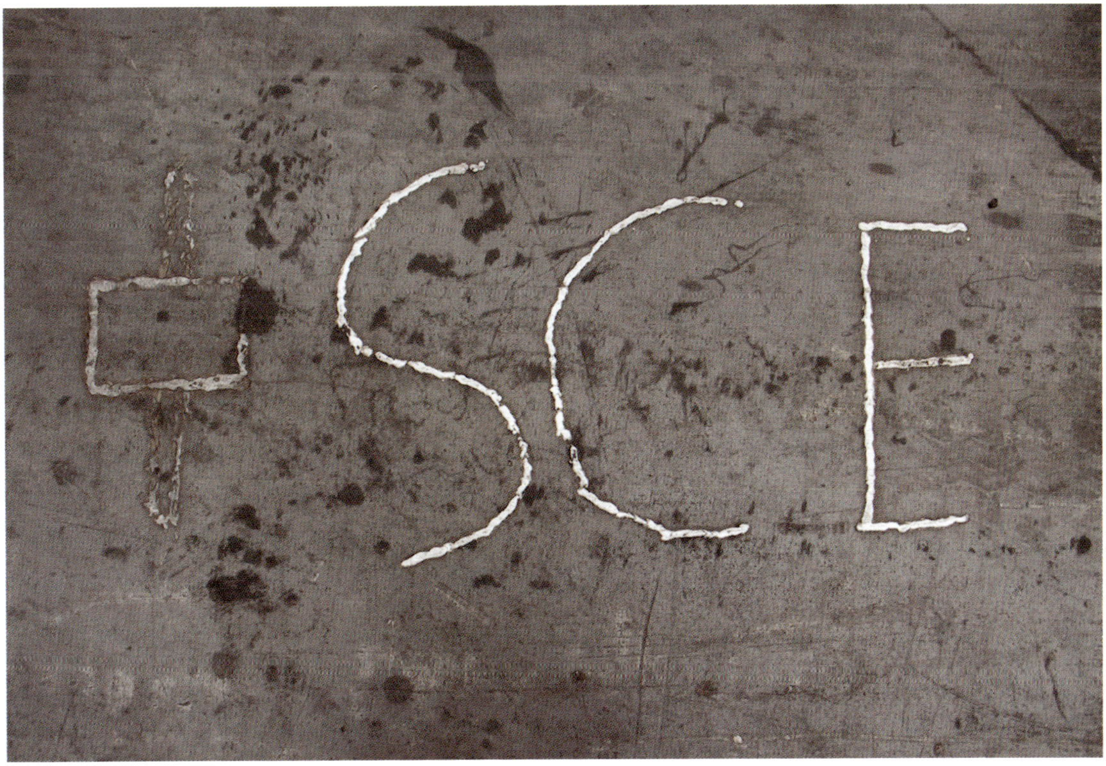

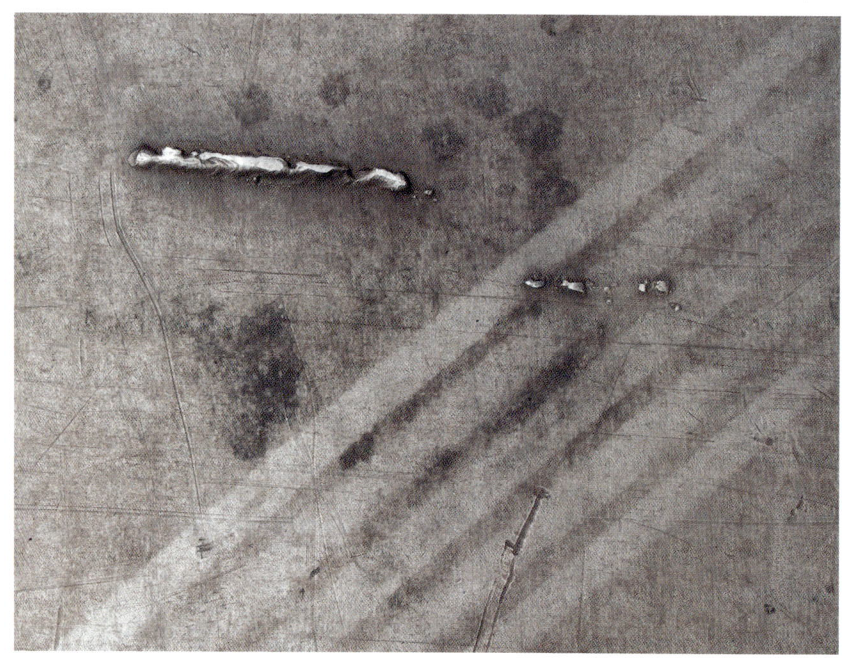

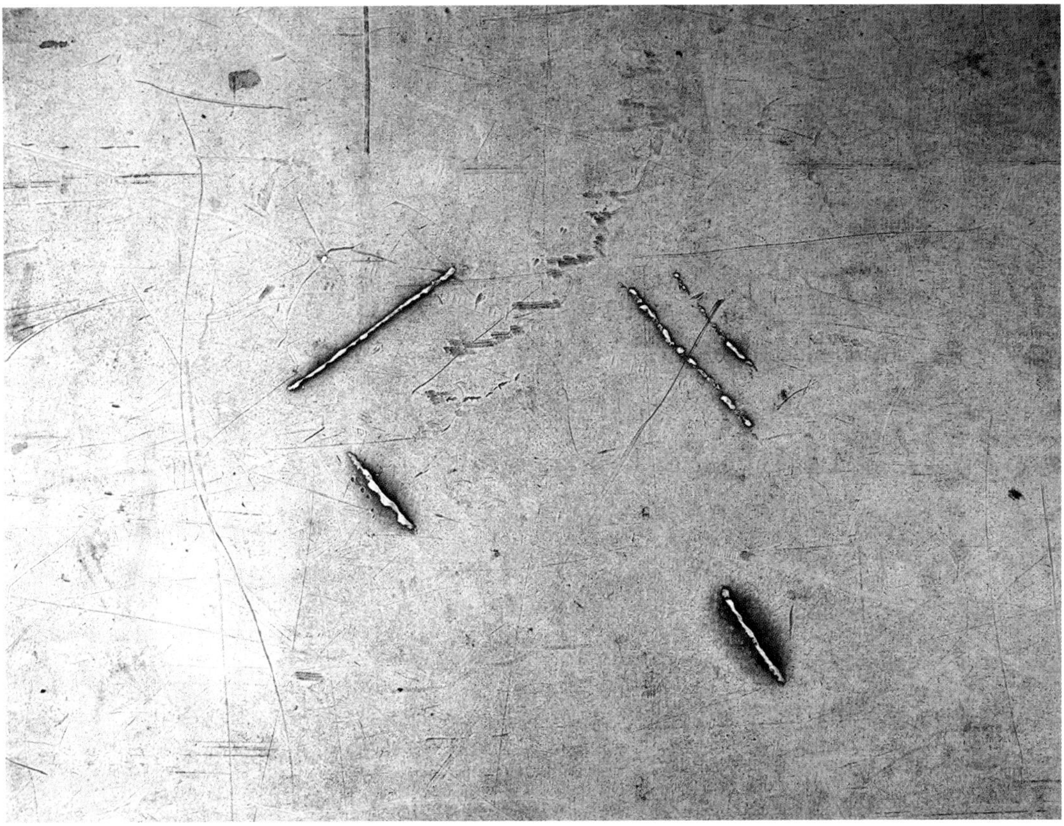

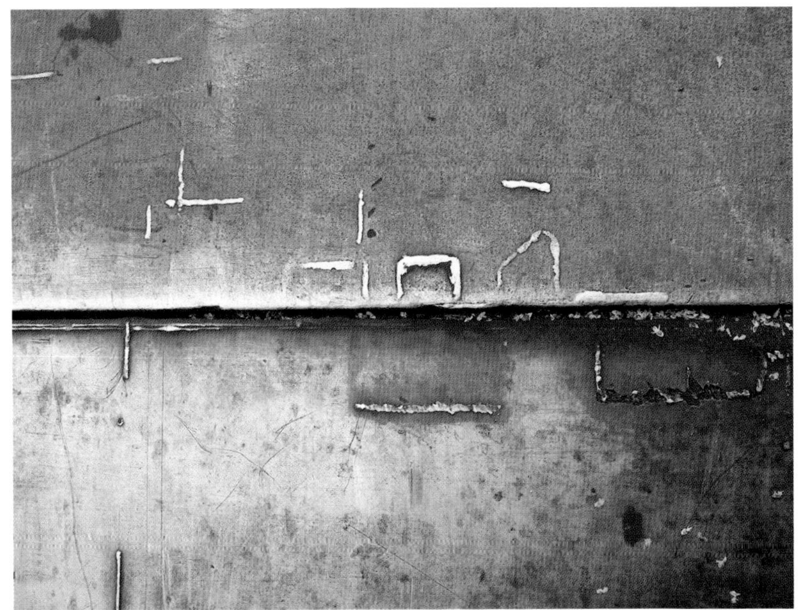

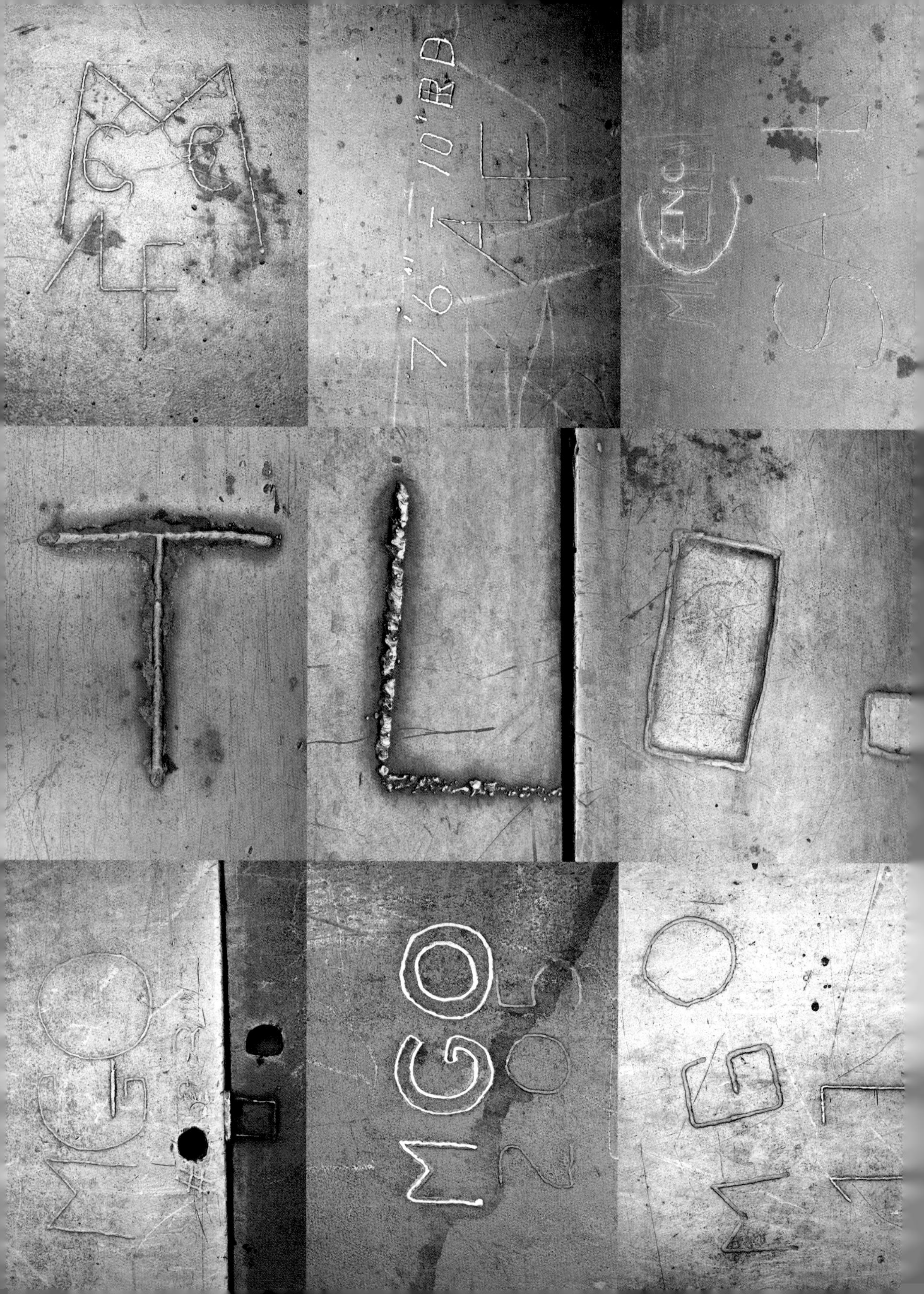

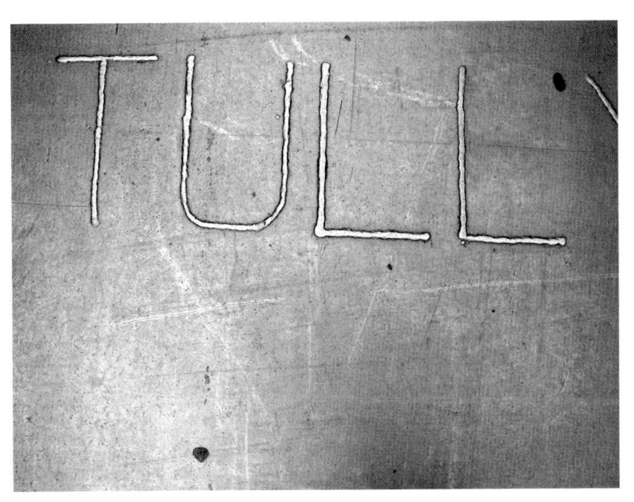
TULL
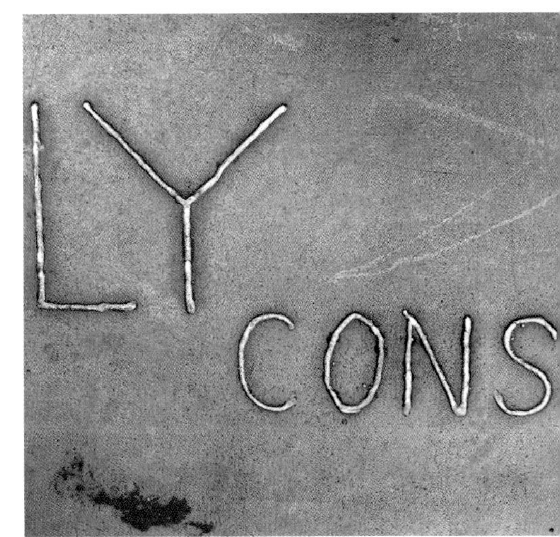
LY
CONS

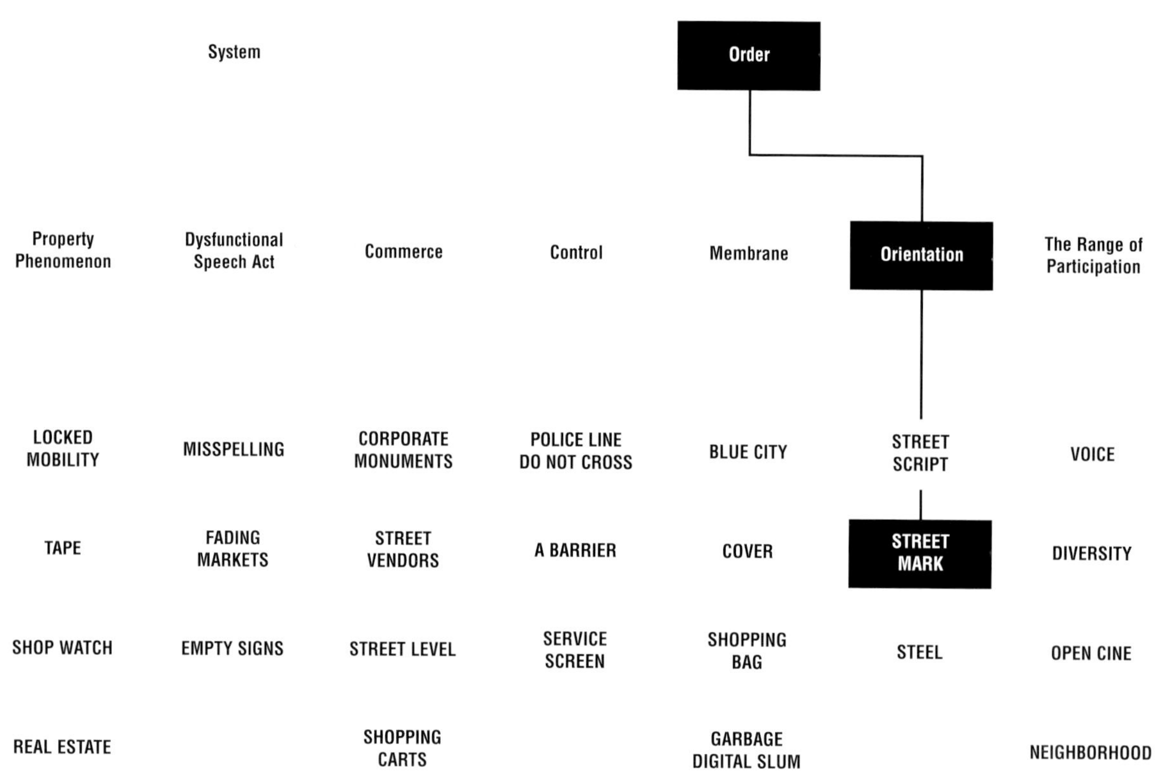
System
Order
Property Phenomenon
Dysfunctional Speech Act
Commerce
Control
Membrane
Orientation
The Range of Participation
LOCKED MOBILITY
MISSPELLING
CORPORATE MONUMENTS
POLICE LINE DO NOT CROSS
BLUE CITY
STREET SCRIPT
VOICE
TAPE
FADING MARKETS
STREET VENDORS
A BARRIER
COVER
STREET MARK
DIVERSITY
SHOP WATCH
EMPTY SIGNS
STREET LEVEL
SERVICE SCREEN
SHOPPING BAG
STEEL
OPEN CINE
REAL ESTATE
SHOPPING CARTS
GARBAGE DIGITAL SLUM
NEIGHBORHOOD

Identity

Alternative Media

Habitual Reinterpretation

STREET MARK

Reading the Street

CAR DOOR

PUBLIC CHAIRS

LABELING.

PLASTIC CRATES

POLE POST

STANDPIPES

PRAY JESUS

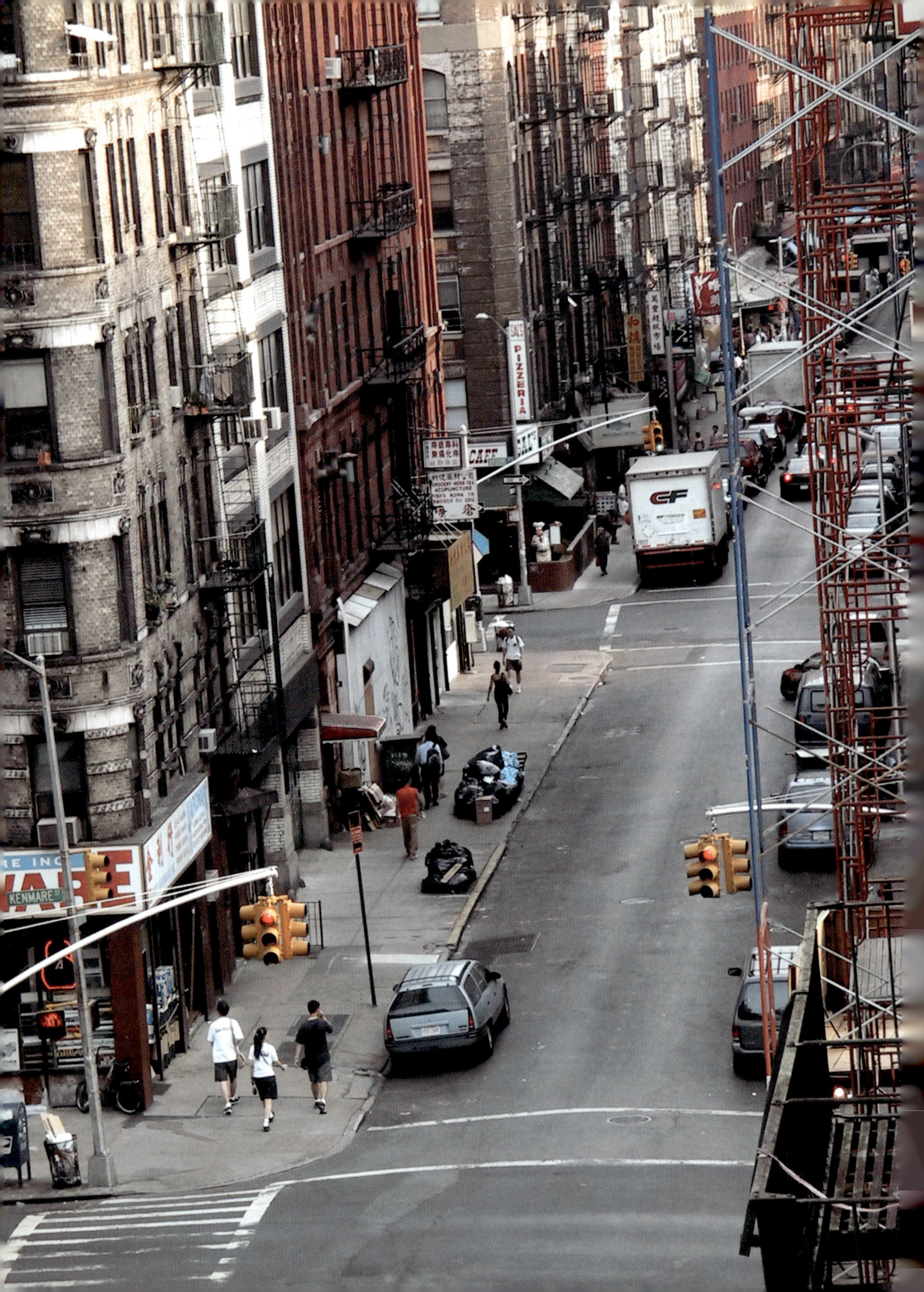
PIZZERIA
CAFE
CF
KENMARE

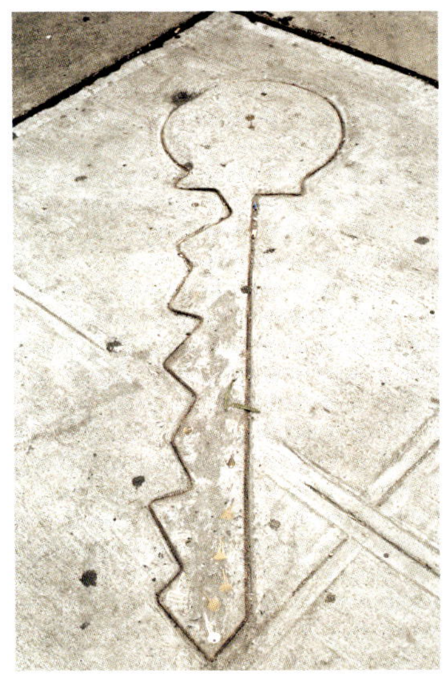

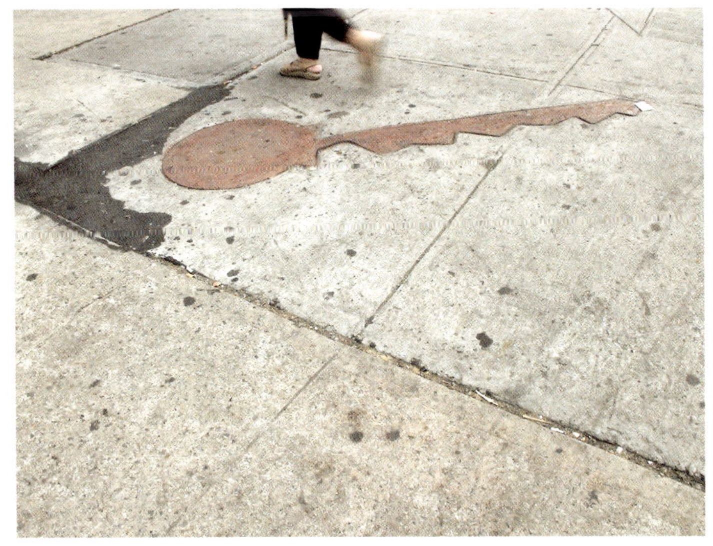

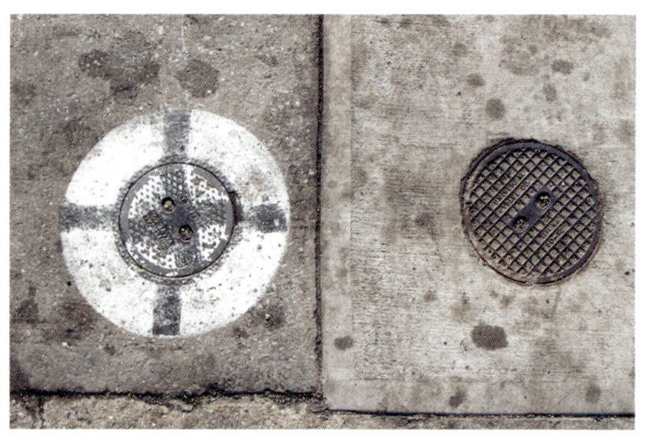
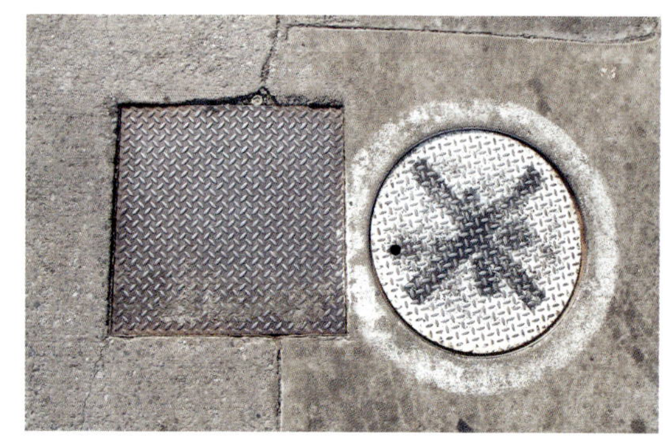
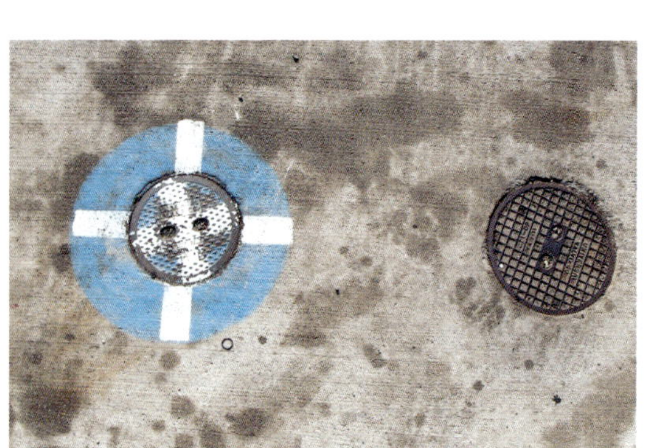
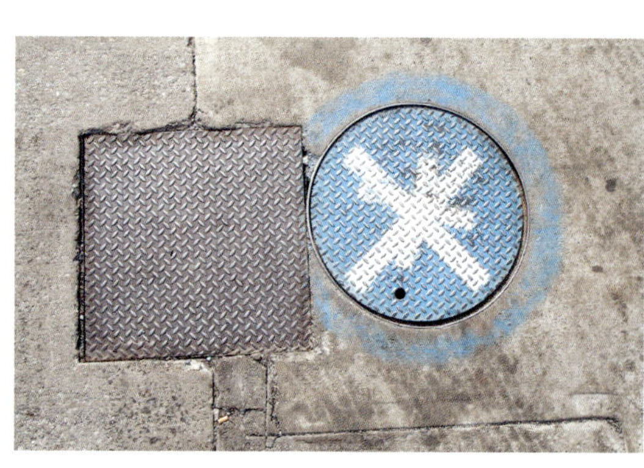
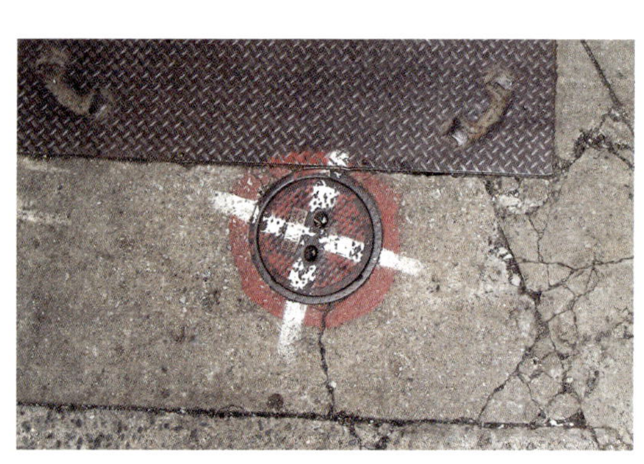
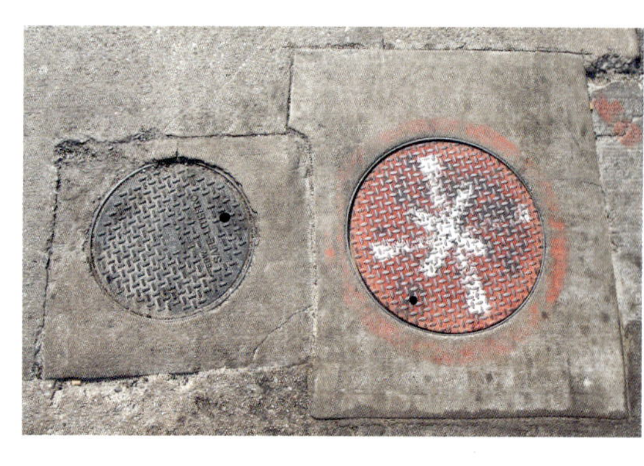
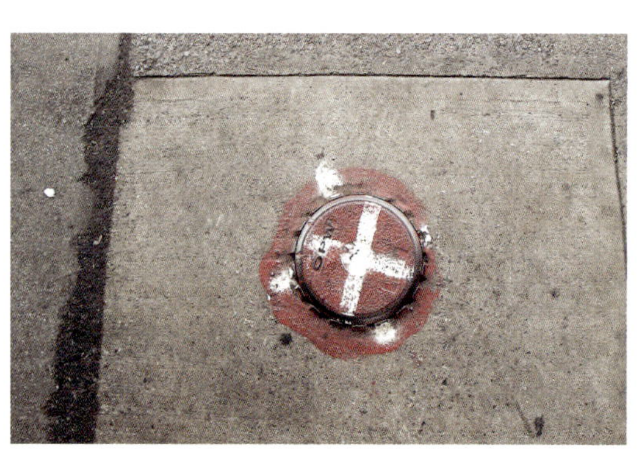
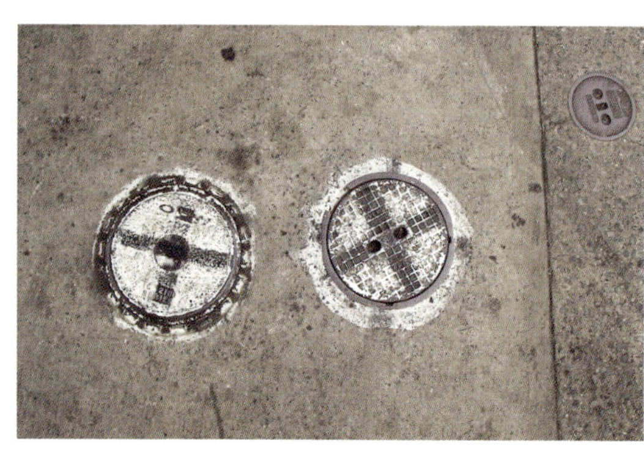

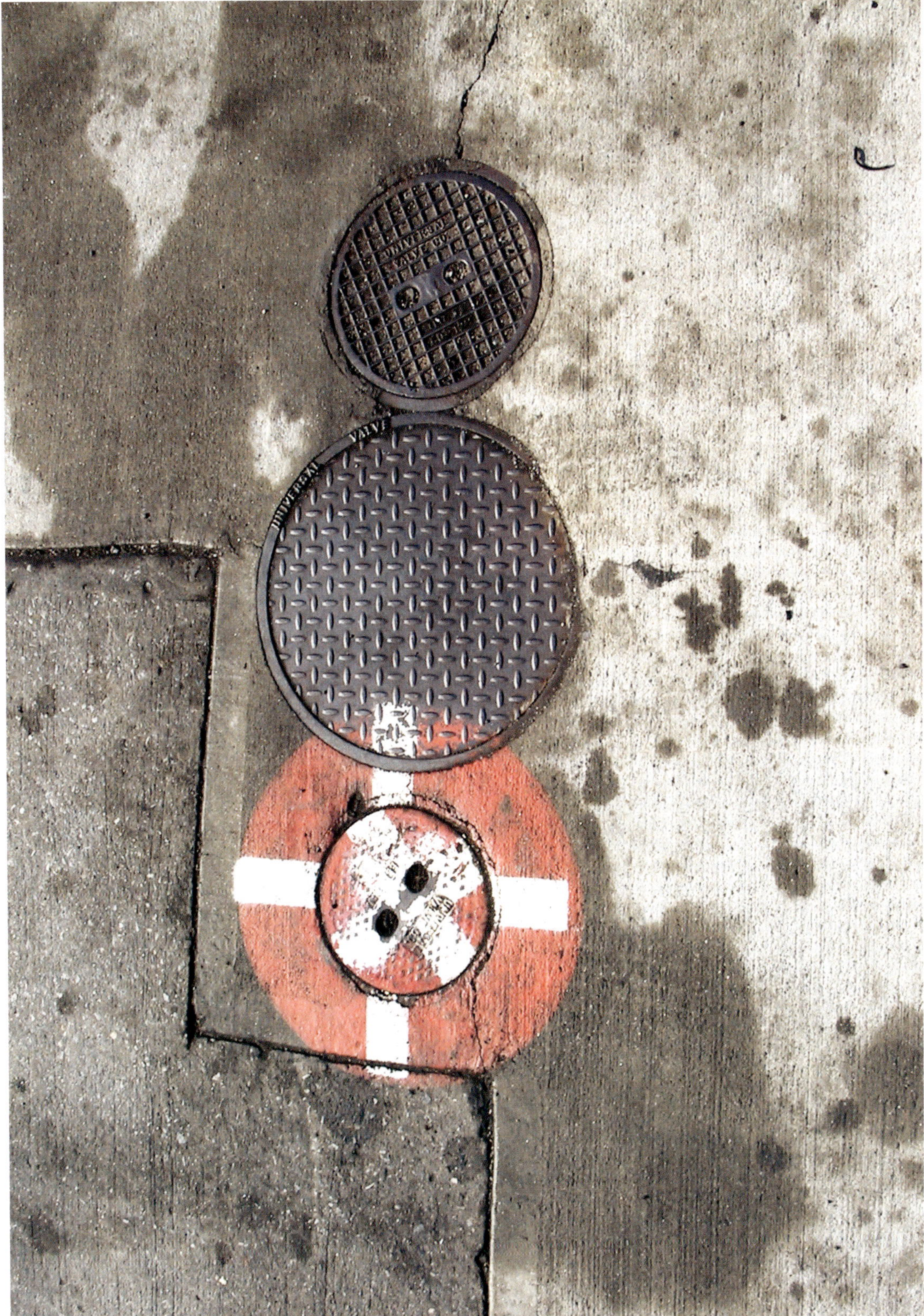
UNIVERSAL VALVE

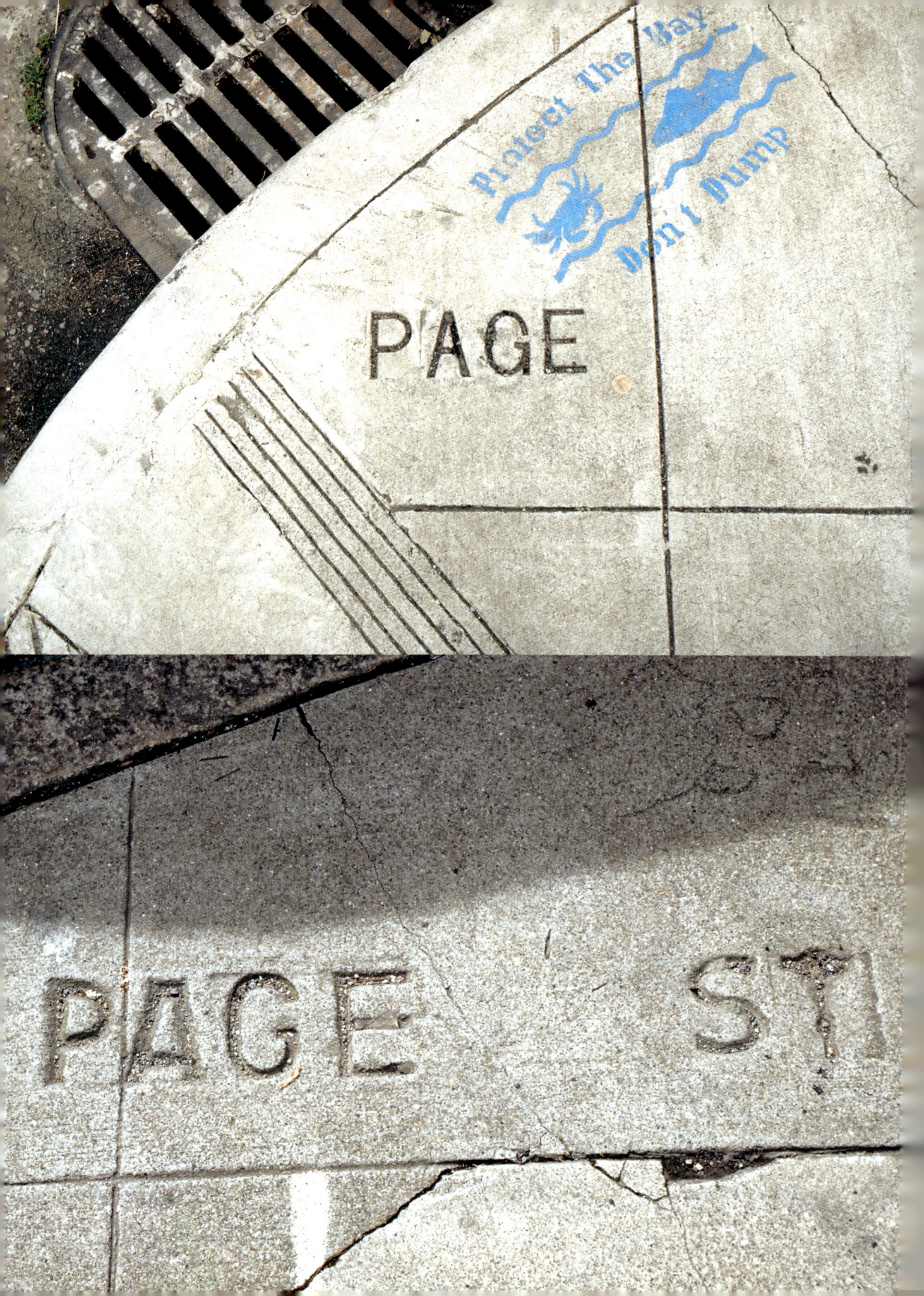
Protect The Bay
Don't Dump
PAGE
PAGE ST

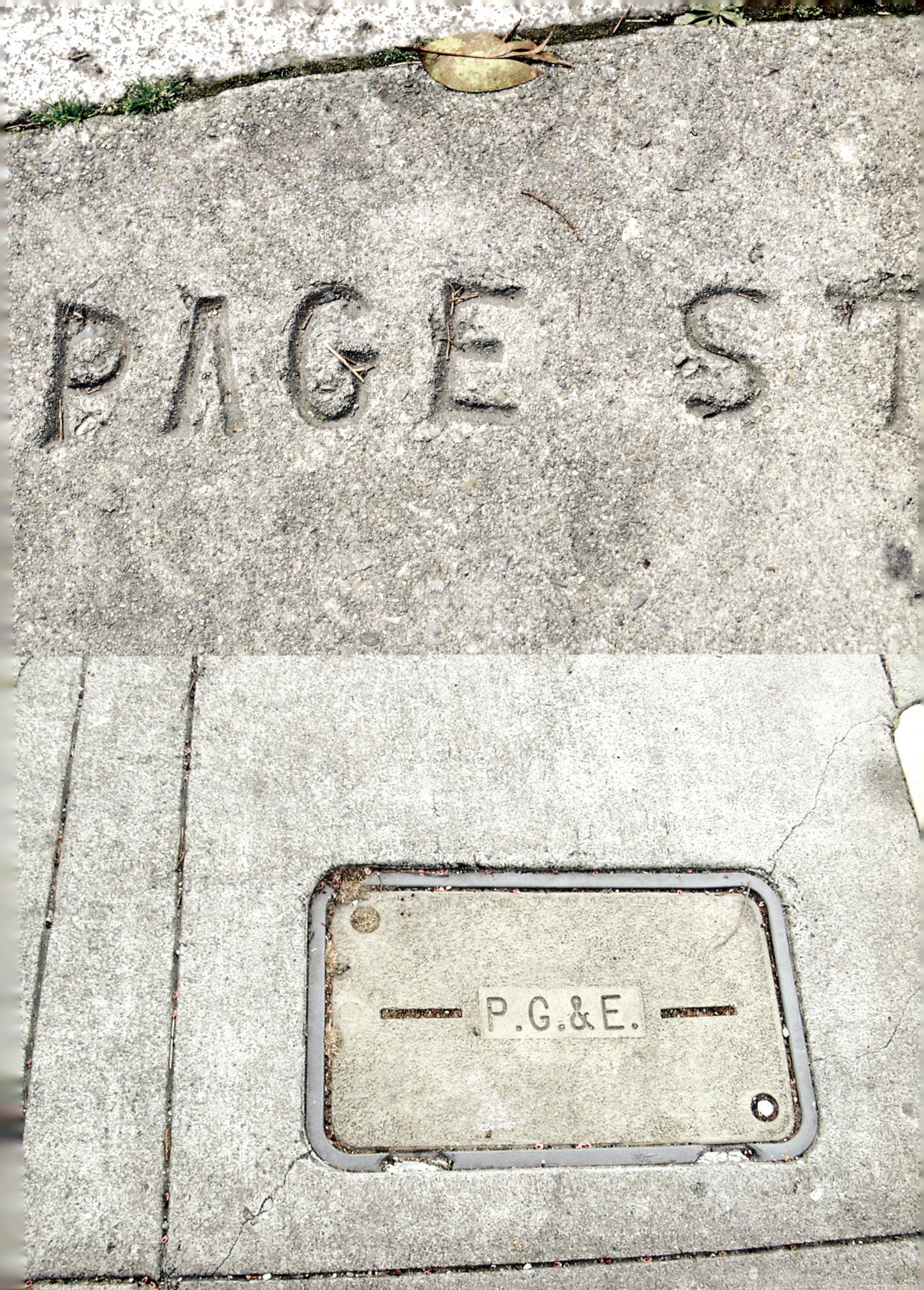
PAGE ST
P.G.&E.

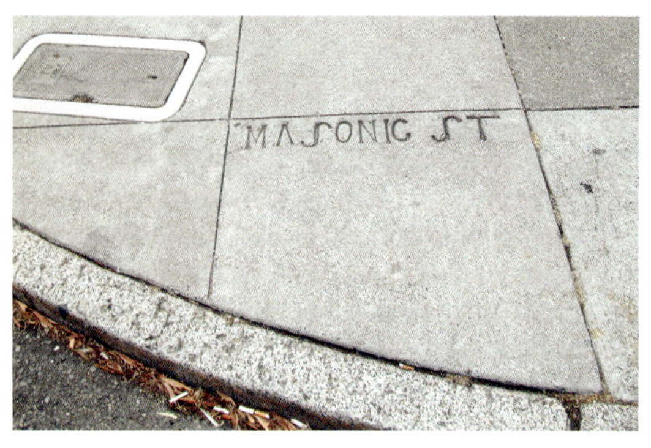
MASONIC ST

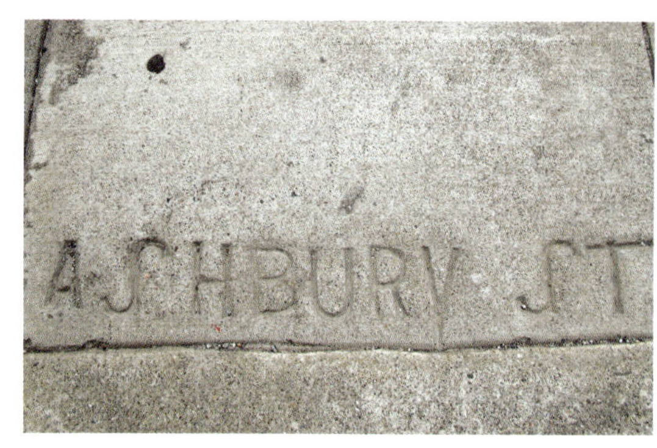
ASHBURY ST

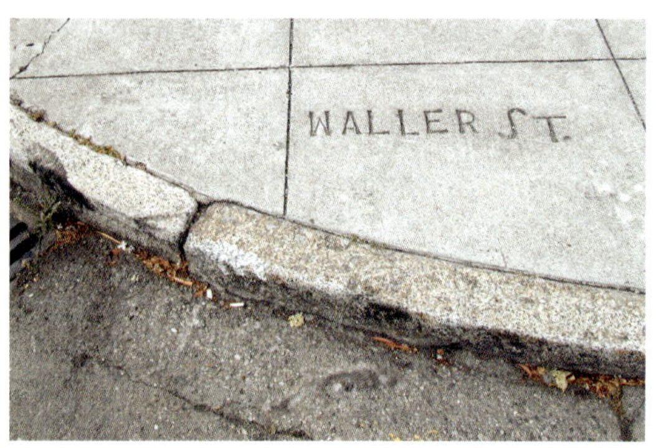
WALLER ST.

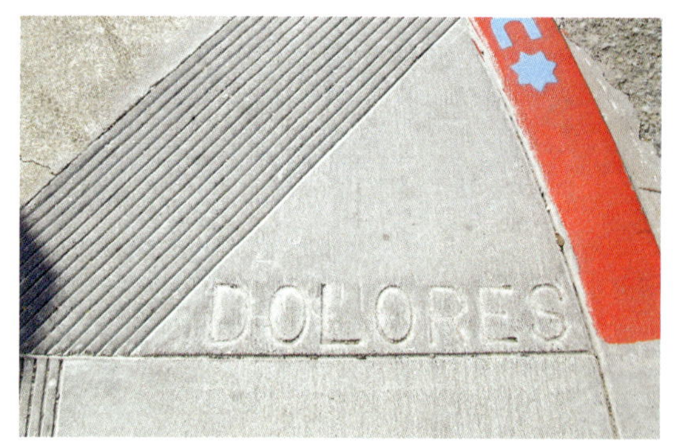
DOLORES

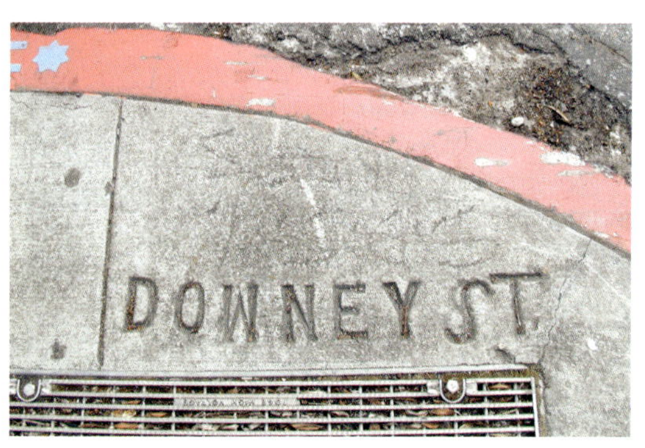
DOWNEY ST

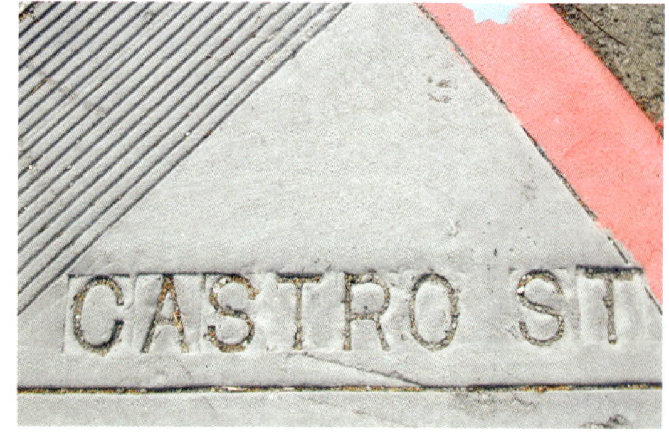
CASTRO ST

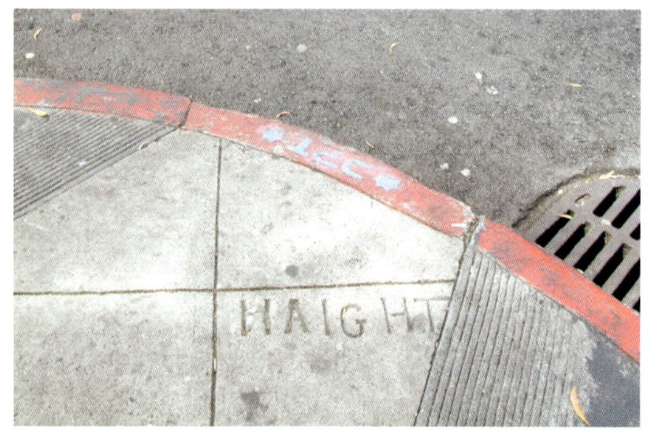
HAIGHT

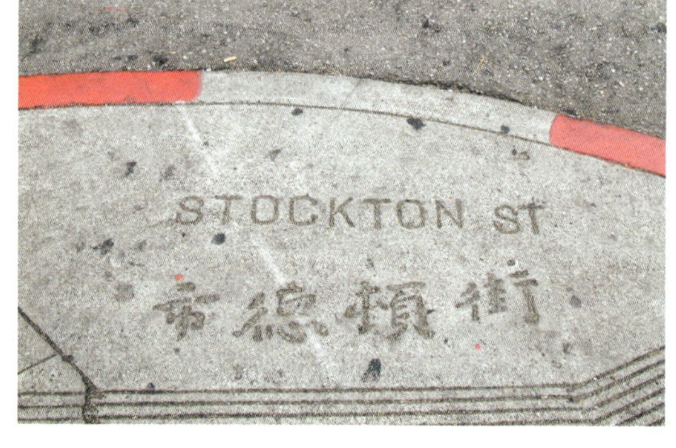
STOCKTON ST

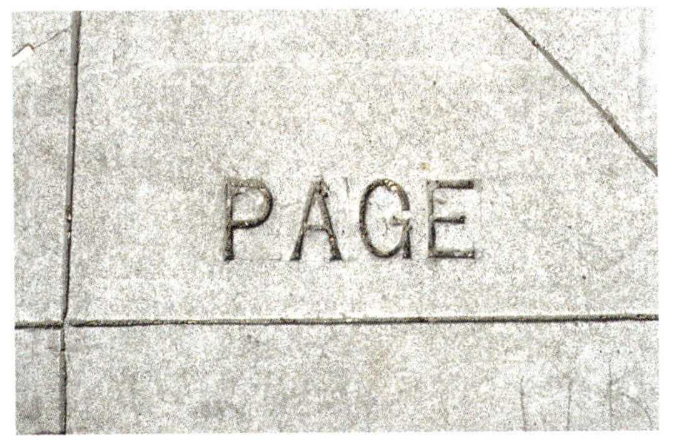
PAGE

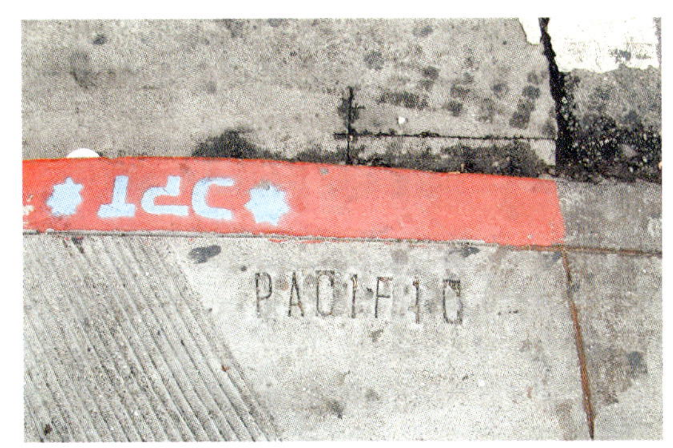
PACIFIC

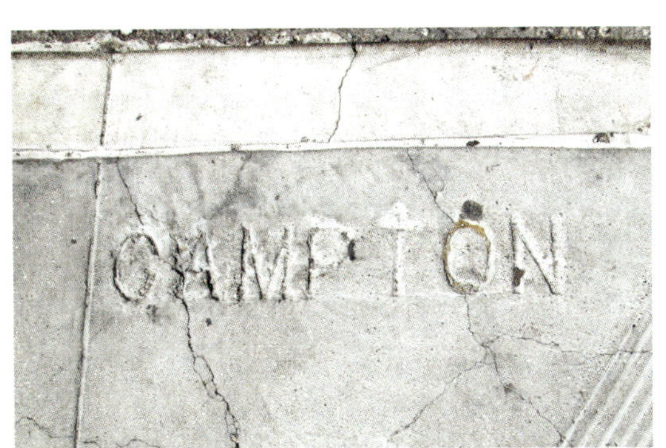
CAMPTON

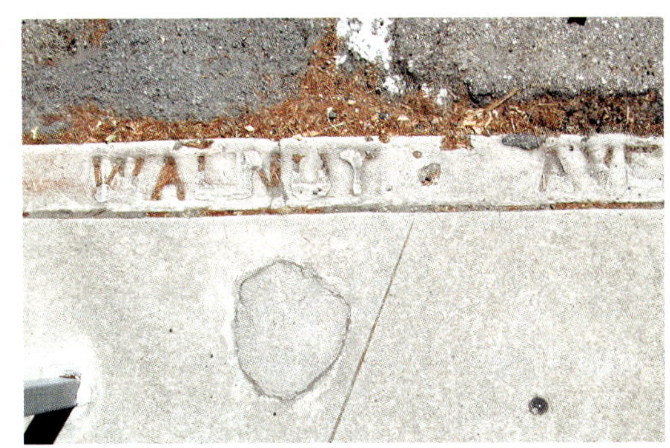
WALNUT AVE

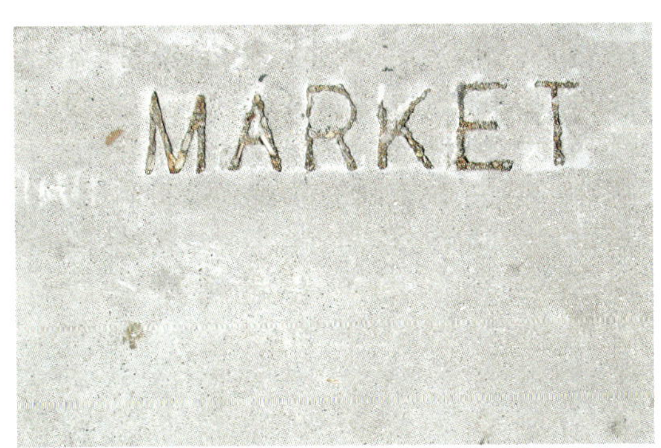
MARKET

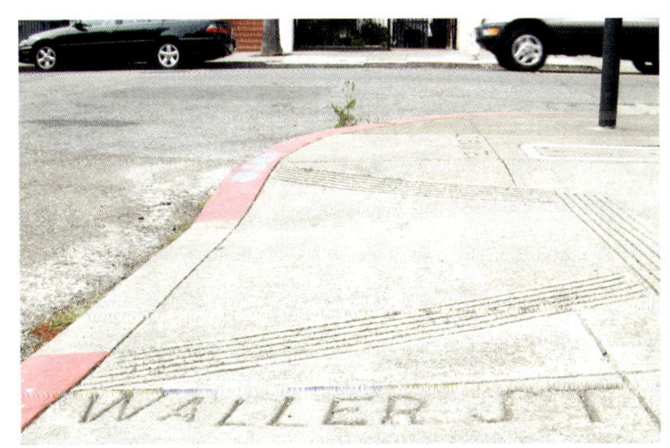
WALLER ST

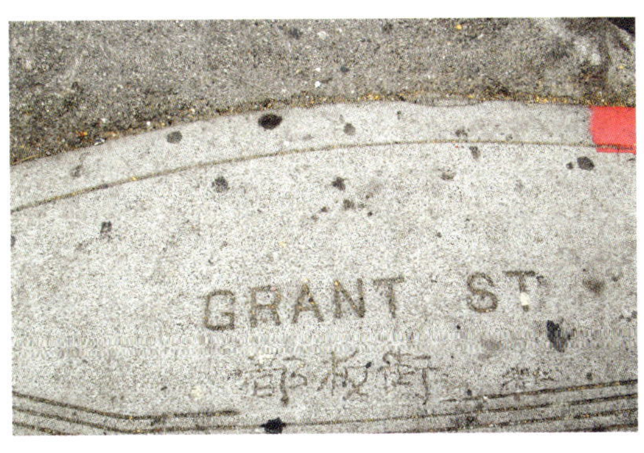
GRANT ST
都板街

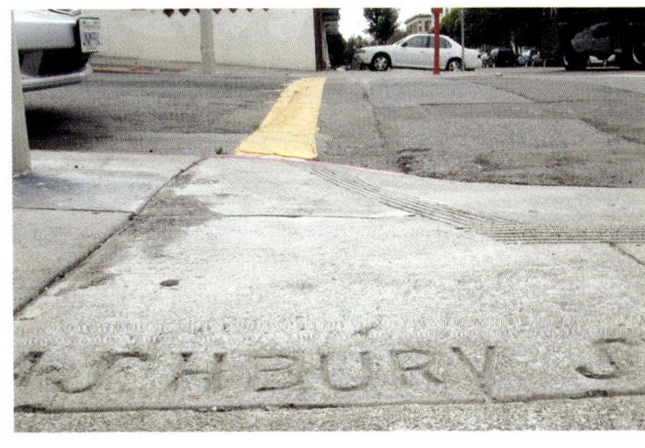

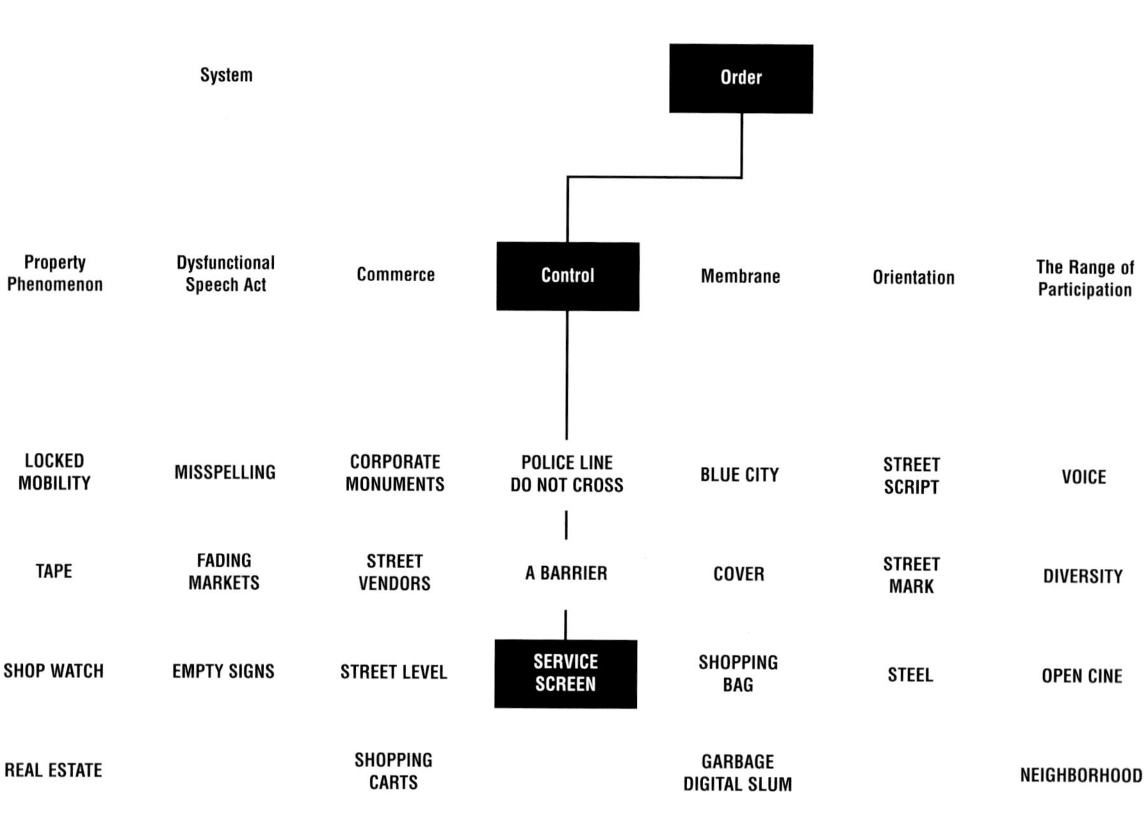
System
Order
Property Phenomenon
Dysfunctional Speech Act
Commerce
Control
Membrane
Orientation
The Range of Participation
LOCKED MOBILITY
MISSPELLING
CORPORATE MONUMENTS
POLICE LINE DO NOT CROSS
BLUE CITY
STREET SCRIPT
VOICE
TAPE
FADING MARKETS
STREET VENDORS
A BARRIER
COVER
STREET MARK
DIVERSITY
SHOP WATCH
EMPTY SIGNS
STREET LEVEL
SERVICE SCREEN
SHOPPING BAG
STEEL
OPEN CINE
REAL ESTATE
SHOPPING CARTS
GARBAGE DIGITAL SLUM
NEIGHBORHOOD

Identity

Alternative Media

Habitual Reinterpretation

SERVICE SCREEN

Word in Private

CAR DOOR

PUBLIC CHAIRS

LABELING.

PLASTIC CRATES

POLE POST

STANDPIPES

PRAY JESUS

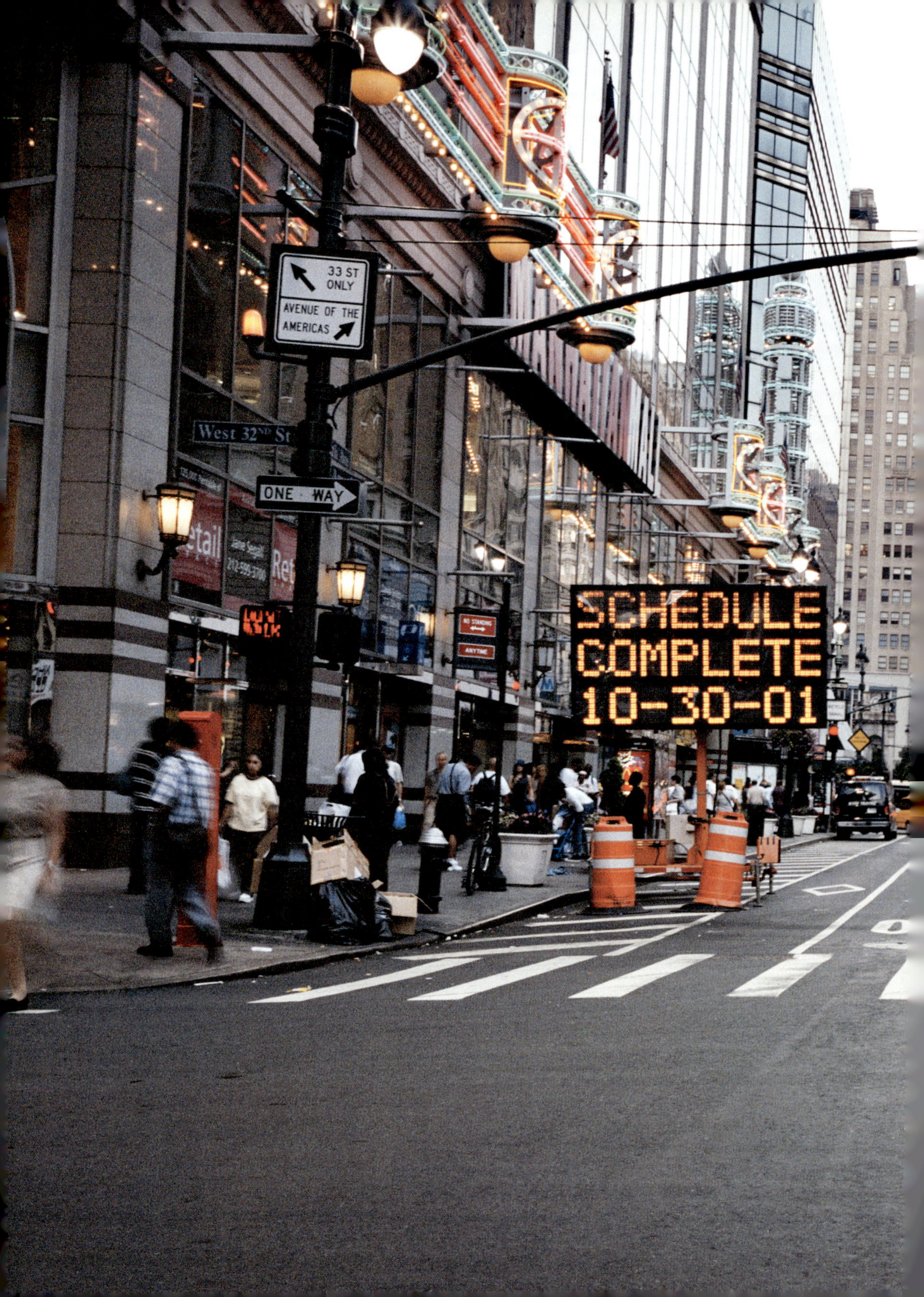
33 ST
ONLY
AVENUE OF THE
AMERICAS
West 32ND St
ONE WAY
SCHEDULE
COMPLETE
10-30-01

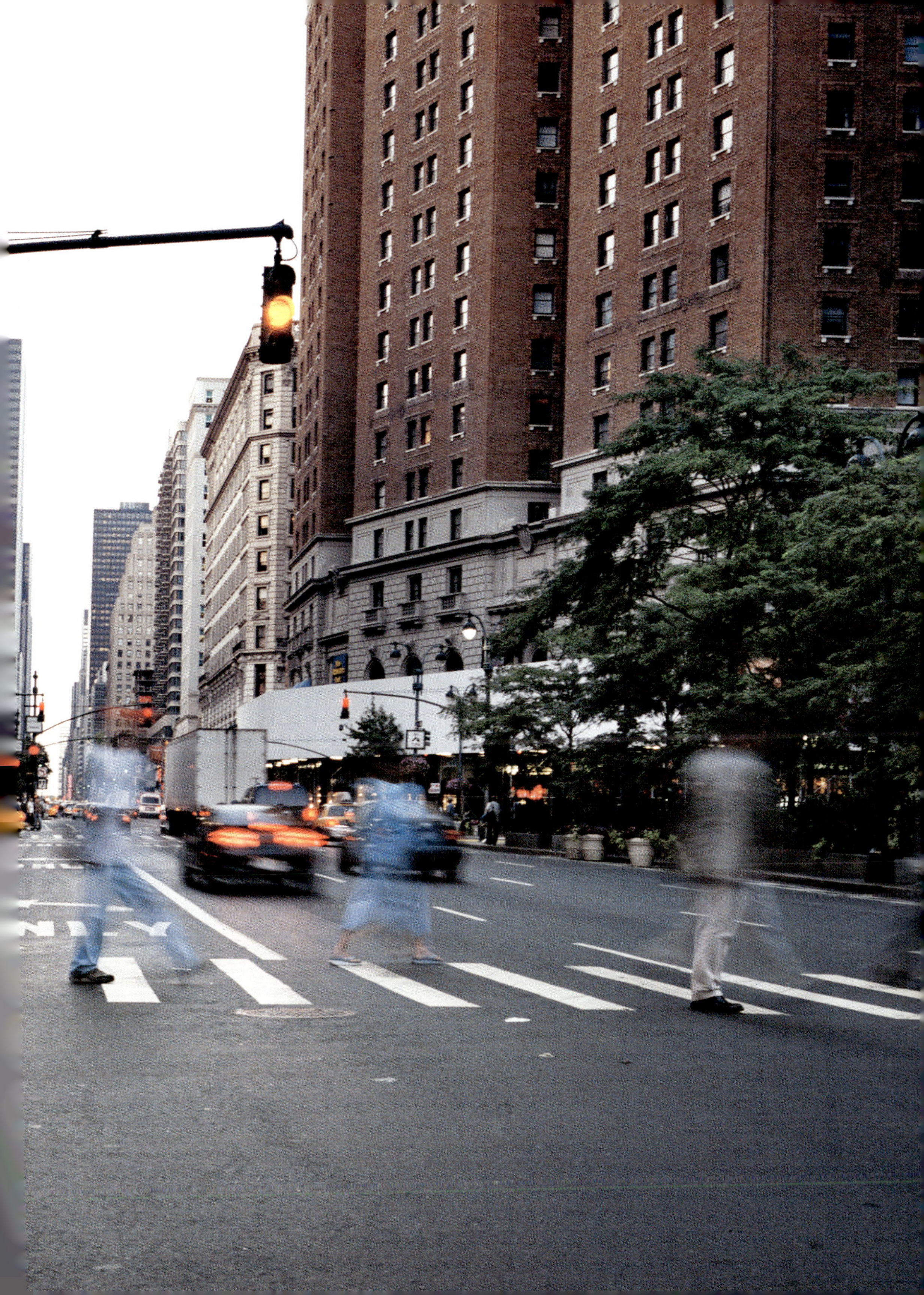

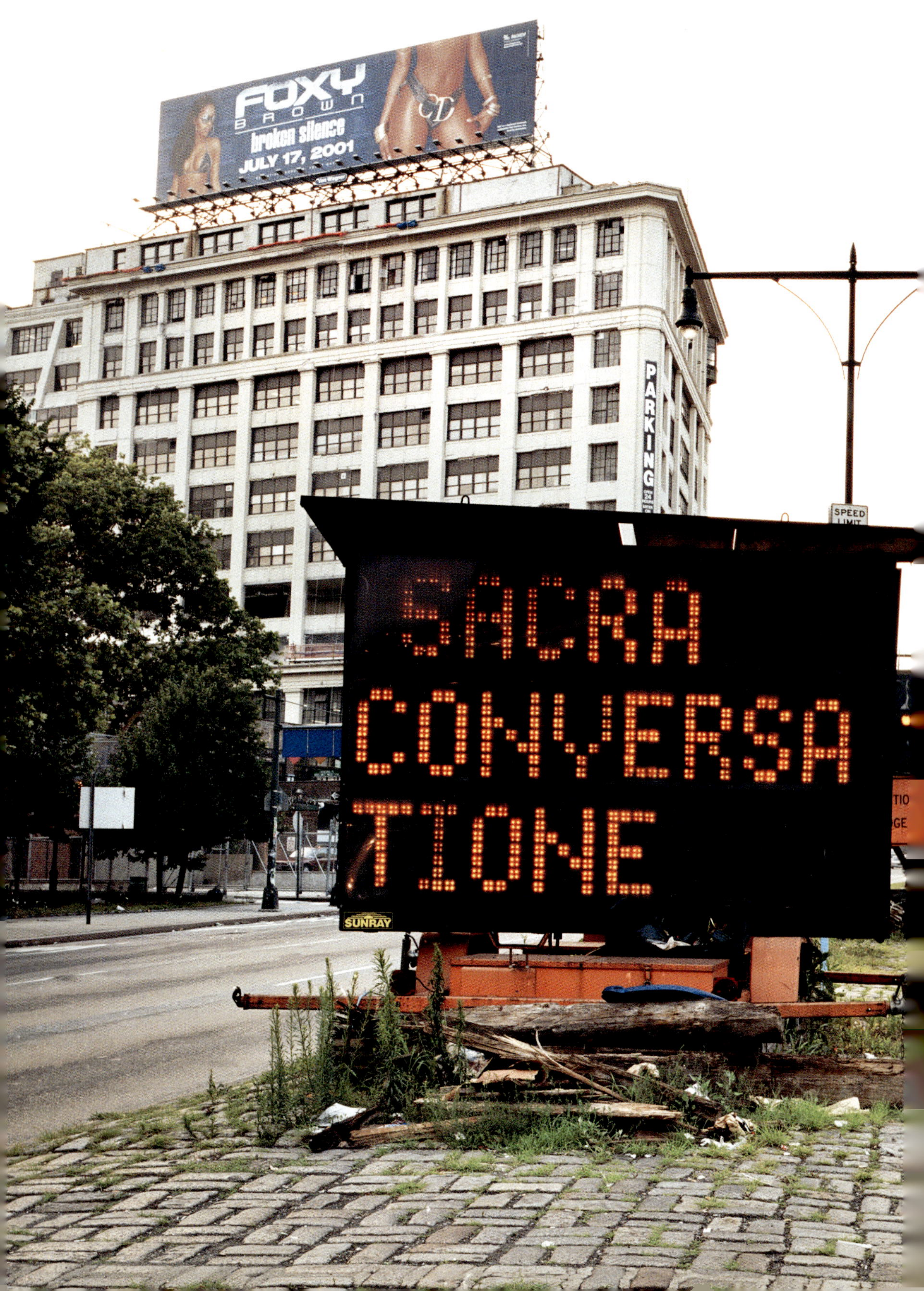
FOXY
BROWN
broken silence
JULY 17, 2001
PARKING
SACRA
CONVERSA
TIONE
SUNRAY
SPEED

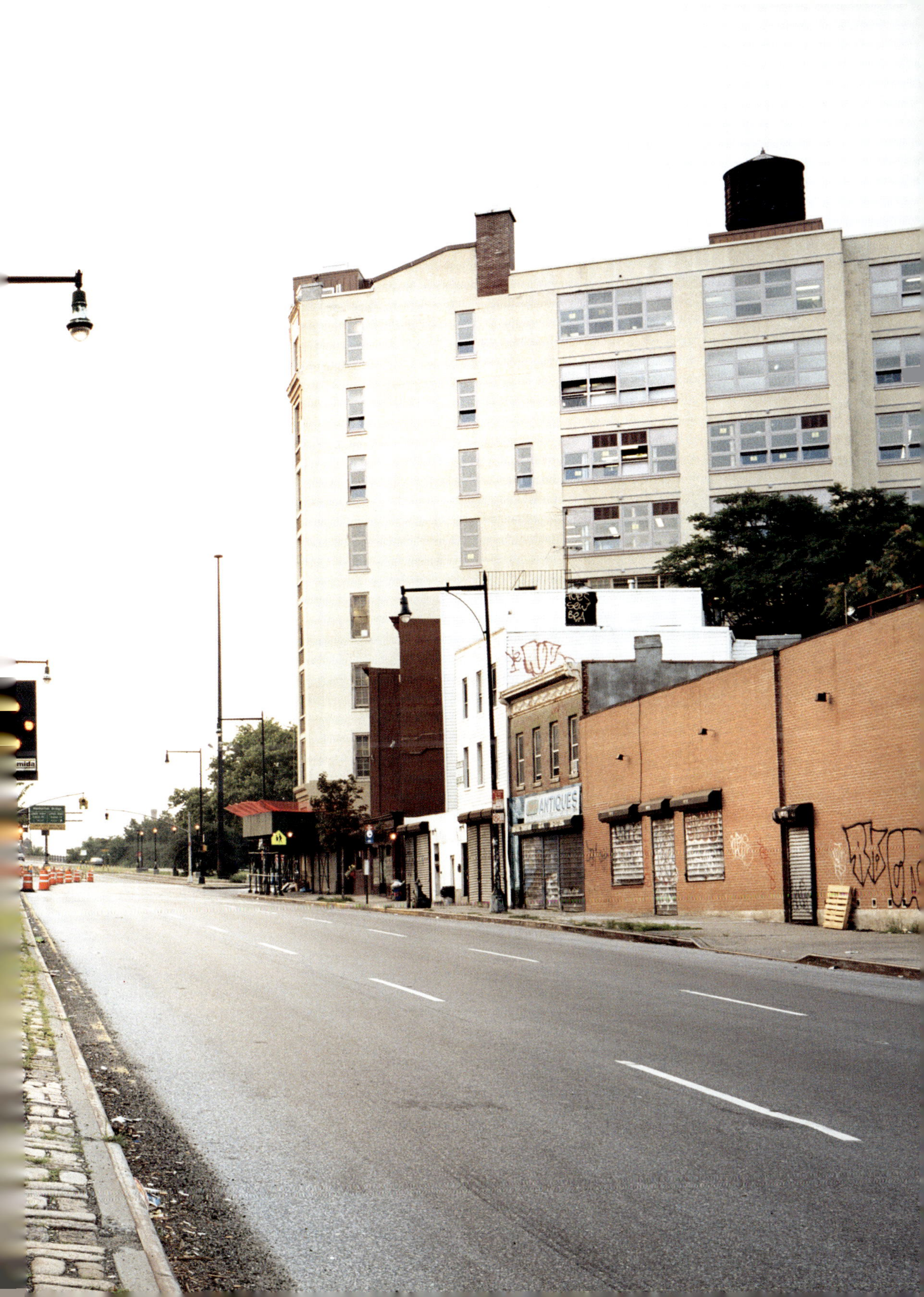
ANTIQUES

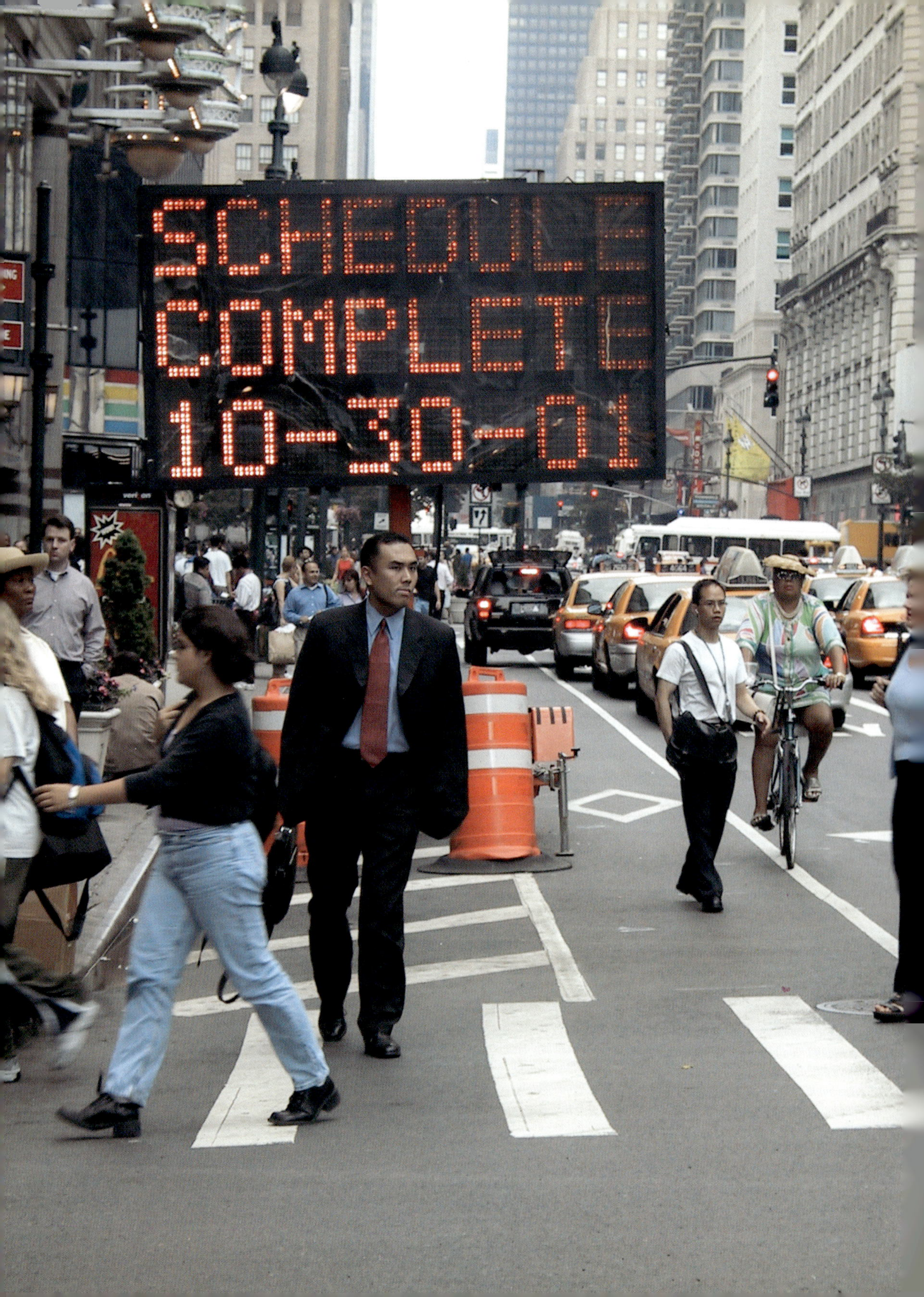
SCHEDULE
COMPLETE
10-30-01

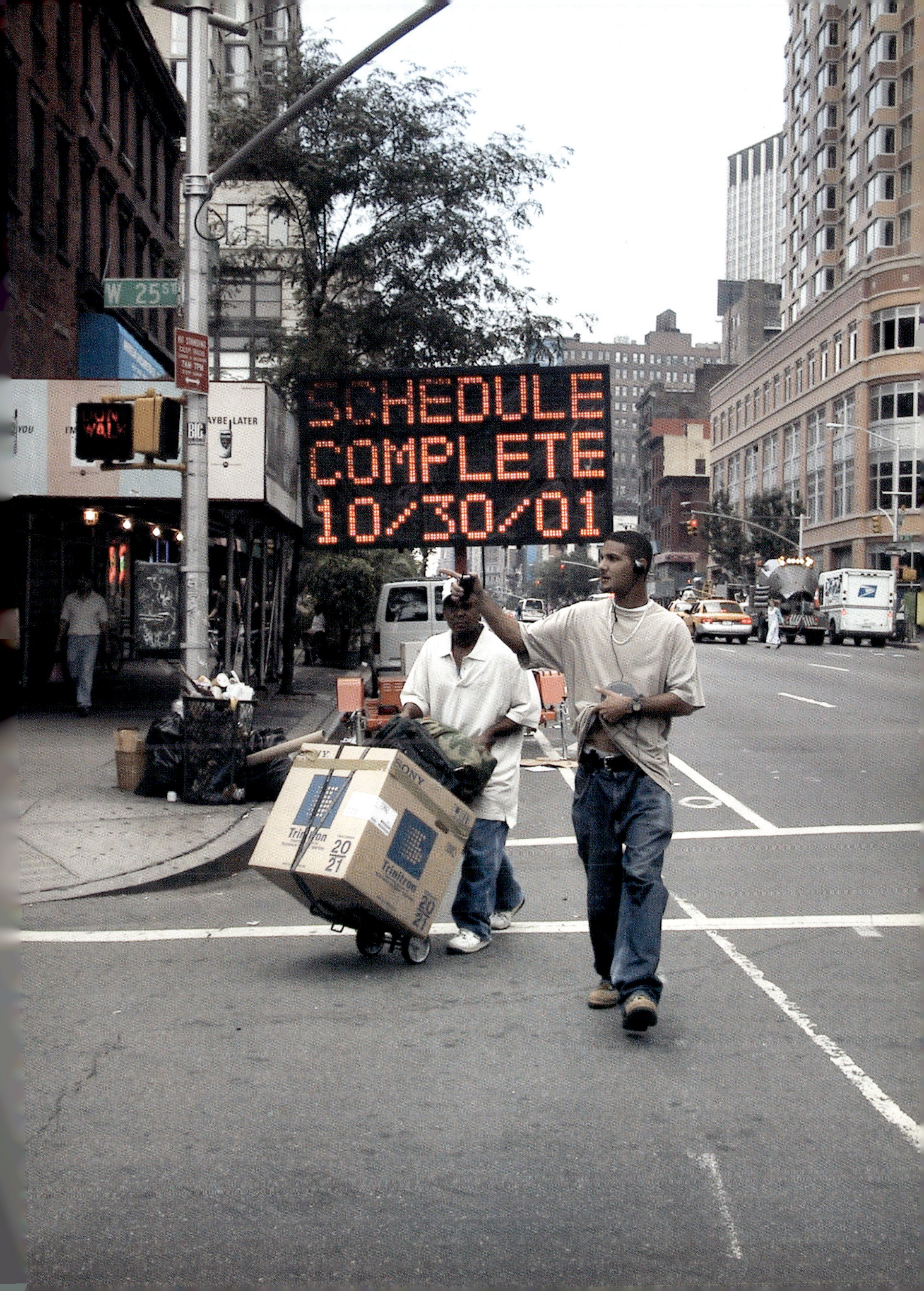

SCHEDULE
COMPLETE
10/30/01
W 25ST
MAYBE LATER
SONY
Trinitron
20
21

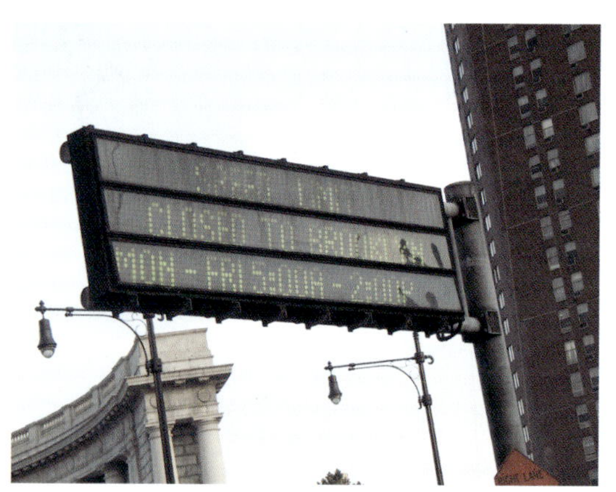

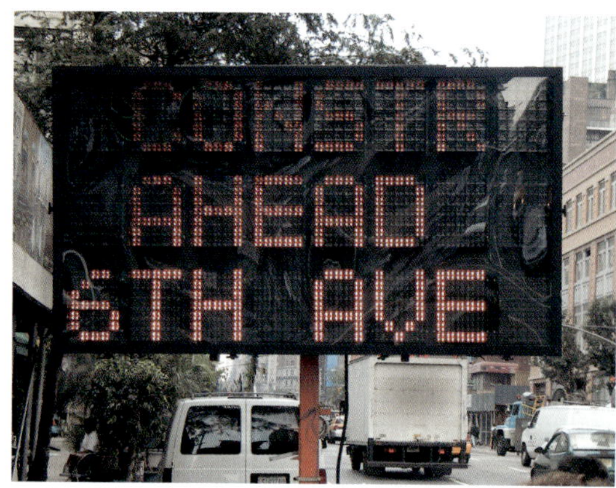

CONSTR
AHEAD
6TH AVE

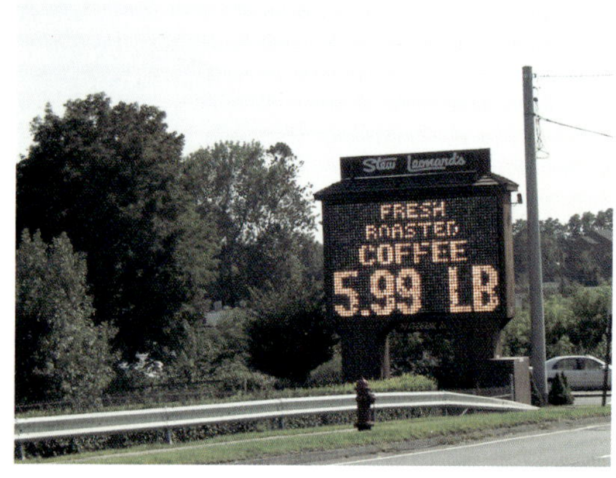

Stew Leonard's
FRESH
ROASTED
COFFEE
5.99 LB

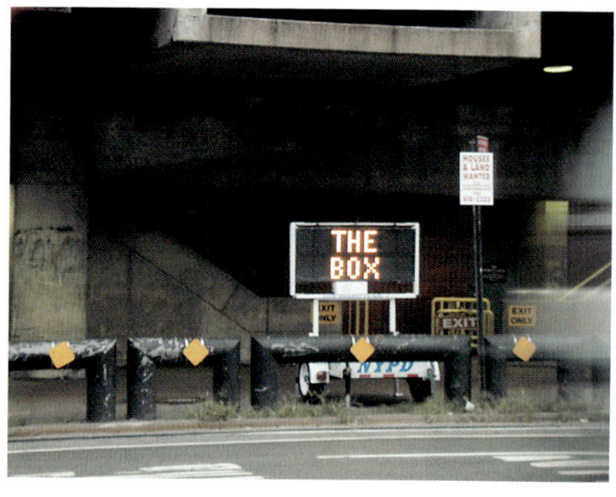

THE
BOX

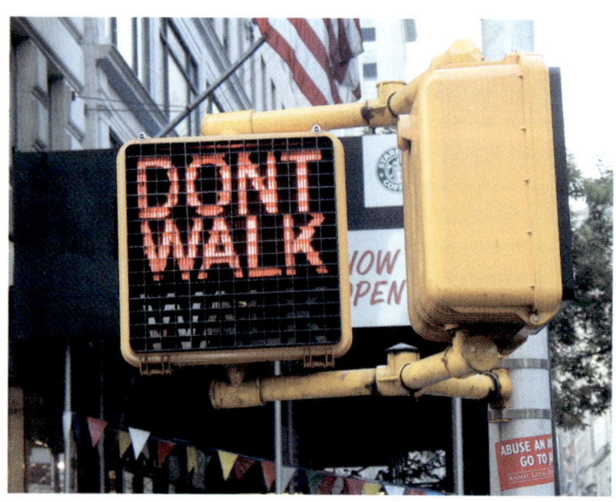

DONT
WALK

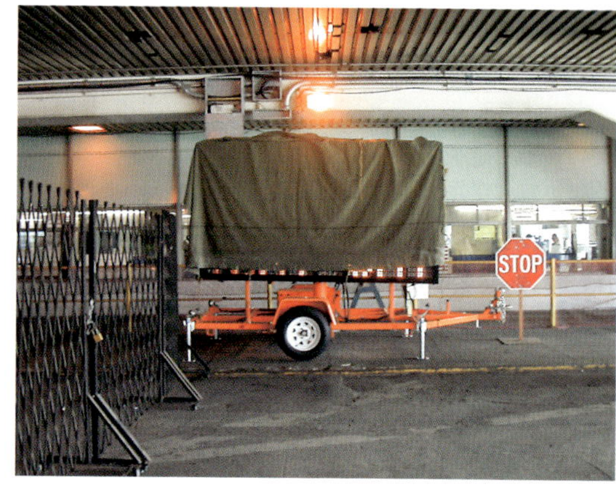

STOP

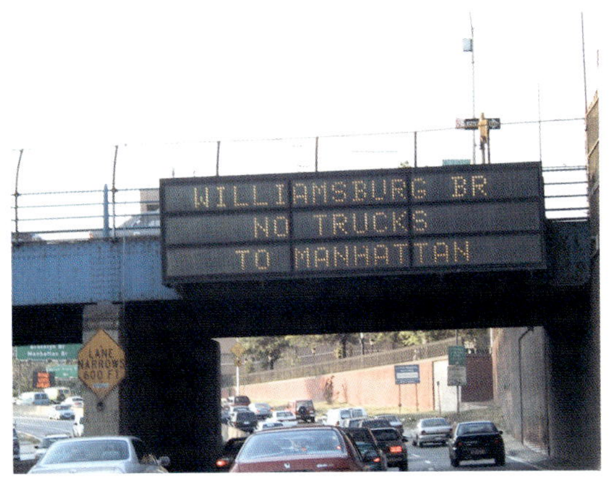
WILLIAMSBURG BR
NO TRUCKS
TO MANHATTAN

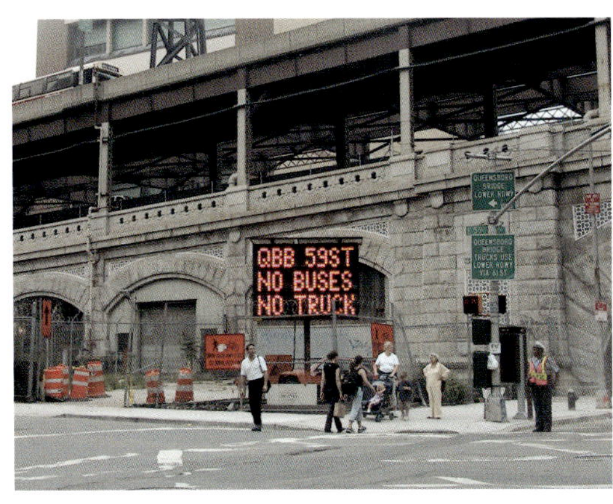
QBB 59ST
NO BUSES
NO TRUCK

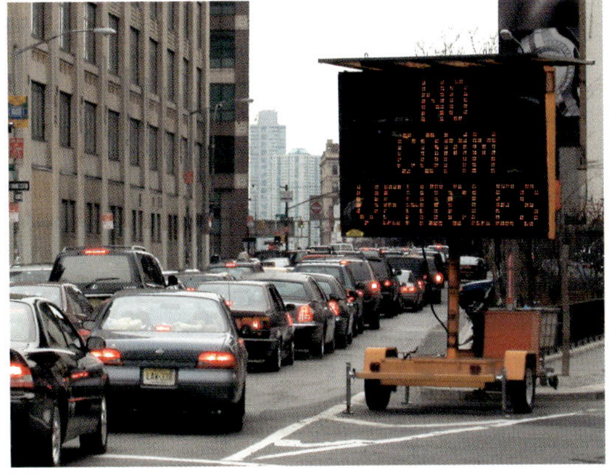
NO
COMM
VEHICLES

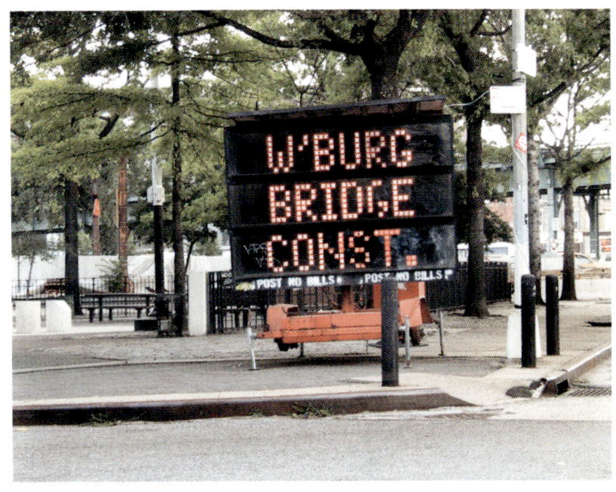
W'BURG
BRIDGE
CONST.
POST NO BILLS

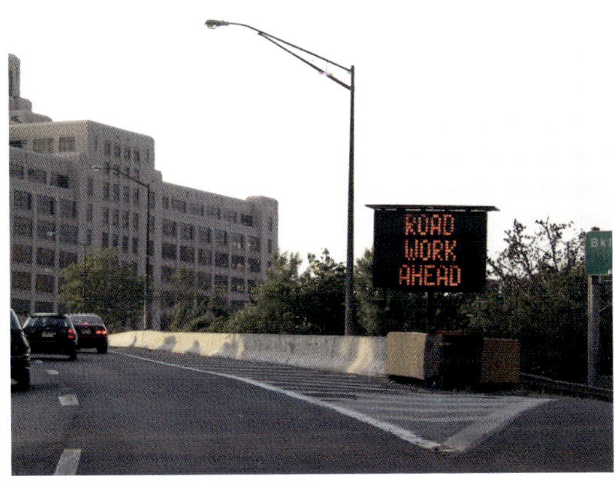
ROAD
WORK
AHEAD

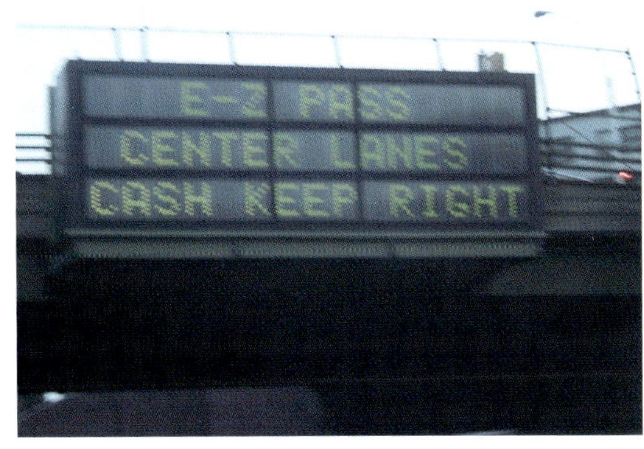
E-Z PASS
CENTER LANES
CASH KEEP RIGHT

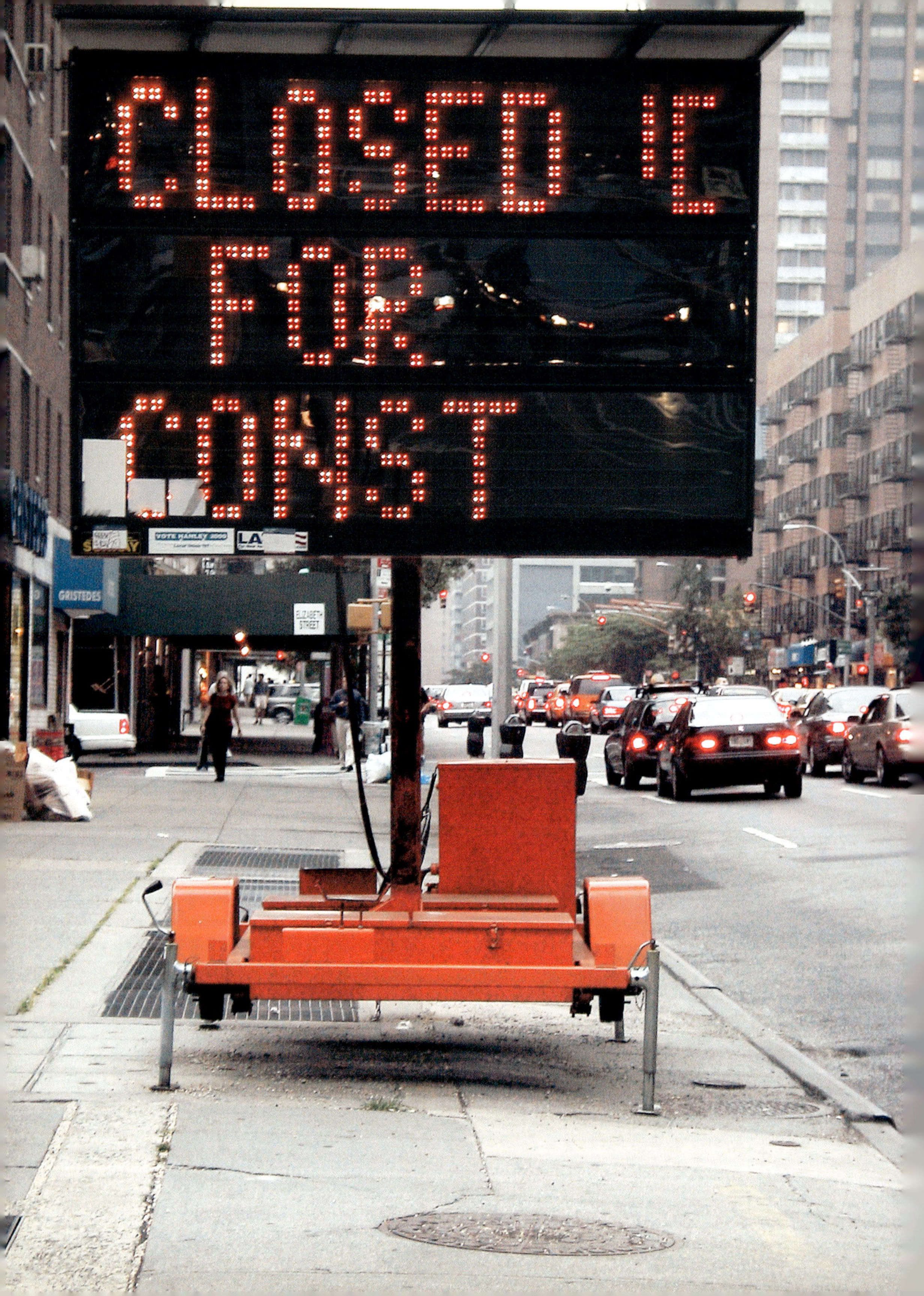
CLOSED
FOR
CONST
GRISTEDES

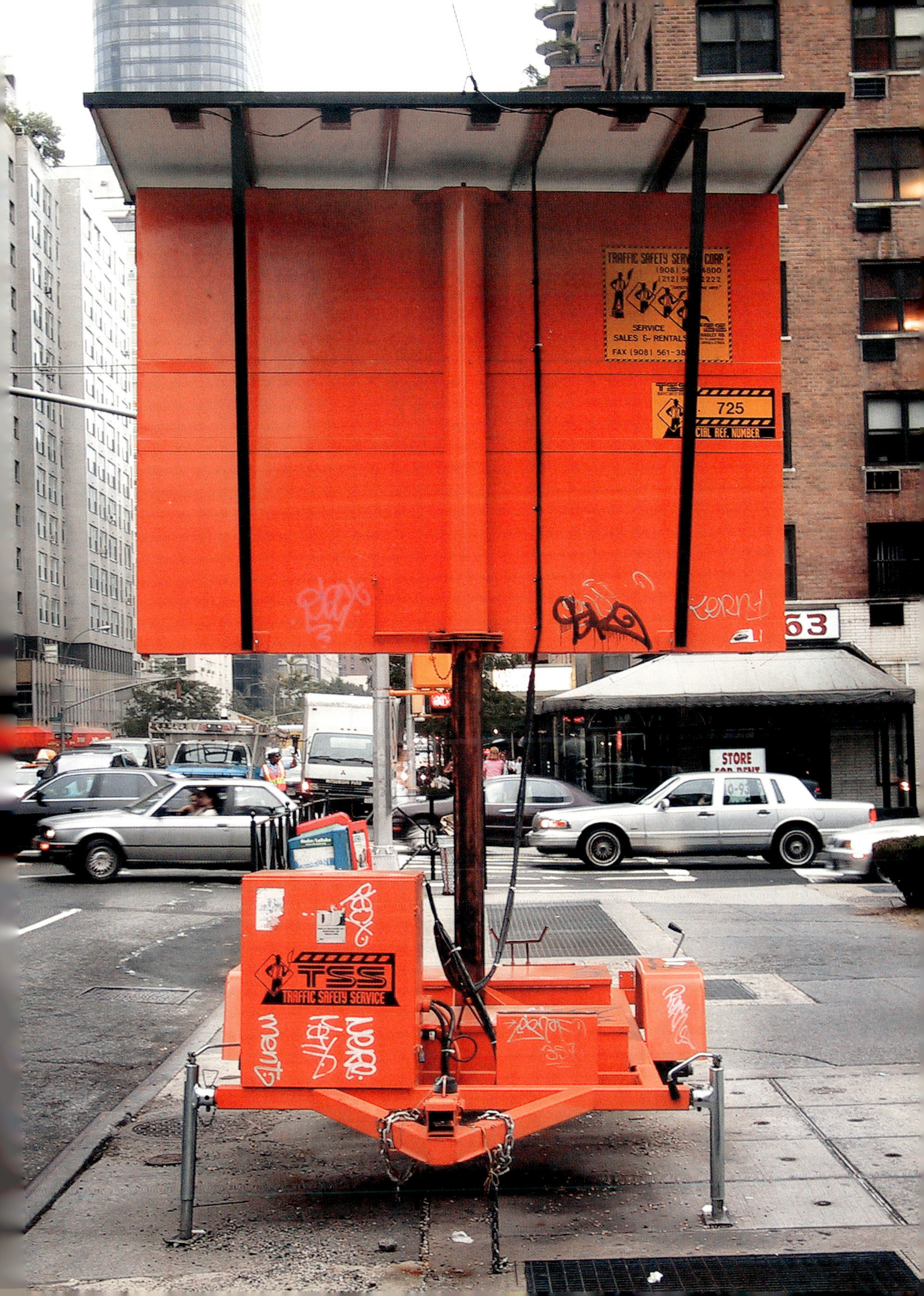
TRAFFIC SAFETY SERVICE CORP
SERVICE
SALES & RENTALS
725
TSS
TRAFFIC SAFETY SERVICE
STORE
63

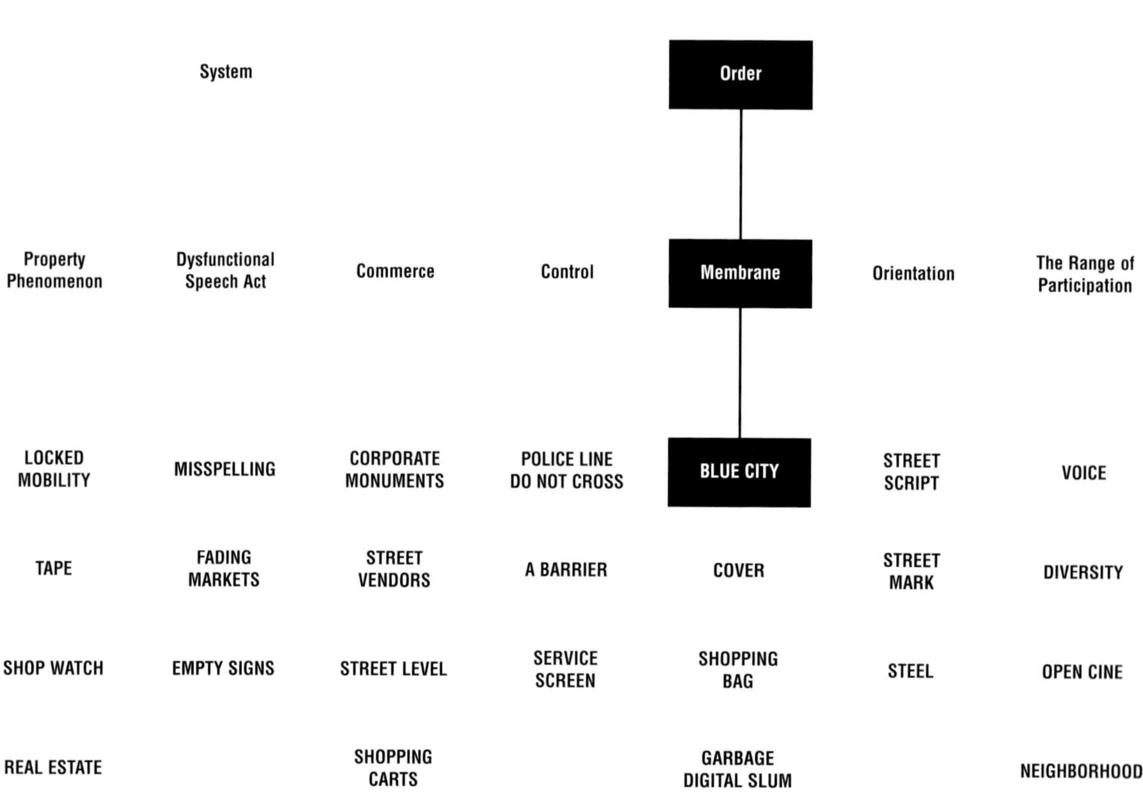

System
Order
Property Phenomenon
Dysfunctional Speech Act
Commerce
Control
Membrane
Orientation
The Range of Participation
LOCKED MOBILITY
MISSPELLING
CORPORATE MONUMENTS
POLICE LINE DO NOT CROSS
BLUE CITY
STREET SCRIPT
VOICE
TAPE
FADING MARKETS
STREET VENDORS
A BARRIER
COVER
STREET MARK
DIVERSITY
SHOP WATCH
EMPTY SIGNS
STREET LEVEL
SERVICE SCREEN
SHOPPING BAG
STEEL
OPEN CINE
REAL ESTATE
SHOPPING CARTS
GARBAGE DIGITAL SLUM
NEIGHBORHOOD

Identity

Alternative Media

Habitual Reinterpretation

BLUE CITY

Cover for the Wound

CAR DOOR

PUBLIC CHAIRS

LABELING.

PLASTIC CRATES

POLE POST

STANDPIPES

PRAY JESUS

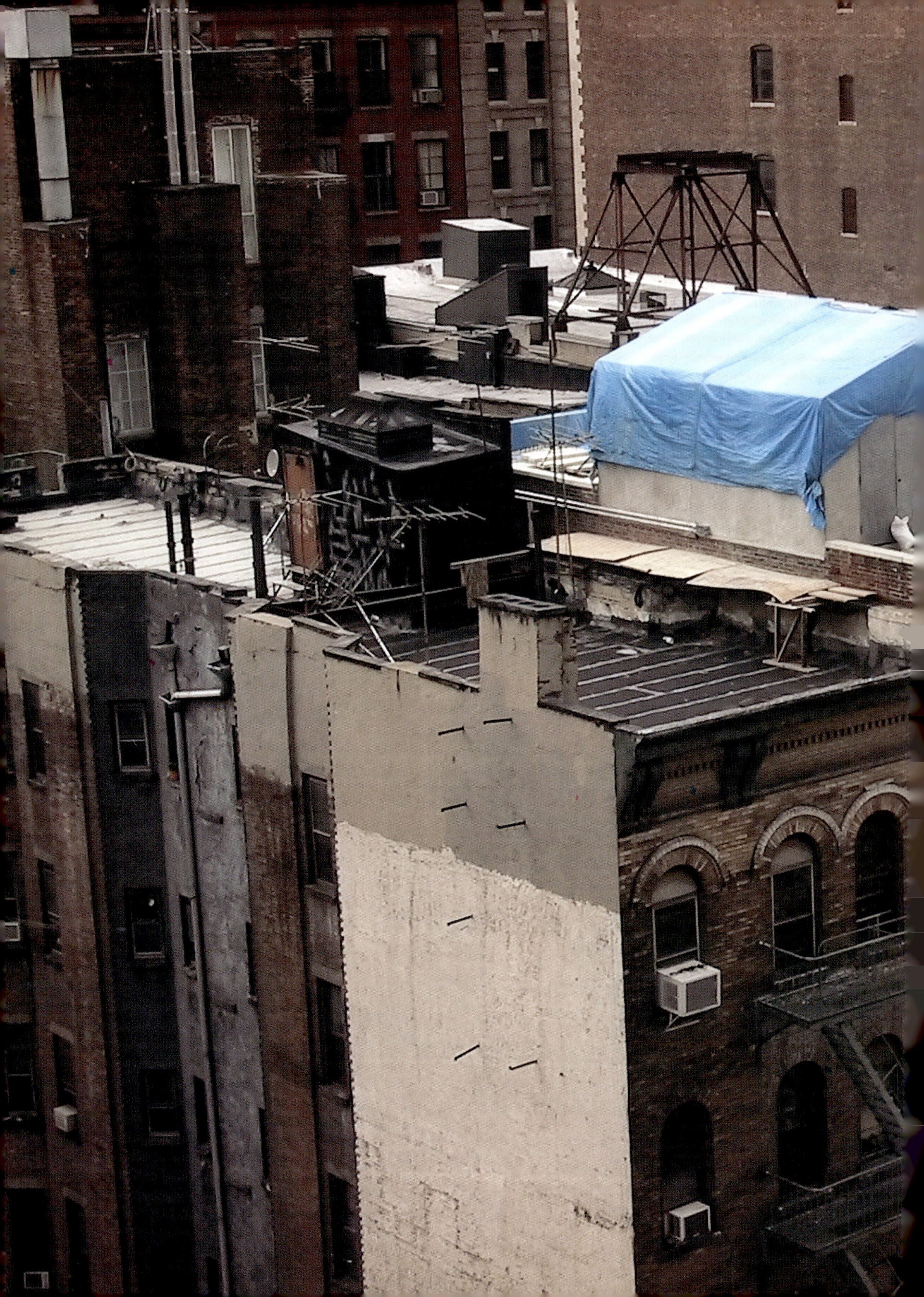

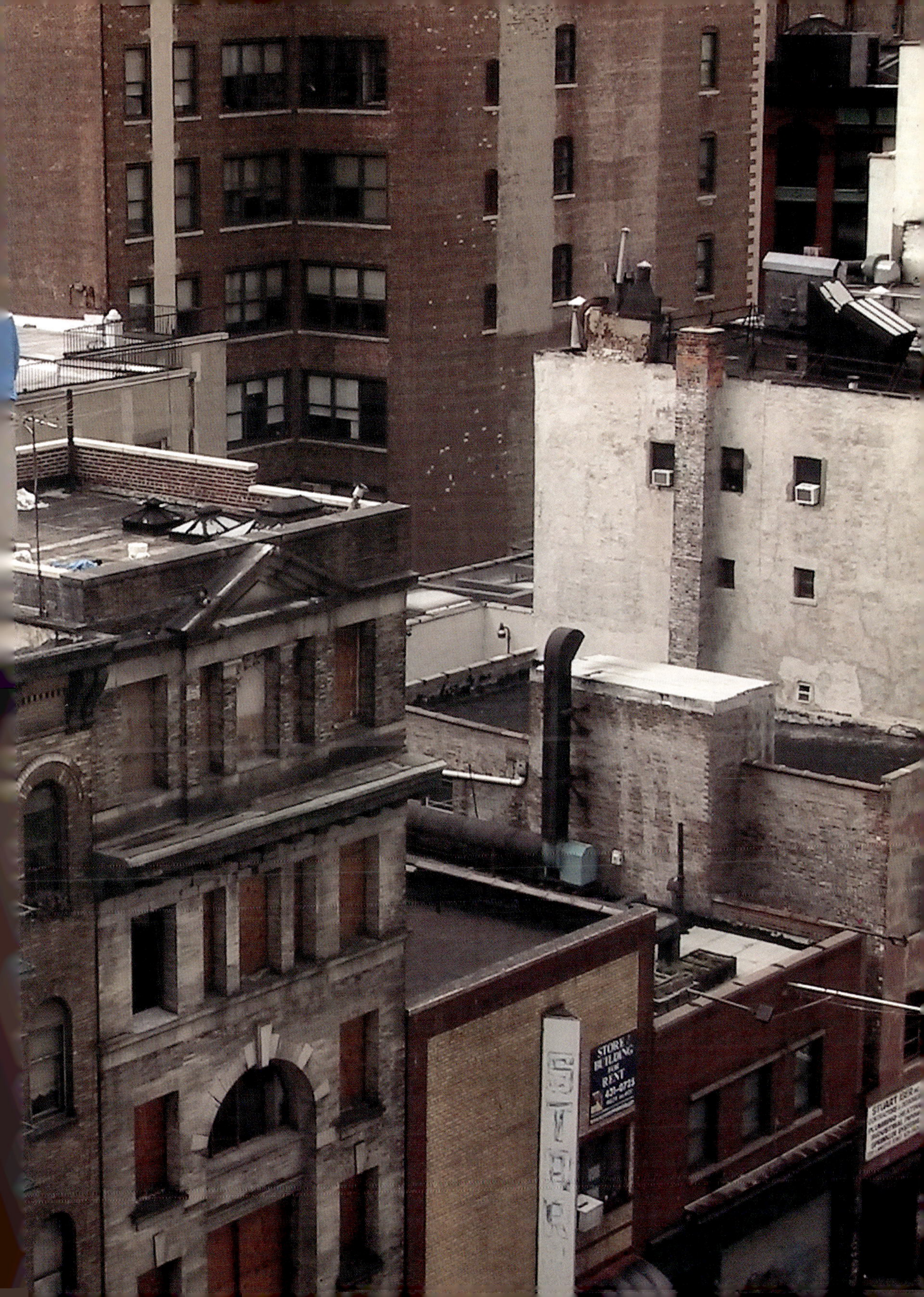
STORE
BUILDING
RENT

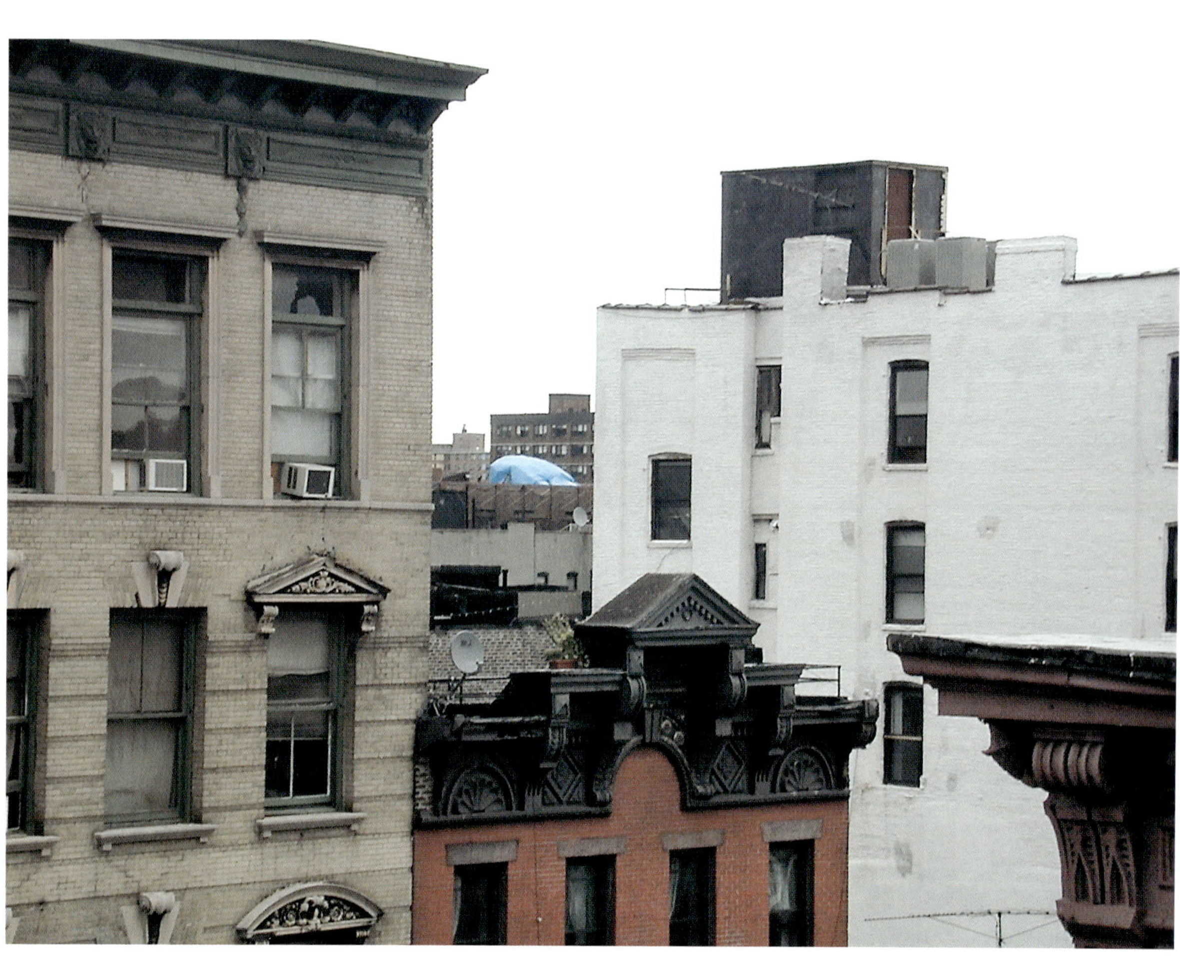

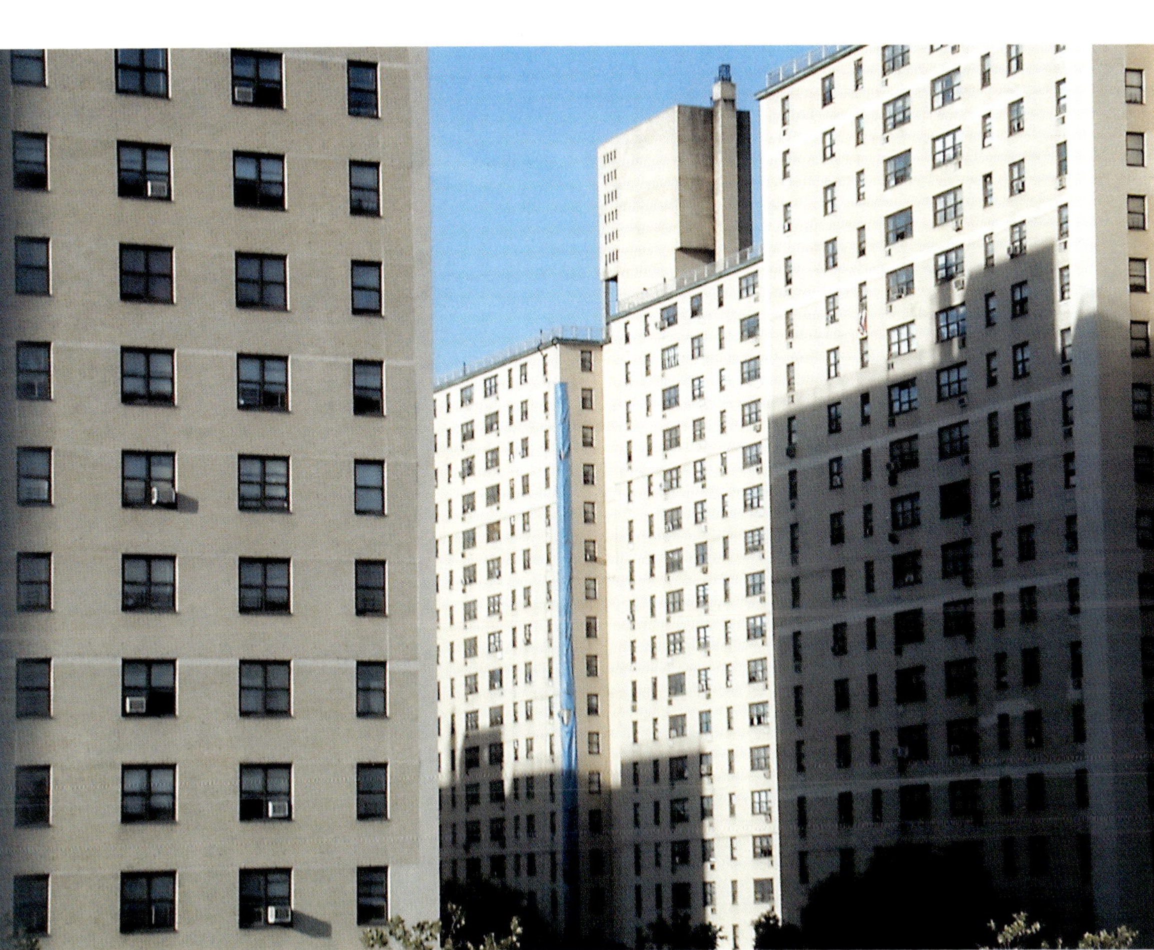

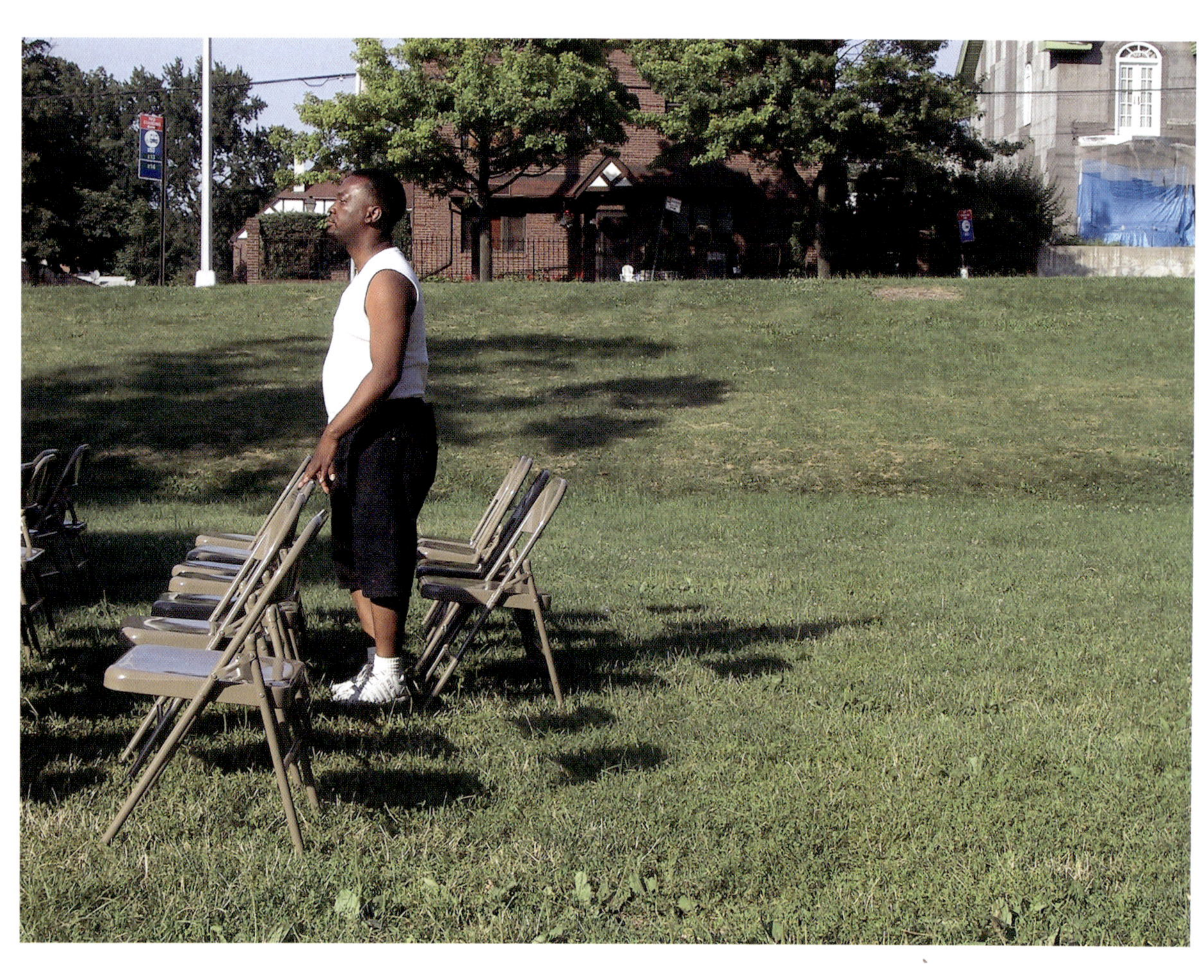

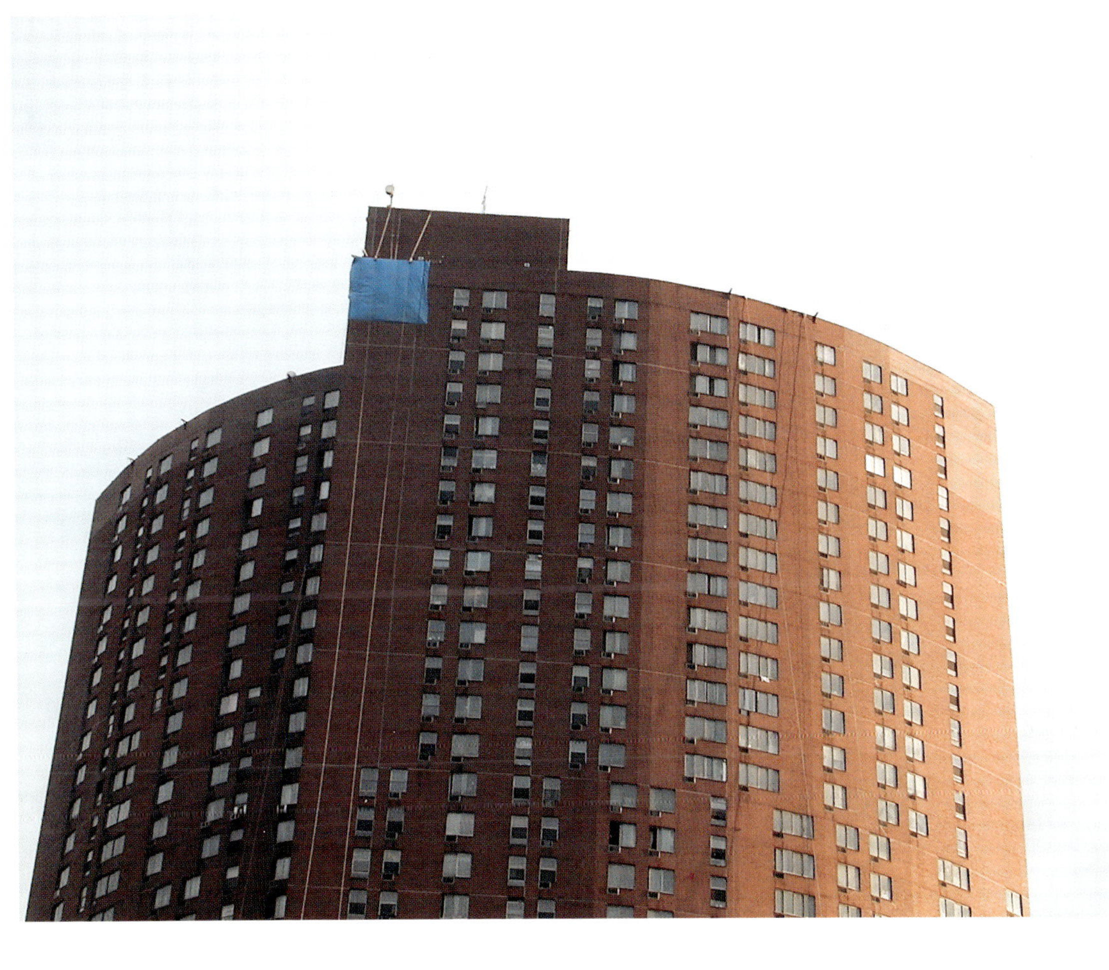

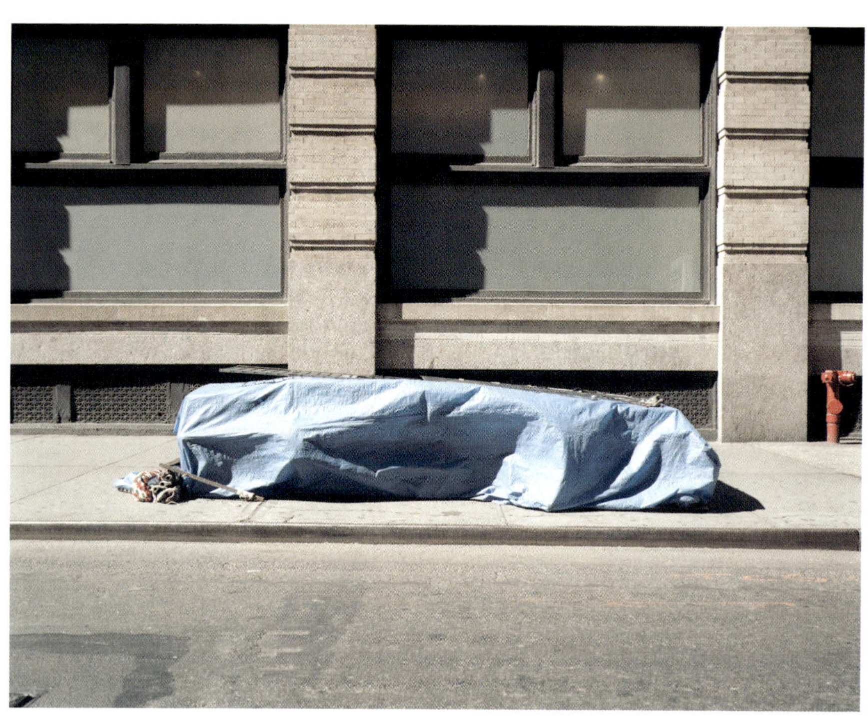

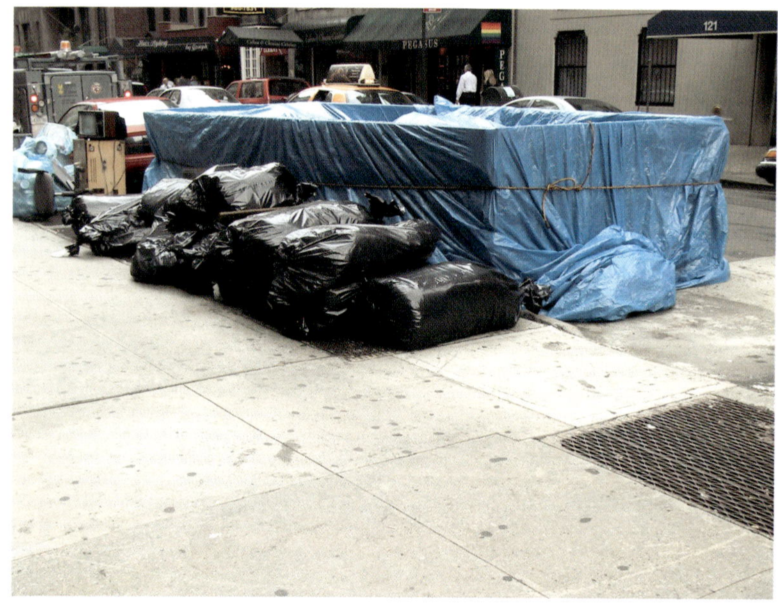
121
PEGASUS

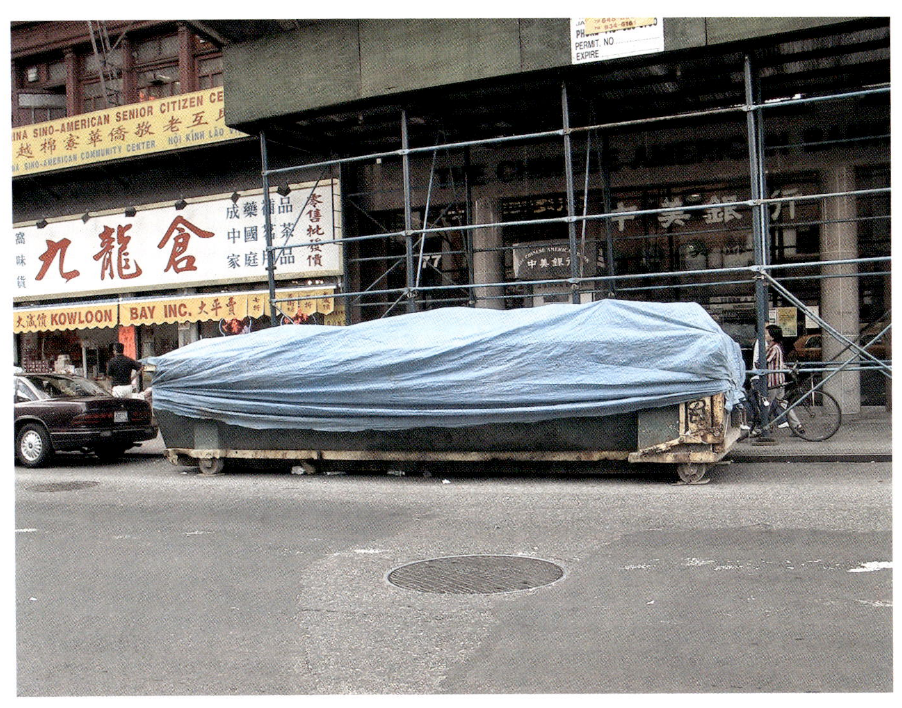
SINO-AMERICAN SENIOR CITIZEN
九龍倉
成藥補品
中國茗茶
家庭用品
KOWLOON
BAY INC.
PERMIT. NO
EXPIRE

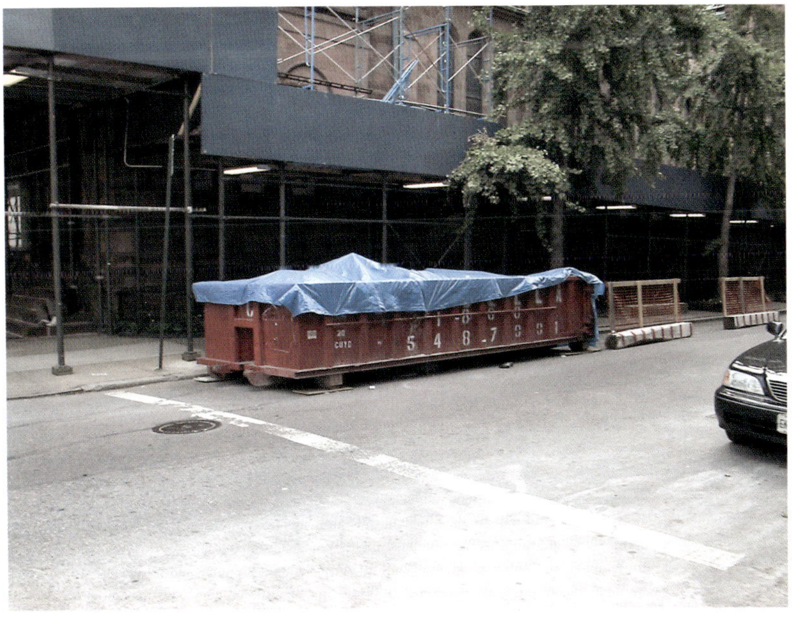

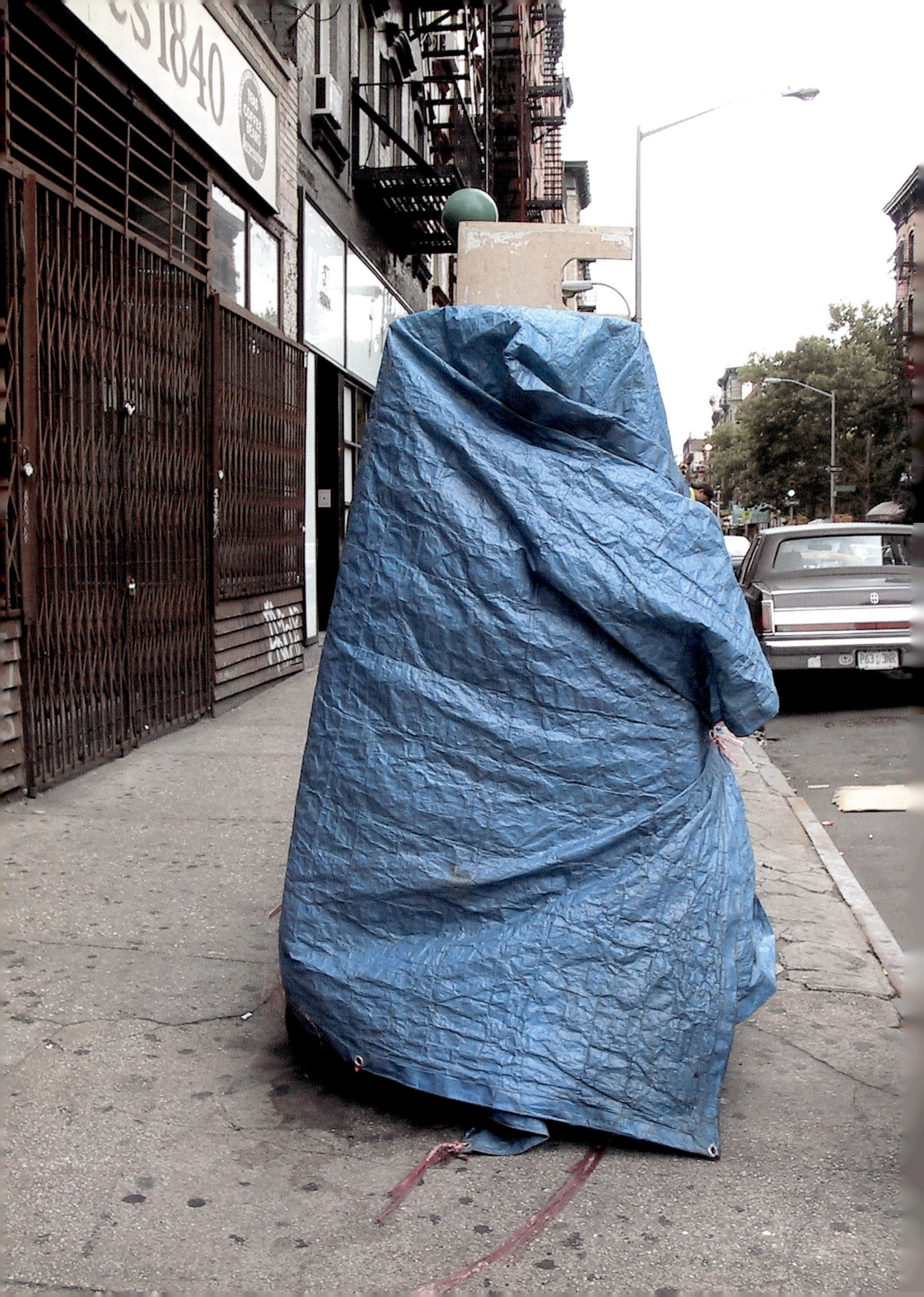
1840

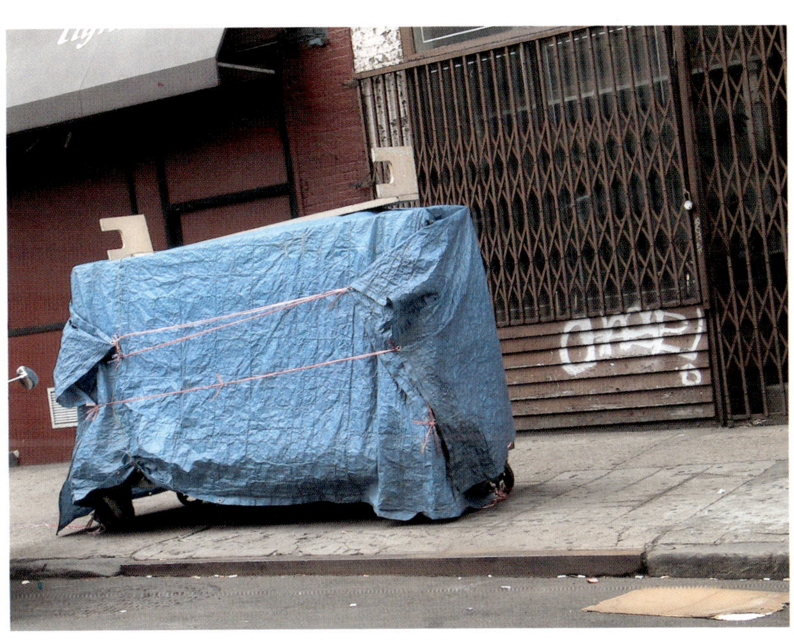

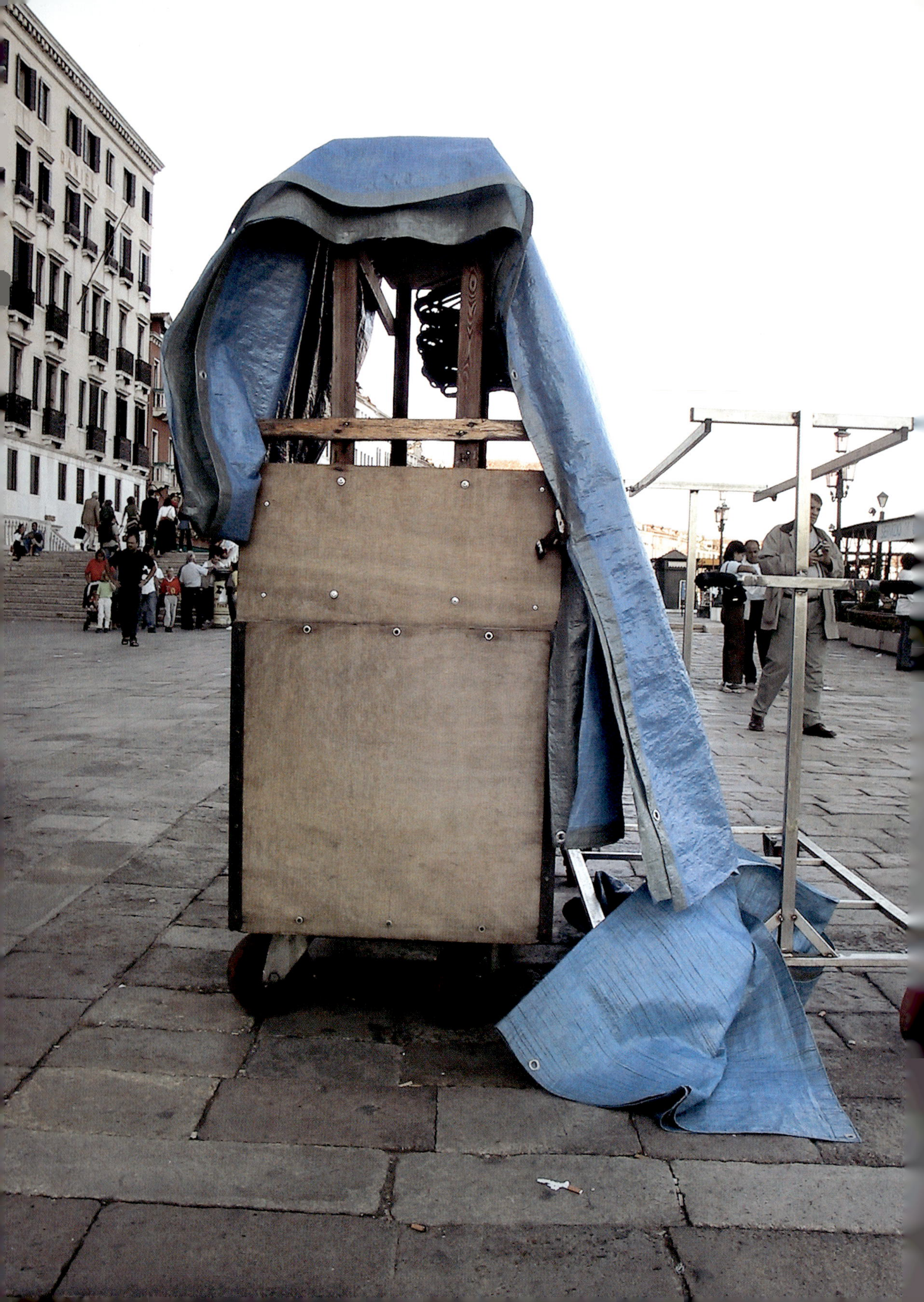

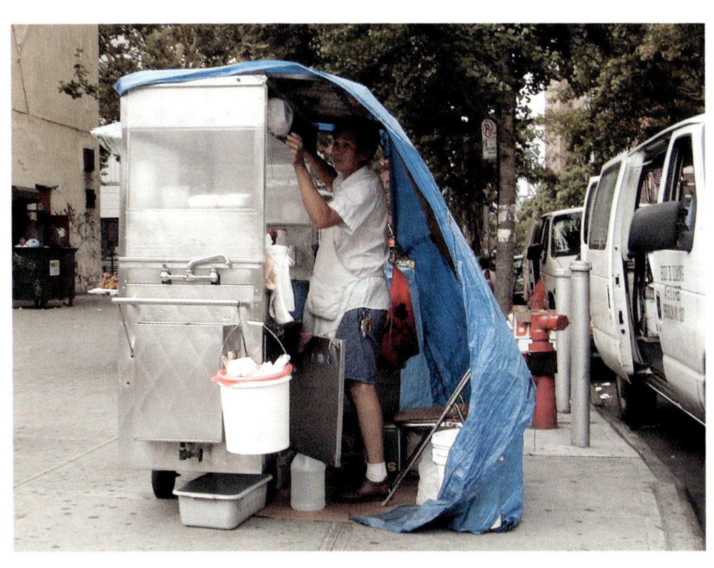

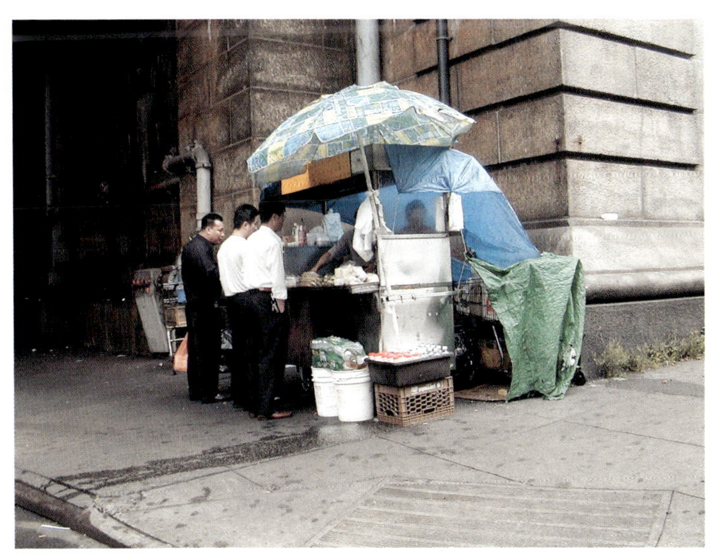

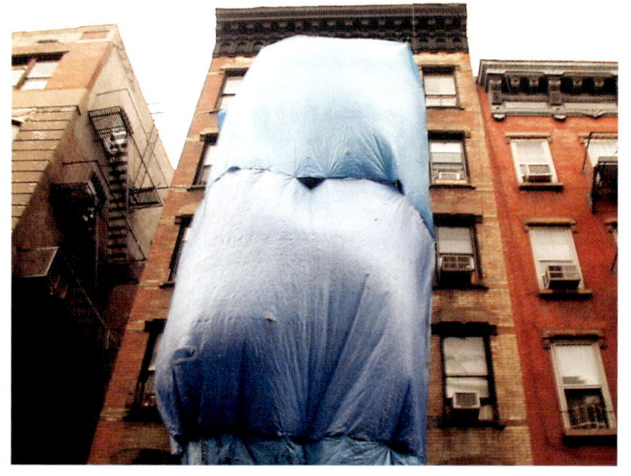

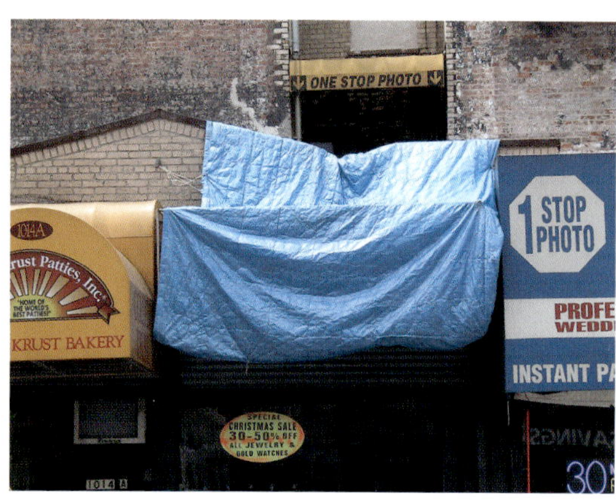
ONE STOP PHOTO
1014A
KRUST BAKERY
1 STOP PHOTO
INSTANT PA
SPECIAL
CHRISTMAS SALE
30-50% OFF
ALL JEWELRY &
GOLD WATCHES

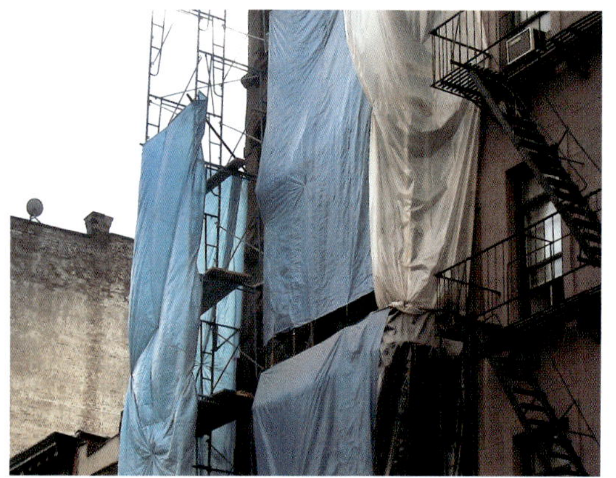

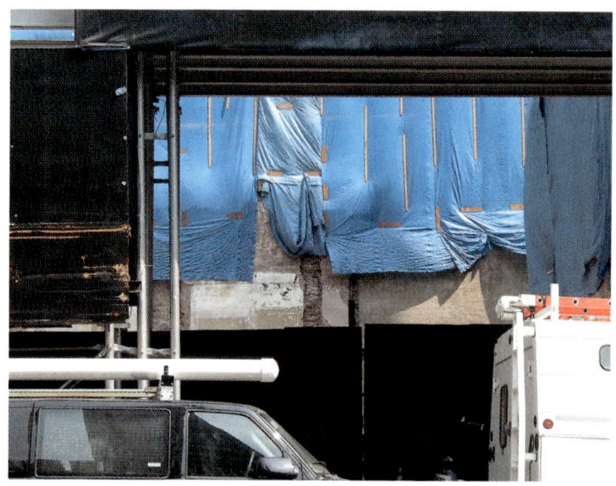

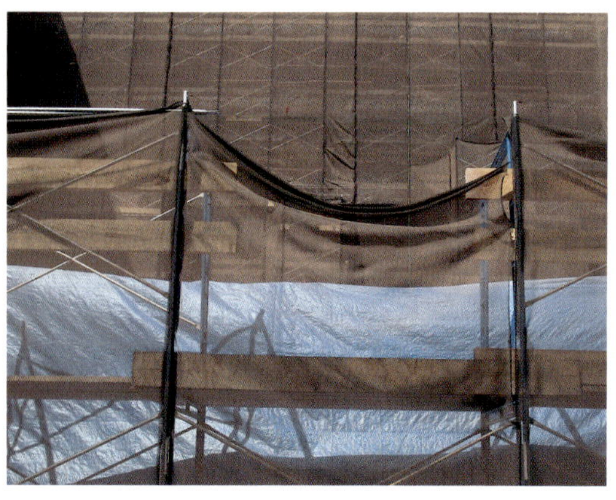

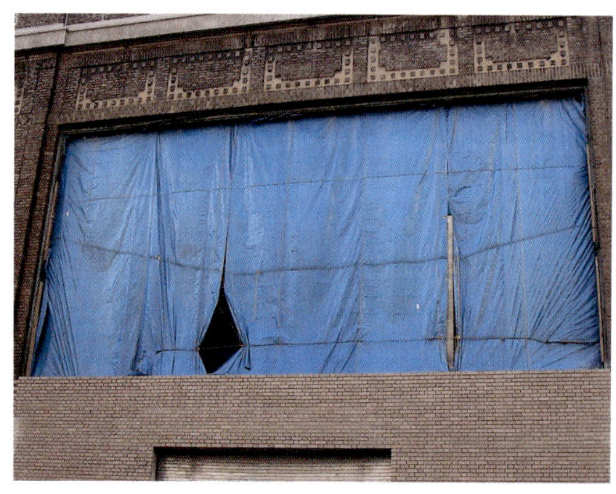

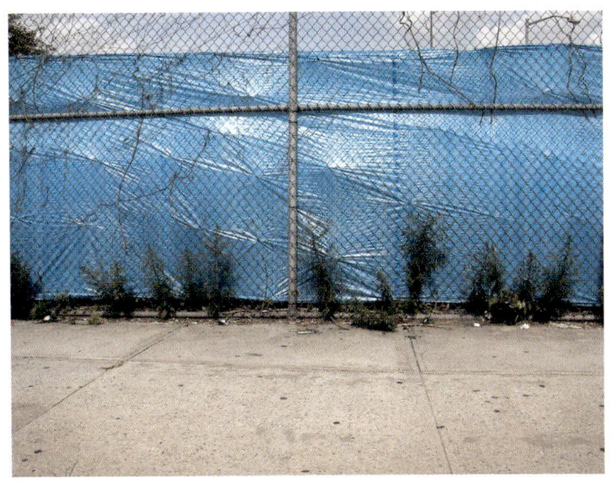

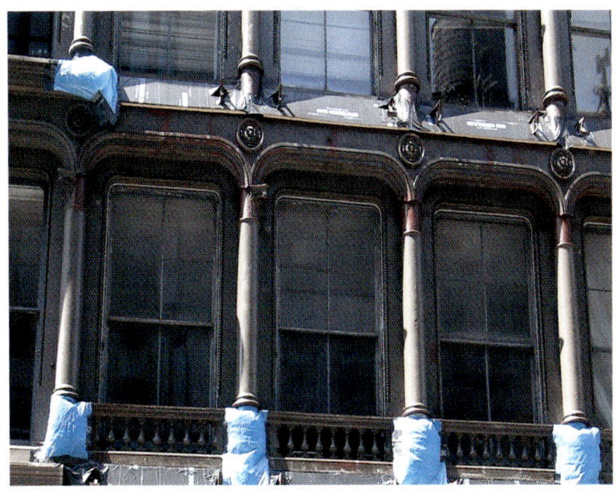

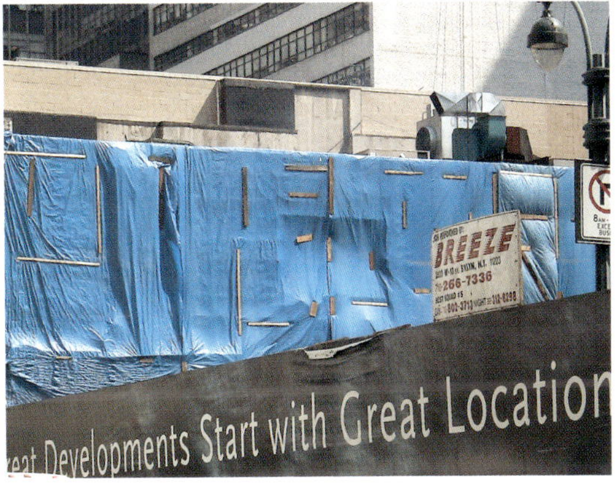
BREEZE
266-7336
eat Developments Start with Great Location

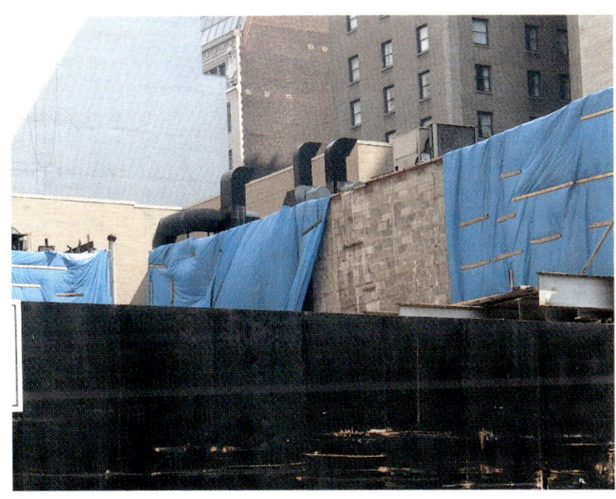

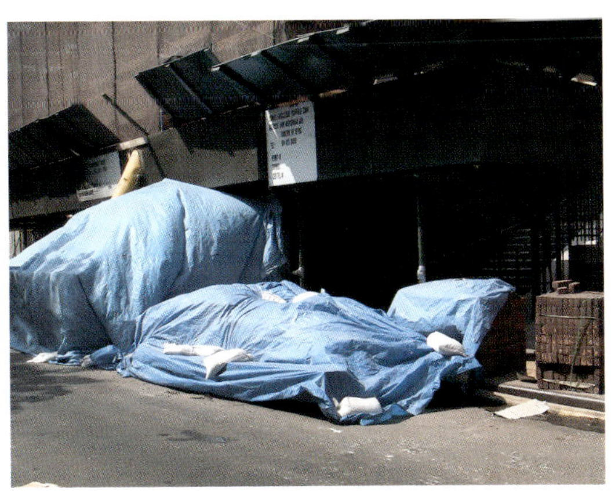

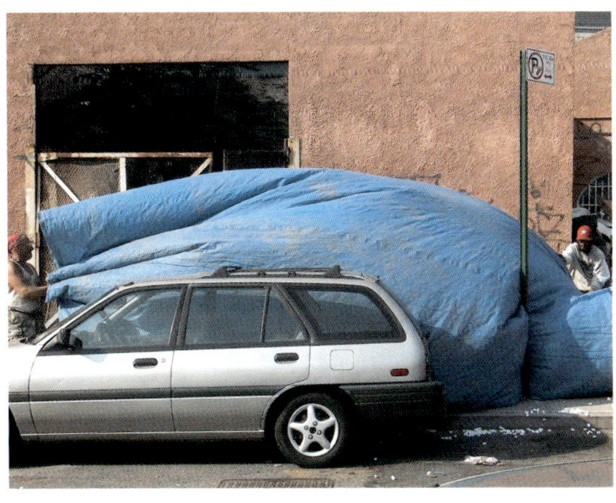

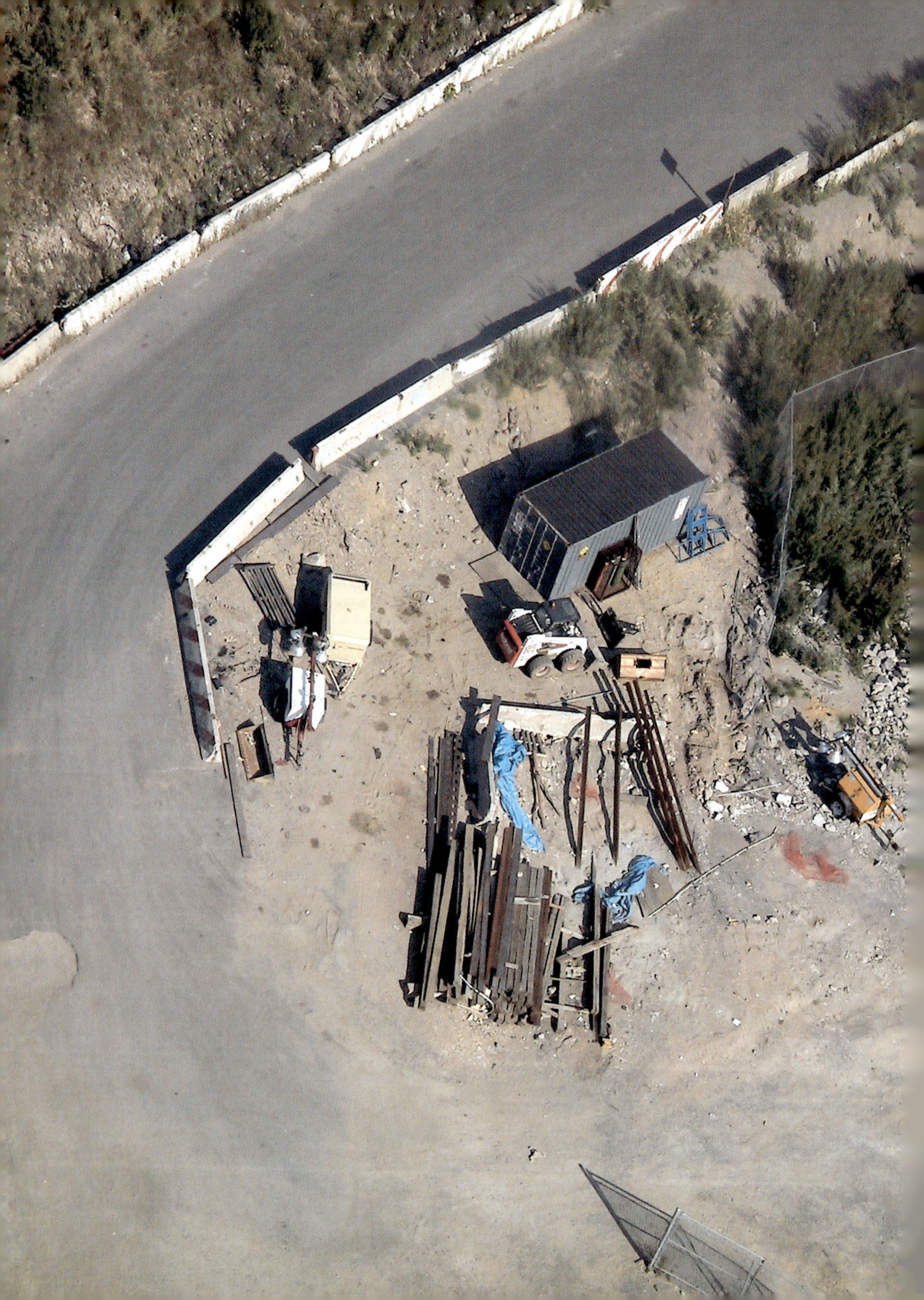

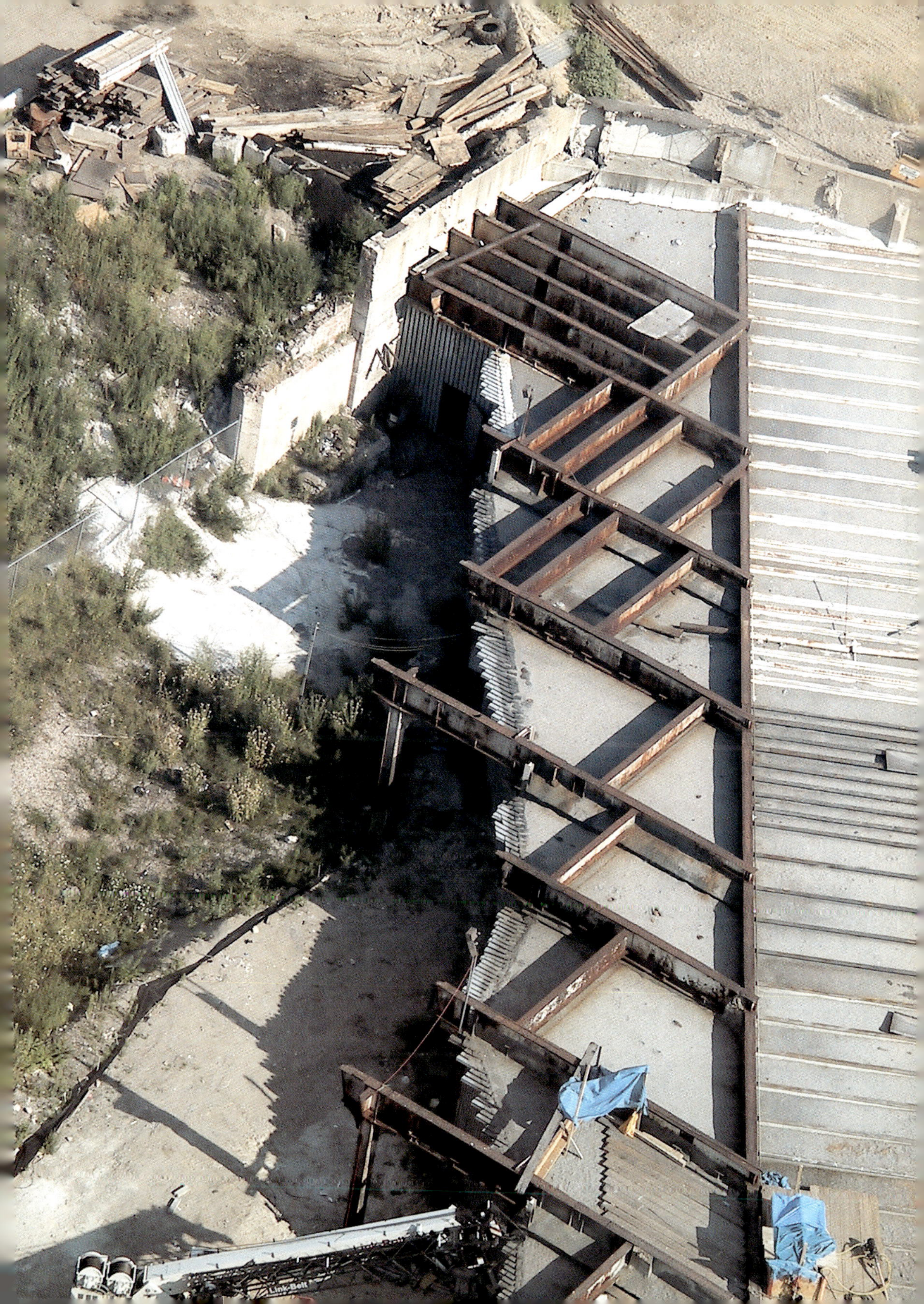
Link-Belt

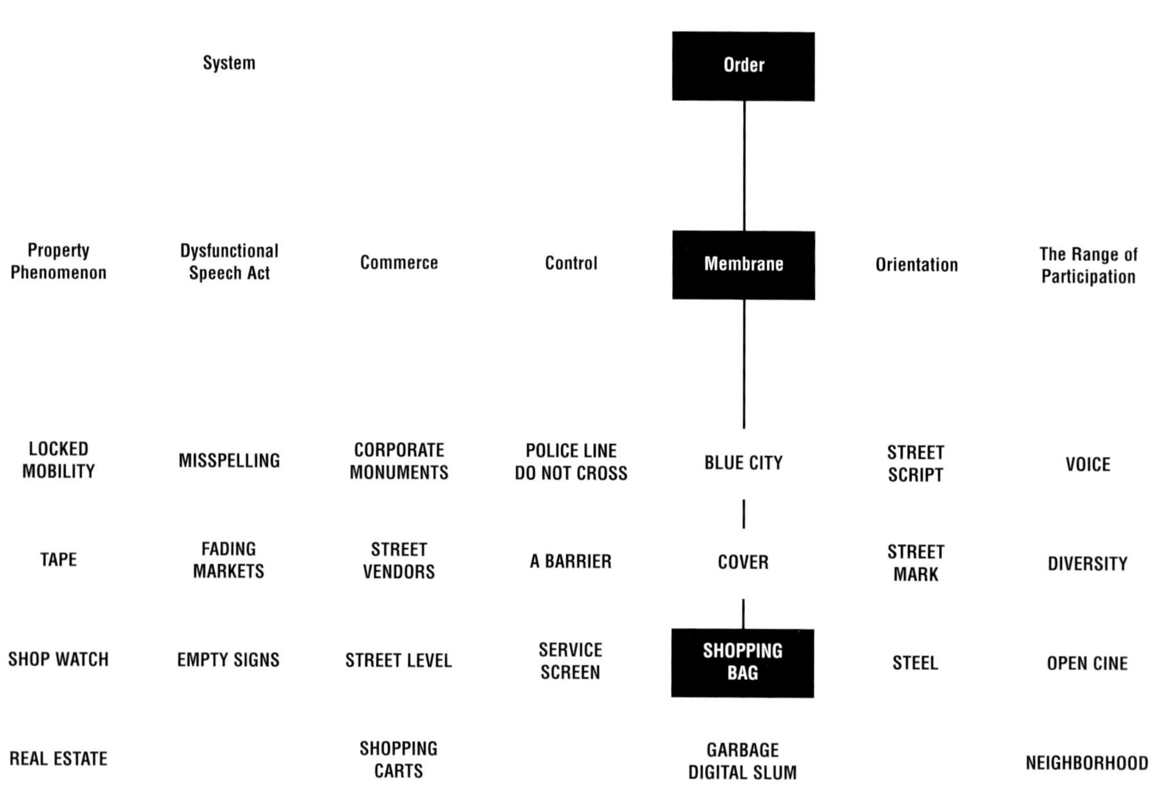
System
Order
Property Phenomenon
Dysfunctional Speech Act
Commerce
Control
Membrane
Orientation
The Range of Participation
LOCKED MOBILITY
MISSPELLING
CORPORATE MONUMENTS
POLICE LINE DO NOT CROSS
BLUE CITY
STREET SCRIPT
VOICE
TAPE
FADING MARKETS
STREET VENDORS
A BARRIER
COVER
STREET MARK
DIVERSITY
SHOP WATCH
EMPTY SIGNS
STREET LEVEL
SERVICE SCREEN
SHOPPING BAG
STEEL
OPEN CINE
REAL ESTATE
SHOPPING CARTS
GARBAGE DIGITAL SLUM
NEIGHBORHOOD

Identity

Alternative Media

Habitual Reinterpretation

SHOPPING BAG

Disposable Packaging Environment

CAR DOOR

PUBLIC CHAIRS

LABELING.

PLASTIC CRATES

POLE POST

STANDPIPES

PRAY JESUS

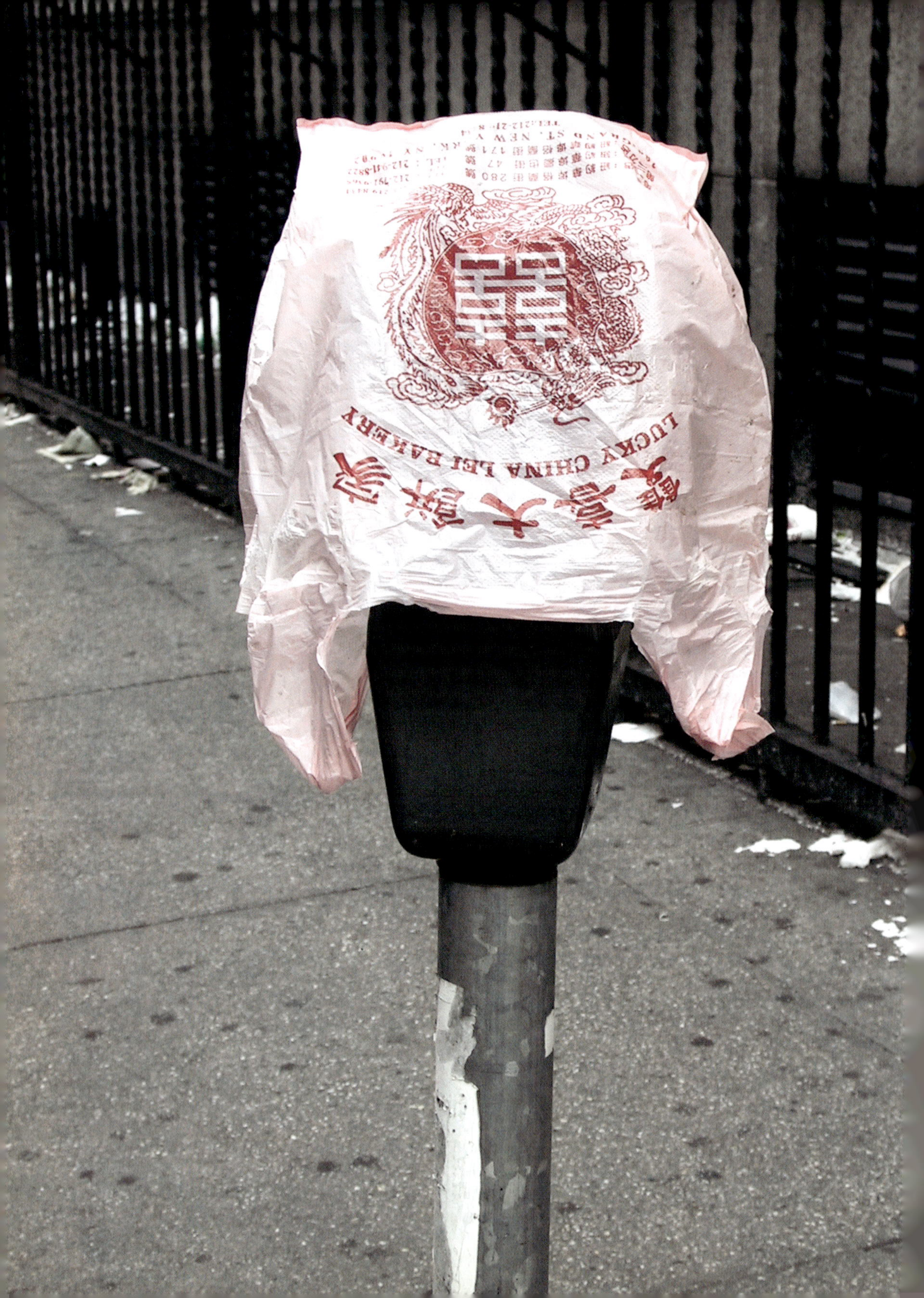
LUCKY CHINA LEI BAKERY

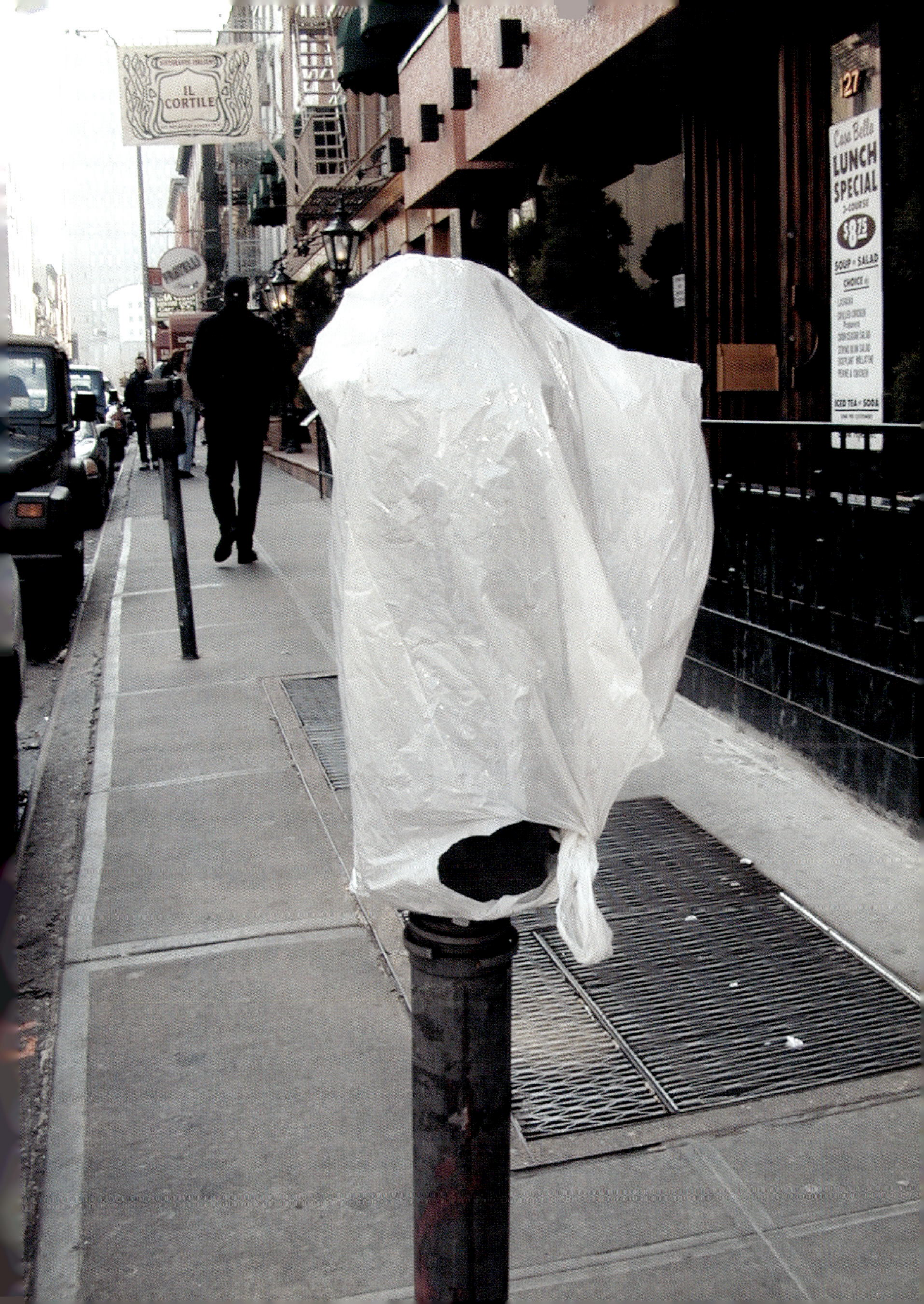
IL CORTILE
FRATELLI
127
Casa Bella
LUNCH SPECIAL
3-COURSE
$8.75
SOUP or SALAD
ICED TEA or SODA

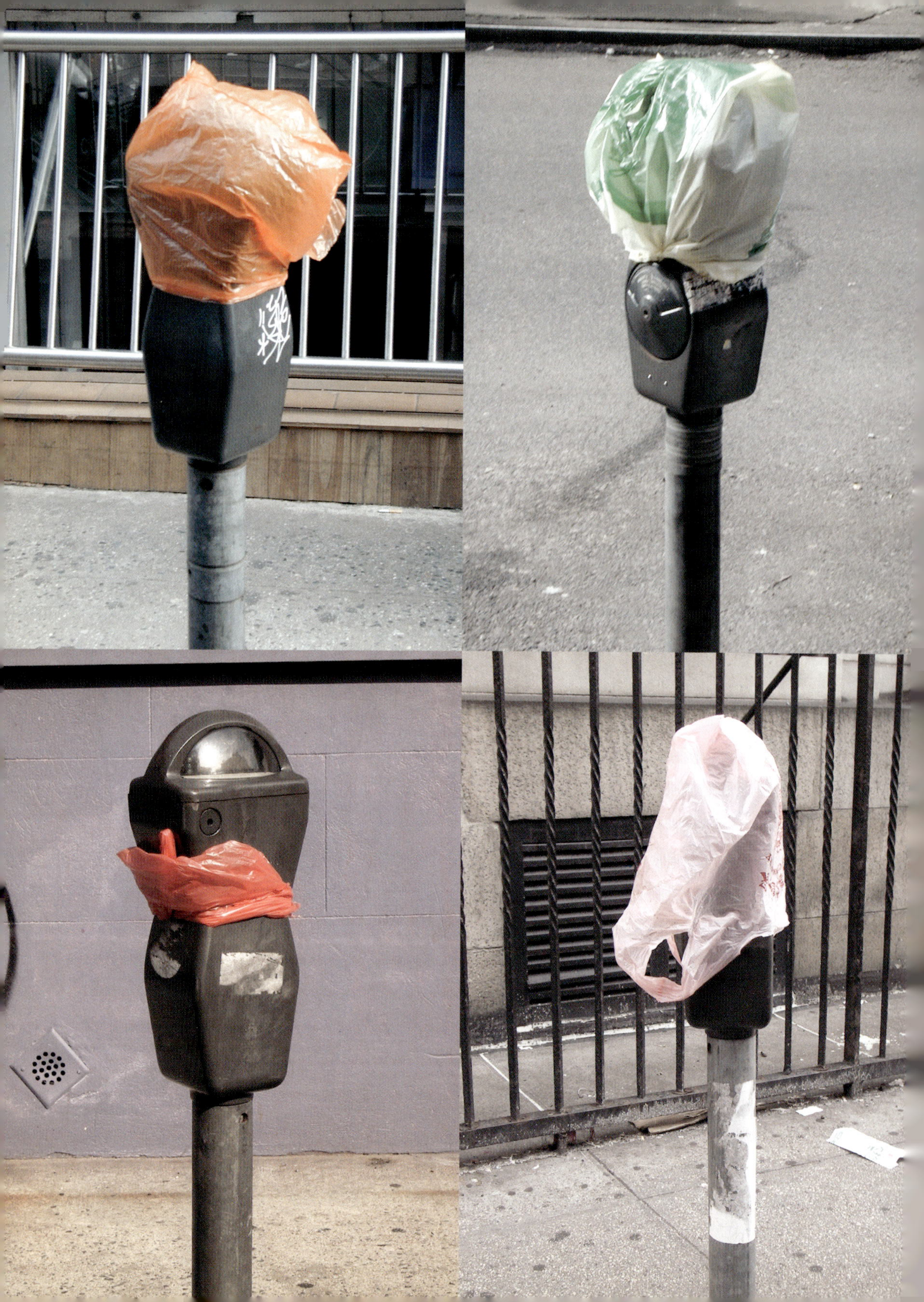

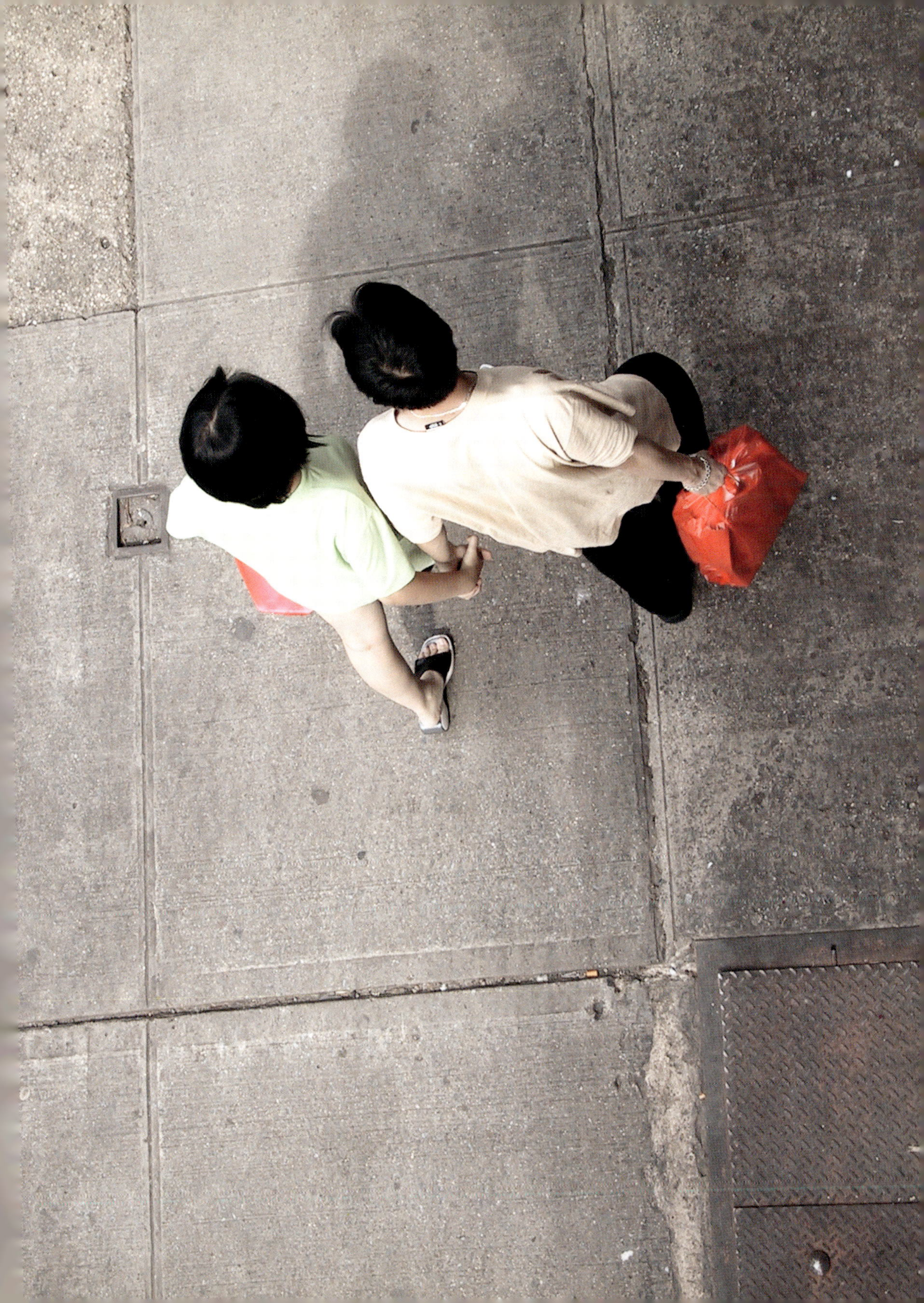

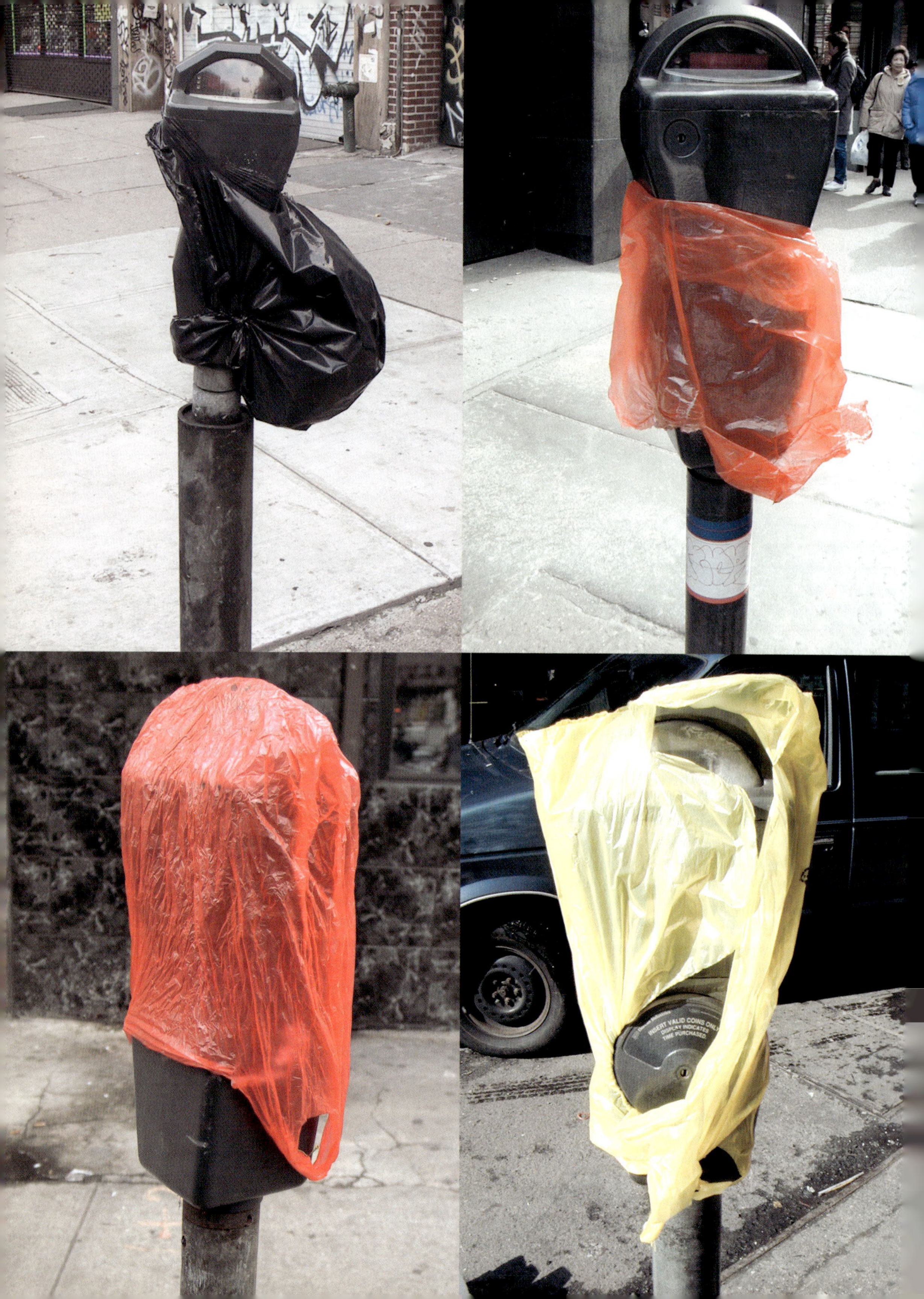
INSERT VALID COINS
DISPLAY INDICATES
TIME PURCHASED

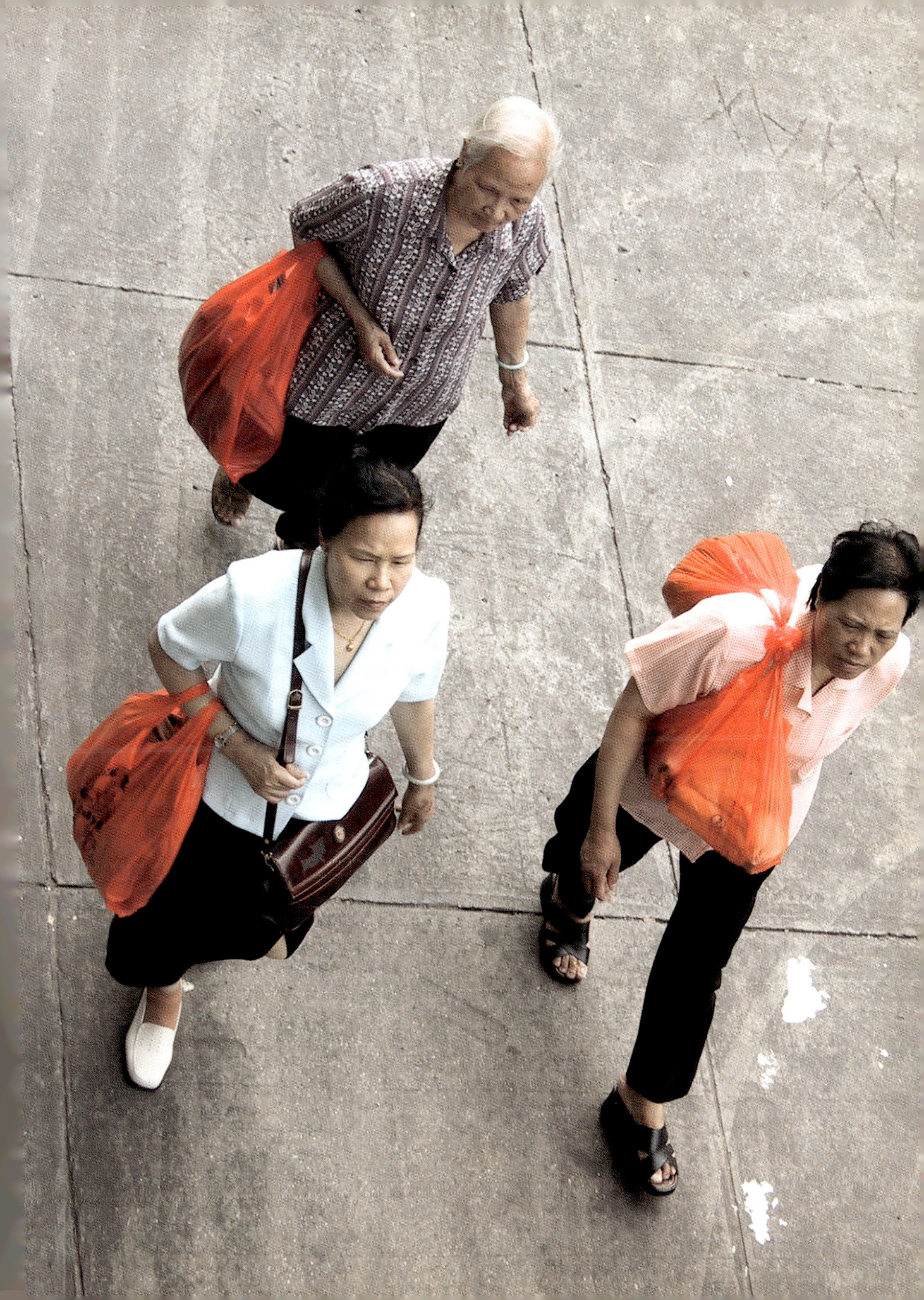

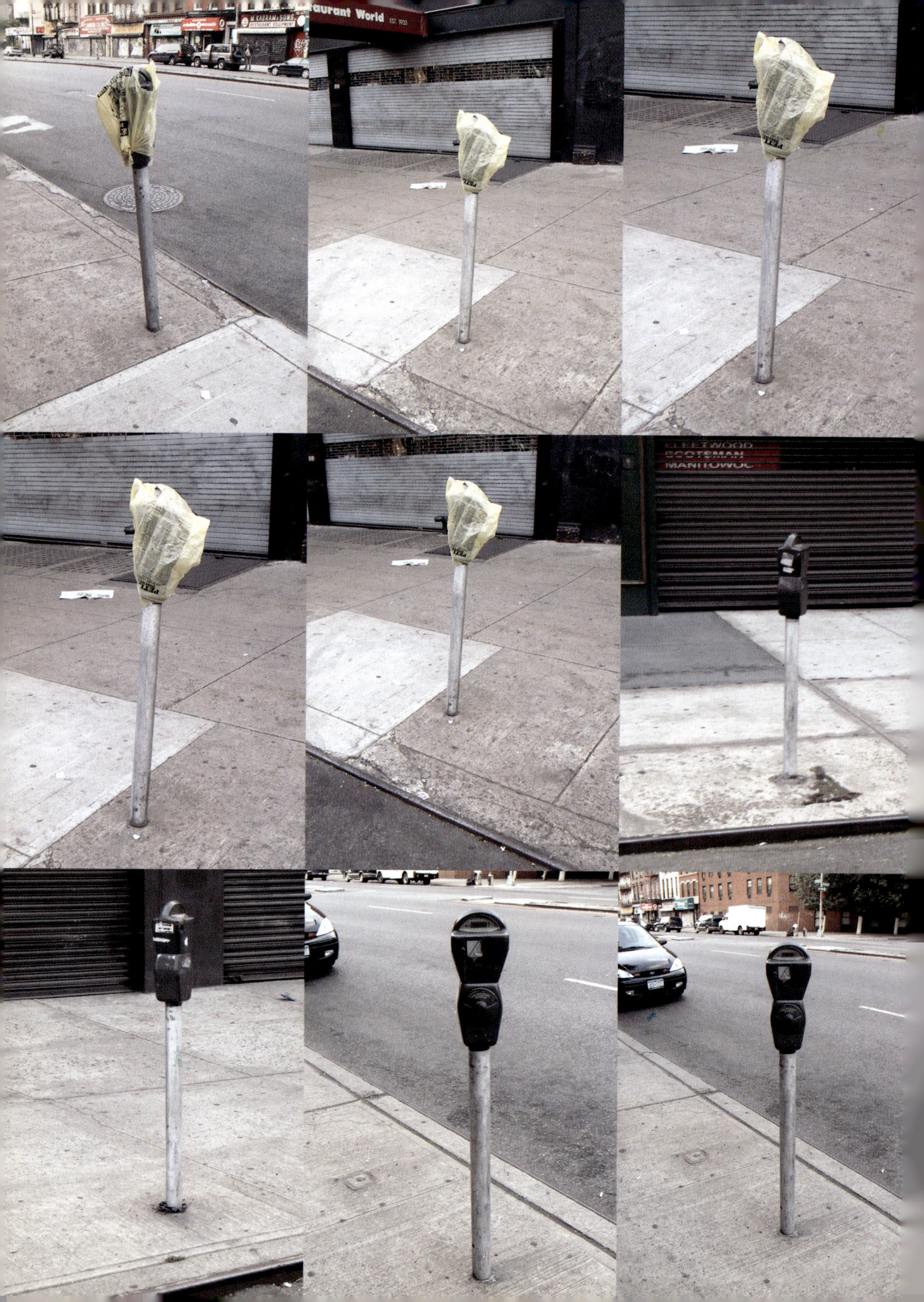

aurant World
SCOTSMAN
MANITOWOC

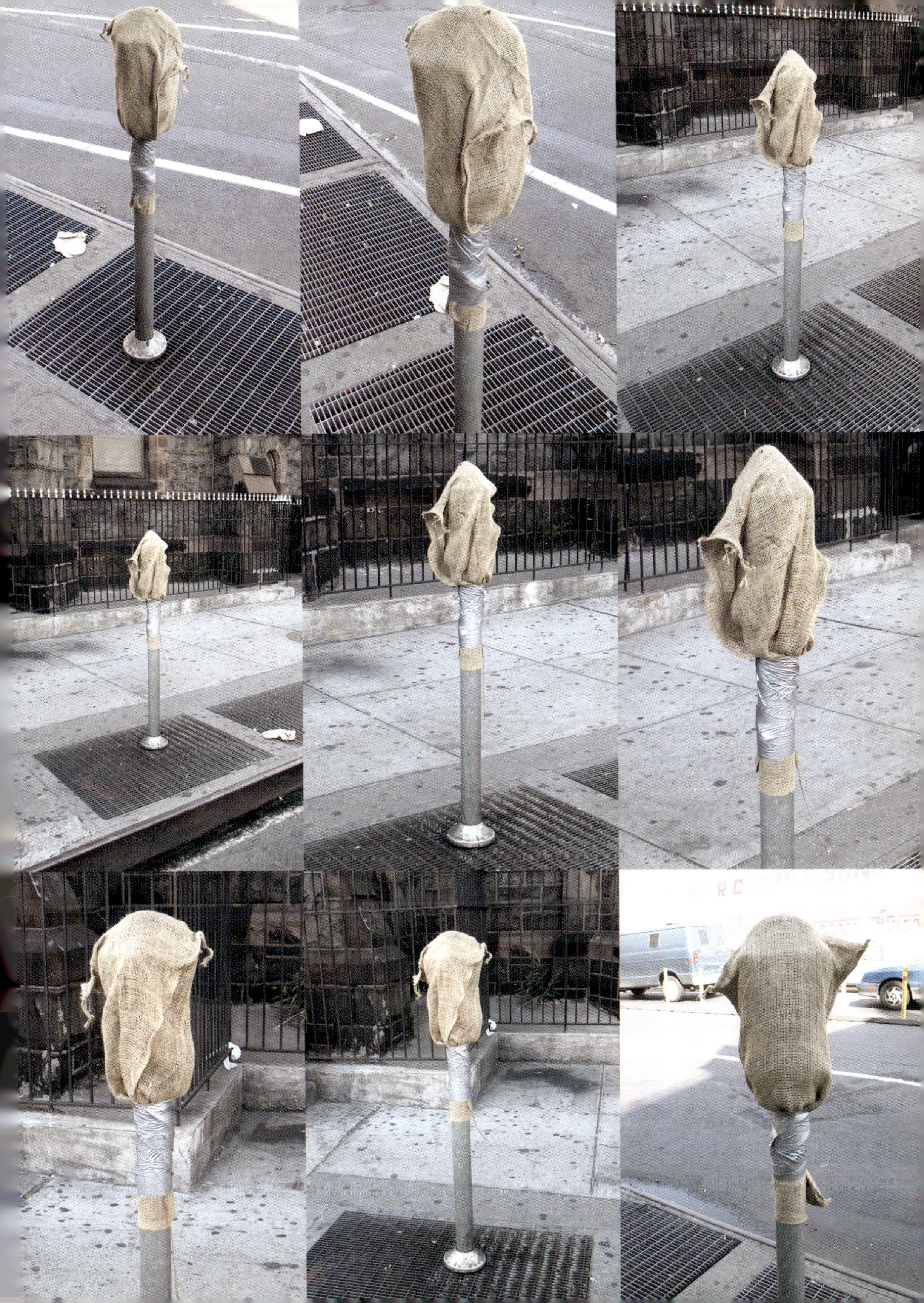

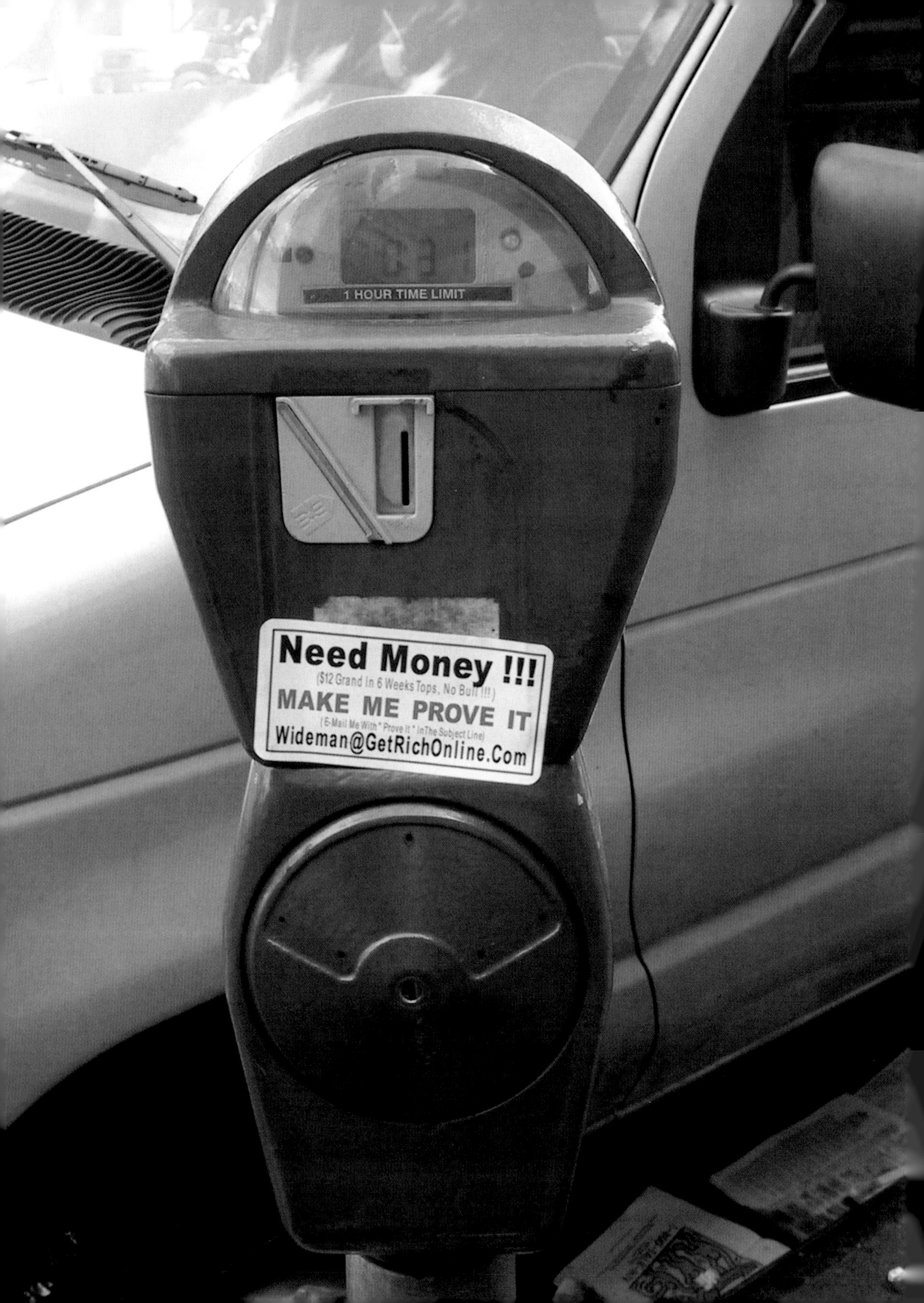
1 HOUR TIME LIMIT
Need Money !!!
($12 Grand In 6 Weeks Tops, No Bull !!!)
MAKE ME PROVE IT
(E-Mail Me With " Prove It " In The Subject Line)
Wideman@GetRichOnline.Com

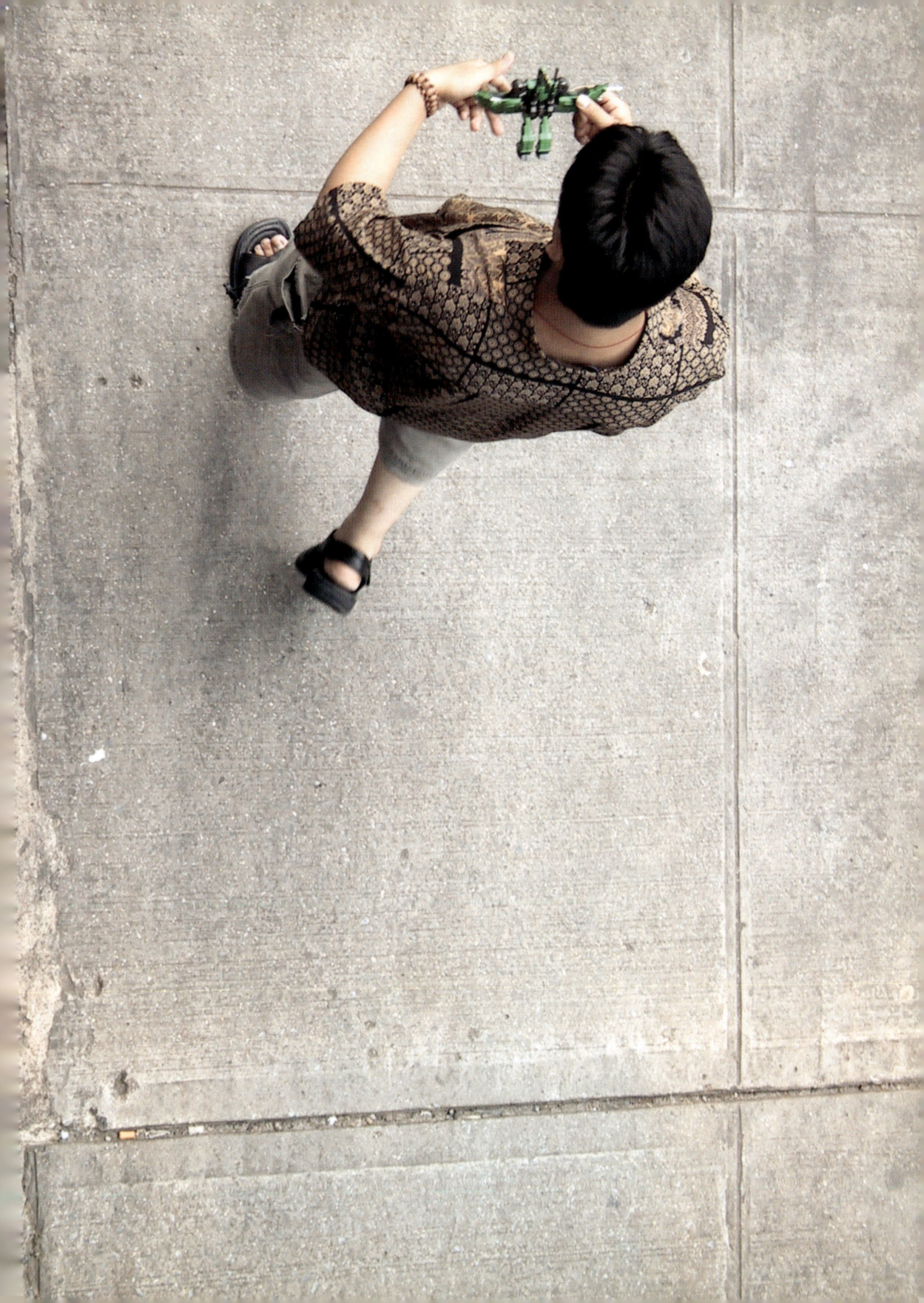

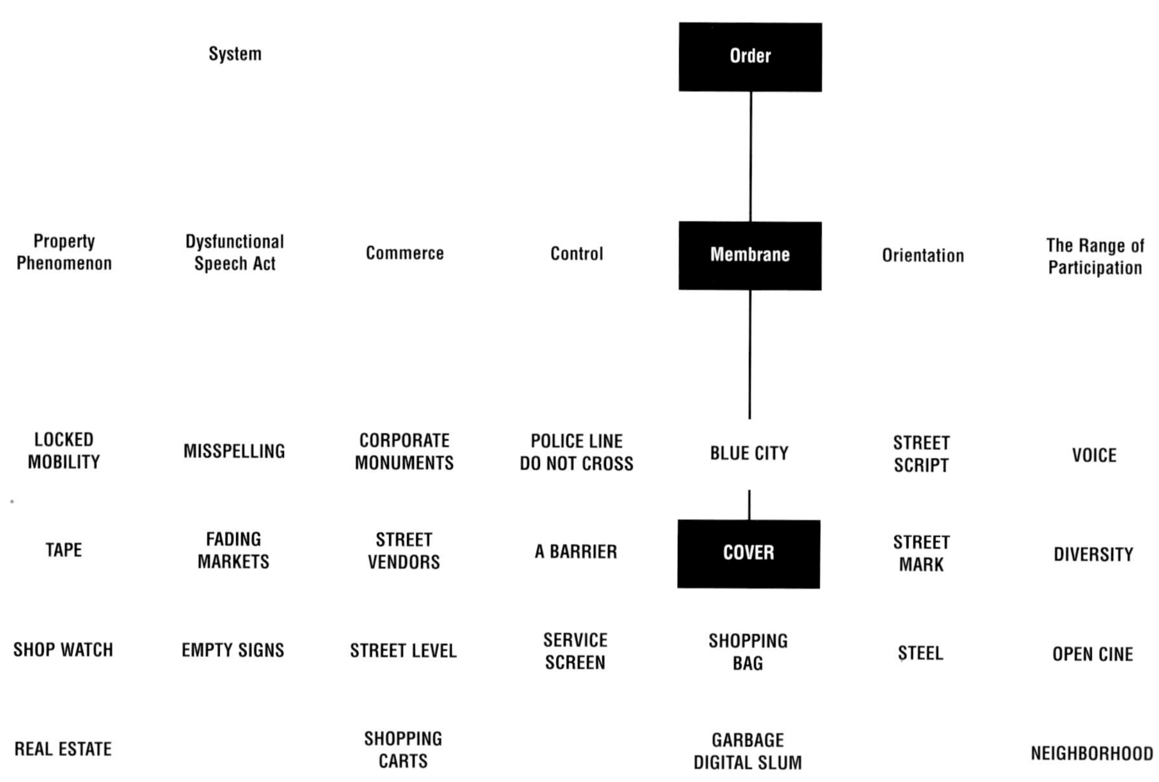
System
Order
Property Phenomenon
Dysfunctional Speech Act
Commerce
Control
Membrane
Orientation
The Range of Participation
LOCKED MOBILITY
MISSPELLING
CORPORATE MONUMENTS
POLICE LINE DO NOT CROSS
BLUE CITY
STREET SCRIPT
VOICE
TAPE
FADING MARKETS
STREET VENDORS
A BARRIER
COVER
STREET MARK
DIVERSITY
SHOP WATCH
EMPTY SIGNS
STREET LEVEL
SERVICE SCREEN
SHOPPING BAG
STEEL
OPEN CINE
REAL ESTATE
SHOPPING CARTS
GARBAGE DIGITAL SLUM
NEIGHBORHOOD

Identity

Alternative Media

Habitual Reinterpretation

COVER

Skin separates Inside from Outside

CAR DOOR

PUBLIC CHAIRS

LABELING.

PLASTIC CRATES

POLE POST

STANDPIPES

PRAY JESUS

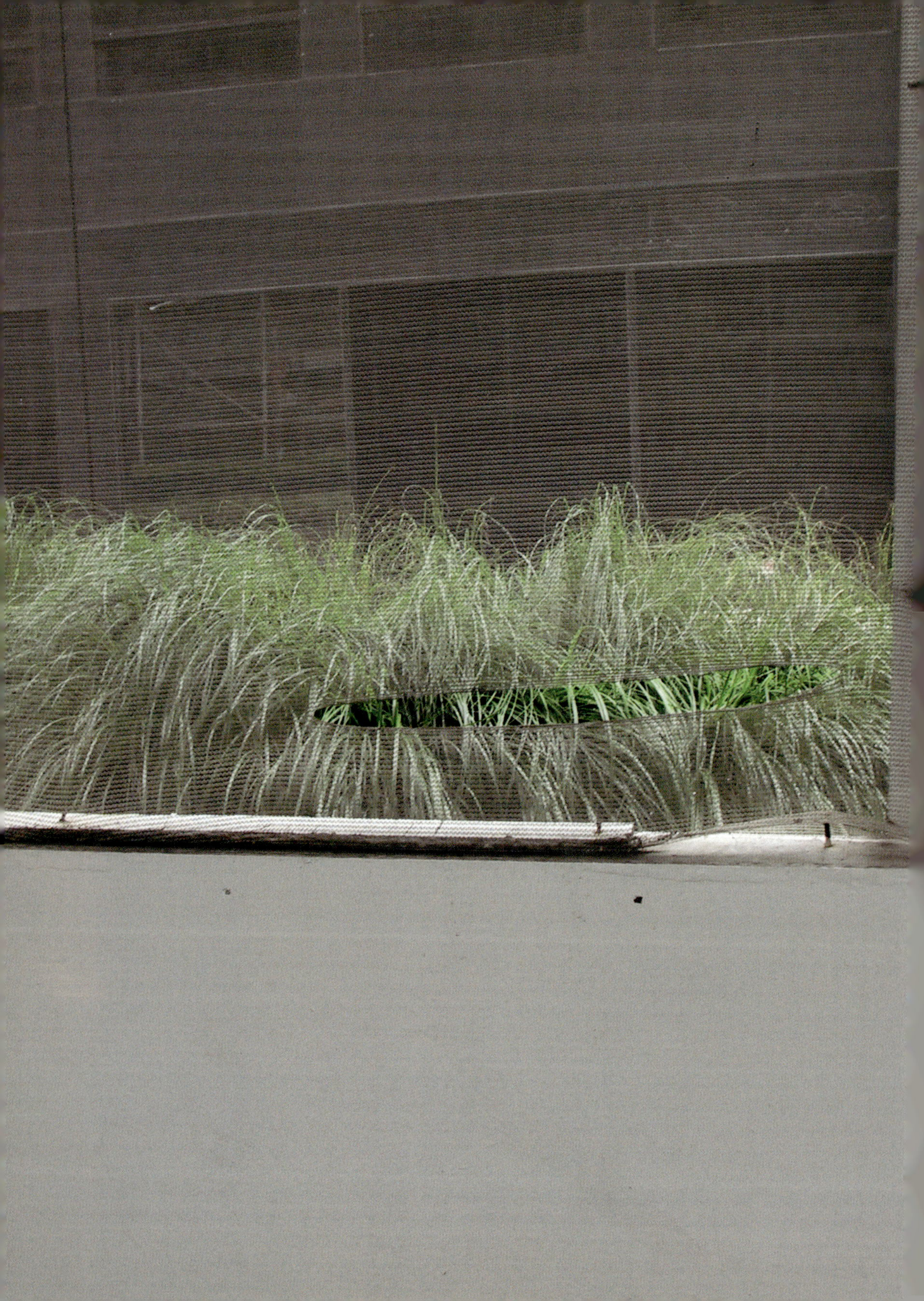

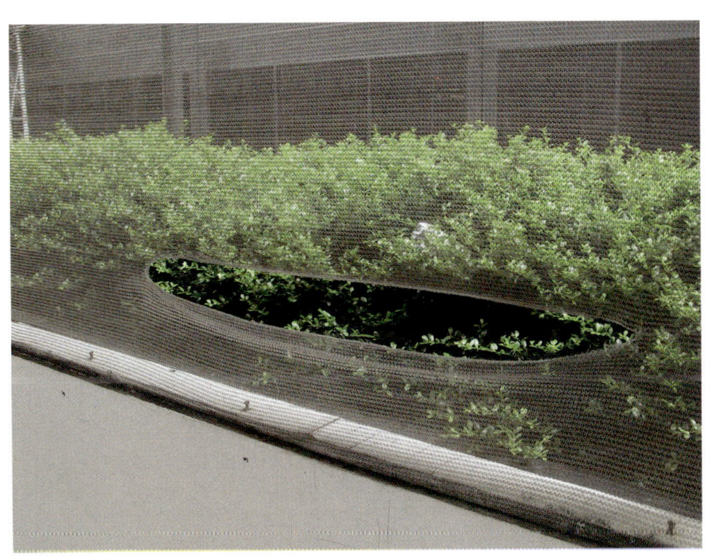

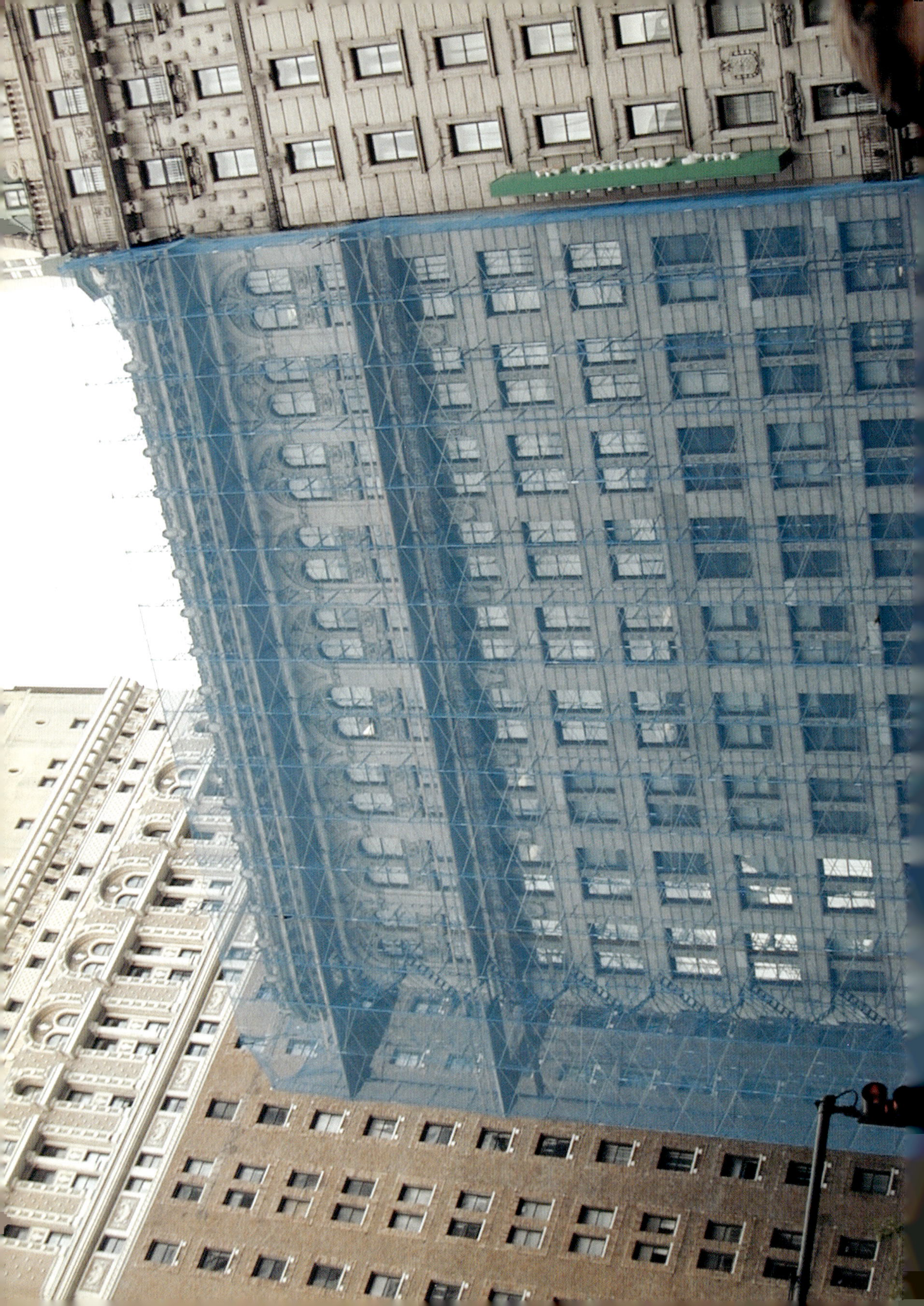

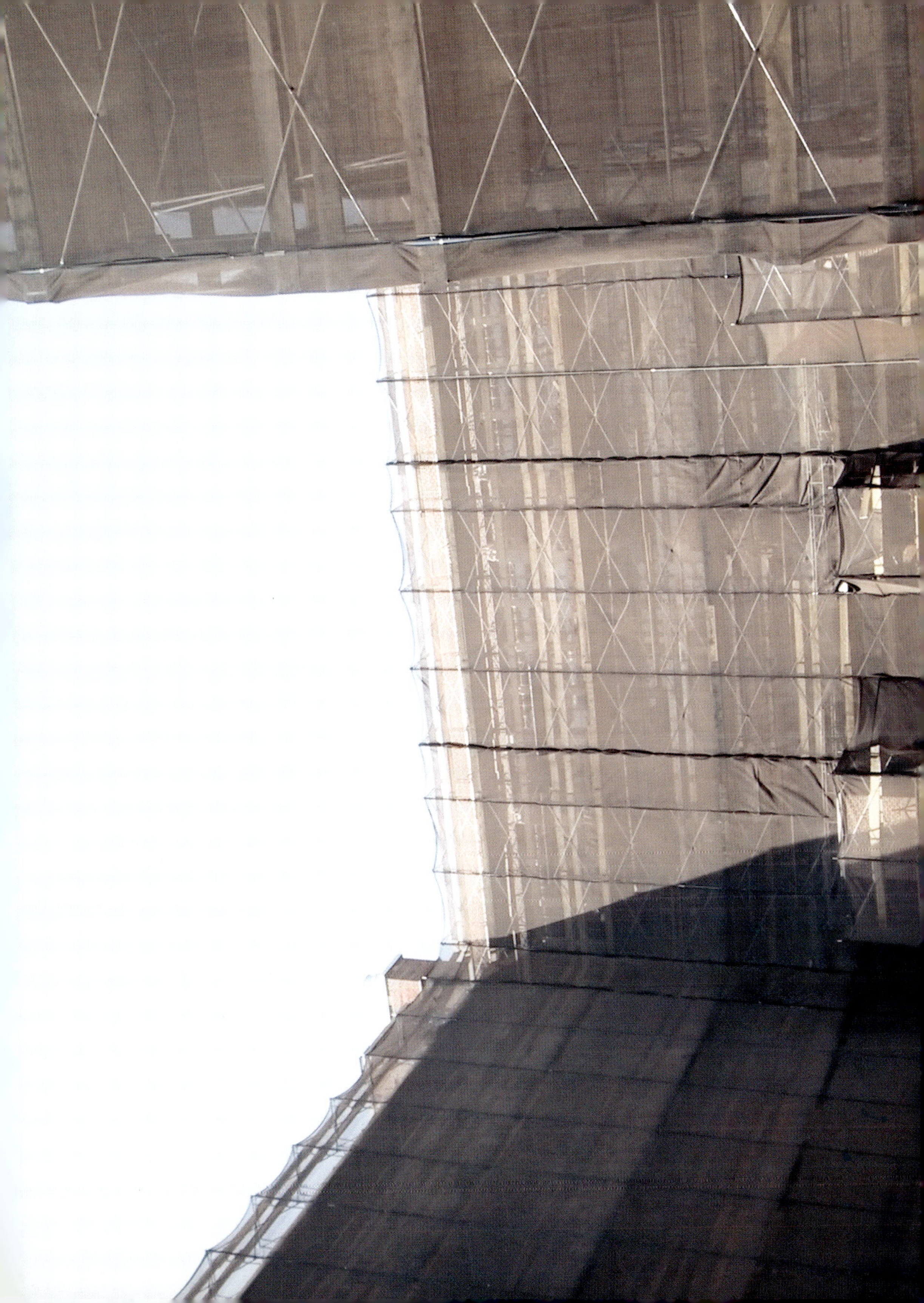

FLORMONT
TAILORS
ALTERATIONS
2ND FLOOR

PIZZA
DELI
ATM
AVAILABLE INSIDE

SINCE 1960
TAILOR
EXPERT TAILORING FOR MEN & LADIES
ALTERATIONS ON:
• SUITS AND SPORTCOATS
• RAIN COATS AND OVER COATS
• LEATHERS AND DENIM
• LADIES GOWNS AND FINE FABRICS
CUSTOM-MADE
TAILORED CLOTHING
SAME DAY SERVICE
AVAILABLE
857 BROADWAY
AT 17th STREET
SUITE 202-A
212 255-2549
OPEN 7-DAYS

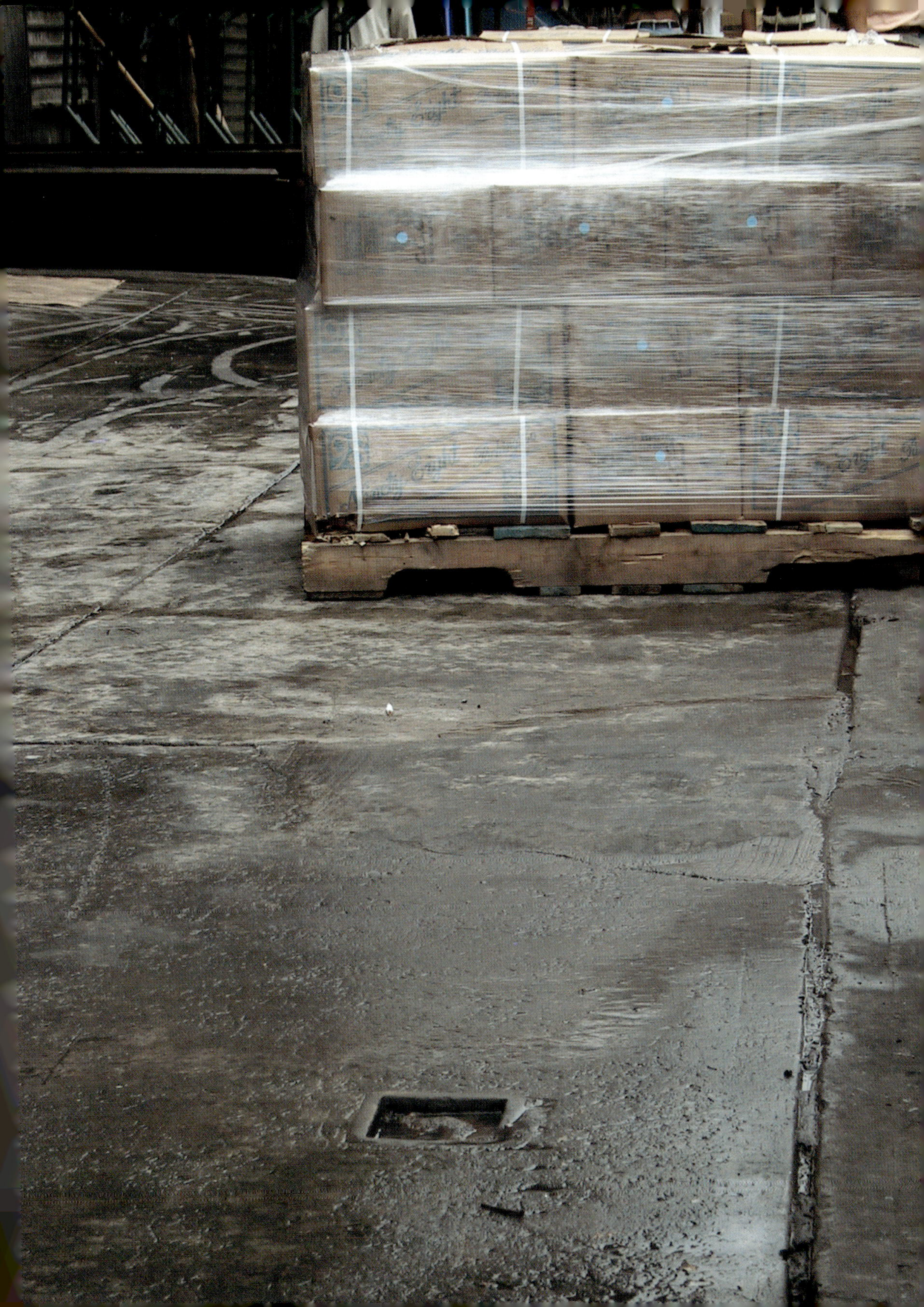

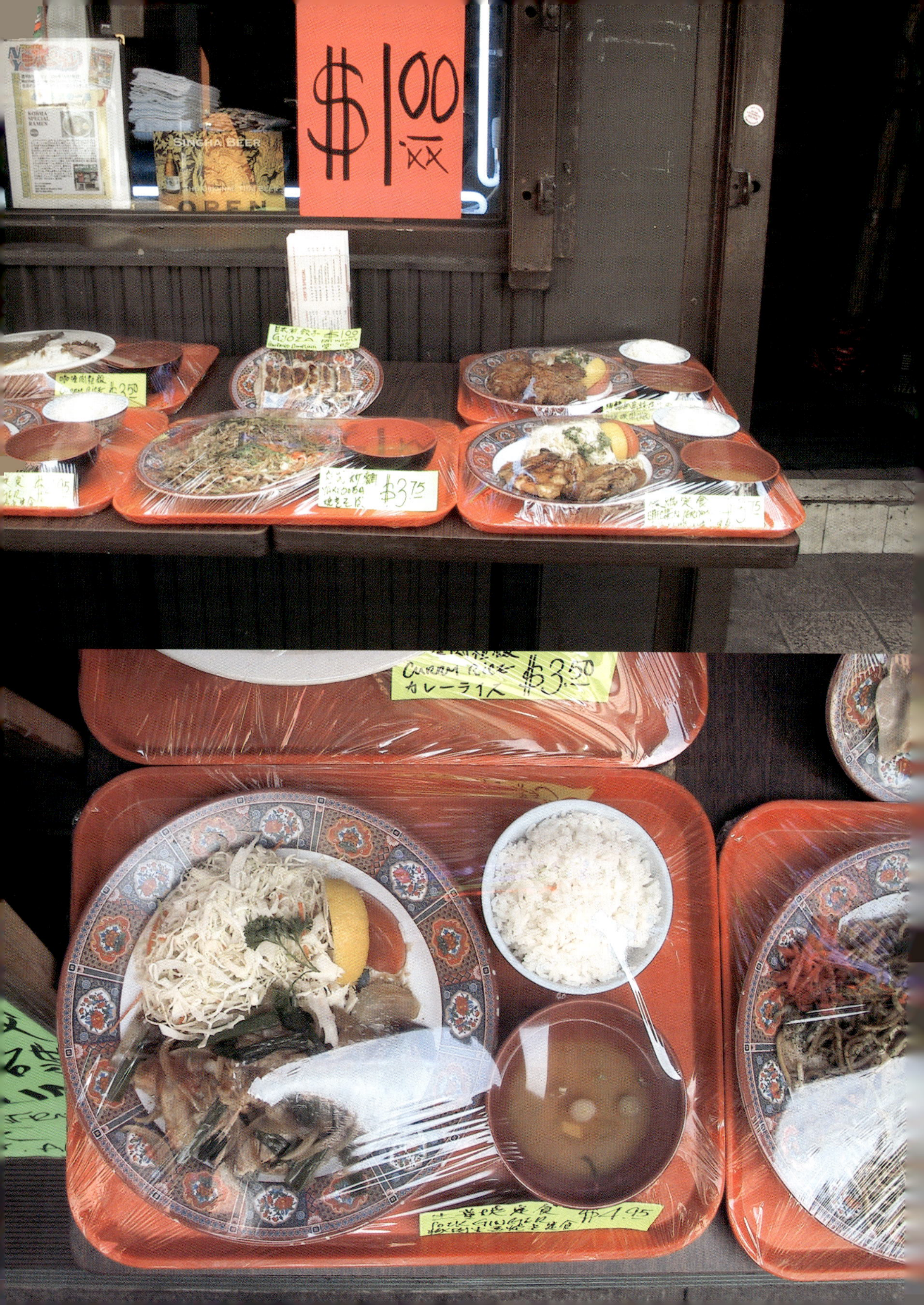
$1.00
SINGHA BEER
$3.75
CURRY RICE $3.50
カレーライス
$4.95

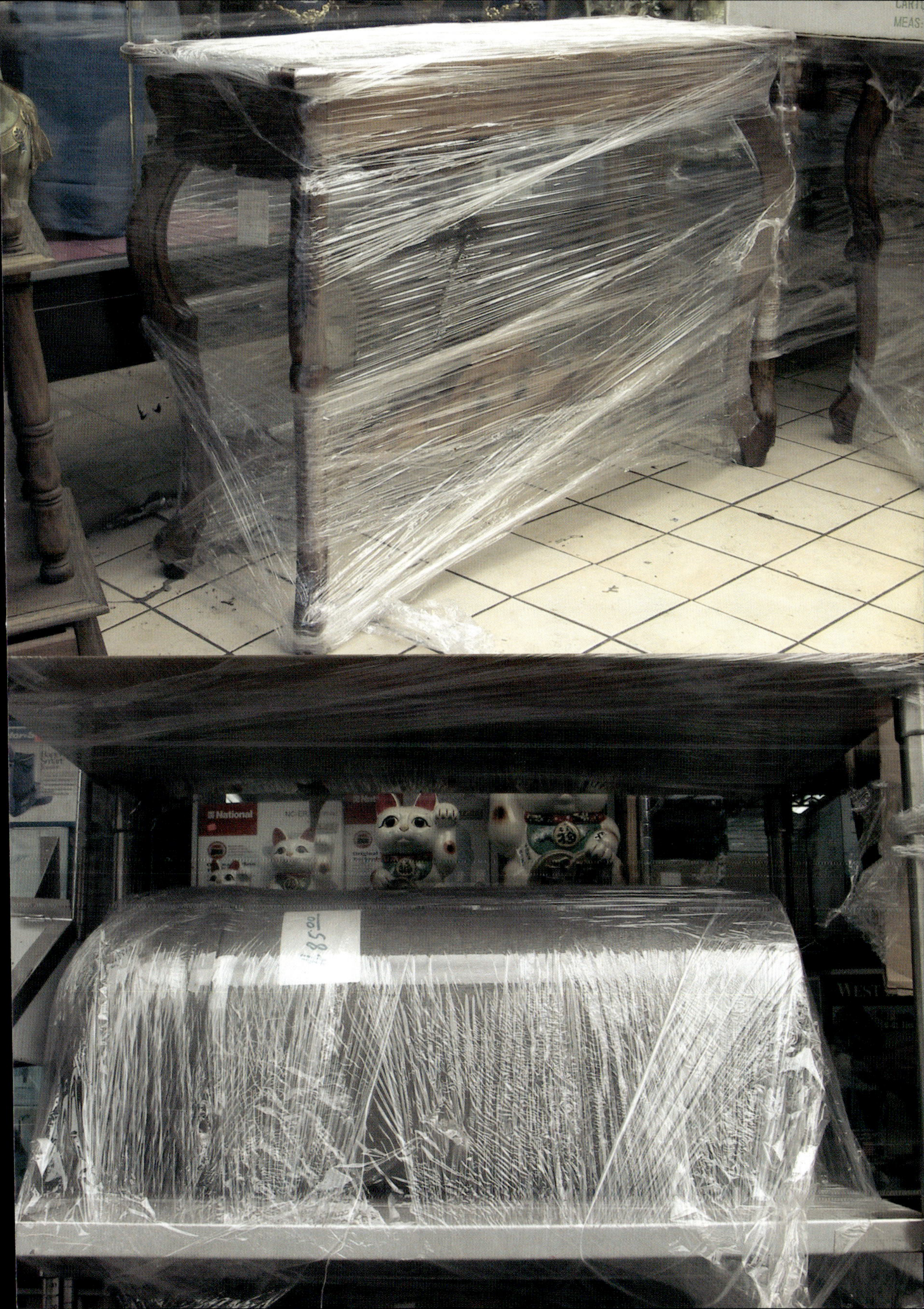
National

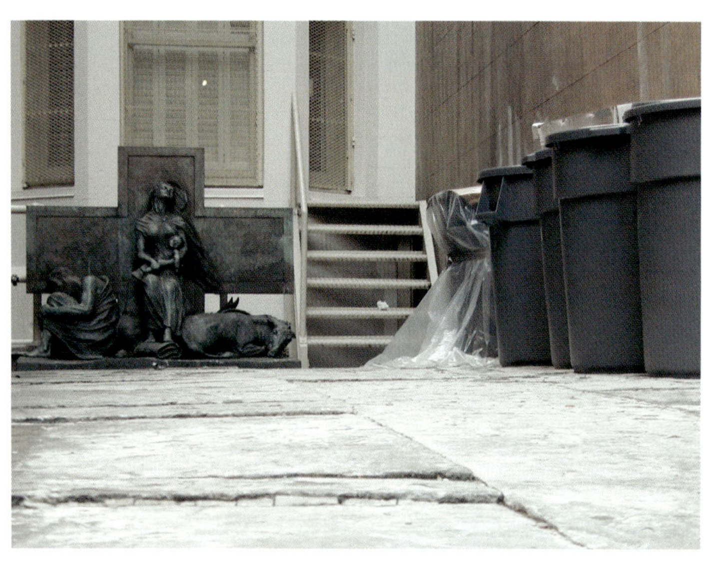

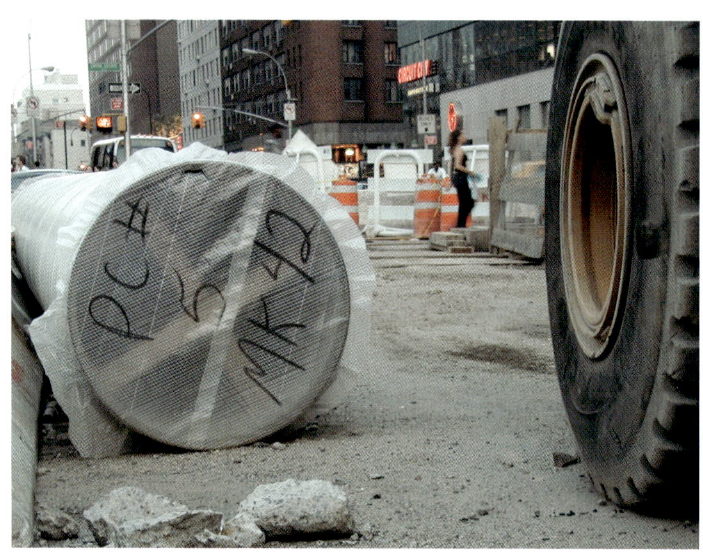
RC#
5
MK42

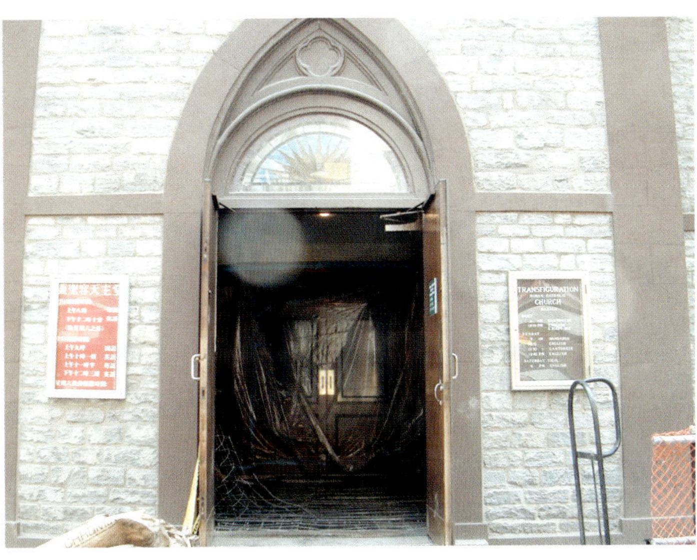
TRANSFIGURATION
CHURCH

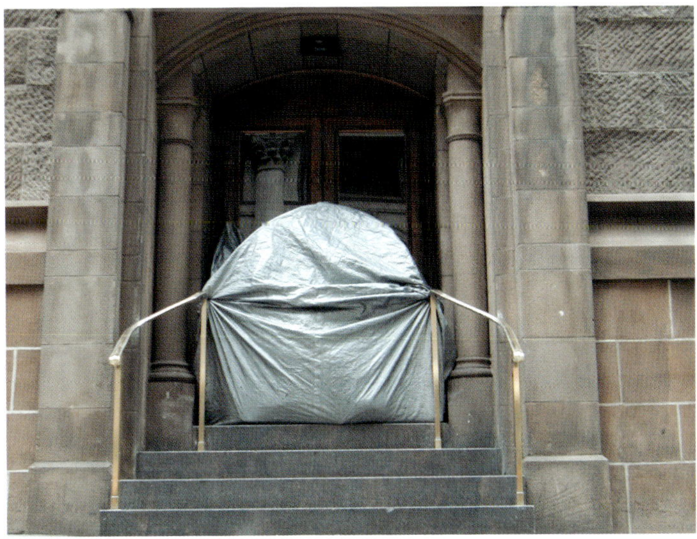

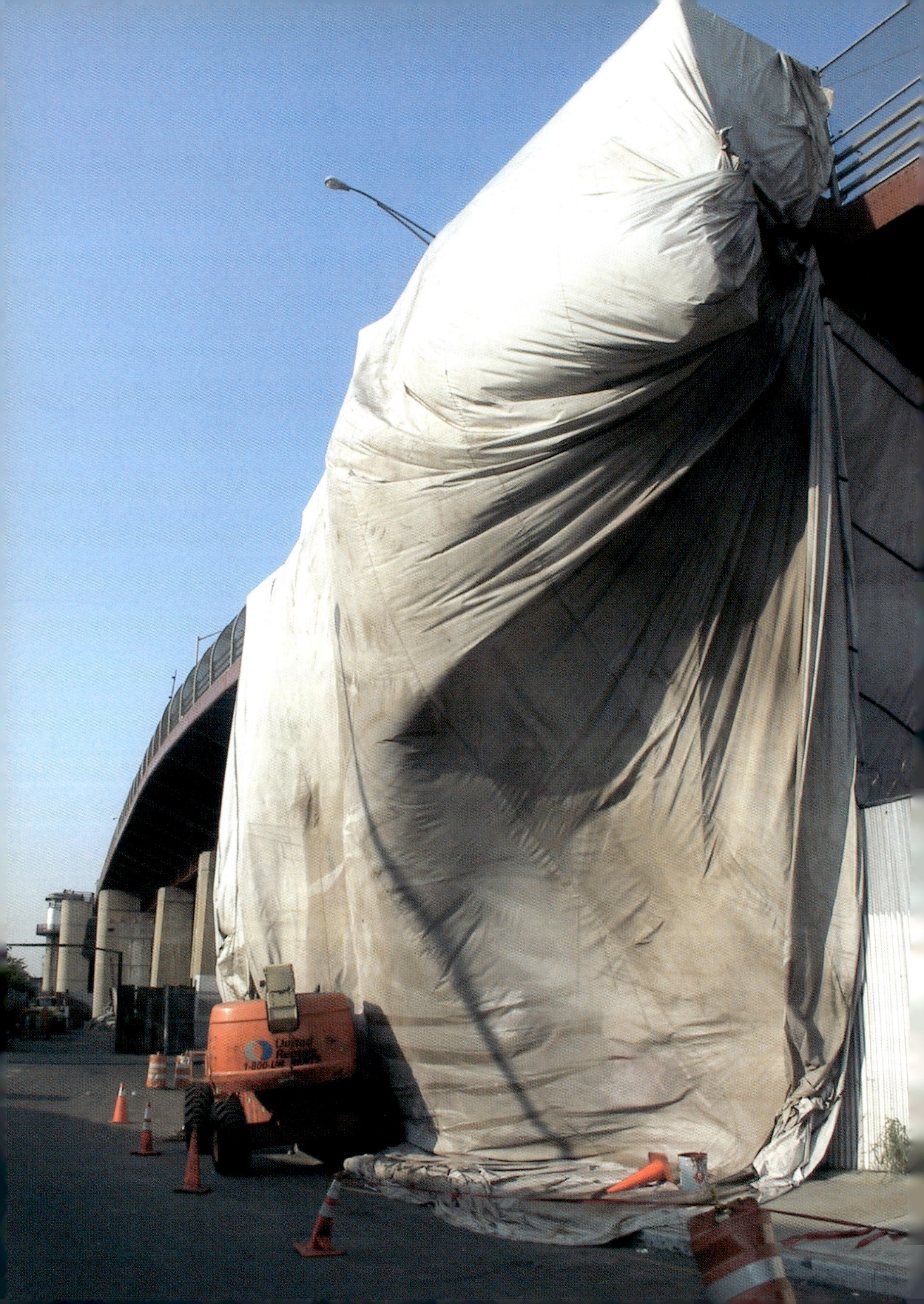
1-800-UR

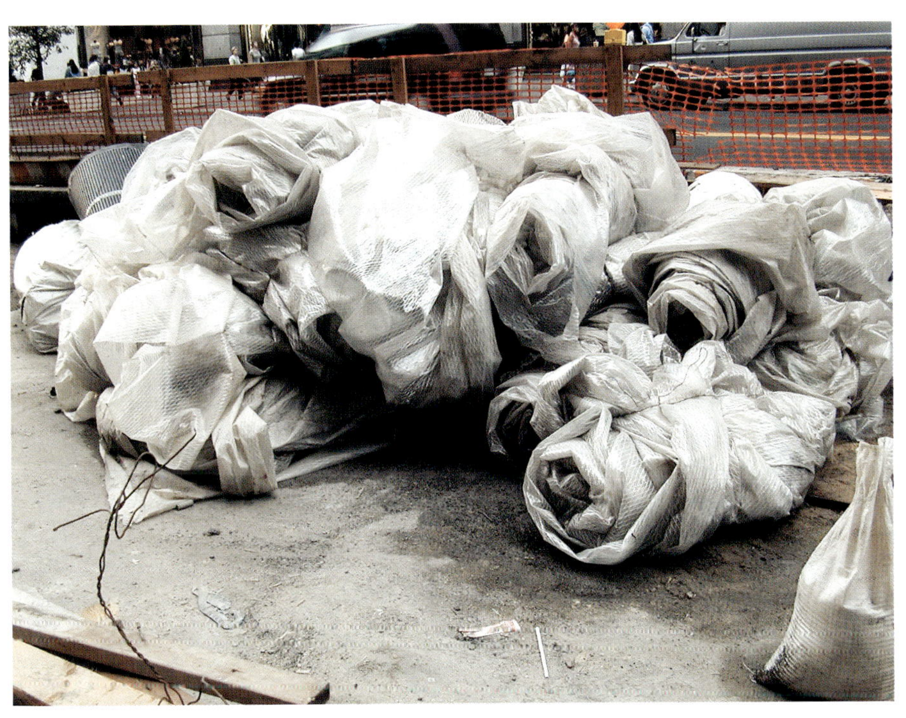

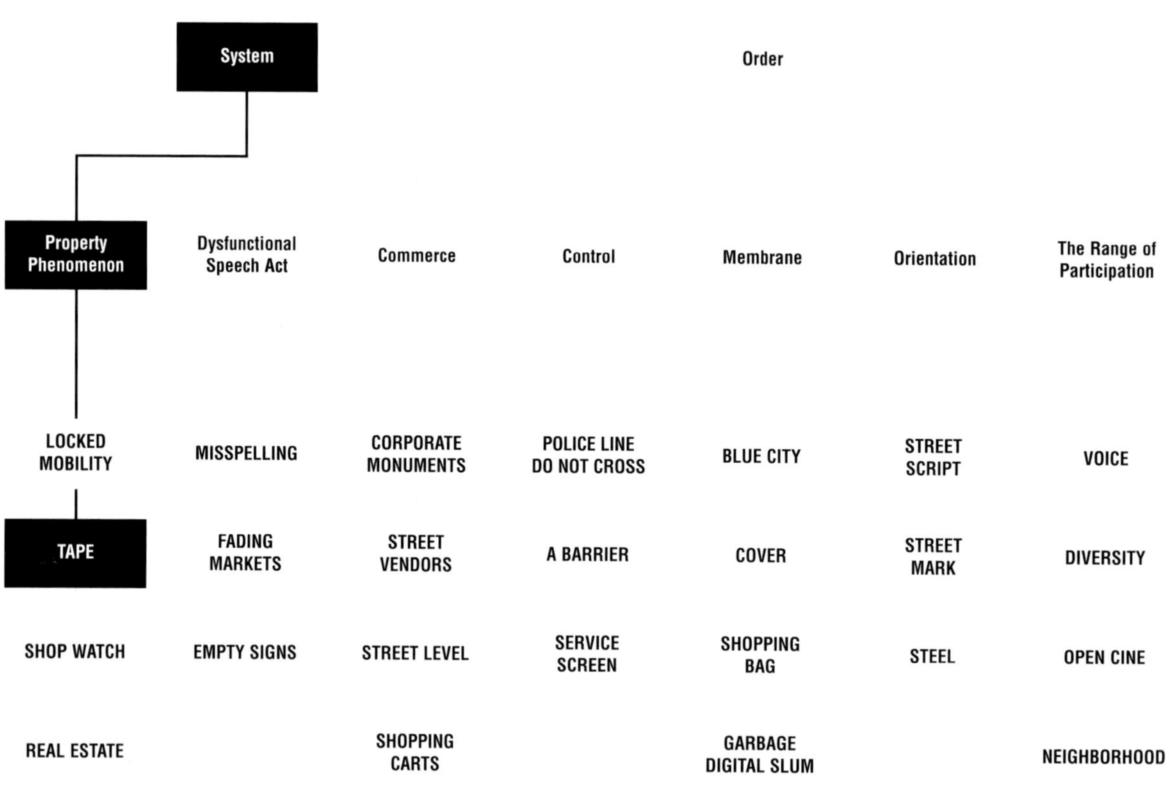
System
Order
Property Phenomenon
Dysfunctional Speech Act
Commerce
Control
Membrane
Orientation
The Range of Participation
LOCKED MOBILITY
MISSPELLING
CORPORATE MONUMENTS
POLICE LINE DO NOT CROSS
BLUE CITY
STREET SCRIPT
VOICE
TAPE
FADING MARKETS
STREET VENDORS
A BARRIER
COVER
STREET MARK
DIVERSITY
SHOP WATCH
EMPTY SIGNS
STREET LEVEL
SERVICE SCREEN
SHOPPING BAG
STEEL
OPEN CINE
REAL ESTATE
SHOPPING CARTS
GARBAGE DIGITAL SLUM
NEIGHBORHOOD

Identity

Alternative Media

Habitual Reinterpretation

TAPE

Protection for and against Possession

CAR DOOR

PUBLIC CHAIRS

LABELING.

PLASTIC CRATES

POLE POST

STANDPIPES

PRAY JESUS

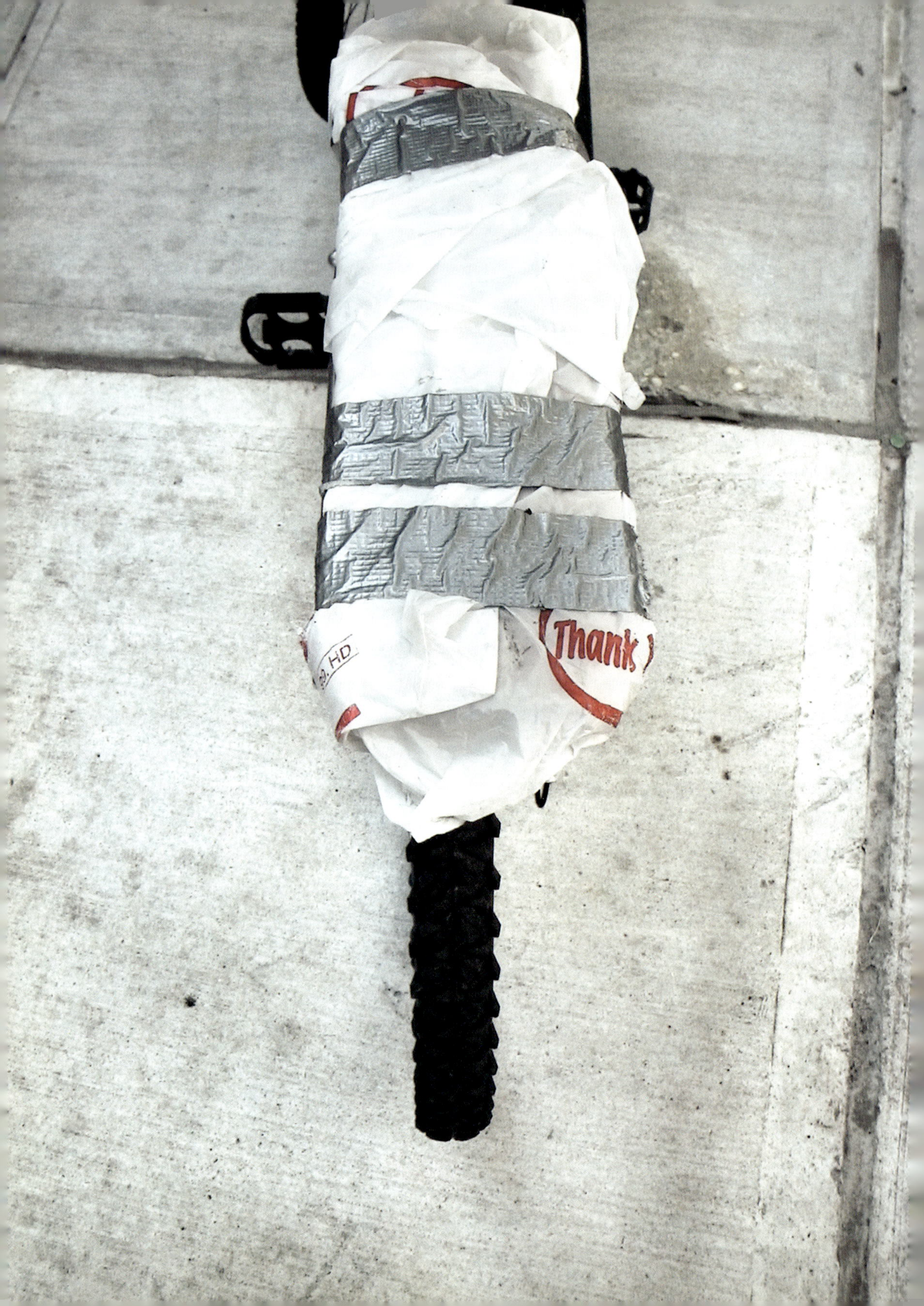
Thank

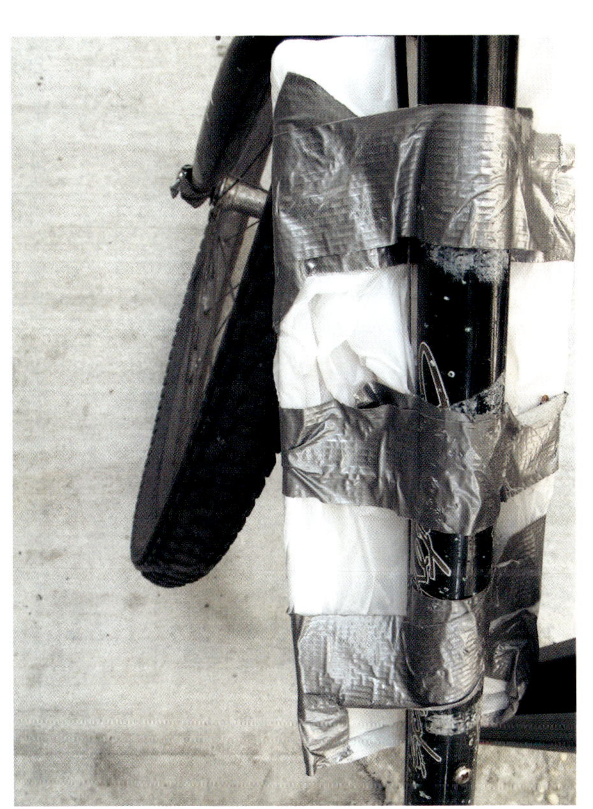

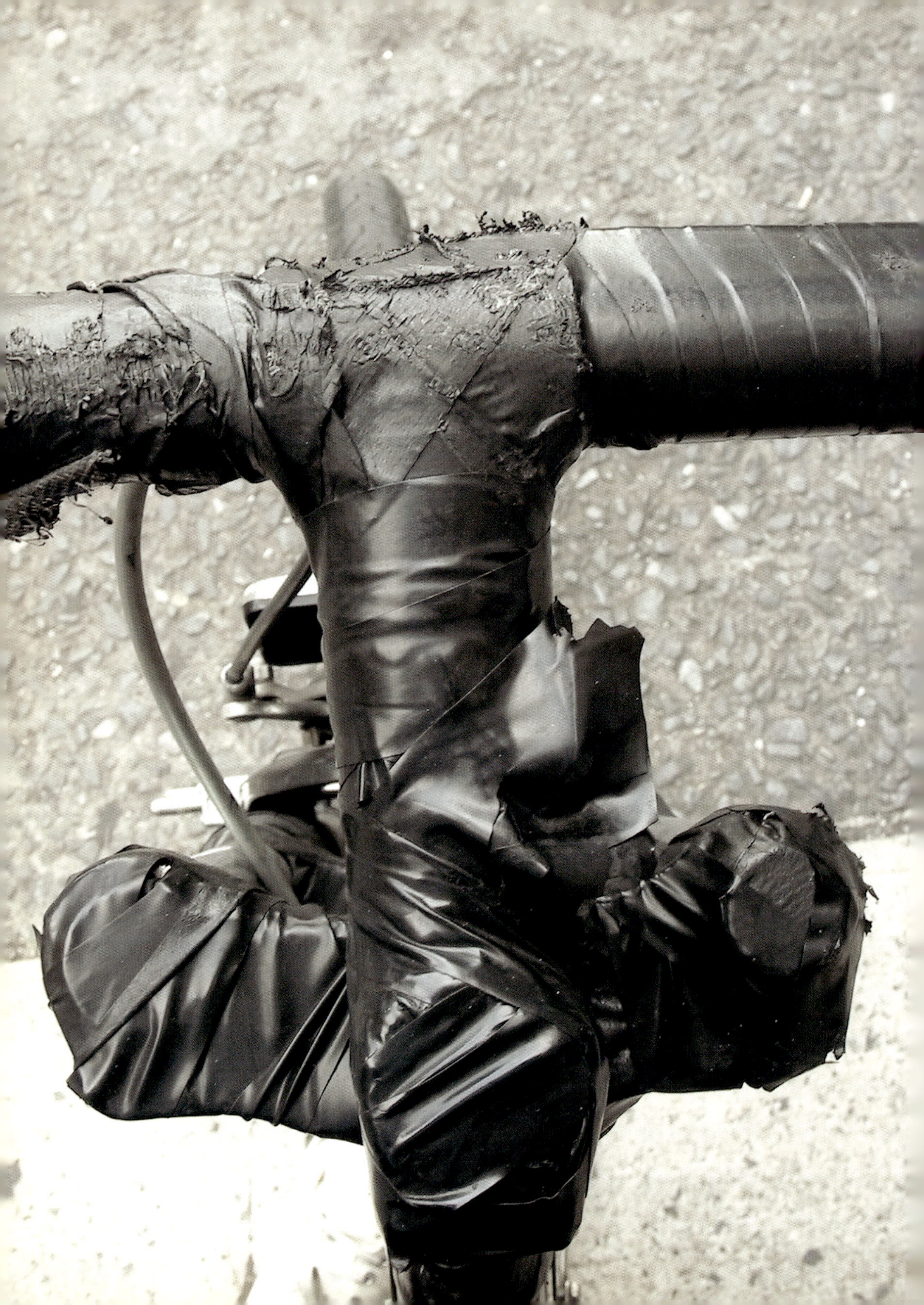

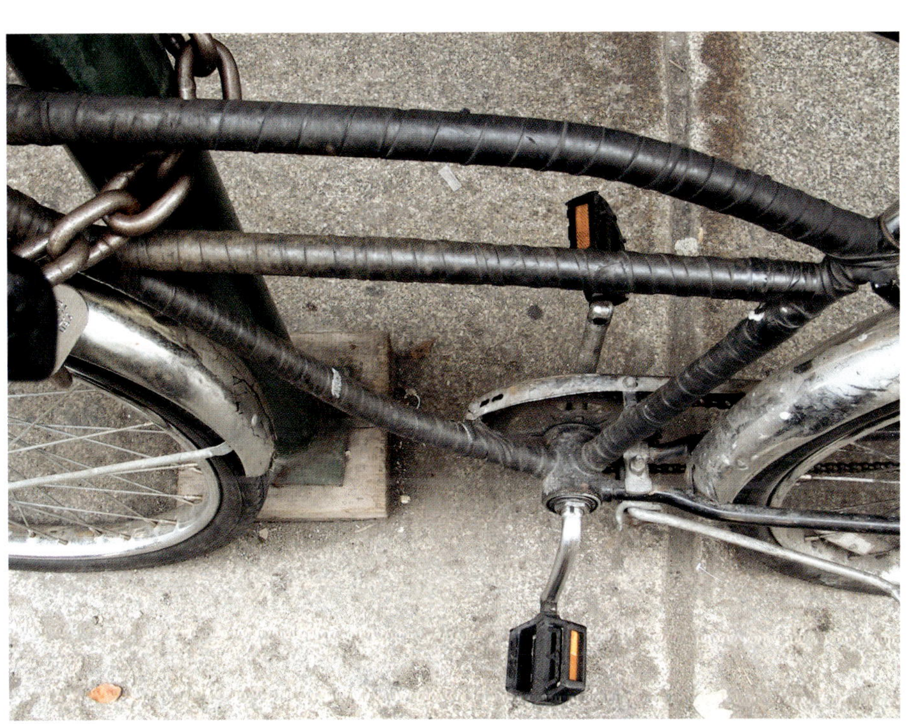

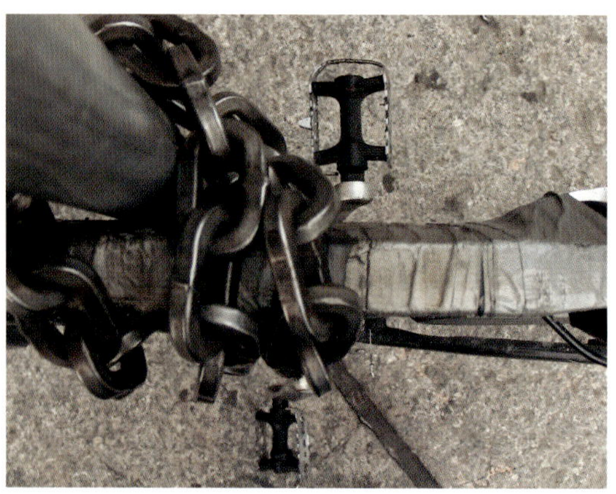
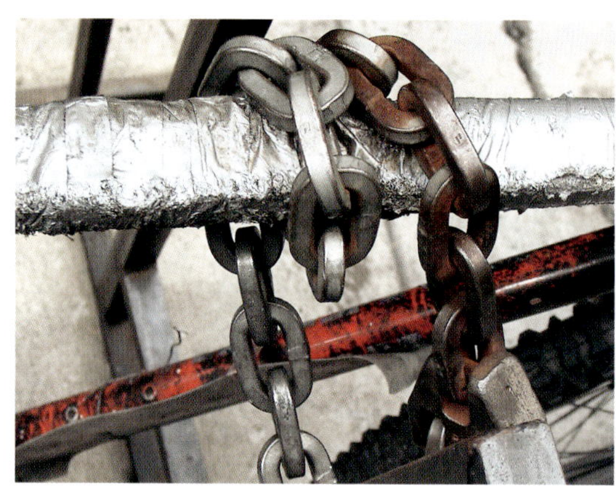
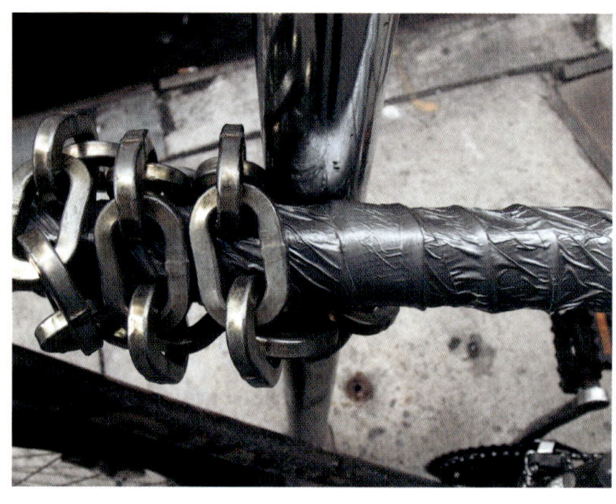
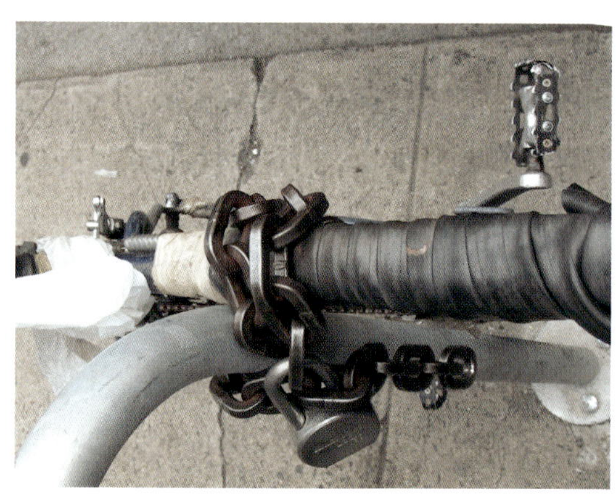
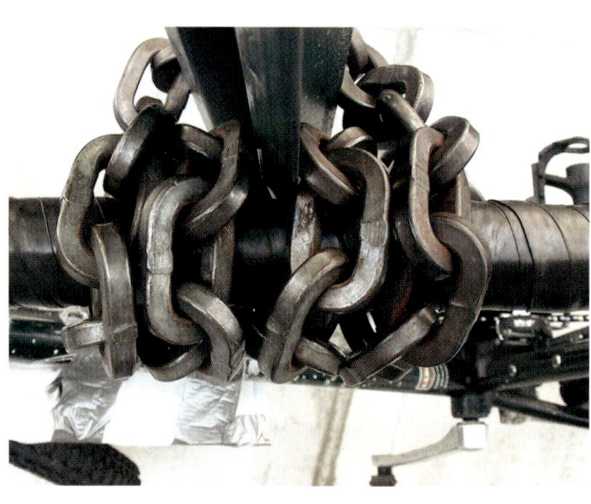
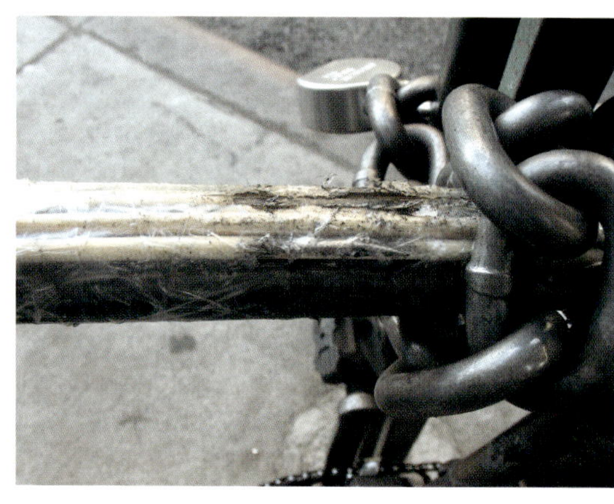

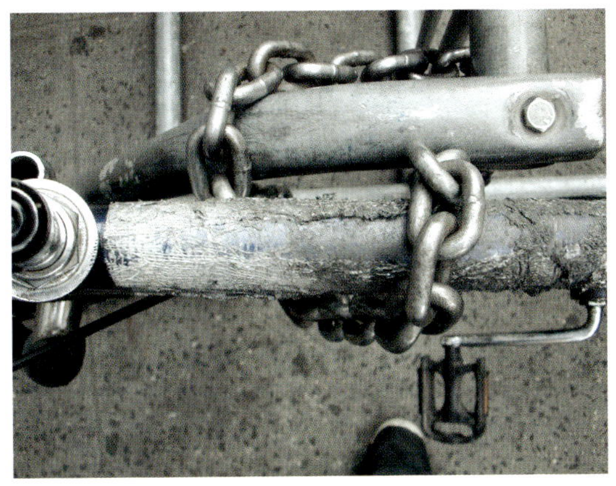

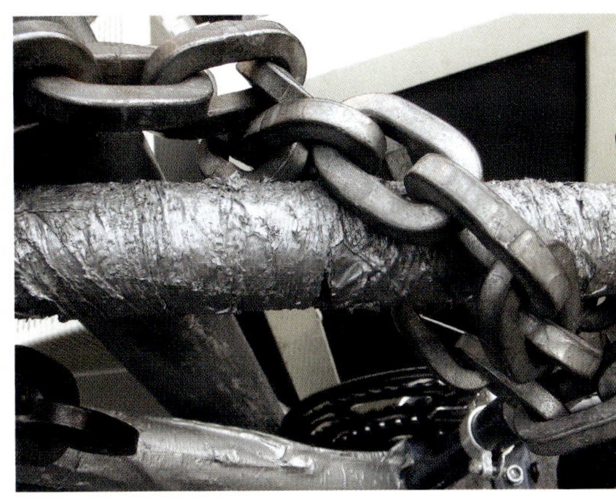

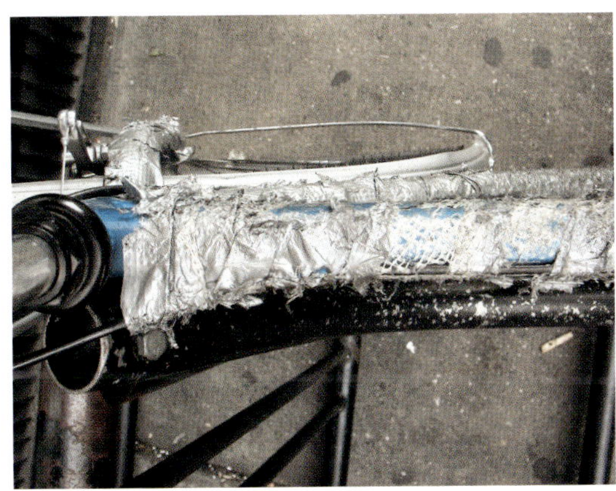

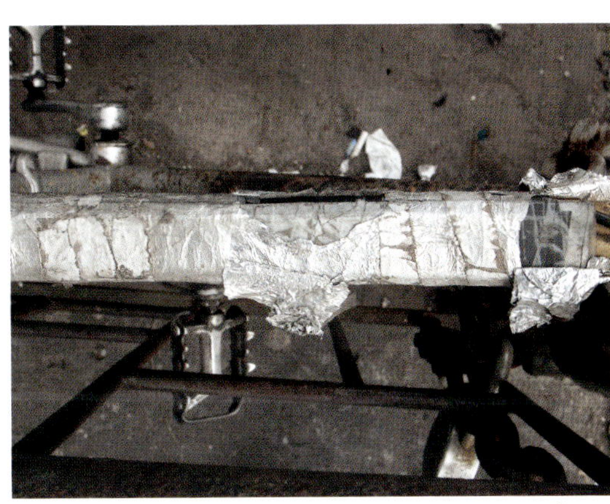

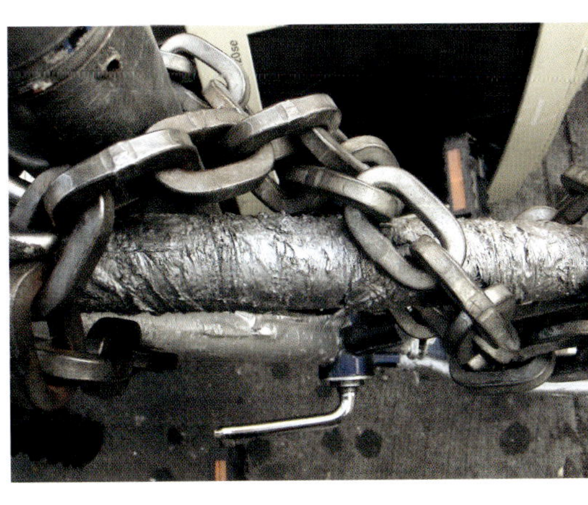

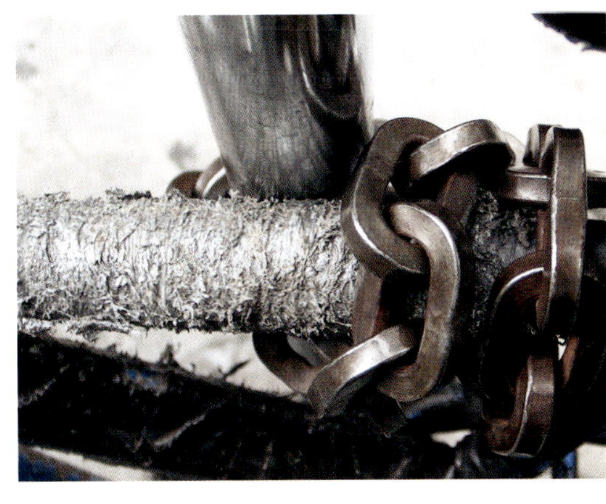

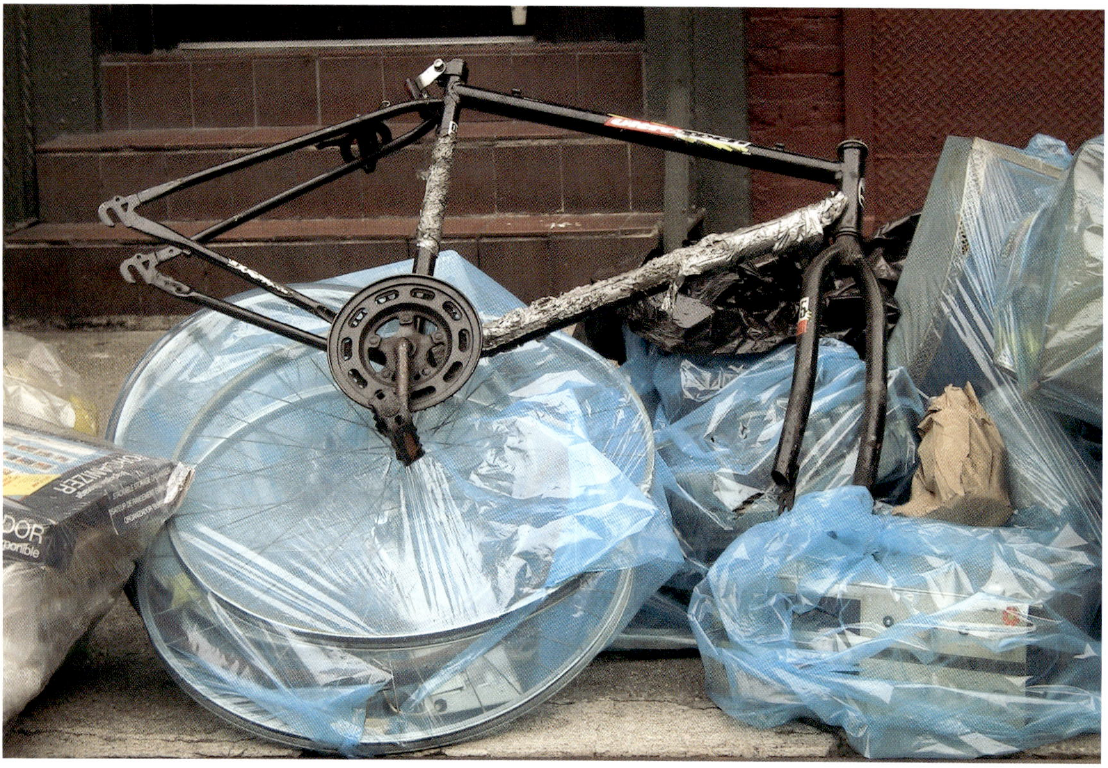

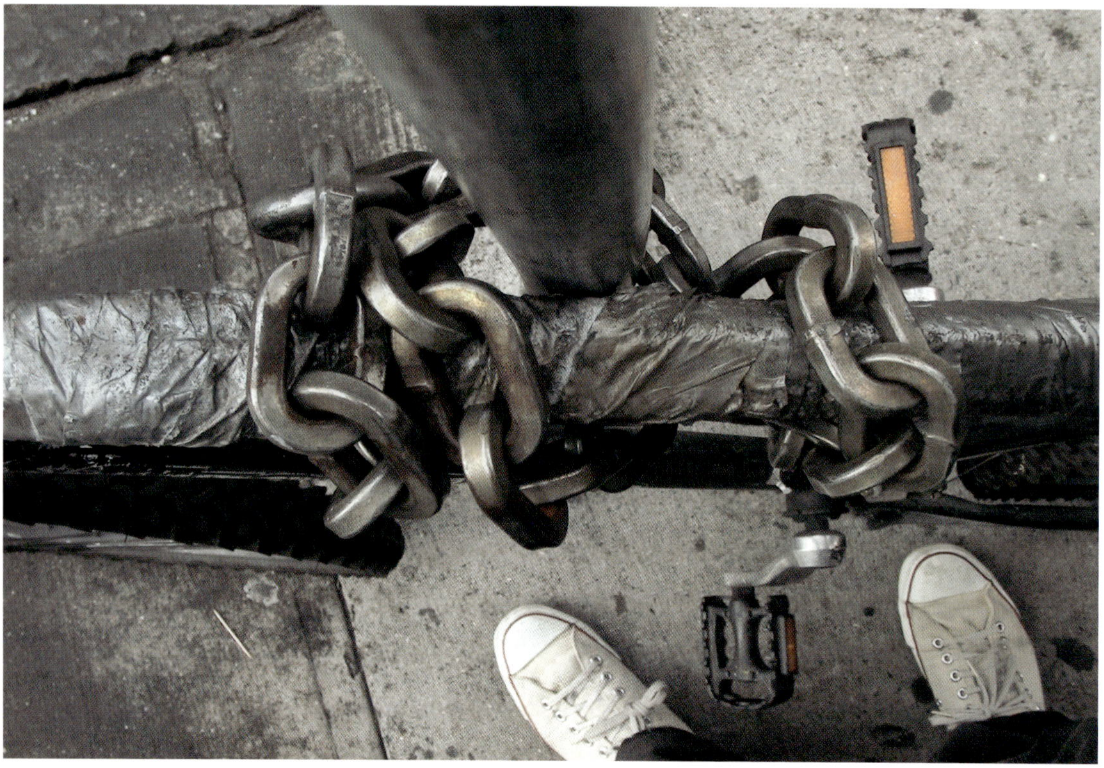

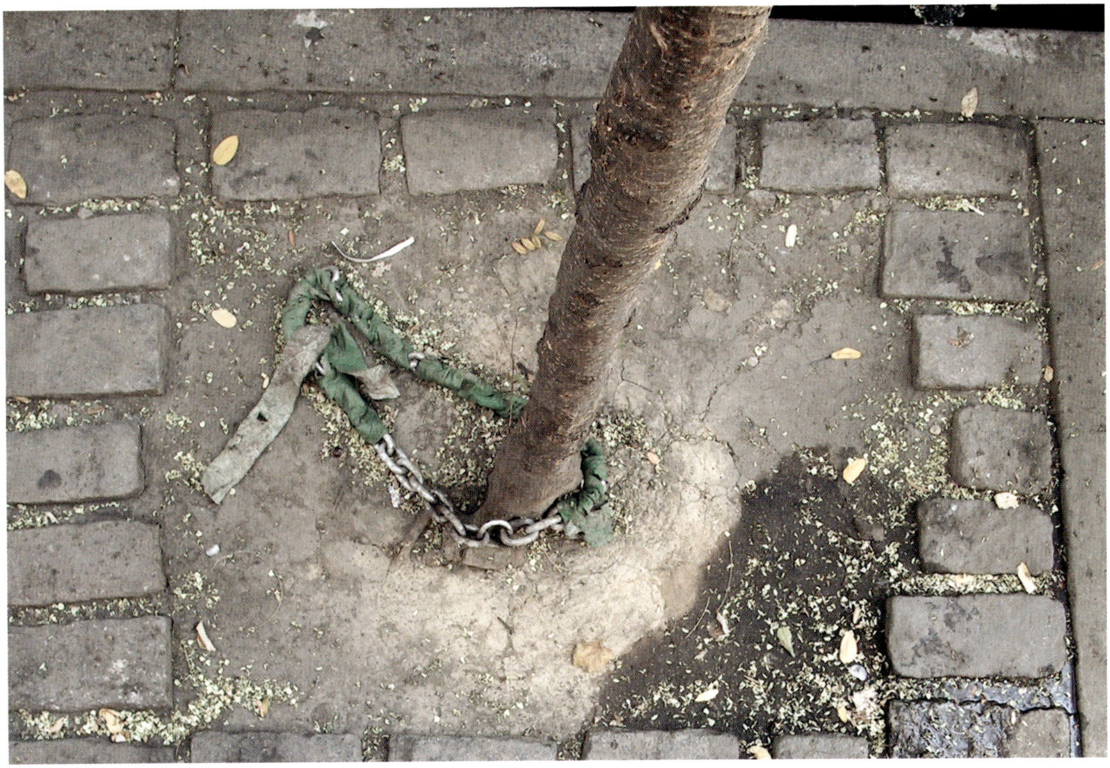

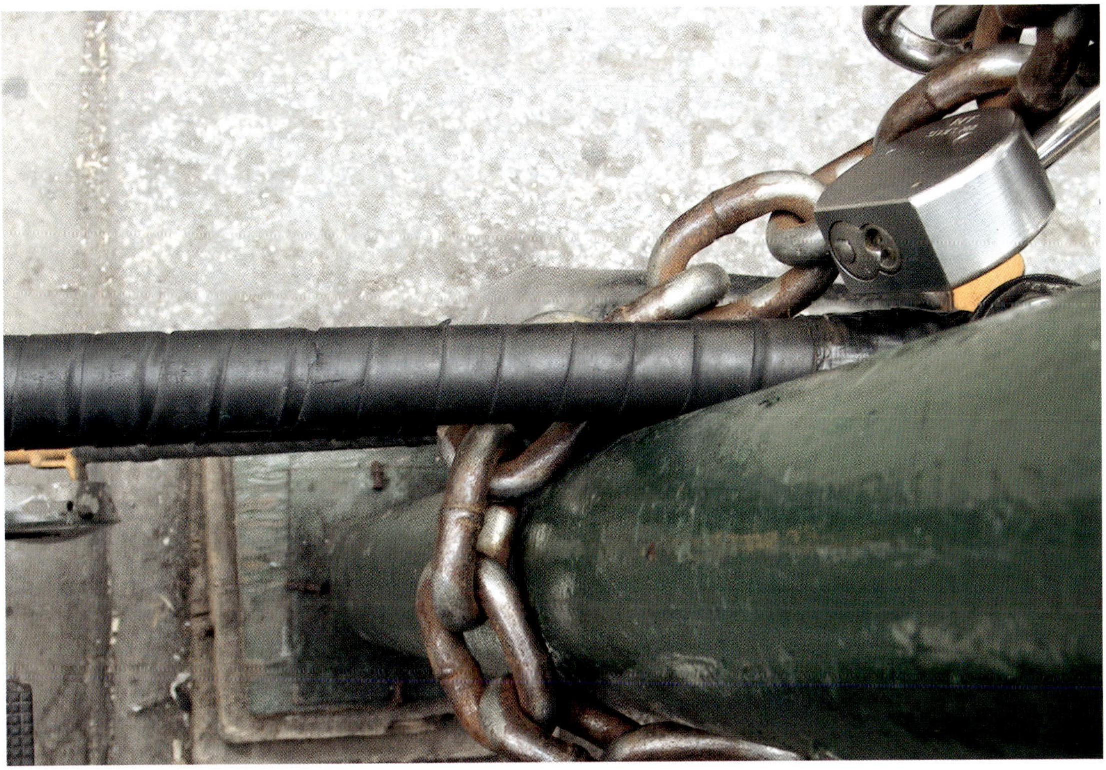

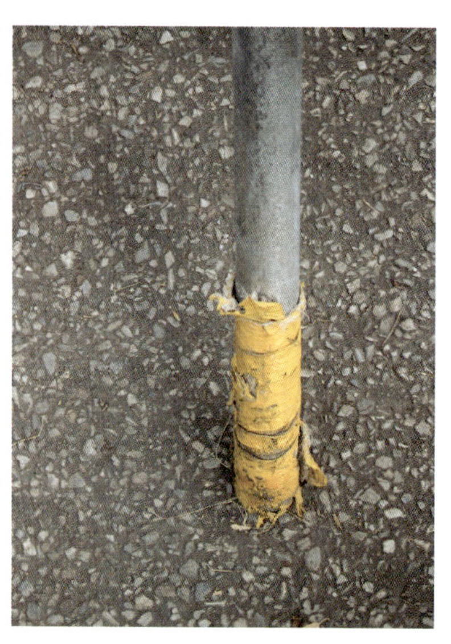

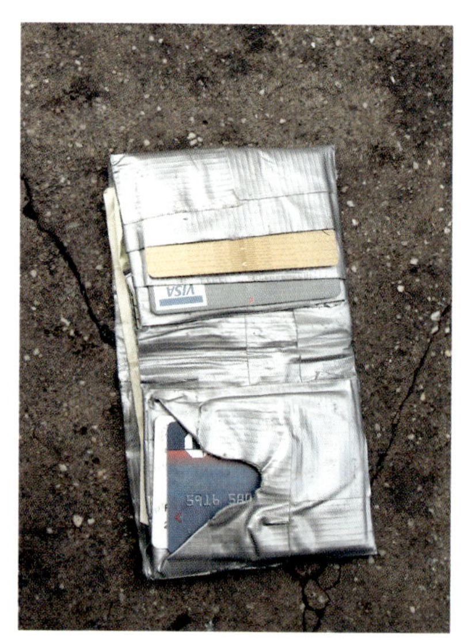
VISA

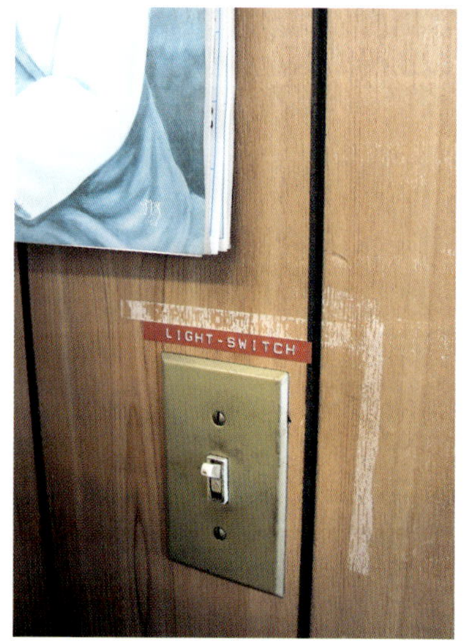
LIGHT-SWITCH

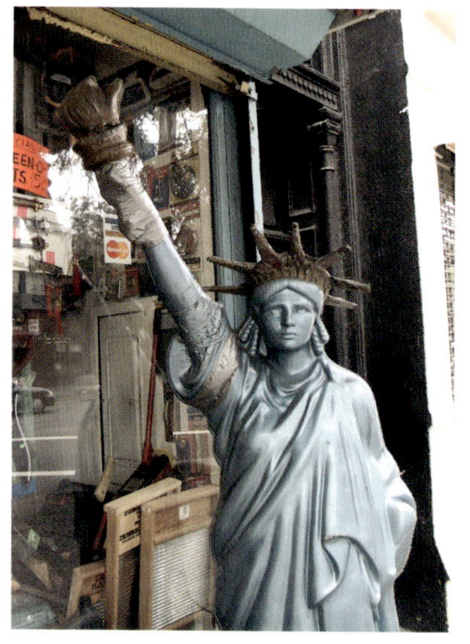

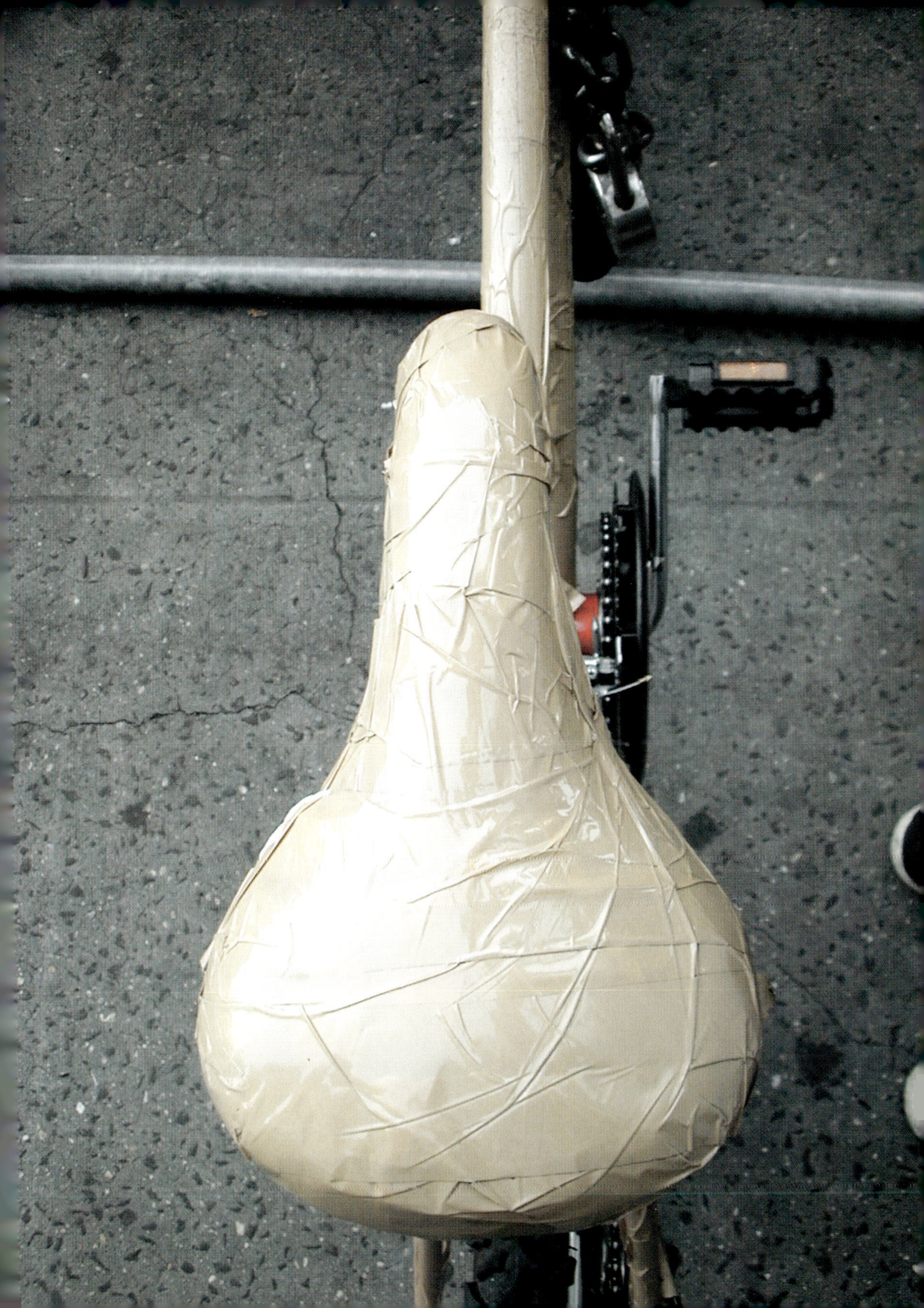

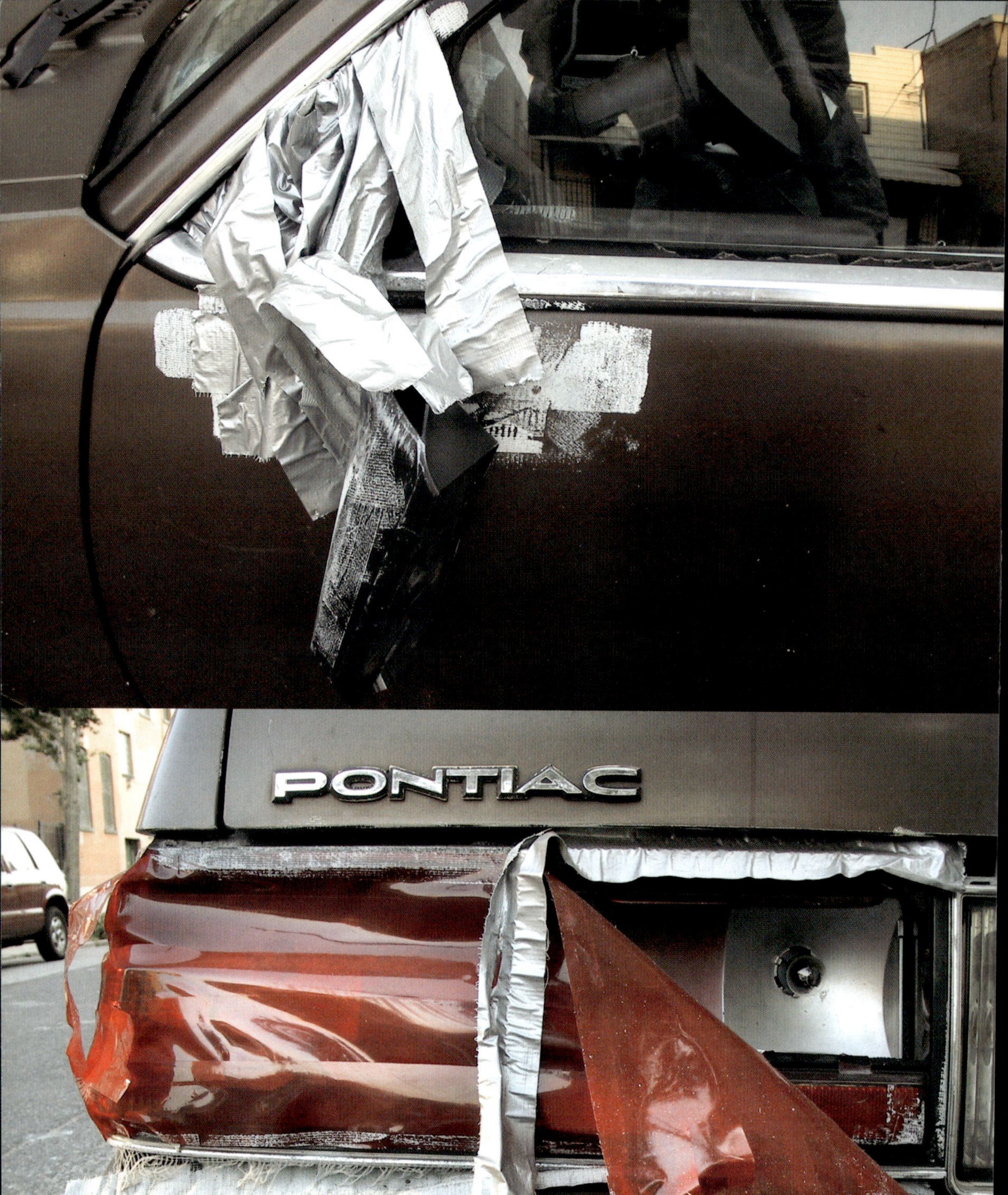
PONTIAC

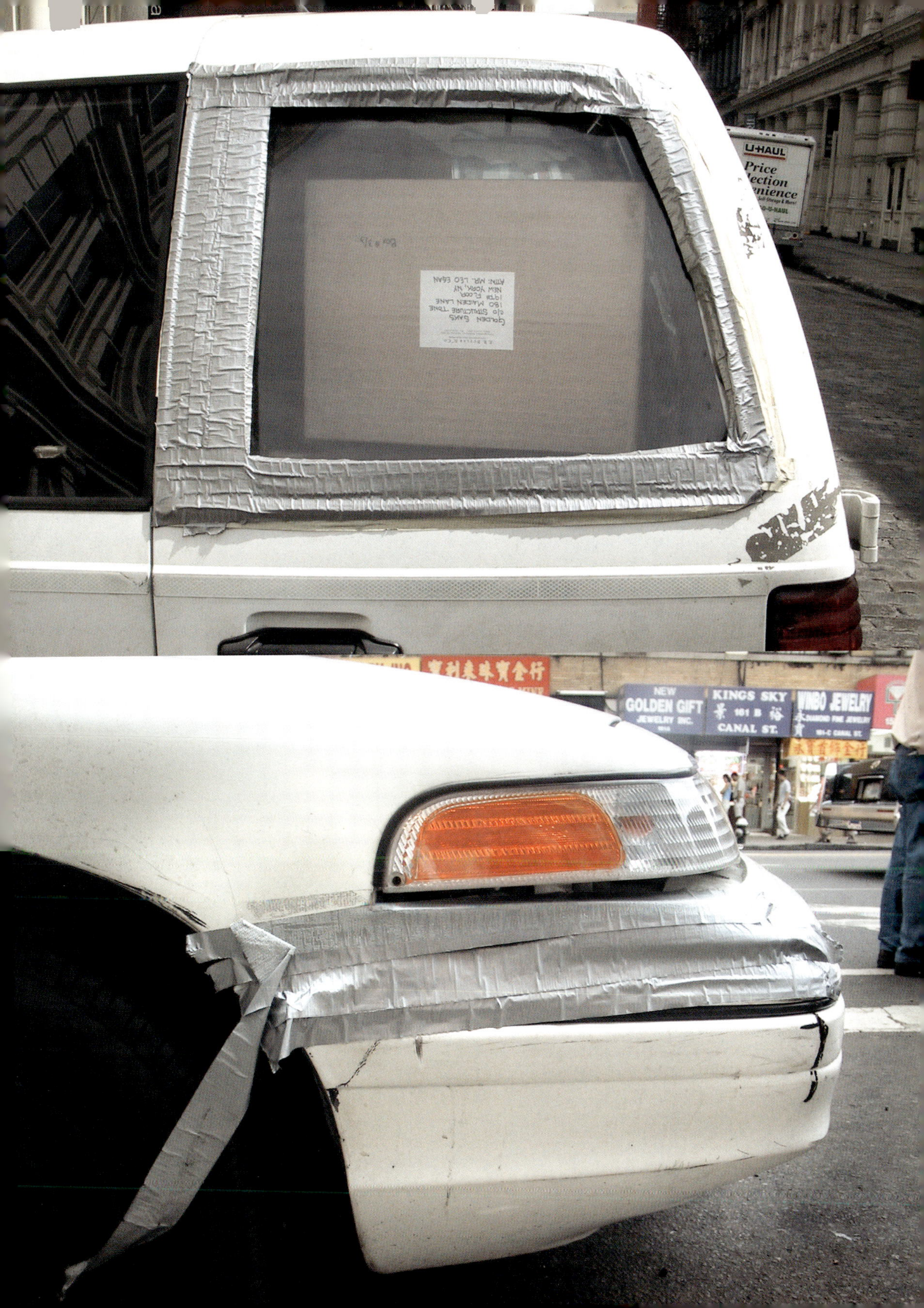
U-HAUL
NEW
GOLDEN GIFT
JEWELRY INC.
KINGS SKY
101 B
CANAL ST.

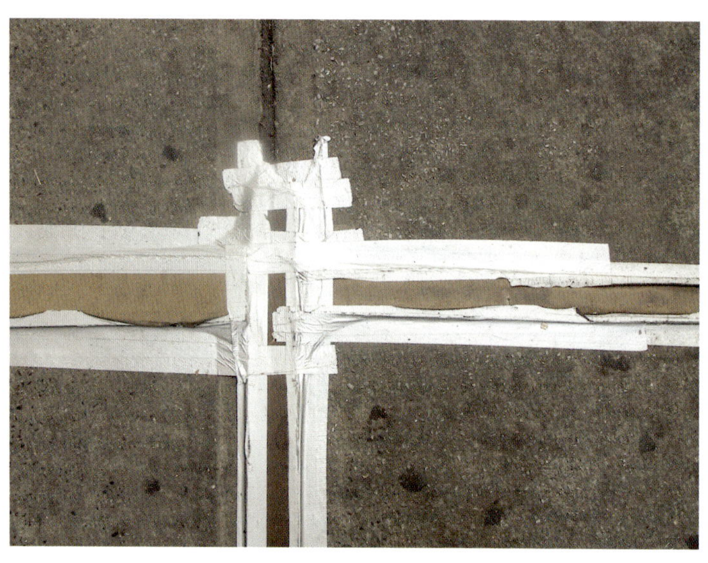

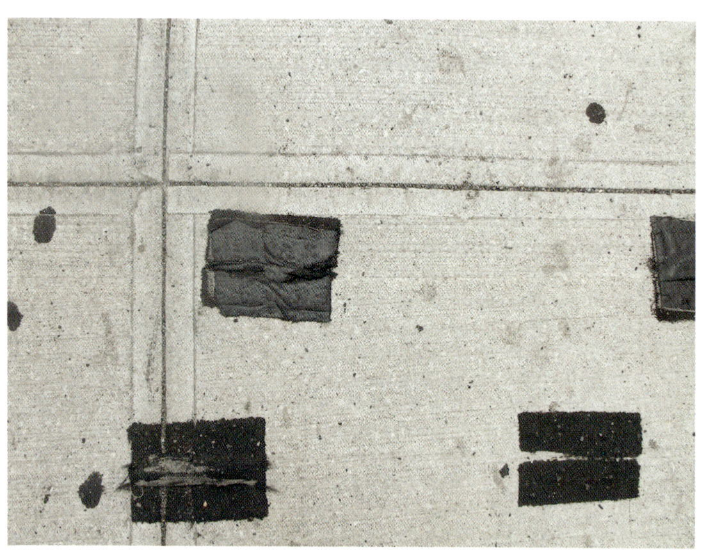

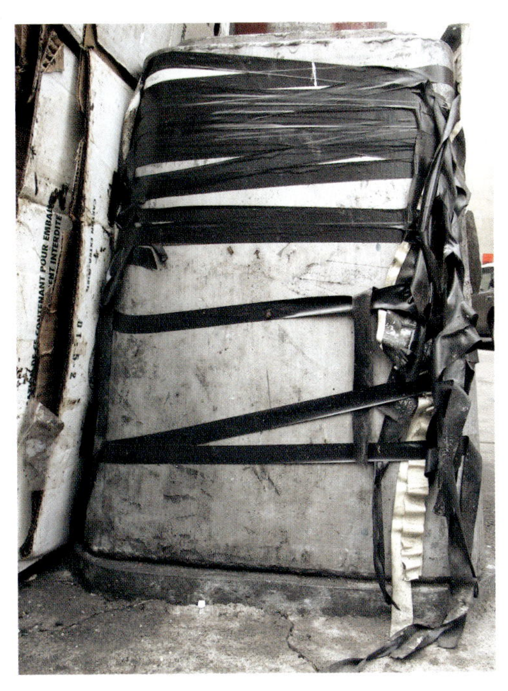

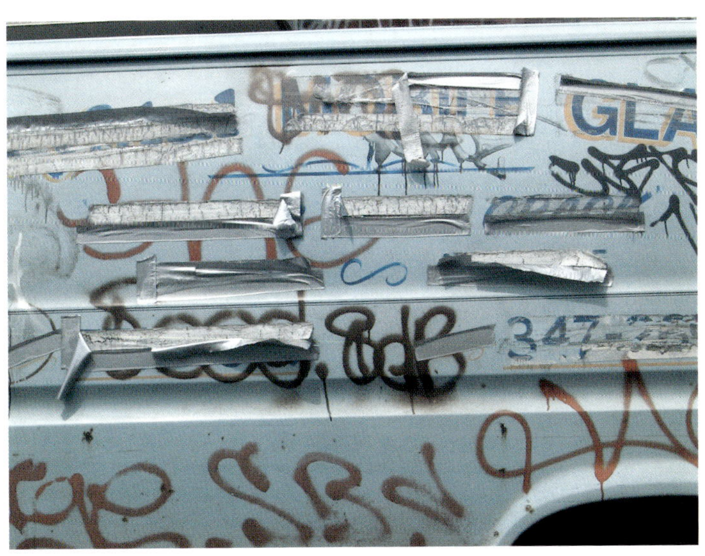

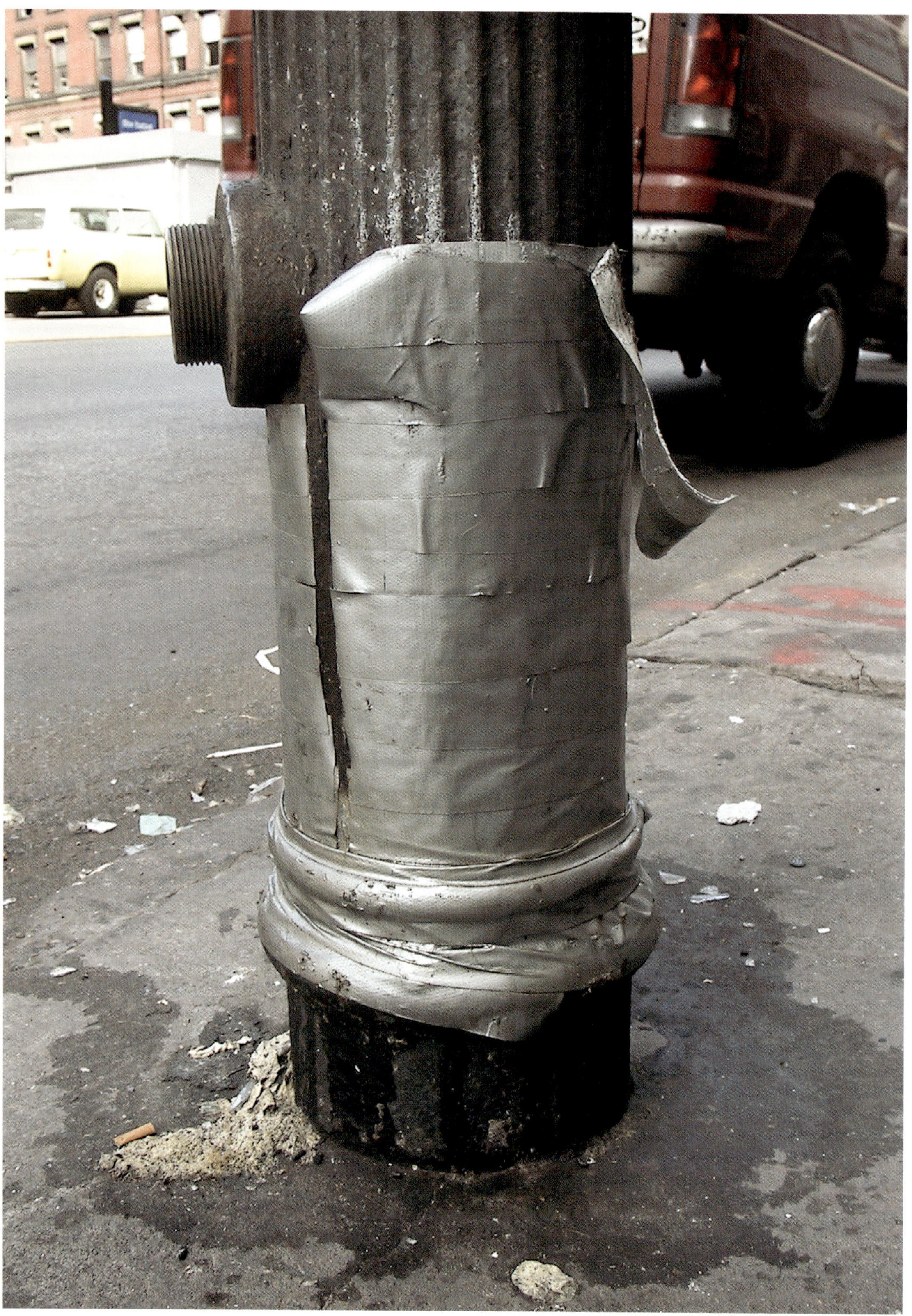

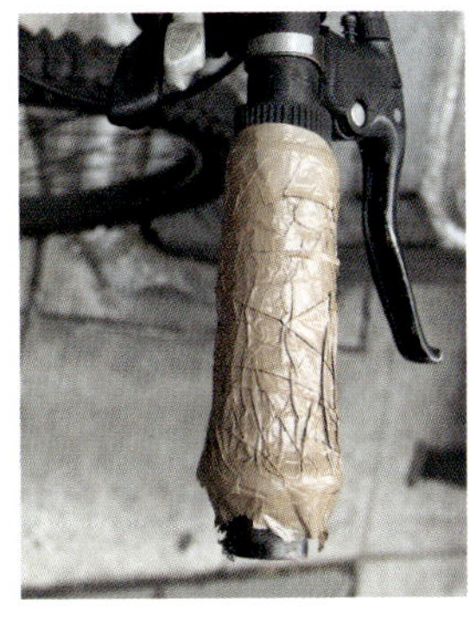
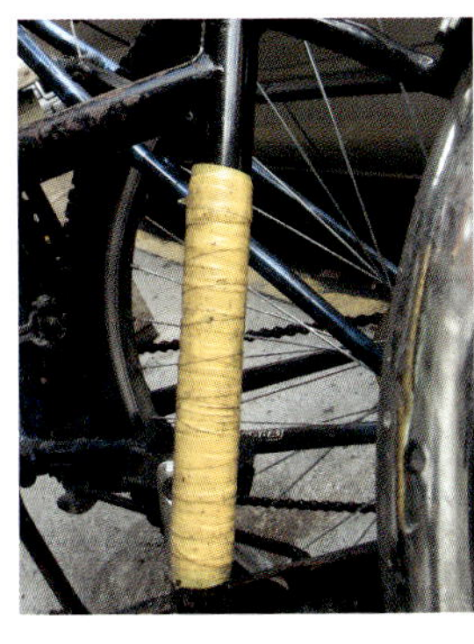
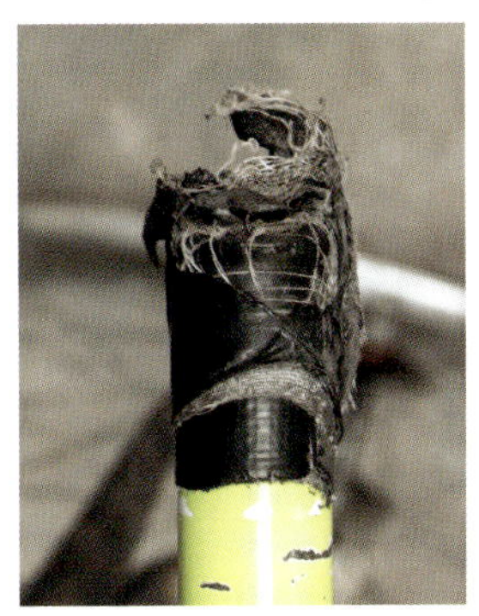
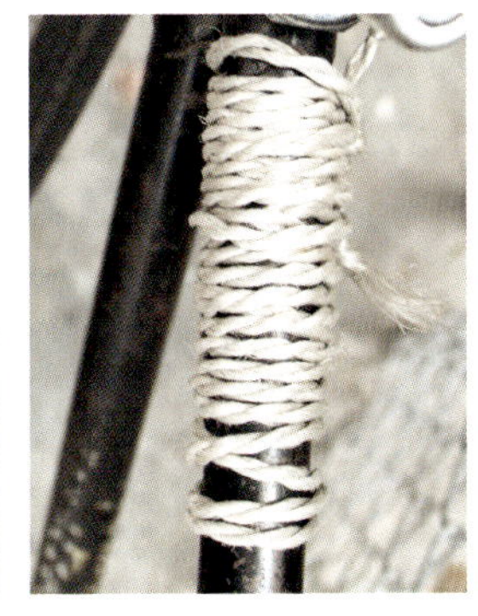
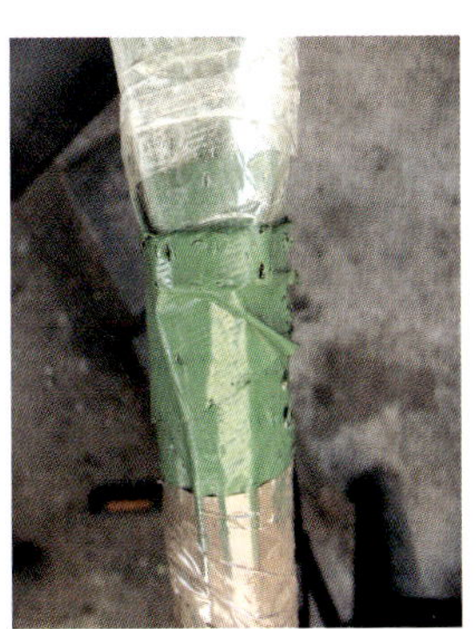
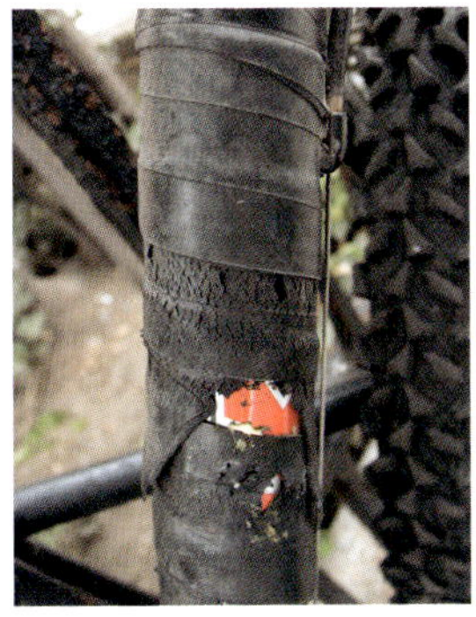
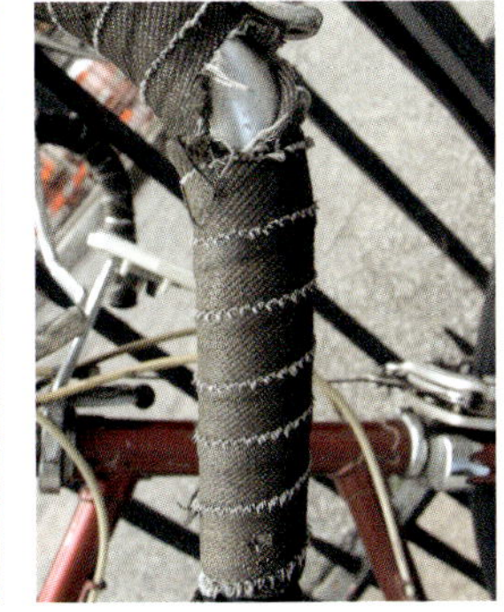
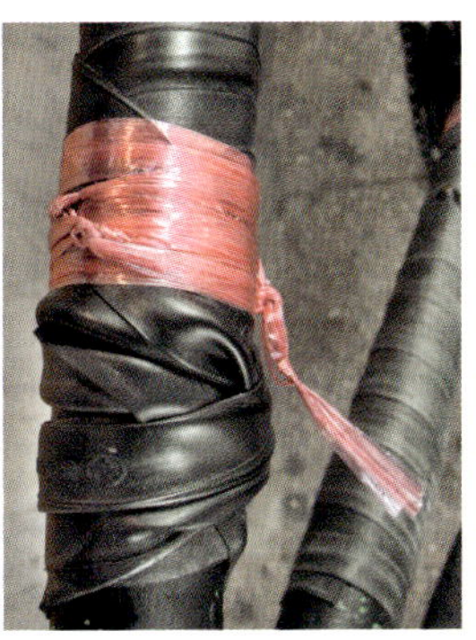
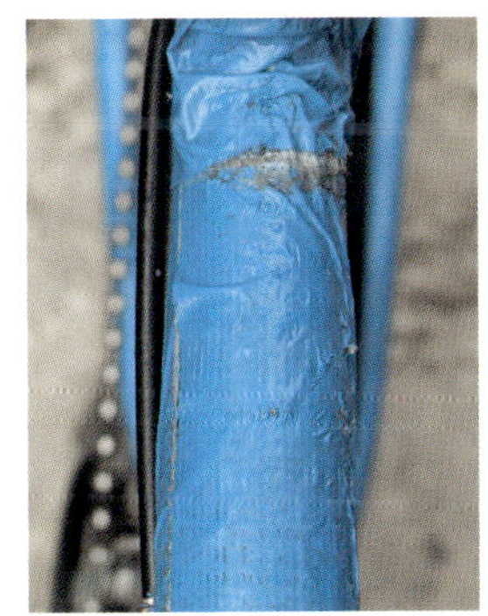
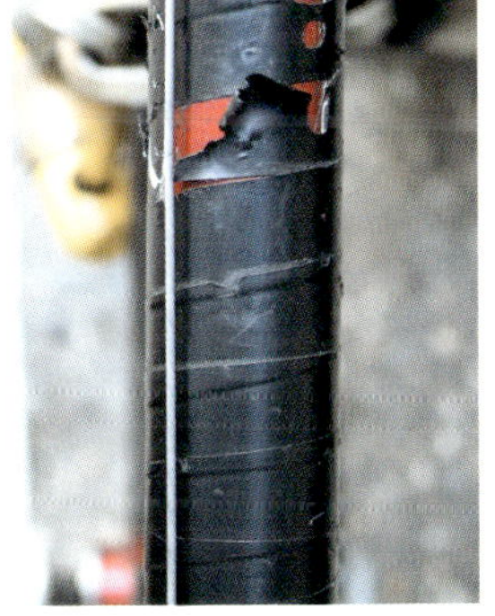
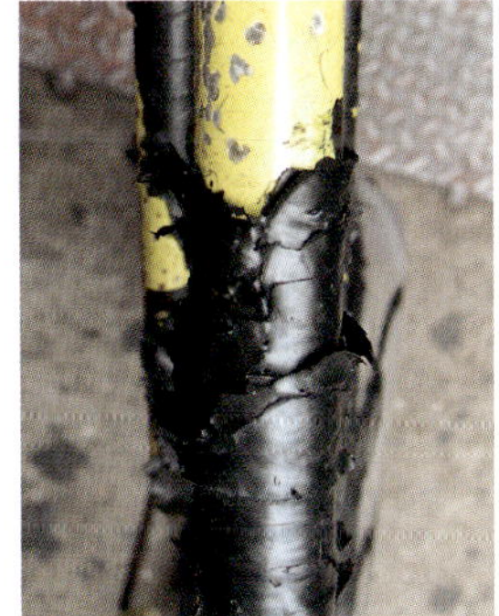
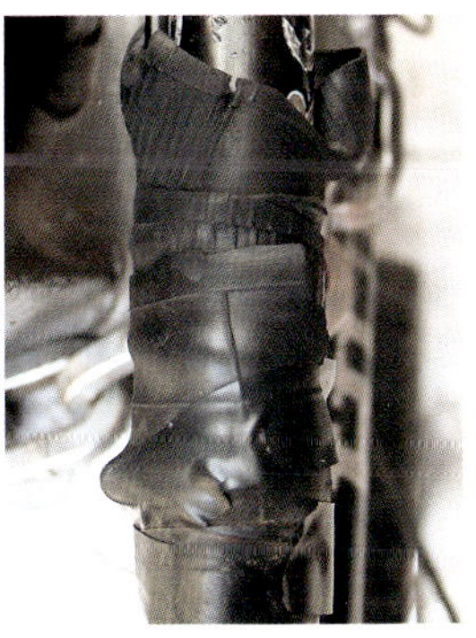
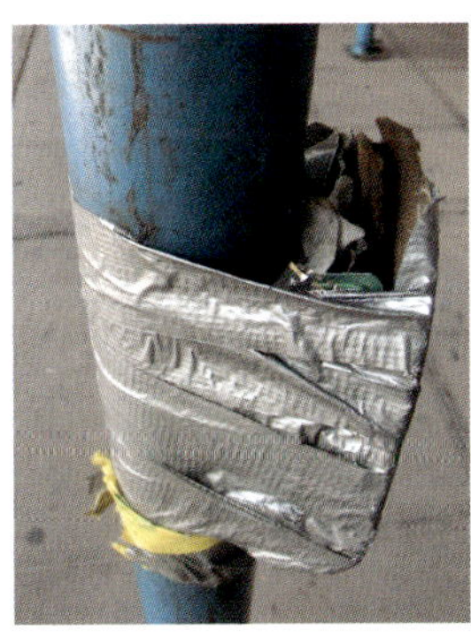
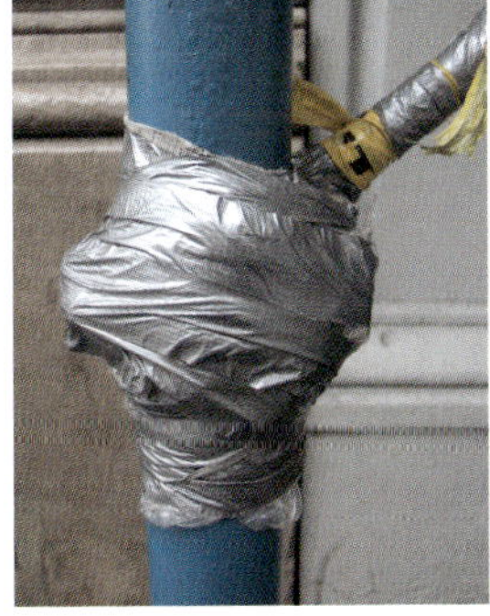
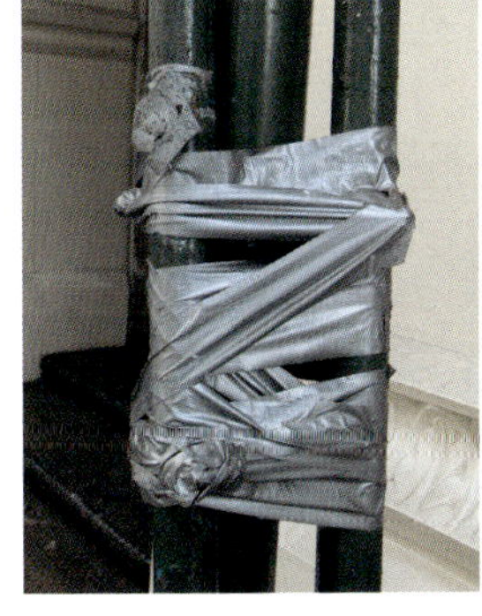
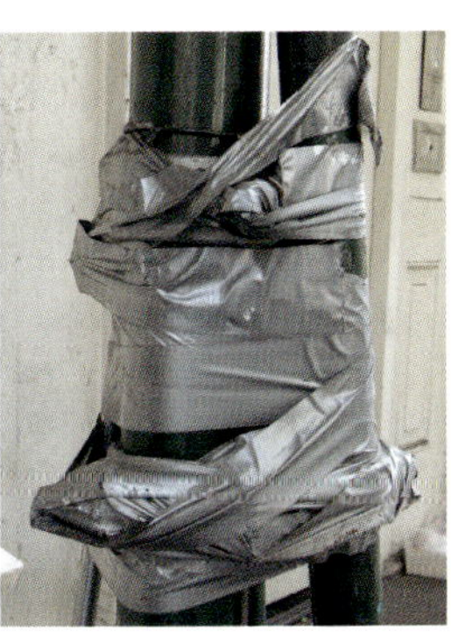

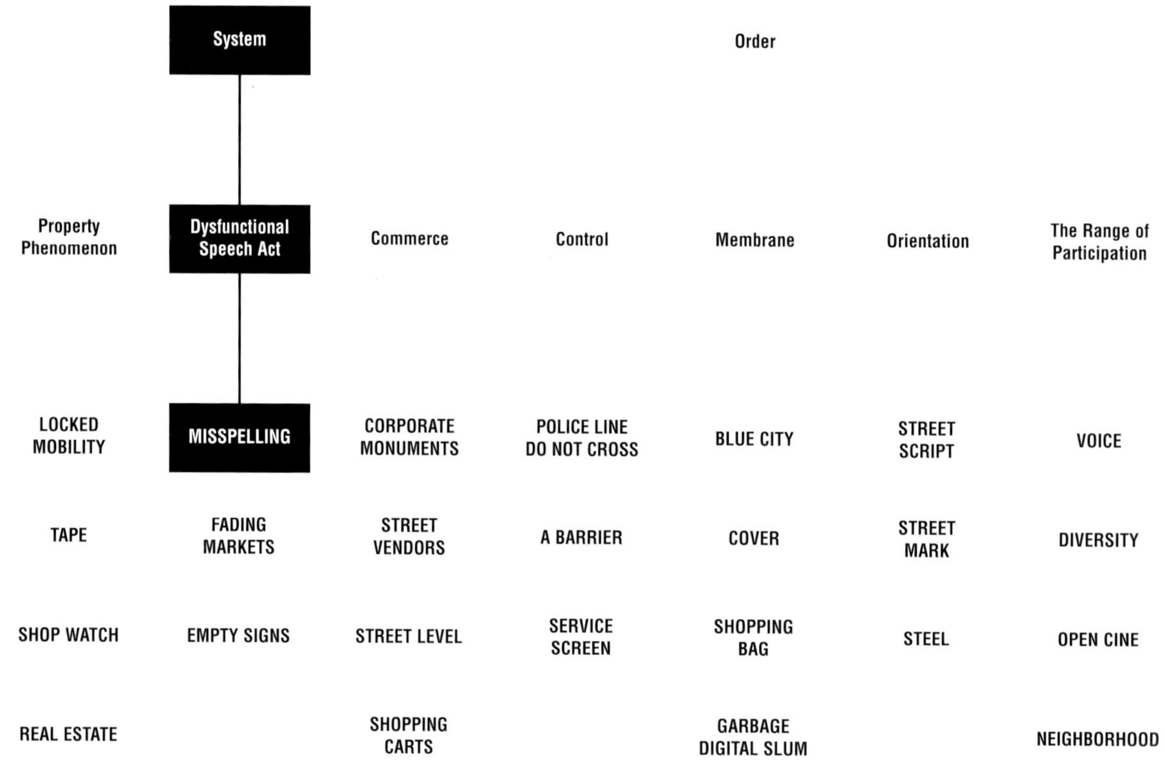
System
Order
Property Phenomenon
Dysfunctional Speech Act
Commerce
Control
Membrane
Orientation
The Range of Participation
LOCKED MOBILITY
MISSPELLING
CORPORATE MONUMENTS
POLICE LINE DO NOT CROSS
BLUE CITY
STREET SCRIPT
VOICE
TAPE
FADING MARKETS
STREET VENDORS
A BARRIER
COVER
STREET MARK
DIVERSITY
SHOP WATCH
EMPTY SIGNS
STREET LEVEL
SERVICE SCREEN
SHOPPING BAG
STEEL
OPEN CINE
REAL ESTATE
SHOPPING CARTS
GARBAGE DIGITAL SLUM
NEIGHBORHOOD

Identity

Alternative Media	Habitual Reinterpretation
CAR DOOR	PUBLIC CHAIRS
LABELING.	PLASTIC CRATES
POLE POST	STANDPIPES
	PRAY JESUS

MISSPELLING

Instant Corporate Identity

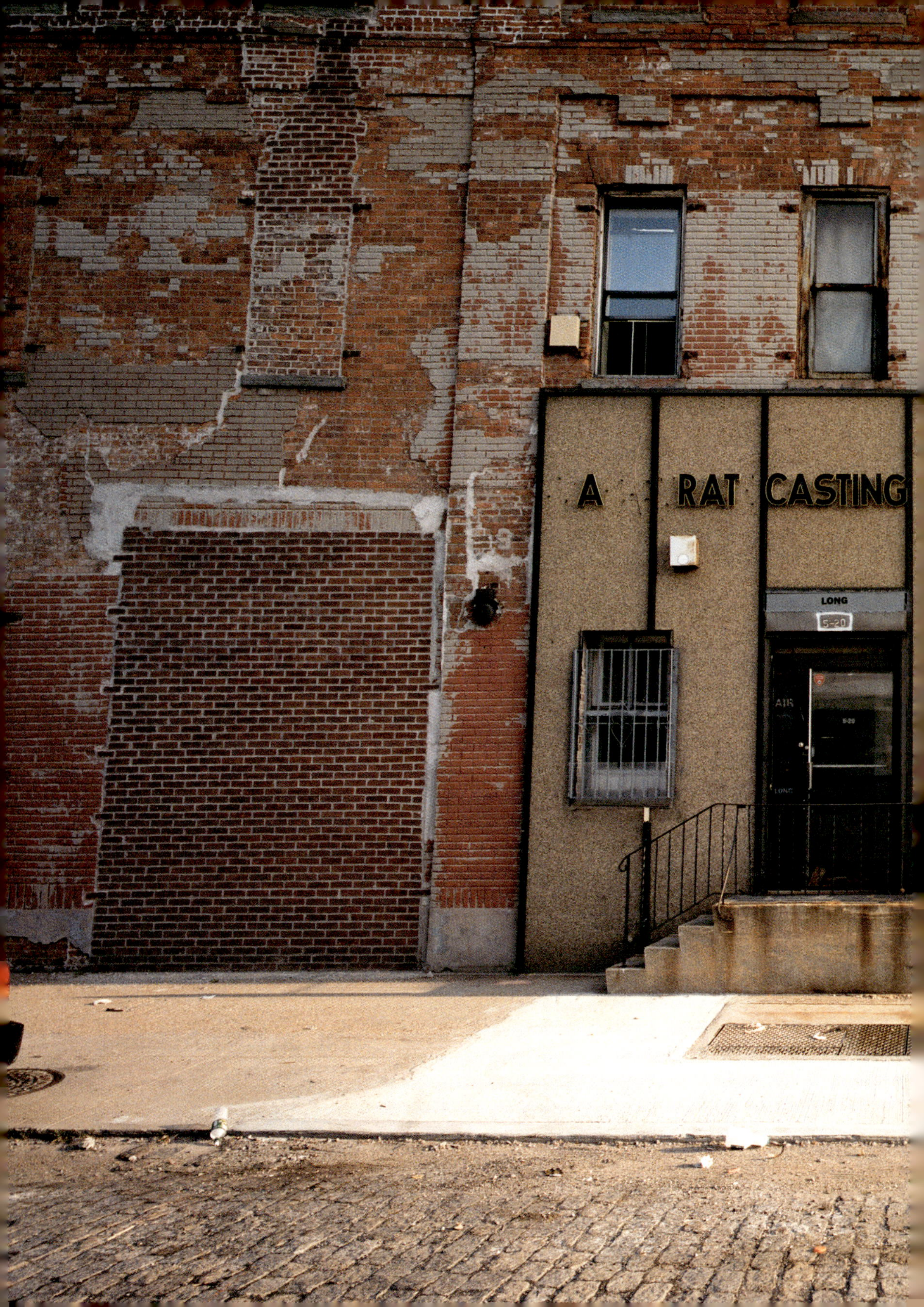
A RAT CASTING
LONG
5-20

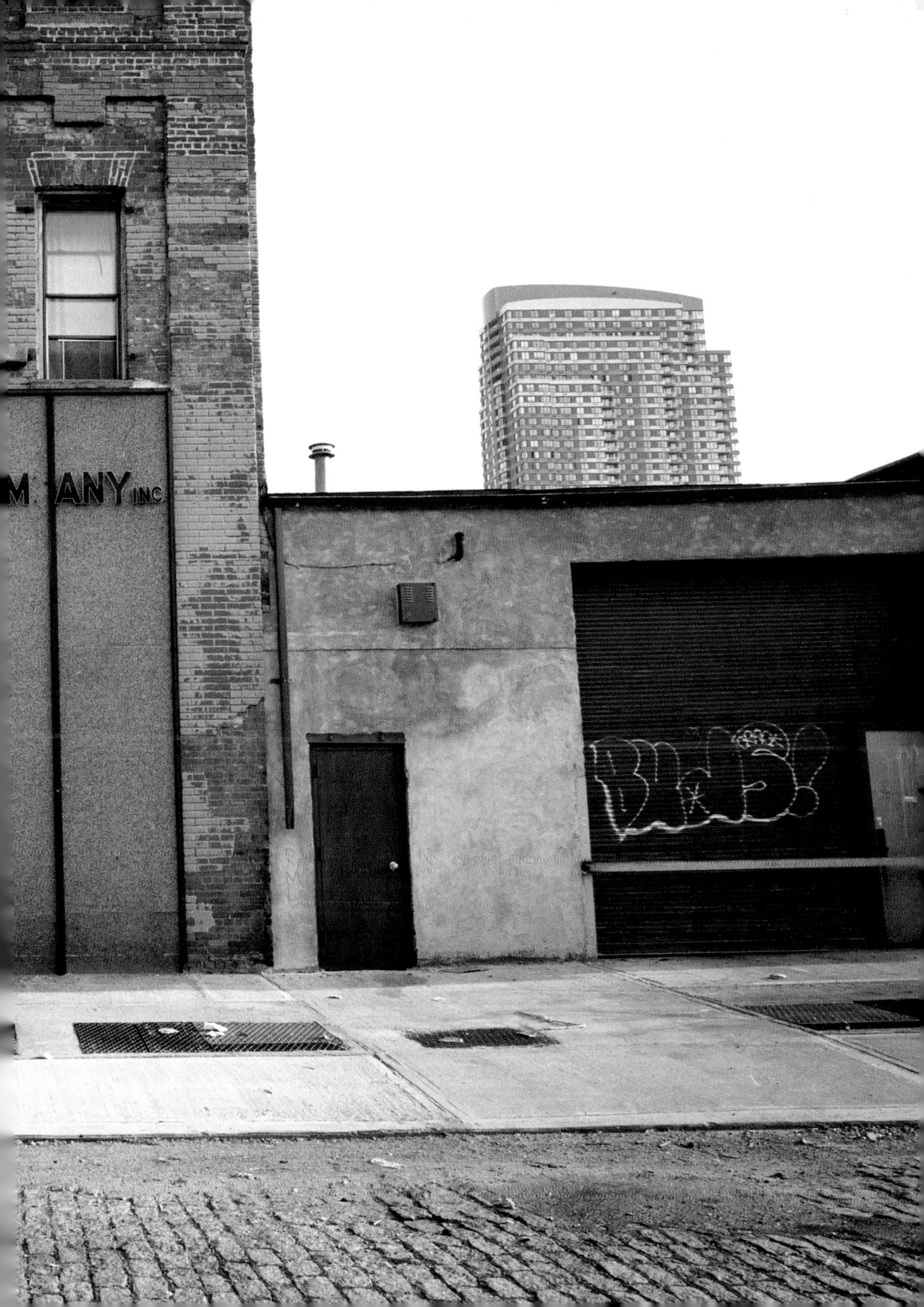
M ANY INC

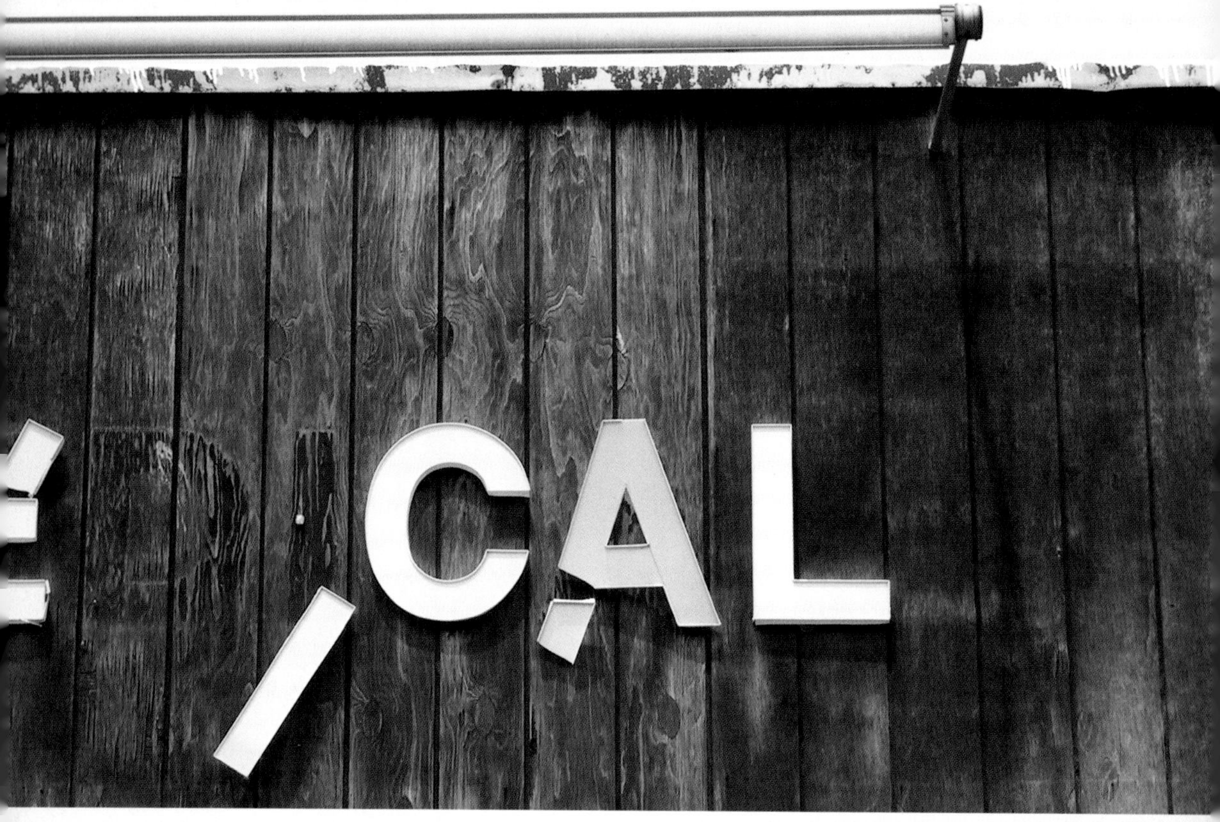

CAL
MÉ CAL 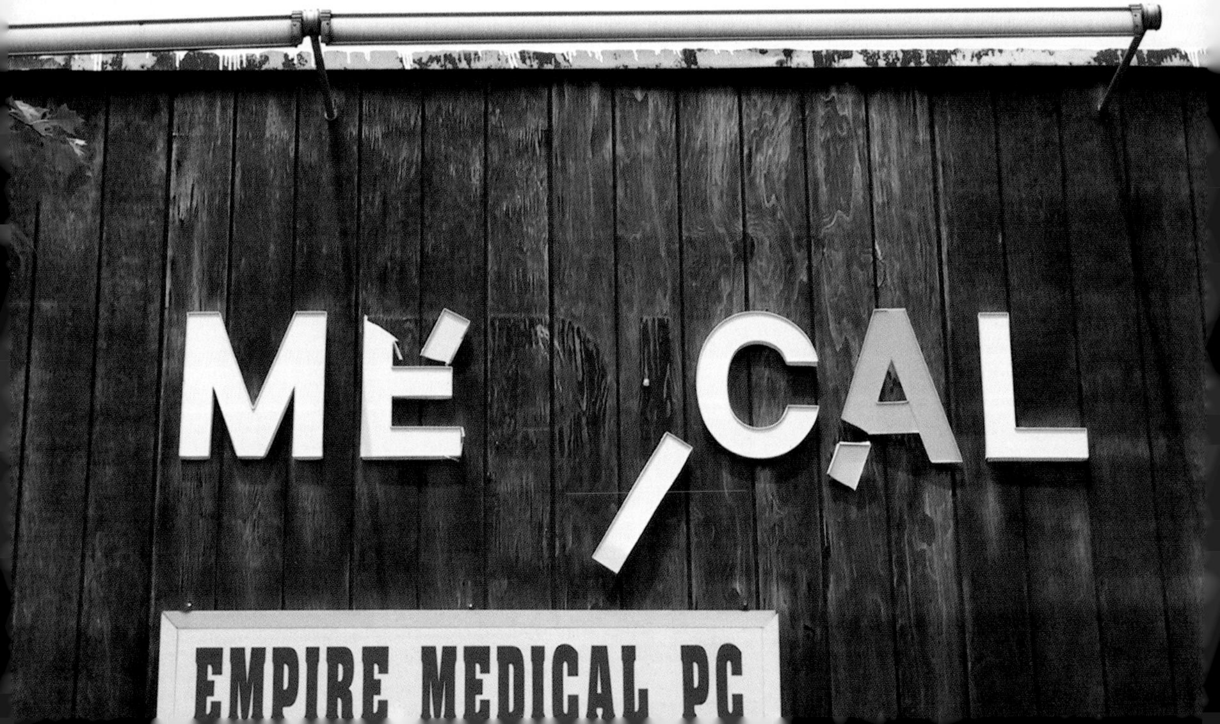
EMPIRE MEDICAL PC

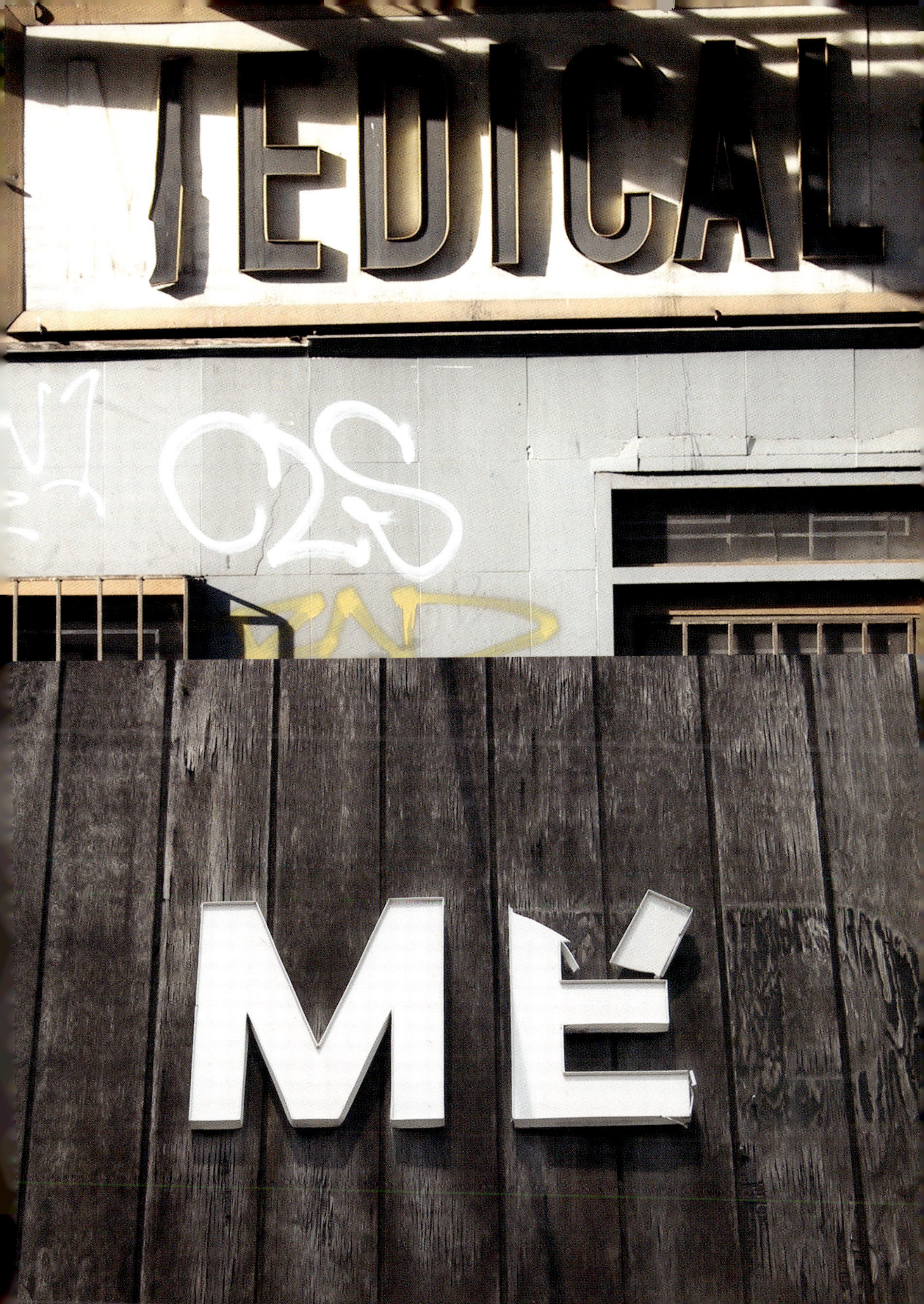
EDICAL
MÉ

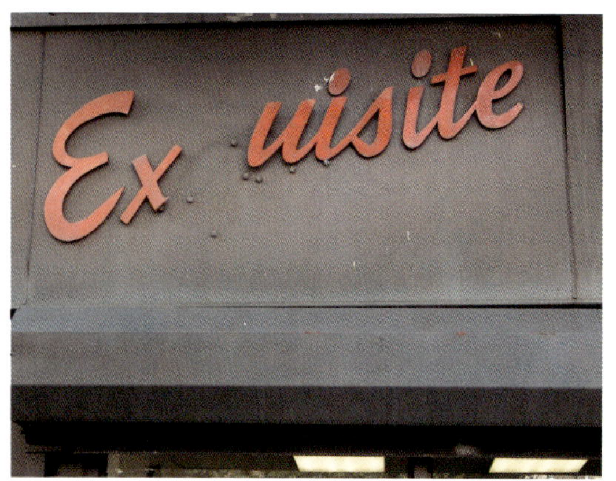
Ex uisite

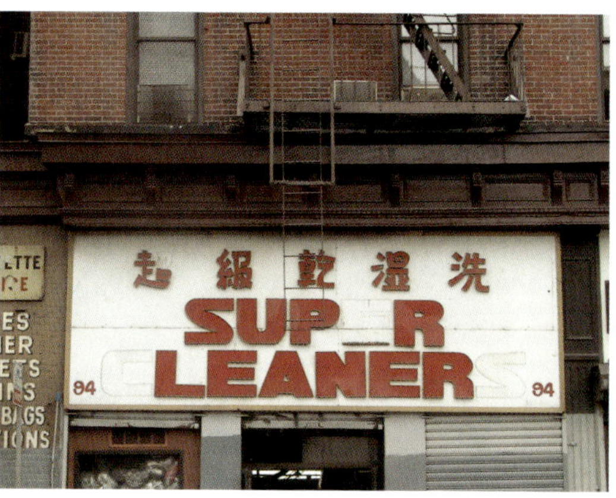
SUP_R
LEANER
94
94

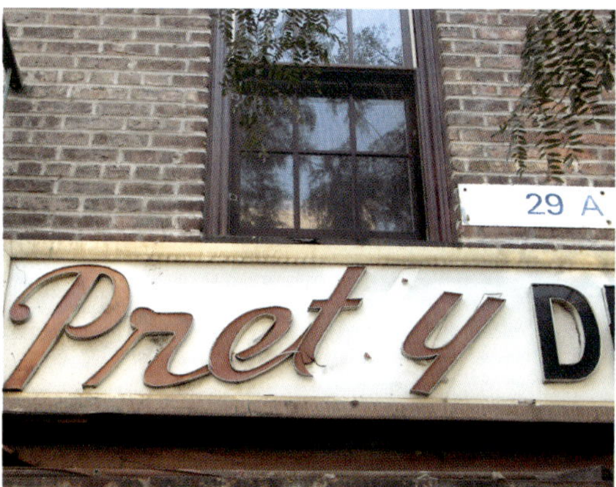
29 A
Pret y D

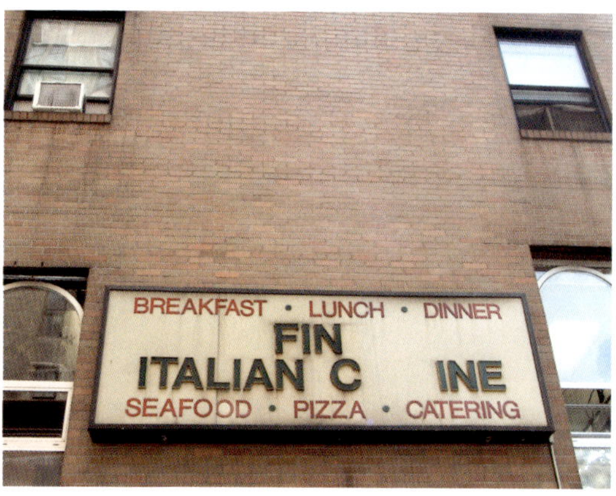
BREAKFAST • LUNCH • DINNER
FIN
ITALIAN C INE
SEAFOOD • PIZZA • CATERING

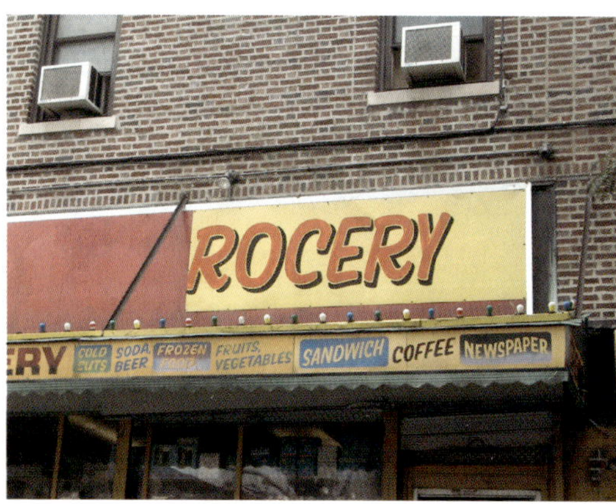
ROCERY
ERY
SODA BEER
FRUITS, VEGETABLES
SANDWICH
COFFEE
NEWSPAPER

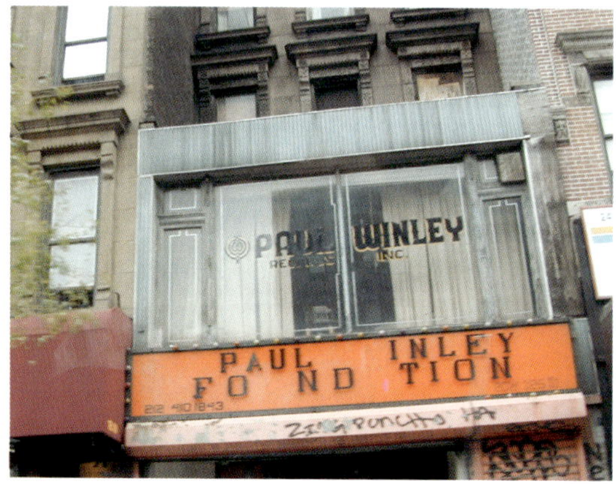
WINLEY
INC.
PAUL INLEY
FO ND TION

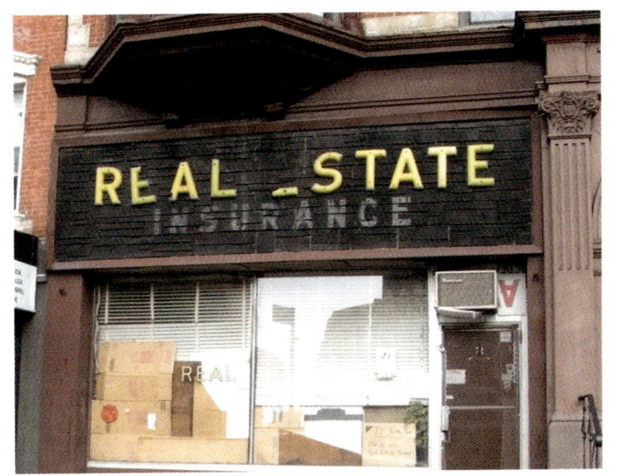
REAL STATE
INSURANCE
REAL

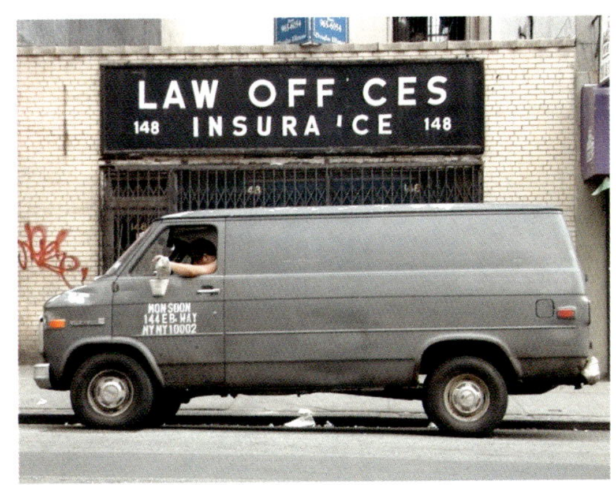
LAW OFF CES
148 INSURA CE 148
MONSOON
144 E B. WAY
NY NY 10002

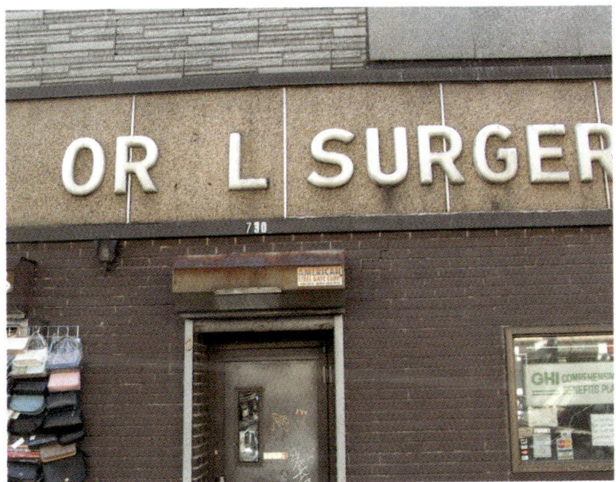
OR L SURGER
790
GHI

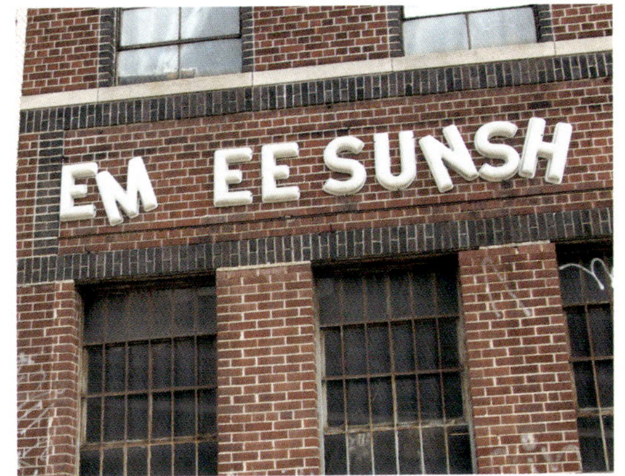
EM EE SUNSH

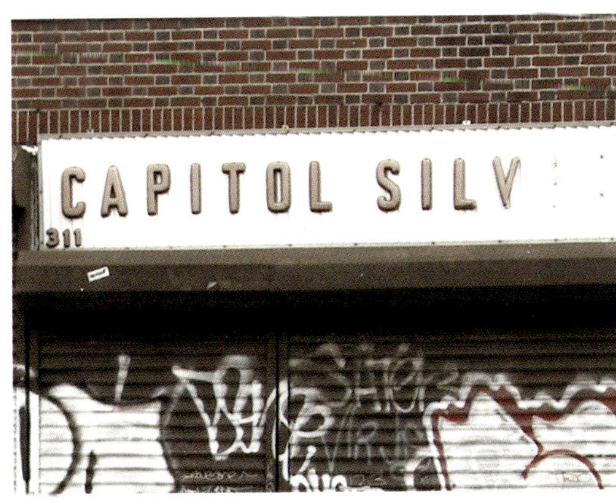
CAPITOL SILV
311

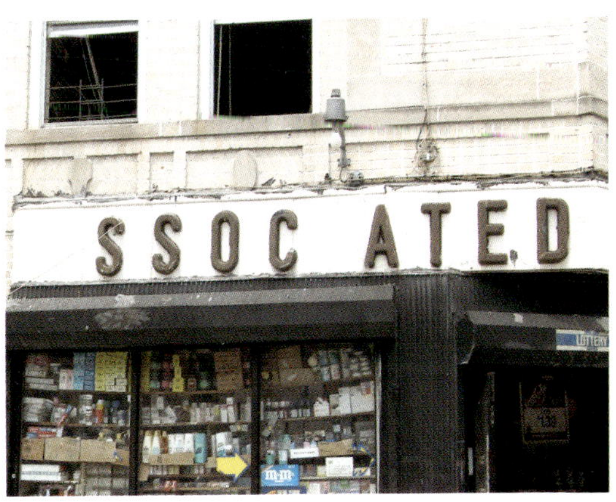
SSOC ATED
LOTTERY

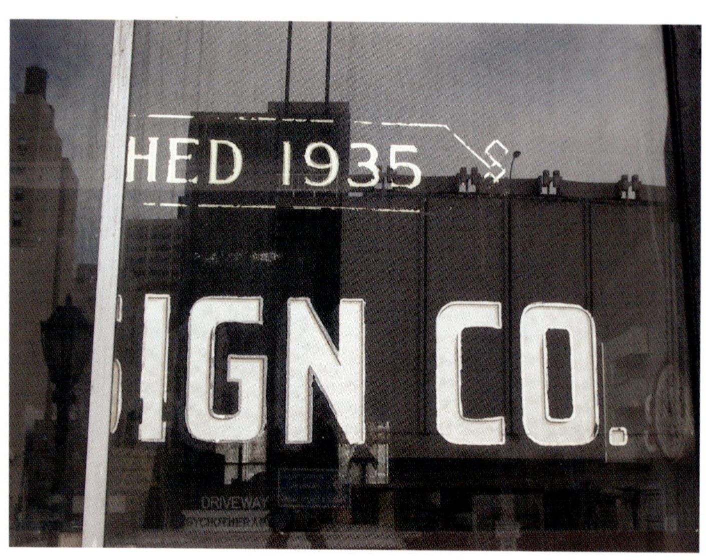
HED 1935
SIGN CO.
DRIVEWAY

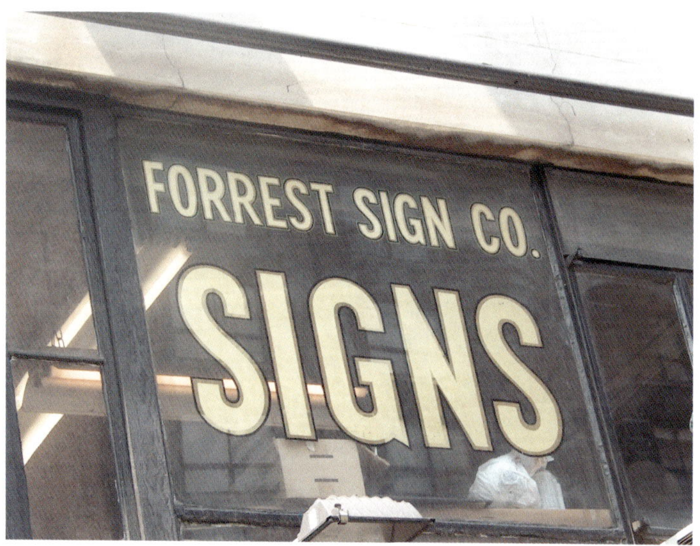
FORREST SIGN CO.
SIGNS

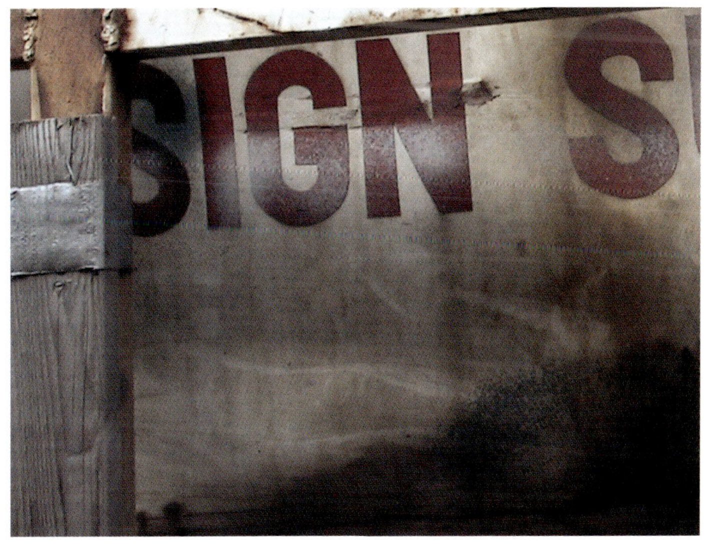
SIGN S

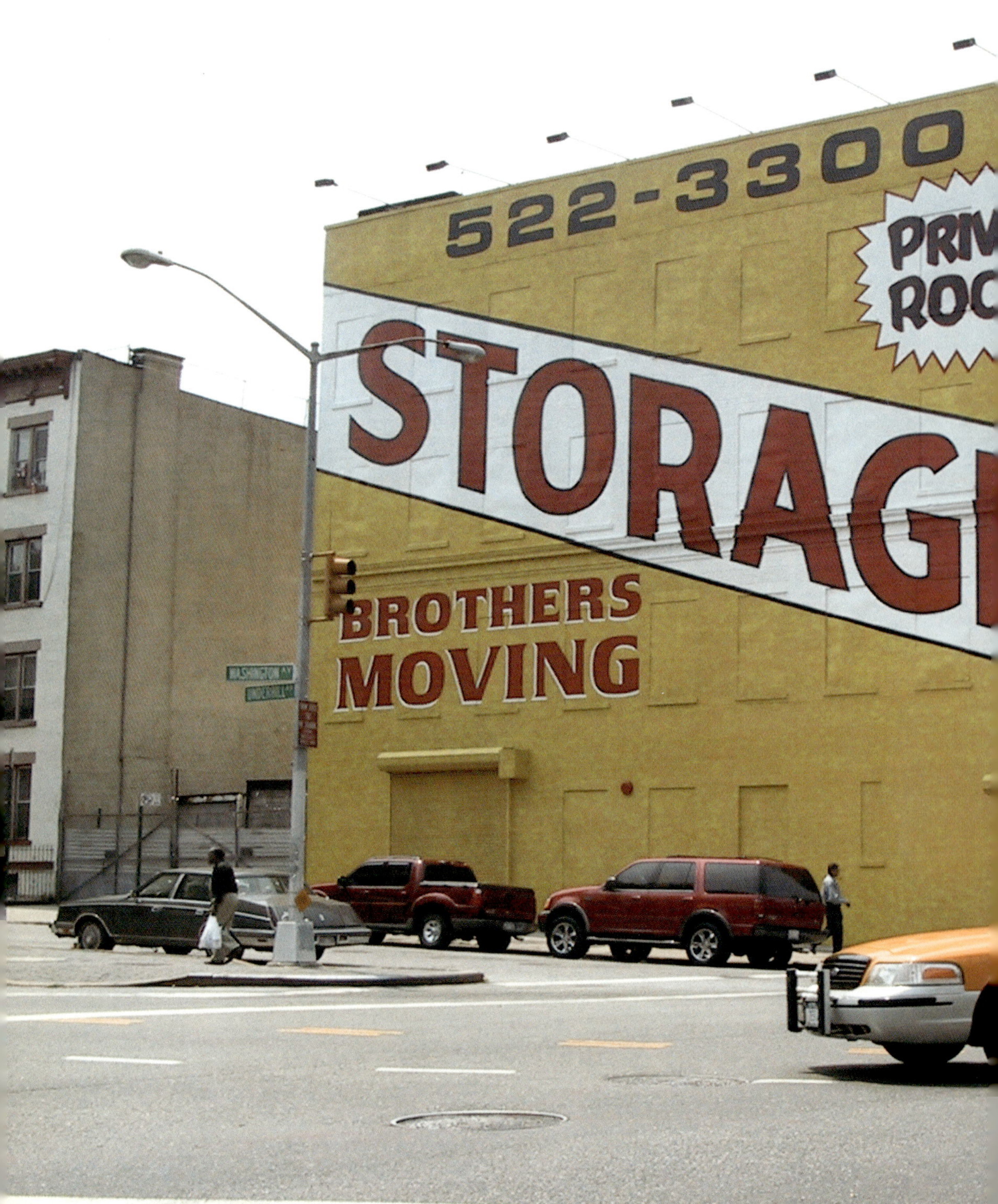
522-3300
BROTHERS
MOVING

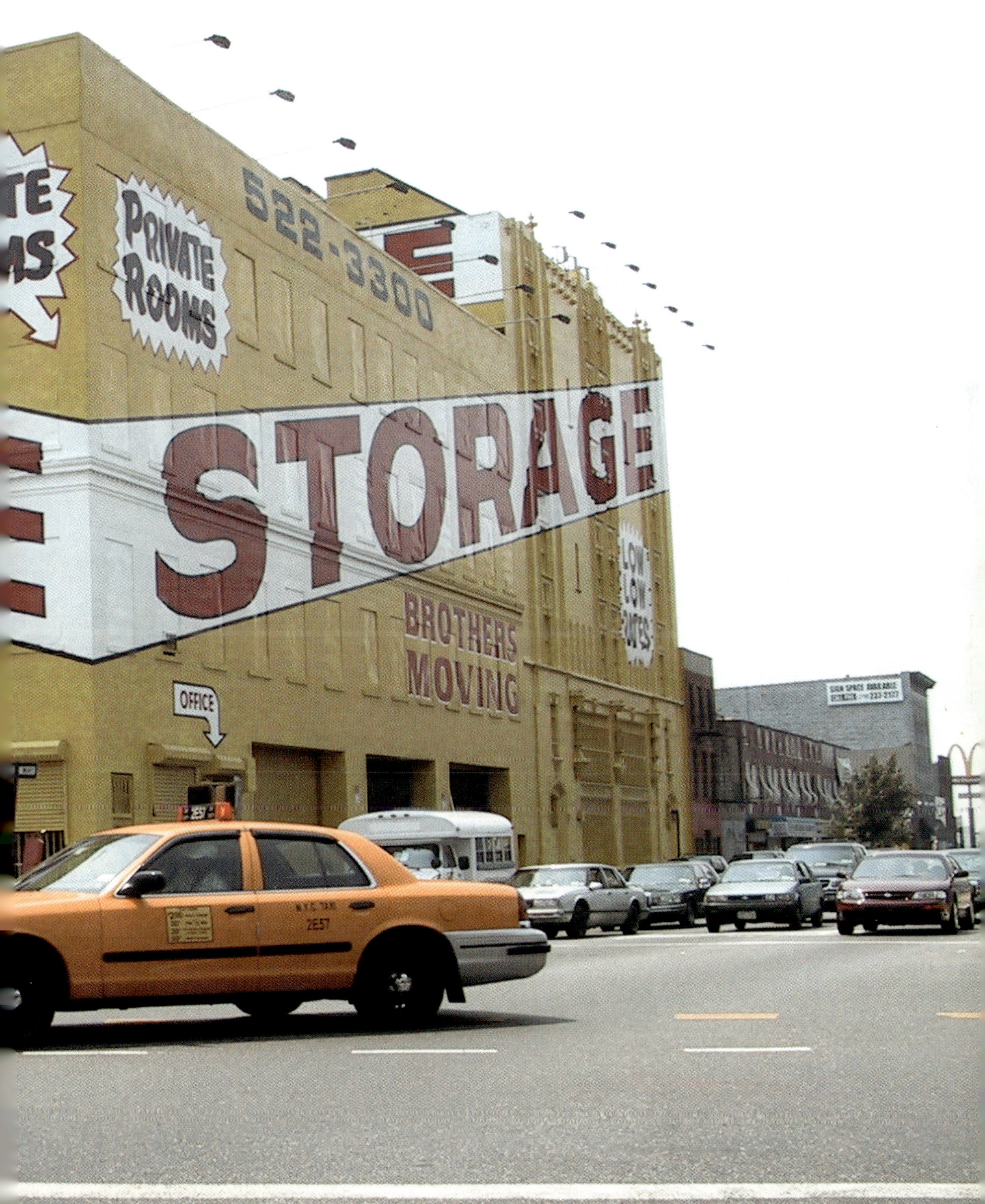
PRIVATE ROOMS
522-3300
STORAGE
BROTHERS MOVING
OFFICE
LOW LOW RATES
N.Y.C. TAXI
2E57

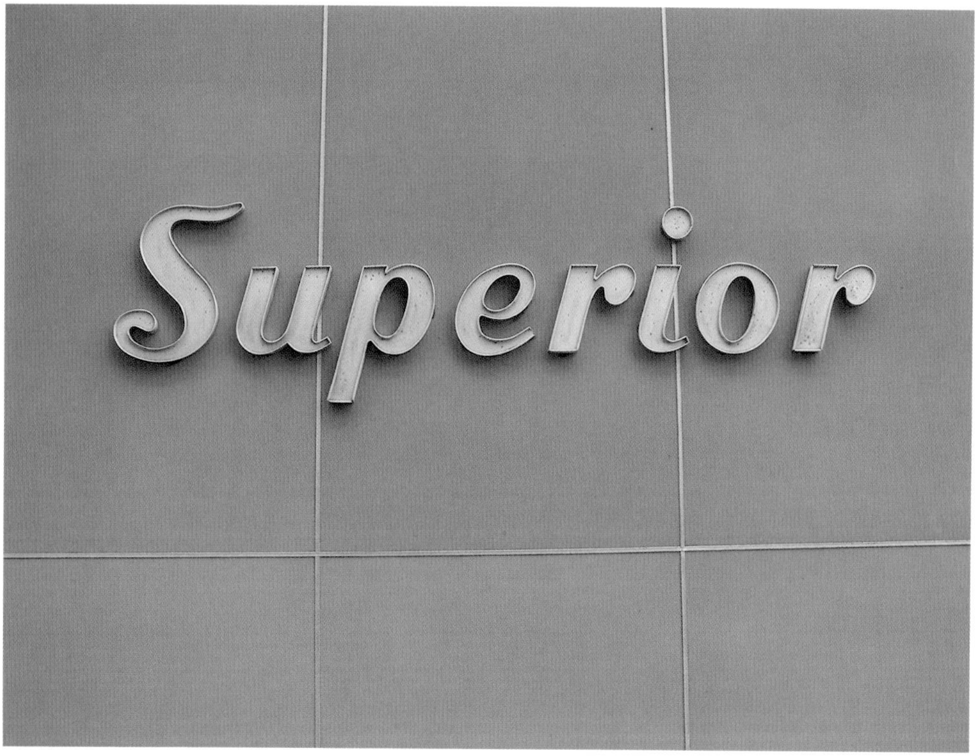

Superior

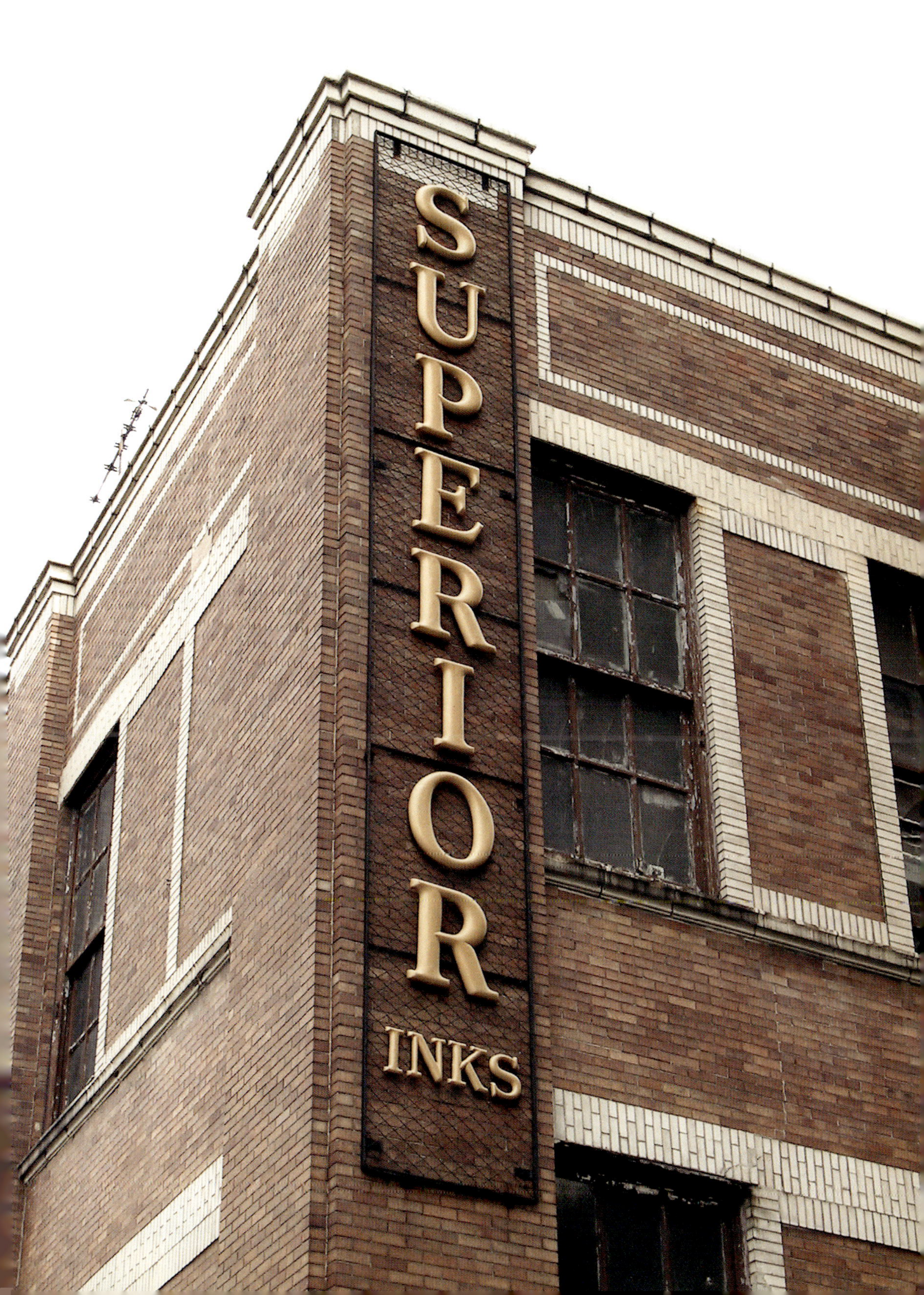
SUPERIOR
INKS

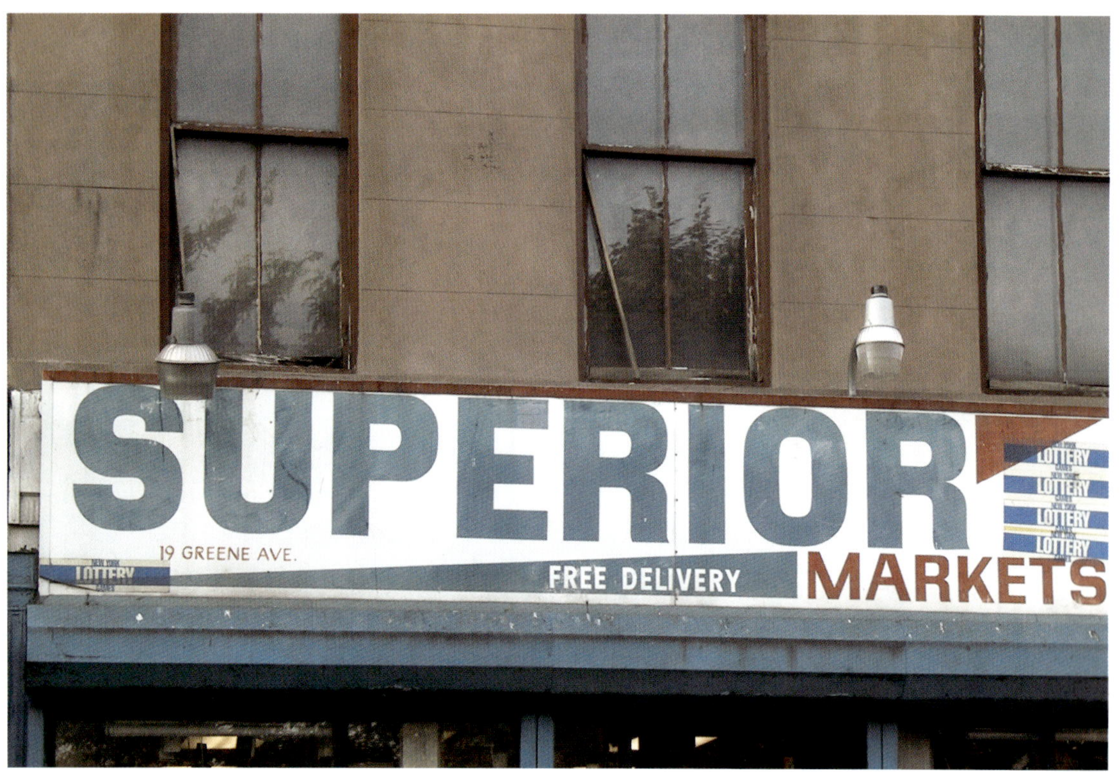

BUSINESS S

Superior Mobile Wash 4175 Cameron St LV 89103 367-4
Superior Mortgage Services
4530 S Eastern Av A3 LV 89119 765-5
Superior Pest Control 656-5
Superior Products Of Nevada
3111 S Valley View Blvd LV 89102 367-2
Superior Radiator Inc 208 W Wyoming Av LV 89102 383-3
Superior Realty 1805 S Eastern Av LV 89104 457-9
Superior Refinishing 388-7
Superior Results Inc 2810 W Charleston Blvd LV 89102 880-7
Superior Satellite Services 877-1
Superior Services 363-1
Superior Services Inc 4450 Grissom Av LV 643-7
Superior Sign 5800 S Valley View Blvd LV 89118 895-9
Superior Sign & Crane 5800 S Valley View Blvd LV 89118 895-9
Superior Sod 3888 W Oquendo Rd LV 89118 798-5
Superior Solid Surfacing 597-2
Superior Tile & Marble Inc 4305 Polaris Av LV 89103 798-7
Superior Tire & Auto Service Centers
2010 E Lake Mead Blvd NLV 89030 649-2
2120 E Warm Springs Rd LV 89119 263-2

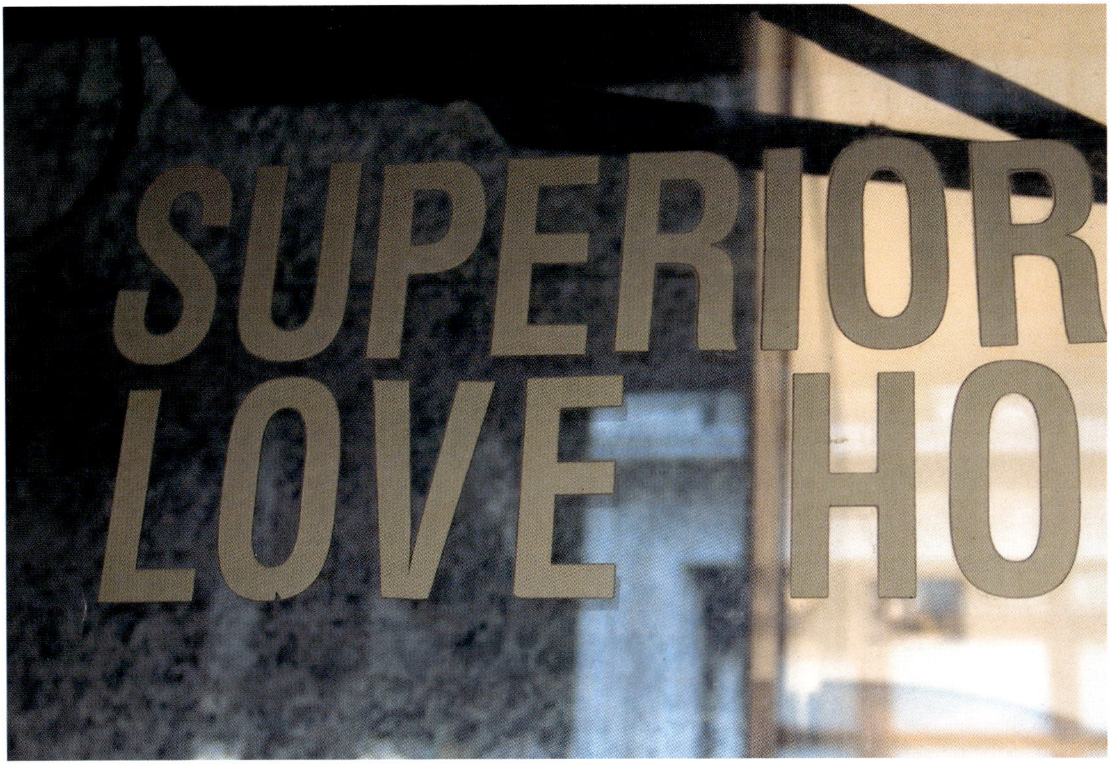

SUPERIOR
LOVE HO

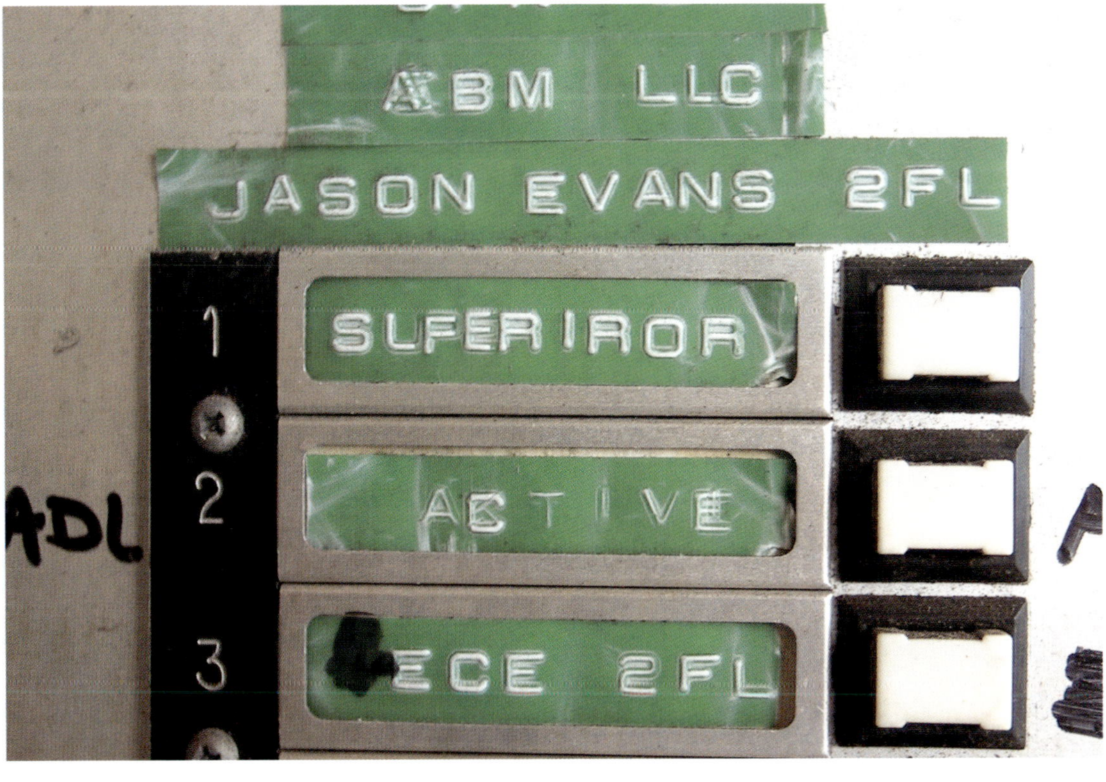

ABM LLC
JASON EVANS 2FL
1 SUPERIROR
2 ACTIVE
3 ECE 2FL
ADL

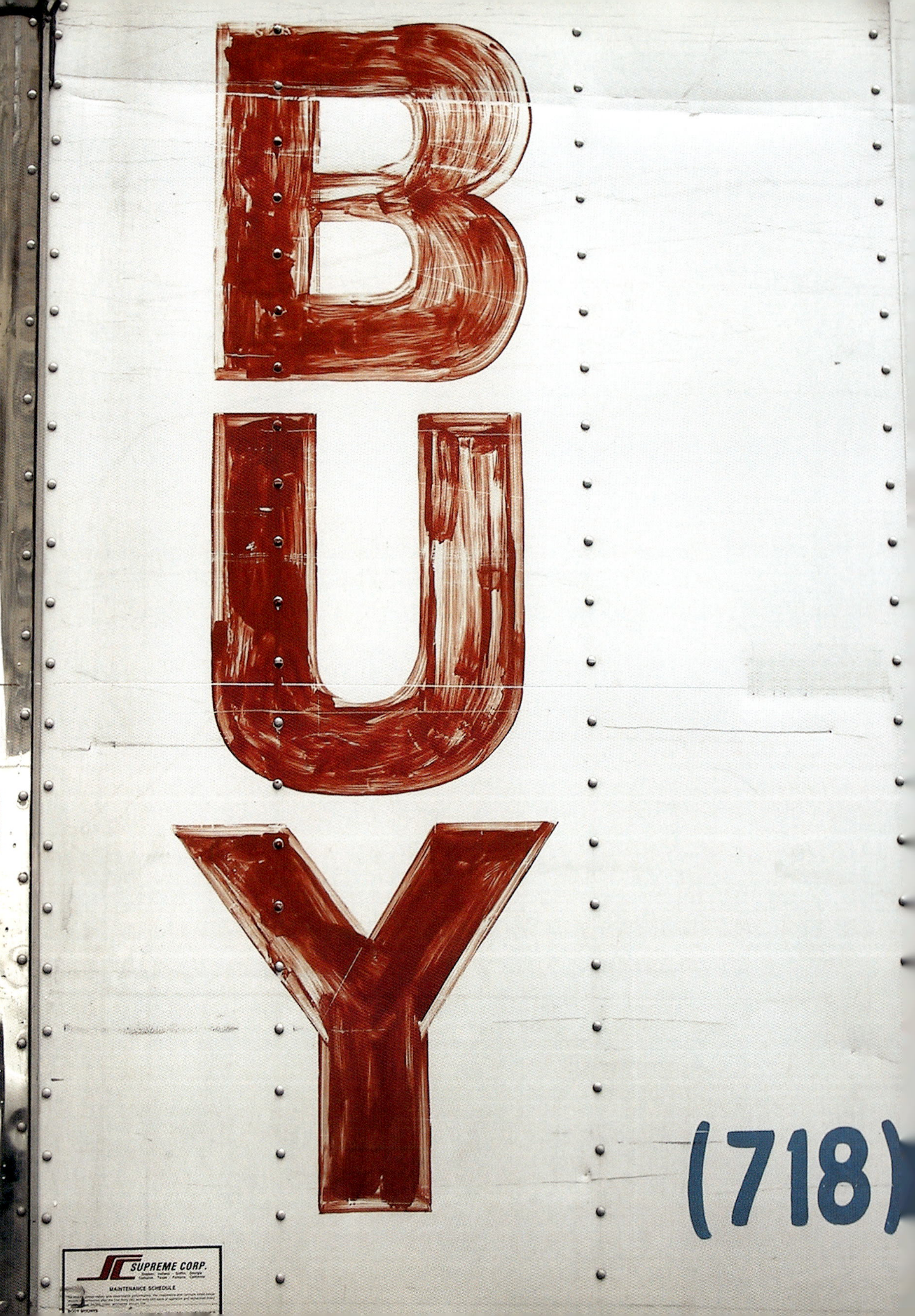
BUY
(718)
SUPREME CORP.
MAINTENANCE SCHEDULE

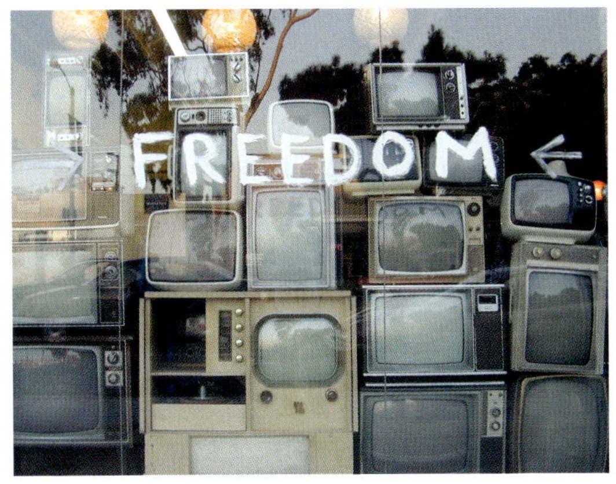
FREEDOM

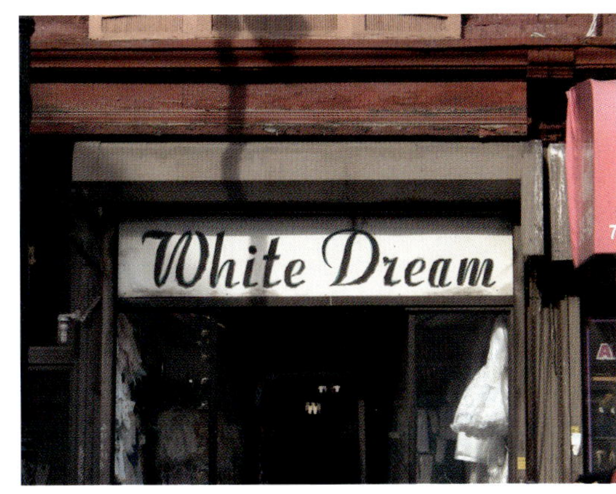
White Dream

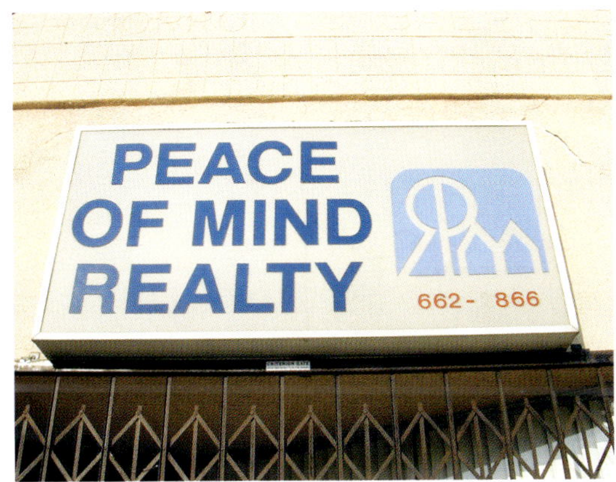
PEACE
OF MIND
REALTY
662- 866

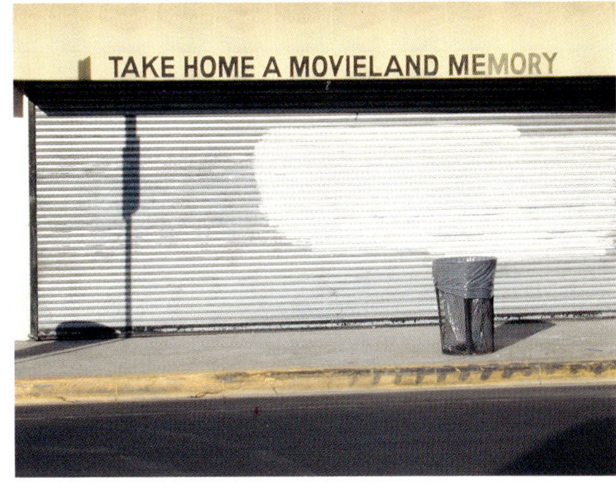
TAKE HOME A MOVIELAND MEMORY

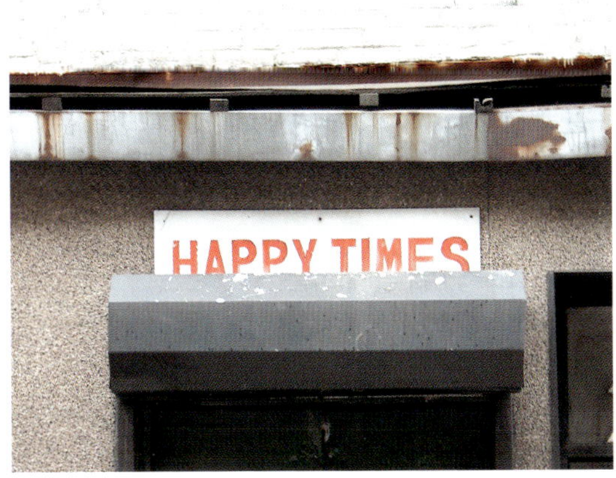
HAPPY TIMES

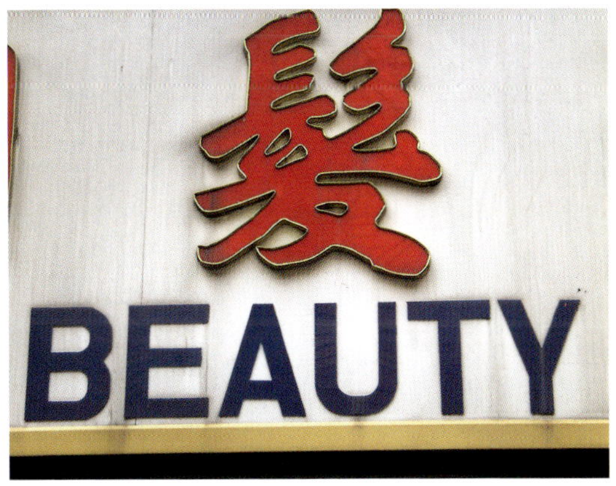
髮
BEAUTY

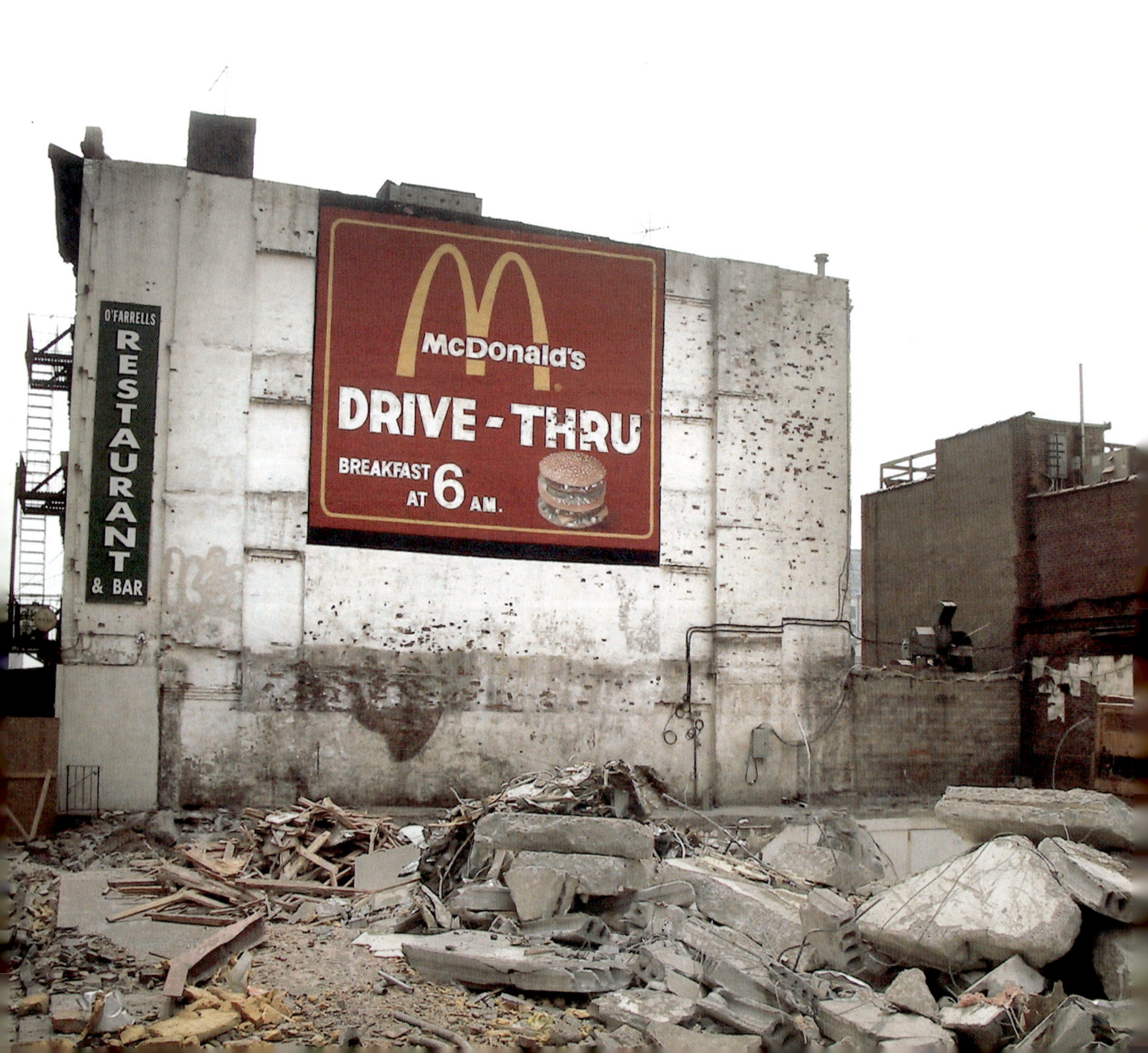
O'FARRELLS
RESTAURANT
& BAR
McDonald's
DRIVE - THRU
BREAKFAST
AT 6 AM.

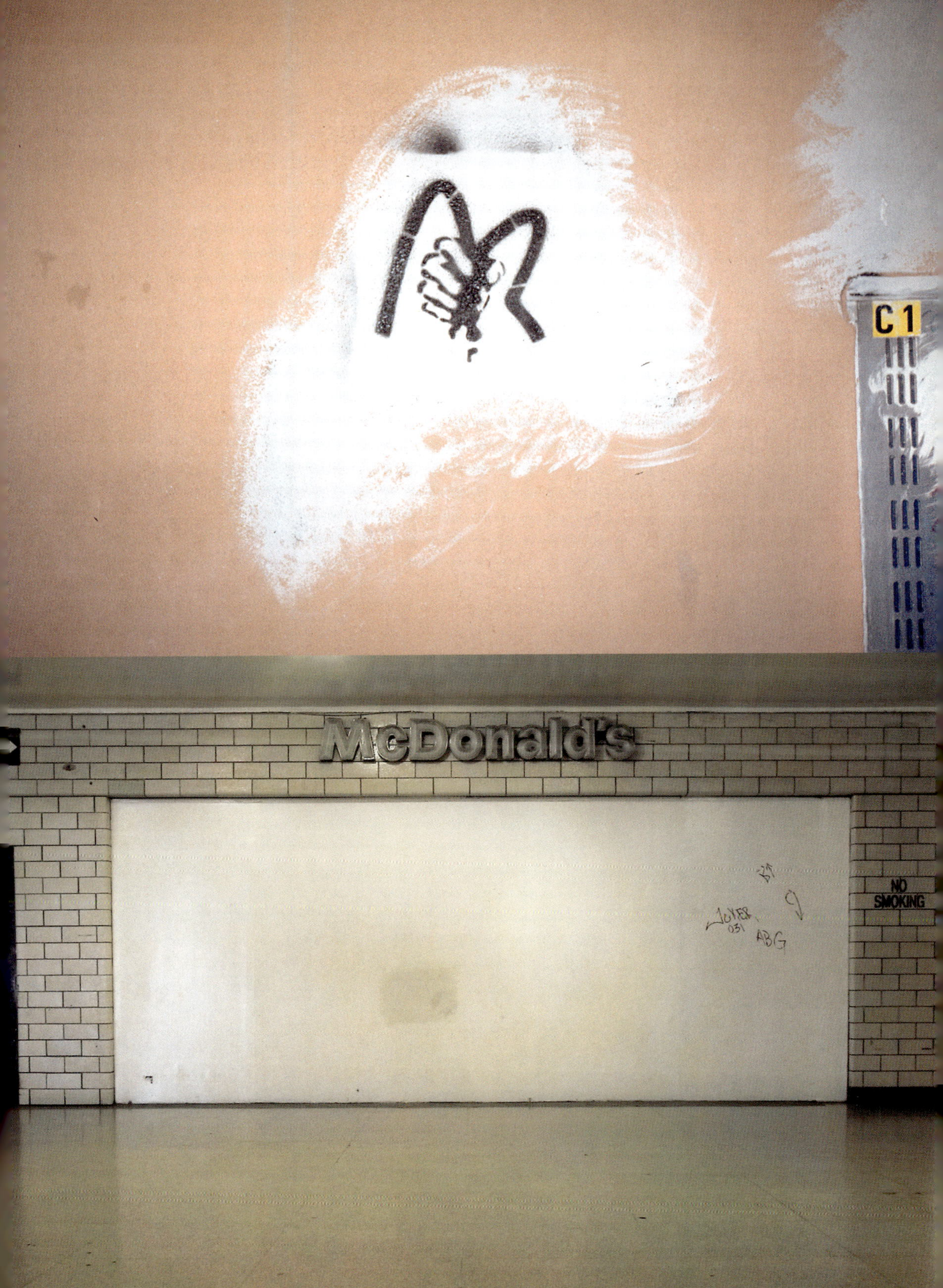
C1
McDonald's
NO SMOKING

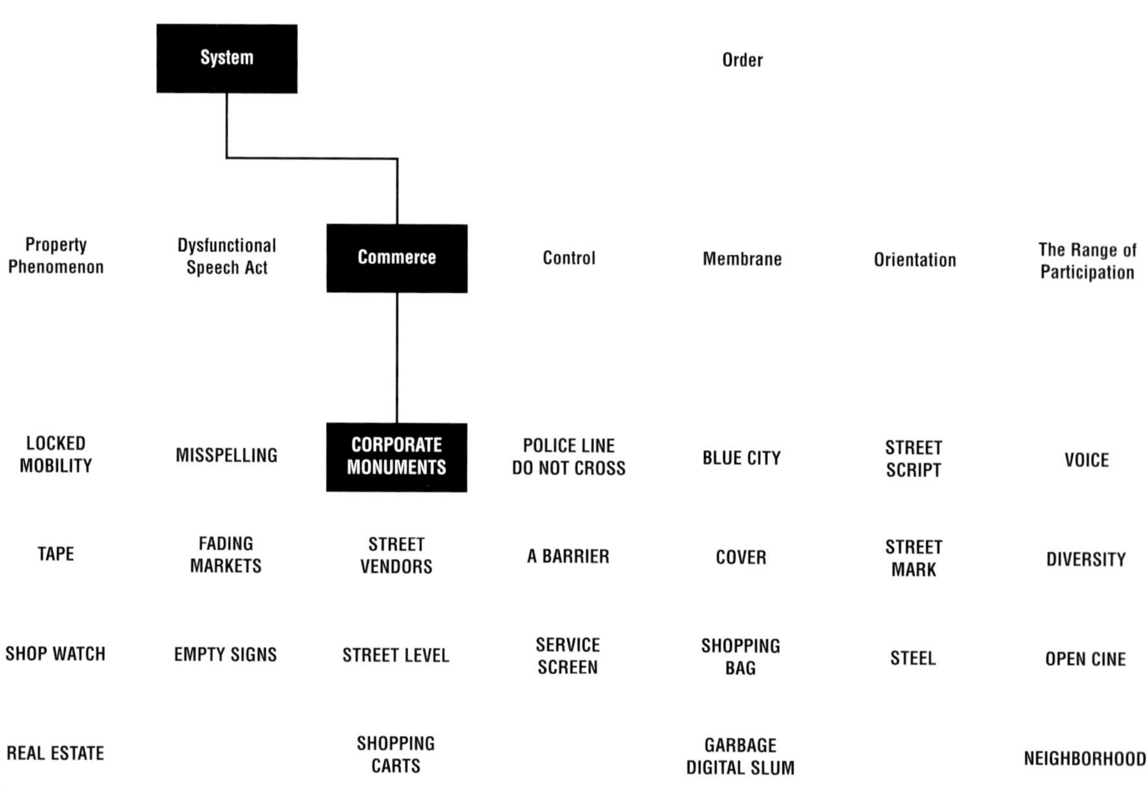
System
Order
Property Phenomenon
Dysfunctional Speech Act
Commerce
Control
Membrane
Orientation
The Range of Participation
LOCKED MOBILITY
MISSPELLING
CORPORATE MONUMENTS
POLICE LINE DO NOT CROSS
BLUE CITY
STREET SCRIPT
VOICE
TAPE
FADING MARKETS
STREET VENDORS
A BARRIER
COVER
STREET MARK
DIVERSITY
SHOP WATCH
EMPTY SIGNS
STREET LEVEL
SERVICE SCREEN
SHOPPING BAG
STEEL
OPEN CINE
REAL ESTATE
SHOPPING CARTS
GARBAGE DIGITAL SLUM
NEIGHBORHOOD

Identity

Alternative Media

Habitual Reinterpretation

CORPORATE MONUMENTS

Global Brands sell Idolatry

CAR DOOR

PUBLIC CHAIRS

LABELING.

PLASTIC CRATES

POLE POST

STANDPIPES

PRAY JESUS

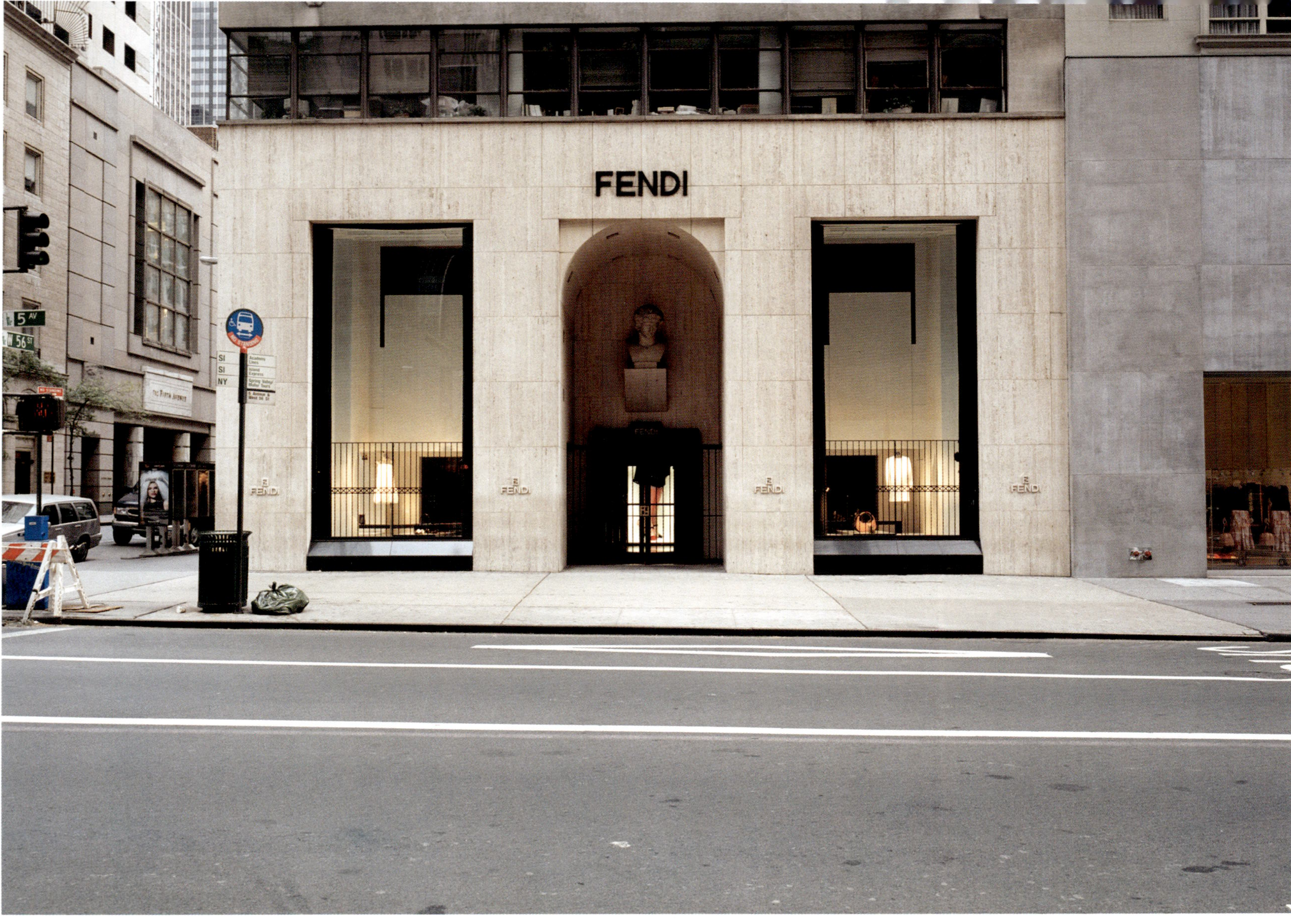
FENDI
5 AV
W 56 ST

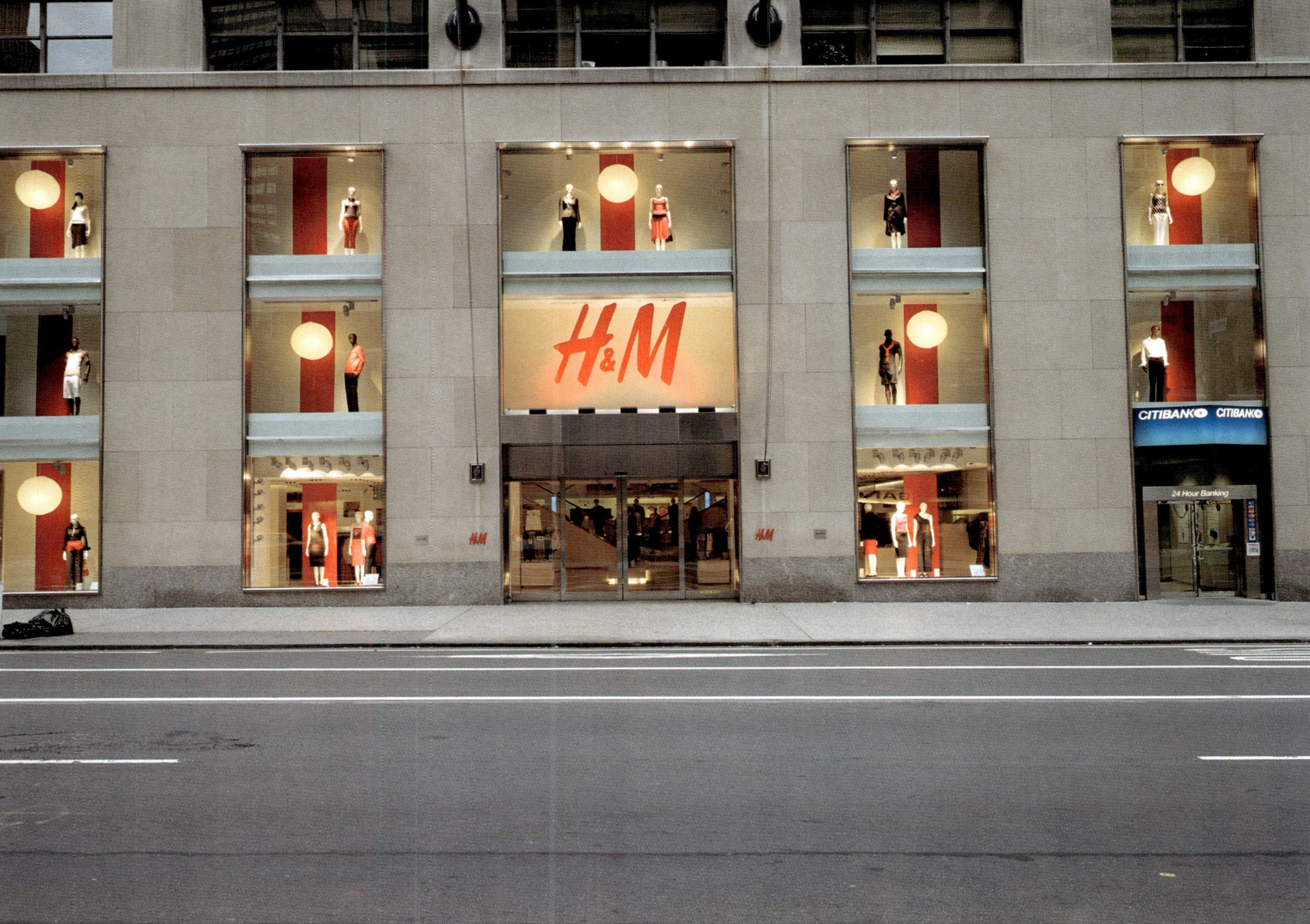
H&M
CITIBANK
CITIBANK
24 Hour Banking

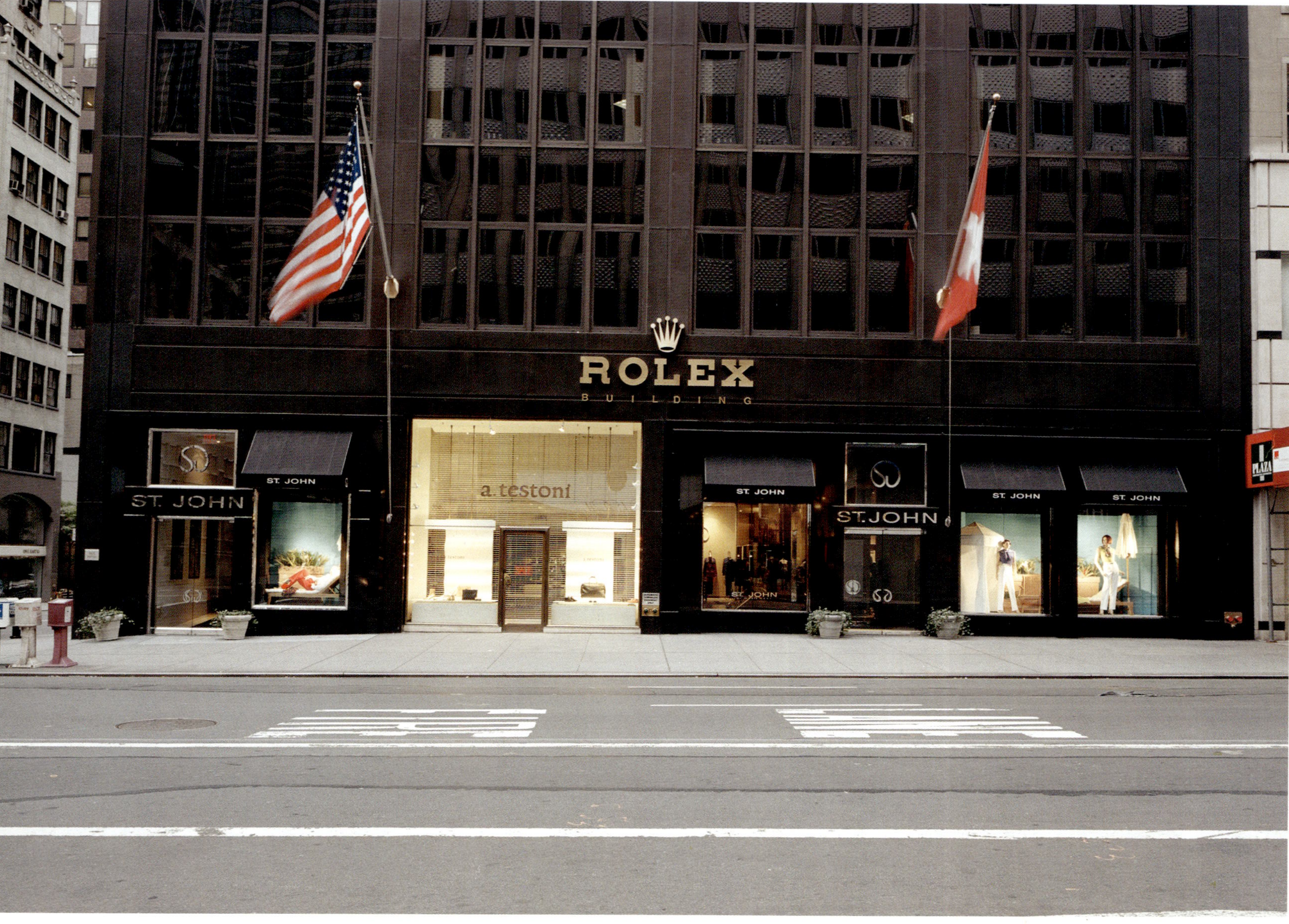
ROLEX
BUILDING
ST. JOHN
ST. JOHN
a. testoni
ST. JOHN
ST. JOHN
ST. JOHN
ST. JOHN

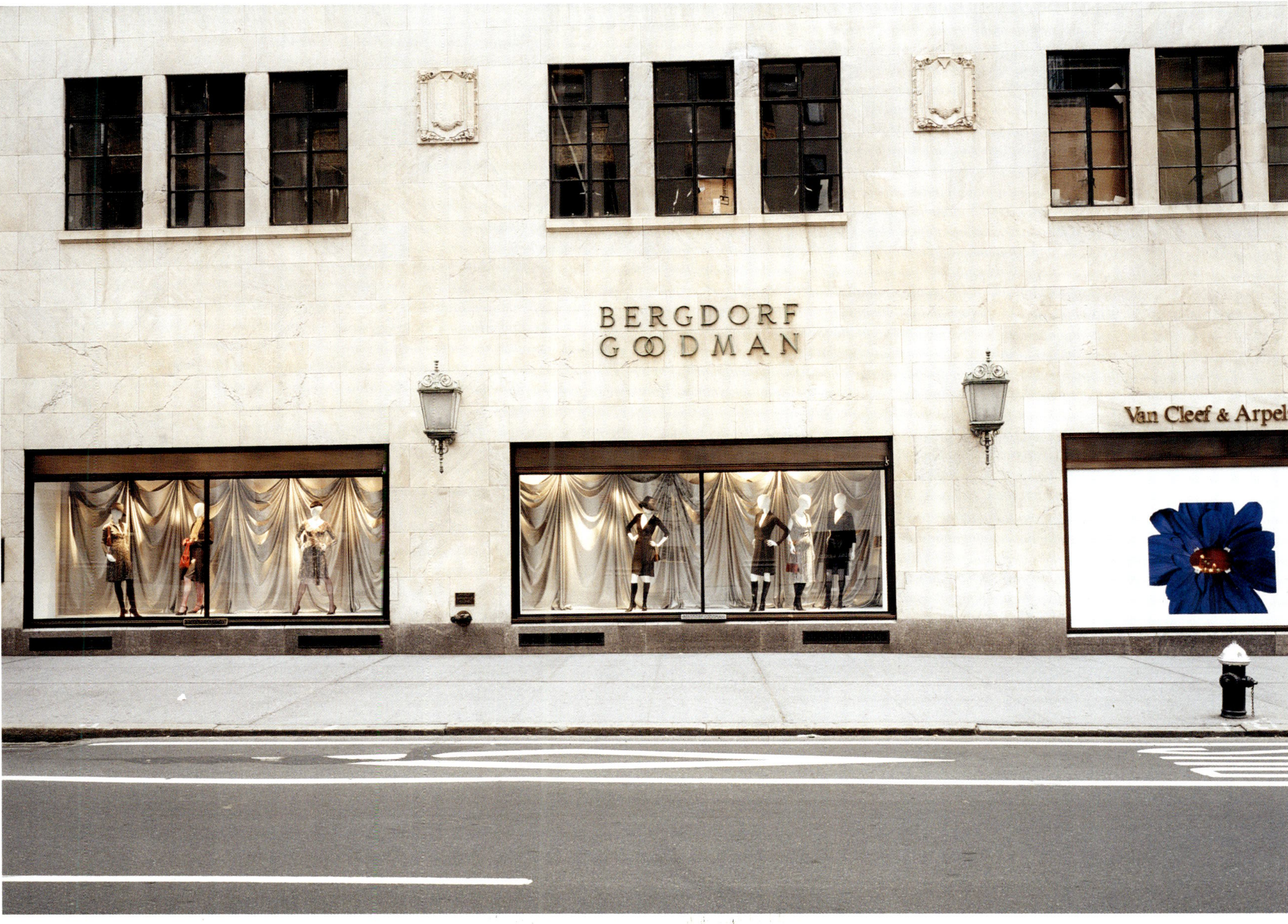
BERGDORF
GOODMAN
Van Cleef & Arpels

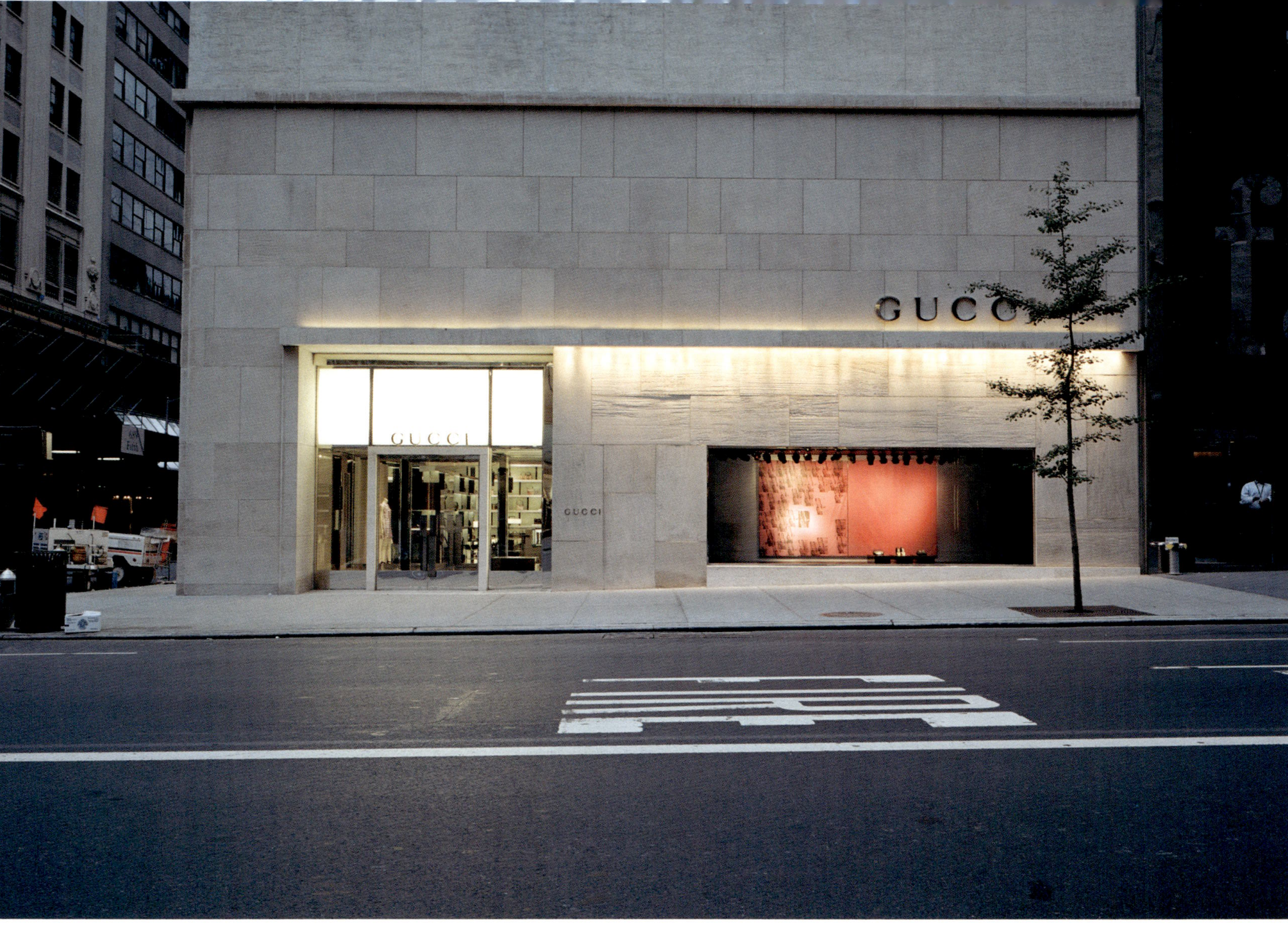
GUCCI
GUCCI

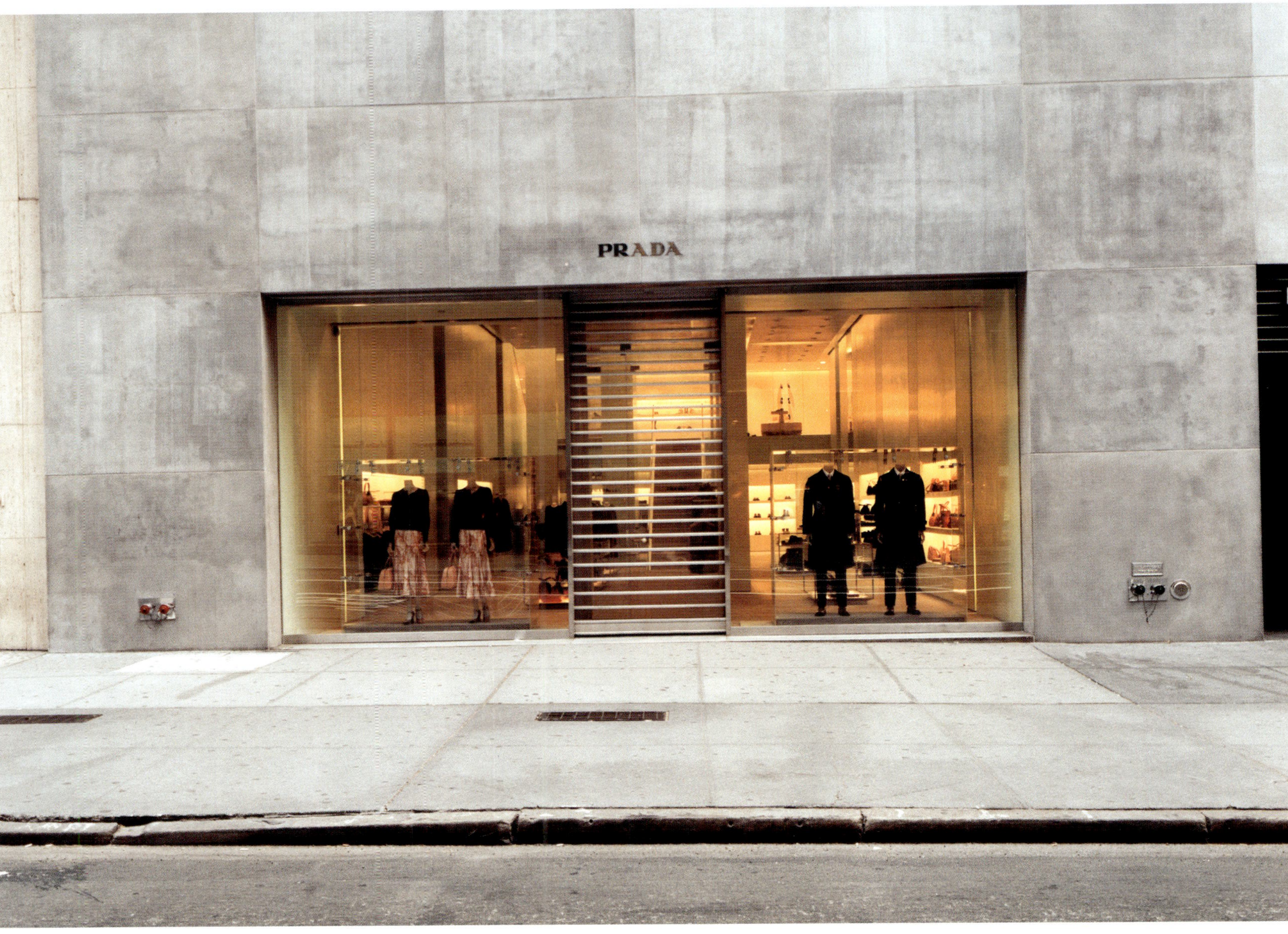
PRADA

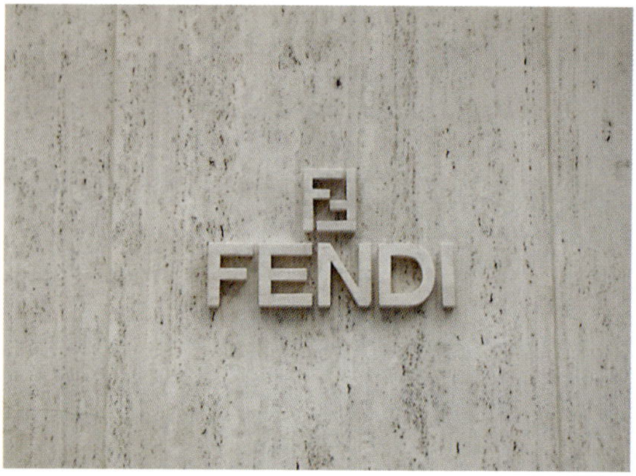

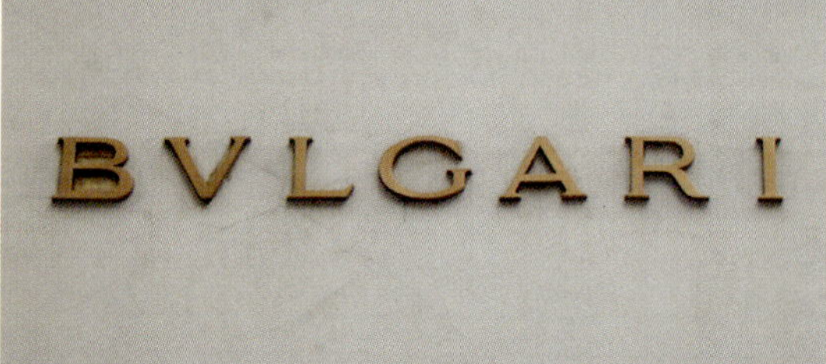
BVLGARI

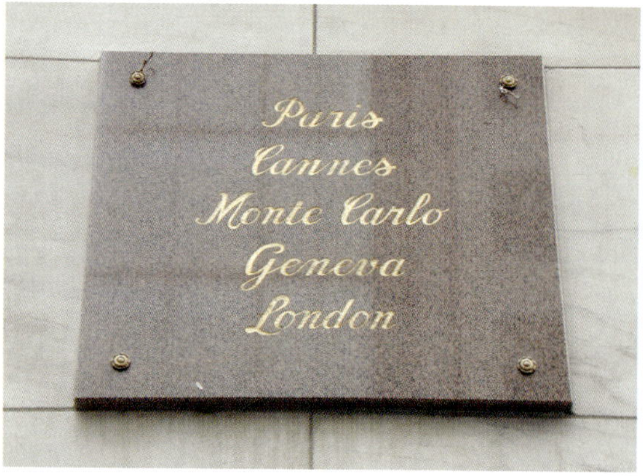

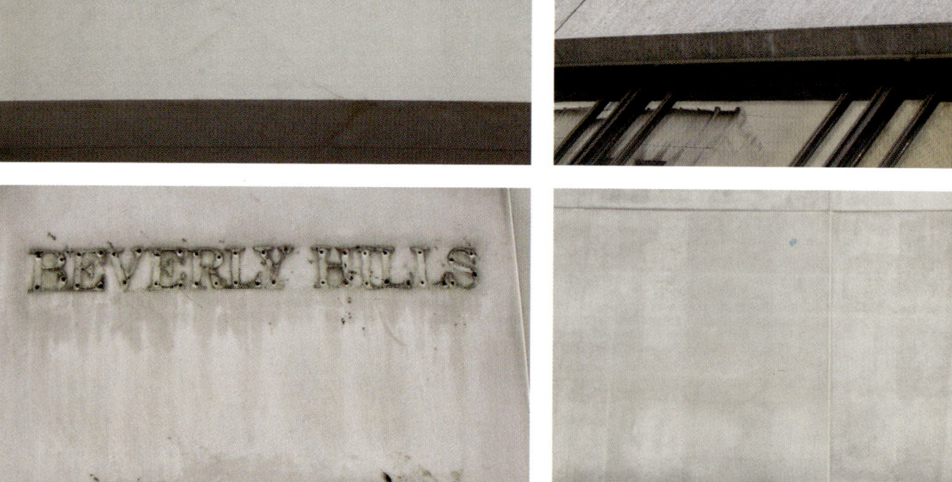
CHANEL
BEVERLY HILLS
HONOLULU
PRADA

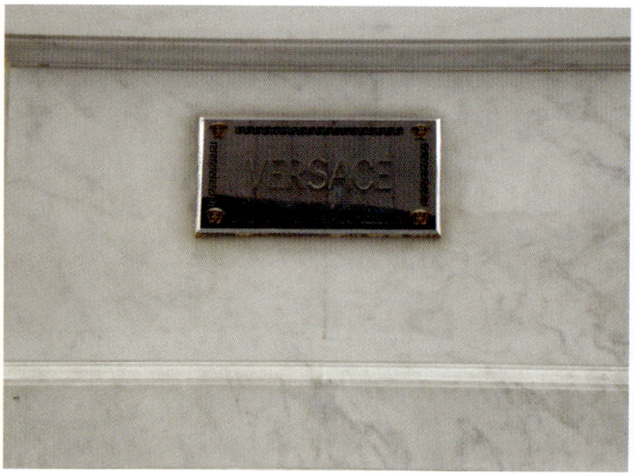

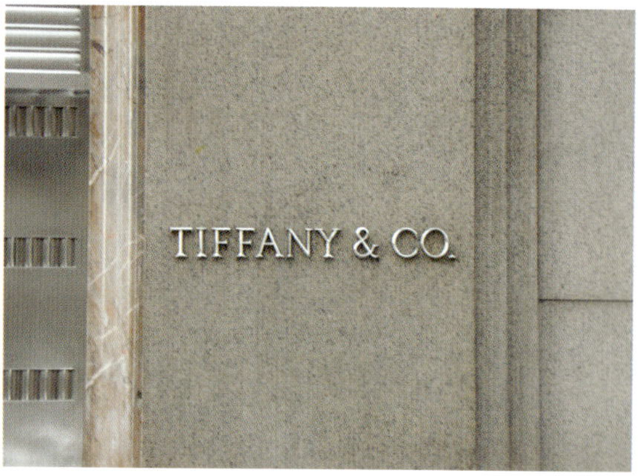

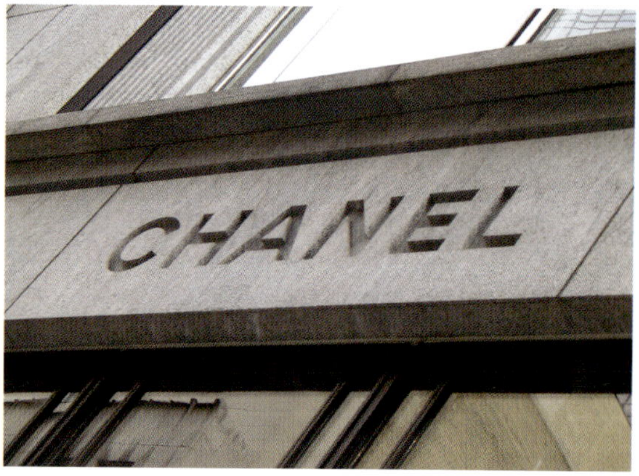

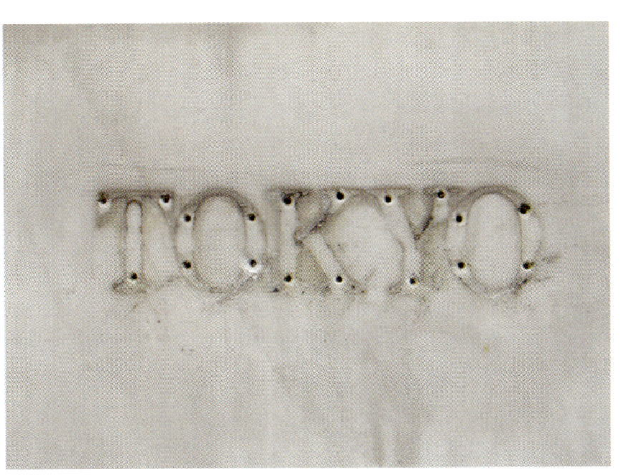
TOKYO
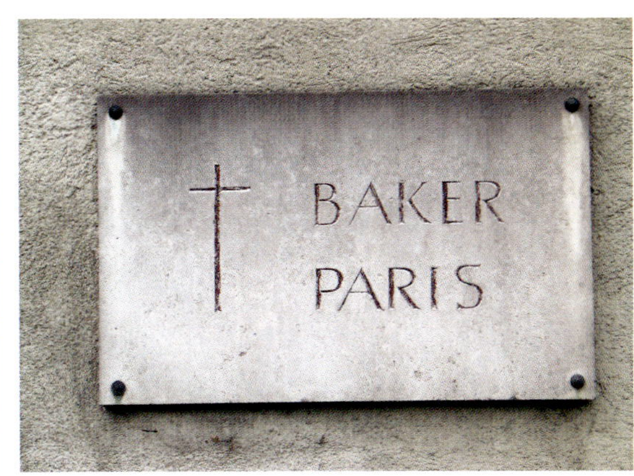
BAKER
PARIS
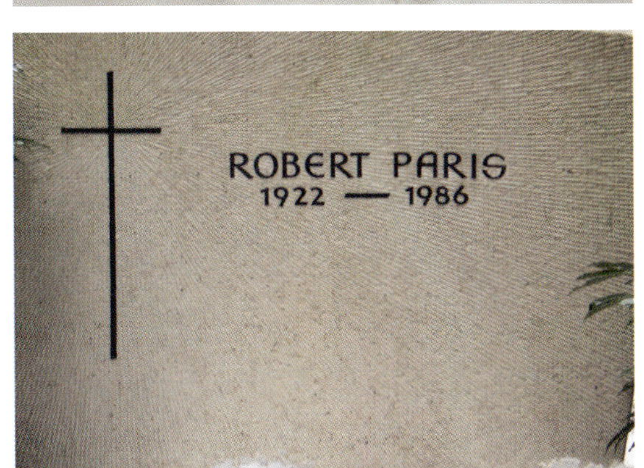
ROBERT PARIS
1922 — 1986
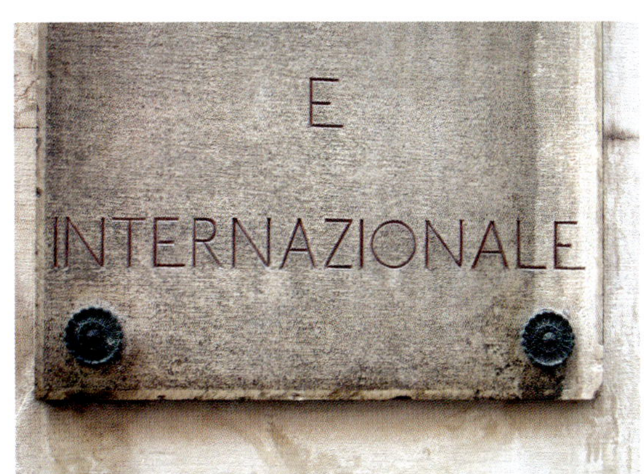
E
INTERNAZIONALE
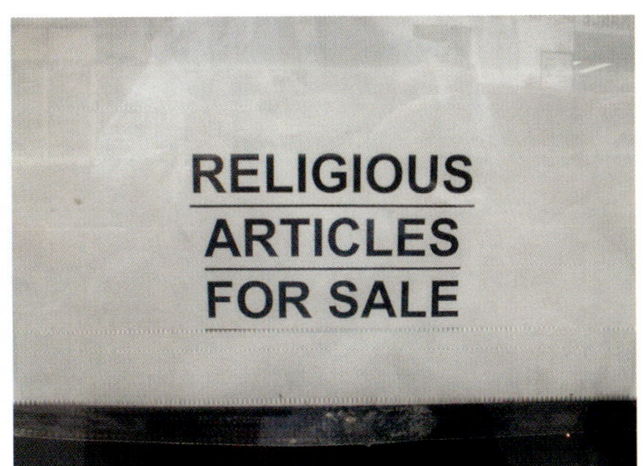
RELIGIOUS
ARTICLES
FOR SALE
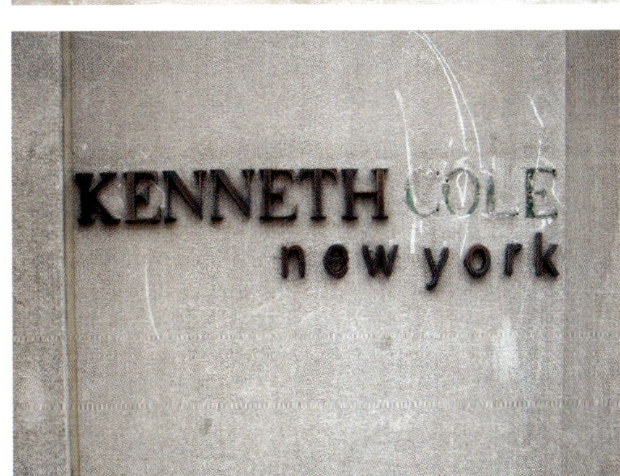
KENNETH COLE
new york
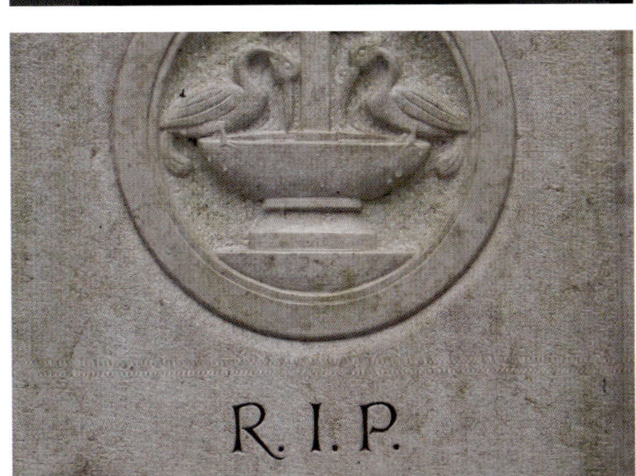
R. I. P.
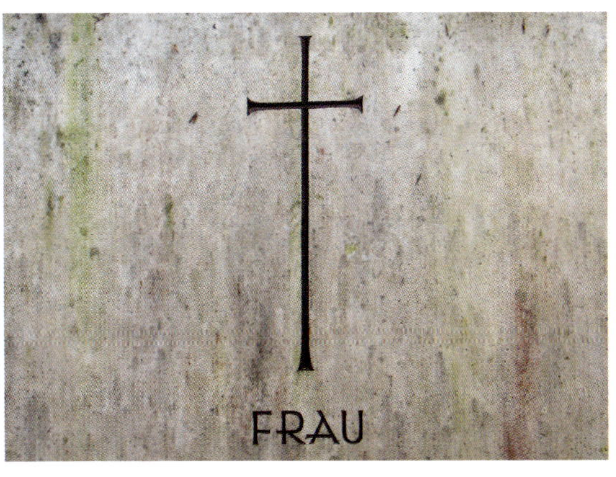
FRAU

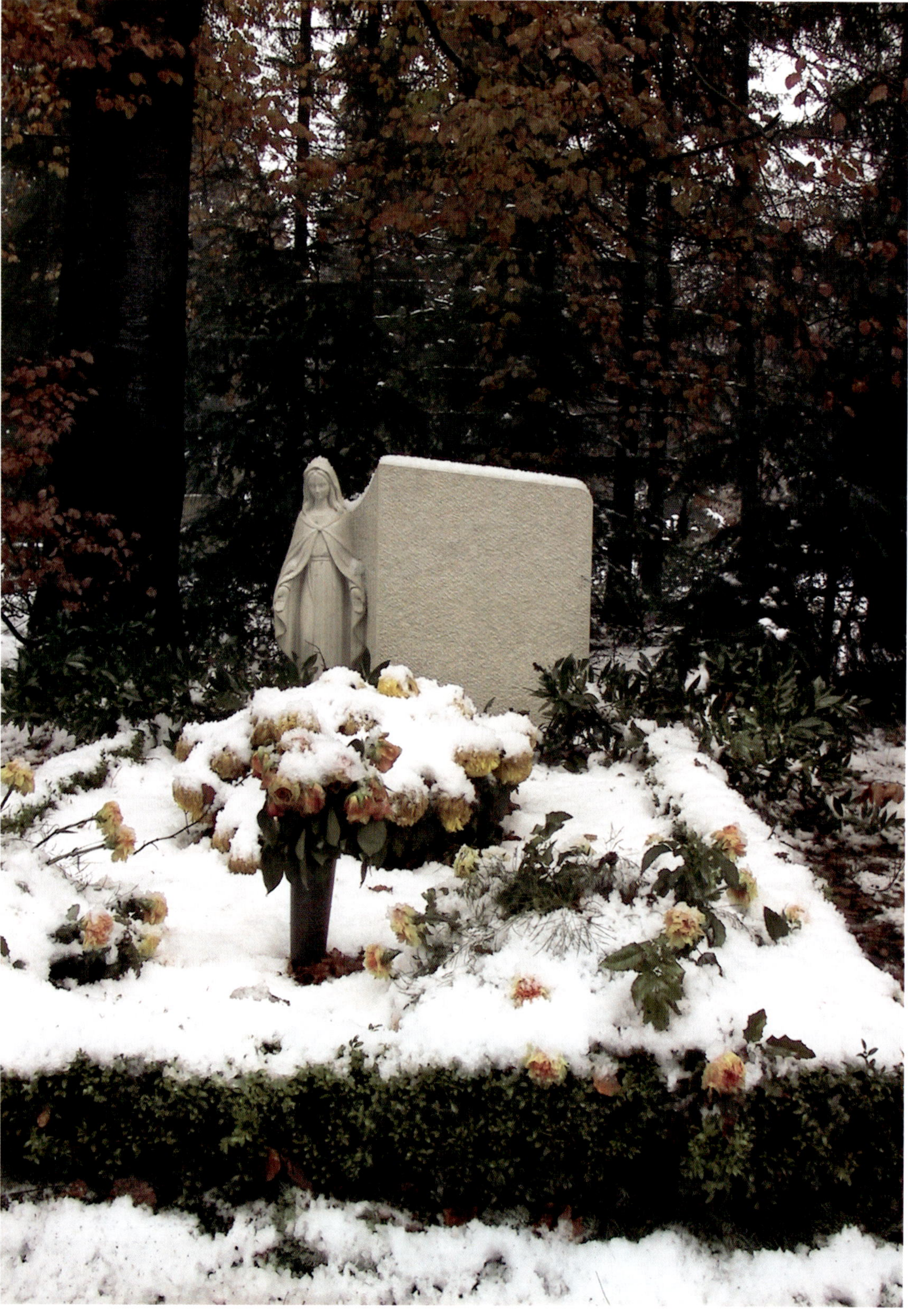

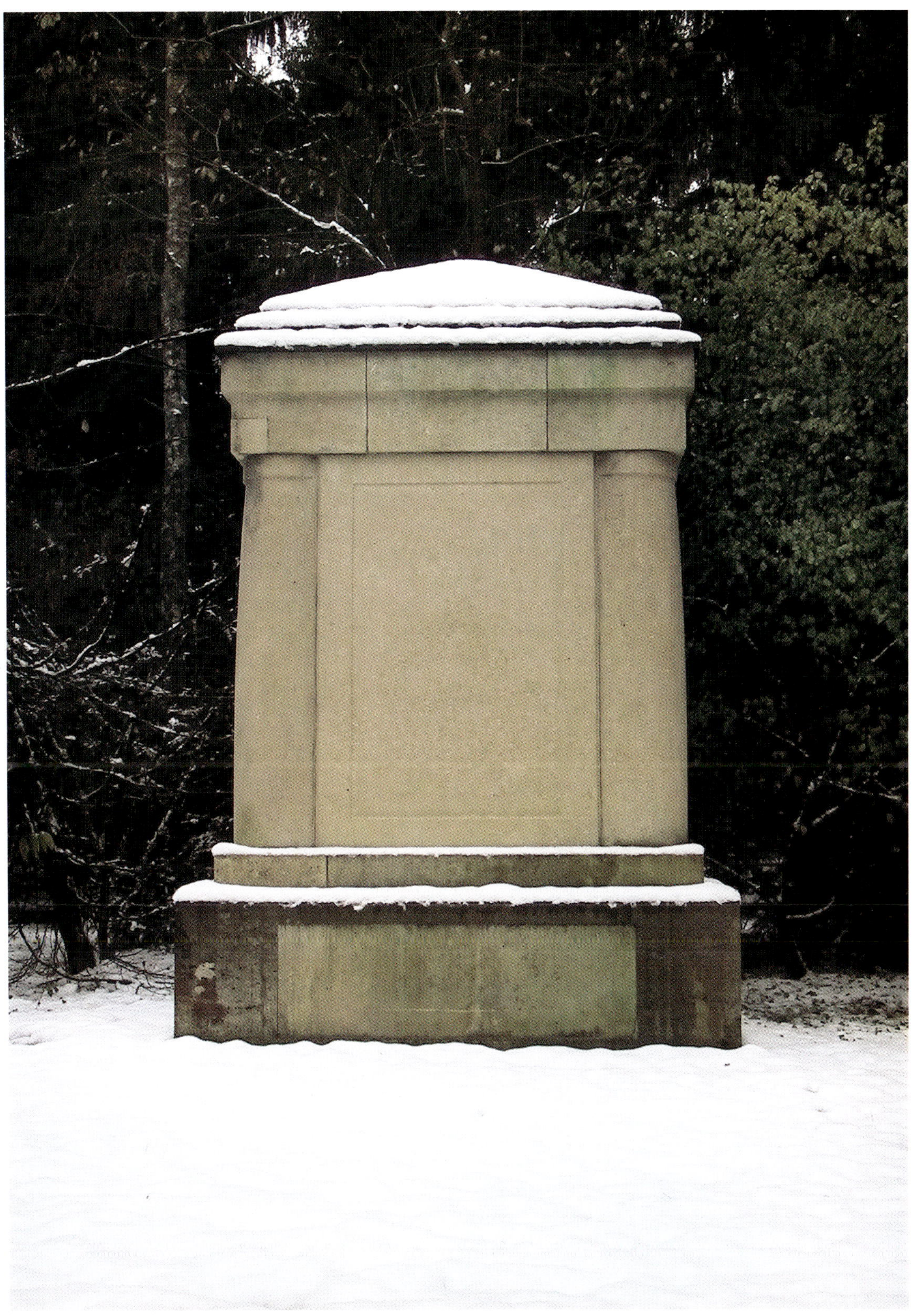

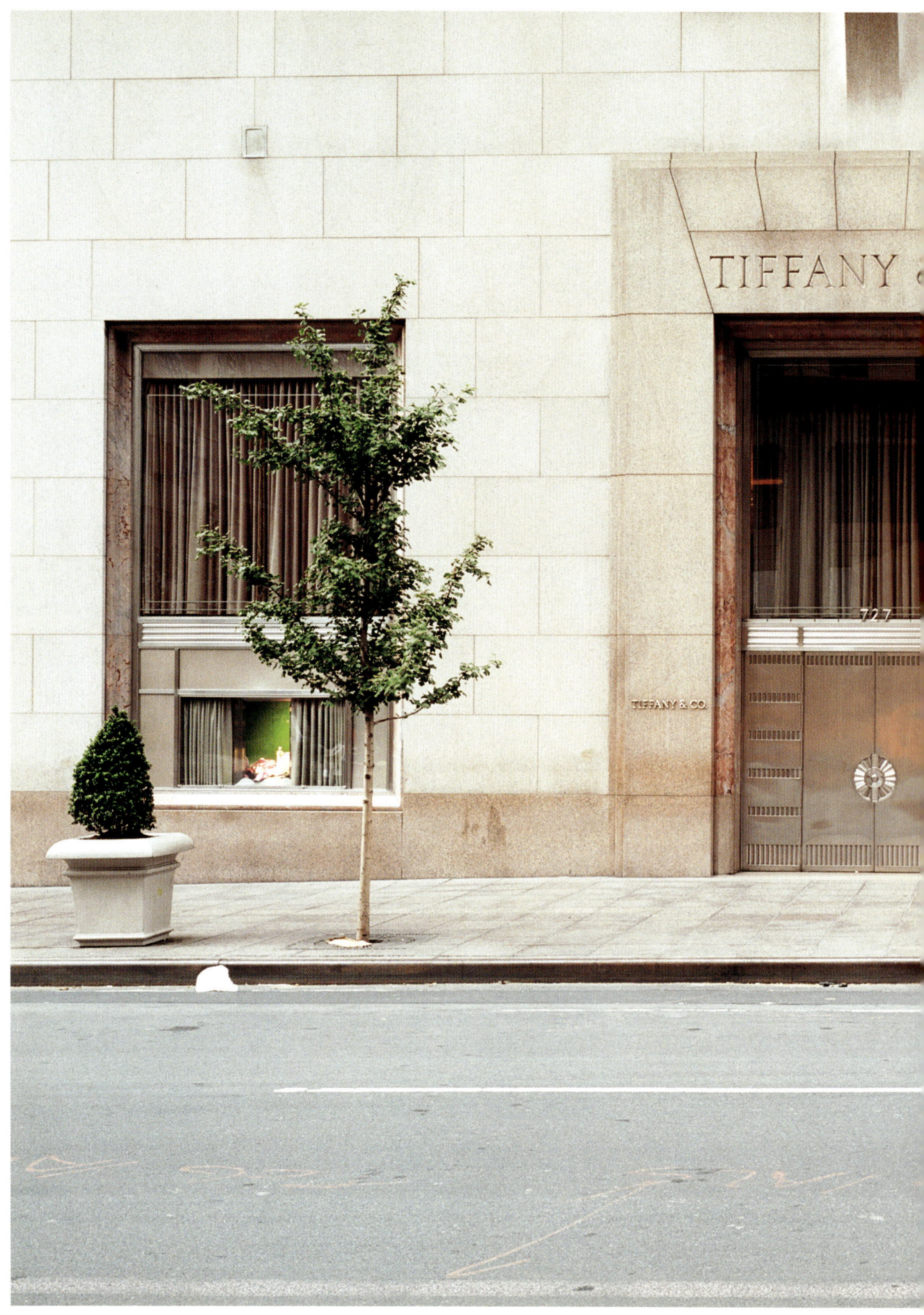
TIFFANY
TIFFANY & CO.
727

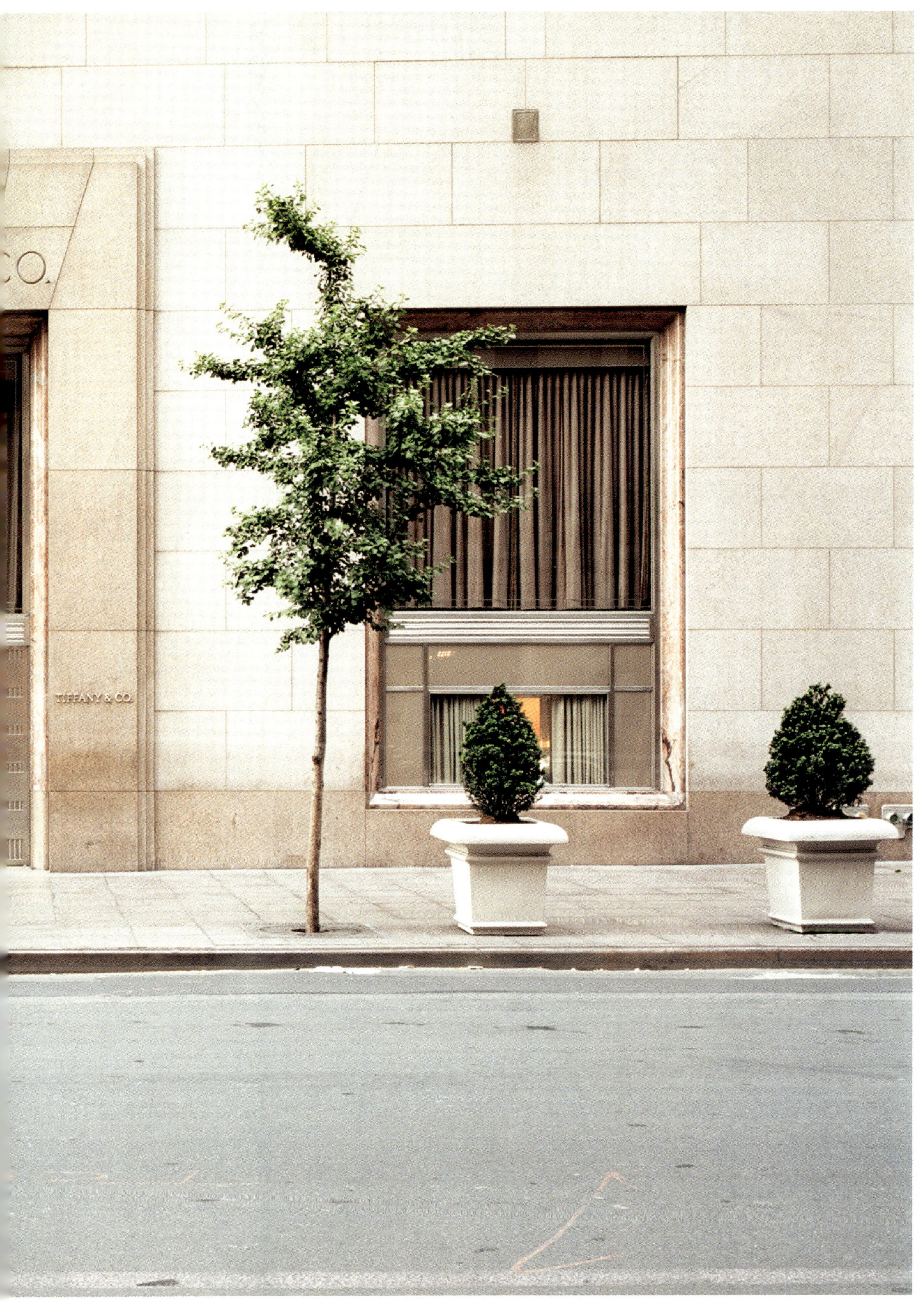
TIFFANY & CO.

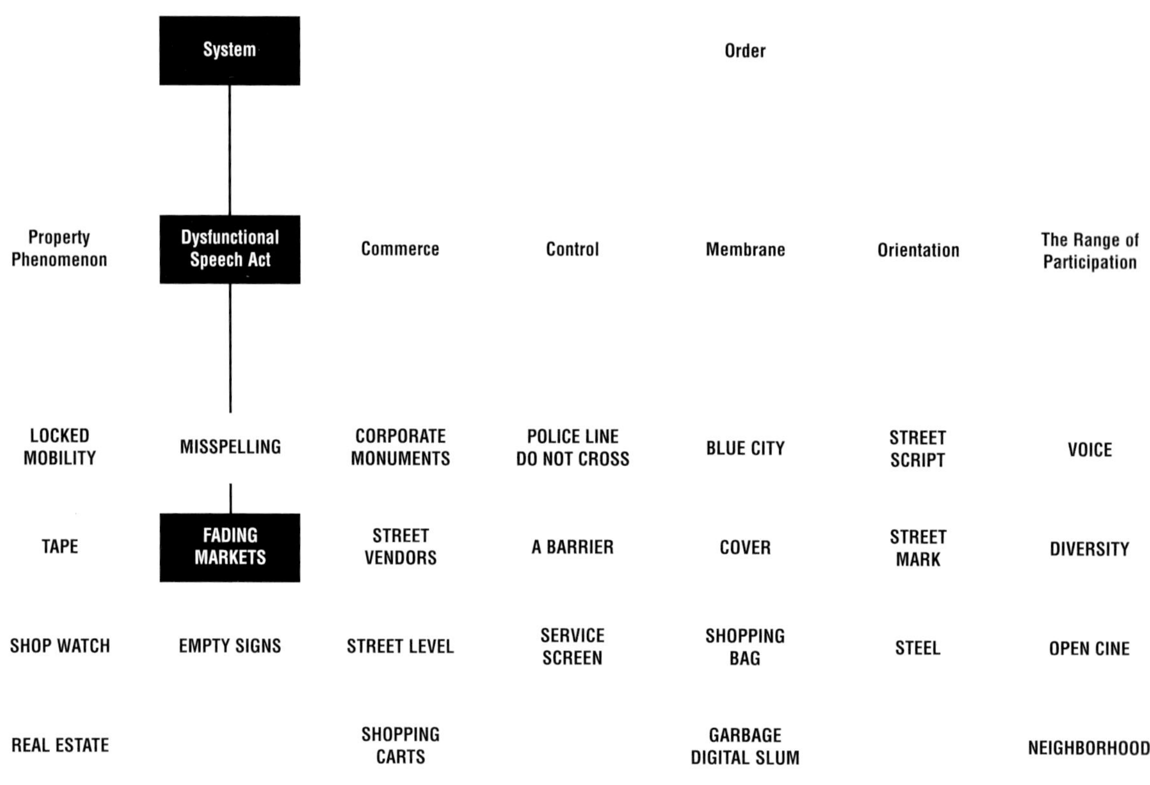
System
Order
Property Phenomenon
Dysfunctional Speech Act
Commerce
Control
Membrane
Orientation
The Range of Participation
LOCKED MOBILITY
MISSPELLING
CORPORATE MONUMENTS
POLICE LINE DO NOT CROSS
BLUE CITY
STREET SCRIPT
VOICE
TAPE
FADING MARKETS
STREET VENDORS
A BARRIER
COVER
STREET MARK
DIVERSITY
SHOP WATCH
EMPTY SIGNS
STREET LEVEL
SERVICE SCREEN
SHOPPING BAG
STEEL
OPEN CINE
REAL ESTATE
SHOPPING CARTS
GARBAGE DIGITAL SLUM
NEIGHBORHOOD

Identity

Alternative Media

Habitual Reinterpretation

FADING MARKETS

Economic Cycle spelled out

CAR DOOR

PUBLIC CHAIRS

LABELING.

PLASTIC CRATES

POLE POST

STANDPIPES

PRAY JESUS

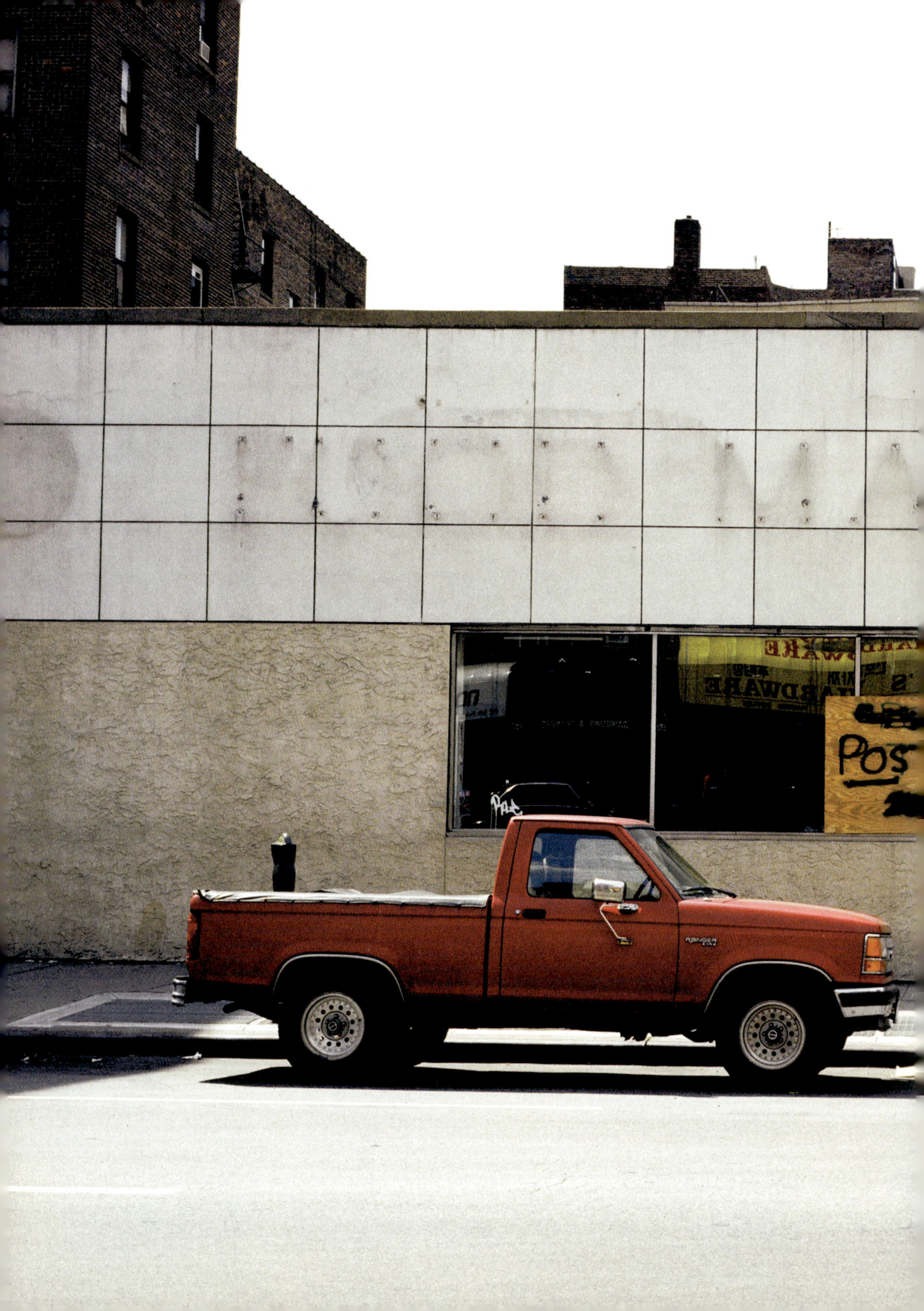
POS

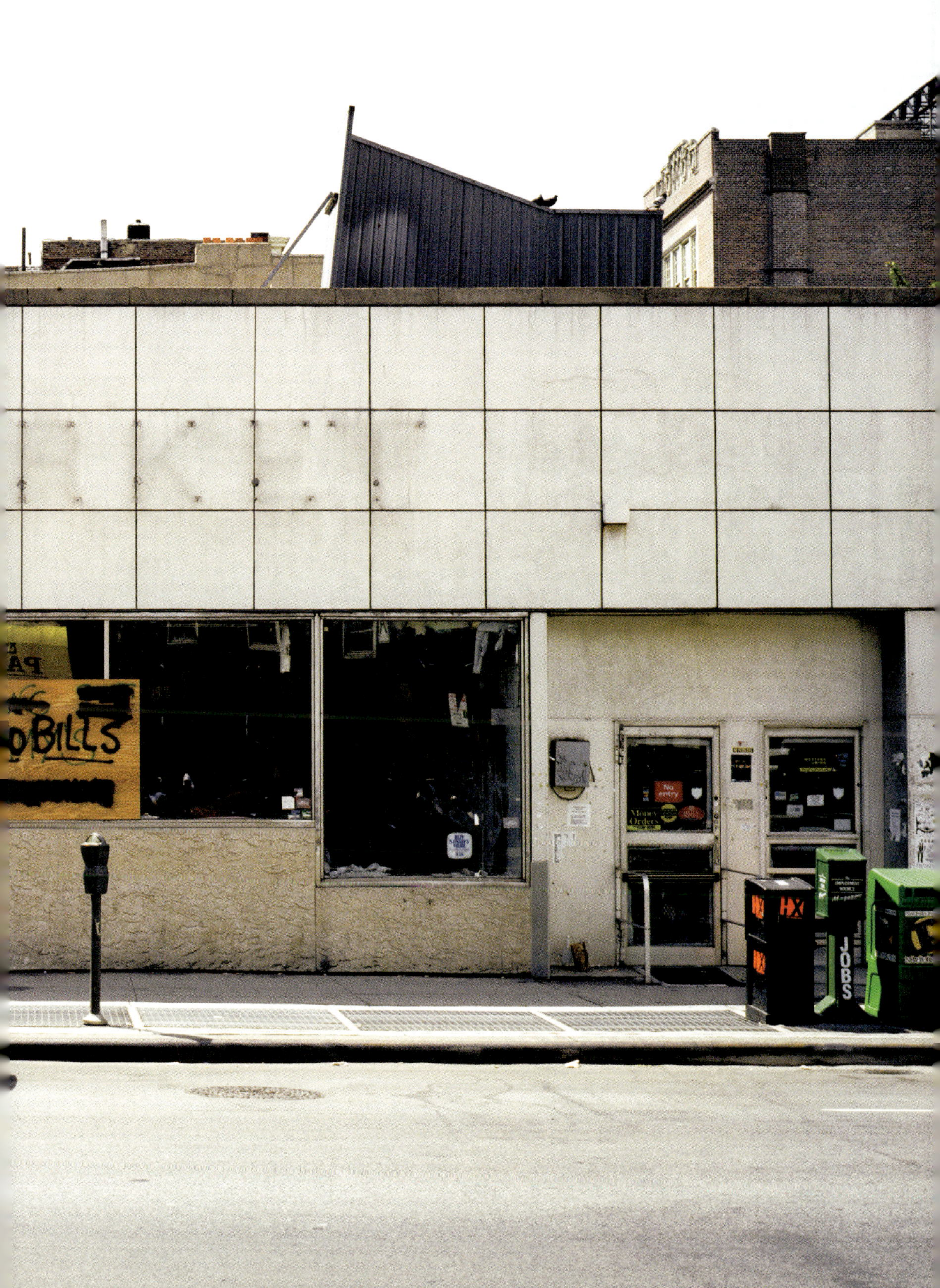
No entry
Money Orders
HX
JOBS

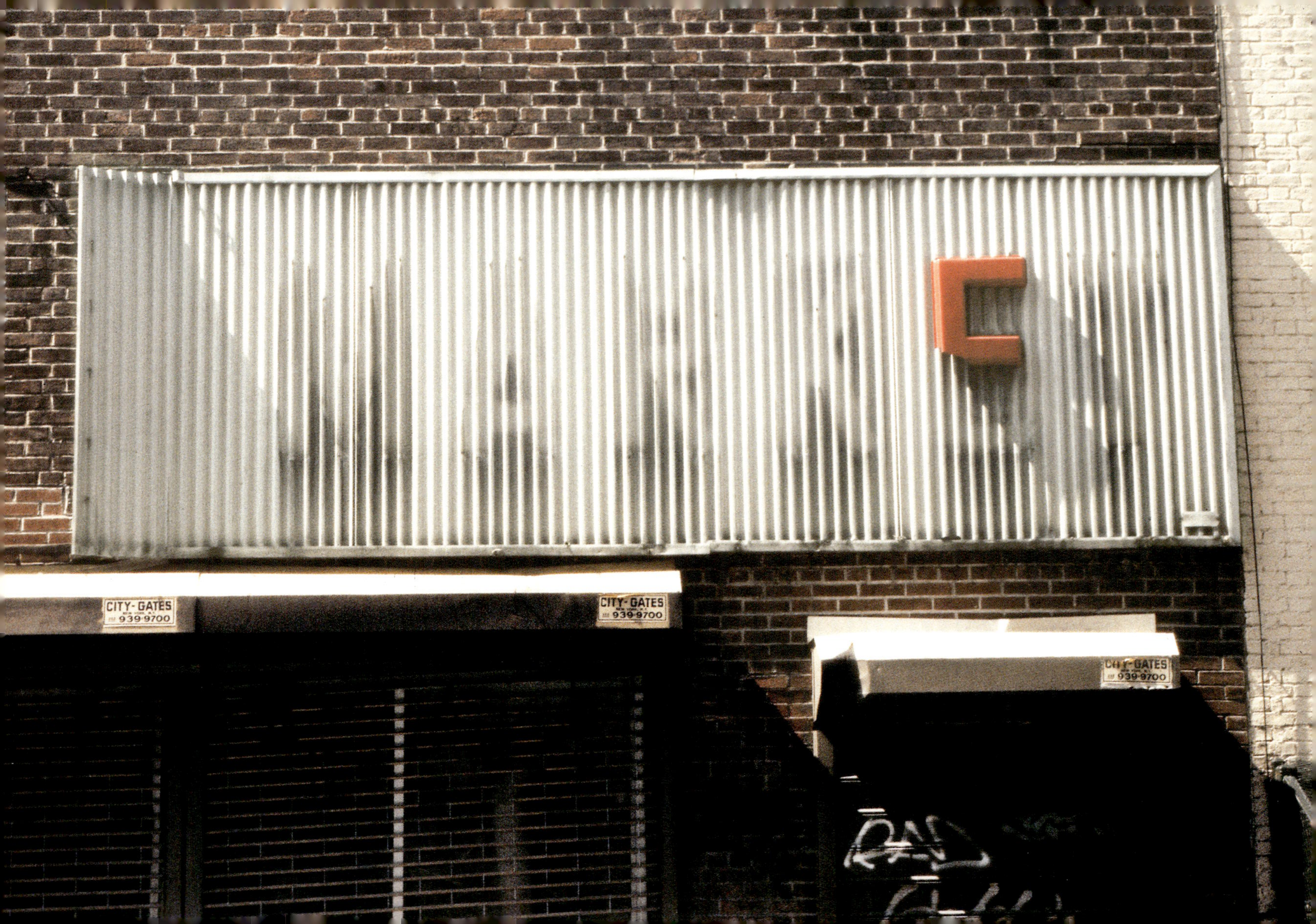
CITY-GATES
939-9700
CITY-GATES
939-9700
CITY-GATES
939-9700

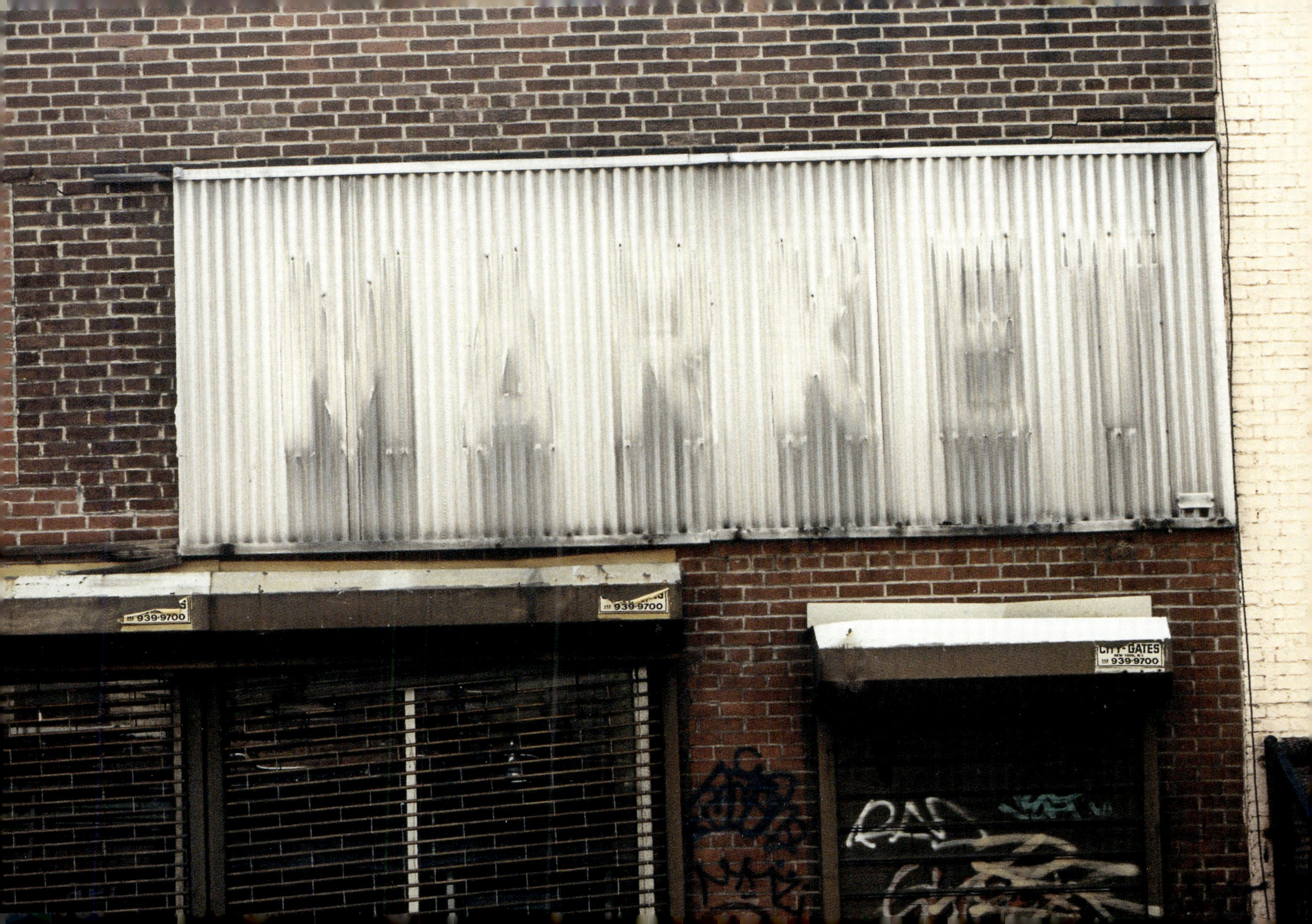
MARKET
939-9700
939-9700
CITY-GATES
939-9700

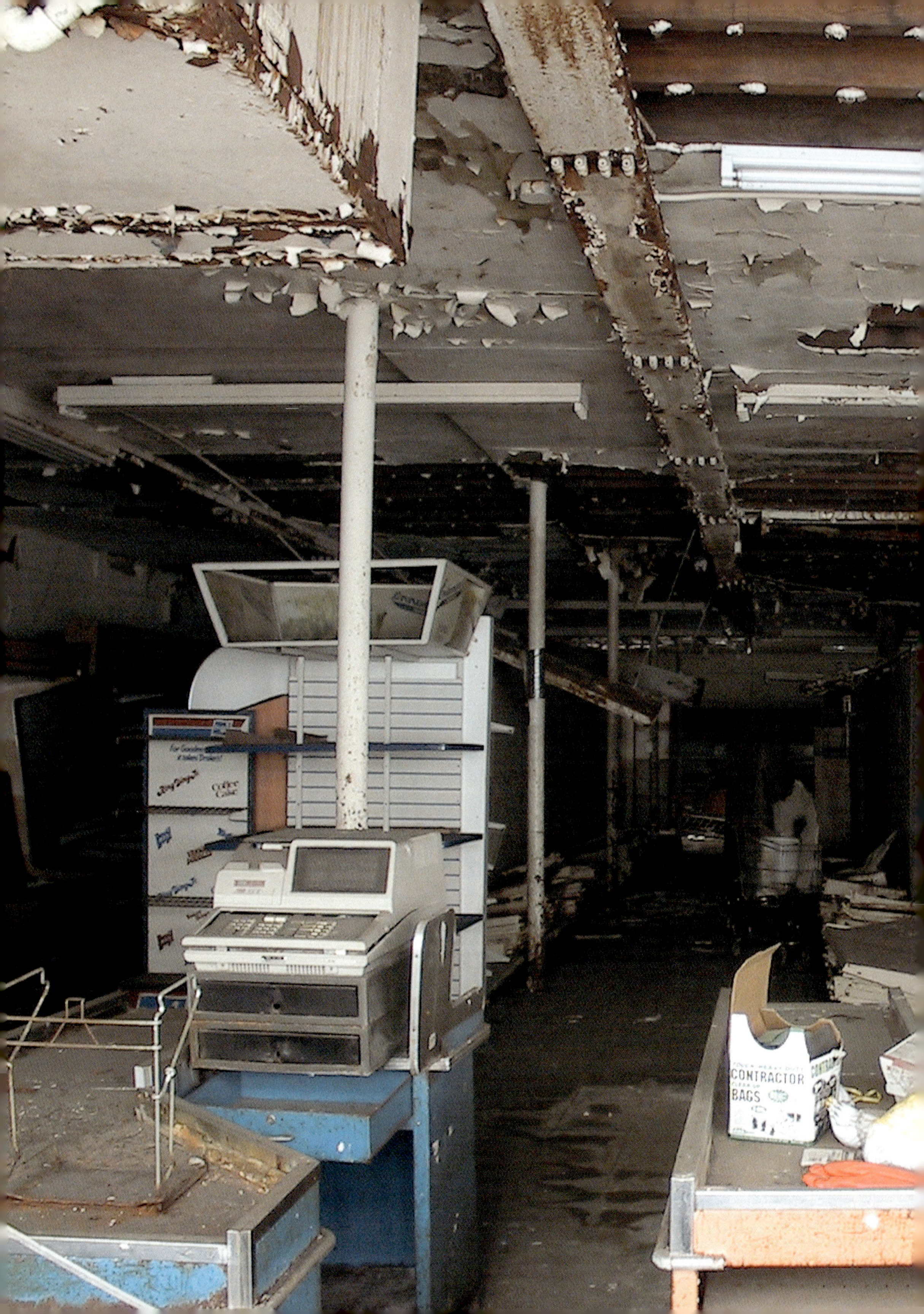
CONTRACTOR
BAGS

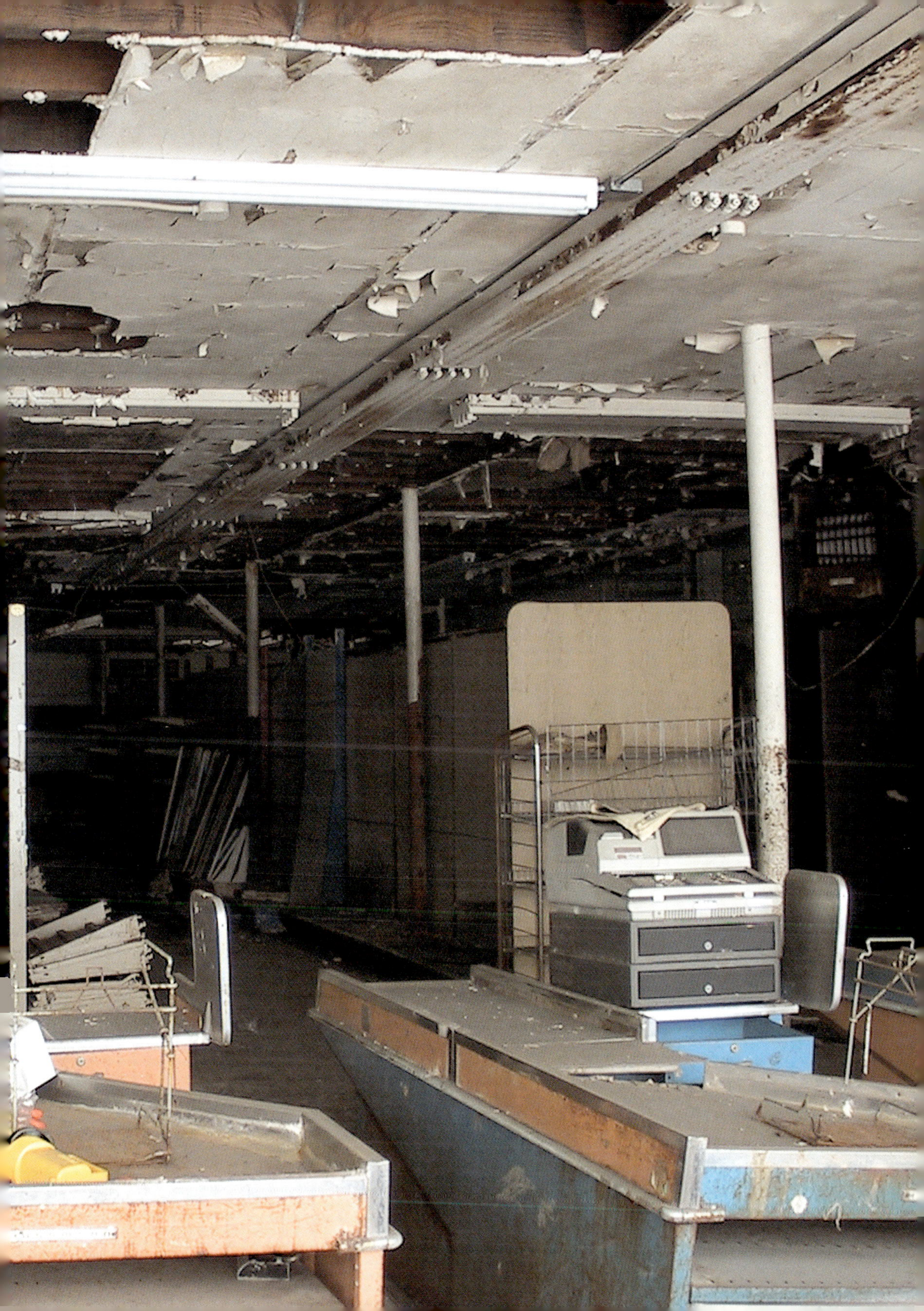

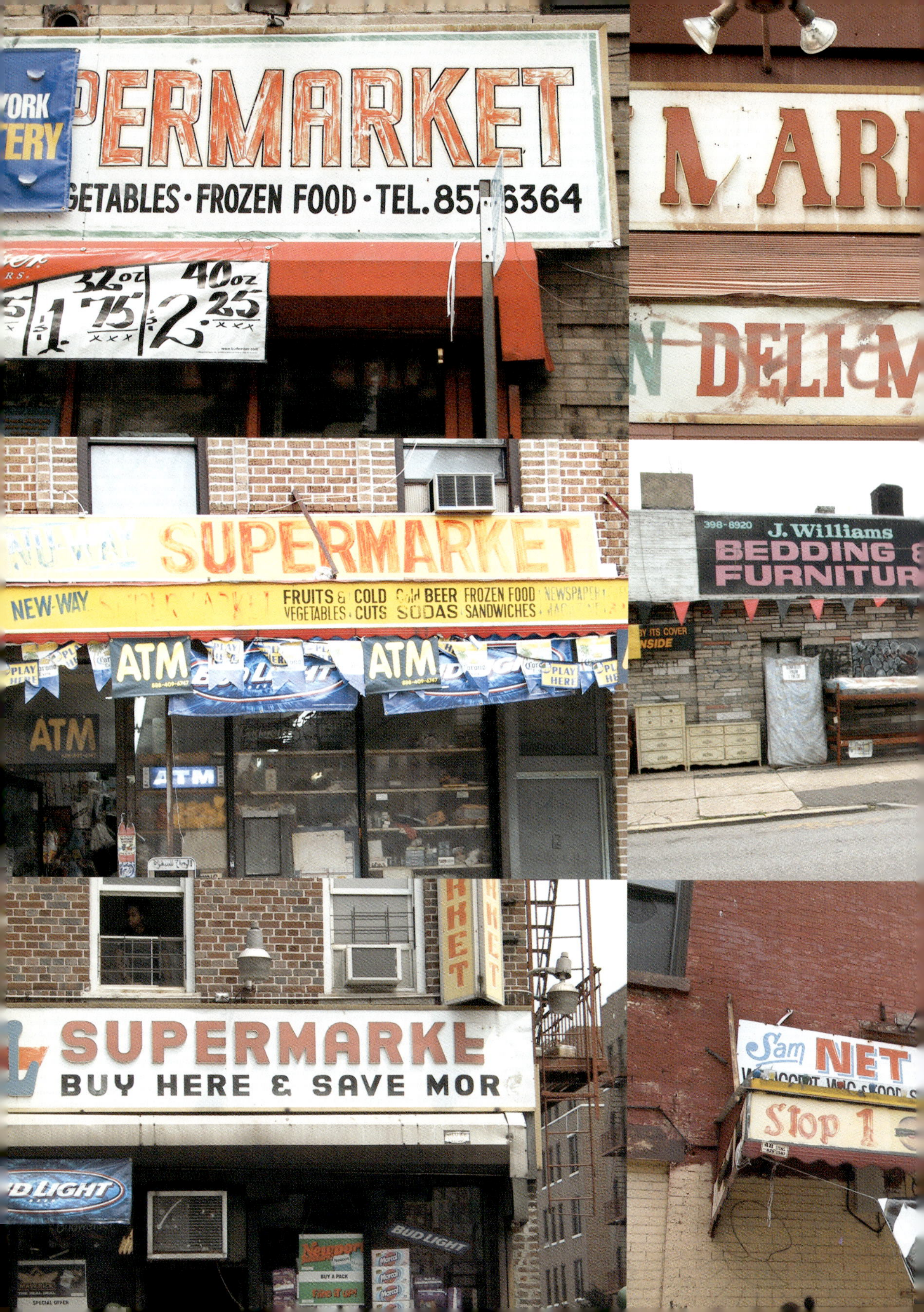

PERMARKET
GETABLES · FROZEN FOOD · TEL. 857 6364
32oz 40oz
$1.75 $2.25
A ARI
N DELI M
SUPERMARKET
NEW-WAY
FRUITS & VEGETABLES
COLD CUTS
Cold BEER SODAS
FROZEN FOOD SANDWICHES
ATM
ATM
ATM
ATM
398-8920
J. Williams
BEDDING &
FURNITUR
SUPERMARKE
BUY HERE & SAVE MOR
BUD LIGHT
BUD LIGHT
Sam NET
Stop 1

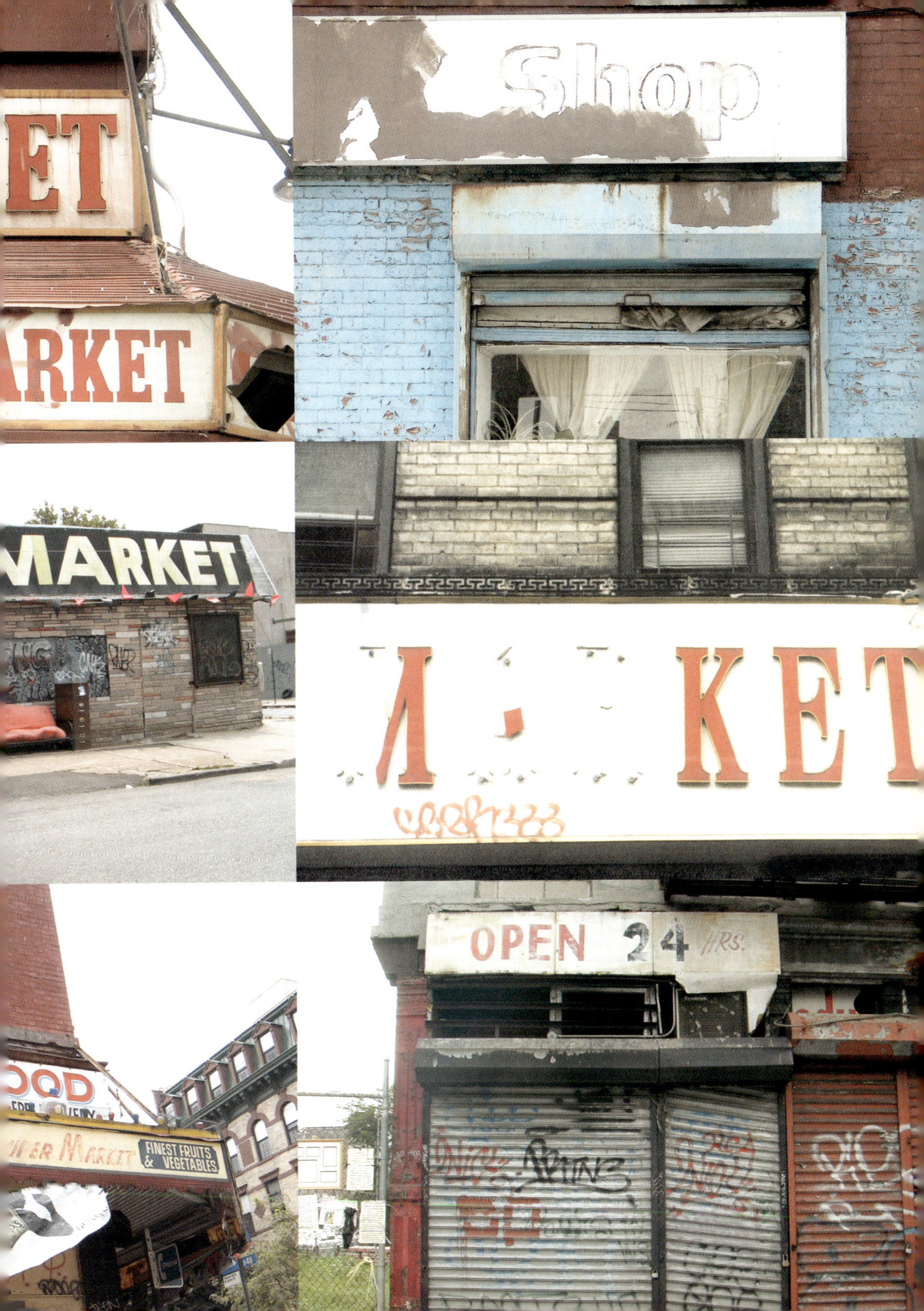

ET
Shop
ARKET
MARKET
KET
OPEN 24 HRS.
OOD
FINEST FRUITS & VEGETABLES

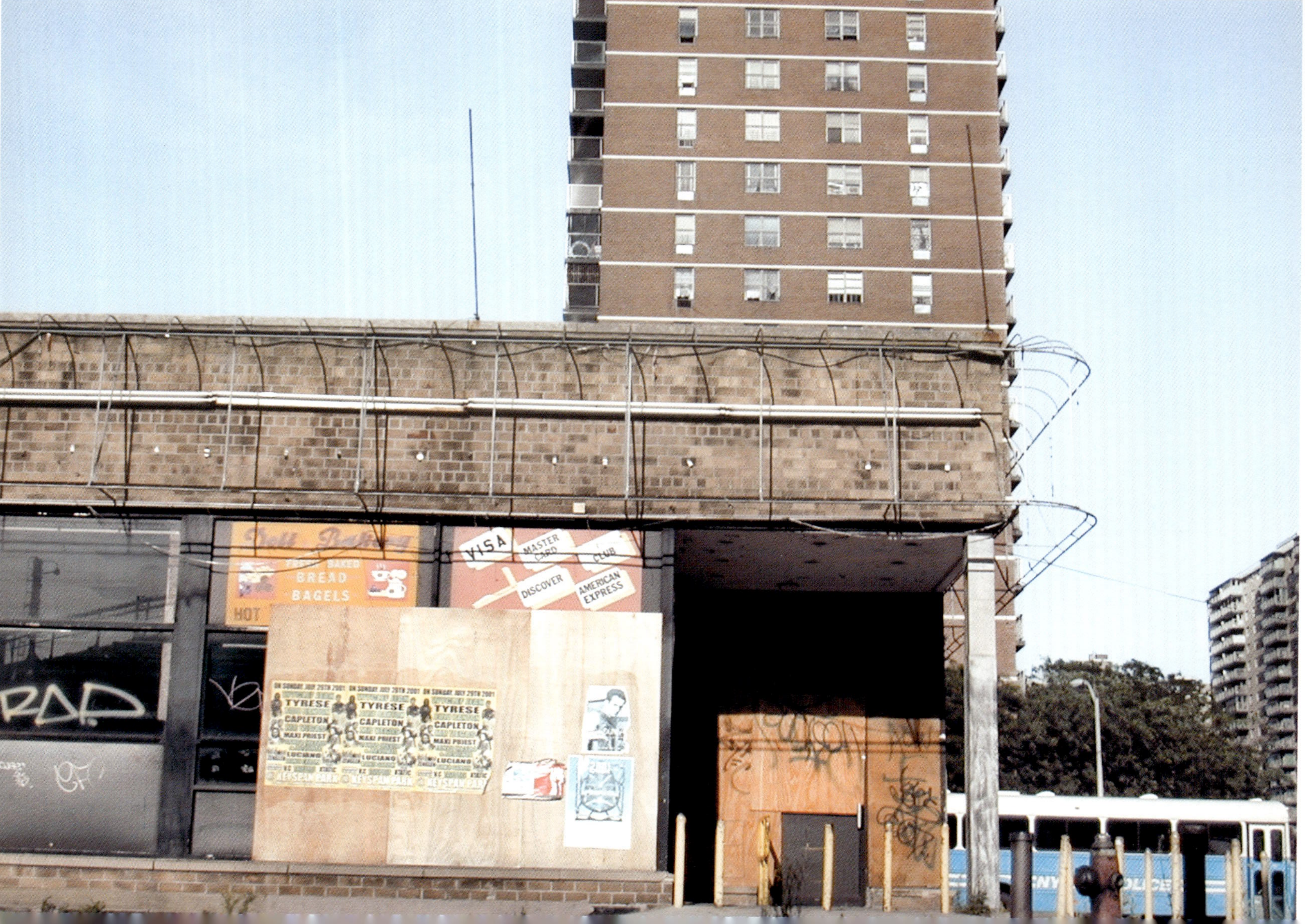
FRESH BAKED
BREAD
BAGELS
HOT
VISA
MASTER CARD
CLUB
DISCOVER
AMERICAN EXPRESS
TYRESE
CAPLETON
MAXI PRIEST
LUCIANO
RAP

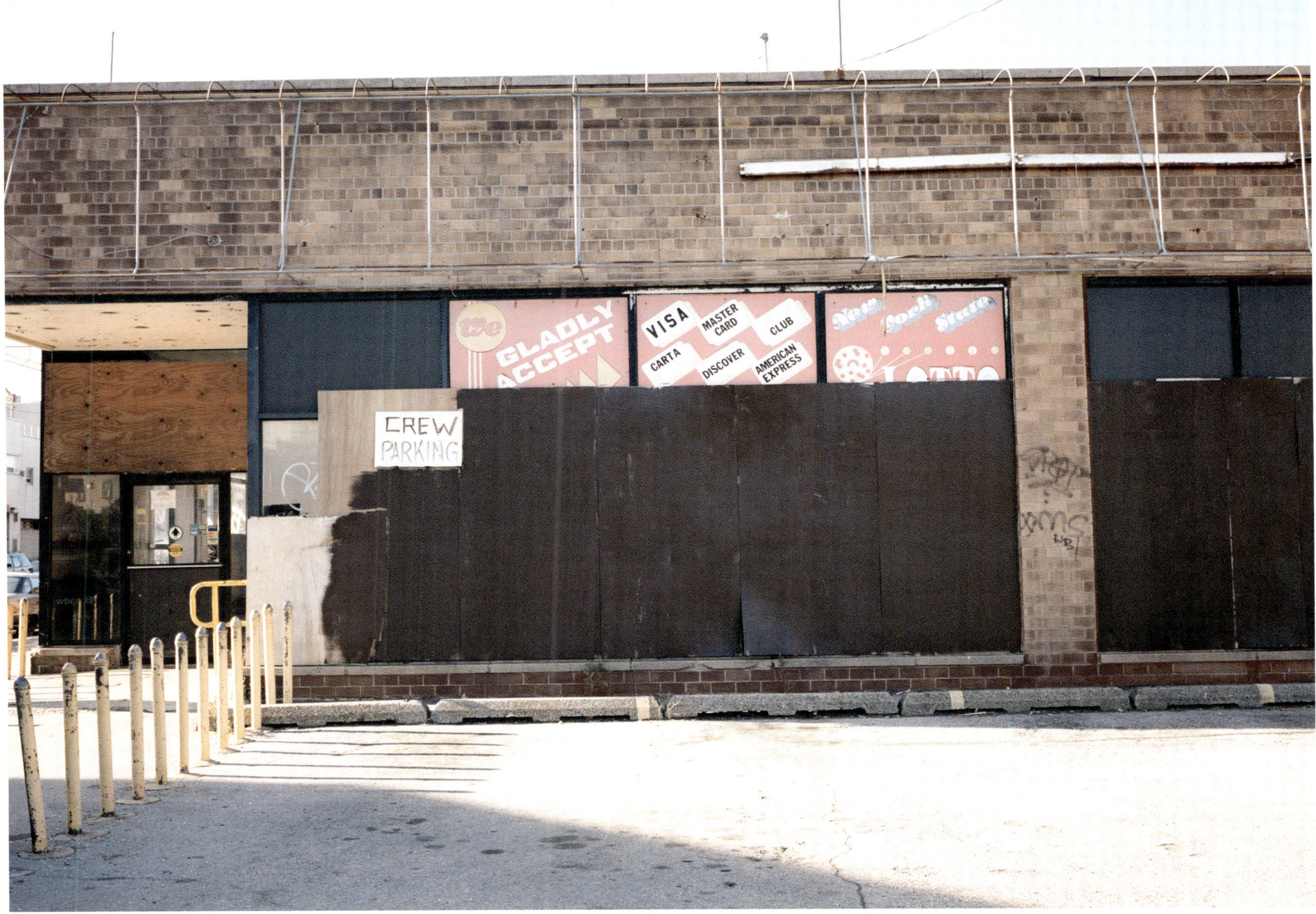

We
GLADLY
ACCEPT
VISA
MASTER CARD
CLUB
CARTA
DISCOVER
AMERICAN EXPRESS
New York State
CREW
PARKING

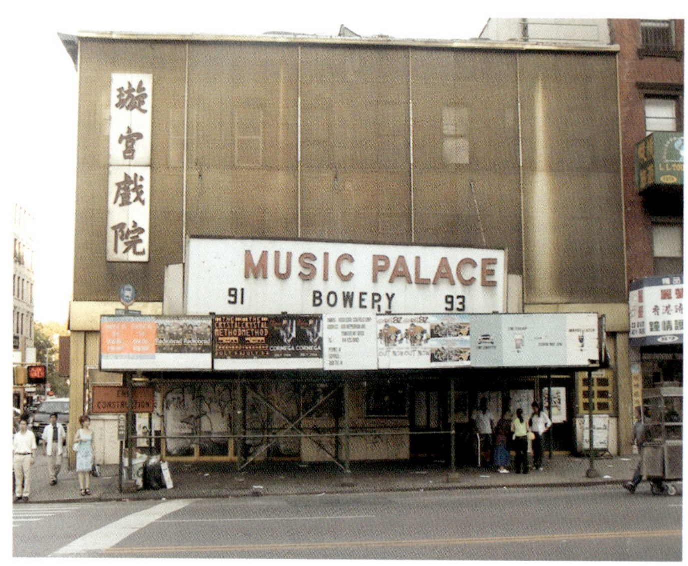
璇宮戲院
MUSIC PALACE
91 BOWERY 93

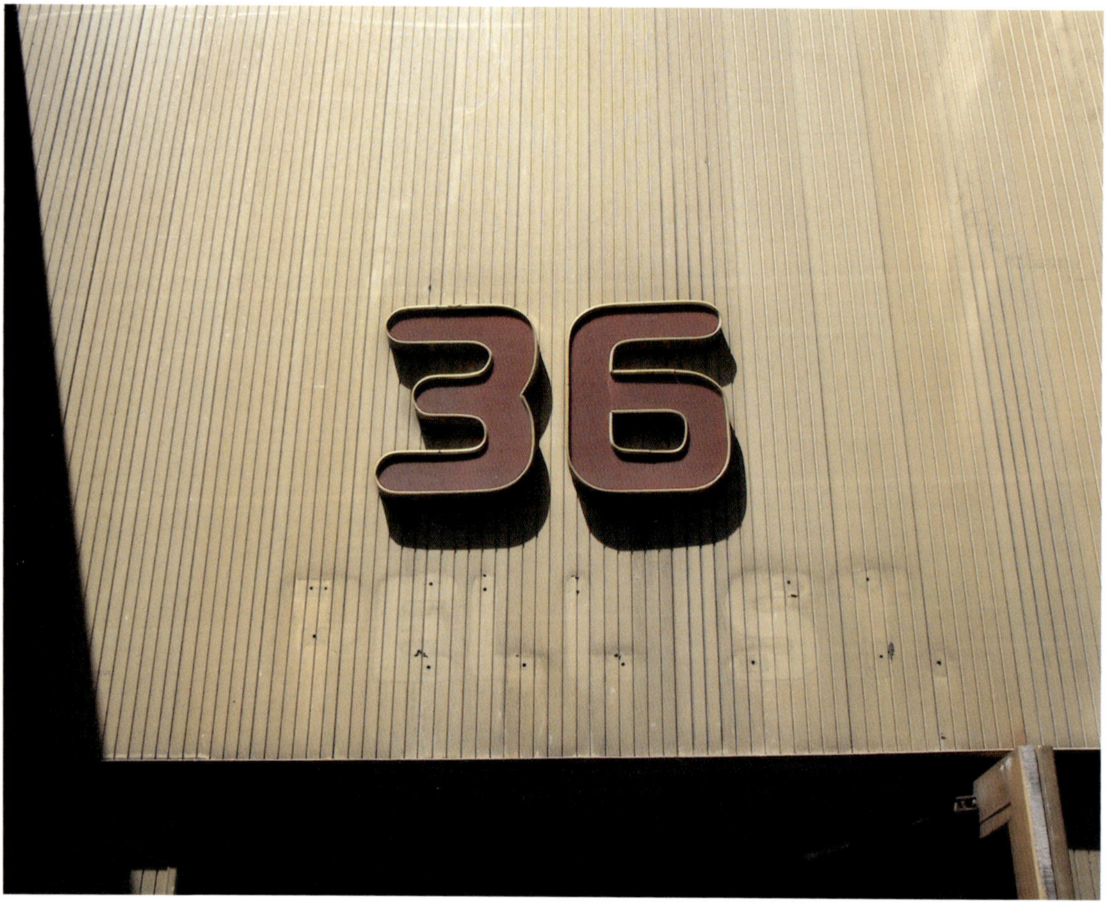

36

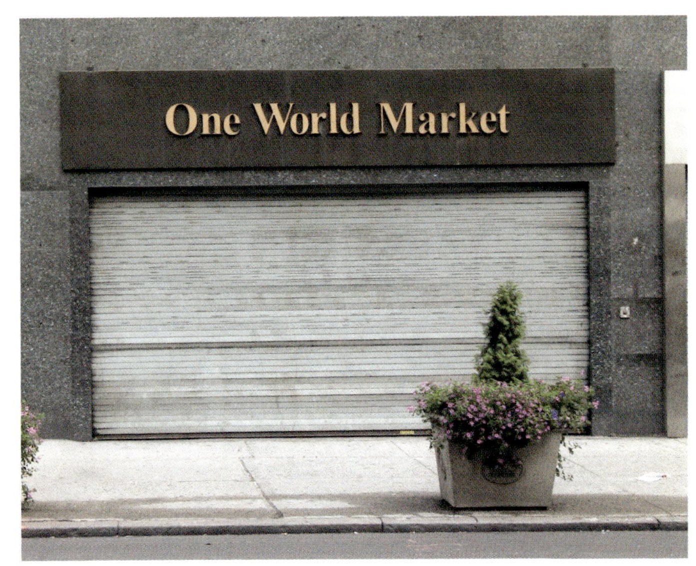
One World Market

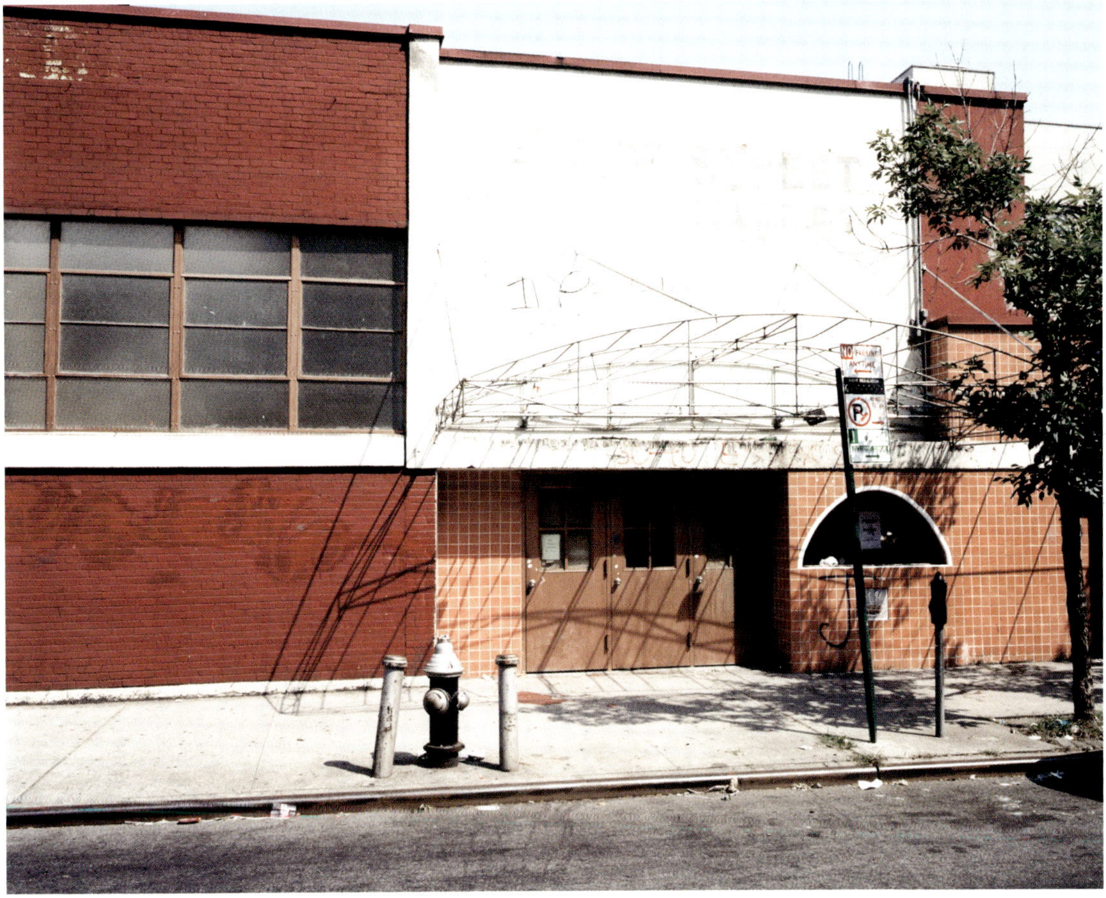

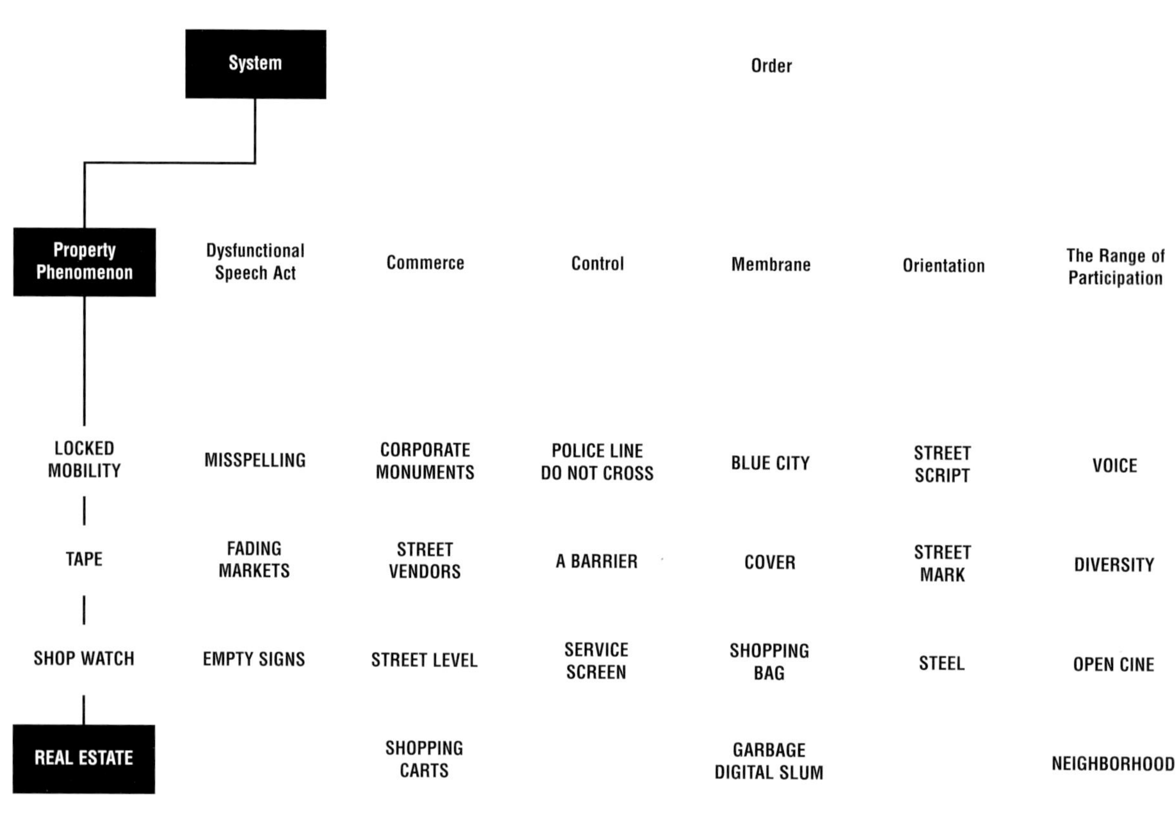
System
Order
Property Phenomenon
Dysfunctional Speech Act
Commerce
Control
Membrane
Orientation
The Range of Participation
LOCKED MOBILITY
MISSPELLING
CORPORATE MONUMENTS
POLICE LINE DO NOT CROSS
BLUE CITY
STREET SCRIPT
VOICE
TAPE
FADING MARKETS
STREET VENDORS
A BARRIER
COVER
STREET MARK
DIVERSITY
SHOP WATCH
EMPTY SIGNS
STREET LEVEL
SERVICE SCREEN
SHOPPING BAG
STEEL
OPEN CINE
REAL ESTATE
SHOPPING CARTS
GARBAGE DIGITAL SLUM
NEIGHBORHOOD

Identity

Alternative Media

Habitual Reinterpretation

REAL ESTATE

Gentrification is Business Gain versus Business Loss

CAR DOOR

PUBLIC CHAIRS

LABELING.

PLASTIC CRATES

POLE POST

STANDPIPES

PRAY JESUS

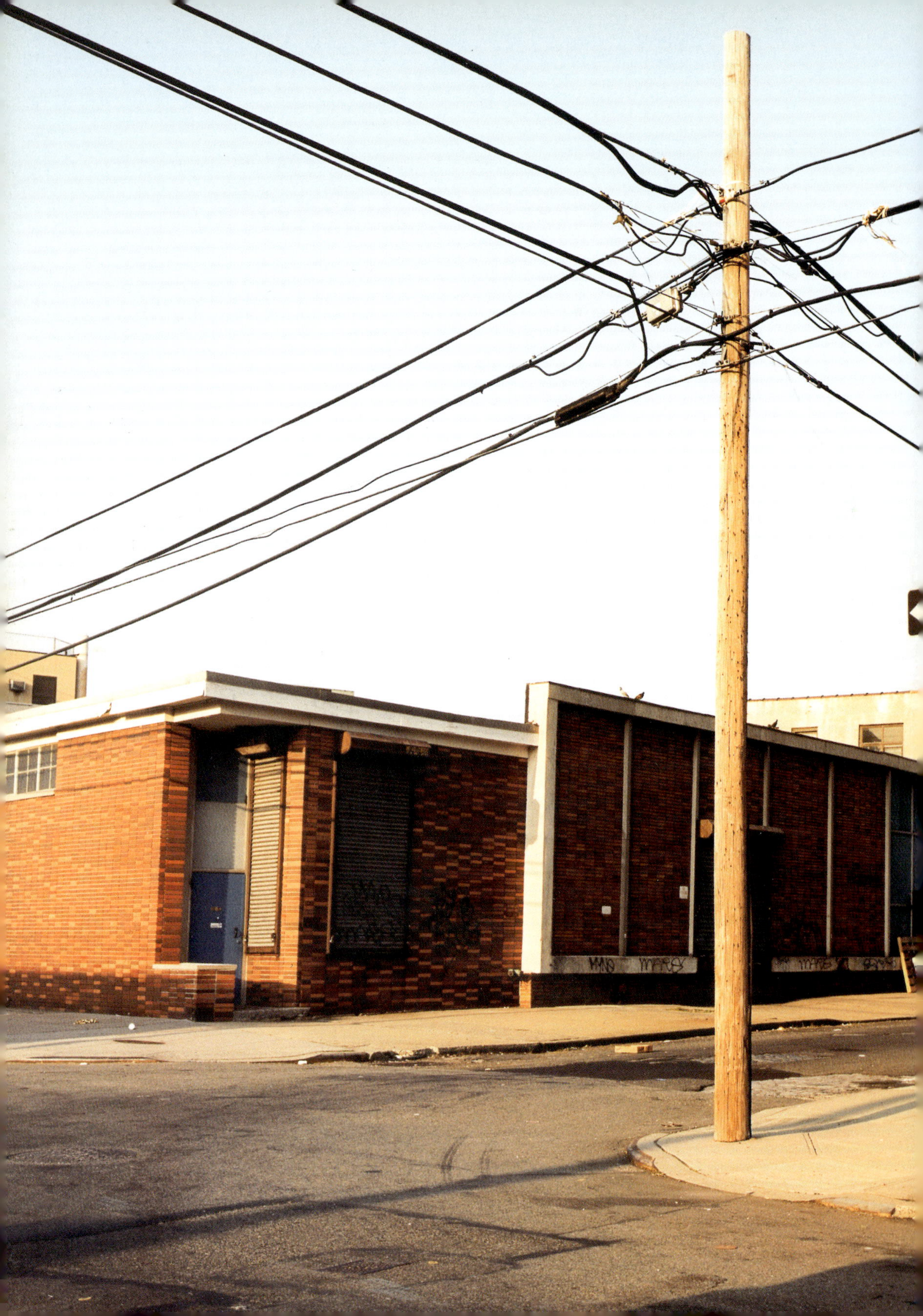

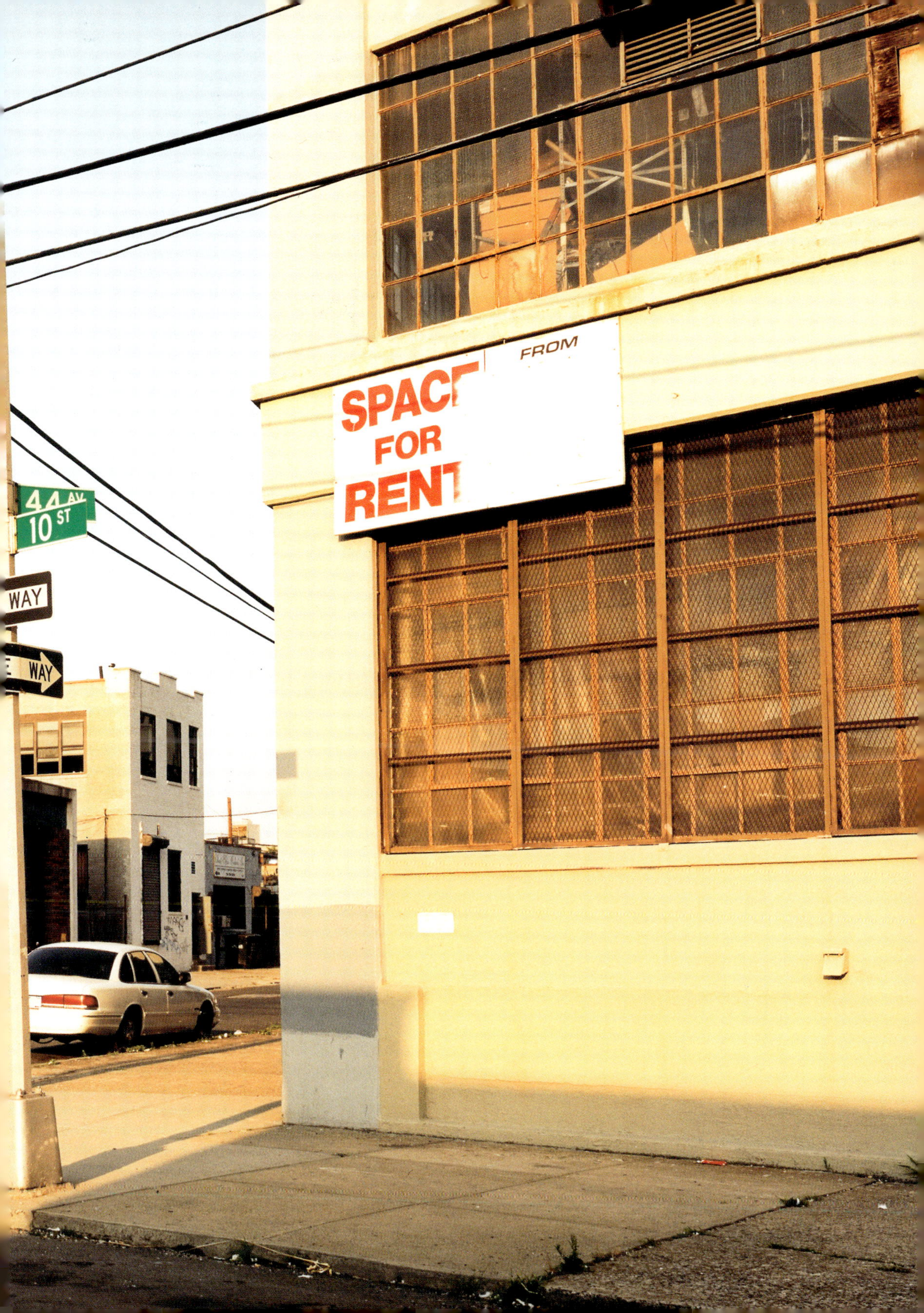

44 AV
10 ST
WAY
WAY
FROM
SPAC
FOR
RENT

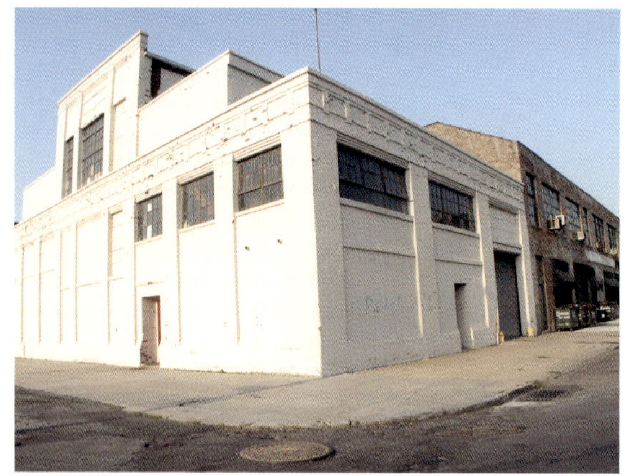

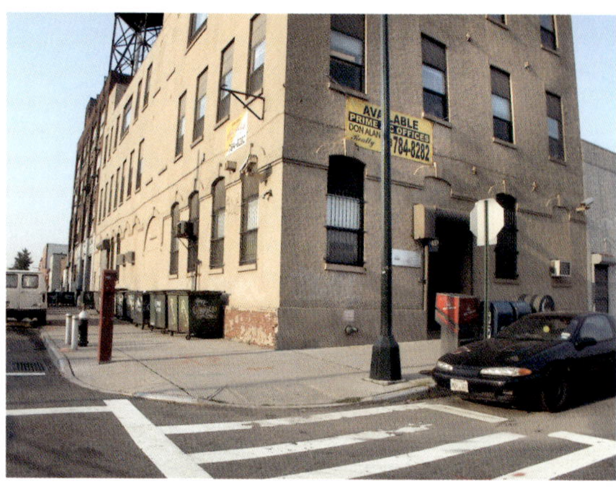
784-8282

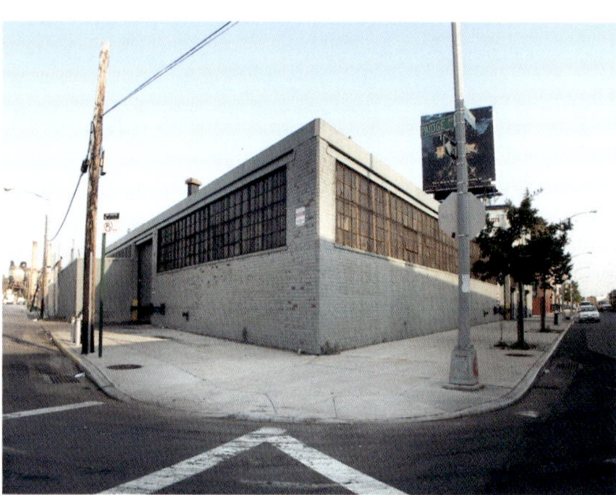

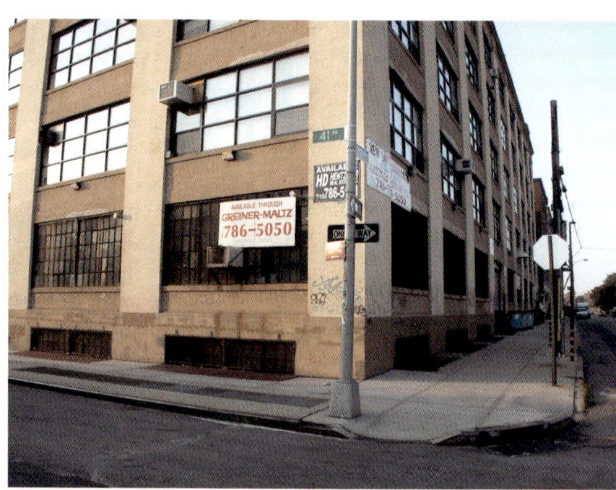
AVAILABLE THROUGH
GREINER-MALTZ
786-5050
ONE WAY

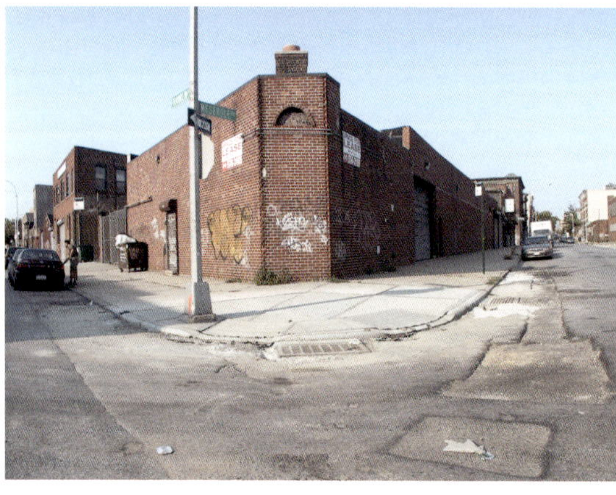

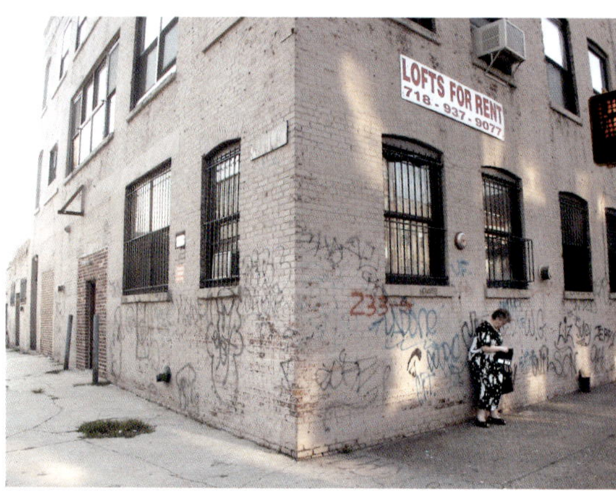
LOFTS FOR RENT
718 · 937 · 9077

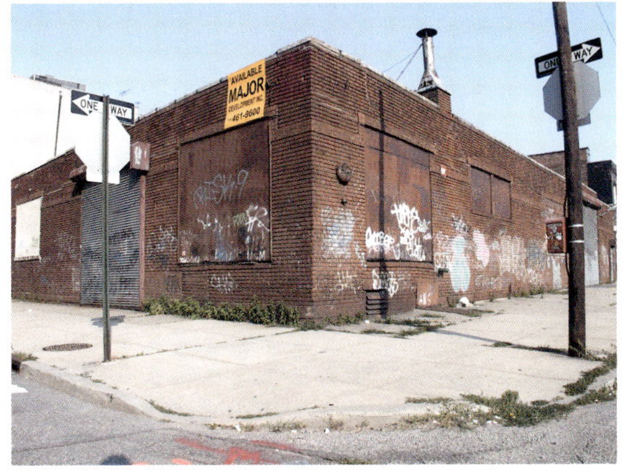
ONE WAY
AVAILABLE
MAJOR
DEVELOPMENT INC.
461-9600
ONE WAY

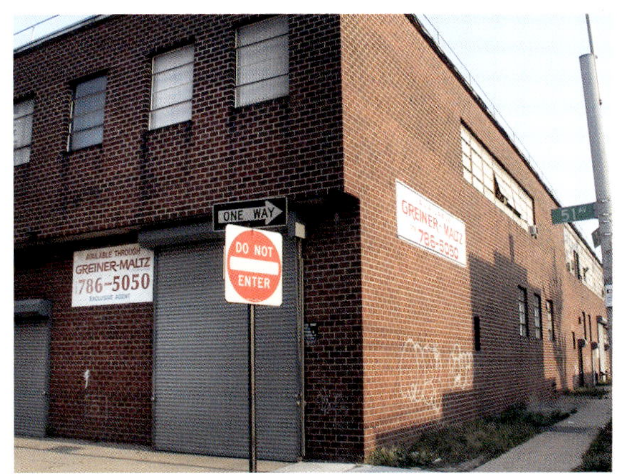
ONE WAY
DO NOT
ENTER
AVAILABLE THROUGH
GREINER-MALTZ
786-5050
EXCLUSIVE AGENT
GREINER-MALTZ
786-5050
51 AV

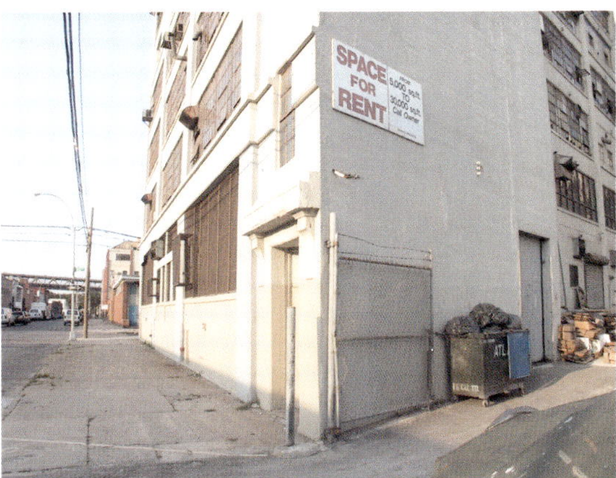
SPACE
FOR
RENT
5,000 sq.ft.
TO
30,000 sq.ft.
Call Owner

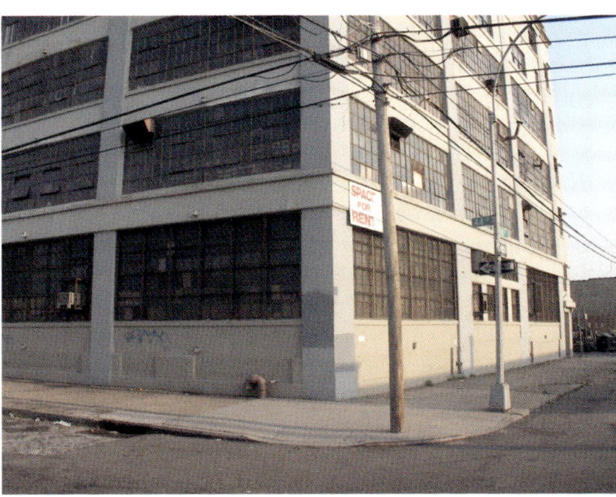
SPACE
FOR
RENT

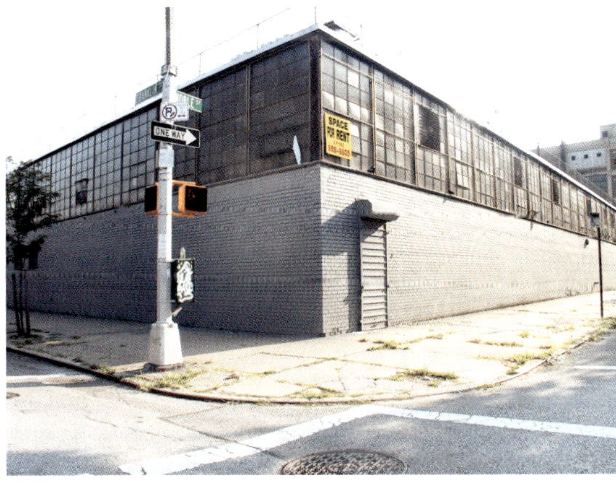
ONE WAY
SPACE
FOR RENT

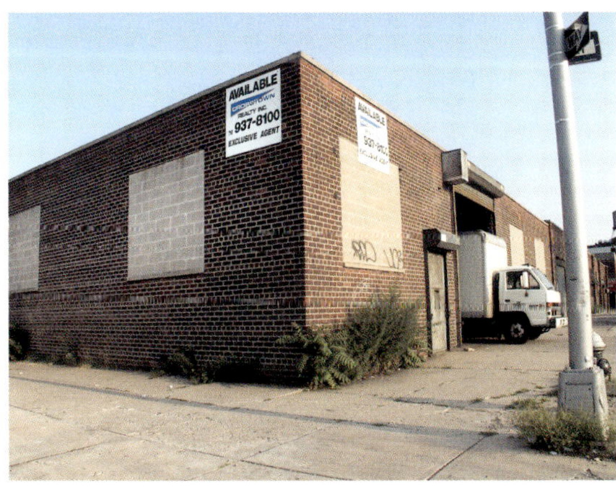
AVAILABLE
REALTY INC.
937-8100
EXCLUSIVE AGENT
AVAILABLE

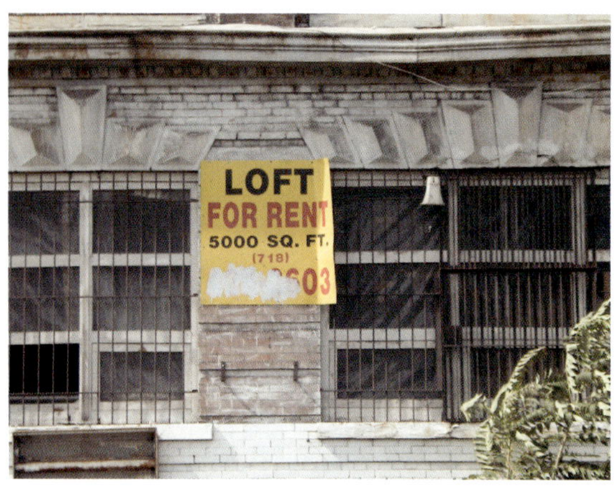
LOFT
FOR RENT
5000 SQ. FT.
(718)

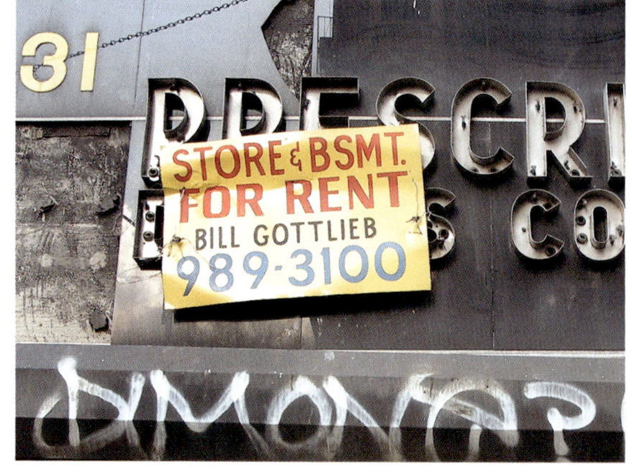
31
STORE & BSMT.
FOR RENT
BILL GOTTLIEB
989-3100

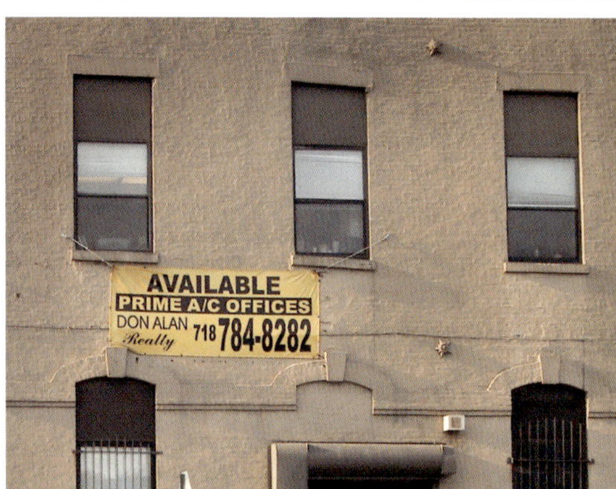
AVAILABLE
PRIME A/C OFFICES
DON ALAN Realty
718 784-8282

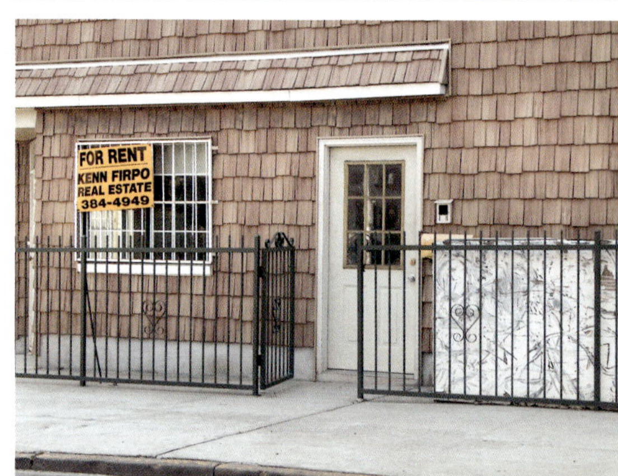
FOR RENT
KENN FIRPO
REAL ESTATE
384-4949

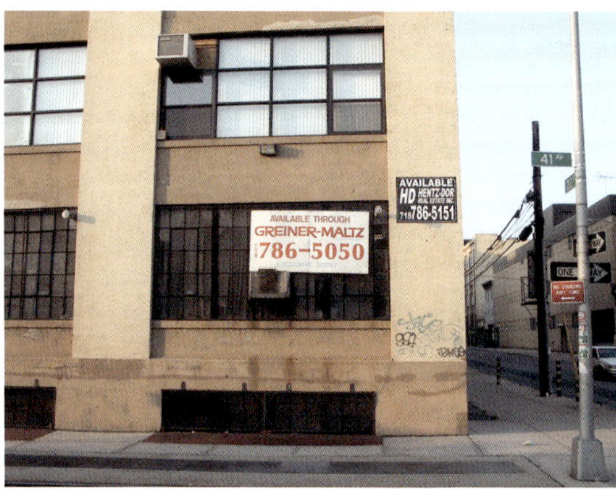
AVAILABLE THROUGH
GREINER-MALTZ
786-5050
AVAILABLE
HD
718 786-5151
41 Av

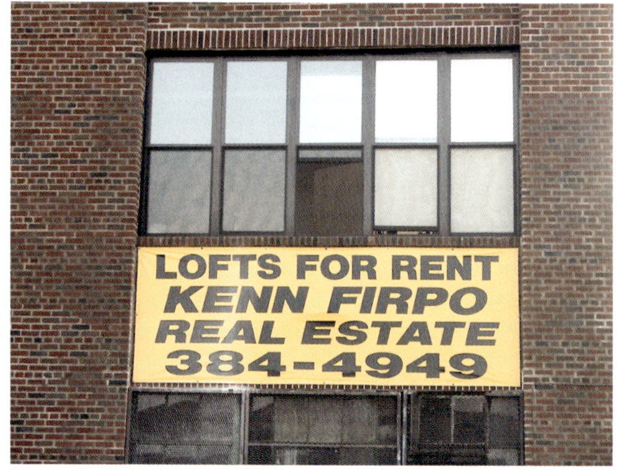
LOFTS FOR RENT
KENN FIRPO
REAL ESTATE
384-4949

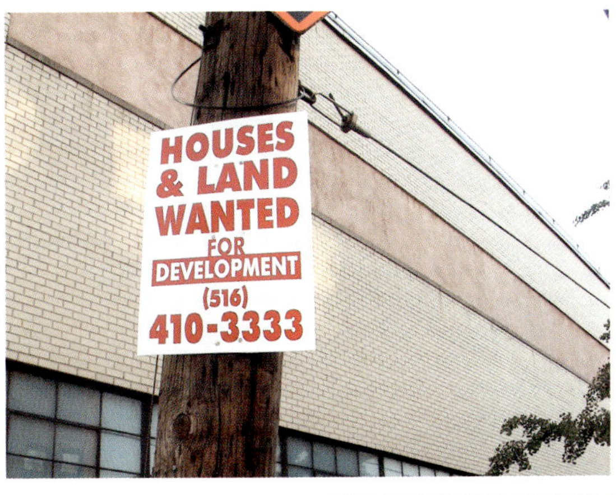
HOUSES
& LAND
WANTED
FOR
DEVELOPMENT
(516)
410-3333

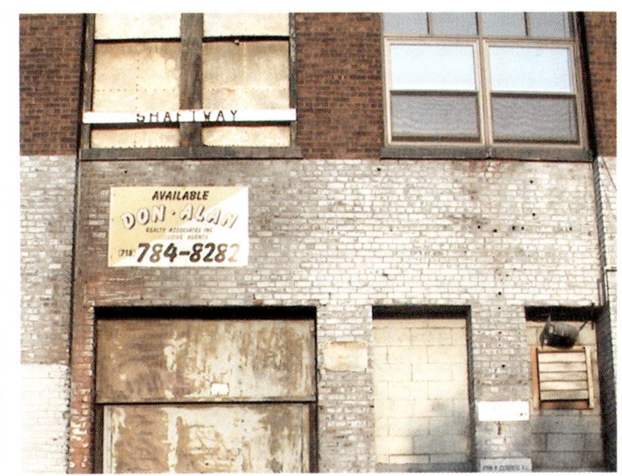
AVAILABLE
DON · ALAN
(718) 784-8282

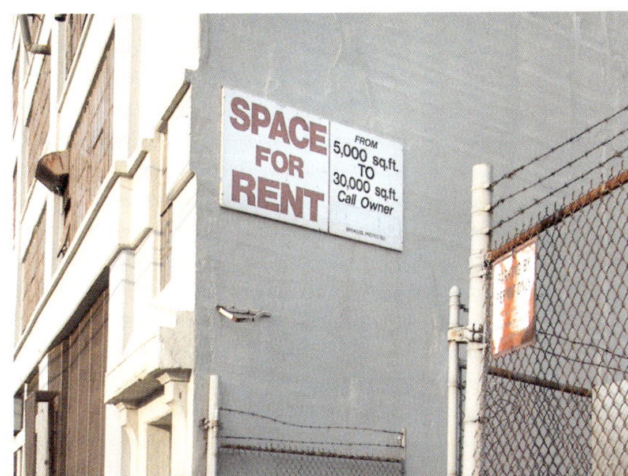
SPACE
FOR
RENT
FROM
5,000 sq.ft.
TO
30,000 sq.ft.
Call Owner

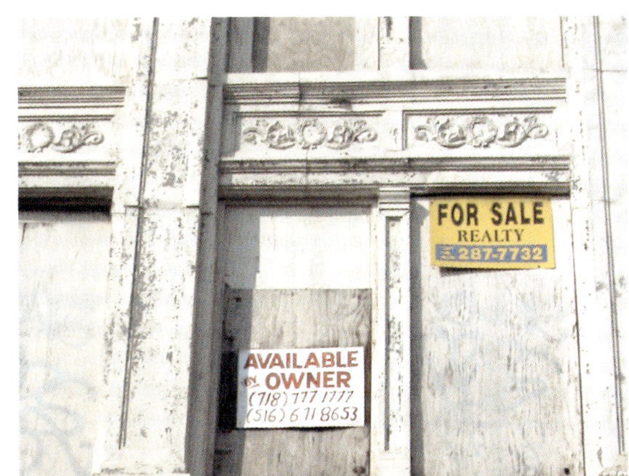
FOR SALE
REALTY
287-7732
AVAILABLE
OWNER
(718) 777 1777
(516) 671 8653

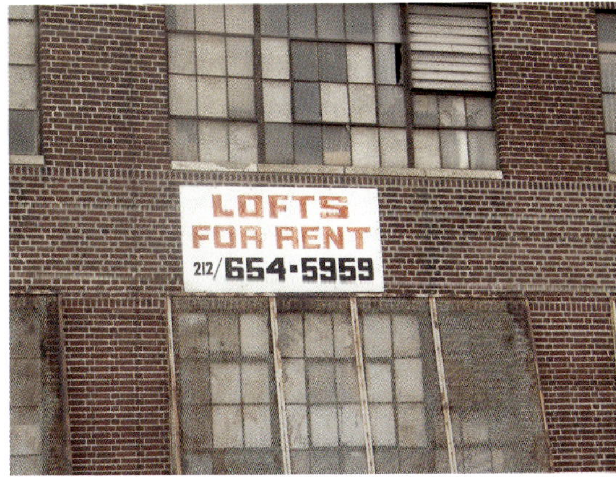
LOFTS
FOR RENT
212/654-5959

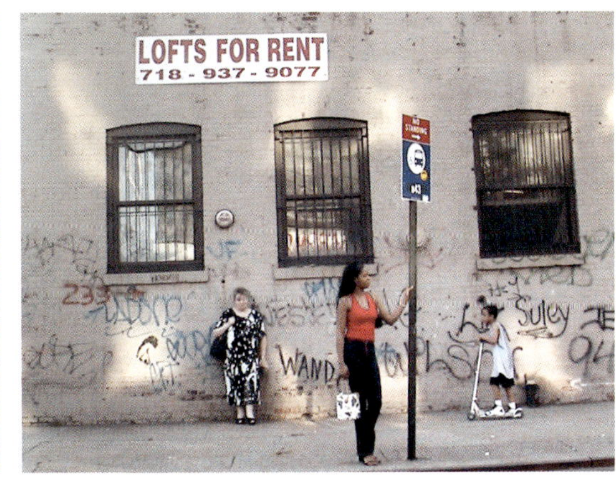
LOFTS FOR RENT
718 - 937 - 9077

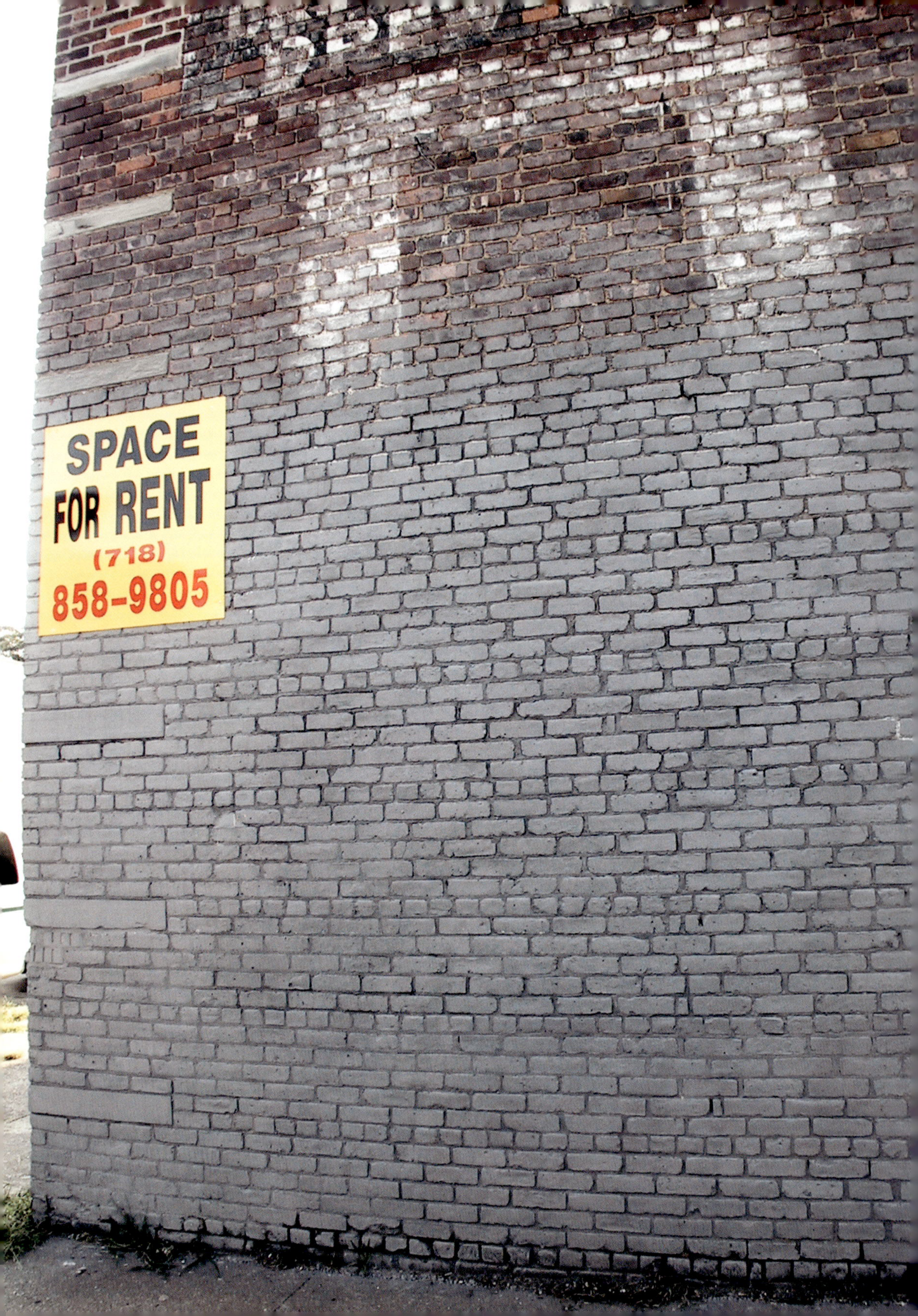
SPACE
FOR RENT
(718)
858-9805

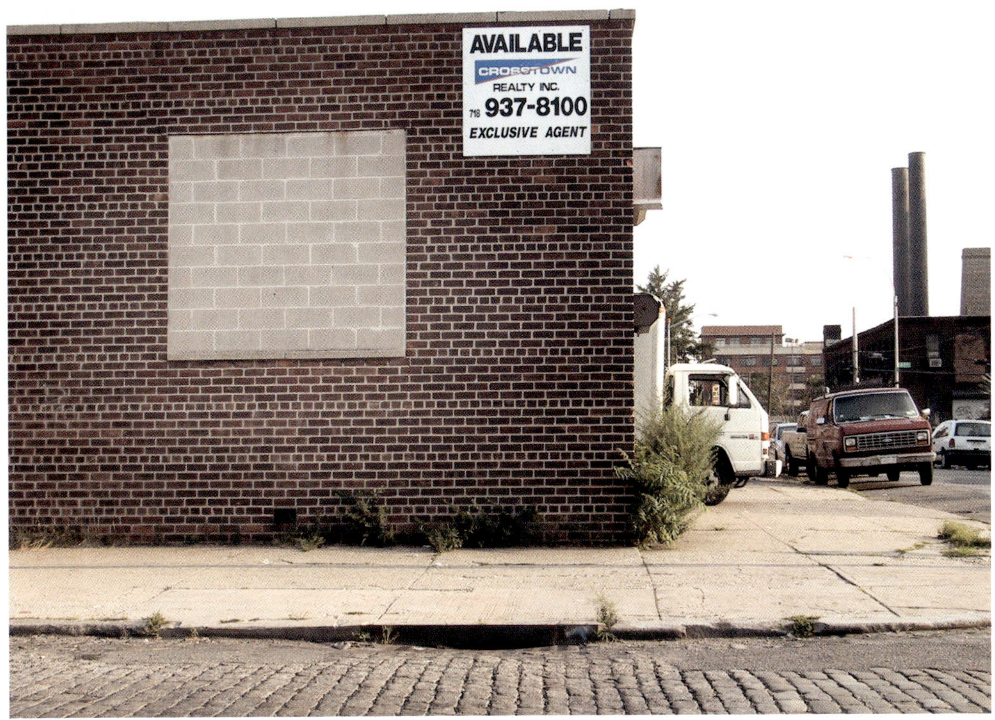
AVAILABLE
CROSSTOWN
REALTY INC.
718 937-8100
EXCLUSIVE AGENT

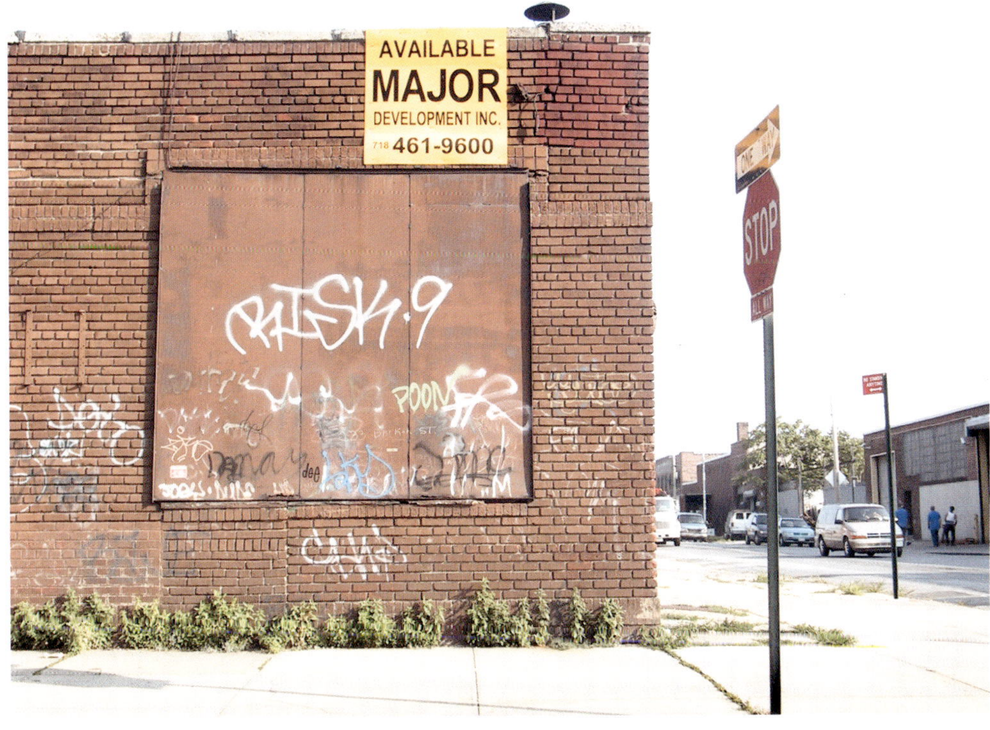
AVAILABLE
MAJOR
DEVELOPMENT INC.
718 461-9600
ONE WAY
STOP

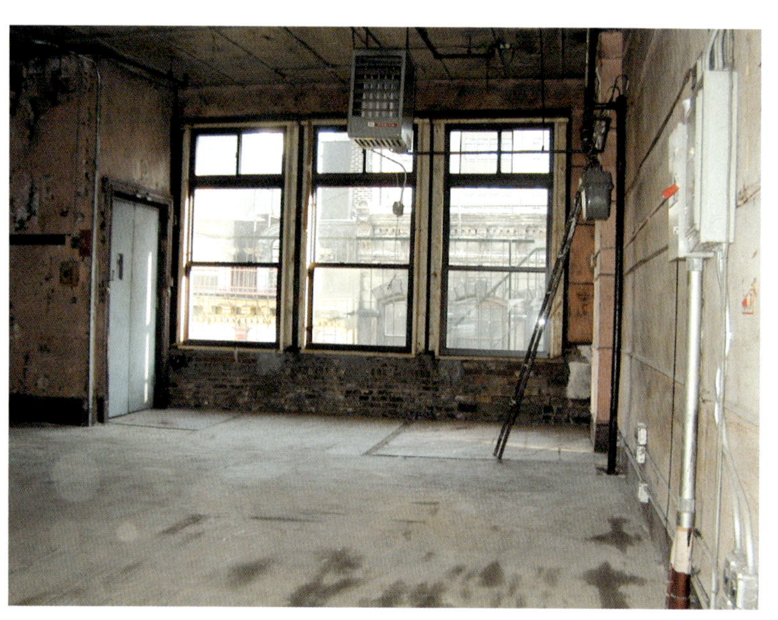

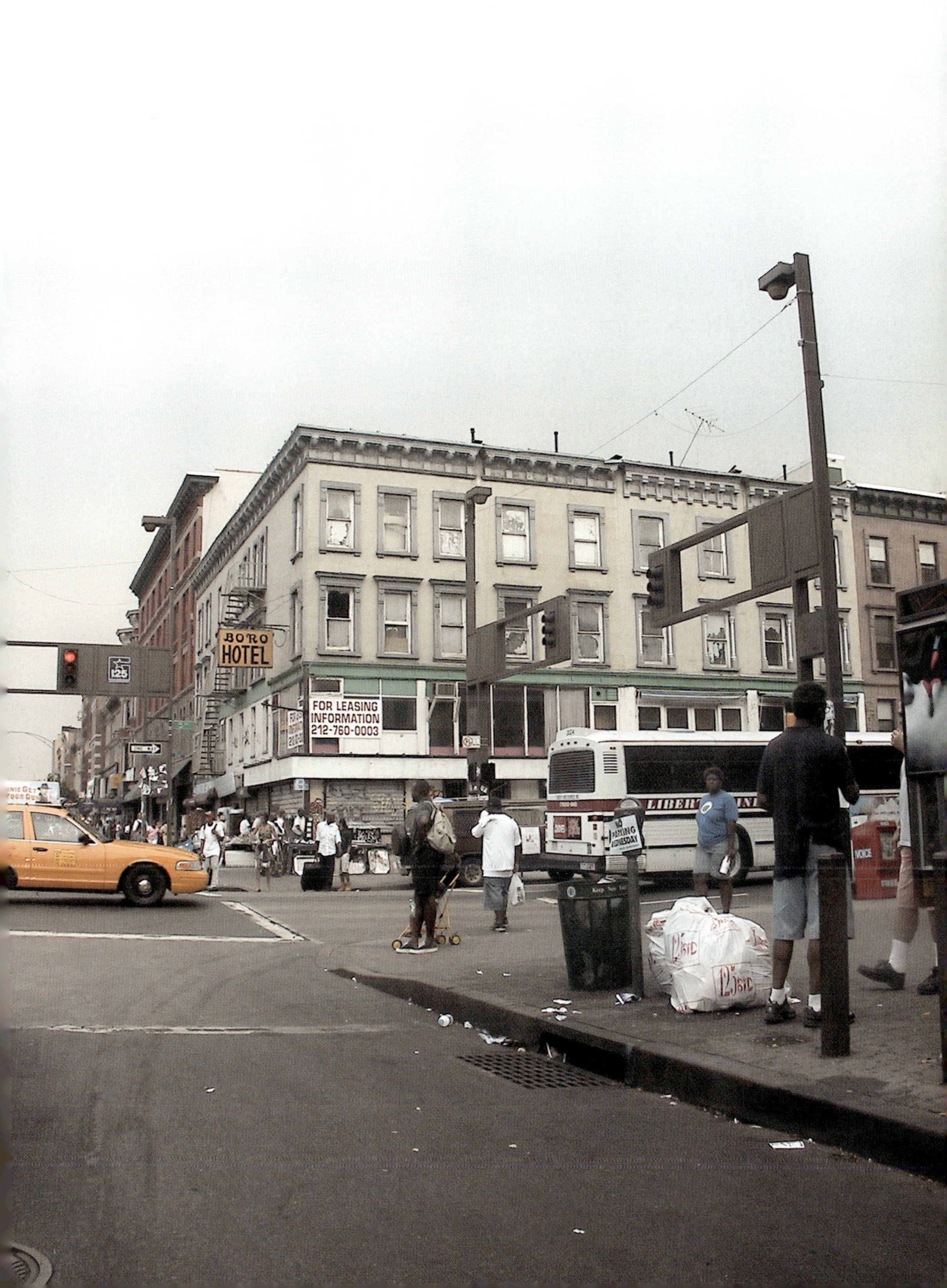

BORO
HOTEL
FOR LEASING
INFORMATION
212-760-0003
ONE WAY
NO PARKING
WEDNESDAY
VOICE

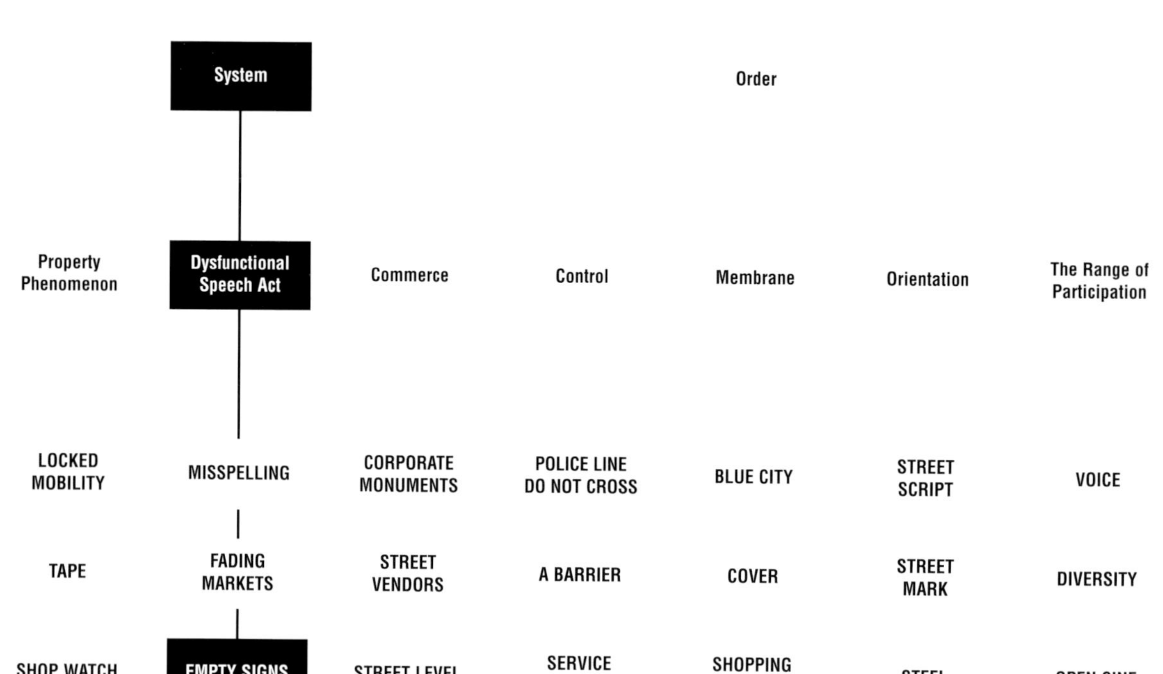

System
Order
Property Phenomenon
Dysfunctional Speech Act
Commerce
Control
Membrane
Orientation
The Range of Participation
LOCKED MOBILITY
MISSPELLING
CORPORATE MONUMENTS
POLICE LINE DO NOT CROSS
BLUE CITY
STREET SCRIPT
VOICE
TAPE
FADING MARKETS
STREET VENDORS
A BARRIER
COVER
STREET MARK
DIVERSITY
SHOP WATCH
EMPTY SIGNS
STREET LEVEL
SERVICE SCREEN
SHOPPING BAG
STEEL
OPEN CINE
REAL ESTATE
SHOPPING CARTS
GARBAGE DIGITAL SLUM
NEIGHBORHOOD

Identity

Alternative Media

Habitual Reinterpretation

EMPTY SIGNS

Signs Signifying Insignificance

CAR DOOR

PUBLIC CHAIRS

LABELING.

PLASTIC CRATES

POLE POST

STANDPIPES

PRAY JESUS

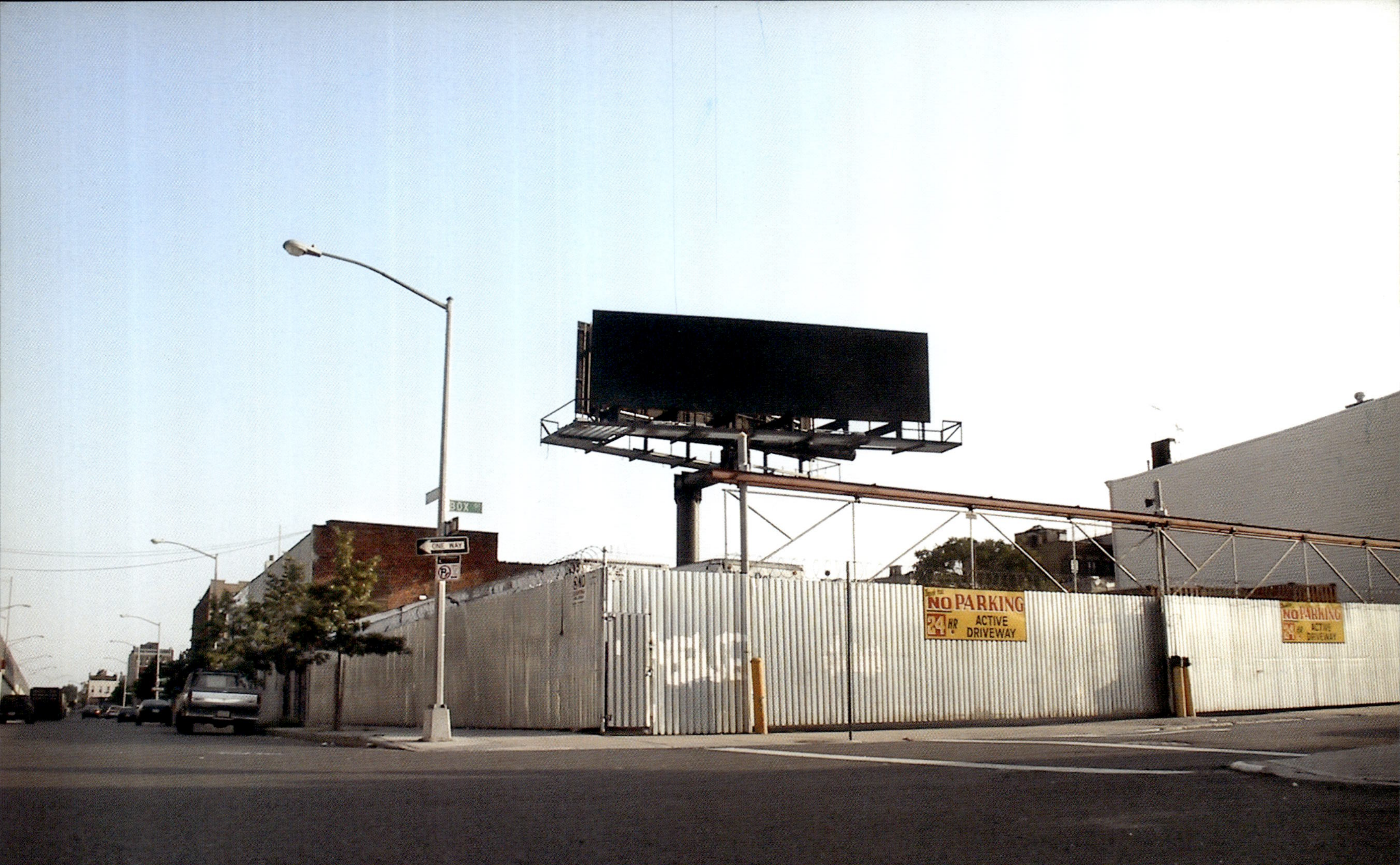
BOX
ONE WAY
NO PARKING
24 HR
ACTIVE
DRIVEWAY
NO PARKING
24 HR
ACTIVE
DRIVEWAY

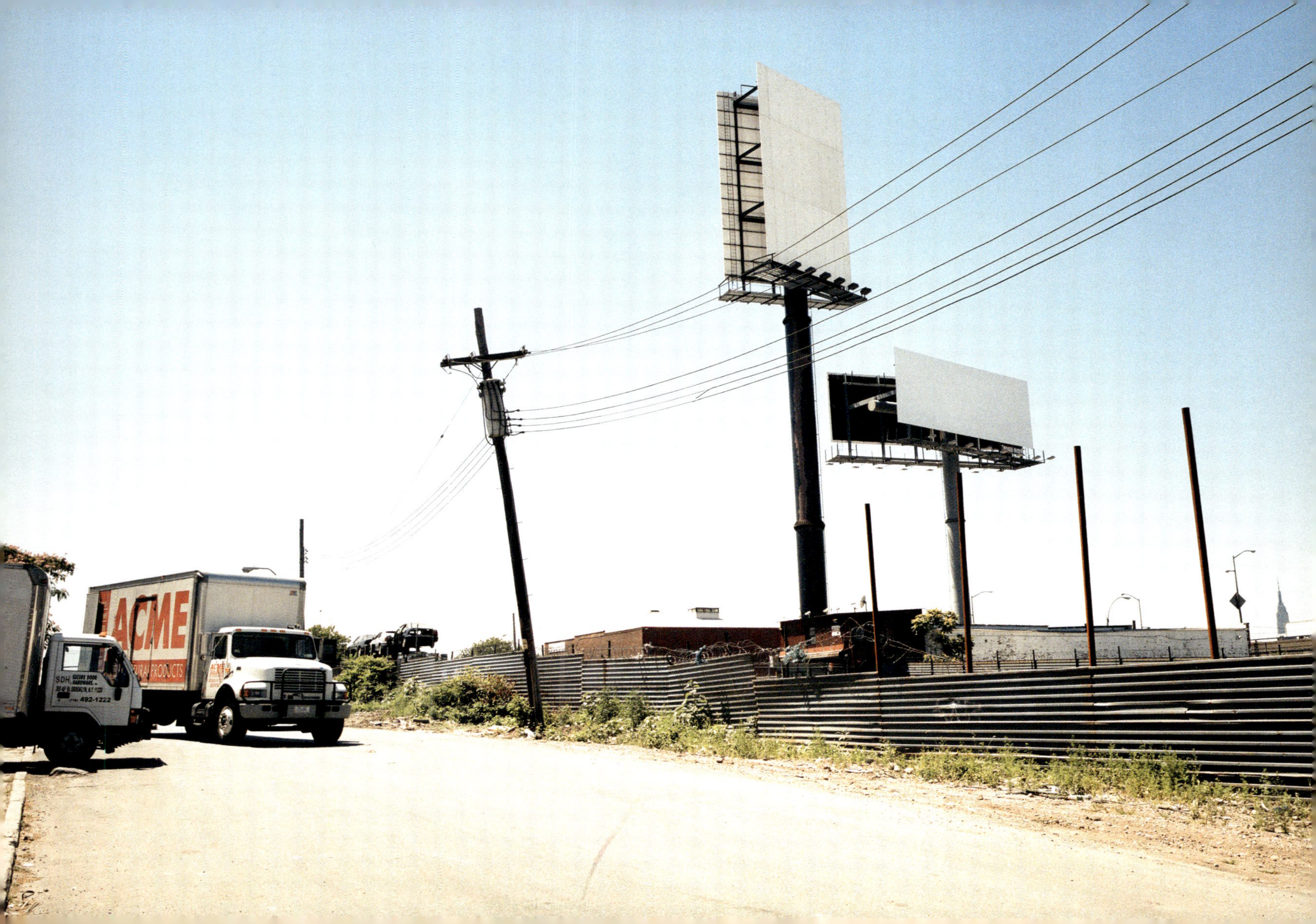
ACME
SDH
492-1222

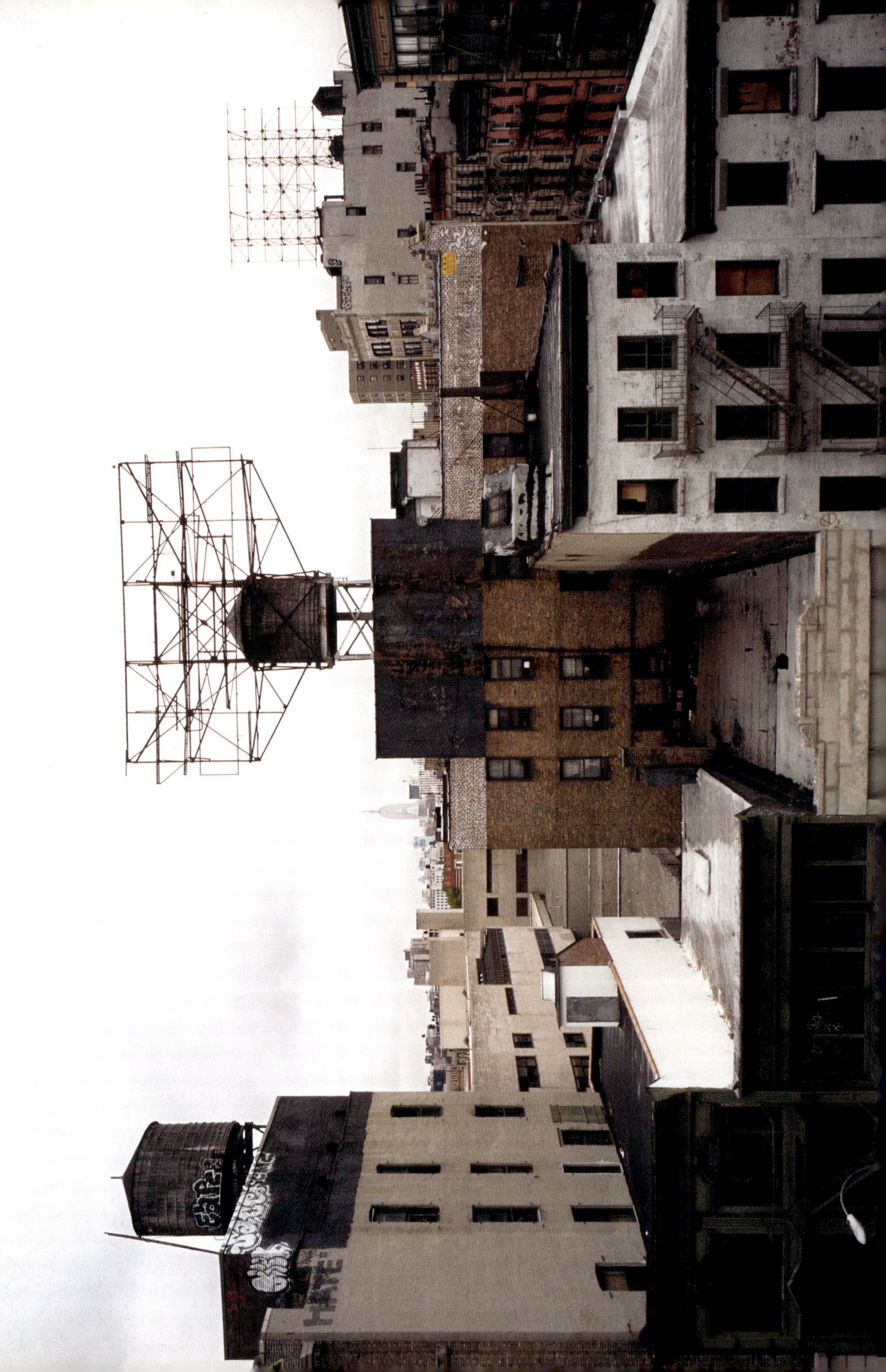

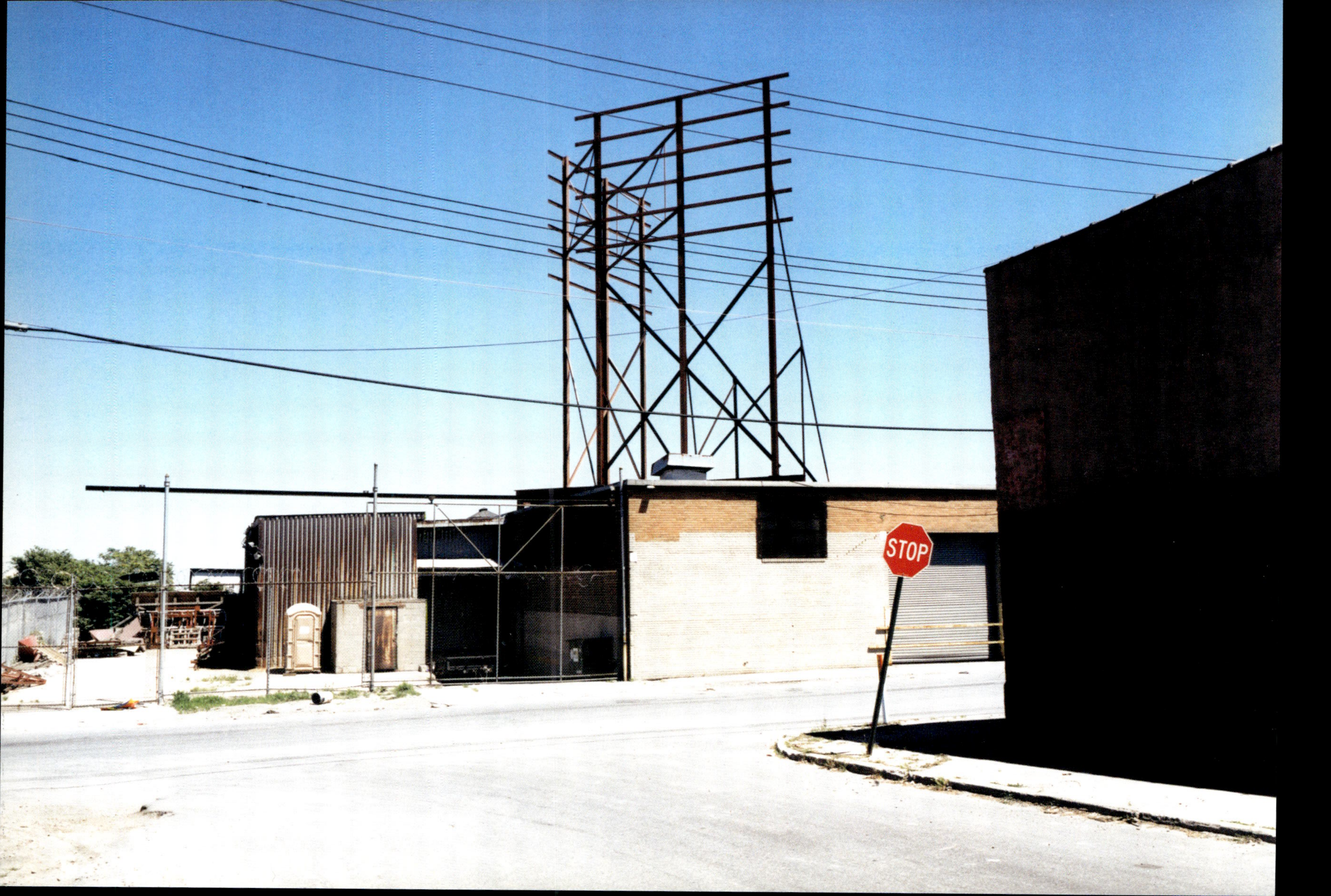
STOP

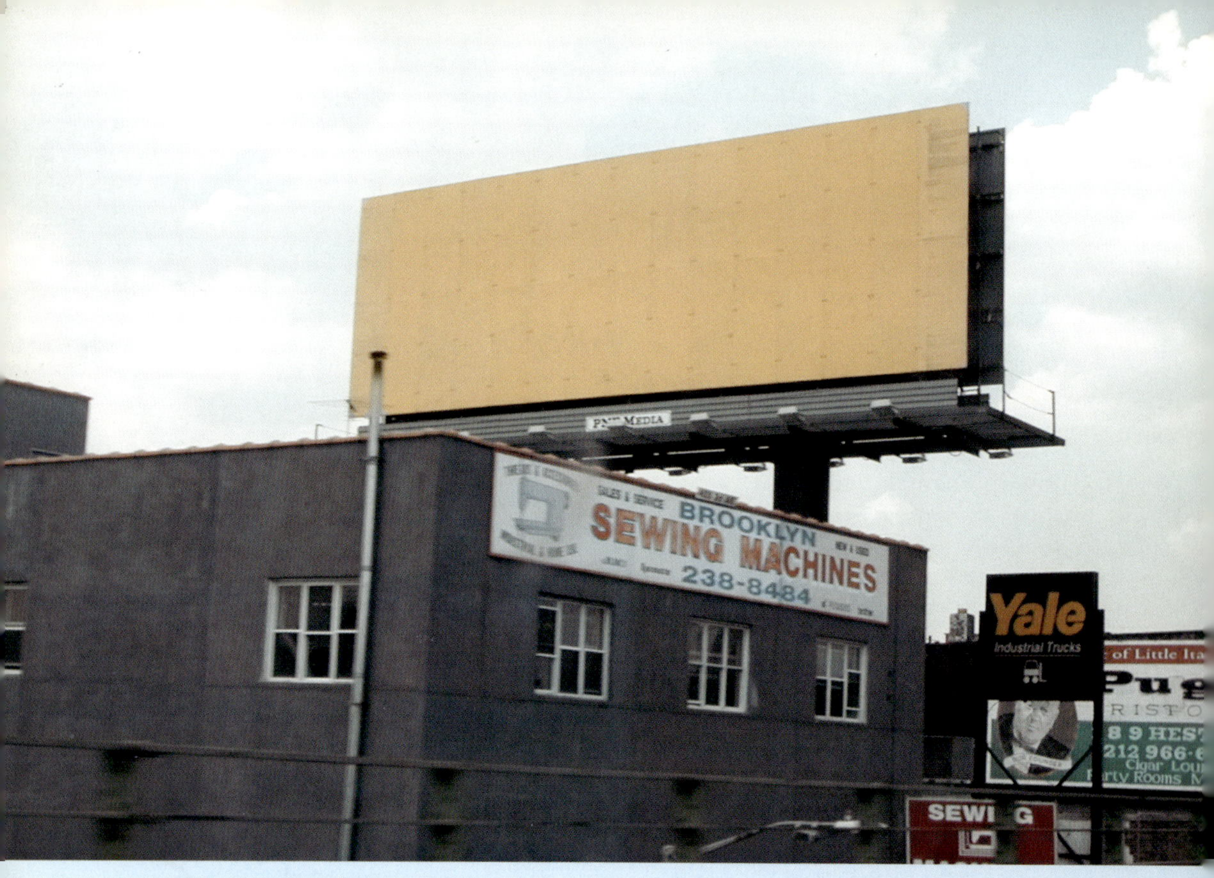

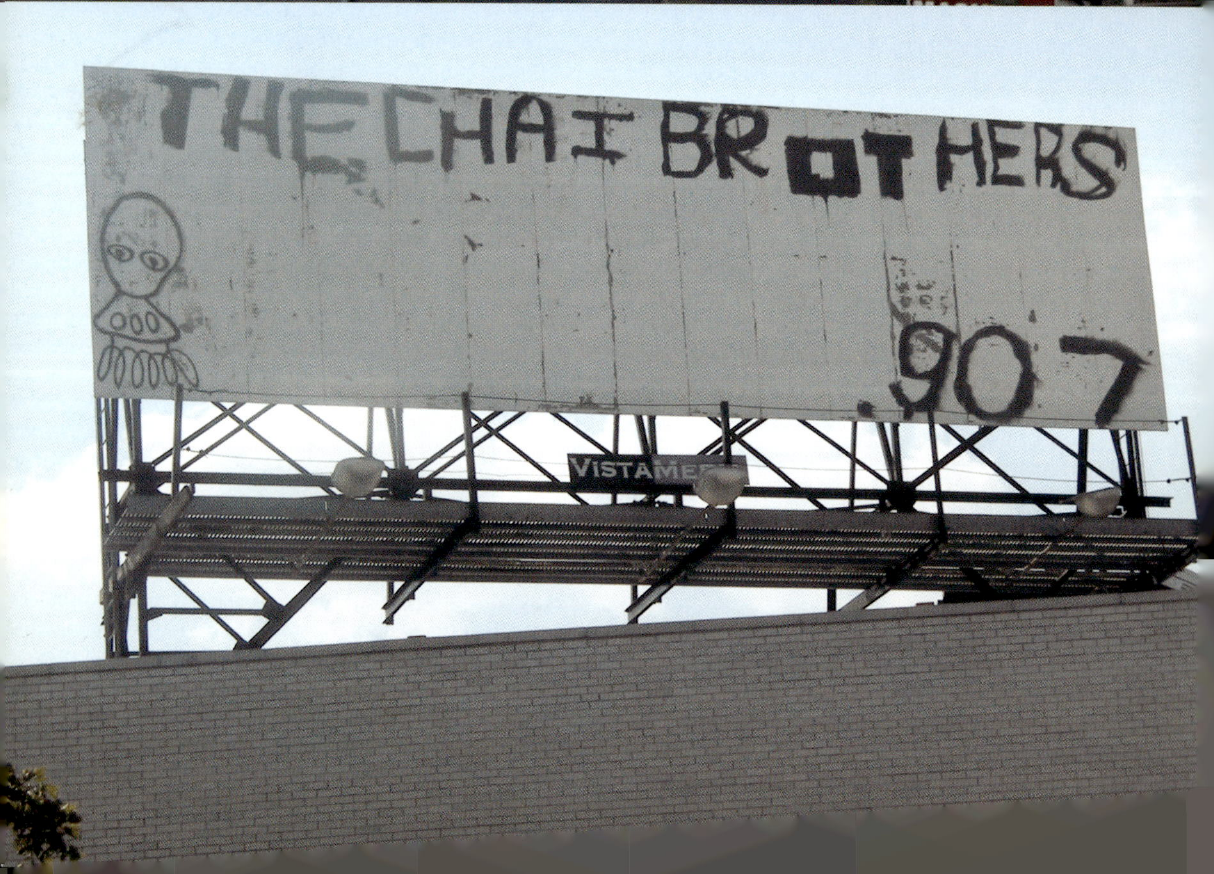

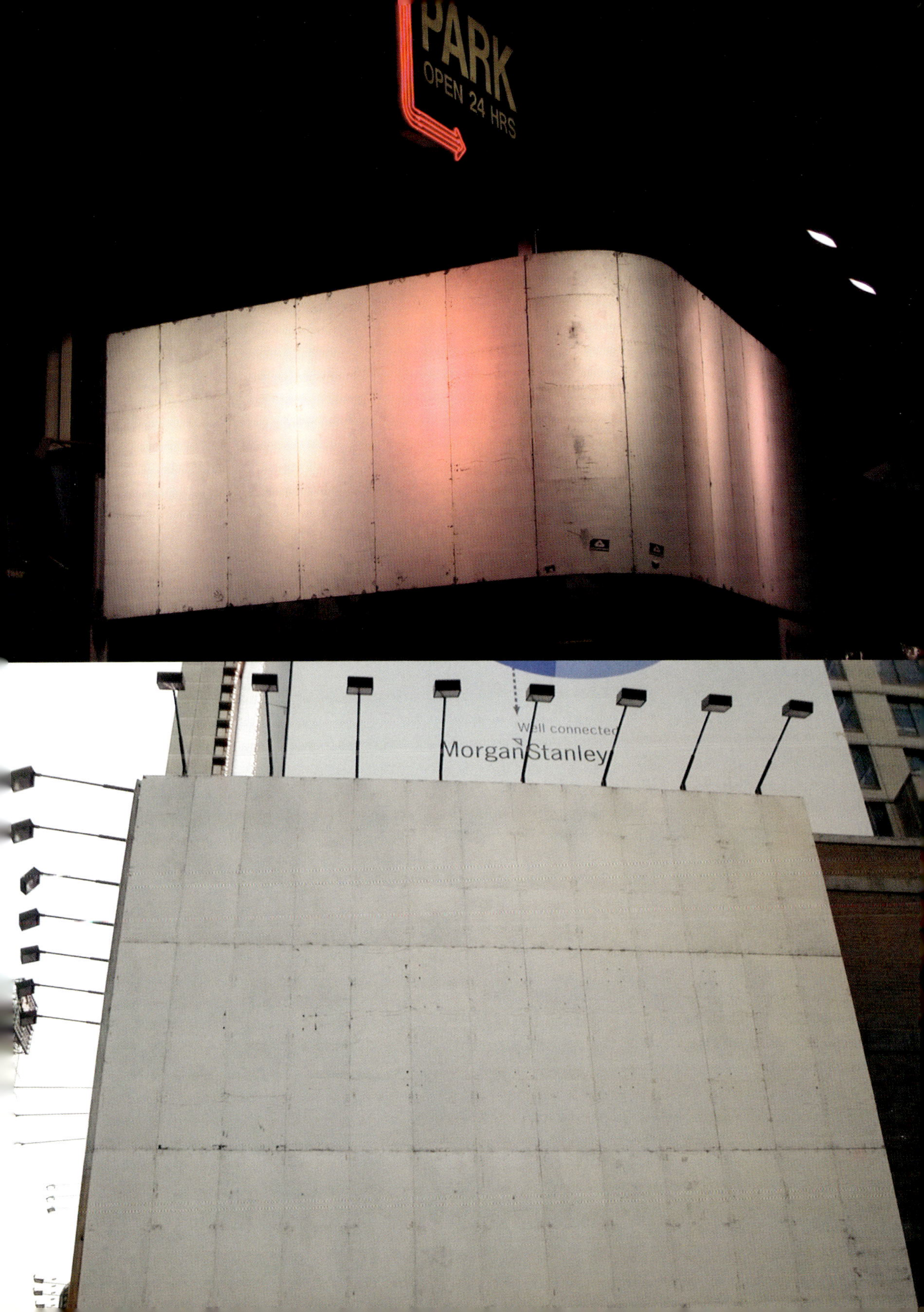
PARK
OPEN 24 HRS
Well connected
Morgan Stanley

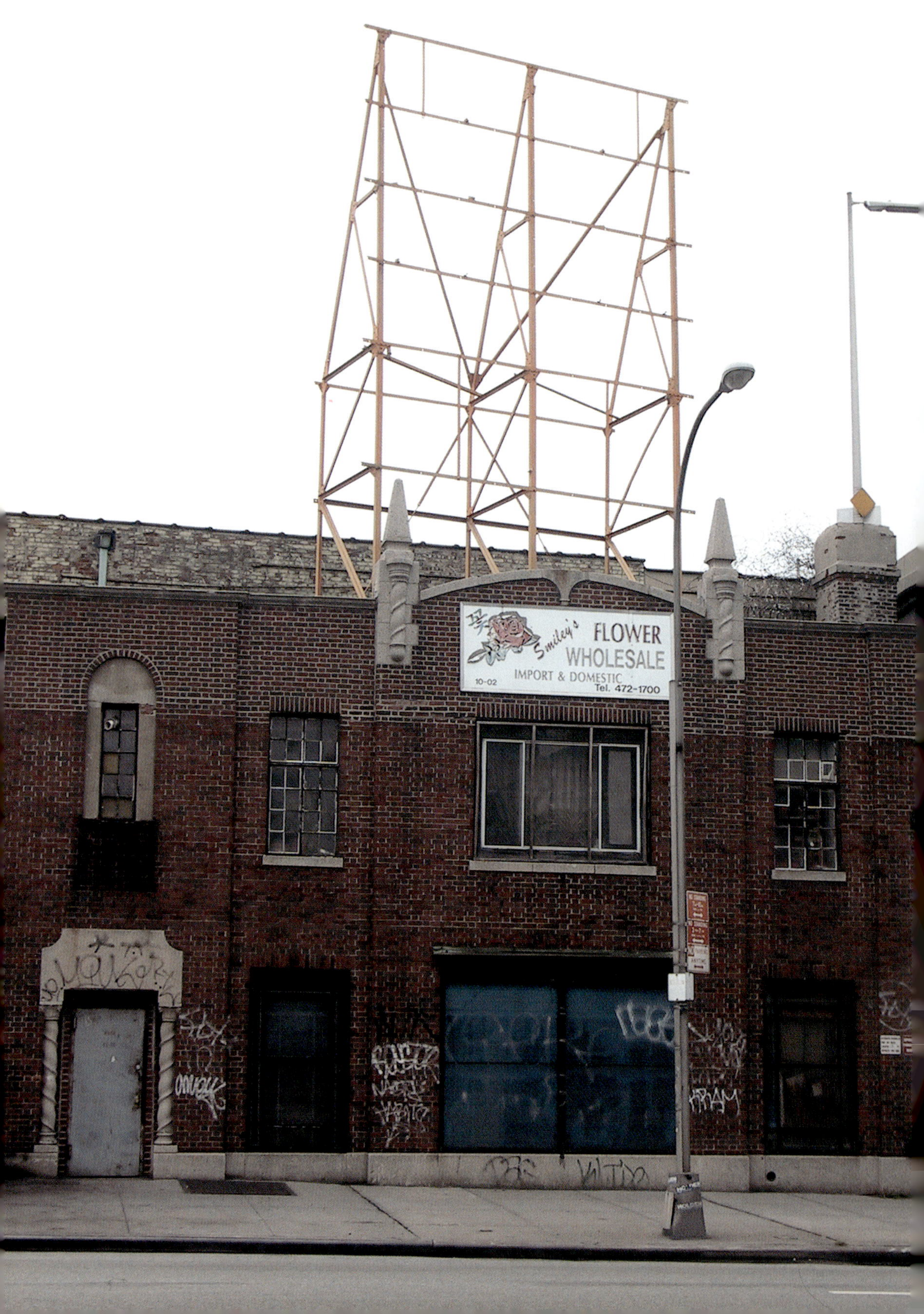
Smiley's
FLOWER
WHOLESALE
IMPORT & DOMESTIC
10-02
Tel. 472-1700

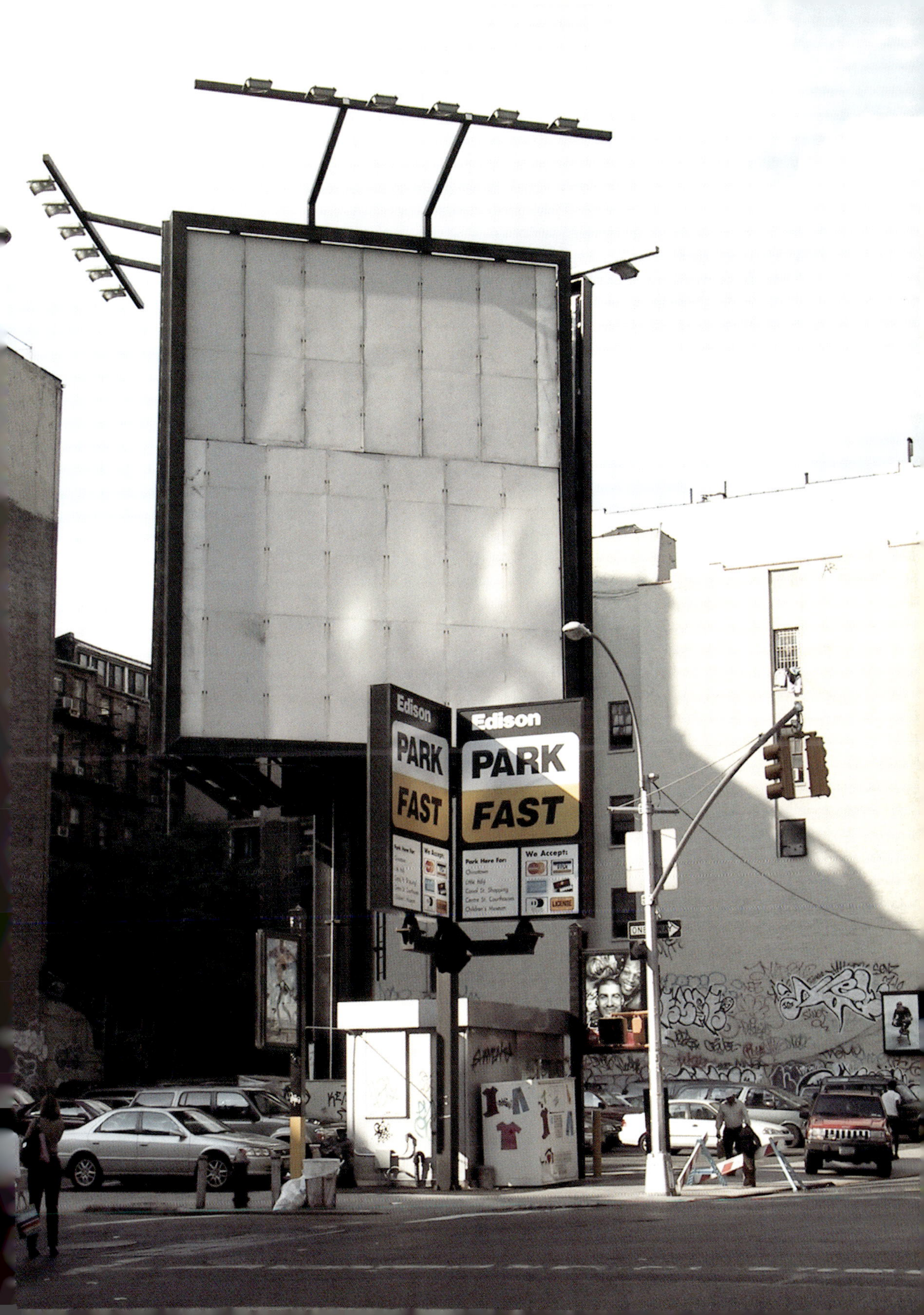
Edison
PARK
FAST
Edison
PARK
FAST
Park Here For:
We Accept:
ONE WAY

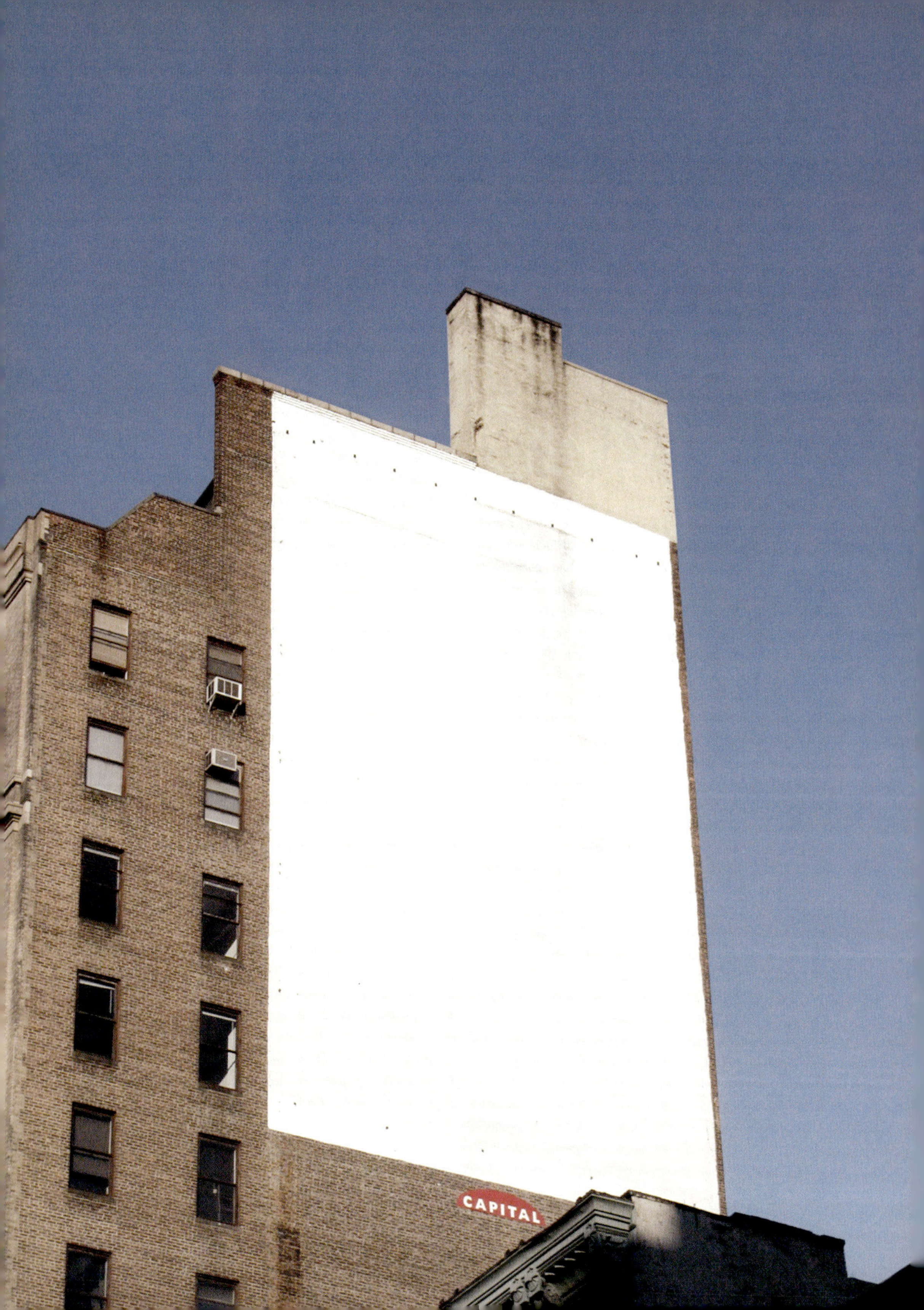
CAPITAL

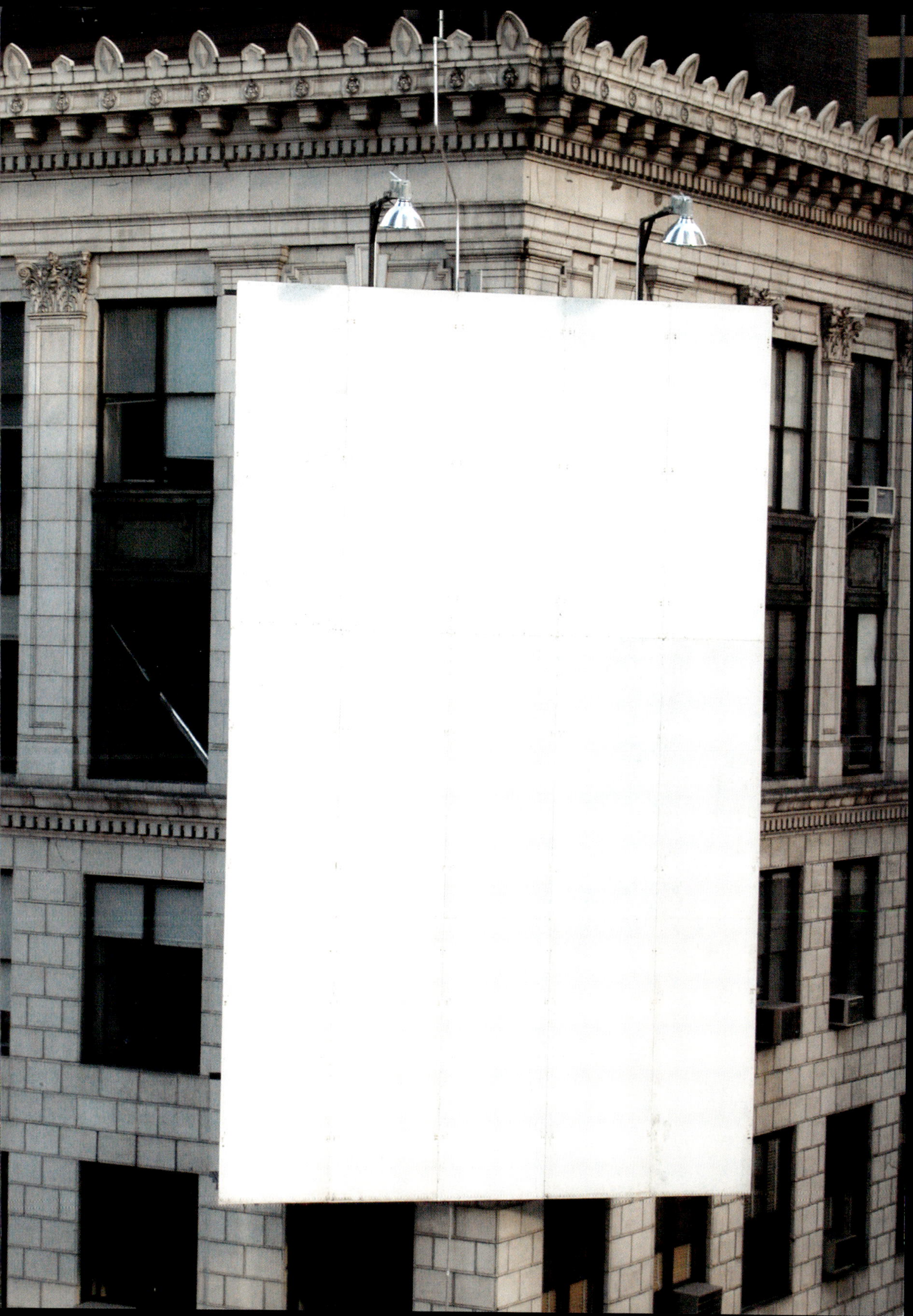

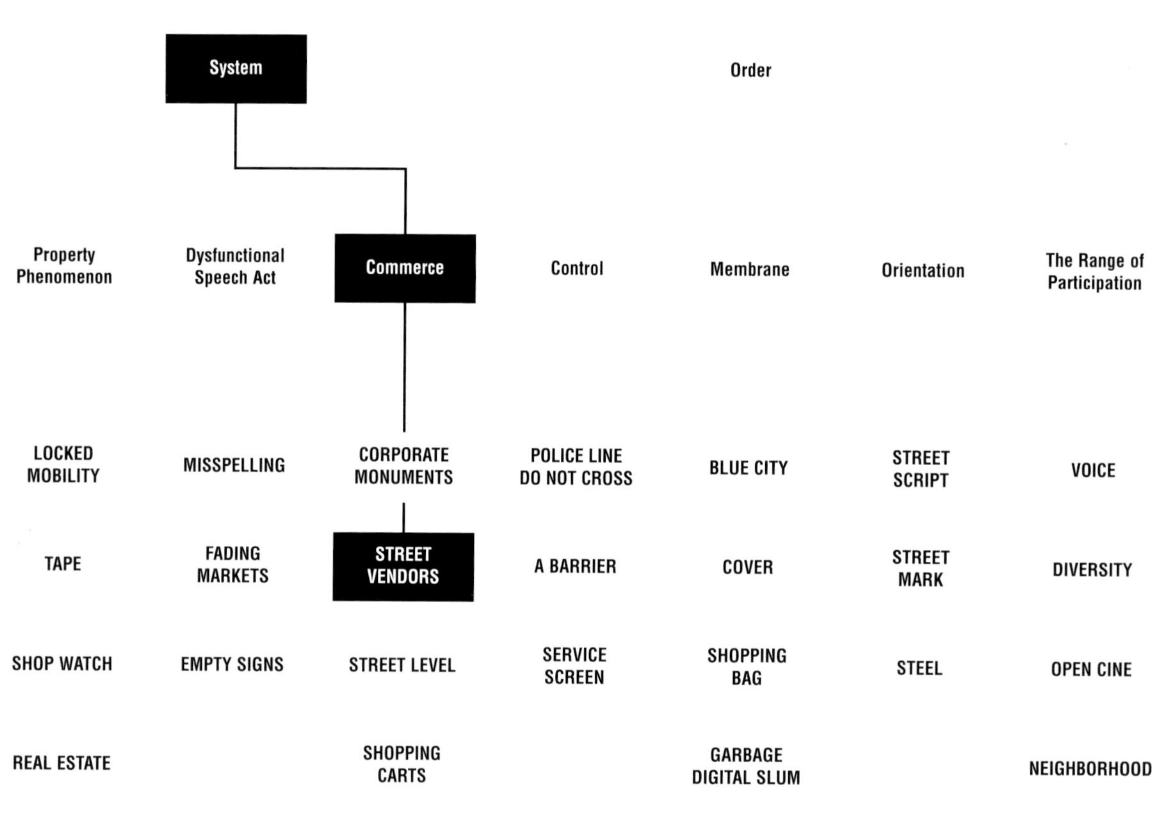
System
Order
Property Phenomenon
Dysfunctional Speech Act
Commerce
Control
Membrane
Orientation
The Range of Participation
LOCKED MOBILITY
MISSPELLING
CORPORATE MONUMENTS
POLICE LINE DO NOT CROSS
BLUE CITY
STREET SCRIPT
VOICE
TAPE
FADING MARKETS
STREET VENDORS
A BARRIER
COVER
STREET MARK
DIVERSITY
SHOP WATCH
EMPTY SIGNS
STREET LEVEL
SERVICE SCREEN
SHOPPING BAG
STEEL
OPEN CINE
REAL ESTATE
SHOPPING CARTS
GARBAGE DIGITAL SLUM
NEIGHBORHOOD

Identity

Alternative Media

Habitual Reinterpretation

STREET VENDORS

Trade Route

CAR DOOR

LABELING.

POLE POST

PUBLIC CHAIRS

PLASTIC CRATES

STANDPIPES

PRAY JESUS

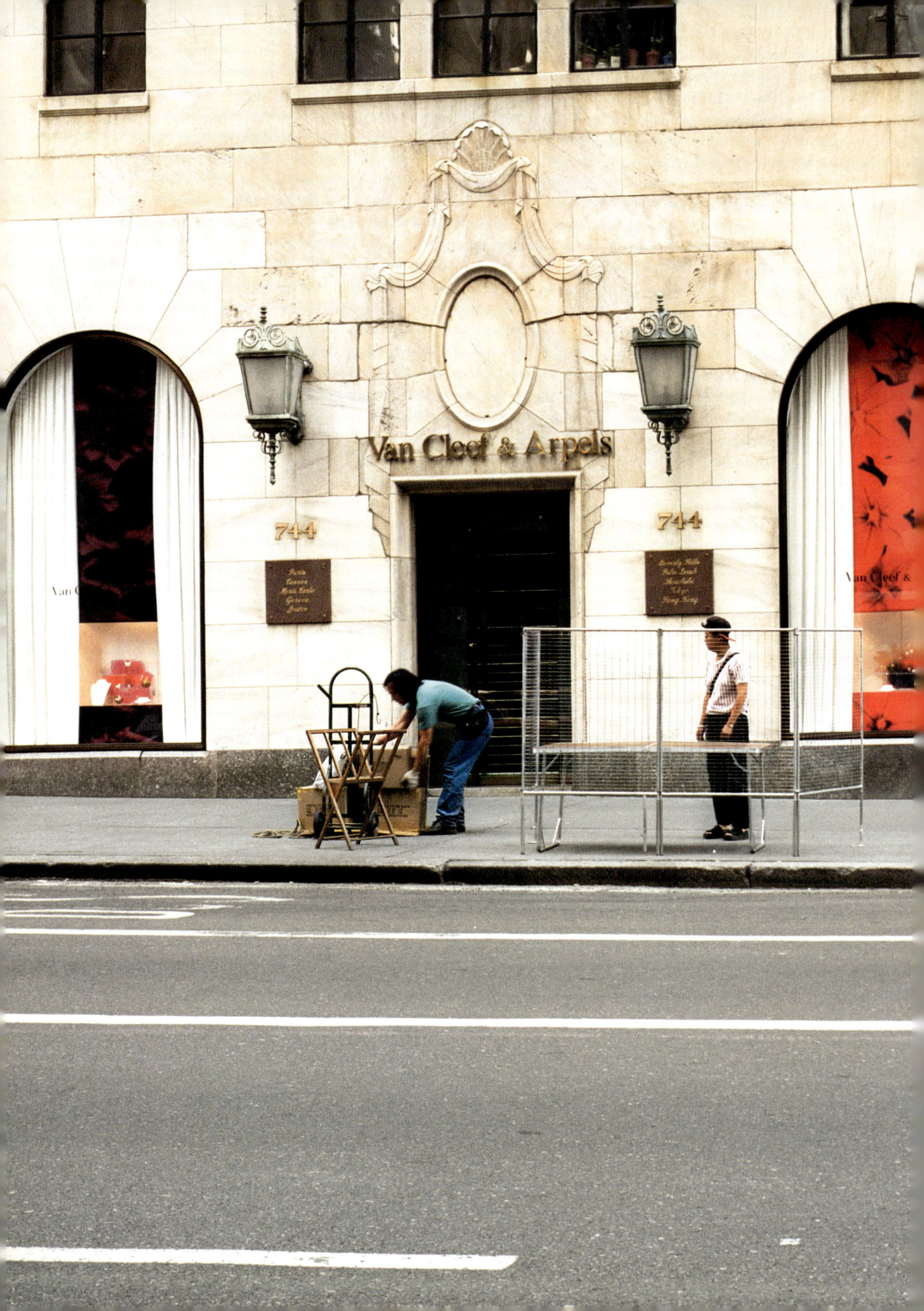
Van Cleef & Arpels
744
744
Van Cleef &

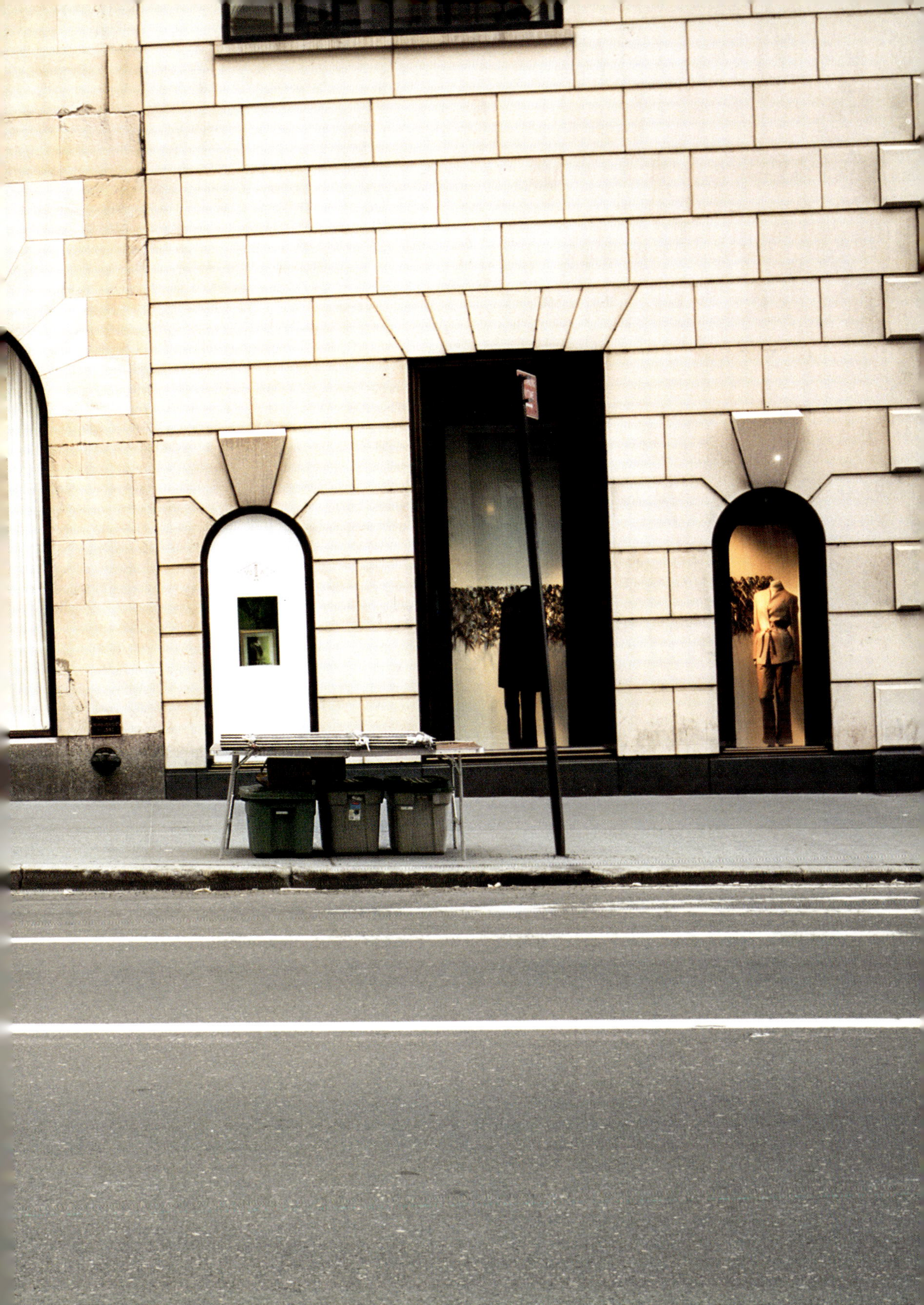

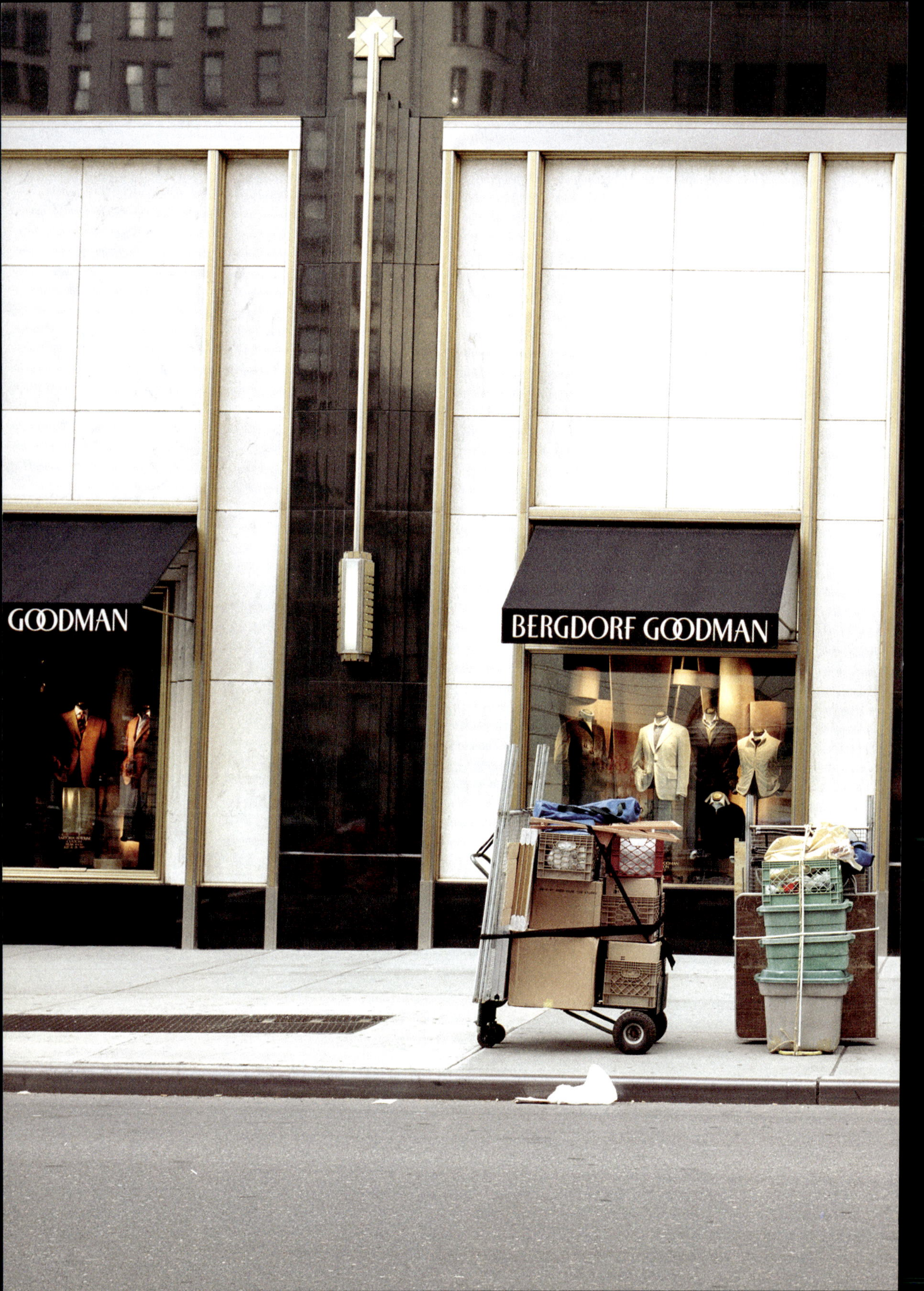
GOODMAN
BERGDORF GOODMAN

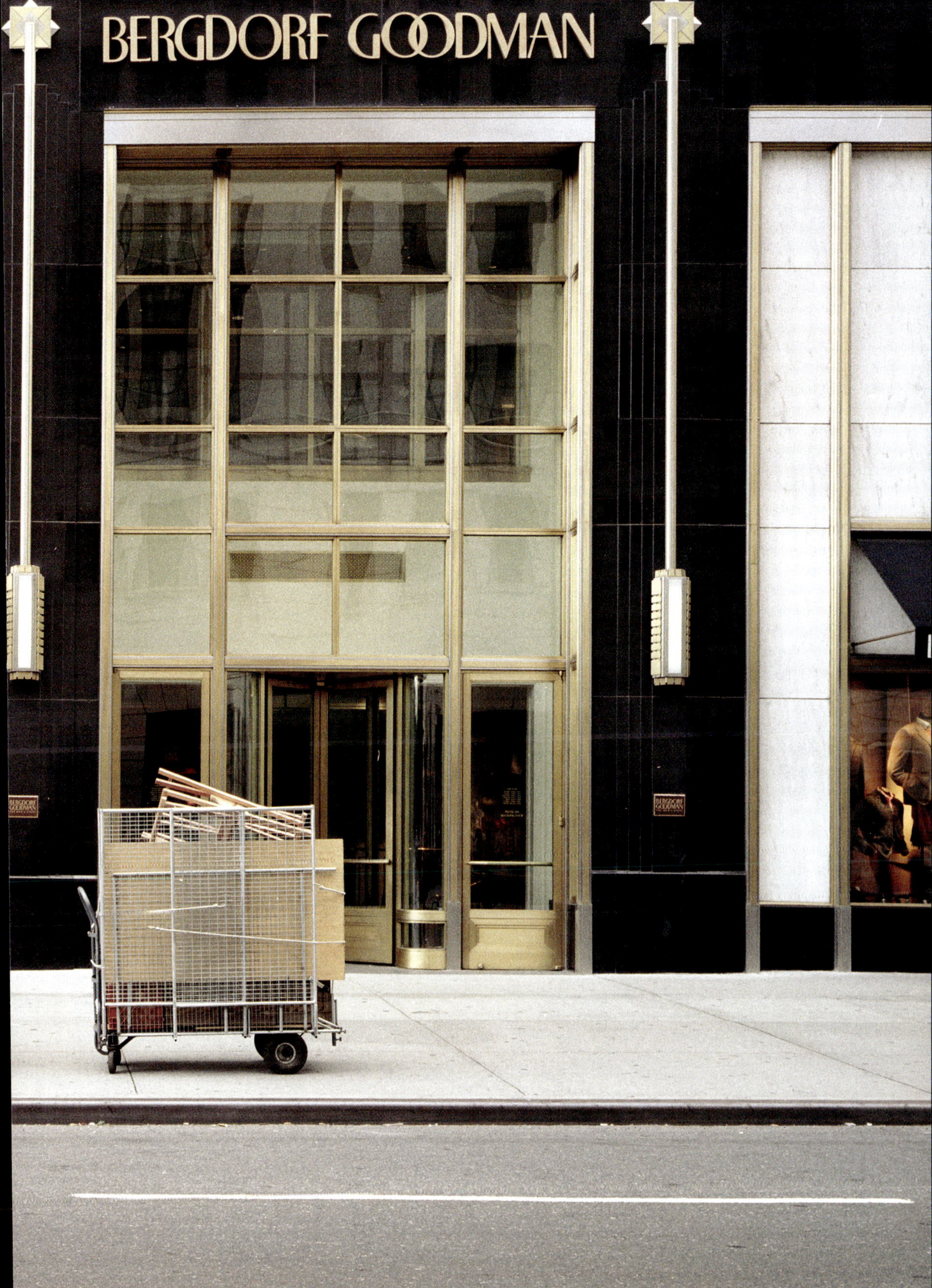
BERGDORF GOODMAN

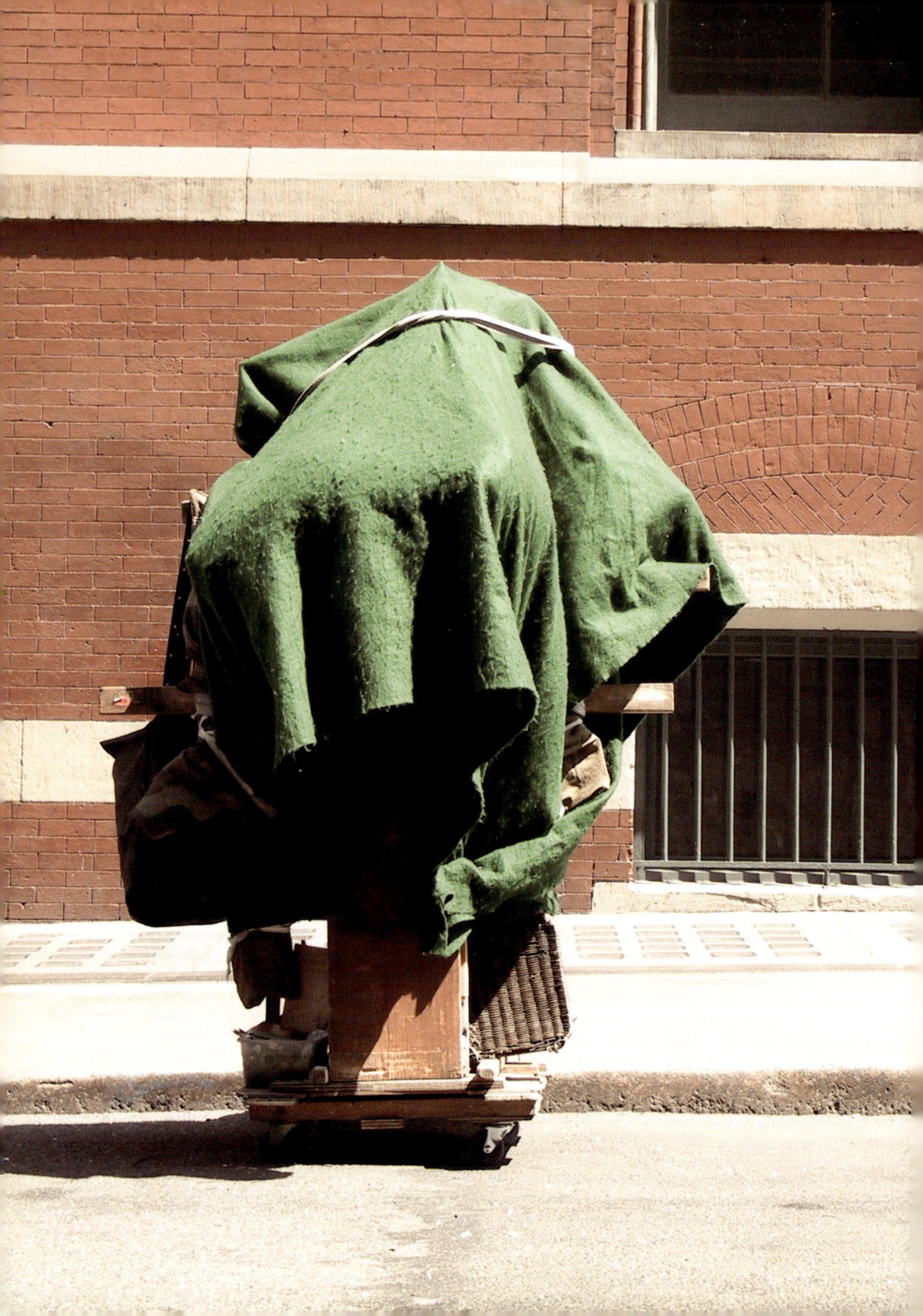

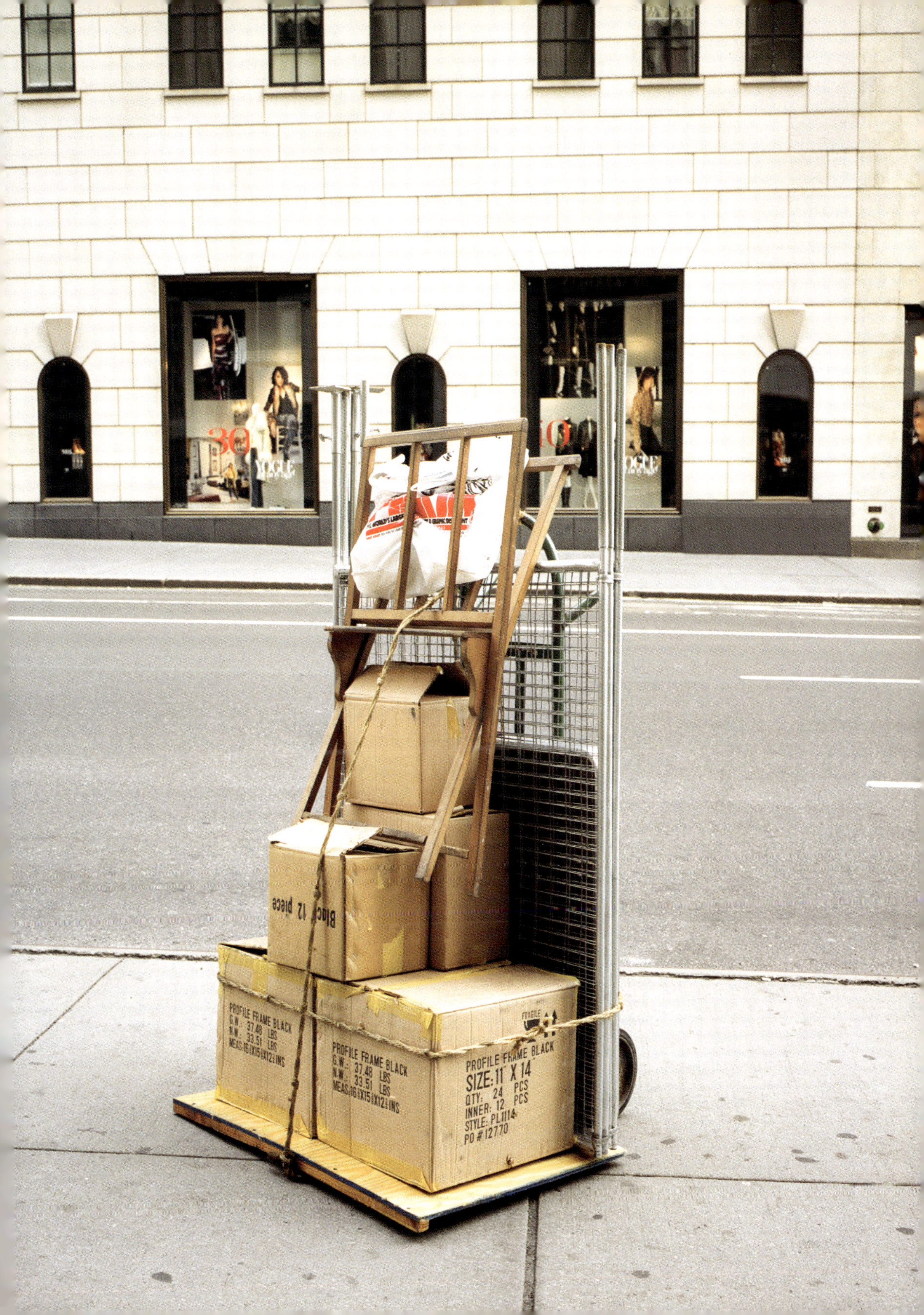
VOGUE
VOGUE
PROFILE FRAME BLACK
G.W.: 37.48 LBS
N.W.: 33.51 LBS
PROFILE FRAME BLACK
G.W.: 37.48 LBS
N.W.: 33.51 LBS
FRAGILE
PROFILE FRAME BLACK
SIZE: 11" X 14"
QTY: 24 PCS
INNER: 12 PCS
STYLE: PL1114
PO # 12770

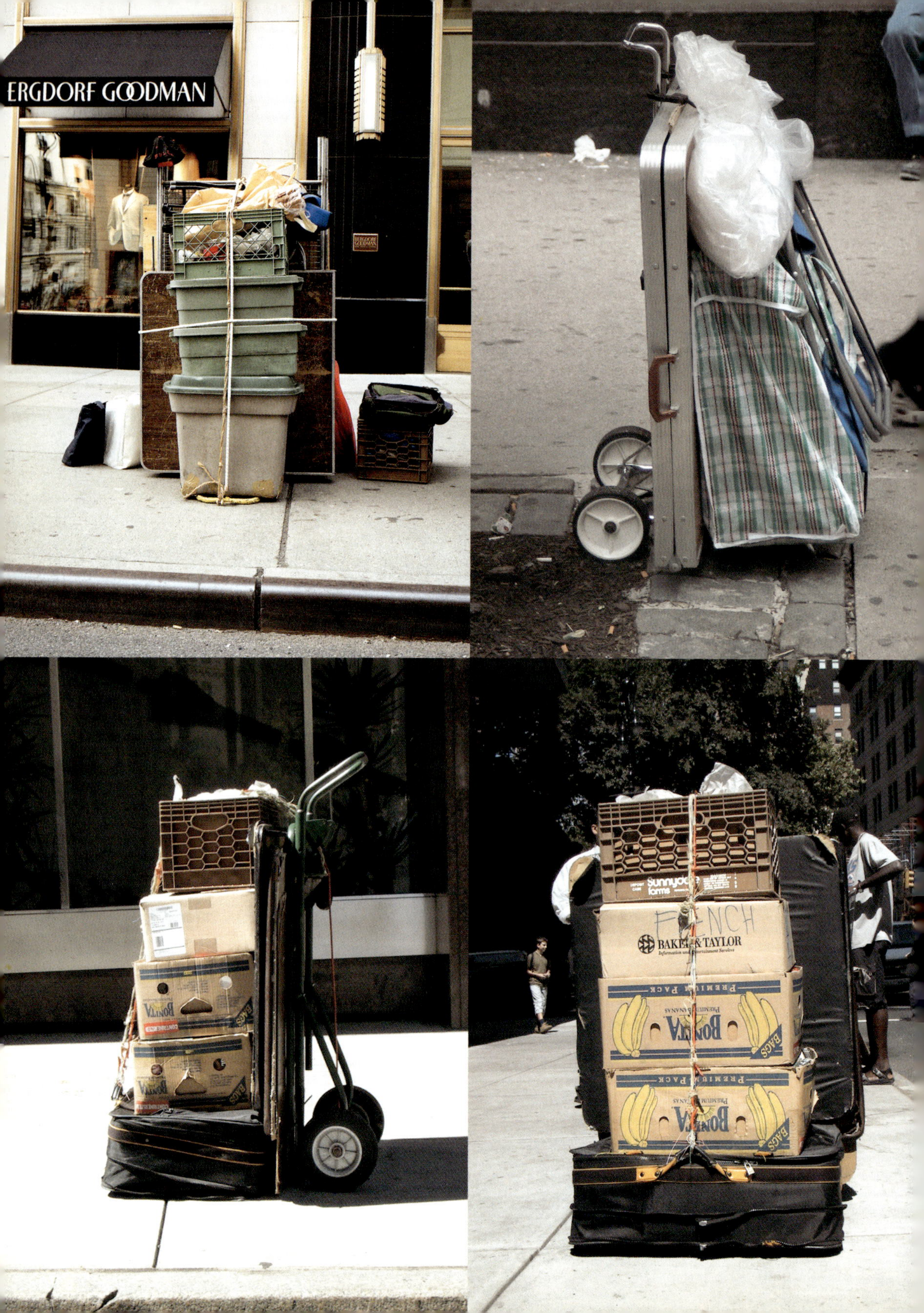
ERGDORF GOODMAN
BAKER & TAYLOR
PREMIUM PACK
BONITA
BAGS

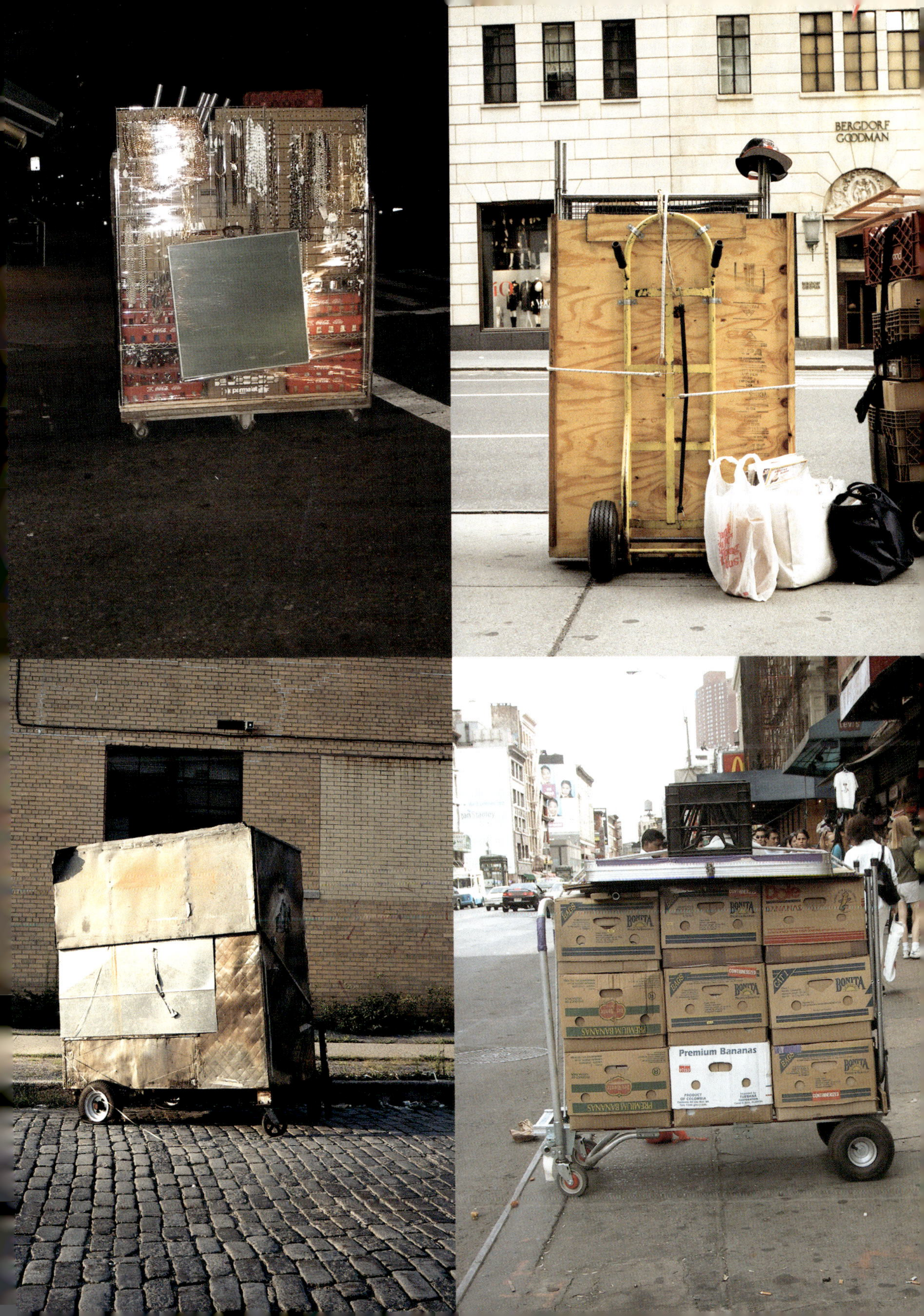

BERGDORF
GOODMAN
Premium Bananas
PREMIUM BANANAS
BONITA
Dole

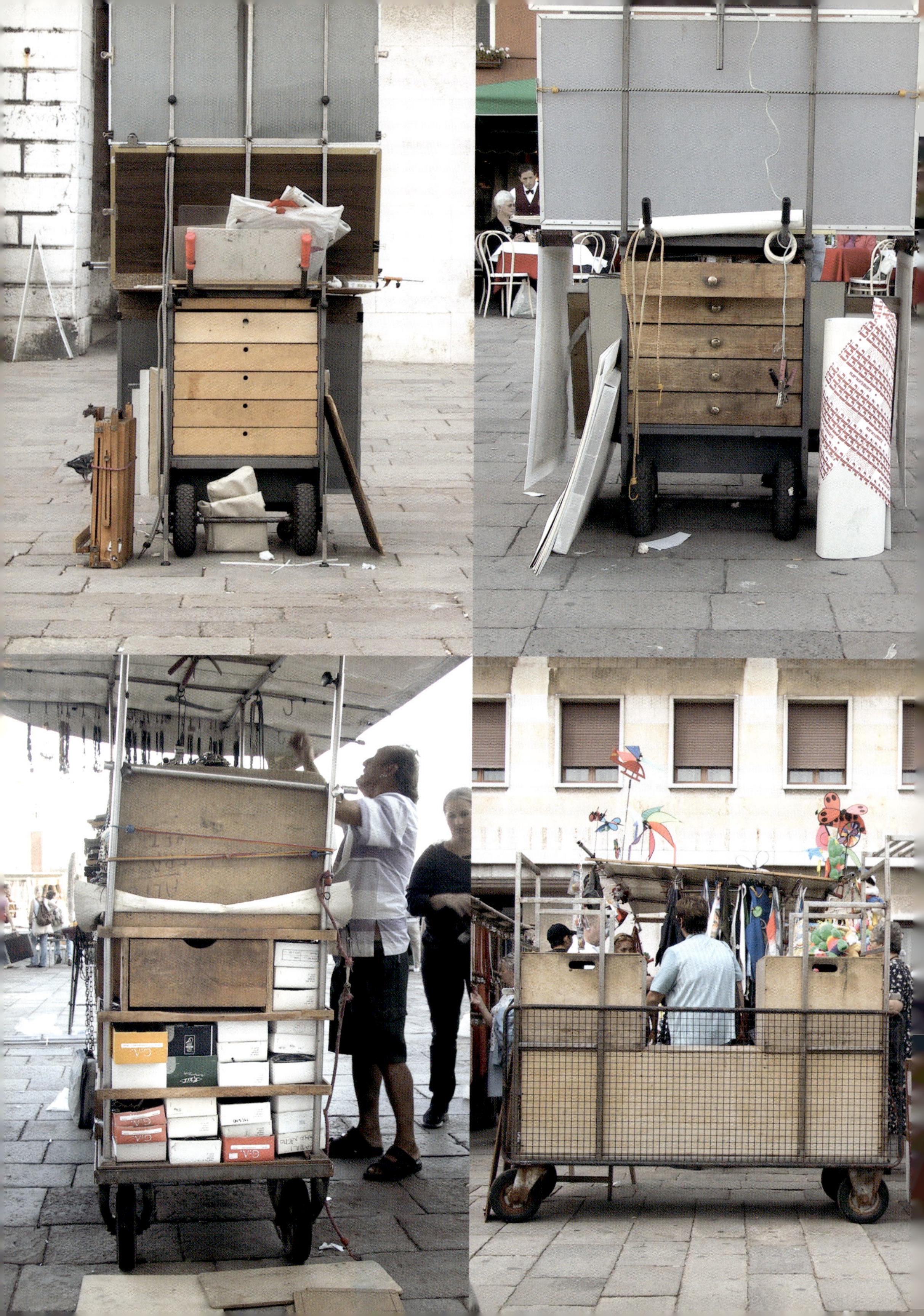

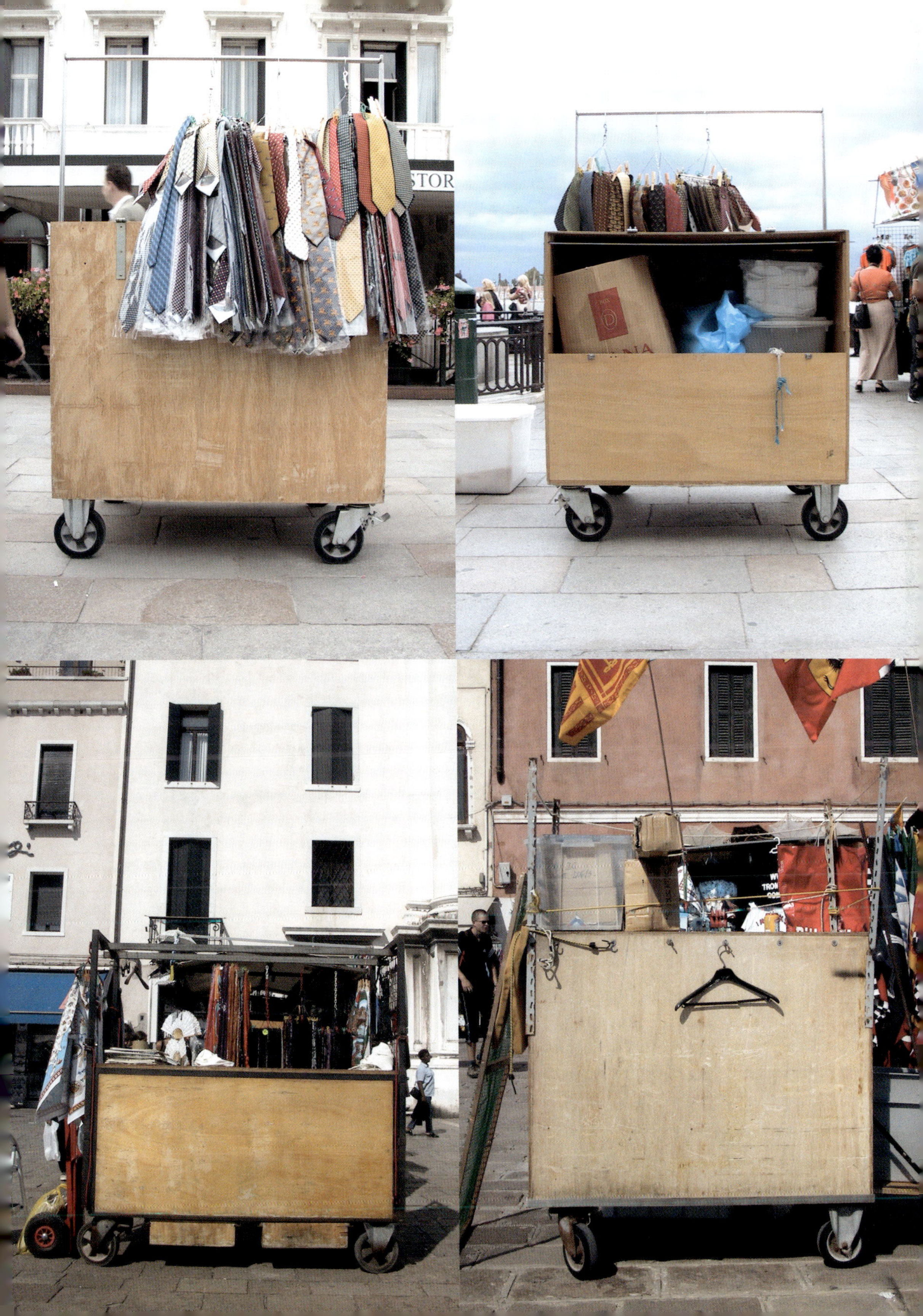
STOR

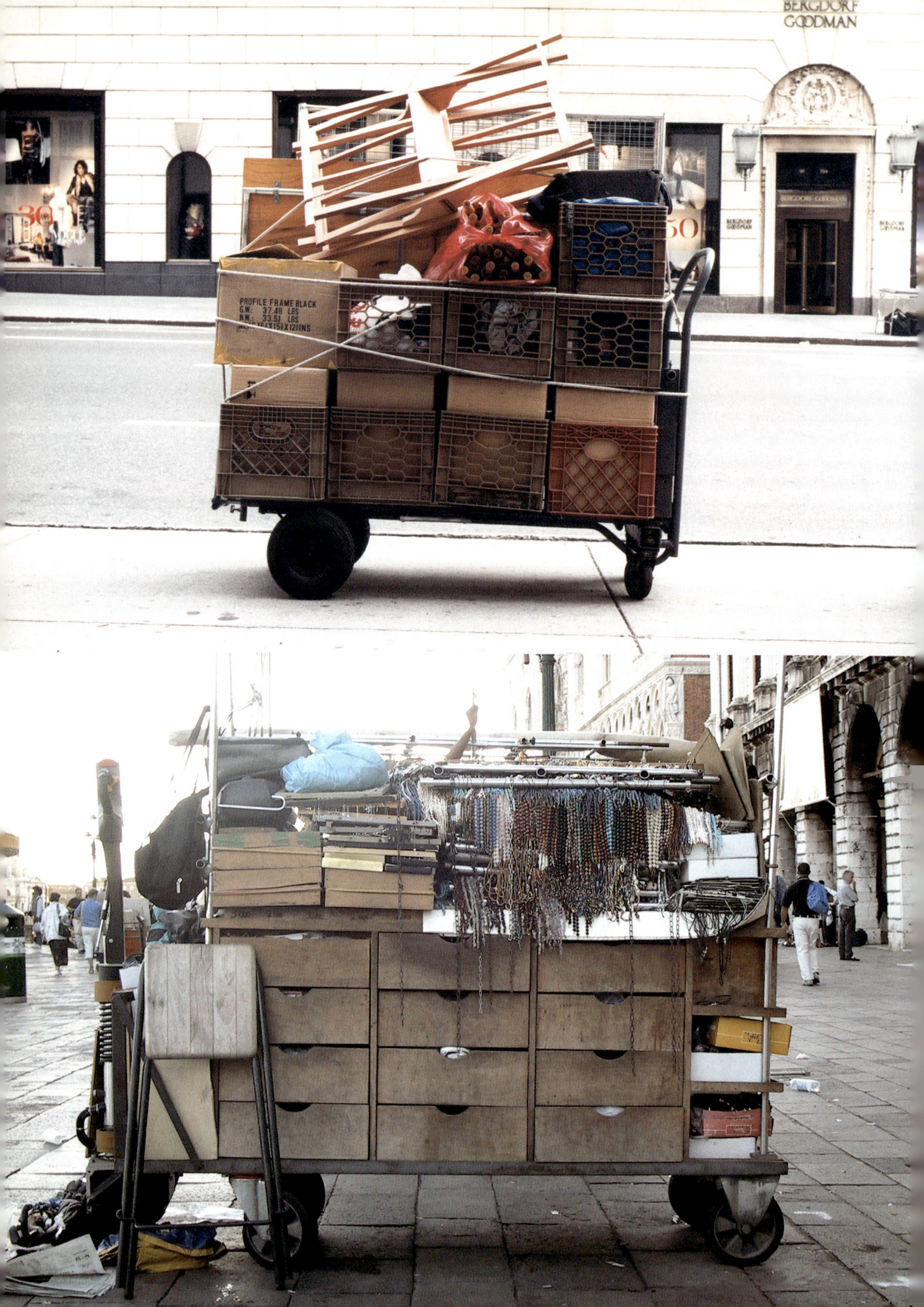
BERGDORF
GOODMAN
PROFILE FRAME BLACK
G.W. 37.48 LBS

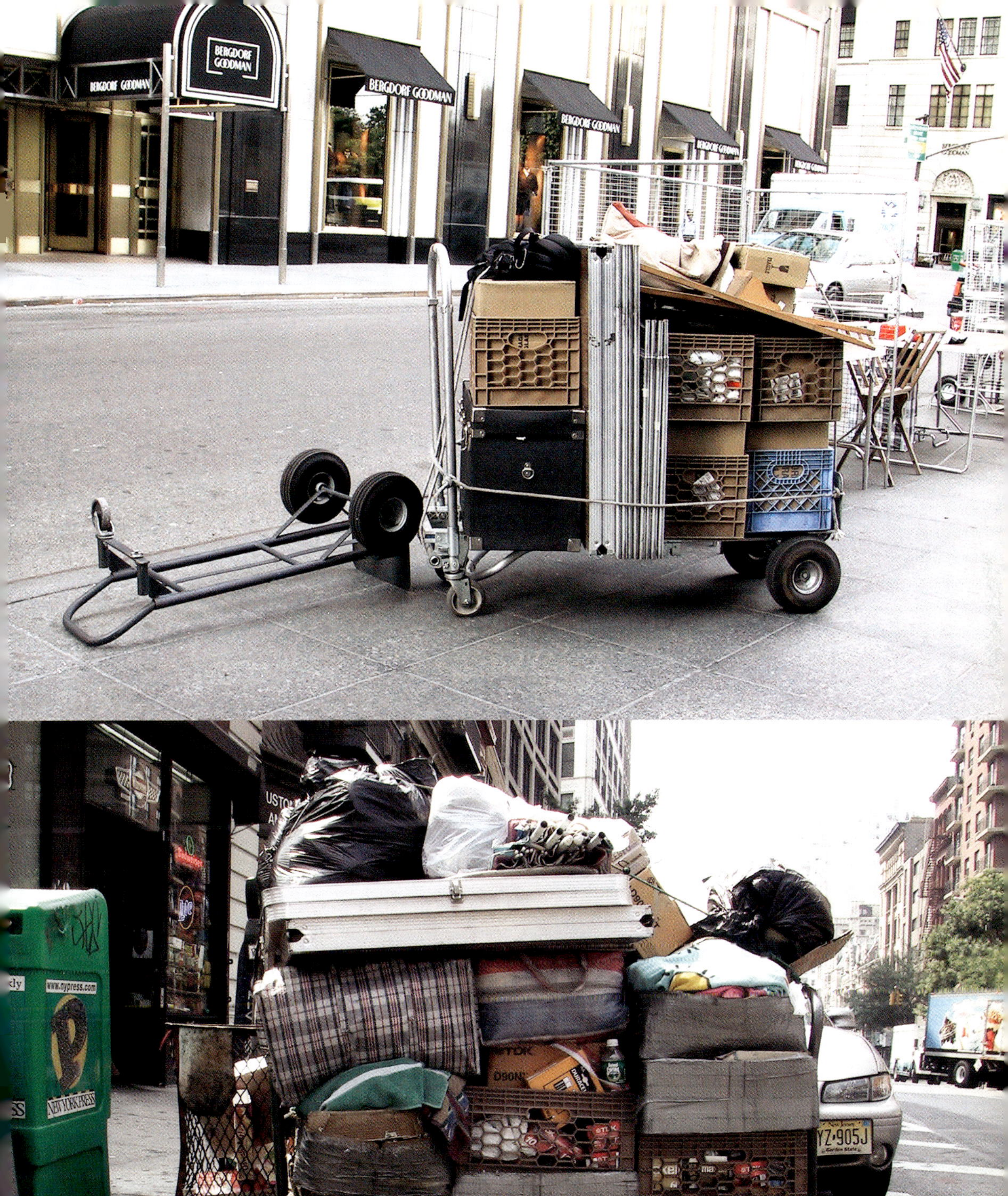
BERGDORF GOODMAN
www.nypress.com
NEW YORK PRESS
TDK
parmalat
YZ 905J

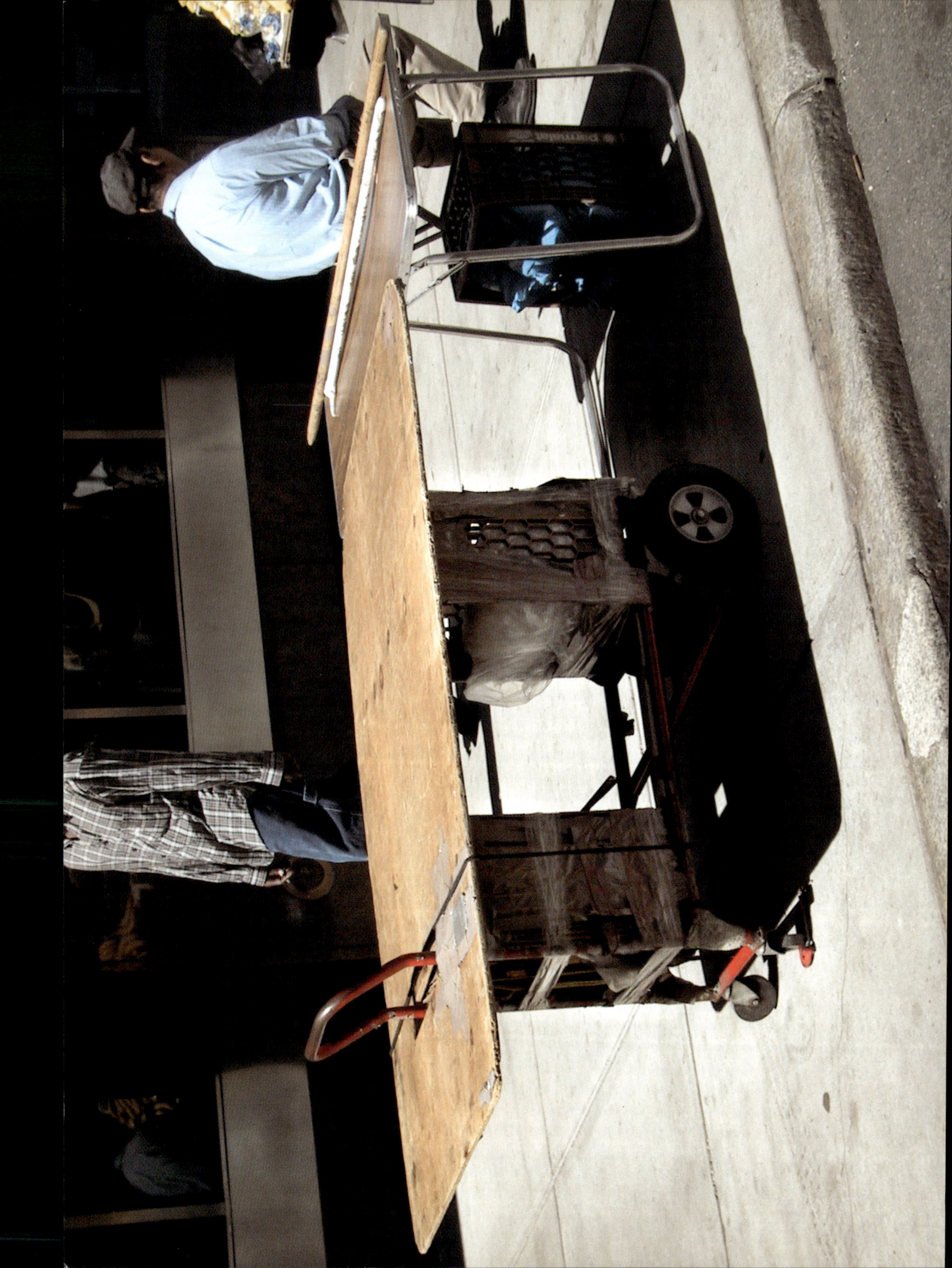

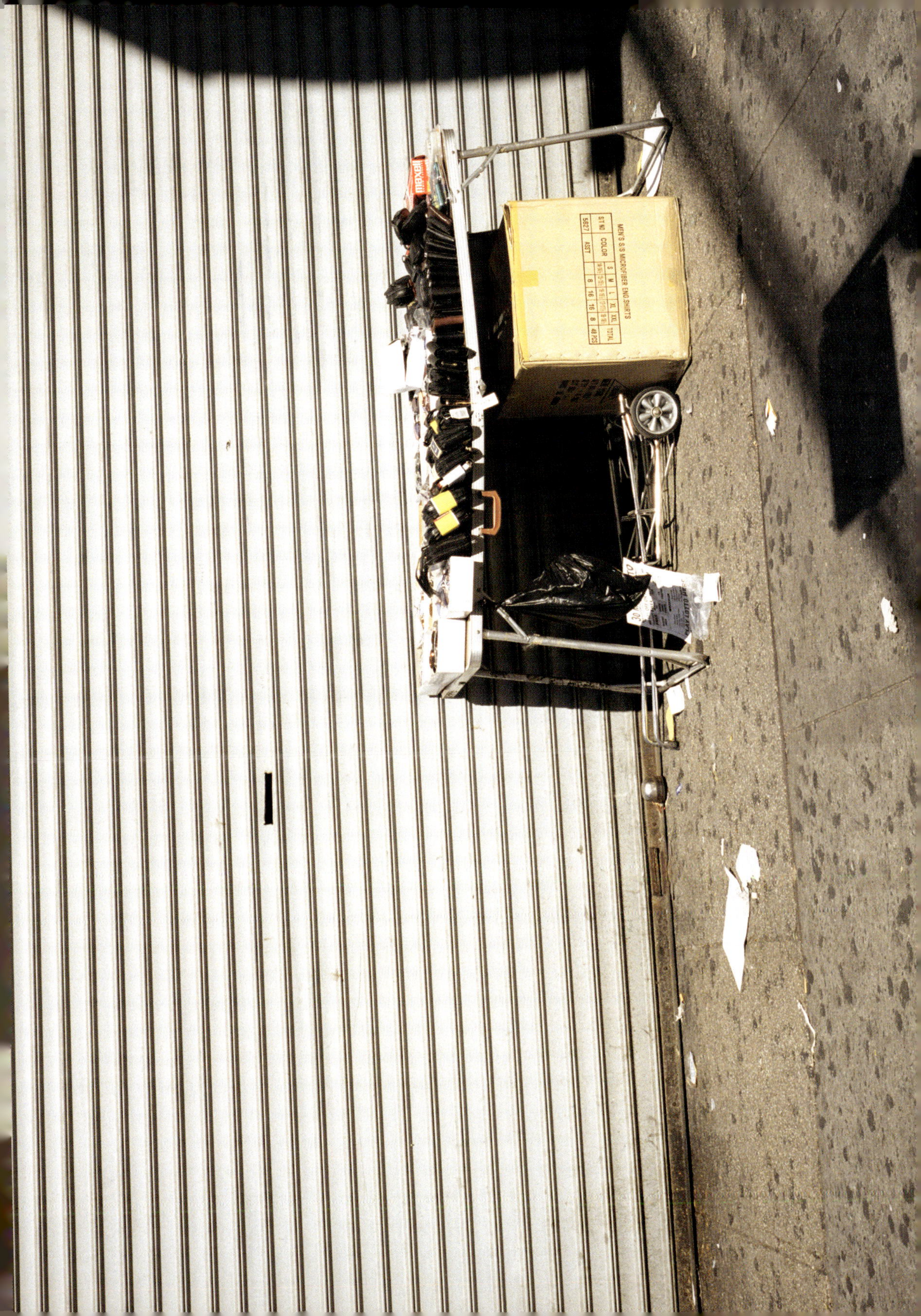
maxell
MEN'S S/S MICROFIBER ENG SHIRTS
ST NO COLOR S M L XL XXL TOTAL
5627 ASST 8 16 16 8 48 PCS

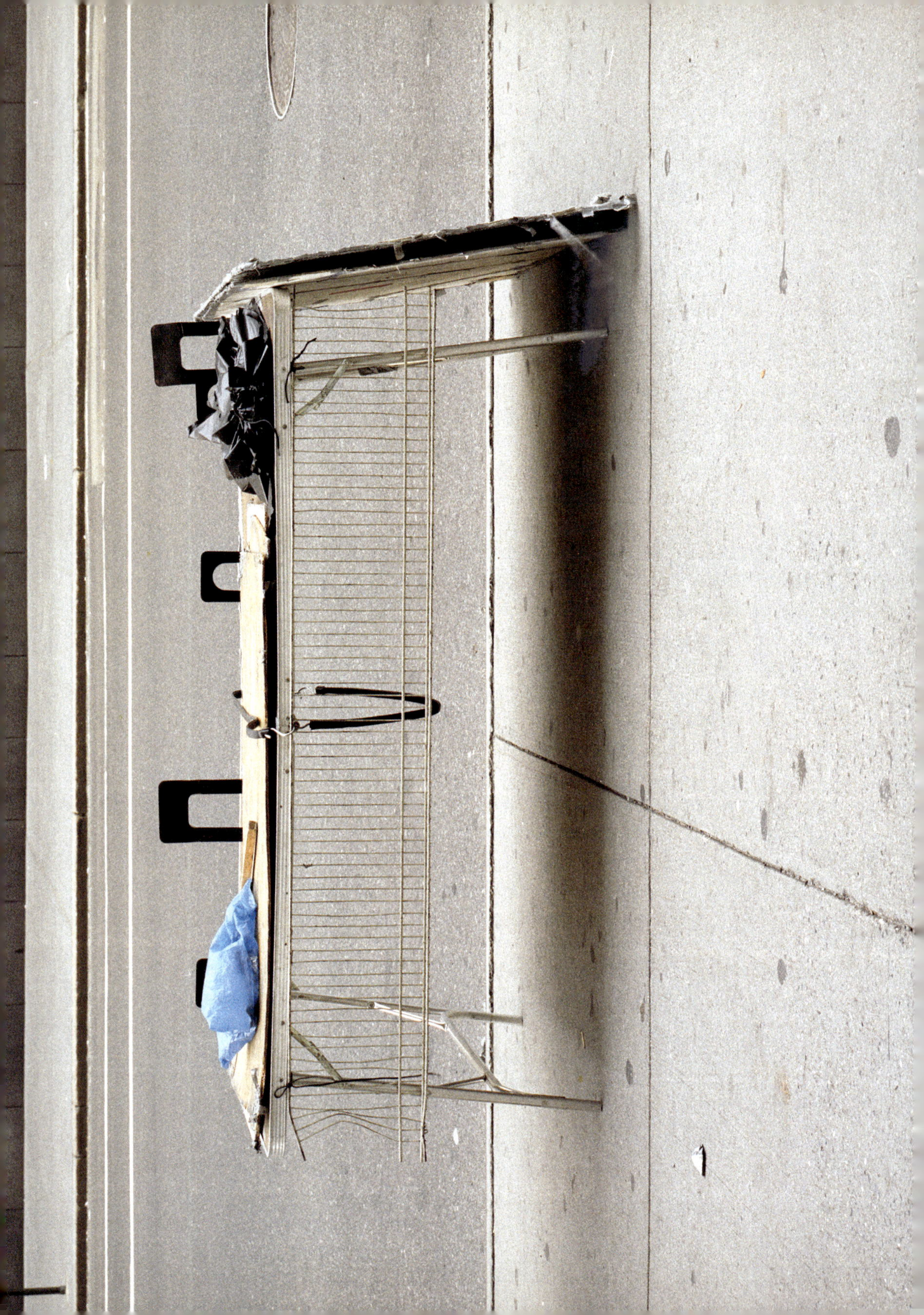

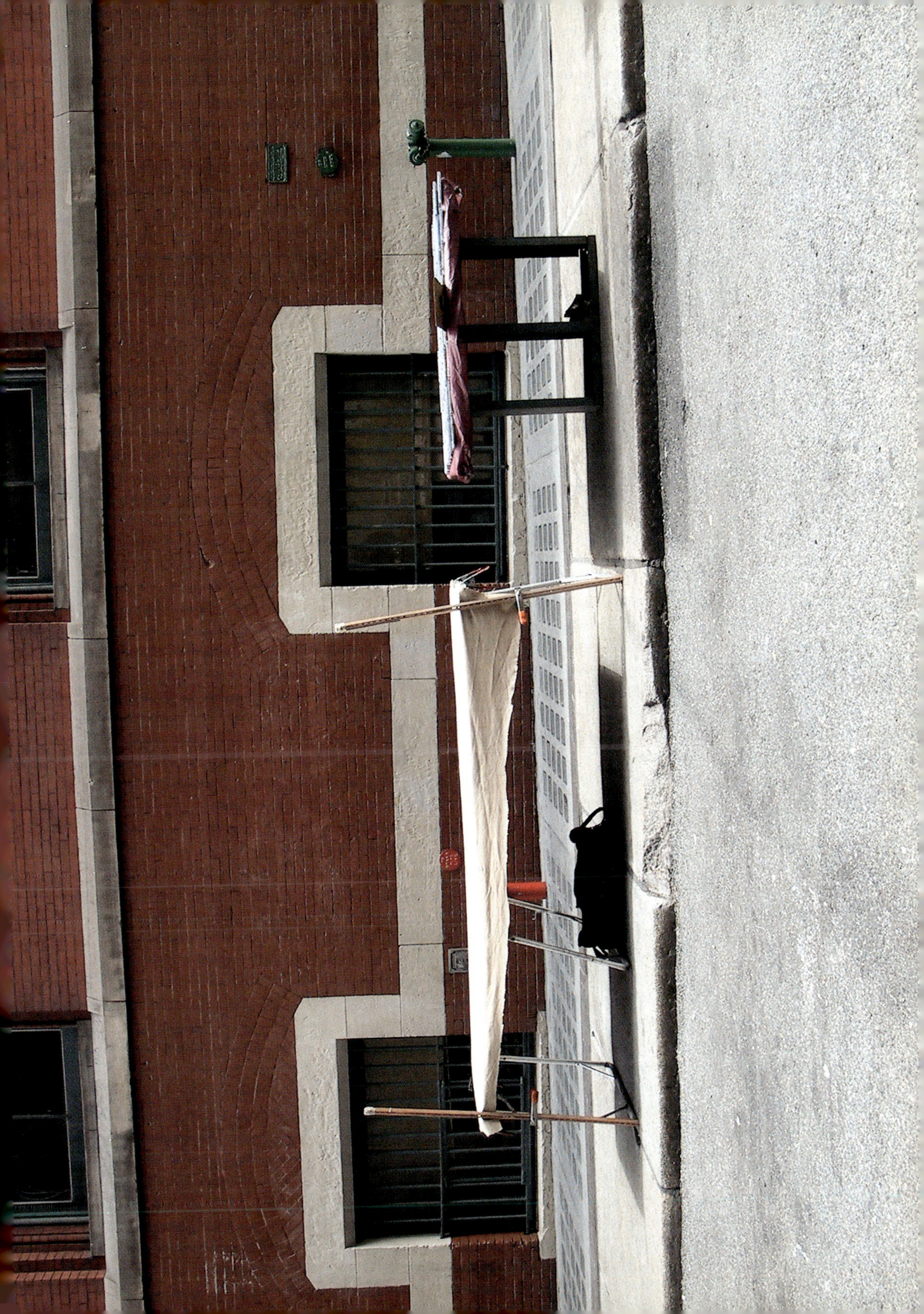

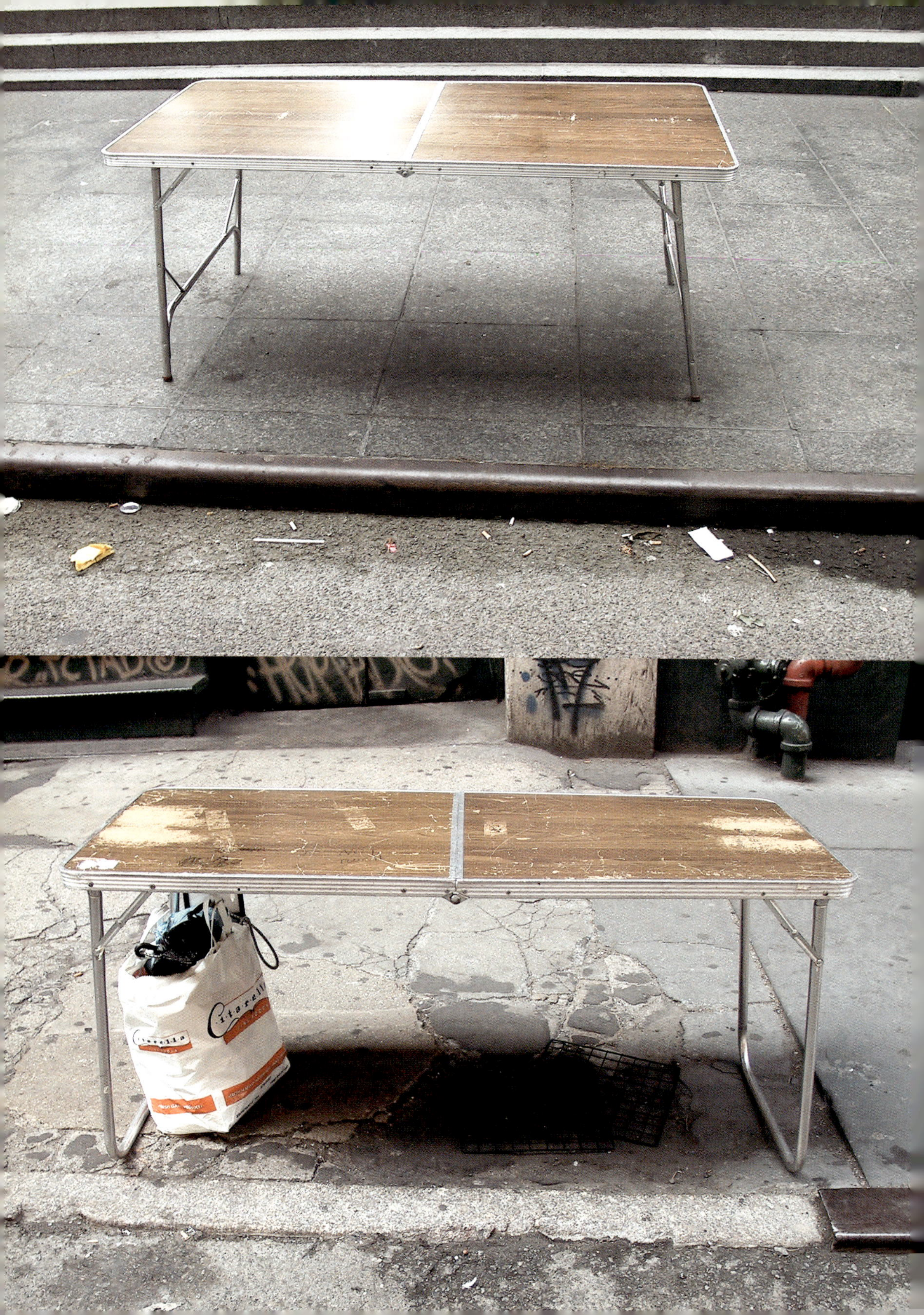

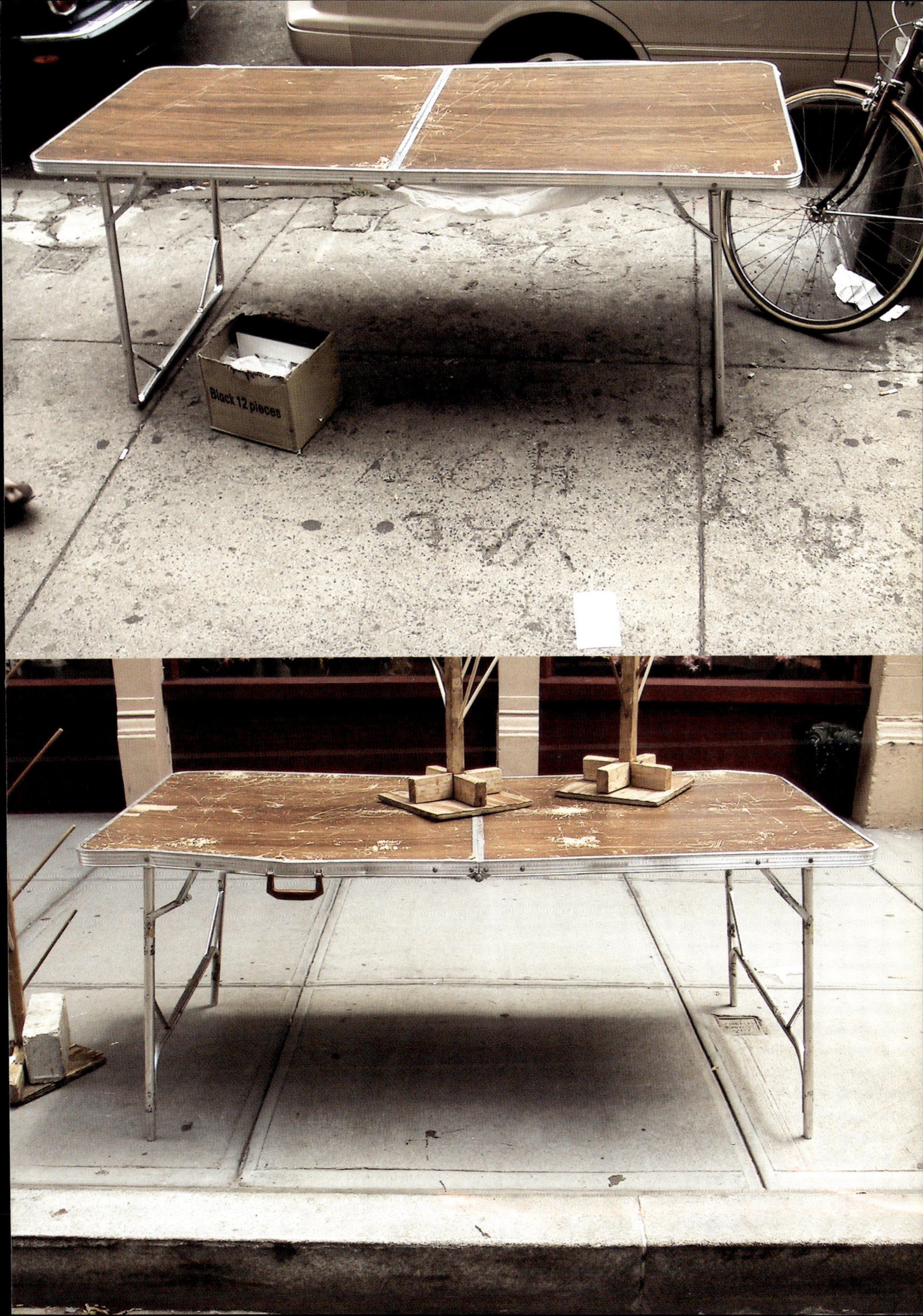
Black 12 pieces

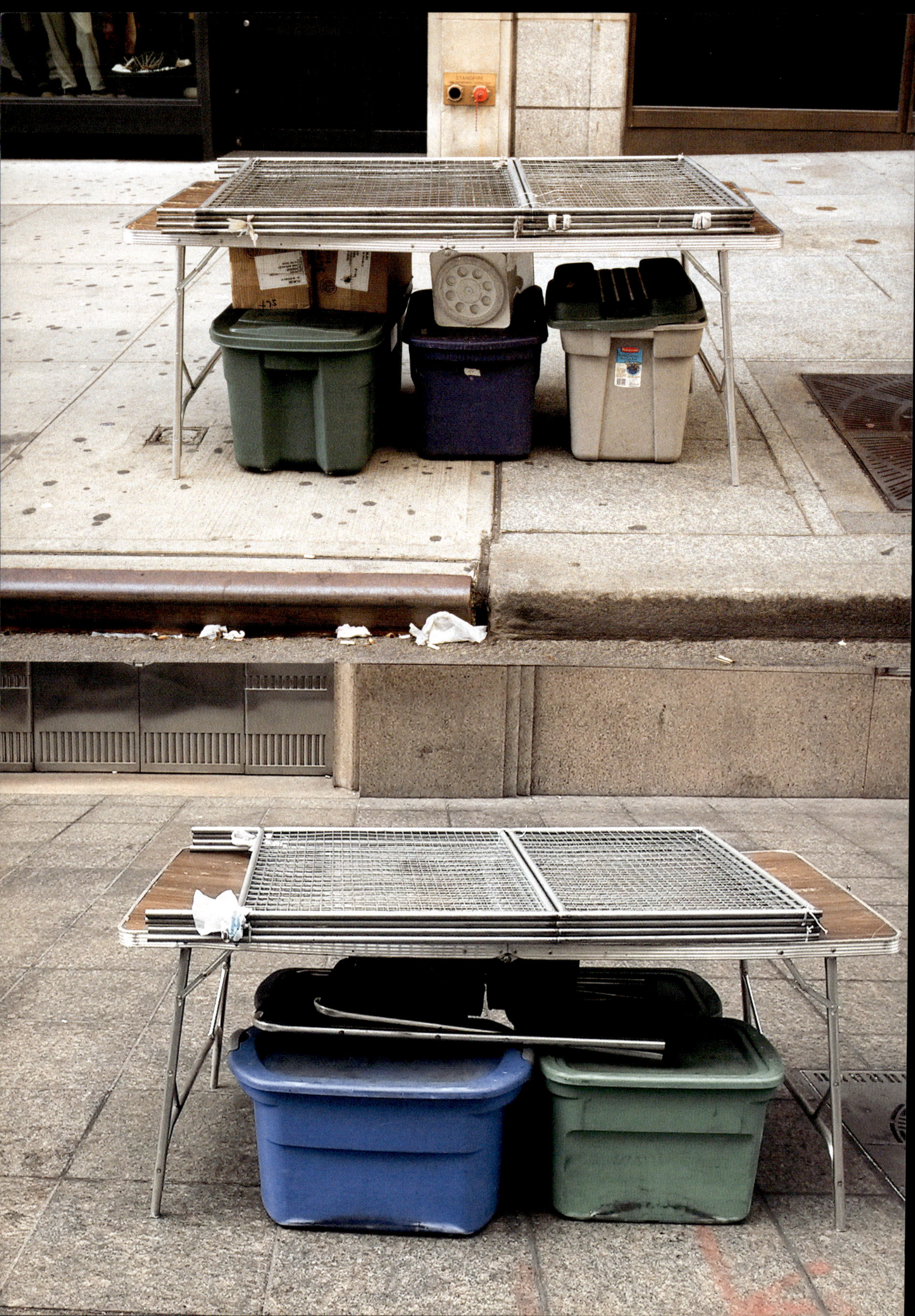

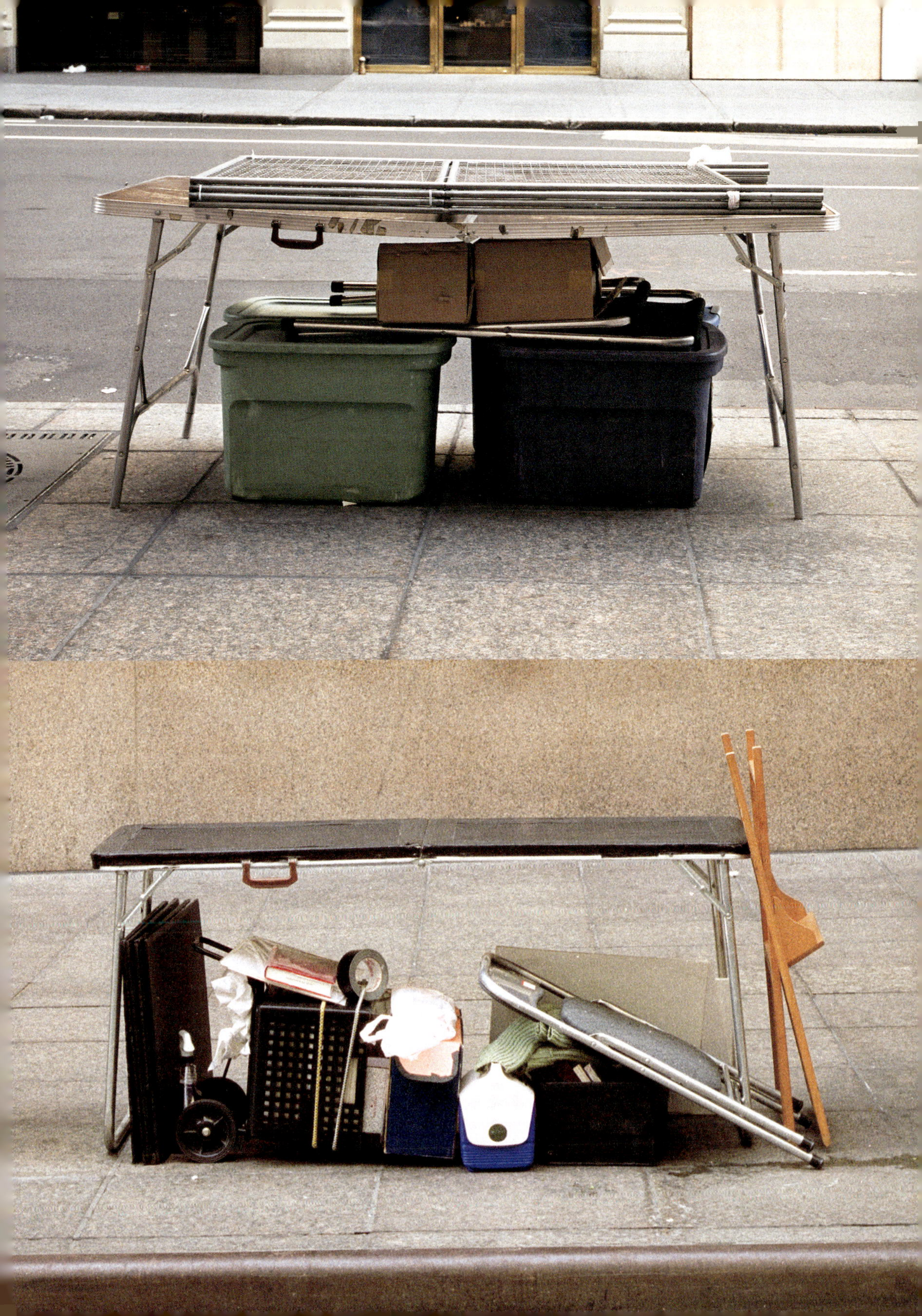

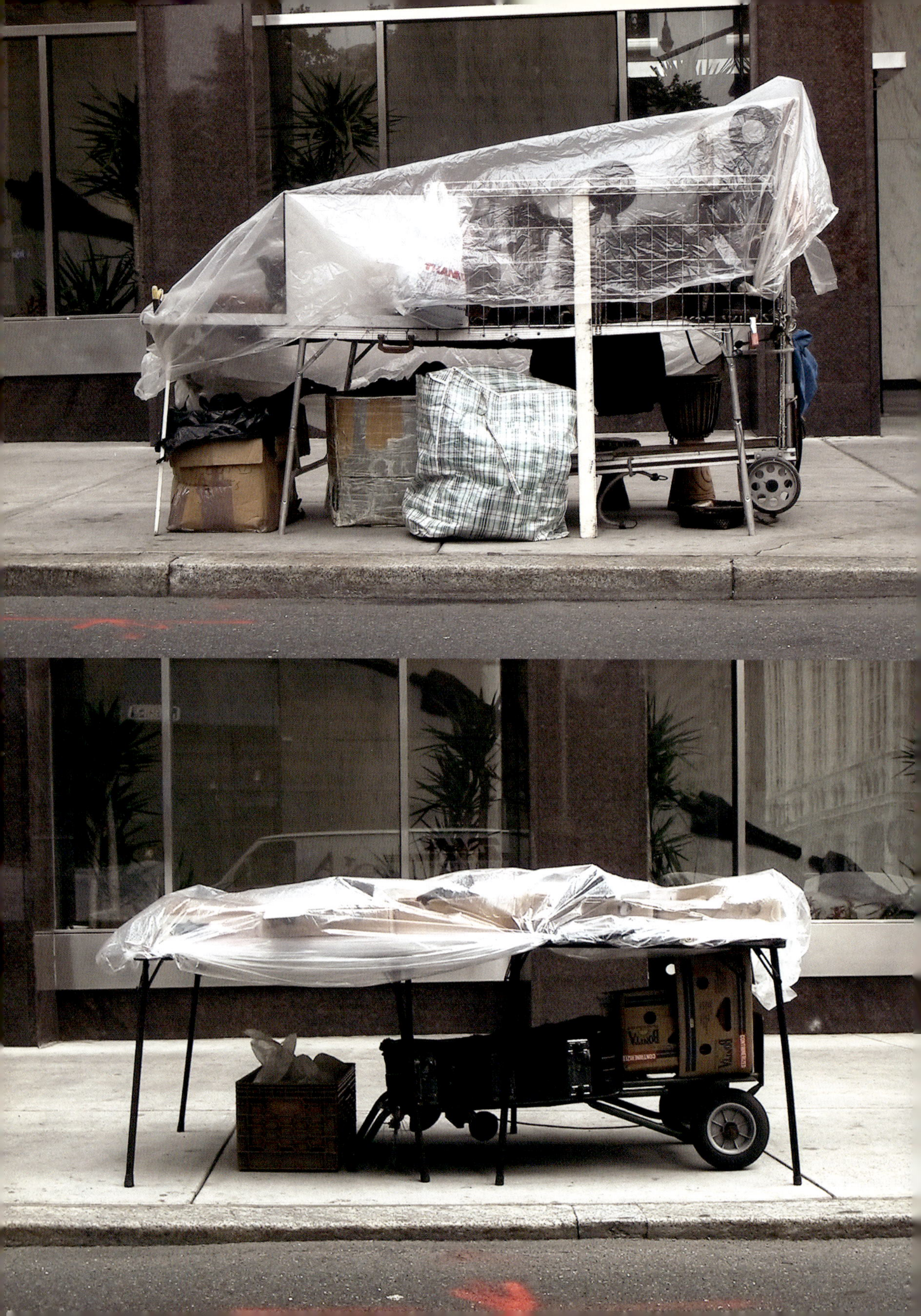

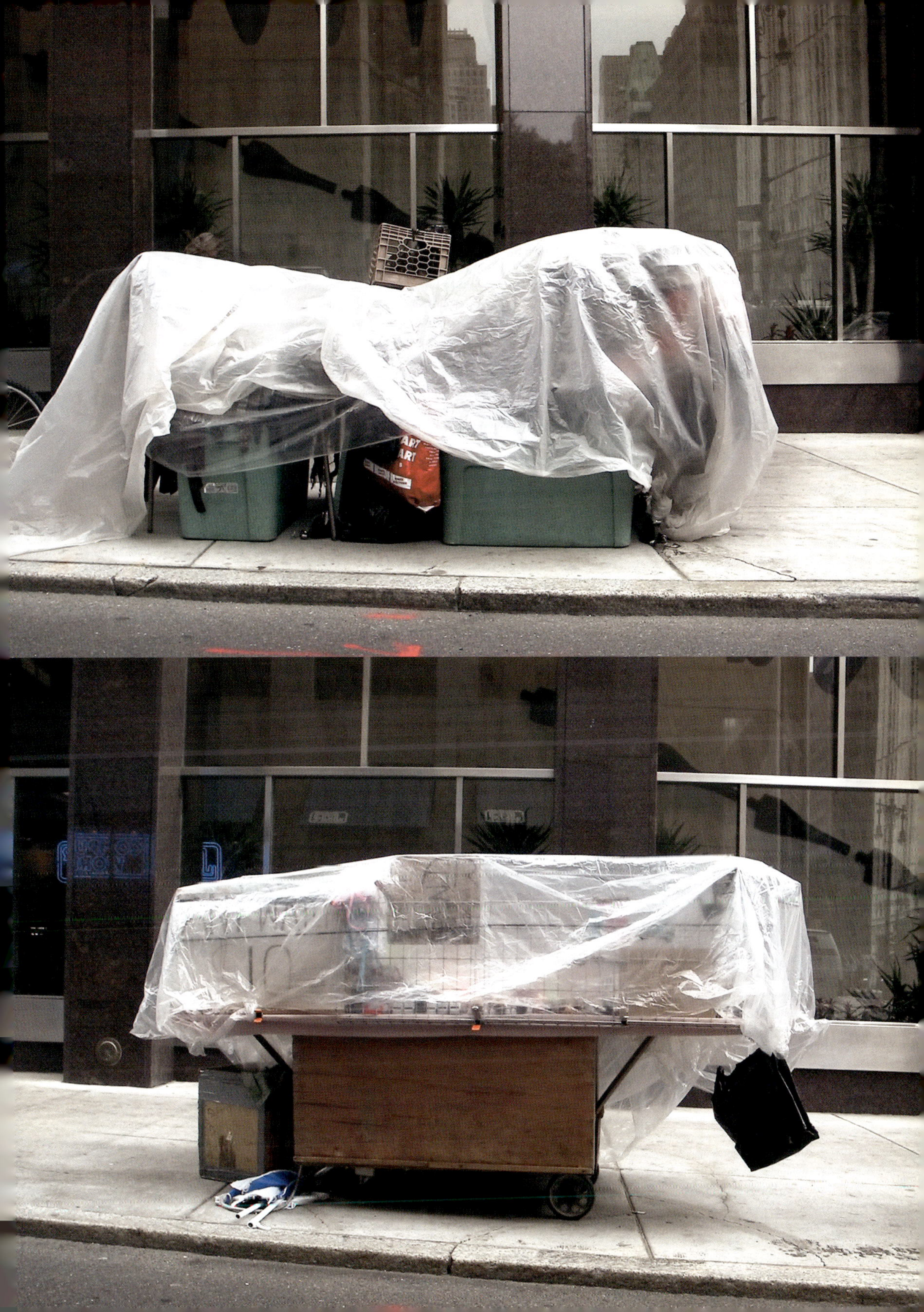

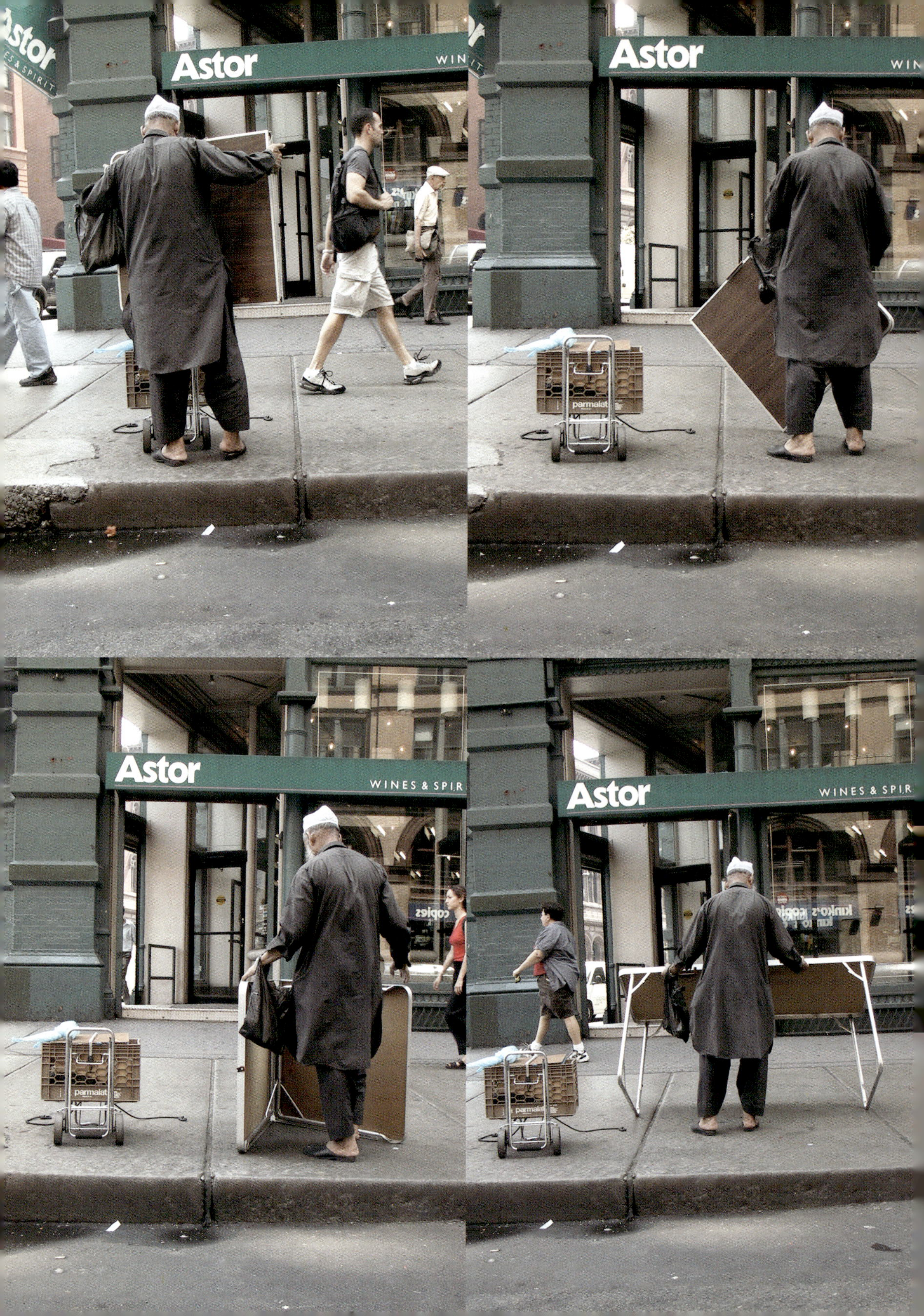
Astor
WINES & SPIR
parmalat
copies

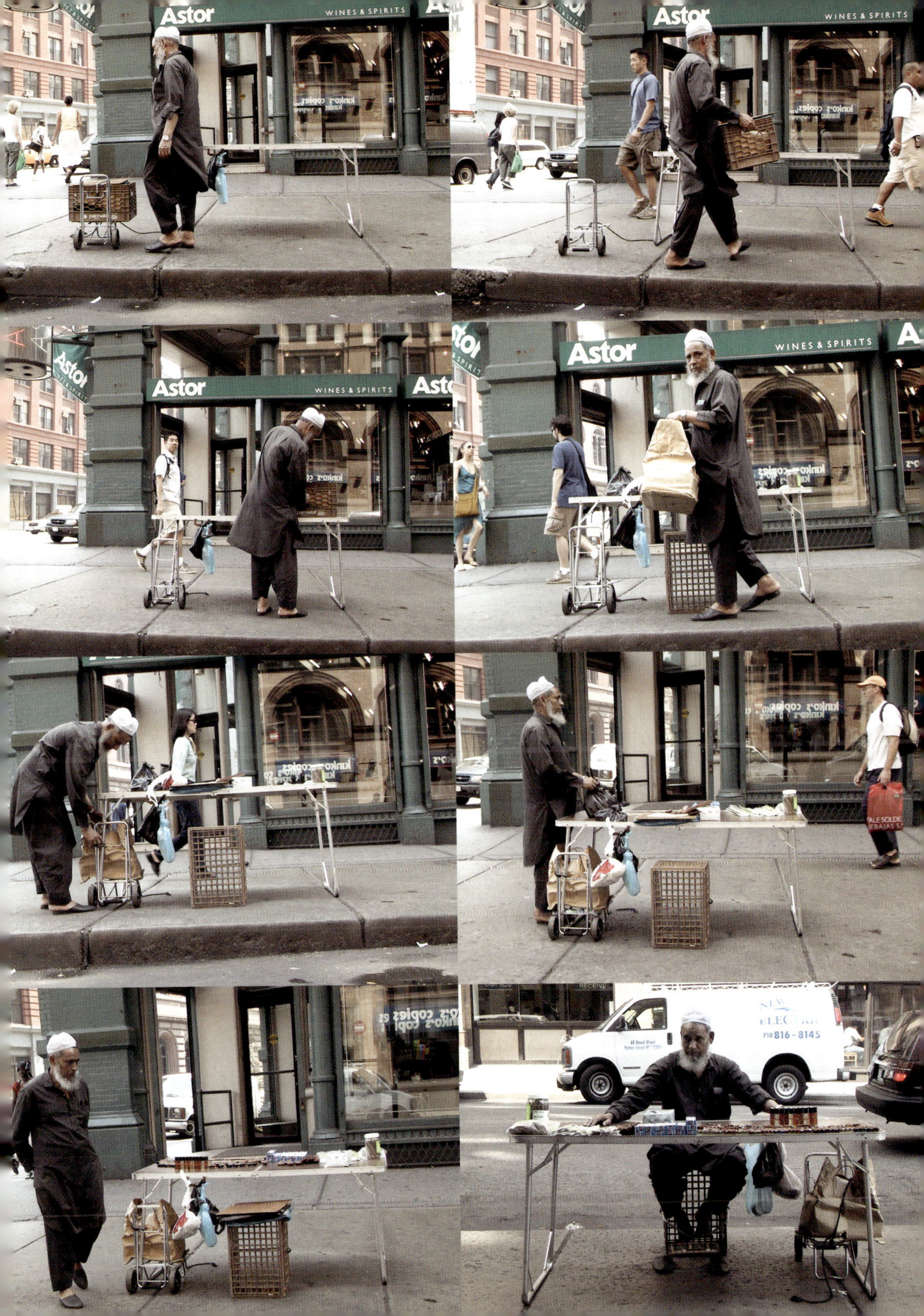
Astor
WINES & SPIRITS
718 816-8145

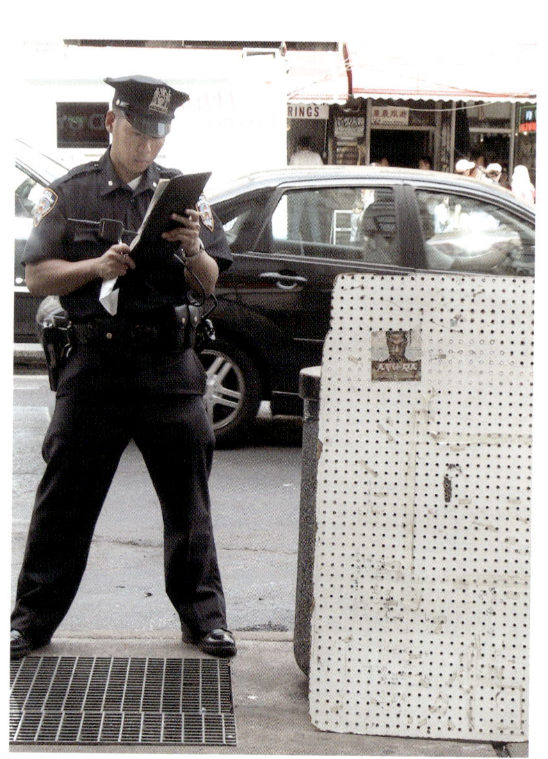

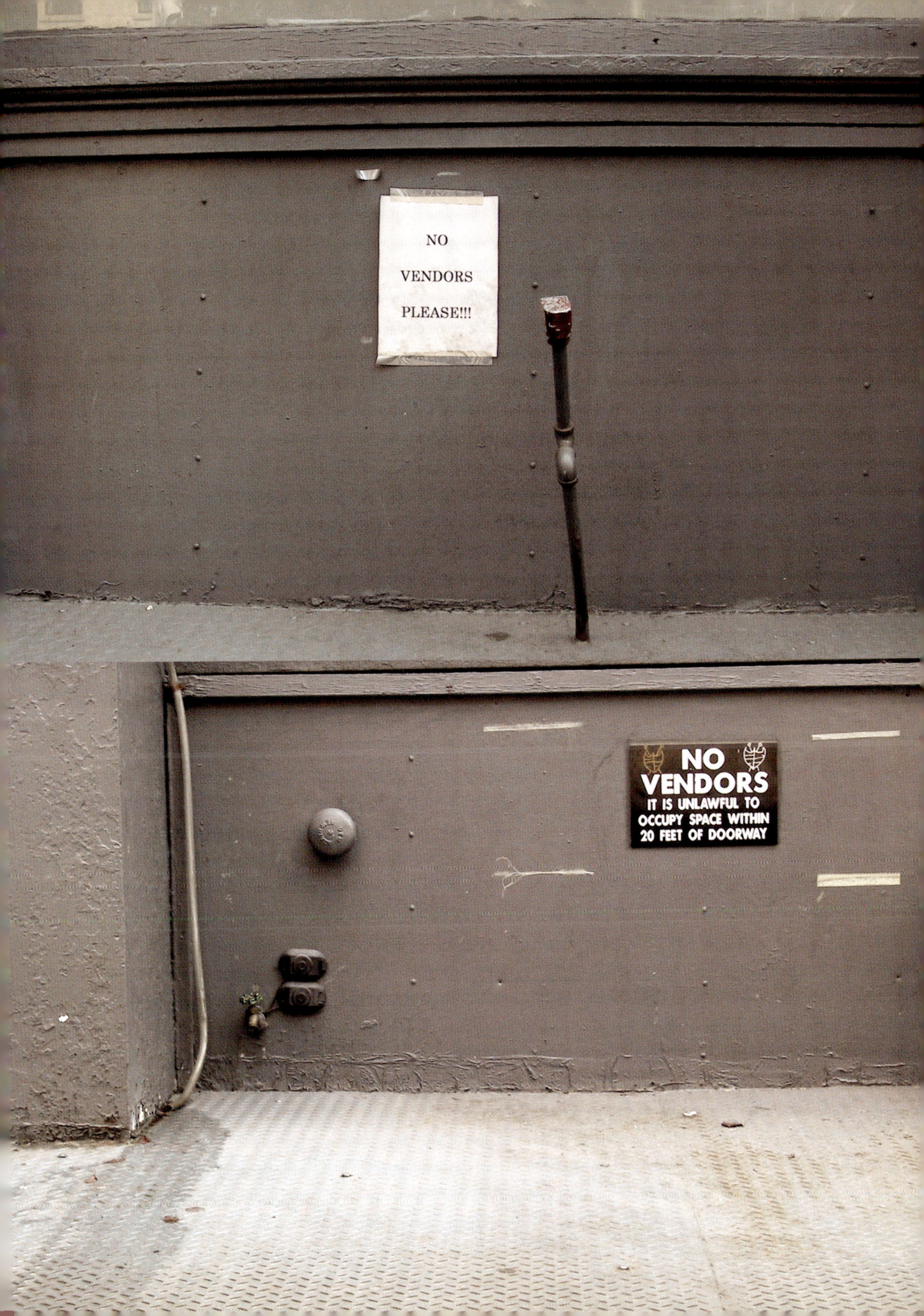
NO
VENDORS
PLEASE!!!
NO
VENDORS
IT IS UNLAWFUL TO
OCCUPY SPACE WITHIN
20 FEET OF DOORWAY

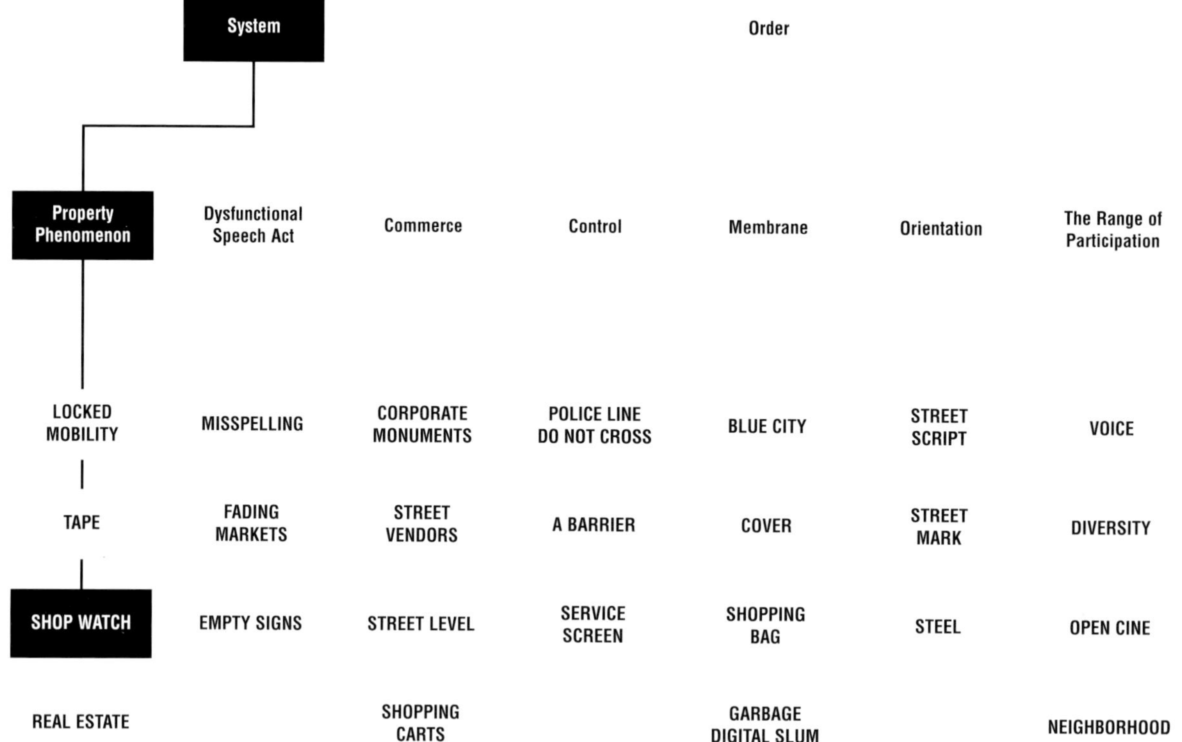

System
Order
Property Phenomenon
Dysfunctional Speech Act
Commerce
Control
Membrane
Orientation
The Range of Participation
LOCKED MOBILITY
MISSPELLING
CORPORATE MONUMENTS
POLICE LINE DO NOT CROSS
BLUE CITY
STREET SCRIPT
VOICE
TAPE
FADING MARKETS
STREET VENDORS
A BARRIER
COVER
STREET MARK
DIVERSITY
SHOP WATCH
EMPTY SIGNS
STREET LEVEL
SERVICE SCREEN
SHOPPING BAG
STEEL
OPEN CINE
REAL ESTATE
SHOPPING CARTS
GARBAGE DIGITAL SLUM
NEIGHBORHOOD

Identity

Alternative Media

Habitual Reinterpretation

SHOP WATCH

Eye with Suspicion

CAR DOOR

PUBLIC CHAIRS

LABELING.

PLASTIC CRATES

POLE POST

STANDPIPES

PRAY JESUS

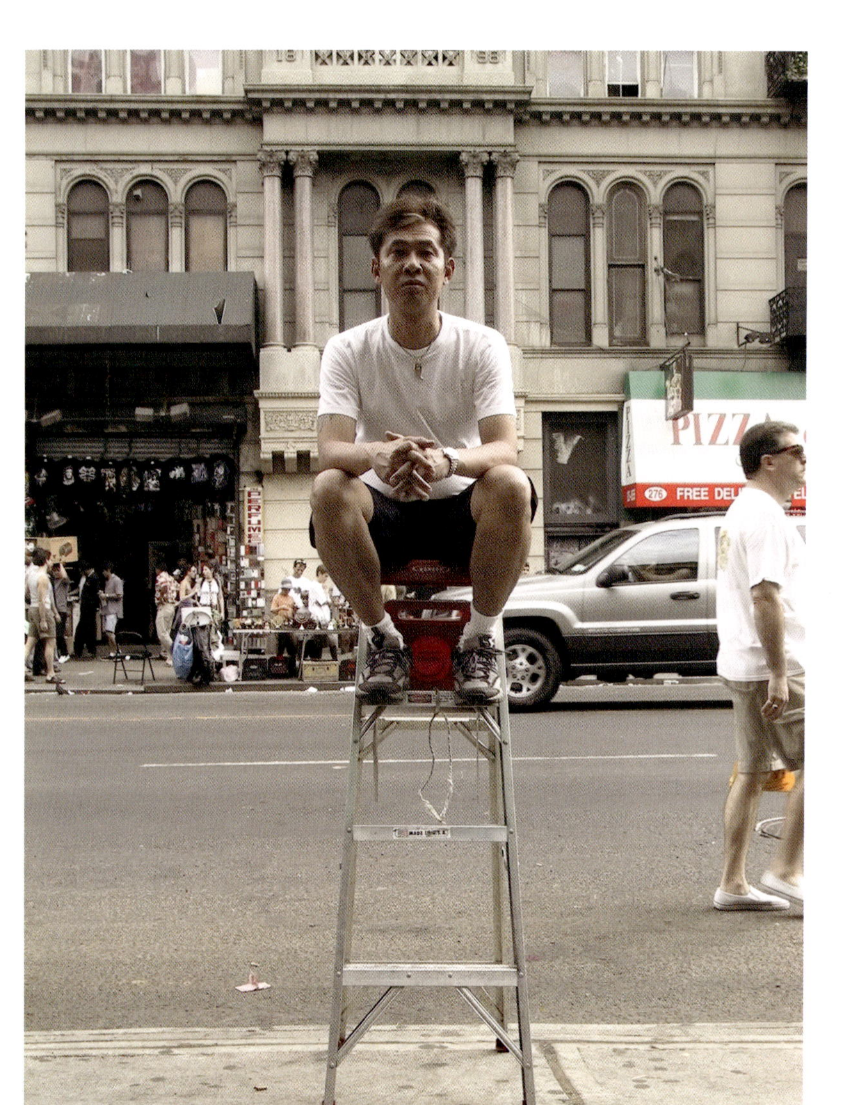
PERFUME
276 FREE

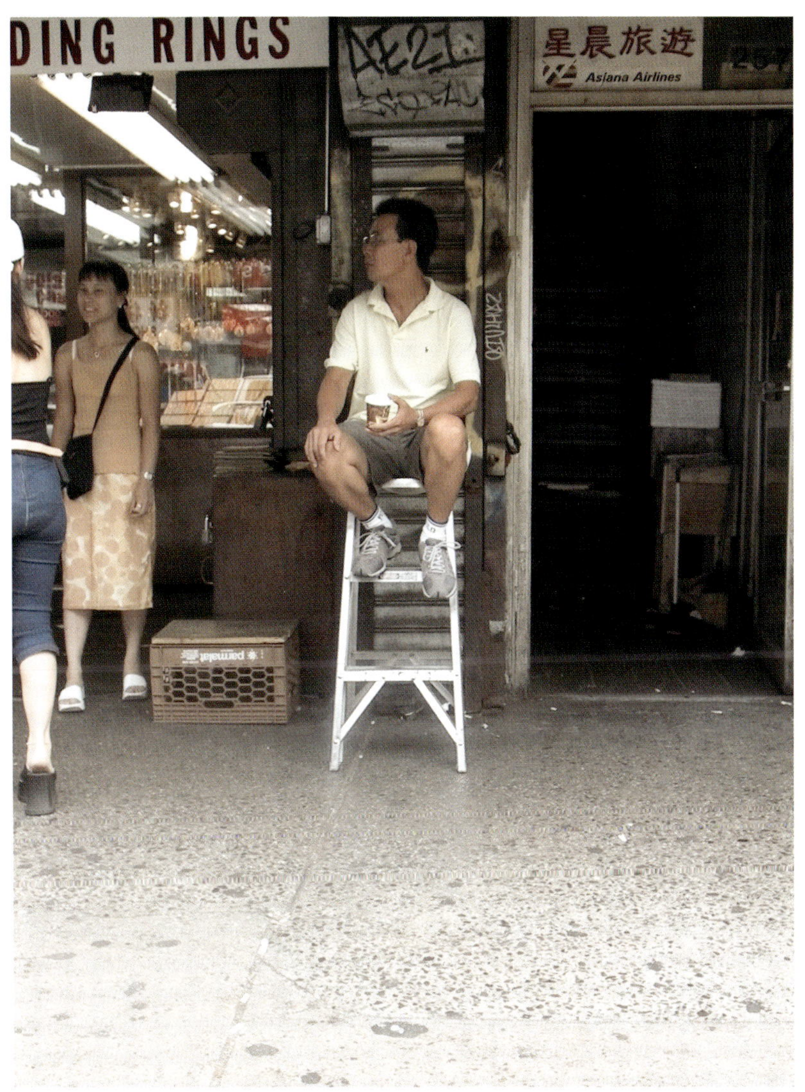
DING RINGS
星晨旅遊
Asiana Airlines
parmalat

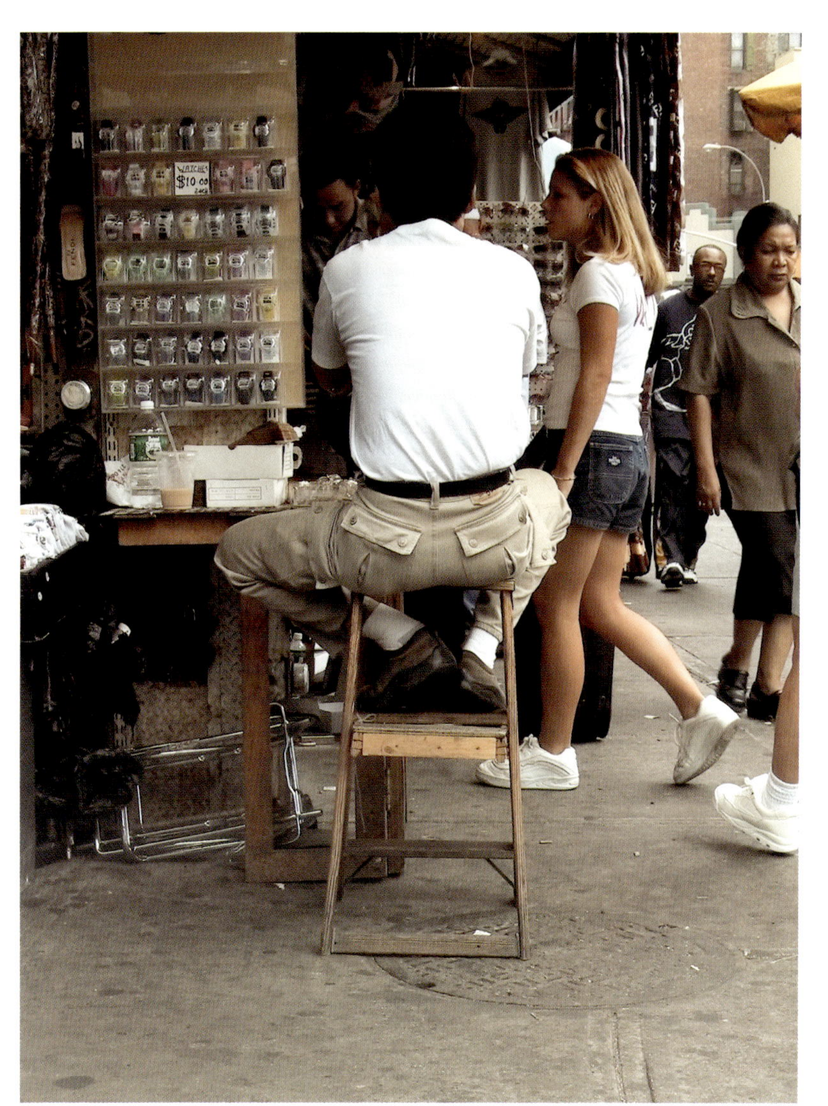
WATCHES
$10.00

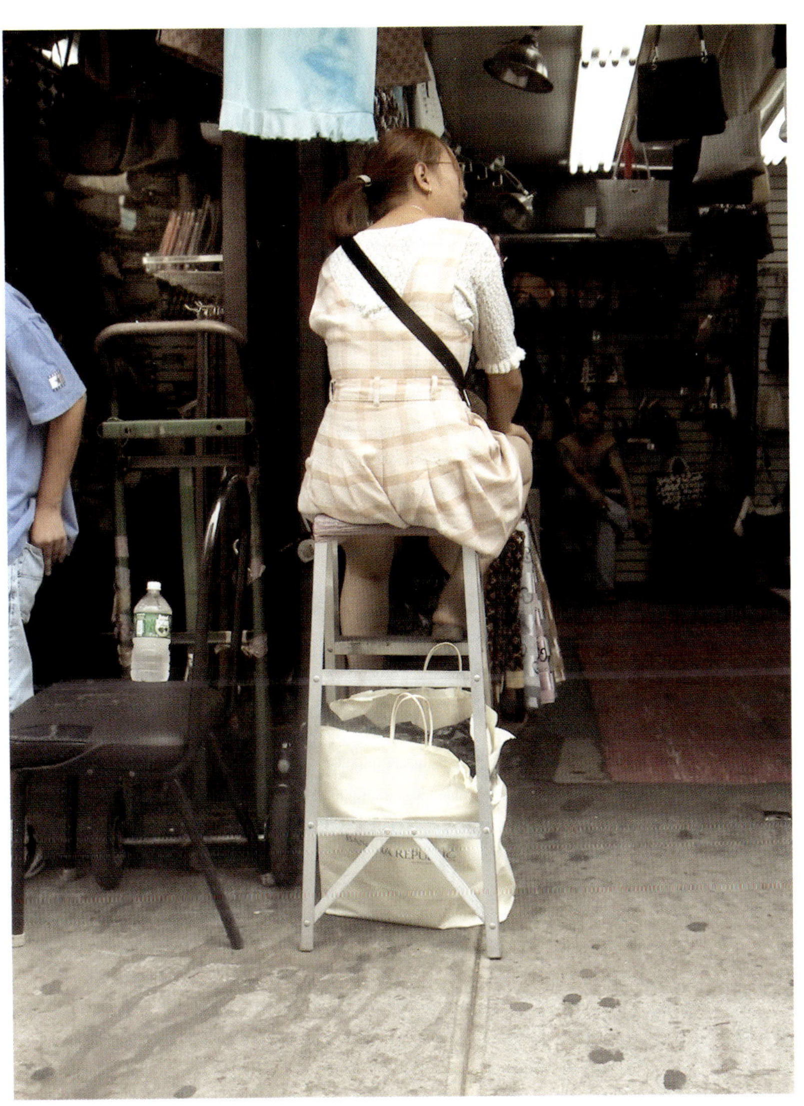

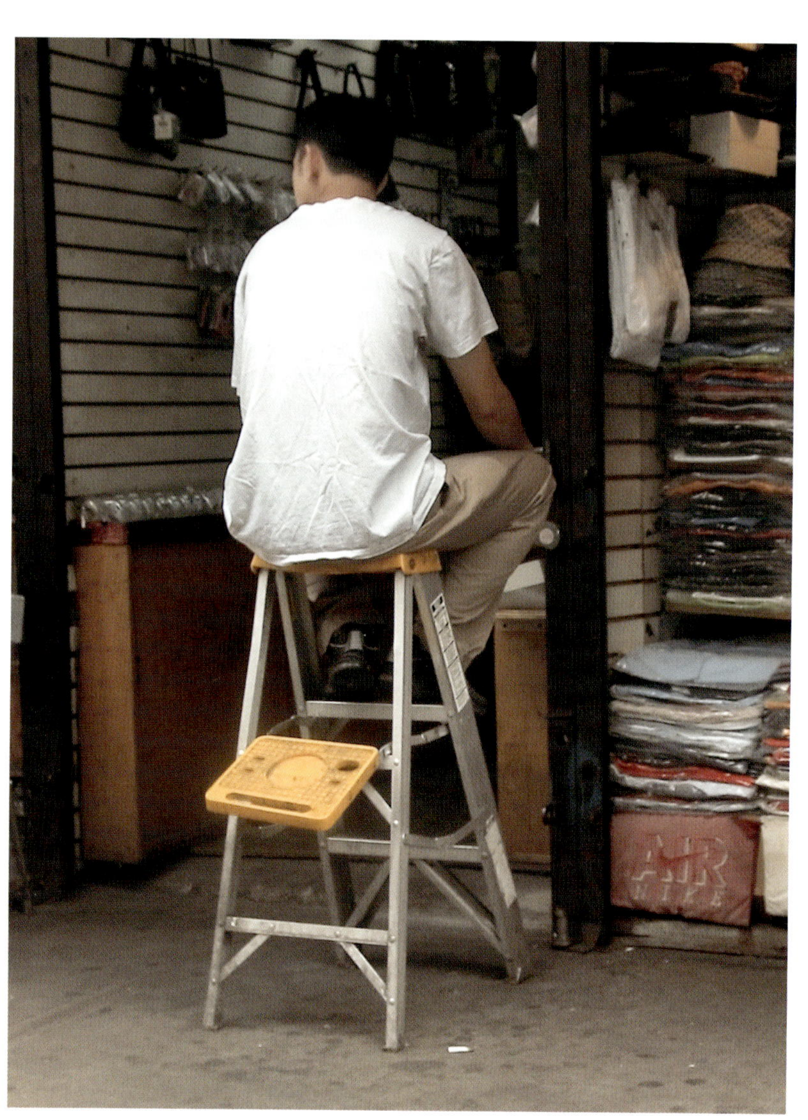
AIR

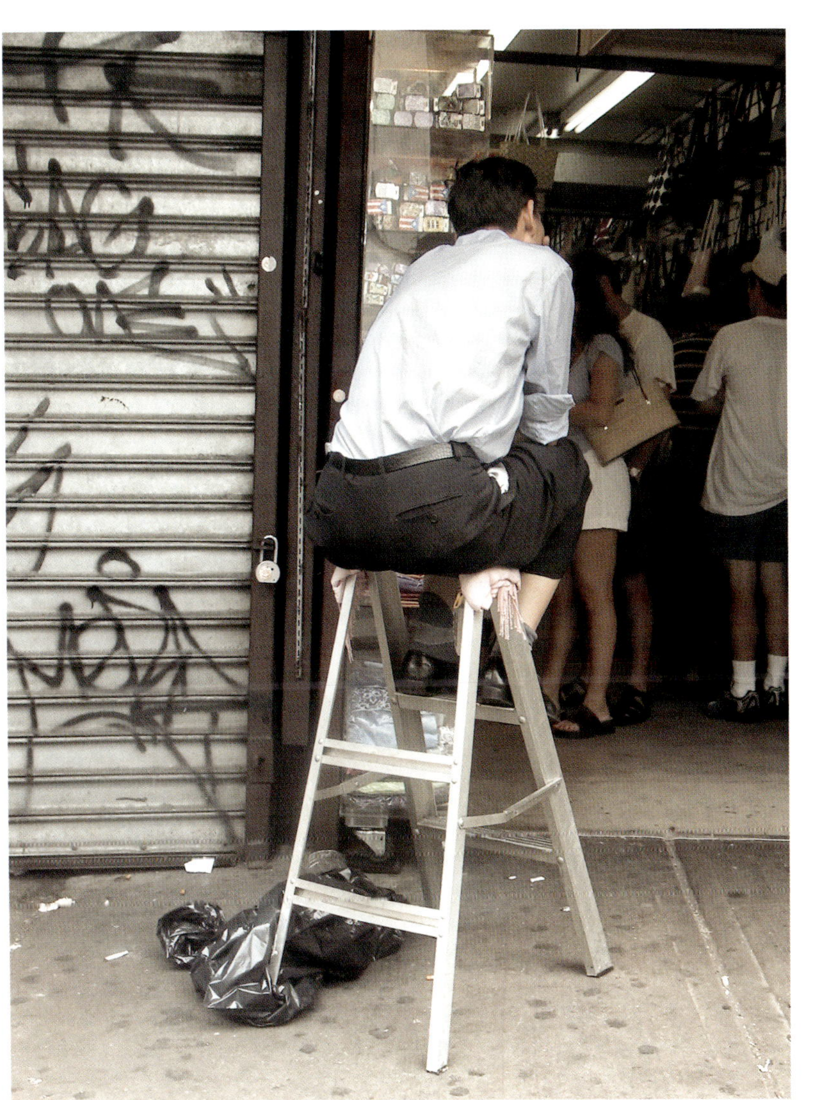

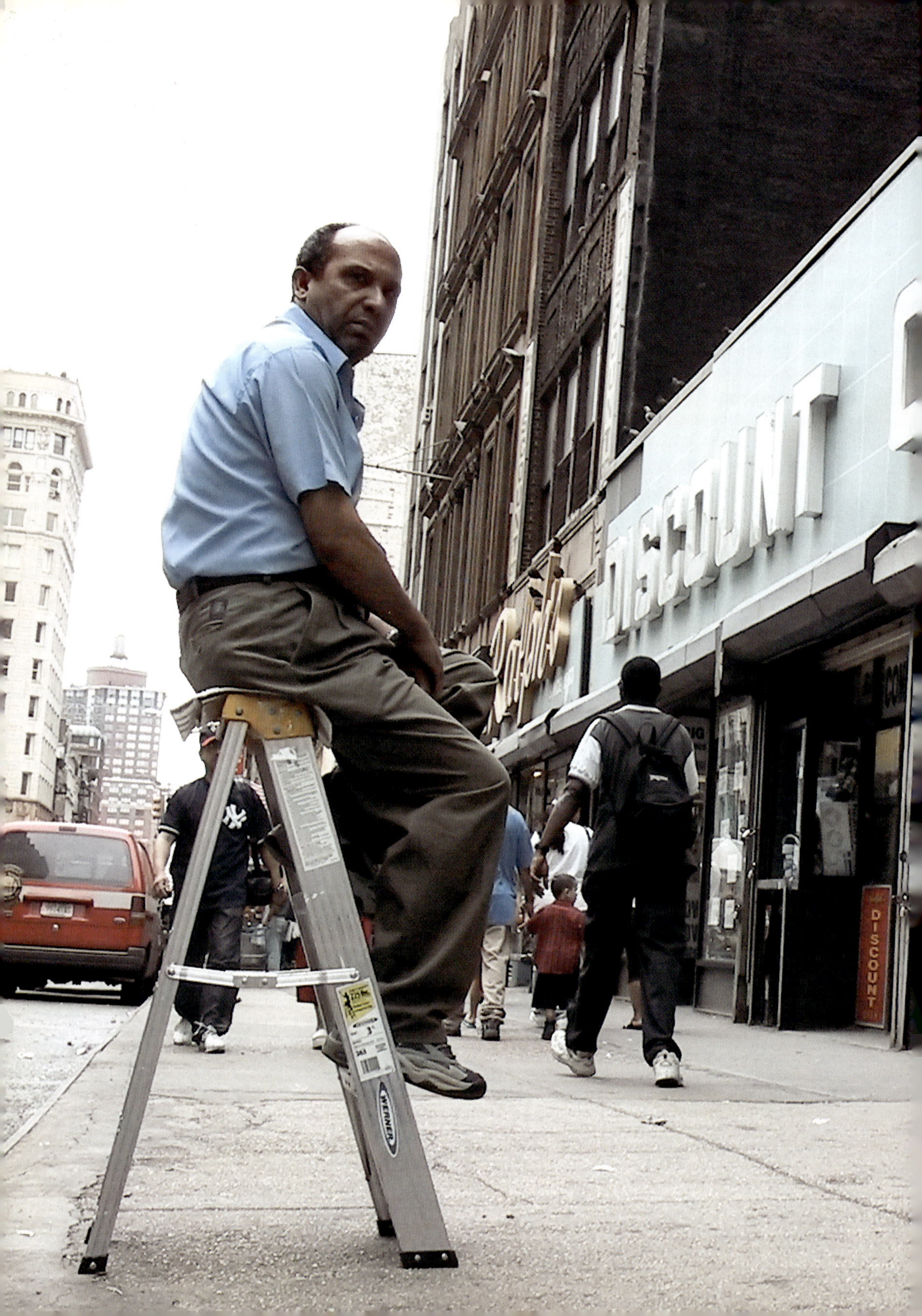
DISCOUNT
DISCOUNT
WERNER

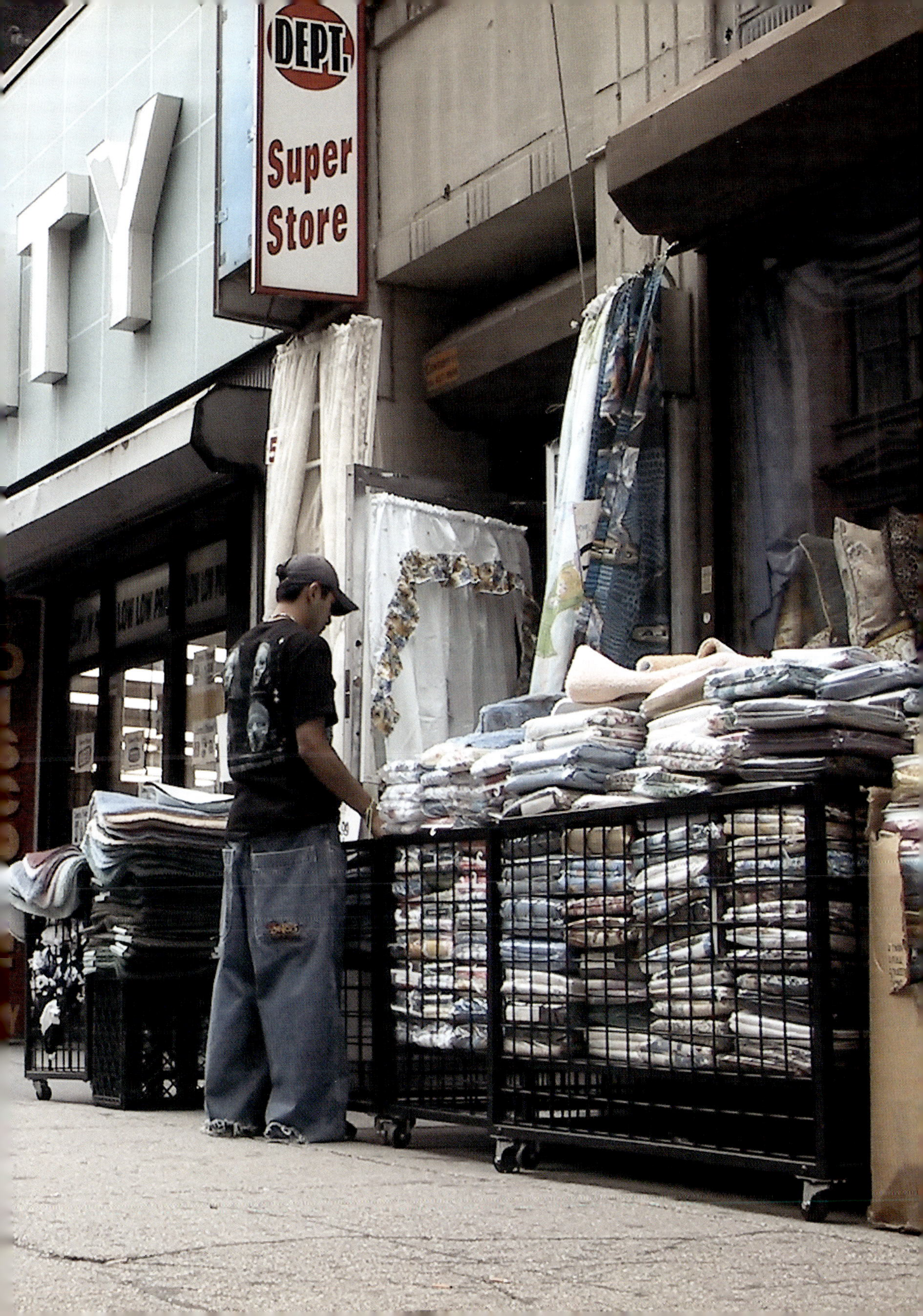
DEPT.
Super
Store

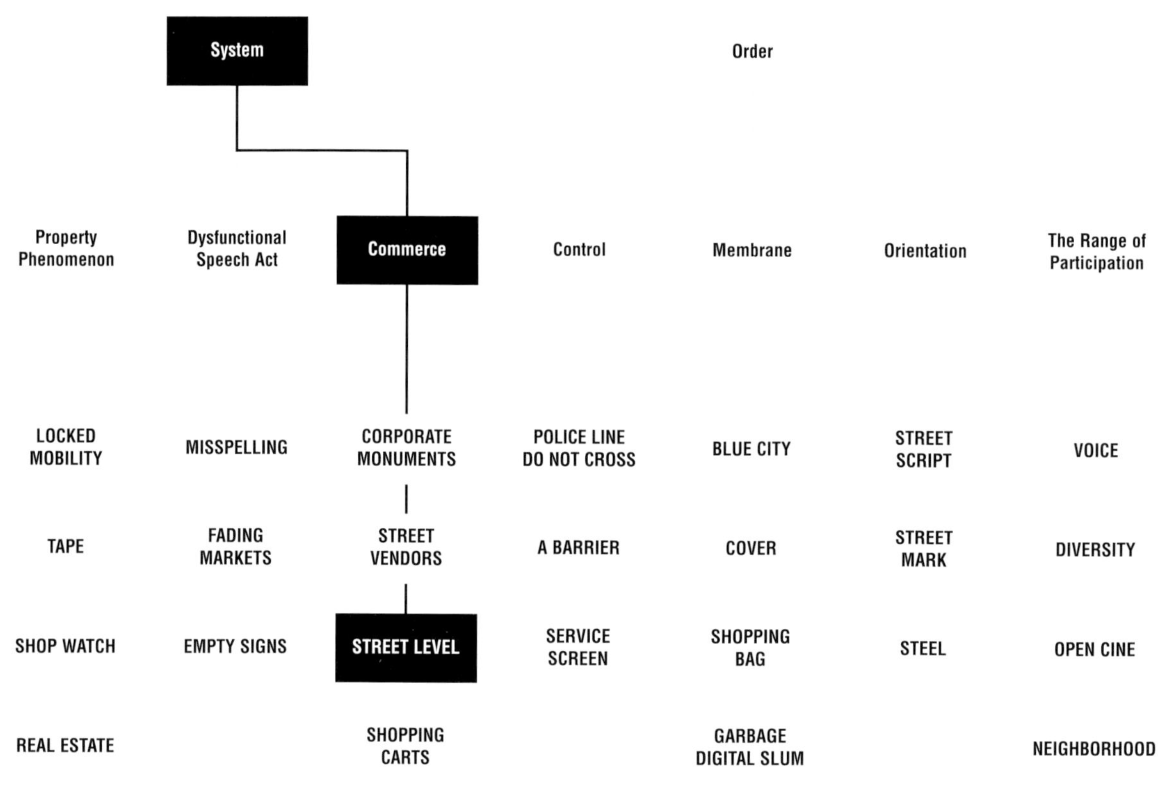
System
Order
Property Phenomenon
Dysfunctional Speech Act
Commerce
Control
Membrane
Orientation
The Range of Participation
LOCKED MOBILITY
MISSPELLING
CORPORATE MONUMENTS
POLICE LINE DO NOT CROSS
BLUE CITY
STREET SCRIPT
VOICE
TAPE
FADING MARKETS
STREET VENDORS
A BARRIER
COVER
STREET MARK
DIVERSITY
SHOP WATCH
EMPTY SIGNS
STREET LEVEL
SERVICE SCREEN
SHOPPING BAG
STEEL
OPEN CINE
REAL ESTATE
SHOPPING CARTS
GARBAGE DIGITAL SLUM
NEIGHBORHOOD

Identity

Alternative Media

Habitual Reinterpretation

STREET LEVEL

Trading Base

CAR DOOR

PUBLIC CHAIRS

LABELING.

PLASTIC CRATES

POLE POST

STANDPIPES

PRAY JESUS

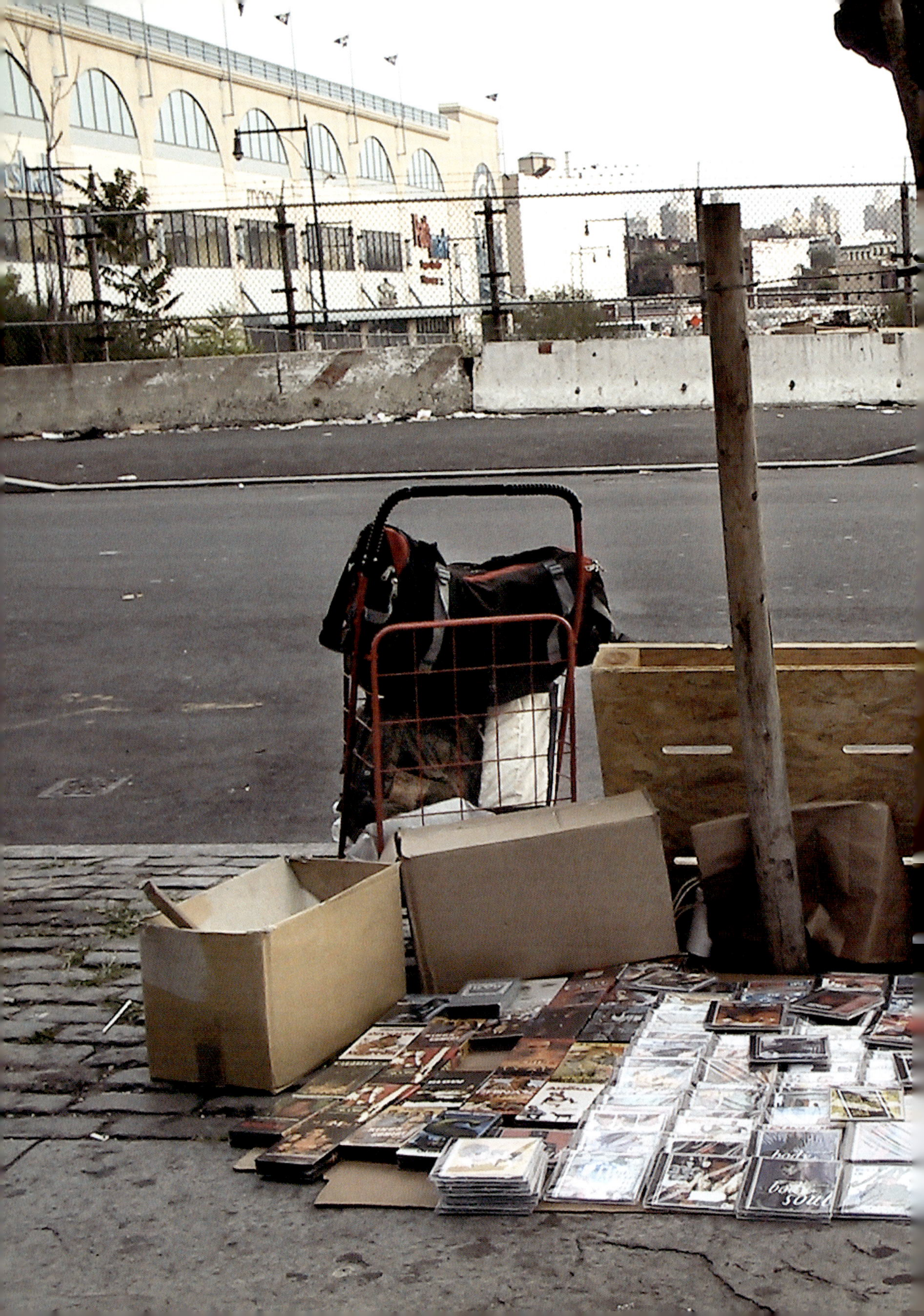

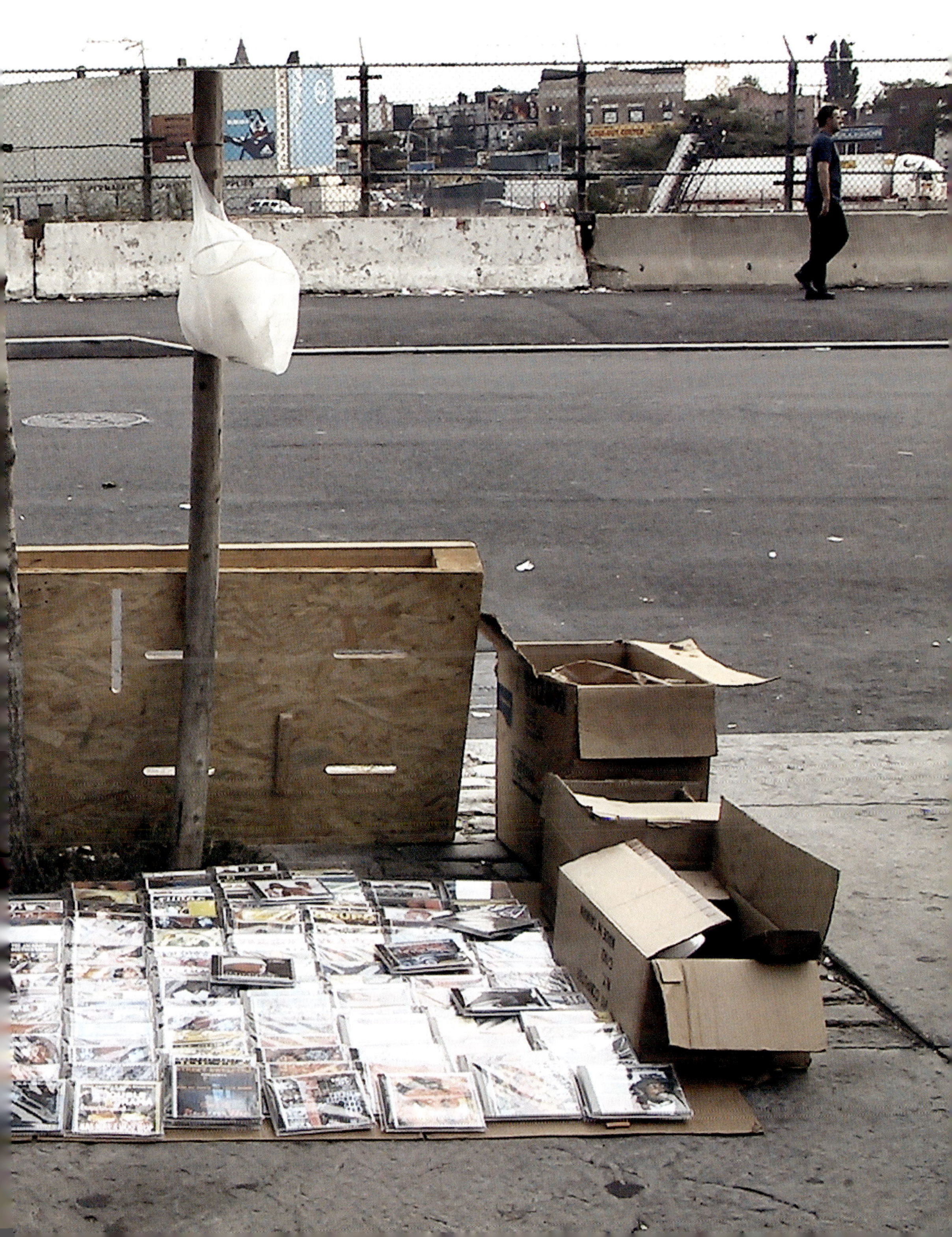

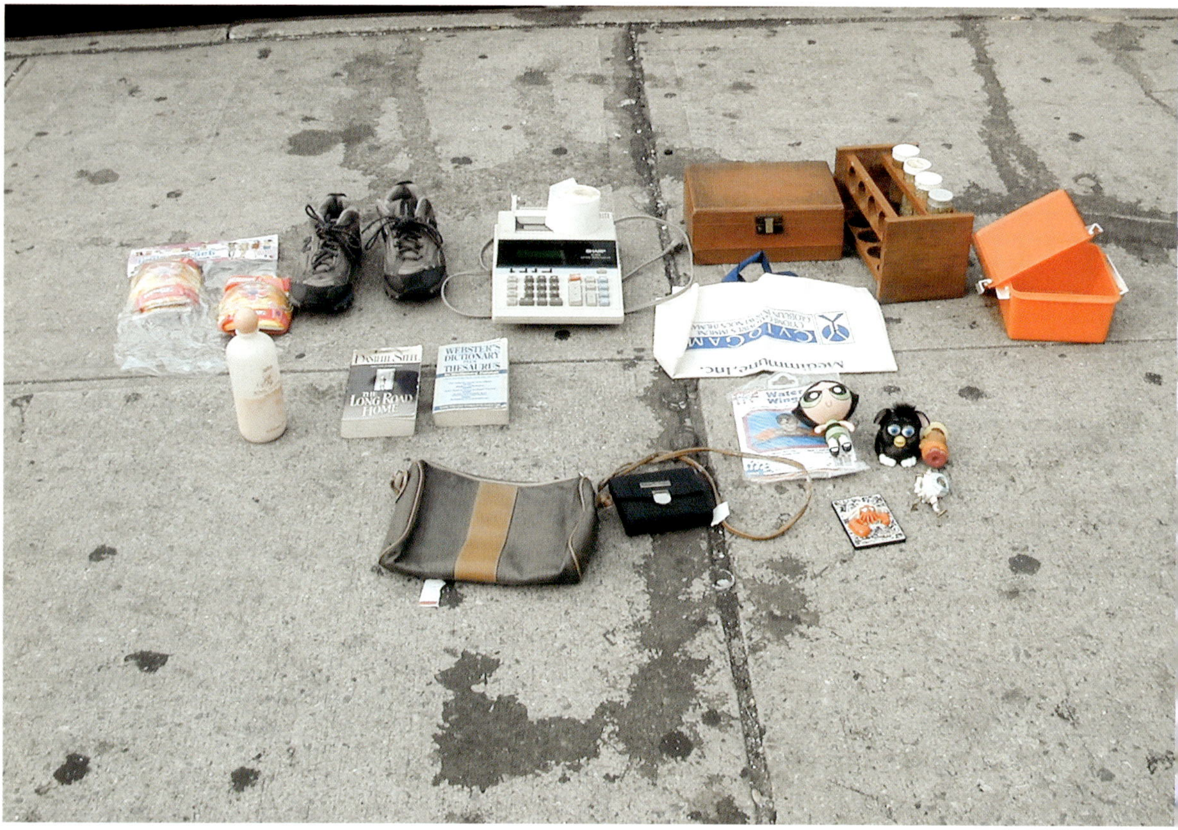
SHARP
WEBSTER'S DICTIONARY
THE LONG ROAD HOME

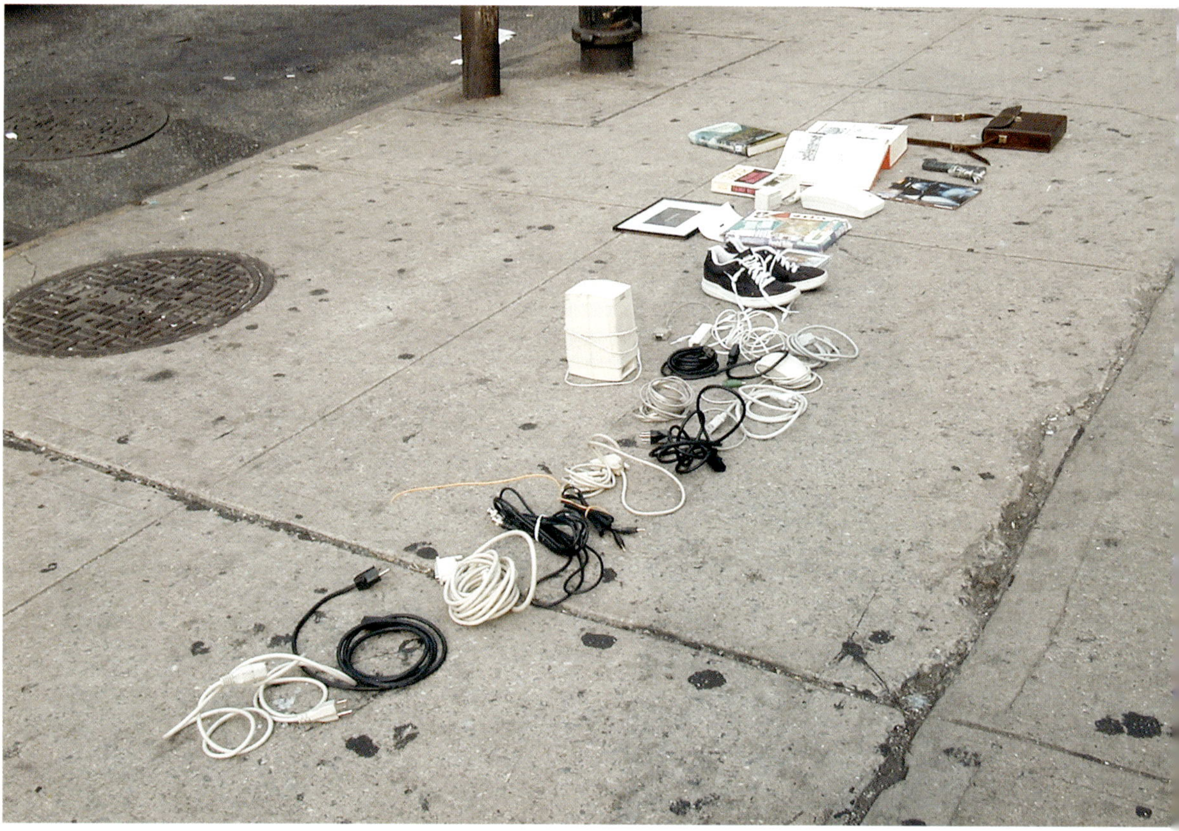

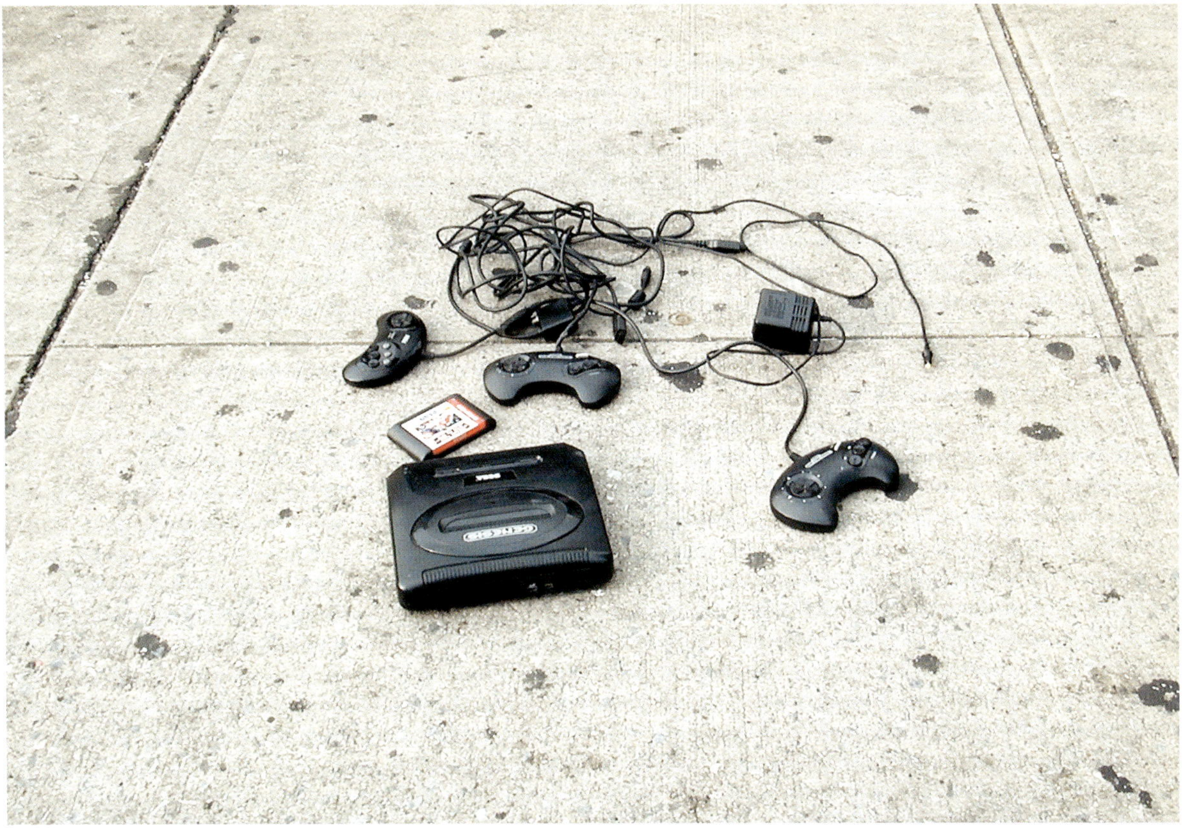

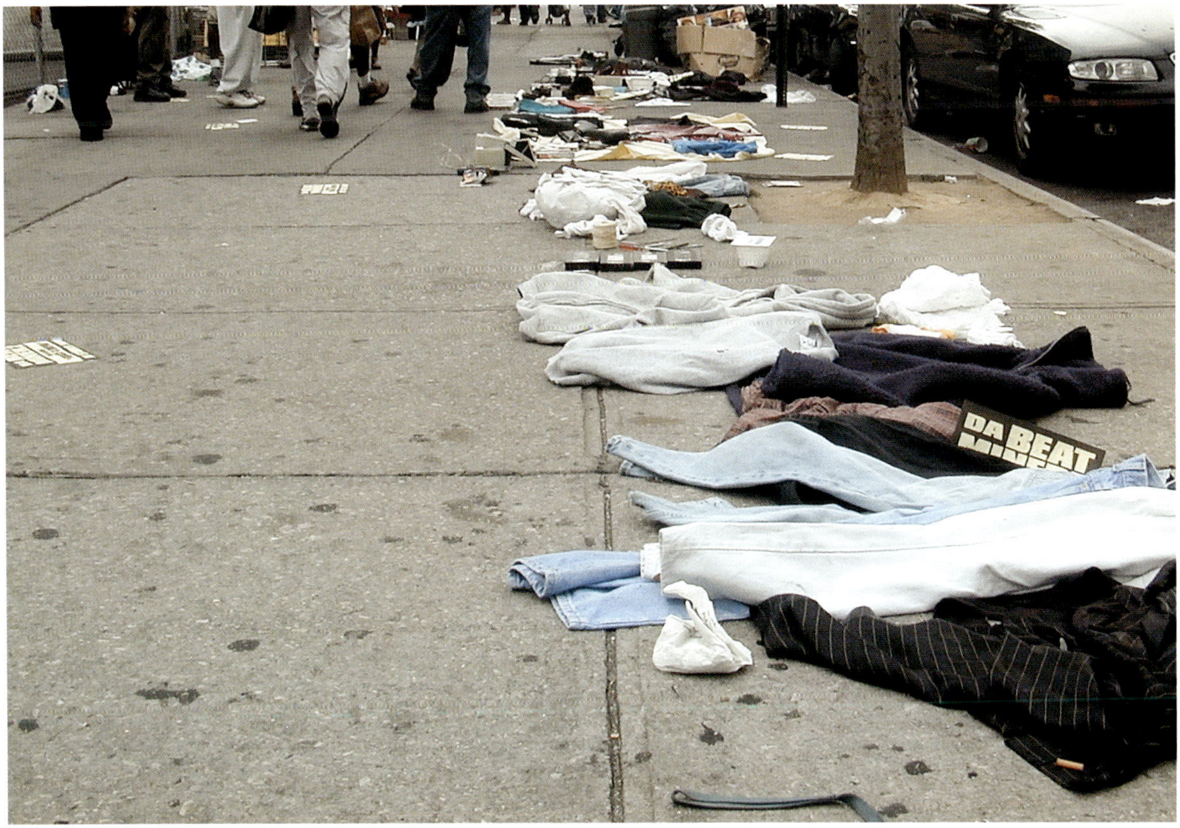

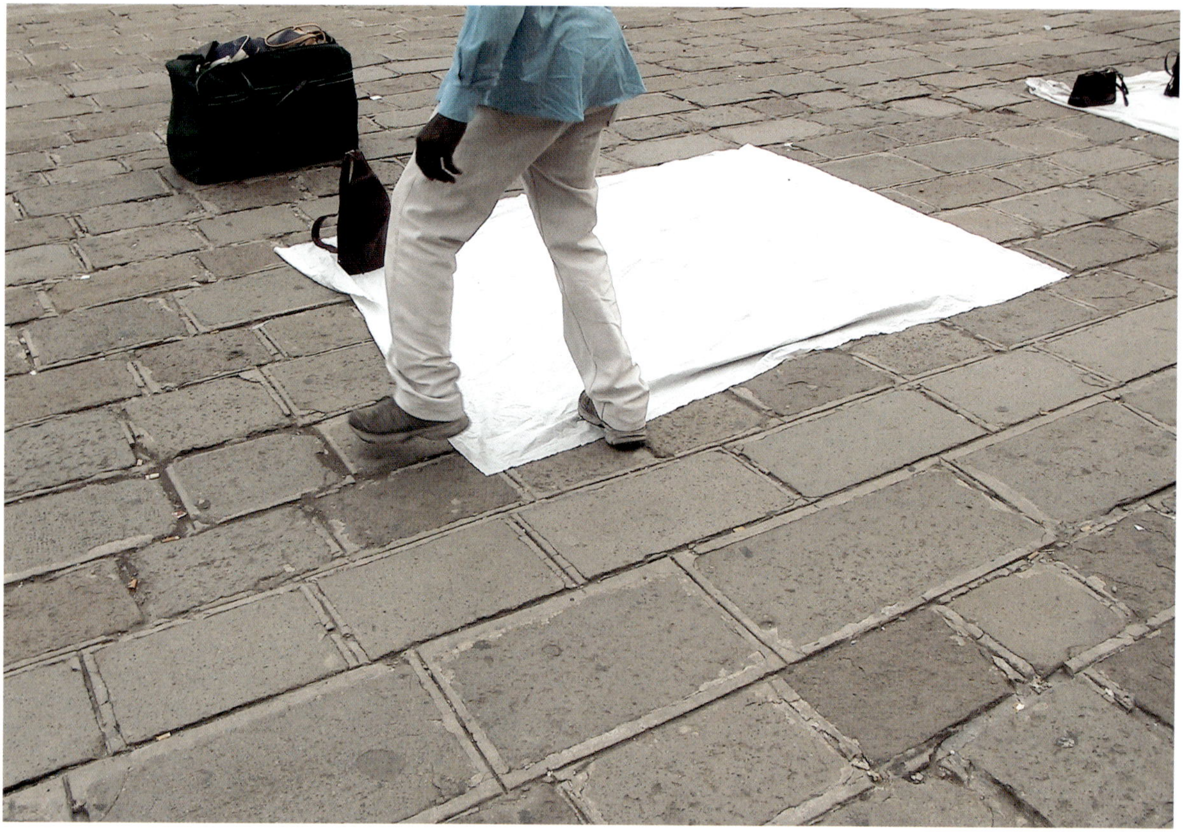

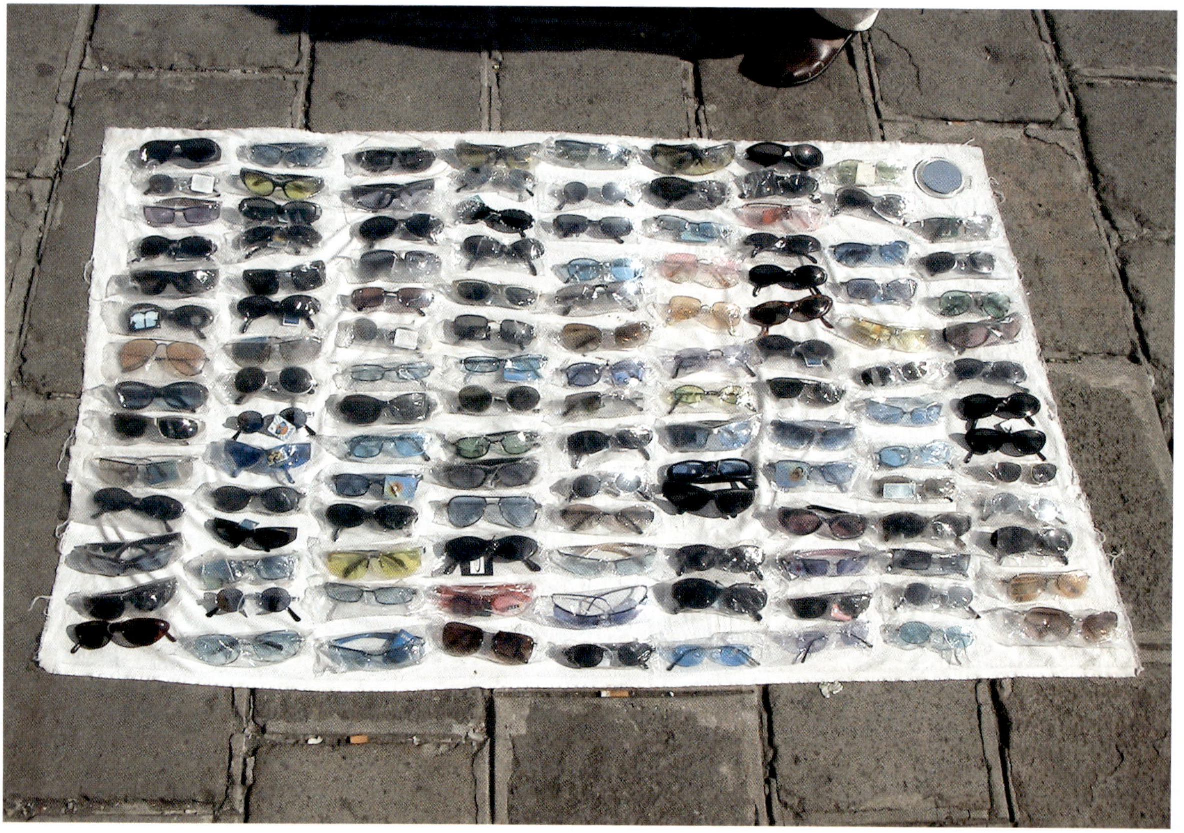

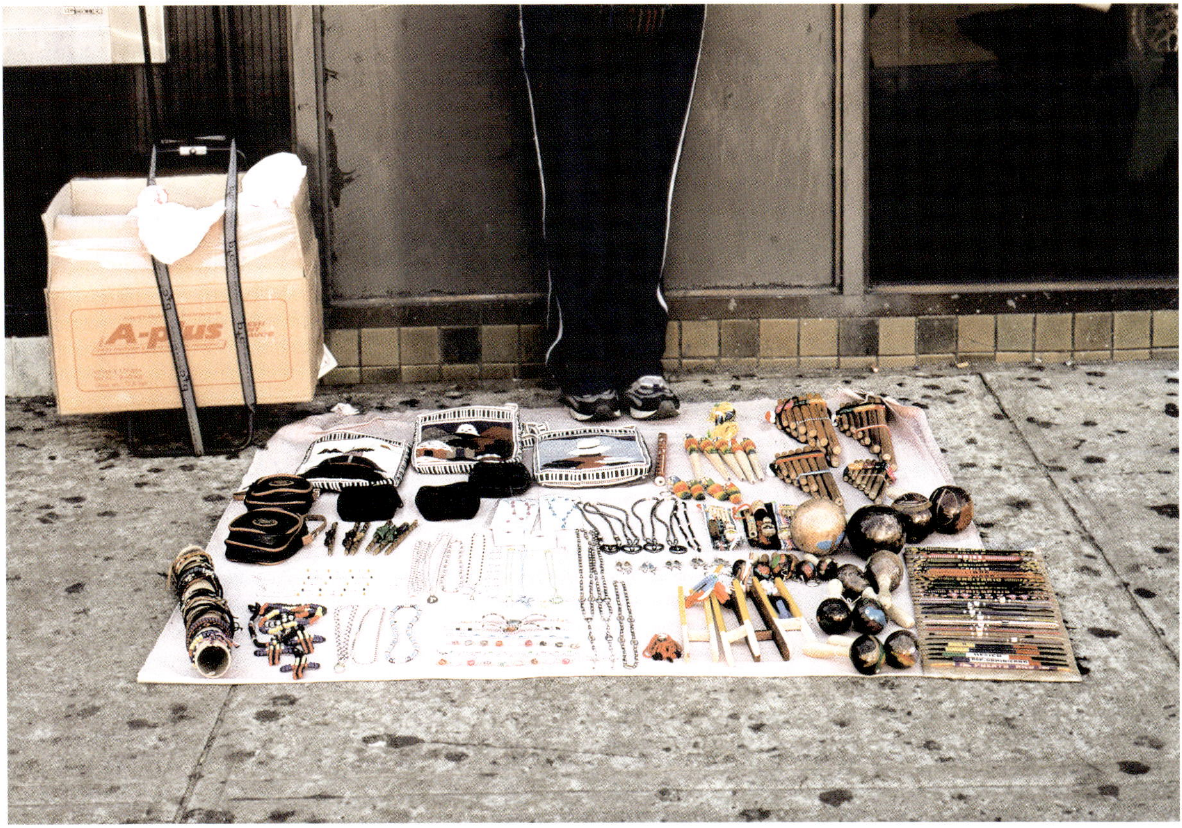

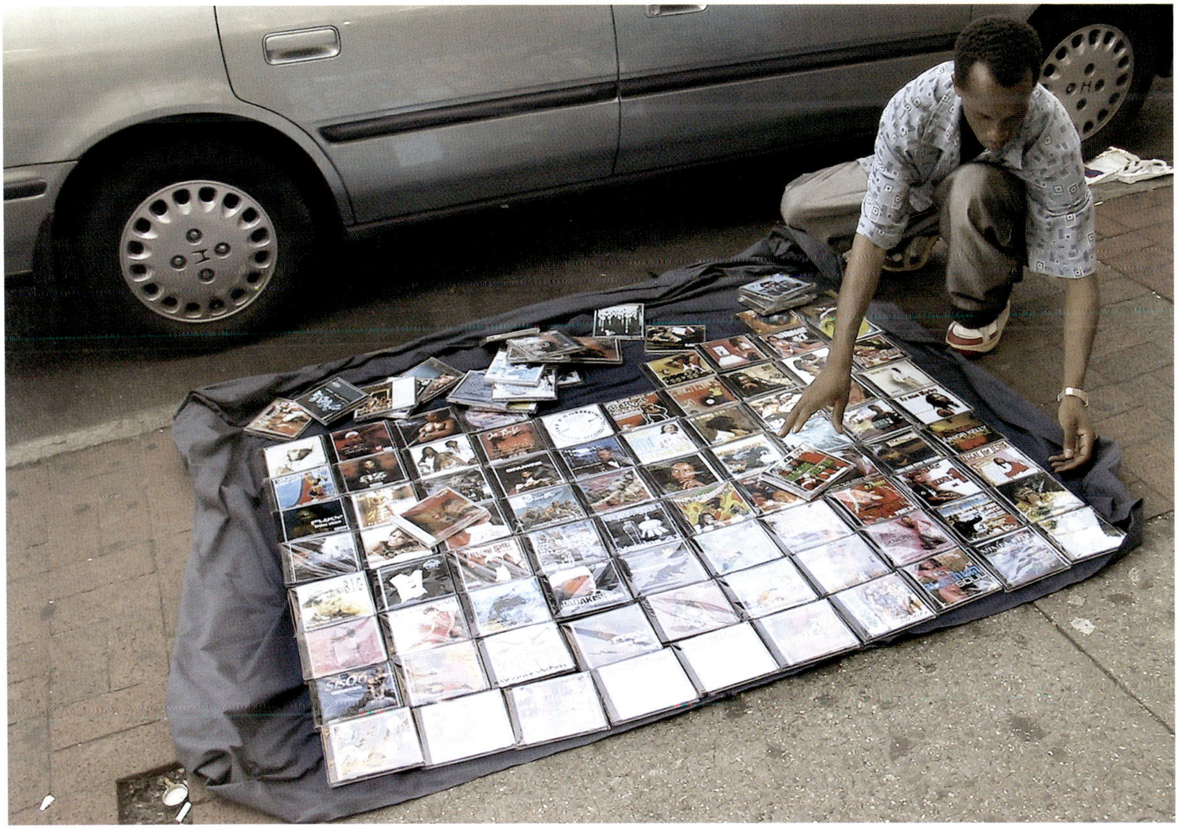

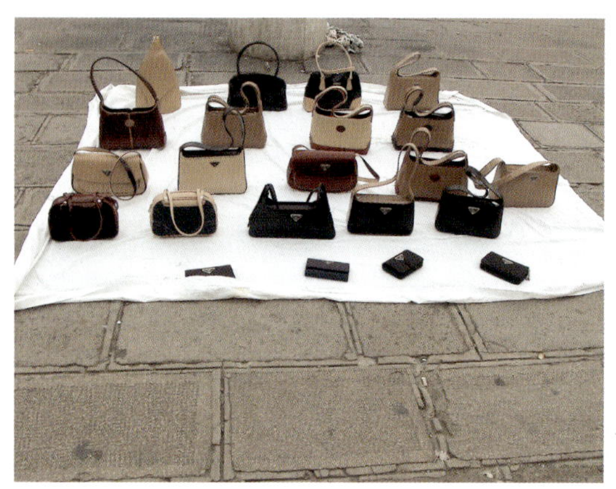
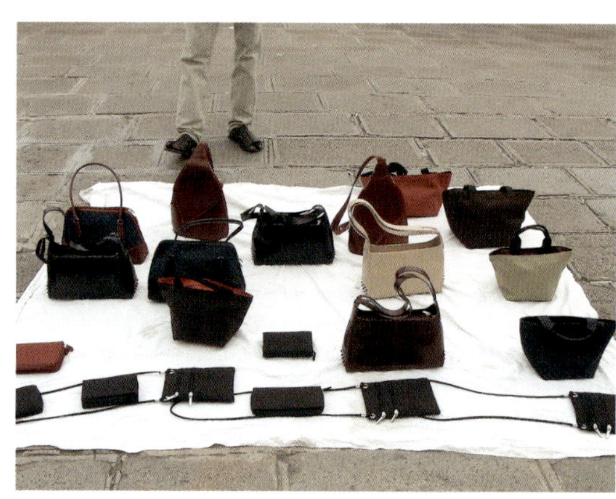
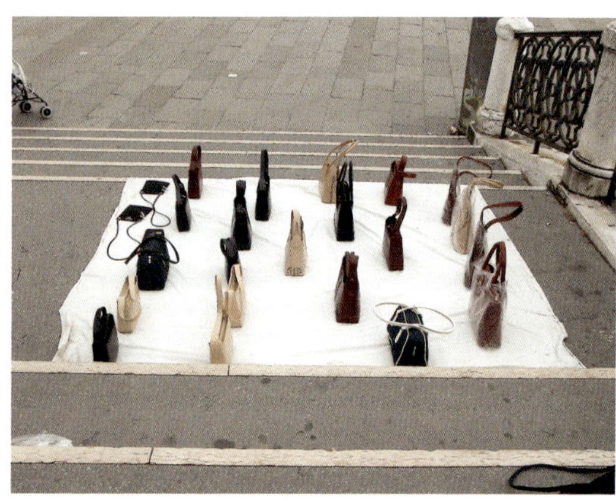
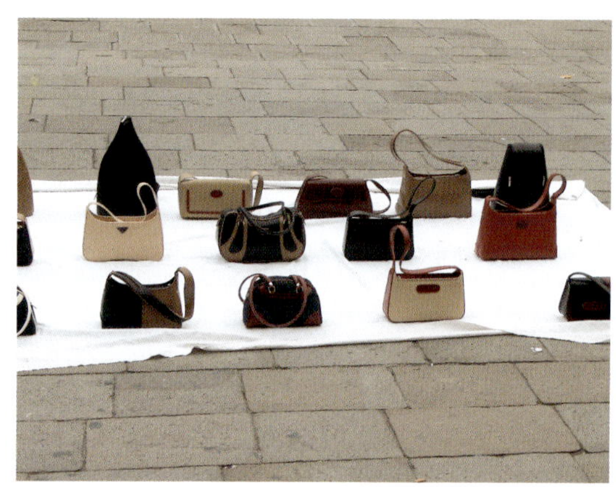
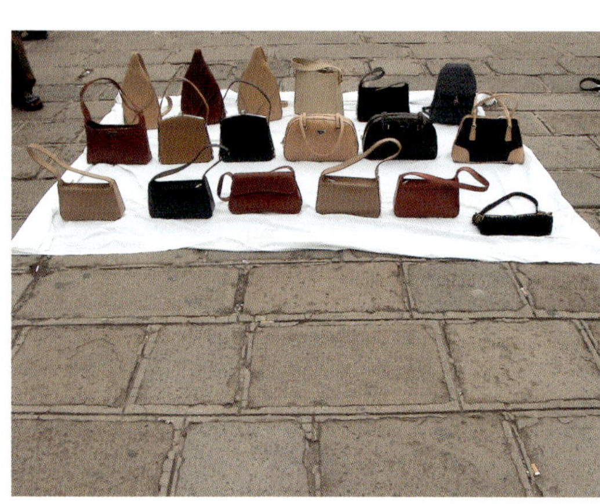
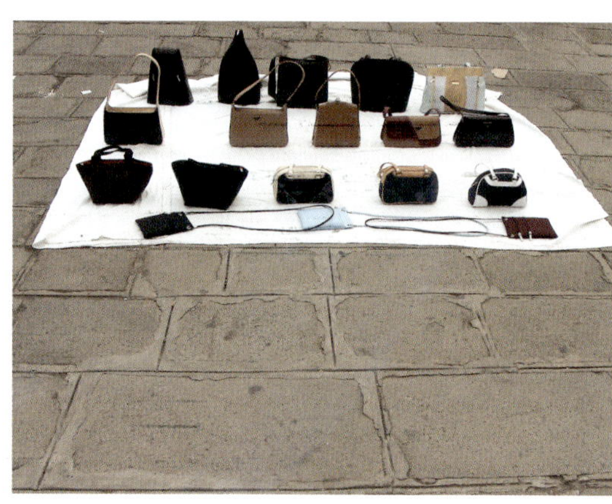

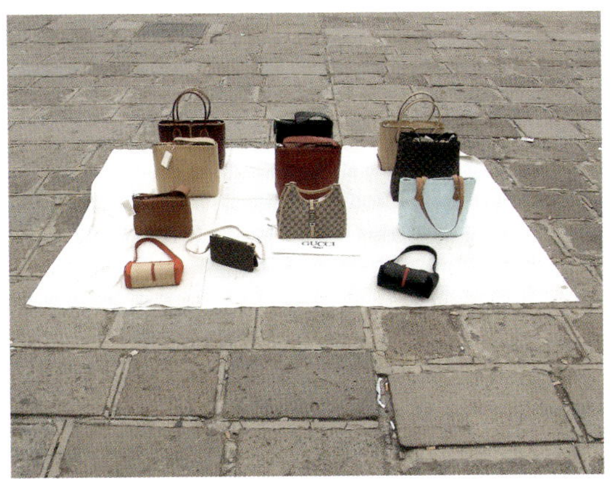
GUCCI

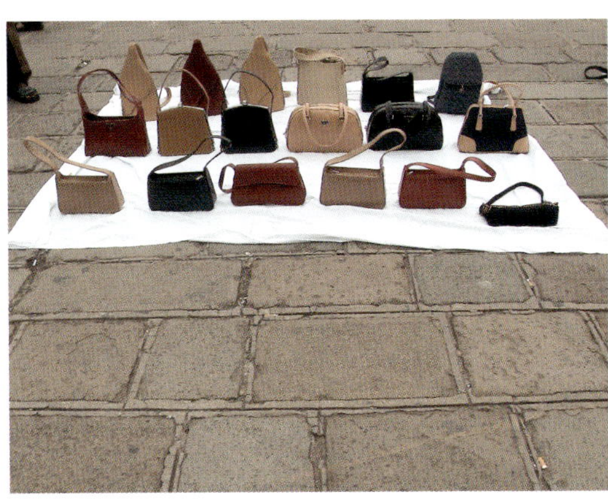

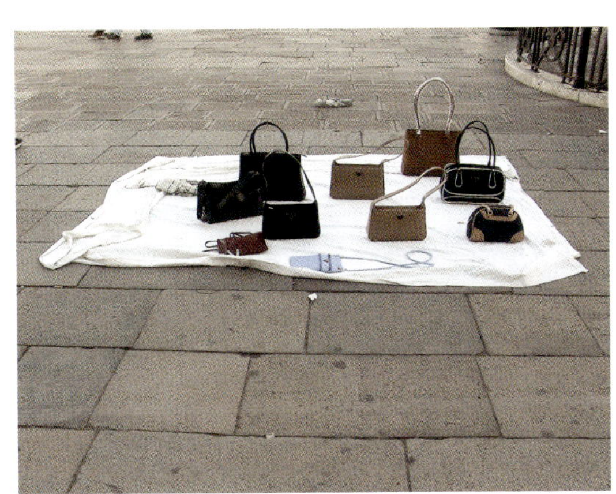

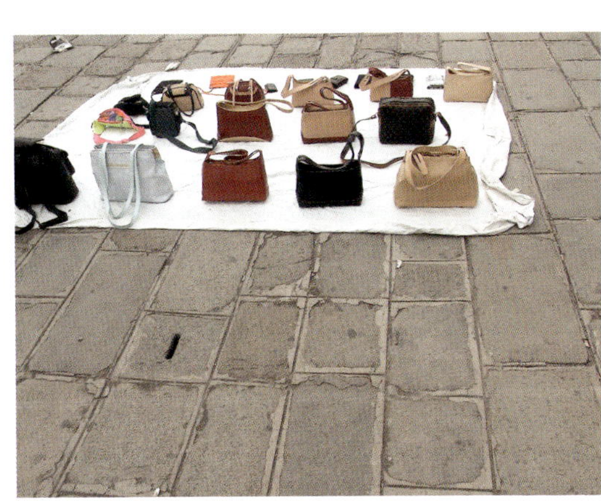

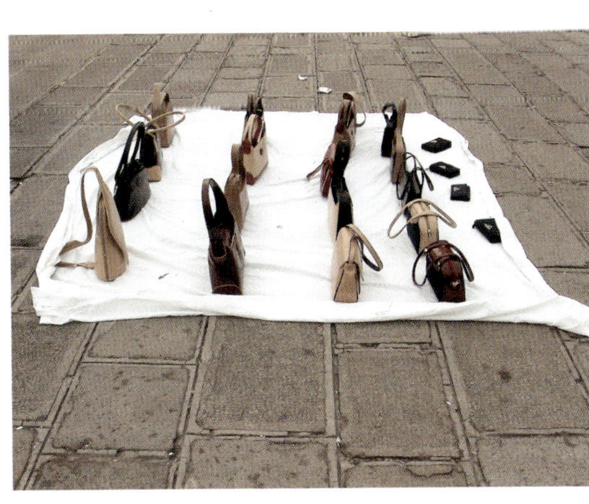

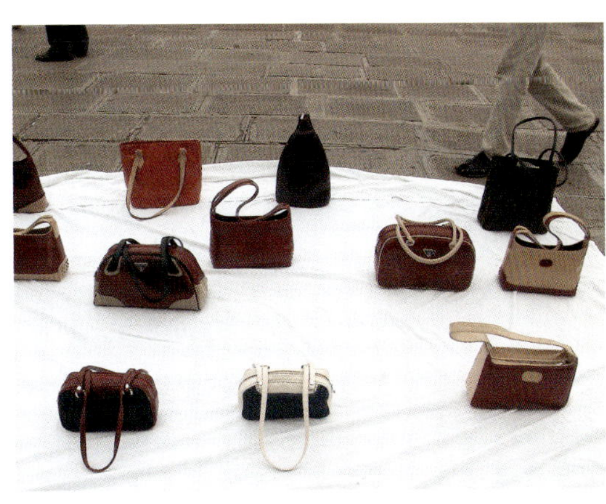

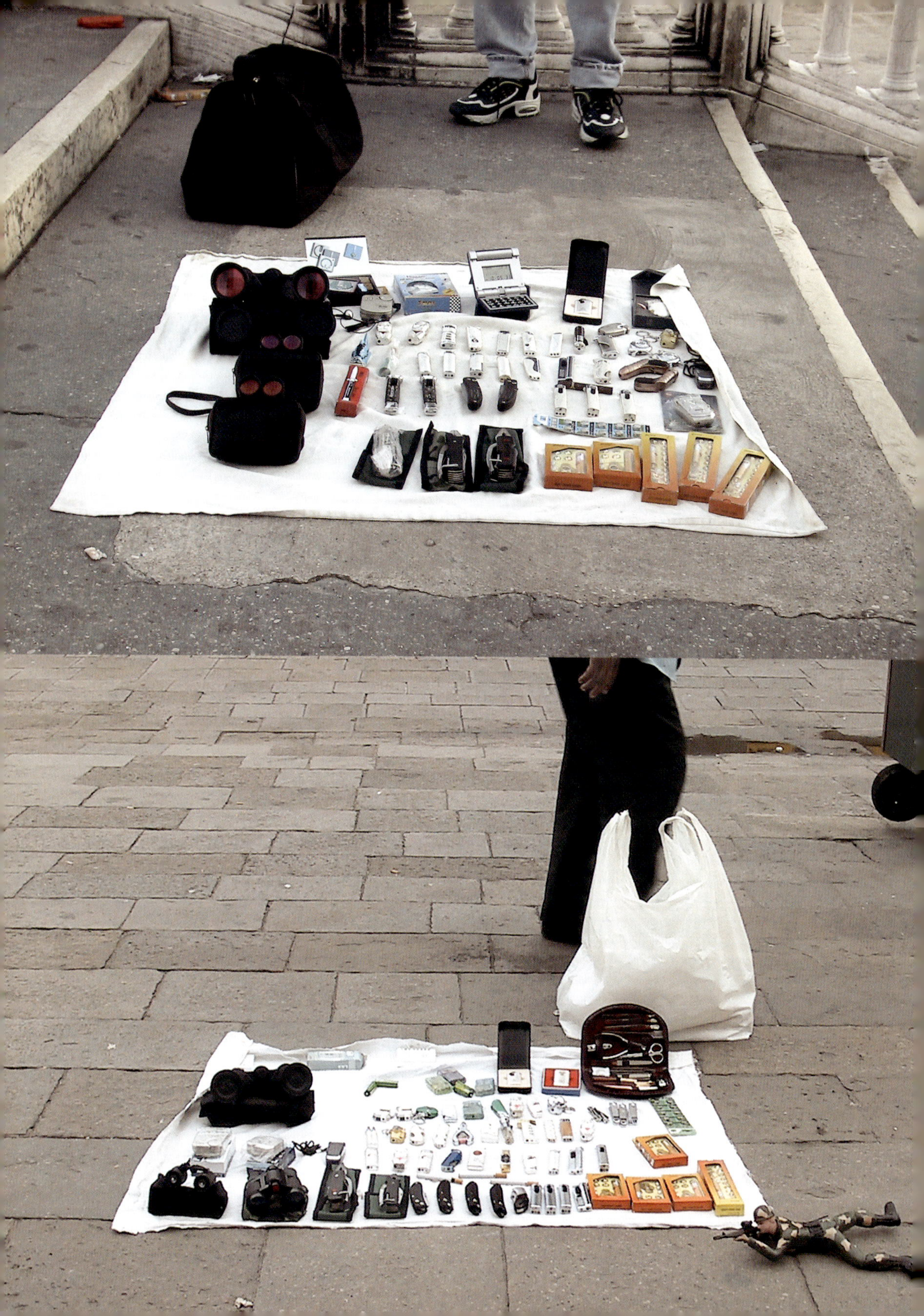

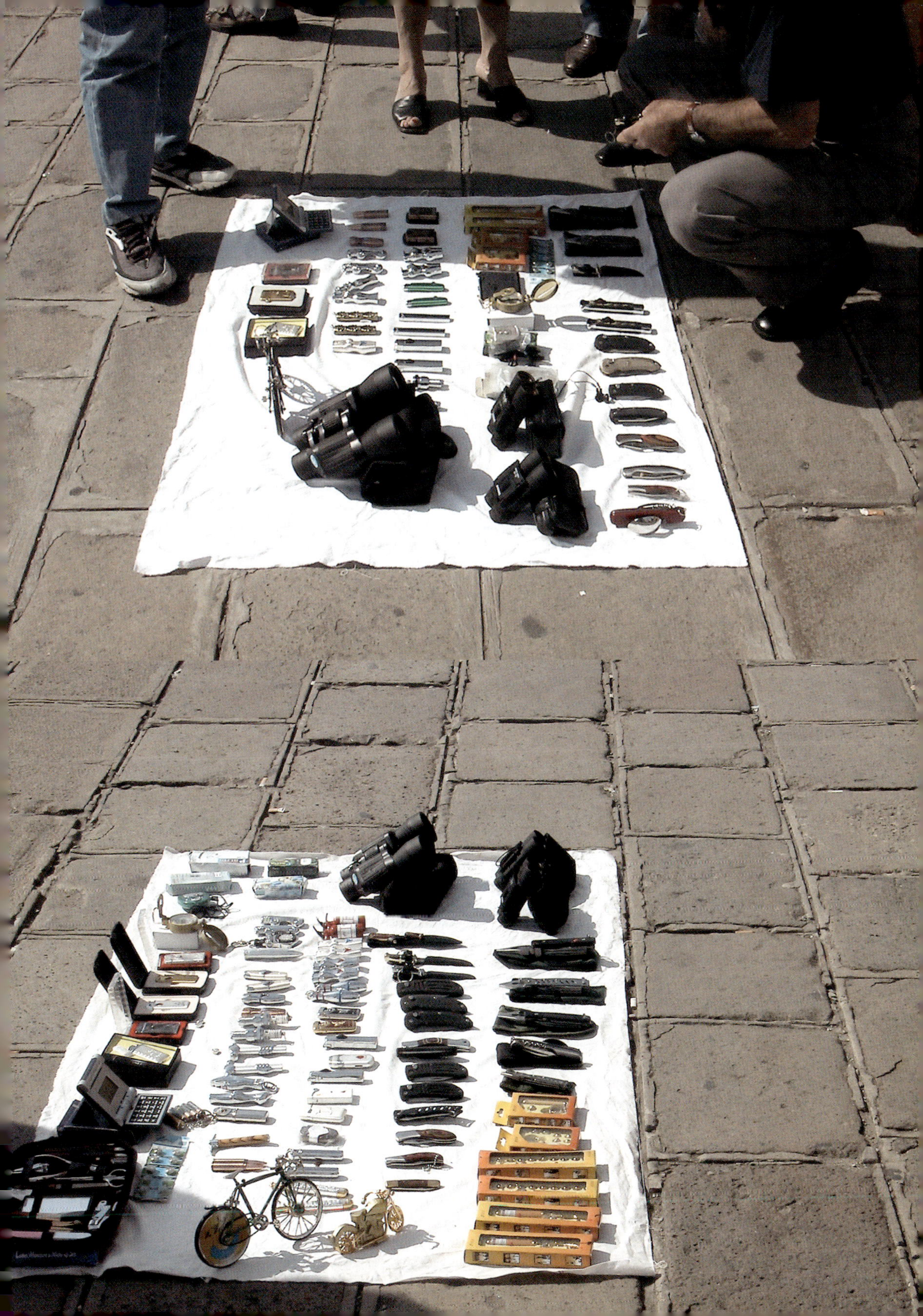

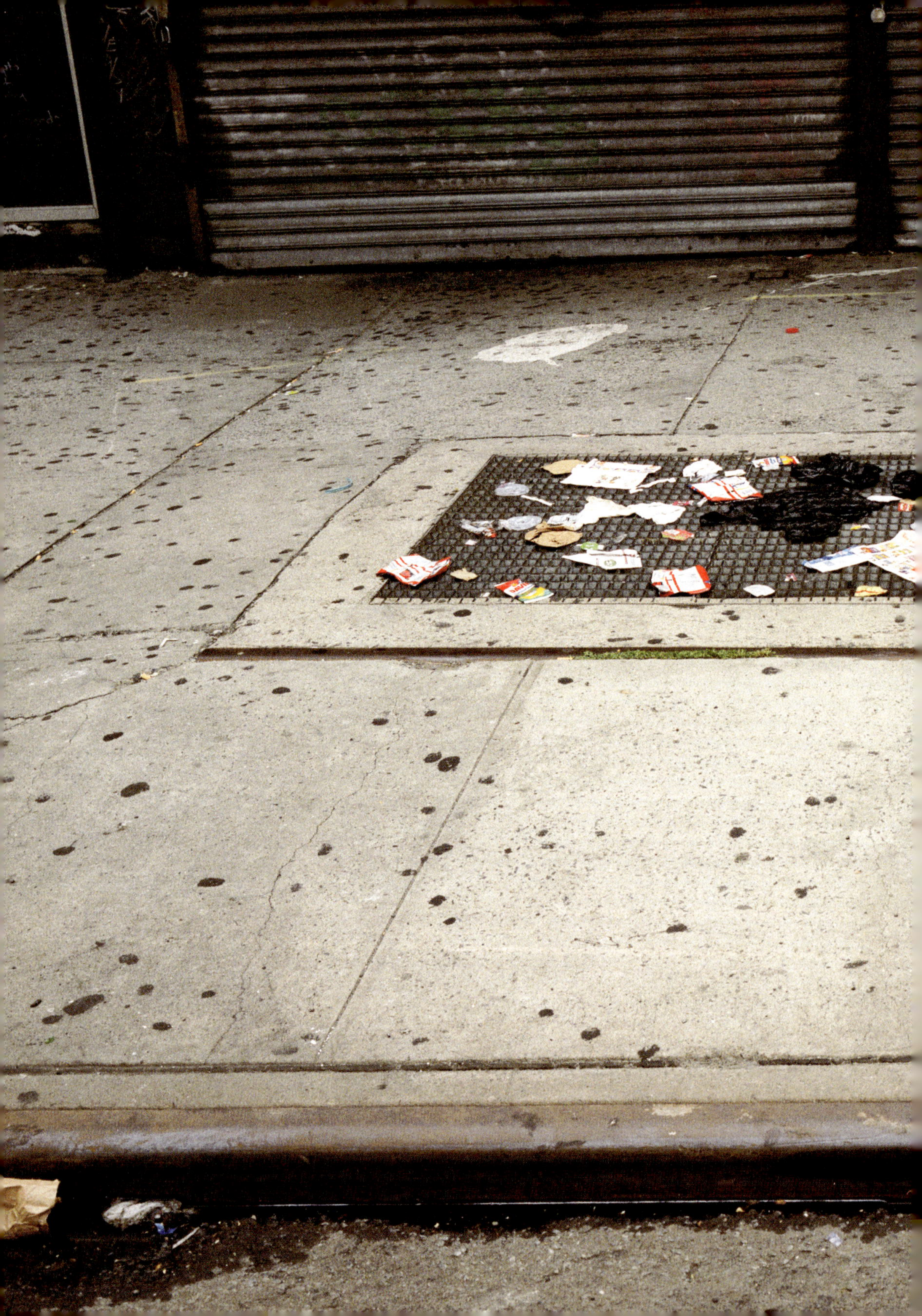

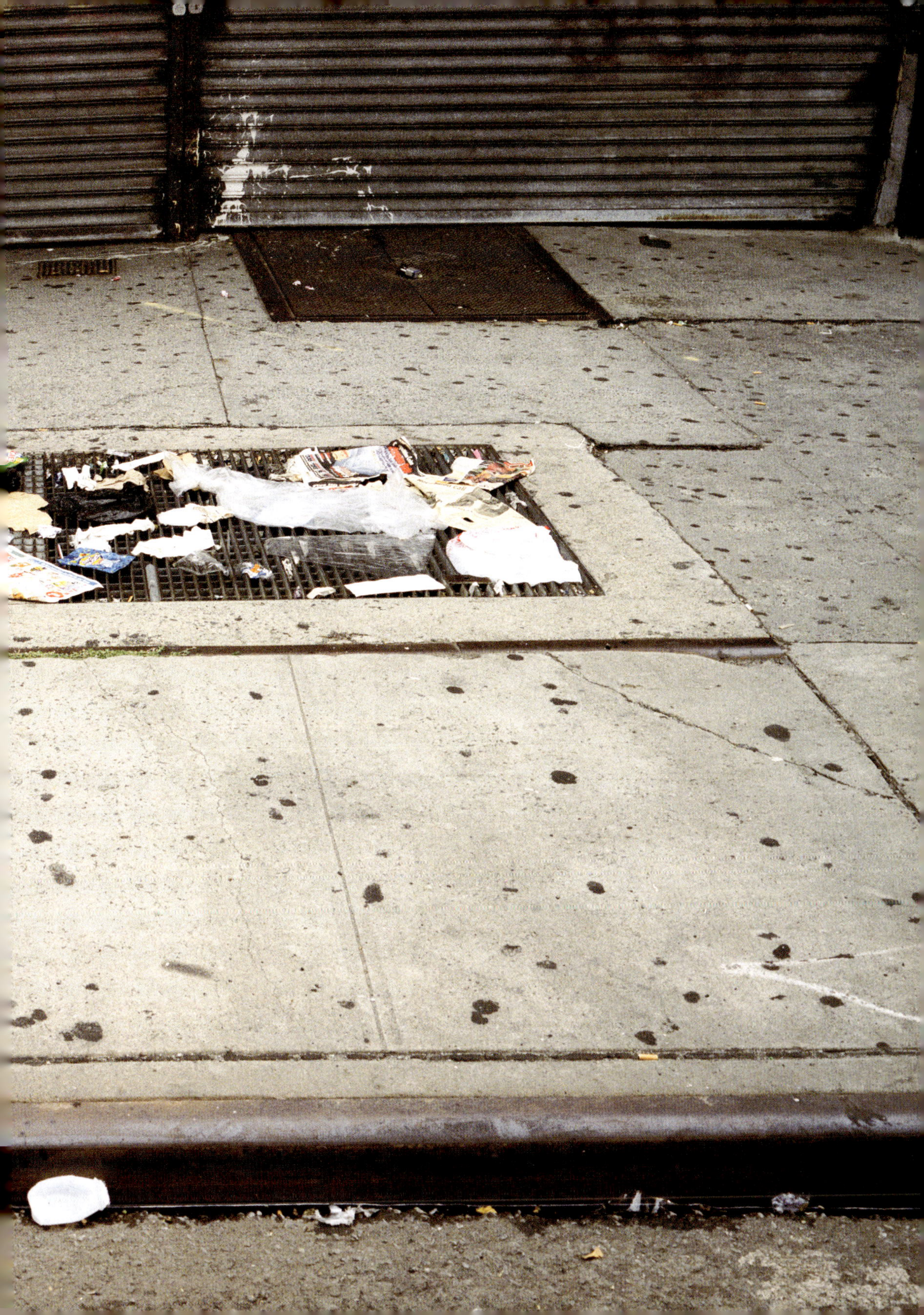

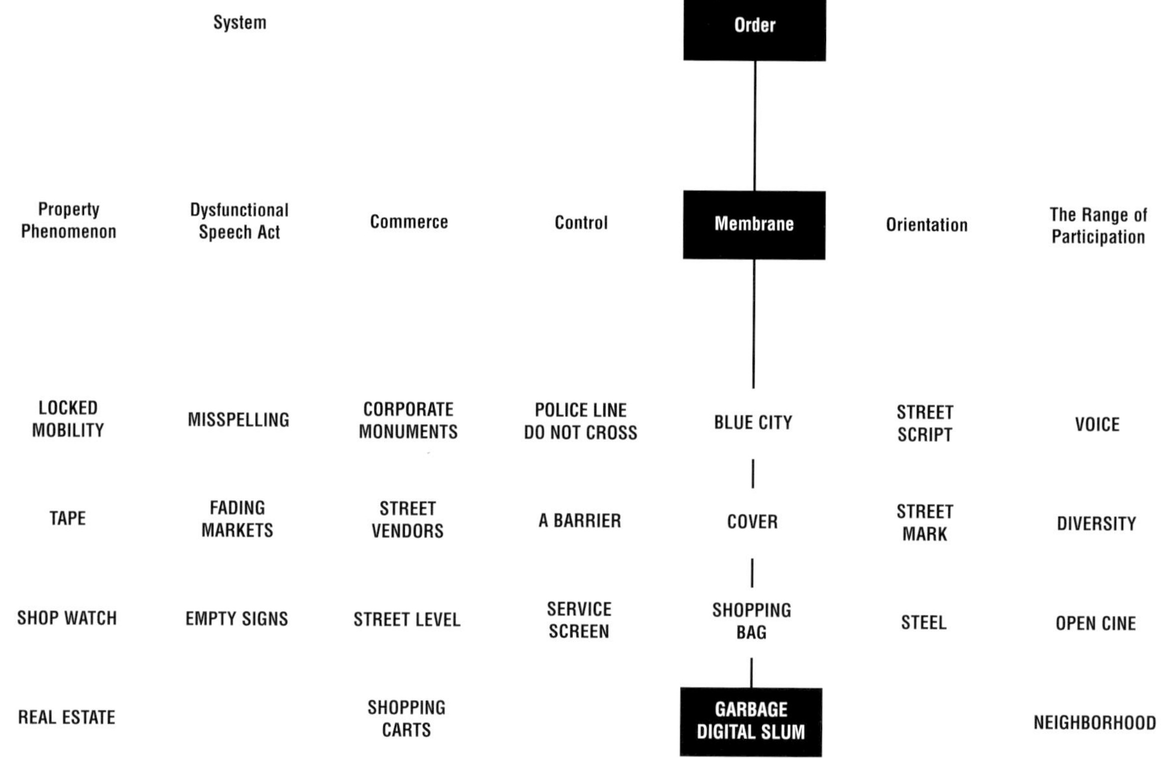
System
Order
Property Phenomenon
Dysfunctional Speech Act
Commerce
Control
Membrane
Orientation
The Range of Participation
LOCKED MOBILITY
MISSPELLING
CORPORATE MONUMENTS
POLICE LINE DO NOT CROSS
BLUE CITY
STREET SCRIPT
VOICE
TAPE
FADING MARKETS
STREET VENDORS
A BARRIER
COVER
STREET MARK
DIVERSITY
SHOP WATCH
EMPTY SIGNS
STREET LEVEL
SERVICE SCREEN
SHOPPING BAG
STEEL
OPEN CINE
REAL ESTATE
SHOPPING CARTS
GARBAGE DIGITAL SLUM
NEIGHBORHOOD

Identity

Alternative Media

Habitual Reinterpretation

GARBAGE / DIGITAL SLUM

Accelerated Cycle of Obsolescence

CAR DOOR

PUBLIC CHAIRS

LABELING.

PLASTIC CRATES

POLE POST

STANDPIPES

PRAY JESUS

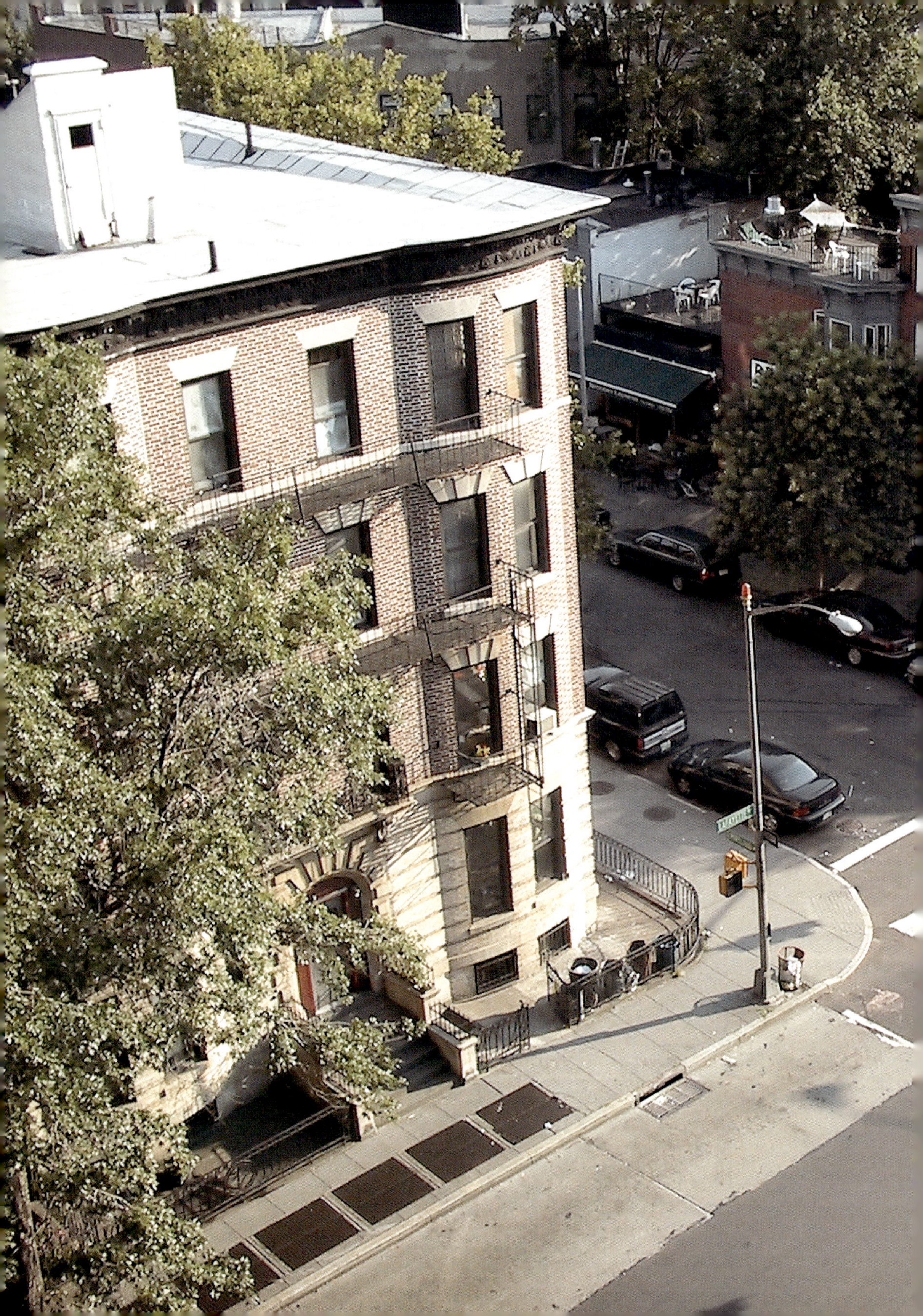

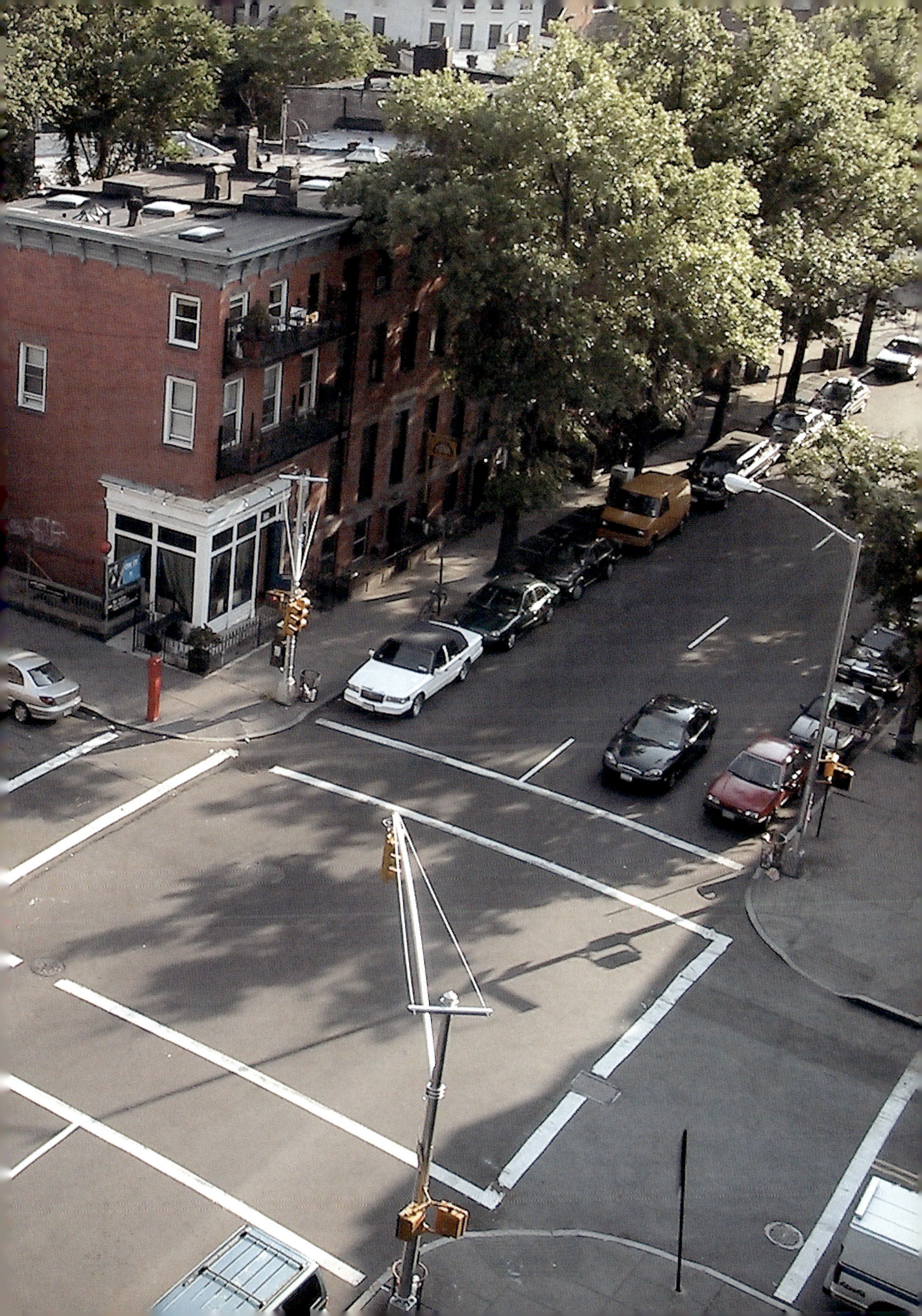

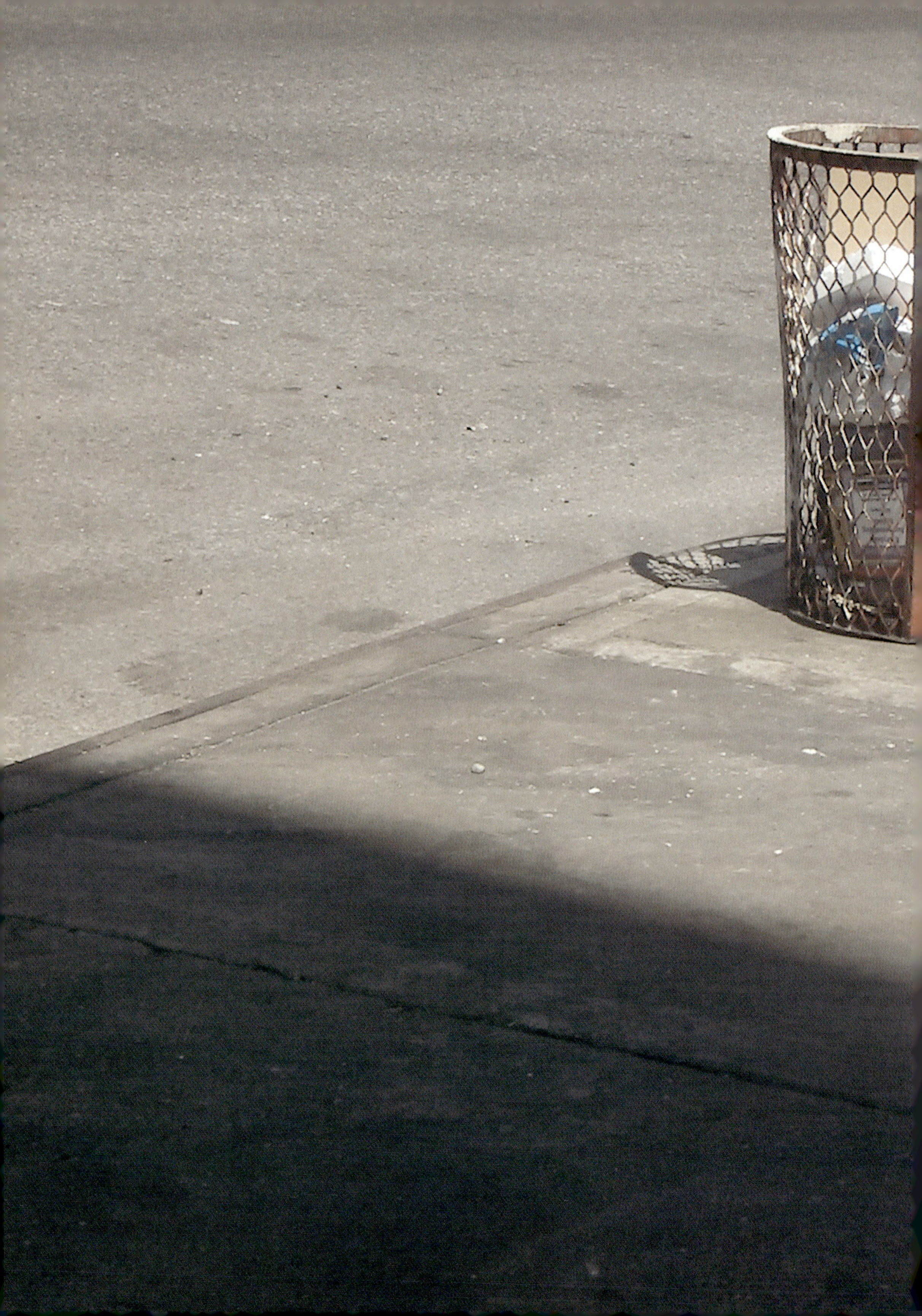

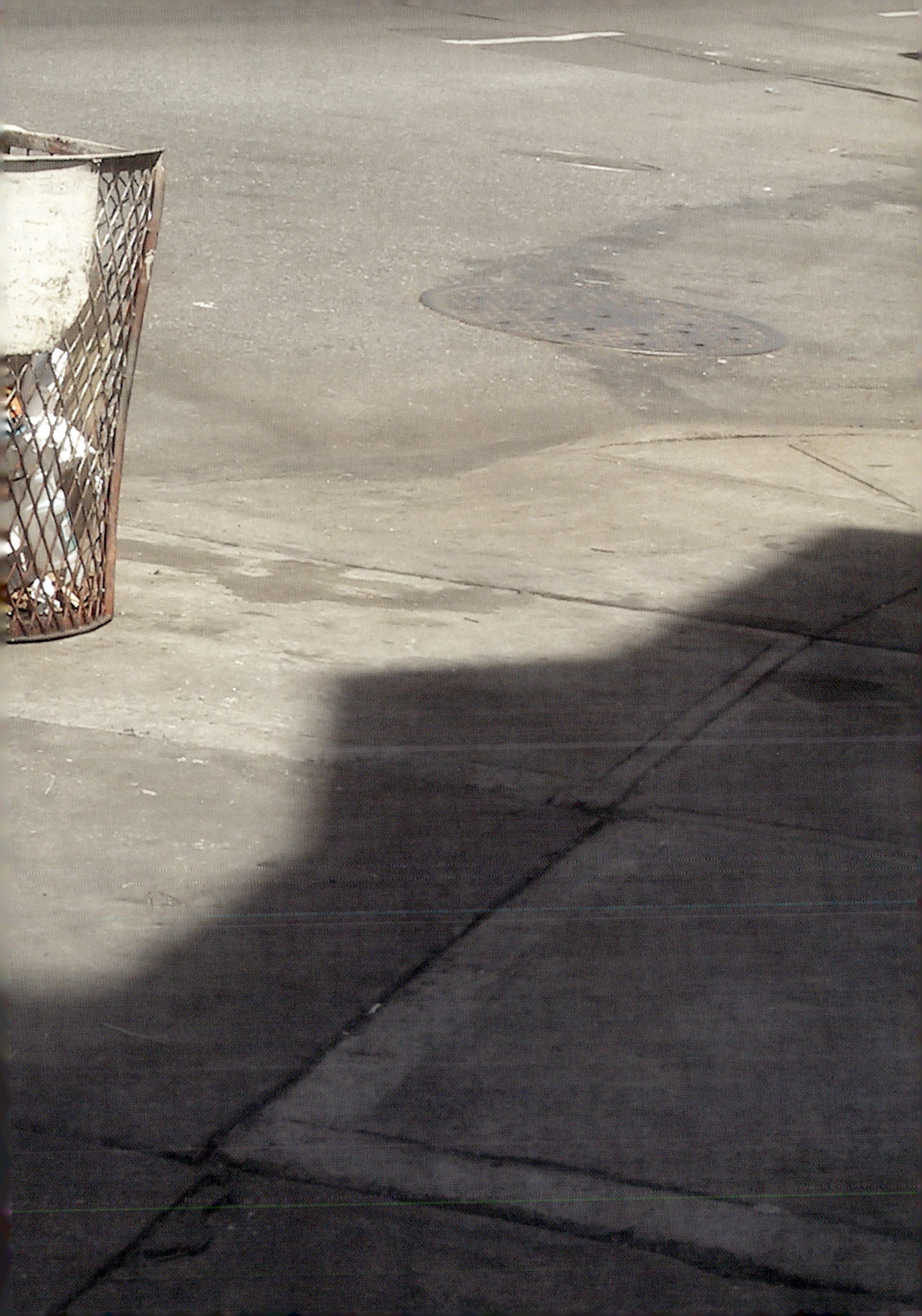

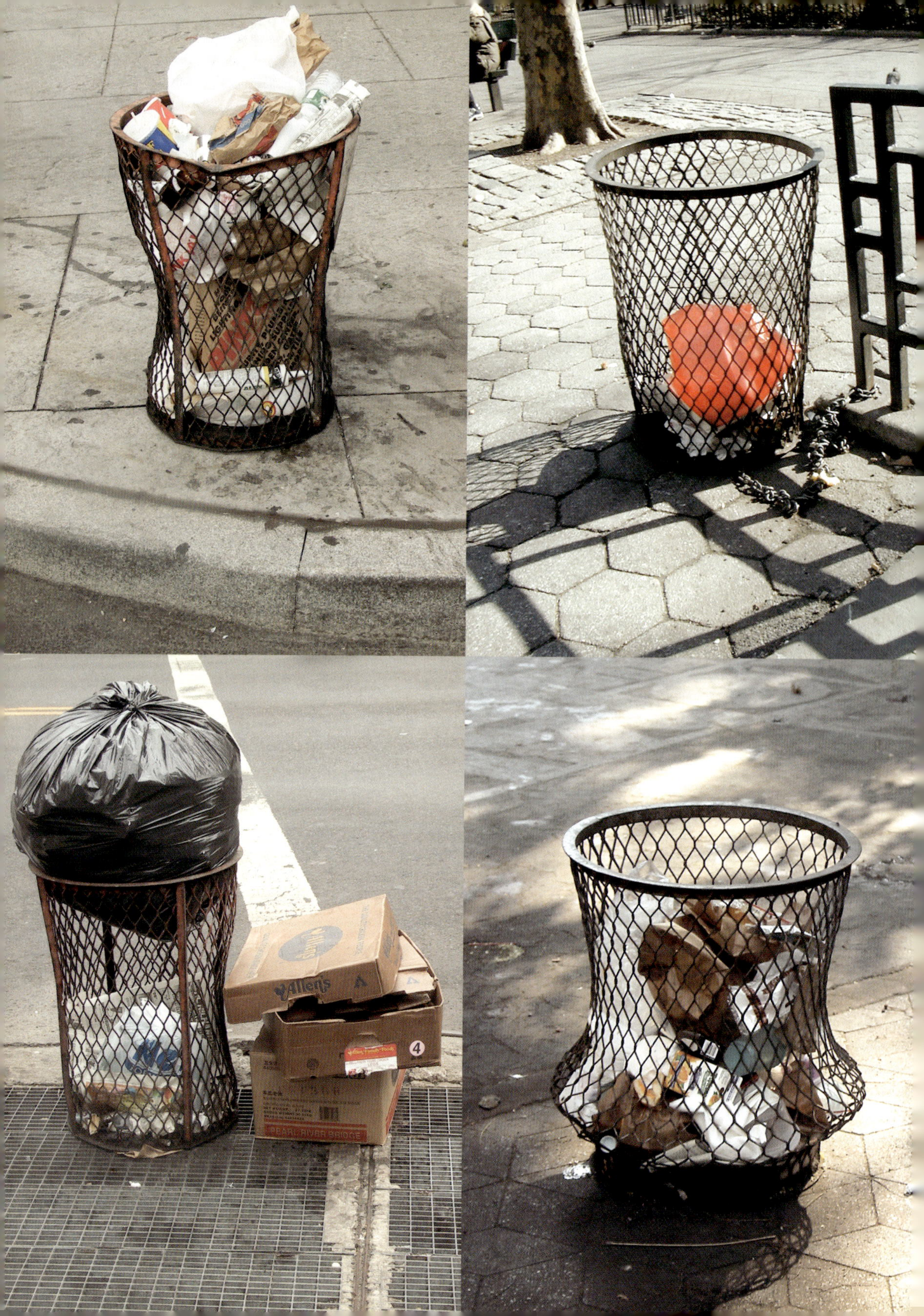
Allens
PEARL RIVER BRIDGE

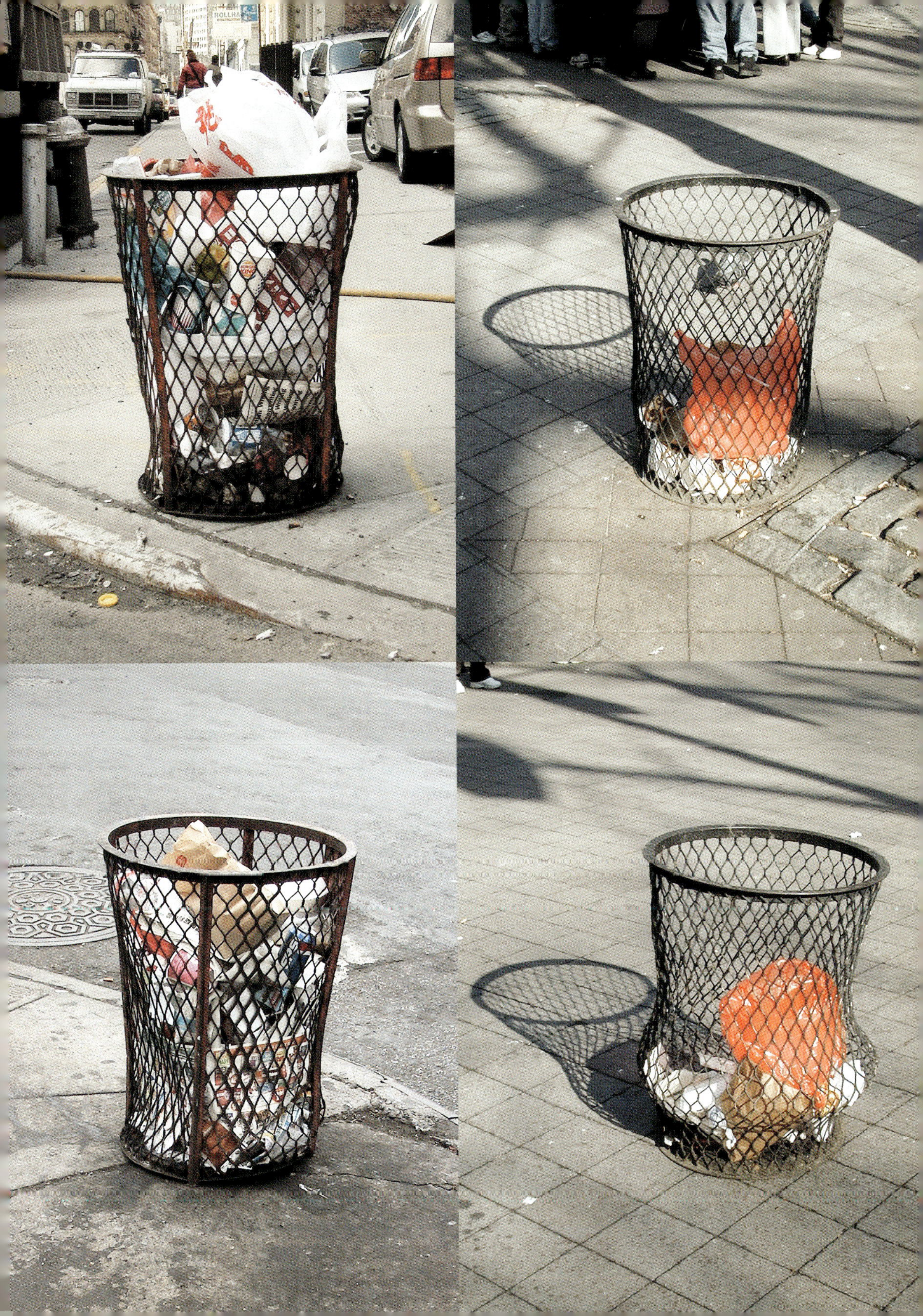

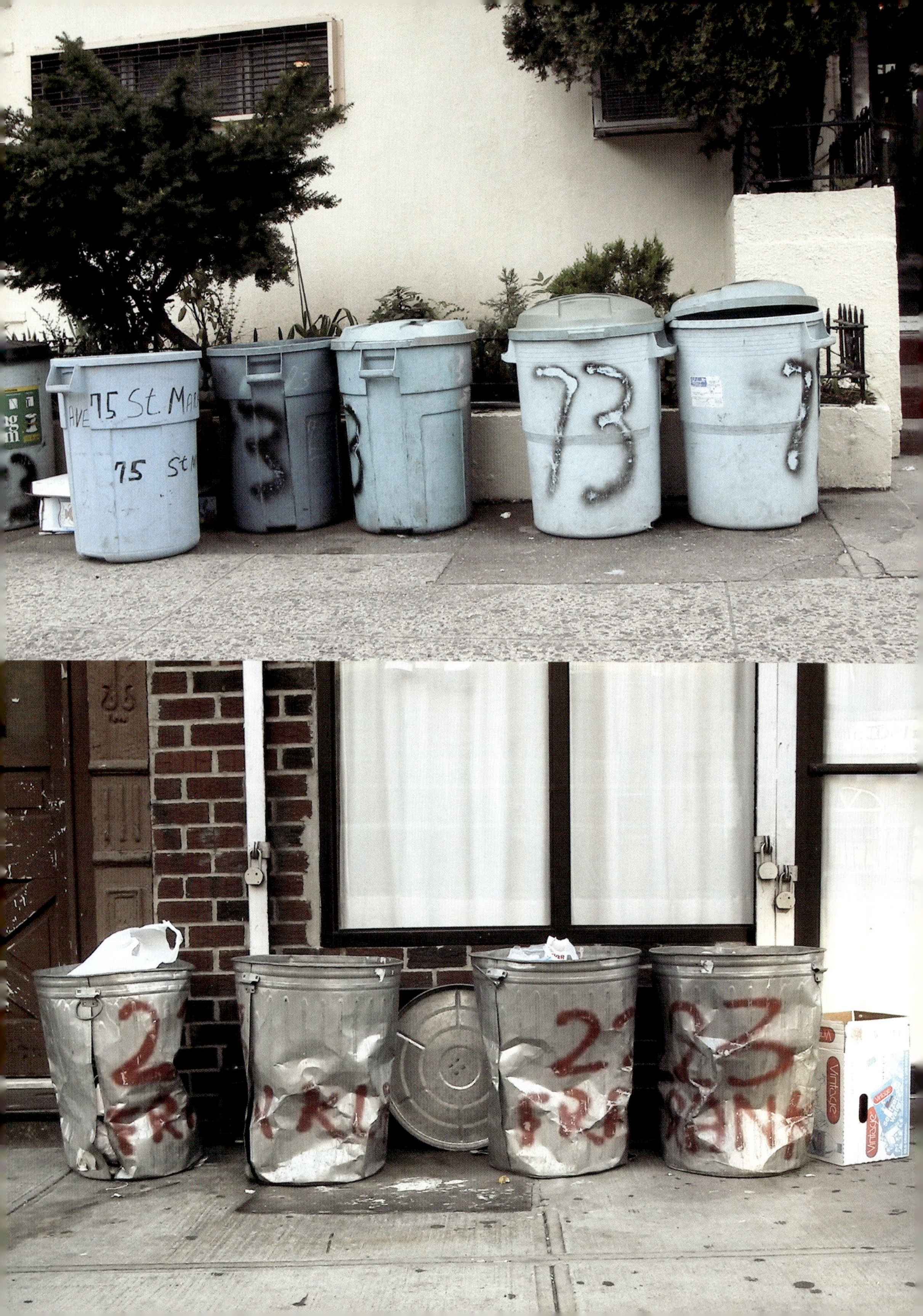

AVE 75 St. Ma
75 St
73
2
23

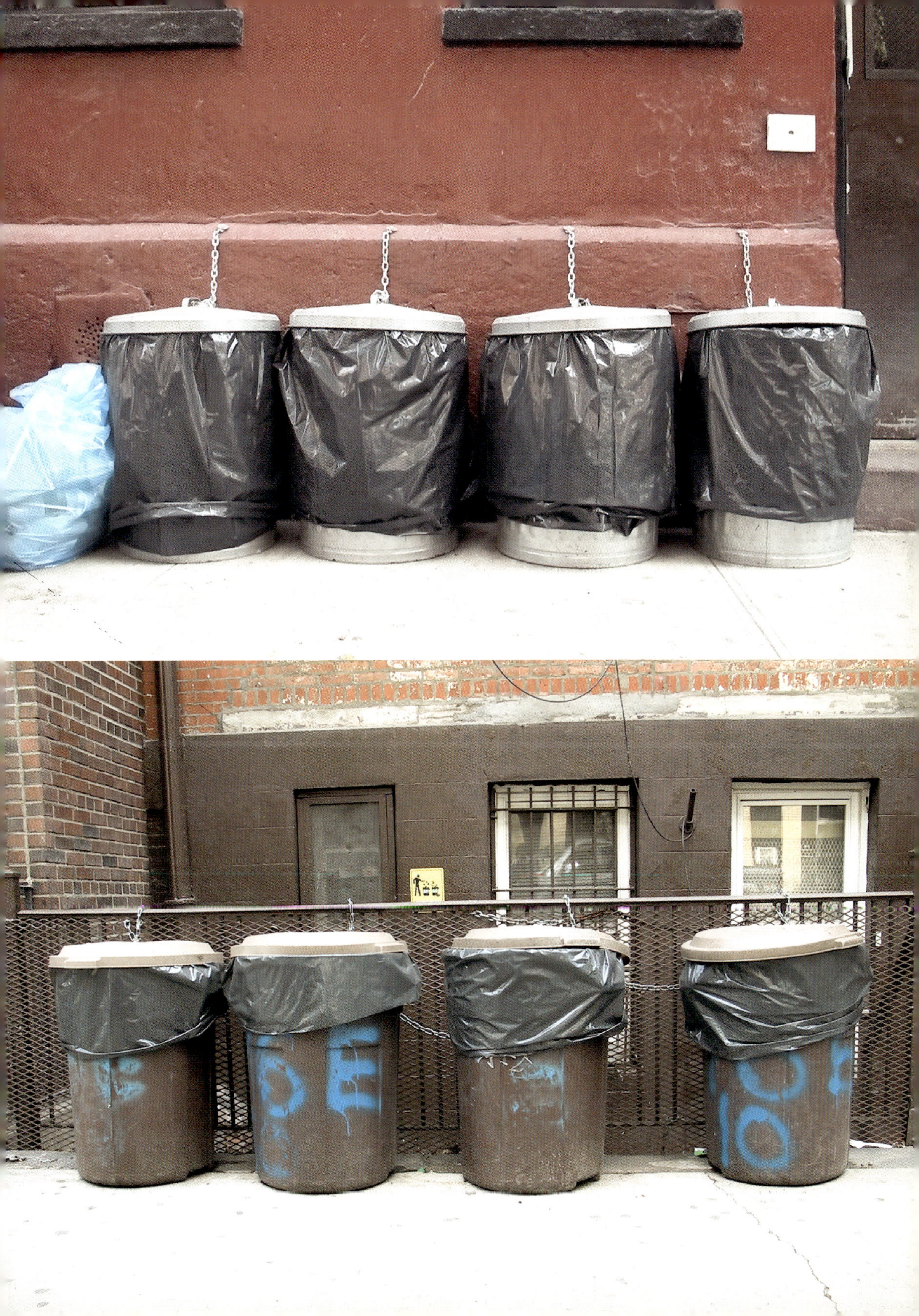

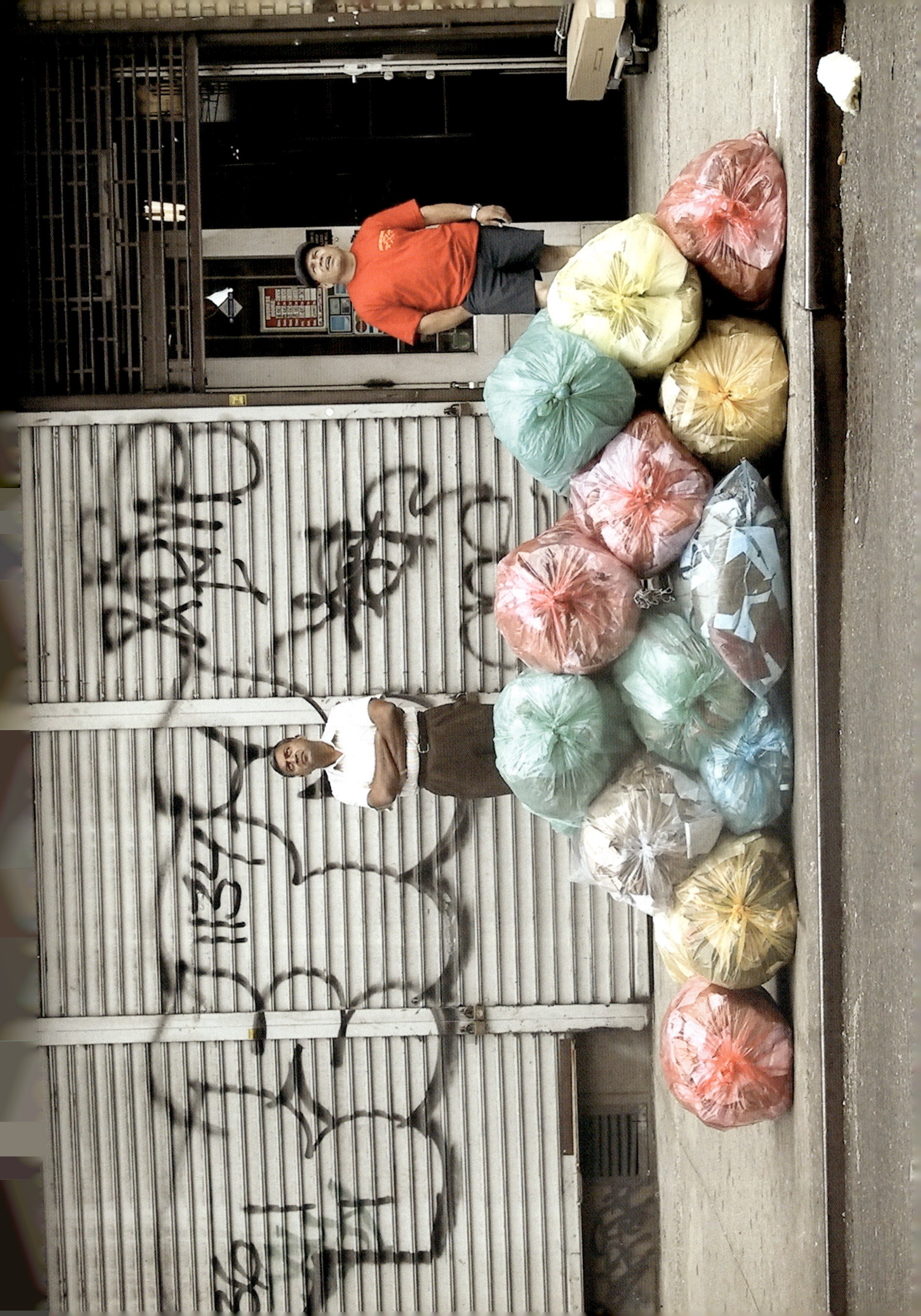

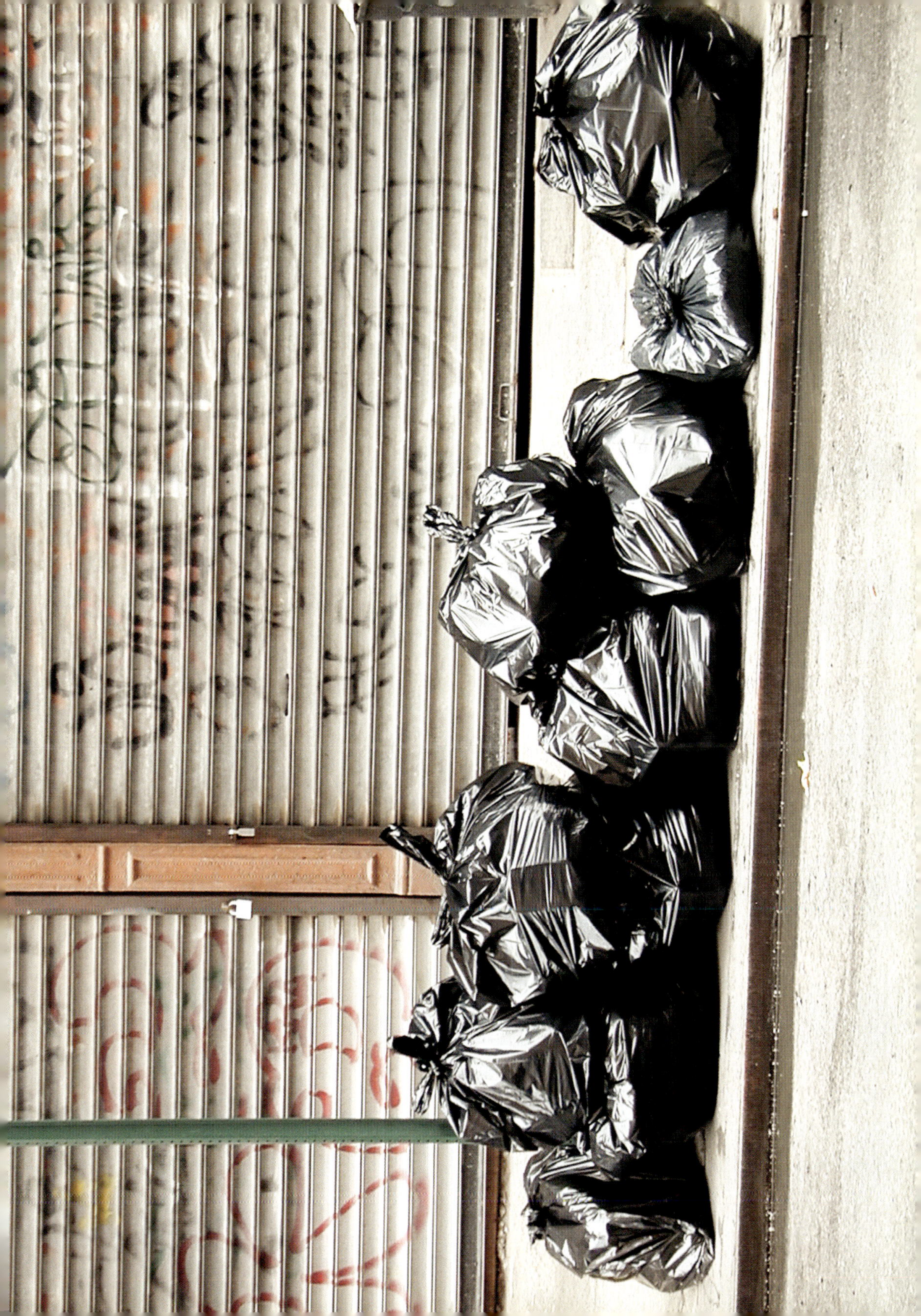

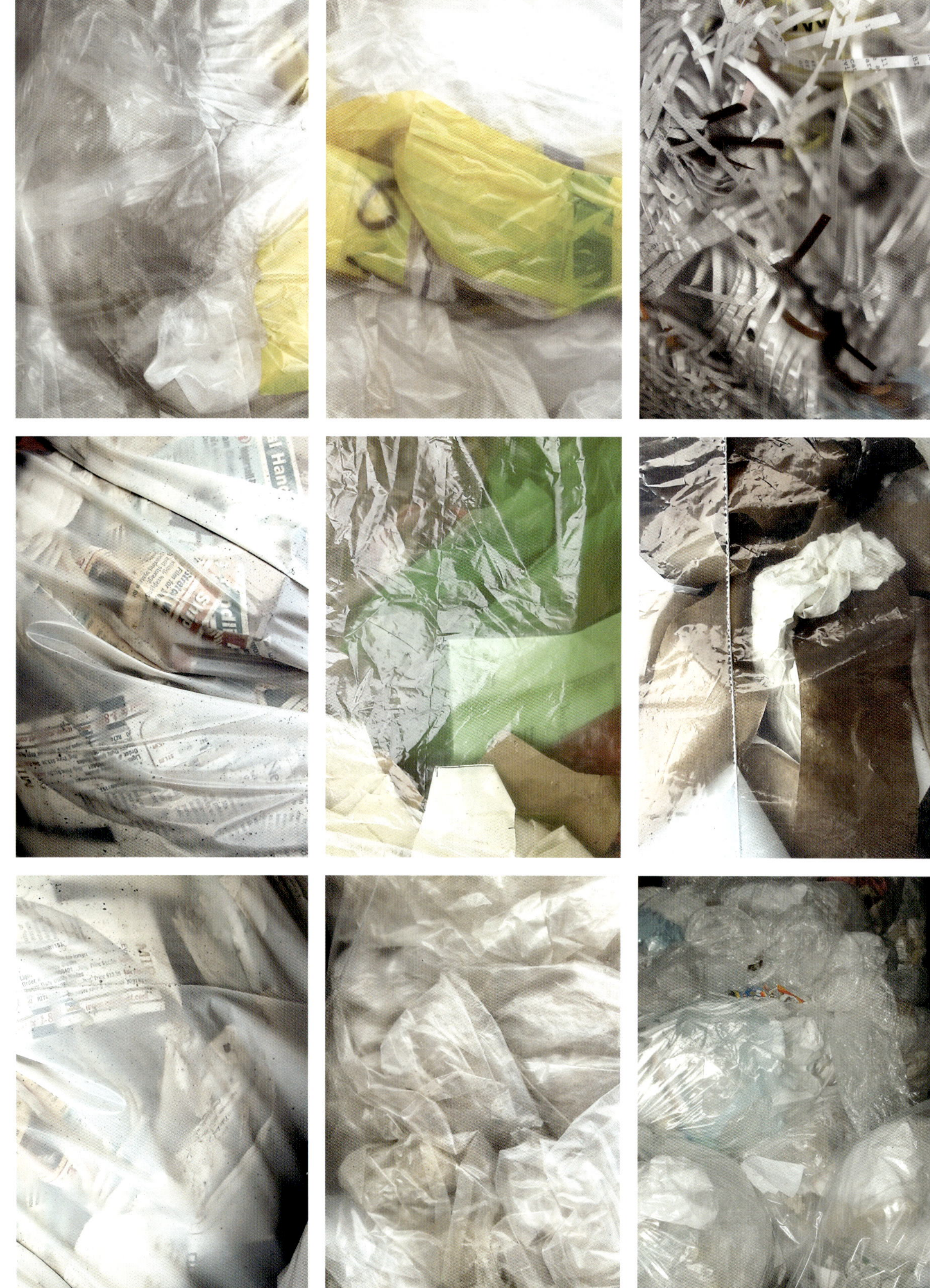

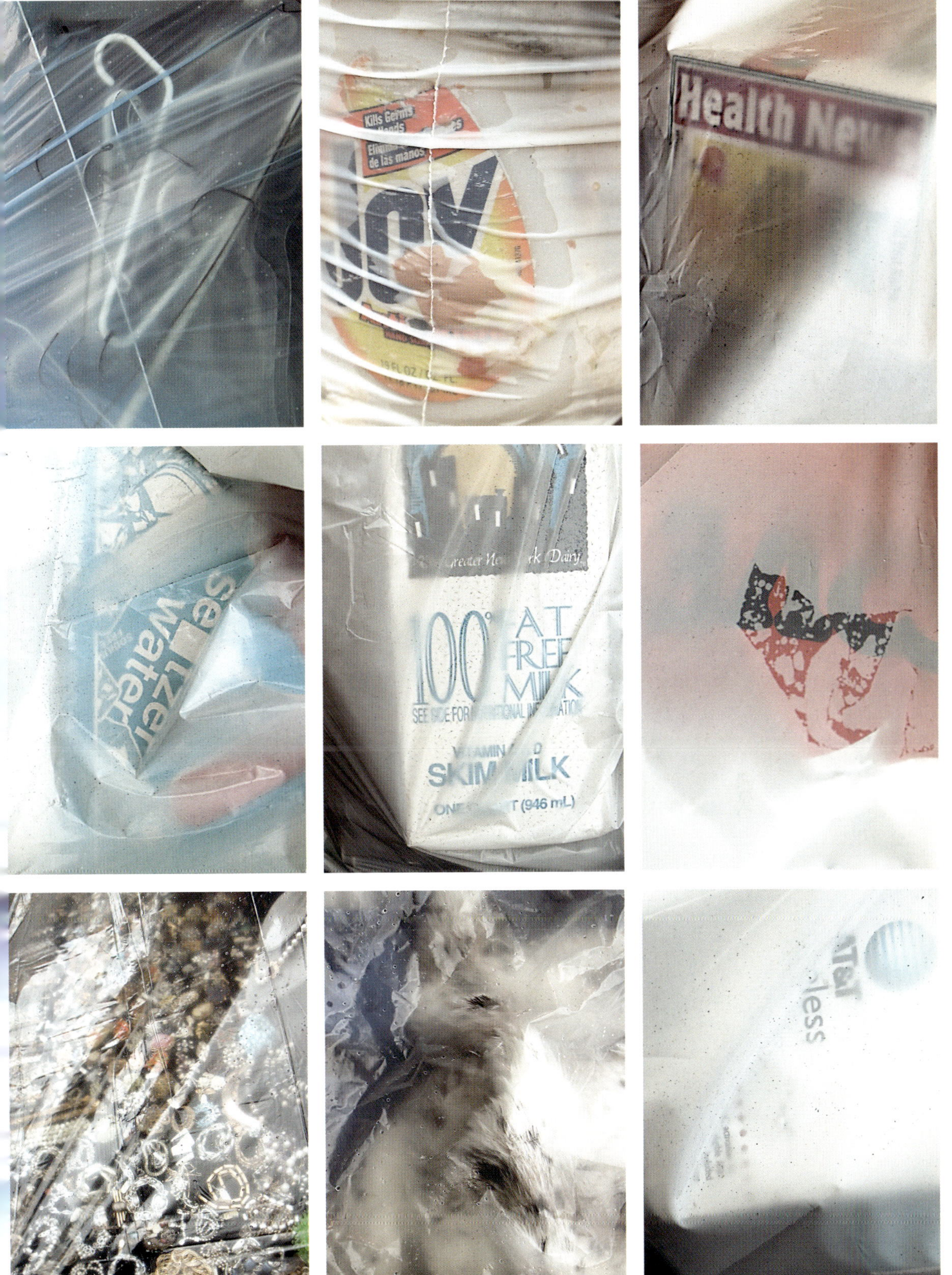
Kills Germs
de las manos
Health Ne
Water
100
FAT
MILK
SKIM
(946 mL)
less

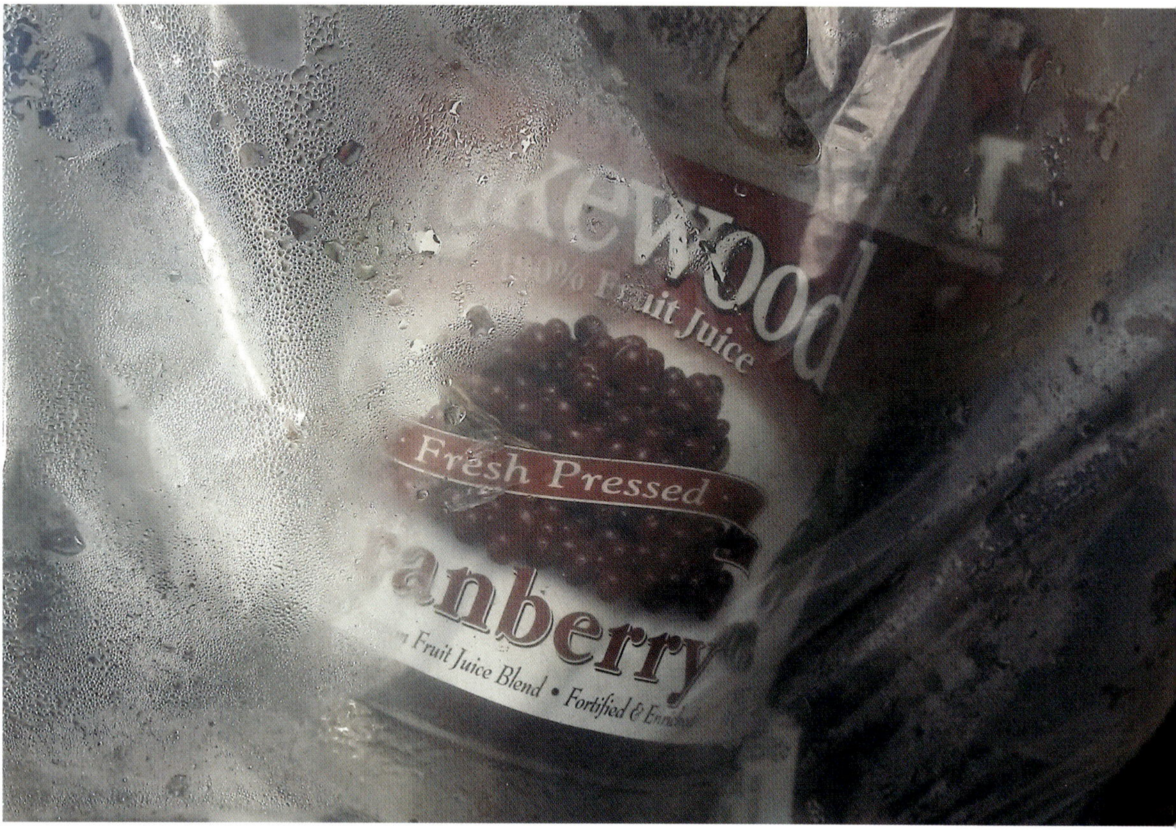

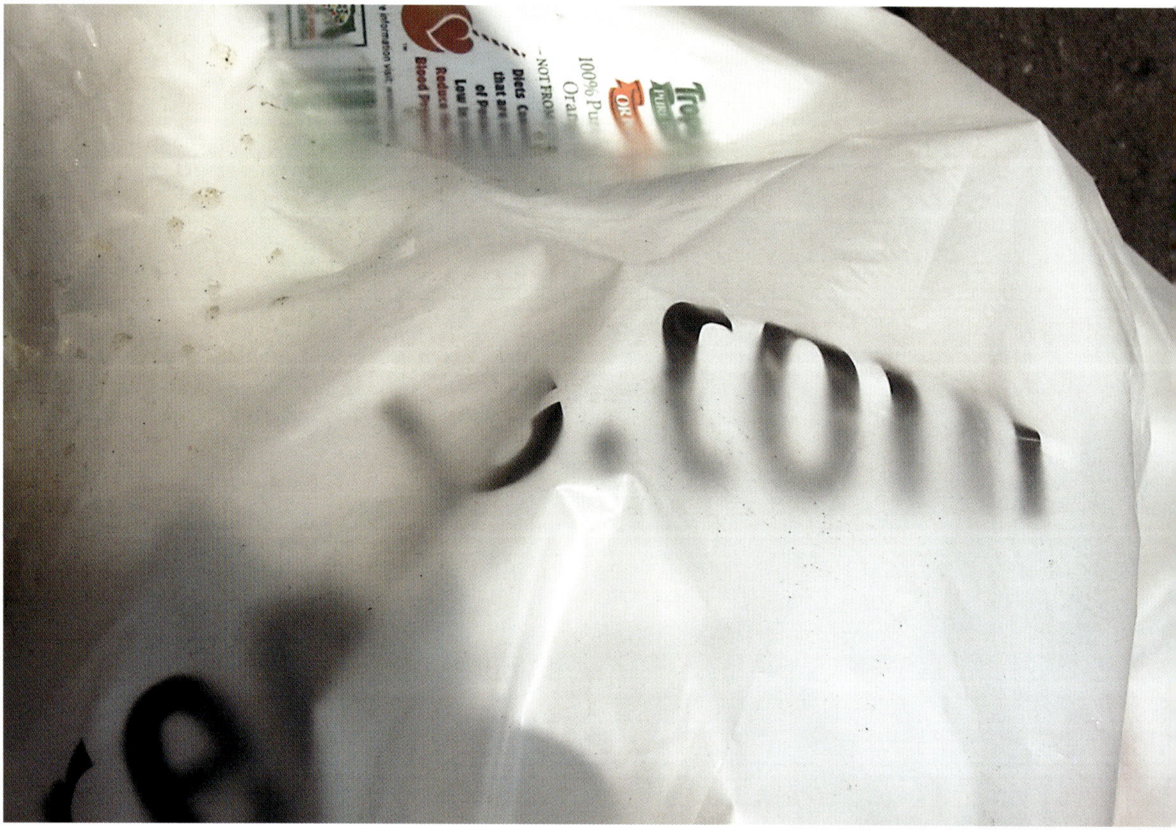

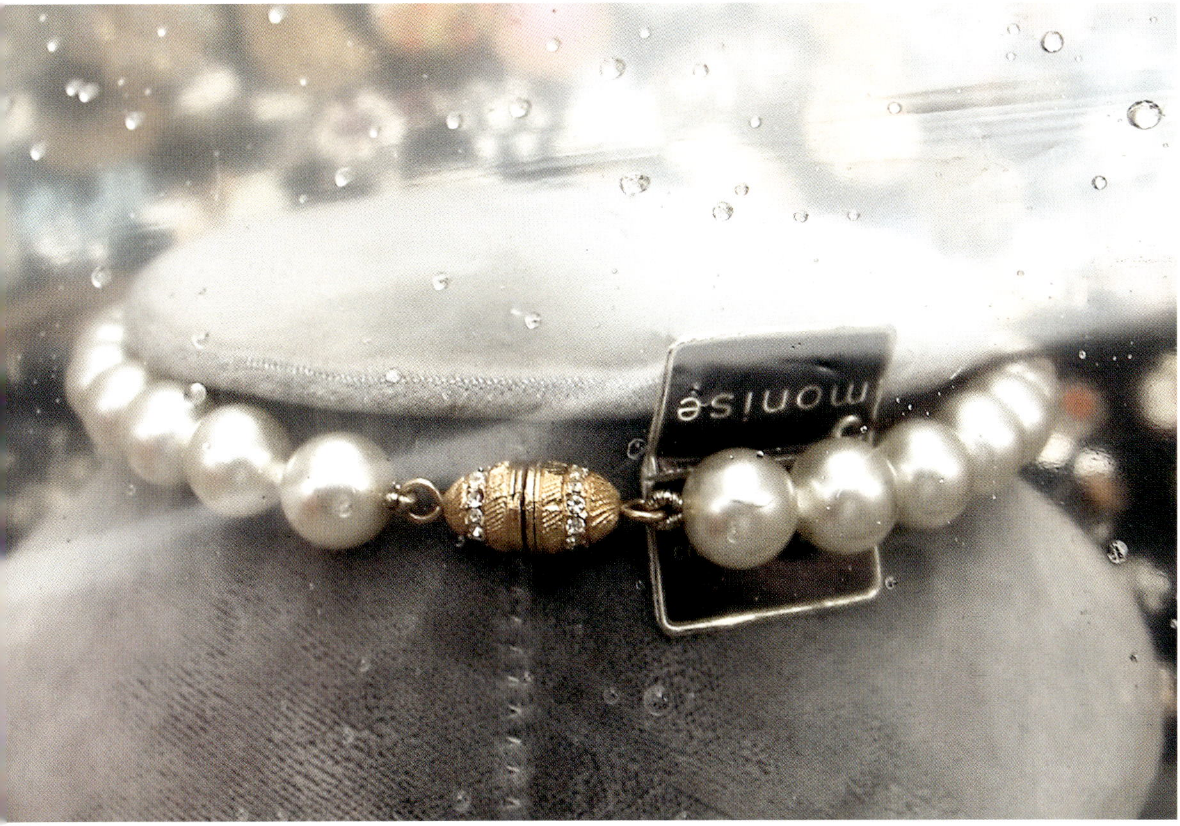

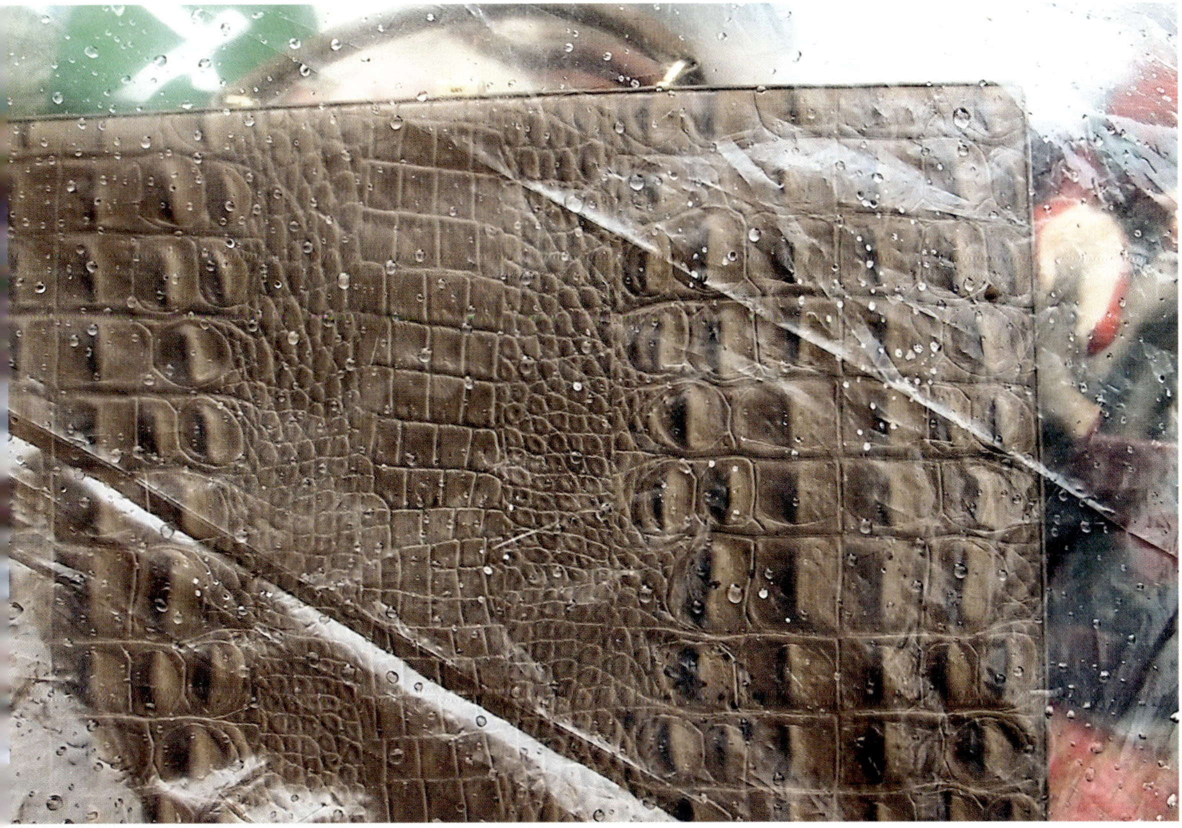

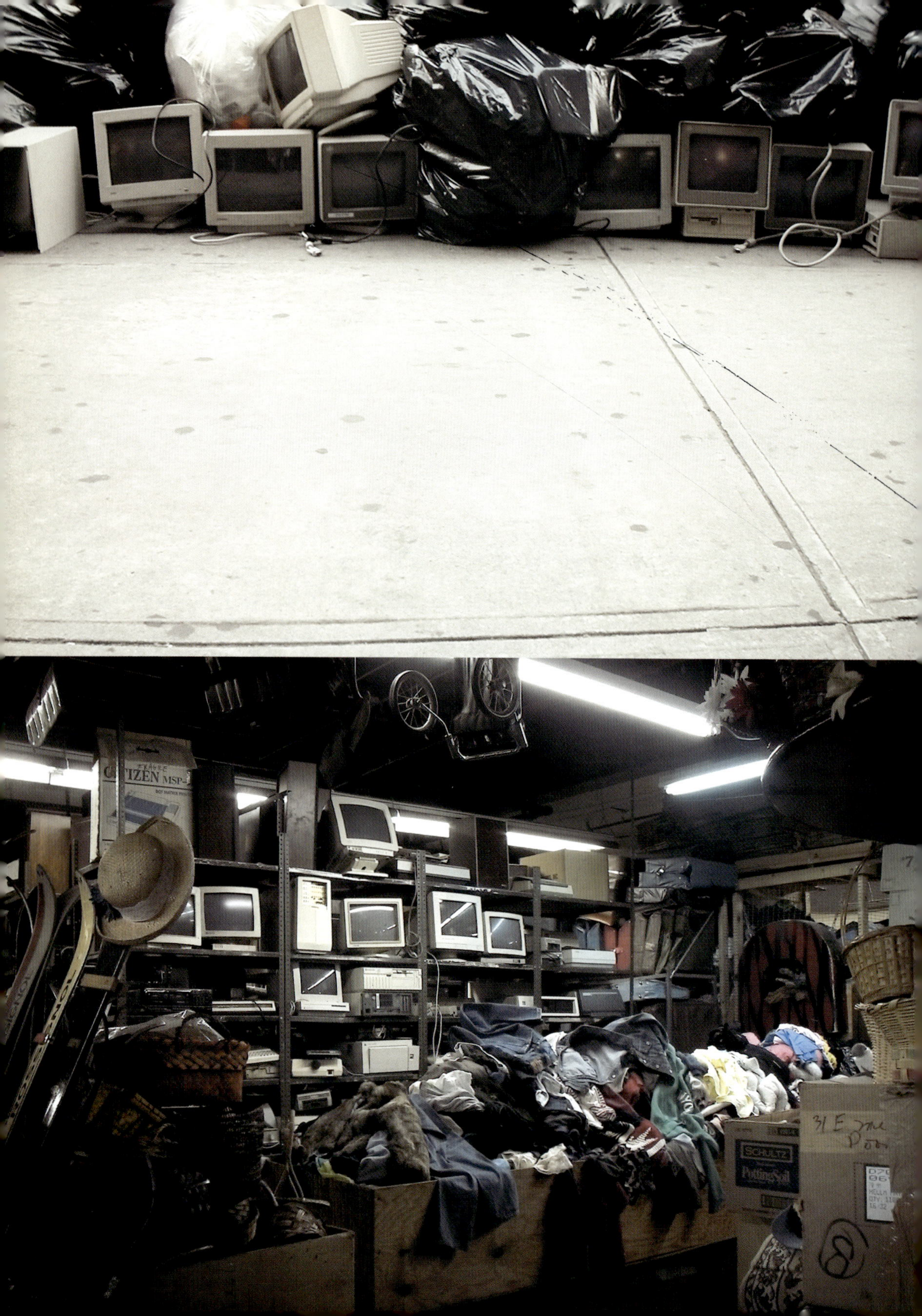
CITIZEN
SCHULTZ

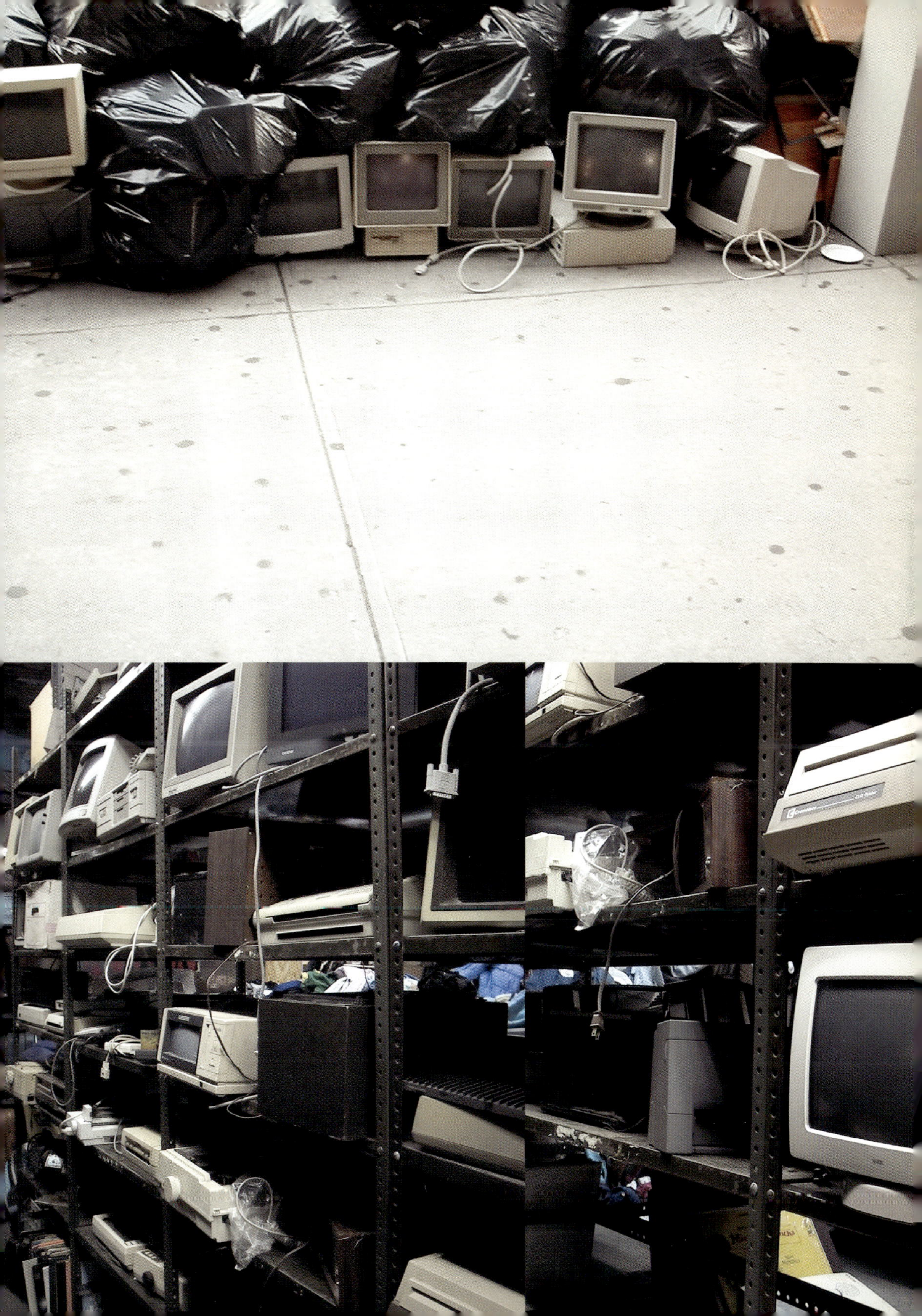

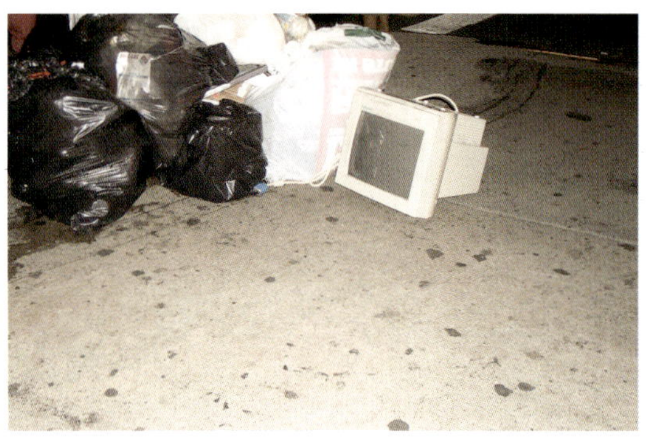
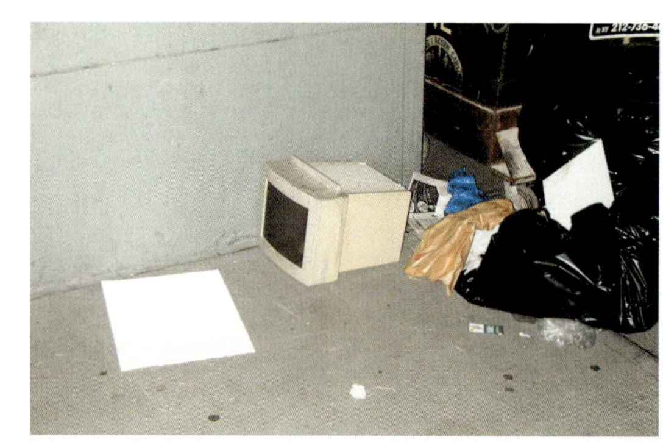
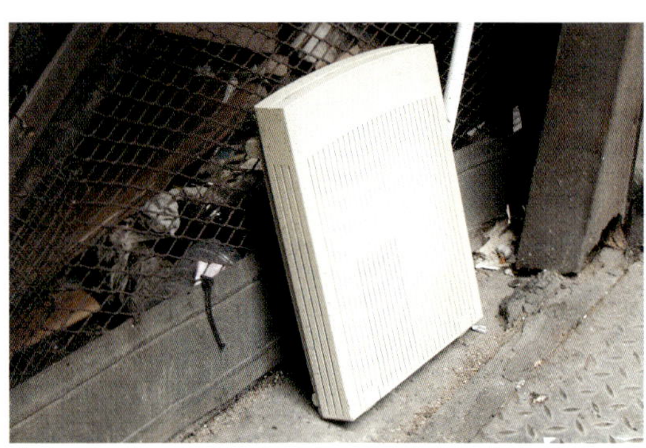
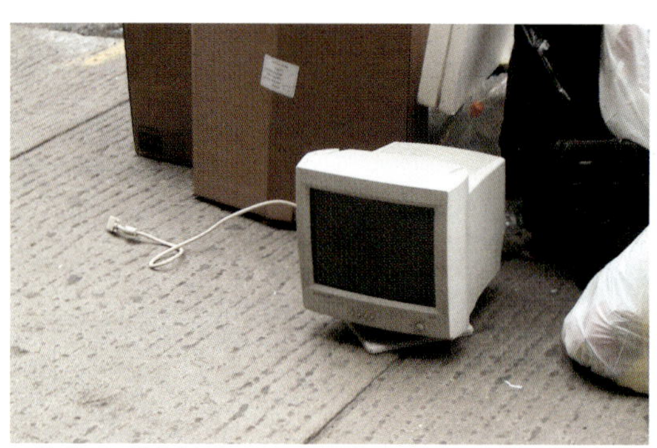
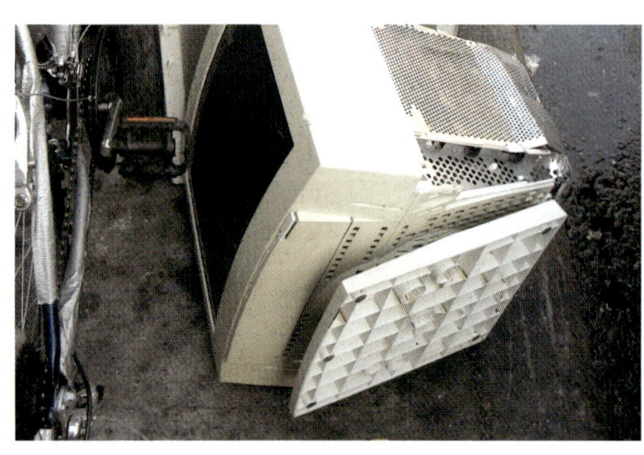
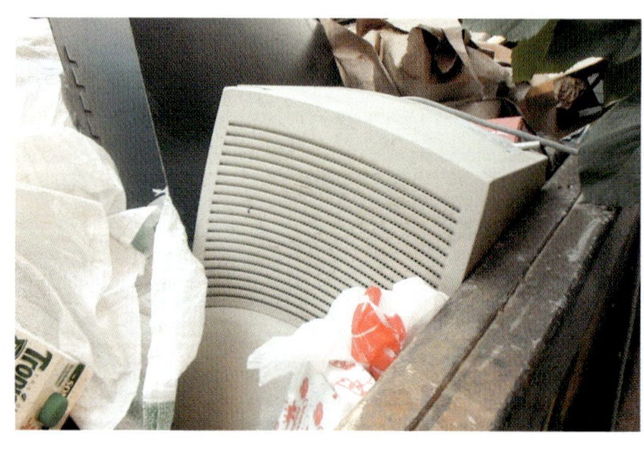
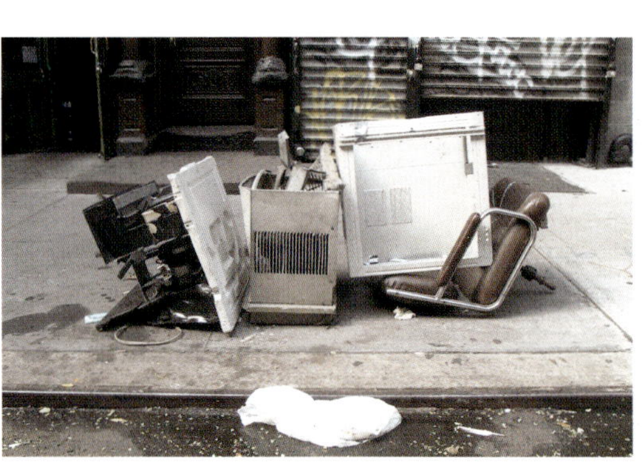
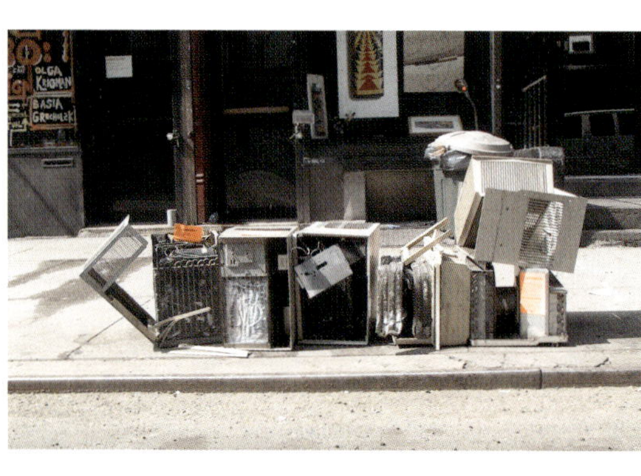

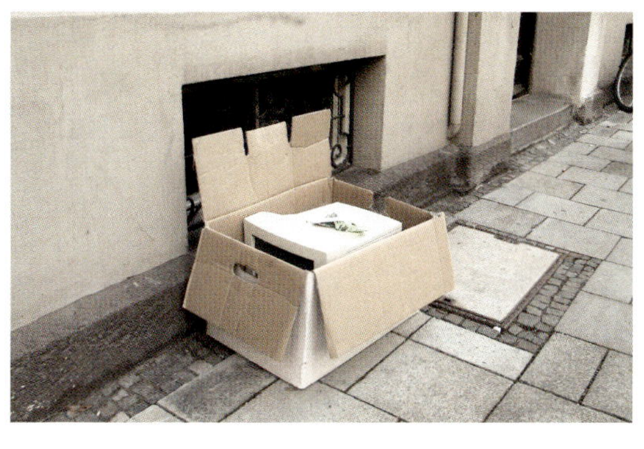
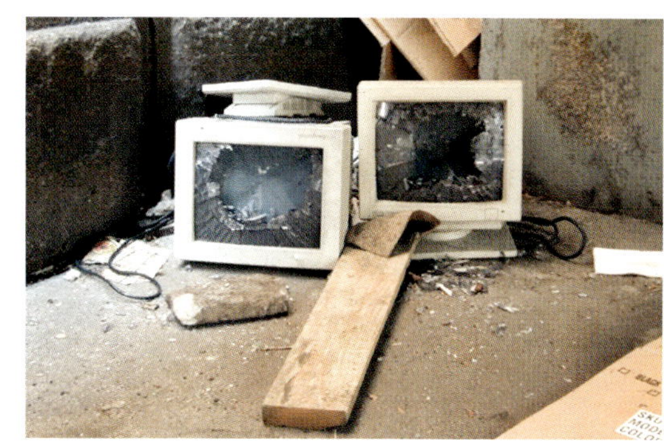
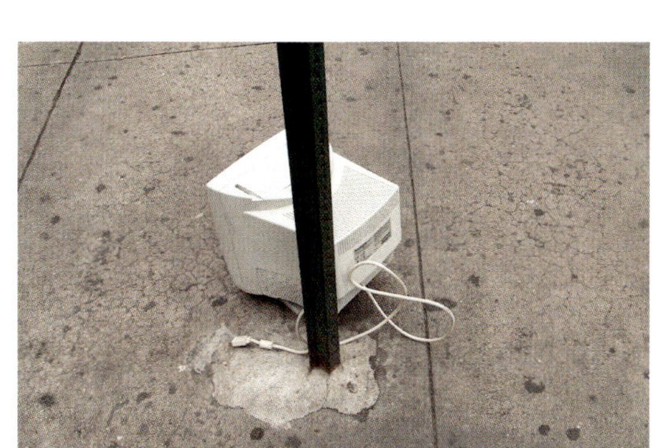
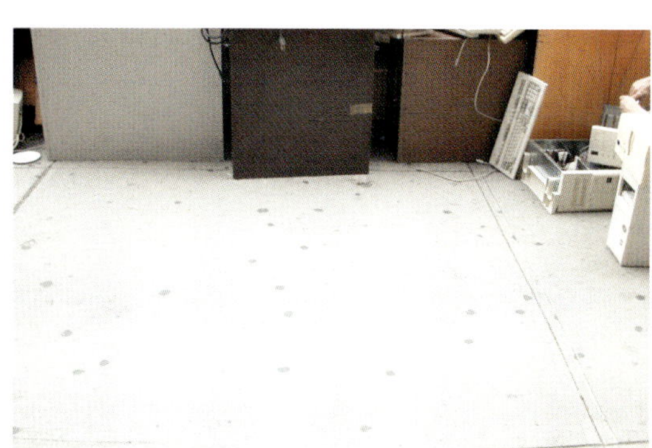
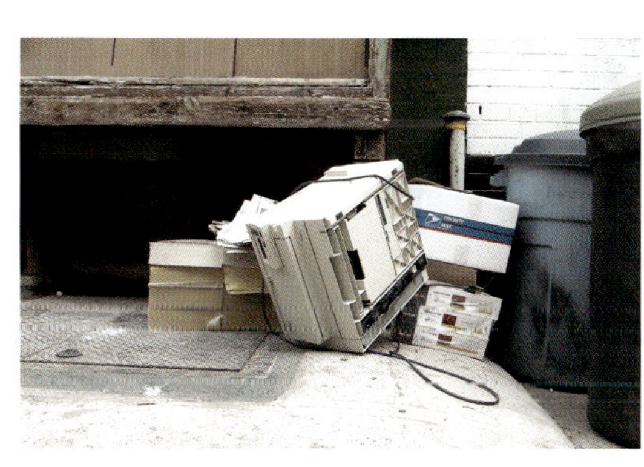
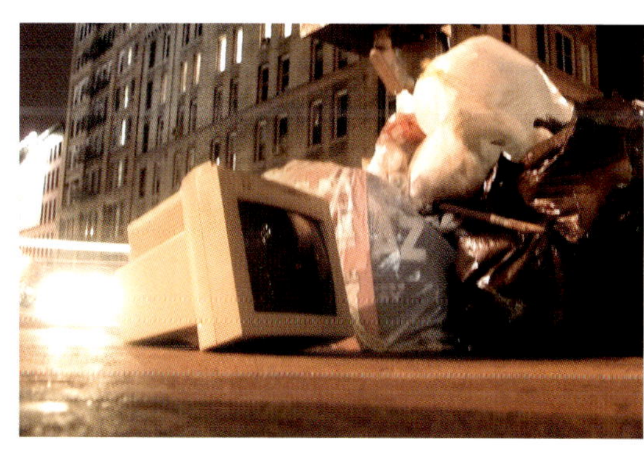
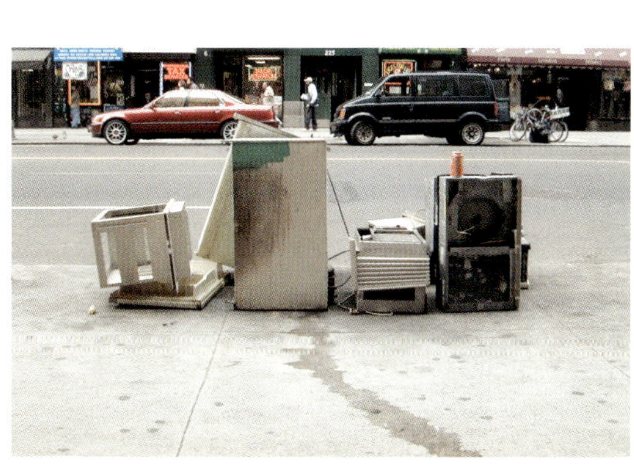
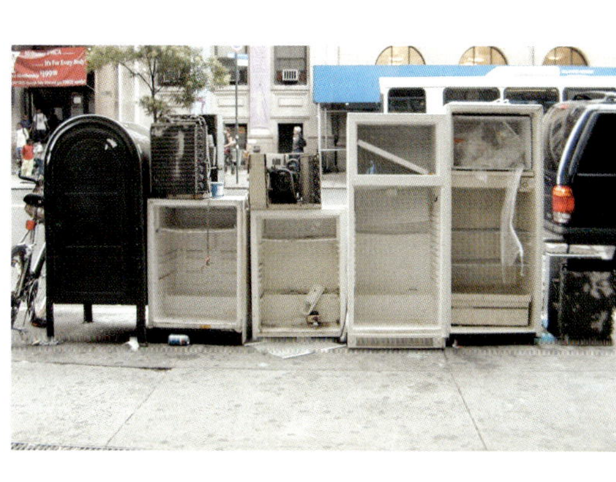

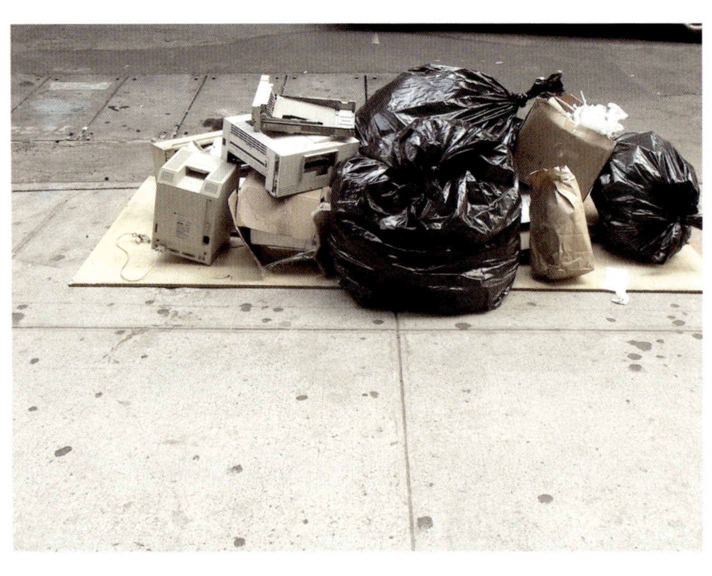

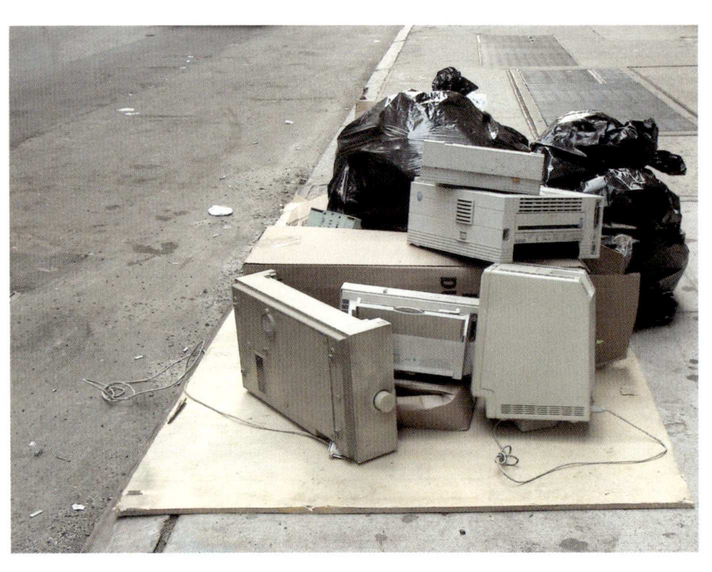

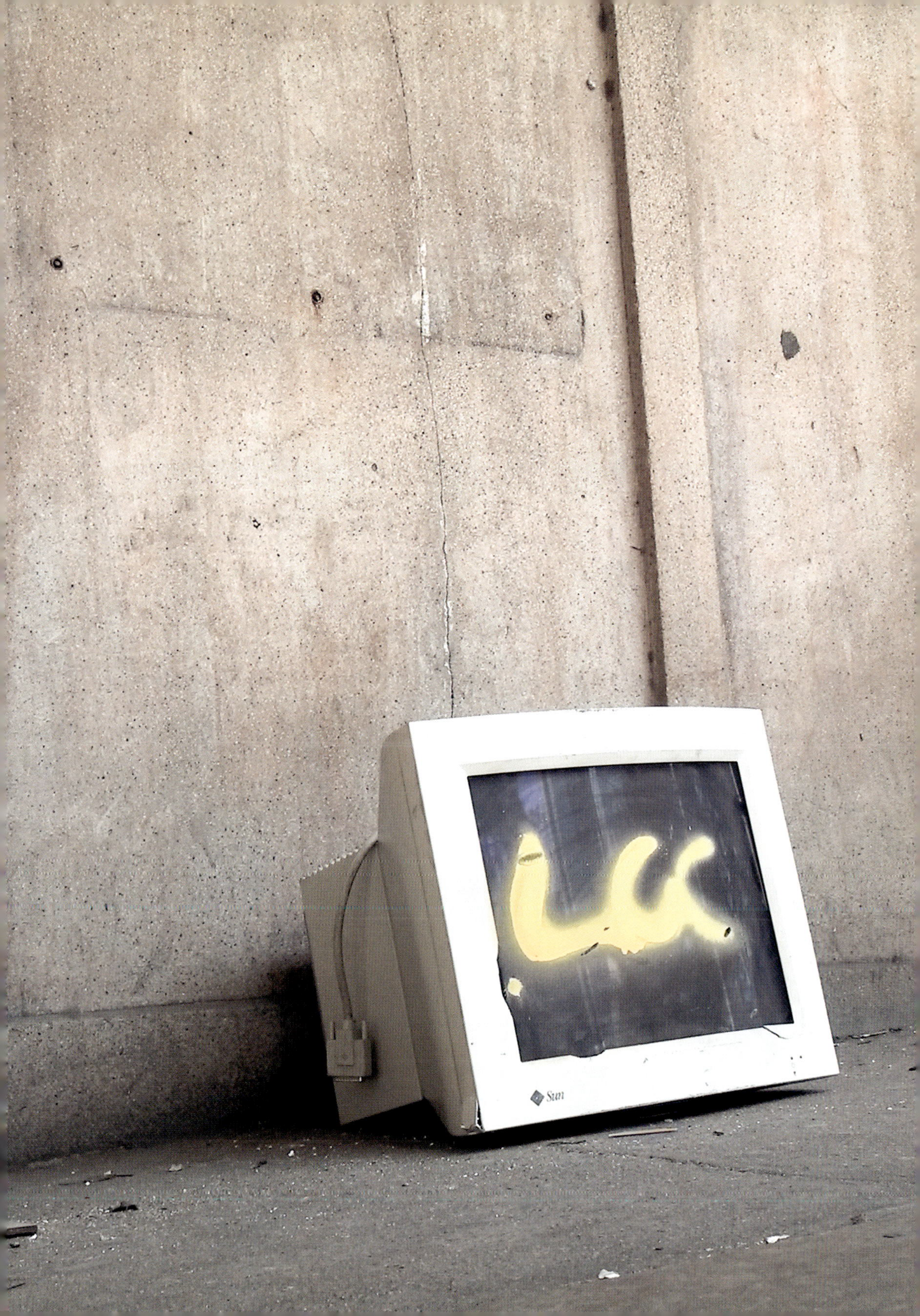
Sun

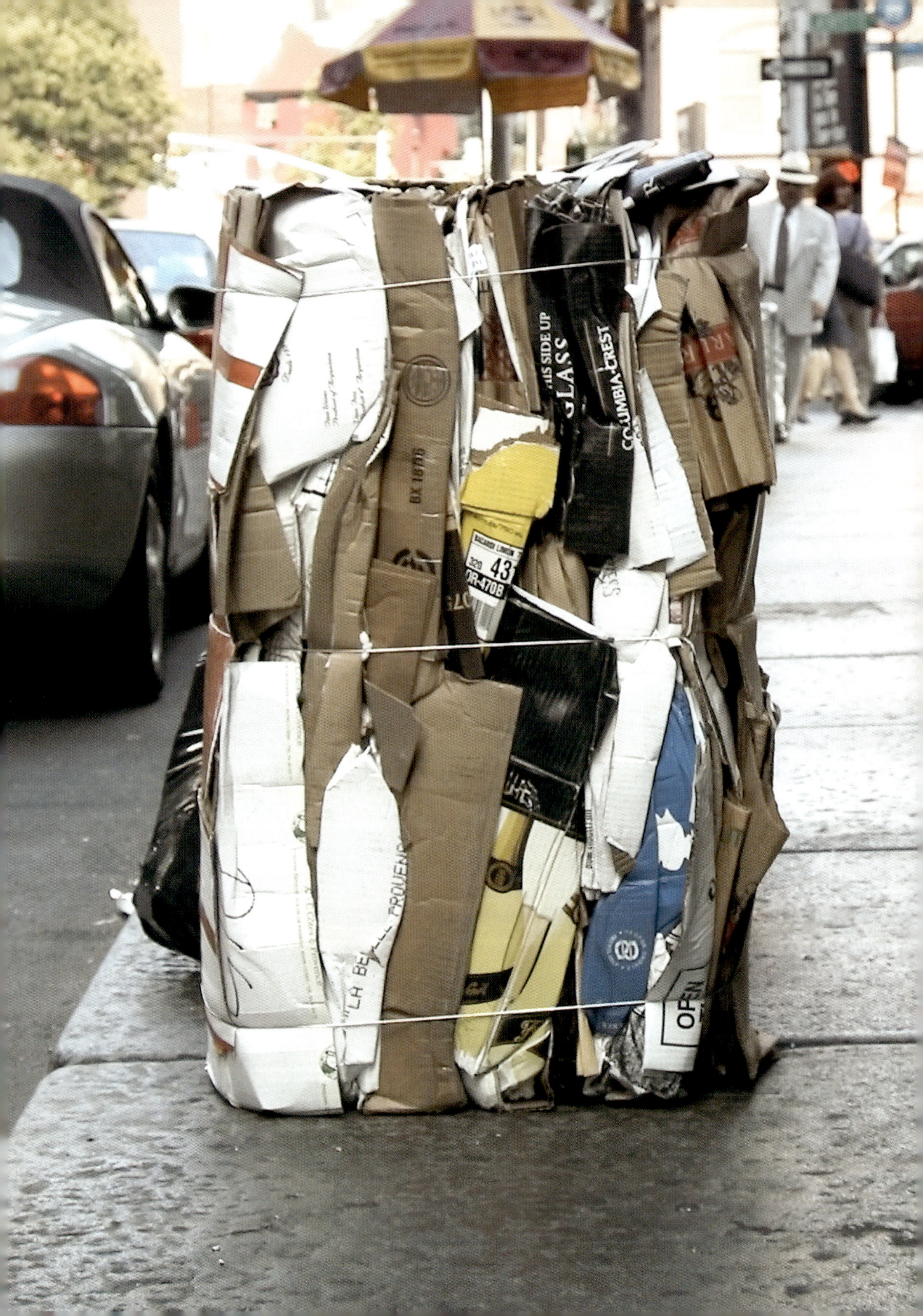
HIS SIDE UP
GLASS
COLUMBIA·CREST
43
OR-470B

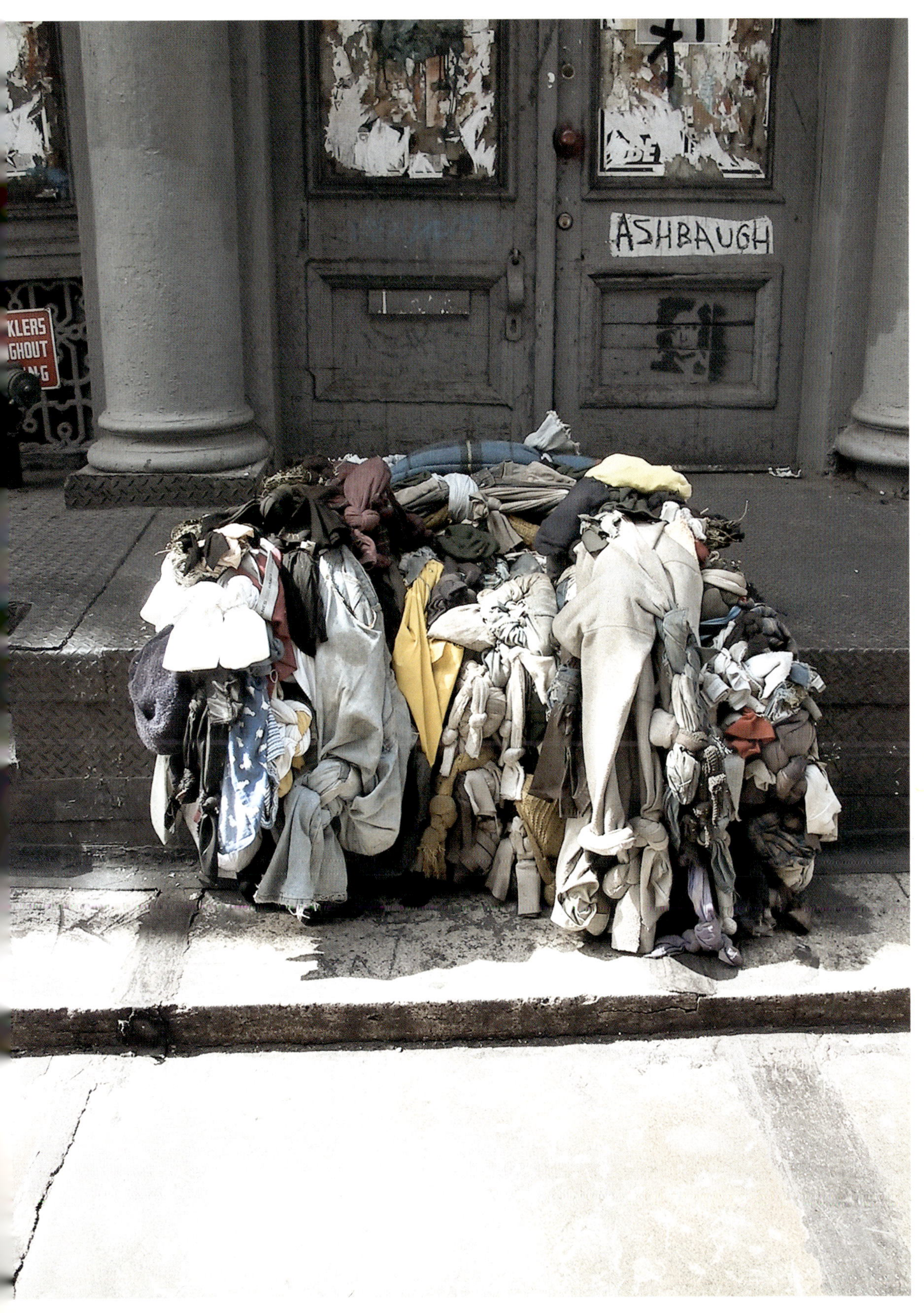
ASHBAUGH

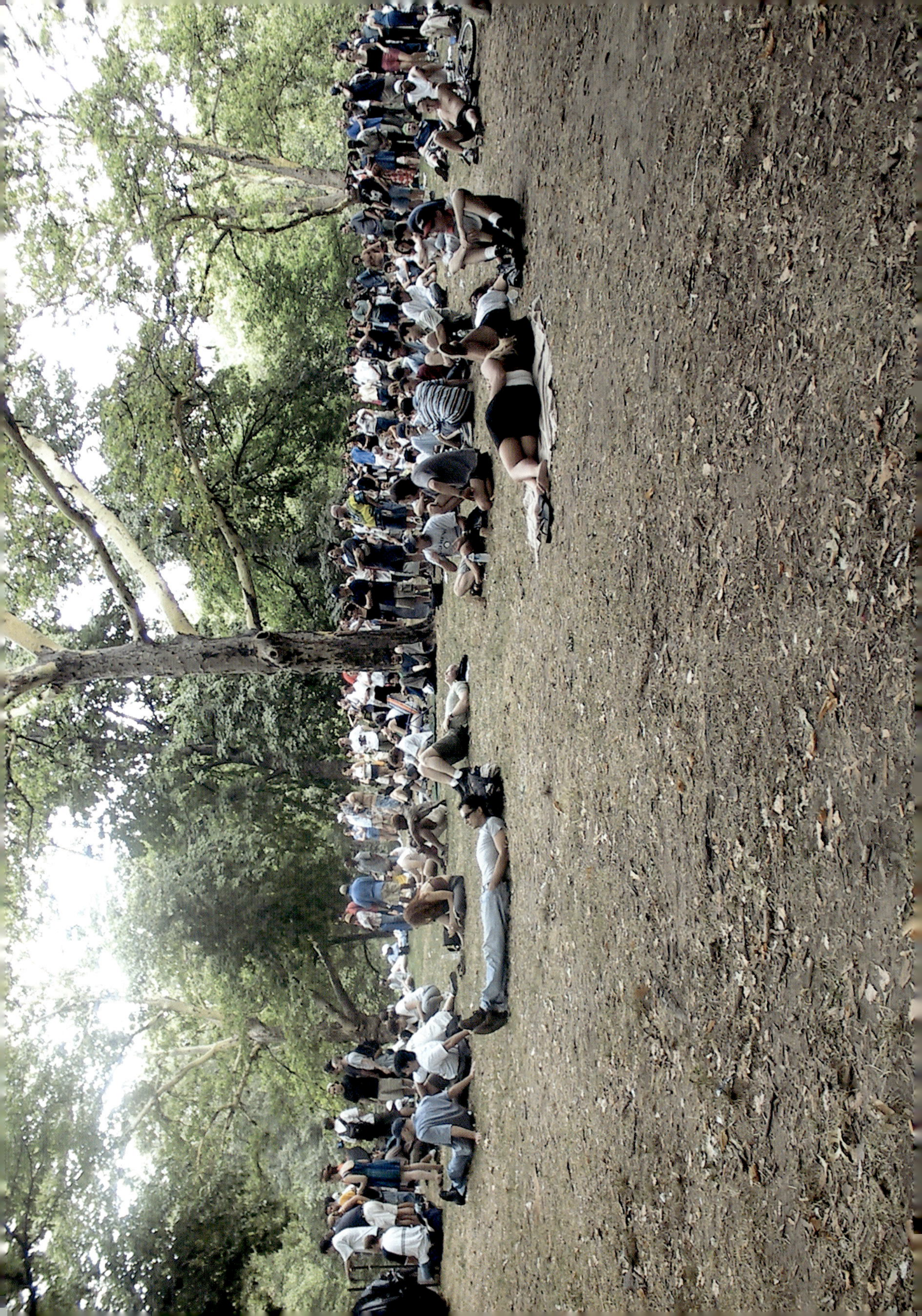

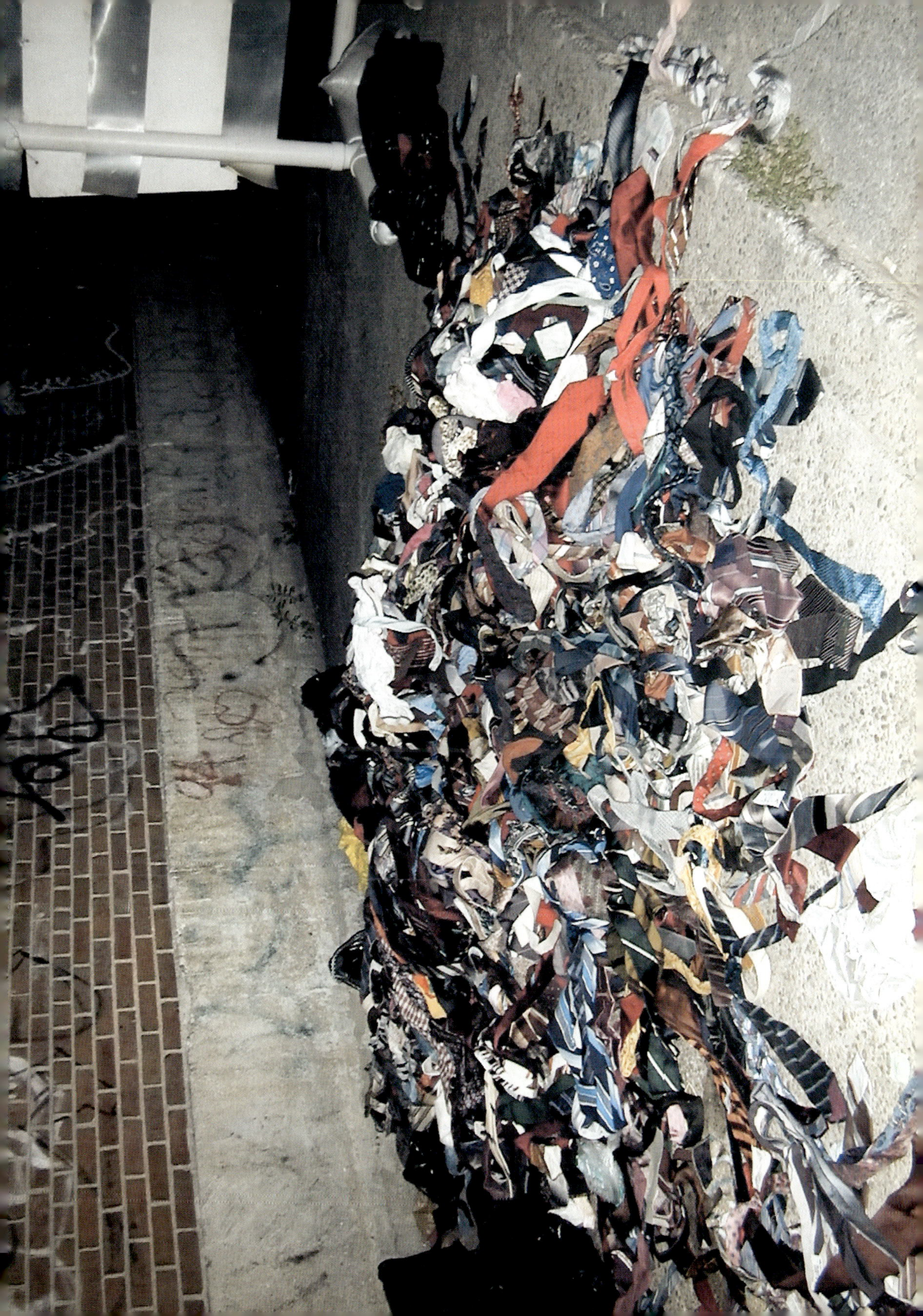

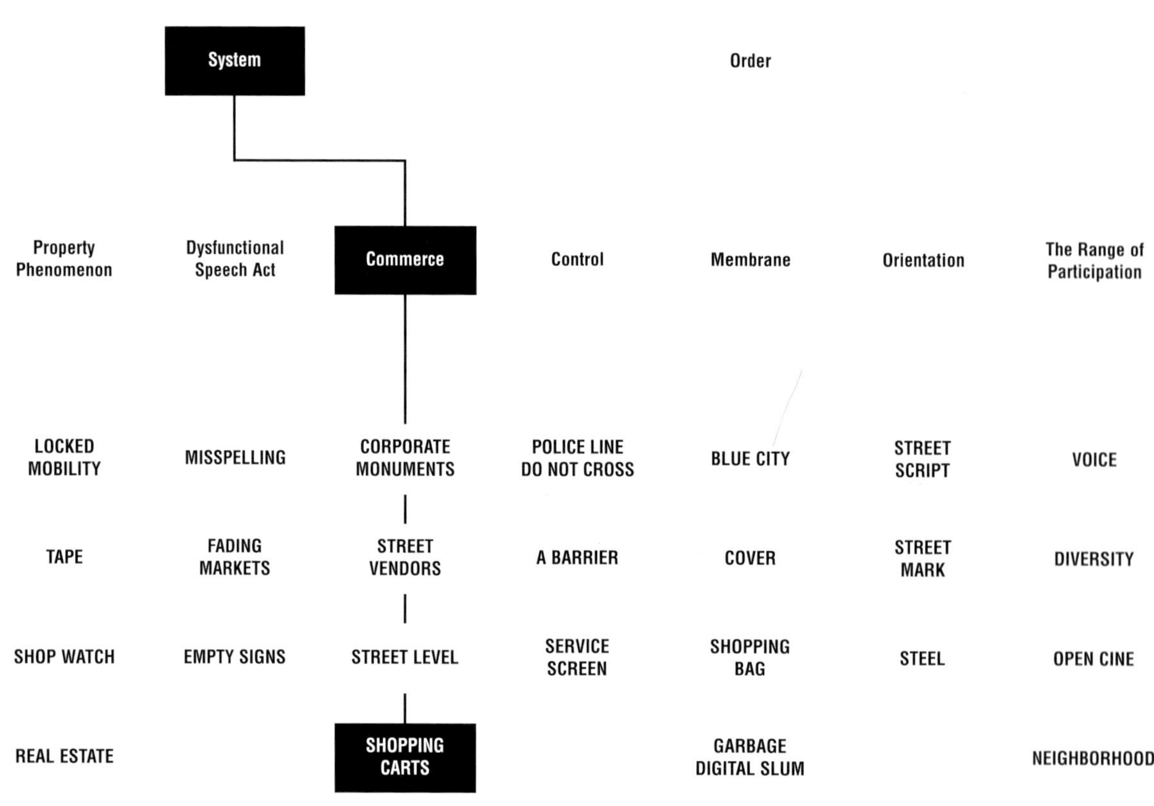
System
Order
Property Phenomenon
Dysfunctional Speech Act
Commerce
Control
Membrane
Orientation
The Range of Participation
LOCKED MOBILITY
MISSPELLING
CORPORATE MONUMENTS
POLICE LINE DO NOT CROSS
BLUE CITY
STREET SCRIPT
VOICE
TAPE
FADING MARKETS
STREET VENDORS
A BARRIER
COVER
STREET MARK
DIVERSITY
SHOP WATCH
EMPTY SIGNS
STREET LEVEL
SERVICE SCREEN
SHOPPING BAG
STEEL
OPEN CINE
REAL ESTATE
SHOPPING CARTS
GARBAGE DIGITAL SLUM
NEIGHBORHOOD

Identity

Alternative Media

Habitual Reinterpretation

SHOPPING CARTS

Mobility and Livelihood

CAR DOOR

PUBLIC CHAIRS

LABELING.

PLASTIC CRATES

POLE POST

STANDPIPES

PRAY JESUS

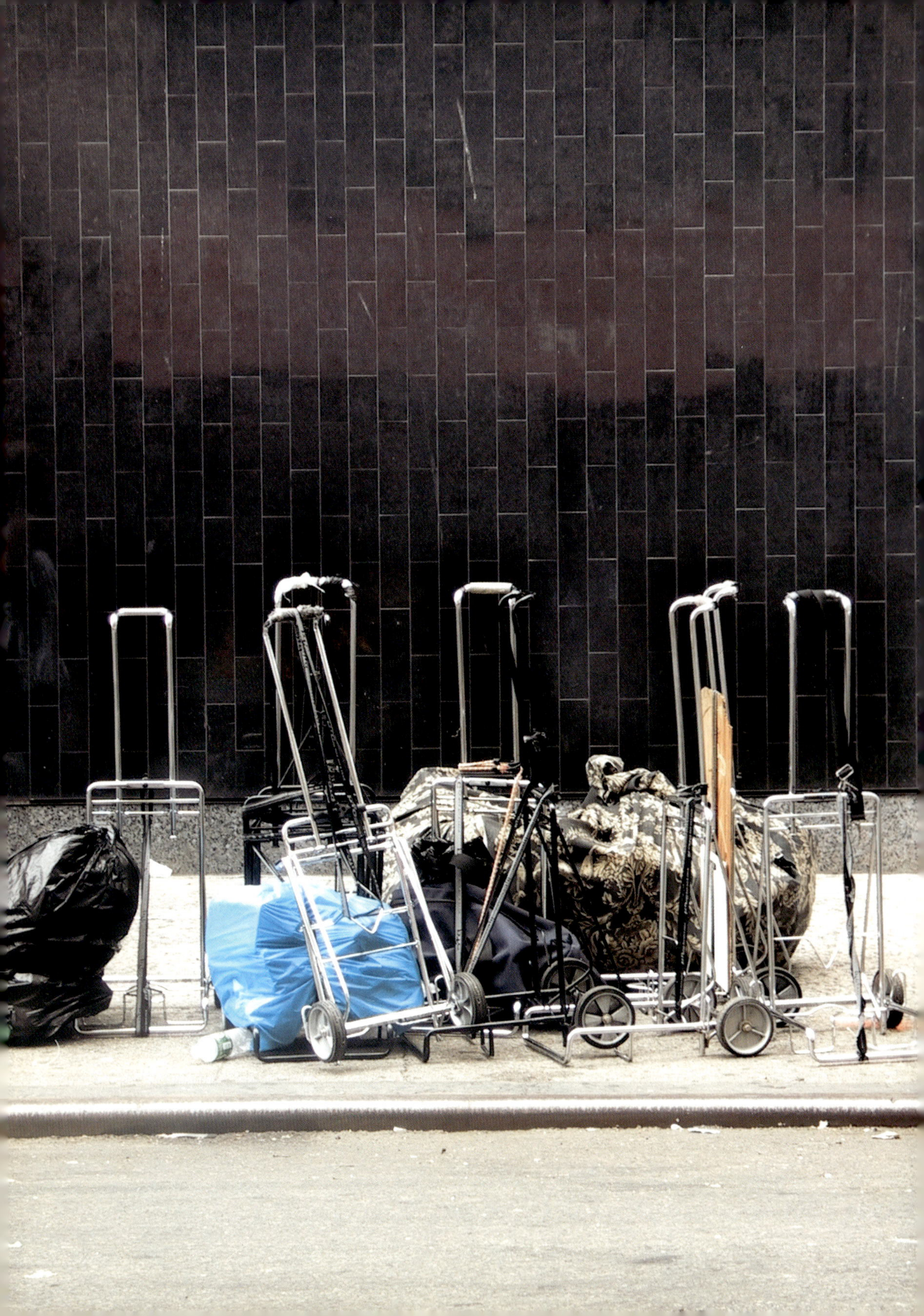

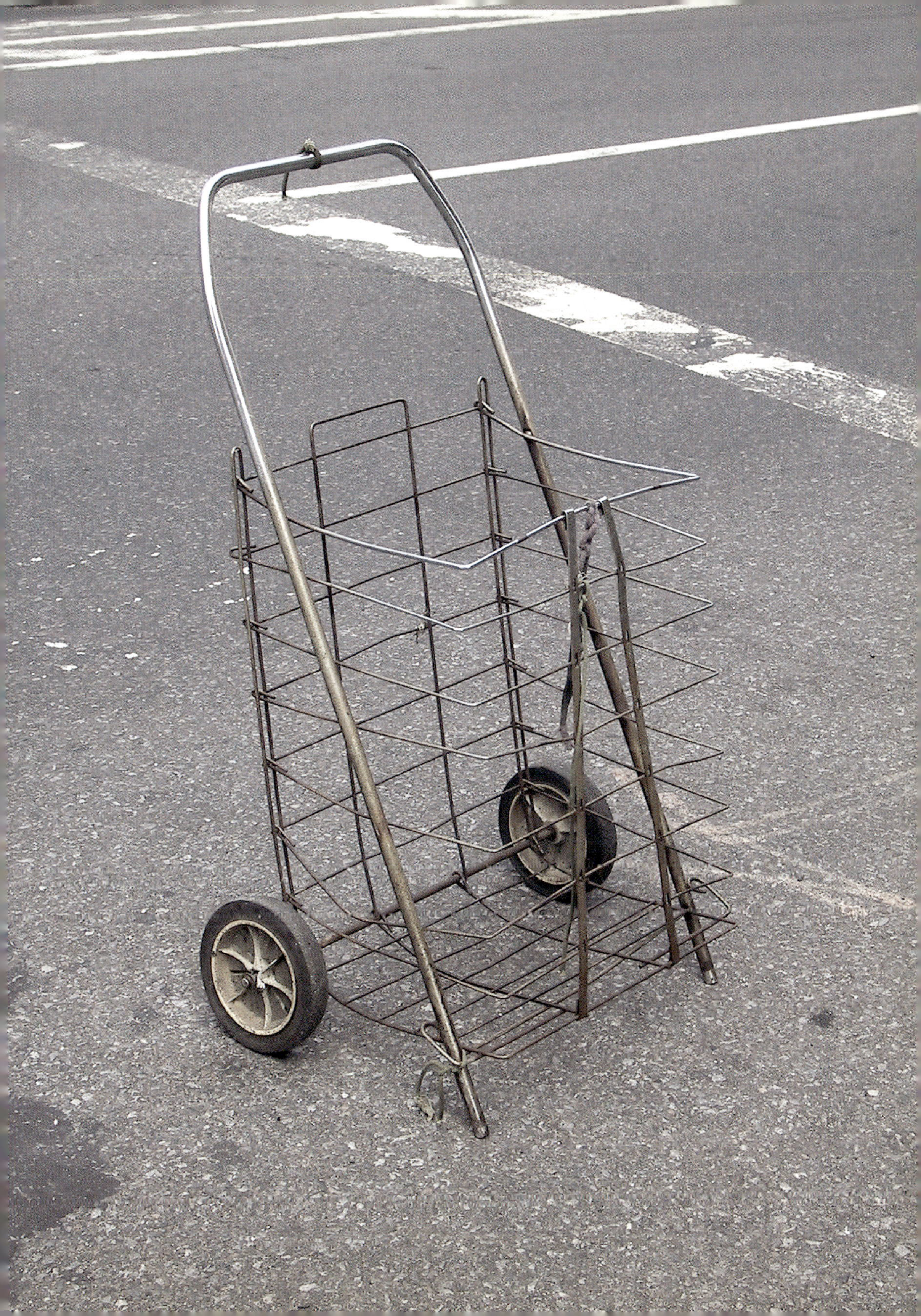

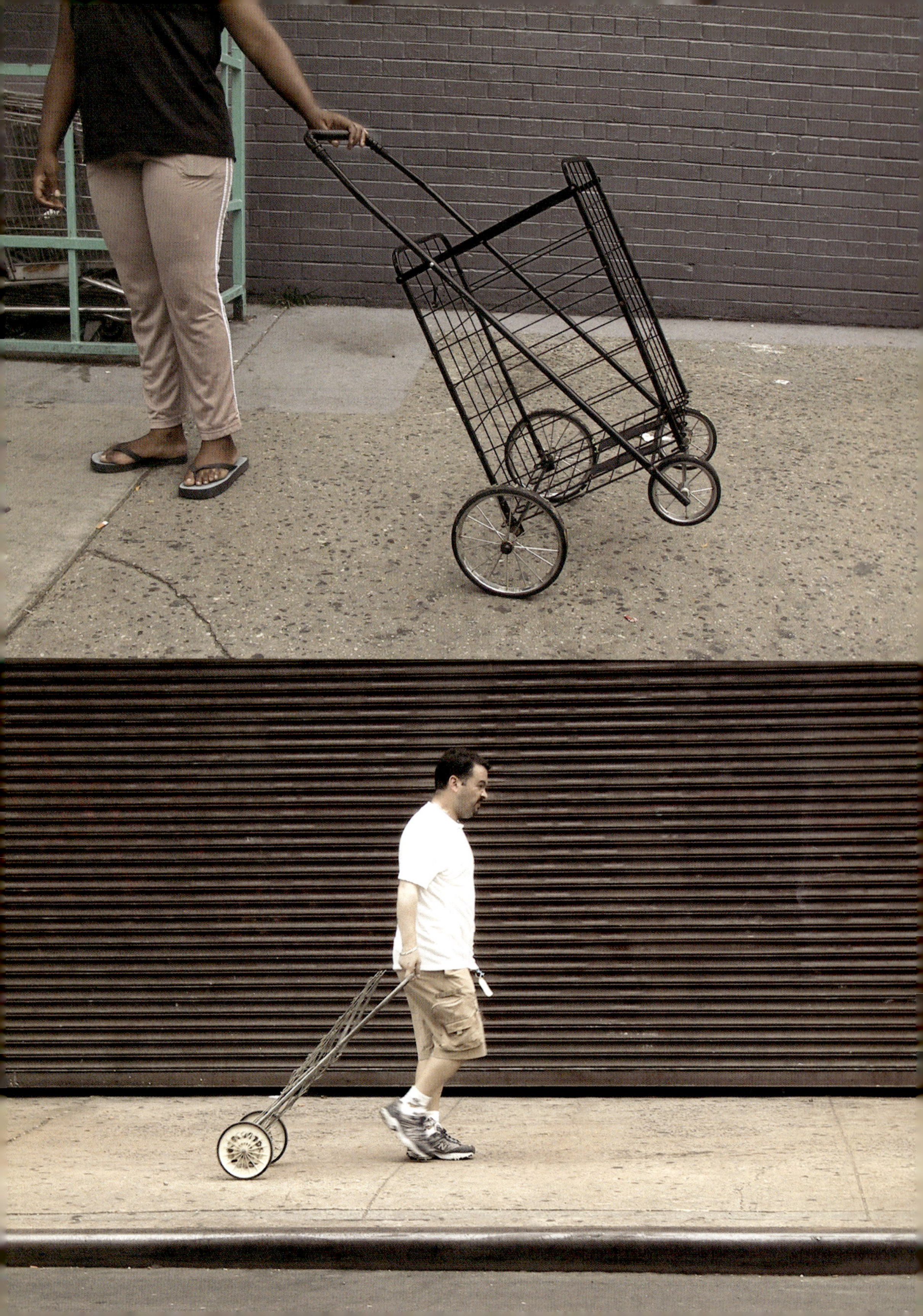

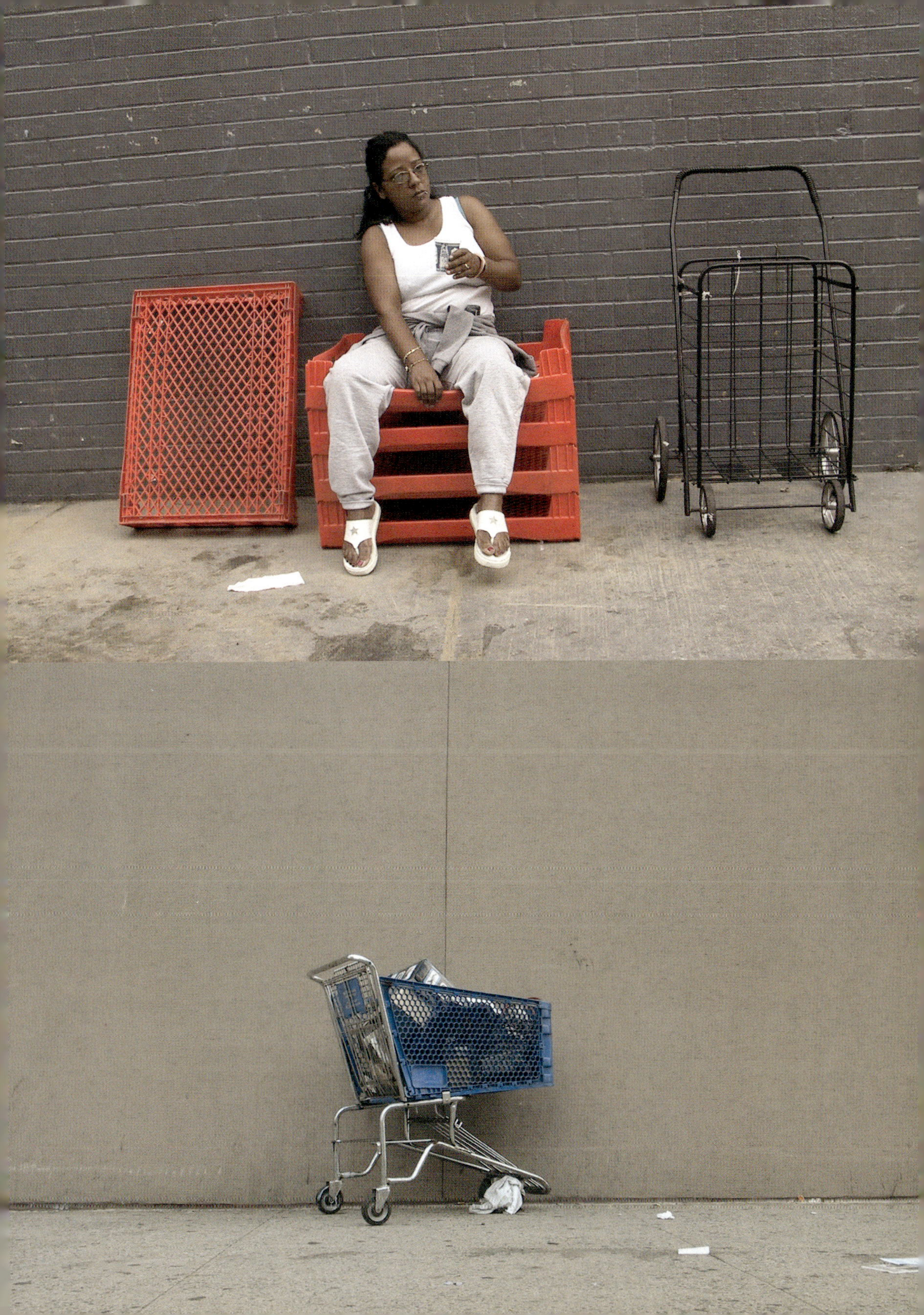

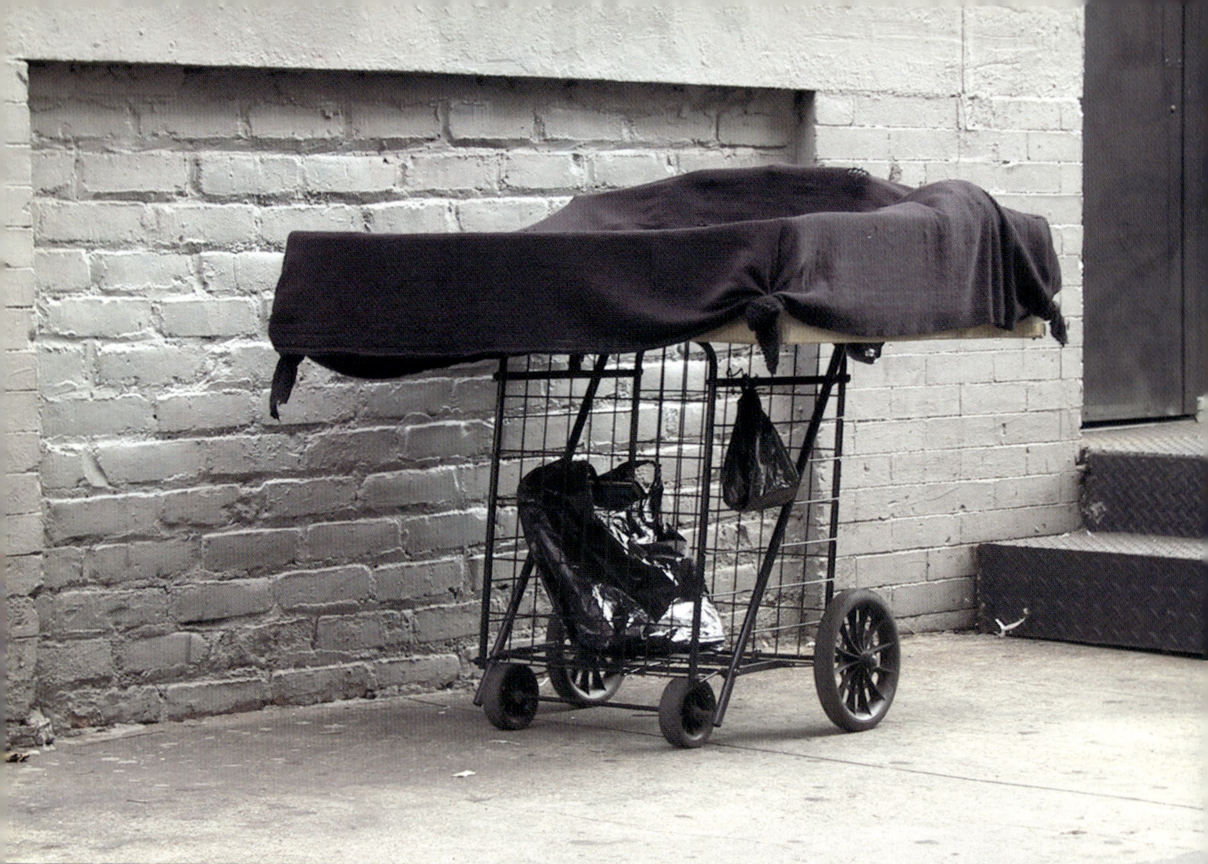

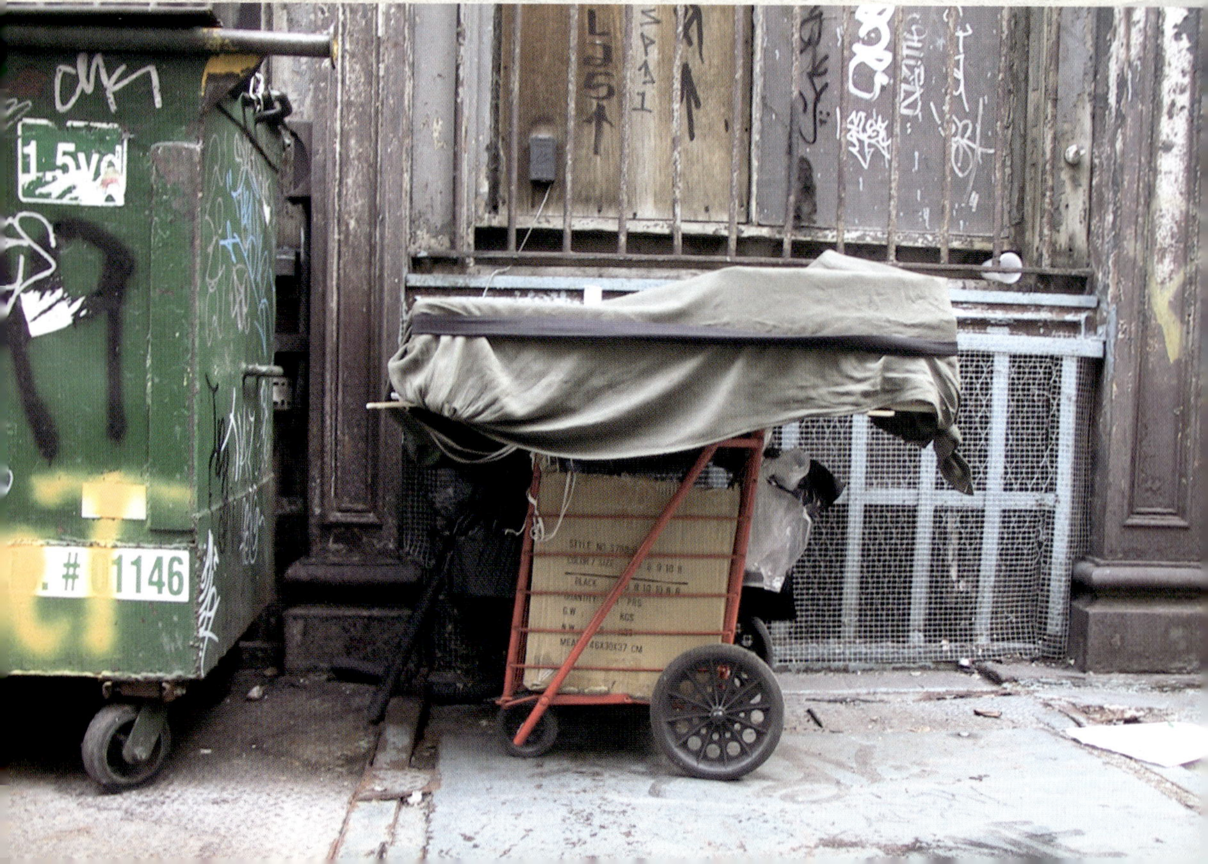

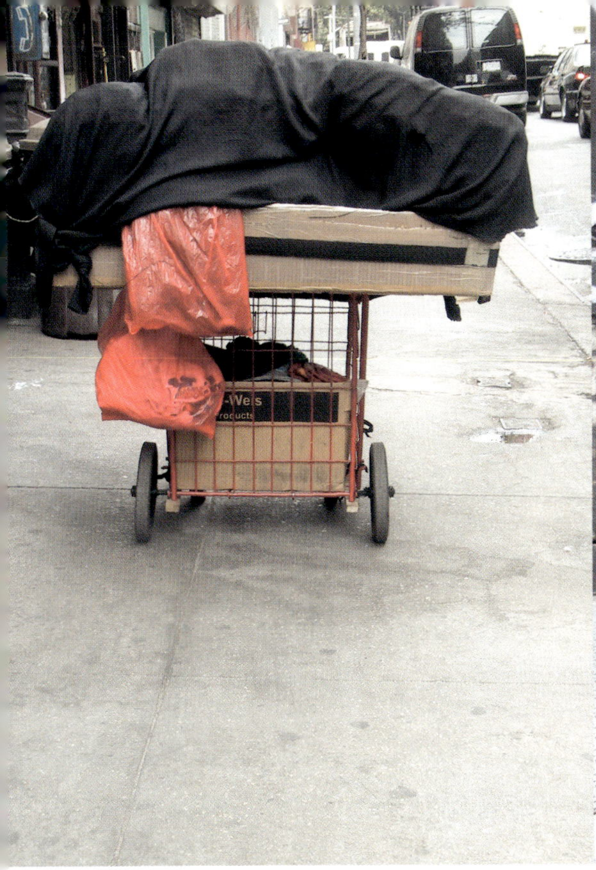

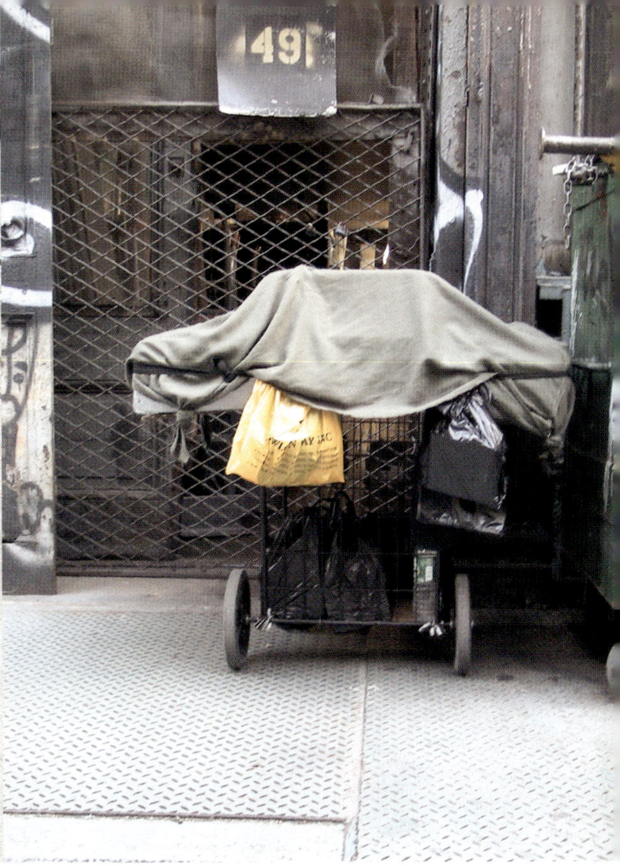

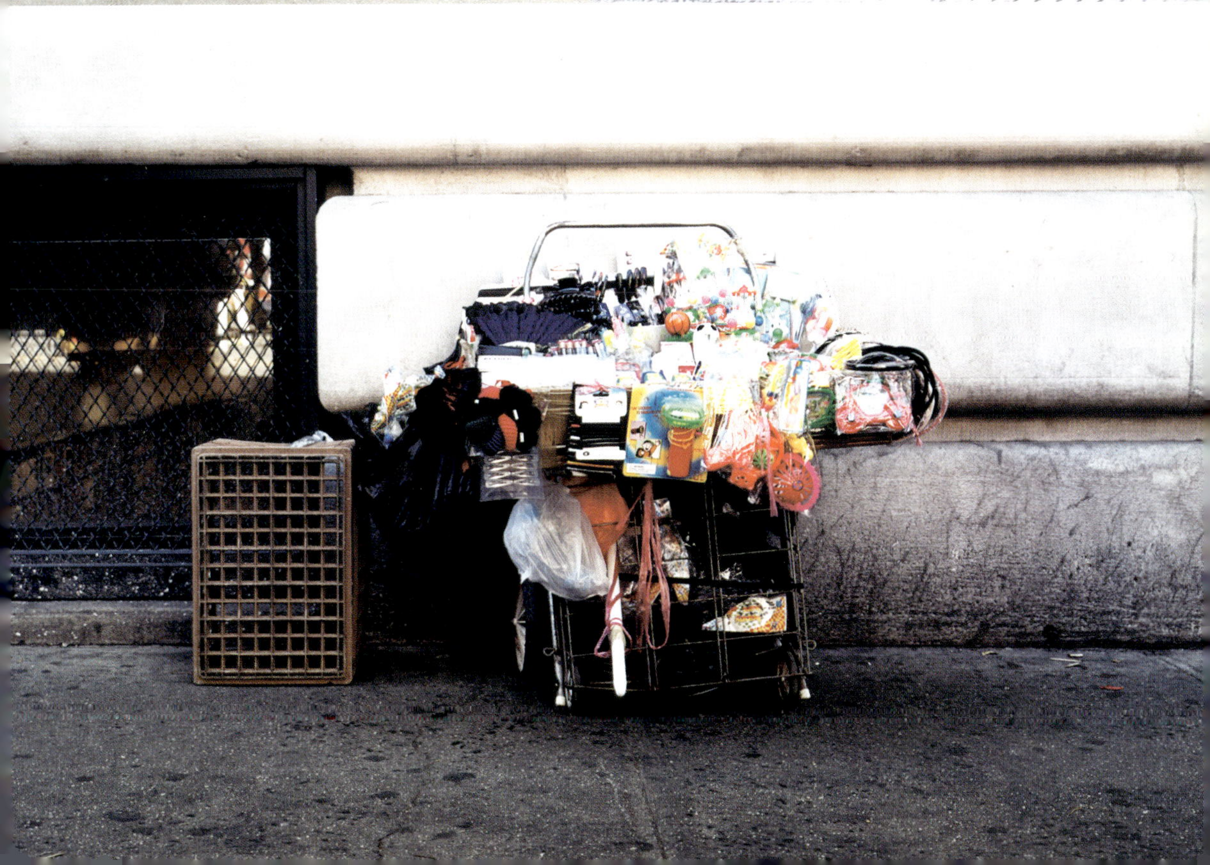

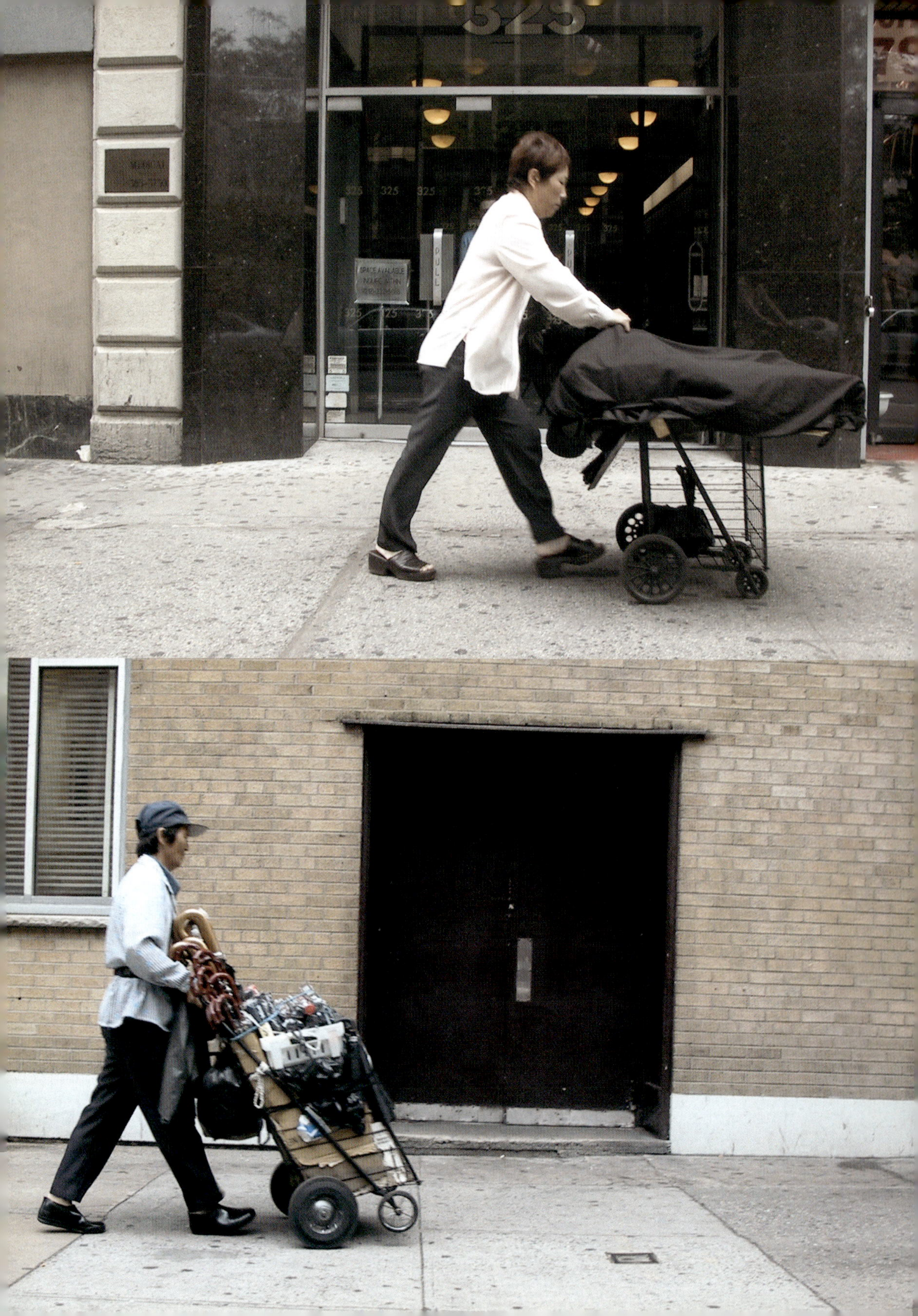
325
PULL

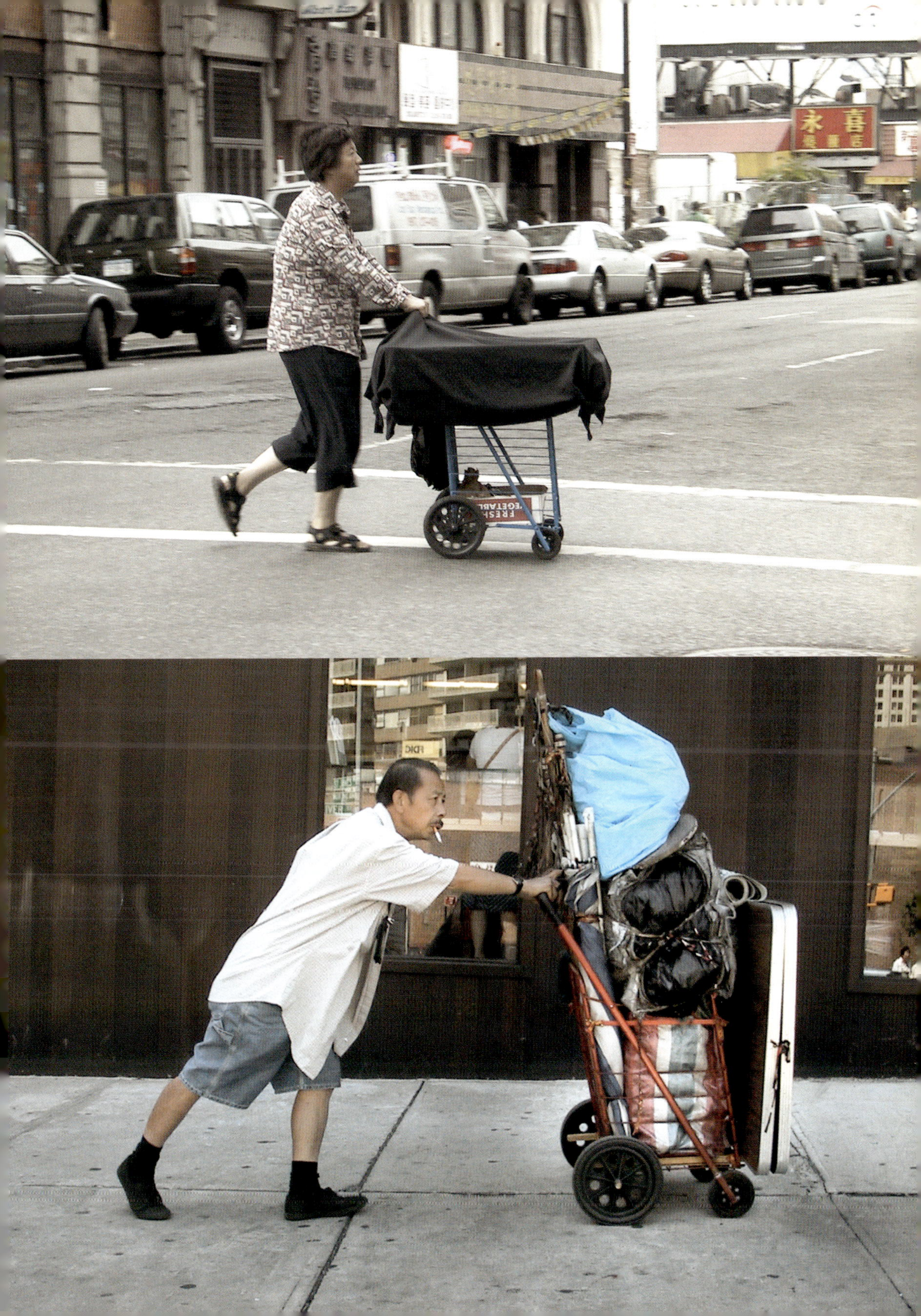
永喜
FDIC

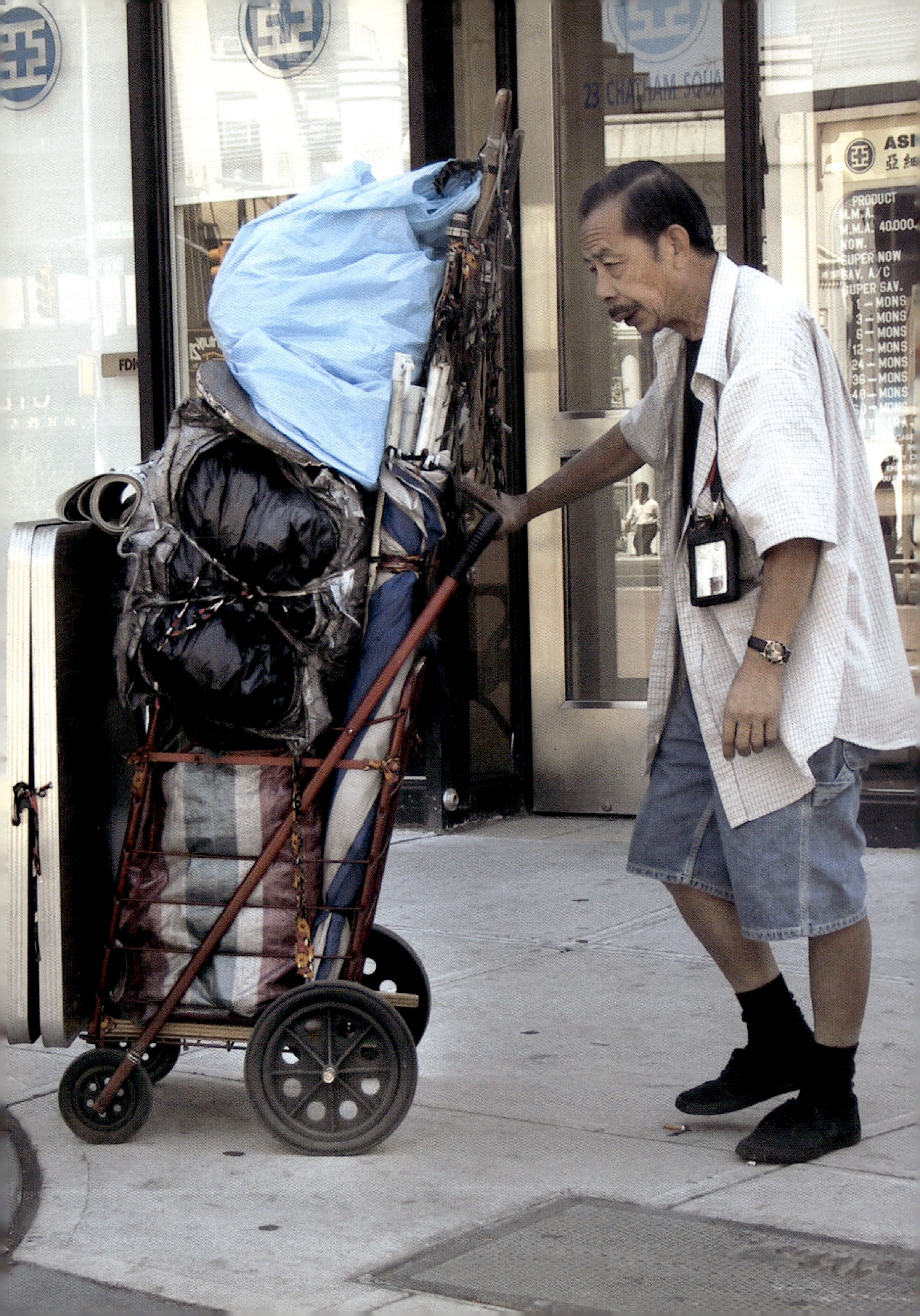

23 CHATHAM SQUA
PRODUCT
M.M.A.
M.M.A. 40,000
NOW.
SUPER NOW
SAV. A/C
SUPER SAV.
1 - MONS
3 - MONS
6 - MONS
12 - MONS
24 - MONS
36 - MONS
48 - MONS

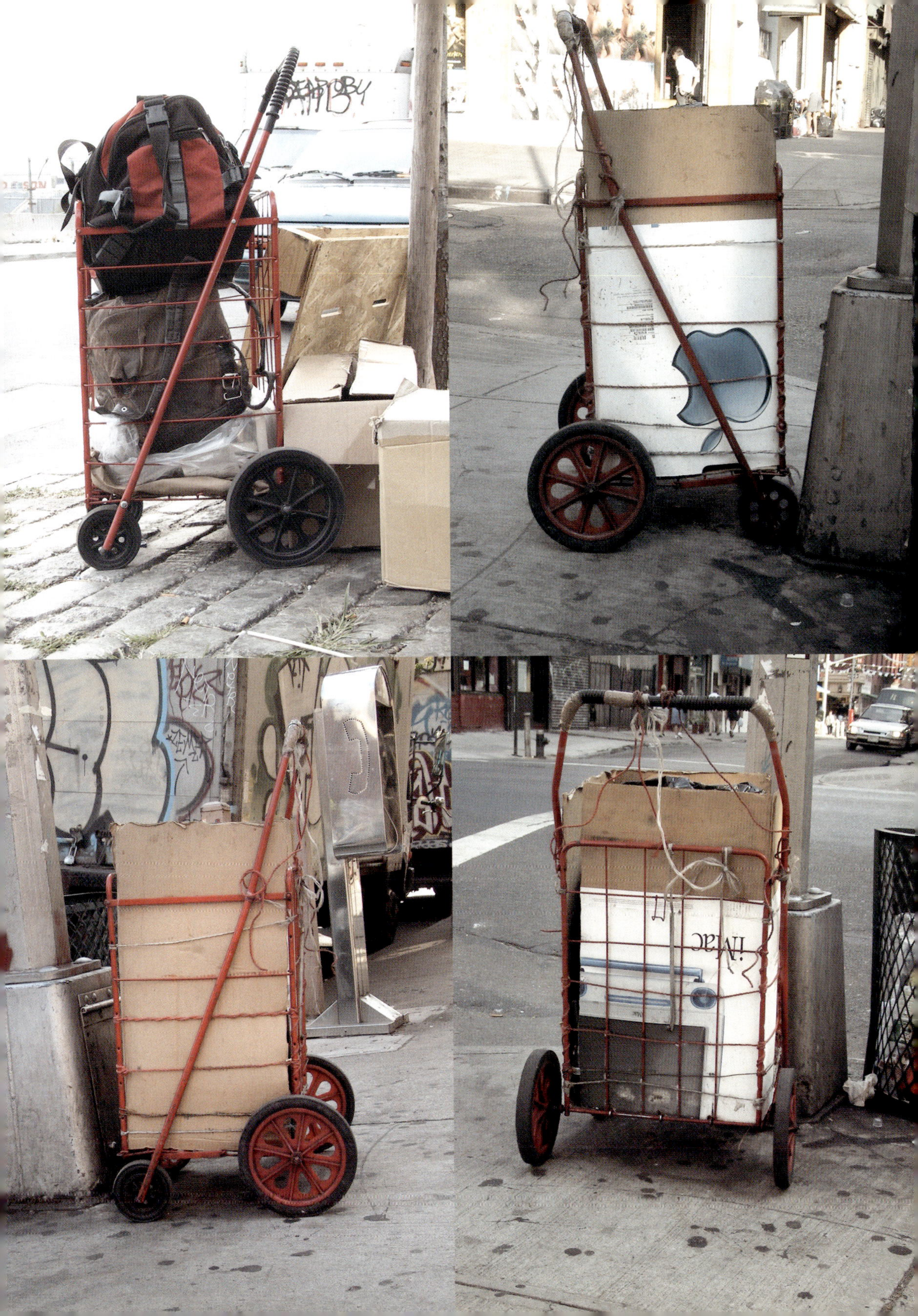

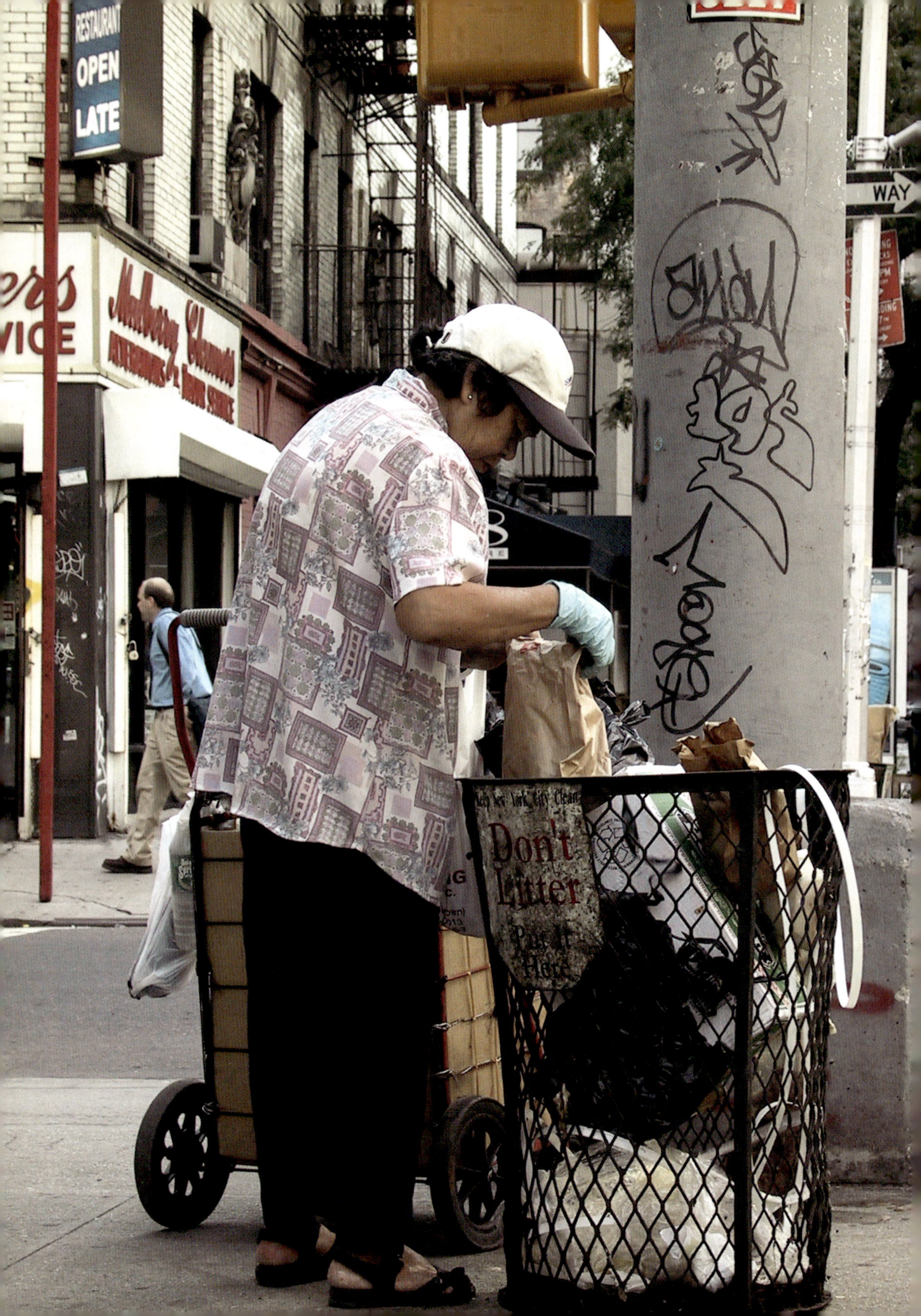
RESTAURANT
OPEN
LATE
WAY
Don't
Litter
Put It
Here

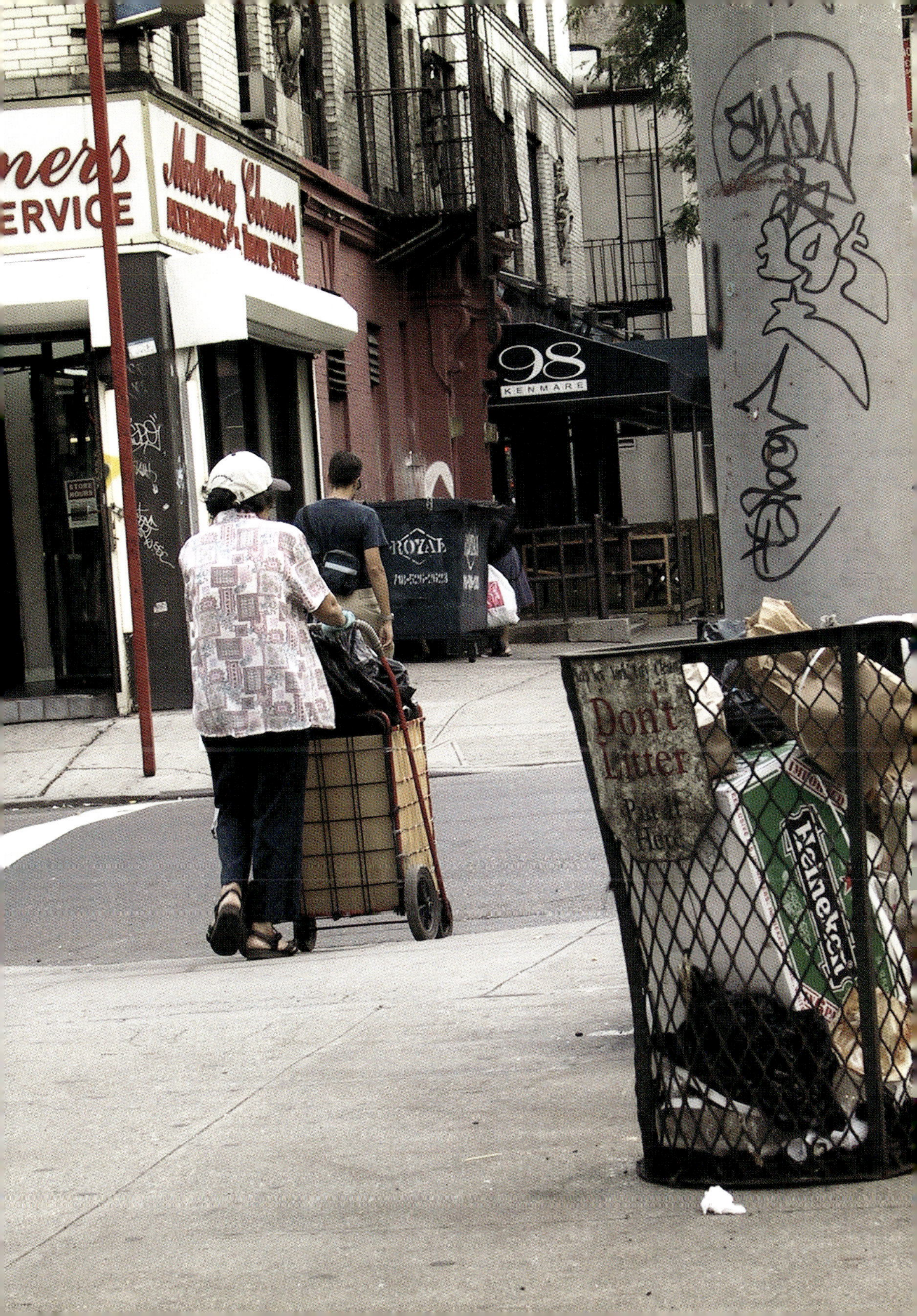

Mulberry Cleaners
98
KENMARE
ROYAL
Don't Litter
Put It Here
Heineken

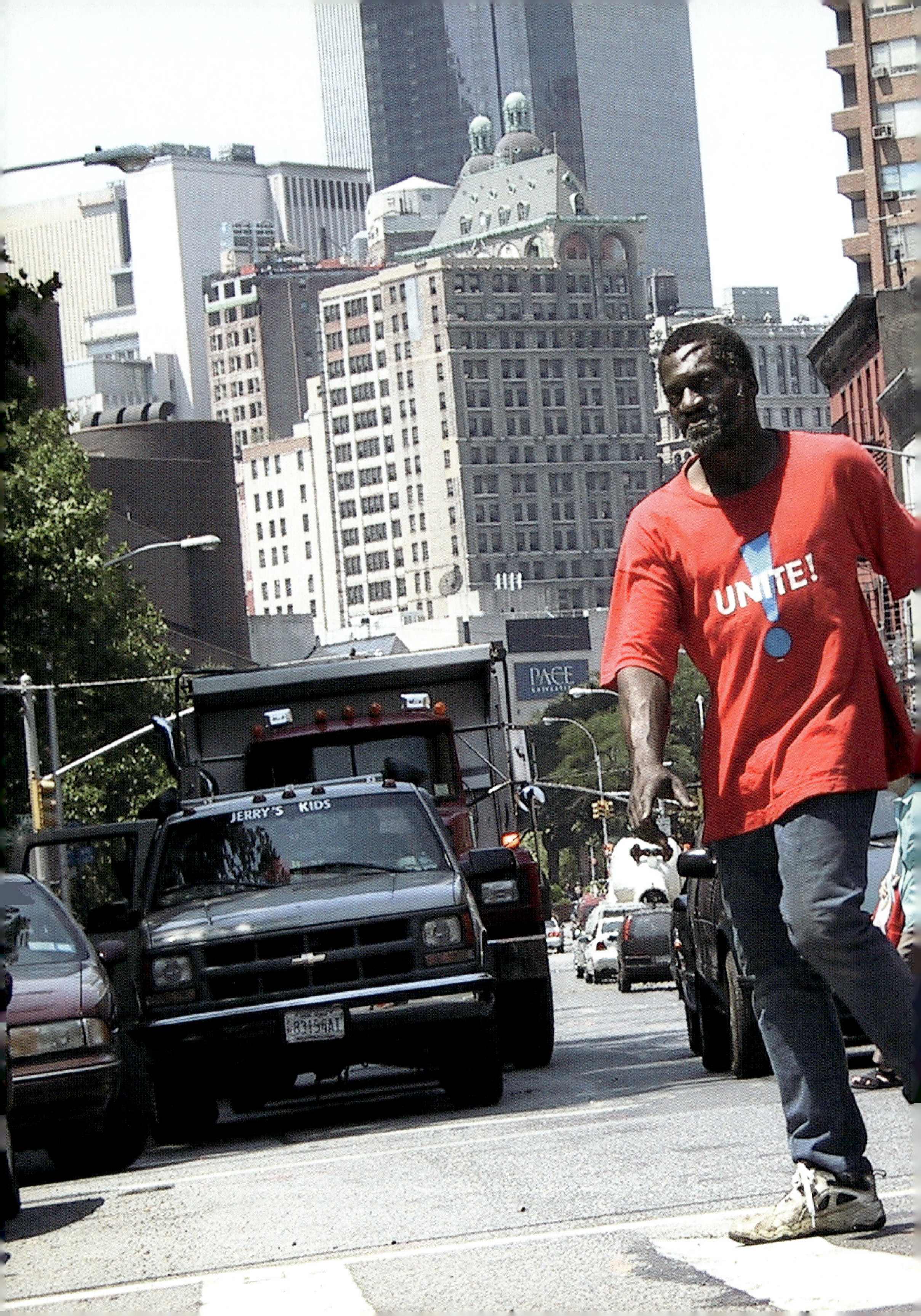
UNITE!
JERRY'S KIDS
PACE

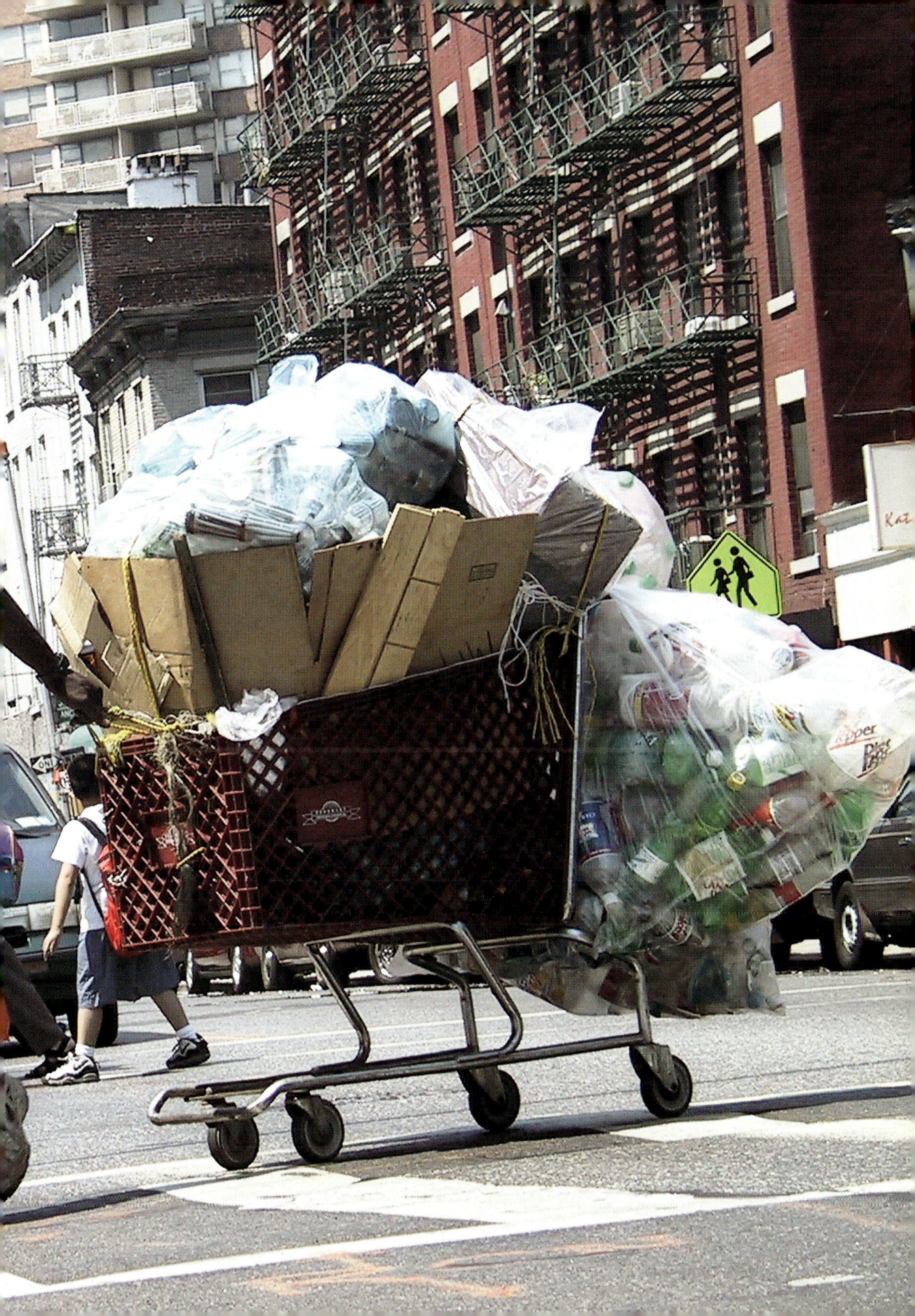

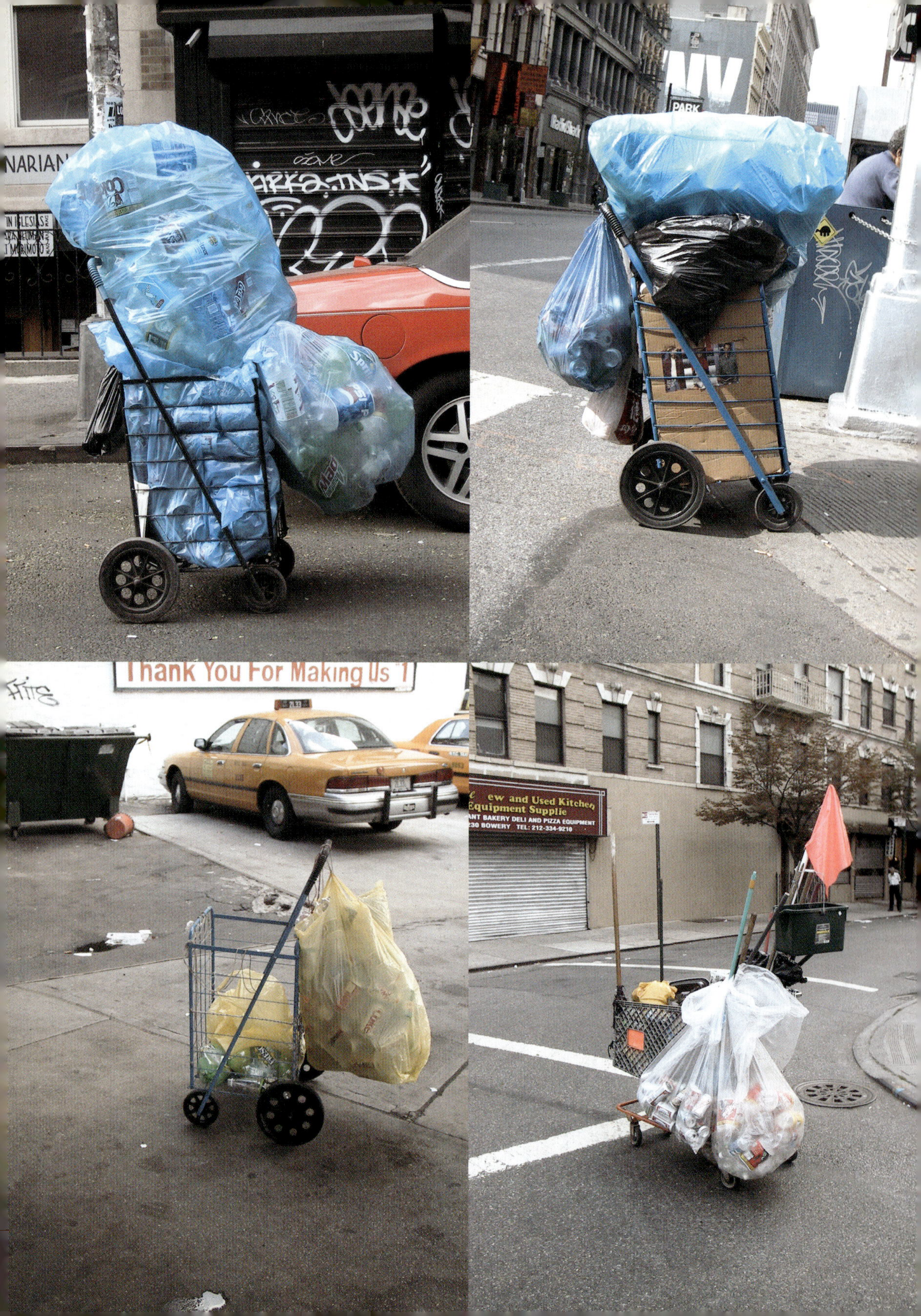
NARIAN
PARK
Thank You For Making Us 1
ew and Used Kitchen
Equipment Supplie
ANT BAKERY DELI AND PIZZA EQUIPMENT
230 BOWERY TEL: 212-334-9210

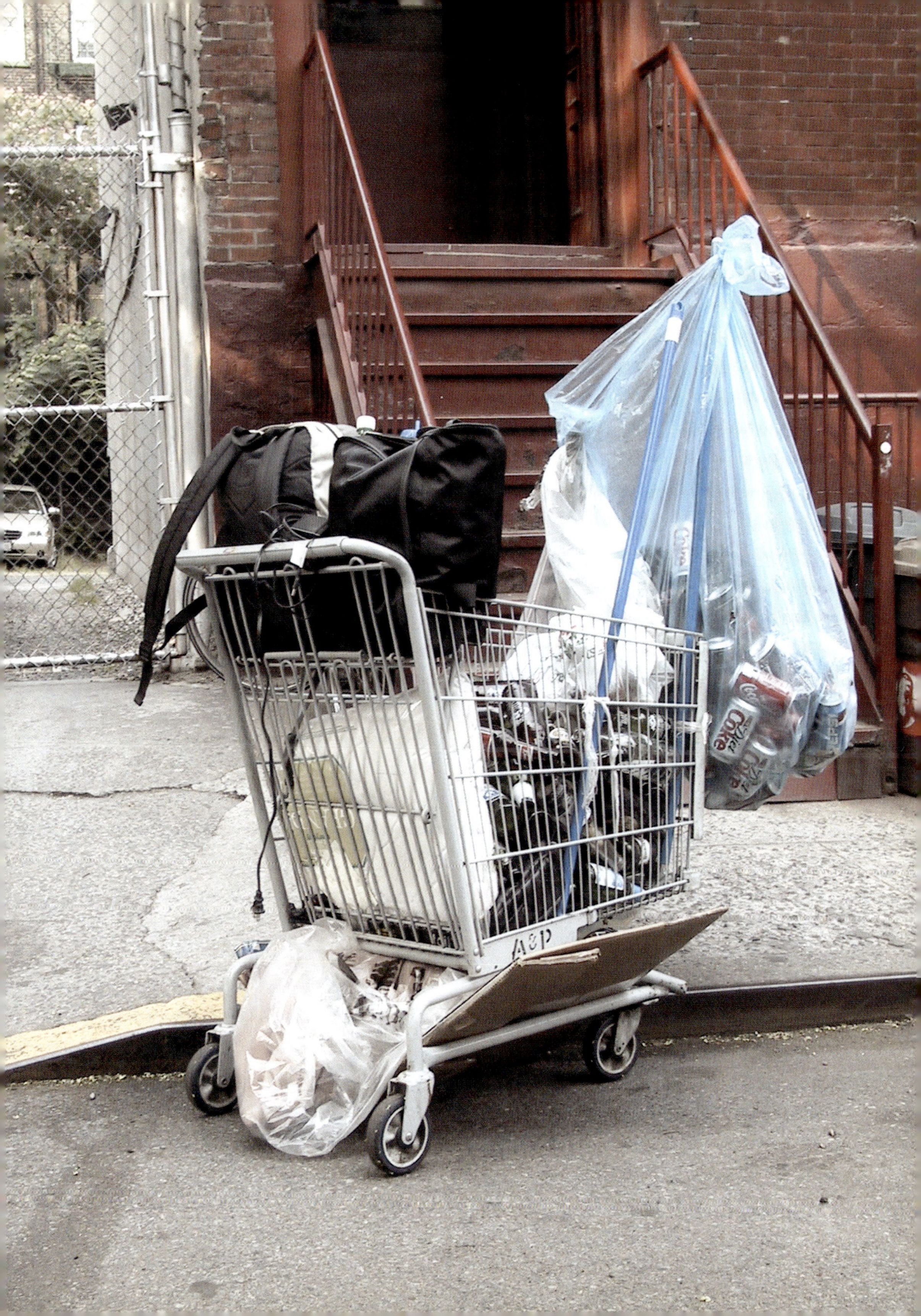
Diet Coke
A&P

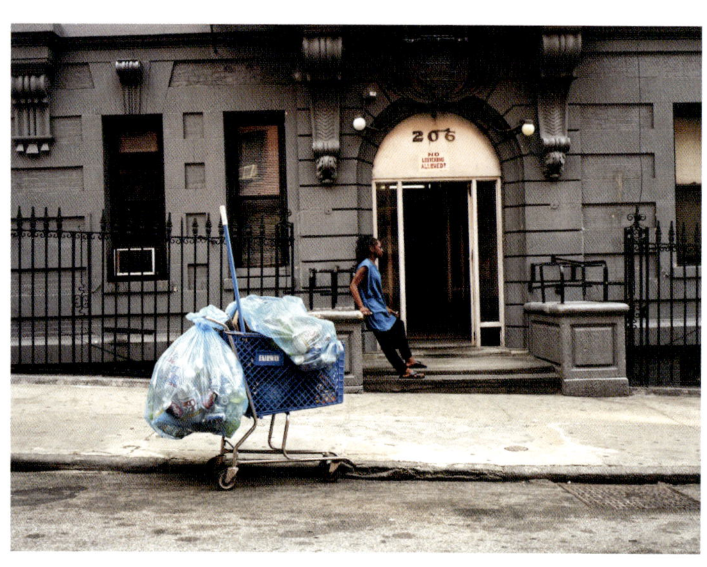
206

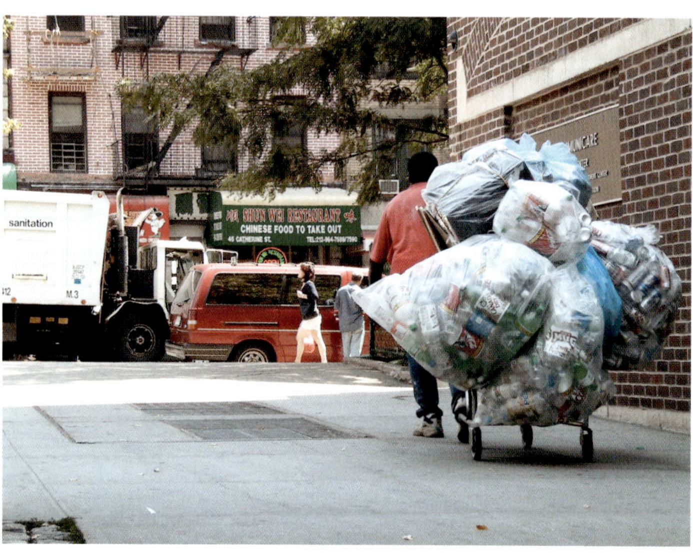
sanitation
SHUN WEI RESTAURANT
CHINESE FOOD TO TAKE OUT

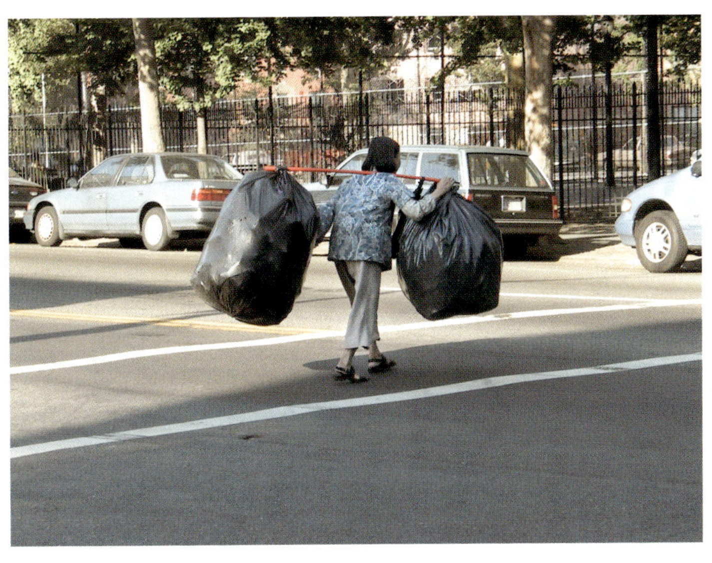

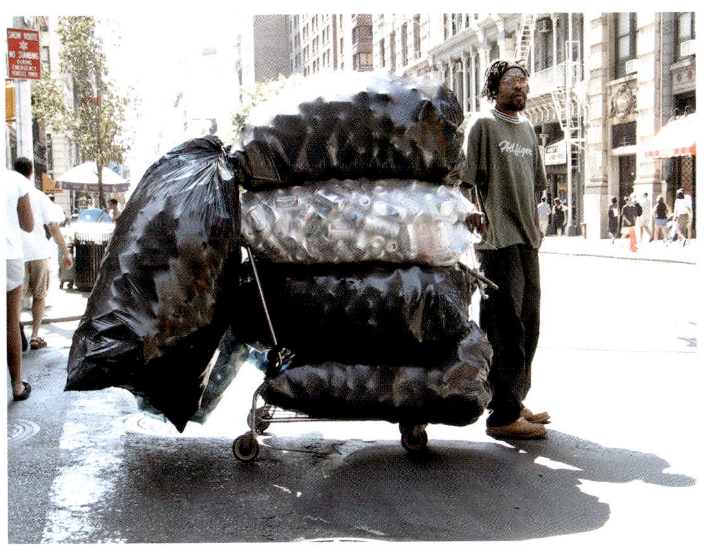
SNOW ROUTE
NO STANDING
DURING
EMERGENCY

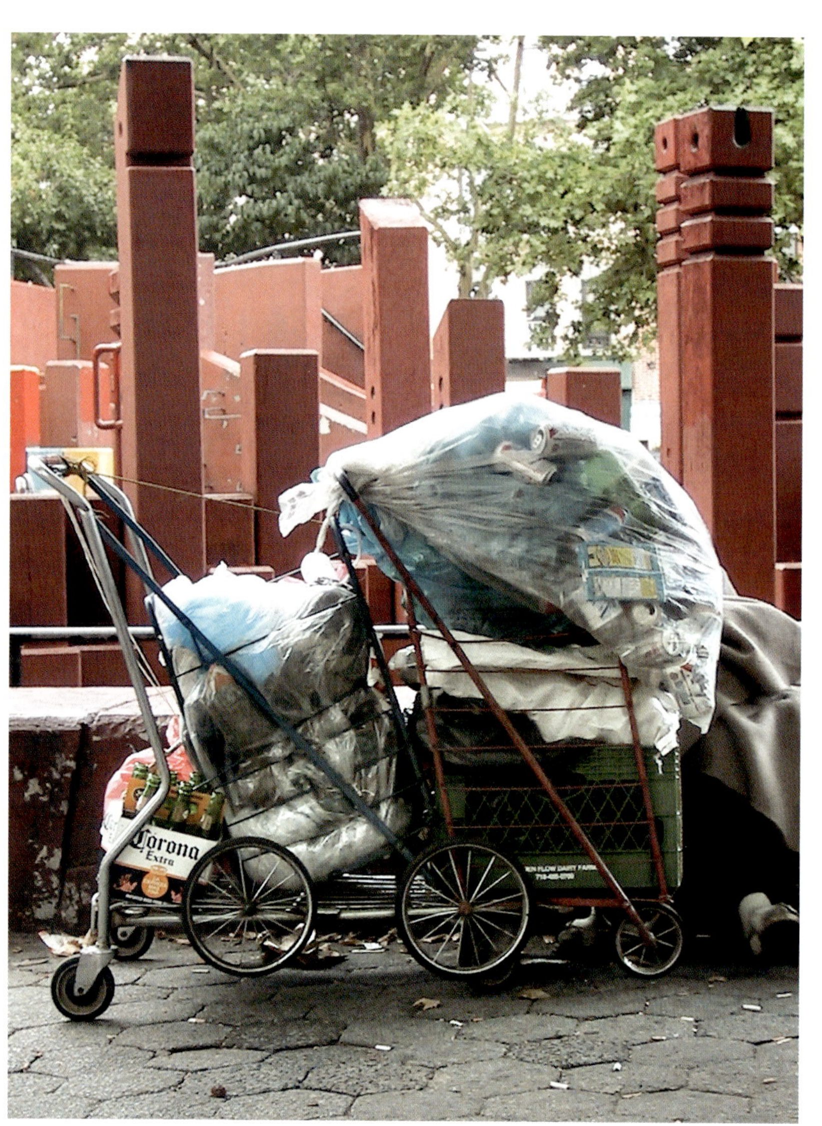
Corona
Extra

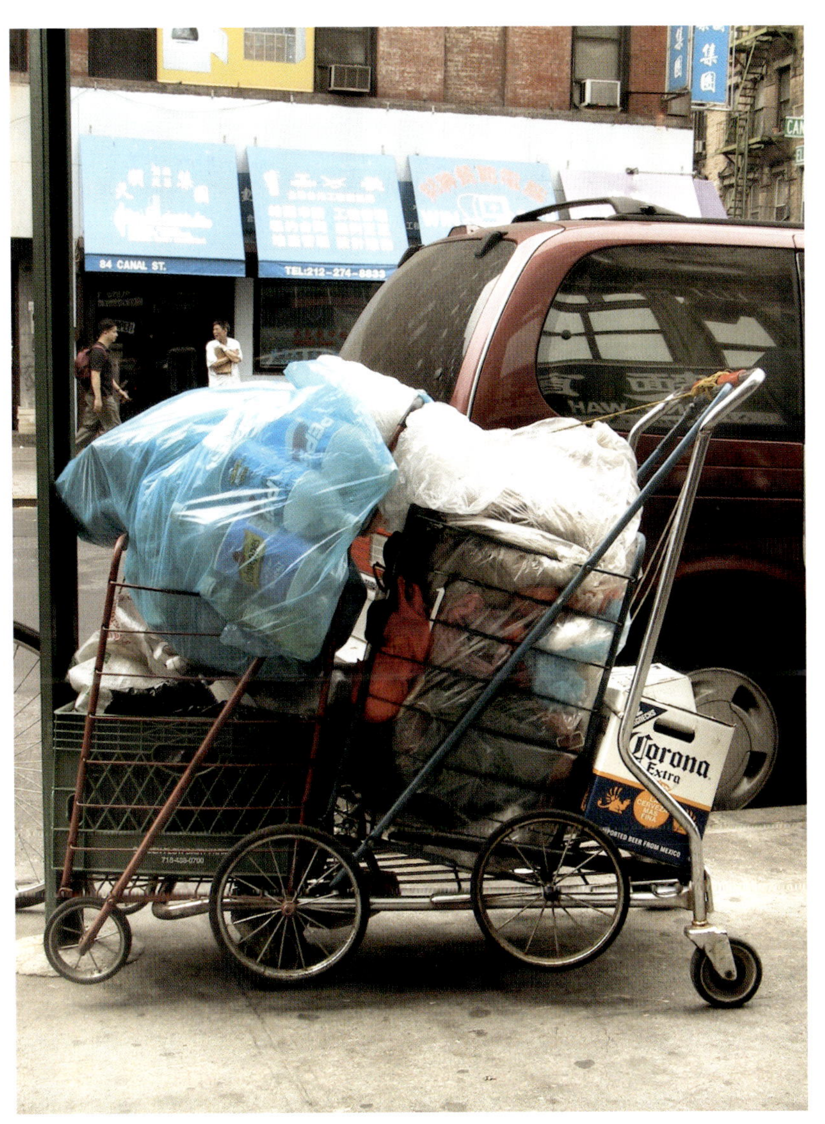
84 CANAL ST.
Corona
Extra

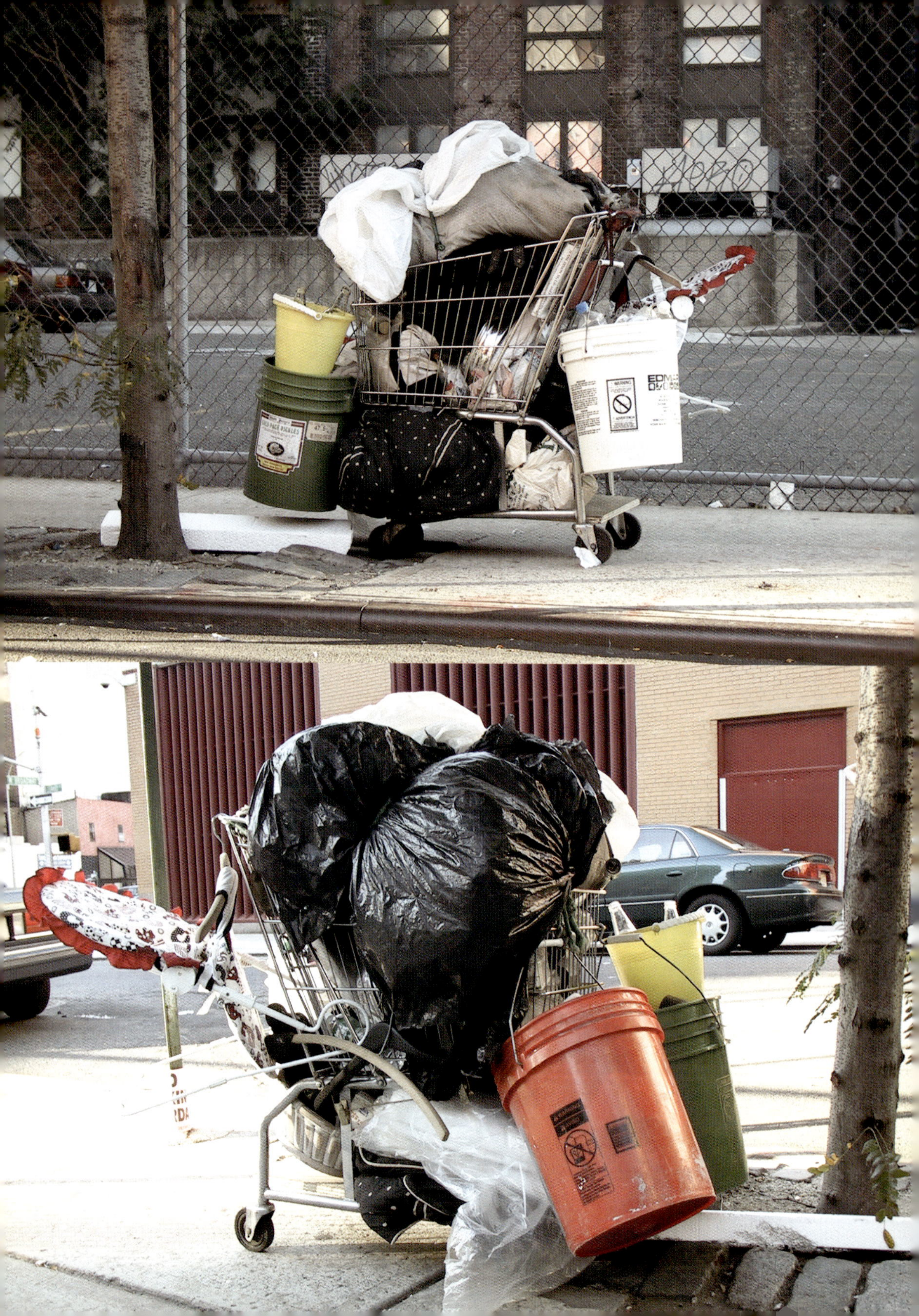
COLD PACK PICKLES
WARNING

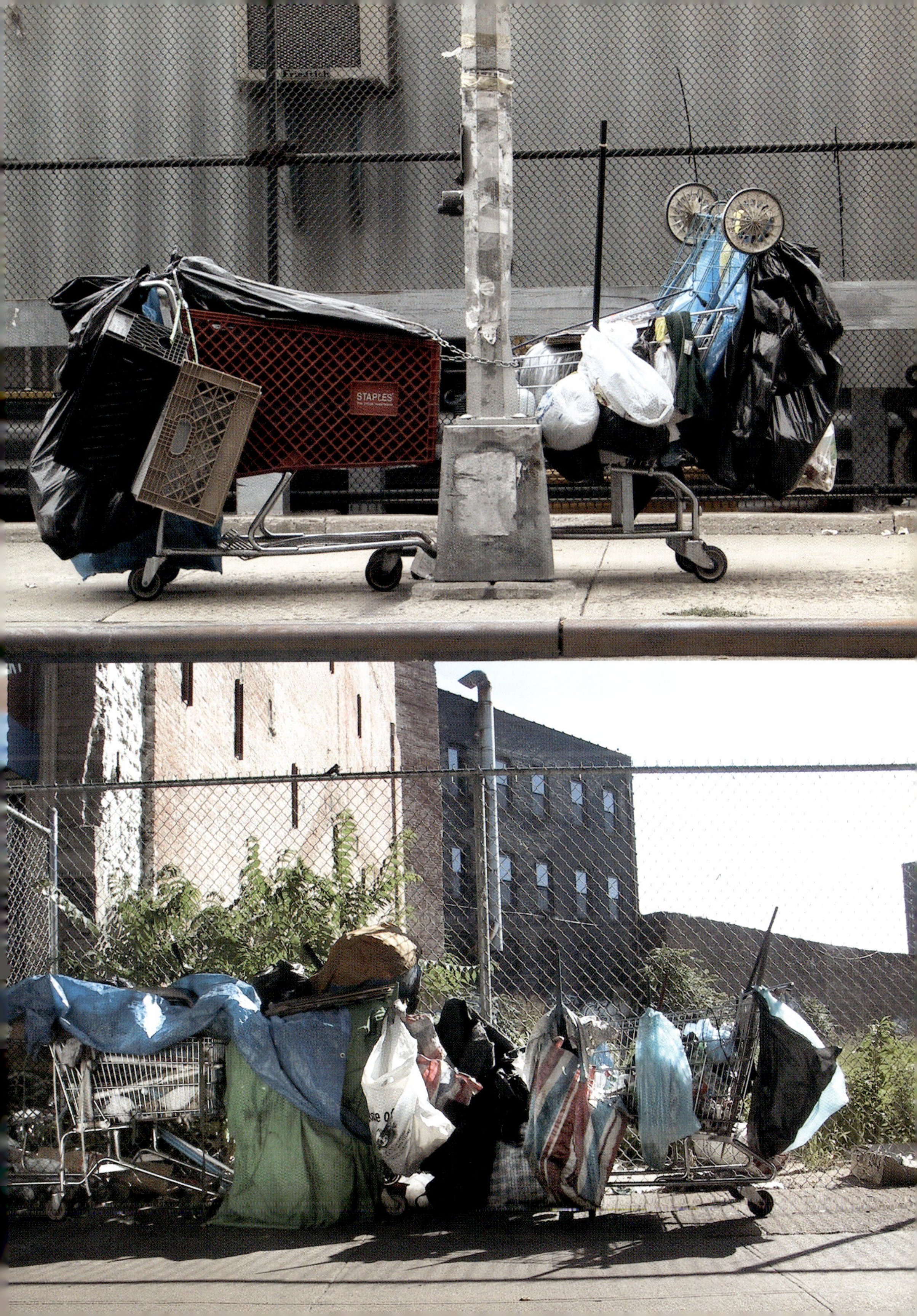
STAPLES

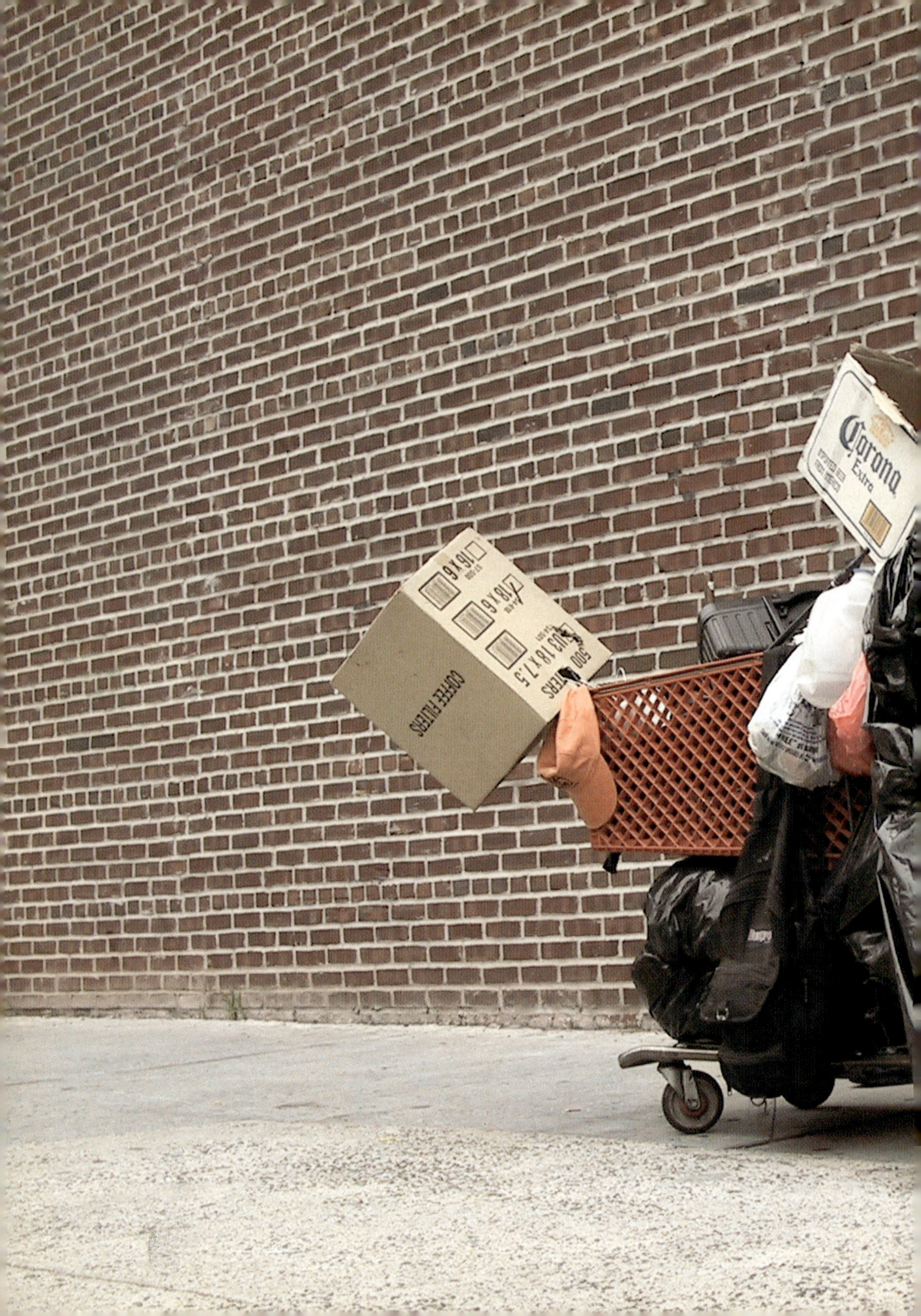
Corona
Extra
COFFEE FILTERS

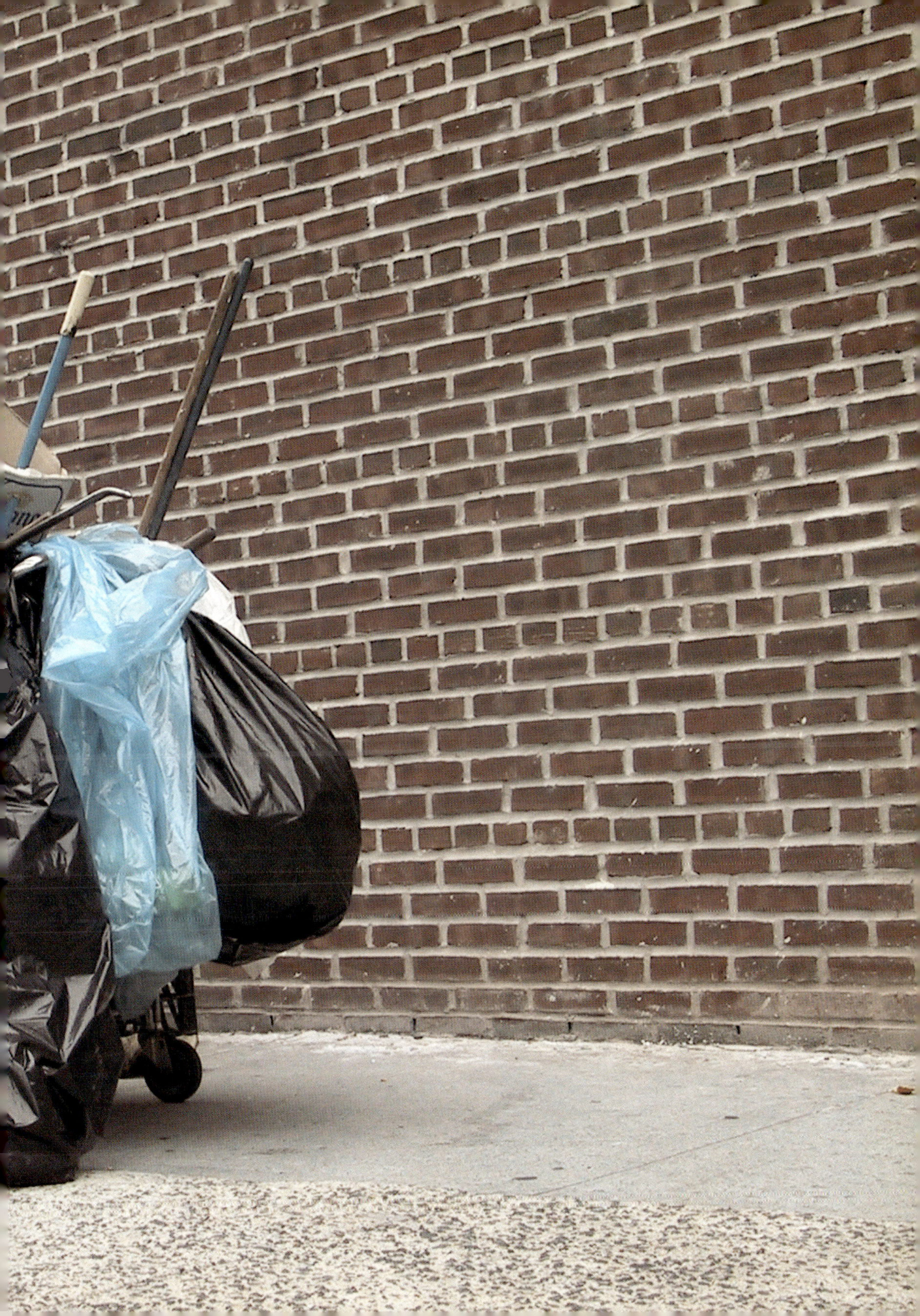

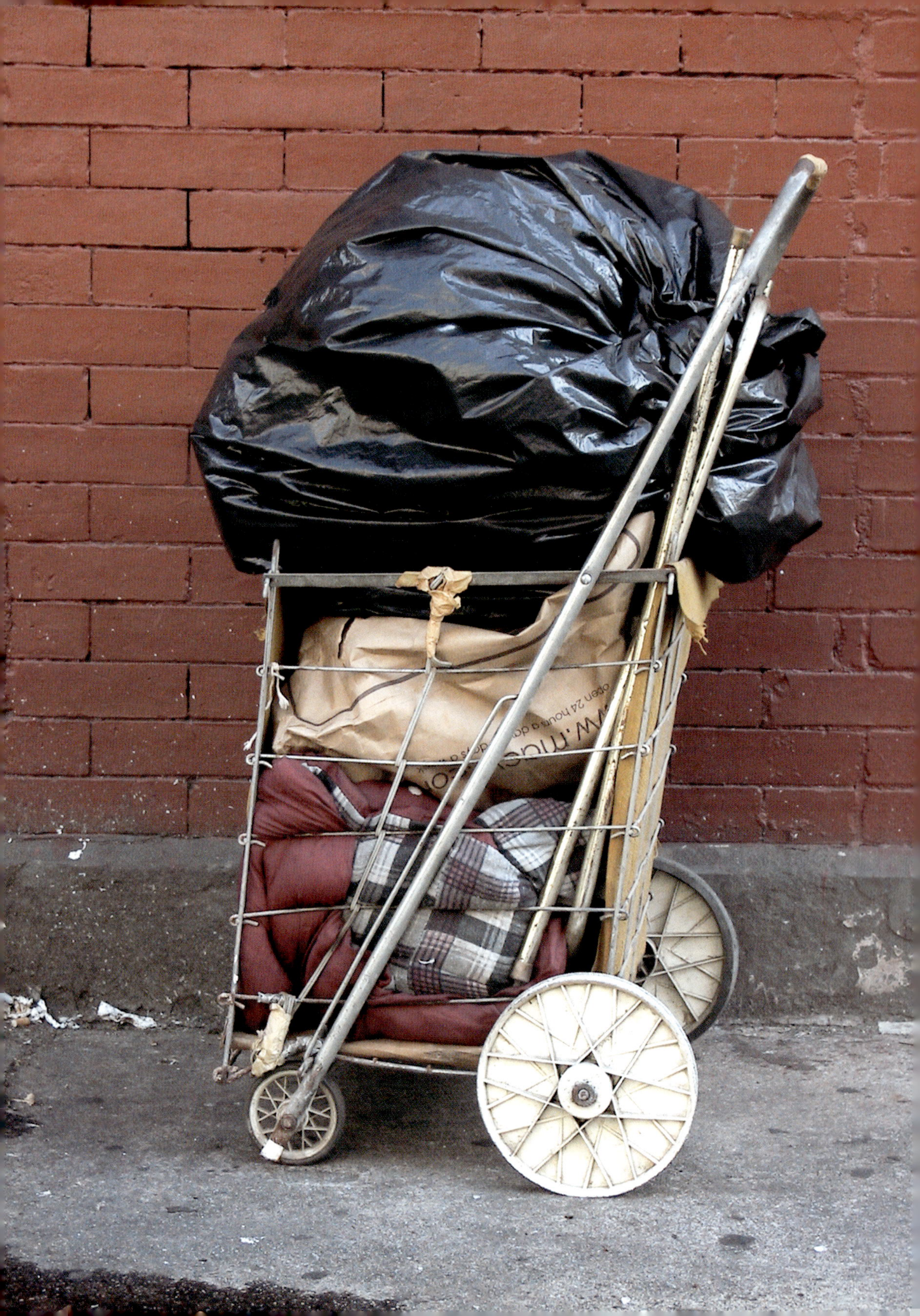

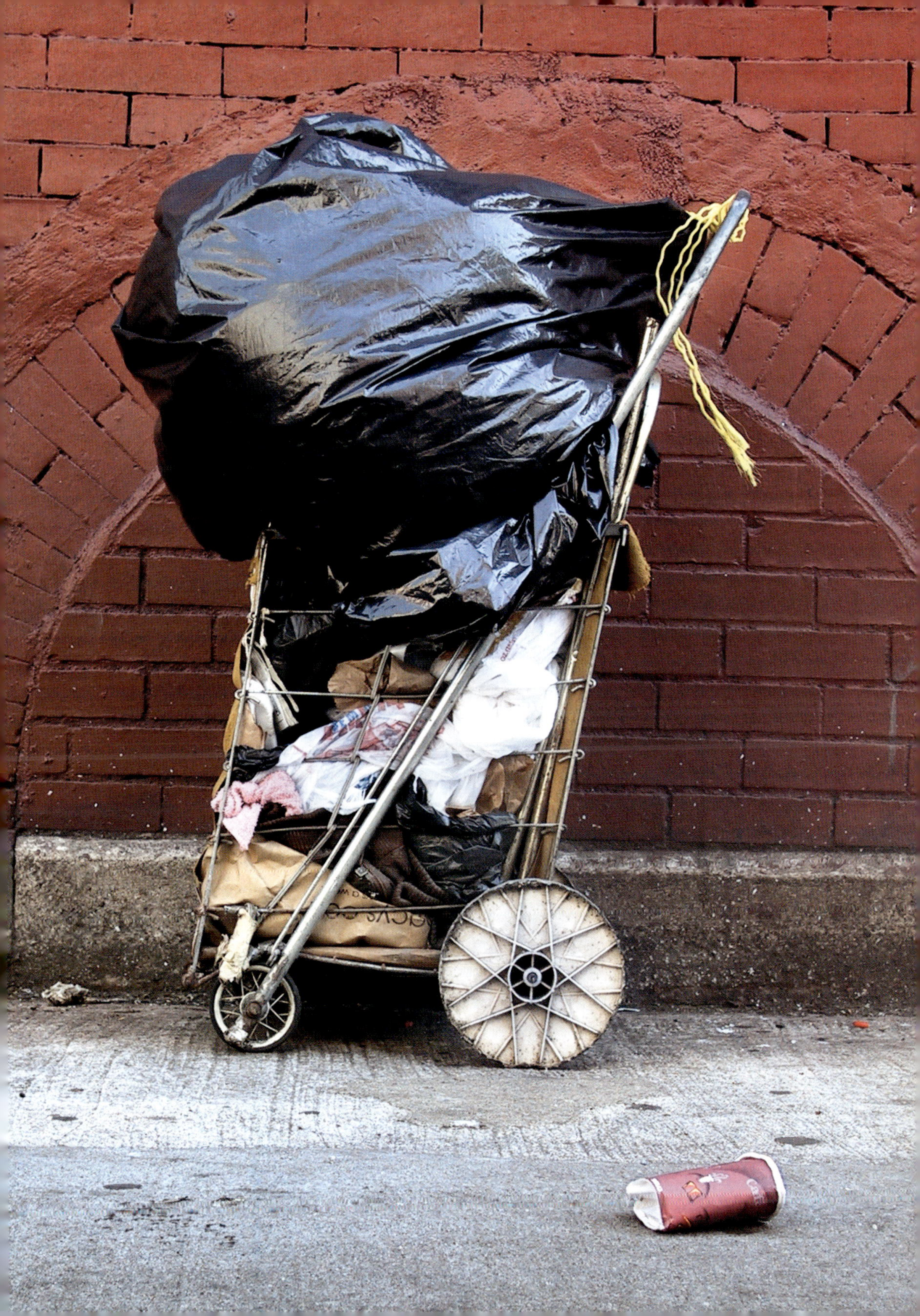

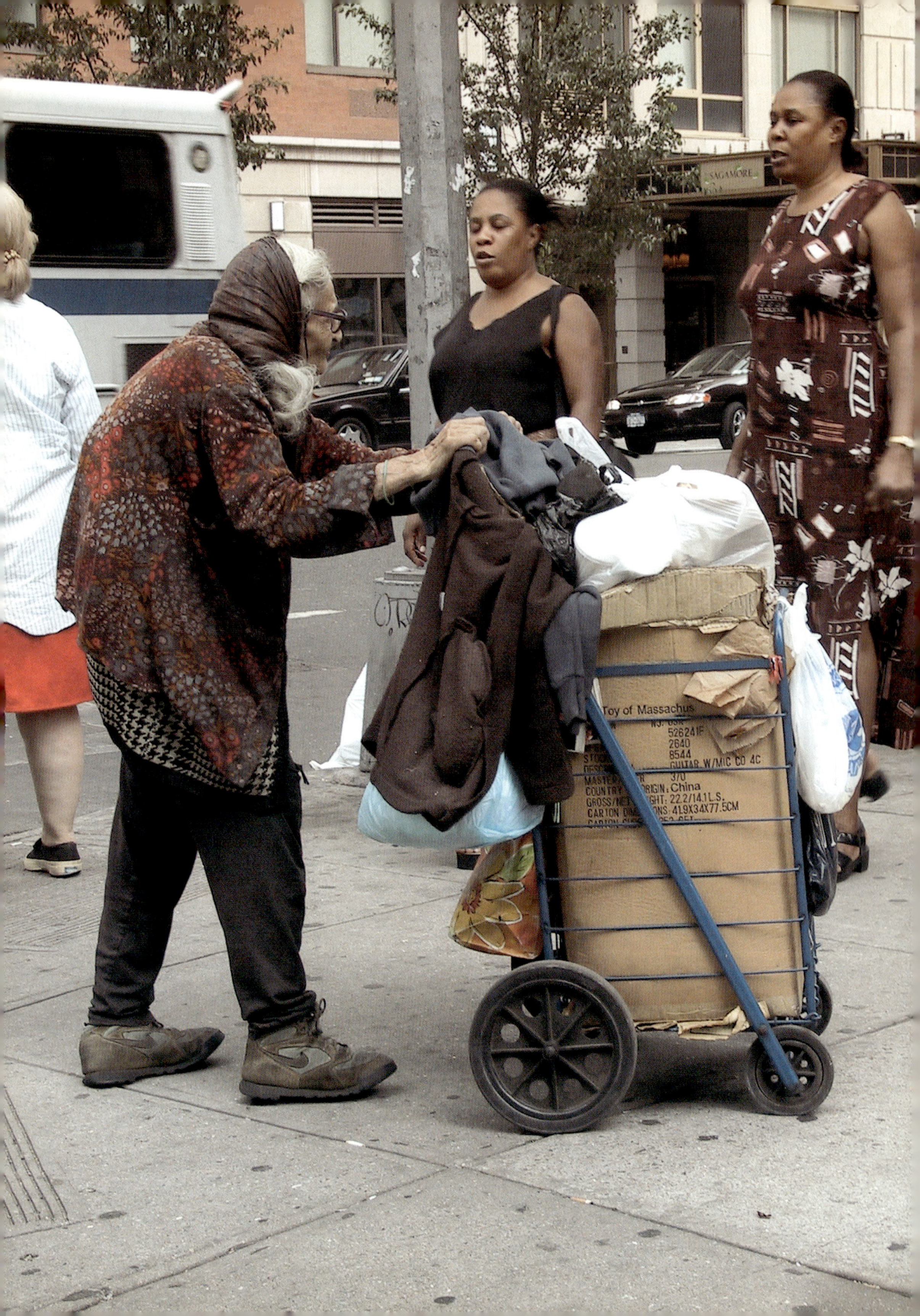
SAGAMORE
Toy of Massachus
526241F
2640
8544
GUITAR W/MIC CO 4C
370
China
22.2/14.1L.S.
41.9X34X77.5CM

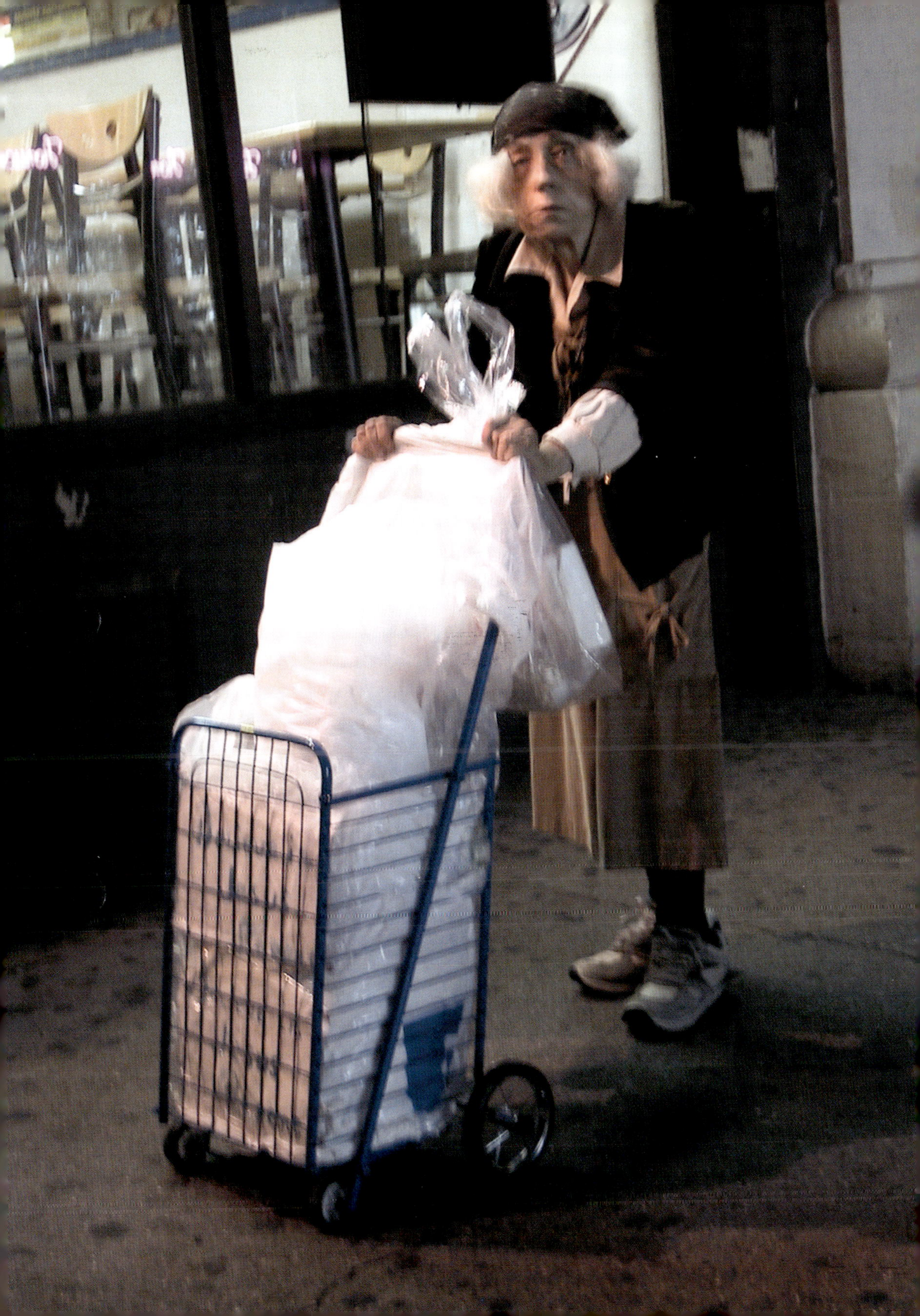

	System			Order		
Property Phenomenon	Dysfunctional Speech Act	Commerce	Control	Membrane	Orientation	The Range of Participation
LOCKED MOBILITY	MISSPELLING	CORPORATE MONUMENTS	POLICE LINE DO NOT CROSS	BLUE CITY	STREET SCRIPT	VOICE
TAPE	FADING MARKETS	STREET VENDORS	A BARRIER	COVER	STREET MARK	DIVERSITY
SHOP WATCH	EMPTY SIGNS	STREET LEVEL	SERVICE SCREEN	SHOPPING BAG	STEEL	OPEN CINE
REAL ESTATE		SHOPPING CARTS		GARBAGE DIGITAL SLUM		NEIGHBORHOOD

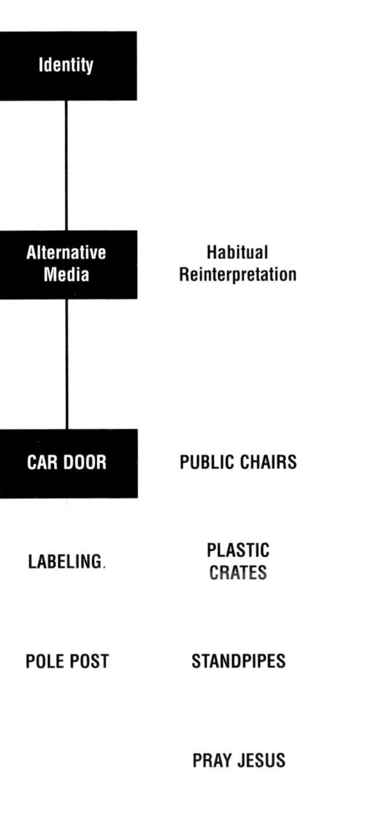

CAR DOOR

Quick Change Identity

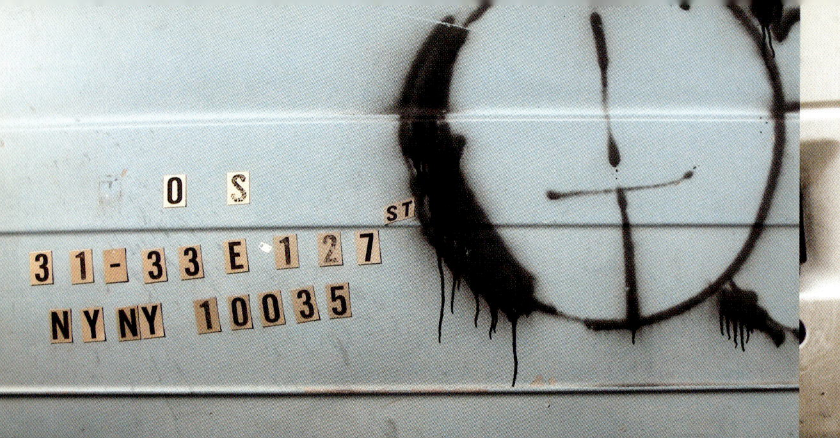
O S
ST
31-33 E 127
NYNY 10035

Goo
Mechanica
74 14T
BROOKLY

ECONOLINE 350
AMANIS
FASHION
71E. B' WAY
N. Y. 10002

ABC
30 JA
N.Y.

BON
34HOWARD ST
NY NY 10013

g
30
ny.n

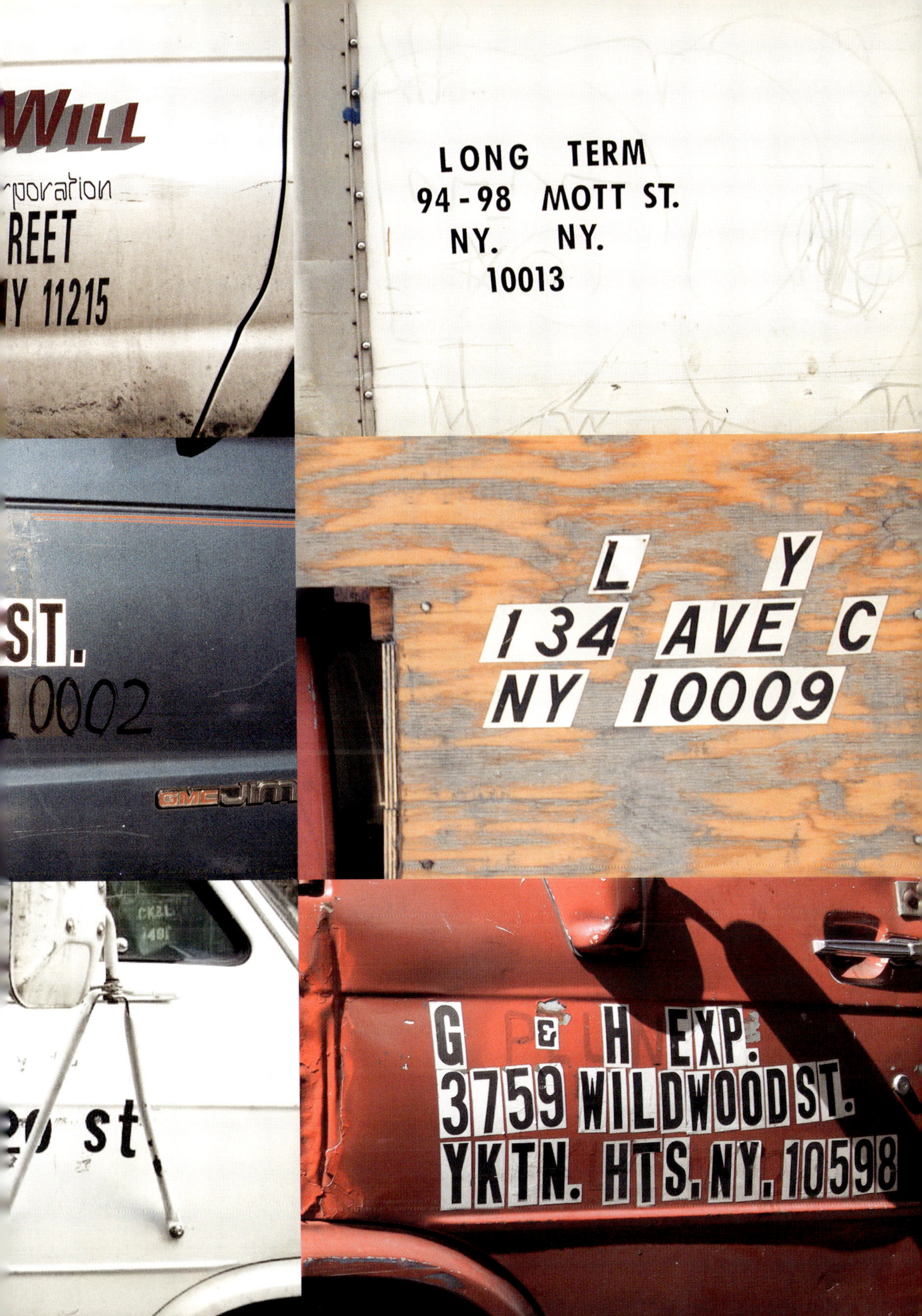
WILL
rporation
REET
Y 11215
LONG TERM
94 - 98 MOTT ST.
NY. NY.
10013
ST.
0002
L Y
134 AVE C
NY 10009
20 st
G & H EXP.
3759 WILDWOOD ST.
YKTN. HTS. NY. 10598

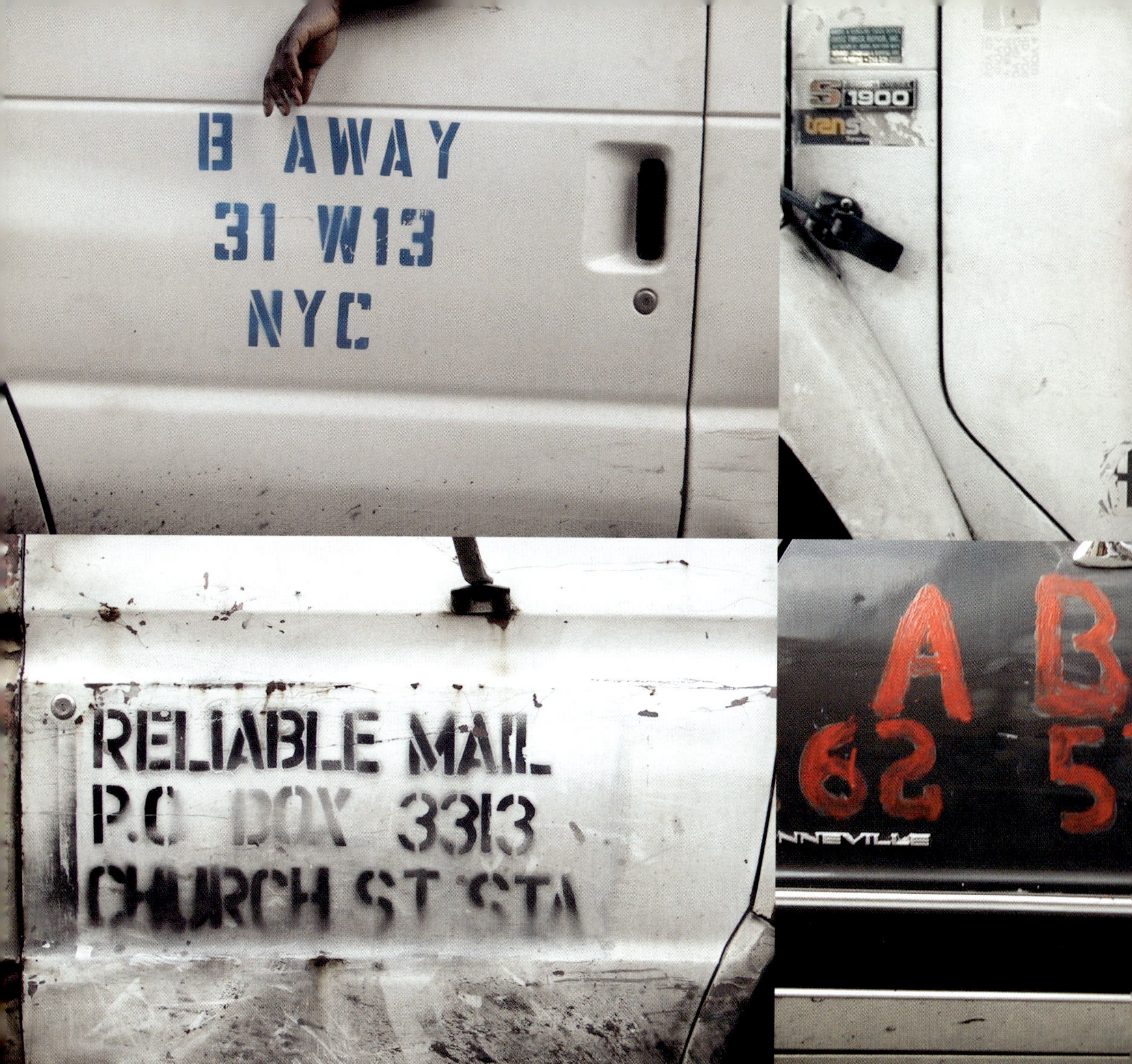
B AWAY
31 W13
NYC
1900
RELIABLE MAIL
P.O BOX 3313
CHURCH ST STA
AB
62 5
NEW YEE'S FARM INC.
192 MOTT STREET
N.Y.C.,N.Y. 10012
TEL (212) 925-3370
JAMT
JAM

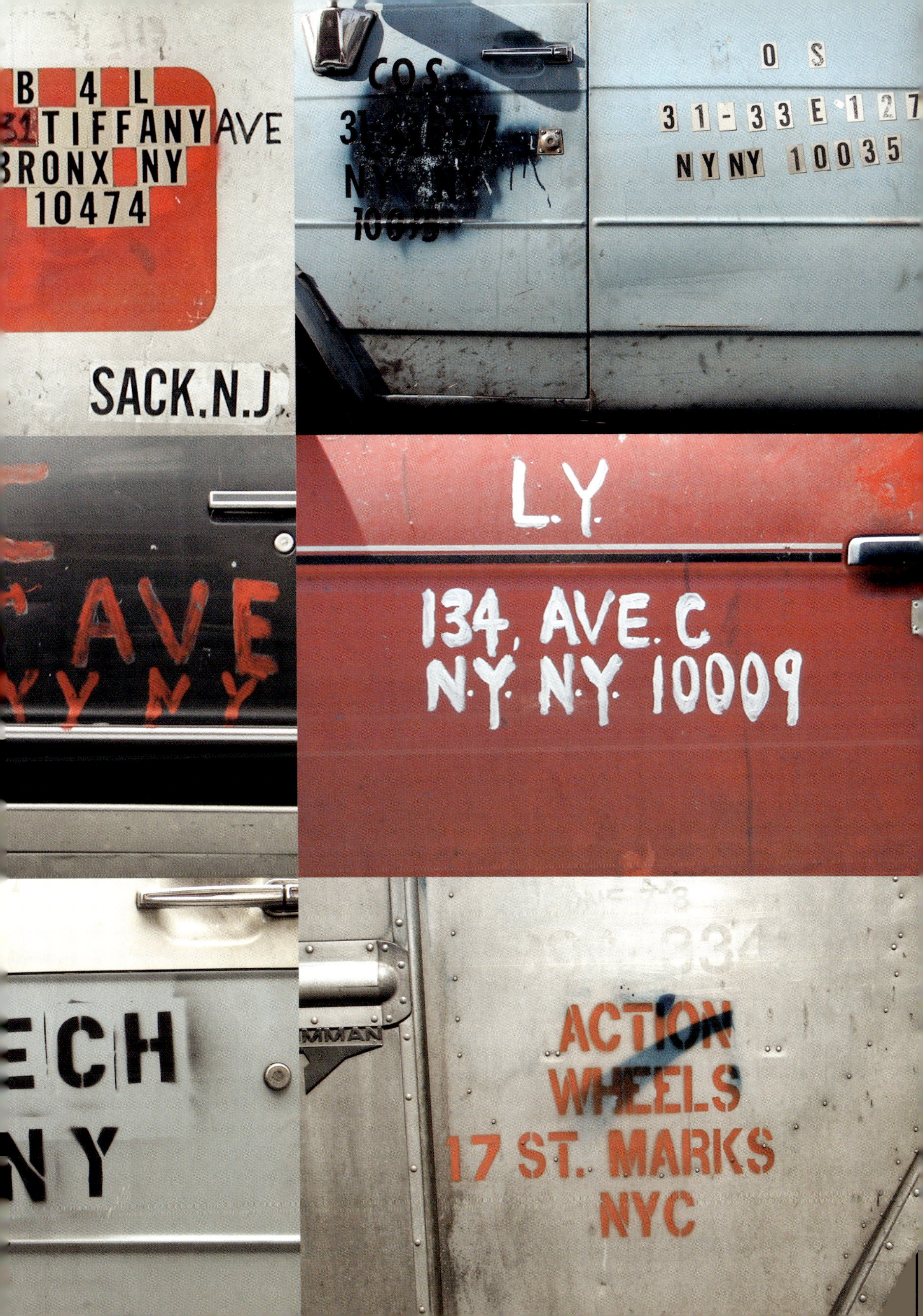
B 4 L
31 TIFFANY AVE
BRONX NY
10474
SACK.N.J
O S
31-33 E 127
NY NY 10035
AVE
L.Y.
134, AVE. C
N.Y. N.Y. 10009
ECH
NY
ACTION
WHEELS
17 ST. MARKS
NYC

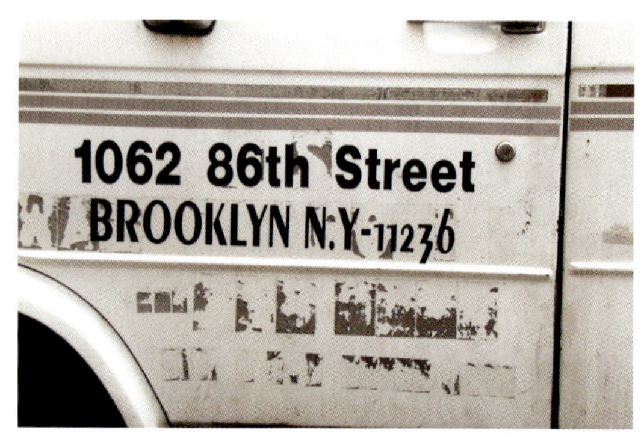
1062 86th Street
BROOKLYN N.Y-11236

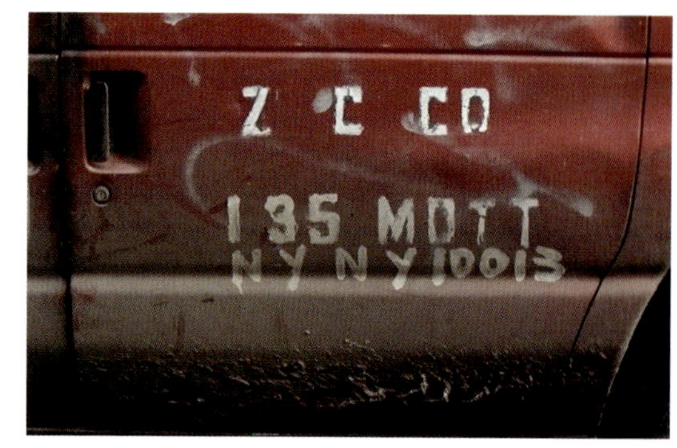
Z C CO
135 MOTT
NY NY 10013

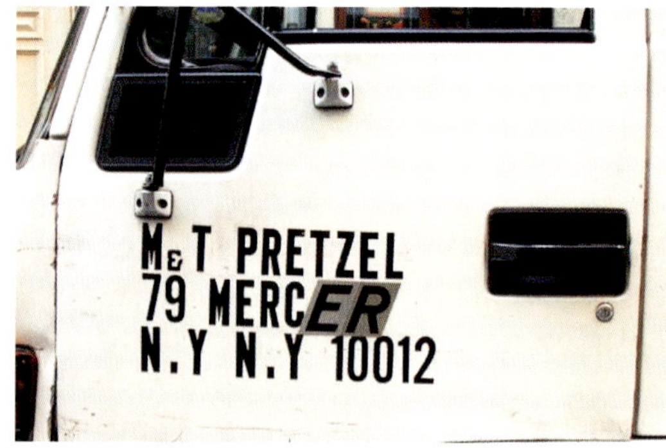
M&T PRETZEL
79 MERCER
N.Y N.Y 10012

HILL-ST
BKLYN-NY-11208
S.A. PRODUCE

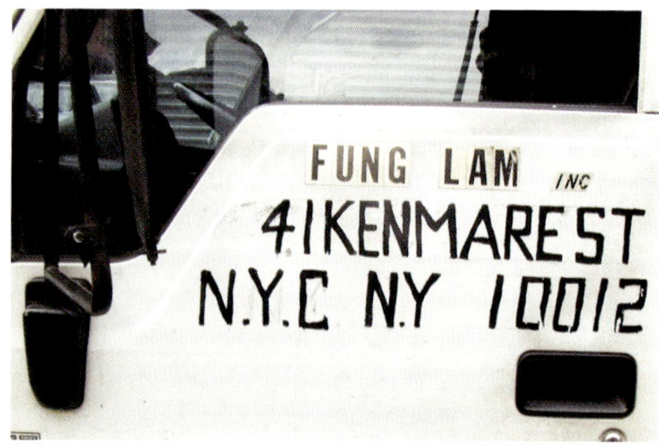
FUNG LAM INC
41KENMARE ST
N.Y.C N.Y 10012

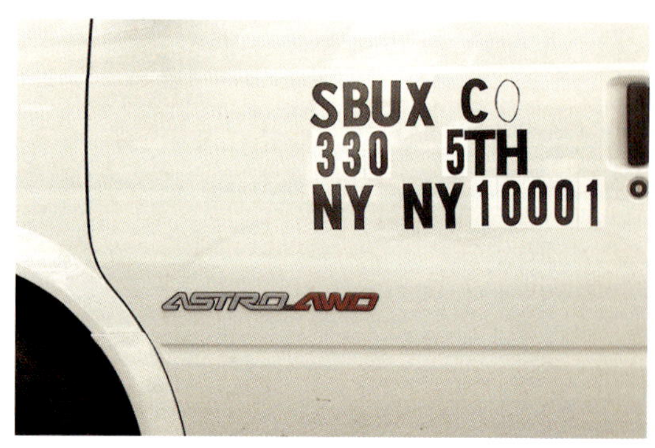
SBUX CO
330 5TH
NY NY 10001
ASTRO AWD

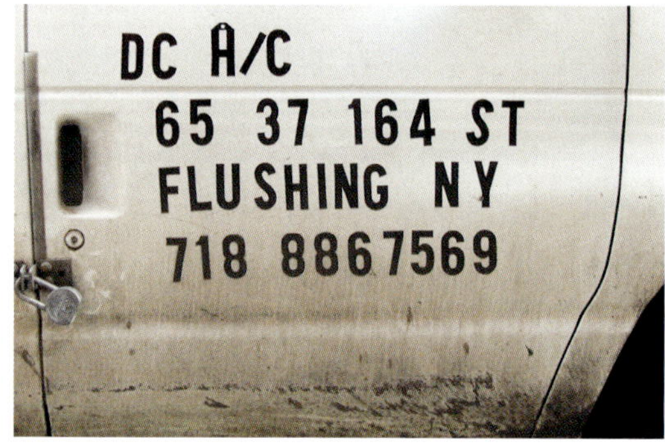
DC A/C
65 37 164 ST
FLUSHING NY
718 8867569

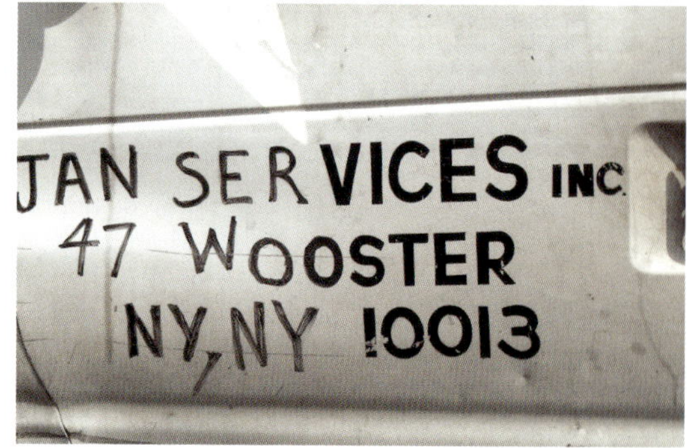
JAN SERVICES INC
47 WOOSTER
NY,NY 10013

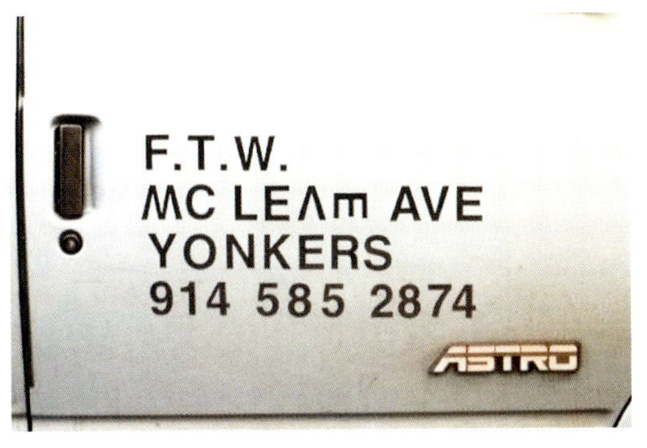
F.T.W.
MC LEAm AVE
YONKERS
914 585 2874
ASTRO

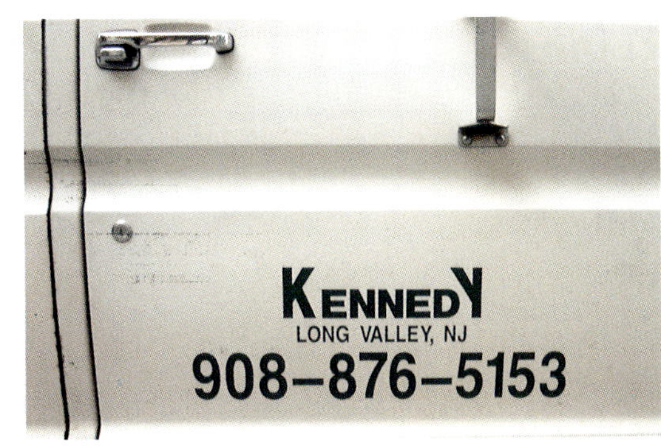
KENNEDY
LONG VALLEY, NJ
908-876-5153

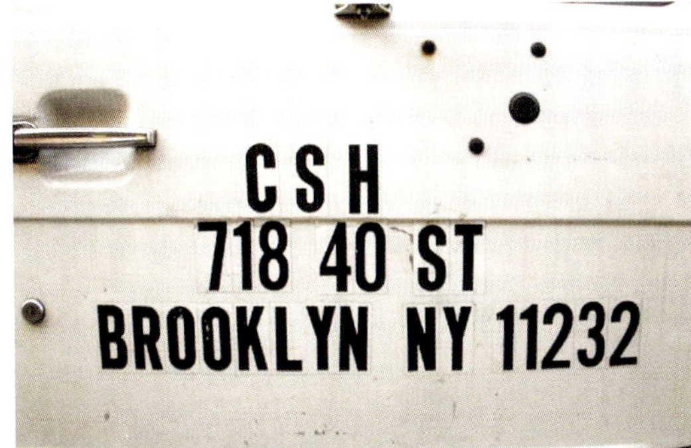
CSH
718 40 ST
BROOKLYN NY 11232

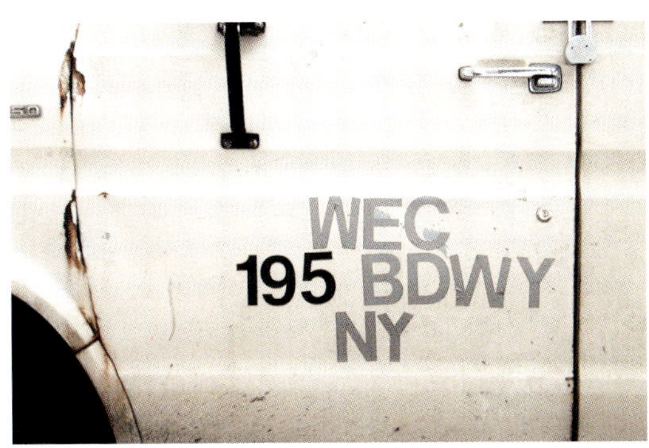
WEC
195 BDWY
NY

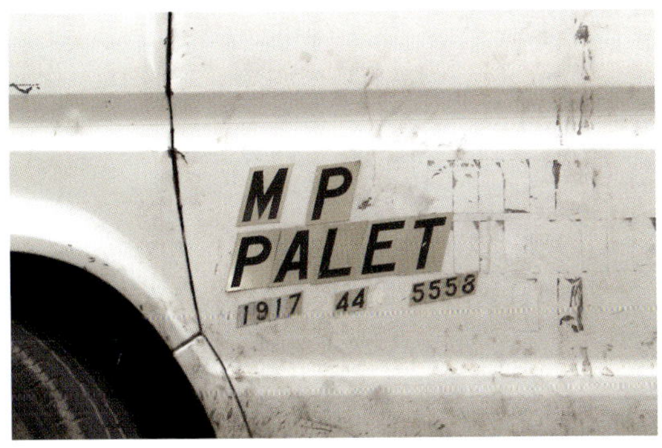
M P
PALET
1917 44 5558

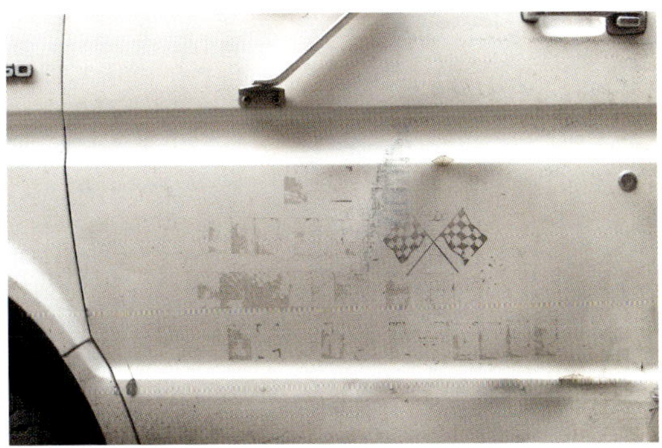

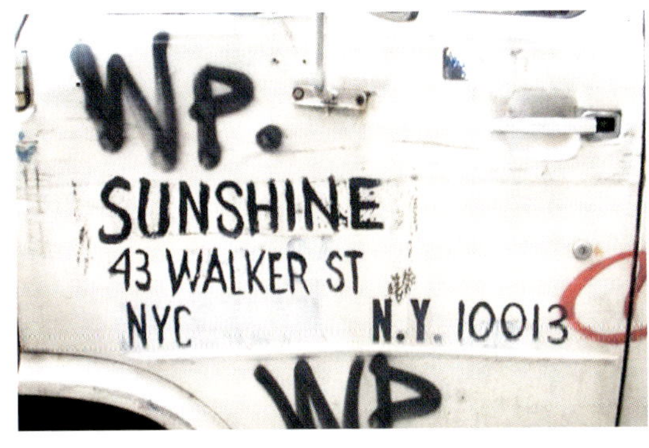
WP.
SUNSHINE
43 WALKER ST
NYC N.Y. 10013
WP

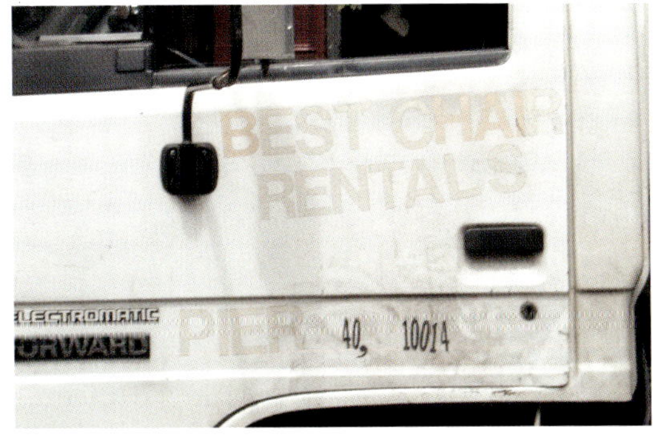
RENTALS
ELECTROMATIC
40, 10014

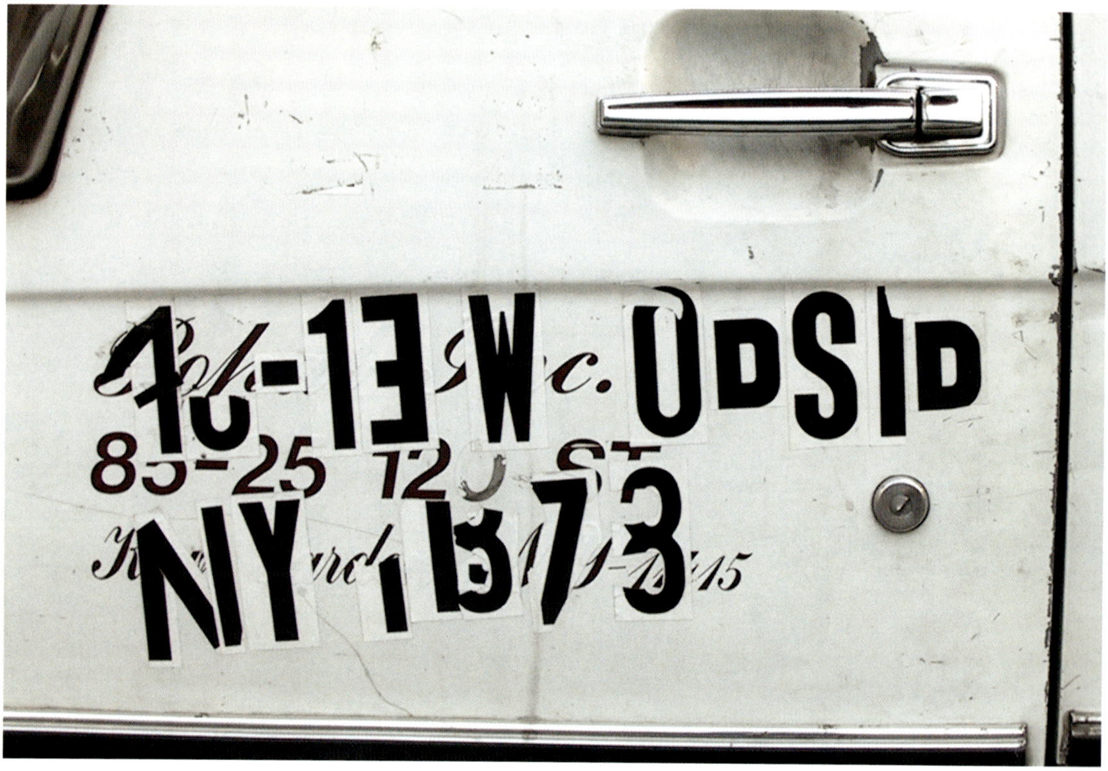

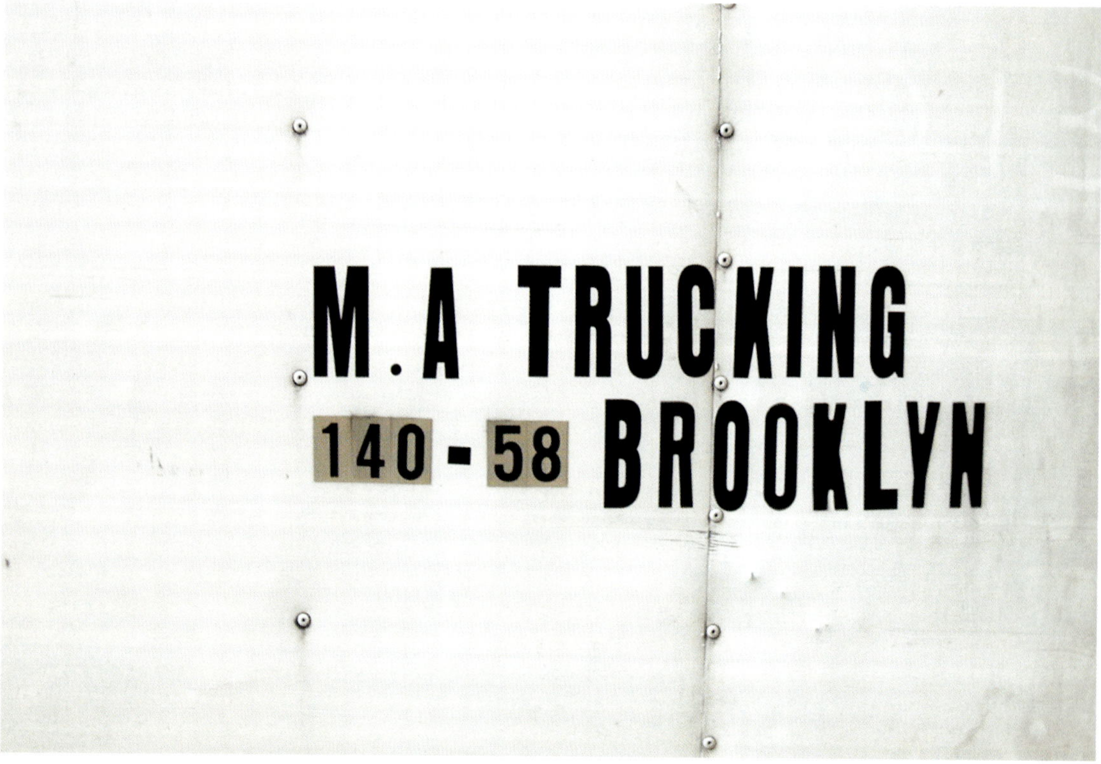

M.A TRUCKING
140-58 BROOKLYN

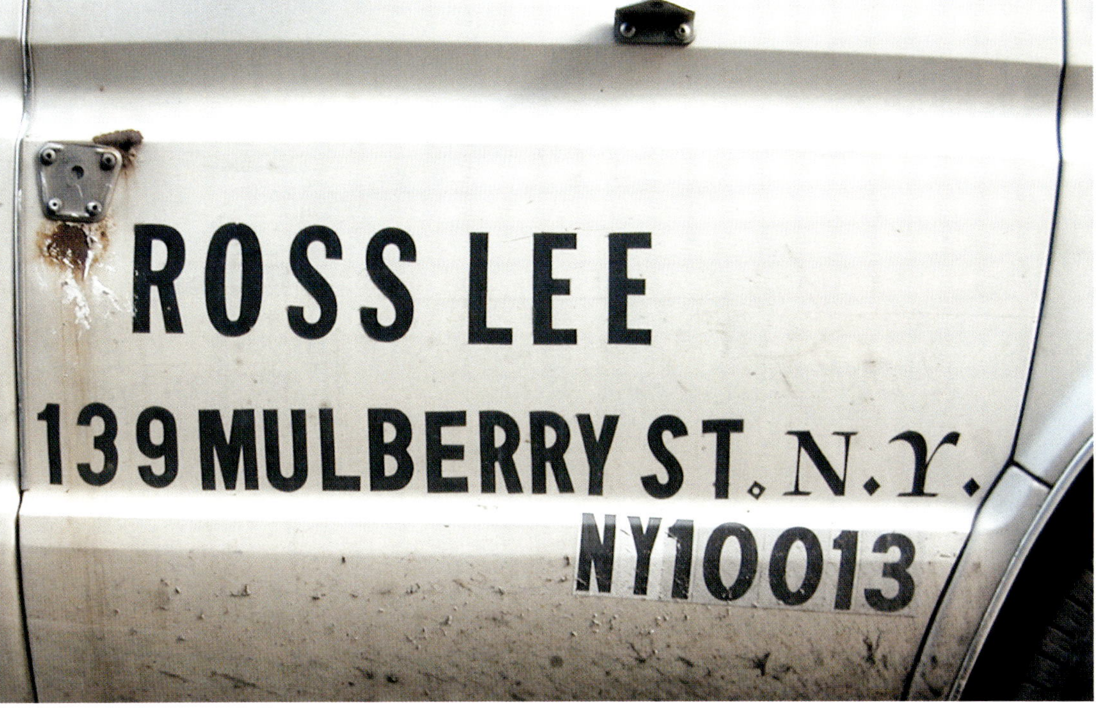
ROSS LEE
139 MULBERRY ST. N.Y.
NY10013

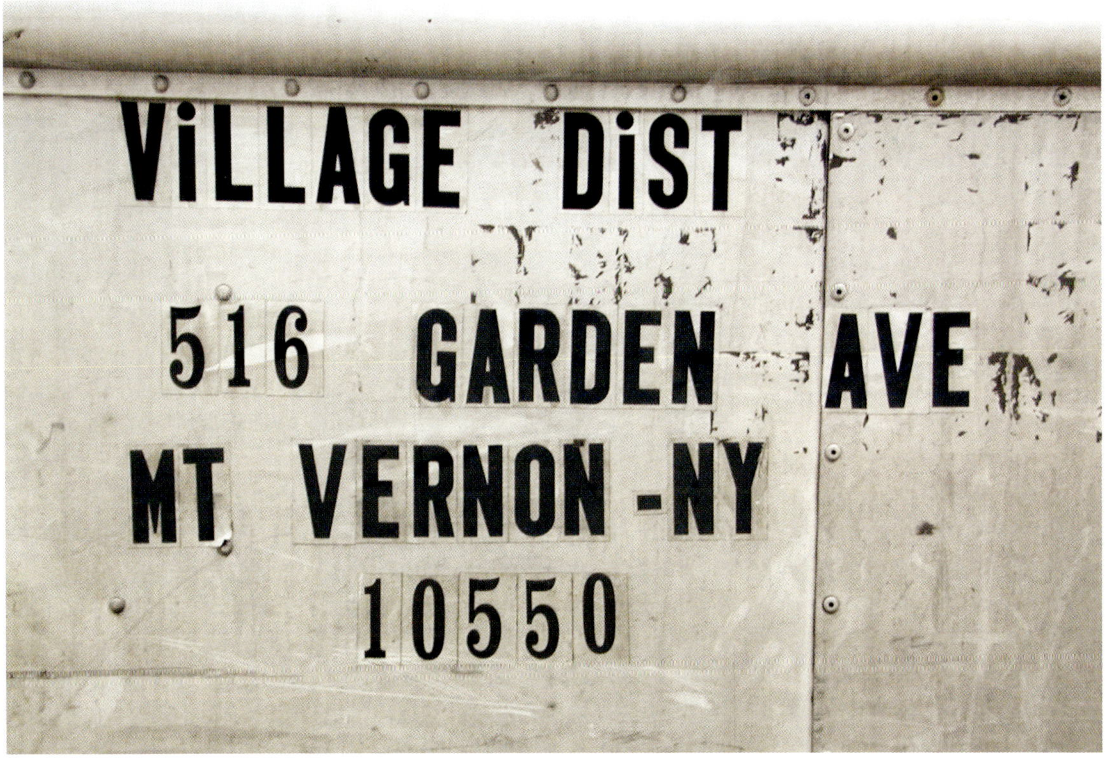

ViLLAGE DiST
516 GARDEN AVE
MT VERNON -NY
10550

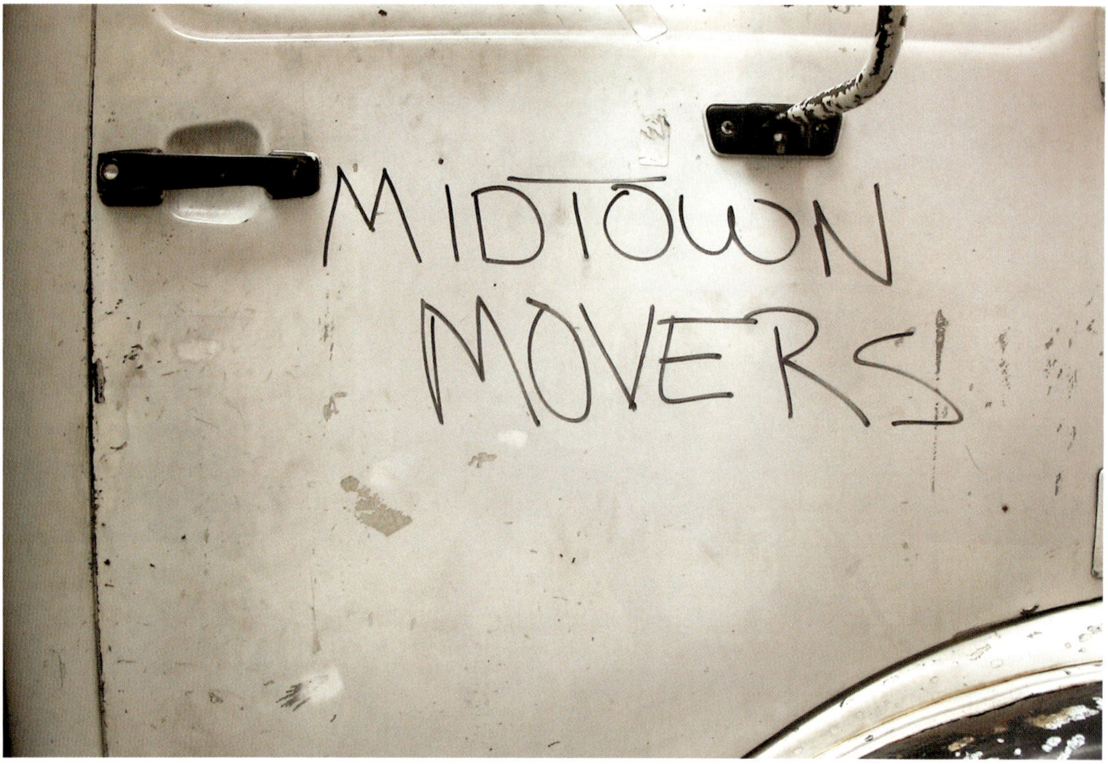

MIDTOWN
MOVERS

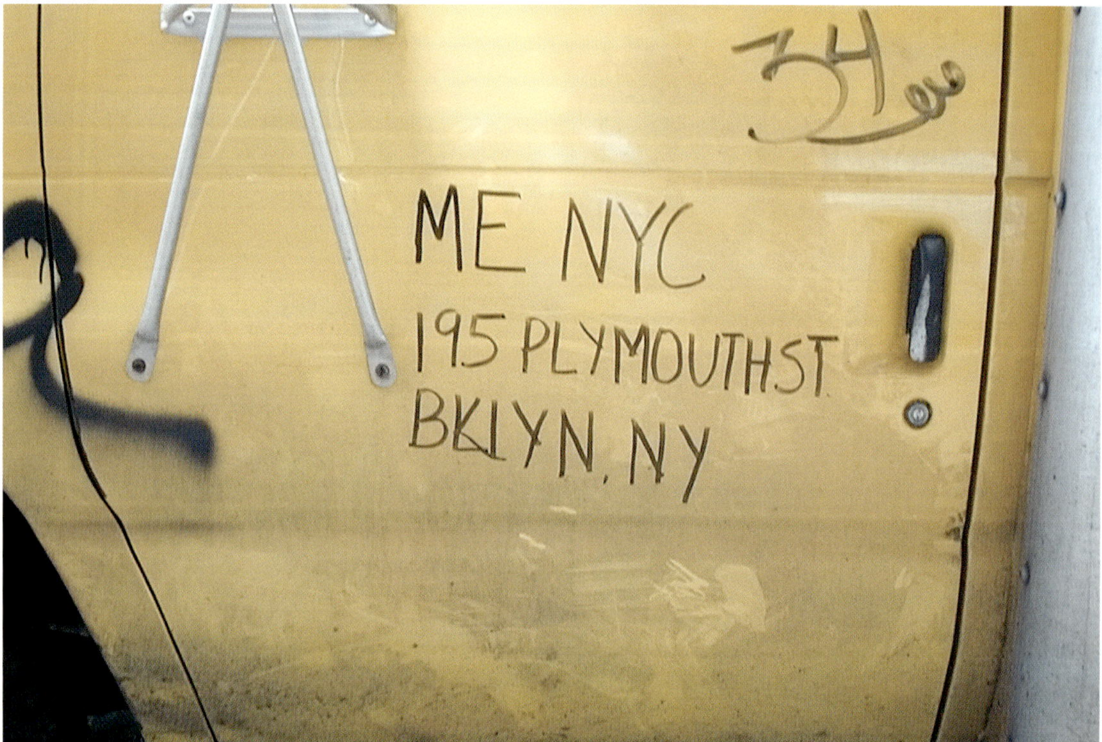

ME NYC
195 PLYMOUTHST
BKLYN, NY

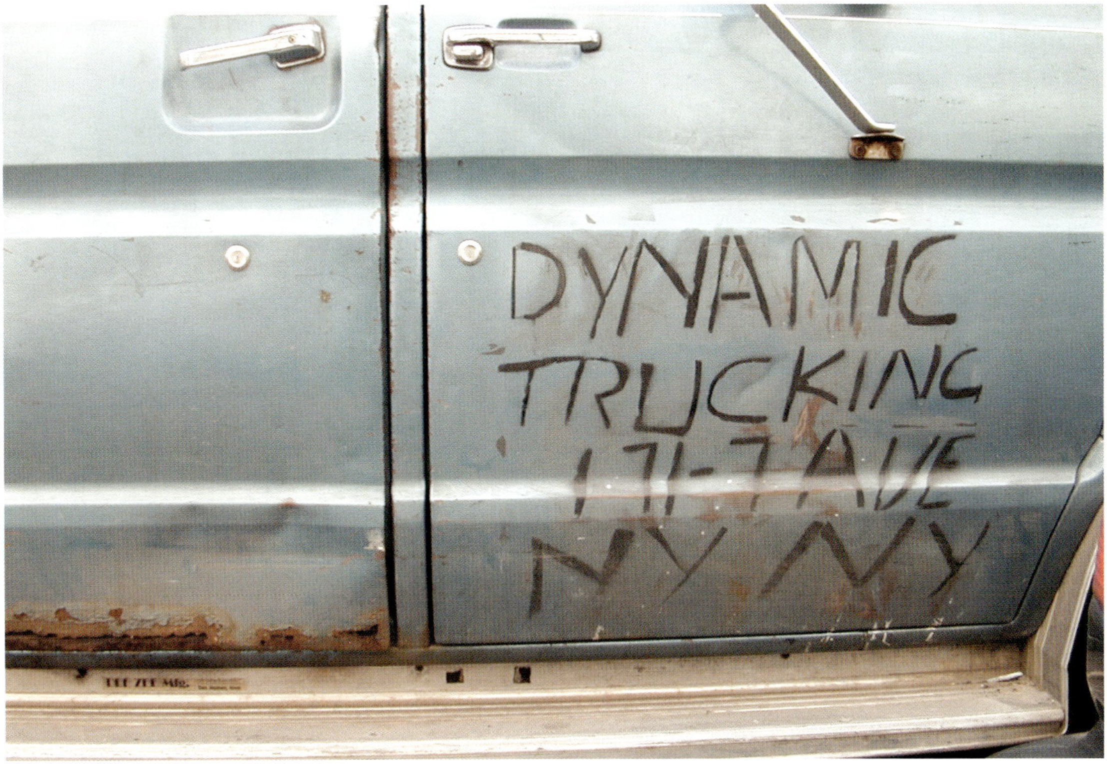

DYNAMIC
TRUCKING
NY NY

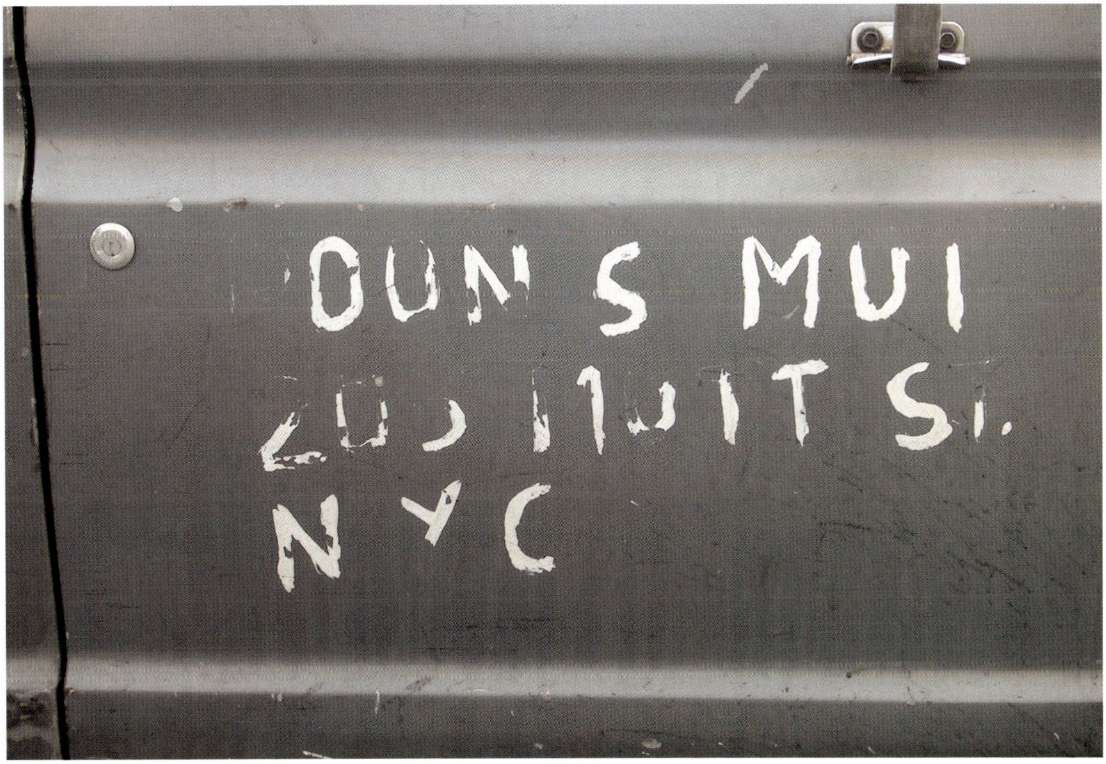

OUN S MUI
NYC

C&G
TRK
I AM NY

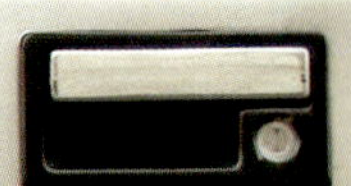

JLLS
8 WARBURTON AVE
YONKERS NY

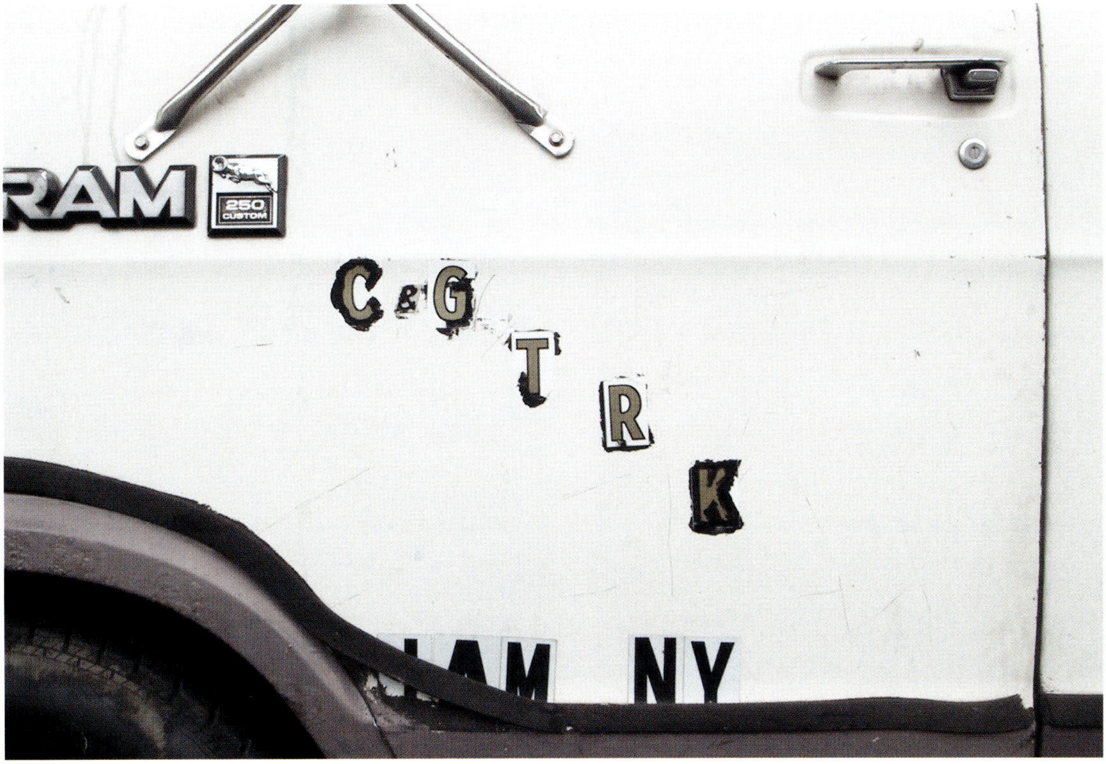

RAM
250
CUSTOM
C&G
T R
K
IAM NY

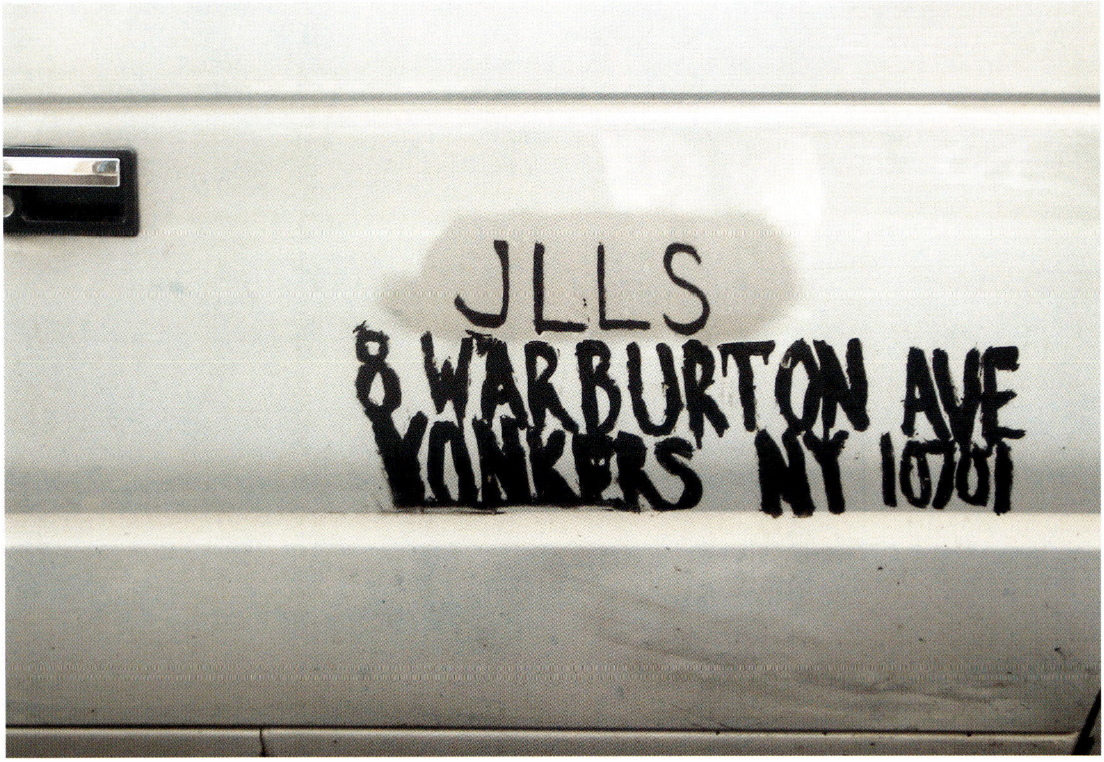

JLLS
8 WARBURTON AVE
YONKERS NY 10701

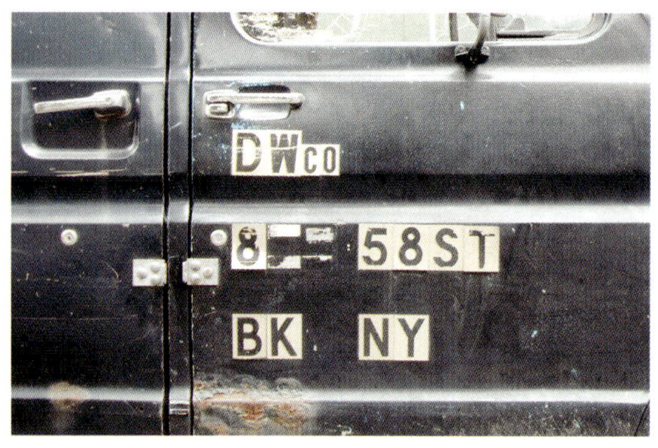
DWCO
8 58ST
BK NY

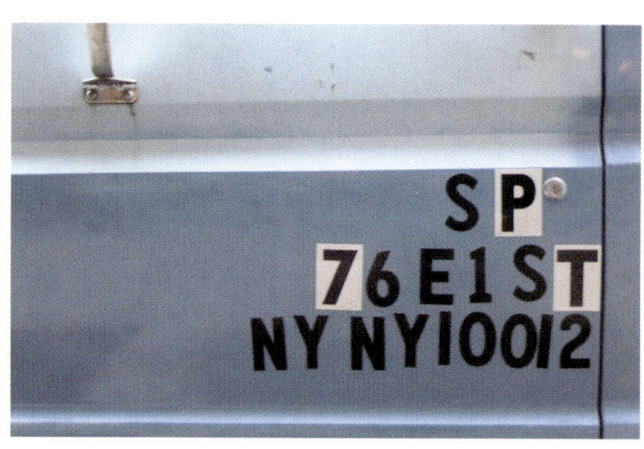
SP
76 E1 ST
NY NY10012

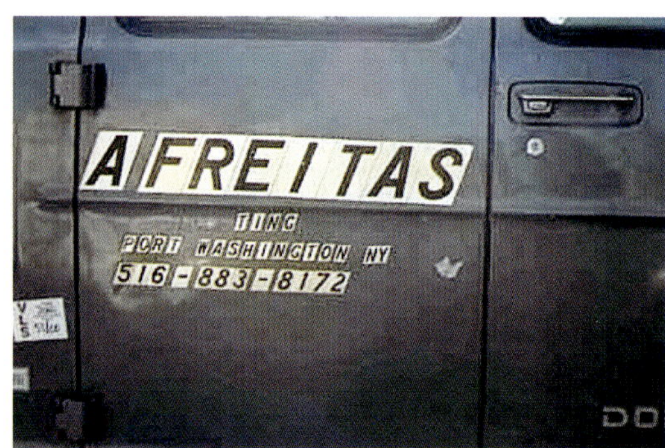
AFREITAS
TING
PORT WASHINGTON NY
516-883-8172

SFC
3 ARCH ST
LIC NY
11101

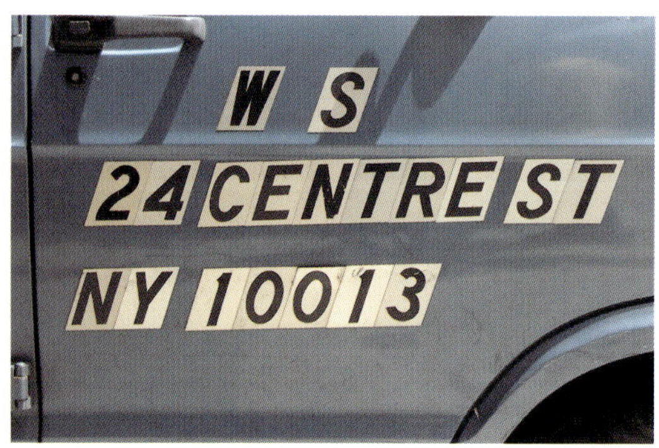
WS
24 CENTRE ST
NY 10013

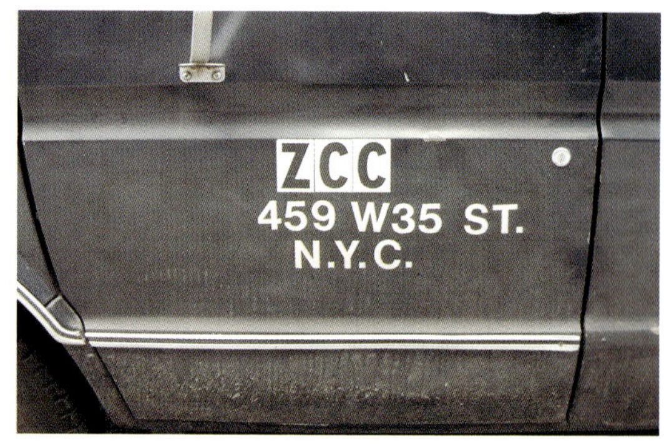
ZCC
459 W35 ST.
N.Y.C.

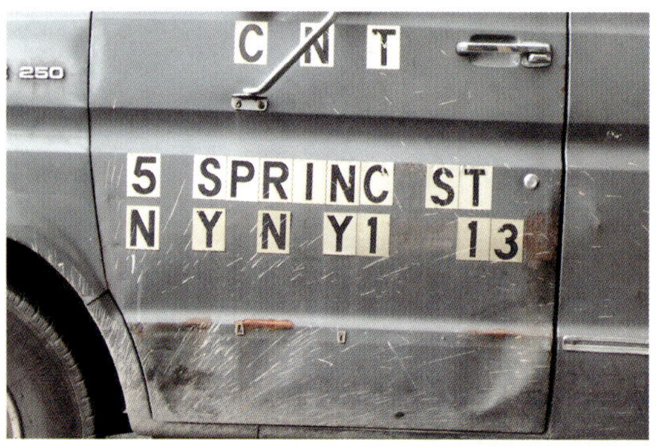
CNT
5 SPRINC ST
NYNY1 13

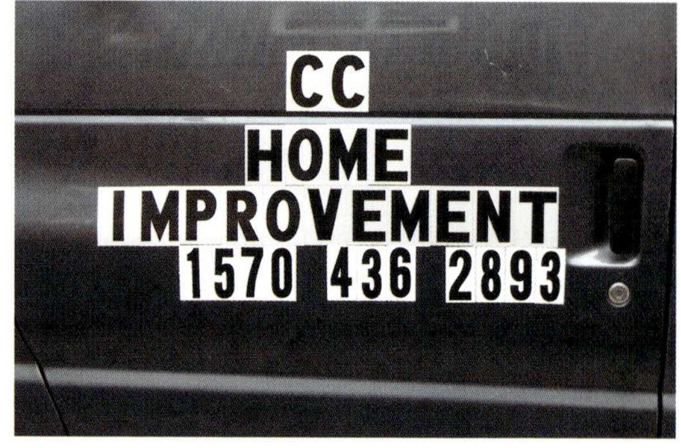
CC
HOME
IMPROVEMENT
1570 436 2893

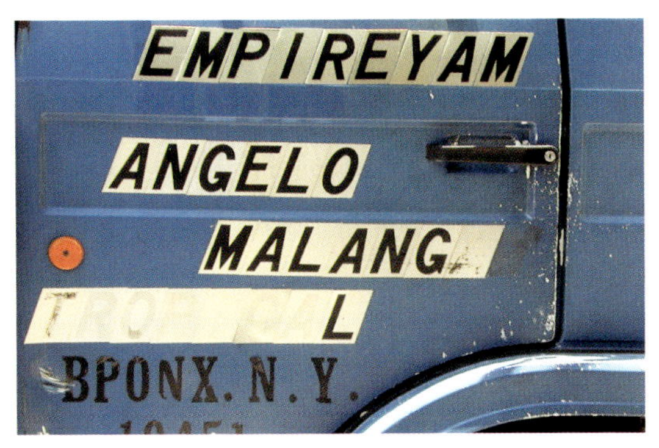
EMPIREYAM
ANGELO
MALANG
BPONX. N. Y.

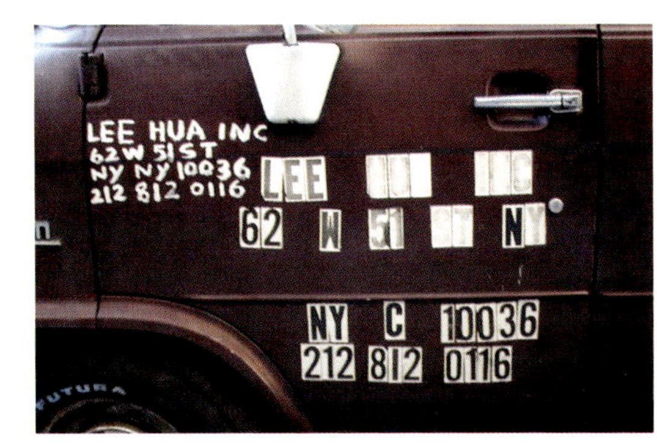
LEE HUA INC
62 W 51 ST
NY NY 10036
212 812 0116
LEE
NY C 10036
212 812 0116

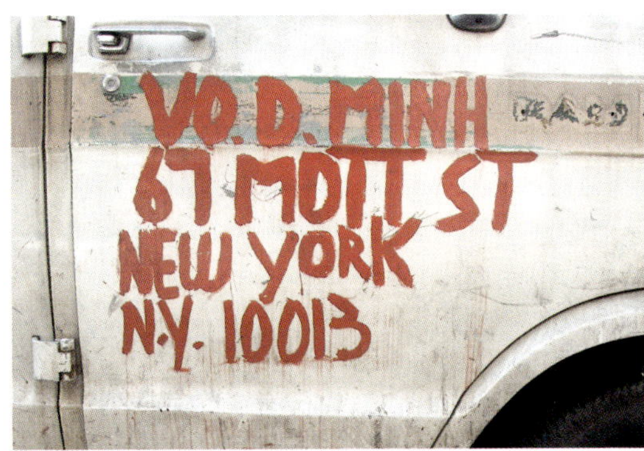
VO.D.MINH
67 MOTT ST
NEW YORK
N.Y. 10013

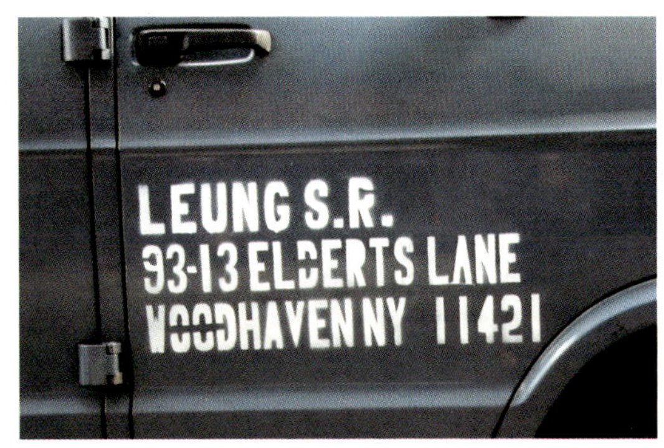
LEUNG S.R.
93-13 ELDERTS LANE
WOODHAVEN NY 11421

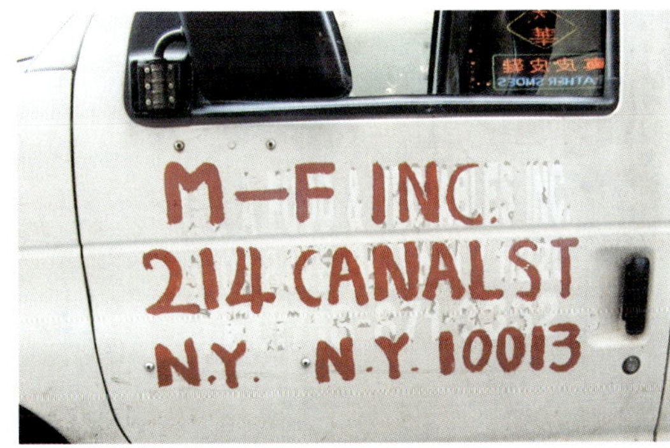
M-F INC.
214 CANAL ST
N.Y. N.Y. 10013

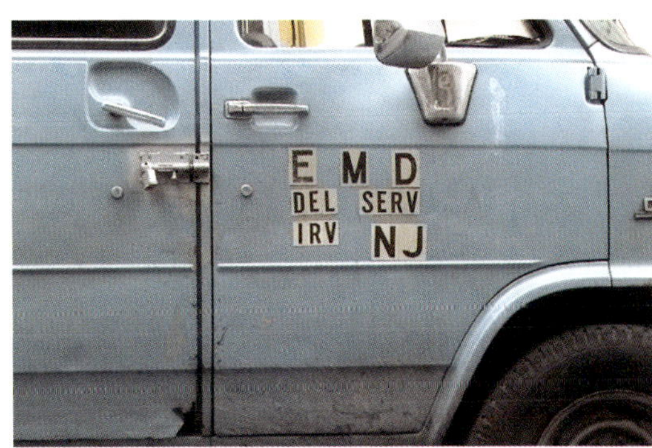
E M D
DEL SERV
IRV NJ

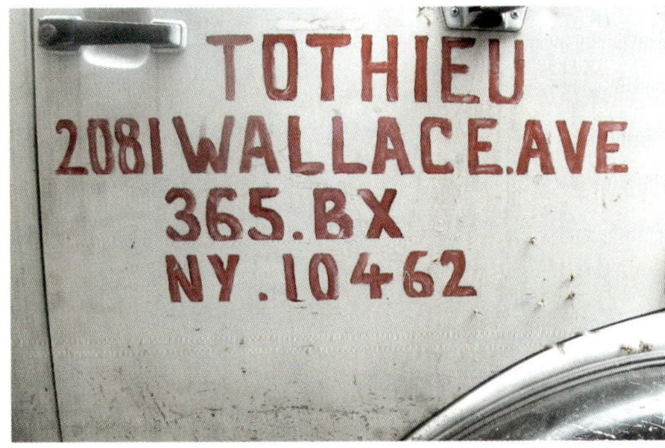
TOTHIEU
2081 WALLACE.AVE
365.BX
NY.10462

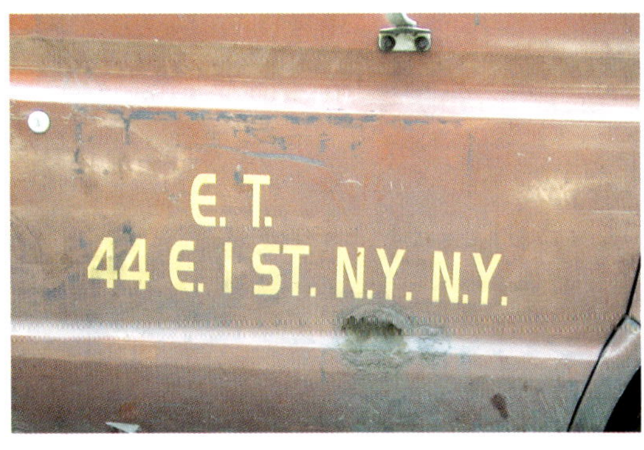
E.T.
44 E. 1 ST. N.Y. N.Y.

	System			Order		
Property Phenomenon	Dysfunctional Speech Act	Commerce	Control	Membrane	Orientation	The Range of Participation
LOCKED MOBILITY	MISSPELLING	CORPORATE MONUMENTS	POLICE LINE DO NOT CROSS	BLUE CITY	STREET SCRIPT	VOICE
TAPE	FADING MARKETS	STREET VENDORS	A BARRIER	COVER	STREET MARK	DIVERSITY
SHOP WATCH	EMPTY SIGNS	STREET LEVEL	SERVICE SCREEN	SHOPPING BAG	STEEL	OPEN CINE
REAL ESTATE		SHOPPING CARTS		GARBAGE DIGITAL SLUM		NEIGHBORHOOD

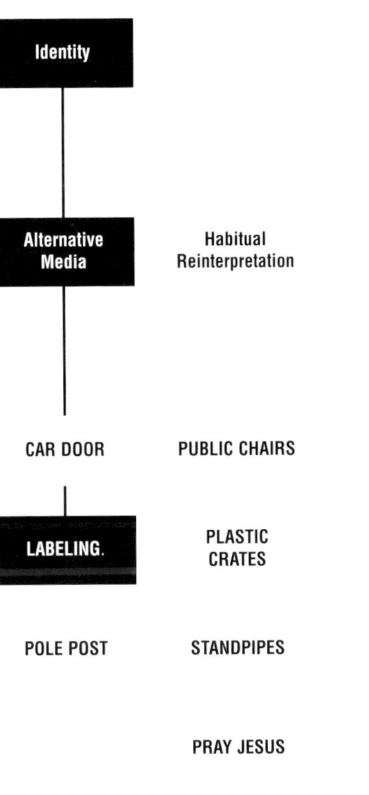

LABELING

Fixed Statements

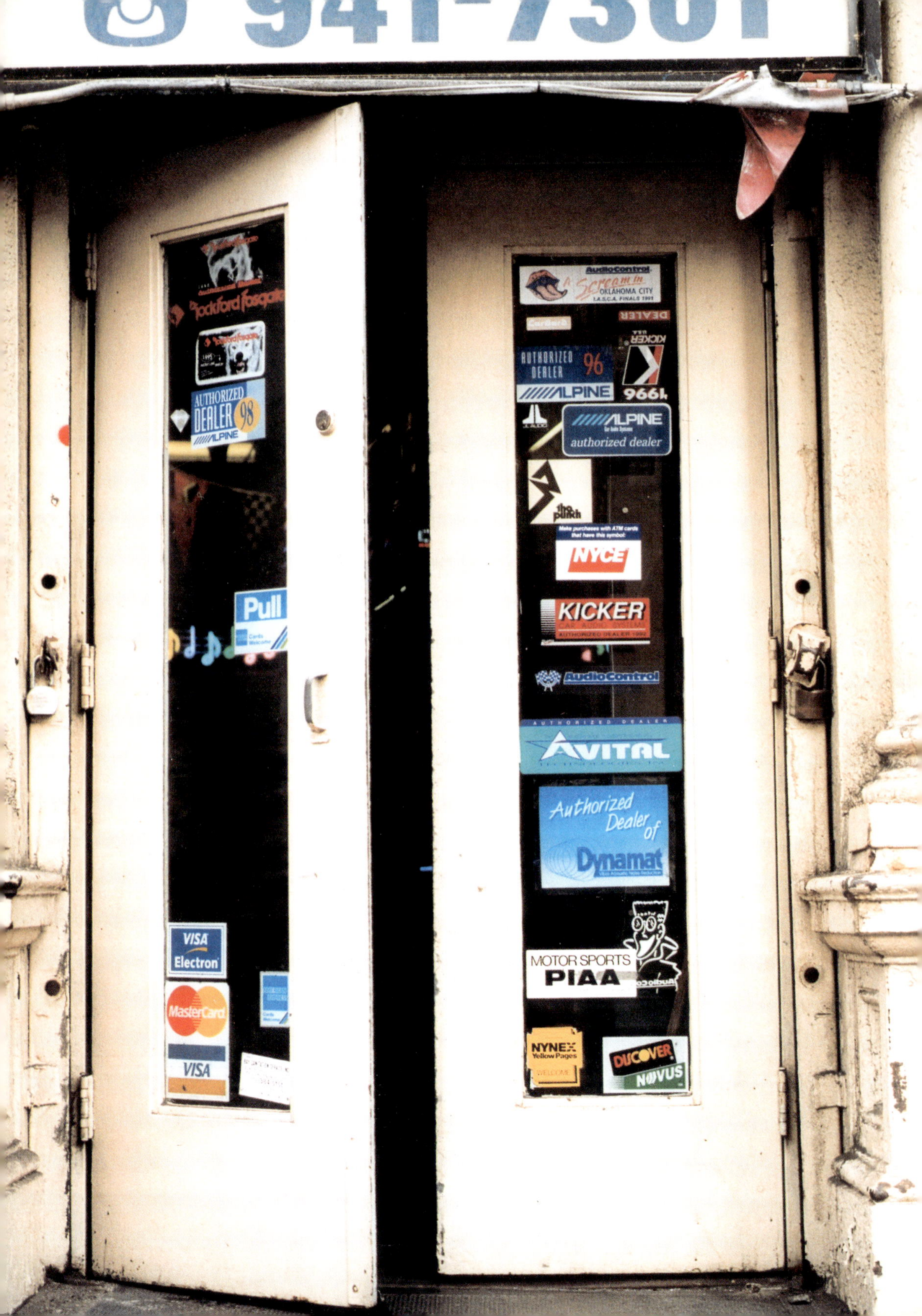

941-7361
Rockford Fosgate
Rockford Fosgate
AUTHORIZED DEALER 98
ALPINE
Pull
VISA Electron
MasterCard
VISA
AudioControl
Scream in
OKLAHOMA CITY
AUTHORIZED DEALER 96
ALPINE
KICKER
ALPINE
authorized dealer
the punch
Make purchases with ATM cards that have this symbol:
NYCE
KICKER
AudioControl
AUTHORIZED DEALER
AVITAL
Authorized Dealer of
Dynamat
MOTOR SPORTS
PIAA
NYNEX
Yellow Pages
DISCOVER
NOVUS

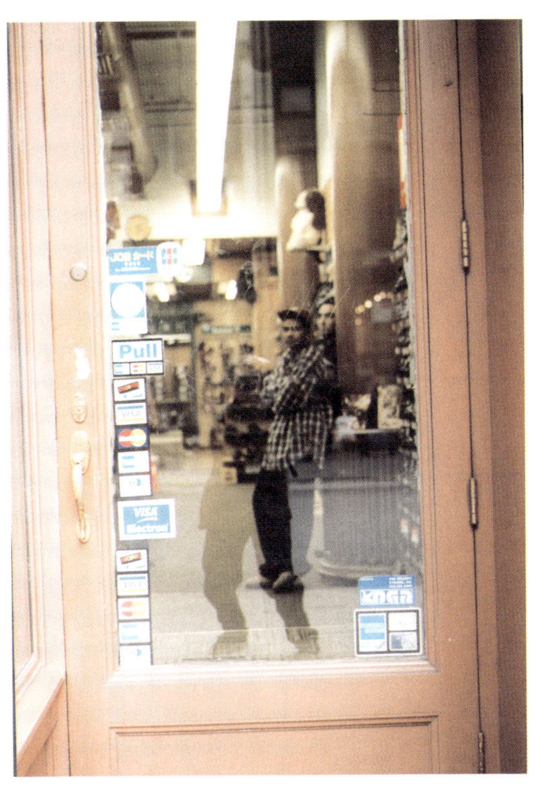
Pull
VISA
Electron

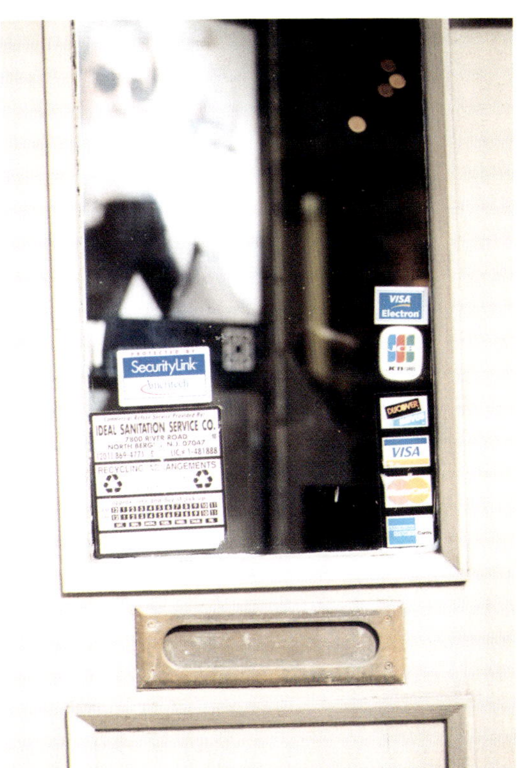
VISA
Electron
SecurityLink
IDEAL SANITATION SERVICE CO.
RECYCLING
VISA

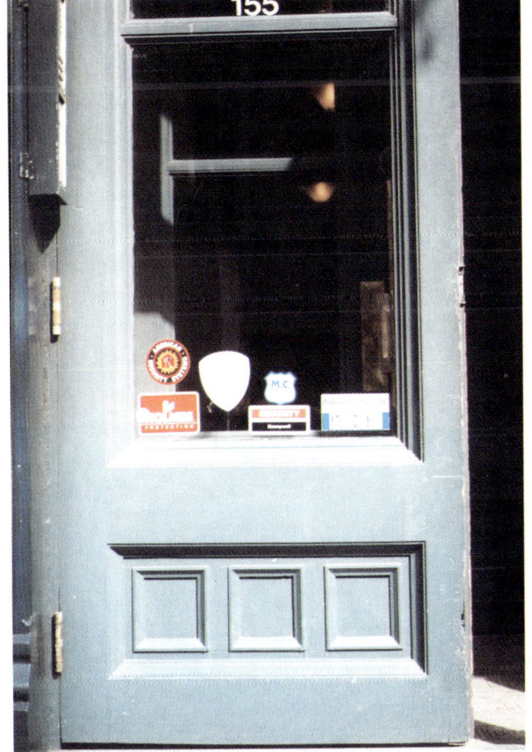
155
MC

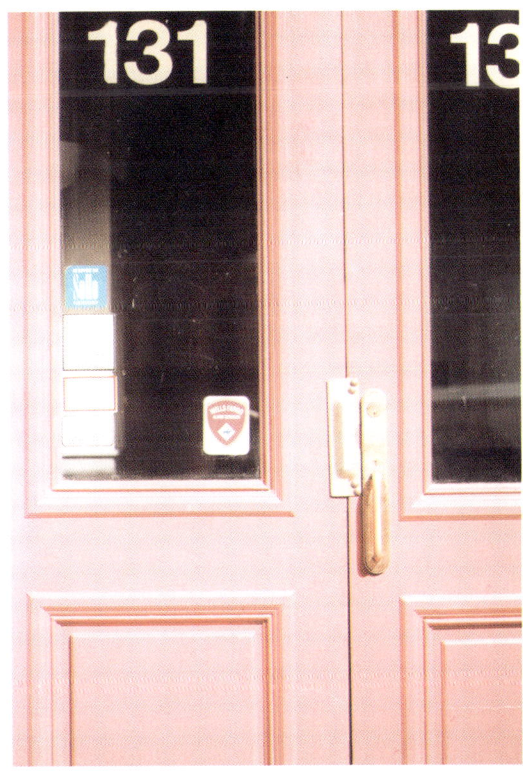
131
13

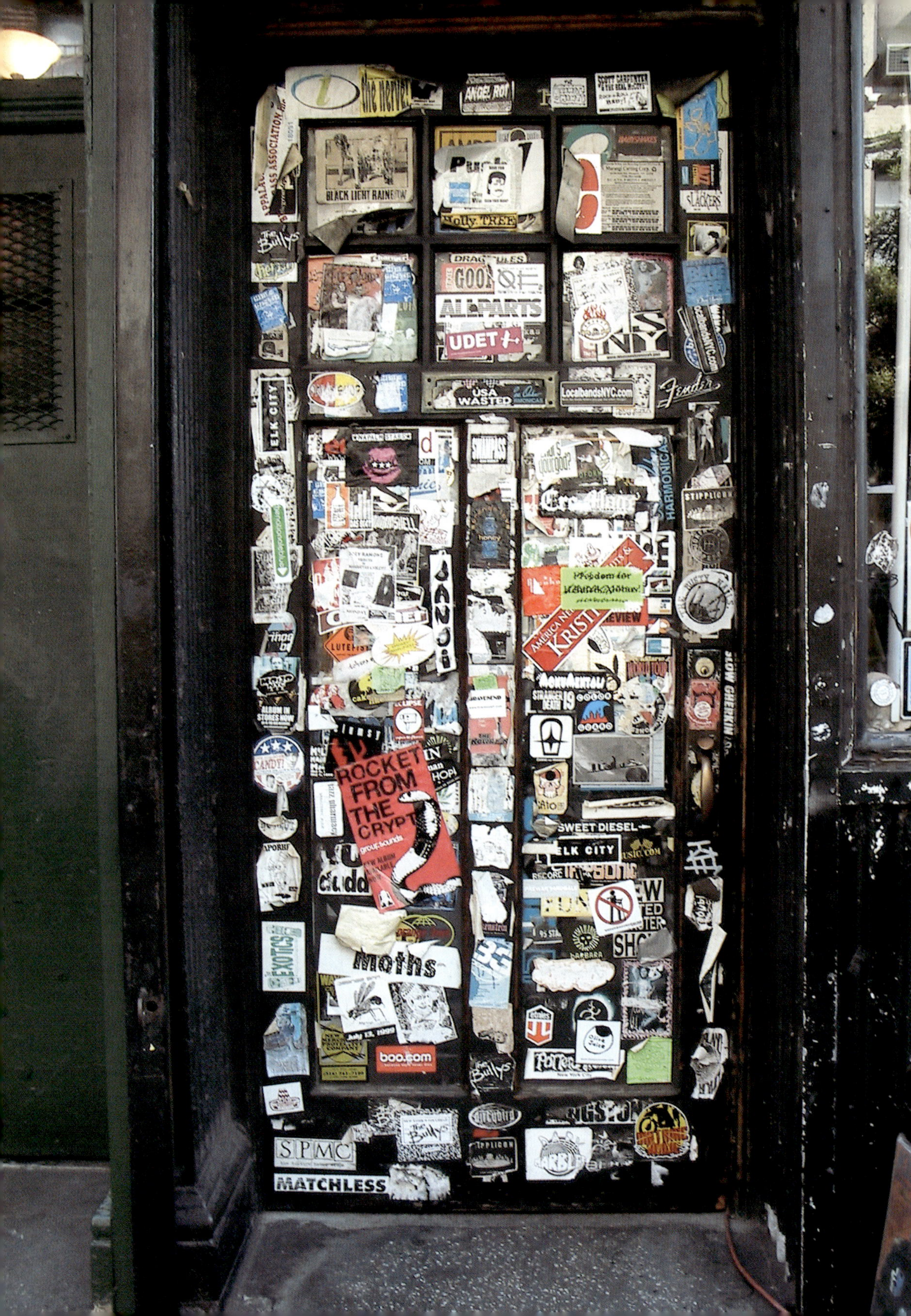
the nerve
BLACK LIGHT RAINBOW
The Bullys
UDET
USA WASTED
LocalbandsNYC.com
Fender
ELK CITY
HARMONICA
KRISTIN
REVIEW
ALBUM IN STORES NOW
ROCKET FROM THE CRYPT
SWEET DIESEL
ELK CITY
moths
July 13, 1999
boo.com
SPMC
MATCHLESS

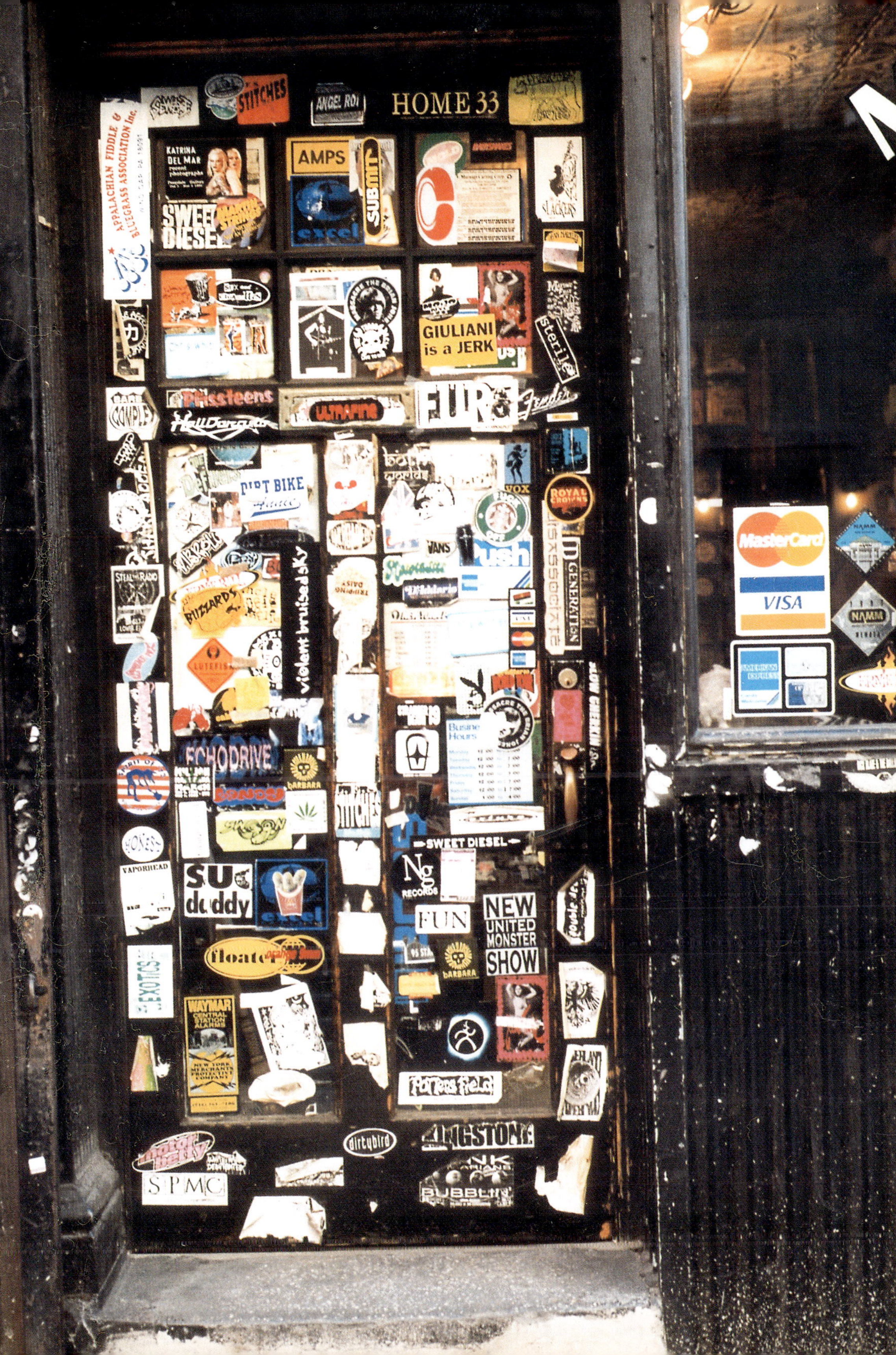

HOME 33
STITCHES
APPALACHIAN FIDDLE & BLUEGRASS ASSOCIATION Inc.
KATRINA DEL MAR
SWEET DIESEL
AMPS
SUBMIT
excel
SLACKERS
GIULIANI is a JERK
sterile
FUR
Fender
DIRT BIKE
violent bruisedsky
BLIZZARDS
Bush
ROYAL CROWNS
VOX
ID GENERATION
VANS
MasterCard
VISA
NAMM
ECHODRIVE
barbara
STITCHES
SWEET DIESEL
Ng RECORDS
FUN
NEW UNITED MONSTER SHOW
VAPORHEAD
SUGAR daddy
floater
EXOTICS
WAYMAR CENTRAL STATION ALARMS
SPMC
dirtybird

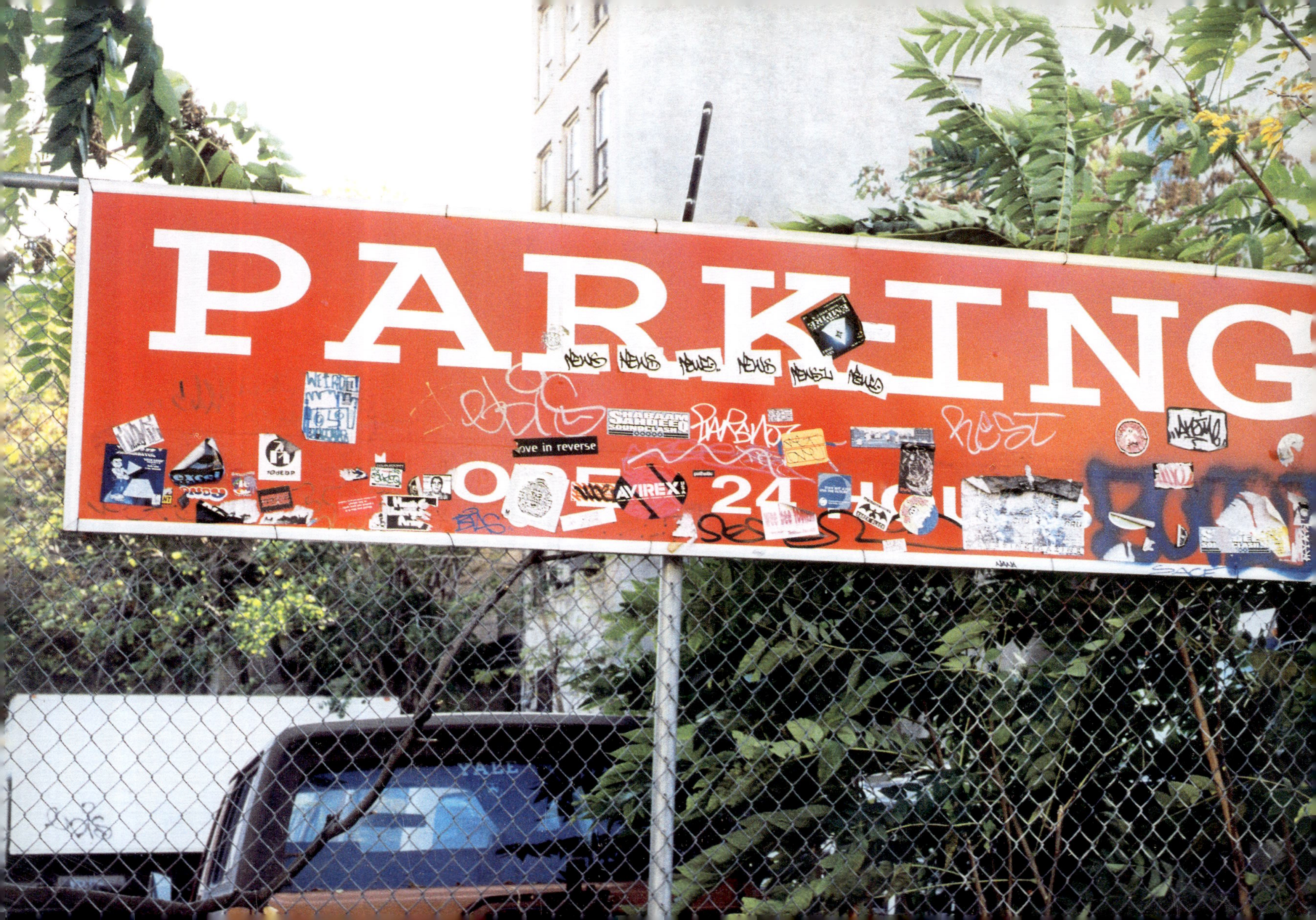
PARKING
love in reverse
AVIREX
24

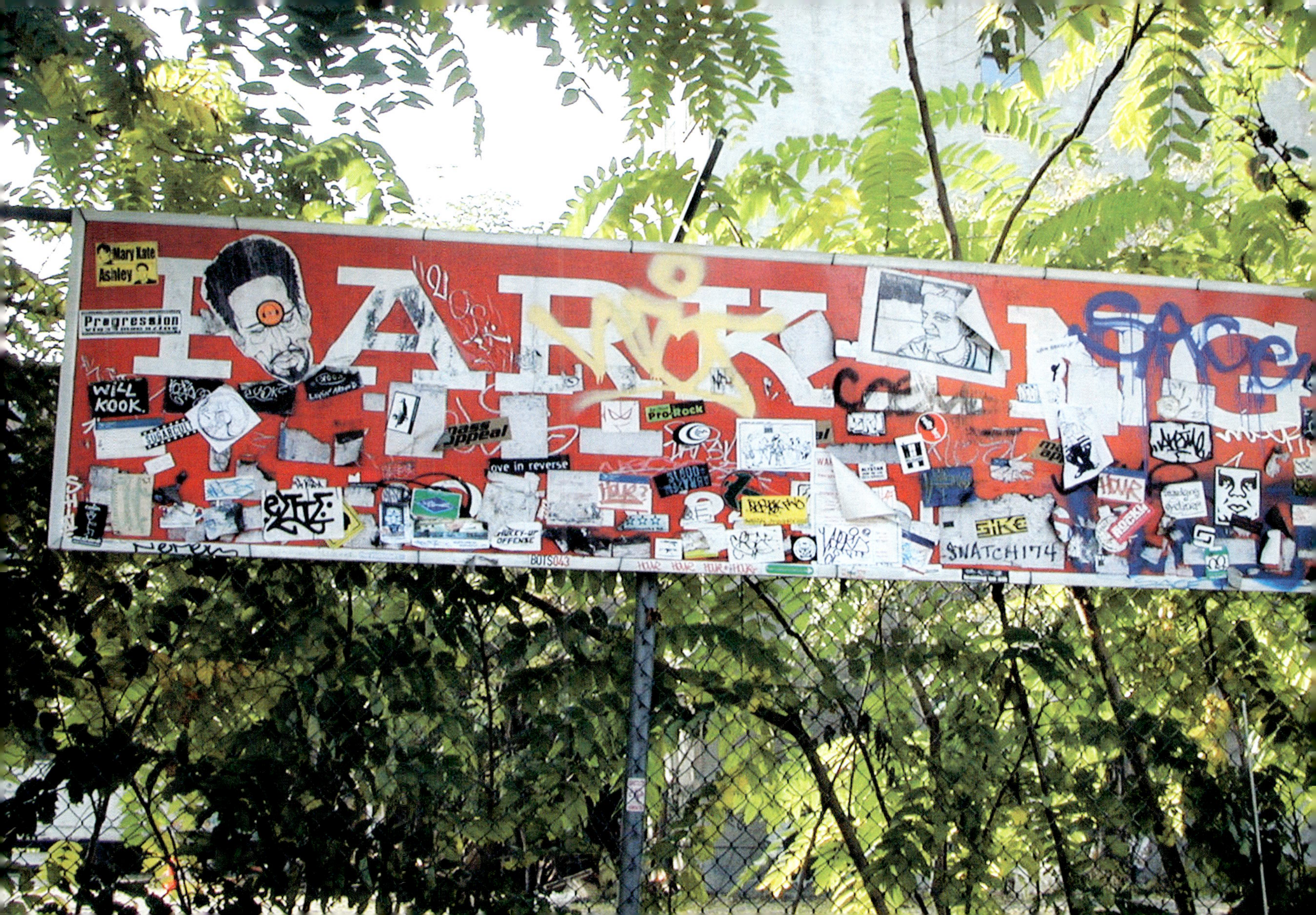
Mary Kate Ashley
Progression
WILL KOOK.
mass appeal
Pro Rock
love in reverse
SIKE
SNATCH174
BOTS043

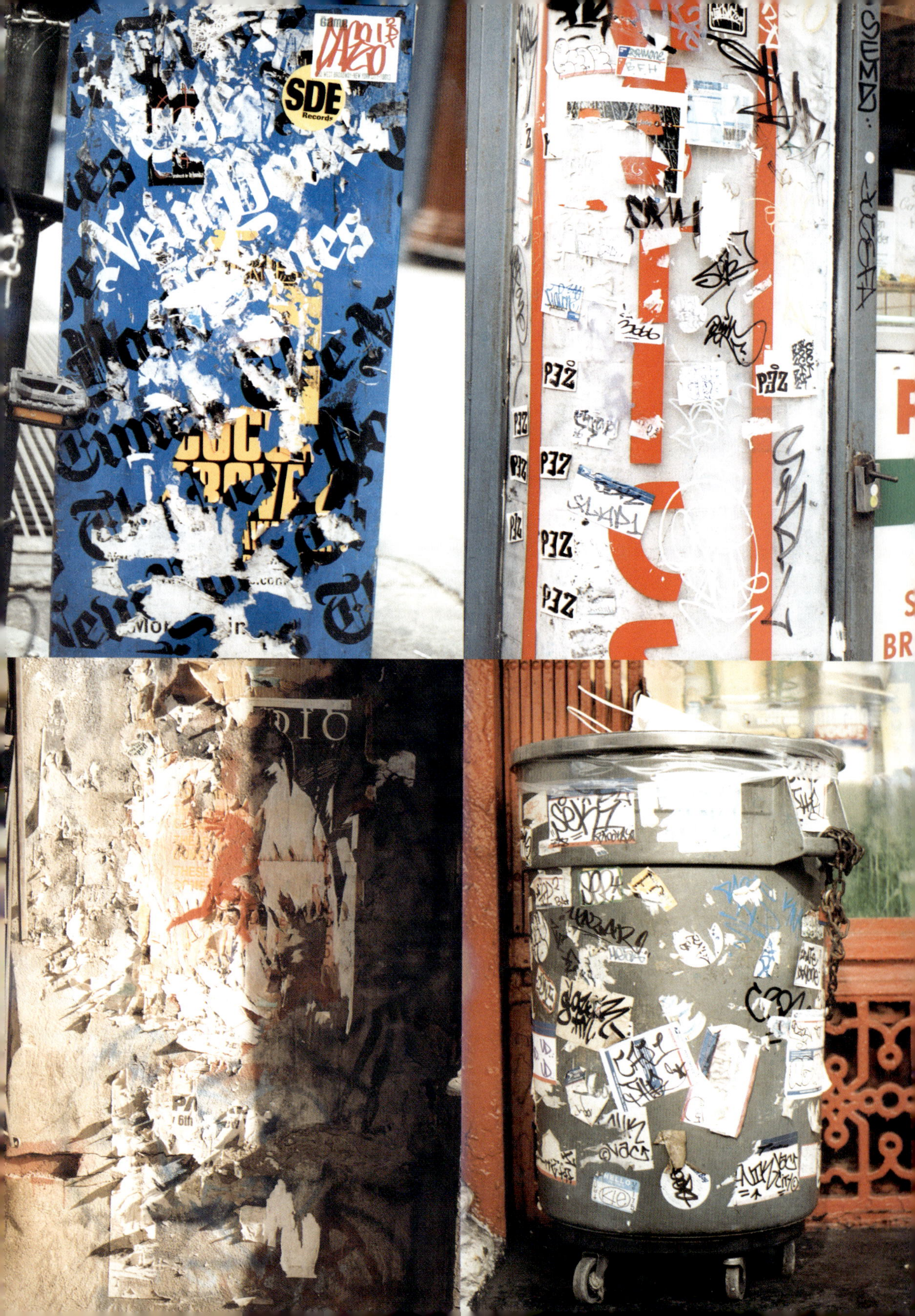

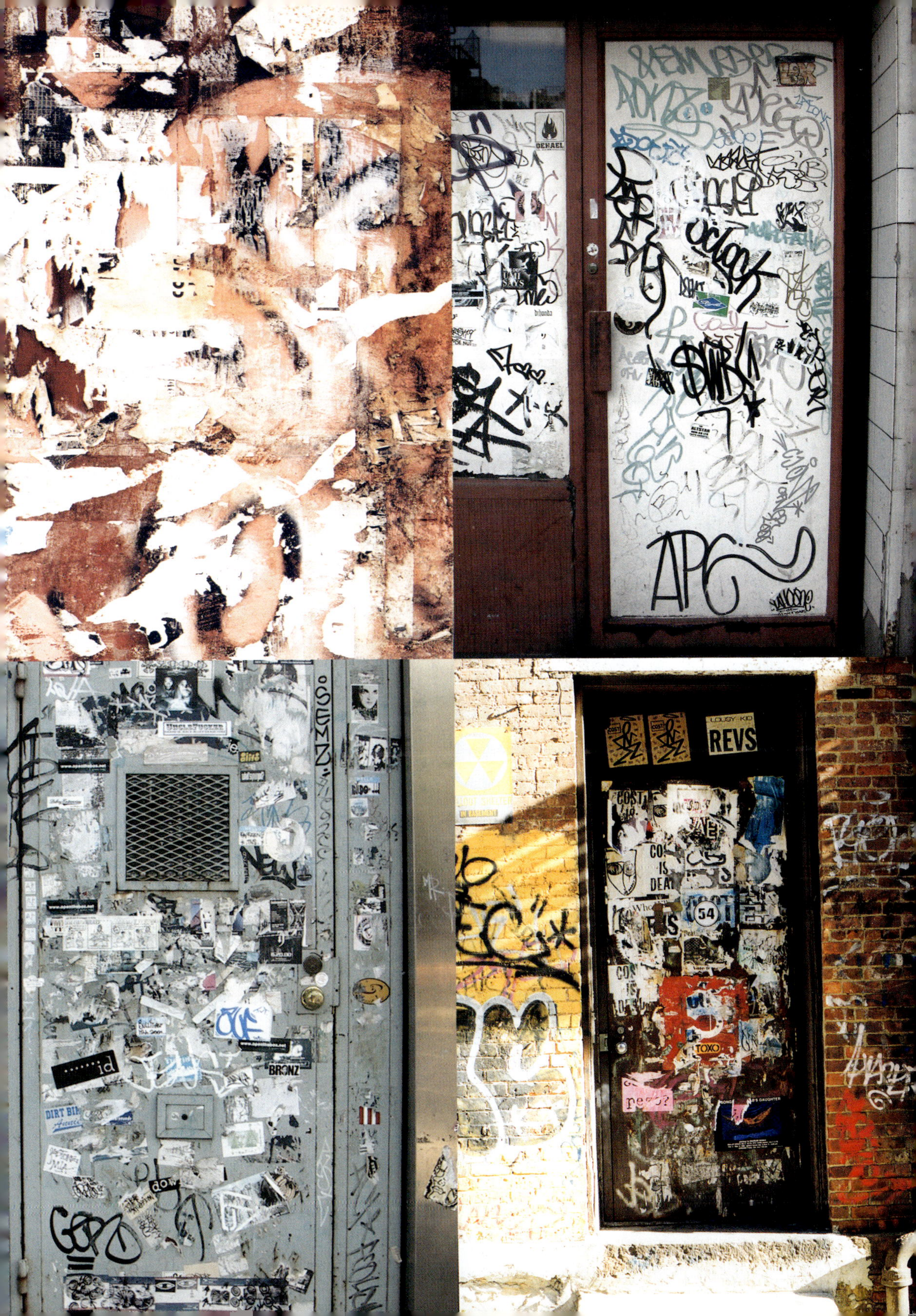
LOUSY KID
REVS
BRONZ
54
TOXO

HELLO
my name is
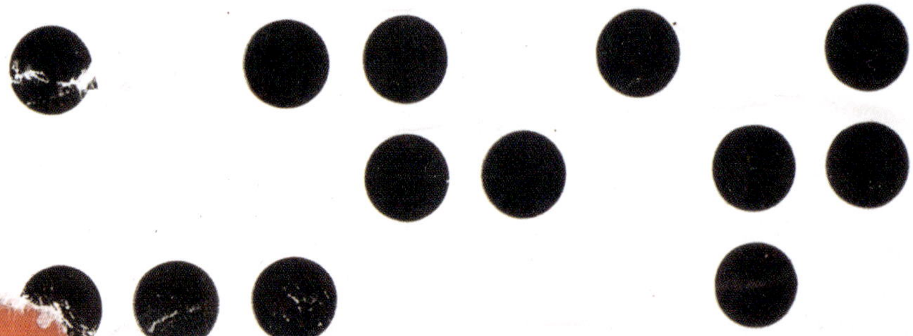
http://www.caipirinha.com/music/unit.html
HELLO
my name is

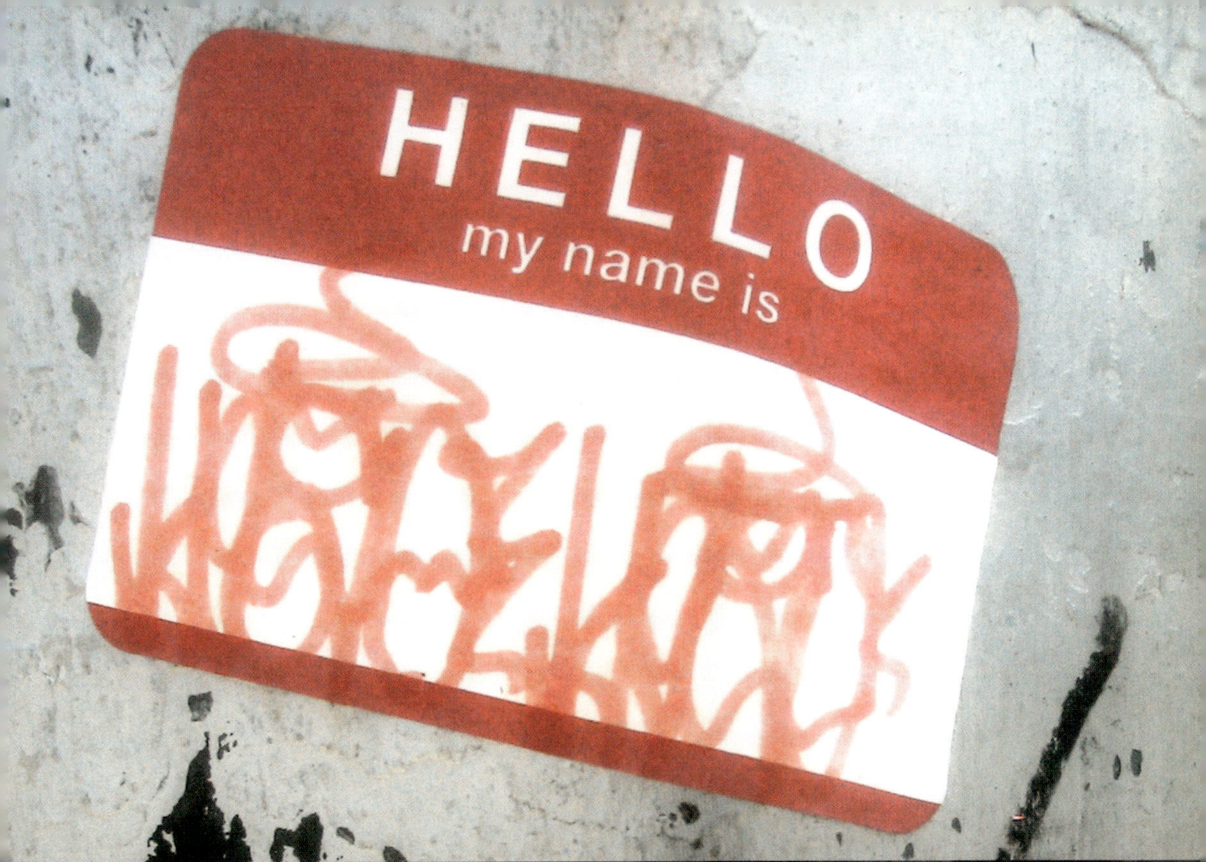

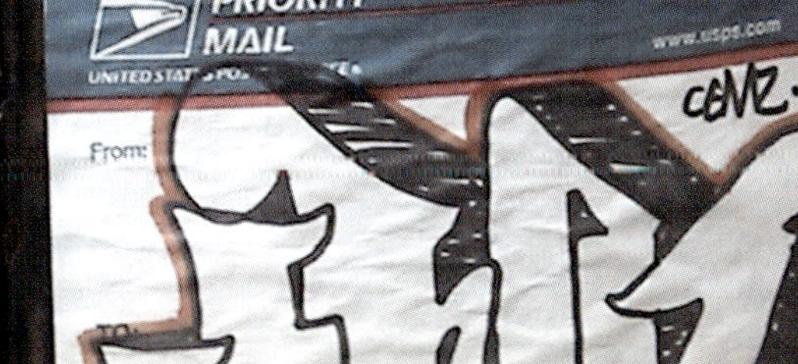
PRIORITY
MAIL
www.usps.com
From:

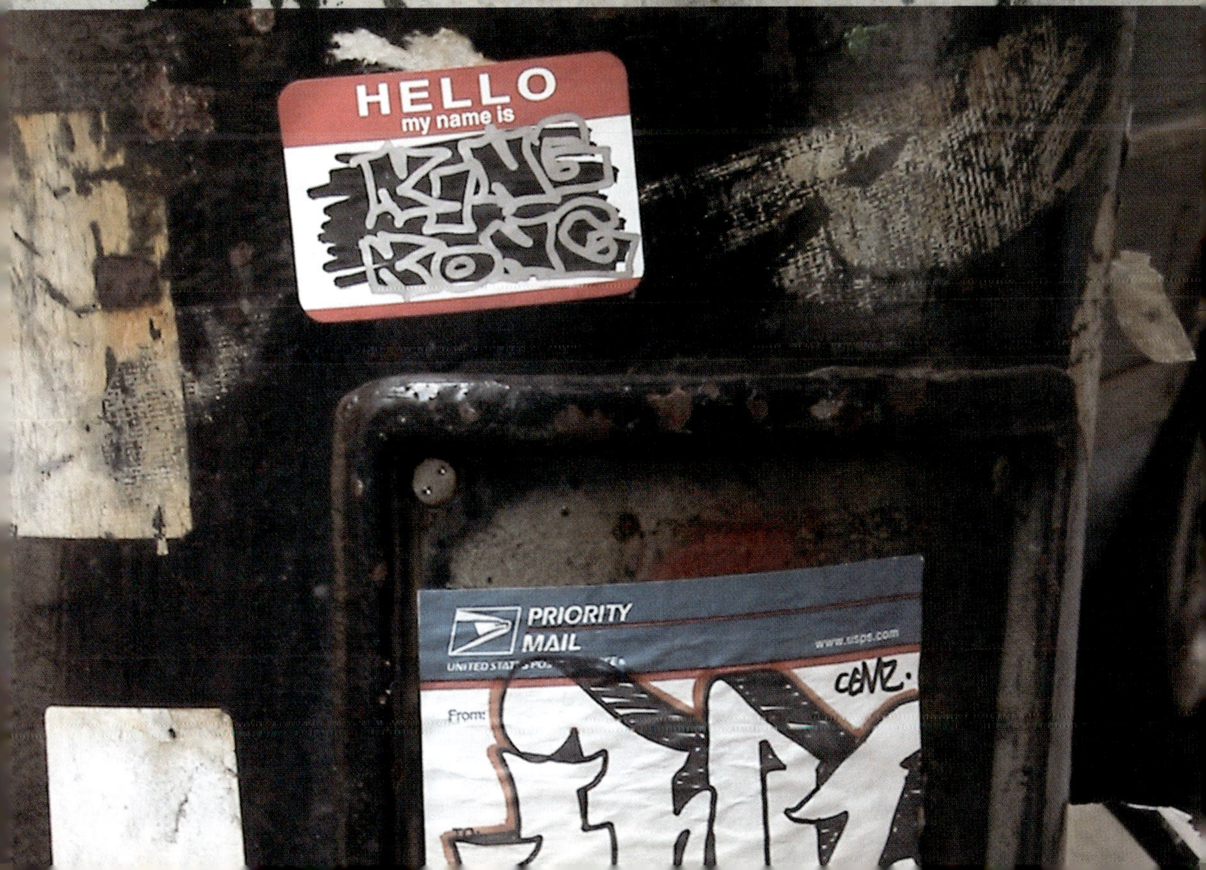

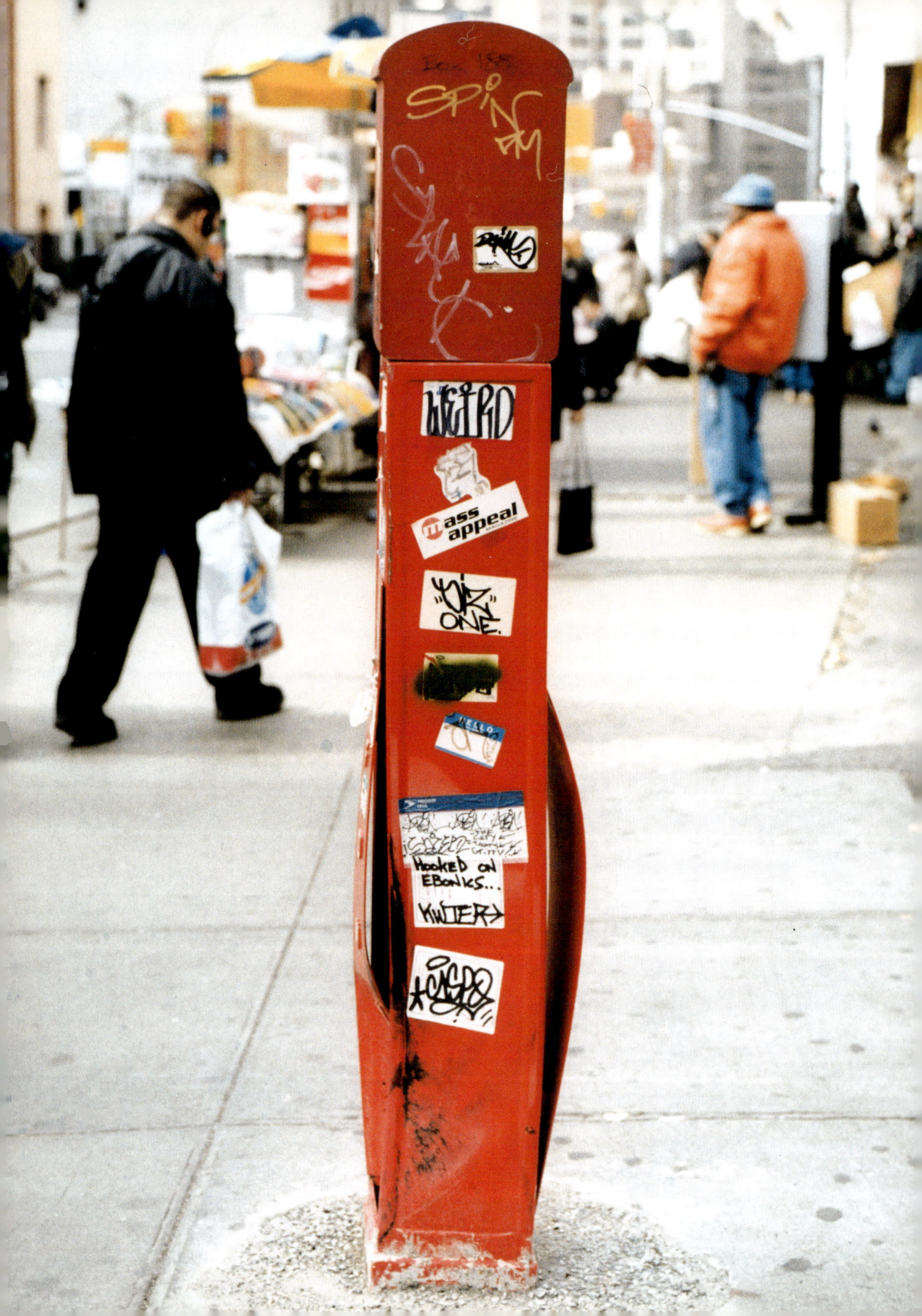

WEIRD
mass appeal
HOOKED ON

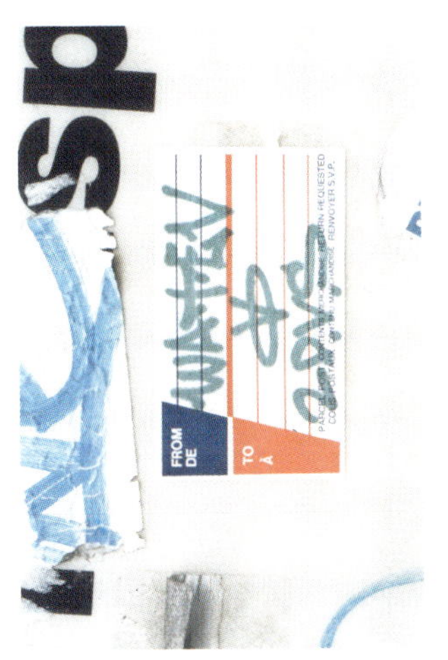
sp
FROM
DE
TO
À

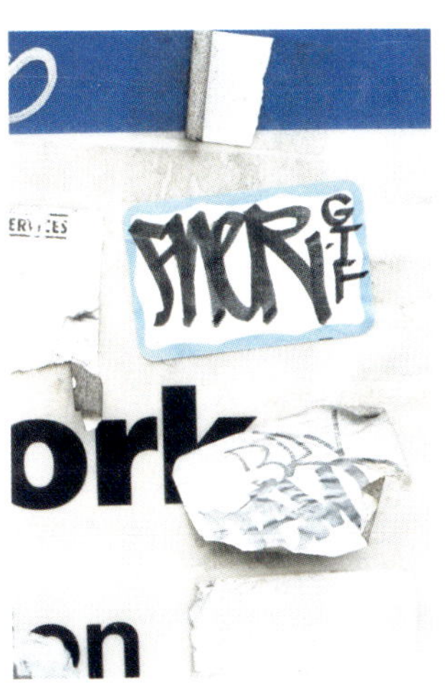
ERVICES
ork
on

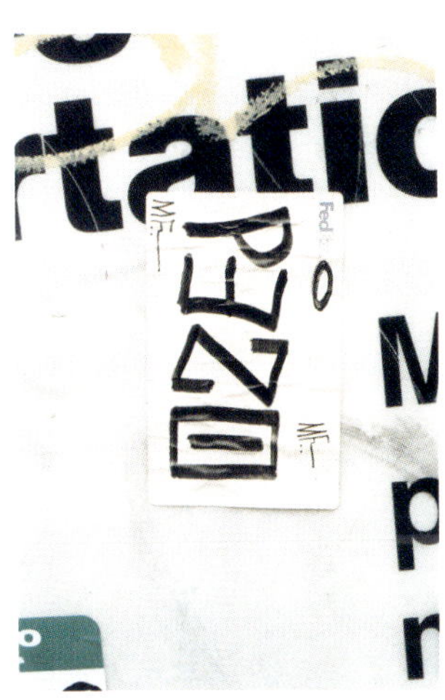
rtatio
M
p
r

	System			Order		
Property Phenomenon	Dysfunctional Speech Act	Commerce	Control	Membrane	Orientation	The Range of Participation
LOCKED MOBILITY	MISSPELLING	CORPORATE MONUMENTS	POLICE LINE DO NOT CROSS	BLUE CITY	STREET SCRIPT	VOICE
TAPE	FADING MARKETS	STREET VENDORS	A BARRIER	COVER	STREET MARK	DIVERSITY
SHOP WATCH	EMPTY SIGNS	STREET LEVEL	SERVICE SCREEN	SHOPPING BAG	STEEL	OPEN CINE
REAL ESTATE		SHOPPING CARTS		GARBAGE DIGITAL SLUM		NEIGHBORHOOD

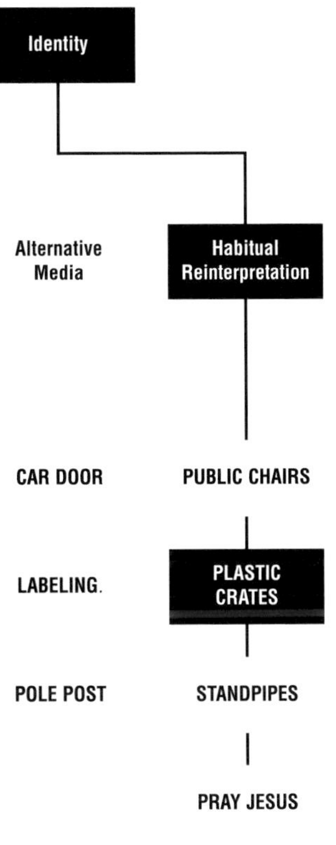

PLASTIC CRATES

In the same Box

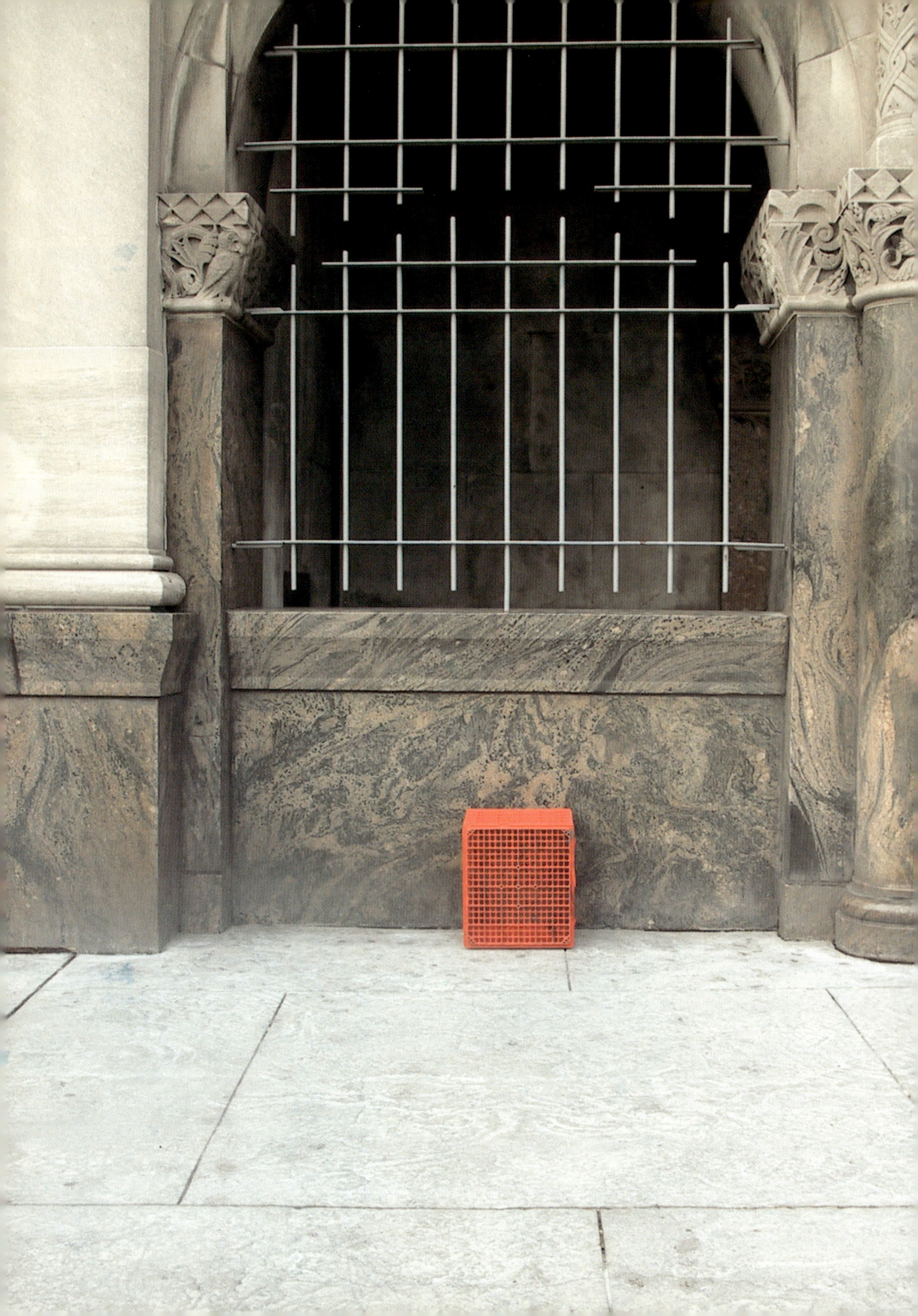

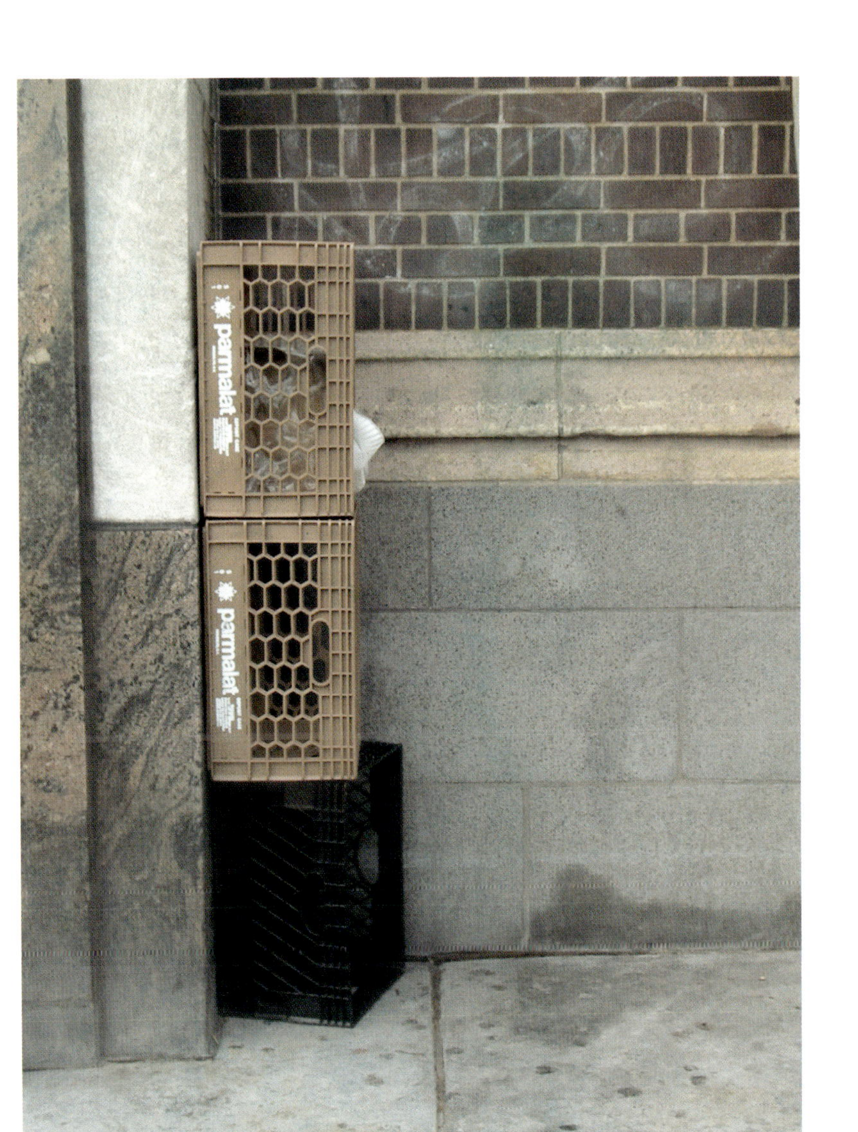
parmalat
parmalat

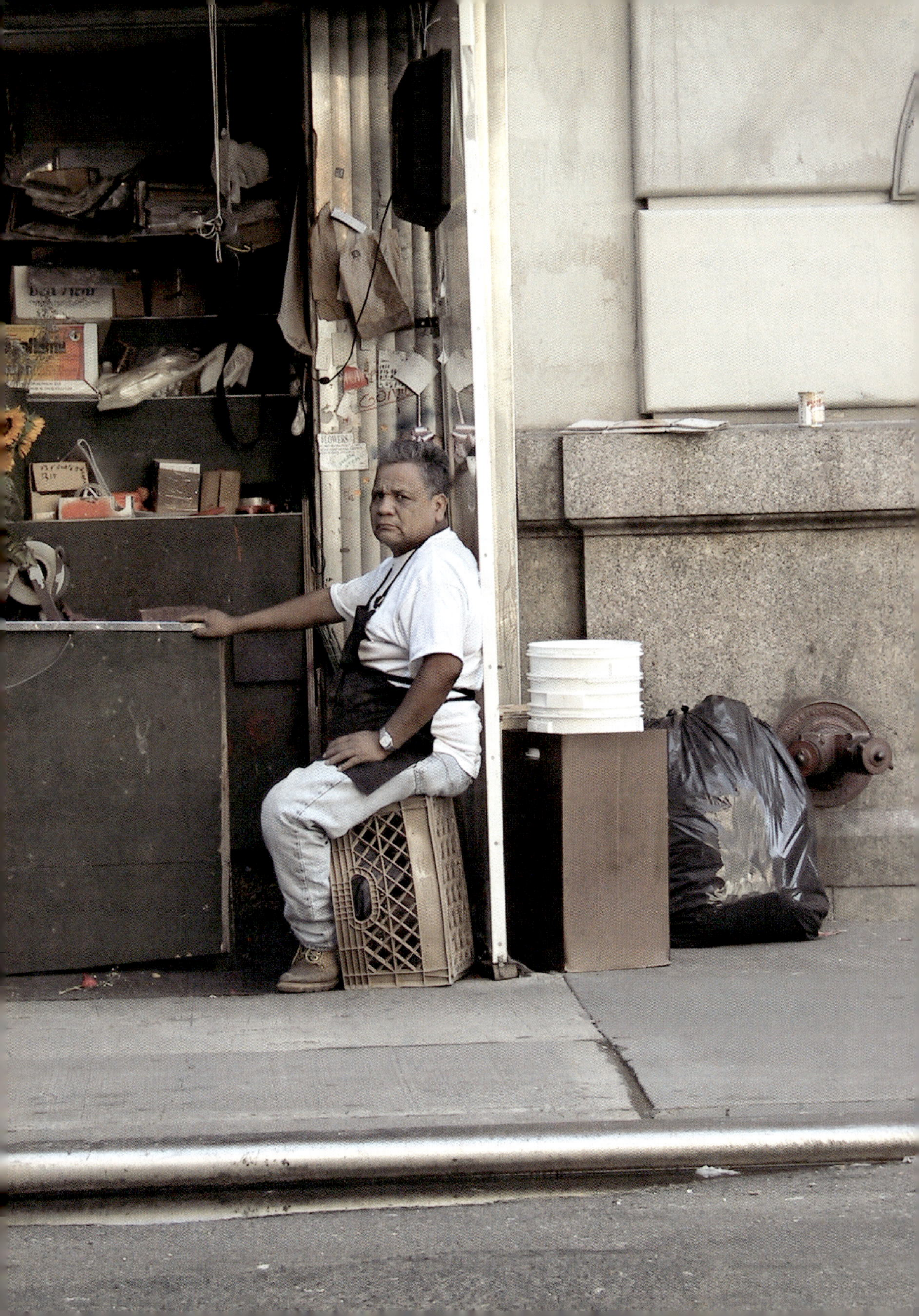
FLOWERS

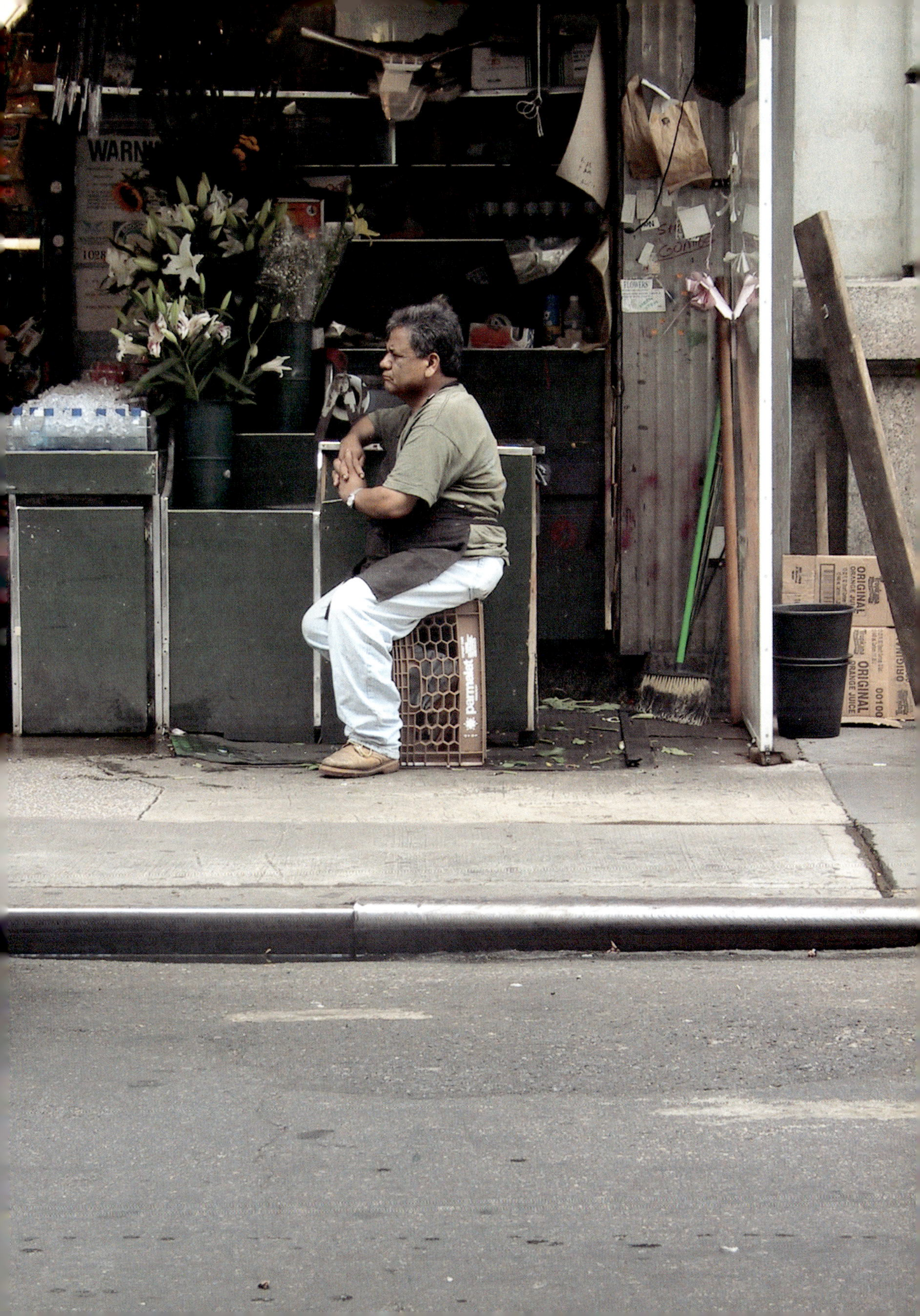
parmalat
ORIGINAL
ORANGE JUICE
00100

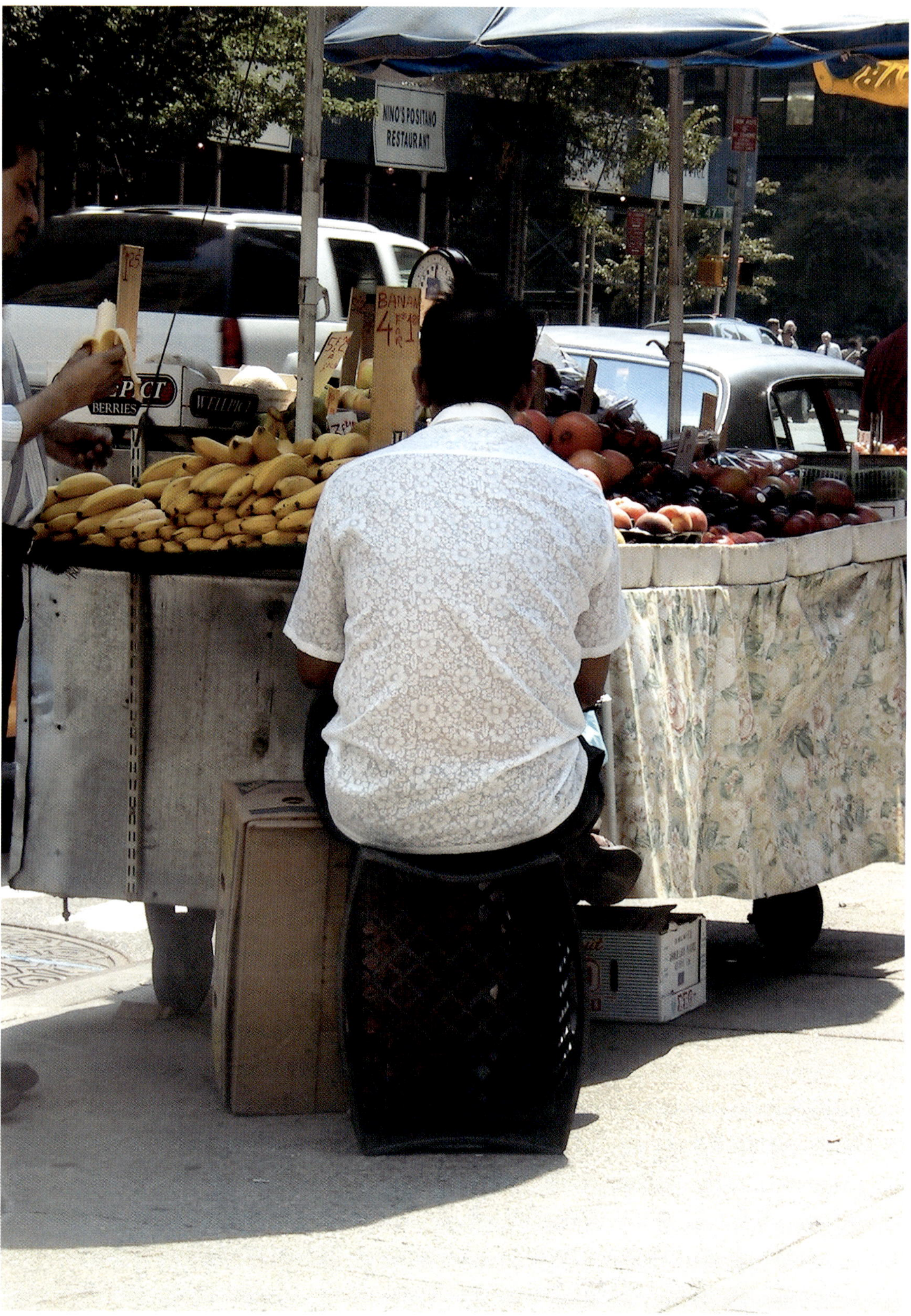
NINO'S POSITANO
RESTAURANT
BERRIES

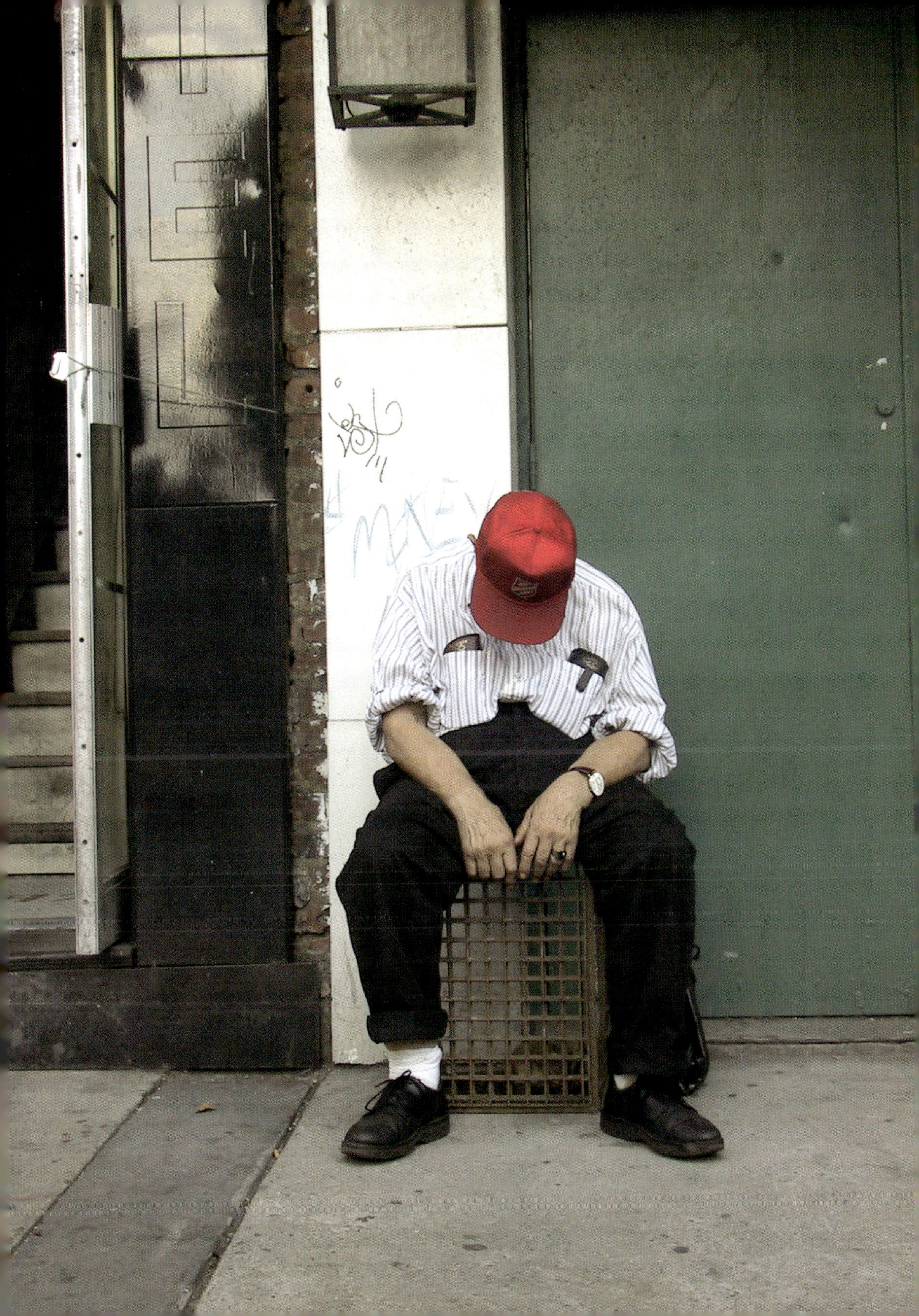

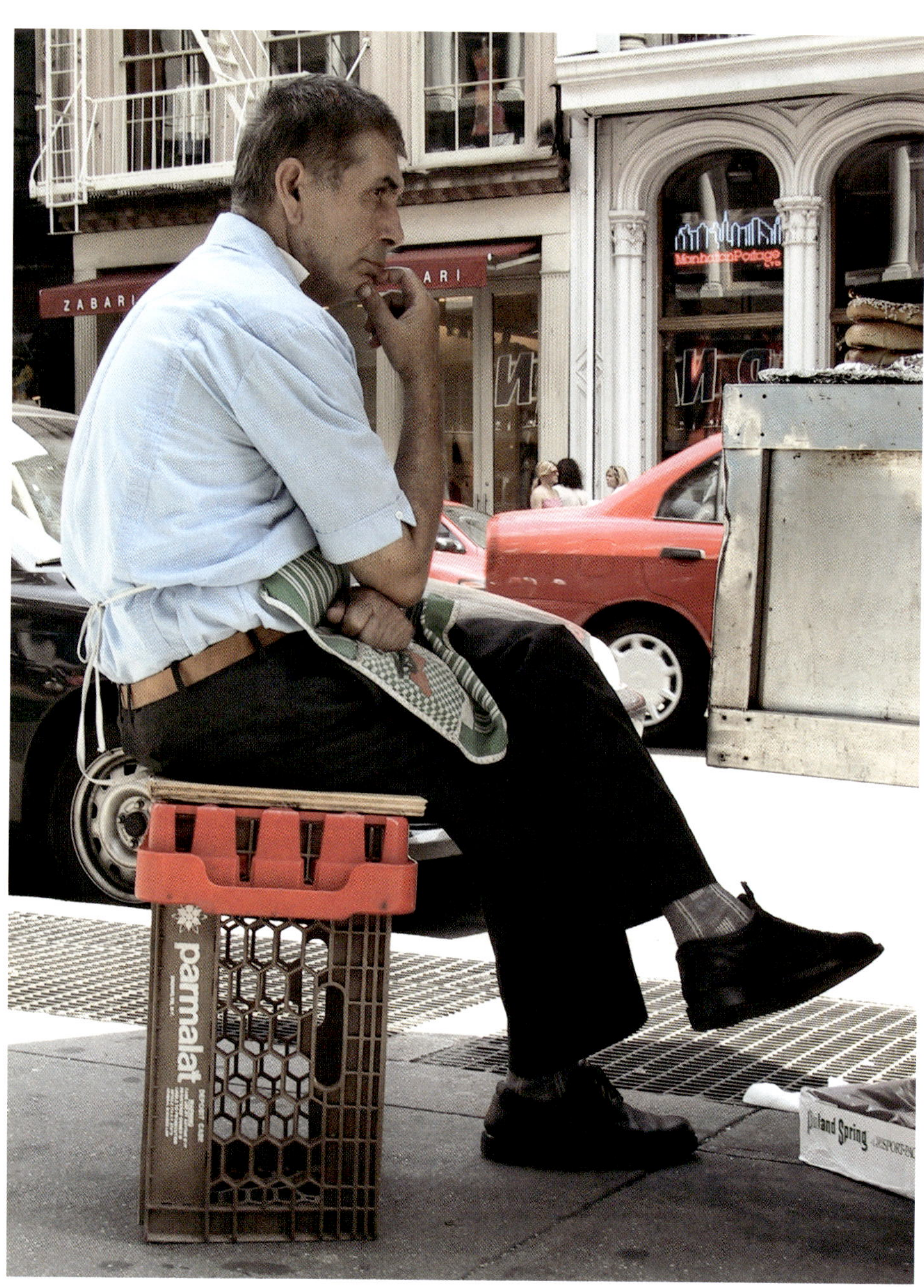
ZABARI
parmalat

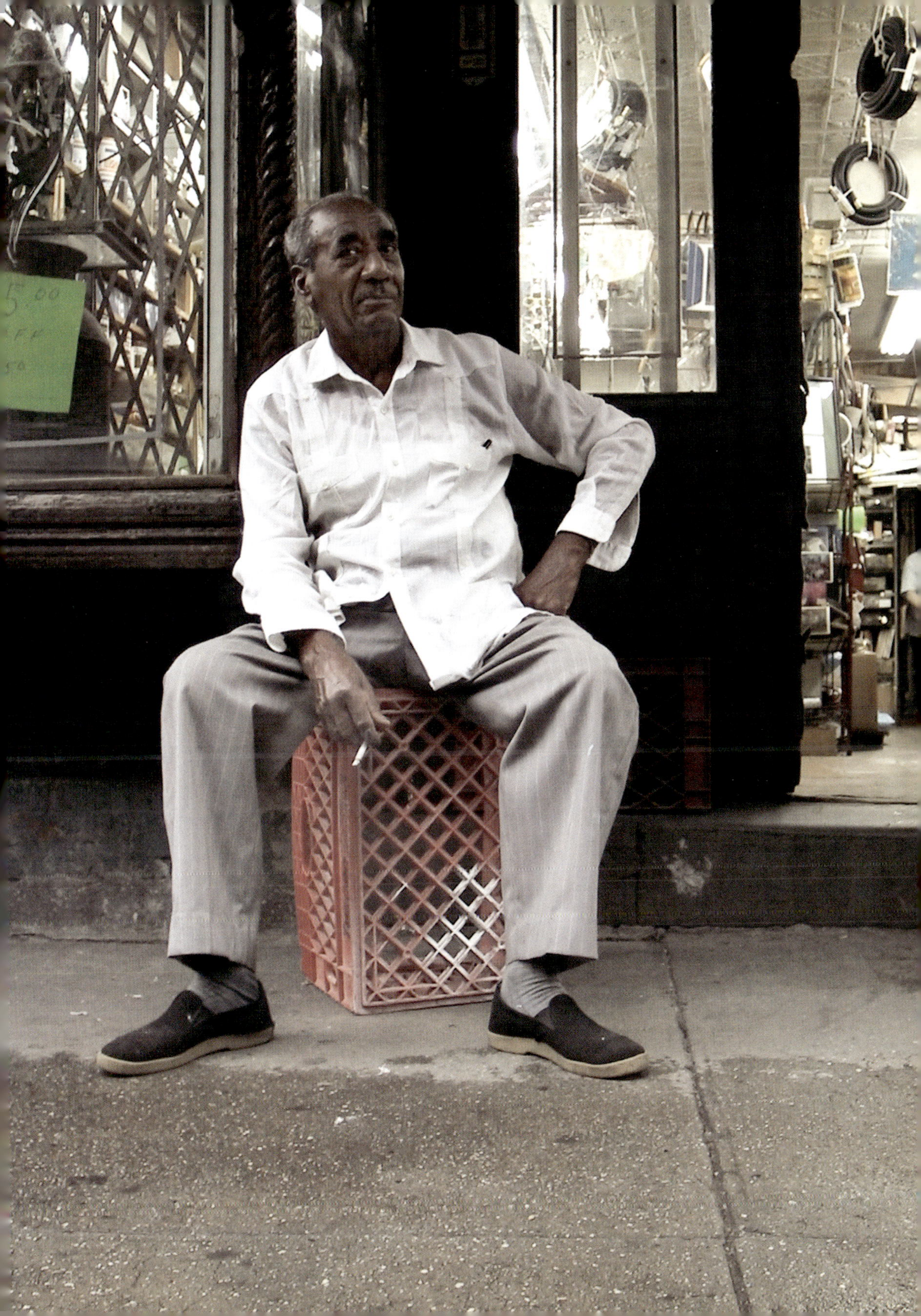

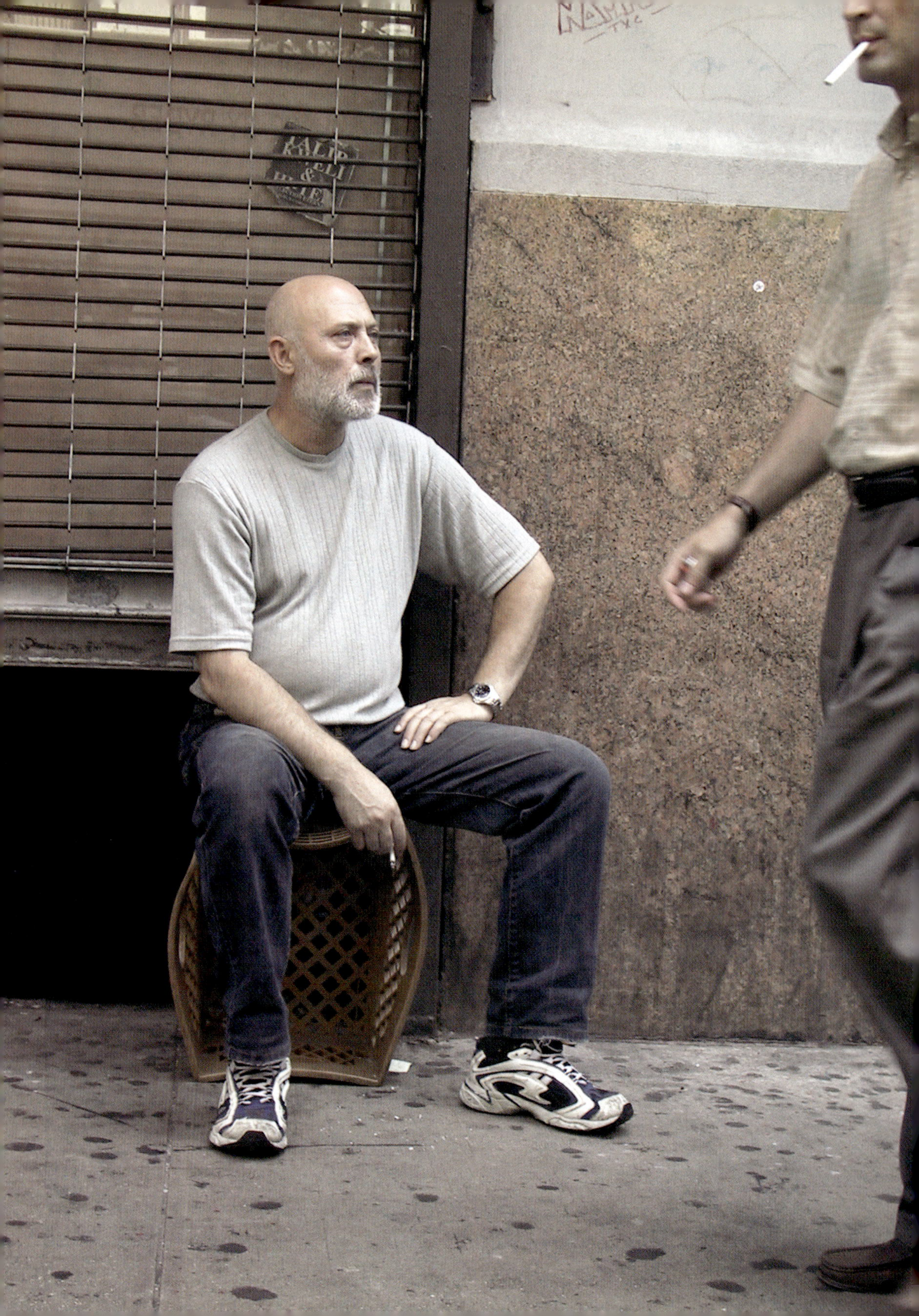

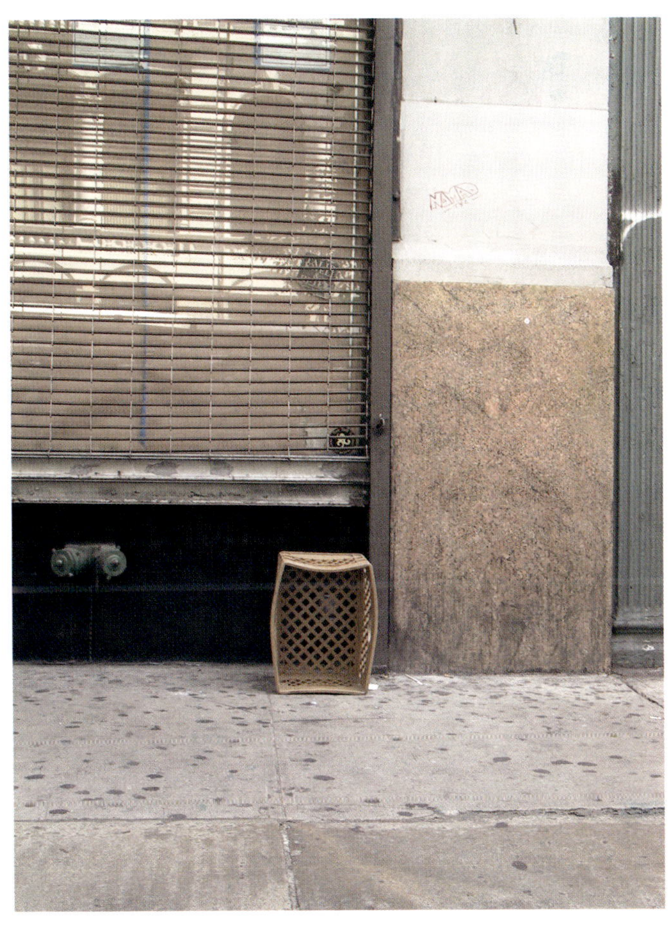

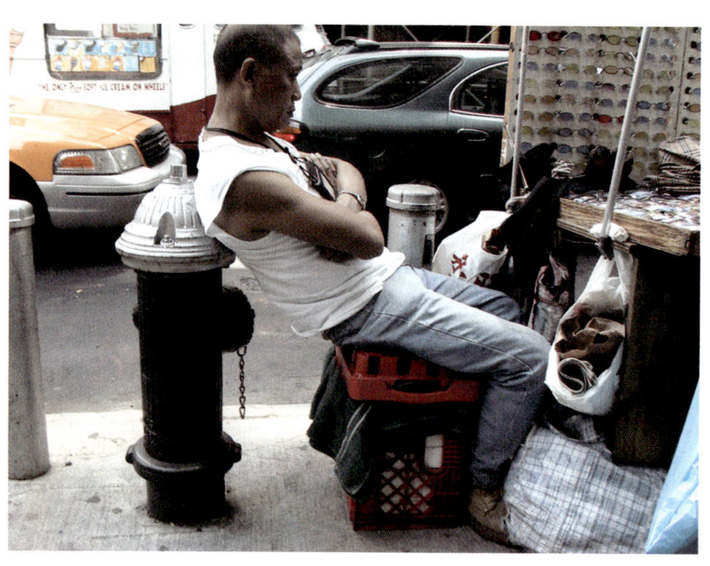

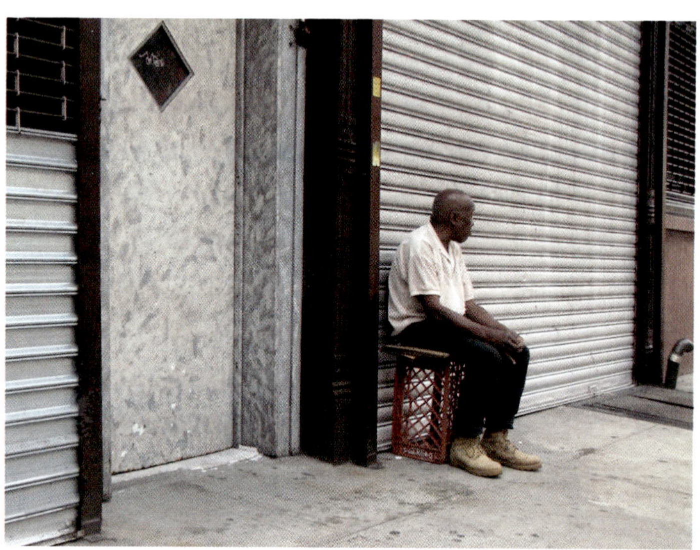

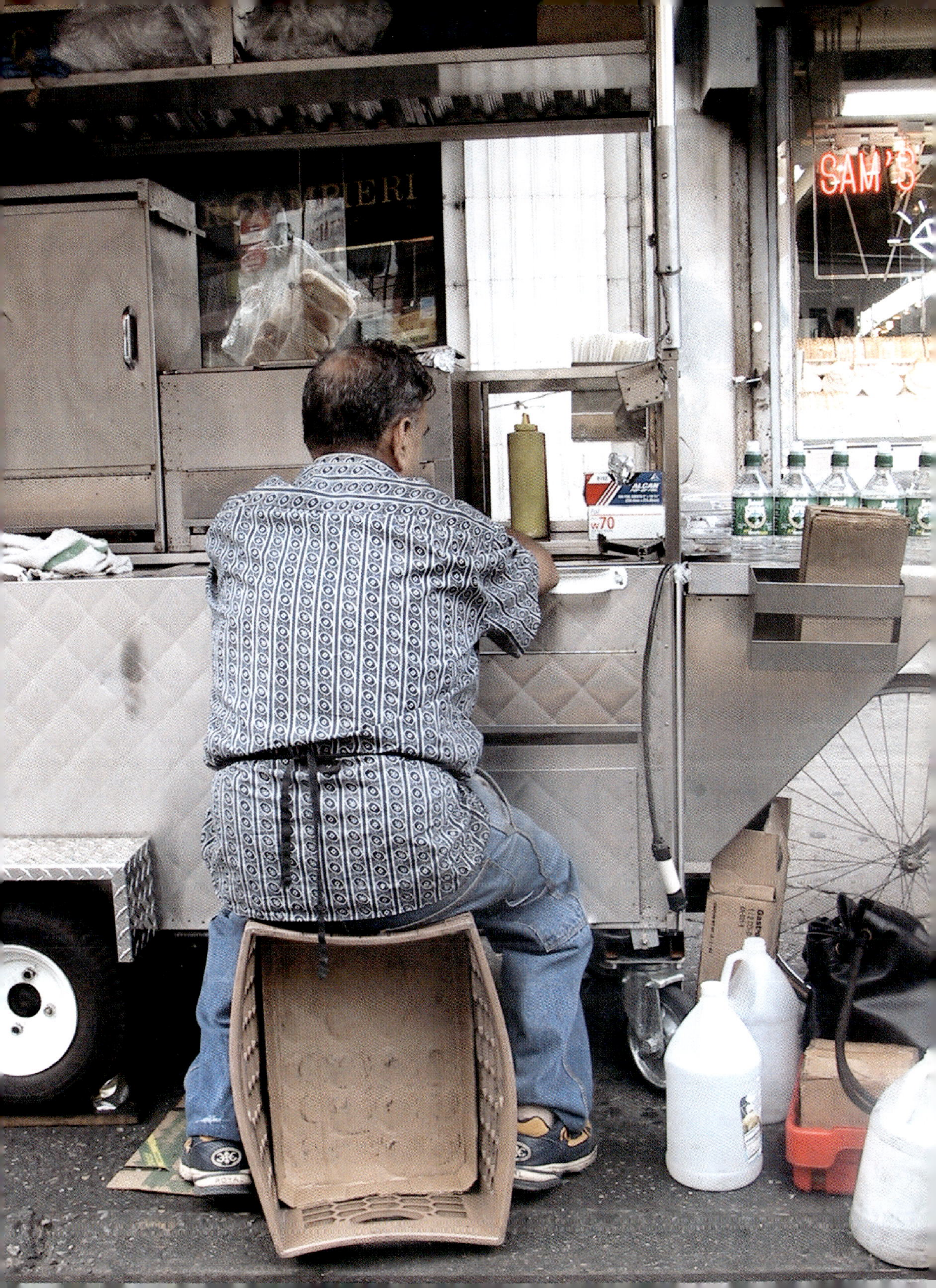
SAM'S
ALCAN
W70

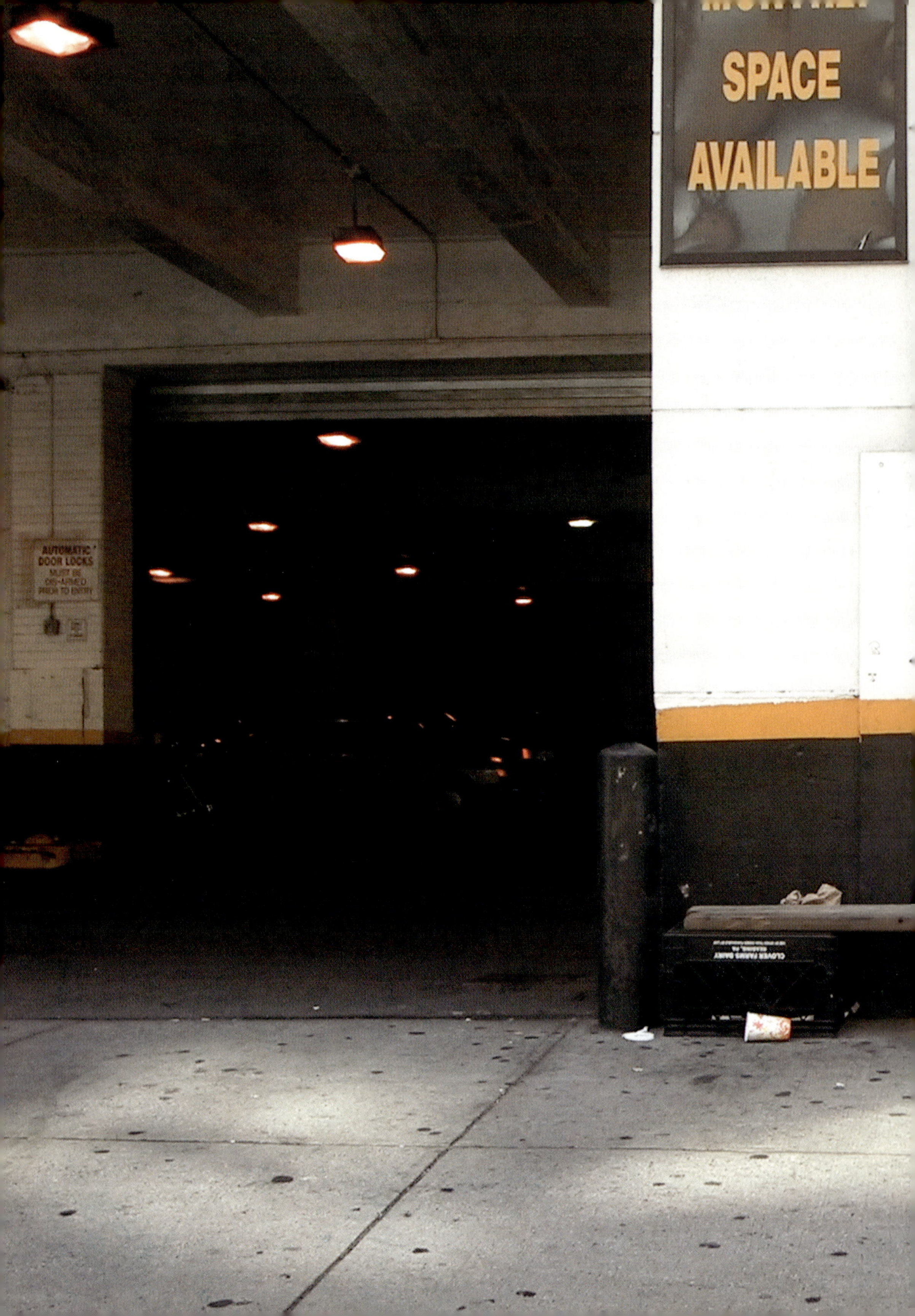
SPACE
AVAILABLE
DOOR LOCKS

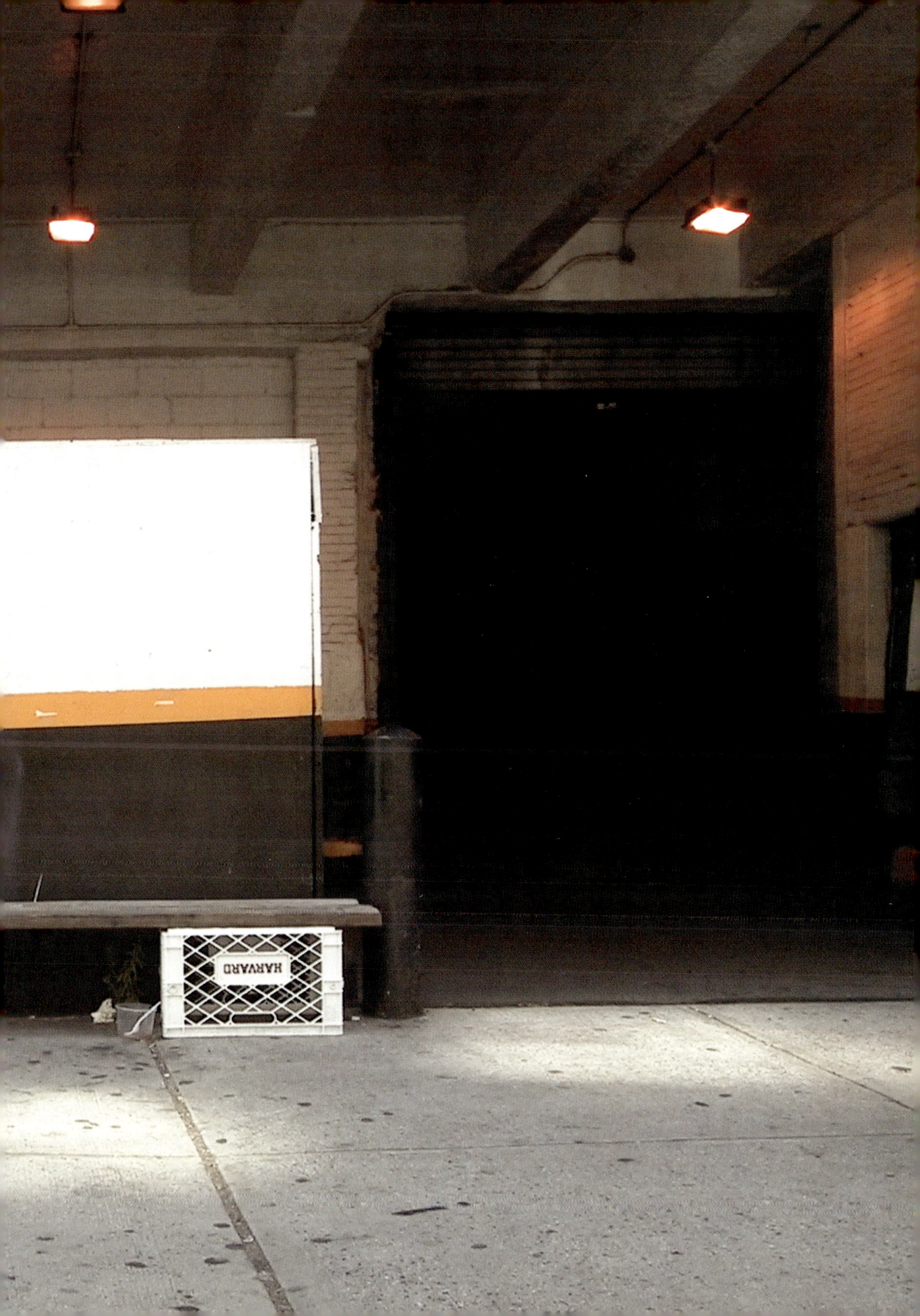
HARVARD

	System			Order		
Property Phenomenon	Dysfunctional Speech Act	Commerce	Control	Membrane	Orientation	The Range of Participation
LOCKED MOBILITY	MISSPELLING	CORPORATE MONUMENTS	POLICE LINE DO NOT CROSS	BLUE CITY	STREET SCRIPT	VOICE
TAPE	FADING MARKETS	STREET VENDORS	A BARRIER	COVER	STREET MARK	DIVERSITY
SHOP WATCH	EMPTY SIGNS	STREET LEVEL	SERVICE SCREEN	SHOPPING BAG	STEEL	OPEN CINE
REAL ESTATE		SHOPPING CARTS		GARBAGE DIGITAL SLUM		NEIGHBORHOOD

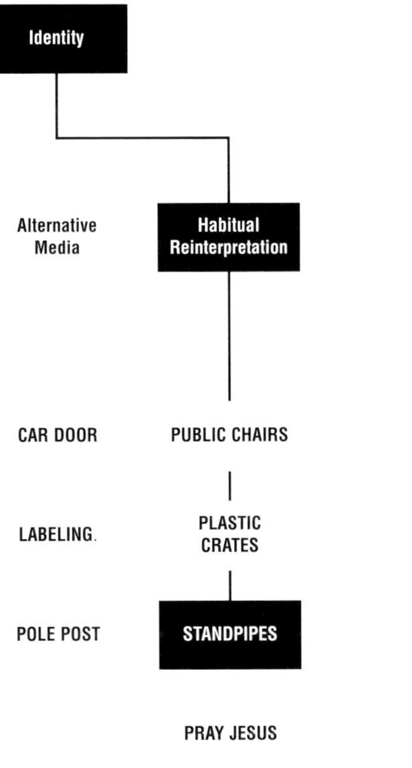

STANDPIPES

Sit on a Matter

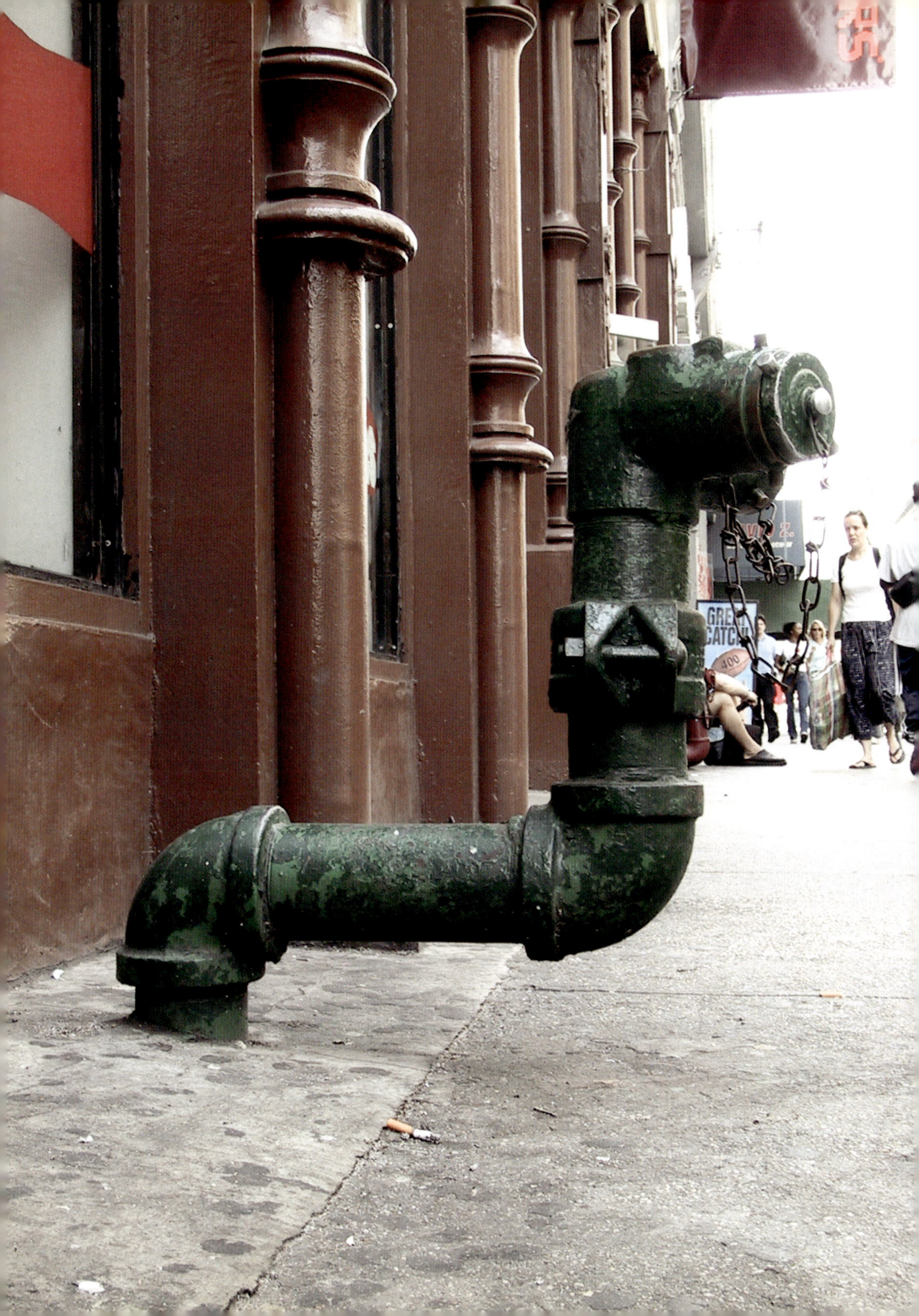
400

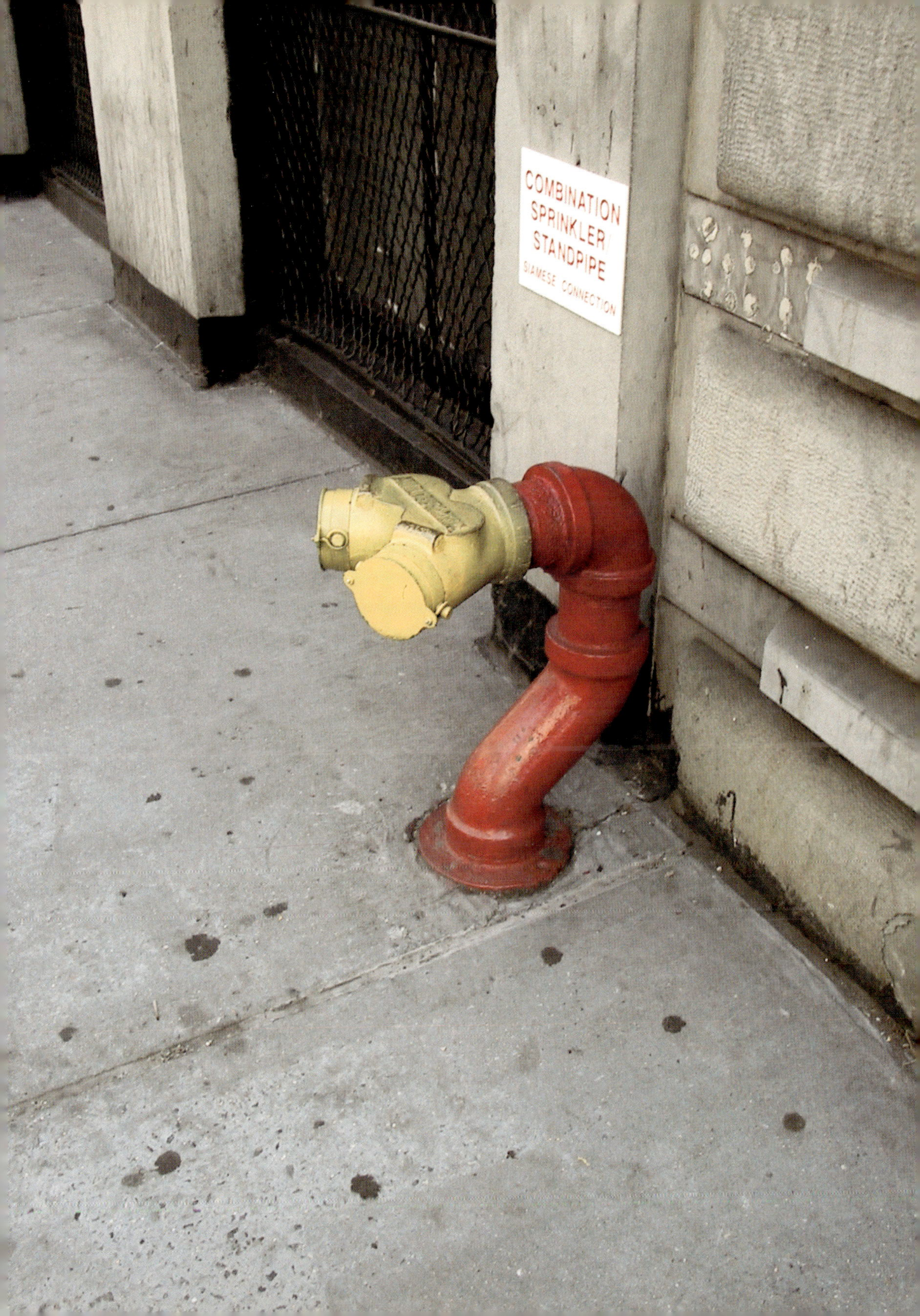
COMBINATION
SPRINKLER/
STANDPIPE
SIAMESE CONNECTION

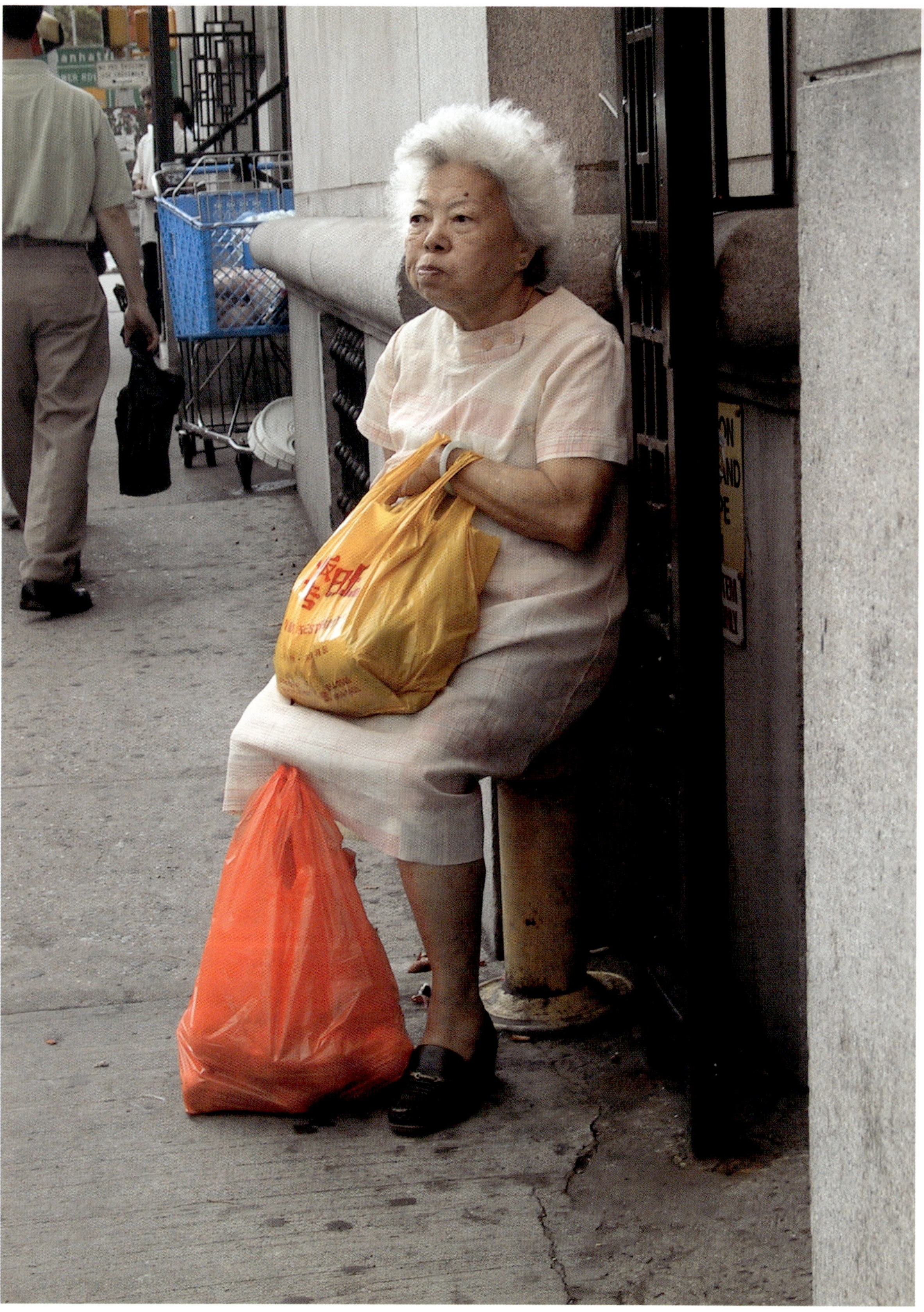

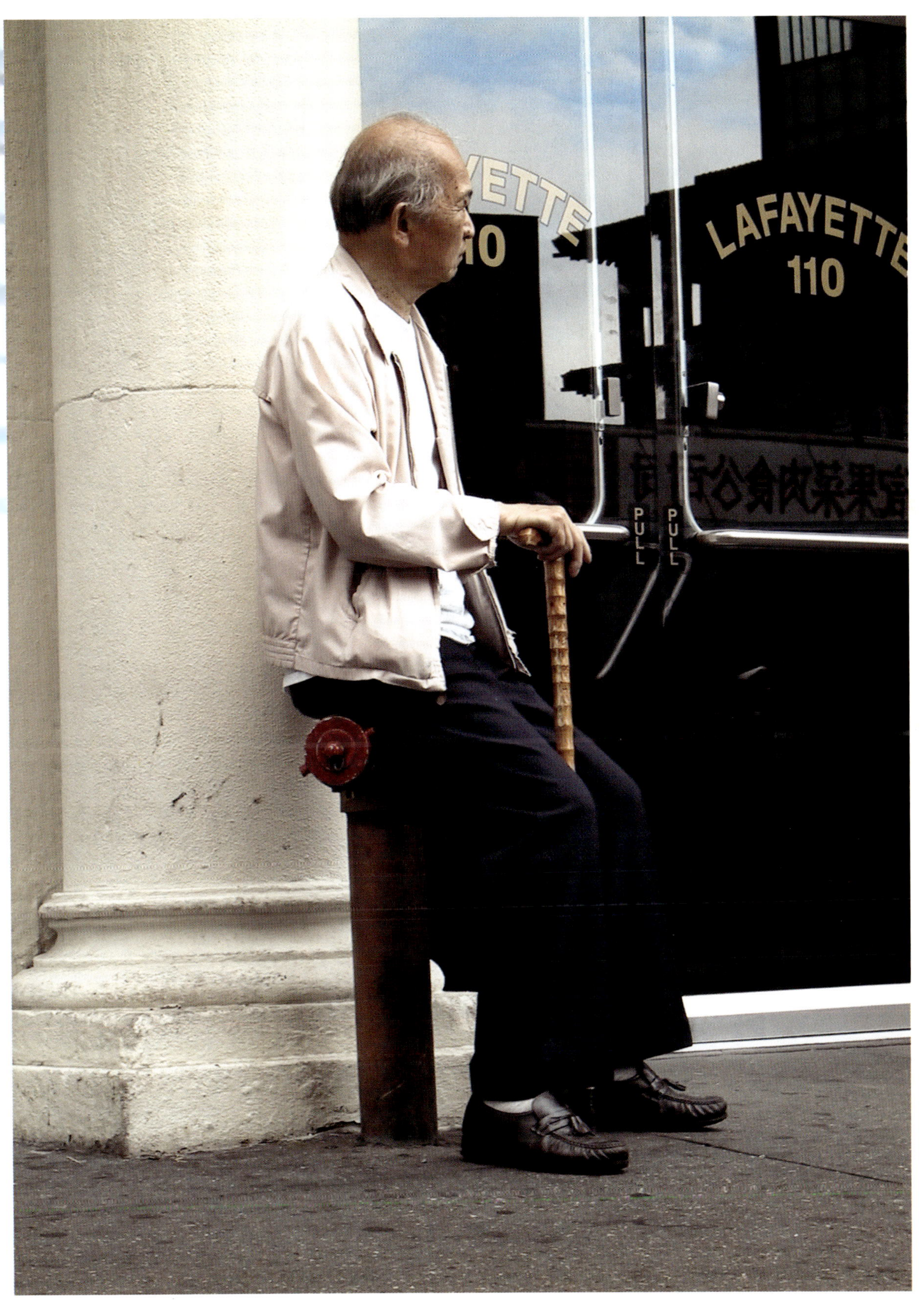
LAFAYETTE
110
PULL
PULL

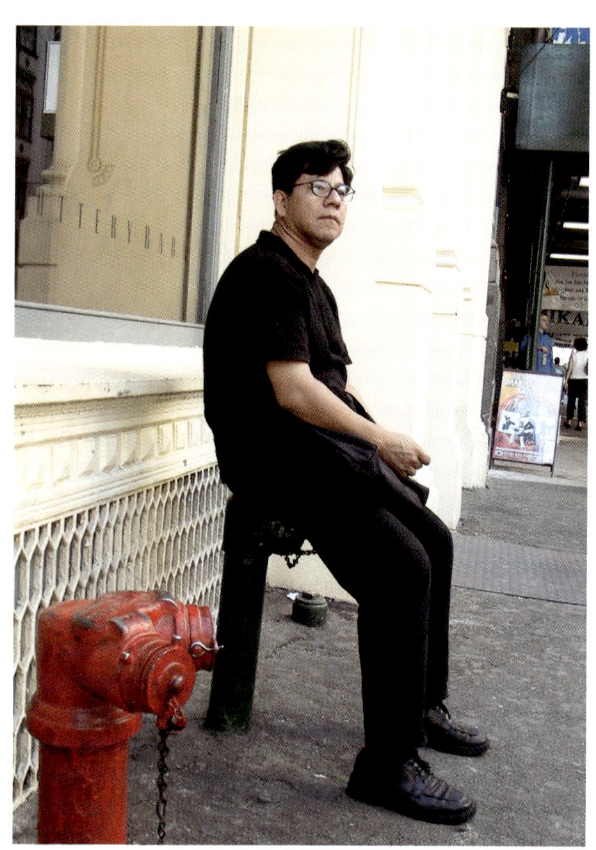

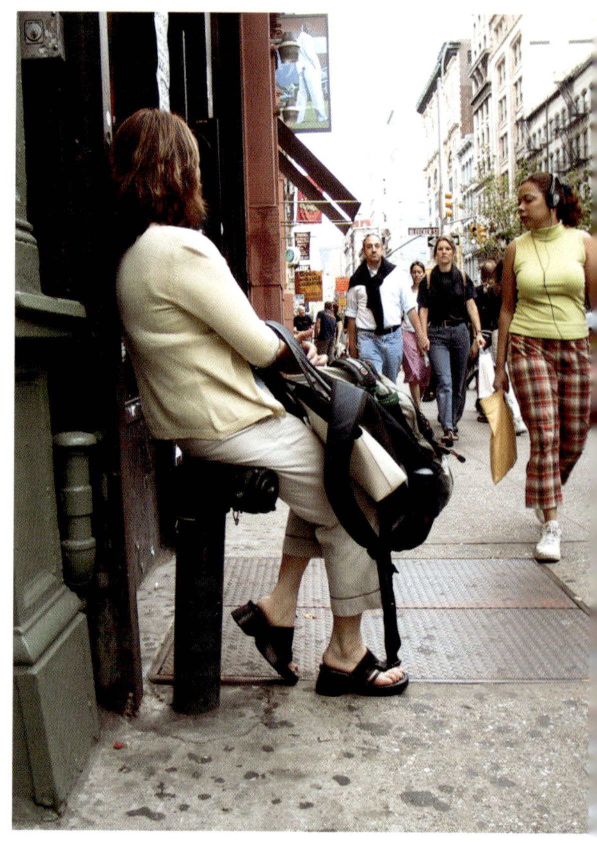

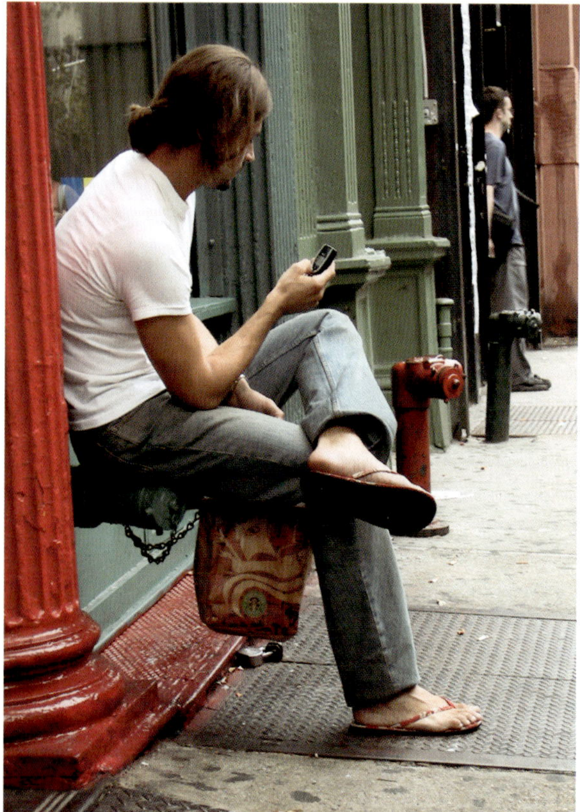

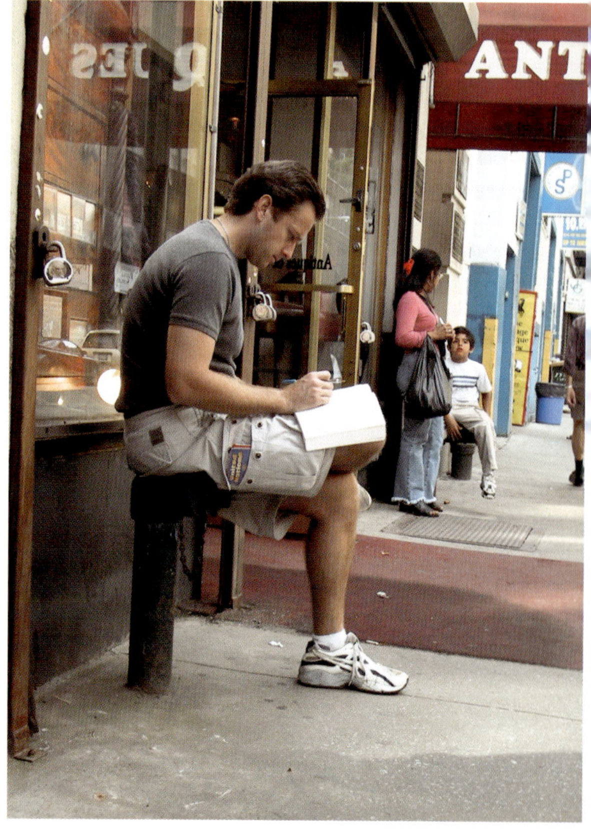
ANT

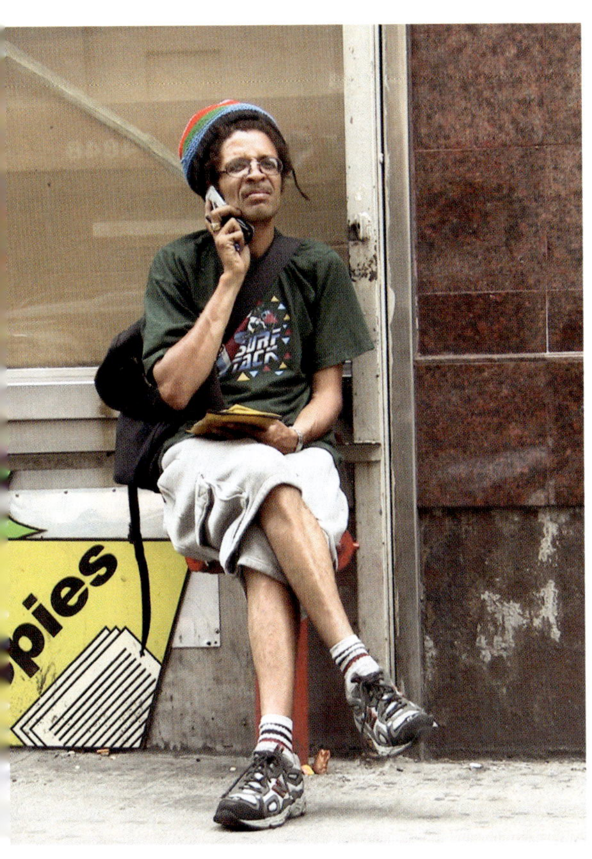
pies

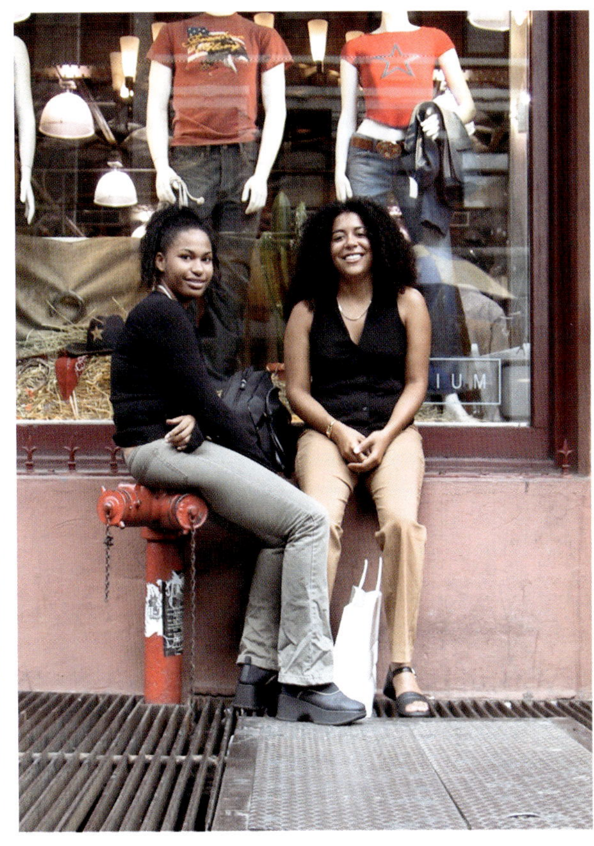
IUM

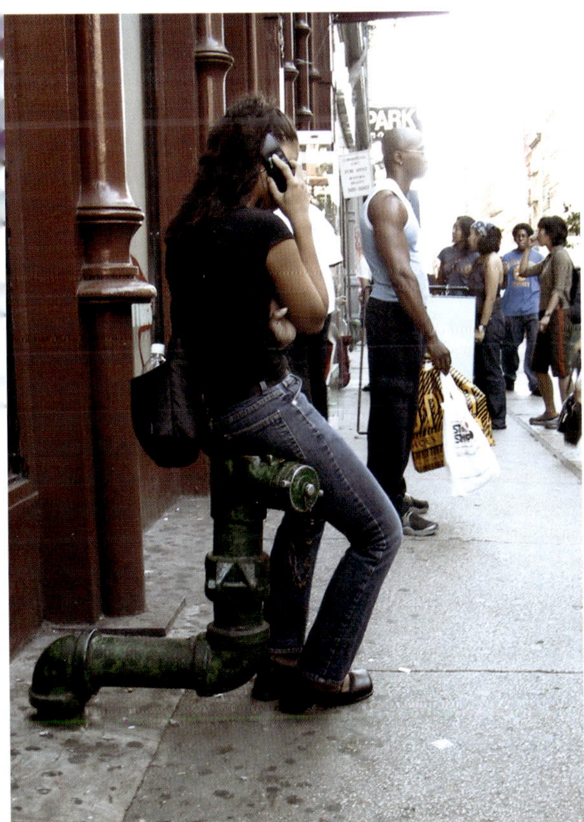
PARK

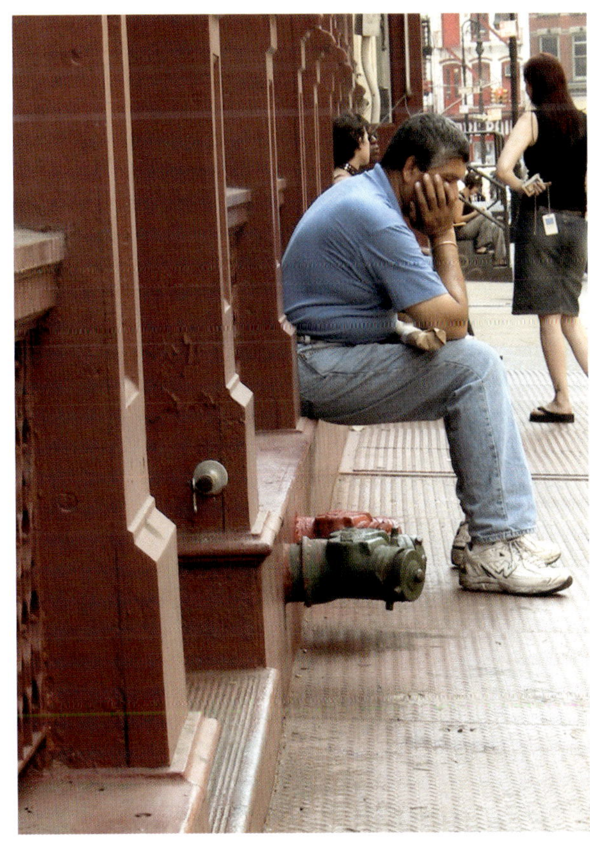

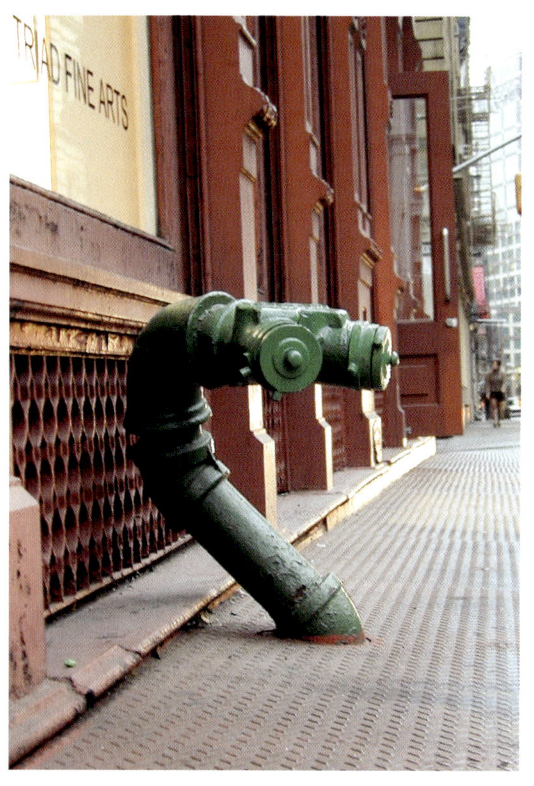
TRIAD FINE ARTS

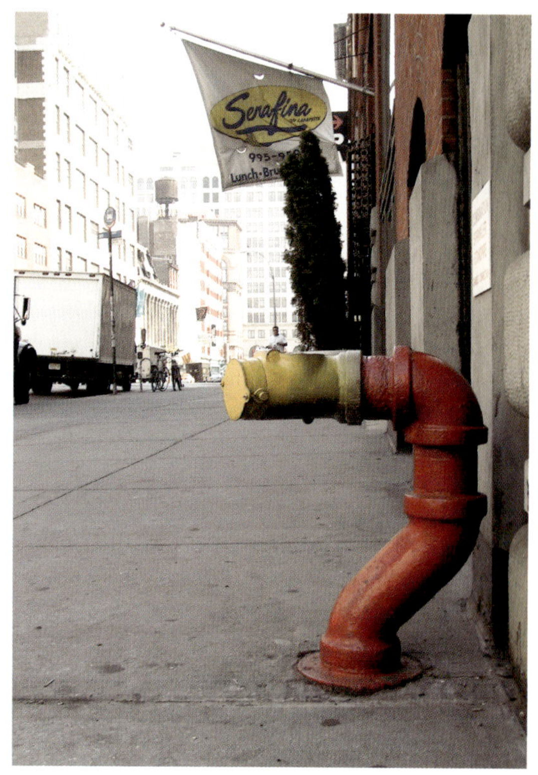
Serafina

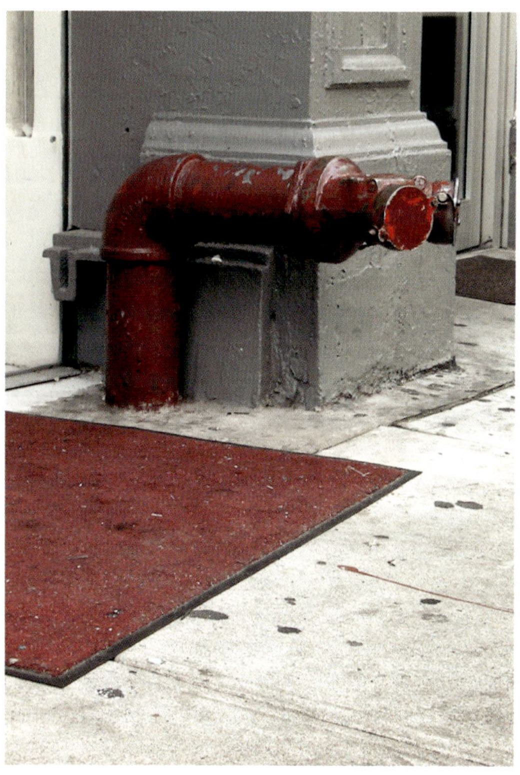

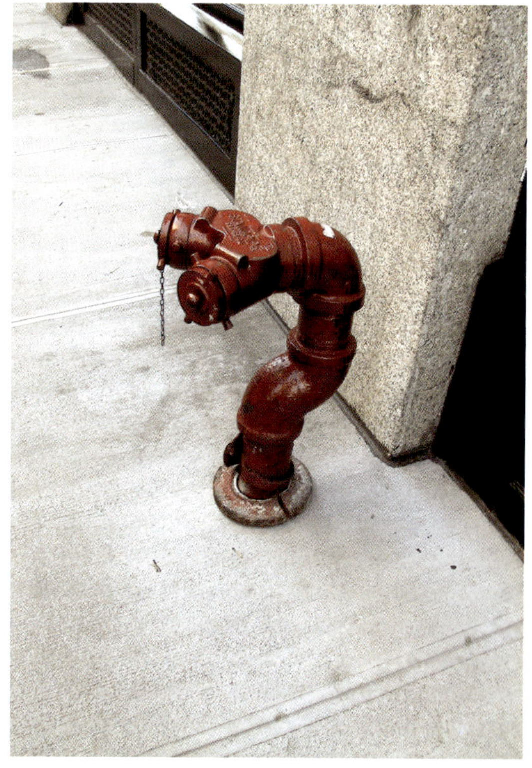

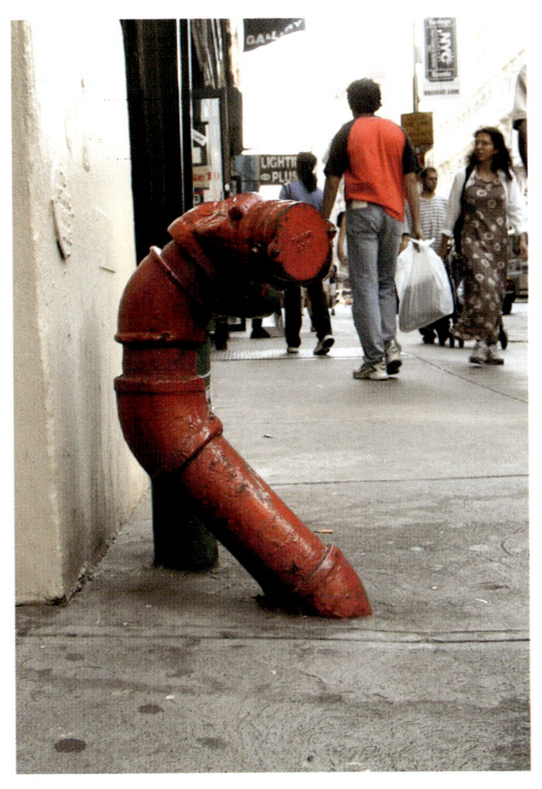
NYC

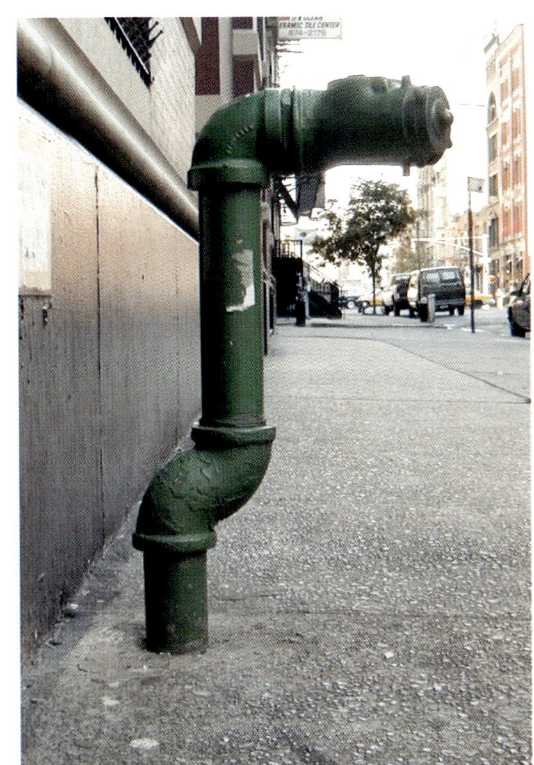

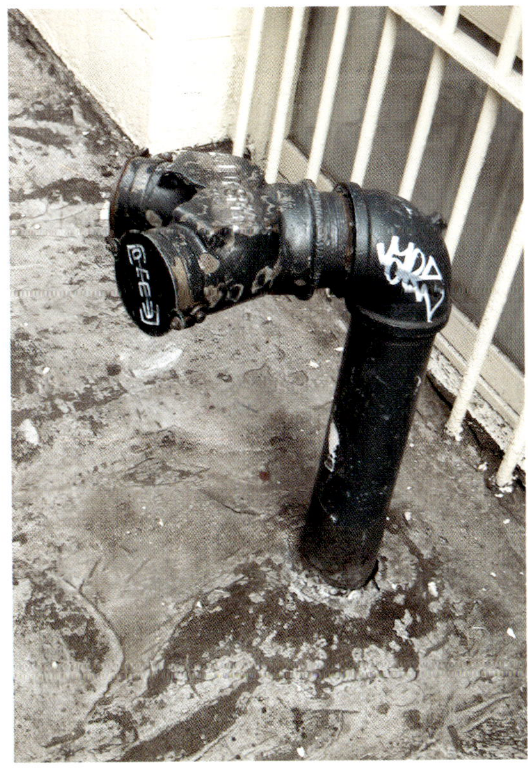

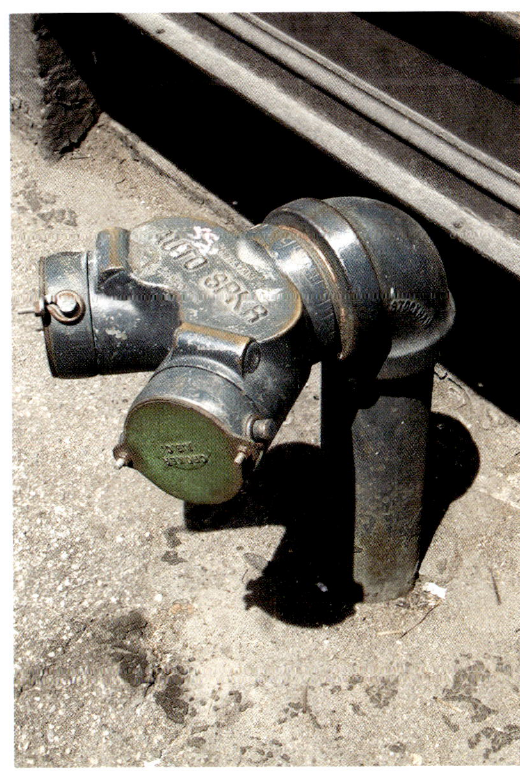
SPKR

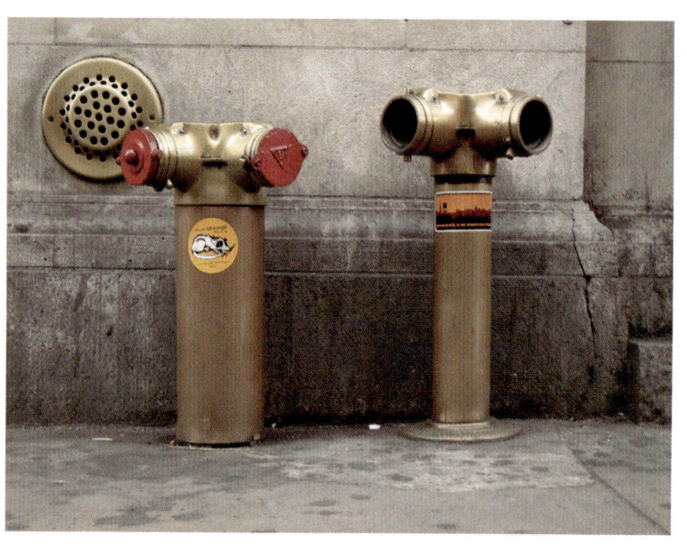

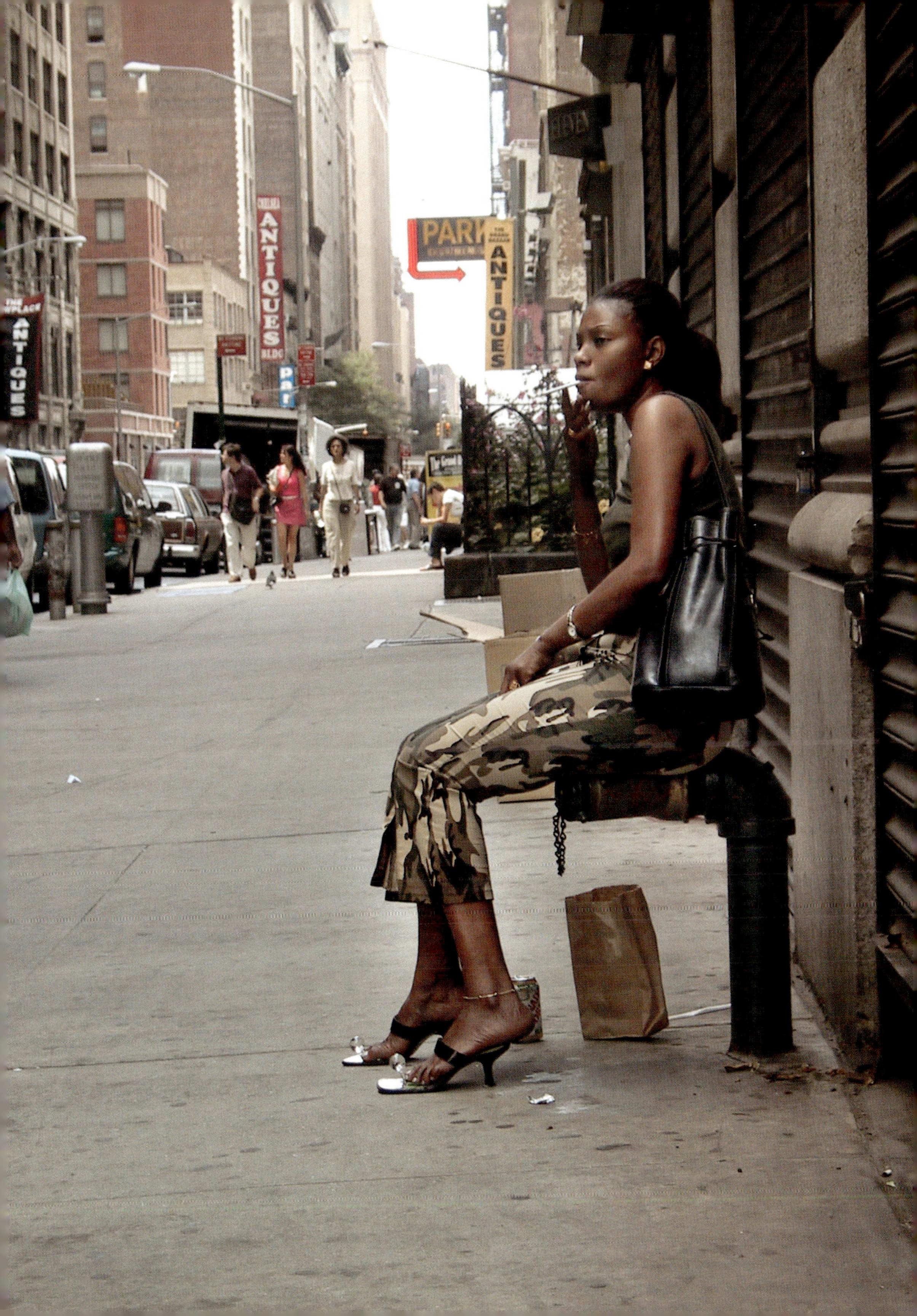
ANTIQUES
ANTIQUES
PARK
ANTIQUES

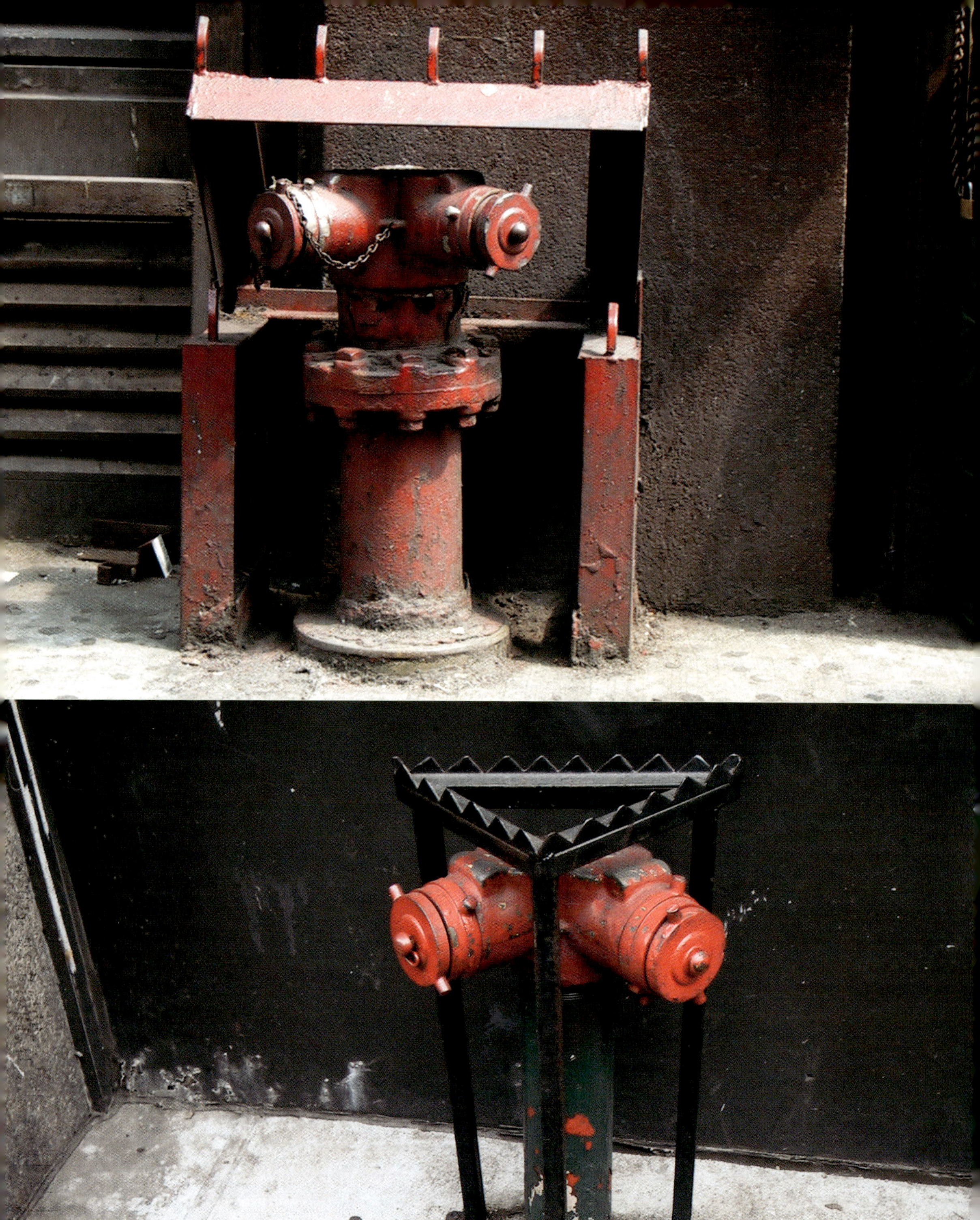

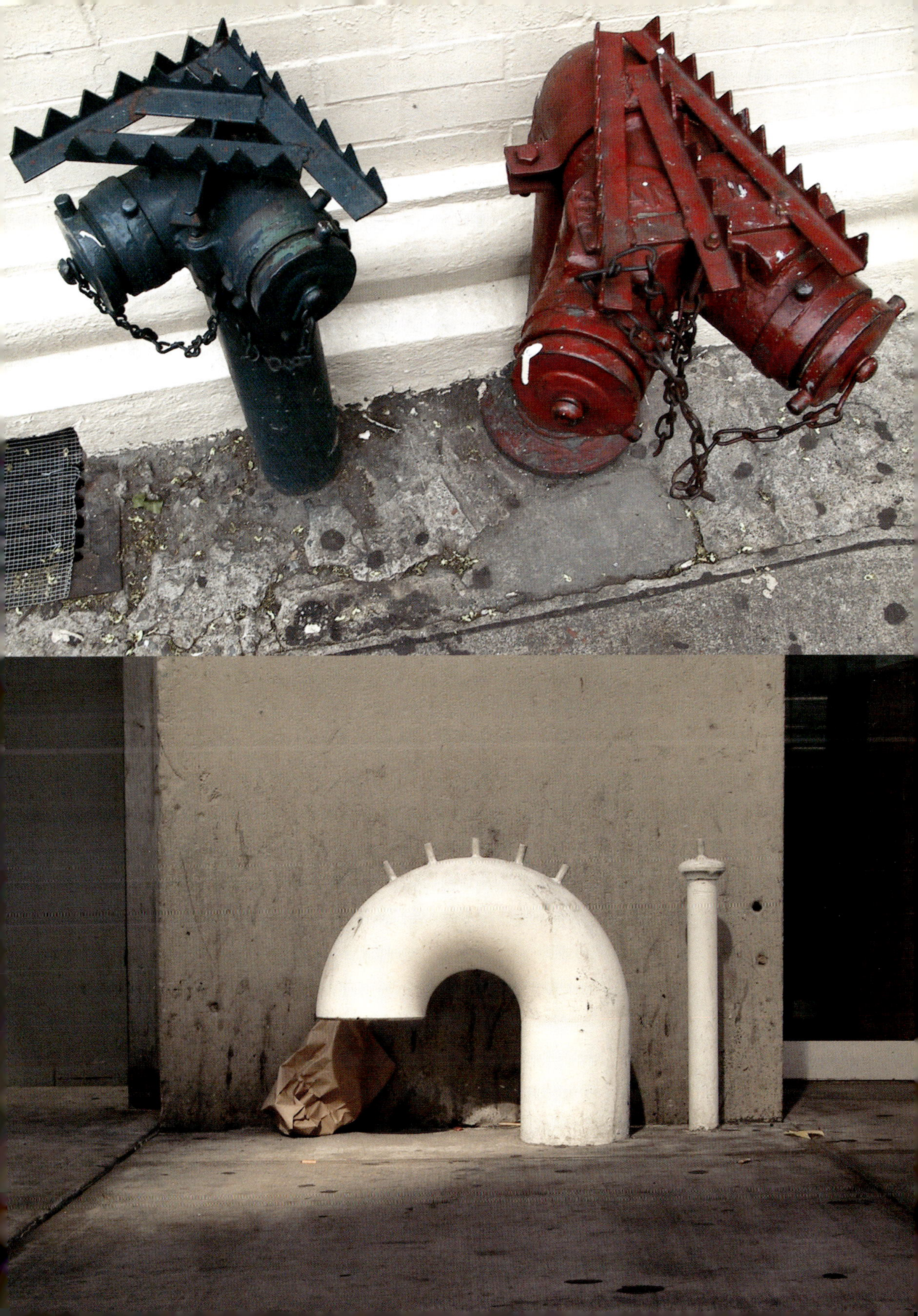

	System			Order		
Property Phenomenon	Dysfunctional Speech Act	Commerce	Control	Membrane	Orientation	The Range of Participation
LOCKED MOBILITY	MISSPELLING	CORPORATE MONUMENTS	POLICE LINE DO NOT CROSS	BLUE CITY	STREET SCRIPT	VOICE
TAPE	FADING MARKETS	STREET VENDORS	A BARRIER	COVER	STREET MARK	DIVERSITY
SHOP WATCH	EMPTY SIGNS	STREET LEVEL	SERVICE SCREEN	SHOPPING BAG	STEEL	OPEN CINE
REAL ESTATE		SHOPPING CARTS		GARBAGE DIGITAL SLUM		NEIGHBORHOOD

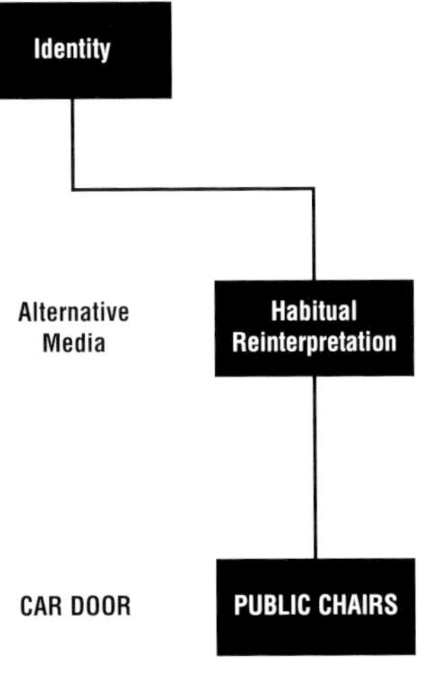

PUBLIC CHAIRS

Sit down in a Town / To be seated

LABELING.

PLASTIC CRATES

POLE POST

STANDPIPES

PRAY JESUS

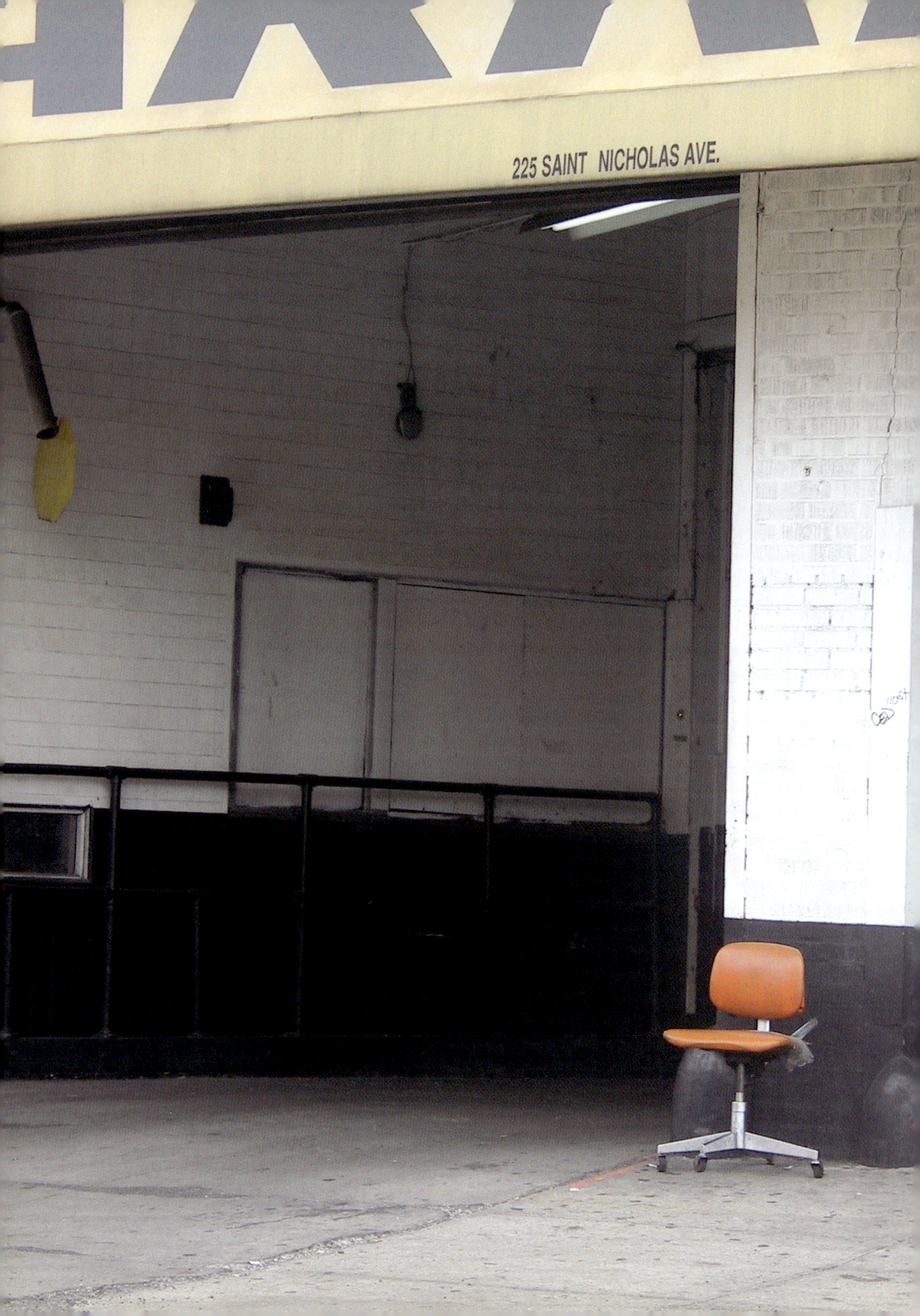
225 SAINT NICHOLAS AVE.

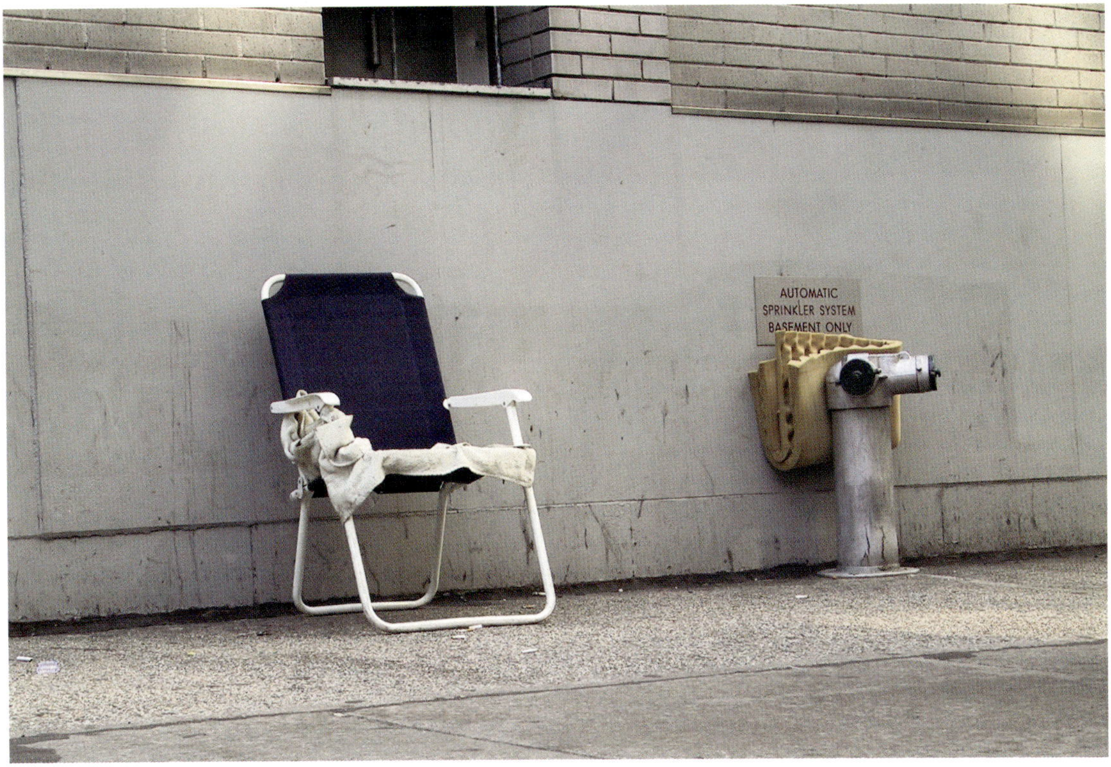

AUTOMATIC
SPRINKLER SYSTEM
BASEMENT ONLY

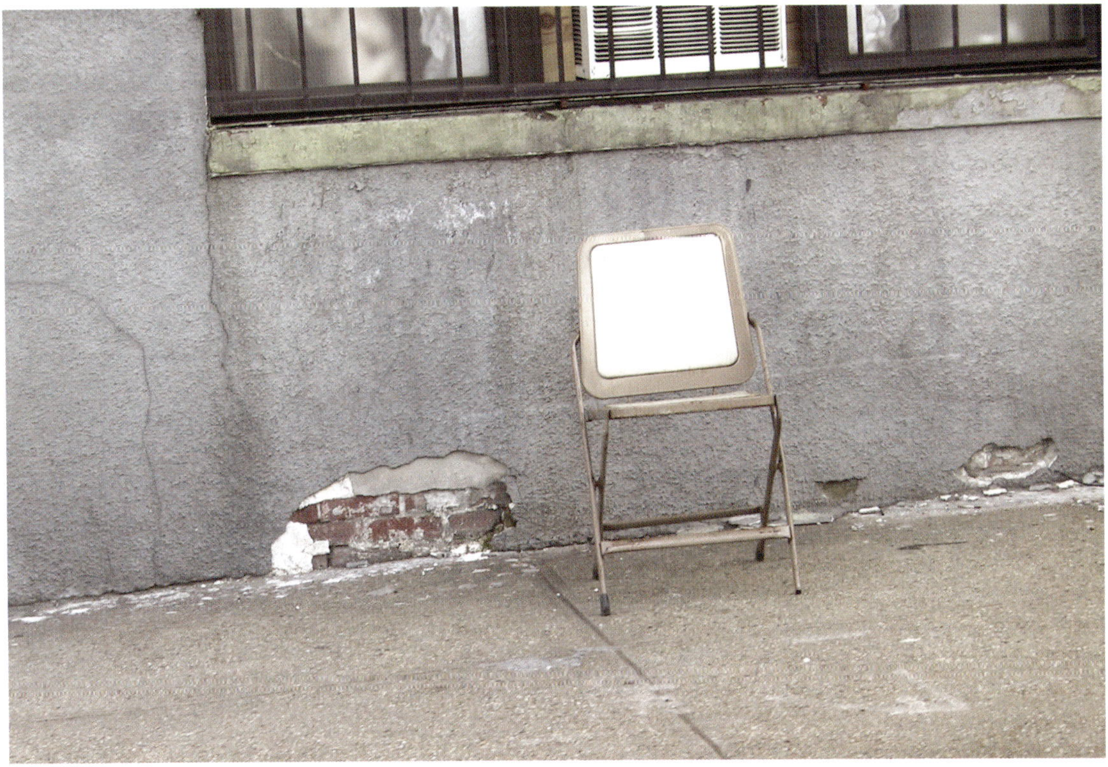

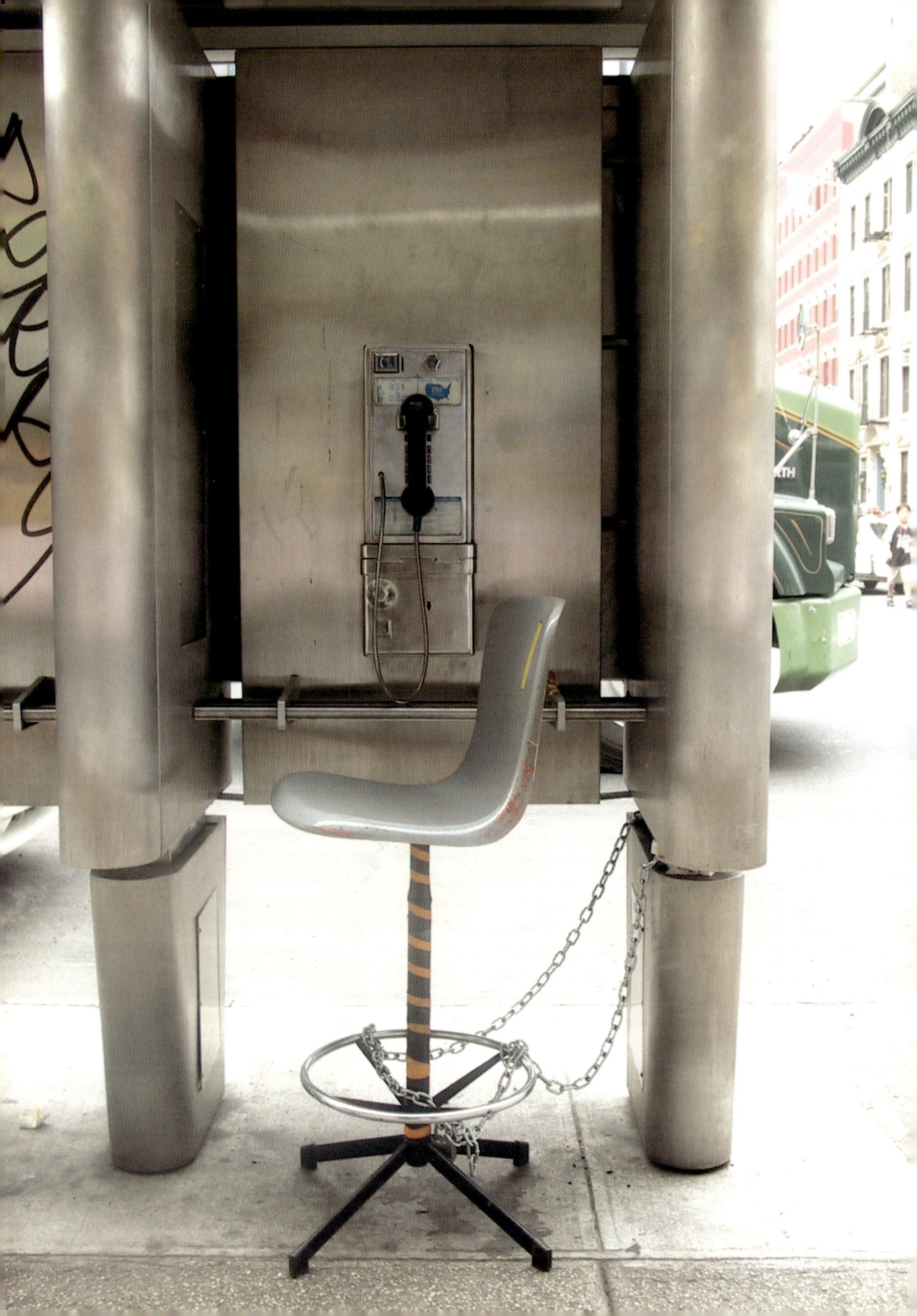

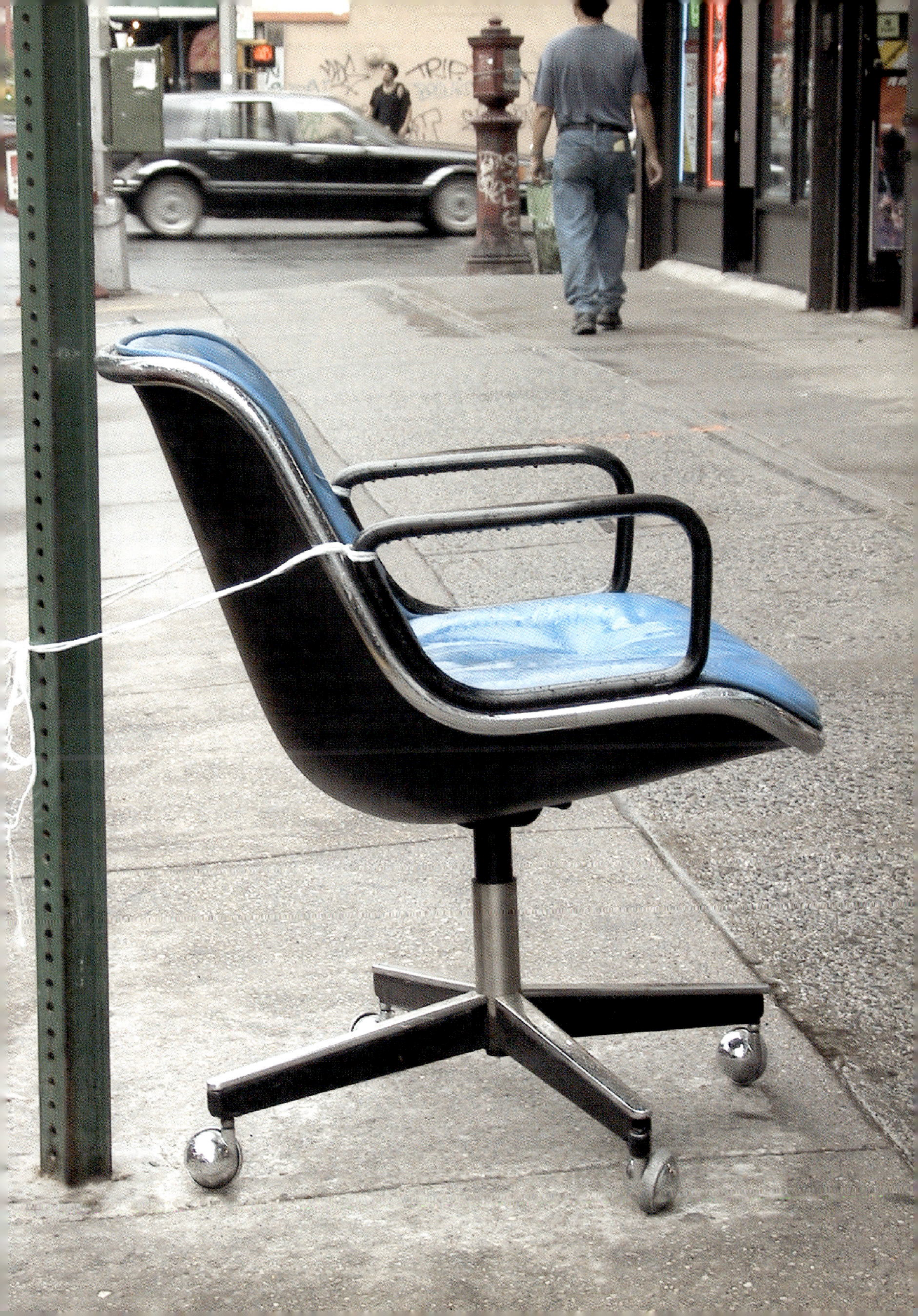

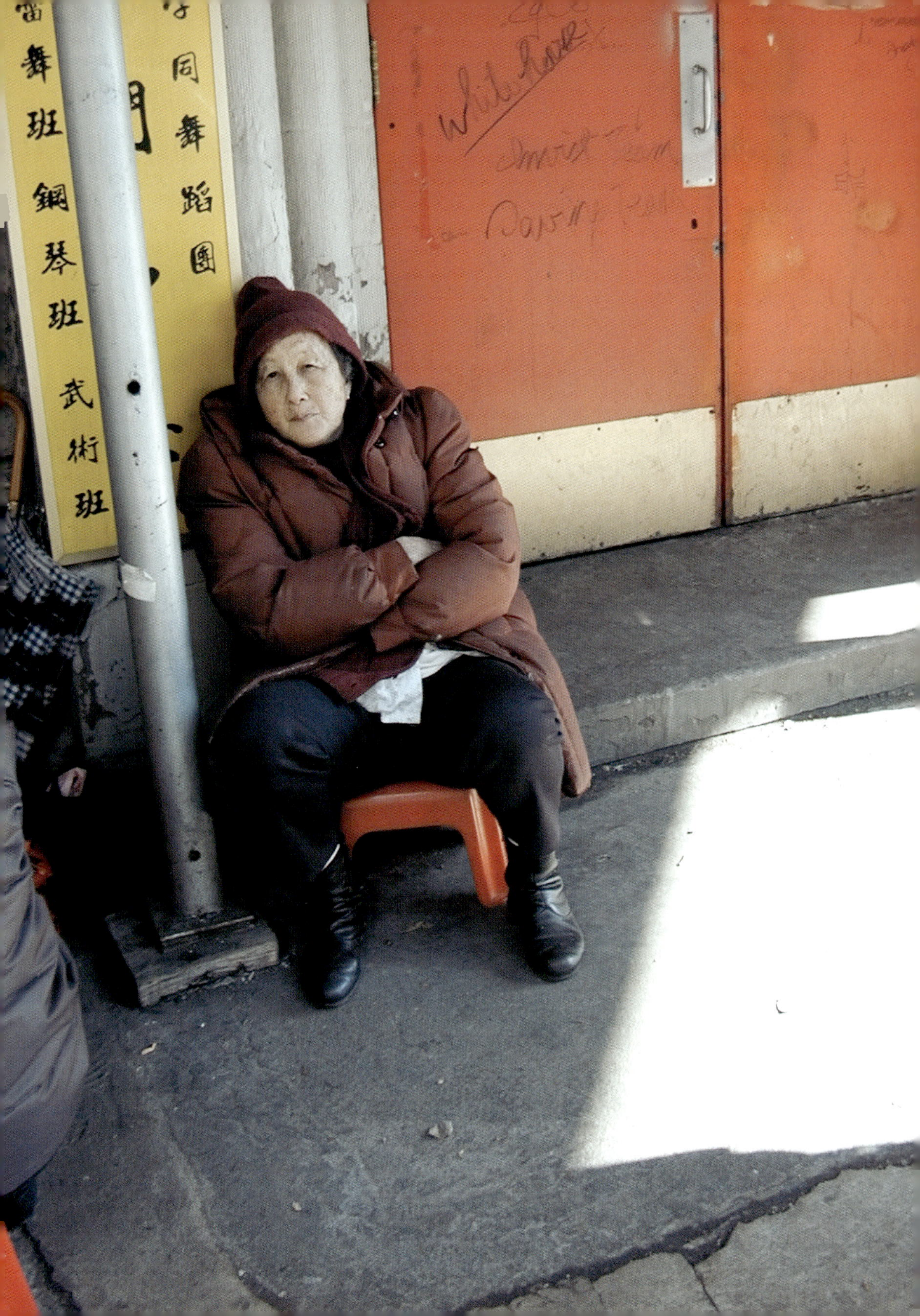
舞班
鋼琴班
武術班
同舞蹈團

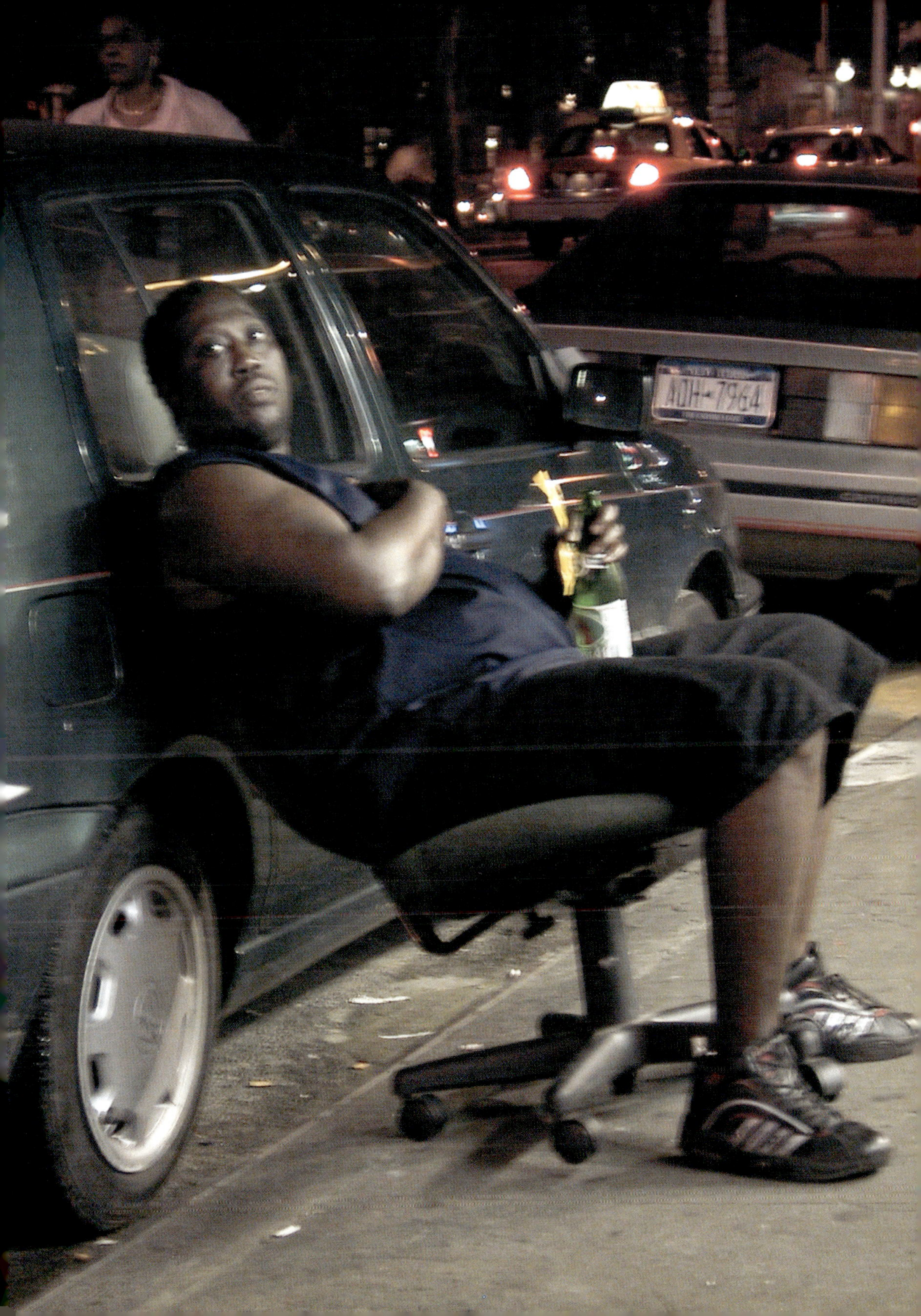

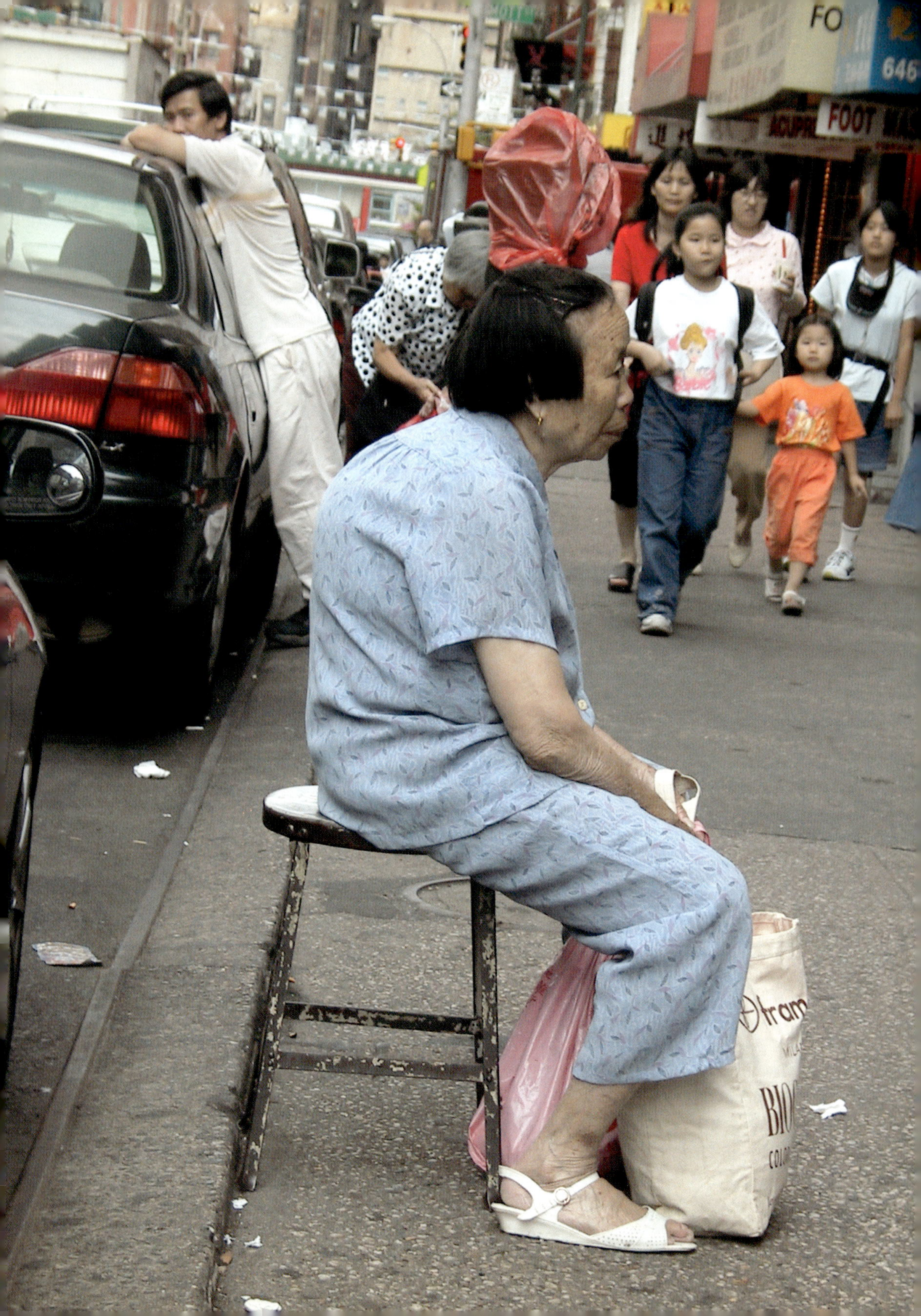
FOOT

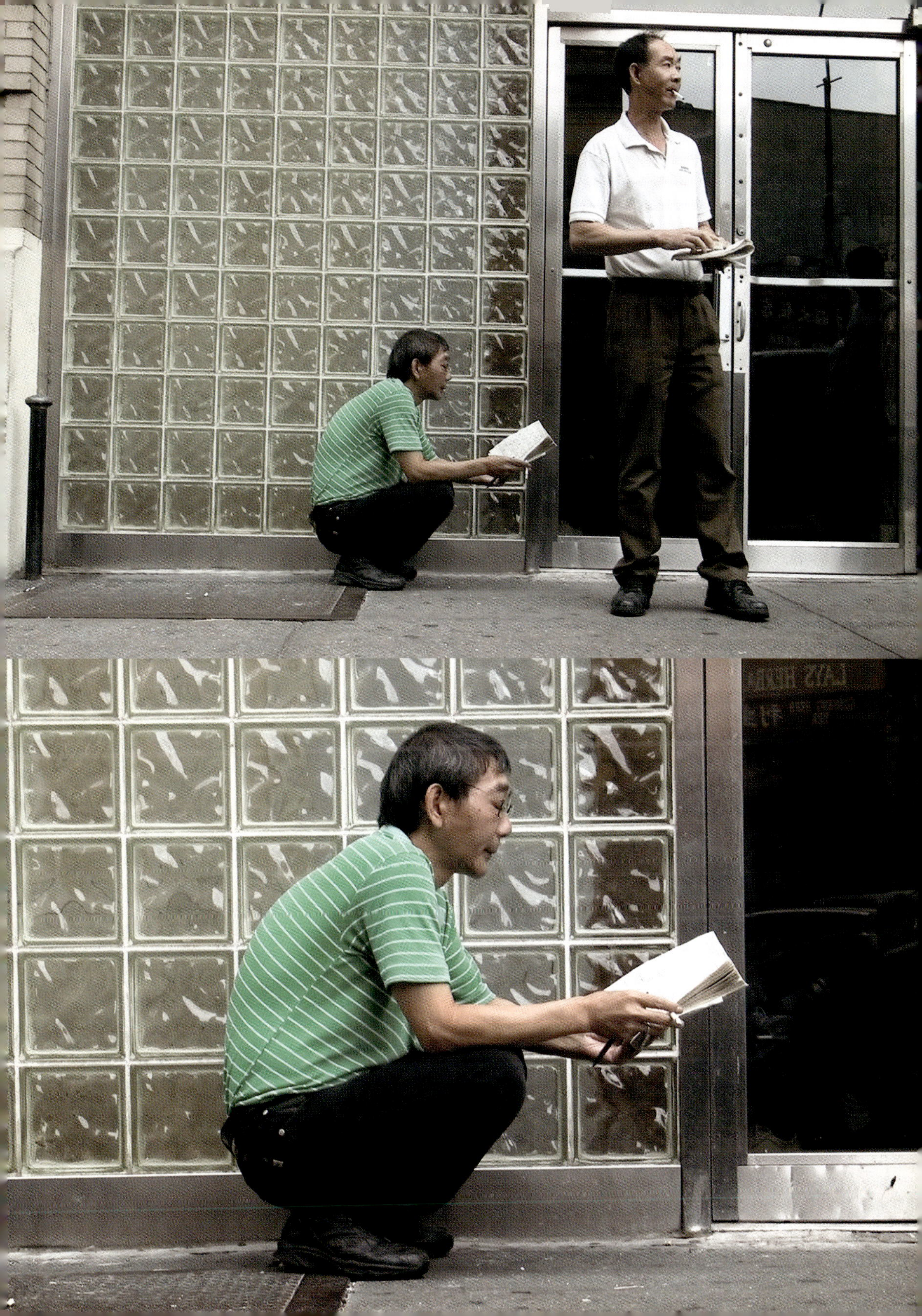

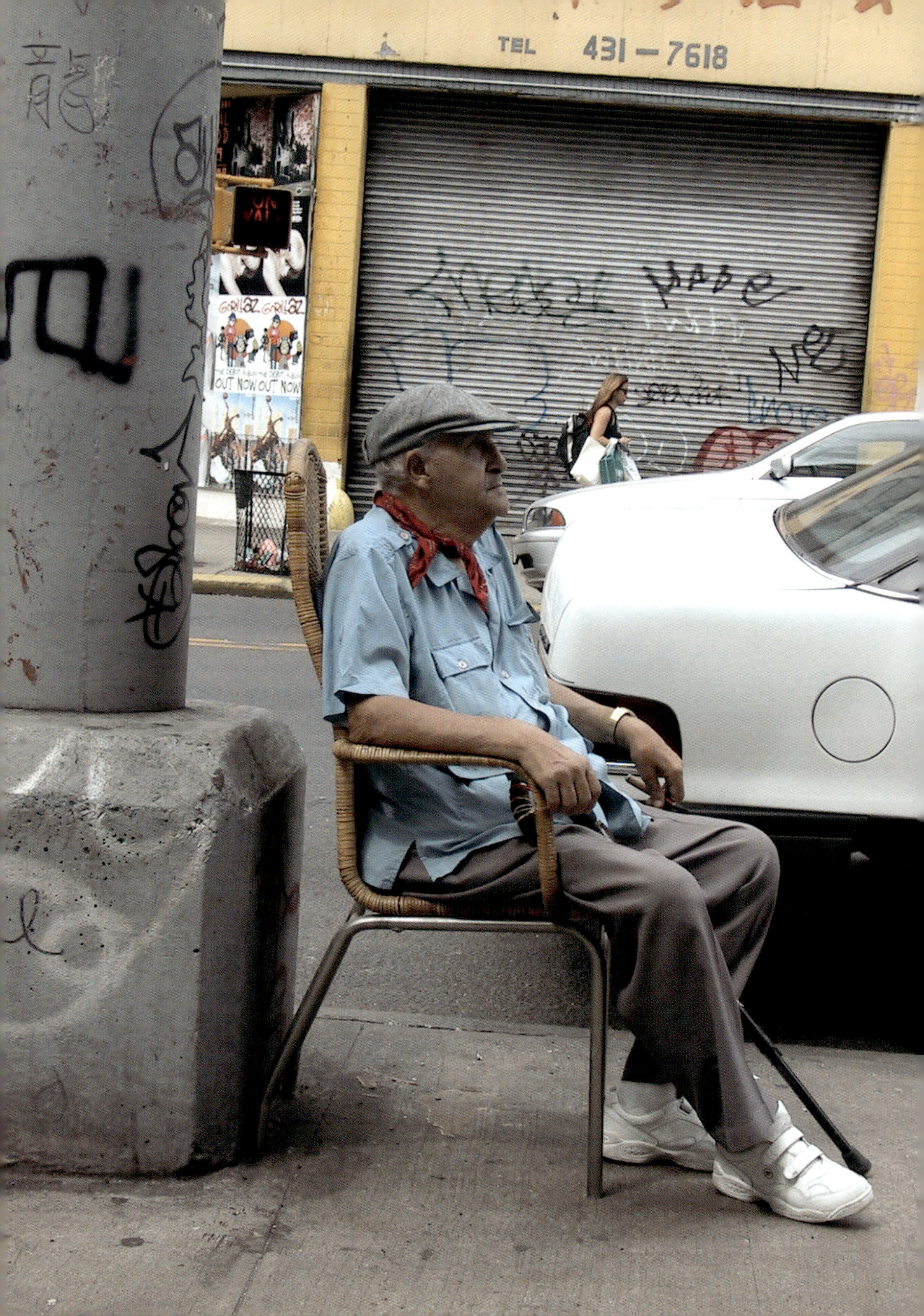
TEL 431 — 7618
GORILLAZ GORILLAZ
OUT NOW OUT NOW

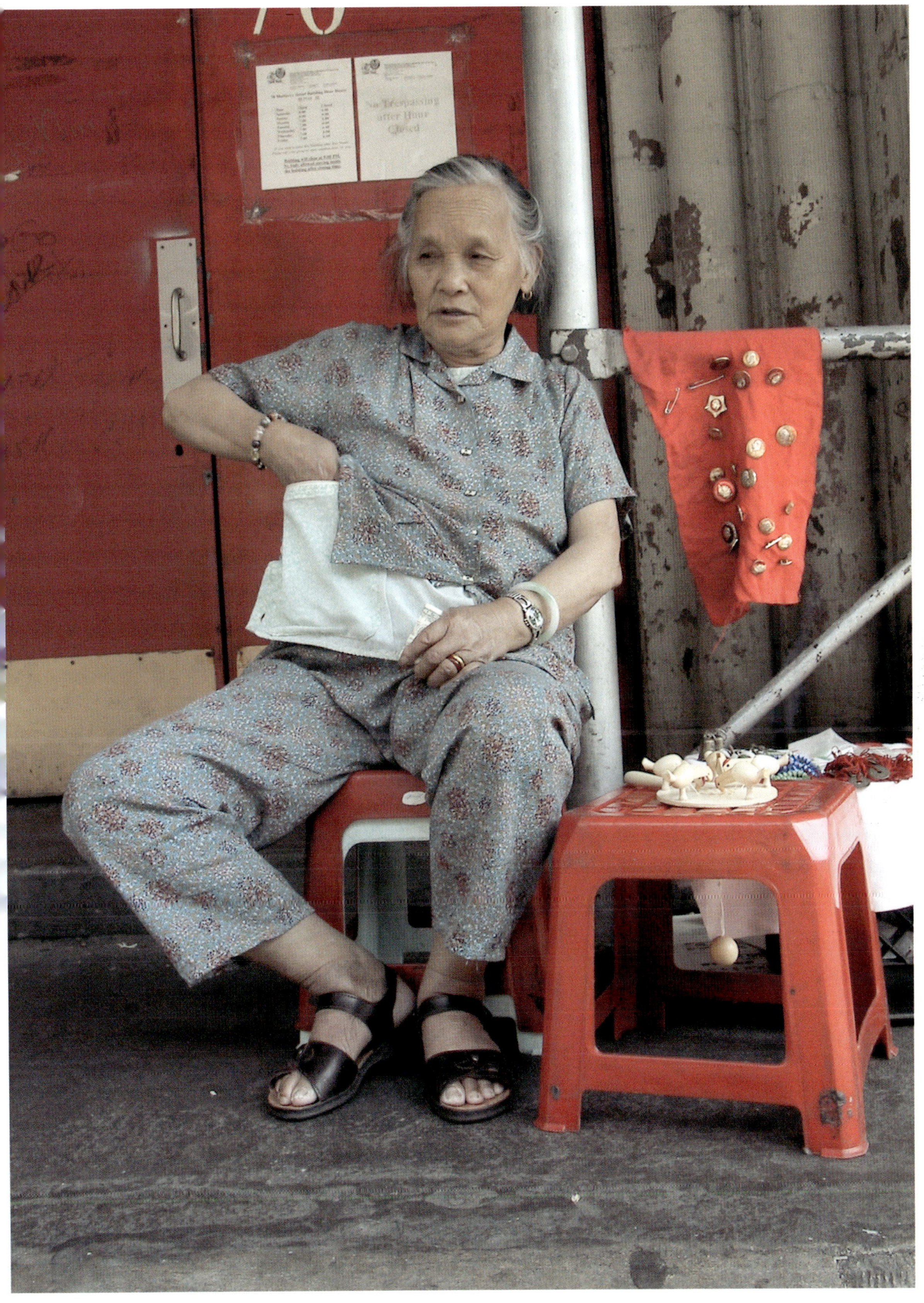

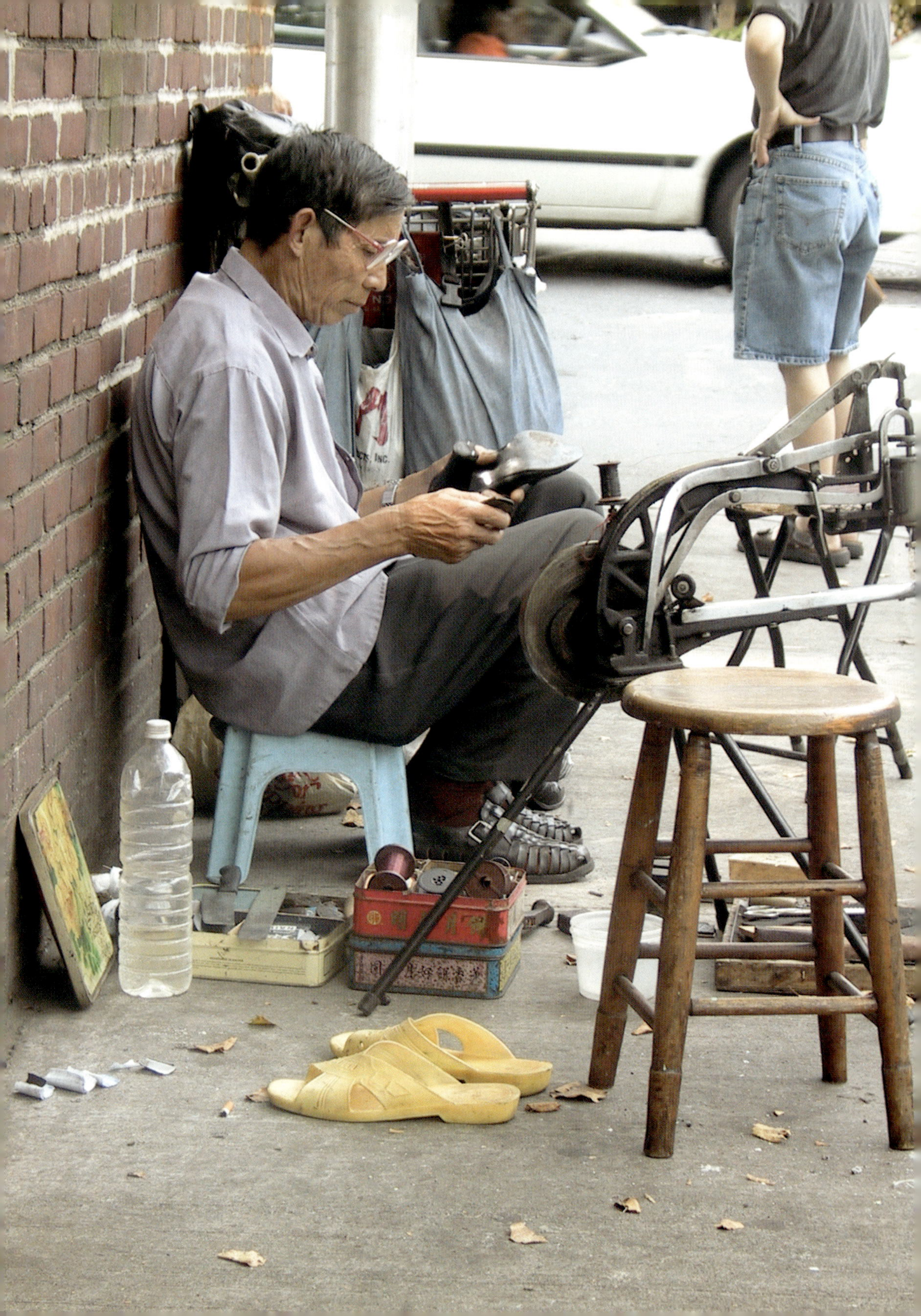

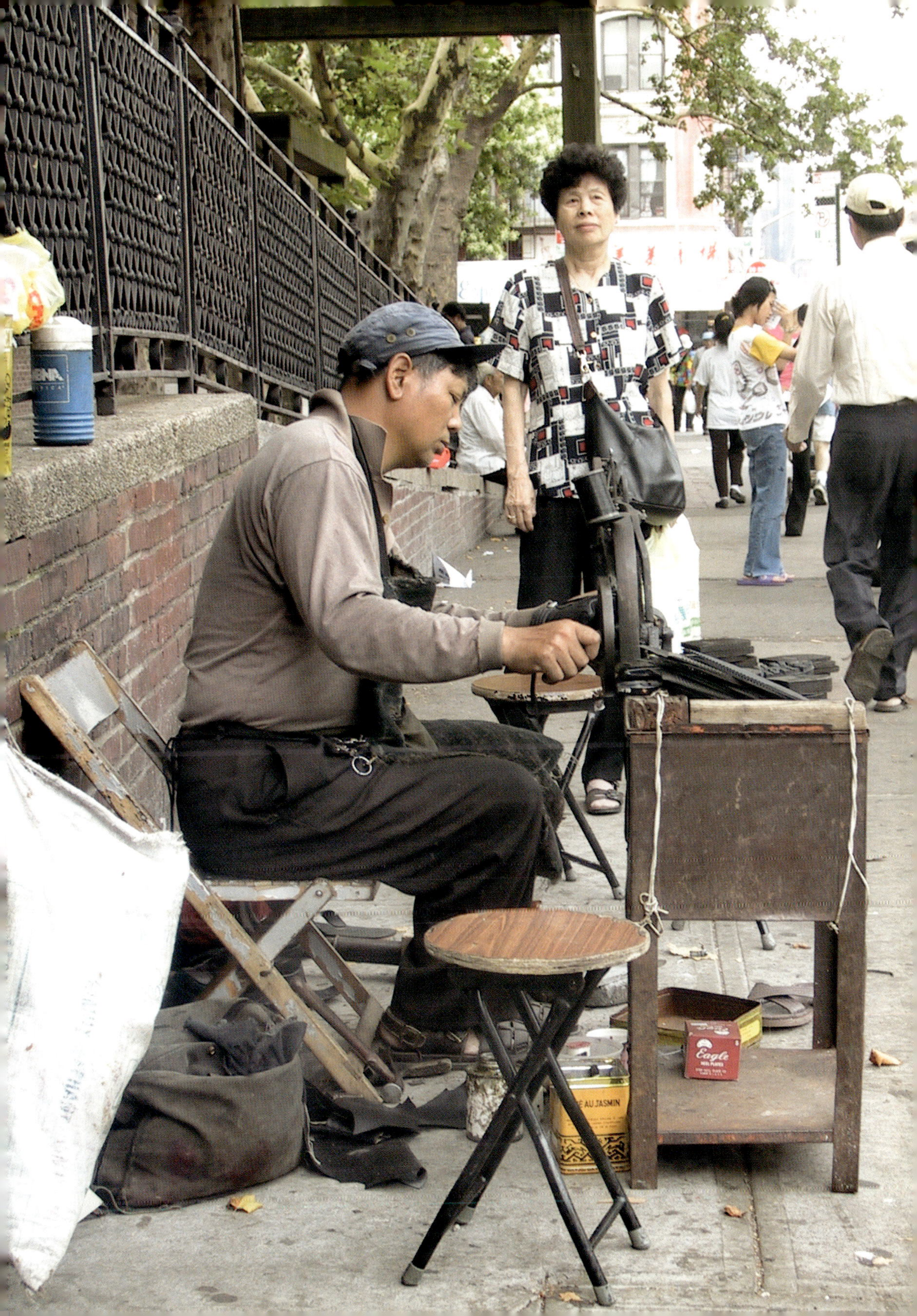
Eagle

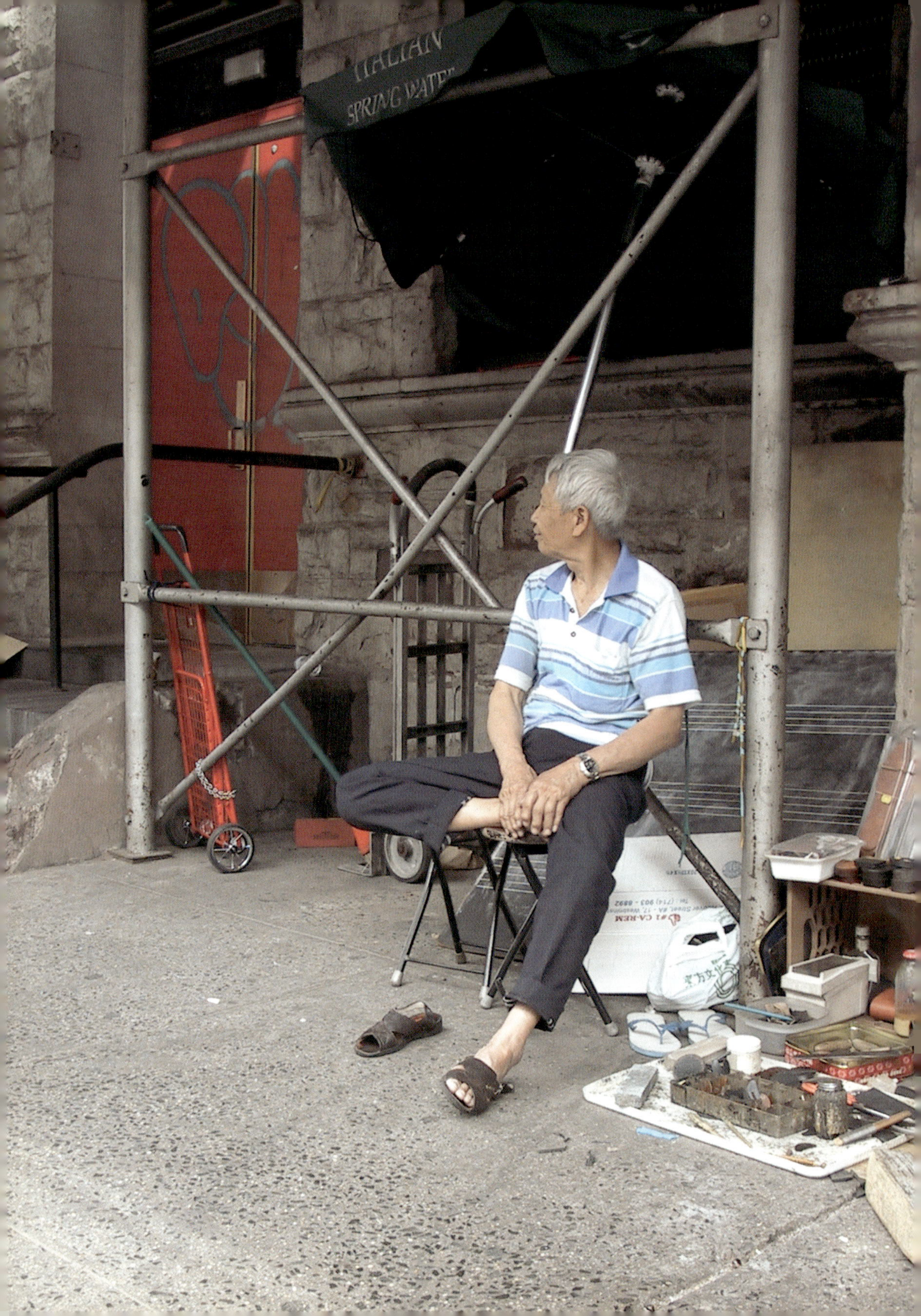
ITALIAN
SPRING

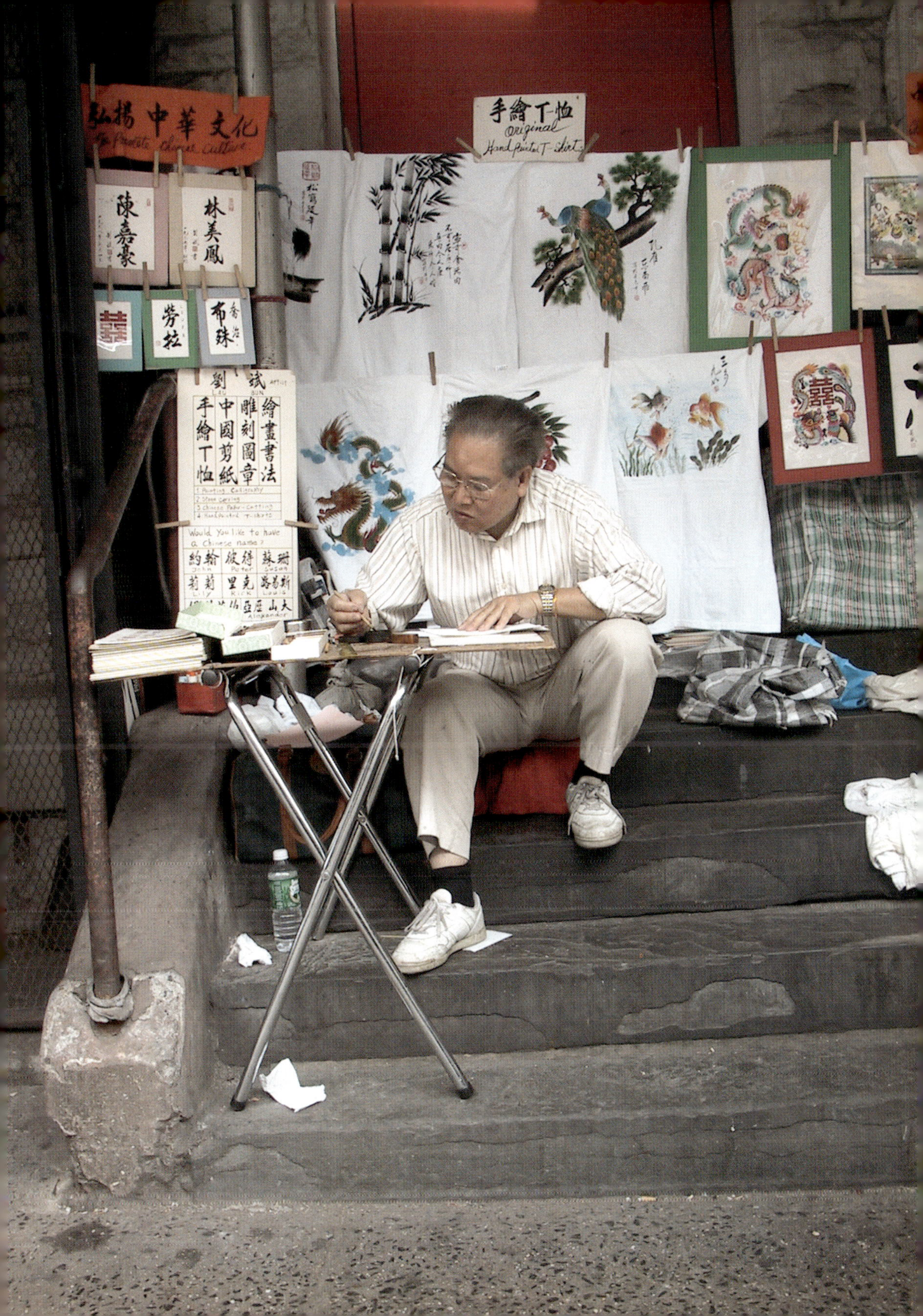

弘揚中華文化
手繪T-恤
Original
陳嘉豪
林美鳳
囍
勞拉
布珠
劉 斌
繪畫書法
雕刻圖章
中國剪紙
手繪T恤
Would you like to have a Chinese name?
約翰
John
彼得
Peter
蘇珊
莉莉
Lily
里克
Rick
亞歷山大

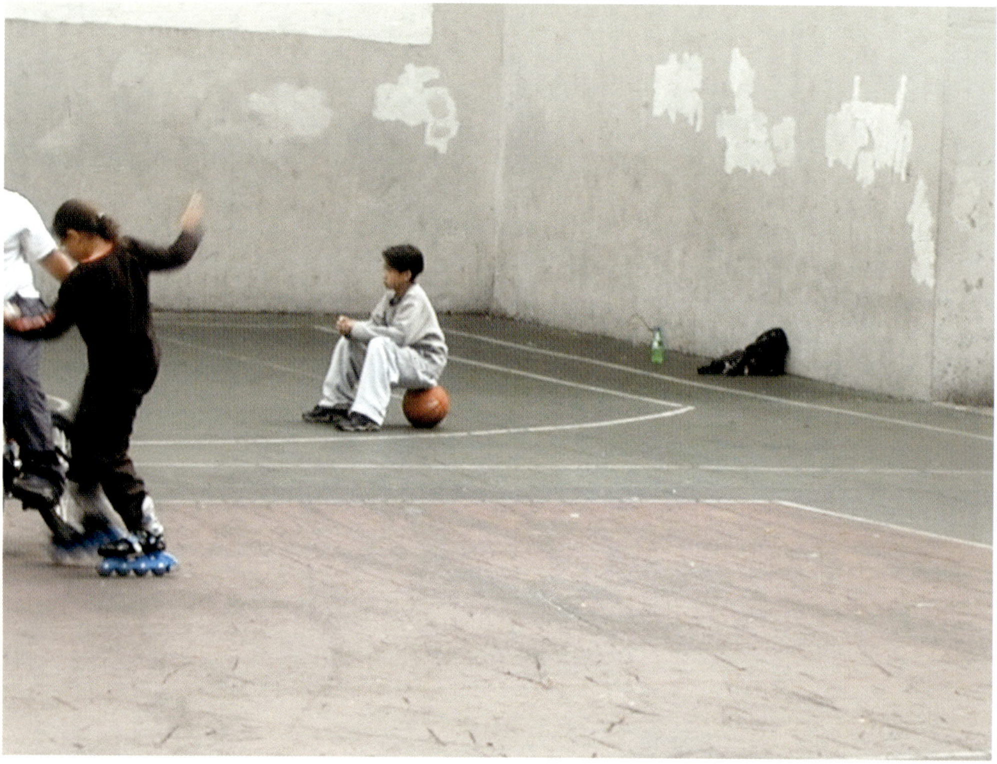

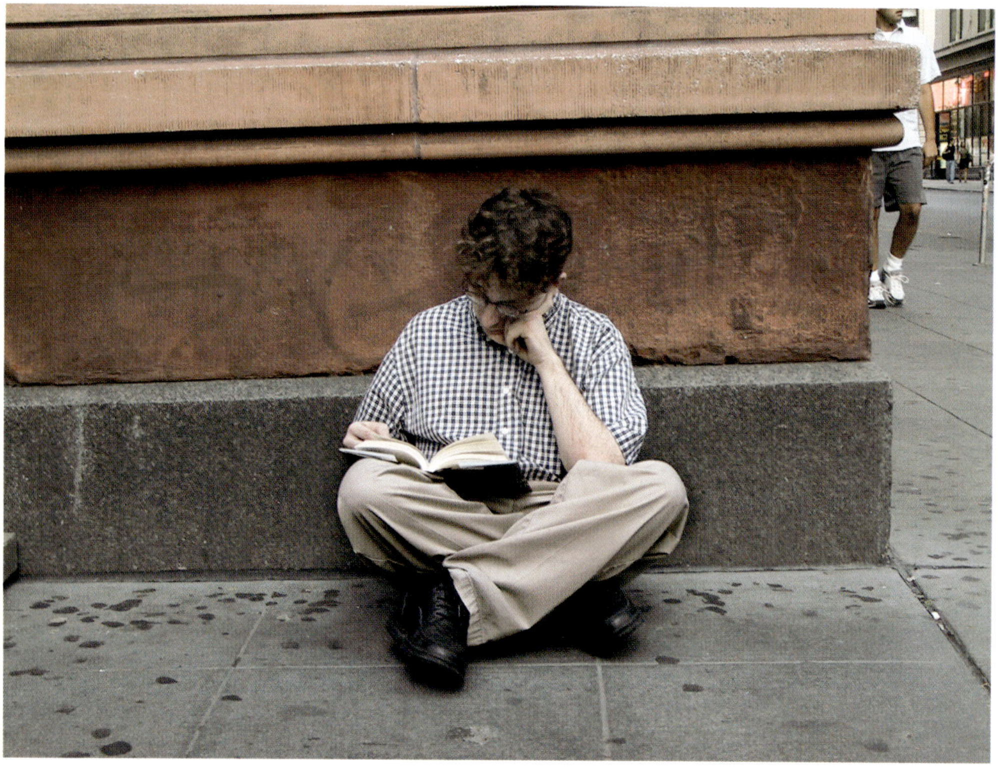

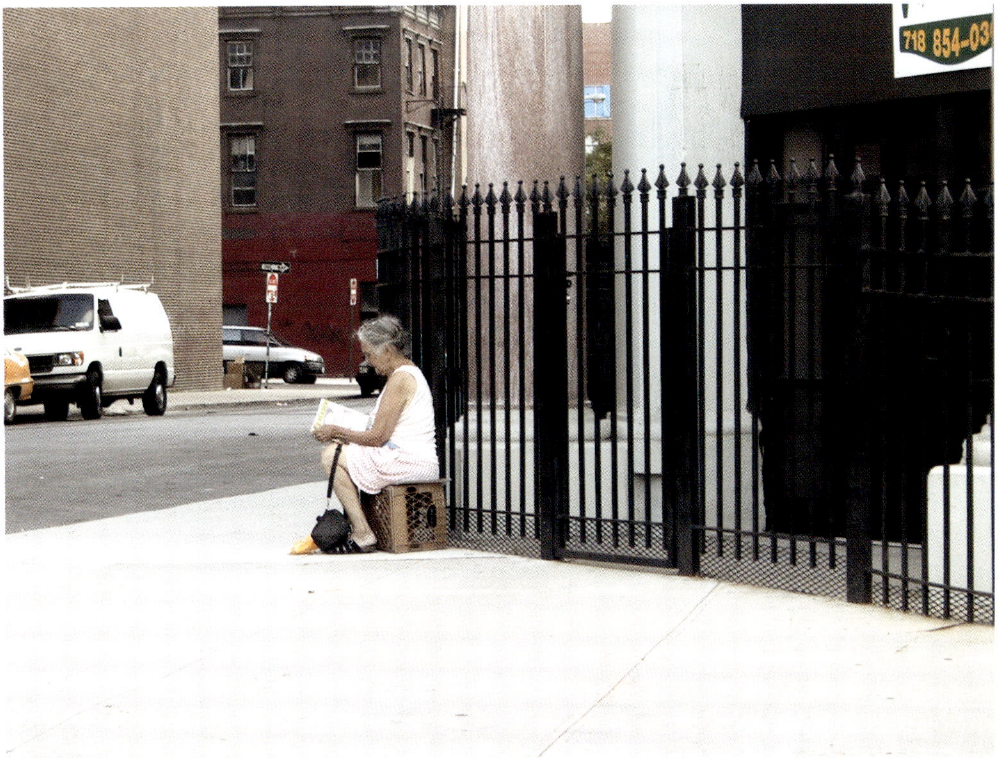

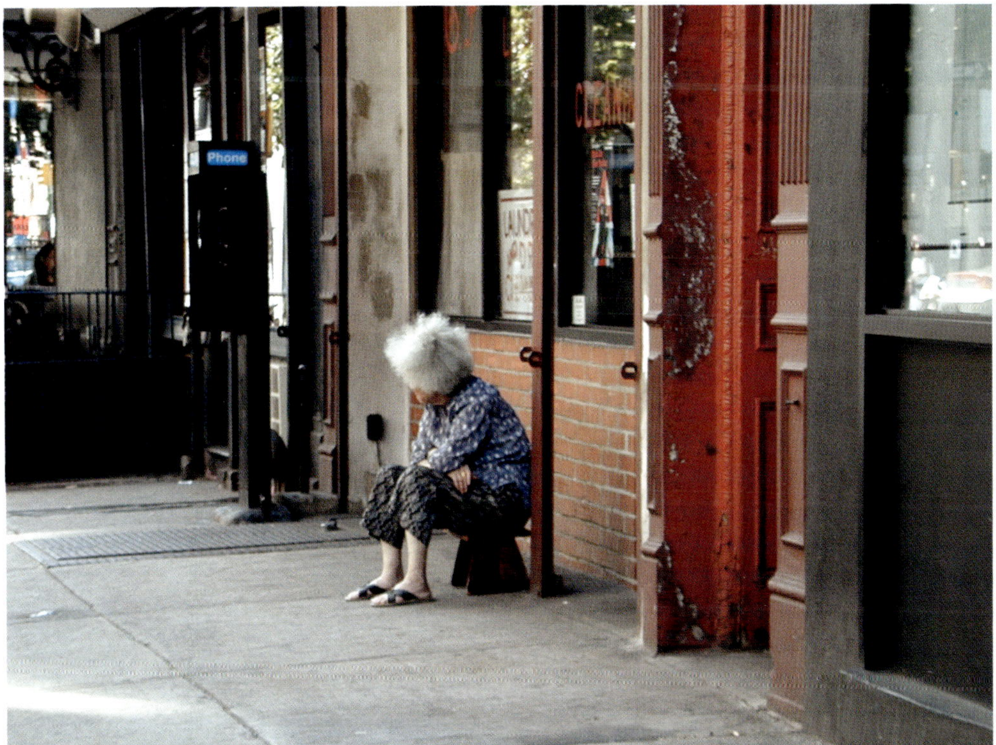

718 854-03

Phone

	System			Order		
Property Phenomenon	Dysfunctional Speech Act	Commerce	Control	Membrane	Orientation	The Range of Participation
LOCKED MOBILITY	MISSPELLING	CORPORATE MONUMENTS	POLICE LINE DO NOT CROSS	BLUE CITY	STREET SCRIPT	VOICE
TAPE	FADING MARKETS	STREET VENDORS	A BARRIER	COVER	STREET MARK	DIVERSITY
SHOP WATCH	EMPTY SIGNS	STREET LEVEL	SERVICE SCREEN	SHOPPING BAG	STEEL	OPEN CINE
REAL ESTATE		SHOPPING CARTS		GARBAGE DIGITAL SLUM		NEIGHBORHOOD

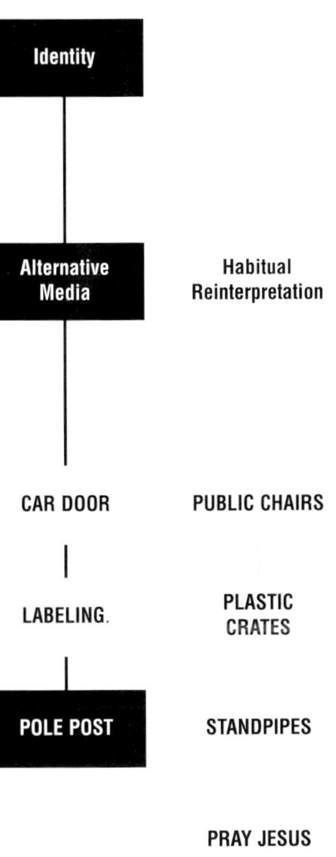

POLE POST

From Pillar to Post

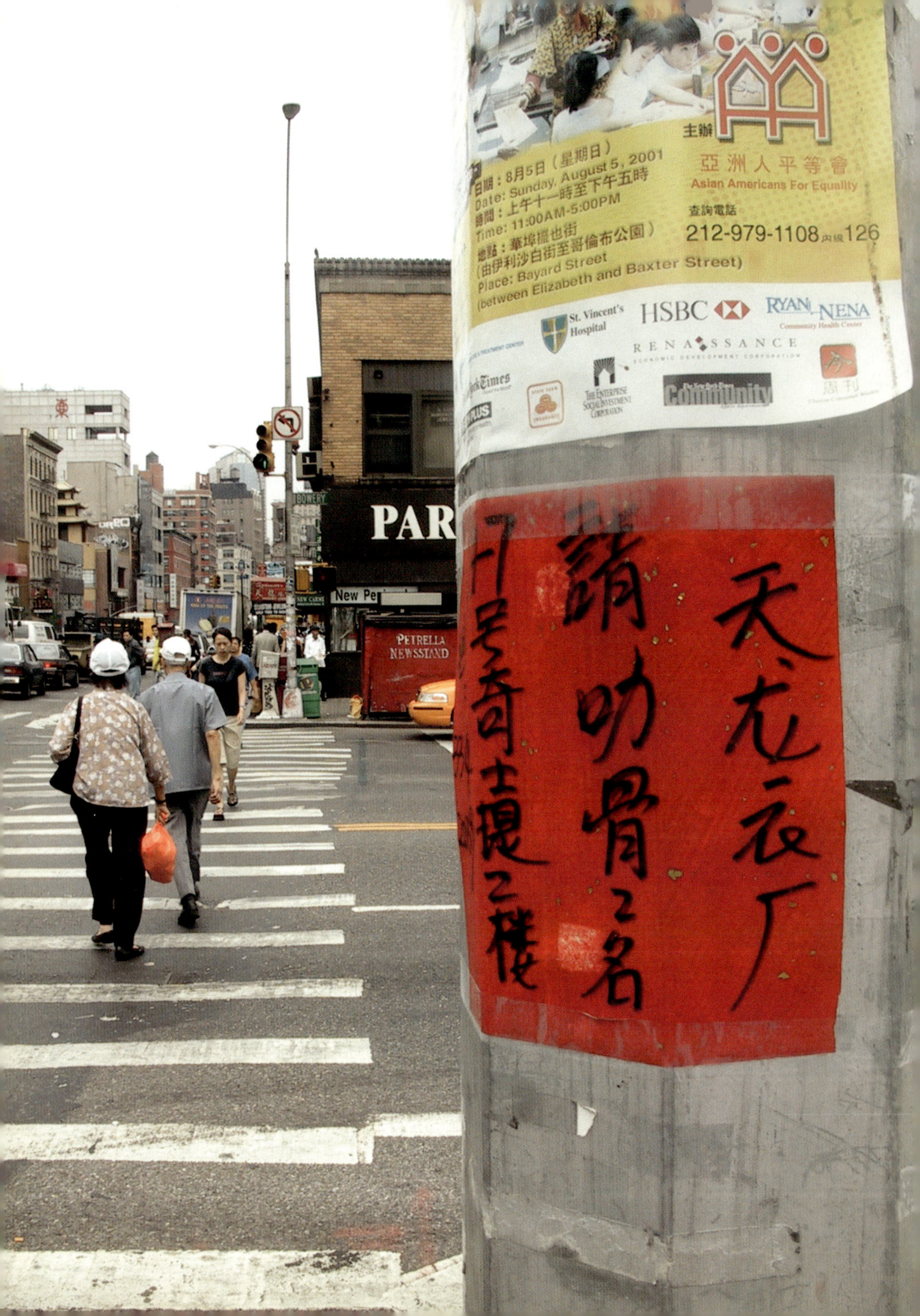

主辦
亞洲人平等會
Asian Americans For Equality
日期：8月5日（星期日）
Date: Sunday, August 5, 2001
時間：上午十一時至下午五時
Time: 11:00AM-5:00PM
地點：華埠擺也街
（由伊利沙白街至哥倫布公園）
Place: Bayard Street
(between Elizabeth and Baxter Street)
查詢電話
212-979-1108 內線 126
St. Vincent's Hospital
HSBC
RYAN NENA
RENAISSANCE
ECONOMIC DEVELOPMENT CORPORATION
THE ENTERPRISE SOCIAL INVESTMENT CORPORATION
Community
BOWERY
PAR
New Pe
PETRELLA NEWSSTAND
天龙衣厂
請叻骨2名
17号奇士提2楼

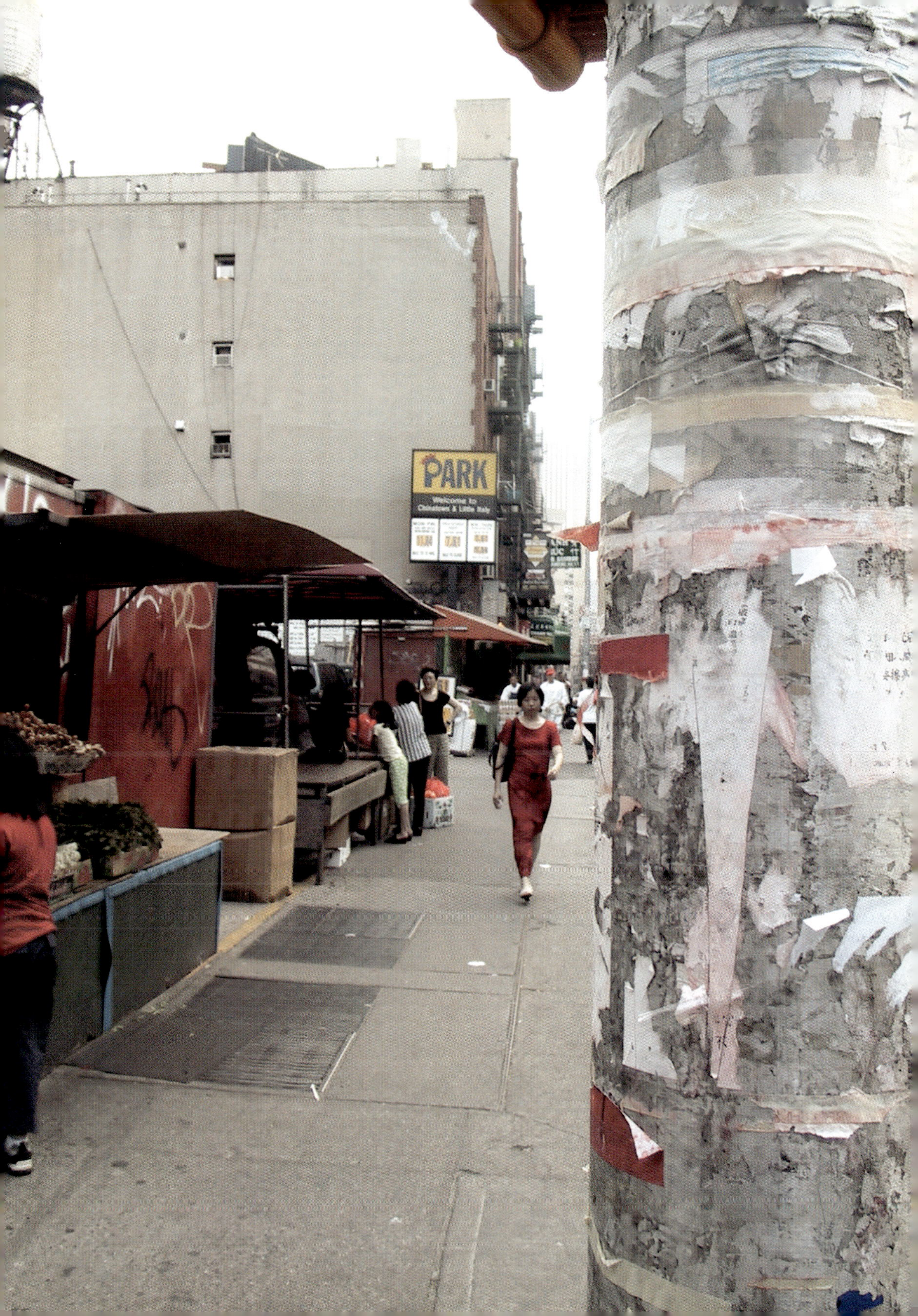
PARK

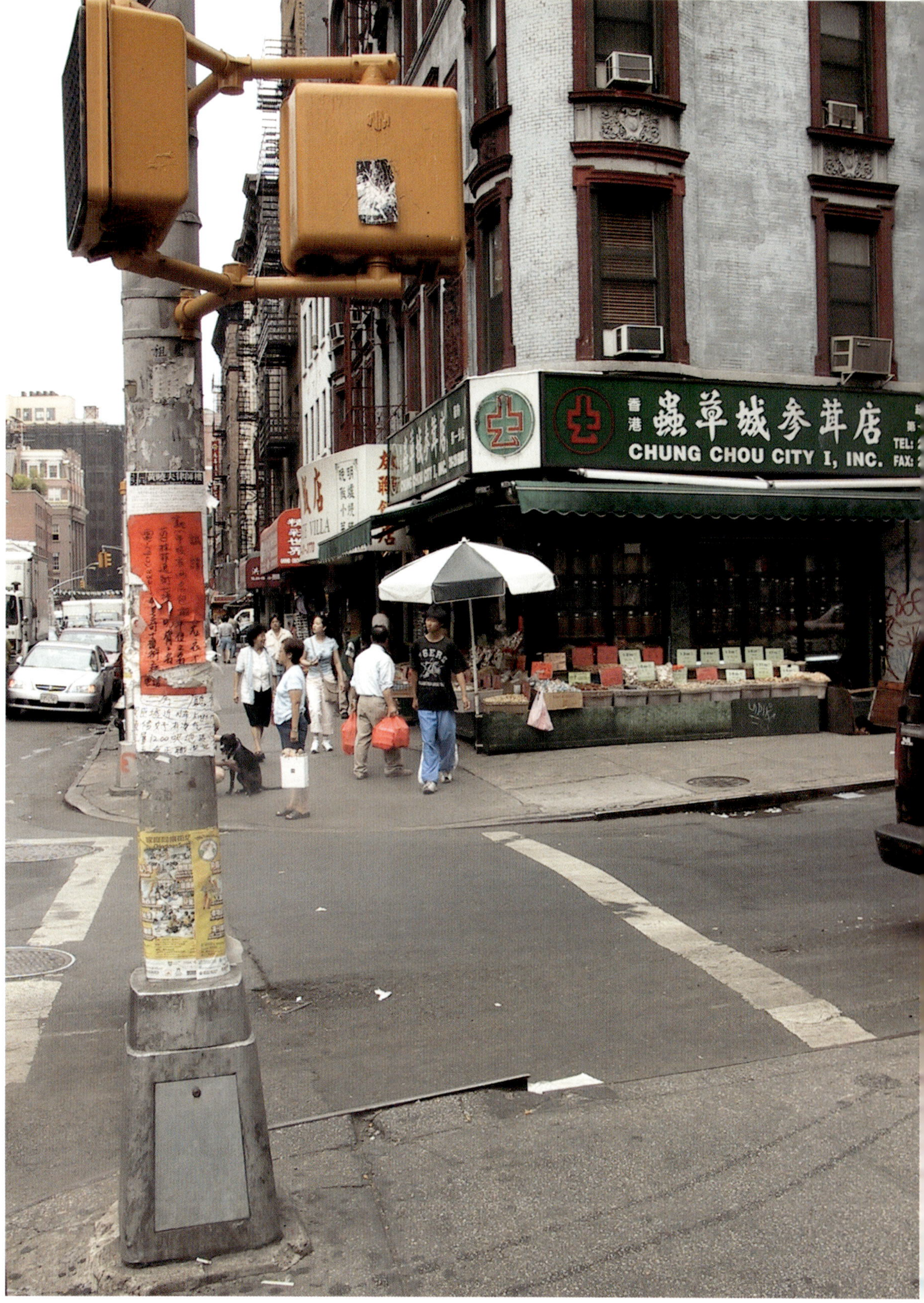

香港
蟲草城參茸店
CHUNG CHOU CITY I, INC.
TEL:
FAX:

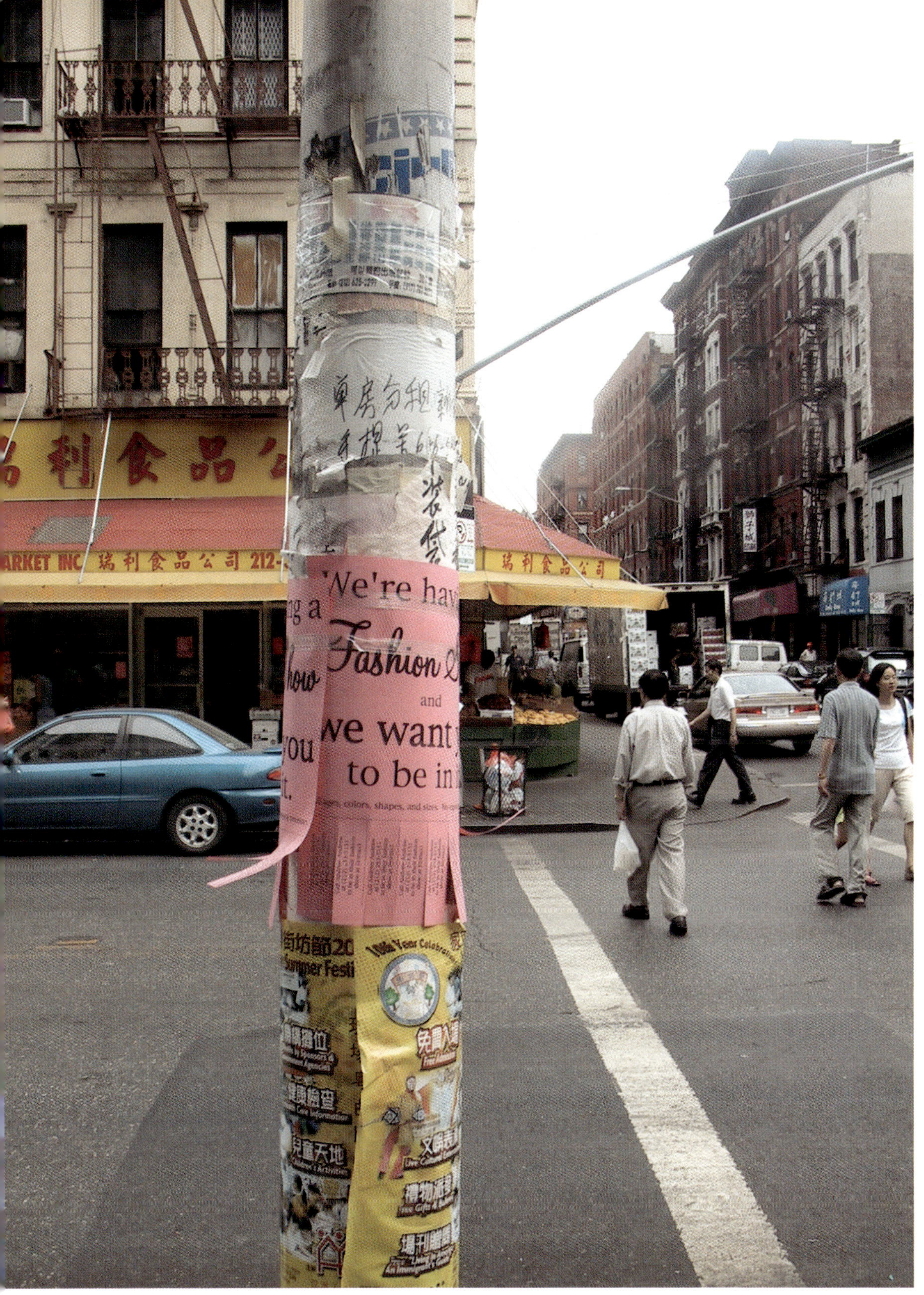

ARKET INC 瑞利食品公司 212-
瑞利食品公司
We're hav
ng a
Fashion
how
and
we want
you
to be in
t.
街坊節20
Summer Festi
免費入場
兒童天地
Children's Activities

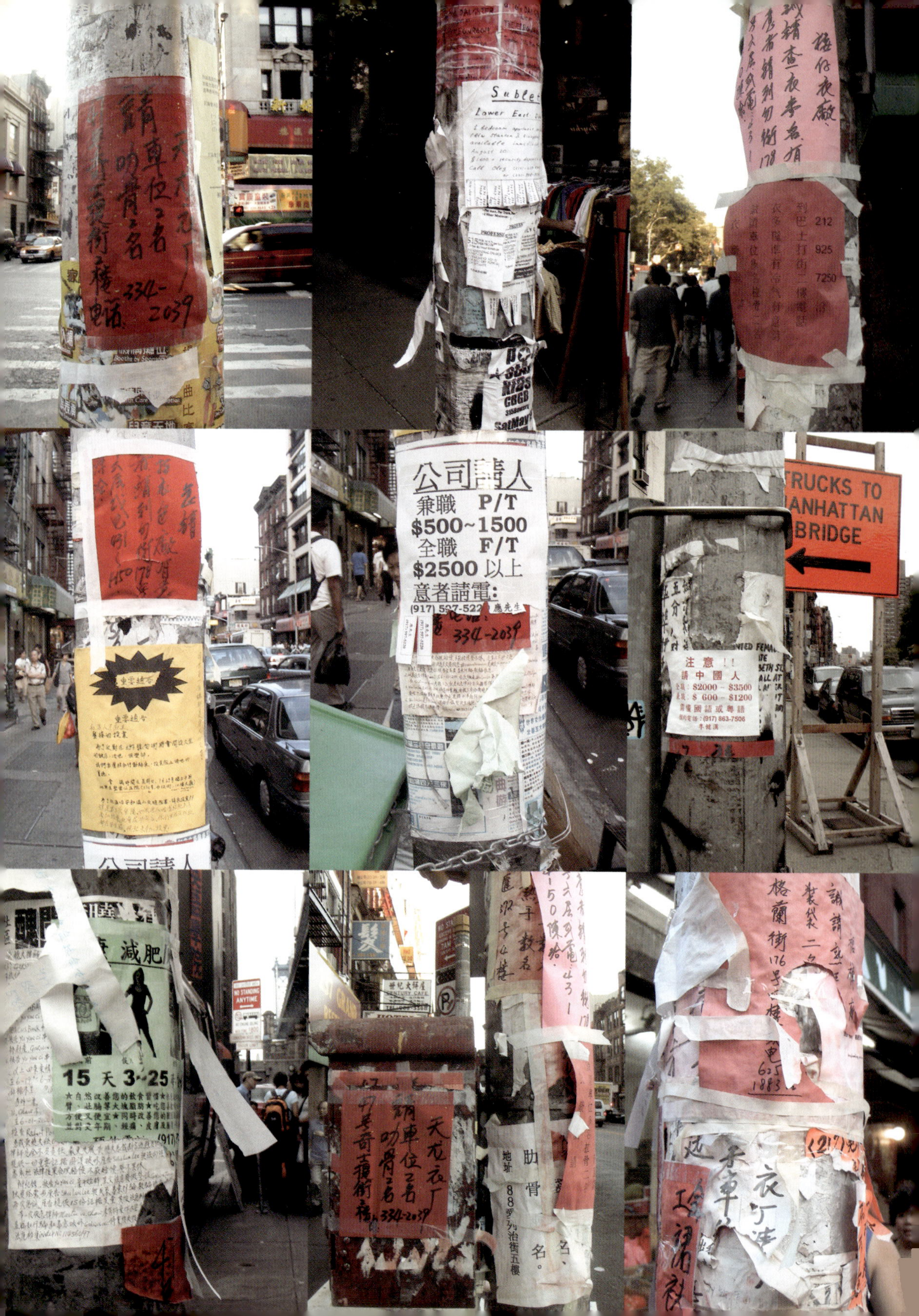

Sublet
公司請人
兼職 P/T
$500~1500
全職 F/T
$2500 以上
意者請電:
334-2039
RUCKS TO
ANHATTAN
BRIDGE
注意！！
請中國人
$2000 – $3500
$ 600 – $1200
212
925
7250
減肥
15 天 3-25
NO STANDING ANYTIME

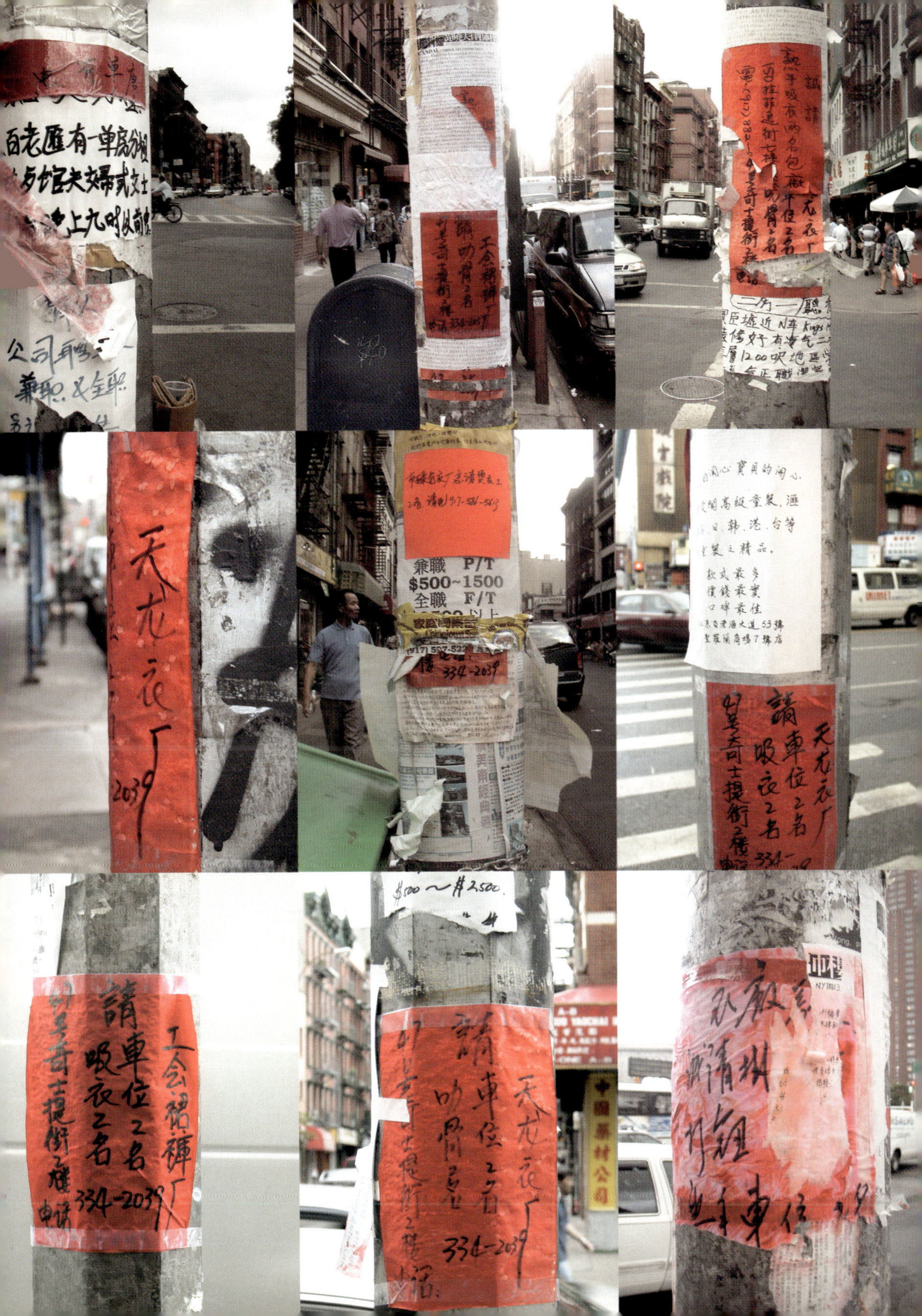

天龙衣厂
2039
兼職 P/T
$500~1500
全職 F/T
334-2039
款式最多
價錢最實
口碑最佳
請車位2名
吸衣2名
天龙衣厂
請車位2名
吸衣2名
工会裙褲厂
334-2039
$500~$2,500
請車位2名
天龙衣厂
334-2039

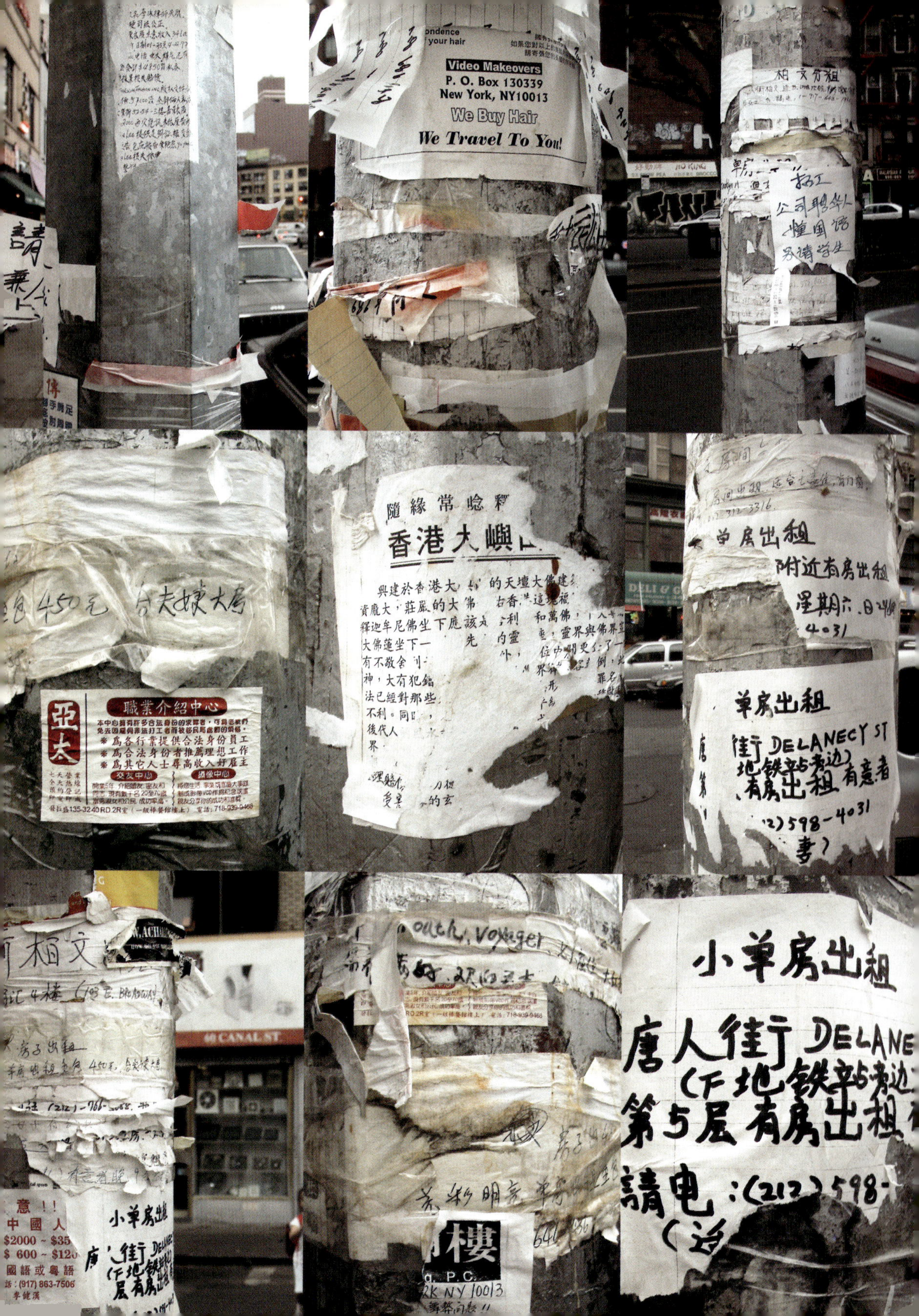

Video Makeovers
P. O. Box 130339
New York, NY10013
We Buy Hair
We Travel To You!
隨緣常唸釋
香港大嶼
職業介紹中心
单房出租
单房出租
DELANECY ST
(212)598-4031
60 CANAL ST
小单房出租
唐人街 DELANE
第5层有房出租

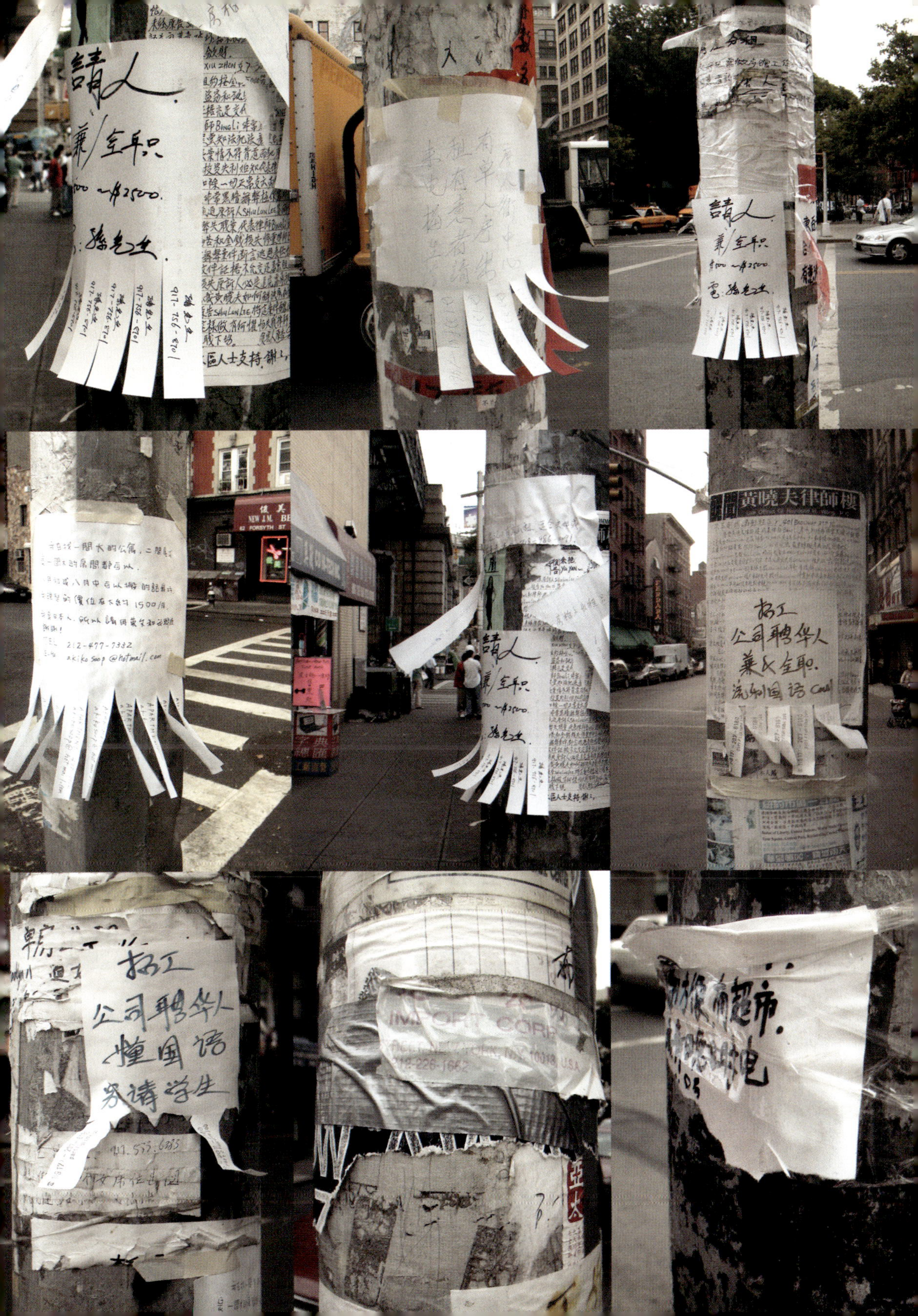
請人
兼/全職
孫先生
請人
兼/全職
孫先生
62 FORSYTH ST
請人
兼/全職
孫先生
黃曉夫律師樓
招工
公司聘华人
兼&全職
流利国语 Call
招工
公司聘华人
懂国语
IMPORT CORP
亞太

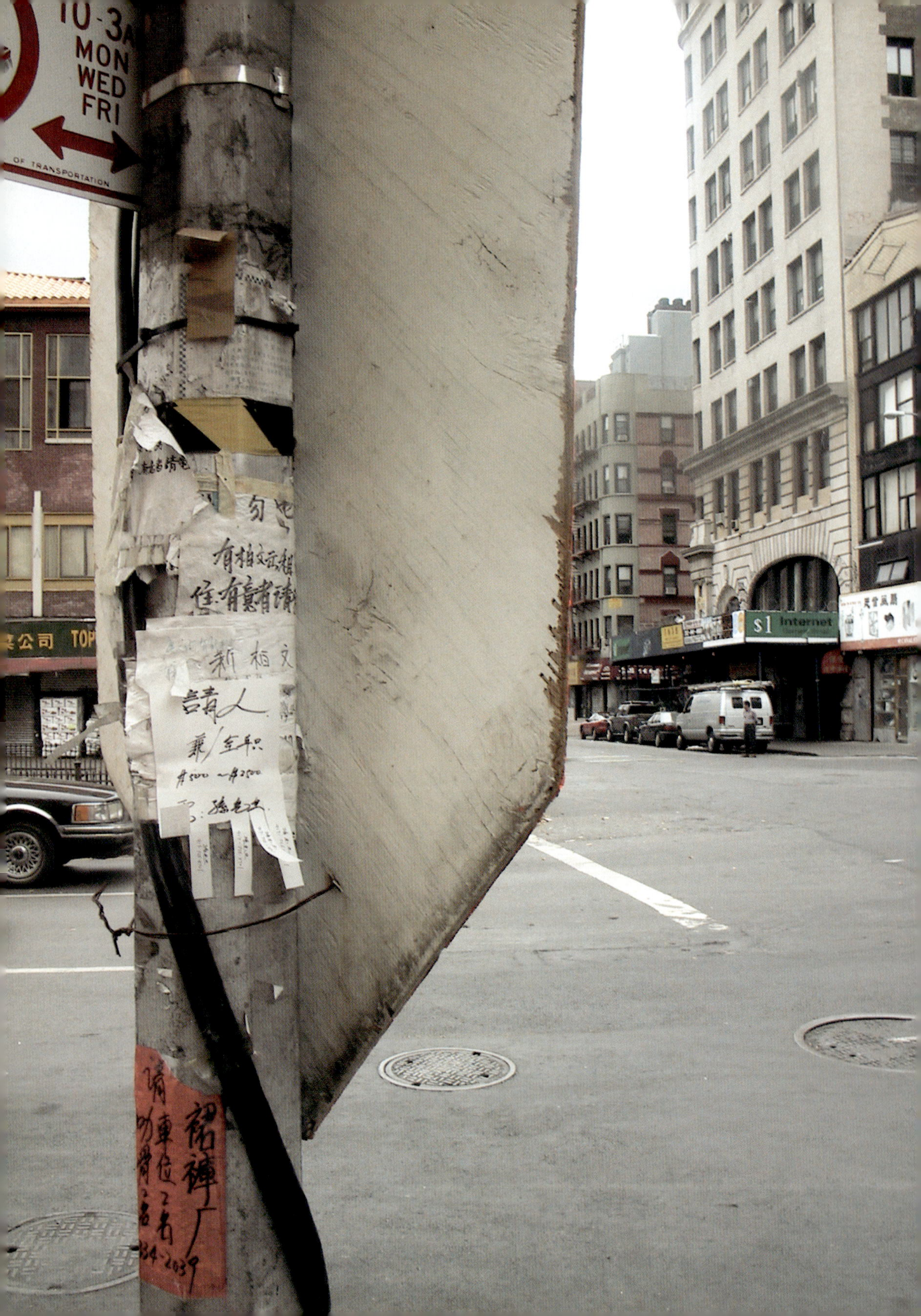
10-3A
MON
WED
FRI
OF TRANSPORTATION
$1 Internet

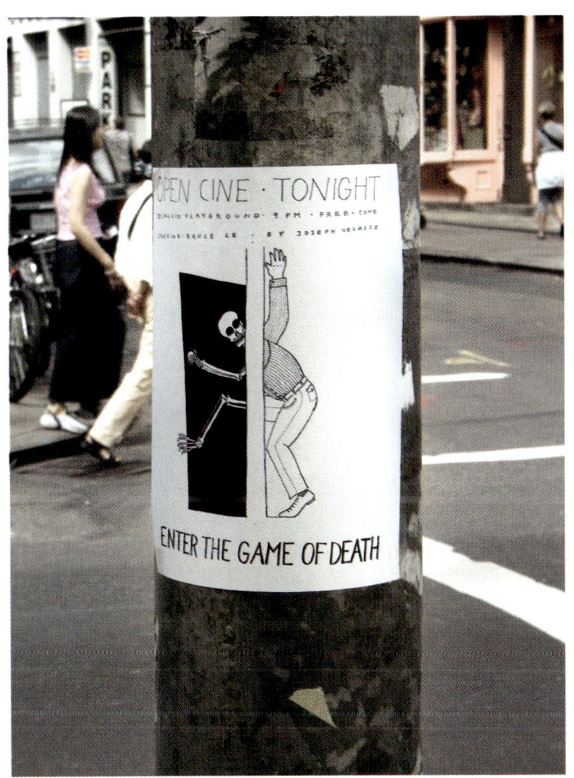
OPEN CINE · TONIGHT
PLAYGROUND · 9 PM · FREE · COME
BRUCE LE : BY JOSEPH
ENTER THE GAME OF DEATH

System				Order		
Property Phenomenon	Dysfunctional Speech Act	Commerce	Control	Membrane	Orientation	**The Range of Participation**
LOCKED MOBILITY	MISSPELLING	CORPORATE MONUMENTS	POLICE LINE DO NOT CROSS	BLUE CITY	STREET SCRIPT	VOICE
TAPE	FADING MARKETS	STREET VENDORS	A BARRIER	COVER	STREET MARK	DIVERSITY
SHOP WATCH	EMPTY SIGNS	STREET LEVEL	SERVICE SCREEN	SHOPPING BAG	STEEL	OPEN CINE
REAL ESTATE		SHOPPING CARTS		GARBAGE DIGITAL SLUM		**NEIGHBORHOOD**

Identity

Alternative Media

Habitual Reinterpretation

NEIGHBORHOOD

Topical Singularity

CAR DOOR

PUBLIC CHAIRS

LABELING.

PLASTIC CRATES

POLE POST

STANDPIPES

PRAY JESUS

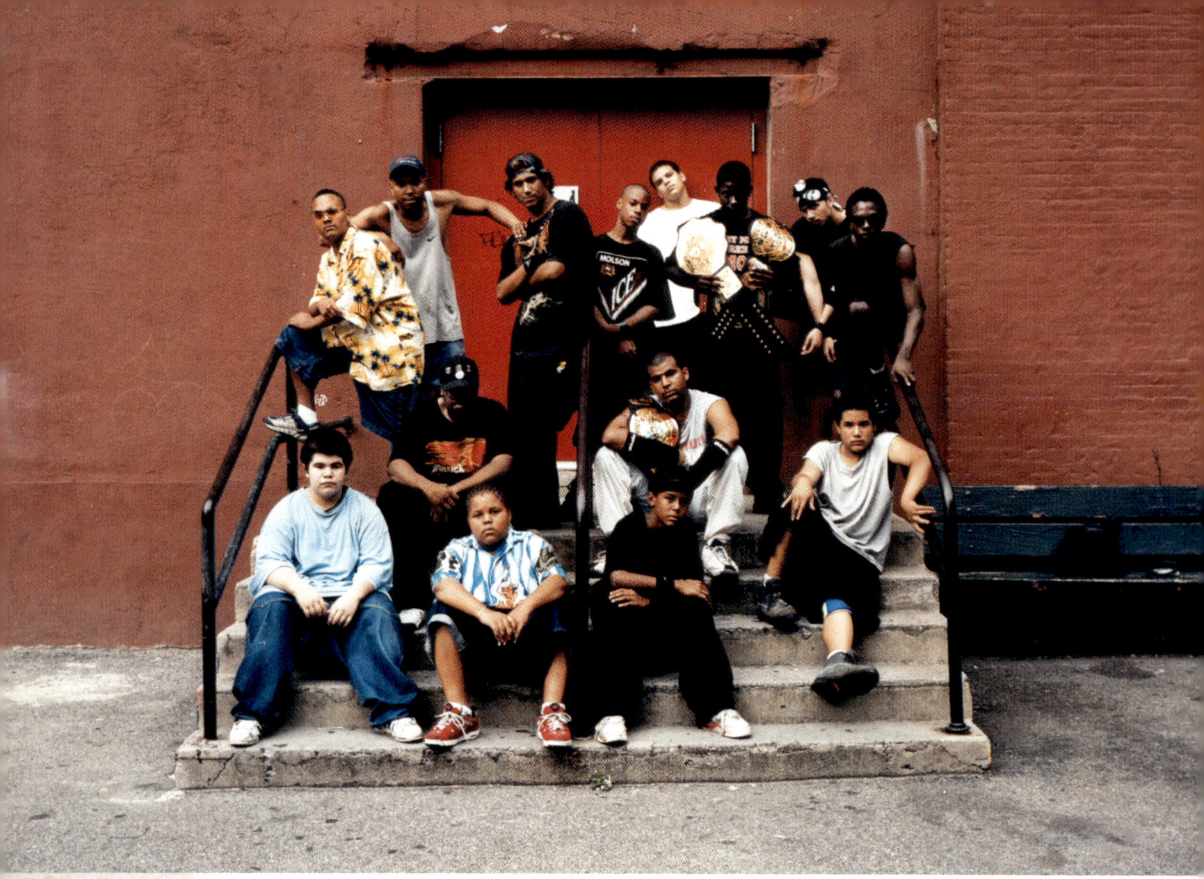

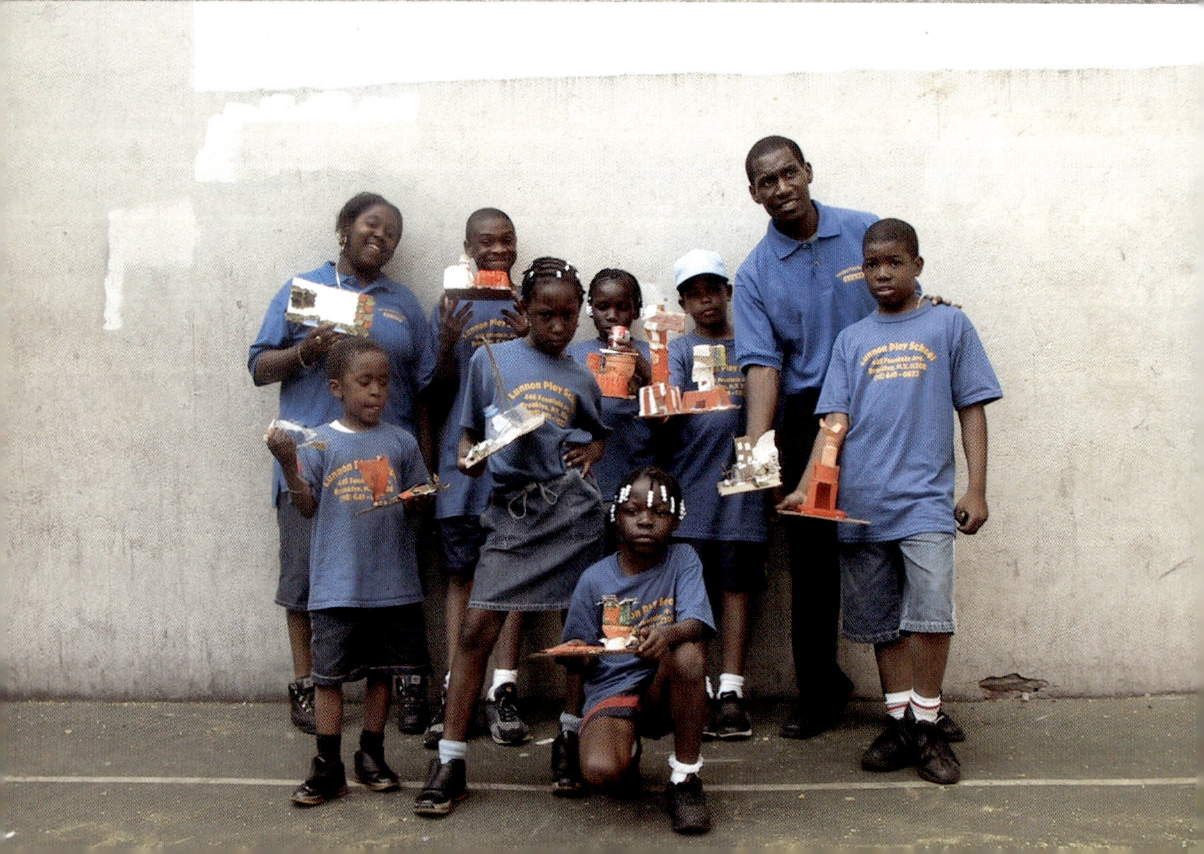

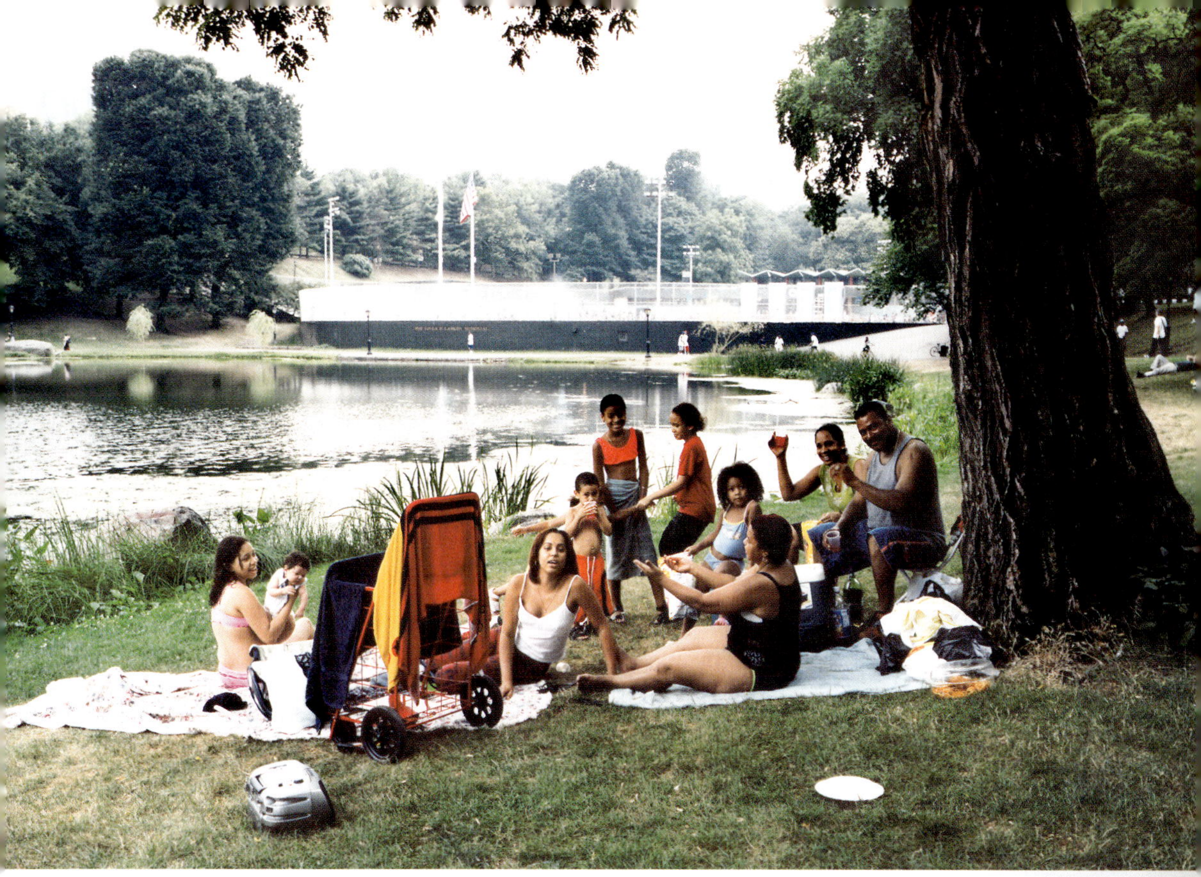

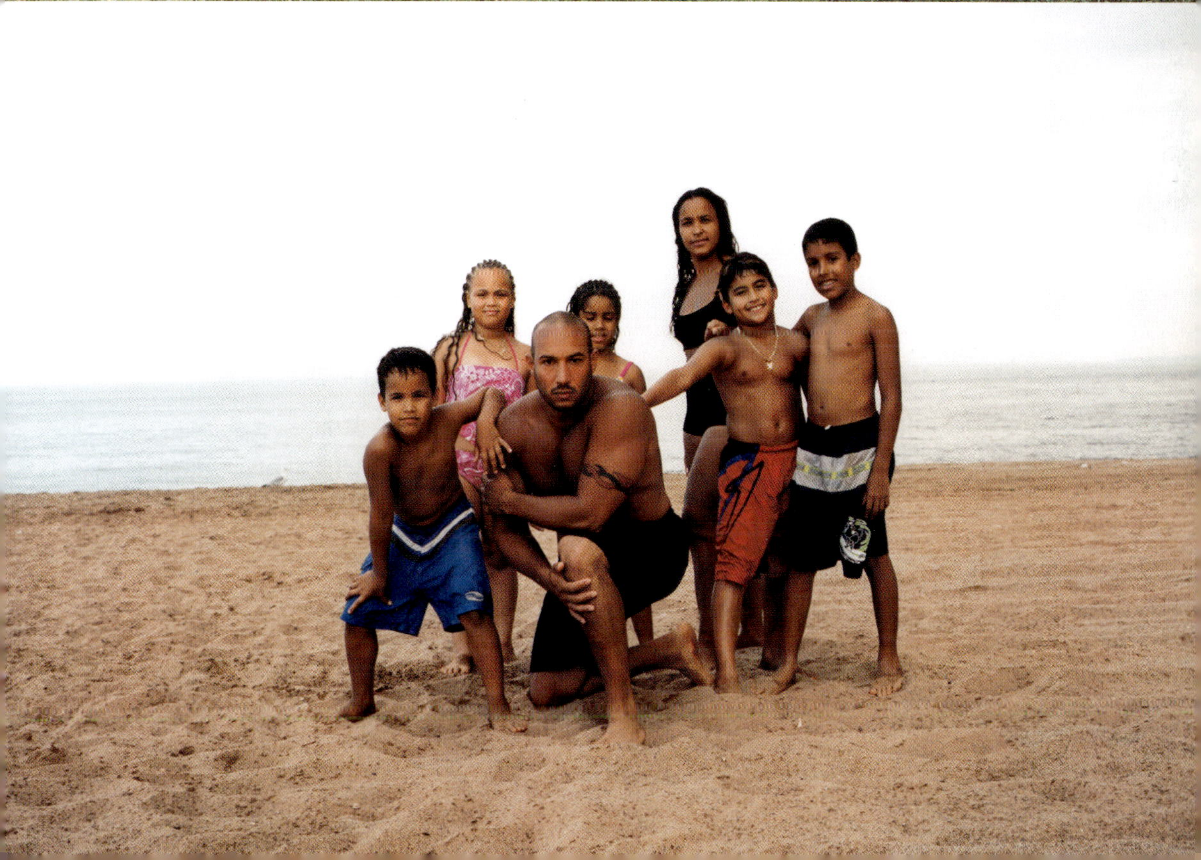

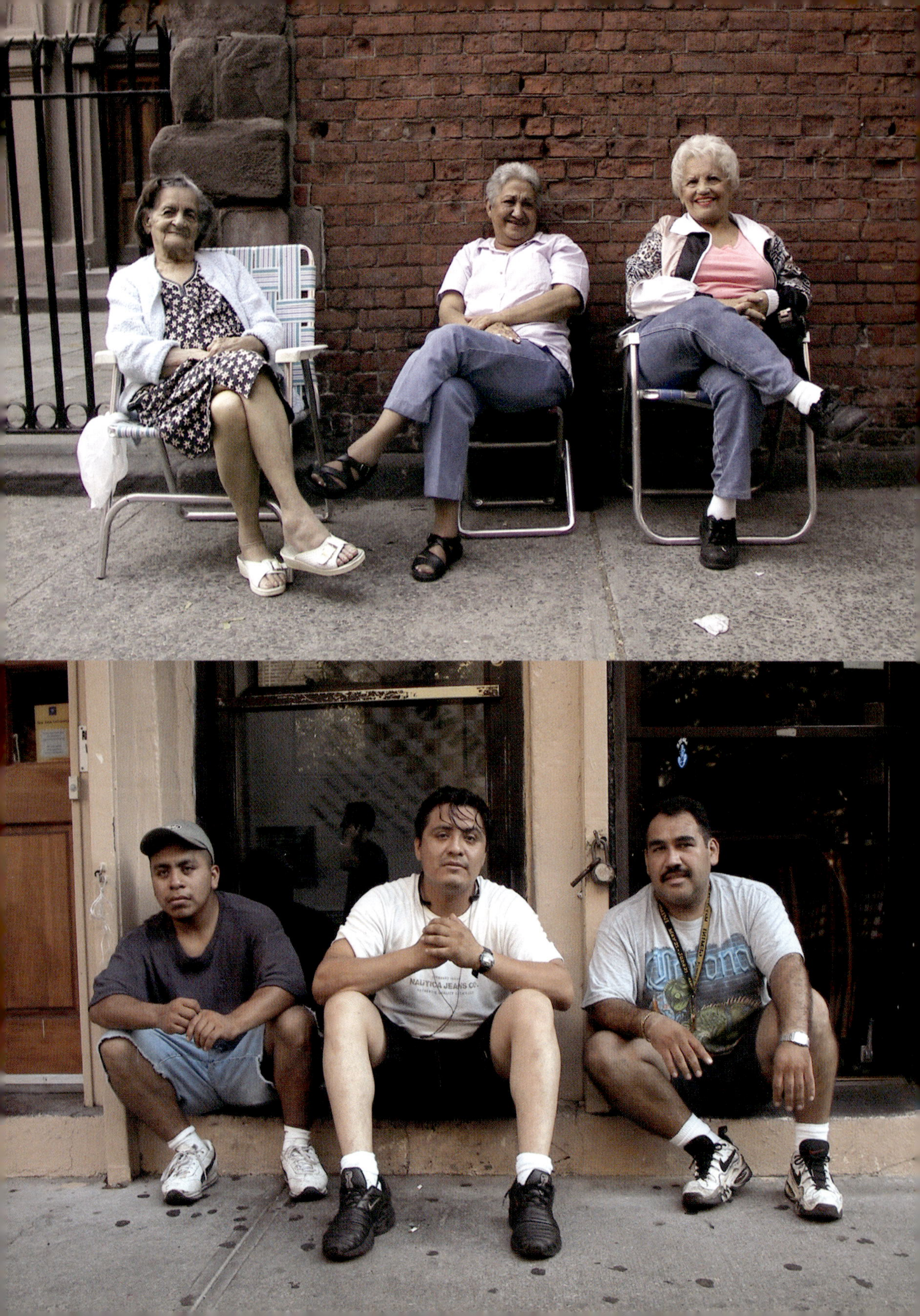
NAUTICA JEANS CO.

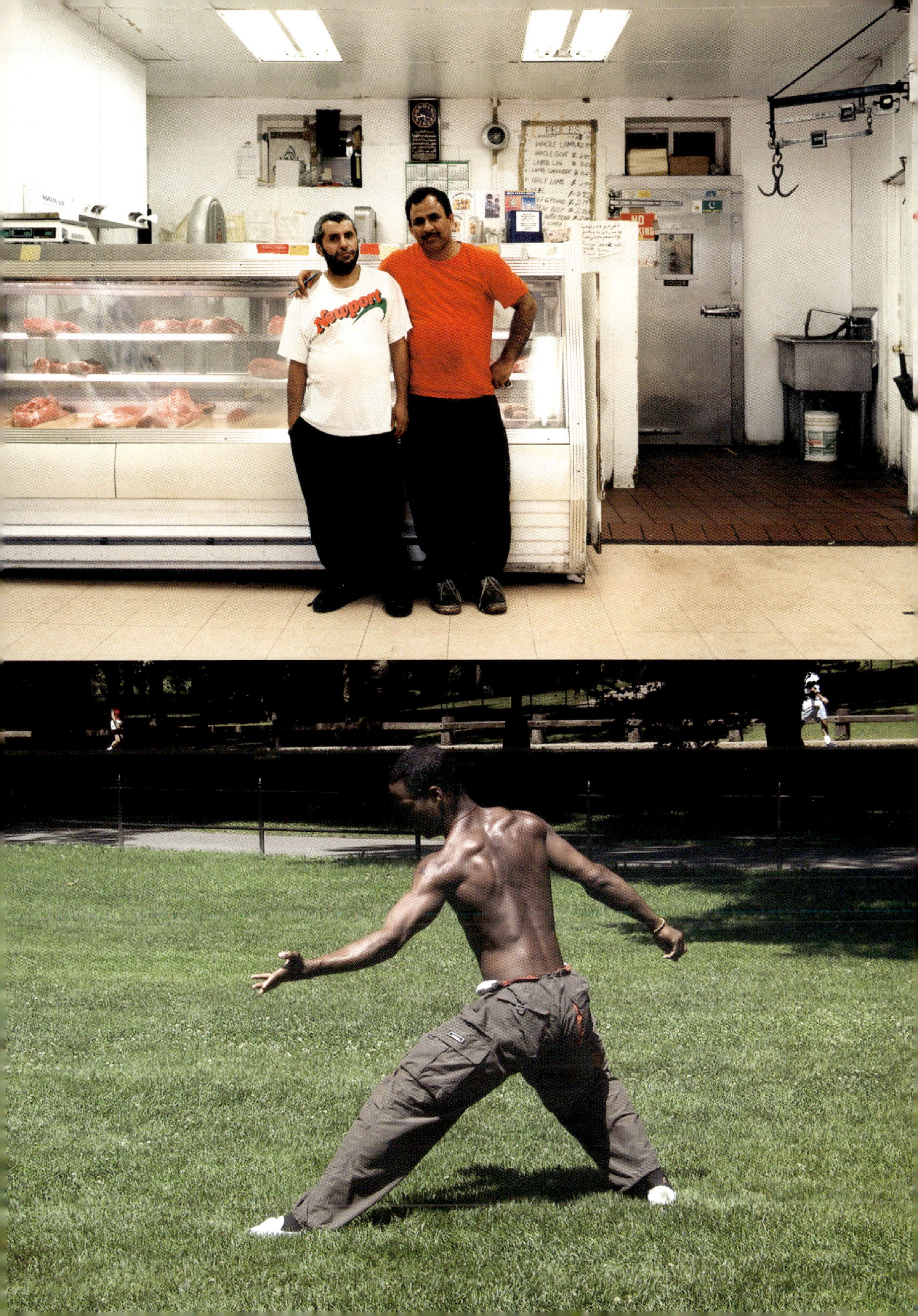
PRICES
WHOLE LAMB
WHOLE GOAT
LABB LEG
HALF LAMB
NO
Newport

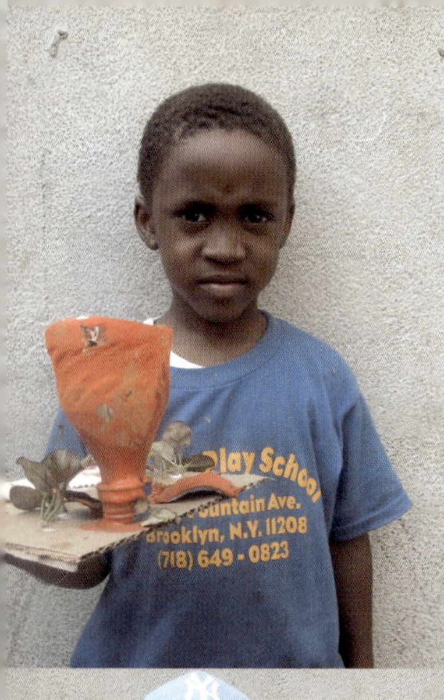
Play School
Fountain Ave.
Brooklyn, N.Y. 11208
(718) 649 - 0823

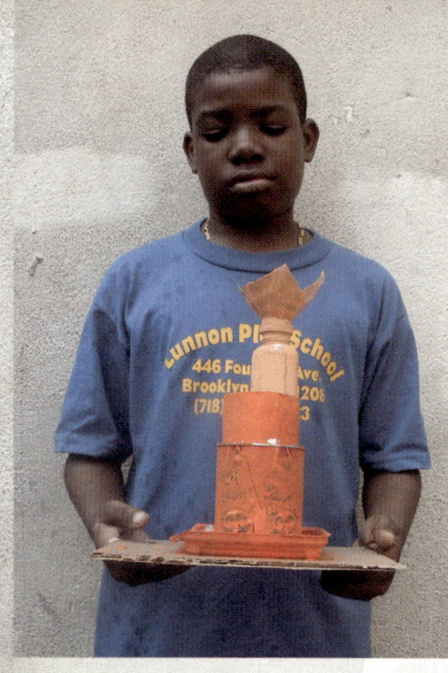

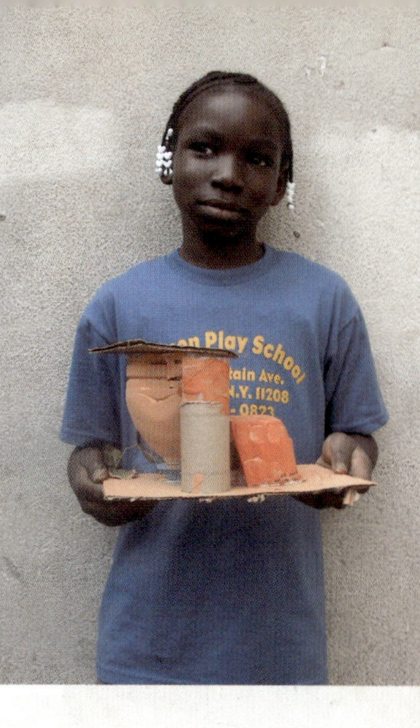
Play School

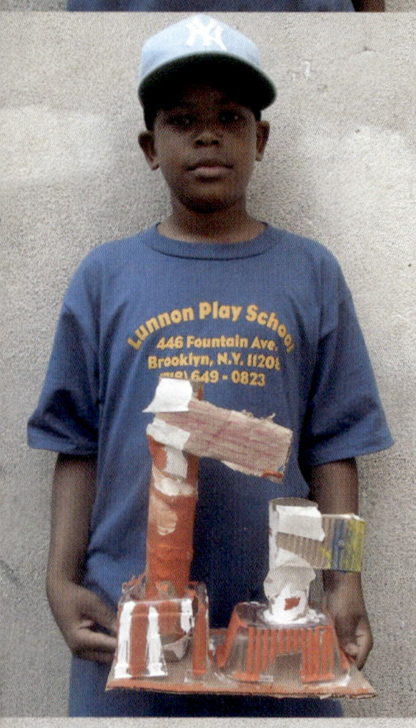
Lunnon Play School
446 Fountain Ave.
Brooklyn, N.Y. 11208
(718) 649 - 0823

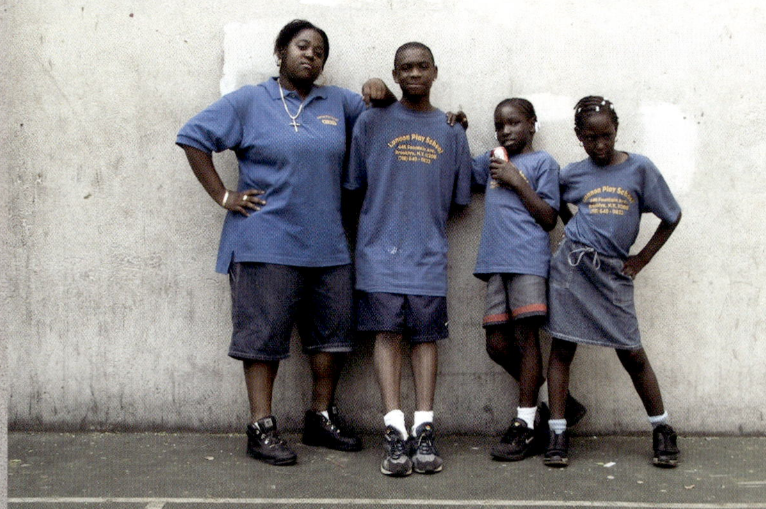

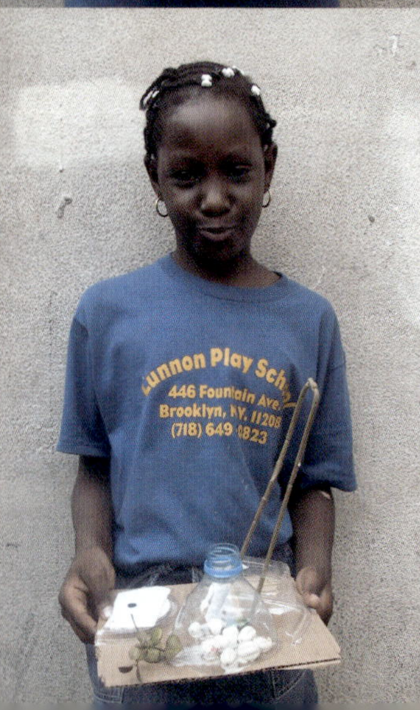
446 Fountain Ave.
Brooklyn, N.Y. 11208
(718) 649 0823

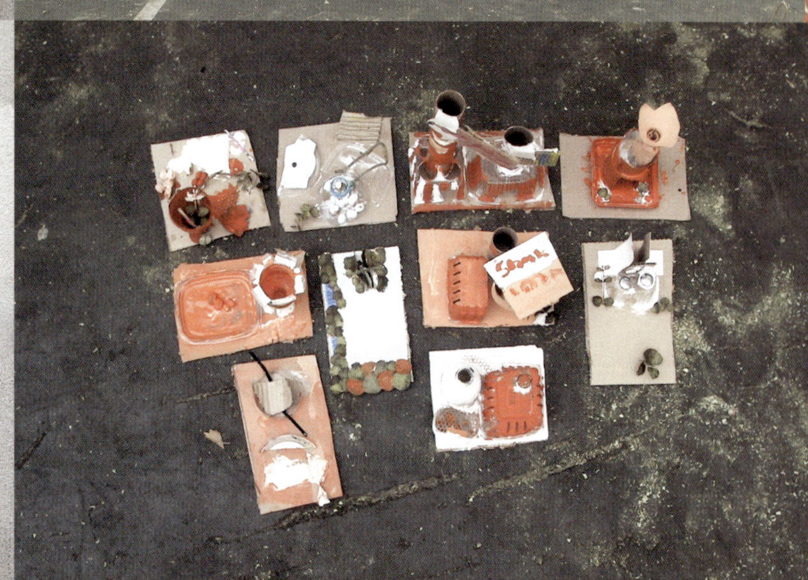

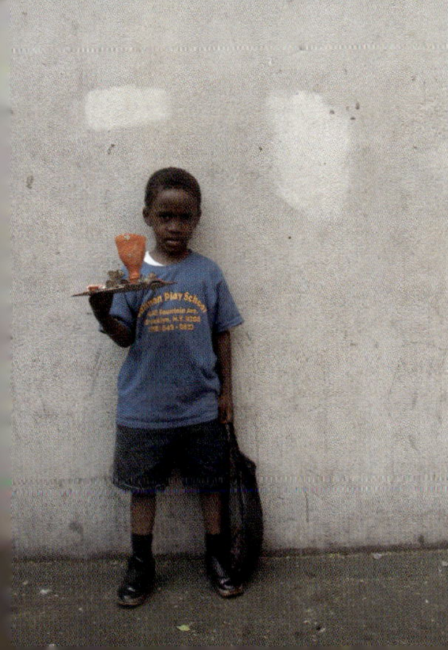

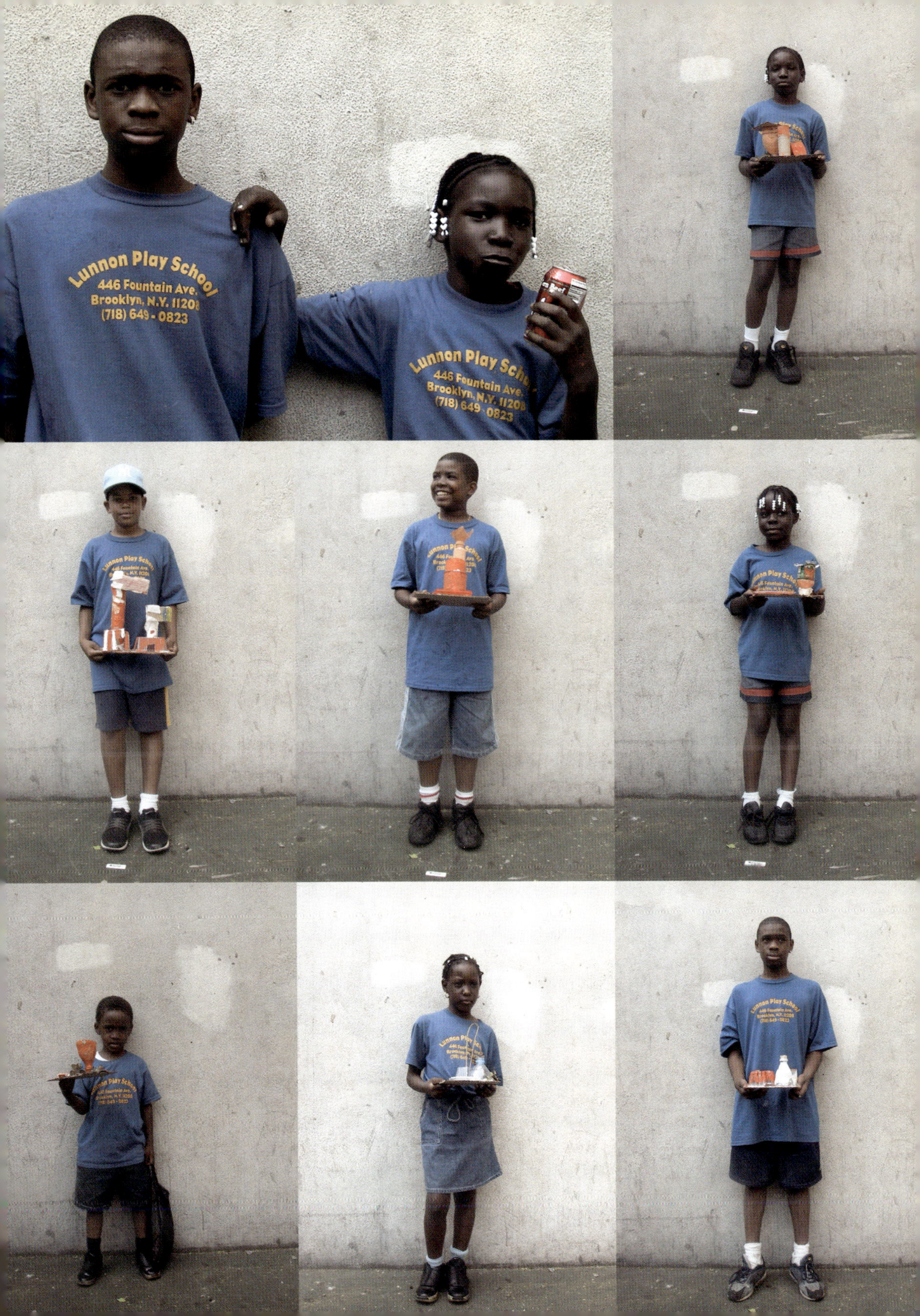

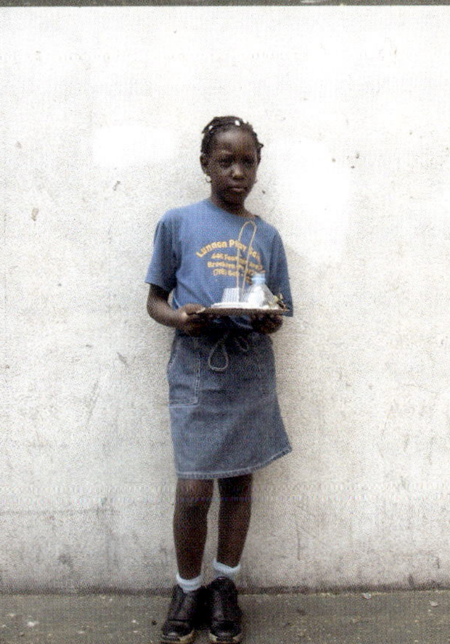

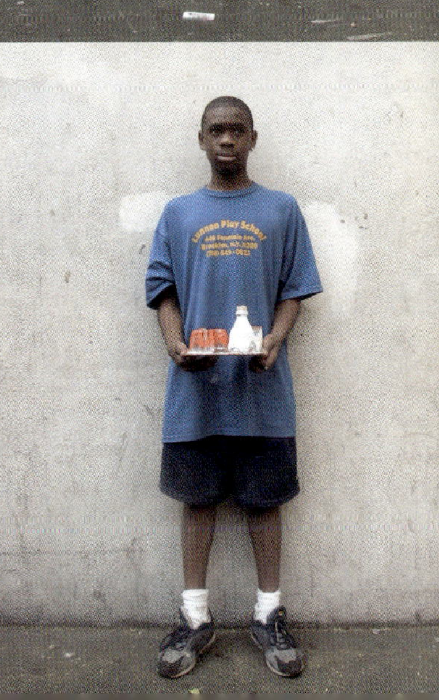

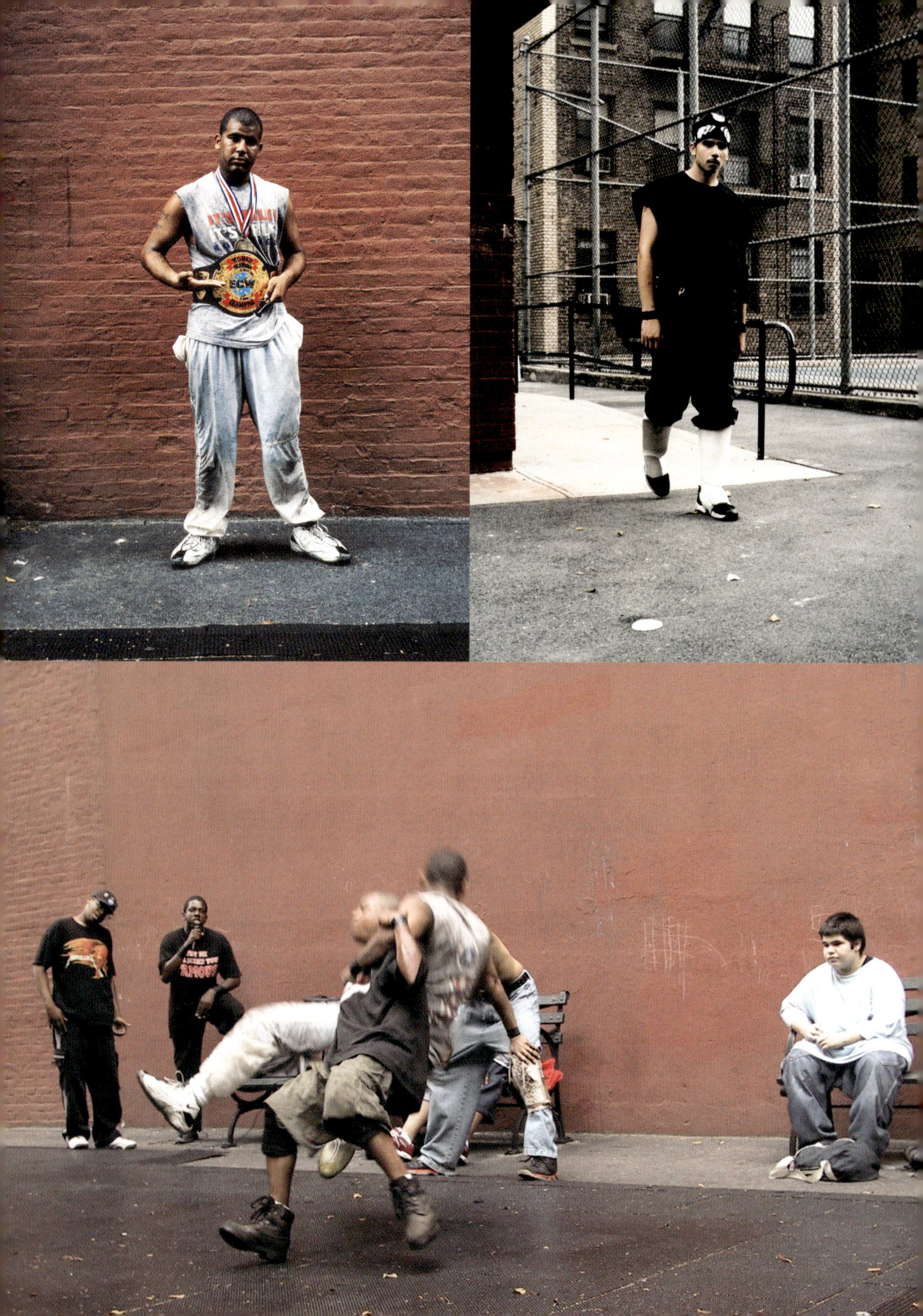
ECW

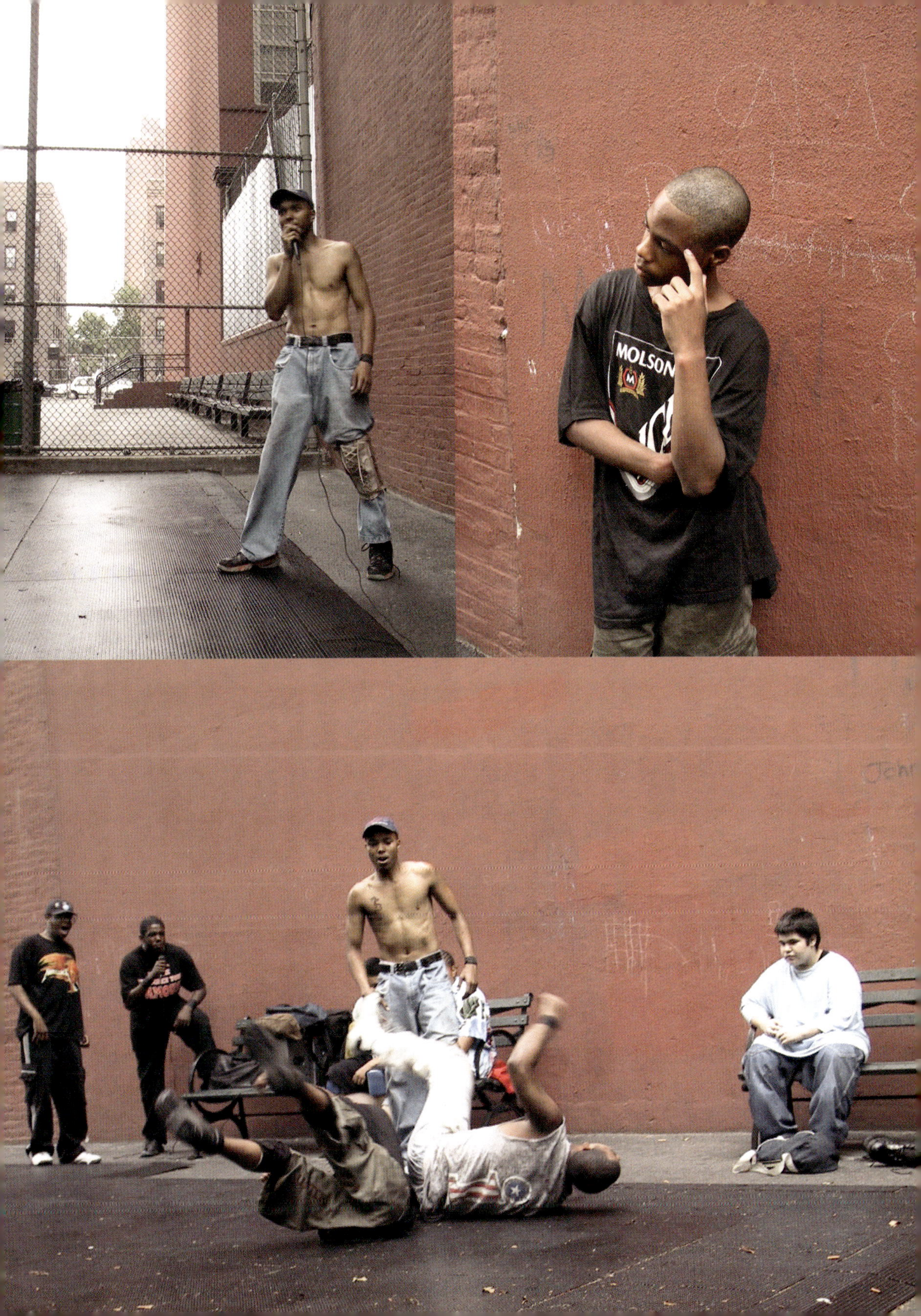
MOLSON

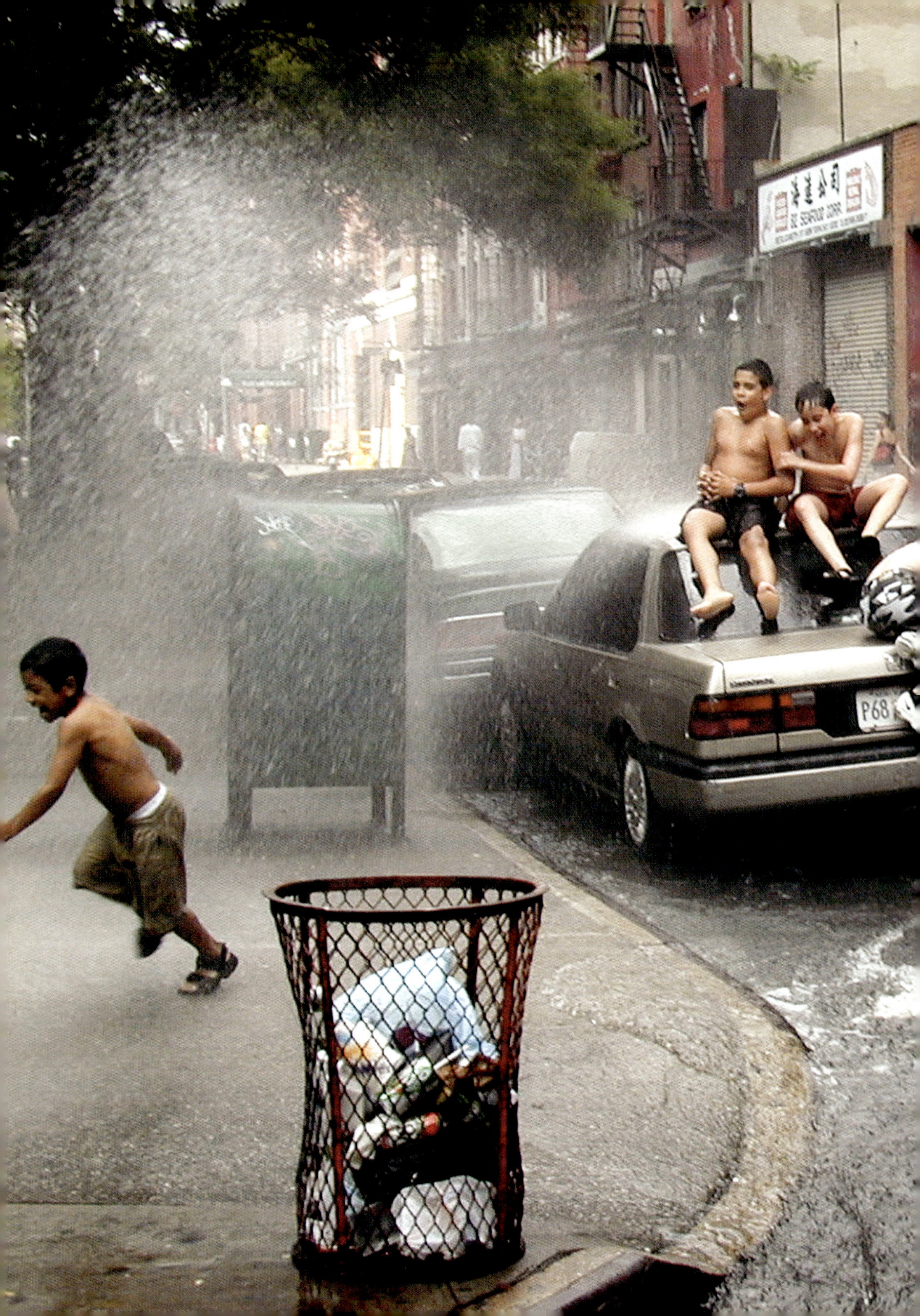

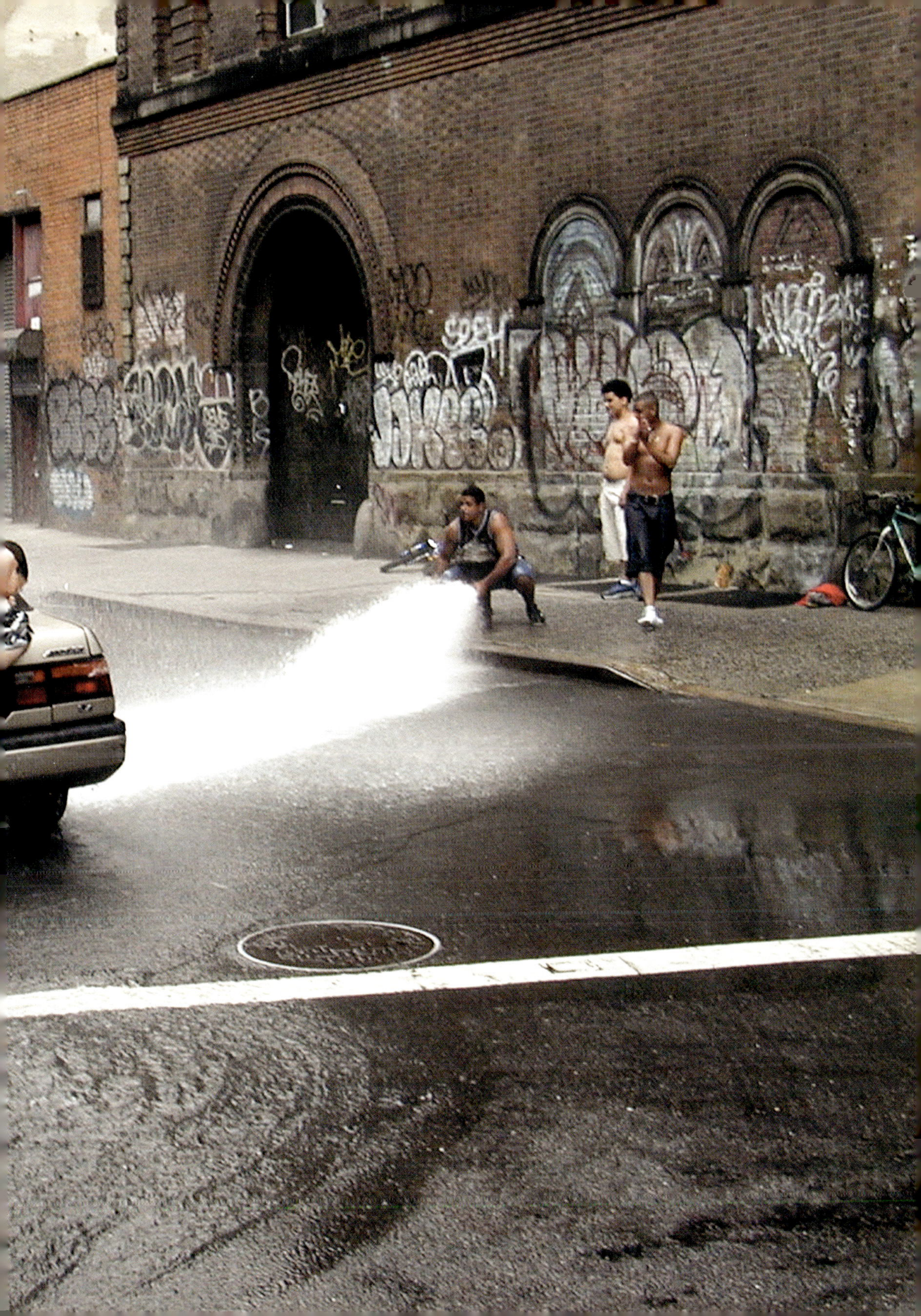

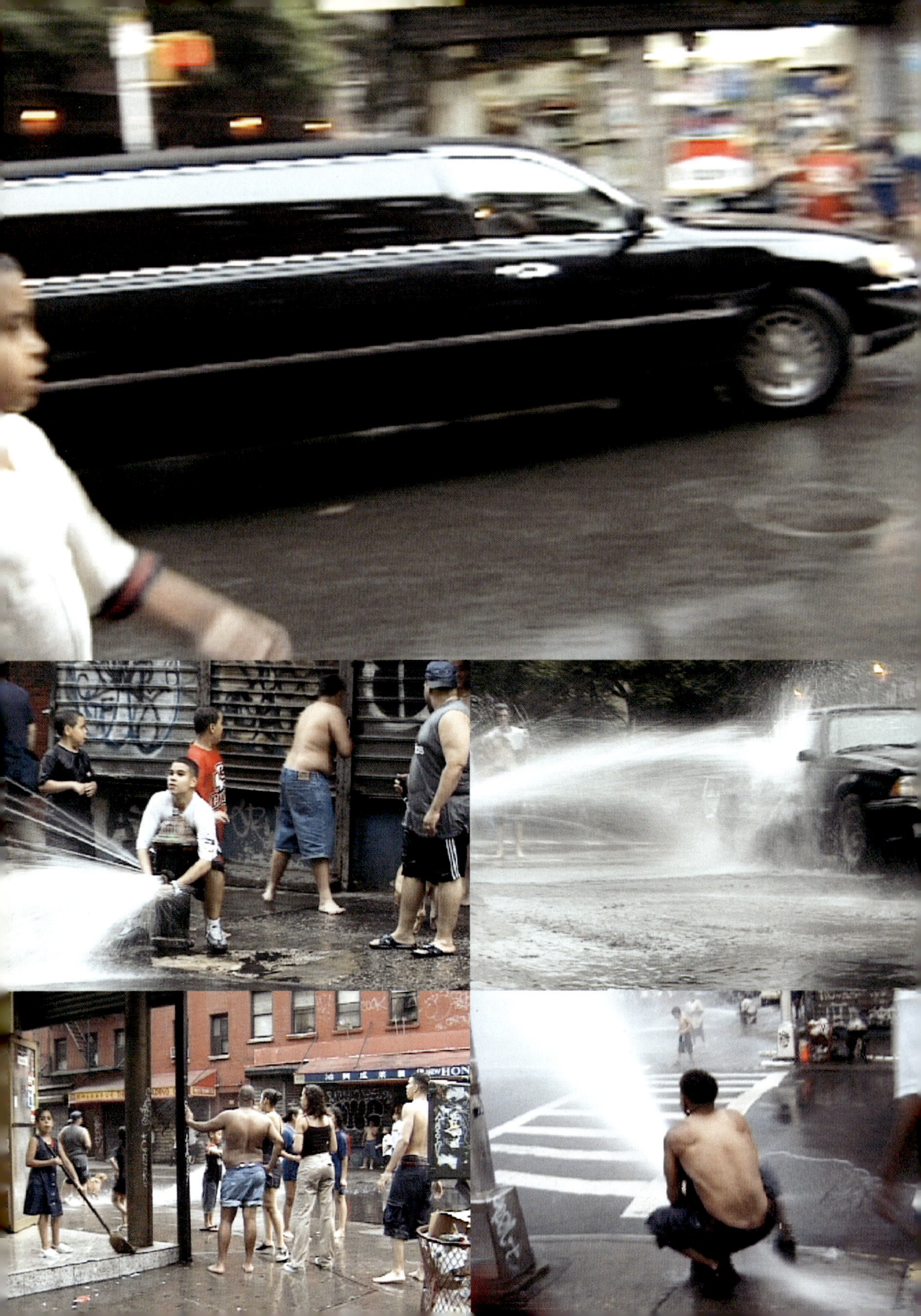

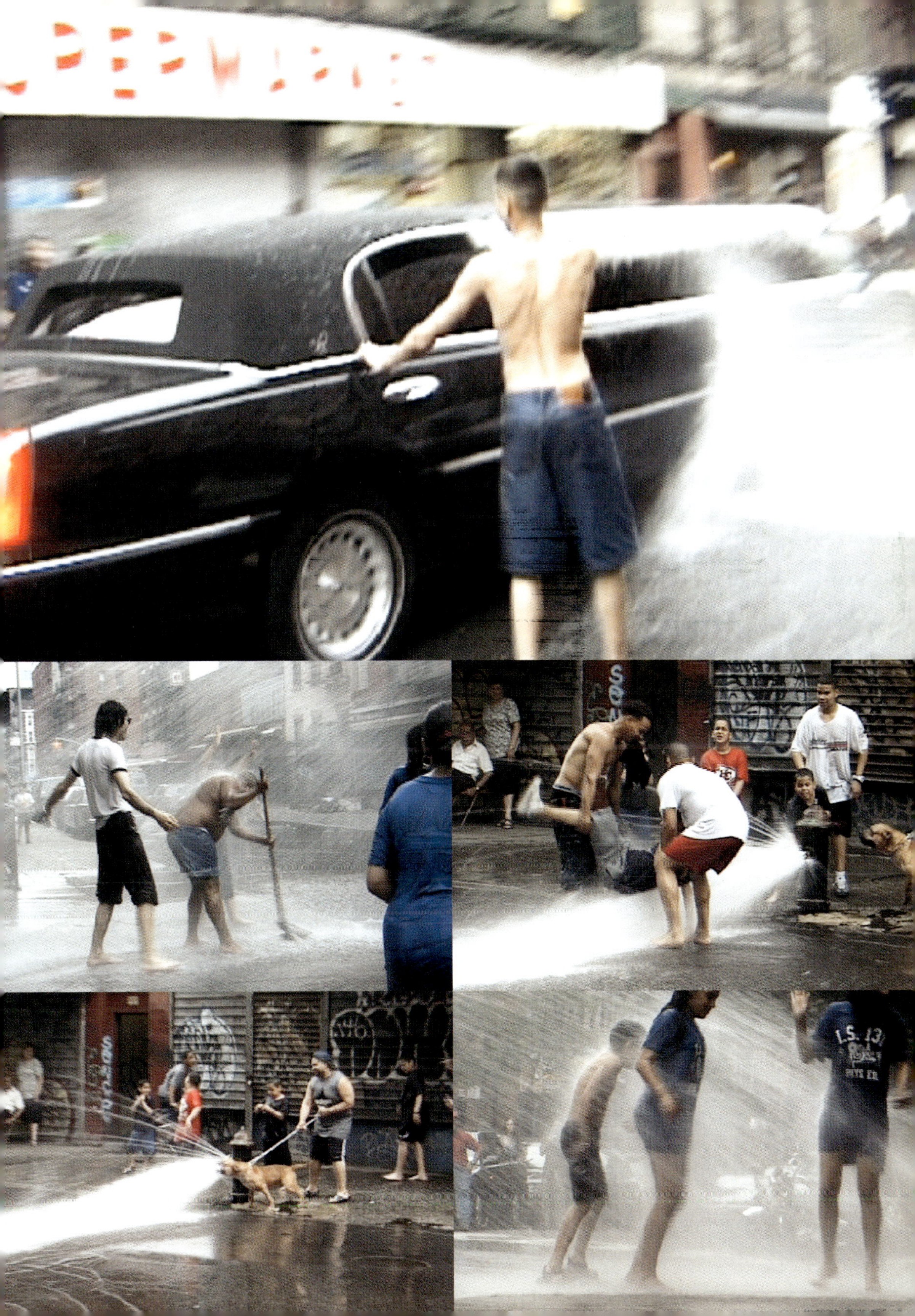

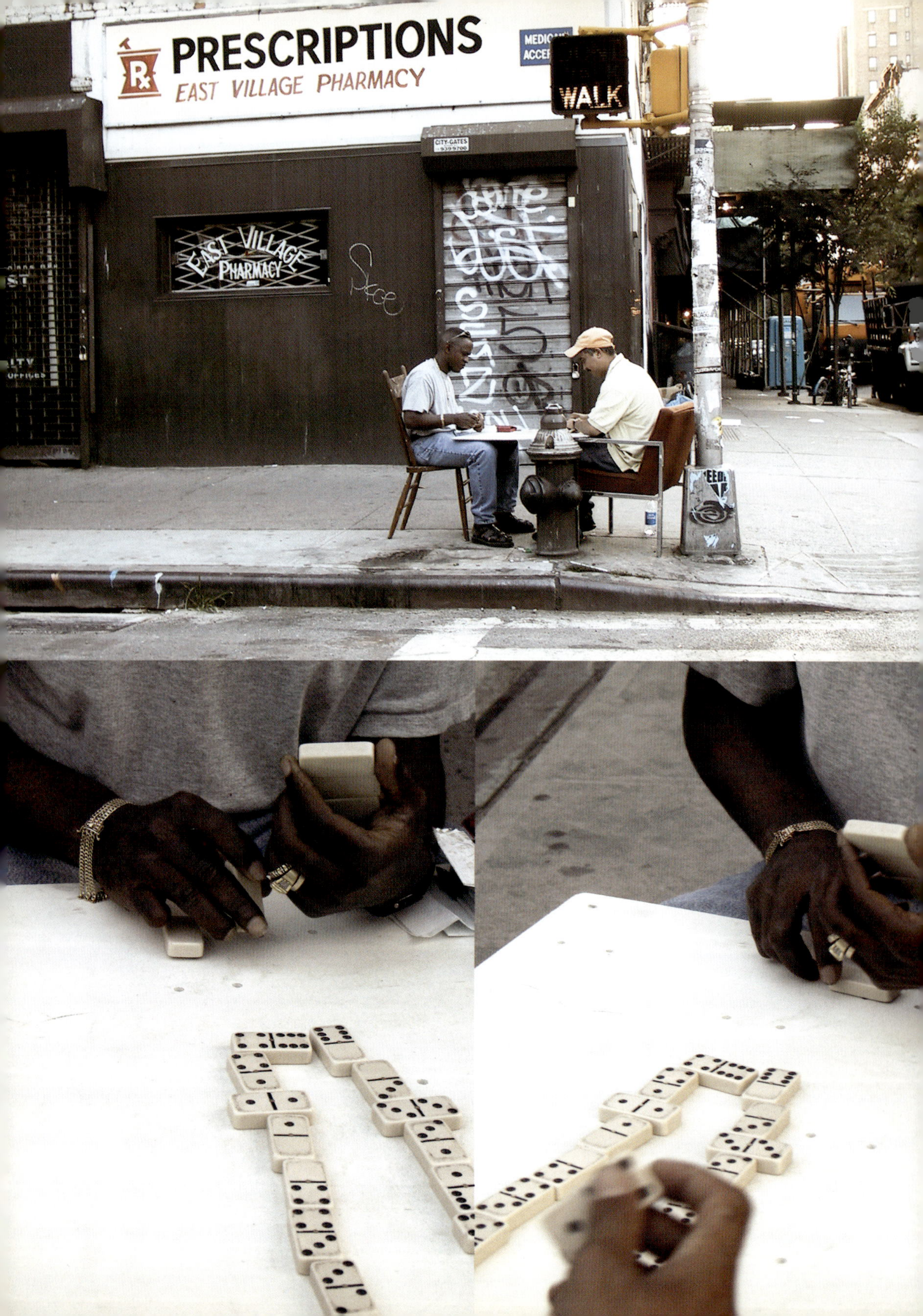

PRESCRIPTIONS
EAST VILLAGE PHARMACY
WALK
EAST VILLAGE
PHARMACY

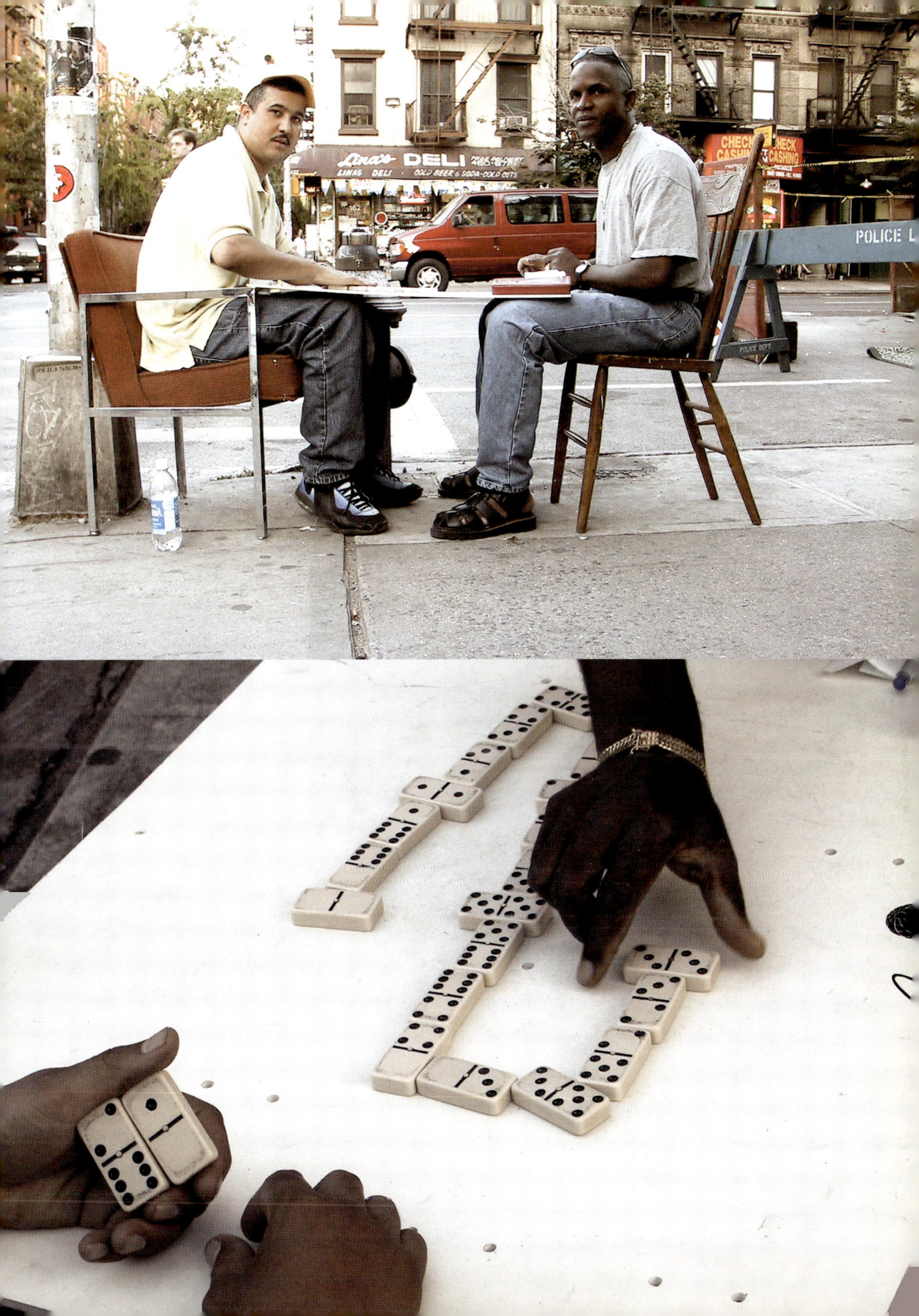
Lina's DELI
COLD BEER & SODA-COLD CUTS
CHECK CASHING
POLICE

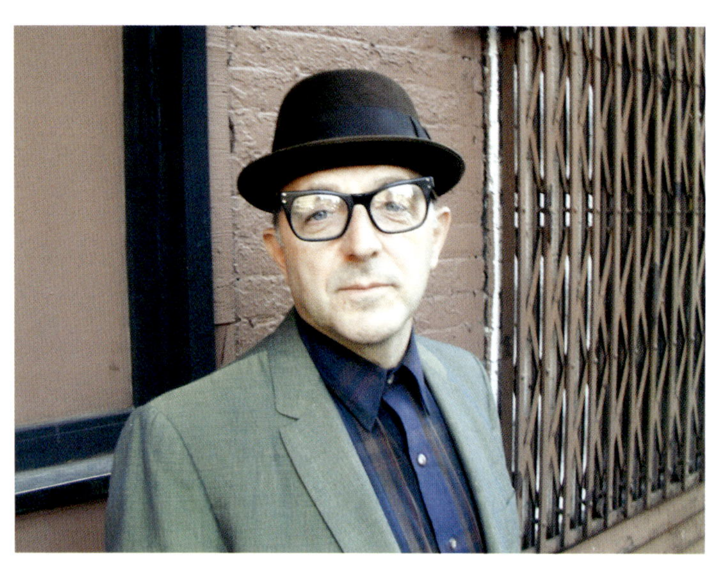

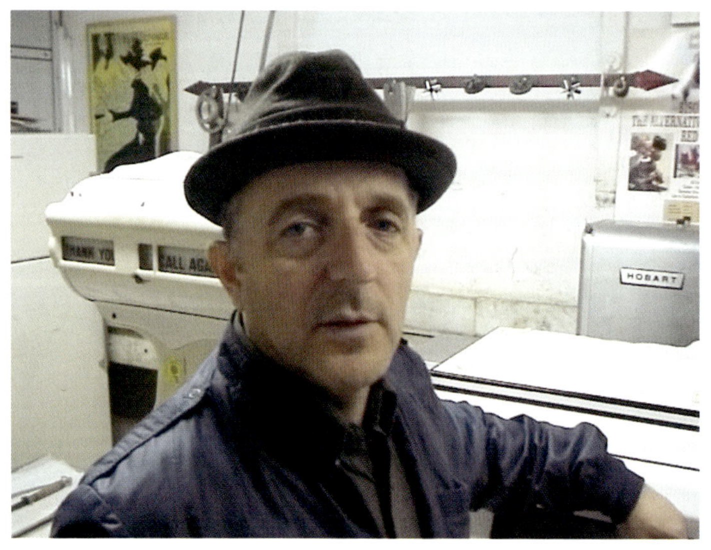
HOBART

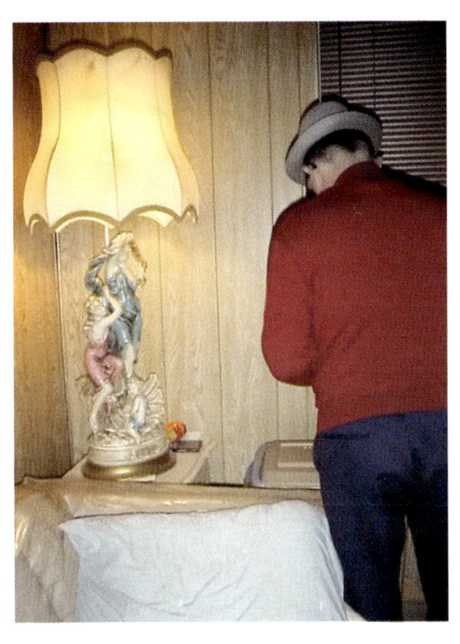
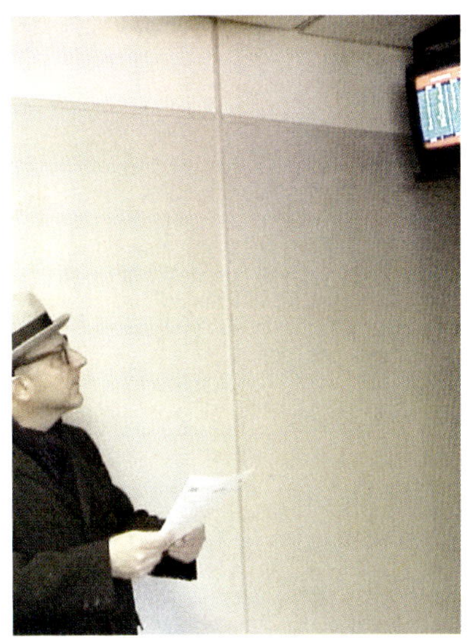
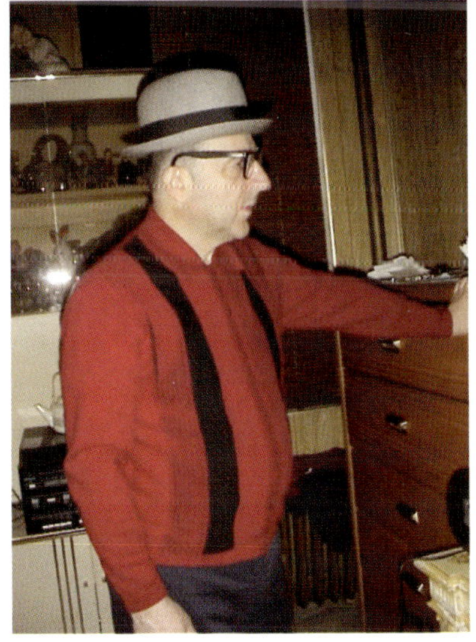
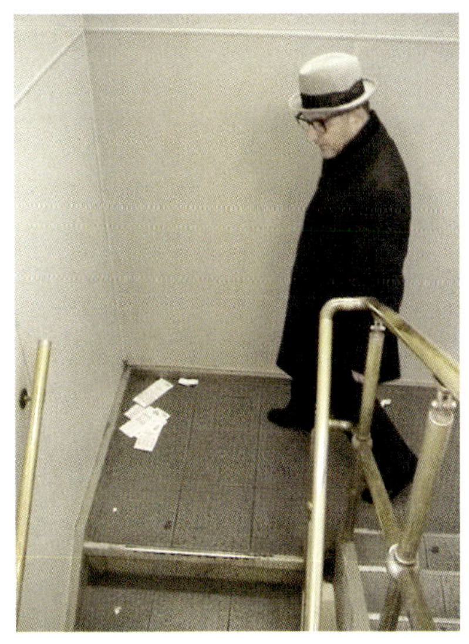

System

Order

Property Phenomenon	Dysfunctional Speech Act	Commerce	Control	Membrane	Orientation	The Range of Participation
LOCKED MOBILITY	MISSPELLING	CORPORATE MONUMENTS	POLICE LINE DO NOT CROSS	BLUE CITY	STREET SCRIPT	VOICE
TAPE	FADING MARKETS	STREET VENDORS	A BARRIER	COVER	STREET MARK	DIVERSITY
SHOP WATCH	EMPTY SIGNS	STREET LEVEL	SERVICE SCREEN	SHOPPING BAG	STEEL	OPEN CINE
REAL ESTATE		SHOPPING CARTS		GARBAGE DIGITAL SLUM		NEIGHBORHOOD

Identity

Alternative Media

Habitual Reinterpretation

OPEN CINE

Projecting Content onto an empty Wall

CAR DOOR

PUBLIC CHAIRS

LABELING.

PLASTIC CRATES

POLE POST

STANDPIPES

PRAY JESUS

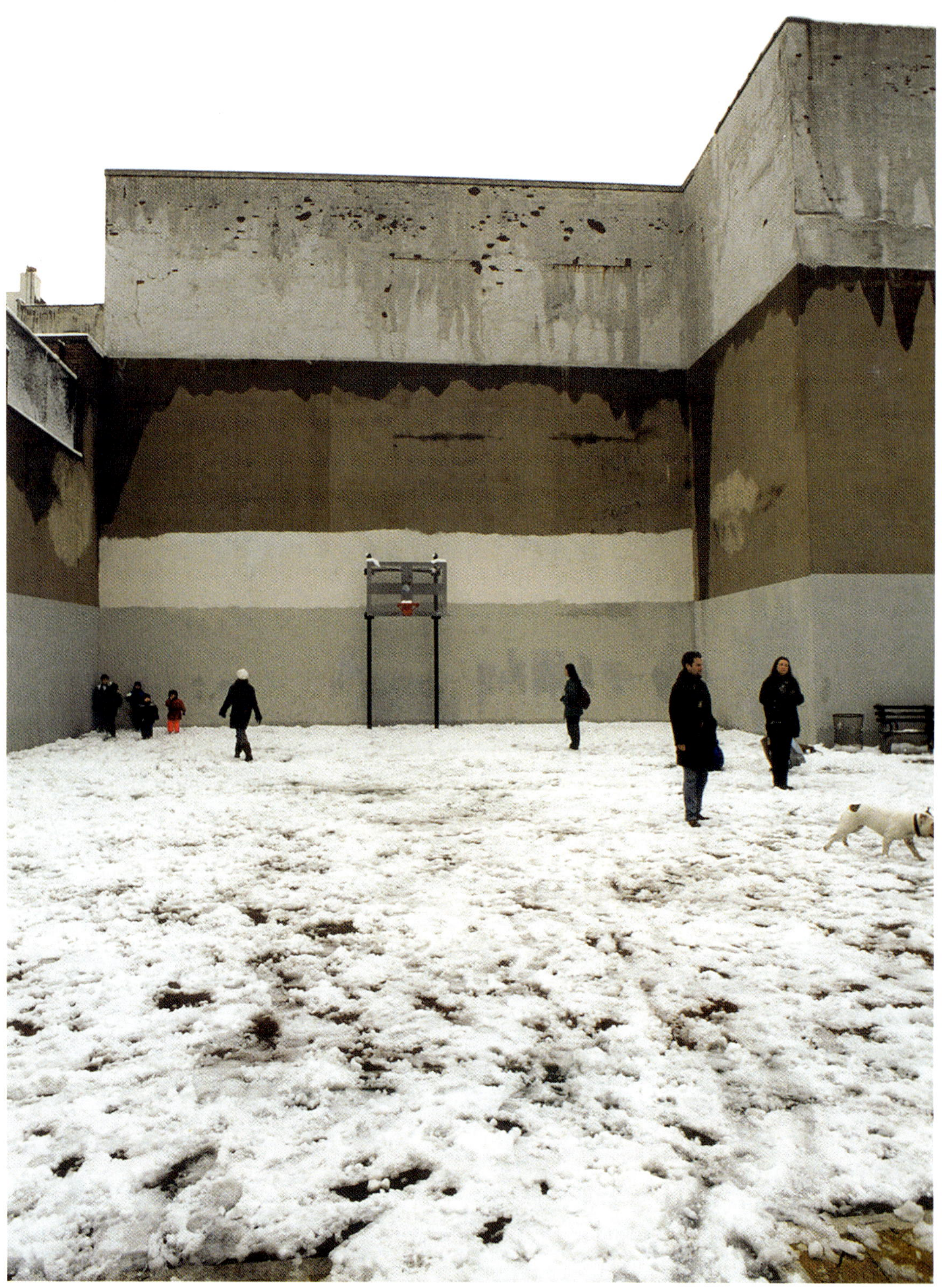

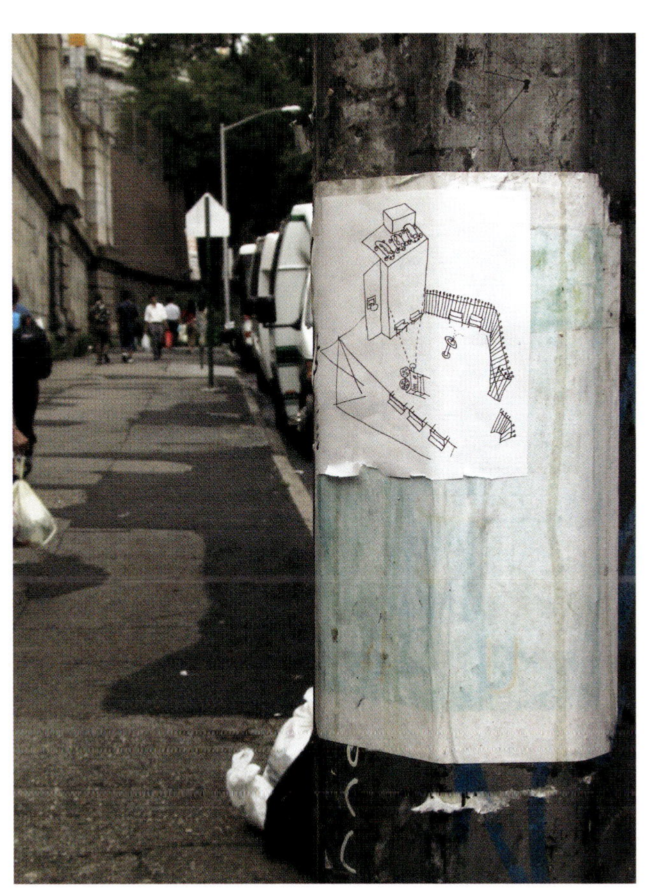

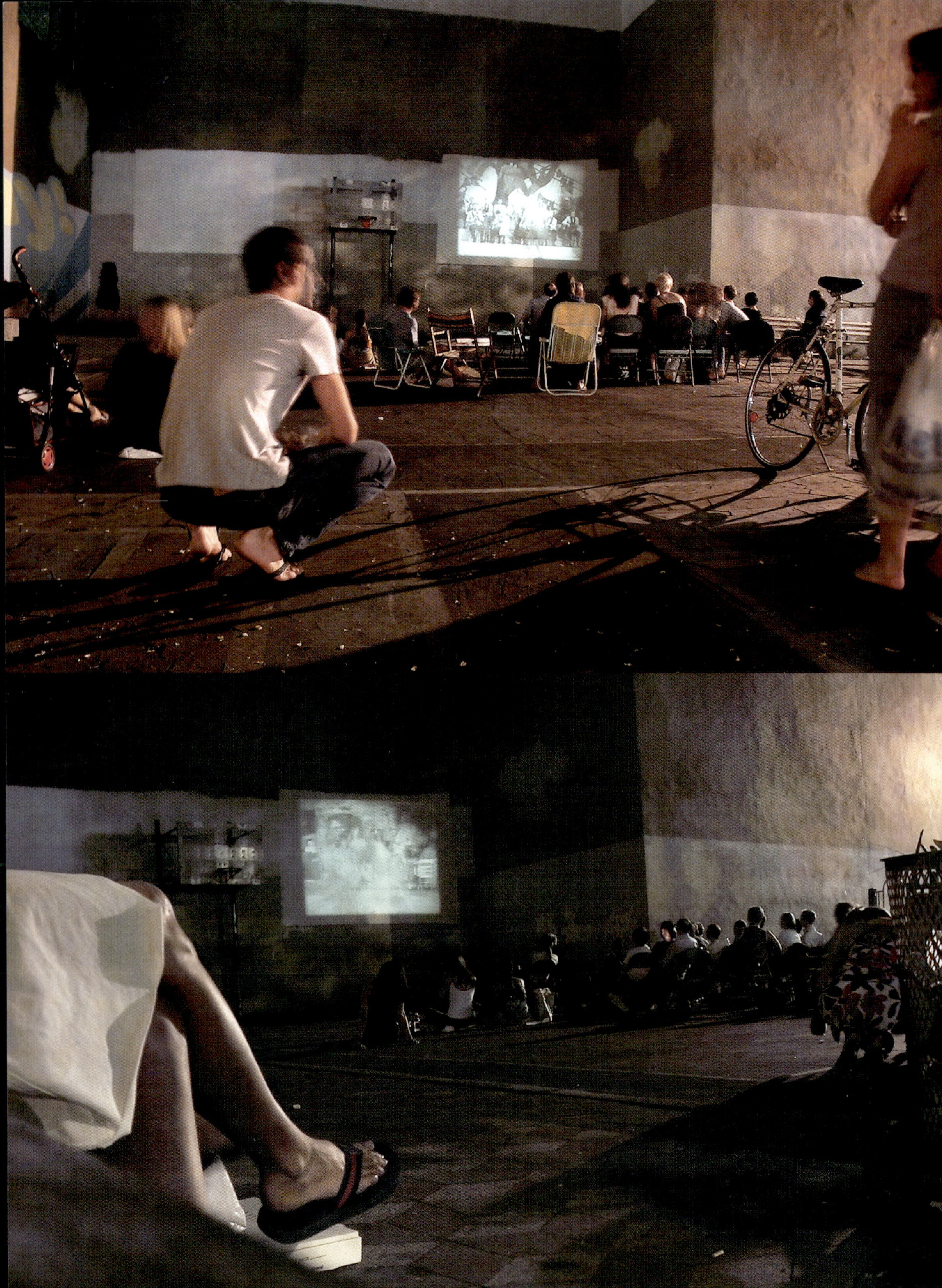

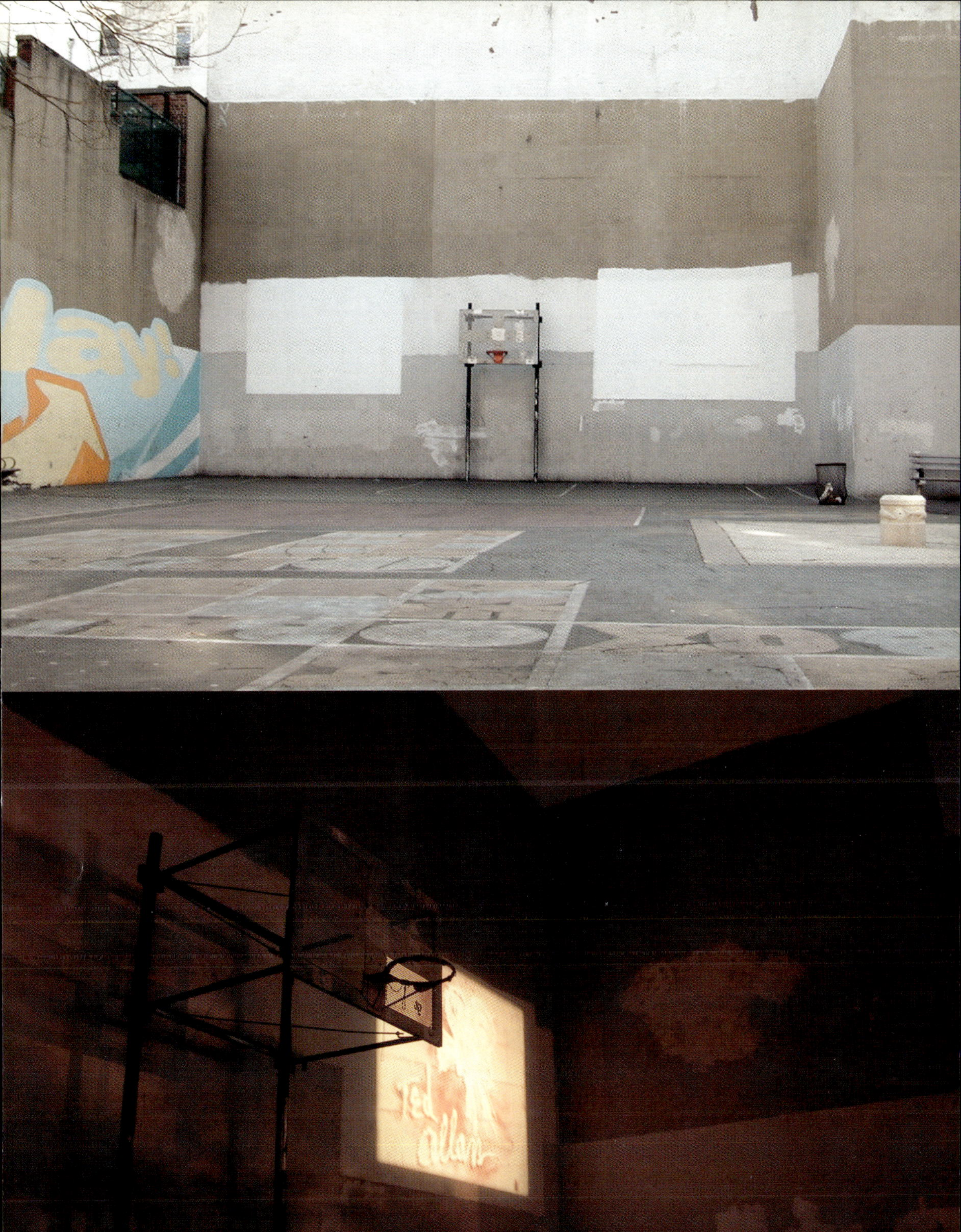

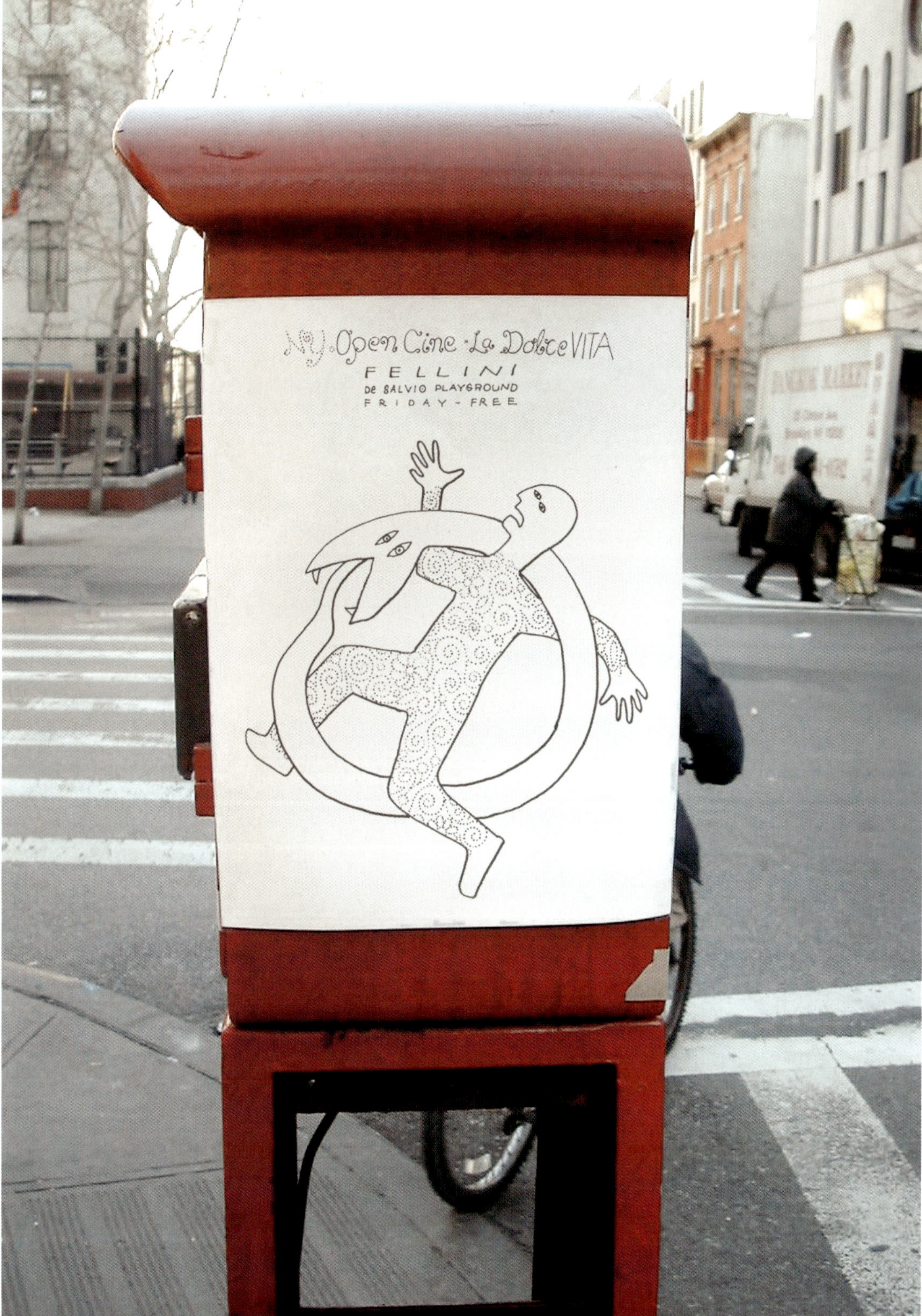
NY · Open Cine · La Dolce VITA
FELLINI
De SALVIO PLAYGROUND
FRIDAY - FREE

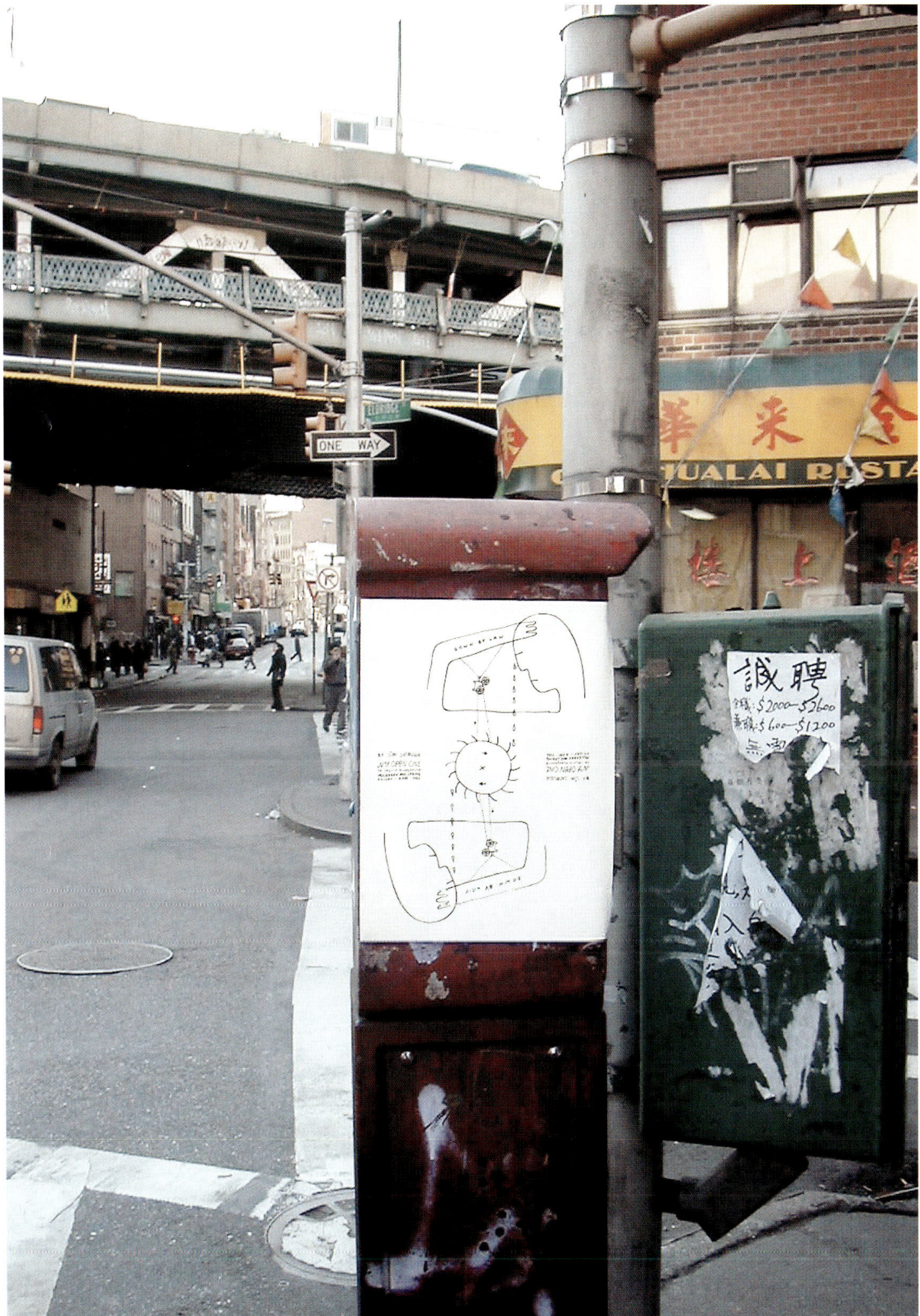
ONE WAY
誠聘
$2000—$2600
$600—$1200

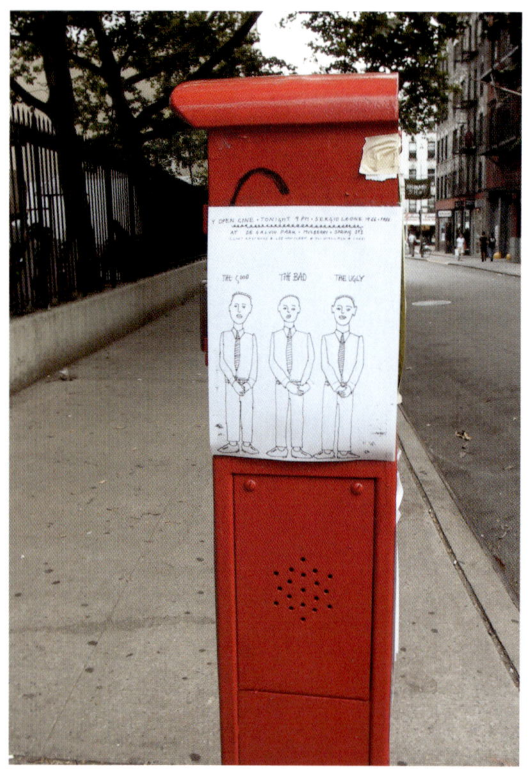
OPEN CINE · TONIGHT 9 PM · SERGIO LEONE 1966 · FREE
AT DE SALVIO PARK · MULBERRY + SPRING STS
THE GOOD
THE BAD
THE UGLY
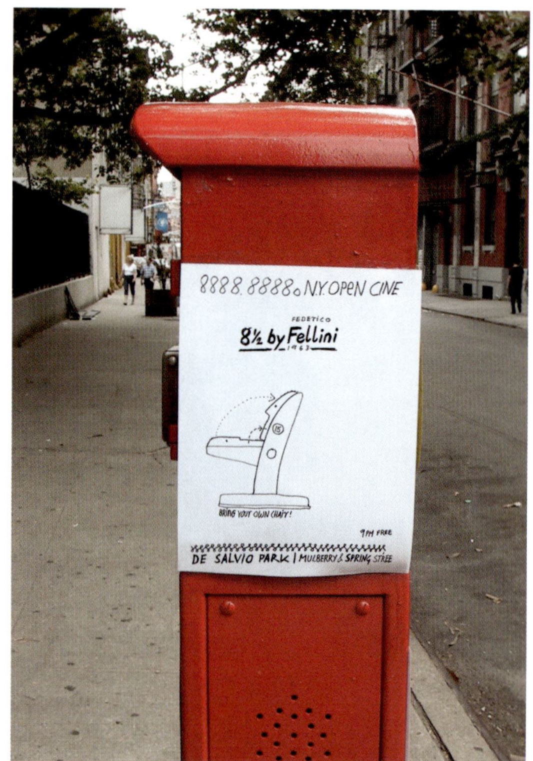
8888.8888 N.Y. OPEN CINE
FEDERICO
8½ by Fellini
1963
BRING YOUR OWN CHAIR!
9PM FREE
DE SALVIO PARK | MULBERRY & SPRING STREE
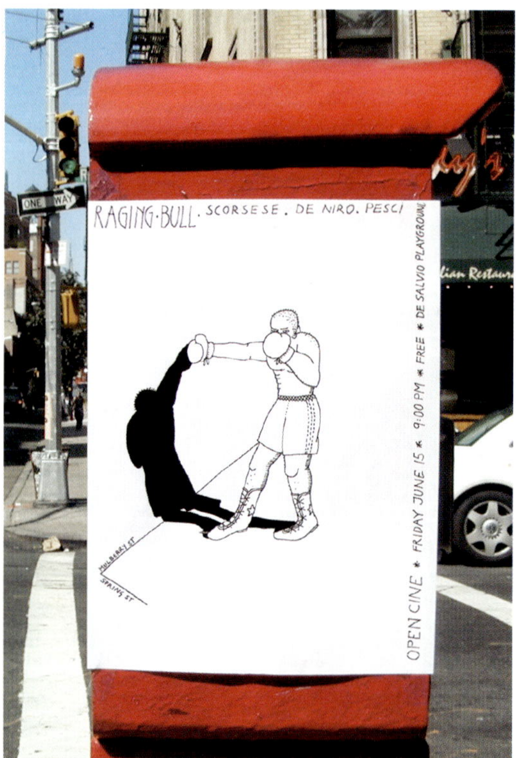
RAGING·BULL · SCORSESE . DE NIRO. PESCI
OPEN CINE ★ FRIDAY JUNE 15 ★ 9:00 PM ★ FREE ★ DE SALVIO PLAYGROUND
MULBERRY ST
SPRING ST
ONE WAY
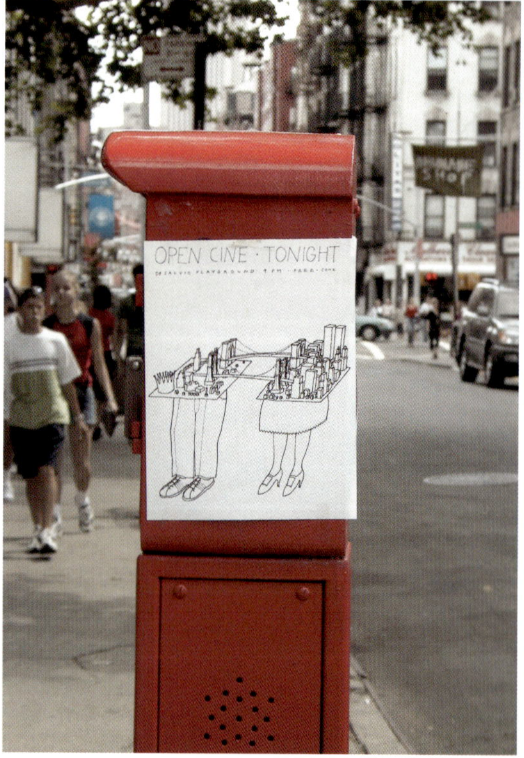
OPEN CINE · TONIGHT

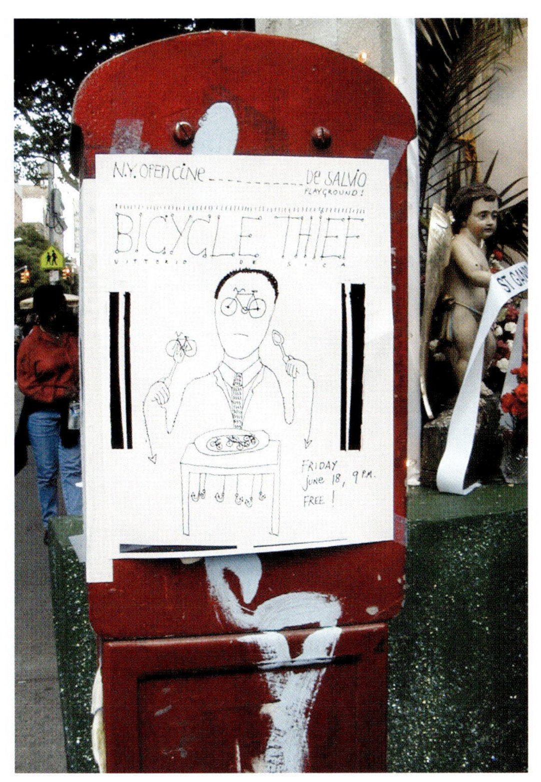
N.Y. Open Cine
De Salvio Playground
BICYCLE THIEF
FRIDAY June 18, 9 P.M.
FREE!

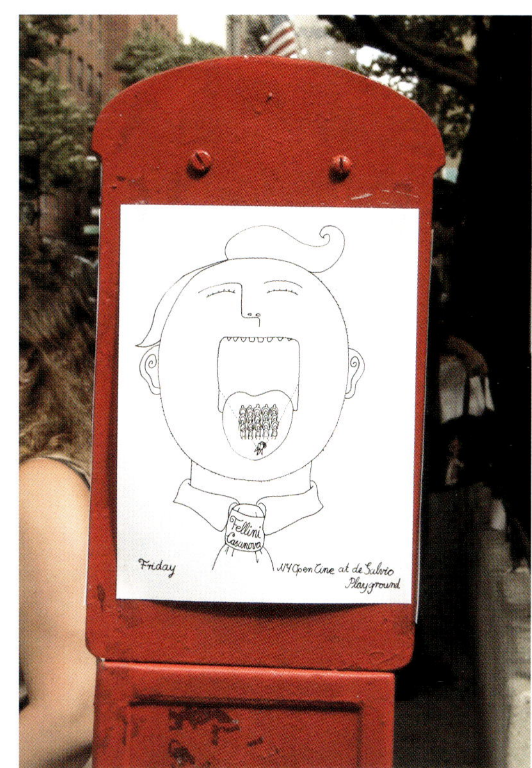
Fellini Casanova
Friday
N.Y. Open Cine at de Salvio Playground

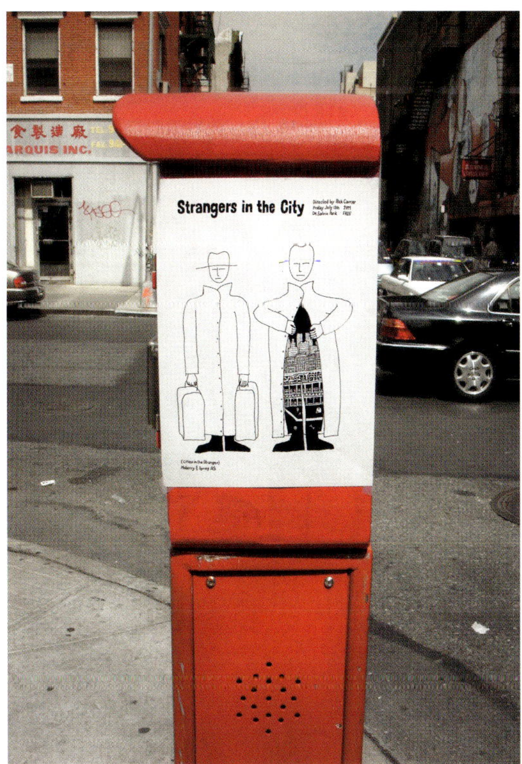
Strangers in the City
Directed by Rick Carrier
De Salvio Park FREE

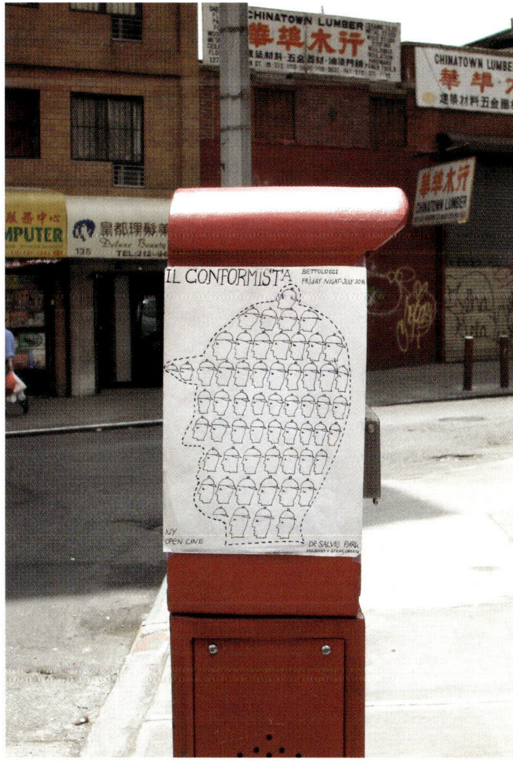
CHINATOWN LUMBER
IL CONFORMISTA
N.Y. OPEN CINE
DE SALVIO PARK

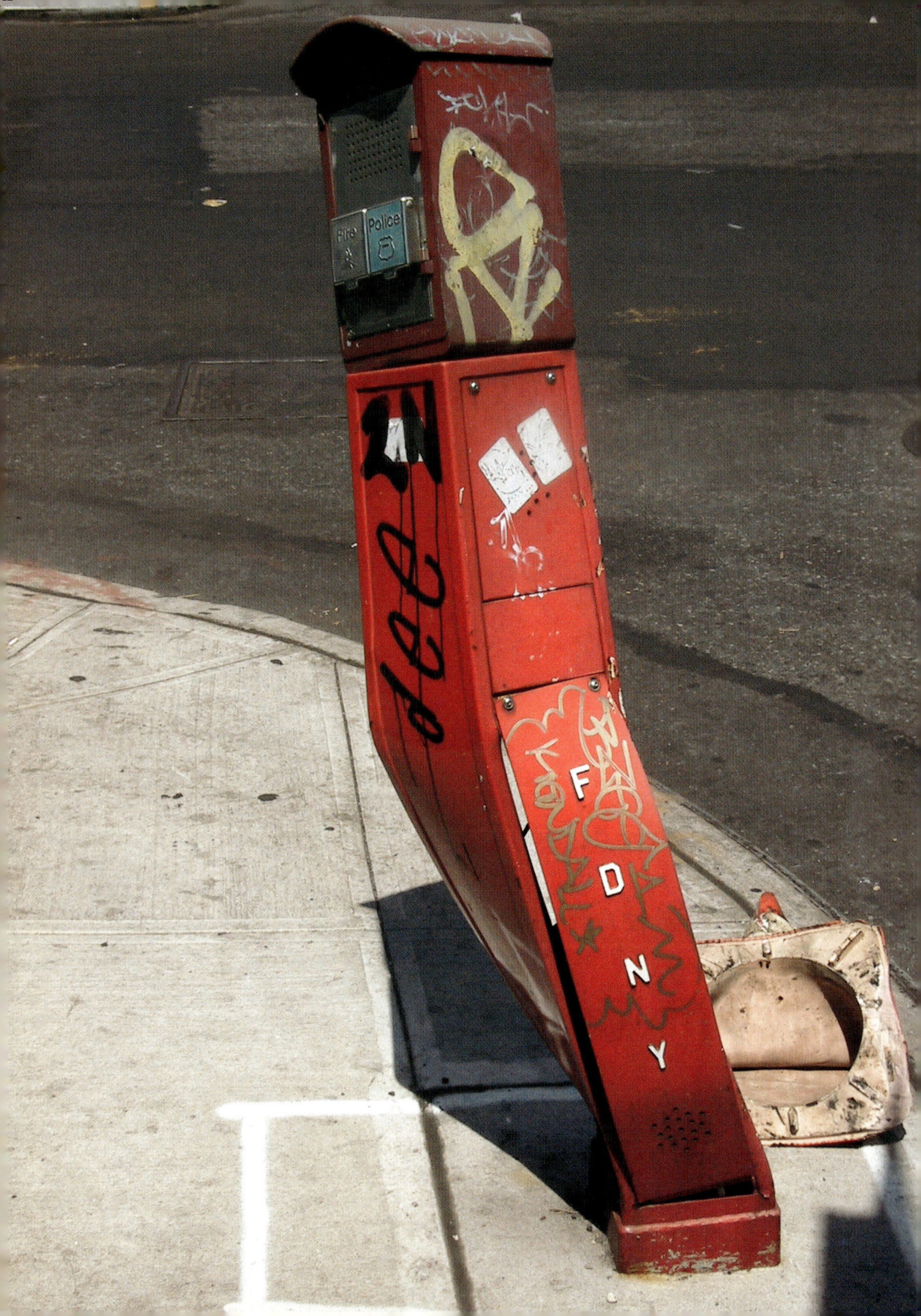
Fire
Police
FDNY

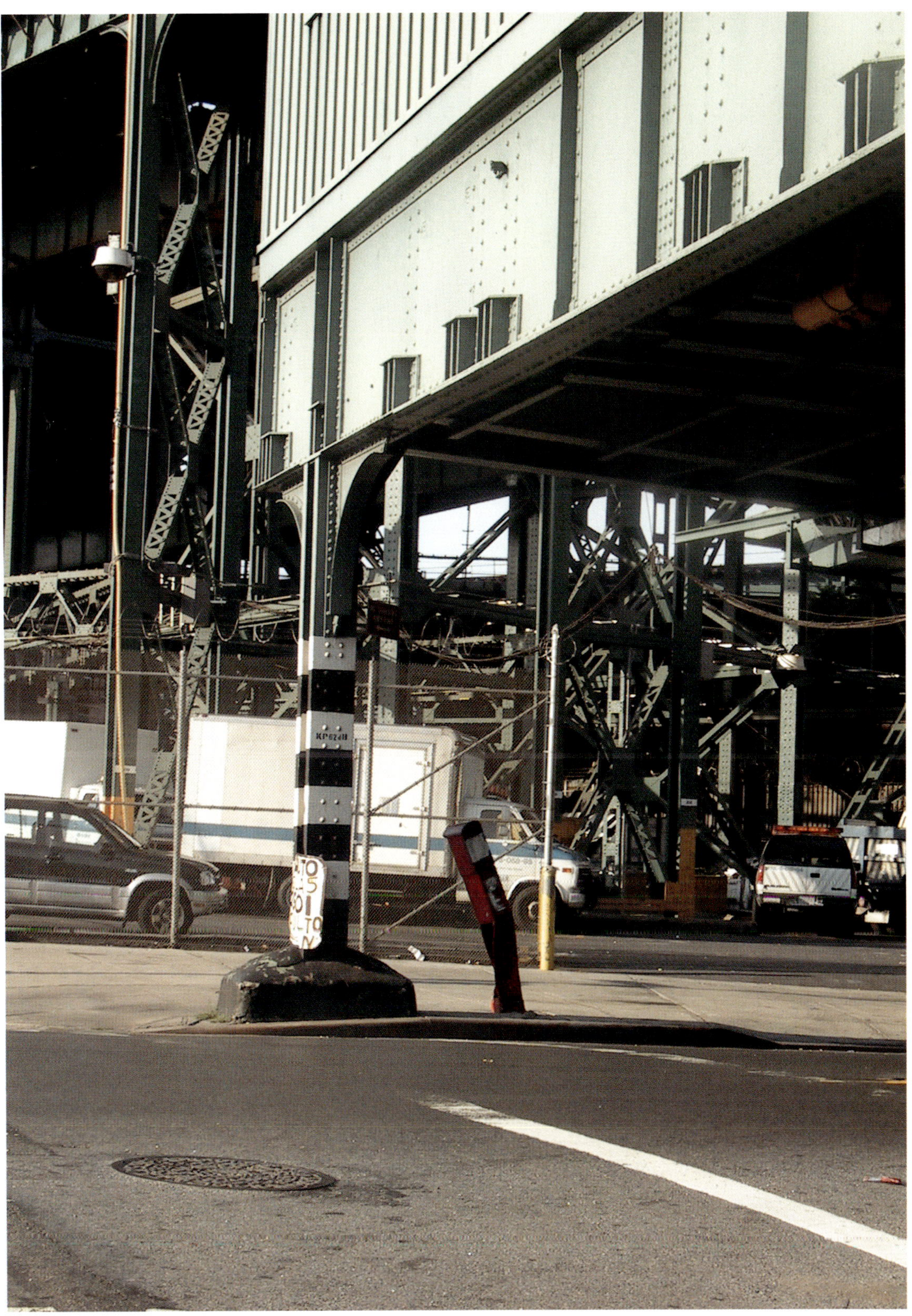

	System			Order		
Property Phenomenon	Dysfunctional Speech Act	Commerce	Control	Membrane	Orientation	**The Range of Participation**
LOCKED MOBILITY	MISSPELLING	CORPORATE MONUMENTS	POLICE LINE DO NOT CROSS	BLUE CITY	STREET SCRIPT	**VOICE**
TAPE	FADING MARKETS	STREET VENDORS	A BARRIER	COVER	STREET MARK	DIVERSITY
SHOP WATCH	EMPTY SIGNS	STREET LEVEL	SERVICE SCREEN	SHOPPING BAG	STEEL	OPEN CINE
REAL ESTATE		SHOPPING CARTS		GARBAGE DIGITAL SLUM		NEIGHBORHOOD

Alternative Media

Habitual Reinterpretation

VOICE

Levels of Volume

CAR DOOR

PUBLIC CHAIRS

LABELING.

PLASTIC CRATES

POLE POST

STANDPIPES

PRAY JESUS

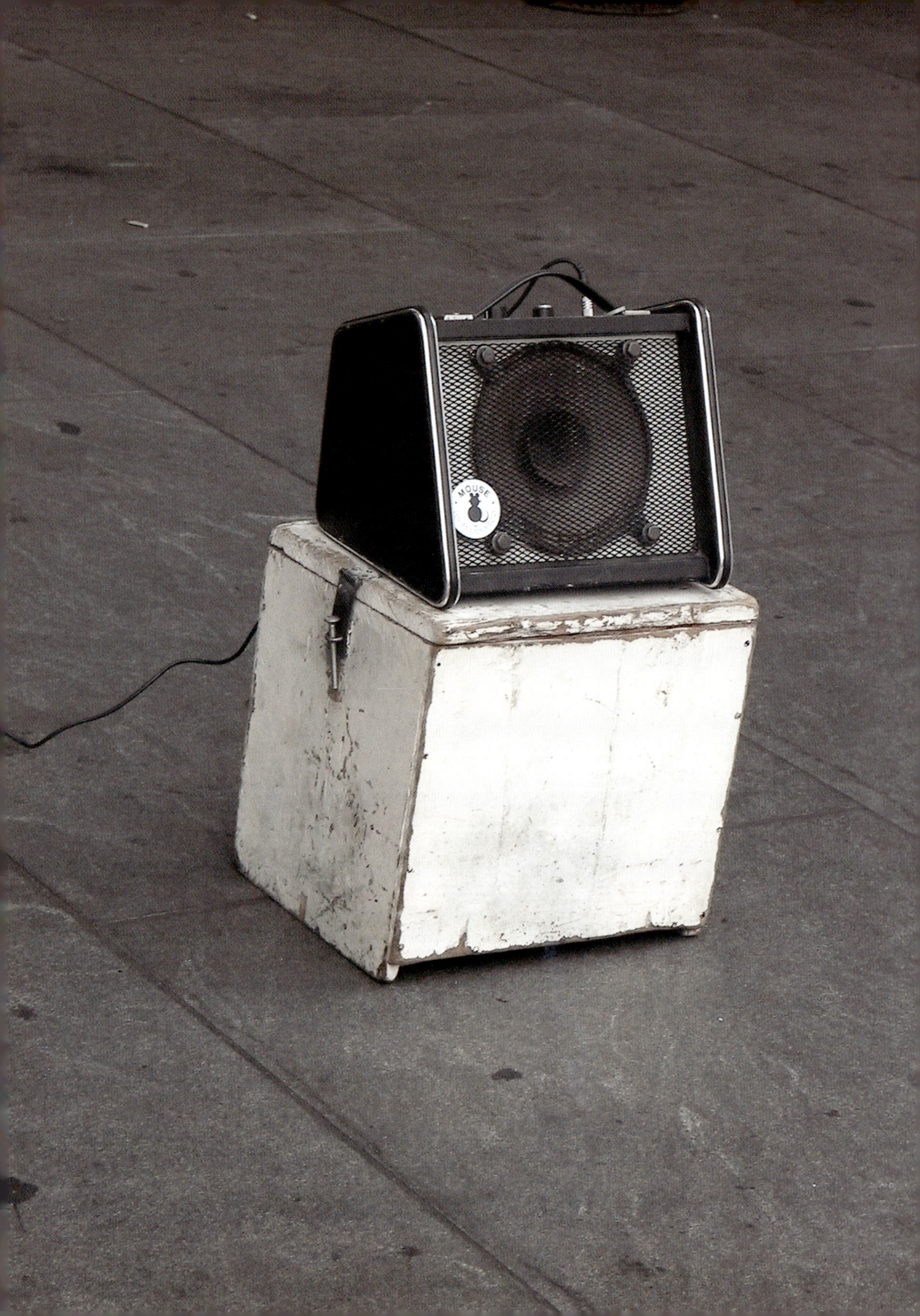
MOUSE

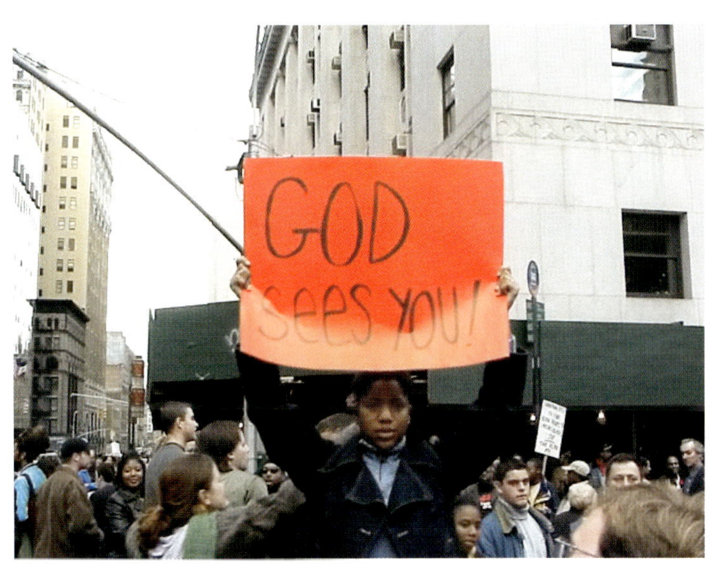
GOD
sees YOU!

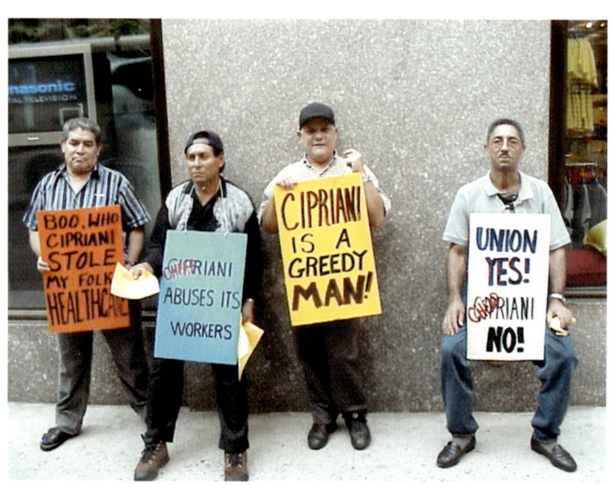

BOO, WHO
CIPRIANI
STOLE
MY FOLK
CIPRIANI
ABUSES ITS
WORKERS
CIPRIANI
IS A
GREEDY
MAN!
UNION
YES!
CIPRIANI
NO!

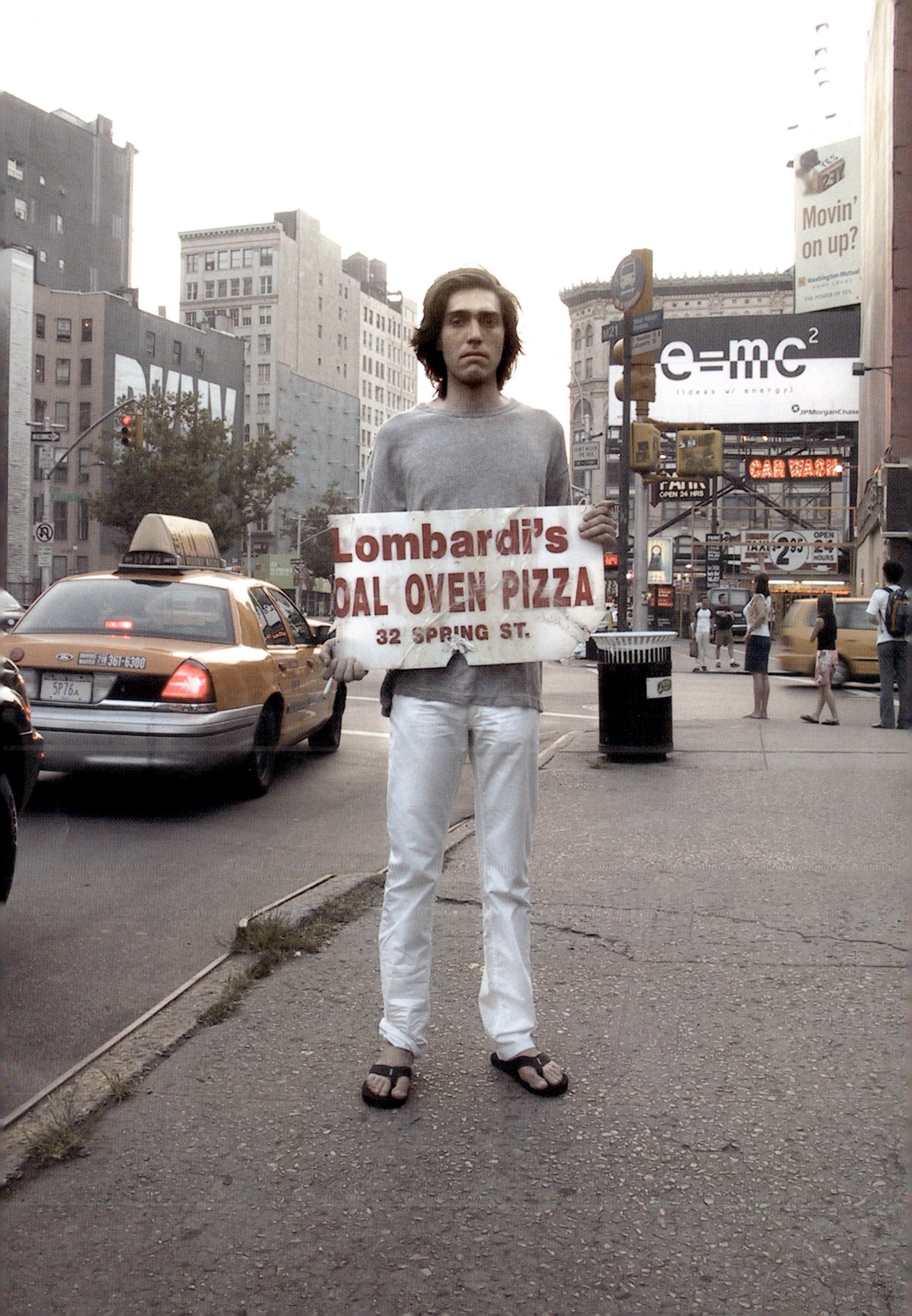
Lombardi's
OAL OVEN PIZZA
32 SPRING ST.
Movin' on up?
e=mc²
(ideas w/ energy)
JPMorganChase
CAR WASH
OPEN 24 HOURS

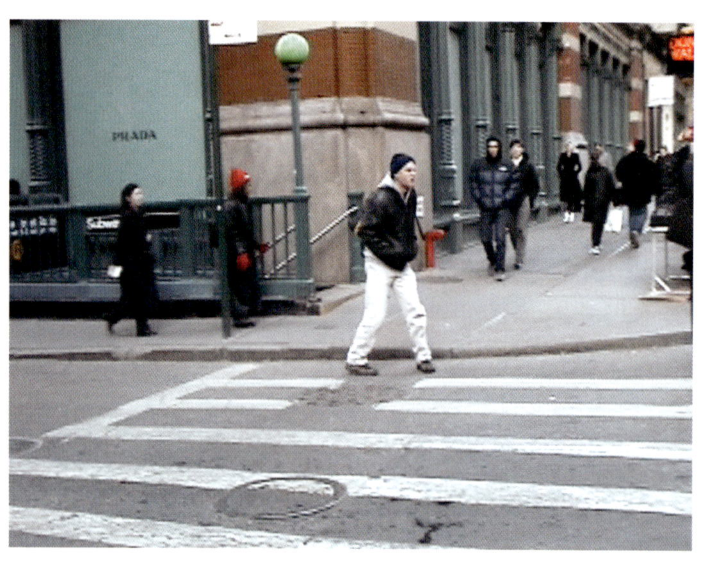
PRADA

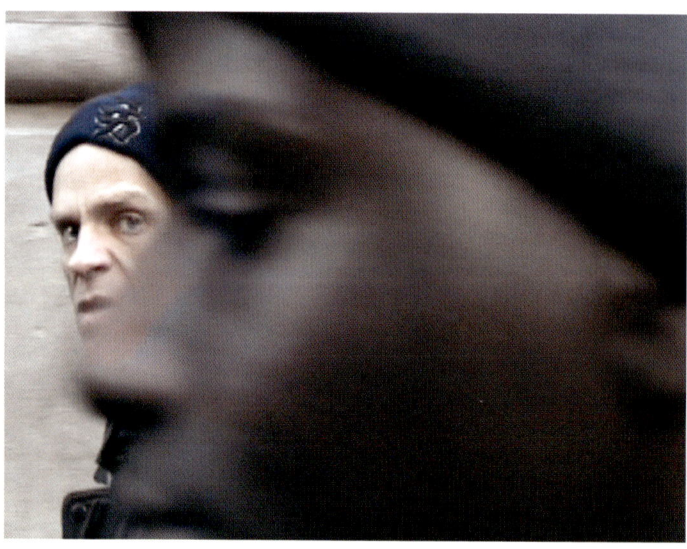

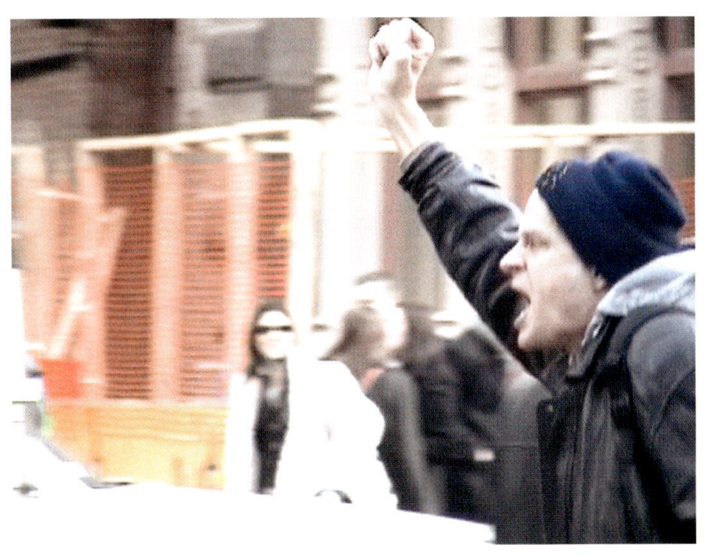

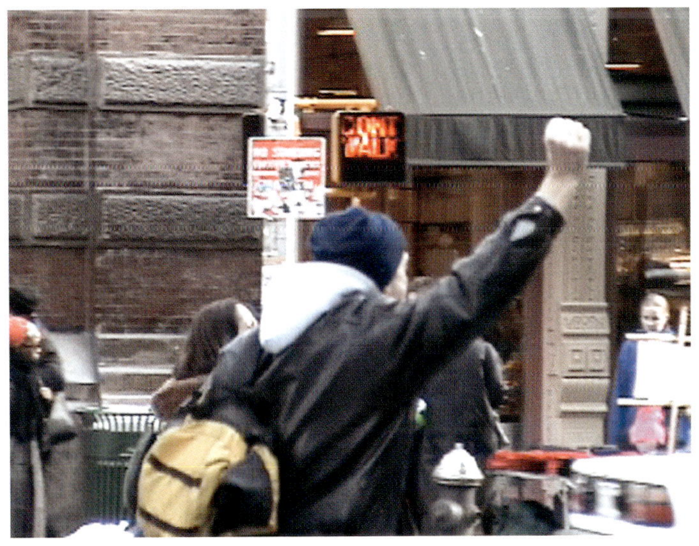

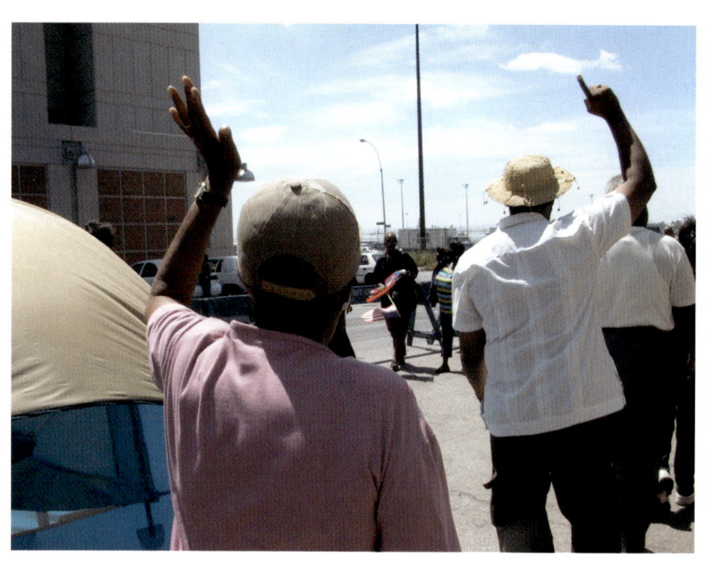

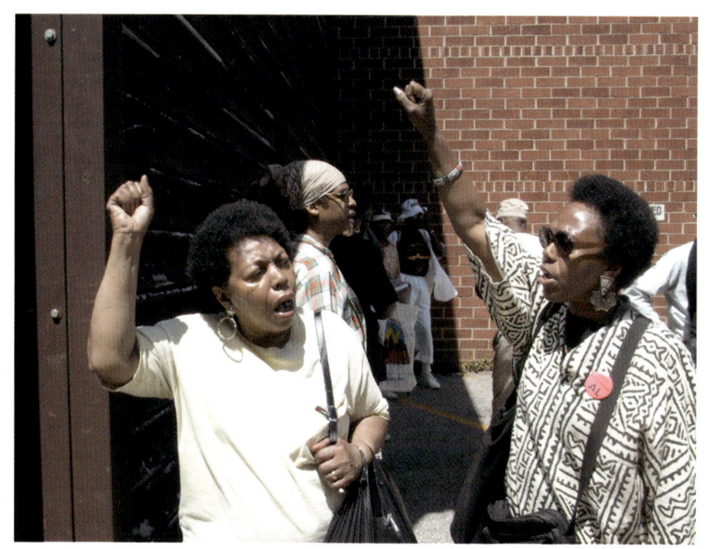

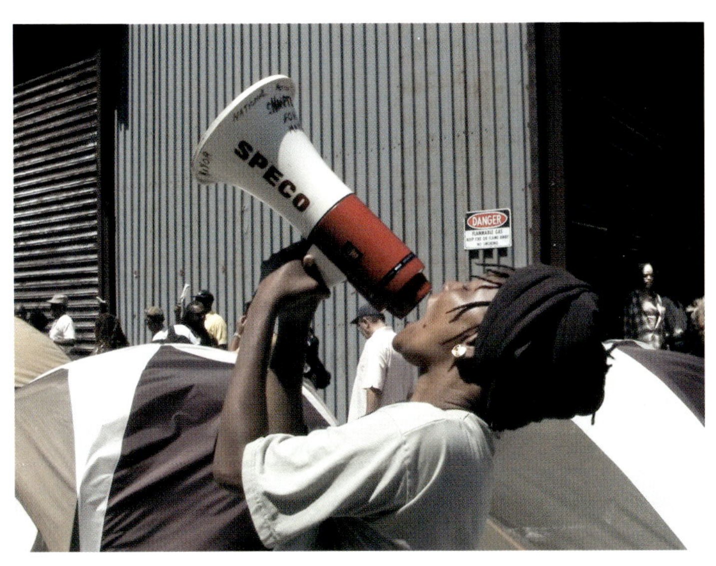
SPECO
DANGER

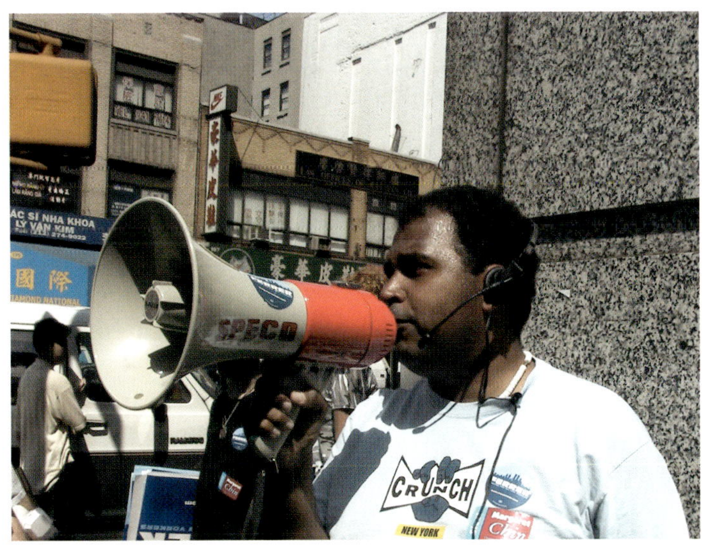
SPECO
CRUNCH
NEW YORK

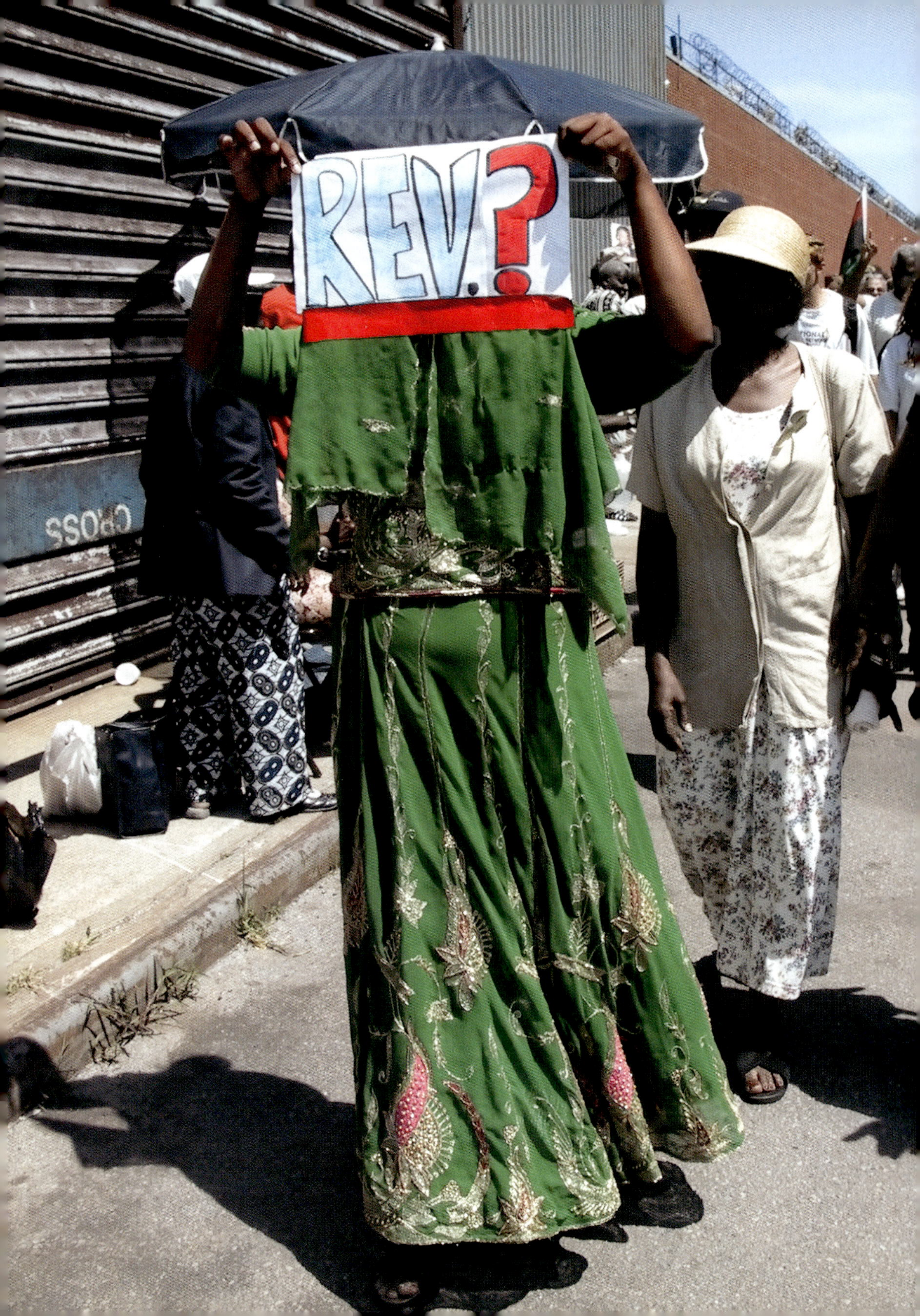
REV.?

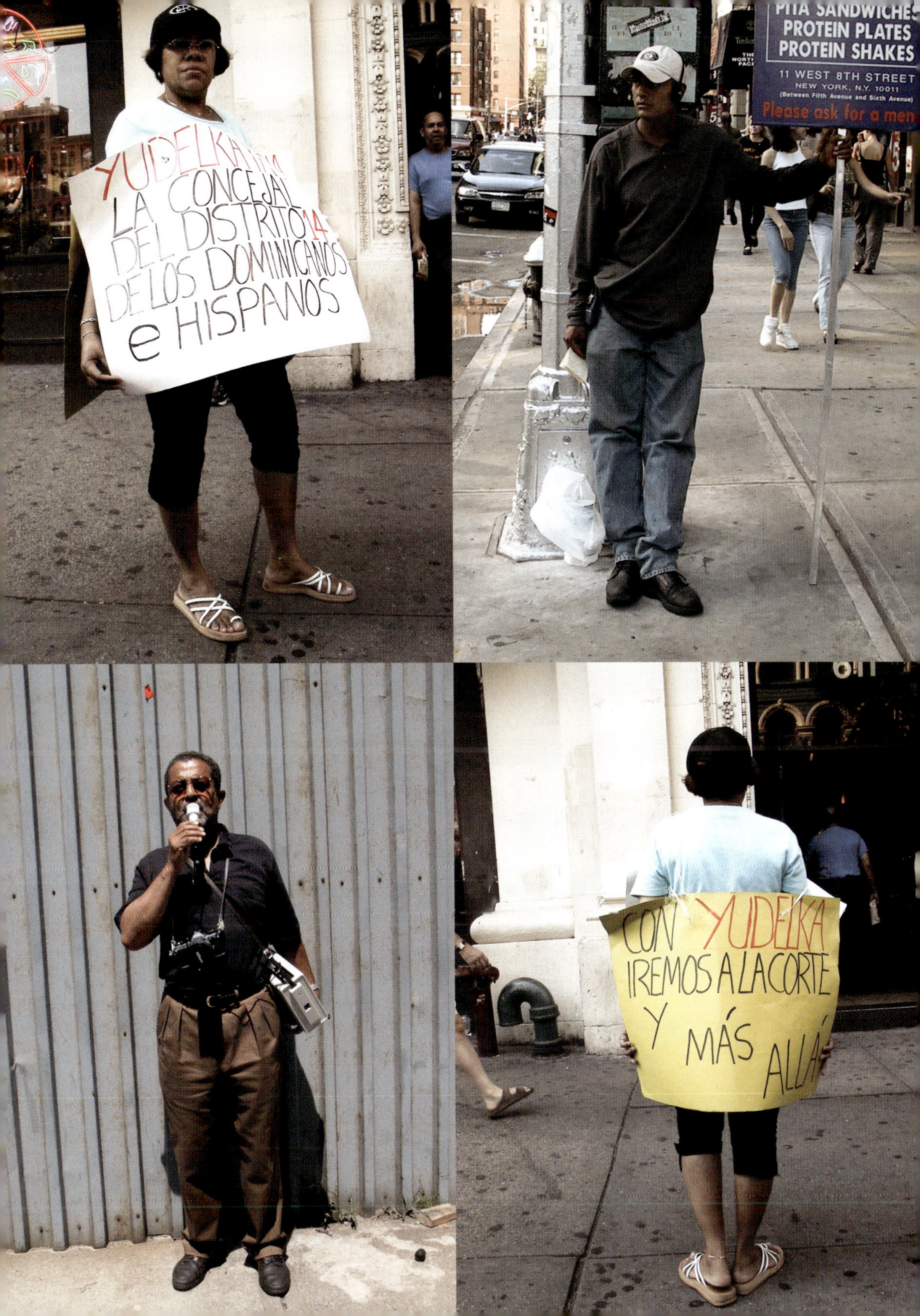
YUDELKA
LA CONCEJAL
DEL DISTRITO 14
DE LOS DOMINICANOS
e HISPANOS
PROTEIN PLATES
PROTEIN SHAKES
11 WEST 8TH STREET
NEW YORK, N.Y. 10011
(Between Fifth Avenue and Sixth Avenue)
Please ask for a
CON YUDELKA
IREMOS A LA CORTE
Y MÁS ALLÁ

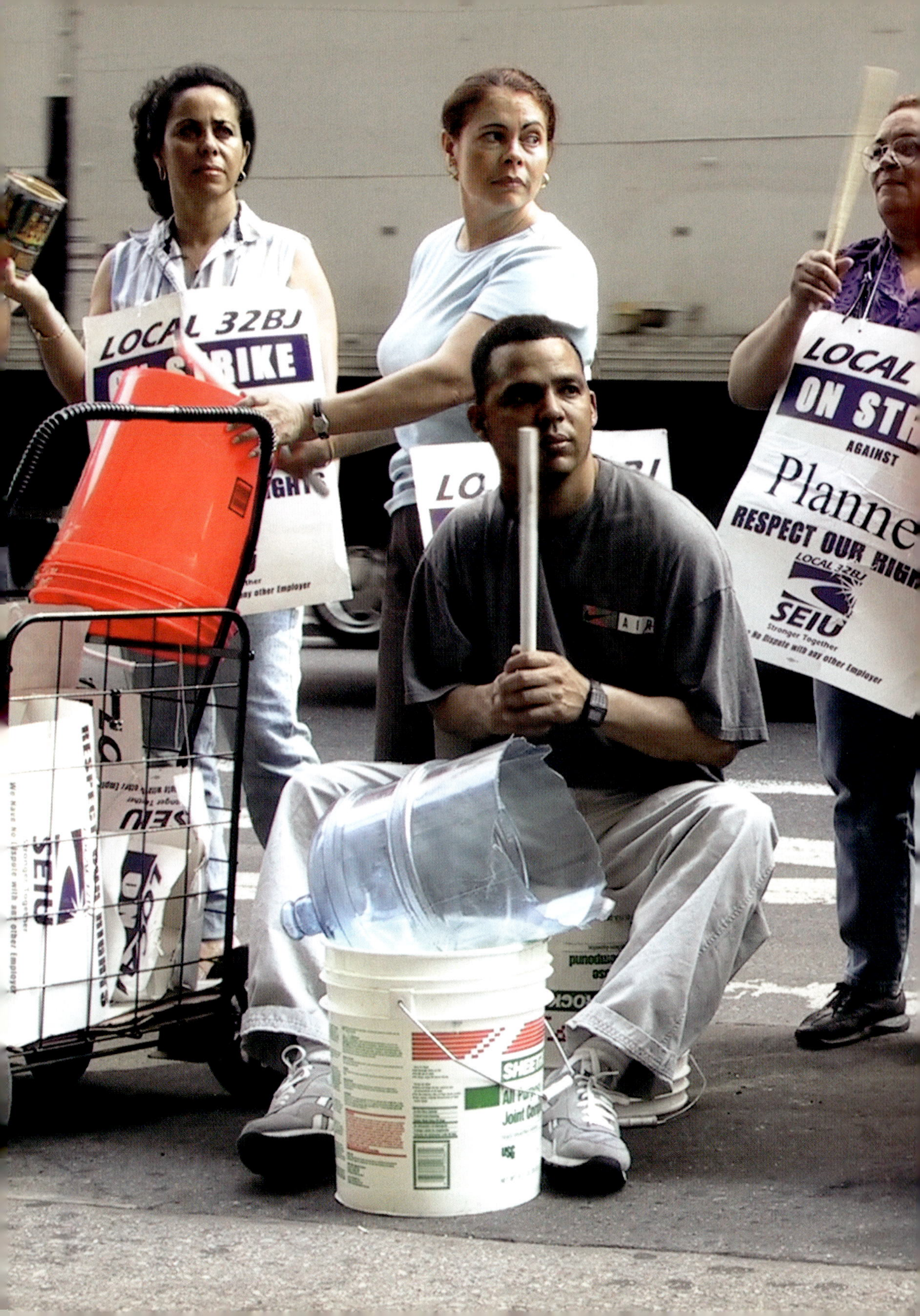
LOCAL 32BJ
LOCAL
AGAINST
LOCAL 32BJ
SEIU
Stronger Together

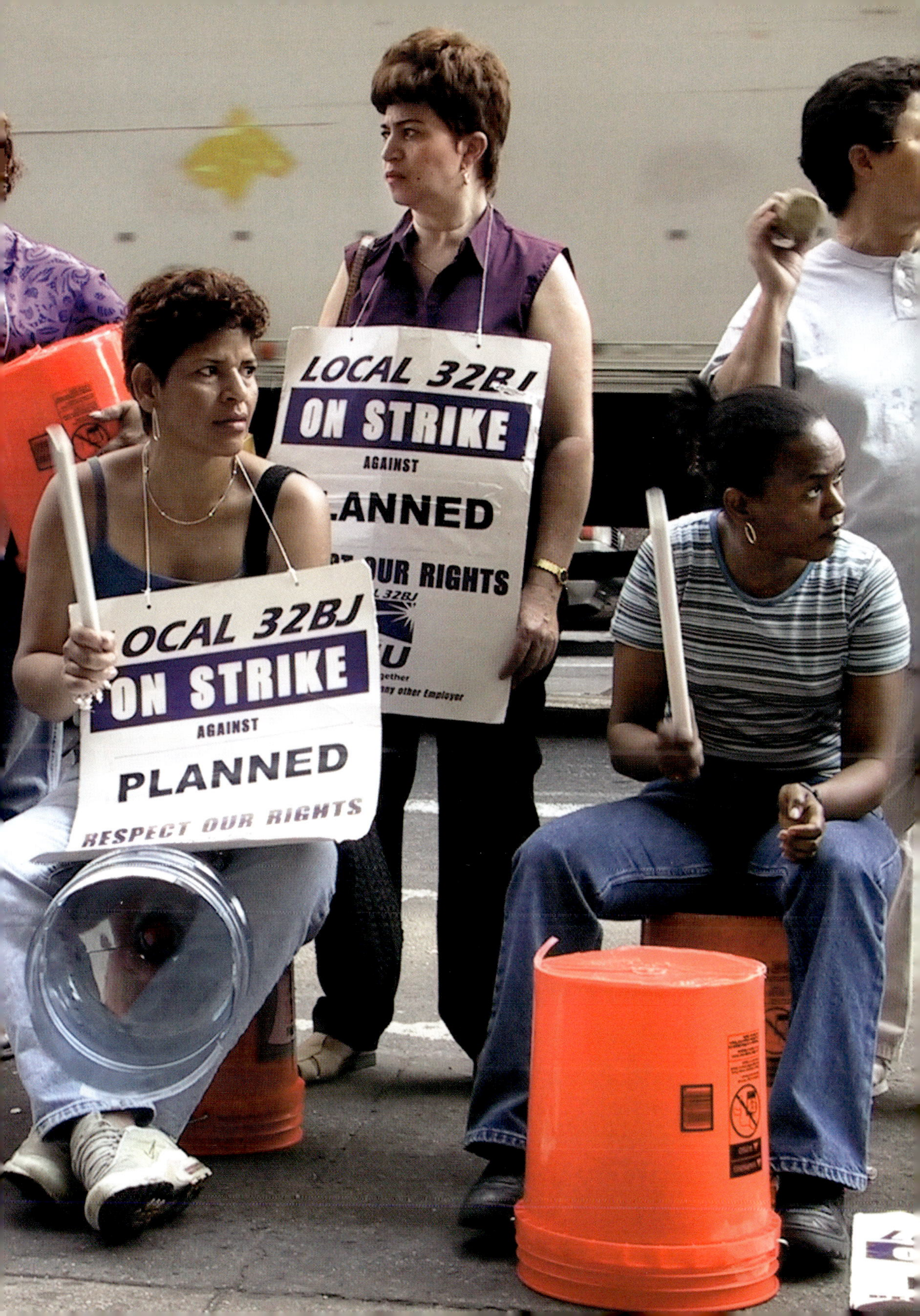
LOCAL 32BJ
ON STRIKE
AGAINST
LANNED
OUR RIGHTS
OCAL 32BJ
ON STRIKE
AGAINST
PLANNED
RESPECT OUR RIGHTS

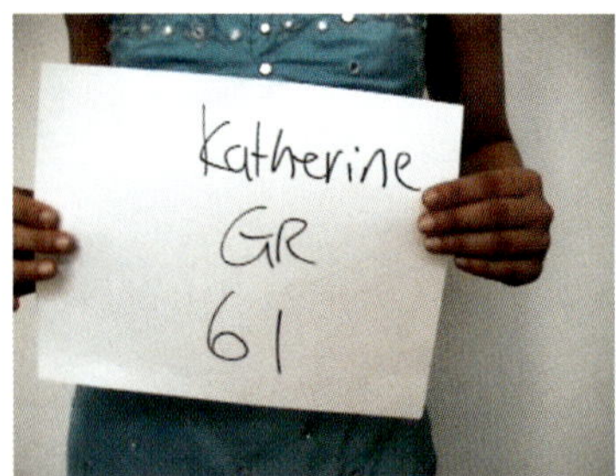
Katherine
GR
61
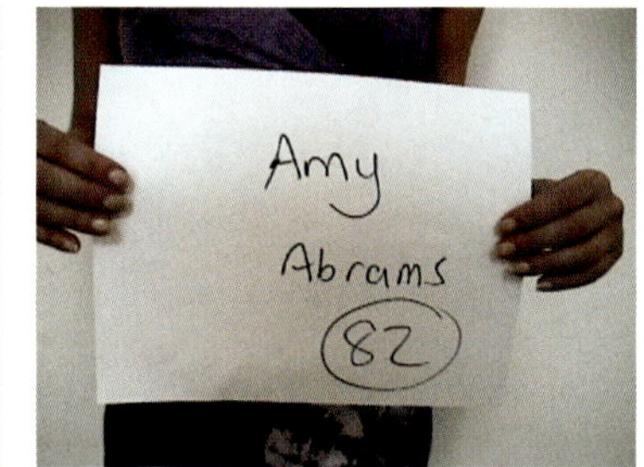
Amy
Abrams
82
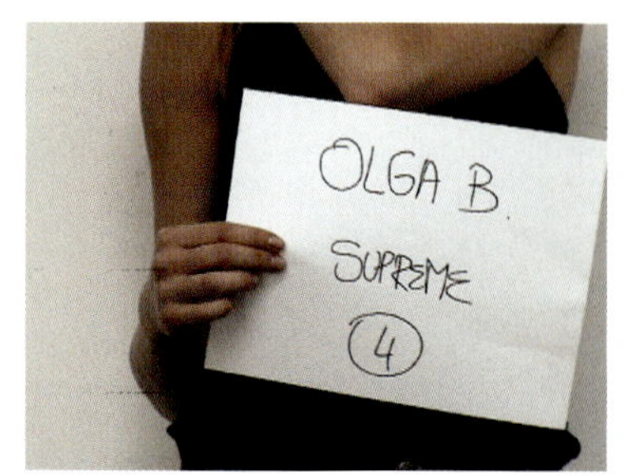
OLGA B.
SUPREME
4
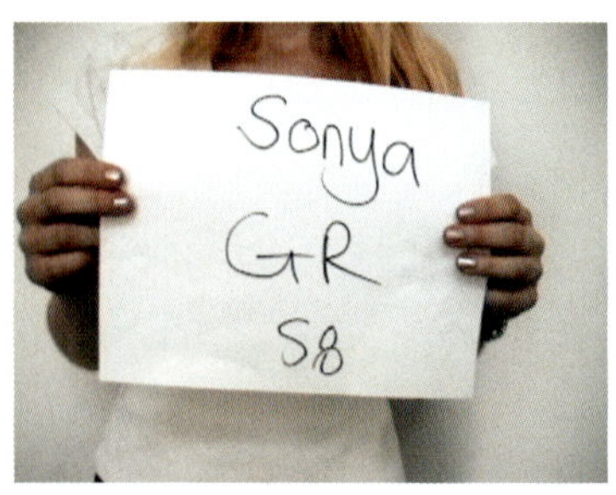
Sonya
GR
58
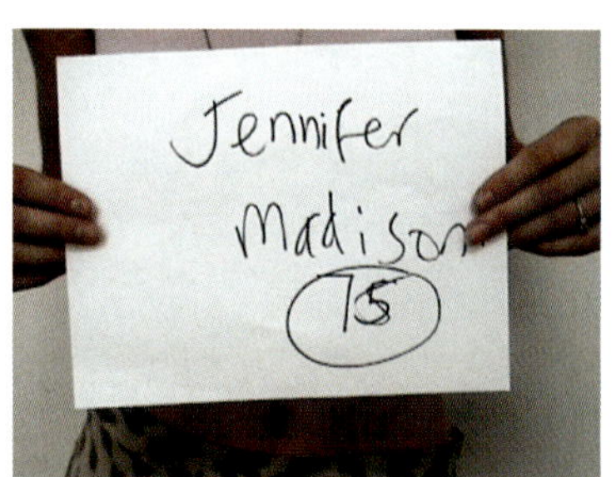
Jennifer
Madison
75
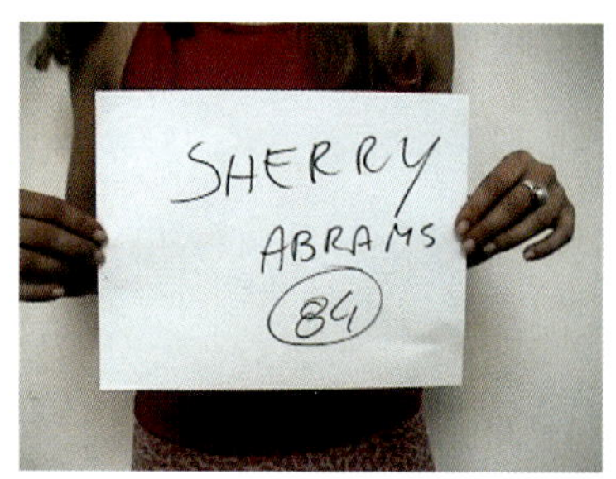
SHERRY
ABRAMS
84
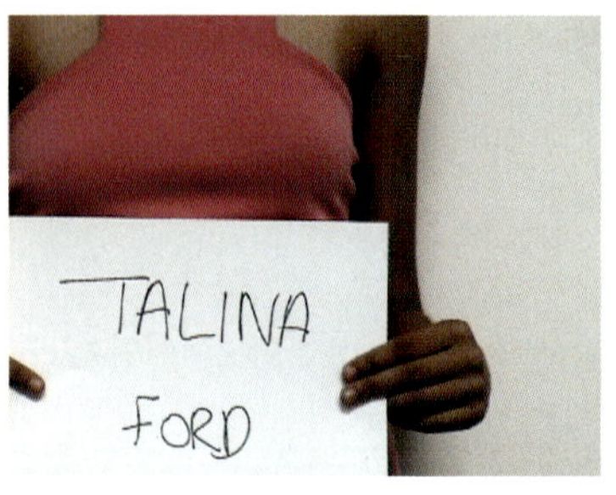
TALINA
FORD
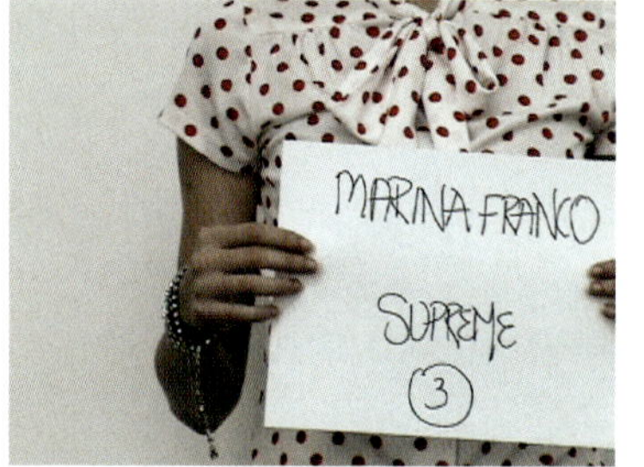
MARINA FRANCO
SUPREME
3
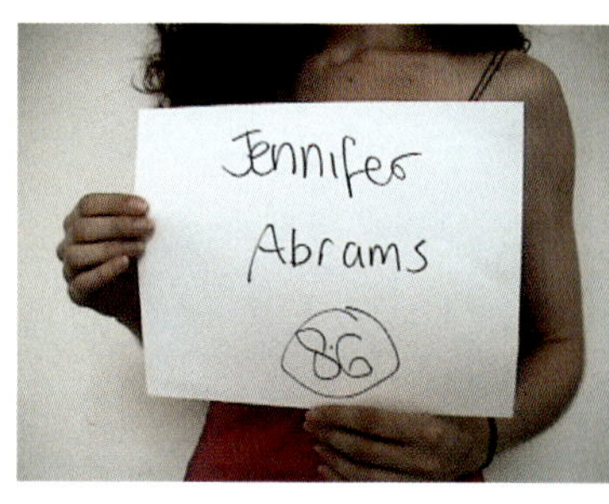
Jennifer
Abrams
86
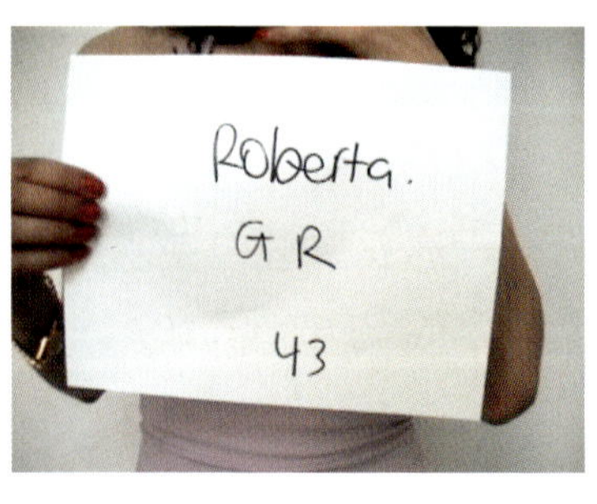
Roberta.
GR
43
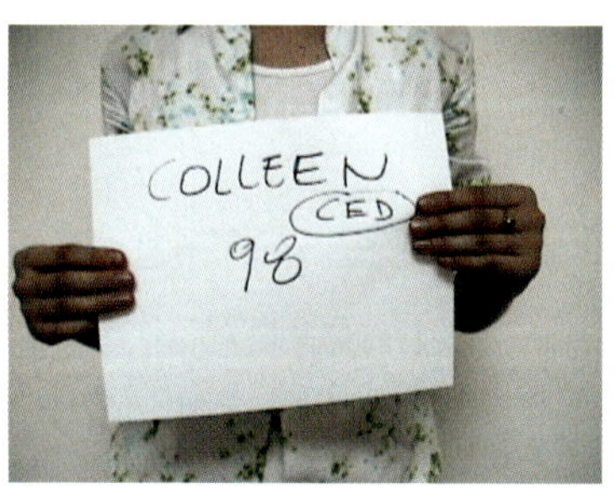
COLLEEN
CED
98
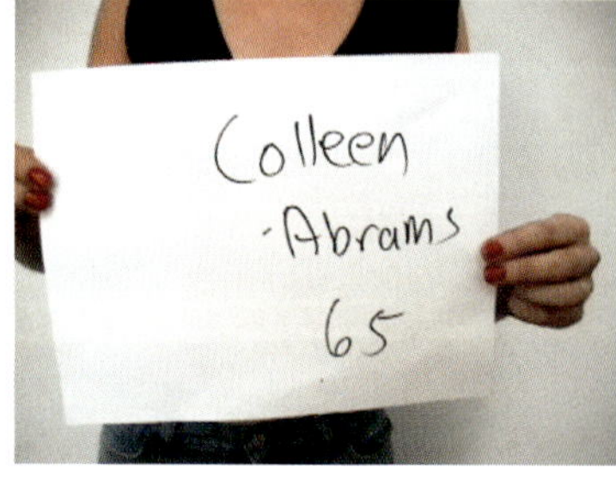
Colleen
Abrams
65
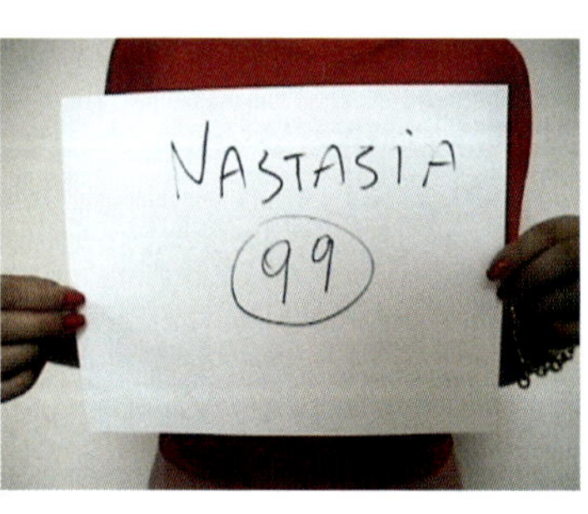
NASTASIA
99
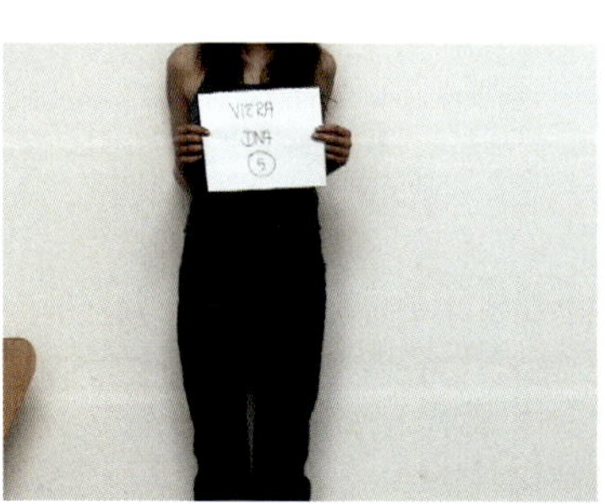
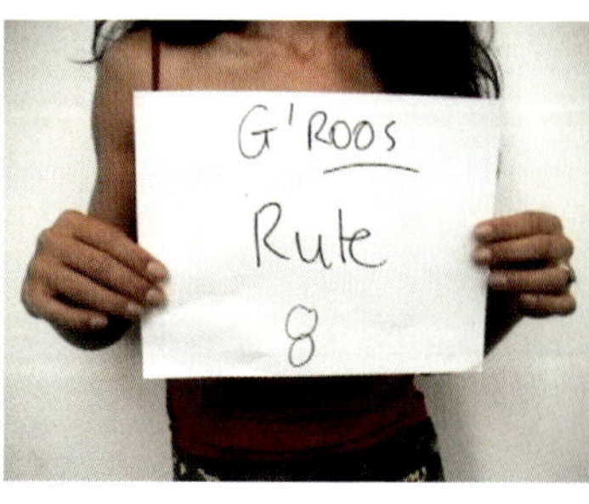
G'ROOS
Rute
8

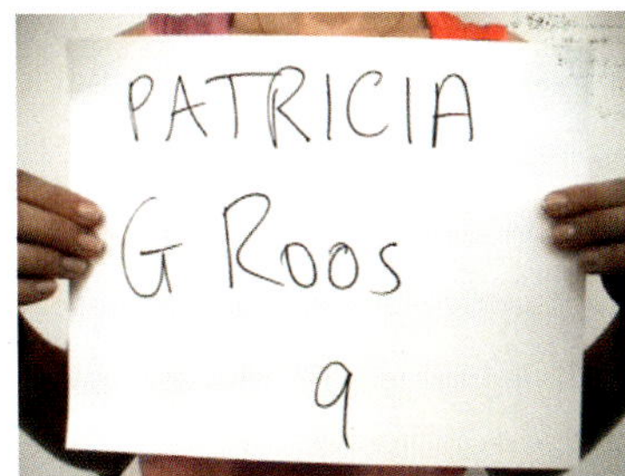
PATRICIA
G Roos
9

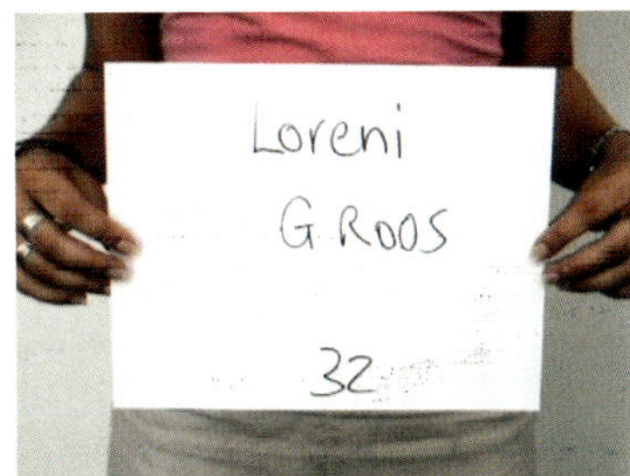
Loreni
G Roos
32

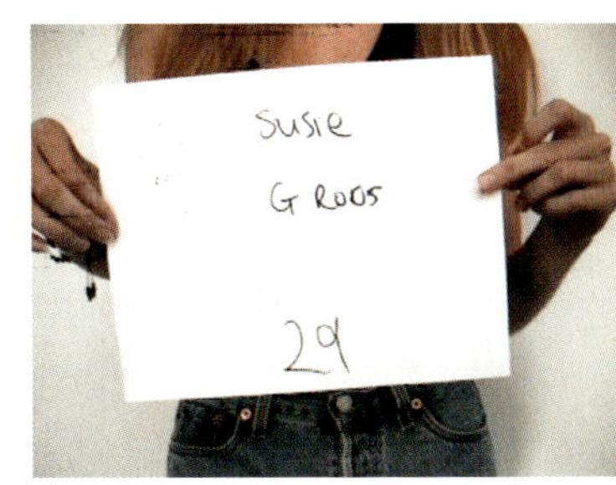
Susie
G Roos
29

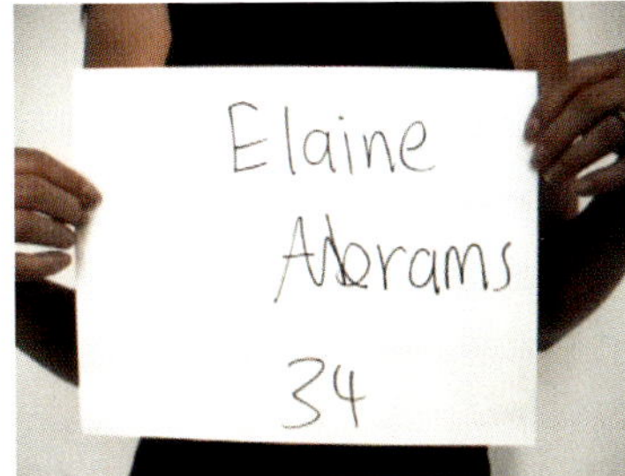
Elaine
Abrams
34

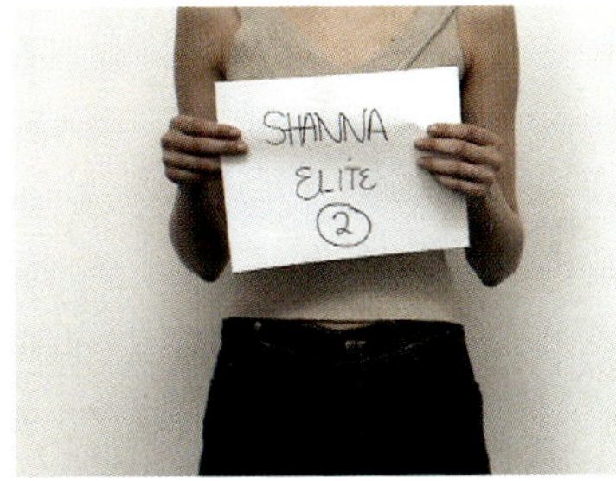
SHANNA
ELITE
2

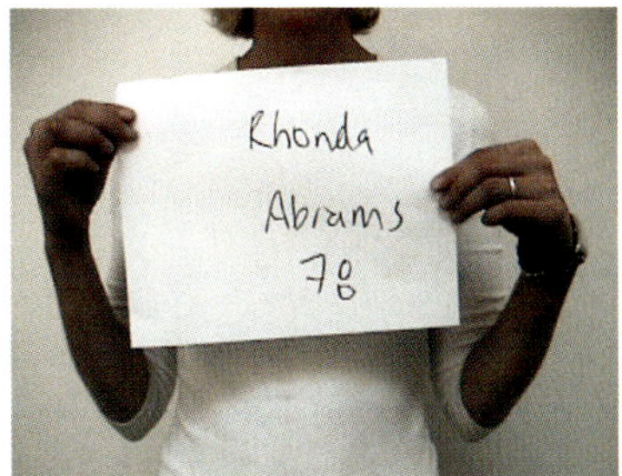
Rhonda
Abrams
78

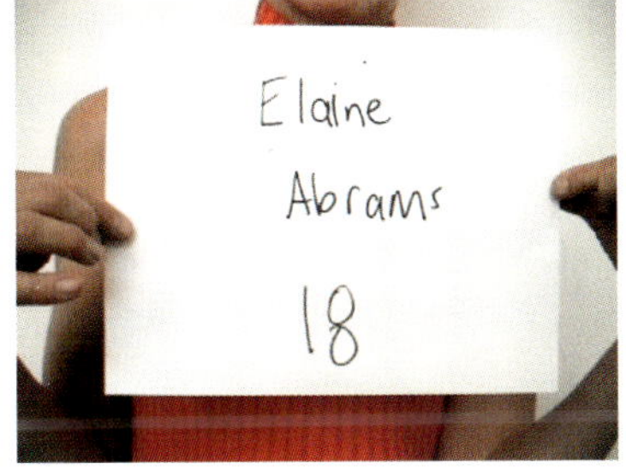
Elaine
Abrams
18

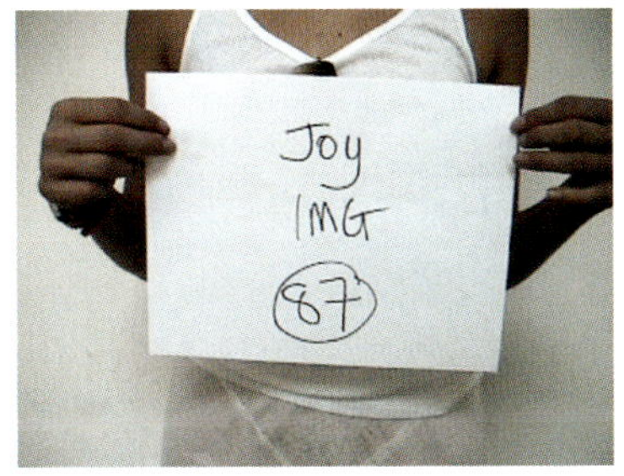
Joy
IMG
87

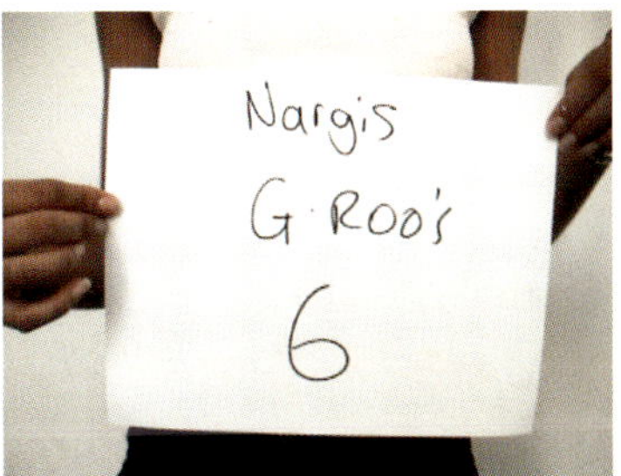
Nargis
G Roo's
6

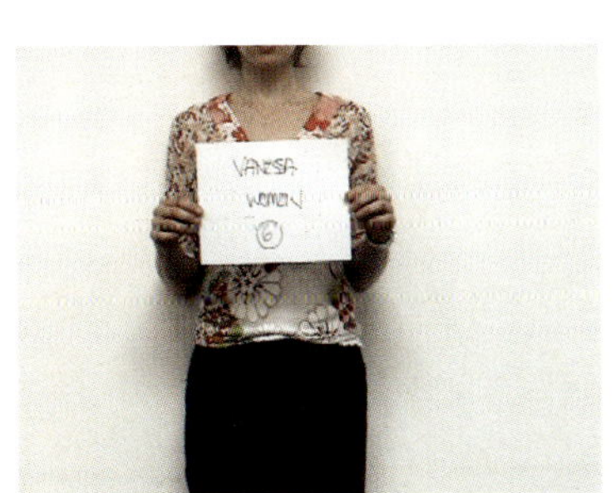
VANESA
WOMEN
6

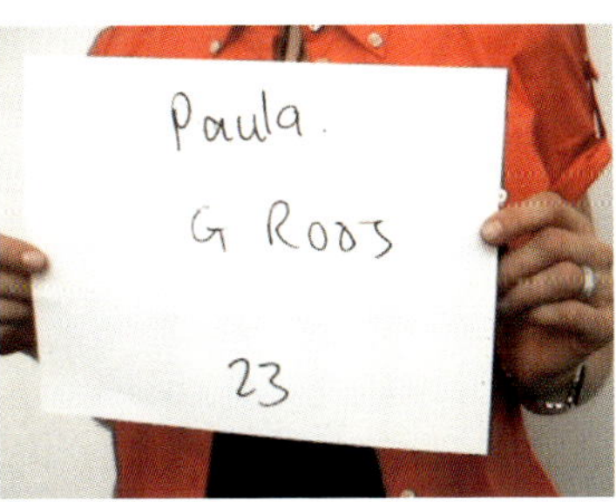
Paula
G Roos
23

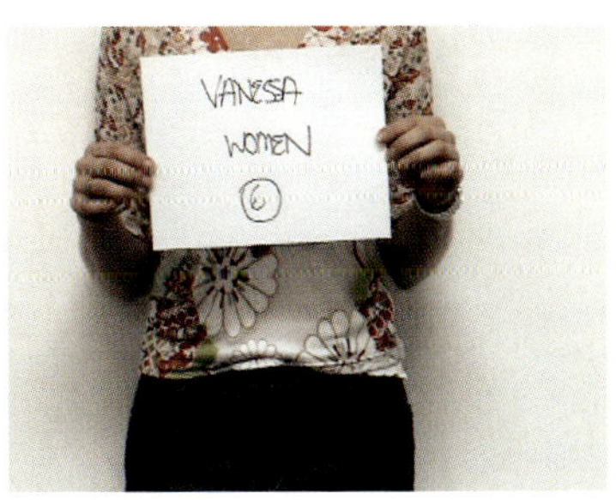
VANESA
WOMEN
6

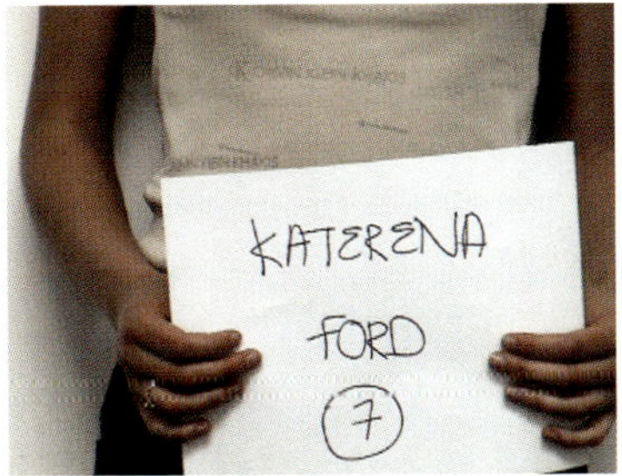
KATERENA
FORD
7

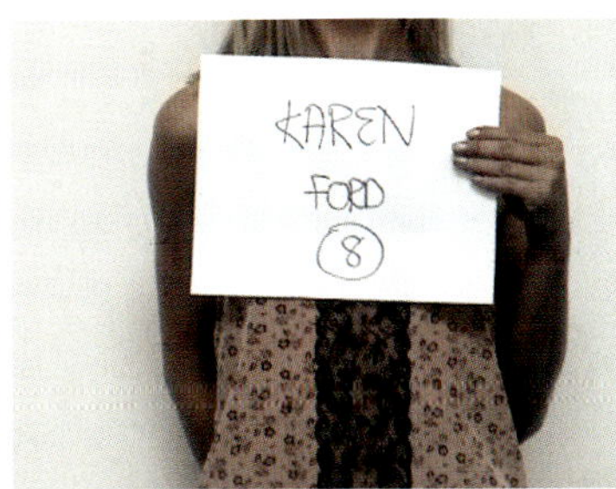
KAREN
FORD
8

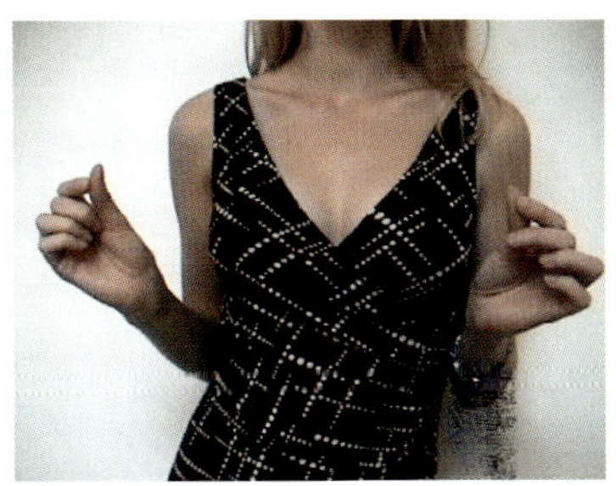

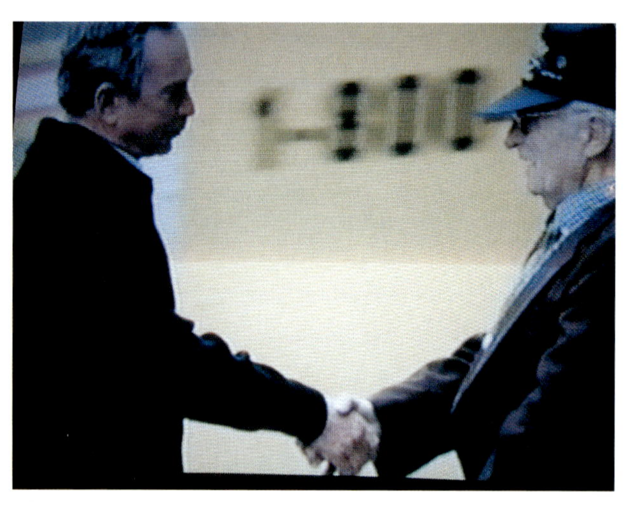
1-800

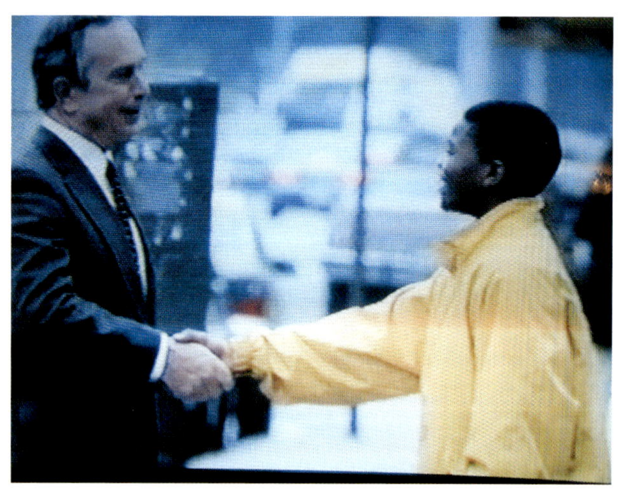

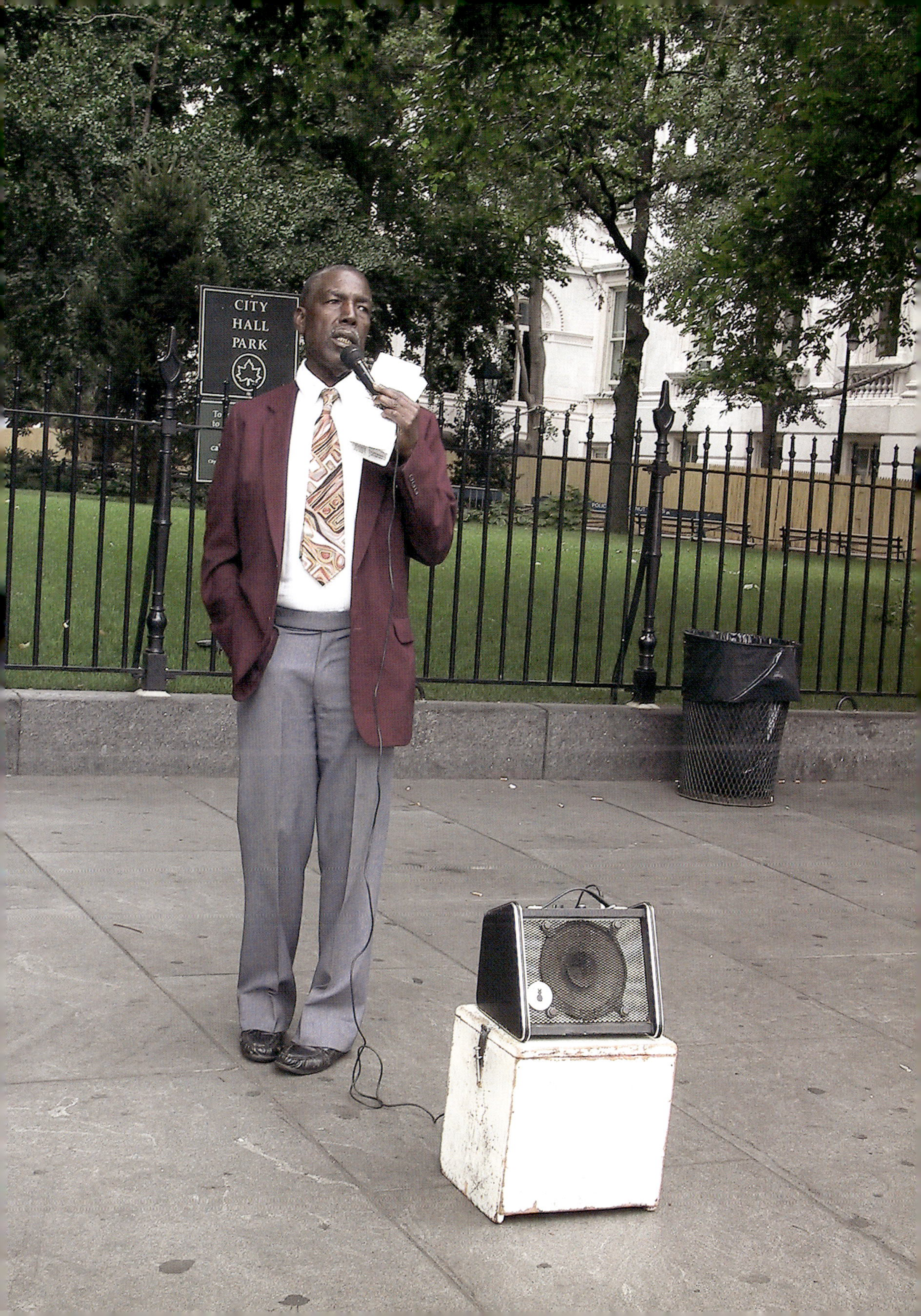
CITY
HALL
PARK

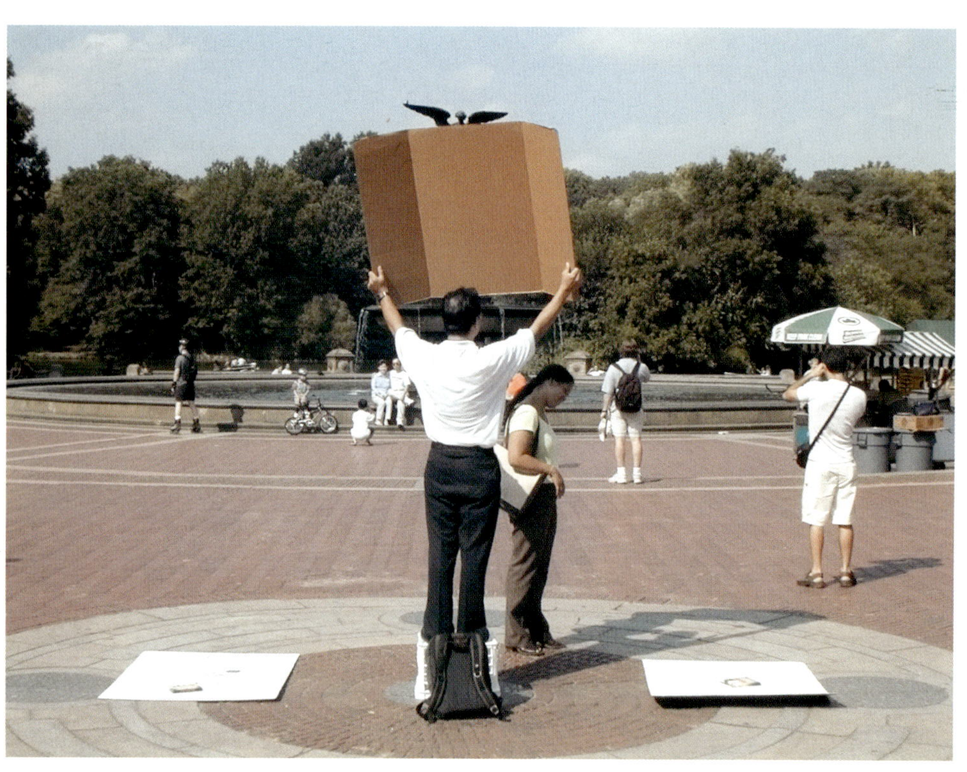

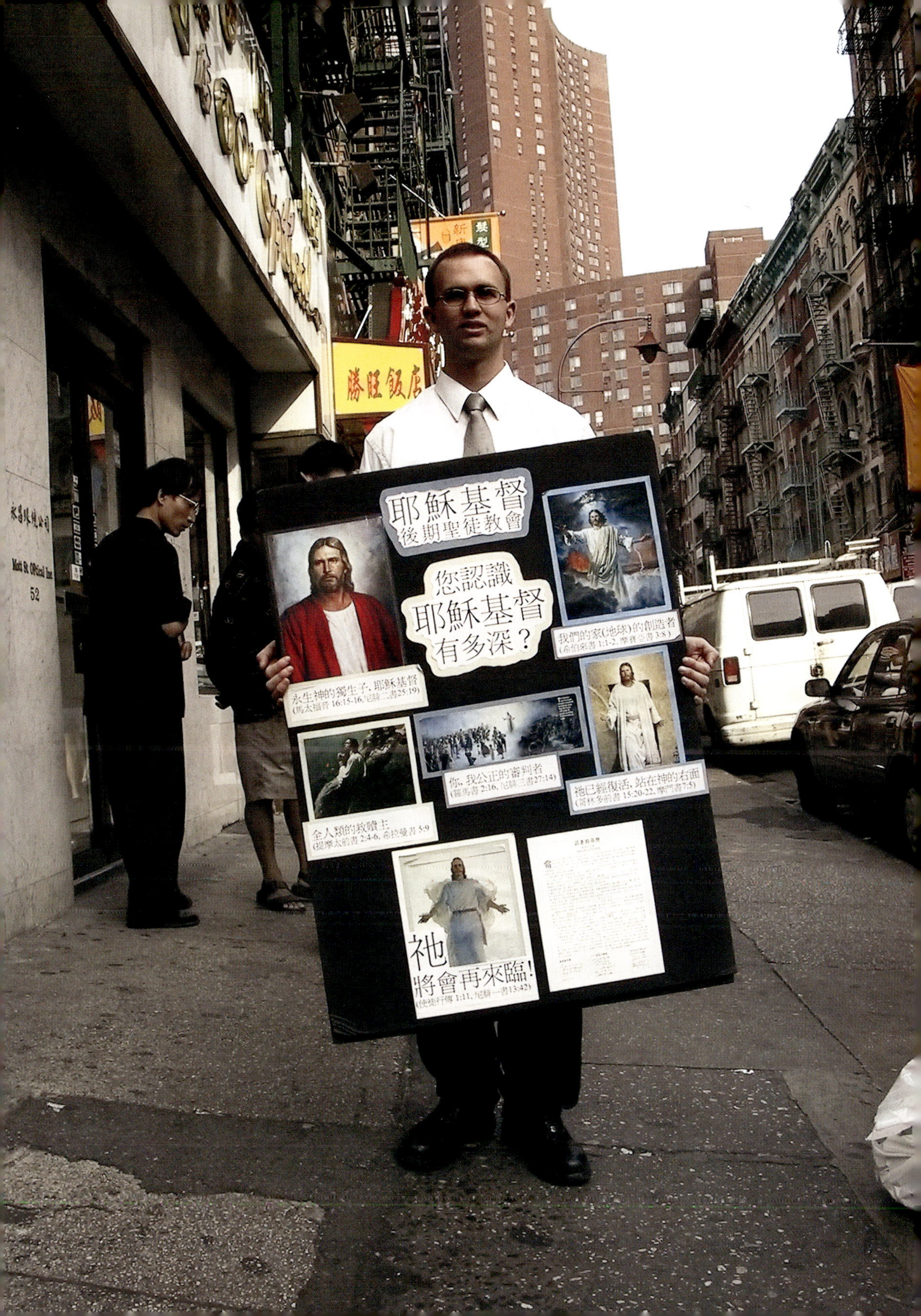
勝旺飯店
耶穌基督
後期聖徒教會
您認識
耶穌基督
有多深？
我們的家(地球)的創造者
(希伯來書 1:1-2, 摩賽亞書 3:8)
永生神的獨生子, 耶穌基督
(馬太福音 16:15-16, 尼腓二書25:19)
你, 我公正的審判者
(羅馬書 2:16, 尼腓三書27:14)
祂已經復活, 站在神的右面
(哥林多前書 15:20-22, 摩門書7:5)
全人類的救贖主
(提摩太前書 2:4-6, 希拉曼書 5:9)
祂
將會再來臨!
(使徒行傳 1:11, 尼腓一書13:42)

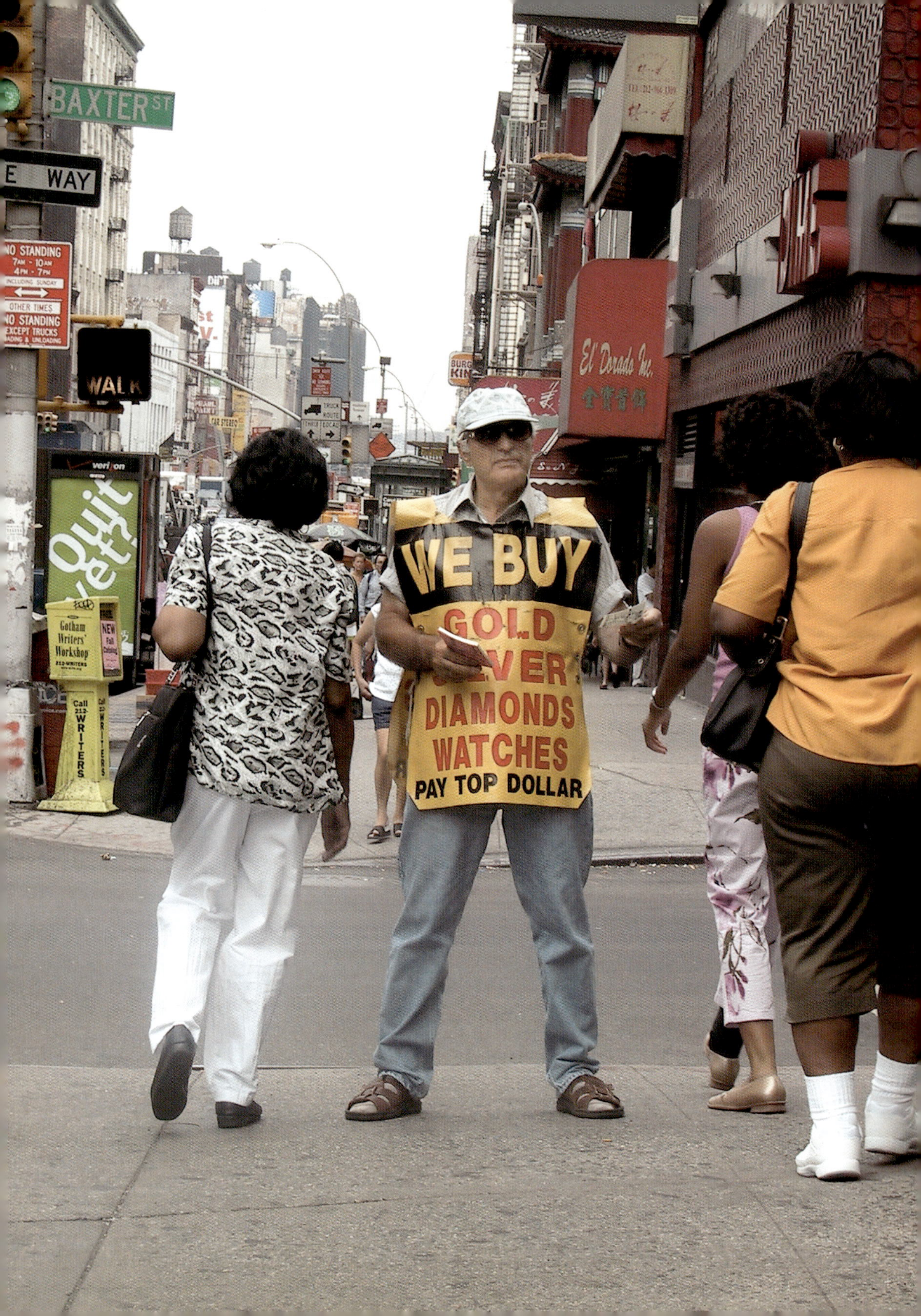

BAXTER ST
WAY
NO STANDING
7AM - 10AM
4PM - 7PM
INCLUDING SUNDAY
OTHER TIMES
NO STANDING
EXCEPT TRUCKS
WALK
verizon
Quit yet?
Gotham Writers' Workshop
NEW Fall Catalog
Call 212-WRITERS
El' Dorado Inc.
WE BUY
GOLD
DIAMONDS
WATCHES
PAY TOP DOLLAR

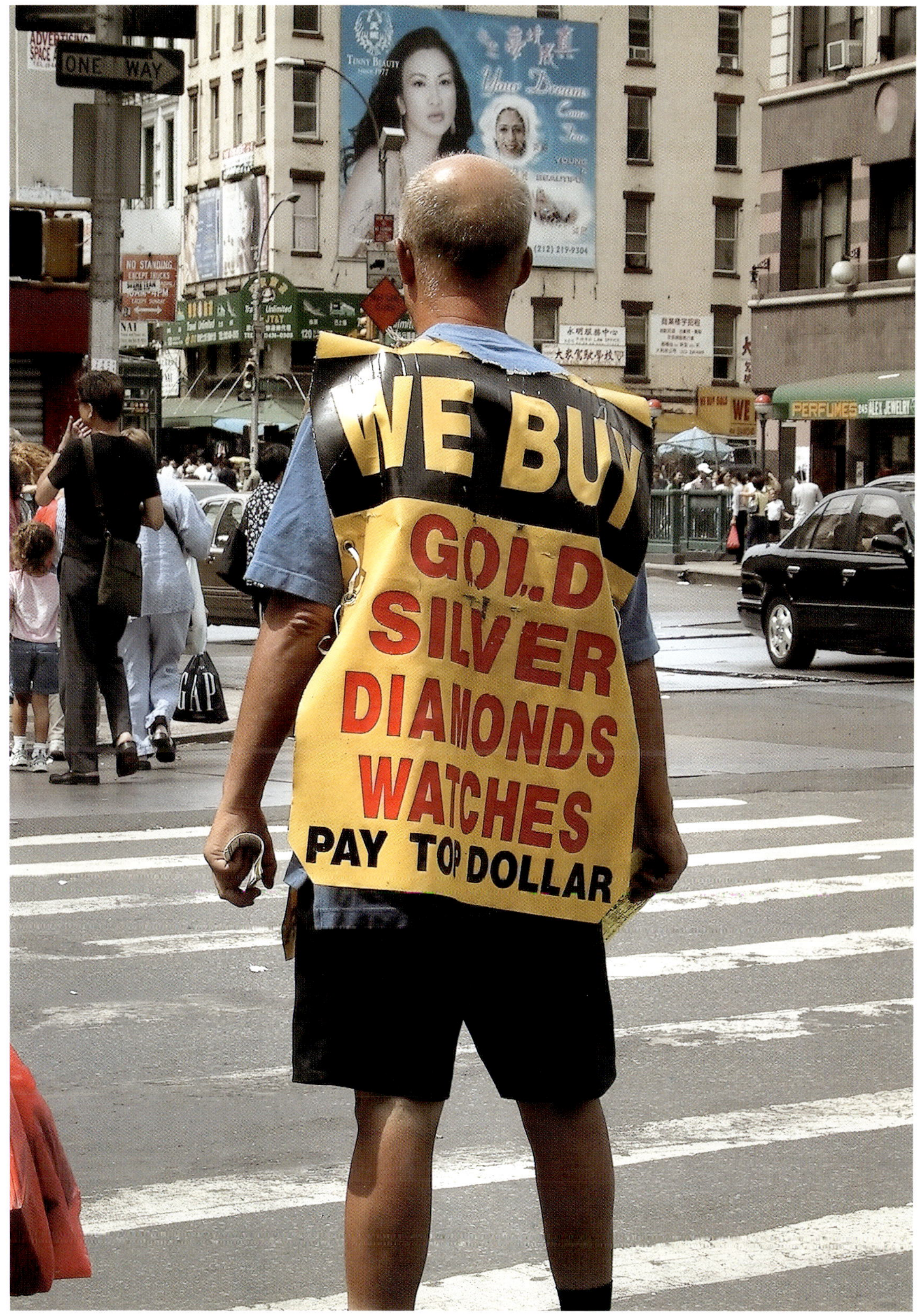
ONE WAY
Tinny Beauty
Your Dreams Come True
YOUNG & BEAUTIFUL
(212) 219-9304
NO STANDING
PERFUMES
ALEX JEWELRY
WE BUY
GOLD
SILVER
DIAMONDS
WATCHES
PAY TOP DOLLAR
GAP

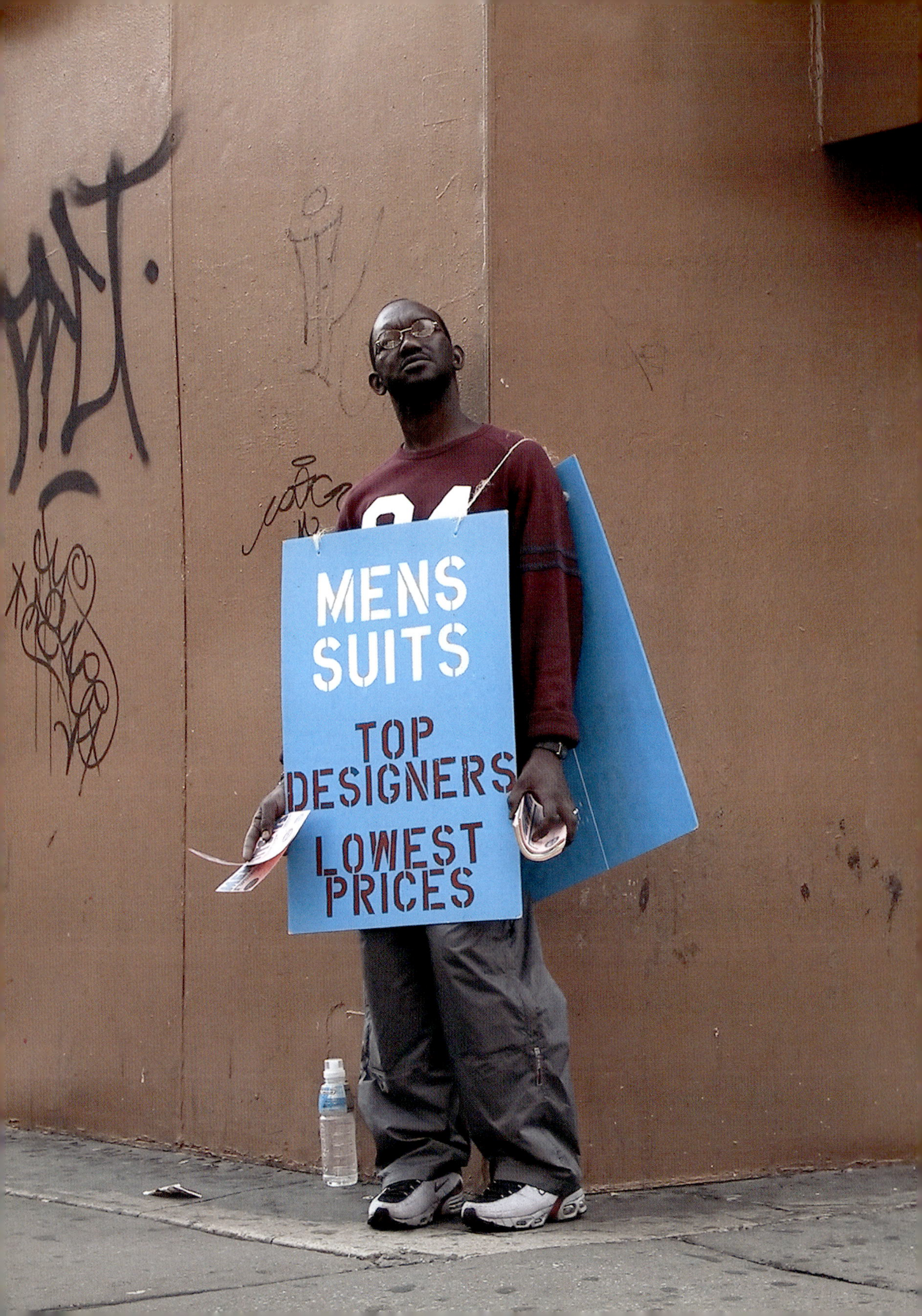
MENS
SUITS
TOP
DESIGNERS
LOWEST
PRICES

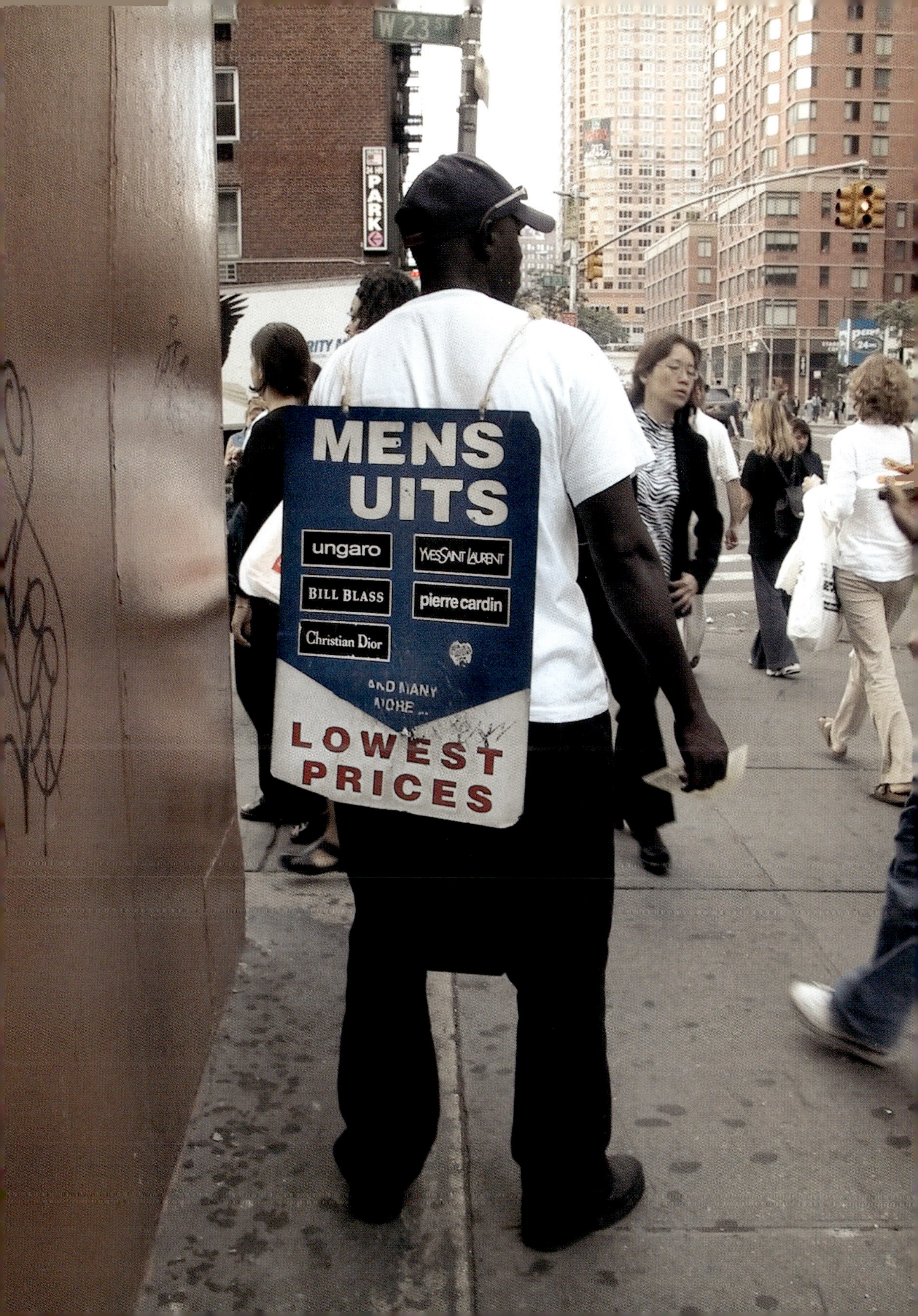
W 23 ST
PARK
MENS
UITS
ungaro
YVES SAINT LAURENT
BILL BLASS
pierre cardin
Christian Dior
AND MANY MORE ...
LOWEST PRICES

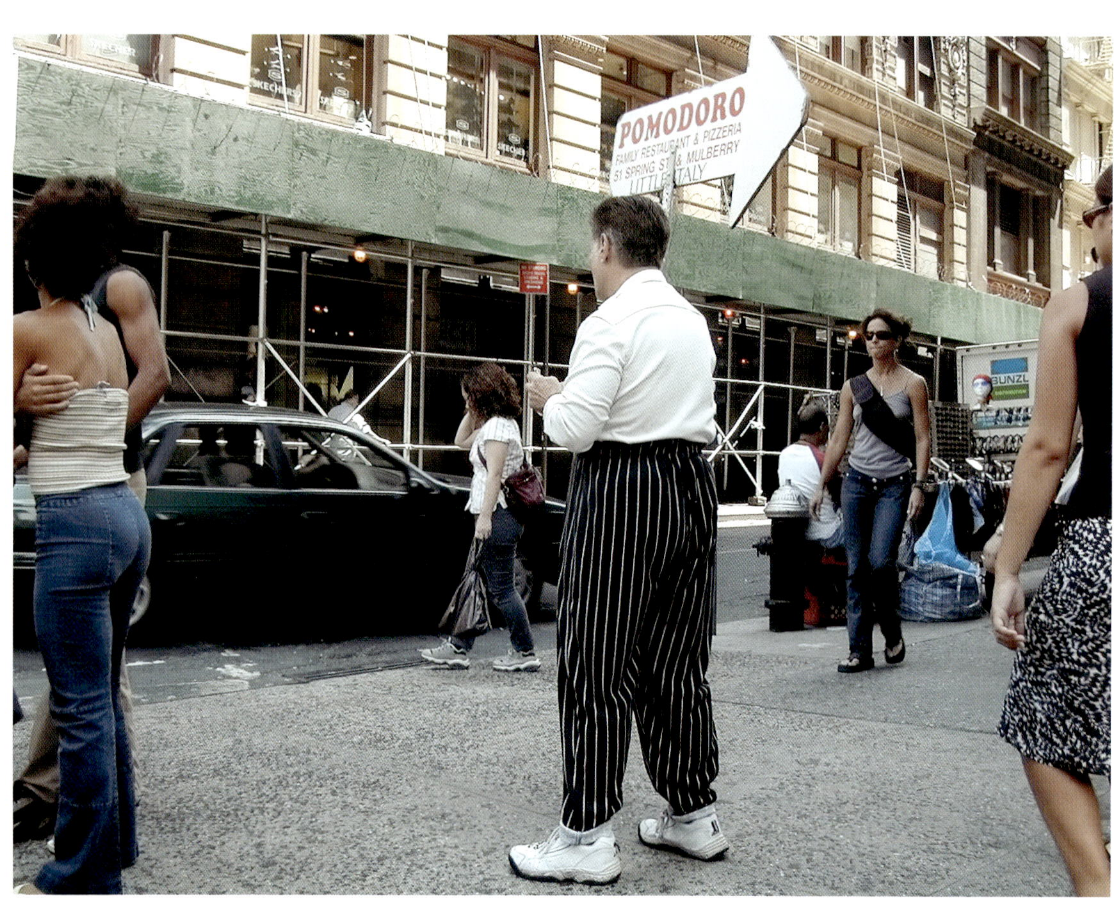
POMODORO
FAMILY RESTAURANT & PIZZERIA
51 SPRING ST & MULBERRY
LITTLE ITALY
BUNZL

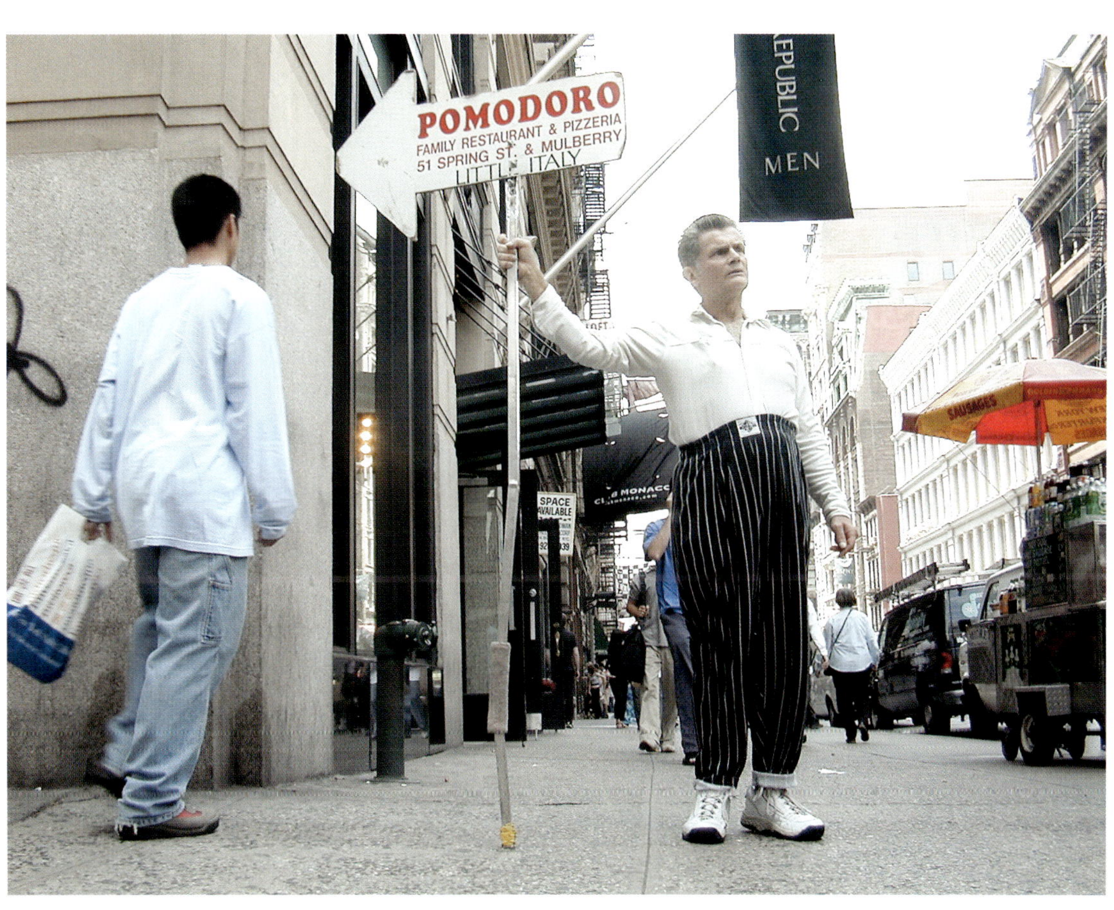
POMODORO
FAMILY RESTAURANT & PIZZERIA
51 SPRING ST. & MULBERRY
LITTLE ITALY
REPUBLIC
MEN
SPACE AVAILABLE
SAUSAGES

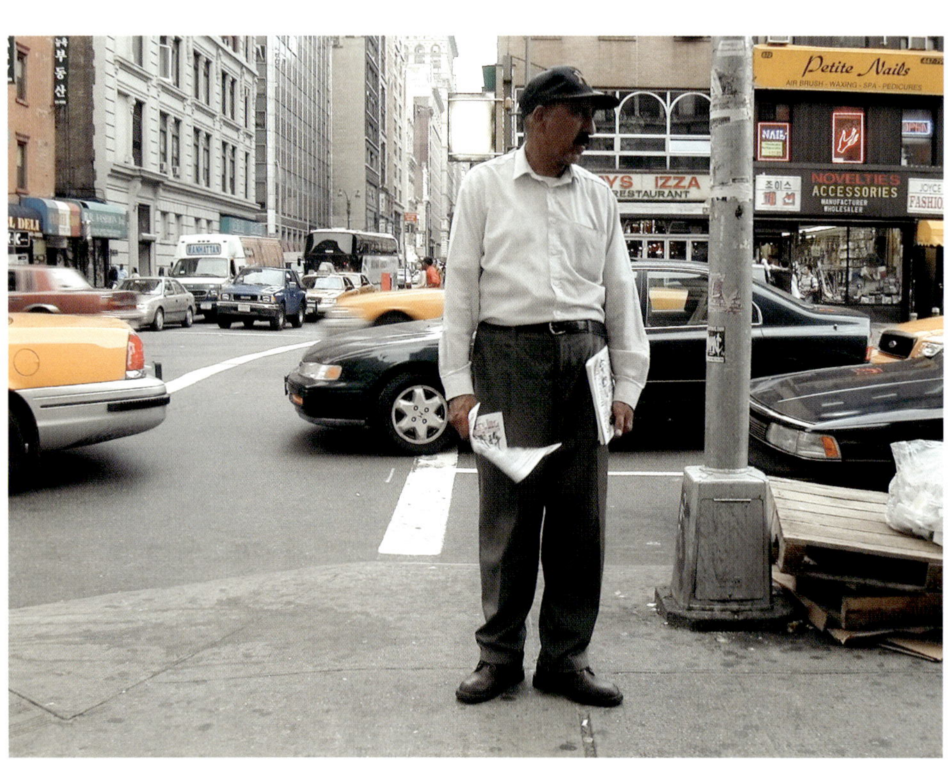
Petite Nails
AIR BRUSH - WAXING - SPA - PEDICURES
NOVELTIE'S
ACCESSORIES
MANUFACTURER
WHOLESALER
RESTAURANT
MANHATTAN

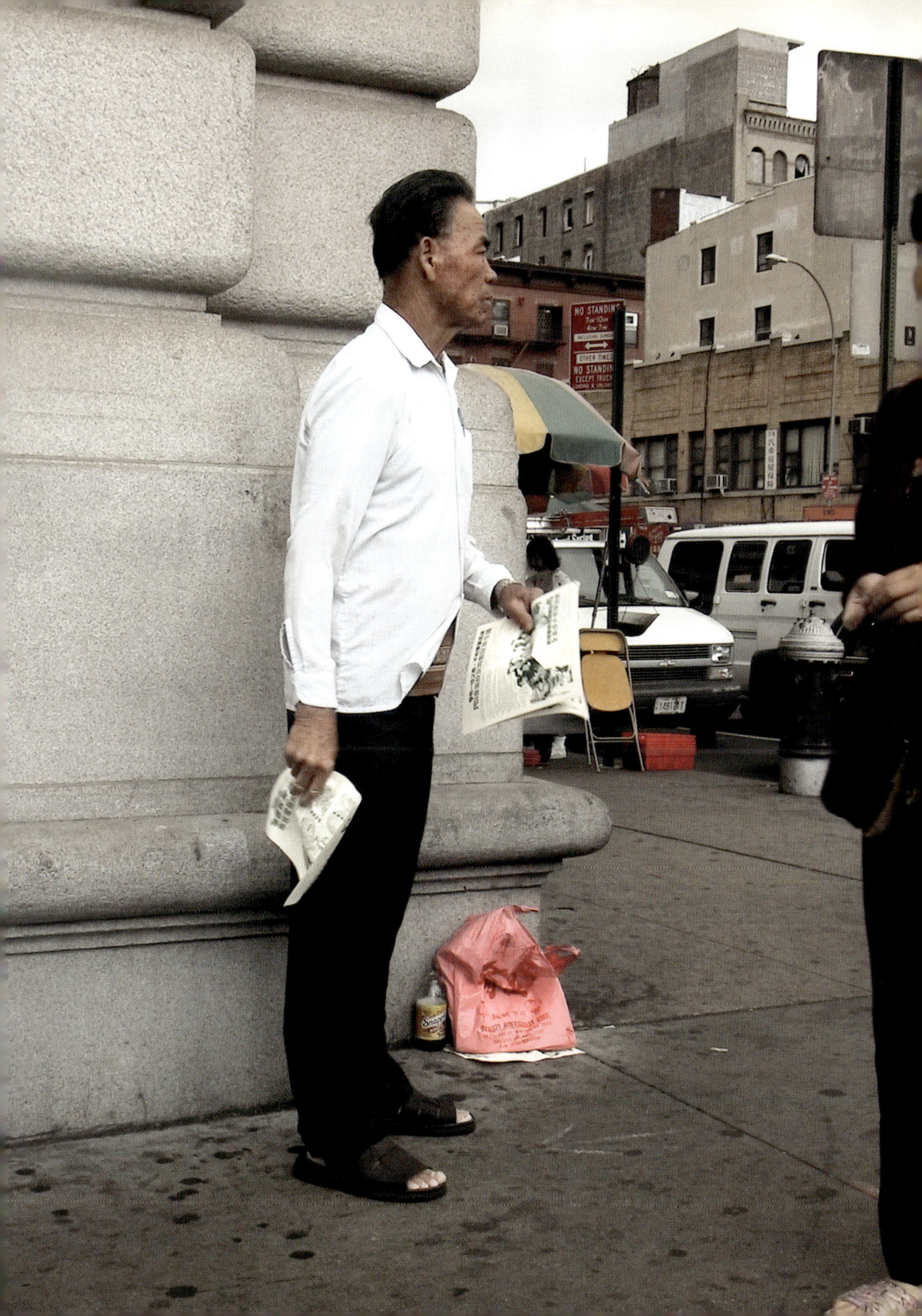

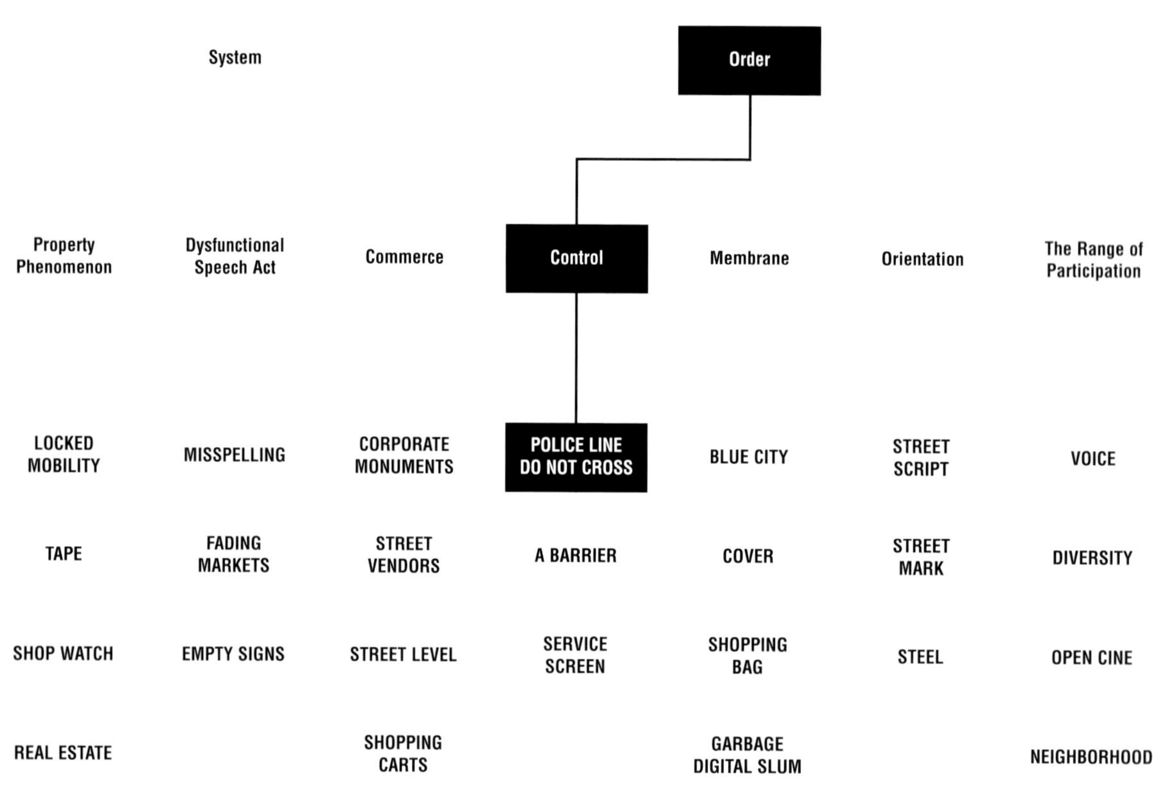

System
Order
Control
Property Phenomenon
Dysfunctional Speech Act
Commerce
Membrane
Orientation
The Range of Participation
LOCKED MOBILITY
MISSPELLING
CORPORATE MONUMENTS
POLICE LINE DO NOT CROSS
BLUE CITY
STREET SCRIPT
VOICE
TAPE
FADING MARKETS
STREET VENDORS
A BARRIER
COVER
STREET MARK
DIVERSITY
SHOP WATCH
EMPTY SIGNS
STREET LEVEL
SERVICE SCREEN
SHOPPING BAG
STEEL
OPEN CINE
REAL ESTATE
SHOPPING CARTS
GARBAGE DIGITAL SLUM
NEIGHBORHOOD

Identity

Alternative Media

Habitual Reinterpretation

POLICE LINE DO NOT CROSS

Exclusion from Wealth requires Force

CAR DOOR

PUBLIC CHAIRS

LABELING.

PLASTIC CRATES

POLE POST

STANDPIPES

PRAY JESUS

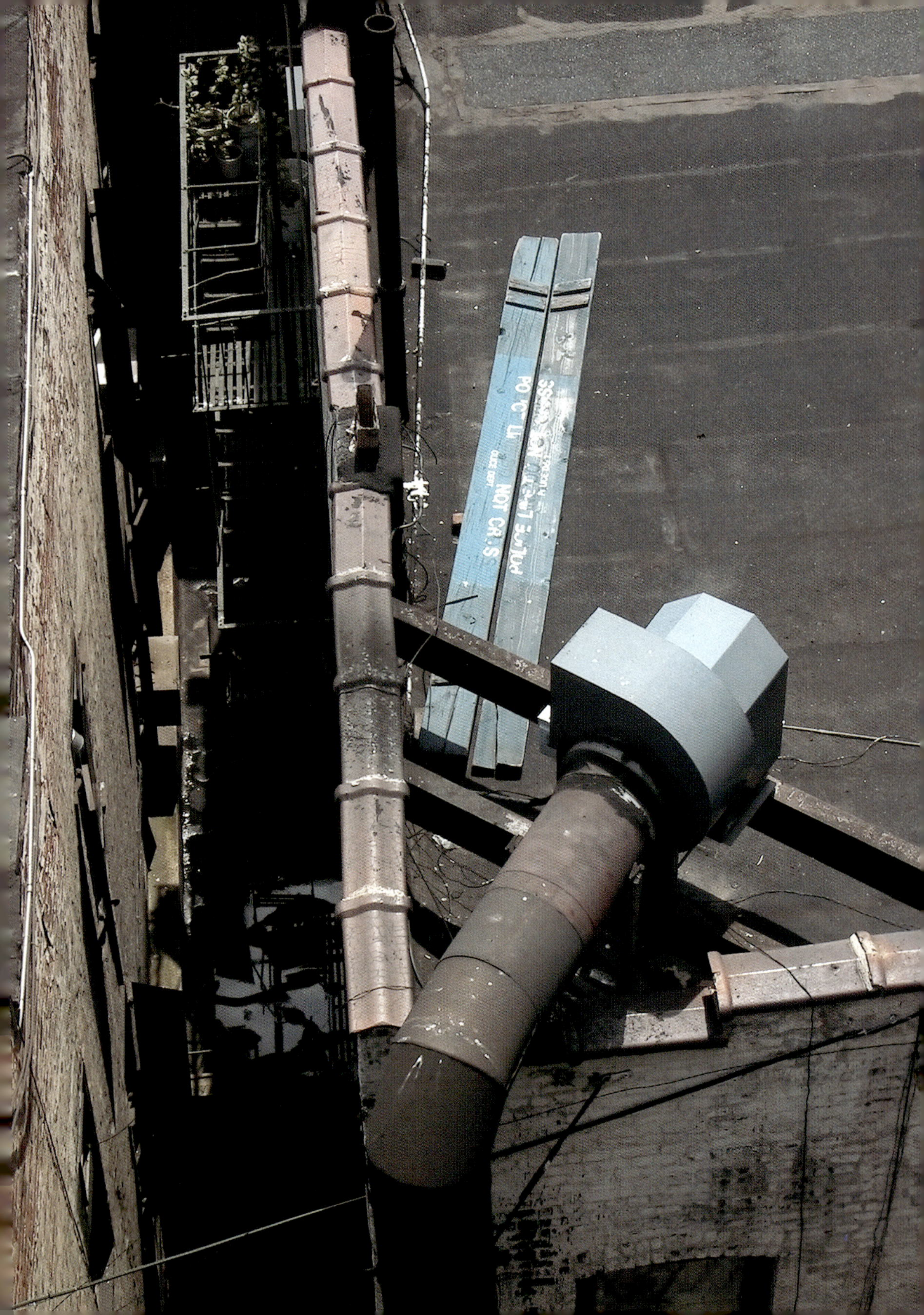

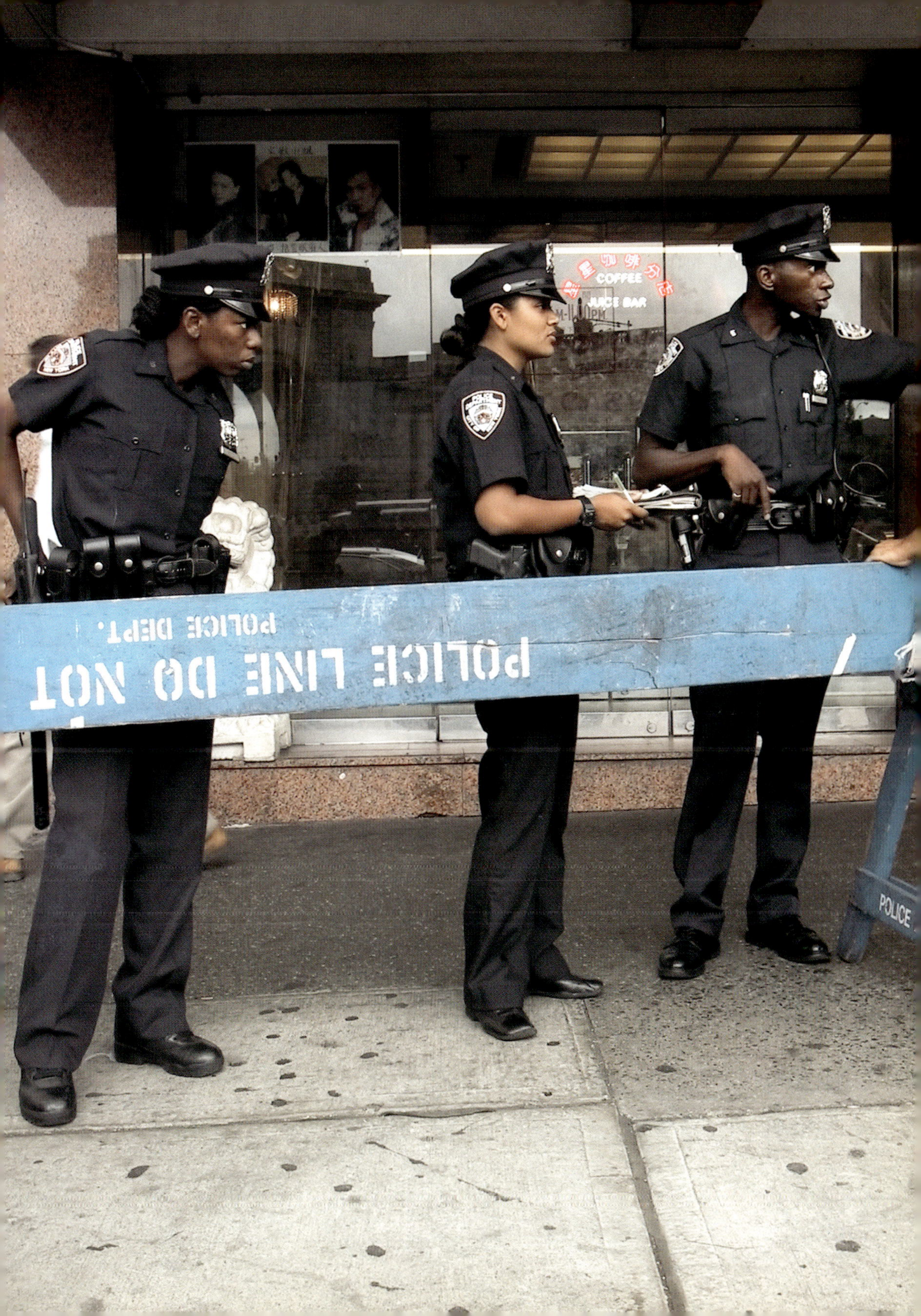
COFFEE
JUICE BAR
POLICE DEPT.
POLICE LINE DO NOT
POLICE

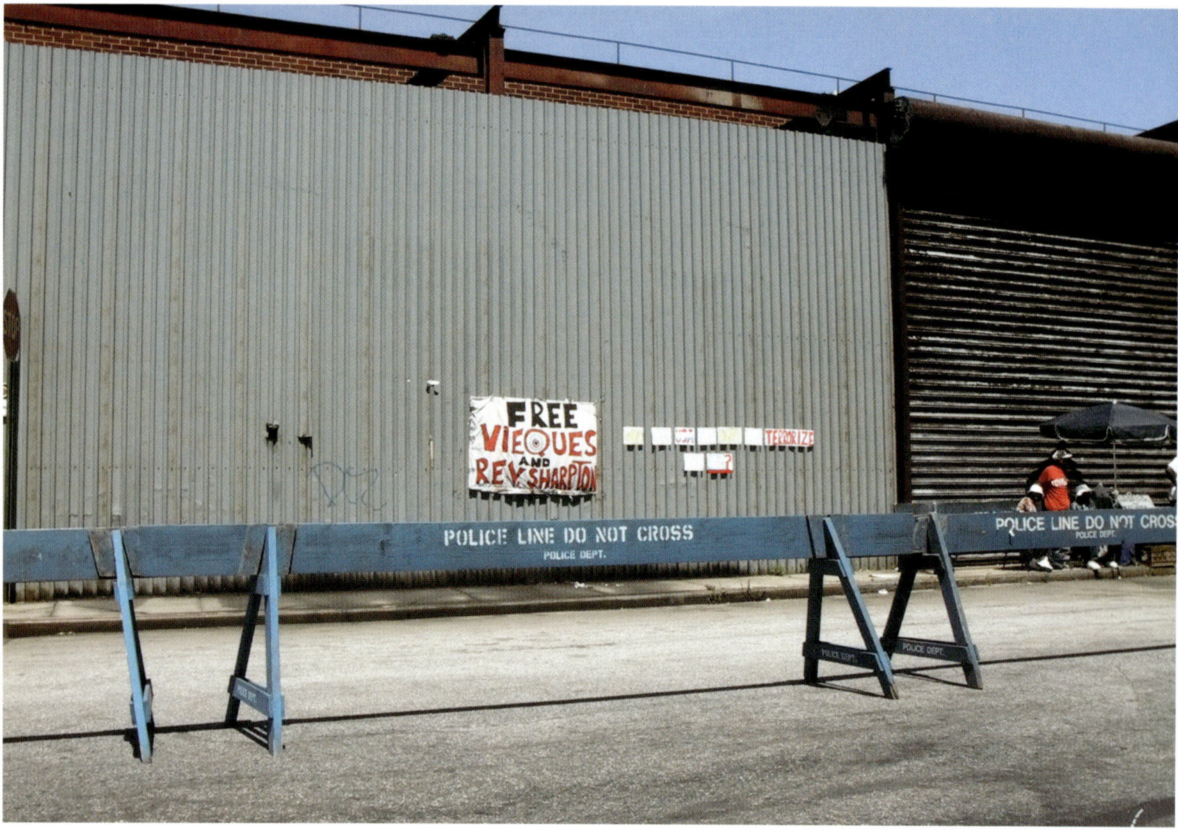

FREE
VIEQUES
AND
REV SHARPTON
TERRORIZE
POLICE LINE DO NOT CROSS
POLICE DEPT.

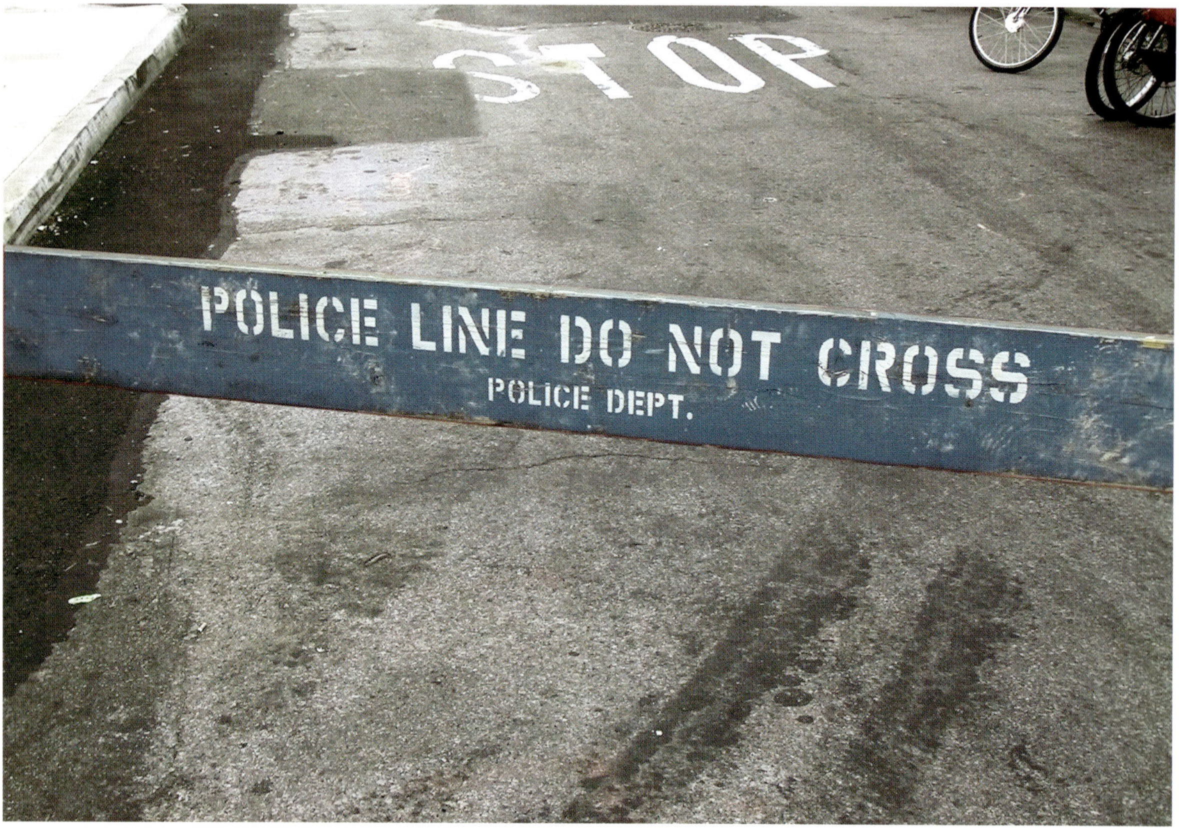

STOP
POLICE LINE DO NOT CROSS
POLICE DEPT.

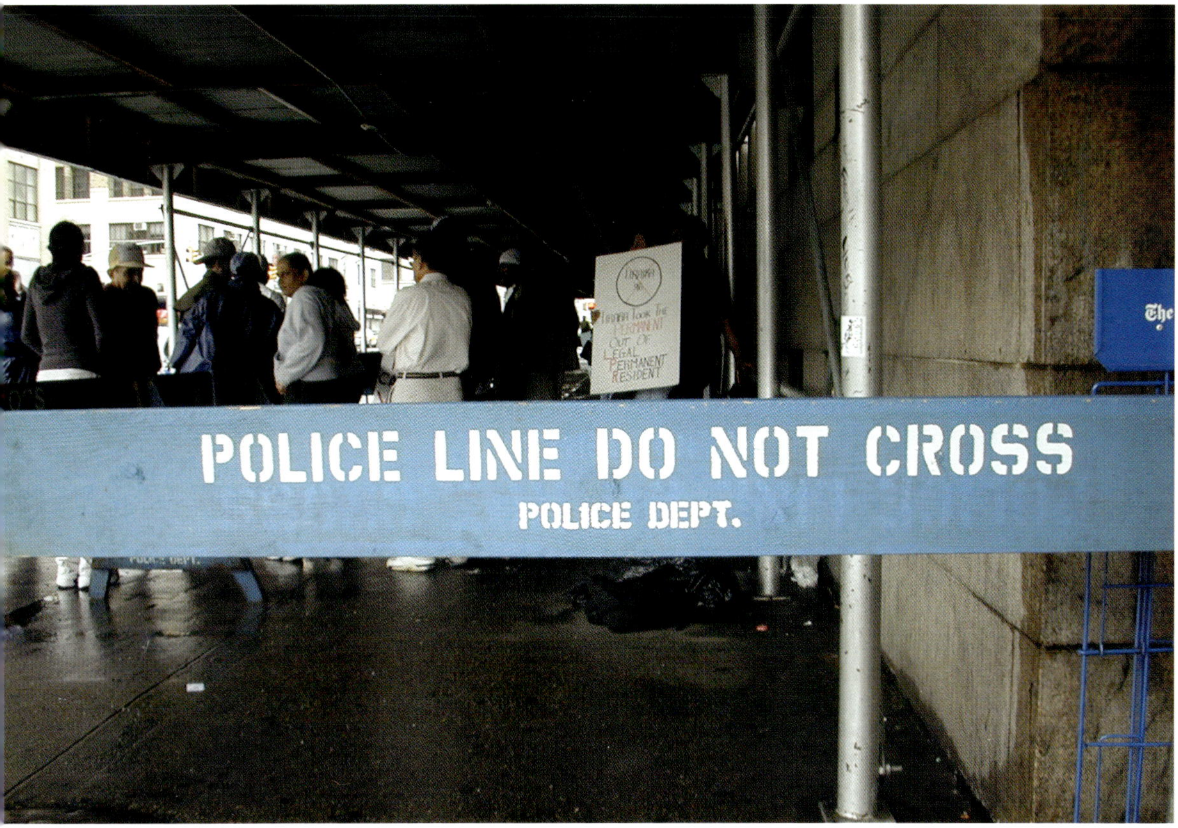

POLICE LINE DO NOT CROSS
POLICE DEPT.

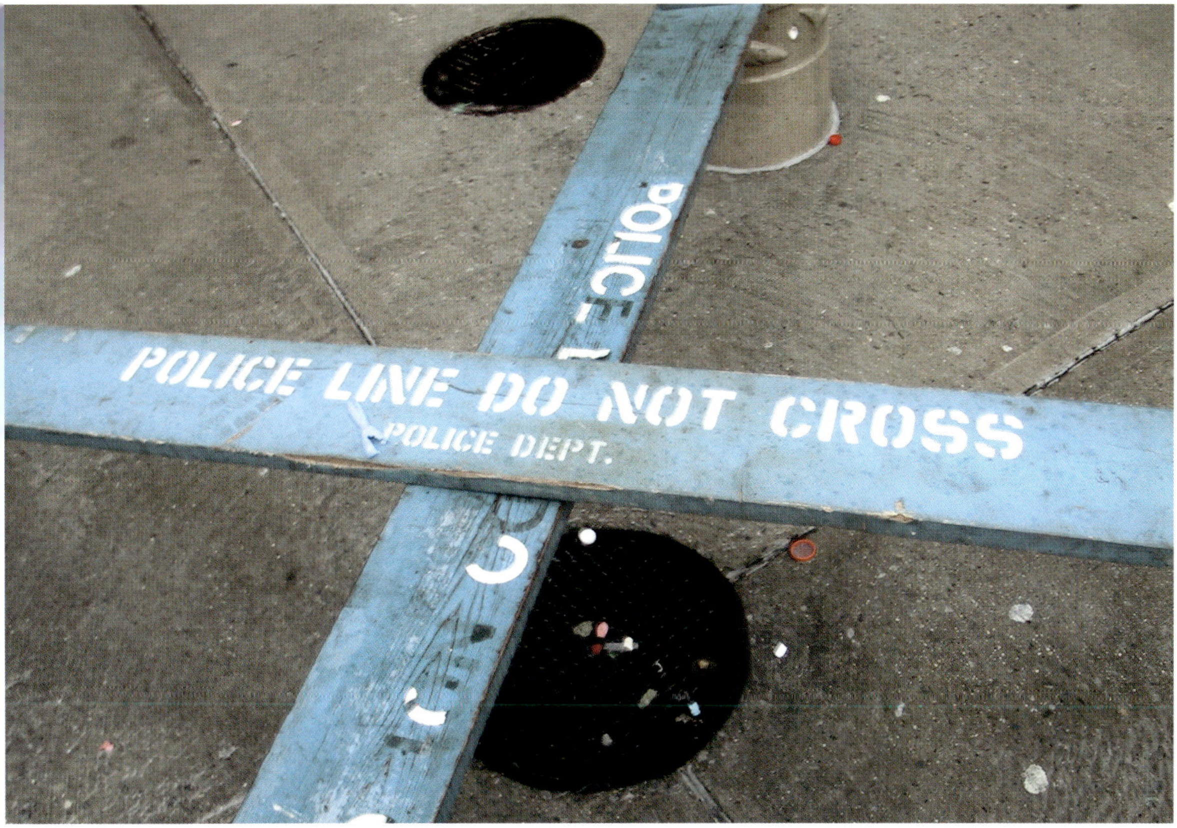

POLICE LINE DO NOT CROSS
POLICE DEPT.

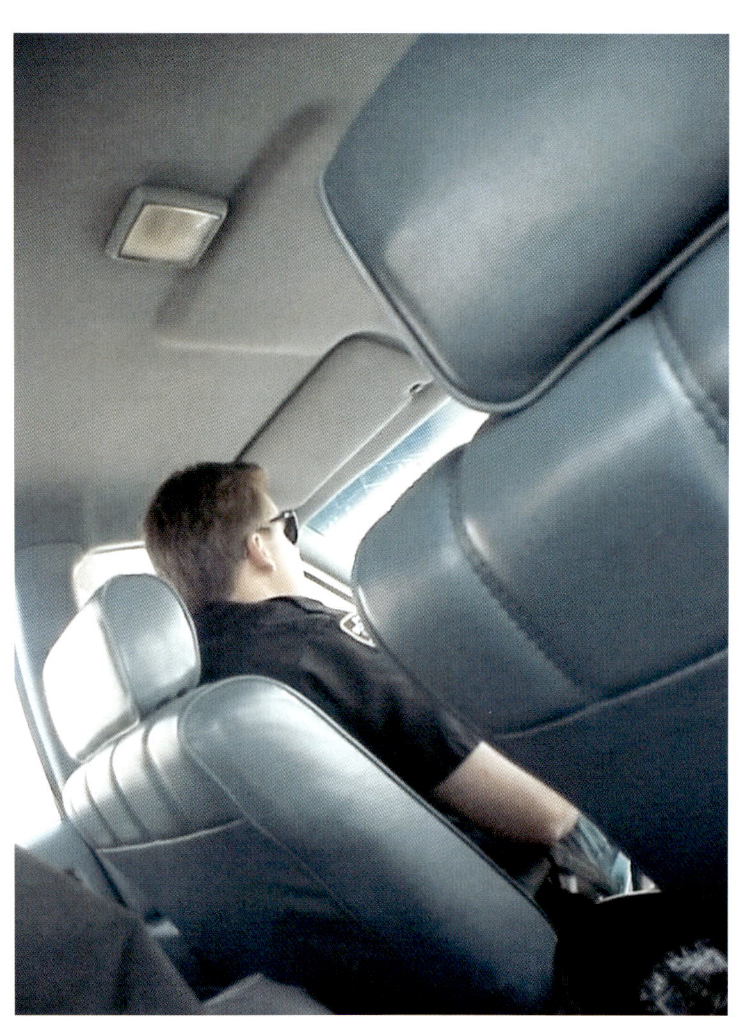

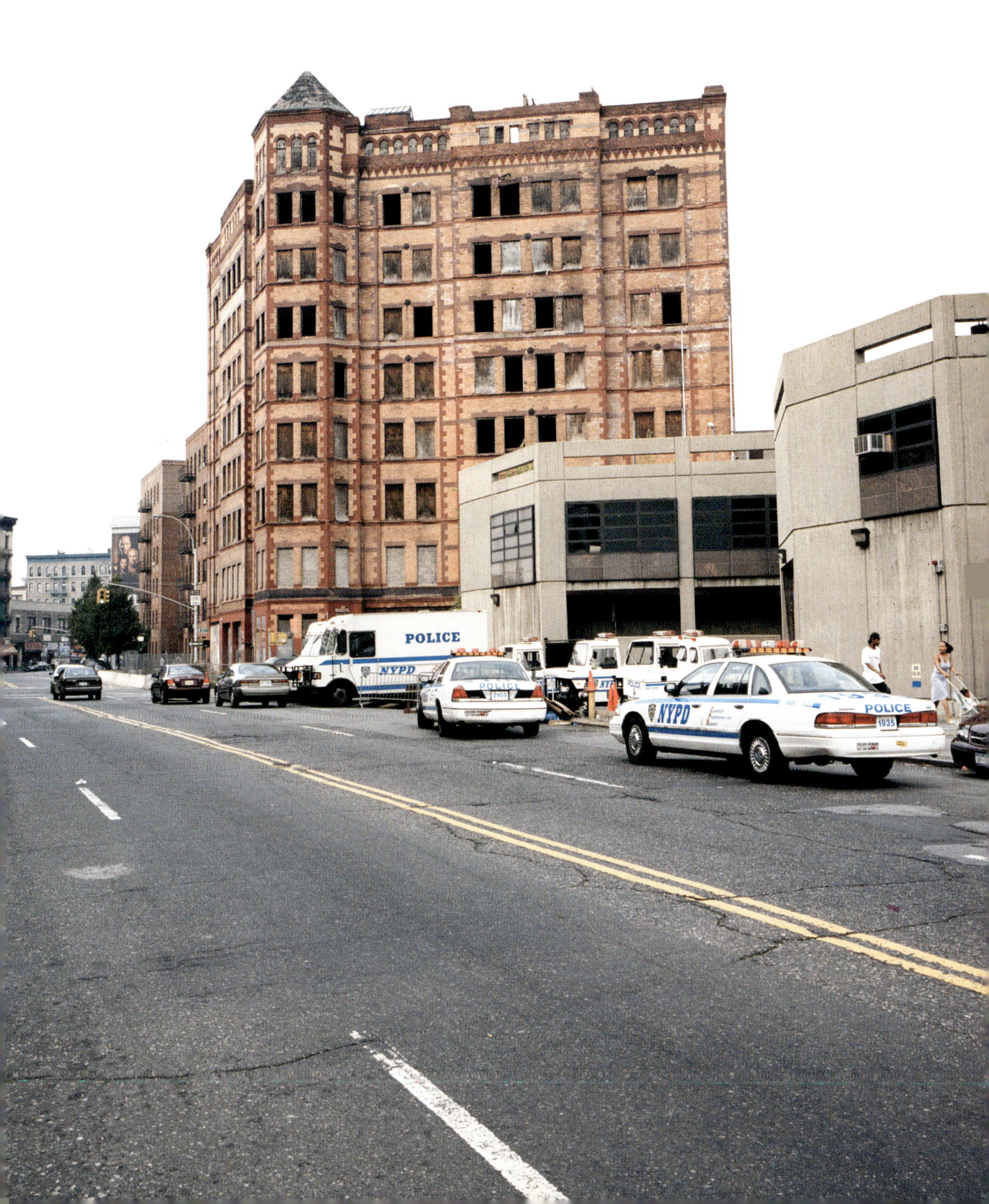
POLICE
NYPD
POLICE
NYPD
POLICE

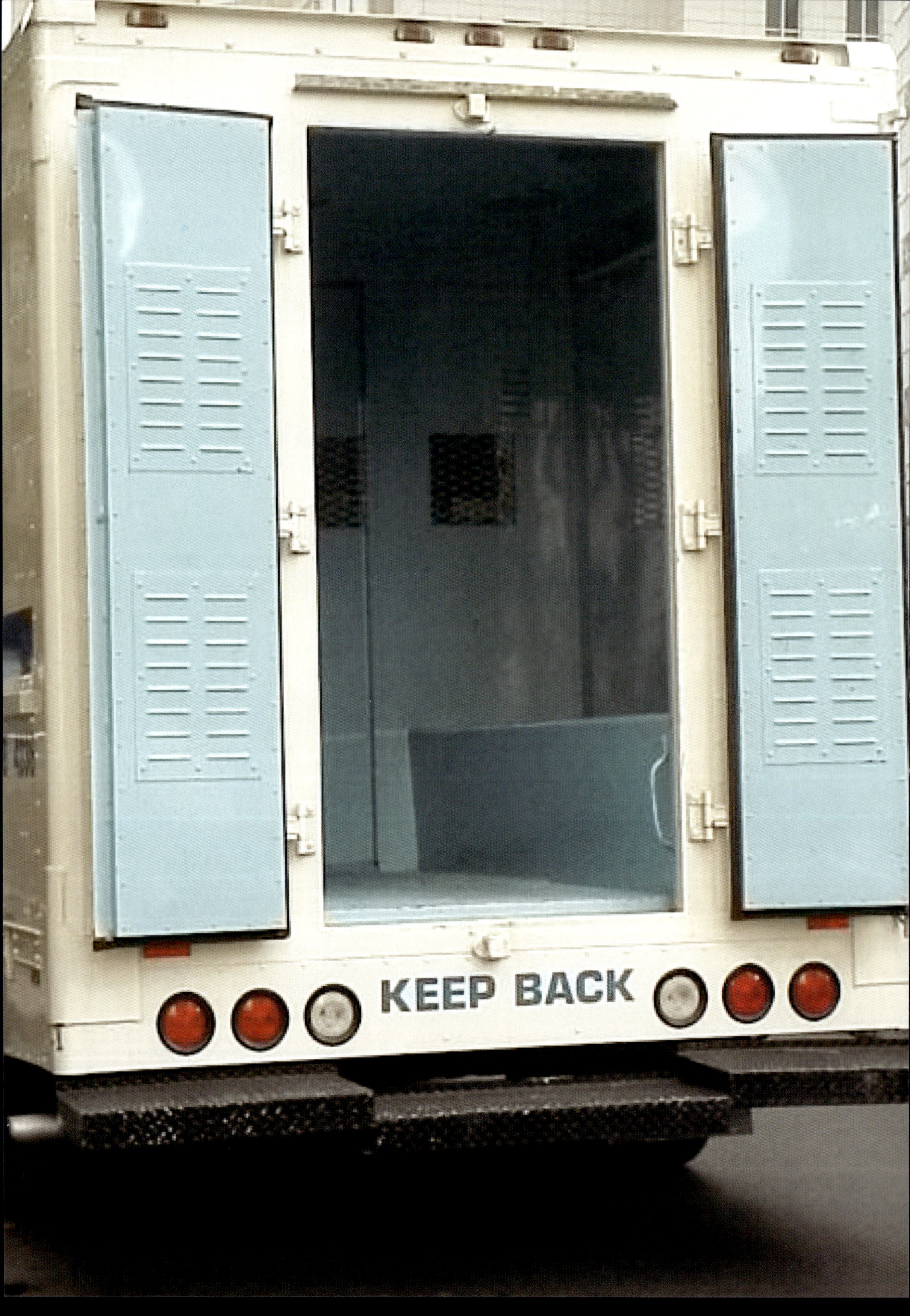
KEEP BACK

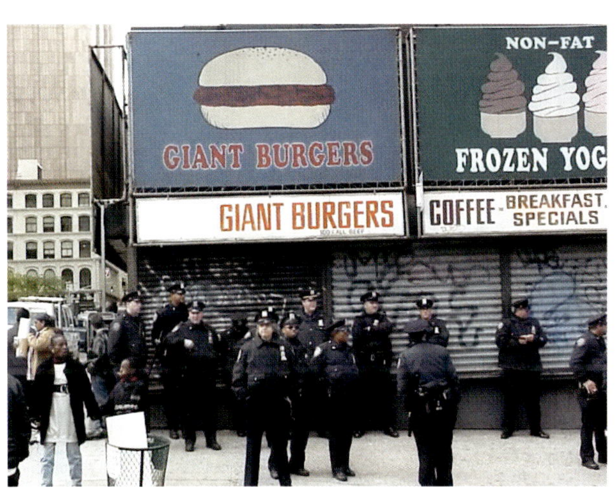
GIANT BURGERS
NON-FAT
FROZEN YOG
GIANT BURGERS
COFFEE
BREAKFAST
SPECIALS

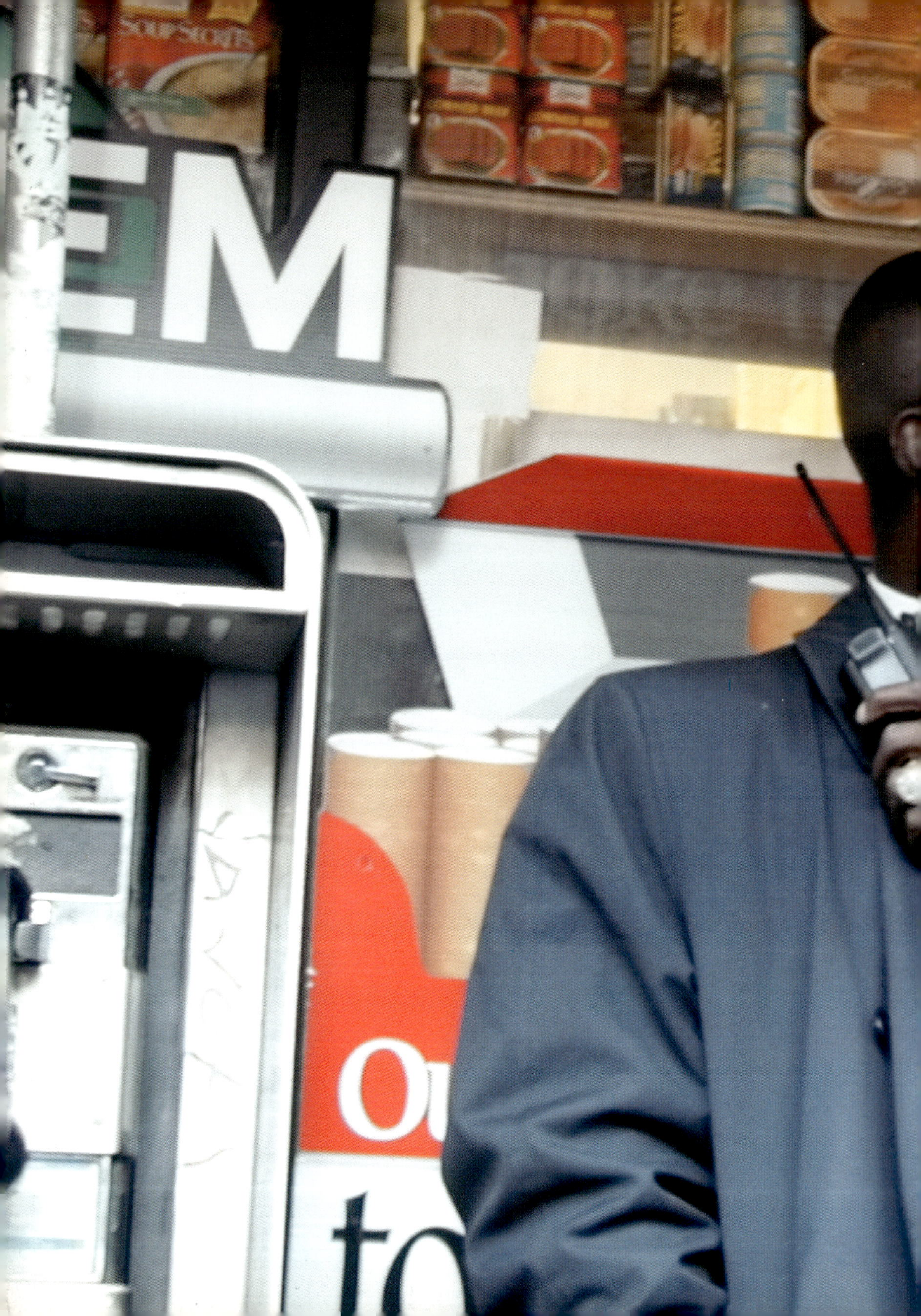
EM
Ou
to

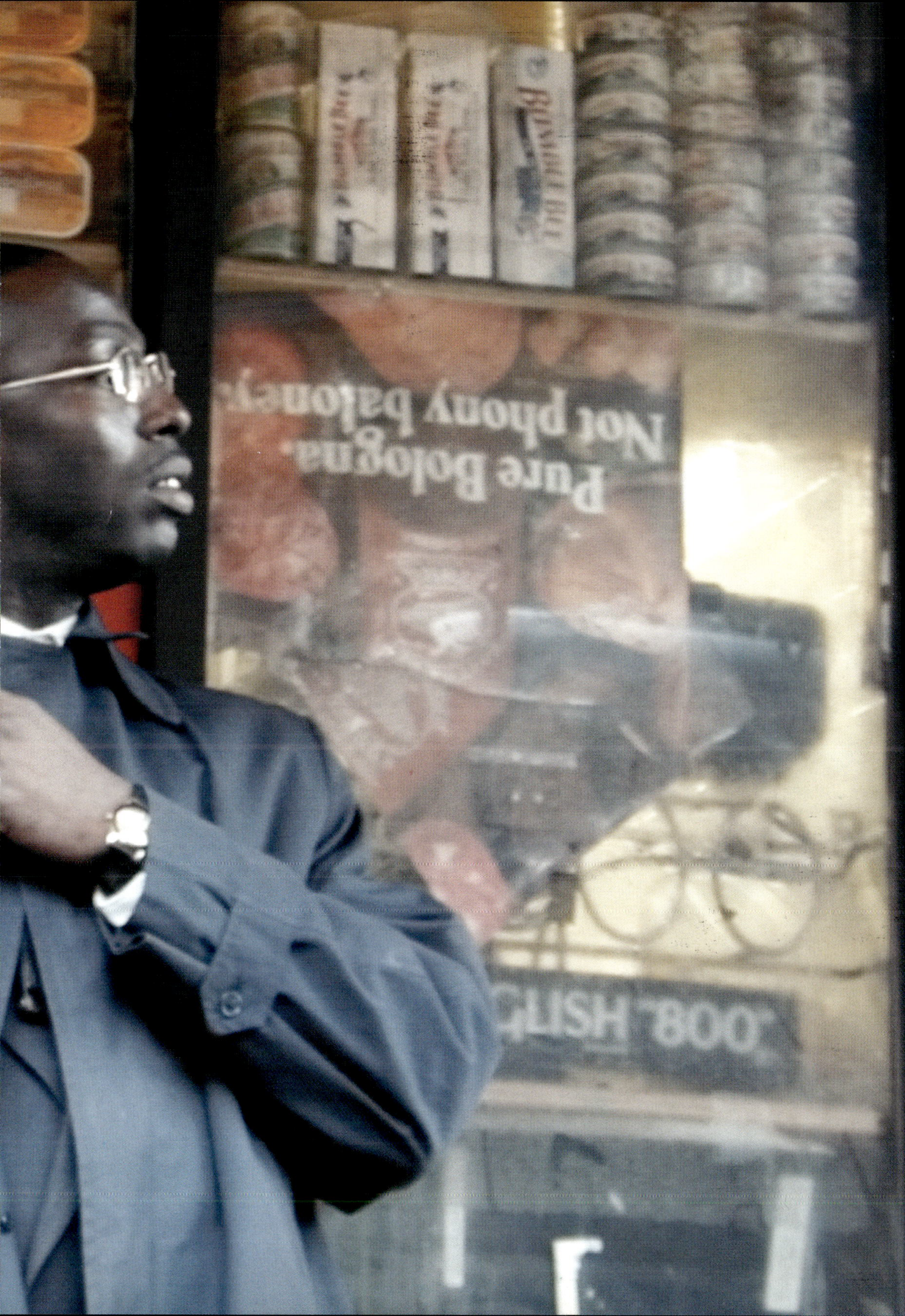
Pure Bologna.
Not phony baloney.

	System			Order		
Property Phenomenon	Dysfunctional Speech Act	Commerce	Control	Membrane	Orientation	**The Range of Participation**
LOCKED MOBILITY	MISSPELLING	CORPORATE MONUMENTS	POLICE LINE DO NOT CROSS	BLUE CITY	STREET SCRIPT	VOICE
TAPE	FADING MARKETS	STREET VENDORS	A BARRIER	COVER	STREET MARK	**DIVERSITY**
SHOP WATCH	EMPTY SIGNS	STREET LEVEL	SERVICE SCREEN	SHOPPING BAG	STEEL	OPEN CINE
REAL ESTATE		SHOPPING CARTS		GARBAGE DIGITAL SLUM		NEIGHBORHOOD

Identity

Alternative Media

Habitual Reinterpretation

DIVERSITY

Identity and Diversity are inseparable

CAR DOOR

PUBLIC CHAIRS

LABELING.

PLASTIC CRATES

POLE POST

STANDPIPES

PRAY JESUS

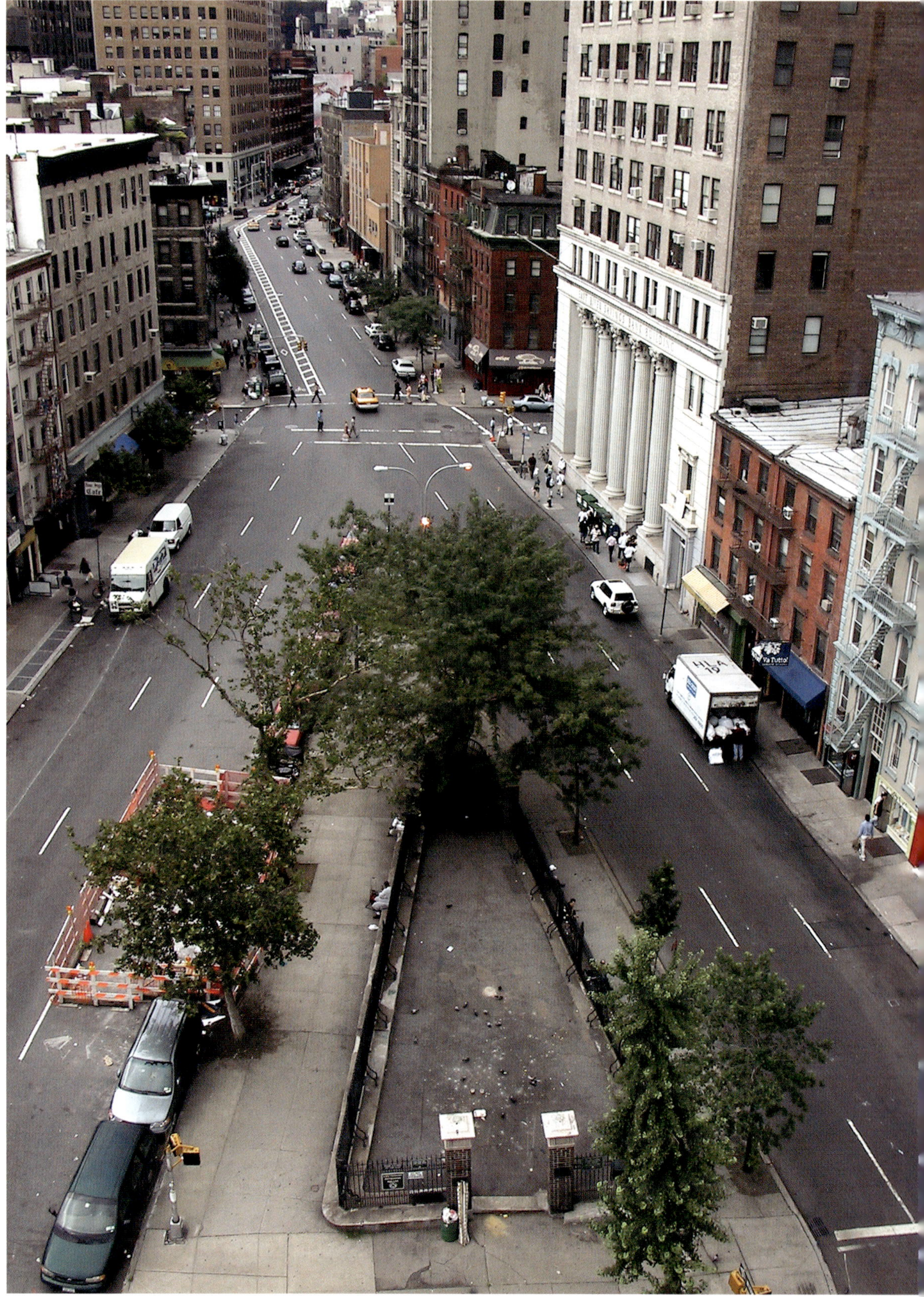
Cafe
Va Tutto!

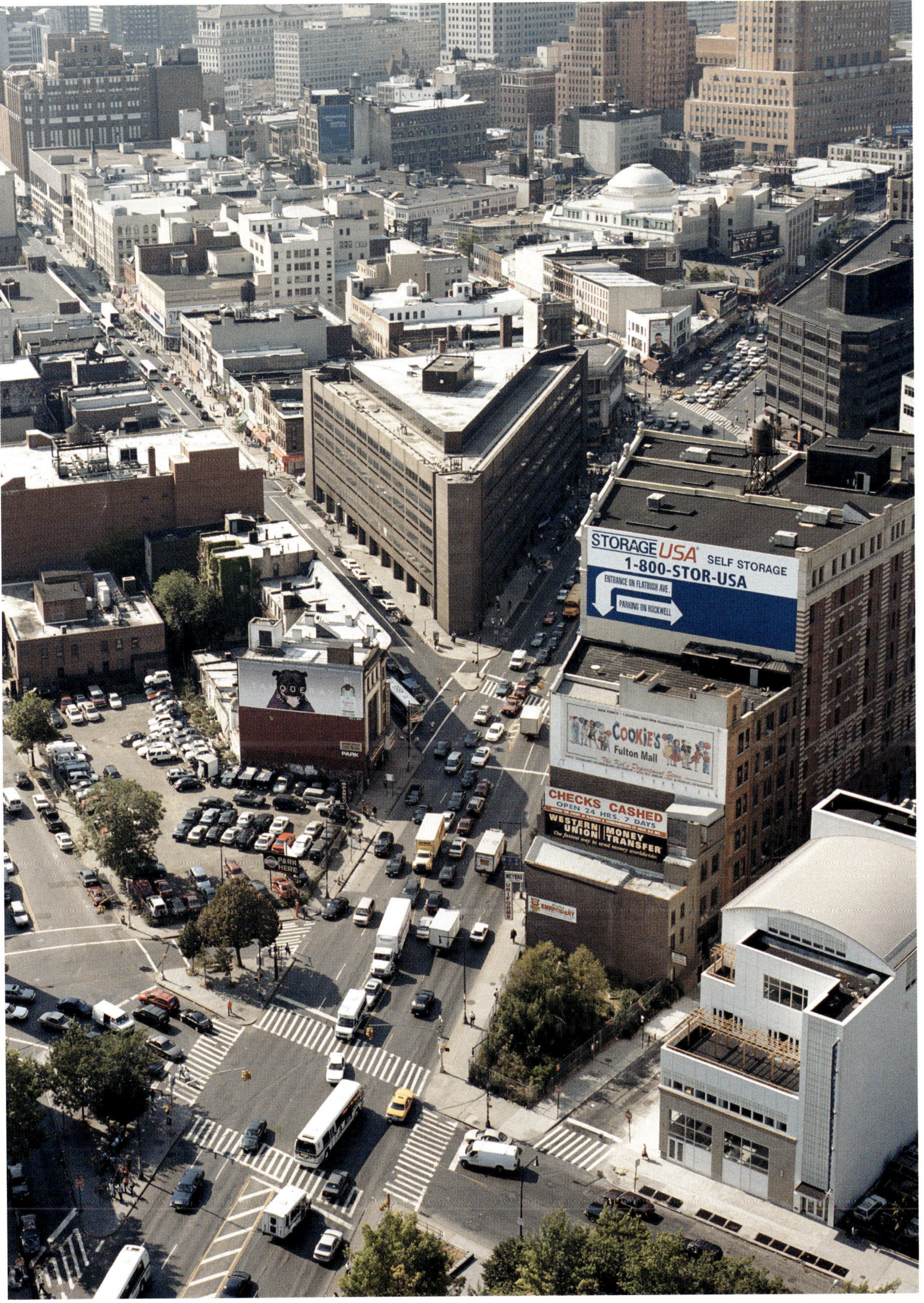
STORAGE USA SELF STORAGE
1-800-STOR-USA
ENTRANCE ON FLATBUSH AVE.
PARKING ON ROCKWELL
COOKIE'S
Fulton Mall
CHECKS CASHED
OPEN 24 HRS. 7 DAYS
WESTERN UNION
MONEY TRANSFER

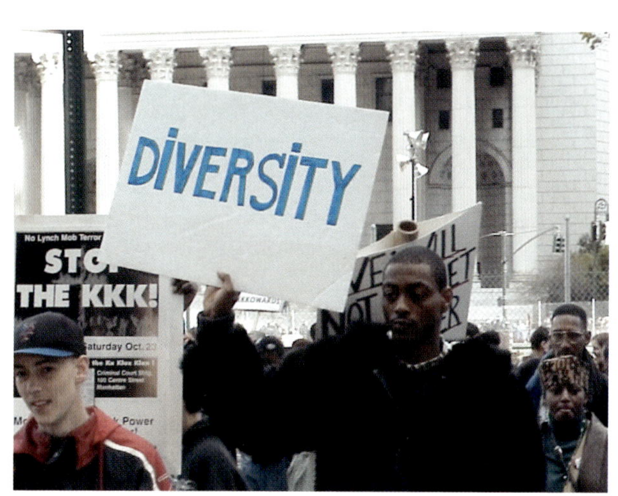
DIVERSITY
No Lynch Mob Terror
THE KKK!

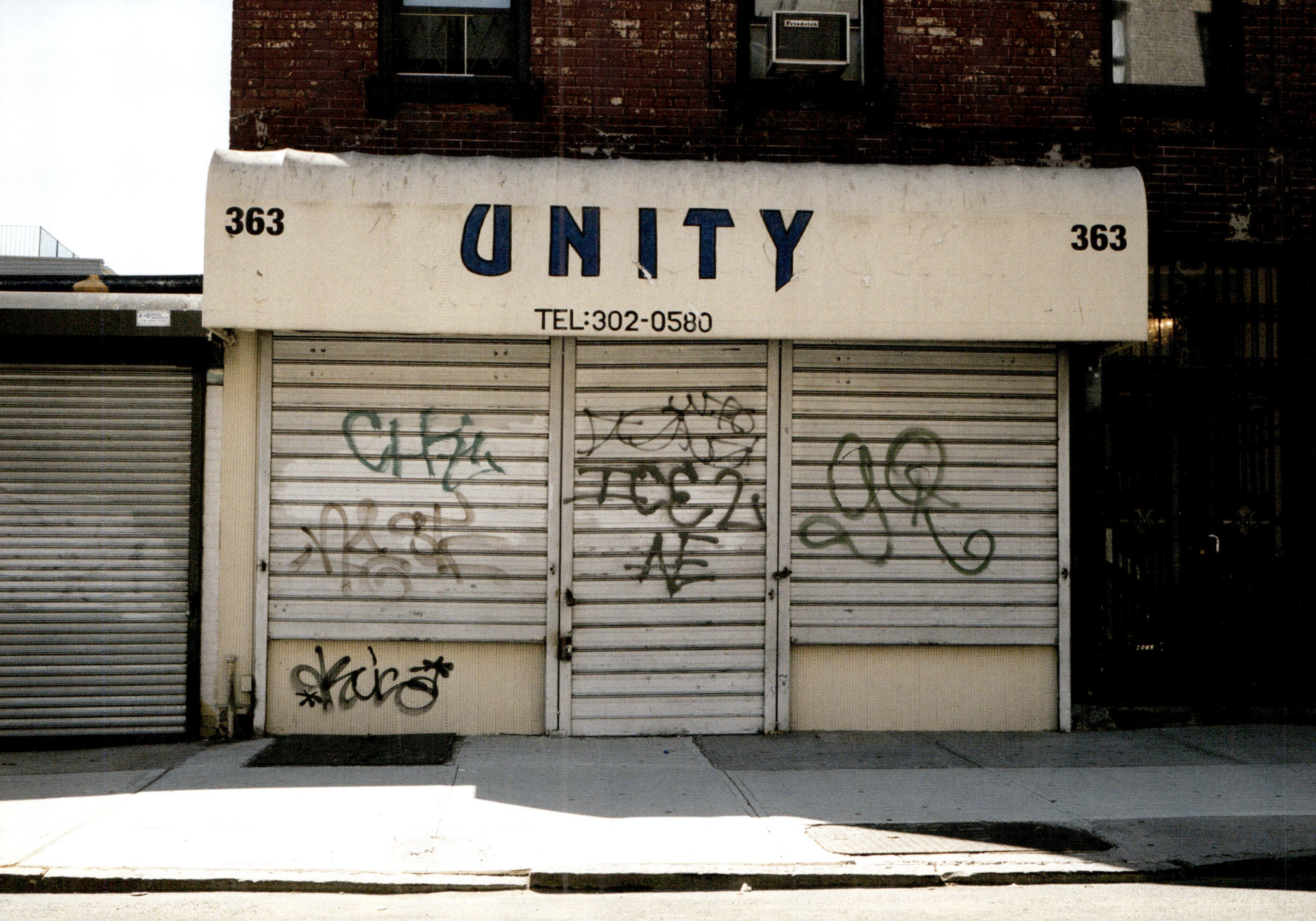
363
UNITY
363
TEL:302-0580

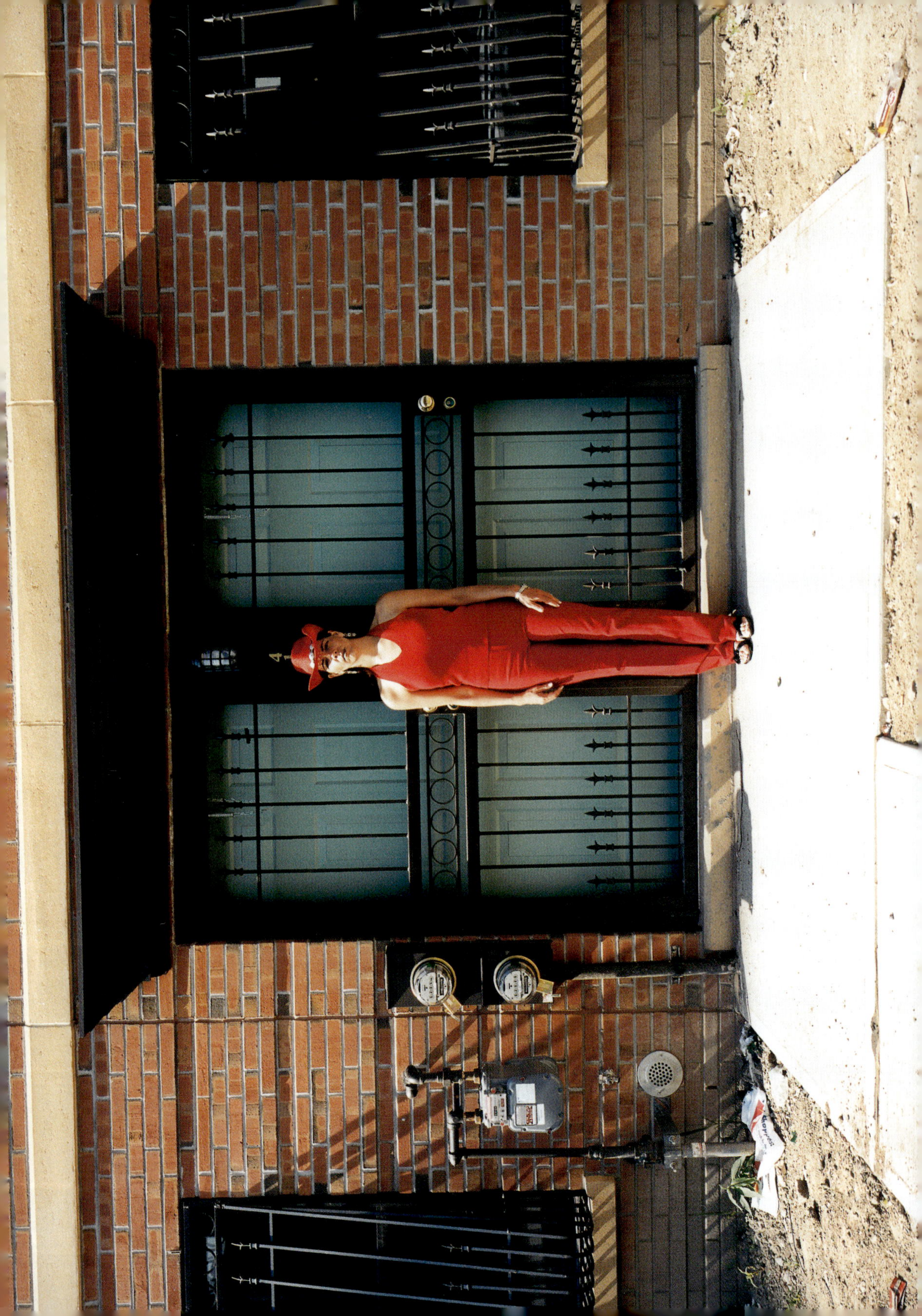

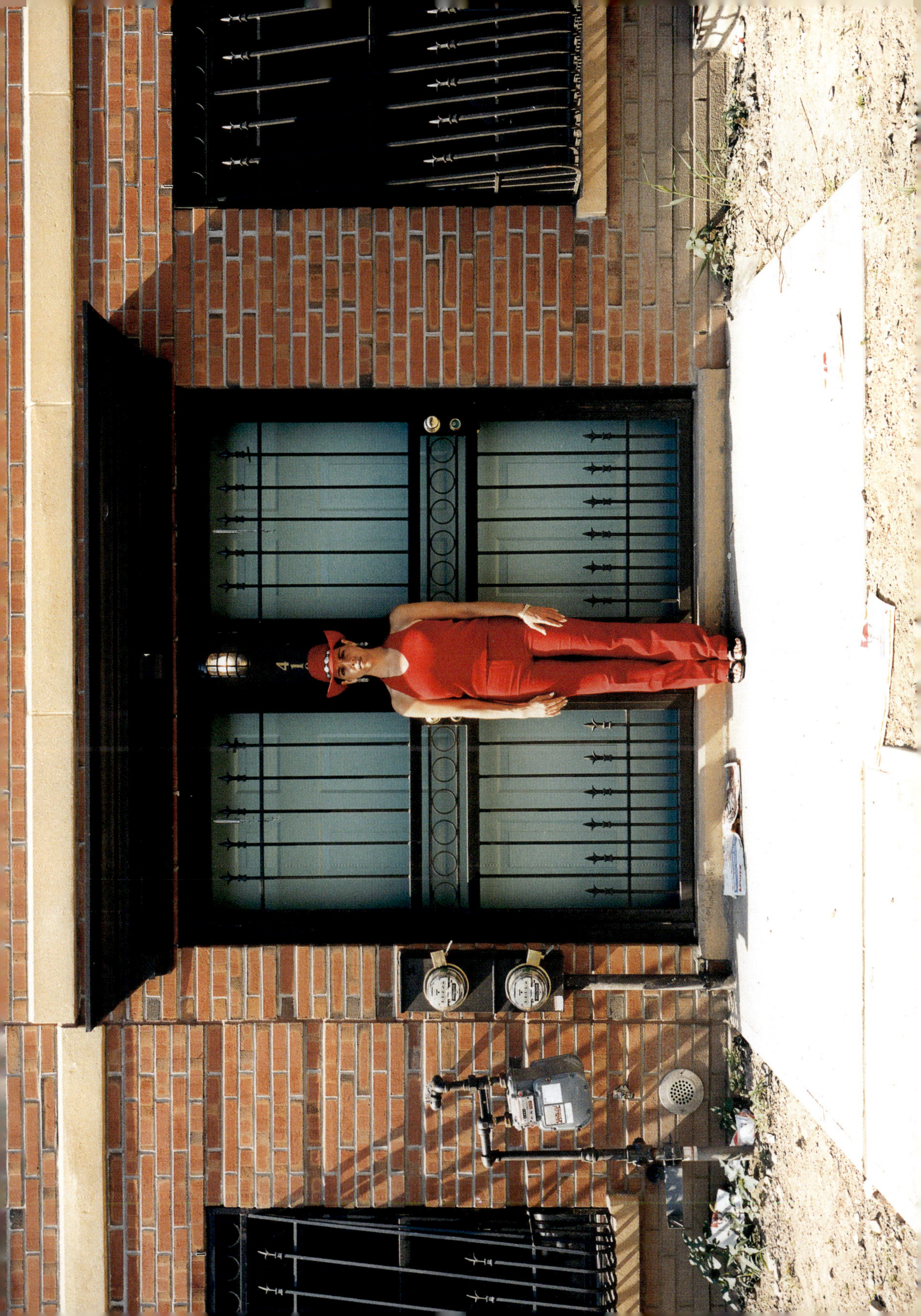

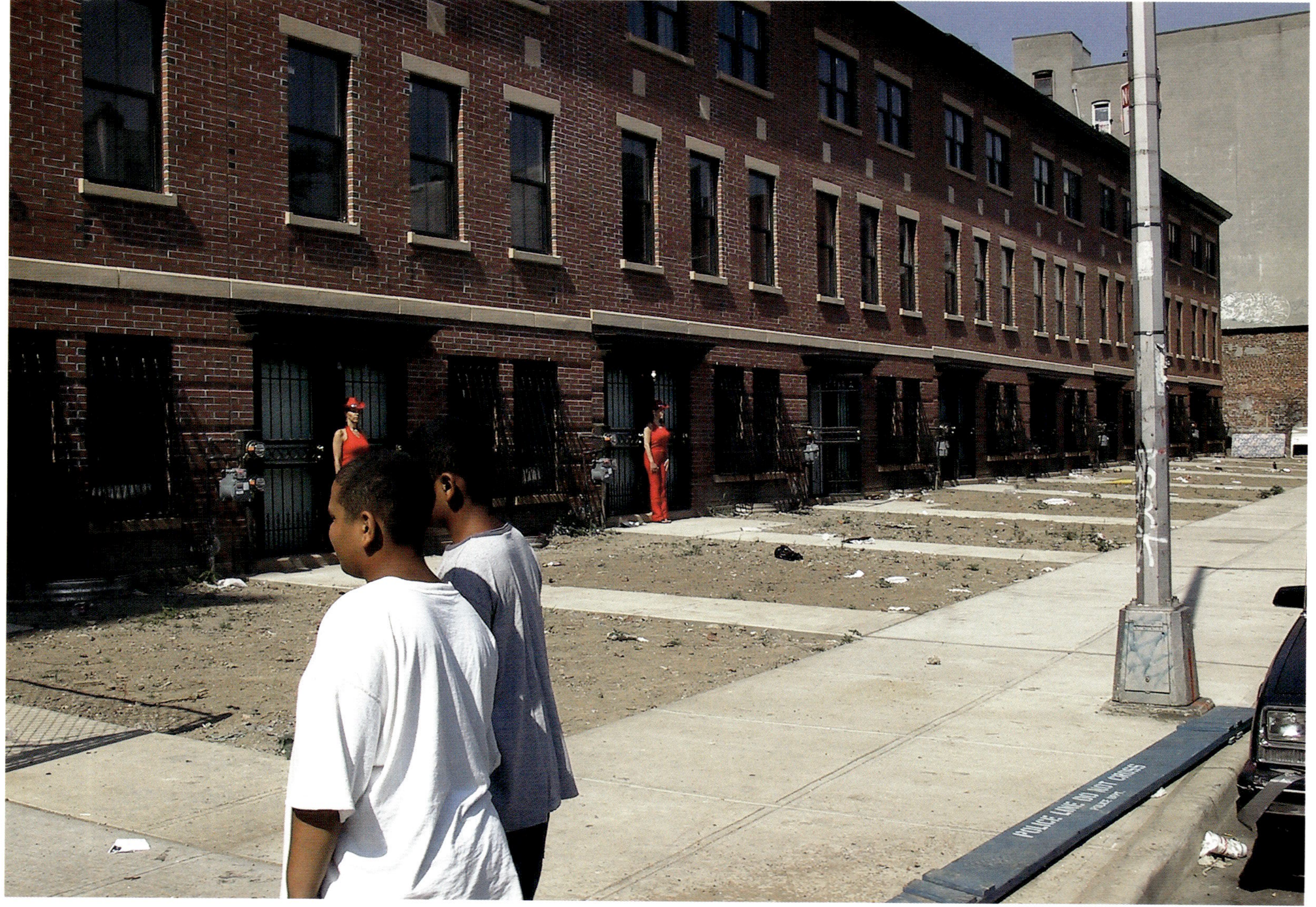
POLICE LINE DO NOT CROSS

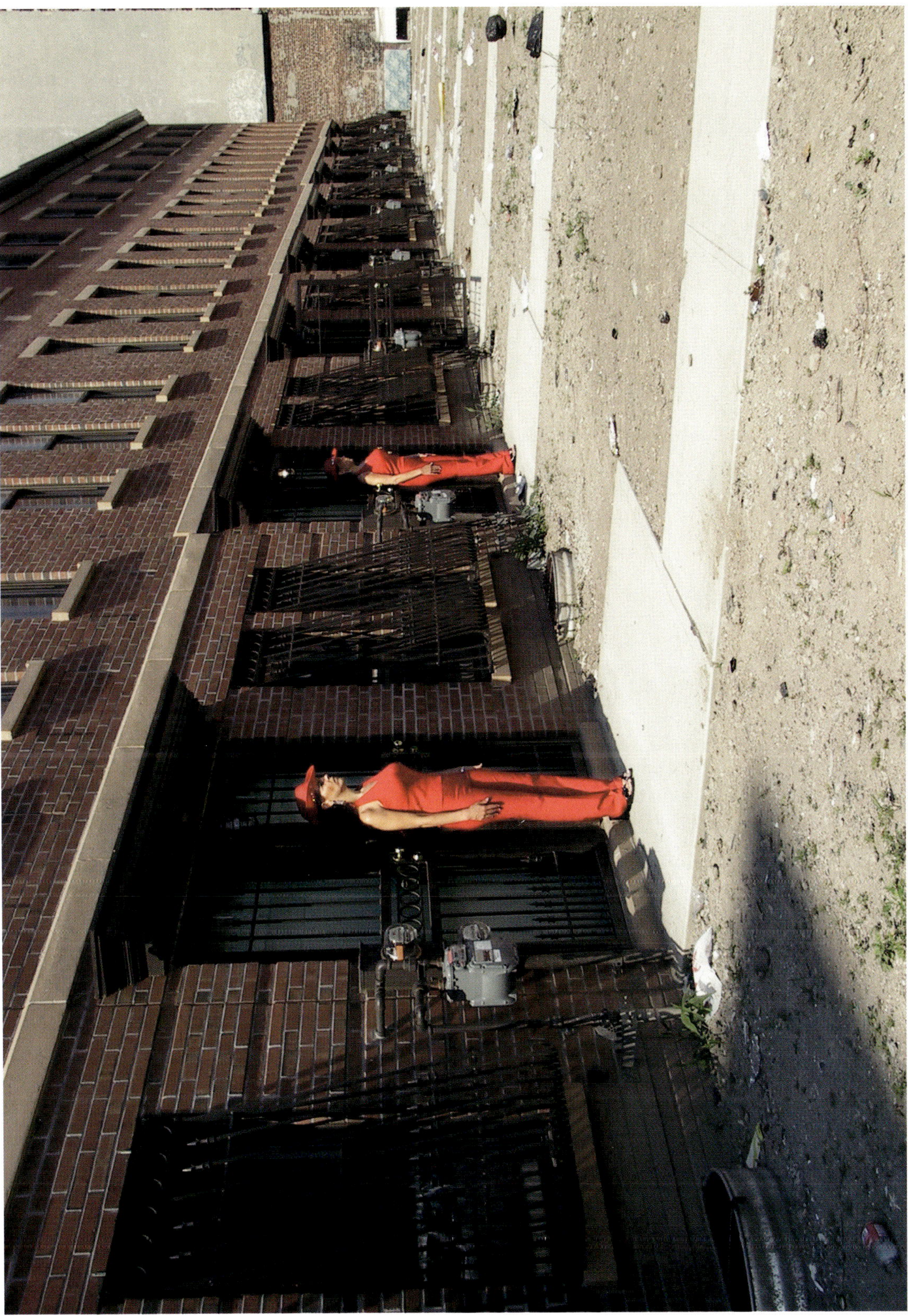

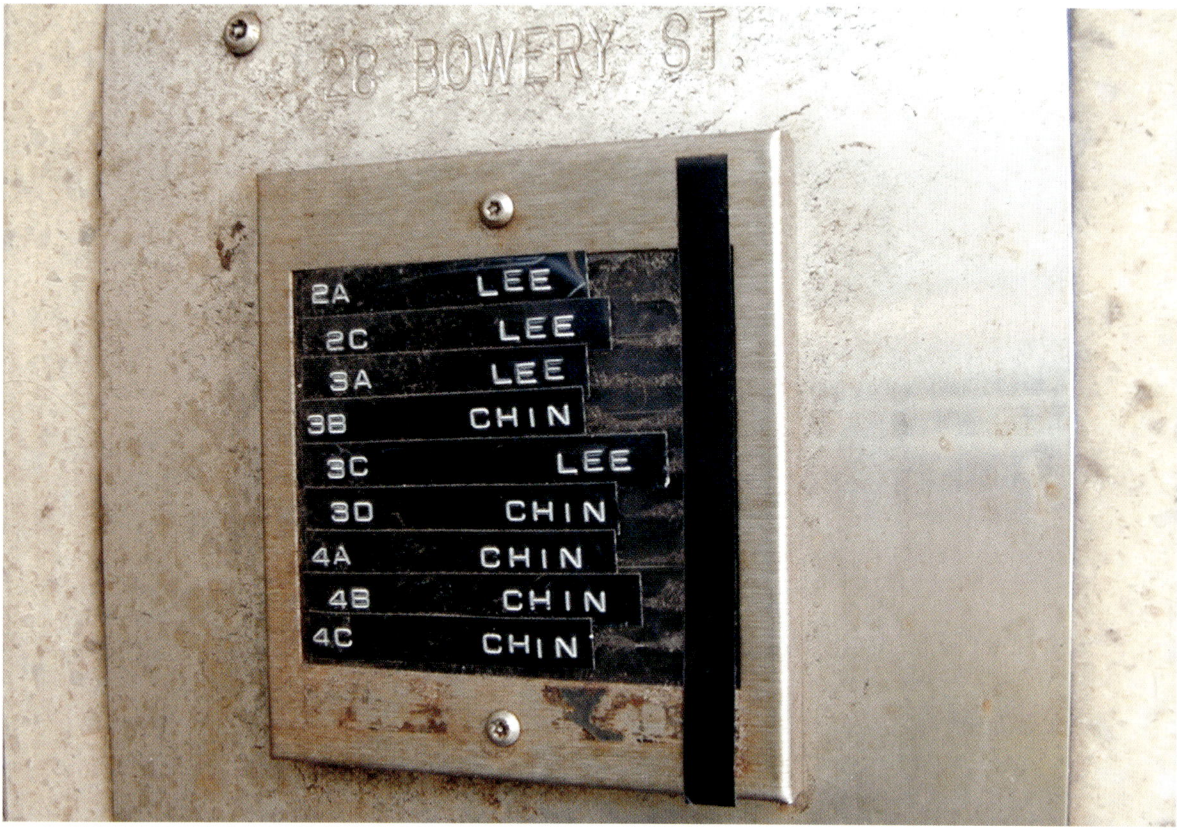

28 BOWERY ST
2A LEE
2C LEE
3A LEE
3B CHIN
3C LEE
3D CHIN
4A CHIN
4B CHIN
4C CHIN

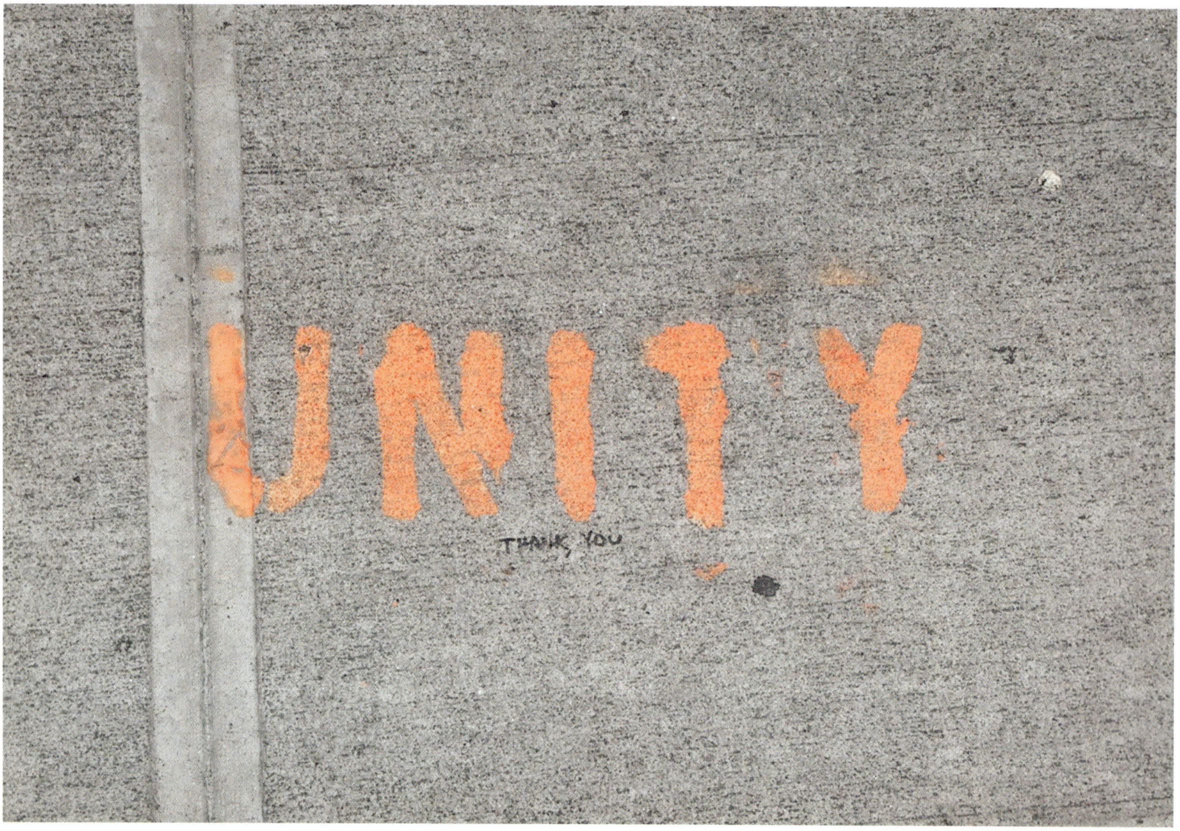

UNITY
THANK YOU

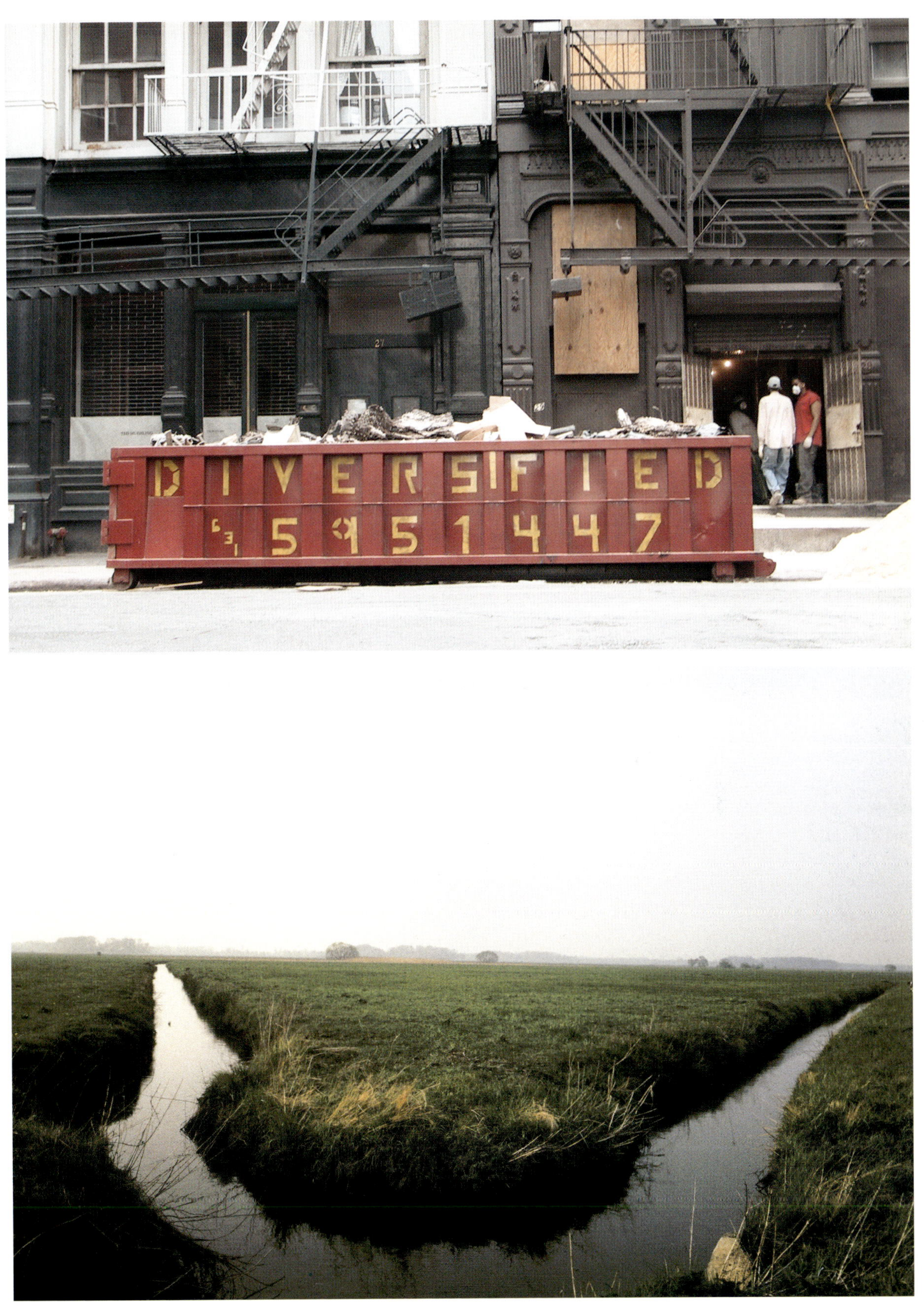
DIVERSIFIED
631 5951447

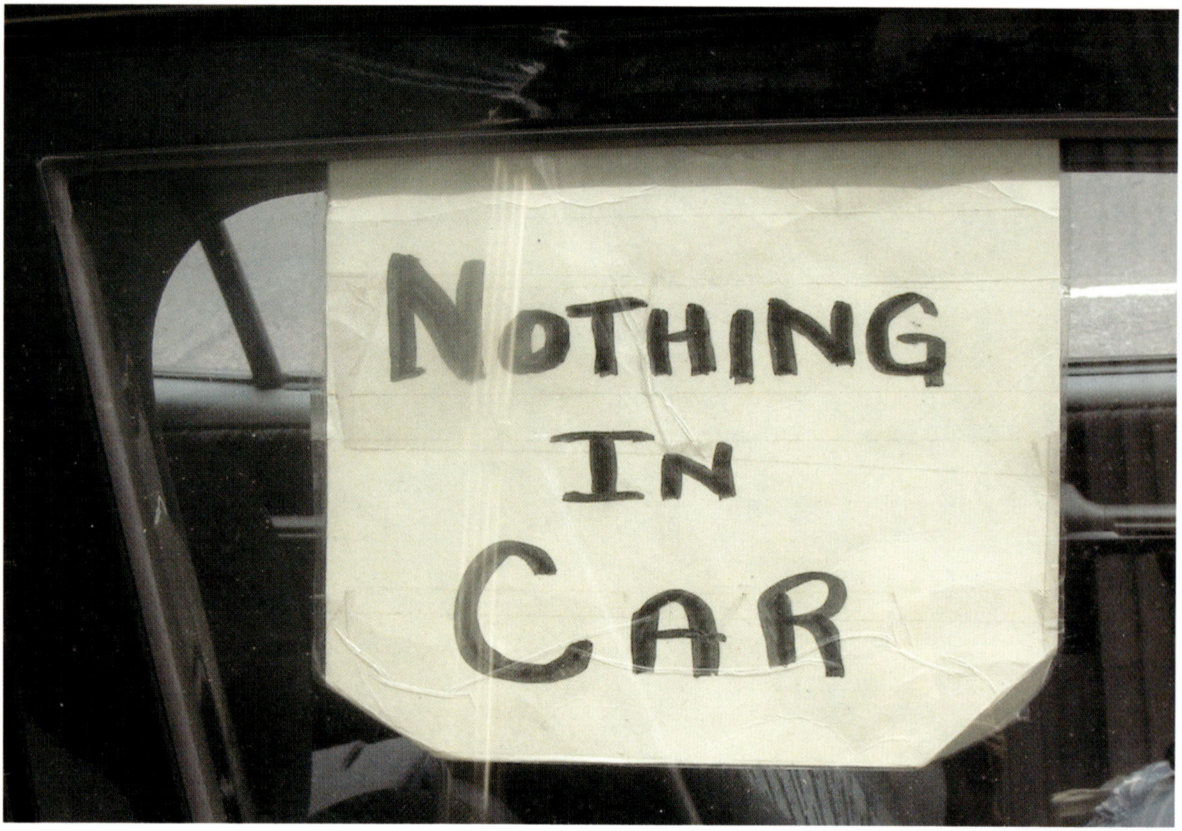

NOTHING
IN
CAR

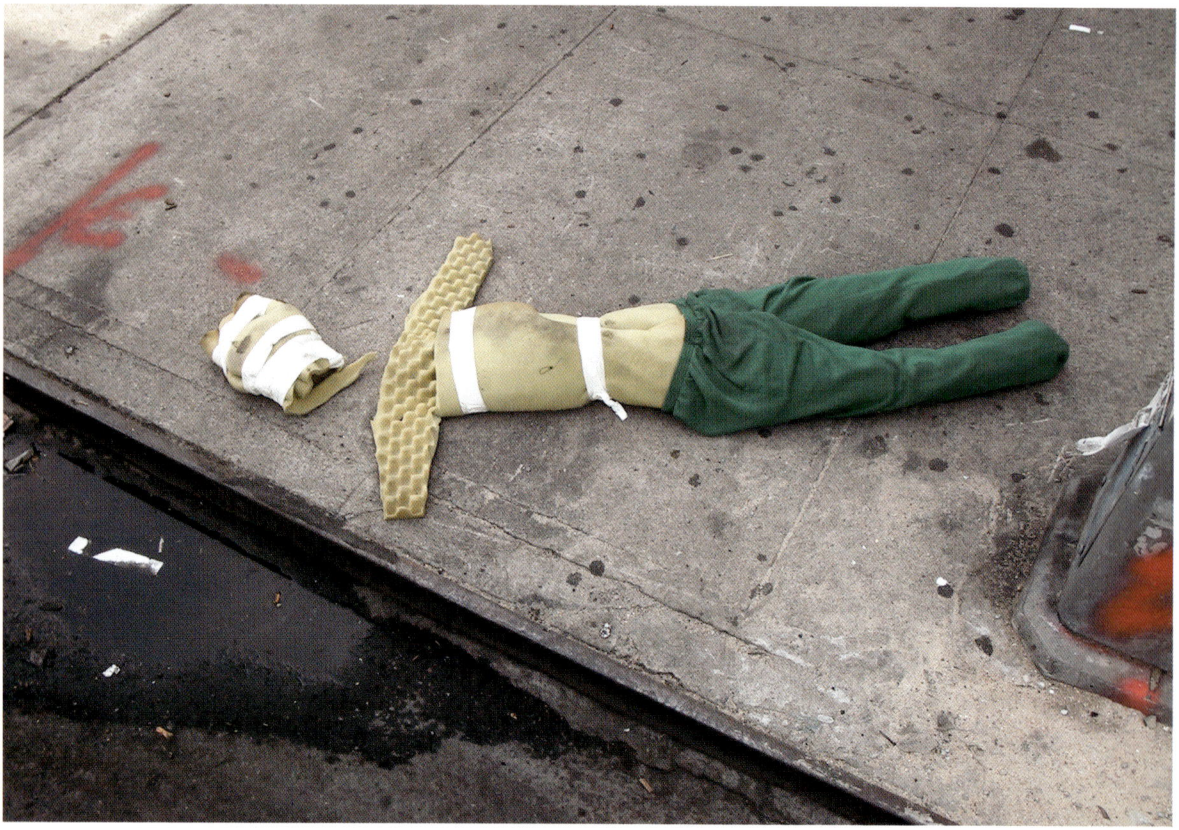

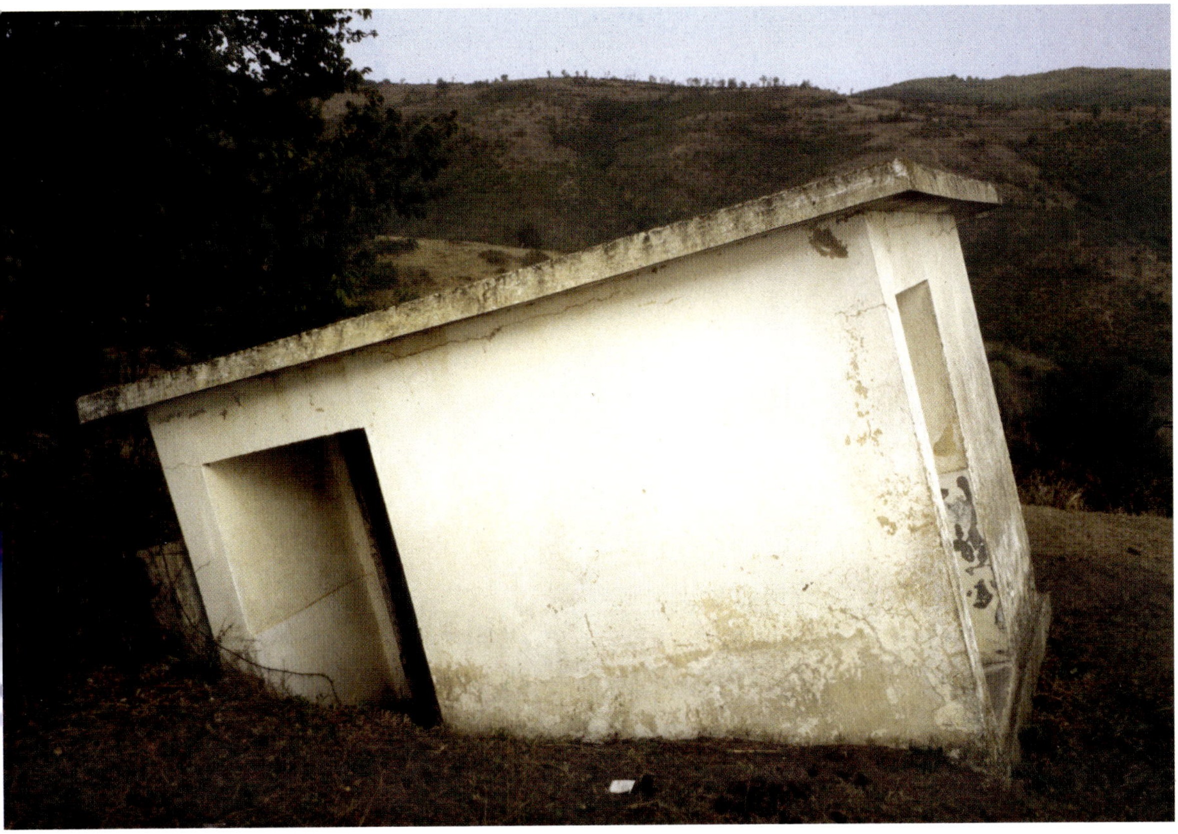

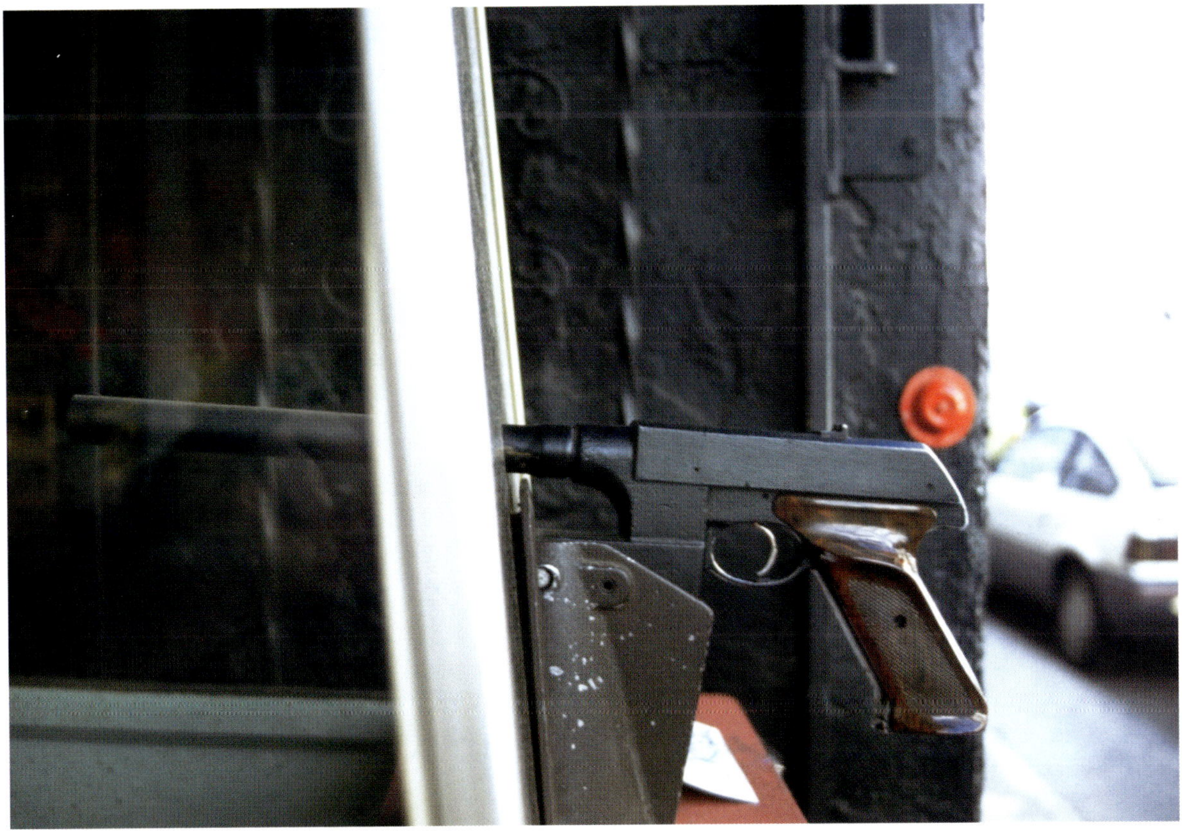

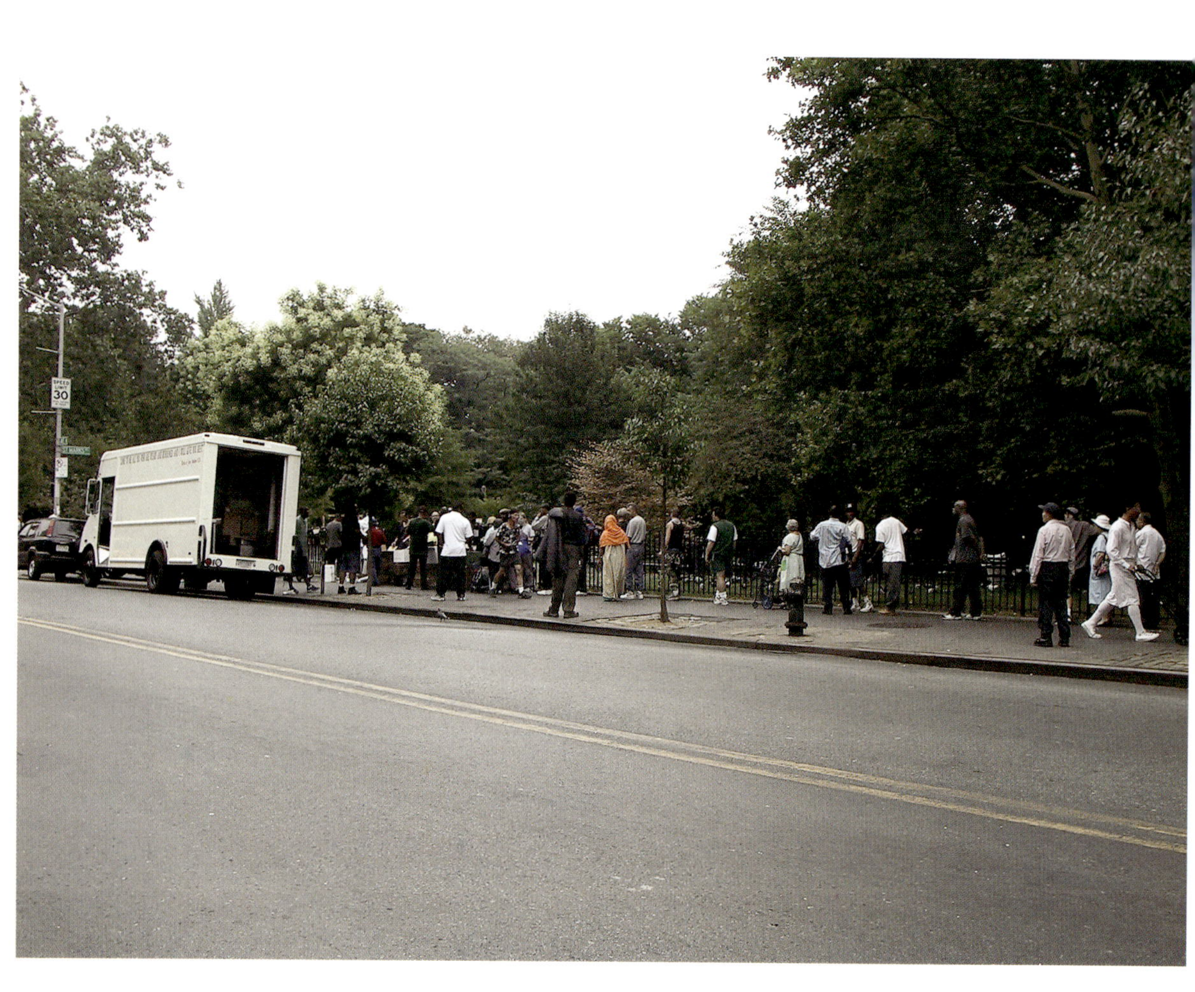
SPEED LIMIT
30

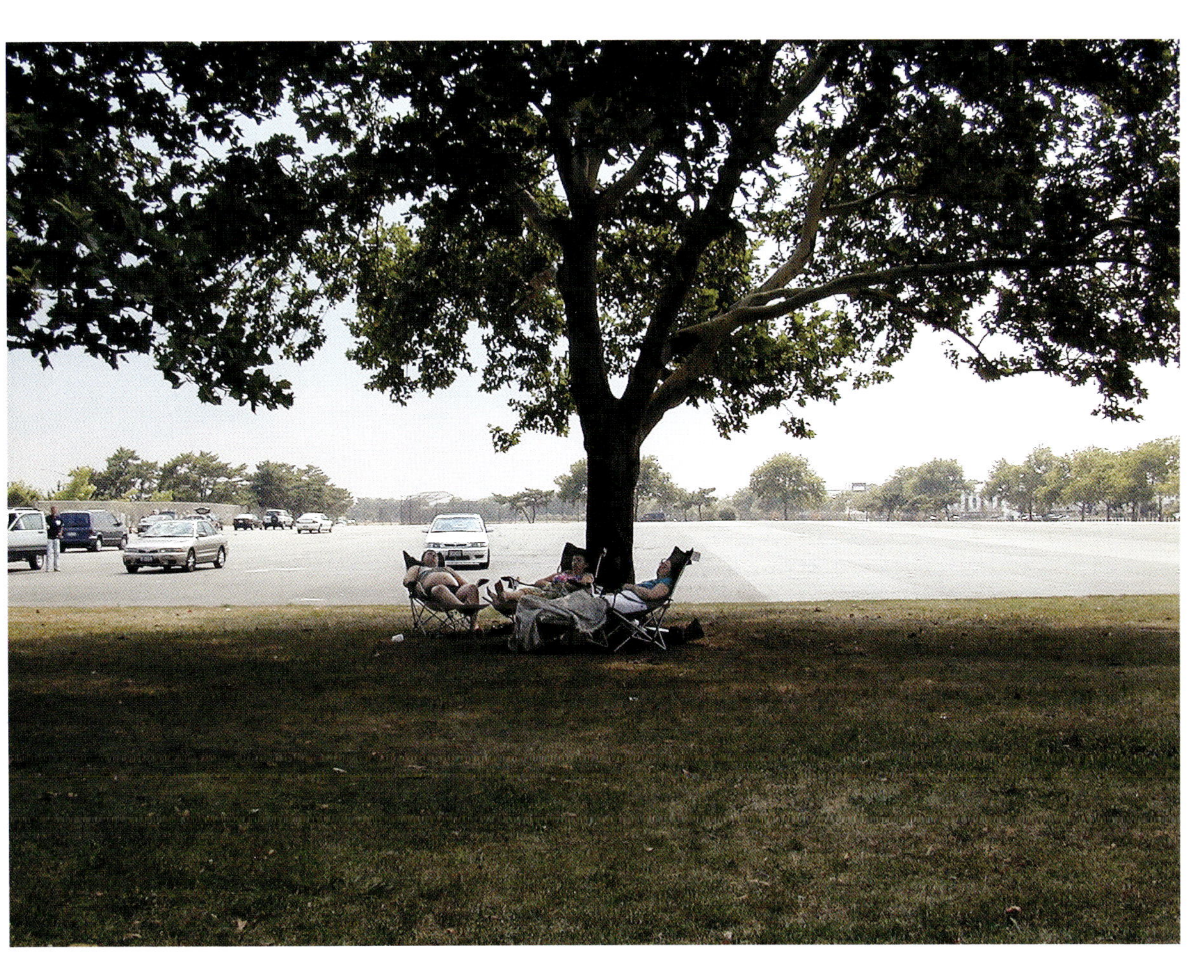

	System			Order		
Property Phenomenon	Dysfunctional Speech Act	Commerce	Control	Membrane	Orientation	The Range of Participation
LOCKED MOBILITY	MISSPELLING	CORPORATE MONUMENTS	POLICE LINE DO NOT CROSS	BLUE CITY	STREET SCRIPT	VOICE
TAPE	FADING MARKETS	STREET VENDORS	A BARRIER	COVER	STREET MARK	DIVERSITY
SHOP WATCH	EMPTY SIGNS	STREET LEVEL	SERVICE SCREEN	SHOPPING BAG	STEEL	OPEN CINE
REAL ESTATE		SHOPPING CARTS		GARBAGE DIGITAL SLUM		NEIGHBORHOOD

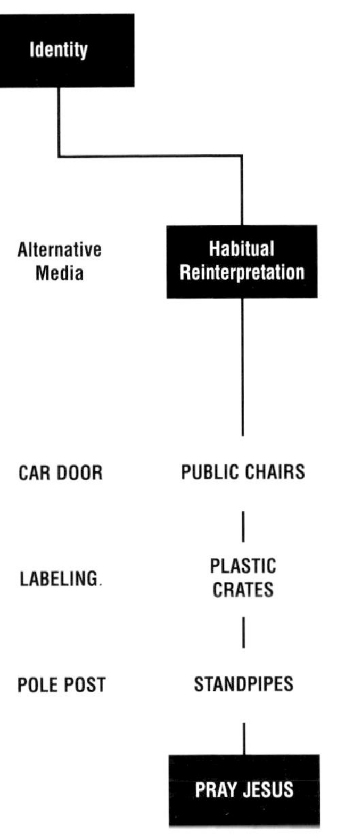

PRAY JESUS

Pay for Eternity / Pay Forever

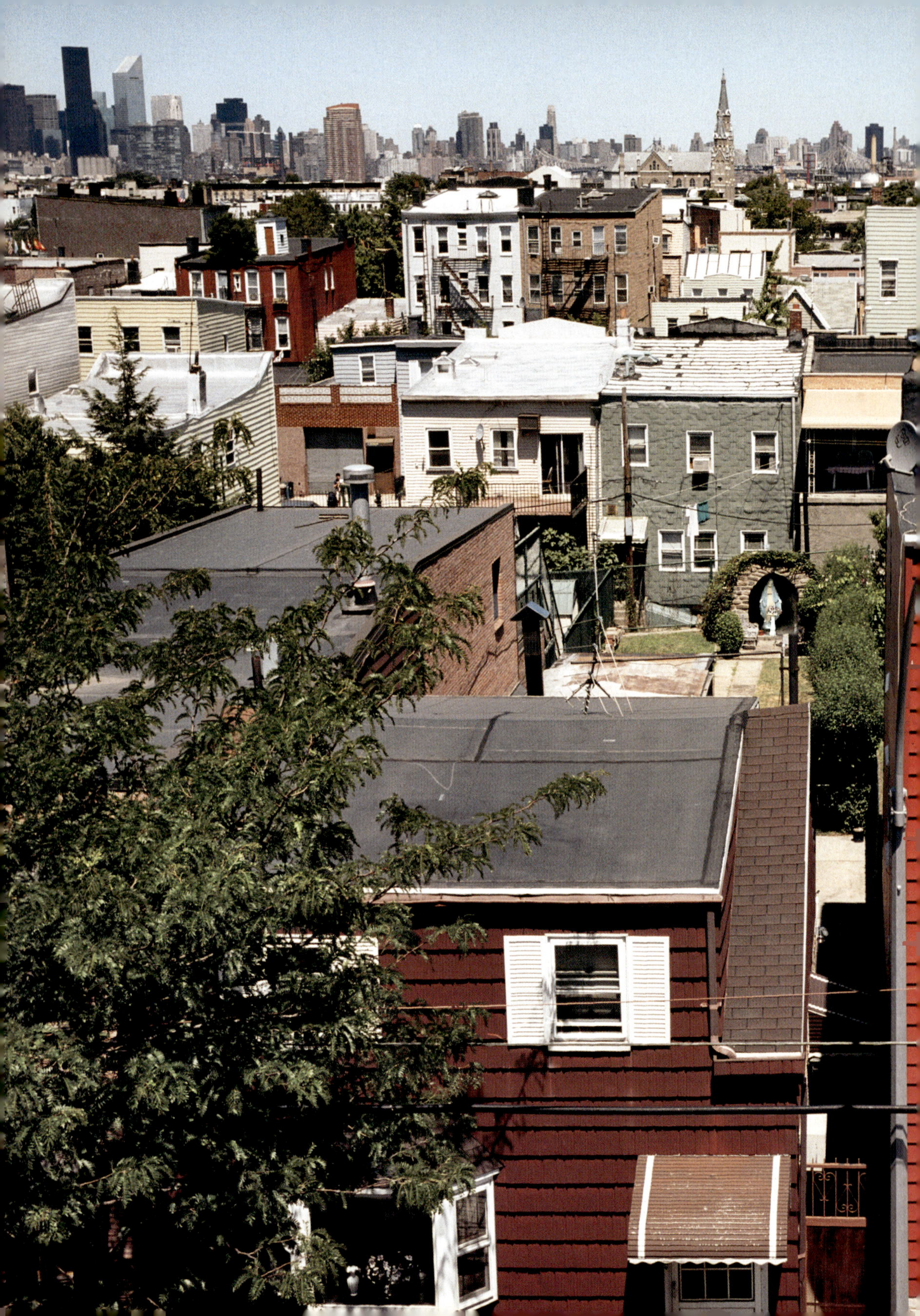

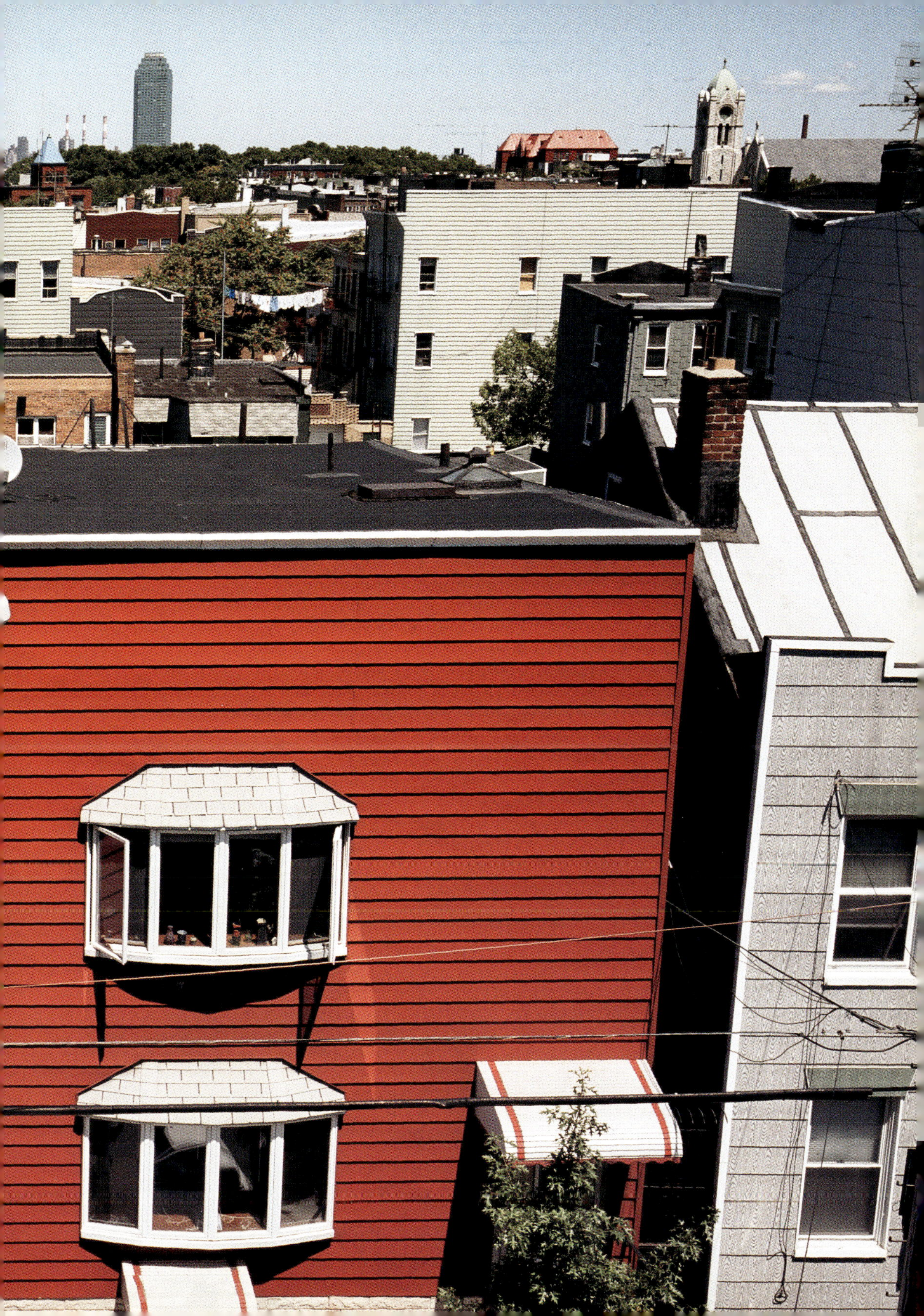

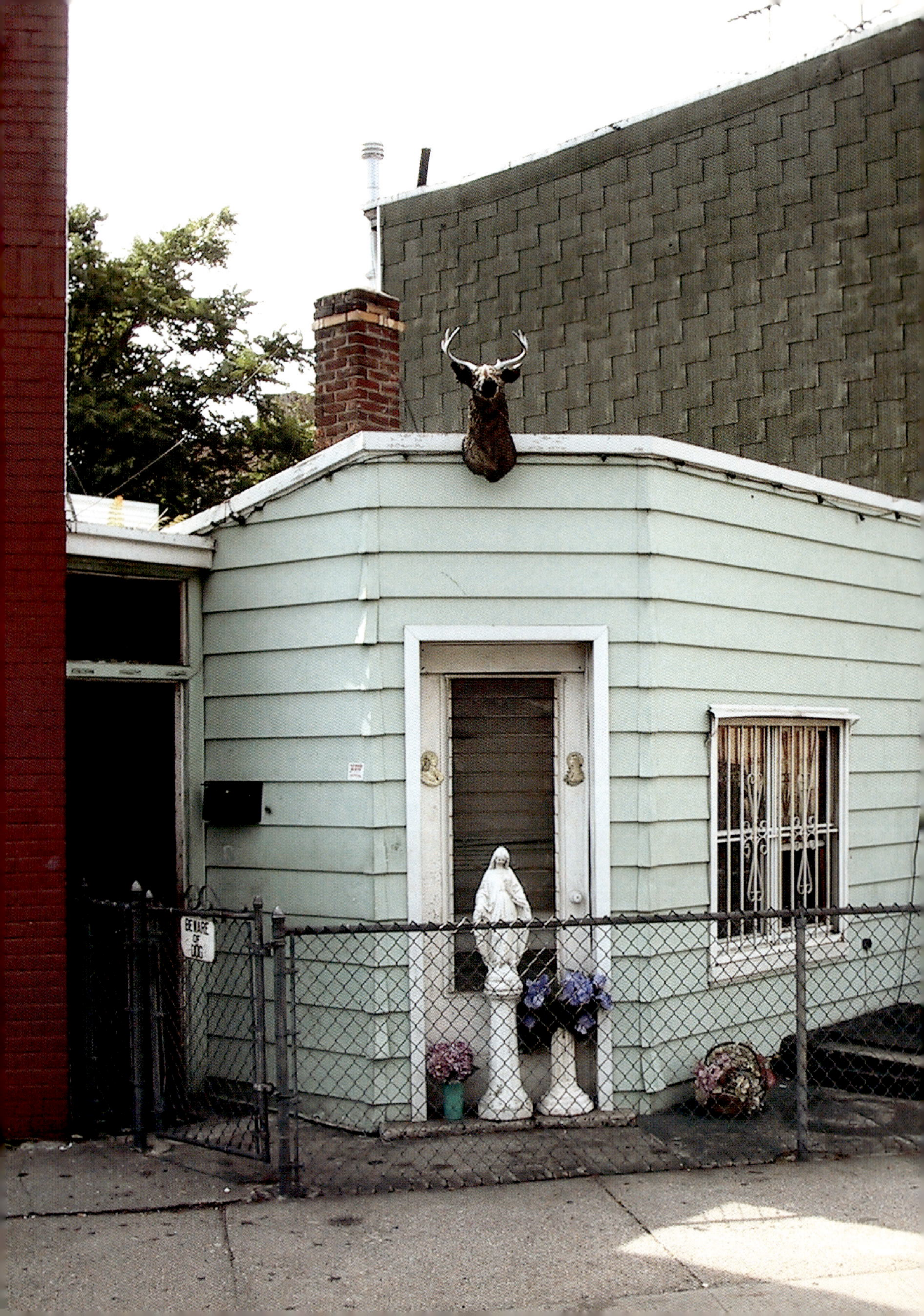
BEWARE
OF
DOG

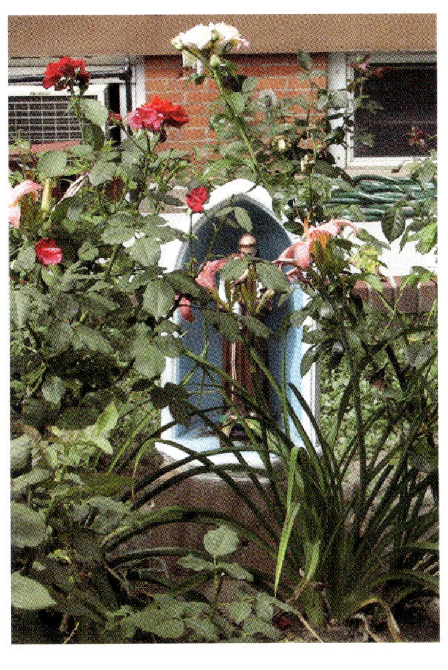

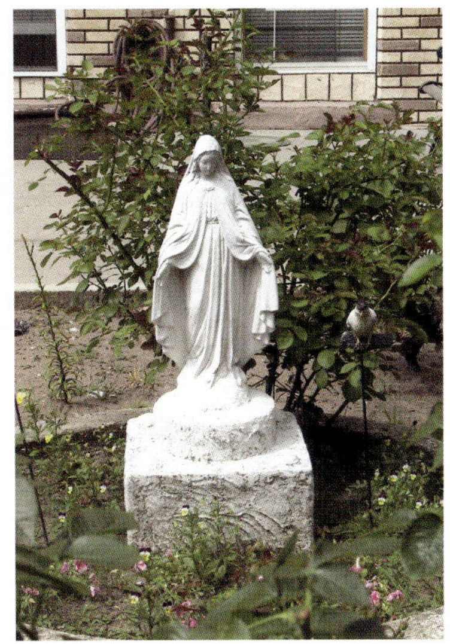

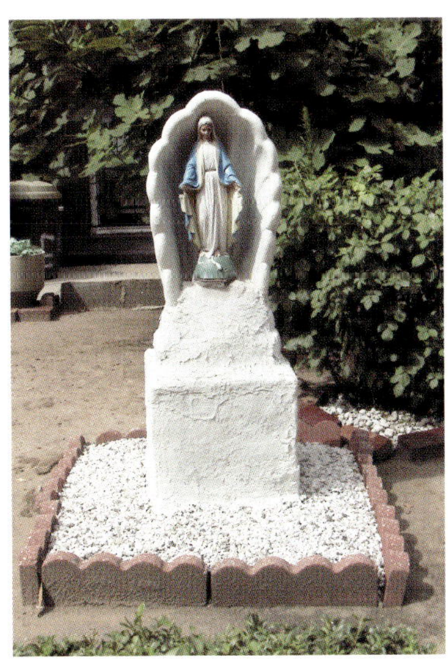

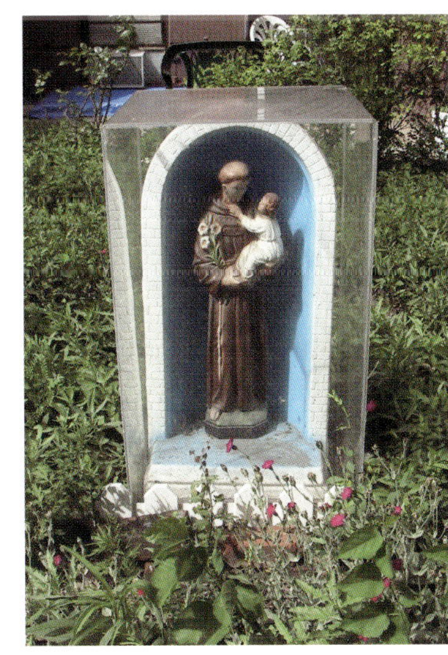

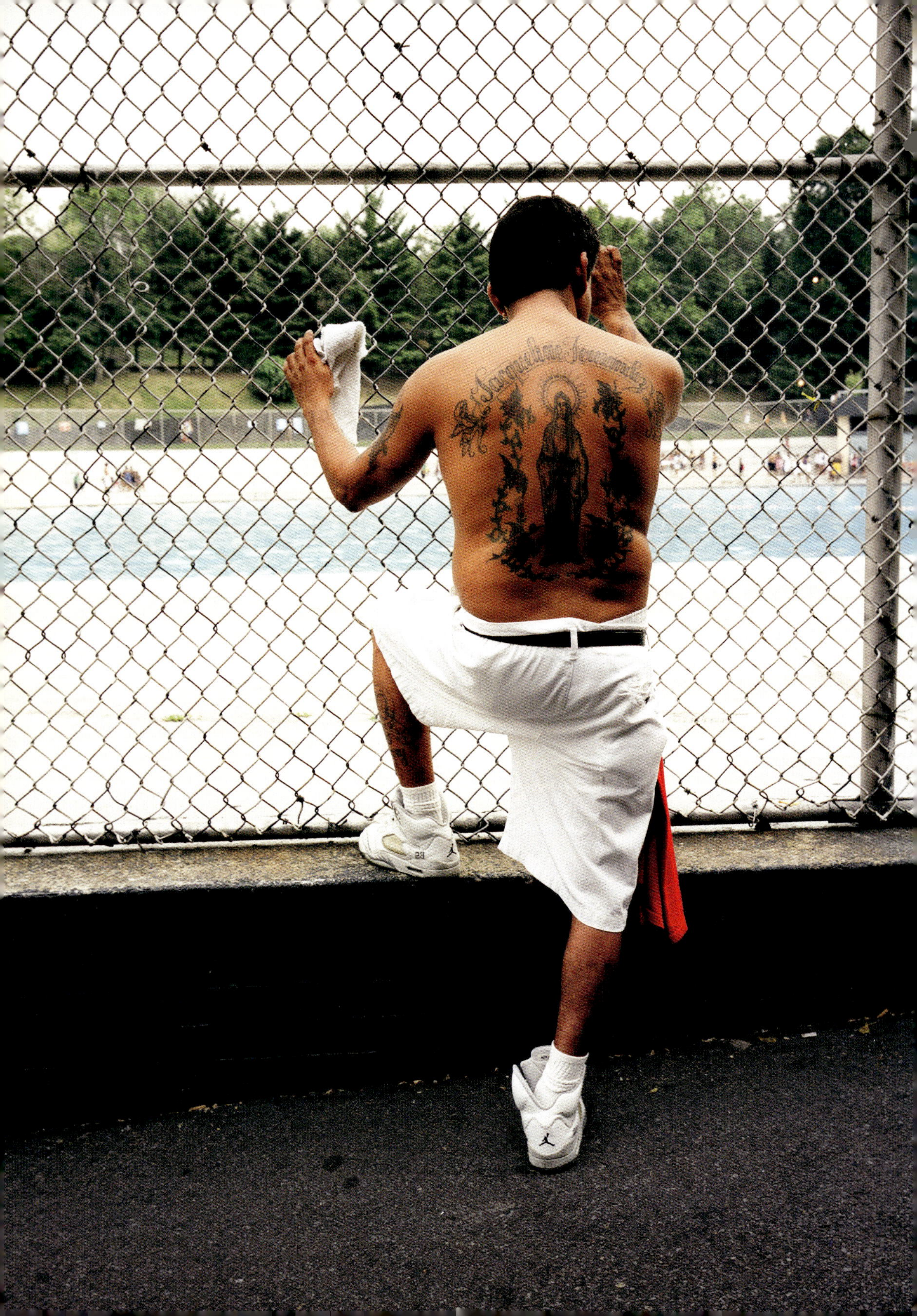

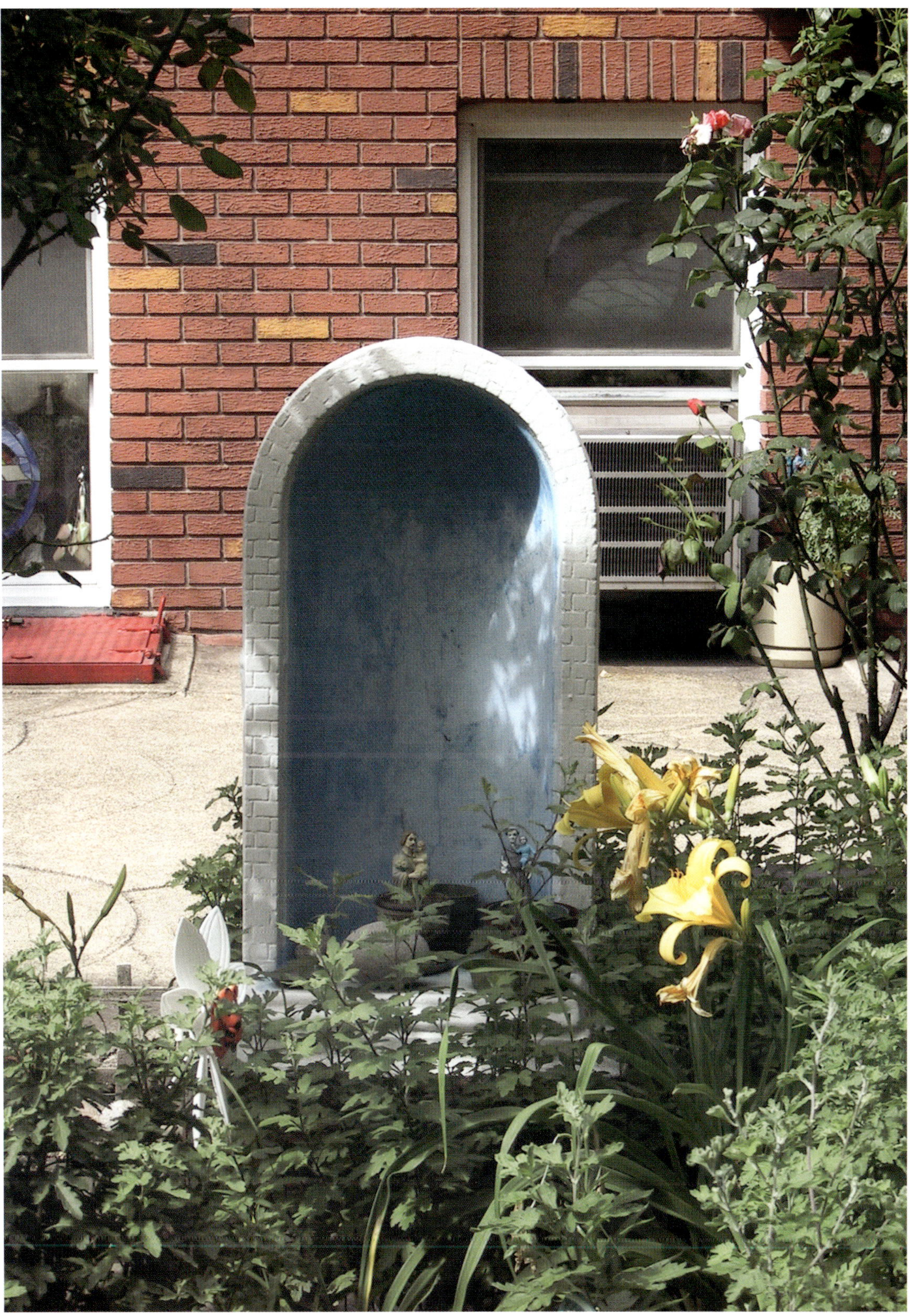

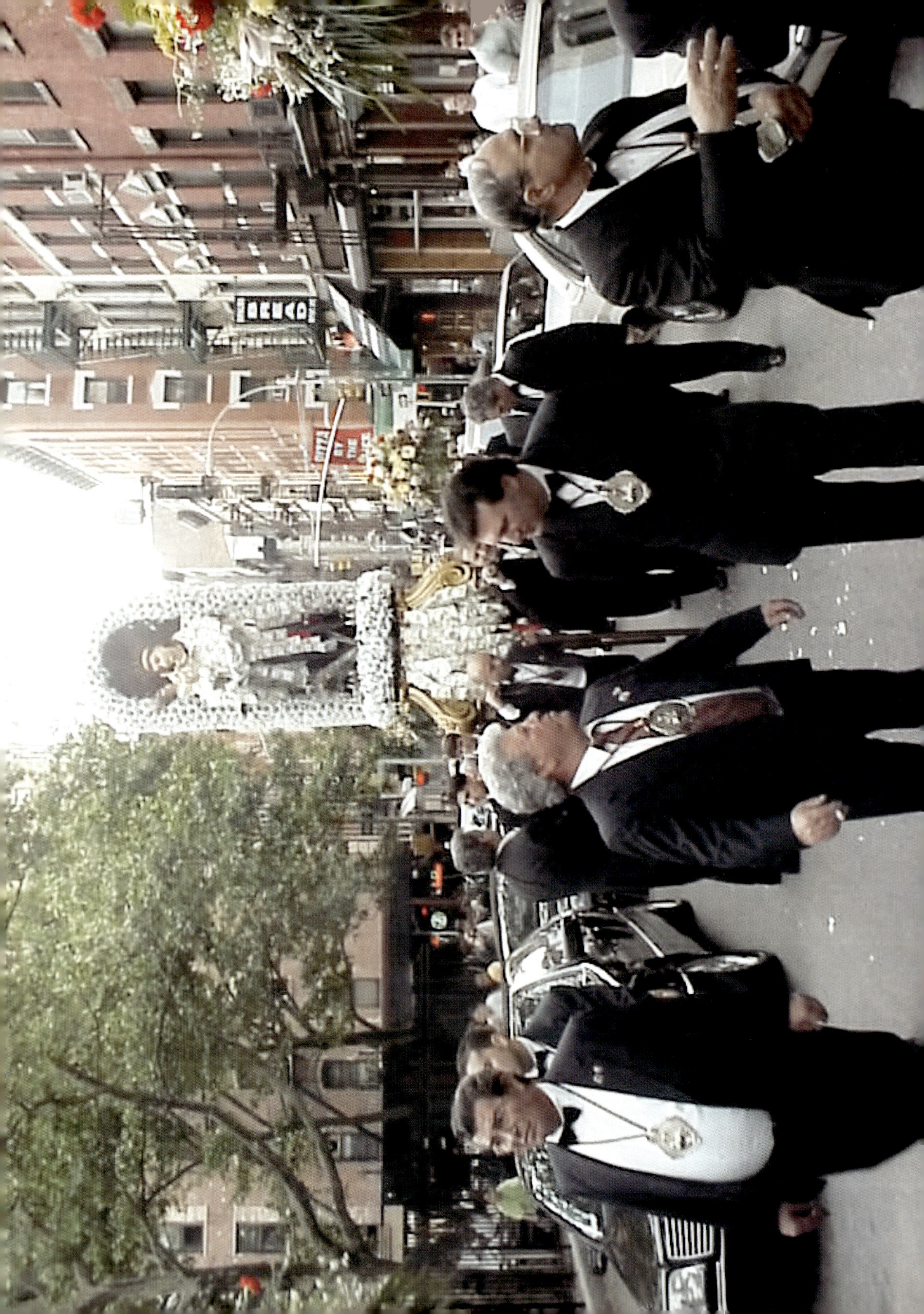

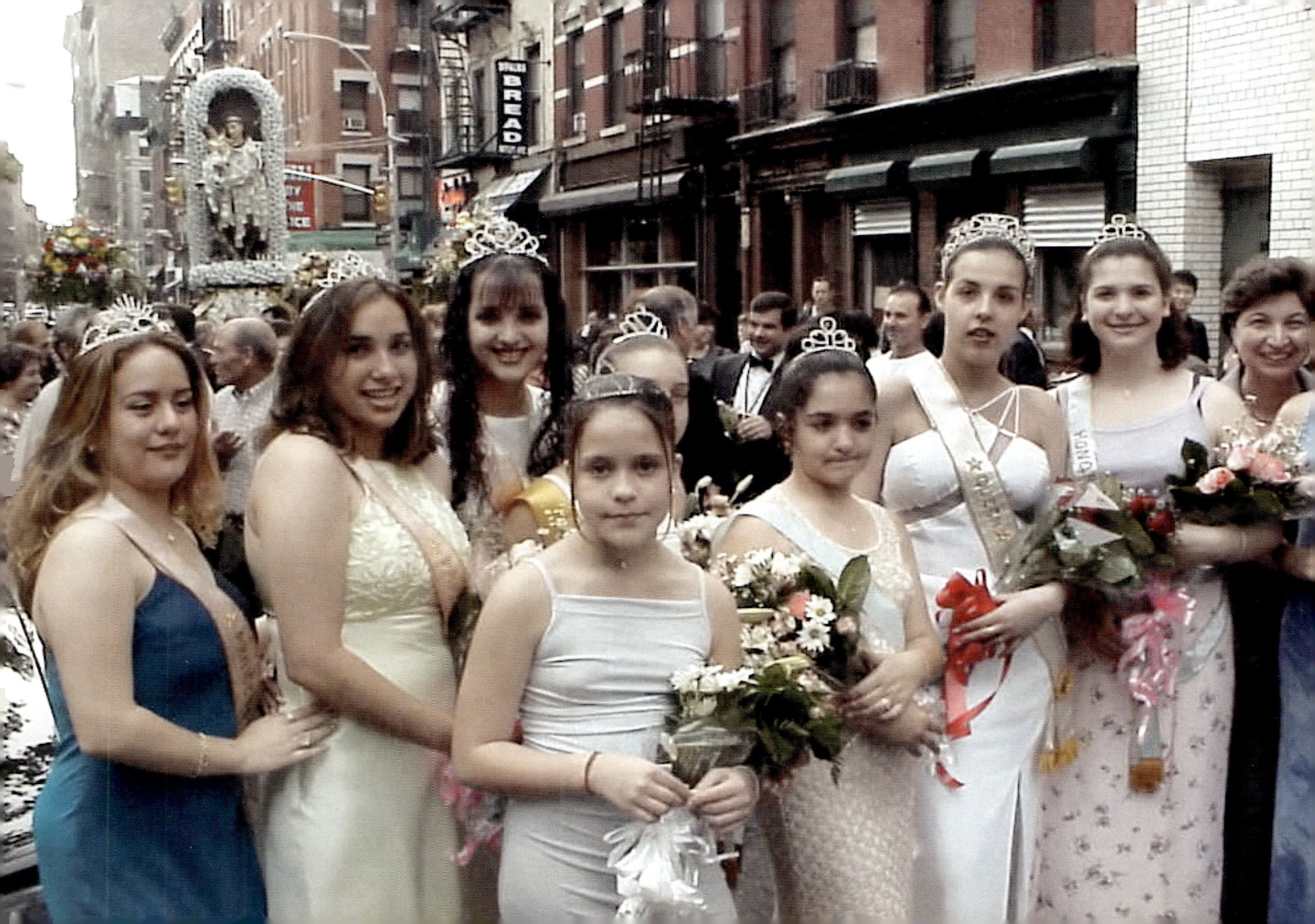
BREAD

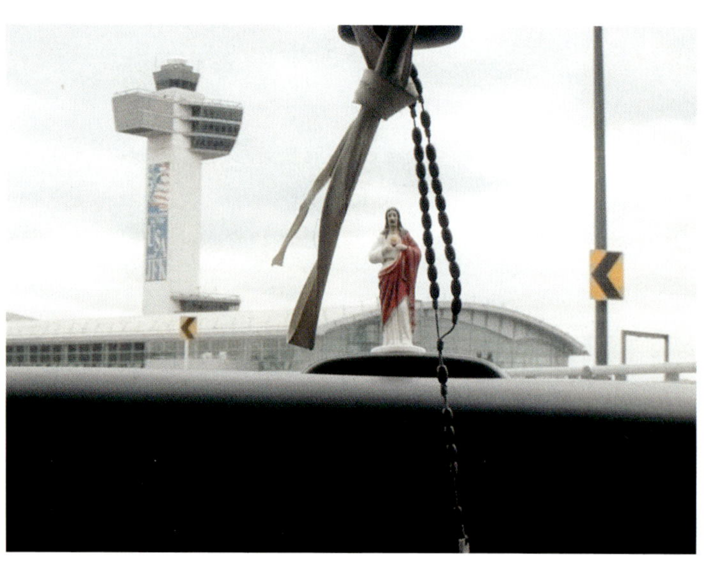

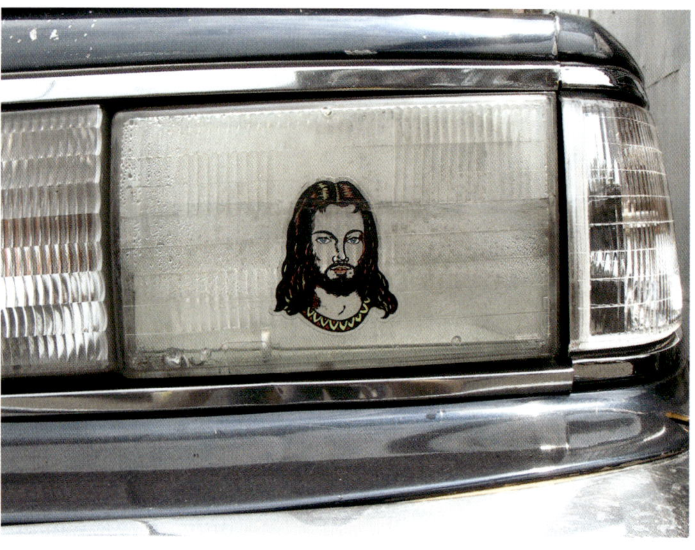

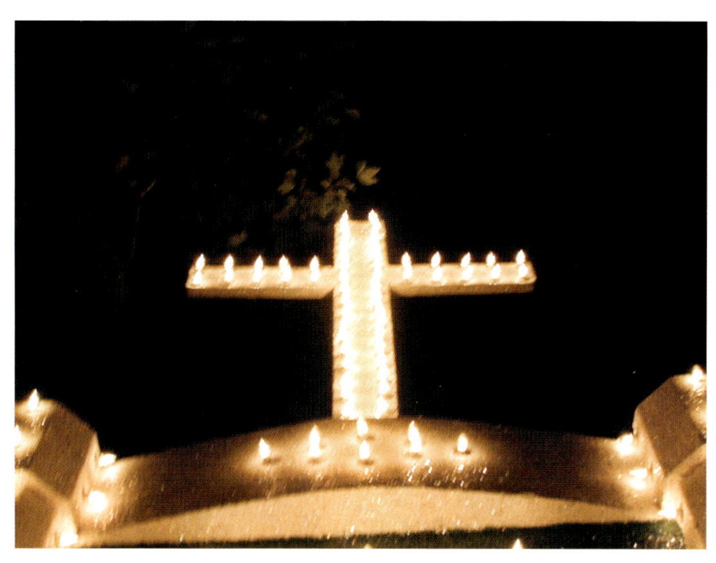

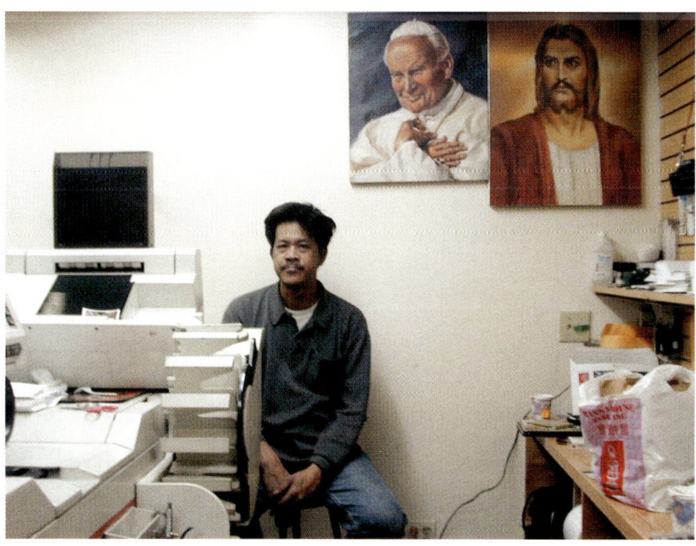

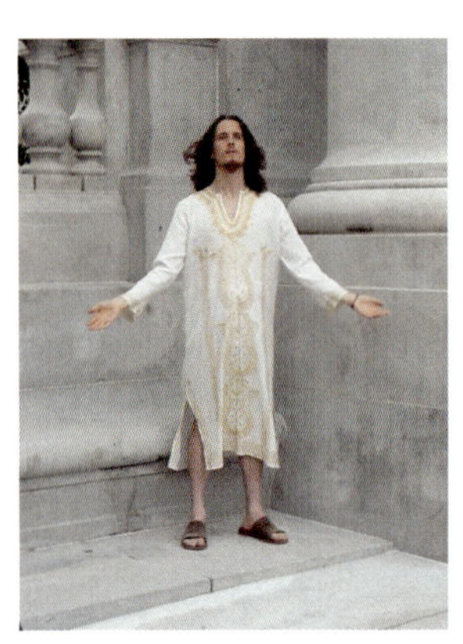

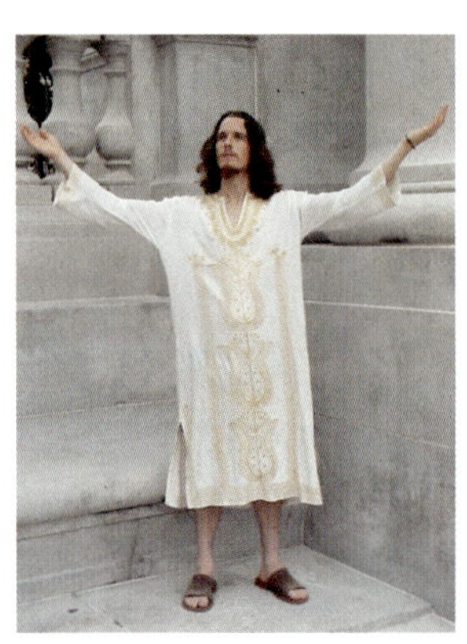

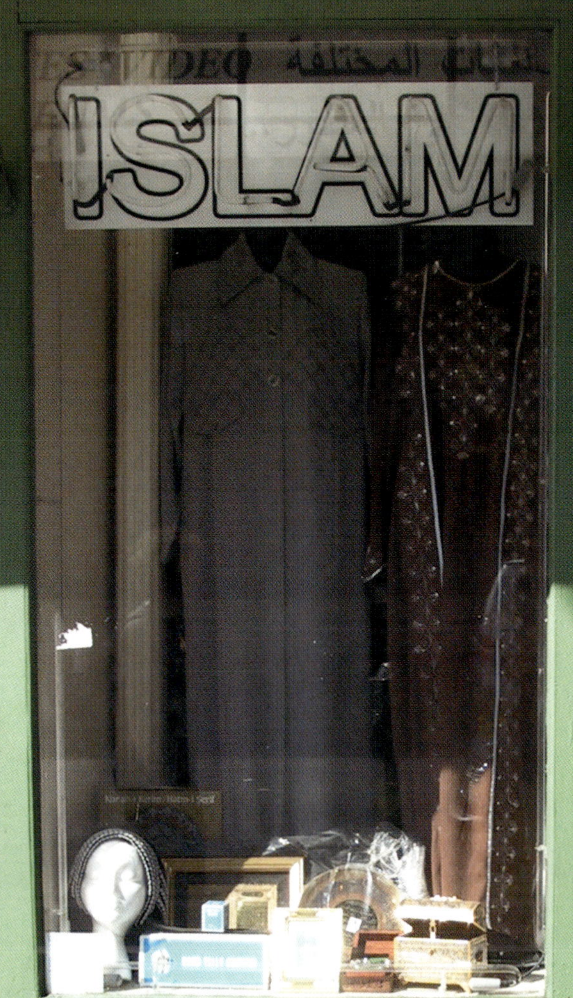
ISLAM
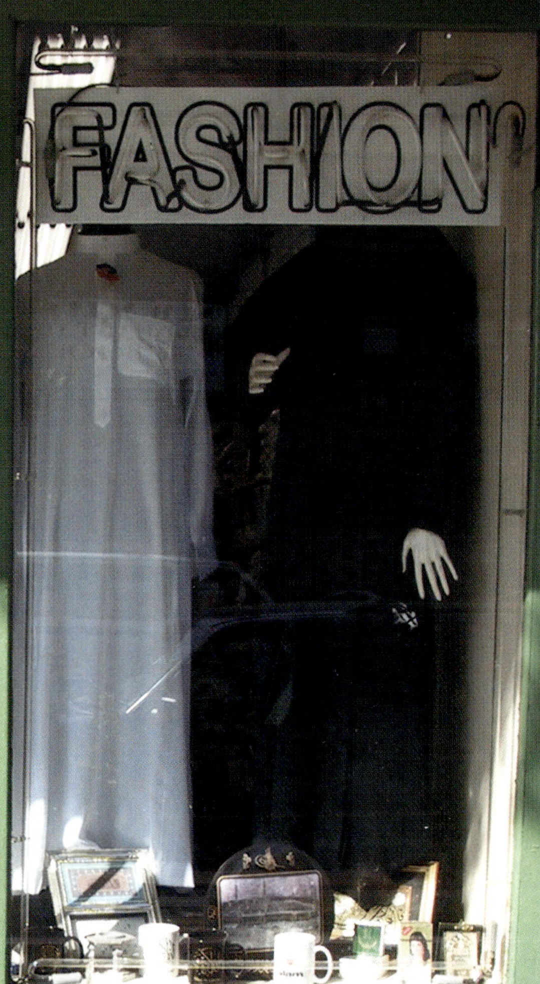
FASHION
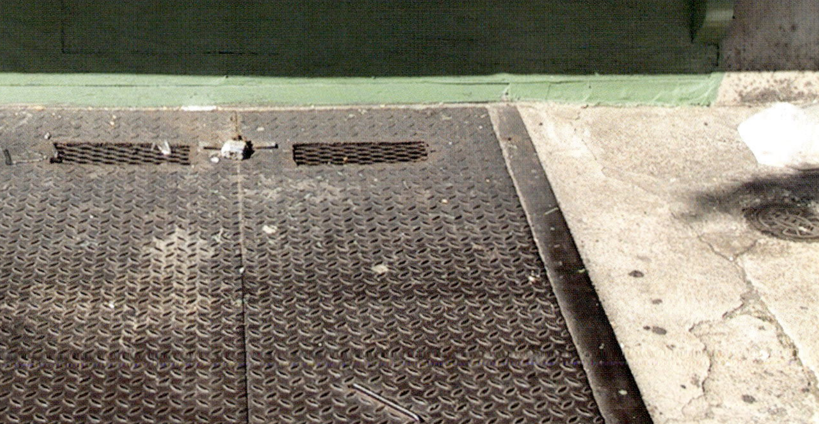

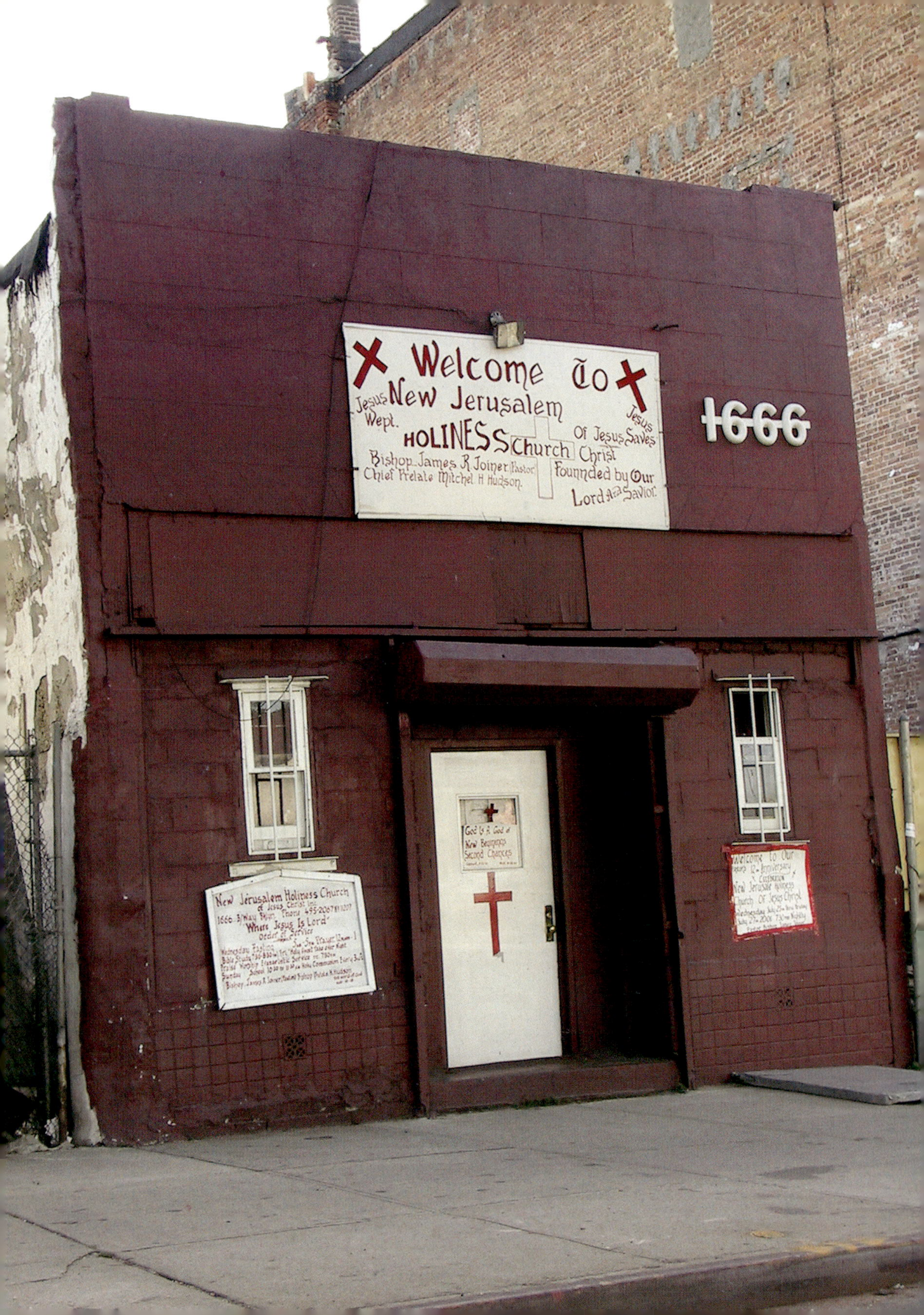
Welcome To
Jesus Wept.
New Jerusalem
HOLINESS Church
Of Jesus Christ
Jesus Saves
Bishop James R. Joiner Pastor
Chief Prelate Mitchel H Hudson
Founnded by Our Lord and Savior
1666
God Is A God of
Second Chances
New Jerusalem Holiness Church
"Where Jesus Is Lord"
Order of Service
Welcome to Our

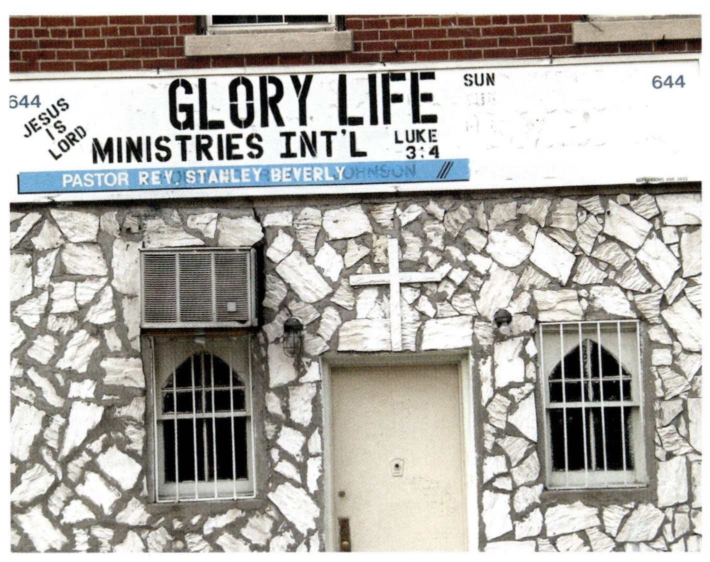
644
JESUS IS LORD
GLORY LIFE
MINISTRIES INT'L
SUN
LUKE 3:4
644
PASTOR REV. STANLEY BEVERLY

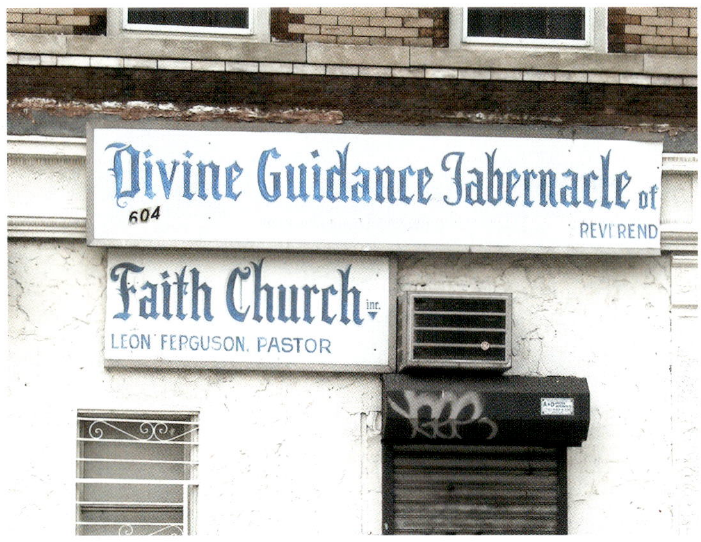
Divine Guidance Tabernacle of
604
REVEREND
Faith Church inc.
LEON FERGUSON, PASTOR

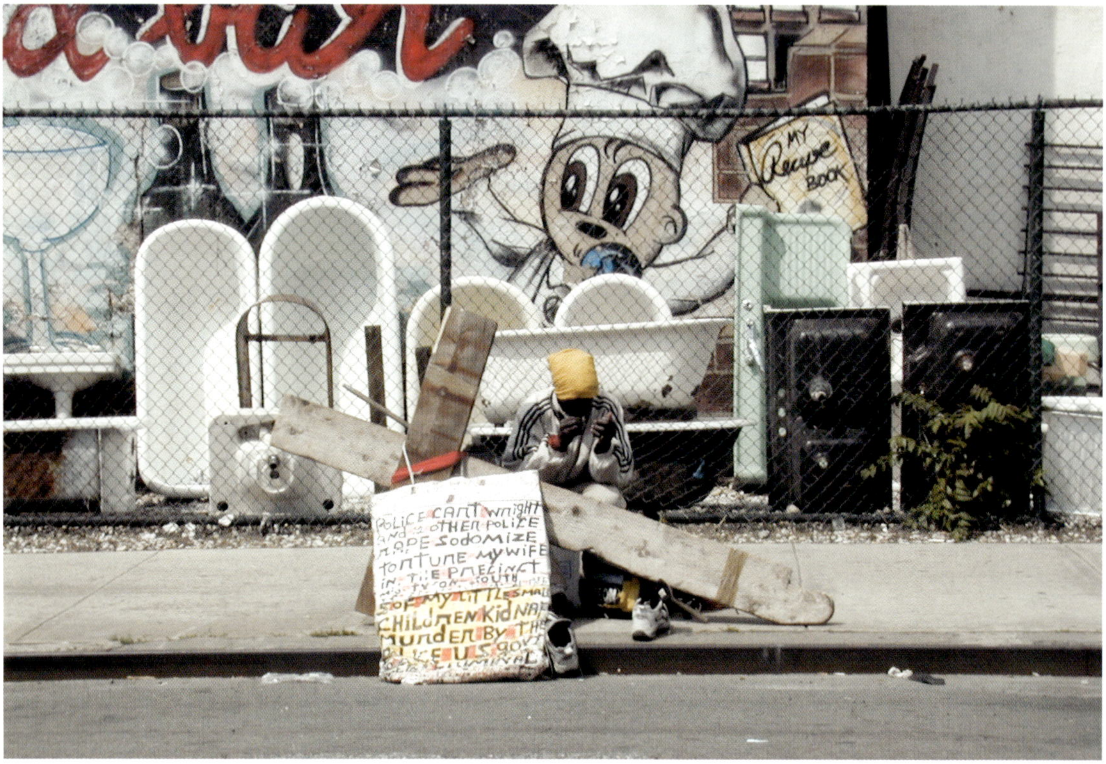
MY
Recipe
BOOK
POLICE CANT WRIGHT
AND OTHER POLIZE
SODOMIZE
MY WIFE
IN THE PRECINCT
MY LITTLE SMA
CHILDREN KIDNA
MURDER BY TH
U.S. GOV

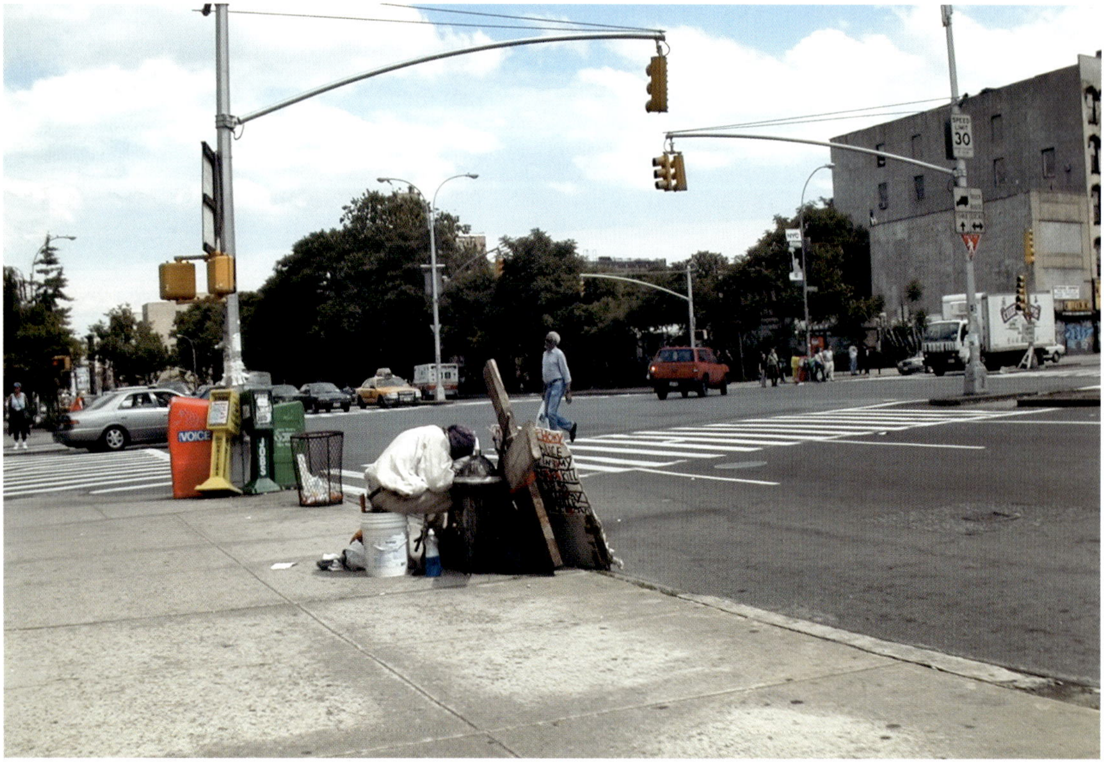
VOICE
SPEED LIMIT
30

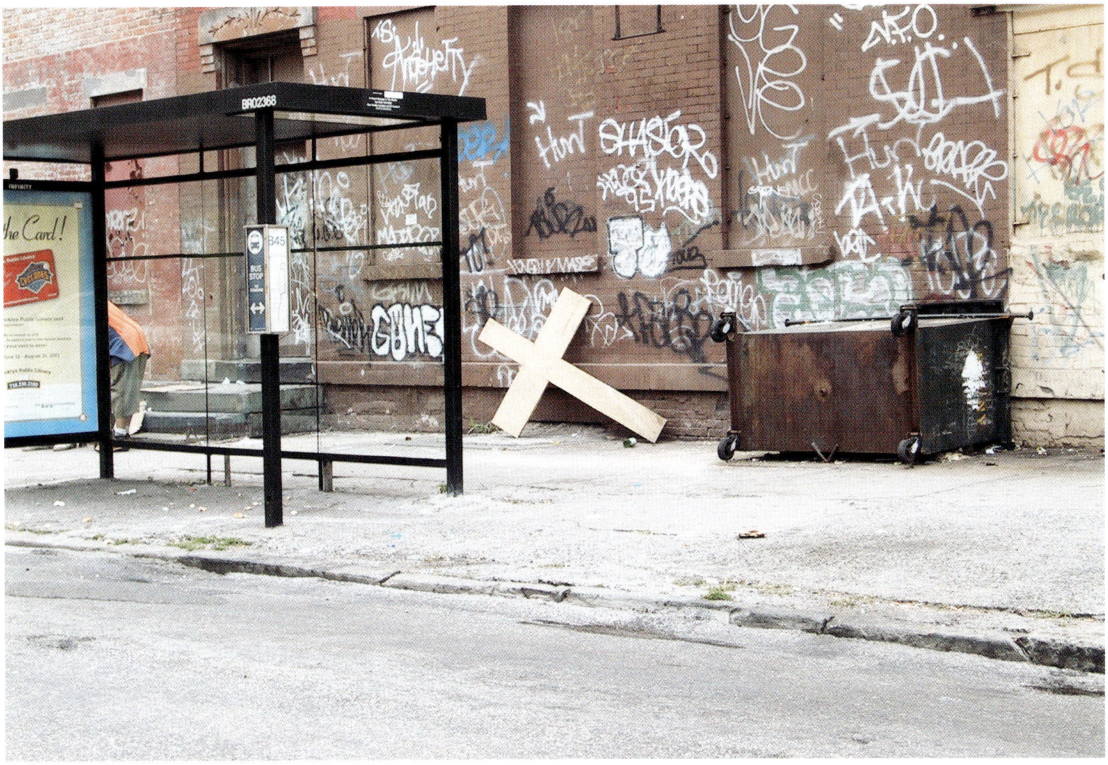

BR02368
BUS STOP 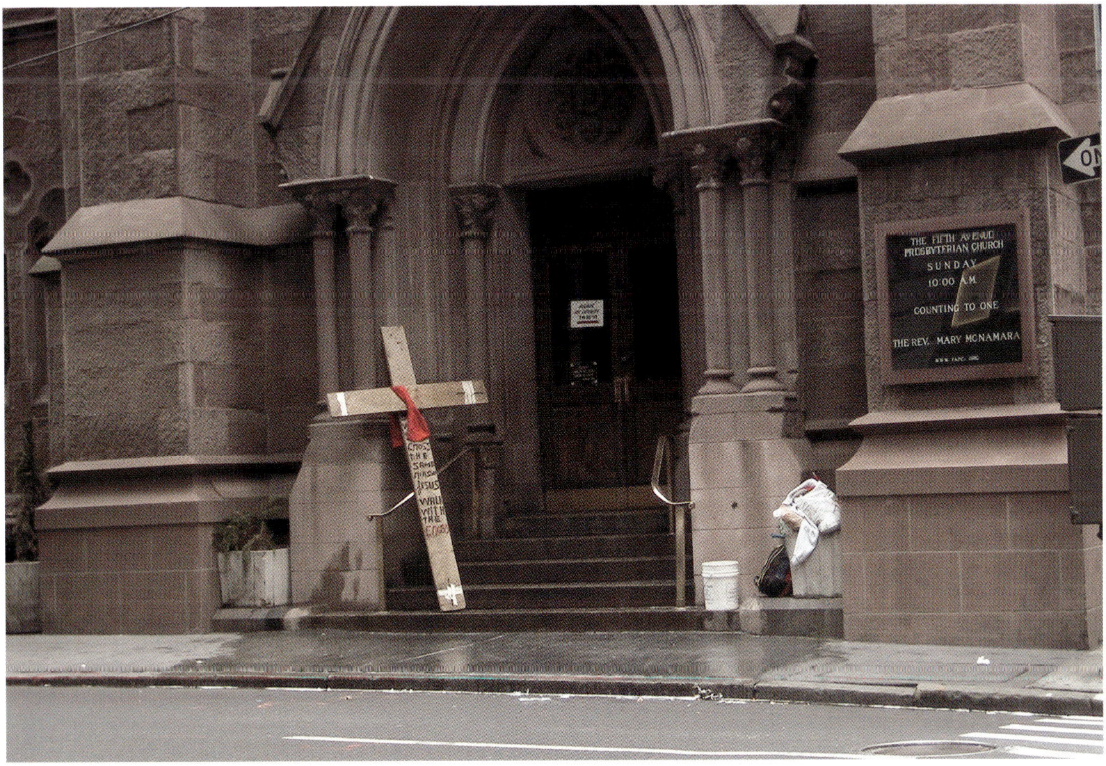
B45
THE FIFTH AVENUE
PRESBYTERIAN CHURCH
SUNDAY
10:00 A.M.
COUNTING TO ONE
THE REV. MARY MCNAMARA

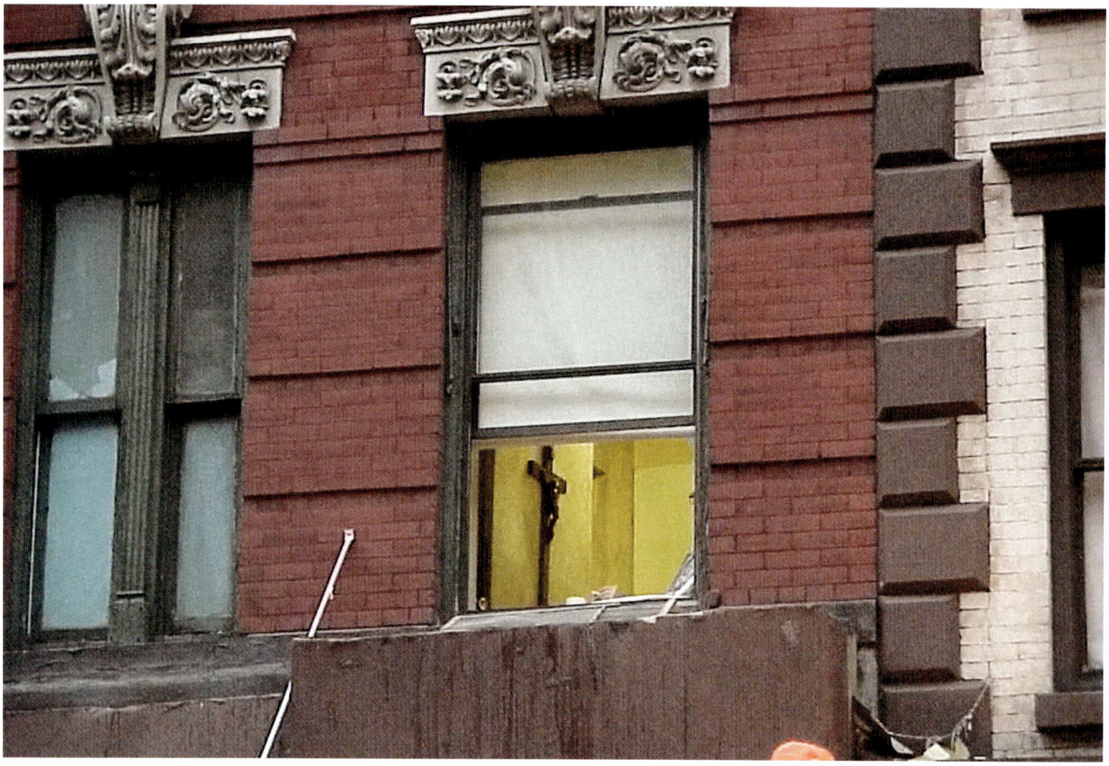

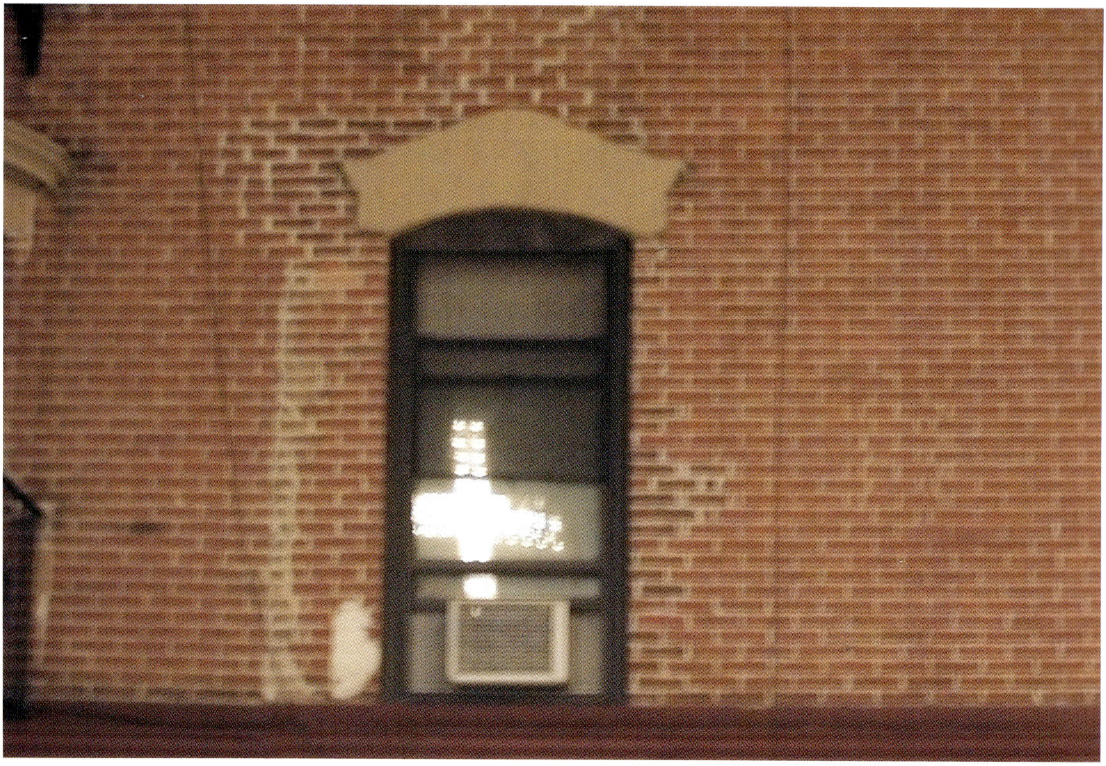

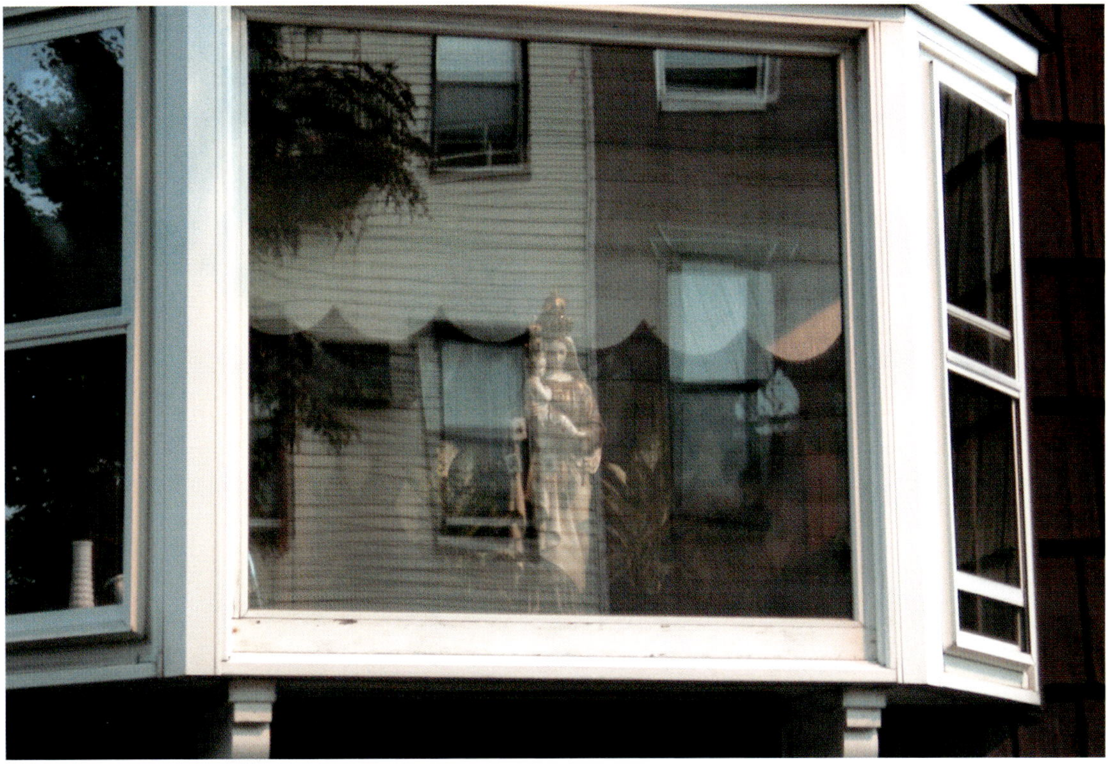

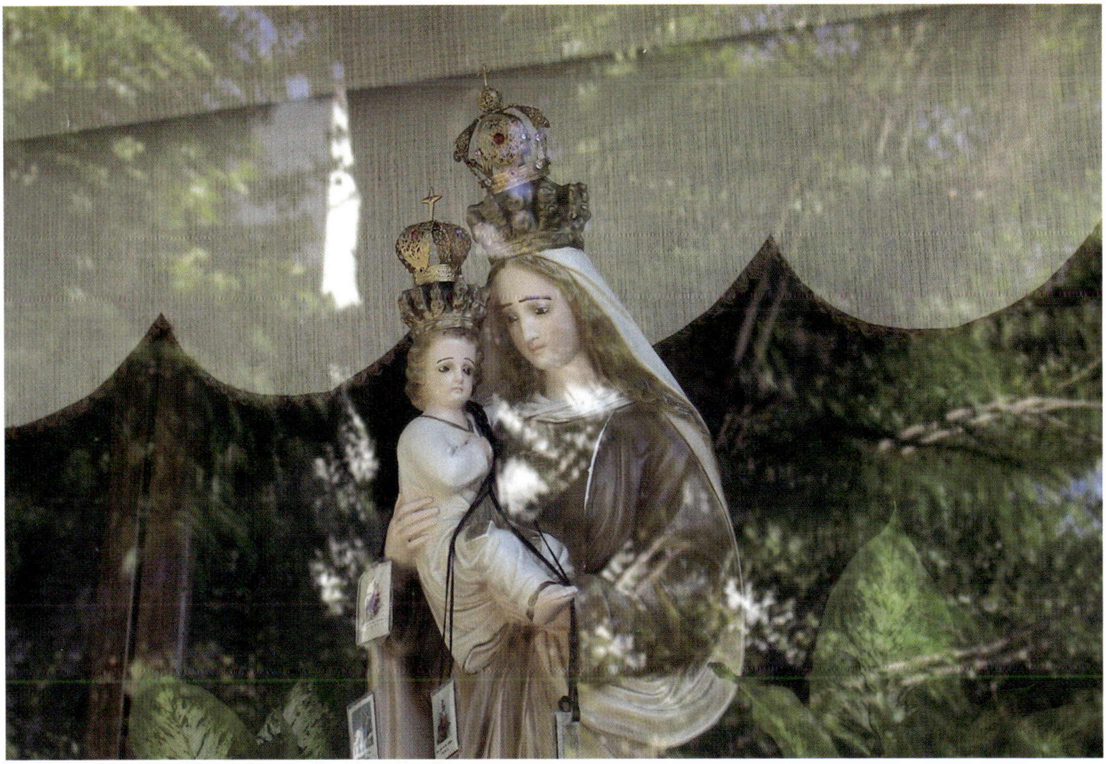

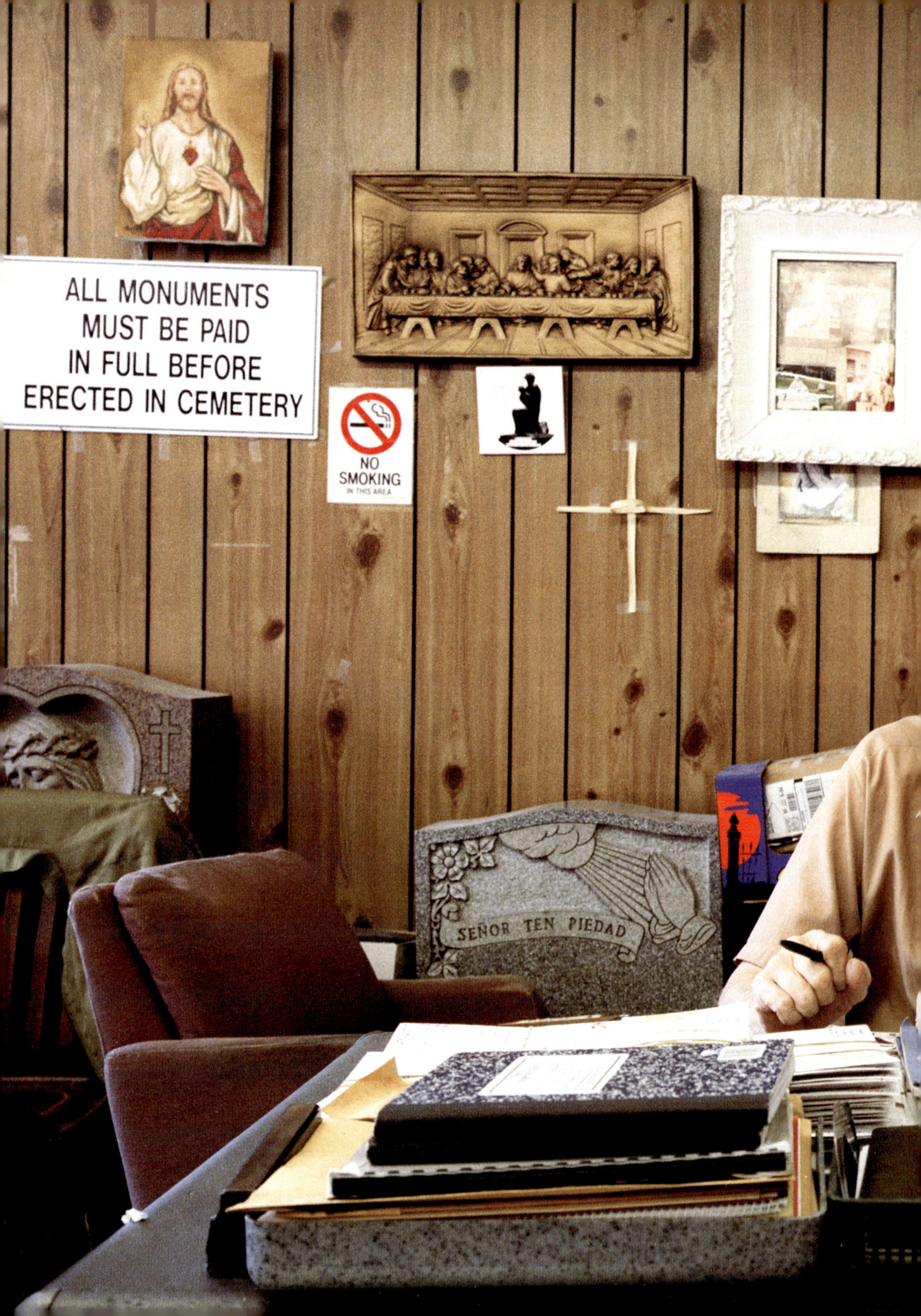
ALL MONUMENTS
MUST BE PAID
IN FULL BEFORE
ERECTED IN CEMETERY
NO
SMOKING
IN THIS AREA
SEÑOR TEN PIEDAD

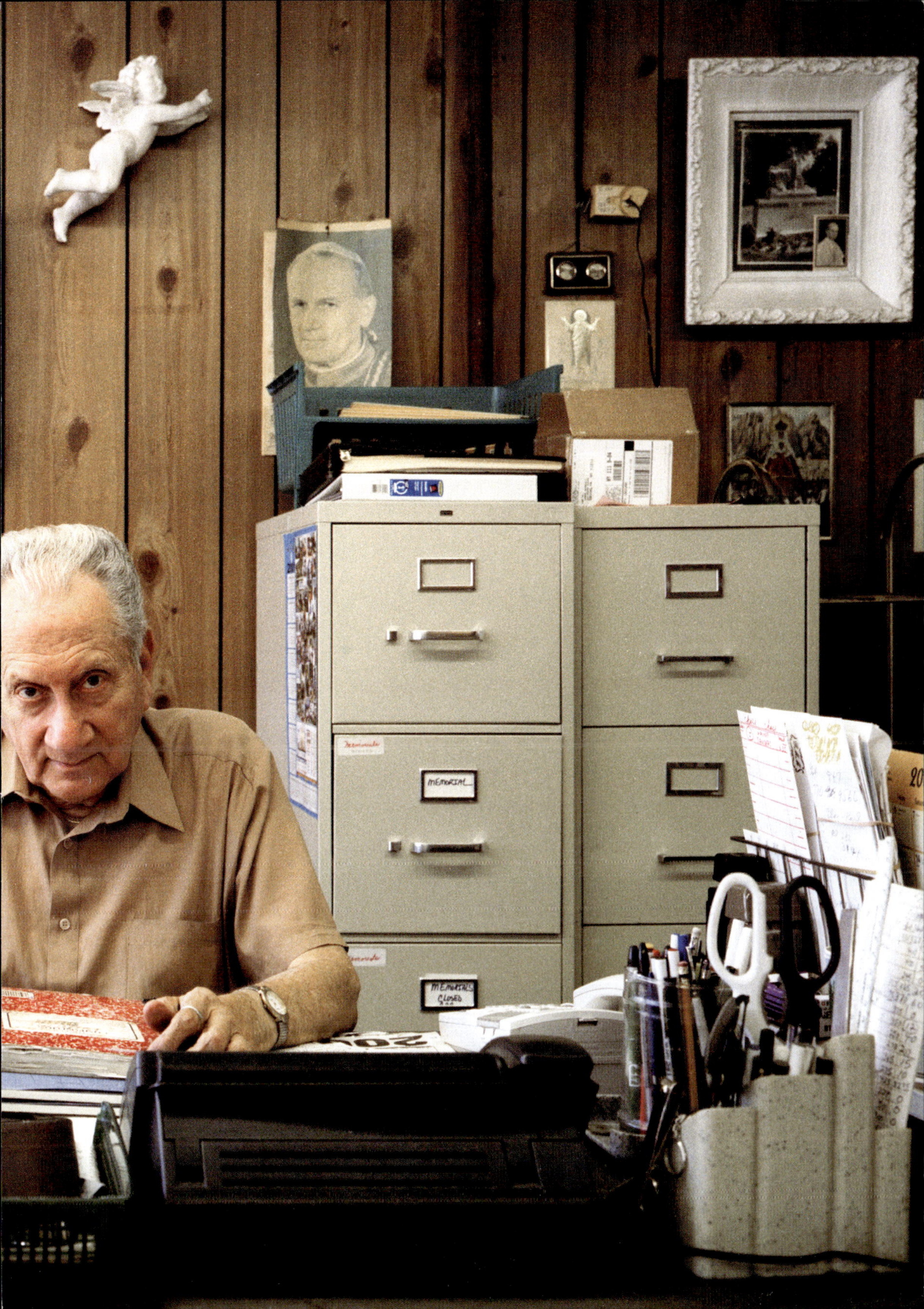
MEMORIAL

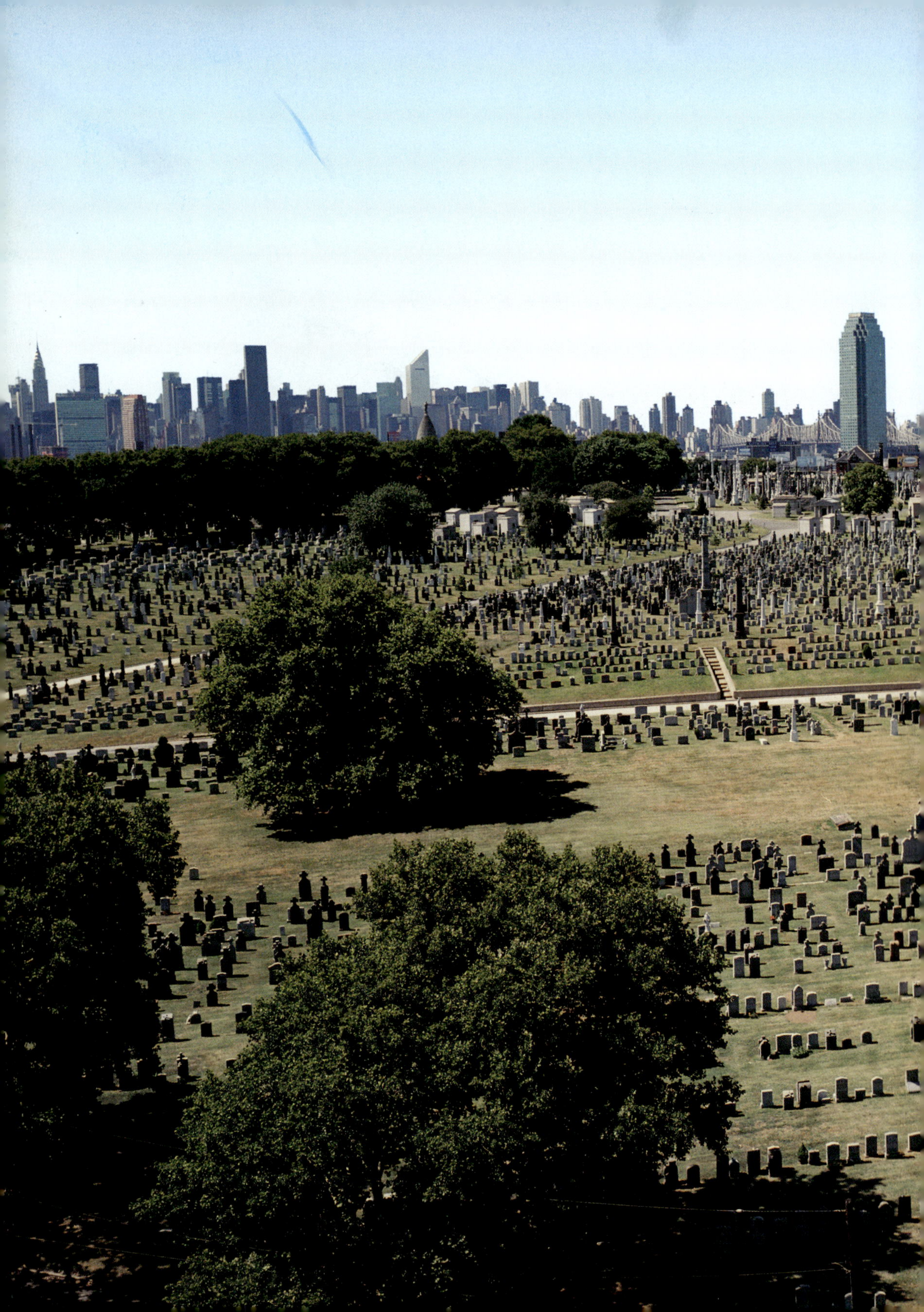

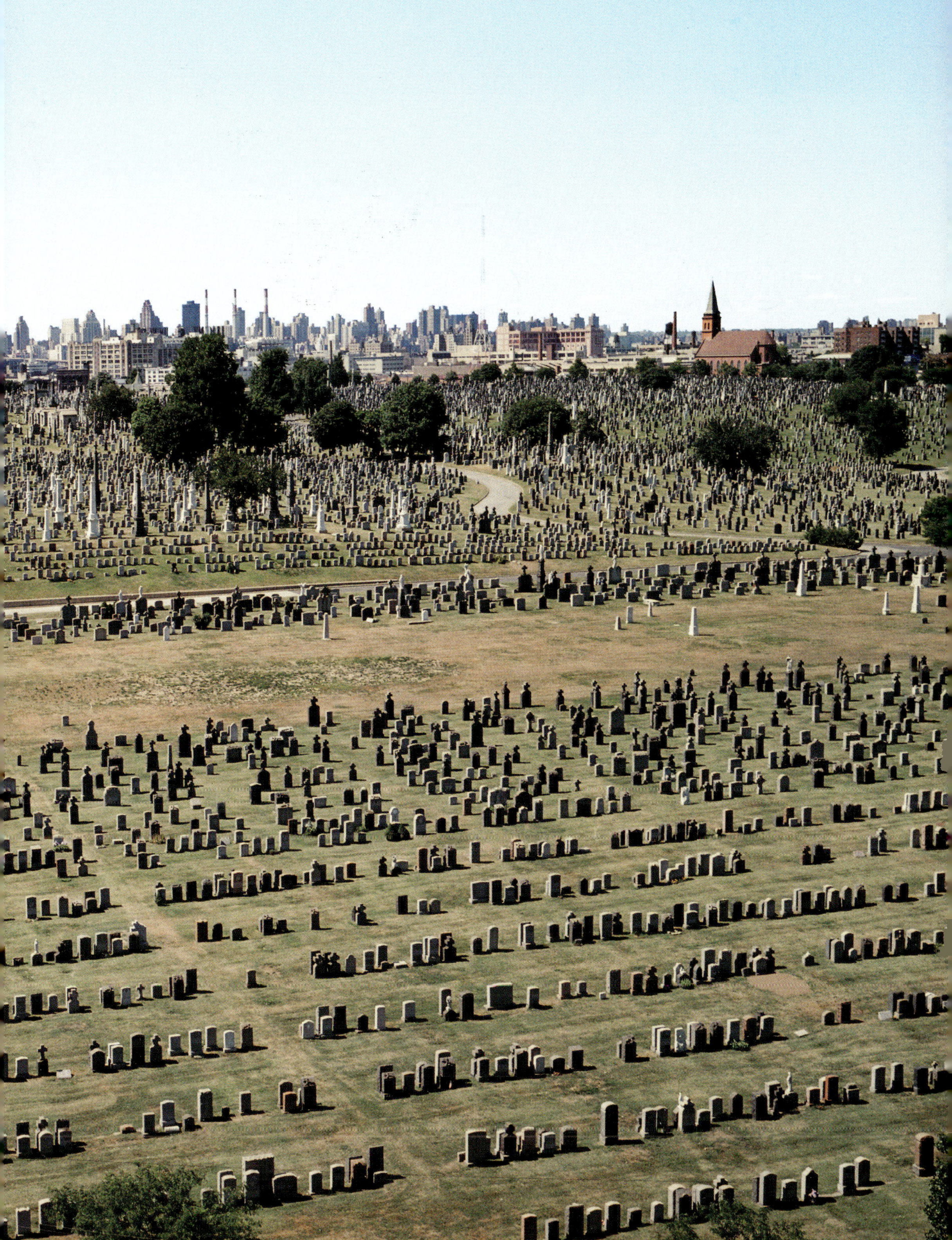

ENDCOMMERCIAL® Reading the City

Edited by Wolfgang Scheppe, Florian Böhm

Produced by SBA / Scheppe Böhm Associates

Art Direction by Wolfgang Scheppe, Florian Böhm

All Photography by Florian Böhm, Luca Pizzaroni, Wolfgang Scheppe

Published by Hatje Cantz Publishers, Senefelderstraße 12, 73760 Ostfildern-Ruit, Germany, www.hatjecantz.com

US Distribution by D.A.P., Distributed Art Publishers, Inc., 155 Ave. of the Americas, New York, NY 10013-1507, USA

ISBN 3-7757-1221-6

Printed in Germany

is a multidisciplinary creative office developing communication and identity strategies for countries, organizations and corporations.

Lindwurmstr. 71, 80337 Munich, Germany, ++49 - 89 - 544 03 588, mail@scheppeboehm.de

New York 32 Spring Street 1, New York, NY 10012, ++1 - 212 - 966 42 31, mail@scheppeboehm.com

Thanks to Ryan Monihan, Elizabeth Franzen, Marie Letz, Judy Payawal, Molly Robinson, Annika Schroeter, Martin Winkler

Additional Picture Commentary www.endcommercial.com
Press Information www.press.endcommercial.com
Daily Output www.digitalslum.com

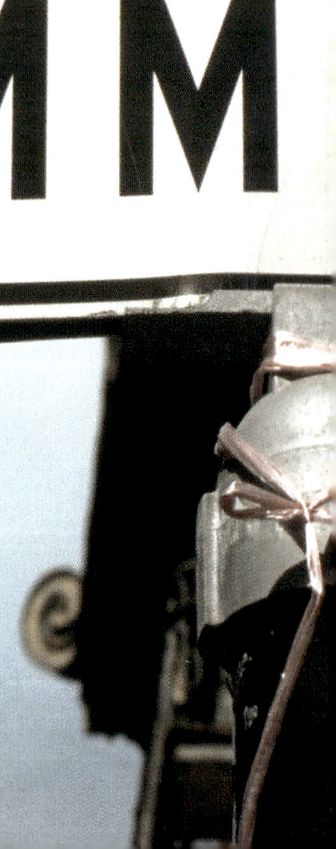
E
COMM

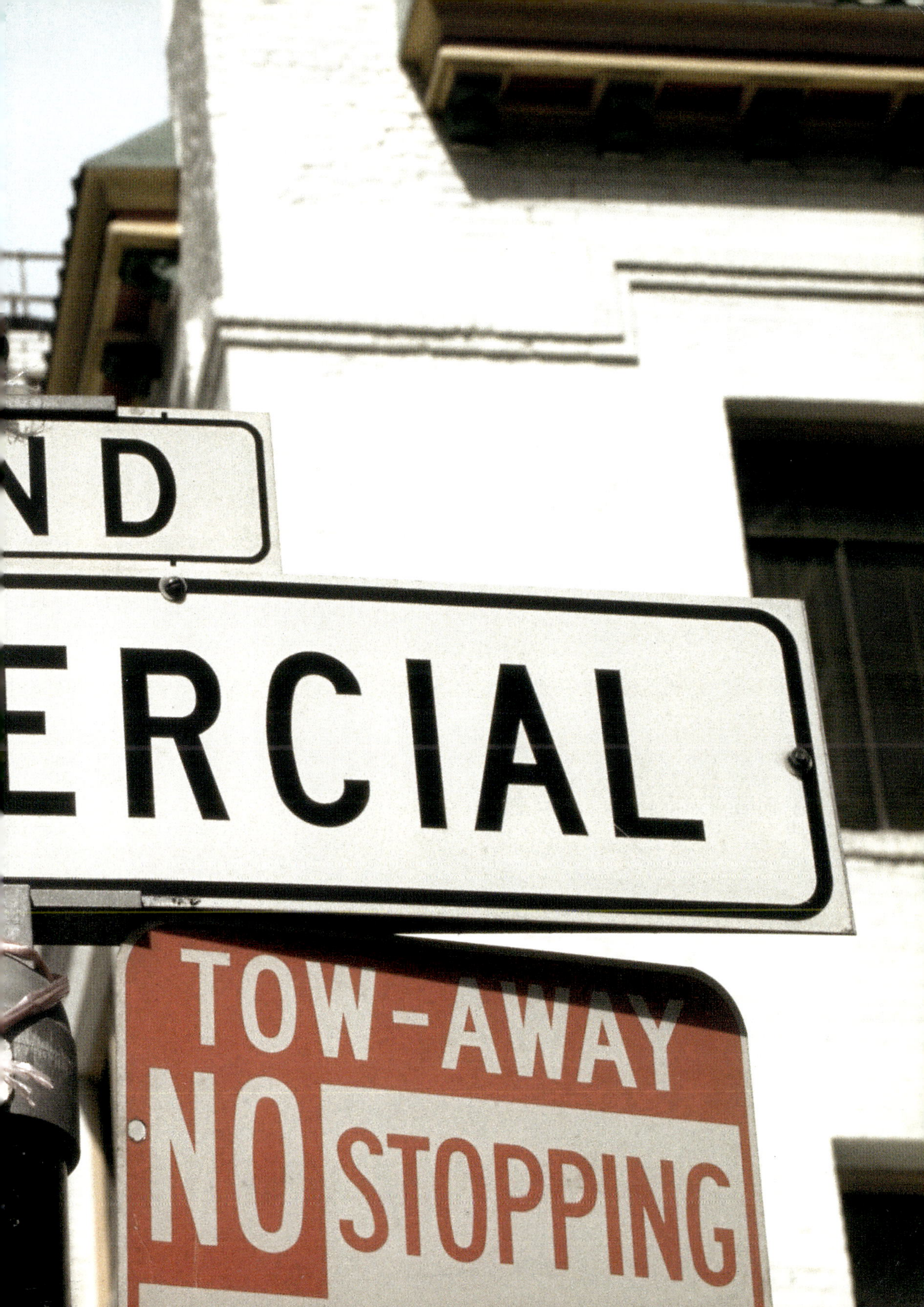
ND
ERCIAL
TOW-AWAY
NO STOPPING

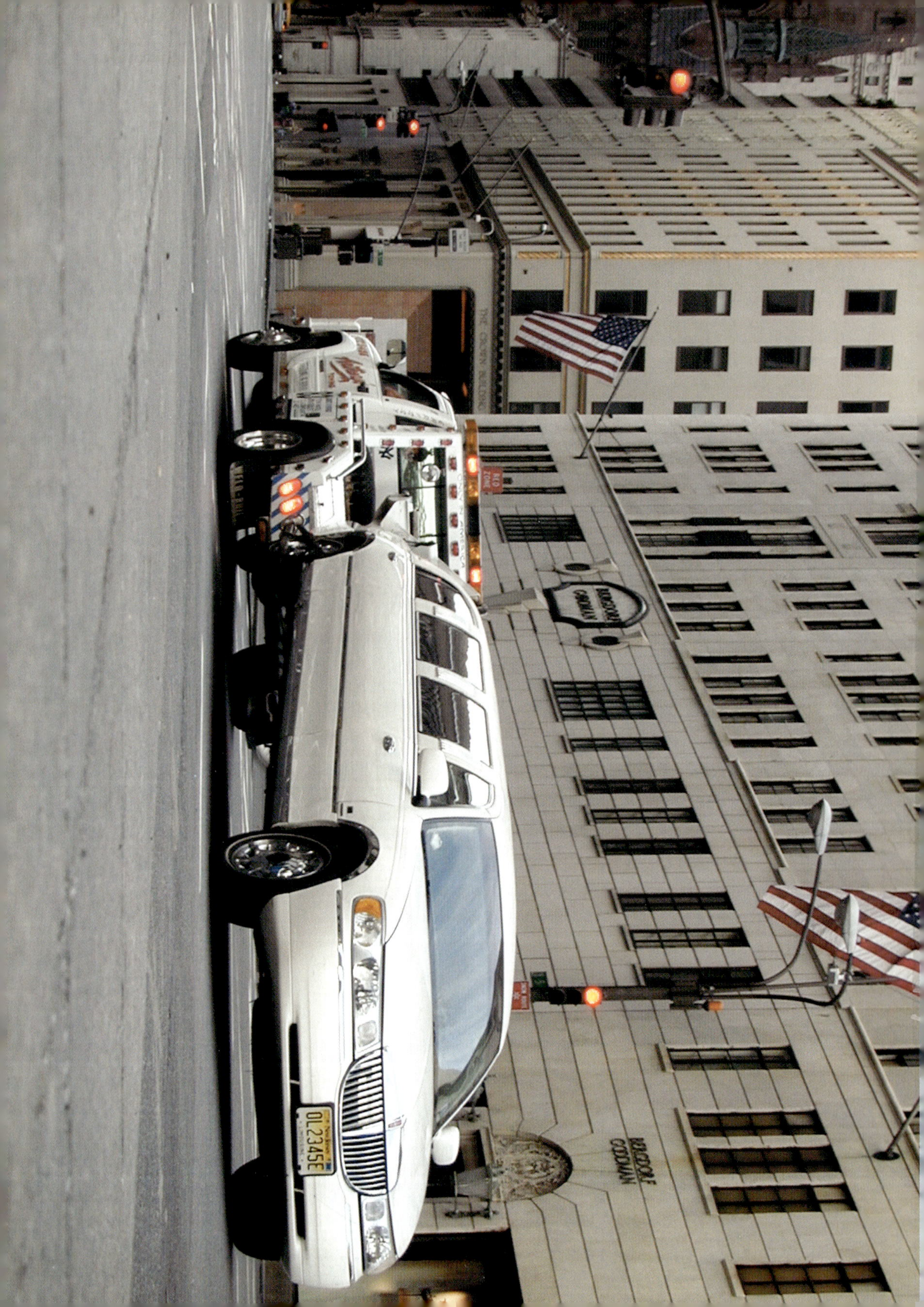

Art Works

••• you must know
•• you should know
• & you really impress if you know

999

Kunstwerke

••• die man kennen muss
•• die man kennen sollte
• & deren Kenntnis beeindruckt

Kunstwerken

••• die je moet kennen
•• die je zou moeten kennen
• en waarmee je indruk maakt als je ze kent

SCALA

62, via Chiantigiana
50012 Bagno a Ripoli
Florence (Italy)

Text and picture research: Sara Bertelli, Mila Magistri
Phrases: Dogma Moguntinae

English translation: Johanna Kreiner
German and Dutch translations: Play sounds and words

Printed in China 2009

ISBN (English): 978-88-8117-800-1
ISBN (German): 978-88-8117-569-7
ISBN (Dutch): 978-88-8117-678-6

Contents

Inhalt

Index

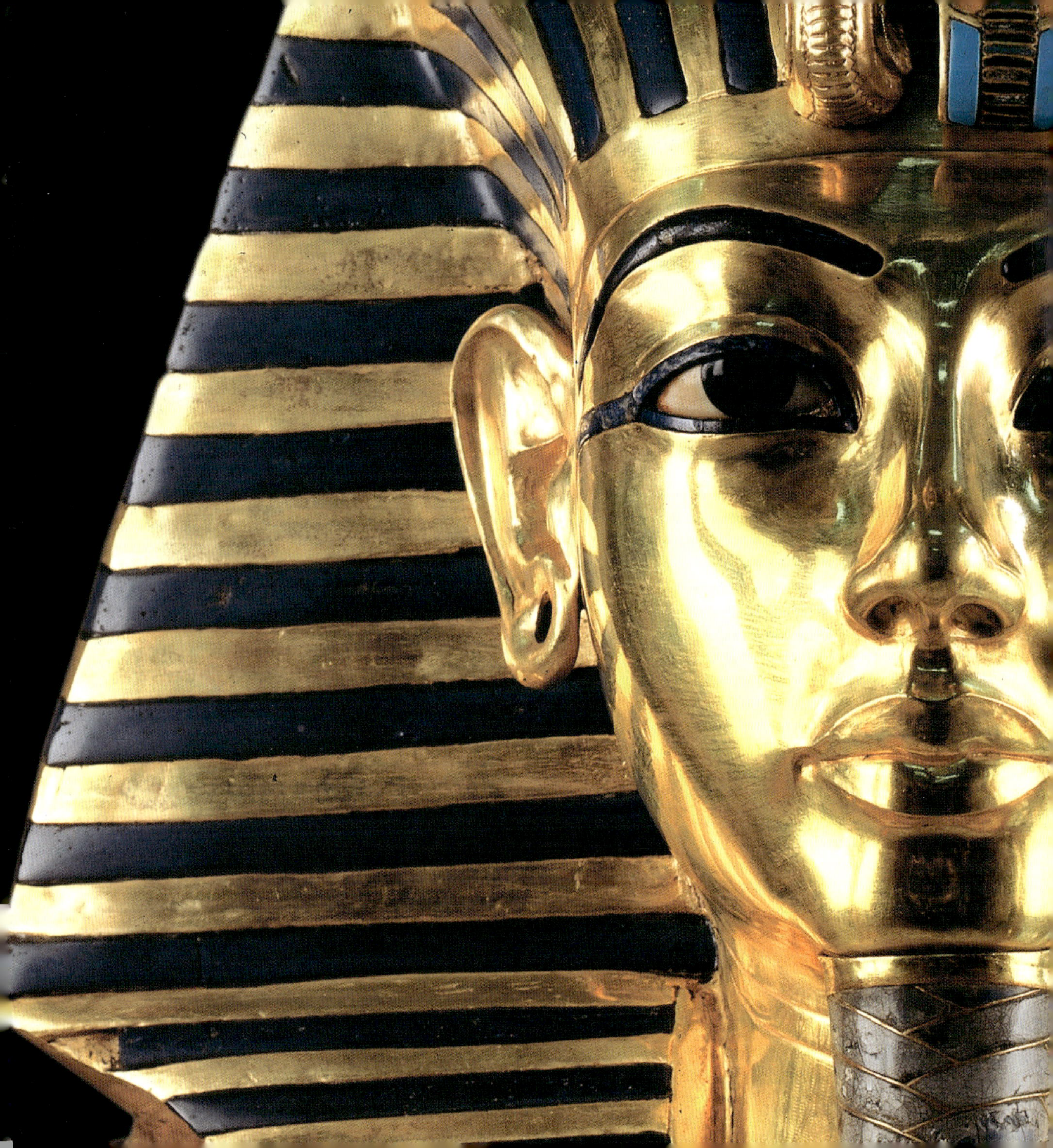

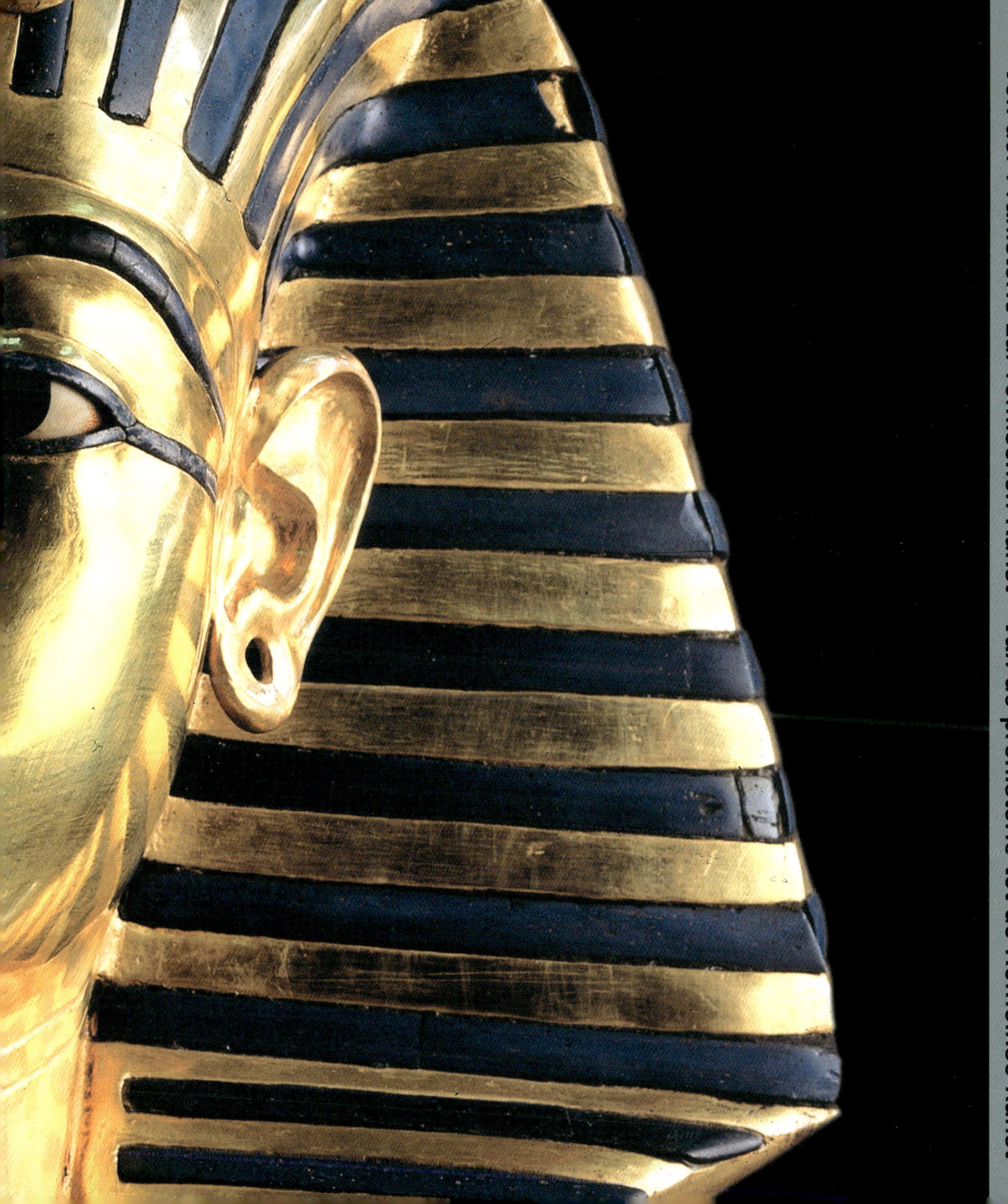

Prehistory to the Roman Empire
Von der Prähistorie zur römischen Kunst • Van de prehistorie tot de Romeinse kunst

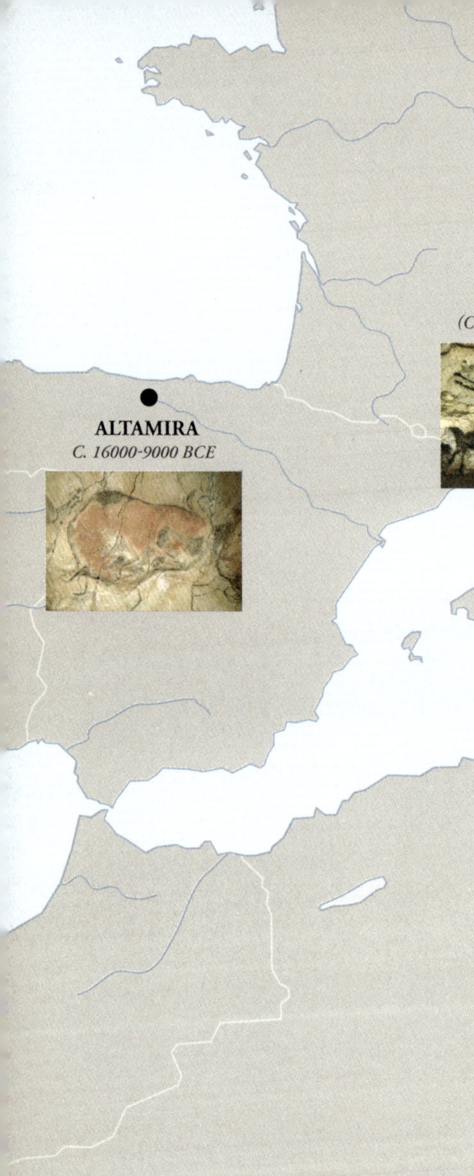

ALTAMIRA
C. 16000-9000 BCE

LASCAUX
(C. 18000-10000 BCE)

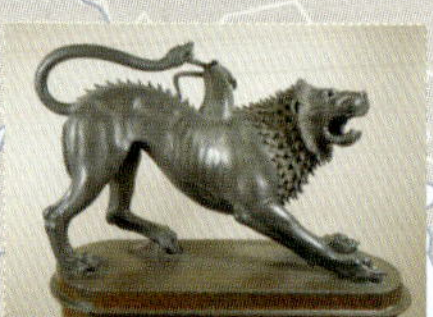

THE ETRUSCANS
DIE ETRUSKER
DE ETRUSKEN
(C. 1000 - C. 250 BCE)

WILLENDORF
(C. 25000 BCE)

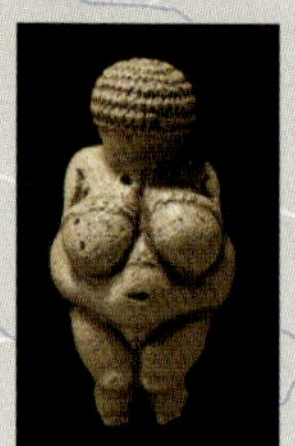

ROMA

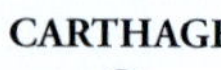

ROMAN EMPIRE
RÖMISCHES REICH
ROMEINSE RIJK
(753 BCE - 476)

MACEDONIAN EMI
ANTIKES GRIECHEN
MACEDONISCHE R
(C. 2500 BCE – 145)

ATHE

MYCENA

CARTHAGE

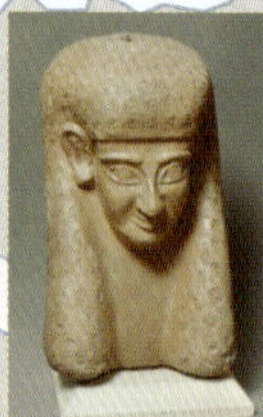

PHOENICIAN EMPIRE
REICH DER PHÖNIZIER
FENICISCHE RIJK
(1200 - 332 BCE)

40.000 YEARS AGO MAN INVENTED ART
VOR 40.000 JAHREN ERFAND DER MENSCH DIE KUNST
40.000 JAREN GELEDEN VOND DE MENS DE KUNST UIT

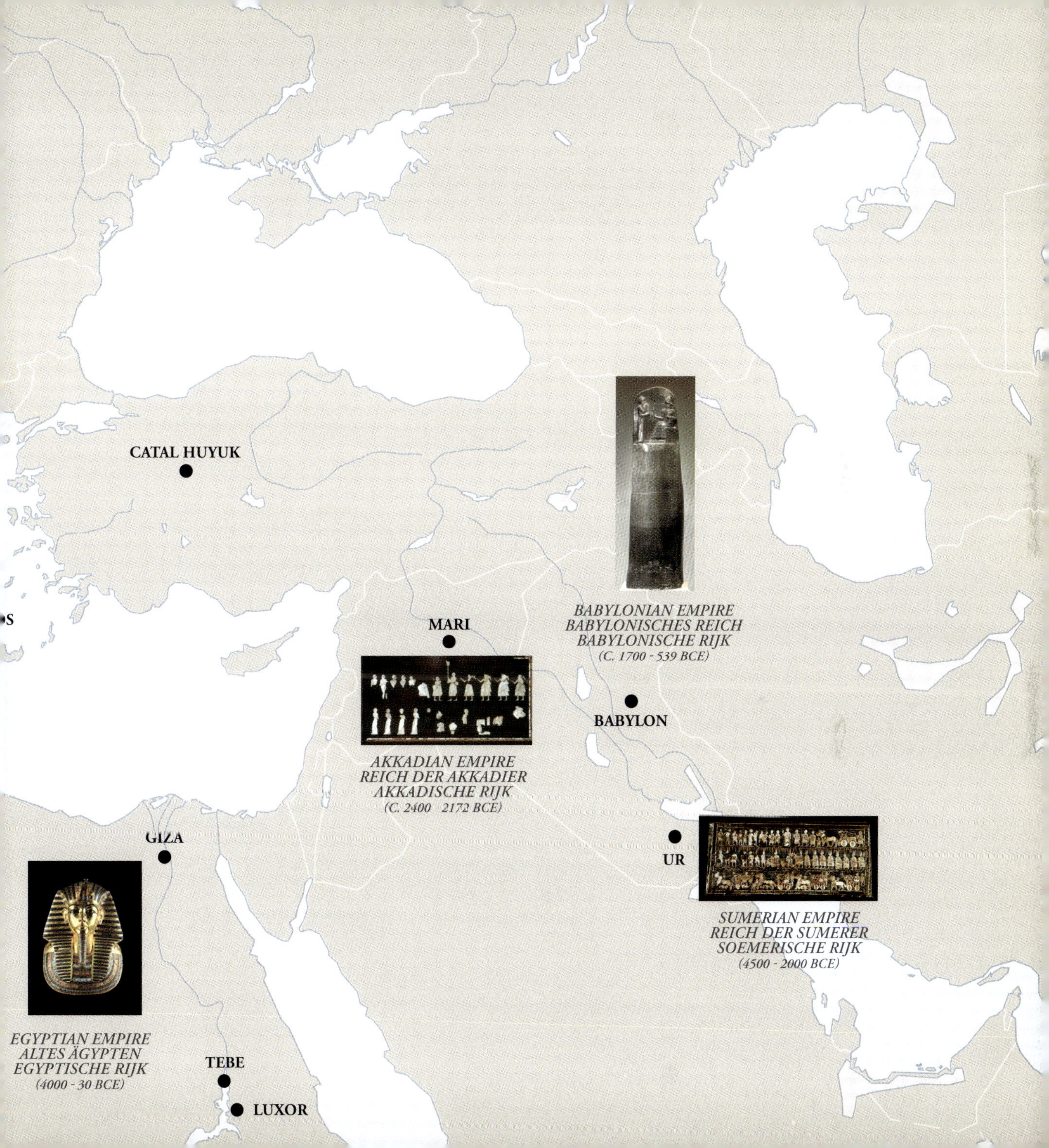

CATAL HUYUK

S

BABYLONIAN EMPIRE
BABYLONISCHES REICH
BABYLONISCHE RIJK
(C. 1700 - 539 BCE)

MARI

BABYLON

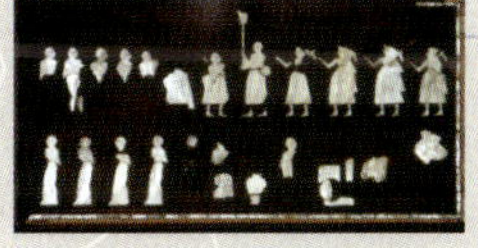

AKKADIAN EMPIRE
REICH DER AKKADIER
AKKADISCHE RIJK
(C. 2400 2172 BCE)

GIZA

UR

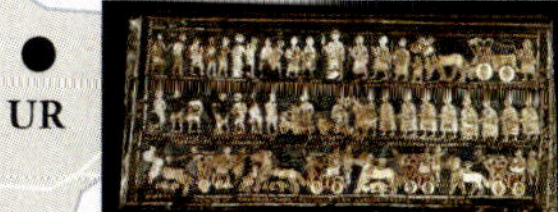

SUMERIAN EMPIRE
REICH DER SUMERER
SOEMERISCHE RIJK
(4500 - 2000 BCE)

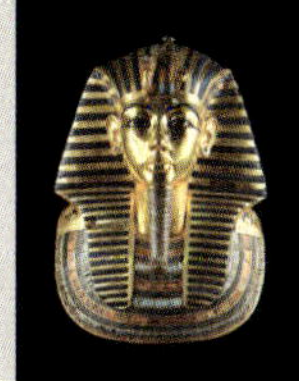

EGYPTIAN EMPIRE
ALTES ÄGYPTEN
EGYPTISCHE RIJK
(4000 - 30 BCE)

TEBE

LUXOR

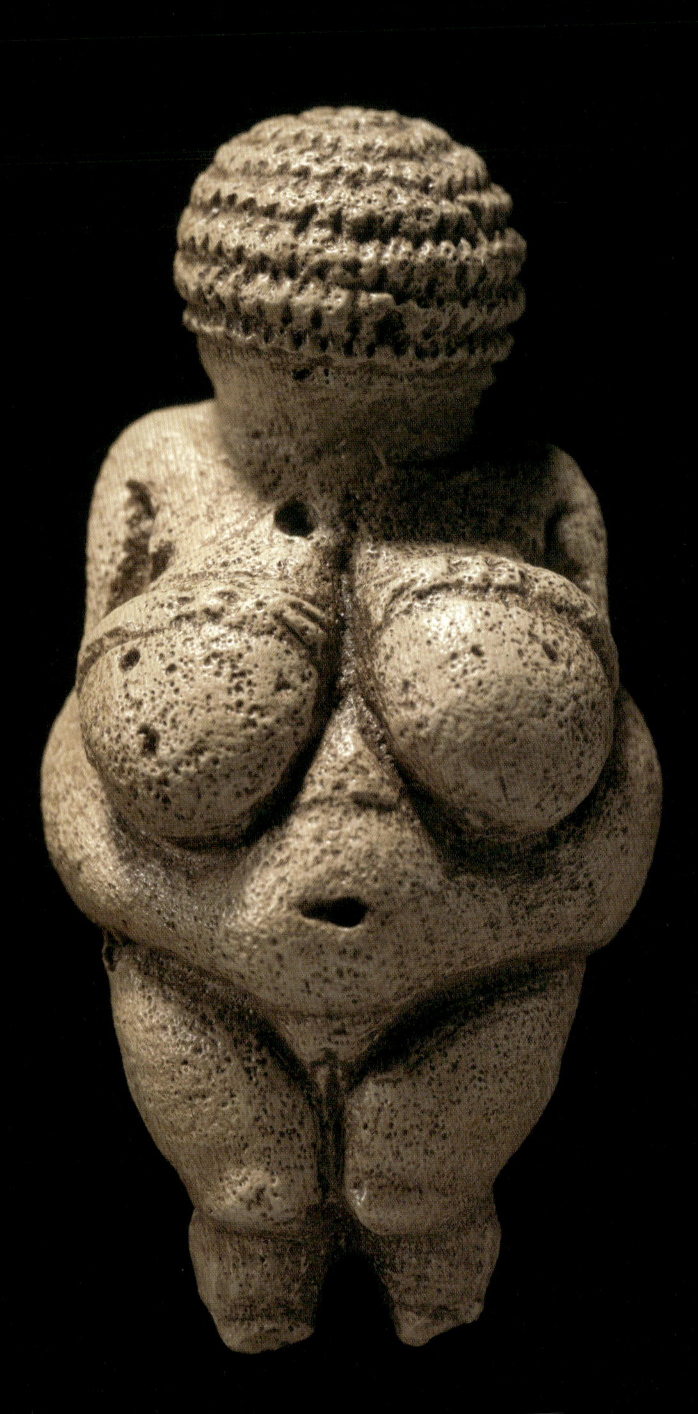

It focuses on fertility...

Im Mittelpunkt steht die Fruchtbarkeit...

In het middelpunt staat de vruchtbaarheid...

Venus of Willendorf
Venus von Willendorf
Venus van Willendorf

●●●

c. 25000 BCE
h. 11 cm / 4.3 in.
Naturhistorisches Museum, Wien

Limestone / Kalkstein / Kalksteen

Venus of Laussel
Venus von Laussel
Venus van Laussel

●

c. 25000-18000 BCE
h. 43 cm / 17 in.
Musée d'Aquitaine, Bordeaux

Limestone / Kalkstein / Kalksteen

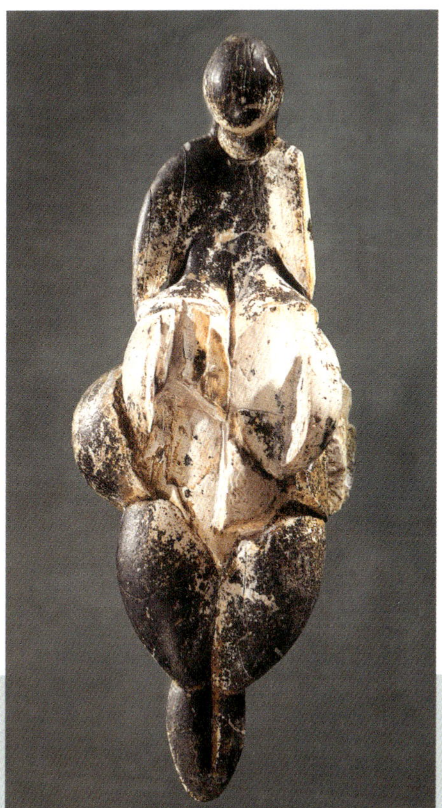

Venus of Lespugue
Venus von Lespugue
Venus van Lespugue

●

c. 25000-18000 BCE
h. 14,6 cm / 5.7 in.
Musée de l'Homme, Paris

Mammoth ivory / Mammut Elfenbein / Mammoet ivoor

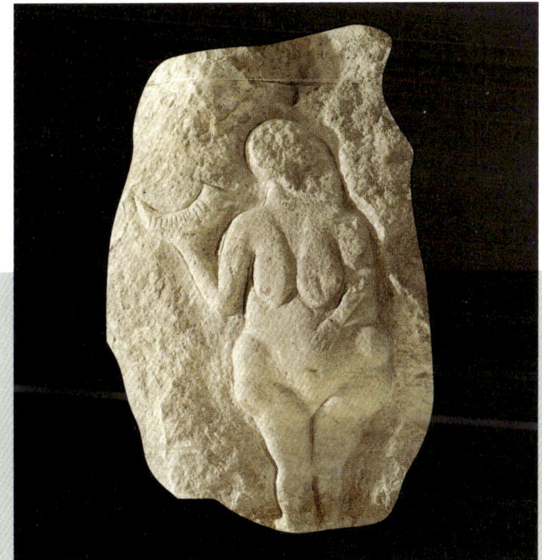

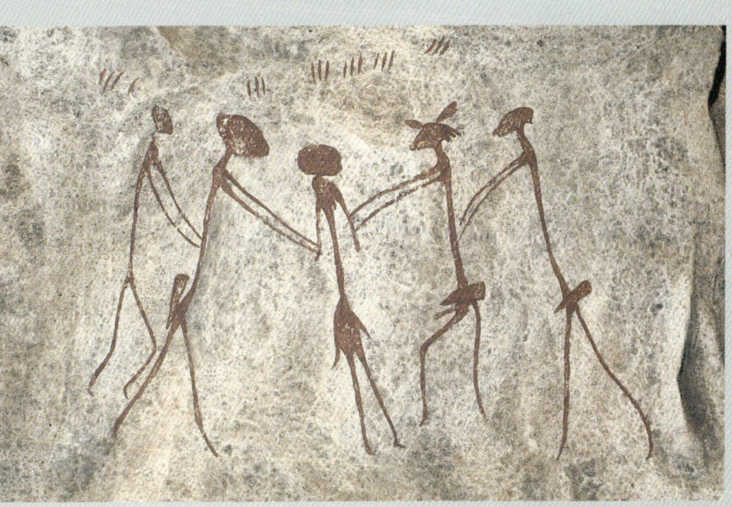

Sandawe Trance Dance
Sandawe Ritual-Tanz
Rituele Sandawe Dans in staat van trance

●

c. 12000-6000 BCE
Tanzania National Museum, Dar es Salaam

Earth pigments / Erdpigmente / Aardekleuren

... and naturally, on the hunt.

... und natürlich die Jagd.

... en natuurlijk de jacht.

Altamira

Bison
Bison
Bizon

●●●

c. 16000-9000 BCE

Earth pigments / Erdpigmente
Aardekleuren

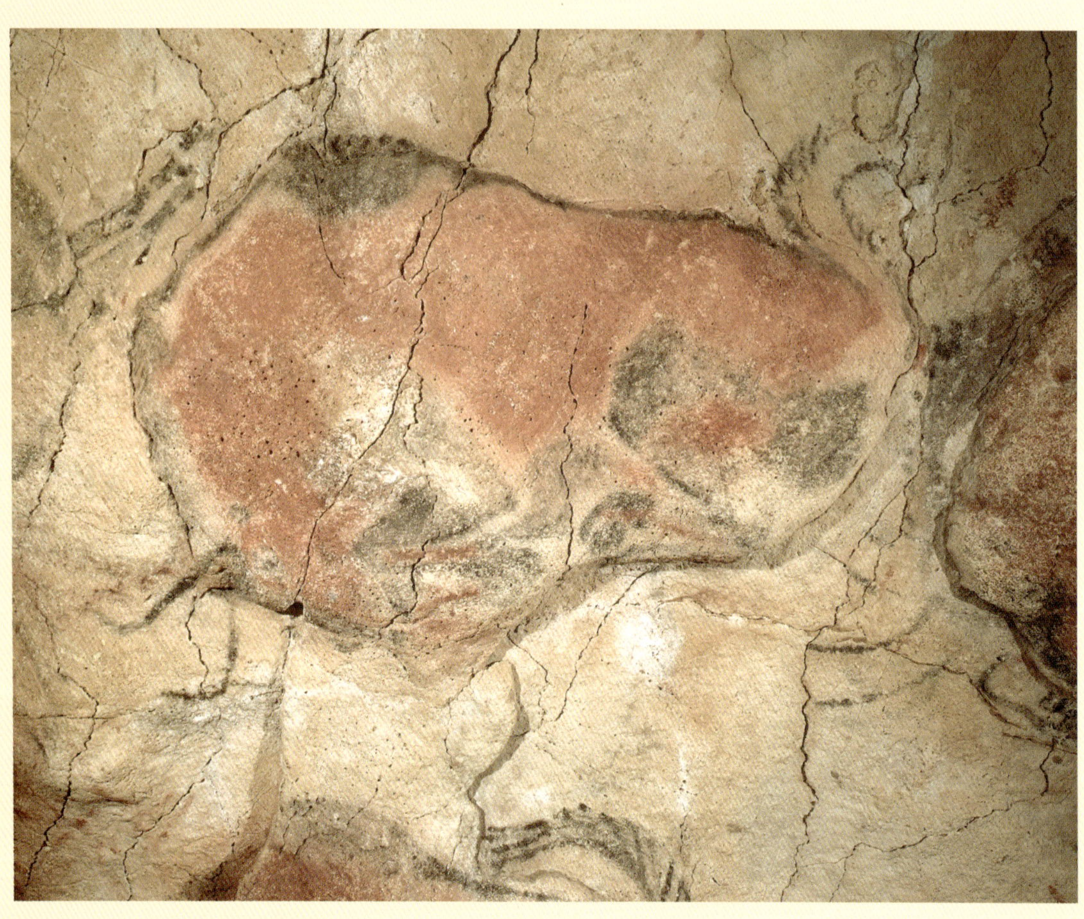

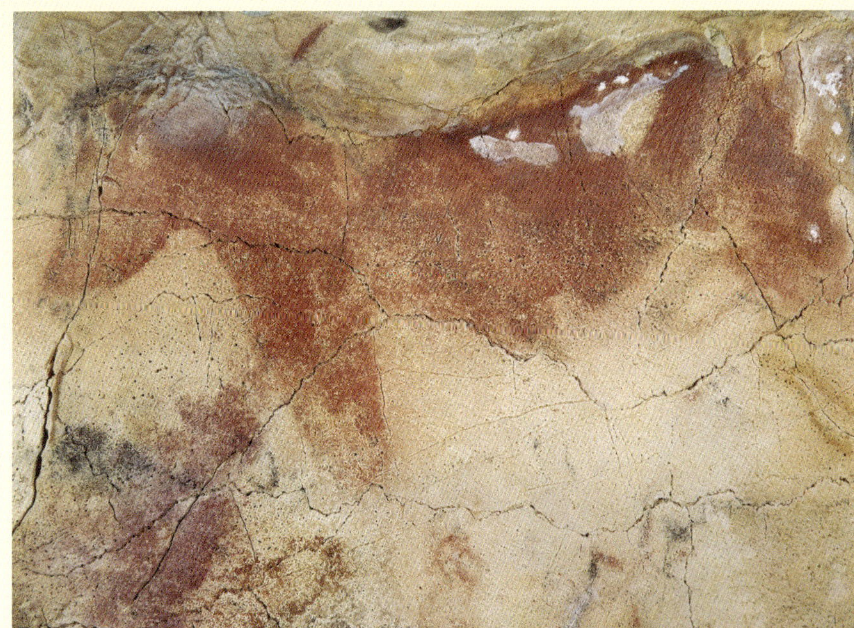

Altamira

Horse
Pferd
Paard

●●●

c. 16000-9000 BCE

Earth pigments / Erdpigmente
Aardekleuren

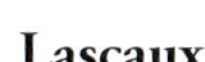

Lascaux

Unicorne
Einhorn
Eenhoorn

●●●

c. 18000-10000 BCE

Earth pigments / Erdpigmente / Aardekleuren

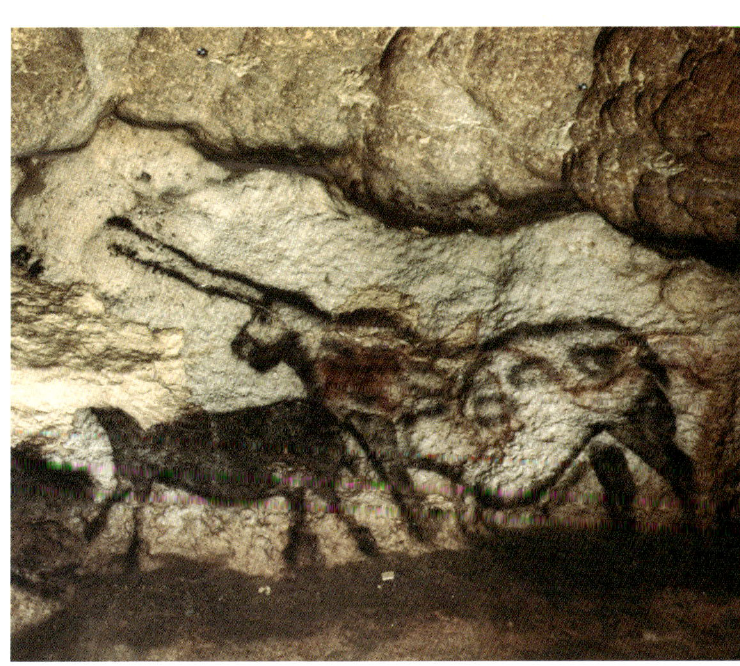

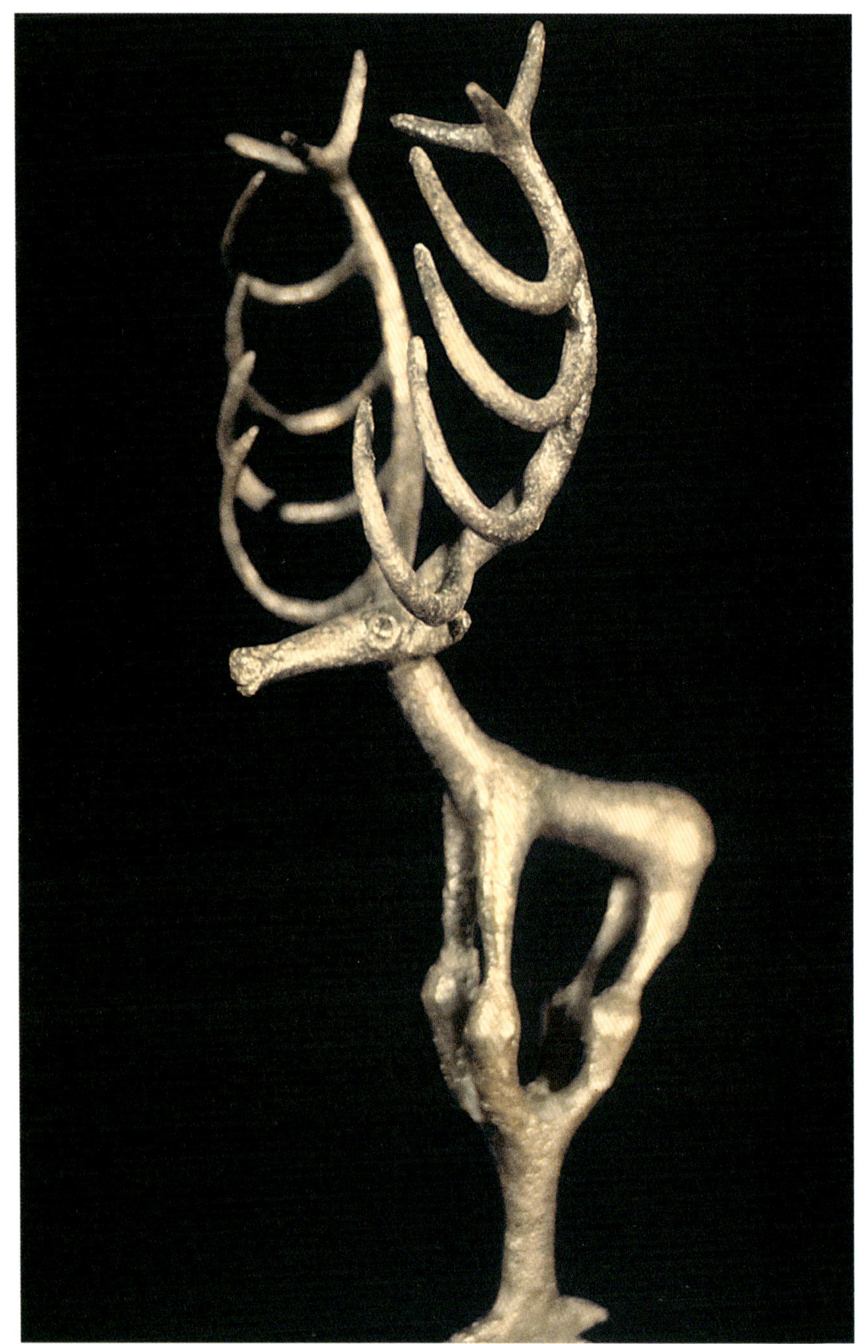

Prehistoric Sculpture from Catal Huyuk in Anatolia
Prähistorischer Fund aus Anatolien, in Catal Huyuk
Prehistorische Anatolische vondst, uit Catal Huyuk

●●

5750 BCE
Archaeological Museum, Istanbul

People start to settle, for example in Anatolia...

Die Völker beginnen sesshaft zu werden, z.B. in Anatolien...

Mensen beginnen zich te vestigen, bijvoorbeeld in Anatolië...

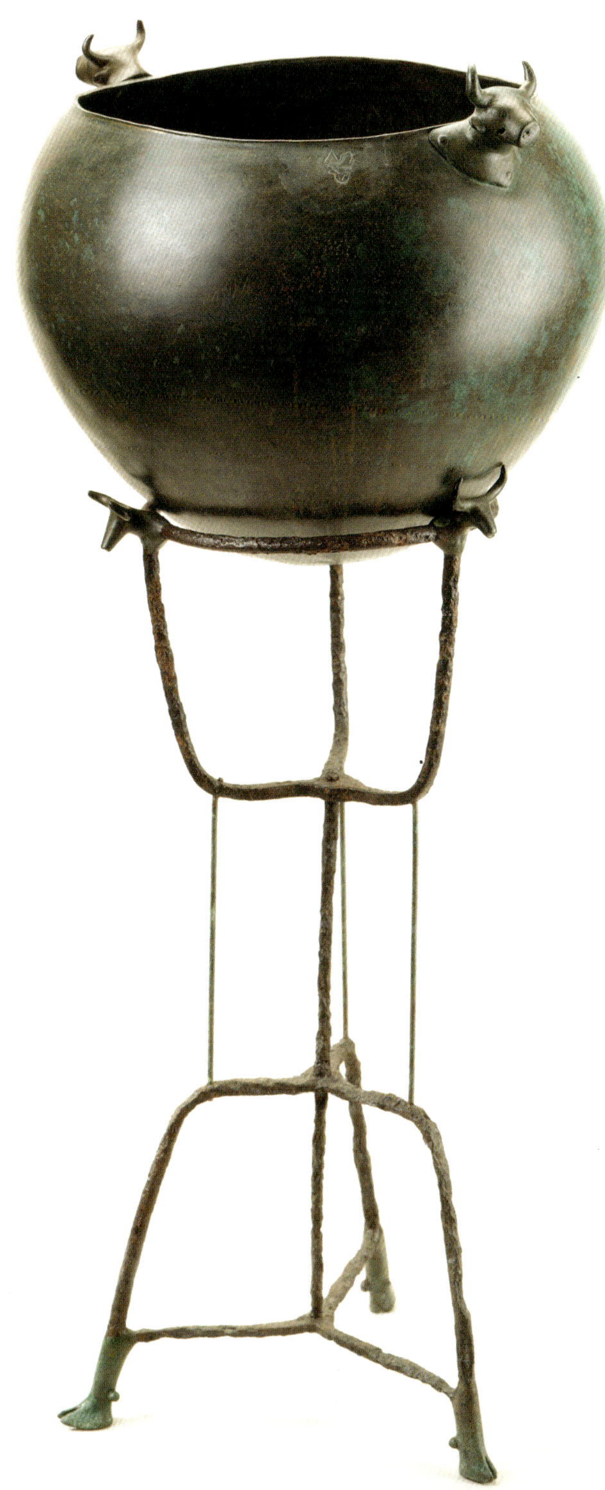

Copper Cauldron, probably from Eastern Anatolia
Kupferkessel, wahrscheinlich aus Ost-Anatolien
Koperen ketel, vermoedelijk afkomstig uit Oost-Anatolië

●●●

900-600 BCE
Museum für Vor- und Frühgeschichte, Staatliche Museen, Berlin

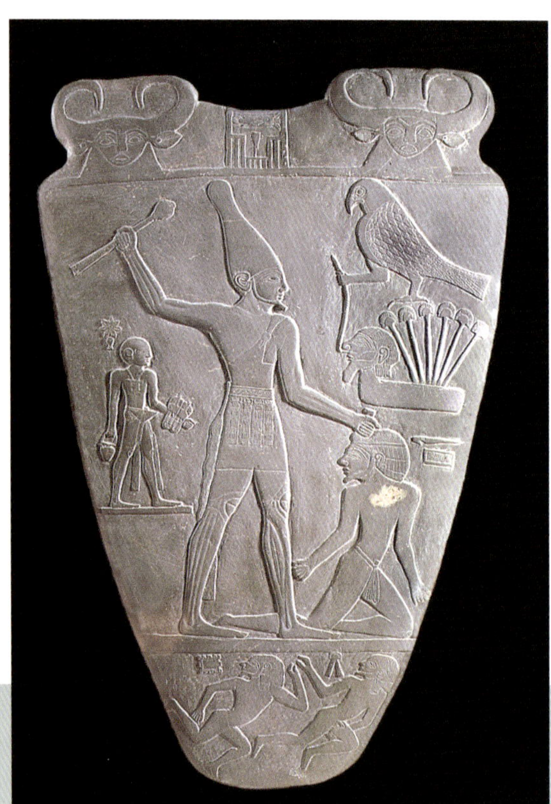

Narmer Palette, verso
Die Palette von König Nàrmer, Rückseite
Narmerpalet, achterzijde
●●●
c. 3100-2850 BCE
h. 64 cm / 25.1 in.
Egyptian Museum, Cairo

Schist / Schiefer / Schiste

Battlefield Palette, recto
Palette des Schlachtfeldes, Vorderseite
Het Slagveld Palet, voorzijde
●
c. 3150 BCE
British Museum, London;
(upper fragment)
Ashmolean Museum, Oxford

Schist / Schiefer / Schiste

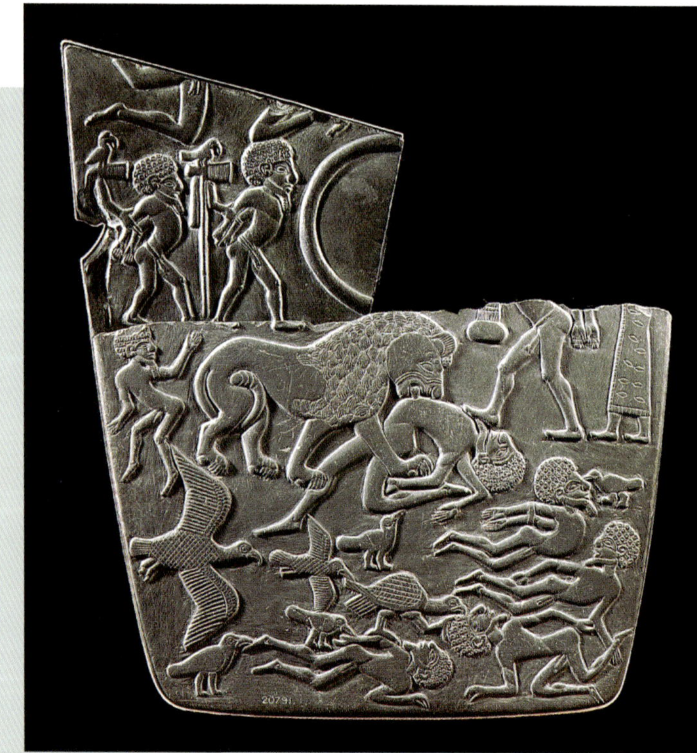

... and settlers found empires.

... und die Siedler gründen Reiche.

... en de gevestigden stichten rijken.

"MacGregor Man"
"MacGregor Mann"

●●

c. 3250 BCE
Ashmolean Museum, Oxford

Basalt

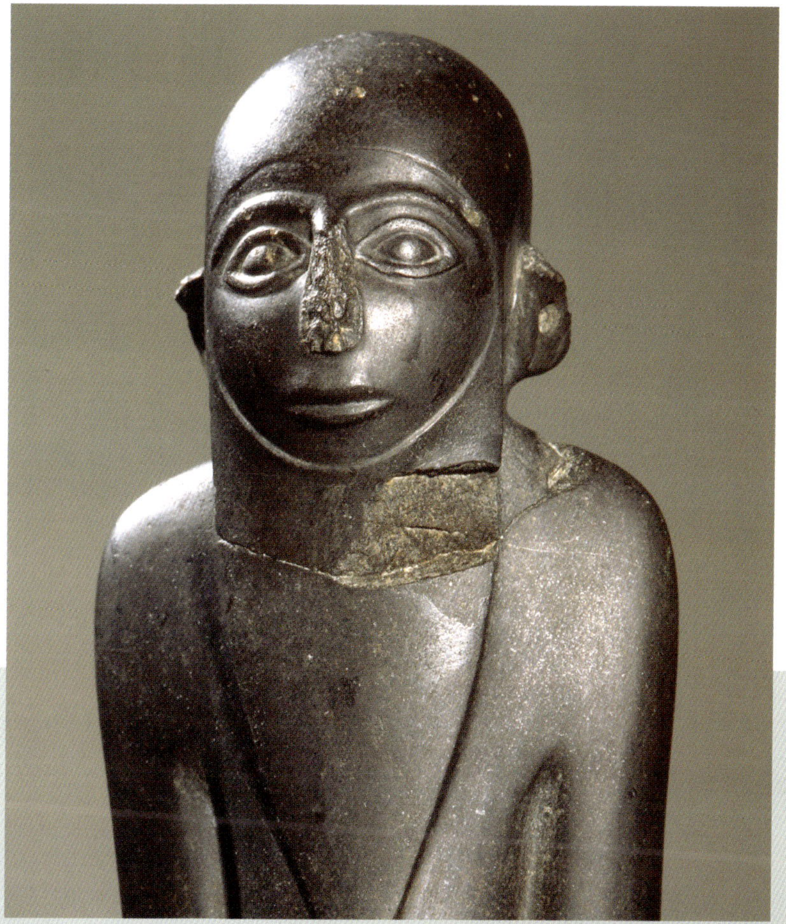

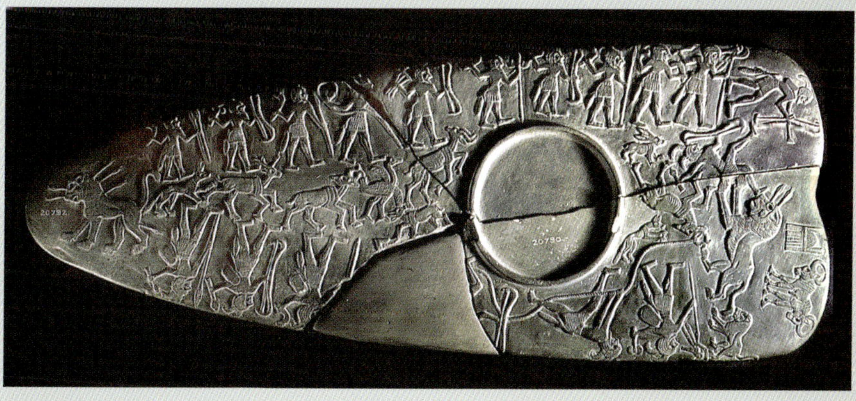

The Hunters' Palette
Die Palette des Jägers
Palet van de jager

●

c. 3000 BCE
30,5 x 14 cm / 12 x 5.6 in.
British Museum, London

Art responds to certain queries: this is what I am, this is what I do...

Kunst erfüllt Aufgaben: Der bin ich, das tue ich...

Kunst vervult de opgave: dit ben ik, dit is wat ik doe...

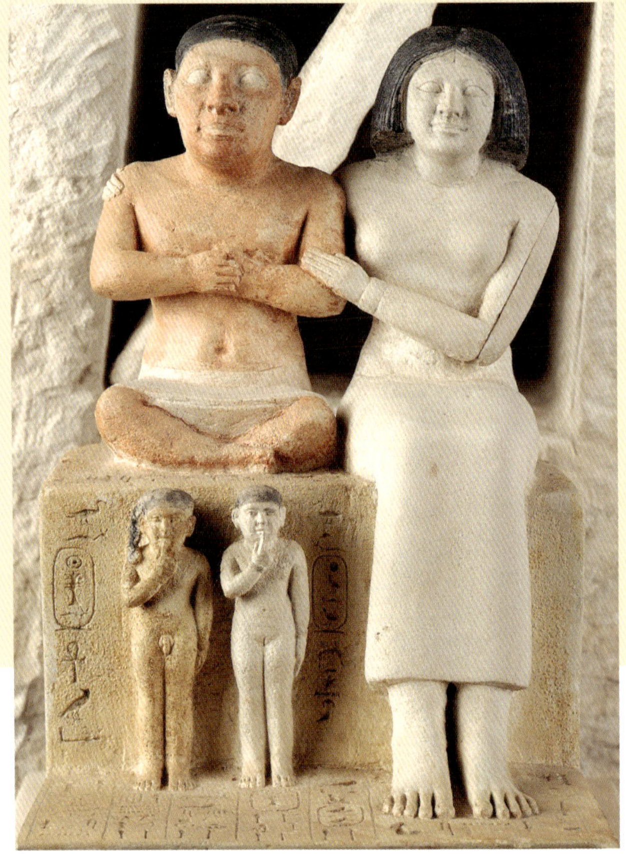

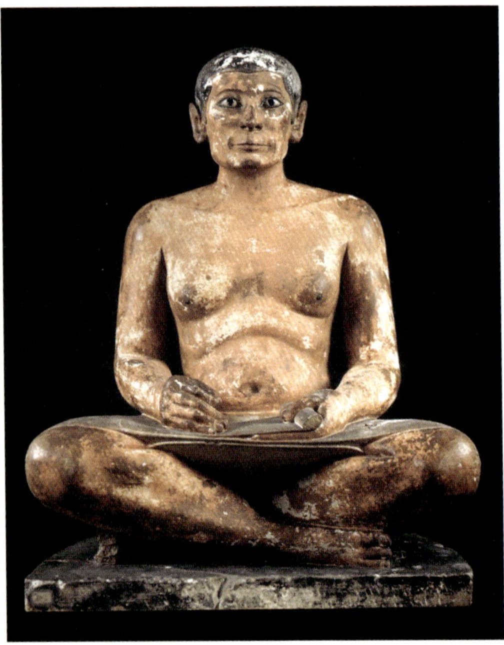

Seated Scribe
Sitzender Schreiber
Zittende schrijver

●●

c. 2613-2494 BCE
h. 53,7 cm / 21.1 in.
Musée du Louvre, Paris

Painted limestone
Bemalter Kalkstein
Beschilderd kalksteen

The Dwarf Seneb and His Family
Der Zwerg Sèneb mit seiner Familie
De dwerg Seneb met zijn gezin

●●

c. 2465-2152 BCE
Egyptian Museum, Cairo

Painted limestone / Bemalter Kalkstein
Beschilderd kalksteen

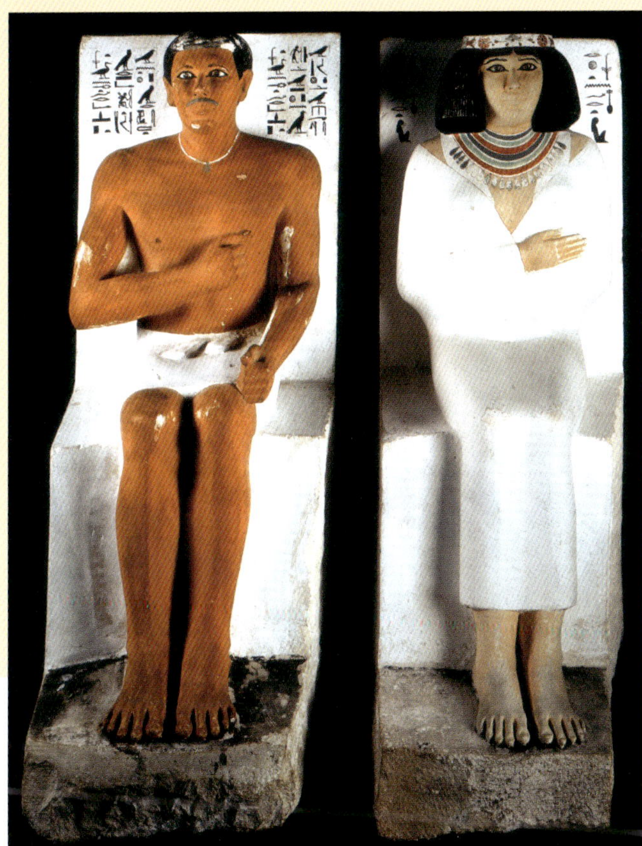

Rahotep and Nofret
Rahotep und Nofret
Rahotep en Nofret

●●

c. 2620 BCE
h. 121 cm / 47.6 in.
Egyptian Museum, Cairo

Painted limestone / Bemalter Kalkstein
Beschilderd kalksteen

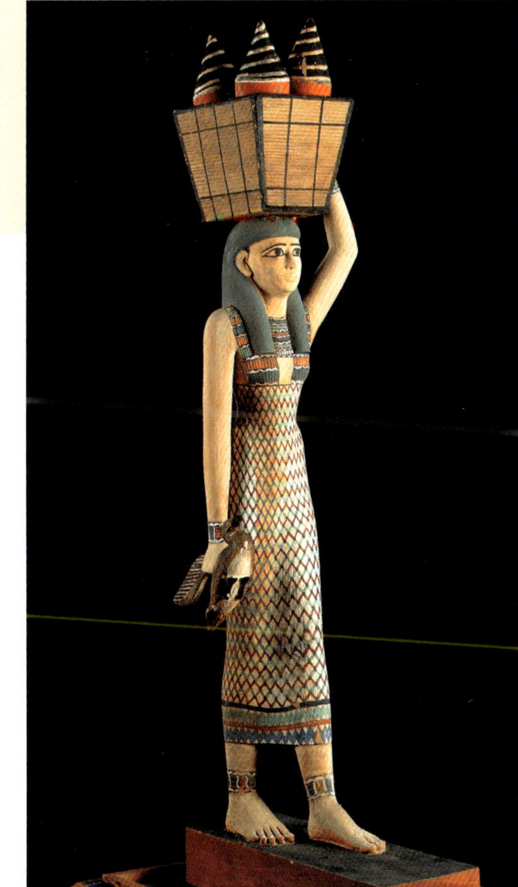

A Woman Bearing Offerings
Frau, die Opfer darbringt
Offerdraagster

●

c. 2040-1640 BCE
Egyptian Museum, Cairo

Painted limestone
Bemalter Kalkstein
Beschilderd kalksteen

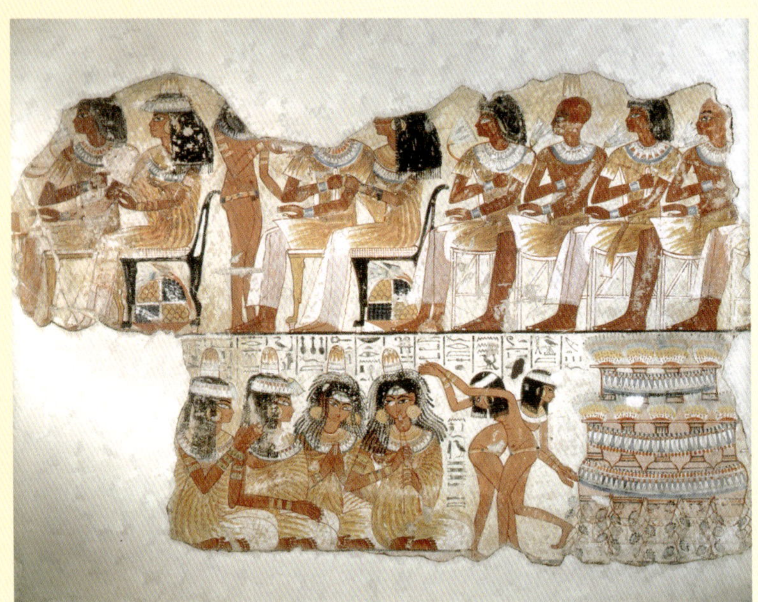

Tomb of Nebamun: Banquet and Hunting Scenes
Grab der Nebamun: Bankett & Jagdszene
Tombe van Nebamun: Banket- en Jachtscène
●●

c. 1390-1352 BCE
British Museum, London

Wall painting / Wandmalerei / Muurschildering

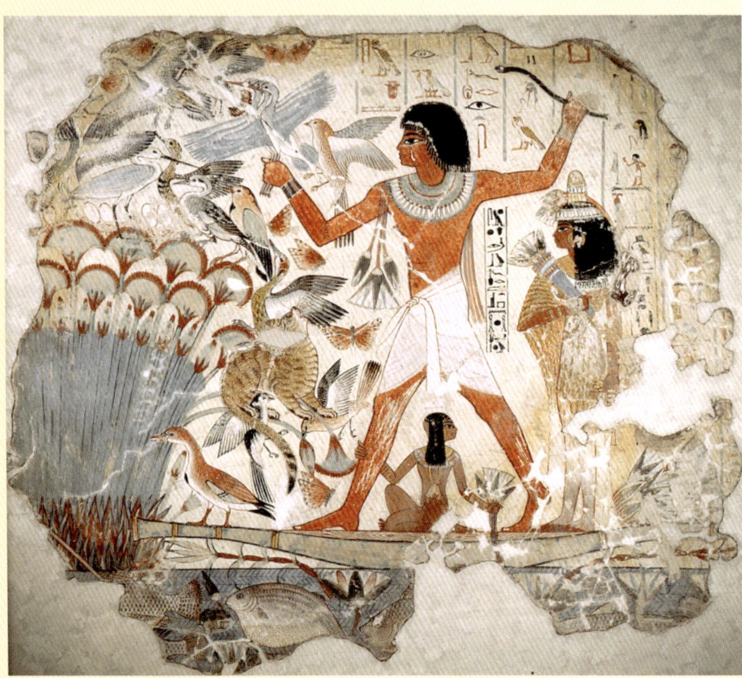

... and this is what I will do after death.

... Und das werde ich auch im Jenseits tun.

... en dit is wat ik ook in het hiernamaals zal doen.

Ploughing with Oxen
Ochsen beim Pflügen
Ploegen met ossen

●

c. 1550-1069 BCE
Deir el-Medina

Wall painting / Wandmalerei
Muurschildering

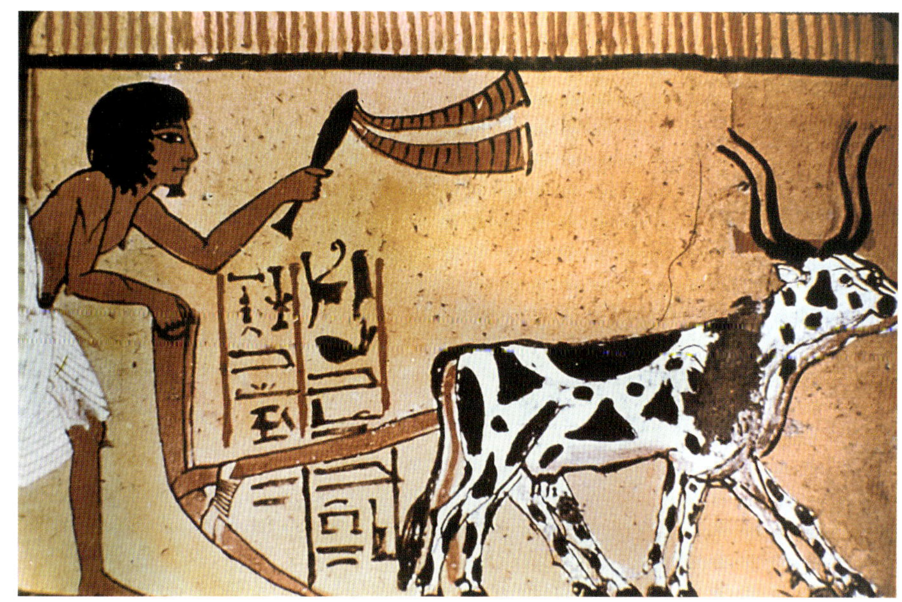

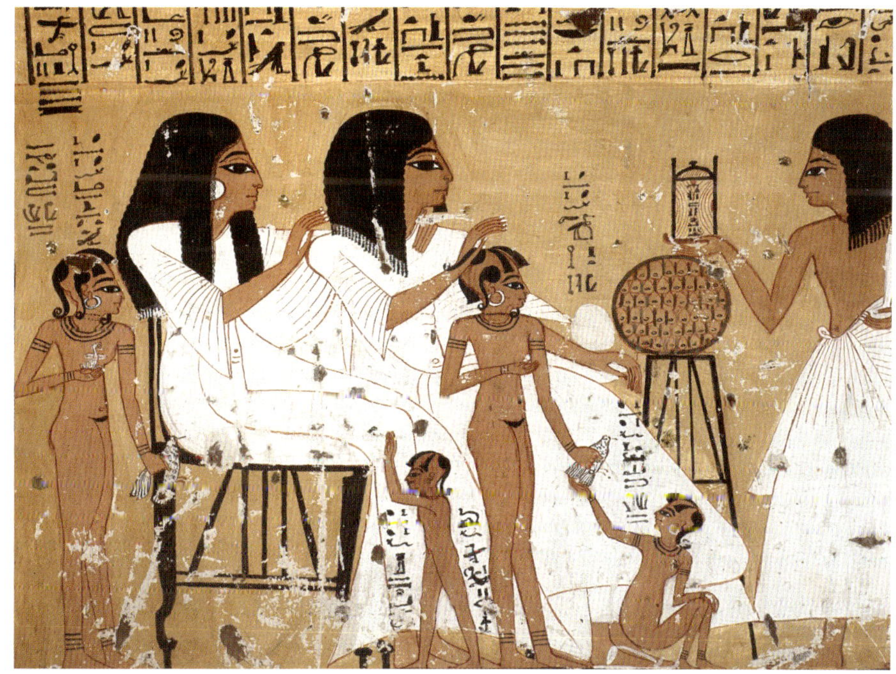

The Deceased with His Wife and Their Children
Der Verstorbene mit seiner Frau und seinen vier Kindern
De overledene met vrouw en vier kinderen

●

c. 1550-1307 BCE
Deir el-Medina

Wall painting / Wandmalerei
Muurschildering

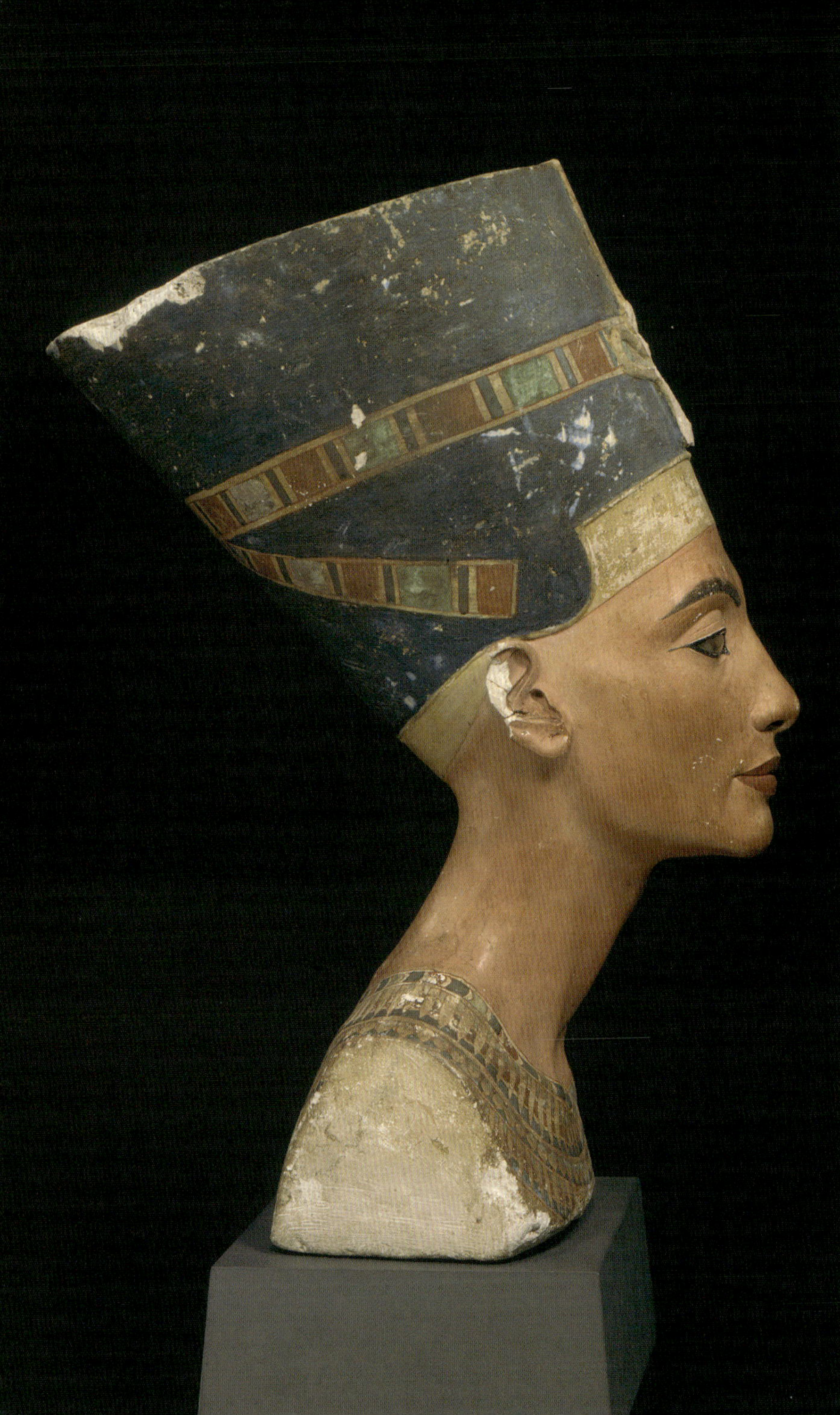

The pharaon is a divine being...

Der Pharao ist Gottmensch...

De farao is een goddelijk weze...

Thutmosis's Workshop
Die Werkstatt von Thutmosis
Werkplaats van Thoetmosis

Bust of Queen Nefertiti
Büste der Königin Nofretete
Buste van koningin Nefertete

●●●

c. 1350 BCE
h. 50 cm / 19.7 in.
Ägyptisches Museum, Staatliche Museen, Berlin

Painted limestone / Bemalter Kalkstein
Beschilderd kalksteen

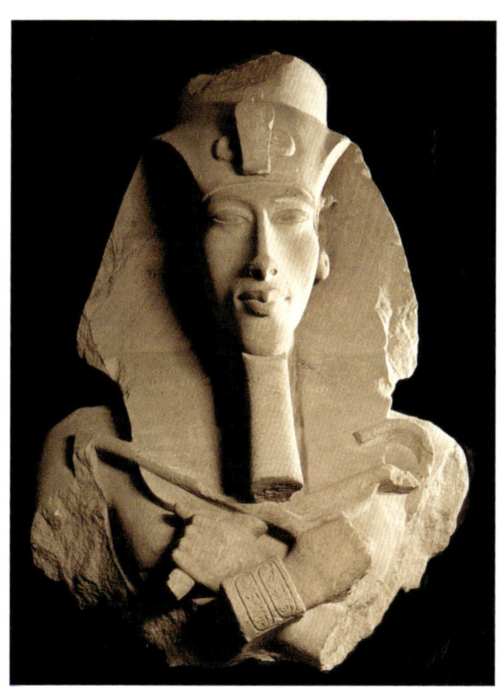

Amenhotep IV and Nefertiti
Amenhotep IV und Nofretete
Amenhotep IV en Nefertiti

●

c. 1345-1337 BCE
h. 22,2 cm / 8.7 in.
Musée du Louvre, Paris

Painted limestone
Bemalter Kalkstein
Beschilderd kalksteen

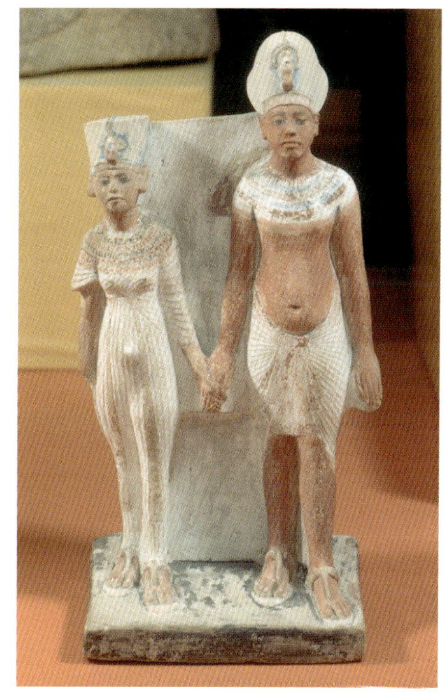

Akhenaten
Echnaton
Achnaton

●

c. 1353-1335 BCE
h. 153 cm / 60.2 in.
Egyptian Museum, Cairo

Sandstone
Sandstein
Zandsteen

Akhenaten and His Family under the Rays of Aton
Echnaton und seine Familie unter den Aton Strahlen
Achnaton en zijn gezin onder de stralen van Aton

●●

c. 1345-1337 BCE
h. 32,5 cm / 12.8 in.
Aegyptisches Museum, Staatliche Museen, Berlin

Painted sandstone / Bemalter Sandstein
Beschilderd zandsteen

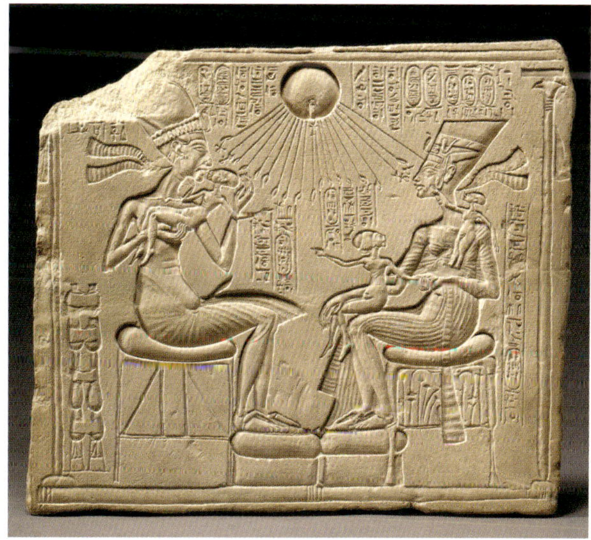

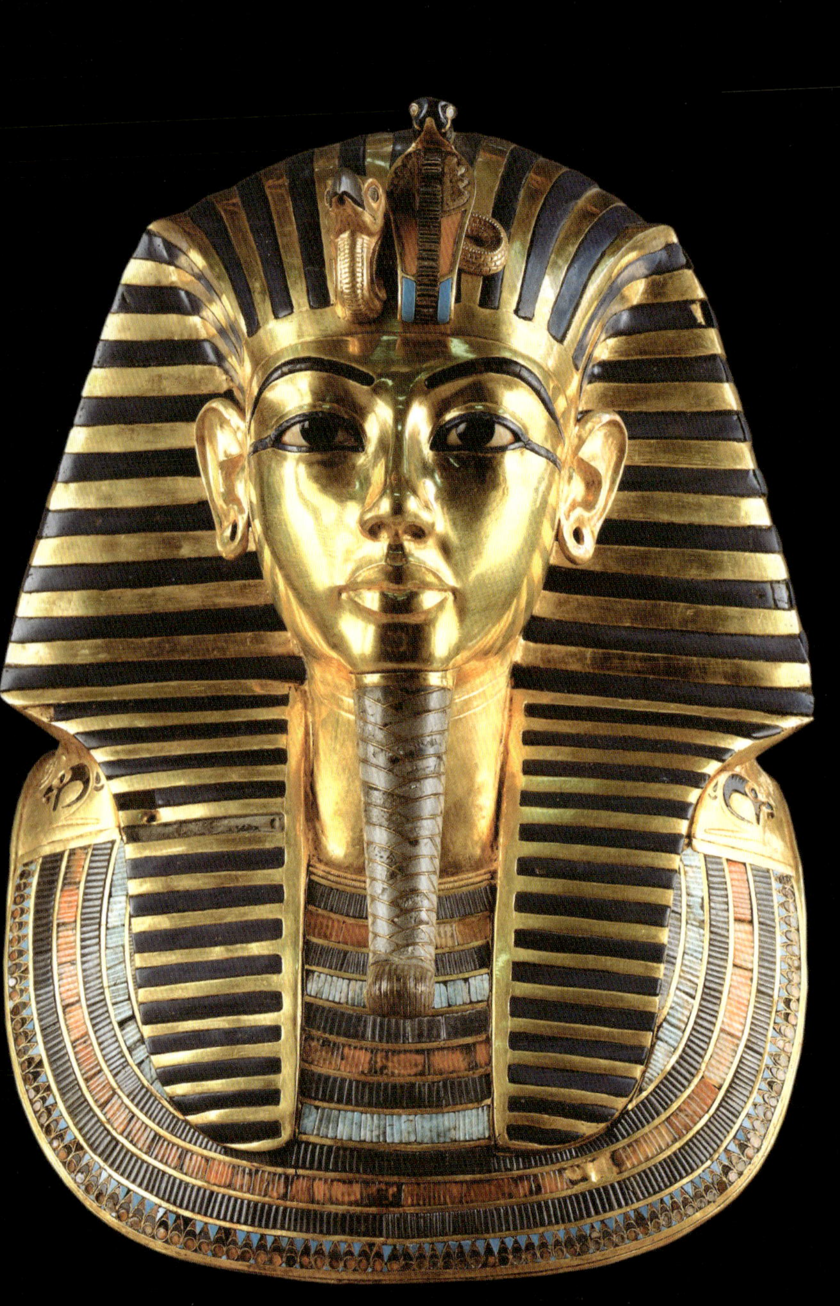

... and thanks to the artistic treasures in his tomb his name will be immortal.

und sein Name wird durch die Kunstschätze in seinem Grab unsterblich.

... en zijn naam wordt onsterfelijk dankzij de kunstschatten van zijn graf.

Tutankhamun's Funerary Mask
Totenmaske von Tutanchamun
Dodenmasker van Toetanchamon

●●●

c. 1330 BCE
Egyptian Museum, Cairo

Gold, stones and glass
Gold, Steine und Glas
Goud, stenen en glas

Pectoral
Pektoral
Pectoraal

●

c. 1333-1323 BCE
Egyptian Museum, Cairo

Gold / Goud

Perfume Vase
Gefäß für Parfüms
Parfumvaas

●

c. 1333-1323 BCE
Egyptian Museum, Cairo

Alabaster / Albast

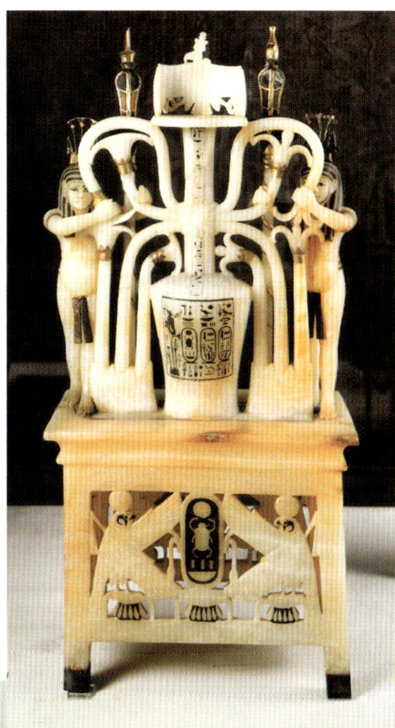

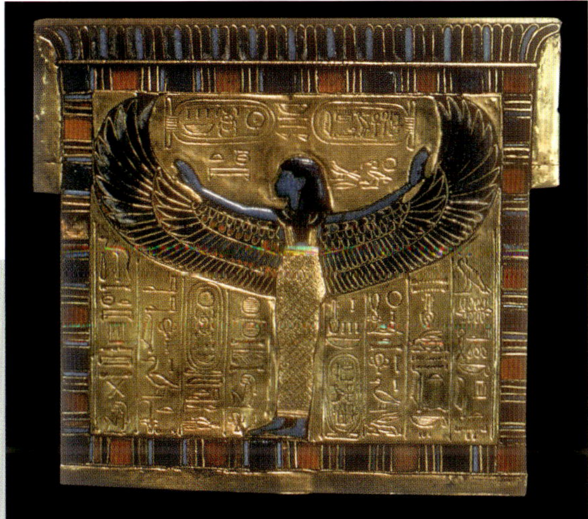

Pectoral
Pektoral
Pectoraal

●●●

c. 1333-1323 BCE
Egyptian Museum, Cairo

Gold / Goud

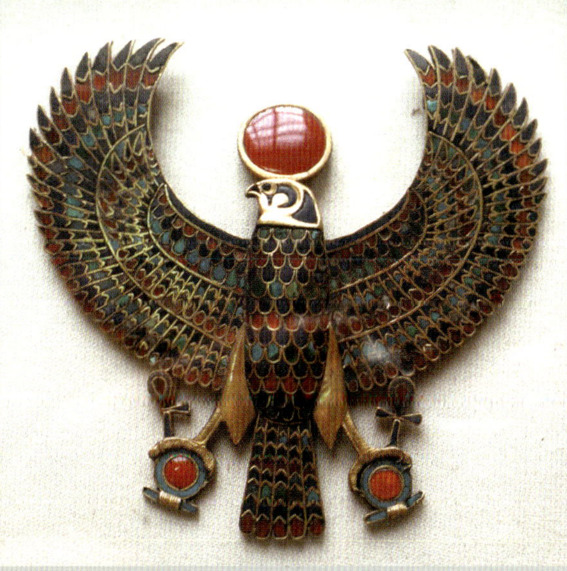

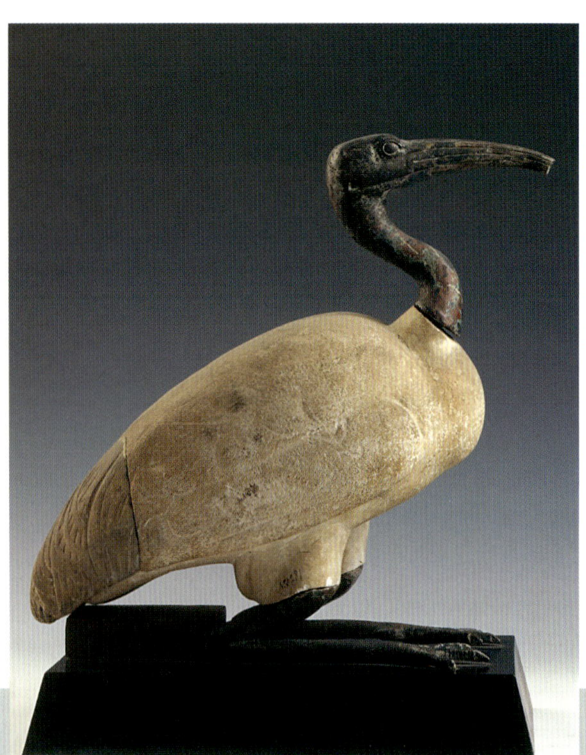

Sacred Ibis
Heiliger Ibis
Heilige Ibis

●

c. 664-525 BCE
h. 34 cm / 13.4 in.
Egyptian Museum, Cairo

Limestone and bronze
Kalkstein und Bronze
Kalksteen en brons

Isis

●

c. 712-332 BCE
h. 27 cm / 10.6 in.
Fondazione Museo
delle Antichità Egizie, Torino

Bronze / Brons

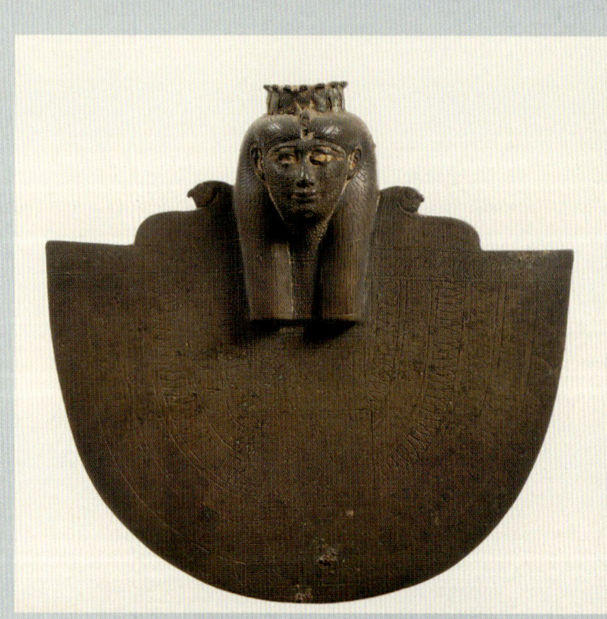

The gods take form.

Die Götter nehmen Gestalt an.

De goden krijgen gestalte.

Horus, the Falcon God
Der Falkengott Horus
Horus, de valkgod

●

c. 664-525 BCE
h. 53 cm / 20.9 in.
Egyptian Museum, Cairo

Basalt

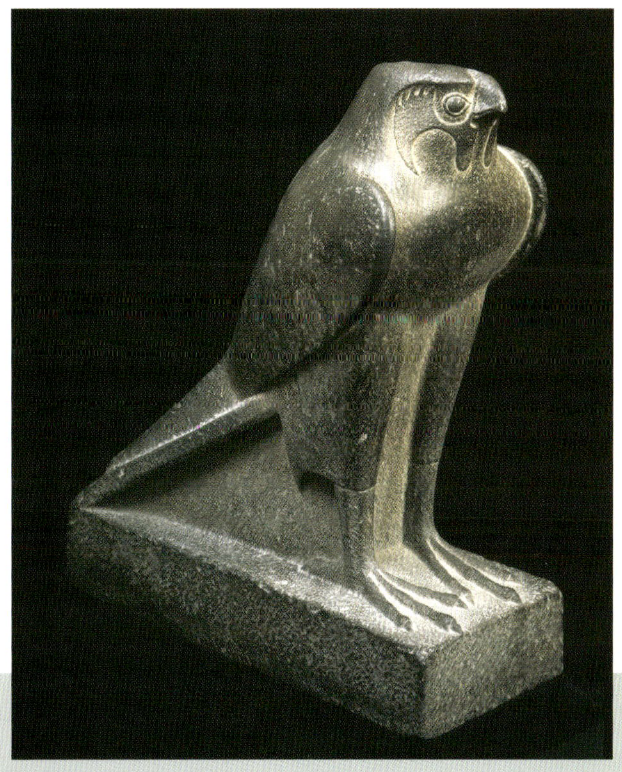

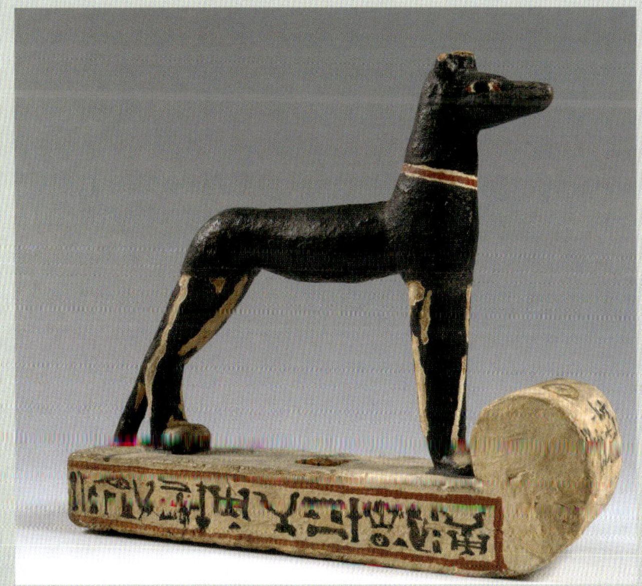

Statuette of the God Anubis in the Form of a Jackal
Statuette des Gottes Anubis als Schakal
Beeldje met weergave van de god Anubis in de vorm van een jakhal

●

399-300 BCE
24,3 x 29,4 x 7 cm / 9.6 x 11.6 x 2.8 in.
Fondazione Museo delle Antichità Egizie, Torino

Painted wood / Bemaltes Holz / Beschilderd hout

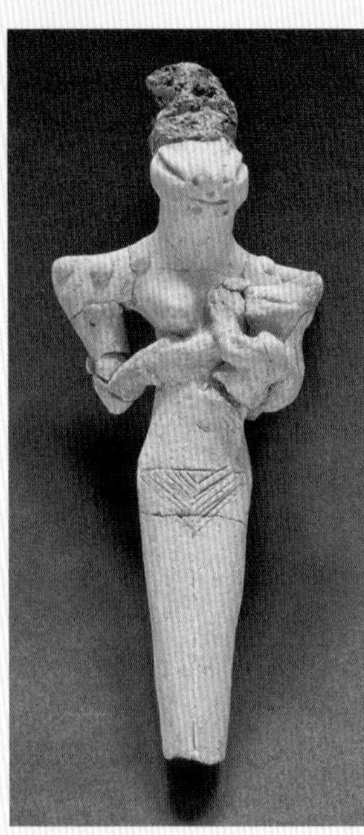

Mother Goddess
Muttergöttin
Moedergodin

●

c. 4000-3000 BCE
h. 14 cm / 5.5 in.
Iraq Museum, Baghdad

Terracotta / Terrakotta

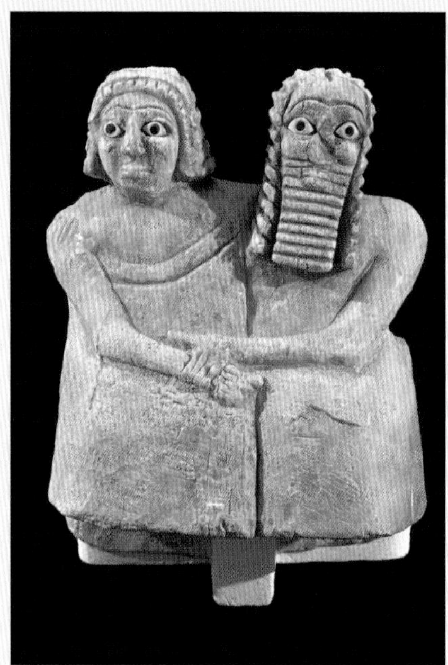

Man and Woman Embracing
Mann und Frau in einer Umarmung
Man en vrouw in omhelzing

●●

c. 3000 BCE
Iraq Museum, Baghdad

Stone and plaster
Stein und Gips
Steen en gips

KARKAMIŠ
NINEVEH
KALḪU
AŠŠUR
KĀR-TUKULTĪ-NINURTA
DŪR KURIGALZU
SIPPAR
BABYLON
SUSA
NIPPUR
URUK
UR

Mesopotamia is another centre of archaic art, the Garden of Eden.

Ein anderes Zentrum der frühen Kunst ist Mesopotamien, das "Paradies".

Een ander centrum van de archaïsche kunst is Mesopotamië, het "paradijs".

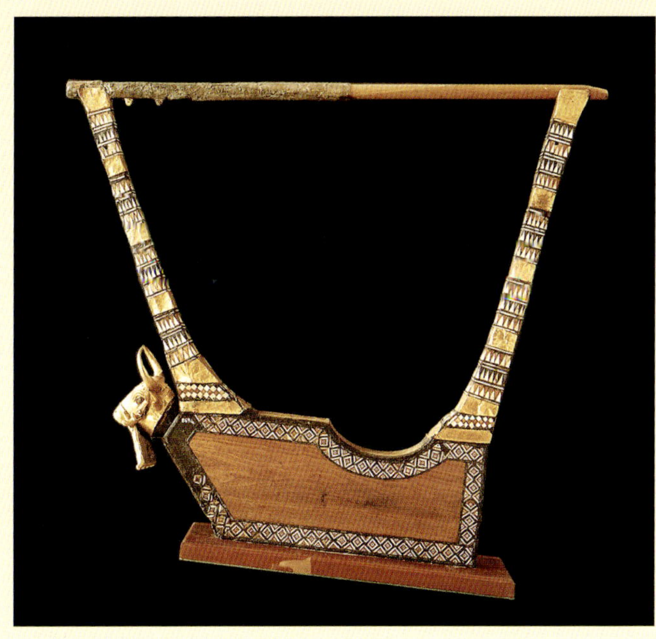

Musical Instrument from Ur
Musikinstrument aus Ur
Muziekinstrumenten uit Ur

c. 2600-2400 BCE
Iraq Museum, Baghdad

Wood / Holz / Hout

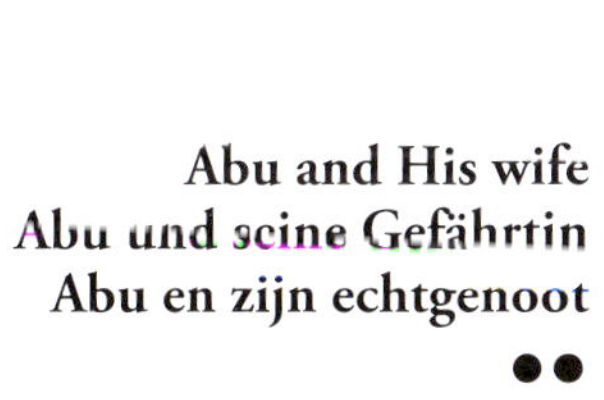

Abu and His wife
Abu und seine Gefährtin
Abu en zijn echtgenoot

●●

c. 2600 BCE
h. 68 cm / 26.78 in.
Iraq Museum, Baghdad

Veined alabaster, tar and shell incrustations
Geäderter Alabaster, Pech, Muschelverkrustungen
Geaderd albast, bitumen, incrustaties van schelpen

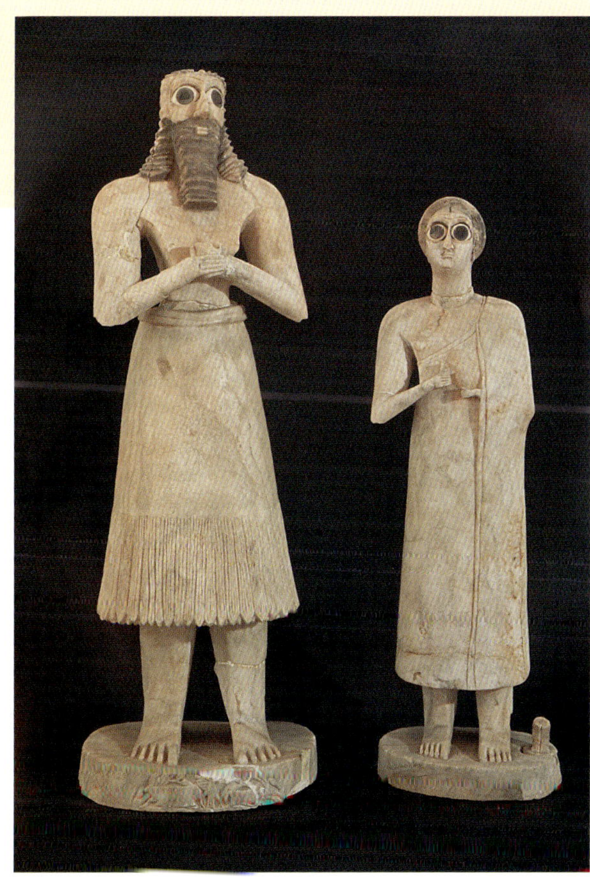

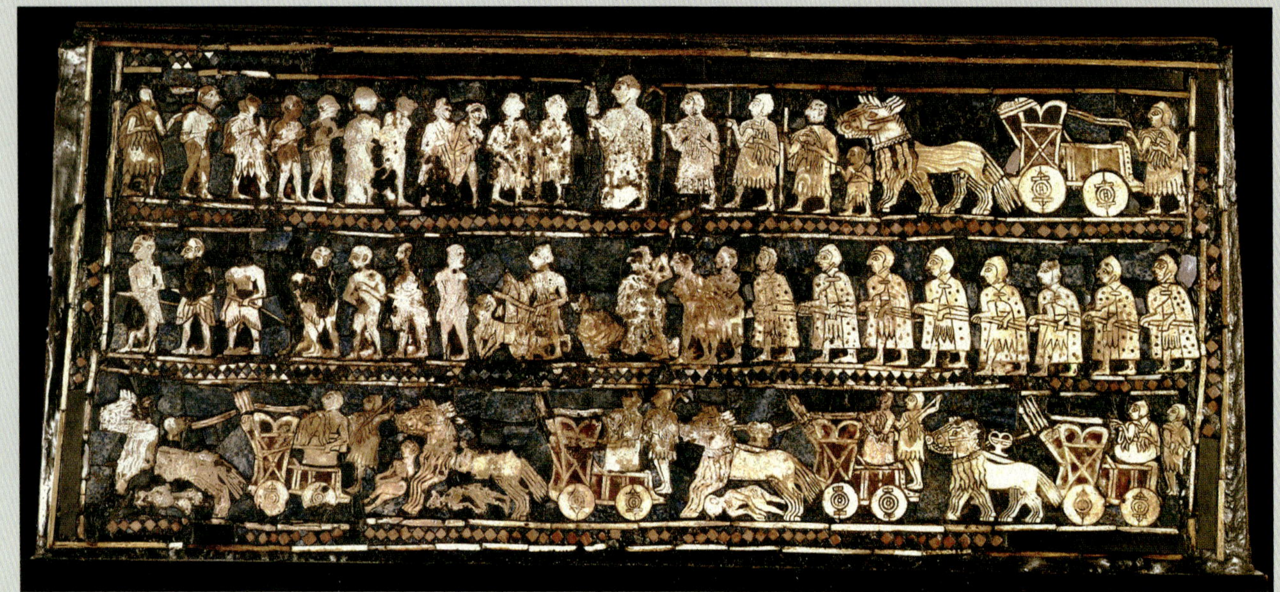

28 **Standard of Ur, the War panel**
Standarte aus Ur, Kriegspaneel
Standaard van Ur, oorlogspaneel

●●●

c. 2500 BCE
British Museum, London

Tesserae of red limestone, shell and lapis lazuli
Mosaiksteine aus rotem Kalkstein, Muschel, Lapislazuli
Mozaïeksteentjes van rood kalksteen, schelp, lapis lazulli

Banners are the chronicles of history.

Standarten sind plastische Chroniken.

Banieren zijn plastische kronieken.

Standard of Mari
Standarte aus Mari
Standaard van Mari

●●

c. 2500-2400 BCE
Musée du Louvre, Paris

Panel of mosaic, shells and schist
Mosaikpaneel, Muscheln und Schiefer
Paneel met mozaïek, schelpen en schist

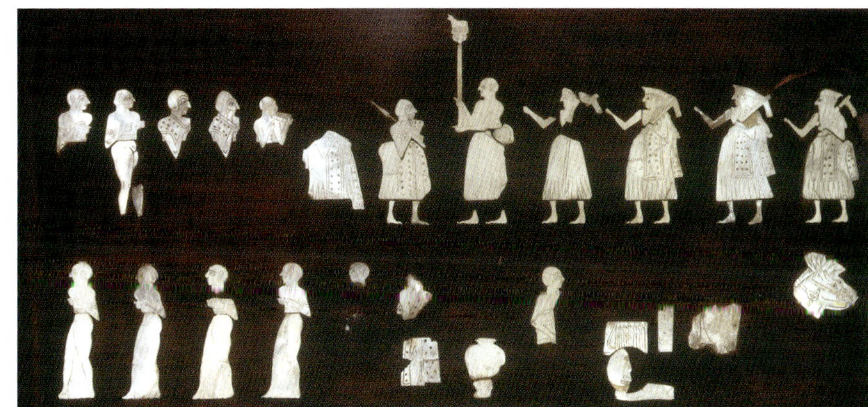

Ur-Nanshe and Family
Ur-Nanshe' und Familie
Ur-Nanshe en zijn gezin

●

c. 2600-2330 BCE
Musée du Louvre, Paris

Stone relief / Steinrelief / Steenreliëf

The Investiture of the Sumerian King Ur-Nammu
Einkleidung des Sumererkönigs Ur-Nammu
Investituur van de Sumerische koning Ur-Nammu

c. 2111-2094 BCE
h. 46 cm / 18.1 in.
University of Pennsylvania Museum of Archaeology and Anthropology, Philadelphia

Limestone / Kalkstein / Kalksteen

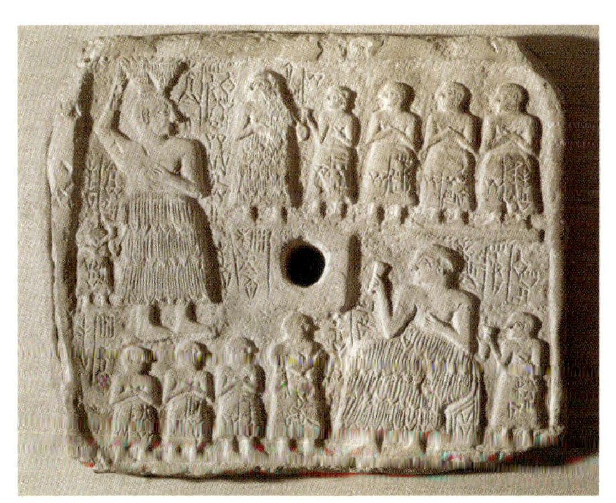

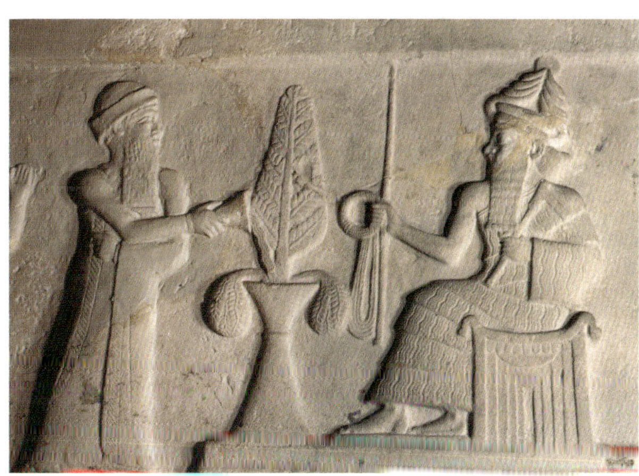

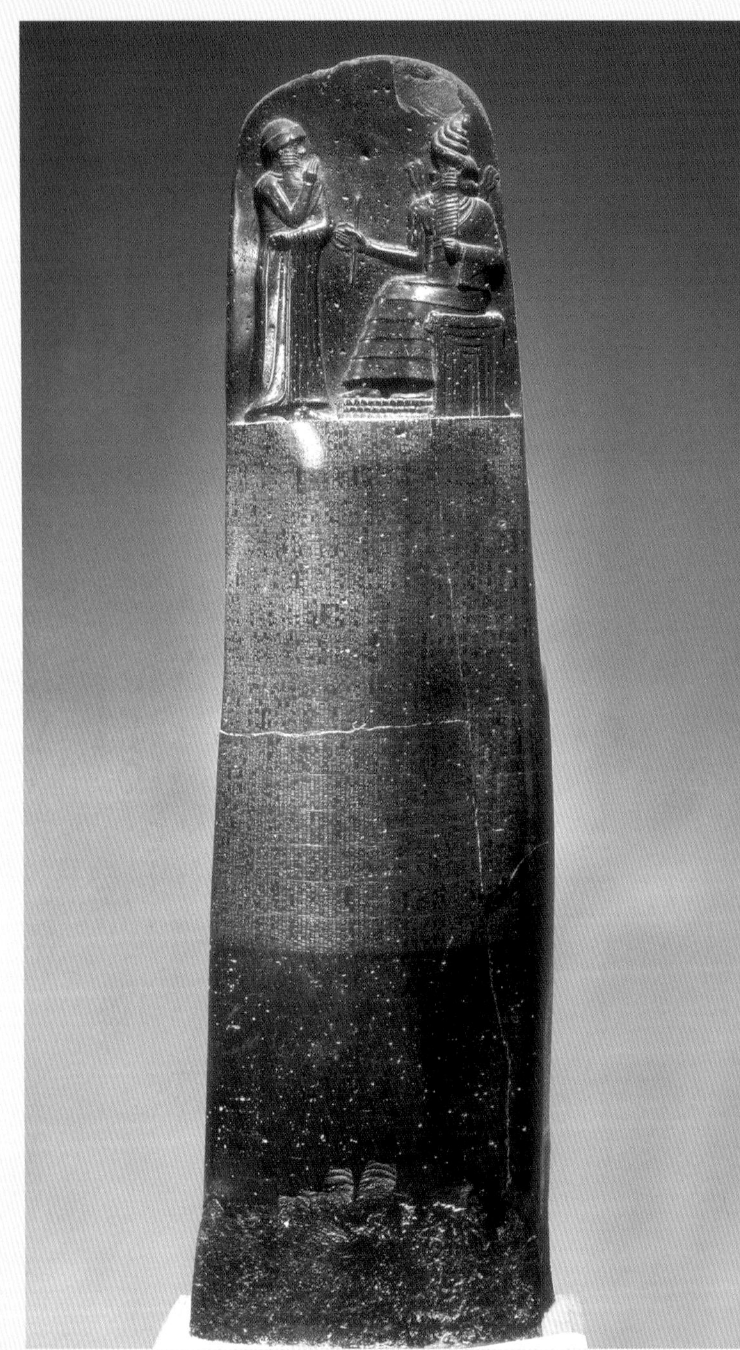

Hammurabi is venerated as the great unifier of the kingdom and the legislator of Babylonia.

Hammurabi wird als großer Reichseiniger und Gesetzgeber Babyloniens verehrt.

Hammurabi wordt geëerd als de grote man die eenheid in het rijk brengt en als wetgever van Babylonië.

Law Code of Hammurabi, King of Babylon
Kodex Hammurabi, König von Babylon
Codex Hammurabi, koning van Babylon

●●●

c. 1792-1750 BCE
h. 225 cm / 88.6 in.
Musée du Louvre, Paris

Diorite / Diorit / Dioriet

Royal Portrait known as the Head of Hammurabi
Königskopf, vermutlich Hammurabi
Koninklijk hoofd, Hammurabi genaamdi

●●

c. 2000 BCE
h. 15 cm / 5.9 in.
Musée du Louvre, Paris

Diorite / Diorit / Dioriet

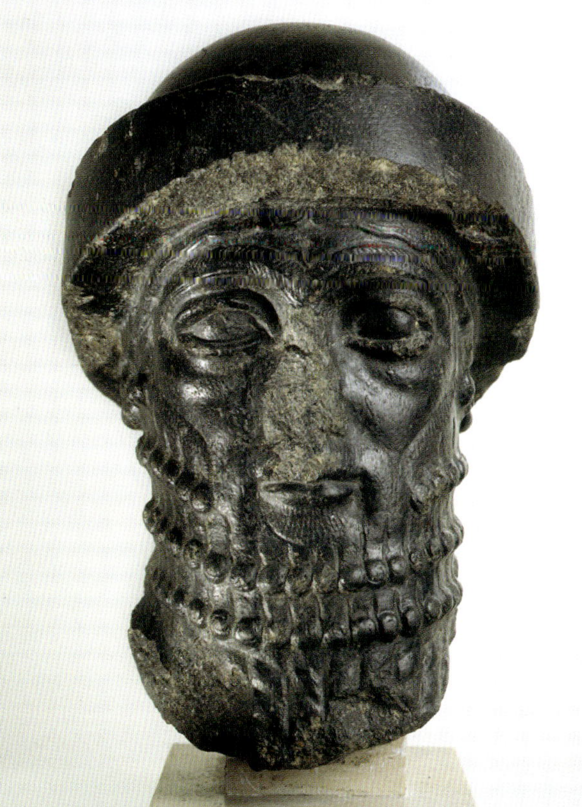

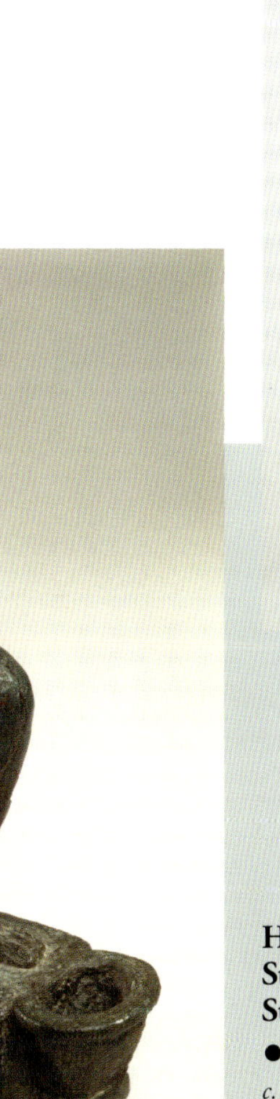

Hammurabi Praying
Statue des betenden Hammurabi
Standbeeld van Hammurabi die bidt

●

c. 2000 BCE
Musée du Louvre, Paris

Stone / Stein / Steen

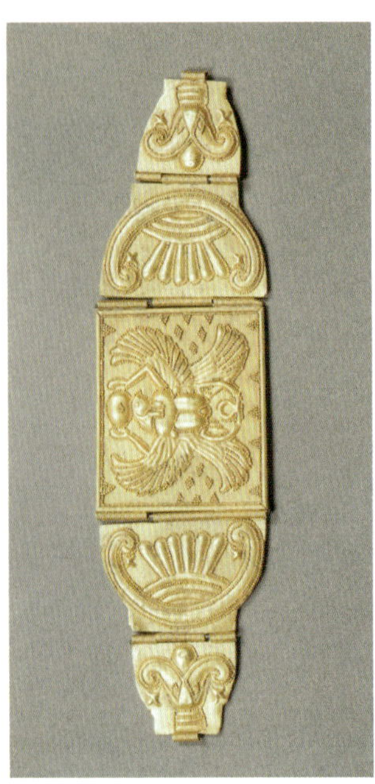

Bracelet
Armschmuck
Armband

●

c. 1200-332 BCE
Museo Archeologico Nazionale di Cagliari, Cagliari

Gold / Goud

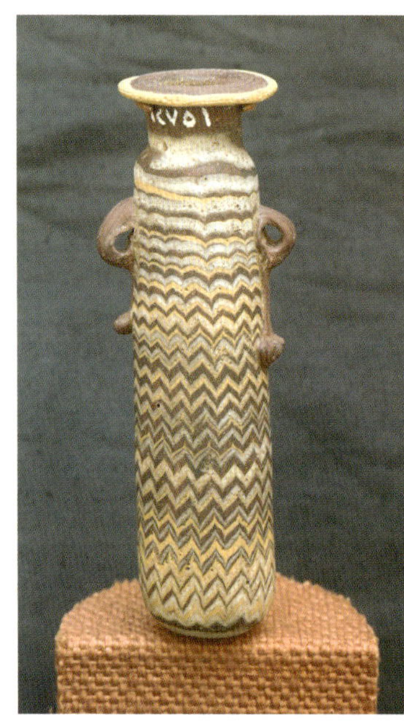

Amphora
Amphore
Amfora

●

c. 1200-332 BCE
The National Museum of Damascus, Damascus

Glass / Glas

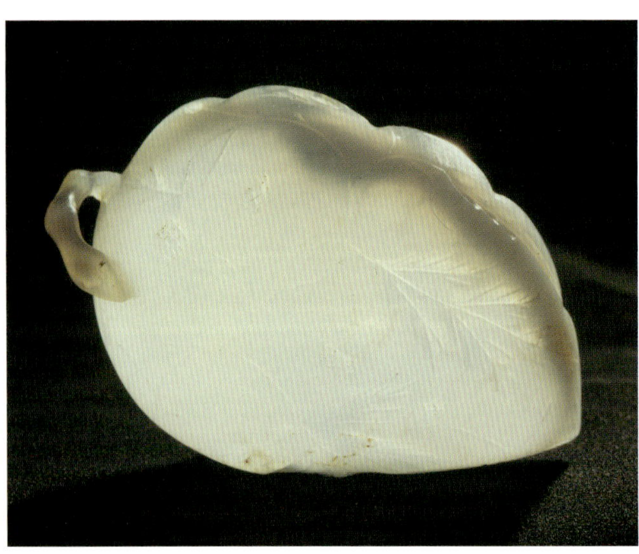

Cup
Schale
Beker

●

c. 1200-332 BCE
Museo Archeologico Nazionale di Cagliari, Cagliari

Chalcedony / Chalzedon / Chalcedoon

The Goddess Tanit
Göttin Tanit
Godin Tanit

●●

Museo Archeologico Nazionale
di Cagliari, Cagliari

Terracotta / Terrakotta

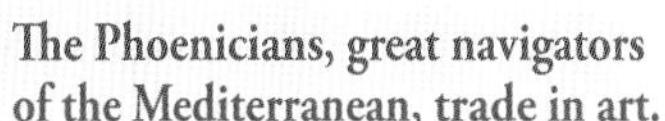

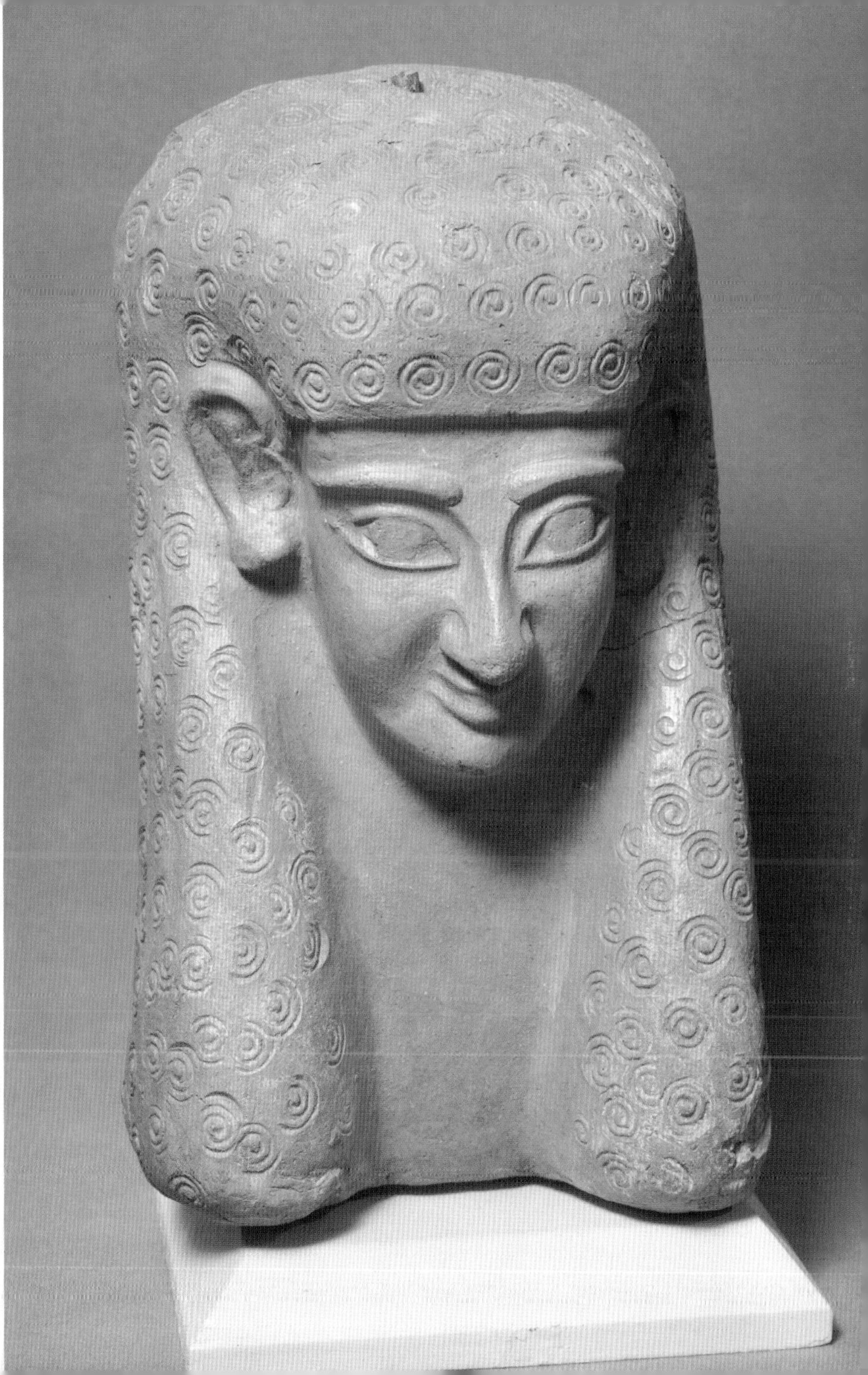

The Phoenicians, great navigators of the Mediterranean, trade in art.

Die Mittelmeerseefahrer Phöniziens handeln mit der Kunst.

De Feniciers, zeevaarders van de Middellandse Zee, handelen in kunst.

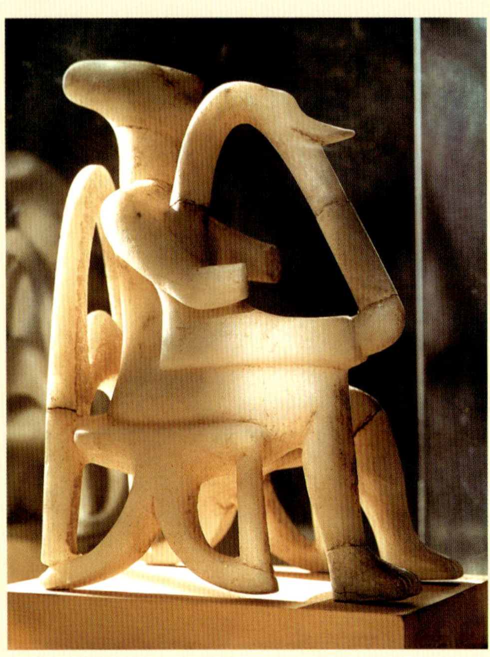

Harp Player
Harfenspieler
Harpspeler

●

c. 2300-2100 BCE
h. 20,3 cm / 7.10 in.
National Archaeological Museum, Athens

Marble / Marmor / Marmer

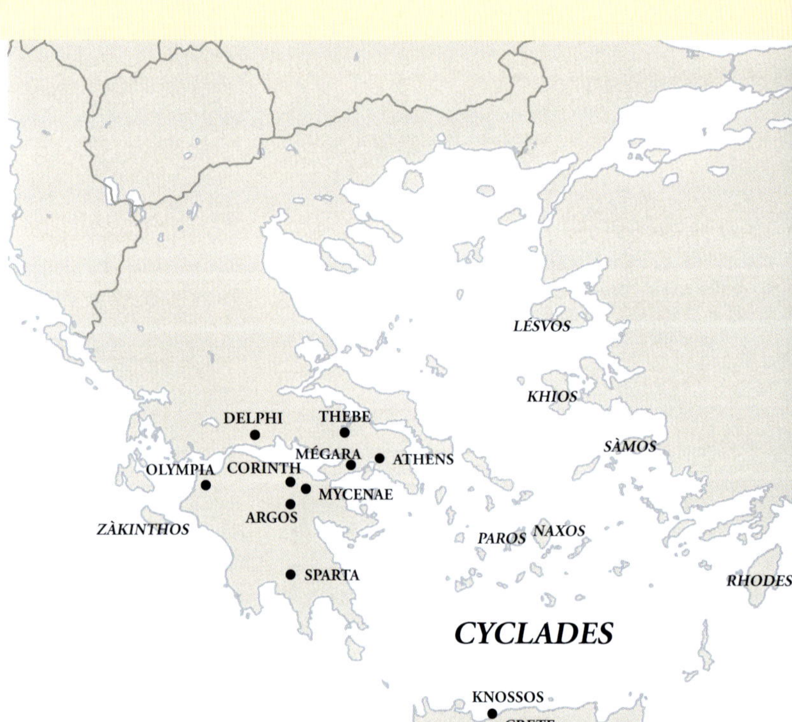

The earliest art of the Cyclades: the first step toward modernity?

Die frühe Kunst der Kykladen: "Anfänge der Moderne"?

De vroegste kunst van de Cycladen: "Het begin van de moderniteit?"

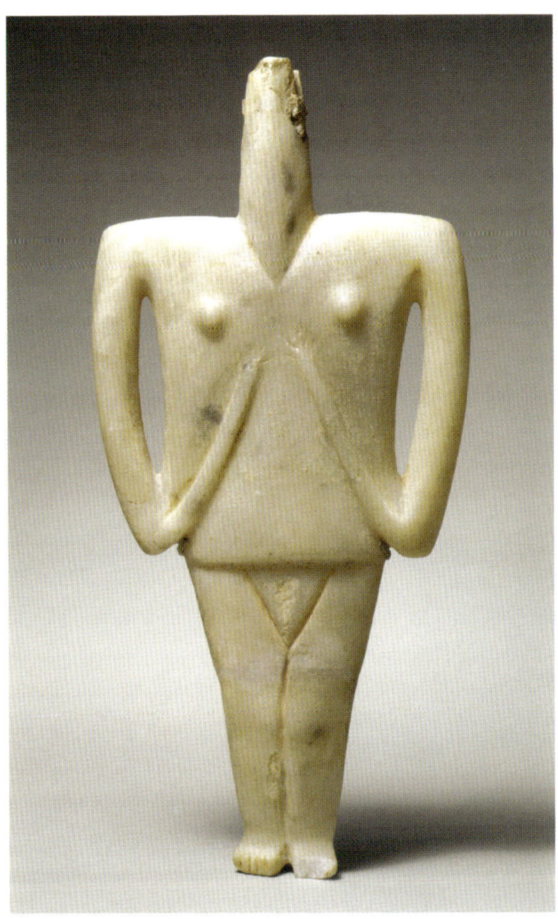

Female Figure
Weibliche Gestalt
Vrouwenfiguur

●

c. 2300-2200 BCE
h. 27,3 cm / 10.7 in.
Metropolitan Museum of Art, New York

Marble / Marmor / Marmer

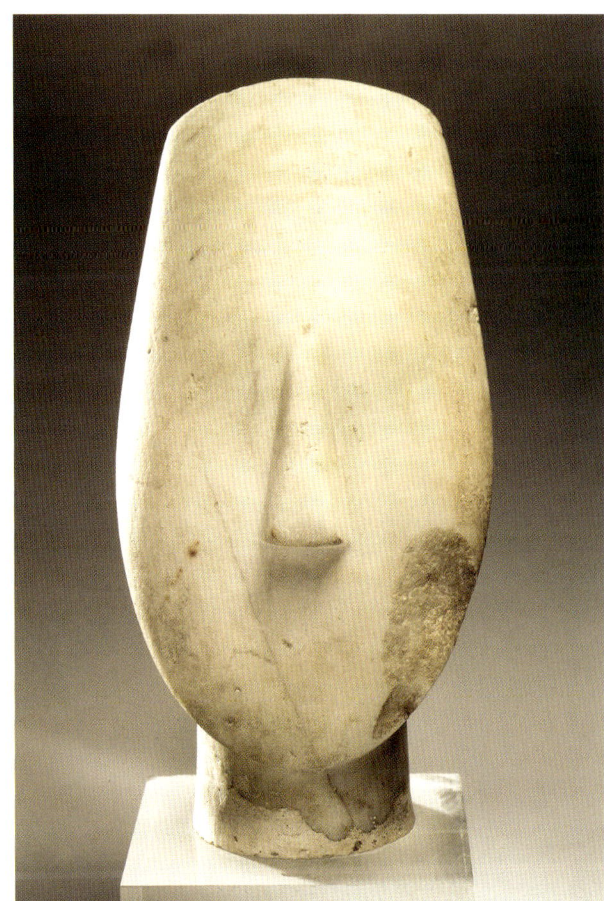

Head of Woman
Frauenkopf
Vrouwenhoofd

●

c. 2700-2300 BCE
Musée du Louvre, Paris

Marble / Marmor / Marmer

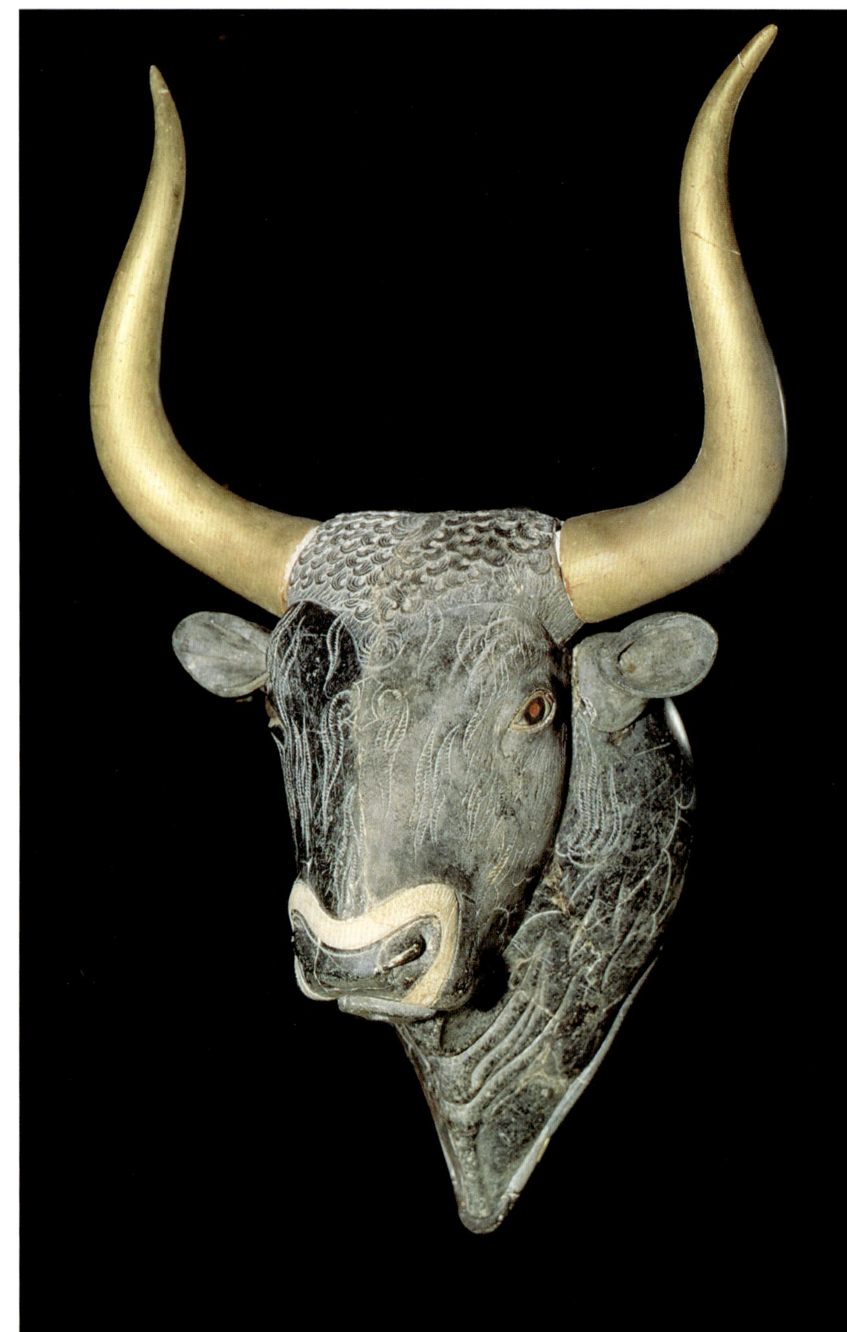

The Minoan culture of Crete is the birthplace of tauromachy.

Die minoische Kultur Kretas ist die Wiege des Stierkampfes.

De Minoische cultuur van Kreta is de wieg van het stierenvechten.

Vase in the Form of a Bull's Head
Stierkopf
Stierenkop

●●●

c. 1700 BCE
Iraklion Museum, Crete

Black steatite
Schwarzer Steatit
Zwart speksteen

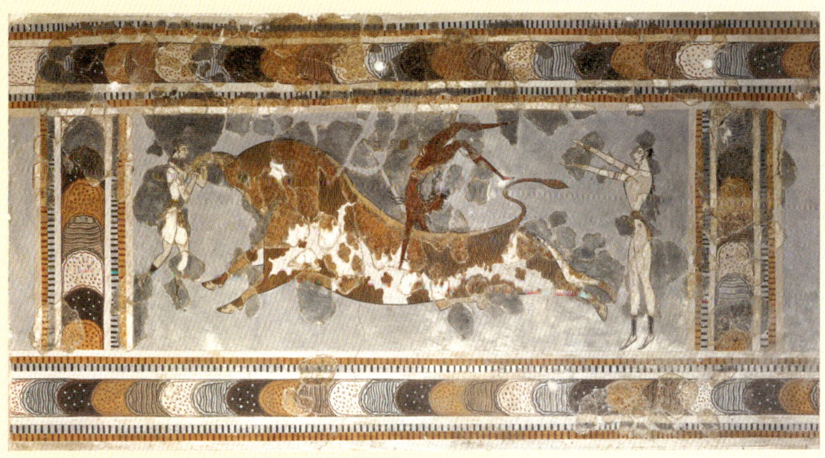

Taurokathapsia,
the bull-leaping ritual
Stierkampf
Stiersprong

●●

c. 1600 BCE
Iraklion Museum, Crete

Fresco / Fresko

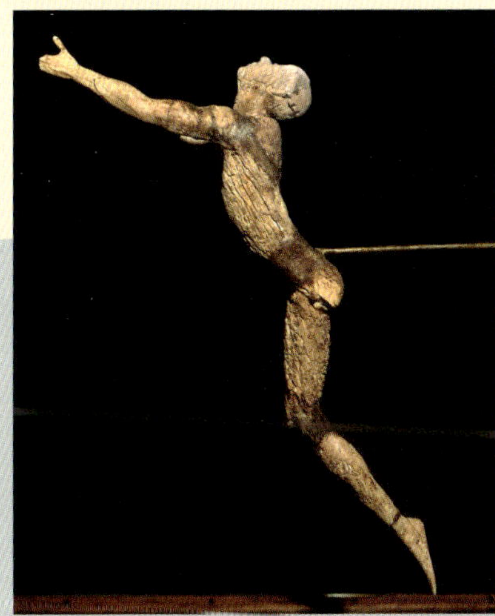

Acrobat
Akrobat
Acrobaat

●●

c. 1600 BCE
h. 29,5 cm / 11.6 in.
Iraklion Museum, Crete

Ivory / Elfenbein / Ivoor

Jug decorated
with sea creatures
Krug mit Meeresmotiven
dekoriert
Kruik gedecoreerd
met zeemotieven

●

c. 1600 BCE
Iraklion Museum, Crete

Ceramic / Keramik / Keramiek

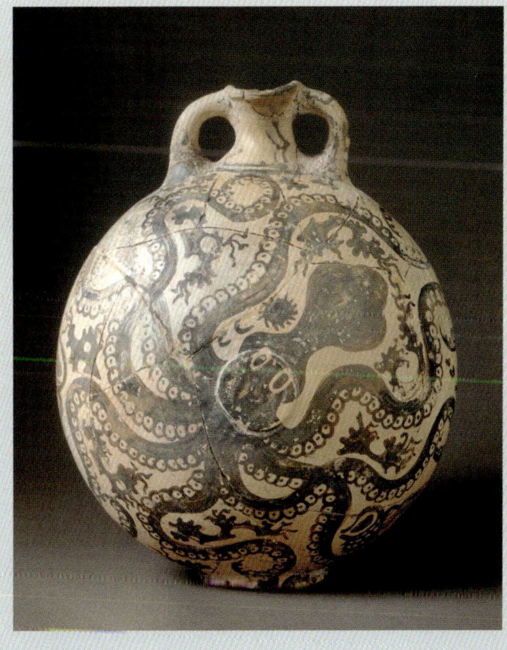

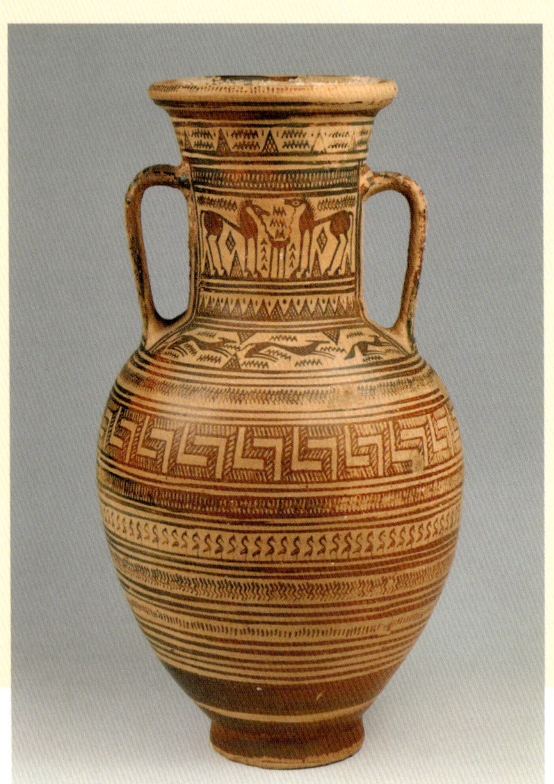

Amphora Decorated with Animals
Amphore mit Tieren
Amfora met dieren

●

c. 720 BCE
h. 43,5 cm / 17.1 in.
Antikensammlung, Staatliche Museen, Berlin

Ceramic / Keramik / Keramiek

Crater with geometric decorations
Krater mit geometrischen Motiven
Krater met geometrische motieven

●

c. 730-720 BCE
h. 50 cm / 19.7 in.
Museo Archeologico e d'Arte della Maremma, Grosseto

Clay / Ton / Klei

Rigorous forms and ornaments characterize the Geometric Period.

Strenge Formen und Dekor bestimmen die Geometrische Periode.

Strenge vormen en ornamenten bepalen de Geometrische periode.

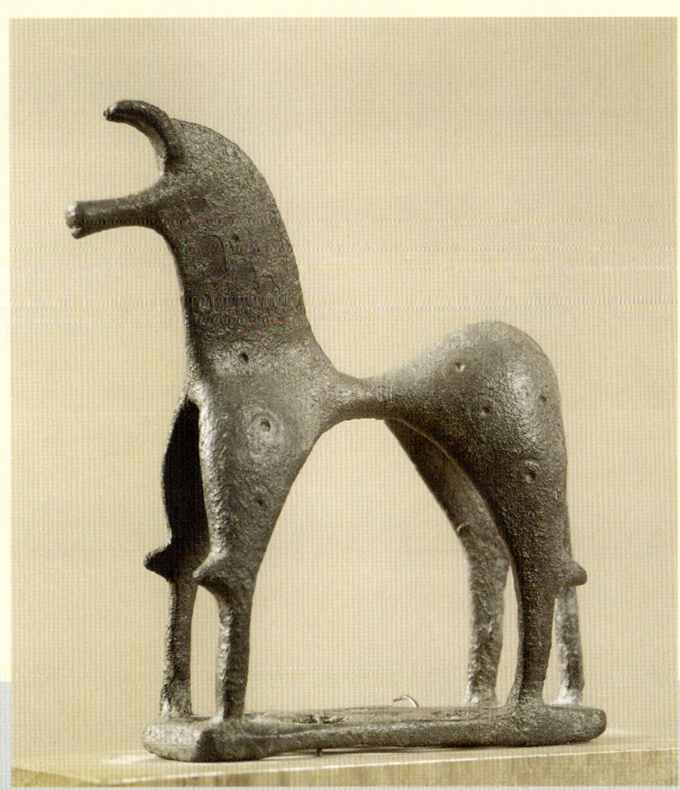

Geometric style horse
Pferd, geometrischer Stil
Paard in geometrische stijl

●●

c. 720 BCE
Museo Archeologico, Siracusa

Bronze / Brons

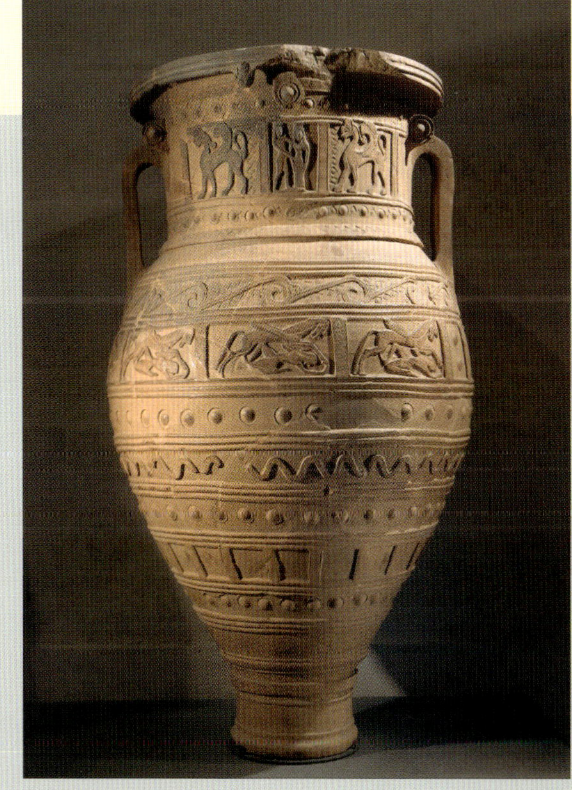

Oriental-style Vase
Orientalisches Gefäß
Oosterse vaas

●

c. 675 BCE
Musée du Louvre, Paris

Ceramic / Keramik / Keramiek

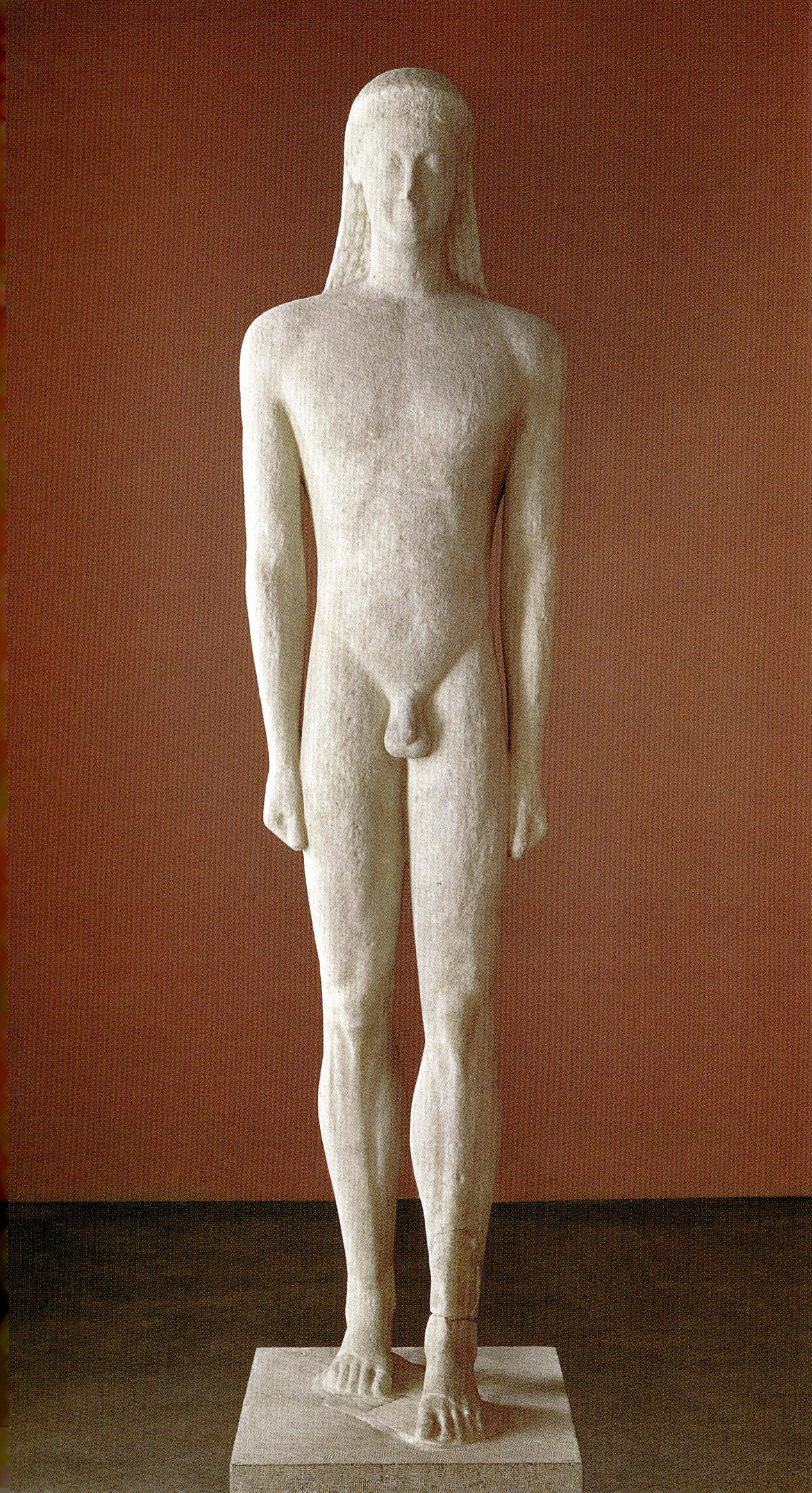

Art of the Archaic Period is forceful, schematic and without ornaments.

Schnörkellos, schematisch und kraftvoll ist die Archaische Periode.

De Archaische periode is schematisch en krachtig en kent geen tierelantijnen

Kouros of Melos
Kouros von Melos
Kouros van Melos

●●●

h. 214 cm / 84.2 in.
National Archaeological Museum, Athens

Marble / Marmor / Marmer

Polymedes of Argos

Kleobis and Biton
Die Kouroi Kleobis und Biton
Kouroi van Kleobis en Biton

●●●

h. 216 cm / 85 in.
Archaeological Museum, Delphi

Marble / Marmor / Marmer

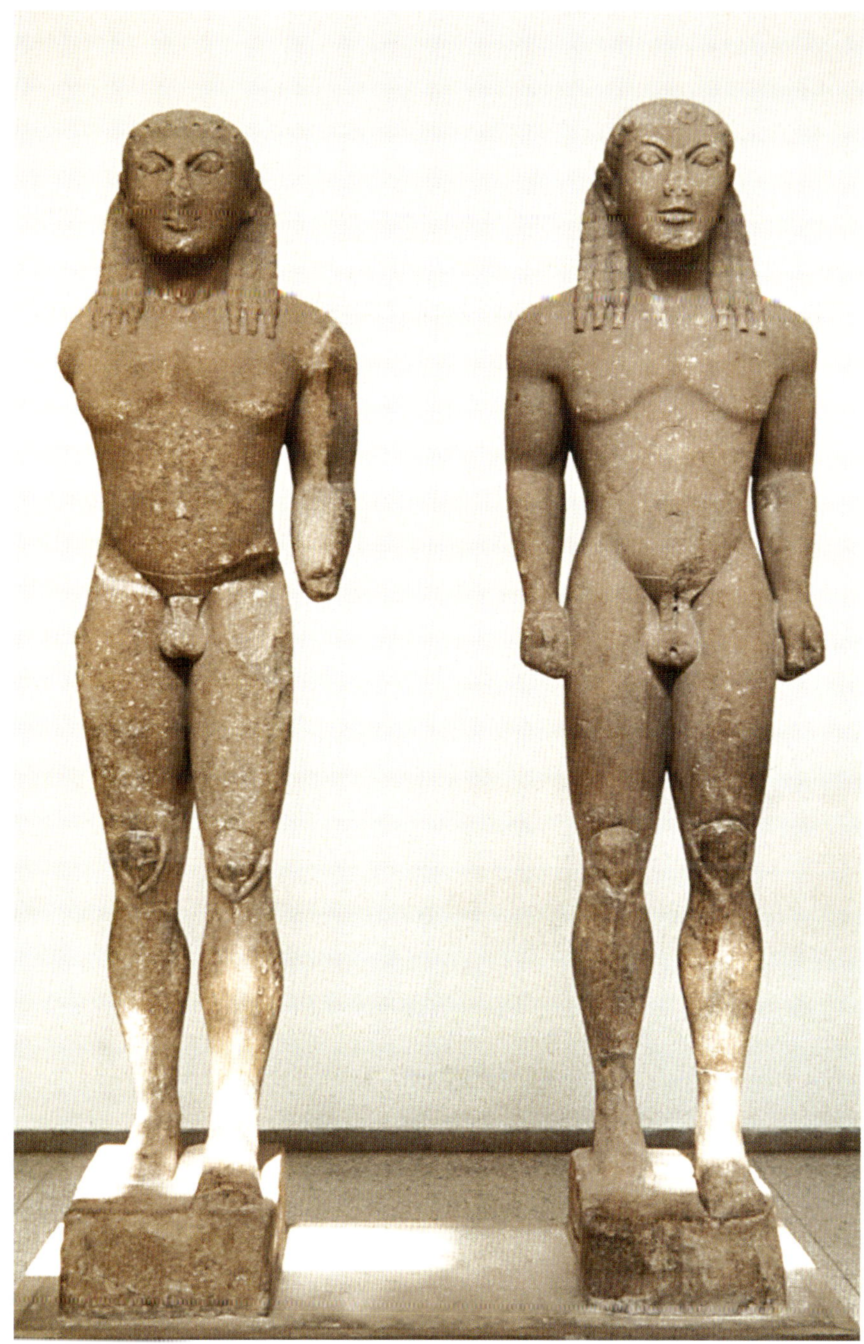

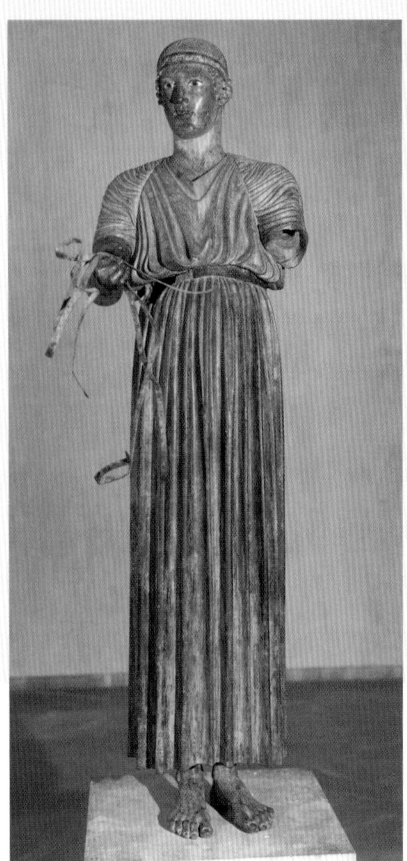

Sòtade

Charioteer of Delphi
Wagenlenker von Delhi
Wagenmenner van Delphi

●

c. 480-470 BCE
h. 180 cm / 70.9 in.
Archaeological Museum,
Delphi

Bronze / Brons

Sòtade

Fallen Warrior
Verletzter Krieger
Gewonde krijger

c. 500-480 BCE
h. 47 cm / 18.5 in.
Staatliche Antikensammlungen
und Glyptothek, Munich

Marble / Marmor / Marmer

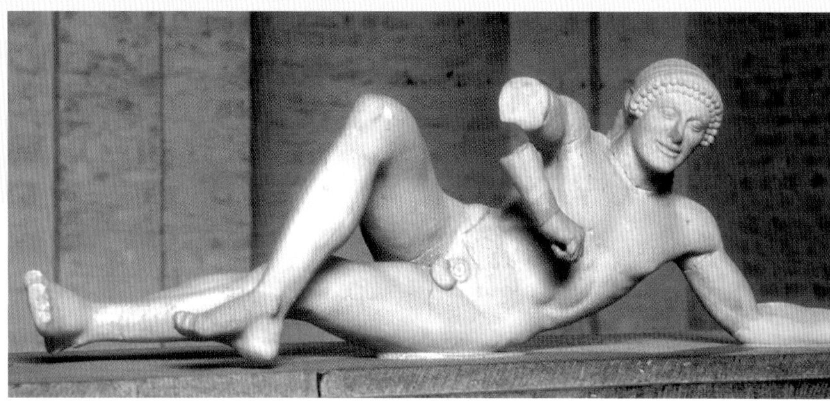

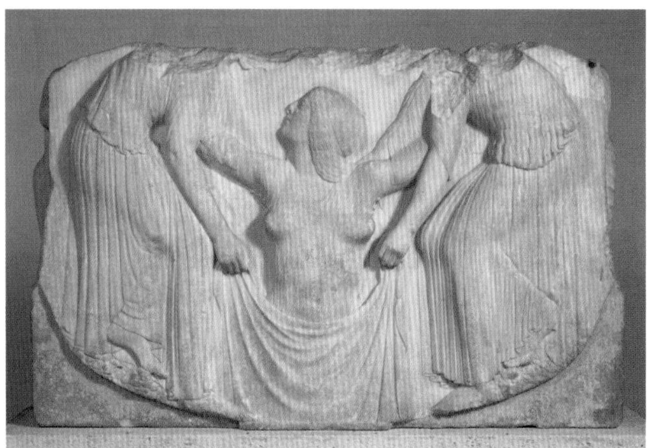

Ludovisi Throne: Birth of Venus
Thron Ludovisi: Geburt der Venus
Ludovisi Troon: Geboorte van Venus

●

c. 460 BCE
h. 110 cm / 43.3 in.
Museo Nazionale Romano, Roma

Marble / Marmor / Marmer

During the Classical Period anatomy and naturalism dominate art.

In der Klsassischen Periode erobern Naturalismus und Anatomie die Kunst.

Tijdens de klassieke periode veroveren het naturalisme en de anatomie de kunst.

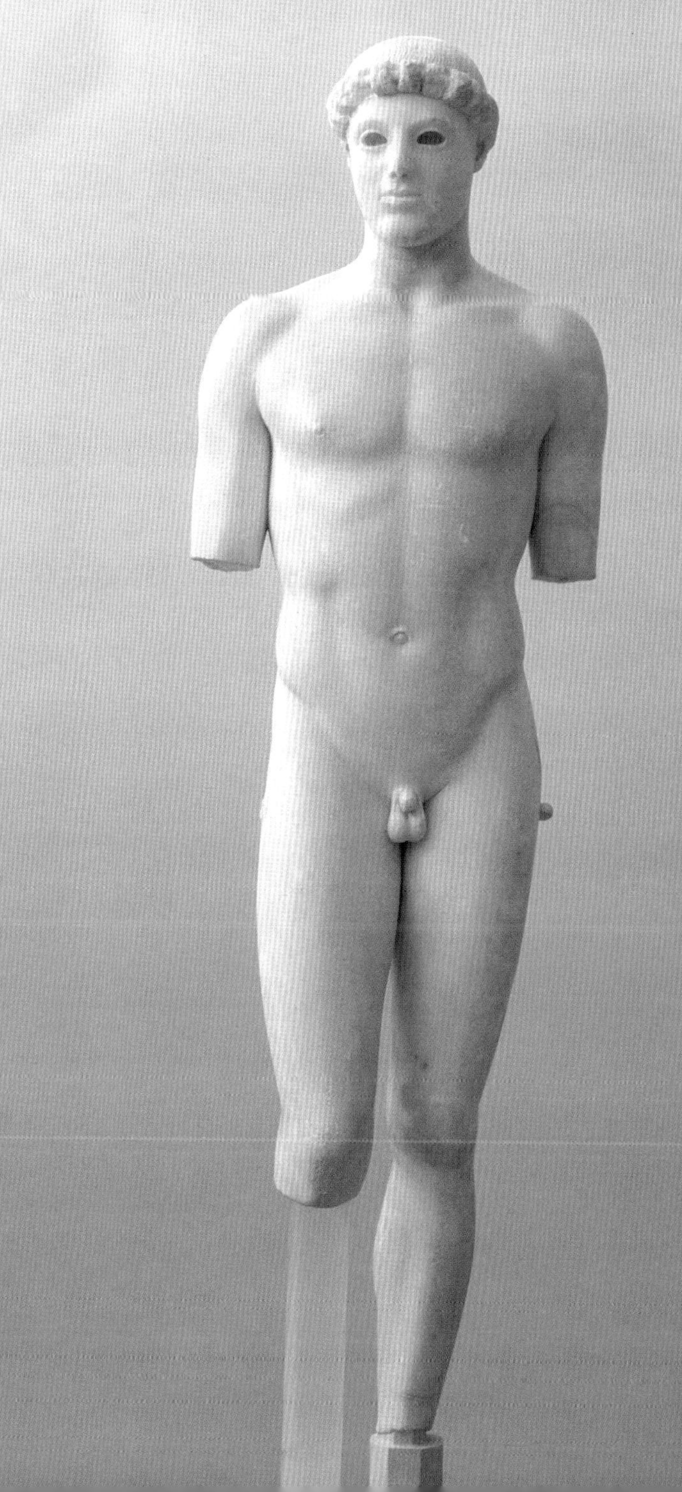

Critius

Ephebos
Ephebe
Efebe

●●●

c. 480 BCE
h. 86 cm / 33.9 in.
Acropolis Museum, Athens

Marble / Marmor / Marmer

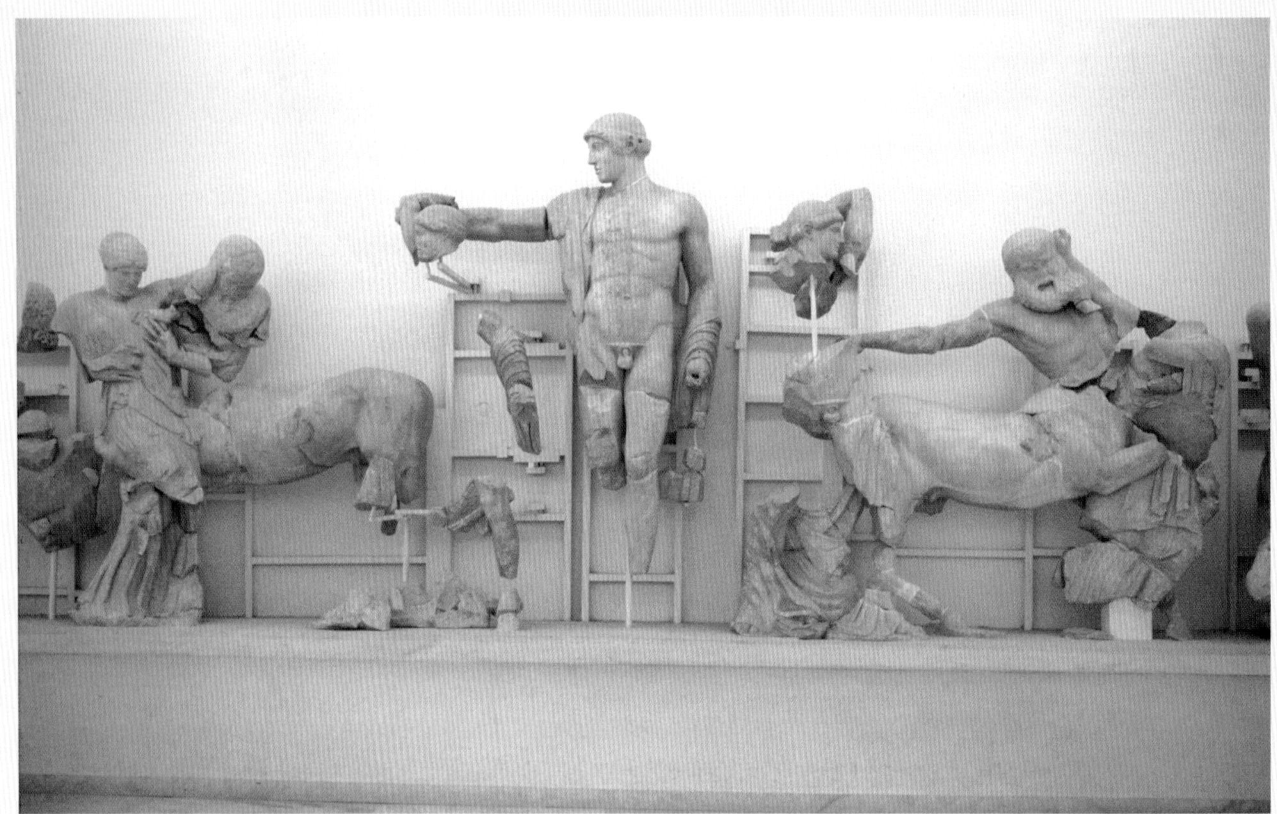

Statues from the West Pediment of the Temple of Zeus
Statuen der Westfront des Zeustempels
Standbeelden van het West-fronton van de Tempel van Zeus

●●●

c. 465-456 BCE
h. 330 cm / 130 in.
Archaeological Museum, Olympia

Marble / Marmor / Marmer

Riace Warriors
Bronzestatuen von Riace
Bronzi di Riace (Bronzen van Riace)

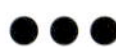

c. 450 BCE
h. 200 cm / 78.8 in.
Museo Nazionale, Reggio Calabria

Bronze / Brons

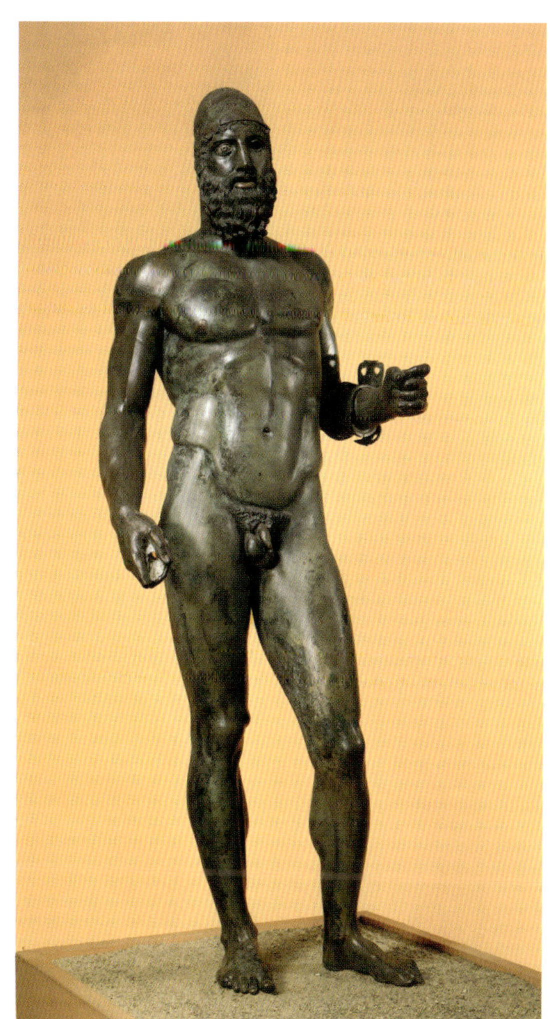

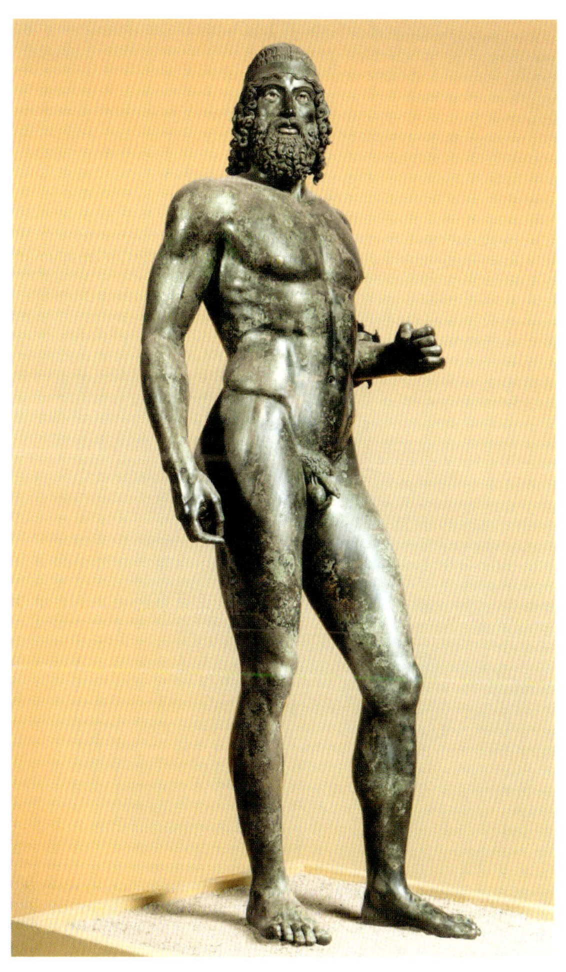

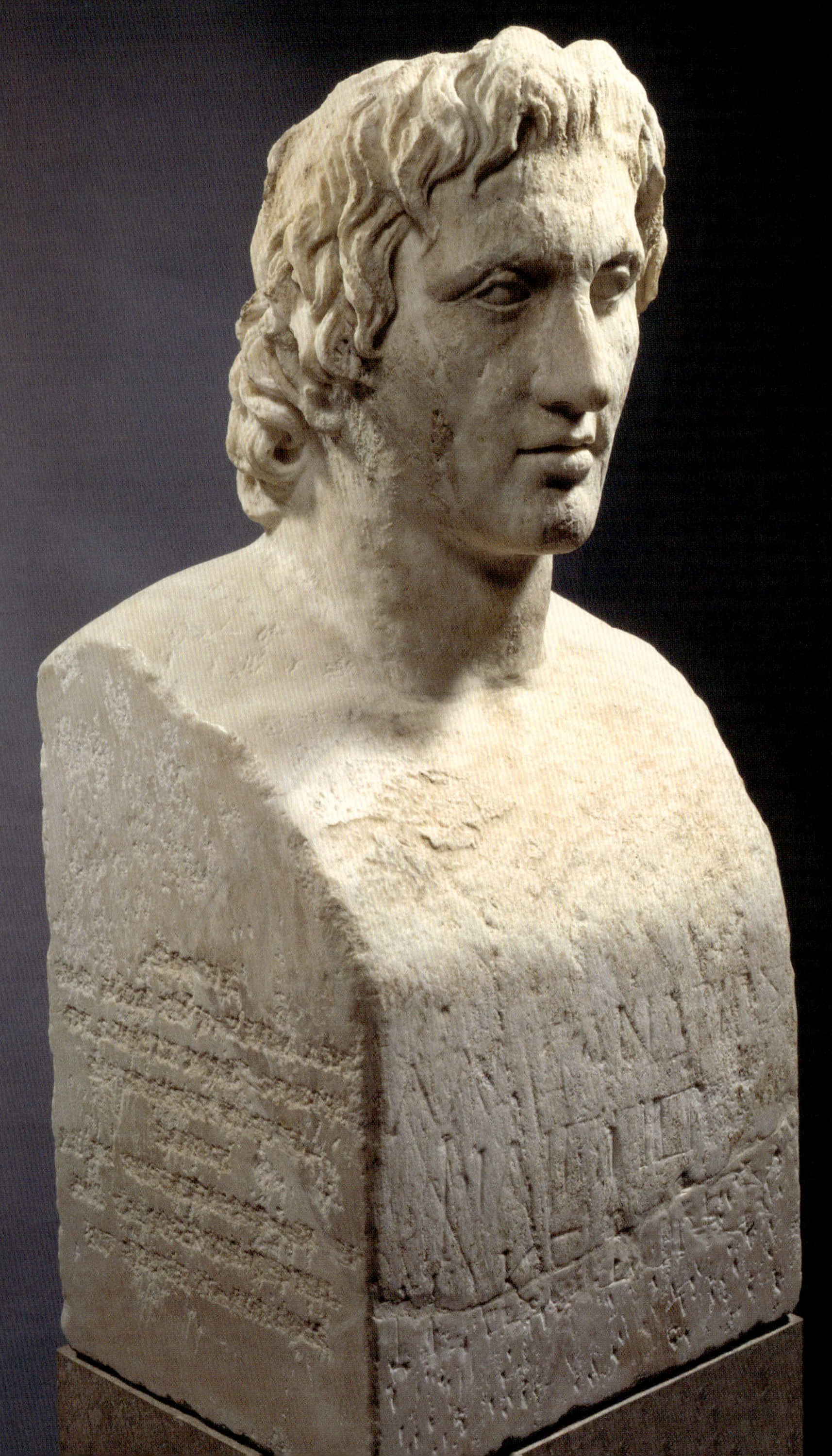

The Hellenistic Period begins with Alexander the Great...

Mit Alexander dem Großen beginnt die Hellenistische Periode...

Met Alexander de Grote begint de Hellenistische periode...

Lysippus

Alexander the Great
Alexander der Große
Alexander de Grote

●●●

c. 335-323 BCE
h. 65 cm / 25.6 in.
Musée du Louvre, Paris

Marble (Roman copy)
Marmor (römische Kopie)
Marmer (Romeinse kopie)

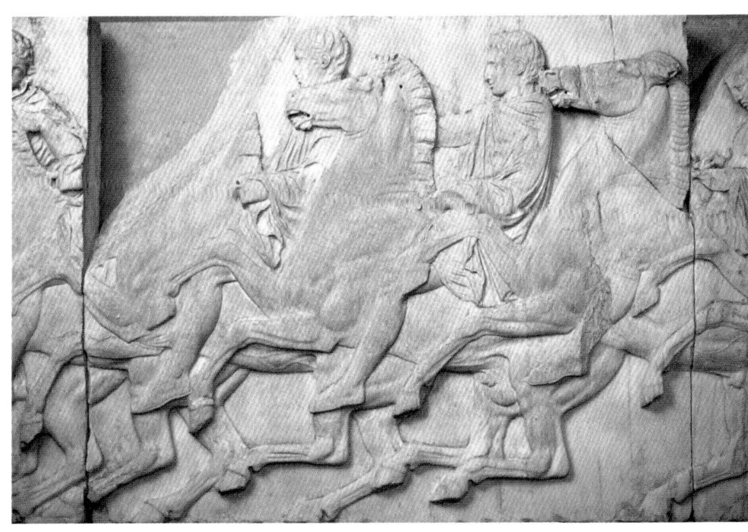

Phidias

Group of Horsemen from the Frieze of the Parthenon
Parthenon-Fries Reitergruppe
Ruitergroep op de Fries van het Parthenon

●

c. 450 BCE
British Museum, London

Marble / Marmor / Marmer

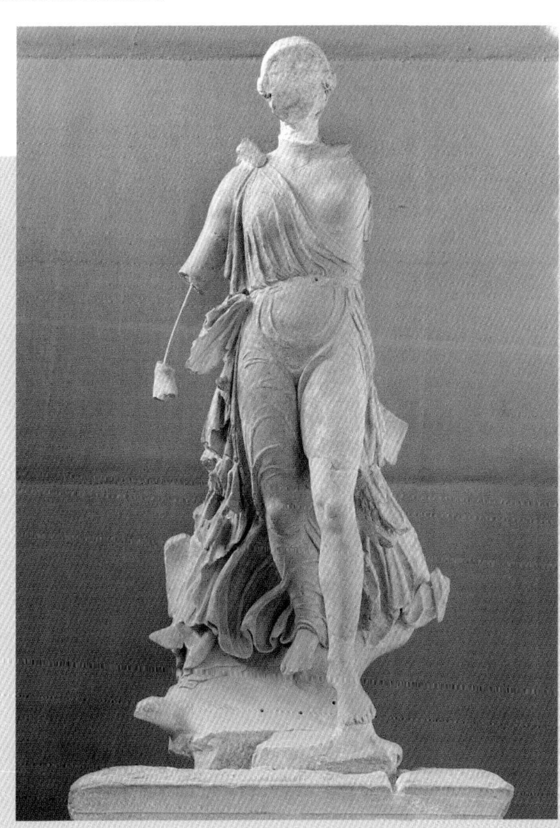

Paeonius of Mende
Paeonius von Mende
Paeonius van Mende

Nike
Nikè

●●●

c. 425 BCE
h. 215 cm / 84.6 in.
Archaeological Museum, Olympia

Marble / Marmor / Marmer

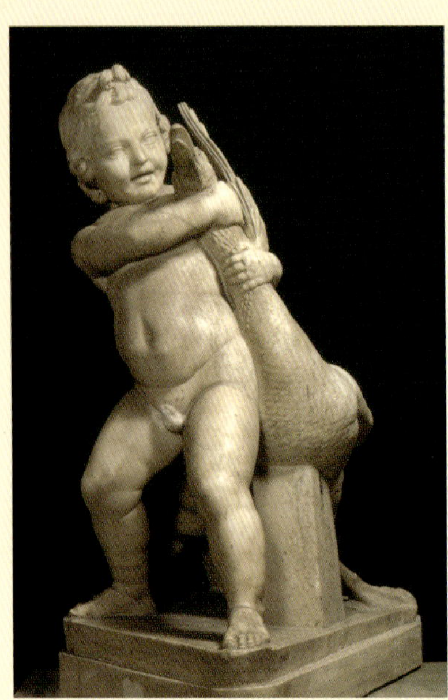

Boethos

Boy with Goose
Knabe mit Gans
Jongen met gans

●

c. 200-100 BCE
h. 82 cm / 32.3 in.
Musei Vaticani,
Città del Vaticano

Marble (Roman copy)
Marmor (römische Kopie) / Marmer (Romeinse kopie)

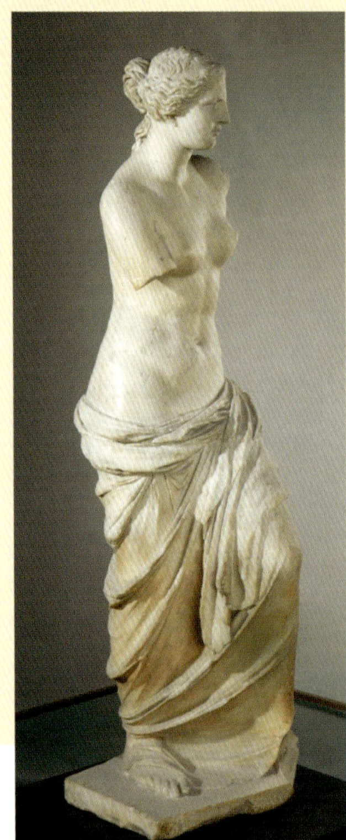

Venus de Milo
Venus von Milo
Venus van Milo

●●●

c. 200-100 BCE
h 204 cm
Musée du Louvre, Paris

Marble
Marmor
Marmer

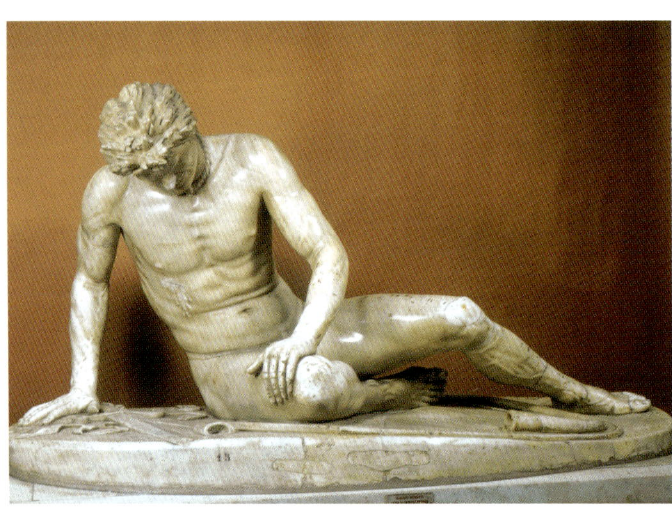

Epigonus

Dying Gaul
Sterbende Galata
Stervende Galliër

●

c. 200-100 BCE
Musei Capitolini, Roma

Marble (Roman copy)
Marmor (römische Kopie)
Marmer (Romeinse kopie)

... and is characterized by emotion and baroque exuberance.

charakterisiert von Emotion und barockem Überschwang.

... gekenmerkt door emotie en barokke exuberantie.

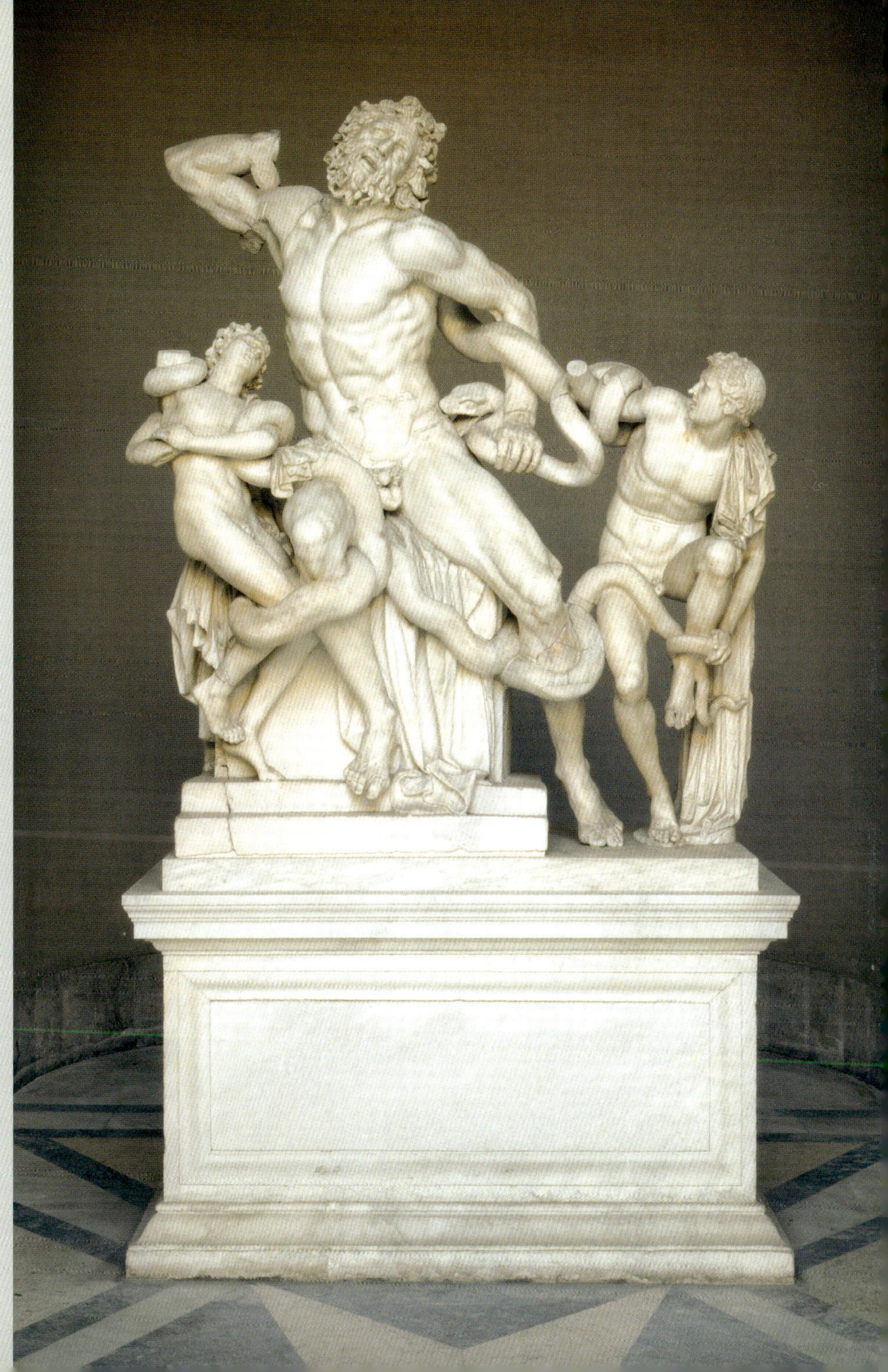

Agesander, Athenodorus, Polydorus

Laocoon
Laokoon
Laocoöngroep

●●●

c. 200-100 BCE
Museo Pio-Clementino, Città del Vaticano

Marble (Roman copy)
Marmor (römische Kopie)
Marmer (Romeinse kopie)

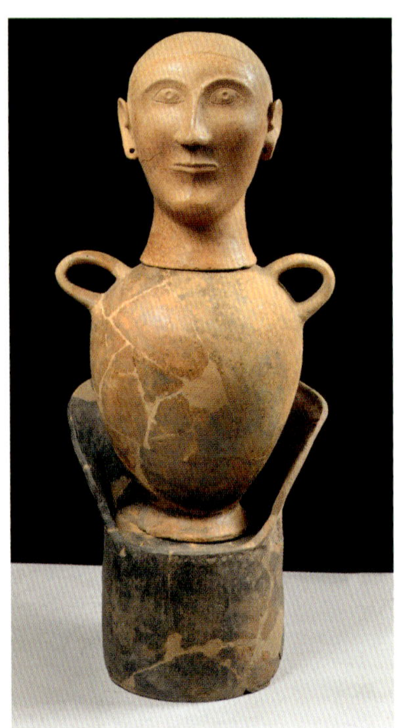

Canopic Jar from Chiusi
Aschenurne aus Chiusi
Asurn uit Chiusi

●

c. 650-600 BCE
h. 45 cm / 17.7 in.
Museo Archeologico Claudio Faina, Orvieto

Terracotta / Terrakotta

Tomb of the Augurs: Wrestlers
Grab der Auguren: Ringer
Tombe van de Auguren: Worstelaars

●

c. 530-520 BCE
Tarquinia

Fresco / Fresko

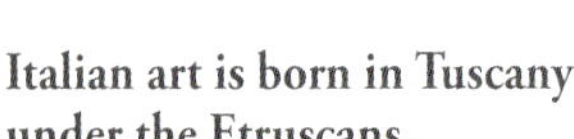

Italian art is born in Tuscany under the Etruscans.

Mit den Etruskern in der Toskana beginnt die italienische Kunst.

Met de Etrusken begint in Toscane de Italiaanse kunst.

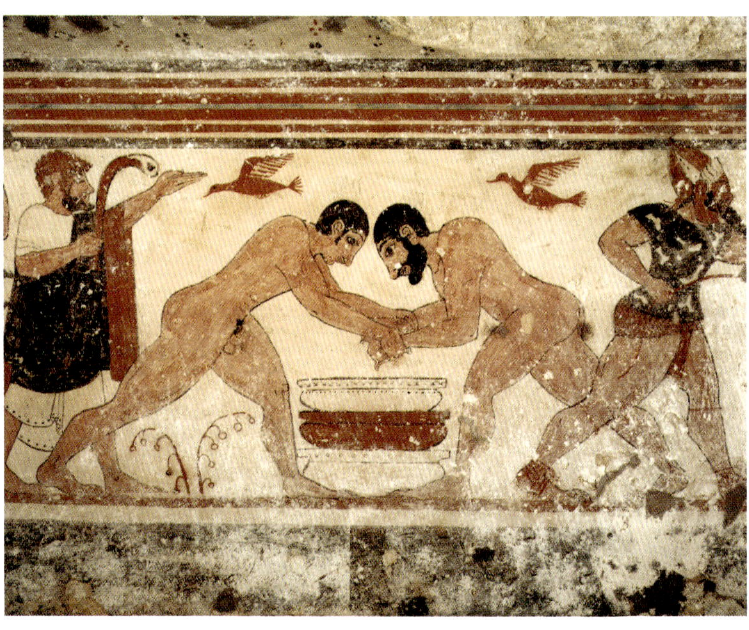

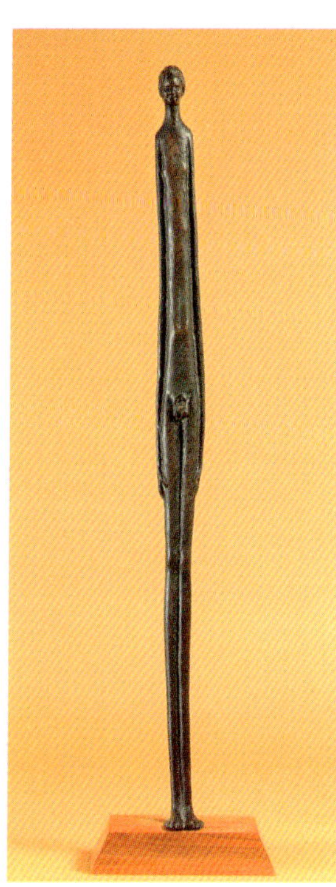

Shadow of the Evening
Abendlicher Schatten
Schaduw van de nacht

●

c. 300-200 BCE
h. 57,5 cm / 22.6 in.
Museo Etrusco Guarnacci, Volterra

Bronze / Brons

Sarcophagus of the Bride and Groom
Sarkophag mit liegendem Paar
Sarcofaag met liggend paar

●●●

c. 525-520 BCE
Museo Nazionale Etrusco di Villa Giulia, Roma

Terracotta / Terrakotta

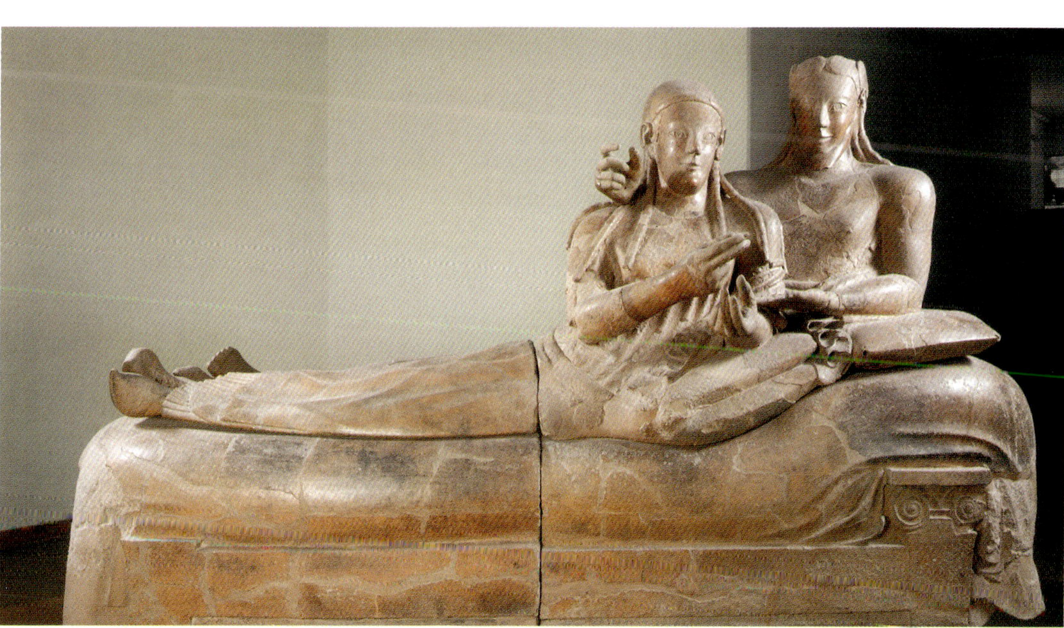

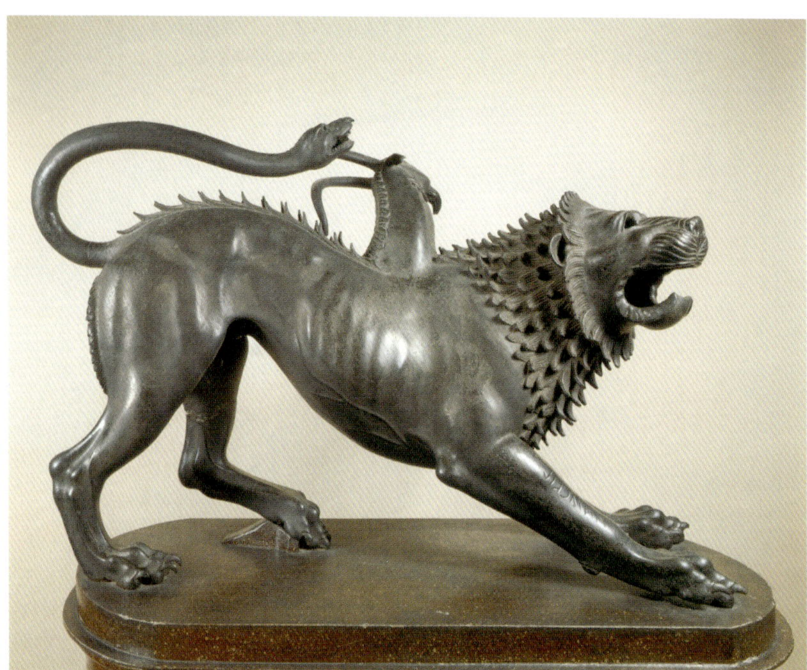

Chimera of Arezzo
Chimäre von Arezzo
Chimaera van Arezzo

●●

c. 490-390 BCE
h. 65 cm / 25.6 in.
Museo Archeologico, Firenze

Bronze / Brons

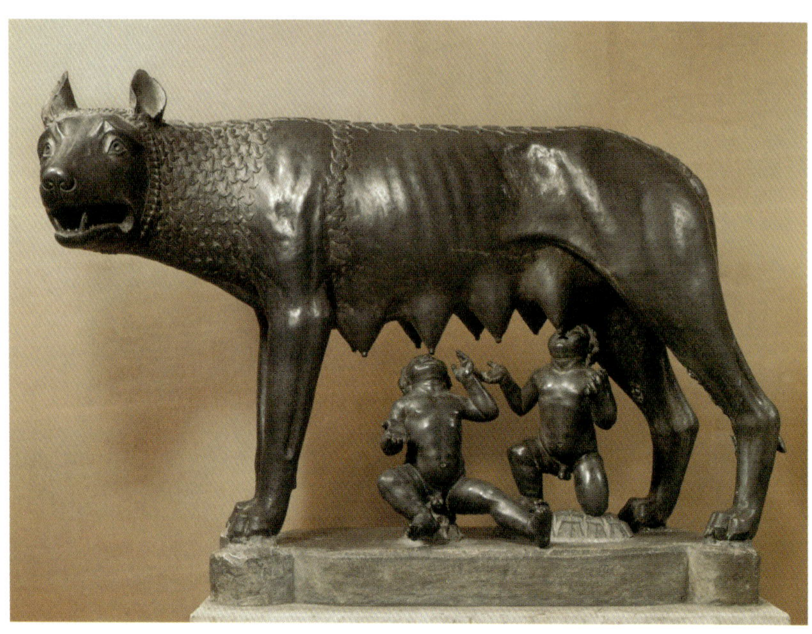

Capitoline Wolf
Die kapitolinische Wölfin
Capitolijnse Wolvin

●●●

c. 490-390 BCE
h. 75 cm / 29.5 in.
Musei Capitolini, Roma

Bronze / Brons

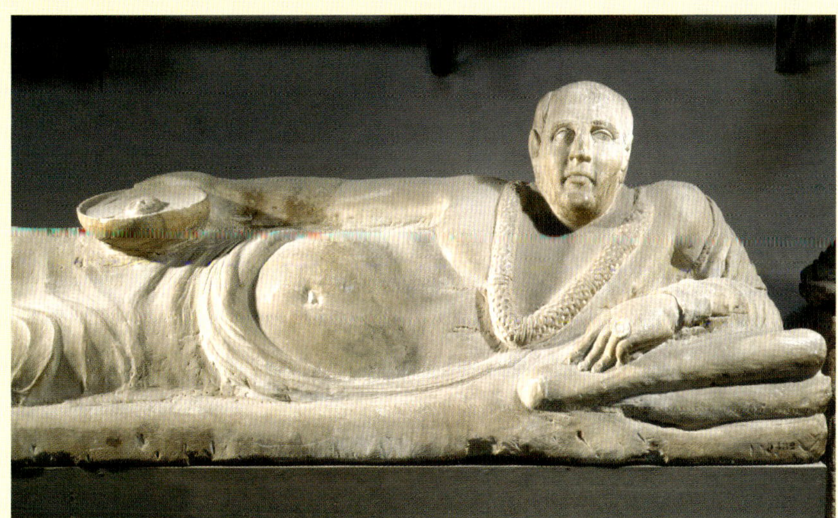

Sarcophagus of the Fat Man
Sarkophag eines dicken Mannes
Sarcofaag van de dikke man

●●

Museo Archeologico, Firenze
c. 200-100 BCE

Terracotta / Terrakotta

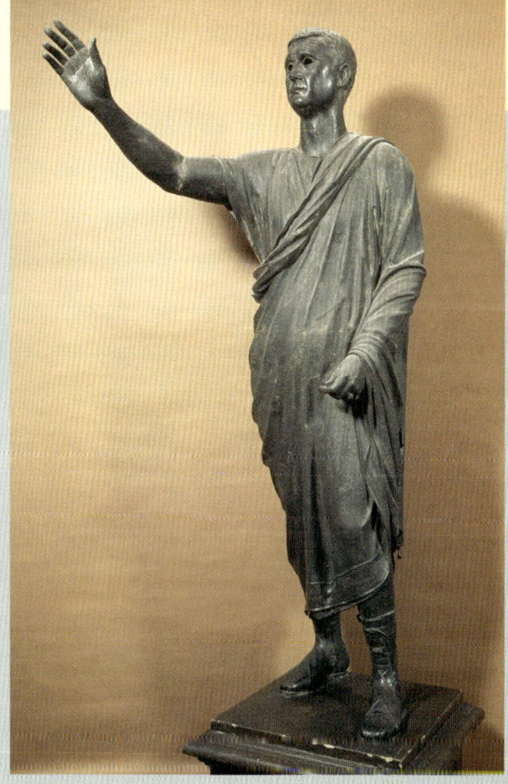

The Orator, Found near Trasimeno Lake
Der Redner, Trasimener See
De Redenaar van het Trasimeense meer

●●●

c. 90 BCE
h. 170 cm / 66.9 in.
Museo Archeologico, Firenze

Bronze / Brons

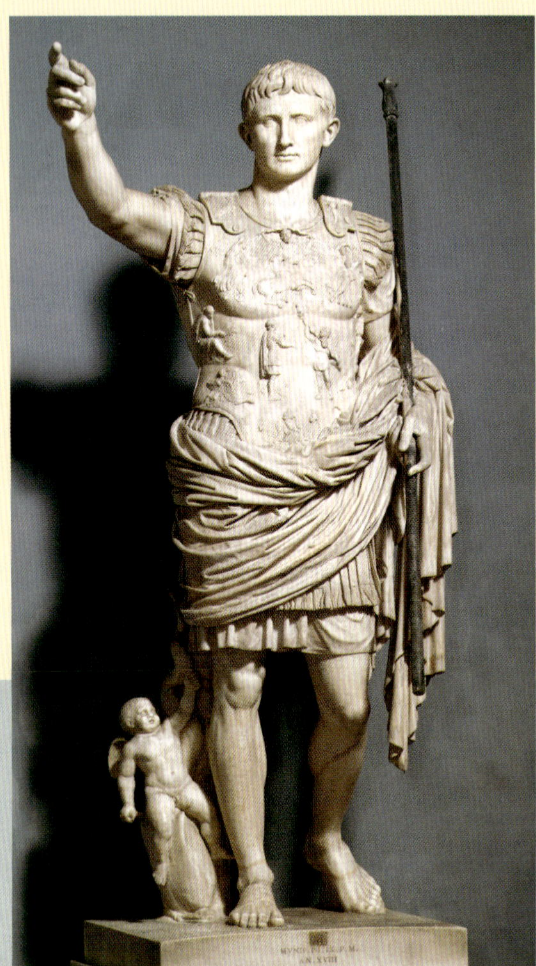

Nero Caesar from the Cartoceto group
Der Kaiser Nero der Cartoceto Gruppe
Keizer Nero van de Cartoceto groep

●●

c. 23-30 CE
Museo Archeologico Nazionale delle Marche, Ancona

Gilded bronze / Vergoldete Bronze / Verguld brons

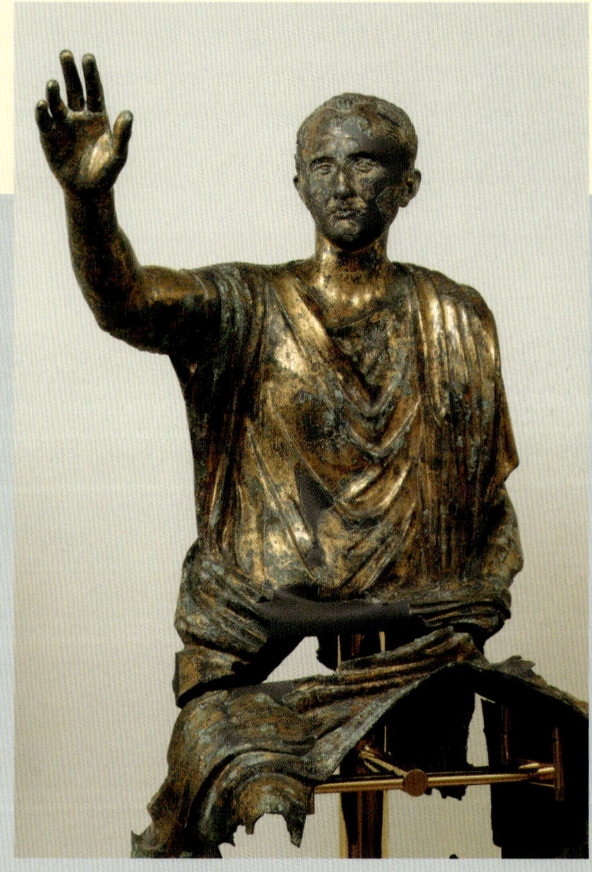

Augustus of Prima Porta
Augustus von Prima Porta
Augustus van Prima Porta

●●

c. 90-80 BCE
h. 240 cm / 94.5 in.
Museo Chiaromonti, Città del Vaticano

Marble / Marmor / Marmer

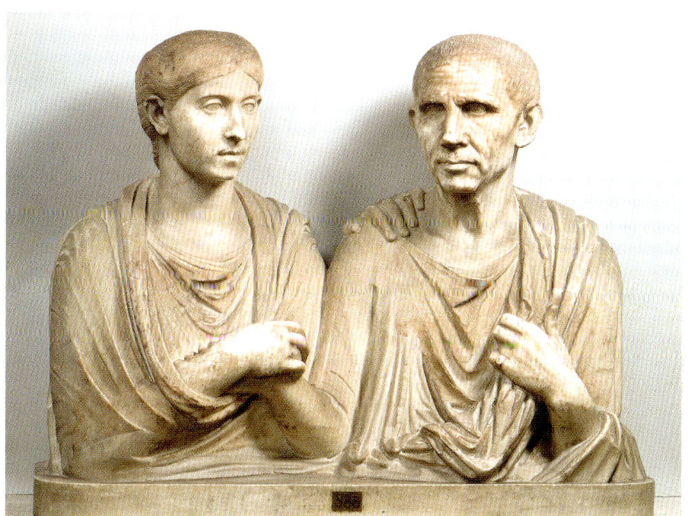

Bust of Cato and Portia
Büste von Cato und Porzia
Buste van Cato en Porcia

●

c. 10-99 CE
Museo Pio-Clementino, Città del Vaticano

Marble / Marmor / Marmer

The golden era of Roman art begins under Augustus.

Mit Augustus beginnt das goldene Zeitalter der römischen Kunst.

Met Augustus begint de Gouden Eeuw van de Romeinse kunst.

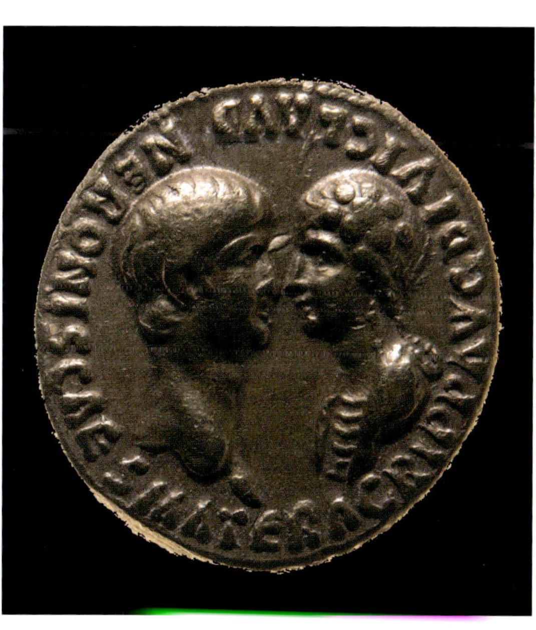

Emperor Claudius and Agrippina, Coin
Münze des Kaisers Tiberius Claudius und Agrippina
Munt van Keizer Tiberius Claudius en Agrippina

●

c. 50-51 CE
Münzkabinett, Staatliche Museen, Berlin

Brass / Messing

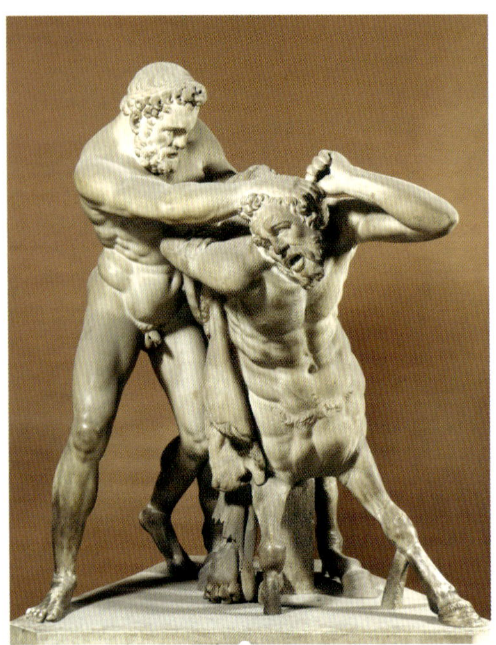

Hercules and Nessus
Herkules und Nessus
Herakles en Nessus

●

Galleria degli Uffizi, Firenze

Marble / Marmor / Marmer

Mithras Killing the Bull
Gott Mithras tötet den Stier
De God Mithras doodt de stier

●

c. 50 CE
Museo Pio-Clementino, Città del Vaticano

Marble / Marmor / Marmer

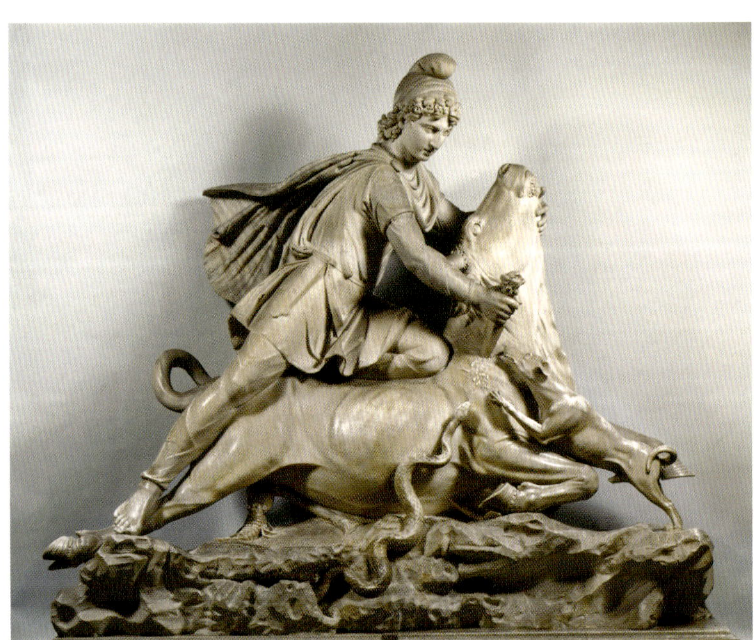

Horses of Saint Mark
Das Viergespann von San Marco
De vierspan van San Marco

●●

c. 150-250 CE
Museo della Basilica di San Marco, Venezia

Gilded bronze / Vergoldete Bronze
Verguld brons

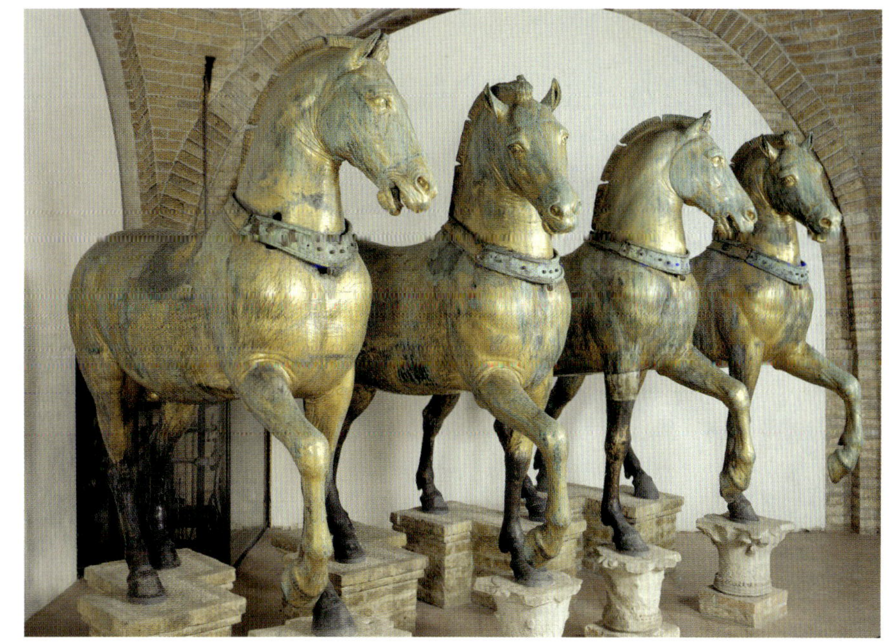

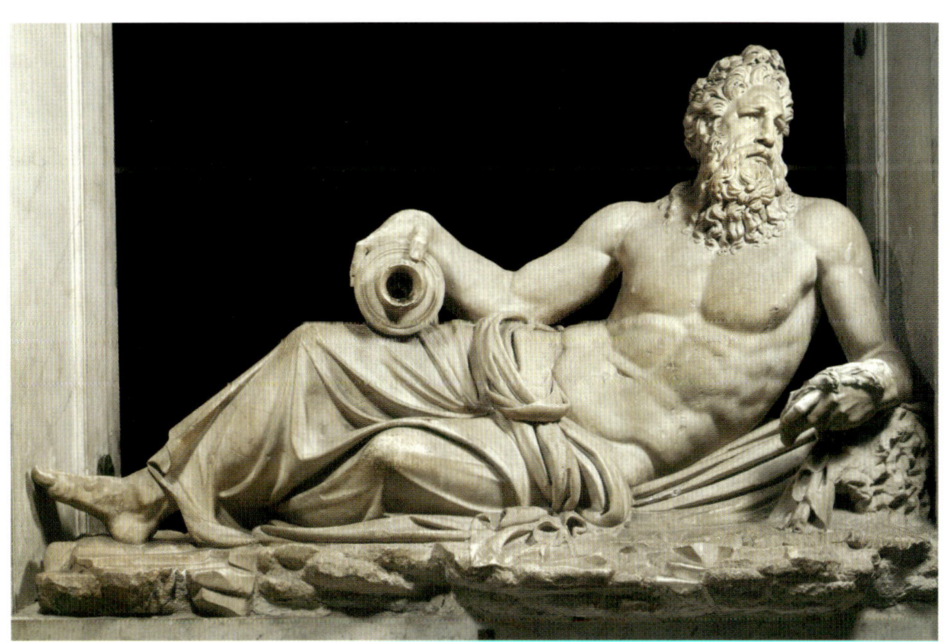

Statue of the River Tigris
Statue des Flusses Tigris
Standbeeld van de rivier de Tigris

●●

Museo Pio-Clementino, Città del Vaticano

Marble / Marmor / Marmer

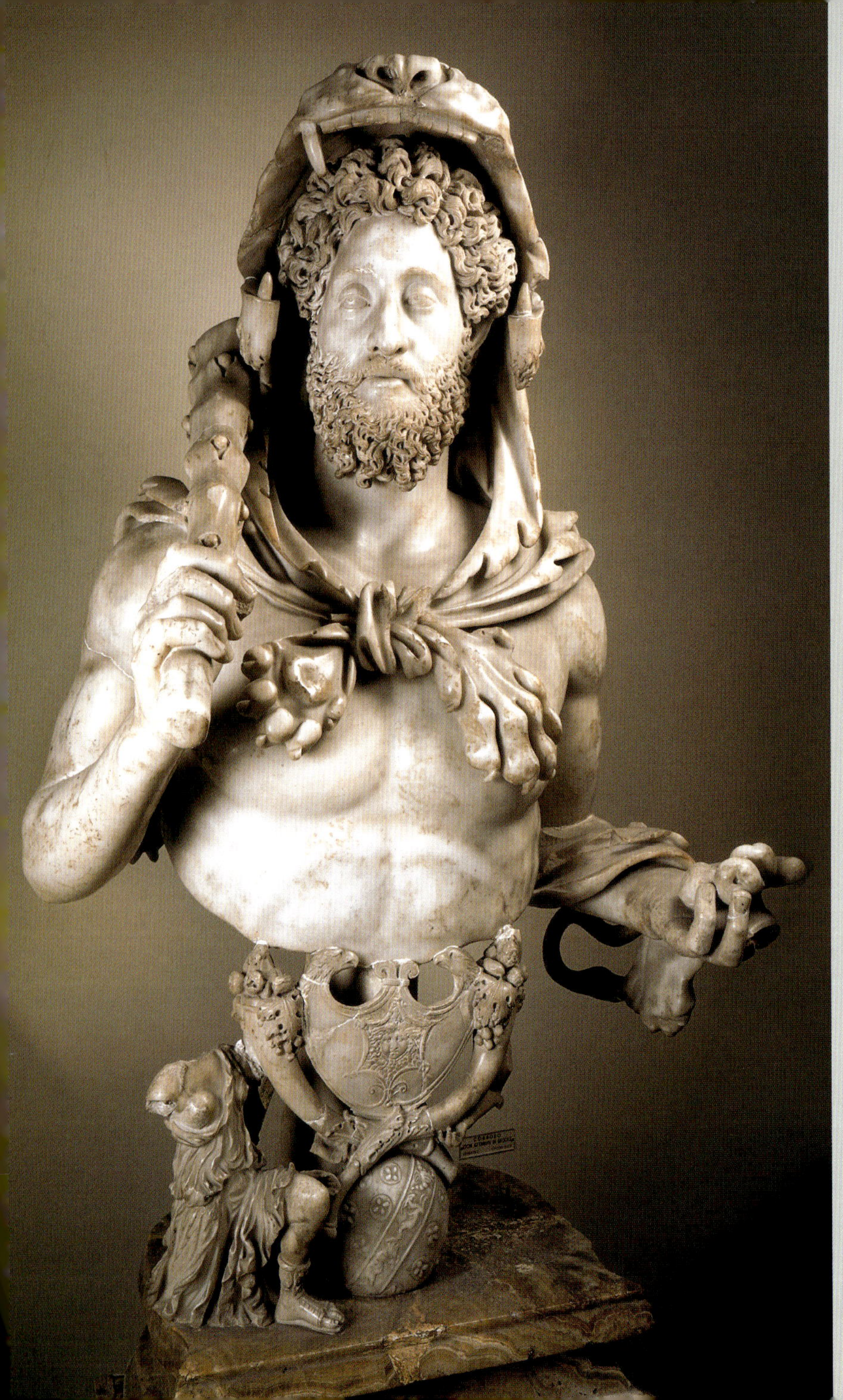

Bust of Commodus as Hercules
Büste des Commodus als Herkules
Buste van Commodus als Hercules

●●●

c. 190-192 CE
h. 118 cm / 46.6 in.
Musei Capitolini, Roma

Marble and alabaster
Marmor und Alabaster
Marmer en albast

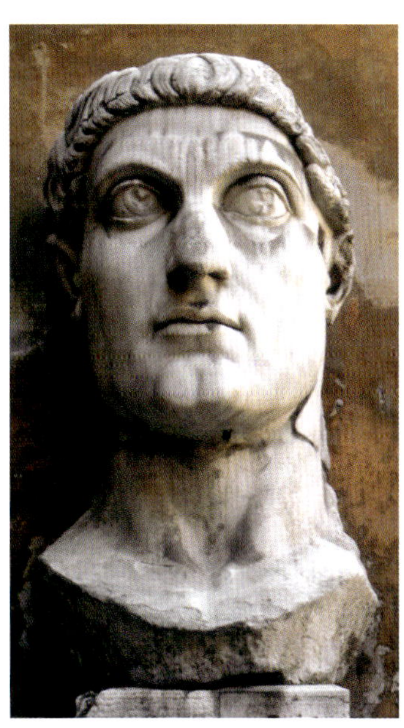

Constantine the Great
Kopf des Kaisers Konstantin
Hoofd van Keizer Constantijn

●

c. 340 CE
Musei Capitolini, Roma

Marble / Marmor / Marmer

Male figure in toga, with the head of Augustus
Darstellung eines Mannes mit Toga und dem Kopf des Augustus
Weergave van een man gekleed in toga, met het hoofd van Augustus

●●

10-100 CE
Galleria Borghese, Roma

Marble / Marmor / Marmer

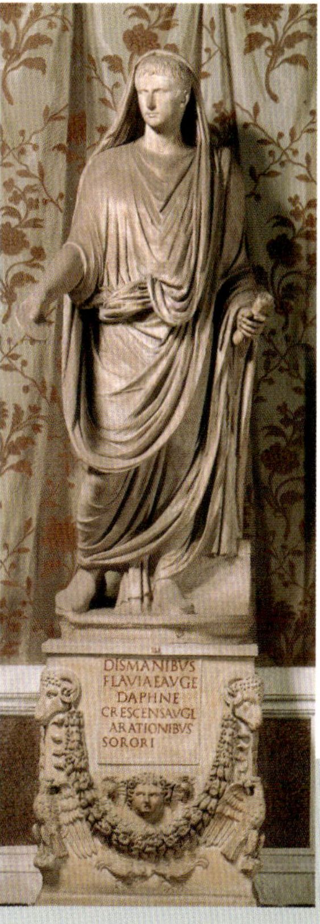

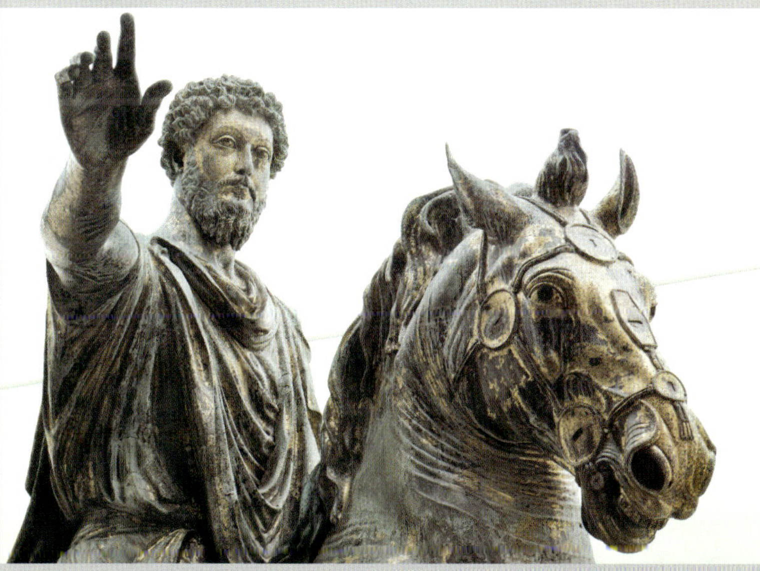

Equestrian Statue of Marcus Aurelius
Reiterstandbild von Mark Aurel
Ruiterstandbeeld van Marcus Aurelius

●●●

c. 180 CE
Musei Capitolini, Roma

Gilded bronze
Vergoldete Bronze
Verguld brons

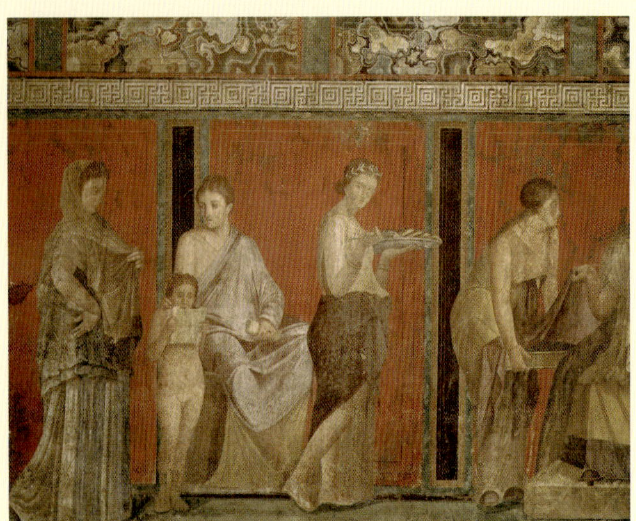

Reading of the Ritual
Das Lesen des Rituals
Het lezen van het ritueel

●●●

c. 30 BCE
Villa dei Misteri, Pompei

Fresco / Fresko

Flora or Spring
Flora oder der Frühling
Flora of Godin van de Lente

●●

c. 50 CE
Museo Archeologico Nazionale, Napoli

Fresco / Fresko

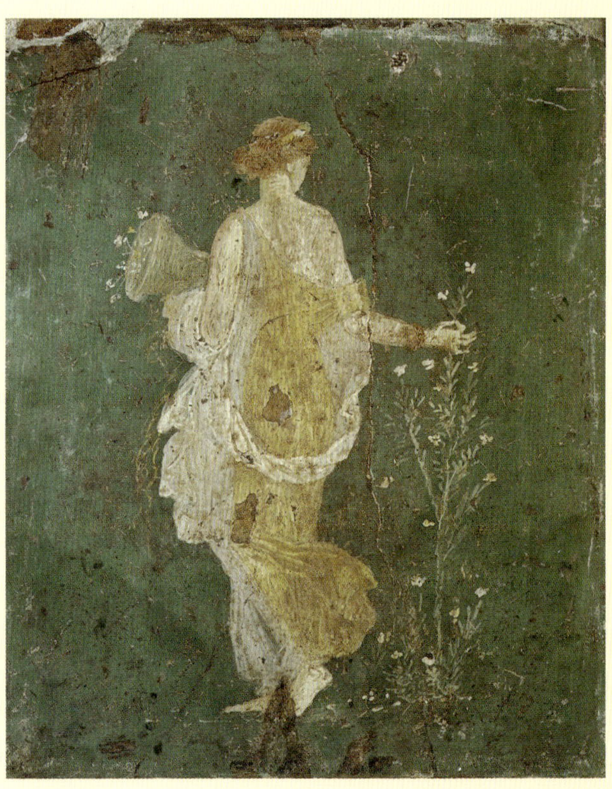

Luxury in the home: the wall paintings at Pompei and Ercolano.

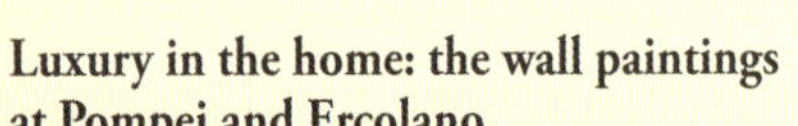

Luxus im eigenen Heim, die Wandmalerei von Pompeji und Herculaneum.

Luxe in het eigen huis, muurschilderingen in Pompeï en Ercolano.

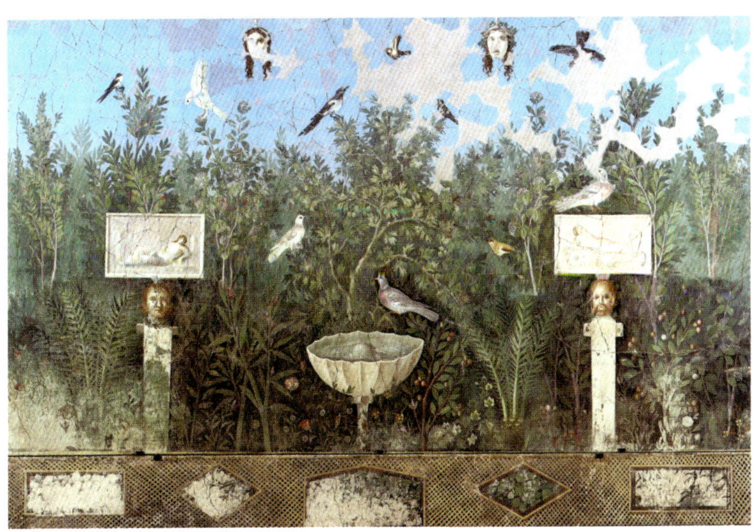

Garden with Herms and Fountain
Garten mit Statuen und Brunnen
Tuin met standbeelden en fontein

●●●

c. 50 CE
Casa del Bracciale d'Oro, Pompei

Fresco / Fresko

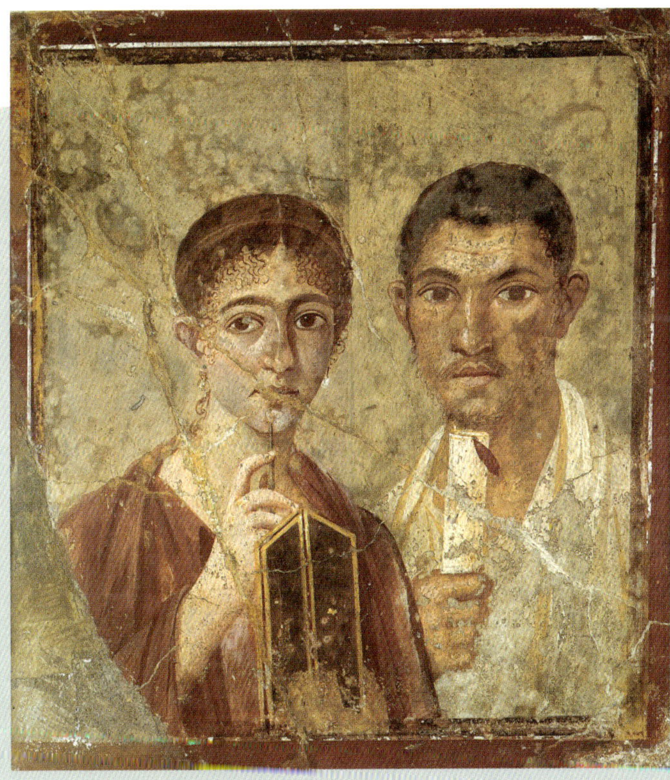

Portrait of Paquius Proculus and His Wife
Bildnis des Paquius Proculus und seiner Frau
Portret van Paquio Proculo en zijn vrouw

●●

c. 50 CE
Museo Archeologico Nazionale, Napoli

Fresco / Fresko

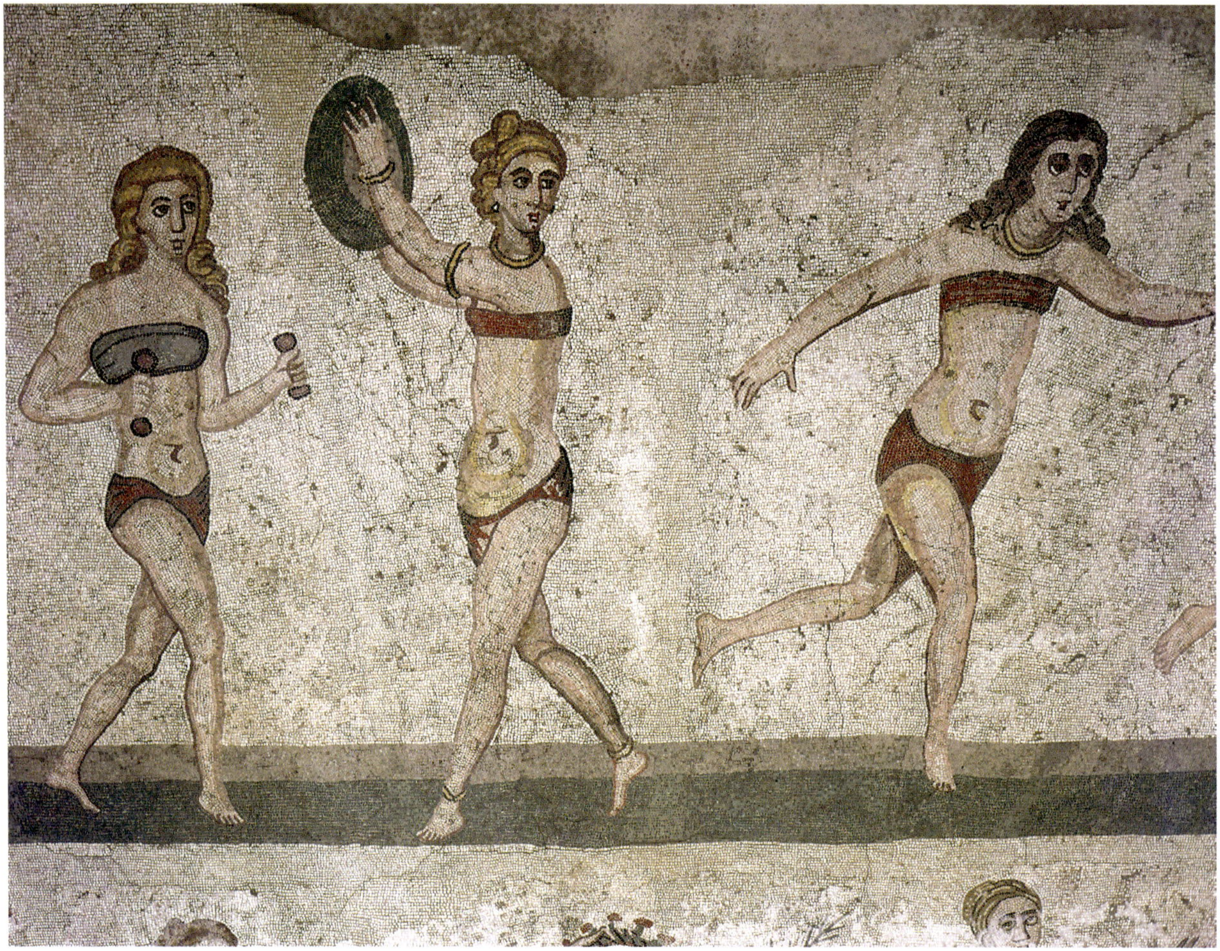

A long lasting status symbol: Roman mosaics.

Strapzierfähiges Statussymbol, das römische Mosaik.

Het Romeinse mozaïek; een resistent statussymbool.

Gymnasts
Turnerinnen
Gymnasten

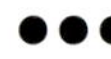

c. 375 CE
Villa del Casale, Piazza Armerina, Sicilia

Mosaic / Mosaik / Mozaïek

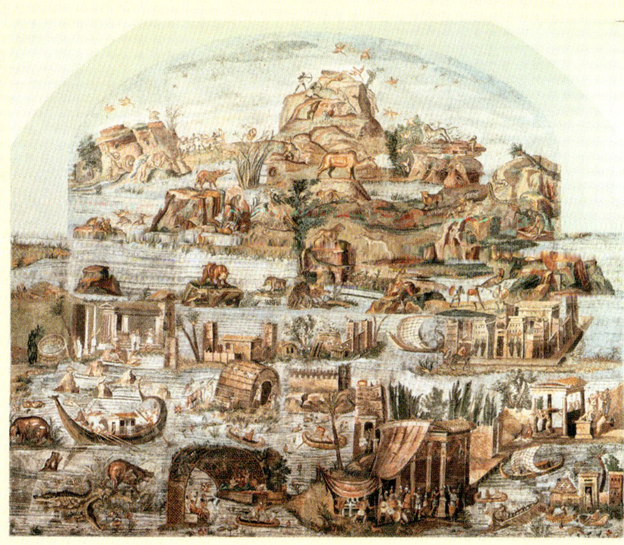

Flooding of the Nile
Nilüberschwemmung
Overstroming van de Nijl

●●

c. 100 BCE
Museo Archeologico,
Palestrina

Mosaic / Mosaik / Mozaïek

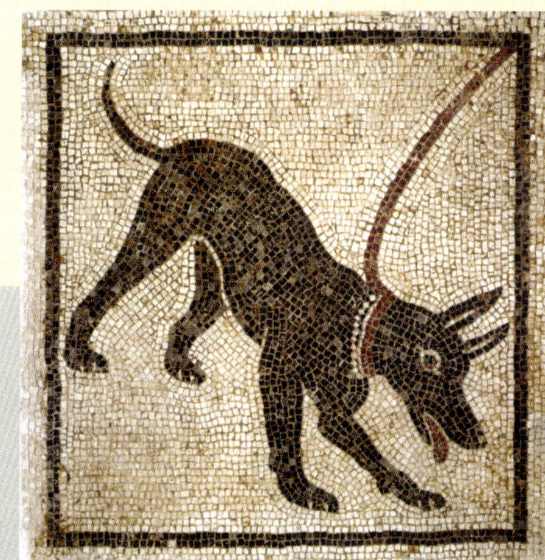

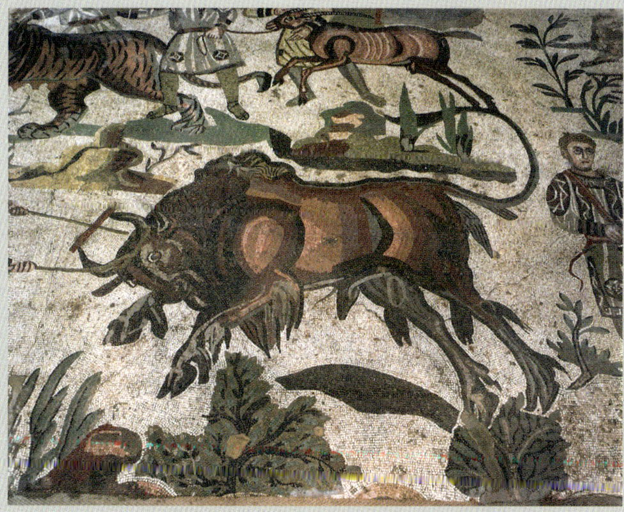

Hunting Scene
Jagdszene
Jachtscène

●

c. 375 CE
Villa del Casale,
Piazza Armerina,
Sicilia

Mosaic / Mosaik / Mozaïek

Cave canem
(beware of the dog)
Cave canem
Cave canem
(Pas op voor de hond)

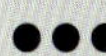

Museo Archeologico
Nazionale, Napoli

Mosaic / Mosaik / Mozaïek

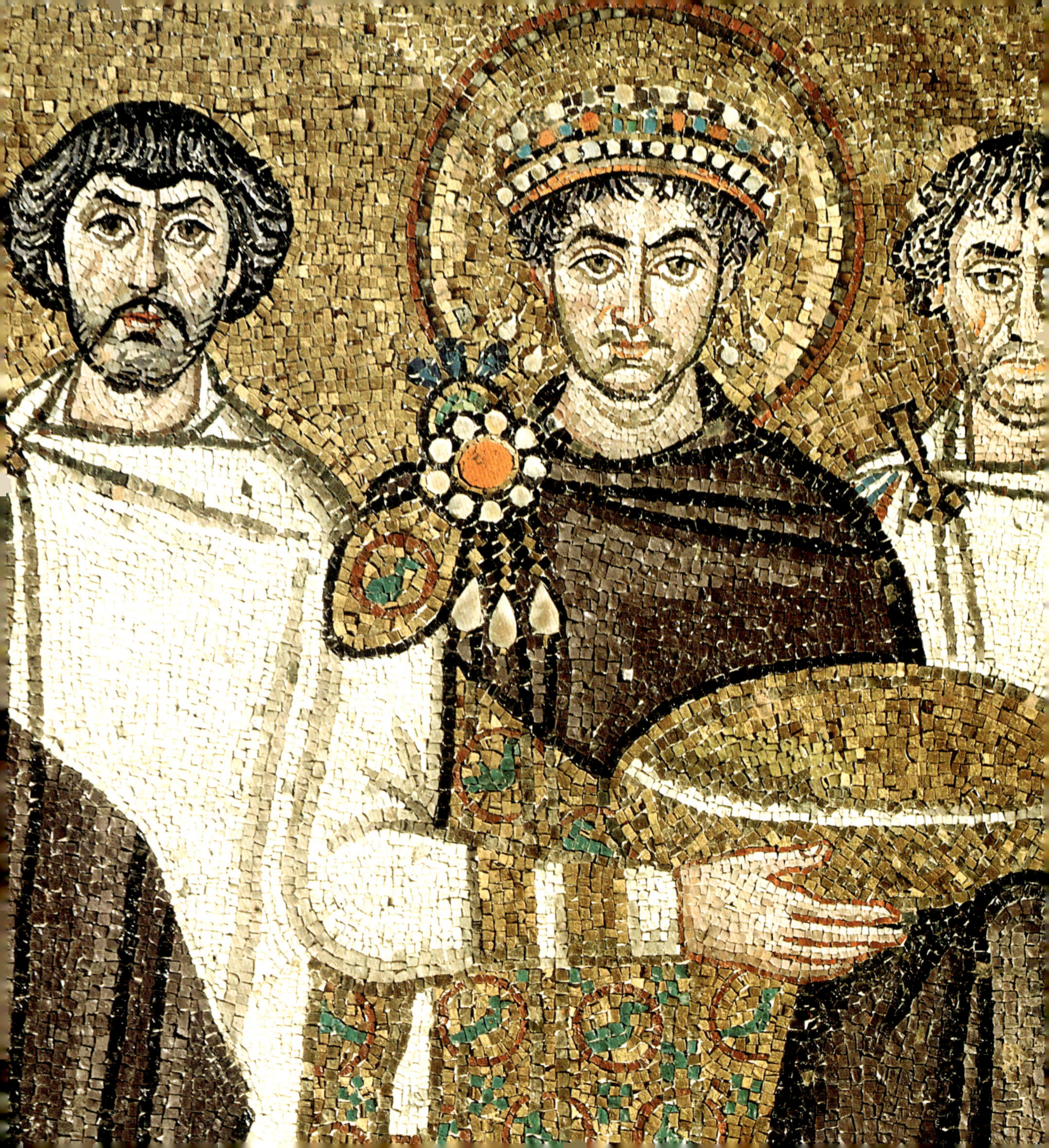

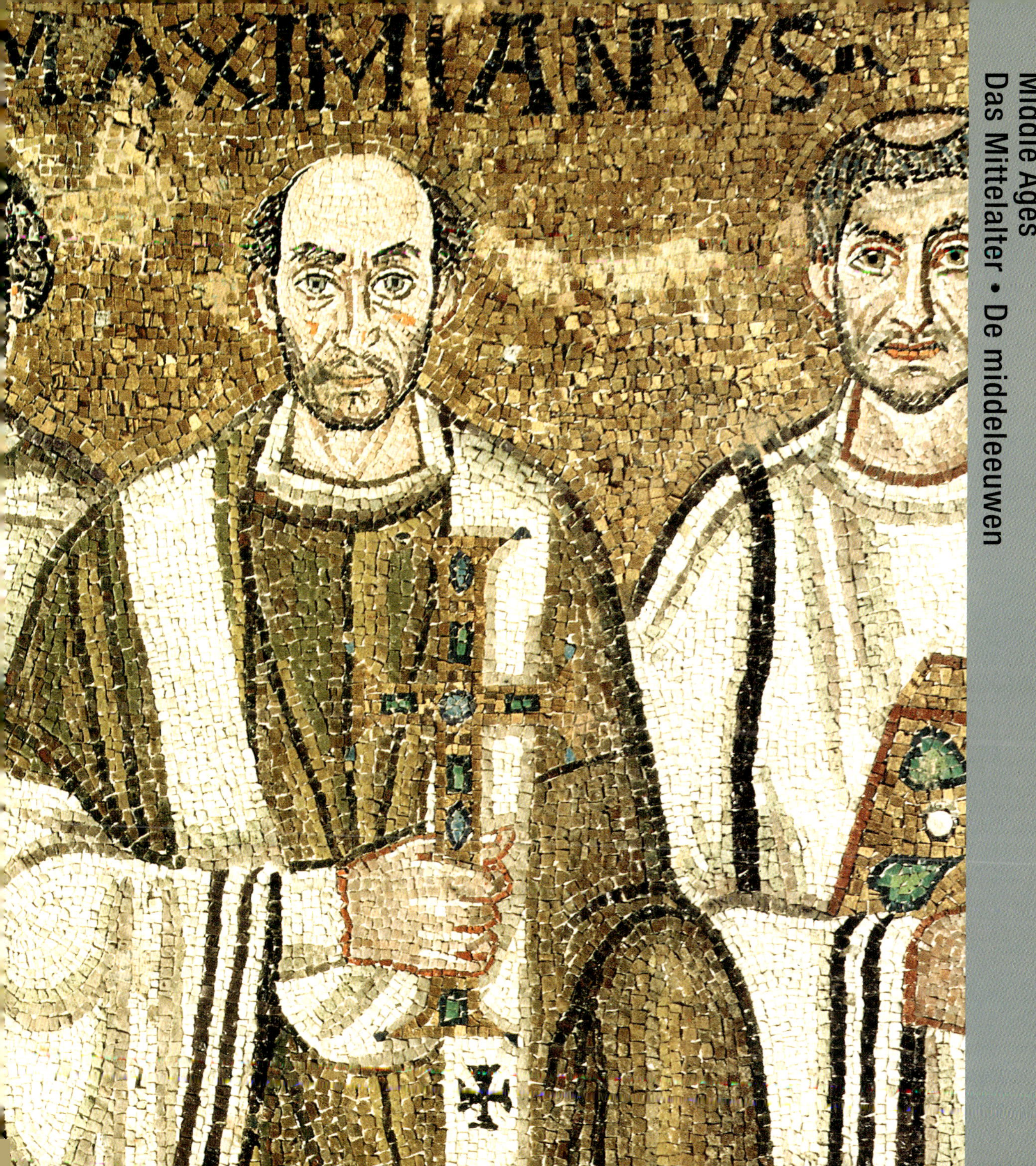

Middle Ages
Das Mittelalter • De middeleeuwen

Art becomes christian
Die Kunst wird Christlich
De kunst wordt christelijk

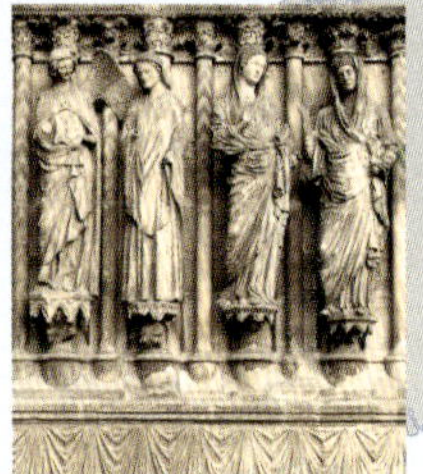

Portal of the Annunciation and the Visitation
Portal der Verkündigung und der Heimsuchung
Poort van de Annunciatie en van de Visitatie
c. 1230

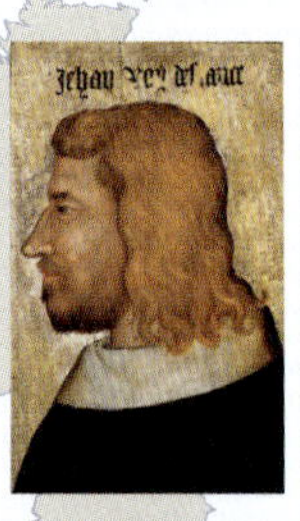

Portrait of Jean le Bon
Portrait Johann des Guten
Portret van Jan II de Goede
c. 1350

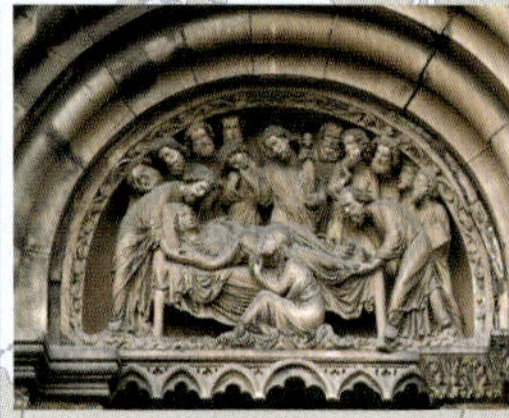

Death of the Virgin
Tod der Jungfrau
Dood van de Maagd
c. 1230

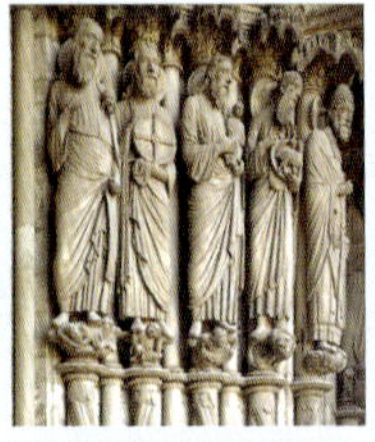

North Portal with Saints
Norportal mit Heiligen
Noordelijke poort met heiligen
1200-1260

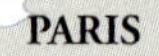

PARIS
REIMS
CHARTRES
STRAßBURG
VEZÉLAY
LINDAU

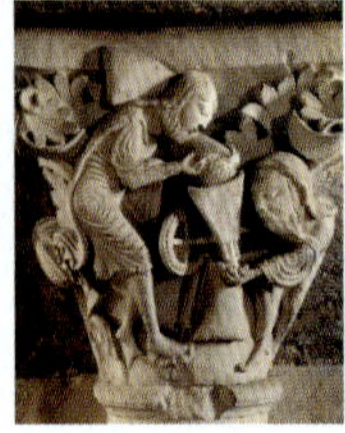

Mystic Wine Press, capital
Kapitell mit Presse für mystischen Wein
Kapiteel met mystieke wijnpers
c. 1120-1132

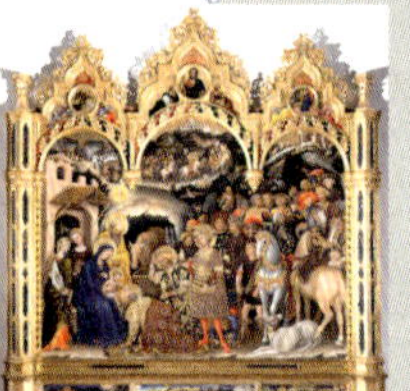

Gentile da Fabriano
Adoration of the Magi
Anbetung der Könige
Aanbidding der drie Koningen
1423

MODENA
RAVENNA
FIRENZE
SIENA
ASSISI

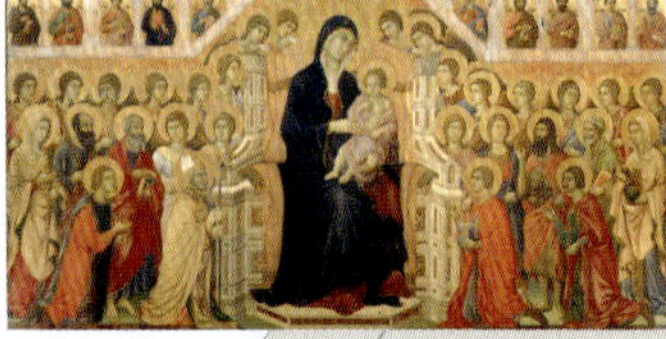

Duccio di Buoninsegna
Maestà
Majestät
Maestà
1285

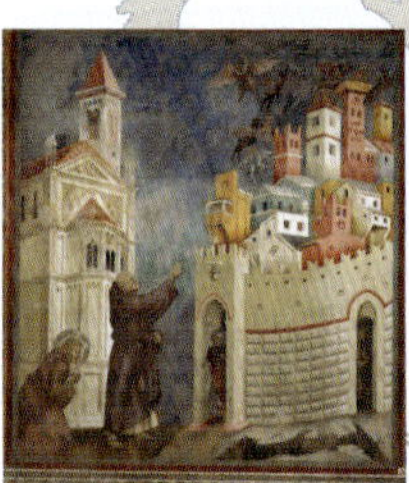

Giotto
Expulsion of the Devils from Arezzo
Vertreibung der Teufel aus Arezzo
Het verdrijven van de duivels uit Arezzo
c. 1296-1300

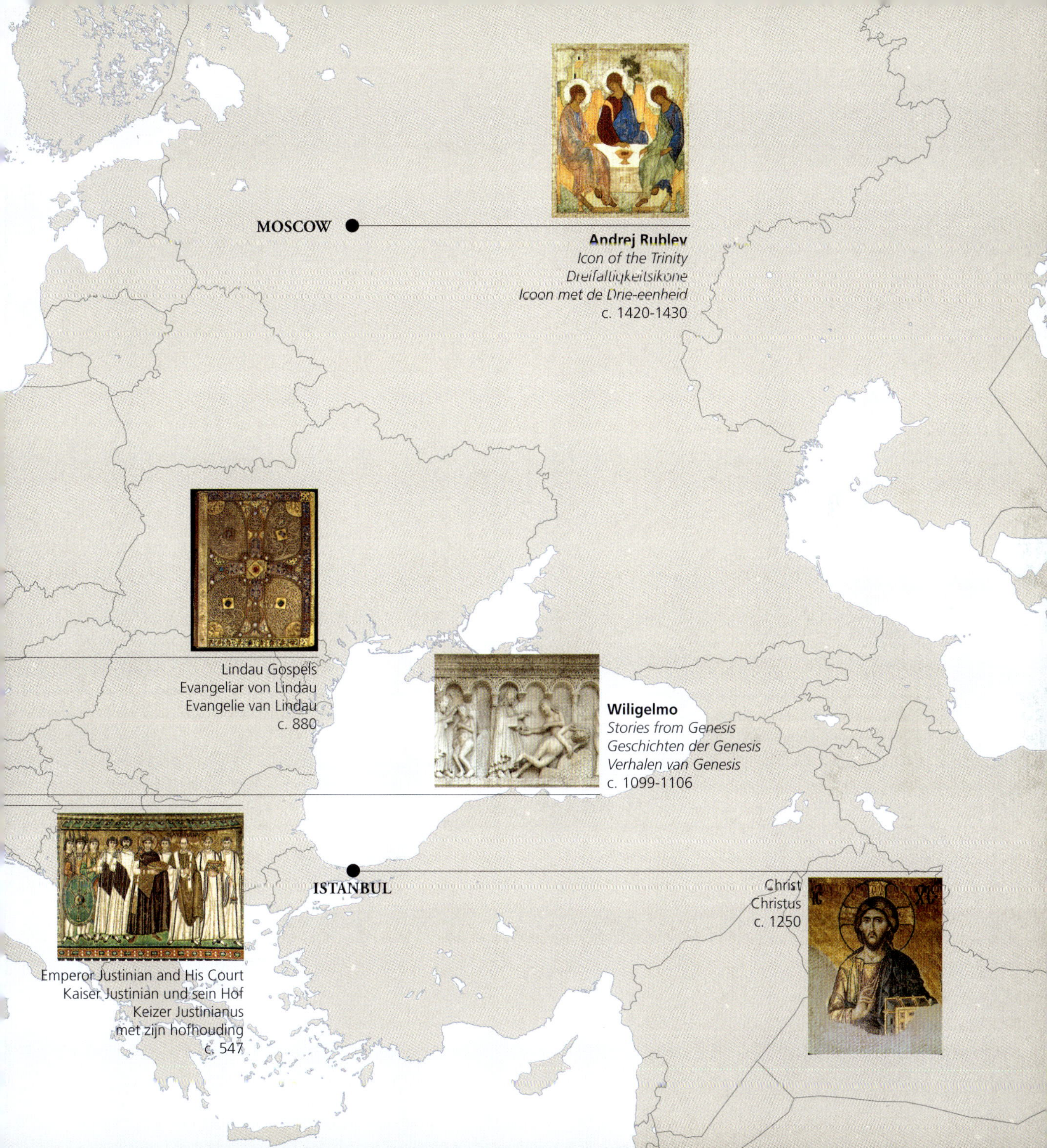

Andrej Rublev
Icon of the Trinity
Dreifaltigkeitsikone
Icoon met de Drie-eenheid
c. 1420-1430

Lindau Gospels
Evangeliar von Lindau
Evangelie van Lindau
c. 880

Wiligelmo
Stories from Genesis
Geschichten der Genesis
Verhalen van Genesis
c. 1099-1106

Christ
Christus
c. 1250

Emperor Justinian and His Court
Kaiser Justinian und sein Hof
Keizer Justinianus
met zijn hofhouding
c. 547

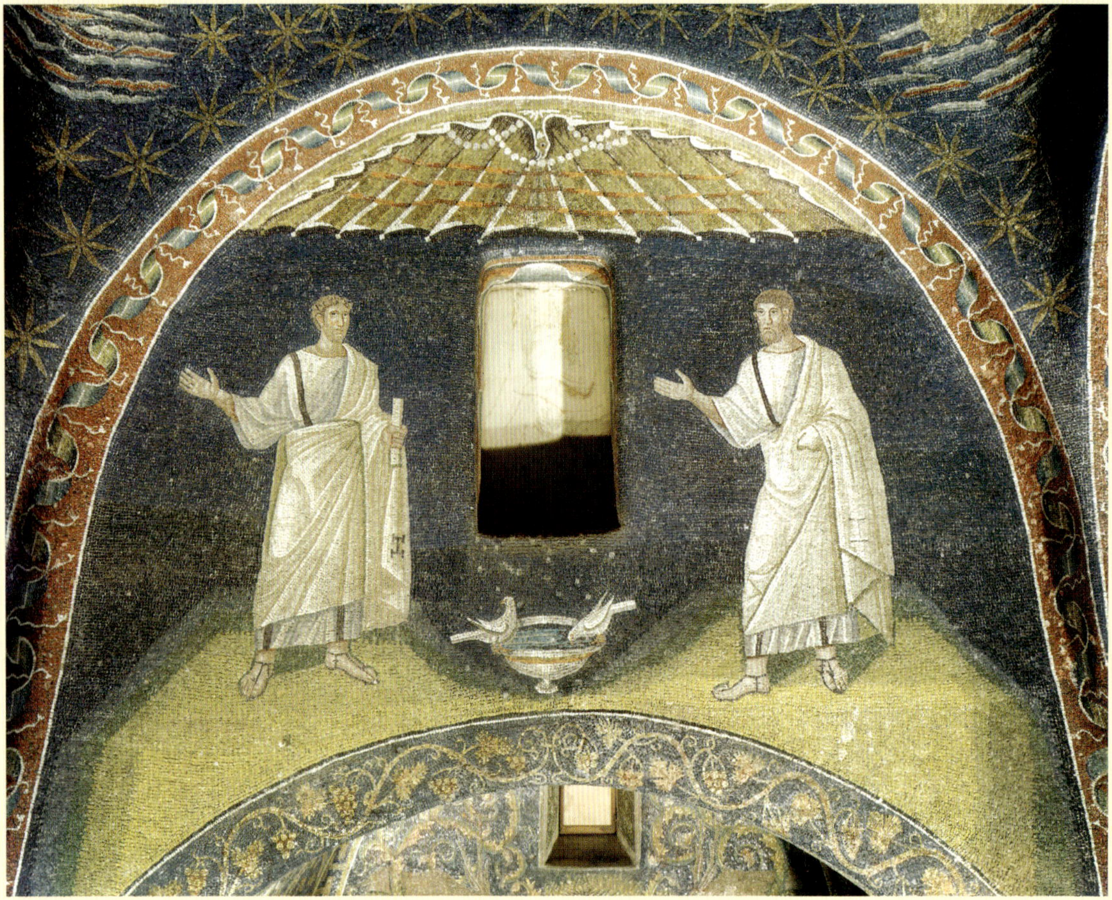

Two Apostles
Zwei Apostel
Twee apostelen

400-500
Mausoleo di Galla Placidia, Ravenna

Mosaic / Mosaik / Mozaïek

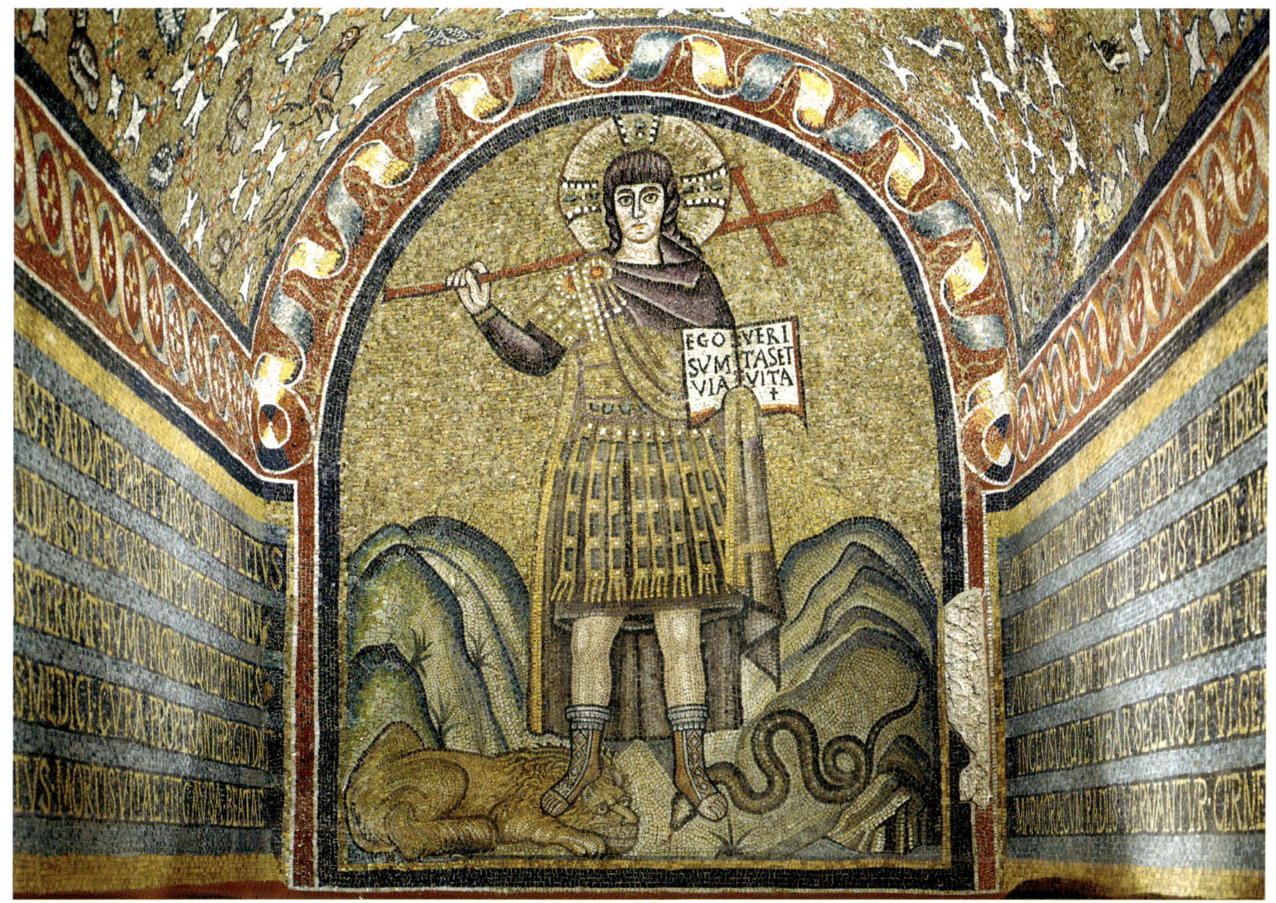

Christ the Warrior
Christus als Krieger
Christus als krijger

●

494-519
Palazzo Arcivescovile, Ravenna

Mosaic / Mosaik / Mozaïek

395 CE: the Roman Empire has fallen and Early Christian and Byzantine art conquers southeastern Europe.

395 AD, das römische Reich existiert nicht mehr, die christlich byzantinische Kunst erobert Südosteuropa.

395 n.Chr.: Het Romeinse rijk bestaat niet meer, de vroeg-christelijke Byzantijnse kunst verovert Zuidoost-Europa.

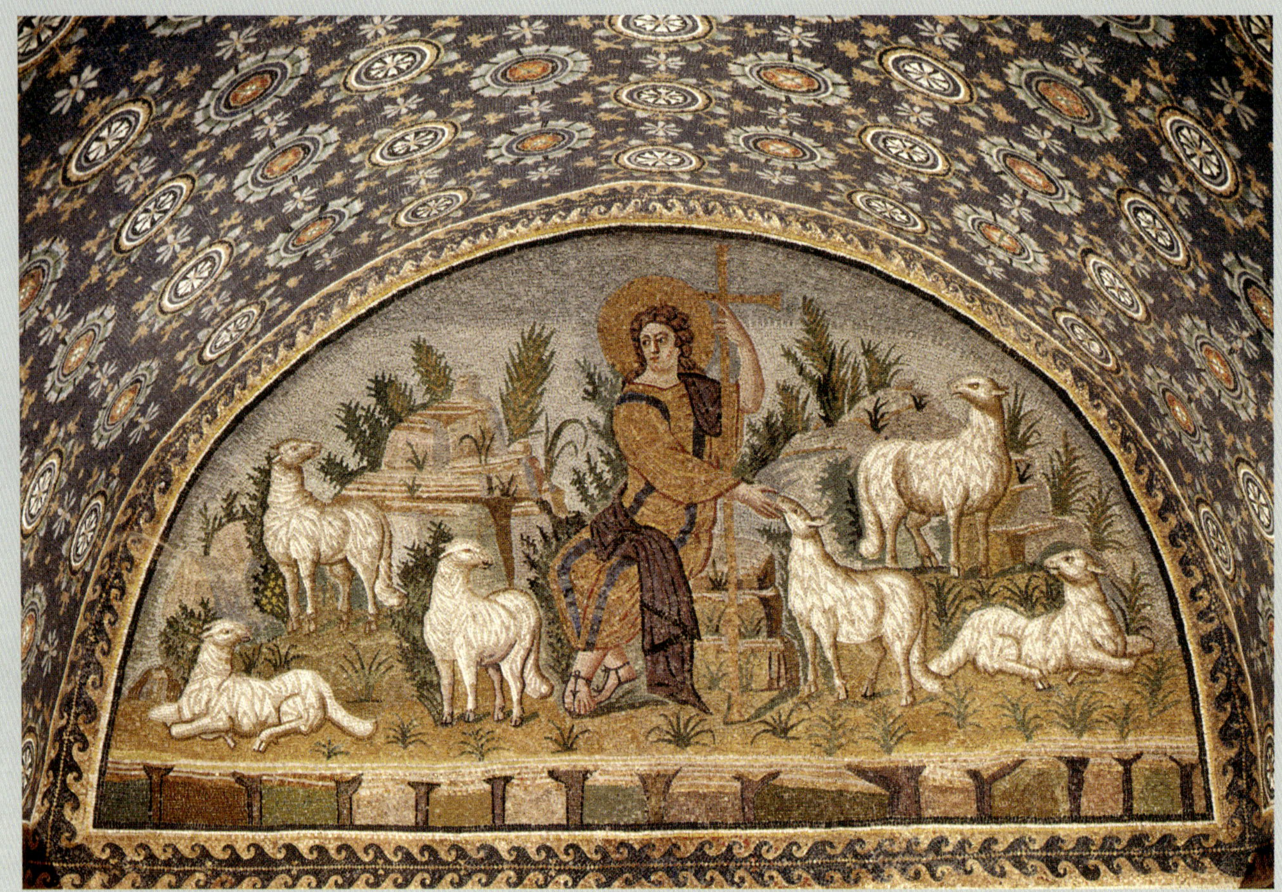

The Good Shepherd
Der Gute Hirte
De Goede Herder

●●

400-500
Mausoleo di Galla Placidia, Ravenna

Mosaic / Mosaik / Mozaïek

Doves Drinking from a Basin
Tauben trinken aus einer Schale
Duiven die uit een kopje drinken

●●

400-500
Mausoleo di Galla Placidia, Ravenna

Mosaic / Mosaik / Mozaïek

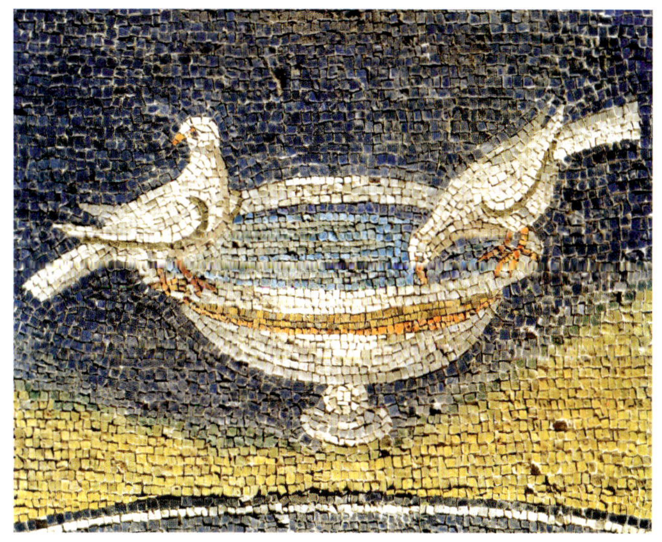

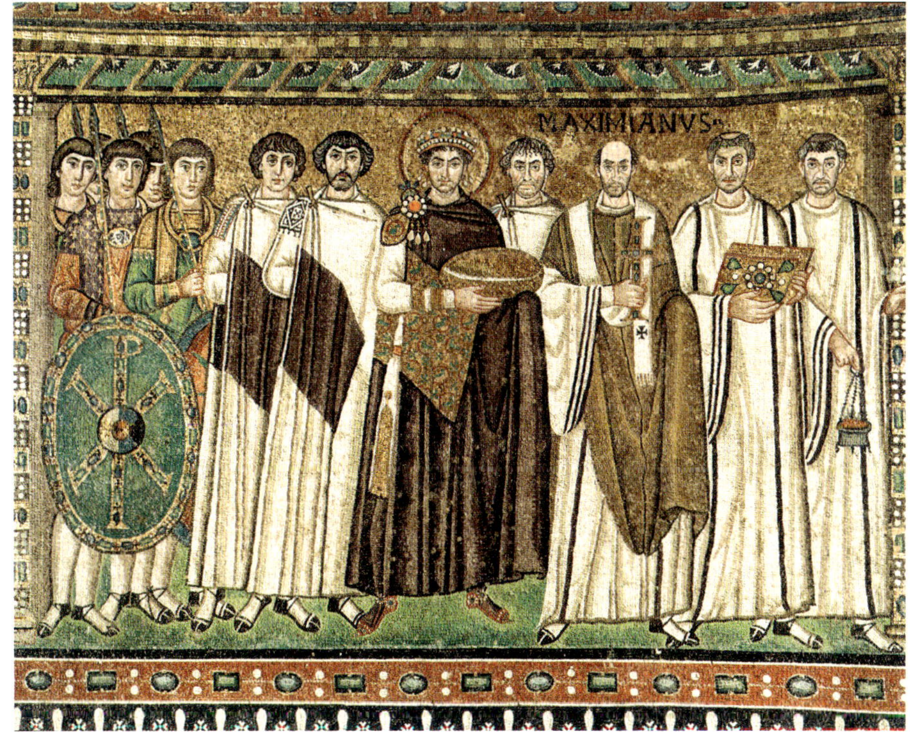

Emperor Justinian and His Court
Kaiscr Justinian und sein Hof
Keizer Justinianus met zijn hofhouding

●●●

c. 547
San Vitale, Ravenna

Mosaic / Mosaik / Mozaïek

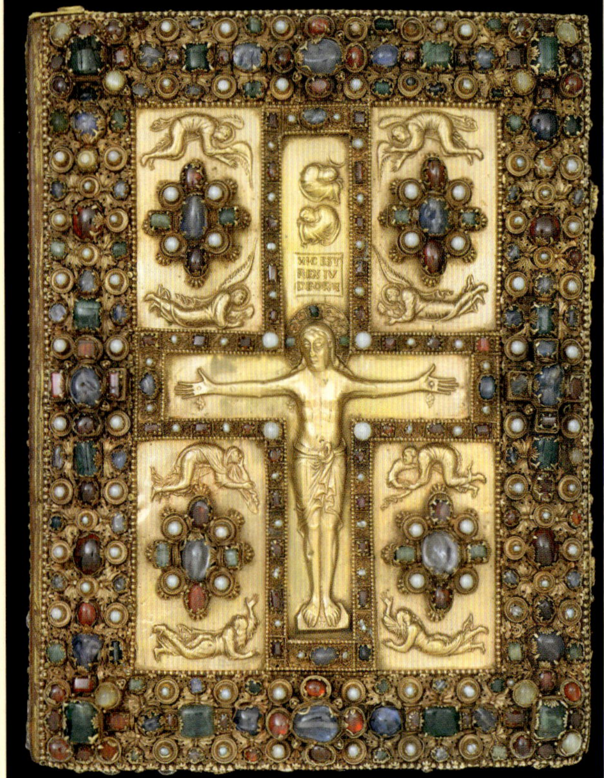

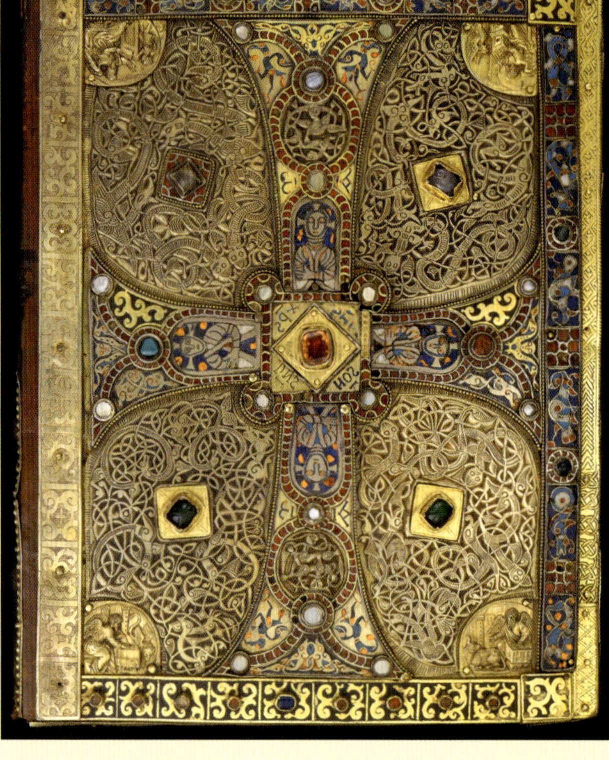

Gospel book: the artistically illustrated books of the New Testament.

Evangeliare sind kunstvoll verzierte Bücher des Neuen Testaments.

De evangeliën zijn de kunstzinnig gedecoreerde boeken van het Nieuwe Testament.

Lindau Gospels
Front and back covers, with the Cross and busts of Christ and the Evangelists
Evangeliar von Lindau
Deckblatt vorne und hinten mit Kreuz, Brustbilder von Christus und den Evangelisten
Evangelie van Lindau
Voor- en achteromslag met Kruisbeeld, bustes van Christus en de Evangelisten

c. 880
The Pierpont Morgan Library, New York

Gilded silver, enamel and precious stones / Vergoldetes Silber, Email und Edelsteine / Verguld zilver, emaille en edelstenen

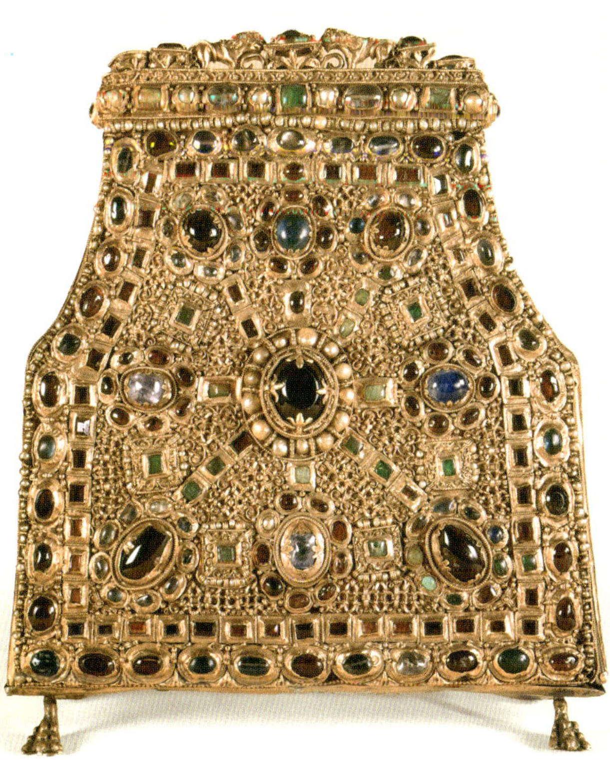

Reliquary for the Tooth of St John
Reliquiar des Zahnes des Hl. Johannes
Reliquarium met de tand van San Giovanni

•

800-900
h. 24 cm / 9.4 in.
Tesoro del Duomo, Monza

Gold, filigree, stones, gems and pearls
Gold, Filigran, Edelsteine, Juwelen und Perlen
Goud, filigraan, stenen, edelstenen en parels

Iron Crown of Lombardy
Eiserne Krone
IJzeren kroon

••

400-900
h. 15 cm / 5.9 in.
Tesoro del Duomo, Monza

Gold, iron, precious stones and enamel
Gold, Eisen, Edelsteine und Email
Goud, ijzer, edelstenen en emailles

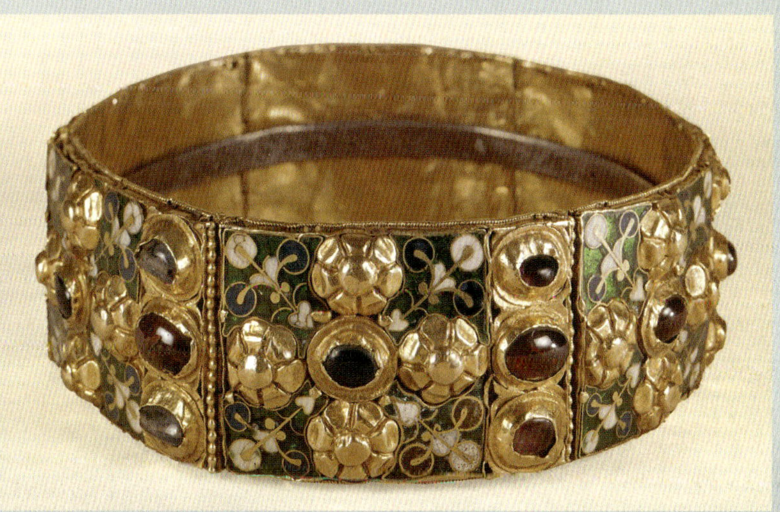

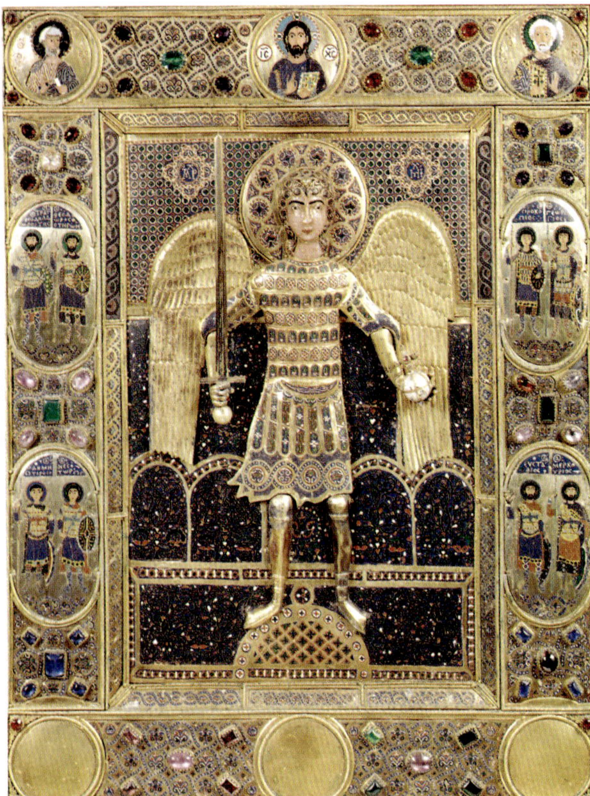

Icon of the Archangel Michael and Other Saints
Ikone des Erzengels Michael und anderer Heilige
Icoon van de Aartsengel Michaël en anderer Heiligen

●

1000-1200
Tesoro della Basilica di San Marco, Venezia

Metal and enamel with precious stones
Metall und Email mit Edelsteinen
Metaal en emaille met edelstenen

Christ Enthroned
Thronender Christus
Christus op de troon

●●

1034-1042
Hagia Sophia, Istanbul

Mosaic / Mosaik / Mozaïek

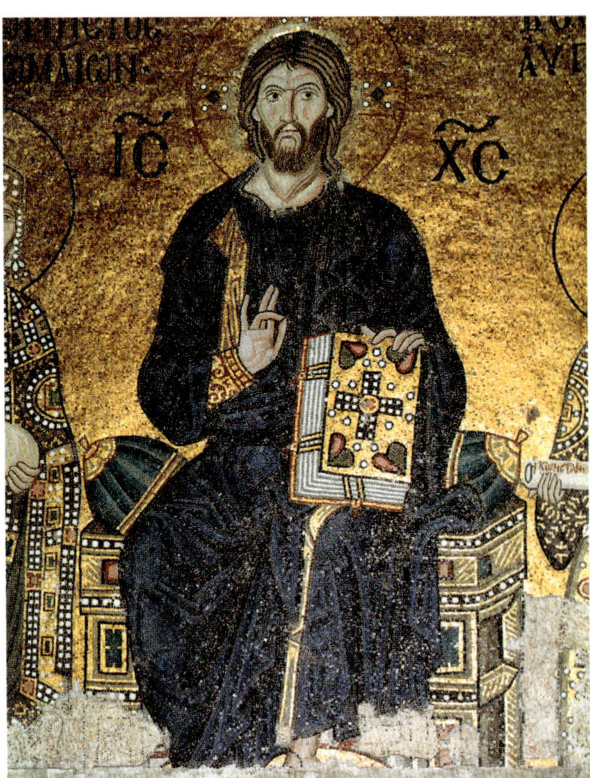

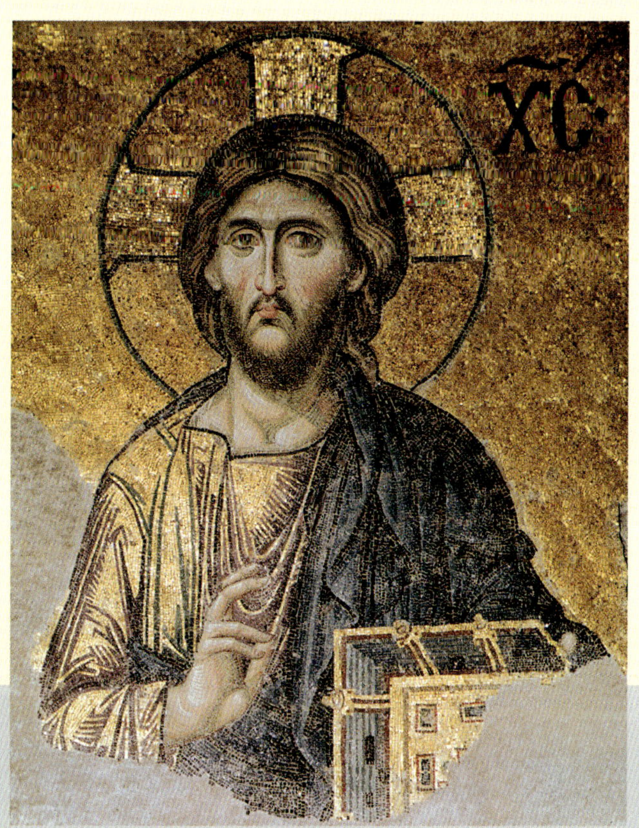

Christ
Christus

●●

c. 1250
Hagia Sophia, Istanbul

Mosaic / Mosaik / Mozaïek

Andrej Rubliev
Icon of the Trinity
Dreifaltigkeitsikone
Icoon met de Drie-eenheid

●●●

c. 1420-1430
Tretyakov State Gallery, Moscow

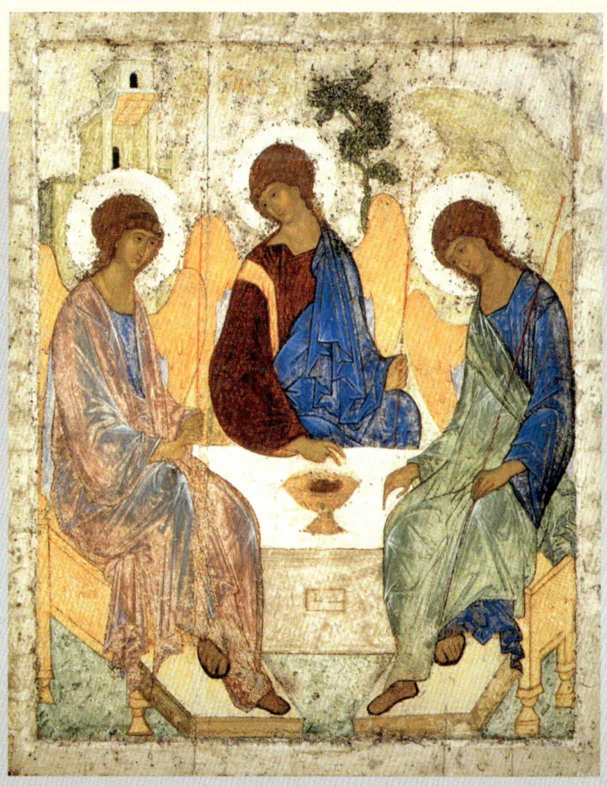

Christ Enthroned with the Symbols of the Evangelists
Thronender Christus mit den Symbolen der Evangelisten
Christus op de troon met de symbolen van de evangelisten

●●

c. 1050-1100
Saint-Sernin, Toulouse

Marble / Marmor / Marmer

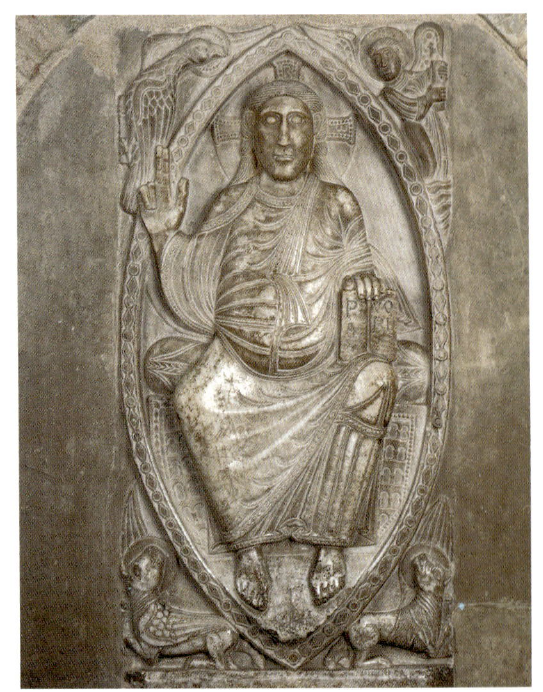

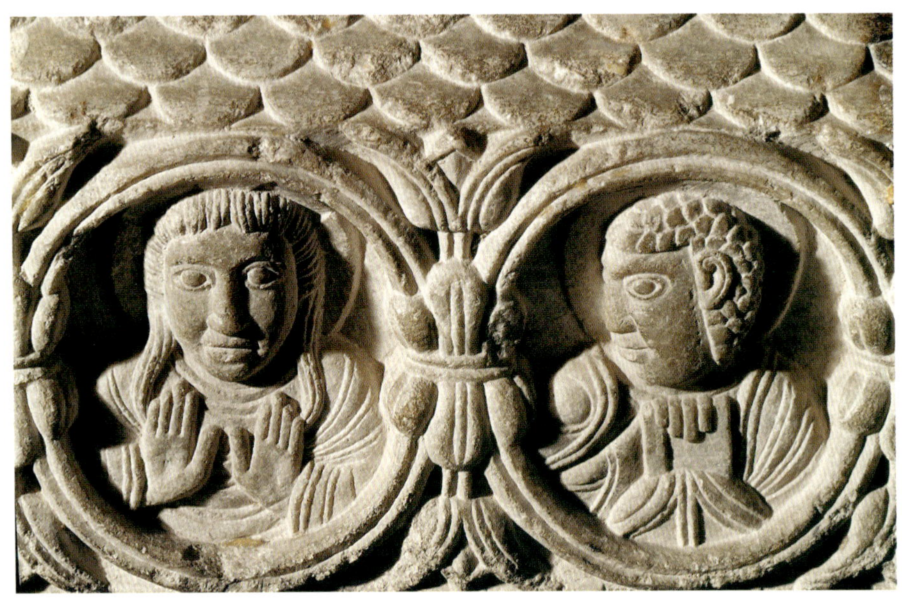

Bernard Gilduin
Two saints
Zwei Heilige
Twee Heiligen

●

1000-1100
Saint-Sernin, Toulouse

Marble / Marmor / Marmer

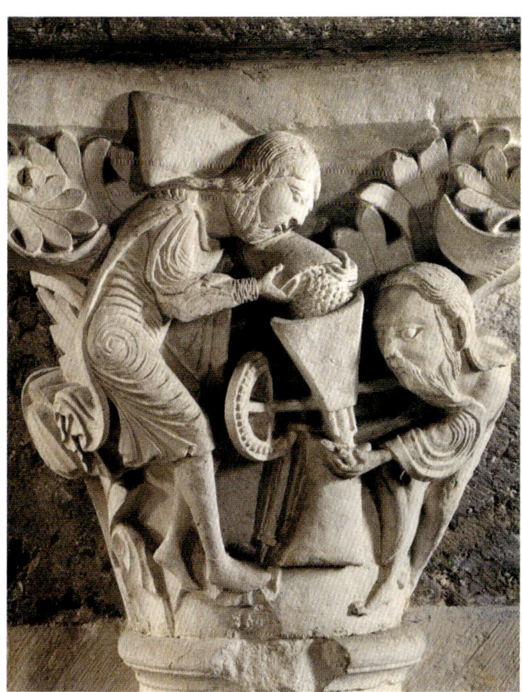

Mystic Wine Press, capital
Kapitell mit Presse für mystischen Wein
Kapiteel met mystieke wijnpers

●●

c. 1120-1132
Sainte-Madeleine, Vézelay

Stone / Stein / Steen

Soldiers, lintel
Architrav mit Soldaten
Architraaf met soldaten

●

c. 1120-1132
Sainte-Madeleine, Vézelay

Marble / Marmor / Marmer

The illiterate read pictures: illustrations of Romanesque stories in stone for the people.

Wer nicht lesen kann soll sehen, romanische Bildgeschichten in Stein für das einfache Volk.

Wie niet lezen kan, moet kijken: geïllustreerde Romeinse verhalen in steen voor het volk

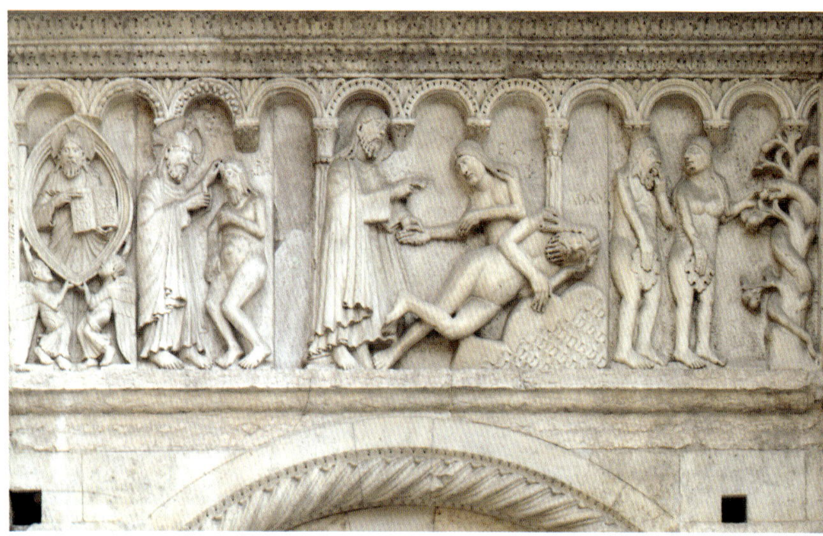

Wiligelmo / Wiligelmus

Stories from Genesis: Creation of Adam, Creation of Eve and the Original Sin
Geschichten der Genesis: Die Erschaffung Adams, die Erschaffung Evas und die Erbsünde
Verhalen uit Genesis: Schepping van Adam, schepping van Eva en de erfzonde

●●●

c. 1099-1106
Cattedrale, Modena

Marble / Marmor / Marmer

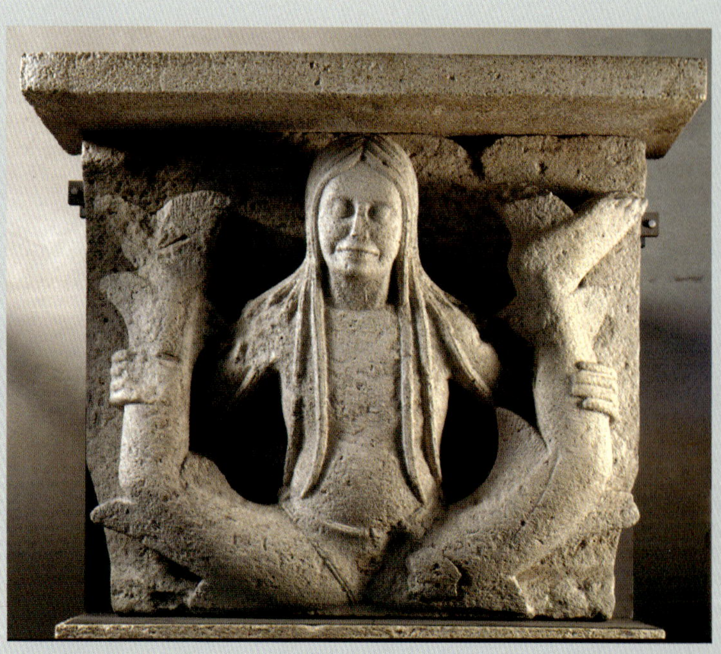

Wiligelmo / Wiligelmus

Double-Tailed Siren, metope
Metopa mit doppelt geschweifter Sirene
Metope met tweestaartige zeemeermin

●

c. 1099-1106
Museo Lapidario del Duomo, Modena

Stone / Stein / Steen

Wiligelmo / Wiligelmus

Relief with Stories from Genesis: Death of Cain, Noah's Ark and Exit from the Ark
Relief mit Geschichten der Genesis: Tod Kains, Arche Noah und Verlassen der Arche
Reliëf met scheppingsverhalen uit het boek Genesis: de dood van Kaïn, de ark van Noach en het verlaten van de ark

●●●

c. 1099-1106
Cattedrale, Modena

Marble / Marmor / Marmer

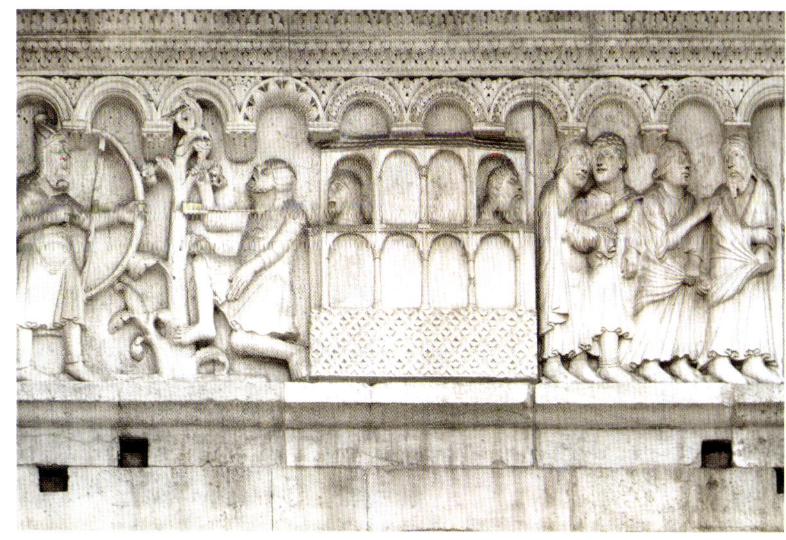

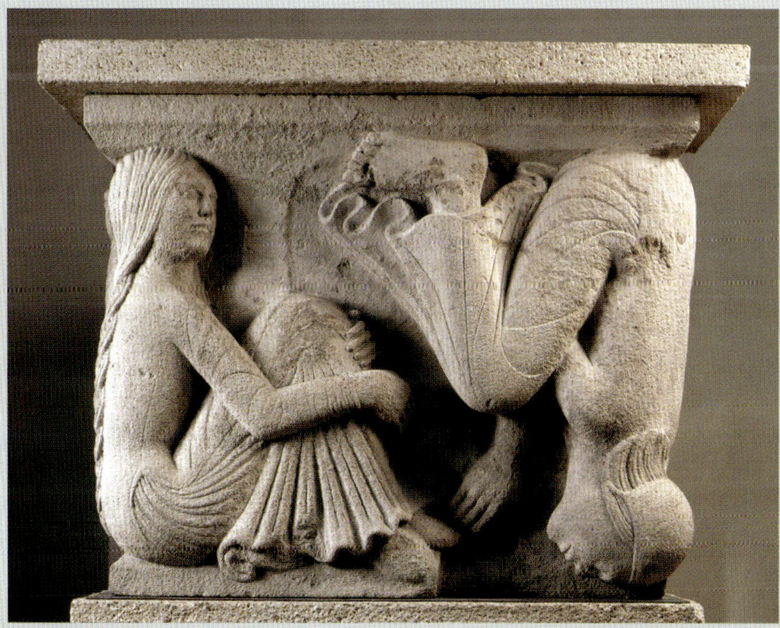

Wiligelmo / Wiligelmus

Opposites, metope
Metopa mit den Antipoden
Metope met de antipoden

●

c. 1099-1106
Museo Lapidario del Duomo, Modena

Marble / Marmor / Marmer

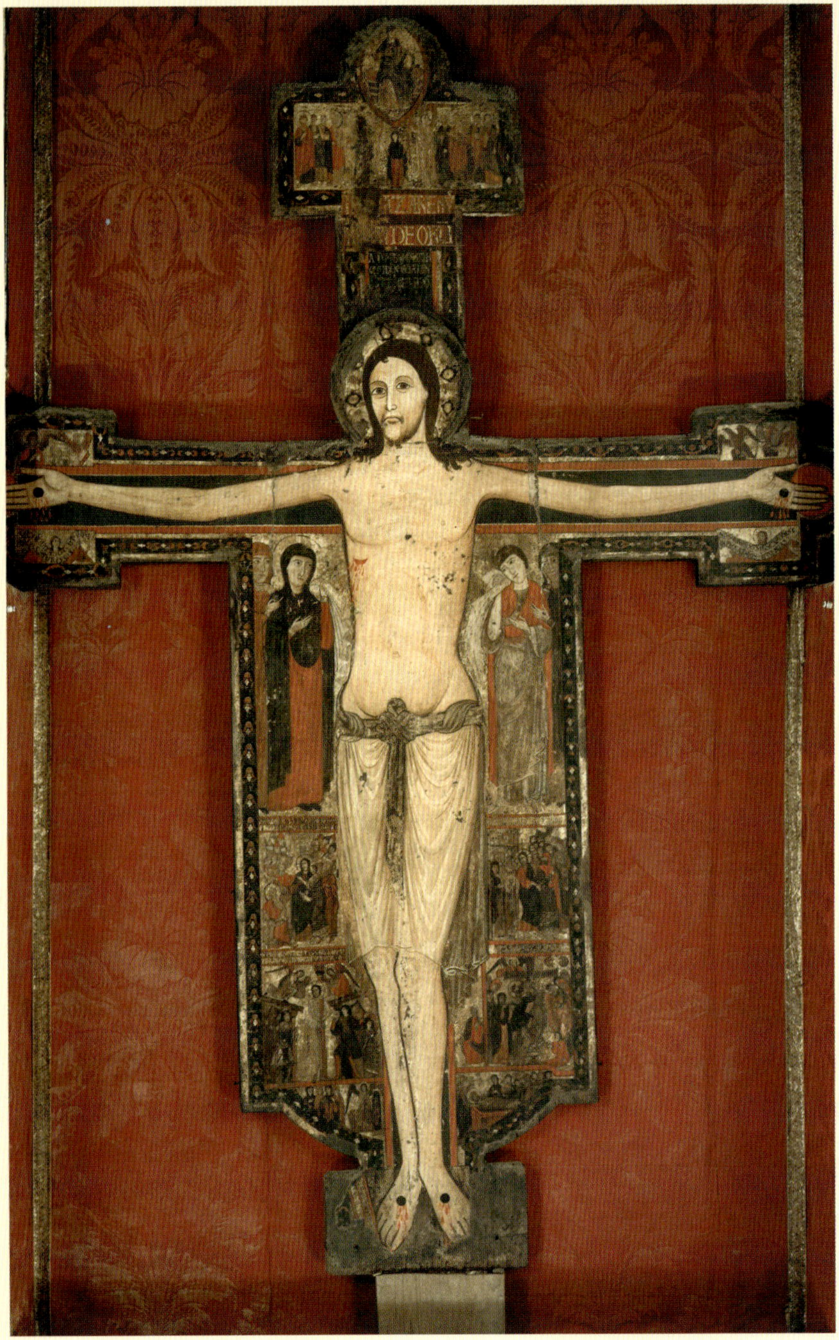

Master of Sarzana
Meister von Sarzana
Meester van Sarzana

Crucifix
Gemaltes Kreuz
Geschilderd Kruisbeeld

1138
h. 300 cm / 118.1 in.
Duomo, Sarzana

Tempera on wood / Tempera auf Tafel
Tempera op paneel

The quintessence of Christianity: the crucifix.

Innbegriff des Christentums, das Kruzifix.

De kwintessens van het christendom: de crucifix.

The Batlló Majesty
Die Majestät von Batlló
Maestà van Batllò

●●

c. 1150
Museu Nacional d'Art de Catalunya, Barcelona

Painted wood
Bemalte Tafel
Beschilderd paneel

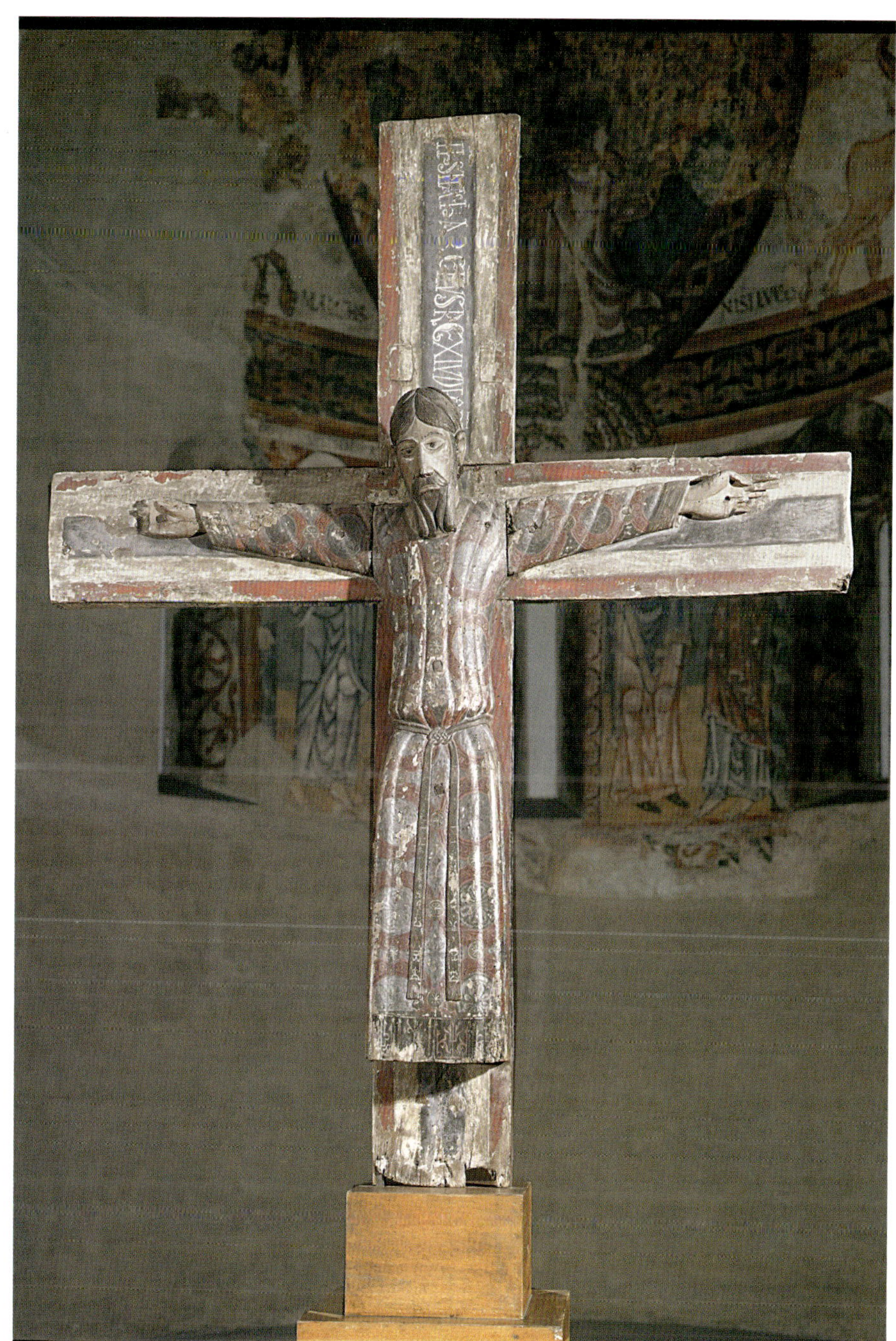

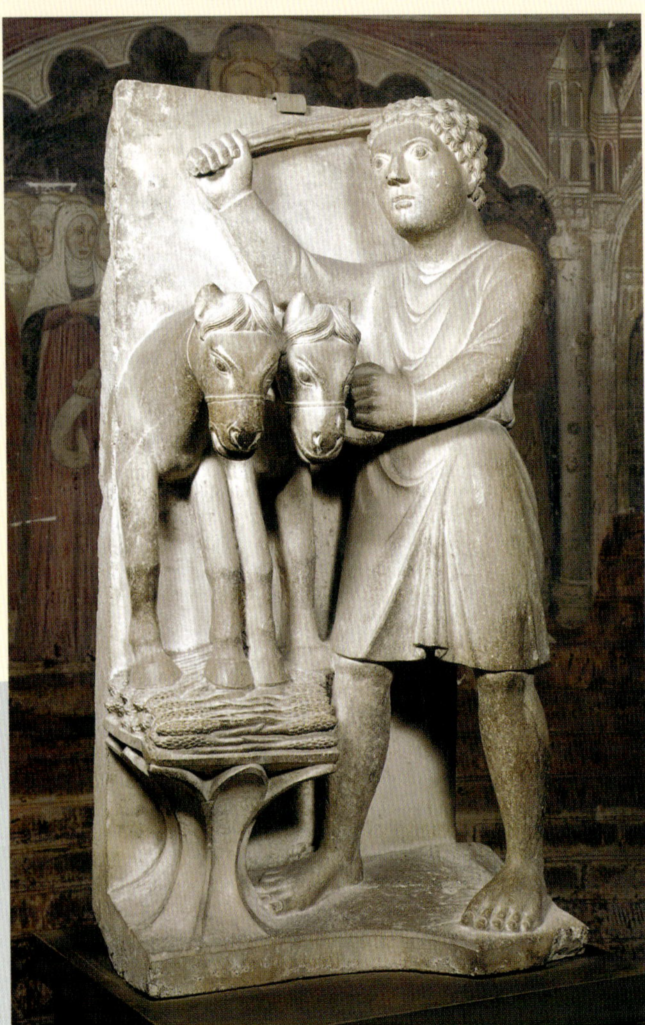

Benedetto Antelami (Val d'Intelvi, 1150 - *c.* 1230)

July: Horses Treading Grain
Der Monat Juli, Pferde stampfen das Korn
De maand juli, paarden die graan verpulveren

●

1196-1219
Battistero, Parma

Stone / Stein / Steen

Benedetto Antelami (Val d'Intelvi, 1150 - *c.* 1230)

September: the Grape Harvest
Der Monat September, die Weinlese
De maand september, de wijnoogst

●

1196-1219
Battistero, Parma

Stone / Stein / Steen

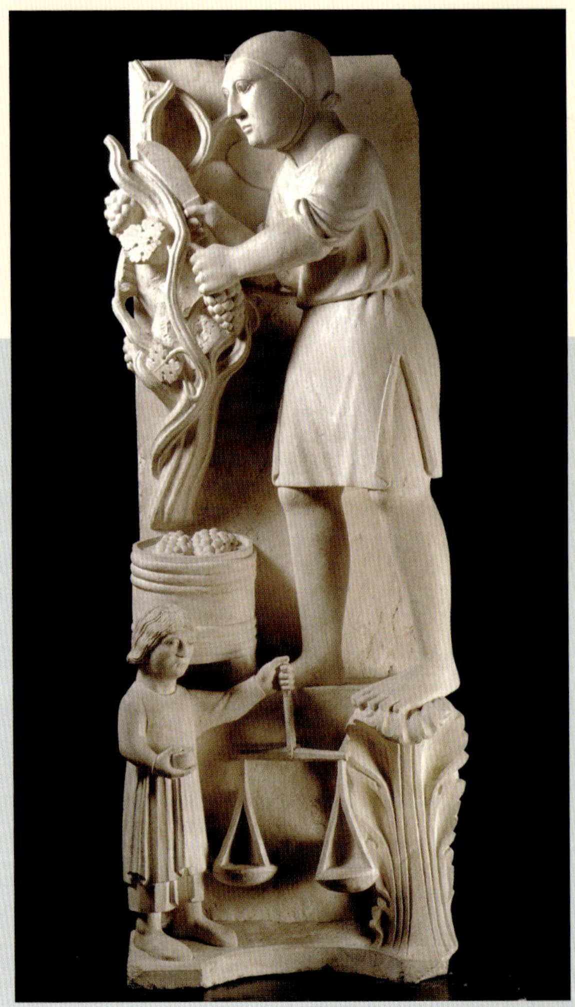

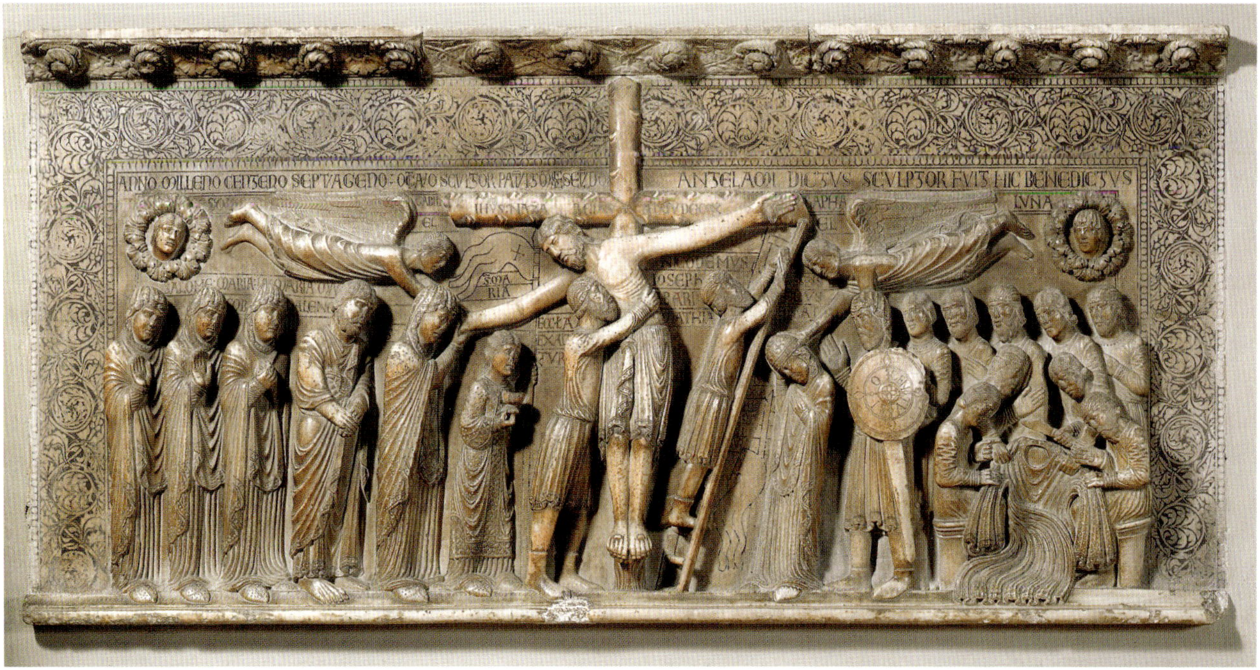

Benedetto Antelami
(Val d'Intelvi, 1150 - *c.* 1230)

Deposition
Kreuzabnahme
De Kruisafneming

1178
Duomo, Parma

Stone / Stein / Steen

Benedetto Antelami, Romanesque sculptor in Parma.

Benedetto Antelami, romanischer Meister der Bildhauerei in Parma.

Benedetto Antelami, Romeinse meester van de beeldhouwkunst in Parma.

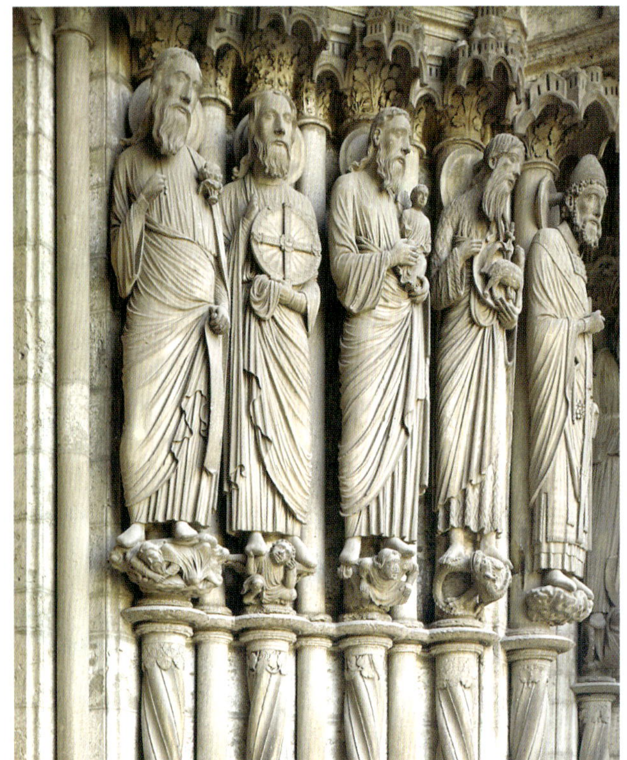

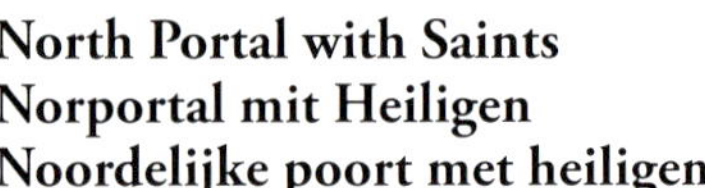

North Portal with Saints
Norportal mit Heiligen
Noordelijke poort met heiligen

1200-1260
Cathédrale de Notre-Dame, Chartres

Stone / Stein / Steen

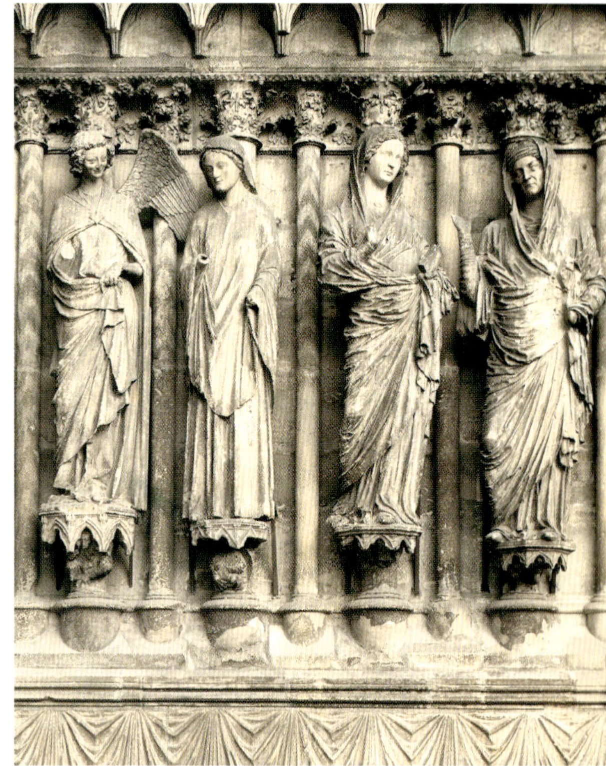

Portal of the Annunciation and the Visitation
Portal der Verkündigung und der Heimsuchung
Poort van de Annunciatie en van de Visitatie

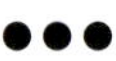

c. 1230
Cathédrale de Notre-Dame, Reims

Stone / Stein / Steen

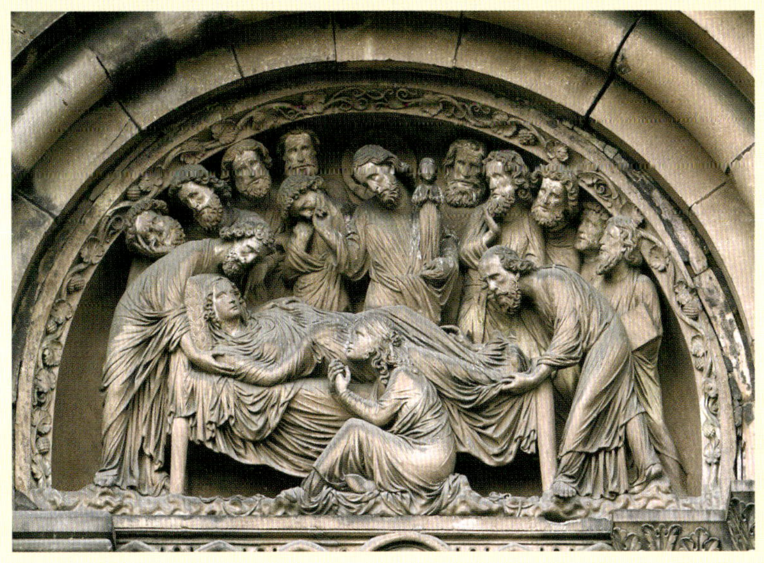

Death of the Virgin
Tod der Jungfrau
Dood van de Maagd

●

c. 1230
Notre-Dame, Strasbourg

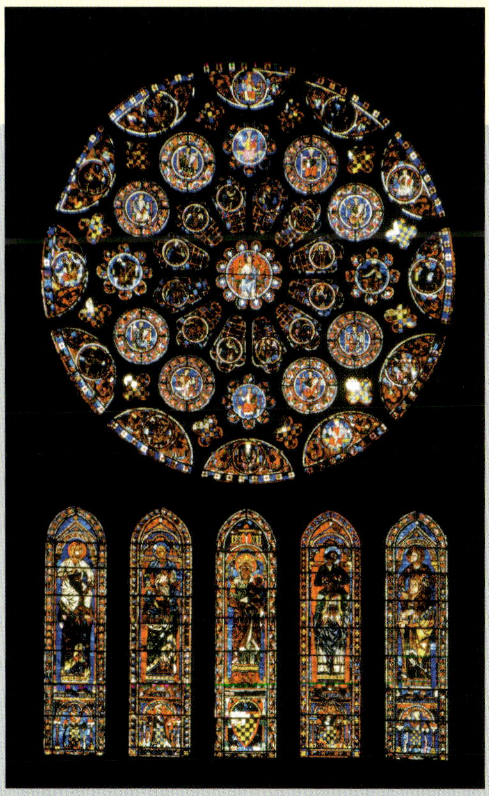

South Rose Window
Glasfenster Nr. 17
Notre-Dame de la Belle Verrière
Raam nr. 17 Notre Dame de la Belle Verrière

●

c. 1220
Cathédrale de Notre-Dame, Chartres

Saints and chimeras: in about 1200 France becomes the centre of Gothic art.

Heilige und Schimären, um 1200 wird Frankreich das Zentrum der Gotik.

Heiligen en chimaera's, rond 1200 wordt Frankrijk het centrum van de gotiek.

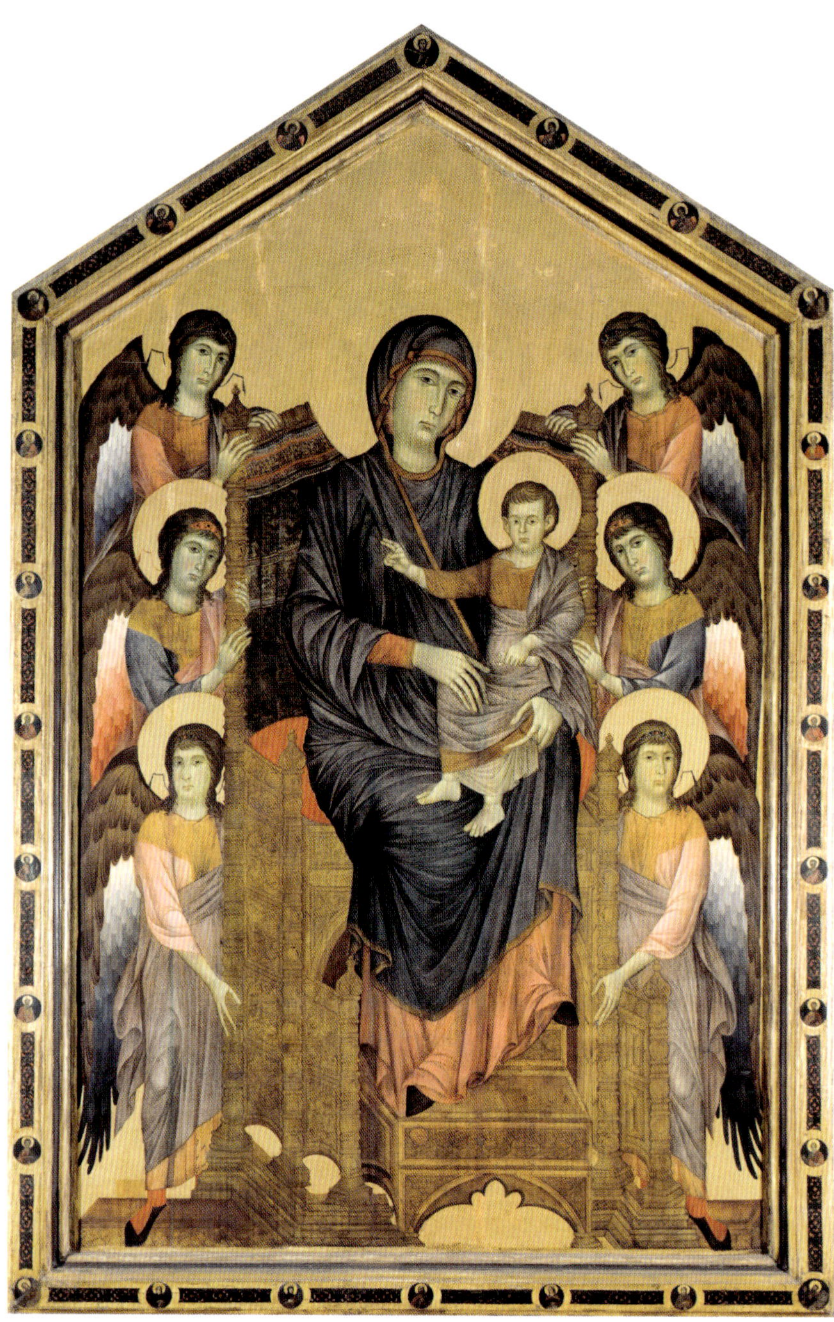

Cimabue renews Byzantine forms in Italy (painting of icons).

Cimabue erneuert die byzantinische Formensprache (Ikonenmalerei) in Italien.

Cimabue vernieuwt in Italië de Byzantijnse vormentaal (het schilderen van iconen).

Cimabue
(Firenze *c.* 1240 - Pisa 1302)

Maestà
Majestät

●●●

c. 1280
427 x 280 cm / 168.1 x 110.2 in.
Musée du Louvre, Paris

Tempera on wood / Tempera auf Tafel
Tempera op paneel

Cimabue
(Firenze *c.* 1240 - Pisa 1302)

Crucifix (before the flood)
Kreuzigung (vor der Restaurierung)
Kruisiging (voor de restauratie)

●●●

c. 1280
448 x 390 cm / 176.4 x 153.5 in.
Museo di Santa Croce, Firenze

Tempera and gold on wood
Tempera und Gold auf Tafel
Tempera en goud op paneel

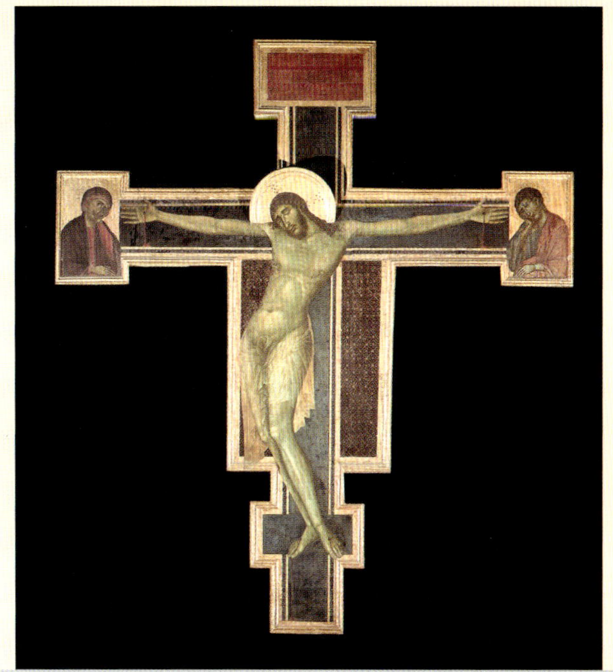

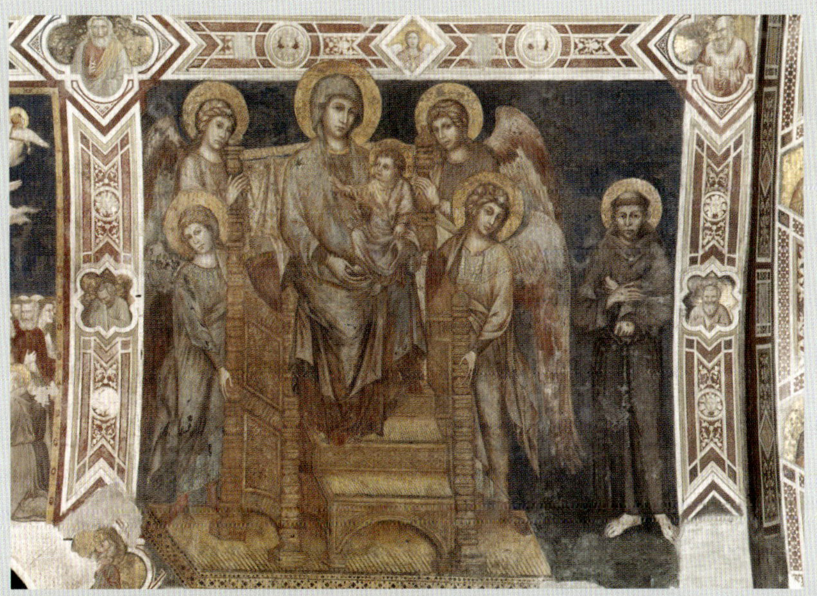

Cimabue
(Firenze *c.* 1240 - Pisa 1302)

Madonna and Child with Angels and St Francis
Madonna mit dem Kind, Engel und der Hl.Franziskus
Madonna met Kind, engelen en Sint Franciscus

●

c. 1280
San Francesco, Assisi

Fresko / Fresco

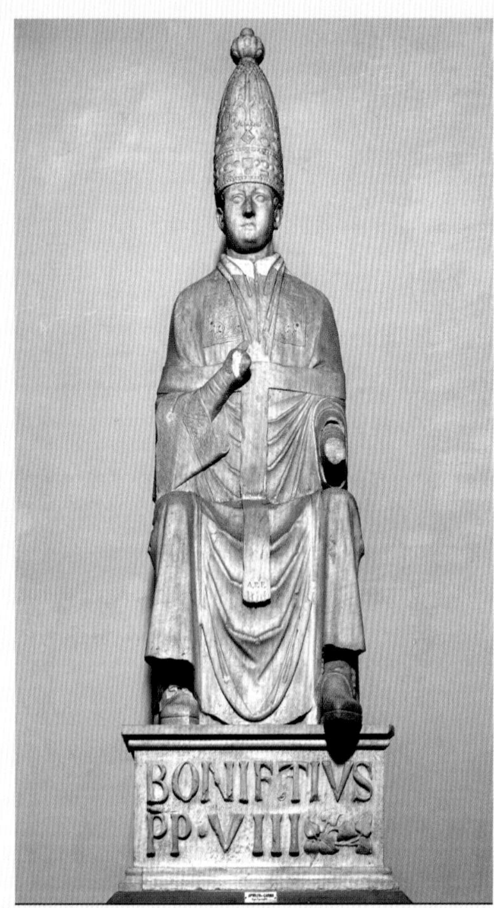

Arnolfo di Cambio
(Colle Val d'Elsa, Siena *c.* 1240 - Firenze *c.* 1302)

Pope Boniface VIII
Papst Bonifaz VIII
Paus Bonifatius VIII

●

c. 1294-1300
h. 280 cm / 110.2 in.
Museo dell'Opera del Duomo, Firenze

Marble / Marmor / Marmer

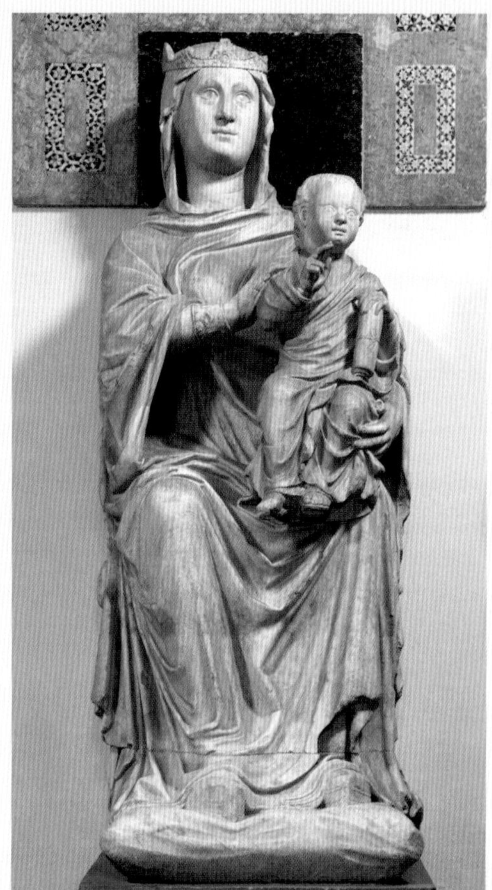

Arnolfo di Cambio
(Colle Val d'Elsa, Siena *c.* 1240 - Firenze *c.* 1302)

Virgin and Child
Madonna mit dem Kind
Madonna met Kind

●

c. 1296-1302
h. 174 cm / 68 in.
Museo dell'Opera del Duomo, Firenze

Marble / Marmor / Marmer

Arnolfo di Cambio
(Colle Val d'Elsa, Siena *c.* 1240 - Firenze *c.* 1302)

Tabernacle
Ziborium
Ciborium

●●

1293
Santa Cecilia in Trastevere, Roma

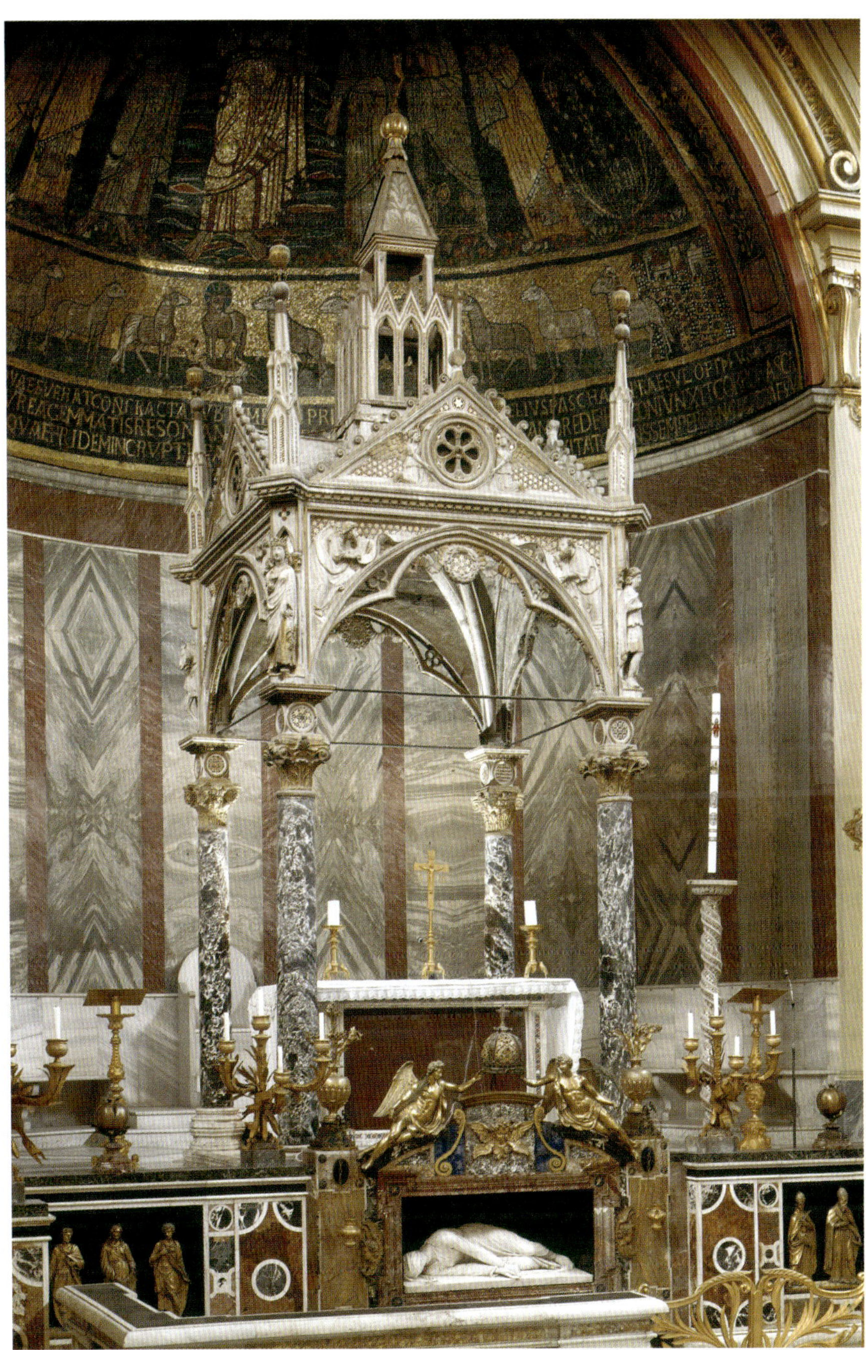

Duccio di Buoninsegna, founder of the school of Siena.

Duccio di Buoninsegna ist Begründer der Sieneser Schule.

Duccio di Buoninsegna sticht de School van Siena.

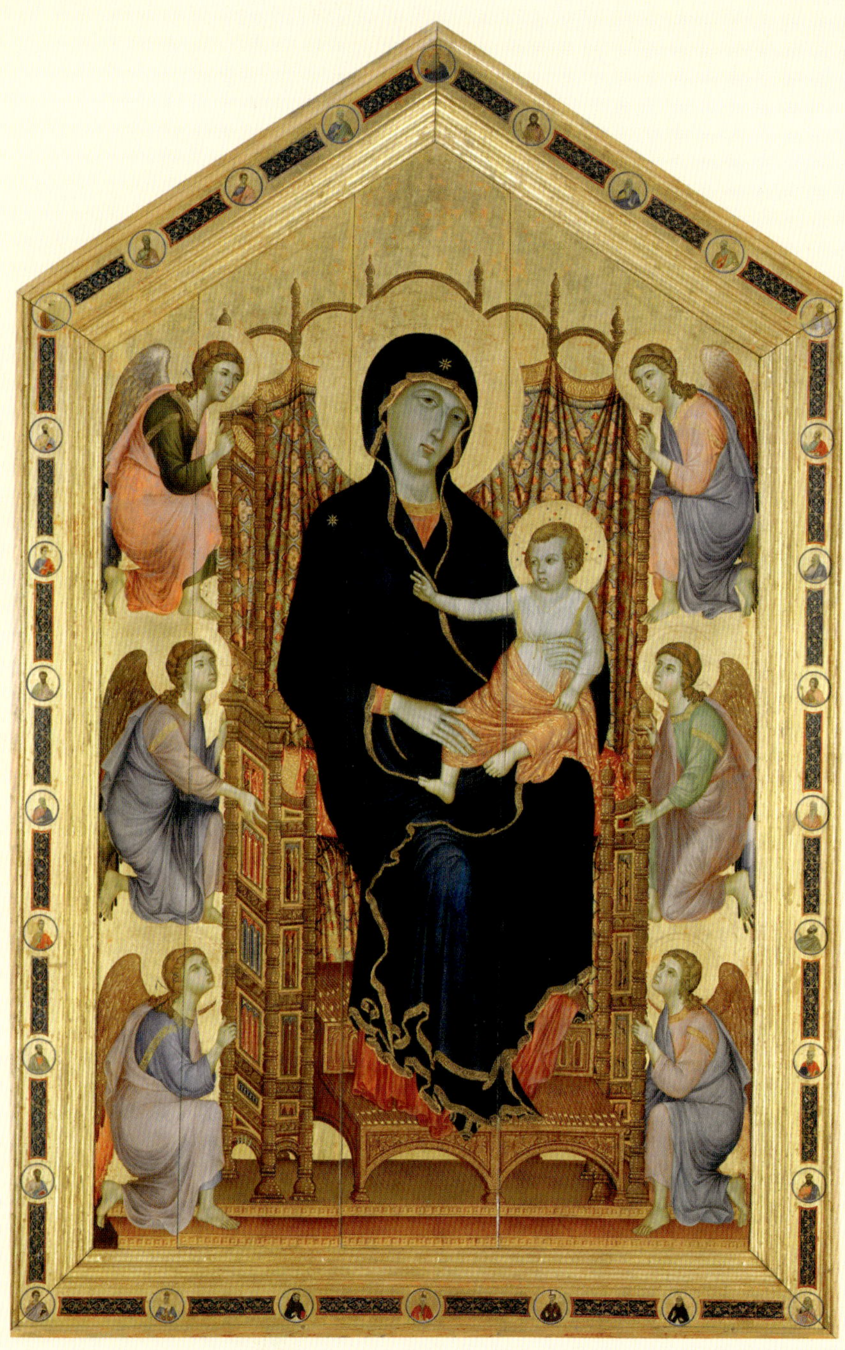

Duccio di Buoninsegna
(Siena *c.* 1255 - *c.* 1319)

Madonna and Child Enthroned (Maestà)
Thronende Madonna
Madonna op troon

●●●

1285
450 x 290 cm / 177.1 x 114.2 in.
Galleria degli Uffizi, Firenze

Tempera on wood / Tempera auf Tafel
Tempera op paneel

Duccio di Buoninsegna
(Siena *c.* 1255 - *c.* 1319)

Triptych
Triptychon
Drieluik

●

c. 1311-1318
61 x 39,4 cm / 24 x 15.5 in.;
45,1 x 19,4 cm / 17.7 x 7.6 in. ;
45,1 x 20,2 cm / 17.7 x 7.9 in.
Museum of Fine Arts, Boston

Tempera on wood / Tempera auf Tafel
Tempera op paneel

Duccio di Buoninsegna
(Siena *c.* 1255 - *c.* 1319)

Maestà (front side)
Majestät (Vorderseite)
Maestà (voorzijde)

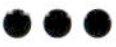

c. 1308-1311
214 x 412 cm / 84.2 x 162.2 in.
Museo dell'Opera della Metropolitana, Siena

Tempera on wood / Tempera auf Tafel
Tempera op paneel

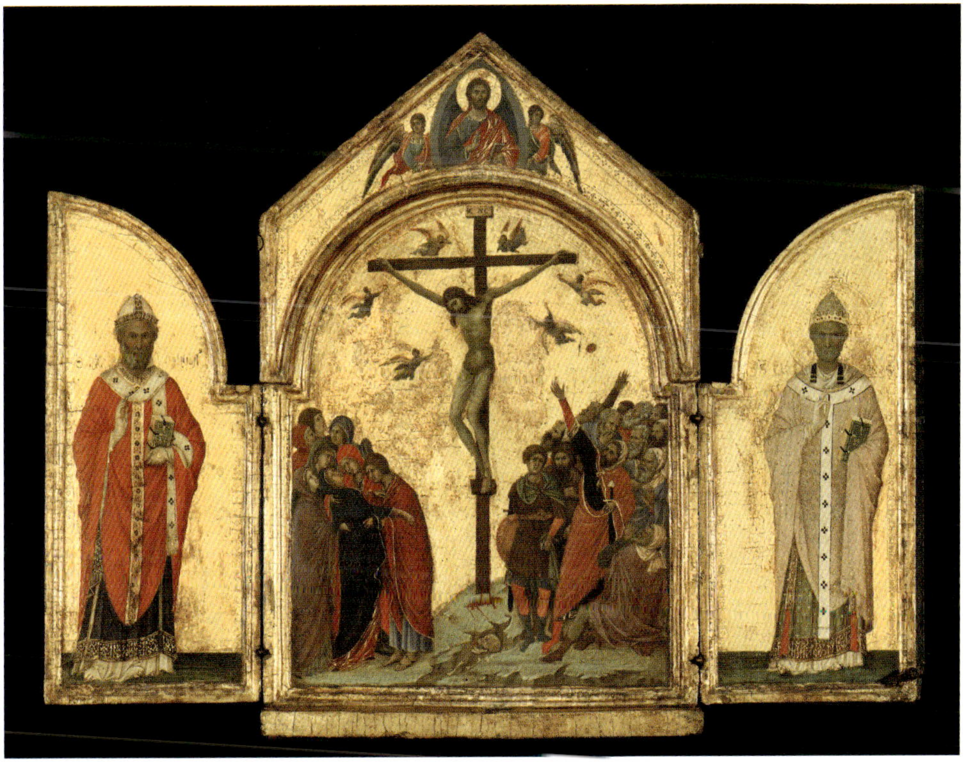

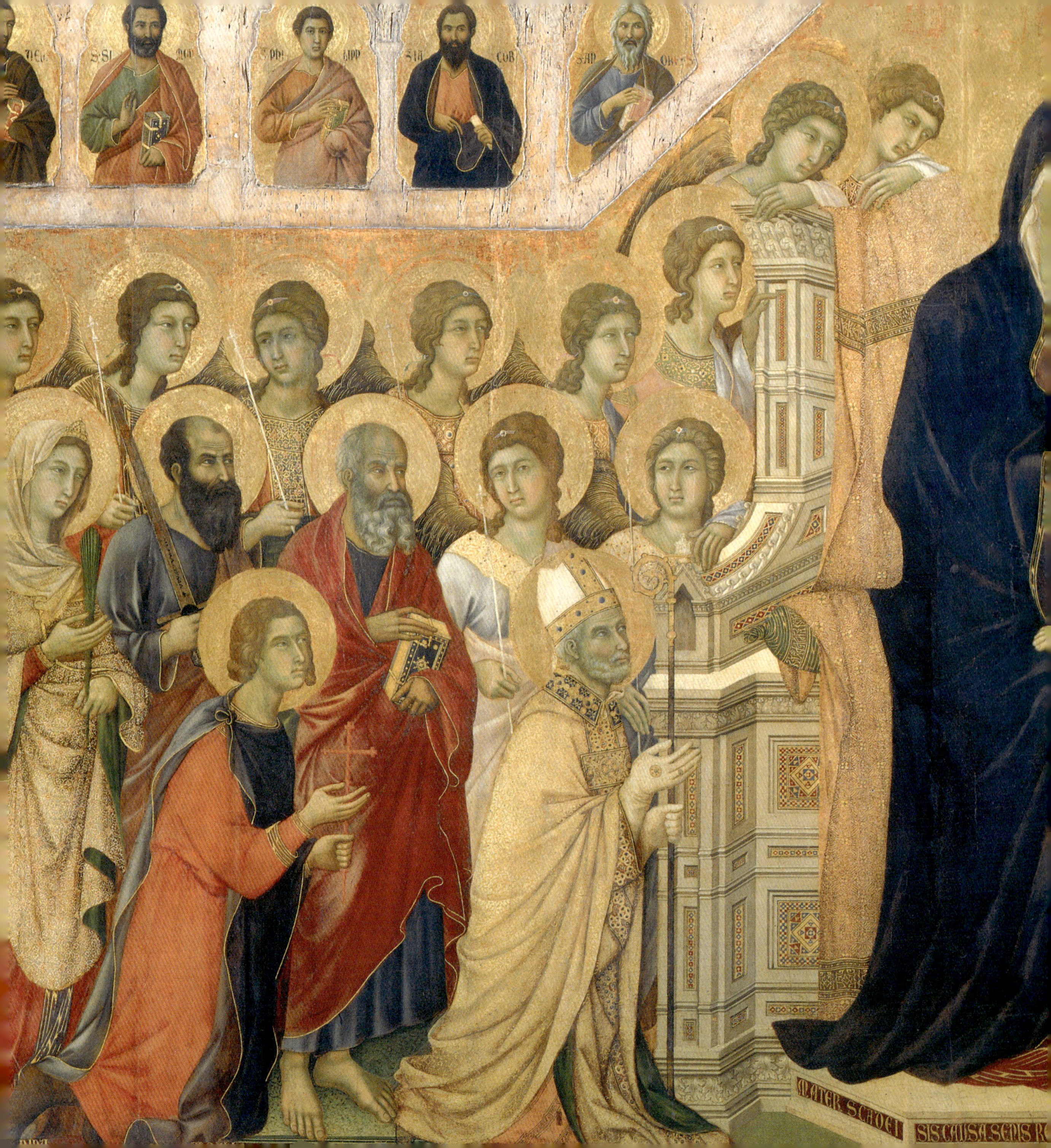
MATER SCA DEI
SIS CAUSA SENIS R

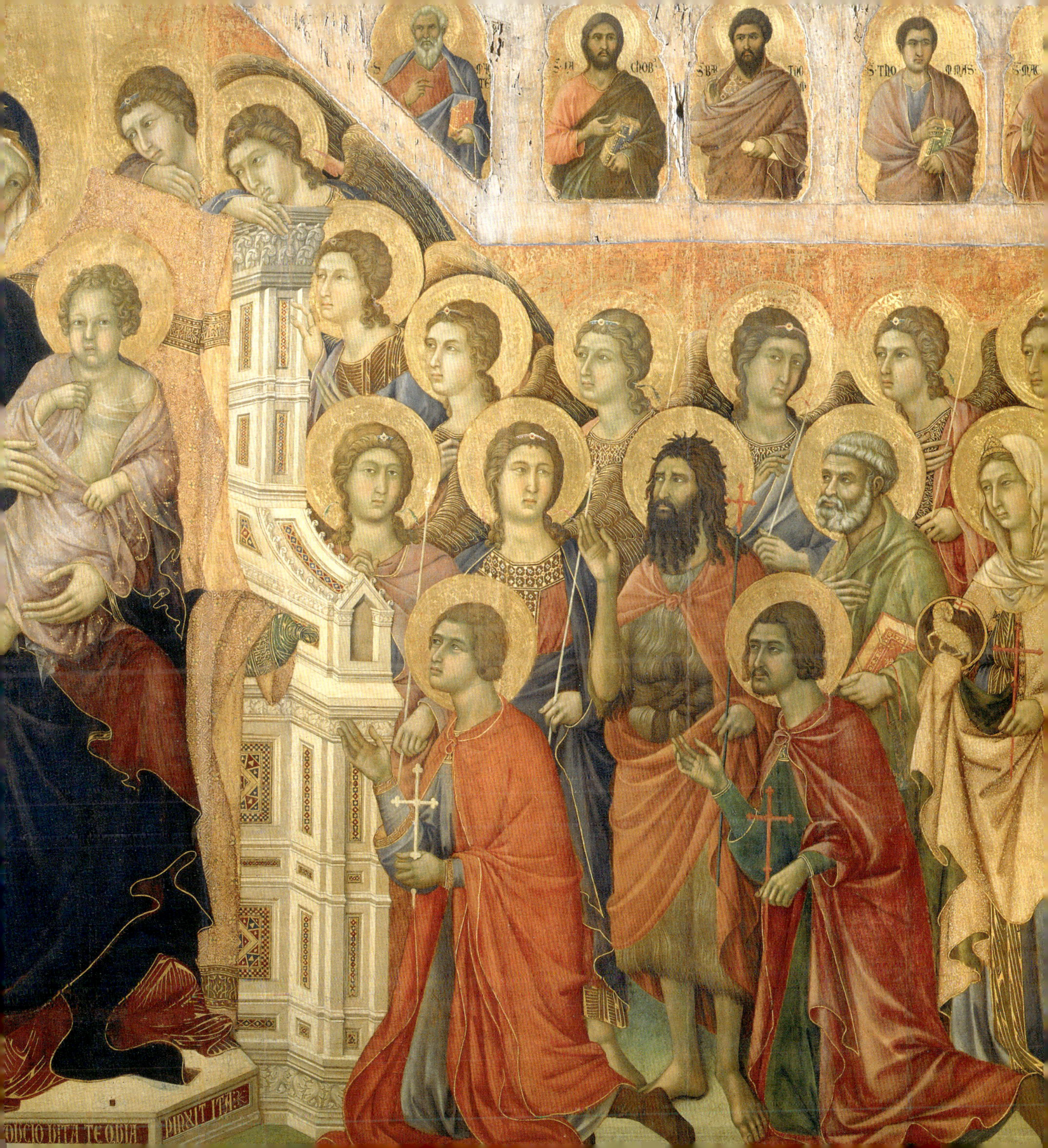
DUCIO VITA TE QUIA
PINXIT ITA

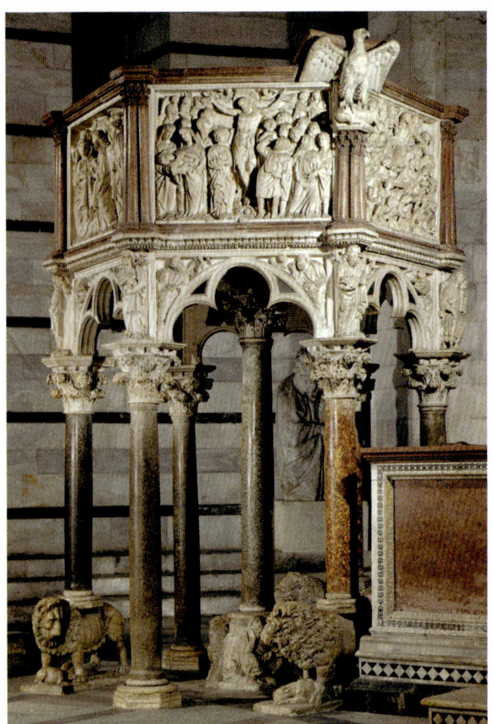

Nicola Pisano adds classical plasticity to Gothic forms through his studies of ancient art...

Nach dem Studium der Antike erfüllt Nicola Pisano die Gotik mit klassischer Plastizität.

Met de bestudering van de Oudheid verrijkt Nicola Pisano de gotiek met klassieke plasticiteit...

Nicola Pisano
(*c.* 1215-1220 - *c.* 1278-1284)

Pulpit and Nativity
Kanzel und Christi Geburt
Preekstoel en Geboorte van Christus

●●

1255-1260
Battistero, Pisa

Marble / Marmor / Marmer

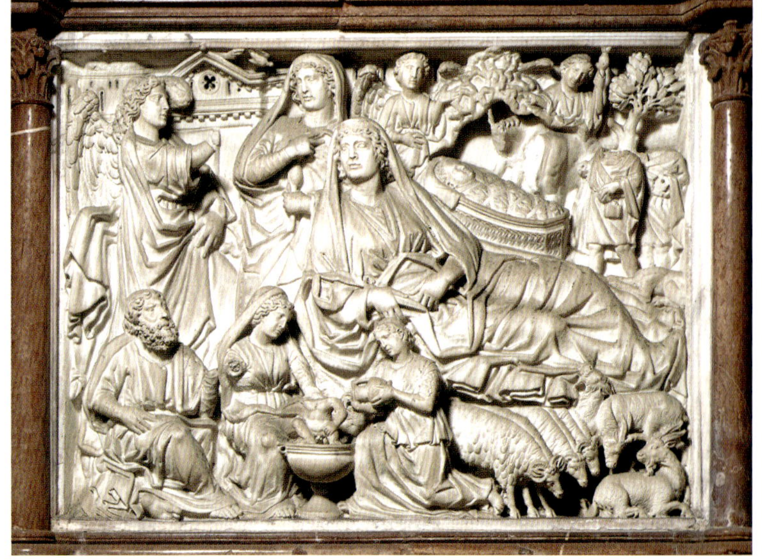

Nicola Pisano
(*c.* 1215-1220 - *c.* 1278-1284)

Pulpit
Kanzel
Preekstoel

●●●

c. 1265-1268
h. 460 cm / 181.1 in.
Duomo, Siena

Marble / Marmor / Marmer

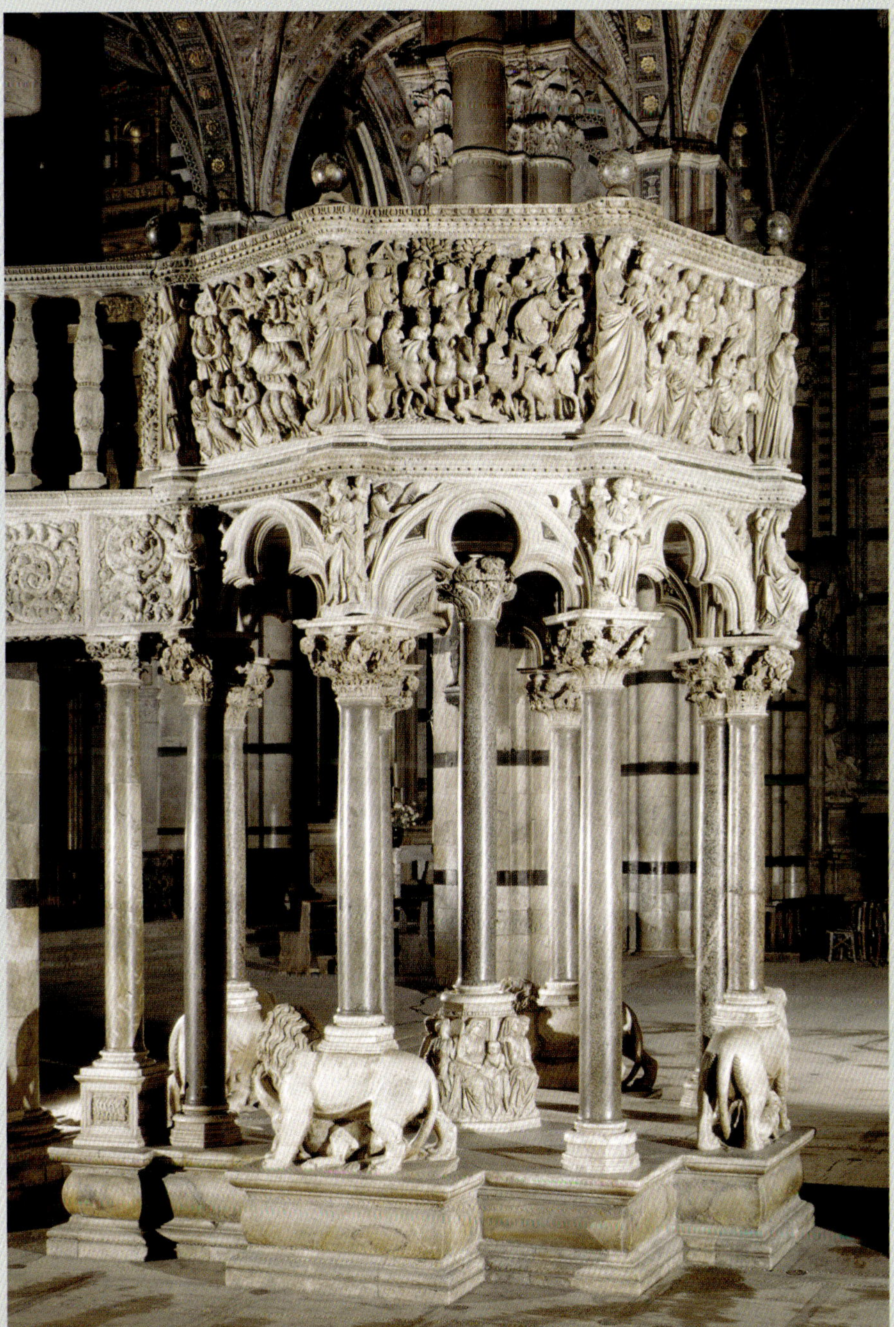

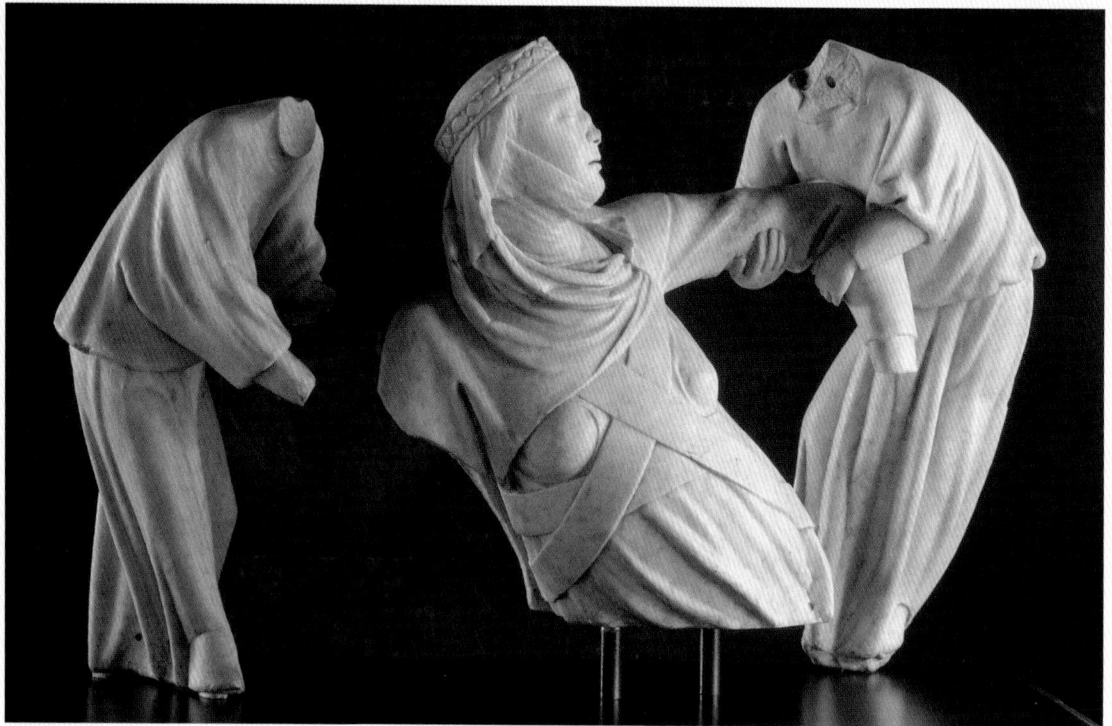

Giovanni Pisano
(Pisa *c.* 1248 - Siena *c.* 1315)

Margaret of Brabant with Two Angels
Margherita von Brabant und zwei Engel
Margaretha van Brabant en twee engelen

●

c. 1311
Museo di Sant'Agostino, Genova

Marble / Marmor / Marmer

... and his family carried on his work.

Seine Familie setzt seine Arbeit fort.

... en zijn familie zet zijn werk voort.

Giovanni Pisano
(Pisa *c.* 1248 - Siena *c.* 1315)

Pulpit
Kanzel
Preekstoel

●●●

c. 1302-1310
Duomo, Pisa

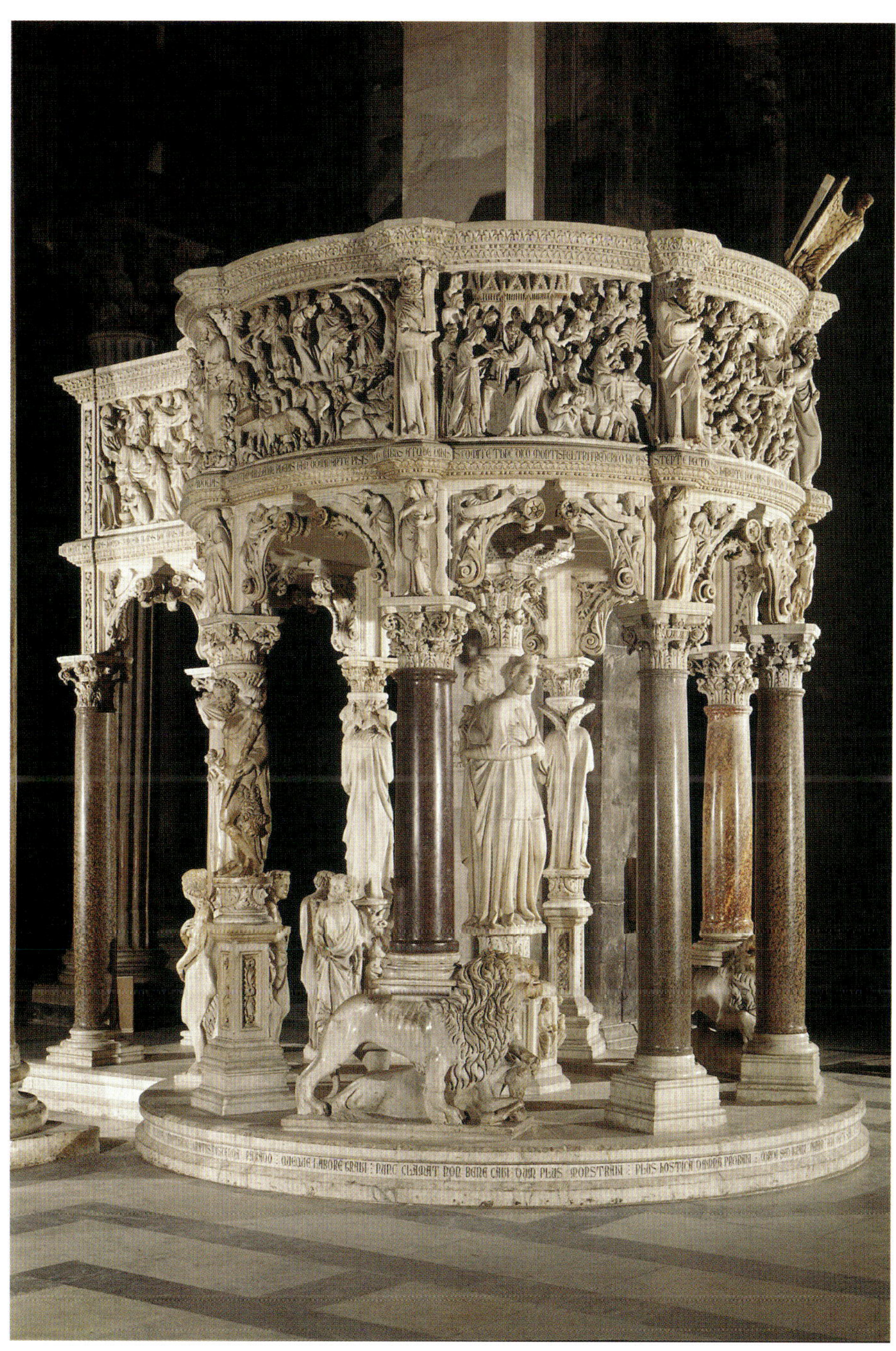

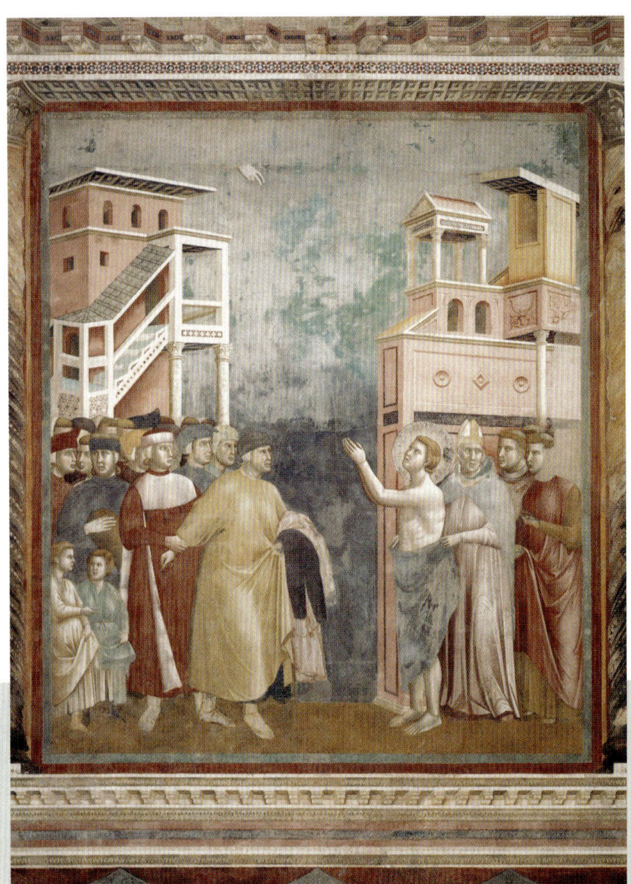

Giotto di Bondone

(Colle di Vespignano, Firenze *c.* 1266 - Firenze 1337)

Stories of St Francis: The Renunciation of Worldly Possessions
Geschichten des Hl. Franziskus: Der Verzicht auf die weltlichen Güter
Legende van St. Franciscus: het afstand doen van de erfenis

●●

c. 1296-1300
San Francesco, Assisi

Fresco / Fresko

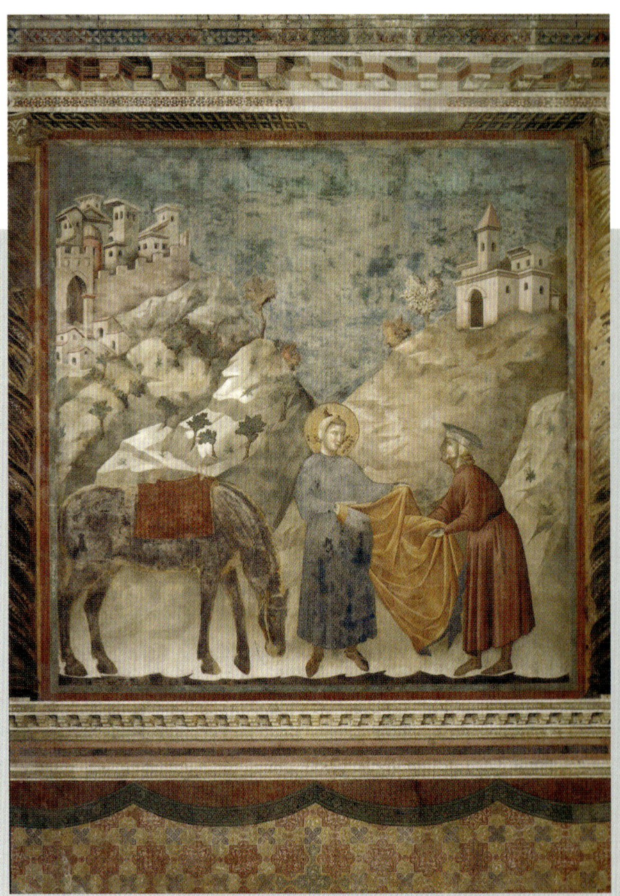

Giotto di Bondone

(Colle di Vespignano, Firenze *c.* 1266 - Firenze 1337)

Stories of St Francis: The Gift of the Mantle
Geschichten des Hl. Franziskus: er verschenkt seinen Mantel
Verhalen van St. Franciscus: het schenken van de mantel

●●

c. 1296-1300
San Francesco, Assisi

Fresco / Fresko

Giotto di Bondone initiates modern painting wit his new interpretations of the human figure and, above all, of space...

Giotto di Bondone begründet mit seiner neuen Auffassung von der Figur und vor allem dem Raum die neuzeitliche Malerei...

Giotto di Bondone geeft aanzet tot de moderne schilderkunst met zijn nieuwe interpretatie van de figuur en vooral van de ruimte...

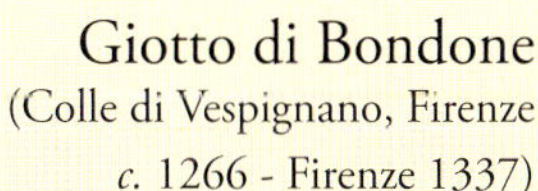

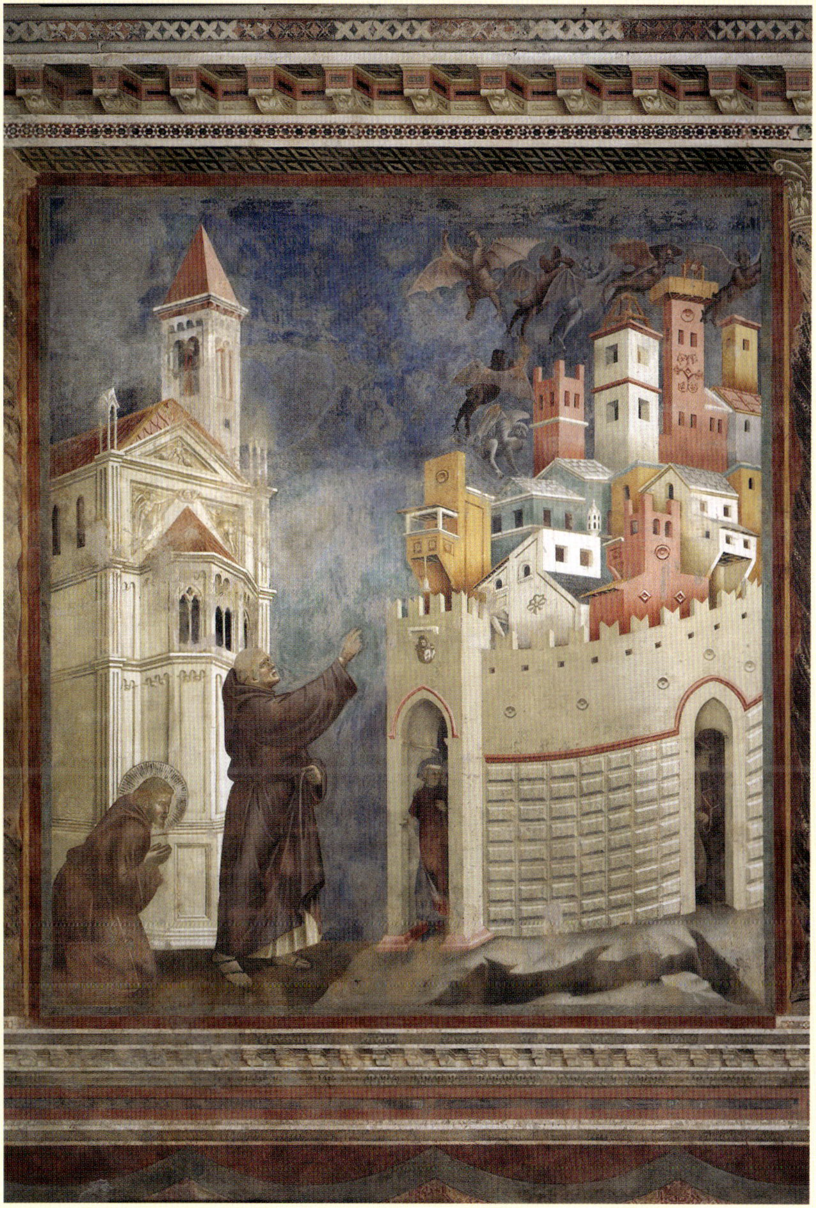

Giotto di Bondone
(Colle di Vespignano, Firenze
c. 1266 - Firenze 1337)

Stories of St Francis: The Expulsion of the Devils from Arezzo
Die Geschichten des Hl. Franziskus: Vertreibung der Teufel aus Arezzo
Legende van St. Franciscus: het verdrijven van de duivels uit Arezzo

●●●

c. 1296-1300
San Francesco, Assisi

Fresco / Fresko

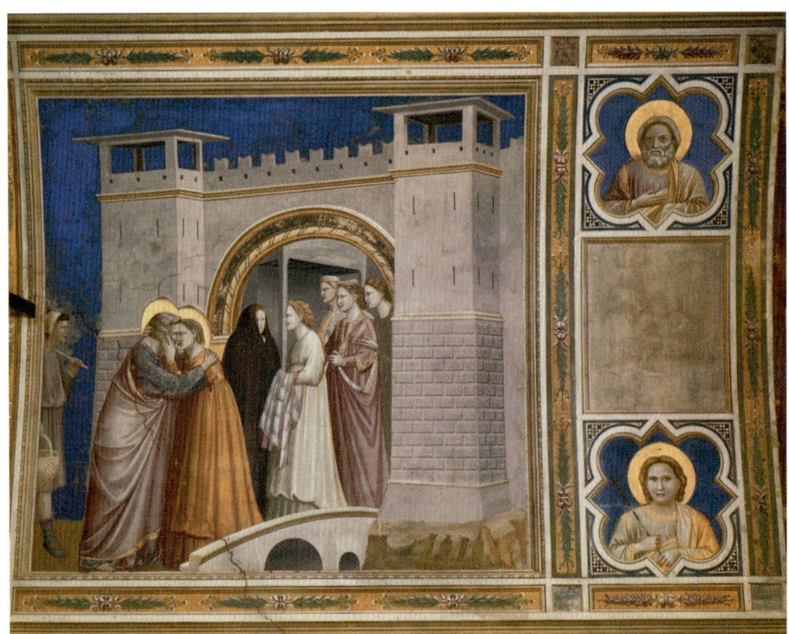

Giotto di Bondone
(Colle di Vespignano, Firenze
c. 1266 - Firenze 1337)

The Meeting at the Golden Gate
Das Treffen an der Porta Aurea
De ontmoeting bij de Porta Aurea (Gouden Poort)

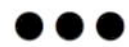

c. 1303-1305
Cappella degli Scrovegni, Padova

Fresco / Fresko

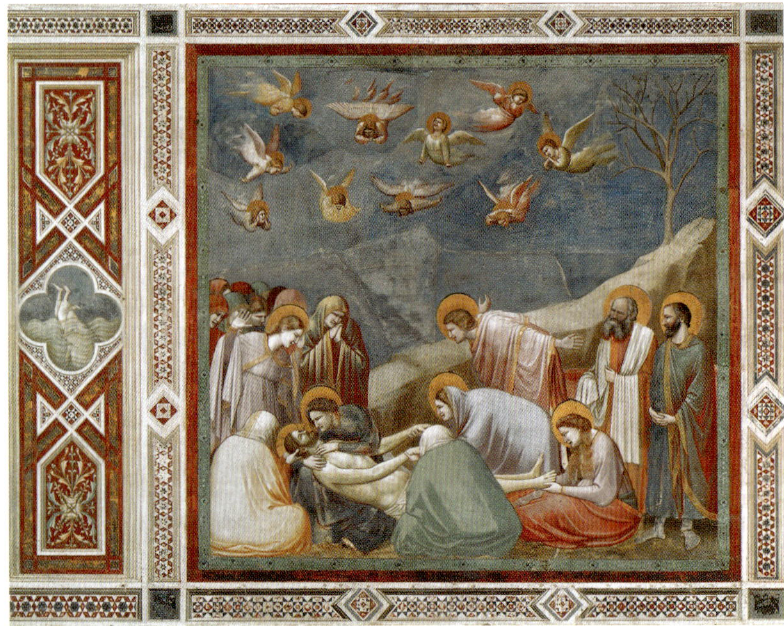

Giotto di Bondone
(Colle di Vespignano, Firenze
c. 1266 - Firenze 1337)

Lamentation over the Dead Christ
Die Klage um den toten Christus
De bewening van de dode Christus

●●

c. 1303-1305
Cappella degli Scrovegni, Padova

Fresco / Fresko

Giotto di Bondone
(Colle di Vespignano, Firenze
c. 1266 - Firenze 1337)

Madonna and Child Enthroned
(Ognissanti Maestà)
Madonna di Ognissanti
Madonna van Allerheiligen

●●●

c. 1310
325 x 204 cm / 128 x 80.3 in.
Galleria degli Uffizi, Firenze

Tempera on wood
Tempera auf Tafel
Tempera op paneel

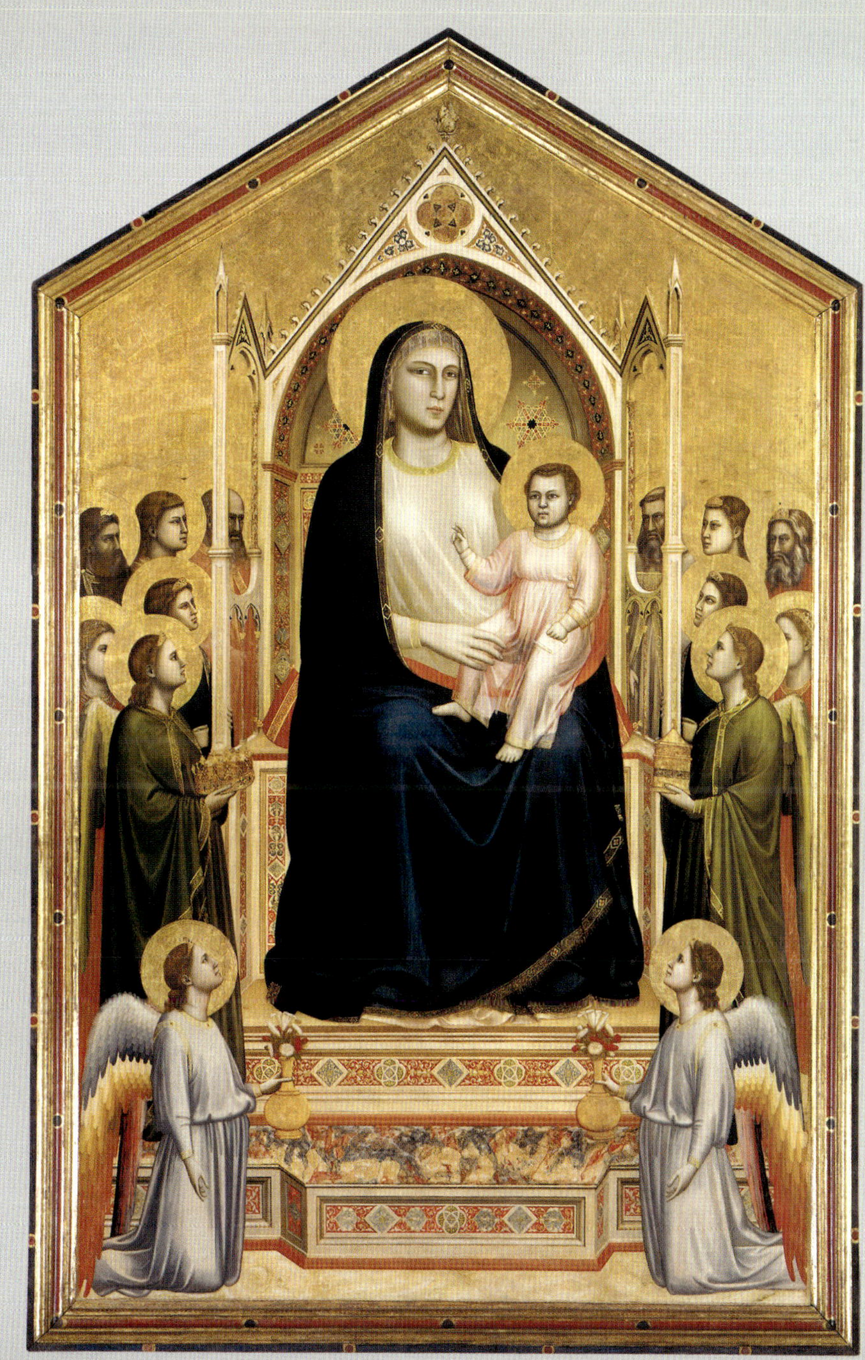

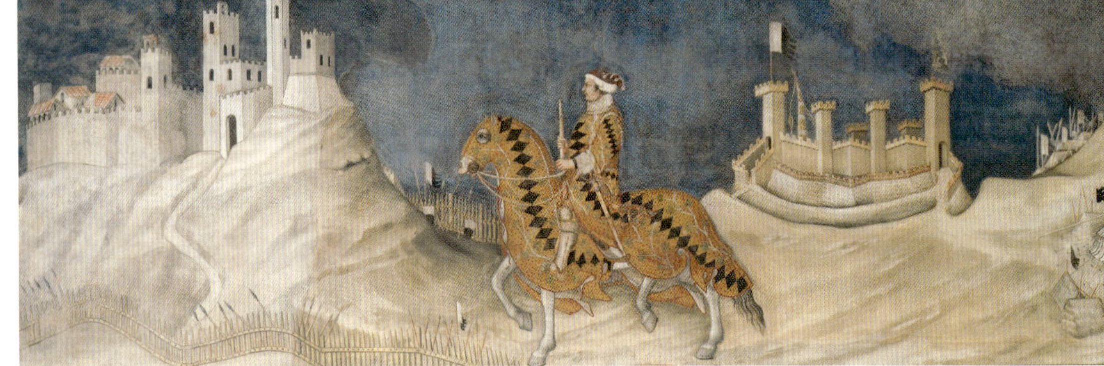

Simone Martini
(Siena *c.* 1284 - Avignon 1344)

Guidoriccio da Fogliano at the Siege of Montemassi
Guidoriccio da Fogliano bei
102 **der Belagerung von Montemassi**
Guidoriccio da Fogliano in de aanval op Montemassi

●●

1328
Palazzo Pubblico, Siena

Fresco / Fresko

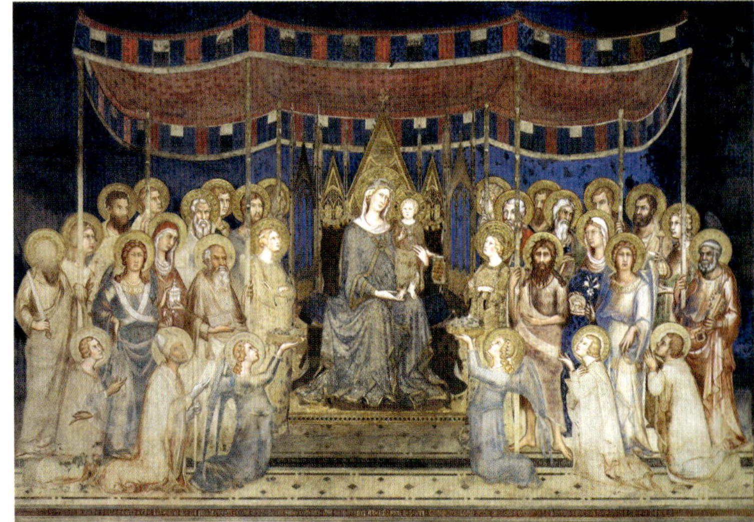

Simone Martini
(Siena *c.* 1284 - Avignon 1344)

Maestà
Majestät

●●

1315
Palazzo Pubblico, Siena

Fresco / Fresko

Simone Martini
(Siena *c.* 1284 - Avignon 1344)

Annunciation
Die Verkündigung
De Annunciatie

●●●

1333
265 x 305 cm / 104.3 x 120 in.
Galleria degli Uffizi, Firenze

Tempera on wood / Tempera auf Tafel
Tempera op paneel

... while Simone Martini lingers in an almost lyrical Gothic style.

... während Simone Martini noch beinahe lyrisch in der Gotik verweilt.

... terwijl Simone Martini zich op bijna lyrische wijze met de gotiek bezighoudt.

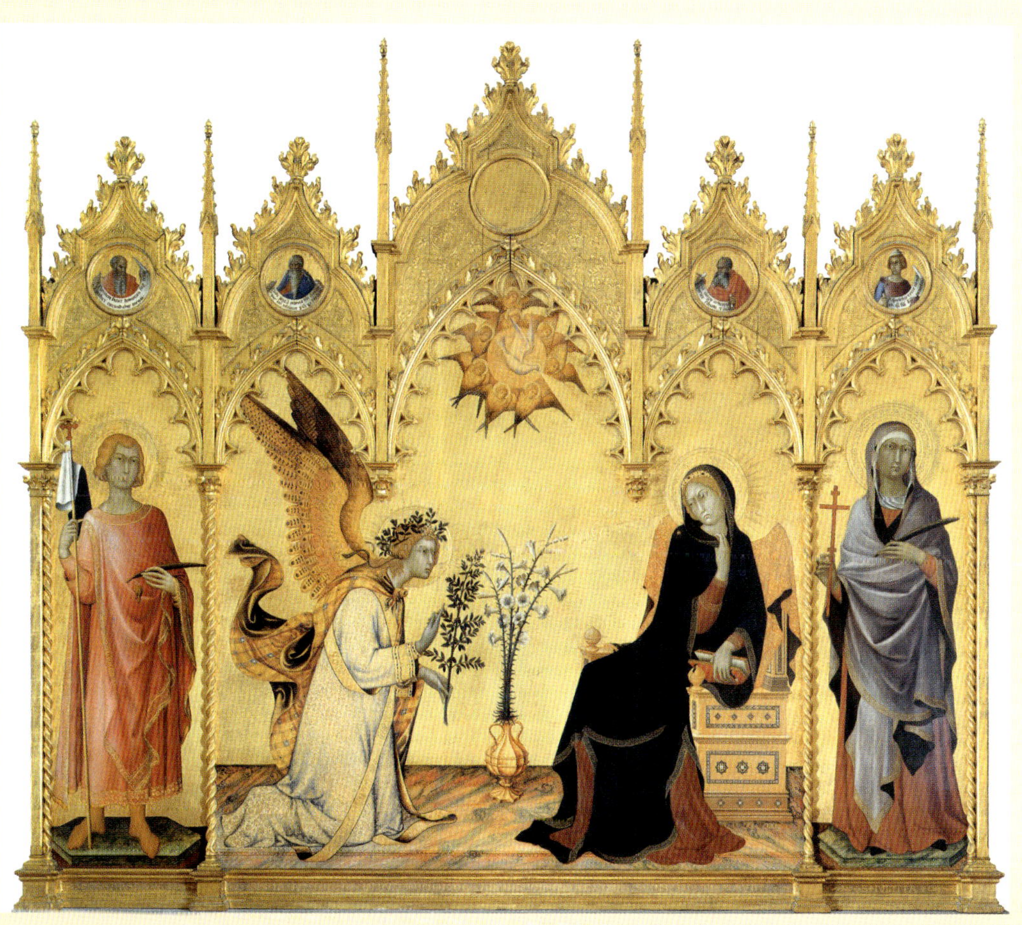

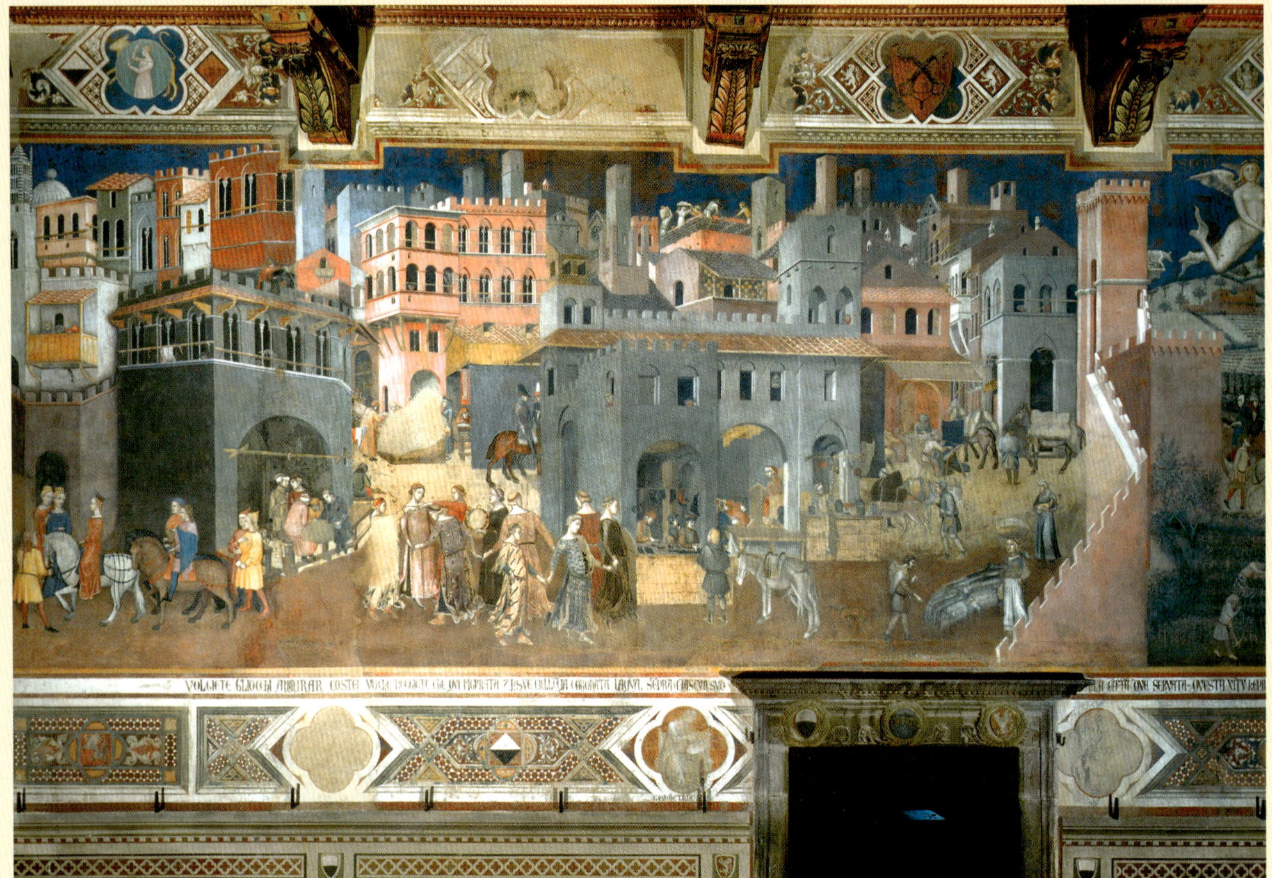

Ambrogio Lorenzetti
(Siena 1285 - 1348)

Allegory of Good Government: in the City and in the Countryside
Effekte des guten Regierens in Stadt und Land
De effecten van Goed Bestuur in stad en land

●●●

c. 1337-1339
Palazzo Pubblico, Siena

Fresco / Fresko

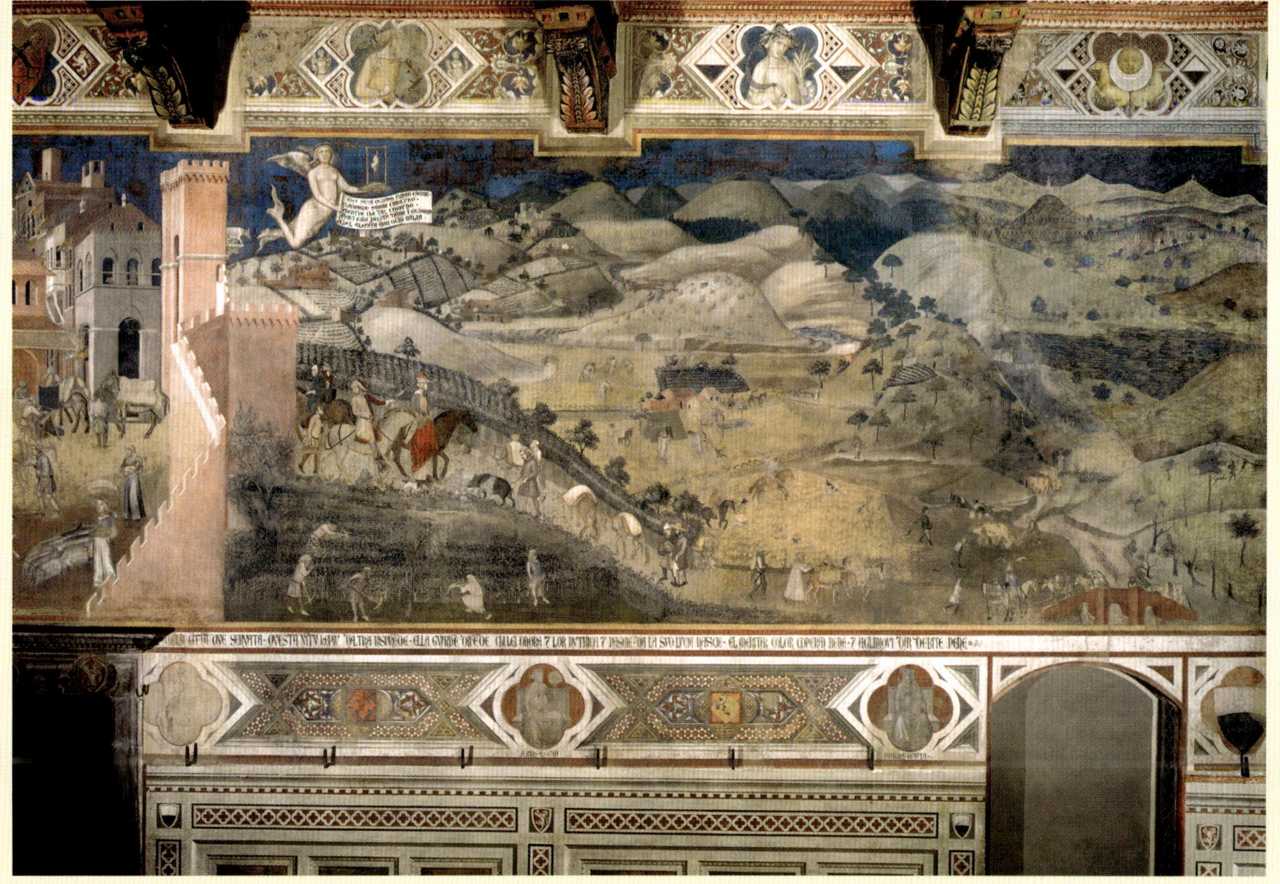

Ambrogio Lorenzetti is the first to portray a real landscape.

Ambrogio Lorenzetti zeigt erstmals eine konkrete Landschaft.

Ambrogio Lorenzetti vertoont als eerste een concreet landschap.

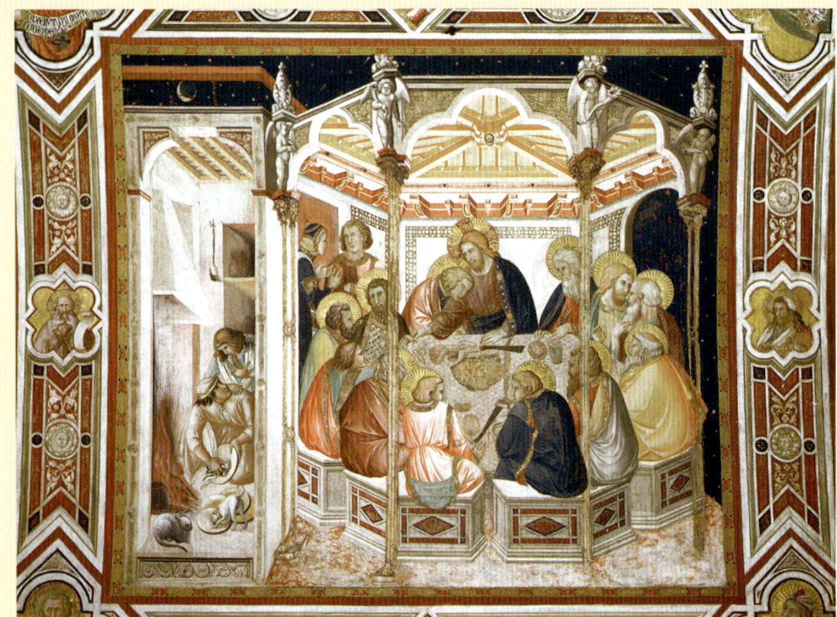

Pietro Lorenzetti
(Siena *c.* 1280 - ? 1348)

Last Supper
Das Letzte Abendmahl
Het Laatste Avondmaal

●

c. 1310-1320
San Francesco, Assisi

Fresco / Fresko

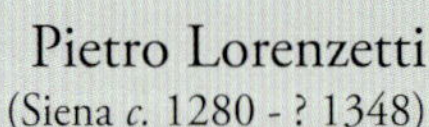

Pietro Lorenzetti
(Siena *c.* 1280 - ? 1348)

Birth of the Virgin
Heimsuchung der Jungfrau
Geboorte van Maria

●●

1335-1342
Museo dell'Opera della Metropolitana, Siena

Tempera on wood / Tempera auf Tafel
Tempera op paneel

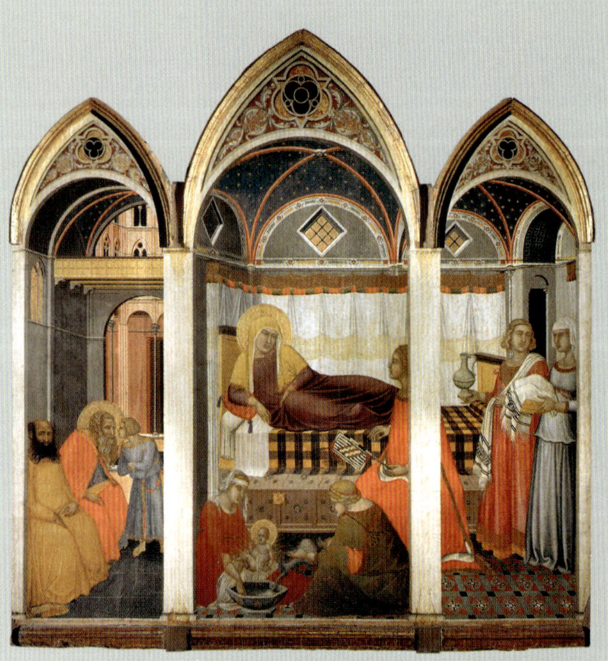

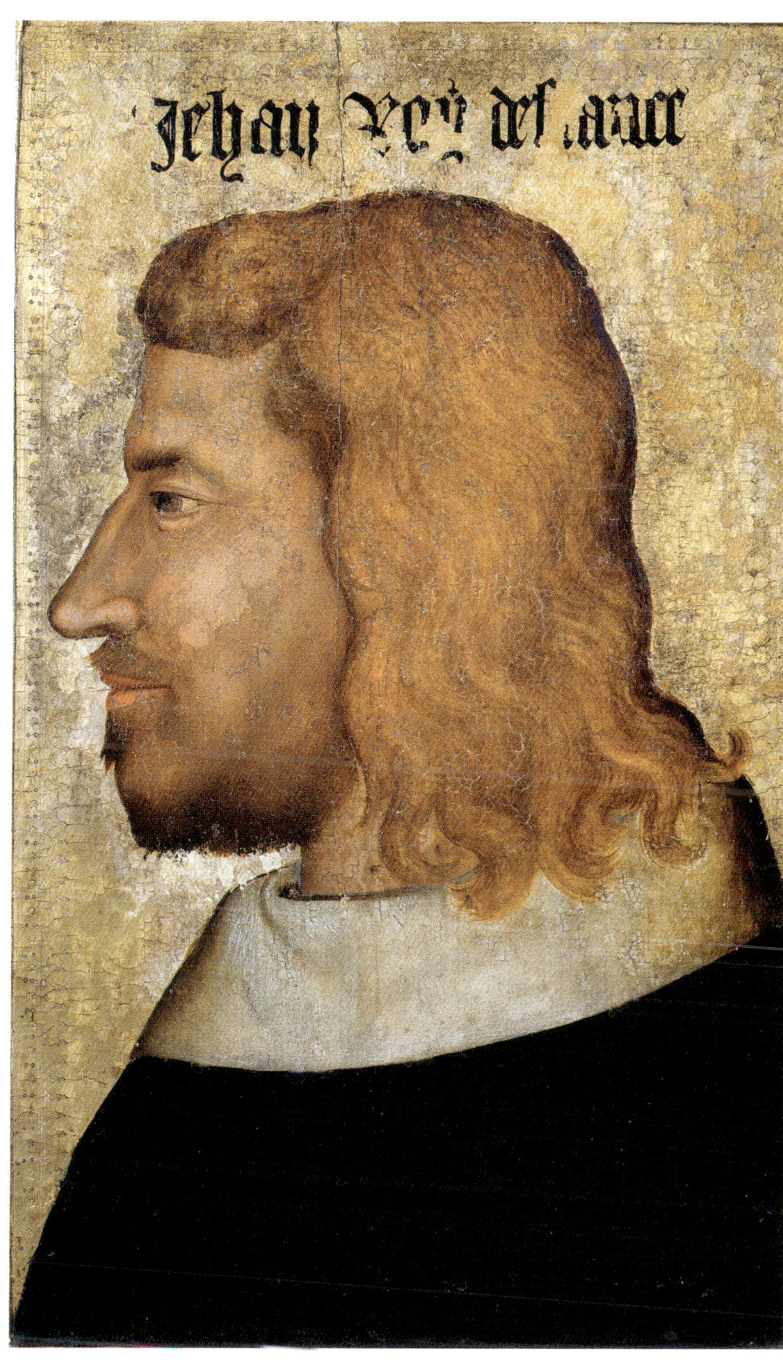

Portrait of Jean le Bon
Portrait Johann des Guten
Portret van Jan II de Goede

●●

c. 1350
Musée du Louvre, Paris

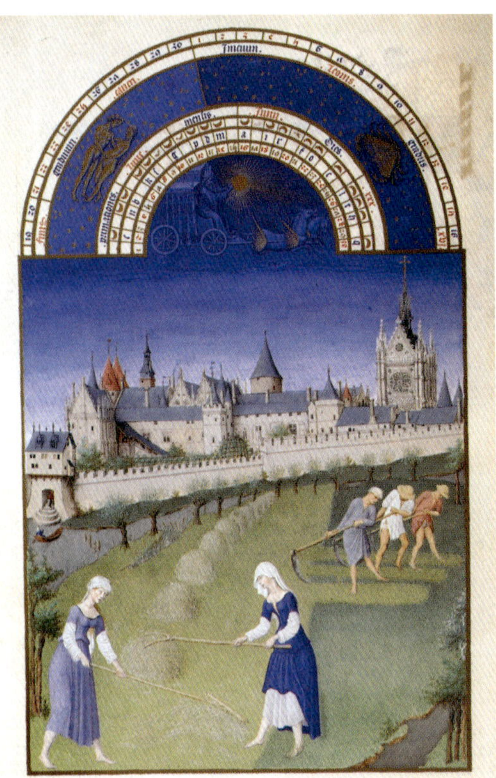

Paul Limbourg

**June: Haymaking,
from 'Le livre des Bonnes mœurs'
Juni: das Heuen,
aus 'Le livre des Bonnes mœurs'
Juni: het hooien,
uit 'Le livre des Bonnes mœurs'**

●●●

1400-1420
Musee Condé, Chantilly

Miniature / Miniatur / Miniatuur

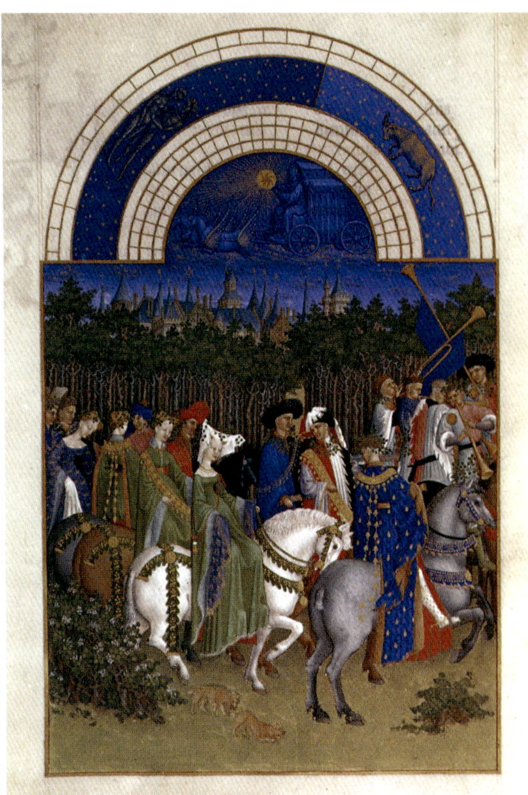

Paul Limbourg

**The Month of May, from Les Très Riches Heures du Duc de Berry
Mai, aus 'Les Très Riches Heures du Duc de Berry'
Mei, uit 'Les Très Riches Heures du Duc de Berry' (De Zeer Rijke Uren van de Hertog van Berry)**

●●●

1412-1416
Musée Condé, Chantilly

Miniature / Miniatur / Miniatuur

Gentile da Fabriano
(Fabriano *c.* 1370 - 1247)

Adoration of the Magi
Anbetung der Könige
Aanbidding der drie Koningen

●●

1423
170 x 220 cm / 67 x 86.6 in.
Galleria degli Uffizi, Firenze

Tempera on wood
Tempera auf Tafel
Tempera op paneel

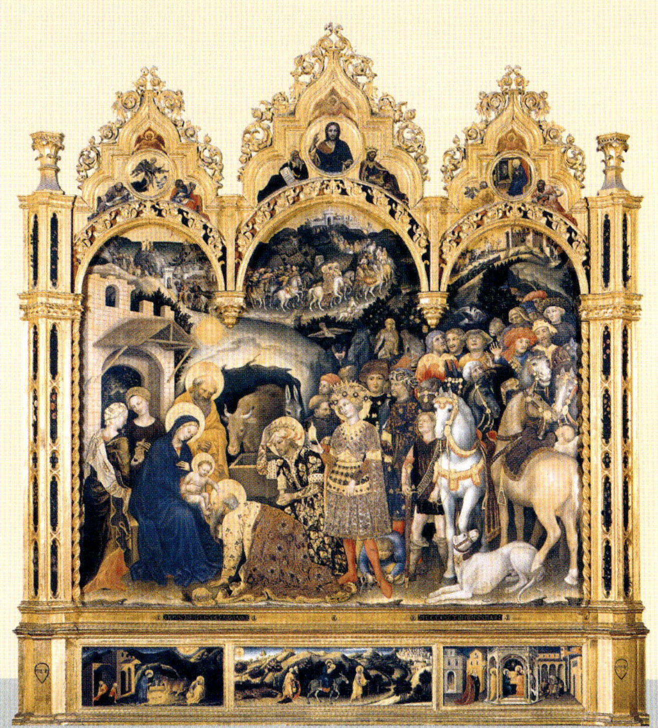

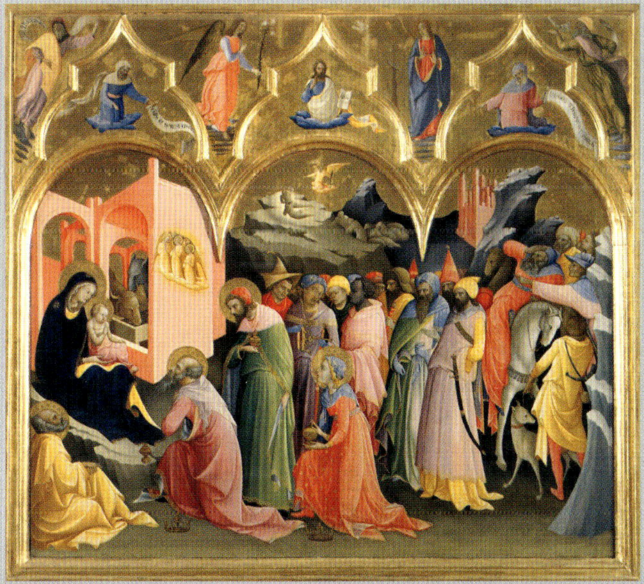

Lorenzo Monaco
(Siena *c.* 1370 - Firenze *c.* 1323)

Adoration of the Magi
Anbetung der Könige
Aanbidding der drie Koningen

●

c. 1421-1422
151 x 170 cm / 59.4 x 67 in.
Galleria degli Uffizi, Firenze

Tempera on wood / Tempera auf Tafel
Tempera op paneel

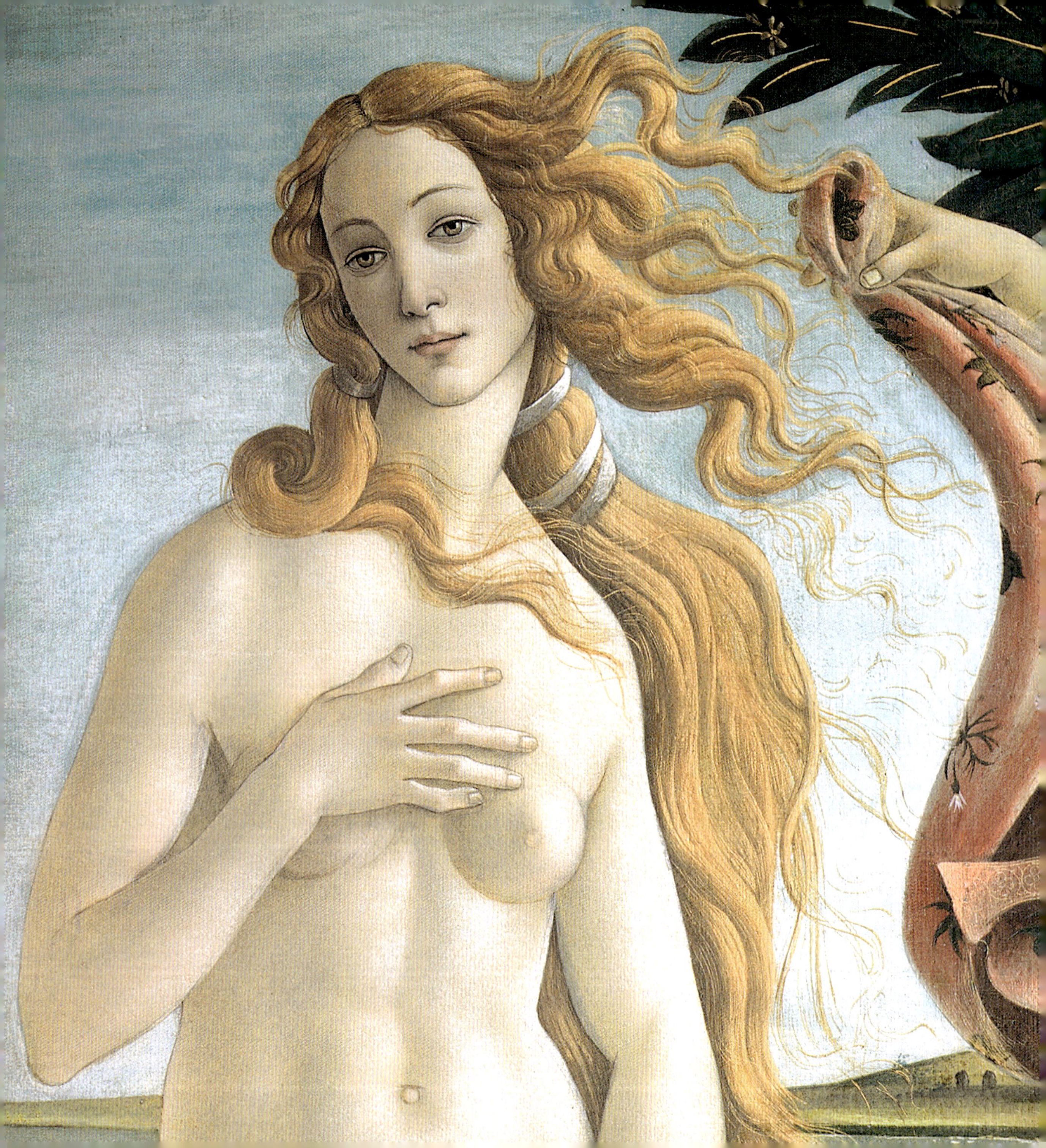

Renaissance
Die Renaissance • De renaissance

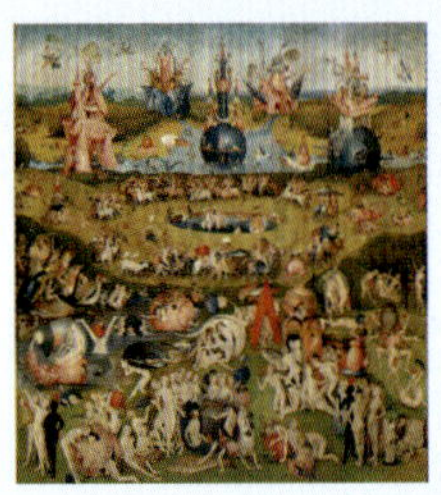

Jan van Eyck (Maastricht c. 1390 - Bruges 1441)
Roger van der Weyden (Tournai c. 1399-1400 - Bruxelles 1464)
Hans Memling (Seligenstadt 1435-1440 - Bruges 1494)
Hugo van der Goes (Gante c. 1440 - Auderghem, Bruxelles 1482)
Hieronymus Bosch (s´Hertogenbosch 1450 - 1516)
Spranger Bartholomaeus (Antwerpen 1546 - Prague 1611)
Quinten Matsijs (Leuven c. 1466 - Antwerpen 1530)
Pieter Bruegel the Elder (Breda of Bree c. 1520 - Bruxelles 1569)

FLANDERS

"Perspective" for the new age
Mit "Durchblick" in die neue Zeit
"In een oogopslag" (perspectief) in een nieuw tijdperk

FRANCE

Robert Campin (Valenciennes c. 1375 - Tournai 1444)
Jean Fouquet (Tours c. 1420 - c. 1477-1481)
Enguerrand Quarton (Laon 1410 - c. 1466)

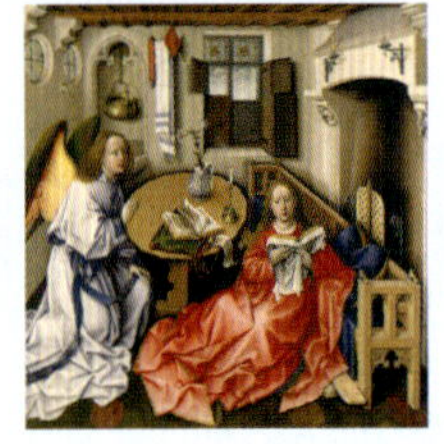

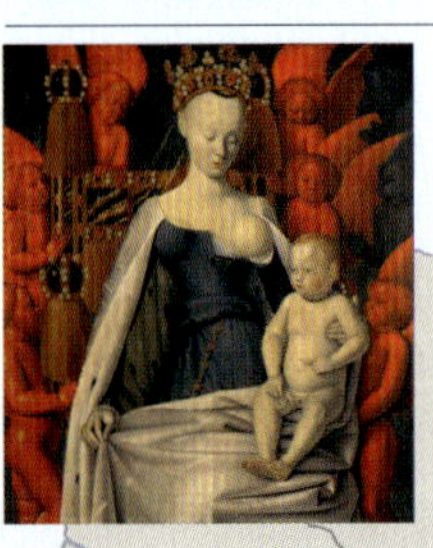

ESPAÑA

Jaime Huguet (Valls 1412 - Barcelona 1492)
Pedro Berruguete (Paredes de Nava, Palencia c. 1450 - 1503)
Alonso Berruguete (Paredes de Nava, Palencia c.1490 - Toledo 1561)
El Greco (Creta 1541 - Toledo 1614)

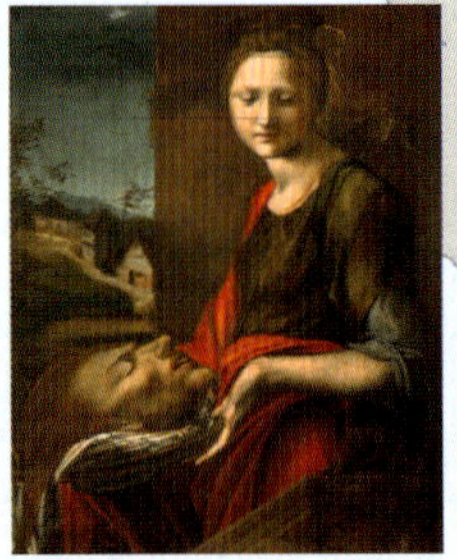

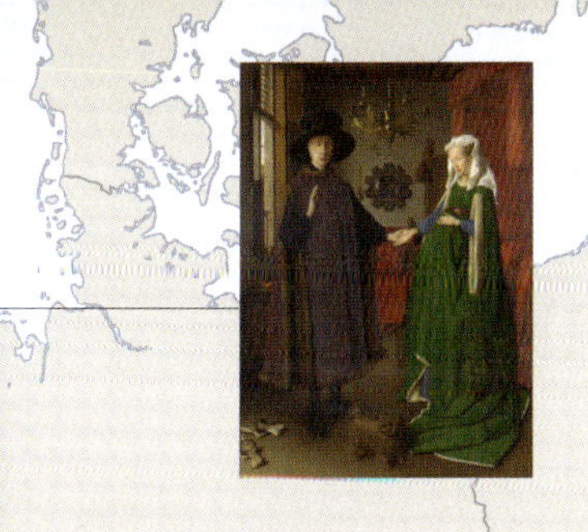

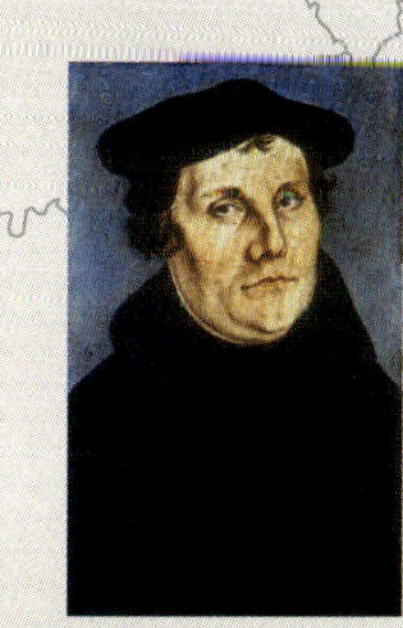

DEUTSCHLAND

Albrecht Dürer (Nürnberg 1471 - 1528)
Matthias Grünewald (Würzburg c. 1475-1480 - Halle an der Saale 1528)
Maarten van Heemskerck (Heemskerck 1498 - Haarlem 1574)
Albrecht Altdorfer (Regensburg 1480 - 1538)
Lucas Cranach the Elder (Kronach 1472 - Weimar 1553)
Hans Holbein (Augsburg 1497/1498 - London 1543)

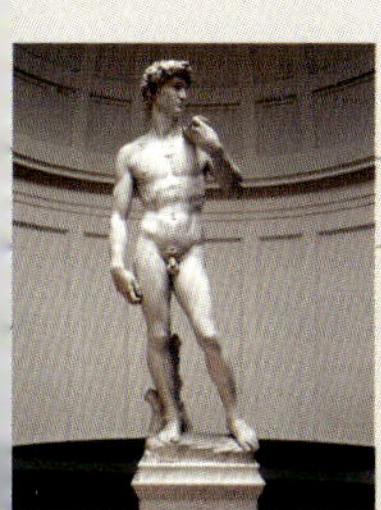

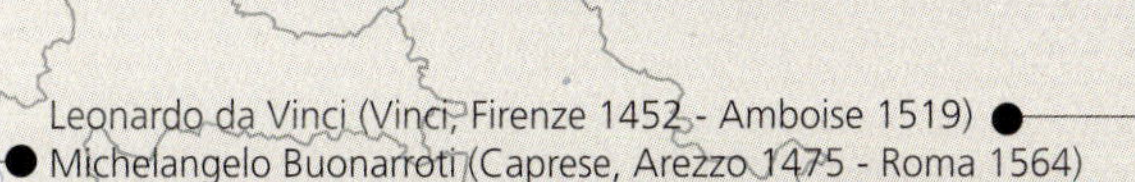

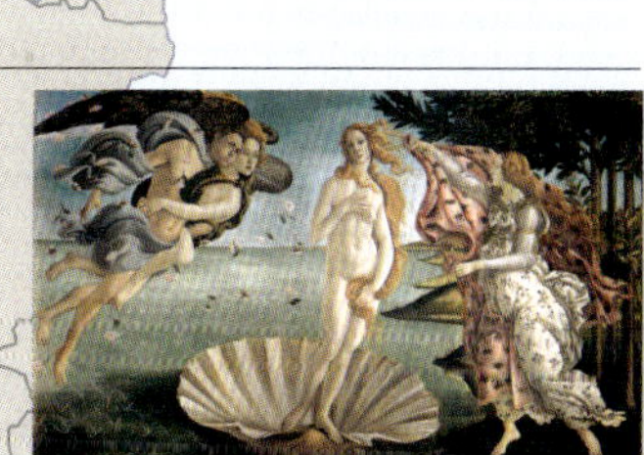

ITALIA

Leonardo da Vinci (Vinci, Firenze 1452 - Amboise 1519)
Michelangelo Buonarroti (Caprese, Arezzo 1475 - Roma 1564)
Sandro Botticelli (Firenze 1445 - 1510)
Piero della Francesca (Arezzo 1410/1420 -1492)
Mantegna (Padova c. 1430 - Mantova 1506)
Raffaello (Urbino 1483 - Roma 1520)
Giorgione (Castelfranco Veneto, 1477 - Venezia 1510)
Jacopo Tintoretto (Venezia 1518 - 1594)
Beato (Fra) Angelico (Firenze c. 1396 - Roma 1455)
Domenico Ghirlandaio (Firenze 1449 - 1494)
Giovanni Bellini (Venezia, c. 1430 - 1516)
Paolo Veronese (Verona 1528 - Venezia 1588)
Giuseppe Arcimboldo (Milano 1527 - 1593)
Antonello da Messina (Messina c. 1423/1430 - 1479)
Filippo Brunelleschi (Firenze 1377 - 1466)
Donatello (Firenze 1386 - 1466)
Masaccio (Arezzo 1401 - Roma 1428)
Paolo Uccello (Firenze 1397 - 1475)
Andrea Verrocchio (Firenze c.1435 - Venezia 1488)
Andrea del Sarto (Firenze 1486 - 1530)
Filippino Lippi (Prato 1457 - Firenze 1504)
Tiziano (Pieve di Cadore, 1490 c. - Venezia 1576)
Correggio (Correggio, Reggio Emilia c. 1489 - 1534)
Pontormo (Pontorme, Empoli 1494 - Firenze 1556-1557)
Lorenzo Ghiberti (Firenze 1378 - 1455)
Luca della Robbia (Firenze 1400 -1482)

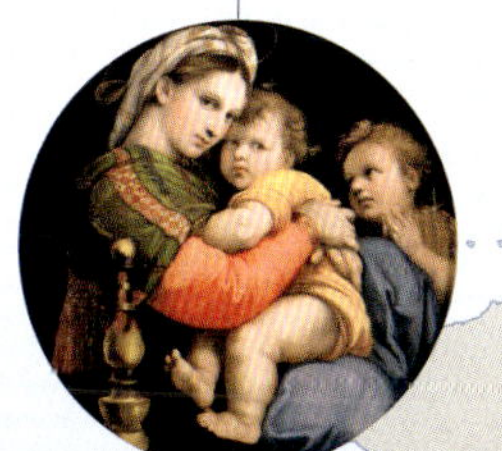

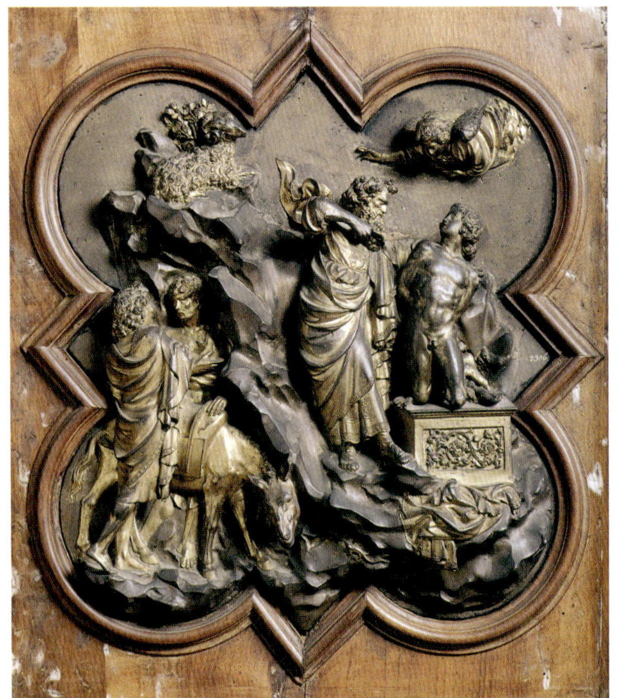

Lorenzo Ghiberti
(Pelago, Firenze 1378 - Firenze 1455)

Sacrifice of Isaac
Isaaks Opfer
Offer van Isaac

1401
45 x 38 cm / 17.7 x 15 in.
Museo Nazionale del Bargello, Firenze

Gilded bronze / Vergoldete Bronze
Verguld brons

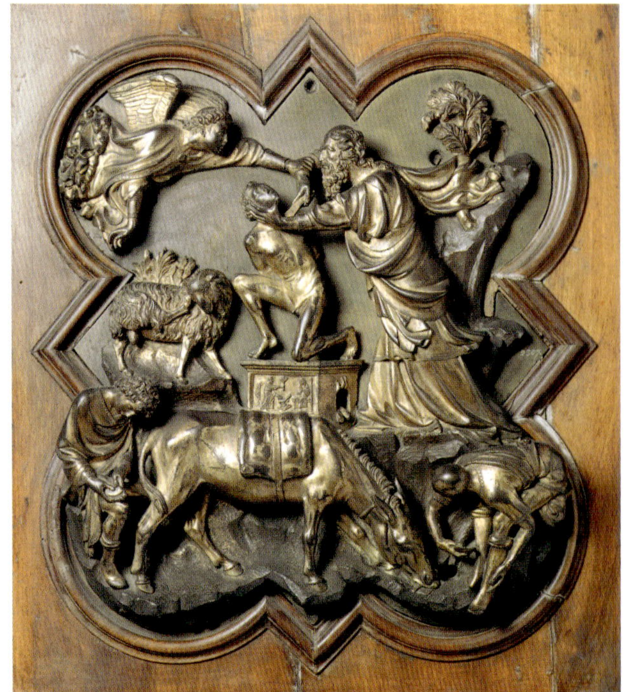

Filippo Brunelleschi
(Firenze 1377 - 1466)

Sacrifice of Isaac
Isaaks Opfer
Offer van Isaac

1401
45 x 38 cm / 17.7 x 15 in.
Museo Nazionale del Bargello, Firenze

Gilded bronze / Vergoldete Bronze
Verguld brons

Firenze and the early Renaissance: Ghiberti wins the competition for the Baptistery doors although Brunelleschi's project is more modern and appears better even today.

Florenz der Frührenaissance, obgleich Brunelleschis Entwurf moderner und aus heutiger Sicht besser ist, setzt sich Ghibertis Entwurf für die Tür des Florentiner Baptisteriums durch.

Het Florence van de vroeg-renaissance. Hoewel Brunelleschi's ontwerp moderner en met huidige blik beter is, wordt het ontwerp van Ghiberti doorgevoerd.

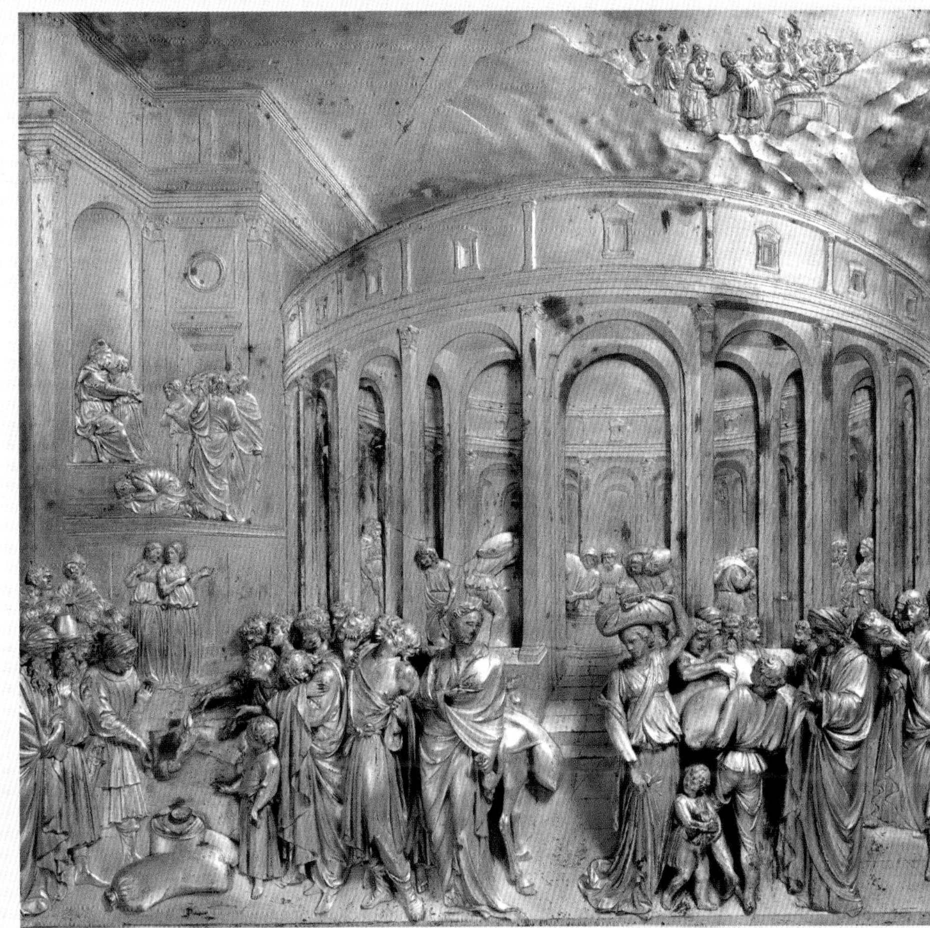

Lorenzo Ghiberti
(Pelago, Firenze 1378 - Firenze 1455)

Stories of Joseph (from the Gates of Paradise)
Geschichten des Joseph (Paradiespforte)
Verhaal van Jozef (van de Paradijspoort)

●●●

1425-1452
Museo dell'Opera del Duomo, Firenze

Gilded bronze / Vergoldete Bronze
Verguld brons

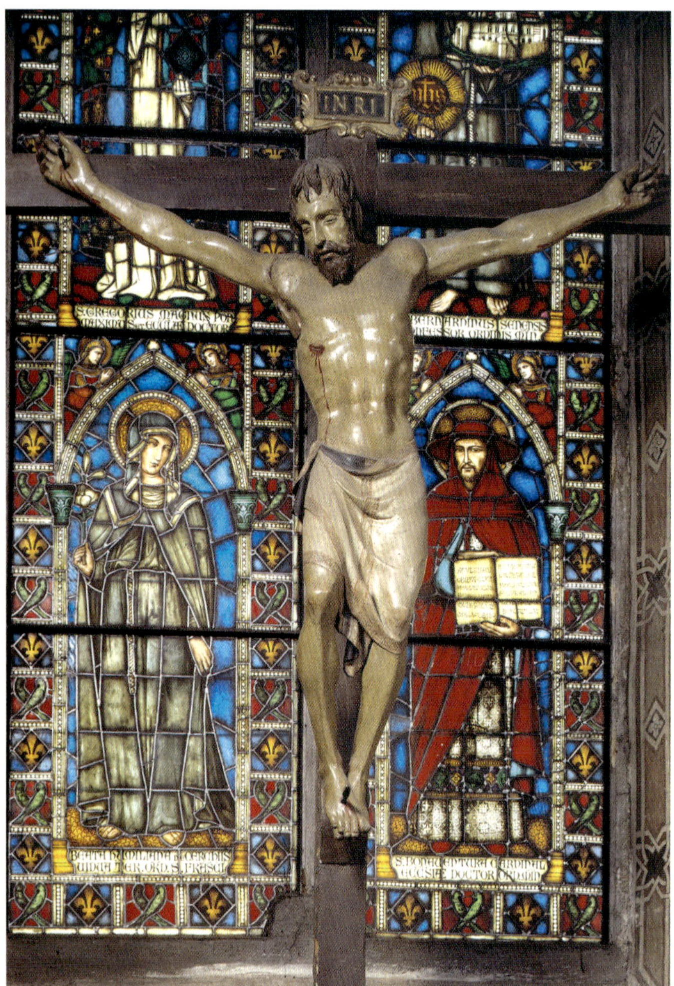

Donatello (Firenze 1386 - 1466)

Crucifix
Kruzifix
Kruisbeeld

●

c. 1412-1413
186 x 173 cm / 73.2 x 68.1 in.
Santa Croce, Firenze

Wood / Holz / Hout

Donatello (Firenze 1386 - 1466)

Jeremiah the Prophet
Der Prophet Jeremias
Profeet Jeremia

●

c. 1425
h. 191 cm / 75.2 in.
Museo dell'Opera del Duomo, Firenze

Marble / Marmor / Marmer

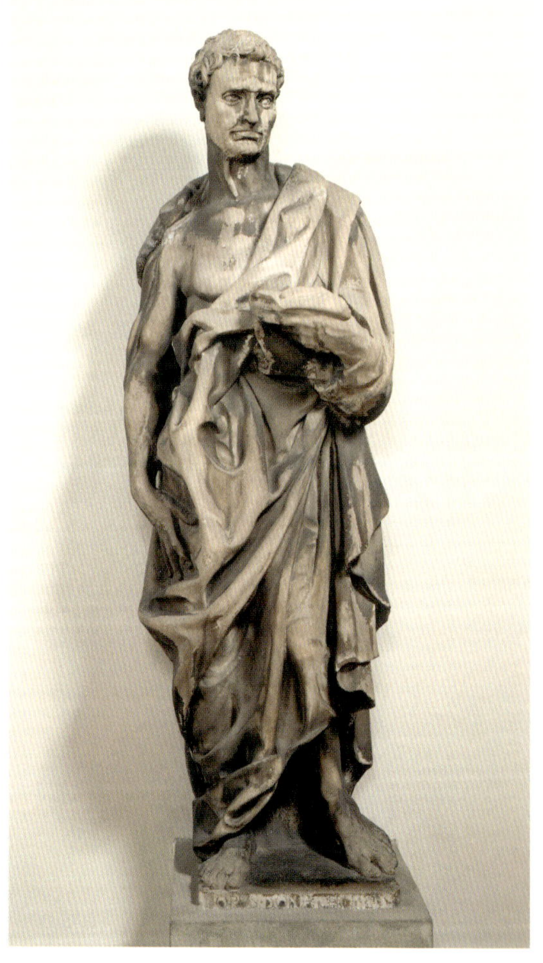

The David of Donatello is the first sculptural nude since ancient times...

Donatellos David ist der erste vollplastische Akt seit der Antike...

De David van Donatello is het eerste naaktbeeld na de Oudheid...

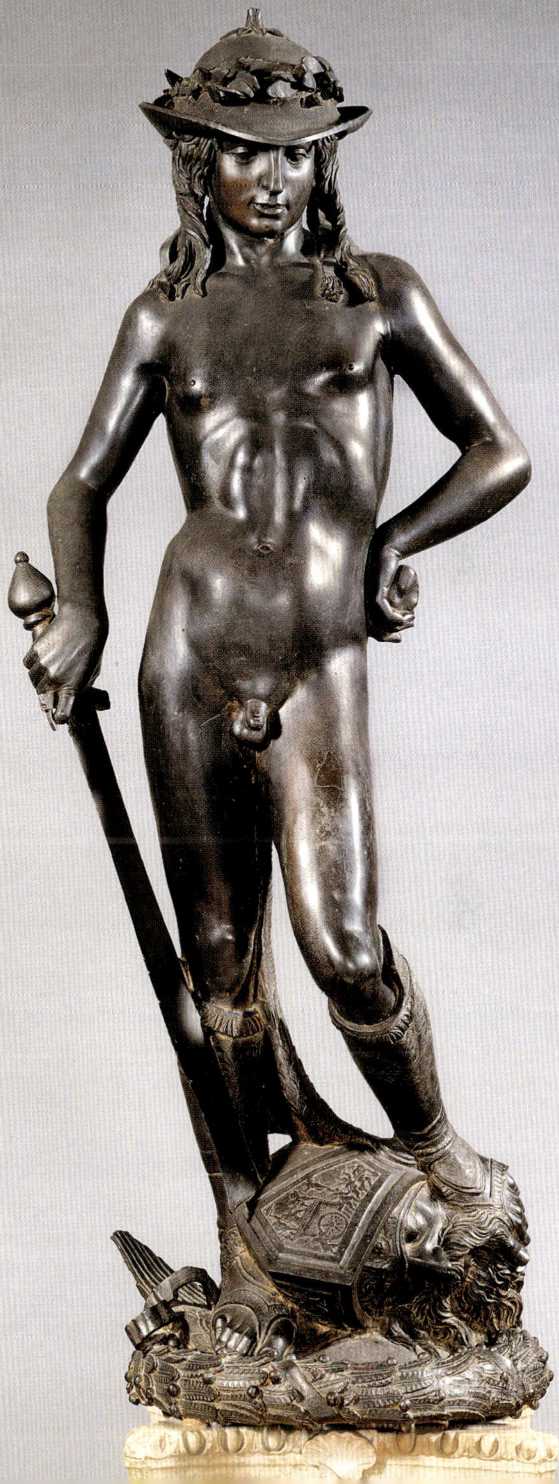

Donatello

(Firenze 1386 - 1466)

David

1440

h.158 cm / 62.2 in.

Museo Nazionale del Bargello, Firenze

Bronze / Brons

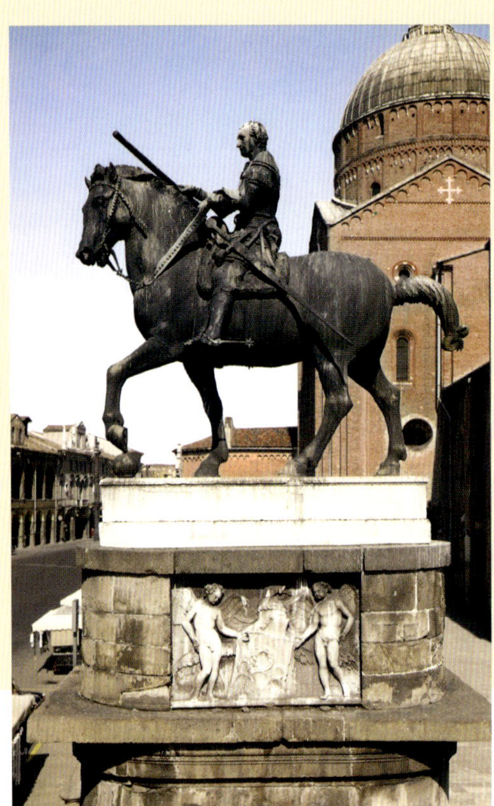

Donatello

(Firenze 1386 - 1466)

Equestrian Monument to Gattamelata
Reiterdenkmal des Gattamelata
Ruiterstandbeeld van Gattamelata

●●

c. 1447-1453
h. 390 cm / 153.5 in.
Piazza del Santo, Padova

Bronze / Brons

... and the same is true for his equestrian monument.

... dies gilt auh für sein Reiterdenkmal.

... dit geldt eveneens voor zijn ruiterstandbeeld.

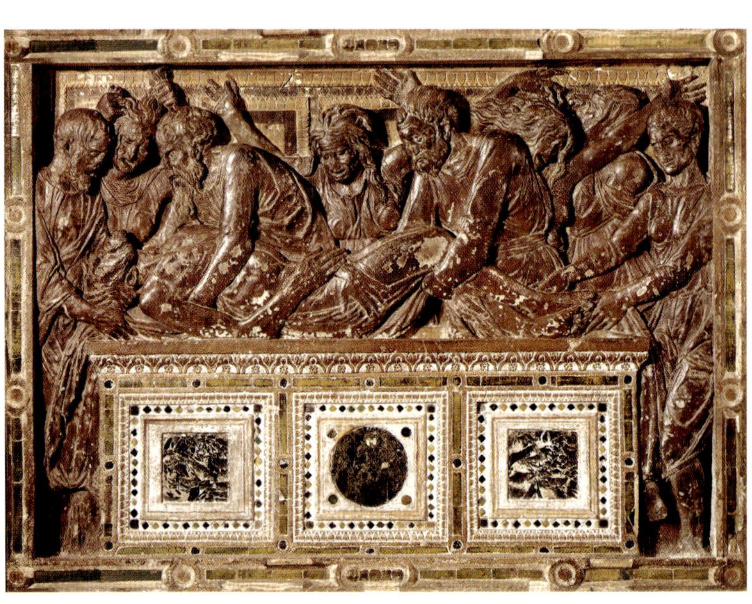

Donatello

(Firenze 1386 - 1466)

Deposition
Kreuzabnahme
Kruisafneming

●

c. 1448
139 x 188 cm / 54.7 x 74 in.
Basilica di Sant'Antonio, Padova

Stone / Stein / Steen

Donatello's figures can even be ugly.

Donatellos Figuren dürfen auch "hässlich" sein.

De figuren van Donatello kunnen ook "lelijk" zijn.

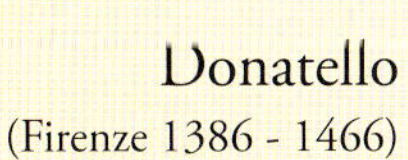

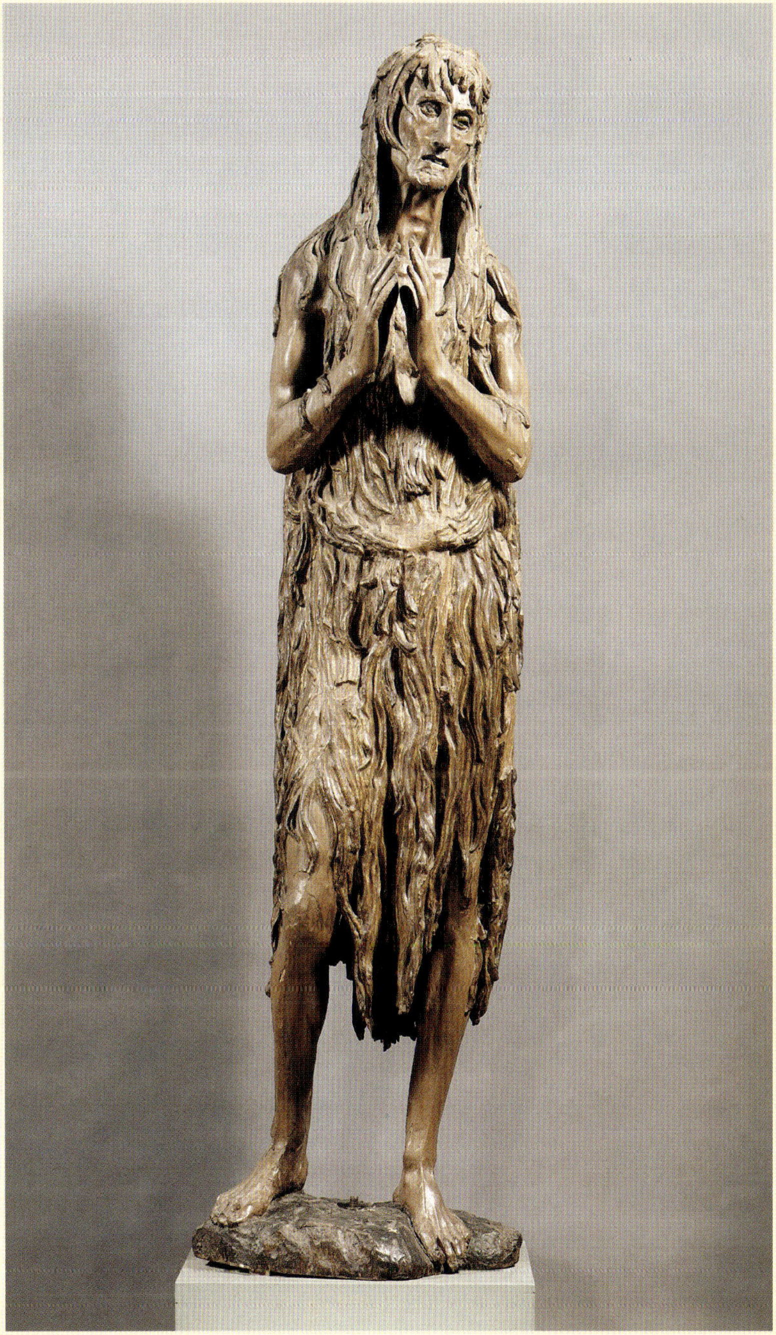

Donatello
(Firenze 1386 - 1466)

Mary Magdalene
Magdalena
Maria Magdalena

●●

c. 1353-1455
h. 188 cm / 74 in.
Museo dell'Opera del Duomo, Firenze

Wood / Holz / Hout

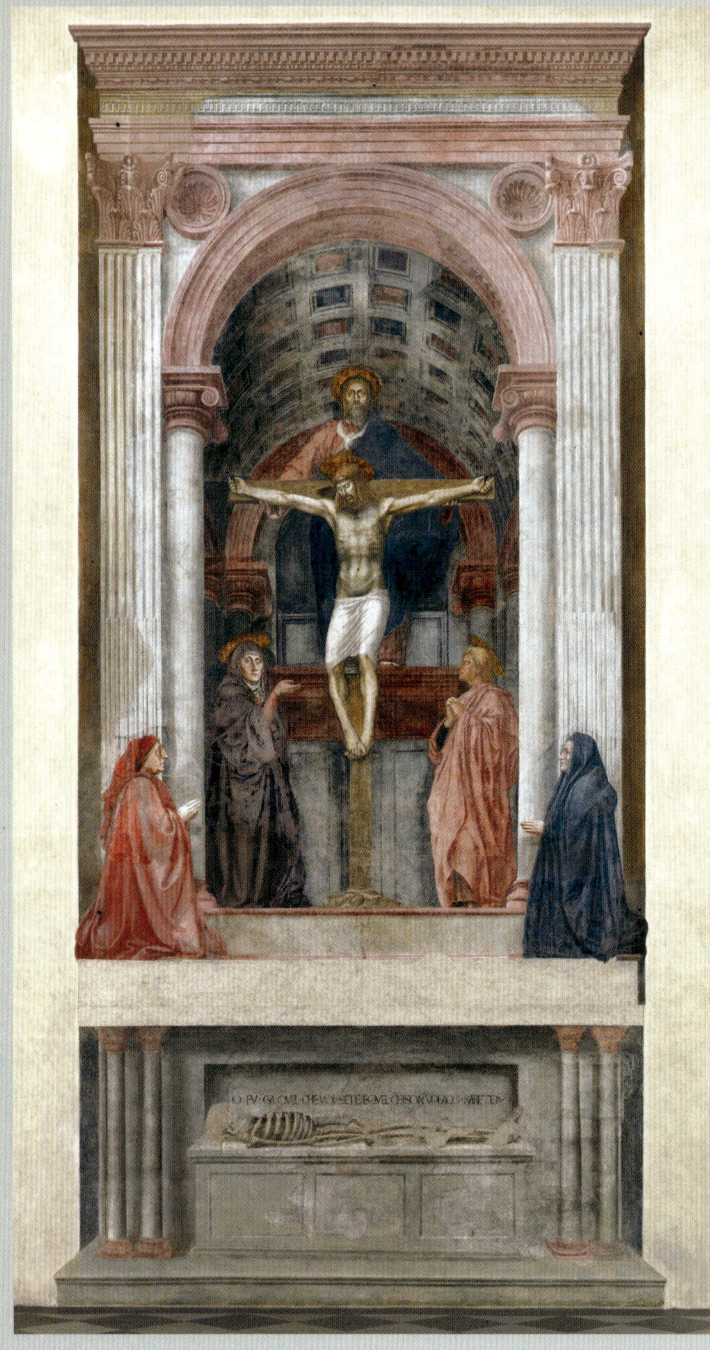

Masaccio created the illusion of space in the Trinity by means of perspective.

In Masaccios Trinität entsteht durch Perspektive ein illusionärer Raum.

In de Drie-eenheid van Masaccio wordt door het perspectief een denkbeeldige ruimte gecreëerd.

Masaccio
(San Giovanni Valdarno,
Arezzo 1401 - Roma 1428)

The Trinity
Die Trinität
De Heilige Drieëenheid

●●●

c. 1425-1427
667 x 317 cm
Santa Maria Novella, Firenze

Fresco / Fresko

Masaccio
(San Giovanni Valdarno,
Arezzo 1401 - Roma 1428)
Masolino
(Panicale, Perugia 1383 - ? c. 1440)

Madonna and Child with Saint Anne
Sant'Anna Metterza
Sint Anna te drieën

●●

1424
h. 174 cm / 68.5 in.
Galleria degli Uffizi, Firenze

Tempera on wood / Tempera auf Tafel
Tempera op paneel

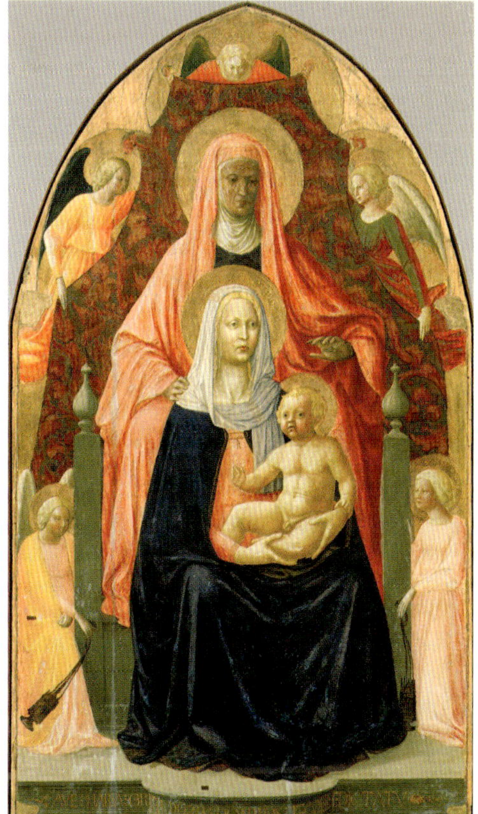

Masaccio
(San Giovanni Valdarno,
Arezzo 1401 - Roma 1428)

The Tribute Money
Der Tribut
De Cijnspenning

●●●

c. 1427
Santa Maria del Carmine,
Cappella Brancacci, Firenze

Fresco / Fresko

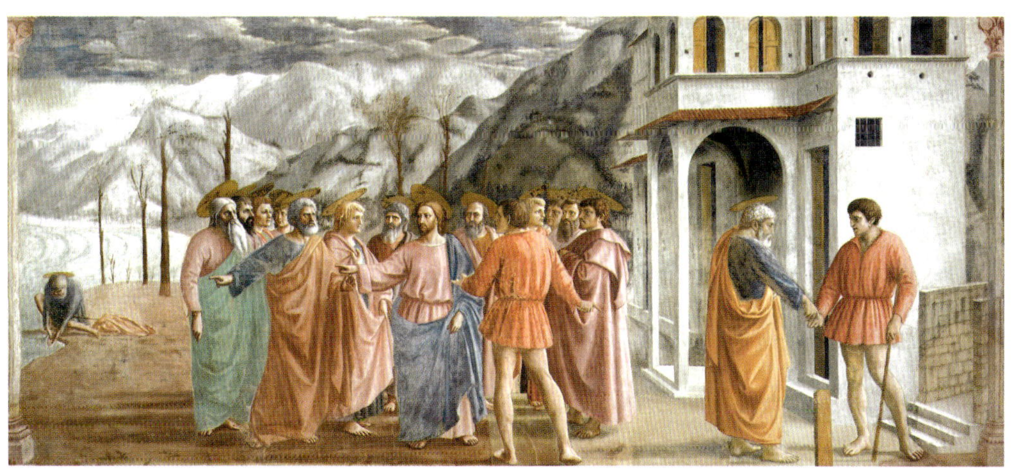

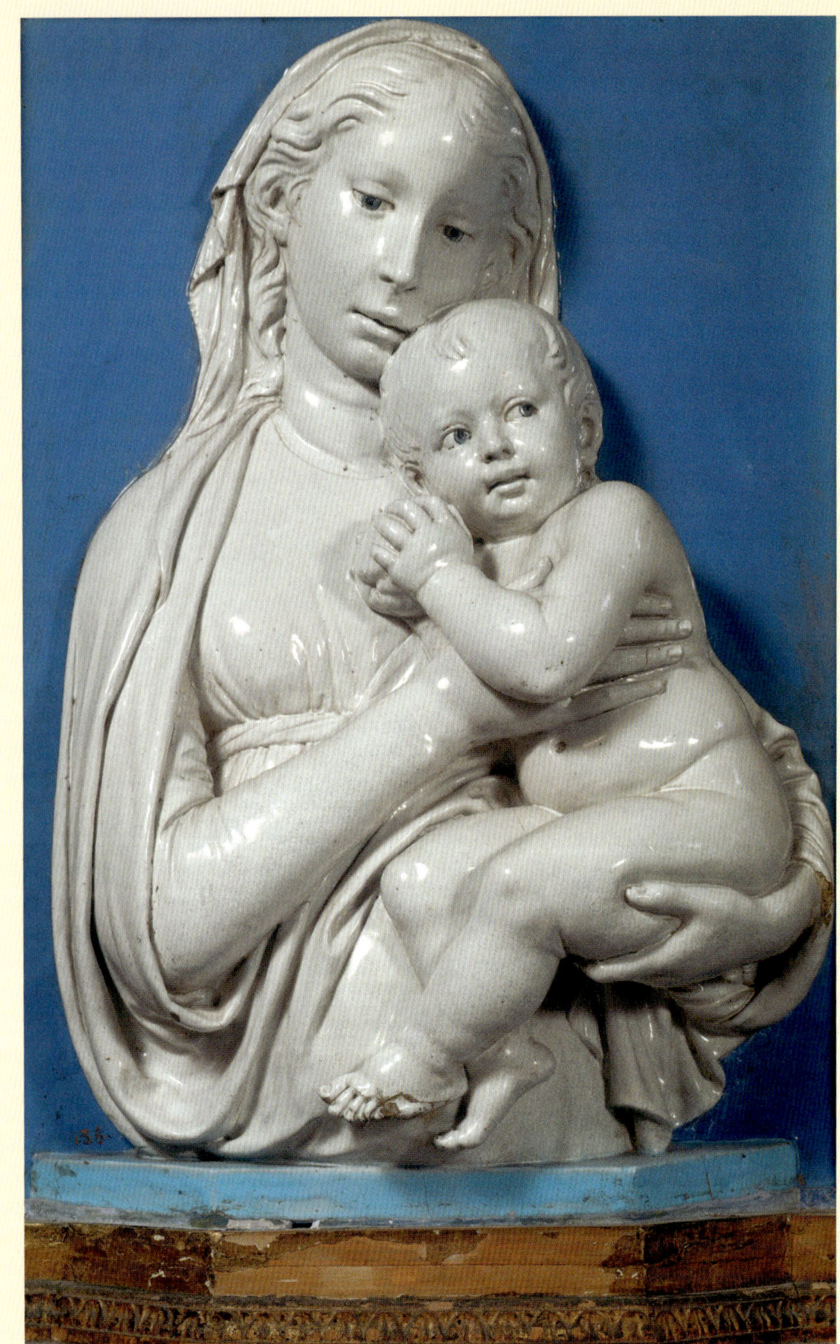

Coloured and glazed ceramics are known as majolicas.

Farbig glasierte Terrakotten bezeichnet man als Majolikas.

De gekleurde, geglazuurde terracotta wordt maiolica.

Luca della Robbia
(Firenze 1400 - 1482)

Madonna of the Apple
Madonna mit dem Apfel
Madonna met de Appel

●●

c. 1450
70 x 52 cm / 27.5 x 20.5 in.
Museo Nazionale del Bargello, Firenze

Glazed terracotta / Glasierte Terrakotta
Geglazuurd terracotta

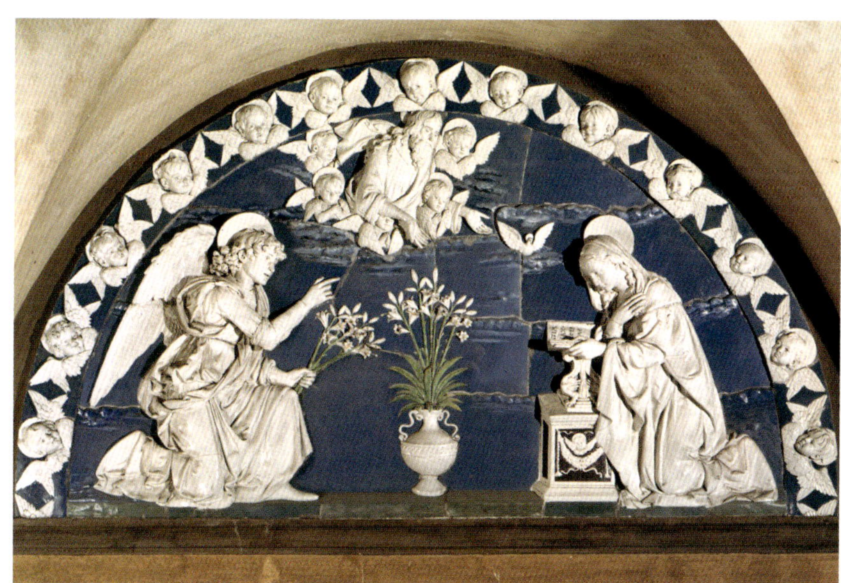

Andrea della Robbia
(Firenze 1435 - 1525)

Annunciation
Verkündigung
Annunciatie

●

*c.*1487
Museo dell'Ospedale degli Innocenti, Firenze

Glazed terracotta / Glasierte Terrakotta
Geglazuurd terracotta

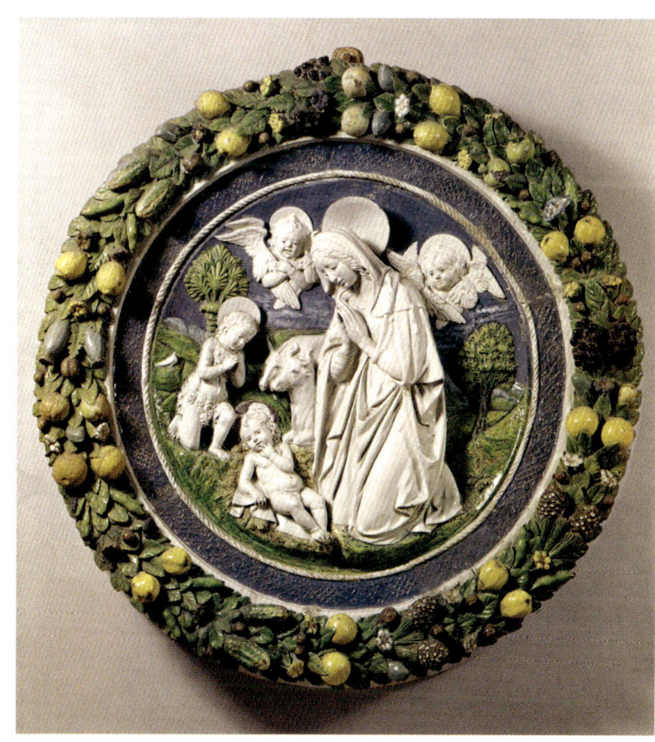

Giovanni della Robbia
(Firenze 1469 - 1529)

Nativity
Geburt Christi
Geboorte van Christus

●

c. 1521
Museo Nazionale del Bargello, Firenze

Glazed terracotta / Glasierte Terrakotta
Geglazuurd terracotta

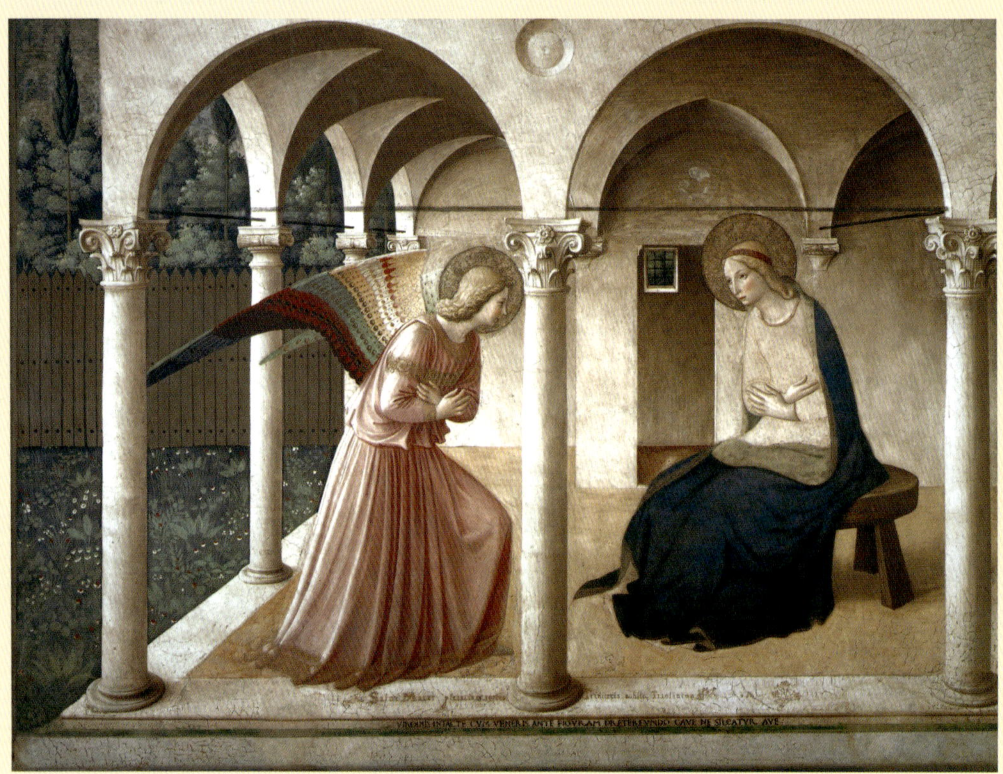

Beato Angelico
(Vicchio di Mugello, Firenze
c. 1396 - Roma 1455)

Annunciation
Verkündigung
Annunciatie

●●●

1435-1440
Museo di San Marco, Firenze

Fresco / Fresko

Fra (Beato) Angelico is considered a painter of outstanding talents (the blessed), still Gothic during the Renaissance.

Fra Angelico gilt als der begnadete (il beato) noch gotische Maler der Frührenaissance.

Fra' Beato Angelico wordt als een zeer getalenteerd (il beato) schilder beschouwd die nog in de gotische stijl van de Renaissance schildert.

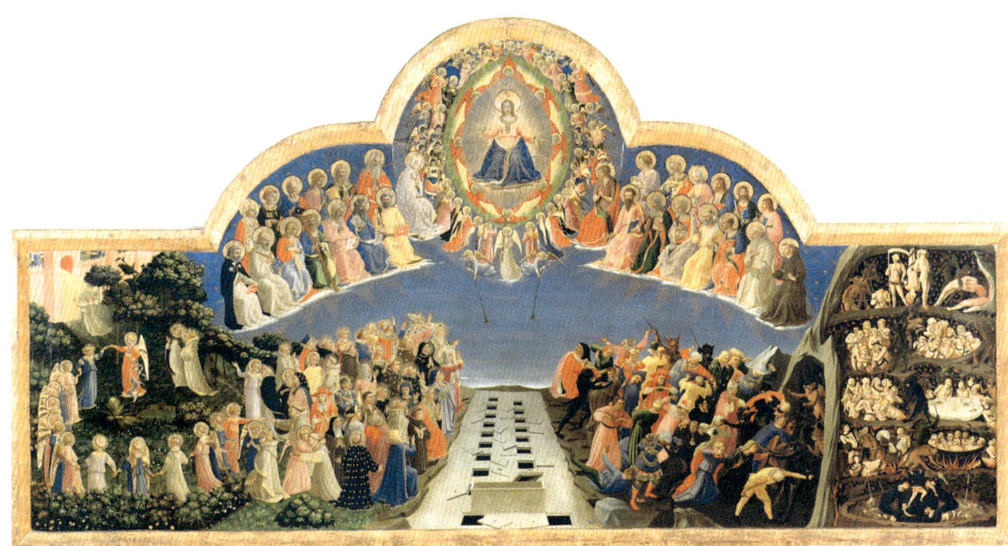

Beato Angelico
(Vicchio di Mugello, Firenze
c. 1396 - Roma 1455)

The Last Judgement
Jüngstes Gericht
Het Laatste Oordeel

●●

c. 1425-1430
105 x 210 cm / 41.3 x 82.7 in.
Museo di San Marco, Firenze

Tempera on wood
Tempera auf Tafel
Tempera op paneel

Beato Angelico
(Vicchio di Mugello, Firenze
c. 1396 - Roma 1455)

Deposition
Kreuzabnahme
Kruisafneming

●●

c. 1440
276 x 285 cm /
108.7 x 112.2 in.
Museo di San Marco,
Firenze

Tempera on wood
Tempera auf Tafel
Tempera op paneel

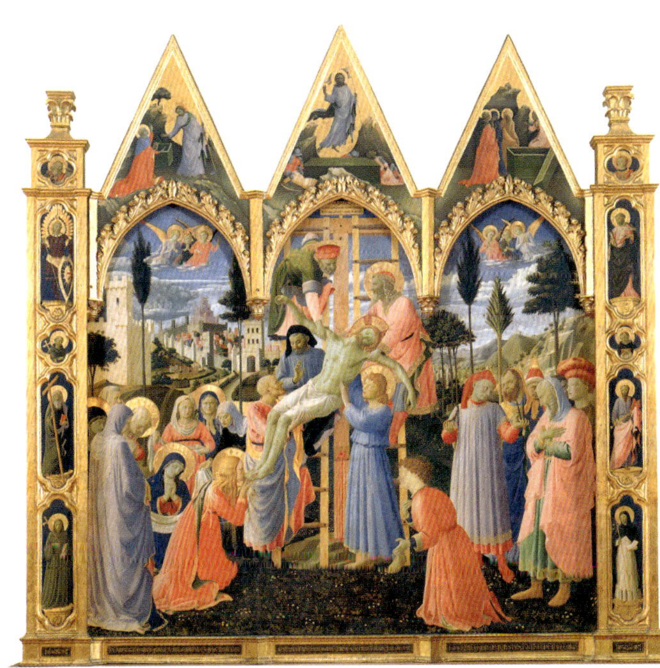

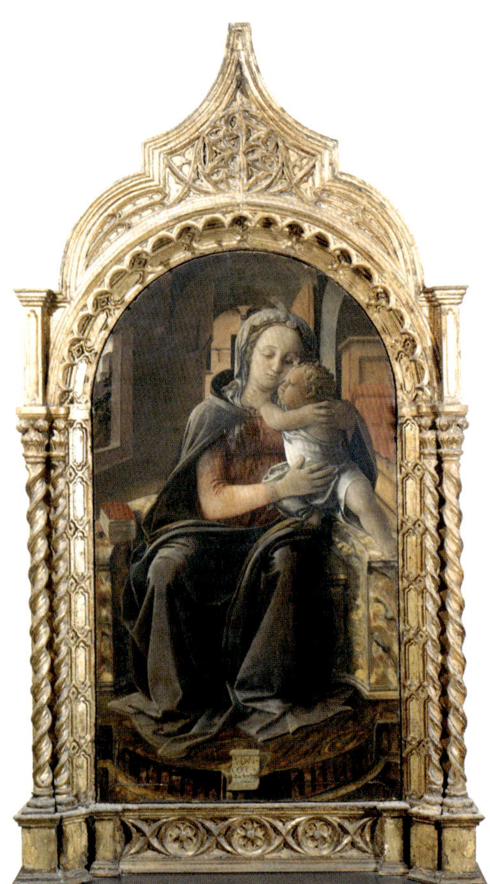

Filippo Lippi
(Firenze 1406 - Spoleto 1469)

Madonna di Tarquinia
Madonna von Tarquinia
Madonna van Tarquinia

●

1437
114 x 65 cm / 108.7 x 25.6 in.
Galleria Nazionale d'Arte Antica, Roma

Tempera on wood / Tempera auf Tafel
Tempera op paneel

Filippo Lippi
(Firenze 1406 - Spoleto 1469)

Virgin and Child
Madonna mit Kind
Madonna met Kind

●

1452
Ø 135 cm / 53.1 in.
Galleria Palatina, Firenze

Tempera on wood
Tempera auf Tafel
Tempera op paneel

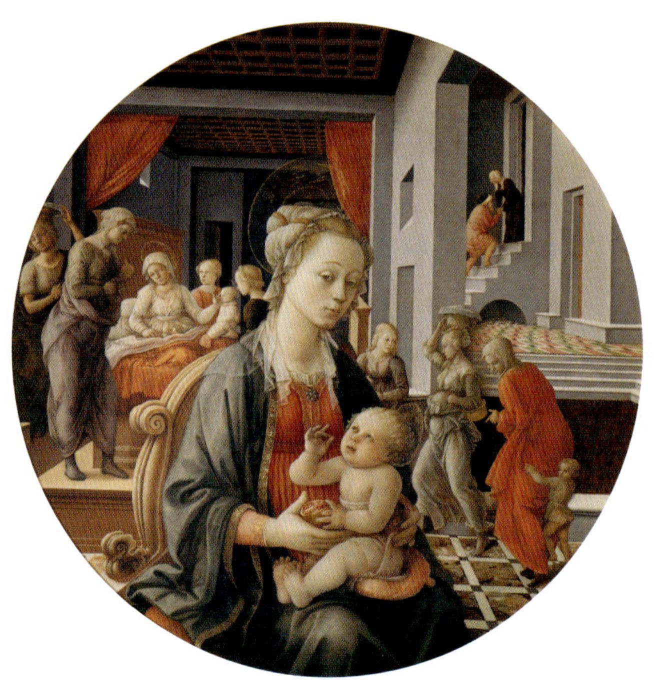

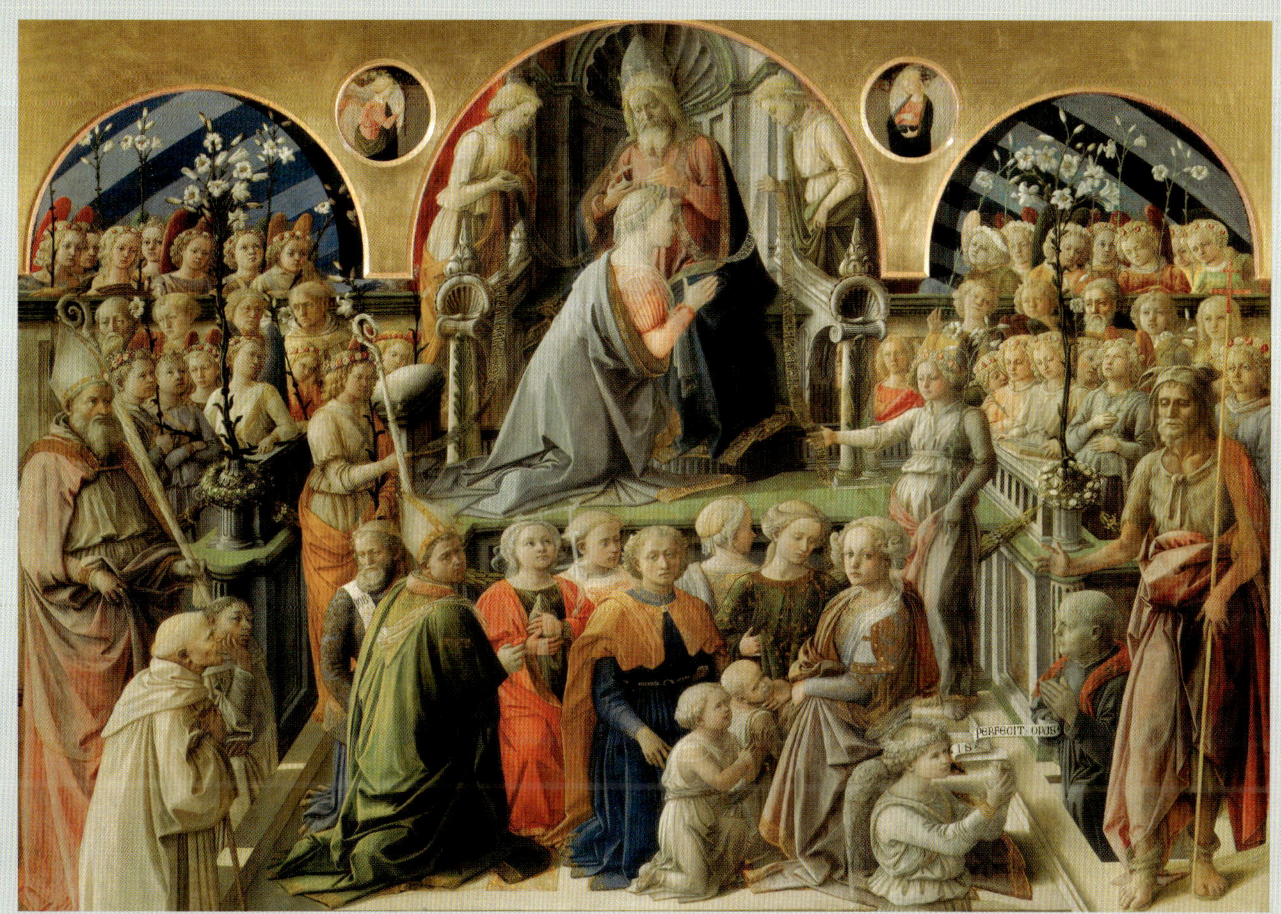

Filippo Lippi
(Firenze 1406 - Spoleto 1469)

Coronation of the Virgin
Krönung der Jungfrau
Kroning van de Maagd

●●

c. 1441-1445
200 x 287 cm / 78.7 x 113
Galleria degli Uffizi, Firenze

Tempera on wood / Tempera auf Tafel / Tempera op paneel

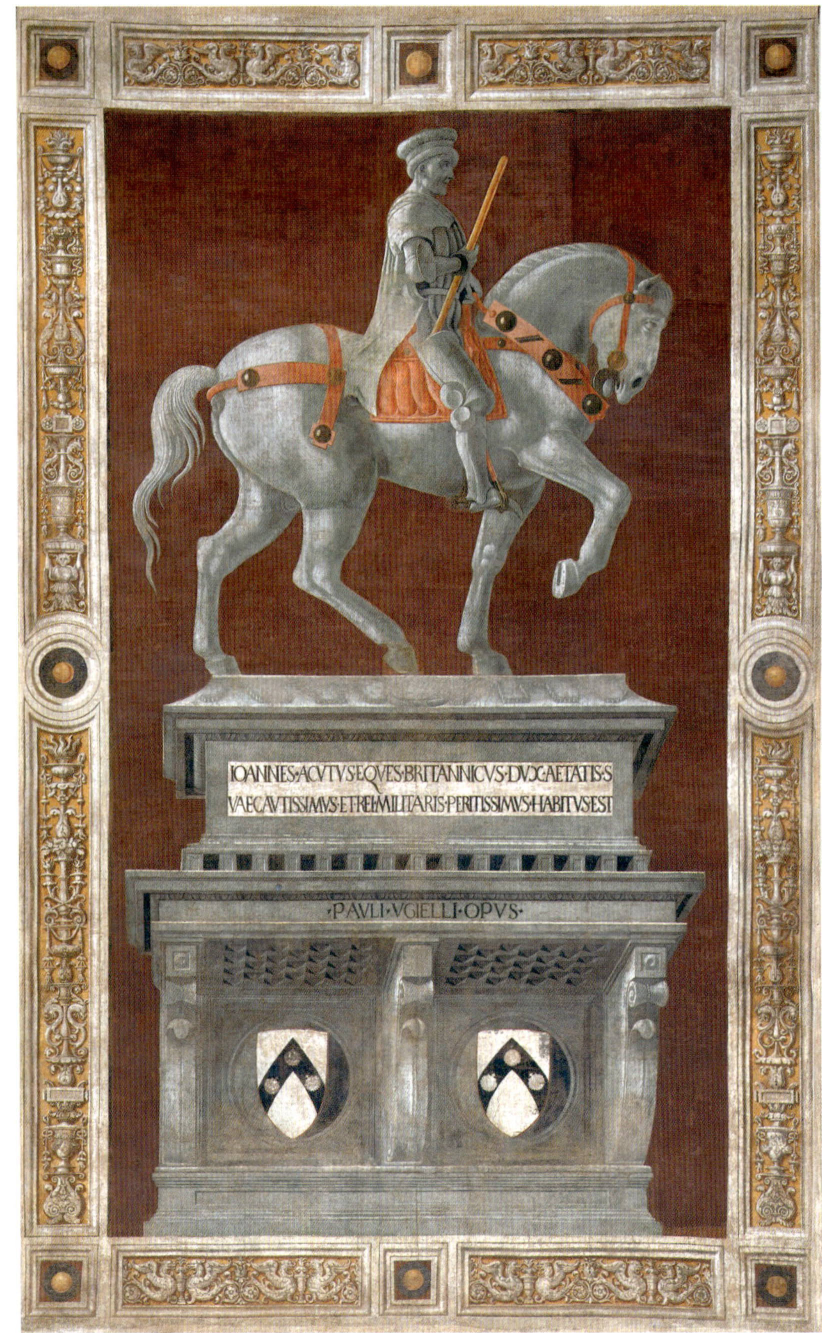

Paolo Uccello is the first to introduce multiple vanishing points in perspectives.

Bei Paolo Uccello erhält die Perspektive erstmals mehrere Fluchtpunkte.

Met Paolo Uccello krijgt het perspectief voor de eerste keer meerdere vluchtpunten.

Paolo Uccello
(Firenze 1397 - 1475)

Equestrian Monument to Sir John Hawkwood
Denkmal für Giovanni Acuto
Mounument voor John Hawkwood

●●

1436
820 x 515 cm / 322.8 x 202.7 in.
Santa Maria del Fiore, Firenze

Fresco transposed to canvas
Fresko, auf Leinwand aufgetragen
Fresco overgebracht op doek

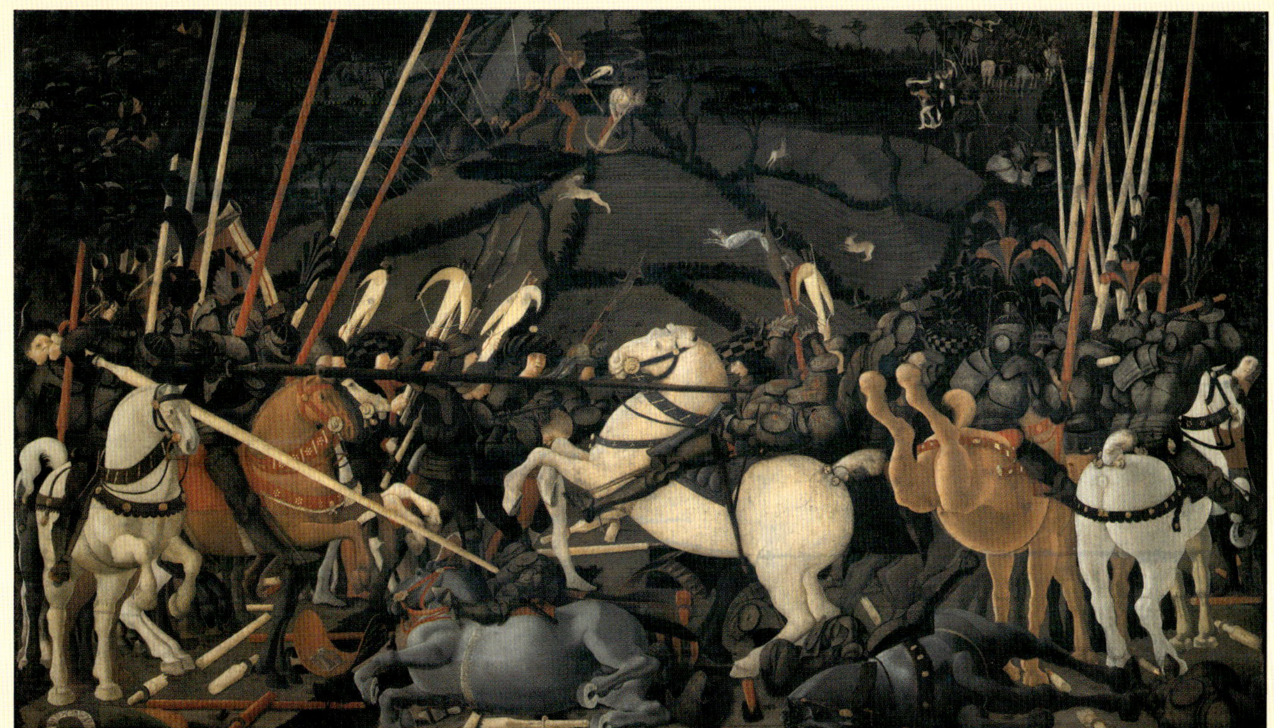

Paolo Uccello
(Firenze 1397 - 1475)

The Battle of San Romano
Die Schlacht zu San Romano
De Slag bij San Romano

●●●

c. 1438
182 x 323 cm / 71.6 x 127.2 in.
Galleria degli Uffizi, Firenze

Tempera on wood / Tempera auf Tafel
Tempera op paneel

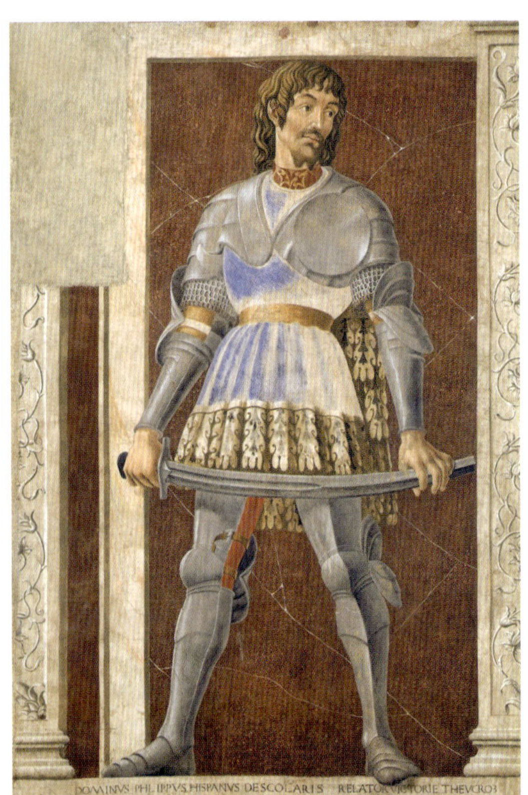

Andrea del Castagno
(Castagno, Firenze *c.* 1421 - Firenze 1457)

Pippo Spano

●

c. 1448
Galleria degli Uffizi, Firenze

Fresco transposed to canvas
Abgelöstes Fresko / Losgemaakt fresco

Andrea del Castagno
(Castagno, Firenze *c.* 1421 - Firenze 1457)

Last Supper
Letztes Abendmahl
Het Laatste Avondmaal

●●

c. 1445-1450
Cenacolo di Sant'Apollonia, Firenze

Fresco / Fresko

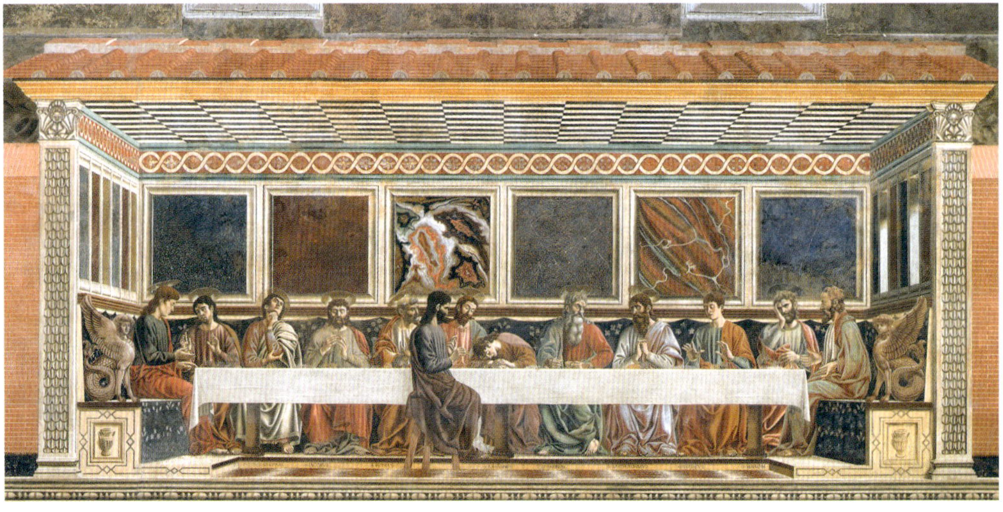

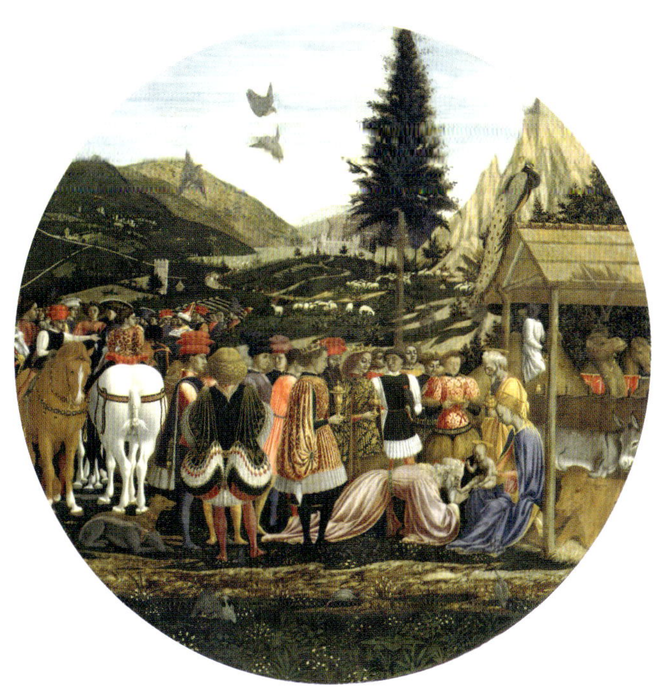

Domenico Veneziano
(Venezia *c.* 1406 - Firenze 1461)

Adoration of the Magi
Anbetung der Könige
Aanbidding der Wijzen

●

1439-1441
Ø 84 cm / 33 in.
Gemäldegalerie, Staatliche Museen, Berlin

Tempera on wood / Tempera auf Tafel / Tempera op paneel

Domenico Veneziano
(Venezia *c.* 1406 - Firenze 1461)

Altarpiece of Santa Lucia dei Magnoli
Altarbild von Santa Lucia dei Magnoli
Altaarstuk van Santa Lucia dei Magnoli

●●

c. 1445-1447
209 x 216 cm / 82.3 x 85 in.
Galleria degli Uffizi, Firenze

Tempera on wood / Tempera auf Tafel / Tempera op paneel

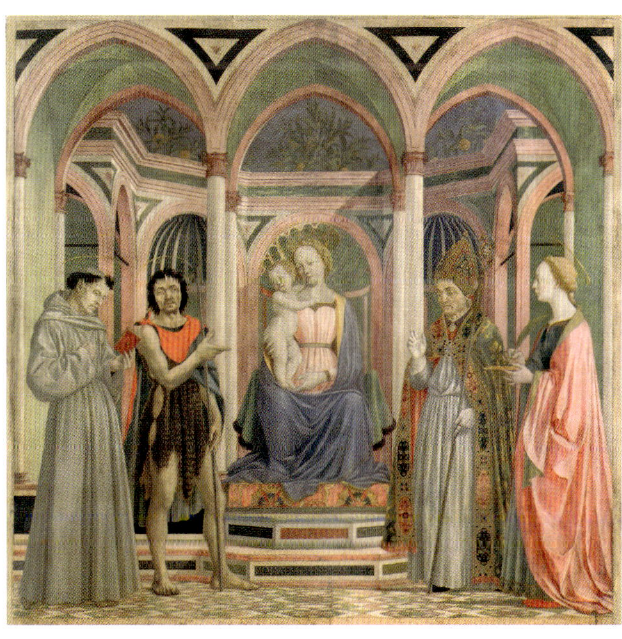

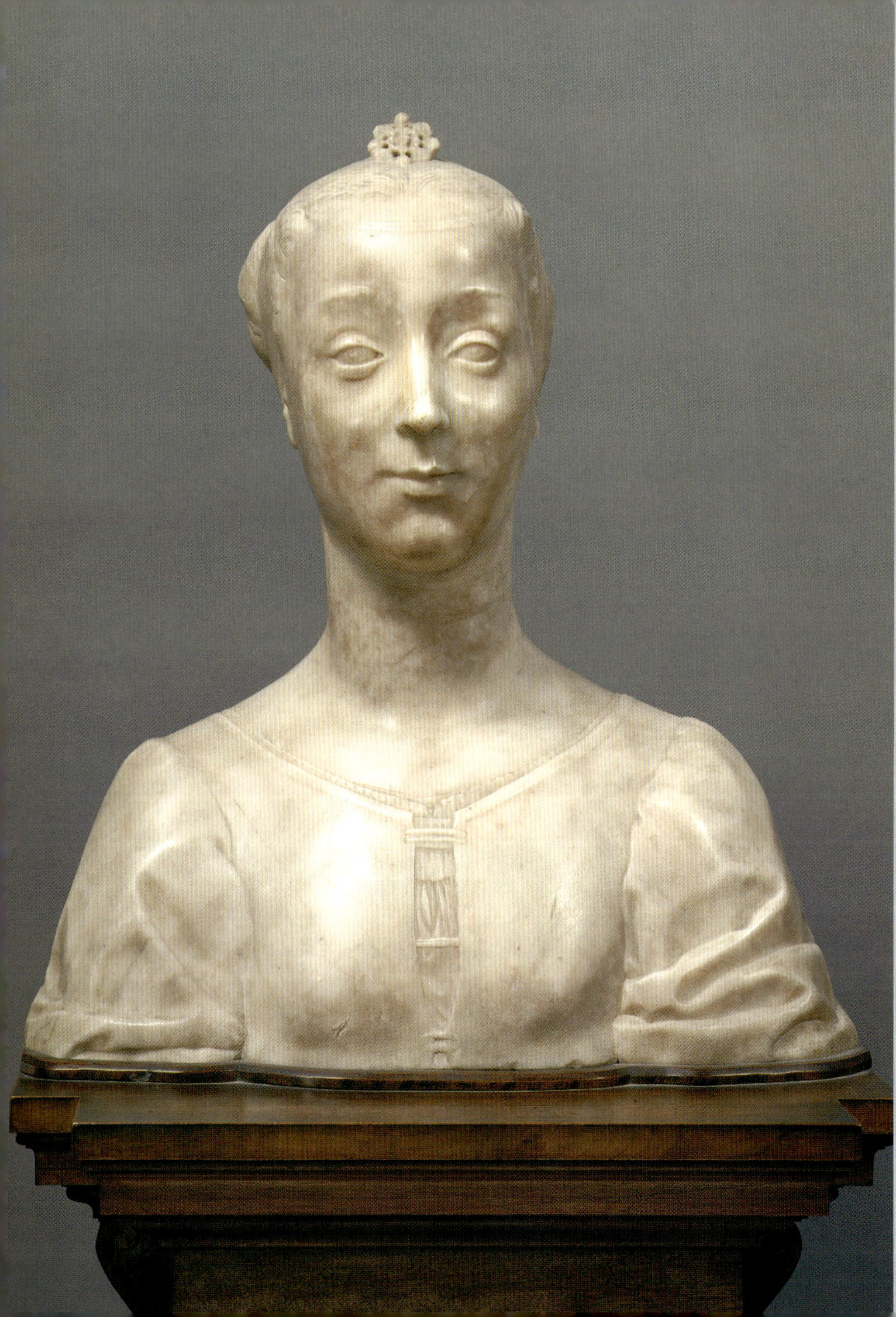

Desiderio
da Settignano
(Settignano, Firenze *c.* 1428 -
Firenze 1464)

Bust of a Lady
Büste einer Edelfrau
Buste van een edelvrouw

1460
Museo Nazionale
del Bargello,
Firenze

Marble / Marmor / Marmer

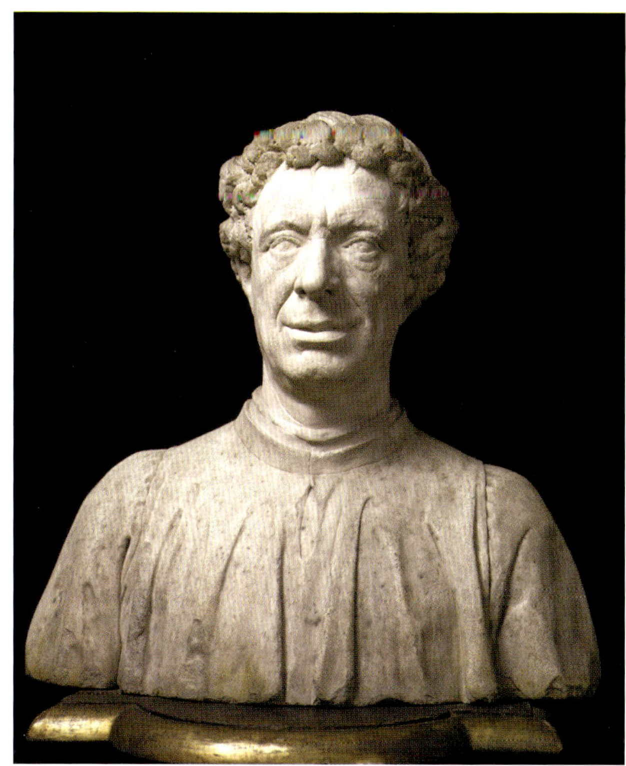

Antonio Rossellino
(Settignano, Firenze 1427 - Firenze 1479)

Bust of Matteo Palmieri
Büste von Matteo Palmieri
Buste van Matteo Palmicri

●

1468
Museo Nazionale del Bargello, Firenze

Marble / Marmor / Marmer

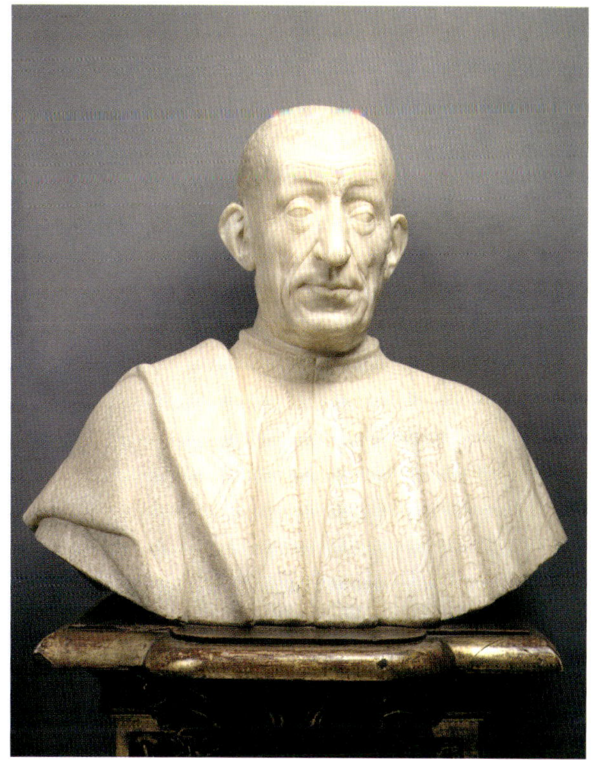

Benedetto da Maiano
(Maiano, Firenze 1442 - Firenze 1497)

Bust of Piero Mellini
Büste von Piero Mellini
Buste van Piero Mellini

c. 1470
h. 55 cm / 21.6 in.
Museo Nazionale del Bargello, Firenze

Marble / Marmor / Marmer

Piero della Francesca experiments with the force of natural light.

Piero della Francesca experimentiert mit der Kraft des natürlichen Lichts.

Piero della Francesca experimenteert met de kracht van het natuurlijk licht.

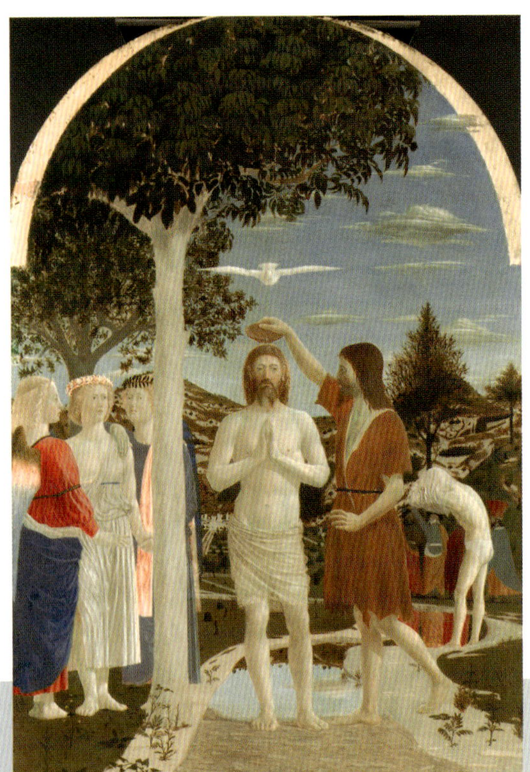

Piero della Francesca
(Borgo San Sepolcro, Arezzo *c.* 1420 - 1492)

Baptism of Christ
Christi Taufe
Doop van Christus

●●●

c. 1448-1450
167 x 116 cm / 65.7 x 45.7 in.
The National Gallery, London

Tempera on wood
Tempera auf Tafel
Tempera op paneel

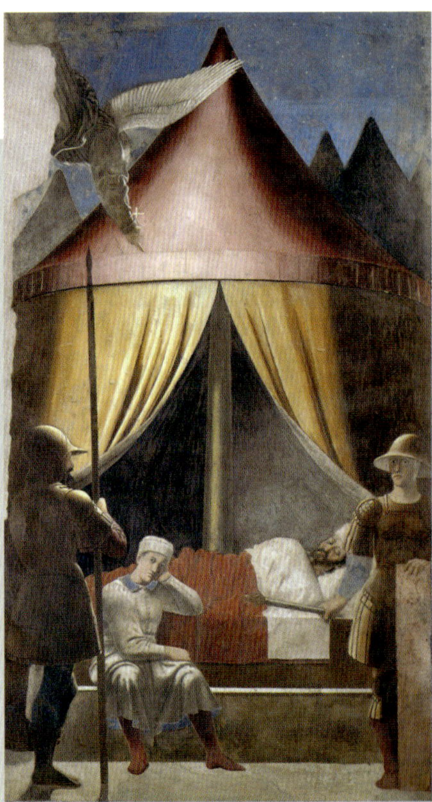

Piero della Francesca
(Borgo San Sepolcro, Arezzo *c.* 1420 - 1492)

Legend of the True Cross: Constantine's Dream
Geschichten vom Kreuz: Traum des Konstantin
Legende van het Ware Kruis: droom van Keizer Constantijn

●●●

c. 1452-1466
San Francesco, Arezzo

Fresco / Fresko

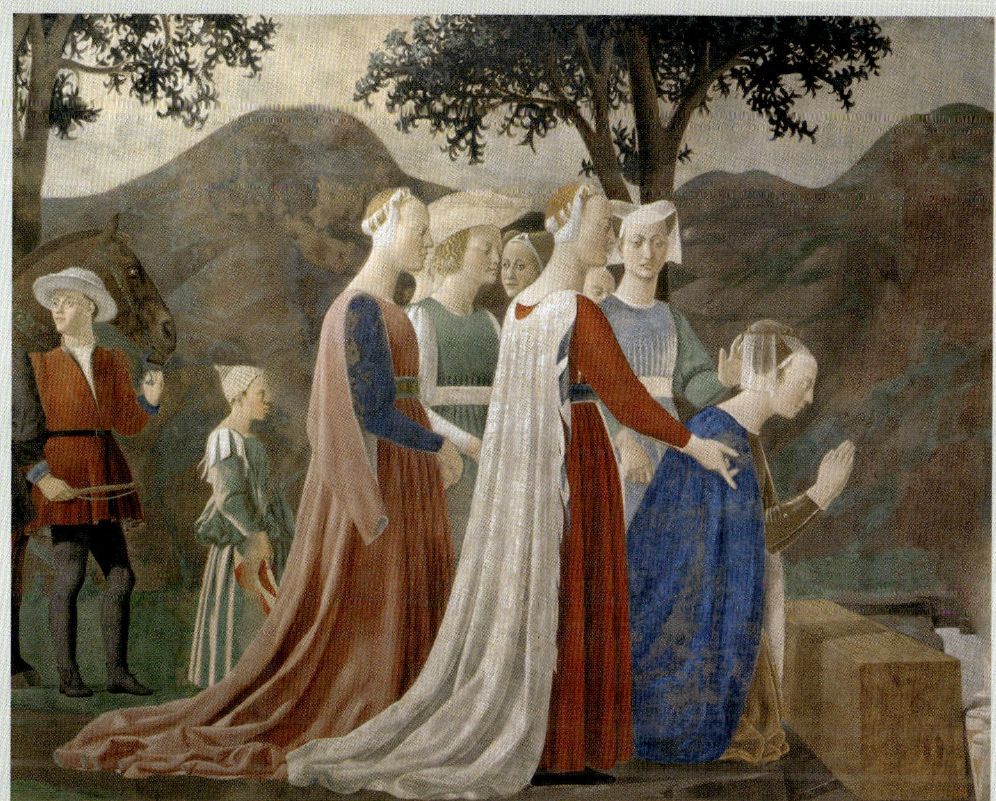

Piero della Francesca
(Borgo San Sepolcro, Arezzo *c.* 1420 - 1492)

Legend of the True Cross: Adoration of the Holy Wood by the Queen of Sheba
Geschichten vom Kreuz: Anbetung des heiligen Holzes durch die Königin von Saba
Legende van het Ware Kruis: aanbidding van het kruishout van de koningin van Sheba

●●

c. 1452-1466
San Francesco, Arezzo

Fresco / Fresko

▸▸

Piero della Francesca
(Borgo San Sepolcro, Arezzo *c.* 1420 - 1492)

Legend of the True Cross: Battle of Heraclius and Khosrau
Die Legende des wahren Kreuzes: Schlacht zwischen Herakleios und Chosroes
Legende van het Heilige Kruis: Strijd van Heraclius en Chosro

●●●

1452-1460
329 x 747 cm / 129.5 x 294.1 in.
San Francesco, Arezzo

Fresco / Fresko

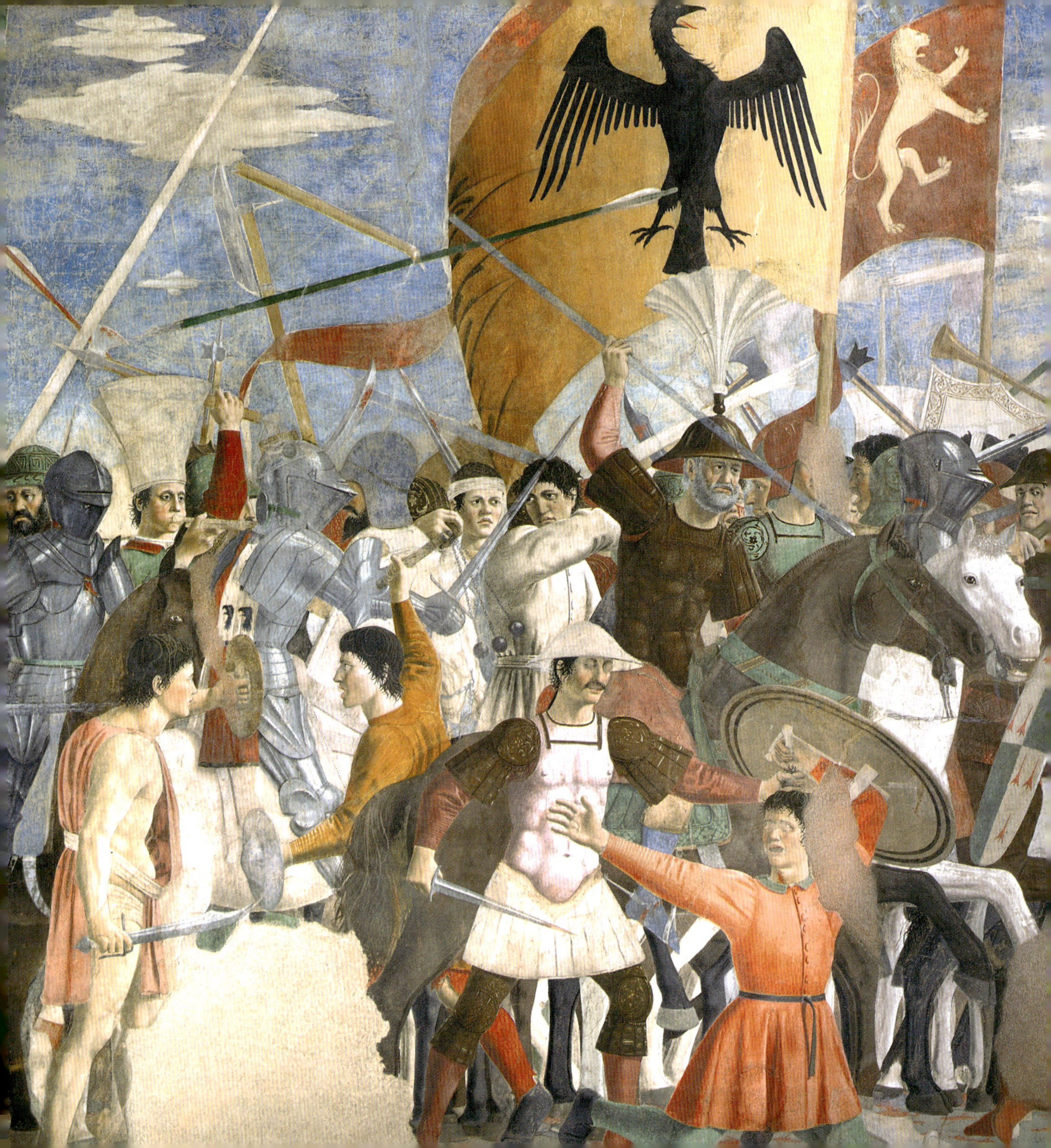

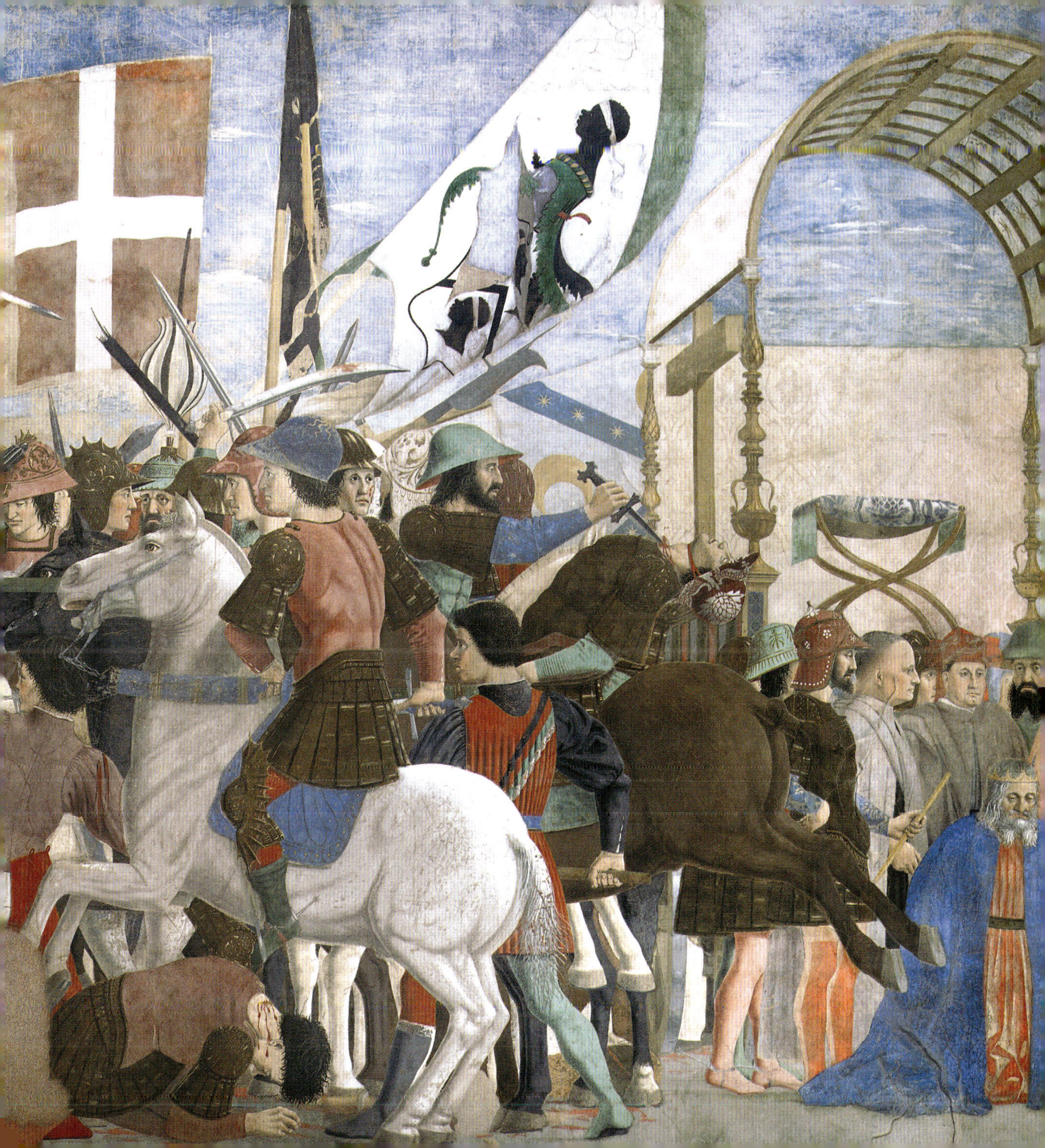

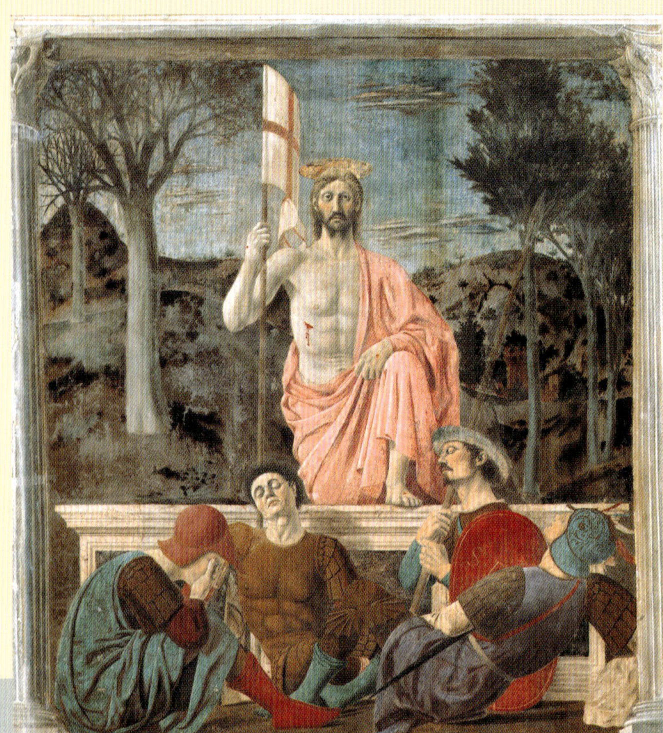

Piero della Francesca
(Borgo San Sepolcro, Arezzo *c.* 1420 - 1492)

Resurrection
Auferstehung
De Opstanding van Christus

●●●

1463-1465
Museo Civico, Sansepolcro

Fresco / Fresko

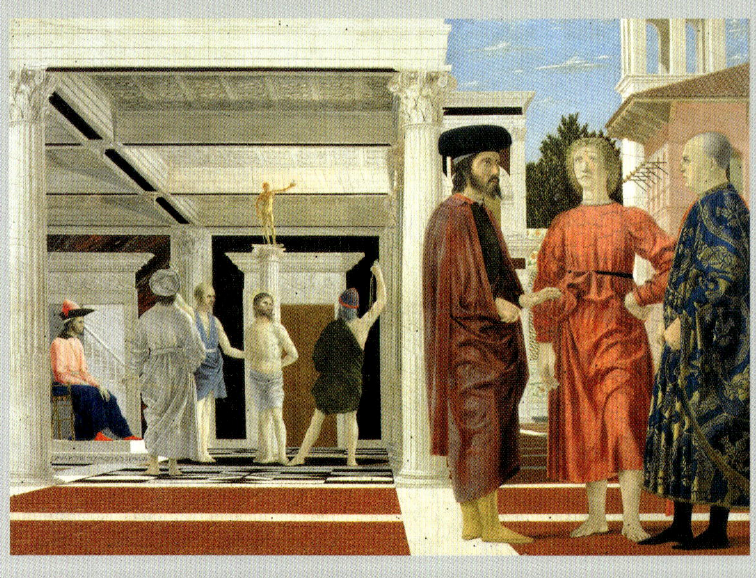

Piero della Francesca
(Borgo San Sepolcro, Arezzo *c.* 1420 - 1492)

The Flagellation
Geißelung
De Geseling

●●●

c. 1460
59 x 81,5 cm / 23.2 x 32 in.
Galleria Nazionale delle Marche, Urbino

Tempera on wood / Tempera auf Tafel
Tempera op paneel

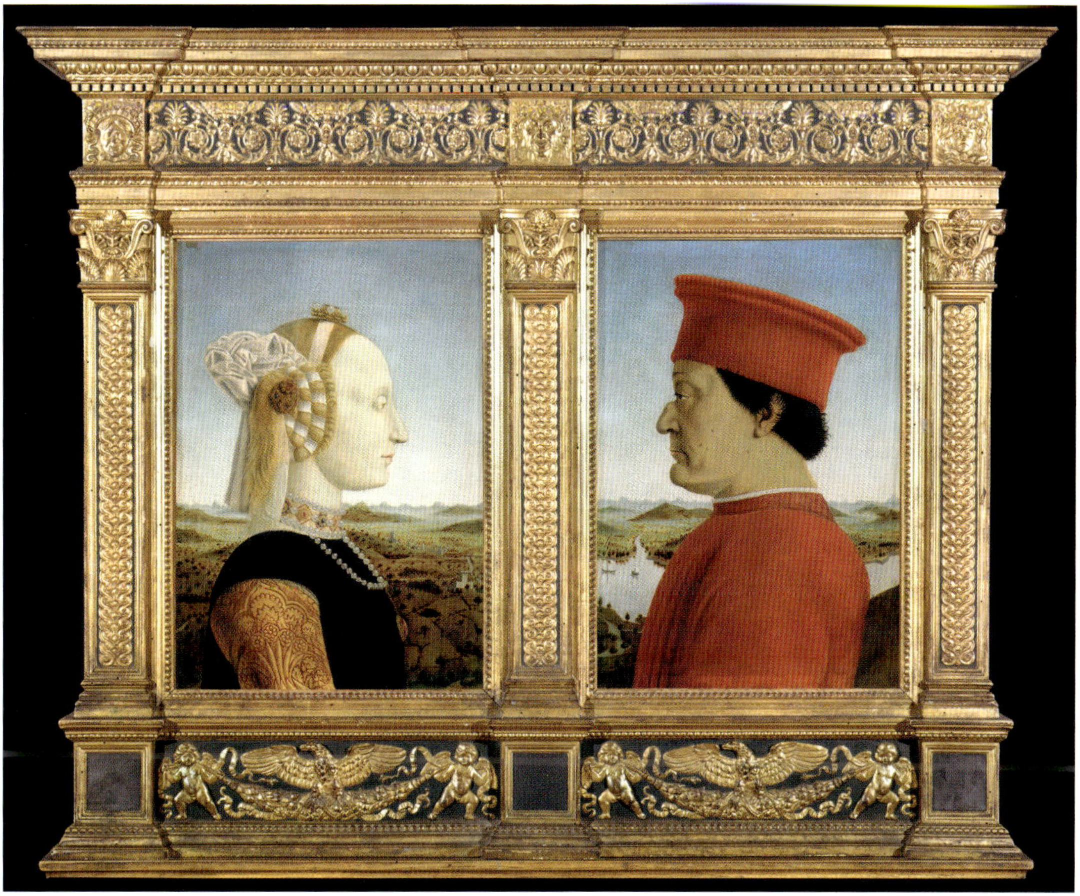

Piero della Francesca
(Borgo San Sepolcro, Arezzo *c.* 1420 - 1492)

**Portrait of Federico da Montefeltro,
Duke of Urbino, and his Wife Battista Sforza
Bildnis der Herzöge von Urbino
Portretten van de hertogen van Urbino**

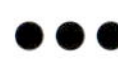

c. 1465
47 x 33 cm / 18.5 x 13 in. each
Galleria degli Uffizi, Firenze

Tempera on wood / Tempera auf Tafel / Tempera op paneel

The Ideal City
Die ideale Stadt
De ideale stad

●●●

c. 1470
60 x 200 cm / 23.6 x 78.7 in.
Galleria Nazionale delle Marche, Urbino

Tempera on wood / Tempera auf Tafel
Tempera op paneel

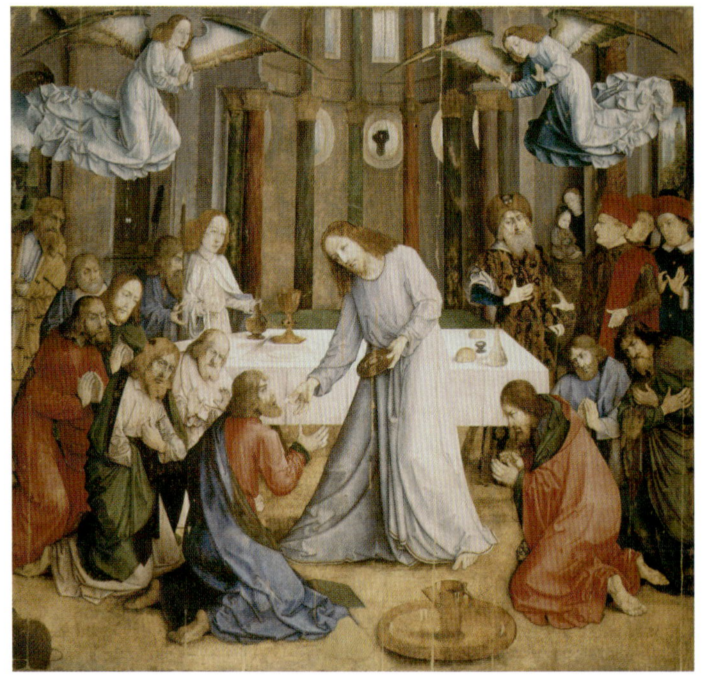

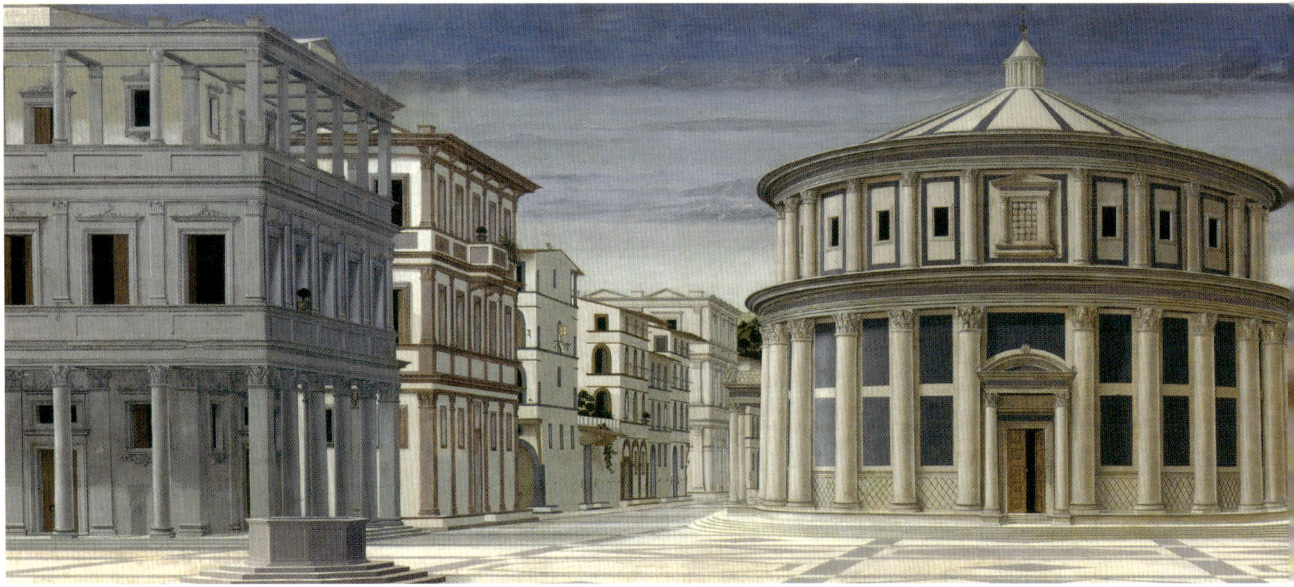

◂ Giusto di Gand
(? *c.* 1430 - ? *c.* 1480)

Communion of the Apostles
Kommunion der Apostel
Communie van de Apostelen

●

c. 1473-1474
288 x 321 cm / 113.4 x 126.4 in.
Galleria Nazionale delle Marche, Urbino

Panel / Tafel / Paneel

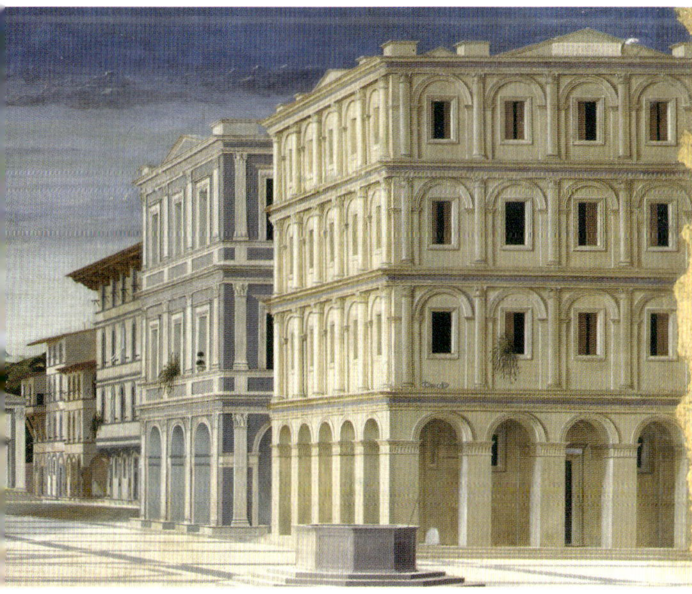

Pedro Berruguete
(Paredes de Nava *c.* 1450 - Avila *c.* 1504)

Federico da Montefeltro

●

c. 1476-1477
134,5 x 75,5 cm / 52.8 x 29.7 in.
Galleria Nazionale delle Marche, Urbino

Oil on wood / Öl auf Tafel
Olieverf op paneel

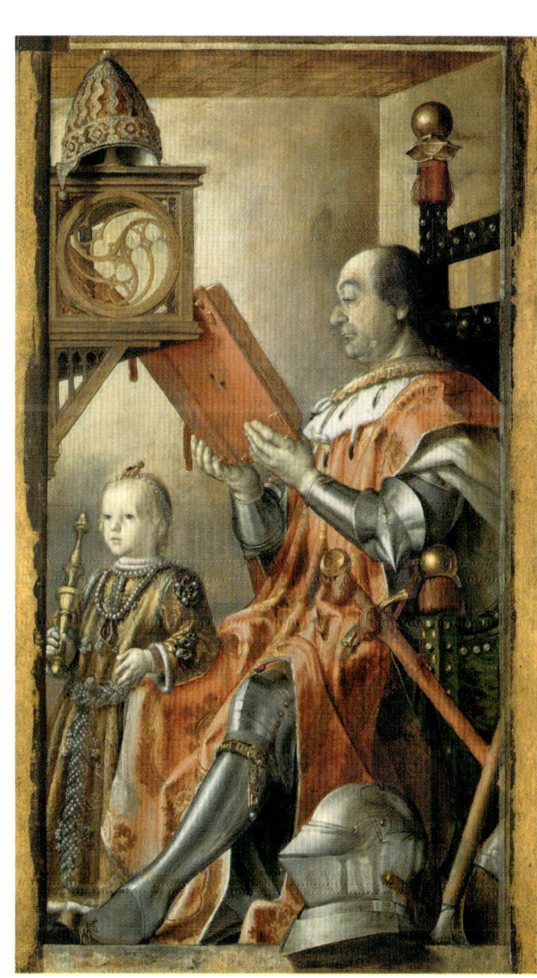

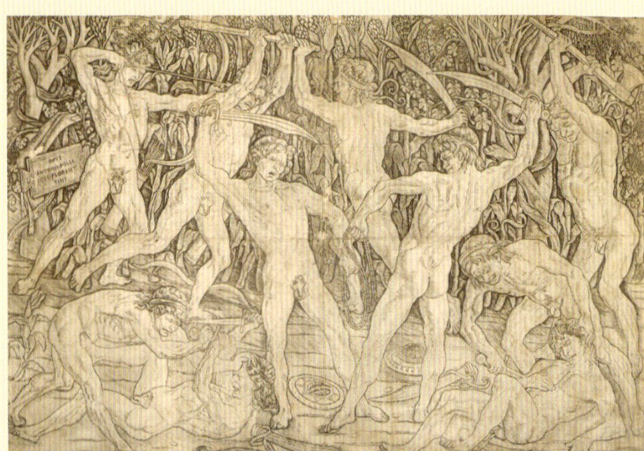

Antonio Pollaiolo
(Firenze *c.* 1431 - Roma 1498)

Battle of the Nudes
Schlacht der Nackten
Strijd der tien naakten

●

c. 1470
40,5 x 58,5 cm / 16 x 23 in.
Galleria degli Uffizi, Gabinetto dei Disegni e delle Stampe, Firenze

Burin engraving / Gravierung
Gravure met graveernaald

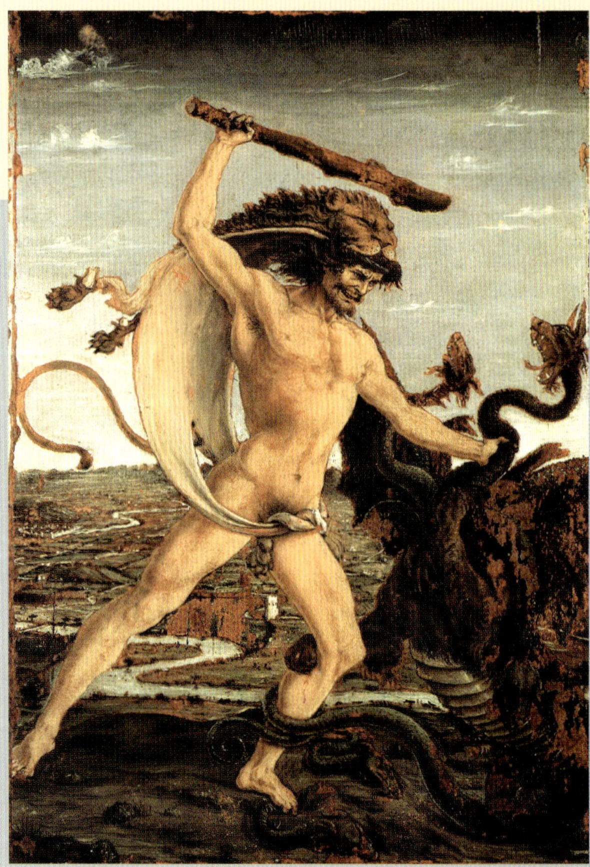

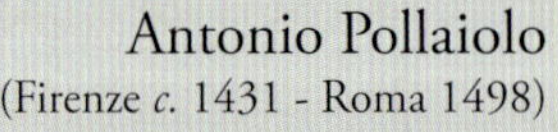

Antonio Pollaiolo
(Firenze *c.* 1431 - Roma 1498)

Hercules and the Hydra
Herkules und Hydra
Herakles en de Hydra

●●

c. 1460-1475
17 x 12 cm / 6.7 x 4.7 in.
Galleria degli Uffizi, Firenze

Wood panel / Tafel / Paneel

Antonio Pollaiolo
(Firenze *c.* 1431 - Roma 1498)

Hercules and Antaeus
Herkules und Antheo
Herakles en Antaios

●

c. 1475
h. 45 cm / 17.7 in.
Museo Nazionale del Bargello, Firenze

Bronze / Brons

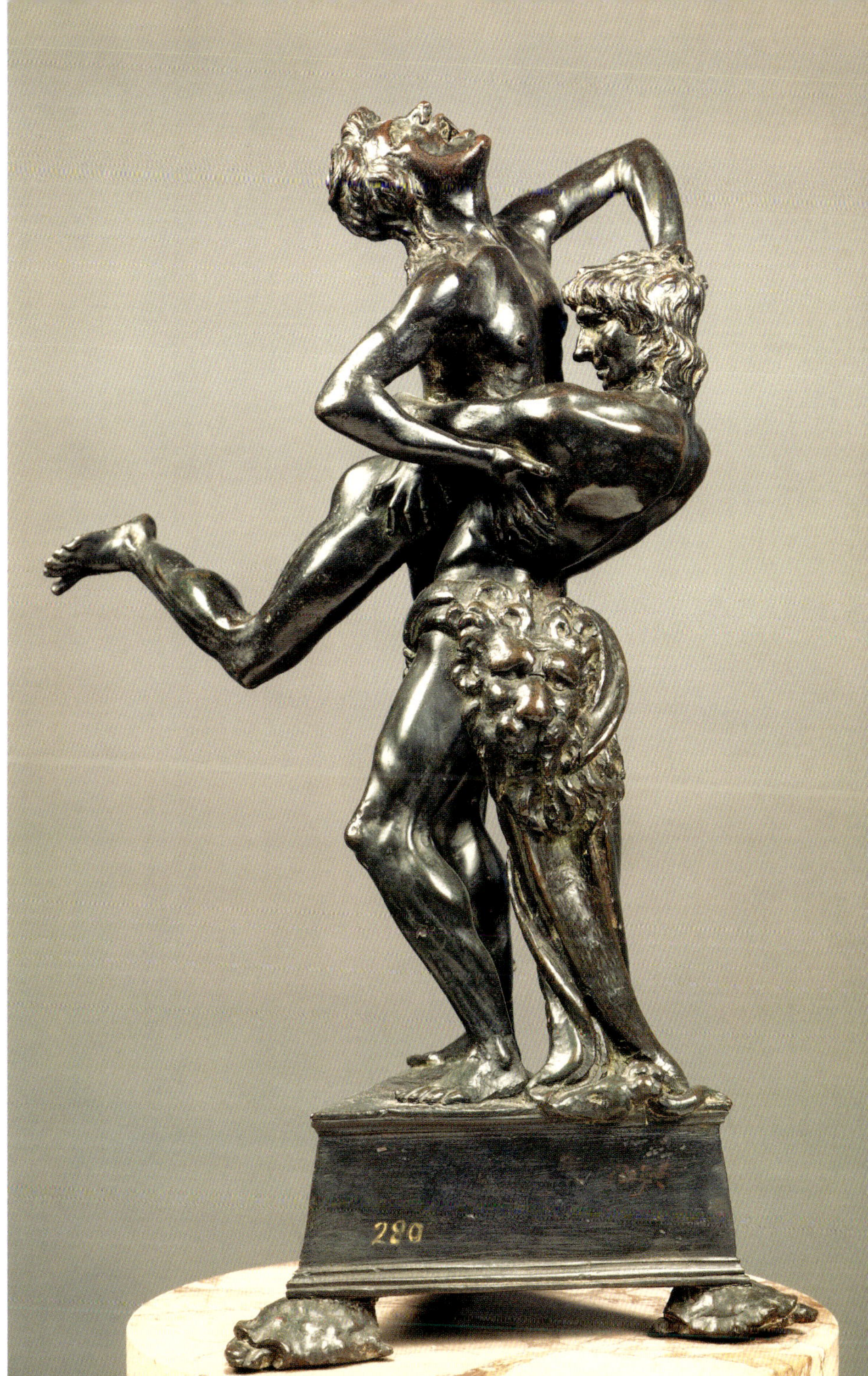

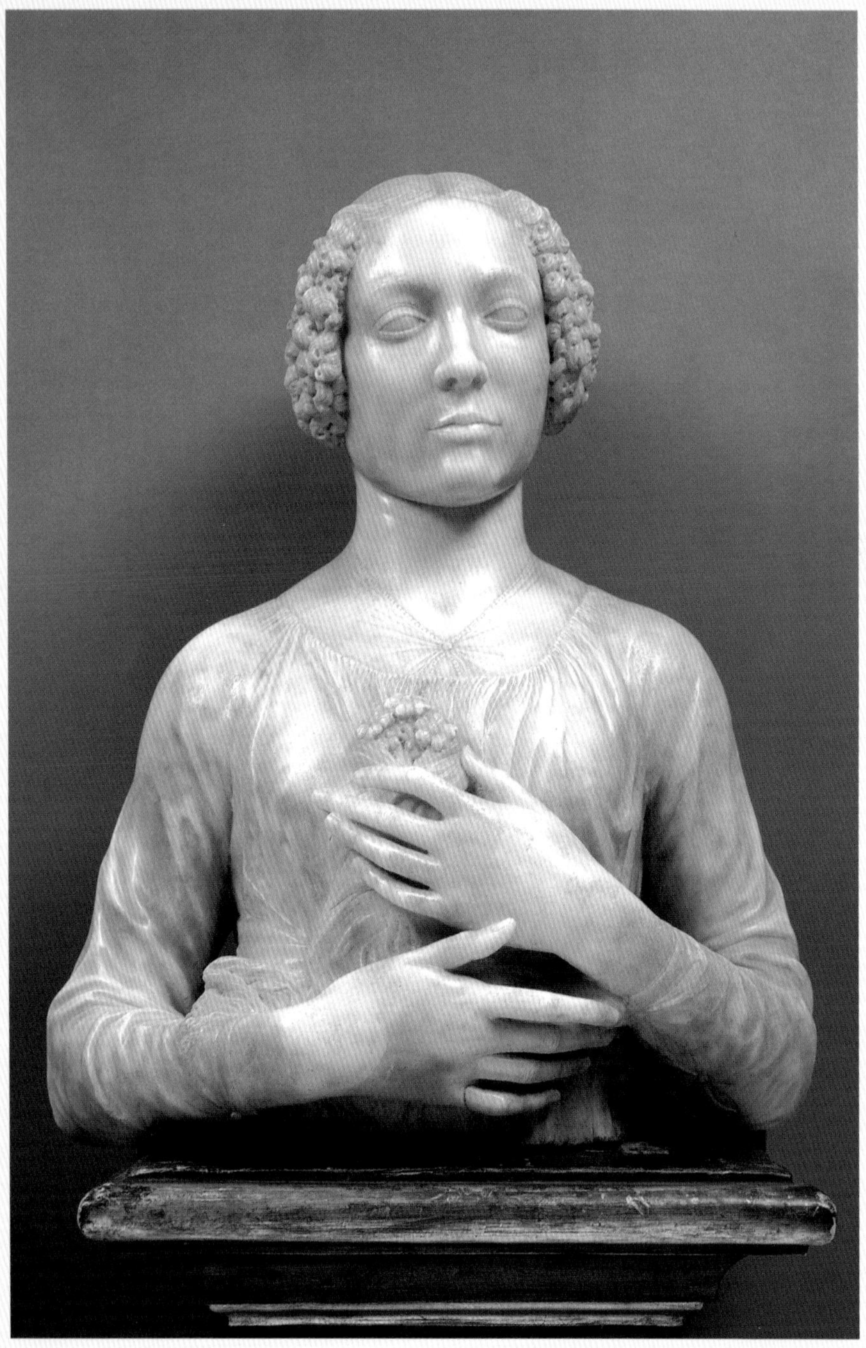

Andrea Verrocchio is the illustrious master of Leonardo da Vinci.

Andrea Verrochio ist wichtiger Lehrmeister Leonardo Da Vincis.

Andrea Verrocchio is de beroemde leermeester van Leonardo Da Vinci.

Andrea Verrocchio
(Firenze *c.* 1435 - Venezia 1488)

Lady with a Bouquet
Dame mit Blumenstrauß
Vrouw met bloemen in de hand

●●

c. 1475
h. 61 cm / 24 in.
Museo Nazionale del Bargello, Firenze

Marble / Marmor / Marmer

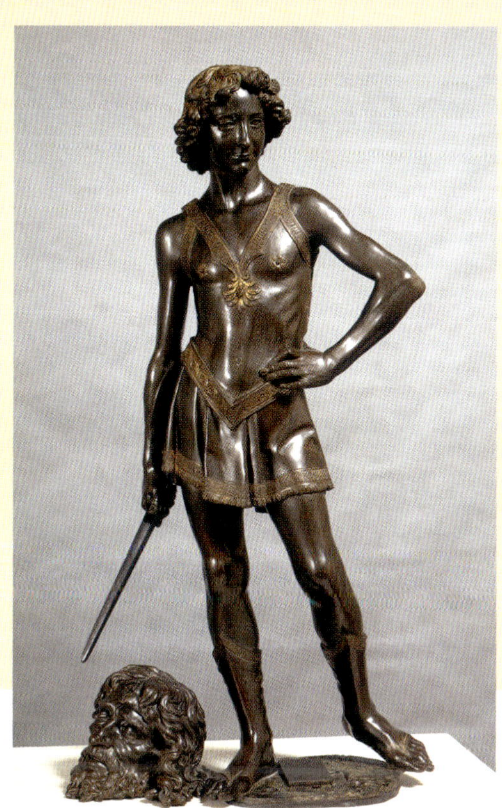

Andrea Verrocchio
(Firenze *c.* 1435 - Venezia 1488)

David

●●

c. 1466
126 cm / 49.6 in.
Museo Nazionale del Bargello, Firenze

Bronze / Brons

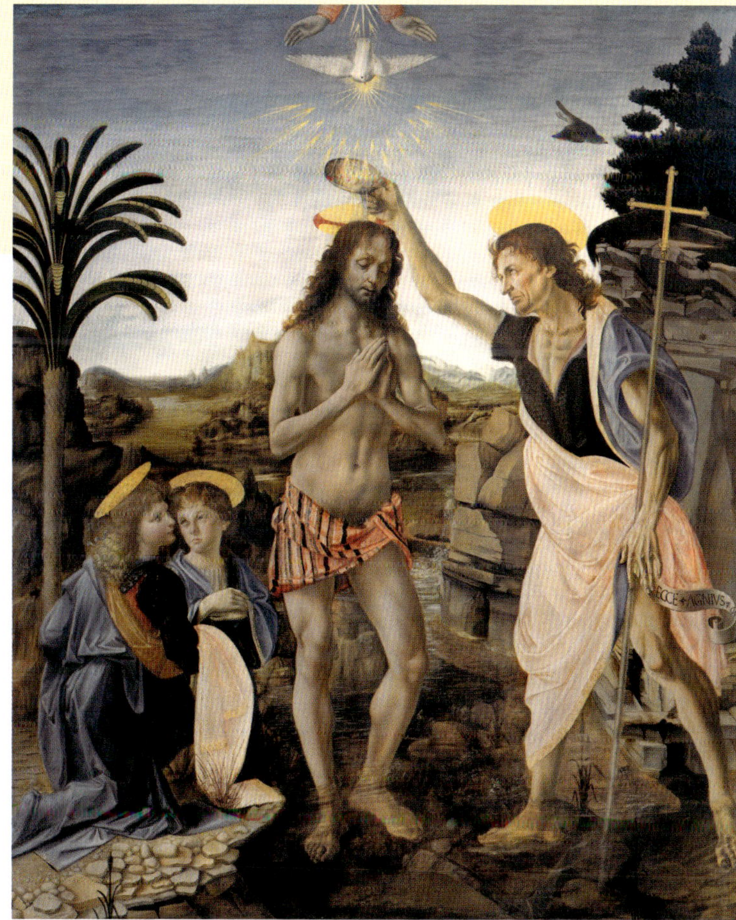

Andrea Verrocchio
(Firenze *c.* 1435 - Venezia 1488)
Leonardo da Vinci
(Vinci, Firenze 1452 - Amboise 1519)

Baptism of Christ
Die Taufe Christi
Doop van Christus

●●

c. 1474
177 x 151 cm / 69.7 x 59.4 in.
Galleria degli Uffizi, Firenze

Oil and tempera on panel / Öl und Tempera auf Tafel / Olieverf en tempera op paneel

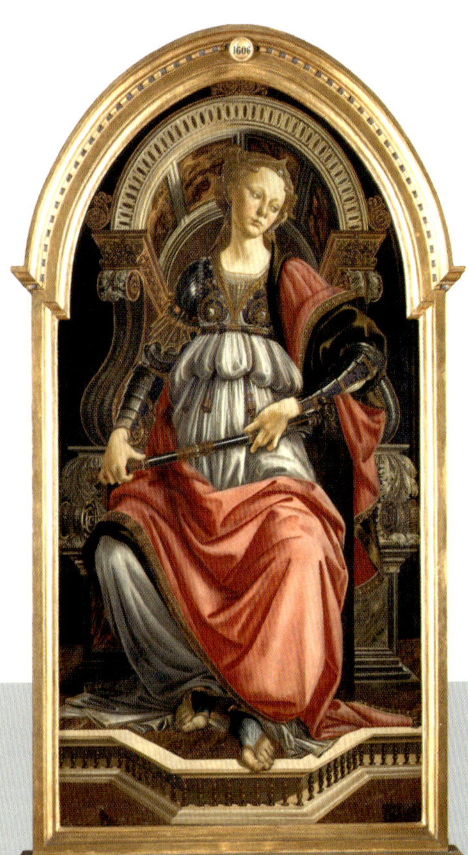

Sandro Botticelli
(Firenze 1445 - 1510)

The Fortress
Fortitudo
La Fortezza (De Standvastigheid)

●●

c. 1470
167 x 87 cm / 65.7 x 34.2 in.
Galleria degli Uffizi, Firenze

Tempera on wood / Tempera auf Tafel
Tempera op paneel

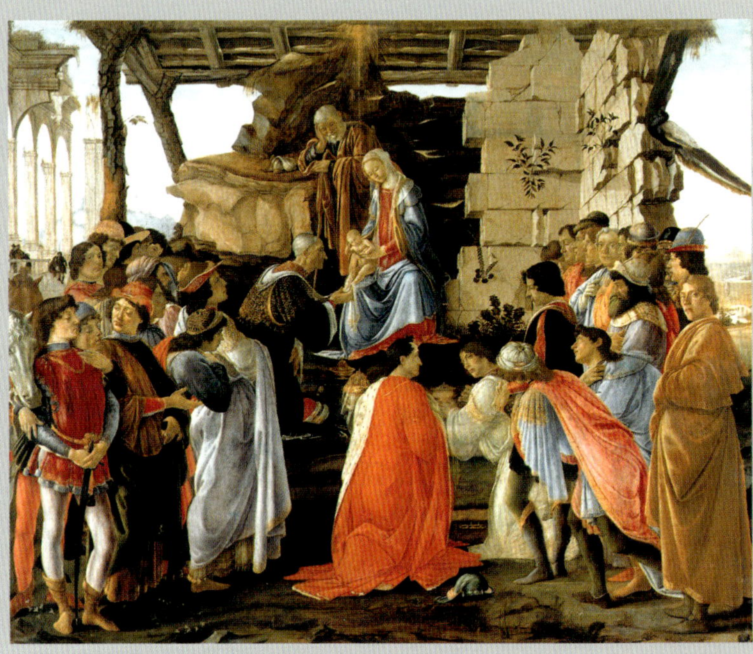

Sandro Botticelli
(Firenze 1445 - 1510)

Adoration of the Magi
Anbetung der Könige
Aanbidding der Wijzen

●●

c. 1475
111 x 134 cm / 43.7 x 52.7 in.
Galleria degli Uffizi, Firenze

Tempera on wood
Tempera auf Tafel
Tempera op paneel

Sandro Botticelli
(Firenze 1445 - 1510)

Portrait of a Man with a Medal
Bildnis eines Mannes mit einer Medaille
Portret van een man met medaille

●

c. 1475
57,5 x 44 cm / 22.6 x 17.3 in.
Galleria degli Uffizi, Firenze

Tempera on wood
Tempera auf Tafel
Tempera op paneel

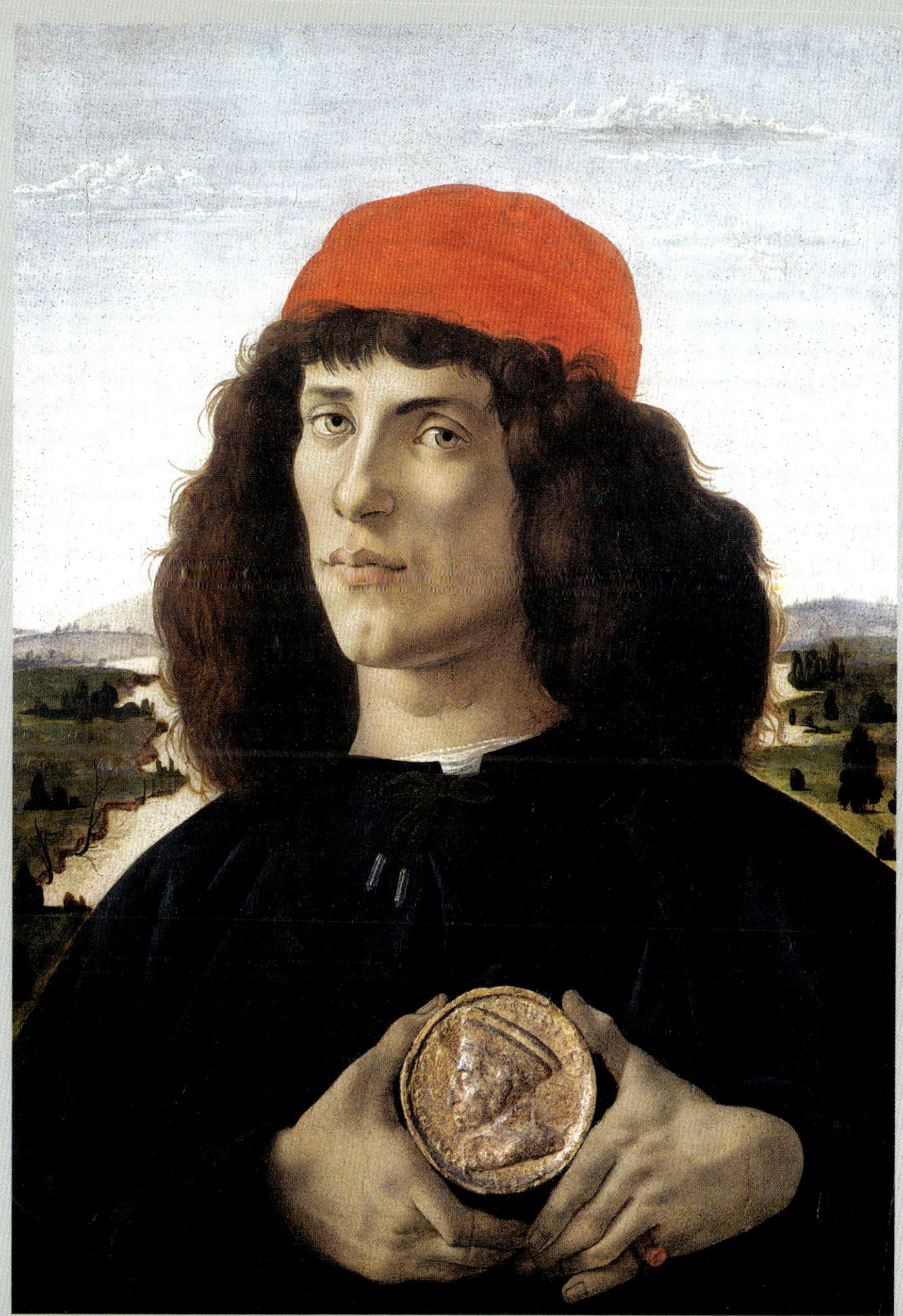

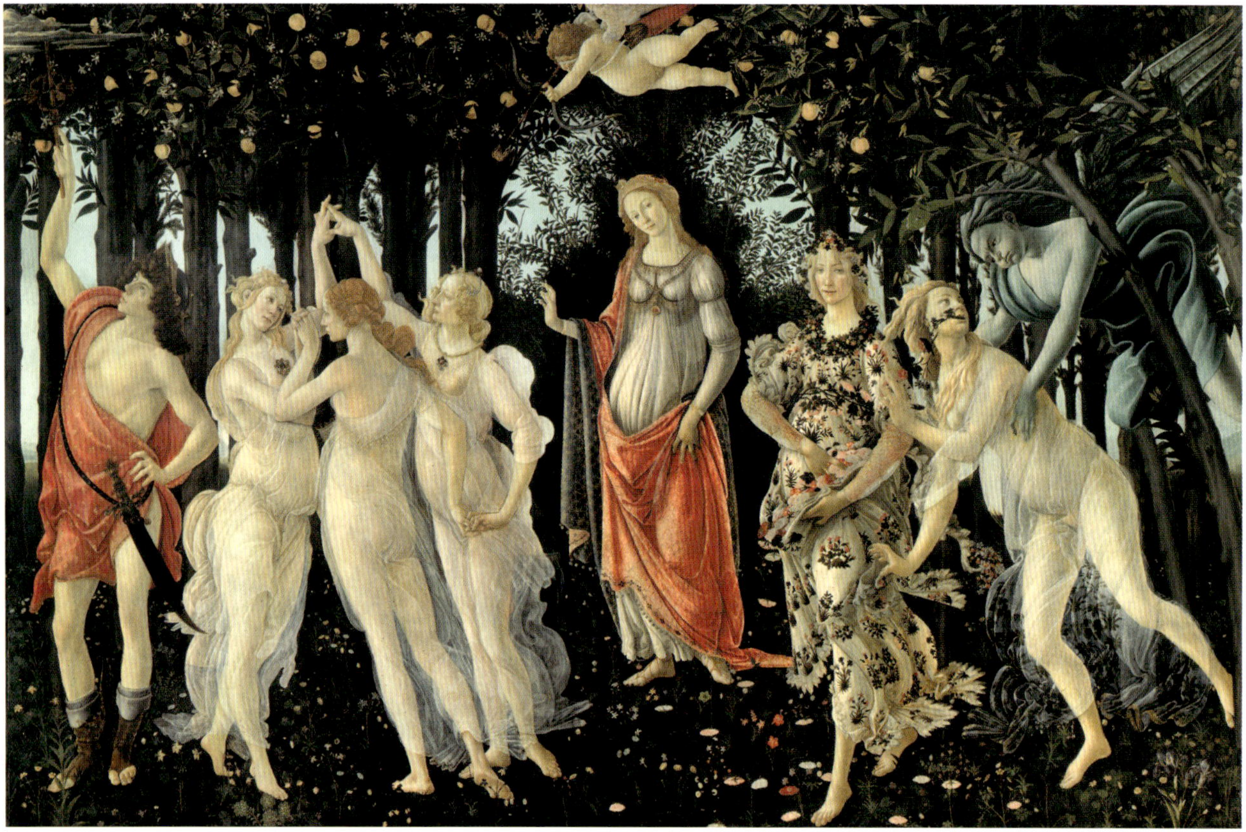

Sandro Botticelli
(Firenze 1445 - 1510)

Spring
Der Frühling
De Lente

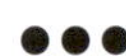

c. 1483-1485
203 x 314 cm / 81.5 x 123.6 in.
Galleria degli Uffizi, Firenze

Tempera on wood / Tempera auf Tafel
Tempera op paneel

Sandro Botticelli brings ancient myths back into art.

Mit Sandro Botticelli kehren antike Mythen in die Kunst zurück.

Met Sandro Botticelli keren de oude mythen terug in de kunst.

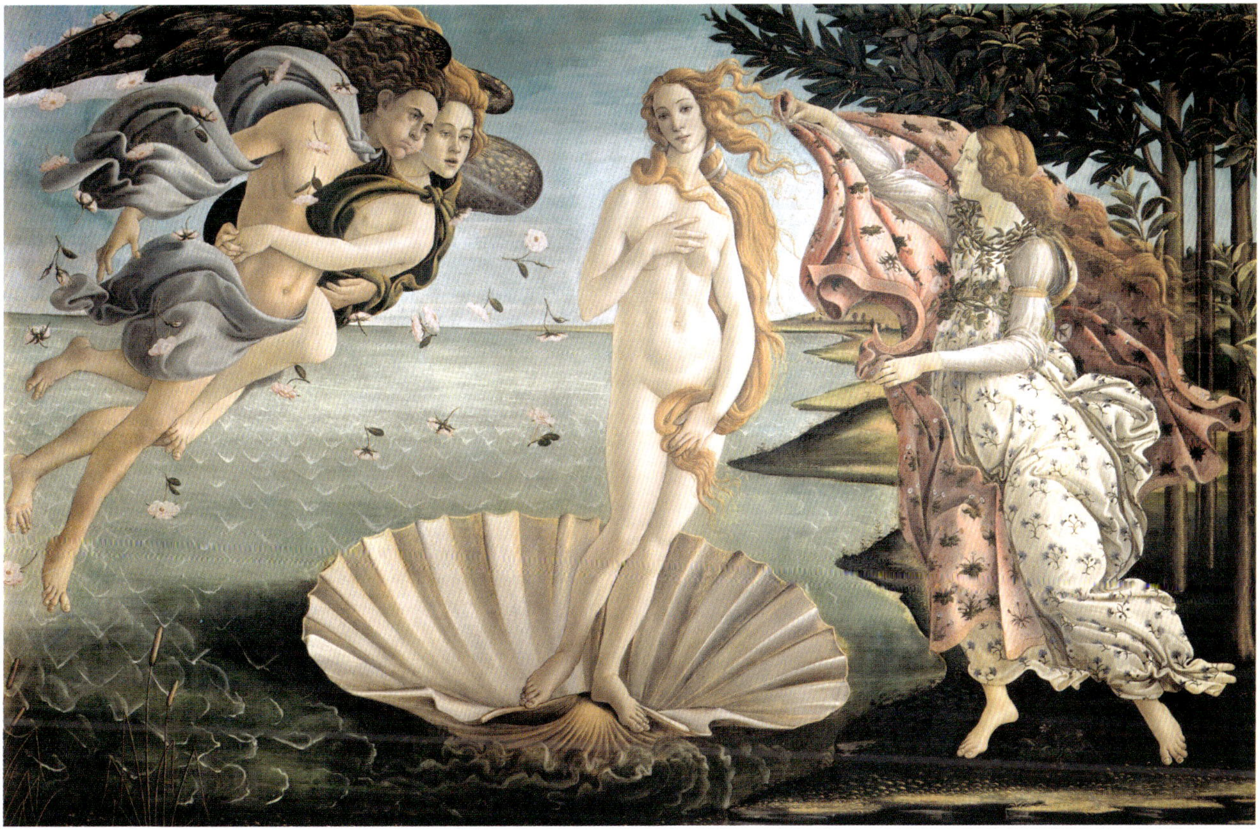

Sandro Botticelli
(Firenze 1445 - 1510)

The Birth of Venus
Die Geburt der Venus
De geboorte van Venus

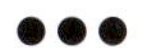

c. 1485
172 x 278 cm / 67.7 x 109.4 in.
Galleria degli Uffizi, Firenze

Tempera on canvas / Tempera auf Leinwand
Tempera op doek

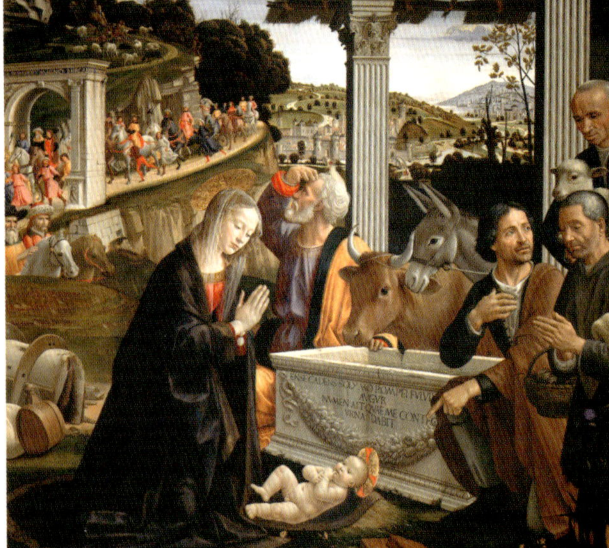

Domenico Ghirlandaio
(Firenze 1449 - 1494)

Adoration of the Shepherds
Anbetung der Hirten
Aanbidding door de Herders

●

1485
167 x 167 cm / 65.7 x 65.7 in.
Chiesa di Santa Trinita, Firenze

Panel / Tafel / Paneel

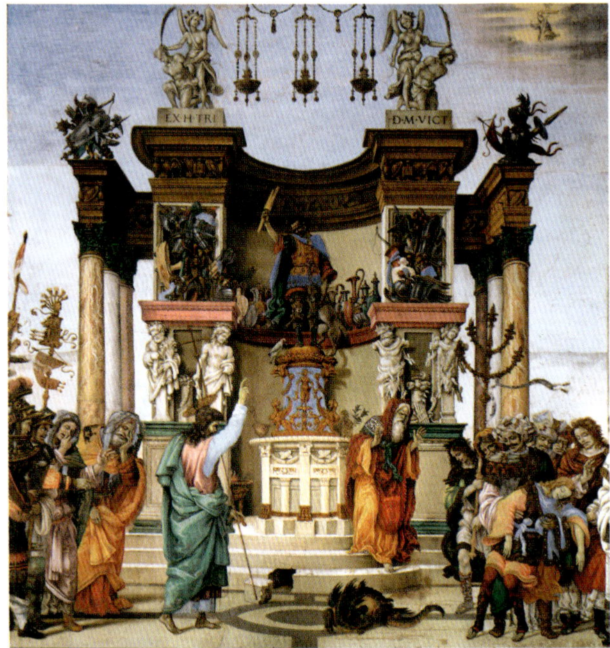

Filippino Lippi
(Prato 1457 - Firenze 1504)

Scenes from the Life of St Philip: The Saint Expelling a Monster from the Temple
Szenen aus dem Leben des Hl. Philipp: Der Heilige vertreibt das Ungeheuer aus dem Tempel
Legende van de Heilige Filippus: De heilige verjaagt de draak uit de tempel

●

1487-1502
Chiesa di Santa Maria Novella, Firenze

Fresco / Fresko

Piero di Cosimo
(Firenze 1461-1462 - 1521)
Simonetta Vespucci
●●
c. 1480-1482
57 x 42 cm / 22.4 x 16.5 in.
Musée Condé, Chantilly

Tempera on wood
Tempera auf Tafel
Tempera op paneel

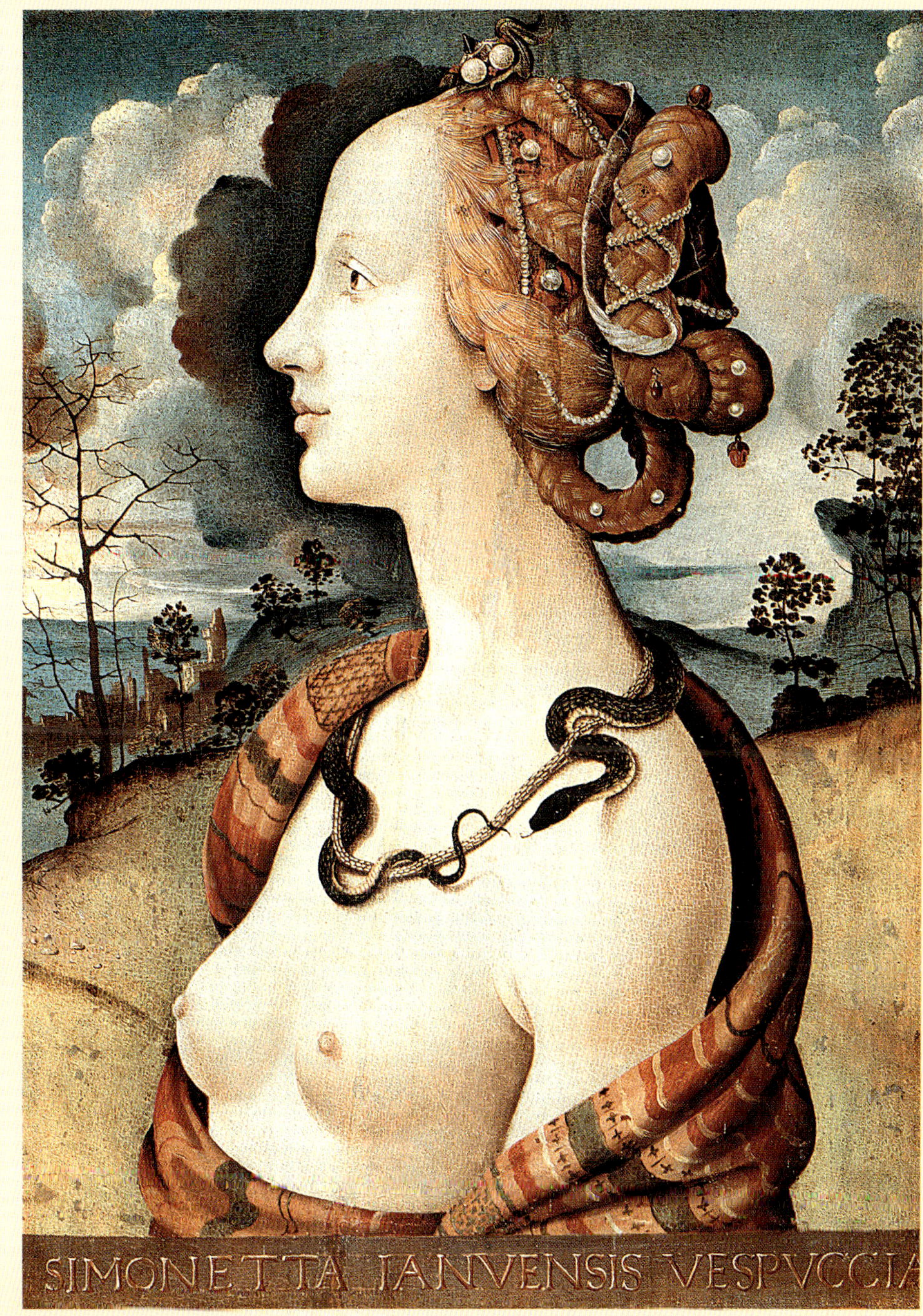

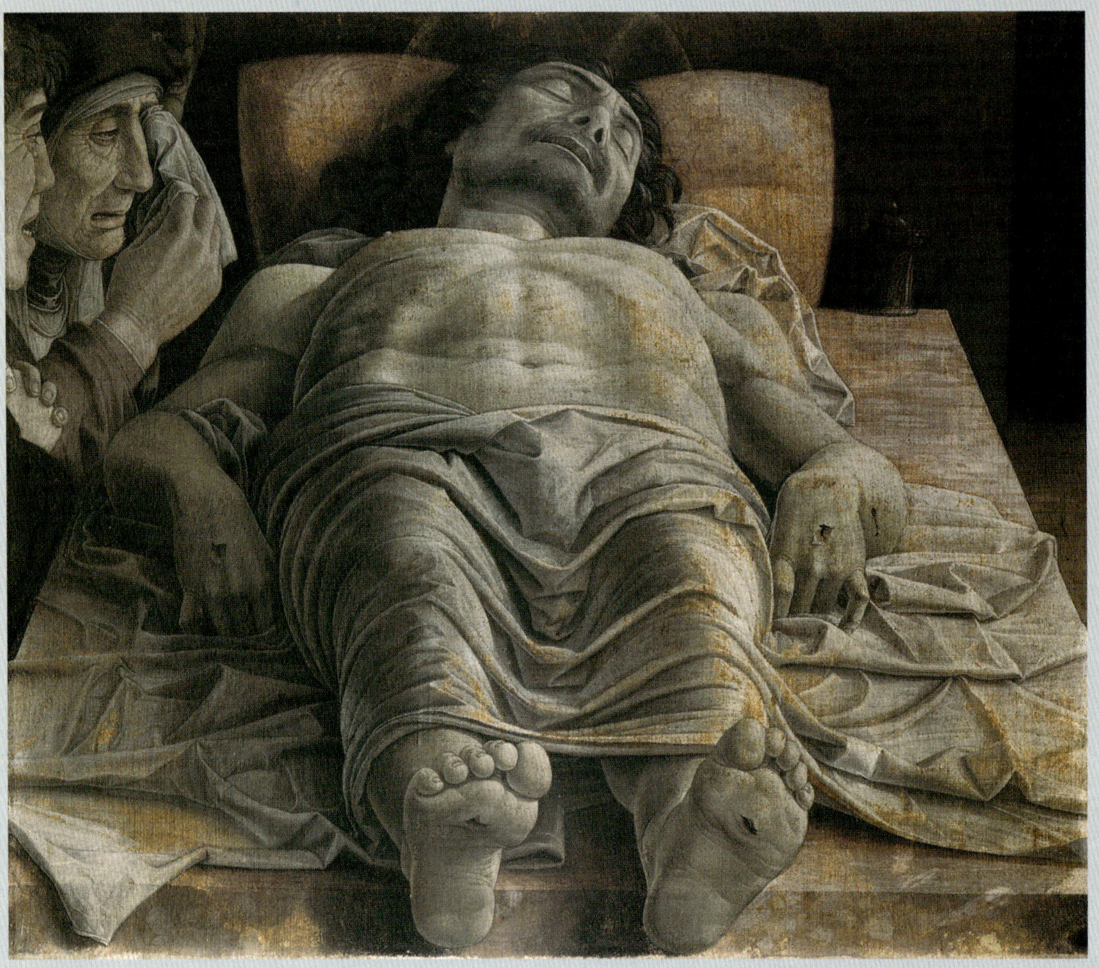

Mantegna
(Isola di Carturo, Padova *c.* 1430 - Mantova 1506)

Dead Christ
Toter Christus
Dode Christus

●●●

c. 1490
68 x 81 cm / 26.8 x 31.9 in.
Pinacoteca di Brera, Milano

Tempera on canvas / Tempera auf Leinwand / Tempera op doek

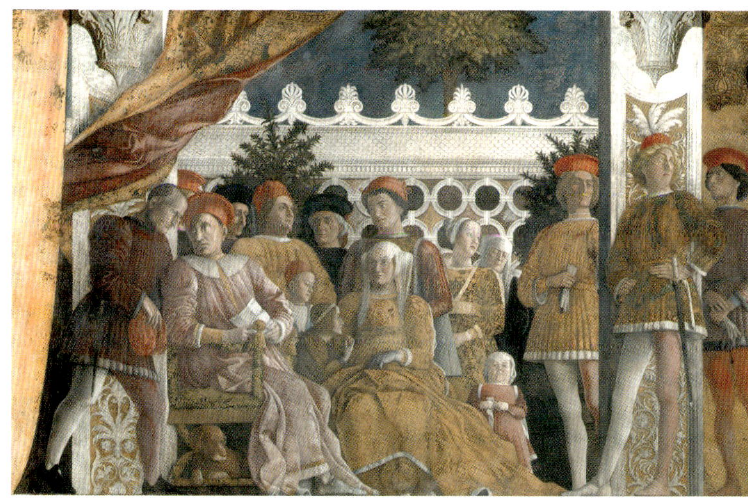

Mantegna
(Isola di Carturo, Padova *c.* 1430 - Mantova 1506)

The Family and Court of Ludovico II Gonzaga
Die Familie und der Hof von Ludovico II Gonzaga
Gezin en hovelingen van Ludovico II Gonzaga

●●●

1465-1474
Camera degli Sposi,
Palazzo Ducale, Mantova

Fresco / Fresko

Mantegna scandalizes his contemporaries with daring perspectives. His Dead Christ never leaves his workshop during his lifetime.

Mantegna schockiert seine Zeitgenossen durch Radikalperspektiven. Der Tote Christus verlässt zu Lebzeiten nie seine Werkstatt.

Mantegna veroorzaakt met zijn radicale perspectieven een schandaal bij zijn tijdgenoten. Zolang hij leeft, verlaat zijn Dode Christus het atelier niet.

Mantegna
(Isola di Carturo, Padova *c.* 1430 - Mantova 1506)

Central Oculus of the Ceiling
Zentraler Oculus an der Decke
Oculus in het midden van het plafond

●●●

1465-1474
Camera degli Sposi,
Palazzo Ducale, Mantova

Fresco / Fresko

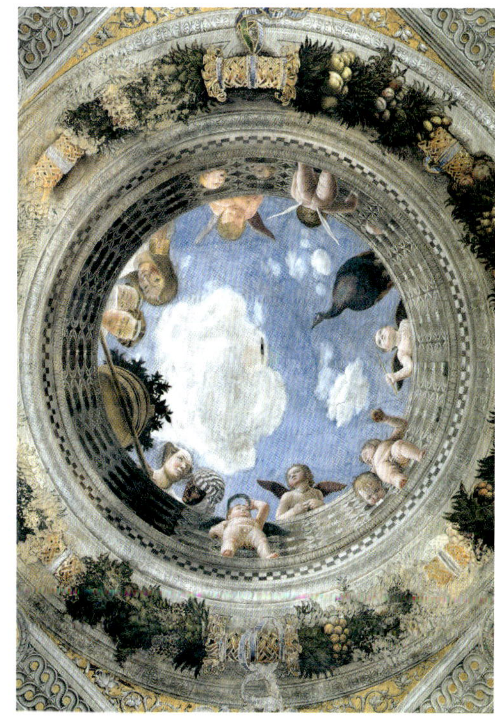

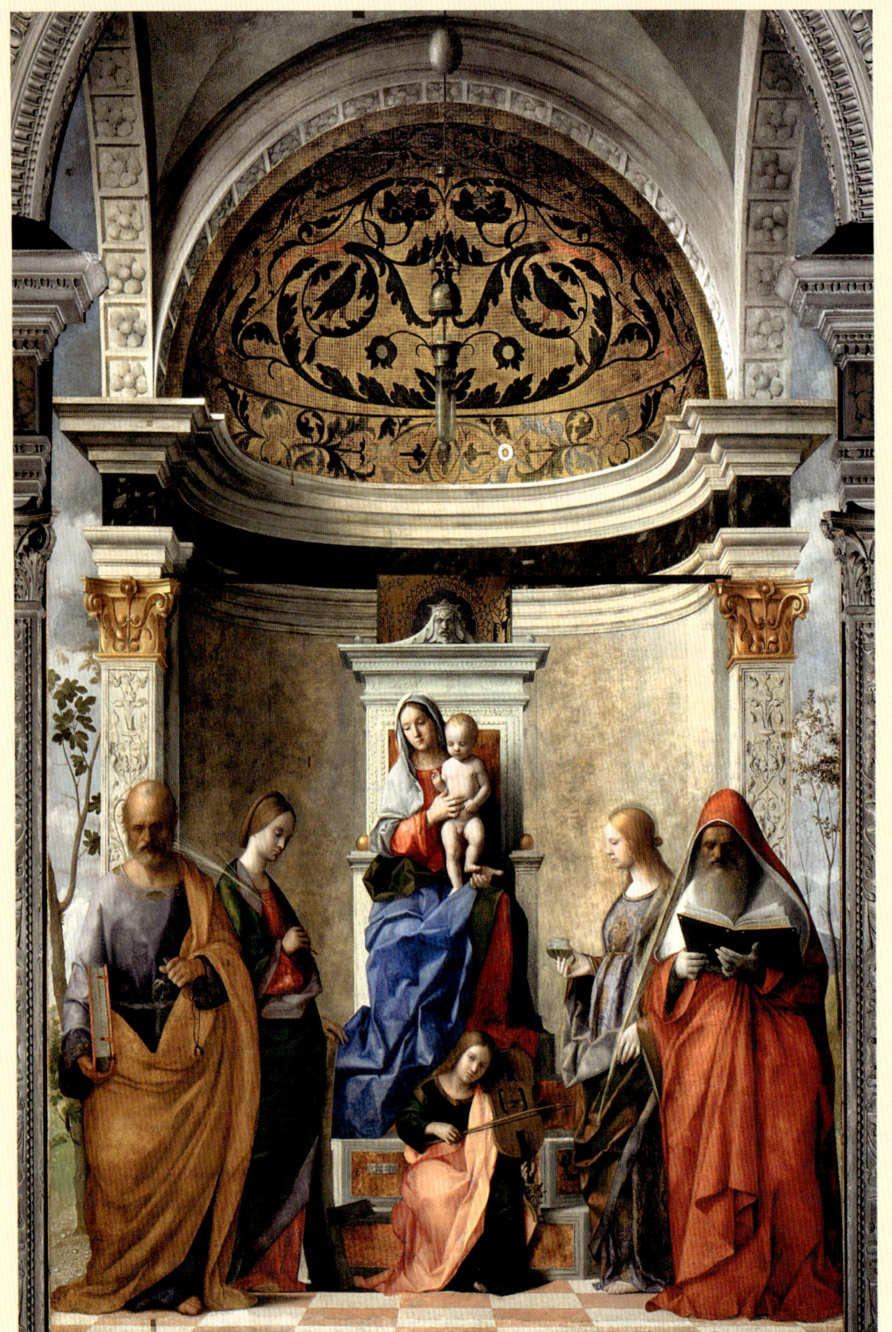

The Bellini family of artists is very influential in Venice.

Die Bellinis sind eine der einflussreichsten Künstlerfamilien in Venedig.

De Bellini's zijn één van invloedrijkste families van Venetië.

Giovanni Bellini
(Venezia, *c.* 1430 - 1516)

Madonna and Child Enthroned with Saints
Madonna mit dem Kind und Heiligen
Madonna op de troon met Kind en heiligen

●●●

1505
500 x 235 cm / 196.8 x 92.5 in.
San Zaccaria, Venezia

Oil on wood / Öl auf Tafel
Olieverf op Paneel

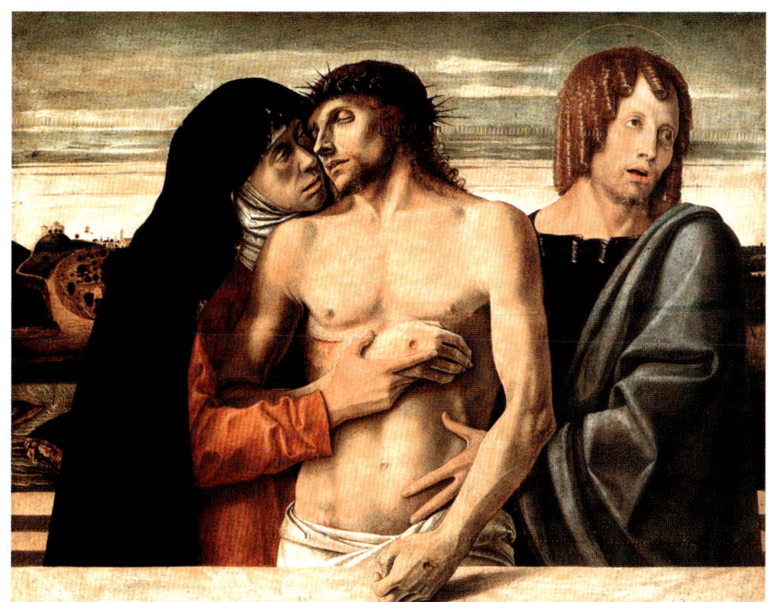

Giovanni Bellini
(Venezia, *c.* 1430 - 1516)

Pietà

c. 1460
86 x 107 cm / 33.8 x 42.1 in.
Pinacoteca di Brera, Milano

Tempera on wood / Tempera auf Tafel
Tempera op paneel

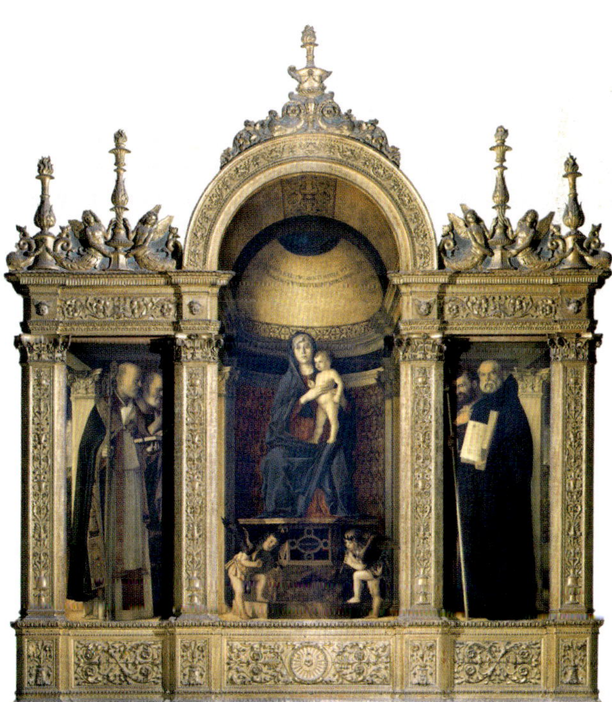

Giovanni Bellini
(Venezia, *c.* 1430 - 1516)

Frari Altarpiece
Frari Tryptichon
Drieluik van Frari

●

1488
Santa Maria Gloriosa dei Frari, Venezia

Oil on wood / Öl auf Tafel / Olieverf op paneel

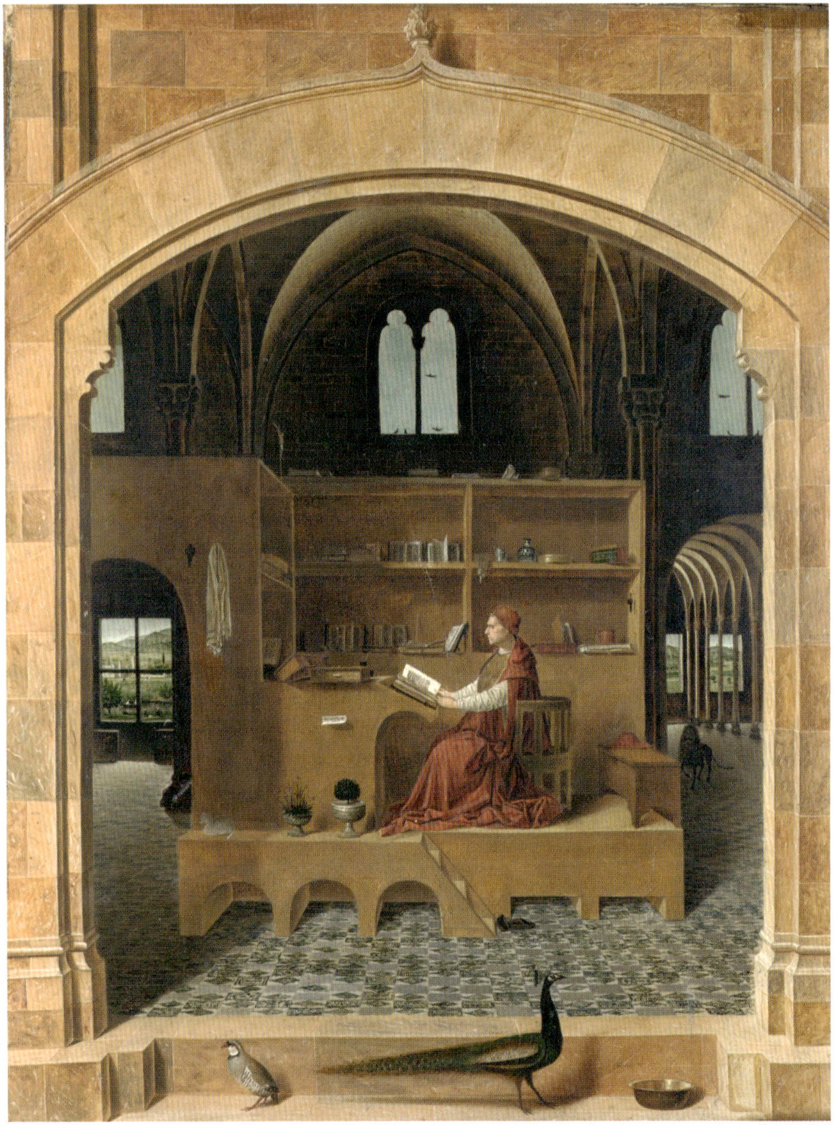

Antonello da Messina introduces the oil painting technique from the Netherlands to Venice.

Mit Antonello da Messina kommt erstmals die niederländische Technik der Ölmalerei nach Venedig.

Met Antonello da Messina bereikt de olieverftechniek Venetië voor de eerste keer.

Antonello da Messina
(Messina *c.* 1423/1430 - 1479)

Saint Jerome in His Study
Der Hl. Hieronymus in seinem Gehäus
De heilige Hiëronymus in zijn studeervertrek

1474
46 x 36,5 cm / 18.1 x 14.4 in.
The National Gallery, London

Oil on wood / Öl auf Tafel
Olieverf op paneel

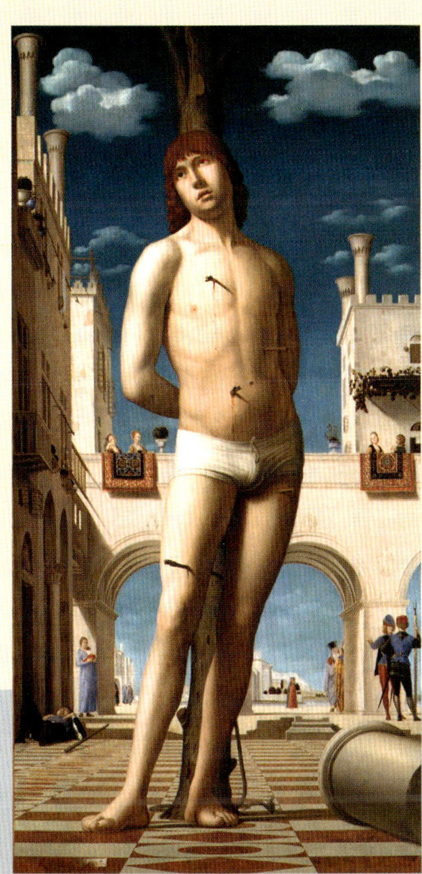

Antonello da Messina
(Messina *c.* 1423/1430 - 1479)

St Sebastian
Hl. Sebastian
Sint Sebastiaan

●●

1478
171 x 85 cm / 67.3 x 33.4 in.
Gemäldegalerie Alte Meister,
Staatliche Kunstsammlungen,
Dresden

Oil on canvas / Öl auf Leinwand
Olieverf op doek

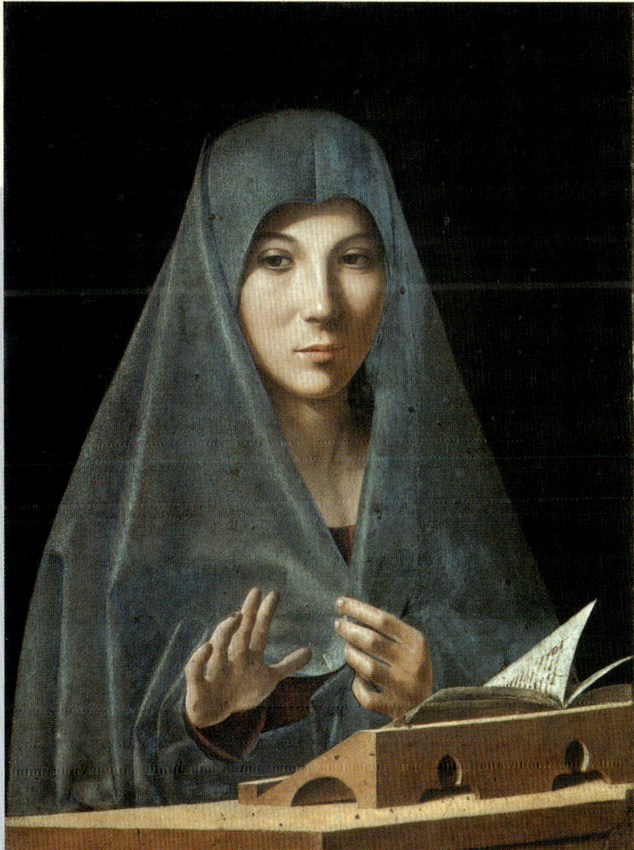

Antonello da Messina
(Messina *c.* 1423/1430 - 1479)

The Virgin Annunciate
Maria der Verkündigung
Maria-boodschap

●●

c. 1476
45 x 34,5 cm / 17.7 x 13.5 in.
Galleria Regionale della Sicilia, Palermo

Tempera and oil on wood
Tempera und Öl auf Holz
Tempera en olieverf op paneel

The revolutionary oil technique, with its microscopic precision, is attributed to the van Eyck brothers.

Die revolutionäre Öltechnik mit ihrer mikroskopischen Genauigkeit wird den Brüdern van Eyck zugeschrieben.

De revolutionaire olieverftechniek, met zijn microscopische precisie, wordt toegeschreven aan de gebroeders van Eyck.

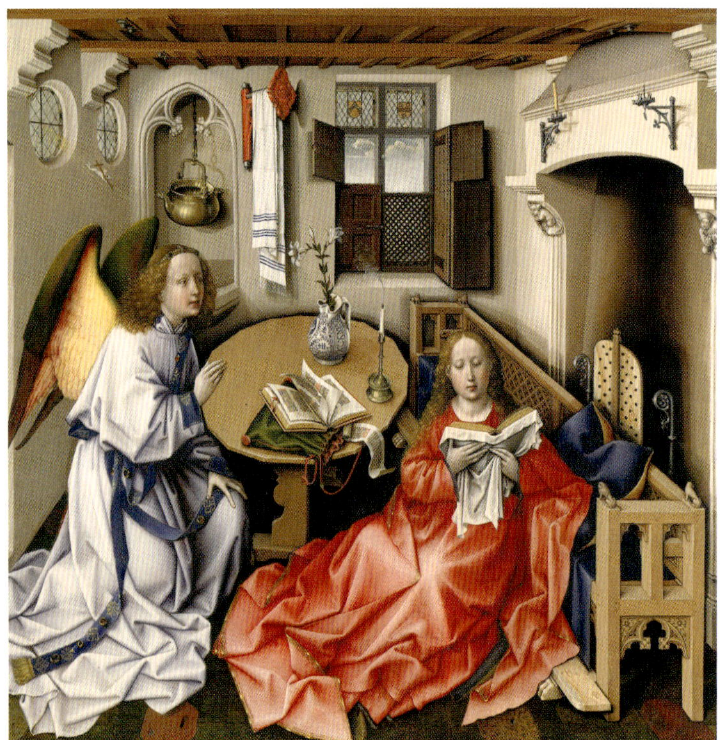

Robert Campin
(Valenciennes *c.* 1375 - Tournai 1444)

Annunciation
Verkündigung
Annunciatie

●

c. 1425-1430
64,1 x 63,2 cm / 25.8 x 24.7 in.
Metropolitan Museum of Art,
New York

Oil on wood
Öl auf Tafel
Olieverf op paneel

Robert Campin
(Valenciennes *c.* 1375 -
Tournai 1444)

Robert de Masmines

●

28,5 x 17,7 cm / 11.2 x 7 in.
Gemäldegalerie, Staatliche Museen,
Berlin

Oil on wood
Öl auf Tafel
Olieverf op paneel

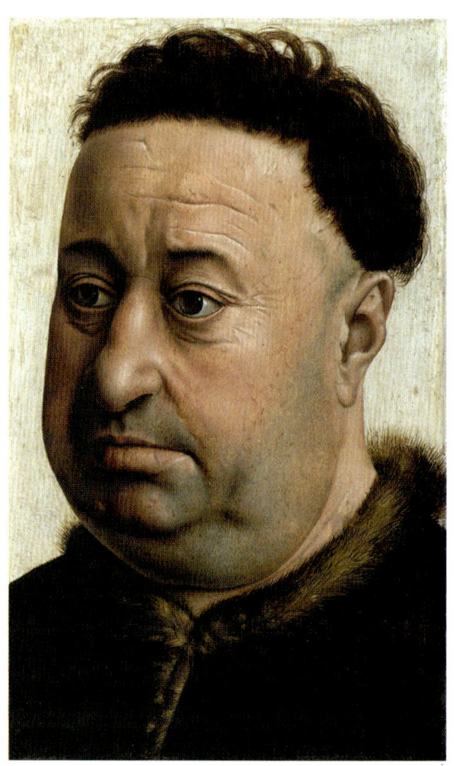

Jan van Eyck
(Maastricht *c.* 1390 -
Bruges 1441)

Portrait of Giovanni Arnolfini and His Wife
Giovanni Arnolfini und seine Frau
Portret van Giovanni Arnolfini en zijn vrouw

●●●

1434
82,20 x 60 cm / 32.4 x 23.6 in.
The National Gallery, London

Oil on wood
Öl auf Tafel
Olieverf op paneel

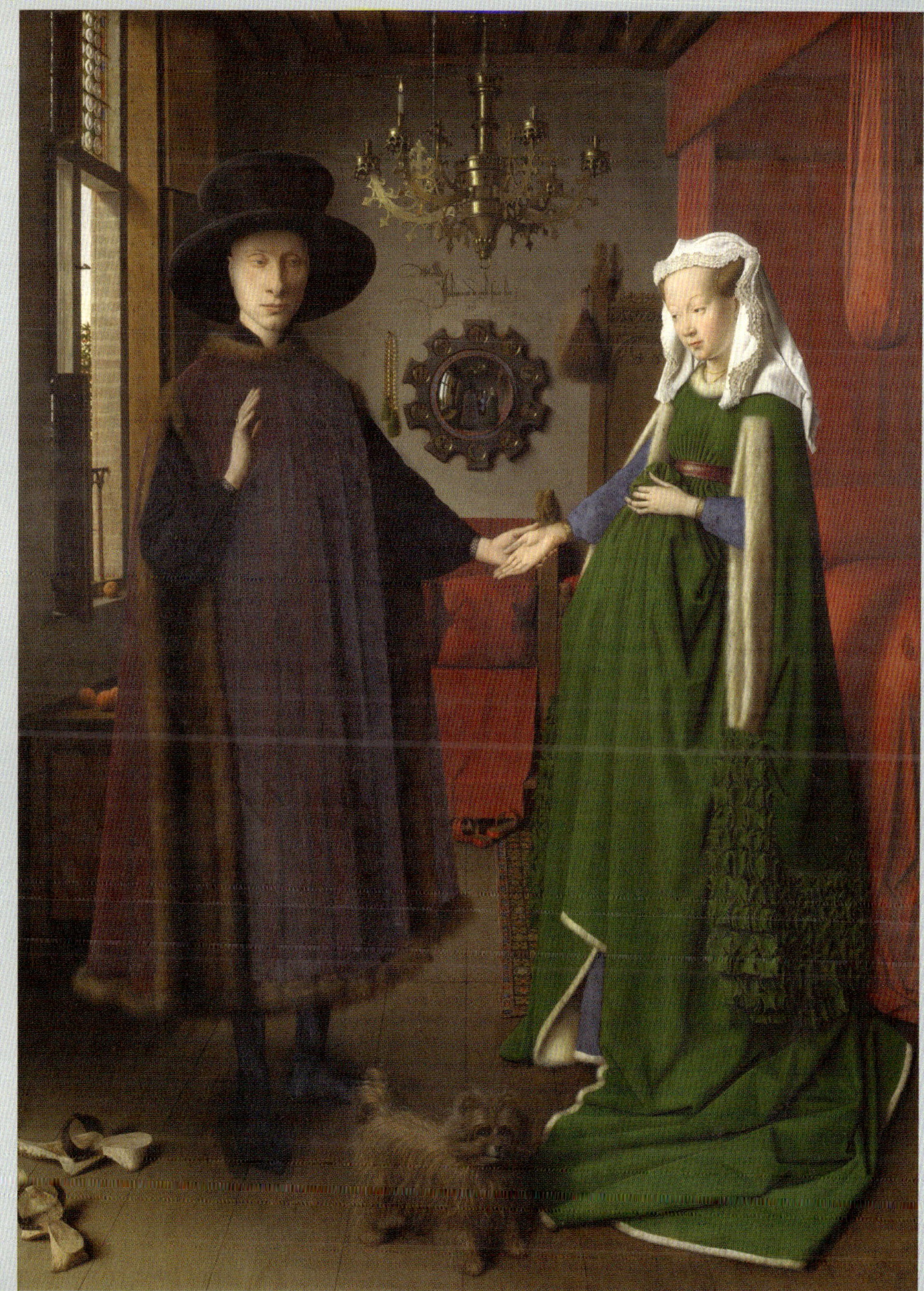

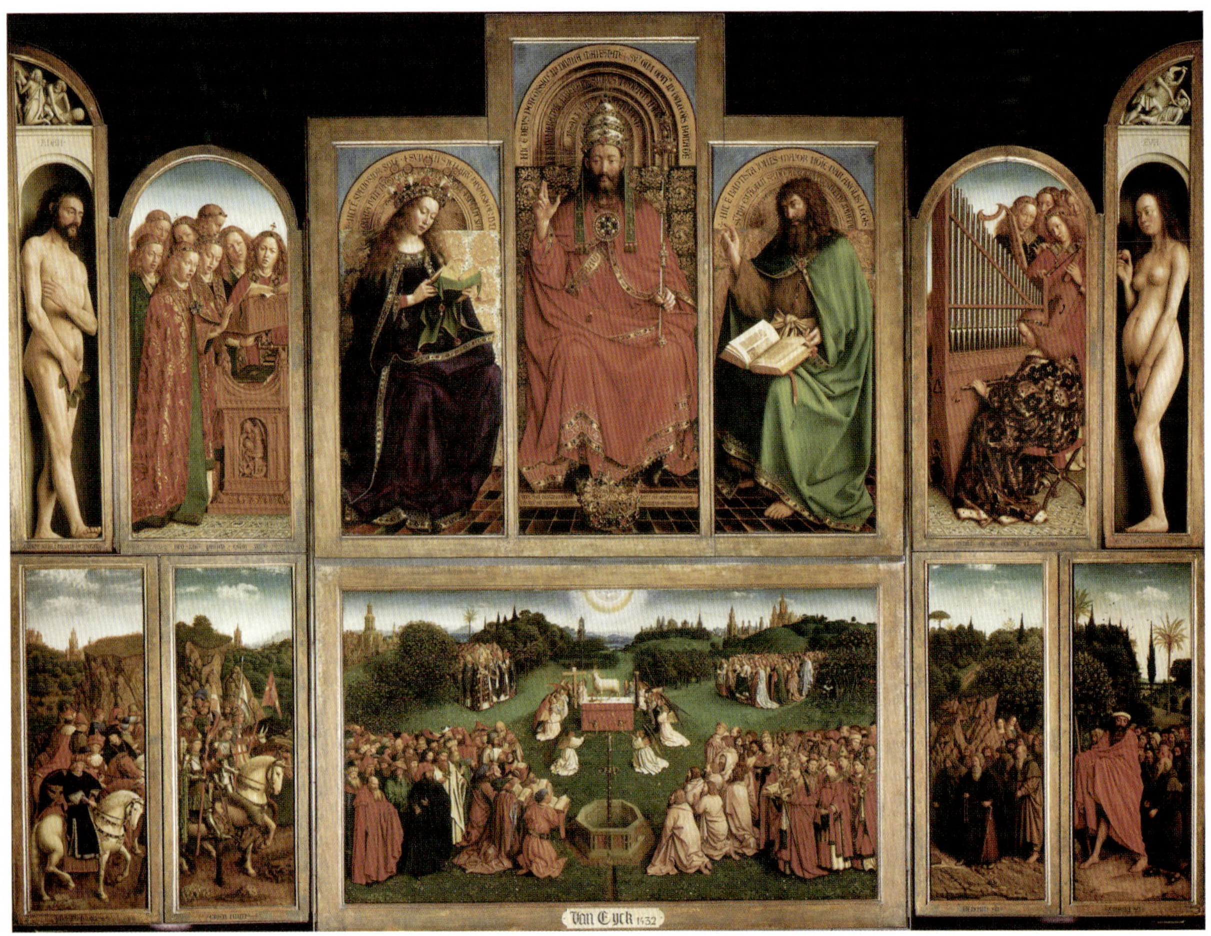

Jan van Eyck
(Maastricht *c.* 1390 - Bruges 1441)
Adoration of the Mystic Lamb (Ghent Altarpice)
Polyptychon des Mystischen Lamms
Veelluik van het Lam Gods
●●●
c. 1432
Saint-Bavon, Gand

Oil on wood / Öl auf Tafel / Olieverf op paneel

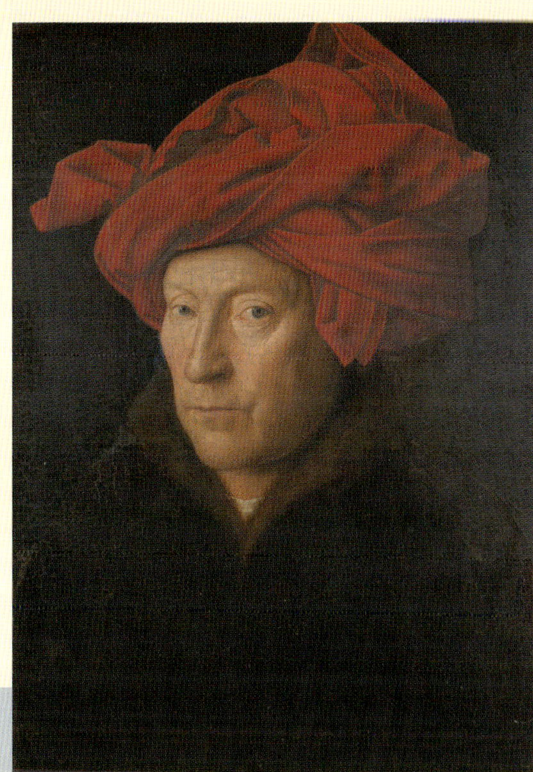

Jan van Eyck
(Maastricht *c.* 1390 - Bruges 1441)

Portait of a Man (Self Portrait?)
Portrait eines Mannes (Selbstportrait?)
Portret van een man (Zelfportret?)

●●●

1433
26 x 19 cm / 10.2 x 7.5 in.
The National Gallery, London

Oil on wood
Öl auf Tafel
Olieverf op paneel

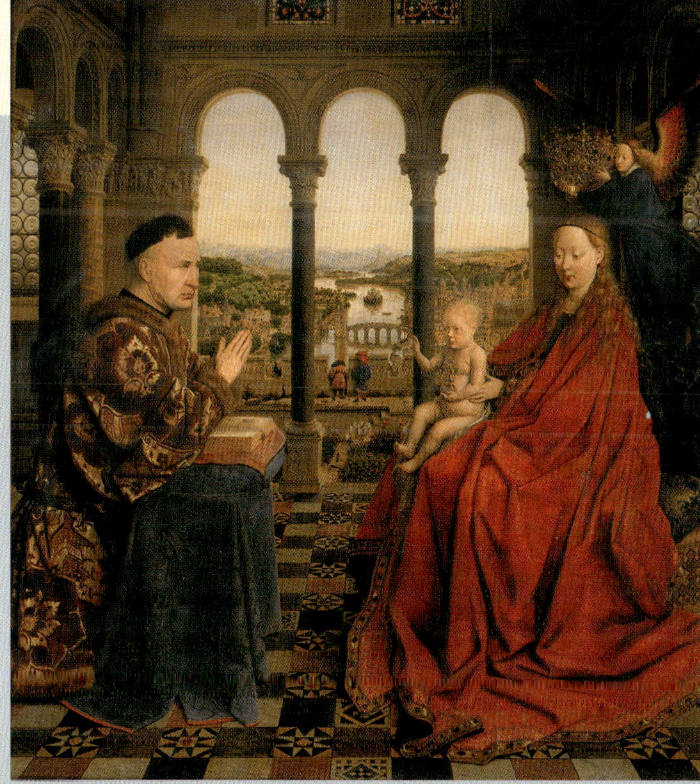

Jan van Eyck
(Maastricht *c.* 1390 - Bruges 1441)

The Rolin Madonna
Madonna des Kanzlers Rolin
Madonna met Kanselier Rolin

●●●

c. 1435
66 x 62 cm / 26 x 24.4 in.
Musée du Louvre, Paris

Oil on wood
Öl auf Tafel
Olieverf op paneel

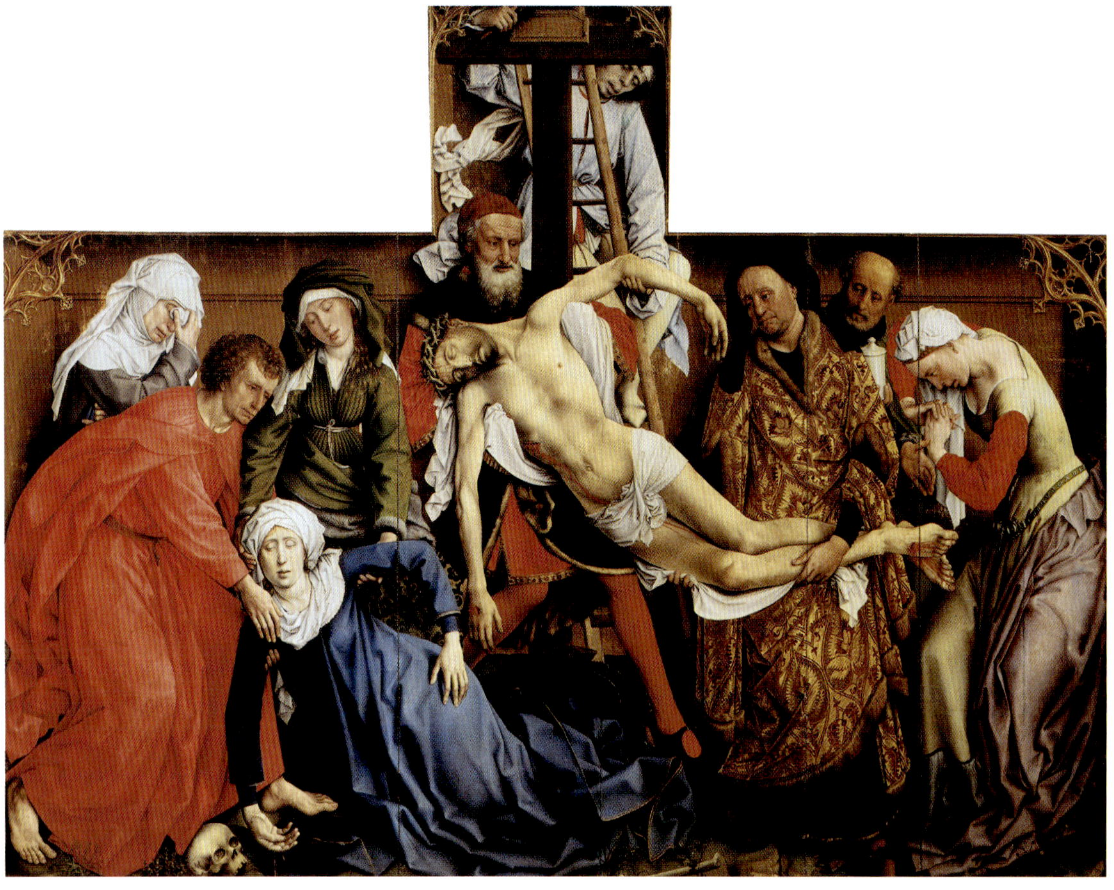

Roger van der Weyden
(Tournai *c.* 1399/1400 - Bruxelles 1464)

Deposition
Kreuzabnahme
De Kruisafneming

●●●

c. 1440
220 x 262 cm / 86.6 x 103.1 in.
Museo Nacional del Prado, Madrid

Oil on wood / Öl auf Tafel
Olieverf op paneel

Colours are applied in numerous transparent layers. New lighting effects are born.

Die Farben werden vielschichtig aufgetragen in durchschimmernden Schichten (Lasuren). Völlig neue Lichtwirkungen entstehen.

Kleuren worden in meerdere transparante lagen toegevoegd. Er ontstaan nieuwe lichteffecten.

Roger van der Weyden
(Tournai *c.* 1399/1400 - Bruxelles 1464)

Deposition in the Tomb
Grablegung Christi
Graflegging

●●

c. 1449-1450
111 x 95 cm / 43. 7 x 37.4 in.
Galleria degli Uffizi, Firenze

Oil on wood
Öl auf Tafel
Olieverf op paneel

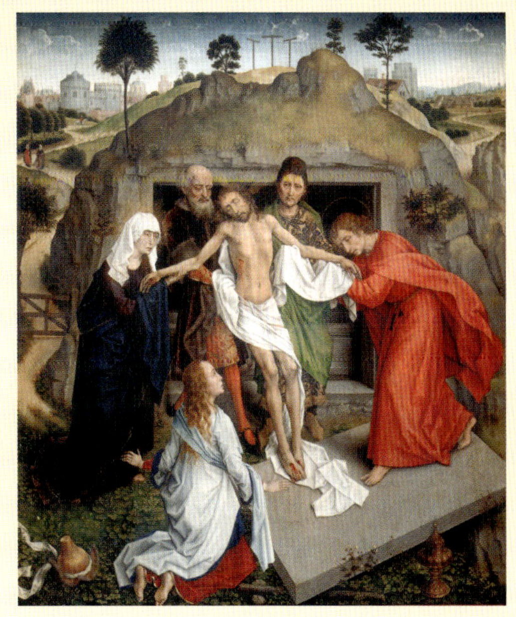

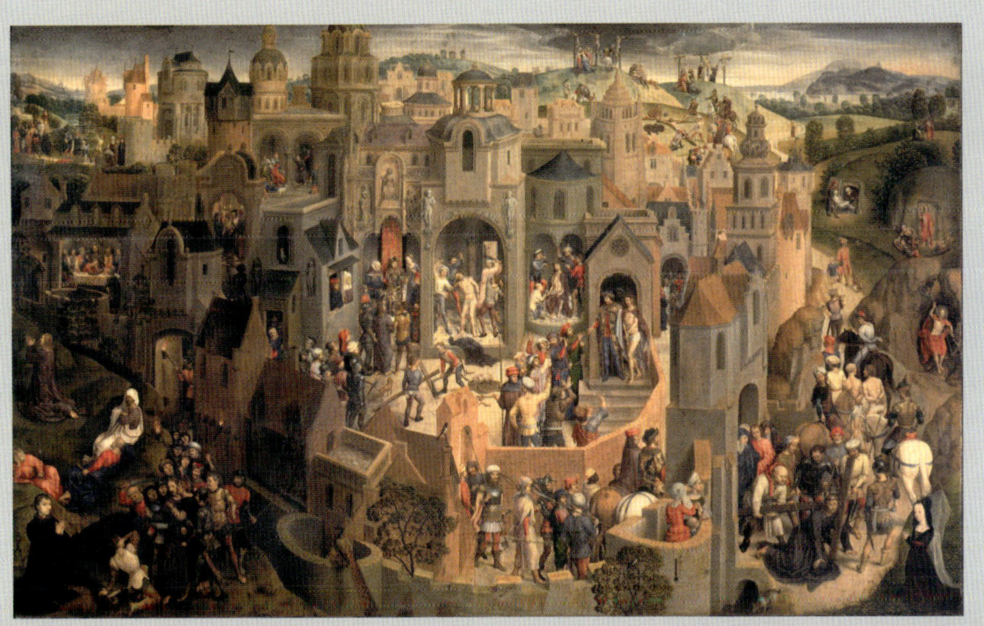

Hans Memling
(Seligenstadt 1435/1440 - Bruges 1494)

Passion of Christ
Die Passion Christi
De Passie van Christus

●●

c. 1470
55 x 90 cm / 21.6 x 35.4 in.
Galleria Sabauda, Torino

Oil on wood
Öl auf Tafel
Olieverf op paneel

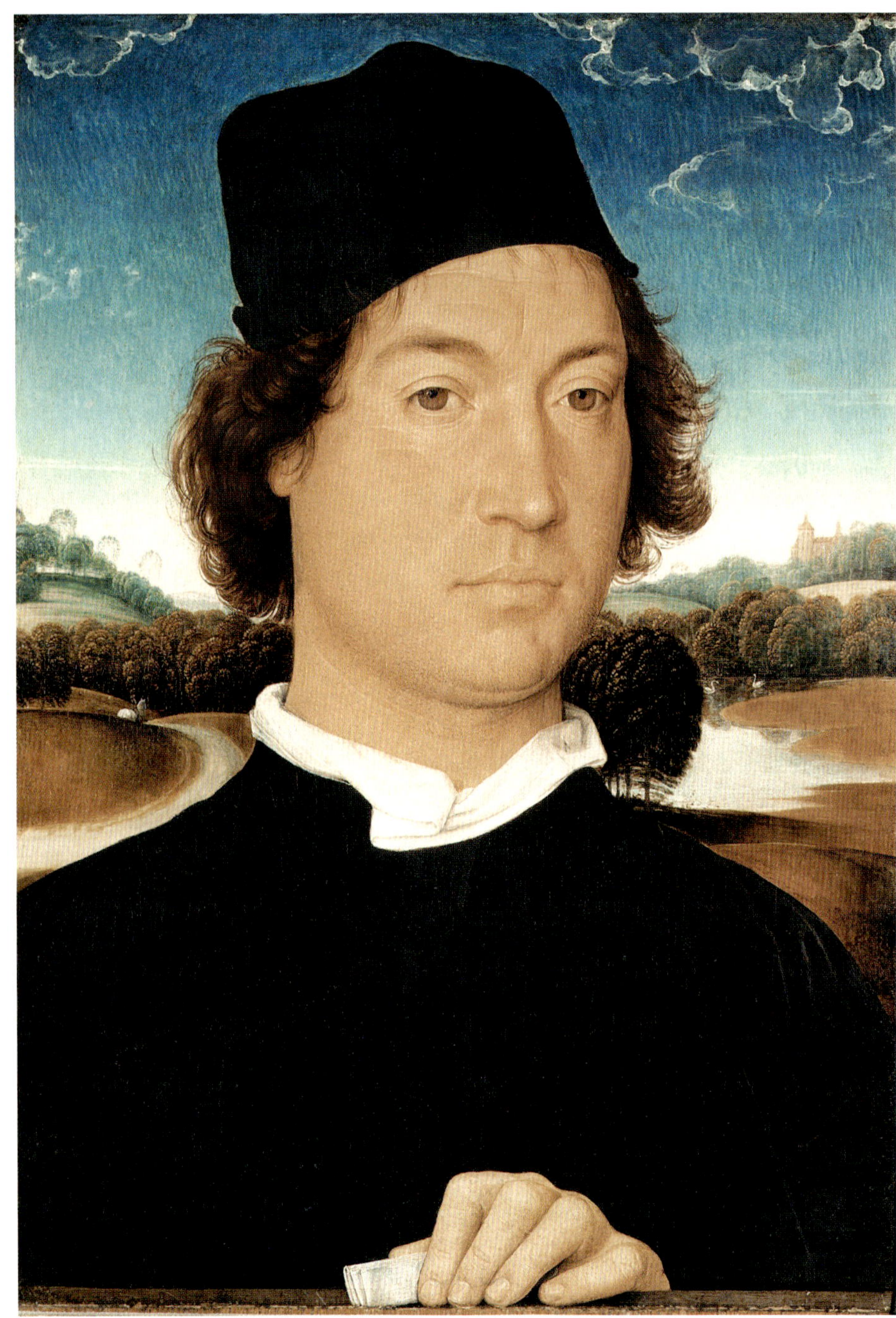

Hans Memling
(Seligenstadt 1435/1440 -
Bruges 1494)

Portrait of a Man
Portrait eines Mannes
Portret van een man

●

c. 1490
33 x 25 cm / 13 x 9.8 in.
Galleria degli Uffizi, Firenze

Oil on wood
Öl auf Tafel
Olieverf op Paneel

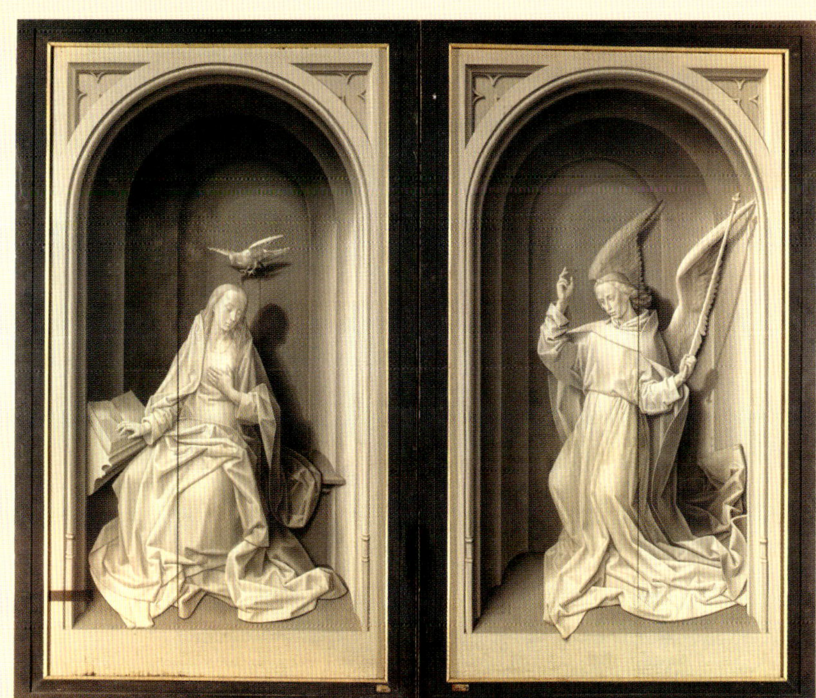

Hugo van der Goes
(Gand *c.* 1440 - Rode Klooster, Bruxelles 1482)

Portinari Triptych
Triptychon Portinari
Portinari triptiek
(Aanbidding der Herders)

●●

c. 1476-1479
249 x 300 cm / 98.3 x 11.8 in.
Galleria degli Uffizi, Firenze

Oil on wood
Öl auf Tafel
Olieverf op paneel

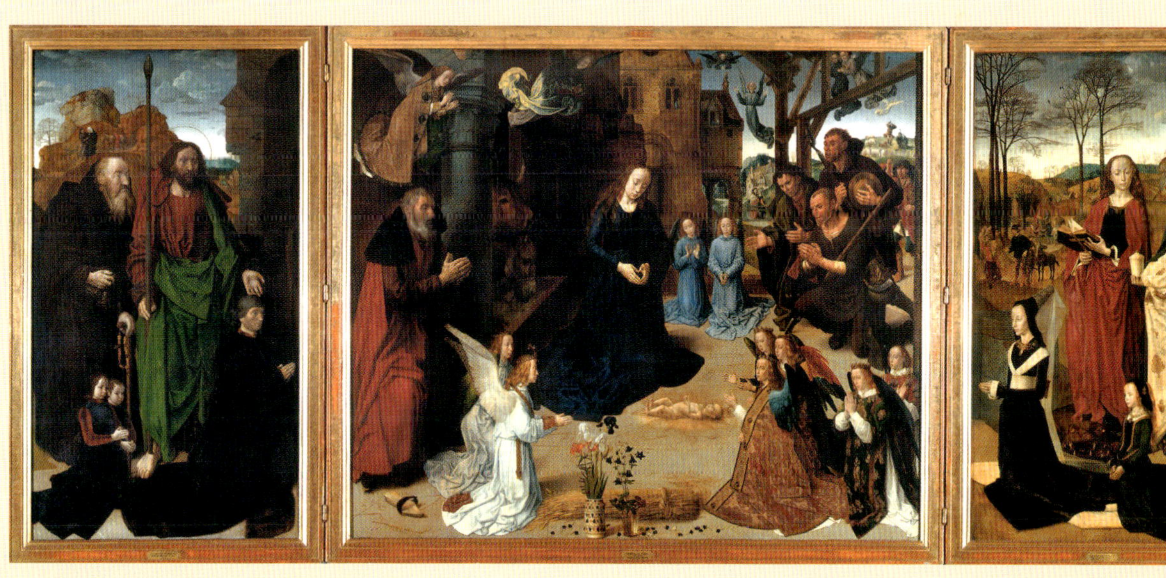

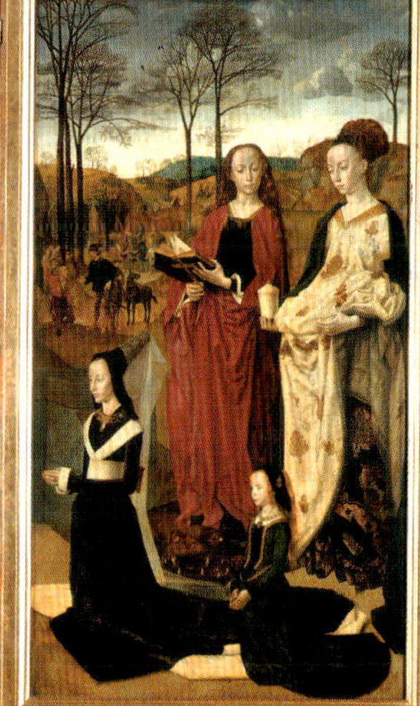

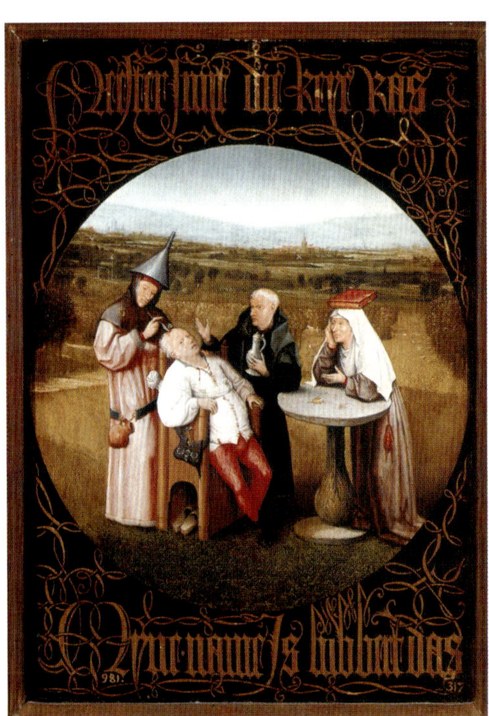

Hieronymus Bosch
(Hertogenbosch 1450 - 1516)

Extraction of the Stone of Madness
Das Steinschneiden
De keisnijding

●

c. 1475-1480
Museo Nacional del Prado, Madrid

Oil on wood
Öl auf Tafel
Olieverf op paneel

Hieronymus Bosch
(Hertogenbosch 1450 - 1516)

Seven Deadly Sins
Die sieben Todsünden
De zeven hoofdzonden

●●●

1485
120 x 150 cm / 47.2 x 59 in.
Museo Nacional del Prado, Madrid

Oil on wood
Öl auf Tafel
Olieverf op paneel

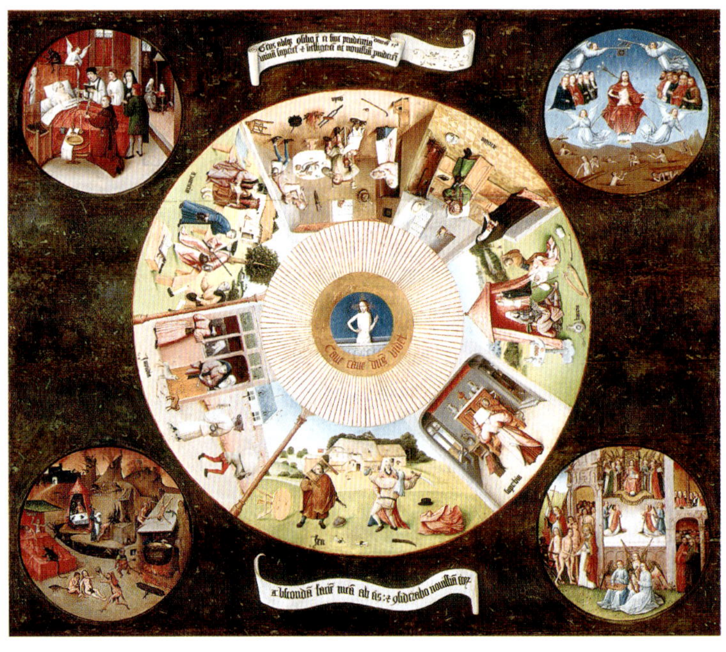

Mythical, allegorical, ecstatic: Hieronymus Bosch is the first "surrealist" in the history of art.

Mystisch, allegorisch, entrückt. Hieronymus Bosch ist der erste "Surrealist" der Kunstgeschichte.

Mythisch, allegorisch en bewonderenswaardig. Hieronymus Bosch is de eerste "surrealist" uit de kunstgeschiedenis.

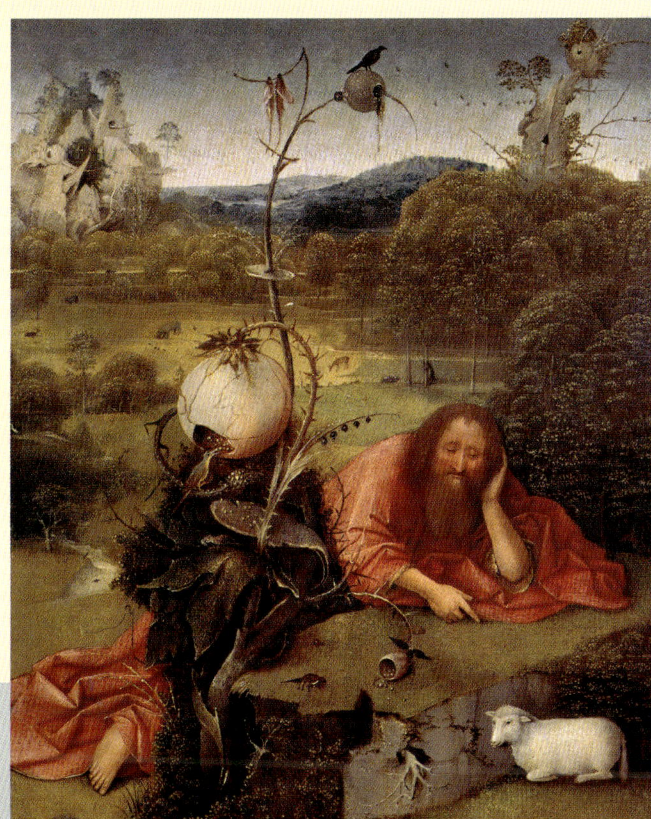

Hieronymus Bosch
(Hertogenbosch 1450 - 1516)

St John the Baptist in the Wilderness
Meditierender Hl. Johannes der Täufer
Johannes de Doper in de wildernis

●●

c. 1489
48,5 x 40 cm / 19.1 x 15.7 in.
Museo Lázaro Galdiano, Madrid

Oil on wood
Öl auf Tafel
Olieverf op paneel

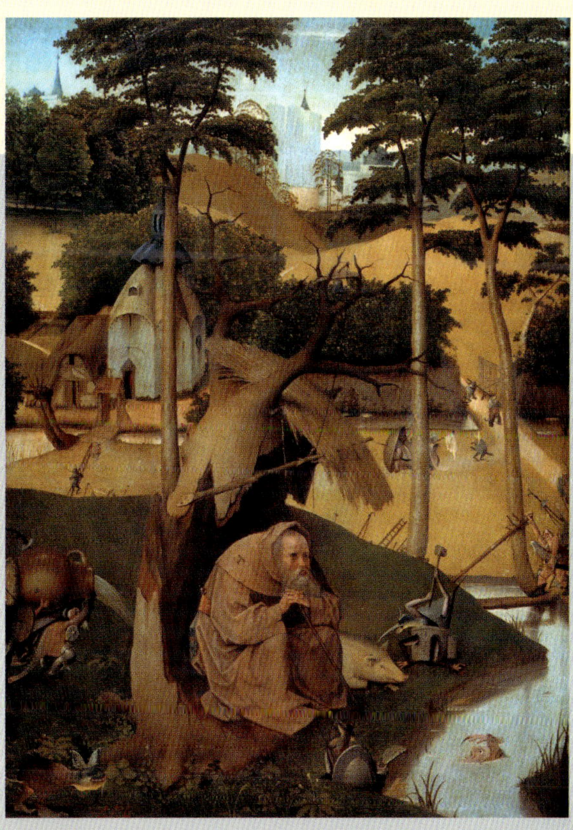

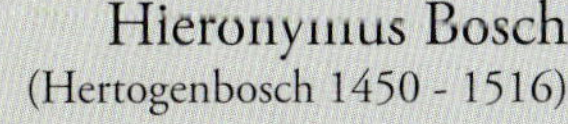

Hieronymus Bosch
(Hertogenbosch 1450 - 1516)

Temptation of St Anthony
Die Versuchung des heiligen Antonius
De verzoeking van de heilige Antonius

●●

1510
70 x 50 cm / 27.6 x 19.7 in.
Museo Nacional del Prado, Madrid

Oil on wood / Öl auf Tafel
Olieverf op paneel

Hieronymus Bosch
(Hertogenbosch 1450 - 1516)

Garden of Earthly Delights
Der Garten der Lüste
De Tuin der Lusten

●●●

c. 1503-1504
220 × 389 cm / 86.6 x 153.1 in.
Museo Nacional del Prado,
Madrid

Oil on wood / Öl auf Tafel
Olieverf op paneel

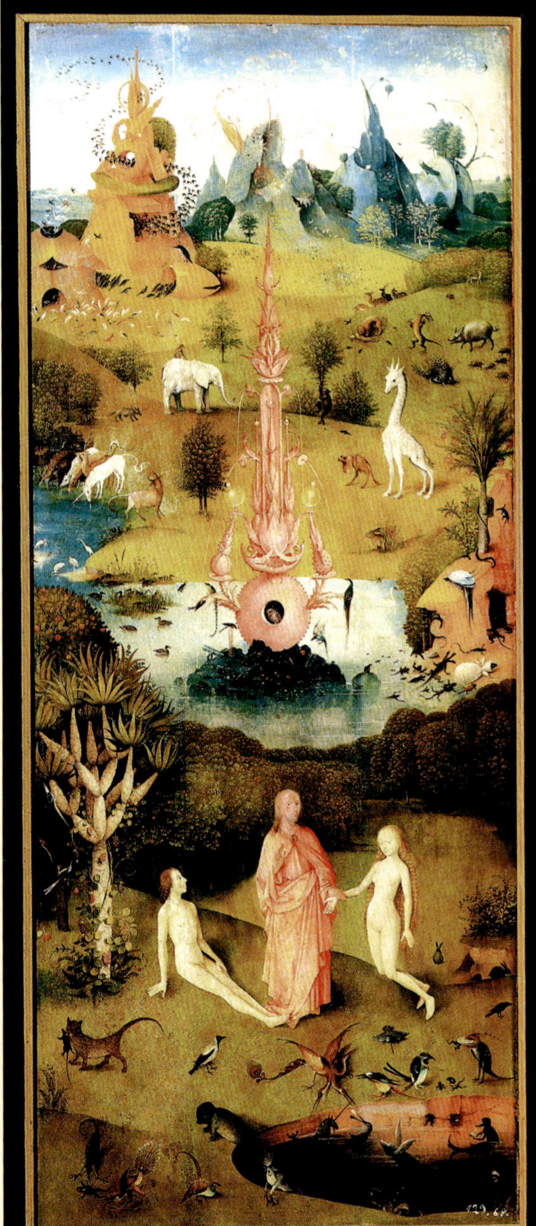

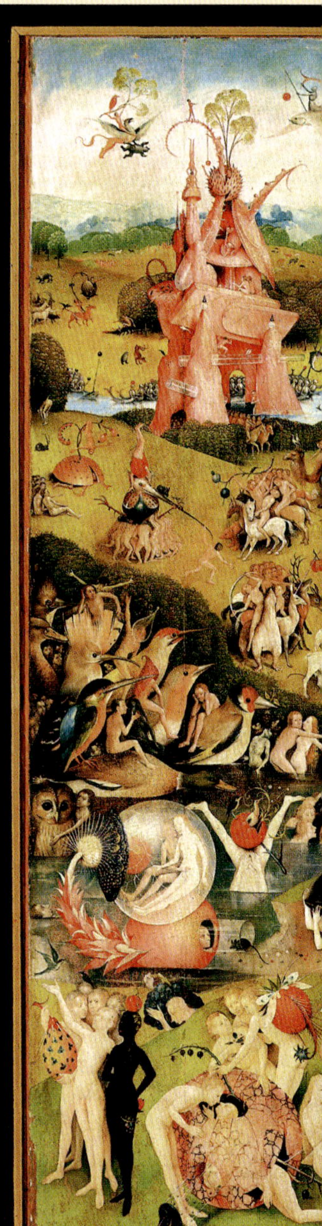

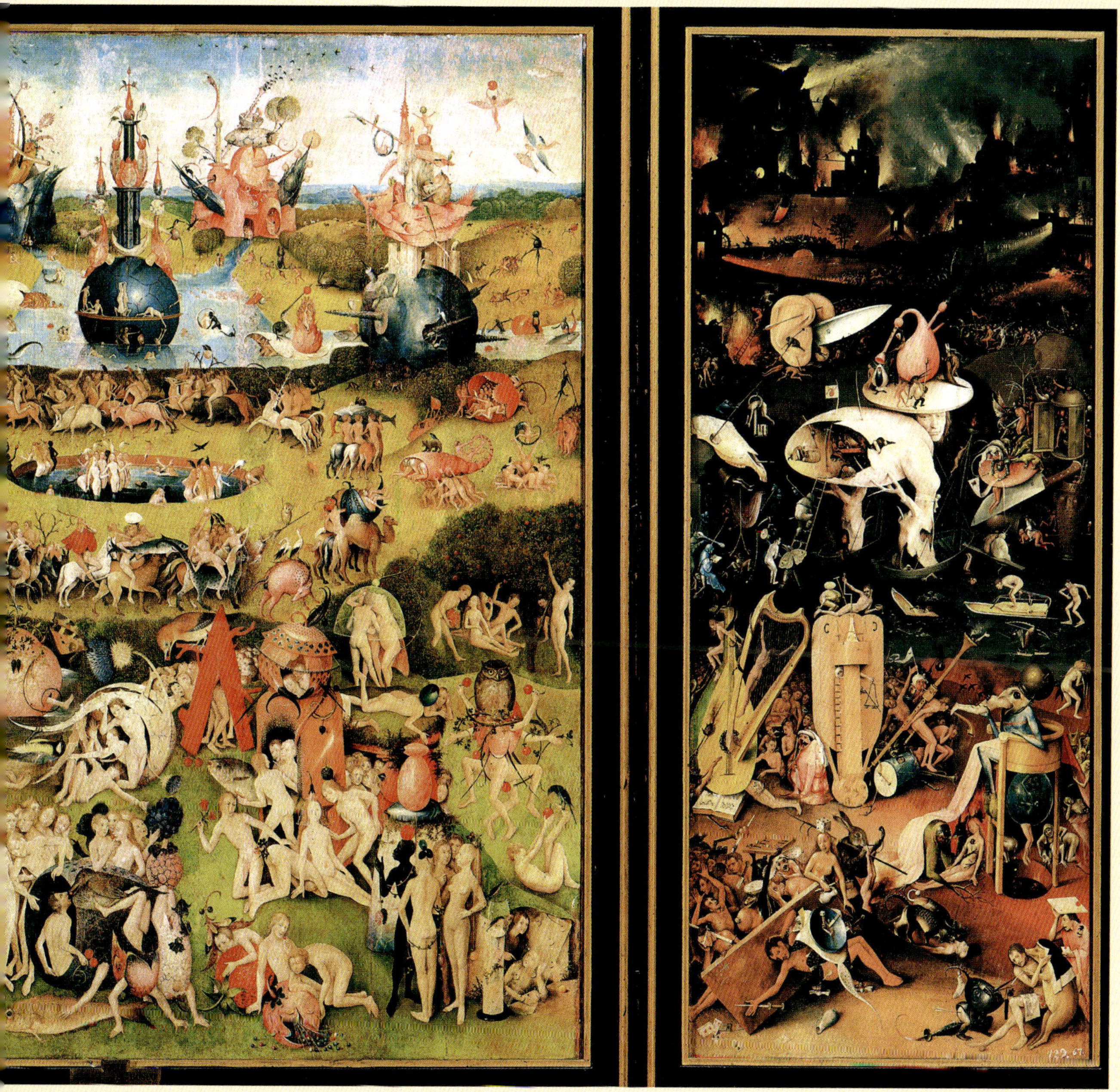

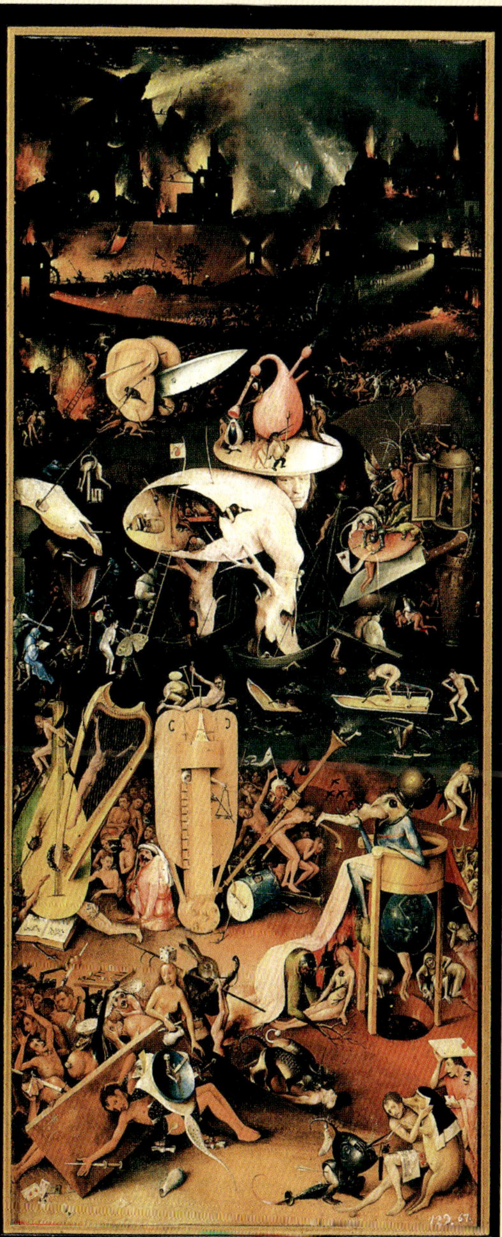

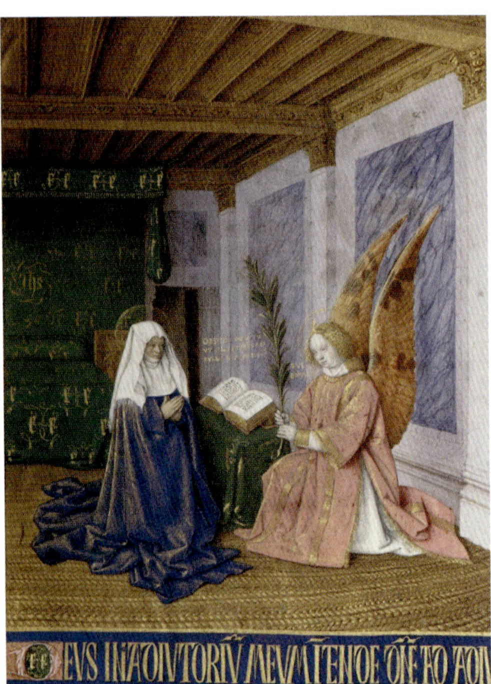

Jean Fouquet
(Tours *c.* 1420 - *c.* 1480)

The Hours of the Virgin: the Second Annunciation
Das Stundenbuch der Jungfrau: Die zweite Verkündigung an Maria
De getijden van de Maagd: aankondiging van de dood van Maria

●●

1445
Musée Condé, Chantilly

Miniature
Miniatur
Miniatuur

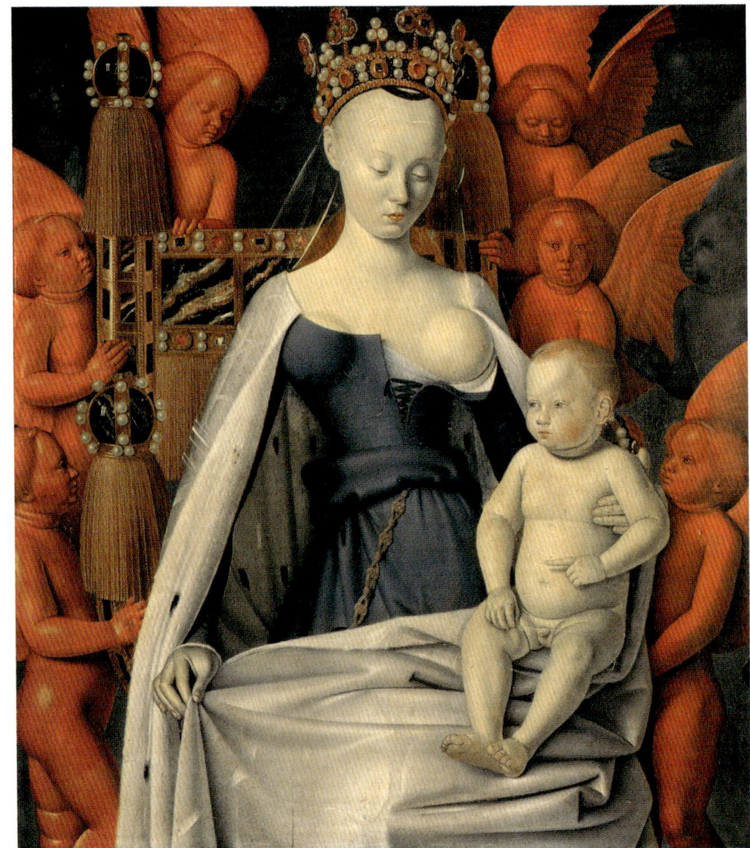

The French Renaissance is still close to the late Gothic tradition.

Die französische Renaissance steht noch in spätgotischer Tradition.

De Franse renaissance valt nog binnen de traditie van de late gotiek

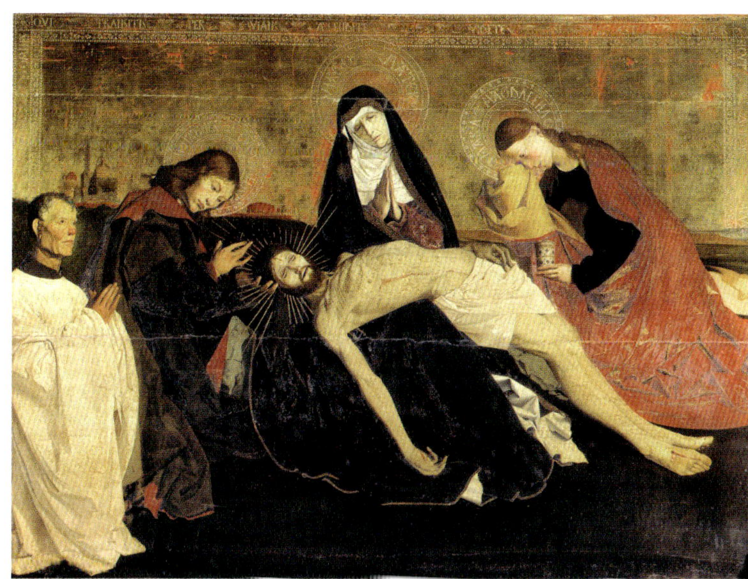

Enguerrand Quarton
(Laon 1410 - *c.* 1466)

The Avignon Pietà
Die Pietà von Villeneuve-lès-Avignon
Pietà uit Villeneuve-lès-Avignon

●●

c. 1455
163 x 218 cm / 64.1 x 85.8 in.
Musée du Louvre, Paris

Tempera on wood / Tempera auf Holz
Tempera op paneel

Jaime Huguet
(Valls 1412 - Barcelona 1492)

The Consecration of St Augustine
Weihe des Hl. Augustinus
Consecratie van Sint Augustinus

●●

c. 1466-1475
272 x 200 cm / 107 x 78.7 in.
Museu Nacional d'Art
de Catalunya,
Barcelona

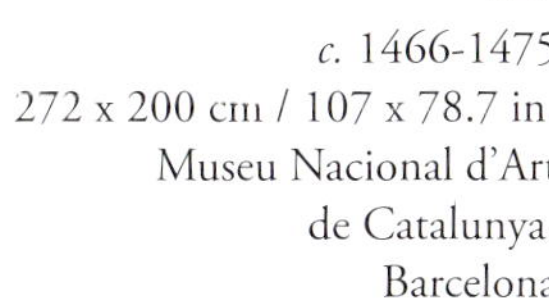

Tempera on wood
Tempera auf Holz
Tempera op paneel

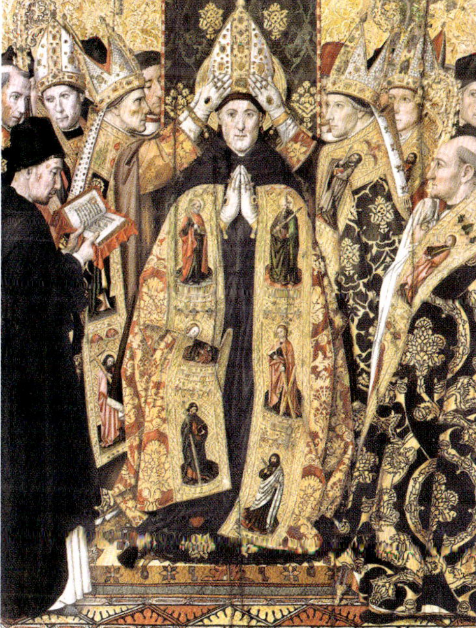

Jean Fouquet
(Tours *c.* 1420 - *c.* 1480)

Melun Diptych
Diptychon von Melun
Diptiek van Melun

●●●

c. 1450
93 x 85 cm / 36.6 x 33.5 in.
Musée royal des Beaux-Arts,
Anvers

Wood panel
Tafel
Paneel

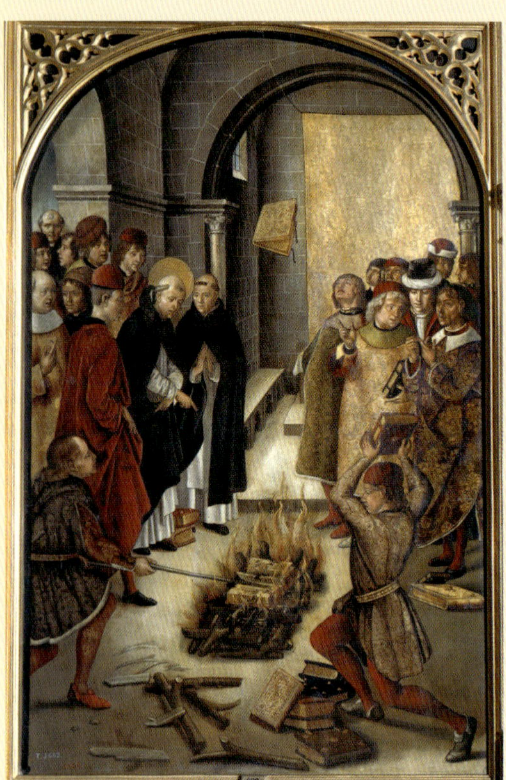

Pedro Berruguete
(Paredes de Nava, Palencia
c. 1450 - 1503)

The Burning of the Books
Der Hl. Dominikus lässt die Schriften der Albigenser verbrennen
Sint Dominicus laat de werken van de Albigenzers verbranden

●

c. 1485-1495
128 x 82 cm / 50.3 x 32.2 in.
Museo Nacional del Prado, Madrid

Oil on wood / Öl auf Tafel
Olieverf op paneel

Pedro Berruguete
(Paredes de Nava, Palencia
c. 1450 - 1503)

Saint Dominic Presides over an Auto-da-Fé
Autodafé unter dem Vorsitz des Hl. Dominikus
Autodafe geleid door Sint Dominicus

●●

c. 1495
154 x 92 cm / 61 x 36.2 in.
Museo Nacional del Prado, Madrid

Wood panel / Tafel / Paneel

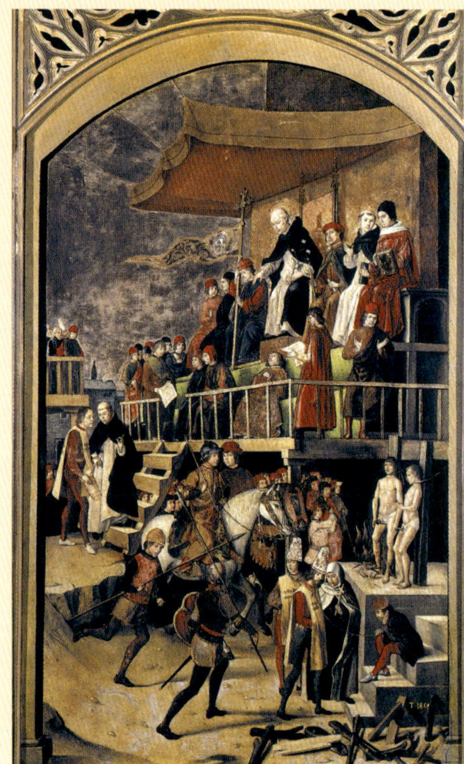

Pedro Berruguete introduces the Renaissance into Spain.

Pedro Berruguete leitet die Renaissance in Spanien ein.

Pedro Berruguete introduceert de renaissance in Spanje.

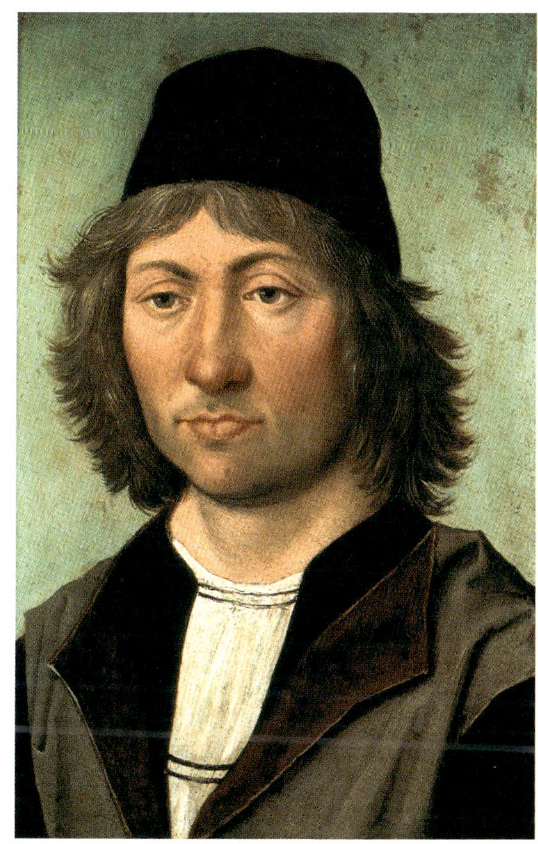

Pedro Berruguete
(Paredes de Nava, Palencia *c.* 1450 - 1503)

Self-Portrait (presumed)
Mutmaßliches Selbstbildnis von Berruguete
Vermoedelijk zelfportret van Berruguete

●

1490
36 x 24 cm / 14.1 x 9.4 in.
Museo Lázaro Galdiano, Madrid

Oil on canvas
Öl auf Leinwand
Olieverf op doek

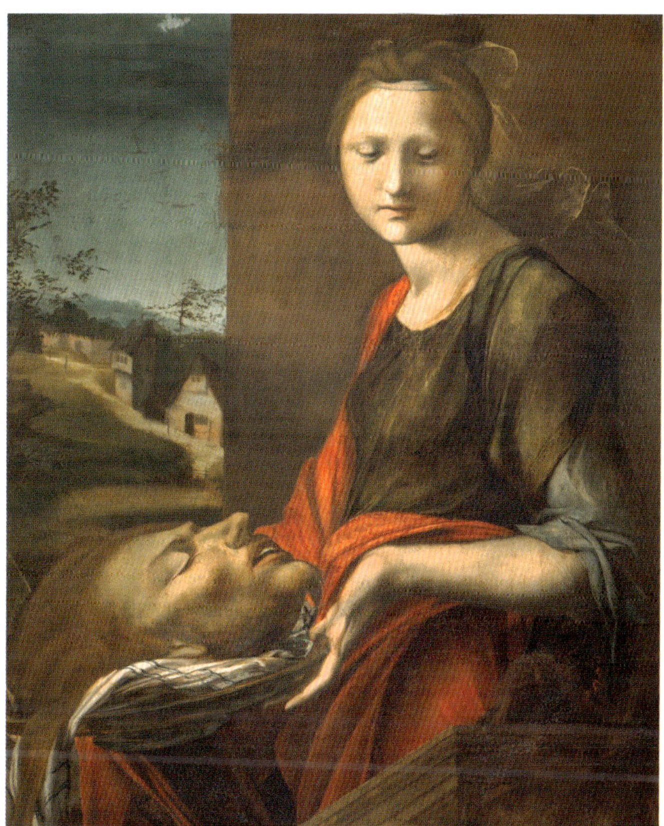

Alonso Berruguete
(Paredes de Nava, Palencia *c.*1490 - Toledo 1561)

Salome with the Head of John the Baptist
Salomé

●●

c. 1512
88 x 71 cm / 34.6 x 28 in.
Galleria degli Uffizi, Firenze

Oil on wood
Öl auf Tafel
Olieverf op paneel

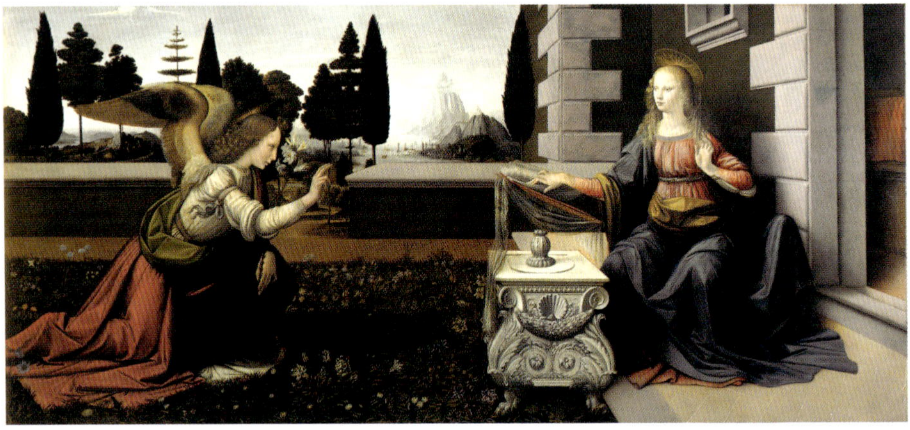

Leonardo da Vinci
(Anchiano da Vinci,
Firenze 1452 - Amboise 1519)

Annunciation
Verkündigung
De Annunciatie

●●

c. 1475
104 x 217 cm / 41 x 85.4 in.
Galleria degli Uffizi, Firenze

Oil on wood / Öl auf Tafel
Olieverf op paneel

Genius, mathematician and inventor: Leonardo da Vinci is the most talented draughtsman of the High Renaissance...

Genie, Mathematiker und Erfinder. Leonardo da Vinci ist der begnadete Zeichner der Hochrenaissance.

Een genie, wiskundige en uitvinder. Leonardo da Vinci is de meest getalenteerde ontwerper van de hoge renaissance.

Leonardo da Vinci
(Anchiano da Vinci,
Firenze 1452 - Amboise 1519)

Adoration of the Magi
Anbetung der Könige
Aanbidding der Wijzen

●●

c. 1481-1482
246 x 243 cm / 97 x 96 in.
Galleria degli Uffizi, Firenze

Wood panel / Tafel / Paneel

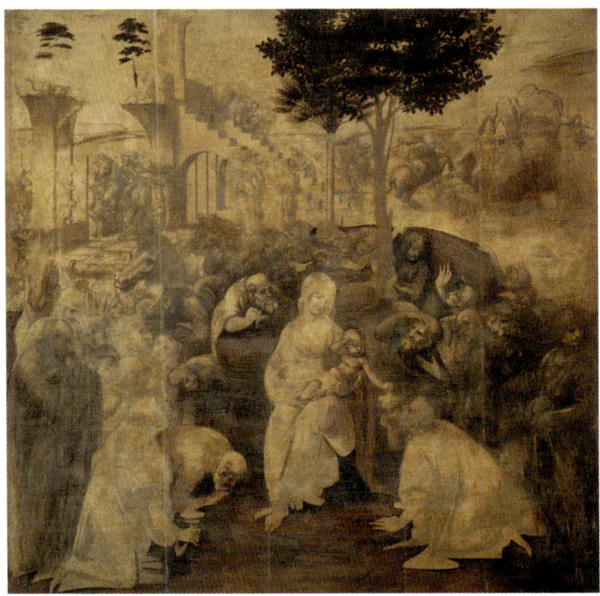

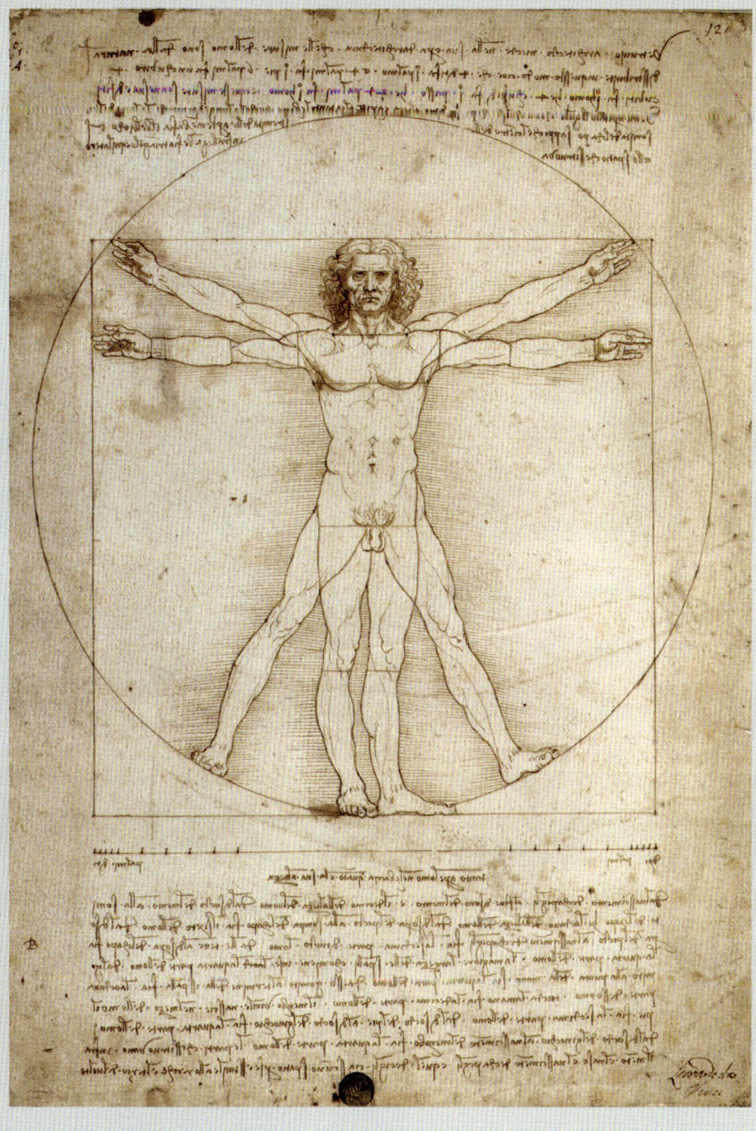

Leonardo da Vinci
(Anchiano da Vinci, Firenze 1452 - Amboise 1519)

Proportions of the Human Body
Die Proportionen des menschlichen Körpers
De proporties van het menselijk lichaam

●●●

c. 1490
34,4 x 24,5 cm / 13.5 x 9.6 in.
Gallerie dell'Accademia, Venezia

Metal graver, pen, ink and watercolour
Metallspitze, Feder und Tinte, Aquarell
Metaalstift, pen en inkt, waterverf

▸▸

Leonardo da Vinci
(Anchiano da Vinci, Firenze 1452 - Amboise 1519)

Last Supper
Das Letzte Abendmahl
Het Laatste Avondmaal

●●●

1494-1498
460 x 880 cm / 181.1 x 346.4 in.
Santa Maria delle Grazie, Milano

Tempera forte on plaster / Seccomalerei
Tempera op muur

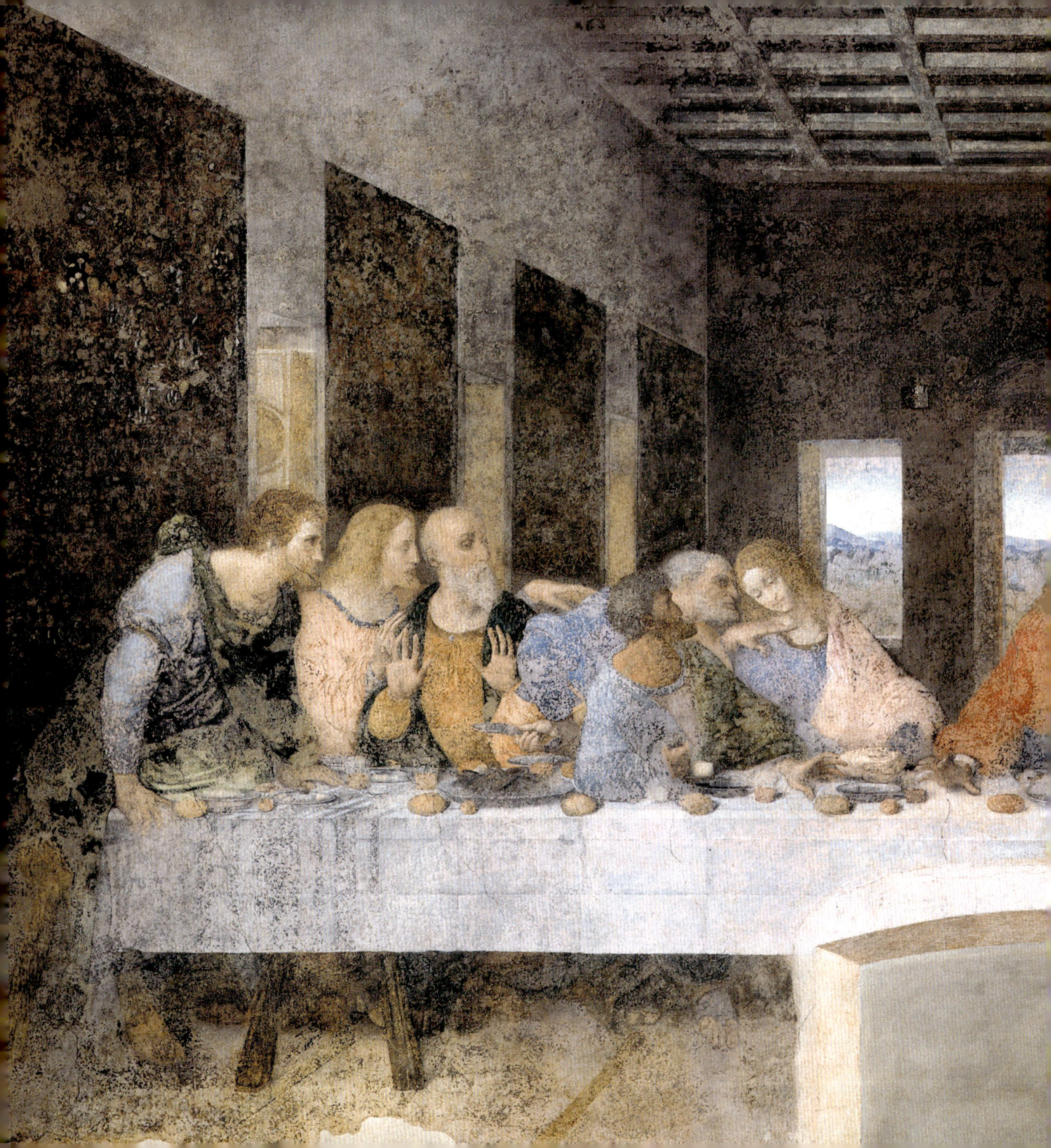

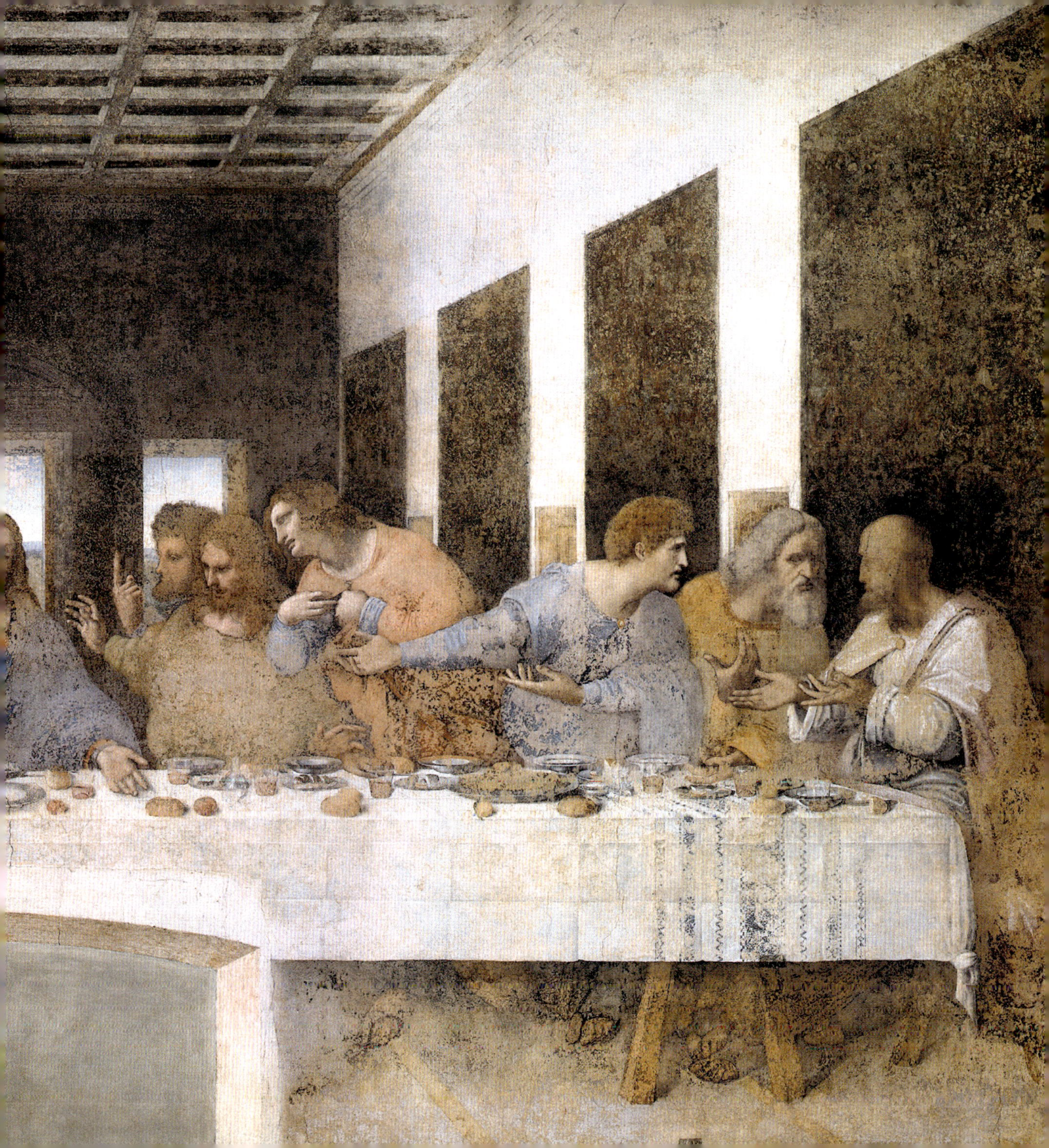

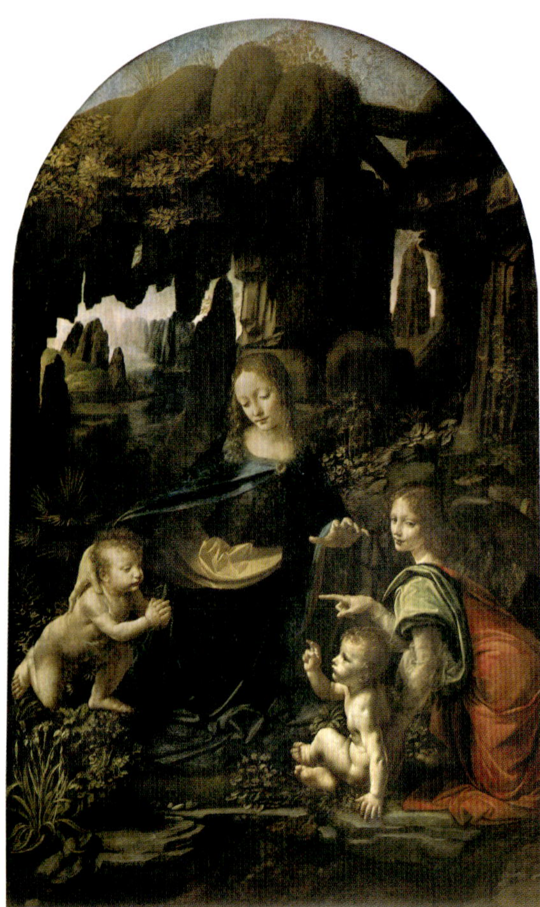

Leonardo da Vinci
(Anchiano da Vinci, Firenze 1452 - Amboise 1519)

Virgin of the Rocks
Felsgrottenmadonna
Maagd op de Rotsen

●●●

c. 1483
198 x 123 cm / 78.3 x 48 in.
Musée du Louvre, Paris

Oil on wood
Öl auf Tafel
Olieverf op paneel

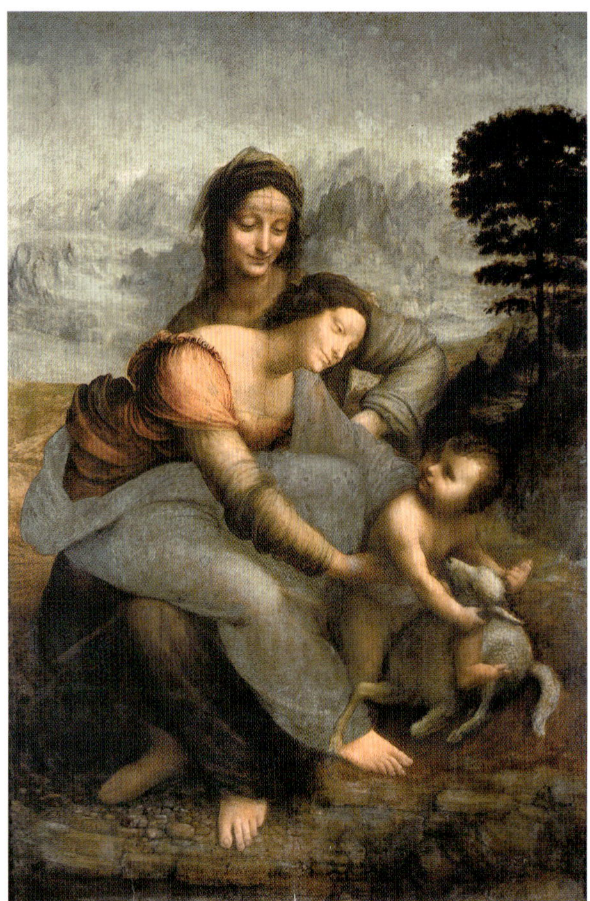

Leonardo da Vinci
(Anchiano da Vinci, Firenze 1452 - Amboise 1519)

Virgin and Child with Saint Anne
Madonna und Kind mit der Hl. Anna
De Maagd en Kind met de Heilige Anna

●●

c. 1506-1513
168 x 130 cm / 66.1 x 51.1 in.
Musée du Louvre, Paris

Oil on wood
Öl auf Tafel
Olieverf op paneel

Leonardo da Vinci
(Anchiano da Vinci, Firenze 1452 - Amboise 1519)

Mona Lisa
Mona Lisa (La Gioconda)

●●●

c. 1505-1514
77 x 53 cm / 30.3 x 20.9 in.
Musée du Louvre, Paris

Oil on wood
Öl auf Tafel
Olieverf op paneel

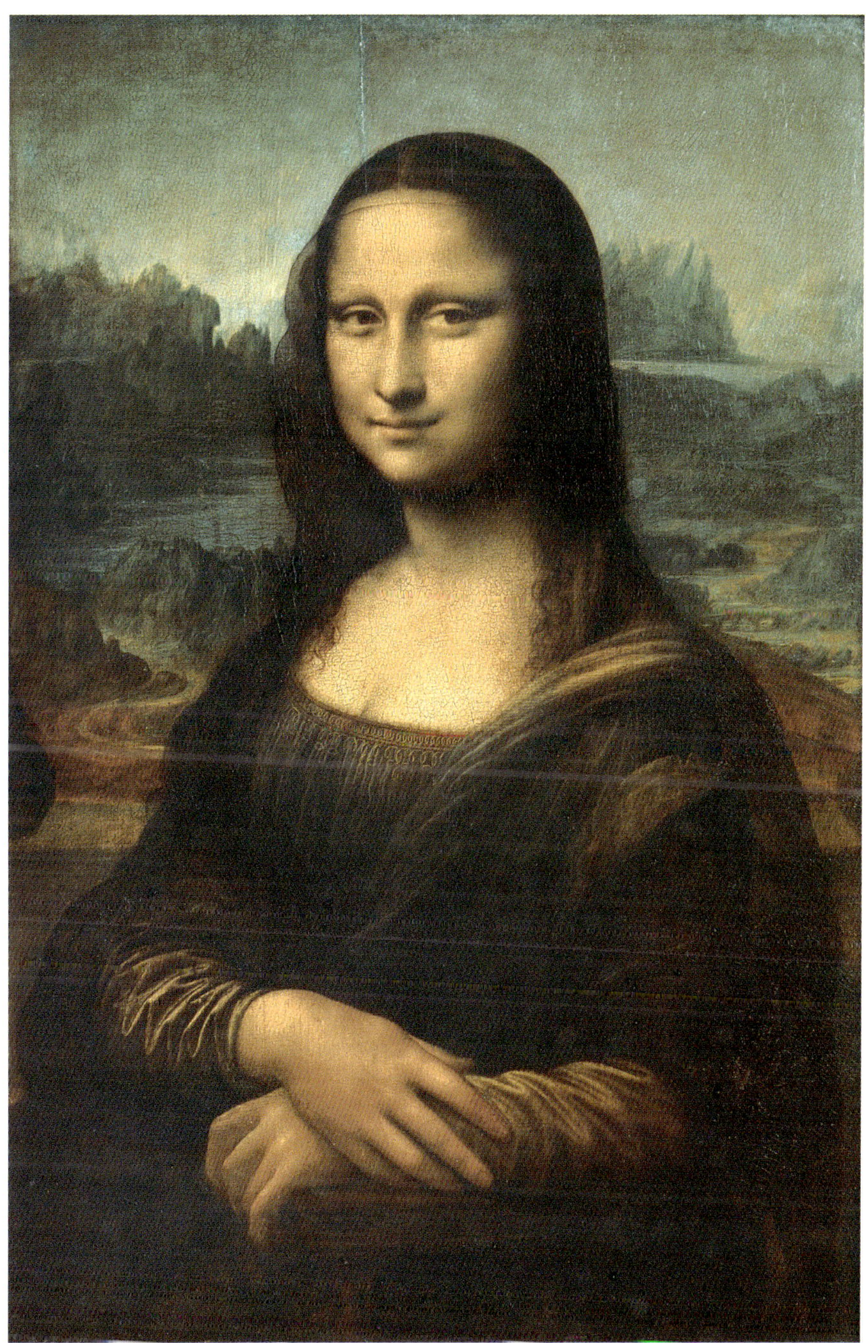

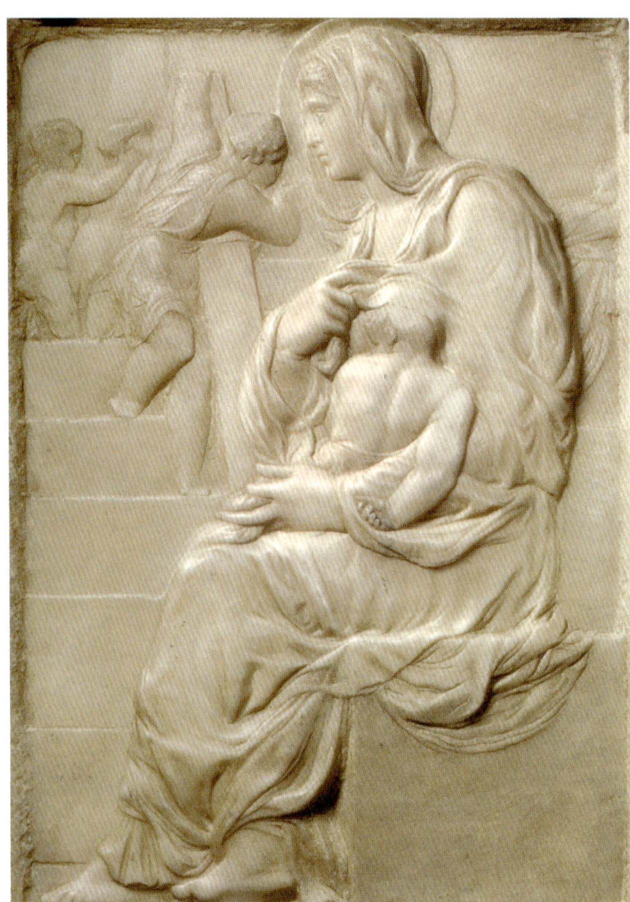

Michelangelo
(Caprese, Arezzo 1475 - Roma 1564)

Madonna of the Stairs
Madonna an der Treppe
Madonna aan de trap

●

c. 1490-1492
55,5 x 40 cm / 21.8 x 15.7 in.
Casa Buonarroti, Firenze

Marble / Marmor / Marmer

Michelangelo
(Caprese, Arezzo 1475 - Roma 1564)

Bacchus

●●

1496-1497
h. 184 cm / 72.4 in.
Museo Nazionale del Bargello, Firenze

Marble / Marmor / Marmer

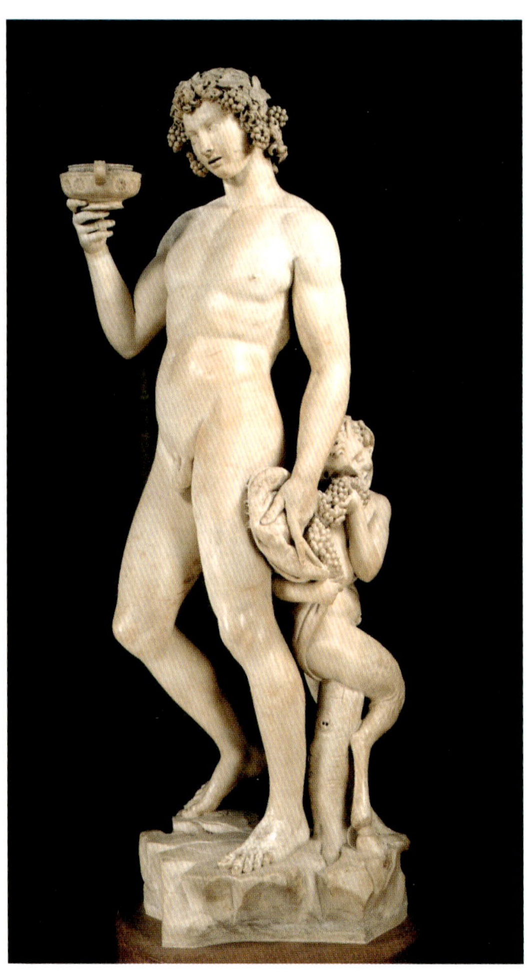

... Michelangelo, on the other hand, is the perfectionist in marble and colour.

Michelangelo hingegen ist Perfektionist in Marmor und Farbe.

... Michelangelo, is daarentegen de perfectionist van het marmer en de kleuren.

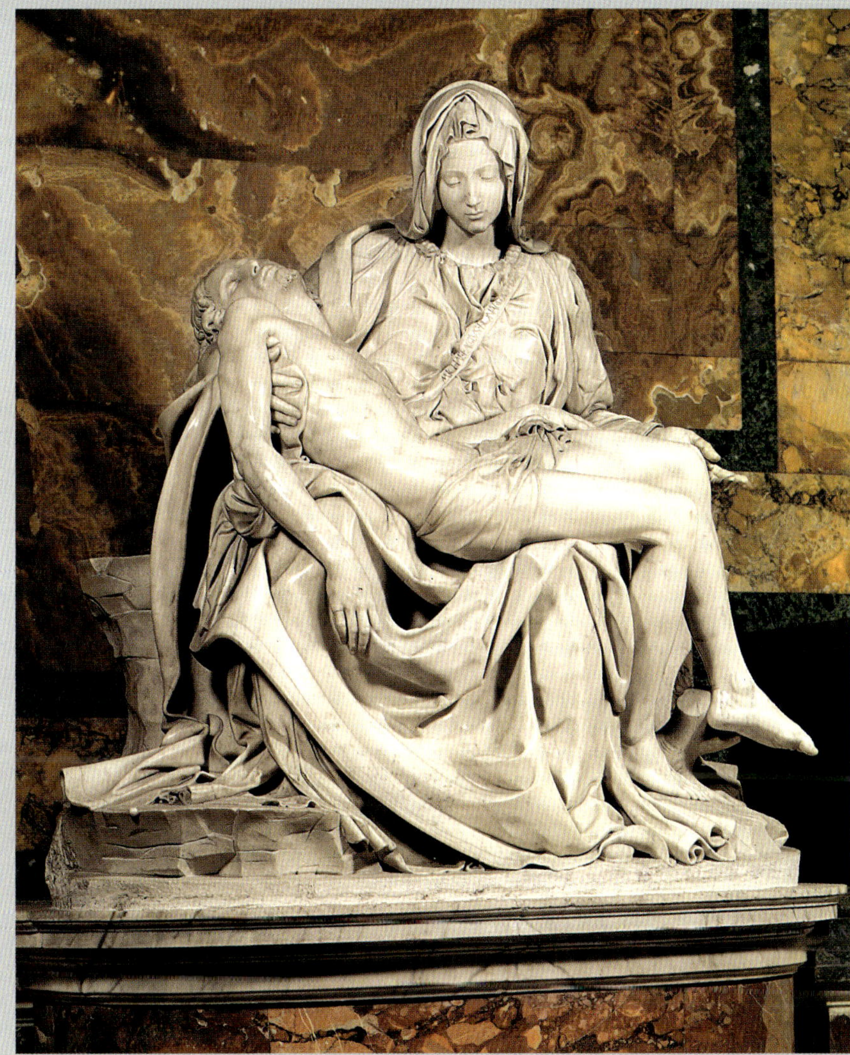

Michelangelo
(Caprese, Arezzo 1475 - Roma 1564)

Pietà

●●●

c. 1498-1499
h. 174 cm / 68.5 in.
Basilica di San Pietro, Città del Vaticano

Marble / Marmor / Marmer

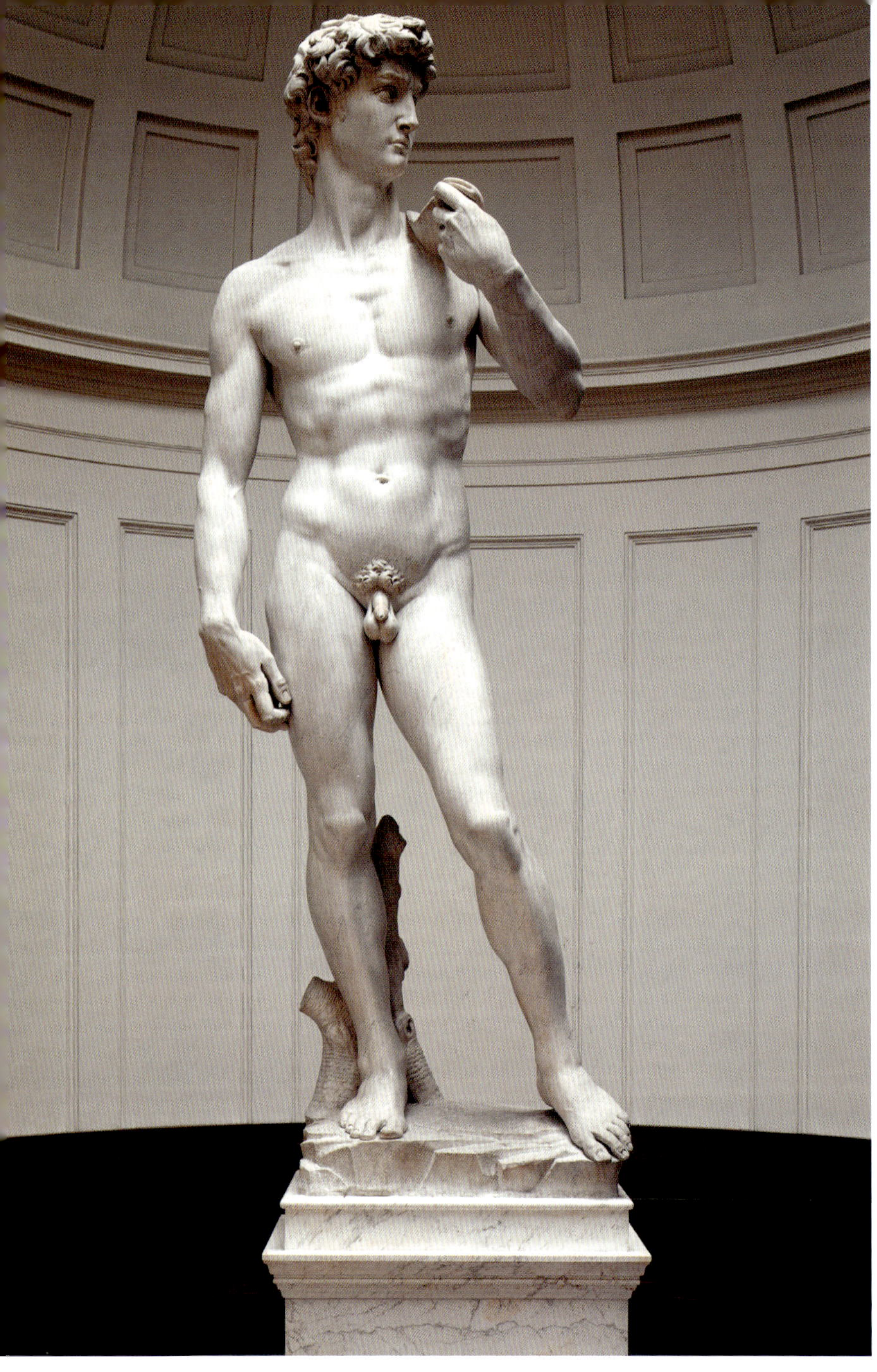

Michelangelo
(Caprese, Arezzo 1475 - Roma 1564)
David
●●●
c. 1501-1504
h. 410 cm / 161.4 in.
Galleria dell'Accademia, Firenze

Marble / Marmor / Marmer

Michelangelo
(Caprese, Arezzo 1475 - Roma 1564)
Holy Family (Tondo Doni)
Tondo Doni
Heilige Familie (Tondo Doni)
●●●
c. 1504-1506
Ø 120 cm / 47.2 in.
Galleria degli Uffizi, Firenze

Tempera on wood
Tempera auf Tafel
Tempera op paneel

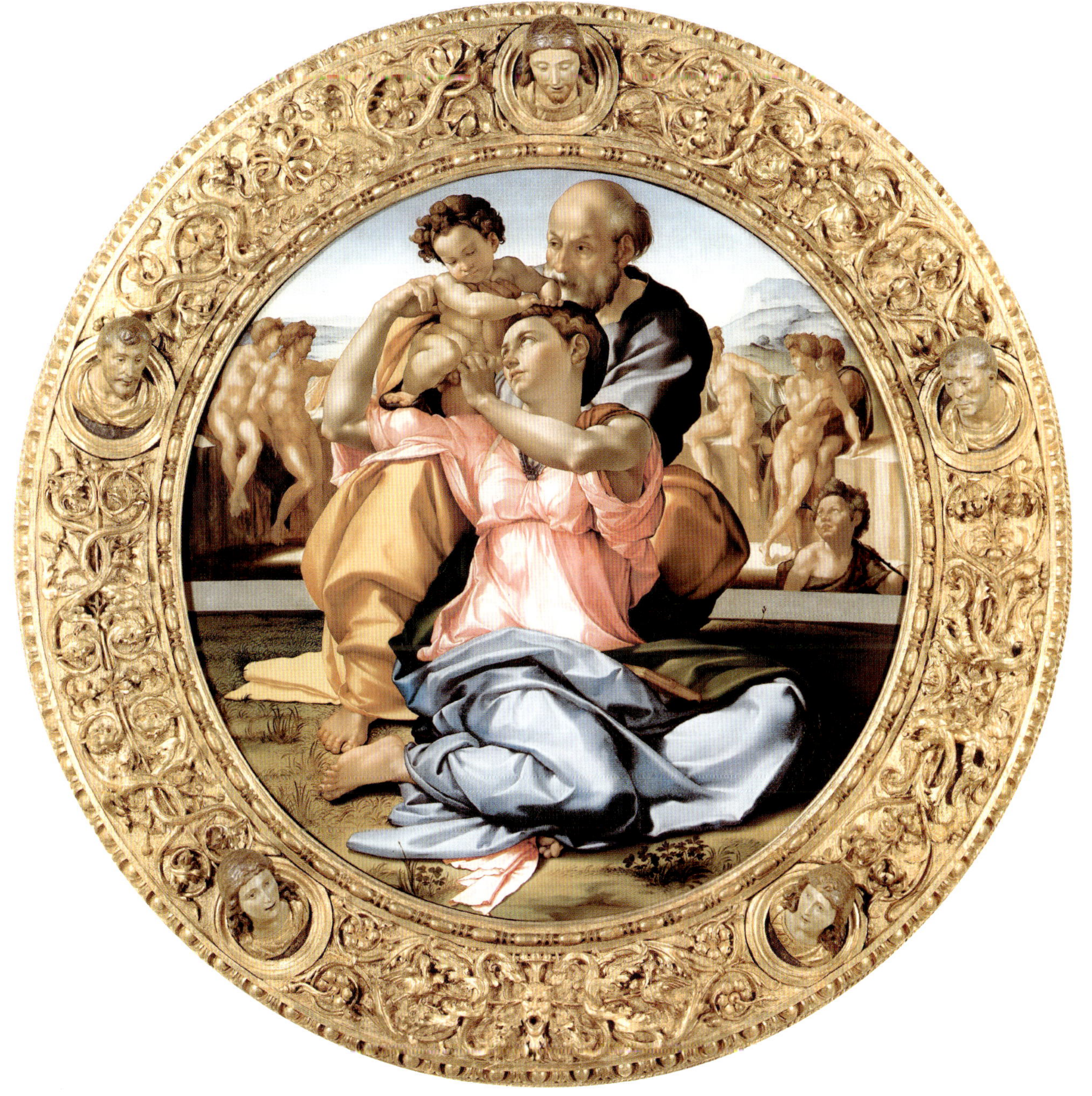

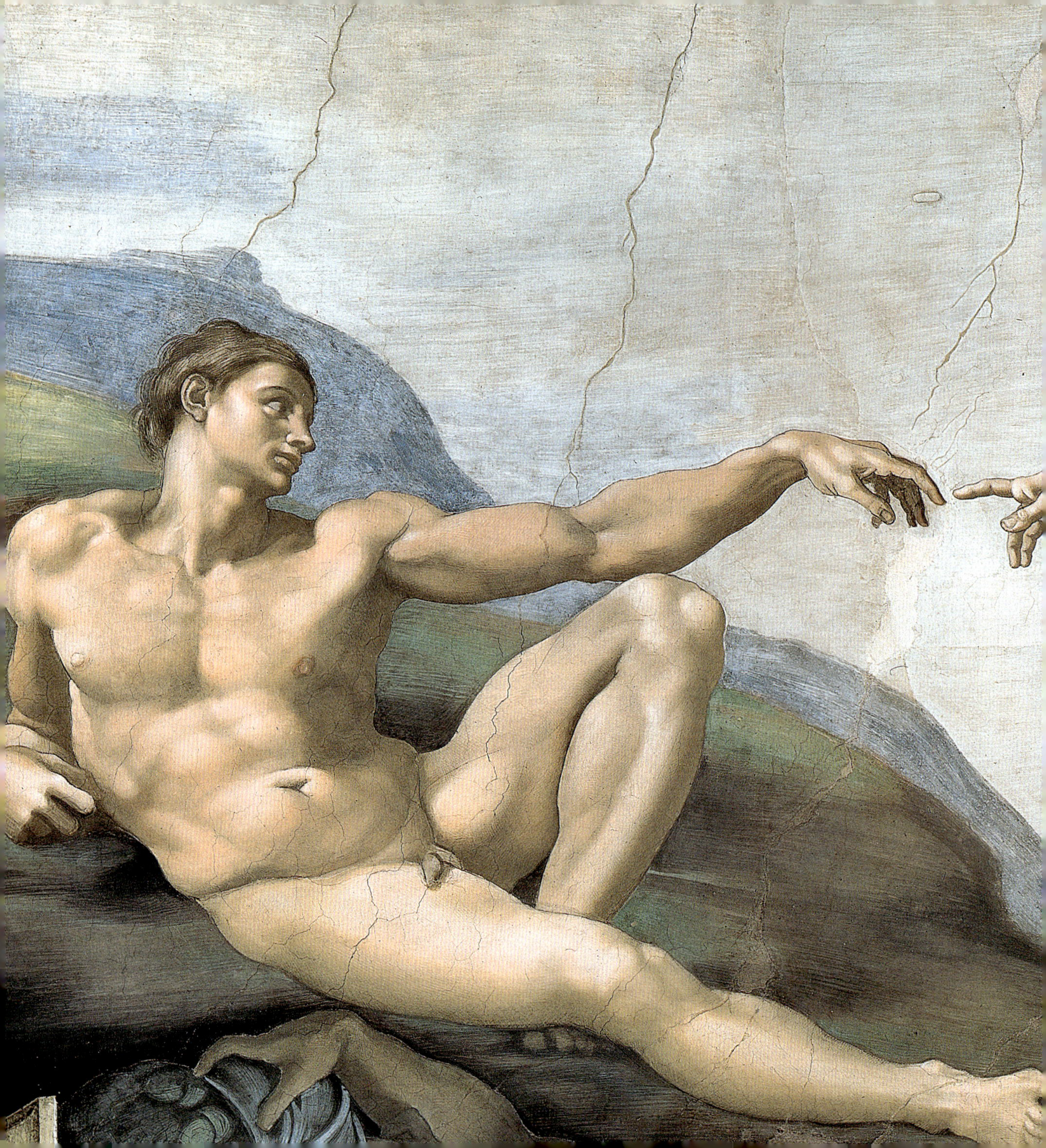

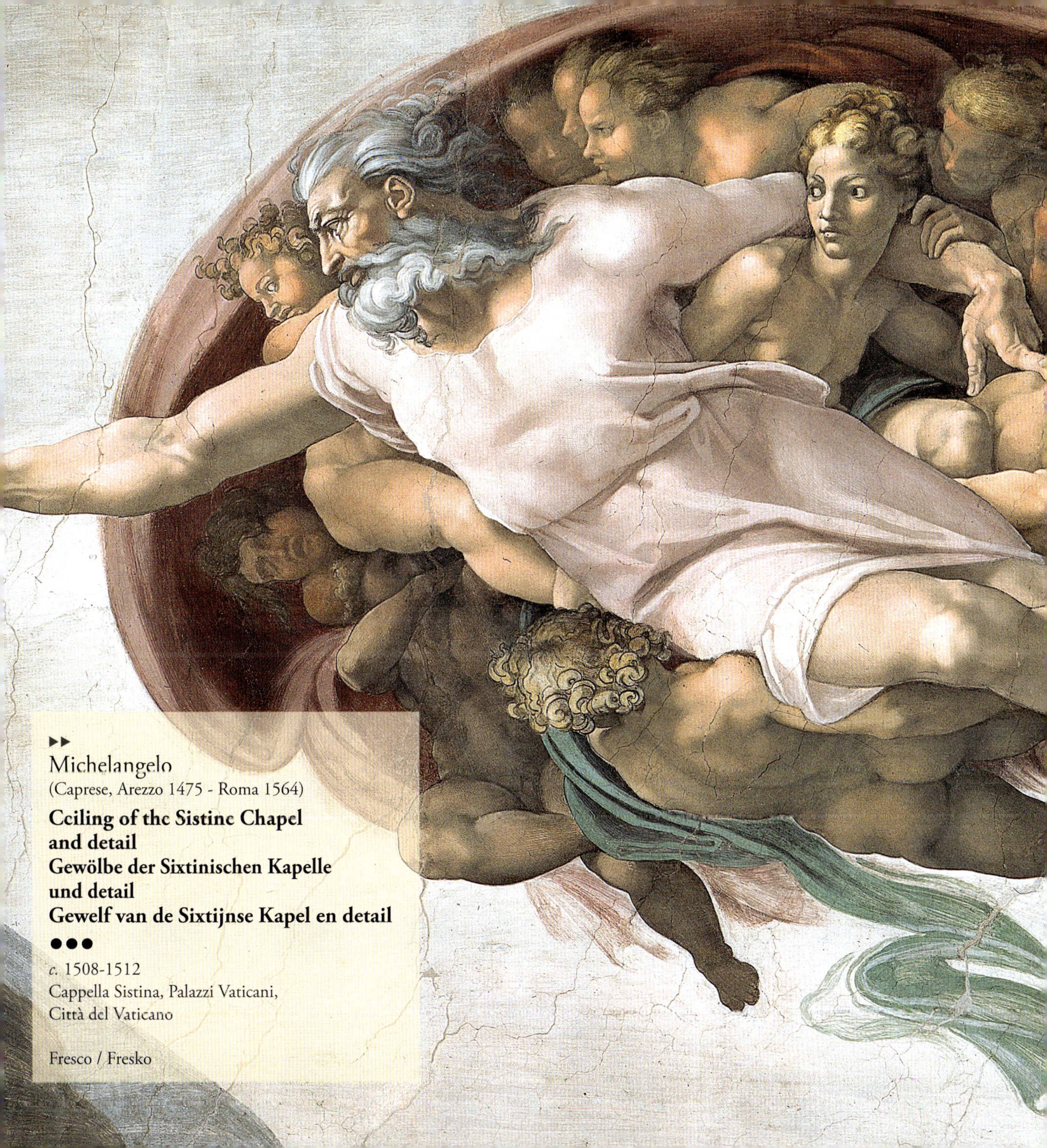

▸▸
Michelangelo
(Caprese, Arezzo 1475 - Roma 1564)
Ceiling of the Sistine Chapel and detail
Gewölbe der Sixtinischen Kapelle und detail
Gewelf van de Sixtijnse Kapel en detail
●●●
c. 1508-1512
Cappella Sistina, Palazzi Vaticani, Città del Vaticano

Fresco / Fresko

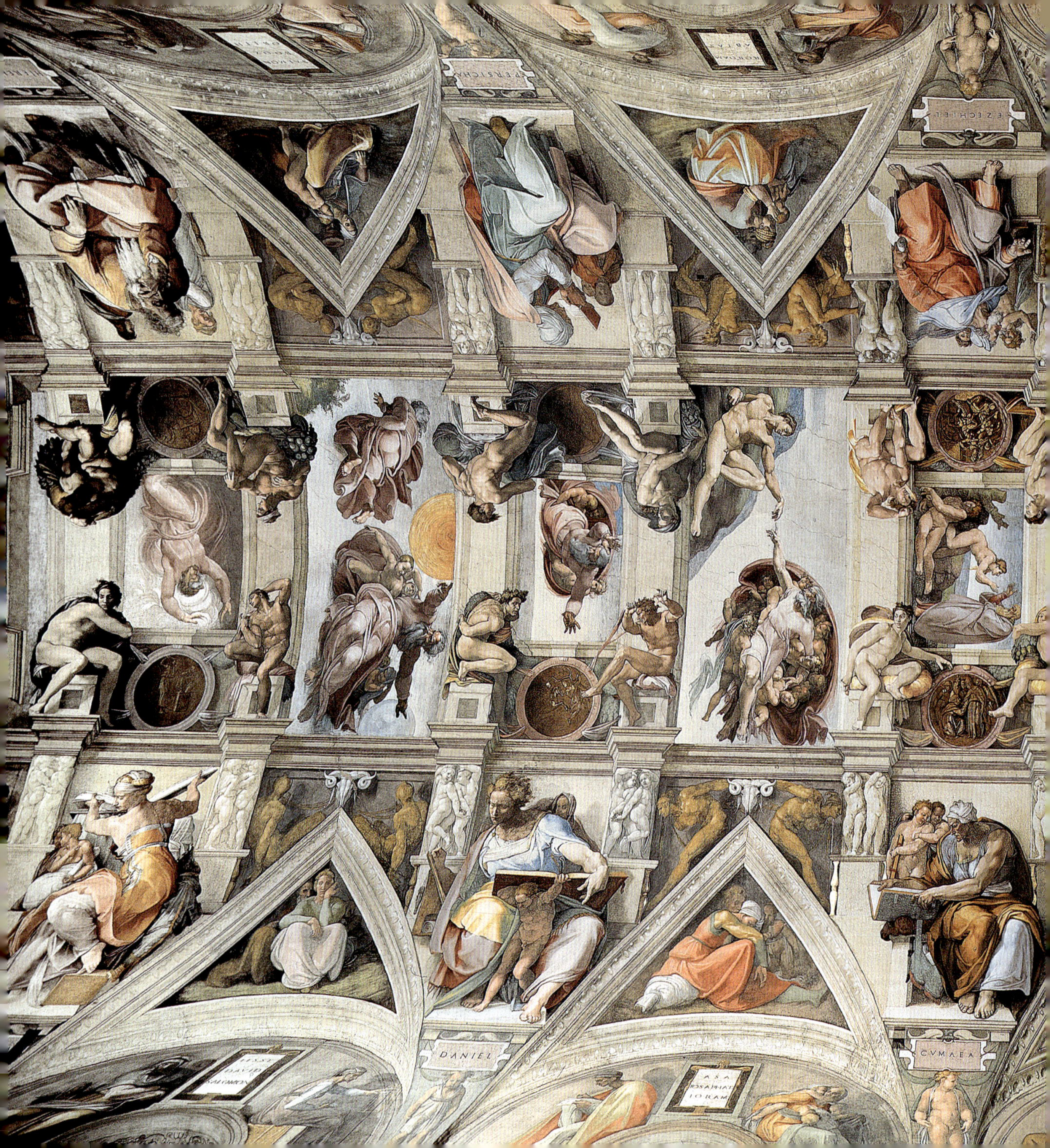

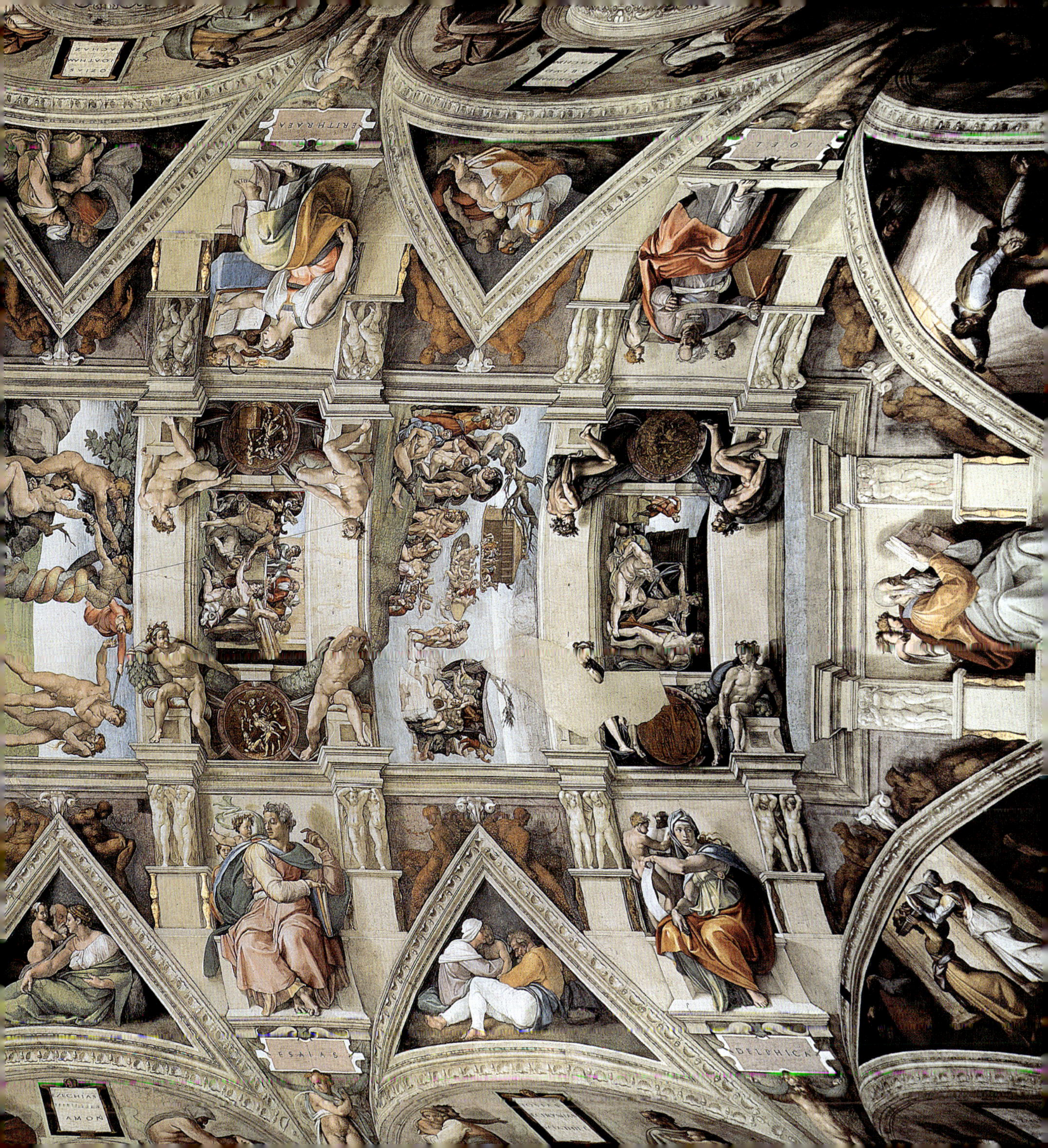

ERITHRAEA
IOEL
ESAIAS
DELPHICA

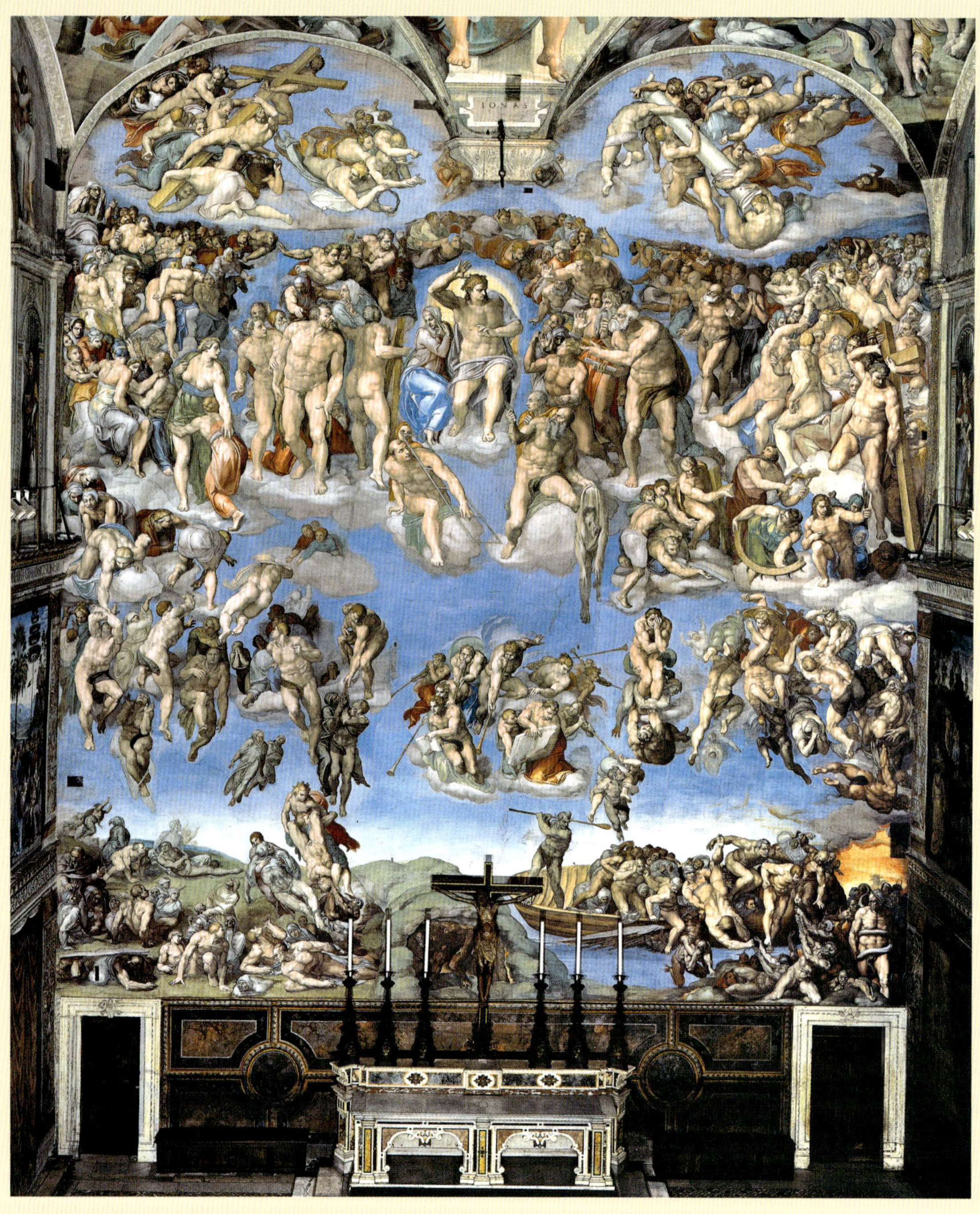
IONAS

Michelangelo
(Caprese, Arezzo 1475 - Roma 1564)

The Last Judgement and detail
Das Jüngse Gericht und detail
Het Laatste Oordeel en detail

●●●

c. 1536-1541
Cappella Sistina, Palazzi Vaticani, Città del Vaticano

Fresco / Fresko

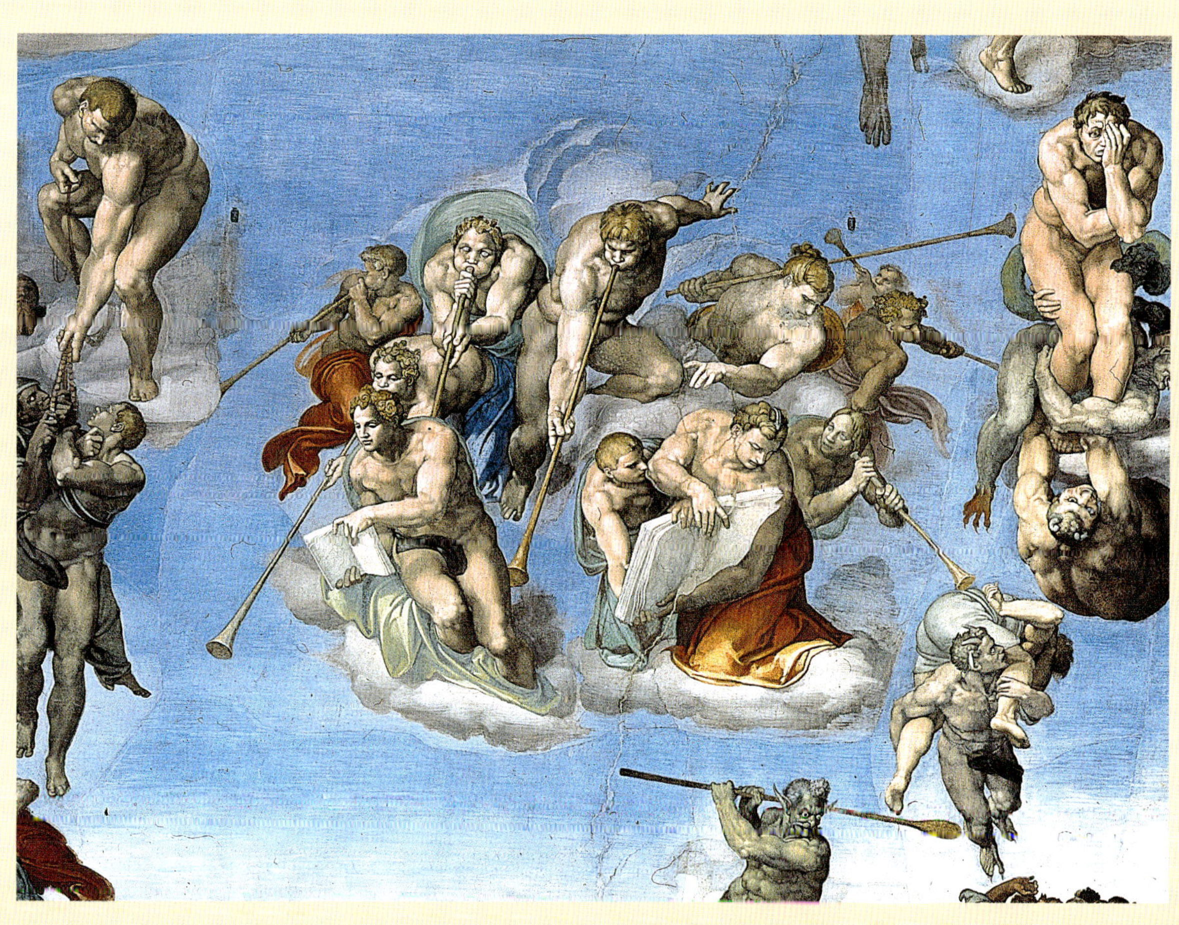

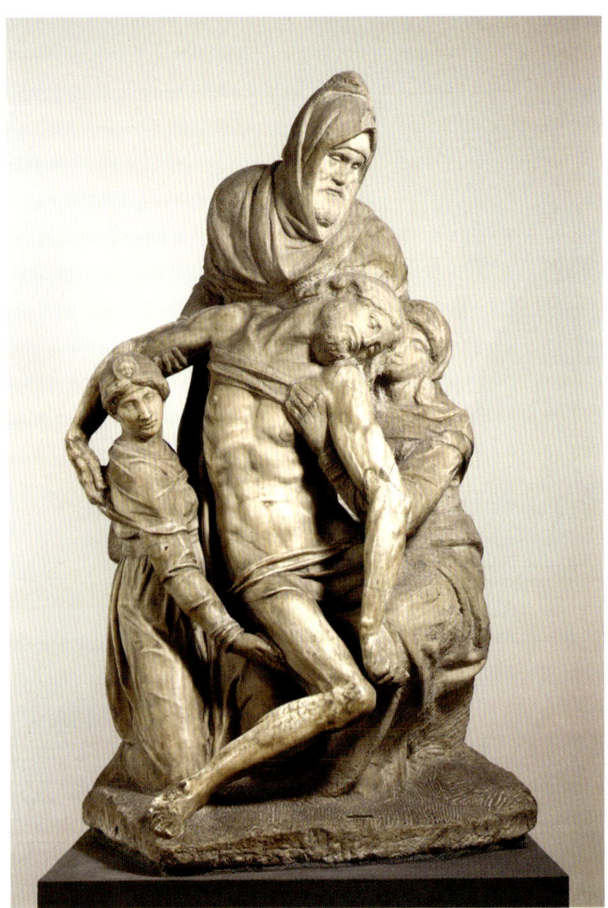

Michelangelo
(Caprese, Arezzo 1475 - Roma 1564)

Pietà

c. 1550-1555
h. 226 cm / 88.9 in.
Museo dell'Opera del Duomo,
Firenze

Marble / Marmor / Marmer

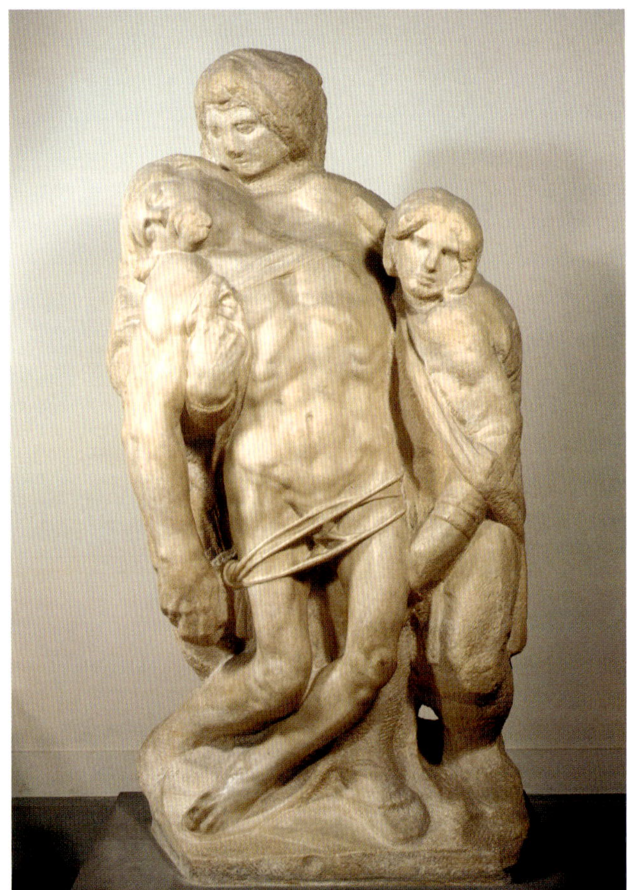

Michelangelo
(Caprese, Arezzo 1475 - Roma 1564)

Pietà di Palestrina

c. 1555
h. 253 cm / 99.6 in.
Galleria dell'Accademia, Firenze

Marble / Marmor / Marmer

The late work of Michelangelo is characterized by doubt. For this reason, some works remain unfinished.

Micehlangelos Spätwerk ist von Zweifeln geprägt. Einige Werke bleiben deshalb unvollendet.

Het late werk van Michelangelo wordt gekenmerkt door twijfel. Daarom blijven enkele werken onvoltooid.

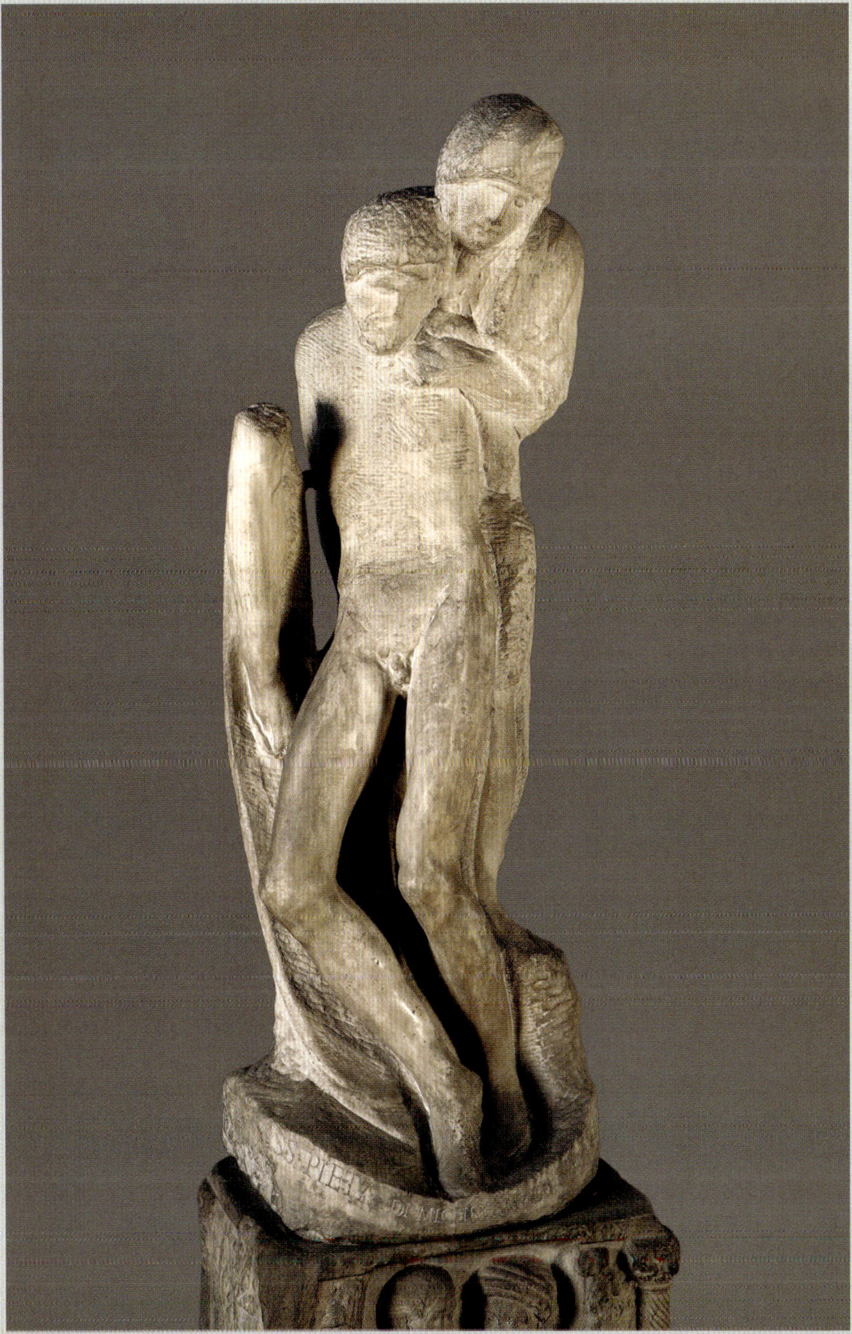

Michelangelo
(Caprese, Arezzo 1475 - Roma 1564)

Pietà Rondanini

●●

c. 1552-1564
h. 195 cm / 76.7 in.
Castello Sforzesco, Milano

Marble / Marmor / Marmer

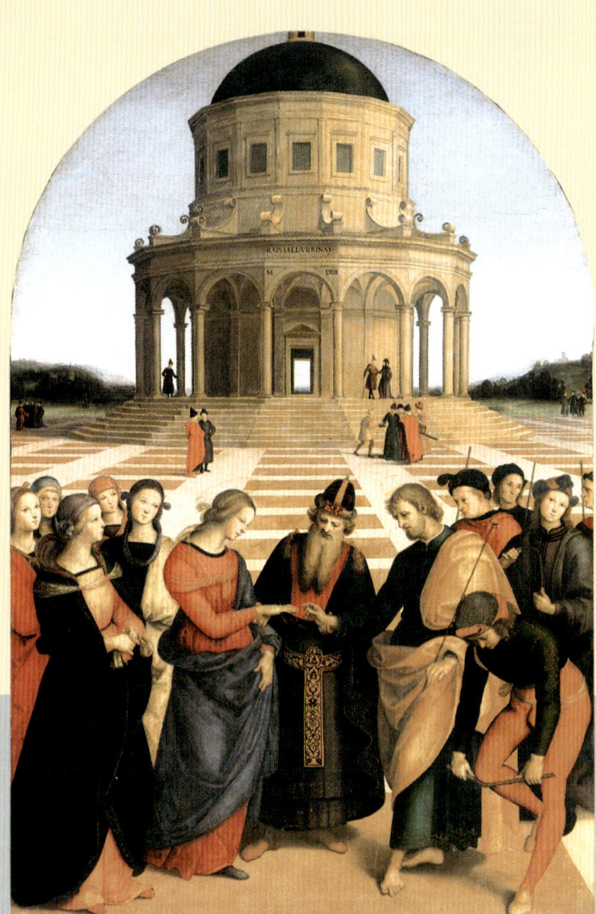

Raphael / Raffaello Sanzio
(Urbino 1483 - Roma 1520)

Marriage of the Virgin
Die Hochzeit der Jungfrau
Het huwelijk van Maria

●●●

1504
170 x 117 cm / 67 x 446 in.
Pinacoteca di Brera, Milano

Oil on wood / Öl auf Tafel
Olieverf op paneel

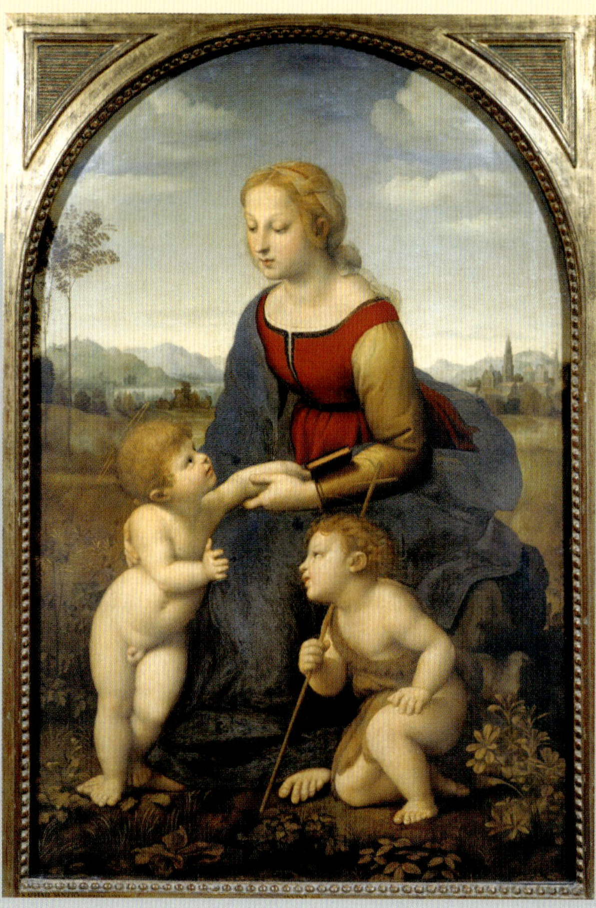

Raphael / Raffaello Sanzio
(Urbino 1483 - Roma 1520)

Mother and Child with St John
(La belle jardinière)
Die schöne Gärtnerin
Maria met Kind en de jonge
Johannes de Doper (La belle jardinière)

●●●

1507
122 x 80 cm / 48 x 31.5 in.
Musée du Louvre, Paris
Oil on wood / Öl auf Tafel / Olieverf op paneel

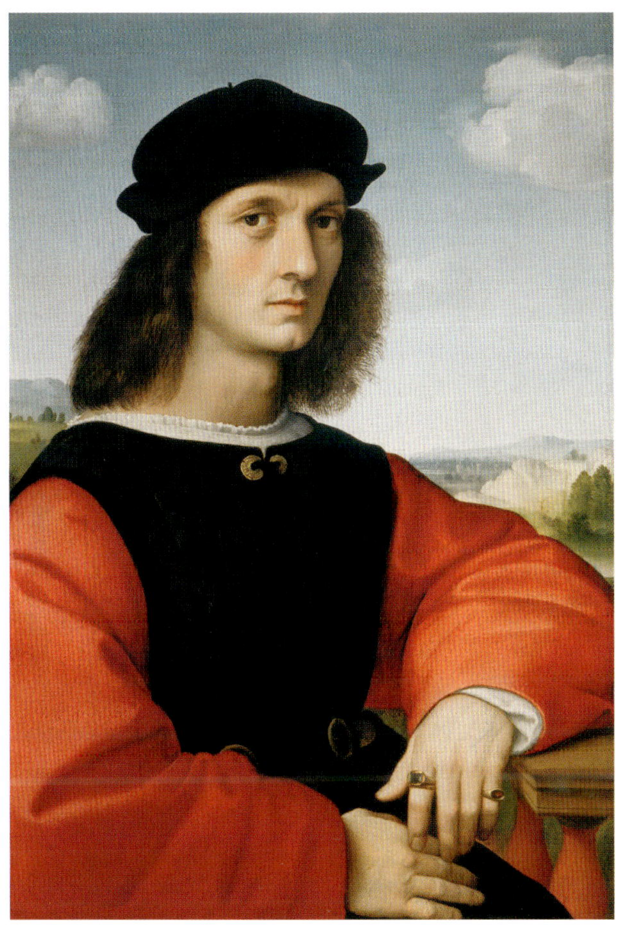

Raphael / Raffaello Sanzio
(Urbino 1483 - Roma 1520)

Agnolo Doni

1506
65 x 45,7 cm / 25.6 x 18 in.
Galleria Palatina, Firenze

Oil on wood
Öl auf Tafel
Olieverf op paneel

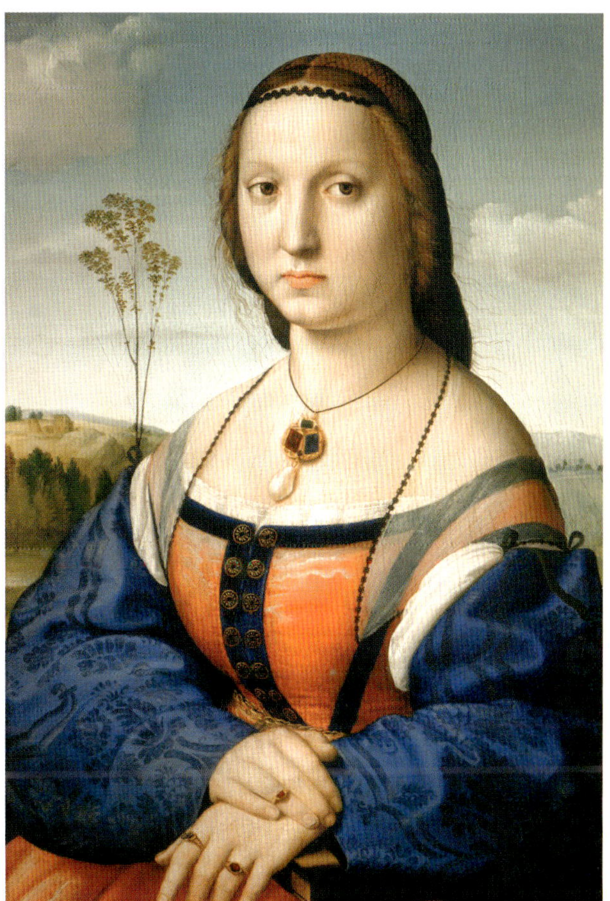

Raphael / Raffaello Sanzio
(Urbino 1483 - Roma 1520)

Maddalena Doni

1506
65 x 45,7 cm / 25.6 x 18 in.
Galleria Palatina, Firenze

Oil on wood
Öl auf Tafel
Olieverf op paneel

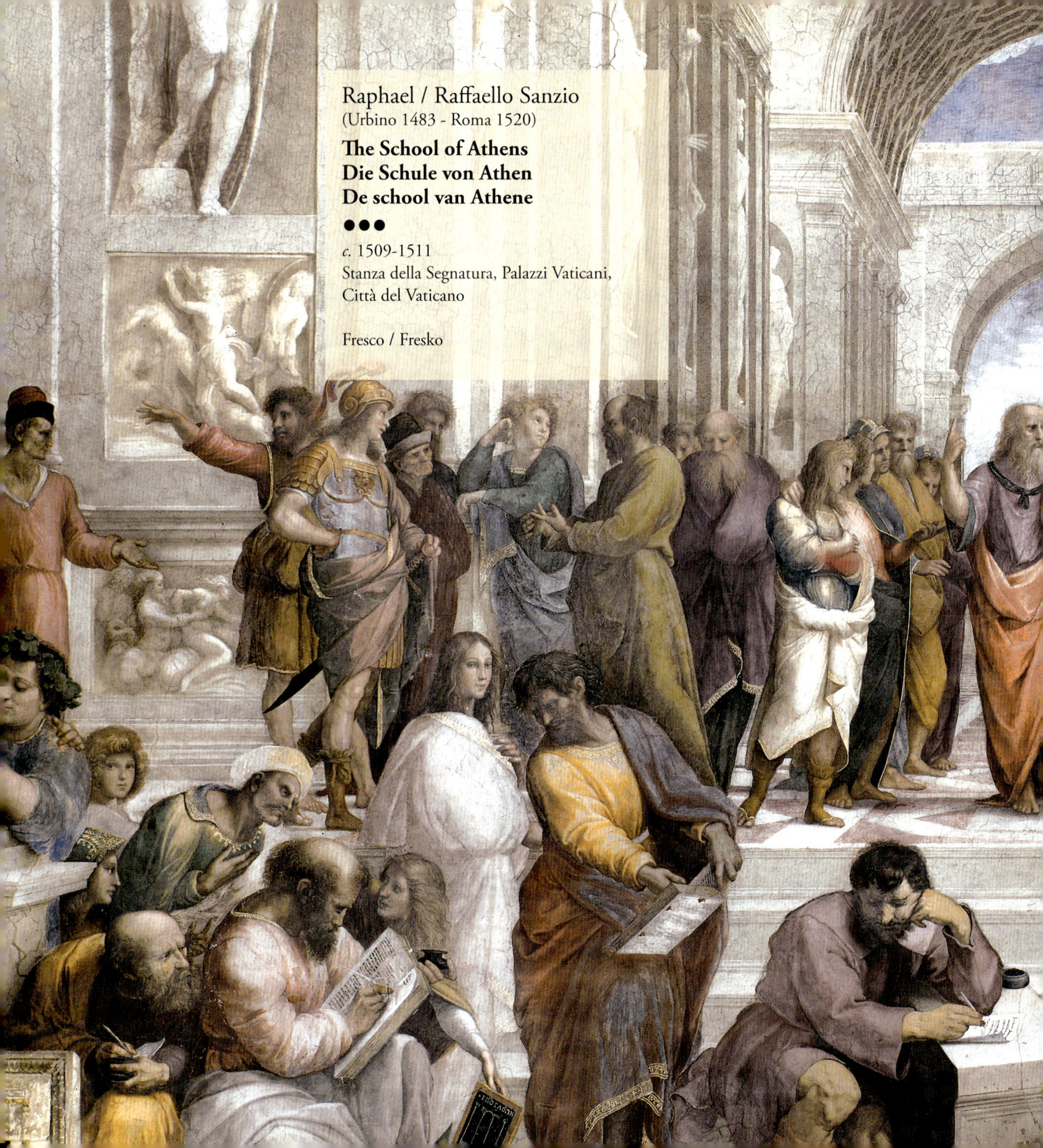

Raphael / Raffaello Sanzio
(Urbino 1483 - Roma 1520)

The School of Athens
Die Schule von Athen
De school van Athene

●●●

c. 1509-1511
Stanza della Segnatura, Palazzi Vaticani,
Città del Vaticano

Fresco / Fresko

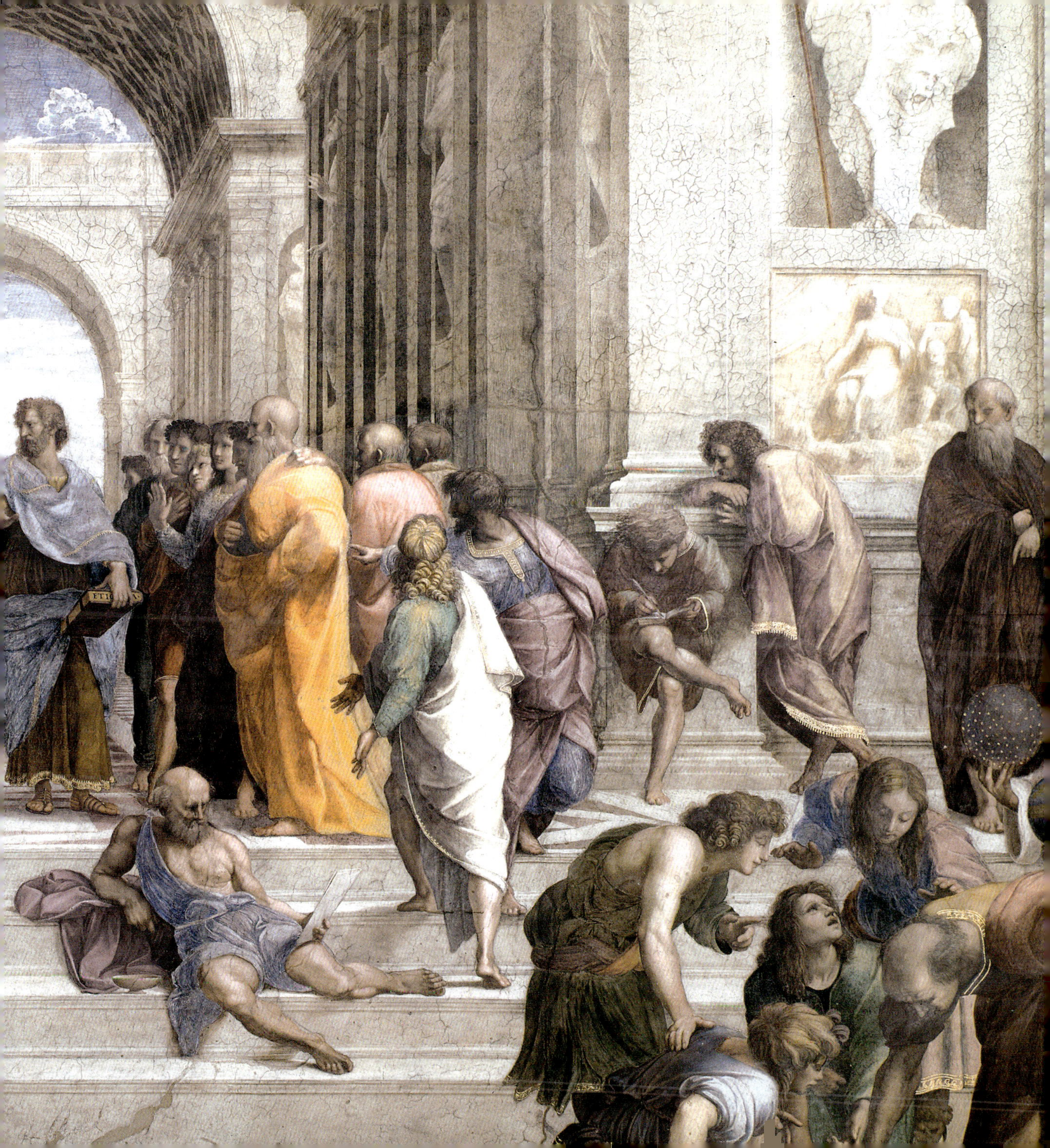

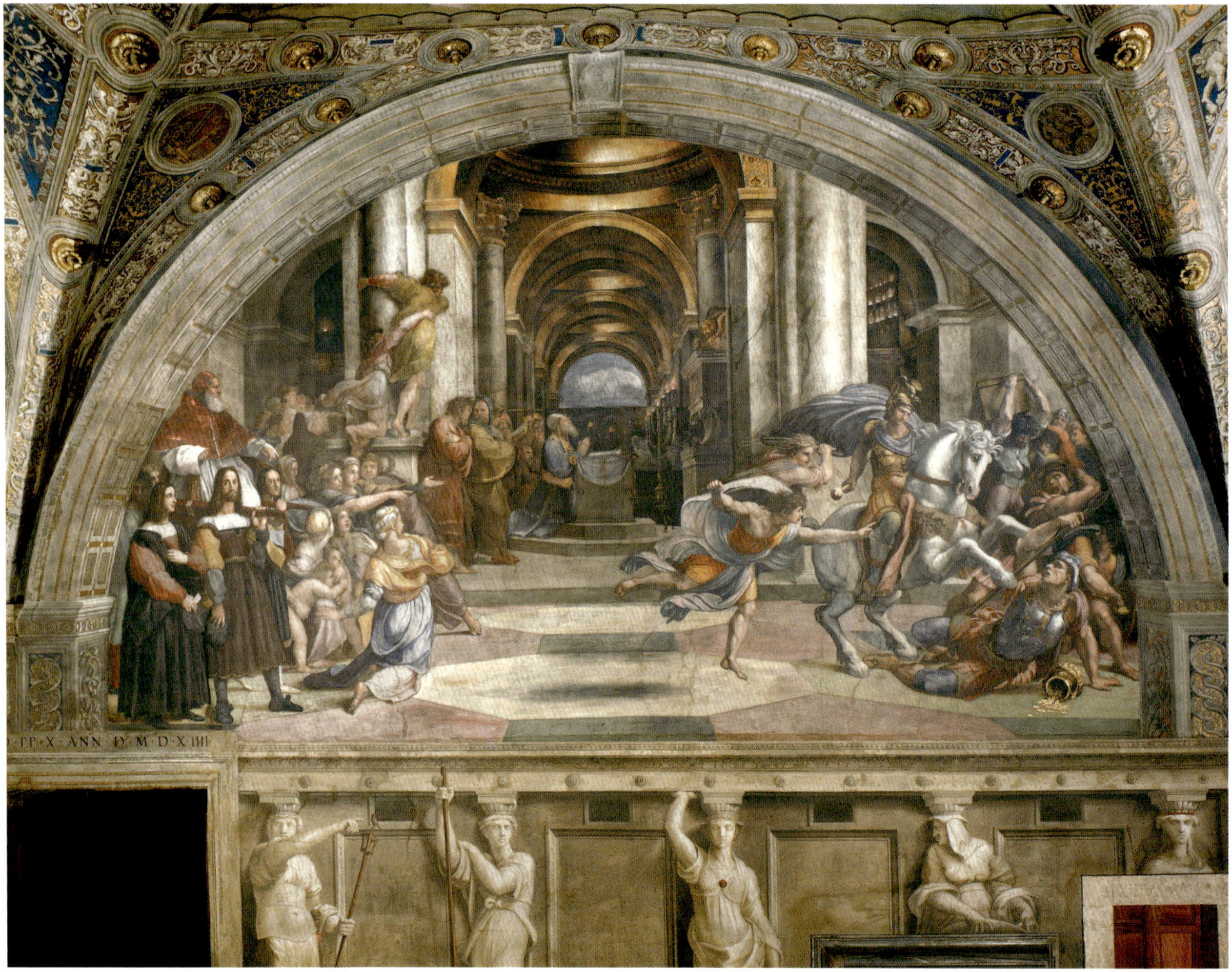

Raphael / Raffaello Sanzio (Urbino 1483 - Roma 1520)

Expulsion of Heliodorus from the Temple
Verjagung Heliodors aus dem Tempel
De verdrijving van Heliodorus uit de Tempel

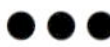

c. 1511-1512
Stanza di Eliodoro, Palazzi Vaticani, Città del Vaticano

Fresco / Fresko

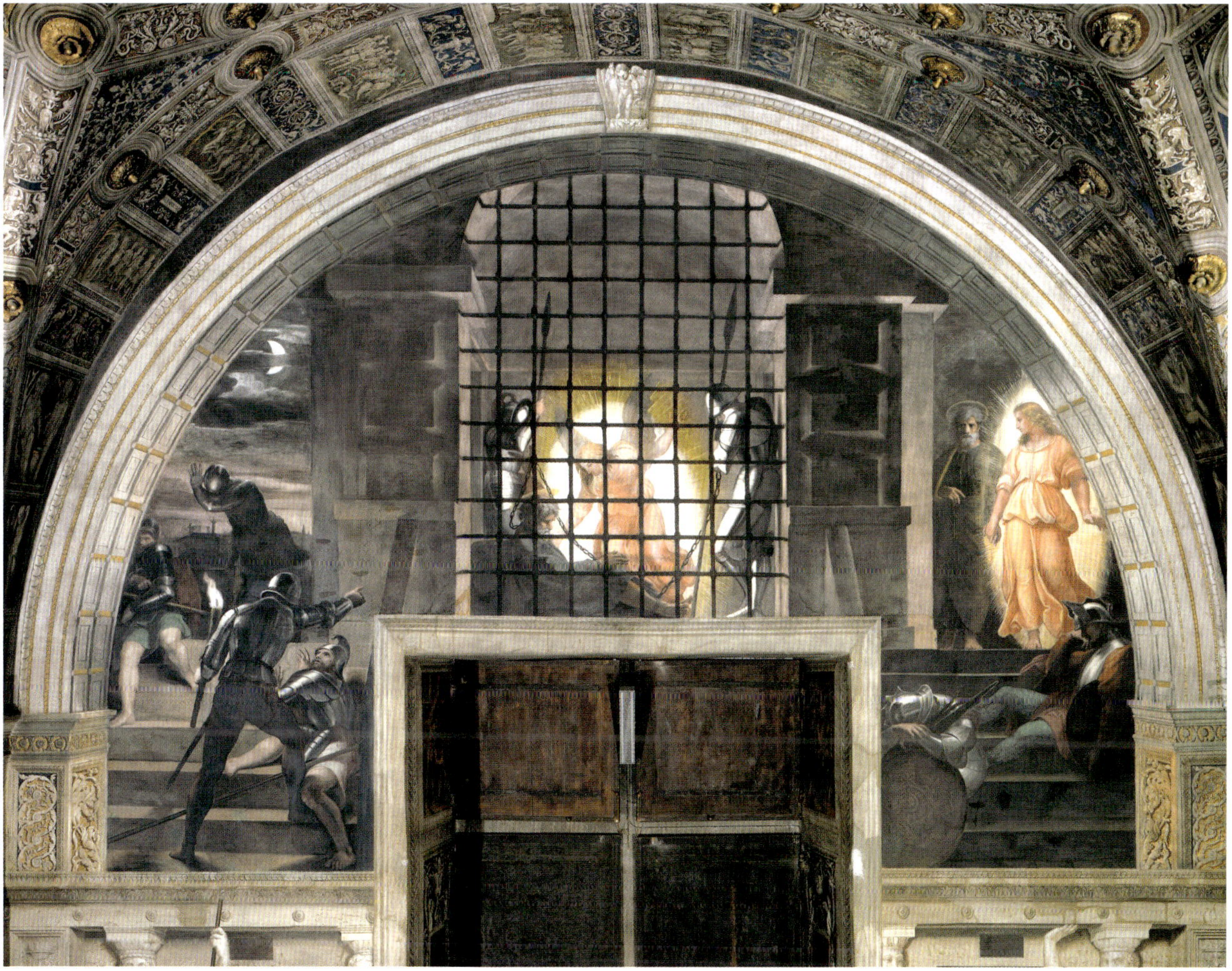

Raphael / Raffaello Sanzio (Urbino 1483 - Roma 1520)

Liberation of St Peter
Befreiung des Hl. Petrus
Bevrijding van de Heilige Petrus

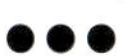

c. 1513-1514
Stanza di Eliodoro, Palazzi Vaticani, Città del Vaticano

Fresco / Fresko

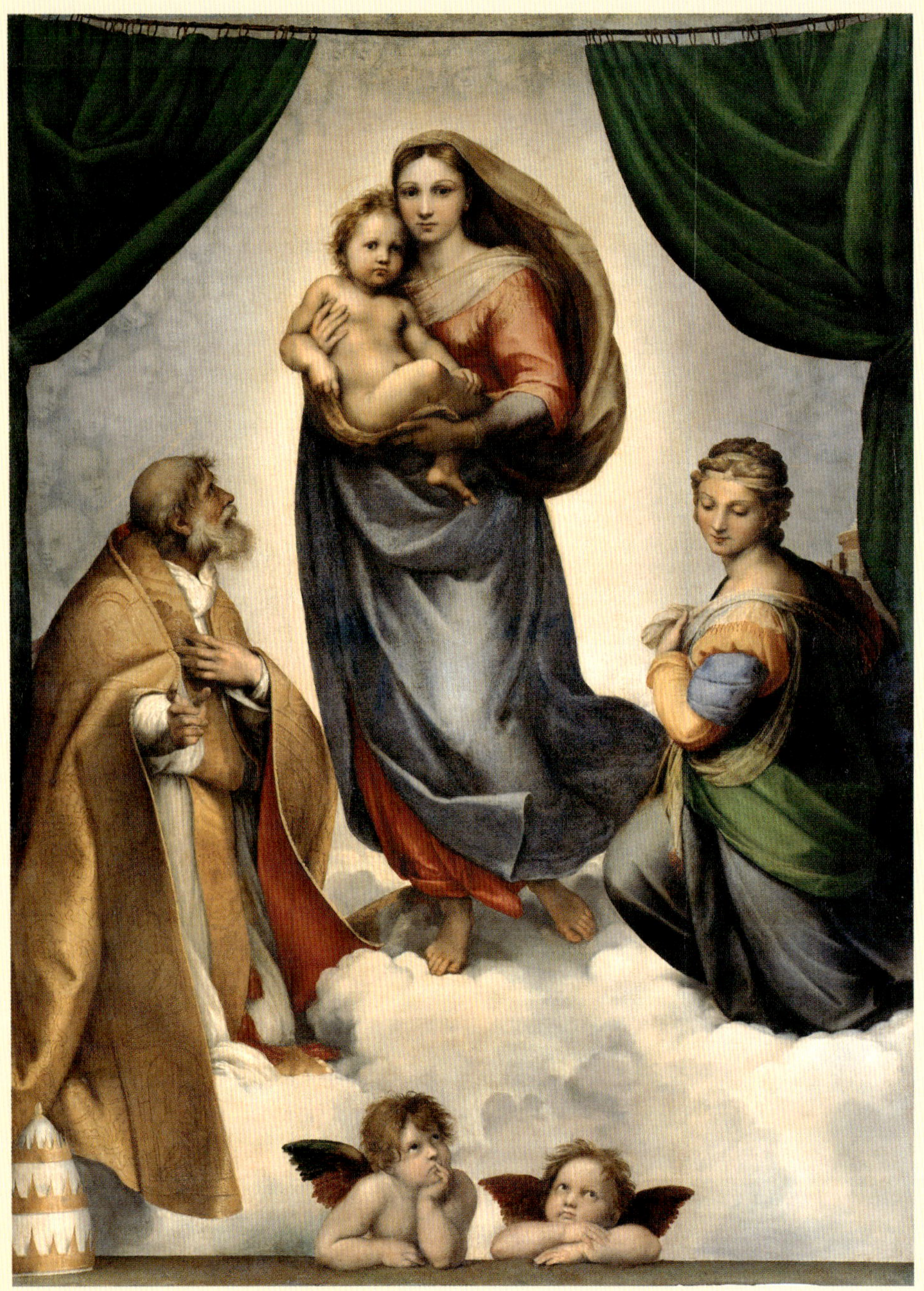

Famous for his gracious Madonnas: Raffaello is already considered a prince of painting and a man of the world in his own time.

Berühmt für seine lieblichen Madonnen. Raphael galt schon zu Lebzeiten als Malerfürst und Lebemann.

Bekend om zijn gracieuze madonna's. Rafaël wordt in zijn tijd als prins van de schilderkunst en man van de wereld gezien.

Raphael / Raffaello Sanzio
(Urbino 1483 - Roma 1520)

The Sistine Madonna
Sixtinische Madonna
Sixtijnse Madonna

●●●

1512-1513
269,5 x 201 cm / 106.1 x 79.1 in.
Gemäldegalerie Alte Meister, Staatliche Kunstsammlungen, Dresden

Oil on wood / Öl auf Leinwand
olieverf op doek

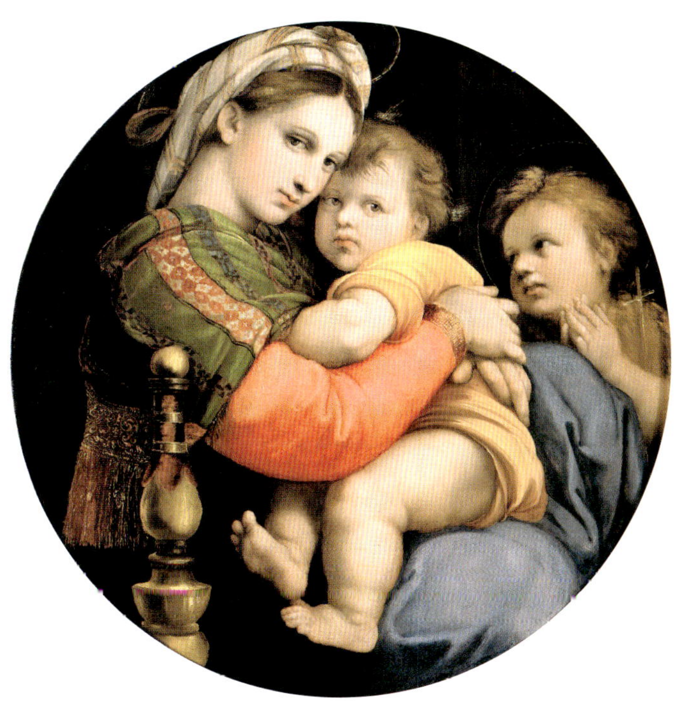

Raphael / Raffaello Sanzio

(Urbino 1483 - Roma 1520)

Madonna of the chair
Madonna auf dem Stuhle
Madonna met de stoel

●●●

c. 1513-1514

Ø 71 cm / 27.9 in.

Galleria Palatina, Firenze

Oil on wood / Öl auf Leinwand / olieverf op doek

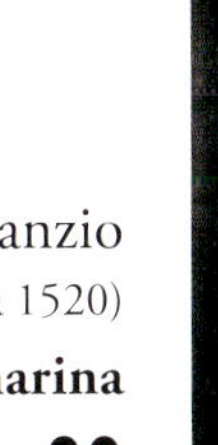

Raphael / Raffaello Sanzio

(Urbino 1483 - Roma 1520)

La Fornarina

●●

c. 1520

87 x 63 cm / 34.2 x 24.8 in.

Galleria Nazionale d'Arte Antica
di Palazzo Barberini, Roma

Oil on canvas / Öl auf Holz / Olieverf op paneel

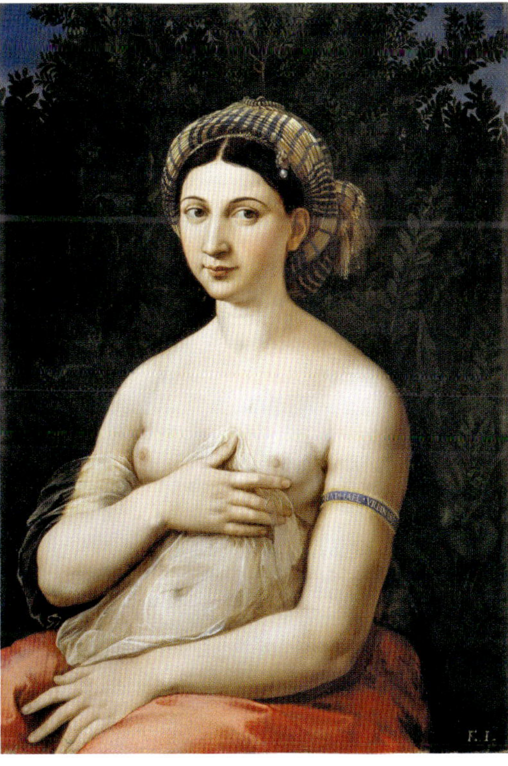

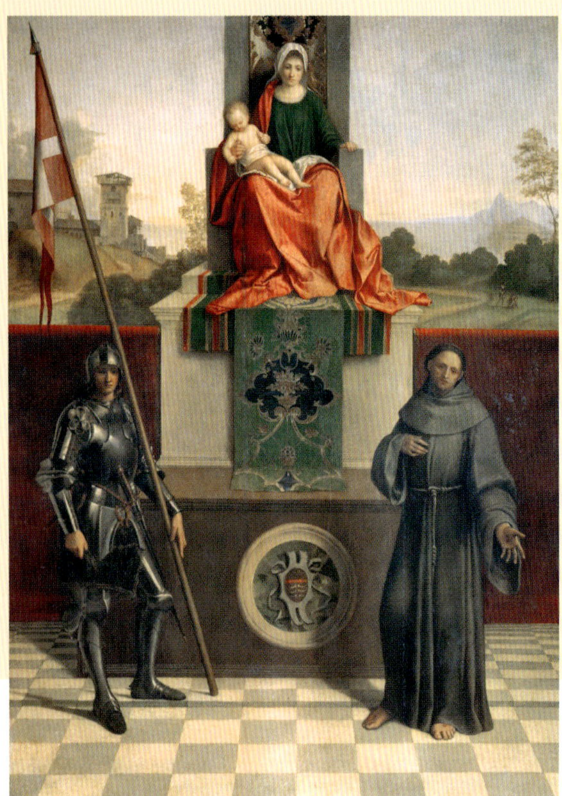

Giorgione
(Castelfranco Veneto 1477/78 - Venezia 1510)

Castelfranco Altarpiece
Altarbild von Castelfranco
Altaarstuk van Castelfranco

●●

c. 1504-1505
202 x 152 cm / 79.52 x 59.84 in
Duomo di San Liberale, Castelfranco Veneto

Tempera on wood
Tempera auf Tafel
Tempera op paneel

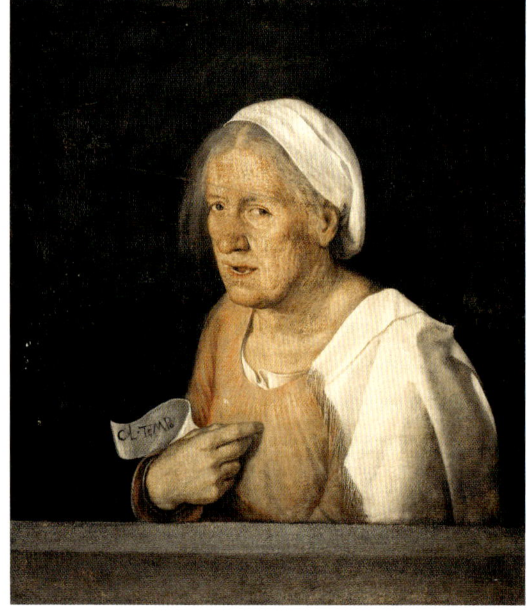

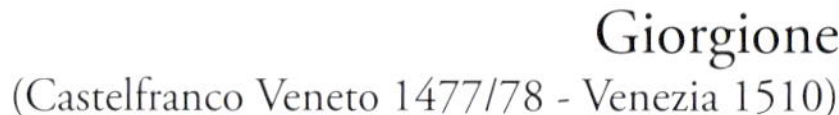

Giorgione
(Castelfranco Veneto 1477/78 - Venezia 1510)

Portrait of an Old Woman
Die Alte
De oude vrouw

●●

c. 1508-1510
68 x 59 cm
Gallerie dell'Accademia, Venezia

Oil on canvas / Öl auf Leinwand
Olieverf op doek

The Tempest by Giorgione is considered one of the most mysterious paintings in the history of art and even today is still enigmatic.

Giorgiones Gewitter ist inhaltlich eines der ungeklärtesten Gemälde der Kunstgeschichte und gibt bis heute Rätsel auf.

De Storm van Giorgione is vanwege zijn inhoud één van de meest mysterieuze schilderijen van de kunstgeschiedenis en tot op de dag van vandaag zijn er omtrent dit schilderij veel raadsels.

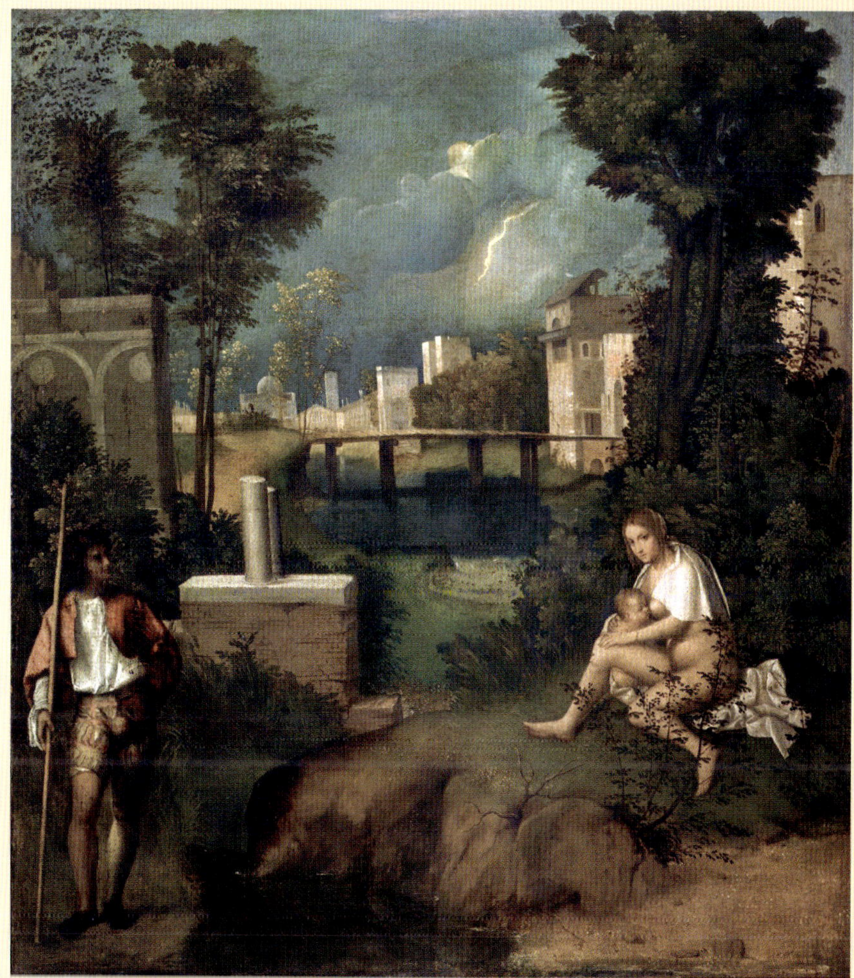

Giorgione
(Castelfranco Veneto 1477/78 - Venezia 1510)
The Tempest
Das Gewitter
La tempesta (Het onweer)
●●●
c. 1506-1508
82 x 73 cm / 32.28 x 28.74 in.
Gallerie dell'Accademia, Venezia

Oil on canvas / Öl auf Leinwand / Olieverf op doek

Titian / Tizian / Titiaan
(Pieve di Cadore, *c.* 1490 - Venezia 1576)

Pastoral Concert
Ländliches Konzert
Landelijk concert

●●

1508-1511
110 x 138 cm / 43.30 x 54.33 in.
Musée du Louvre, Paris

Oil on canvas / Öl auf Leinwand
Olieverf op doek

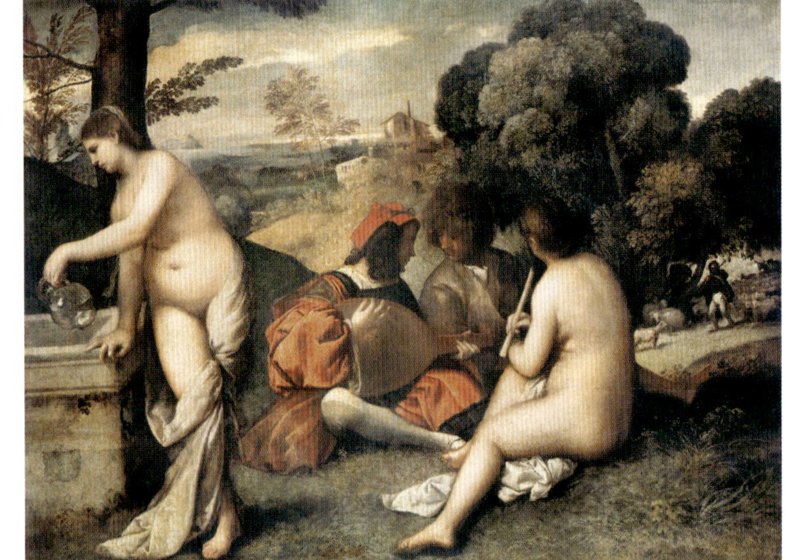

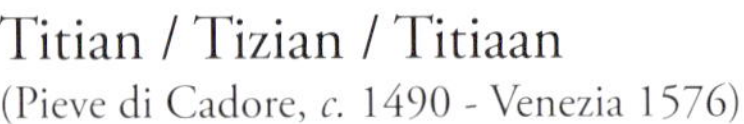

Titian / Tizian / Titiaan
(Pieve di Cadore, *c.* 1490 - Venezia 1576)

Sacred and Profane Love
Himmlische und irdische Liebe
Hemelse en Aardse Liefde

●●●

1514
118 x 280 cm / 46.45 x 110.23 in.
Galleria Borghese, Roma

Oil on canvas / Öl auf Leinwand / Olieverf op doek

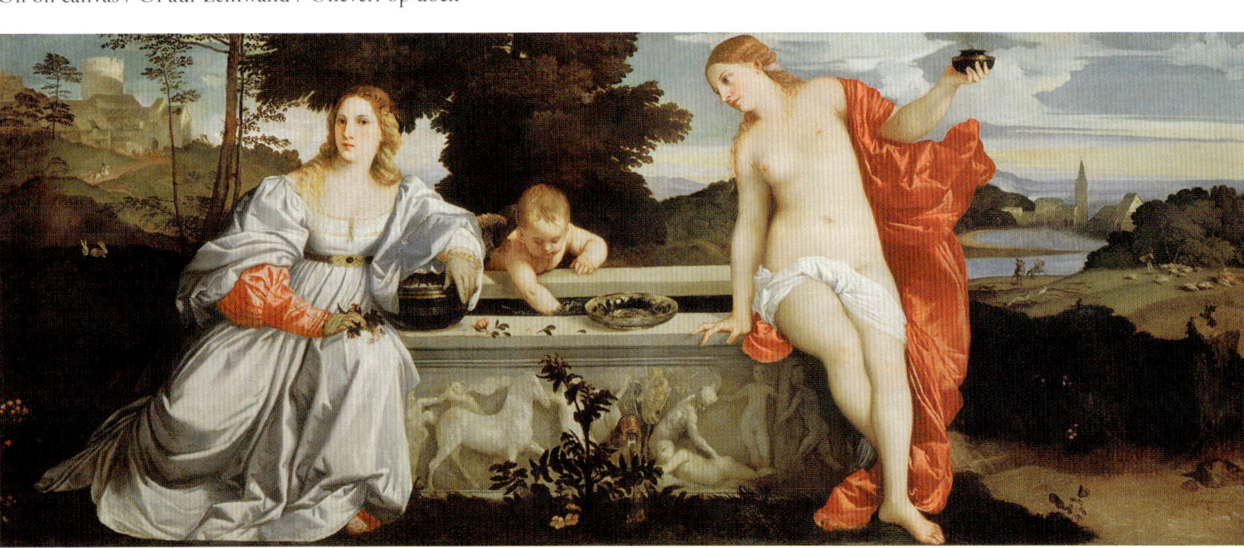

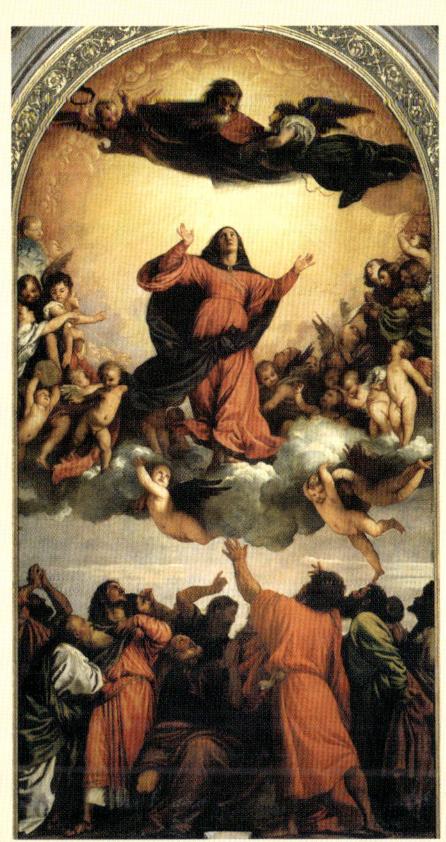

Titian / Tizian / Titiaan
(Pieve di Cadore,
c. 1490 - Venezia 1576)

Assumption of the Virgin
Assunta
Maria-Tenhemelopneming

●●●

1516-1518
690 x 360 cm /
271.65 x 141.73 in.
Santa Maria Gloriosa dei Frari,
Venezia

Oil on wood
Öl auf Tafel
Olieverf op paneel

Titian / Tizian / Titiaan
(Pieve di Cadore,
c. 1490 - Venezia 1576)

Bacchus and Ariadne
Bacchus und Ariadne
Bacchus en Ariadne

●●

c. 1520-1523
176.5 x 191 cm /
69.48 x 75.19 in.
The National Gallery,
London

Oil on canvas
Öl auf Leinwand
Olieverf op doek

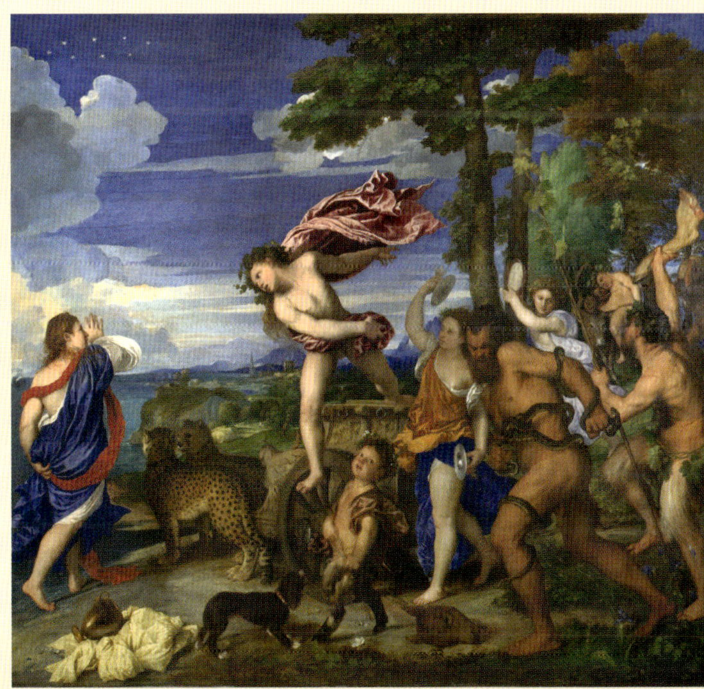

Titian: a major portraitist and an example for Baroque artists.

Tizian ist wichtiger Porträtmaler und Vorbild des Barock.

Titiaan: belangrijk portrettist en voorbeeld voor de barok.

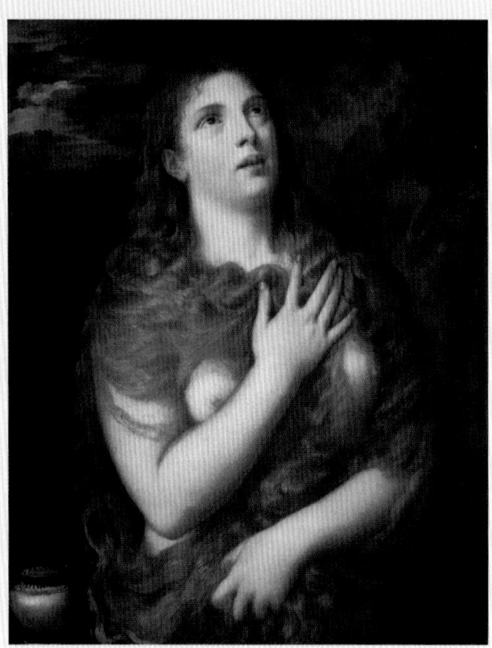

Titian / Tizian / Titiaan
(Pieve di Cadore, 1490 *c.* - Venezia 1576)

The Penitent Magdalene
Büßende Hl.Magdalena
Boetende Maria Magdalena

●

1533
85 x 68 cm / 33.46 x 26.77 in.
Galleria Palatina, Firenze

Oil on canvas
Öl auf Leinwand
Olieverf op doek

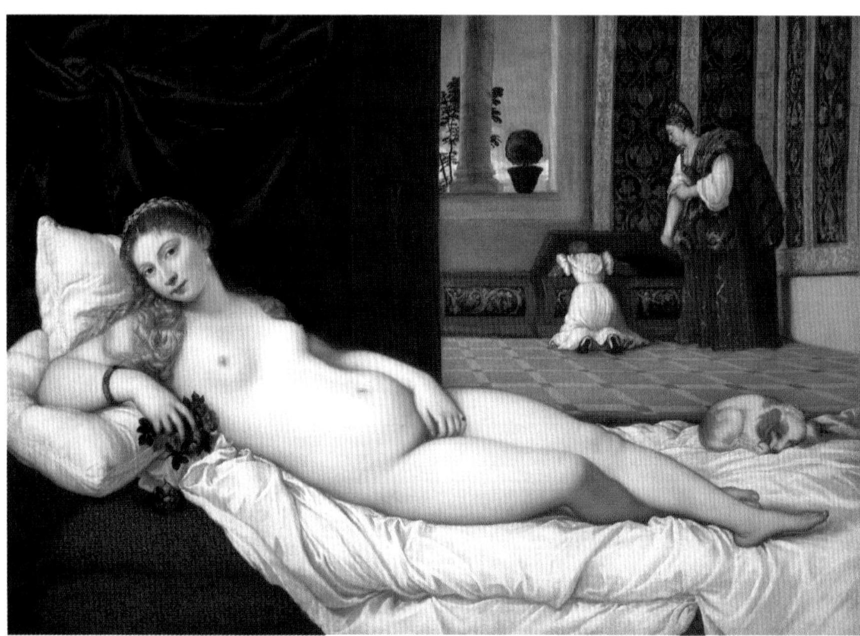

Titian / Tizian / Titiaan
(Pieve di Cadore, 1490 *c.* - Venezia 1576)

Venus of Urbino
Venus von Urbino
Venus van Urbino

●●●

1538
119 x 165 cm / 46.85 x 64.96 in.
Galleria degli Uffizi, Firenze

Oil on canvas
Öl auf Leinwand
Olieverf op doek

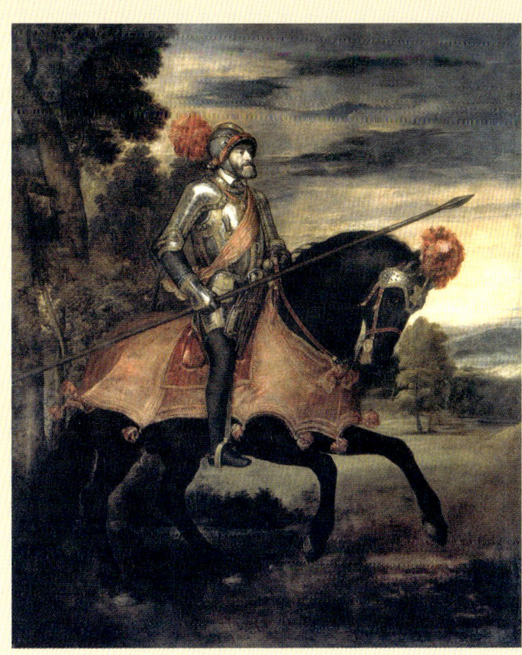

Titian / Tizian / Titiaan
(Pieve di Cadore, 1490 *c.* - Venezia 1576)

Charles V on Horseback
Karl V
Karel V

●●

1548
332 x 279 cm / 130.70 x 109.84 in.
Museo Nacional del Prado, Madrid

Oil on canvas
Öl auf Leinwand
Olieverf op doek

Titian / Tizian / Titiaan
(Pieve di Cadore, 1490 *c.* - Venezia 1576)
Palma the Younger
Palma der Jüngere
Palma de Jonge
(Venezia 1548 - 1628)

Pietà

●●

c. 1570-1576
351 x 389 cm / 138.18 x 153.14 in.
Gallerie dell'Accademia, Venezia

Oil on canvas
Öl auf Leinwand
Olieverf op doek

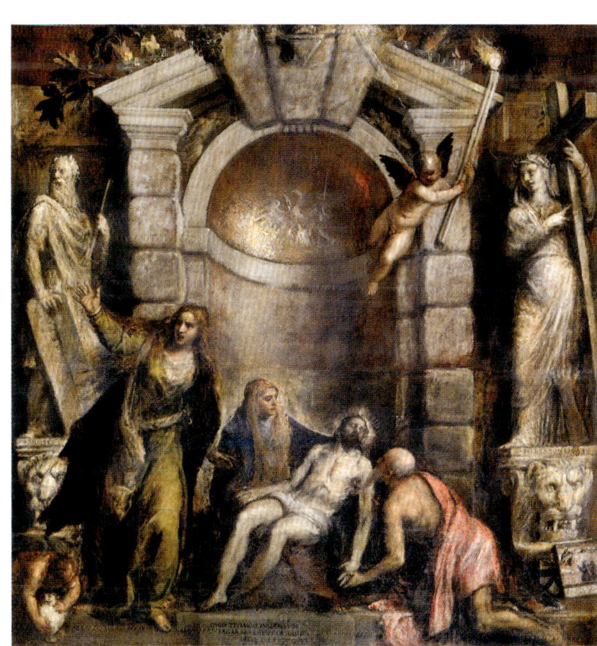

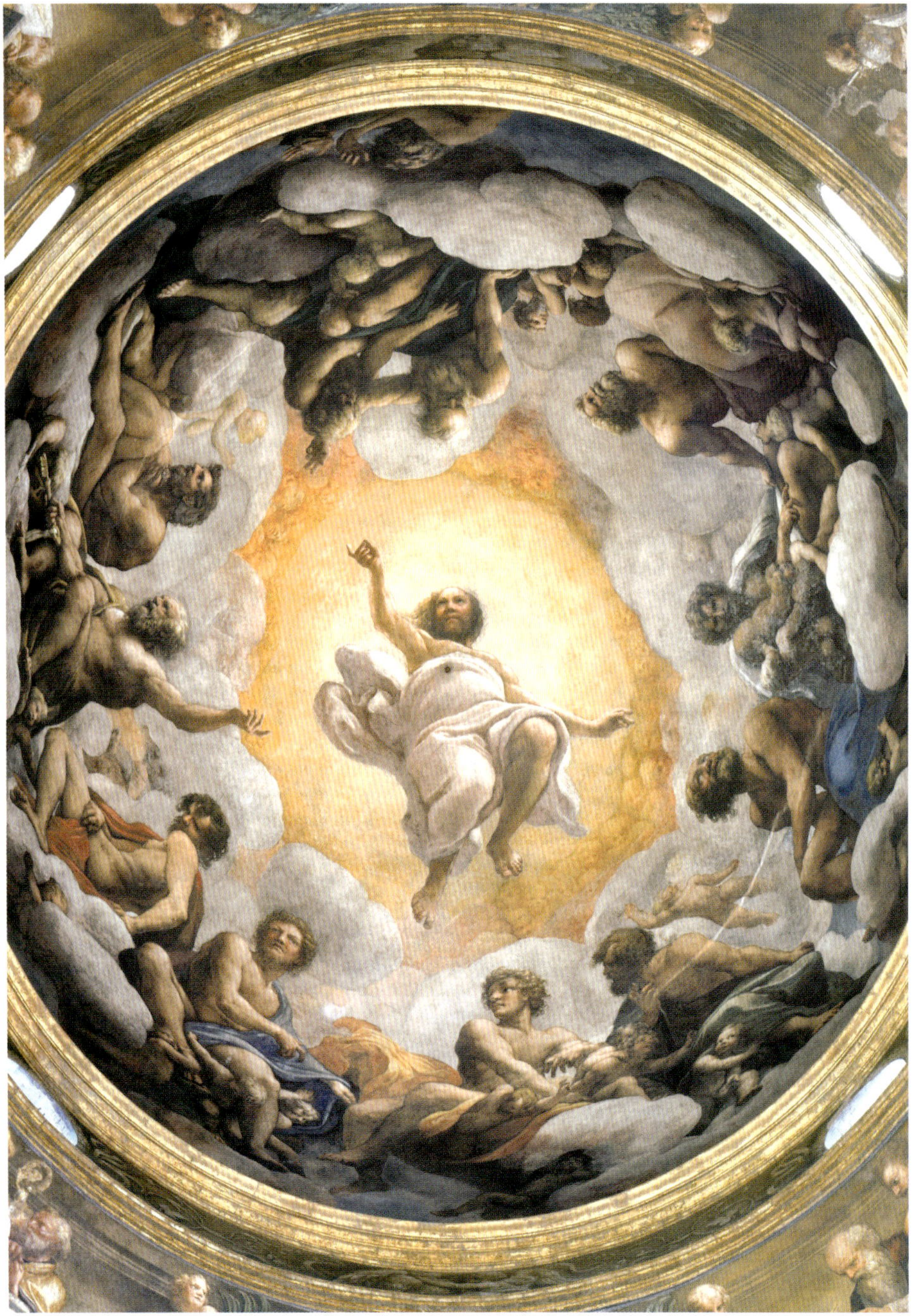

Correggio
(Correggio, Reggio Emilia
c. 1489 - 1534)

Vision of St John the Evangelist
Die Vision des Hl.Johannes
Visioen van Johannes de Evangelist

c. 1520-1521
San Giovanni Evangelista, Parma

Fresco / Fresko

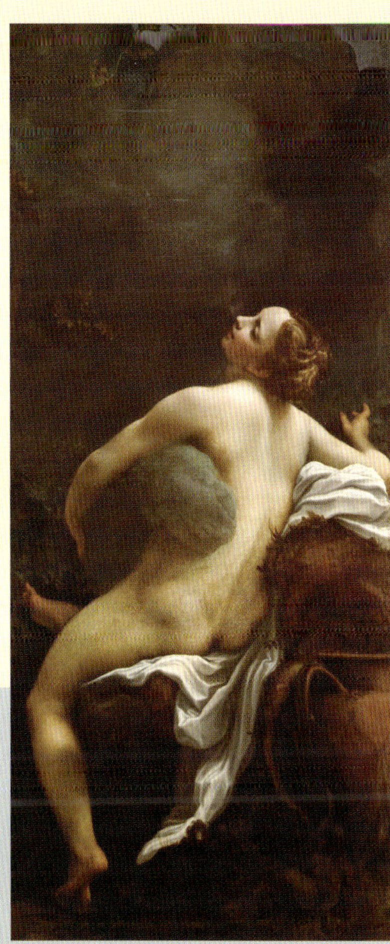

Correggio
(Correggio, Reggio Emilia *c.* 1489 - 1534)

Jupiter and Io
Jupiter und Io
Jupiter en Io

●

c. 1531-1532
162 x 73,5 cm / 63,8 x 73,5 in.
Kunsthistorisches Museum, Wien

Oil on canvas
Öl auf Leinwand
Olieverf op doek

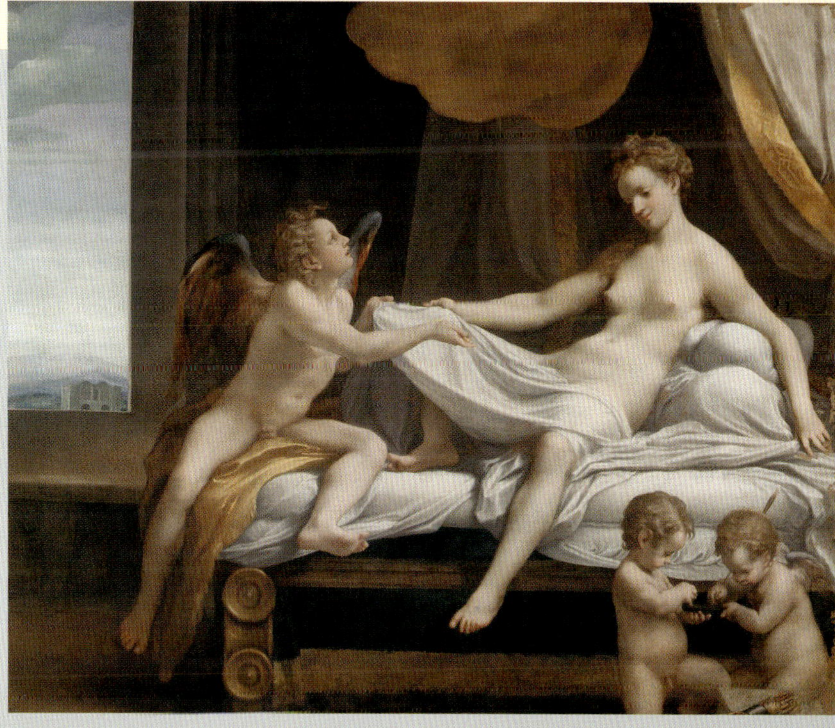

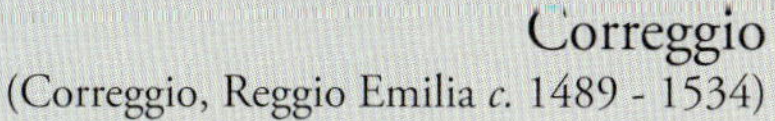

Correggio
(Correggio, Reggio Emilia *c.* 1489 - 1534)

Danae
Dànae

●●

c. 1530-1531
161 x 193 cm / 63.38 x 75.98 in.
Galleria Borghese, Roma

Oil on canvas / Öl auf Leinwand
Olieverf op doek

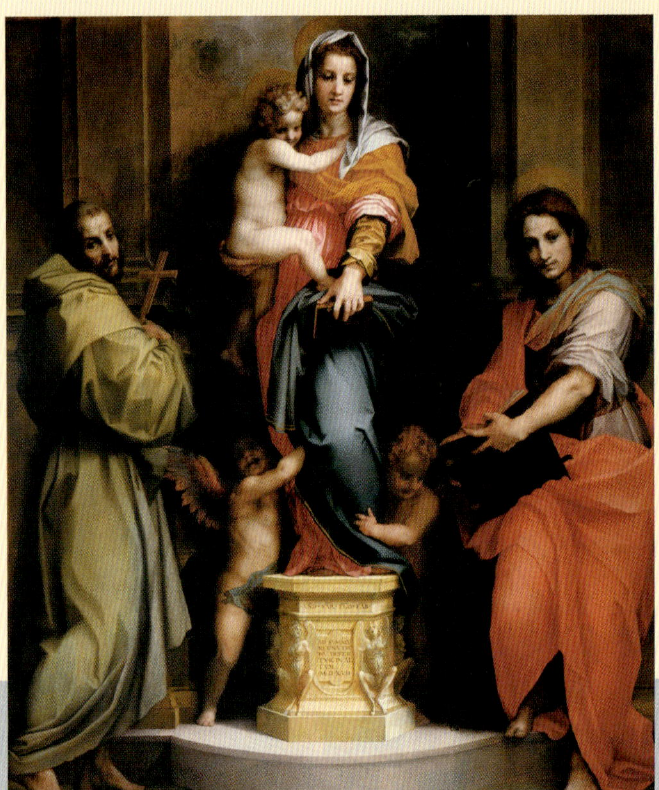

Andrea del Sarto
(Firenze 1486 - 1530)

Madonna delle Arpie (Madonna of the Harpies)
Die Madonna mit den Harpyien
Madonna van de Harpijen

●●

c. 1517
208 x 178 cm / 81.88 x 70.07 in.
Galleria degli Uffizi, Firenze

Oil on wood / Öl auf Tafel
Olieverf op paneel

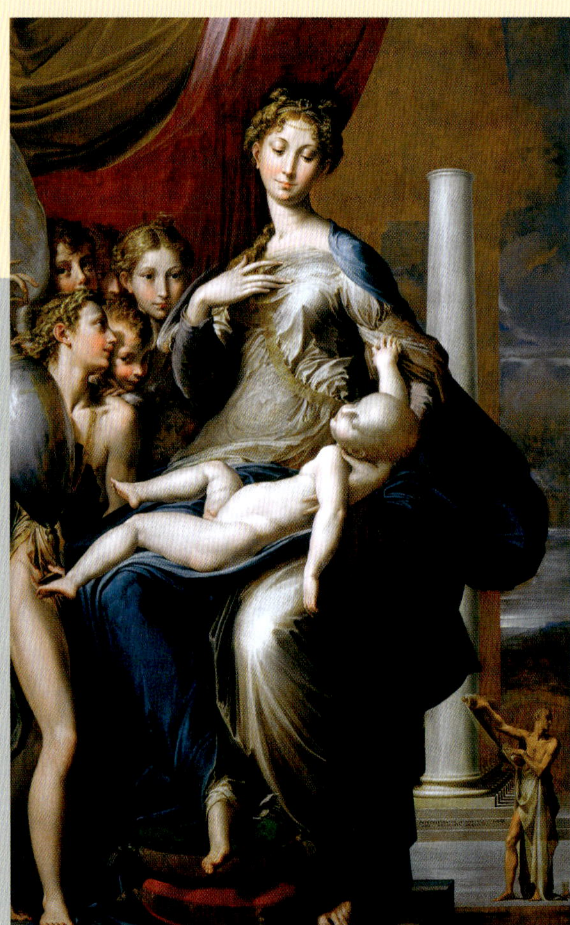

Parmigianino
(Parma 1503 - Casalmaggiore, Cremona 1540)

Madonna with the Long Neck
Madonna mit dem langen Hals
Madonna met de lange hals

●●

c .1535
216 x 132 cm / 85 x 52 in.
Galleria degli Uffizi, Firenze

Oil on panel / Öl auf Tafel / Olieverf op paneel

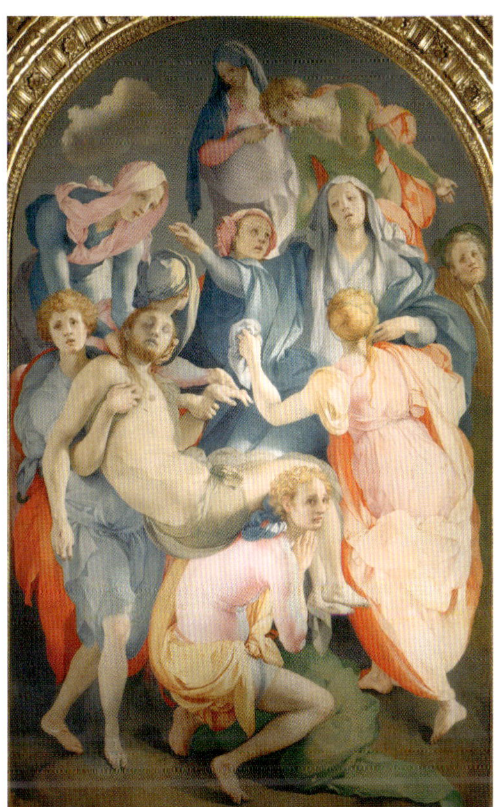

Pontormo
(Pontorme, Empoli 1494 - Firenze *c.* 1556-1557)

Deposition
Kreuzabnahme
Kruisafneming

●●

c. 1528
313 x 192 cm / 123.22 x 75.59
Santa Felicita, Firenze

Oil on wood
Öl auf Tafel
Olieverf op paneel

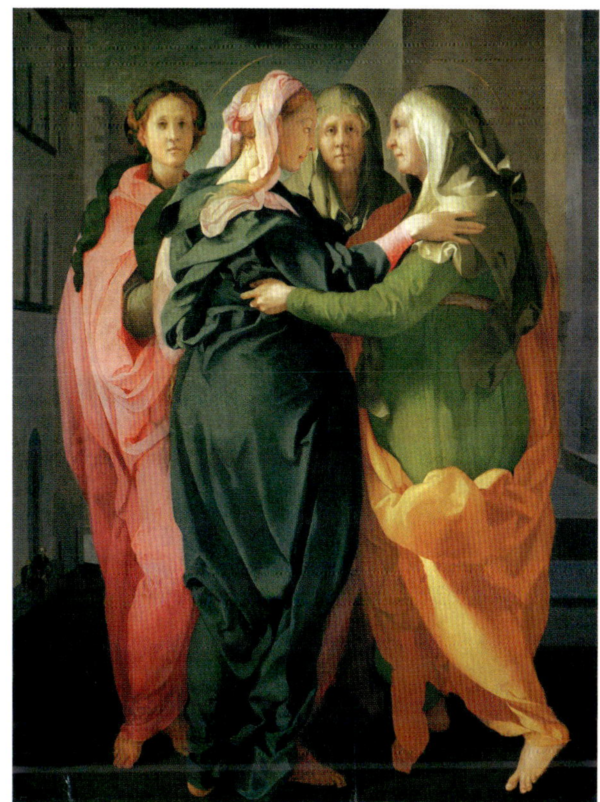

Pontormo
(Pontorme, Empoli 1494 - Firenze *c.* 1556-1557)

Visitation
Der Besuch
Visitatie

●

c. 1528-1529
202 x 156 cm / 79.5 x 61.4 in.
San Michele, Carmignano

Oil on wood
Öl auf Tafel
Olieverf op paneel

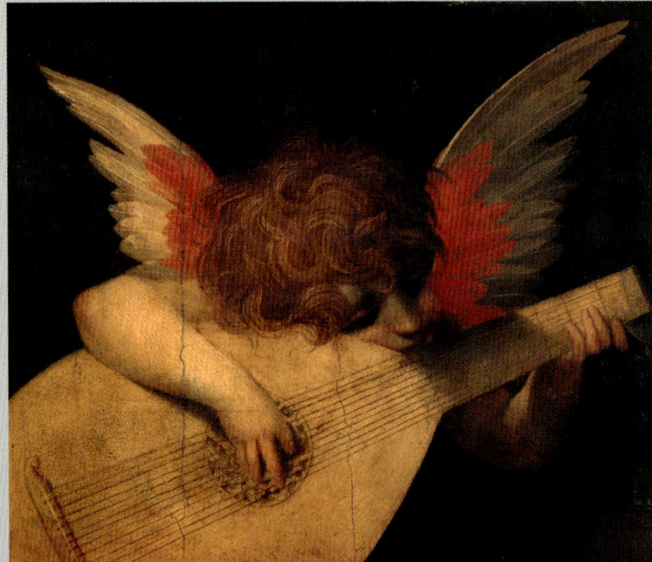

Rosso Fiorentino
(Firenze 1495 - Fontainebleau 1540)

Deposition
Kreuzabnahme
Kruisafneming

●●

1521
375 x 196 cm / 147.6 x 77.1 in.
Pinacoteca Comunale, Volterra

Oil on wood / Öl auf Tafel
Olieverf op paneel

Rosso Fiorentino
(Firenze 1495 - Fontainebleau 1540)

Angel
Engel
Musicerende Engel

●●●

c. 1520
39 x 47 cm / 15.35 x 18.50 in.
Galleria degli Uffizi, Firenze

Oil on wood
Öl auf Tafel
Olieverf op paneel

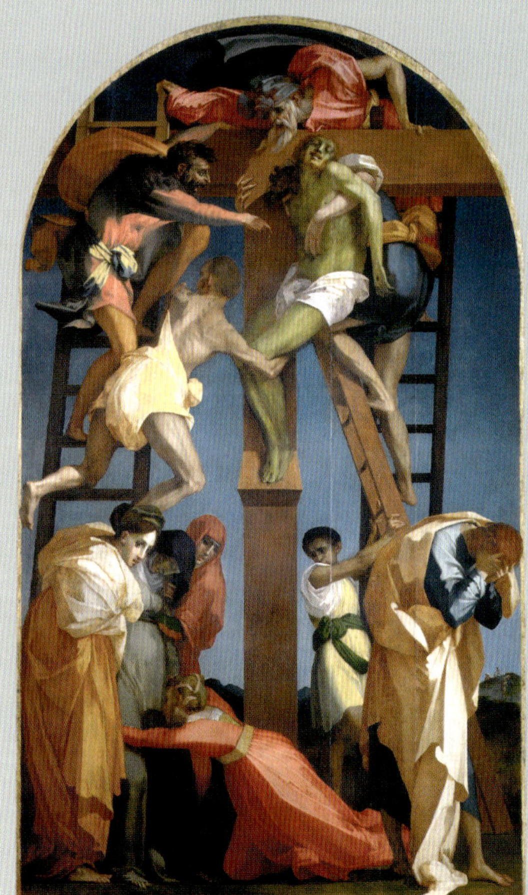

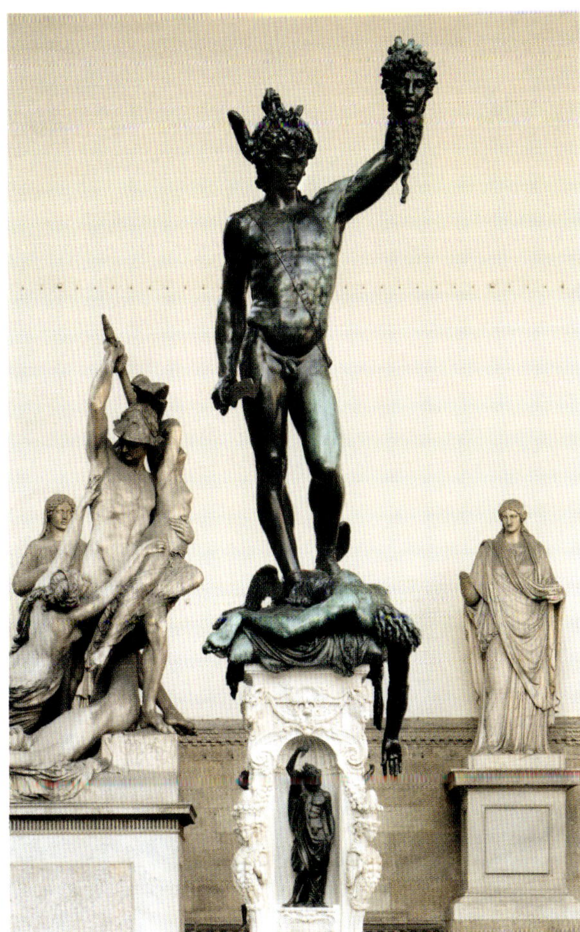

Benvenuto Cellini
(Firenze 1500 - 1571)

Perseus

●●●

c. 1545-1554
h. 5.19 m / 204.33 in.
Loggia dei Lanzi, Firenze

Bronze / Brons

Jean Boulogne
(Douai 1529 - Firenze 1608)

Rape of the Sabines
Der Raub der Sabinerinnen
De Sabijnse maagdenroof

●●

c. 1580-1583
h. 410 cm / 161.41 in.
Loggia dei Lanzi, Firenze

Marble / Marmor / Marmer

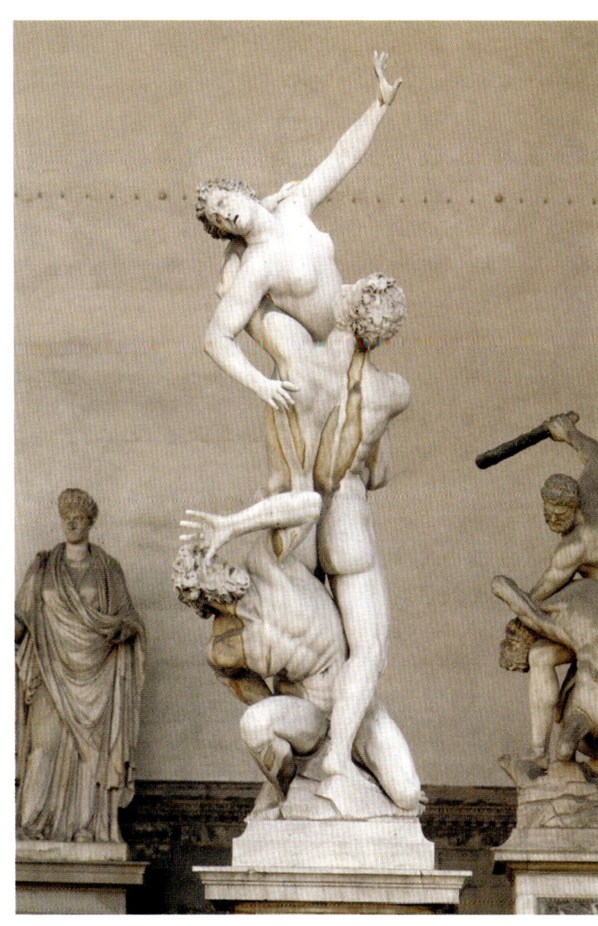

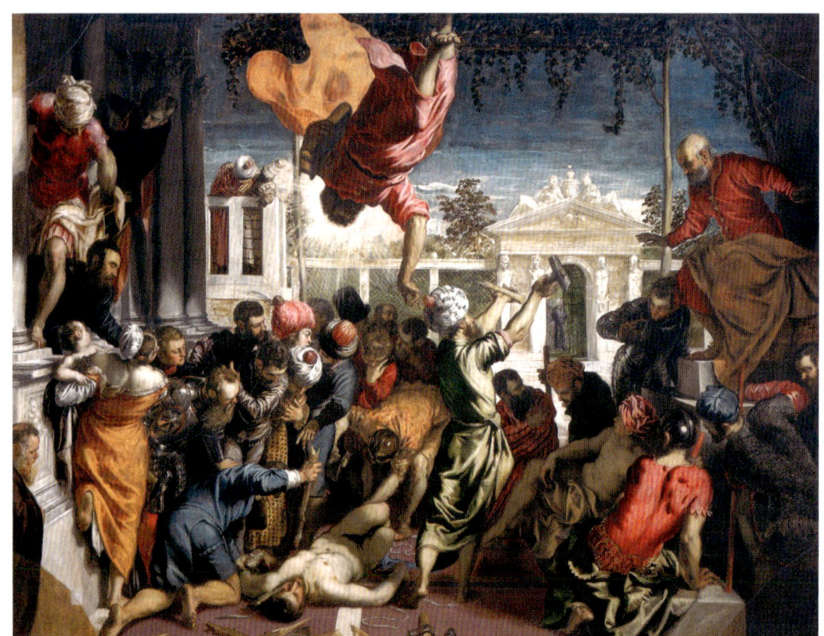

Tintoretto
(Venezia 1518 - 1594)

Miracle of St Mark Freeing the Slave
Wunder des Hl.Markus, der einen Sklaven befreit
Het wonder van Sint-Marcus die de slaaf bevrijdt

●

1548
415 x 541 cm / 164.4 x 213 in.
Gallerie dell'Accademia, Venezia

Oil on canvas / Öl auf Leinwand
Olieverf op doek

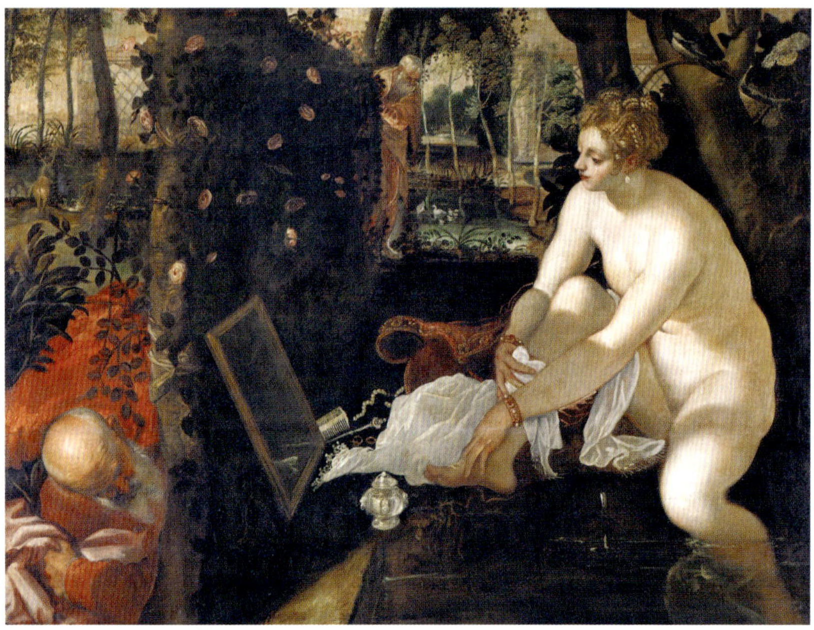

Tintoretto
(Venezia 1518 - 1594)

Susanna in the Bath
Susanna im Bade
Susanna in bad

●

c. 1560
146 x 193.6 cm / 57.48 x 76.22 in.
Kunsthistorisches Museum, Wien

Oil on canvas / Öl auf Leinwand
Olieverf op doek

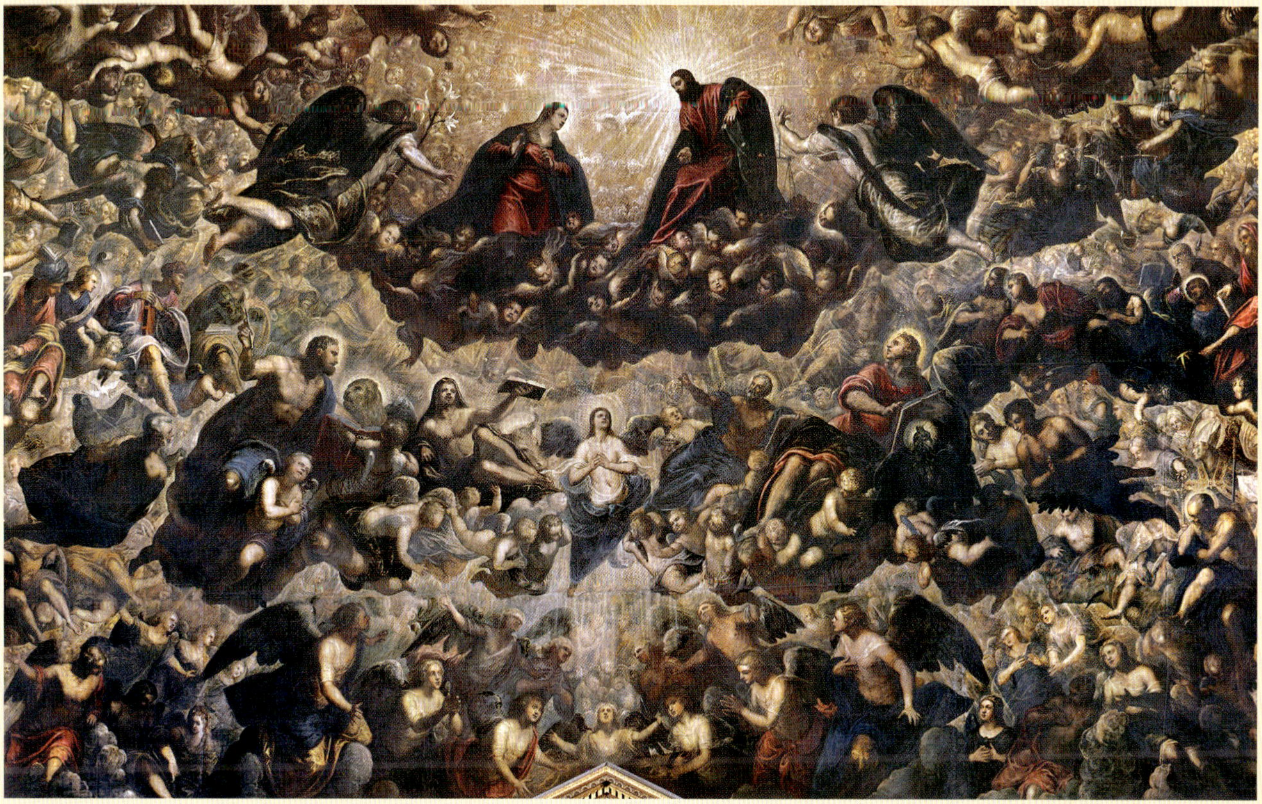

Tintoretto
(Venezia 1518 - 1594)

Paradise
Das Paradies
Het Paradijs

c. 1588-1592
700 x 220 cm / 275.59 x 866.14 in.
Palazzo Ducale, Venezia

Oil on canvas / Öl auf Leinwand
Olieverf op doek

Elegant composition, effects of depth and lighting: Tintoretto is considered one of the first Mannerists.

Raffinierte Komposition, Tiefenwirkung und Lichtgebung. Tintoretto gilt früher Meister des Manierismus.

Geraffineerde compositie, dieptewerking en lichteffecten. Tintoretto wordt als een van de eerste meesters van het maniërisme beschouwd.

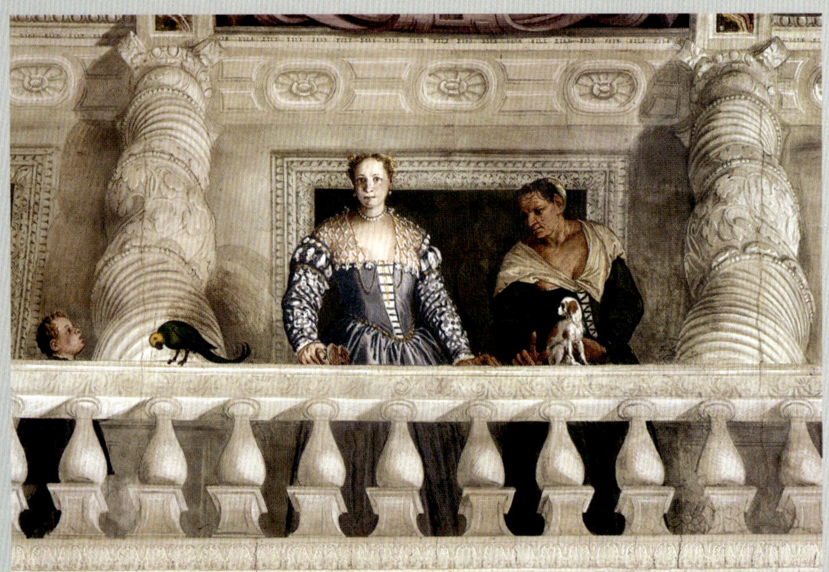

Paolo Veronese
(Verona 1528 - Venezia 1588)

Giustiniana Barbaro and Her Nurse
Giustiana Barbaro und ihre Krankenschester
Giustiniana Barbaro en haar min & Klein meisje aan de deur

●●

c. 1560-1562
Villa Barbaro, Maser

Fresco / Fresko

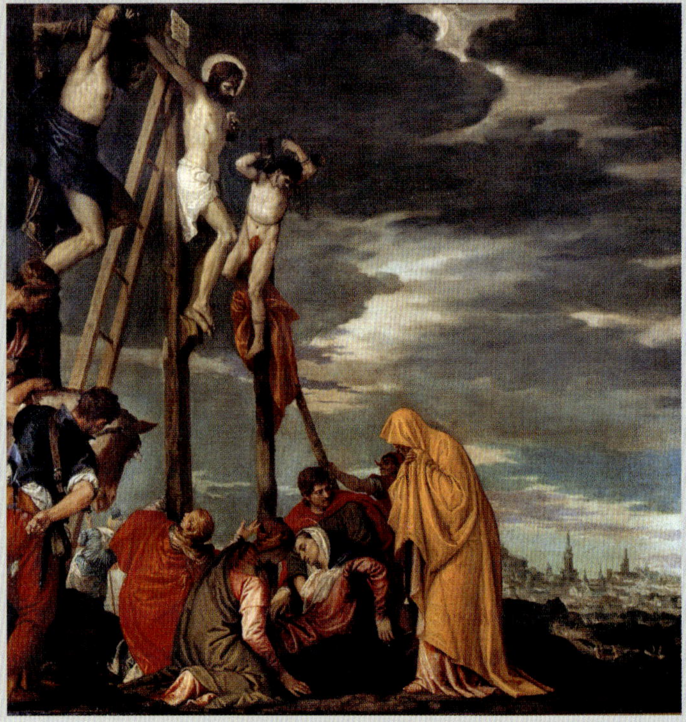

Paolo Veronese
(Verona 1528 - Venezia 1588)

Calvary
Kreuzweg
Kruisiging

●●

●

c. 1570-1580
102 x 102 cm/ 40.15 x 40.15 in.
Musée du Louvre, Paris

Oil on canvas / Öl auf Leinwand
Olieverf op doek

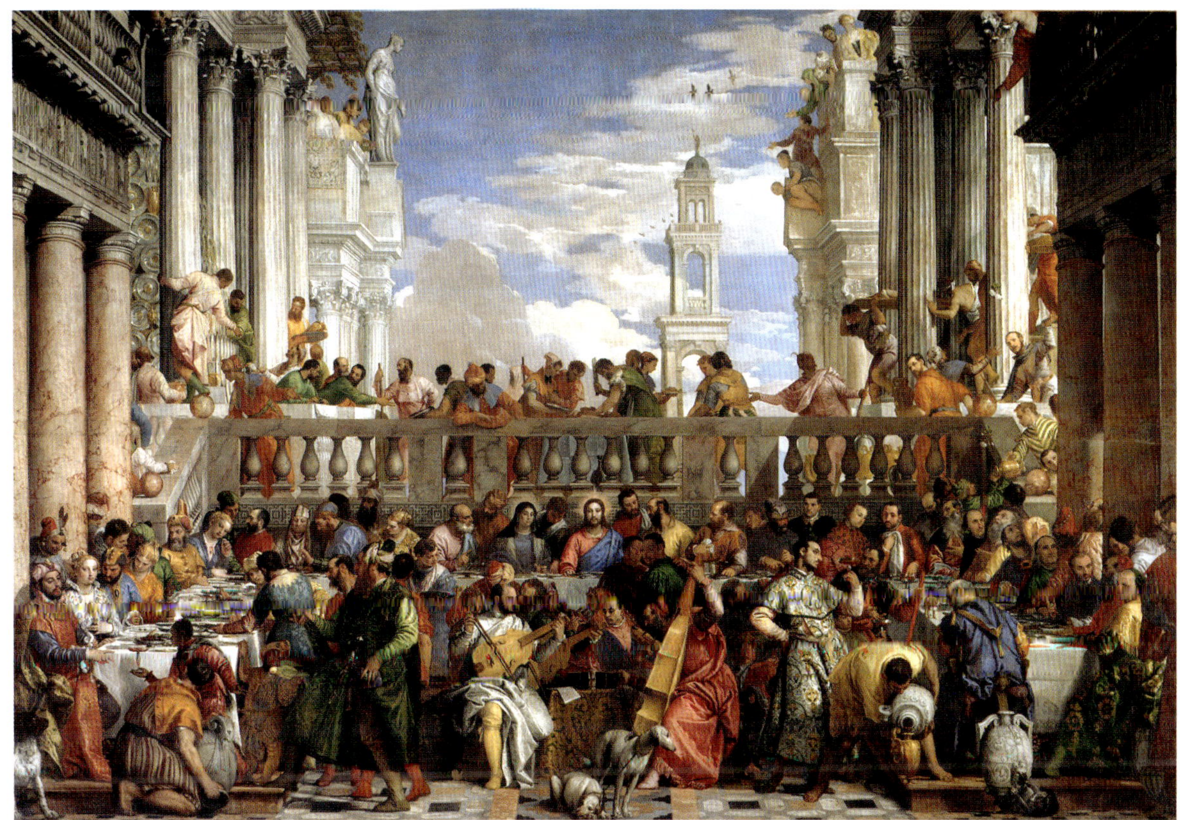

Paolo Veronese
(Verona 1528 - Venezia 1588)

The Marriage at Cana
Hochzeit von Kanaa
Brulloft te Kana

●●●

1563
677 x 994 cm / 266.5 x 391.3 in.
Musée du Louvre, Paris

Oil on canvas / Öl auf Leinwand
Olieverf op doek

After a conflict with the Inquisition, Veronese calls his paintings of the Last Supper simply "Supper in the House of Levi".

Nach einem Streit mit der Inquisition nannte Veronese sein Abendmahlgemälde einfach "das Nachtmahl im Hause des Levi".

Na een onenigheid met de Inquisitie, noemt Veronese zijn schilderijen van het Laatste Avondmaal eenvoudigweg "Maaltijd in het huis van Levi".

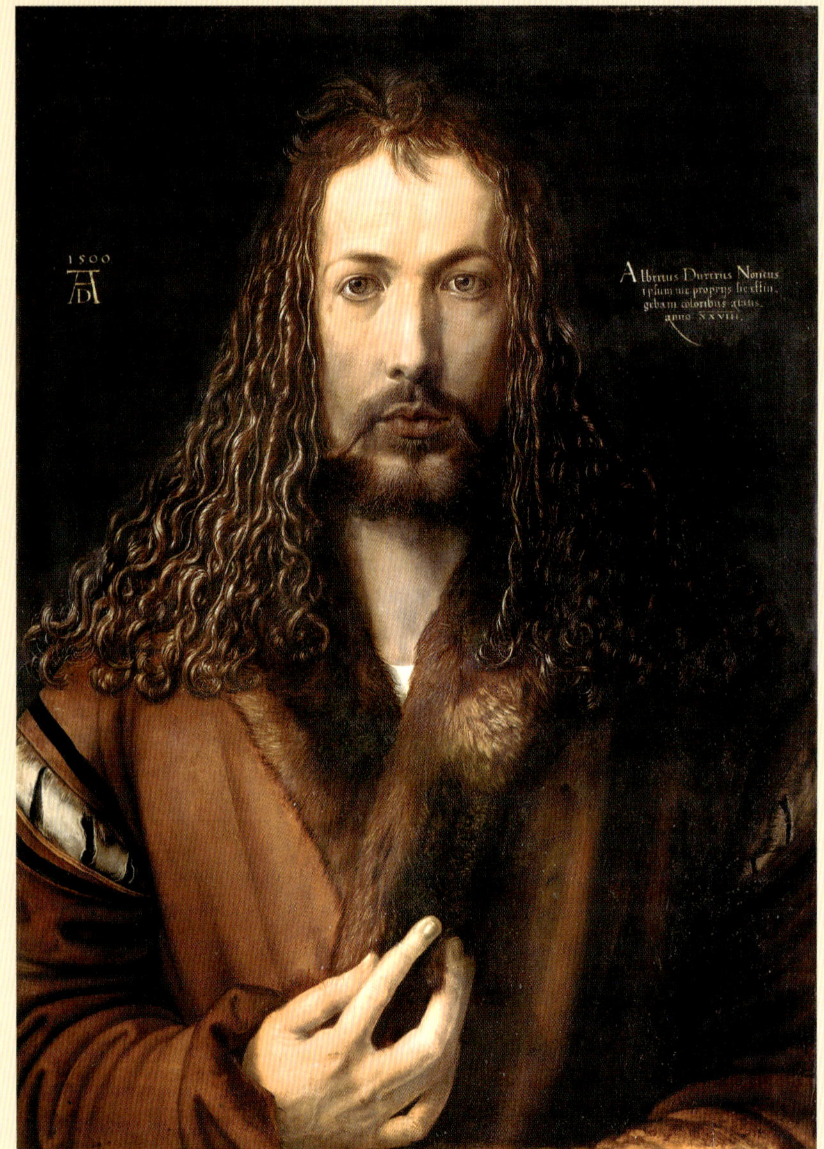

Albrecht Dürer
(Nürnberg 1471 - 1528)

Self-Portrait
Selbstbildnis
Zelfportret

●●●

1500
67.3 x 49.5 cm / 26.49 x 19.48 in.
Alte Pinakothek, München

Oil on wood
Öl auf Tafel
Olieverf op paneel

Dürer is one of the first artists to paint a self-portrait.

Dürer ist einer der ersten Künstler, der sich selbst porträtierte.

Dürer is een van de eerste kunstenaars die zijn eigen portret schildert.

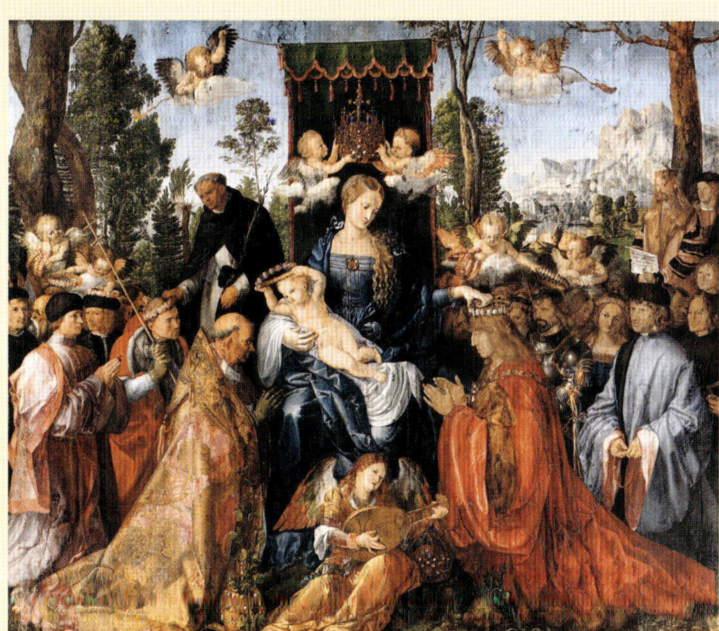

Albrecht Dürer
(Nürnberg 1471 - 1528)

Feast of the Rose Garlands
Das Rosenkranzfest
Rozenkransfeest

●

1506
162 x 194,5 cm / 63.7 x 76.6 in.
Národní Museum, Prague

Oil on wood
Öl auf Tafel
Olieverf op Paneel

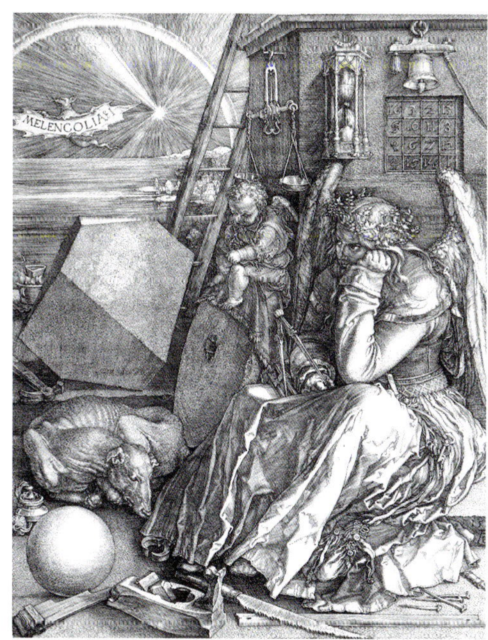

Albrecht Dürer
(Nürnberg 1471 - 1528)

Melancholy
Melancholie

●●

c. 1514
24 x 19 cm / 9.44 x 7.48 in.
Fondazione Magnani Rocca,
Traversetolo, Parma

Engraving/ Stich / Gravure

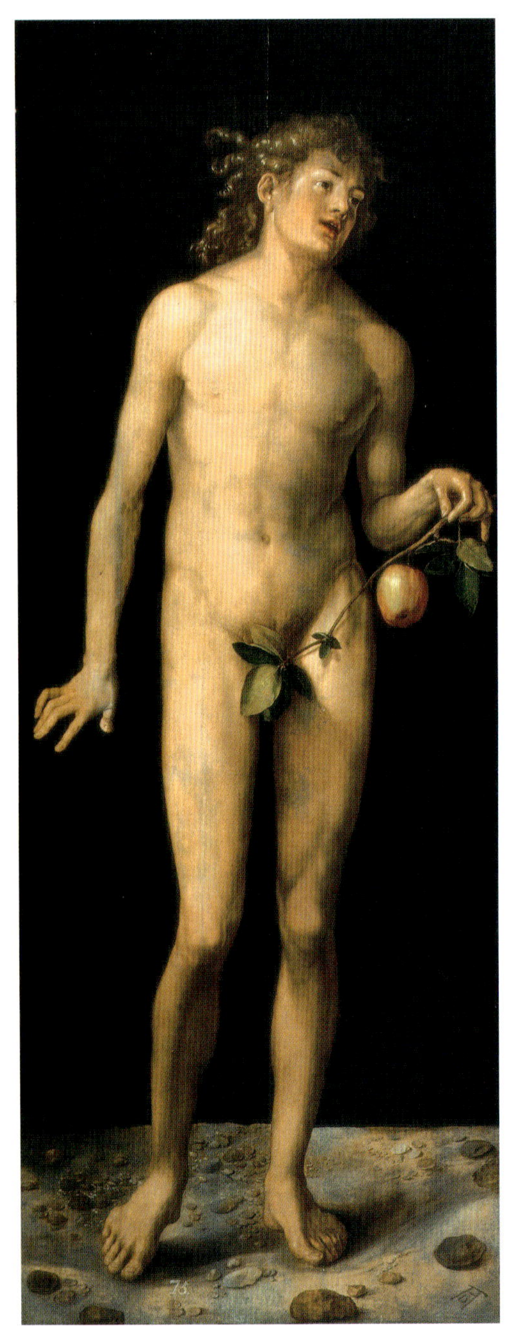

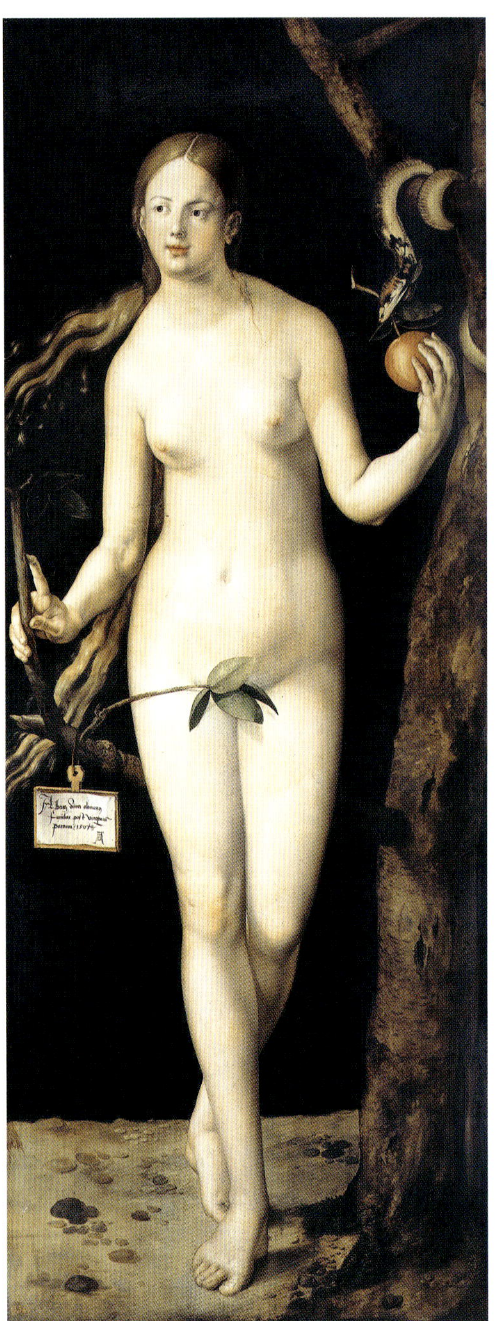

Albrecht Dürer
(Nürnberg 1471 - 1528)

Adam and Eve
Adam und Eva
Adam en Eva

●●

1507
209 x 81 cm -
209 x 83 cm
82.28 x 31.88
82.28 x 32.67 in.
Museo Nacional
del Prado, Madrid

Oil on wood
Öl auf Tafel
Olieverf op paneel

Albrecht Dürer
(Nürnberg 1471 - 1528)

Four Apostles
Die Vier Apostel
Vier apostelen

●●●

1526
1526
215.5 x 76 cm -
214.5 x 76 cm
84.84 x 29.92 -
84.44 x 29.92 in.
Alte Pinakothek,
München

Oil on wood
Öl auf Tafel
Olieverf op paneel

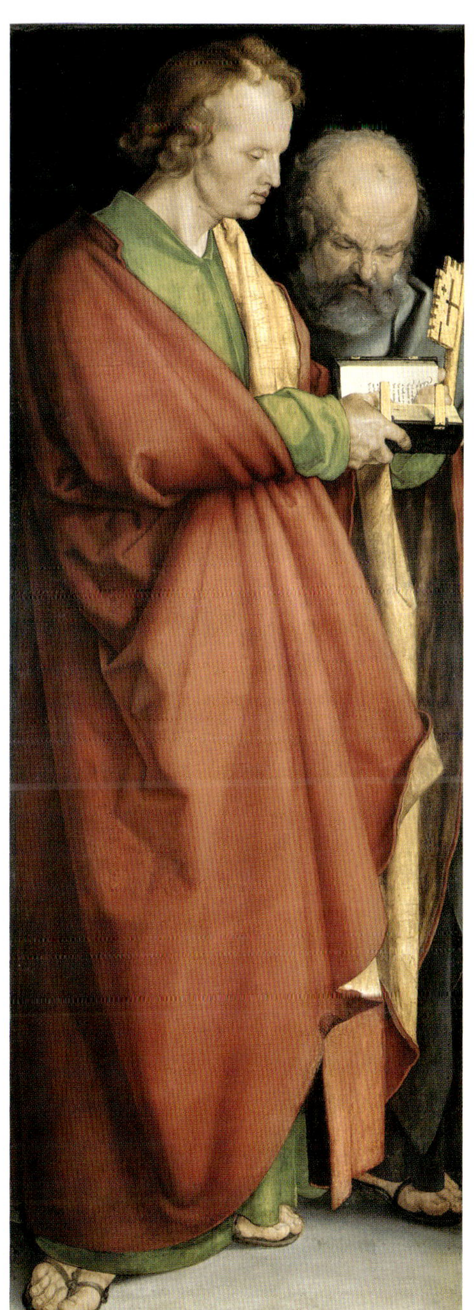

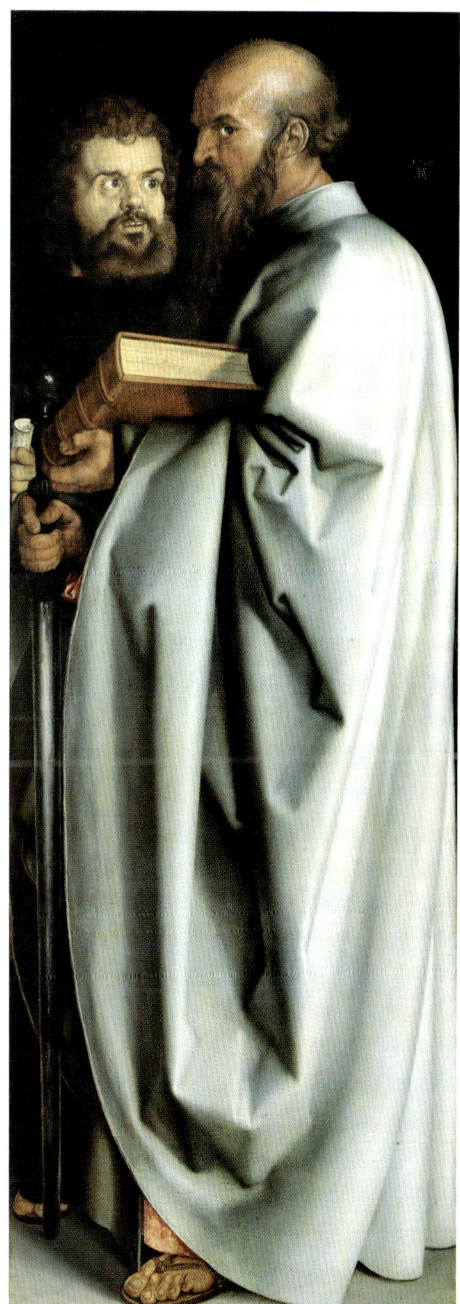

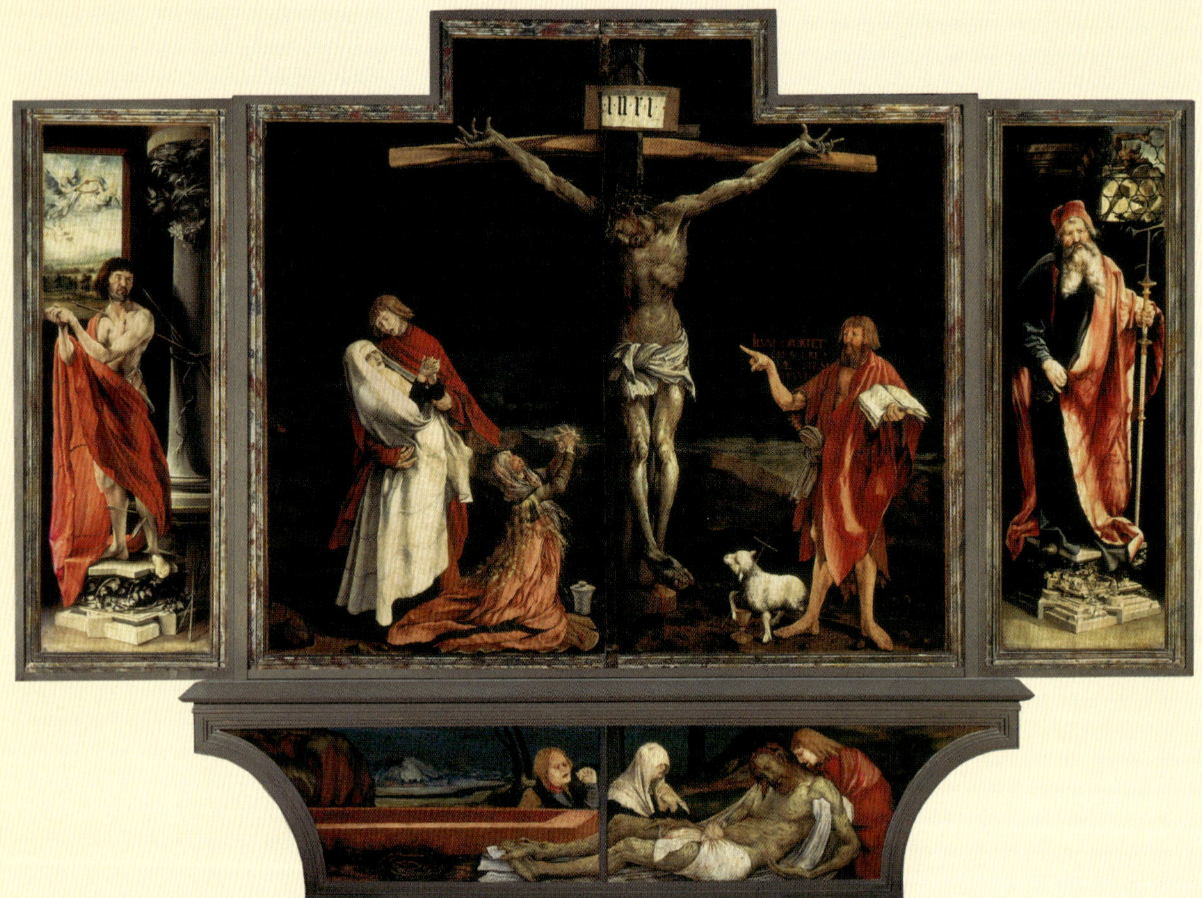

Matthias Grünewald
(Würzburg c. 1475-1480 - Halle an der Saale 1528)

Isenheim Altarpiece: The Crucifixion
Isenheimer Altar: Die Kreuzigung
Isenheimer Altaar: De Kruisiging

●●

1512-1516
345 x 458 cm / 135.8 x 180.3 in.
Musée d'Unterlinden, Colmar

Oil on wood / Öl auf Holz / Olieverf op paneel

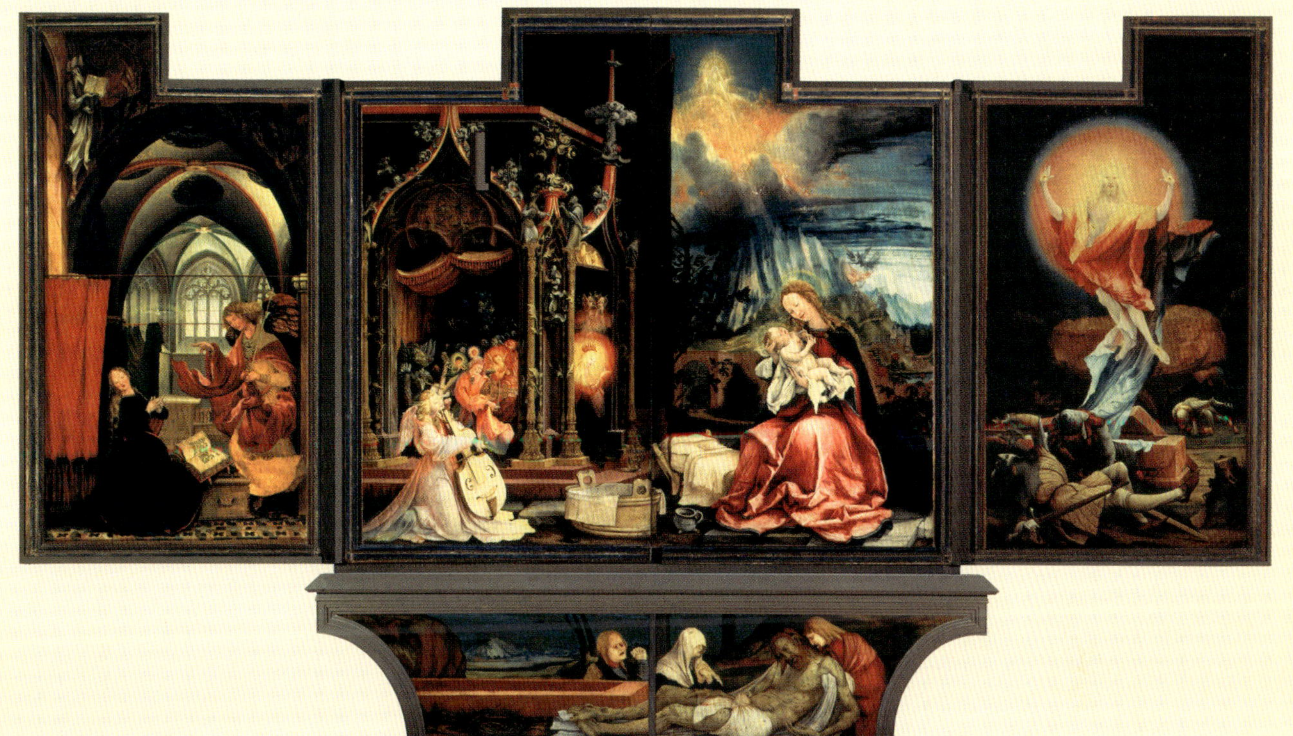

Matthias Grünewald
(Würzburg c. 1475-1480 - Halle an der Saale 1528)

Isenheim Altarpiece: Allegory of the Nativity
Isenheimer Aktar: Allegorie der Geburt
Isenheimer Altaar: Allegorie van de Geboorte van Christus

●●

1512-1516
345 x 458 cm / 135.8 x 180.3 in.
Musée d'Unterlinden, Colmar

Oil on wood / Öl auf Holz / Olieverf op paneel

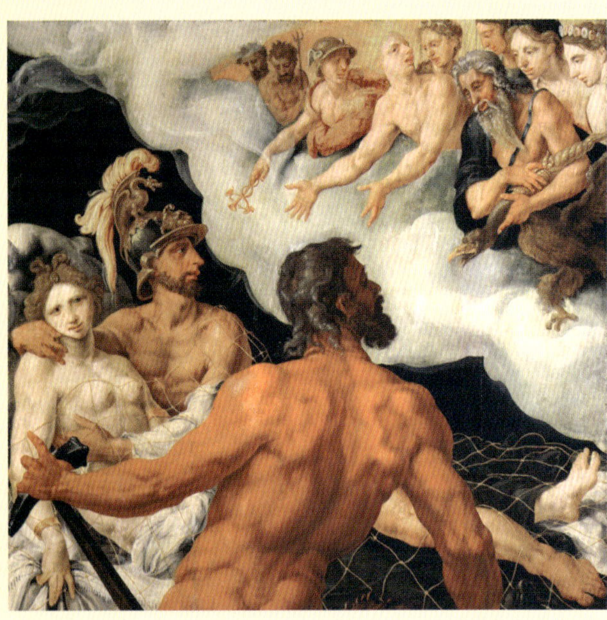

Maarten van Heemskerck
(Heemskerck, Utrecht 1498 - Haarlem 1574)

Venus and Mars in Vulcan's Net Shown to the Gods
Vulkan fängt Venus und Mars in seinem Netz und zeigt sie den Göttern
Vulcanus vangt Venus en Mars in een net en toont ze aan de goden

●

1540
96 x 99 cm / 37.8 x 39 in
Kunsthistorisches Museum, Wien

Oil on oakwood / Öl auf Eichenholz / Olieverf op eikenhout

Giuseppe Arcimboldo
(Milano 1527 - 1593)

Summer
Der Sommer
De Zomer

●●●

1573
76 x 64 cm / 29.9 x 25.1 in.
Musée du Louvre, Paris

Oil on canvas / Öl auf Leinwand
Olieverf op doek

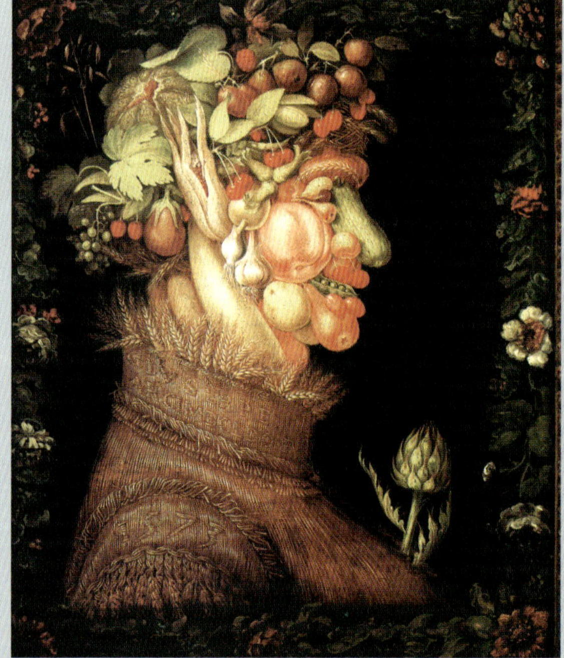

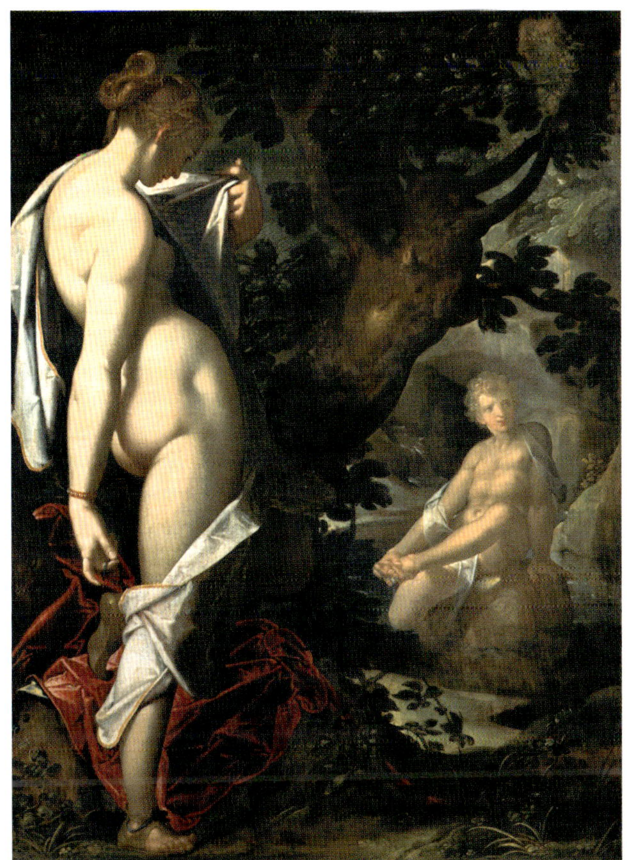

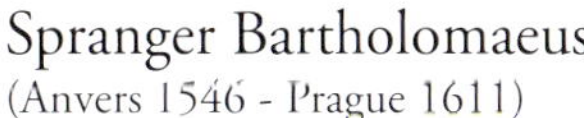

Spranger Bartholomaeus
(Anvers 1546 - Prague 1611)

Hermaphrodite with the Nymph Salmacide
Hermaphrodit und die Nymphe Salamacis
Hermaphroditus en de nimf Salmacis

●

1580-1582
110 x 81 cm / 43.3 x 31.9 in.
Kunsthistorisches Museum, Wien

Oil on canvas
Öl auf Leinwand
Olieverf op doek

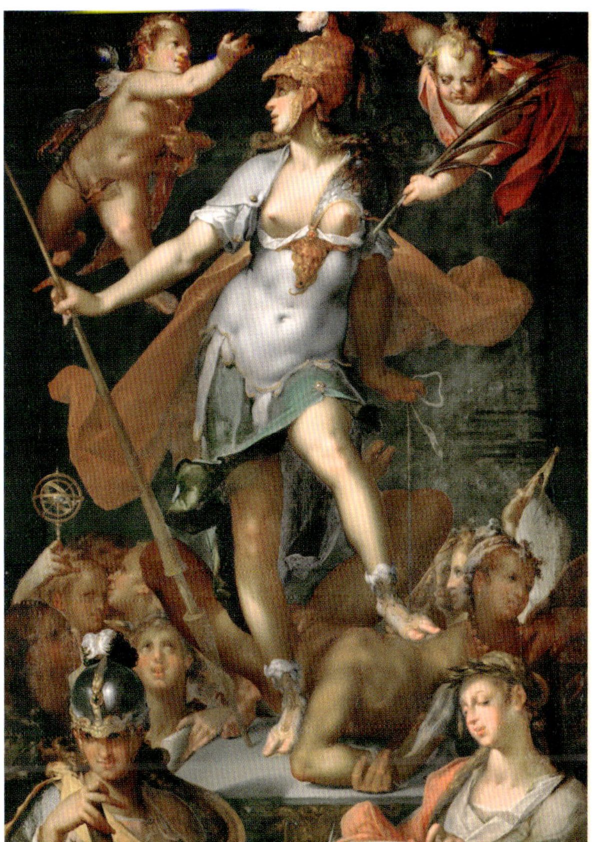

Spranger Bartholomaeus
(Anvers 1546 - Prague 1611)

Minerva Victorious over Ignorance
Minerva als Siegerin über die Unwissenheit
Minerva overwint de Onwetendheid

●

1591
163 x 117 cm / 64.2 x 46 in.
Kunsthistorisches Museum, Wien

Oil on canvas
Öl auf Leinwand
Olieverf op doek

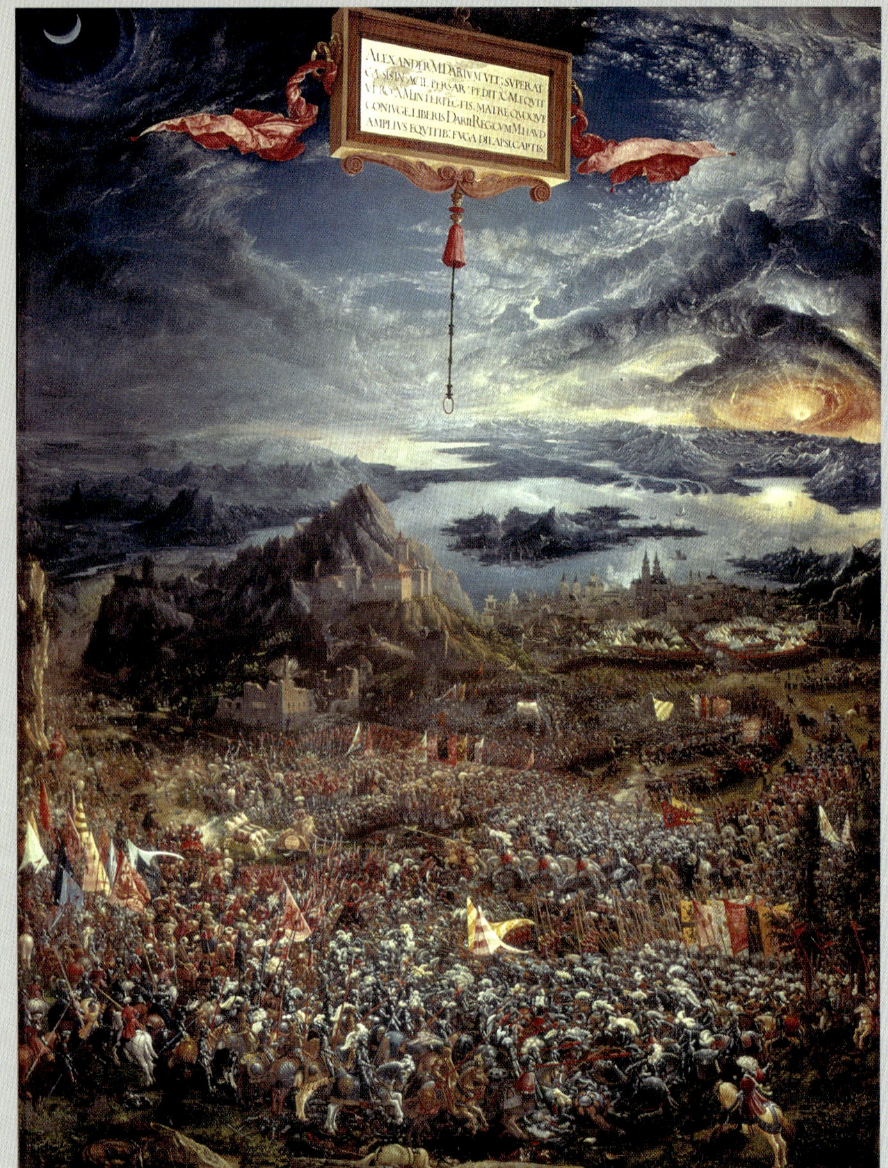

Albrecht Altdorfer
(Regensburg 1480 - 1538)

The Battle of Alexander at Issus
Die Alexanderschlacht
Veldslag van Alexander tegen Darius (Alexanderslag)

●●●

1529
158 × 120 cm / 62.20 x 47.24 in.
Alte Pinakothek, München

Oil on wood / Öl auf Tafel
Olieverf op paneel

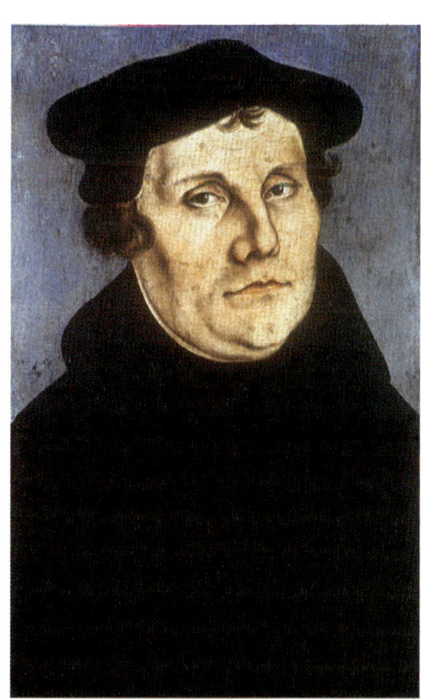

Lucas Cranach the Elder
Lucas Cranach der Ältere
Lucas Cranach de Oude
(Kronach 1472 - Weimar 1553)

Martin Luther
Maarten Luther

●●●

1529
37 x 23 cm / 14.56 x 9.05 in.
Galleria degli Uffizi, Firenze

Oil on wood
Öl auf Tafel
Olieverf op paneel

Lucas Cranach the Elder
Lucas Cranach der Ältere
Lucas Cranach de Oude
(Kronach 1472 - Weimar 1553)

Venus and Cupid with a Bee Hive
Venus und Amor
Venus en Cupido die de honingraat draagt

●●

c. 1525
170 x 67 cm / 66.92 x 26.37 in.
Galleria Borghese, Roma

Oil on wood
Öl auf Tafel
Olieverf op paneel

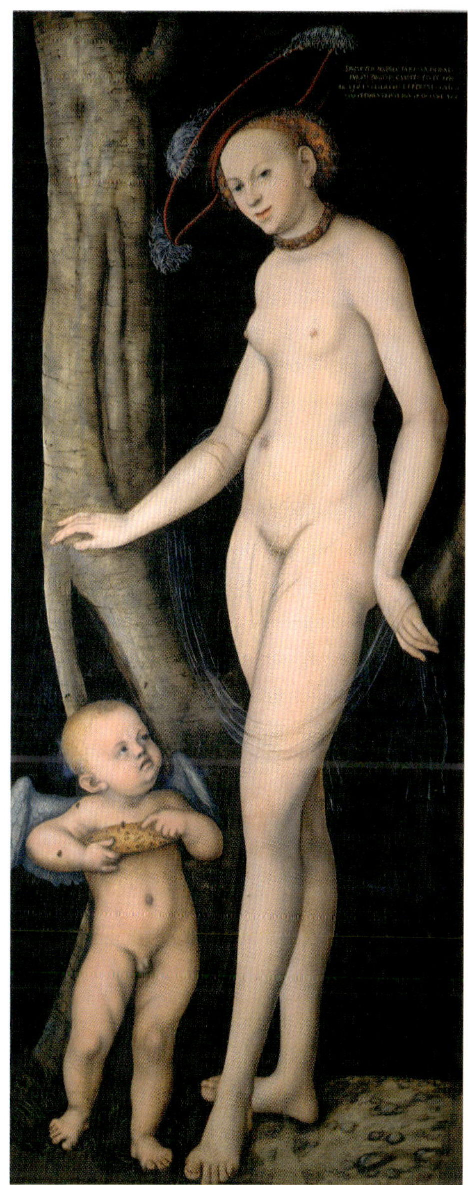

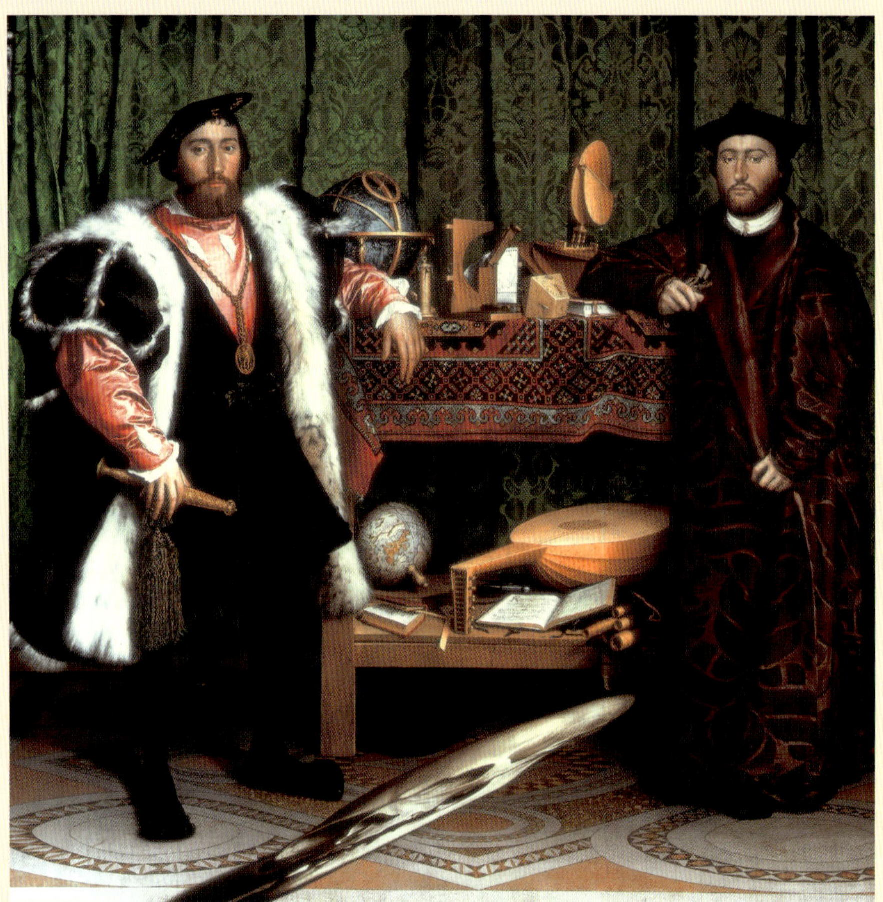

Hans Holbein
(Augsburg 1497/1498 - London 1543)

The Ambassadors
Die Botschafter
De Ambassadeurs

●●

1533
207 x 209,5 cm / 81.4 x 82.4 in.
National Gallery, London

Oil on wood / Öl auf Holz / Olieverf op paneel

Cosmopolitan Hans Holbein is admired for his characteristic portraits and becomes court painter to Henry VIII.

Der Kosmopolit Hans Holbein begeistert mit seinen charaktervollen Portraits und wird Hofmaler Heinrich VIII.

De kosmopoliet Hans Holbein krijgt enthousiaste reacties op zijn karaktervolle portretten en wordt hofschilder van Hendrik VIII.

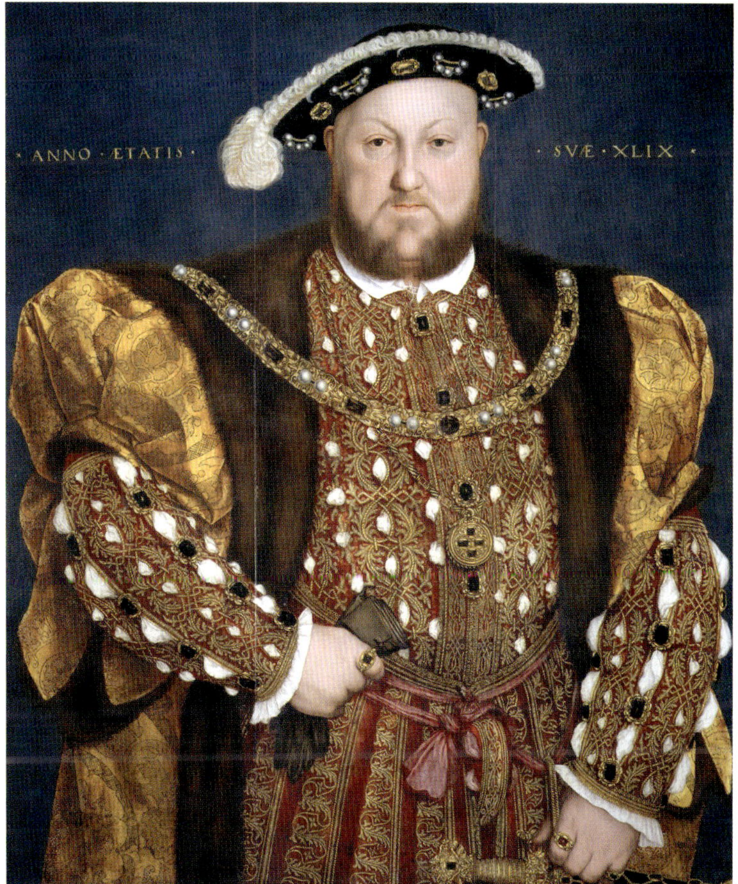

Hans Holbein
(Augsburg 1497/1498 London 1543)

Portrait of Henry VIII
Porträt von Heinrich VIII
Portret van Hendrik VIII

●●●

c. 1540
88,5 x 74,5 cm / 34.8 x 29.3 in.
Galleria Nazionale di Arte Antica di Palazzo Barberini, Roma

Oil on wood / Öl auf Holz / Olieverf op paneel

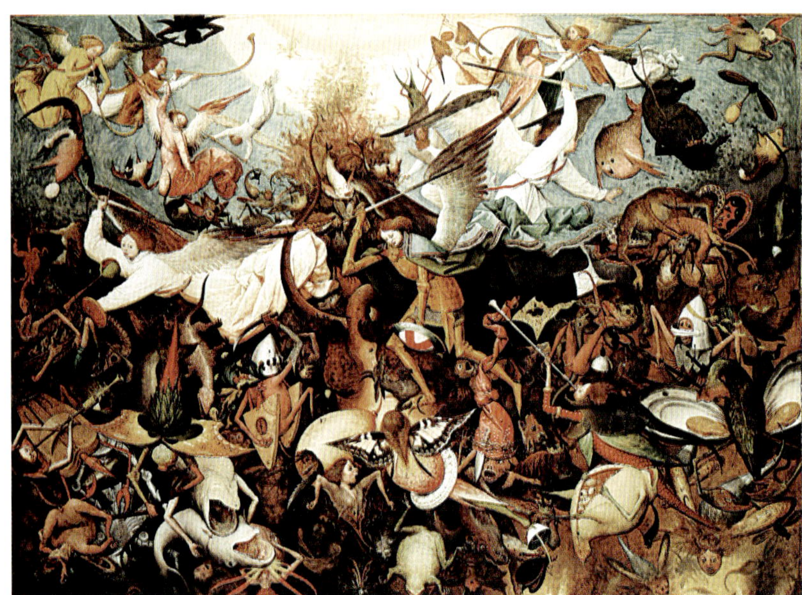

Pieter Bruegel the Elder
Pieter Bruegel der Ältere
Pieter Bruegel de Oude
(Breda *c.* 1525/1530 - Bruxelles 1569)

Fall of the Rebel Angels
Fall der Engel
De val van de opstandige engelen

●●

1562
117 x 162 cm / 46.06 x 63.77 in.
Musées Royaux des Beaux-Arts, Bruxelles

Oil on wood
Öl auf Tafel
Olieverf op paneel

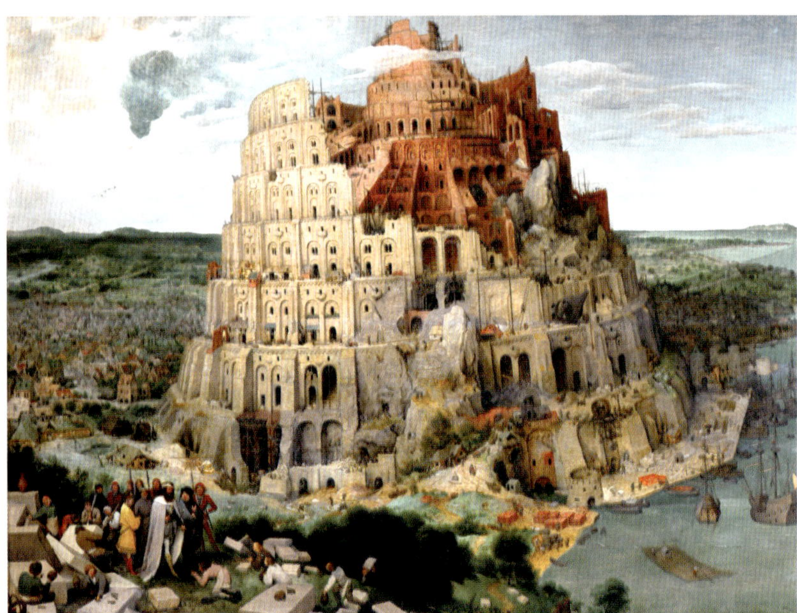

Pieter Bruegel the Elder
Pieter Bruegel der Ältere
Pieter Bruegel de Oude
(Breda *c.* 1525/1530 - Bruxelles 1569)

The Tower of Babel
Der Turmbau zu Babel
De toren van Babel

●●●

1563
114 x 155 cm / 44.8 x 61
Kunsthistorisches Museum, Wien

Oil on wood
Öl auf Holz
Olieverf op paneel

Pieter Bruegel the Elder
Pieter Bruegel der Ältere
Pieter Bruegel de Oude
(Breda *c.* 1525/1530 - Bruxelles 1569)

Peasants Dancing
Der Bauerntanz
Boerendans

●●●

1568
114 x 164 cm / 44.9 x 64.6 in.
Kunsthistorisches Museum, Wien

Oil on oakwood
Öl auf Eichenholz
Olieverf op eikenhout

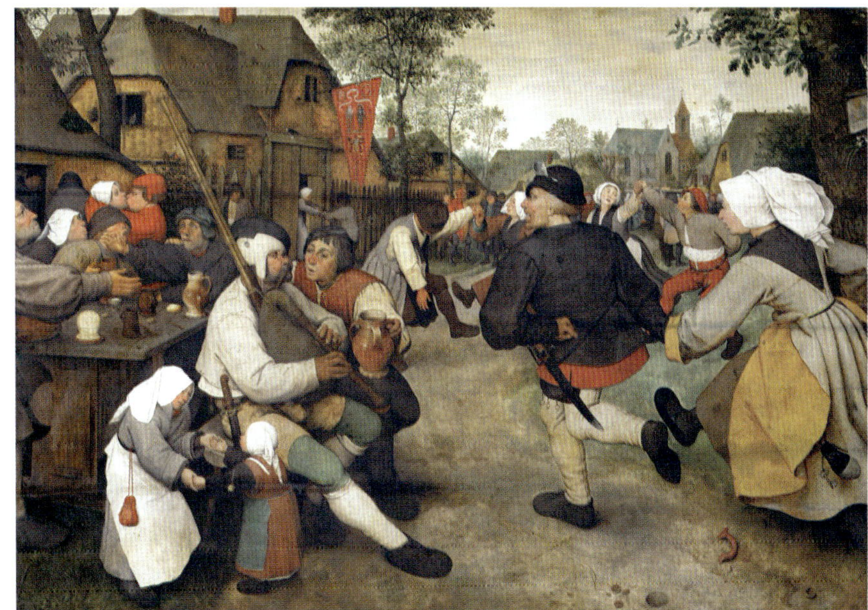

Pieter Bruegel the Elder
Pieter Bruegel der Ältere
Pieter Bruegel de Oude
(Breda *c.* 1525/1530 - Bruxelles 1569)

The Parable of the Blind
Parabel der Blinden
Parabel van de blinden

●●●

1568
86 x 154 cm / 33.9 x 60.6 in.
Museo Nazionale di Capodimonte, Napoli

Tempera on canvas
Tempera auf Leinwand
Tempera op doek

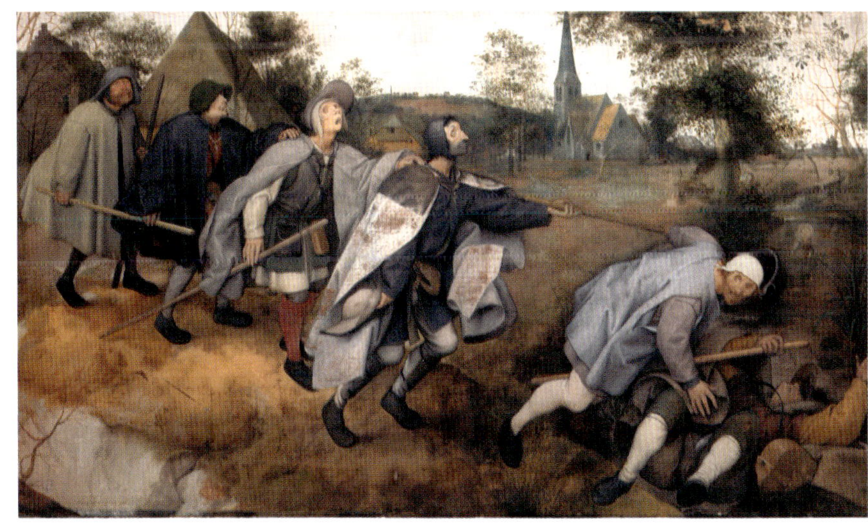

230

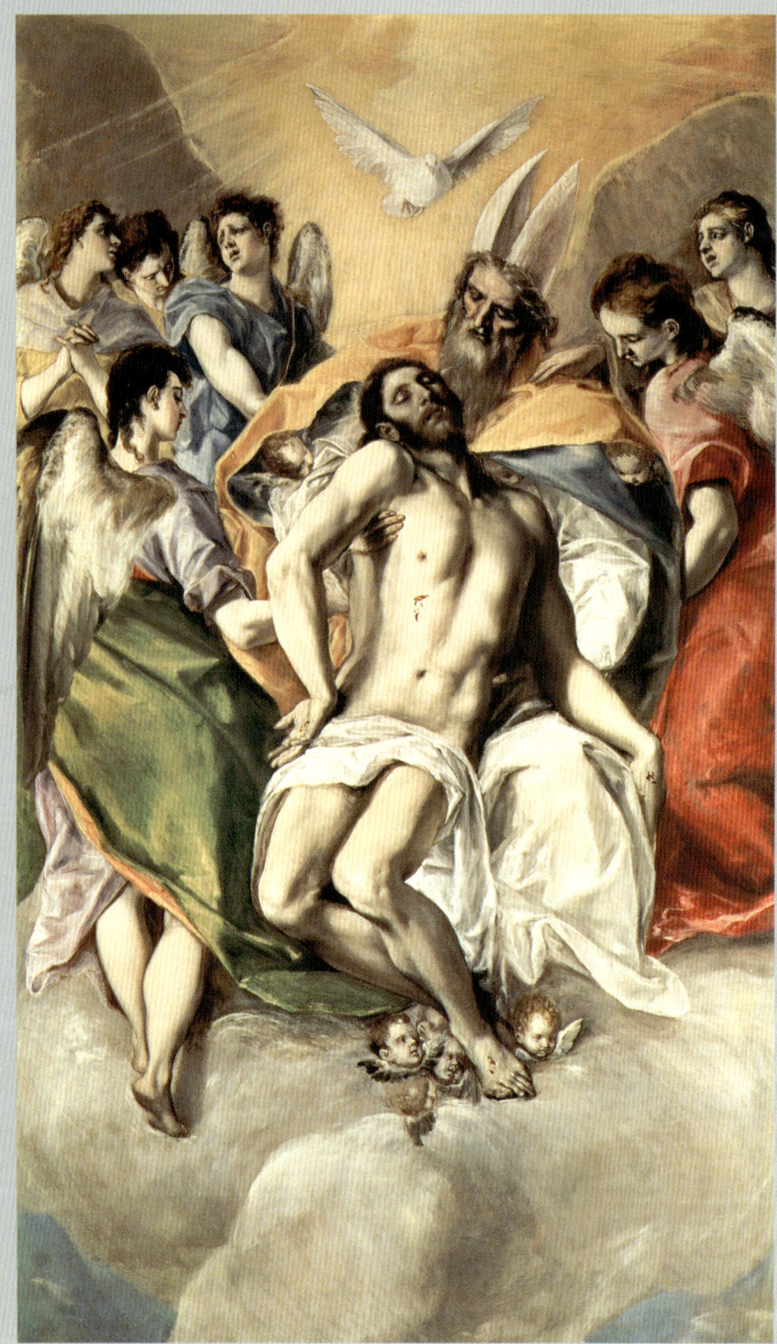

Excessive expansion and lengthening are typical of Mannerism. In this style, between the Renaissance and the Baroque, the head-to-body proportion can easily reach 1 to 12, while the normal ratio is about 1 to 7.

Überdehnung und Überlängung sind Hauptmerkmale des Manierismus. Das Kopf-Körper Verhältnis beträgt in diesem Stil zwischen Renaissance und Barock leicht 1 zu 12, normal ist etwa 1 zu 7.

Dilatatie en excessieve verlenging zijn de belangrijkste kenmerken van het maniërisme. In deze stijl, tussen renaissance en barok, bedraagt de verhouding hoofd-lichaam gemakkelijk 1 op 12, normaliter is dit ongeveer 1 op 7.

El Greco
(Candía, Crete 1541 - Toledo 1614)

Trinity
Trinität
Drie-eenheid

●●

c. 1577-1579
300 x 179 cm / 118.11 x 70.47 in.
Museo Nacional del Prado, Madrid

Oil on canvas / Öl auf Leinwand
Olieverf op doek

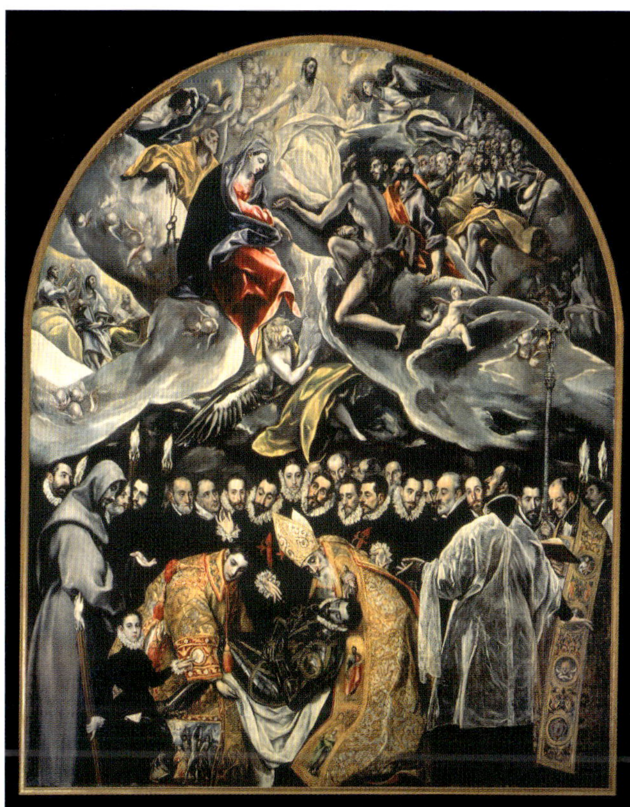

El Greco
(Candía, Crete 1541 - Toledo 1614)

Burial of the Count of Orgaz
Das Begräbnis des Grafen Orgaz
Begrafenis van de graaf van Orgaz

●●●

c. 1586-1588
460 x 360 cm / 187.40 x 141.73 in.
Santo Tomé, Toledo

Oil on canvas / Öl auf Leinwand
Olieverf op doek

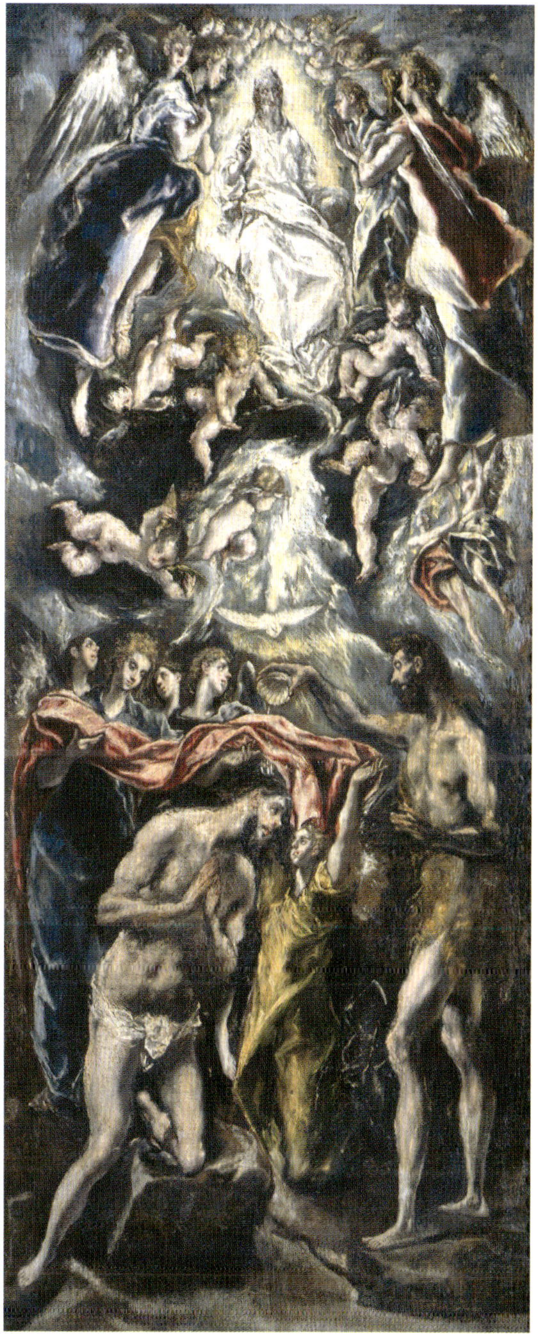

El Greco
(Candía, Crete 1541 - Toledo 1614)

Baptism of Christ
Taufe Christi
De Doop van Christus

●

1545 - 1548
111 x 47 cm / 43.7 x 18.5 in.
Galleria Nazionale d'Arte Antica
di Palazzo Barberini, Roma

Oil on canvas / Öl auf Leinwand
Olieverf op doek

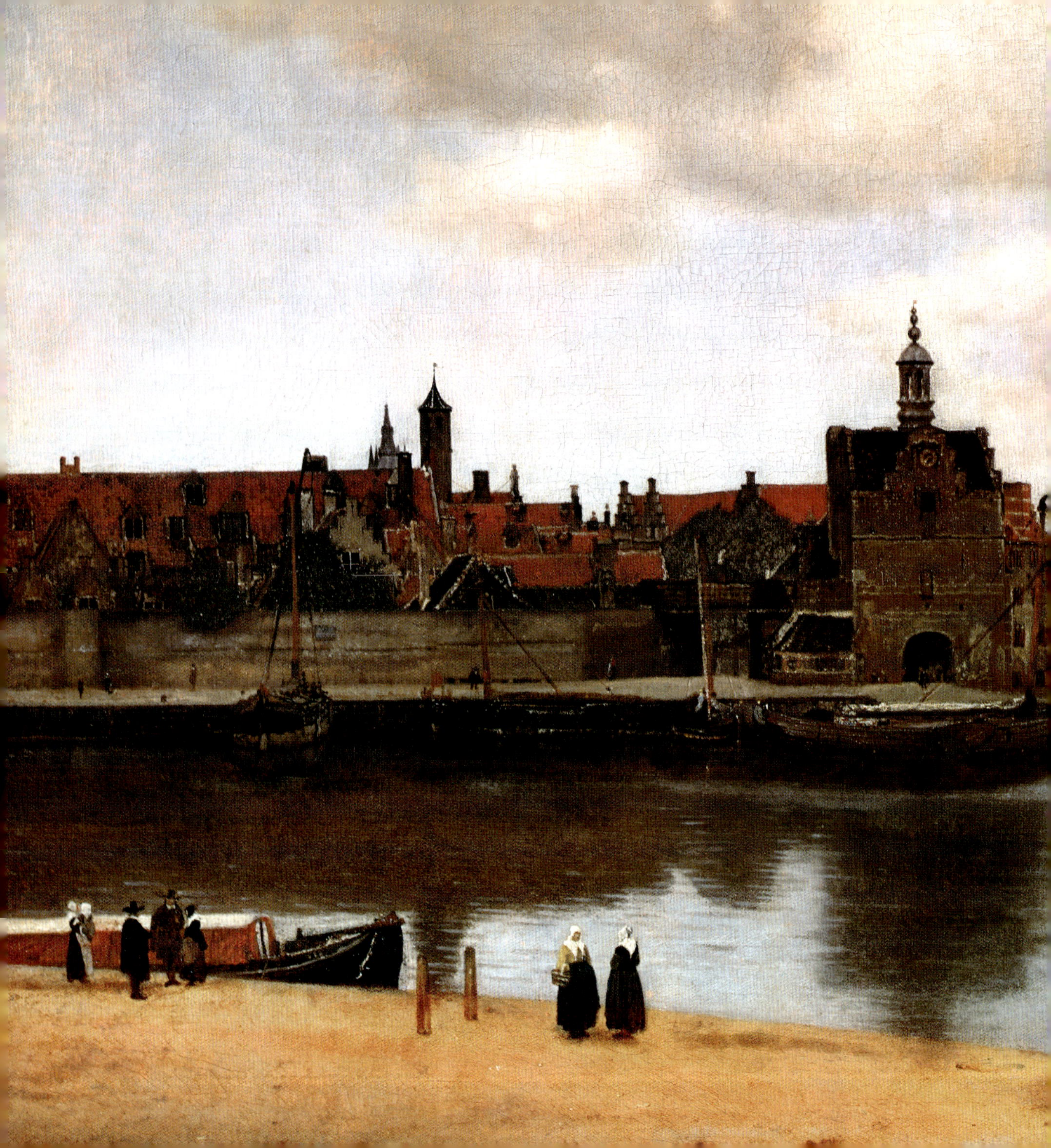

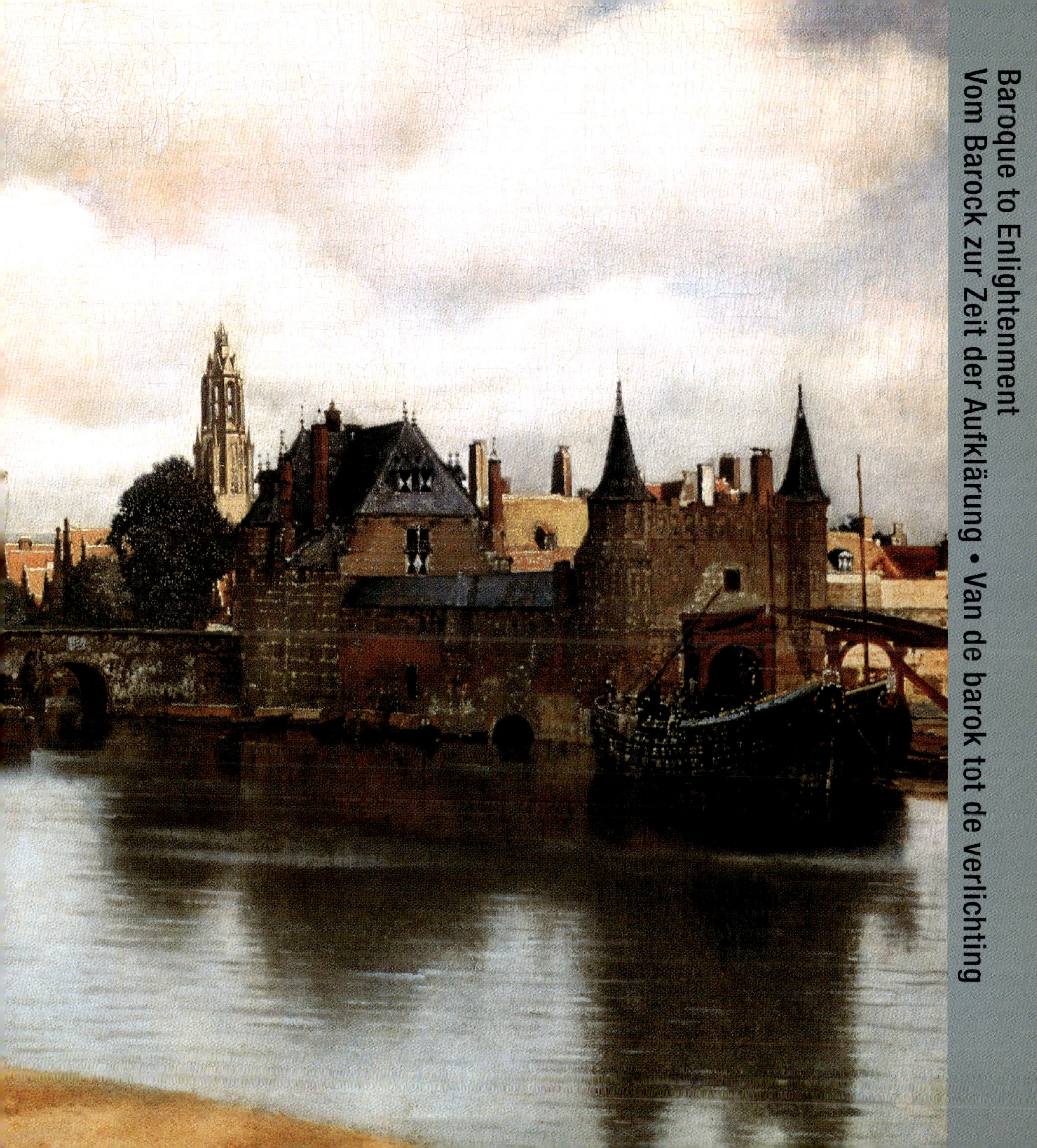
Baroque to Enlightenment
Vom Barock zur Zeit der Aufklärung • Van de barok tot de verlichting

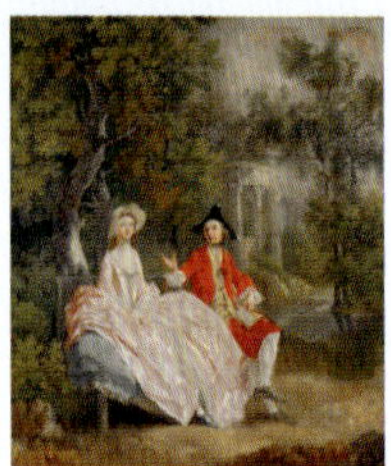

GREAT BRITAIN

Thomas Gainsborough (Sudbury 1727 - London 1788)
Joshua Reynolds (Plympton 1723 - London 1792)
William Hogarth (London 1697 - 1764)

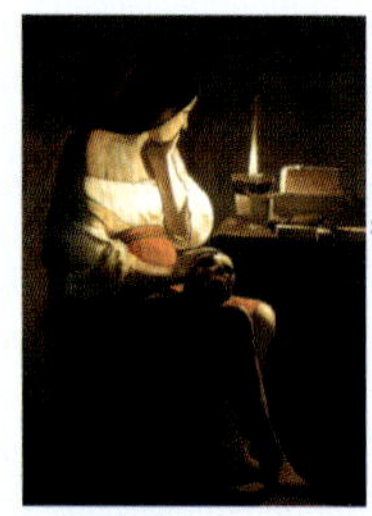

NEDERLAND

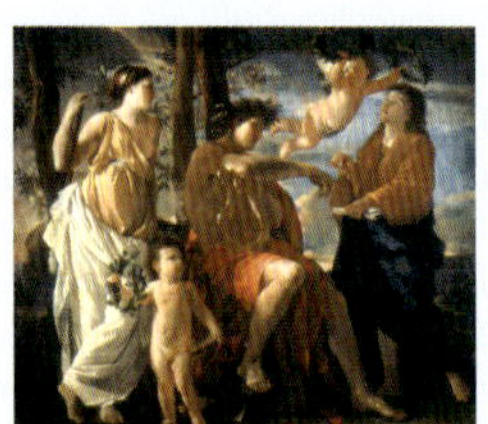

FRANCE

Georges De La Tour (Vic-sur-Seille 1593 - Lunéville 1652)
Valentin de Boulogne (Coulommiers 1591 - Roma 1632)
Nicolas Poussin (Les Andelys 1594 - Roma 1665)
Claude Lorrain (Chamagne 1600 - Roma 1682)
Pierre Puget (Marseille 1620 - Marseille 1694)
Hyacinthe Rigaud (Perpignan 1659 - Paris 1743)
Antoine Coysevox (Lyon 1640 - Paris 1720)
Jean-Antoine Watteau (Valenciennes 1684 - Nogent-sur-Marne 1721)
Jean Baptiste Siméon Chardin (Paris 1699 - 1779)
François Boucher (Paris 1703 - 1770)
Carle van Loo (Nice 1705 - Paris 1765)
Jean Baptiste Pigalle (Paris 1714 - Paris 1785)
Jean Antoine Houdon (Versailles 1741 - Paris 1828)
Jean-Baptiste Greuze (Tournus 1725 - Parigi 1805)
Elisabeth Vigée-Lebrun (Paris 1755 - 1842)

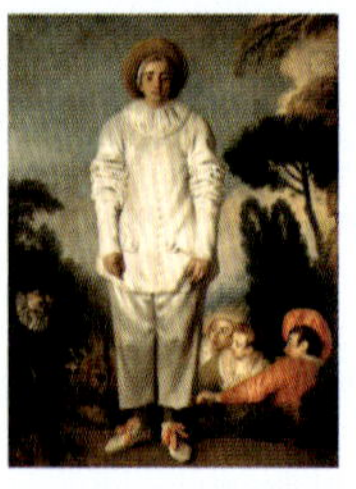

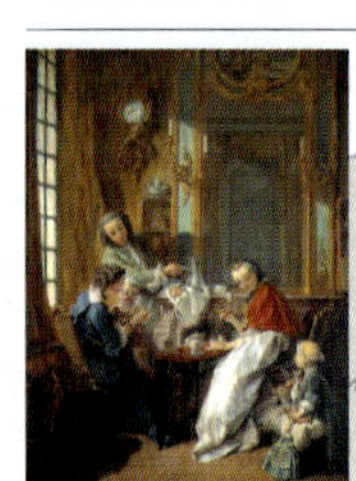

ESPAÑA

Jusepe de Ribera (Xàtiva 1591 - Napoli 1652)
Diego Velázquez (Sevilla 1599 - Madrid 1660)

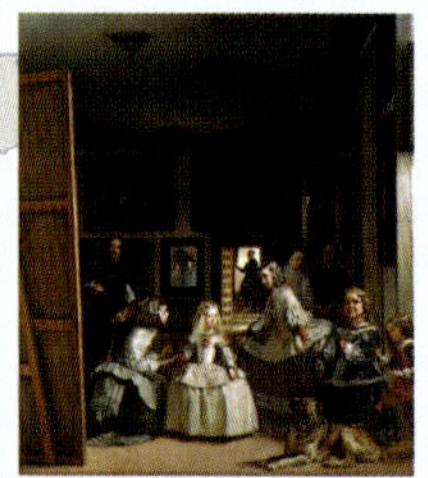

Courtly art serving self-portrayal
Höfische Kunst im Dienst der Selbstdarstellung
De kunst van het hof in dienst van de zelfverheerlijking

DANMARK

Bertel Thorvaldsen (Copenhagen 1770 - 1844)

Pieter Paul Rubens (Siegen 1577 - Anvers 1640)
Antoon van Dyck (Antwerpen 1599 - London 1641)
François Duquesnoy (Bruxelles 1597 - Livorno 1643)
Rembrandt (Leiden 1606 - Amsterdam 1669)
Michael Sweerts (Bruxelles 1618 - Goa 1664)
Bamboccio (Pieter van Laer) (Haarlem 1599 - ? 1642)
Jan Vermeer (Delft 1632 - 1675)
Jan Steen (Leiden 1626 - Leiden 1679)
Jan van der Heyden (Gorinchem 1637 - Amsterdam 1712)
Gerard ter Borch II (Zwolle 1617 - Deventer 1681)
Gerrit Berckheyde (Haarlem 1638 - Haarlem 1698)

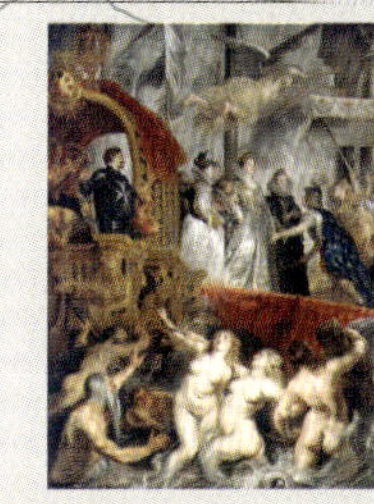

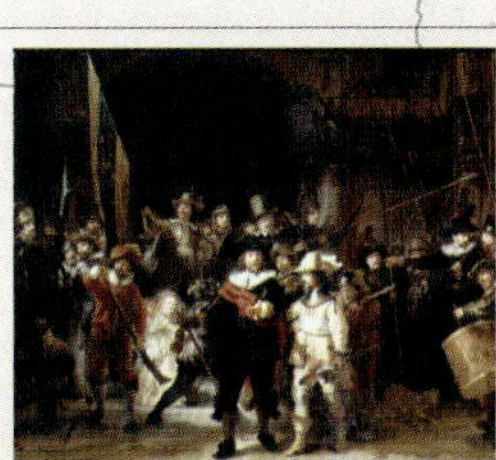

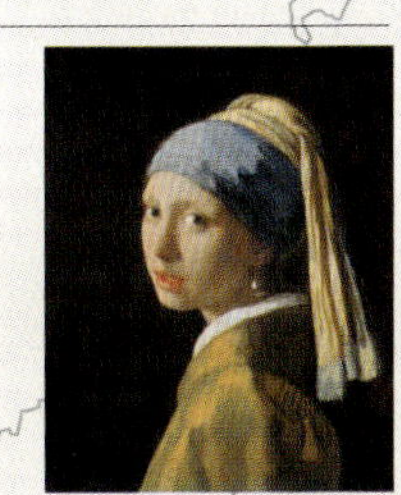

DEUTSCHLAND

Johann Heinrich Wilhelm Tischbein (Haina1751 - Eutin 1829)
Emil Wolff (Berlin 1802 - Roma 1879)

SCHWEIZ

Angelica Kauffmann (Chur, 1741 - Roma 1807)

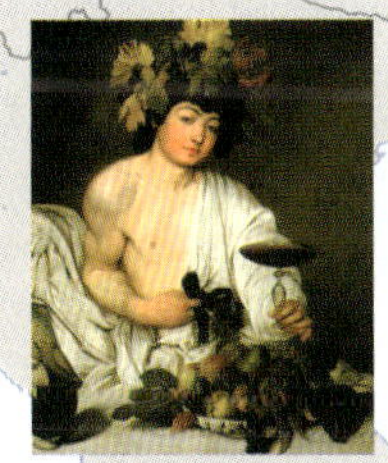

ITALIA

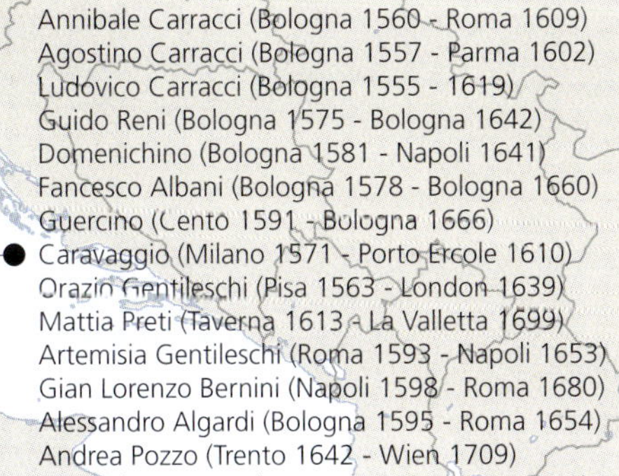

Annibale Carracci (Bologna 1560 - Roma 1609)
Agostino Carracci (Bologna 1557 - Parma 1602)
Ludovico Carracci (Bologna 1555 - 1619)
Guido Reni (Bologna 1575 - Bologna 1642)
Domenichino (Bologna 1581 - Napoli 1641)
Fancesco Albani (Bologna 1578 - Bologna 1660)
Guercino (Cento 1591 - Bologna 1666)
Caravaggio (Milano 1571 - Porto Ercole 1610)
Orazio Gentileschi (Pisa 1563 - London 1639)
Mattia Preti (Taverna 1613 - La Valletta 1699)
Artemisia Gentileschi (Roma 1593 - Napoli 1653)
Gian Lorenzo Bernini (Napoli 1598 - Roma 1680)
Alessandro Algardi (Bologna 1595 - Roma 1654)
Andrea Pozzo (Trento 1642 - Wien 1709)
Pietro da Cortona (Cortona 1596 - Roma 1669)
Canaletto (Venezia 1697 - 1768)
Francesco Guardi (Venezia 1712 - 1793)
Giacomo Ceruti (Milano 1698 - 1767)
Giuseppe Maria Crespi (Bologna 1665 - Bologna 1747)
Giambattista Tiepolo (Zianigo 1696 - Madrid 1770)
Giandomenico Tiepolo (Zianigo 1727 - Venezia 1804)
Pietro Longhi (Venezia 1701 - 1785)
Giovanni Battista Piranesi (Mogliano Veneto 1720 – Roma 1778
Rosalba Carriera (Chioggia 1675 - Venezia 1757)
Antonio Canova (Possagno 1757 - Venezia 1822)

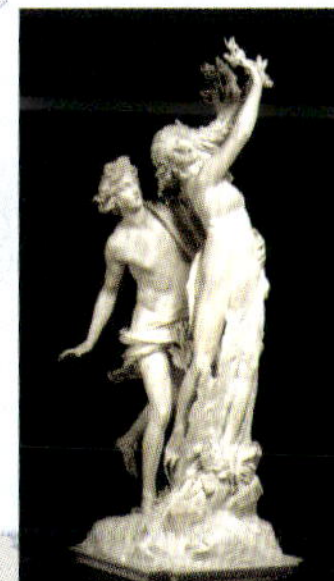

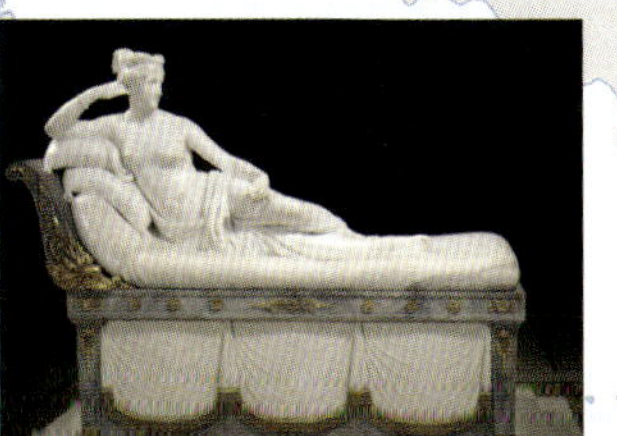

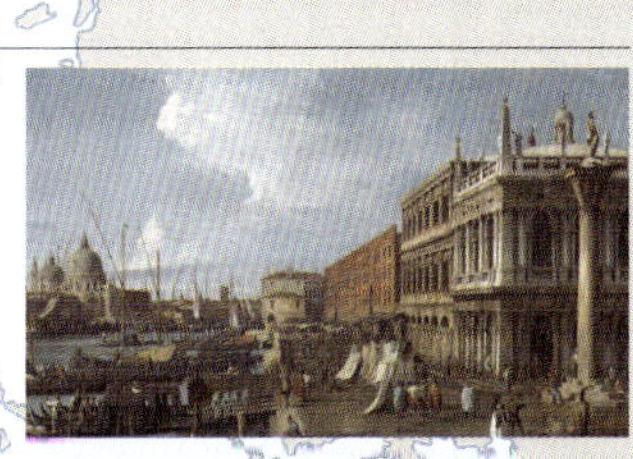

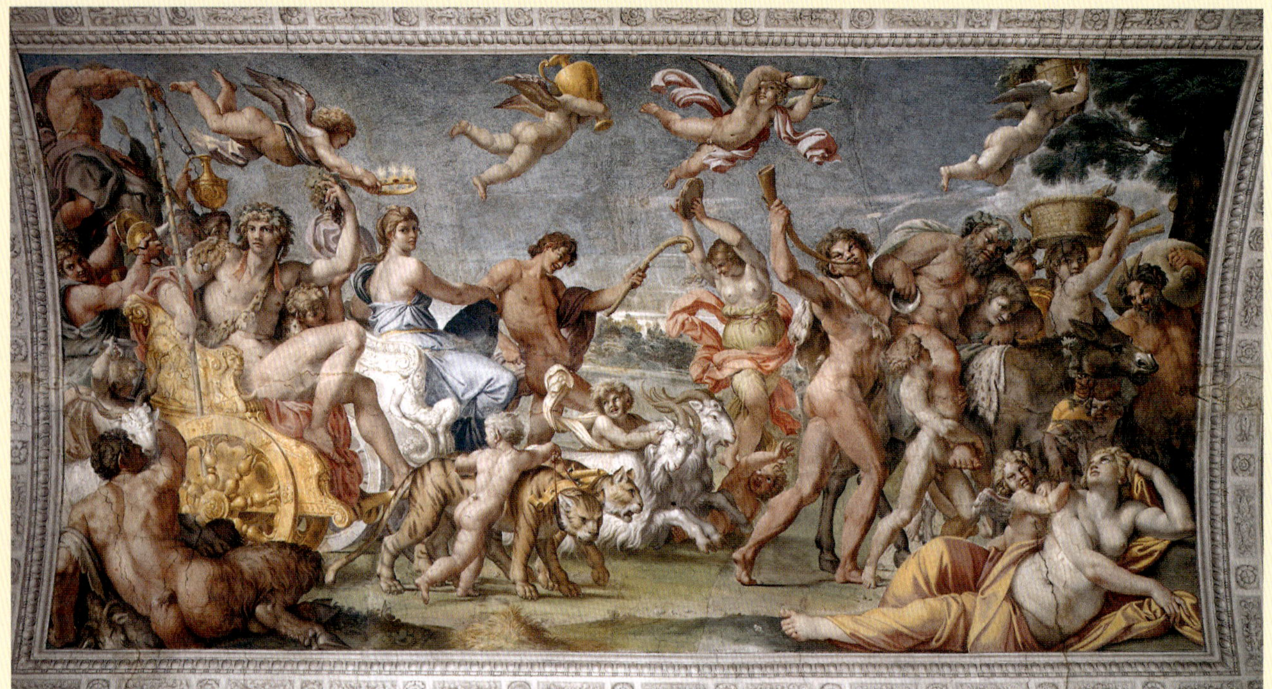

Annibale Carracci
(Bologna 1560 - Roma 1609)

Triumph of Bacchus and Ariadne
Der Triumph von Bacchus und Ariadne
Triomf van Bacchus en Ariadne

●●

1597-1601
Palazzo Farnese, Roma

Fresko / Fresco

Early Baroque art in Bologna: idealism and pathos in the ancient paradise of the gods. The works of the Carracci family become on export success.

Frühbarock in Bologna, Idealismus und Pathos im antiken Götterhimmel. Die Werke der Familie Caracci entwickeln sich zum Exportschlager.

De vroege barok in Bologna, idealisme en pathos in de godenhemel. De kunstwerken van de familie Carracci worden een exportsucces.

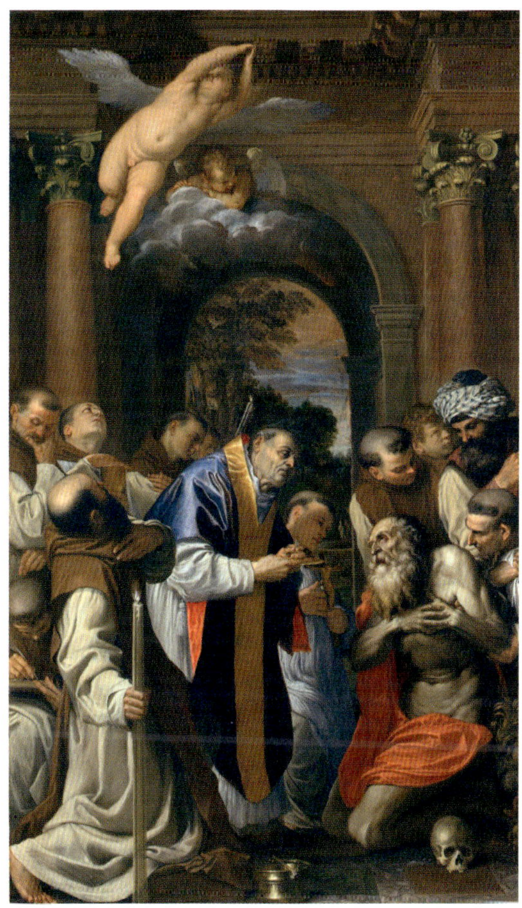

Agostino Carracci
(Bologna 1557 - Parma 1602)

Communion of St Jerome
Die Kommunion des Hl.Hieronymus
Communie van de Heilige Hiëronymus

●

1592
376 x 224 cm / 148.03 x 88.18 in.
Pinacoteca Nazionale, Bologna

Oil on canvas / Öl auf Leinwand / Olieverf op doek

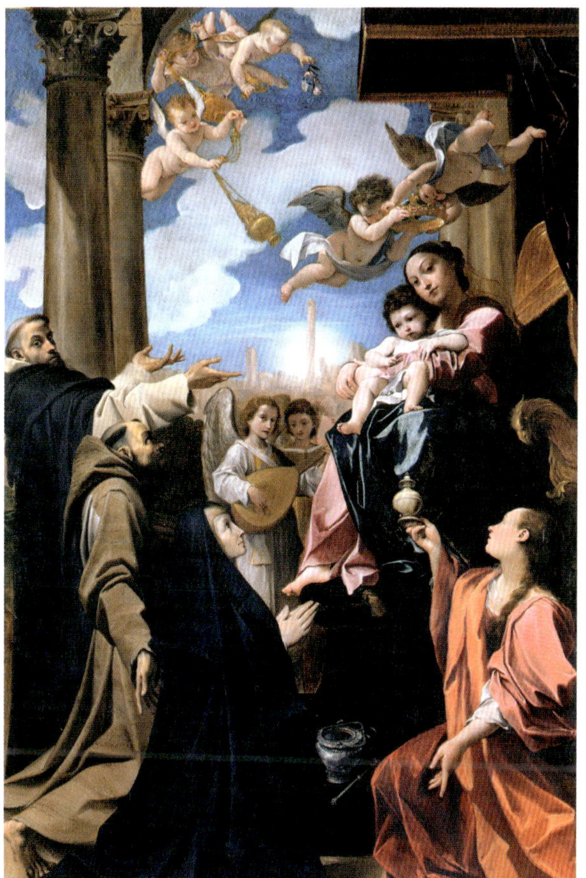

Ludovico Carracci
(Bologna 1555 - 1619)

Bargellini Madonna

●

1588
282 x 188 cm / 111.02 x 74.01 in.
Pinacoteca Nazionale, Bologna

Oil on canvas / Öl auf Leinwand / Olieverf op doek

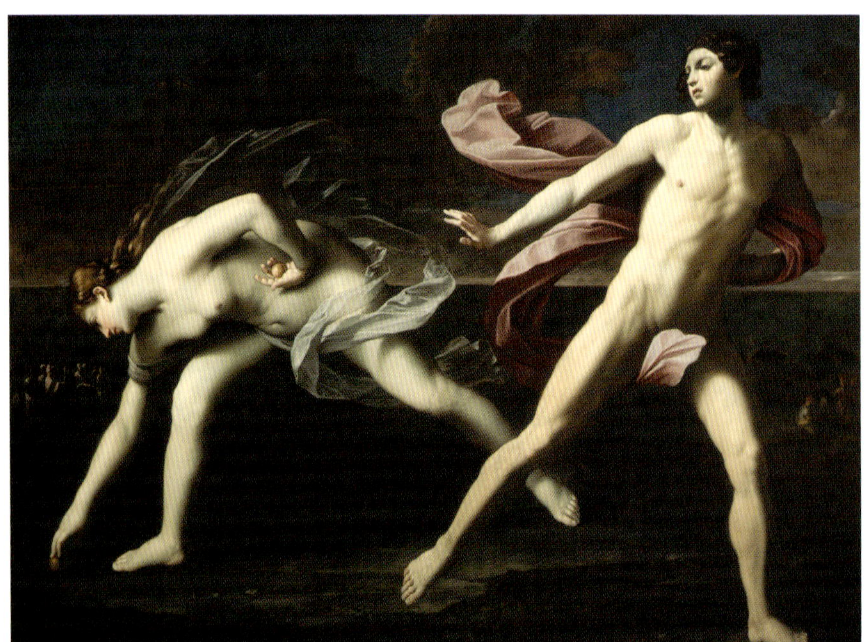

Guido Reni
(Bologna 1575 - Bologna 1642)

Atalanta and Hippomenes
Atalante und Hippomenes
Atalanta en Hippomenes

●●

c. 1625
206 x 297 cm / 81.10 x 116.92 in.
Museo Nazionale di Capodimonte, Napoli

Oil on canvas / Öl auf Leinwand
Olieverf op doek

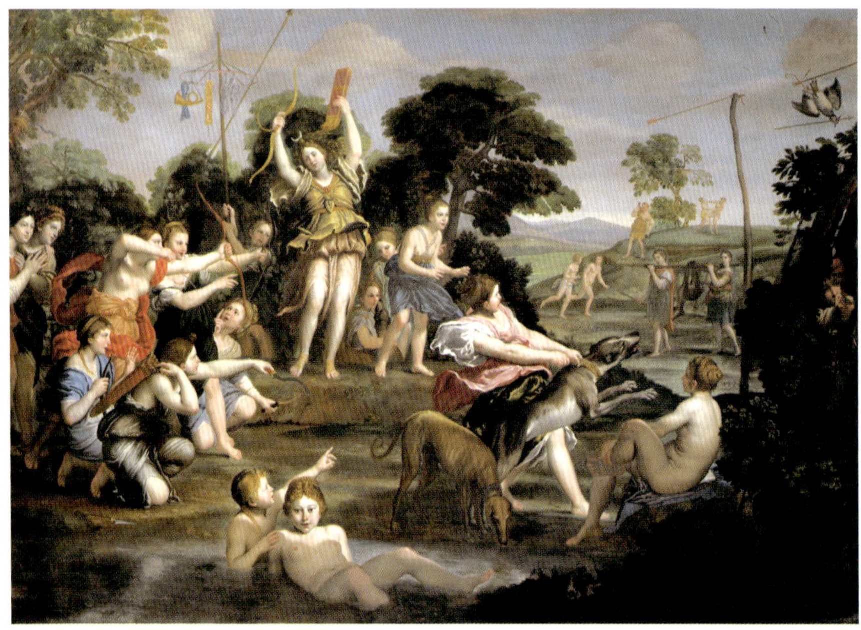

Domenichino
(Bologna 1581 - Napoli 1641)

Diana at the Hunt
Die Jagd der Diana
Jacht van Diana

●●

c. 1616-1617
225 x 320 cm / 88.58 x 125.98 in.
Galleria Borghese, Roma

Oil on canvas / Öl auf Leinwand
Olieverf op doek

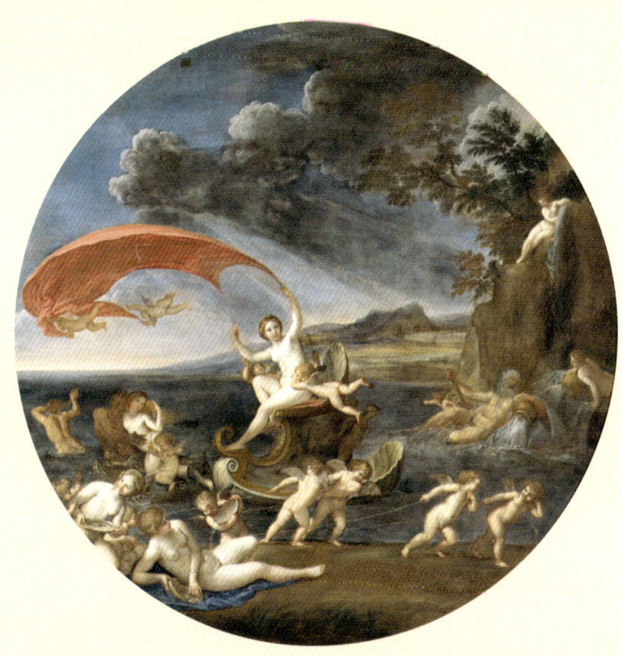

Francesco Albani
(Bologna 1578 - Bologna 1660)

Allegory of Water: the Four Elements
Allegorie des Wassers: Vier Elemente
Allegorie van het Water: de Vier Elementen

●

c. 1627
Ø 180 cm / 70.86 in.
Galleria Sabauda, Torino

Oil on canvas / Öl auf Leinwand / Olieverf op doek

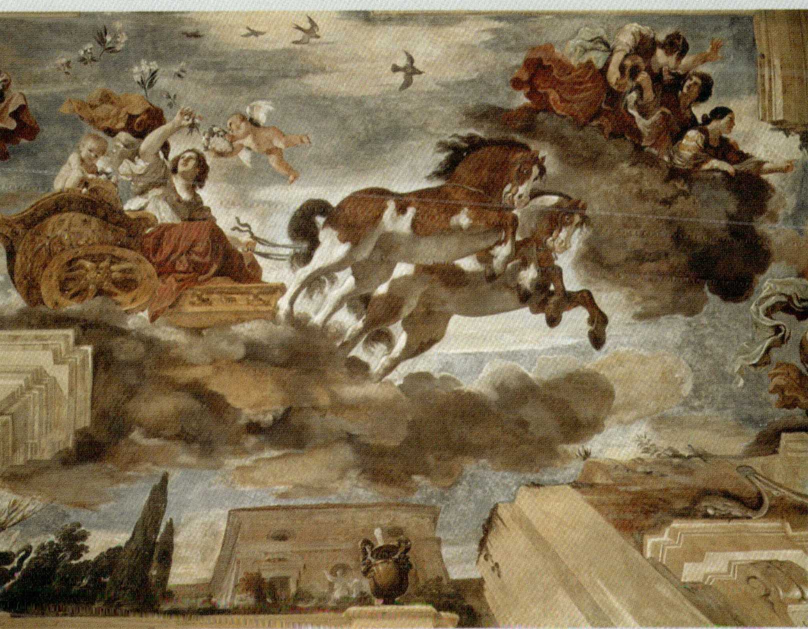

Guercino
(Cento 1591 - Bologna 1666)

Aurora (Dawn), detail
Aurora, Detail
De Dageraad, detail

●

1621
Casino Ludovisi, Roma

Fresco / Fresko

A biblical story with no dignity? Caravaggio's models come from the street. Many clients refuse to purchase his works.

Biblische Geschichte ohne "Würde"? Caravaggio's Modelle sind von der Straße. Vielen Kunden verweigern die Abnahme.

Bijbelse geschiedenis zonder "waardigheid"? De modellen van Caravaggio worden van straat geplukt. Veel klanten weigeren schilderijen af te nemen.

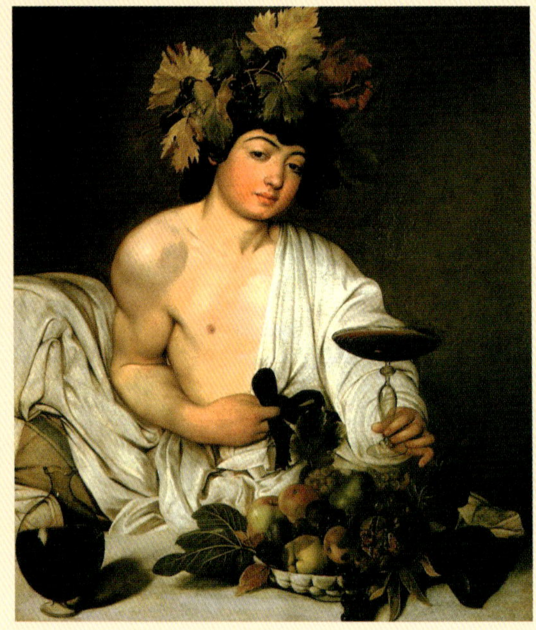

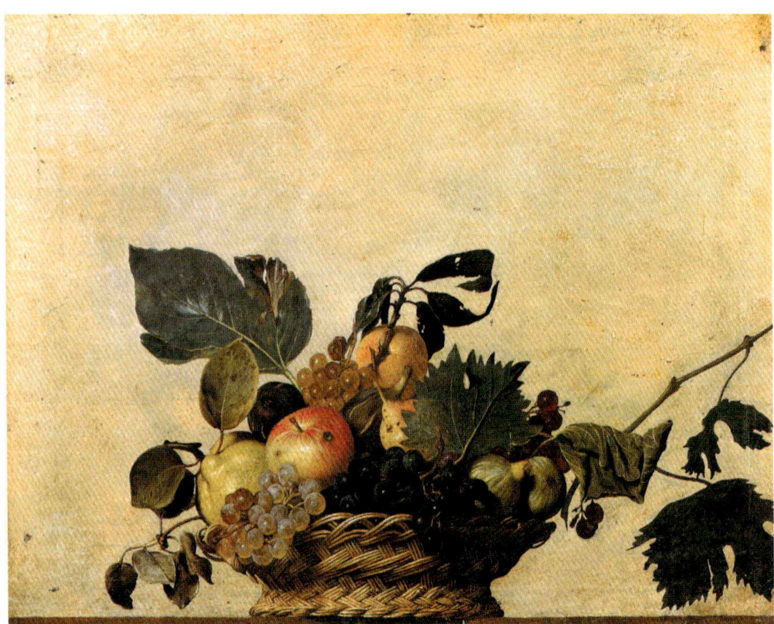

Caravaggio
(Milano 1571 - Porto Ercole 1610)

Basket of Fruit
Obstkorb
Mand met fruit

●●●

1596
46 x 64,5 cm / 18.11 x 25.39 in.
Pinacoteca Ambrosiana, Milano

Oil on canvas / Öl auf Leinwand
Olieverf op doek

Caravaggio
(Milano 1571 - Porto Ercole 1610)

Bacchus

●●●

c. 1602
95 x 85 cm / 37.4 x 33.5 in.
Galleria degli Uffizi, Firenze

Oil on canvas / Öl auf Leinwand
Olieverf op doek

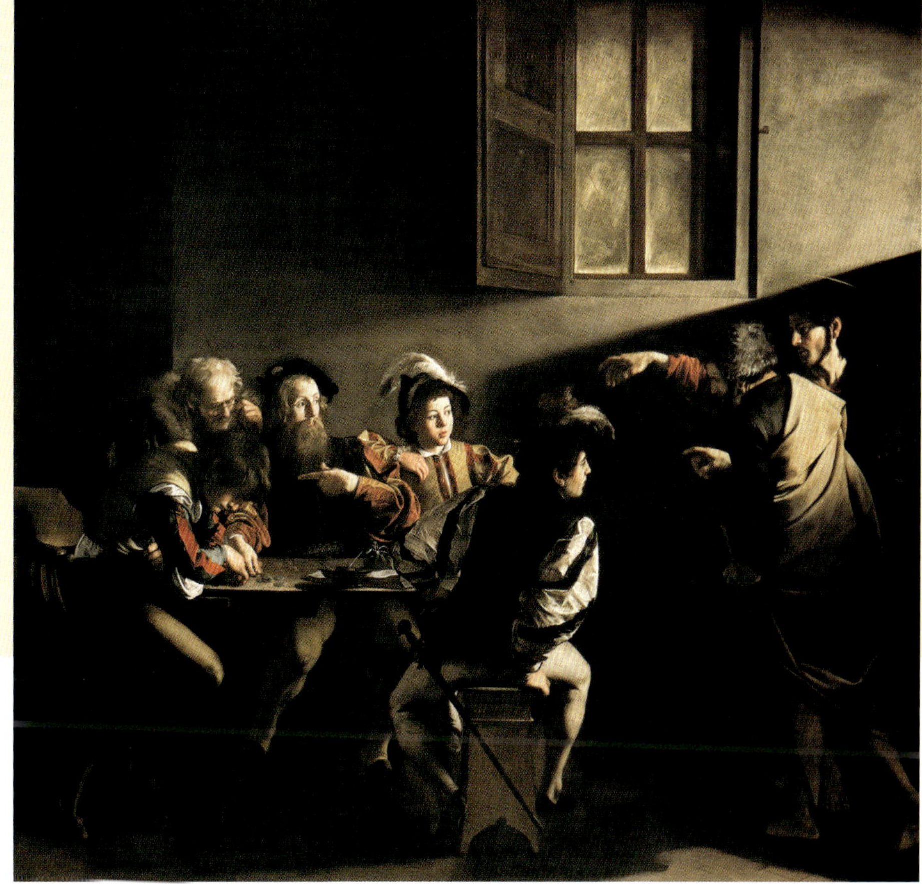

Caravaggio
(Milano 1571 - Porto Ercole 1610)

Calling of St Matthew
Die Berufung des Hl.Matthäus
De roeping van Mattheus

●●

c. 1599-1600
322 x 340 cm / 126.77 x 133.85 in.
San Luigi dei Francesi, Roma

Oil on canvas / Öl auf Leinwand
Olieverf op doek

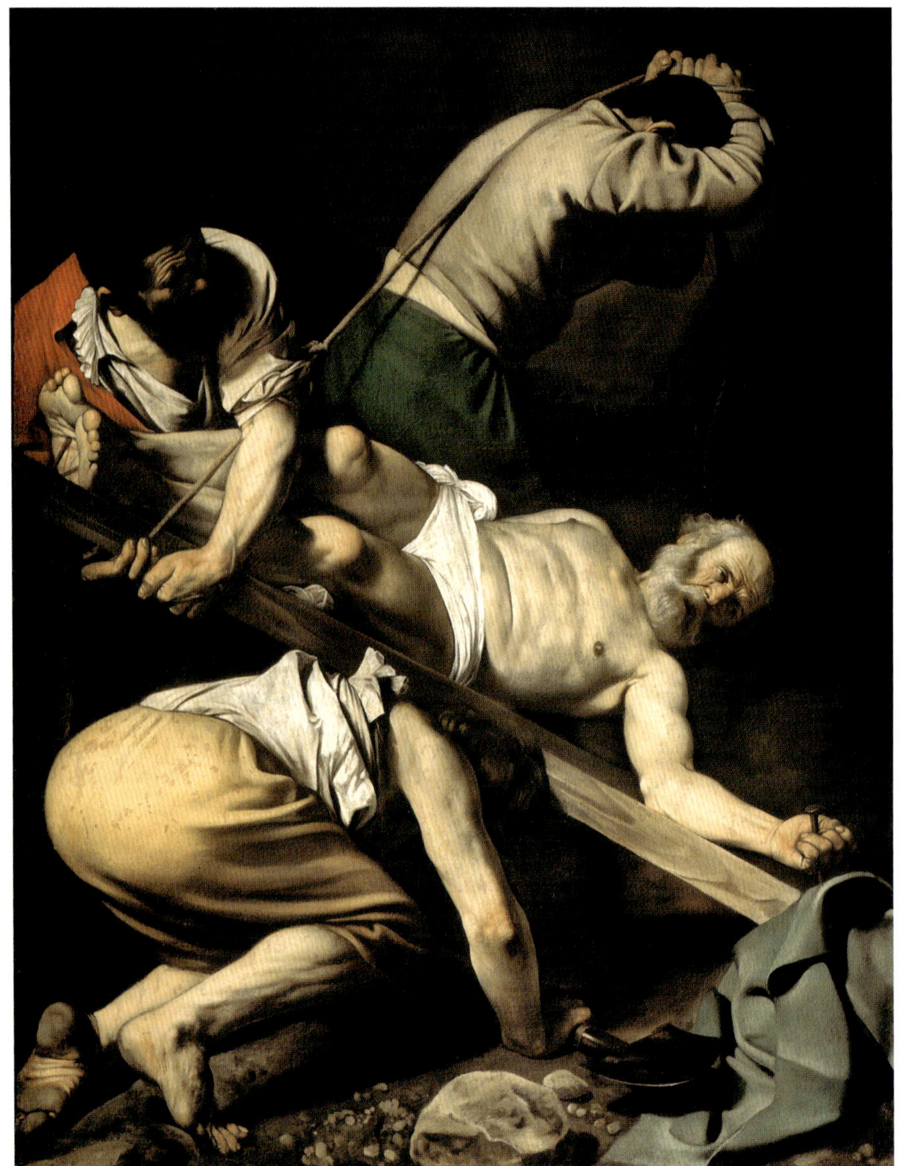

Caravaggio
(Milano 1571 - Porto Ercole 1610)

Crucifixion of St Peter
Kreuzigung des Hl.Petrus
Kruisiging van Sint Petrus

●●

c. 1600-1601
230 x 175 cm / 90.55 x 68.89 in.
Santa Maria del Popolo, Roma

Oil on canvas / Öl auf Leinwand
Olieverf op doek

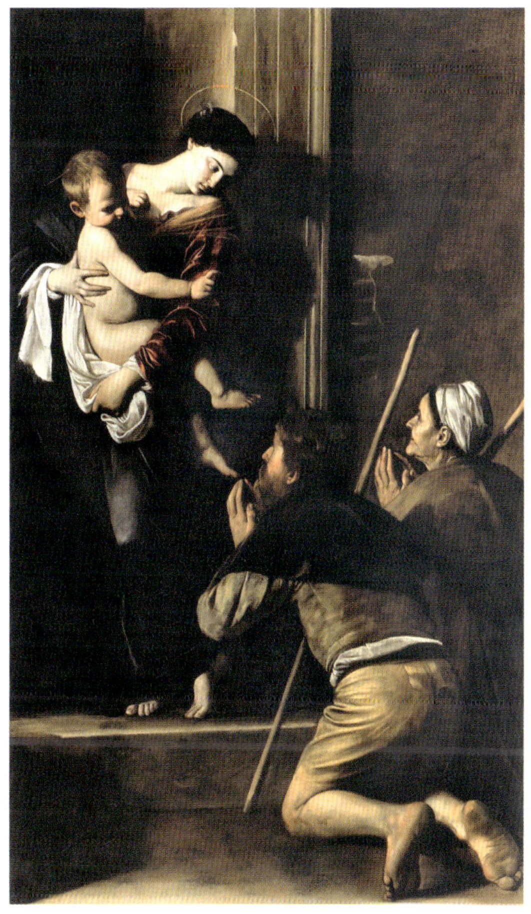

Caravaggio
(Milano 1571 - Porto Ercole 1610)

Madonna of the Pilgrims
Madonna der Pilger
Madonna van de pelgrims

●●

c. 1604 -1606
260 × 150 cm / 102.36 x 59.05 in.
Sant'Agostino, Roma

Oil on canvas / Öl auf Leinwand / Olieverf op doek

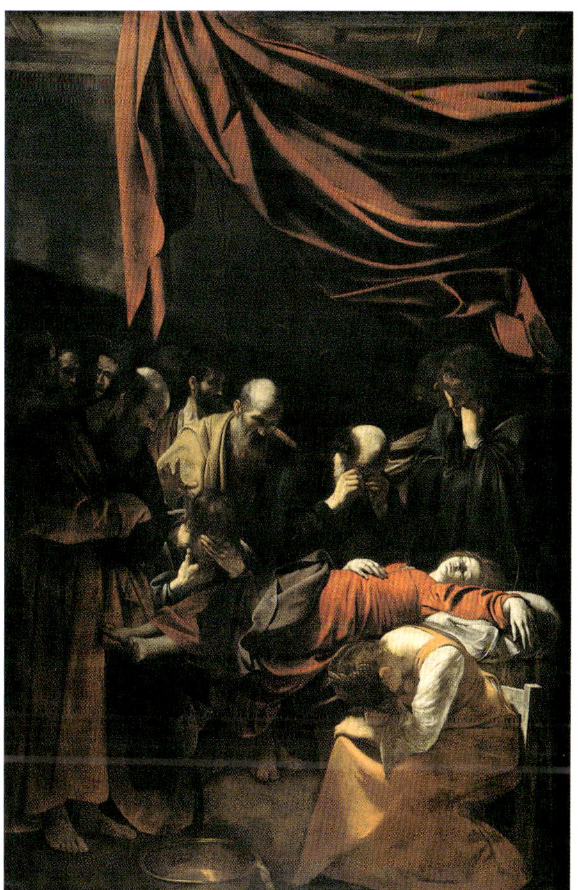

Caravaggio
(Milano 1571 - Porto Ercole 1610)

Death of the Virgin
Tod Mariä
De dood van Maria

●●●

c. 1605 -1606
369 x 245 cm / 145.27 x 96.45 in.
Musée du Louvre, Paris

Oil on canvas / Öl auf Leinwand / Olieverf op doek

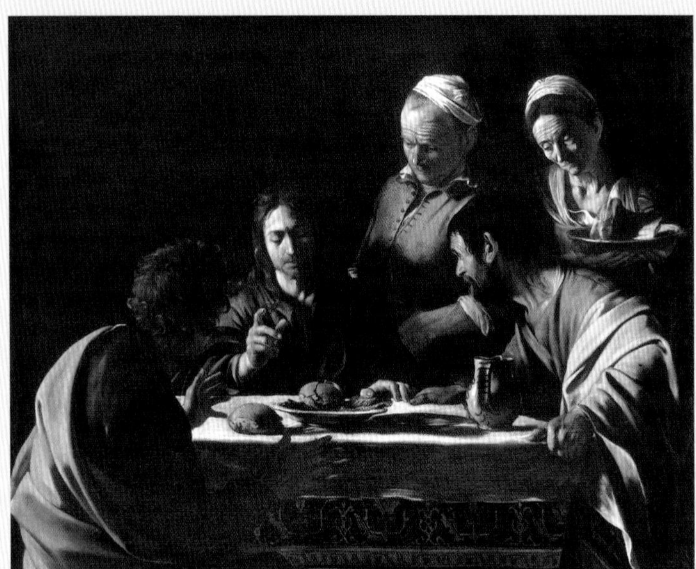

Caravaggio
(Milano 1571 - Porto Ercole 1610)

Supper at Emmaus
Abendmahl in Emmaus
Avondmaal te Emmaüs

●●●

1606
141 x 175 cm / 55.51 x 68.89 in.
Pinacoteca di Brera, Milano

Oil on canvas / Öl auf Leinwand / Olieverf op doek

Caravaggio
(Milano 1571 - Porto Ercole 1610)

Victorious Cupid
Amor siegt über alles
Omnia vincit Amor
(Liefde overwint alles)

●●

c. 1602
156 x 113 cm / 61.4 x 44.5 in.
Gemäldegalerie, Staatliche Museen, Berlin

Oil on canvas / Öl auf Leinwand / Olieverf op doek

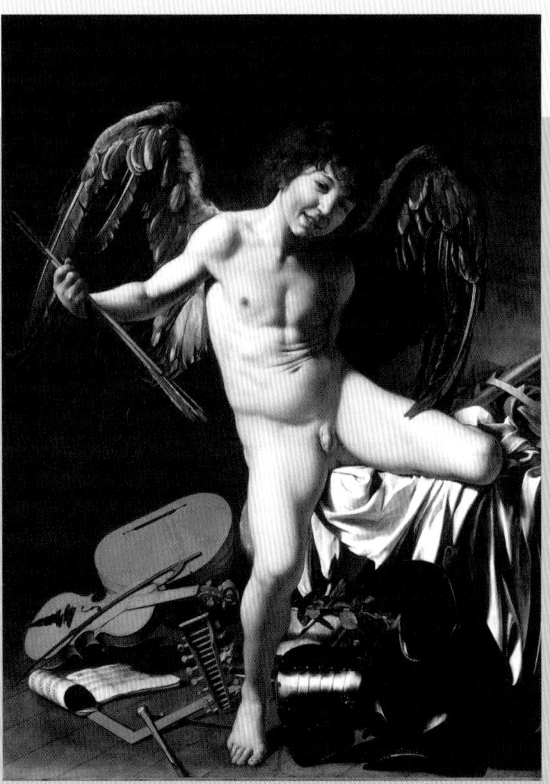

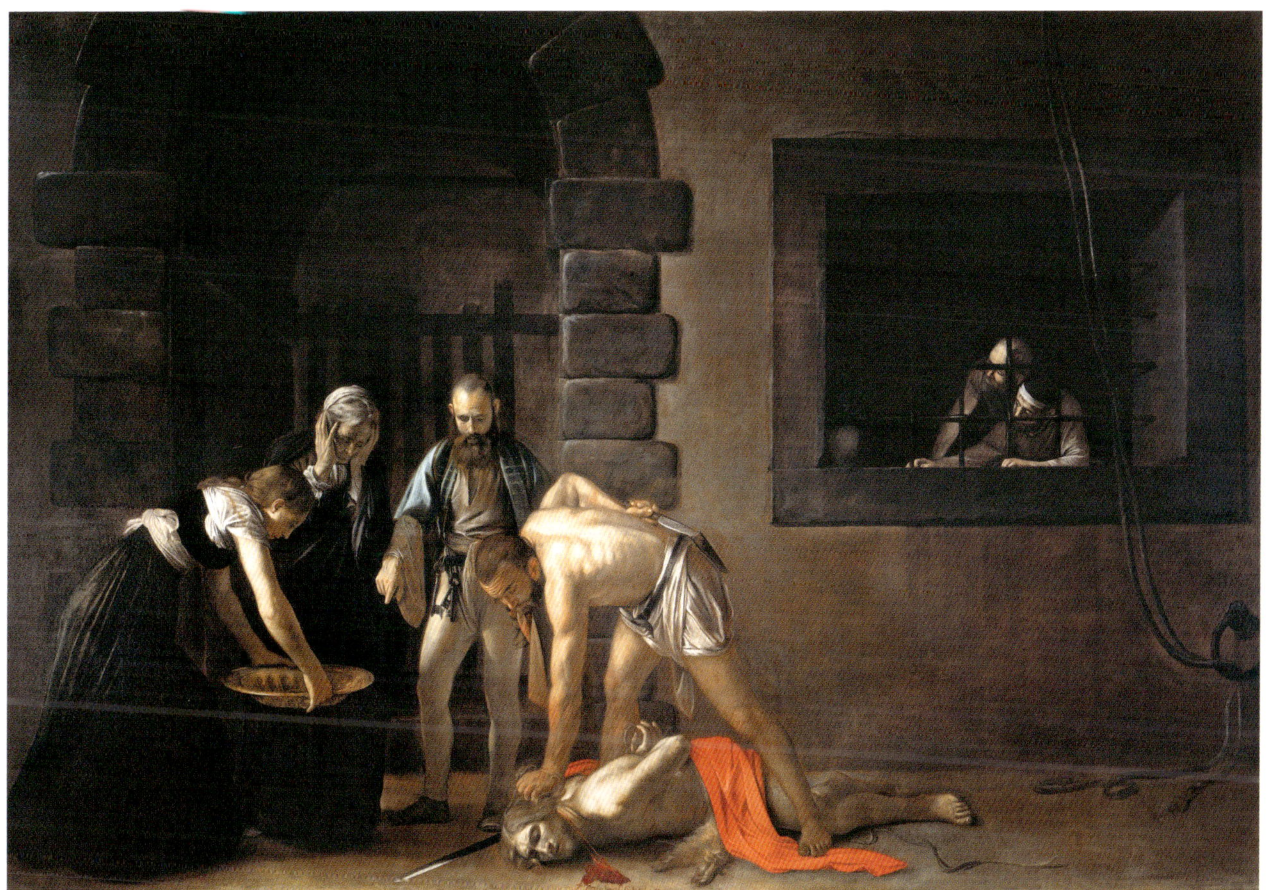

Caravaggio
(Milano 1571 - Porto Ercole 1610)

Beheading of St John the Baptist
Die Enthauptung Johannes des Täufers
De onthoofding van Johannes de Doper

●●

1608
360 x 520 cm / 141.73 x 204.72 in.
San Giovanni, La Valletta

Oil on canvas / Öl auf Leinwand / Olieverf op doek

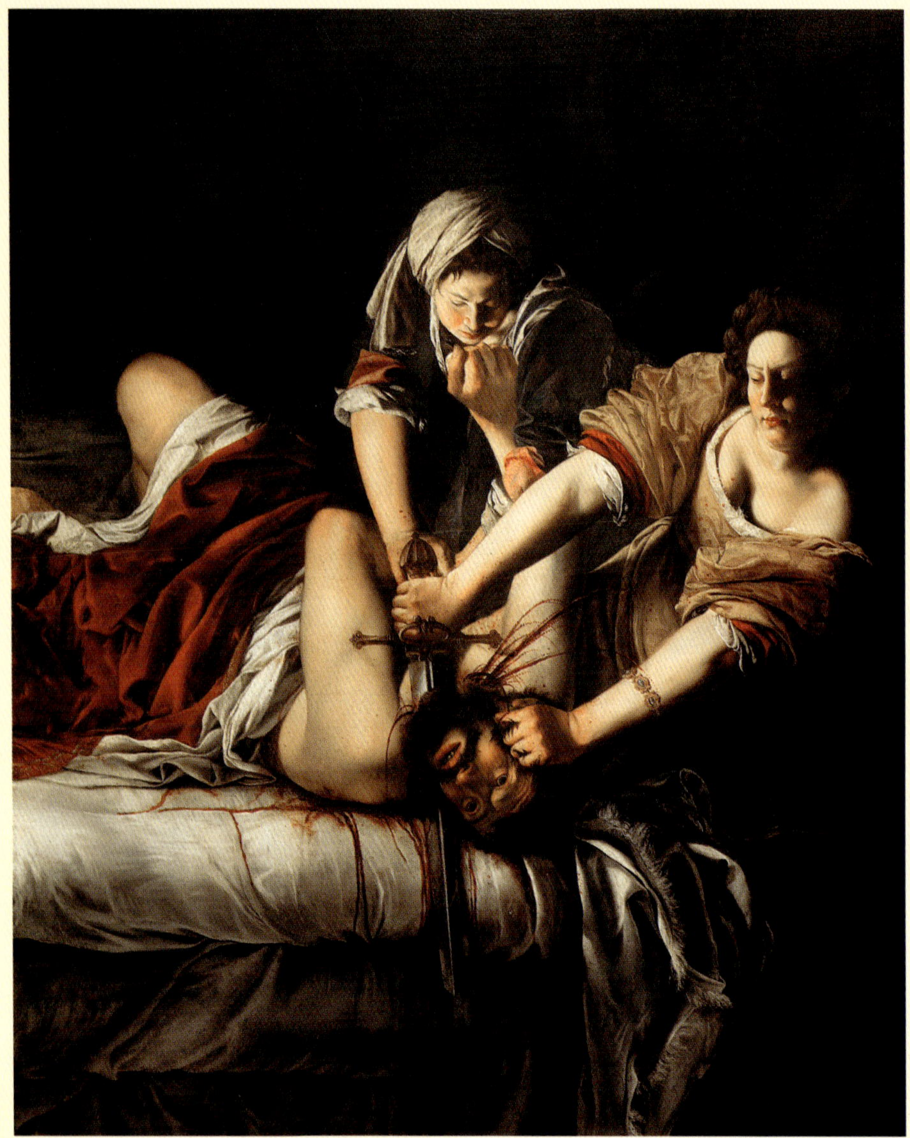

Artemisia Gentileschi is an energetic painter who has a preference for biblical scenes with strong female figures.

Kraftvolle Malerin, Artemisia Gentileschi sucht biblische Szenen mit starken Frauengestalten.

Artemisia Gentileschi, krachtige schilderes, heeft een voorkeur voor bijbelscènes met sterke vrouwenfiguren.

Artemisia Gentileschi
(Roma 1593 - Napoli 1653)

Judith and Holofernes
Judith und Holofernes
Judith en Holofernes

●●

c. 1620
200 x 162 cm / 78.74 x 63.67 in.
Galleria degli Uffizi, Firenze

Oil on canvas / Öl auf Leinwand
Olieverf op doek

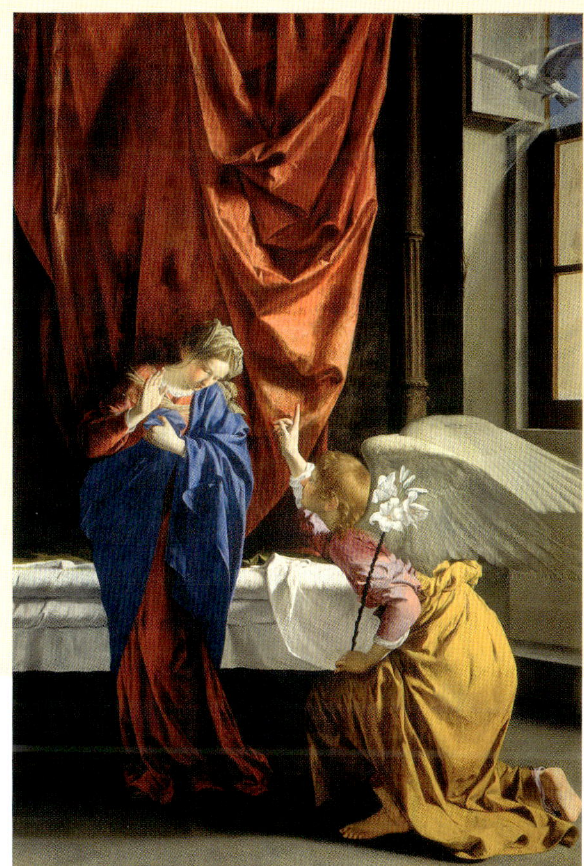

Orazio Gentileschi
(Pisa 1563 - London 1639)

Annunciation
Verkündigung
Annunciatie

●

1623
289 x 198 cm
Galleria Sabauda, Torino

Oil on canvas / Öl auf Leinwand
Olieverf op doek

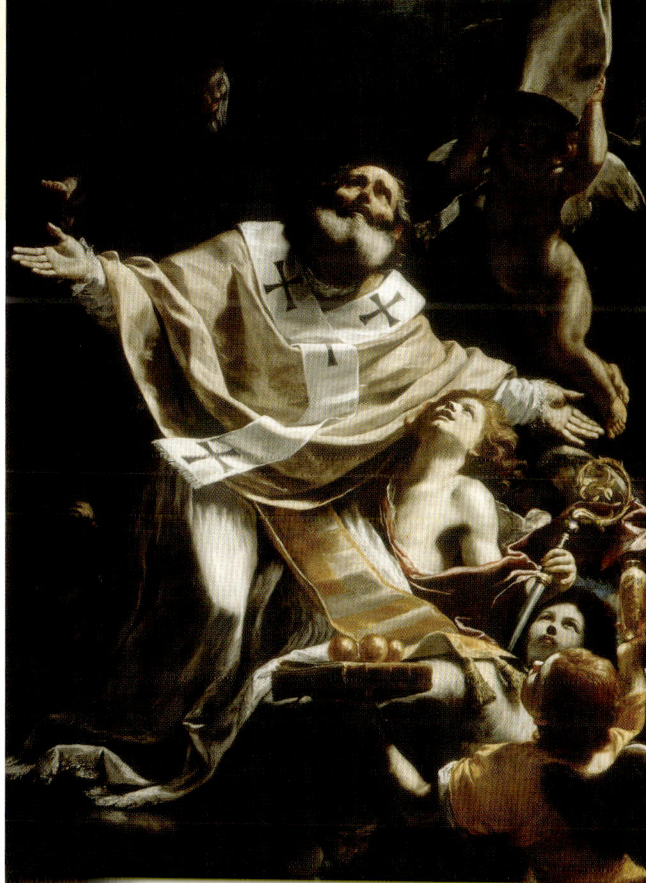

Mattia Preti
(Taverna, Catanzaro 1613 - La Valletta 1699)

Ecstasy of St Nicholas of Bari
Ekstase des Hl.Nikolaus von Bari
De extase van Sint Nicolaas van Bari

●

c. 1653
217 x 156 cm / 85.43 x 61.41 in.
Museo Nazionale di Capodimonte, Napoli

Oil on canvas / Öl auf Leinwand / Olieverf op doek

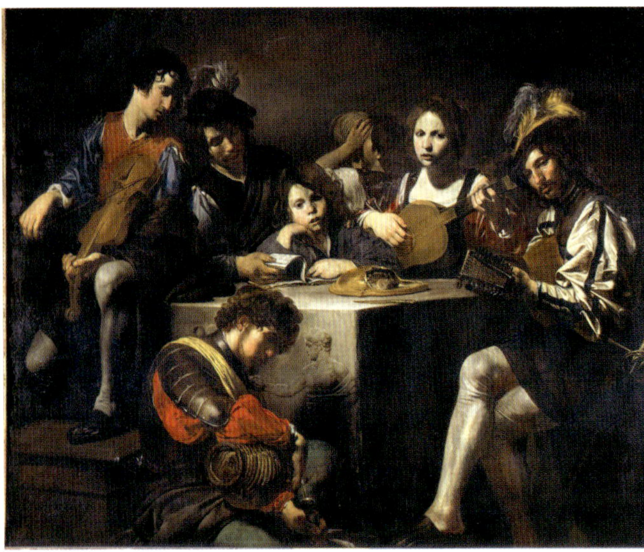

Valentin de Boulogne
(Coulommiers 1591 - Roma 1632)

The Concert
Das Konzert
Concert

●

1628-1630
175 x 216 cm / 69.29 x 85.03 in.
Musée du Louvre, Paris

Nocturnes with artificial lighting.

Nachtstücke mit künstlicher Beleuchtung.

Nachtschilderijen met een kunstmatige verlichting.

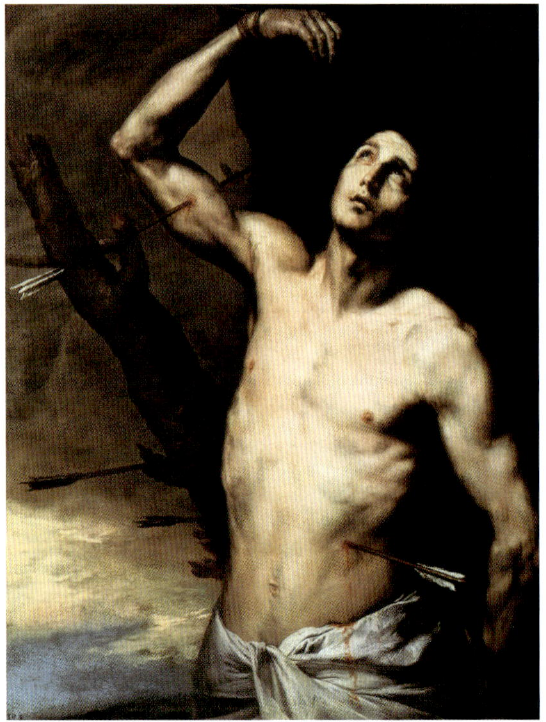

Jusepe de Ribera
(Xàtiva 1591 - Napoli 1652)

St Sebastian
Der Hl. Sebastian
De Heilige Sebastiaan

1636
127 x 100 cm / 49.9 x 39.37 in.
Museo Nacional del Prado,
Madrid

Oil on canvas / Öl auf Leinwand / Olieverf op doek

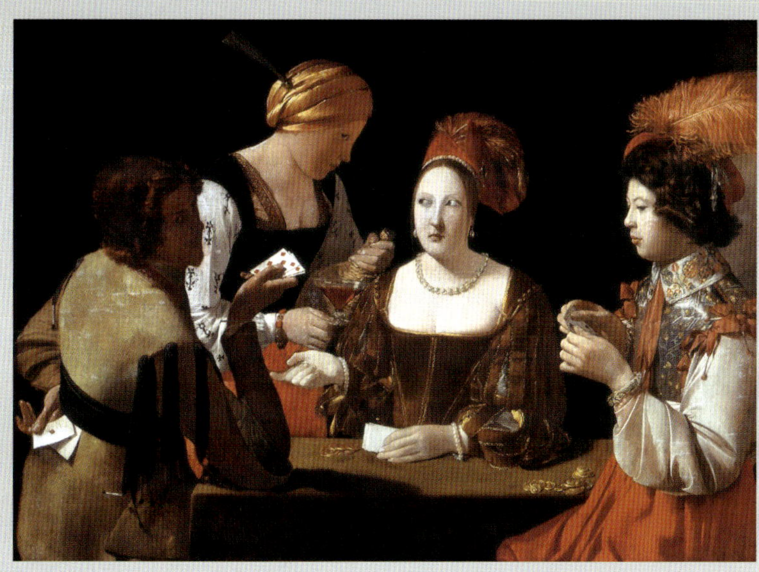

Georges De La Tour
(Vic-sur-Seille 1593 - Lunéville 1652)

The Card Sharp whit Ace of Diamonds
Der Falschspieler
De valsspeler

●●

1630-1634
106 x 146 cm / 41.73 x 57.48 in.
Musée du Louvre, Paris

Oil on canvas / Öl auf Leinwand
Olieverf op doek

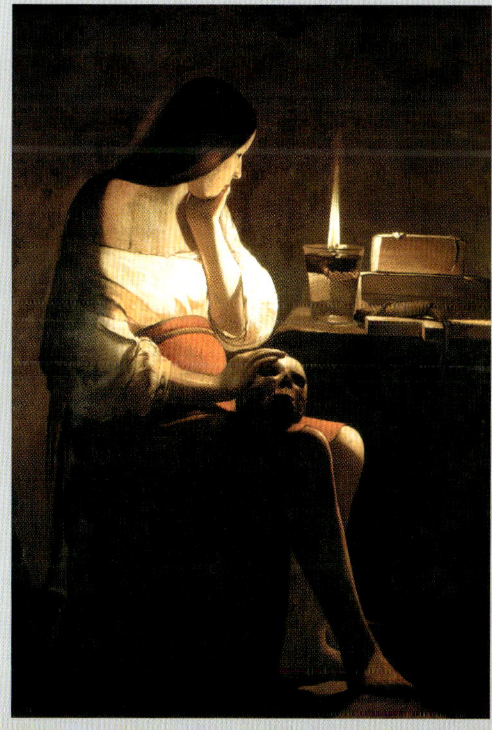

Georges De La Tour
(Vic-sur-Seille 1593 - Lunéville 1652)

Penitence of Mary Magdalene
Büßende Magdalena
Magdalena met het nachtlicht

●●●

c. 1640-1645
128 x 94 cm / 50.39 x 37 in.
Musée du Louvre, Paris

Oil on canvas / Öl auf Leinwand / Olieverf op doek

Landscape as a backdrop for pathos and poetry.

Landschaft als Bühne für Pathos und Poesie.

Het landschap vormt het toneel voor de pathos en de poëzie.

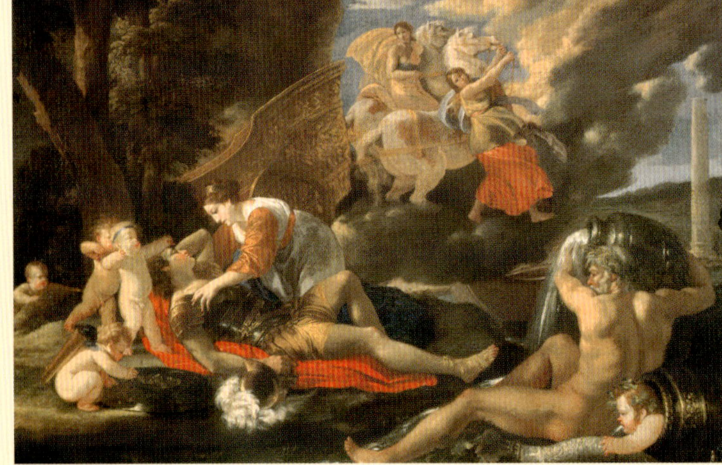

Nicolas Poussin
(Les Andelys 1594 - Roma 1665)

Rinaldo and Armida
Rinaldo und Armida
Rinaldo en Armida

●

1625
95 x 133 cm / 37.40 x 52.36 in.
Pushkin Museum, Moscow

Oil on canvas / Öl auf Leinwand
Olieverf op doek

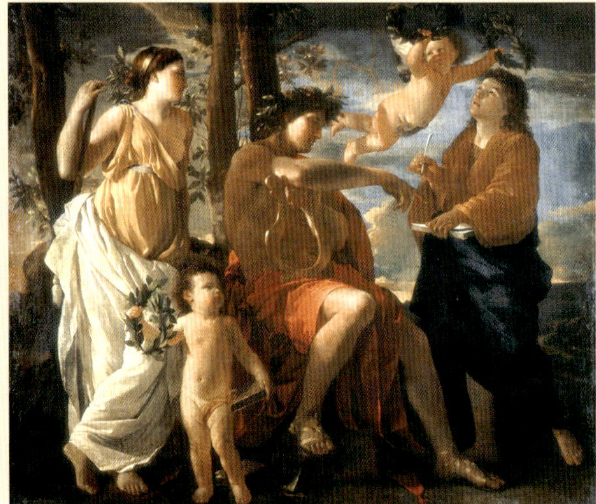

Nicolas Poussin
(Les Andelys 1594 - Roma 1665)

Inspiration of the Poet
Inspiration des Dichters
De inspiratie van de dichter

●●

1630
184 x 214 cm / 72.44 x 84.25 in.
Musée du Louvre, Paris

Oil on canvas / Öl auf Leinwand
Olieverf op doek

Claude Lorrain
(Chamagne 1600 - Roma 1682)

Sea Port at Sunset
Hafen bei Sonnenuntergang
Zeehaven bij zonsondergang

●●●

1639
137 x 103 cm / 53.39 x 40.55 in.
Musée du Louvre, Paris

Oil on canvas / Öl auf Leinwand
Olieverf op doek

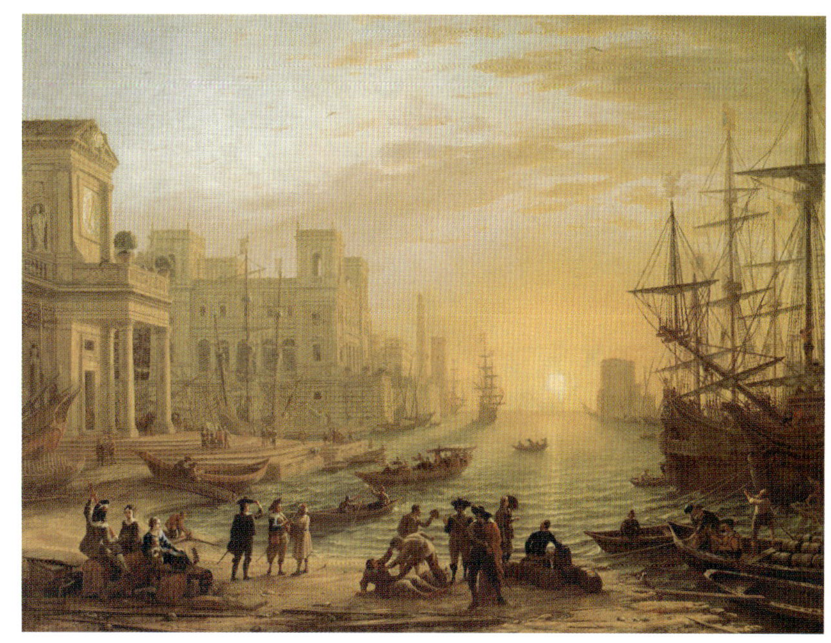

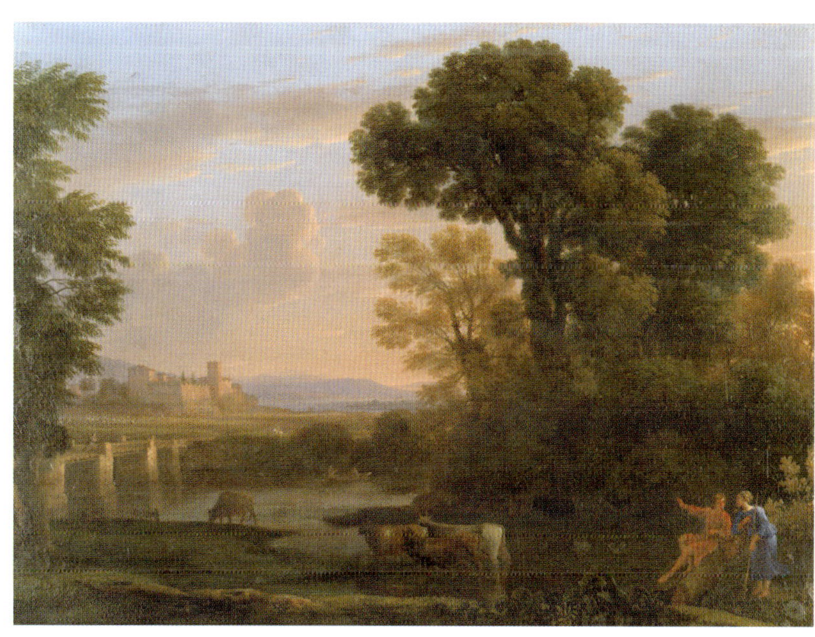

Claude Lorrain
(Chamagne 1600 - Roma 1682)

Pastoral Landscape
Landschaft mit Hirten
Pastoraal landschap

●

1648
39 x 53 cm / 15.35 x 20.86 in.
Yale University Art Gallery, New Haven

Oil on copper / Öl auf Kupfer
Olieverf op koper

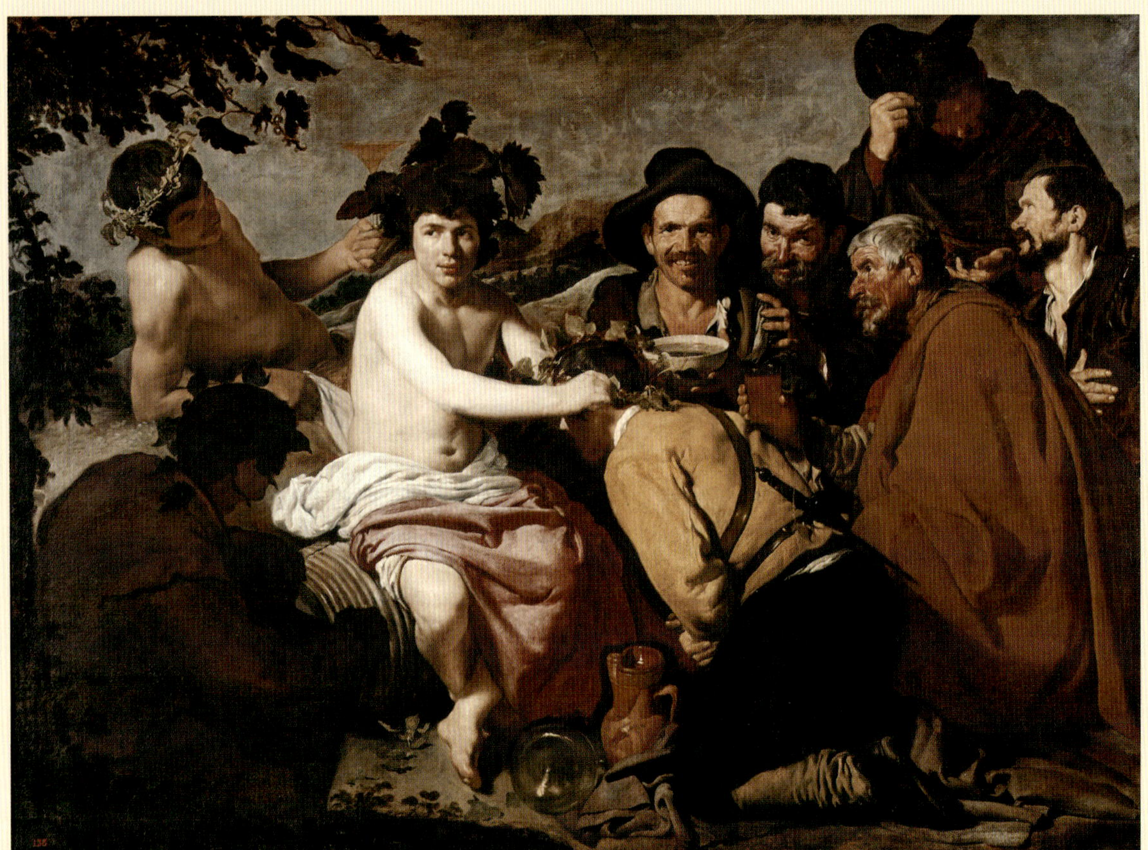

Diego Velázquez
(Sevilla 1599 - Madrid 1660)

Triumph of Bacchus (The Drinkers)
Triumph des Bacchus (DieTrinker)
Triomf van Bacchus (De Drinkers)

●●●

c. 1628-1629
165 x 227 cm / 64.96 x 89.36 in.
Museo Nacional del Prado, Madrid

Oil on canvas / Öl auf Leinwand / Olieverf op doek

Popes, aristocrats, dwarfs and drinkers: Velázquez is the protagonist of the Spanish Baroque.

Päpste, Adelige, Zwerge und Trinker, Velazquez ist der Hauptvertreter des spanischen Barock.

Pausen, edelen, dwergen en drinkers, Velázquez is de belangrijkste vertegenwoordiger van de Spaanse barok.

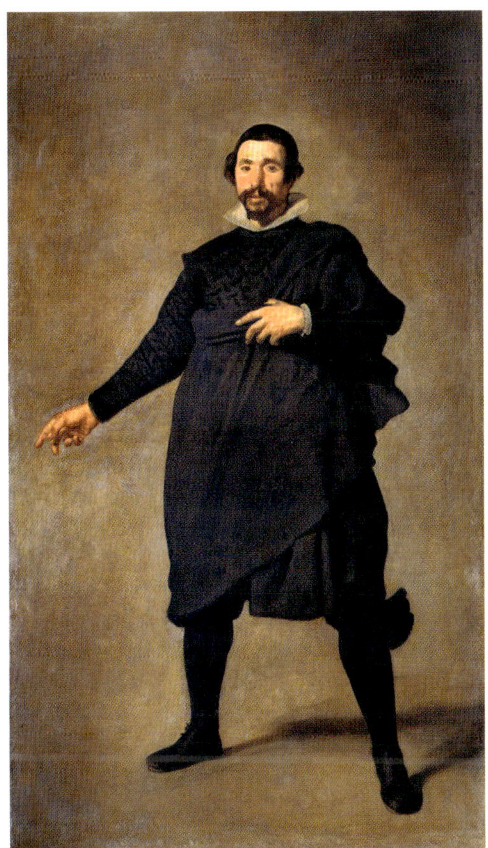

Diego Velázquez
(Sevilla 1599 - Madrid 1660)

Pablo de Valladolid

●

c. 1635-1637
209 x 123 cm / 82.28 x 48.42 in.
Museo Nacional del Prado, Madrid

Oil on canvas / Öl auf Leinwand
Olieverf op doek

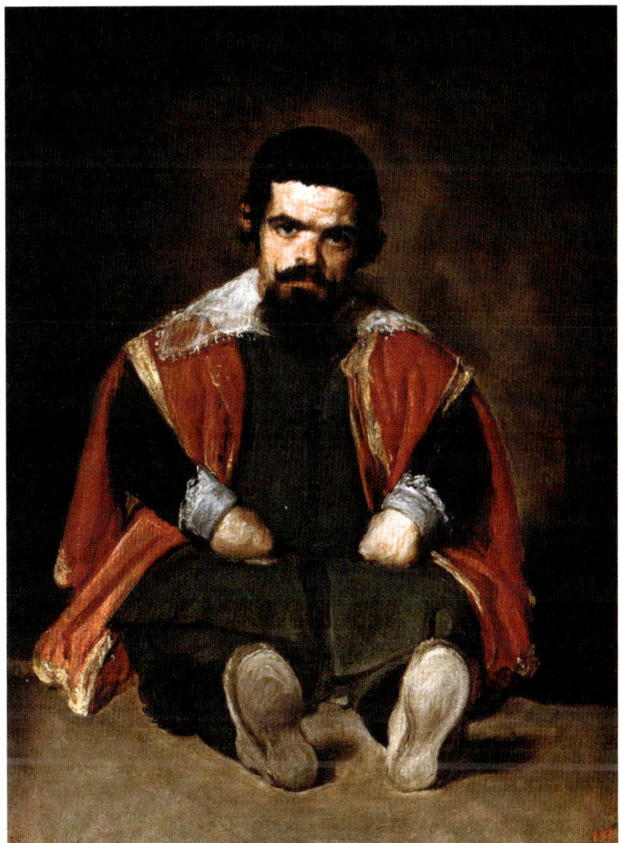

Diego Velázquez
(Sevilla 1599 - Madrid 1660)

The Jester Sebastian de Morra
Porträt des Hofnarren Sebastian de Morra
Portret van de hofdwerg don Sebastián de Morra

1643-1644
106 x 81 cm / 41.73 x 31.88 in.
Museo Nacional del Prado, Madrid

Oil on canvas / Öl auf Leinwand / Olieverf op doek

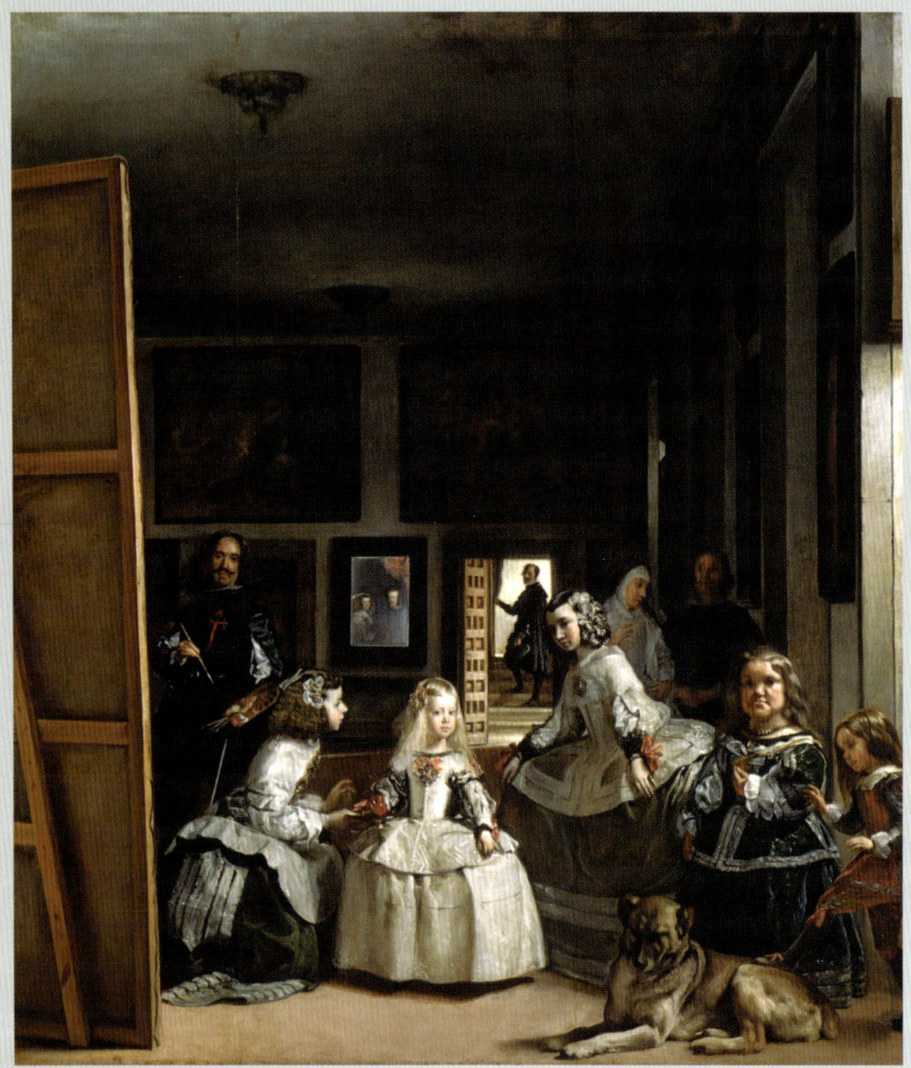

Different points of view: Velázquez depicts the royal couple (reflected in the mirror) while the damsels and the Infanta look on, all seen from the royal couple's point of view.

Verschiedene Blickwinkel. Velazquez portraitiert das Königspaar (im Spiegel zu sehen). Die "Hoffräulein" und die Infantin schauen zu. Wir betrachten das Bild aus Sicht des Königspaars.

Verschillende gezichtspunten. Velázquez portretteert het koninklijk paar (zichtbaar in de spiegel). De "hofdames" en de infant kijken toe, het koninklijk paar vormt ons gezichtspunt.

Diego Velázquez
(Sevilla 1599 - Madrid 1660)

Las Meninas
Las Meninas (Die Hoffräulein)
Las Meniñas (De Hofdames)

●●●

1656
318 x 276 cm / 125.19 x 108.66 in.
Museo Nacional del Prado, Madrid

Oil on canvas / Öl auf Leinwand
Olieverf op doek

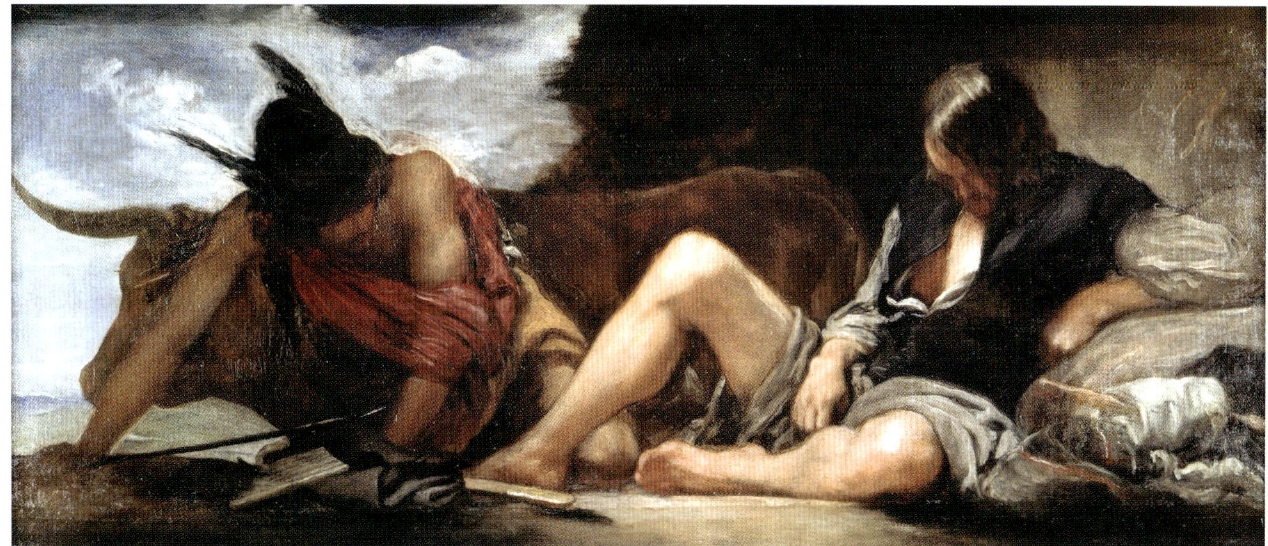

Diego Velázquez
(Sevilla 1599 - Madrid 1660)

Mercury and Argos
Merkur und Argus
Mercurius en Argus

●●

1659
127 x 248 cm / 49.99 x 97.63 in.
Museo Nacional del Prado,
Madrid

Oil on canvas
Öl auf Leinwand
Olieverf op doek

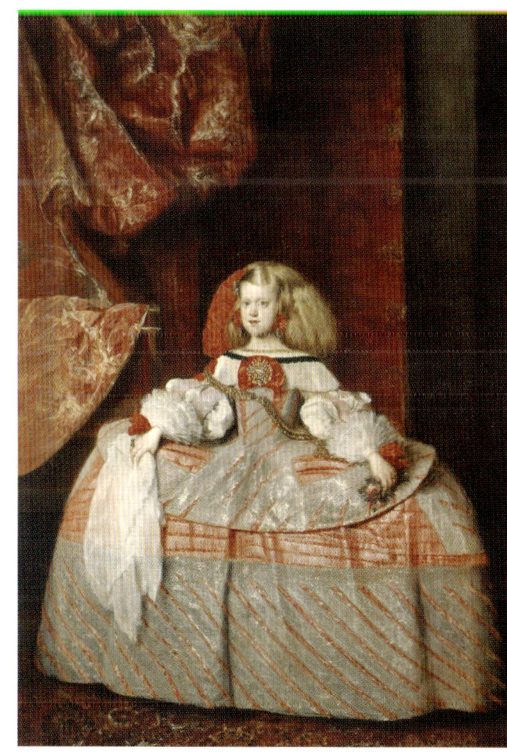

Diego Velázquez
(Sevilla 1599 - Madrid 1660)

Portrait of the Infanta Margarita Teresa
Die Infantin Margarita von Österreich
Infanta Margaretha van Oostenrijk

●●●

1660
212 x 147 cm / 83.46 x 57.87 in.
Museo Nacional del Prado, Madrid

Oil on canvas / Öl auf Leinwand
Olieverf op doek

The artist as an entrepreneur: Peter Paul Rubens sketches and the workshop carries out. The master gives the last flourish and sells his works with success to the cream of the aristocracy.

Der Künstler als Unternehmer. Peter Paul Rubens entwirft, die Werkstatt führt aus. Der Meister gibt den letzten Schliff und verkauft seine Werke erfolgreich an den Hochadel.

De kunstenaar als ondernemer. Peter Paul Rubens maakt schetsen, de werkplaats voert uit. De meester legt er de laatste hand aan en verkoopt met succes zijn schilderijen aan de aristocratie.

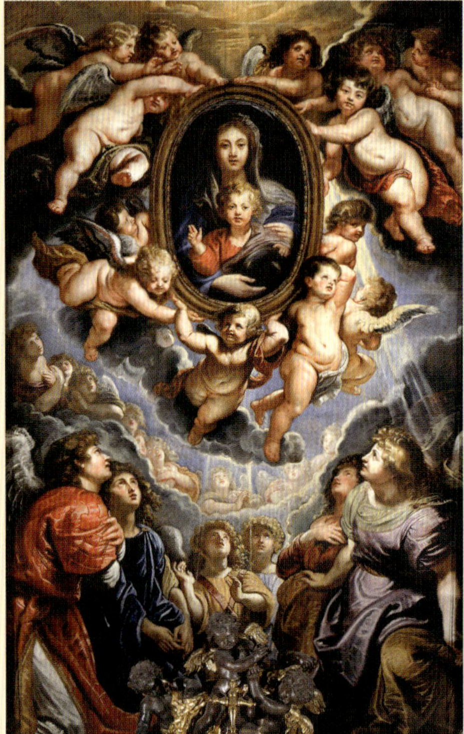

Peter Paul Rubens
(Siegen 1577 - Anvers 1640)

Virgin and Child with Angels
Jungfrau mit Engeln
Maagd met engelen

●●

1606-1608
425 x 250 cm
167.32 x 98.42 in.
Santa Maria in Vallicella, Roma

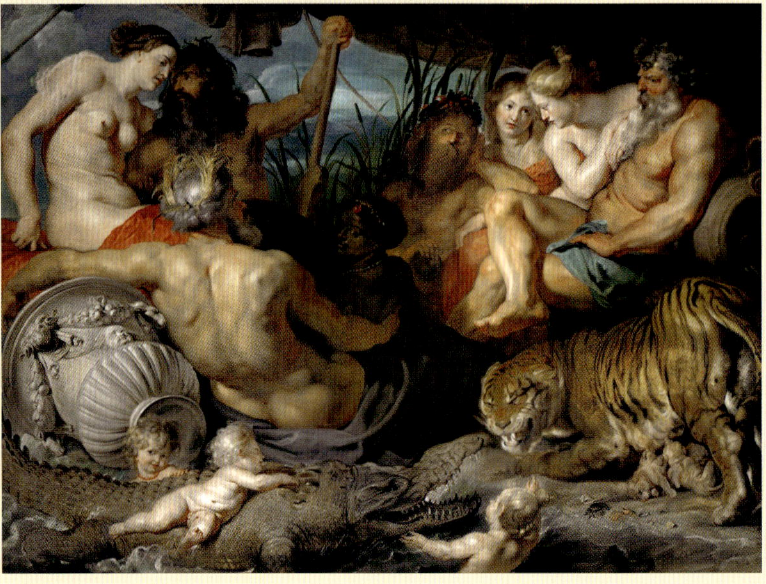

Peter Paul Rubens
(Siegen 1577 - Anvers 1640)

The Four Continents
Die vier Kontinente
De vier continenten

●●

c. 1615
209 x 284 cm / 82.28 x 111.81 in.
Kunsthistorisches Museum, Wien

Oil on canvas
Öl auf Leinwand
Olieverf op doek

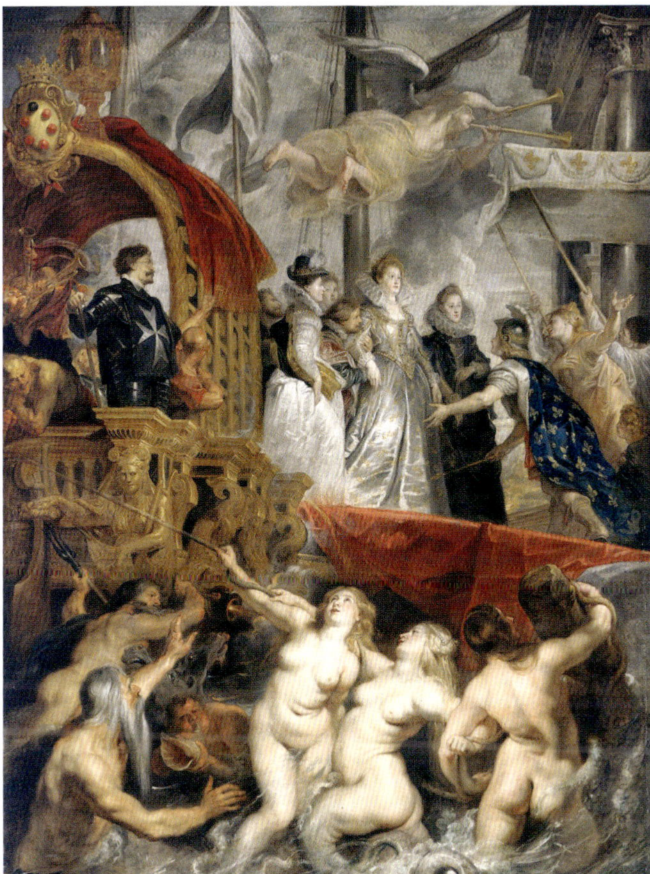

Peter Paul Rubens (Siegen 1577 - Anvers 1640)

Landing of Maria de' Medici at Marseilles
Ausschiffung der Maria von Medici in Marseille
Aankomst van Maria de Medici; ontscheping in de haven van Marseille

●●●

1622-1625
394 x 295 cm / 155.11 x 116.14 in.
Musée du Louvre, Paris

Oil on canvas / Öl auf Leinwand / Olieverf op doek

Peter Paul Rubens
(Siegen 1577 - Anvers 1640)

Saturn Devouring One of His Sons
Saturn verschlingt seine Kinder
Saturnus verslindt één van zijn kinderen

●

1636-1638, 180 x 87 cm / 70.86 x 34.25 in.
Museo Nacional del Prado, Madrid
Oil on canvas / Öl auf Leinwand
Olieverf op doek

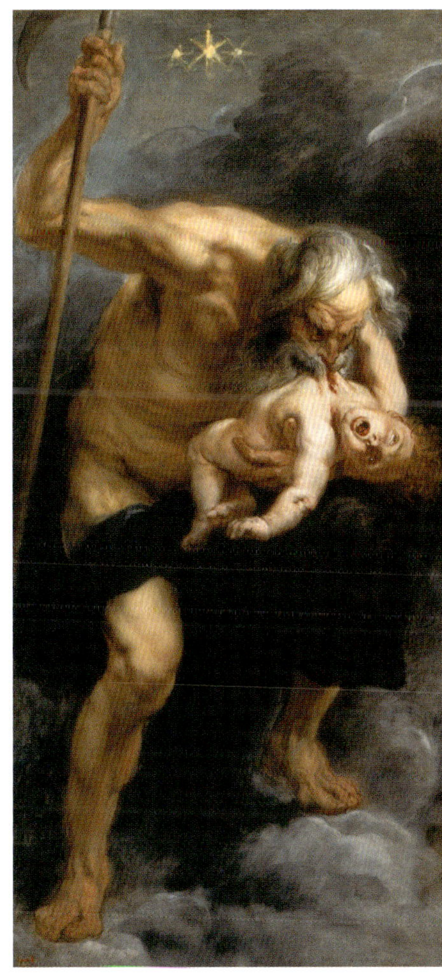

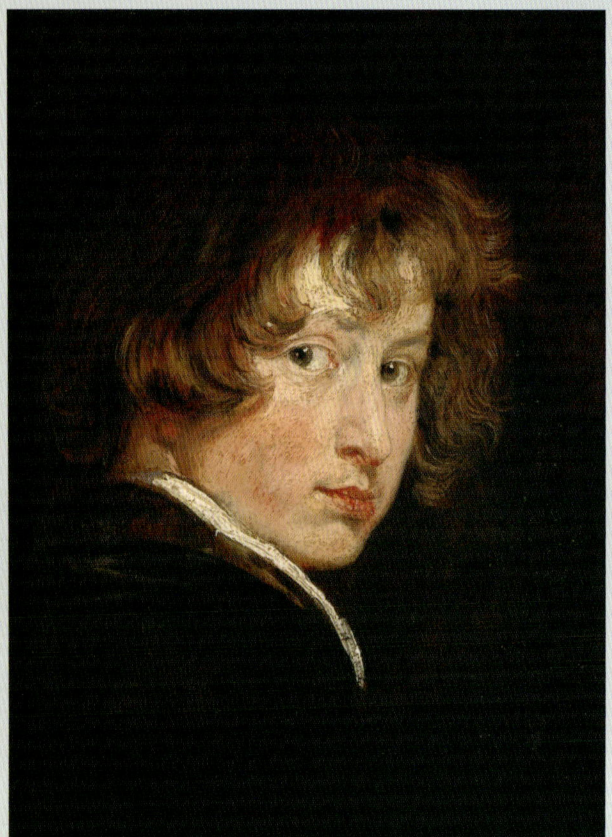

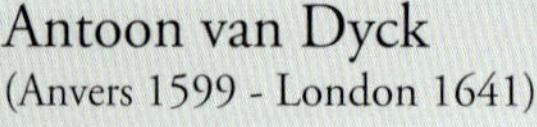

Antoon van Dyck
(Anvers 1599 - London 1641)

Self-Portrait
Selbstportrait
Zelfportret

c. 1613-1614
258 x 195 cm / 101.57 x 76.77 in.
Kunsthistorisches Museum, Wien

Oil on canvas / Öl auf Leinwand / Olieverf op doek

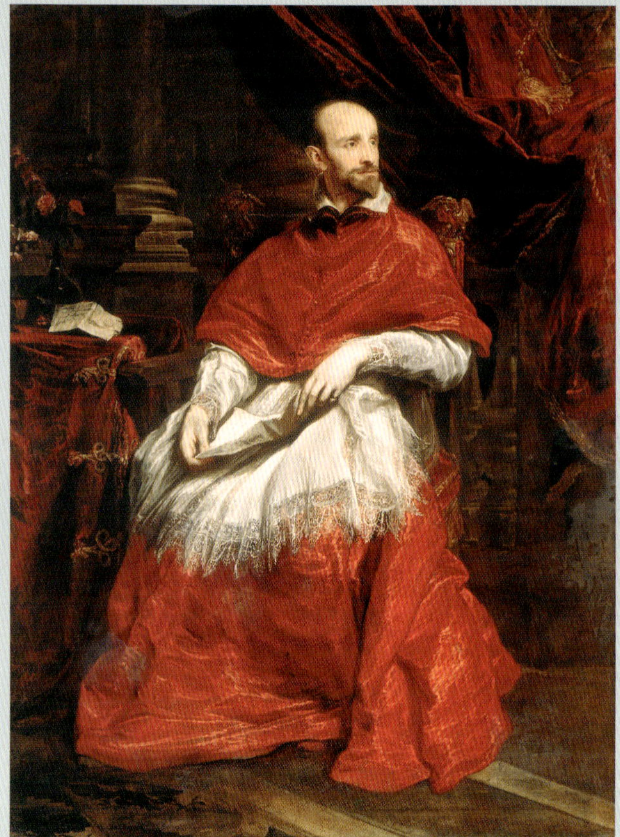

Antoon van Dyck
(Anvers 1599 - London 1641)

Portrait of Cardinal Guido Bentivoglio
Kardinal Guido Bentivoglio
Kardinaal Guido Bentivoglio

1623
196 x 145 cm / 77.16 x 57.08 in.
Galleria Palatina, Firenze

Oil on canvas / Öl auf Leinwand / Olieverf op doek

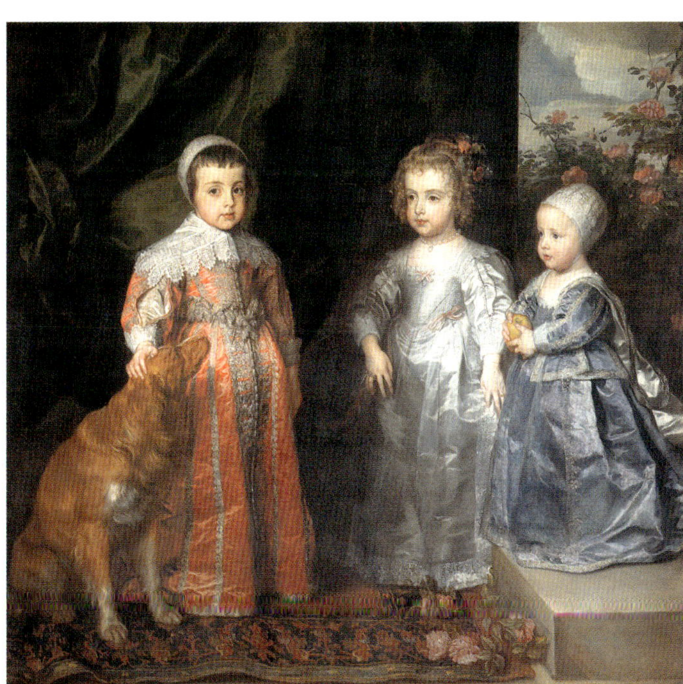

Antoon van Dyck
(Anvers 1599 - London 1641)

The Children of Charles I of England
Die Kinder Karl I von England
De kinderen van Karel I van Engeland

●●

1635
151 x 154 cm / 59.44 x 60.62 in.
Galleria Sabauda, Torino

Oil on canvas / Öl auf Leinwand / Olieverf op doek

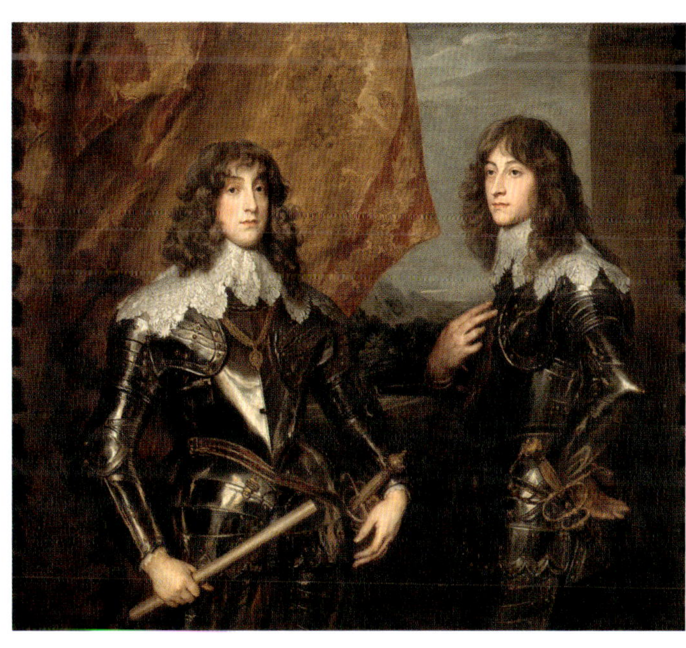

Antoon van Dyck
(Anvers 1599 - London 1641)

Double Portrait of the Palatine Princes
Portrait der Palatin Prinzen
Portret van de prinsen van de Palts

●●

1637
132 x 152 cm / 51.98 x 59.84 in.
Musée du Louvre, Paris

Oil on canvas / Öl auf Leinwand / Olieverf op doek

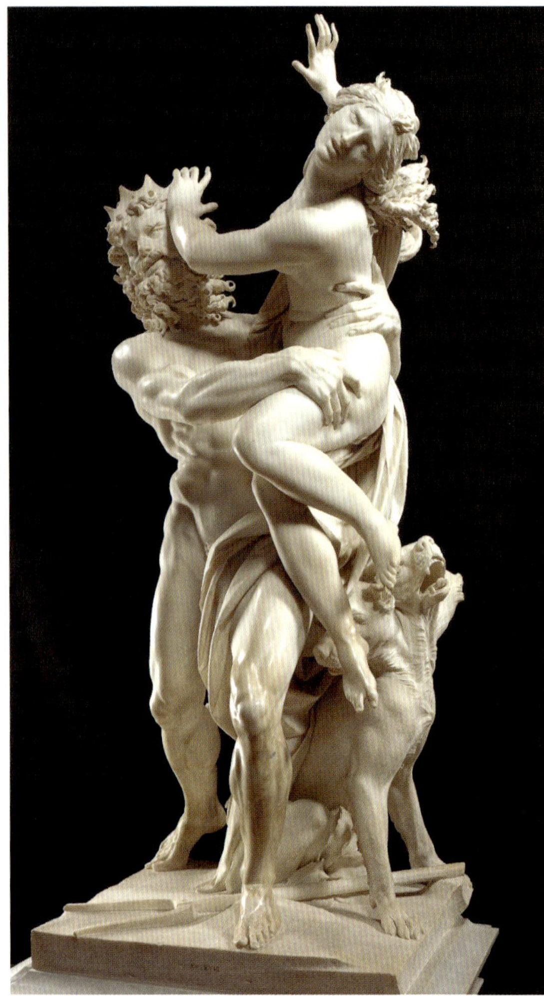

Gian Lorenzo Bernini (Napoli 1598 - Roma 1680)

The Rape of Proserpina
Der Raub der Proserpina
De Roof van Proserpina

●●

1621-1622
h. 295 cm / 116.14 in.
Galleria Borghese, Roma

Marble / Marmor / Marmer

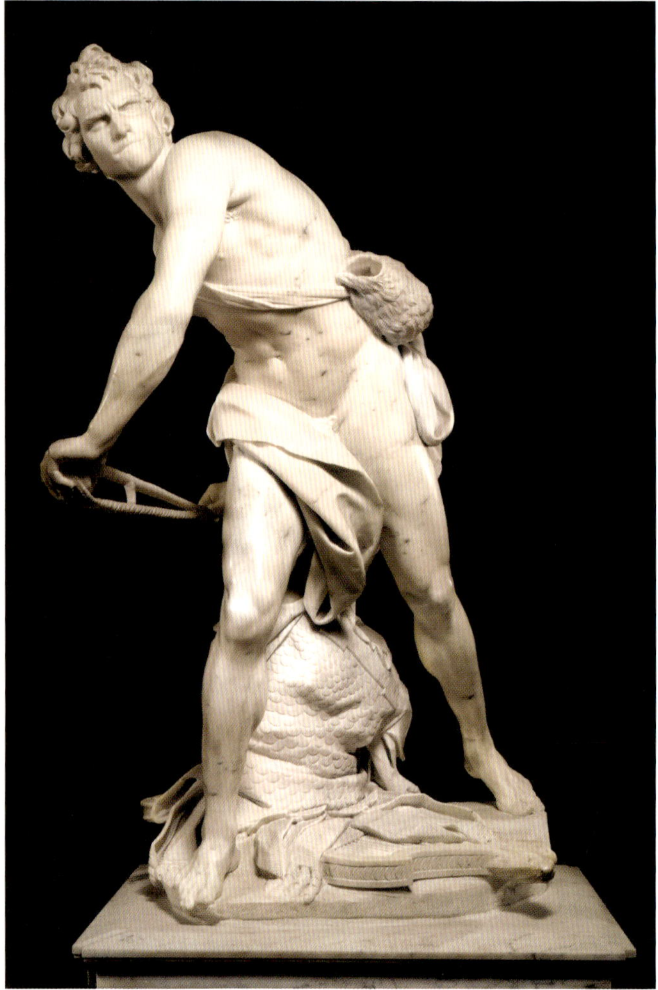

Gian Lorenzo Bernini (Napoli 1598 - Roma 1680)

David

●●

1623-1624
h. 190 cm / 74.80 in.
Galleria Borghese, Roma

Marble / Marmor / Marmer

Greek models are recalled in the sculptures of Gian Lorenzo Bernini...

Erinnerungen an hellenistische Vorbilder werden wach bei den Skulpturen Gian Lorenzo Berninis...

Herinneringen aan Hellenistische modellen ontwaken bij de beelden van Gian Lorenzo Bernini...

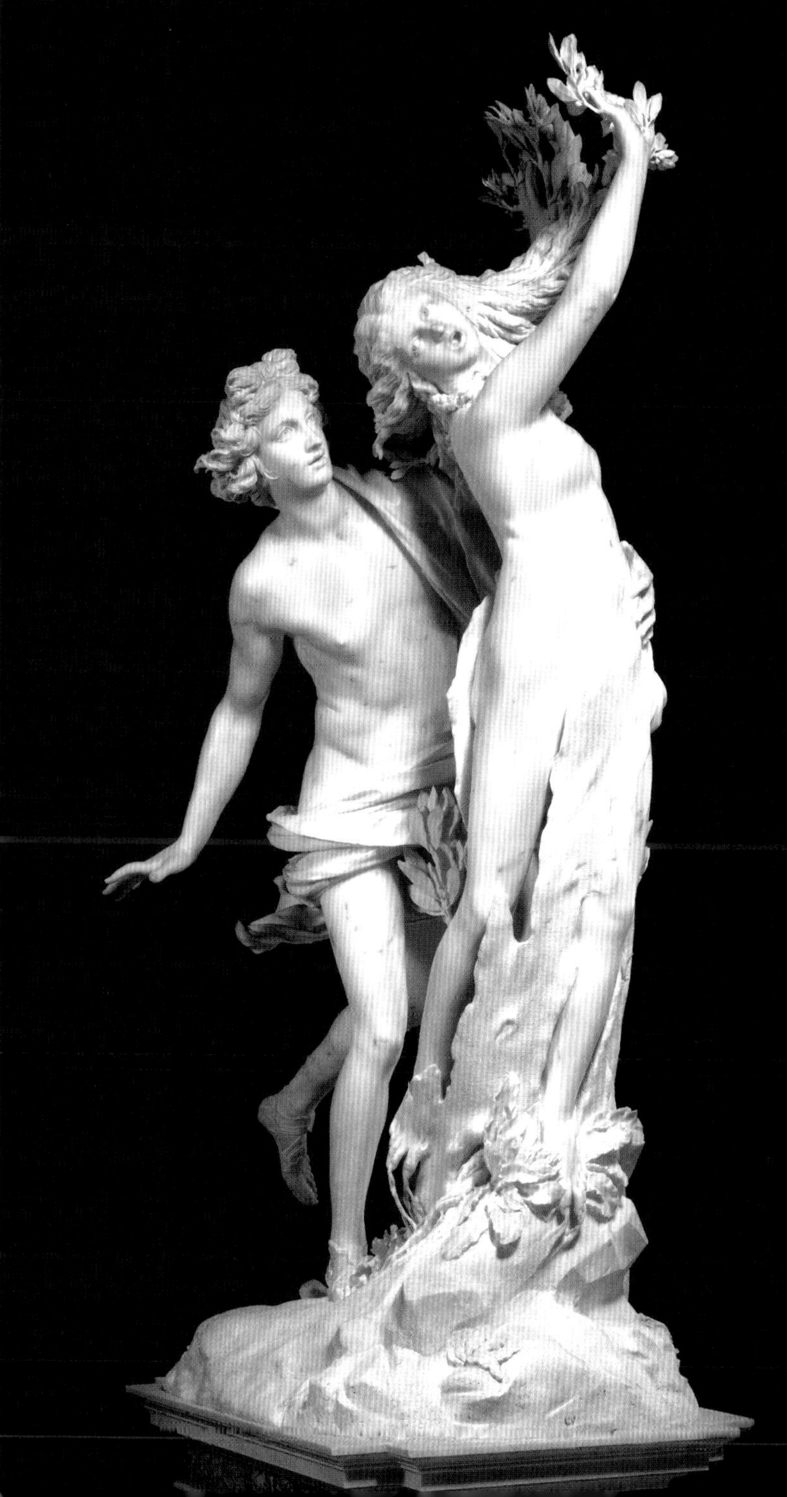

Gian Lorenzo Bernini
(Napoli 1598 - Roma 1680)

Apollo and Daphne
Apollon und Daphne
Apollo en Daphne

●●●

c. 1622-1624
h. 243 cm / 95.66 in.
Galleria Borghese, Roma

Marble / Marmor / Marmer

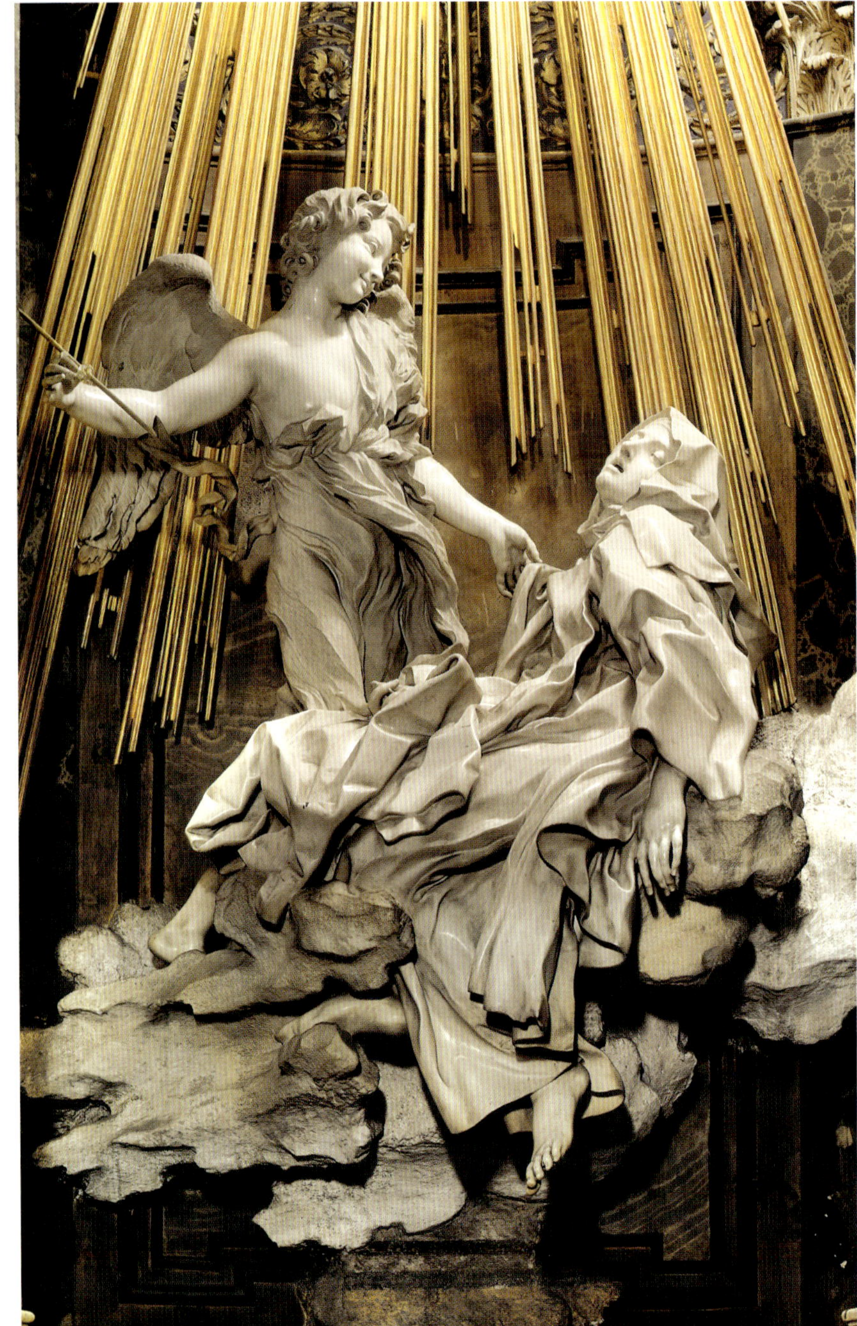

... while he becomes famous throughout the world as an architect, above all for the canopy in the cathedral of St Peter.

... der auch als Architekt und insbesondere durch den Baldachin im Petersdom zu Weltruhm gelangt.

... die ook wereldberoemd wordt als architect, vooral vanwege het baldakijn in de basiliek van de Sint Pieter.

Gian Lorenzo Bernini
(Napoli 1598 - Roma 1680)

Ecstasy of St Teresa
Ekstase der Hl. Theresa
De Extase van Theresia

●●●

c. 1647-1652
h. 350 cm / 137.79 in.
Santa Maria della Vittoria, Roma

Marble / Marmor / Marmer

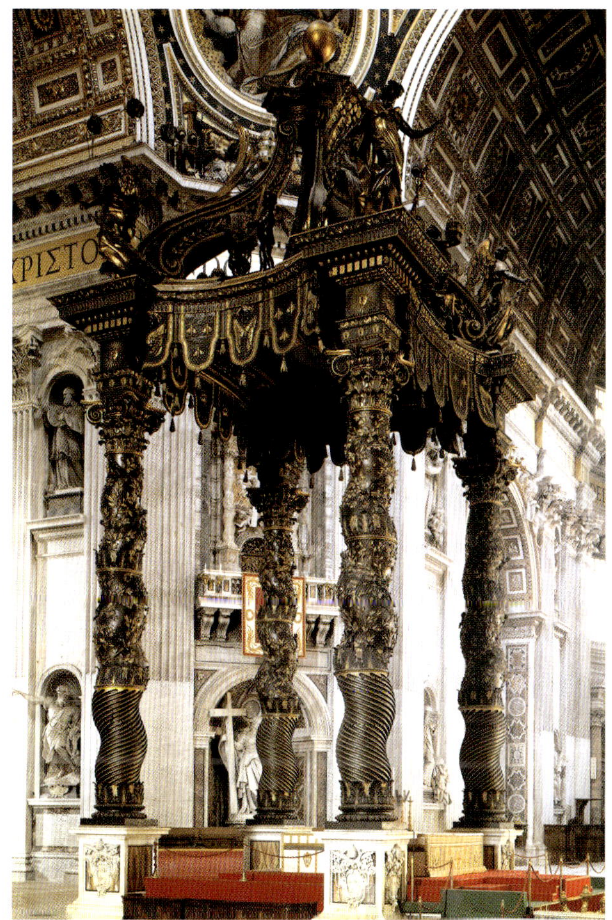

Gian Lorenzo Bernini
(Napoli 1598 - Roma 1680)

Canopy of St Peter
Baldachin des Hl.Petrus
Baldakijn van Petrus

●●●

1624-1633
h. 15 m / 590.55 in.
Basilica di San Pietro,
Città del Vaticano

Bronze / Brons

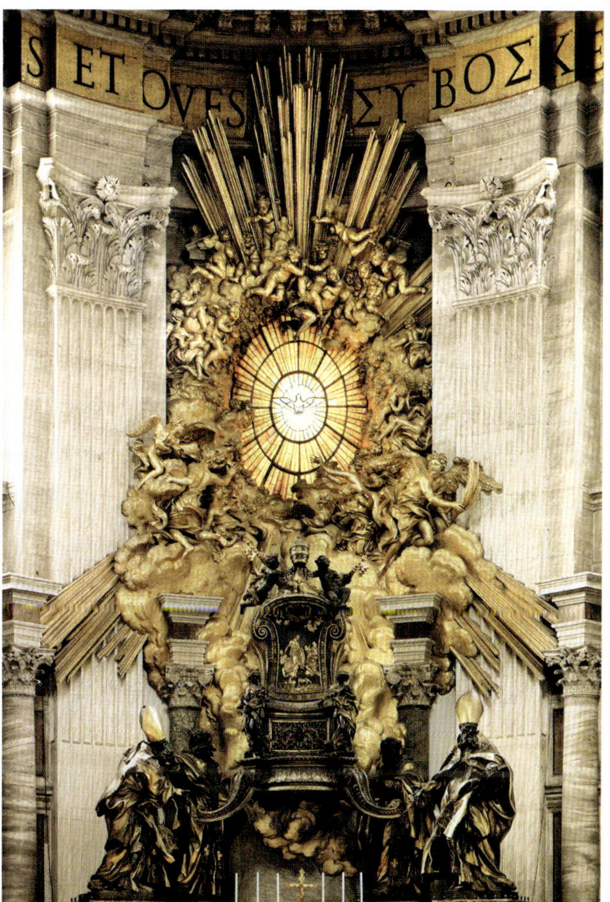

Gian Lorenzo Bernini
(Napoli 1598 - Roma 1680)

Throne of St Peter
Cathedra Petri
Cathedra van Petrus

●●

1656-1665
Basilica di San Pietro,
Città del Vaticano

Wood, bronze and stucco / Holz, Bronze, Stuck
Hout, Brons, Pleister

Pierre Puget
(Marseille 1620 - 1694)

St Sebastian
Hl. Sebastian
Sint Sebastiaan

●

1668
h. c. 300 cm / 118.10 in.
Santa Maria Assunta in Carignano, Genova

Marble / Marmor / Marmer

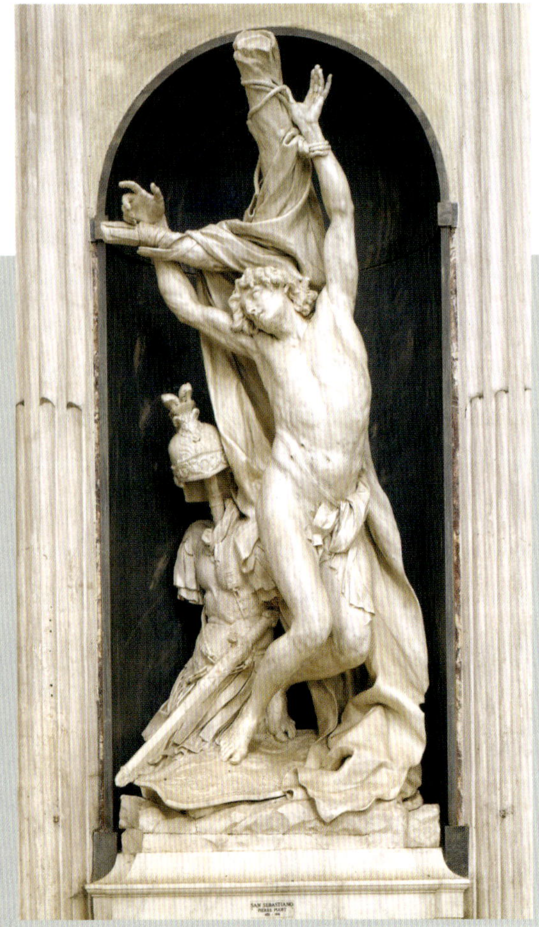

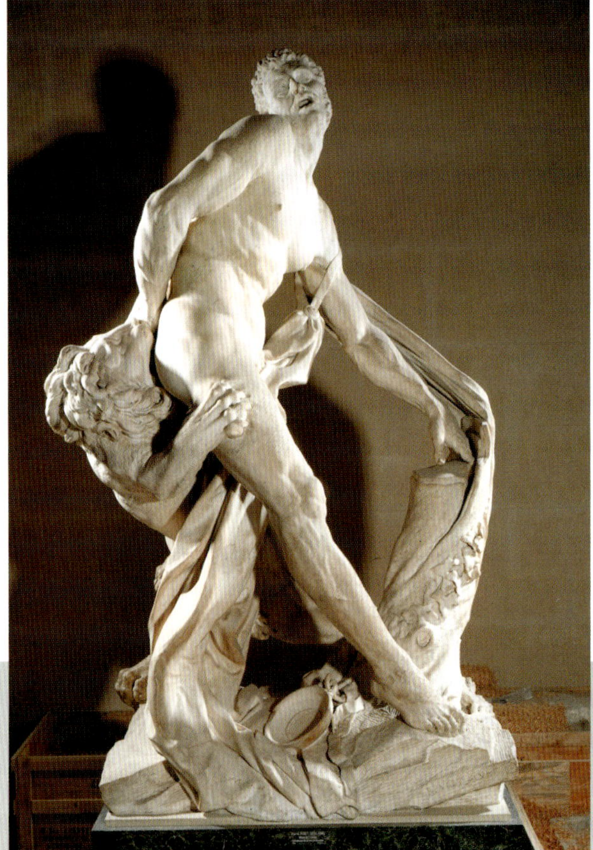

Pierre Puget
(Marseille 1622 - 1694)

Milo of Croton
Milon von Kroton
Milo van Croton

●●

c. 1682
h. 269 cm / 105.90 in.
Musée du Louvre, Paris

Marble / Marmor / Marmer

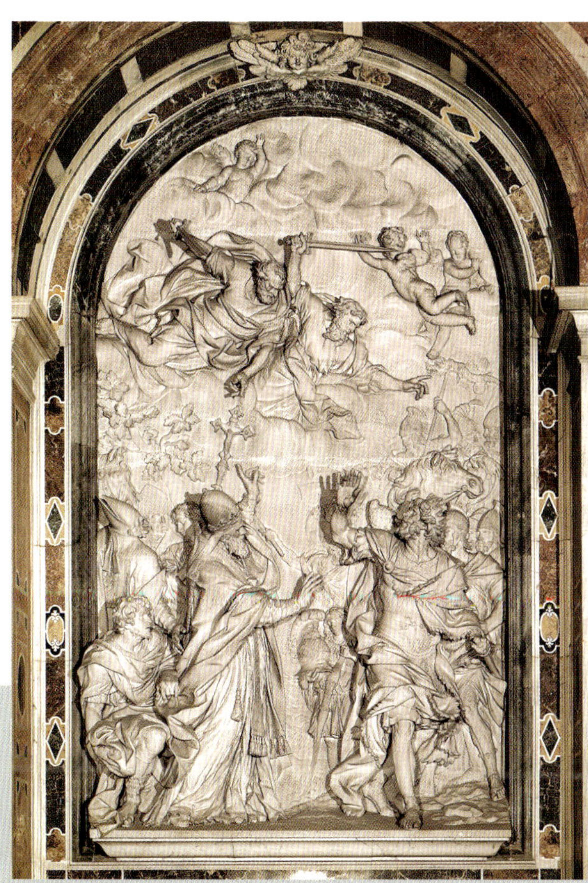

François Duquesnoy
(Bruxelles 1597 - Livorno 1643)

St Susanna
Hl. Susanne
Heilige Susanna

●

c. 1629-1633
h. 200 cm / 78.74 in.
Santa Maria di Loreto, Roma

Marble / Marmor / Marmer

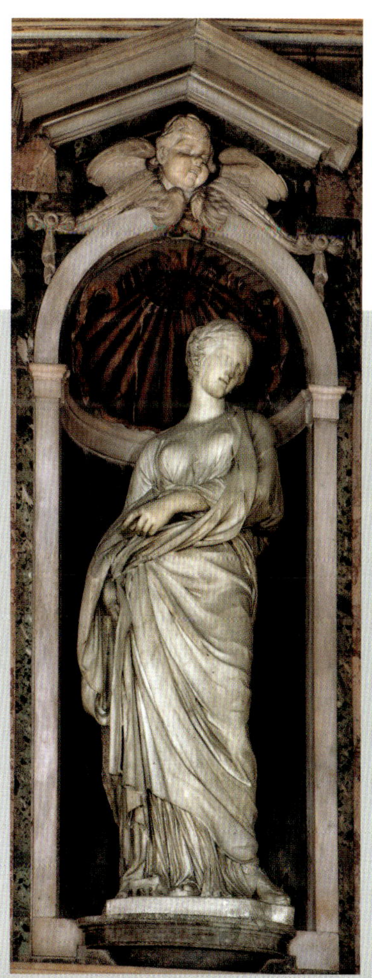

Alessandro Algardi
(Bologna 1595 - Roma 1654)

Meeting of Leo the Great and Attila
Begegnung von Leo dem Großen und Attila
Ontmoeting tussen Leo I de Grote en Atilla

●

1646-1653
h. 750 cm / 295.27 in.
Basilica di San Pietro, Città del Vaticano

Marble / Marmorrelief / Marmer

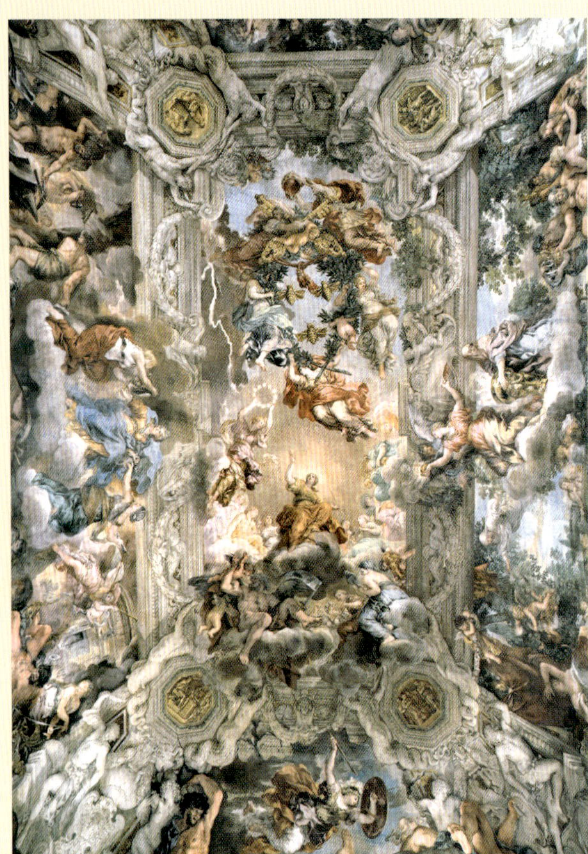

Pietro da Cortona
(Cortona 1596 - Roma 1669)

The Triumph of Divine Providence
Triumph der Göttlichen Vorsehung
Triomf van de Goddelijke Voorzienigheid

●●●

c. 1633-1639
Palazzo Barberini, Roma

Fresco / Fresko

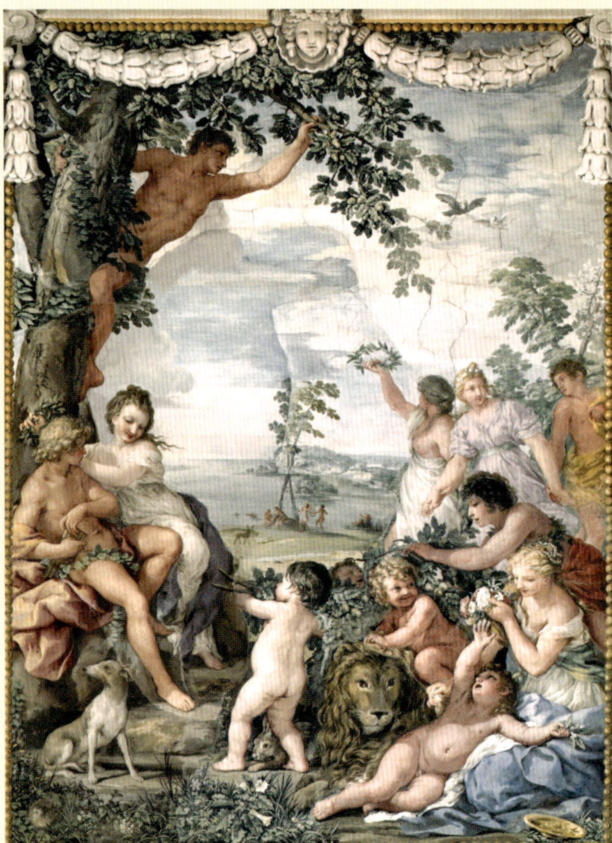

Pietro da Cortona
(Cortona 1596 - Roma 1669)

The Golden Age
Das Goldene Zeitalter
Het Gouden Tijdperk

●●

1637
Palazzo Pitti, Firenze

Fresco / Fresko

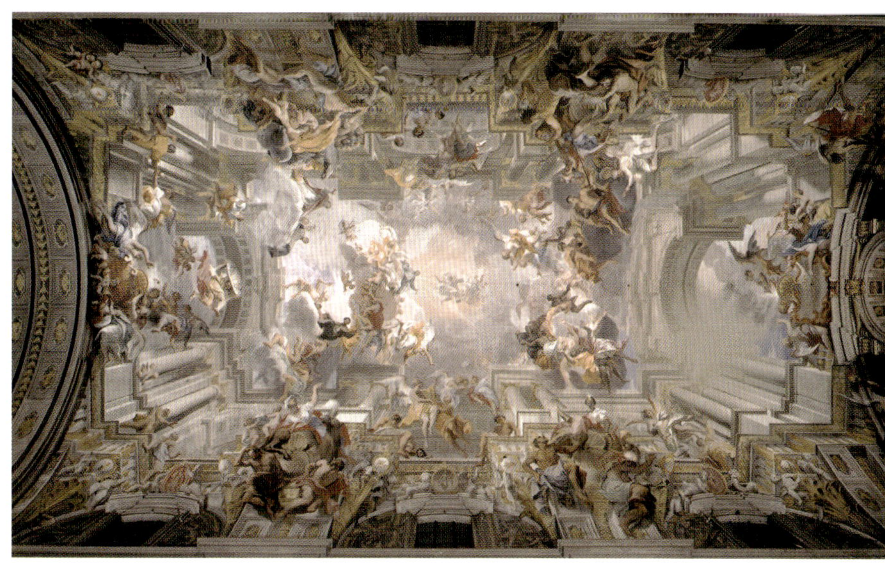

Andrea Pozzo
(Trento 1642 - Wien 1709)

Entrance of St Ignatius into Paradise
Die Aufnahme des Hl.Ignatius ins Paradies
Betreding van het Paradijs door Sint Ignatius

●●

1685
Sant'Ignazio di Loyola, Roma

Fresco / Fresko

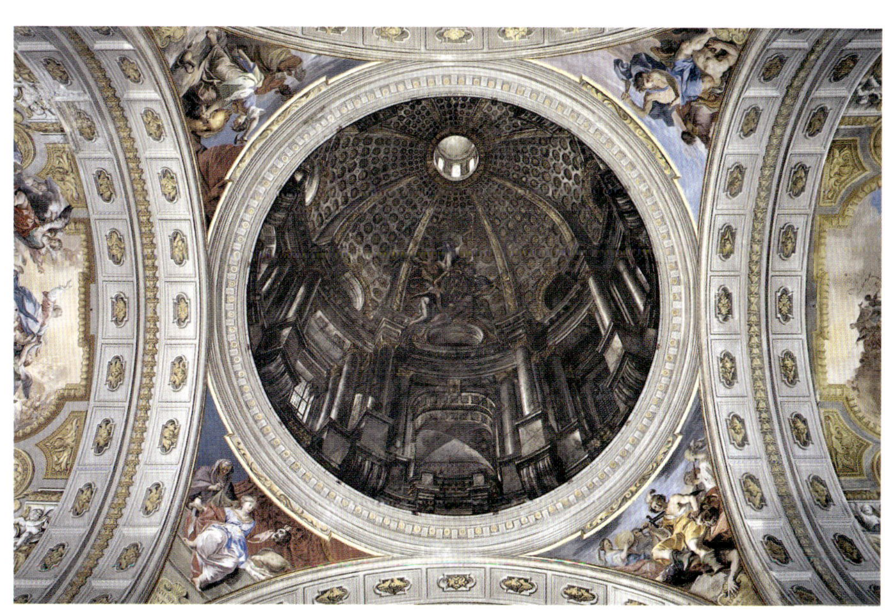

Andrea Pozzo
(Trento 1642 - Wien 1709)

Trompe l'oeil dome
"Falsche" Kuppel
"Valse" Koepel

●

1685
Sant' Ignazio di Loyola, Roma

Fresco / Fresko

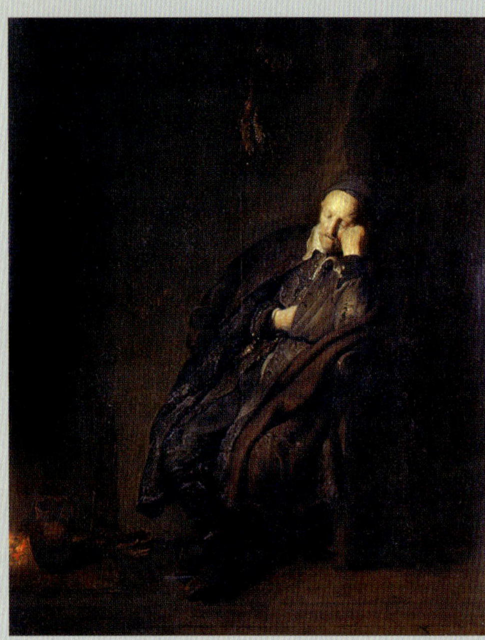

Rembrandt
(Leiden 1606 - Amsterdam 1669)

Old Man Sleeping
Schlafender alter Mann
Slapende oude man

●

c. 1629
51,9 x 40,8 cm / 20.43 x 16.06 in.
Galleria Sabauda, Torino

Oil on wood / Öl auf Holz
olieverf op paneel

Rembrandt
(Leiden 1606 - Amsterdam 1669)

Belshazzar's Feast
Belsazar
Belsazar's Feest

●●●

1635
168 x 209 cm / 66.14 x 82.28 in.
The National Gallery, London

Oil on canvas / Öl auf Leinwand
Olieverf op doek

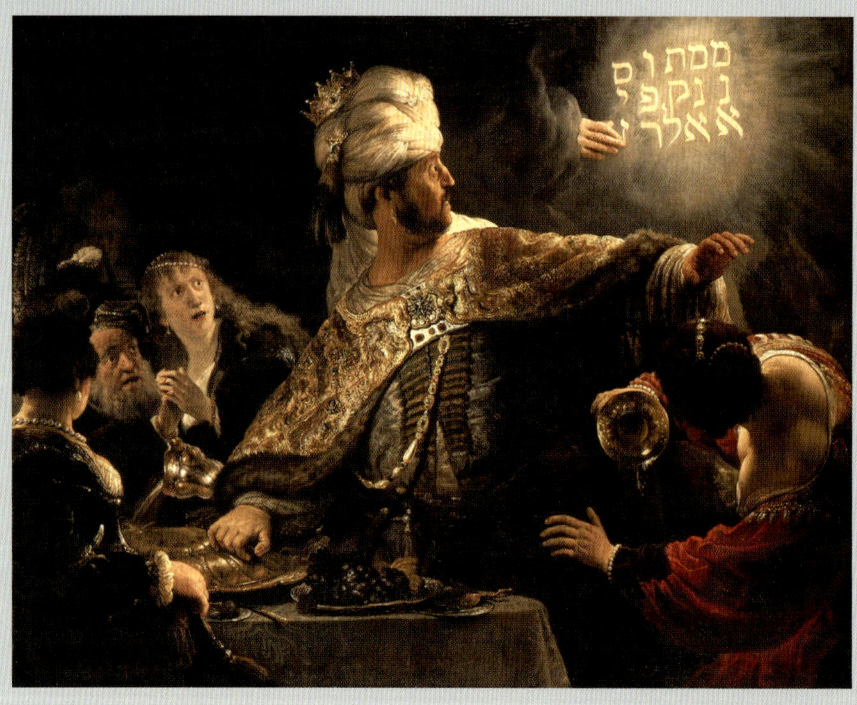

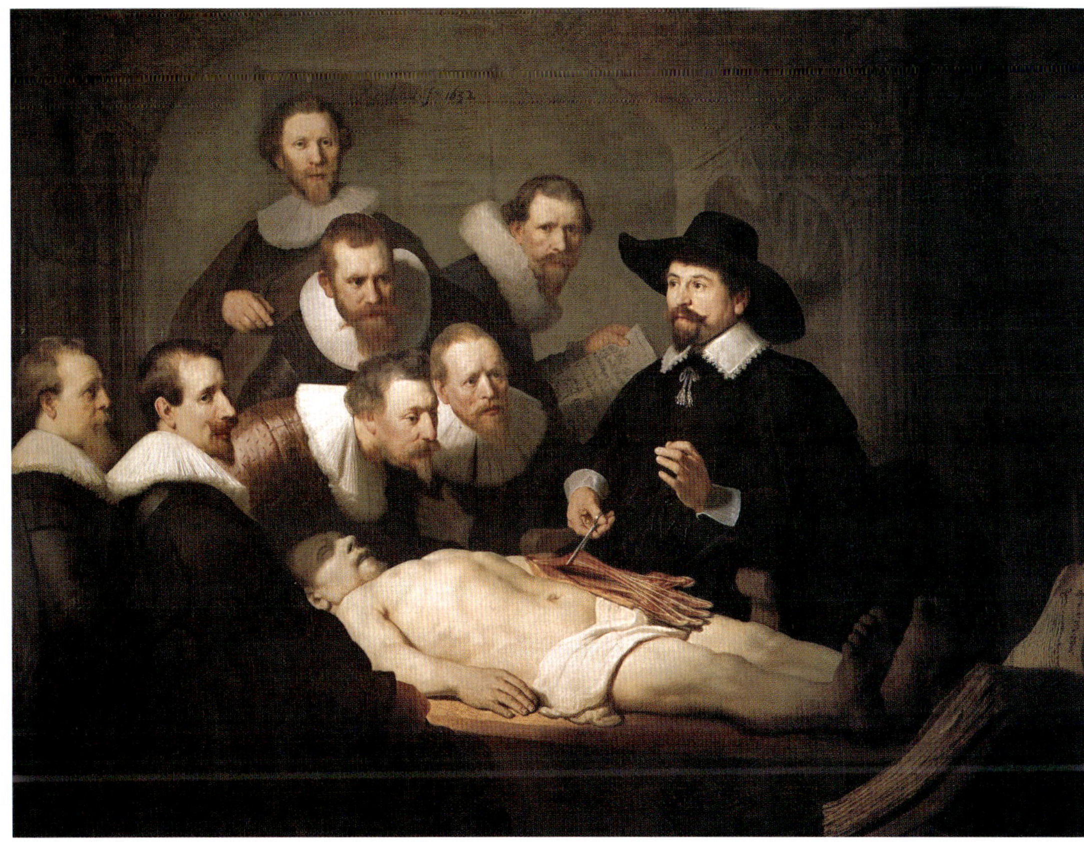

Rembrandt
(Leiden 1606 - Amsterdam 1669)

The Anatomy Lesson of Dr. Nicolaes Tulp
Die Anatomie des Dr. Nicolacs Tulp
De Anatomische les van Dr. Nicolaes Tulp

●●●

1632
169 x 216 cm / 66.53 x 85.03 in.
Mauritshuis, The Hague

Oil on canvas / Öl auf Leinwand / Olieverf op doek

Rembrandt, a Protestant, strews light and shadows like Caravaggio.

Der protestantische Rembrandt streut Licht und Schatten wie Caravaggio.

De protestant Rembrandt strooit licht en schaduw zoals Caravaggio.

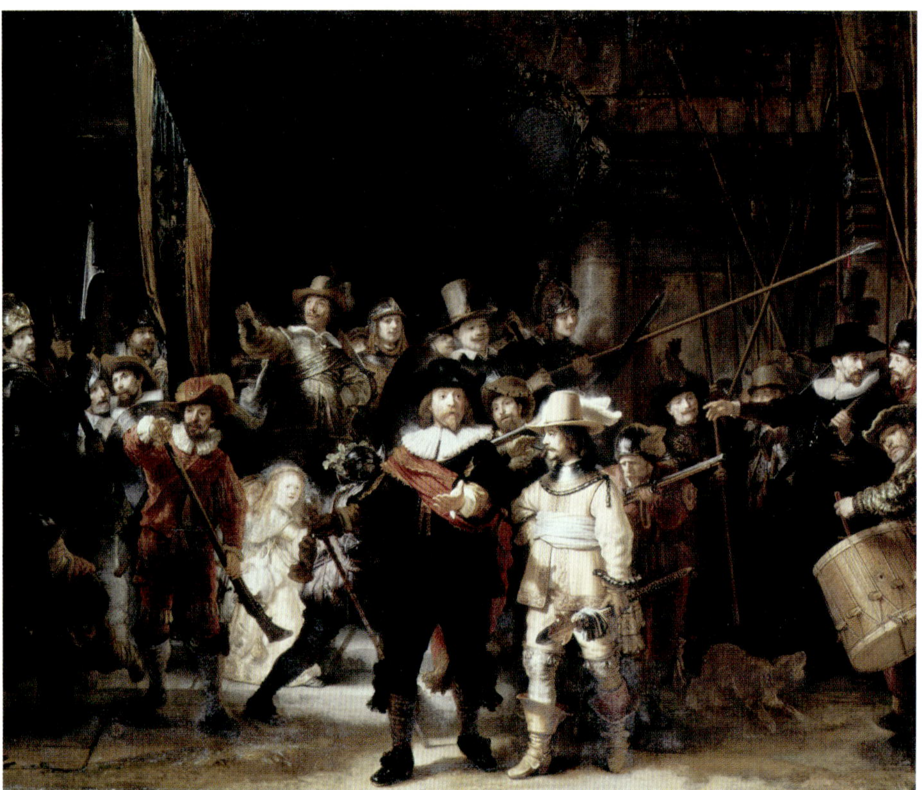

Rembrandt
(Leiden 1606 - Amsterdam 1669)

The Night Watch (Company of Frans Banning Cocq and Willem van Ruytenburch)
Die Nachtwache (Die Schützenkompanie des Kapitäns Frans Banning Cocq)
De Nachtwacht (De Compagnie van kapitein Frans Banning Cocq en luitenant Willem van Ruytenburgh)

●●●

1642
363 x 437 cm / 142.91 x 172.04 in.
Rijksmuseum, Amsterdam

Oil on canvas / Öl auf Leinwand / Olieverf op doek

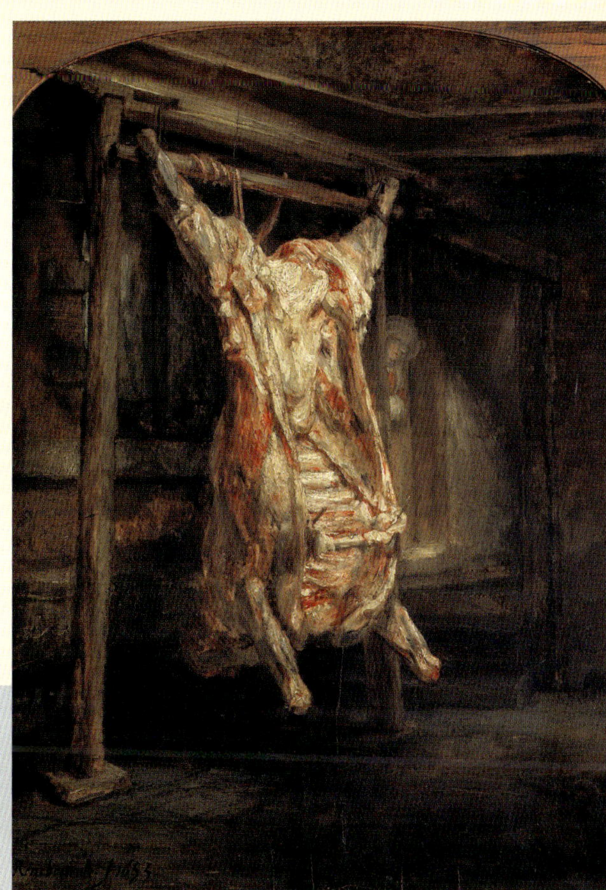

Rembrandt
(Leiden 1606 - Amsterdam 1669)

The Slaughtered Ox
Geschlachteter Ochse
Geslachte os

●●●

1655
94 × 69 cm / 37 x 27.16 in.
Musée du Louvre, Paris

Oil on canvas / Öl auf Leinwand / Olieverf op doek

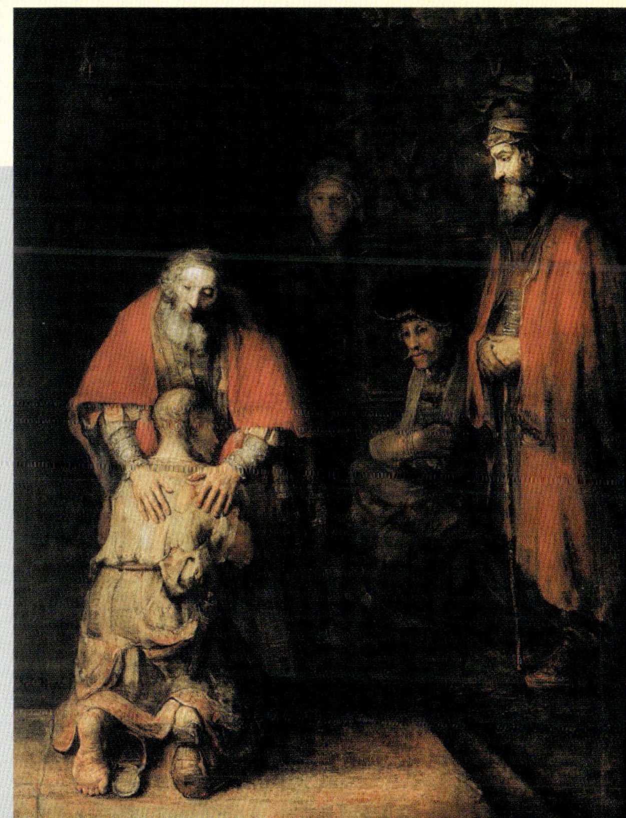

Rembrandt
(Leiden 1606 - Amsterdam 1669)

The Return of the Prodigal Son
Die Rückkehr des Verlorenen Sohnes
De terugkeer van de Verloren Zoon

●●

1666
262 x 206 cm / 103.14 x 81.10 in.
The State Hermitage Museum, St. Petersburg

Oil on canvas / Öl auf Leinwand / Olieverf op doek

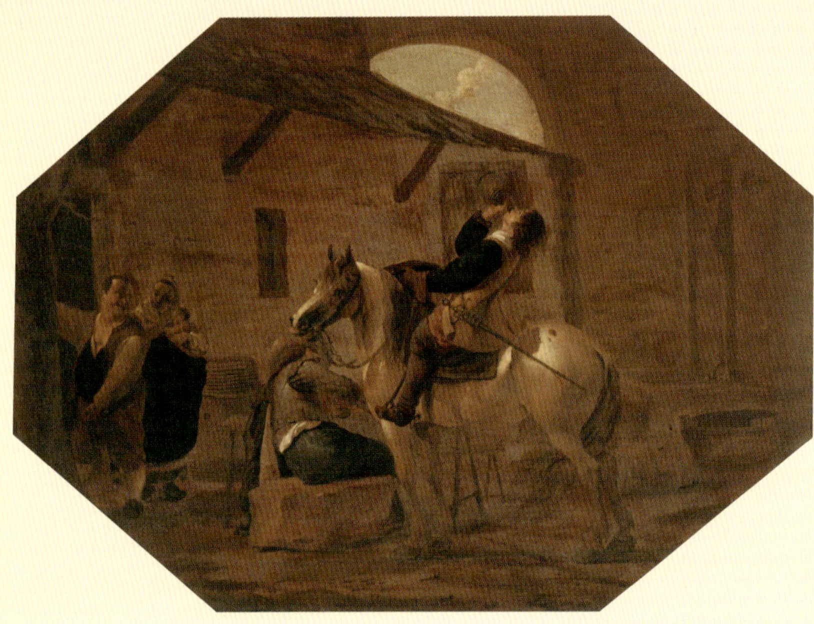

Bamboccio (Pieter van Laer)
(Haarlem 1599 - ? 1642)

Stopping at the Tavern
Abfahrt von einer Gaststätte
Stop bij de taverne

●

c. 1625-1639
35 x 49 cm / 13.77 x 19.29 in.
Galleria Spada, Roma

Oil on canvas / Öl auf Leinwand
Olieverf op doek

Michelangelo Cerquozzi
(Roma 1602 - 1660)

The Uprising of Masaniello
Revolte von Masaniello
Opstand van Masaniello

●

1648
97 x 134 cm / 38.18 x 52.75 in.
Galleria Spada, Roma

Oil on canvas / Öl auf Leinwand
Olieverf op doek

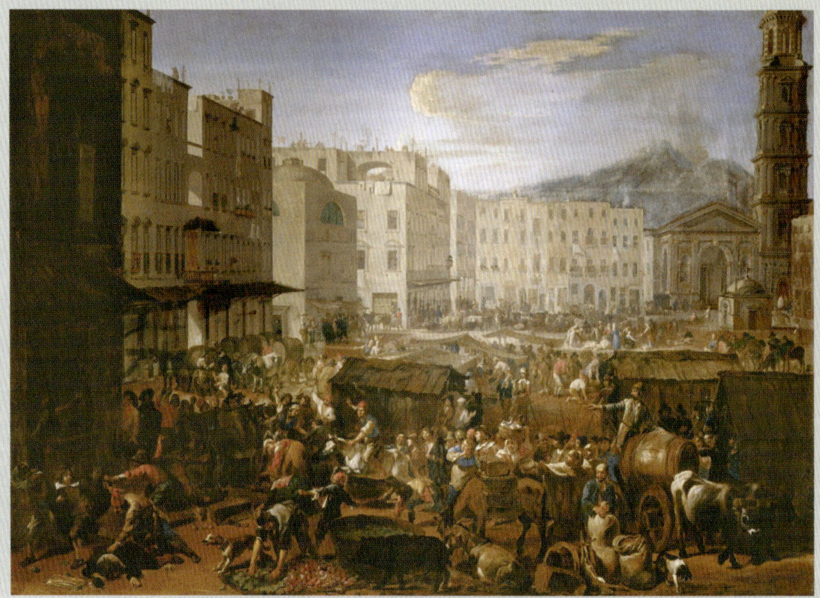

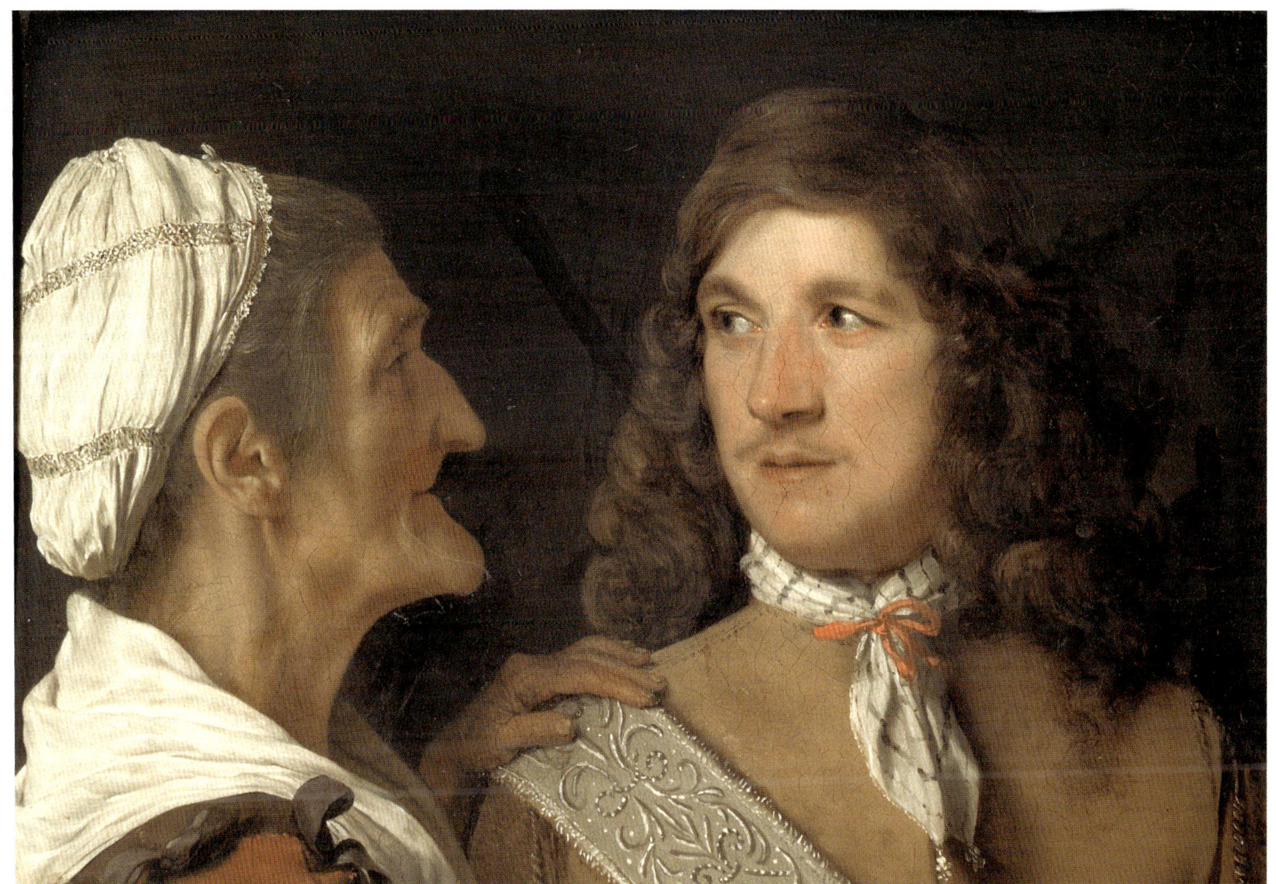

Michael Sweerts
(Bruxelles 1618 - Goa 1664)

Young Man and the Procuress
Junger Mann mit einer Kupplerin
Jonge man met oude vrouw

●

c. 1660
27 x 19 cm / 10.62 x 7.48 in.
Musée du Louvre, Paris

Oil on brass / Öl auf Messing / Olieverf op koper

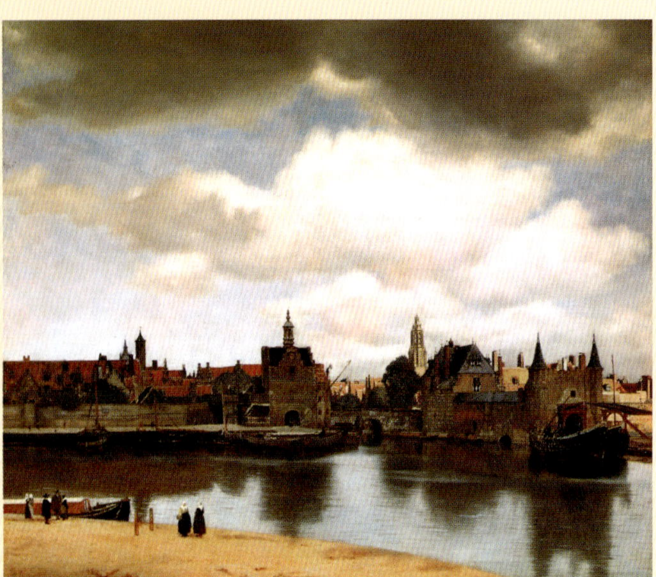

Jan Vermeer
(Delft 1632 - 1675)

View of Delft
Ansicht von Delft
Gezicht op Delft

●●

c. 1661
96,5 x 117 cm / 37.99 x 46.06 in.
Mauritshuis, The Hague

Oil on canvas / Öl auf Leinwand / Olieverf op doek

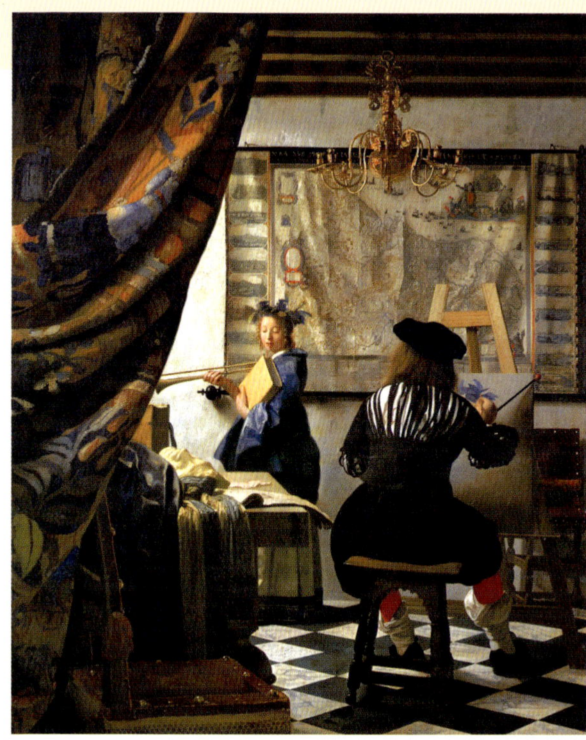

Jan Vermeer
(Delft 1632 - 1675)

The Art of Painting (Self-Portrait with his Model as Clio)
Der Maler und sein Modell als Klio
De schilder en zijn model als Clio

●●●

c. 1664-1673
100 x 120 cm / 39.37 x 47.24 in.
Kunsthistorisches Museum, Wien

Oil on canvas / Öl auf Leinwand / Olieverf op doek

Jan Vermeer depicts bourgeois comfort. Van Gogh admires his lemon yellows and pale blues.

Jan Vermeer schildert bürgerliche Behaglichkeit. Van Gogh bewundert seine Farben Zitronengelb und Blassblau.

Johannes Vermeer schildert de burgerlijke behaaglijkheid. Van Gogh bewondert zijn citroengele en bleekblauwe kleuren.

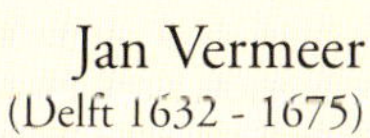

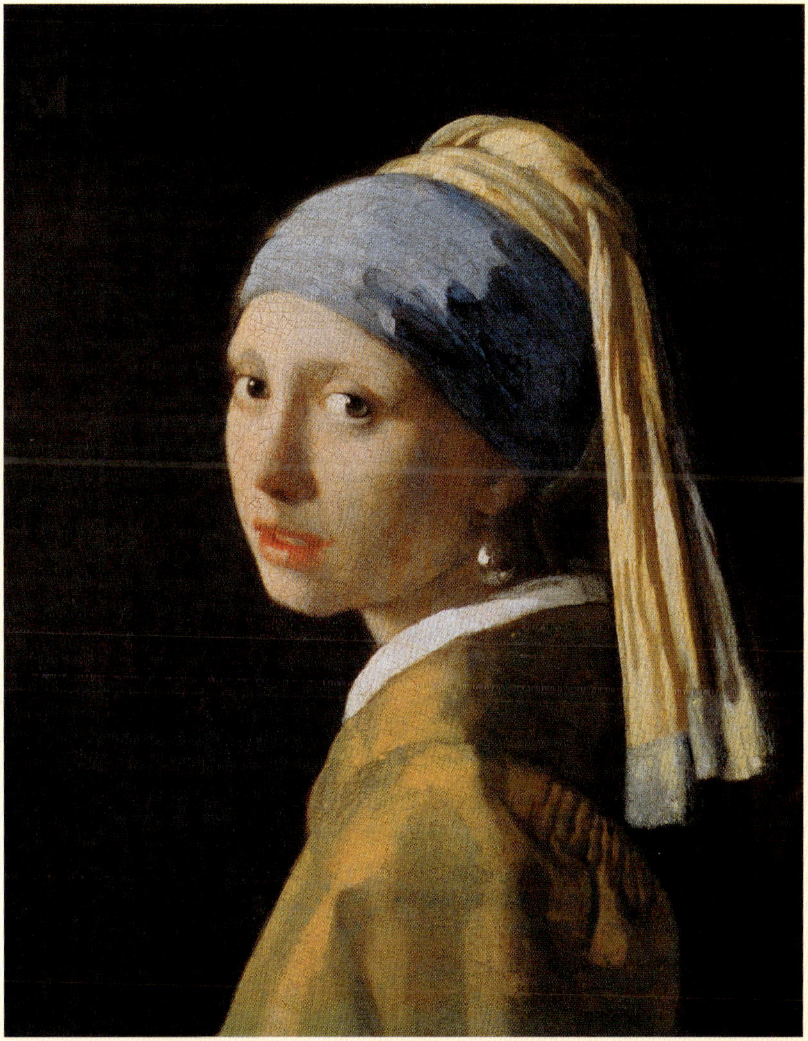

Jan Vermeer
(Delft 1632 - 1675)

Girl with a Turban
(Girl with a Pearl Earring)
Das Mädchen mit demTurban
(Das Mädchen mit dem Perlenohrring)
Meisje met de tulband
(Het meisje met de parel)

●●●

c. 1665
46.5 x 40 cm / 18.30 x 15.74 in.
Mauritshuis, The Hague

Oil on canvas / Öl auf Leinwand
Olieverf op doek

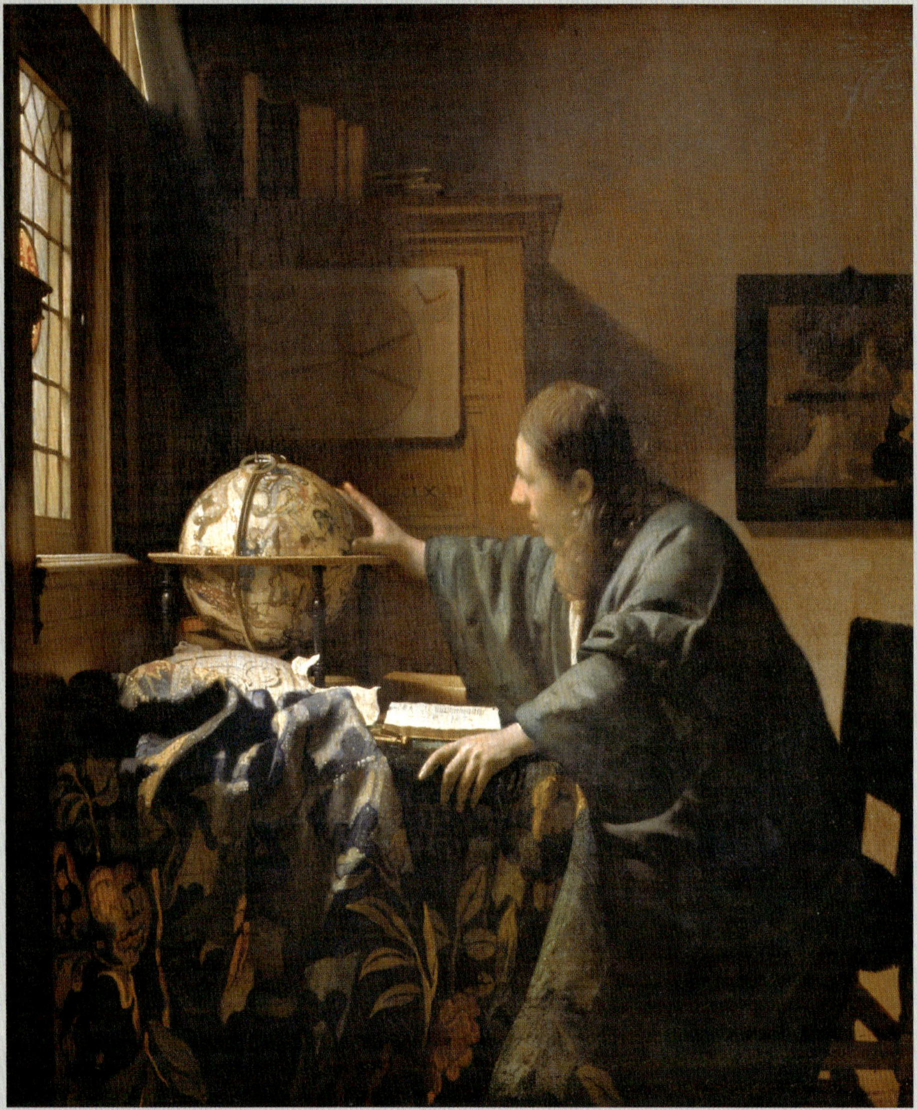

Jan Vermeer
(Delft 1632 - 1675)

The Astronomer
Der Astronom
De Astronoom

●●●

1668
50 x 45 cm / 19.68 x 17.71 in.
Musée du Louvre, Paris

Oil on canvas / Öl auf Leinwand
Olieverf op doek

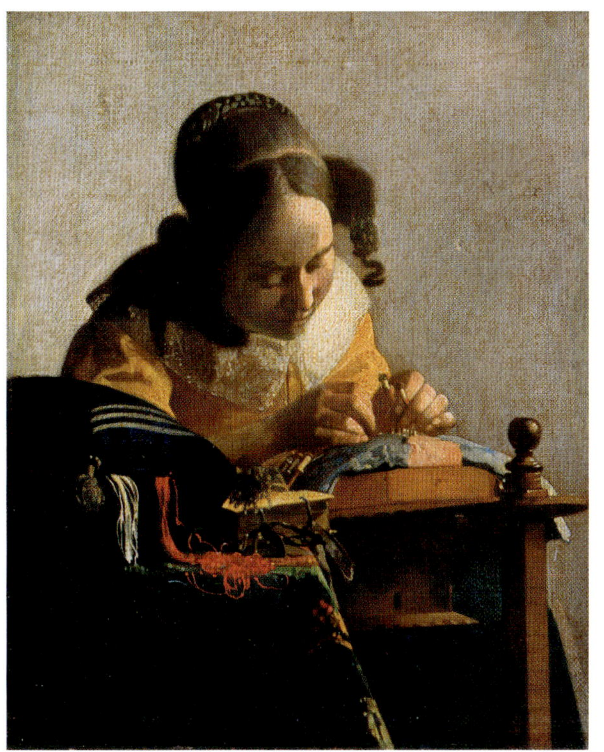

Jan Vermeer
(Delft 1632 - 1675)

The Lace Maker
Die Spitzenklöpplerin
De Kantklosster

●●●

1669
34 x 20,5 cm / 13.38 x 8.07 in.
Musée du Louvre, Paris

Oil on canvas / Öl auf Leinwand
Olieverf op doek

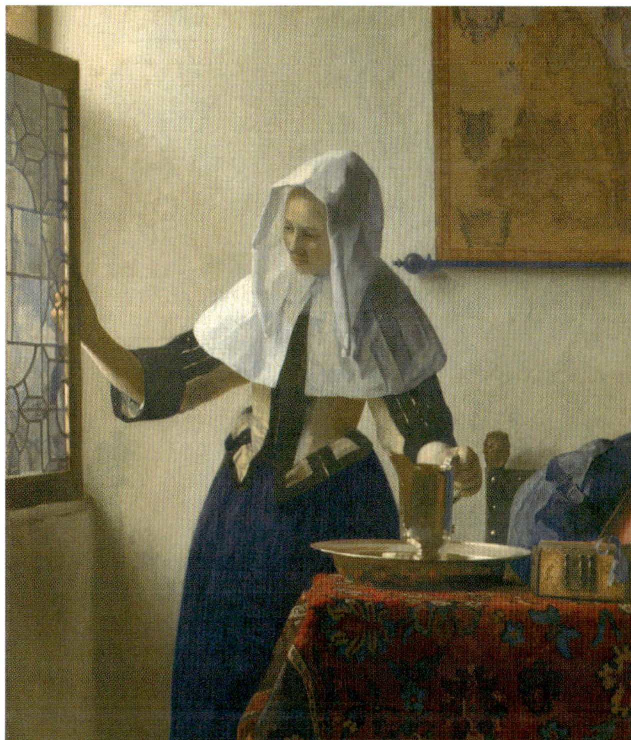

Jan Vermeer
(Delft 1632 - 1675)

Young Woman with a Water Pitcher
Junge Frau mit einem Wasserkrug
Vrouw met waterkan

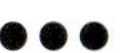

c. 1662
45.7 x 40.6 cm / 17.99 x 15.98 in.
Metropolitan Museum of Art, New York

Oil on canvas / Öl auf Leinwand / Olieverf op doek

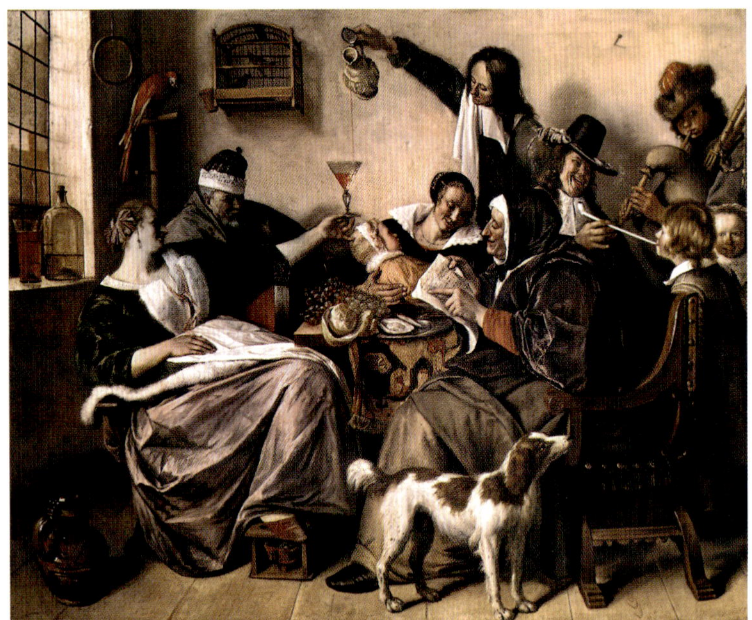

Jan Steen
(Leiden 1626 - 1679)

The Cheerful Companions (The way you hear it, is the way you sing it)
Fröhliche Gesellschaft
'Soo voer gesongen, soo na gepepen'

●

c. 1663
134 x 163 cm / 52.75 x 64.17 in.
Mauritshuis, The Hague

Oil on canvas / Öl auf Leinwand
Olieverf op doek

Gerard ter Borch
(Zwolle 1617 - Deventer 1681)

The Flea Catcher
Knabe floht seinen Hund
Jongen vlooit zijn hond

●

c. 1665
35 x 27 cm / 13.77 x 10.62 in.
Alte Pinakothek, Munchen

Oil on canvas / Öl auf Leinwand / Olieverf op doek

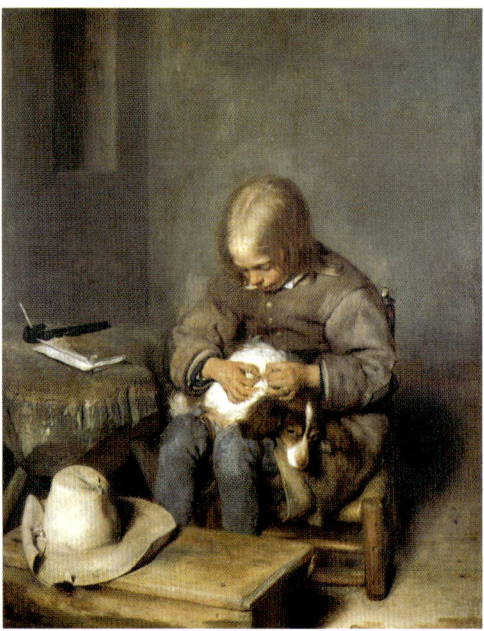

Jan van der Heyden
(Gorinchem 1637 - Amsterdam 1712)

City Hall of Amsterdam
Das Stadthaus zu Amsterdam
Het Stadhuis van Amsterdam

●

1667
Galleria degli Uffizi, Firenze

Oil on canvas / Öl auf Leinwand
Olieverf op doek

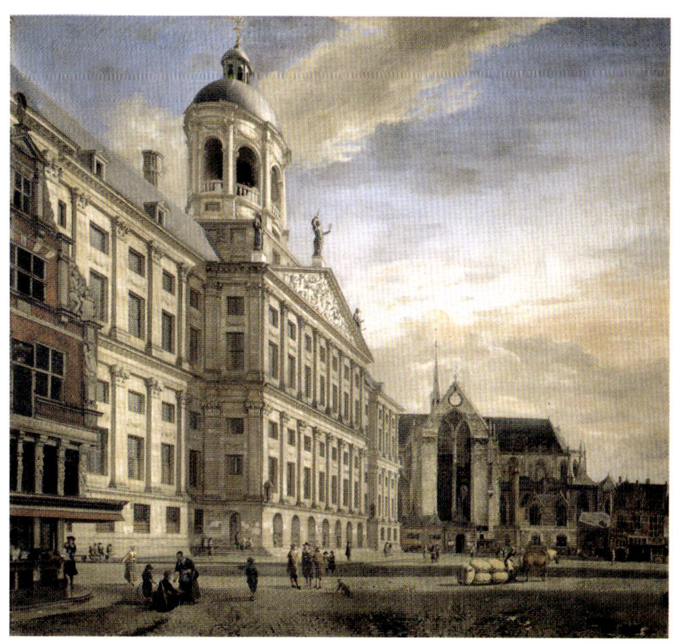

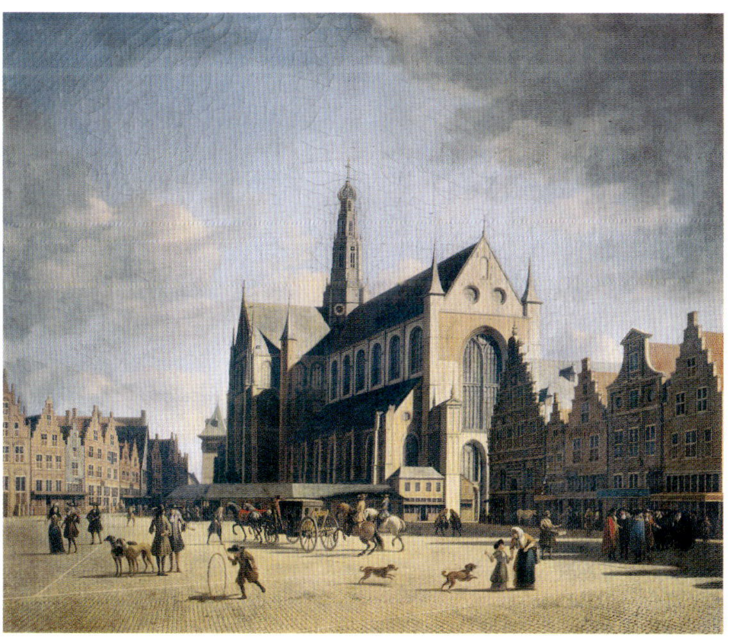

Gerrit Berckheyde
(Haarlem 1638 - 1698)

Market of Haarlem
Der Große Markt in Haarlem
De Grote Markt te Haarlem

●

1693
56 x 64 cm / 22.04 x 25.19 in.
Galleria degli Uffizi, Firenze

Oil on canvas / Öl auf Leinwand
Olieverf op doek

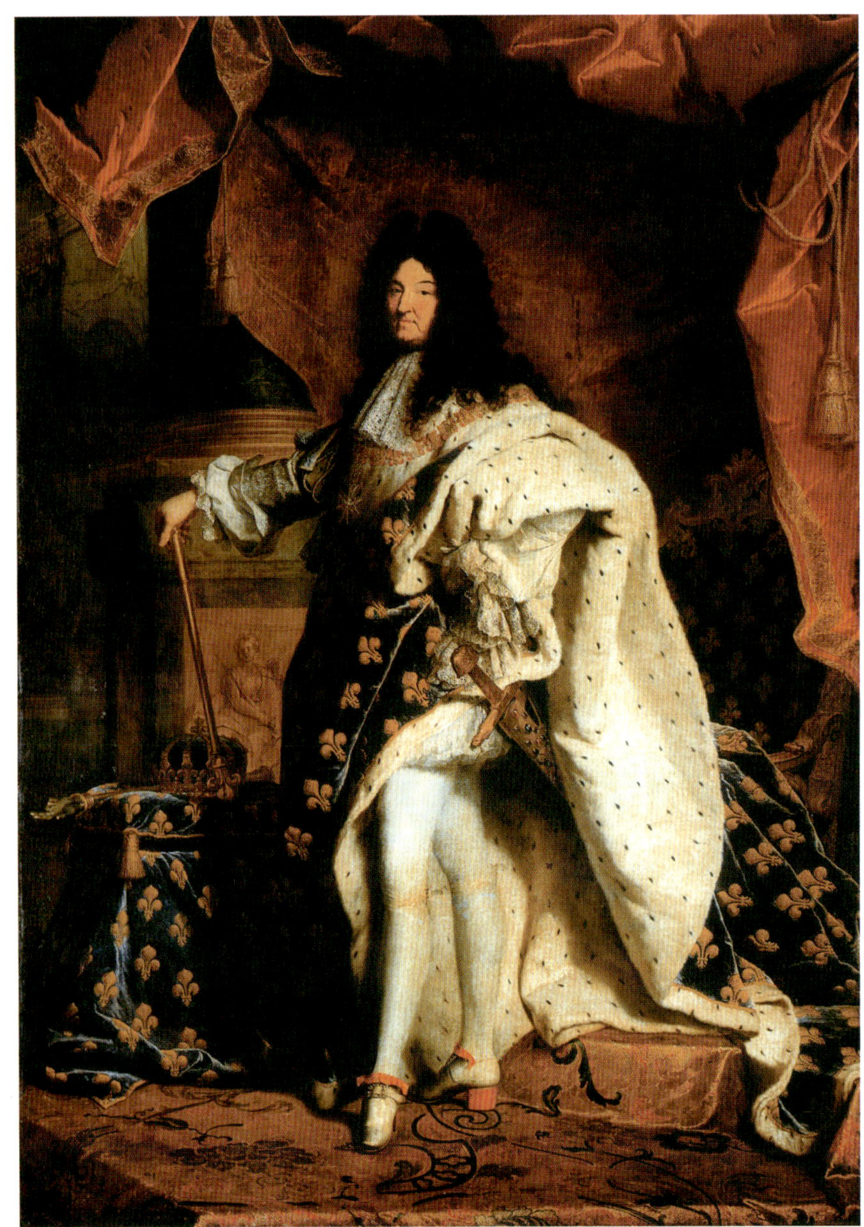

The absolute apex of the Baroque.

Der absolutistische Höhepunkt des Barock.

Het absolutist hoogtepunt van de barok.

Hyacinthe Rigaud
(Perpignan 1659 - Paris 1743)

Louis XIV
Ludwig XIV
Lodewijk XIV

●●

1701
274 x 194 cm / 107.76 x 76.44 in.
Musée du Louvre, Paris

Oil on canvas / Öl auf Leinwand
Olieverf op doek

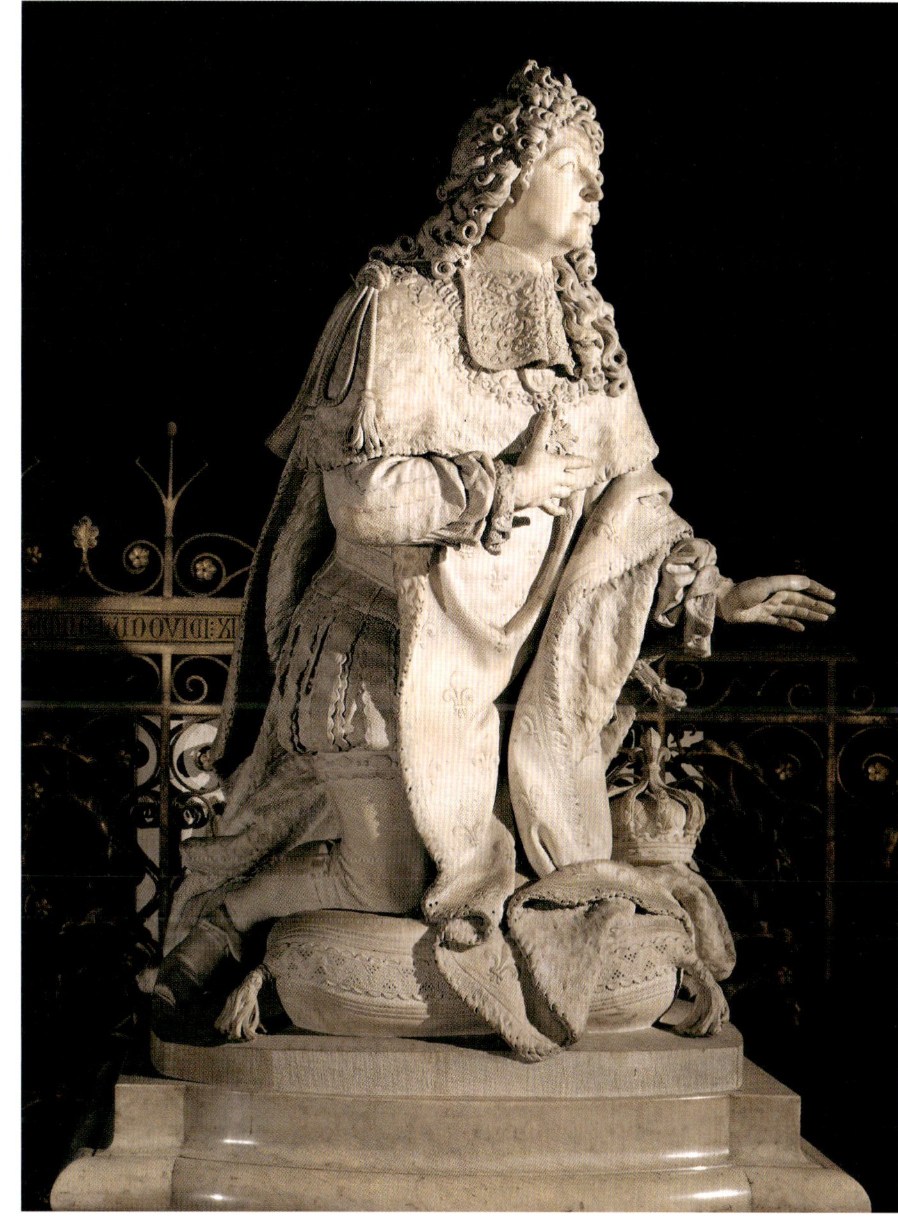

Antoine Coysevox
(Lyon 1640 - Paris 1720)

Louis XIV, King of France
Ludwig XIV,
König von Frankreich
Lodewijk XIV,
koning van Frankrijk

●

c. 1713-1715
170 cm / 66.98 in.
Notre Dame, Paris

Marble / Marmor / Marmer

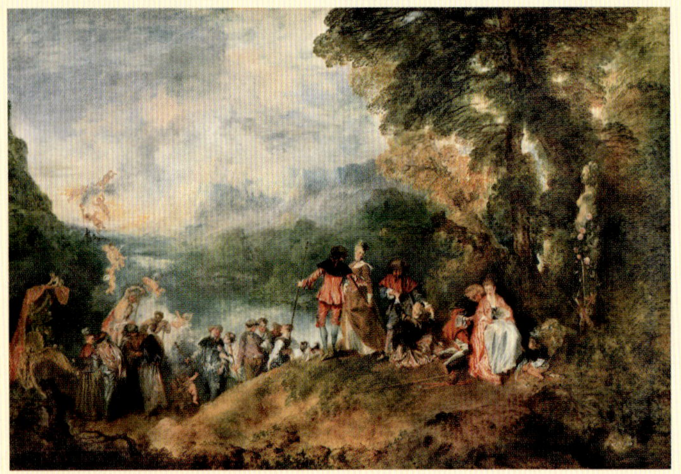

Life as a game: Watteau is the principal protagonist of the French Rococo, the link between the Baroque and Neo-Classicism.

Leben als Spiel. Watteau ist der Hauptvertreter des französischen Rokoko, der Übergangsepoche vom Barock zum Klassizismus.

Het leven als spel. Watteau is de belangrijkste vertegenwoordiger van de Franse rococo, de overgang de tussen barok en het neoclassicisme.

Jean-Antoine Watteau
(Valenciennes 1684 - Nogent-sur-Marne 1721)

Pilgrimage to the Isle of Cythera
Einschiffung nach Cythera
Pelgrimstocht naar Cythera

●●

1717
130 x 194 cm / 51.22 x 76.44 in.
Musée du Louvre, Paris

Oil on canvas / Öl auf Leinwand / Olieverf op doek

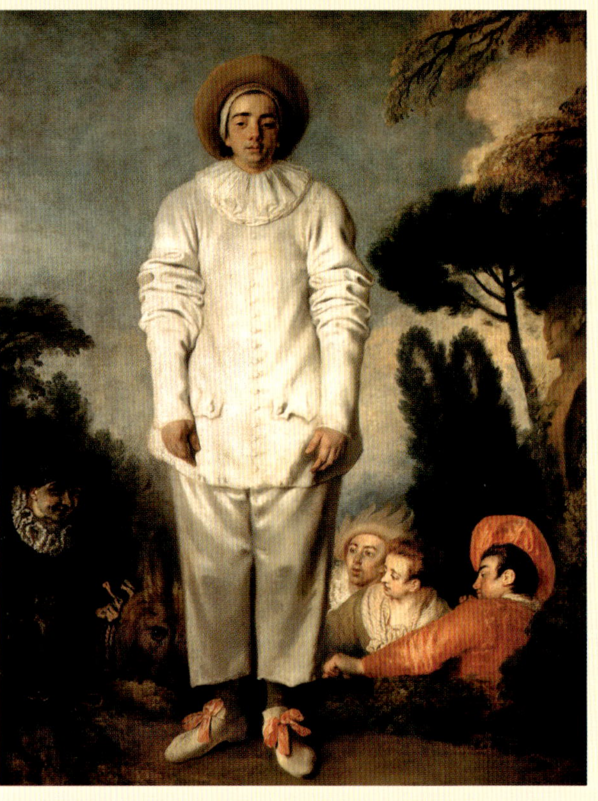

Jean-Antoine Watteau
(Valenciennes 1684 - Nogent-sur-Marne 1721)

Pierrot

●●●

c. 1718-1719
165 x 150 cm / 65.01 x 59.1 in.
Musée du Louvre, Paris

Oil on canvas / Öl auf Leinwand / Olieverf op doek

Jean-Antoine Watteau
(Valenciennes 1684 - Nogent-sur-Marne 1721)

At the Sign of Gersaint
Die Gersaint Insignien
L'Enseigne de Gersaint (Het uithangbord van Gersaint)

●●

1720
163 x 360 cm / 64.22 x 141.84 in.
Schloss Charlottenburg, Berlin

Oil on canvas / Öl auf Leinwand
Olieverf op doek

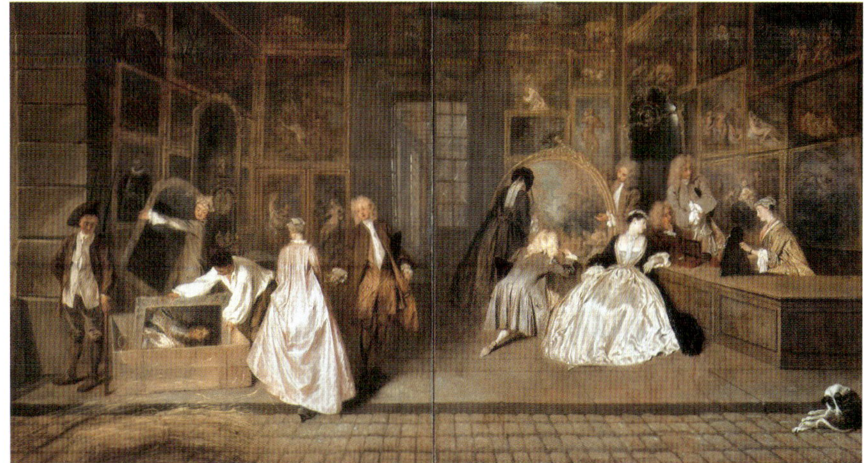

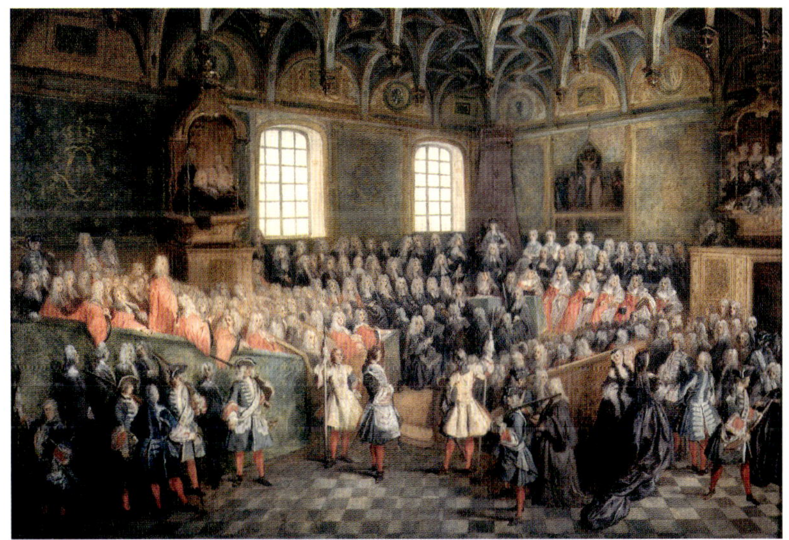

Nicolas Lancret
(Paris 1690 - 1743)

Meeting of the Parliament on 22nd February 1723 on the occasion of Louis XV attaining his legal majority
Feierliche Parlamentssitzung anlässlich der Volljährigkeit Ludwig XV (22. Februar 1723)
Koninklijke zetel van het Parlement voor de verklaring van meerderjarigheid van Lodewijk XV (22 februari 1723)

●

c. 1723
56 x 81 cm / 22.04 x 31.9
Musée du Louvre, Paris

Oil on canvas / Öl auf Leinwand
Olieverf op doek

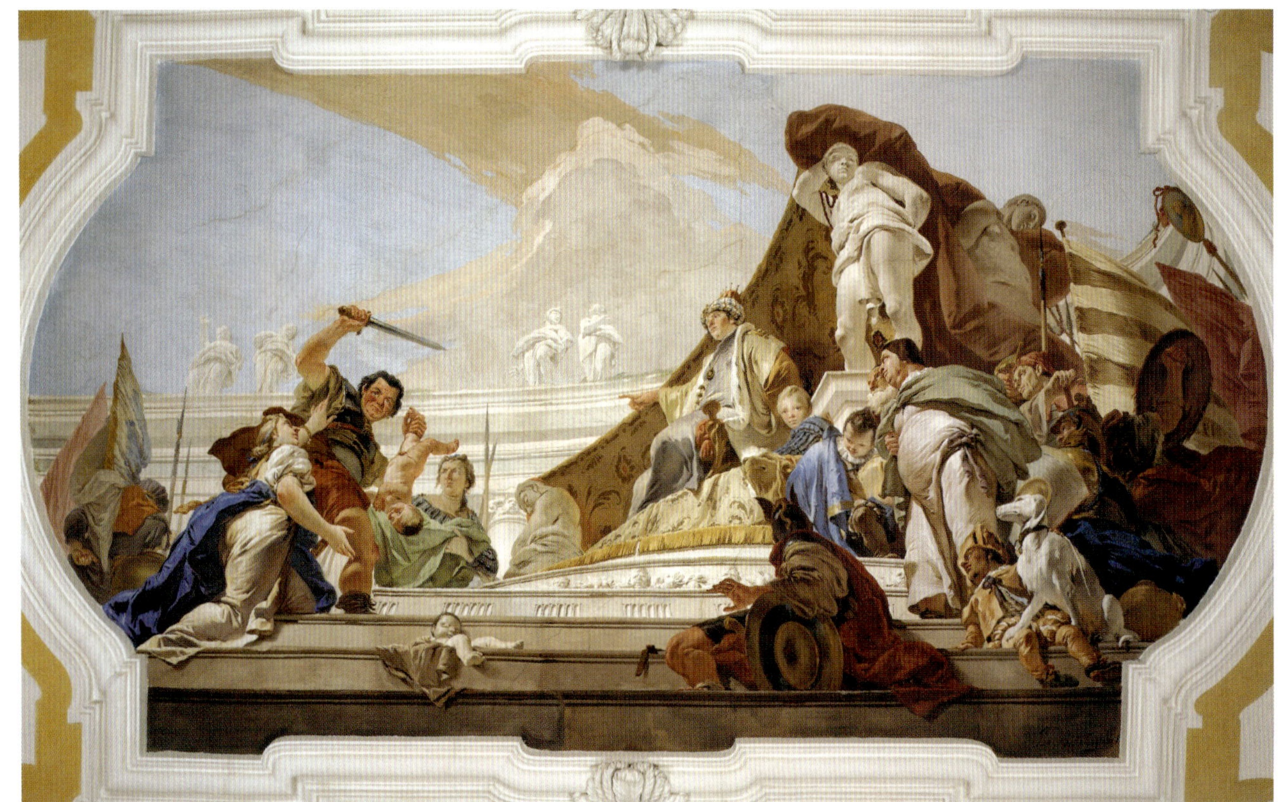

Giambattista Tiepolo
(Zianigo 1696 - Madrid 1770)

Judgement of Solomon
Urteil des Salomon
Oordeel van Salomo

●

c. 1726-1728
Palazzo Arcivescovile, Udine

Fresco / Fresko

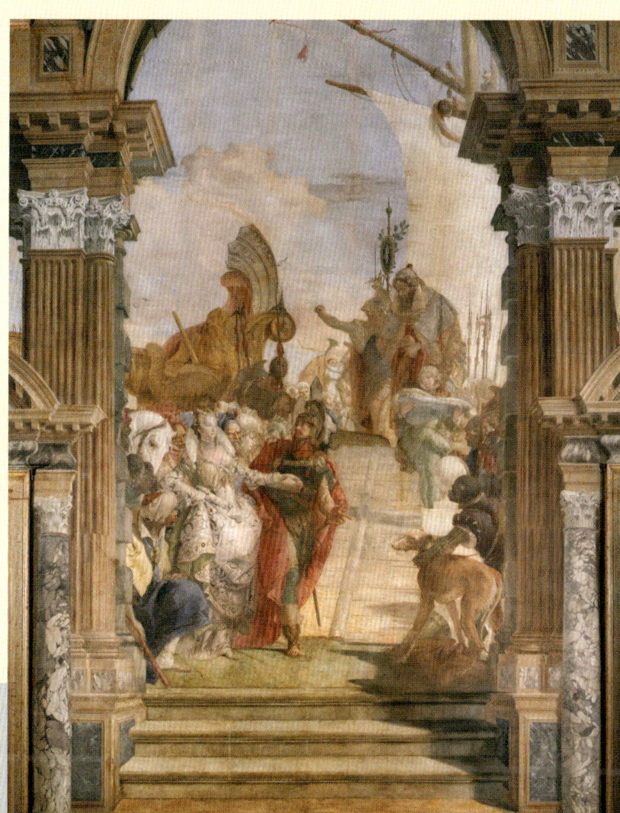

Giambattista Tiepolo
(Zianigo 1696 - Madrid 1770)

Meeting of Anthony and Cleopatra
Die Begegnung von Antonius und Kleopatra
De ontmoeting tussen Antonius en Cleopatra

●●●

1746-1747
Palazzo Labia, Venezia

Fresco / Fresko

Giambattista Tiepolo
(Zianigo 1696 - Madrid 1770)

The Investiture of Herold
Einkleidung des Bischofs Aroldo
Inhuldiging van de bisschop Aroldo

●●

1750-1752
Kaisersaal
Würzburger Residenz, Würzburg

Fresco / Fresko

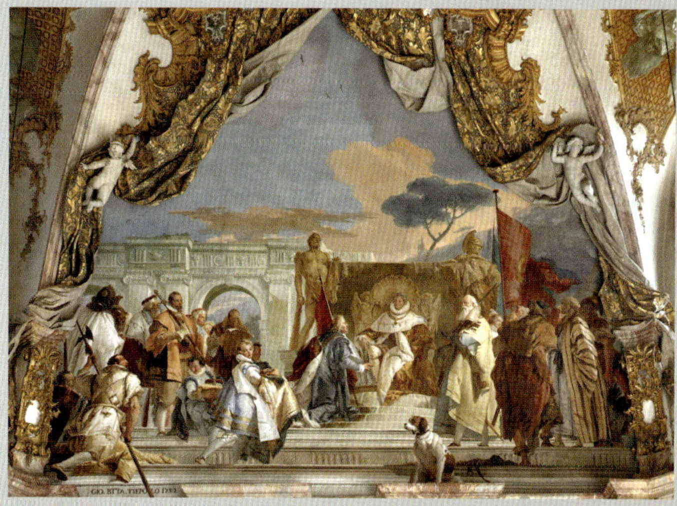

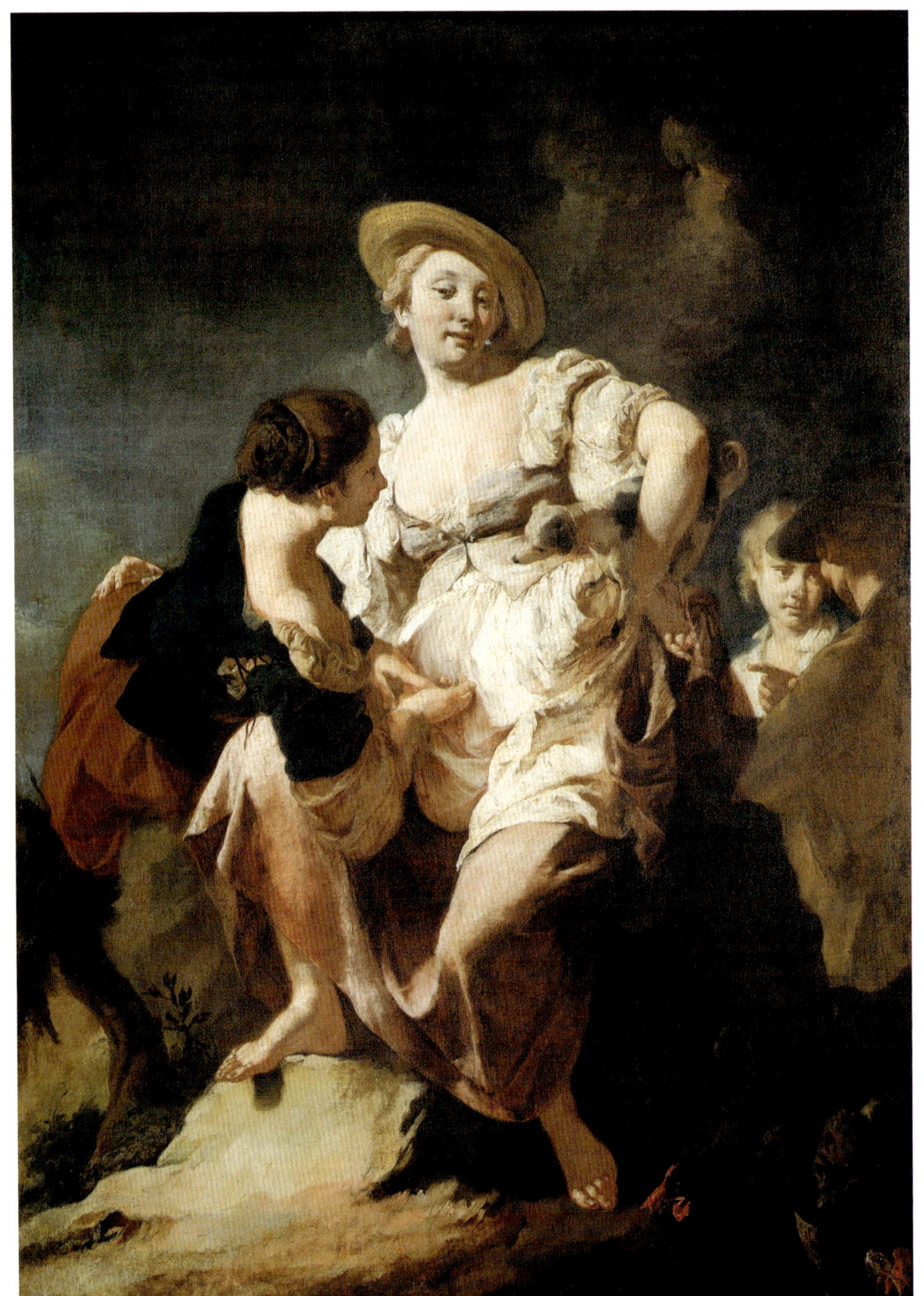

Giovan Battista Piazzetta
(Venezia 1683 - 1754)

The Soothsayer
Die Wahrsagerin
De waarzegster

●●

c. 1740
154 x 114 cm / 60.68 x 44.92 in.
Gallerie dell'Accademia, Venezia

Oil on canvas / Öl auf Leinwand
Olieverf op doek

Giandomenico Tiepolo
(Zianigo 1727 - Venezia 1804)

A Dance in the Country
Tanz auf dem Lande
Een dans op het platteland

●

c. 1755
76 x 120 cm / 29.94 x 47.28 in.
Metropolitan Museum of Art, New York

Oil on canvas / Öl auf Leinwand
Olieverf op doek

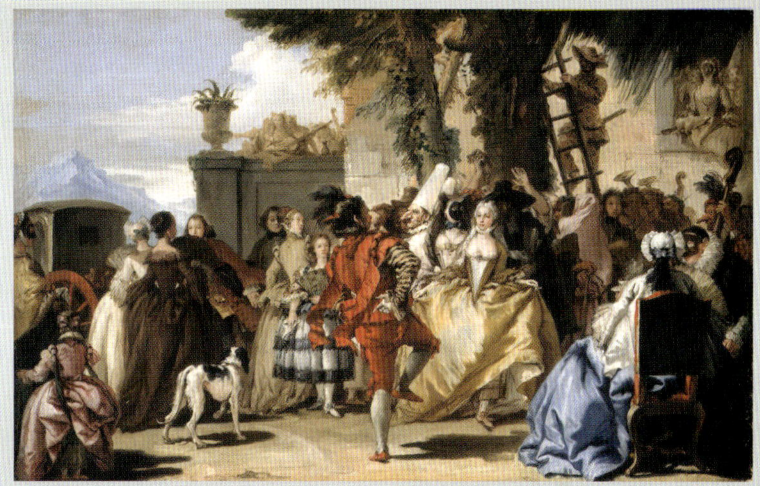

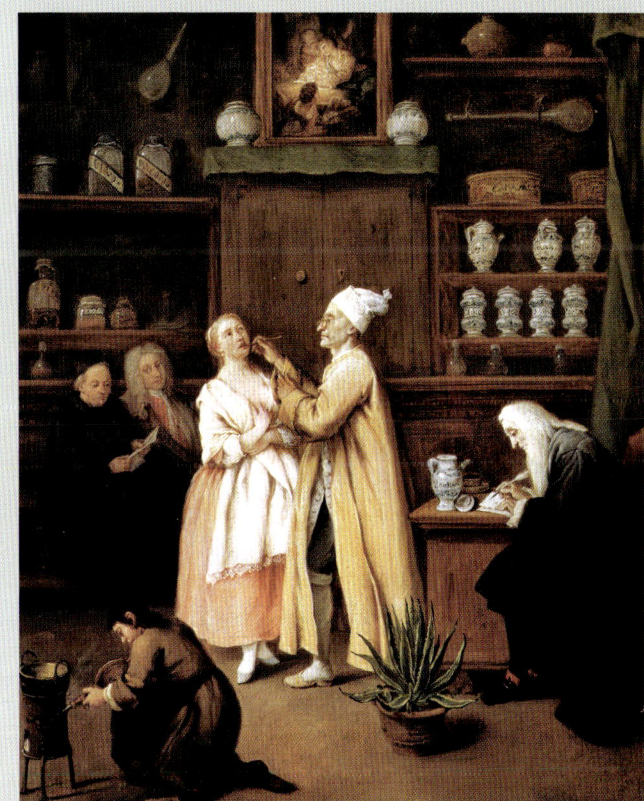

Pietro Longhi
(Venezia 1701 - 1785)

The Pharmacist
Der Apotheker
De apotheker

●●●

c. 1752
60 x 48 cm / 23.64 x 18.91 in.
Gallerie dell'Accademia, Venezia

Oil on canvas / Öl auf Leinwand
Olieverf op doek

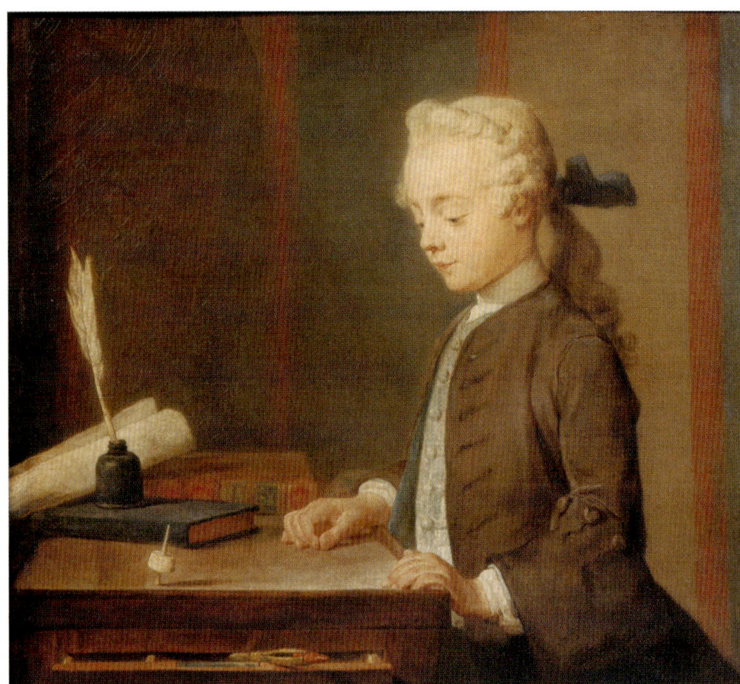

Jean-Baptiste
Siméon Chardin
(Paris 1699 - 1779)

Boy with a Top
Der Knabe mit dem Kreisel
Jongen met tol

●●

c. 1735
67 x 76 cm / 26.4 x 29.94 in.
Musée du Louvre, Paris

Oil on canvas / Öl auf Leinwand
Olieverf op doek

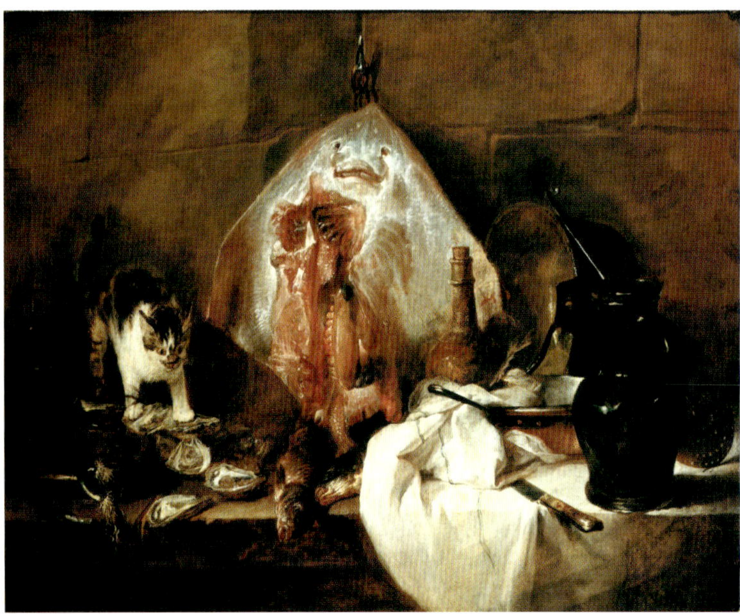

Jean-Baptiste
Siméon Chardin
(Paris 1699 - 1779)

The Skate
Der Rochen
De rog

●●

1725-1726
114 x 146 cm / 44.88 x 57,48 in.
Musée du Louvre, Paris

Oil on canvas / Öl auf Leinwand
Olieverf op doek

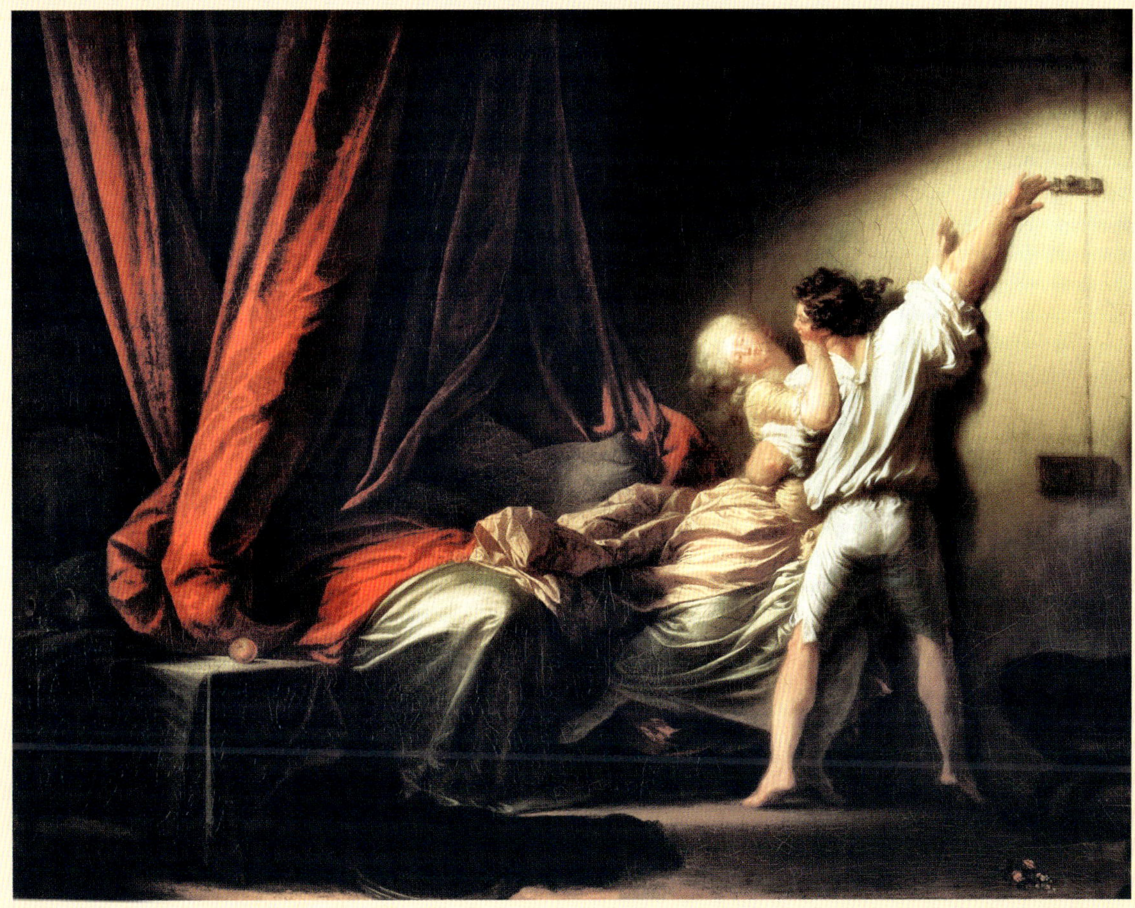

289

Jean-Honoré Fragonard
(Grasse 1732 - Paris 1806)

The Bolt
Der Riegel
De grendel

●●

c. 1775-1777
74 x 94 cm / 29.13 x 37.01 in.
Musée du Louvre, Paris

Oil on wood / Öl auf Tafel
Olieverf op paneel

Chercher l'Amour: stunning tableaus of amorous trysts.

Chercher l'Amour. Galanterien werden effektvoll in Szene gesetzt.

Chercher l'Amour. Effectvol geënsceneerde galanterieën.

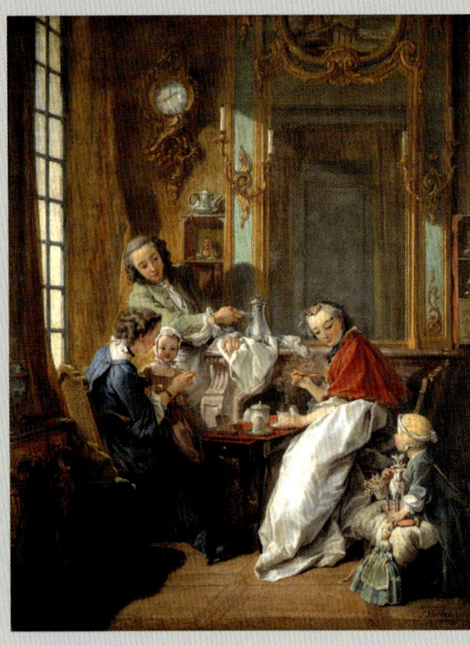

François Boucher
(Paris 1703 - 1770)

Morning Coffee
Das Frühstück
De lunch

●●

1739
81 x 65 cm / 31.91 x 25.61 in.
Musée du Louvre, Paris

Oil on canvas / Öl auf Leinwand
Olieverf op doek

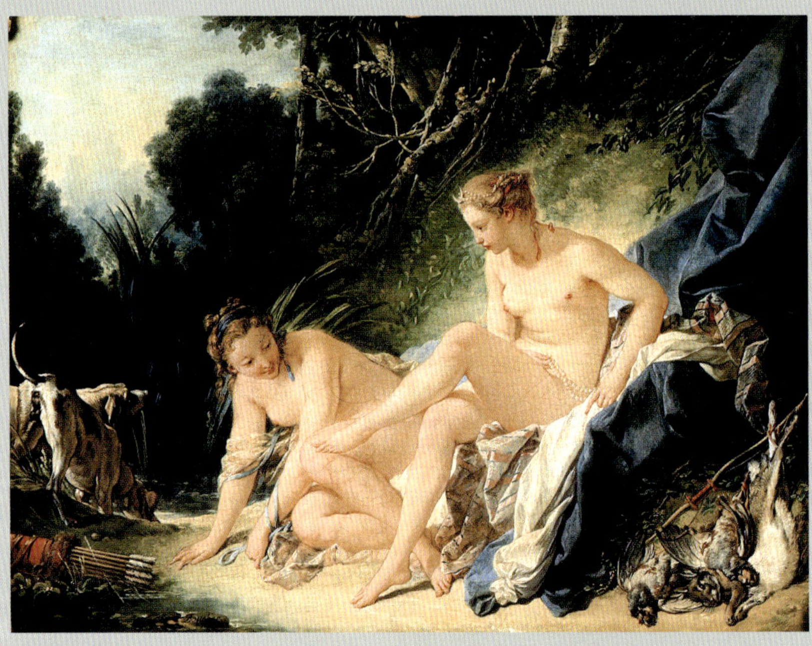

François Boucher
(Paris 1703 - 1770)

Diana Leaving Her Bath
Diana im Bade
Badende Diana

●●●

1742
56 x 73 cm / 22 x 28.7 in.
Musée du Louvre, Paris

Oil on canvas / Öl auf Leinwand
Olieverf op doek

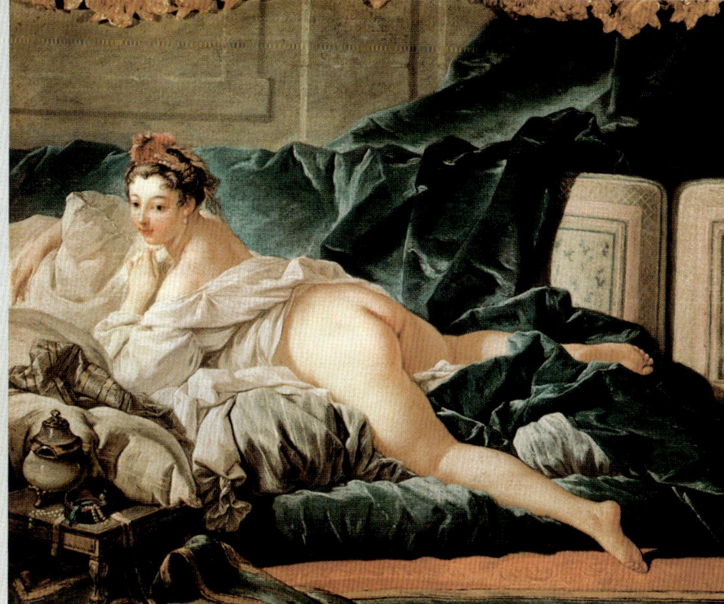

François Boucher
(Paris 1703 - 1770)

Odalisque
Odaliske
Odalisk

●

1745
53 x 64 cm / 20.87 x 25.20 in.
Musée du Louvre, Paris

Oil on canvas / Öl auf Leinwand
Olieverf op doek

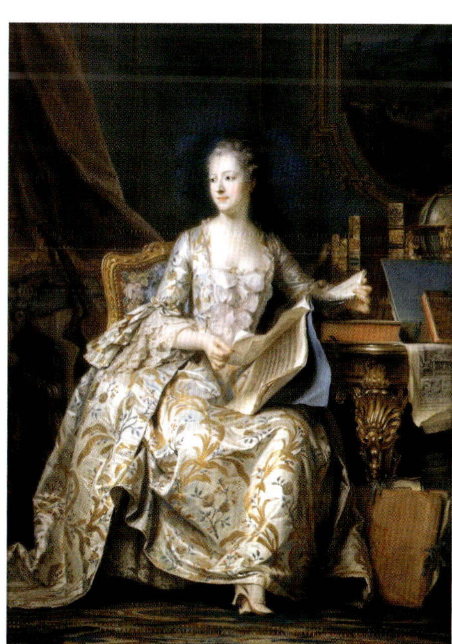

Maurice Quentin de La Tour
(Saint Quentin 1704 - 1788)

Madame de Pompadour

●

1755
175 x 128 cm /
68.95 x 50.43 in.
Musée du Louvre, Paris

Oil on canvas / Öl auf Leinwand
Olieverf op doek

Thomas Gainsborough. A precursor of Impressionism?

Thomas Gainsborough. Vorläufer des Impressionismus?

Thomas Gainsborough. Voorloper van het impressionisme?

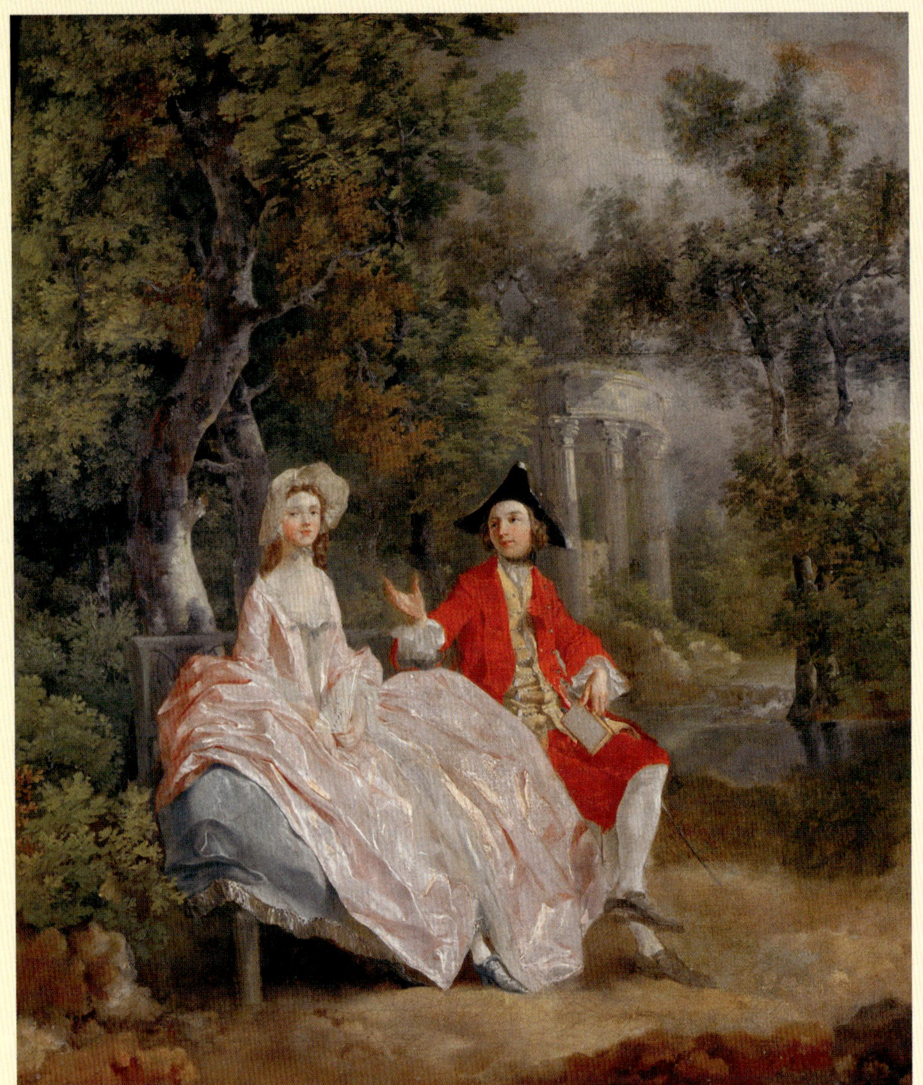

Thomas Gainsborough
(Sudbury 1727 - London 1788)

Conversation in the Park
Plauderei im Park
Conversatie in een park

●●

c. 1746
73 x 67 cm / 28.76 x 26.4 in.
Musée du Louvre, Paris

Oil on canvas / Öl auf Leinwand
Olieverf op doek

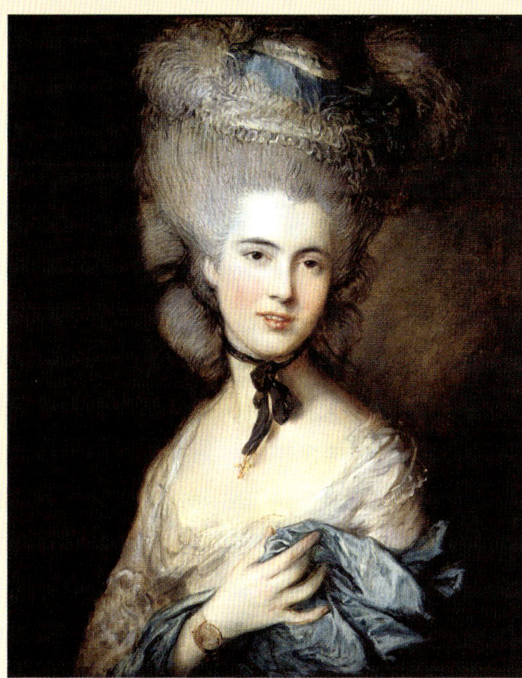

Thomas Gainsborough
(Sudbury 1727 - London 1788)

Woman in Blue (Portrait of the Duchess of Beaufort)
Bildnis der Herzogin Beaufort
Portret van de hertogin van Beaufort

●●●

1775-1780
76 x 65 cm / 29.92 x 25.59 in.
The State Hermitage Museum, St. Petersburg

Oil on canvas / Öl auf Leinwand / Olieverf op doek

Joshua Reynolds
(Plympton 1723 - London 1792)

George Clive and His Family with an Indian Maid
George Clive und seine Familie mit Kindermädchen
George Clive en zijn gezin met een Indiaanse bediende

●

1765
171 x 140 cm / 67.37 x 55.16 in.
Gemäldegalerie, Staatliche Museen, Berlin

Oil on canvas / Öl auf Leinwand / Olieverf op doek

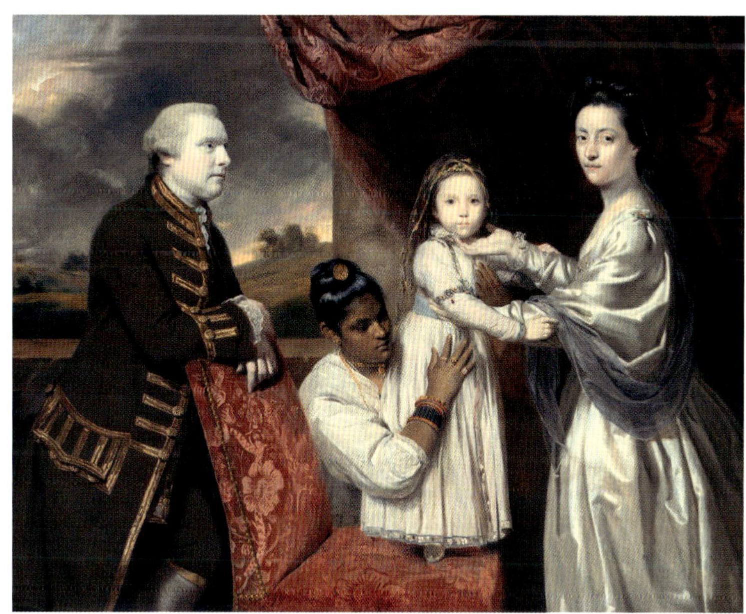

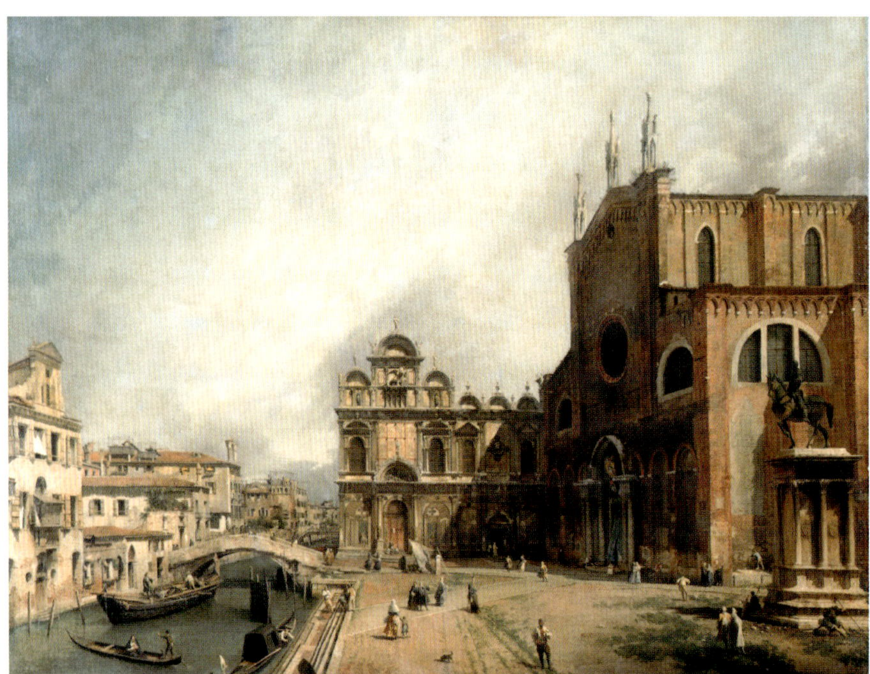

Canaletto
(Venezia 1697 - 1768)

Campo Santi Giovanni e Paolo in Venezia
Campo Santi Giovanni e Paolo in Venedig
Campo Santi Giovanni e Paolo te Venetië

●

c. 1725
125 x 165 cm / 49.25 x 65.01 in.
Gemäldegalerie Alte Meister, Staatliche Kunstsammlungen, Dresden

Oil on canvas / Öl auf Leinwand
Olieverf op doek

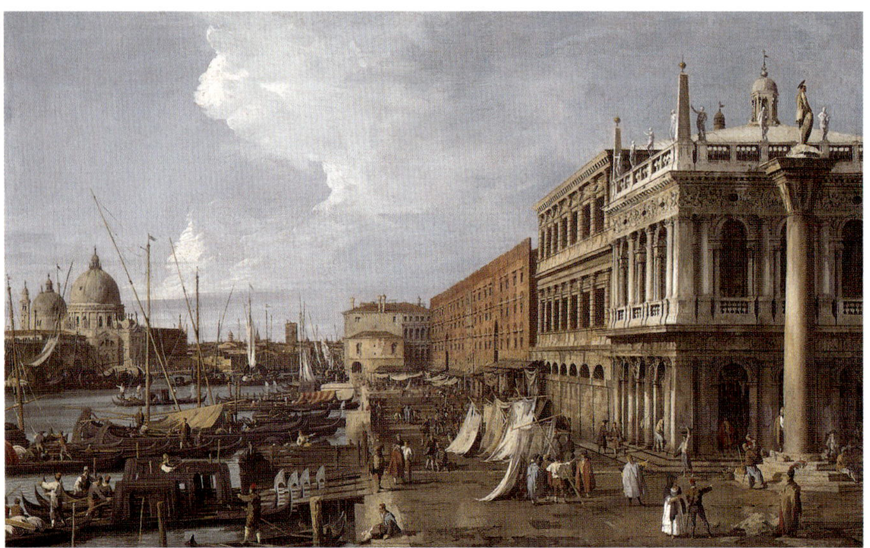

Canaletto
(Venezia 1697 - 1768)

The Pier in Venice
Die Mole, Venedig
De Molo, Venetië

●●

c. 1735
62 x 101 cm / 24.43 x 39.79 in.
Kimbell Art Museum, Fort Worth

Oil on canvas / Öl auf Leinwand
Olieverf op doek

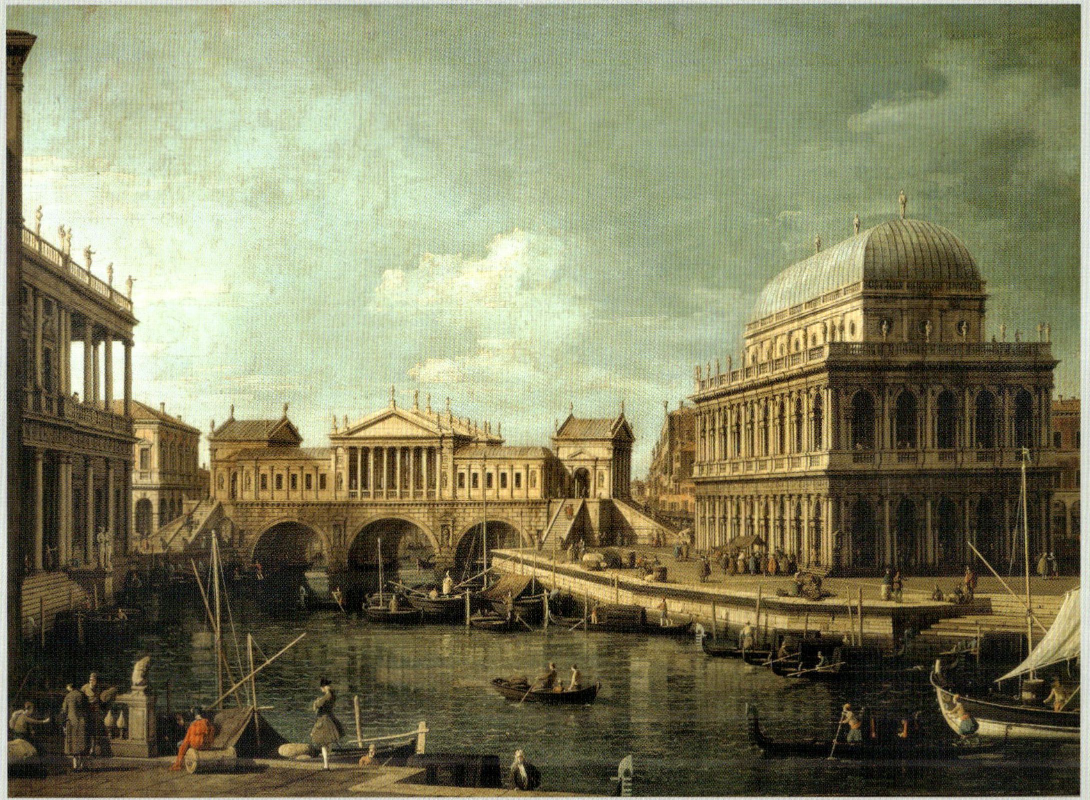

Canaletto
(Venezia 1697 - 1768)

Capriccio Palladiano
Capriccio mit Palladio Gebäuden
Capriccio met Palladiaans gebouw

c. 1759
59 x 79 cm / 23.25 x 31.13 in.
Galleria Nazionale, Parma

Oil on canvas / Öl auf Leinwand / Olieverf op doek

Architectural views full of the finest details: Canaletto is already making use of the camera obscura.

Architekturtreue Ansichten bis ins Detail. Canaletto nutzt schon die Camera Obskura, einen innen schwarzen Lochkasten mit transparenter Rückwand.

Tot in detail getrouwe architectonische aanzichten. Canaletto maakt al gebruik van de camera obscura, een zwarte doos met een gat en een transparante achterwand.

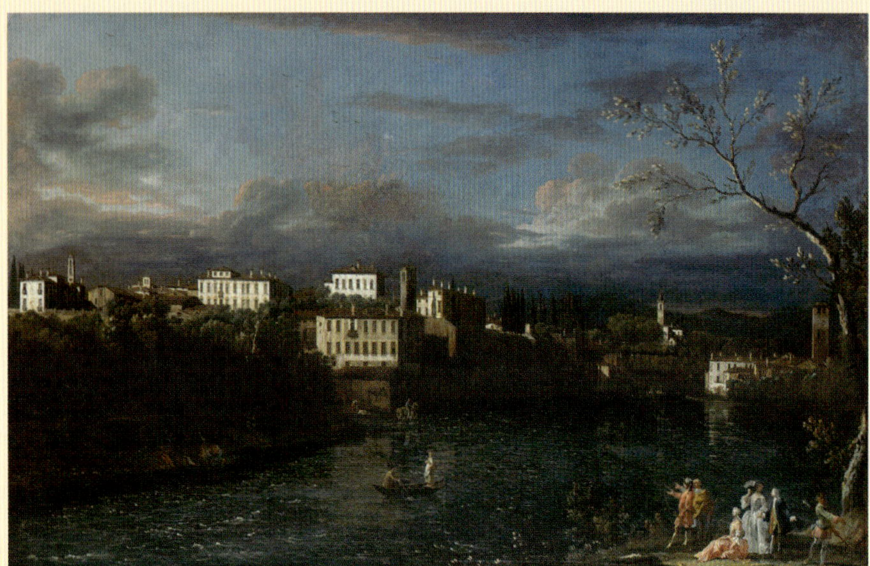

Bernardo Bellotto
(Venezia 1721 - Warszawa 1780)

Vaprio d'Adda

●

1744
64 x 100 cm / 25.22 x 39.4 in.
Metropolitan Museum of Art,
New York

Oil on canvas / Öl auf Leinwand
Olieverf op doek

Luca Carlevarijs
(Udine 1663 - Venezia 1730)

The Pier and the Ducal Palace
Die Mole mit dem Dogenpalast
Het Dogenpaleis aan de Molo

●

c. 1726
70 x 118 cm / 27.58 x 46.49 in.
The State Hermitage Museum,
St. Petersburg

Oil on canvas / Öl auf Leinwand
Olieverf op doek

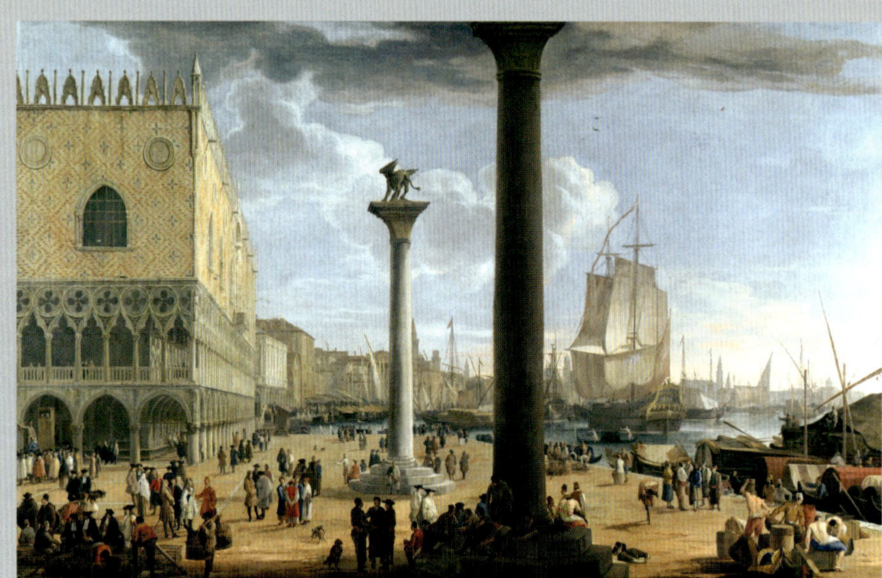

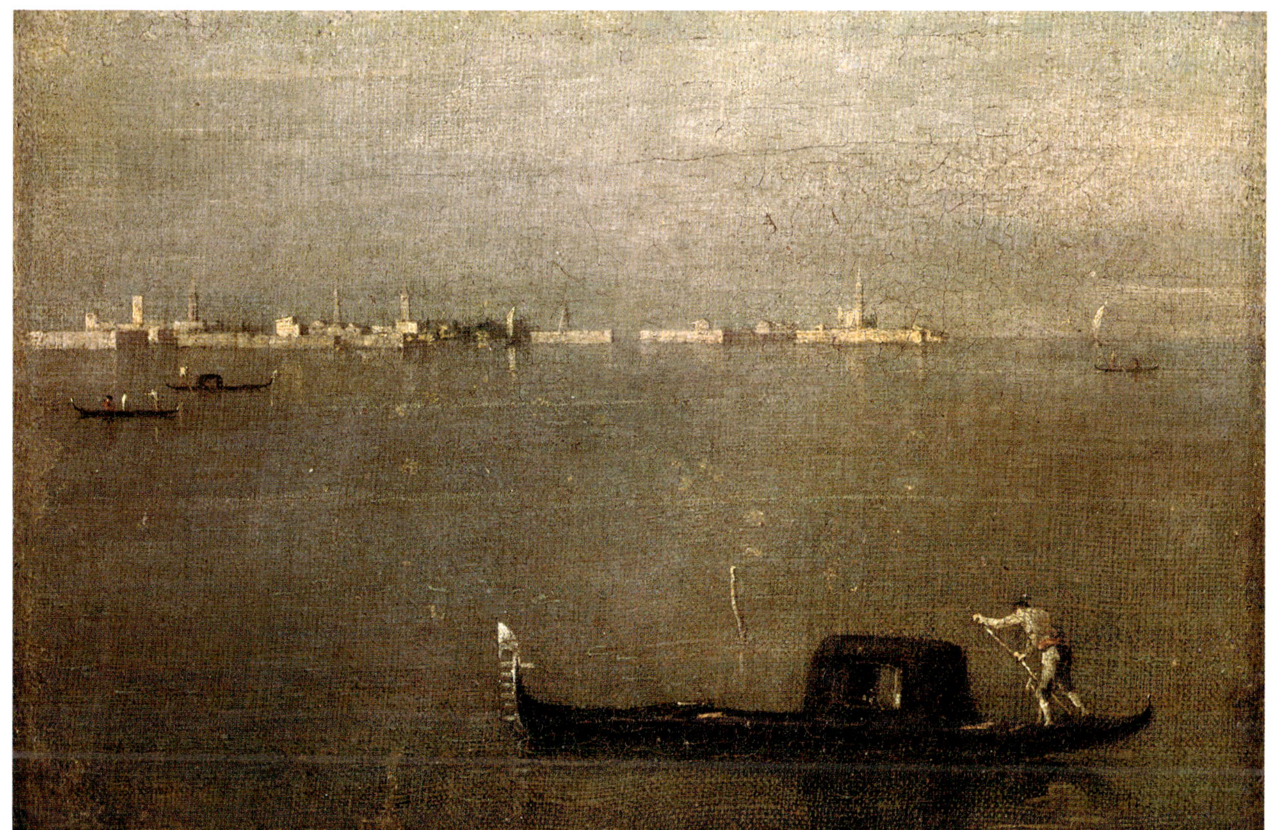

Francesco Guardi
(Venezia 1712 - 1793)

Gondolas on the Lagoon
Die Lagune mit Gondeln
Gondels op de lagune

●●

c. 1780
25 x 38 cm / 9.85 x 14.97 in.
Museo Poldi Pezzoli, Milano

Oil on canvas / Öl auf Leinwand
Olieverf op doek

Landscapes and cityscapes (veduta): travel souvenirs before the discovery of photography.

Landschafts und Stadtansichten (Veduten): Reiseandenken vor der Erfindung der Fotografie.

Landschappen en stadsgezichten: reissouvenirs van voor de uitvinding van de fotografie.

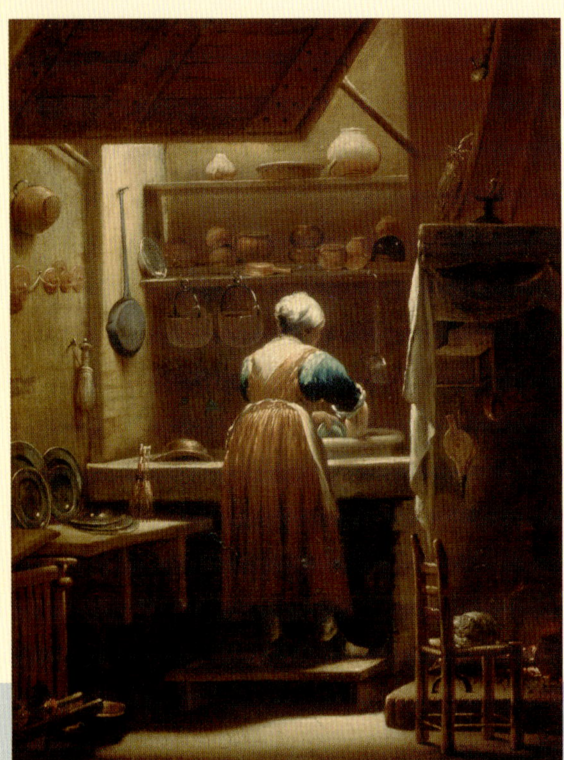

Giuseppe Maria Crespi
(Bologna 1665 - 1747)

The Cook
Die Köchin
De kokkin

●

c. 1725
56 x 44 cm / 22.06 x 17.34 in.
Galleria degli Uffizi, Firenze

Oil on canvas / Öl auf Leinwand
Olieverf op doek

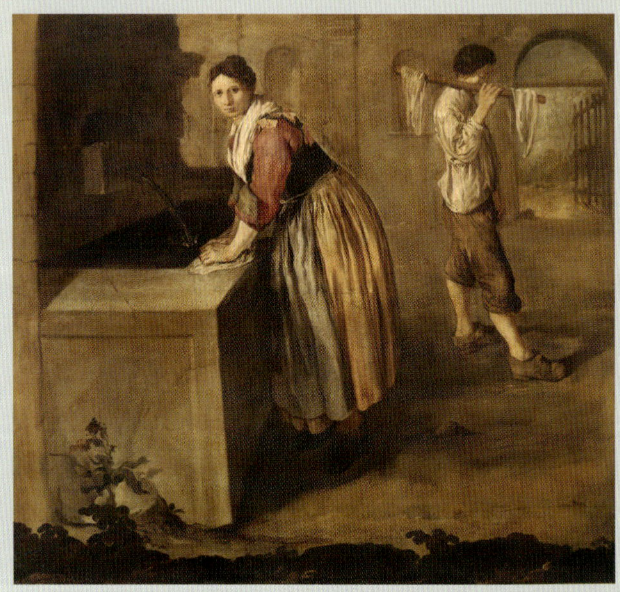

Giacomo Ceruti
(Milano 1698 - 1767)

The Laundress
Die Wäscherin
De wasvrouw

●

c. 1740
131 x 145 cm / 51.61 x 57.13 in.
Pinacoteca Civica Tosio Martinengo, Brescia

Oil on canvas / Öl auf Leinwand
Olieverf op doek

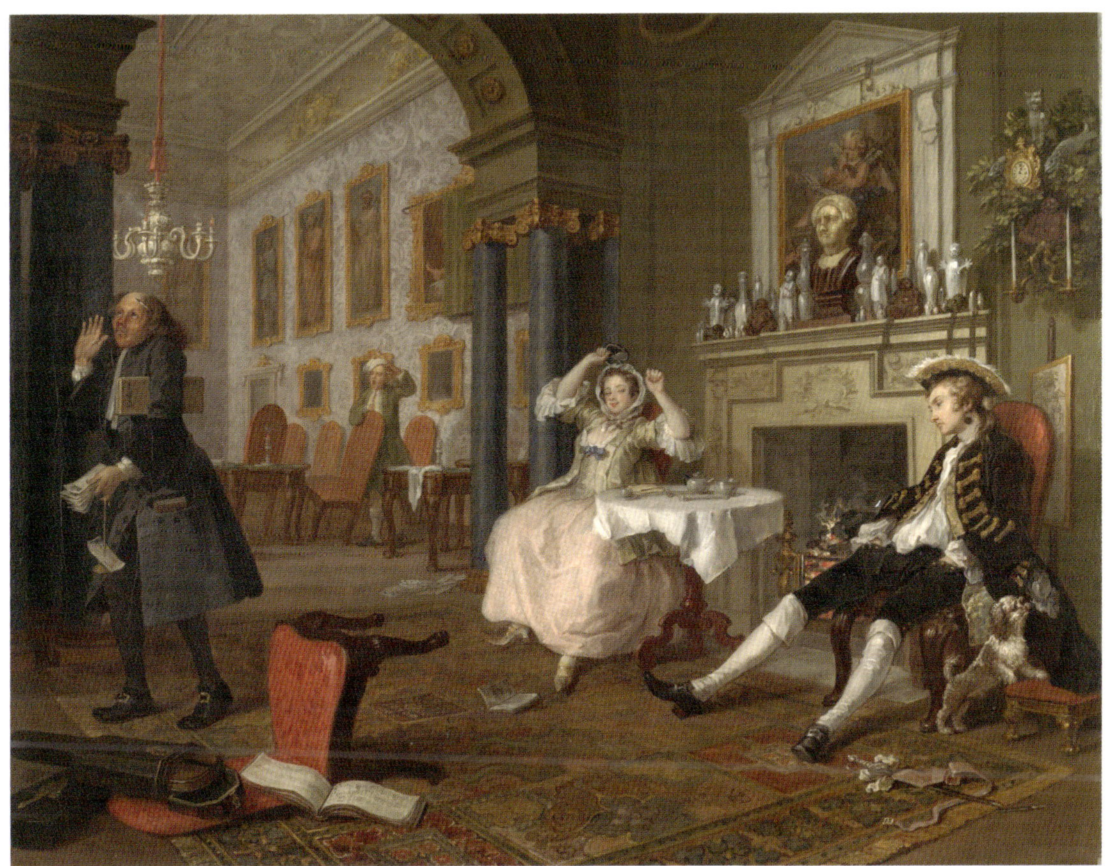

William Hogarth
(London 1697 - 1764)

Marriage A-la-Mode: The 'Tête à Tête'
Moderne Ehe: das Tête-à-Tête
Huwelijk à la mode: de tête-à-tête

●●●

c. 1743
70 x 91 cm / 27.58 x 35.85 in.
National Gallery, London

Oil on canvas / Öl auf Leinwand / Olieverf op doek

300

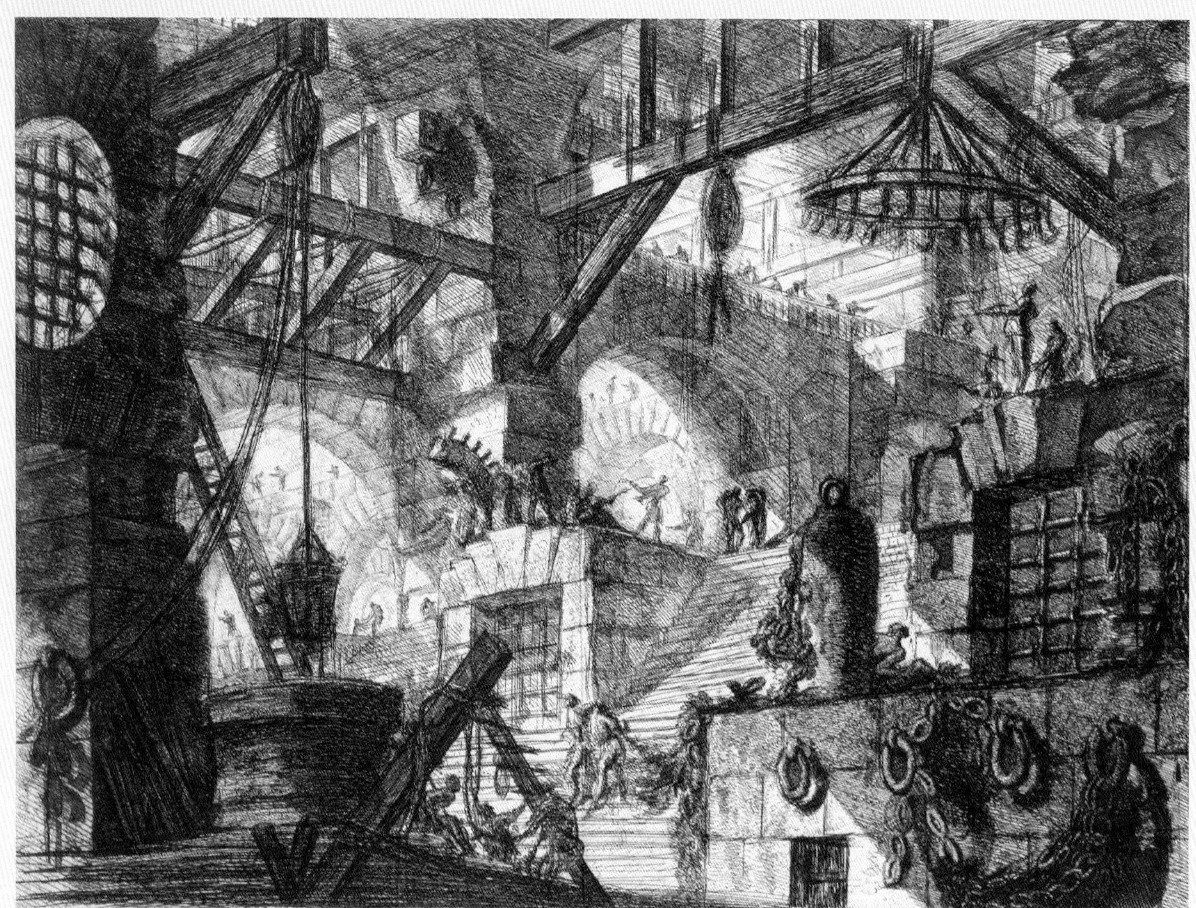

Giovan Battista Piranesi
(Mogliano Veneto 1720 - Roma 1778)

Imaginary Prisons: the Well
Erfundene Kerker: Der Brunnen
Carceri d'invenzione: il pozzo (Imaginaire Kerkers)

●●

1750
Kupferstichkabinett, Staatliche Museen, Berlin

Engraving / Stich / Ets

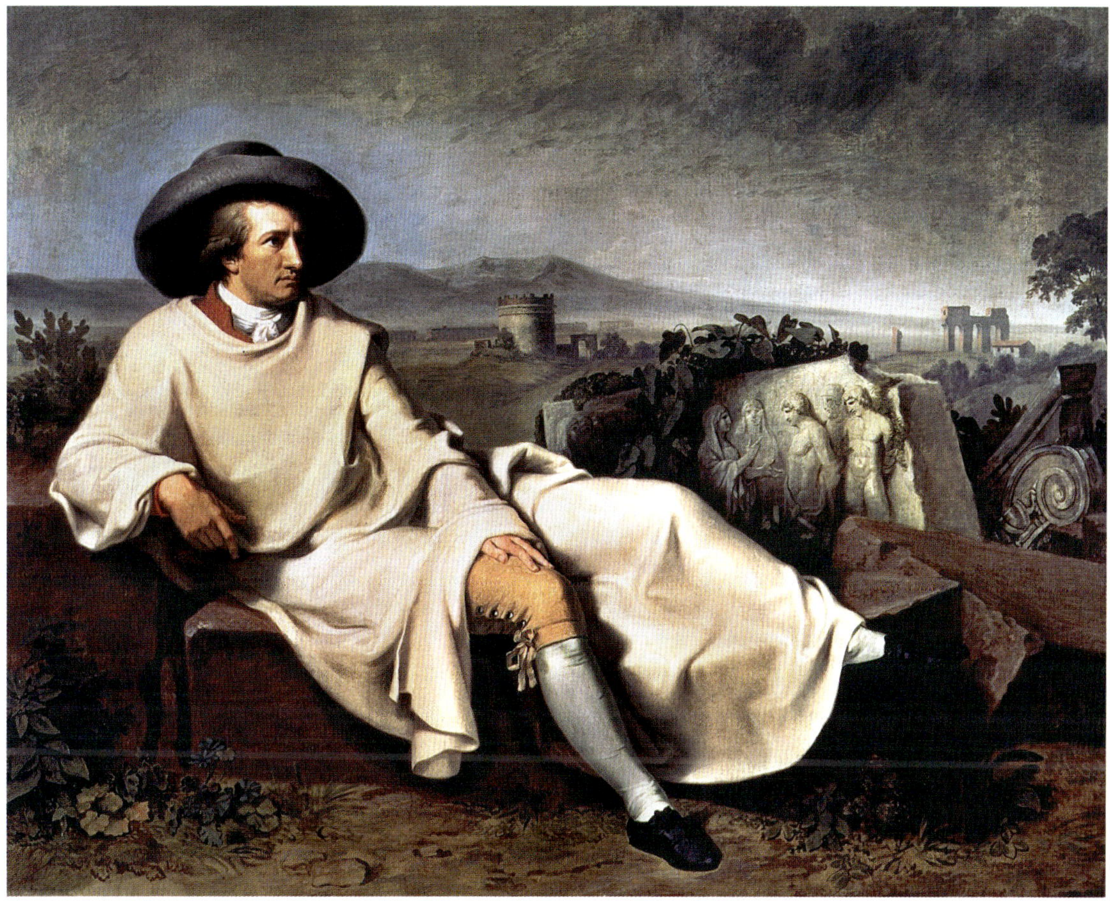

Johann Heinrich Wilhelm Tischbein
(Haina 1751 - Eutin 1829)

Goethe in the Countryside of Rome
Goethe in der römischen Campagna
Goethe in de campagna romana

●●●

c. 1786-1787
164 x 206 cm / 64.62 x 81.16 in.
Städelsches Kunstinstitut, Frankfurt am Main

Oil on canvas / Öl auf Leinwand / Olieverf op doek

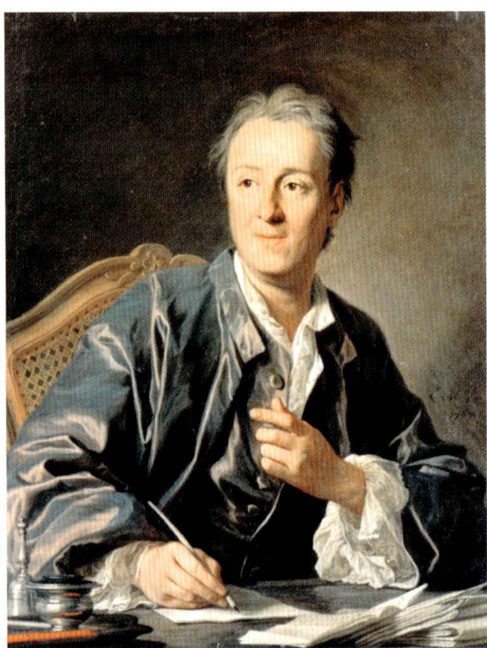

Jean-Baptiste Pigalle
(Paris 1714 - 1785)

Voltaire

●●

1776
h. 150 cm / 59.1 in.
Musée du Louvre, Paris

Marble / Marmor
Marmer

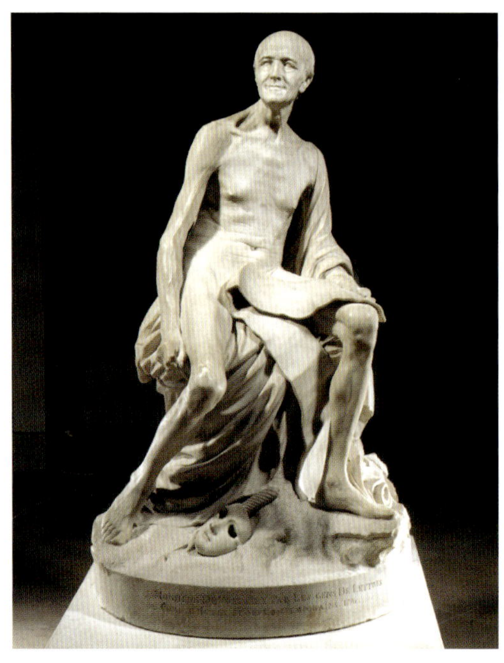

Carle van Loo
(Nice 1705 - Paris 1765)

Portrait of Diderot
Portrait von Diderot
Portret van Diderot

●

1767
65 x 81 cm / 25.61 x 31.91 in.
Musée du Louvre, Paris

Oil on canvas / Öl auf Leinwand
Olieverf op doek

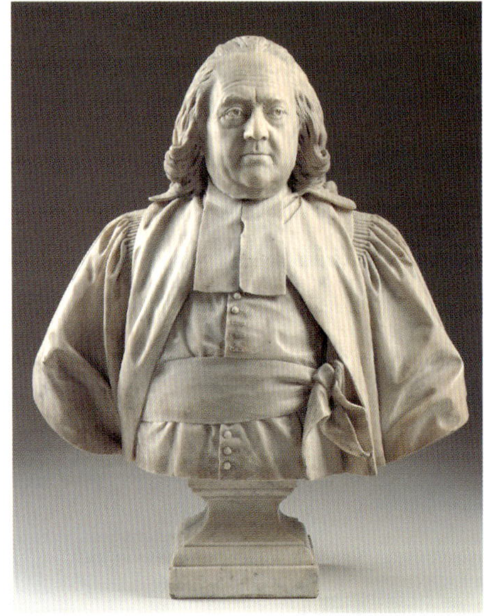

Jean Antoine Houdon
(Versailles 1741 - Paris 1828)

Aymard-Jean de Nicolay

●

1779
h. 60 cm / 23.64 in.
Kimbell Art Museum, Fort Worth

Marble / Marmor / Marmer

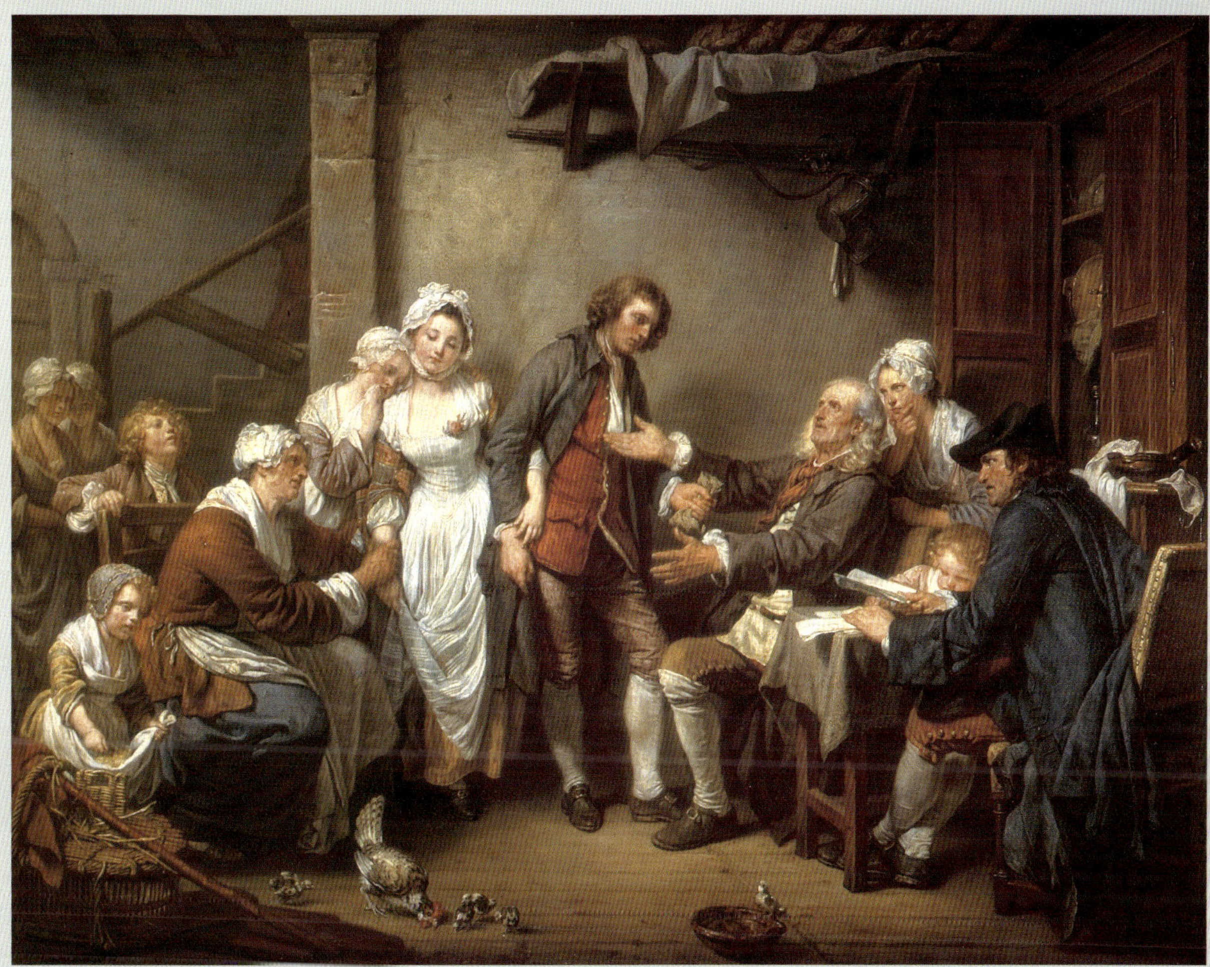

Jean-Baptiste Greuze
(Tournus 1725 - Paris 1805)

The Marriage Contract
Verlobung im Dorfe
De huwelijksakte

●●

1761
92 x 117 cm / 362.2 x 46.06 in.
Musée du Louvre, Paris

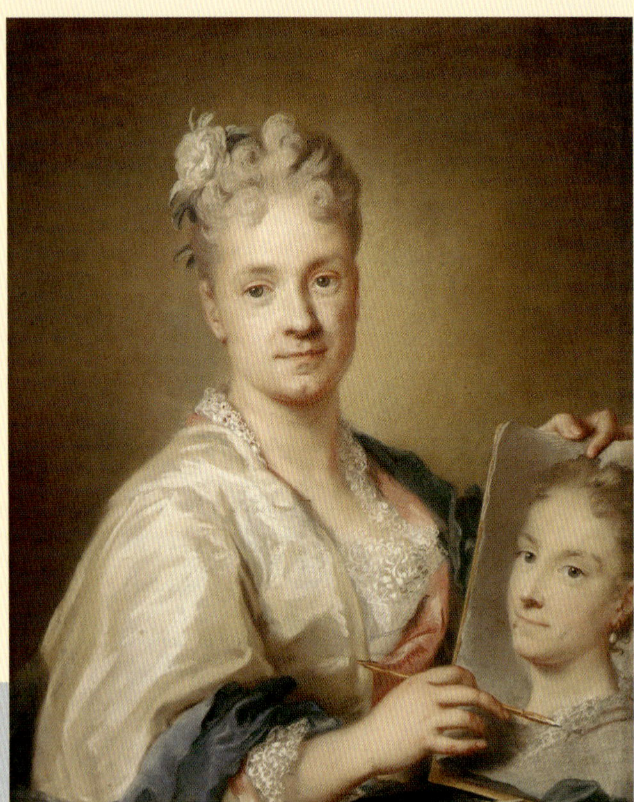

Rosalba Carriera
(Chioggia 1675 - Venezia 1757)

Self-Portrait Holding a Portrait of Her Sister
Selbstbildnis mit dem
Portrait ihrer Schwester
Zelfportret met portret van haar zus

●

1715
Galleria degli Uffizi, Firenze

Oil on canvas / Öl auf Leinwand / Olieverf op doek

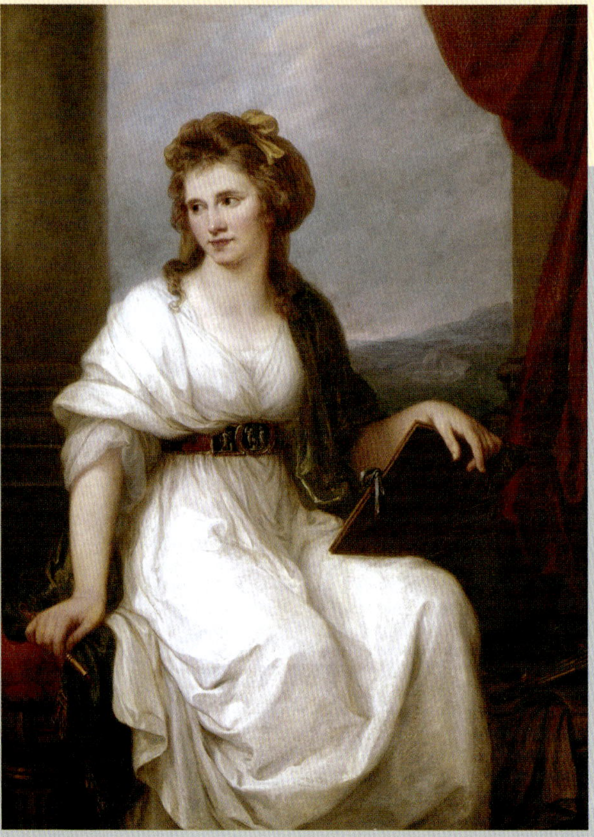

Angelica Kauffmann
(Chur 1741 - Roma 1807)

Self-Portrait
Selbstbildnis
Zelfportret

●

1787
93 x 128 cm / 36.64 x 50.43 in.
Galleria degli Uffizi, Firenze

Oil on canvas
Öl auf Leinwand
Olieverf op doek

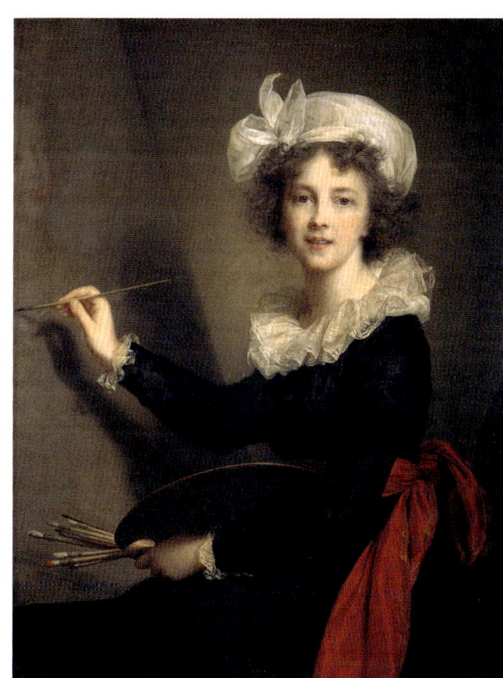

Elisabeth Vigée-Lebrun
(Paris 1755 - 1842)

Self-Portrait
Selbstbildnis
Zelfportret

●●

1790
81 x 100 cm / 31.91 x 39.4 in.
Galleria degli Uffizi, Firenze

Oil on canvas / Öl auf Leinwand
Olieverf op doek

Adélaïde Labille-Guiard
(Paris 1749 - 1803)

Self-portrait with Two Pupils
Selbstbildnis mit zwei Schülerinnen
Zelfportret met twee leerlingen

●

1785
211 x 151 cm / 83.13 x 59.49 in.
Metropolitan Museum of Art, New York

Oil on canvas / Öl auf Leinwand / Olieverf op doek

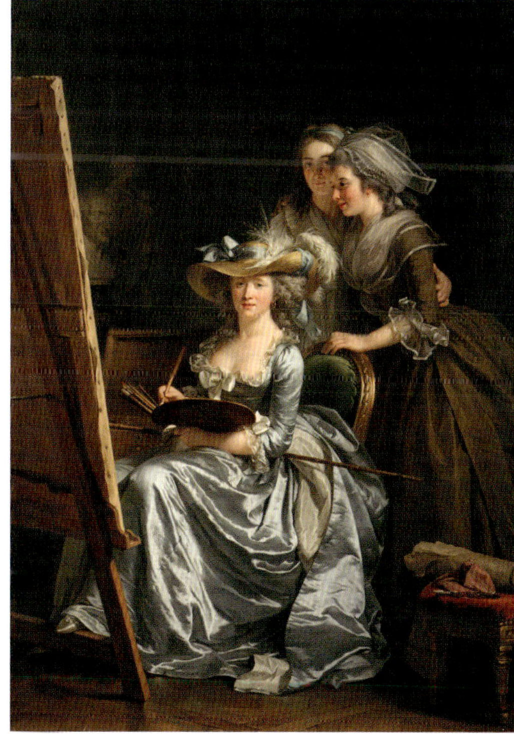

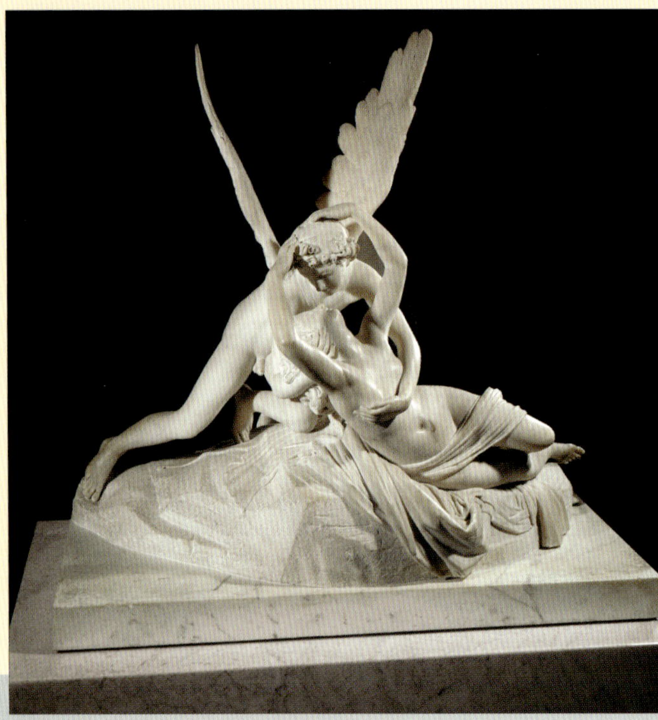

Antonio Canova
(Possagno 1757 - Venezia 1822)

Amor and Psyche
Amor und Psyche
Amor en Psyche

●●●

1787
h. 155 cm / 61.07 in.
Musée du Louvre, Paris

Marble / Marmor / Marmer

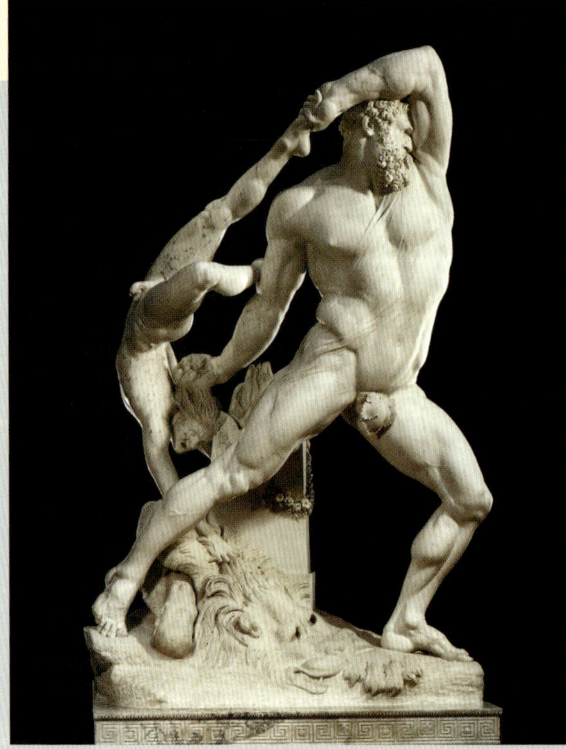

Antonio Canova
(Possagno 1757 - Venezia 1822)

Hercules and Lycus
Herkules und Lichas
Herakles en Lycus

●

1795-1815
h. 335 cm / 131.89 in.
Galleria Nazionale d'Arte Moderna, Roma

Marble / Marmor / Marmer

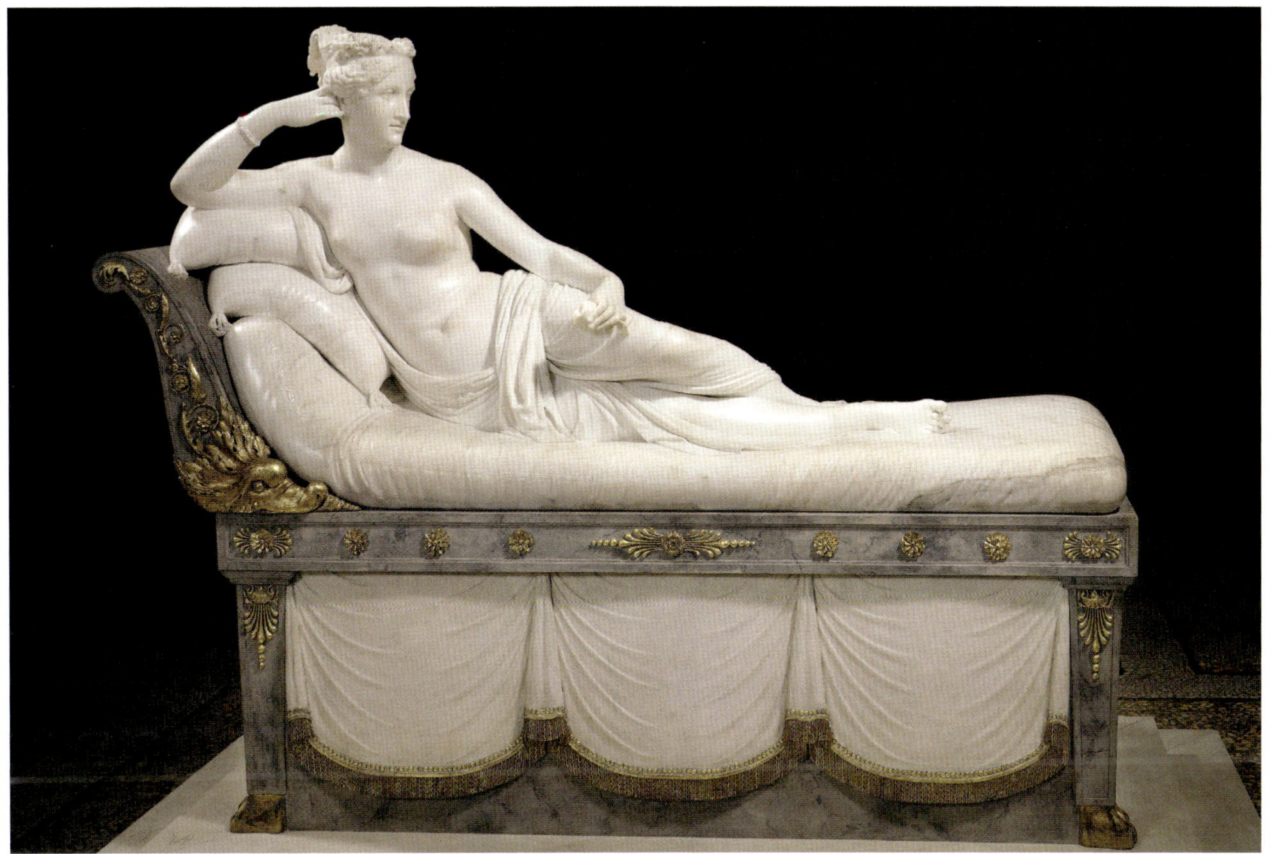

Antonio Canova
(Possagno 1757 - Venezia 1822)

Paolina Borghese

●●●

c. 1805-1808
160 x 192 cm / 63 x 75.6 in.
Galleria Borghese, Roma

Marble / Marmor / Marmer

Antonio Canova: marble modeled delicately according to ancient ideals.

Delikat modellierter Marmor nach antikem Vorbild. Antonio Canova.

Fijn gemodelleerd marmer naar voorbeeld van het klassieke ideaal. Antonio Canova.

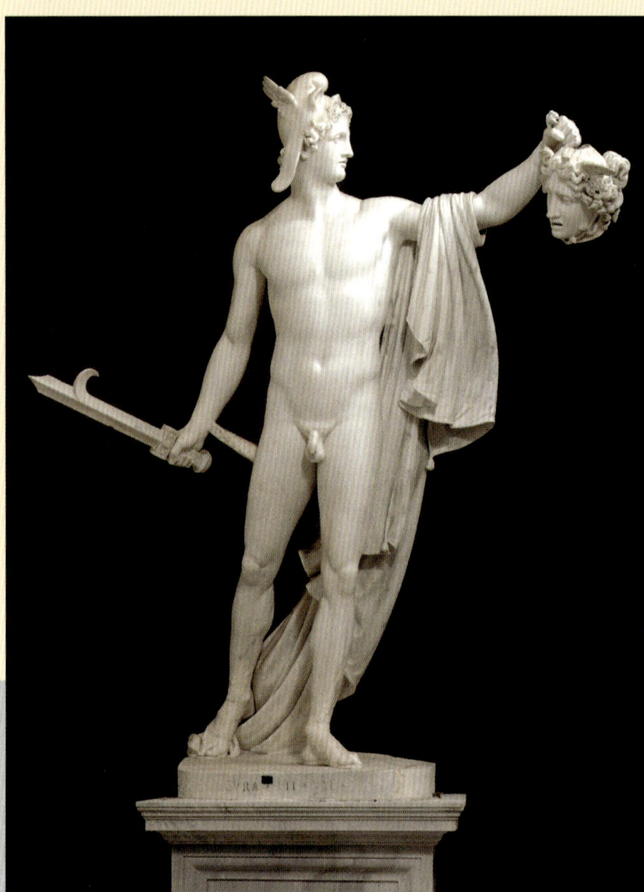

Antonio Canova
(Possagno 1757 - Venezia 1822)

Perseus with the Head of Medusa
Perseus mit dem Haupte der Medusa
Perseus met het hoofd van Medusa

●●

1797-1801
h. 235 cm / 92.52 in.
Museo Pio-Clementino, Città del Vaticano

Marble / Marmor / Marmer

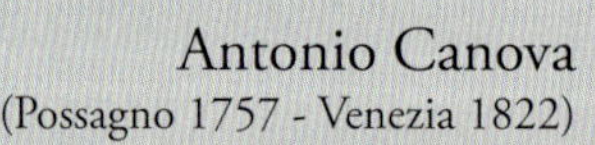

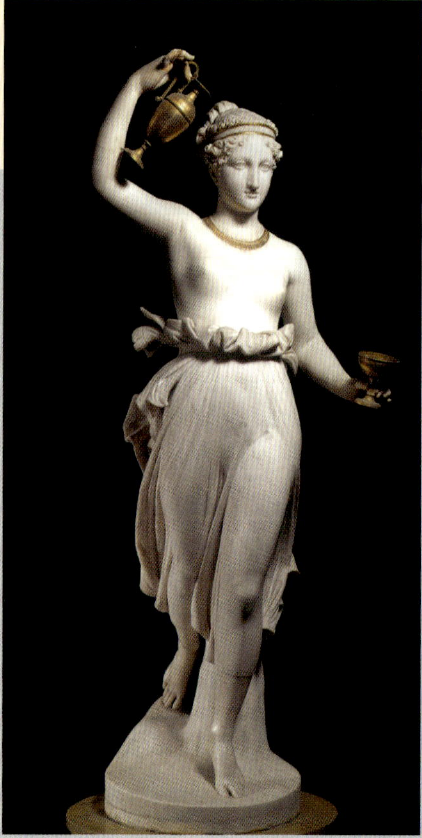

Antonio Canova
(Possagno 1757 - Venezia 1822)

Ebe
Hebe

●●

1816-1817
h. 158 cm / 62.20 in.
Pinacoteca Comunale, Forlì

Marble and gilded bronze / Marmor und vergoldete Bronze / Marmer en verguld brons

Antonio Canova
(Possagno 1757 - Venezia 1822)

The Three Graces
Die Drei Grazien
De drie gratiën

●●●

c. 1814-1817
h. 173 cm / 68.1 in.
Victoria and Albert Museum, London

Marble / Marmor / Marmer

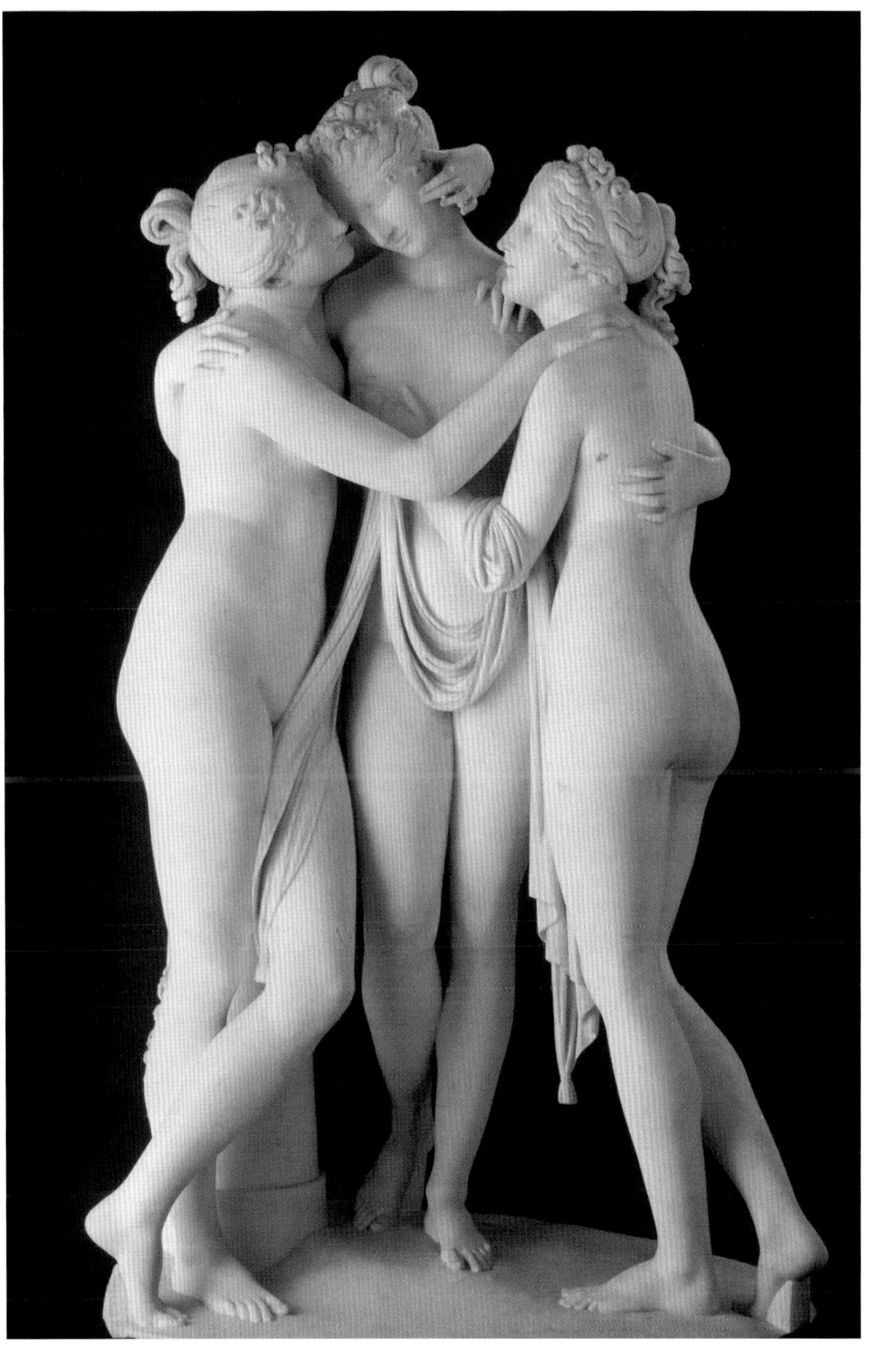

Purity, beauty, delicacy: Thorvaldsen brings Neo-Classicism to northern Europe.

Reinheit, Schönheit, Zartheit. Mit Thorvaldsen erreicht der Klassizismus Nordeuropa.

Zuiverheid, schoonheid, delicaatheid. Met Thorvaldsen arriveert het neoclassicisme in Noord-Europa

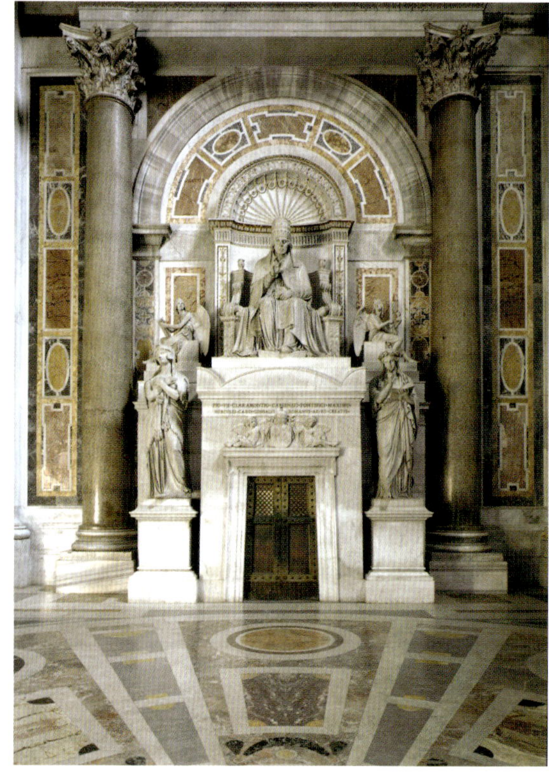

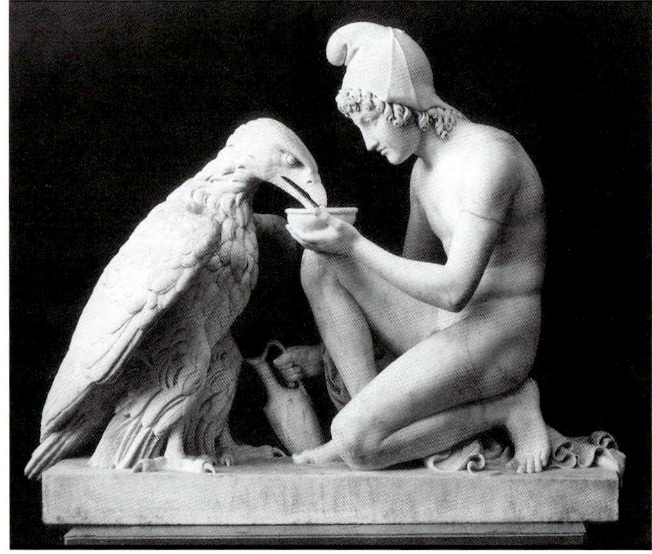

Bertel Thorvaldsen
(Copenhagen 1770 - 1844)

Ganymede and the Eagle
Ganymed mit Jupiters Adler
Ganymedes en de adelaar

●●

1817
89.6 x 119.3 cm / 35.3 x 47 in.
Museum der bildenden Künste, Leipzig

Marble / Marmor / Marmer

◂ Bertel Thorvaldsen
(Copenhagen 1770 - 1844)

Tomb of Pope Pius VII
Grabmal von Papst Pius VII
Tombe van paus Pius VII

●

1825 - 1831
Basilica di San Pietro,
Città del Vaticano

Marble / Marmor / Marmer

Emil Wolff
(Berlin 1802 - Roma 1879)

Nereid
Nereide
Nereïde

●

1840
h. 1.24 m / 48.86 in.
Nationalgalerie, Staatliche Museen, Berlin

Marble / Marmor / Marmer

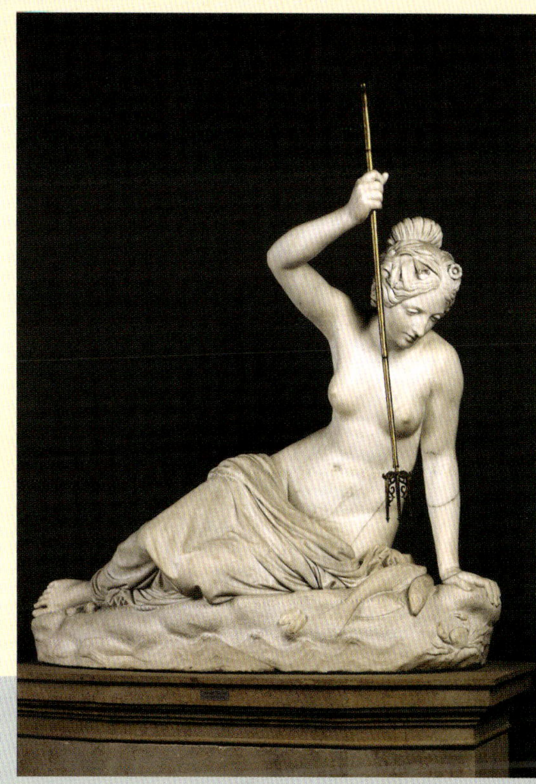

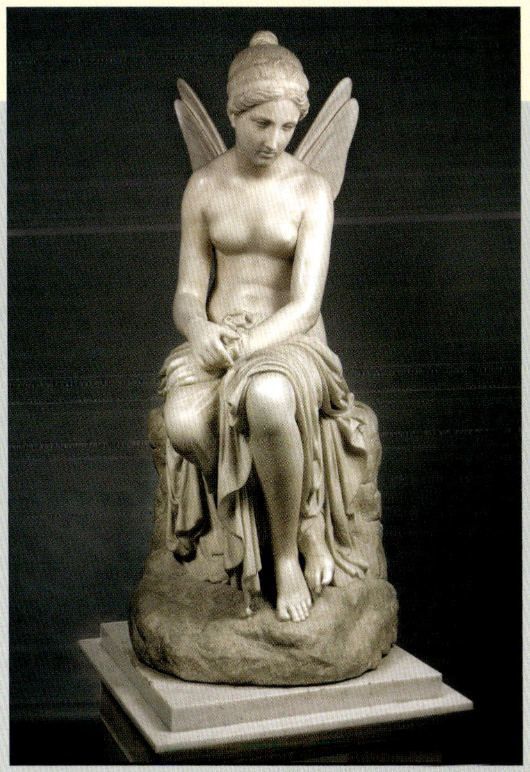

Pietro Tenerani
(Carrara 1789 - Roma 1869)

Psyche Abandoned
Verlassene Psyche
Achtergelaten Psyche

●

c. 1818
Galleria d'Arte Moderna, Firenze

Marble / Marmor / Marmer

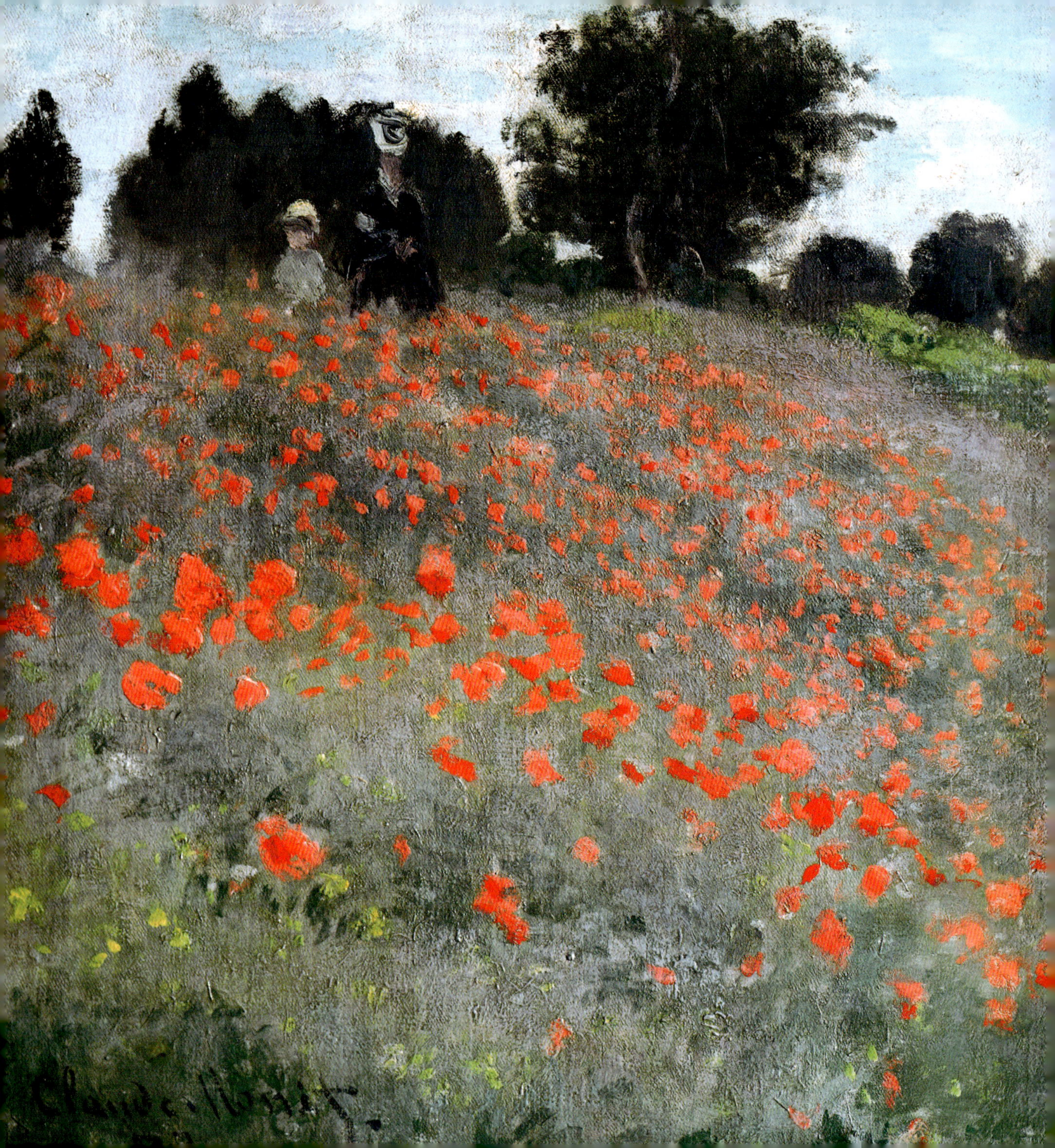

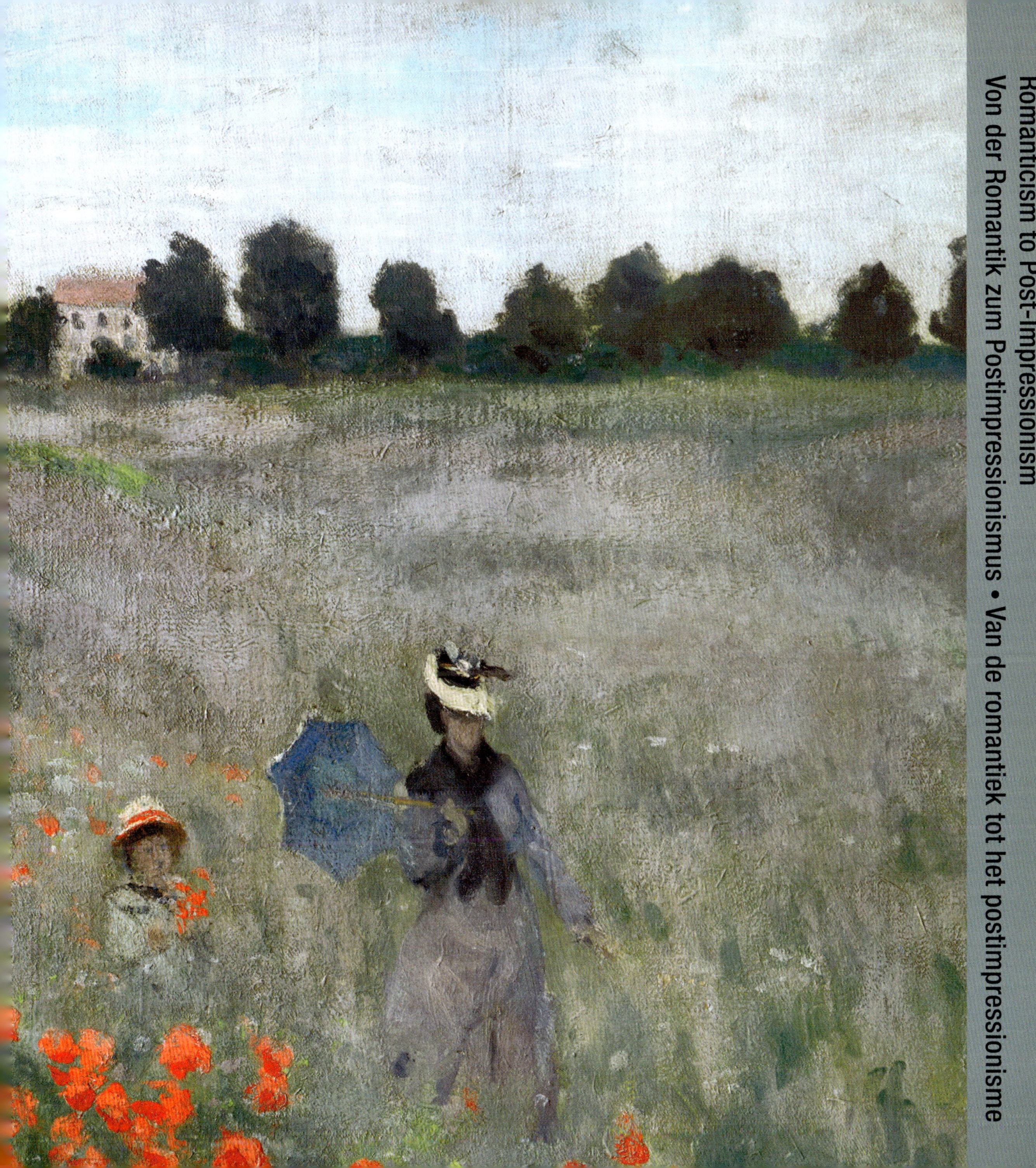

Romanticism to Post-Impressionism

Von der Romantik zum Postimpressionismus • Van de romantiek tot het postimpressionisme

Diversity of style
Vielfalt der Stile
Een veelvoud aan stijlen

GREAT BRITAIN

William Blake (London 1757 - 1827)
Joseph Turner (London 1775 - 1851)
John Constable (East Berghol 1776 - London 1837)
William Holam Hunt (London 1827 - 1910)
Dante Gabriele Rossetti (London 1828 - Birchington 1882)
John Everett Millais (Southampton 1829 - London 1896)
Frederick Leighton (Scarborough 1830 - London 1896)
Edward Coley Burne-Jones (Birmingham 1833 - Fulham 1898)
James Abbott Whistler (Lowell 1834 - London 1903)
Alfred Sisley (Paris 1839 - Monet-sur-Loing 1899)
John Singer Sargent (Firenze 1856 - London 1925)

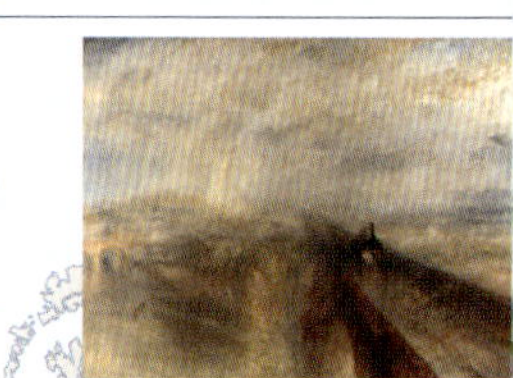

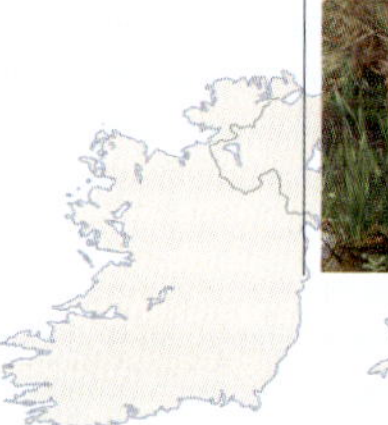

USA

George Catlin (Wilkes-Barres 1796 - New York 1872)
Thomas Cole (Bolton 1801 - Catskill NY 1848)
Frederic Edwin Church (Hartford 1826 - 1900)
Mary Cassat (Allegheny City 1844 - Chat. De Beaufresne 1926)

BELGIQUE

James Ensor (Oostende 1860 - 1949)

FRANCE

Jacques-Louis David (Paris 1748 - Bruxelles 1825)
Pierre-Paul Prud'hon (Cluny 1758 - Paris 1823)
Francois Gérard (Roma 1770 - Paris 1837)
Antoine-Jean Gros (Paris 1771 - 1835)
Jean-Auguste-Dominique Ingres (Montauban 1780 - Paris 1867)
Jean-Louis Théodore Géricault (Rouen 1791 - Paris 1824)
Camille Corot (Paris 1796 - Ville-d'Avray 1875)
Eugène Delacroix (St-Maurice 1798 - Paris 1863)
Honoré Daumier (Marseille 1808 - Paris 1879)
Hippolyte Flandrin (Lyon 1809 - Roma 1864)
Théodore Rousseau (Paris 1812 - Barbizon 1867)
Jean-Francois Millet (Gréville-Hague 1814 - Barbizon 1875)
Charles-Francois Daubigny (Paris 1817 - 1878)
Gustave Courbet (Ornans 1819 - La Tour-de-Peilz 1877)
Alexandre Cabanel (Montpellier 1823 - Paris 1889)
Jean-Leon Gerome (Vésoul 1824 - Paris 1904)
Pierre Puvis de Chavannes (Lyon 1824 - Paris 1898)
William-Adolph Bouguereau (la Rochelle 1825 - 1905)
Gustave Moreau (Paris 1826 - 1898)
Camille Pissarro (St-Thomas 1830 - Paris 1903)
Édouard Manet (Paris 1832 - 1883)
Edgar Degas (Paris 1834 - 1917)
Paul Cézanne (Aix-en-Provence 1839 - 1906)
Claude Monet (Paris 1840 - Giverny 1926)
Odilon Redon (Bordeaux 1840 - Paris 1926)

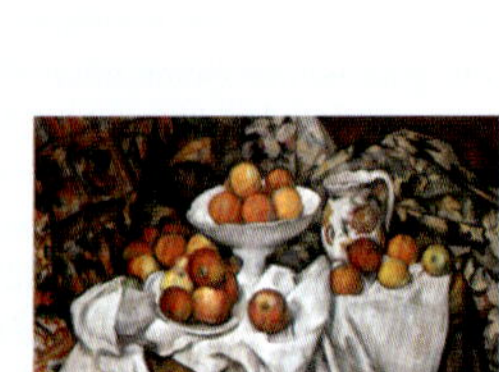

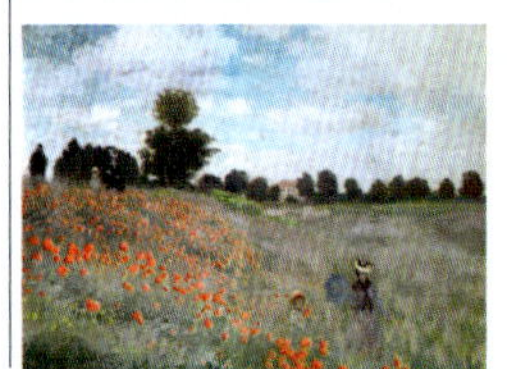

Auguste Rodin (Paris 1840 - Meudon 1917)
Frédéric Bazille (Montpellier 1841 - Beaune-la-Rolande 1870)
Berthe Morisot (Bourges 1841 - Paris 1895)
August Renoir (Limoges 1841 - Cagnes-sur-Mer 1919)
Henri Rousseau (Laval 1844 - Paris 1910)
Paul Gauguin (Paris 1848 - Hiva Oa 1903)
Gustave Caillebotte (Paris 1848 - Gennevillier 1894)
Georges Seurat (Paris 1859 - Gravelines 1891)
Paul Signac (Paris 1863 - 1935)
Henri de Toulouse-Lautrec (Albi 1864 - Chat. Malromé 1901)
Pierre Bonnard (Fontenay-aux-Roses 1867 - Le Cannet 1947)
Édouard Vuillard (Cuiseaux 1869 - La Baule 1940)
Maurice Denis (Granville 1870 - Paris 1943)

ESPAÑA

Francisco de Goya
(Fuendetodos 1746 - Bordeaux 1828)

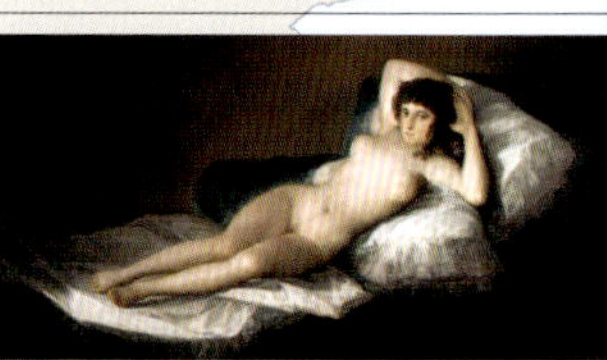

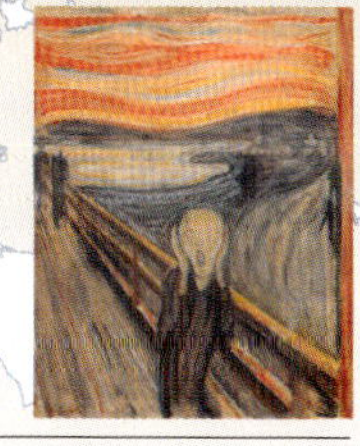

NORGE

Edvard Munch (Loten 1863 - Ekeley 1944)
Johan Christian Dahl (Bergen 1788 - Dresden 1857)

RUSSIA

Ilya Repin (Chuhuiv 1844 - Kuokkala 1930)
Valentin Serov (St. Petersburg 1865 - Moscow 1911)

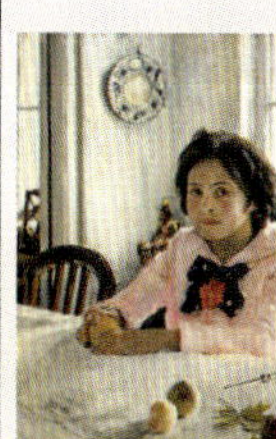

NEDERLAND

Vincent van Gogh (Zundert 1853 - Auvers-sur-Oise 1890)

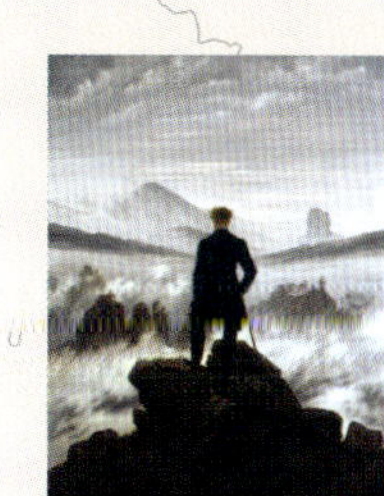

DEUTSCHLAND

Caspar David Friedrich (Greifswald 1774 - Dresden 1814)
Peter v. Cornelius (Düsseldorf 1783 - Berlin 1867
Friedrich Wilhelm v. Schadow (Berlin 1788 - Düsseldorf 1862)
Friedrich Overbeck (Lübeck 1789 - Roma 1869)
Adolph v. Menzel (Breslau 1815 - Berlin 1905)
Anselm Feuerbach (Speyer 1829 - Venezia 1880)
Hans v. Marées (Elberfeld 1837 - Roma 1887)
Max Liebermann (Berlin 1847 - 1935)

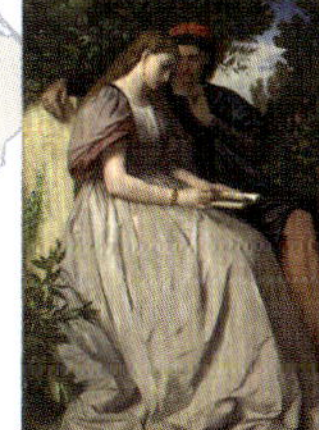

SCHWEIZ

Johann-Heinrich Füssli (Zürich 1741 - Putney Hill 1825)
Felix Vallotton (Lausanne 1865 - Paris 1925)
Arnold Böcklin (Basel 1827 - San Domenico di Fiesole 1901)

ITALIA

Francesco Hayez (Venezia 1791 - Milano 1882)

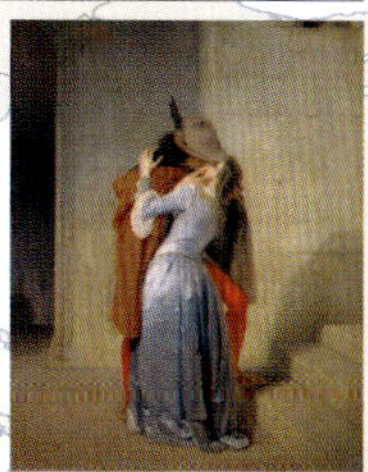

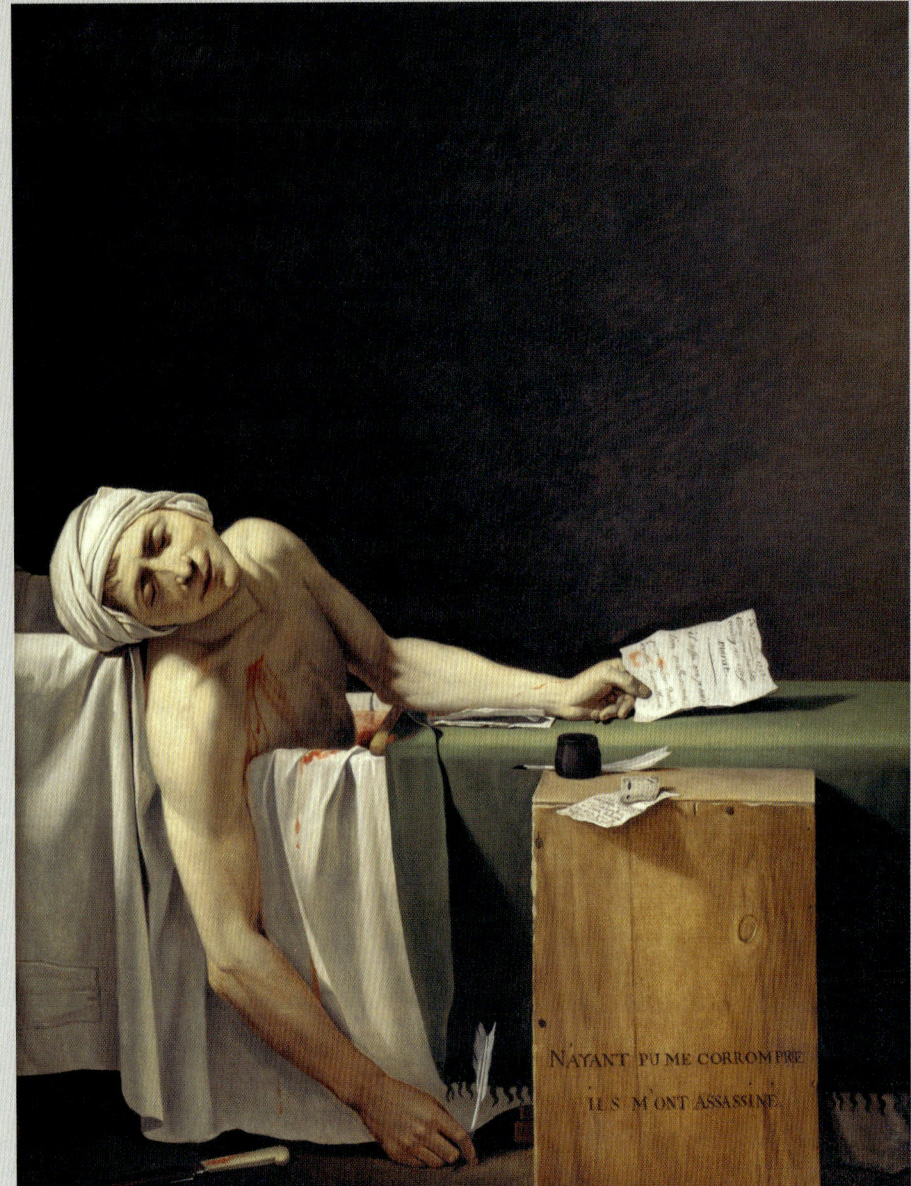

The Neo-Classical sycophant: Jacques-Louis David first painted for Louis XVI, then for the revolutionaries and finally for Napoléon.

Klassizister Wendehals. Jacques-Louis David malt zunächst für Ludwig XVI., dann für die Revolutionäre und dann für Napoleon.

Jacques-Louis David: de voortrekker van het neoclassicisme schildert eerst voor Louis XVI, daarna voor de revolutionairen en ten slotte voor Napoleon.

Jacques-Louis David
(Paris 1748 - Bruxelles 1825)

The Death of Marat
Der Tod des Marat
De dood van Marat

●●●

1793
165 x 128 cm / 64.96 x 50.39 in.
Musée Royaux des Beaux-Arts, Bruxelles

Oil on canvas / Öl auf Leinwand
Olieverf op doek

Jacques-Louis David
(Paris 1748 - Bruxelles 1825)

Oath of the Tennis Court
Der Schwur im Jeu de Paume
De eed op de Kaatsbaan

●

1789
65 x 88 cm / 25.59 x 34.6 in.
Musée Carnavalet, Paris

Oil on canvas
Öl auf Leinwand
Olieverf op doek

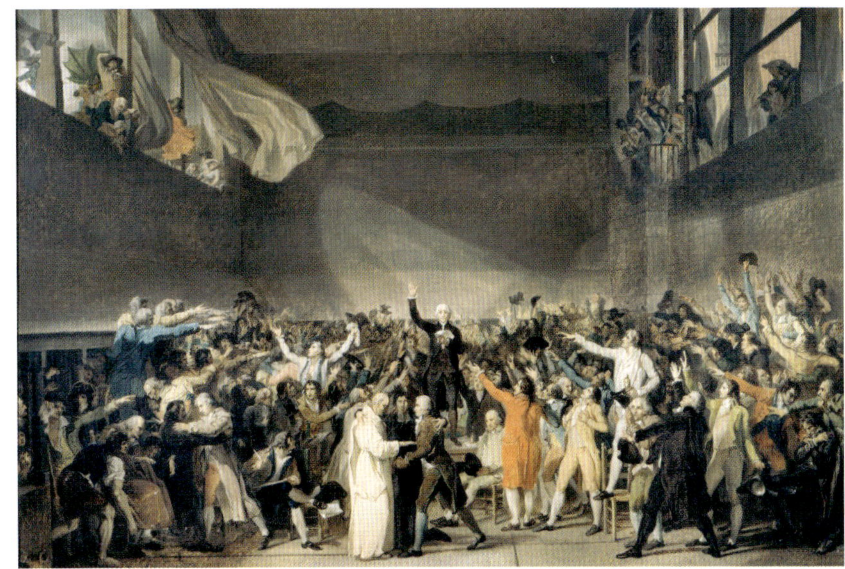

Jacques-Louis David
(Paris 1748 - Bruxelles 1825)

Intervention of the Sabine Women
Die Sabinerinnen
De tussenkomst door de Sabijnse vrouwen

●●●

1794-1799
385 x 522 cm / 151.87 x 205.51 in.
Musée du Louvre, Paris

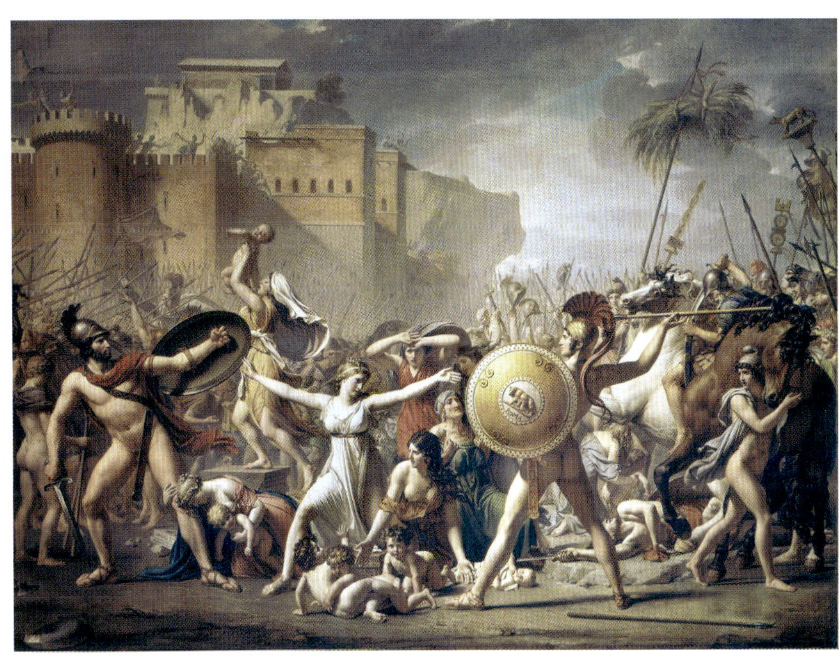

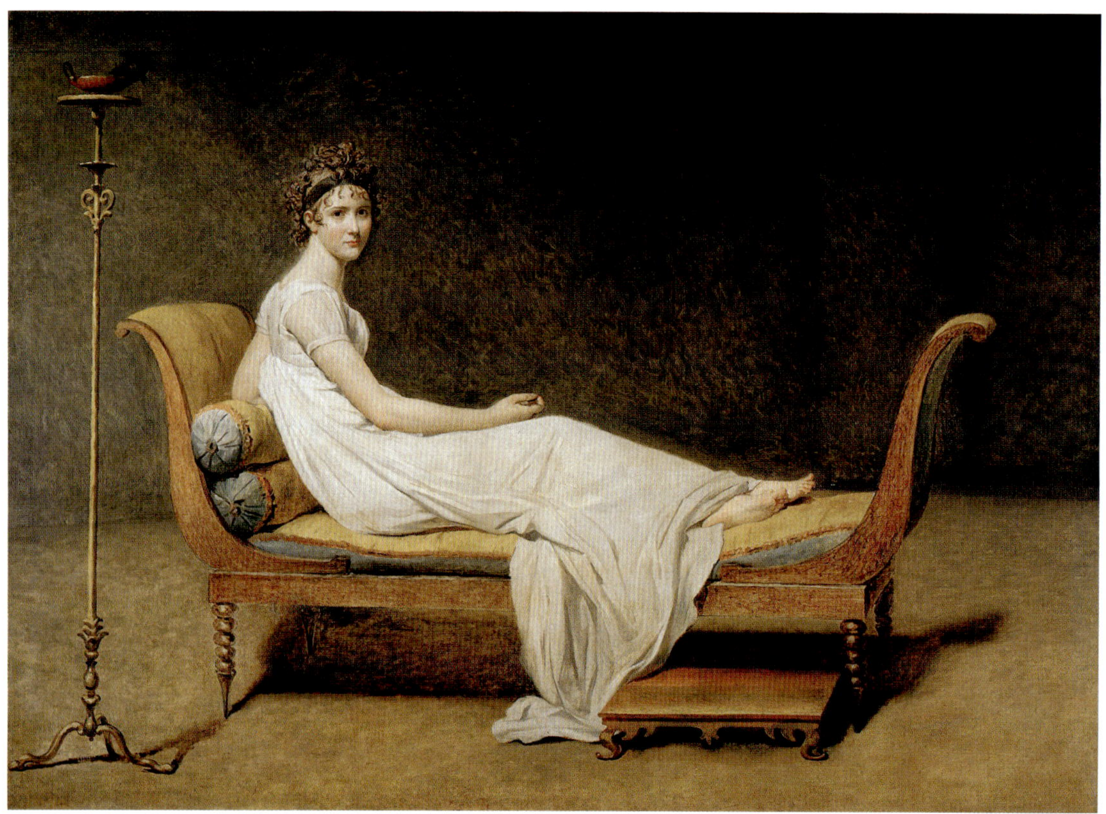

Jacques-Louis David
(Paris 1748 - Bruxelles 1825)

Portrait of Madame Récamier
Bildnis der Madame Récamier
Portret van Madame Récamier

●●

1800
174 x 244 cm / 68.50 x 96.06 in.
Musée du Louvre, Paris

Oil on canvas
Öl auf Leinwand
Olieverf op doek

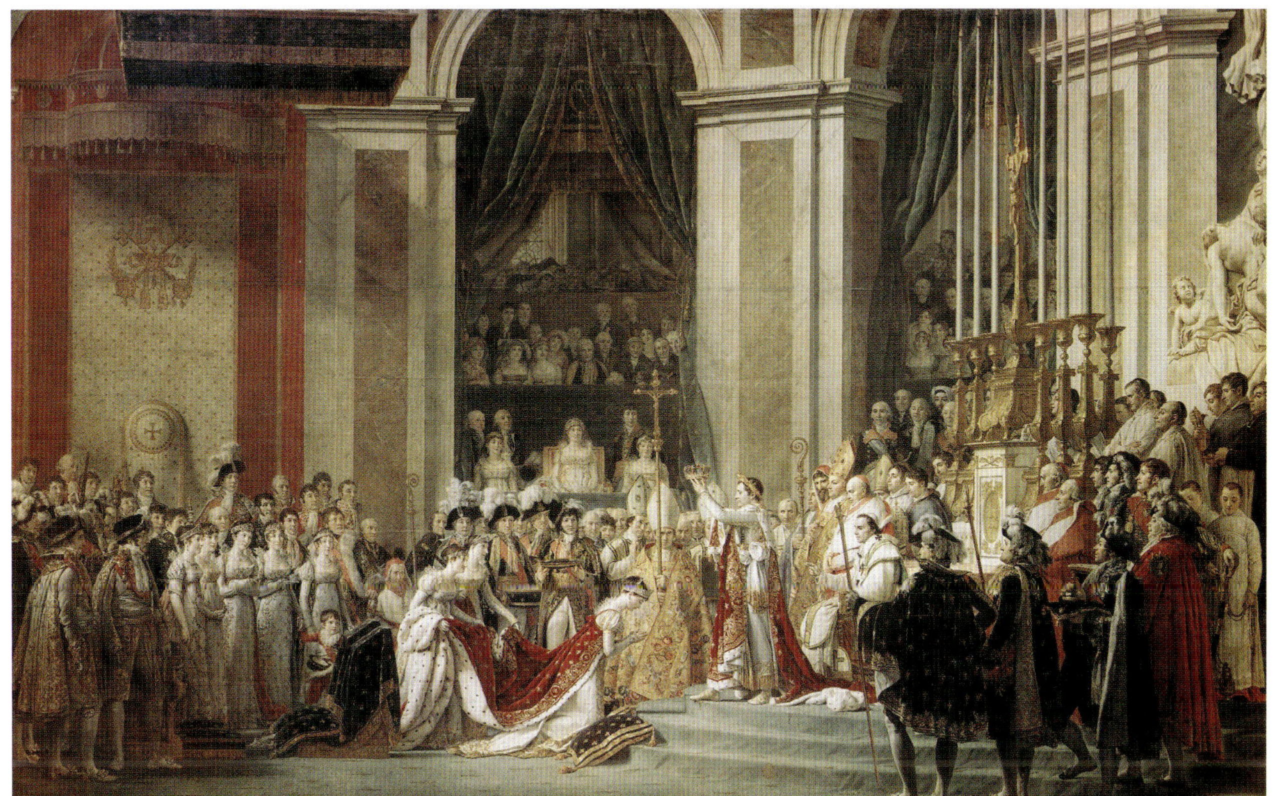

Jacques-Louis David
(Paris 1748 - Bruxelles 1825)

Coronation of Napoleon
Die Krönung Napoleons
De kroning van Napoleon

●●

1805-1807
690 x 927 cm / 271.65 x 364.95 in.
Musée du Louvre, Paris

Oil on canvas
Öl auf Leinwand
Olieverf op doek

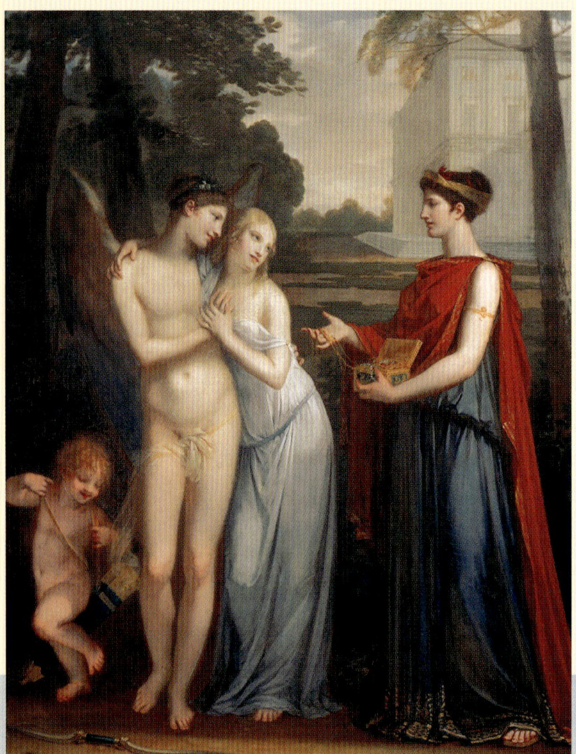

Pierre-Paul Prud'hon
(Cluny 1758 - Paris 1823)

Innocence Prefers Love to Wealth
Die Unschuld bevorzugt dem Reichtum die Liebe
De Onschuld verkiest Liefde boven Rijkdom

●

1804
The State Hermitage Museum, St. Petersburg

Oil on canvas
Öl auf Leinwand
Olieverf op doek

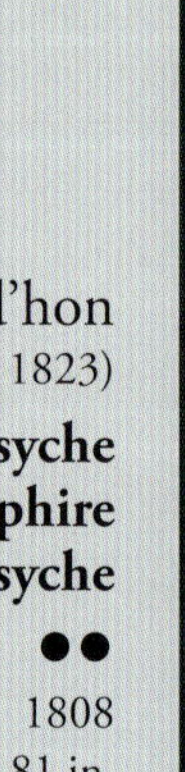

Pierre-Paul Prud'hon
(Cluny 1758 - Paris 1823)

The Abduction of Psyche
Entführung der Psyche durch die Zephire
De ontvoering van Psyche

●●

1808
195 x 157 cm / 76.77 x 61.81 in.
Musée du Louvre, Paris

Oil on canvas
Öl auf Leinwand
Olieverf op doek

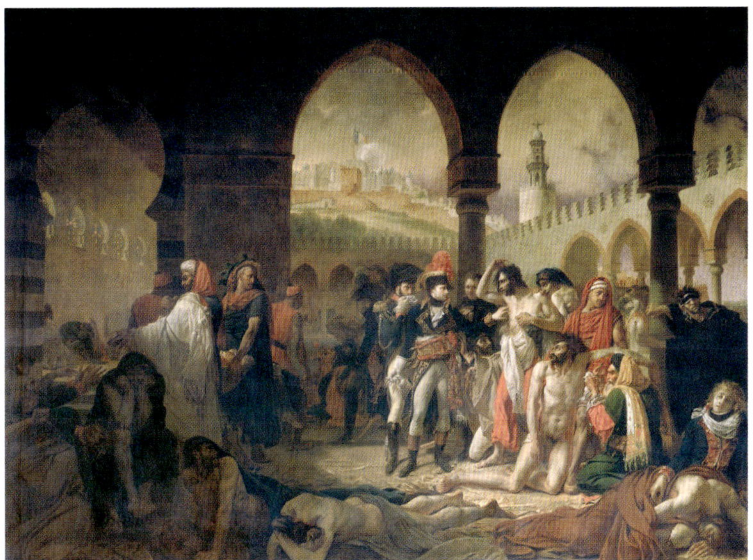

Antoine-Jean Gros
(Paris 1771 -1835)

Napoleon Visiting the Pesthouse at Jaffa
Napoleon bei den Pestkranken von Jaffa
Napoleon bezoekt het pesthuis in Jaffa

●

1804
532 x 720 cm / 209.05 x 283.46 in.
Musée du Louvre, Paris

Oil on canvas
Öl auf Leinwand
Olieverf op doek

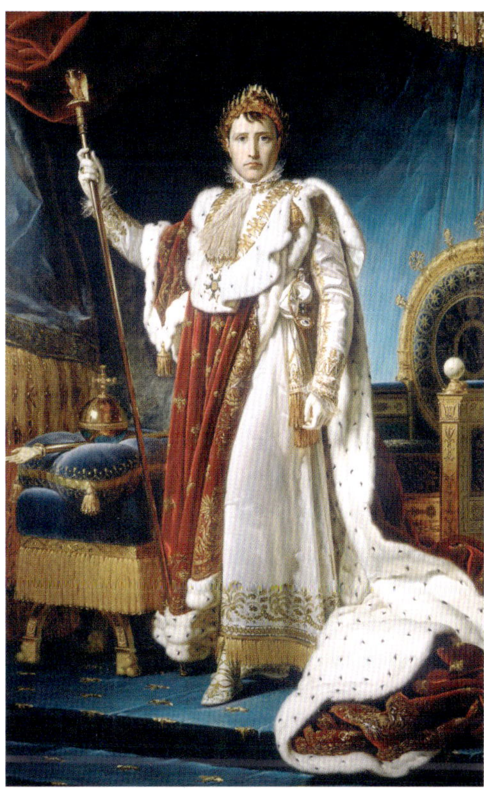

François Gérard
(Roma 1770 - Paris 1837)

Portrait of Napoleon Bonaparte
Portrait von Napoleon Bonaparte
Portret van Napoleon Bonaparte

1807
Museo Nazionale di Capodimonte, Napoli

Oil on canvas
Öl auf Leinwand
Olieverf op doek

Oriental erotic dreams seen through the keyhole: furtive pleasures for the owners of Ingres'nudes.

Erotische Träume vom Orient durchs Schlüsselloch gesehen. Ingres Akte erfreuen deren Besitzer im Verborgenen.

Erotische dromen uit de Oriënt, gezien door het sleutelgat. De naakten van Ingres vormen geheime geneugten voor de bezitter.

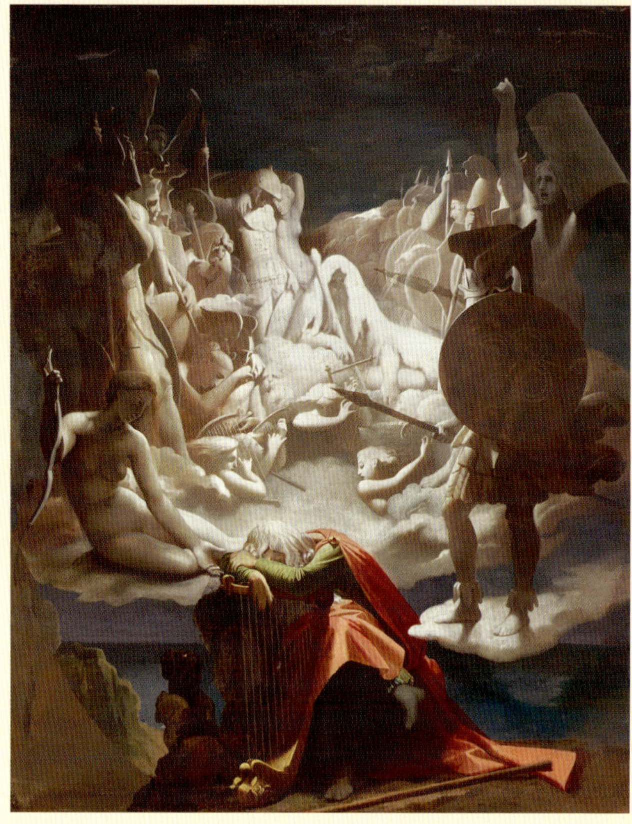

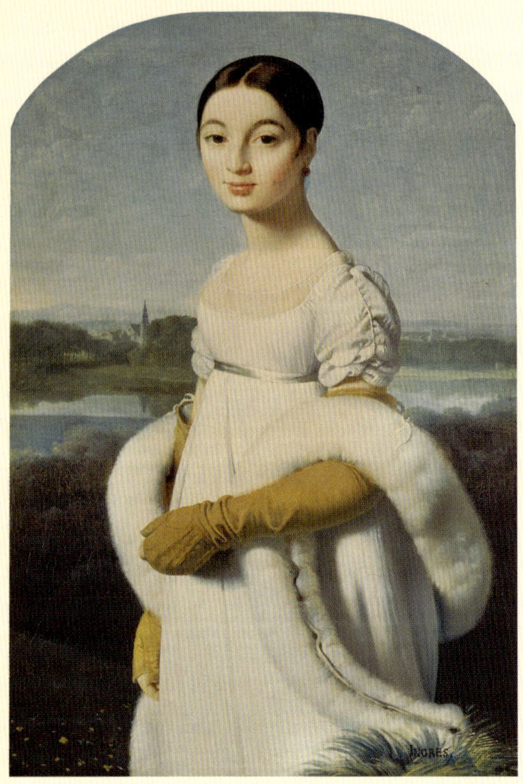

Jean-Auguste-Dominique Ingres (Montauban 1780 - Paris 1867)

Portrait of Mademoiselle Rivière
Portrait von Mademoiselle Rivière
Portret van Mademoiselle Rivière

●●

1806
100 x 70 cm / 39.37 x 27.55 in.
Musée du Louvre, Paris
Oil on canvas / Öl auf Leinwand
Olieverf op doek

Jean-Auguste-Dominique Ingres (Montauban 1780 - Paris 1867)

The Dream of Ossian
Der Traum des Ossian
De droom van Ossian

●

1813
348 x 275 cm / 137 x 108.26 in.
Musée Ingres,
Montauban

Oil on canvas
Öl auf Leinwand
Olieverf op doek

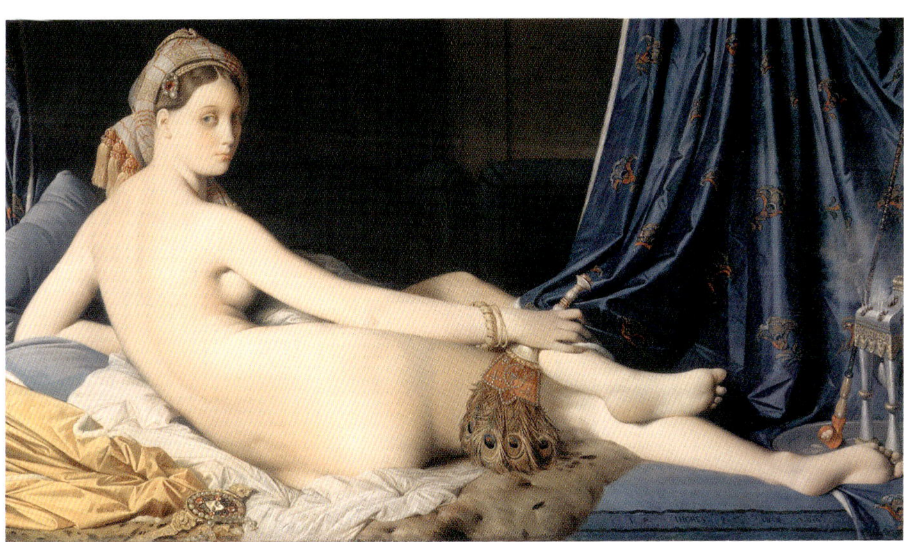

Jean-Auguste-Dominique Ingres (Montauban 1780 - Paris 1867)

The Grand Odalisque
Die große Odaliske
De grote Odalisk

●●●

1814
91 x 162 cm / 35.82 x 63.77 in.
Musée du Louvre, Paris

Oil on canvas /Öl auf Leinwand
Olieverf op doek

Jean-Auguste-Dominique Ingres
(Montauban 1780 - Paris 1867)

The Turkish Bath
Türkisches Bad
Het Turkse bad

●●●

1862
Ø 108 cm / Ø 42.51 in.
Musée du Louvre, Paris

Oil on canvas / Öl auf Leinwand
Olieverf op doek

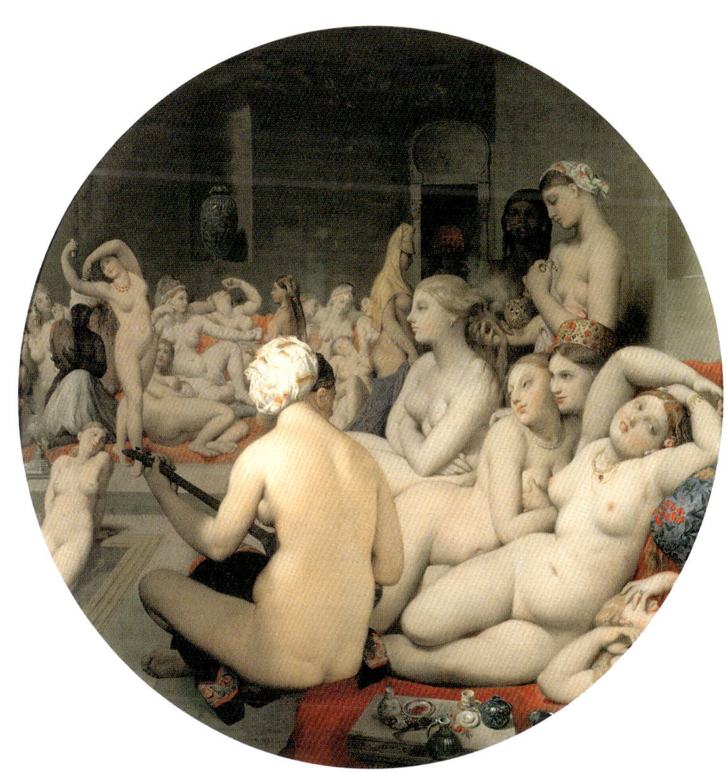

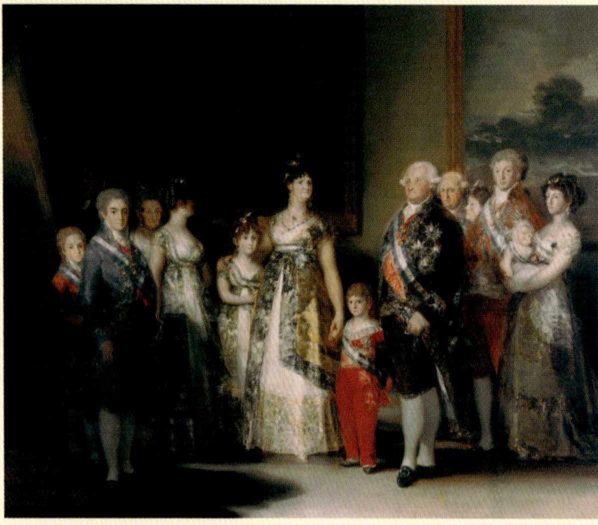

Protection against the Inquisition: Goya hides the Nude Maya behind the clothed version of the same painting.

Schutz vor der Inquisition. Goya versteckt die nackte Maya hinter der formatgleichen bekleideten Version.

Bescherming tegen de Inquisitie. Goya verbergt de naakte Maya achter de geklede versie van hetzelfde schilderij.

Francisco de Goya
(Fuendetodos 1746 - Bordeaux 1828)

The Family of Carlos IV

Die Familie Karl IV.
De familie van Karel IV

●●●

1800
280 x 336 cm
110.23 x 132.28 in.
Museo Nacional del Prado, Madrid

Oil on canvas / Öl auf Leinwand
Olieverf op doek

Francisco de Goya
(Fuendetodos 1746 - Bordeaux 1828)

Equestrian Portrait of Ferdinando VII
Ferdinand VII. zu Pferde
Ferdinand VII te paard

●●

1808
286,5 x 207 cm / 112.8 x 81.5 in.
Real Academia de Bellas Artes de San Fernando, Madrid

Oil on canvas / Öl auf Leinwand
Olieverf op doek

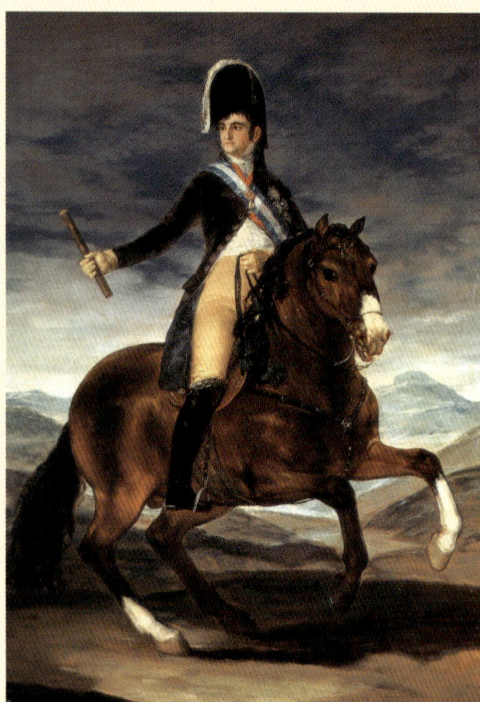

Francisco de Goya
(Fuendetodos 1746
- Bordeaux 1828)

La maja desnuda
Die nackte Maja
De naakte Maja

●●●

1795
98 x 191 cm
38.58 x 75.19 in.
Museo Nacional
del Prado, Madrid

Oil on canvas
Öl auf Leinwand
Olieverf op doek

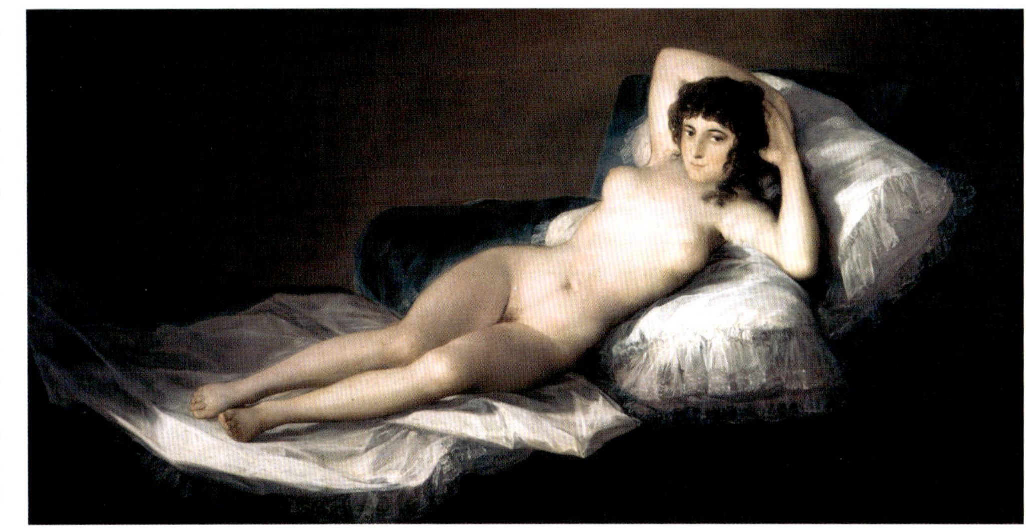

Francisco de Goya
(Fuendetodos 1746 -
Bordeaux 1828)

La maja vestida
Die angekleidete Maja
De geklede Maja

●●●

1800
95 x 190 cm
37.40 x 74.80 in.
Museo Nacional del Prado,
Madrid

Oil on canvas
Öl auf Leinwand
Olieverf op doek

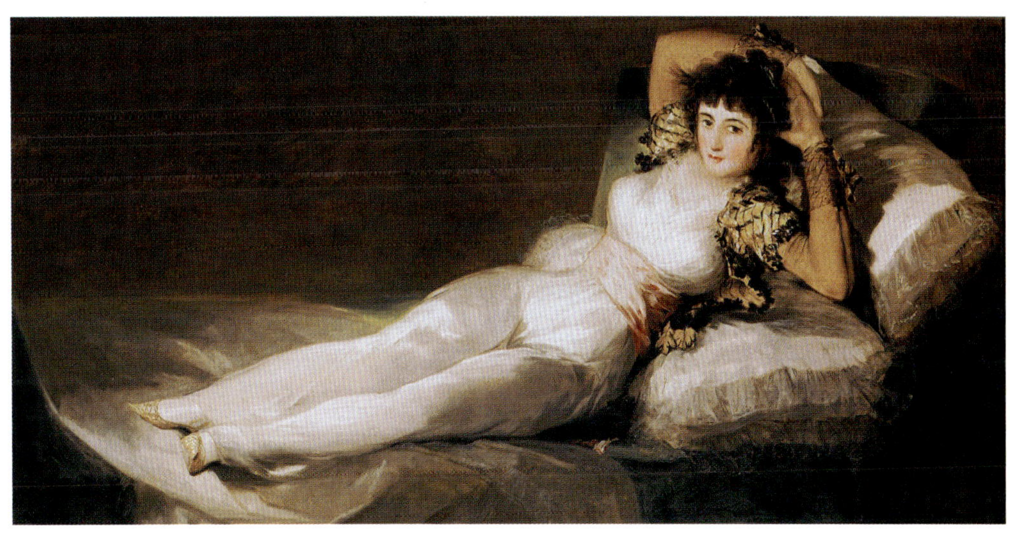

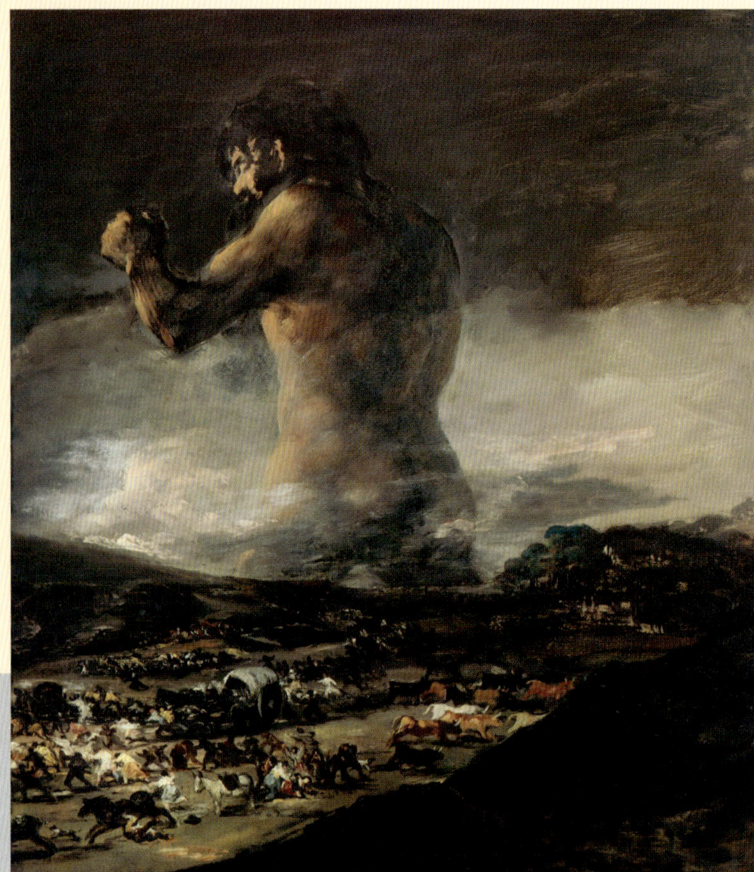

Francisco de Goya
(Fuendetodos 1746 - Bordeaux 1828)

The Colossus
Der Koloss
De kolos

●●

c. 1808
116 x 105 cm / 45.66 x 41.33 in.
Museo Nacional del Prado, Madrid

Oil on canvas
Öl auf Leinwand
Olieverf op doek

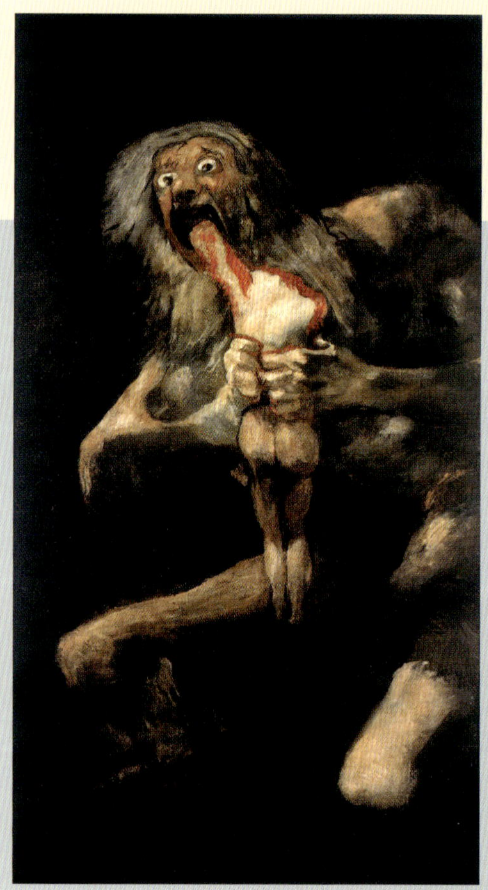

Francisco de Goya
(Fuendetodos 1746 - Bordeaux 1828)

Saturn Devouring One of His Sons
Saturn verschlingt seine Kinder
Saturnus verslindt één van zijn kinderen

●●

c. 1821-1823
146 × 83 cm / 57.48 x 32.67 in.
Museo Nacional del Prado, Madrid

Oil on canvas
Öl auf Leinwand
Olieverf op doek

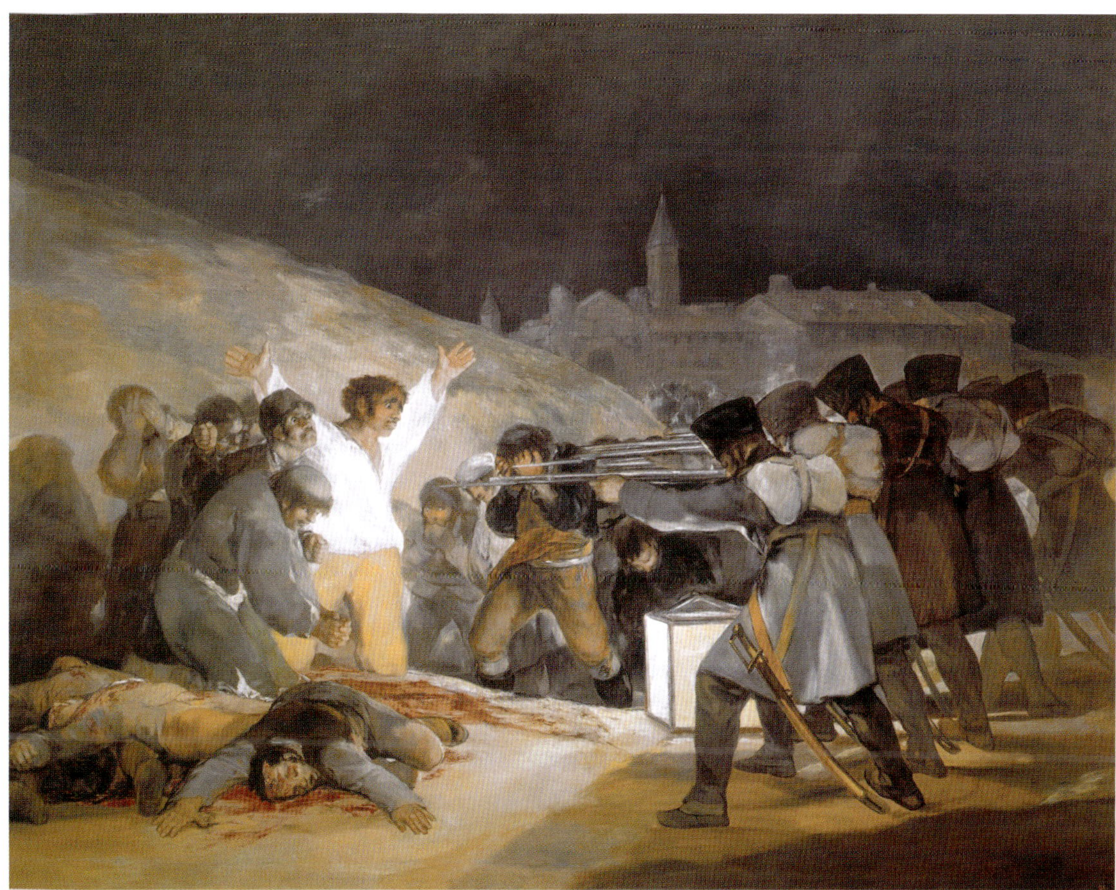

Francisco de Goya
(Fuendetodos 1746 - Bordeaux 1828)

The Shootings of May 3rd
Die Erschießung der Aufständigen am 3. Mai
Beschieting op 3 mei 1808

●●●

1814
266 x 345 cm / 104.72 x 135.82 in.
Museo Nacional del Prado, Madrid

Oil on canvas / Öl auf Leinwand
Olieverf op doek

In his late works Goya abandons court painting to express a critical vision of his times.

Im Spätwerk entwickelt sich Goya vom Hofmaler zum expressiven Zeitkritiker.

In zijn latere werk neemt Goya afstand van de hofschilderkunst en wordt een criticus van zijn tijd.

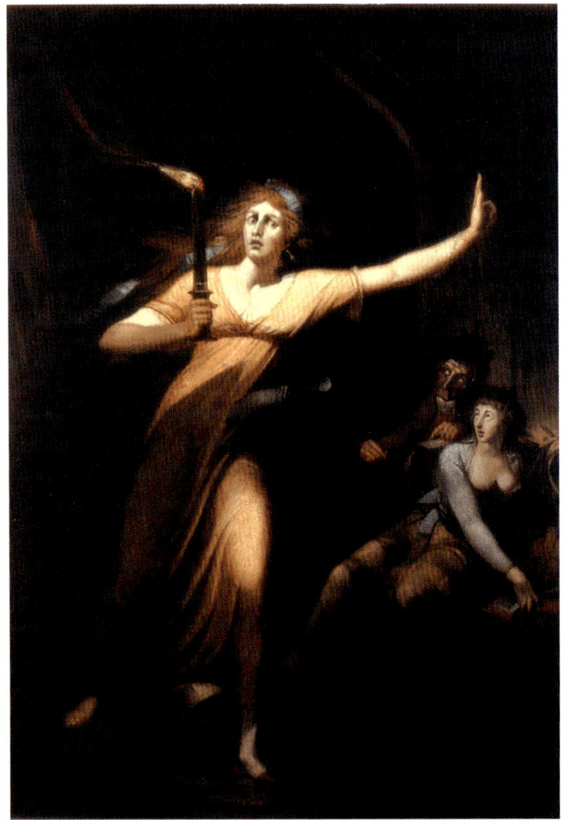

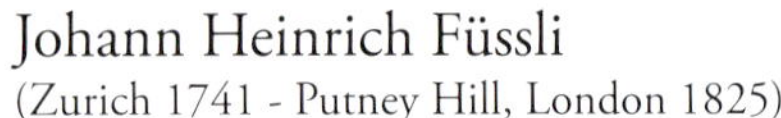

Johann Heinrich Füssli
(Zurich 1741 - Putney Hill, London 1825)

Lady Macbeth Sleepwalking
Die schlafwandelnde Lady Macbeth
Lady Macbeth slaapwandelend

*c.*1784
221 x 160 cm / 62.99 x 87 in.
Musée du Louvre, Paris

Oil on canvas
Öl auf Leinwand
Olieverf op doek

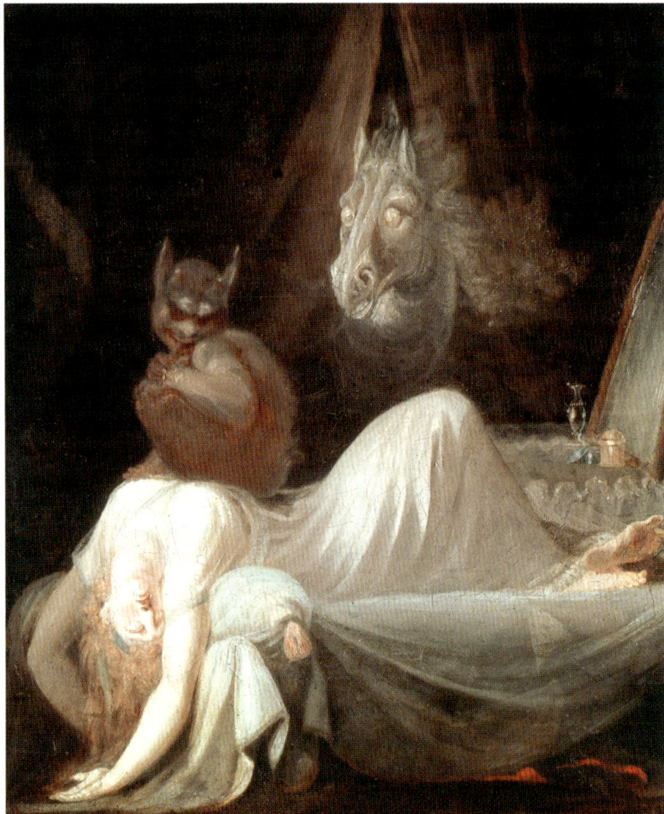

Johann Heinrich Füssli
(Zurich 1741 - Putney Hill, London 1825)

The Nightmare
Der Nachtmahr
De nachtmerrie

c. 1790
64 x 75 cm / 25.19 x 29.52 in.
Goethe-Museum, Frankfurt Am Main

Oil on canvas
Öl auf Leinwand
Olieverf op doek

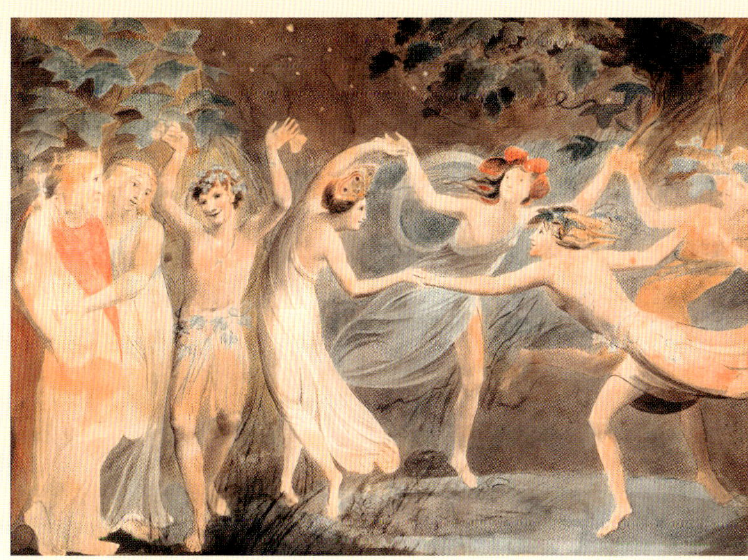

William Blake
(London 1757 - 1827)

Oberon, Titania and Puck with Fairies Dancing
Oberon, Titania und Puck mit tanzenden Feen
Oberon, Titania en Puck met dansende elfen

●

c. 1786
Tate Gallery, London

Watercolour on paper
Acquarell auf Papier
Acquarell auf Papier

Fantastical visions.

Fantastische Visionen.

Fantastische visioenen.

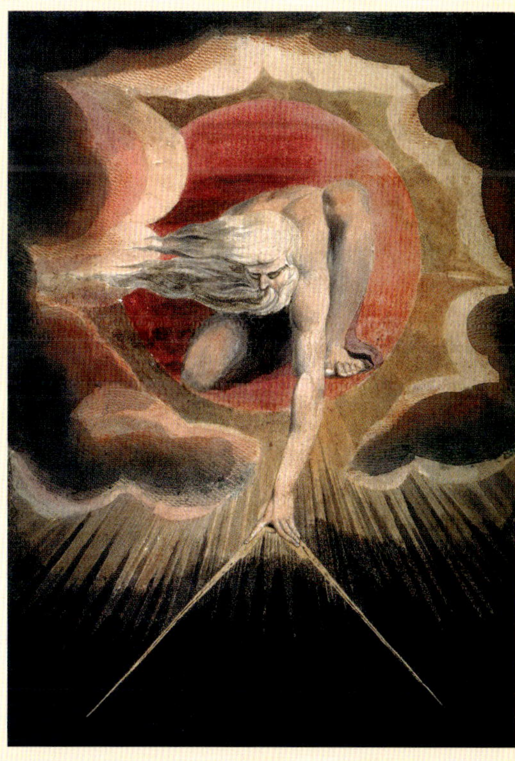

William Blake
(London 1757 - 1827)

Ancient of days
Der Alte der Tage
Het begin der tijden

●●

1794
18 x 22 cm / 7.08 x 8.66 in.
Pierpont Morgan Library, New York

Acquaforte etching / Acquaforte / Aquatint

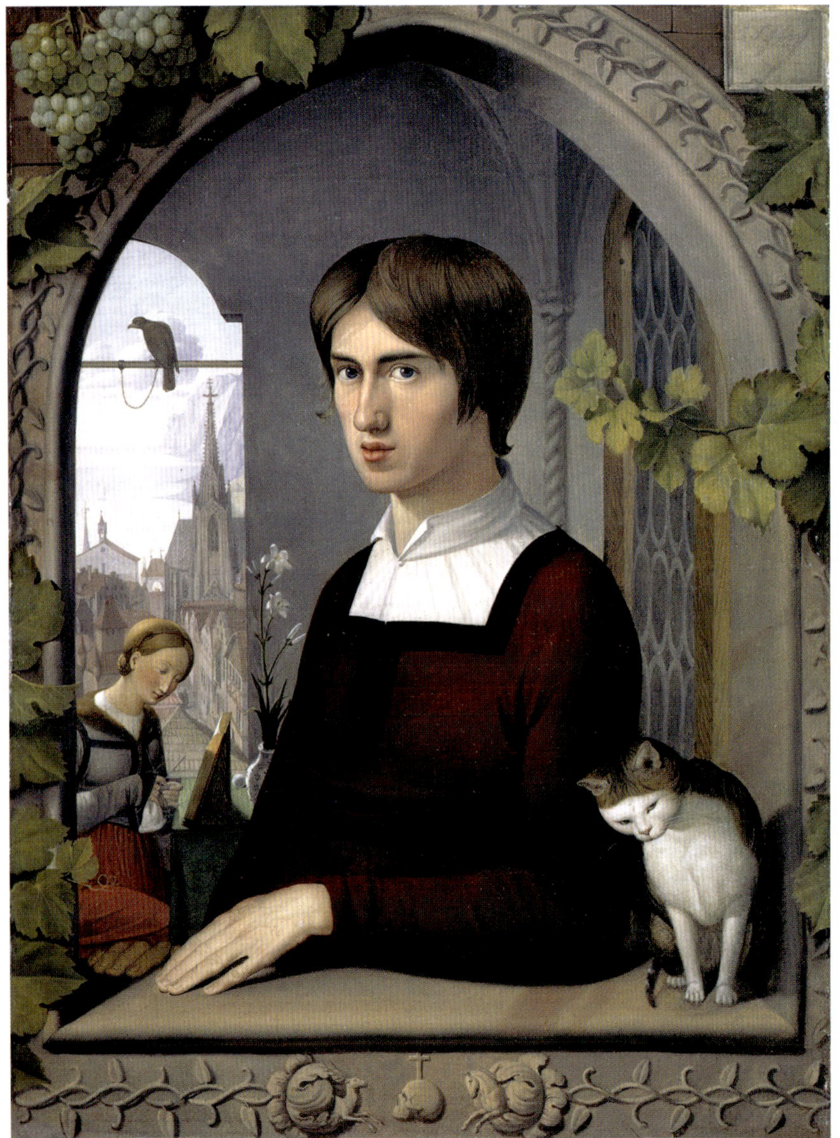

The Nazarenes: a Catholic order of artists who wear their hair like Jesus.

Die Nazarener: eine katholische Künstlerbruderschaft mit Jesusfrisur.

De Nazarenen; een katholieke kunstenaarsgroep met de haardracht van Jezus.

Friedrich Overbeck
(Lübeck 1789 - Roma 1869)

Portrait of the Painter Franz Pforr
Portrait das Malers Franz Pforr
Portret van de schilder Franz Pforr

●●

1810
62 x 47 cm / 24.40 x 18.50 in.
Alte Nationalgalerie, Staatliche Museen, Berlin

Oil on canvas
Öl auf Leinwand
Olieverf op doek

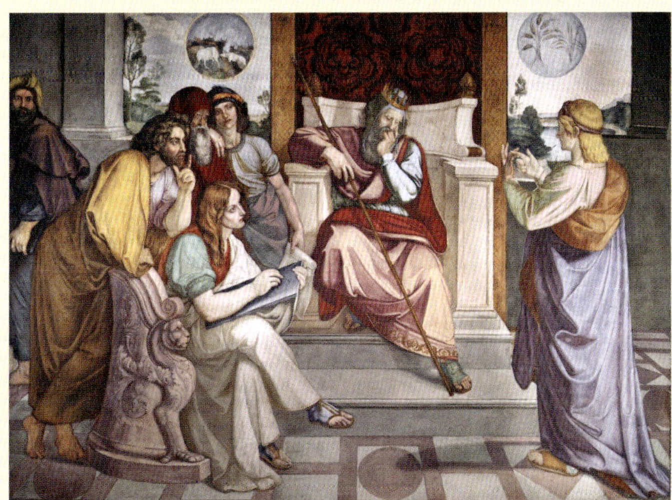

Peter von Cornelius
(Düsseldorf 1783 - Berlin 1867)

Joseph Explaining the Pharaoh's Dreams
Joseph deutet die Träume des Pharao
Jozef verklaart de dromen van de Farao

●

c. 1816-1817
Nationalgalerie, Staatliche Museen zu Berlin, Berlin

Detached fresco
Abgelöstes Fresko
Los Fresco

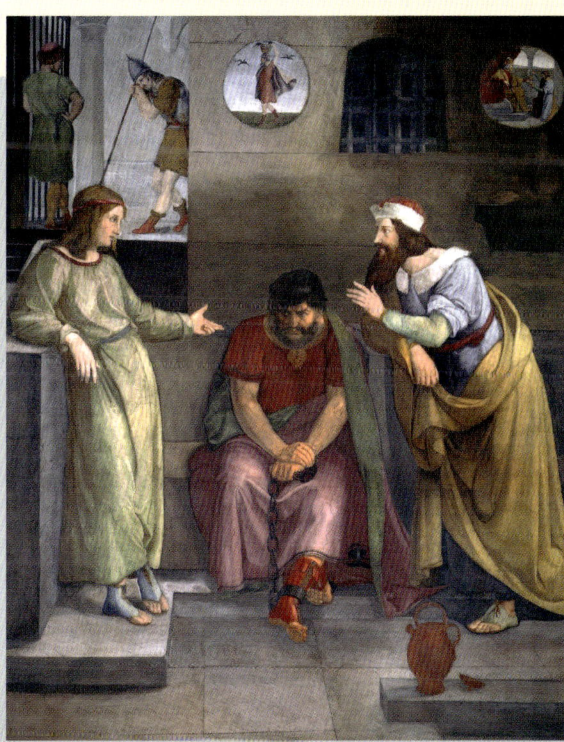

Friedrich Wilhelm von Schadow
(Berlin 1788 - Düsseldorf 1862)

Joseph in Prison
Joseph im Gefängnis
Jozef in de gevangenis

●

1817
Nationalgalerie,
Staatliche Museen, Berlin

Detached fresco
Abgelöstes Fresko
Los Fresco

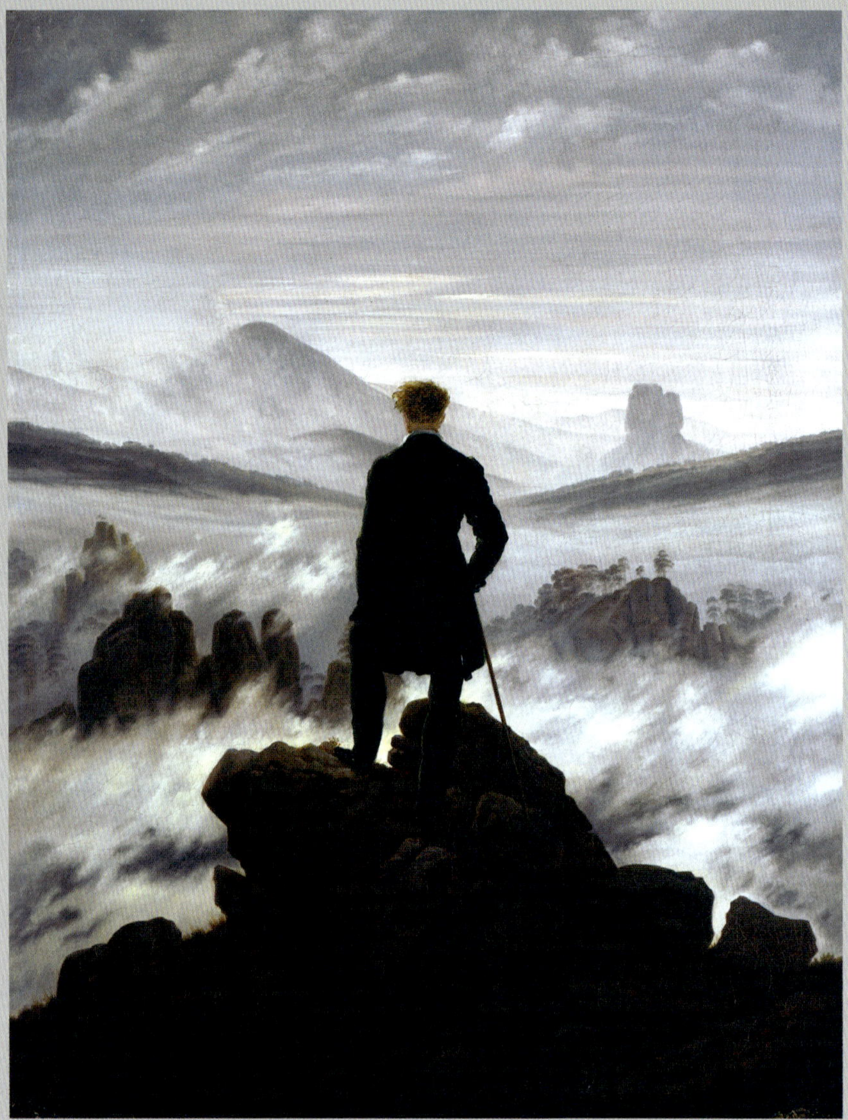

The landscape becomes an altarpiece: Caspar David Friedrich lead the way to Romanticism, a new religious fervour independent of the religious denominations.

Die Landschaft wird zum Altarbild. Caspar David Friedrich ist der Hauptvertreter des neuen Gefühls von überkonfessioneller Religiosität, der Romantik.

Het landschap wordt een altaarstuk. Caspar David Friedrich is de belangrijkste vertegenwoordiger van een nieuw religieus gevoel dat boven de religies staat; de romantiek.

Caspar David Friedrich
(Greifswald 1774 - Dresden 1840)

Wanderer above the Sea of Fog
Der Wanderer über dem Nebelmeer
De wandelaar boven een zee van mist

●●●

c. 1817
98 × 74 cm / 38.58 x 29.13 in.
Hamburger Kunsthalle, Hamburg

Oil on canvas
Öl auf Leinwand
Olieverf op doek

Caspar David Friedrich
(Greifswald 1774 - Dresden 1840)

Abbey in an Oak Forest
Abtei im Eichwald
Abdij in het eikenbos

●●

1809-1810
110,4 x 171 cm / 43.46 x 67.32 in.
Nationalgalerie, Staatliche Museen zu Berlin, Berlin

Oil on canvas
Öl auf Leinwand
Olieverf op doek

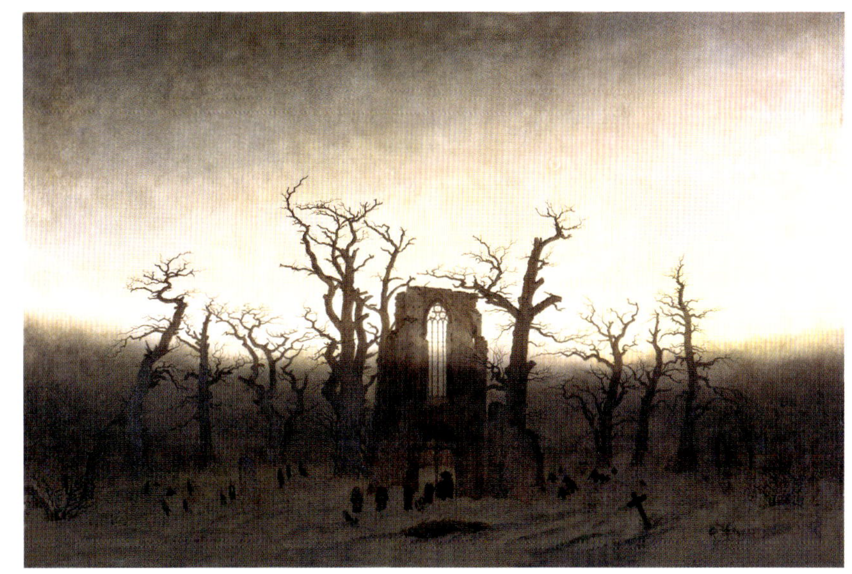

Caspar David Friedrich
(Greifswald 1774 - Dresden 1840)

The Wreck of the Hope
Das Eismeer
De IJszee

●●

c. 1823-1824
97 x 127 cm / 38.18 x 49.99 in.
Hamburger Kunsthalle, Hamburg

Oil on canvas
Öl auf Leinwand
Olieverf op doek

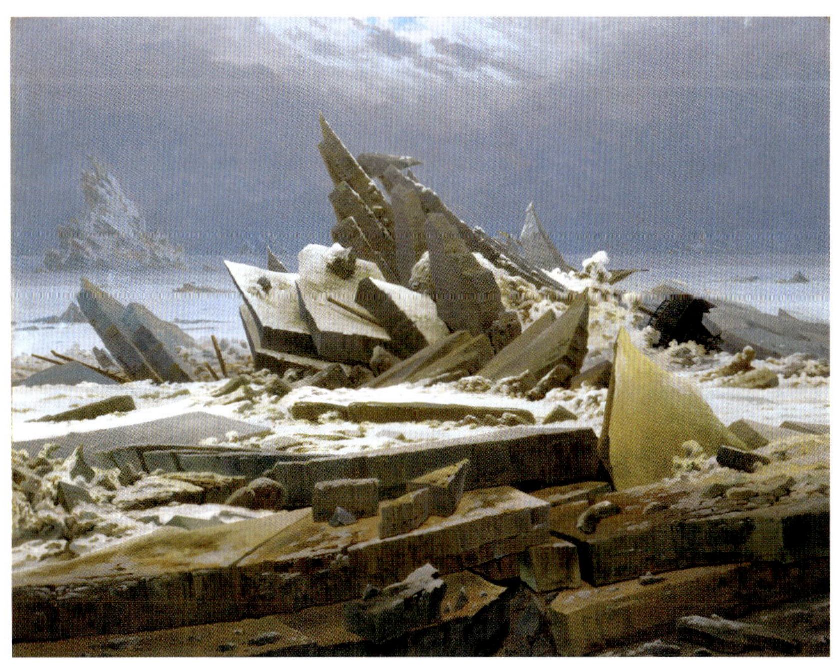

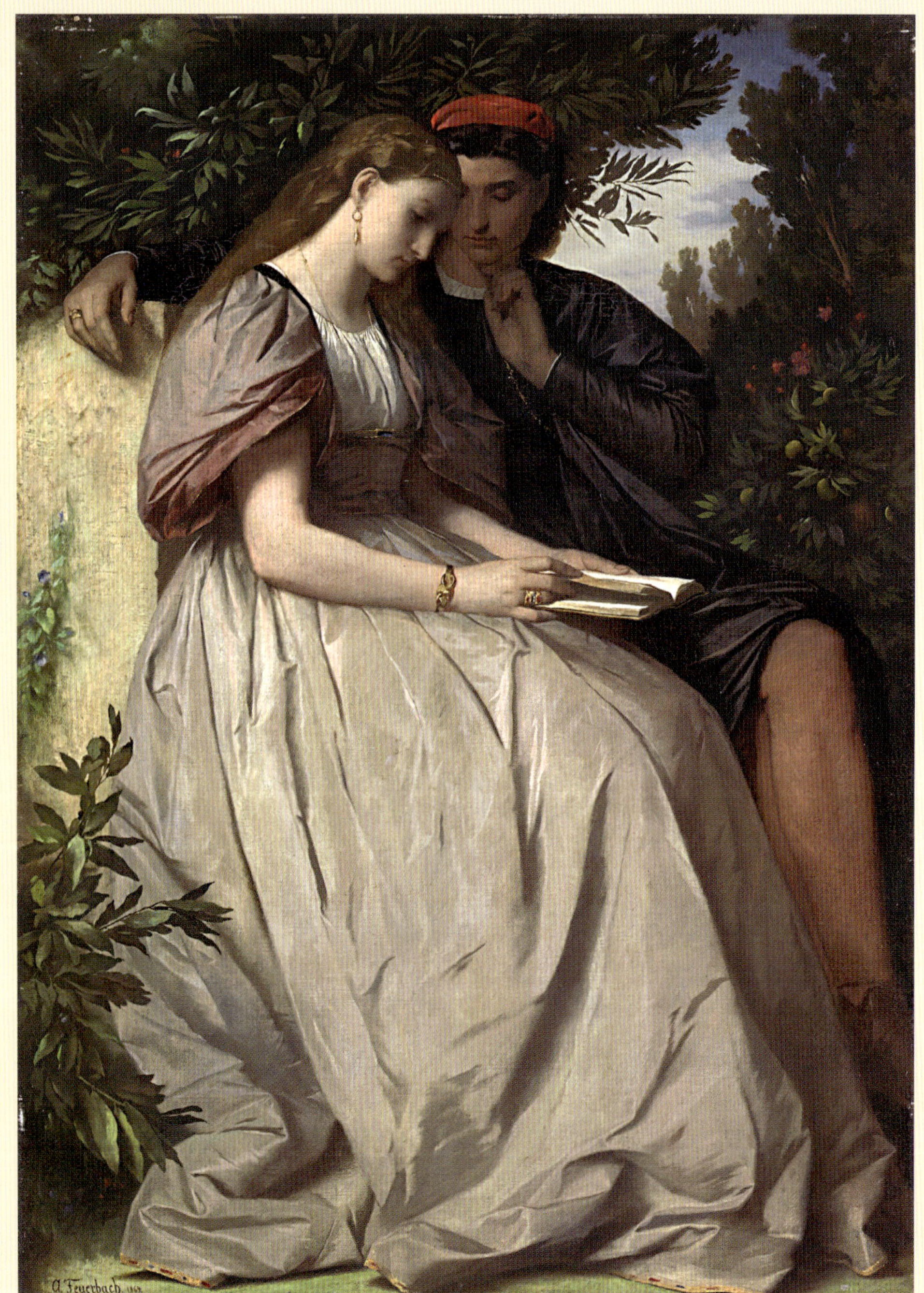

Anselm Feuerbach
(Speyer 1829 - Venezia 1880)

Paolo and Francesca
Paolo und Francesca
Paolo en Francesca

●●

1864
137 x 99.5 cm
53.93 x 39.17 in.
Schack-Galerie, Munich

Oil on canvas
Öl auf Leinwand
Olieverf op doek

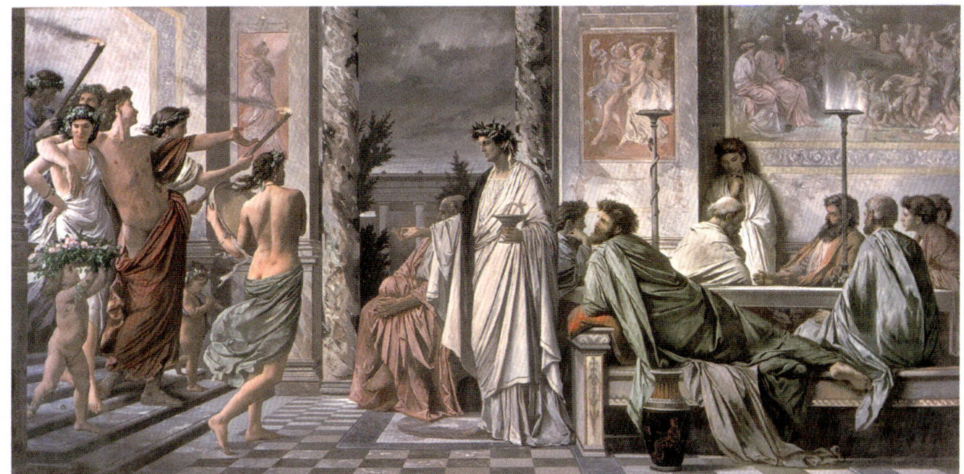

Anselm Feuerbach
(Speyer 1829 - Venezia 1880)

Plato's Symposium
Gastmahl des Plato
Het gastmaal van Plato

●

1869
295 x 598 cm / 116.14 x 235.43 in.
Staatliche Kunsthalle, Karlsruhe

Oil on canvas
Öl auf Leinwand
Olieverf op doek

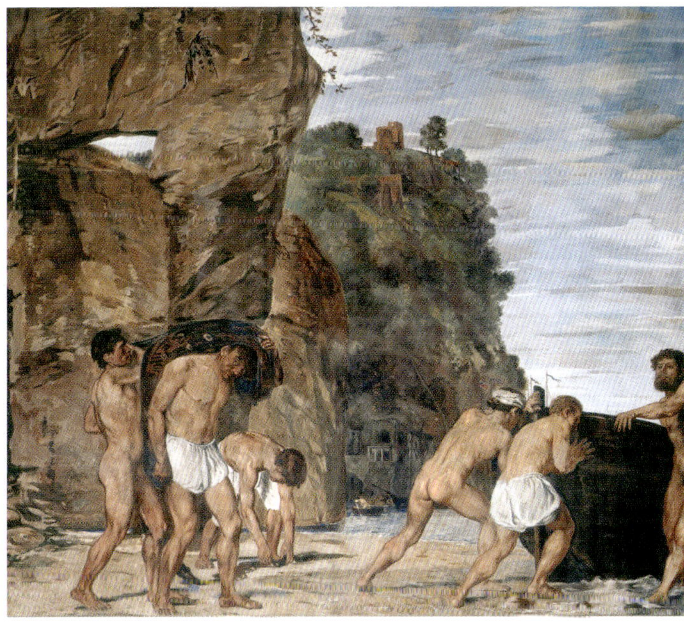

Hans von Marées
(Elberfeld 1837 - Roma 1887)

Fishermen Launching their Boat
Ausfahrt der Fischer
Vissers die een boot de zee opduwen

●●

1873
Stazione Zoologica, Napoli

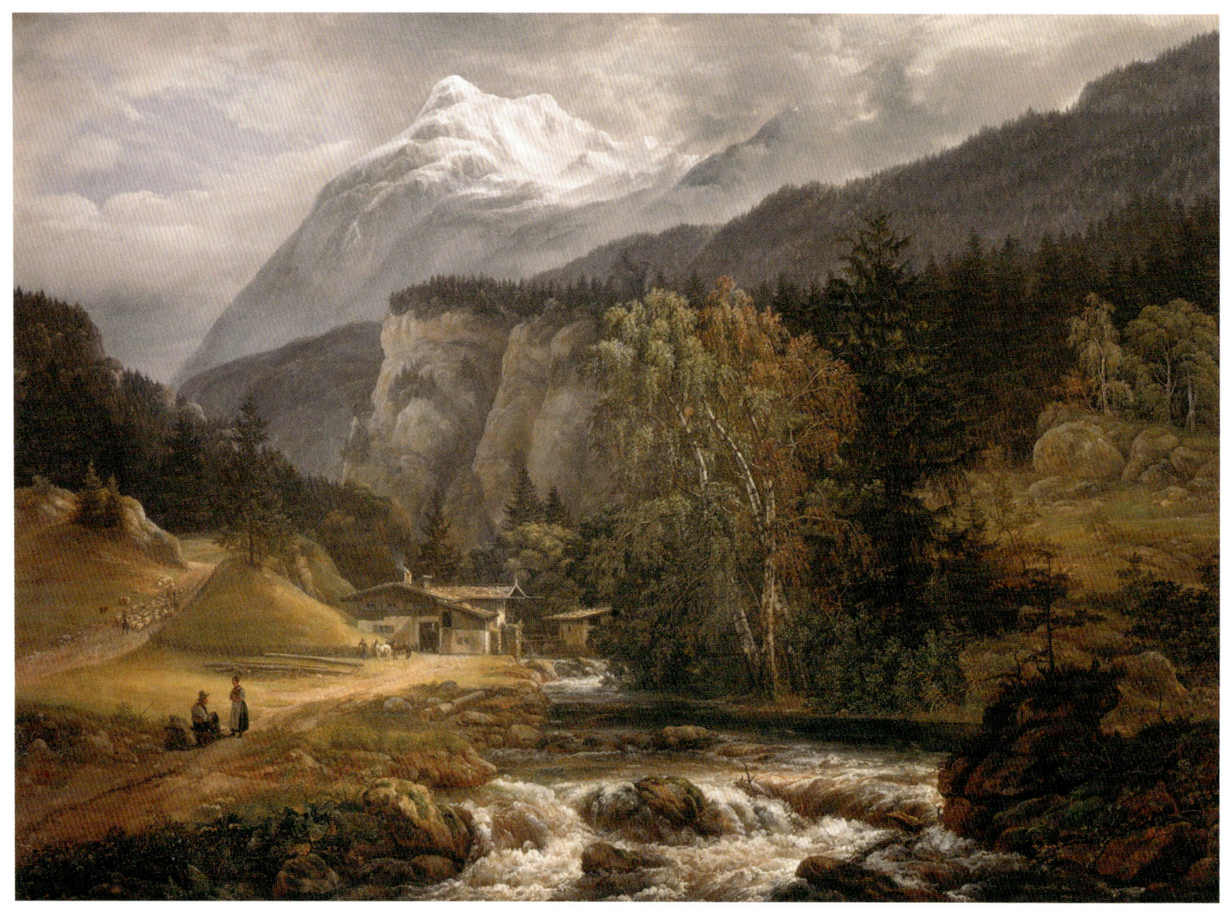

Johan Christian Dahl
(Bergen 1788 - Dresden 1857)

Alpine Landscape
Alpenlandschaft
Alpenlandschap

●

1821
Germanisches Nationalmuseum,
Nürnberg

Oil on canvas
Öl auf Leinwand
Olieverf op doek

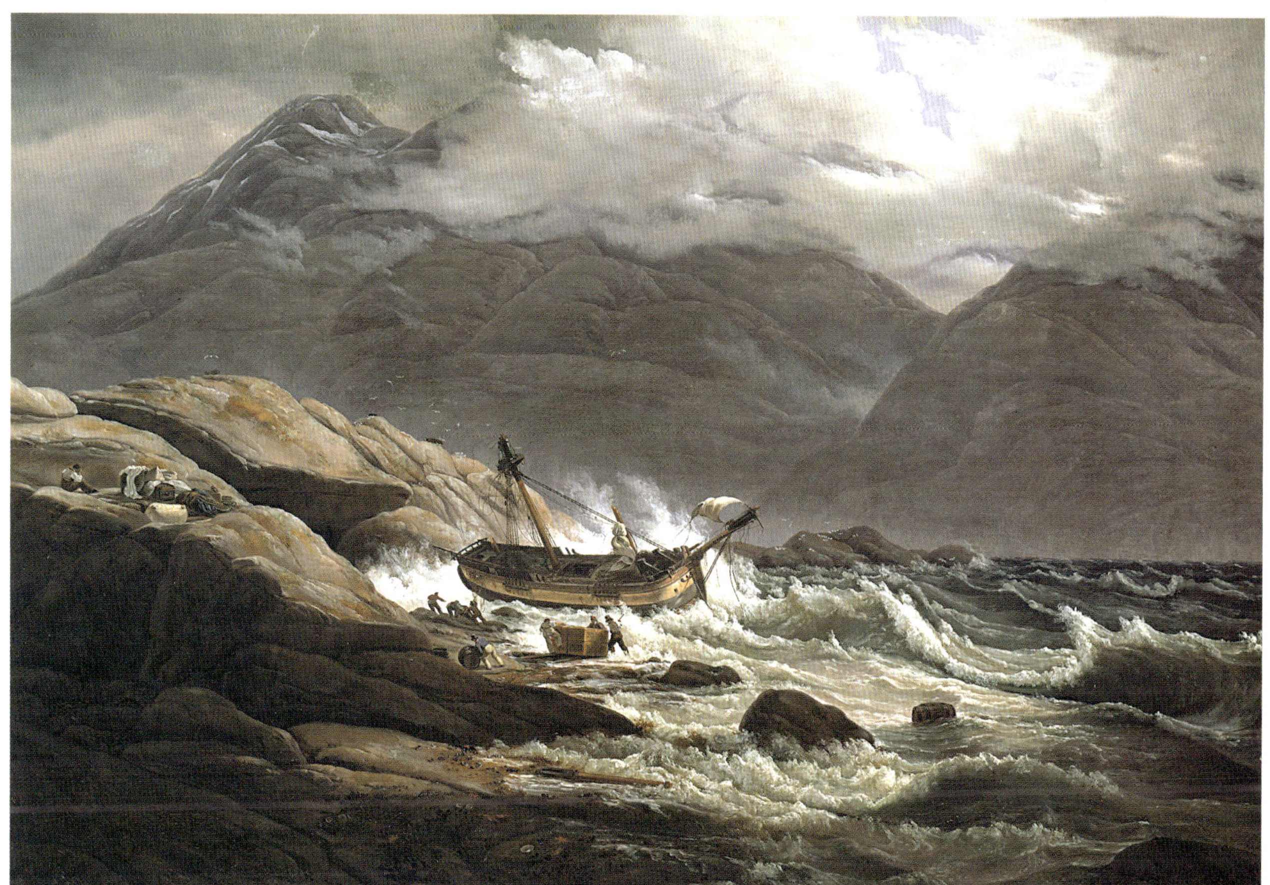

Johan Christian Dahl
(Bergen 1788 - Dresden 1857)

Shipwreck on the Norwegian Coast
Vor der Norwegischen Küste
Schipbreuk aan de Noorse kust

●

1831
78,9 x 114,6 cm / 31.06 x 45.11 in.
Hamburger Kunsthalle, Hamburg

Oil on canvas
Öl auf Leinwand
Olieverf op doek

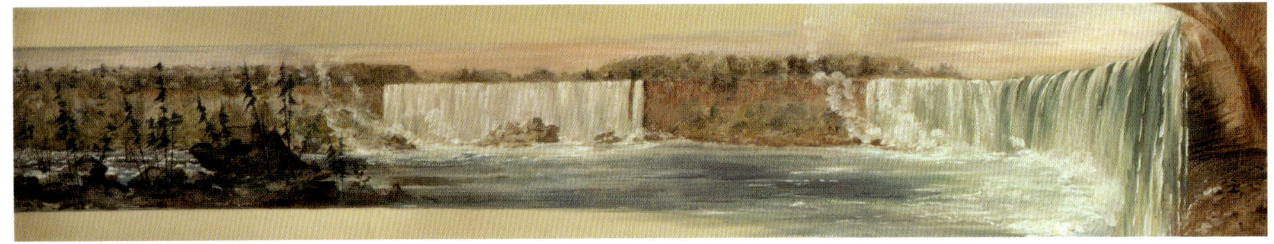

George Catlin
(Wilkes-Barres 1796 - New York 1872)

Niagara Falls

●

c. 1827-1828
41 x 217 cm / 18.50 x 85.43 in.
Smithsonian American Art Museum,
Washington D.C.

Oil on canvas
Öl auf Leinwand
Olieverf op doek

Thomas Cole
(Bolton 1801 - Catskill, New York 1848)

The Pilgrim of the Cross at the End of His Journey
Der Pilger vor dem Kreuz am Ende seiner Reise
Pelgrim voor het Kruis aan het einde van zijn reis

●●

c. 1846-1848
Smithsonian American Art Museum,
Washington D.C.

Oil on canvas / Öl auf Leinwand / Olieverf op doek

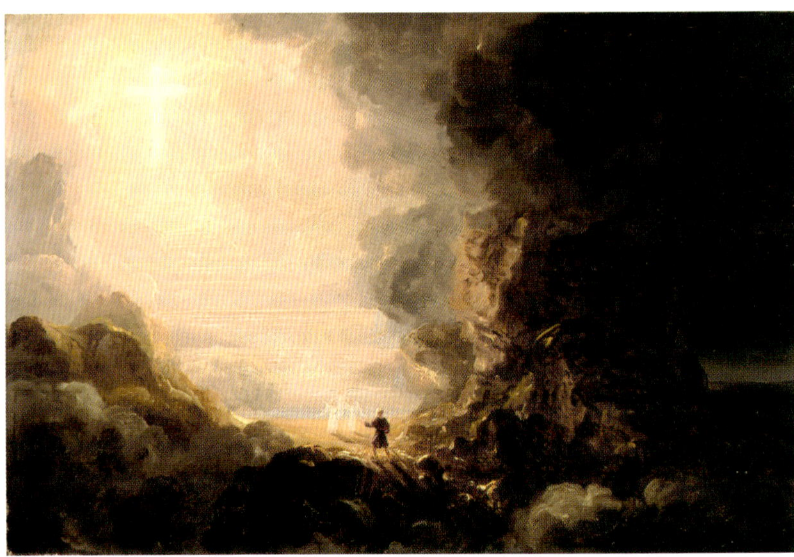

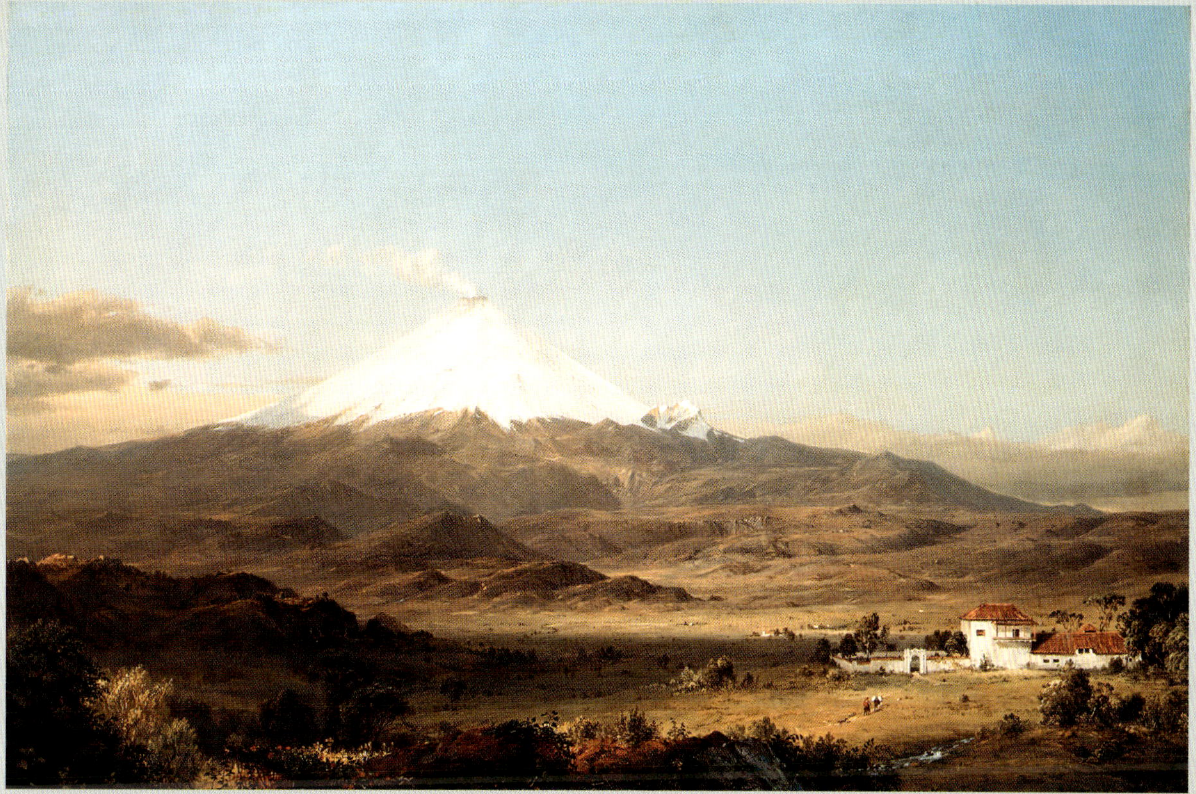

Frederic Edwin Church
(Hartford 1826 - 1900)

Cotopaxi

1855
71,1 x 106,8 cm / 27.99 x 42.04 in.
Smithsonian American Art Museum,
Washington D.C.

Oil on canvas / Öl auf Leinwand
Olieverf op doek

New World Romanticism: the majesty of the American landscape is exalted in painting.

**Romantik der Neuen Welt.
Die Grandiosität der amerikanischen Landschaft wird in der Malerei noch gesteigert.**

**De romantiek van de Nieuwe Wereld.
De grootsheid van het Amerikaanse landschap wordt in de schilderkunst nog groter.**

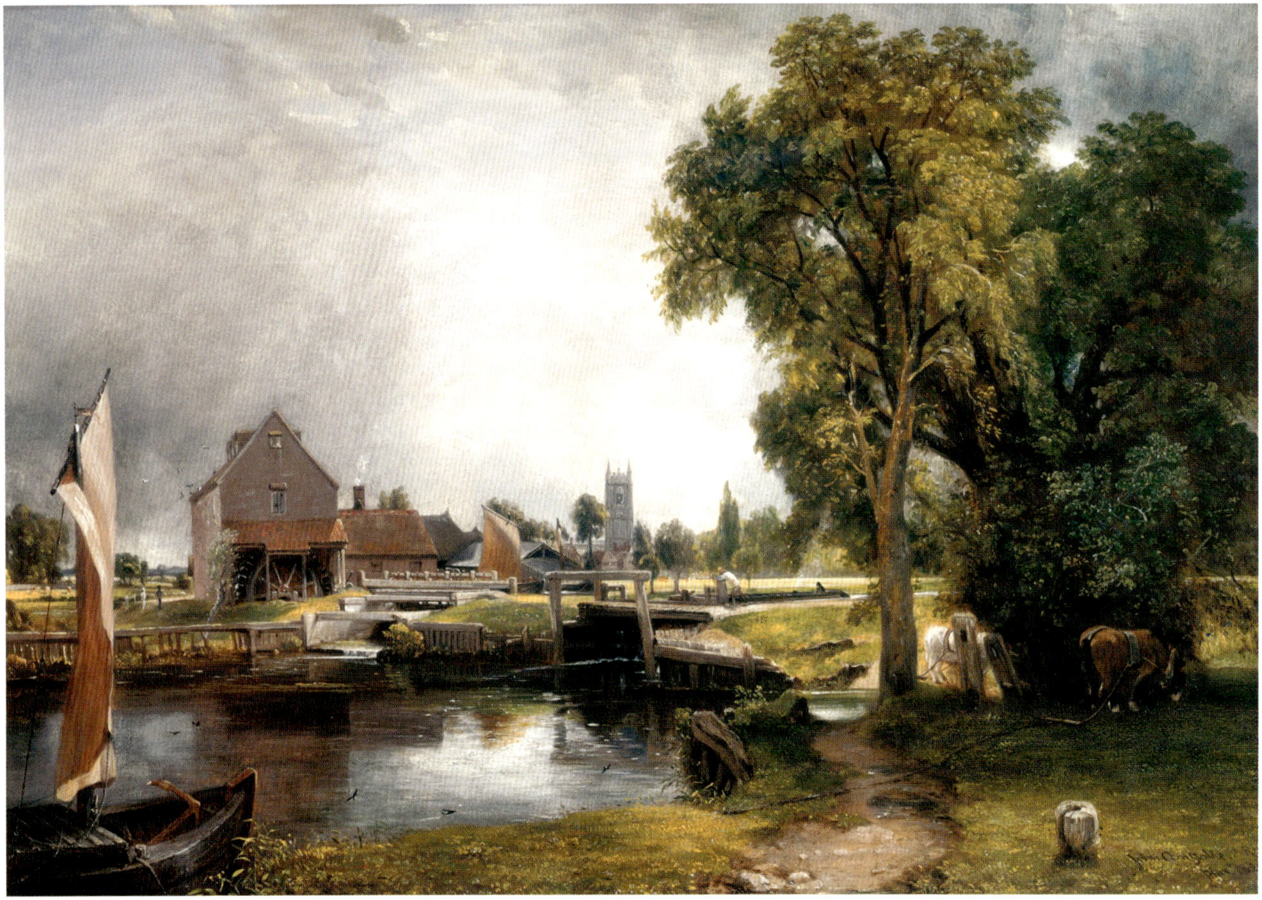

John Constable
(East Berghol 1776 - London 1837)

Dedham Lock and Mill
Der Damm und die Mühle von Dedham
De dijk en de molen van Dedham

●●

1820
53,7 x 76,2 cm / 21.14 x 29.99 in.
Victoria & Albert Museum, London

Oil on canvas
Öl auf Leinwand
Olieverf op doek

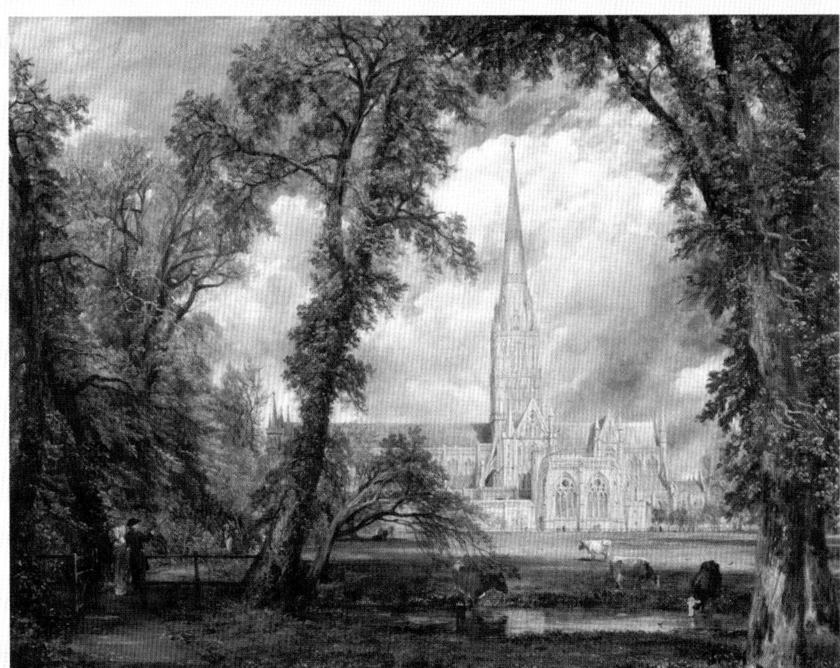

John Constable
(East Berghol 1776 - London 1837)

View of Salisbury Cathedral from the Bishop's House
Die Kathedrale von Salisbury vom Garten des Bischofs aus gesehen
Zicht op de Kathedraal van Salisbury vanaf de weilanden

●●●

1823
87,6 x 111,8 cm / 34.48 x 44.01 in.
Victoria & Albert Museum, London

Oil on canvas
Öl auf Leinwand
Olieverf op doek

John Constable
(East Berghol 1776 - London 1837)

Windmill near Brighton
Eine Windmühle nahe Brighton
Windmolen nabij Brighton

●

1824
Victoria & Albert Museum, London

Oil on canvas
Öl auf Leinwand
Olieverf op doek

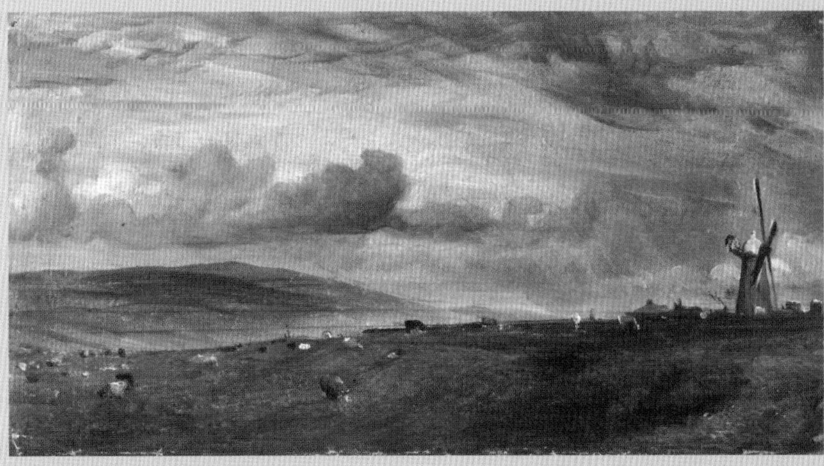

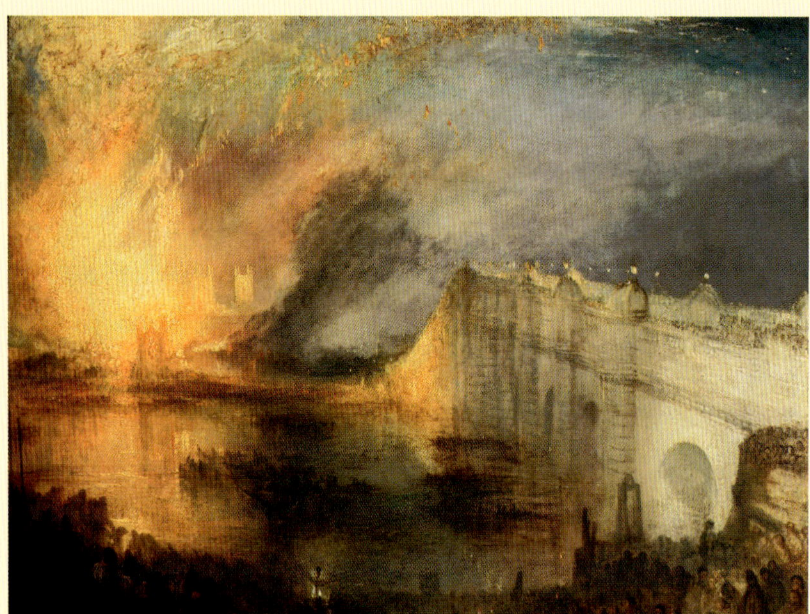

Joseph Turner
(London 1775 - 1851)

The Burning of the Houses of Lords and Commons
Brand des Parlamentsgebäudes
De brand van het Hoger- en Lagerhuis

●●

1835
92 x 123 cm / 36.22 x 48.42 in.
Philadelphia Museum of Art, Philadelphia

Oil on canvas
Öl auf Leinwand
Olieverf op doek

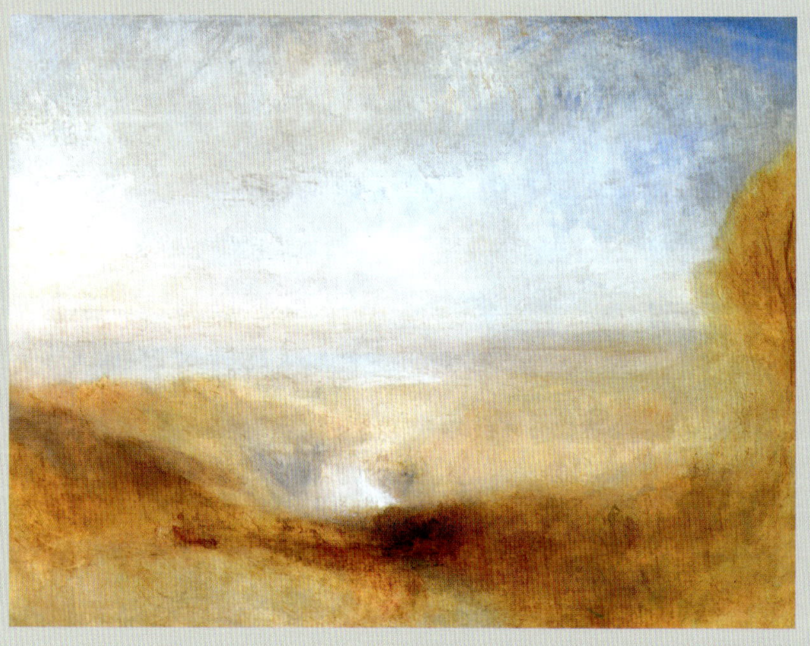

Joseph Turner
(London 1775 - 1851)

Landscape with River and Bay in the Background
Landschaft mit einem Fluss und einer Bucht in der Ferne
Landschap met rivier en baai op de achtergrond

●●

c. 1845
93 x 123 cm / 36.61 x 48.42 in.
Musée du Louvre, Paris

Oil on canvas
Öl auf Leinwand
Olieverf op doek

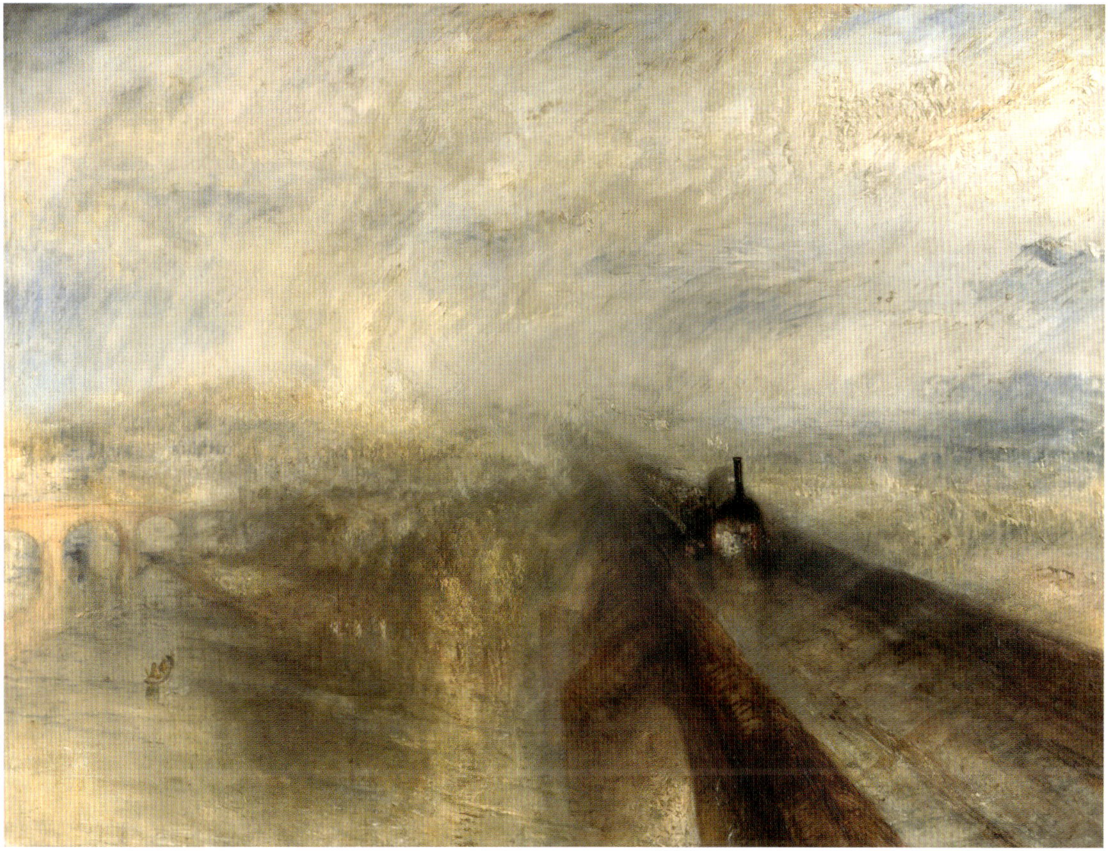

Joseph Turner
(London 1775 - 1851)

Rain, Steam and Speed
Regen, Dampf und Geschwindigkeit
Regen, stoom en snelheid

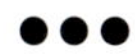

1844
89 x 122 cm / 35.03 x 48.03 in.
The National Gallery, London

Oil on canvas / Öl auf Leinwand
Olieverf op doek

Joseph Turner: the English precursor of Impressionism whose works often depictes dramatic weather conditions.

Joseph Turner englischer Vorgriff auf den Impressionismus mit teilweise dramatischen Wettersituationen.

Joseph Turner, een Engelse voorloper van het Impressionisme, wiens werk soms wordt gekenmerkt door dramatische weersomstandigheden.

A group of English artists recognize veracity in Italian painting before Raphael and call themselves Pre-Raphaelites.

In der italienischen Malerei vor Raphael erkennt die englische Künstlergruppe Wahrhaftigkeit und nennt sich Präraphaeliten.

Een Engelse kunstenaarsgroep erkent de waarachtigheid in de Italiaanse schilderkunst van Rafaël en noemt zich Prerafaëlieten.

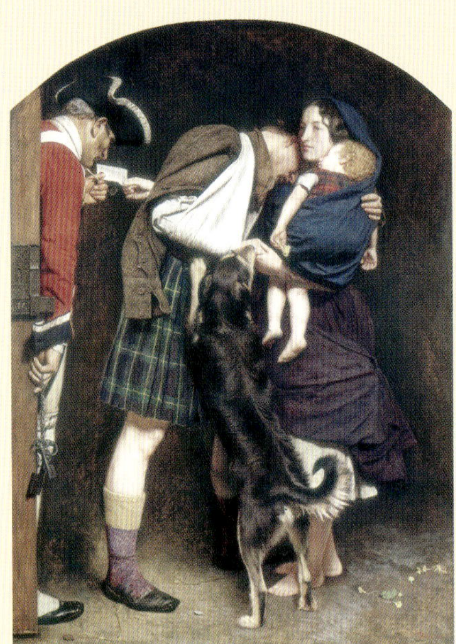

John Everett Millais
(Southampton 1829 - London 1896)

The Order of Release, 1746
Der Befehl zur Freilassung, 1746
Het bevel tot vrijlating, 1746

●

1852-1853
150,5 x 121 cm / 59.25 x 47.64 in.
Tate Gallery, London

Oil on canvas / Öl auf Leinwand
Olieverf op doek

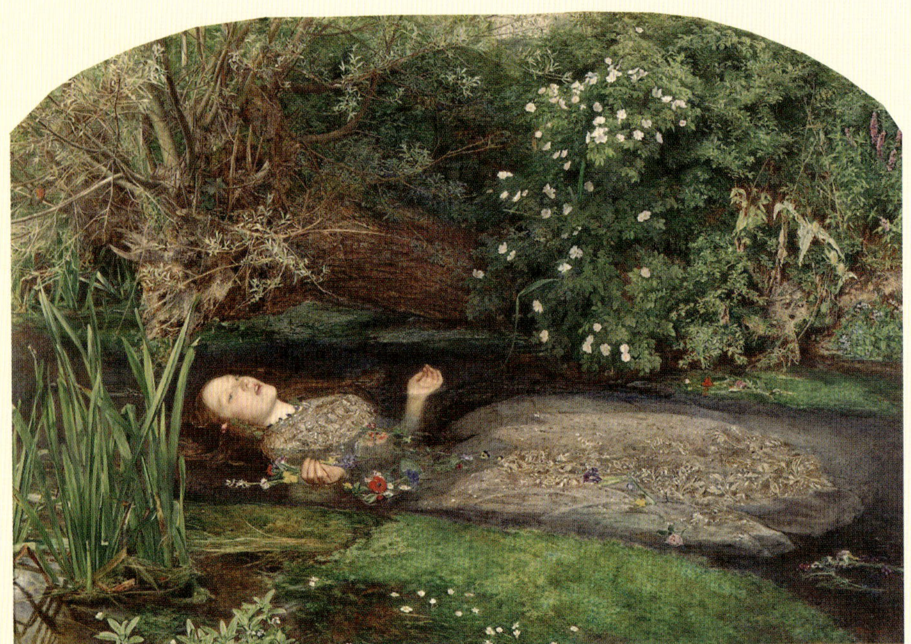

John Everett Millais
(Southampton 1829 - London 1896)

Ophelia

●●●

1852
Tate Gallery, London

Oil on canvas
Öl auf Leinwand
Olieverf op doek

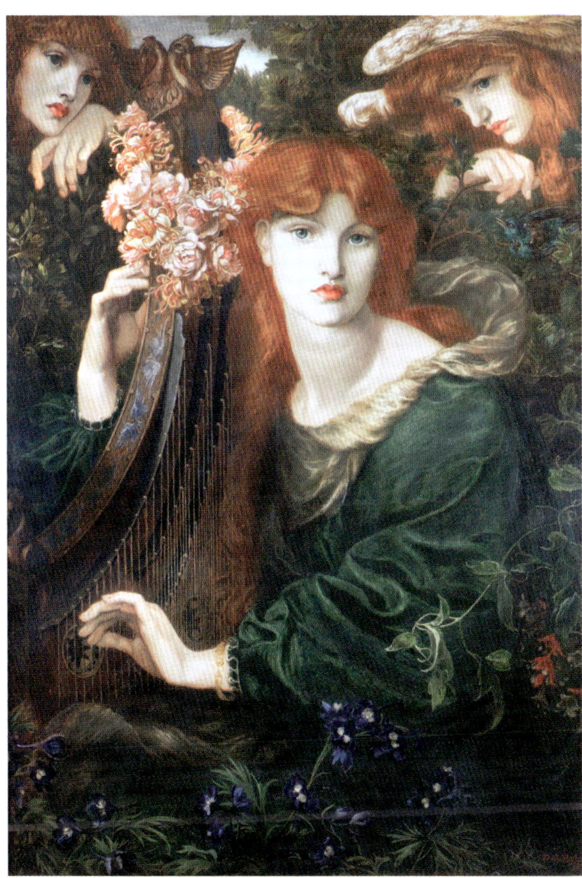

Dante Gabriele Rossetti
(London 1828 - Birchington 1882)

La Ghirlandata

●●

1873
Guildhall Library and Art Gallery, London

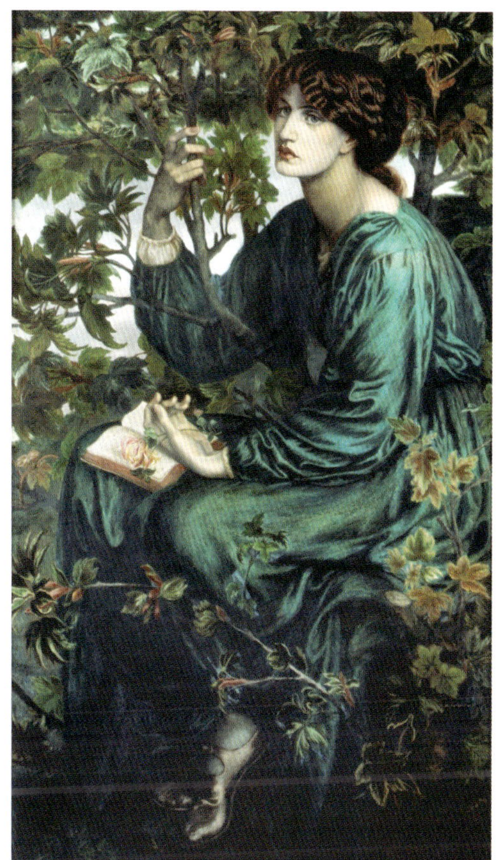

Dante Gabriele Rossetti
(London 1828 - Birchington 1882)

The Day Dream
Der Tagtraum
De dagdroom

●●●

1880
158,7 x 92,7 cm / 62.48 x 36.5 in.
Victoria & Albert Museum, London

Oil on canvas
Öl auf Leinwand
Olieverf op doek

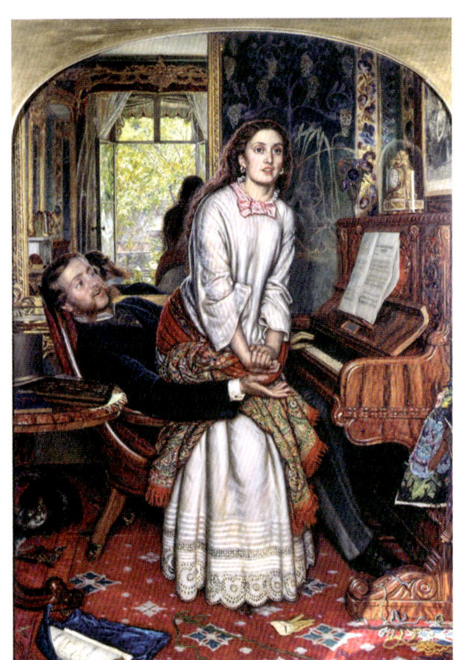

William Holman Hunt
(London 1827 - 1910)

Awakening Conscience
Das erwachende Gewissen
Het ontwakend bewustzijn

●

1853
76 x 55 cm / 29.92 x 21.65 in.

Private Collection / Privatsammlung
Privécollectie

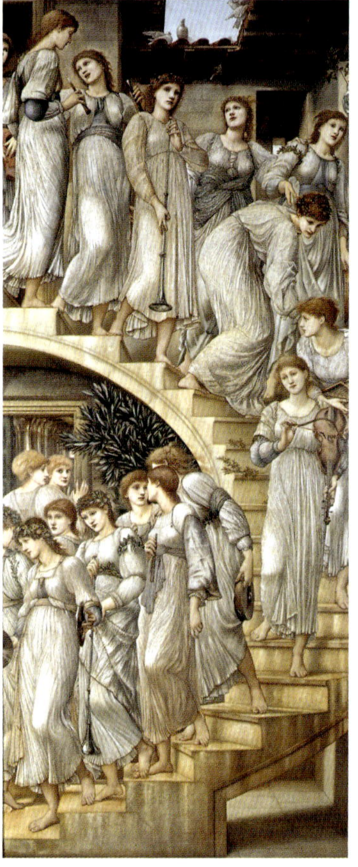

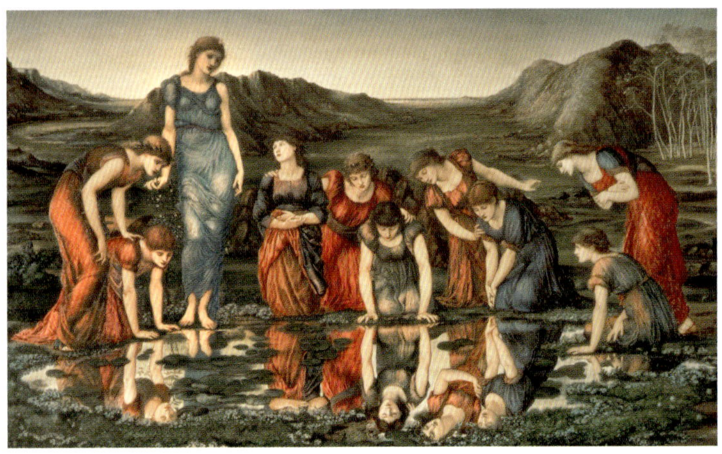

Edward Coley Burne-Jones
(Birmingham 1833 - Fulham 1898)

The Mirror of Venus
Der Spiegel der Venus
De Spiegel van Venus

●

1898
Museu Calouste Gulbenkian, Lisboa

Oil on canvas / Öl auf Leinwand
Olieverf op doek

◂ Edward Coley Burne-Jones
(Birmingham 1833 - Fulham 1898)

The Golden Stairs
Die golden Treppe
De gouden trap

●

1880
269,2 x 116,8 cm / 105.98 x 45.98 in.
Tate Gallery, London

Oil on canvas
Öl auf Leinwand
Olieverf op doek

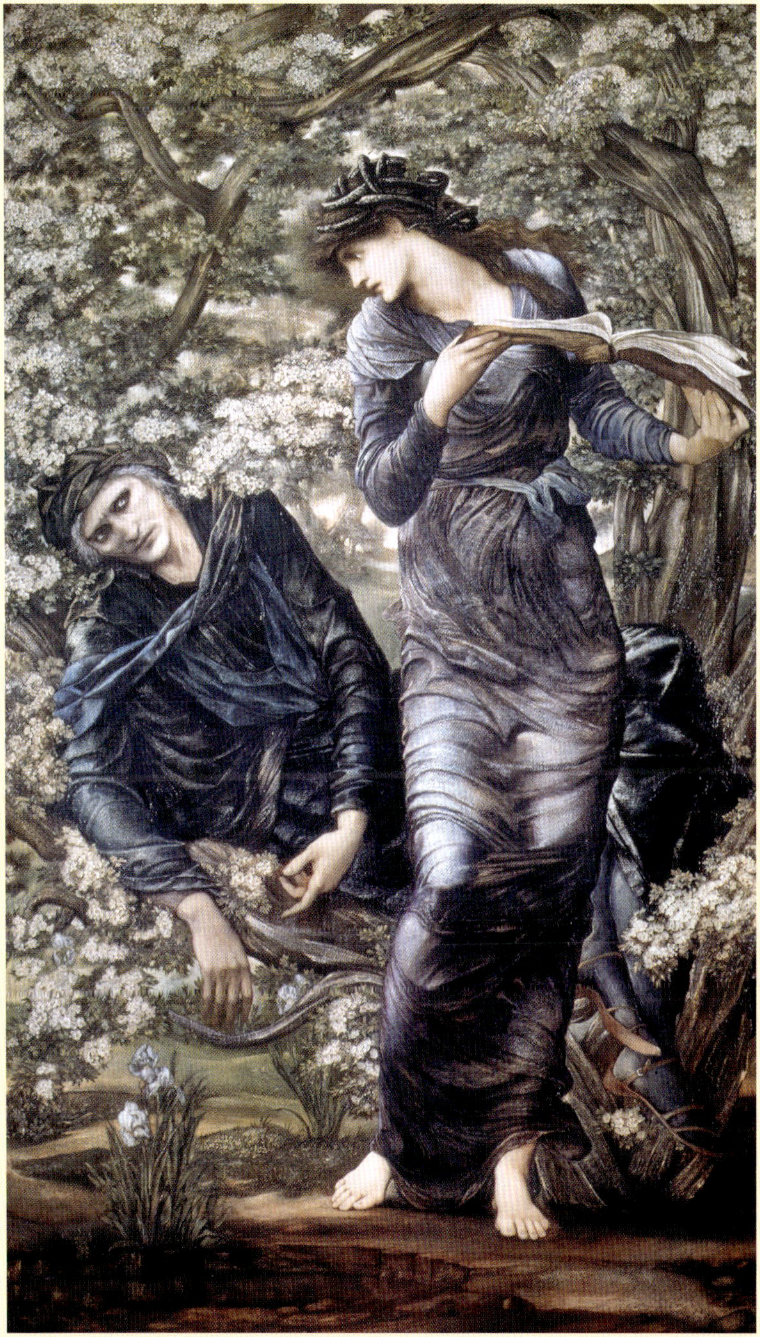

Edward Coley Burne-Jones
(Birmingham 1833 - Fulham 1898)

The Beguiling of Merlin
Die Verzauberung Merlins
De verleiding van Merlijn

●

1874

Private Collection / Privatsammlung
Privécollectie

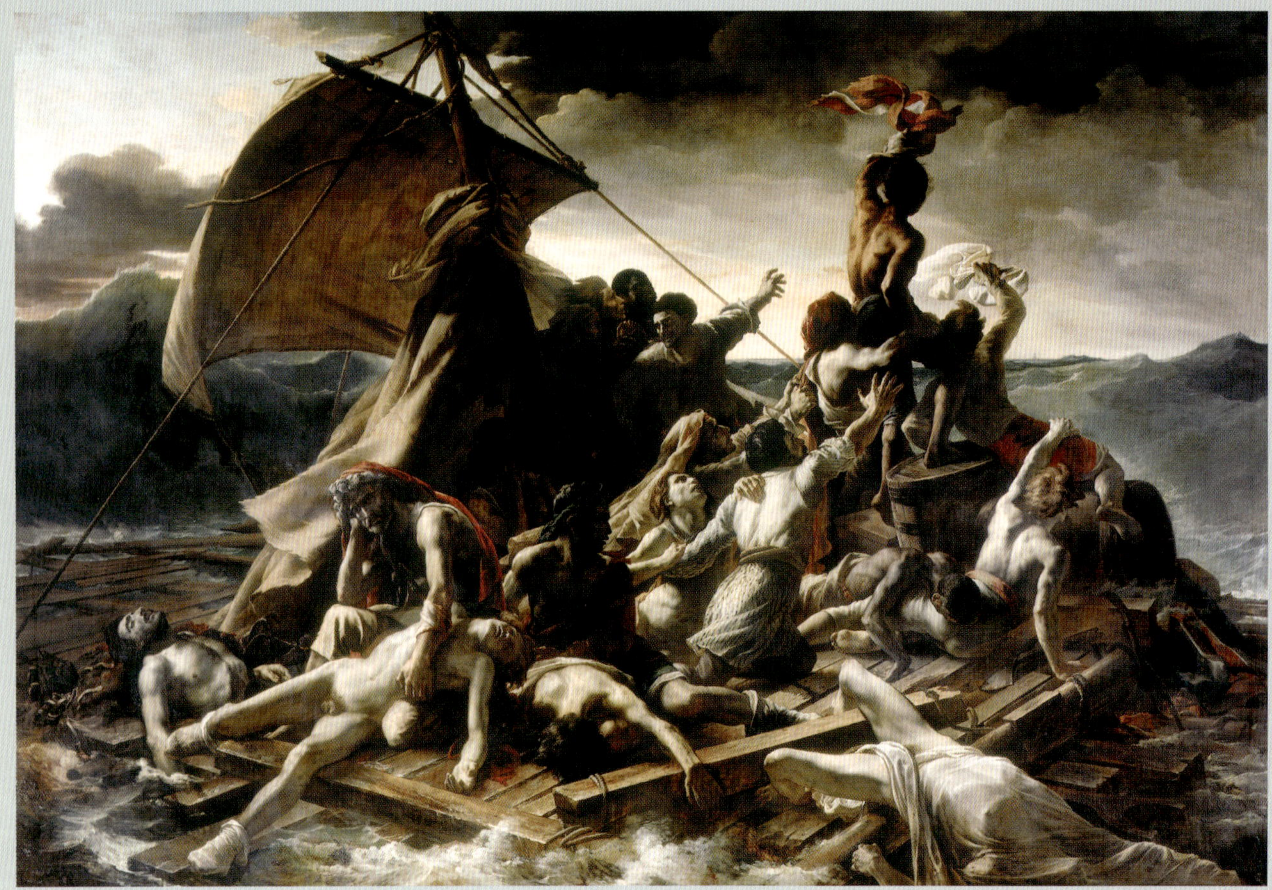

348

Jean-Louis Théodore Géricault
(Rouen 1791 - Paris 1824)

The Raft of the Medusa
Das Floß der Medusa
Het vlot van de Medusa

●●●

c. 1819-1819
491 x 716 cm / 193.30 x 281.88 in.
Musée du Louvre, Paris

Oil on canvas
Öl auf Leinwand
Olieverf op doek

French Romanticism, unlike the German, takes a political stance.

Die französische Romantik bezieht im Gegensatz zur deutschen politisch Stellung.

De Franse romantiek neemt, in tegenstelling tot de Duitse, politieke stellingname in.

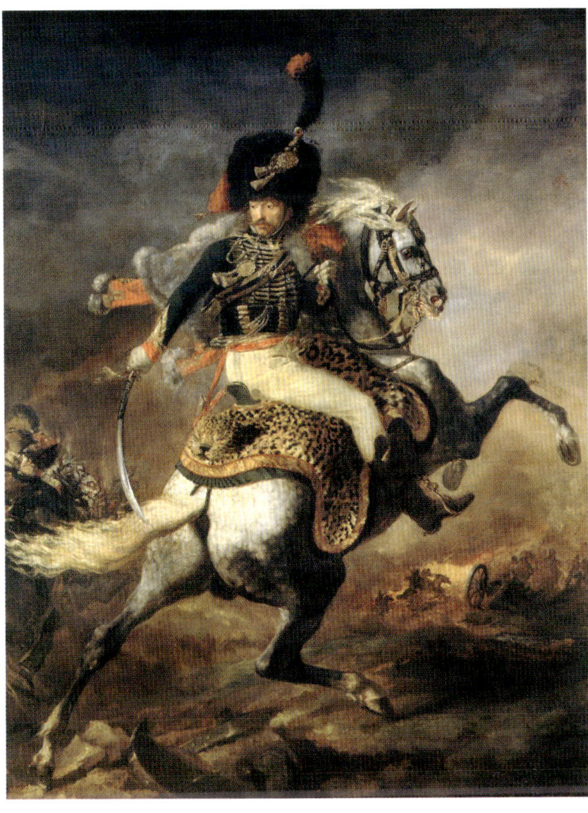

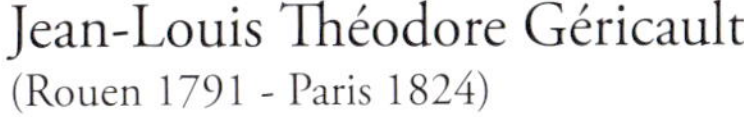

Jean-Louis Théodore Géricault
(Rouen 1791 - Paris 1824)

Officer of the Chasseurs Commanding a Charge
Offizier der Gardejäger beim Angriff
Officier van de Keizerlijke ruiterij in de aanval

●

1812
292 x 194 cm / 114.96 x 76.37 in.
Musée du Louvre, Paris

Oil on canvas
Öl auf Leinwand
Olieverf op doek

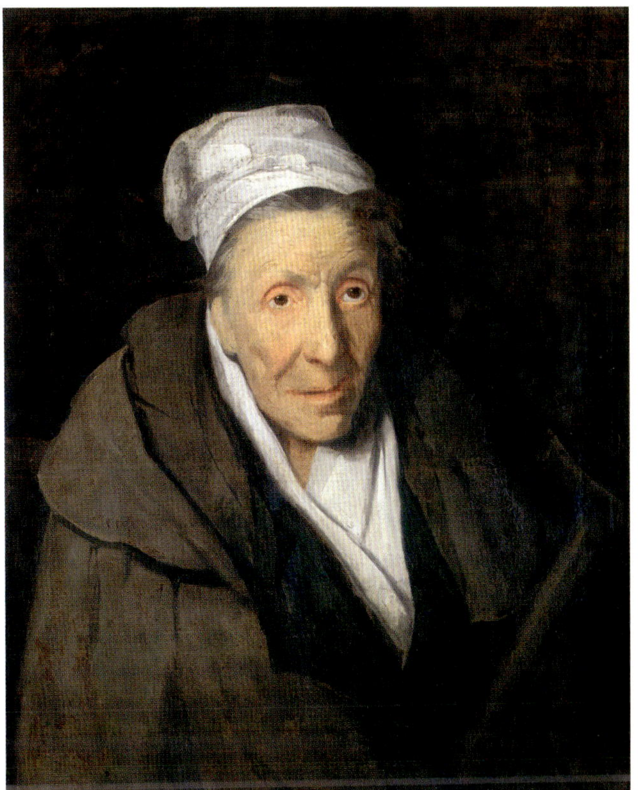

Jean-Louis Théodore Géricault
(Rouen 1791 - Paris 1824)

Woman with a Gambling Mania
Die Irre
De gokverslaafde

●●

c. 1819-1824
77 x 64 cm / 30.31 x 25.19 in.
Musée du Louvre, Paris

Oil on canvas
Öl auf Leinwand
Olieverf op doek

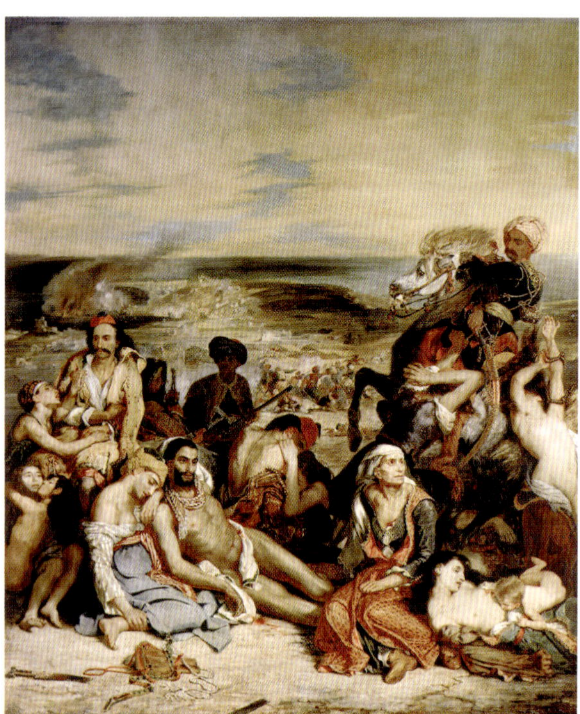

Eugène Delacroix
(Saint-Maurice 1798 - Paris 1863)

The Massacre at Chios
Das Massaker in Scio (Chios)
De Slachting op Chios

●●

1824
422 x 352 cm / 166.14 x 138.58 in.
Musée du Louvre, Paris

Oil on canvas
Öl auf Leinwand
Olieverf op doek

Eugène Delacroix
(Saint-Maurice 1798 - Paris 1863)

Death of Sardanapalus
Der Tod des Sardanapal
De dood van Sardanapalus

●●

1827
395 x 495 cm / 155.51 x 194.88 in.
Musée du Louvre, Paris

Oil on canvas / Öl auf Leinwand
Olieverf op doek

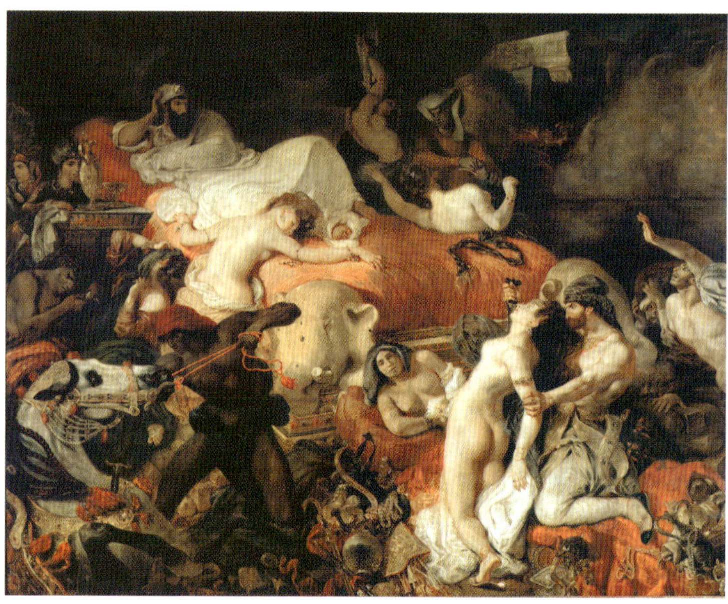

Eugène Delacroix
(Saint-Maurice 1798 - Paris 1863)

Liberty Leading the People
Die Freiheit führt das Volk
De Vrijheid leidt het volk

●●●

1830
260 x 325 cm / 102.36 x 127.95 in.
Musée du Louvre, Paris

Oil on canvas
Öl auf Leinwand
Olieverf op doek

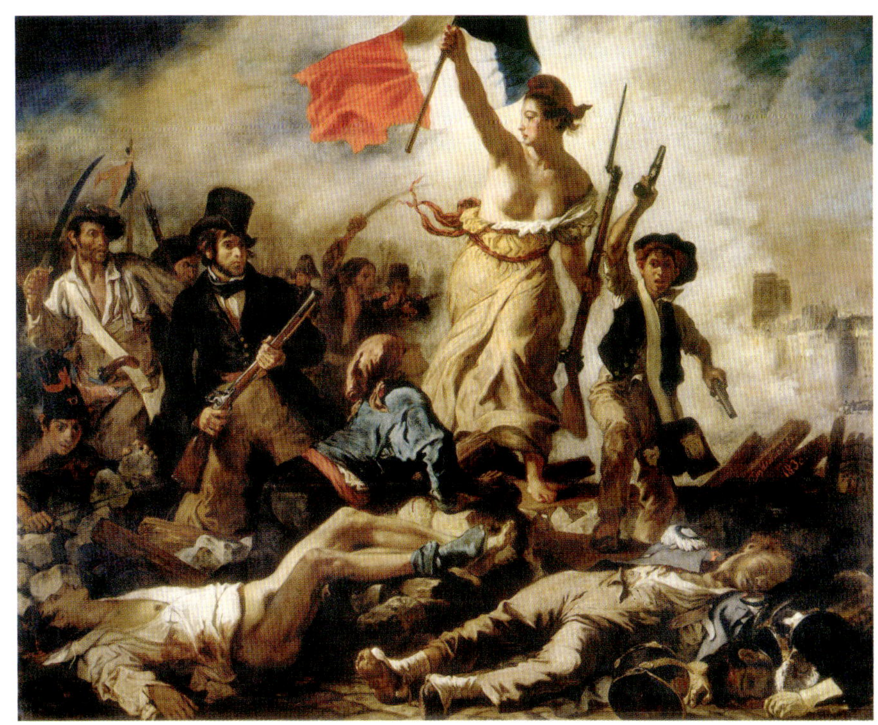

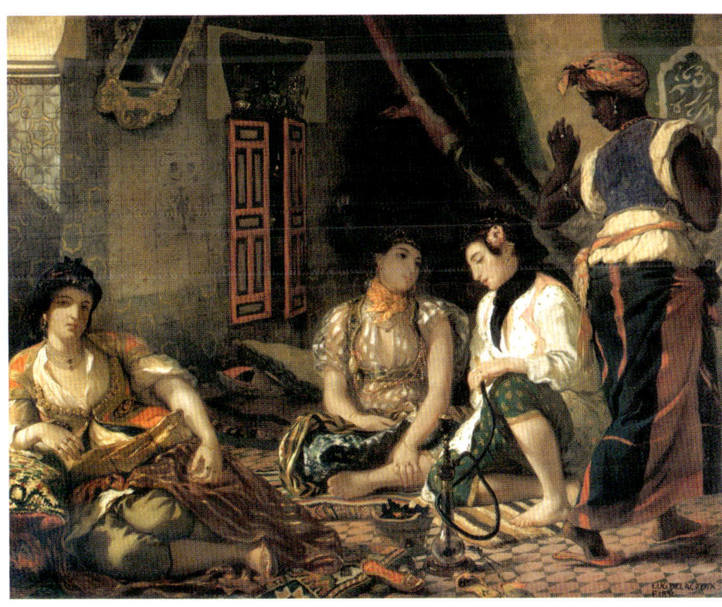

Eugène Delacroix
(Saint-Maurice 1798 - Paris 1863)

The Women of Algiers
Die Frauen von Algier in ihrem Gemach
De vrouwen van Algiers

●●●

1834
180 x 229 cm / 70.86 x 90.15 in.
Musée du Louvre, Paris

Oil on canvas / Öl auf Leinwand
Olieverf op doek

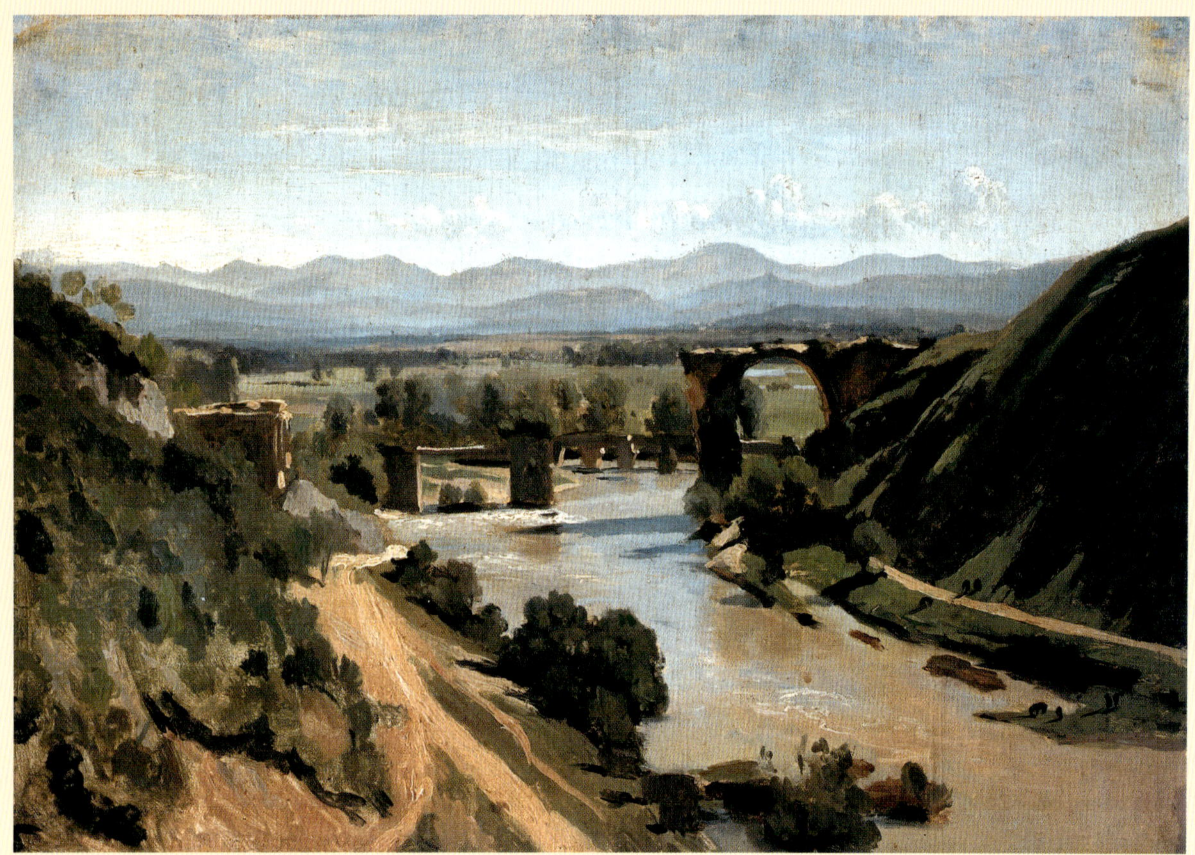

Jean-Baptiste Camille Corot
(Paris 1796 - Ville-d'Avray 1875

The Bridge at Narni
Brücke bei Narni
De brug bij Narni

●●

1826
34 x 48 cm / 13.38 x 18.89 in.
Musée du Louvre, Paris

Oil on canvas
Öl auf Leinwand
Olieverf op doek

The painter moved outdoors: "Plein Air" painting begins with Camille Corot.

Der Maler zieht ins Freie. Mit Camille Corot beginnt die "Pleine Air" Malerei.

De schilder trekt het vrije veld in. Met Camille Corot begint de "Plein Air" schilderkunst.

Jean-Baptiste Camille Corot
(Paris 1796 - Ville-d'Avray 1875

Cathedral of Chartres
Die Kathedrale von Chartres
De kathedraal van Chartres

●●

1830
64 x 51 cm / 25.2 x 20.08 in.
Musée du Louvre, Paris

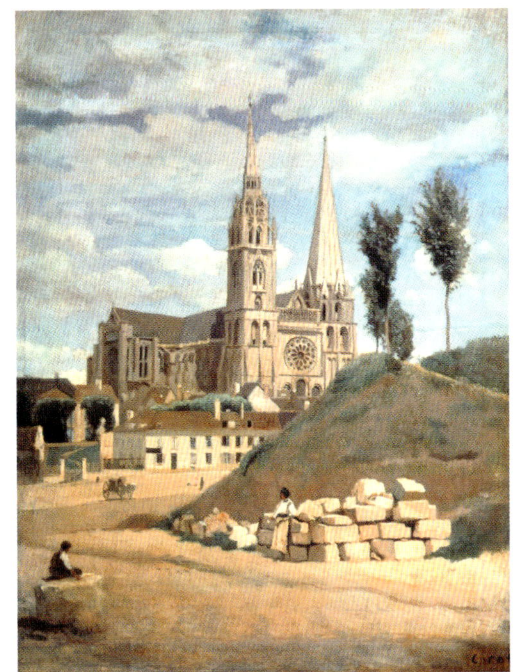

Jean-Baptiste Camille Corot
(Paris 1796 - Ville-d'Avray 1875

Recollection of Mortefontaine
Erinnrung an Mortefontaine
Herinnering aan Mortefontaine

●●

1864
64 x 88 cm / 25.19 x 34.64 in.
Musée du Louvre, Paris

Oil on canvas
Öl auf Leinwand
Olieverf op doek

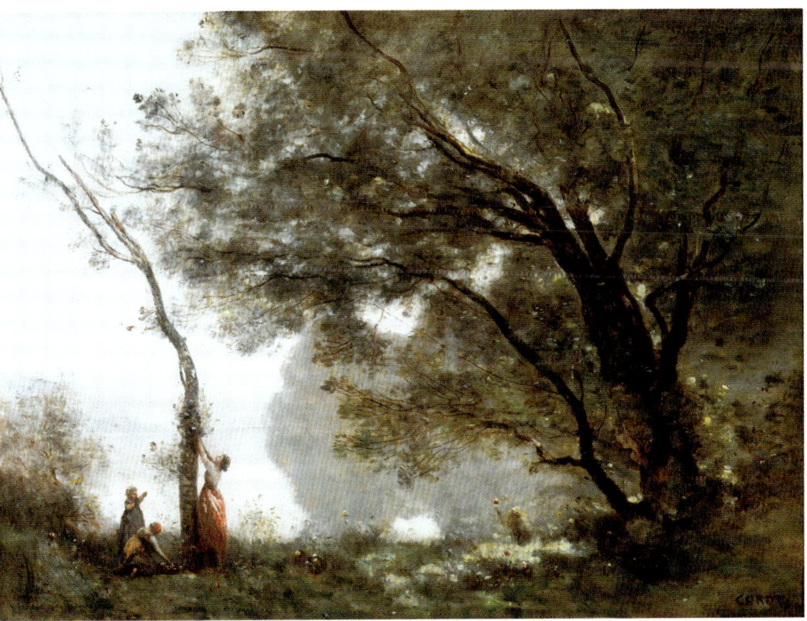

Théodore Rousseau
(Paris 1812 - Barbizon 1867)

The Edge of the Forest at Fontainebleau, Sunset
Im Wald von Fontainebleau, Sonnenuntergang
Uitgang van het bos van Fontainebleau, zonsondergang

●

1848
Musée du Louvre, Paris

Oil on canvas
Öl auf Leinwand
Olieverf op doek

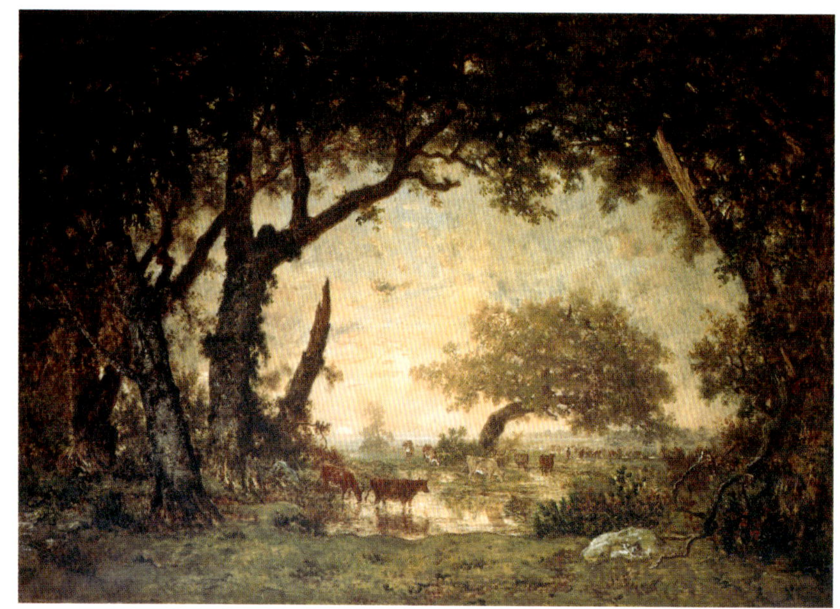

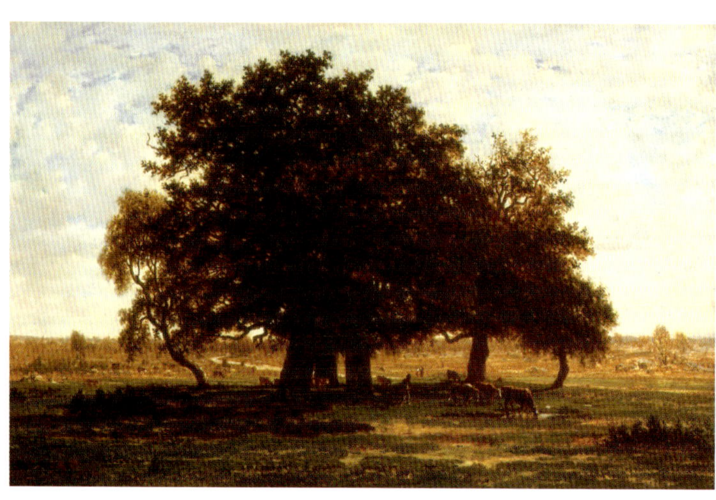

Théodore Rousseau
(Paris 1812 - Barbizon 1867)

Oak Trees near Apremont
Die Eichen des Aspromonte
Groep eiken, Aspromonte

●

1852
63.5 x 99.5 cm / 24.99 x 39.17 in.
Musée du Louvre, Paris

Oil on canvas
Öl auf Leinwand
Olieverf op doek

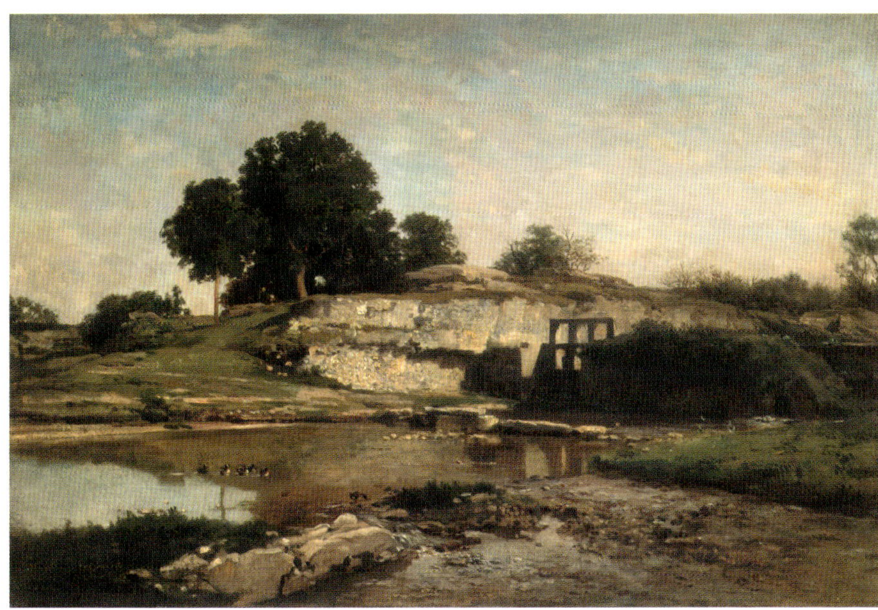

Charles-François Daubigny
(Paris 1817 - 1878)

Flood Gate at Optevoz
Die Schleuse von Optevoz
De dijk van Optevoz

●

1855
Musée du Louvre, Paris

Oil on canvas
Öl auf Leinwand
Olieverf op doek

Charles-François Daubigny
(Paris 1817 - 1878)

Spring
Frühling
Lente

●

1857
94 x 193 cm / 37 x 75.98 in.
Musée du Louvre, Paris

Oil on canvas
Öl auf Leinwand
Olieverf op doek

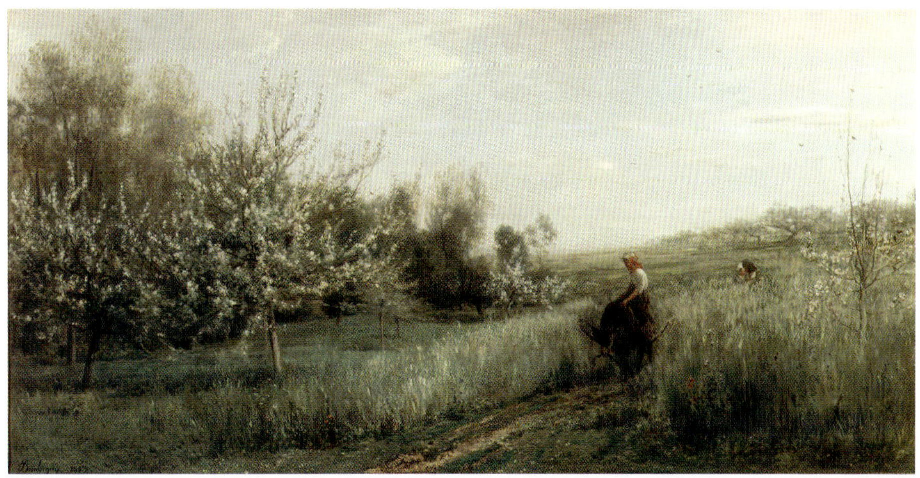

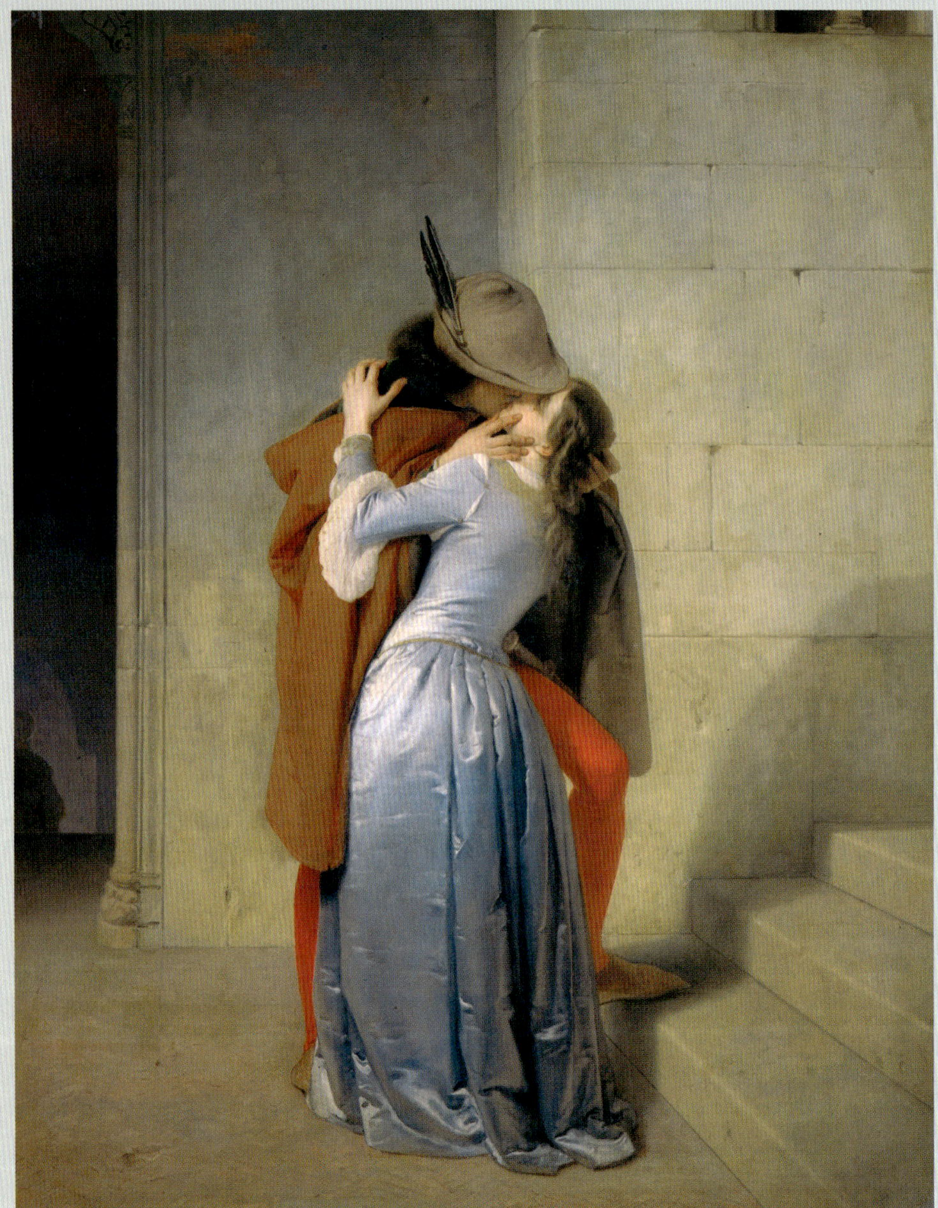

Portraits and castle views: Francesco Hayez is the protagonist of Italian Romanticism.

Burgszenen und Porträts, Hayez ist der Hauptvertreter der italienischen Romantik.

Kasteelscènes en portretten, Hayez is de belangrijkste vertegenwoordiger van de Italiaanse romantiek.

Francesco Hayez
(Venezia 1791 - Milano 1882)

The Kiss
Der Kuss
De kus

●●

1859
112 x 88 cm / 44.09 x 34.64 in.
Pinacoteca di Brera, Milano

Oil on canvas
Öl auf Leinwand
Olieverf op doek

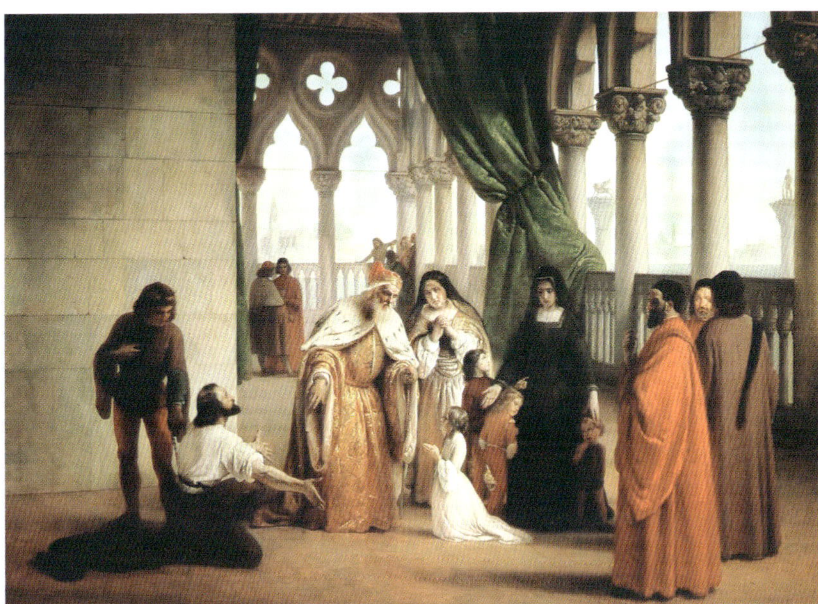

Francesco Hayez
(Venezia 1791 - Milano 1882)

The Two Foscari
Die beiden Foscari
De twee Foscari's

●

1842
120 x 167 cm / 47.24 x 65.74 in.
Galleria d'Arte Moderna, Firenze

Oil on canvas
Öl auf Leinwand
Olieverf op doek

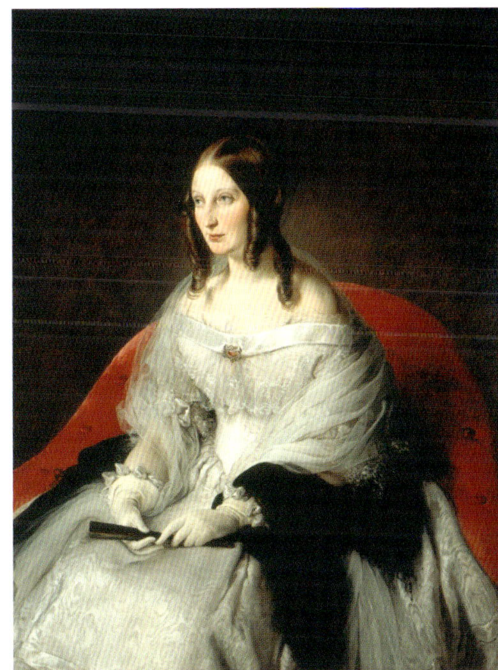

Francesco Hayez
(Venezia 1791 - Milano 1882)

Portrait of the Princess of Sant'Antimo
Portrait der Prinzessin von Sant'Antimo
Portret van de prinses van Sant'Amtimo

●●

1840-1844
225 x 300 cm / 88.6 x 118.2 in.
Museo di San Martino, Napoli

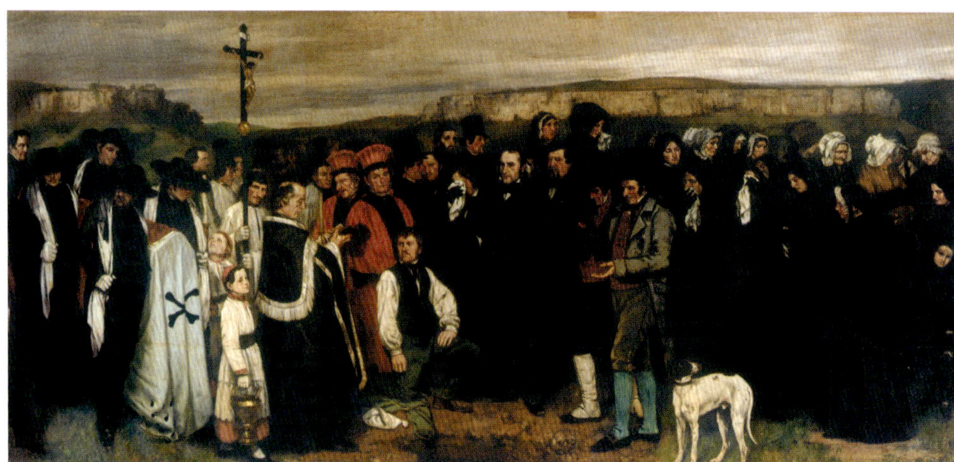

Gustave Courbet
(Ornans 1819 - La Tour-de-Peilz 1877)

Funeral at Ornans
Begräbnis in Ornans
Begrafenis te Ornans

●

c. 1849-1850
314 x 663 cm /
123.62 x 261.02 in.
Musée d'Orsay, Paris

Oil on canvas
Öl auf Leinwand
Olieverf op doek

Gustave Courbet
(Ornans 1819 - La Tour-de-Peilz 1877)

The Meeting, or Bonjour Monsieur Courbet
Treffen zwischen Alfred Bruyas und Gustave Courbet
Ontmoeting tussen Alfred Bruyas en Gustave Courbet

●

c. 1854
129 x 149 cm / 50.78 x 58.66 in.
Musée Fabre, Montpellier

Oil on canvas
Öl auf Leinwand
Olieverf op doek

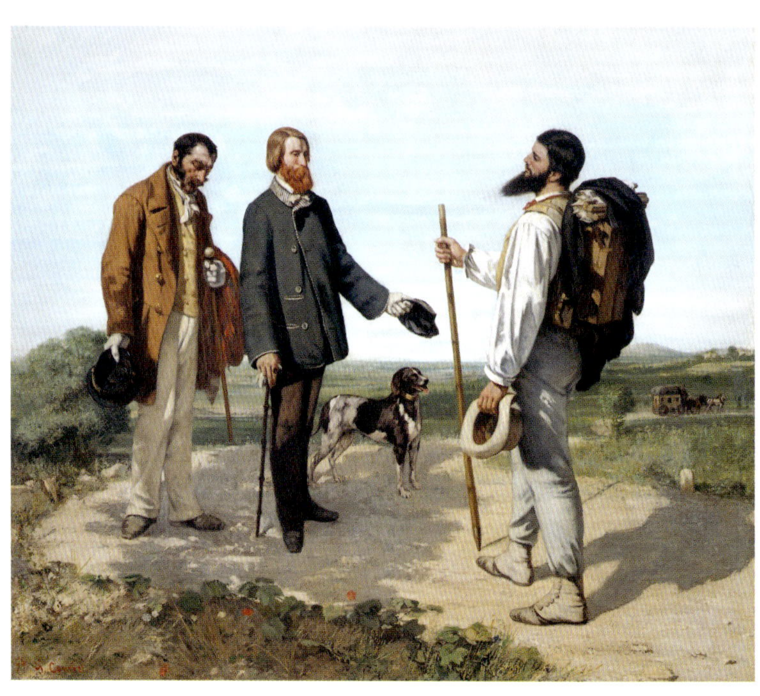

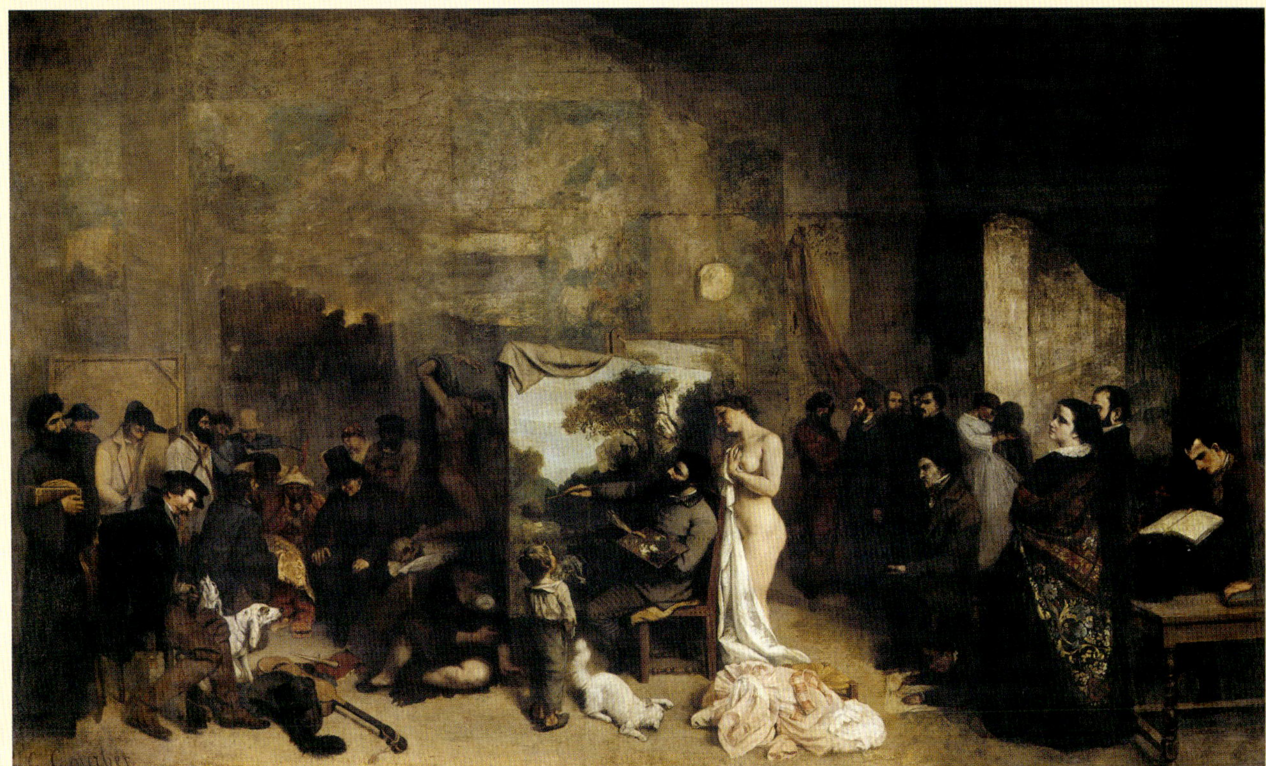

Gustave Courbet
(Ornans 1819 - La Tour-de-Peilz 1877)

The Painter's Studio
Das Maleratelier
Het atelier van de schilder

●

1854-1855
361 x 598 cm / 142.12 x 235.43 in.
Musée d'Orsay, Paris

Oil on canvas
Öl auf Leinwand
Olieverf op doek

Gustave Courbet is excluded from the Salon of Paris due to his controversial subjects.

Gustave Courbet, wird wegen seiner brisanten Themen vom Pariser Kunst Salon ausgeschlossen.

Gustave Courbet wordt vanwege zijn explosieve thema's geweerd uit de Salon van Parijs.

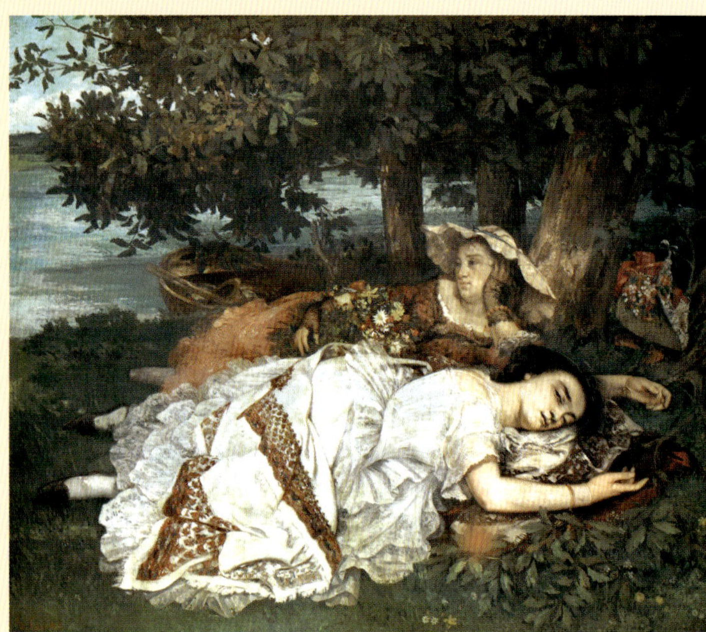

Gustave Courbet
(Ornans 1819 - La Tour-de-Peilz 1877)

Young Ladies on the Bank of the Seine
Fräulein am Ufer der Seine
Jongedames aan de oevers van de Seine

●●

1857
174 x 206 cm / 68.50 x 81.10 in.
Musée du Petit Palais, Paris

Oil on canvas / Öl auf Leinwand
Olieverf op doek

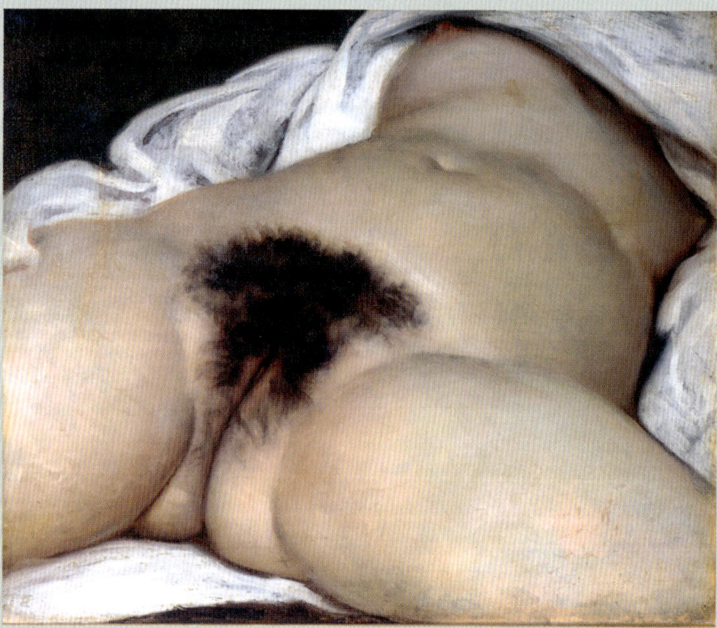

Gustave Courbet
(Ornans 1819 - La Tour-de-Peilz 1877)

The Origin of the World
Der Ursprung der Welt
De oorsprong van de wereld

●●●

1866
46 x 55 cm / 18.11 x 21.65 in.
Musée d'Orsay, Paris

Oil on canvas / Öl auf Leinwand
Olieverf op doek

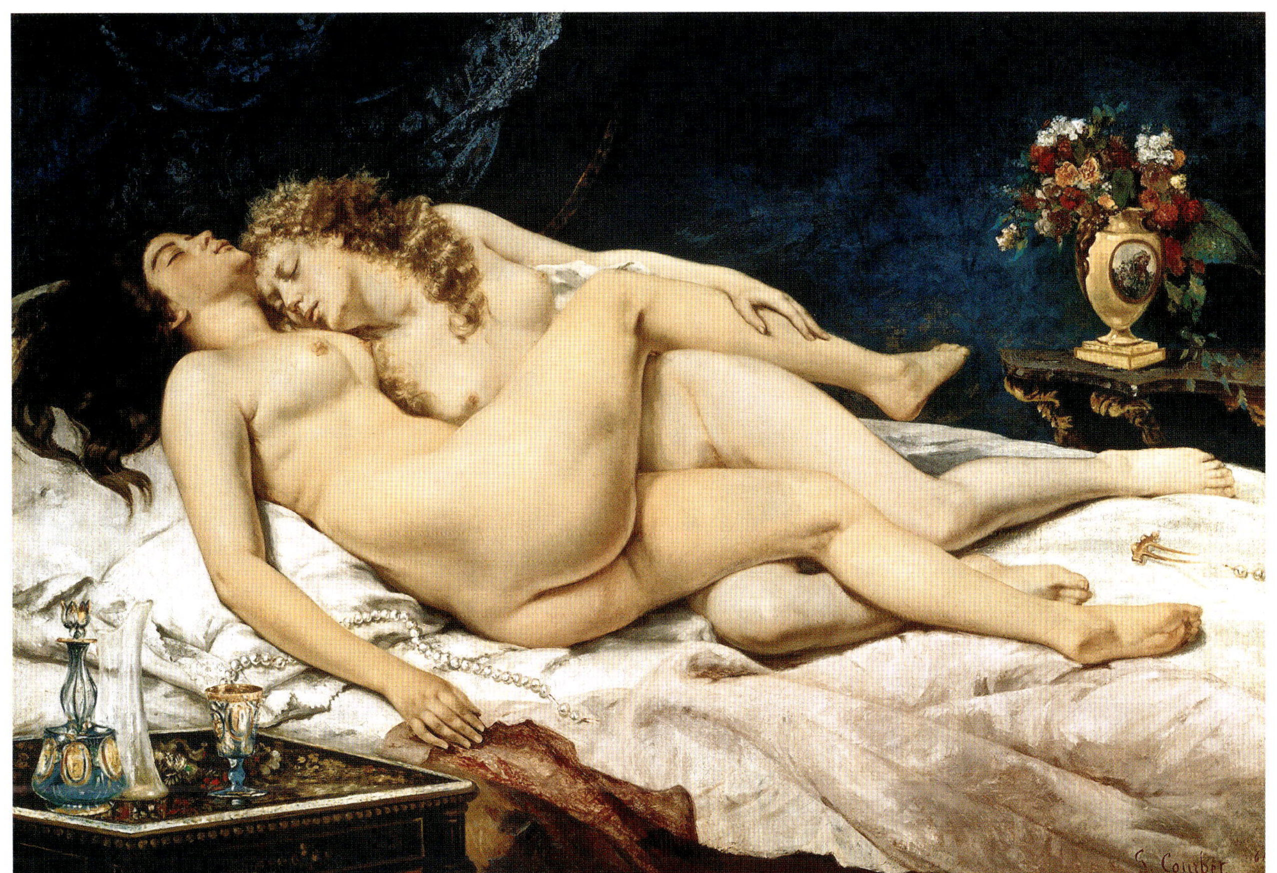

Gustave Courbet
(Ornans 1819 - La Tour-de-Peilz 1877)

Sleep
Der Schlaf
De slaap

●●●

1866
135 x 200 cm / 53.14 x 78.74 in.
Musée du Petit Palais, Paris

Oil on canvas / Öl auf Leinwand
Olieverf op doek

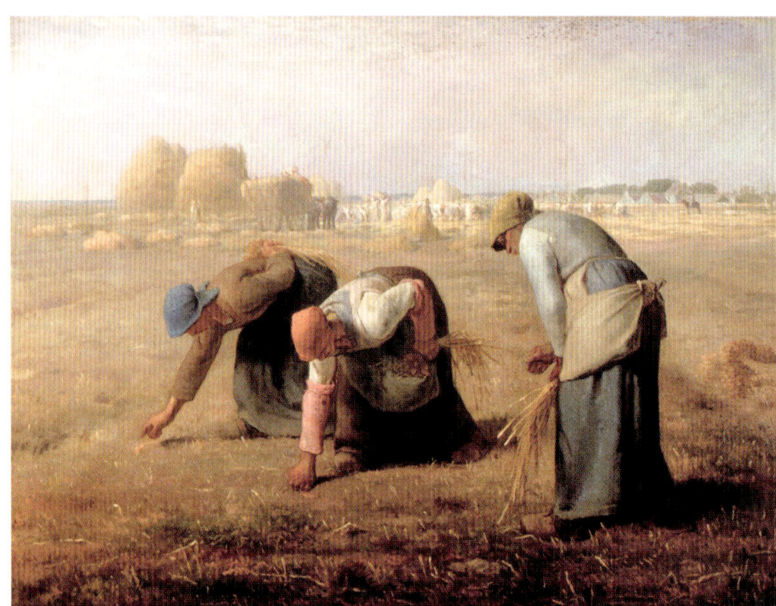

Jean-François Millet
(Gréville-Hague 1814 - Barbizon 1875)

The Gleaners
Die Ährenleserinnen
De arenleesters

●●

1857

84 x 112 cm / 33.07 x 44.09 in.
Musée d'Orsay, Paris

Oil on canvas
Öl auf Leinwand
Olieverf op doek

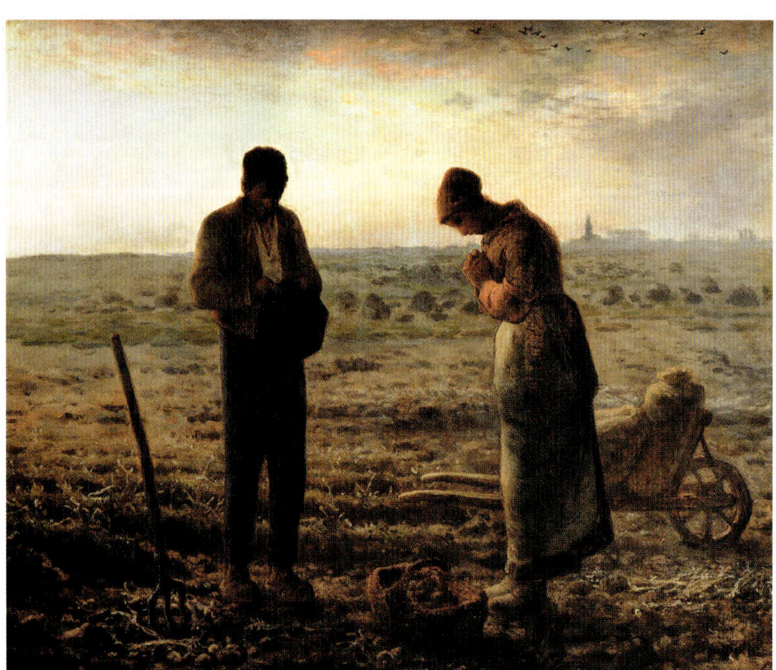

Jean-François Millet
(Gréville-Hague 1814 - Barbizon 1875)

Angelus
Het Angelus

●●

c. 1857-1859
55.5 x 66 cm / 21.85 x 26 in.
Musée d'Orsay, Paris

Oil on canvas
Öl auf Leinwand
Olieverf op doek

In his caricatures Daumier expresses an opinion on almost all social issues.

Daumier nimmt in seinen Karrikaturen zu fast allen gesellschaftlichen Themen Stellung.

Daumier neemt in zijn karikaturen stelling ten opzichte van bijna alle maatschappelijke thema's.

Honoré Daumier
(Marseille 1808 - Paris 1879)

The Laundress
Die Wäscherin
De wasvrouw

●●

1863
49 x 33,5 cm / 19.29 x 13.19 in.
Musée d'Orsay, Paris

Oil on wood
Öl auf Tafel
Olieverf op paneel

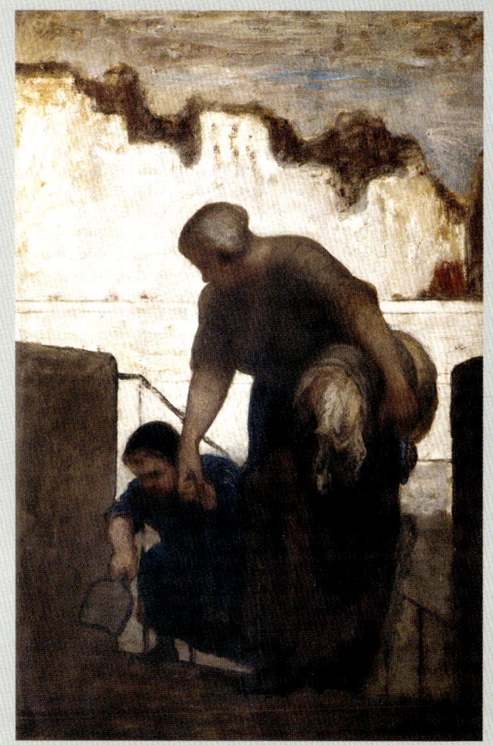

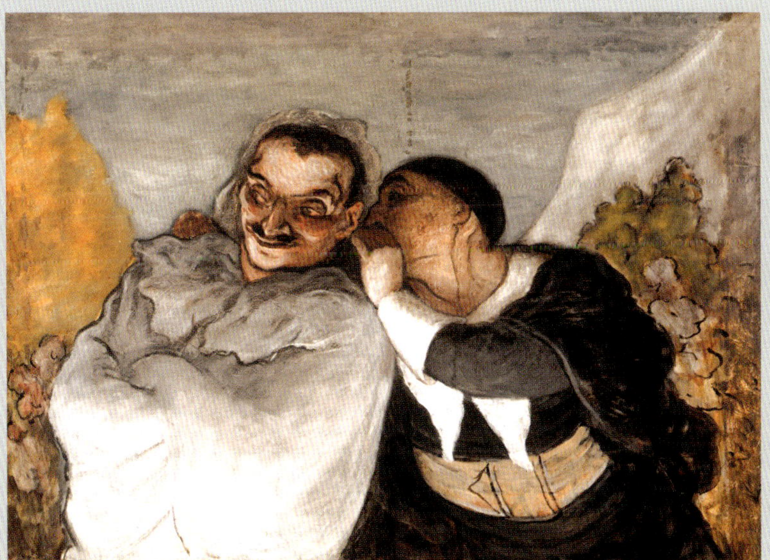

Honoré Daumier
(Marseille 1808 - Paris 1879)

Crispin and Scapin
Crispin und Scapin
Crispin en Scapin

●●●

c. 1858-1860
55,2 x 81,9 cm / 21.73 x 32.24 in.
Musée d'Orsay, Paris

Oil on canvas
Öl auf Leinwand
Olieverf op doek

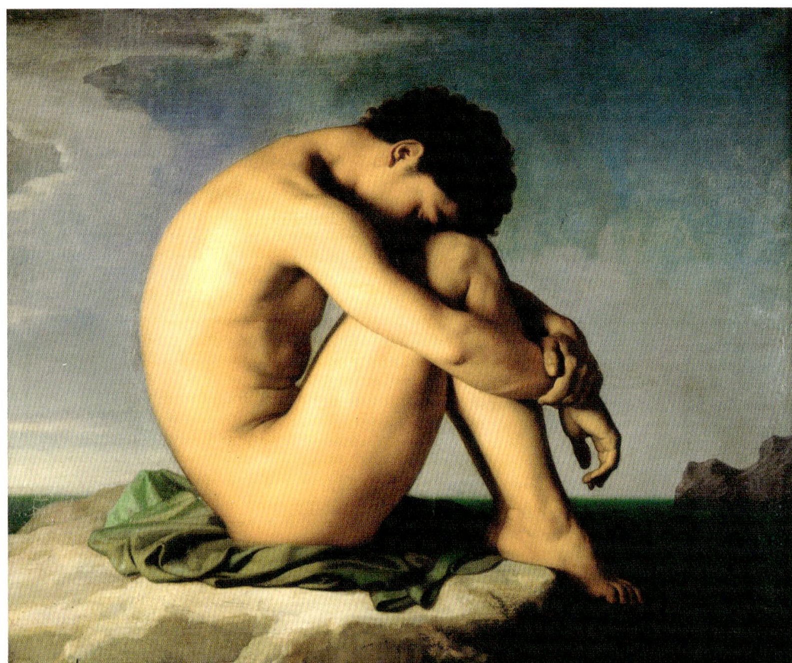

Hippolyte Flandrin
(Lyon 1809 - Roma 1864)

Young Man beside the Sea
Nackter junger Mann am Meeresstrand
Jongen aan zee

●

1835
98 x 124 cm / 38.58 x 48.82 in.
Musée du Louvre, Paris

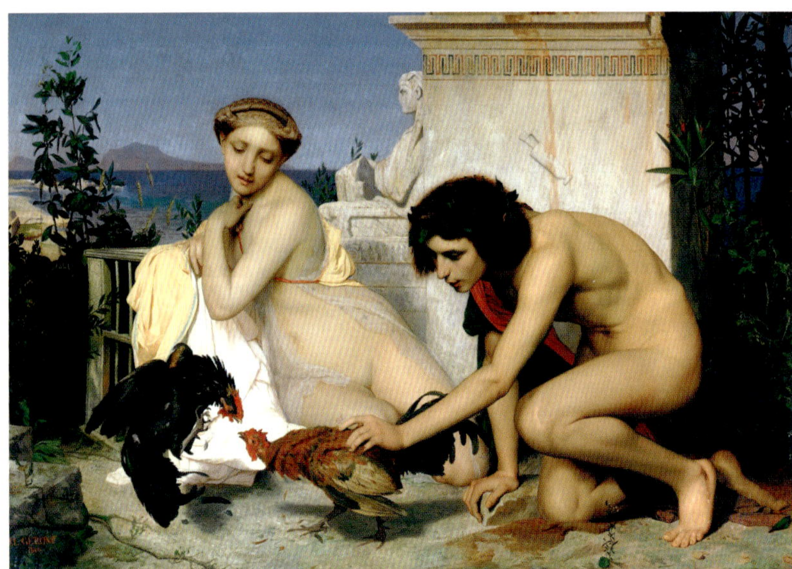

Jean-Léon Gérôme
(Vésoul, Haute-Saône 1824 - Paris 1904)

Cock Fight
Hahnenkampf
Hanengevecht

●

1847
143 x 204 cm / 56.3 x 80.31 in.
Musée d'Orsay, Paris

Oil on canvas
Öl auf Leinwand
Olieverf op doek

Alexandre Cabanel
(Montpellier 1823 - Paris 1889)

Birth of Venus
Geburt der Venus
De geboorte van Venus

●

1863
130 x 225 cm / 51.18 x 88.58 in.
Musée d'Orsay, Paris

Oil on canvas
Öl auf Leinwand
Olieverf op doek

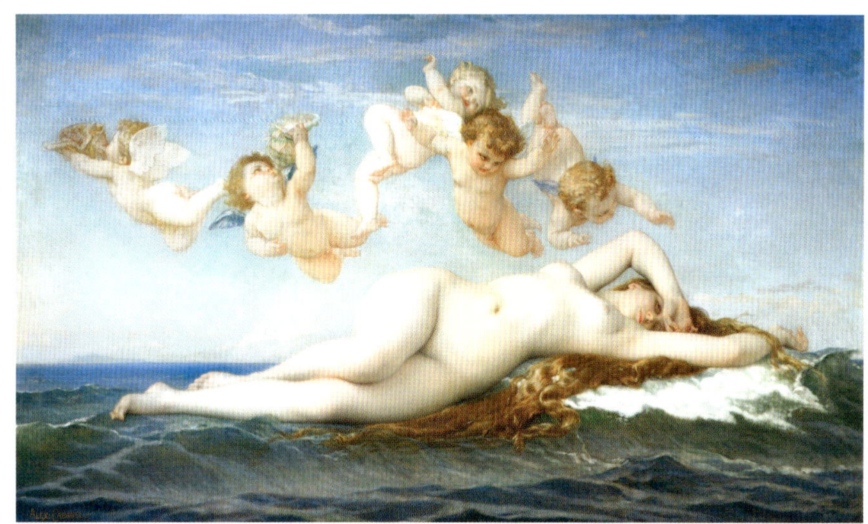

Accepted by 18th century society and publicly promoted at the time, today the paintings of the Salons look like erotic kitsch.

Von der Gesellschaft des 19. Jahrhunderts akzeptiert. Die öffentlich geförderte Salonmalerei mutet heute kitschig erotisch an.

De salonschilderkunst van de groepen uit de 19e eeuw die destijds door het publiek werd geaccepteerd, doet tegenwoordig aan als erotische kitsch.

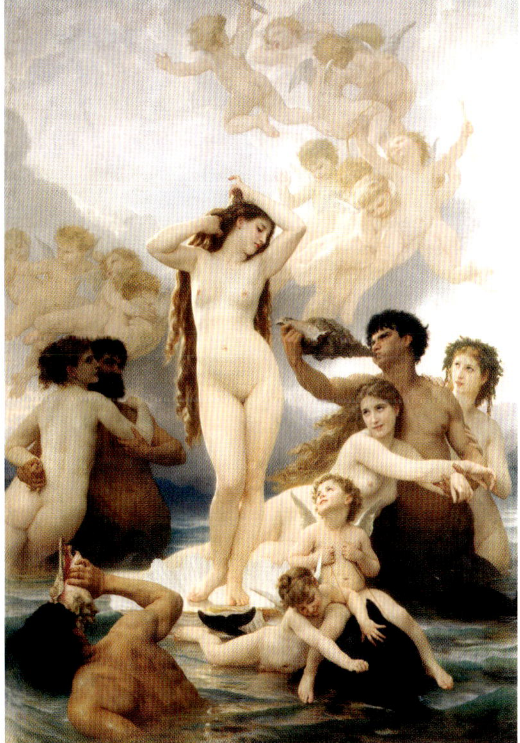

William-Adolph
Bouguereau
(La Rochelle 1825 - 1905)

The Birth of Venus
Geburt der Venus
De geboorte van Venus

●

1879
300 x 215 cm
118.11 x 84.65 in.
Musée d'Orsay, Paris

Oil on canvas
Öl auf Leinwand
Olieverf op doek

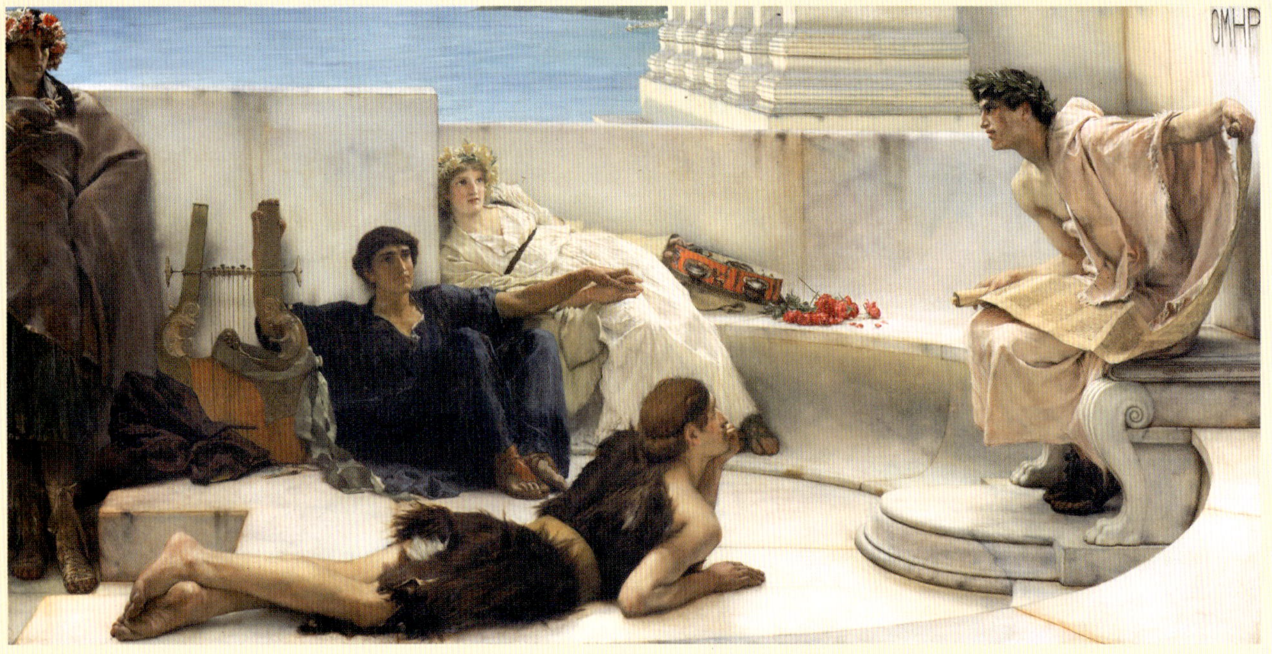

366

Lawrence Alma-Tadema
(Dronrijp 1836 - Wiesbaden 1912)

A Reading from Homer
Lesung aus dem Homer
Lezing uit Homerus

●

1885
91,8 x 183,5 cm / 36.14 x 72.24 in.
Philadelphia Museum of Art, Philadephia

Oil on canvas
Öl auf Leinwand
Olieverf op doek

Frederick Leighton
(Scarborough 1830 - London 1896)

Miss May Sartoris

●

c. 1860
152,1 x 90,2 cm / 59.88 x 35.51 in.
Kimbell Art Museum,
Fort Worth, Texas

Oil on canvas / Öl auf Leinwand
Olieverf op doek

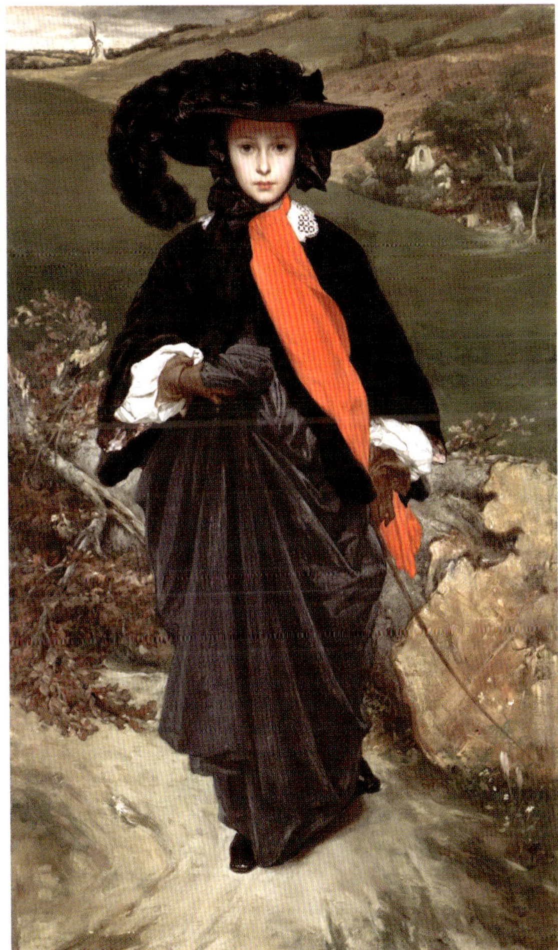

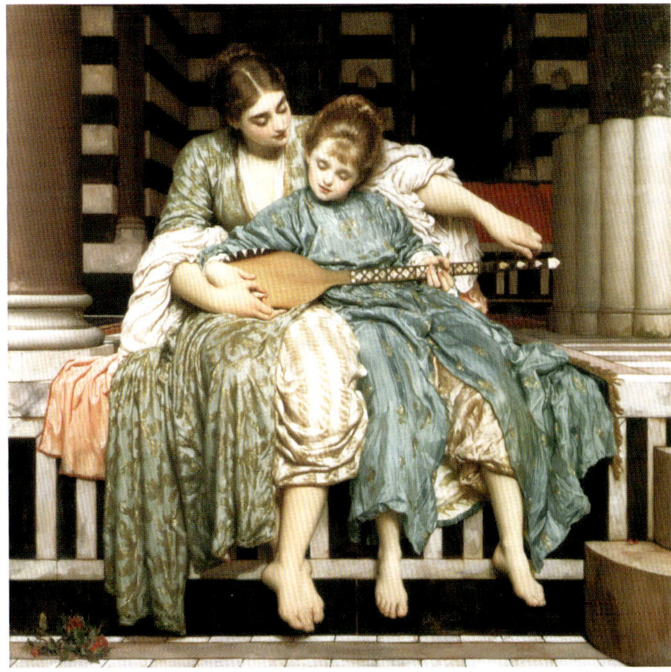

Frederick Leighton
(Scarborough 1830 - London 1896)

The Music Lesson
Die Musikstunde
De muziekles

●

1877
Guildhall Library and Art Gallery,
London

Oil on canvas
Öl auf Leinwand
Olieverf op doek

Édouard Manet is the founder of modern art and a precursor of Impressionism.

Manet ist Begründer der modernen Kunst und Wegbereiter des Impressionismus.

Manet is de grondlegger van de moderne kunst en wegbereider van het impressionisme.

Édouard Manet
(Paris 1832 - 1883)

The Fifer
Pfeifer
De fluitspeler

●●●

1866
160 x 98 cm / 62.99 x 38.58 in.
Musée d'Orsay, Paris

Oil on canvas
Öl auf Leinwand
Olieverf op doek

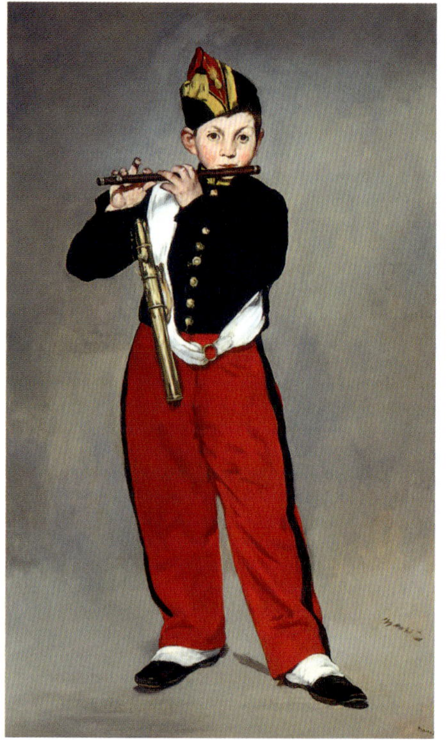

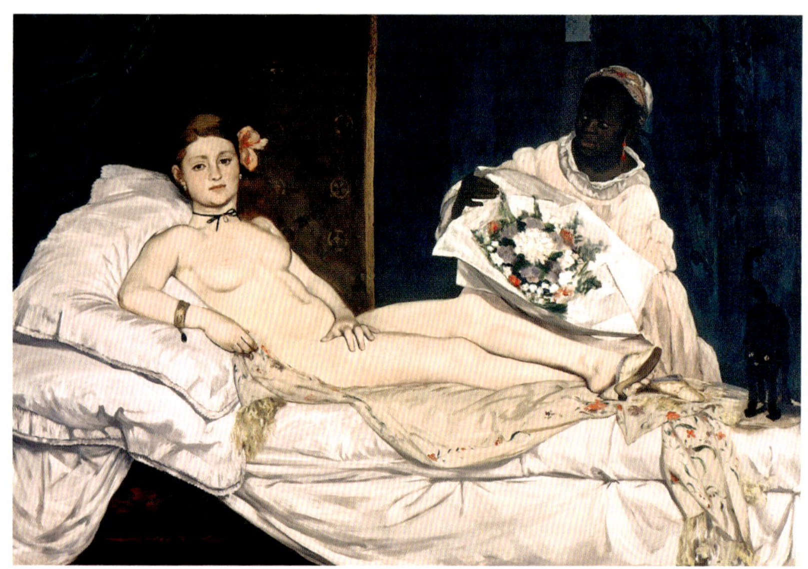

Édouard Manet
(Paris 1832 - 1883)

Olympia

●●●

1863
131 x 190 cm / 51.57 x 74.80 in.
Musée d'Orsay, Paris

Oil on canvas / Öl auf Leinwand
Olieverf op doek

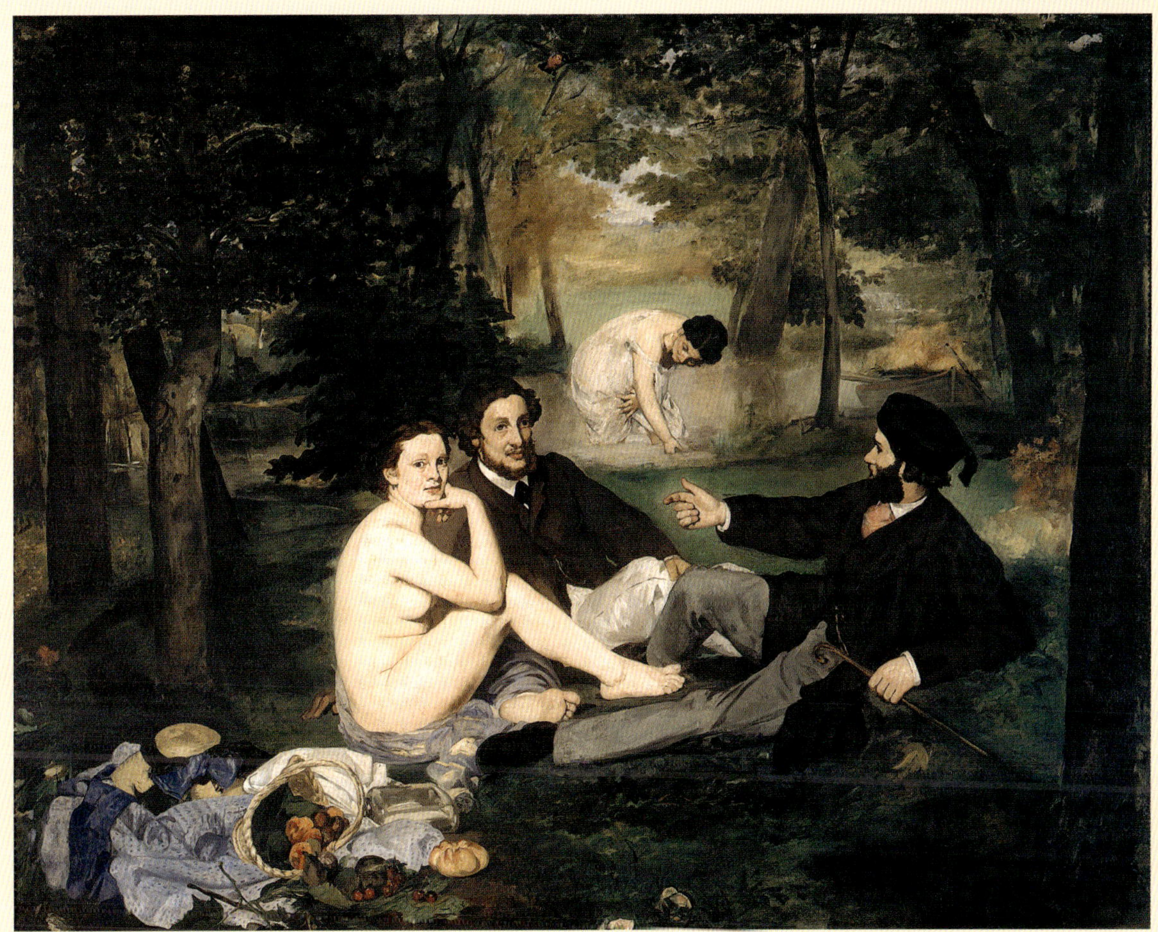

Édouard Manet
(Paris 1832 - 1883)

Luncheon on the Grass
Frühstück im Grünen
Lunch op het gras

●●●

1863
208 x 264 cm / 110.23 x 107.87 in.
Musée d'Orsay, Paris

Oil on canvas / Öl auf Leinwand / Olieverf op doek

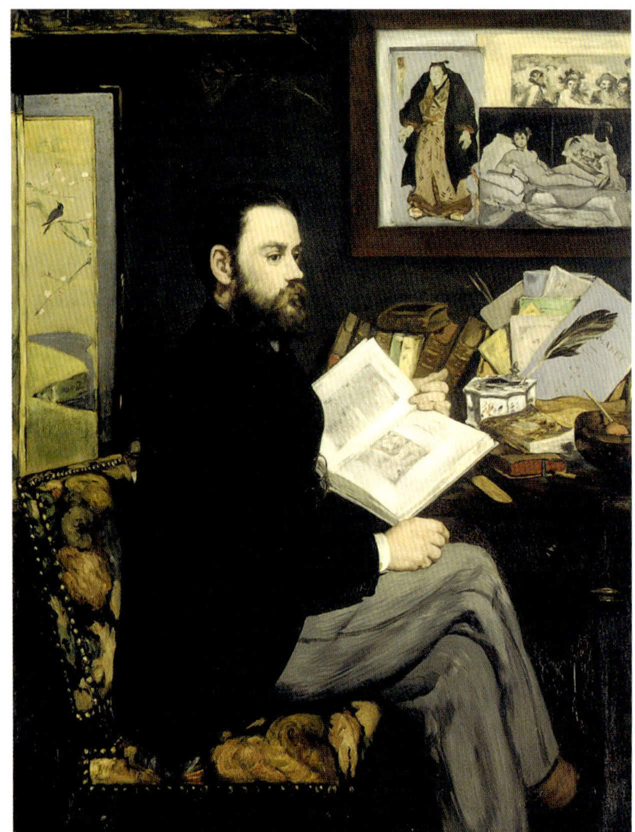

Édouard Manet
(Paris 1832 - 1883)

Émile Zola

1867-1868
146 x 114 cm / 57.48 x 44.88 in.
Musée d'Orsay, Paris

Oil on canvas
Öl auf Leinwand
Olieverf op doek

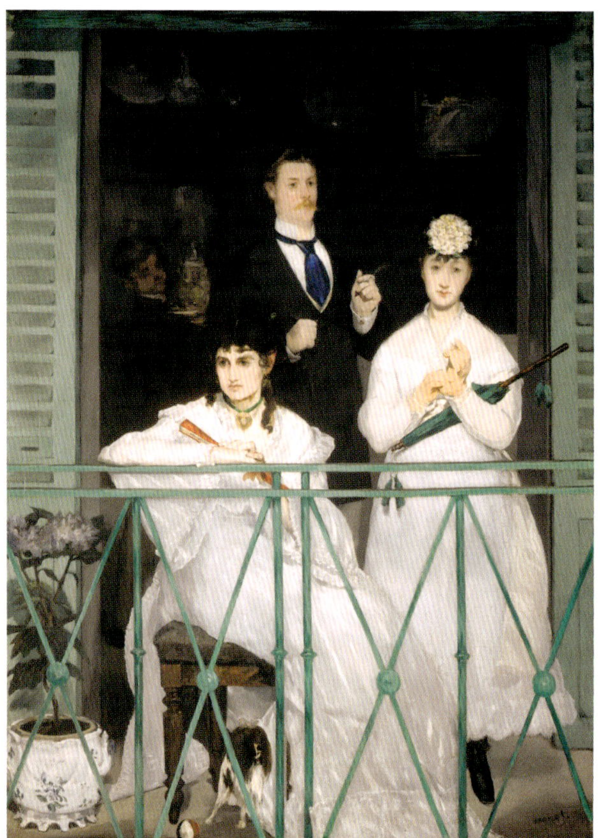

Édouard Manet
(Paris 1832 - 1883)

The Balcony
Der Balkon
Het balkon

●●●

c. 1868-1869
170 x 124,5 cm / 66.92 x 49.01 in.
Musée d'Orsay, Paris

Oil on canvas
Öl auf Leinwand
Olieverf op doek

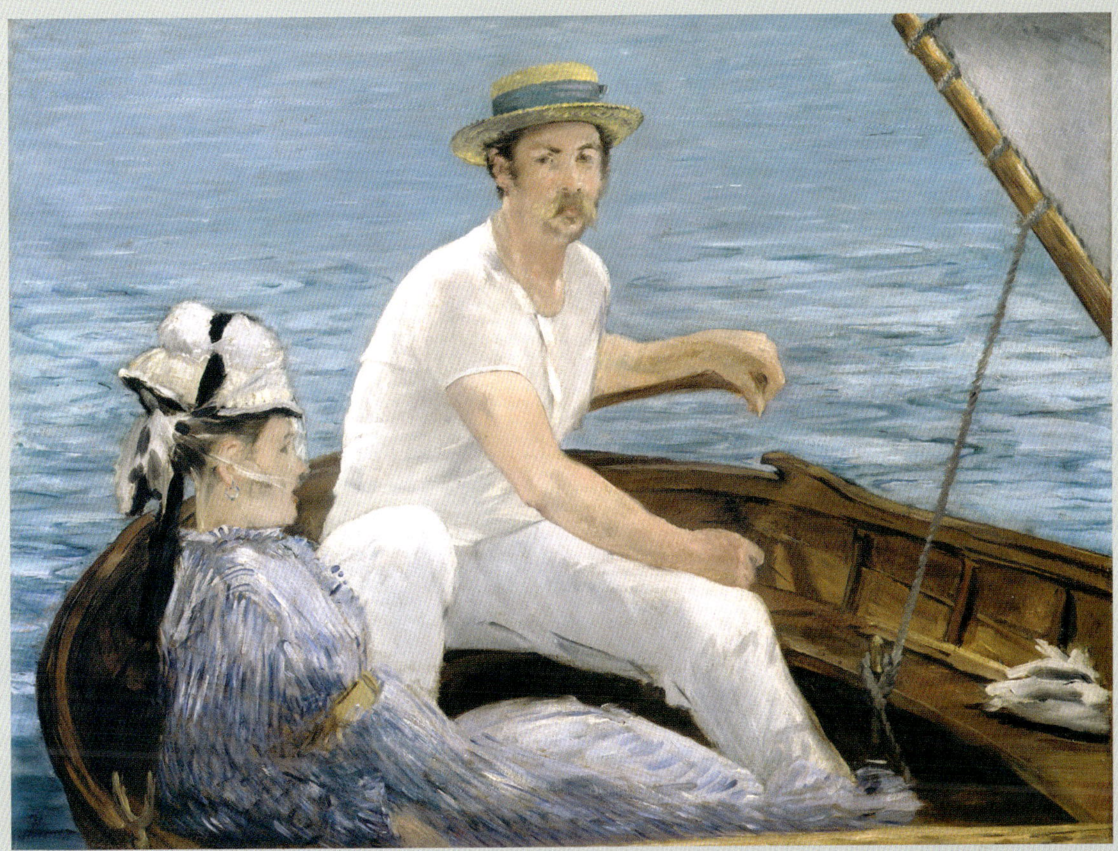

Édouard Manet
(Paris 1832 - 1883)

Boating
Im Boot
Op de boot

●●●

1874
97,2 x 130,2 cm / 38.26 x 51.25 in.
Metropolitan Museum of Art, New York

Oil on canvas
Öl auf Leinwand
Olieverf op doek

A rival of photography: Manet's snapshots of Parisian bourgeois life.

Konkurrenz zur Fotografie: Manets Momentaufnahmen des bürgerlichen Lebens in Paris.

Concurrentie voor de fotografie: de momentopnamen van Manet van het burgerlijke leven in Parijs.

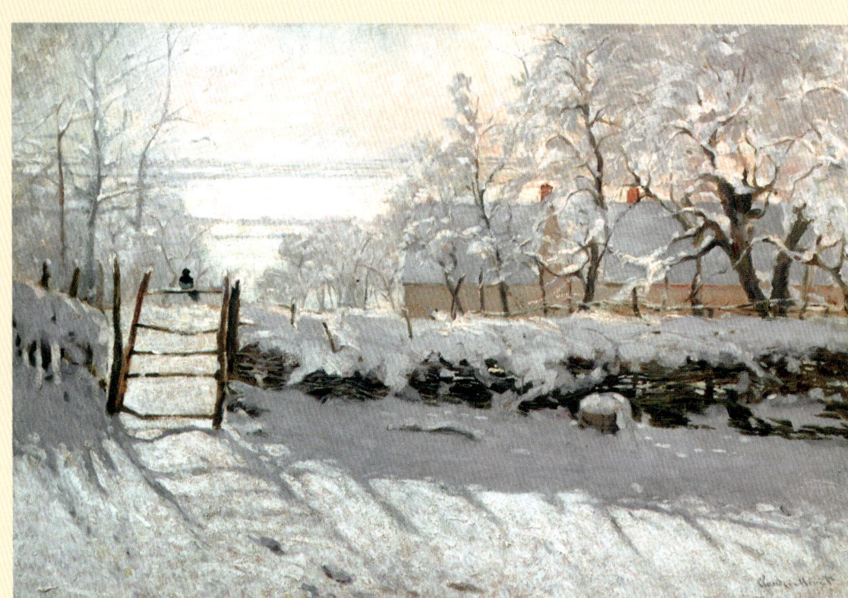

Claude Monet
(Paris 1840 - Giverny 1926)

The Magpie
Die Elster
De ekster

●

c. 1868-1869
83,8 x 130,2 cm / 32.99 x 51.25 in.
Musée d'Orsay, Paris

Oil on canvas
Öl auf Leinwand
Olieverf op doek

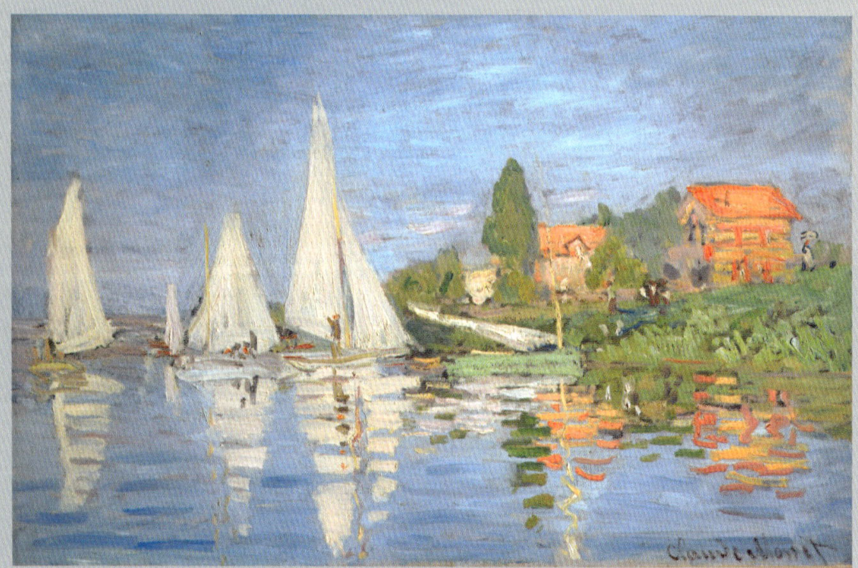

Claude Monet
(Paris 1840 - Giverny 1926)

Regatta at Argenteuil
Regatta in Argenteuil
Zeilwedstrijd bij Argenteuil

●

c. 1872
48 x 75 cm / 18.89 x 29.52 in.
Musée d'Orsay, Paris

Oil on canvas
Öl auf Leinwand
Olieverf op doek

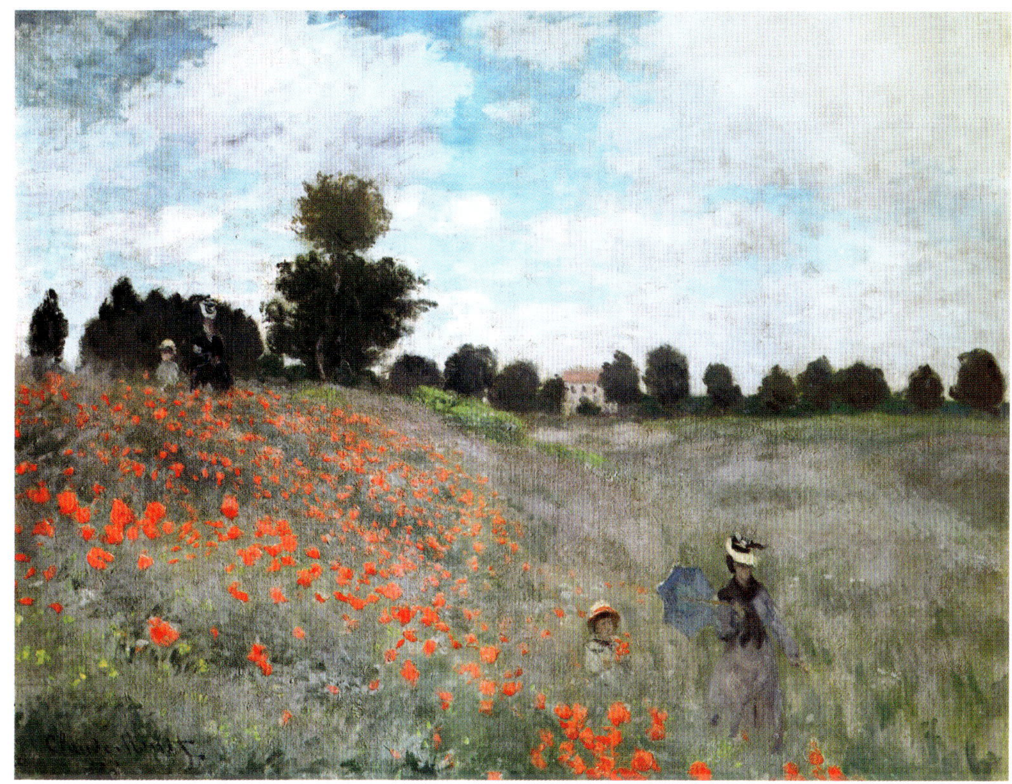

373

Claude Monet
(Paris 1840 - Giverny 1926)

Poppy Field
Mohnblumenfeld
Papaverveld

●●●

1873
50 x 65 cm / 19.7 x 25.6 in.
Musée d'Orsay, Paris

Oil on canvas
Öl auf Leinwand
Olieverf op doek

The painting as a fleeting impression of light and colour: Claude Monet the Impressionist favours landscapes...

Das Bild als flüchtiger Eindruck von Licht und Farbe. Der Impressionist Monet bevorzugt die Landschaftsmalerei...

Het schilderij als vluchtige impressie van licht en kleur. De impressionist Monet geeft de voorkeur aan de landschapschilderkunst...

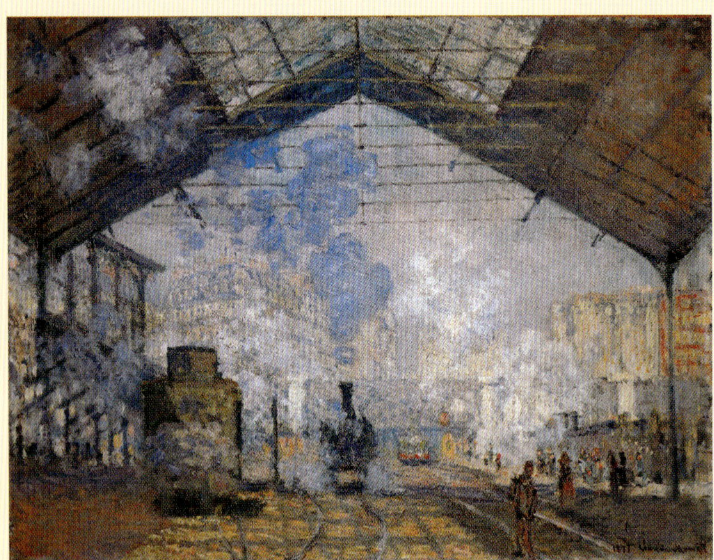

Claude Monet
(Paris 1840 - Giverny 1926)

Saint-Lazare Train Station
Der Bahnhof Saint-Lazare
Het station Saint-Lazare

●●

1877
75,6 x 104 cm / 29.76 x 40.94 in.
Musée d'Orsay, Paris

Oil on canvas
Öl auf Leinwand
Olieverf op doek

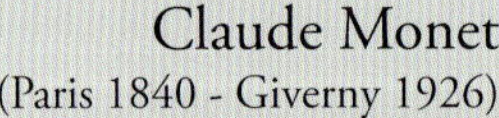

Claude Monet
(Paris 1840 - Giverny 1926)

Rouen Cathedral in Full Sunlight
Die Kathedrale von Rouen bei strahlender Sonne
Kathedraal van Rouen bij stralende zon

●●●

1893
107 x 73 cm / 42.12 x 28.74 in.
Musée d'Orsay, Paris

Oil on canvas / Öl auf Leinwand / Olieverf op doek

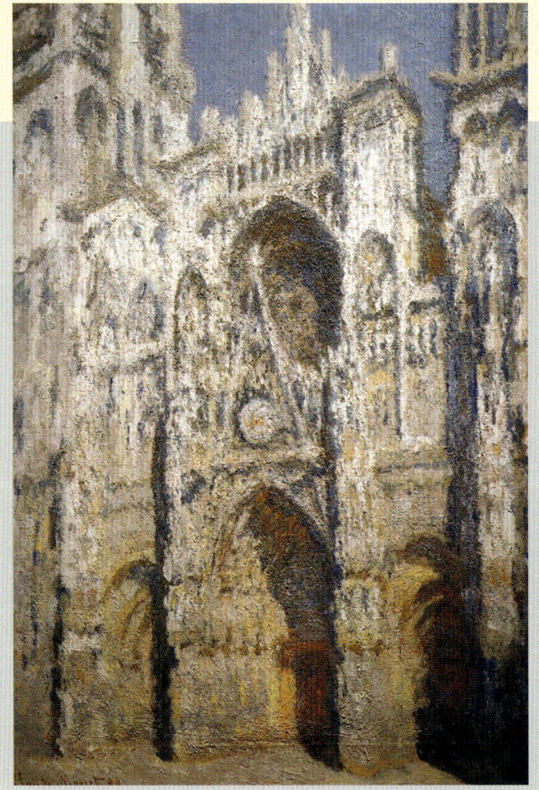

Claude Monet
(Paris 1840 - Giverny 1926)

Water-Lily Pond, Green Harmony
Seerosen, grüne Harmonie
Waterlelievijver, groene harmonie

●●●

1899
89 x 93,5 cm / 35.03 x 36.81 in.
Musée d'Orsay, Paris

Oil on canvas
Öl auf Leinwand
Olieverf op doek

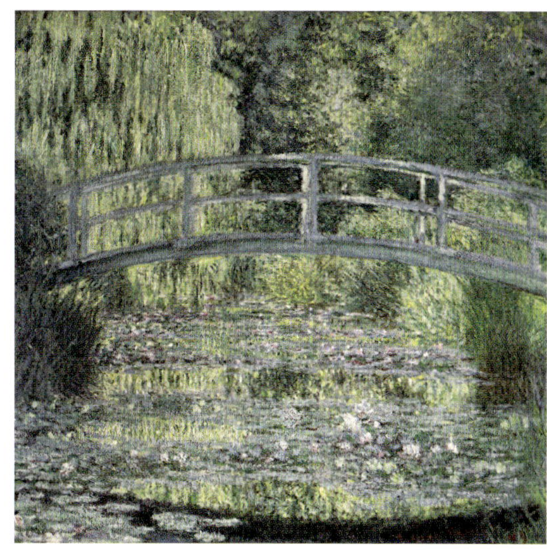

Claude Monet
(Paris 1840 - Giverny 1926)

Waterlilies, Green Reflection
Seerosen, grüne Reflektion
De waterlelies, groene reflectie

●●●

Diptych, left part / Diptychon, linker Teil
Diptiek, linker deel
1914-1926
200 x 425 cm / 78.74 x 167.32 in.
Musée de l'Orangerie, Paris

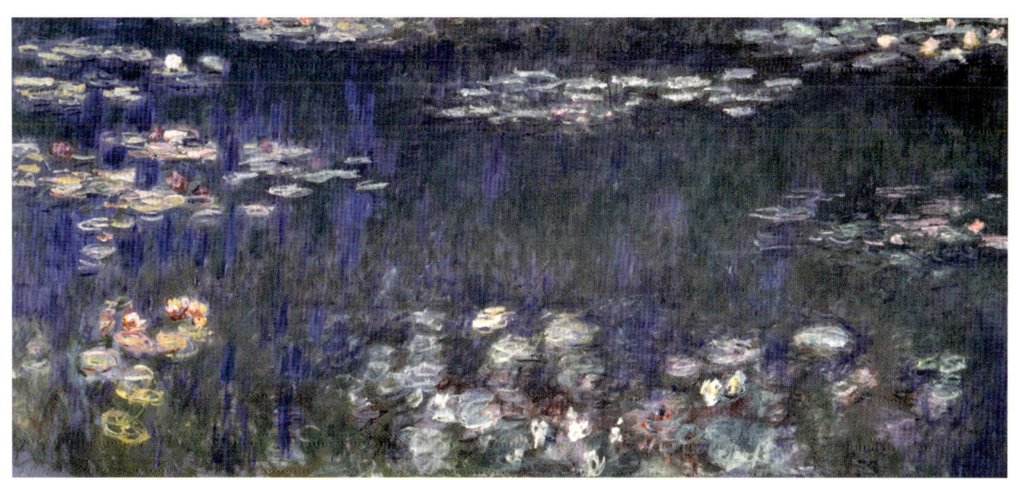

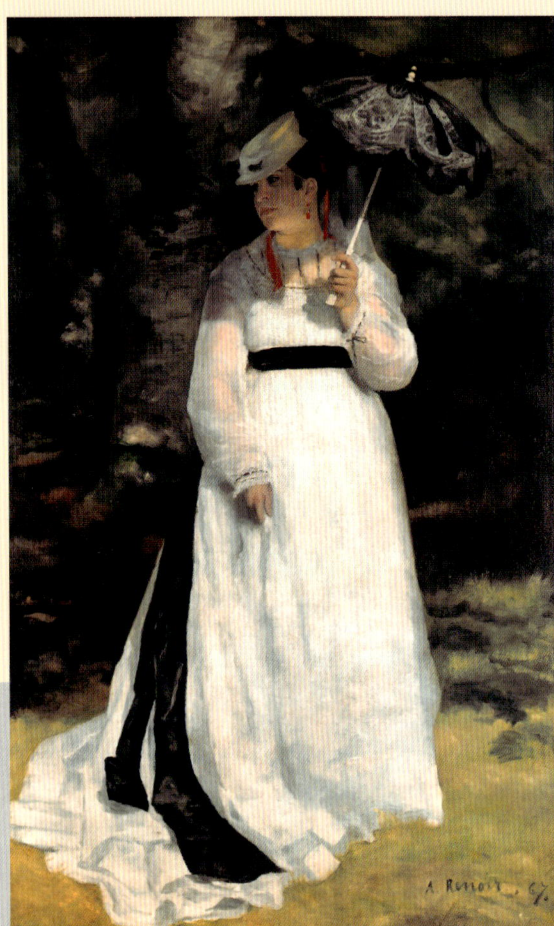

Pierre-Auguste Renoir
(Limoges 1841 - Cagnes-sur-Mer 1919)

Lisa with Parasol
Lise mit Sonnenschirm
Lise met de parasol

●●

c. 1868
184 x 115 cm / 72.44 x 45.27 in.
Folkwang Museum, Essen

Oil on canvas / Öl auf Leinwand
Olieverf op doek

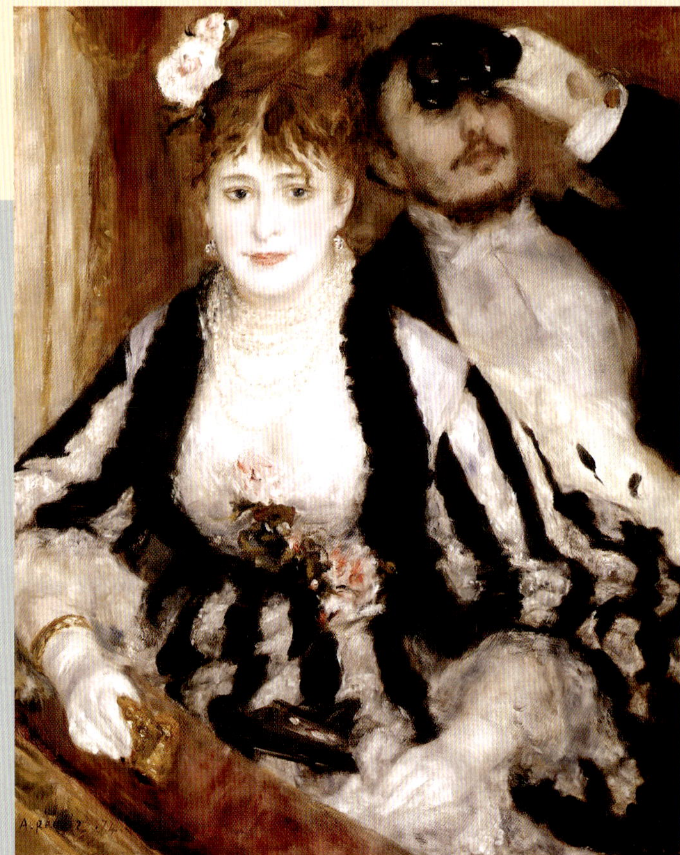

Auguste Renoir
(Limoges 1841 - Cagnessur-Mer 1919)

The Theatre Box
Die Loge
De Loge

●●

c. 1875
80 x 63,5 cm / 31.49 x 24.99 in.
The Courtauld Institute Galleries, London

Oil on canvas / Öl auf Leinwand
Olieverf op doek

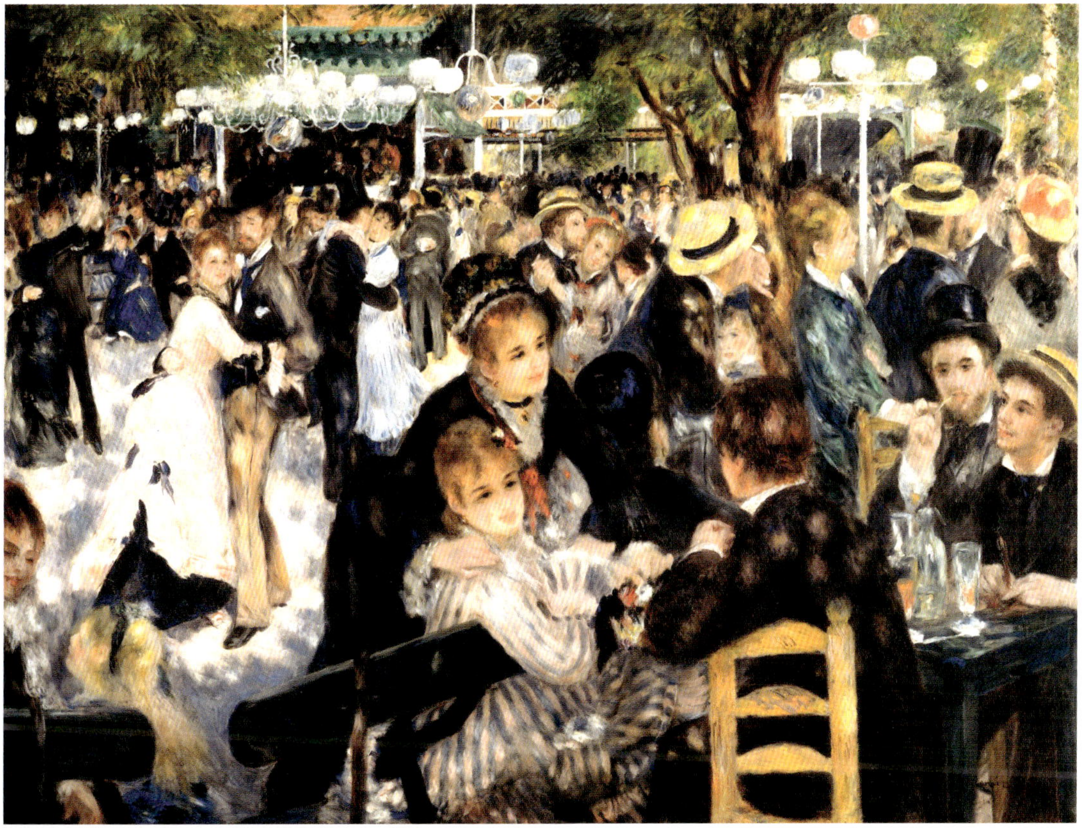

Auguste Renoir
(Limoges 1841 - Cagnessur-Mer 1919)

Dance at the Moulin Galette
Tanz im Moulin de la Galette
Bal in de Moulin de la Galette

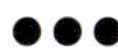

1876
131 x 175 cm / 51.57 x 68.89 in.
Musée d'Orsay, Paris

Oil on canvas / Öl auf Leinwand
Olieverf op doek

... while Auguste Renoir focuses on people.

... während sich Auguste Renoir eher dem Menschen widmet.

... terwijl Auguste Renoir zich vooral met de mens bezighoudt.

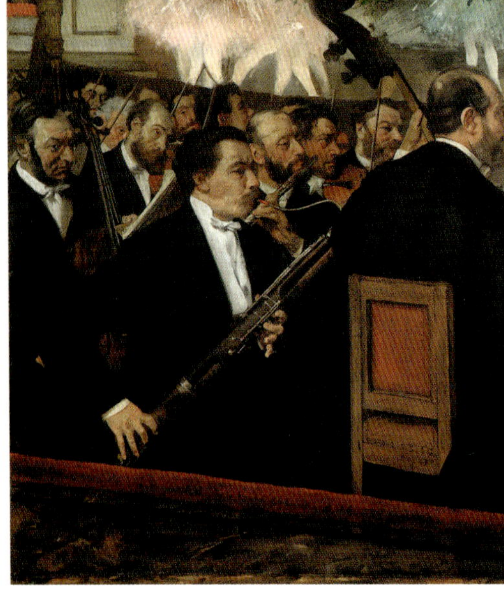

"They call me the painter of dancers. However, they don't understand that for me dancers represent an opportunity to depict beautiful fabrics and to capture movement": Edgar Degas.

"Man nennt mich den Maler der Tänzerinnen. Dabei versteht man nicht, dass ich die Tänzerin nur zum Anlass nehme, schöne Stoffe zumalen und Bewegung zu zeigen" Edgar Degas.

"Men noemt mij de danseressenschilder. Men begrijpt niet dat voor mij de danseressen een aanleiding zijn om mooie stoffen te schilderen en de beweging vast te leggen", Edgar Degas.

378

Edgar Degas
(Paris 1834 - 1917)

Orchestra at the Opéra
Das Orchester der Opera
Het orkest van de Opera

●●

c. 1870
56,5 x 46 cm / 22.24 x 18.11 in.
Musée d'Orsay, Paris

Oil on canvas / Öl auf Leinwand
Olieverf op doek

Edgar Degas
(Paris 1834 - 1917)

The Dance Lesson
Tanzstunde
Balletles

●●●

1873-1876
85 x 75 cm / 33.46 x 29.53 in.
Musée d'Orsay, Paris

Oil on canvas
Öl auf Leinwand
Olieverf op doek

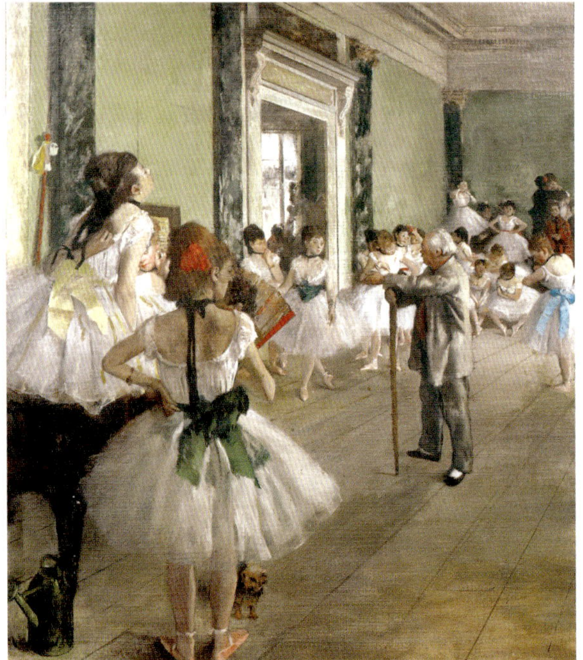

Edgar Degas
(Paris 1834 - 1917)

Absinthe Drinker
Der Absinth
De Absintdrinkster

●●●

c. 1875-1876
92 x 68 cm / 36.22 x 26.77 in.
Musée d'Orsay, Paris

Oil on canvas
Öl auf Leinwand
Olieverf op doek

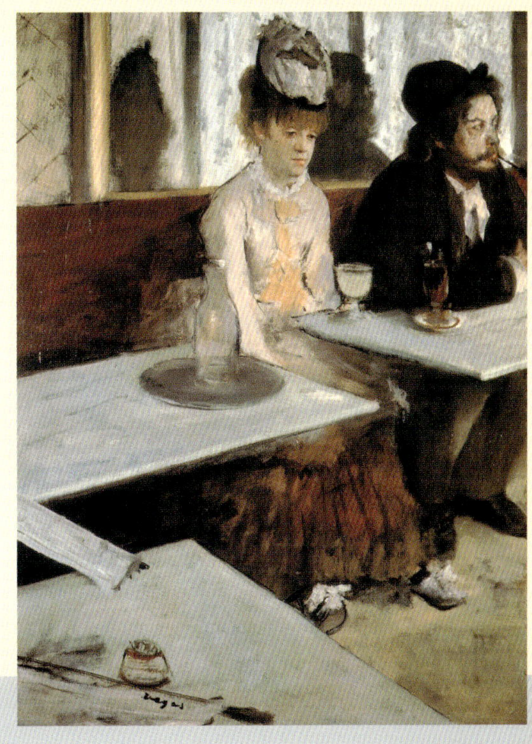

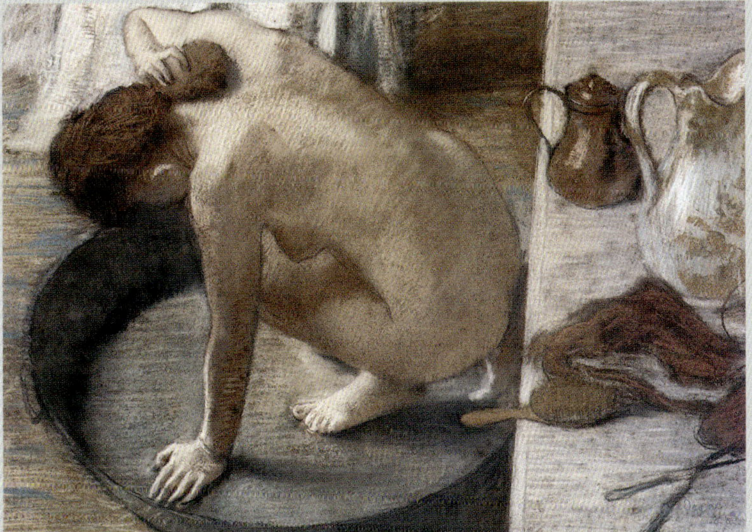

Edgar Degas
(Paris 1834 - 1917)

The tub
Der Waschbottich
De tobbe

●●

1886
60 x 83 cm / 23.62 x 32.67 in.
Musée d'Orsay, Paris

Pastel on paper
Pastell auf Papier
Pastel op papier

Theorist and spokesman of the Impressionists: Camille Pissarro is famous for his street scenes of Paris ...

Theoretiker und Wortführer der Impressionisten. Pissarro ist berühmt durch seine Pariser Straßenszenen ...

Theoreticus en woordvoerder van de impressionisten. Pisarro is bekend vanwege zijn straatscènes in Parijs ...

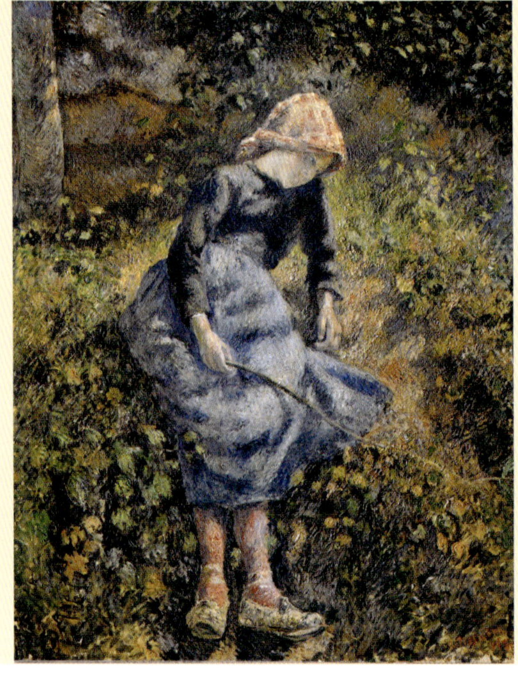

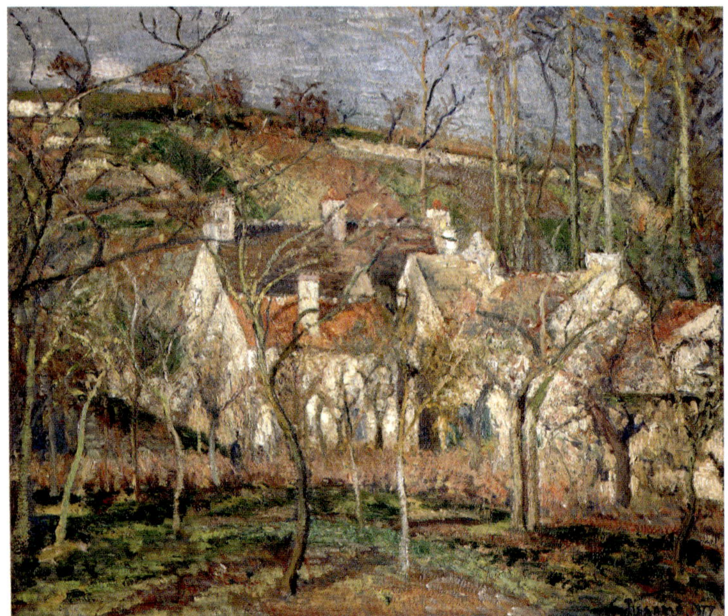

Camille Pissarro
(Saint-Thomas 1830 - Paris 1903)

Red Roofs
Die roten Dächer
De rode daken

●●

1877
54,5 x 65,6 cm / 21.5 x 25.9 in.
Musée d'Orsay, Paris

Oil on canvas
Öl auf Leinwand
Olieverf op doek

◂ Camille Pissarro
(Saint-Thomas 1830 - Paris 1903)

The Shephardess
Die Hirtin
Het herderinnetje

●

1881
81 x 64,7 cm / 31.89 x 25.47 in.
Musée d'Orsay, Paris

Oil on canvas / Öl auf Leinwand / Olieverf op doek

Camille Pissarro
(Saint-Thomas 1830 - Paris 1903)

Boulevard Montmartre, Paris

●●●

1897
74 x 92.8 cm / 29.13 x 36.53 in.
The State Hermitage Museum, St. Petersburg

Oil on canvas
Öl auf Leinwand
Olieverf op doek

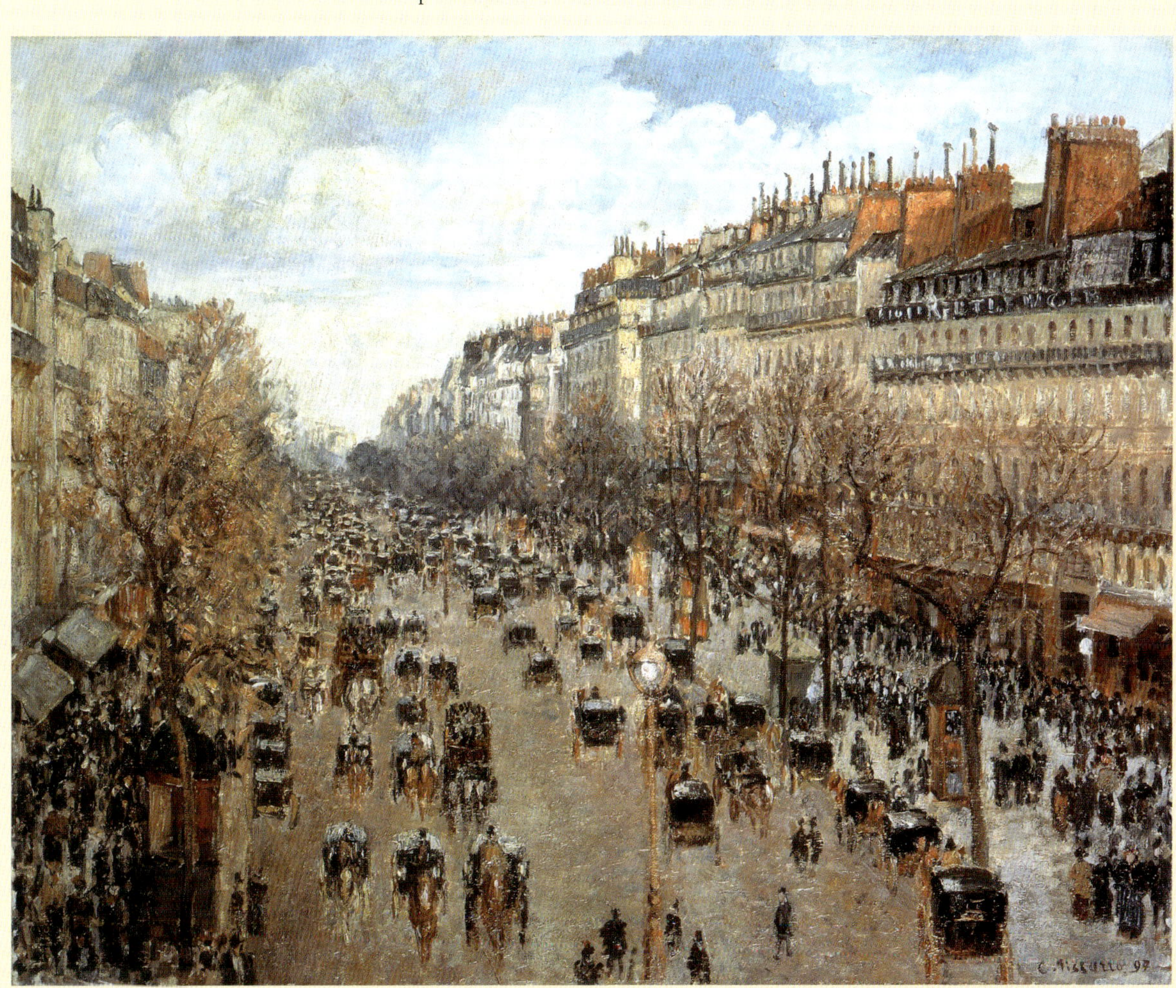

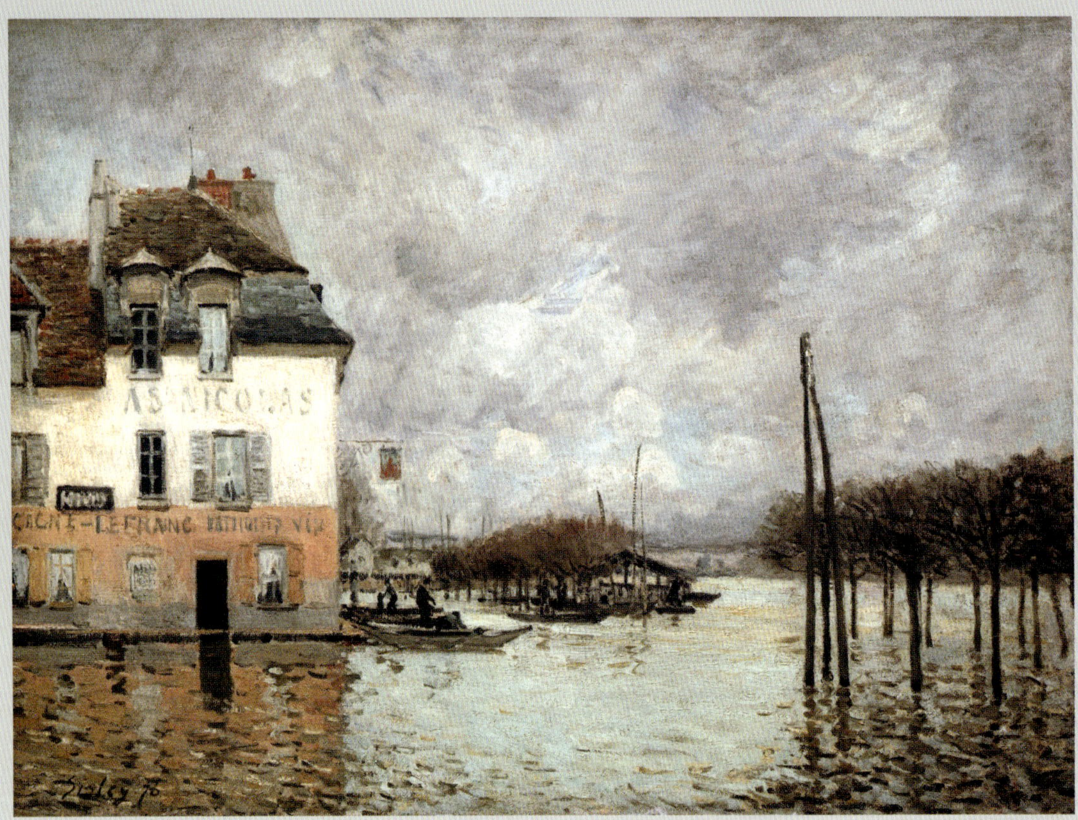

Alfred Sisley
(Paris 1839 - Moret-sur-Loing 1899)

Flood at Port-Marly
Überschwemmung von Port-Marly
De overstroming, Port-Marly

●●

1876
60 x 81 cm / 23.62 x 31.88 in.
Musée d'Orsay, Paris

Oil on canvas
Öl auf Leinwand
Olieverf op doek

...while Alfred Sisley, an Englishman born in Paris, is fascinated by carefree landscapes.

...dagegen faszinieren den in Paris geborenen Engländer Alfred Sisley die heiteren Landschaften.

...Alfred Sisley de Engelsman die in Parijs is geboren, wordt daarentegen gefascineerd door zorgeloze landschappen.

Alfred Sisley
(Paris 1839 - Moret-sur-Loing 1899)

The Seine at Bougival
Die Seine bei Bougival
De Seine bij Bougival

●

1872-1873
46 x 65 cm / 18.11 x 25.59 in.
Musée d'Orsay, Paris

Oil on canvas
Öl auf Leinwand
Olieverf op doek

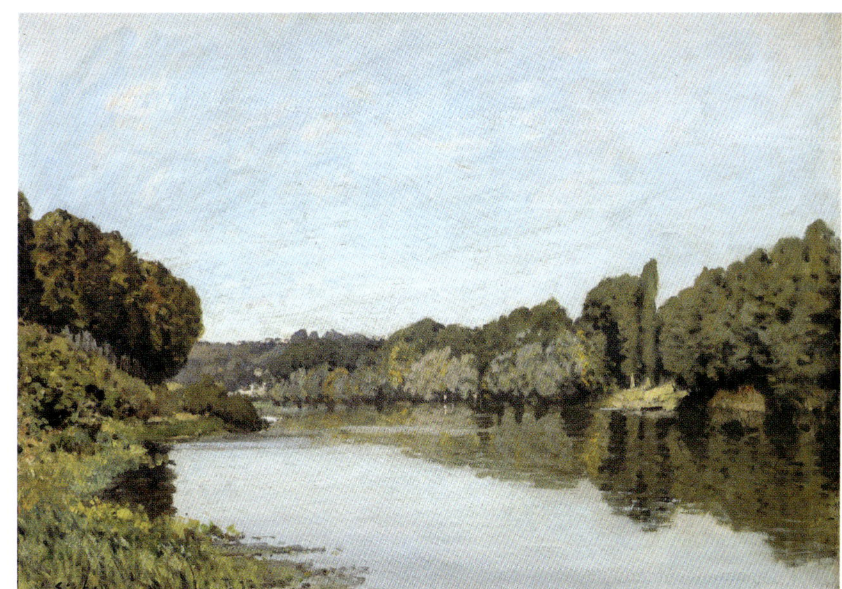

Alfred Sisley
(Paris 1839 - Moret-sur-Loing 1899)

Barges at Billancourt
Etladen der Fähre in Billancourt
Het lossen van de vrachtschepen bij Billancourt

●

1877
62 x 47 cm / 24.40 x 18.50 in.
The Ordrugaard Collection, Copenhagen

Oil on canvas
Öl auf Leinwand
Olieverf op doek

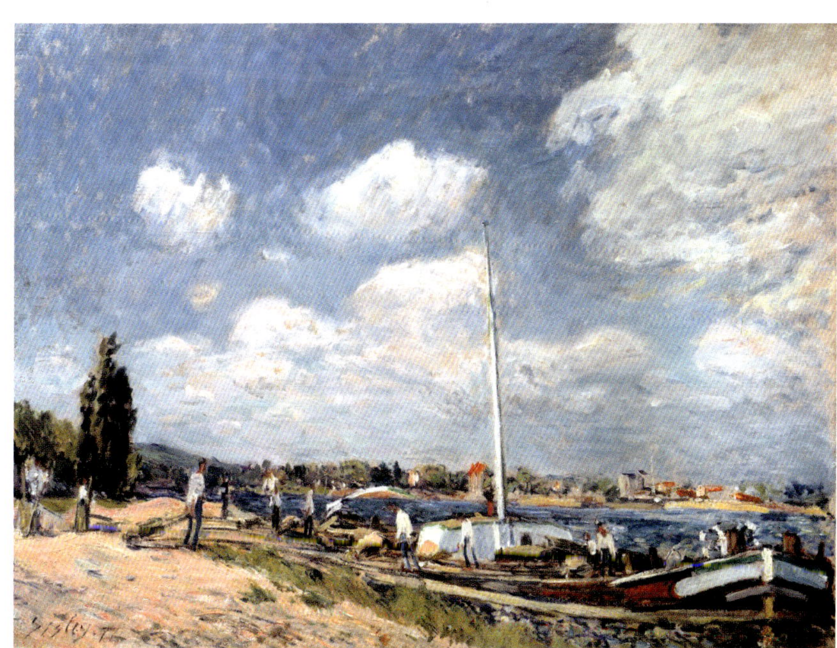

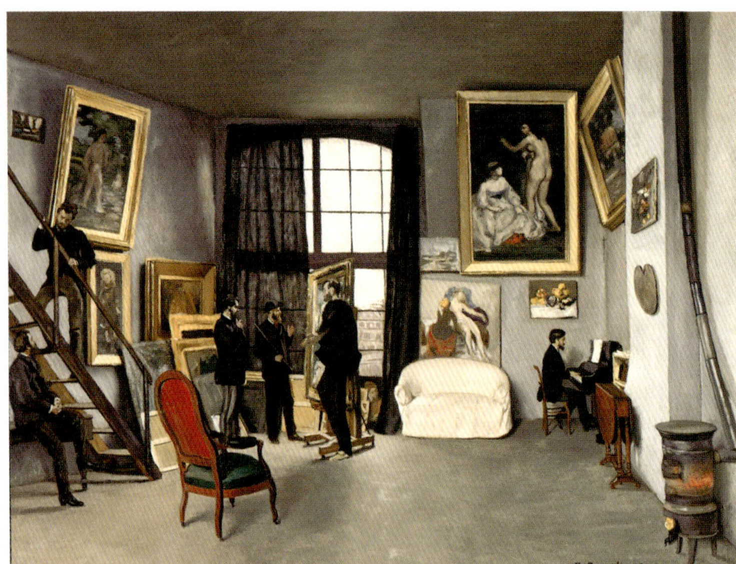

Frédéric Bazille
(Montpellier 1841 - Beaune-la-Rolande 1870)

Studio on the rue de la Condamine
Das Atelier des Künstlers in der Rue de la Condamine
Atelier in Rue de la Condamine

●

1870
98 x 128,5 cm / 38.58 x 50.59 in.
Musée d'Orsay, Paris

Oil on canvas
Öl auf Leinwand
Olieverf op doek

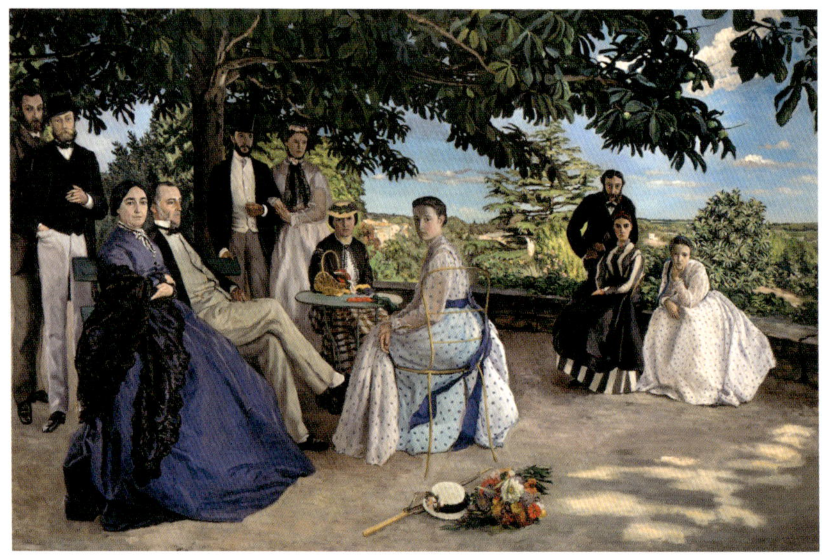

Frédéric Bazille
(Montpellier 1841 - Beaune-la-Rolande 1870)

Family Gathering
Familientreffen
Familiereünie

●

1867
152 x 230 cm / 59.84 x 90.55 in.
Musée d'Orsay, Paris

Oil on canvas
Öl auf Leinwand
Olieverf op doek

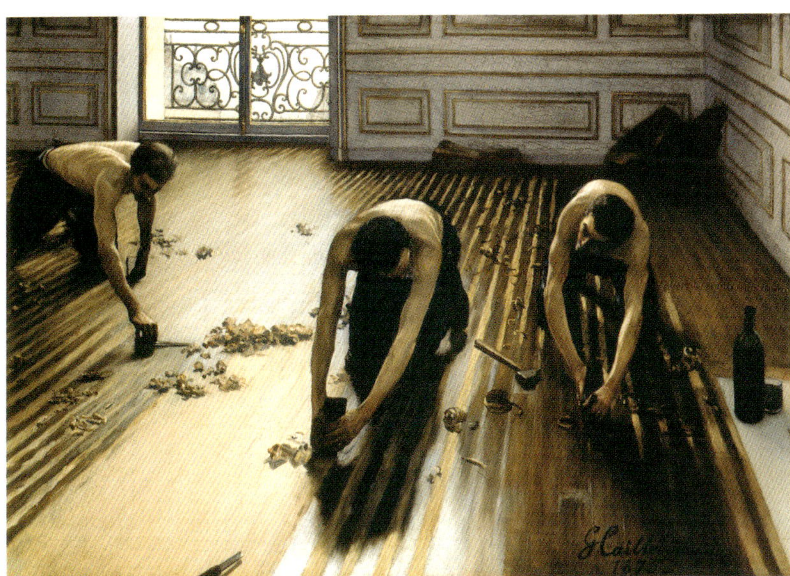

Gustave Caillebotte
(Paris1848 - Gennevilliers 1894)

The Floor Scrapers
Die Parkettschleifer
De Parketschavers

●●

1875
102 x 146 cm / 40.15 x 57.48 in.
Musée d'Orsay, Paris

Oil on canvas
Öl auf Leinwand
Olieverf op doek

Berthe Morisot
(Bourges 1841 - Paris 1895)

The Crib
Die Wiege
De wieg

●●

56 x 46 cm / 22.04 x 18.11 in.
Musée d'Orsay, Paris

Oil on canvas
Öl auf Leinwand
Olieverf op doek

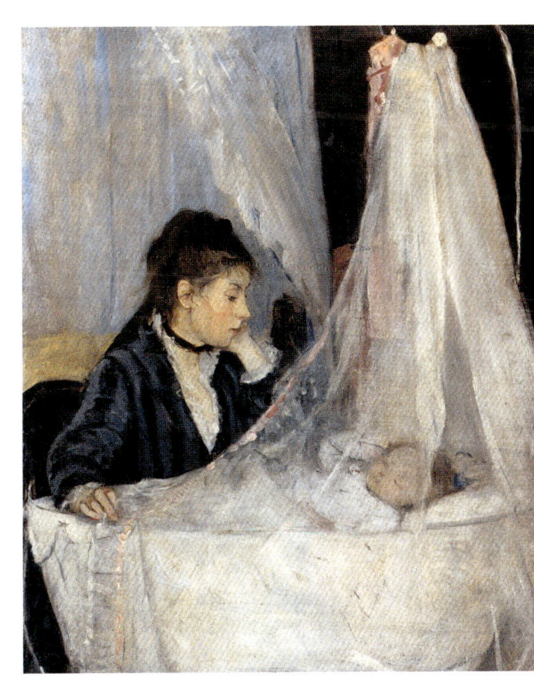

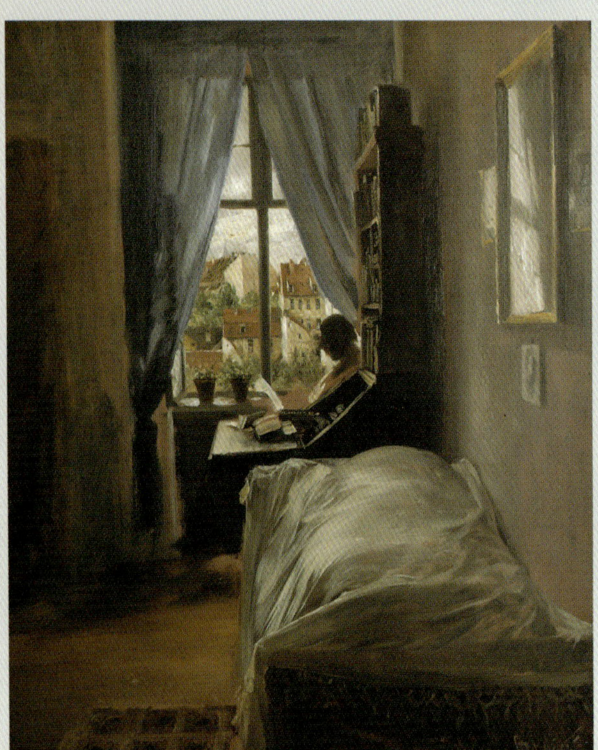

Adolph von Menzel
(Breslau 1815 - Berlin 1905)

The Artist's Bedroom
Das Schlafzimmer des Künstlers
Slaapkamer van de kunstenaar

●●

1847
56 x 46 cm / 22.05 x 18.11 in.
Nationalgalerie, Staatliche Museen, Berlin

Oil on cardboard / Öl auf Karton / Olieverf op karton

Adolph von Menzel
(Breslau 1815 - Berlin 1905)

Studio Wall
Atelierwand
Wand in het atelier van de kunstenaar

●

1872
111 x 79,3 cm / 47.7 x 31.22 in.
Hamburger Kunsthalle, Hamburg

Oil on canvas
Öl auf Leinwand
Olieverf op doek

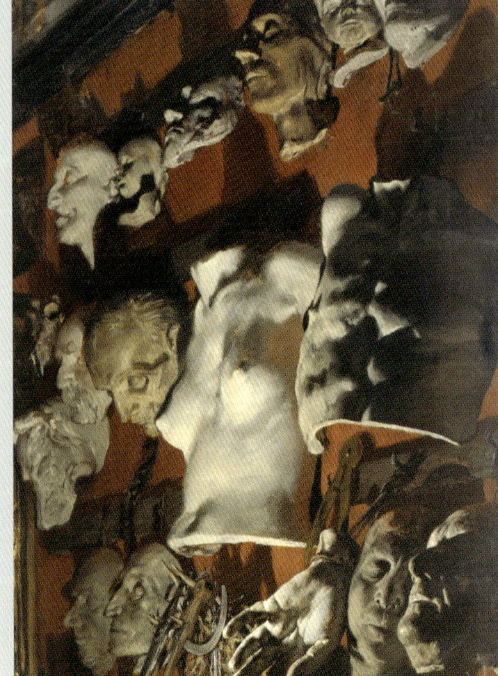

German Realism with a touch of Impressionism.

Deutscher Realismus mit impressionistischen Tendenzen.

Duits realisme met impressionistische tendensen.

Max Liebermann
(Berlin 1847- 1935)

Plucking Geese
Die Gänserupferinnen
Vrouwen die ganzen plukken

●●

c. 1871-1872
119,5 x 170,5 cm / 47.04 x 67.12 in.
Nationalgalerie, Staatliche Museen, Berlin

Oil on canvas
Öl auf Leinwand
Olieverf op doek

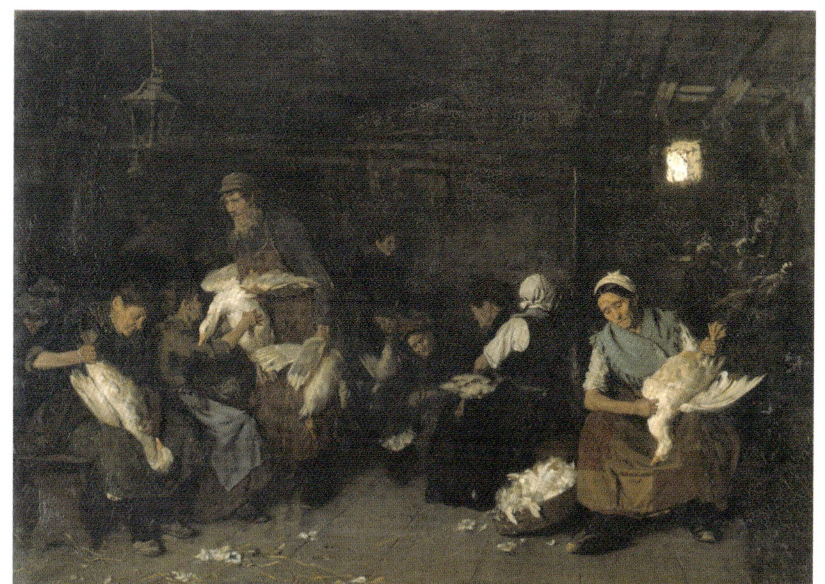

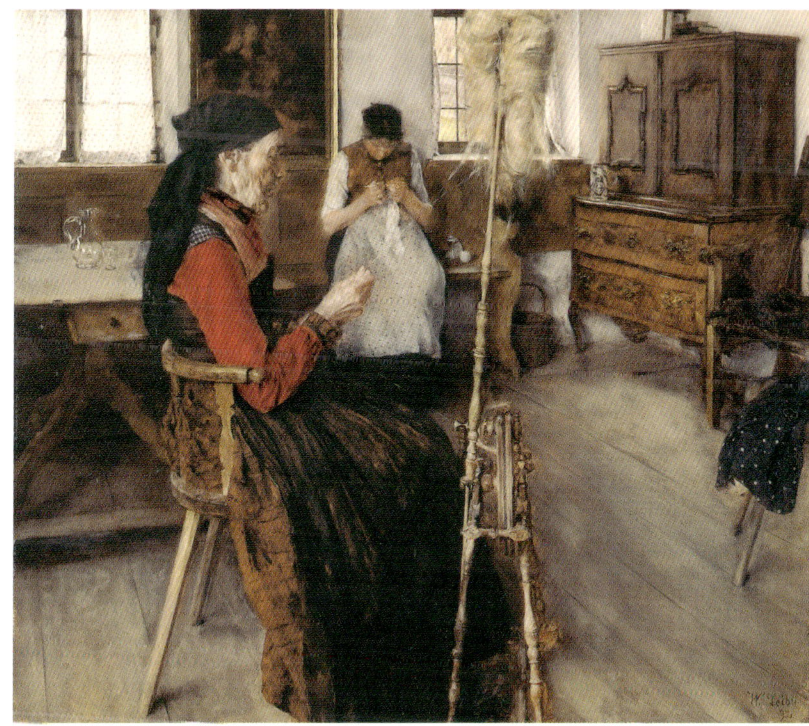

Wilhelm Leibl
(Köln 1844 - Würzburg 1900)

The Spinstress
Die Spinnerin
De Spinster

●

1892
65 x 74 cm / 25.59 x 29.13 in.
Museum der bildenden Künste, Leipzig

Théo van Rysselberghe
(Ghent 1862 - 1926)

Man at the Helm
Der Mann am Ruder
De man aan het roer

●

1892
60 x 80 cm / 23.62 x 31.49 in.
Musée d'Orsay, Paris

Oil on canvas
Öl auf Leinwand
Olieverf op doek

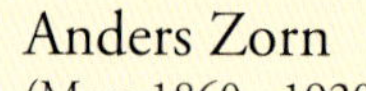

Anders Zorn
(Mora 1860 - 1920)

Maja

●

1900
91,5 x 53,5 cm / 36.02 x 21.06 in.
Nationalgalerie, Staatliche Museen, Berlin
Berlin

Oil on canvas
Öl auf Leinwand
Olieverf op doek

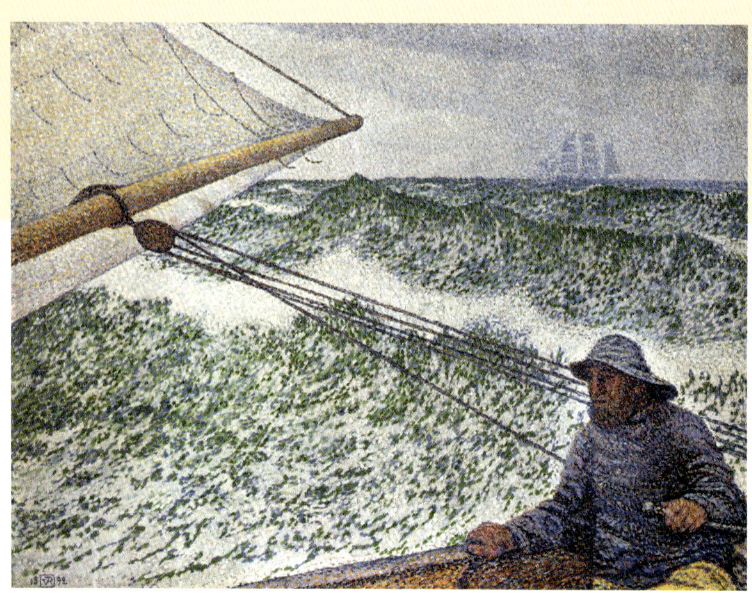

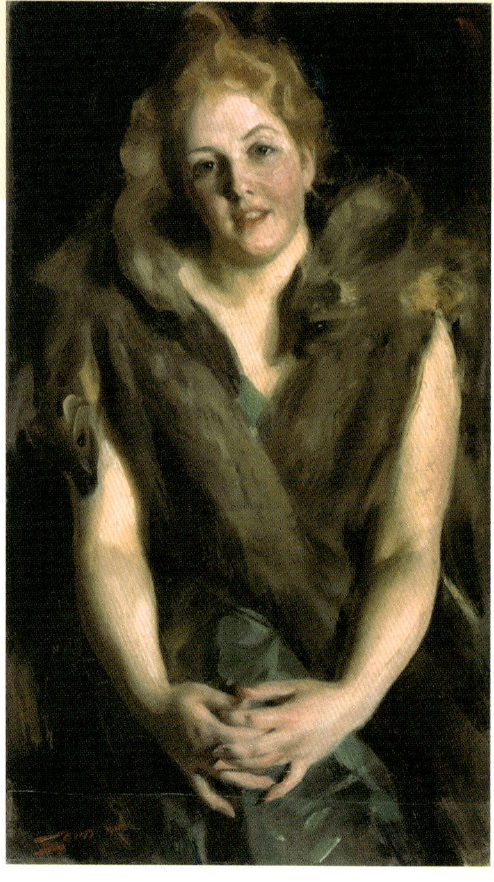

Valentin Serov
(Saint Petersburg 1865 - Moscow 1911)

Girl with Peaches
Mädchen mit Pfirsichen
Meisje met perzikken

●

1887
Tret'jakov Gallery, Moscow

Oil on canvas
Öl auf Leinwand
Olieverf op doek

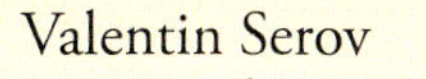

Valentin Serov
(Saint Petersburg 1865 - Moscow 1911)

Madame Lwoff

●

1895
90 x 59 cm / 35.43 x 23.22 in.
Musée d'Orsay, Paris

Oil on canvas
Öl auf Leinwand
Olieverf op doek

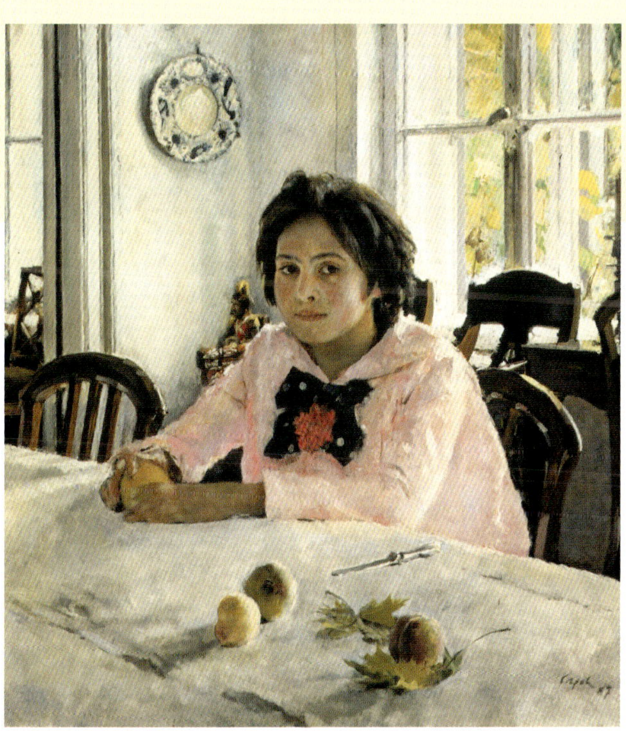

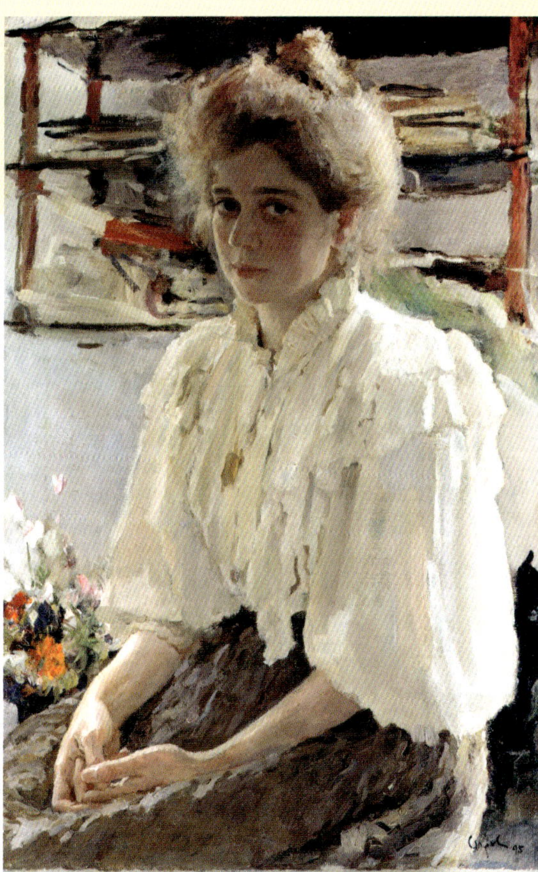

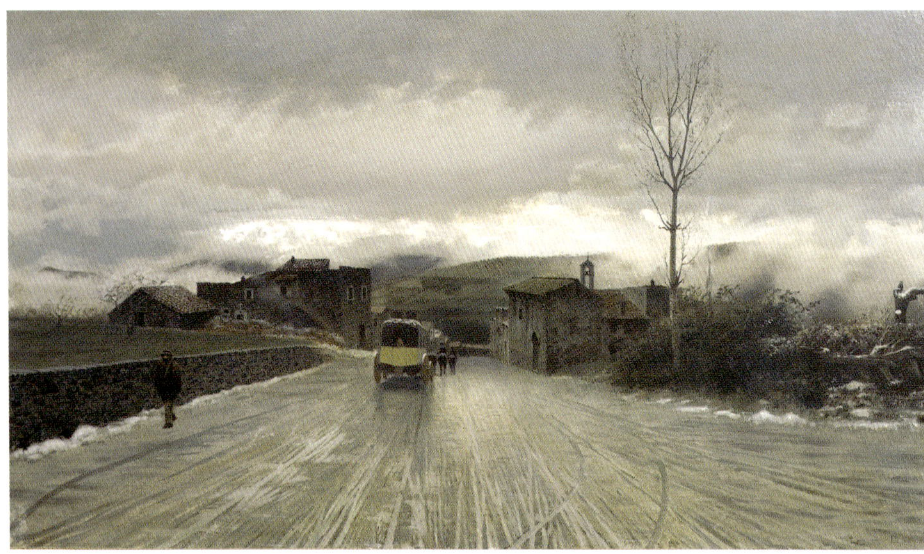

Giuseppe De Nittis
(Barletta 1846 - Saint-Germain-en-Laye 1884)

The Appenine Pass
Die Durchquerung des Apennin
De doorgang in de Apennijnen

●●

1867
Museo Nazionale
di Capodimonte, Napoli

Giovanni Boldini
(Ferrara 1842 - Paris 1931)

Portrait of Giuseppe Verdi
Portrait von Giuseppe Verdi
Portret van Giuseppe Verdi

●●●

1886
65 x 54 cm / 25.59 x 21.25 in.
Galleria Nazionale d'Arte Moderna, Roma

Pastel on paper
Pastell auf Papier
Pastel op papier

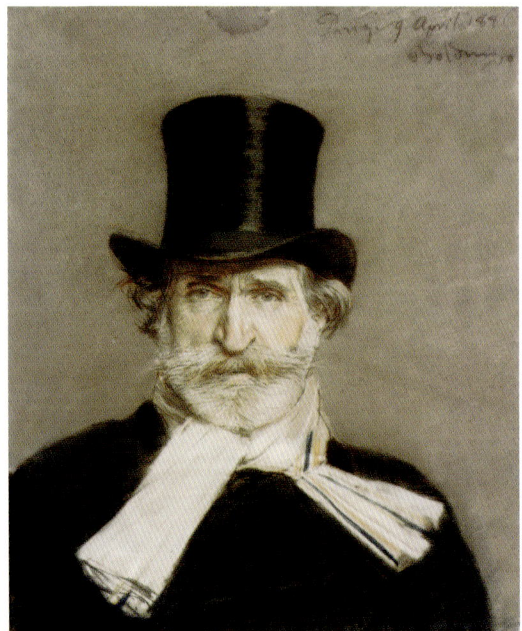

Ignacio Zuloaga
(Eibar 1870 - Madrid 1945)

Mountains of Calatayud
Der Berg von Calatayud
Berg van Calatayud

●

Museo Nacional Centro
de Arte Reina Sofía,
Madrid

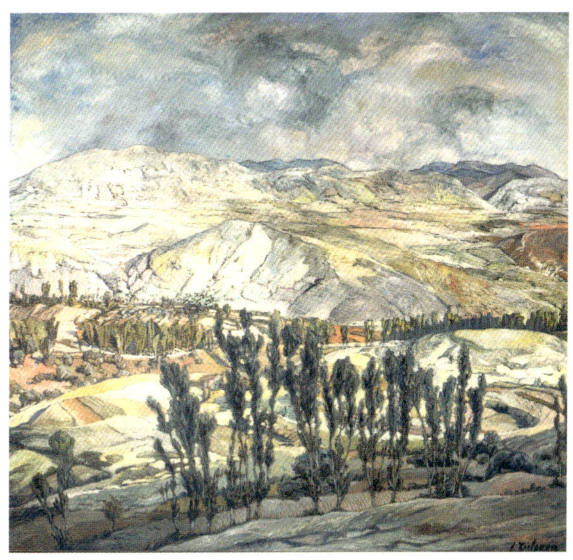

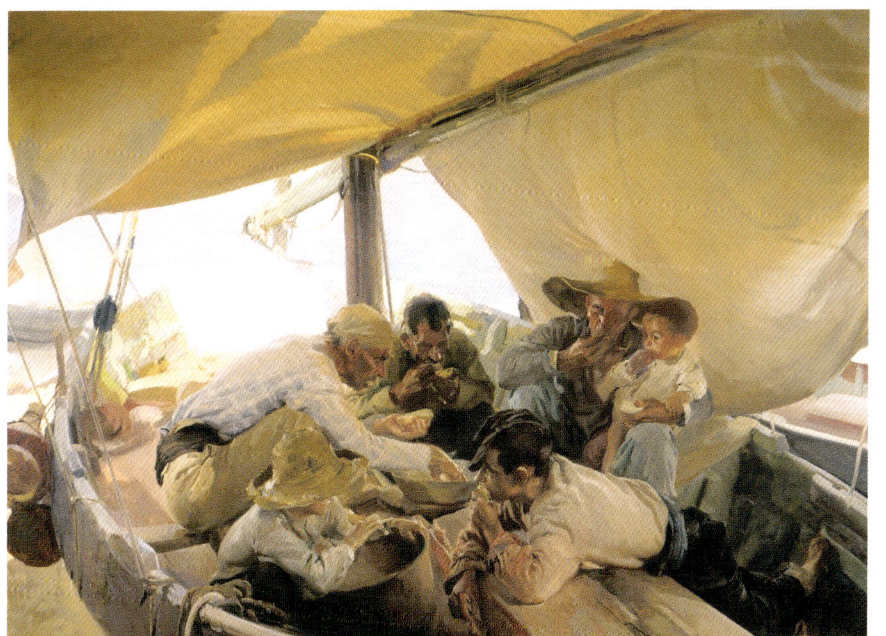

Joaquín Sorolla y Bastida
(Valencia 1863 - Cercedilla 1923)

A Meal on the Boat
Essen im Boot
Eten op de boot

●

c. 1895
Museo de la Real Academia
de Bellas Artes de San Fernando,
Madrid

Oil on canvas
Öl auf Leinwand
Olieverf op doek

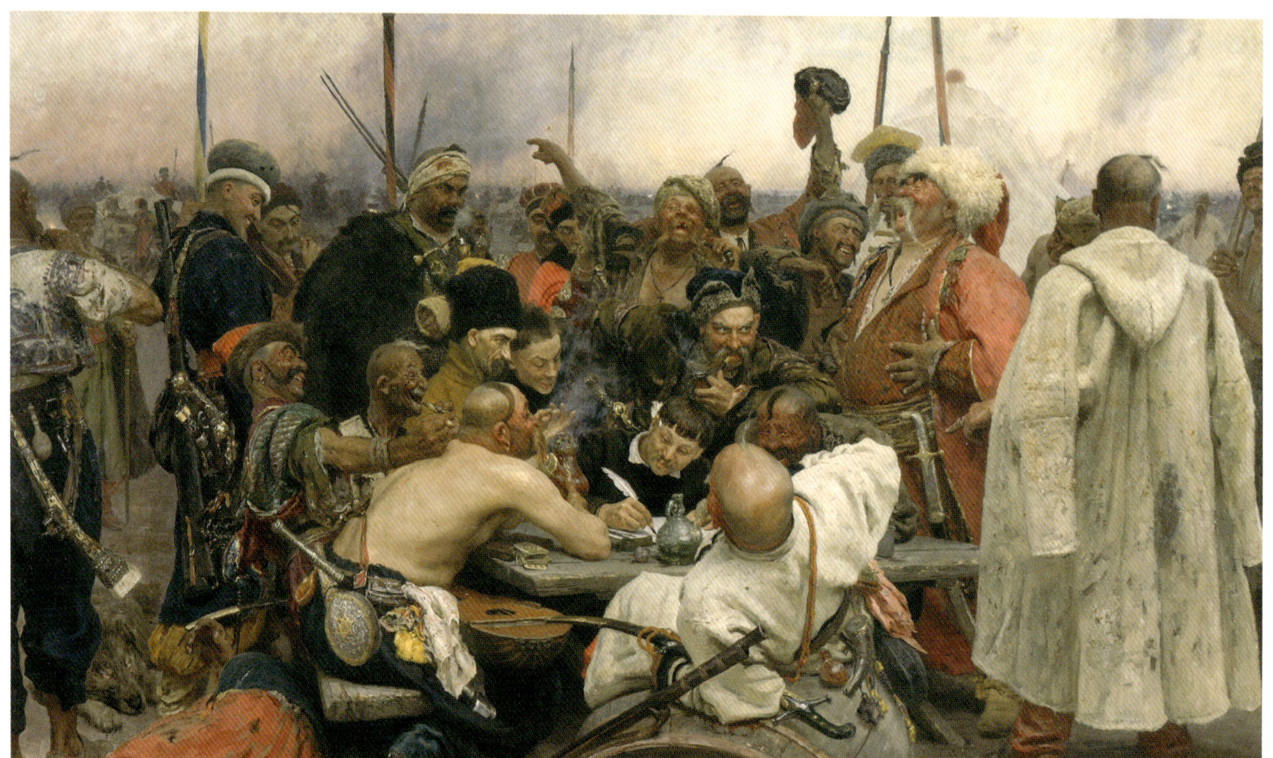

Ilya Repin
(Chuhuiv 1844 - Kuokkala 1930)

The Zaporizhzhya Cossacks Write to the Turkish Sultan
Die Saporoper Kosaken schreiben dem Türkischen Sultan einen Brief
De Kozakken van Zaporozje schrijven een brief aan de Turkse Sultan

●●

c. 1880-1891
203 x 358 cm / 79.92 x 140.94 in.
State Russian Museum, St. Petersbourg

Oil on canvas / Öl auf Leinwand / Olieverf op doek

The drama of the decisive moment: Ilya Repin is the leading protagonist of Russian Realism

Die Dramatik des entscheidenden Augenblicks. Ilya Repin ist der Hauptvertreter der russischen Realismus.

De dramatiek van het beslissende moment. Ilya Repin is de belangrijkste vertegenwoordiger van het Russische realisme.

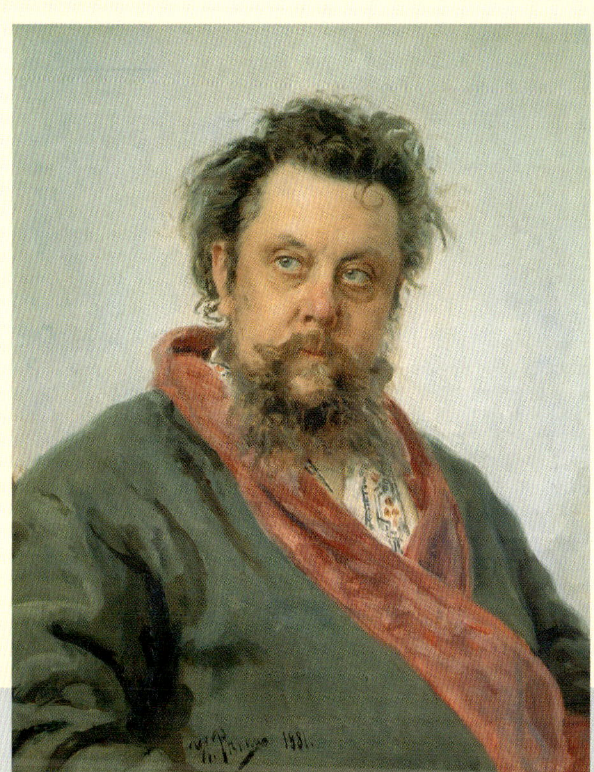

Ilya Repin
(Chuhuiv 1844 - Kuokkala 1930)

Modest Mussorgsky
Portrait vom bescheidenen Mussorgsky

●●●

1881
69 x 57 cm / 27.16 x 22.44 in.
Tret'jakov Gallery, Moscow

Oil on canvas / Öl auf Leinwand / Olieverf op doek

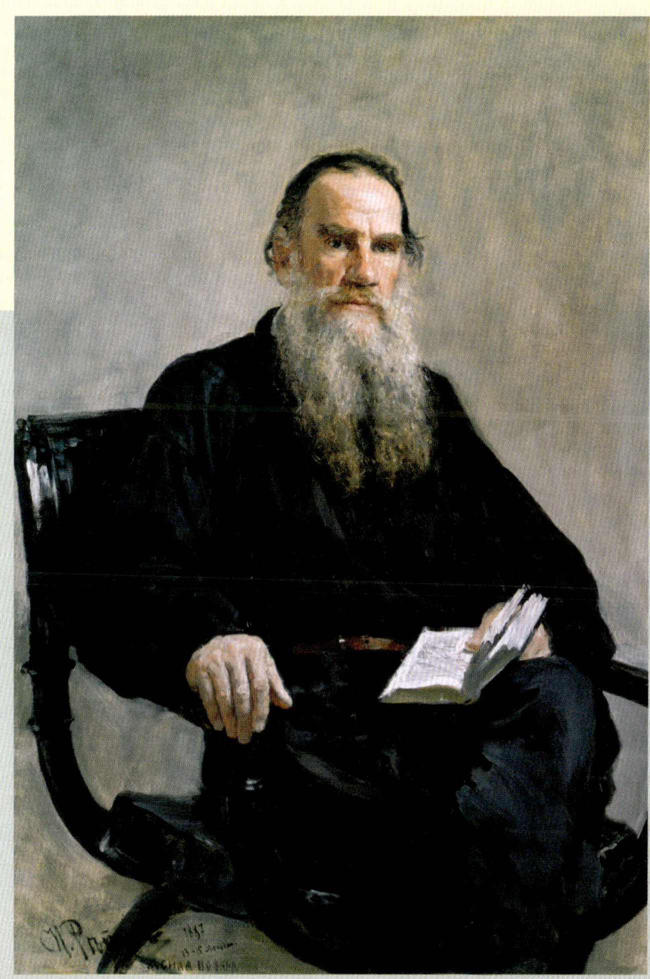

Ilya Repin
(Chuhuiv 1844 - Kuokkala 1930)

Leo Tolstoy

●●

1887
124 x 88 cm / 48.81 x 34.64 in.
Tret'jakov Gallery, Moscow

Oil on canvas
Öl auf Leinwand
Olieverf op doek

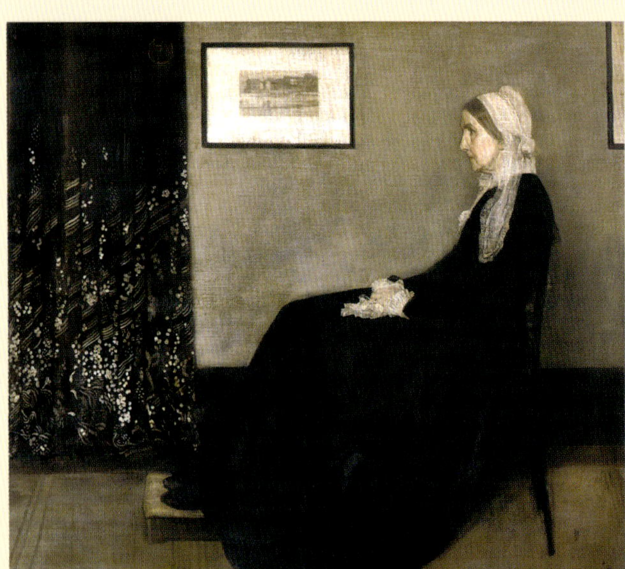

James Abbott McNeill Whistler
(Lowell 1834 - London 1903)

Arrangement in Grey and Black:
The Artist's Mother
Arrangement in Grau und Schwarz.
Portrait der Mutter des Künstlers
Arrangement in grijs en zwart.
Portret van de moeder van de kunstenaar

●●

1871
144,3 x 162,5 cm / 56.81 x 63.97 in.
Musée d'Orsay, Paris

Oil on canvas / Öl auf Leinwand / Olieverf op doek

Americans in Impressionist Europe.

Amerikaner im impressionistischen Europa.

Amerikanen in het impressionistische Europa.

Mary Cassatt
(Allegheny City 1844 -
Château de Beaufresne 1926)

The bath
Das Bad
Het bad

●●

1893
100,3 x 66,1 cm / 39.48 x 26.02 in.
Art Institute of Chicago, Chicago

Oil on canvas
Öl auf Leinwand
Olieverf op doek

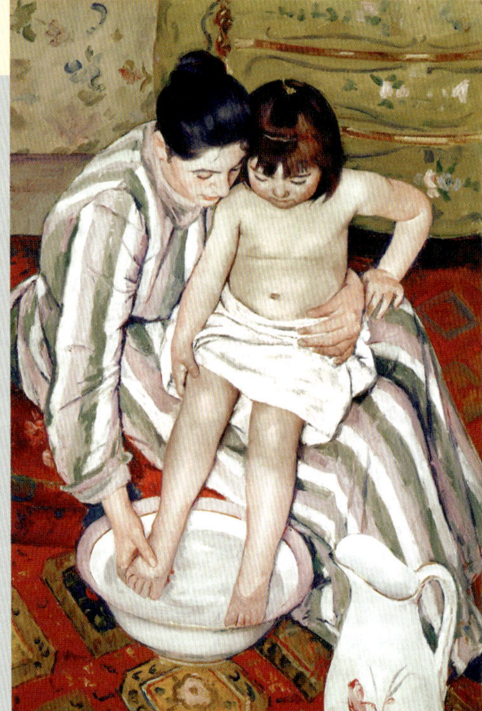

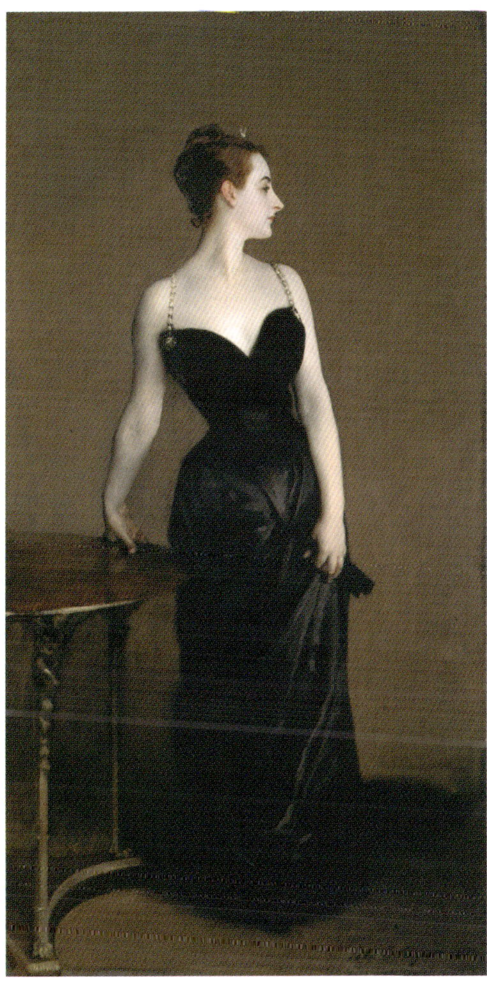

John Singer Sargent
(Firenze 1856 - London 1925)

Madame X

●

1883-1884
208,6 x 109,9 cm / 82.13 x 43.27 in.
Metropolitan Museum of Art, New York

Oil on canvas
Öl auf Leinwand
Olieverf op doek

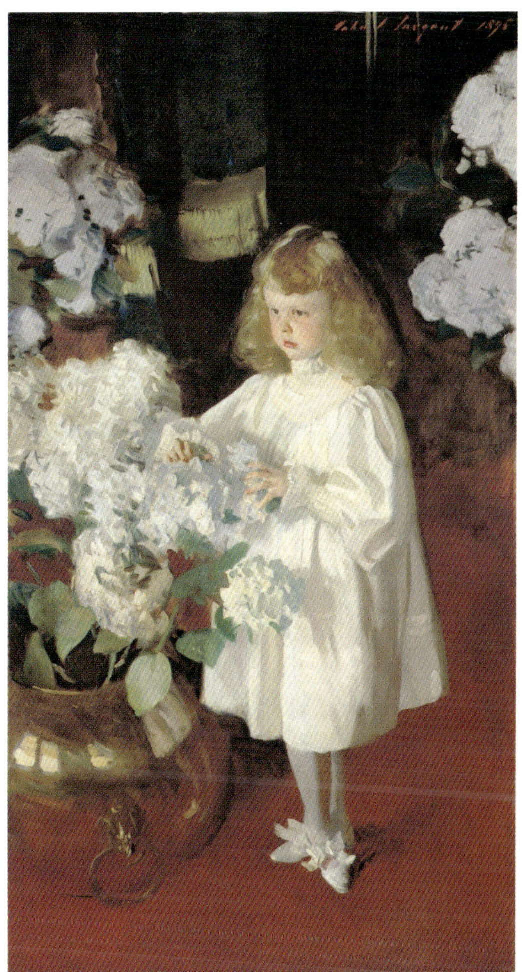

John Singer Sargent
(Firenze 1856 - London 1925)

Helen Sears

1895
167,3 x 91,4 cm / 65.87 x 36 in.
Museum of Fine Arts, Boston

Oil on canvas
Öl auf Leinwand
Olieverf op doek

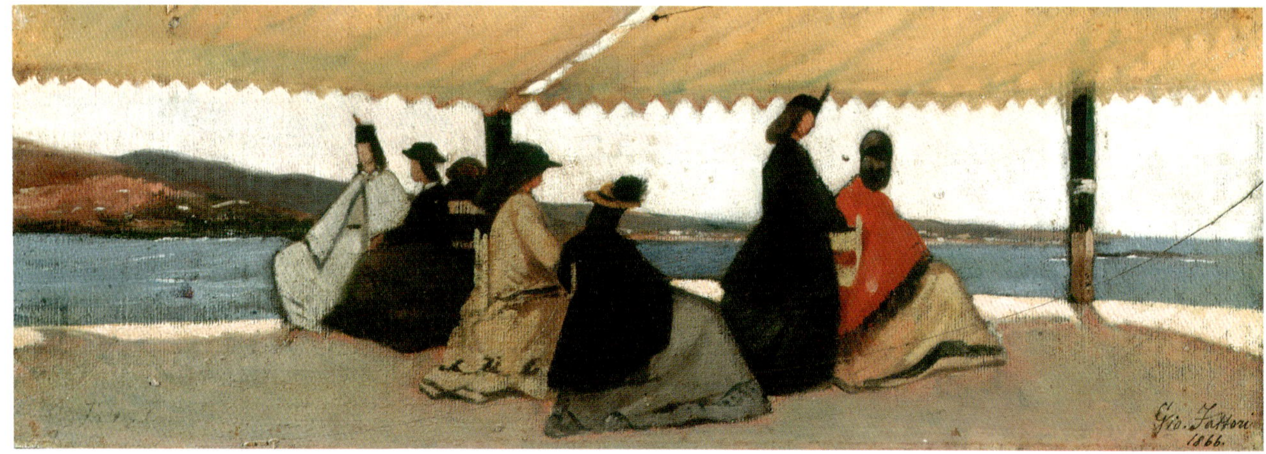

Giovanni Fattori
(Livorno 1825 - Firenze 1908)

The Rotunda at Palmieri
Die Rotonde von Palmieri
De Rotonda di Palmieri

●●

1866
12 x 35 cm / 4.72 x 13.77 in.
Galleria Nazionale d'Arte Moderna, Firenze

Oil on canvas
Öl auf Leinwand
Olieverf op doek

Giovanni Fattori
(Livorno 1825 - Firenze 1908)

The Rest
Die Rast
De rust

●

c. 1870
88 x 179 cm / 34.64 x 70.47 in.
Pinacoteca Nazionale di Brera, Milano

Oil on canvas
Öl auf Leinwand
Olieverf op doek

Protagonists of Italian Impressionism.

Meister des italienischen Impressionismus.

Meesters van het Italiaanse impressionisme.

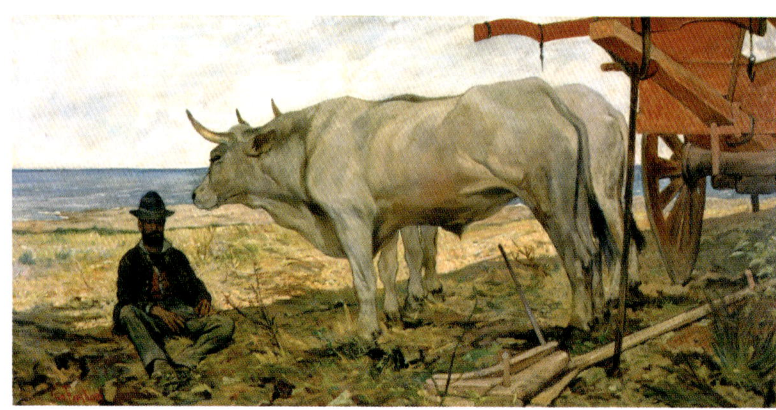

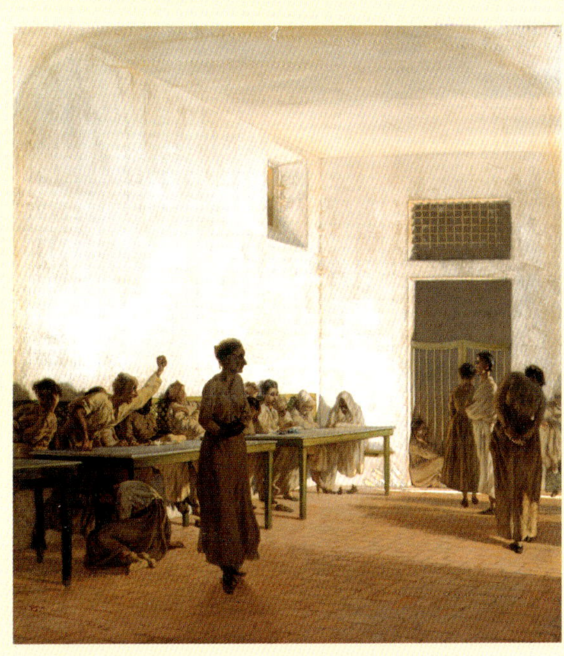

Telemaco Signorini
(Firenze 1835 - 1901)

The Madhouse
Der Saal der Tobsüchtigen
Afdeling voor gewelddadige geesteszieke vrouwen

●

1865
66 x 59 cm / 25.98 x 23.22 in.
Galleria d'Arte Moderna di Ca' Pesaro, Venezia

Oil on canvas
Öl auf Leinwand
Olieverf op doek

Silvestro Lega
(Modigliana, Forlì 1826 - Firenze 1895)

The Wine Bower
Die Pergola
De pergola

●

1868
75 x 93,5 cm / 29.52 x 36.81 in.
Pinacoteca Nazionale di Brera, Milano

Oil on canvas / Öl auf Leinwand
Olieverf op doek

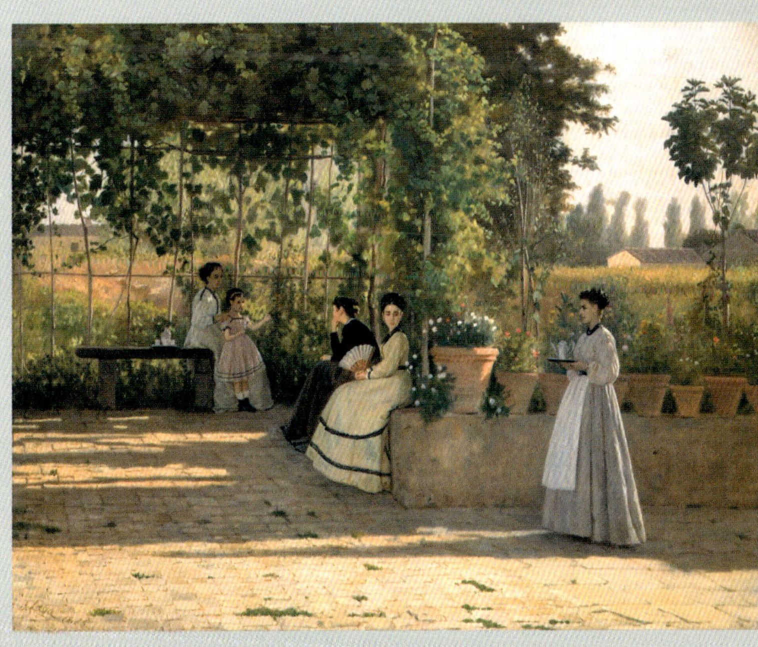

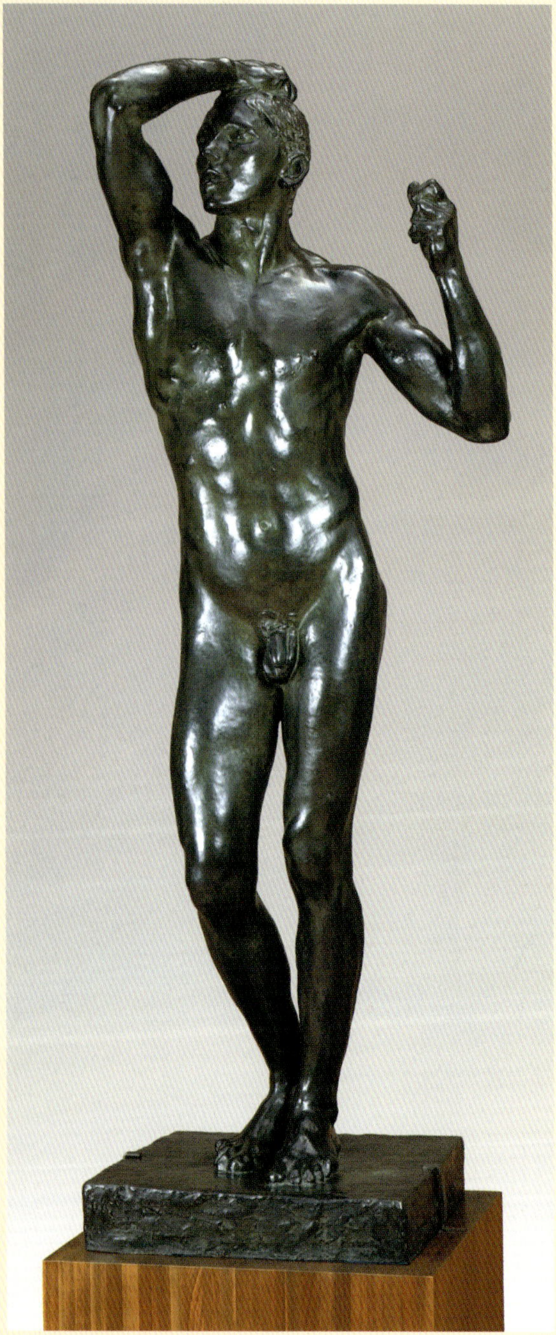

Auguste Rodin
(Paris 1840 - Meudon 1917)

The Age of Bronze
Das Bronzezeitalter
De Bronstijd

●●

1876
h. 182,9 cm / 72 in.
Metropolitan Museum of Art,
New York

Bronze / Brons

Auguste Rodin
(Paris 1840 - Meudon 1917)

The Thinker
Der Denker
De denker

●●●

1880
h. 200,7 cm / 79.01 in.
Rodin Museum,
Philadelphia

Bronze / Brons

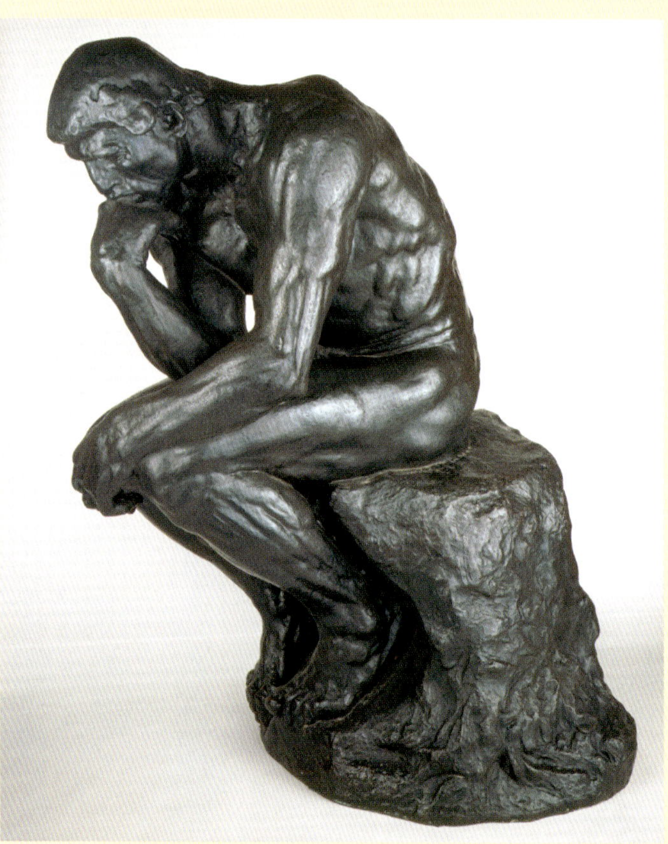

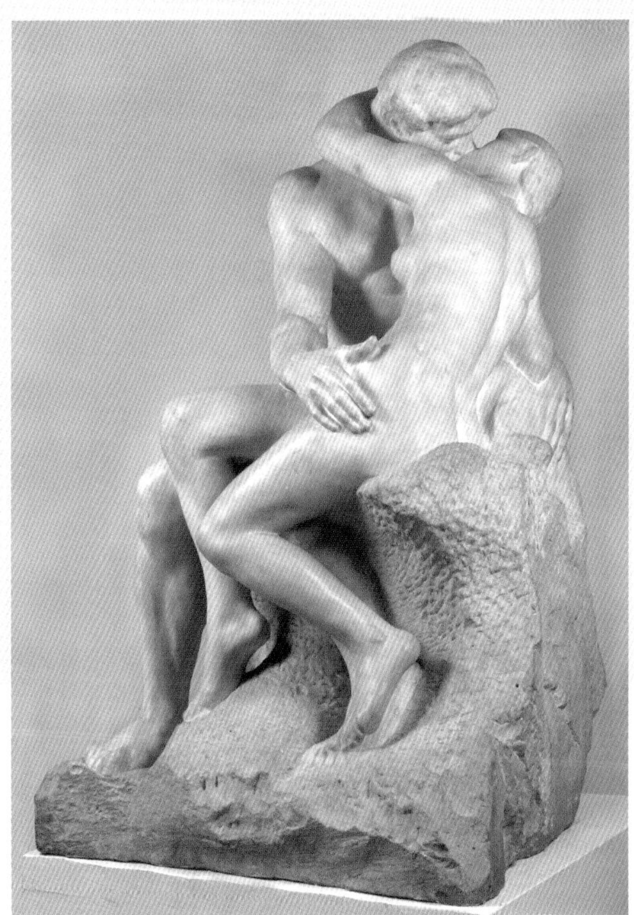

Auguste Rodin
(Paris 1840 - Meudon 1917)

The Kiss
Der Kuss
De kus

●●●

1888 -1889
181,5 x 112,3 x 117 cm /
71.46 x 44.21 x 46.06 in.
Musée Rodin, Paris

Marble
Marmor
Marmer

Medardo Rosso
(Torino 1858 - Milano 1828)

The Concierge
Die Hausmeisterin
De conciërge

●●

1883
h. 36,8 cm / 14.48 in.
Museum of Modern Art
(MoMA), New York

Wax on plaster
Wachs auf Gips
Was op gips

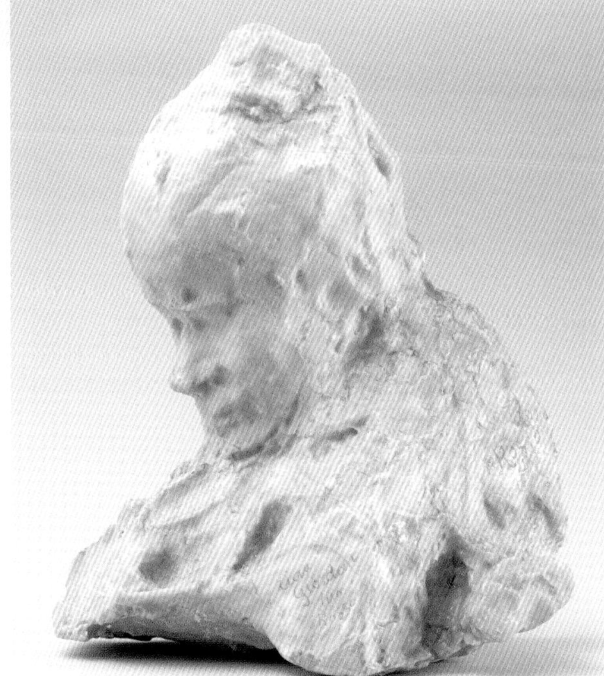

Impressionism in bronze, marble and wax.

Impressionismus in Bronze, Stein und Wachs.

Impressionisme in brons, steen en was.

Paul Cézanne
(Aix-en-Provence 1839 - 1906)

The Hanged Man's House
Das Haus des Gehängten
Het huis van de gehangene

●●●

1873
55 x 66 cm / 21.65 x 25.98 in.
Musée d'Orsay, Paris

Oil on canvas
Öl auf Leinwand
Olieverf op doek

Paul Cézanne: capturing the fleeting moment.

Cézanne: das Flüchtige dauerhaft machen.

Cézanne: het vluchtige duurzaam maken.

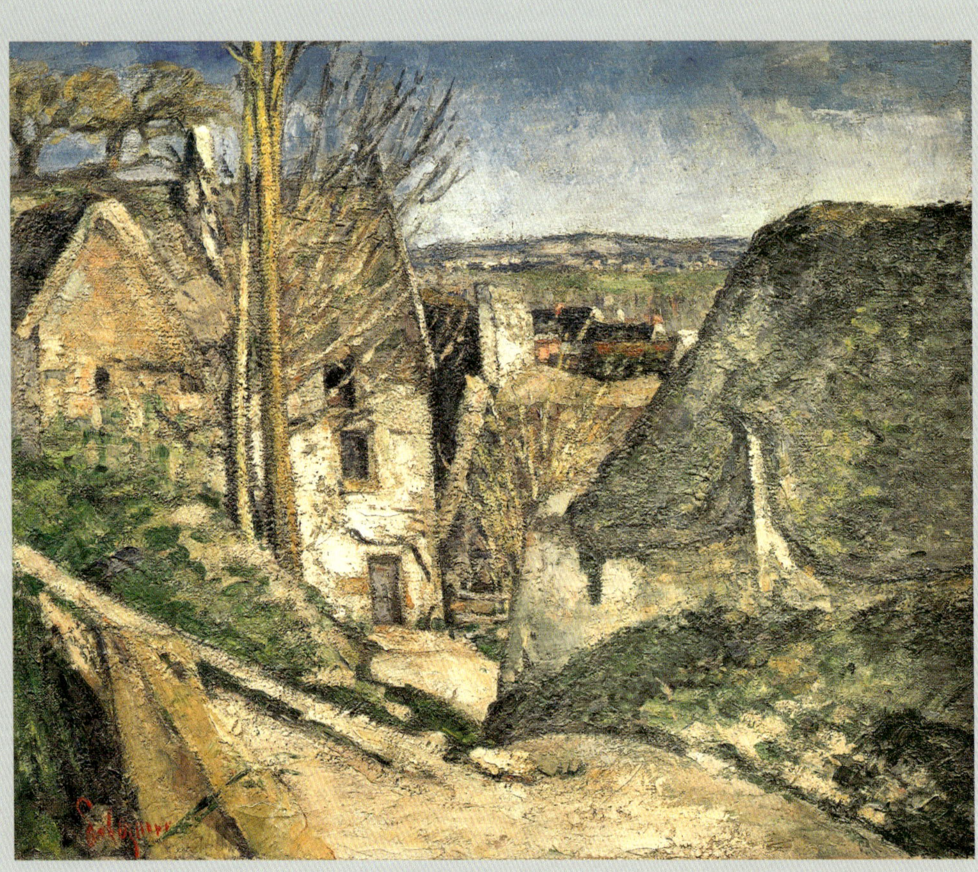

Paul Cézanne
(Aix-en-Provence 1839 - 1906)

Estaque

●●

c. 1882-1885
58 x 72,7 cm / 22.83 x 28.62 in.
Musée d'Orsay, Paris

Oil on canvas
Öl auf Leinwand
Olieverf op doek

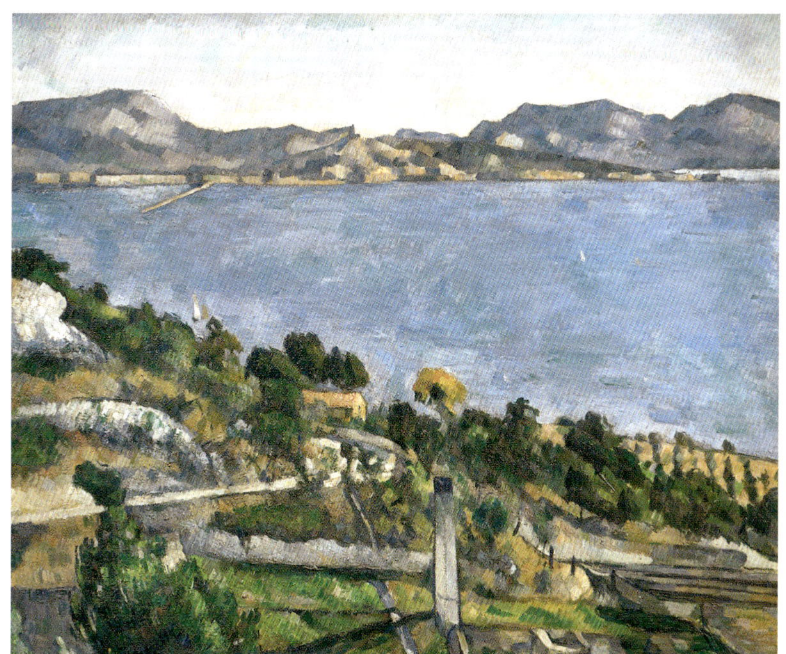

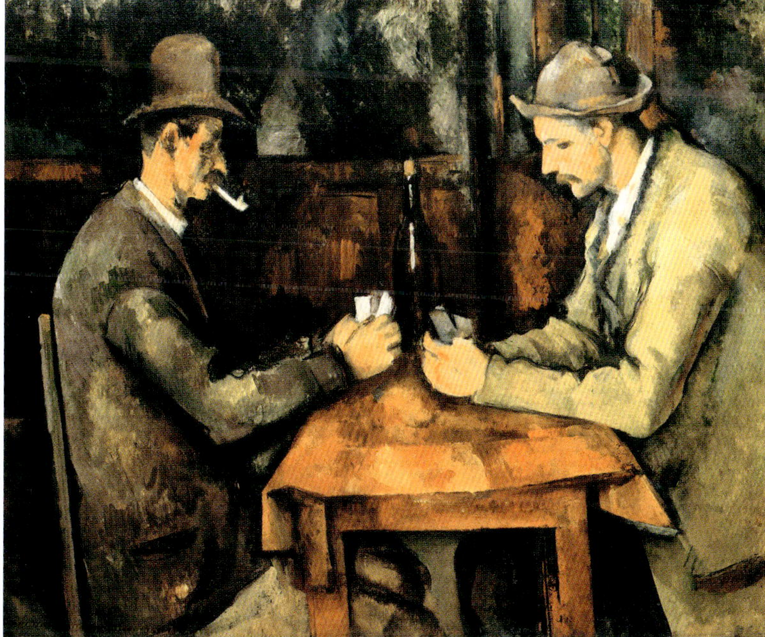

Paul Cézanne
(Aix-en-Provence 1839 - 1906)

Card Players
Die Kartenspieler
De kaartspelers

●●●

1890-1895
57,5 x 57 cm / 18.7 x 22.44 in.
Musèe d'Orsay, Paris
Oil on canvas
Öl auf Leinwand
Olieverf op doek

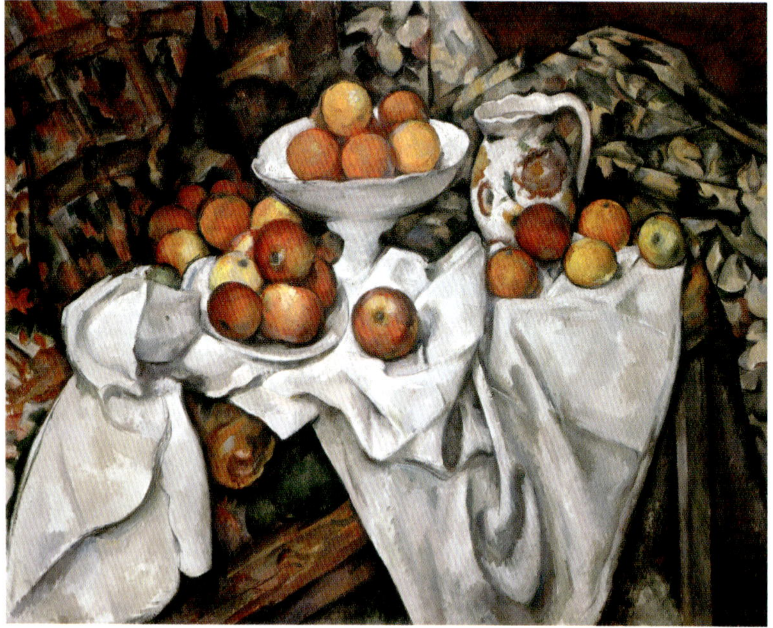

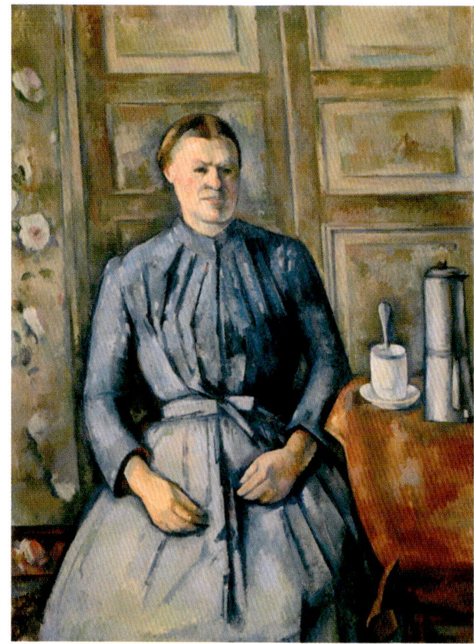

Paul Cézanne
(Aix-en-Provence 1839 - 1906)

Still Life with Apples and Oranges
Stillleben mit Äpfeln und Orangen
Stilleven met appels en sinaasappels

c. 1899
74 x 93 cm / 29.13 x 36.61 in.
Musée d'Orsay, Paris

Oil on canvas
Öl auf Leinwand
Olieverf op doek

Paul Cézanne
(Aix-en-Provence 1839 - 1906)

Woman with a Coffee Pot
Frau mit Kaffeemaschine
Vrouw met koffiepot

c. 1890-1894
130 x 96,5 cm / 51.18 x 37.99 in.
Musée d'Orsay, Paris

Oil on canvas
Öl auf Leinwand
Olieverf op doek

Paul Cézanne
(Aix-en-Provence 1839 - 1906)

Mont Sainte-Victoire

●●●

c. 1902-1904
74 x 93 cm / 29.13 x 36.61 in.
Philadelphia Museum of Art, Philadelphia

Oil on canvas
Öl auf Leinwand
Olieverf op doek

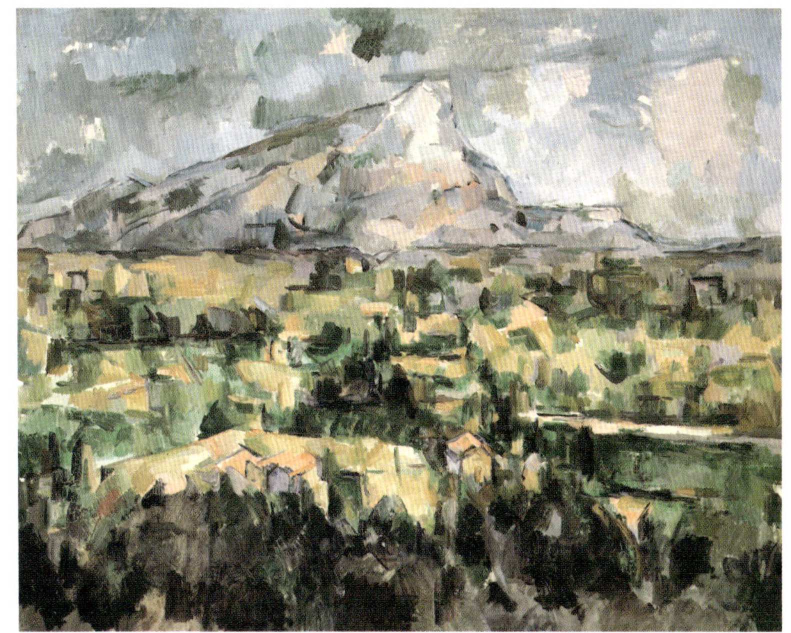

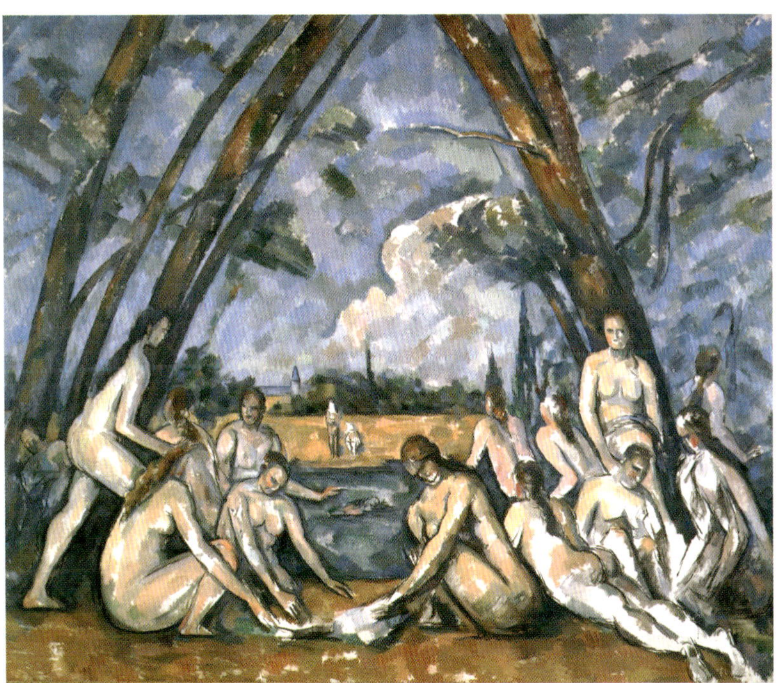

Paul Cézanne
(Aix-en-Provence 1839 - 1906

The Large Bathers
Badende
Grote baadsters

●●●

1906
2.10 x 2.50 m / 82.67 x 98.42 in.
Philadelphia Museum of Art, Philadelphia

Oil on canvas
Öl auf Leinwand
Olieverf op doek

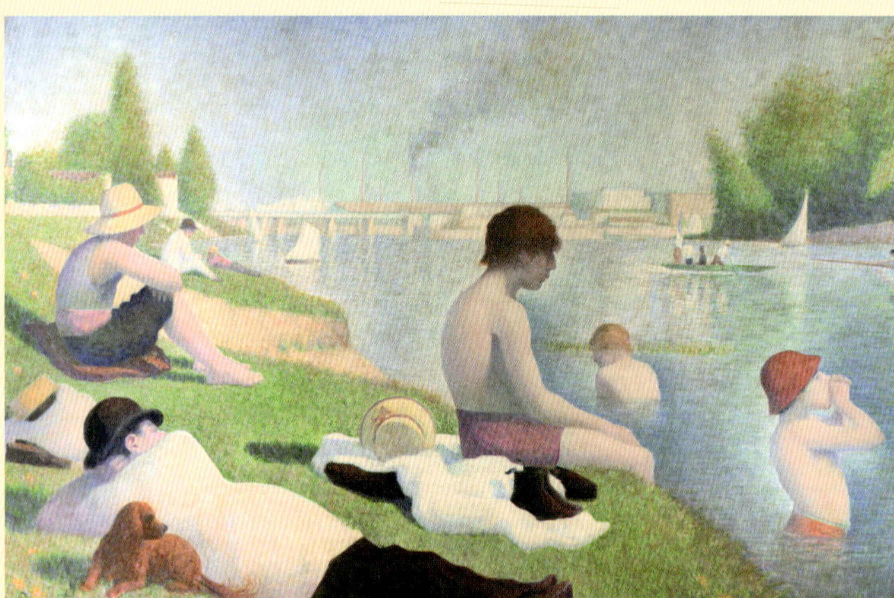

Georges Seurat
(Paris 1859 - Gravelines 1891)

Bathers at Asnières
Badeplatz in Asnières
Une baignade à Asnières

●●●

1884
201 x 300 cm / 79.13 x 118.11 in.
National Gallery, London

Oil on canvas
Öl auf Leinwand
Olieverf op doek

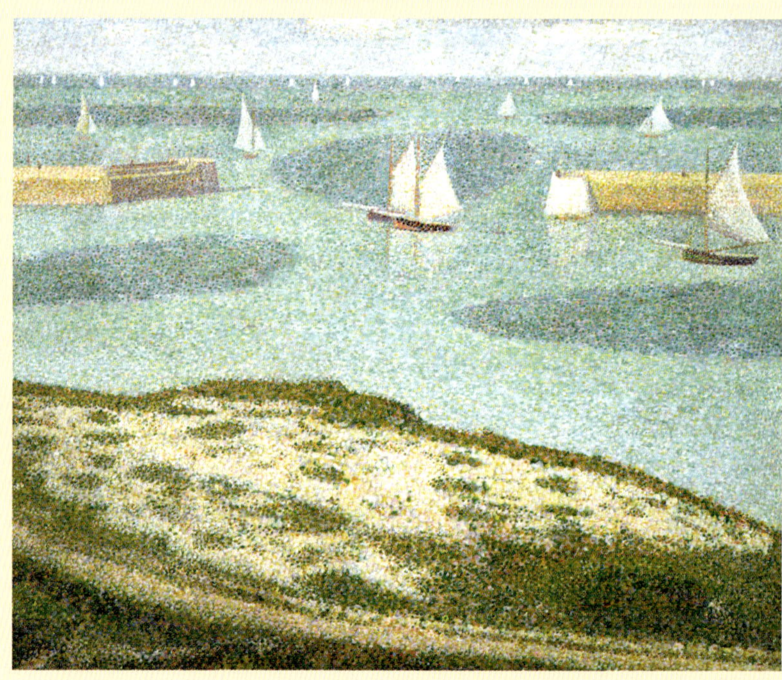

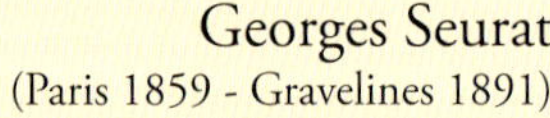

Georges Seurat
(Paris 1859 - Gravelines 1891)

Port-en-Bessin

●●

1888
54,9 x 65,1 cm / 21.61 x 25.62 in.
Museum of Modern Art (MoMA), New York

Oil on canvas
Öl auf Leinwand
Olieverf op doek

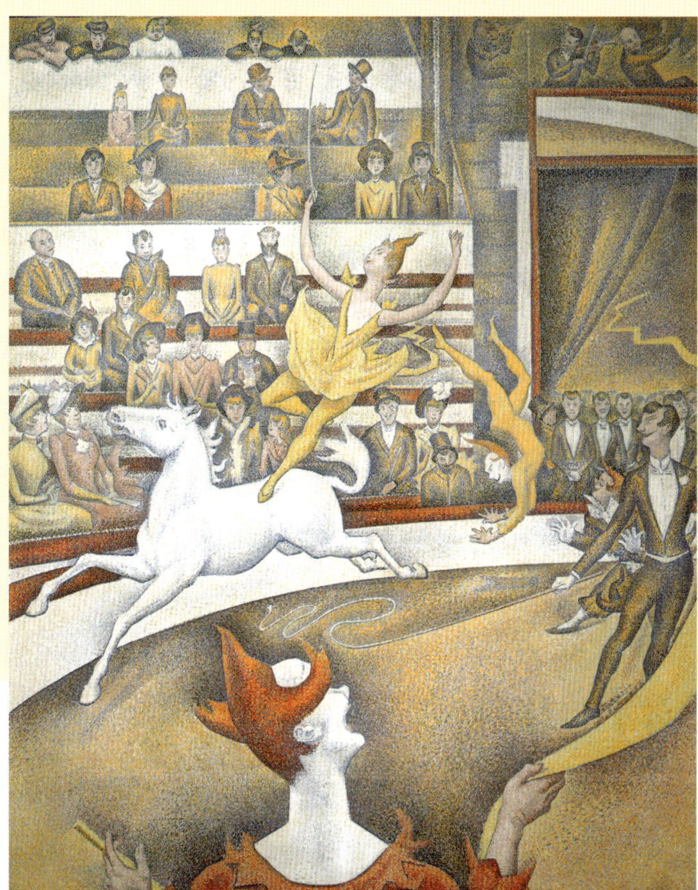

Georges Seurat
(Paris 1859 - Gravelines 1891)

The Circus
Der Zirkus
Het circus

●●●

c. 1890-1891
185 x 152 cm / 72.83 x 59.84 in.
Musée d'Orsay, Paris

Oil on canvas
Öl auf Leinwand
Olieverf op doek

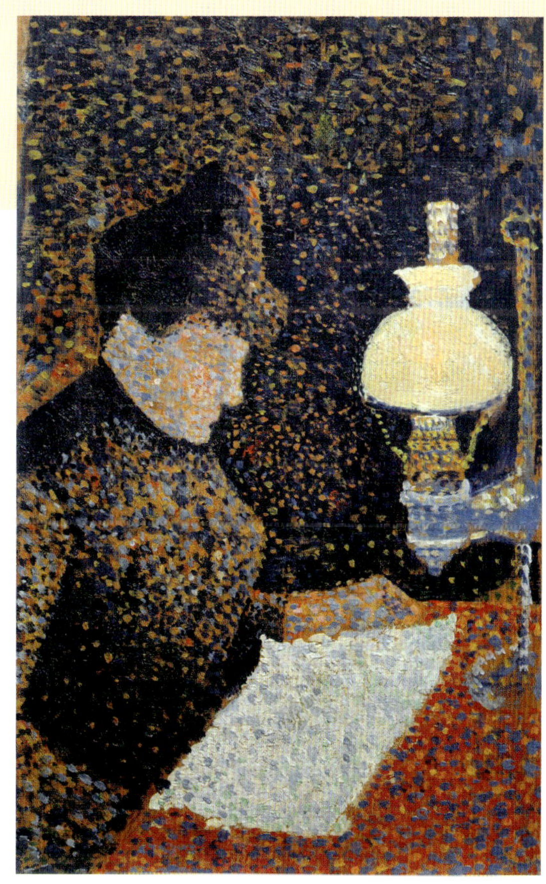

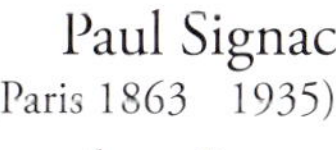

Paul Signac
(Paris 1863 1935)

Woman by a Lamp
Frau unter der Lampe
Vrouw onder het lamplicht

●

1890
25,5 x 15 cm / 9.6 x 6 in.
Musée d'Orsay, Paris

Oil on canvas
Öl auf Leinwand
Olieverf op doek

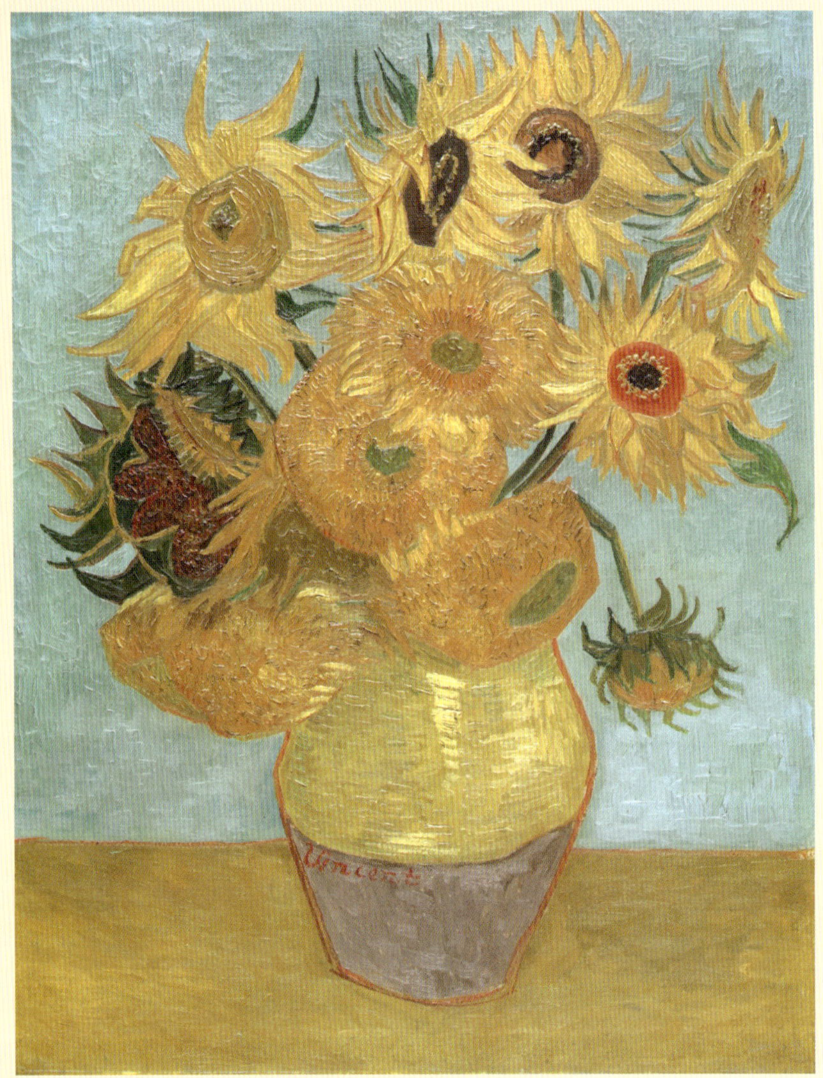

Painting on the brink of folly: Vincent van Gogh's creative ecstasy in southern France produces orgies of colour and whirling brushstrokes.

Malerei am Rande des Wahnsinns. Vincent van Goghs extatisches Schaffen in Südfrankreich produziert Farborgien mit wirbelnden Pinselzügen im Stundentakt.

Schilderkunst op de grens van de waanzin. De esthetische creativiteit van Vincent van Gogh in Zuid-Frankrijk produceert orgiën van kleuren met wervelende penseelstreken.

Vincent van Gogh
(Zundert 1853 - Auvers-sur-Oise 1890)

Sunflowers
Die Sonnenblumen
Zonnebloemen

●●●

c. 1888-1889
92 x 71 cm / 36.22 x 27.95 in.
Philadelphia Museum of Art, Philadelphia

Oil on canvas
Öl auf Leinwand
Olieverf op doek

Vincent van Gogh
(Zundert 1853 - Auvers-sur-Oise 1890)

Starry Night
Sternen-Nacht
Sterrennacht

●●●

1889
73 x 92 cm / 28.74 x 36.22 in.
Museum of Modern Art (MoMA), New York

Oil on canvas
Öl auf Leinwand
Olieverf op doek

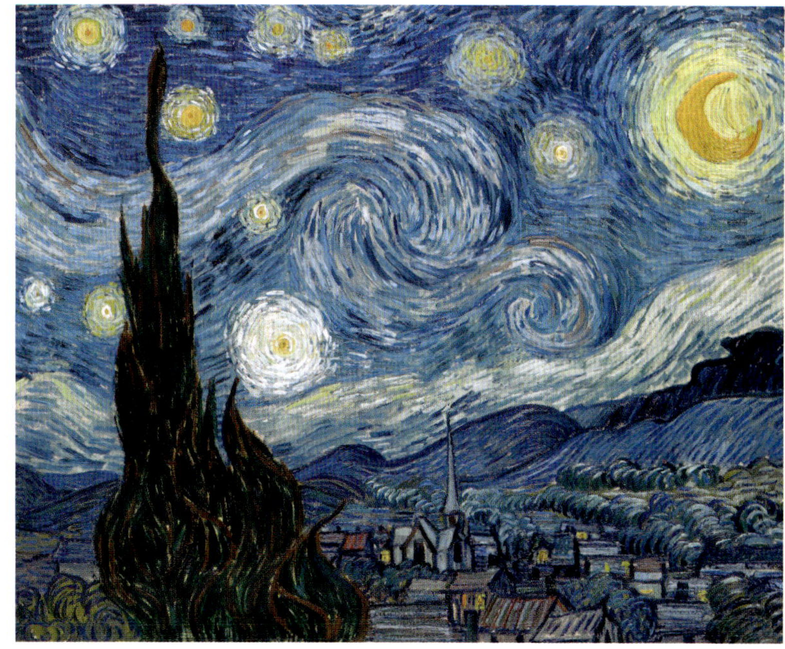

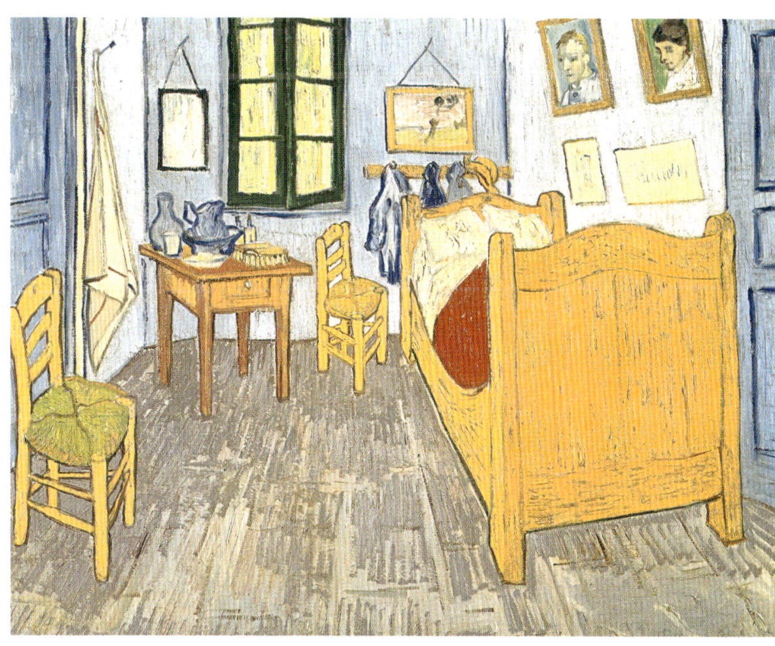

Vincent van Gogh
(Zundert 1853 - Auvers-sur-Oise 1890)

Van Gogh's Room at Arles
Das Schlafzimmer des Künstlers in Arles
De slaapkamer van Van Gogh in Arles

●●●

1889
56,5 x 74 cm / 22.24 x 29.13 in.
Musée d'Orsay, Paris

Oil on canvas
Öl auf Leinwand
Olieverf op doek

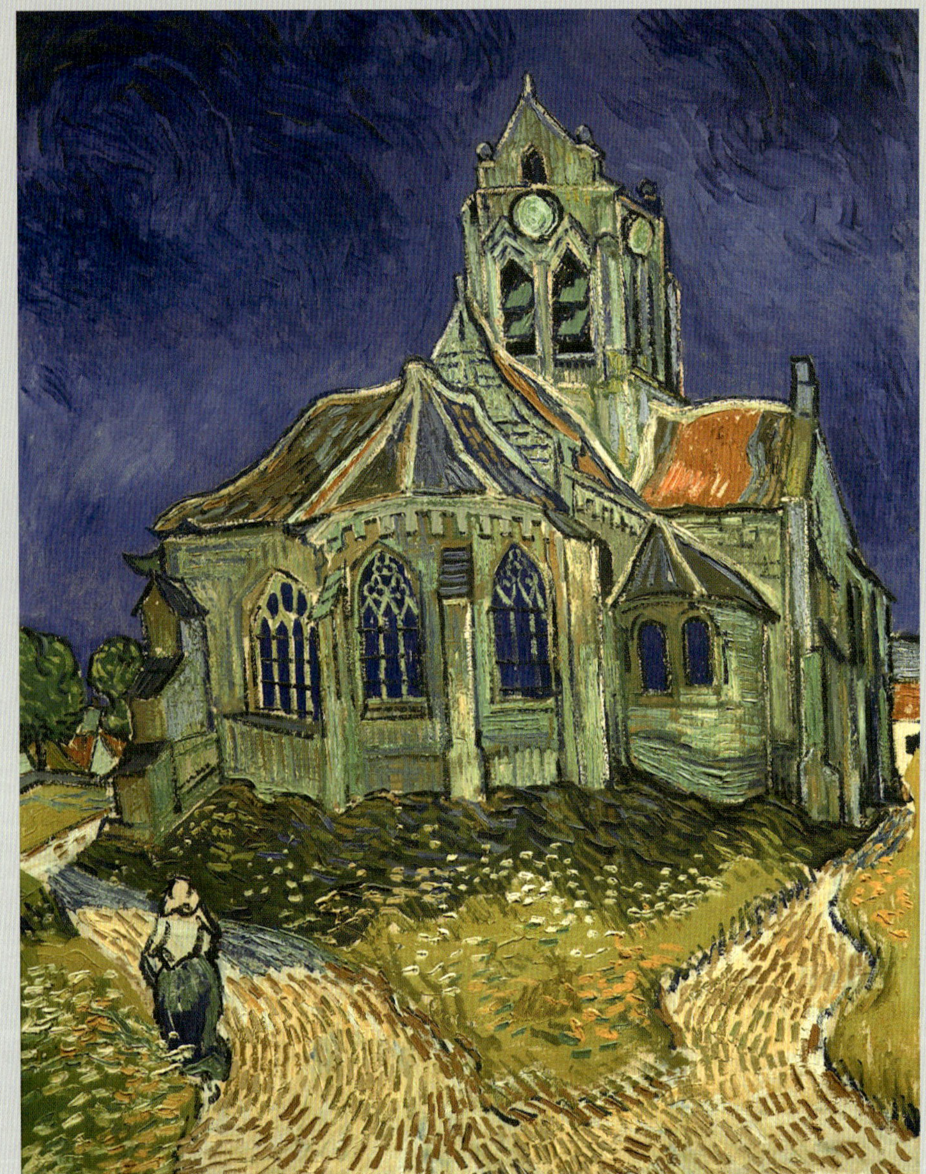

Vincent van Gogh
(Zundert 1853 - Auvers-sur-Oise 1890)

The Church at Auvers
Die Kirche von Auvers
De kerk van Auvers

●●●

1890
94 x 74 cm / 37 x 29.13 in.
Musée d'Orsay, Paris

Oil on canvas
Öl auf Leinwand
Olieverf op doek

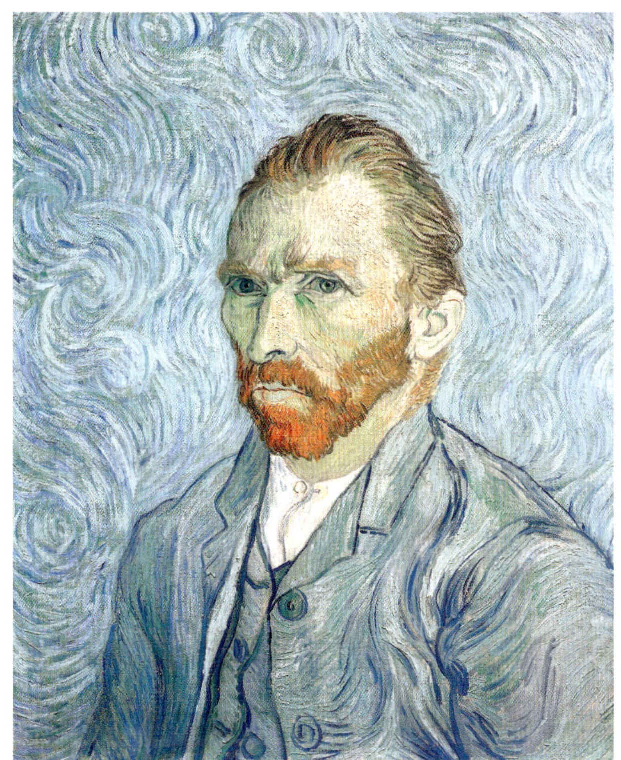

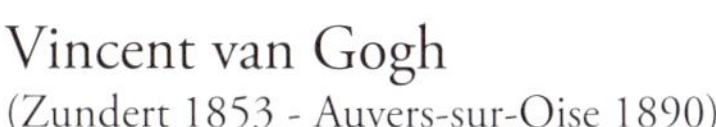

Vincent van Gogh
(Zundert 1853 - Auvers-sur-Oise 1890)

Self-Portrait
Selbstportrait
Zelfportret

●●●

1889
65 x 54 cm / 25.59 x 21.25 in.
Musée d'Orsay, Paris

Oil on canvas
Öl auf Leinwand
Olieverf op doek

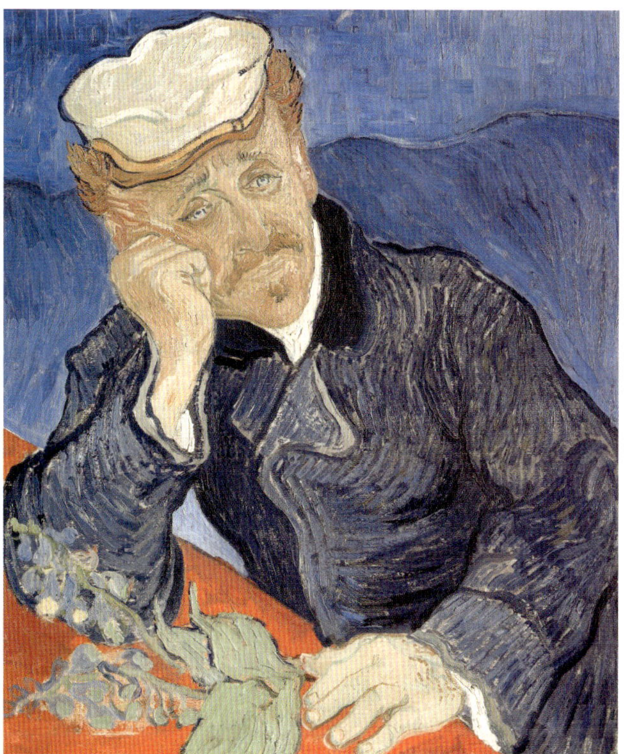

Vincent van Gogh
(Zundert 1853 - Auvers-sur-Oise 1890)

Portrait of Doctor Gachet
Portrait des Doktor Gachet
Portret van dokter Gachet

●●●

1890
67,9 x 50,9 cm / 26.73 x 20.03 in.
Musée d'Orsay, Paris

Oil on canvas
Öl auf Leinwand
Olieverf op doek

Paul Gauguin
(Paris 1848 - Hiva Oa 1903)

Women of Tahiti
Frauen auf Tahiti
Vrouwen van Tahiti

●●●

1891
69 x 91,5 cm / 27.16 x 36.02 in.
Musée d'Orsay, Paris

Oil on canvas
Öl auf Leinwand
Olieverf op doek

Disappointed ambitions: former banker Paul Gauguin seeks the idyll of the south seas in the French colonies but it had ceased to exist.

Enttäuschter Aussteiger. Der ehemalige Banker Paul Gauguin sucht in seinen Bildern Südsee Idylle, die es in den inzwischen französischen Kolonien längst nicht mehr gibt.

Teleurgestelde yup. De ex-bankier Paul Gauguin is in zijn schilderijen van de zuidelijke zeeën op zoek naar idylles die ondertussen niet meer bestaan in de Franse koloniën.

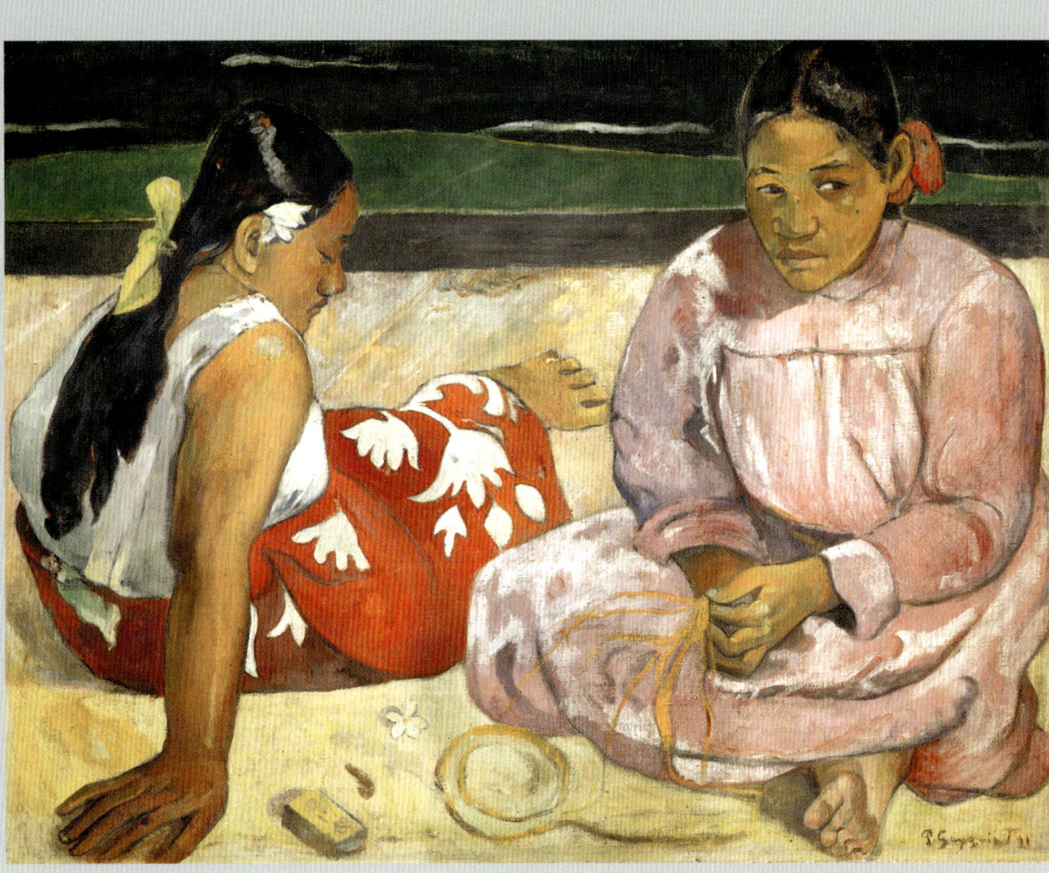

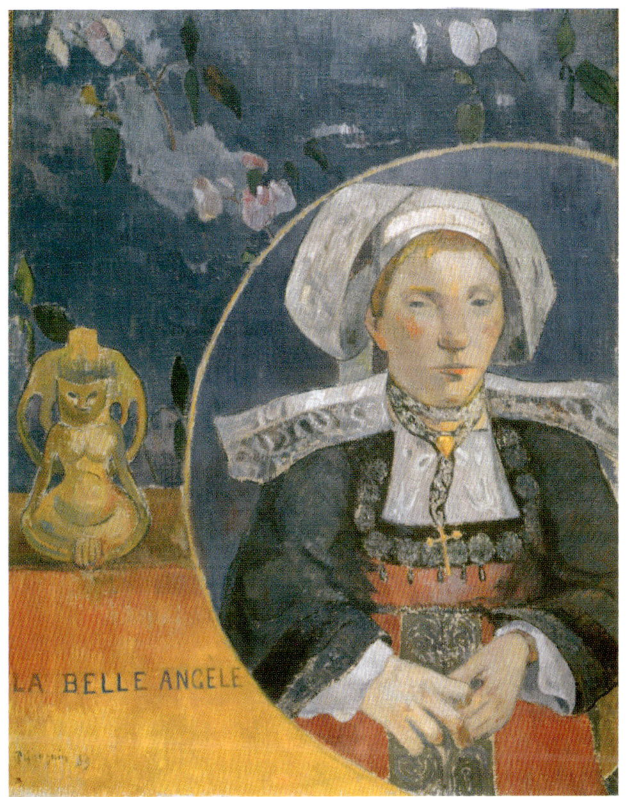

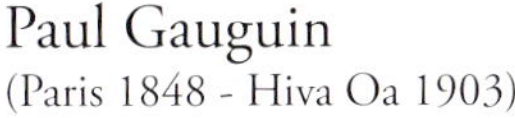
Paul Gauguin
(Paris 1848 - Hiva Oa 1903)

La Belle Angèle (The Beautiful Angèle)
Die Schöne Angèle
La Belle Angèle

1889
92 x 73 cm / 36.22 x 28.74 in.
Musée d'Orsay, Paris

Oil on canvas / Öl auf Leinwand / Olieverf op doek

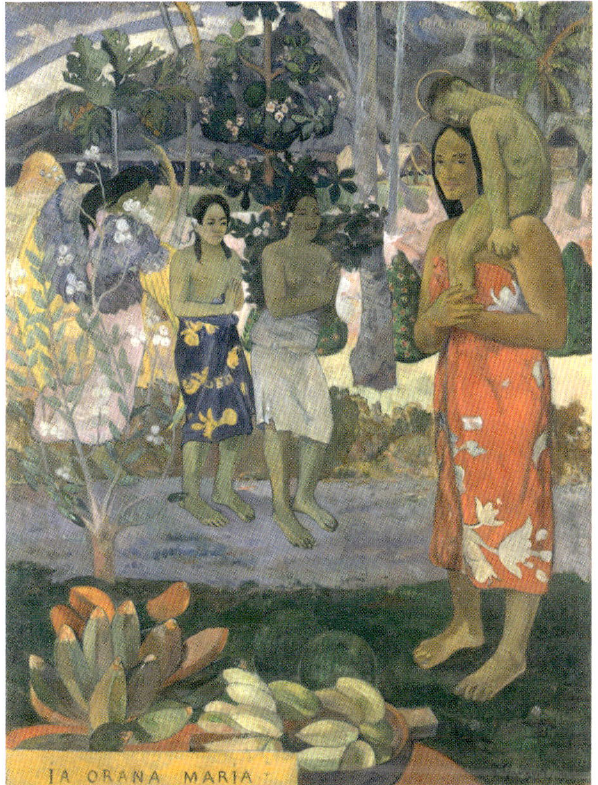

Paul Gauguin
(Paris 1848 - Hiva Oa 1903)

Ia Orana Maria (Hail Mary)
Gegrüßet seist Du, Maria (Ave Maria)
Ia Orana Maria (Ave Maria)

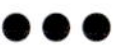

1891
113,7 x 87,6 cm
Metropolitan Museum of Art, New York

Oil on canvas / Öl auf Leinwand / Olieverf op doek

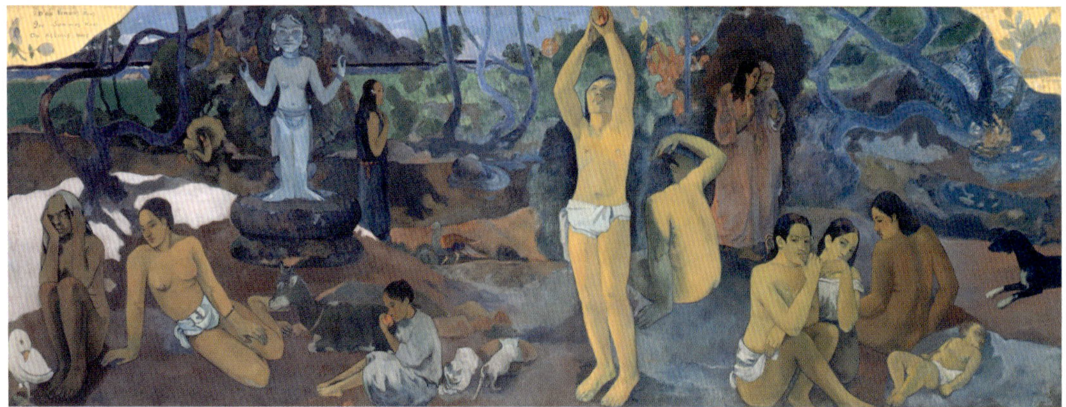

Paul Gauguin
(Paris 1848 - Hiva Oa 1903)

Where Do We Come From? What Are We? Where Are We Going?
Woher kommen wir? Wer sind wir? Wohin gehen wir?
Waar komen wij vandaan? Wie zijn wij? Waar gaan we naar toe?

●●●

1897
141 x 376 cm / 55.51 x 148.03 in.
Museum of Fine Arts, Boston

Oil on canvas / Öl auf Leinwand / Olieverf op doek

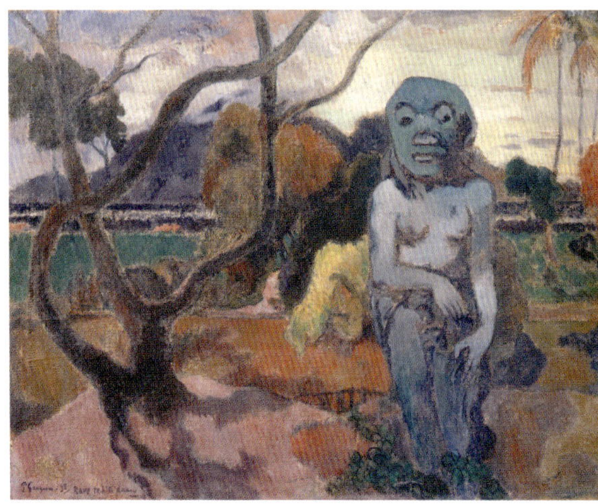

Paul Gauguin
(Paris 1848 - Hiva Oa 1903)

Rave te hiti aamu (The Idol)
Rave te hiti ramu (Der böse Geist)
Rave te hiti ramu (Verschijning van de kwade demon)

●

c. 1898
73,5 x 92 cm / 28.93 x 36.22 in.
The State Hermitage Museum, St. Petersburg

Oil on canvas / Öl auf Leinwand / Olieverf op doek

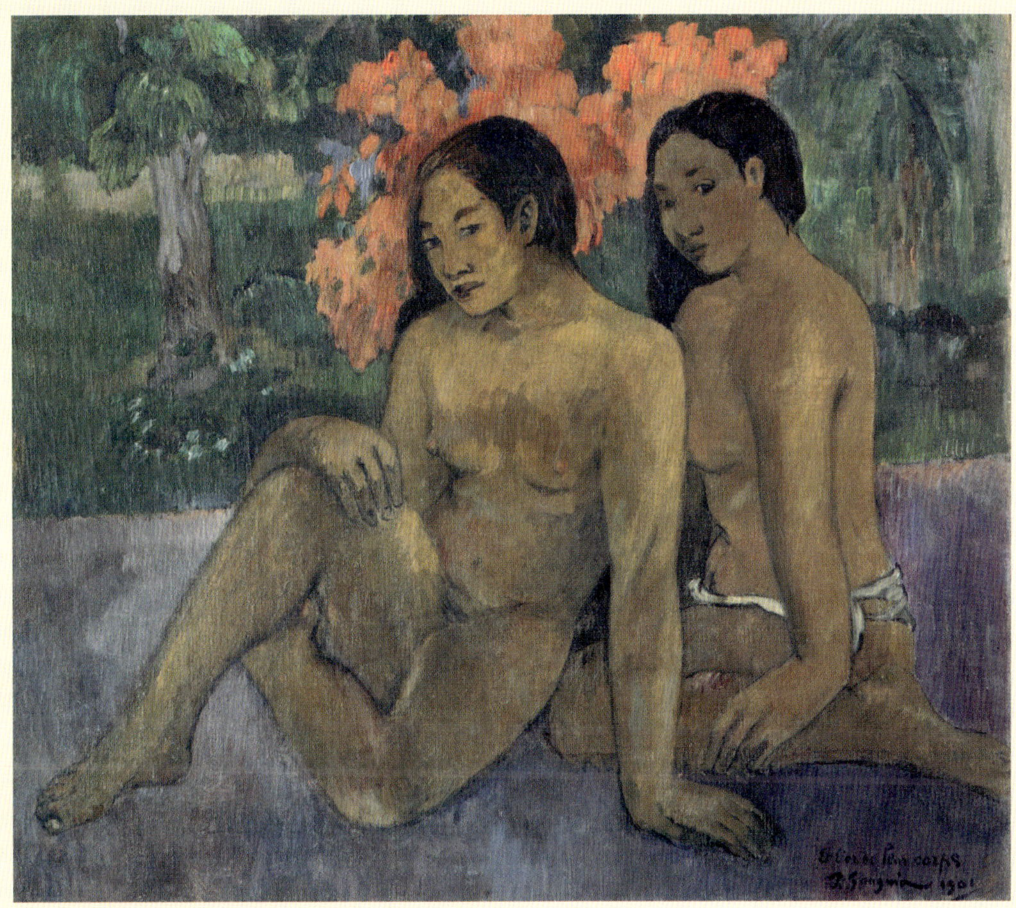

Paul Gauguin
(Paris 1848 - Hiva Oa 1903)

And the Gold of their Bodies
Und das Gold ihrer Körper
En het goud van hun lichamen

●●●

1901
67 x 76 cm / 26.37 x 29.92 in.
Musée d'Orsay, Paris

Oil on canvas / Öl auf Leinwand / Olieverf op doek

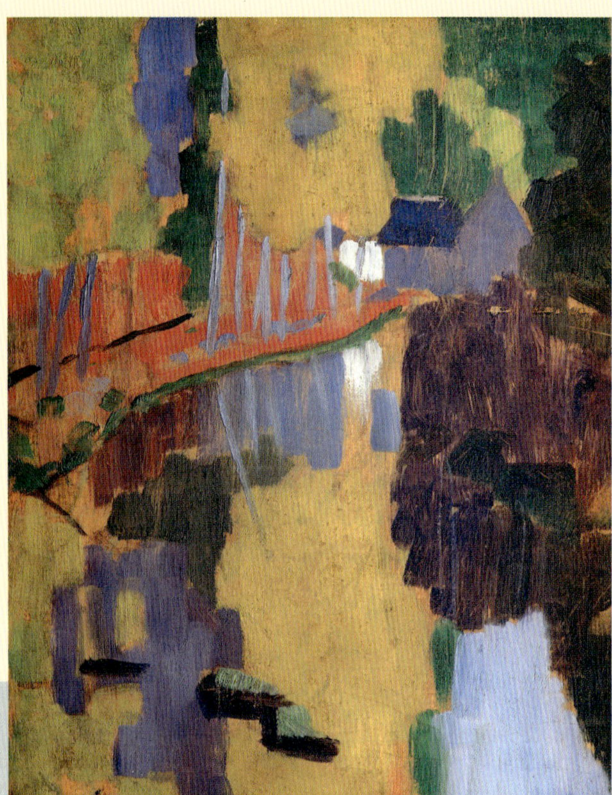

Paul Sérusier
(Paris 1864 - Morlaix 1927)

The Talisman
Der Talisman
De talisman

●

1888
27 x 21 cm / 10.63 x 8.27 in.
Musée d'Orsay, Paris

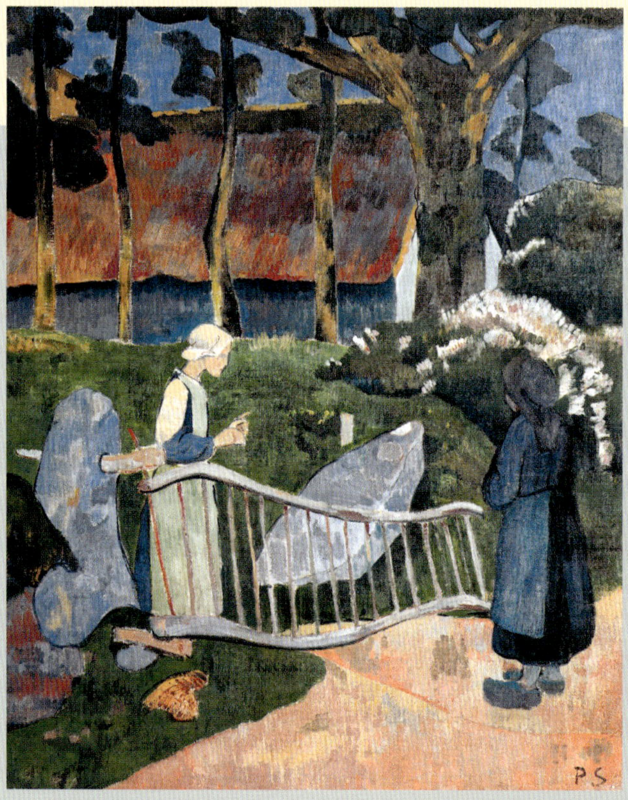

Paul Sérusier
(Paris 1864 - Morlaix 1927)

The Flowered Hedge
Blühende Hecke
Bloeiende haag

●

1889
Musée d'Orsay, Paris

Oil on canvas
Öl auf Leinwand
Olieverf op doek

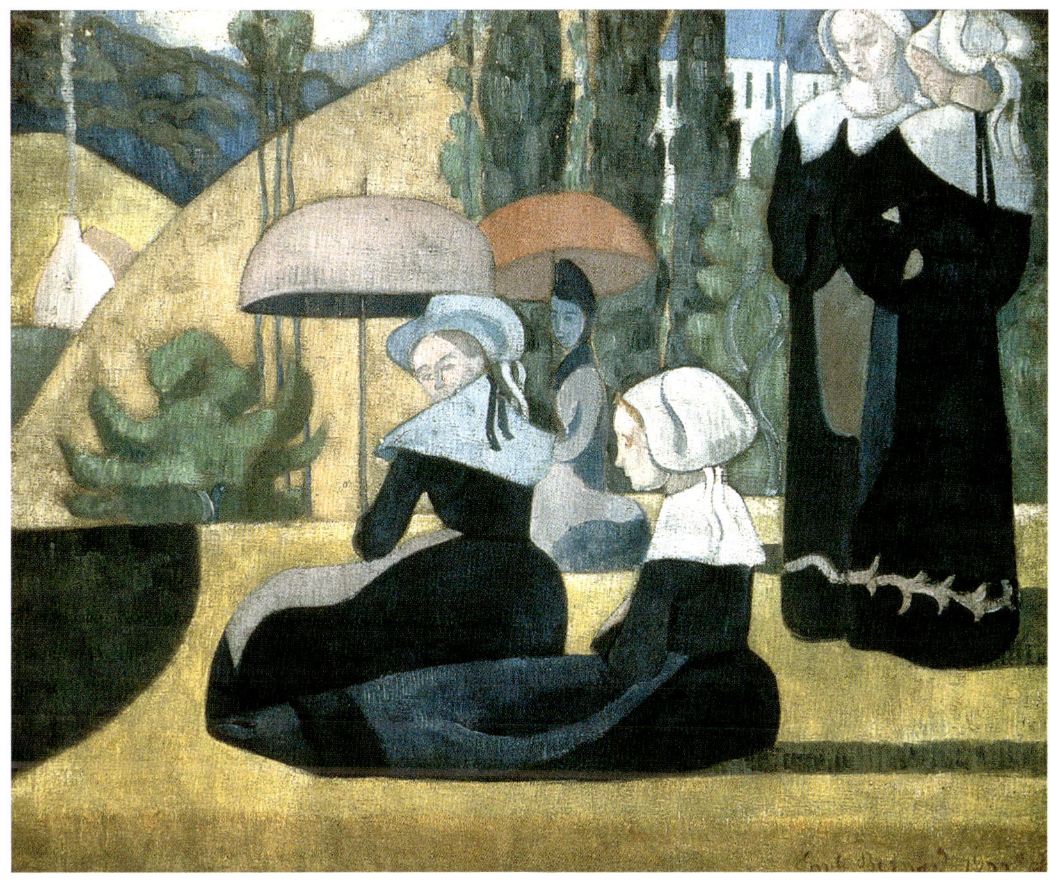

Émile Bernard
(Lille 1868 - Paris 1941)

Breton Women with Umbrellas
Bretoninnen mit Sonnenschirm
Bretonse vrouwen met paraplu's

●

1892
85 x 105 cm / 33.46 x 41.33 in.
Musée d'Orsay, Paris

Oil on canvas / Öl auf Leinwand / Olieverf op doek

Gauguin's friends of the school of Pont-Aven and the cloisonné technique.

Gauguins Freunde der Schule von Pont-Aven in der Technik des Cloisonismus.

Vrienden van de school van Pont-Aven en de techniek van het "cloisonnisme".

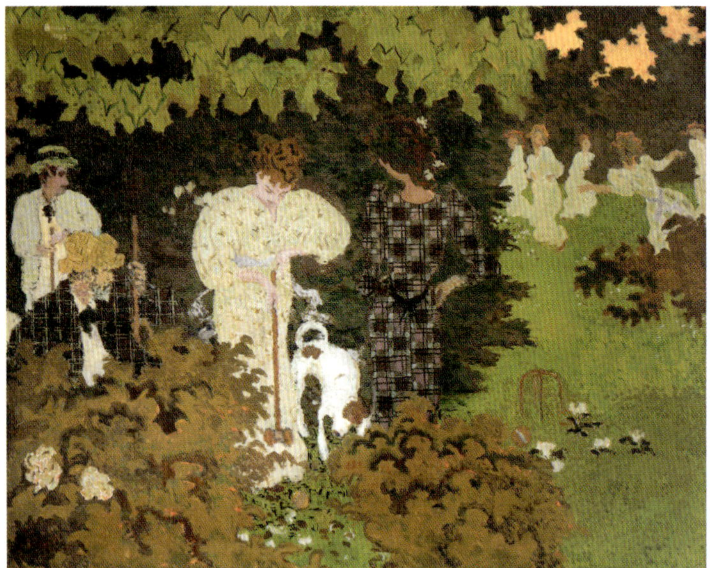

The Nabis, self-declared prophets of modern art, also originate from the school of Gauguin.

Auch die Nabis (selbsternannte “Propheten” der Moderne) entstammen der Schule Gauguins.

Ook de Nabis (die zichzelf hebben uitgeroepen tot “profeten” van de moderne kunst) komen voort uit de school van Gauguin.

Pierre Bonnard
(Fontenay-aux-Roses 1867 - Le Cannet 1947)

Twilight, also called The Game of Croquet
Die Krocketpartie
Het croquetspel

●

1892
130 x 162,5 cm
51.18 x 63.98 in.
Musée d’Orsay, Paris

Oil on canvas
Öl auf Leinwand
Olieverf op doek

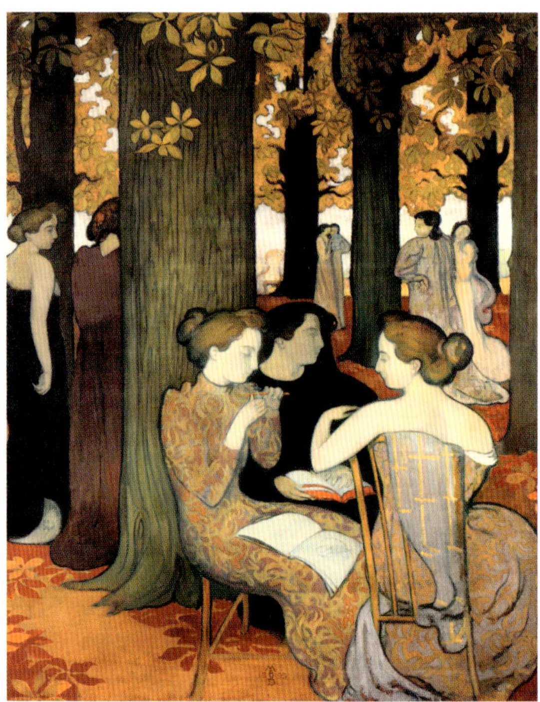

Maurice Denis
(Granville 1870 - Paris 1943)

The Muses
Die Musen
De Muzen

●

1893
171,5 x 137,5 cm
67.51 x 54.13 in.
Musée d’Orsay, Paris

Oil on canvas
Öl auf Leinwand
Olieverf op doek

Édouard Vuillard
(Cuiseaux, Saône et Loire 1868 - La Baule 1940)

Public Gardens
Öffentliche Gärten
Het park

•

1894
213,5 x 154 cm / 84.06 x 60.63 in.
Musée d'Orsay, Paris

Oil on canvas
Öl auf Leinwand
Olieverf op doek

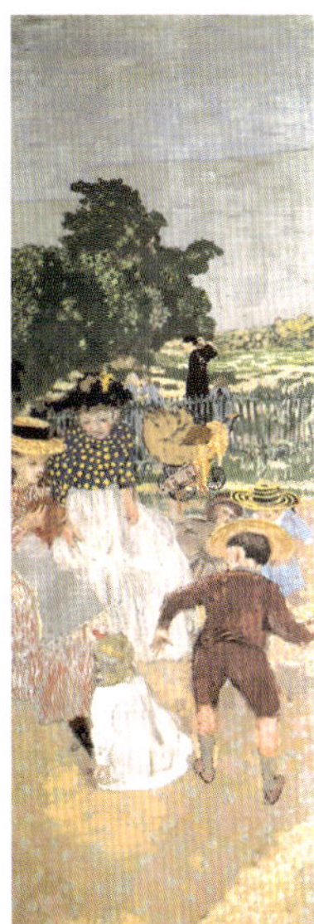
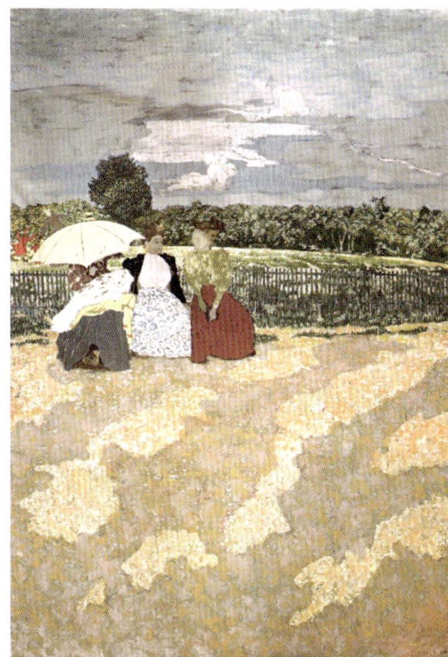
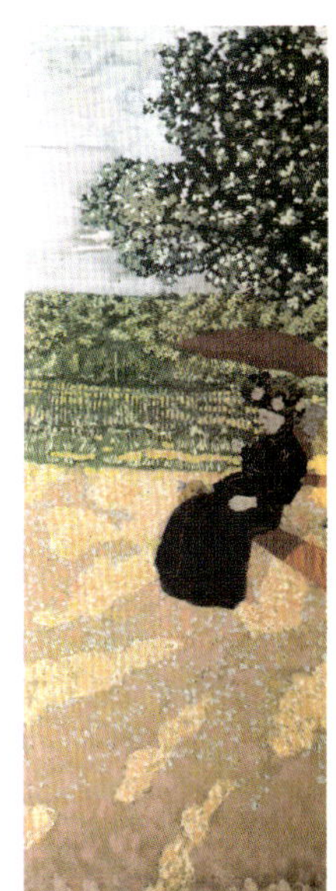

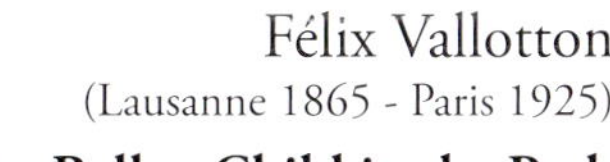

Félix Vallotton
(Lausanne 1865 - Paris 1925)

The Ball: a Child in the Park
Der Ball
Kind dat met een bal speelt

•

1899
48 x 61 cm
Musée d'Orsay, Paris

Oil on canvas
Öl auf Leinwand
Olieverf op doek

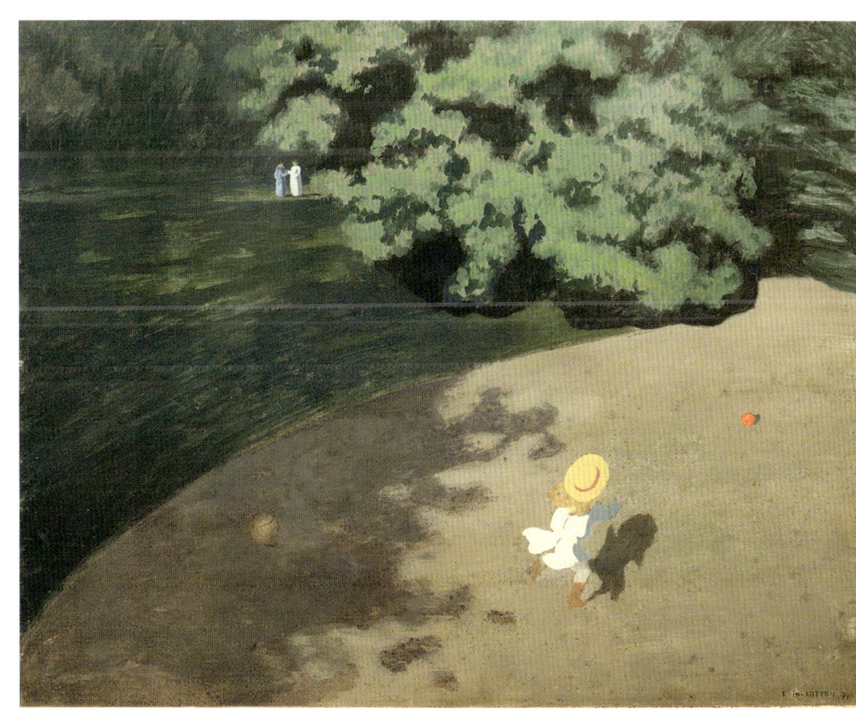

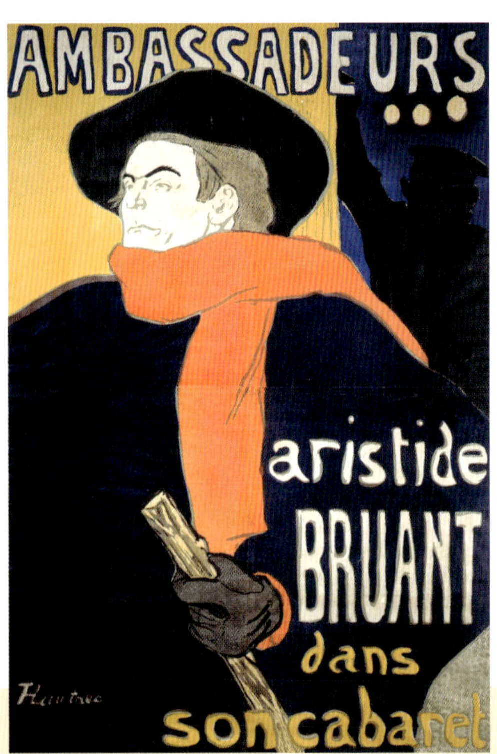

Henri de Toulouse-Lautrec
(Albi 1864 - Château Malromé 1901)

Ambassadeurs
(Os embaixadores)

●●●

1892
141 x 98 cm / 55.51 x 38.58 in.
Musée d'Ixelles, Bruxelles

Lithograph / Litographie / Lithografie

Henri de Toulouse-Lautrec
(Albi 1864 - Château Malromé 1901)

Moorish Dance
Maurischer Tanz
De Moorse dans

●●

1895
298 x 316 cm / 117.92 x 124.40 in.
Musée d'Orsay, Paris

Drawing / Zeichnung / Tekening

Toulouse Lautrec is considered to be the inventor of posters.

Toulouse Lautrec, körperlich behinderter Maler der Bordelle gilt als Erfinder des Plakats.

Toulouse Lautrec, gehandicapte schilder van bordelen, wordt beschouwd als de uitvinder van het affiche.

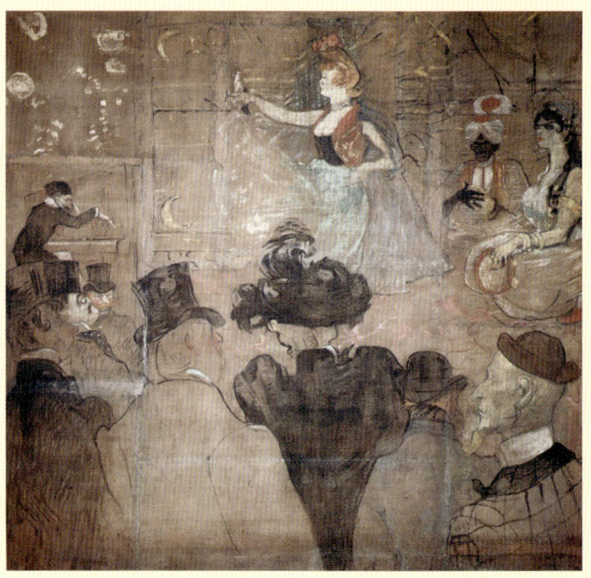

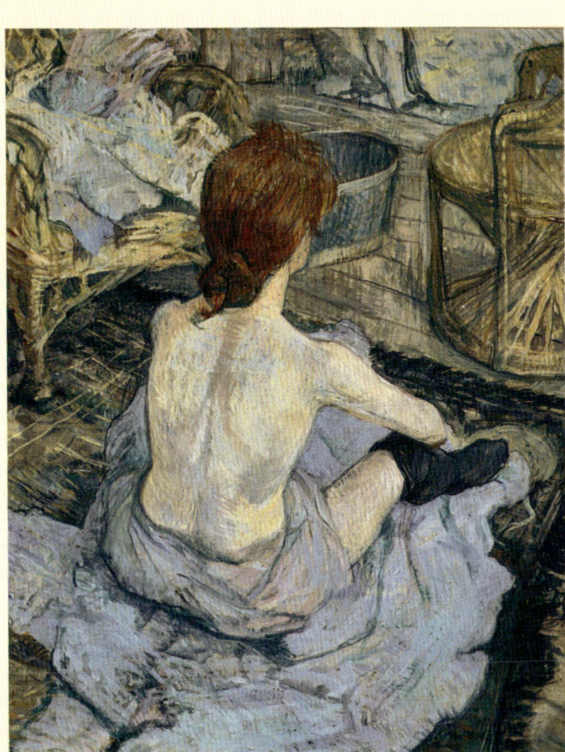

Henri de Toulouse-Lautrec
(Albi 1864 - Château Malromé 1901)

The Toilette
Die Toilette
Het toilet

●●●

1896
67 x 54 cm / 26.37 x 21.25 in.
Musée d'Orsay, Paris

Oil on cardboard
Öl auf Karton
Olieverf op karton

Henri de Toulouse-Lautrec
(Albi 1864 - Château Malromé 1901)

Crouching Woman with Red Hair
Femme rousse nue accroupie
(Kauernde Frau mit rotem Haar)

●●

1897
San Diego Museum of Art, San Diego

Oil / Öl / Olieverf

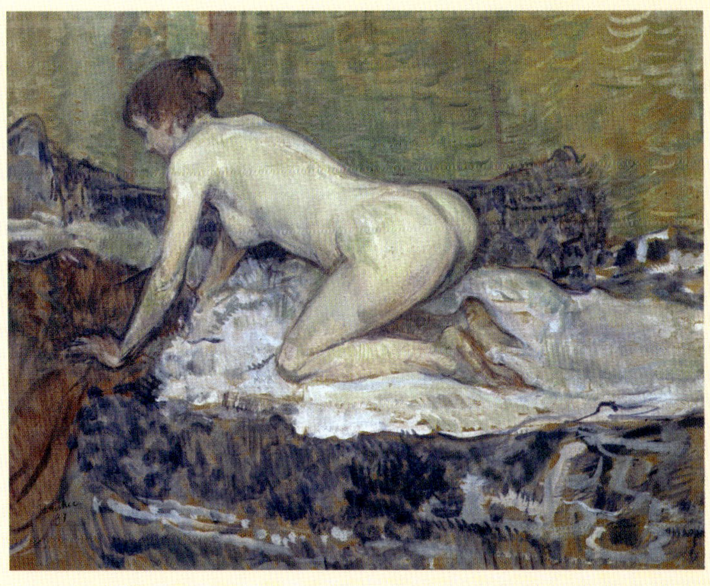

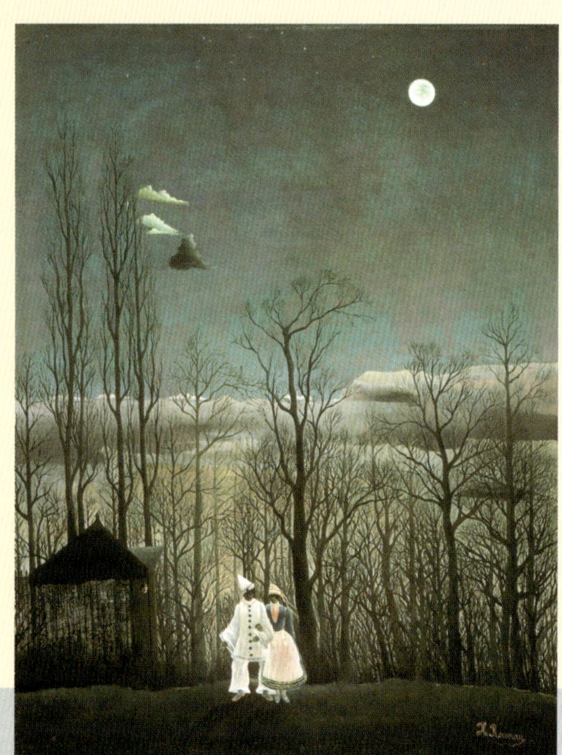

Henri Julien Félix Rousseau
(Laval 1844 - Paris 1910)

Carnival Evening
Karnevalsabend
Carnavalsavond

●●

1886
117.3 x 89.5 cm / 46.18 x 35.23 in.
Philadelphia Museum of Art, Philadelphia

Oil on canvas
Öl auf Leinwand
Olieverf op doek

Henri Julien Félix Rousseau
(Laval 1844 - Paris 1910)

Surprised
Überrascht
Verrast

●●●

1891
129,8 x 161,9 cm / 51.10 x 63.74 in.
National Gallery, London

Oil on canvas
Öl auf Leinwand
Olieverf op doek

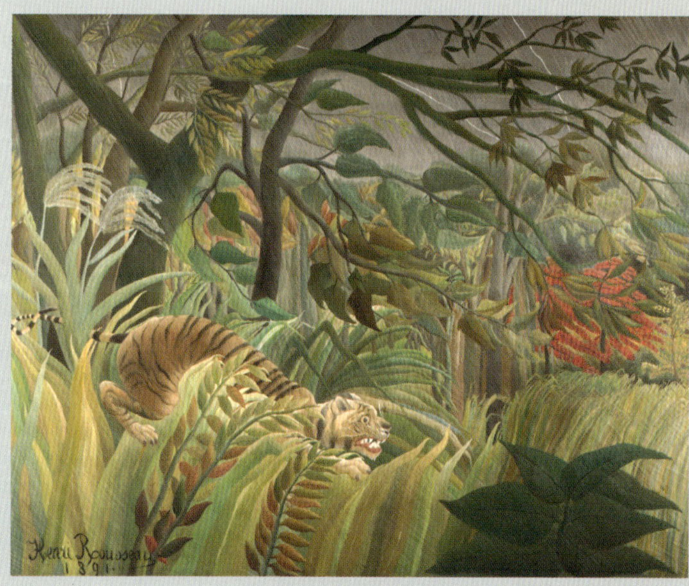

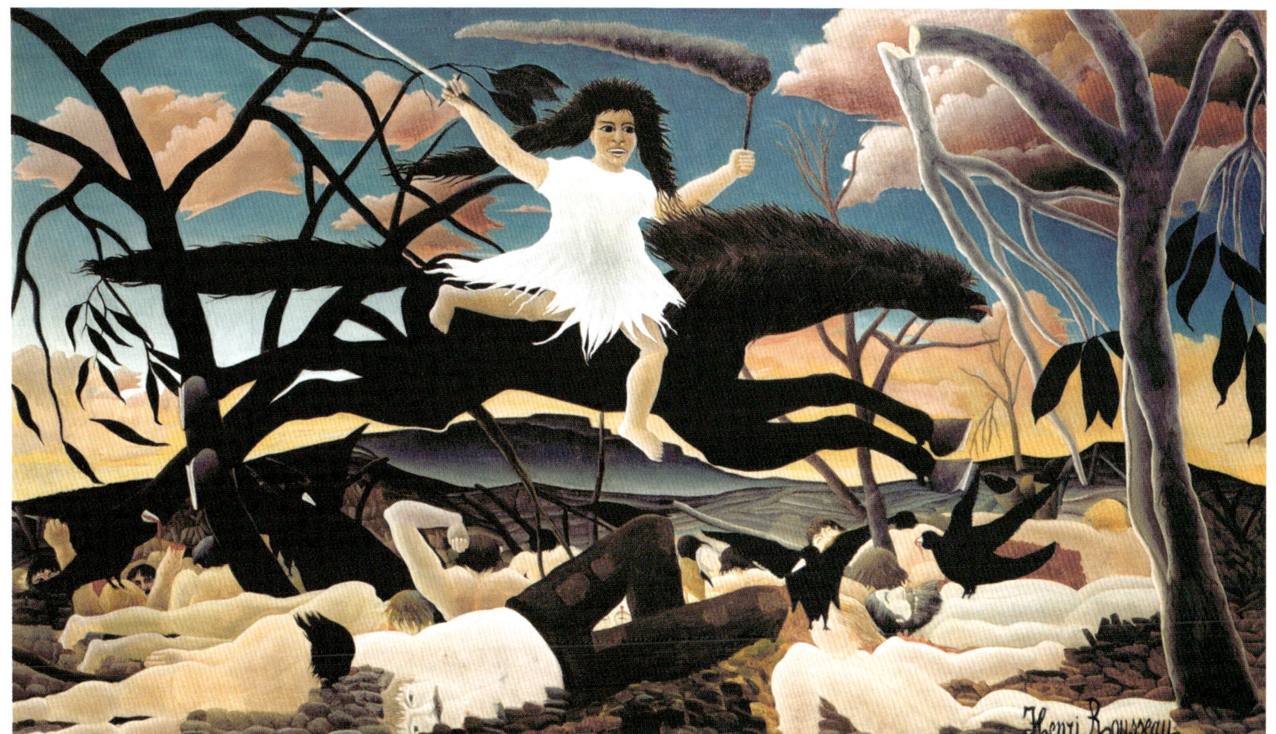

Henri Julien Félix Rousseau
(Laval 1844 - Paris 1910)

War
Der Krieg
De oorlog

●●●

c. 1894
114 x 195 cm / 44.88 x 76.77 in.
Musée d'Orsay, Paris

Oil on canvas
Öl auf Leinwand
Olieverf op doek

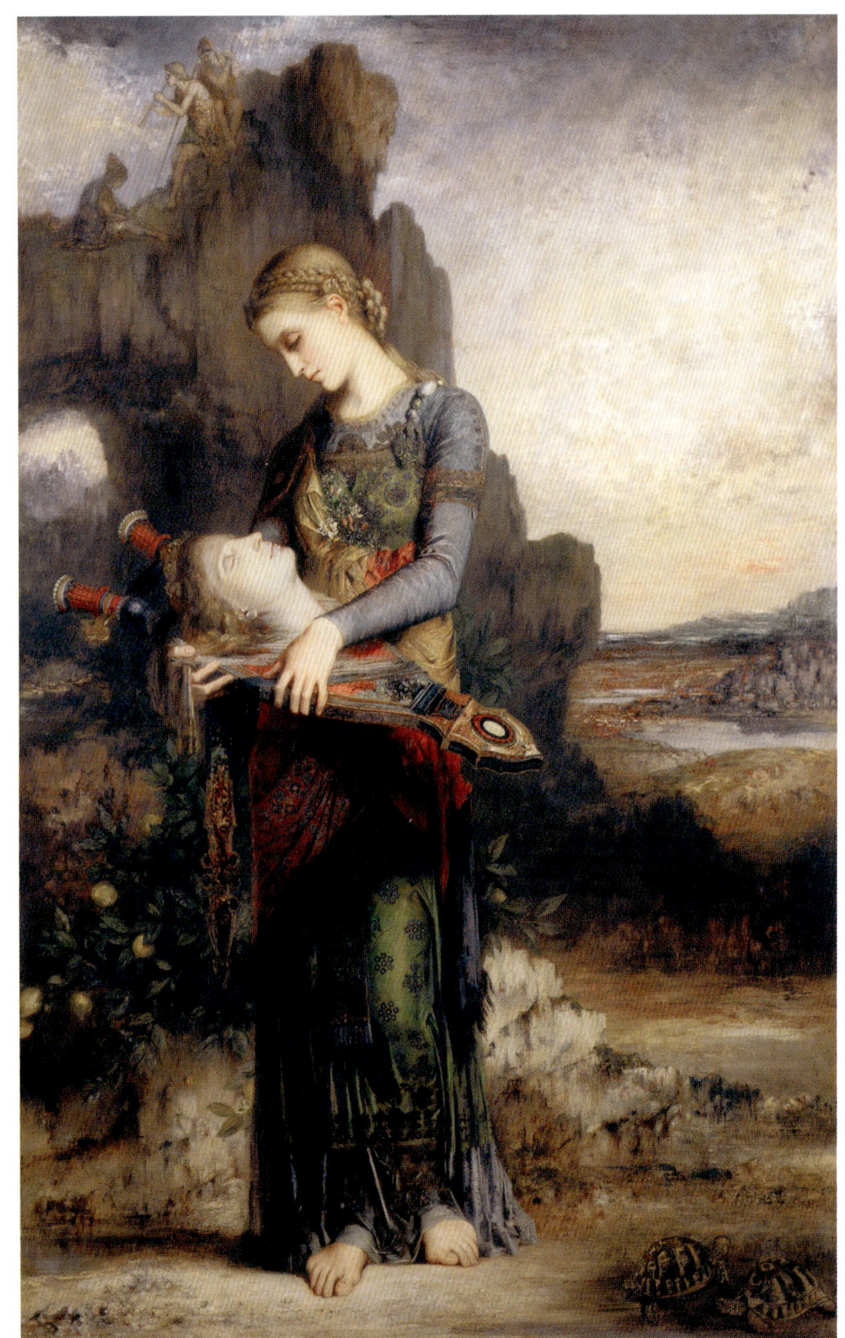

Gustave Moreau
(Paris 1826 - 1898)

Orpheus

●●

1865
154 x 101 cm / 60.62 x 39.76 in.
Musée d'Orsay, Paris

Oil on canvas / Öl auf Leinwand
Olieverf op doek

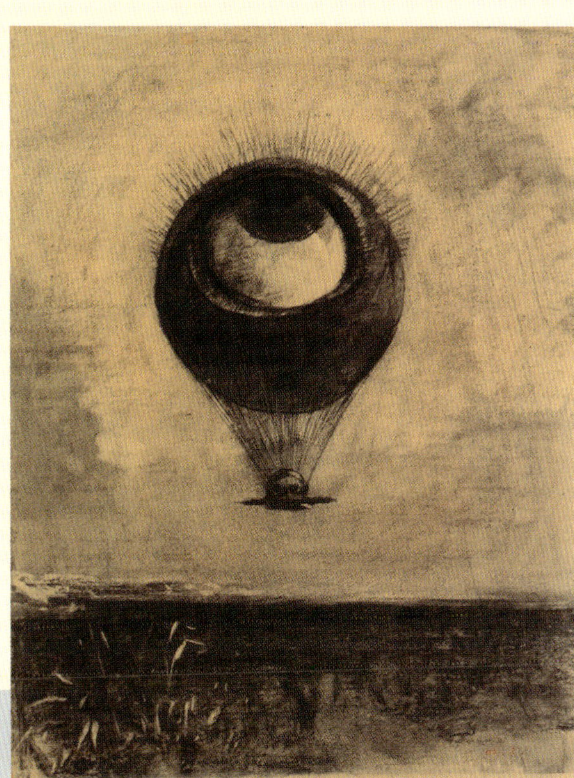

Odilon Redon
(Bordeaux 1840 - Paris 1916)

The Eye Like a Strange Balloon Mounts Toward Infinity
Wie ein bizarre Ballon wendet sich das Auge an die Unendlichkeit
Het oog stijgt als een vreemde ballon op naar het oneindige

●

1878
42,2 x 33,2 cm / 16 x 13 in.
Museum of Modern Art (MoMA), New York

Charcoal on paper / Kohle auf Papier / Houtskool op papier

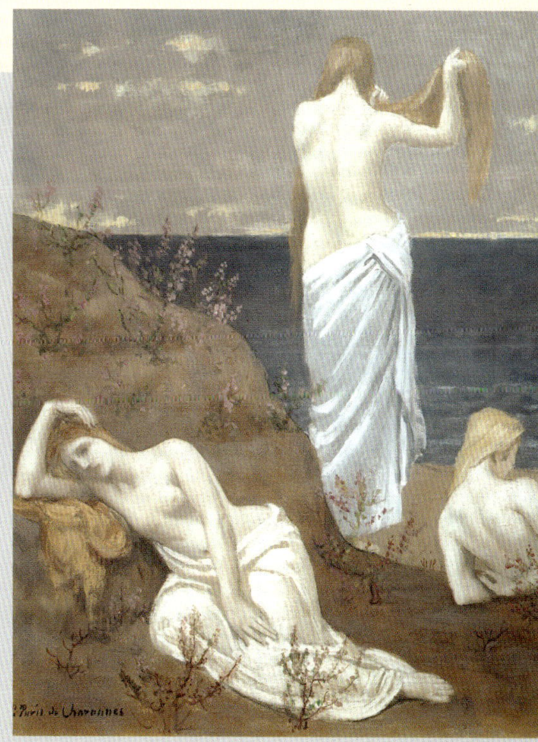

Pierre Puvis de Chavannes
(Lyon 1824 - Paris 1898)

Young Girls by the Sea
Junge Mädchen am Meer
Jonge meisjes aan de waterkant

●

1879
61 x 47 cm / 24.01 x 18.50 in.
Musée d'Orsay, Paris

Oil on canvas
Öl auf Leinwand
Olieverf op doek

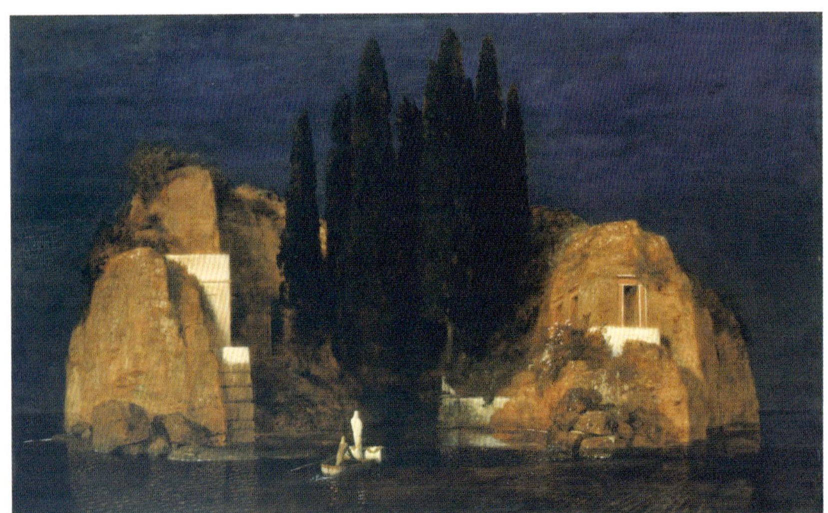

Arnold Böcklin
(Bâle 1827 - San Domenico di Fiesole 1901)

Isle of the Dead
Die Toteninsel
Het dodeneiland

●●

1880
73,3 x 121,9 cm / 28.85 x 47.99 in.
Metropolitan Museum of Art, New York

Oil on canvas
Öl auf Leinwand
Olieverf op doek

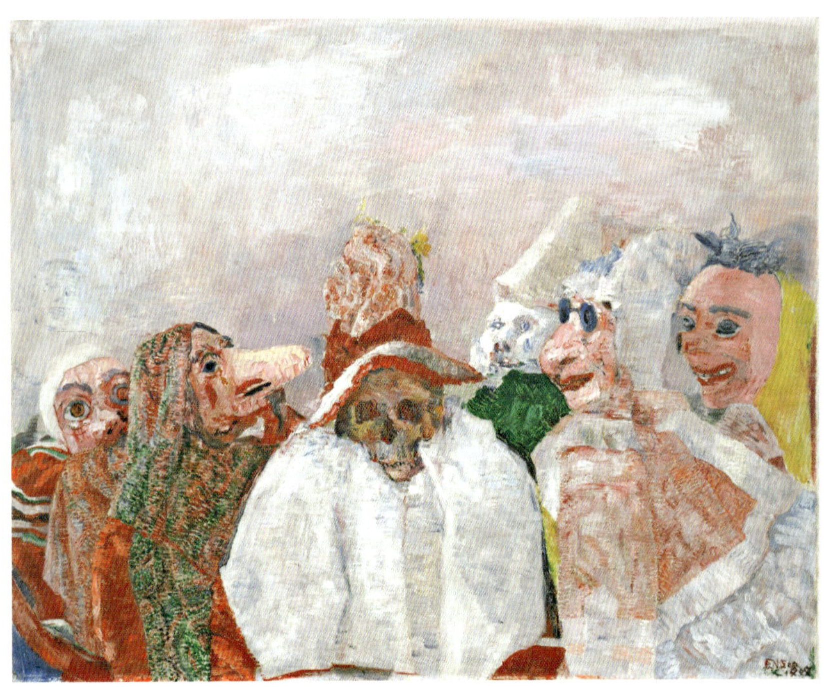

James Ensor
(Ostende 1860 - 1949)

Masks Confronting Death
Masken und Tod
Maskers tarten de dood

●●

c. 1890
81,3 x 100,3 cm / 32 x 39.48 in.
Museum of Modern Art (MoMA), New York

Oil on canvas
Öl auf Leinwand
Olieverf op doek

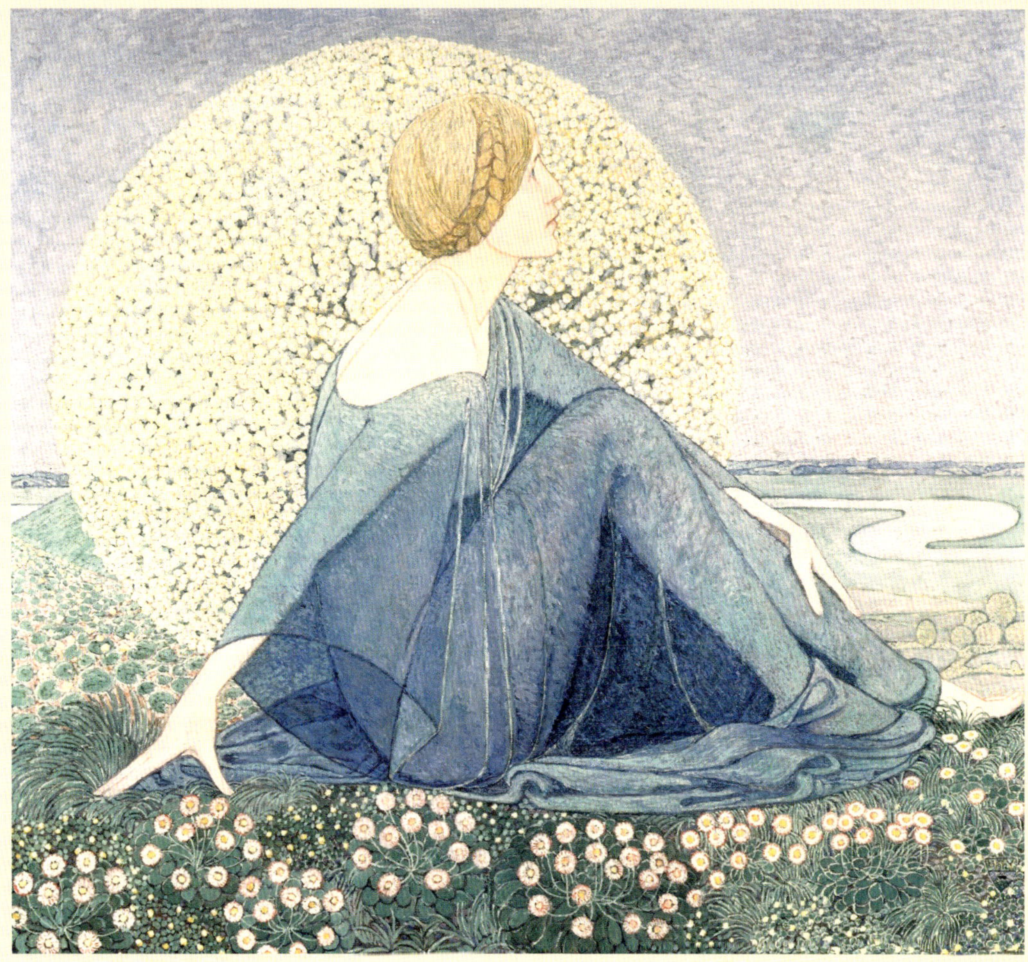

425

Heinrich Vogeler
(Bremen 1872 - Kolchos 1942)

The Dream
Der Traum
De droom

●●

Germanisches Nationalmuseum, Nürnberg

Oil on canvas
Öl auf Leinwand
Olieverf op doek

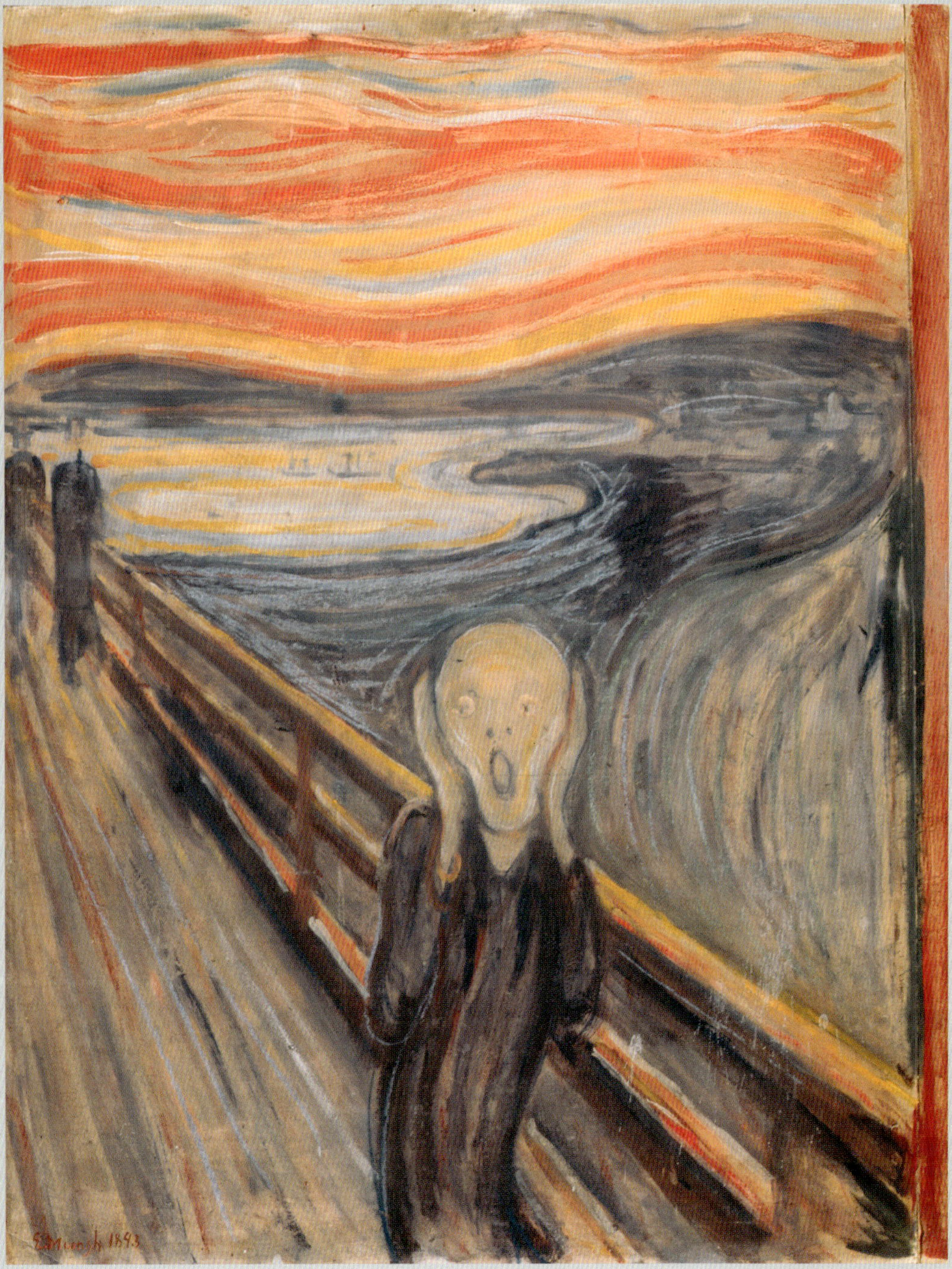

Edward Munch
(Løten 1863 - Ekeley 1944)

The Scream
Der Schrei
De schreeuw

●●●

1893
91 x 73,5 cm
35.82 x 28.93 in.
National Gallery, Oslo

Oil on canvas
Öl auf Leinwand
Olieverf op doek

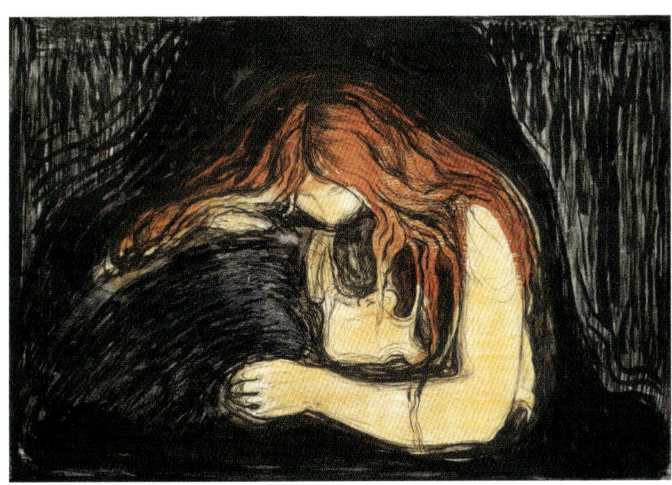

Edward Munch
(Løten 1863 - Ekeley 1944)

Vampire
Vampir
Vampier

●

c. 1893-1894
Munch Museum, Oslo

Oil on canvas
Öl auf Leinwand
Olieverf op doek

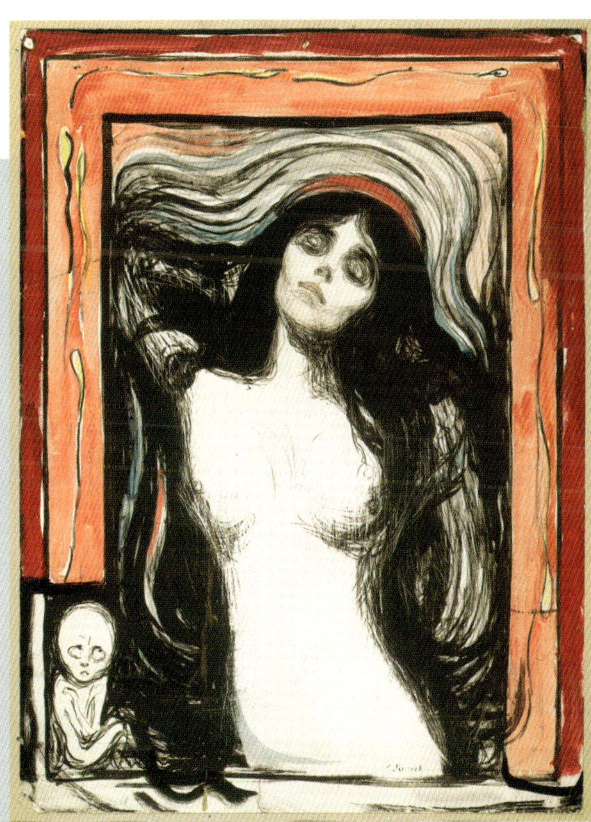

Edward Munch
(Løten 1863 - Ekeley 1944)

Madonna

●●●

c. 1893-1894
Munch Museum, Oslo

Oil on canvas
Öl auf Leinwand
Olieverf op doek

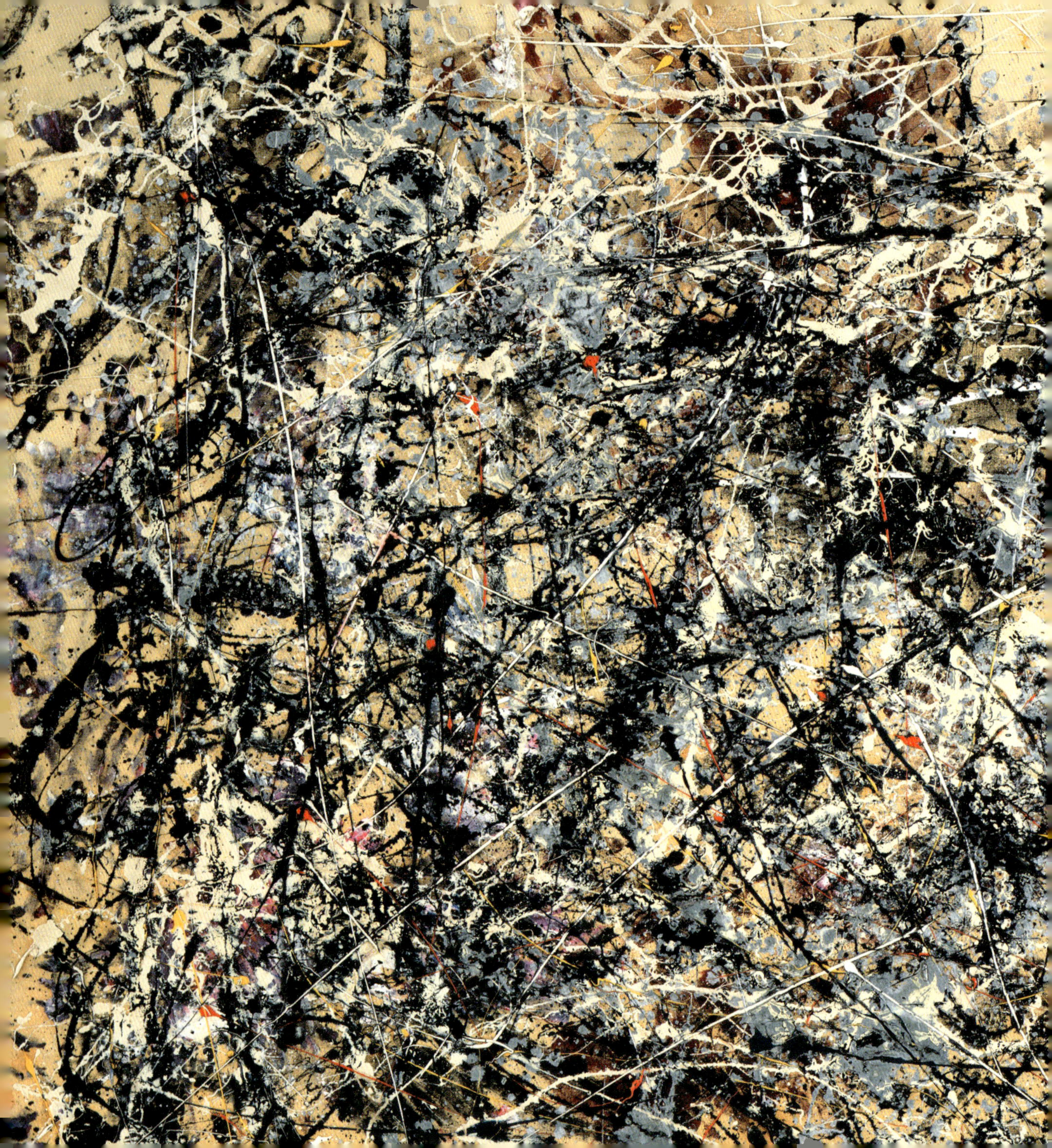

20th Century
Die Kunst des 20. Jahrhunderts • Kunst van de twintigste eeuw

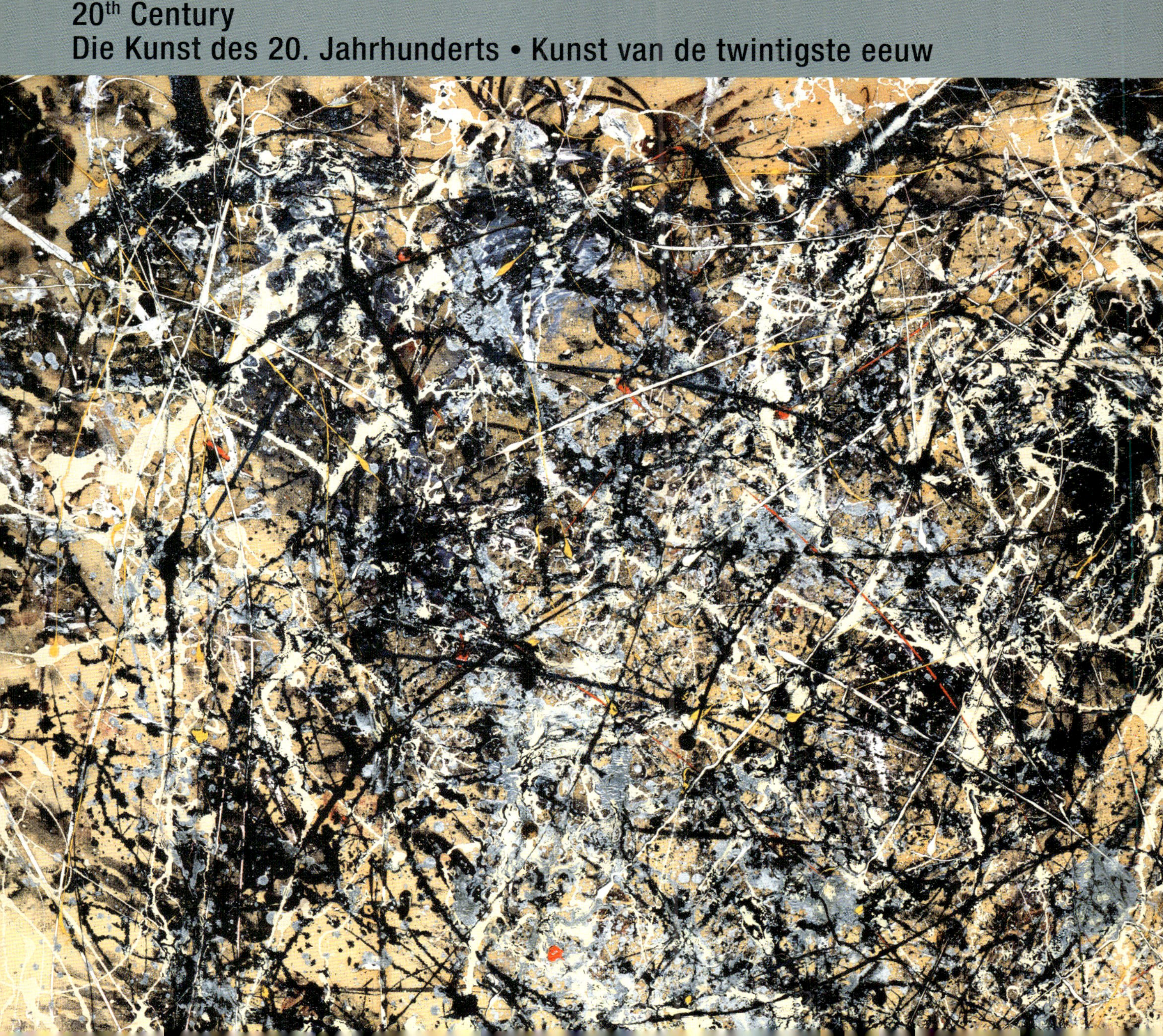

The art of unlimited possibilities, art without limits
Kunst der unbegrenzten Möglichkeiten, grenzenlose Kunst
Kunst van de onbegrensde mogelijkheden, kunst zonder grenzen

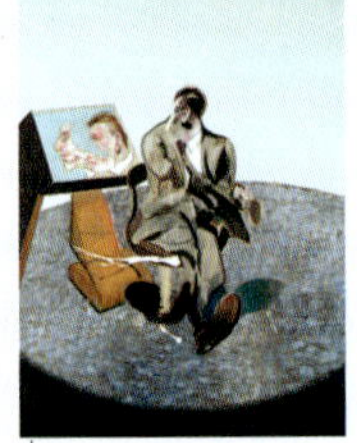

IRELAND

Francis Bacon (Dublin 1909 - Madrid 1992)

GREAT BRITAIN

Henry Moore (Castelford, Leeds 1898 - London 1986)
David Hockney (Bradford 1937)
Richard Hamilton (London 1922)
Eduardo Paolozzi (Leith 1924 - London 2005)

NEDERLAND

Kees van Dongen (Delfshaven 1877 - 1968)
Pieter Mondrian (Amersfoort 1872 - New York 1944)
Willem de Kooning (Rotterdam 1904 - New York 1997)

BELGIQUE

René Magritte (Lessines 1898 - Bruxelles

FRANCE

Maurice de Vlaminck (Paris 1876 - Rueil-la-Gadelière Eure-et-Loir 1958)
André Derain (Chatou 1880 - Garches 1954)
Henri Matisse (Cateau-Cambrésis 1869 - Nice 1954)
Georges Braque (Argenteuil 1882 - Paris 1963)
Fernand Léger (Argentan 1881 - Gif-sur-Yvette 1955)
Raymond Duchamp-Villon (Damville 1876 - Cannes 1918)
Hans Arp (Strasbourg 1886 - Bâle 1966)
Marcel Duchamp (Blainville-Crevon 1887 - Neuilly-sur-Seine 1968)
Yves Tanguy (Paris 1900 - Woodbury 1955)
Maurice Utrillo (Paris 1883 - Dax 1955)
Georges Rouault (Paris 1871 - 1958)
Jean Dubuffet (Havre 1901 - Paris 1985)
Jean Fautrier (Paris 1898 - Châtenay-Malabry 1964)
Yves Klein (Nice 1928 - Paris 1962)
César (Marseille 1921 - Paris 1998)
Arman (Nice 1928 - New York 2005)

S
Pa
Al

MEXICO

Diego Riveira (Guanajuato 1886 - Ciudad de Mexico 1957)
Frida Kahlo (Coyoacan 1907 - 1954)

ARGENTINA

Lucio Fontana (Rosario 1899 - Milano 1968)

USA

Edward Hopper (Nyack 1882 - New York 1967)
Jackson Pollock (Cody 1912 - Long Island 1956)
Barnett Newman (New York 1905 - 1970)
Ad Reinhardt (Buffalo 1913 - New York 1967)
Franz Kline (Wilkes-Barre 1910 - New York 1962)
Robert Rauschenberg (Port Arthur 1925 - Captiva 2008)
Jim Dine (Cincinnati 1935)
Roy Lichtenstein (New York 1923 - 1997)
Robert Indiana (New Castle 1928)
Andy Warhol (PittsBurgh 1928 - New York 1987)
Neil Jenney (Torrington, 1945).
David Salle (Norman 1952)
Susan Rothenberg (Buffalo 1945)
Richard Estes (Kewanee 1932)
Ray Charles (Chicago 1953)
Chuck Close (Monroe, Washington 1940)
Duane Hanson (Alexandria 1925 - Boca Raton 1996)
Robert Morris (Kansas City 1931)
Richard Serra (San Francisco 1939)
Sol LeWitt (Hartford 1928 - New York 2007)

ESPAÑA

Pablo Picasso (Málaga 1881 - Mougins 1973)
Juan Gris (Madrid 1887 - Boulogne-Billancourt 1927)
Salvador Dalí (Figueres 1904 - 1989)
Joan Miró (Barcelona 1893 - Palma de Mallorca 1983)

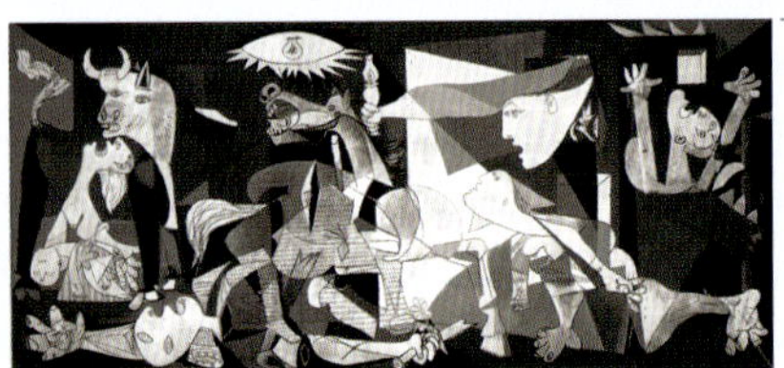

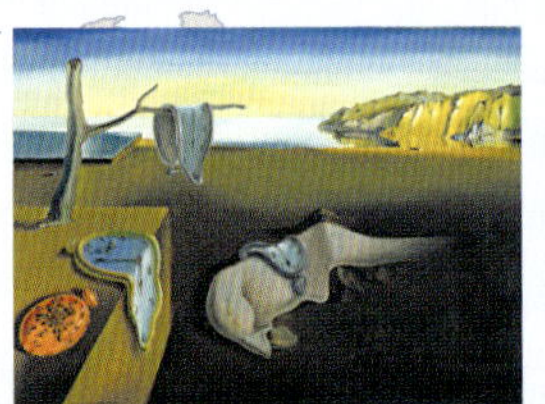

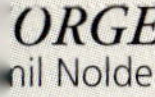

ORGE
nil Nolde (Nolde 1867 - Seebüll 1956)

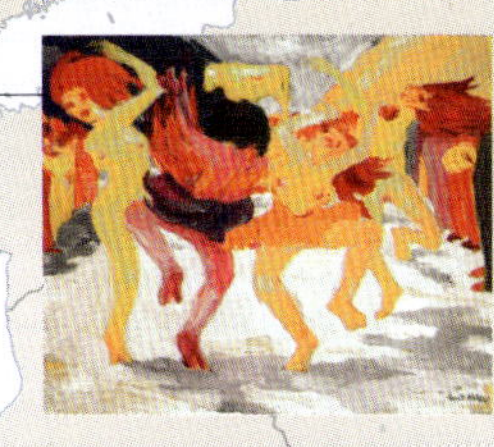

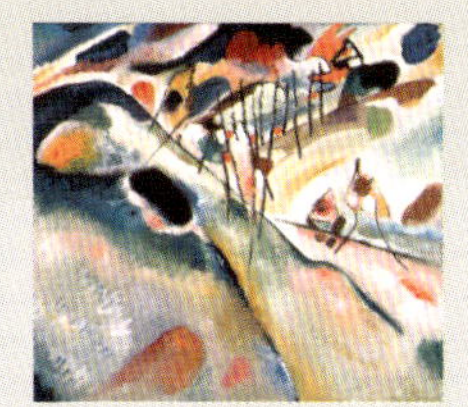

SVERIGE
Claes Oldenburg (Stockholm 1929)

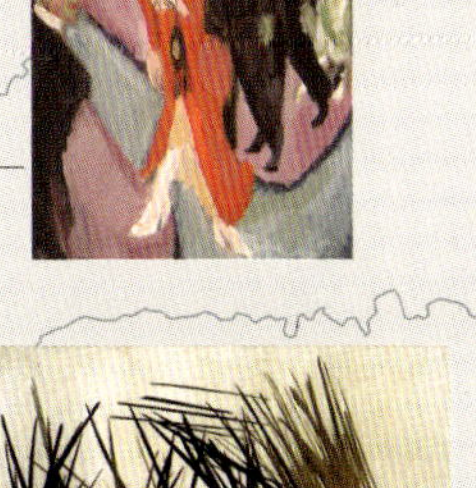

RUSSIA
Alexander Archipenko (Kiev 1887 - New York 1964)
Jacques Lipchitz (Druskininkai 1891 - Capri 1973)
Wassily Kandinsky (Moscow 1866 - Neuilly-sur-Seine 1944)
Michel Larionov (Tiraspol Moldavie 1881 - Fontenay-aux-Roses 1964)
Kazimir Malevich (Kiev 1878 - Saint Petersburg 1935)
Alexander Rodchenko (Saint Petersburg 1891 - Moscow 1958)
Vladimir Tatlin (Kharkhov 1885 - Moscow 1953)
Anton Pevsner (Orel 1886 - Paris 1962)
Marc Chagall (Vitebsk 1887 - Saint-Paul de Vence 1985)

UTSCHLAND
Heckel (Döbeln 1883 - Rudolfzell 1970)
: Ludwig Kirchner (Aschaffenburg 1880 - Davos 1938)
Schmidt-Rottluff (Rottluff 1884 - Berlin 1976)
z Marc (München 1880 - Verdun 1916)
Schwitters (Hannover 1887 - Ambleside 1948)
nah Höch (Gotha 1889 - 1978)
Ernst (Brühl 1891 - Paris 1976)
Dix (Gera 1891 - Singen 1969)
ge Grosz (Berlin 1893 - 1959)
Beckmann (Leipzig 1884 - New York 1950)
(Berlin 1913 - Paris 1951)
Hartung (Leipzig 1904 - Antibes 1989)
er Johns (Augusta 1930)
g Baselitz (Deutschbaselitz 1938)
Penck (Dresden 1939)
lm Kiefer (Donaueschingen 1945)

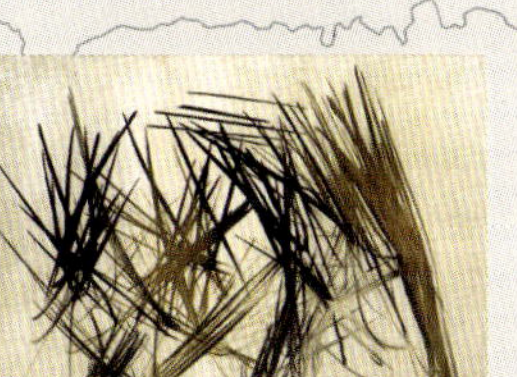

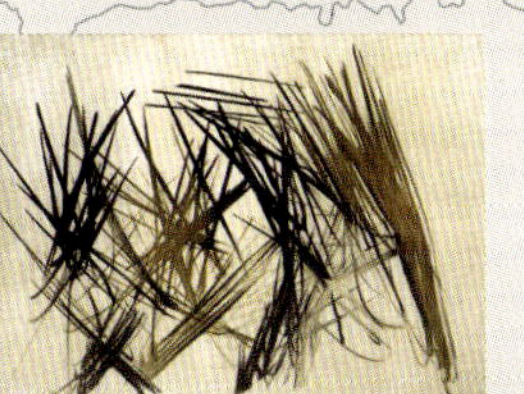

MAGYAR
László Moholy-Nagy (Bàcs-Borsod 1895 - Chicago 1946)

ÖSTERREICH
Gustav Klimt (Baumgarten 1862 - Wien 1918)
Oskar Kokoschka (Pöchlarn 1886 - Montreux 1980)
Egon Schiele (Tulln 1890 - Wien 1918)

ROMÂNIA
Constantin Brâncuşi (Peştişani 1876 - Paris 1957)
Daniel Spoerri (Galaţi 1930)

chenbuchsee, Bern 1879 - Muralto 1940)
etti (Stampa 1901 - Coire 1966)

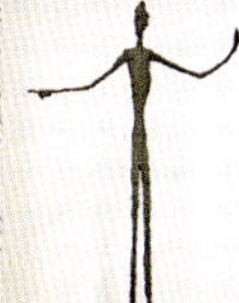

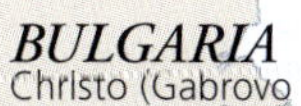

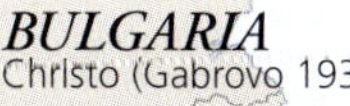

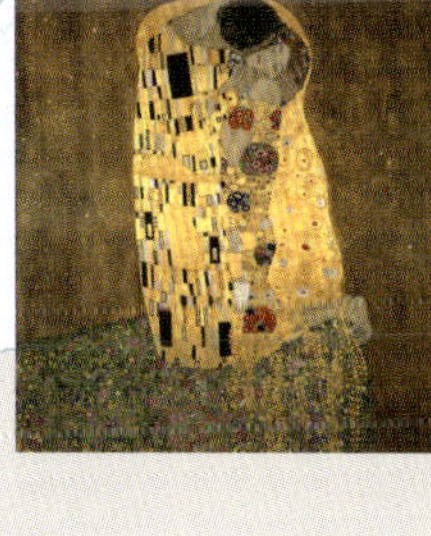

BULGARIA
Christo (Gabrovo 1935)

ITALIA
Umberto Boccioni (Reggio Calabria 1882 - Verona 1916)
Carlo Carrà (Quargnento, Alessandria 1881 - Milano 1966)
Giorgio de Chirico (Volo 1888 - Roma 1978)
Amedeo Modigliani (Livorno 1884 - Paris 1920)
Felice Casorati (Novara 1886 - Torino 1963)
Alberto Burri (Città di Castello 1915 - Nice 1995)
Piero Manzoni (Soncino 1933 - Milano 1963)

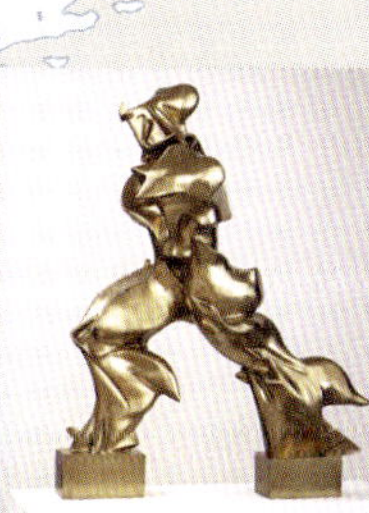

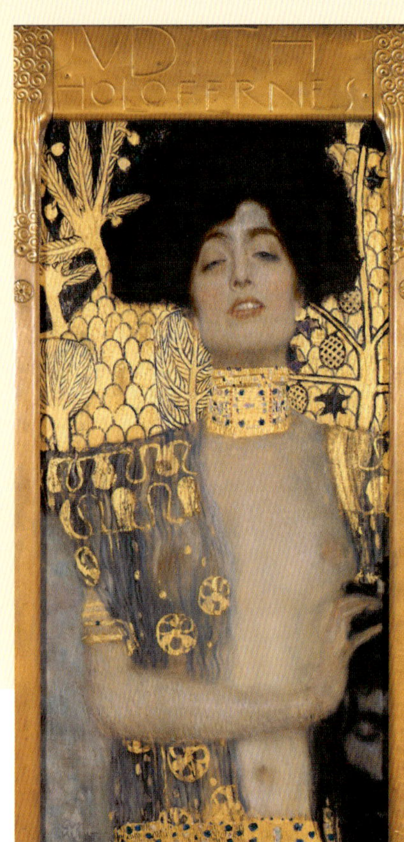

Gustav Klimt
(Baumgarten 1862 - Wien 1918)

Judite
Judith

●●●

1901
84 x 42 cm / 33.07 x 16.53 in.
Österreichische Galerie Belvedere,
Wien

Oil on canvas
Öl auf Leinwand
Olieverf op doek

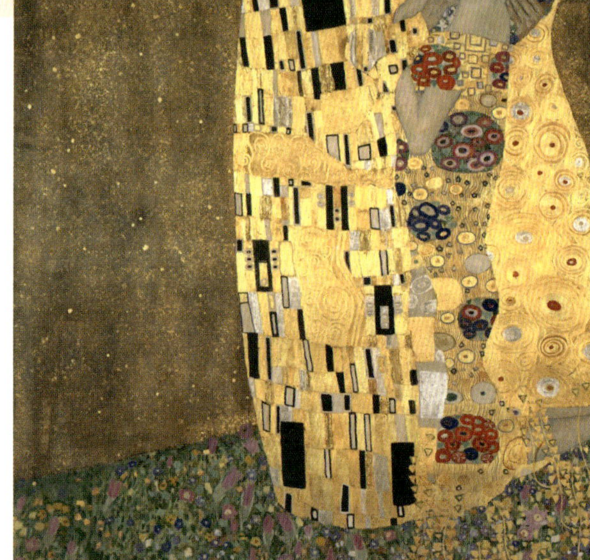

Gustav Klimt
(Baumgarten 1862 - Wien 1918)

The Kiss
Der Kuss
De kus

●●●

1901
180 x 180 cm / 70.86 x 70.86 in.
Österreichische Galerie Belvedere, Wien

Oil on canvas
Öl auf Leinwand
Olieverf op doek

Vienna Secession (Jugendstil): the visions of Gustav Klimt are collages composed of portraits, ornaments, monochromes and gilding.

Wiener Sezession (Jugendstil). Gustav Klimt Traumbilder sind eine "Collage" aus Porträt, Ornament, Monochromie (Einfarbigkeit) und Vergoldung.

De Wiener Sezession (Jugendstil). De visioenen van Gustav Klimt zijn een collage van portretten, ornamenten, monochromieën en verguldsels.

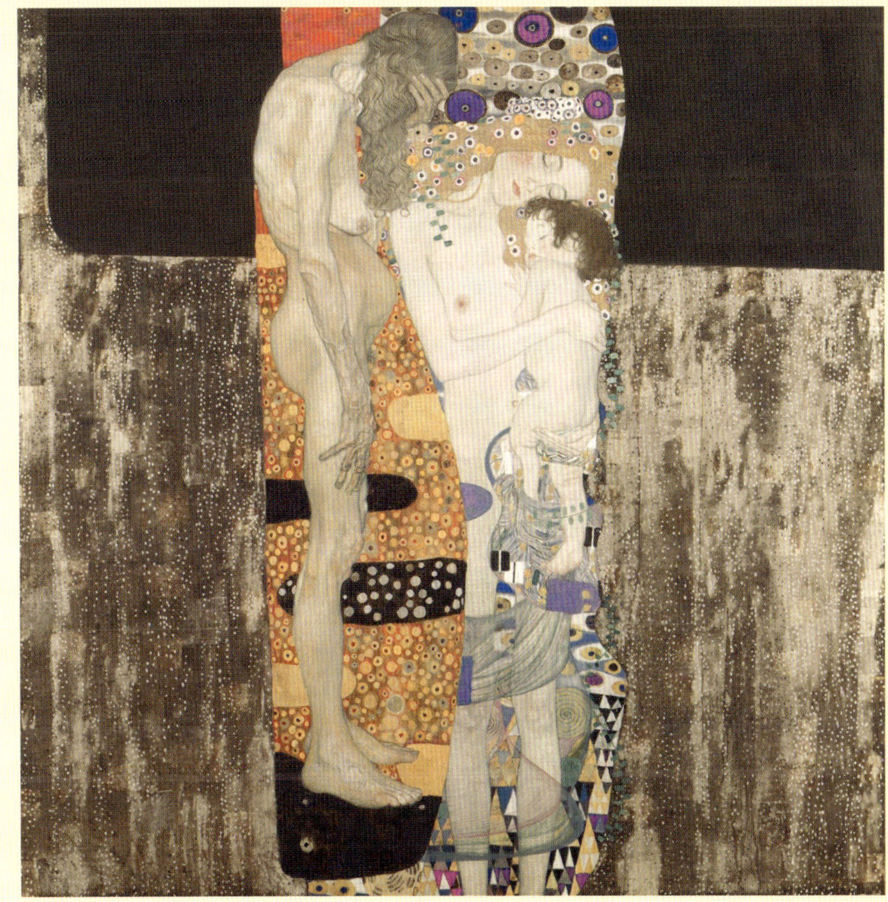

Gustav Klimt
(Baumgarten 1862 - Wien 1918)

The Three Ages of Woman
Die Drei Lebensalter
De drie levensfasen

●●●

1905
180 x 180 cm / 70.86 x 70.86 in.
Galleria Nazionale d'Arte Moderna, Roma

Oil on canvas
Öl auf Leinwand
Olieverf op doek

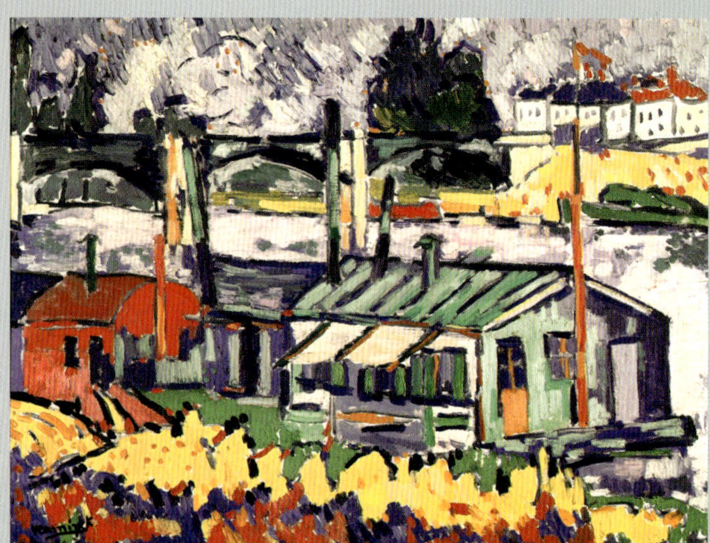

Maurice de Vlaminck
(Paris 1876 - Rueil-la-Gadelière Eure-et-Loir 1958)

The Bridge at Chatou
Die Brücke von Chatou
De brug van Chatou

●●

1905
Musée de l'Annonciade, Saint-Tropez

Oil on canvas
Öl auf Leinwand
Olieverf op doek

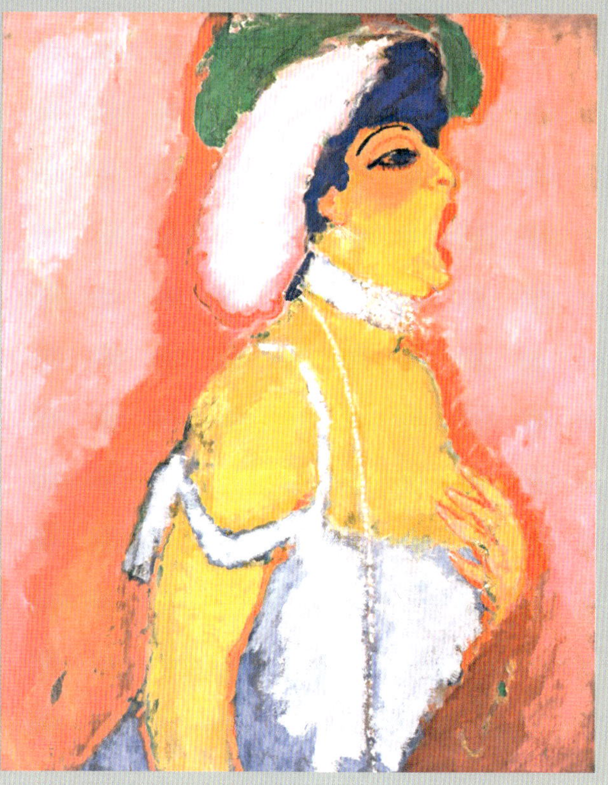

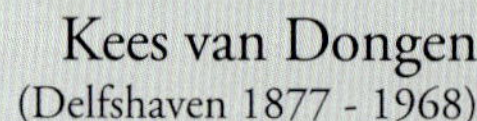

Kees van Dongen
(Delfshaven 1877 - 1968)

Modjesko

●●

1908
81 x 100 cm / 39 x 32 in.
Museum of Modern Art (MoMA), New York

Oil on canvas
Öl auf Leinwand
Olieverf op doek

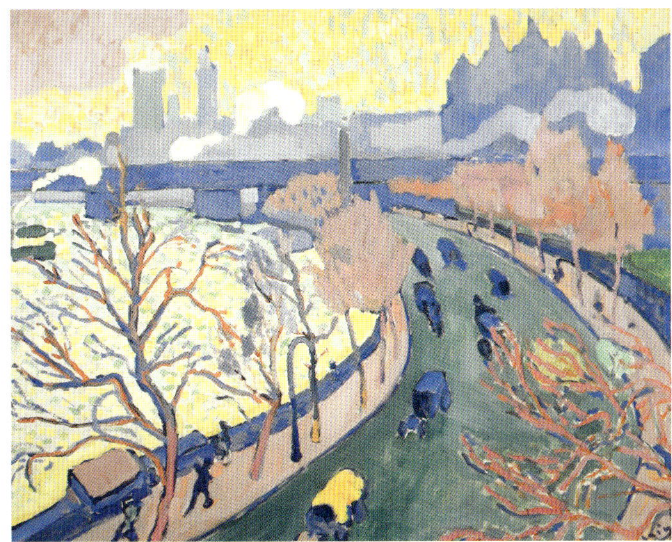

André Derain
(Chatou 1880 - Garches 1954)

Charing Cross Bridge
Die Brücke von Charing Cross
De brug van Charing Cross

●

c. 1906
81 x 100 cm / 31.88 x 39.37 in.
Musée d'Orsay, Paris

Oil on canvas
Öl auf Leinwand
Olieverf op doek

André Derain
(Chatou 1880 - Garches 1954)

Harlequin with Guitar
Harlekin mit Gitarre
Harlekijn met gitaar

●●

1924
Musée de l'Orangerie, Paris

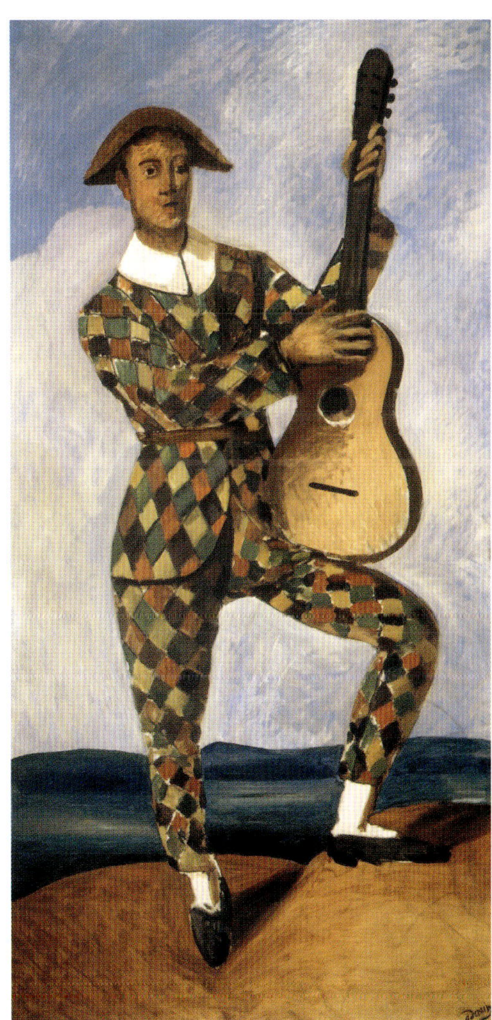

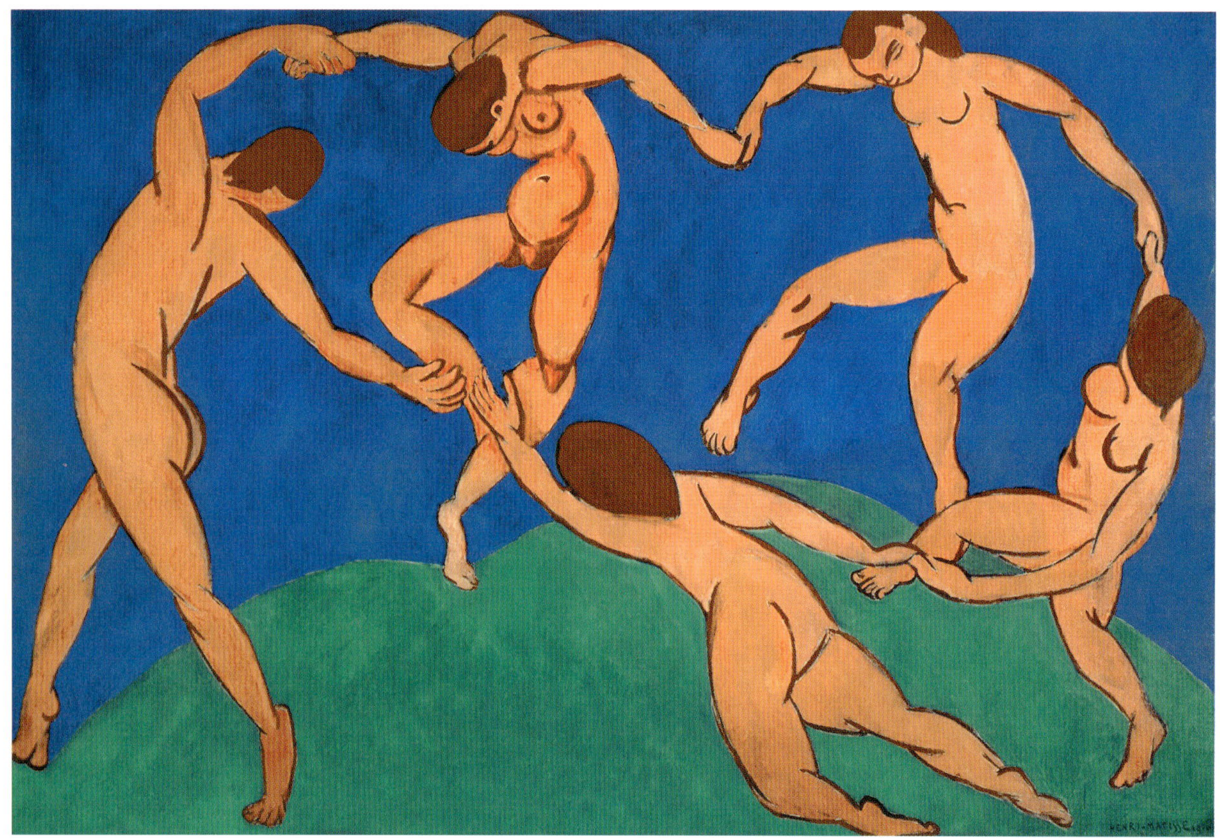

Henri Matisse
(Cateau-Cambrésis 1869 - Nice 1954)

The Dance II
Der Tanz II
De dans II

●●●

1910
260 x 392 cm / 102.36 x 154.33 in.
The State Hermitage Museum, St. Petersburg

Oil on canvas
Öl auf Leinwand
Olieverf op doek

Rhythmically balanced compositions with decorative elements: Henri Matisse is considered the master of colour of classical modern art.

Rhythmisch ausgewogene Kompositionen mit dekorativen Elementen. Henri Matisse gilt als der Meister der Farbe der klassischen Moderne.

Ritmisch evenwichtige composities met decoratieve elementen. Henri Matisse wordt als meester van de kleur van de klassieke moderne kunst beschouwd.

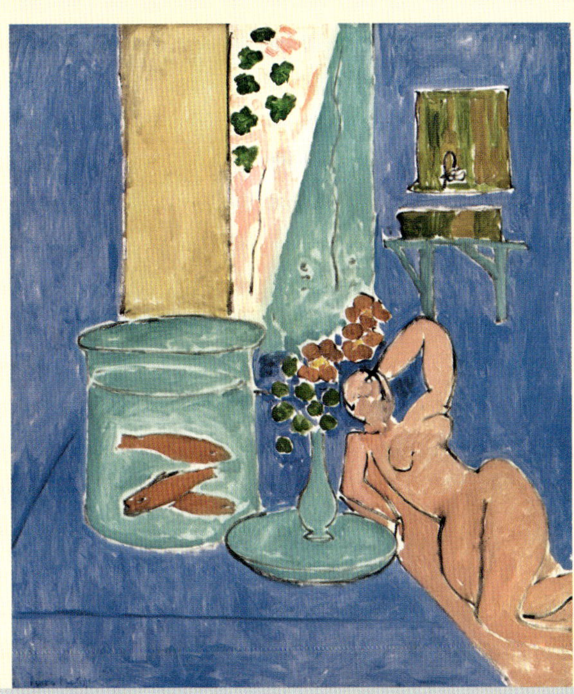

Henri Matisse
(Cateau-Cambrésis 1869 - Nice 1954)

Goldfish and Sculpture Issy-les Moulineaux
Goldfische und Skulptur Issy-les Moulineaux
Issy-les Moulineaux, rode vissen met beeld

●●

1912
116 x 110 cm / 45.66 x 43.30 in.
Museum of Modern Art (MoMA), New York

Oil on canvas / Öl auf Leinwand / Olieverf op doek

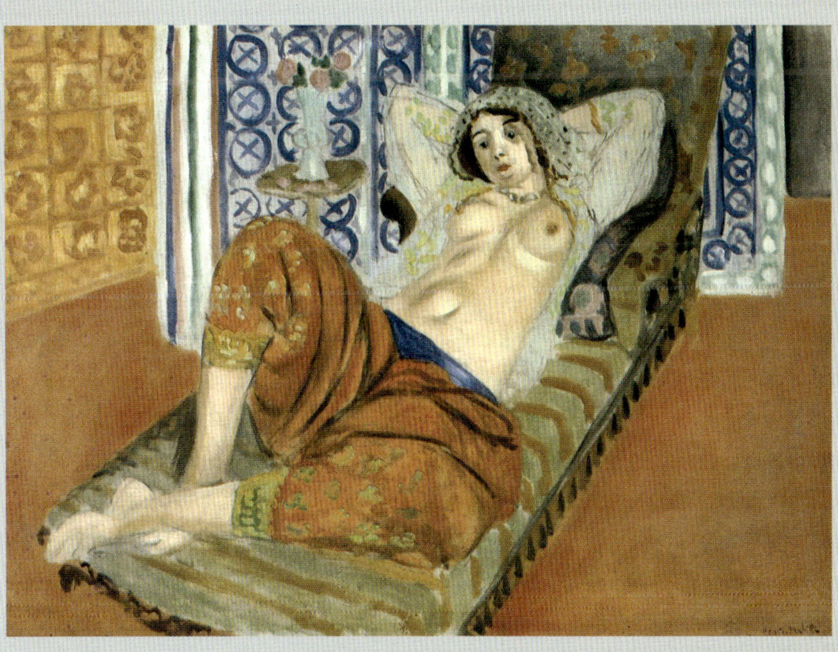

Henri Matisse
(Cateau-Cambrésis 1869 - Nice 1954)

Odalisque in Red Trousers
Odaliske mit roten Hosen
Odalisk in rode broek

●●●

1921
67 x 84 cm / 26.37 x 33.07 in.
Musée National d'Art Moderne - Centre Pompidou, Paris

Oil on canvas
Öl auf Leinwand
Olieverf op doek

Pablo Picasso (Málaga 1881 - Mougins 1973)
La Vie (Life)
Das Leben
La vie

●●

1903
196,8 x 129,5 cm / 77.48 x 50.98 in.
Cleveland Museum of Art, Cleveland

Oil on canvas / Öl auf Leinwand / Olieverf op doek

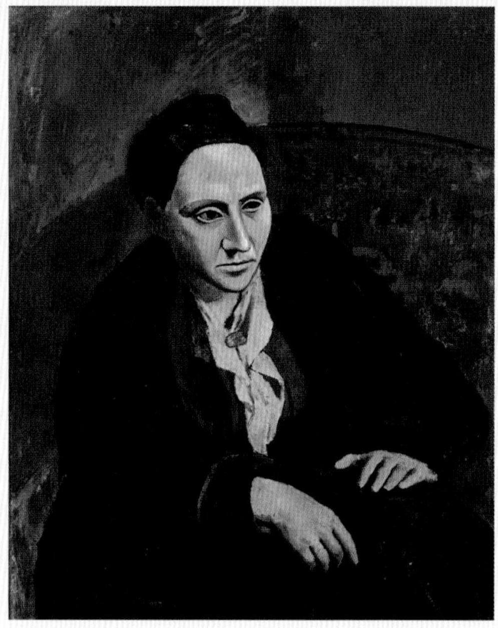

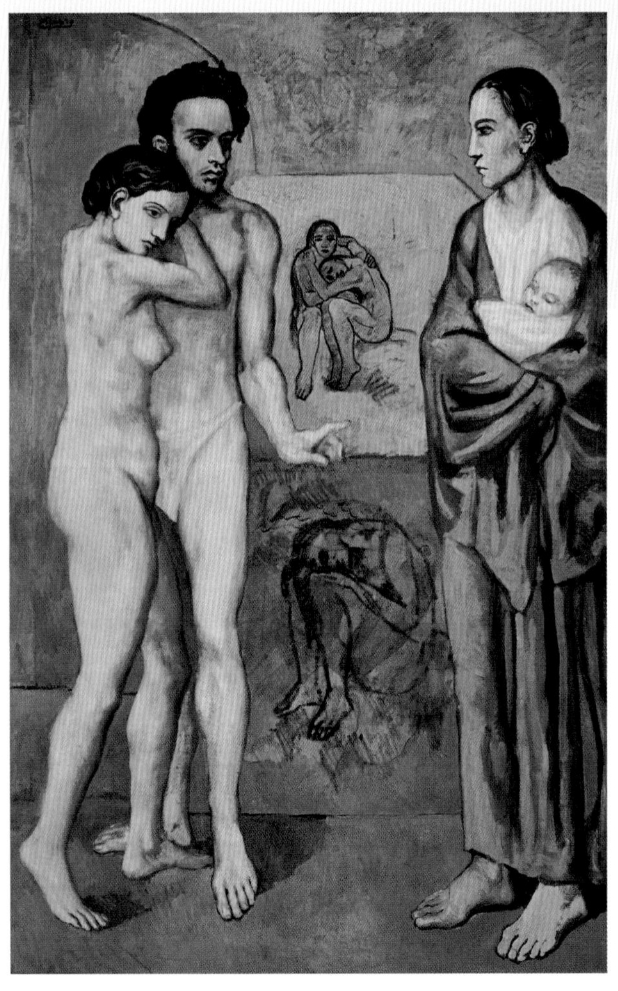

In the early works Picasso borrows and experiments. The works of his Blue (1901-1904) and Rose (1905-1906) periods seem to follow a Mannerist aesthetic.

Der frühe Picasso entlehnt und probiert aus. Manieristisch überdehnt wirken seine Werke der blauen (1901-1904) und rosa (1905-1906) Periode.

De vroege Picasso leent en experimenteert. Zijn werk uit de Blauwe periode (1910-1940) en Roze periode (1905-1906) lijkt maniëristisch uitgerekt.

◂ Pablo Picasso
(Málaga 1881 - Mougins 1973)

Gertrude Stein

●●

1906
100 x 81,3 cm / 39.37 x 32 in.
Metropolitan Museum of Art,
New York

Oil on canvas
Öl auf Leinwand
Olieverf op doek

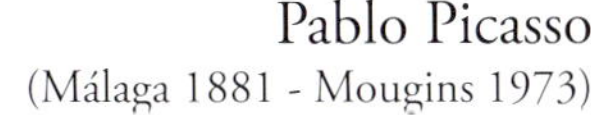

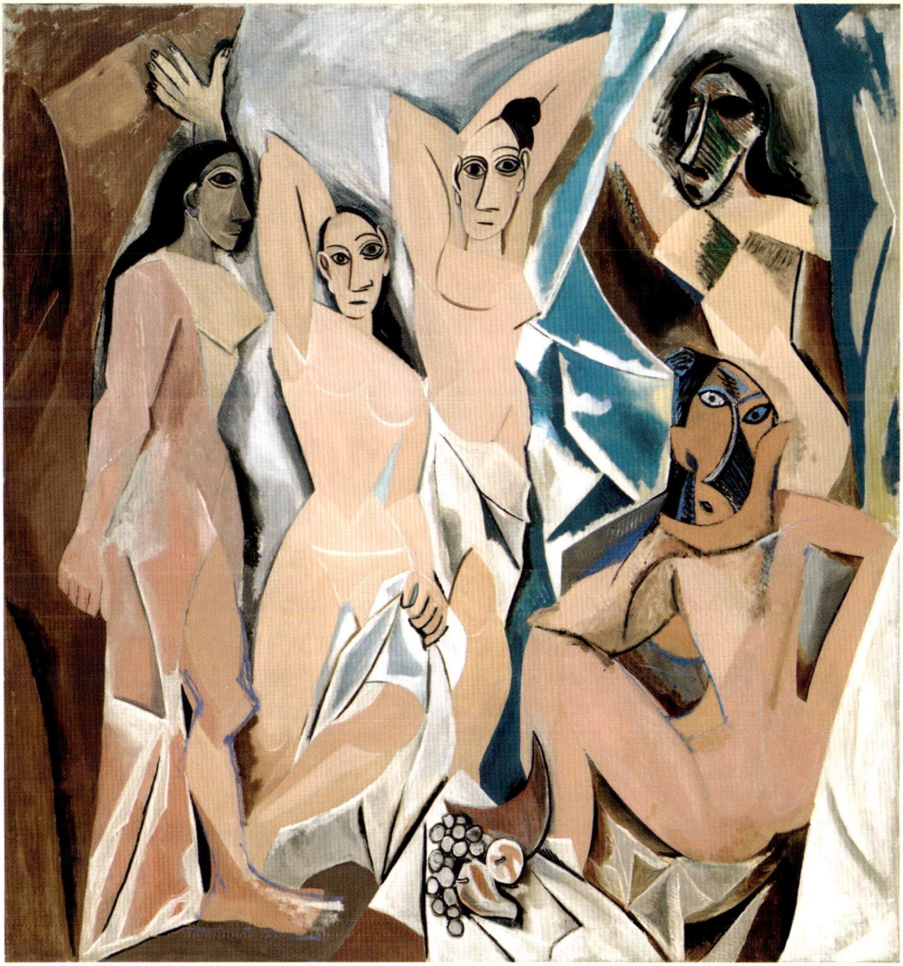

Pablo Picasso
(Málaga 1881 - Mougins 1973)

Les demoiselles d'Avignon
Demoiselles d'Avignon
Les Demoiselles d'Avignon
(De jongedames van Avignon)

●●●

1907
243,9 x 233,7 cm / 96 x 92 in.
Museum of Modern Art (MoMA),
New York

Oil on canvas
Öl auf Leinwand
Olieverf op doek

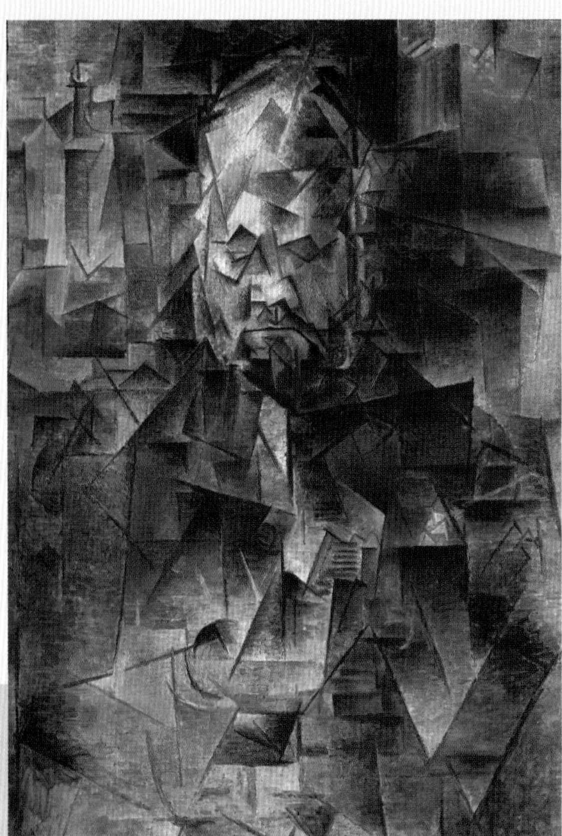

Pablo Picasso
(Málaga 1881 - Mougins 1973)

Ambroise Vollard

●●

c. 1909-1910
92 x 65 cm / 36.22 x 25.59 in.
Pushkin Museum of Fine Arts, Moscow

Oil on canvas
Öl auf Leinwand
Olieverf op doek

Pablo Picasso
(Málaga 1881 - Mougins 1973)

Still Life with Straw-Bottomed Chair
Stillleben mit Flechtstuhl
Stilleven met rieten stoel

●

1912
29 x 37 cm / 11.41 x 14.56 in.
Musée Picasso, Paris

Oil on canvas
Öl auf Leinwand
Olieverf op doek

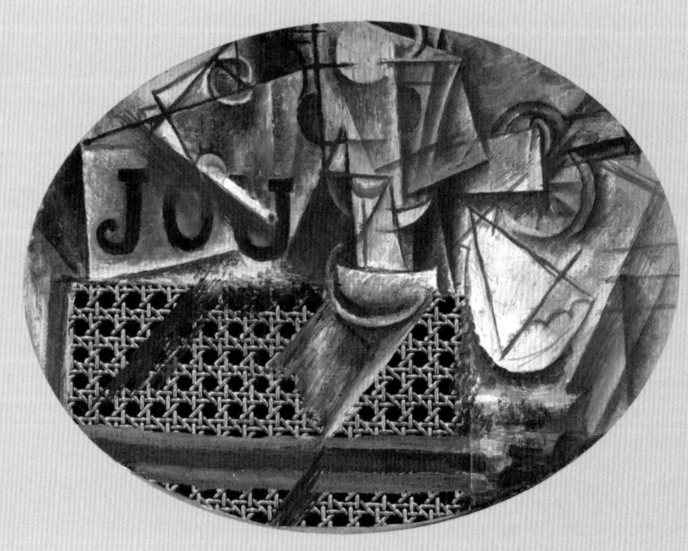

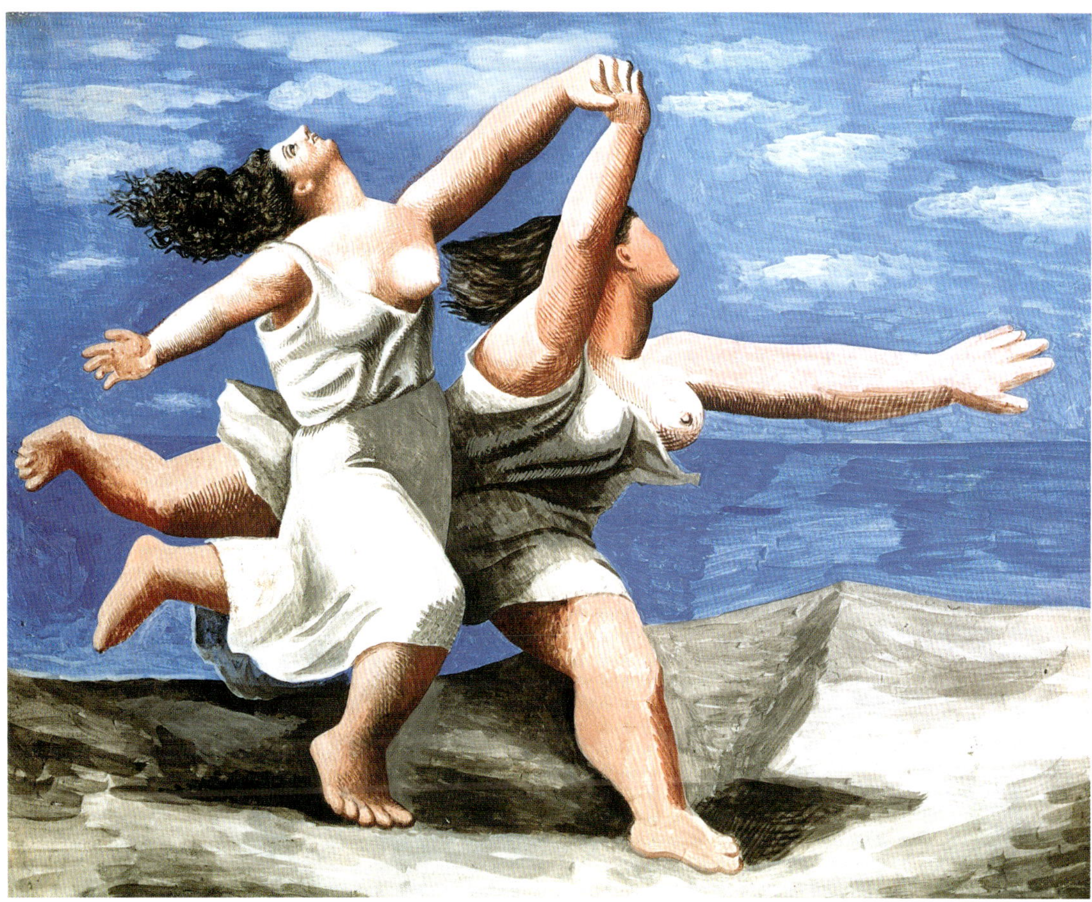

Pablo Picasso
(Málaga 1881 - Mougins 1973)

Two Women Running on the Beach
Zwei Frauen am Strand laufend
Twee rennende vrouwen op het strand

●●●

1922
34 x 42 cm / 13.38 x 16.53 in.
Musée Picasso, Paris

Oil on fibreboard / Öl auf Hartfaserplatte
Olieverf op fibreboard

▸▸

Pablo Picasso
(Málaga 1881 - Mougins 1973)

Guernica

●●●

1937
351 x 782 cm / 138.18 x 307.87 in.
Museo Nacional Centro de Arte Reina Sofía, Madrid

Oil on canvas
Öl auf Leinwand
Olieverf op doek

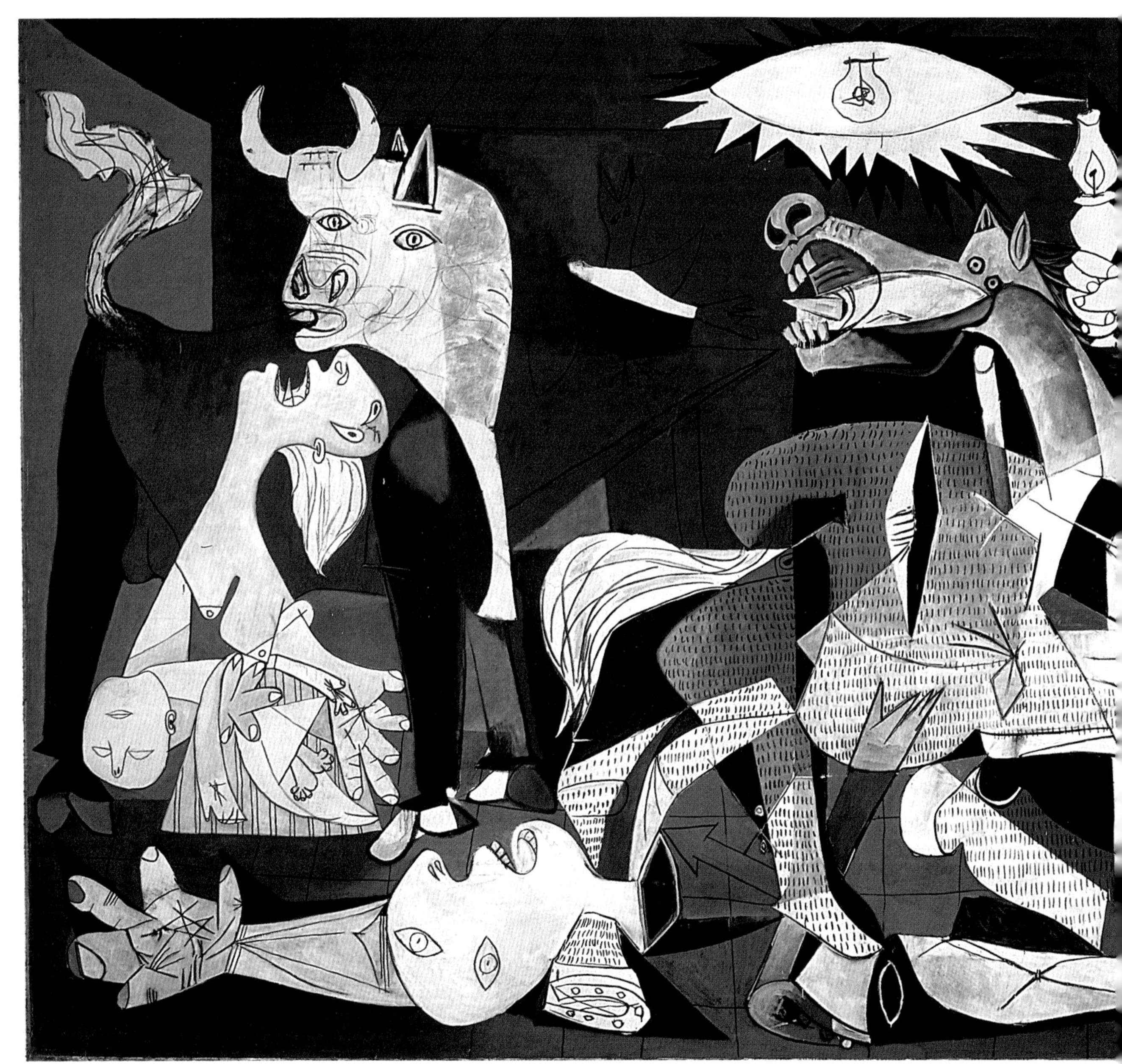

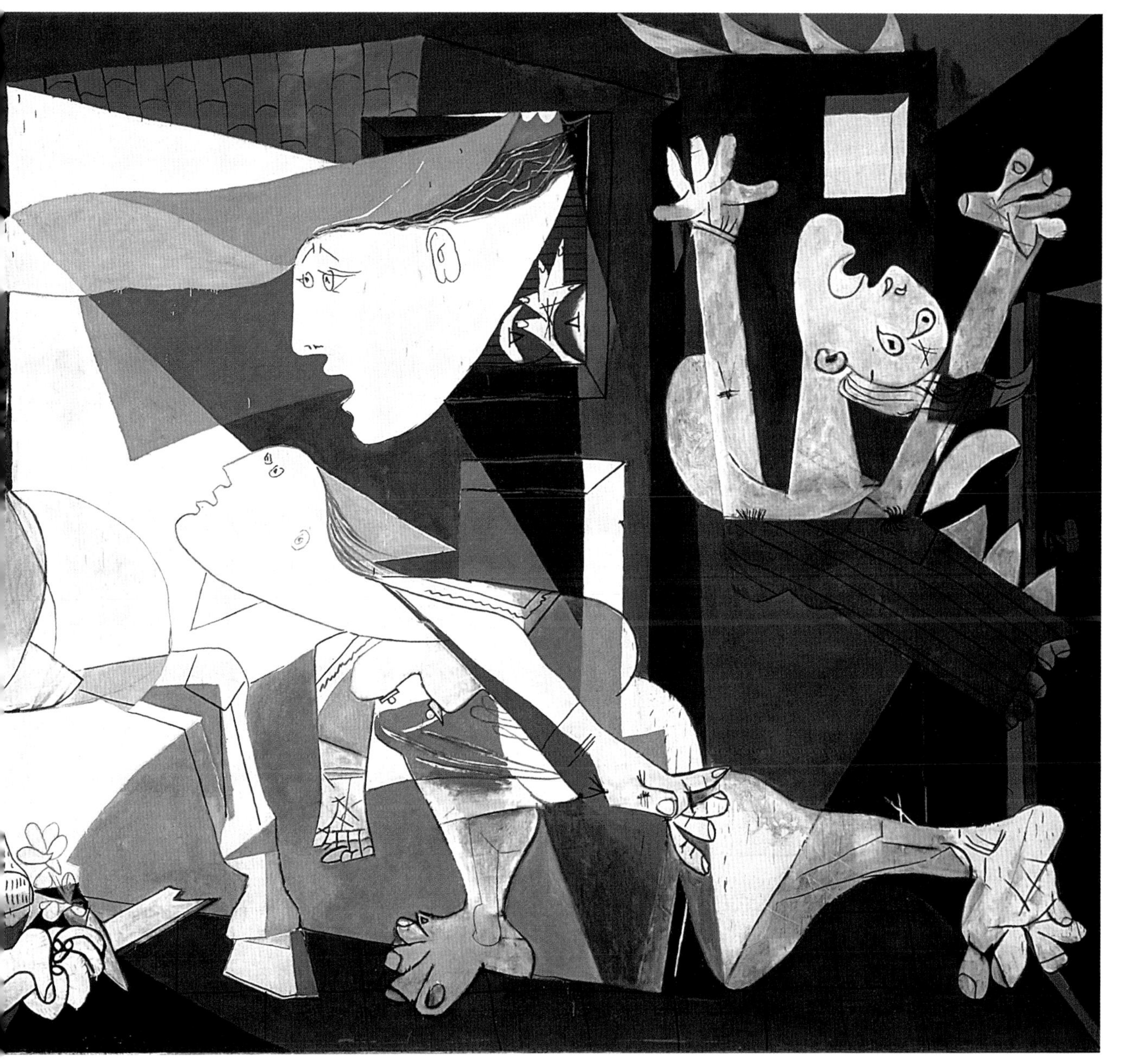

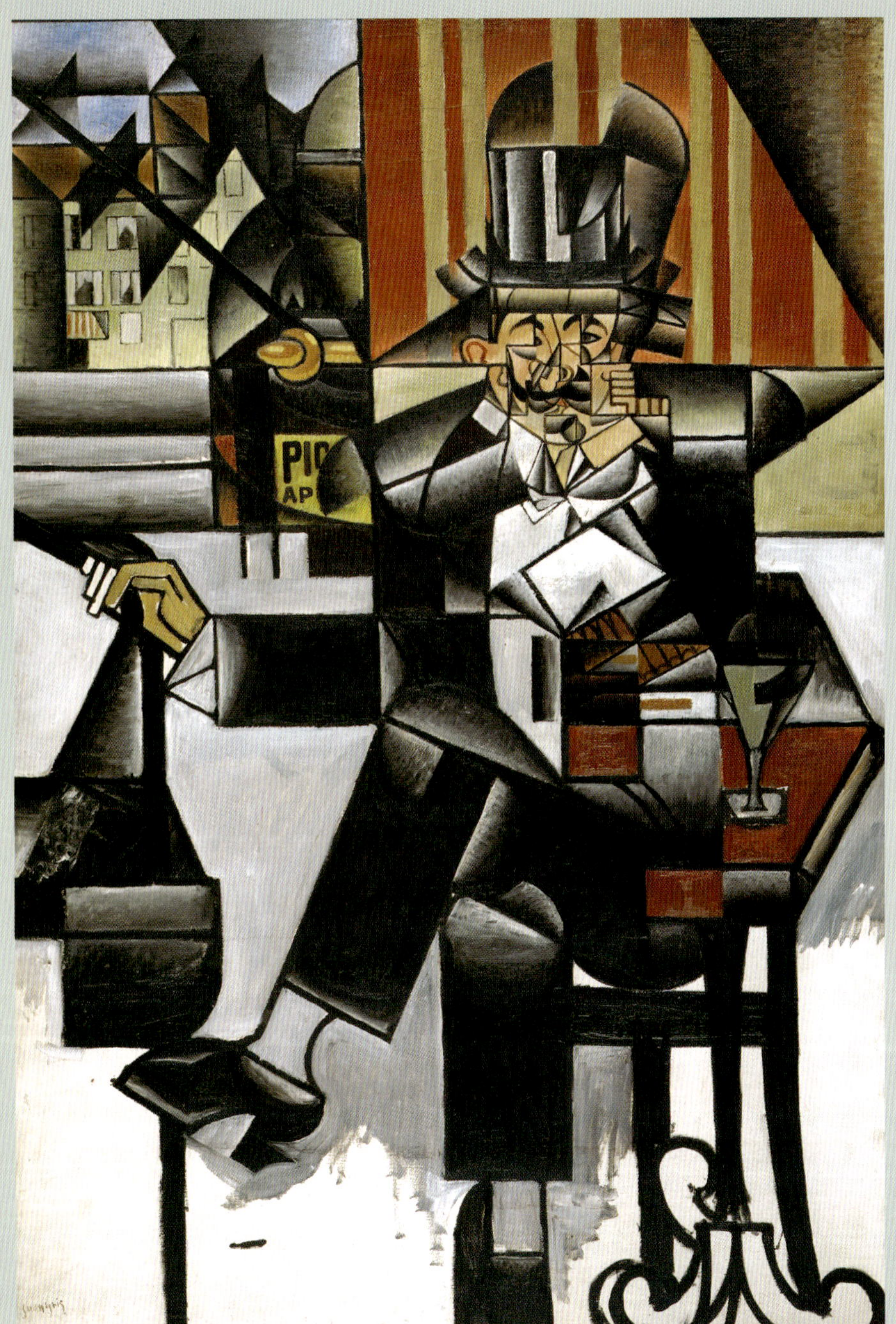

Cubism becomes a European style...

Der Kubismus wird ein europäischer Stil...

Het kubisme wordt een Europese stijl...

444

Juan Gris
(Madrid 1887 - Boulogne-Billancourt 1927)

Man in a Café
Mann in einem Kaffeehaus
Man in een café

●

1912
127,6 x 88,3 cm / 50.23 x 34.76 in.
Philadelphia Museum of Art, Philadelphia

Oil on canvas
Öl auf Leinwand
Olieverf op doek

Georges Braque
(Argenteuil 1882 - Paris 1963)

Glass and Newspaper
Glas und Zeitung
Glas en krant

●●

1913
98,7 x 72,5 cm / 38.85 x 28.54 in.
Nationalgalerie, Museum Berggruen, Staatliche Muséen, Berlin

Chalk, charcoal and oil on canvas
Kreide, Kohle, Öl auf Leinwand
Krijt, houtskool, olieverf op doek

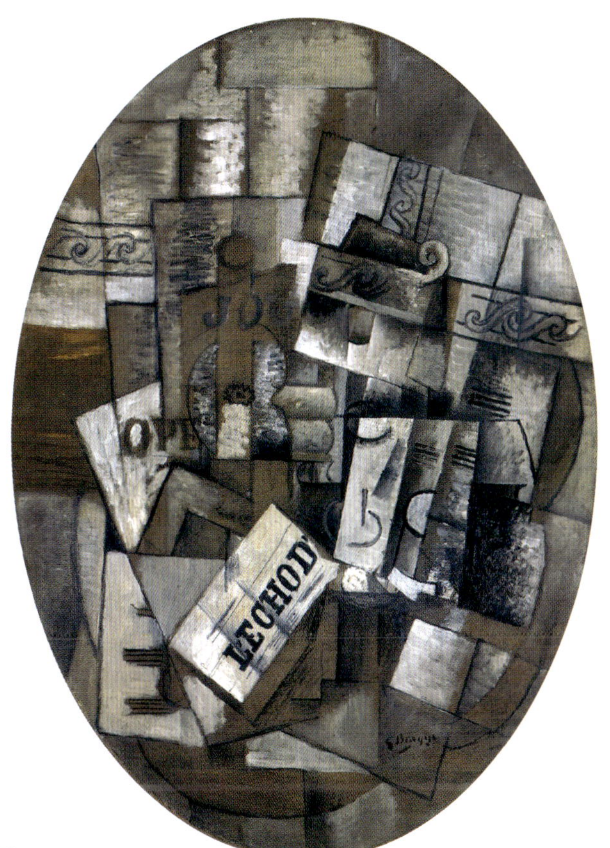

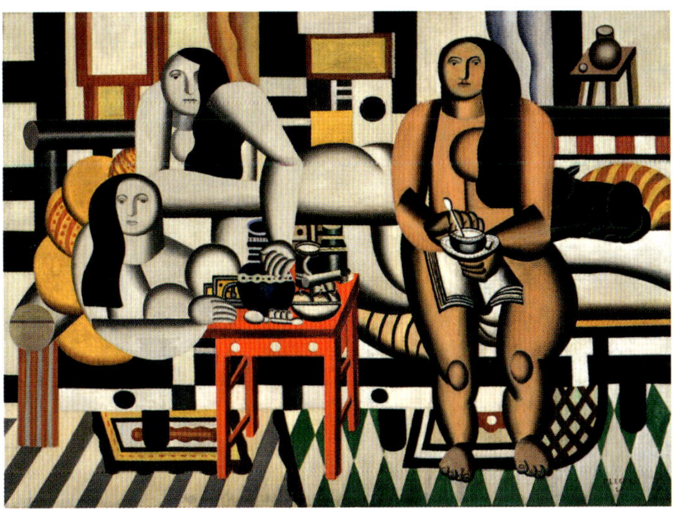

Fernand Léger
(Argentan 1881 - Gif-sur-Yvette 1955)

Three Women
Drei Frauen
Drie vrouwen

●●●

1921
183,5 x 251,5 cm / 72.24 x 99 in.
Museum of Modern Art (MoMA), New York

Oil on canvas
Öl auf Leinwand
Olieverf op doek

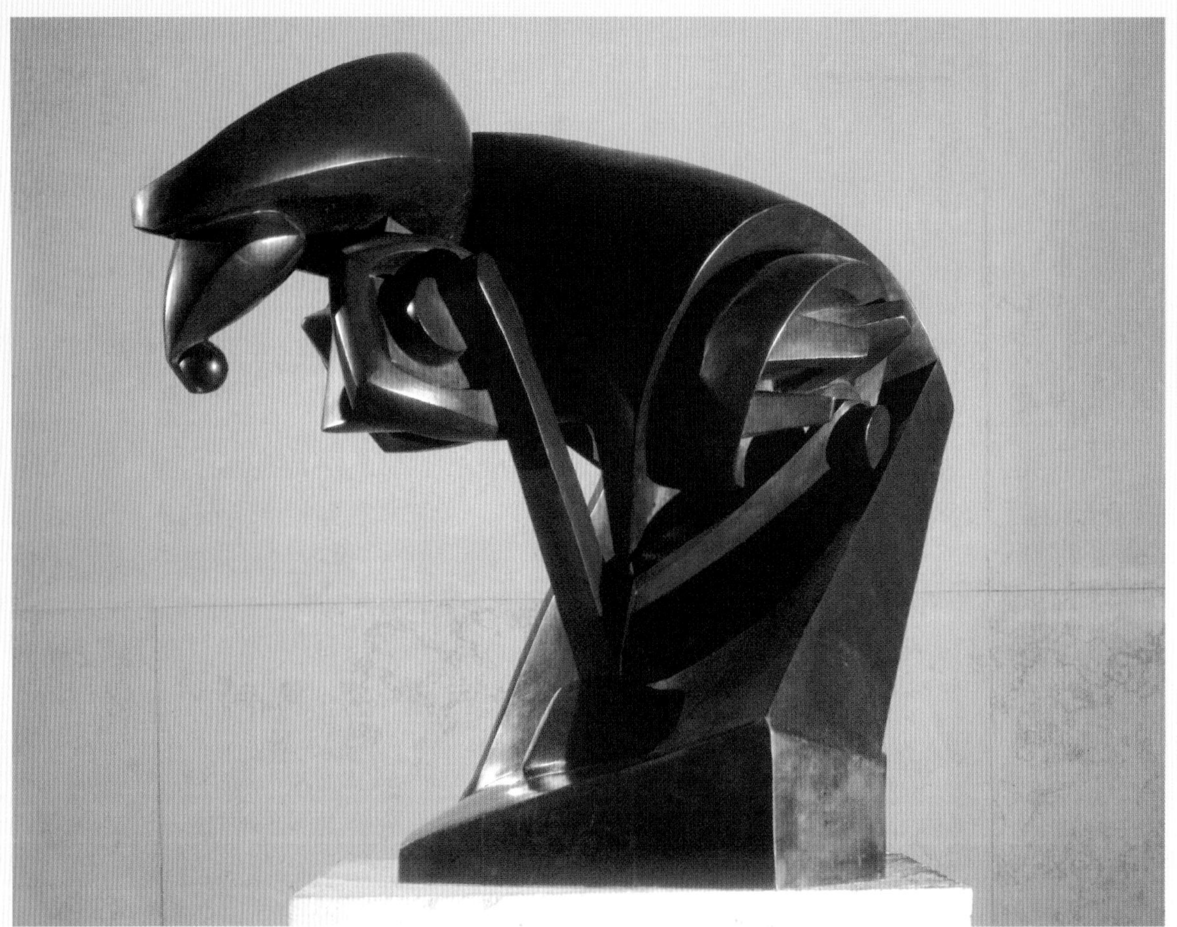

Raymond Duchamp-Villon
(Damville 1876 - Cannes 1918)

Horse
Großes Pfed
Het Grote Paard

●

1914
Art Institute of Chicago, Chicago

Bronze / Brons

... and also influences sculpture.

... und beeinflusst auch die Bildhauerei.

... en beïnvloedt ook de beeldhouwkunst.

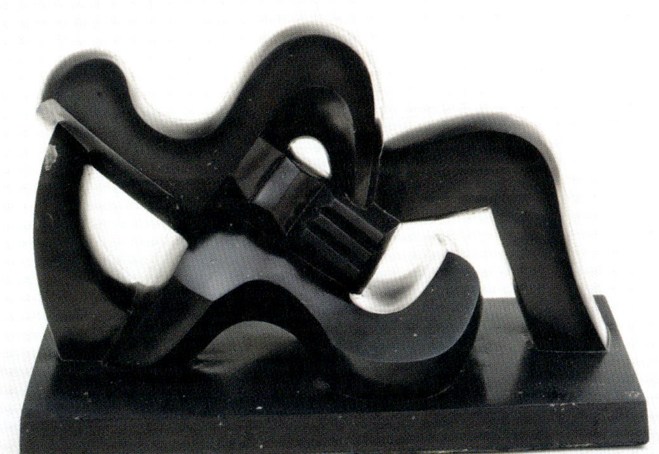

Jacques Lipchitz
(Druskininkai 1891 - Capri 1973)

Reclining Nude with Guitar
Ruhender Akt mit Gitarre
Liggend naakt met gitaar

●

1928
h. 41,6 cm / 16.37 in.
Museum of Modern Art (MoMA), New York

Bronze / Brons

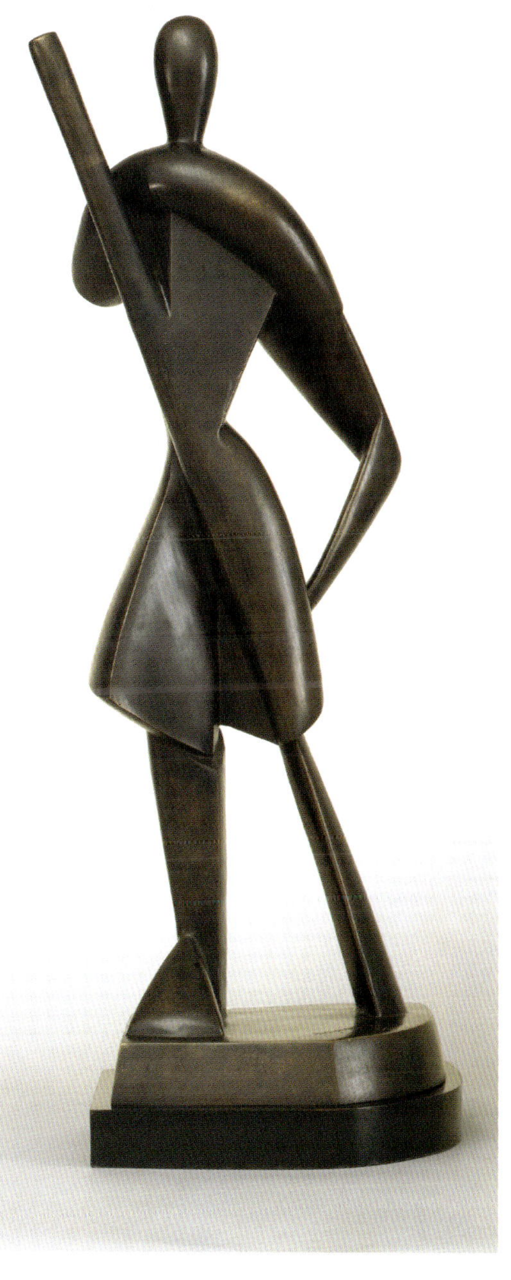

Alexander Archipenko
(Kiev 1887 - New York 1964)

Gondolier
De gondelier

●

1914
h. 83,8 cm / 33 in.
Museum of Modern Art (MoMA), New York

Bronze / Brons

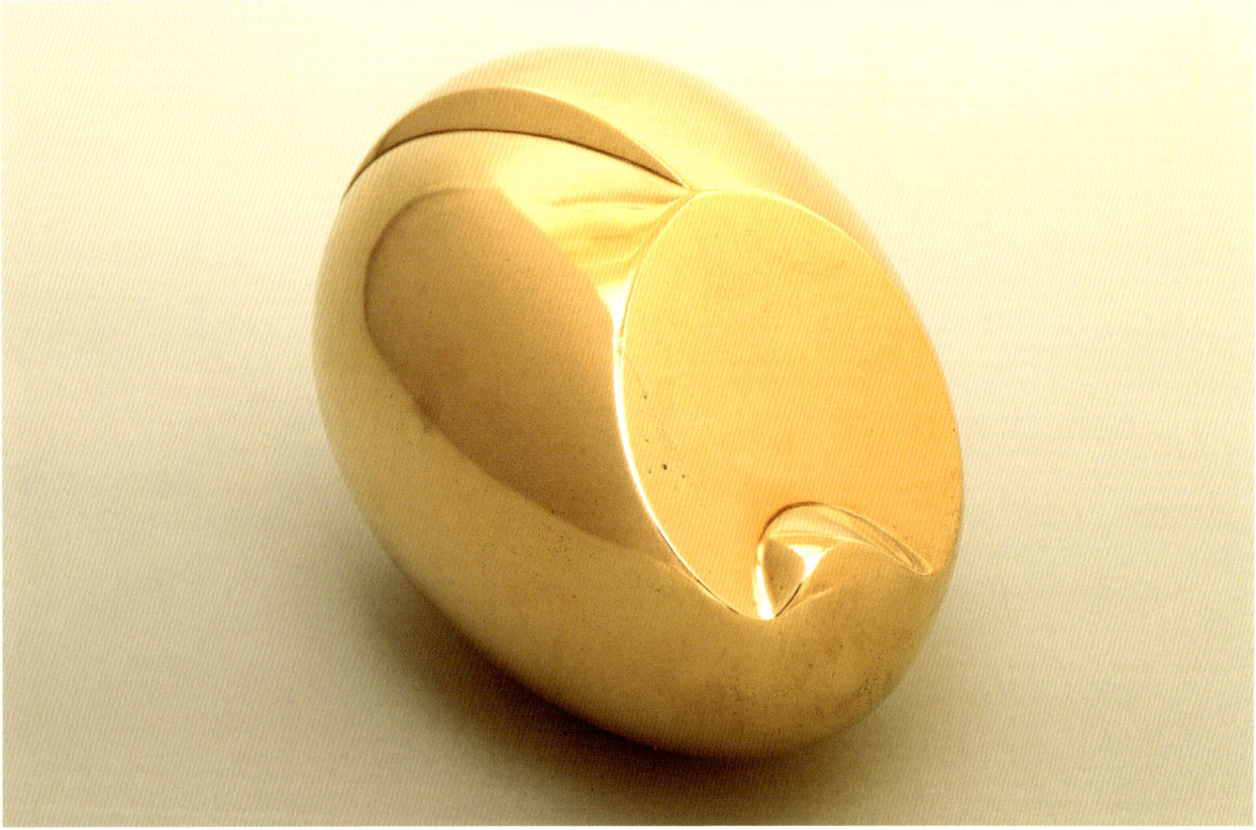

Constantin Brancusi
(Peştişani 1876 - Paris 1957)

The Newborn, version I
Neugeborener, Version I
Pasgeborene, versie I

1920
14,6 x 21 x 14,6 cm / 5.74 x 8.3 x 5.74 in.
Museum of Modern Art (MoMA), New York

Bronze / Brons

The small still form characterizes the works of the Rumanian Constantin Brancusi.

Reduzierte, in sich ruhende Form kennzeichnet das Werk des Rumänen Constantin Brancusi.

De onbeweeglijke, gereduceerde vorm kenmerkt ook het werk van de Roemeen Constantin Brancusi.

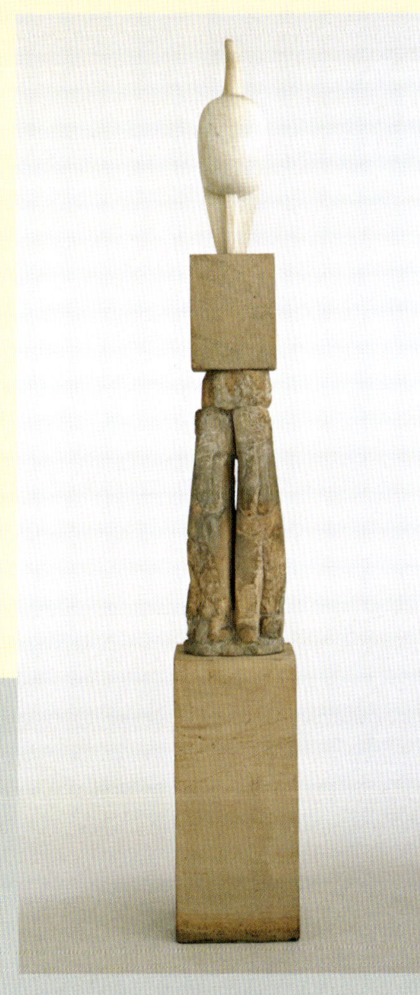

Constantin Brancusi
(Peştişani 1876 - Paris 1957)

Magic Bird (Pasarea Maiastra)
Mythischer Vogel (Pasarea Maiastra)
Magische Vogel (Pasarea Maiastra)

●●

c. 1910 - 1912
h. 233,7 cm / 92 in.
Museum of Modern Art (MoMA), New York

Marble / Marmor / Marmer

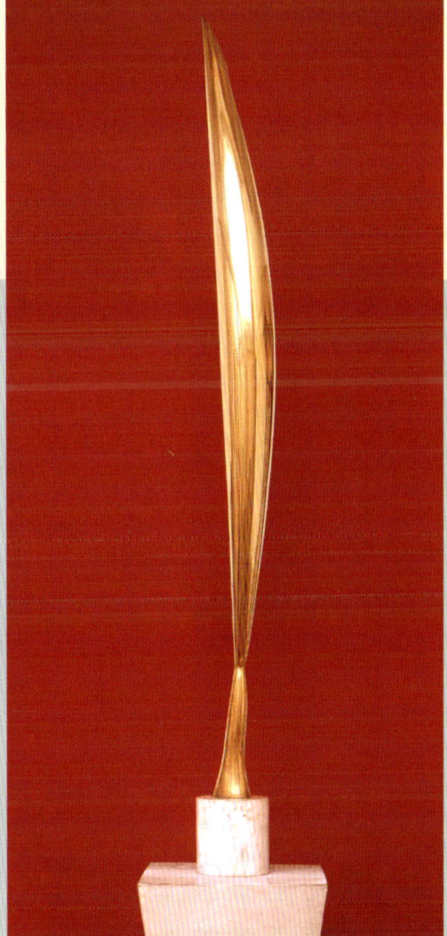

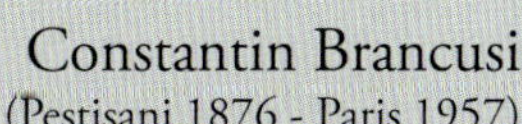

Constantin Brancusi
(Peştişani 1876 - Paris 1957)

Bird in Space
Vogel im Raum
Vogel in de ruimte

●●●

c. 1931-1936
h. 39 cm / 15.35 in.
Musée National d'Art Moderne - Centre Pompidou, Paris

Bronze / Brons

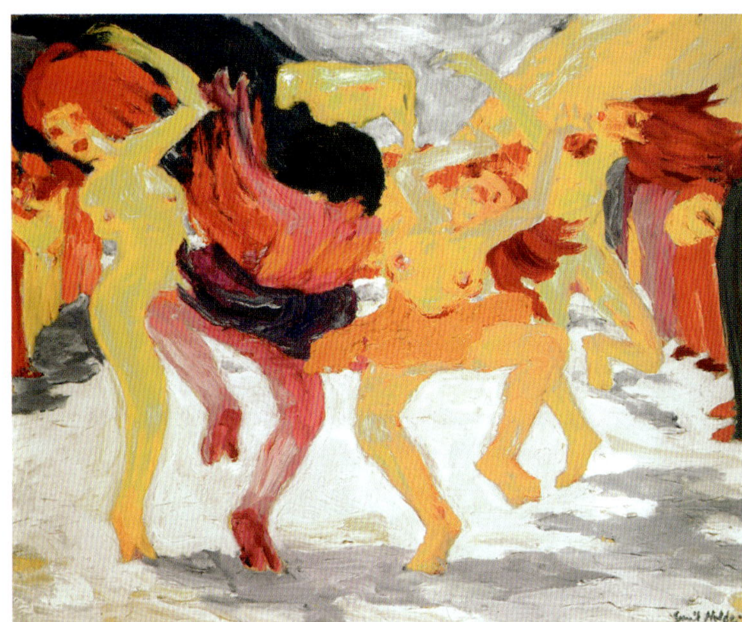

Emil Nolde
(Nolde 1867 - Seebüll 1956)

Dance around the Golden Calf
Der Tanz um das Goldene Kalb
Dans rond het gouden kalf

●●

1910
88 x 106 cm / 34.64 x 41.73 in.
Neue Pinakothek, München

Oil on canvas
Öl auf Leinwand
Olieverf op doek

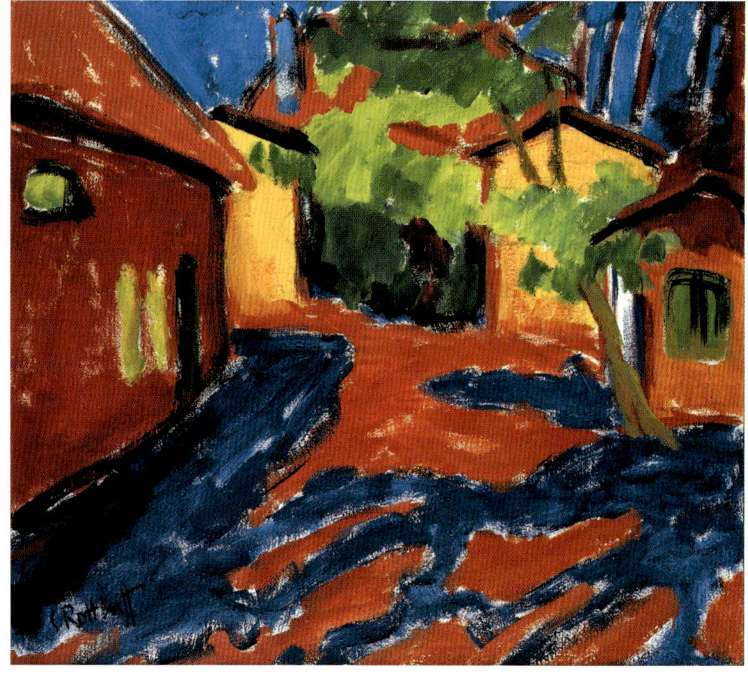

Karl Schmidt-Rottluff
(Rottluff 1884 - Berlin 1976)

Manor House at Dangast
Das Haus in Dangast
Verblijf in Dangast

●

1910
86,5 x 94,5 cm / 34.05 x 37.20 in.
Nationalgalerie, Staatliche Museen, Berlin

Oil on canvas
Öl auf Leinwand
Olieverf op doek

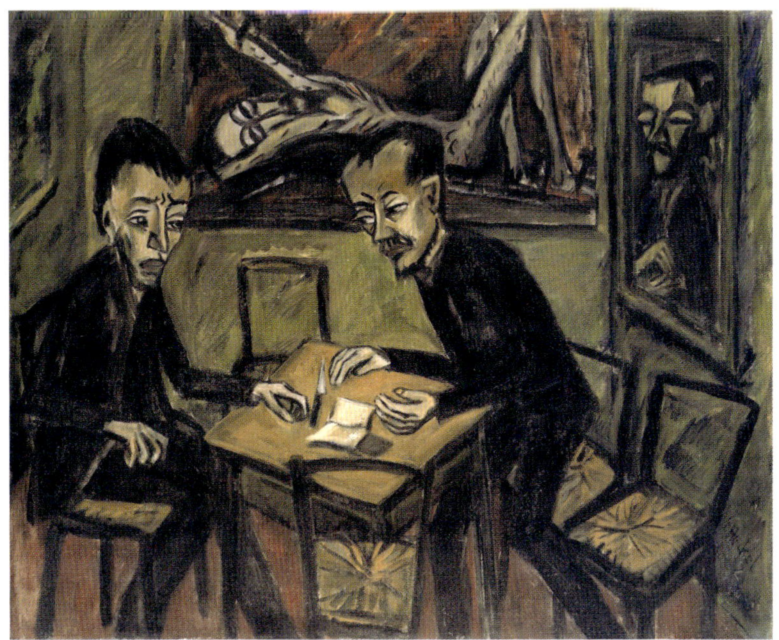

In Expressionism colours and forms represent a subjective expression of the artist.

Im Expressionismus sind Farben und Formen subjektiver "Ausdruck" des Künstlers.

In het expressionisme zijn kleuren en vormen een subjectieve "expressie" van de kunstenaar.

Erich Heckel
(Döbeln 1883 - Rudolfzell 1970)

Two Artists Seated at a Table
Zwei Männer am Tisch
Twee kunstenaars aan tafel

●●

1912
97 x 120 cm / 38.18 x 47.24 in.
Hamburger Kunsthalle,
Hamburg

Oil on canvas
Öl auf Leinwand
Olieverf op doek

Ernst Ludwig Kirchner
(Aschaffenburg 1880 - Davos 1938)

Street Scene in Berlin with a Tart in Red
Straße mit roter Kokotte
Straatscène in Berlijn met rode prostituee

●●

1914-1925
125 x 90,5 cm / 49.21 x 35.62 in.
Museo Thyssen-Bornemisza, Madrid

Oil on canvas
Öl auf Leinwand
Olieverf op doek

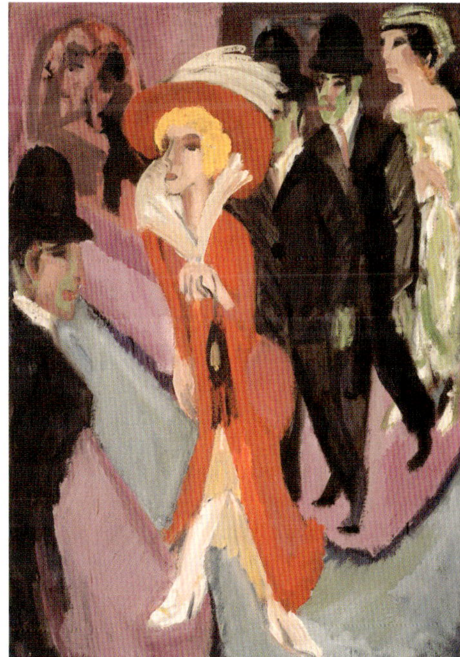

Oskar Kokoschka
(Pöchlarn 1886 - Montreux 1980)

Pietà

●

1907
18,1 x 76,2 cm / 7.12 x 30 in.
Museum of Modern Art (MoMA),
New York

Lithograph
Litographie
Lithografie

Oskar Kokoschka
(Pöchlarn 1886 - Montreux 1980)

Lovers with a Cat
Liebespaar mit Katze
Geliefden met kat

●

Kunsthaus, Zürich

Oil on canvas
Öl auf Leinwand
Olieverf op doek

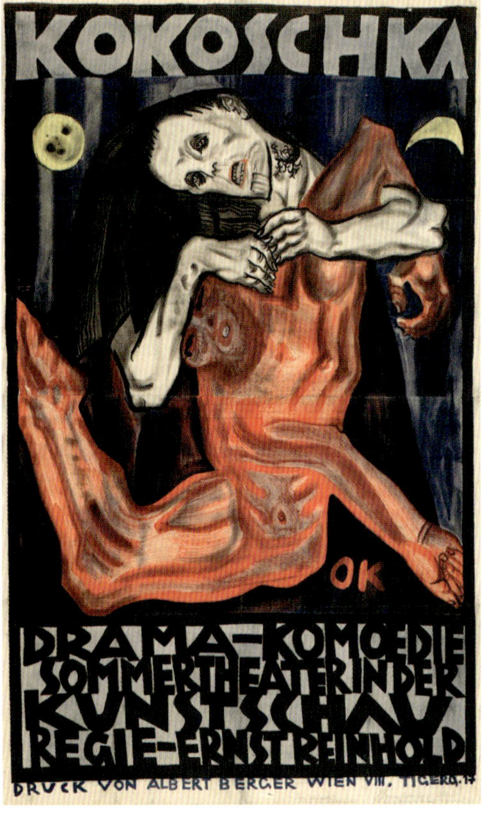

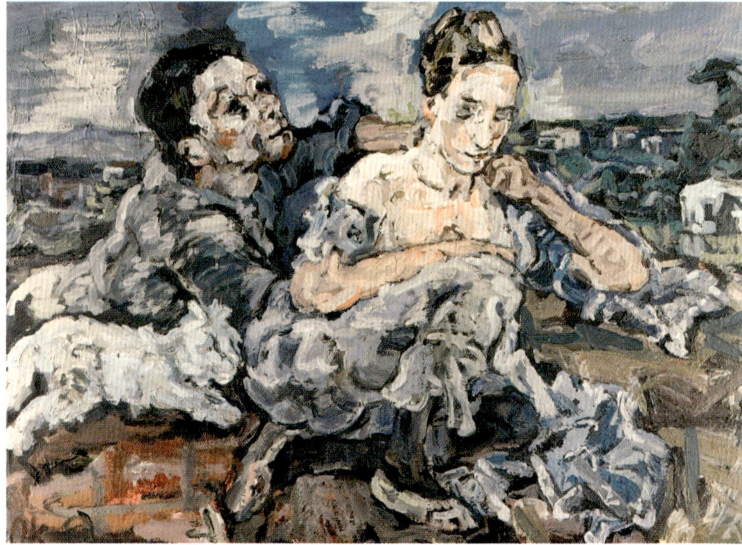

Egon Schiele
(Tulln 1890 - Wien 1918)

Self-Portrait with Spread Fingers
Selbstakt mit gespreizten Fingern
Zelfportret met gespreide vingers

●●●

1911
27,5 x 34 cm / 10.8 x 13.4 in.
Historisches Museum der Stadt Wien, Wien

Oil on wood
Öl auf Tafel
Olieverf op paneel

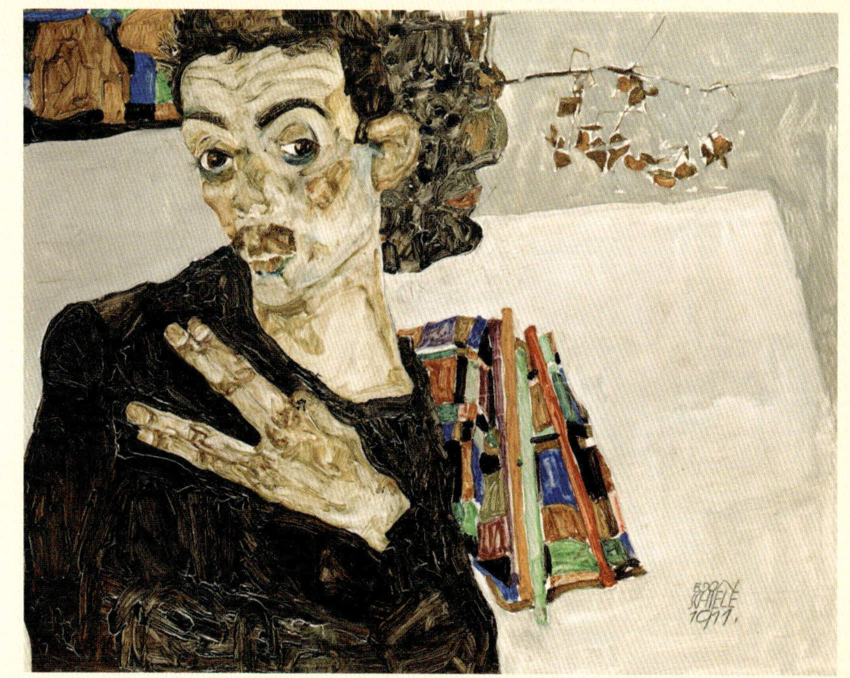

453

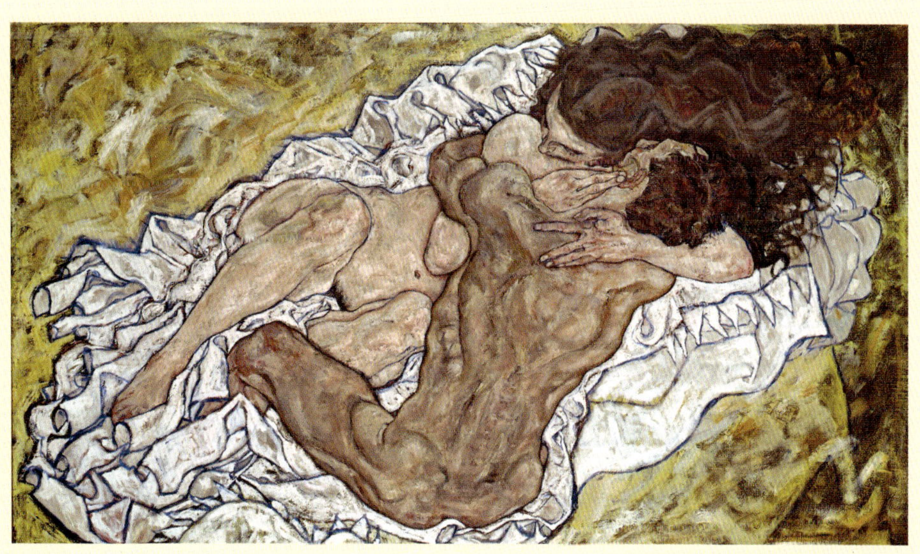

Egon Schiele
(Tulln 1890 - Wien 1918)

The Embrace - Lovers II
Die Umarmung
(Die Liebenden II)
De Omhelzing Geliefden II

●●

1917
100 x 70 cm / 39.37 x 27.55 in.
Österreichische Galerie Belvedere, Wien

Oil on canvas
Öl auf Leinwand
Olieverf op doek

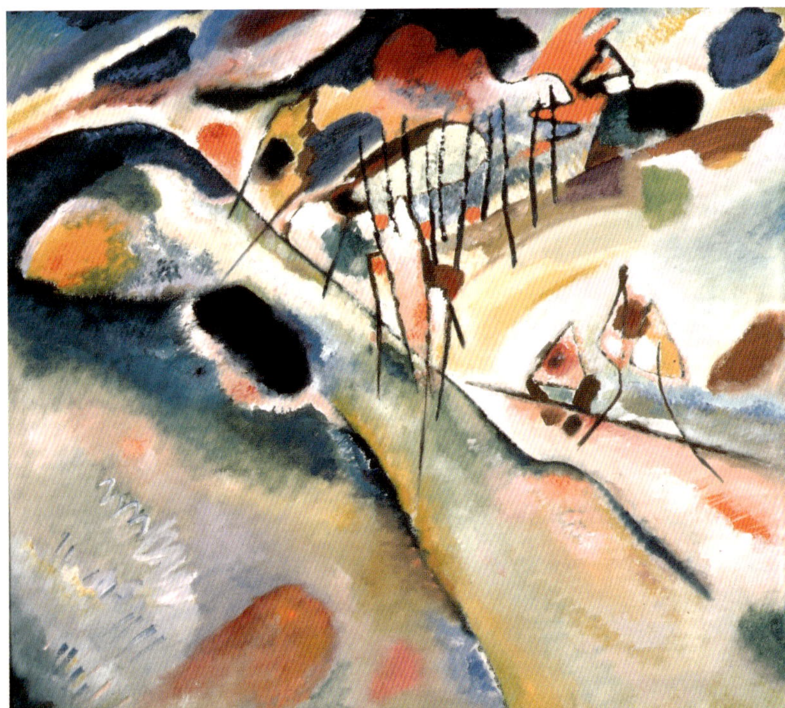

Vasilij Kandinskij
(Moscow 1866 - Neuilly-sur-Seine 1944)

Landscape
Landschaft
Landschap

●●

1913
88 x 100 cm / 34.64 x 39.37 in.
State Hermitage Museum, St. Petersburg

Oil on canvas
Öl auf Leinwand
Olieverf op doek

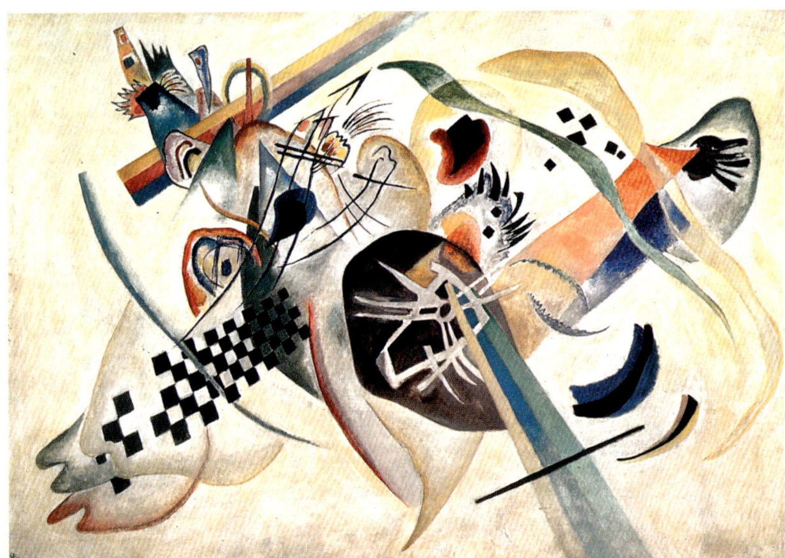

Vasilij Kandinskij
(Moscow 1866 - Neuilly-sur-Seine 1944)

On White
Auf Weiß
Op wit

●●

1920
80 x 73 cm / 31.5 x 28.7 in.
Russian Museum, St. Petersburg

Oil on wood
Öl auf Tafel
Olieverf op paneel

From expression
to abstraction.

Von der Expression
zur Abstraktion.

Van expressie
naar abstractie.

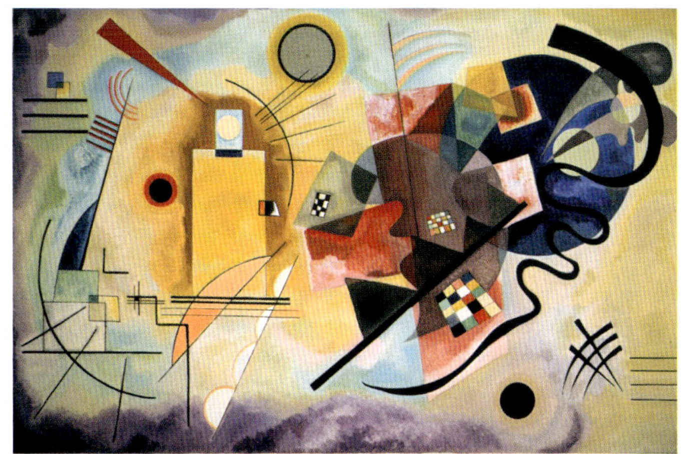

Vasilij Kandinskij
(Moscow 1866 - Neuilly-sur-Seine 1944)

Yellow, Red, Blue
Gelb, Rot, Blau
Geel, rood, blauw

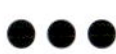

1925
128 x 210 cm / 50.4 x 82.7 in.
Musée National d'Art Moderne - Centre Pompidou, Paris

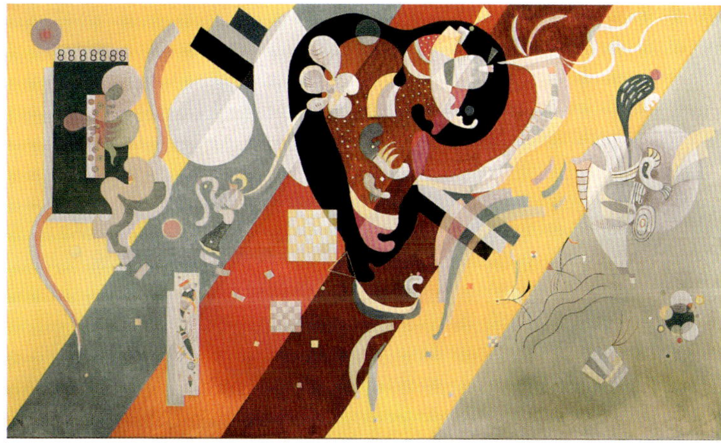

455

Vasilij Kandinskij
(Moscow 1866 - Neuilly-sur-Seine 1944)

Composition IX
Komposition IX
Compositie 19

1936
113,5 x 195 cm / 44.68 x 76.77 in.
Musée National d'Art Moderne - Centre Pompidou, Paris

Oil on canvas / Öl auf Leinwand / Olieverf op doek

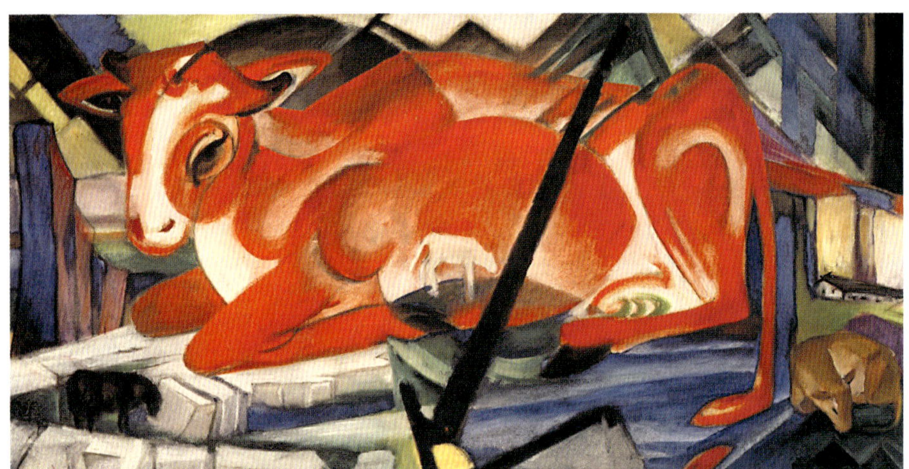

Franz Marc
(München 1880 - Verdun, Frankreich 1916)

The World Cow
Die Weltenkuh
De Wereldkoe

●●

1913
70.7 x 141.3 cm / 27.83 x 55.62 in.
Museum of Modern Art (MoMA), New York

Oil on canvas
Öl auf Leinwand
Olieverf op doek

Paul Klee
(Münchenbuchsee, Bern 1879 - Muralto 1940)

Static-Dynamic Gradation
Statisch-dynamische Farbenabstufung
Statische-Dynamische Gradatie

●

1923
38,1 x 26,1 cm / 15 x 10.27 in.
Metropolitan Museum of Art, New York

Oil and gouache on paper
Öl und Gouache auf Papier
Olieverf en gouache op papier

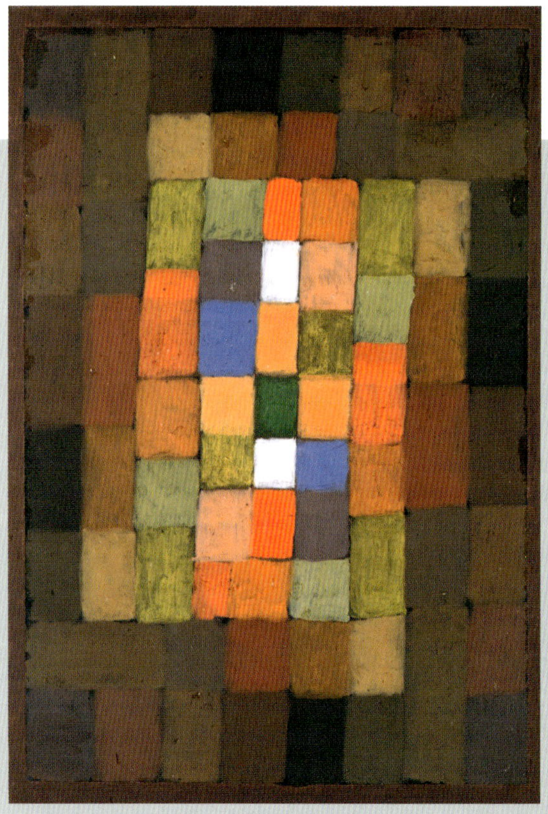

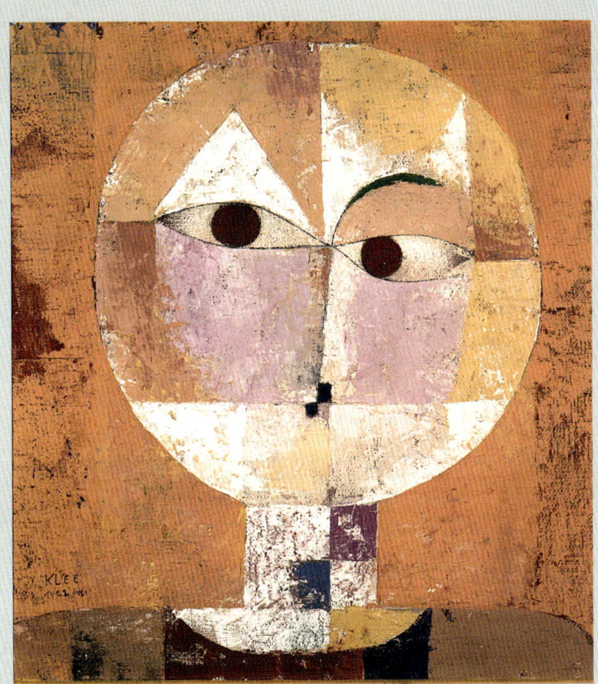

Paul Klee
(Münchenbuchsee, Bern 1879 - Muralto 1940)

Senecio
Baldgreis (Senecio)
Senecio (Oude man)

●●

1922
40,5 x 38 cm / 15.94 x 14.96 in.
Kunsthalle, Basel

Oil on canvas / Öl auf Leinwand / Olieverf op doek

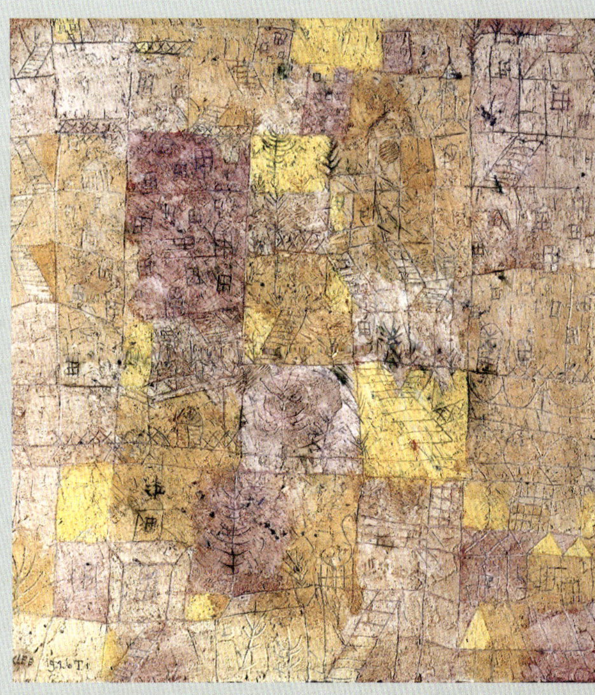

Paul Klee
(Münchenbuchsee, Bern 1879 - Muralto 1940)

Garden City Idyll
Idylle einer Gartenstadt
Tuinstad idylle

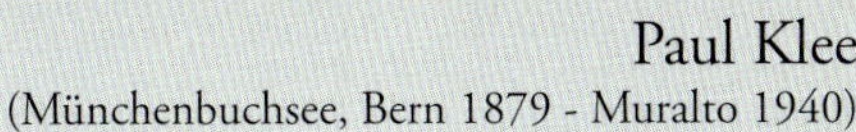

●●

1926
Kunsthalle, Basel

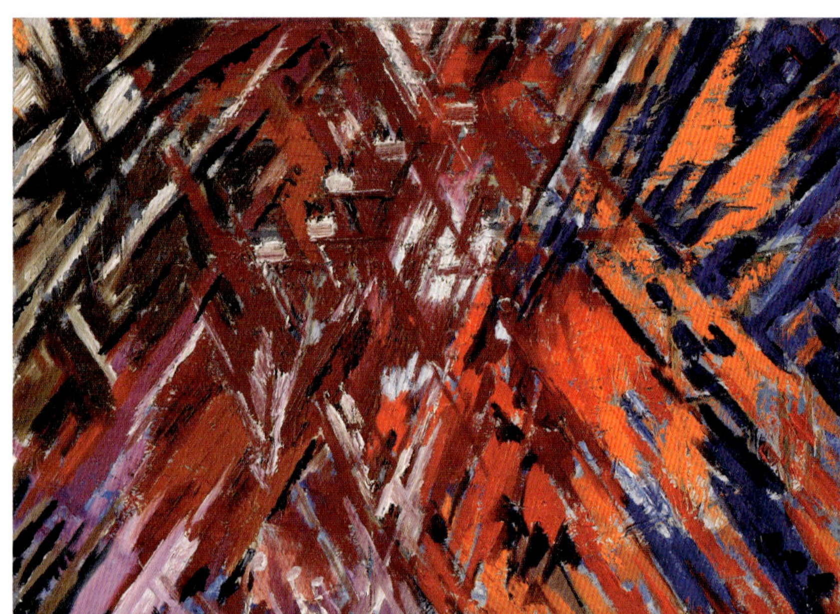

Michel Larionov
(1881-1964)

Domination of red
Dominierendes Rot
Dominantie van rood

●

1911
52,7 x 72,4 cm / 20.74 x 28.50 in.
Museum of Modern Art (MoMA), New York

Oil on canvas
Öl auf Leinwand
Olieverf op doek

László Moholy-Nagy
(Bàcs-Borsod 1895 - Chicago 1946)

Q 1 Suprematistic

●

1923
95,2 x 95,2 cm / 37.48 x 37.48 in.
Museum of Modern Art (MoMA), New York

Oil on canvas
Öl auf Leinwand
Olieverf op doek

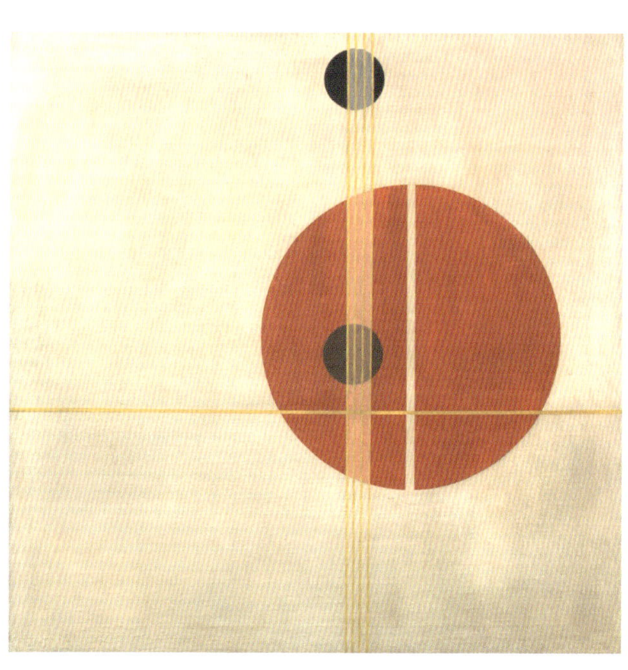

Kazimir Malevič
(Kiev 1878 - Saint Petersburg 1935)

Black square
Schwarzes Quadrat
Zwart vierkant

●●●

c. 1923
106 x 106 cm / 41.73 x 41.73 in.
Russian State Museum,
St. Petersburg

Oil on canvas
Öl auf Leinwand
Olieverf op doek

Malevič conceives the black square as the purest dominating form of figurative art.

Malevič sieht im schwarzen Quadrat die Suprematie (Vorherrschaft) der reinen Form in der bildenen Kunst.

Malevič ziet in het zwarte vierkant de suprematie (oppergezag) van de pure vorm in de figuratieve kunst.

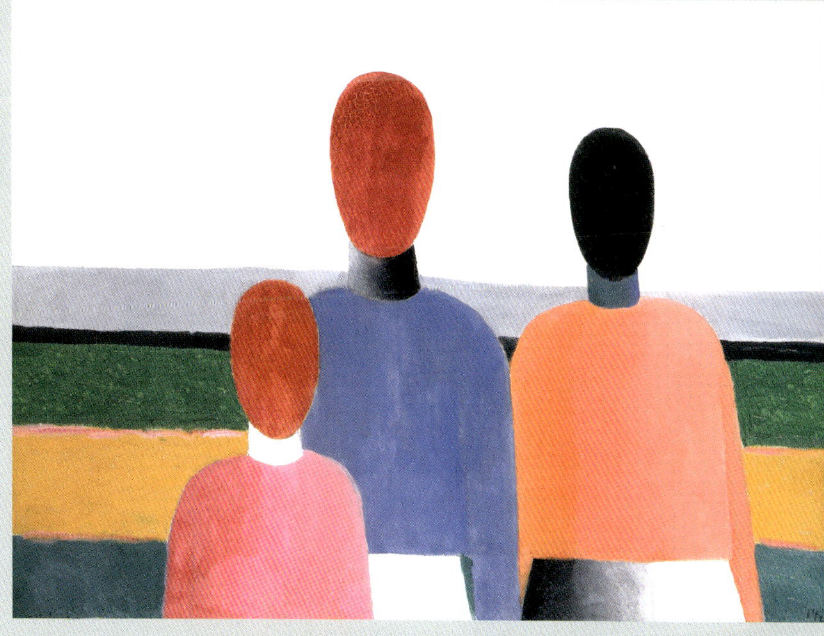

Kazimir Malevič
(Kiev 1878 - Saint Petersburg 1935)

Three female figures
Drei Frauen
Drie vrouwenfiguren

●●●

c. 1928
47 x 63,5 cm / 18.50 x 25 in.
Russian State Museum,
St. Petersburg

Oil on canvas
Öl auf Leinwand
Olieverf op doek

Alexander Rodchenko
(St. Petersburg 1891 - Moscow 1958)

Advertisement: "Books!"
Plakat: "Bücher!"
Advertentie: "Boeken!"

●●●

1925
Rodchenko Archives, Moscow

Print / Druck / Prent

Avant-garde artists are enthusiastic about the Russian Revolution.

Avantgarde Künstler begeistern sich für die russische Revolution.

Kunstenaars van de avant-garde zijn enthousiast over de Russische revolutie.

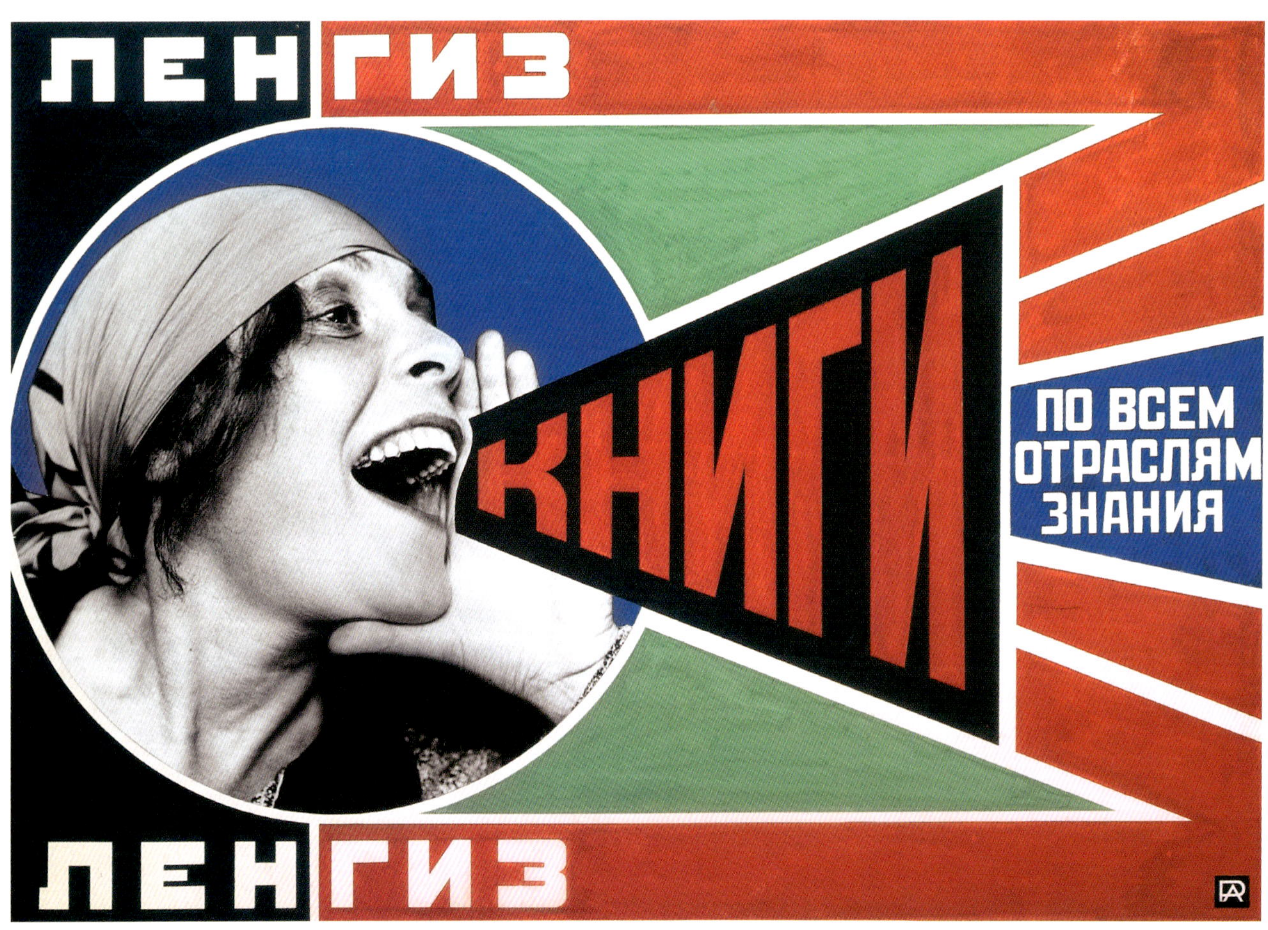

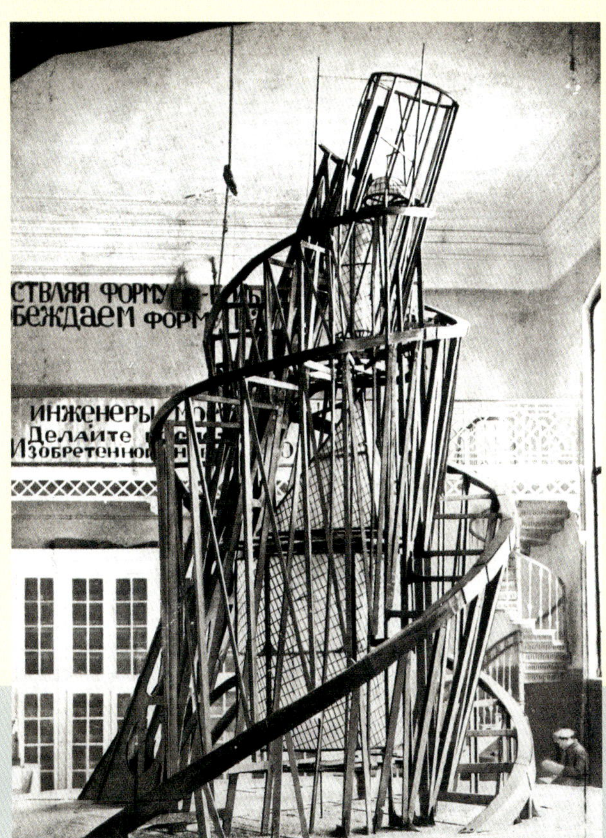

Vladimir Tatlin
(Kharkhov 1885 - Moscow 1953)

Model of the Monument to the Third International
Modell vom Monument der Dritten Internationalen
Een model voor het Monument voor de Derde Internationale

●●●

1920
Museum of Modern Art (MoMA), New York

Various materials / Verschiedene Materialien / Verschillende materialen

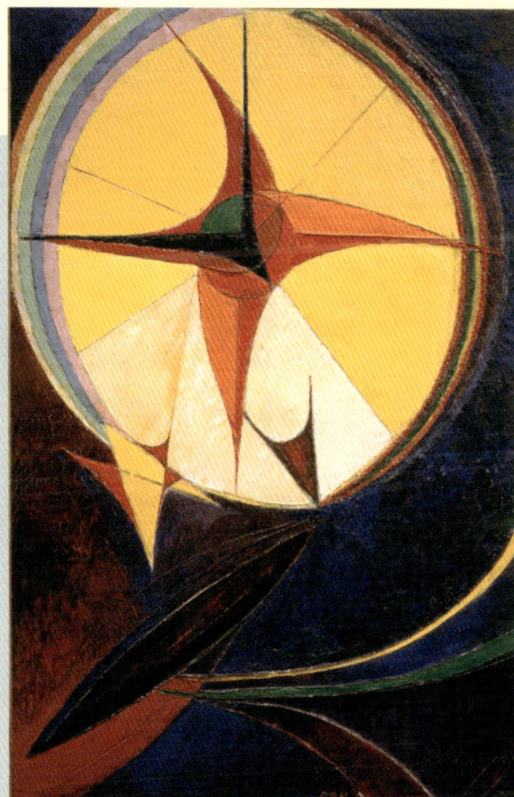

Anton Pevsner
(Orel 1886 - Paris 1962)

A Meeting of Planets
Begegnung der Planeten
Ontmoeting van de planeten

●

1961
Musée National d'Art Moderne - Centre Pompidou, Paris

Oil on canvas
Öl auf Leinwand
Olieverf op doek

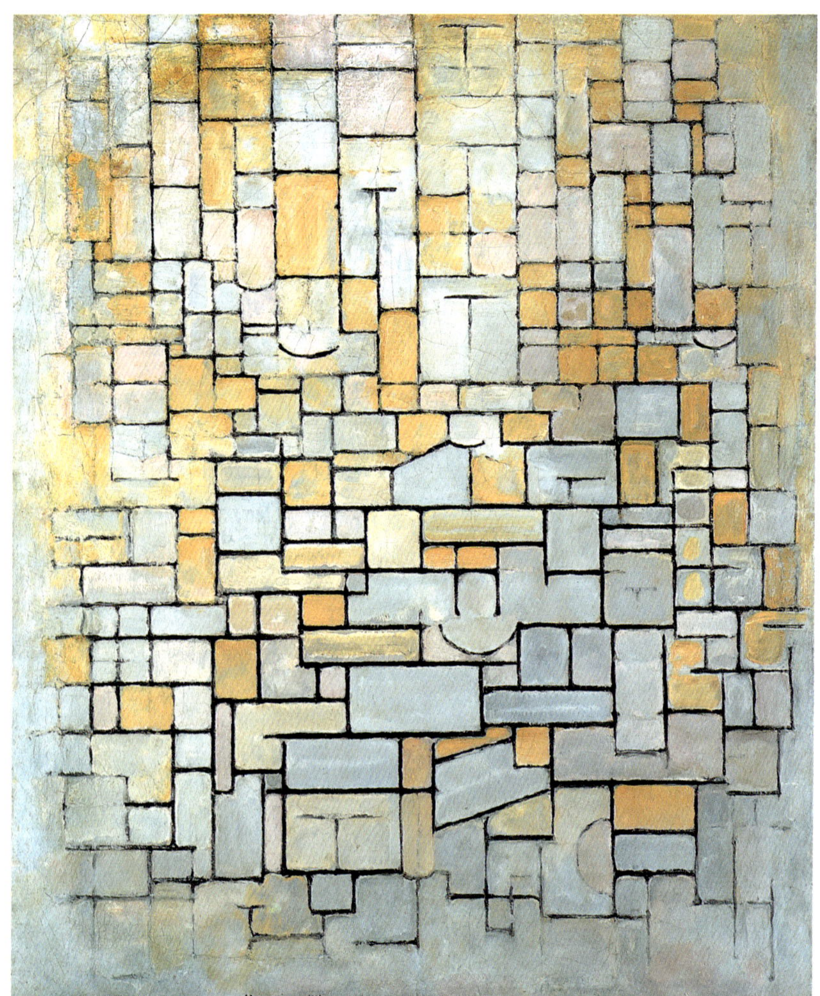

Piet Mondrian reduces his paintings to primary colors and the absence of color (black and white), lines and right angles.

Piet Mondrian reduziert die Malerei auf die Grundfarben,die Nichtfarben (schwarz und weiß), Geraden und rechte Winkel.

Piet Mondriaan reduceert de schilderkunst tot primaire kleuren, non-kleuren (zwart en wit), de lijn en de rechte hoek.

Piet Mondrian
(Amersfoort 1872 - New York 1944)
Tableau No. 1 / Composition No. 1 / Compositie 7, 1914
●●
119 x 101 cm / 47 x 40 in.
Kimbell Art Museum, Fort Worth, Texas

Oil on canvas / Öl auf Leinwand
Olieverf op doek

Piet Mondrian
(Amersfoort 1872 - New York 1944)
Tableau 3, with Orange-Red, Yellow, Black, Blue and Grey, 1921
Tableau 3, mit Orange-Rot, Gelb, Schwarz, Blau und Grau, 1921
Tableau 3, met oranje-rood, geel, zwart, blauw en grijs, 1921
●●●
49,5 x 41,5 cm / 19.5 x 16.3
Kunsthalle Basel, Basel

Oil on canvas / Öl auf Leinwand
Olieverf op doek

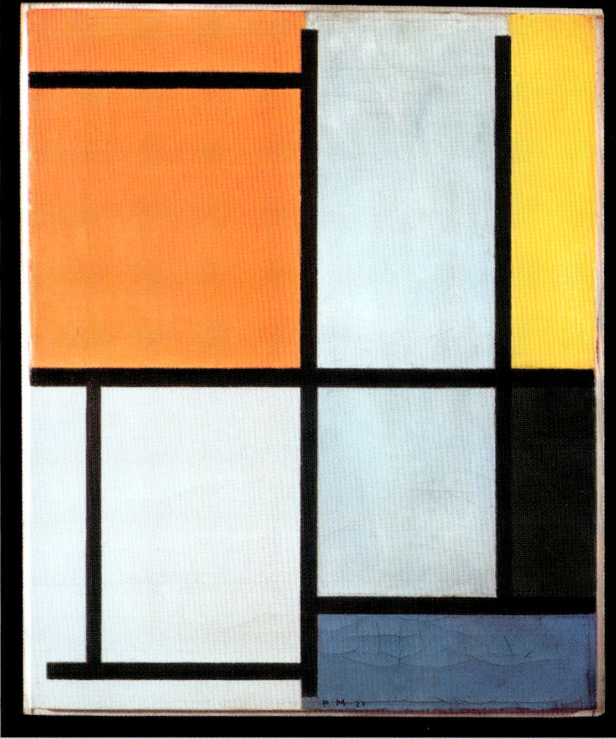

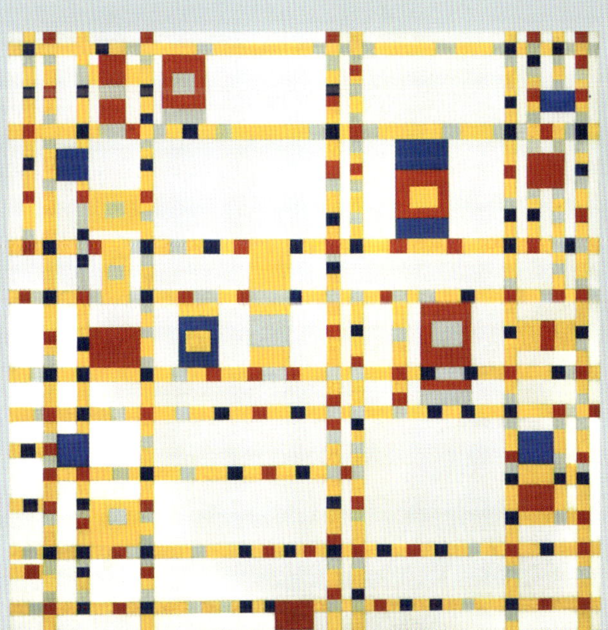

Piet Mondrian
(Amersfoort 1872 - New York 1944)
Broadway Boogie Woogie, 1942-1943
●●
127 x 127 cm / 50 x 50 in.
Museum of Modern Art (MoMA), New York

Oil on canvas / Öl auf Leinwand
Olieverf op doek

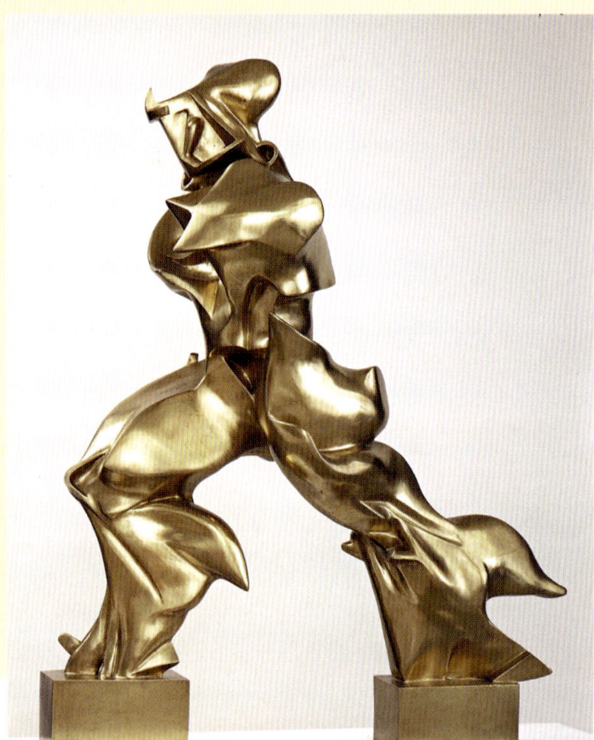

Umberto Boccioni
(Reggio Calabria 1882 - Verona 1916)

Unique Forms of Continuity in Space
Einzigartige Formen in der Kontinuität im Raum
Unieke vormen van de continuïteit in de ruimte

●●

1913
h. 111,2 cm / 42.77 in.
Museum of Modern Art (MoMA), New York

Bronze / Brons

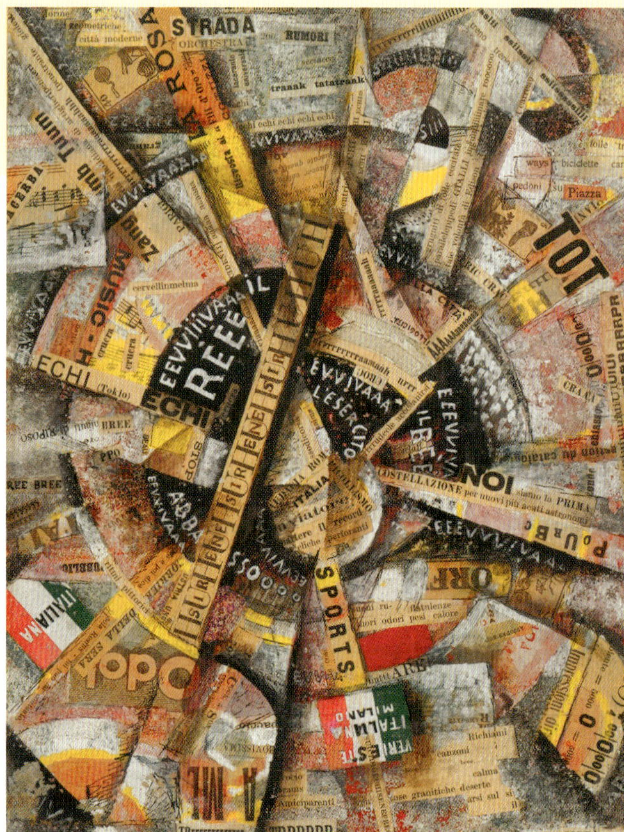

Carlo Carrà
(Quargnento, Alessandria 1881 - Milano 1966)

Interventist Demonstration
Interventionistische Manifestation
Interventionistische demonstratie

●

1914
38,5 x 30 cm / 15.15 x 11.81 in.
Private collection
Privatsammlung
Privécollectie

Collage on cardboard
Collage auf Karton
Collage op karton

Futurism and metaphysical painting: movement against statics, two important styles of early Italian modern art.

Futurismus und Pittura Metafisica (Metaphysische Malerei), Bewegung gegen Statik, zwei Hauptstile der frühen italienischen Moderne.

Het futurisme en de metafysische schilderkunst, beweging tegen de stabiliteit, zijn twee hoofdstijlen van de eerste moderne Italiaanse kunst.

Giorgio de Chirico
(Volo 1888 - Roma 1978)

The Disturbing Muses
Die beunruhigenden Musen
De verontrustende muzen

●●●

1916
97 x 66 cm / 38.18 x 25.98 in.
Private collection
Privatsammlung
Privécollectie

Oil on canvas
Öl auf Leinwand
Olieverf op doek

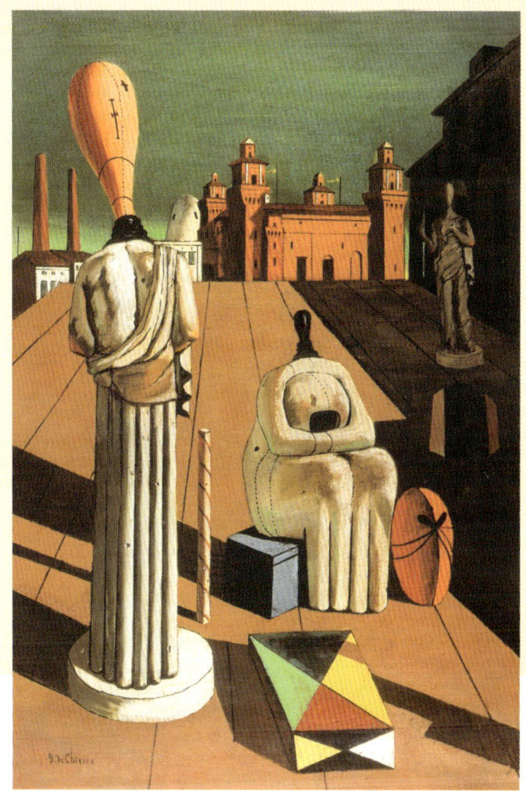

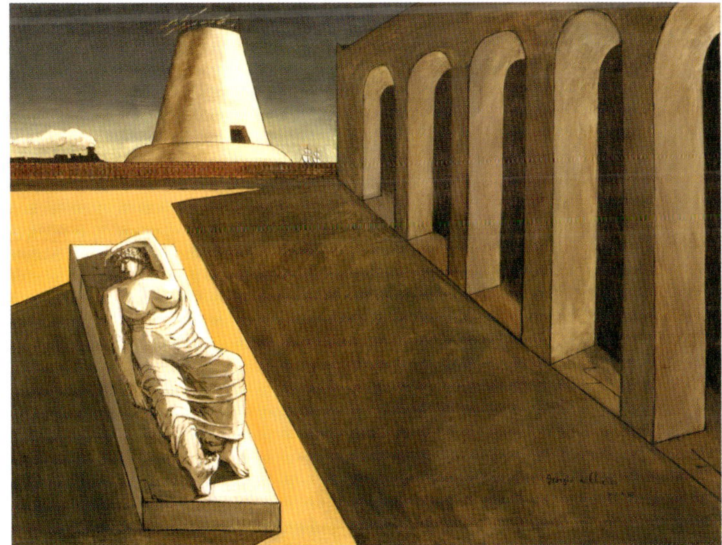

Giorgio de Chirico
(Volo 1888 - Roma 1978)

Arianna
Ariadne

●

1913
135,6 x 180,3 cm / 53.38 x 70.98 in.
Metropolitan Museum of Art, New York

Oil and graphite on canvas
Öl und Graphit auf Leinwand
Olieverf en grafiet op doek

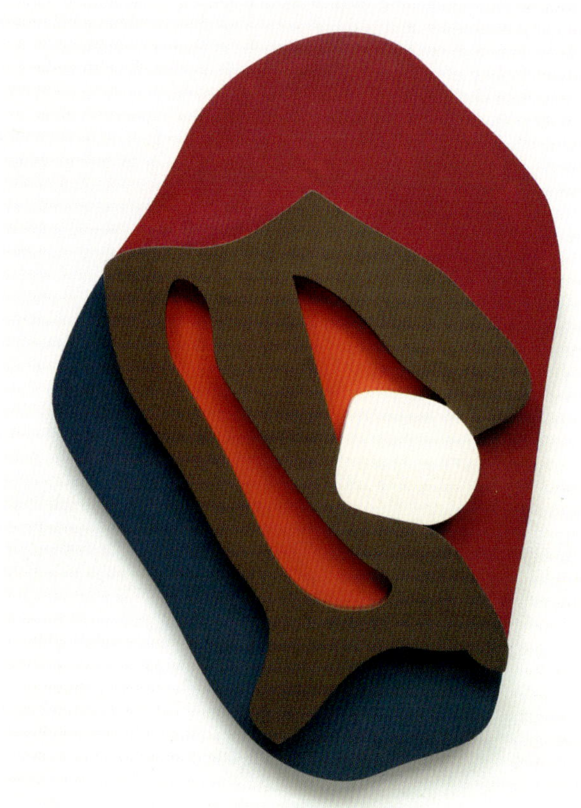

Hans Arp
(Strasbourg 1886 - Bâle 1966)

Enak's Tears (Terrestrial Forms)
Irdische Formen
Aardse vormen

●

1917
86,2 x 58,5 cm / 33.93 x 23.03 in.
Museum of Modern Art (MoMA), New York

Painted wood
Bemaltes Holz
Beschilderd hout

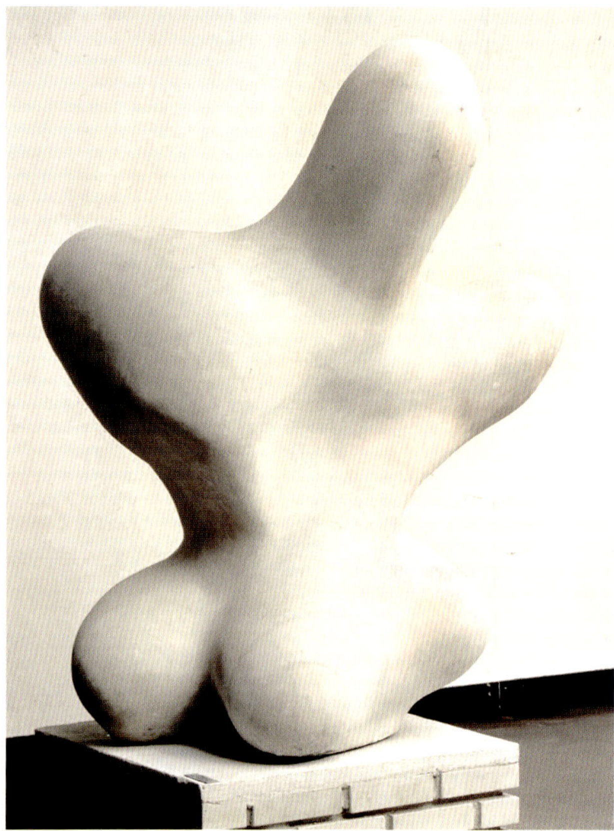

Hans Arp
(Strasbourg 1886 - Bâle 1966)

Giant Pip
Le Pepin Geant
Grote Pip

1937
162 x 127 x 77 cm / 63.7 x 49.9 x 30.3 in.
Musée National d'Art Moderne - Centre Pompidou, Paris

Marble / Marmor / Marmer

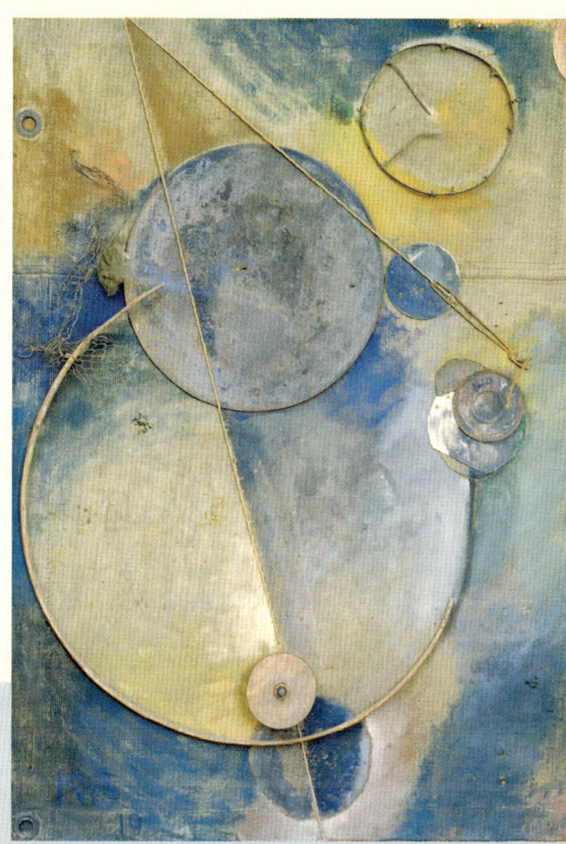

Kurt Schwitters
(Hannover 1887 - Ambleside 1948)

Revolving
Das Kreisen
Draaiing (Das Kreisen)

●

1919
122,7 x 88,7 cm / 48.30 x 34.92 in.
Museum of Modern Art (MoMA), New York

Relief with various materials
Relief aus verschiedenen Materialien
Reliëf met verschillende materialen

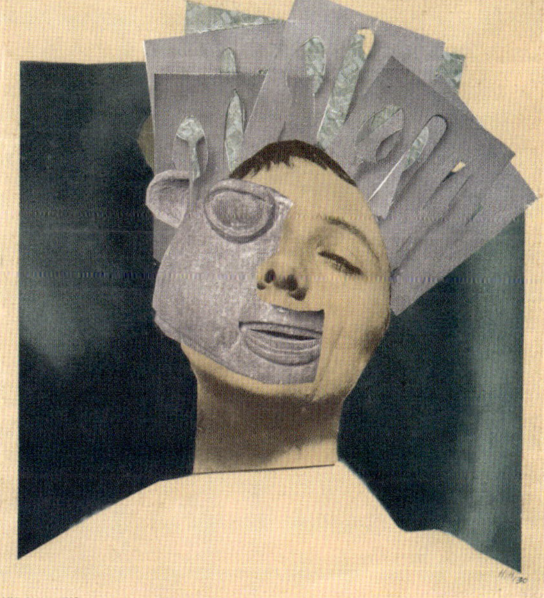

Hannah Höch
(1889 - 1978)

Indian Dancer
Indische Tänzerin
Indiase danseres

●

1930
25,7 x 22,4 cm / 10.11 x 8.81 in.
Museum of Modern Art (MoMA), New York

Various materials
Verschiedene Materialien
Verschillende materialen

Dada: derision of middle class obtusity.

Verspottung bürgerlicher Borniertheit: Dadaismus.

Dadaïsme: bespotting van burgerlijke bekrompenheid.

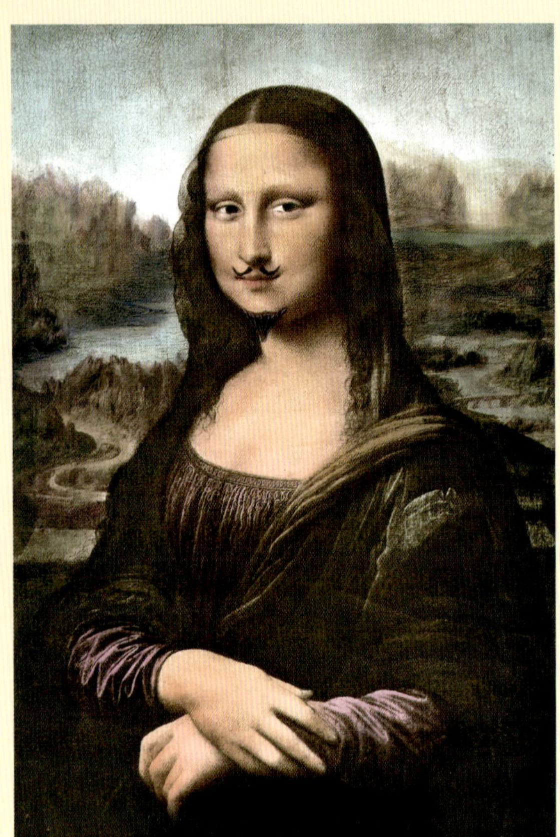

Marcel Duchamp
(Blainville-Crevon 1887 - Neuilly-sur-Seine 1968)

L.H.O.O.Q.

●●●

1919
19,7 x 12,4 cm / 7.75 x 4.88 in.
Private collection
Privatsammlung
Privécollectie

Print / Druck / Prent

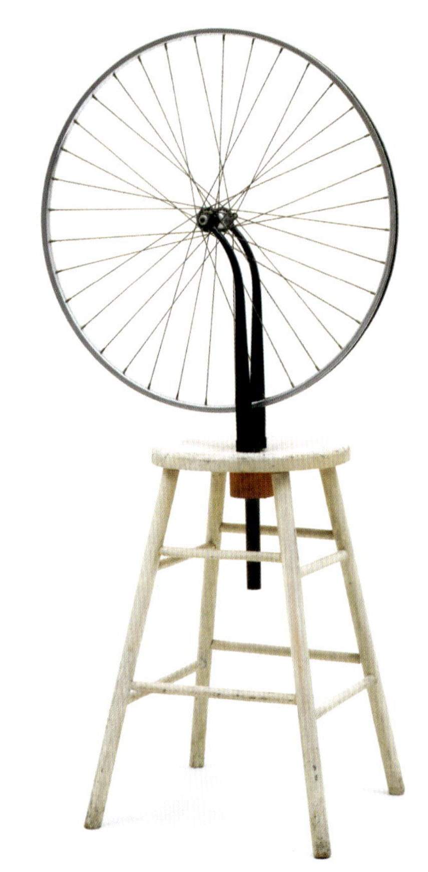

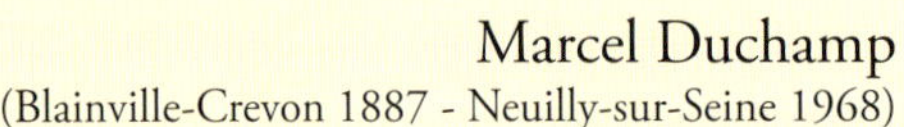

Marcel Duchamp
(Blainville-Crevon 1887 - Neuilly-sur-Seine 1968)

Bicycle Wheel
Fahrrad-Rad
Fietswiel

●●●

1951
h. 128,3 cm / 50.51 in.
Museum of Modern Art (MoMA), New York

Assemblage / Ready-made

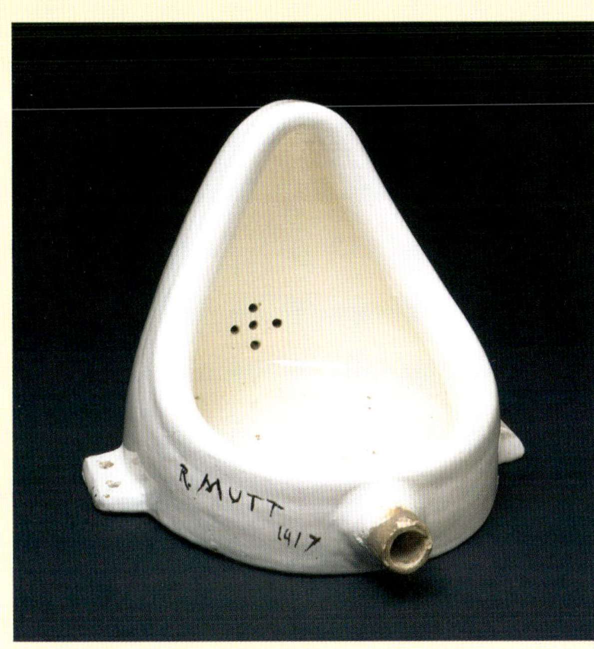

Marcel Duchamp
(Blainville-Crevon 1887 - Neuilly-sur-Seine 1968)

Fountain

1950
h. 60 cm / 23.62 in.
Philadelphia Museum of Art, Philadelphia

Porcelain / Porzellan / Porselein

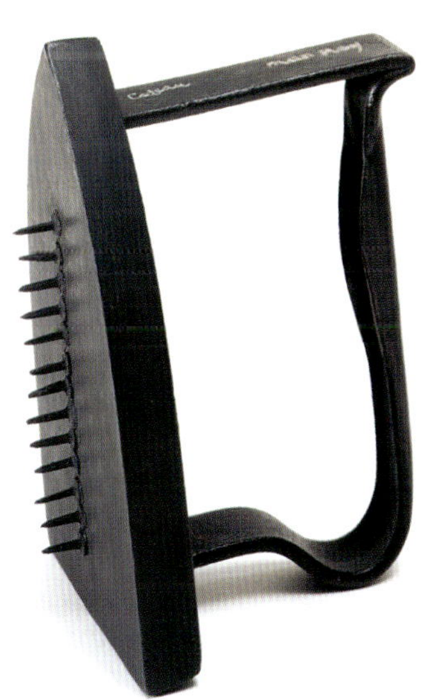

Man Ray
(Philadelphia 1890 - Paris 1976)

Gift
Cadeau

●●

c. 1958
15,3 x 9 x 11,4 cm / 6 x 3 x 4 in.
Museum of Modern Art (MoMA), New York

A painted iron
Bemaltes Bügeleisen
Beschilderd strijkijzer

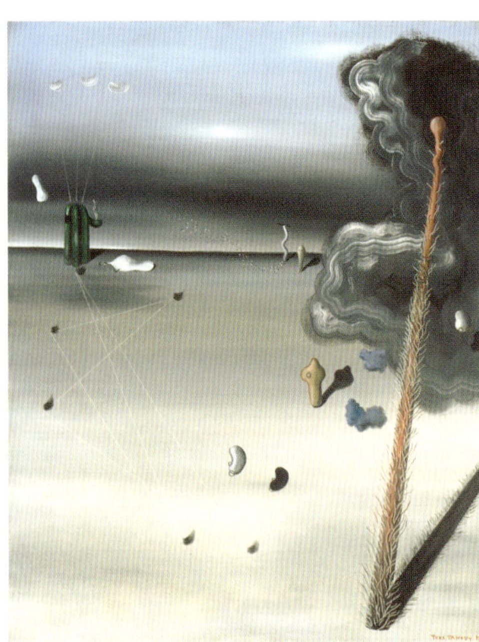

Yves Tanguy
(Paris 1900 - Woodbury 1955)

Mama, Papa is Wounded!
Mama, Papa ist verletzt!
Mama, papa is gewond!

●●

1927
92,1 x 73 cm / 36.25 x 28.74 in.
Museum of Modern Art (MoMA), New York

Oil on canvas
Öl auf Leinwand
Olieverf op doek

Max Ernst
(Brühl, Rheinland 1891 - Paris 1976)

Chimera
Chimäre
Chimaera

●

1928
Musée National d'Art Moderne - Centre Pompidou, Paris

Oil on canvas
Öl auf Leinwand
Olieverf op doek

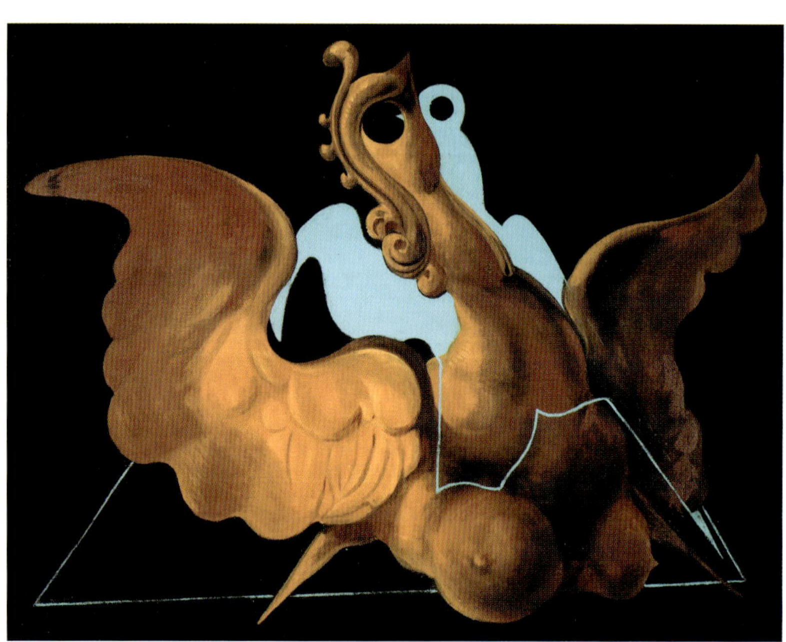

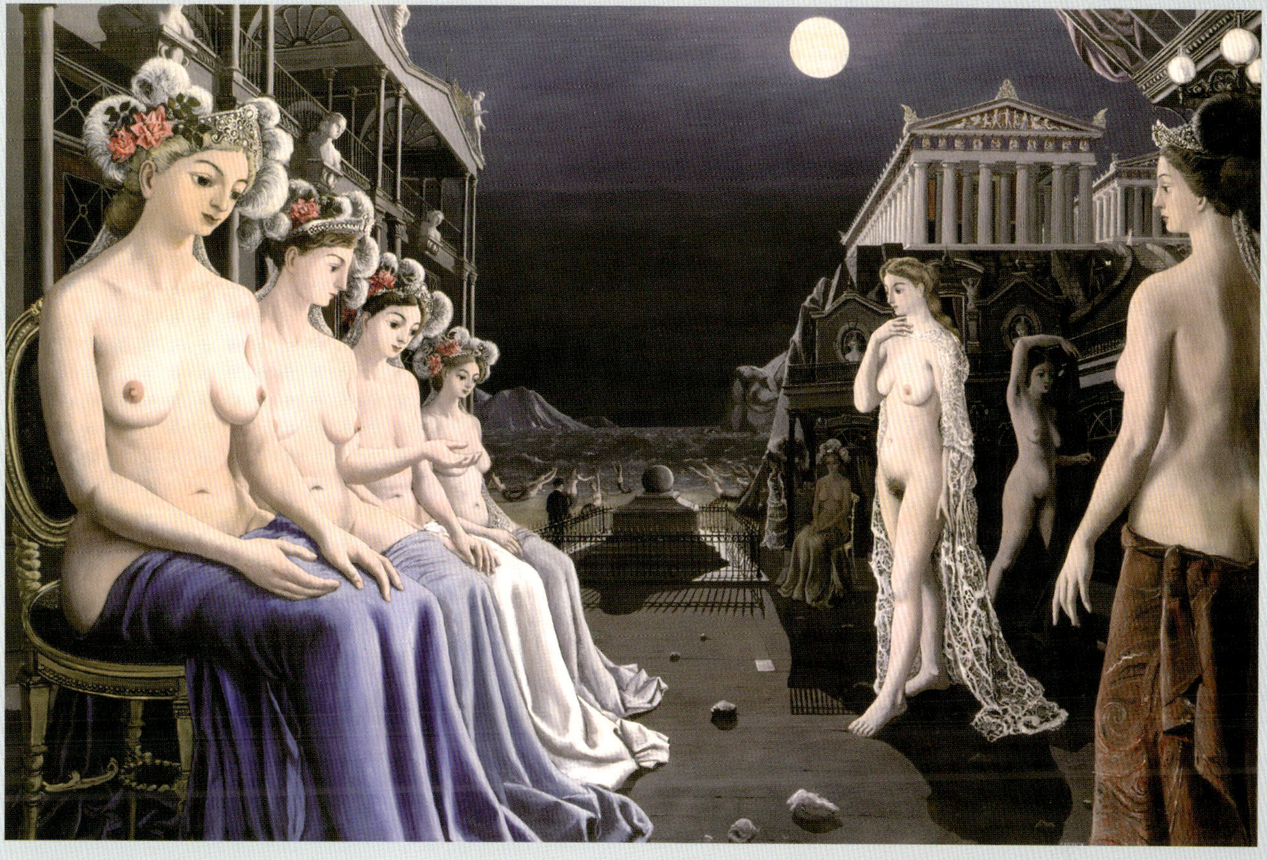

Paul Delvaux
(Antheit 1897 - Furnes 1994)

The Great Sirens
Die großen Sirenen
De grote sirenen

1947
203 x 305 cm / 79.92 x 120.07 in.
Metropolitan Museum of Art,
New York

Oil on canvas
Öl auf Leinwand
Olieverf op doek

The unofficial motto of the Surrealists: As beautiful as the casual meeting of an umbrella with a sewing machine on a morgue table.

"Schön wie die zufällige Begegnung eines Regenschirms und einer Nähmaschine auf einem Seziertisch", das inoffizielle Motto der Surrealisten.

Het onofficiële motto van de surrealisten: "Mooi als de toevallige ontmoeting van een paraplu en een naaimachine op de ontleedtafel".

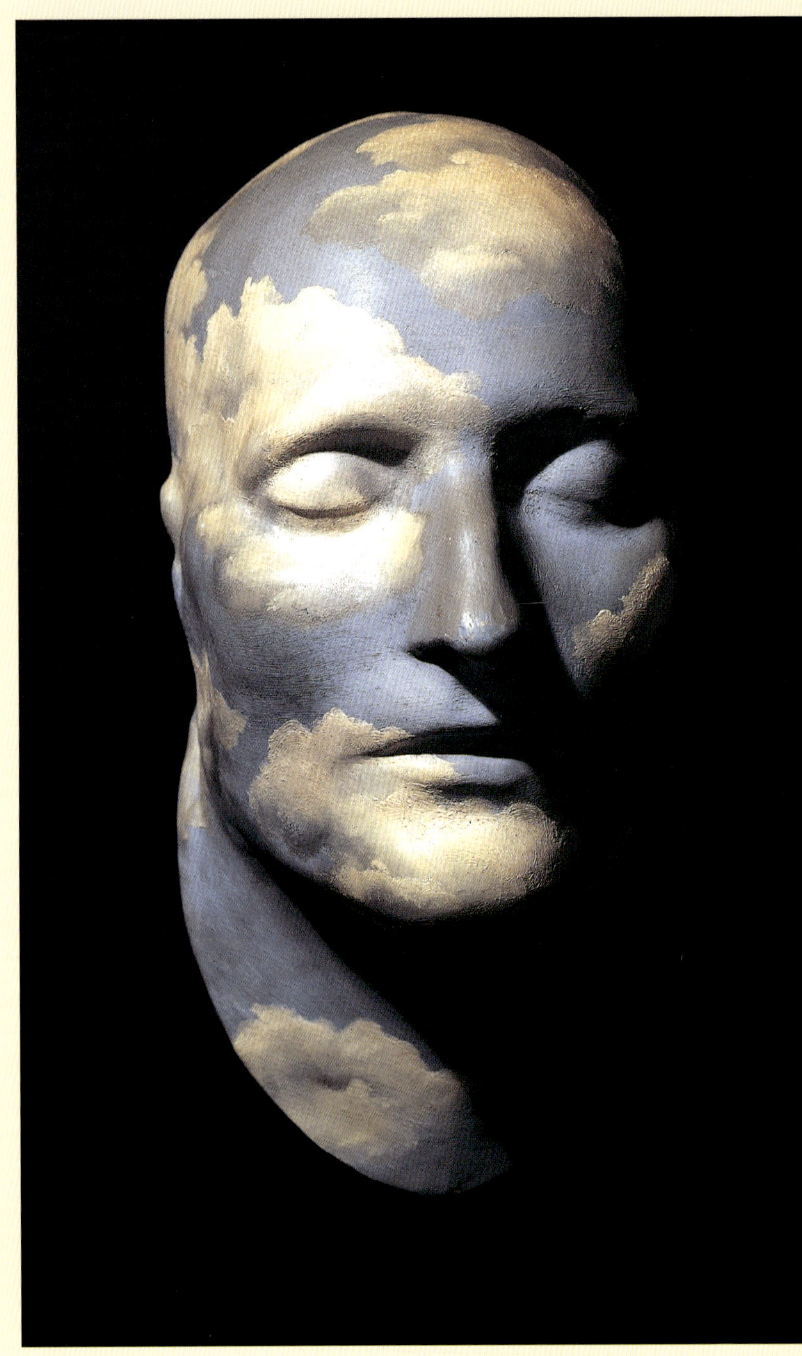

Alienation induced by an unreal composition, a title often impossible to deduce from the contents: René Magritte is the intellectual of the Surrealists.

Verfremdung durch unwirkliche Zusammenstellung, aus dem Bildinhalt häufig nicht ableitbare Bildtitel: René Magritte ist der Intellektuelle unter den Surrealisten.

Vervreemding door een onwerkelijke compositie, de titel van het schilderij is vaak niet af te leiden van de inhoud: René Magritte is de intellectueel van de surrealisten.

René Magritte
(Lessines 1898 - Bruxelles 1967)

The Future of Statues
L'avenir des statues
De toekomst der standbeelden

●

1932
h. 32 cm / 12.59 in.
Wilhelm Lehmbruck Museum, Duisburg

Oil on plaster
Öl auf Gips
Olieverf op gips

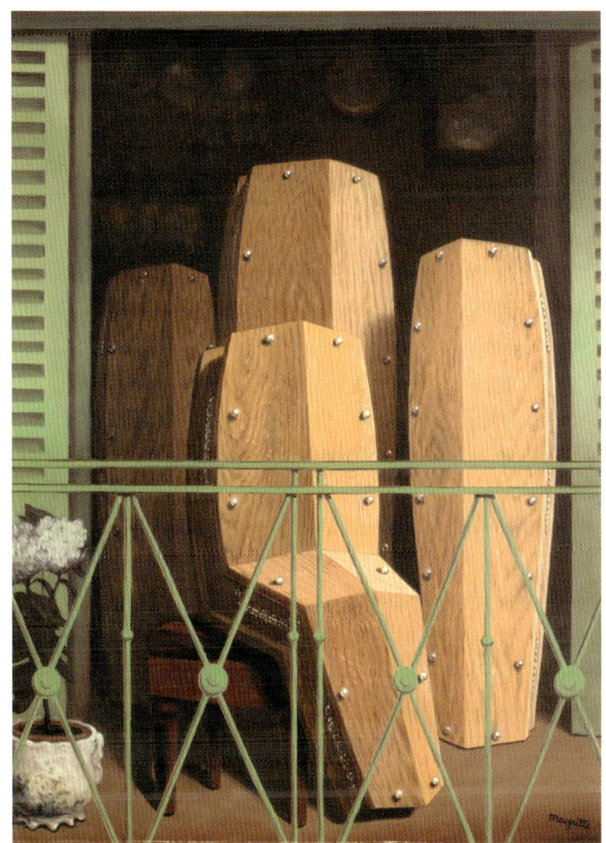

René Magritte
(Lessines 1898 - Bruxelles 1967)

Perspective II. Manet's Balcony
Perspektive II. Der Balkon von Manet
Perspectief II. Balkon van Manet

●●

1950
80 x 60 cm / 31.49 x 23.62 in.
Museum voor Schone Kunsten, Gand

Oil on canvas / Öl auf Leinwand / Olieverf op doek

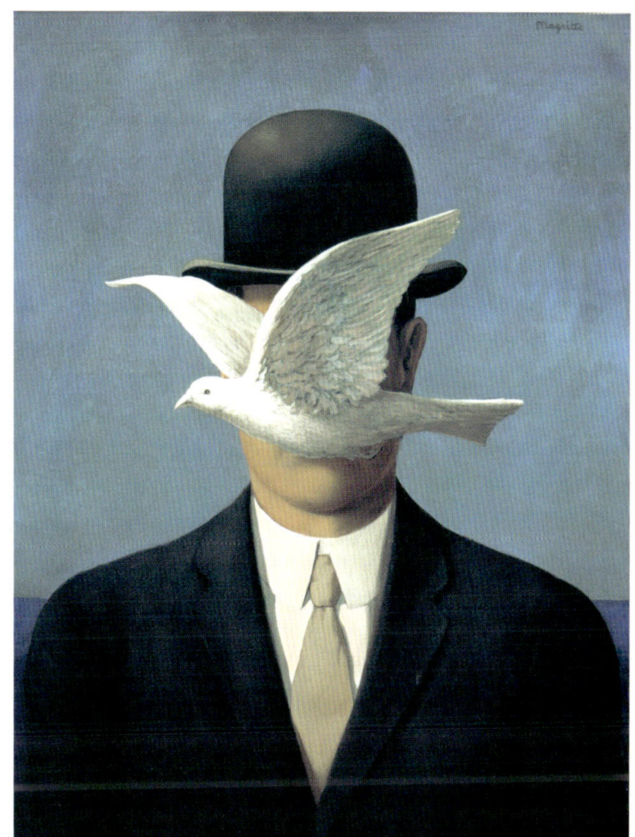

René Magritte
(Lessines 1898 - Bruxelles 1967)

Man in Bowler Hat
Der Mann mit der Melone
Man met bolhoed

●●●

Private collection / Privatsammlung / Privécollectie

Oil on canvas / Öl auf Leinwand / Olieverf op doek

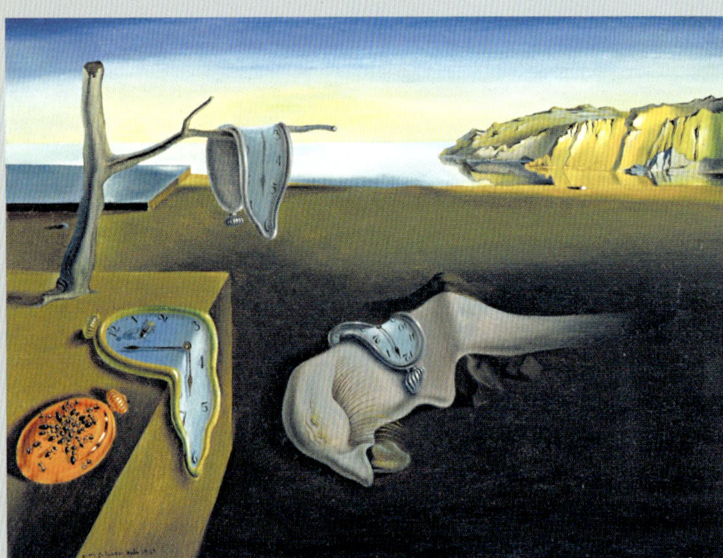

Salvador Dalí
(Figueres 1904 - 1989)

The Persistence of Memory
Die Beständigkeit der Erinnerung
De volharding der herinnering

●●●

1931
24,1 x 33 cm / 9.48 x 13 in.
Museum of Modern Art (MoMA), New York

Oil on canvas
Öl auf Leinwand
Olieverf op doek

Salvador Dalí
(Figueres 1904 - 1989)

Soft Construction with Boiled Beans (Premonition of Civil War)
Konstruktion mit gekochten Bohnen (Vorahnung des Bürgerkriegs)
Weke constructie met gekookte bonen (Voorgevoel van de burgeroorlog)

●●

1936
99,9 x 100 cm / 39.33 x 39.34 in.
Philadelphia Museum of Art, Philadelphia

Oil on canvas / Öl auf Leinwand / Olieverf op doek

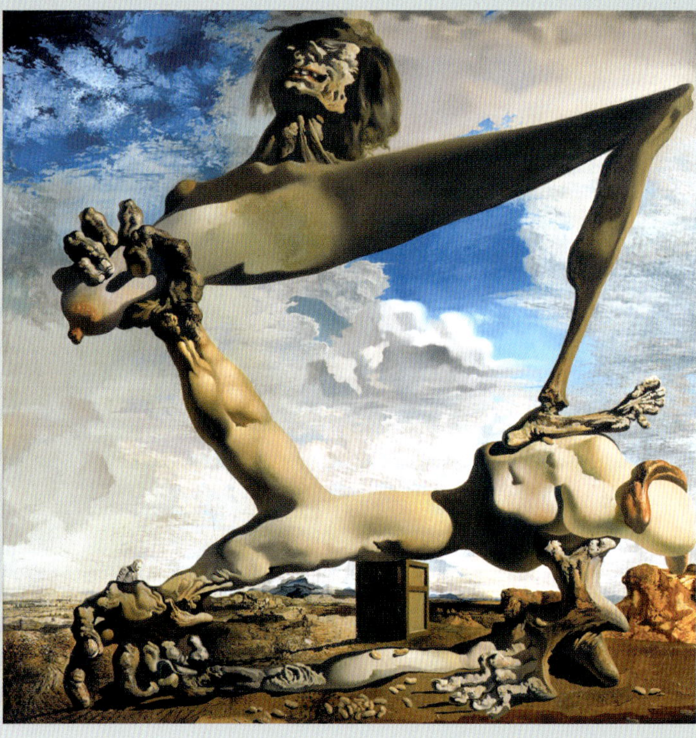

Painting with the "critical-paranoiac method".

Malen mit der "paranoisch-kritischen Methode".

Schilderen volgens de "paranoia-kritische methode".

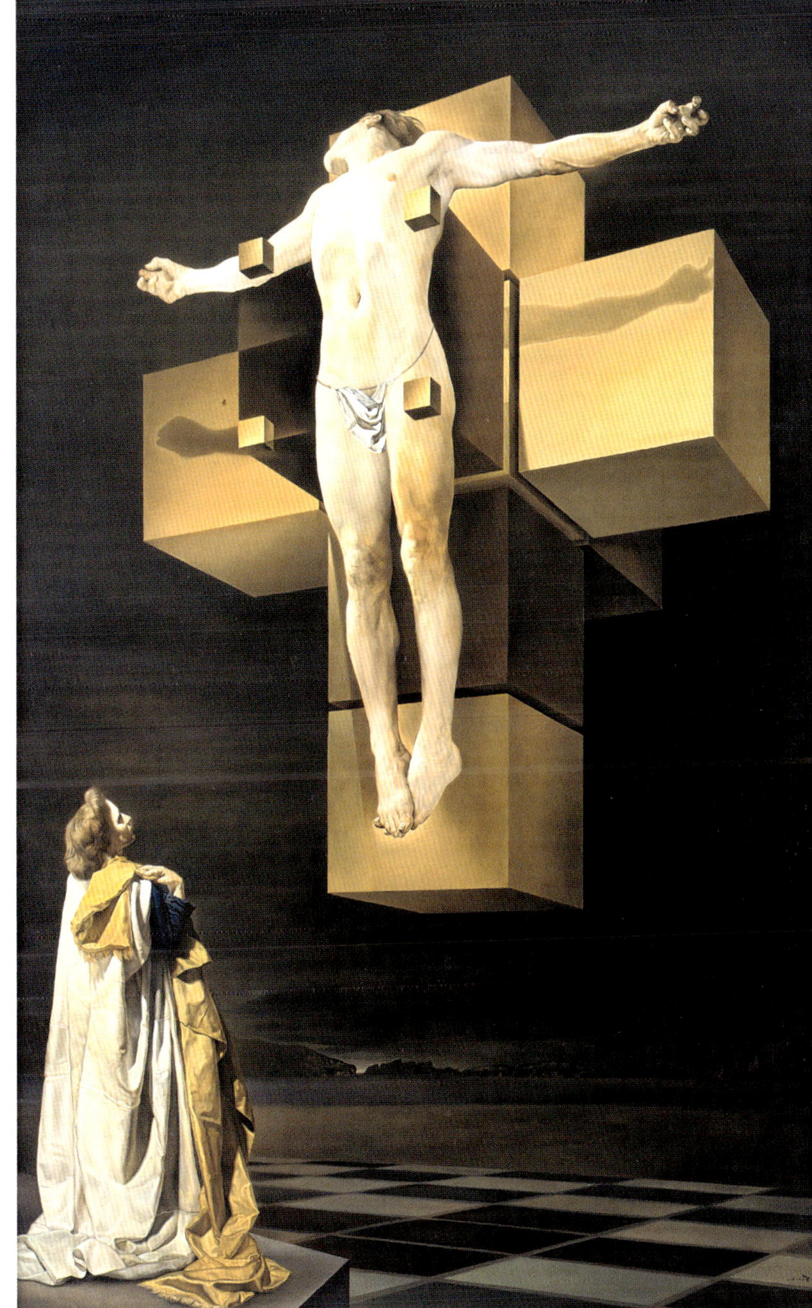

Salvador Dalí
(Figueres 1904 - 1989)

Crucifixion (Corpus Hypercubus)
Kreuzigung (Corpus Hypercubus)
Kruisiging (Corpus Hypercubus)

●●●

1954
Metropolitan Museum of Art, New York

Oil on canvas
Öl auf Leinwand
Olieverf op doek

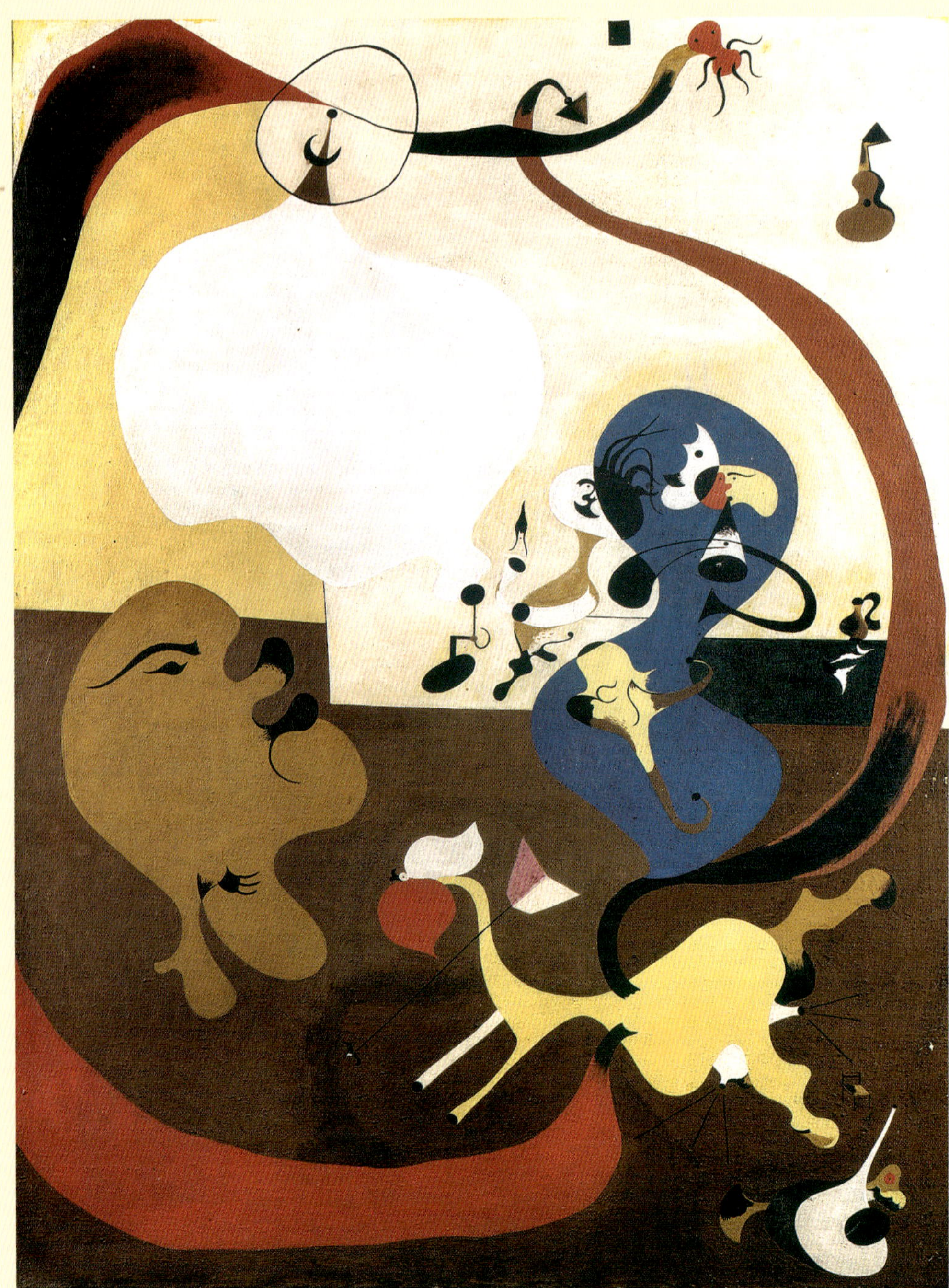

Composition of biomorphic forms that look like hieroglyphics.

Komposition aus biomorphen Formen die wie heitere Hieroglyphen wirken.

Compositie van biomorfe vormen die op vrolijke hiërogliefen lijken.

Joan Miró
(Barcelona 1893 - Palma de Mallorca 1983)

Dutch Interior II
Holländisches Interieur II
Hollands interieur II

●●●

1928
73 x 92 cm
28.74 x 36.22 in.
Collezione Peggy Guggenheim, Venezia

Oil on canvas
Öl auf Leinwand
Olieverf op doek

Joan Miró
(Barcelona 1893 - Palma de Mallorca 1983)

People in the Night
Personen in der Nacht
Personages in de nacht

●

1950
Zadok Collection, New York

Oil on canvas
Öl auf Leinwand
Olieverf op doek

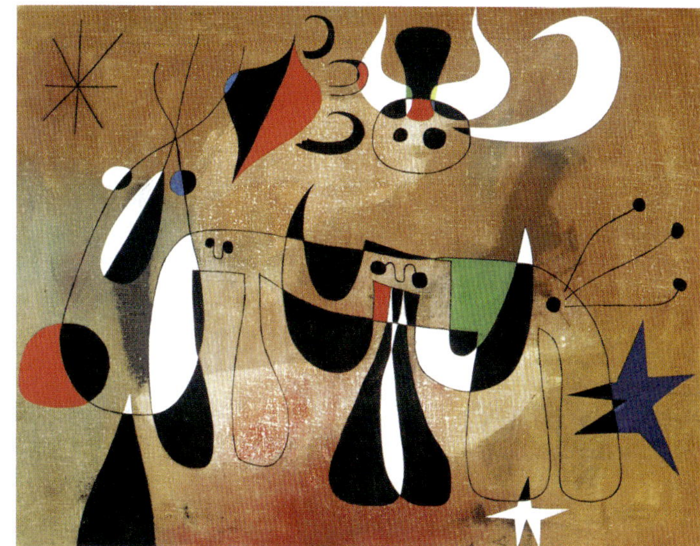

Joan Miró
(Barcelona 1893 - Palma de Mallorca 1983)

Mural Painting
Wandmalerei
Muurschildering

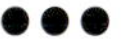

c. 1950-1951
188,8 x 593,8 cm / 74.73 x 233.77 in.
Museum of Modern Art (MoMA), New York

Oil on canvas
Öl auf Leinwand
Olieverf op doek

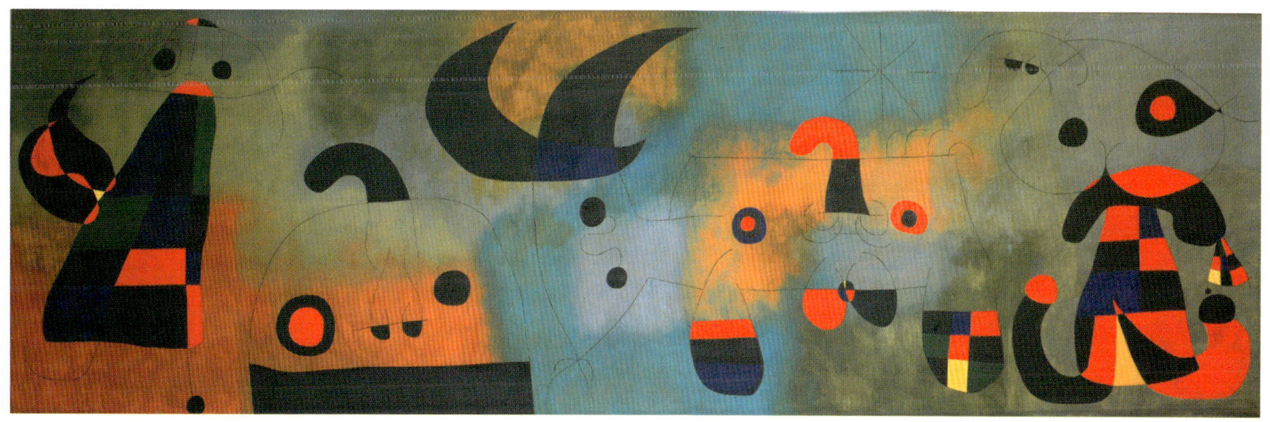

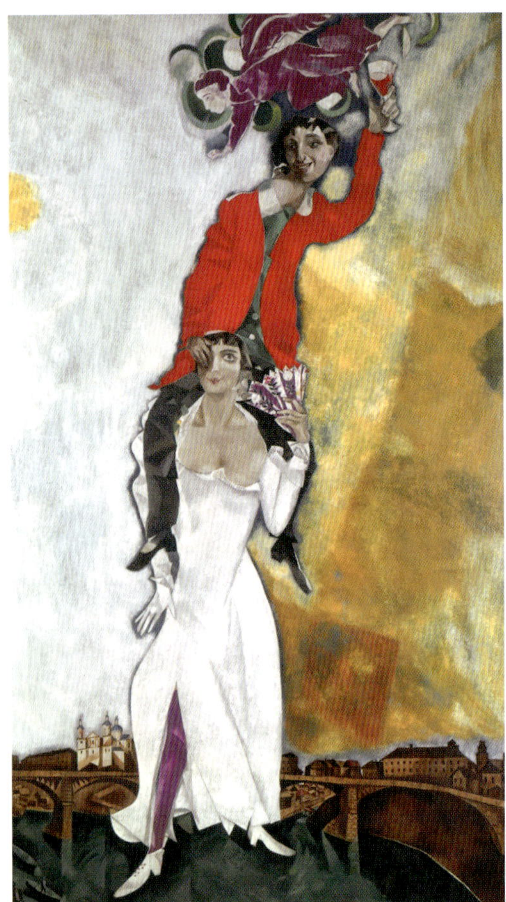

Marc Chagall
(Vitebsk 1887 - Saint-Paul de Vence 1985)

Double Portrait with a Glass of Wine
Doppelportrait auf Weinglas
Dubbelportret met glas wijn

●●●

1917-1918
Musée National d'Art Moderne - Centre Pompidou, Paris

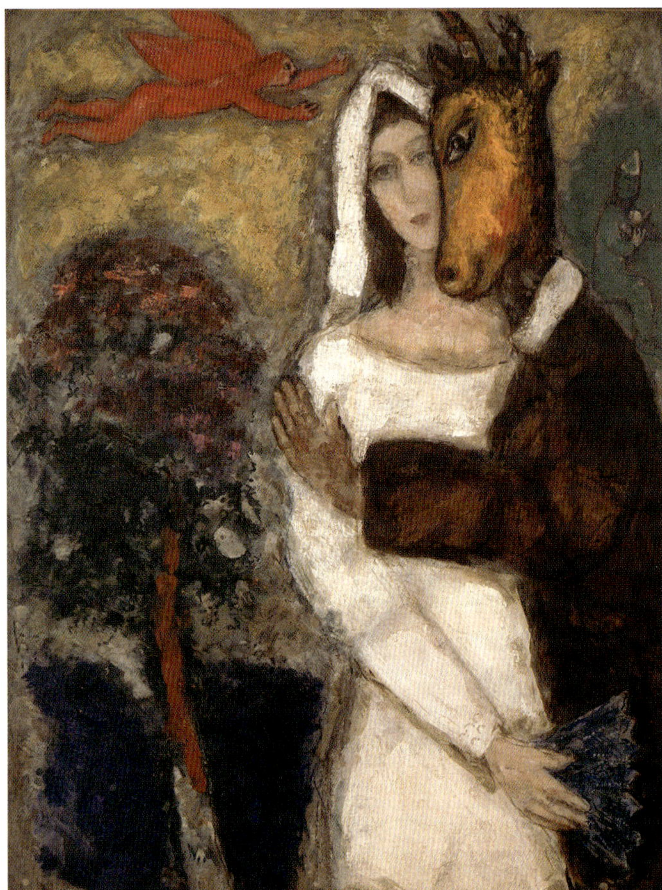

Marc Chagall
(Vitebsk 1887 - Saint-Paul de Vence 1985)

Midsummer Night's Dream
Der Traum in einer Sommernacht
Droom van een zomernacht

●●

1939
116,5 x 89 cm / 45.86 x 35.03 in.
Musée de Grenoble, Grenoble

Oil on canvas / Öl auf Leinwand / Olieverf op doek

Amedeo Modigliani
(Livorno 1884 - Paris 1920)

Reclining Nude
Liegender Akt
Liggend naakt

●●●

1917
60 x 92 cm / 23.62 x 36.22 in.
Private collection
Privatsammlung
Privécollectie

Oil on canvas
Öl auf Leinwand
Olieverf op doek

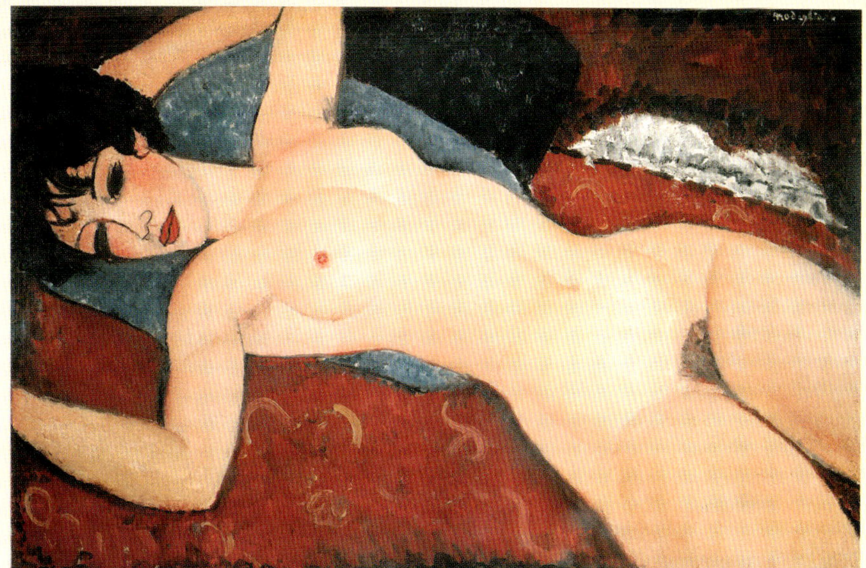

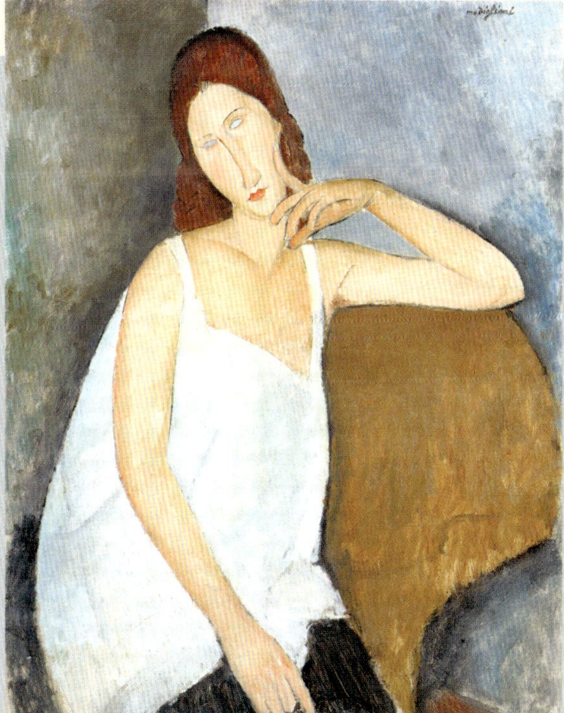

Amedeo Modigliani
(Livorno 1884 - Paris 1920)

Jeanne Hébuterne

●●

1919
Metropolitan Museum of Art,
New York

Oil on canvas
Öl auf Leinwand
Olieverf op doek

Chagall and Modigliani: two examples of individualism in modern art.

Chagall und Modigliani sind zwei Beispiele für den Individualismus in der Moderne.

Chagall en Modigliani: twee voorbeelden van individualisme in de moderne kunst.

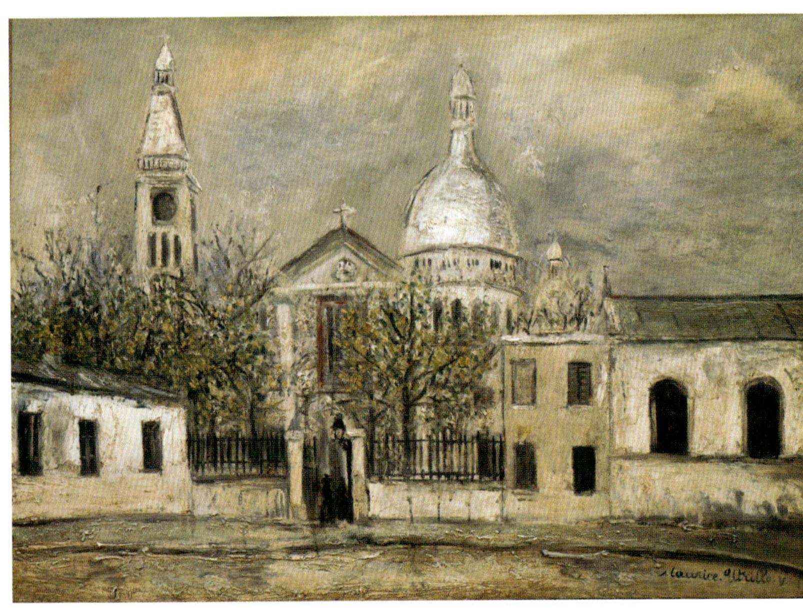

Maurice Utrillo
(Paris 1883 - Dax 1955)

The Church of St Peter
Die Kirche St. Peter
De Sint-Pieter kerk

●

c. 1914
Musée de l'Orangerie, Paris

Oil on cardboard
Öl auf Karton
Olieverf op karton

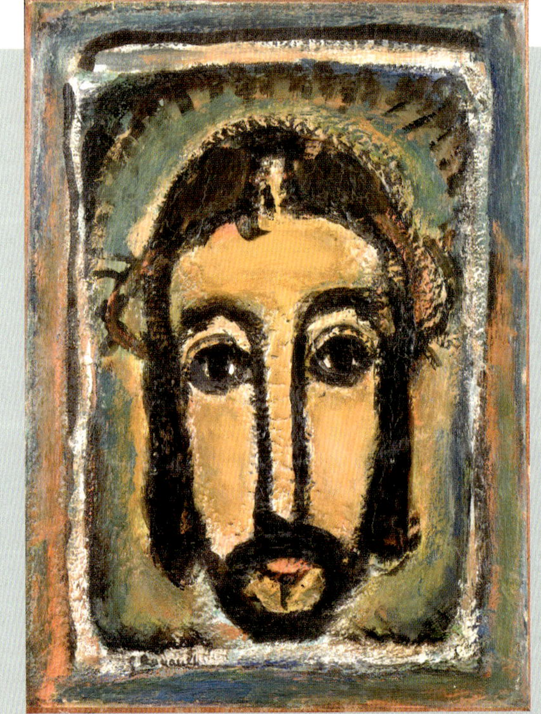

Georges Rouault
(Paris 1871 - 1958)

Christ
Christus

●●

Collezione d'Arte Religiosa Moderna,
Città del Vaticano

Oil on canvas
Öl auf Leinwand
Olieverf op doek

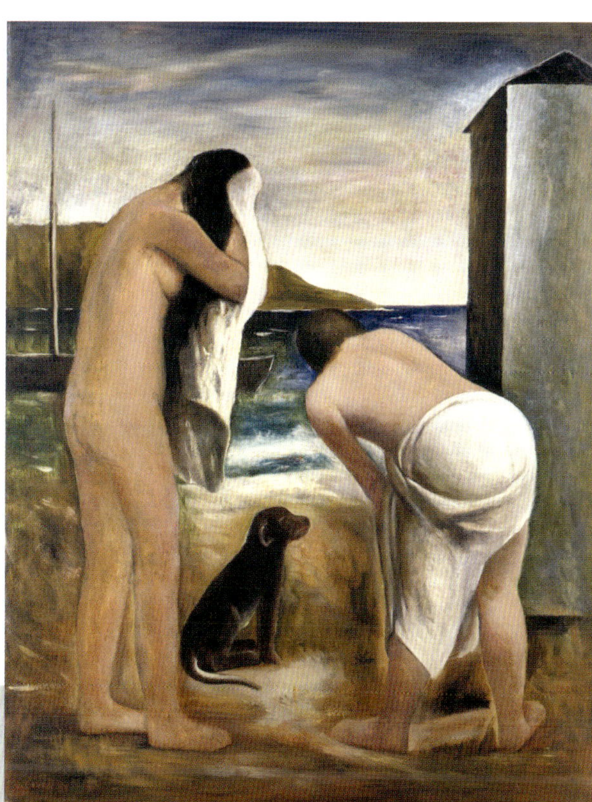

Carlo Carrà
(Quargnento 1881 - Milano 1966)

Summer
Sommer
Zomer

●

1930
165 x 121 cm / 64.96 x 47.63 in.
Galleria d'Arte Moderna, Milano

Oil on canvas
Öl auf Leinwand
Olieverf op doek

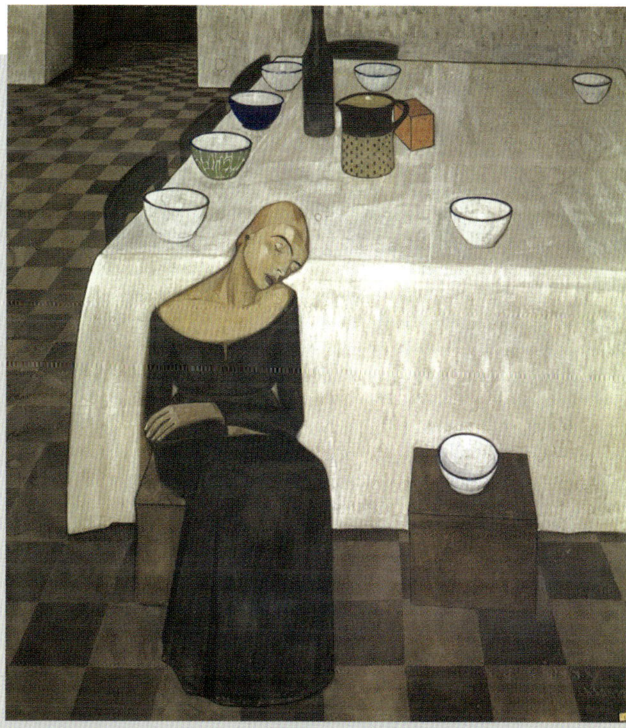

Felice Casorati
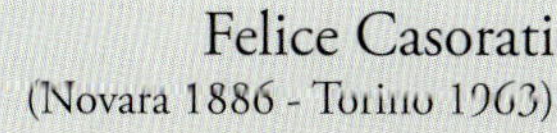
(Novara 1886 - Torino 1963)

A Woman (Waiting)
Eine Frau (Warten)
Een vrouw (Het Wachten)

●

1921
137 x 127 cm / 53.93 x 50 in.
Collezione Menzio, Torino

Tempera on canvas
Tempera auf Leinwand
Tempera op doek

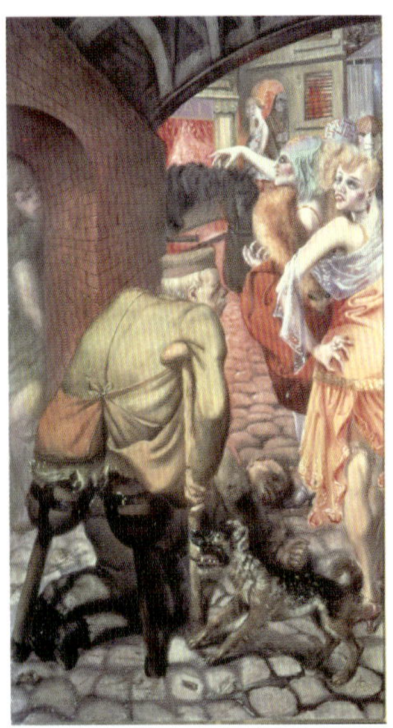
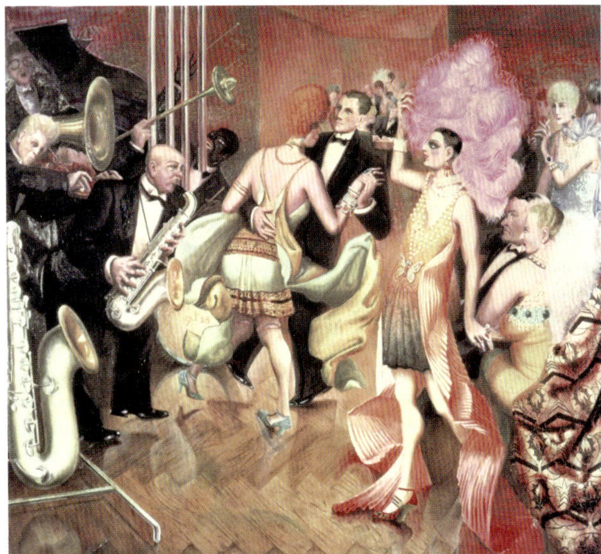
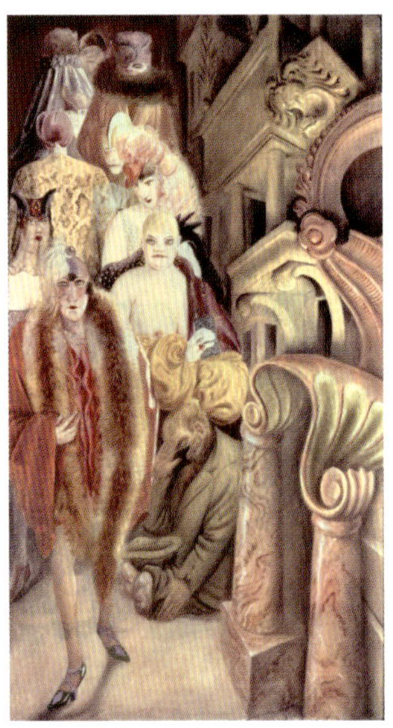

Otto Dix
(Gera 1891 - Singen 1969)

482 **Big City Triptych**
Triptychon Großstadt
Drieluik: De grote stad

●●

c. 1927-1928
181 x 400 cm / 71.25 x 157.48 in.
Staatsgalerie, Stuttgart

Oil on wood
Öl auf Tafel
Olieverf op paneel

Bitter caricatures and late Expressionism: the true face of Germany during the 1920s in the images of the new realism.

Das wahre Gesicht der goldenen Zwanziger in Deutschland im Bild der Neuen Sachlickeit, der beissenden Karrikatur und dem späten Expressionismus.

Bijtende satire en laat expressionisme: het ware gezicht van de jaren twintig in Duitsland in het beeld van de Nieuwe Zakelijkheid.

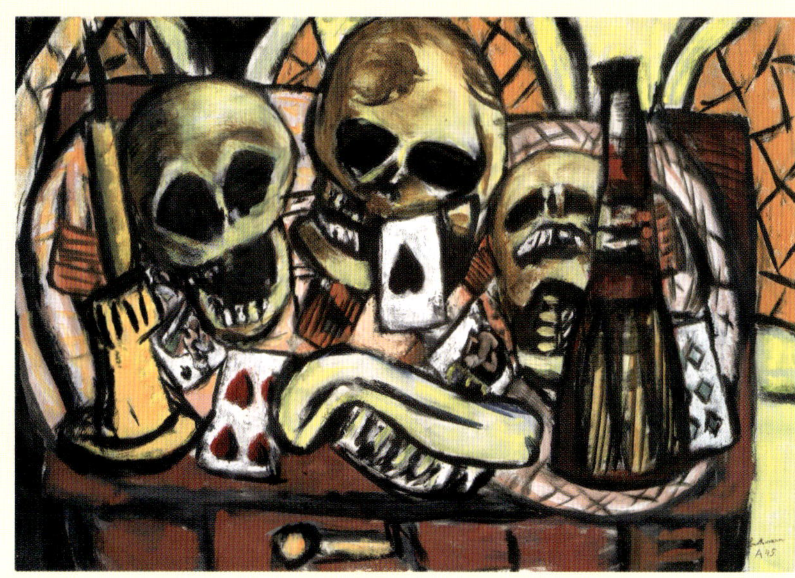

Max Beckmann
(Leipzig 1884 - New York 1950)

Still Life with Three Skulls
Stillleben mit drei Schädeln
Stilleven met drie schedels

●●

55,2 x 89,5 cm / 21.73 x 35.23 in.
Museum of Fine Arts, Boston

Oil on canvas
Öl auf Leinwand
Olieverf op doek

George Grosz
(Berlin 1893 - 1959)

The Convict
Der Gefangene
De gevangene

●●●

1920
41,9 x 30,5 cm / 16.49 x 12 in.
Museum of Modern Art
(MoMA), New York

Mixed technique
Miischtechnik
Verschillende technieken

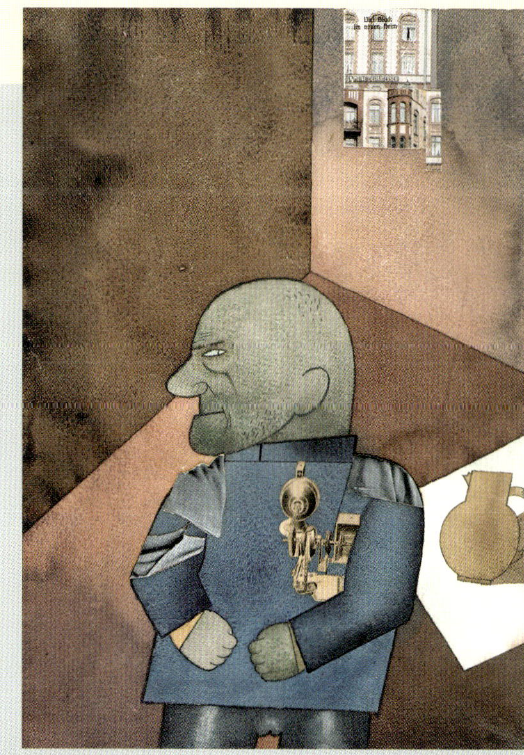

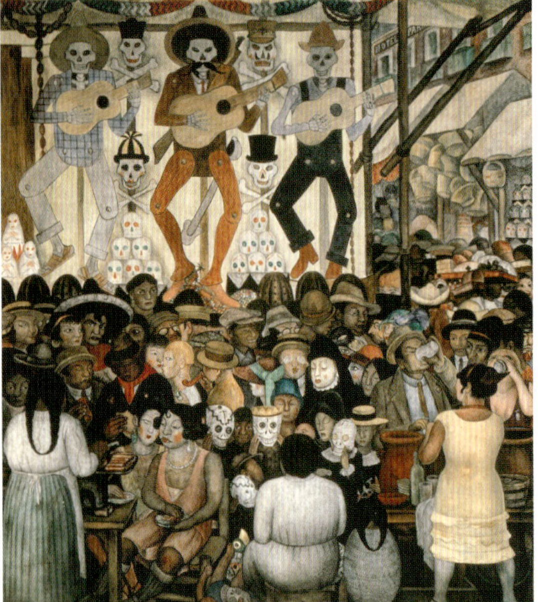

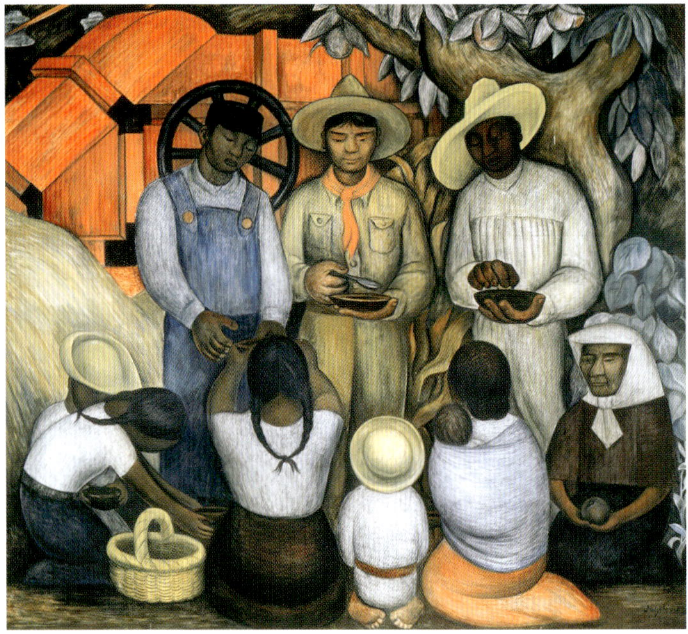

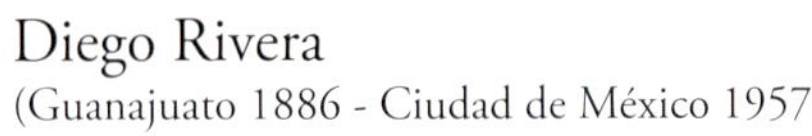

Diego Rivera
(Guanajuato 1886 - Ciudad de México 1957)

The Fair on All Souls'Day
Allerseelen - Straßenfest
Dodendag - Feest op straat

●

1923-1924
417 x 375 cm / 164,2 x 147.6 in.
Secretaría de Educación Pública, Ciudad de México

Mural / Wandmalerei / Muurschildering

Diego Rivera
(Guanajuato 1886 - Ciudad de México 1957)

Triumph of the Revolution,
Distribution of Food
Triumph der Revolution,
Verteilung der Speisen
Triomf van de Revolutie, voedseldistributie

●●

c. 1926-1927
Universidad Autónoma, Chapingo

Mural / Wandmalerei / Muurschildering

Frida Kahlo
(Coyoacán 1907 - 1954)

The Two Fridas
Die zwei Fridas
De twee Frida's

●●●

1939
67 x 67 cm / 26.3 x 26.3 in.
Museo Nacional de Arte Moderno, Ciudad de México

Oil on canvas
Öl auf Leinwand
Olieverf op doek

Frida Kahlo
(Coyoacán 1907 - 1954)

Broken Column
Die gebrochene Säule
De gebroken zuil

●●

1944
Fundación Dolores Olmedo, Ciudad de México

Oil on canvas
Öl auf Leinwand
Olieverf op doek

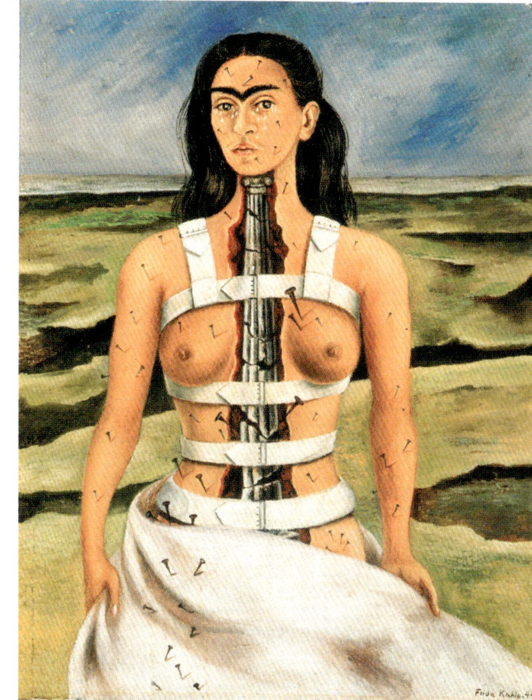

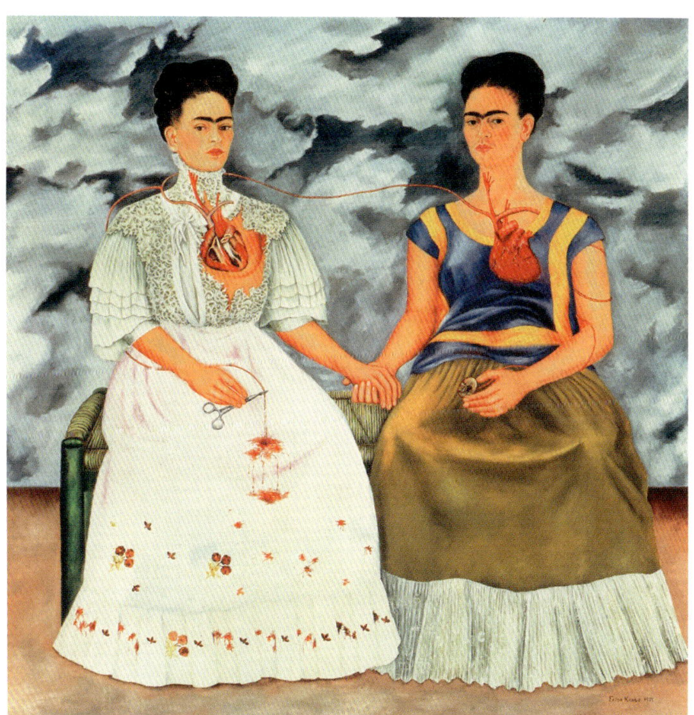

Art as therapy: Frida Kahlo, the wife of Rivera, elaborates her own suffering in her art after a serious accident.

Kunsttherapie, Frida Kahlo, Gattin Riveras, verarbeitet in ihrer Kunst ihre Leidensgeschichte nach einem schweren Unfall.

Kunst als therapie: Frida Kahlo, vrouw van Diego Rivera, verwerkt met haar kunst haar lijdensweg na een ernstig ongeluk.

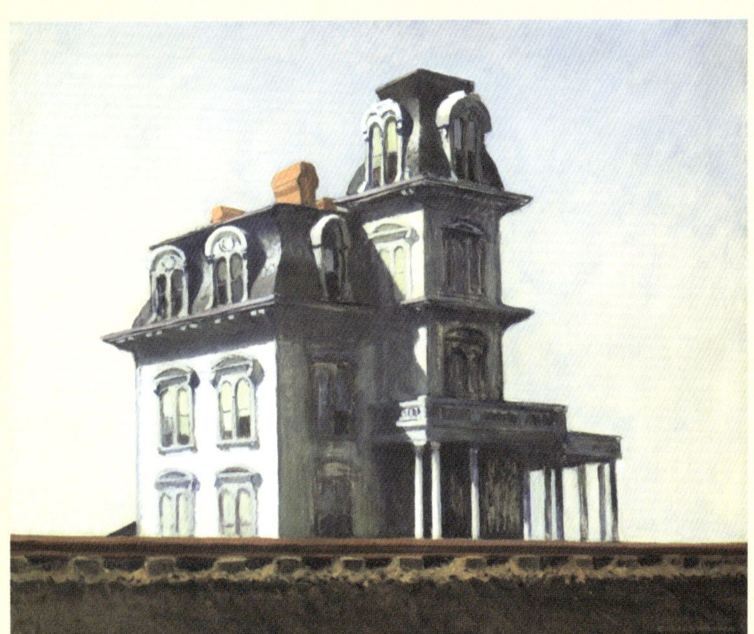

Edward Hopper
(Nyack 1882 - New York 1967)

House by the Railroad
Haus am Bahndamm
Huis bij het treinstation

●●●

1925
61 x 73,7 cm / 24 x 29 in.
Museum of Modern Art (MoMA), New York

Oil on canvas
Öl auf Leinwand
Olieverf op doek

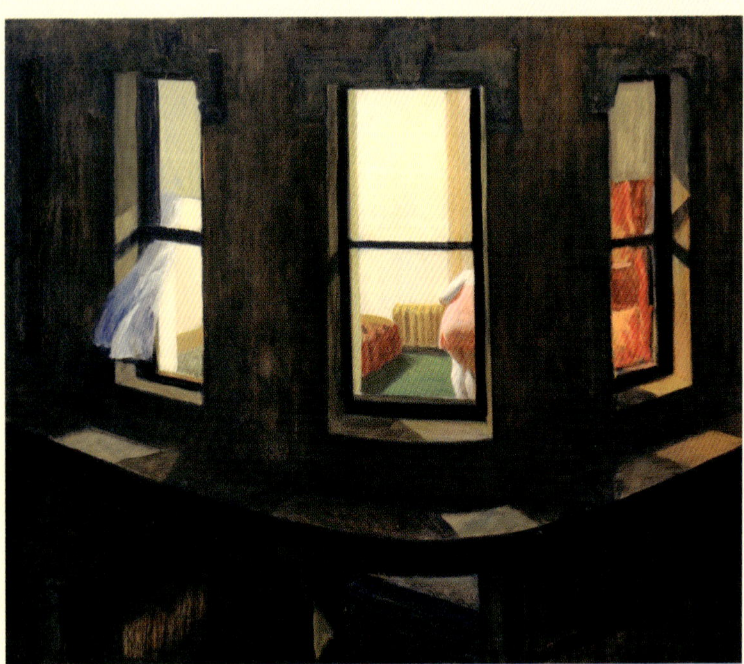

Edward Hopper
(Nyack 1882 - New York 1967)

Night Windows
Das Nachtfenster
Nachtvensters

●●

1928
73,7 x 86,4 cm / 29.01 x 34.01 in.
Museum of Modern Art (MoMA), New York

Oil on canvas
Öl auf Leinwand
Olieverf op doek

Edward Hopper
(Nyack 1882 - New York 1967)

Hotel Room
Hotelzimmer
Hotelkamer

●●●

1931
152,4 x 165,7 cm / 60 x 65.2 in.
Museo Thyssen-Bornemisza,
Madrid

Oil on canvas
Öl auf Leinwand
Olieverf op doek

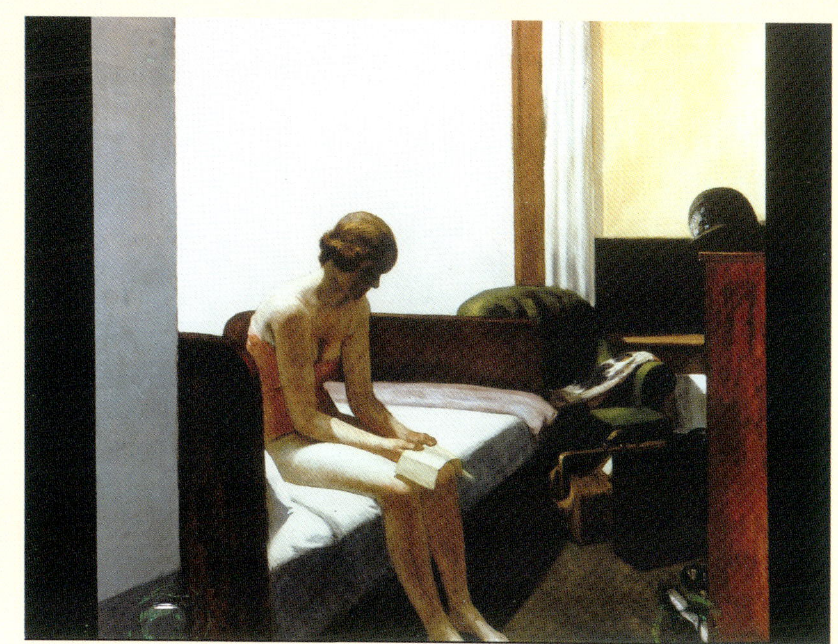

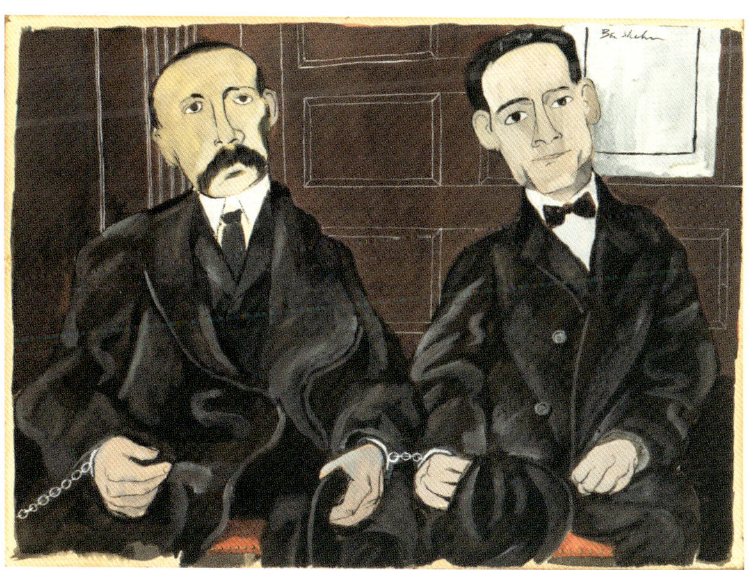

Ben Shahn
(Kovno 1898 - New York 1969)

Bartolomeo Vanzetti and Nicola Sacco
Bartolomeo Vanzetti und Nicola Sacco
Bartolomeo Vanzetti en Nicola Sacco

●

c. 1931-1932
26,7 x 36,8 cm / 10 x 14 in.
Museum of Modern Art (MoMA), New York

Tempera on paper
Tempera auf Papier
Tempera op papier

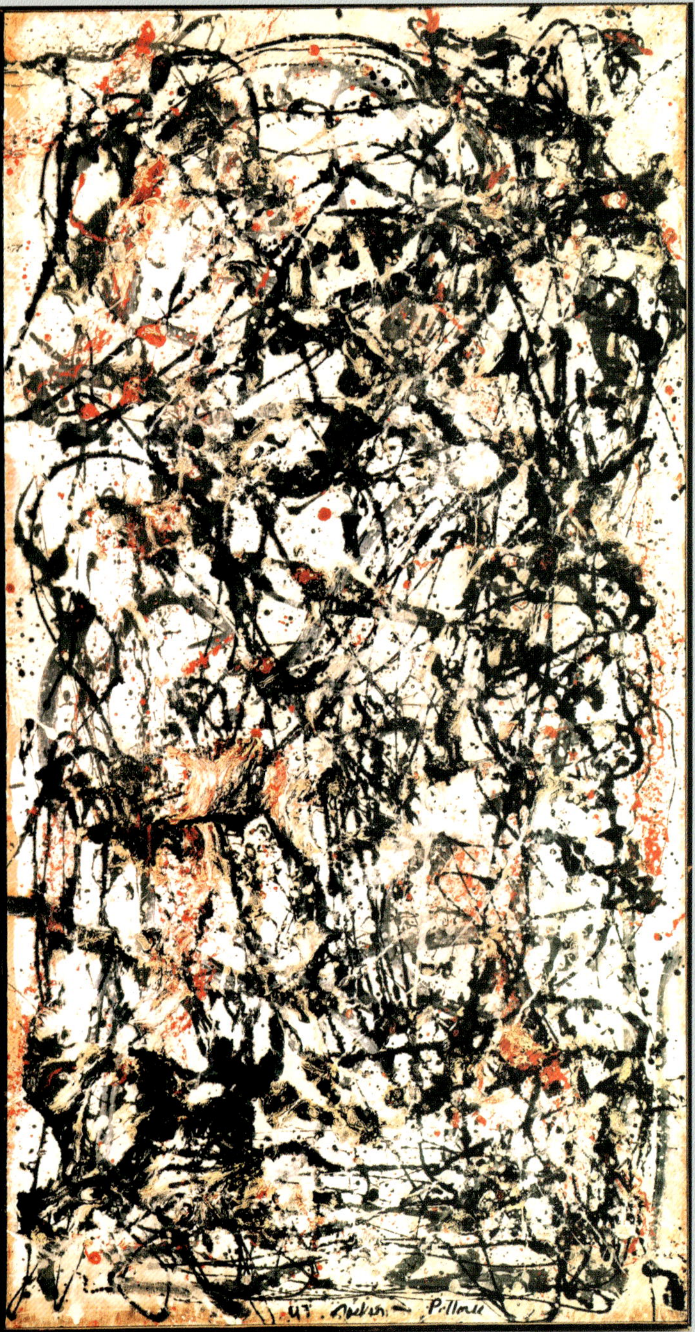

Pollock's Action Painting: colours are dripped from tins over the canvas stretched out on the floor.

Pollocks Action painting: Über die am Boden liegende Leinwand pendeln Dosen, aus denen Farbe tropft (Dripping).

Pollock's Action Painting: kleur drupt uit blikken die boven het op de grond liggende doek hangen (Dripping).

Jackson Pollock
(Cody 1912 - Long Island 1956)

Enchanted Forest
Zauberwald
Het betoverde woud

●●●

1947
221,3 x 114,6 cm
Peggy Guggenheim Collection, Venezia

Mixed technique
Mischtechnik
Verschillende technieken

Jackson Pollock
(Cody 1912 - Long Island 1956)

Number 4
Nummer 4

●●

1949
90,2 x 87,3 cm / 35.51 x 34.37 in.
Yale University Art Gallery,
New Haven

Mixed technique
Mischtechnik
Verschillende technieken

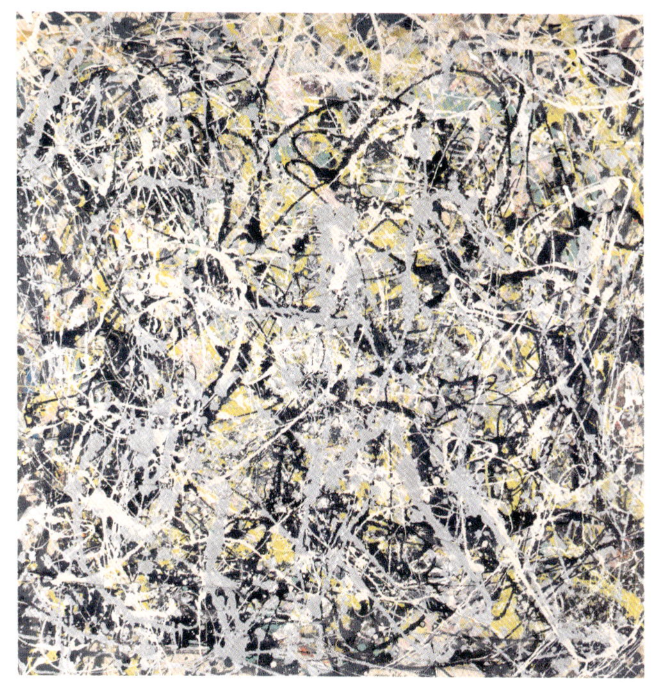

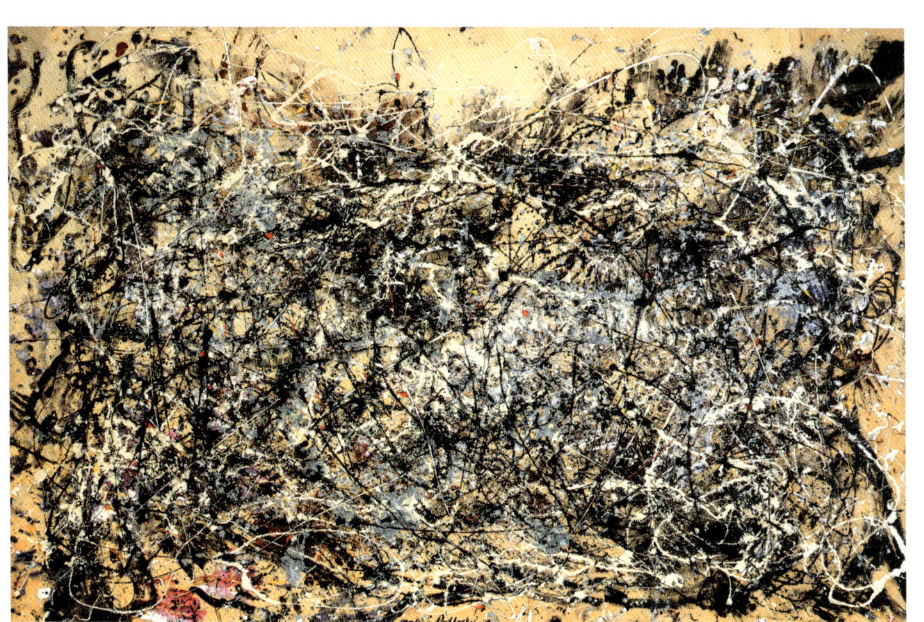

Jackson Pollock
(Cody 1912 - Long Island 1956)

One: Number 31
Eins: Nummer 31
Één: Nummer 31

●●●

1950
269,5 x 530,8 cm
104.62 x 208.97 in.
Museum of Modern Art (MoMA),
New York

Mixed technique
Mischtechnik
Verschillende technieken

Barnett Newman
(New York 1905 - 1970)

Vir Heroicus Sublimis

●●

c. 1950-1951
242,2 x 541,7 cm / 95.35 x 213.26 in.
Museum of Modern Art (MoMA),
New York

Oil on canvas
Öl auf Leinwand
Olieverf op doek

Abstract Expressionism
Abstrakter Expressionismus
Abstract expressionisme

Ad Reinhardt
(Buffalo 1913 - New York 1967)

Painting
Malerei
Schilderij

1956
203,8 x 109,5 cm
80.23 x 43.11 in.
Yale University Art Gallery,
New Haven

Oil on canvas
Öl auf Leinwand
Olieverf op doek

Willem de Kooning
(Rotterdam 1904 - New York 1997)

Woman I
Frau I
Vrouw I

●●●

1950-1952
192,7 x 147,3 cm / 75.86 x 58 in.
Museum of Modern Art (MoMA), New York

Oil on canvas
Öl auf Leinwand
Olieverf op doek

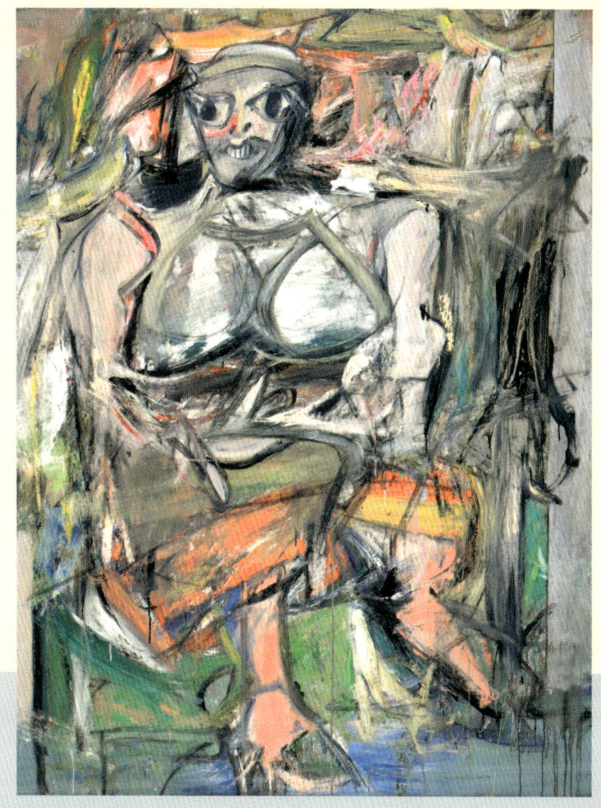

Franz Kline
(Wilkes-Barre 1910 - New York 1962)

Merce C
Merce

●●

1961
93 x 74 cm / 36.61 x 29.13 in.
Smithsonian American Art Museum, Washington DC

Oil on canvas
Öl auf Leinwand
Olieverf op doek

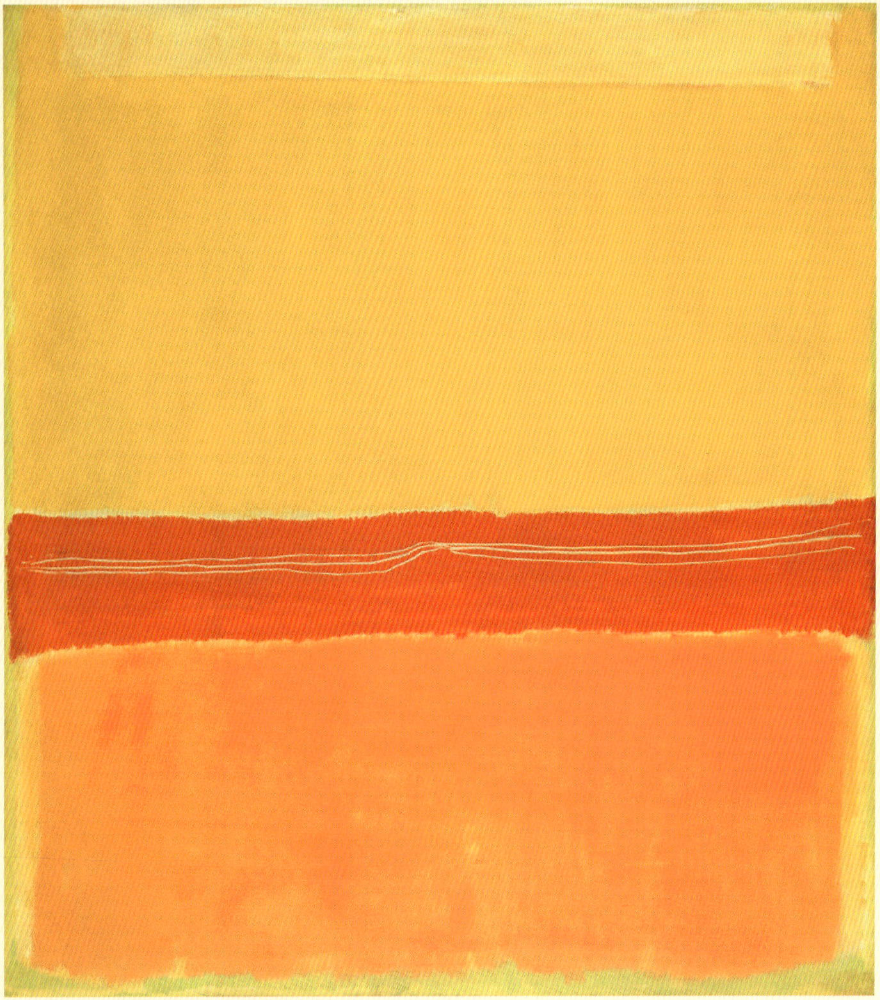

Lyrical and meditative chromatic harmonies: Rothko is the protagonist of Color Field Painting.

Lyrische meditative Farbharmonien. Rothko ist Hauptvertreter des Color Field Painting.

Lyrische en meditatieve harmonieën. Rothko is de belangrijkste vertegenwoordiger van de Color Field Painting.

Mark Rothko
(Dvinsk 1903 - New York 1970)

Number 5/Number 22
Nummer 5/Nummer 22

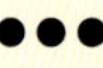

1949
297 x 272 cm / 116.9 x 107.08 in.
Museum of Modern Art (MoMA), New York

Oil on canvas
Öl auf Leinwand
Olieverf op doek

Mark Rothko

(Dvinsk 1903 - New York 1970)

Horizontals, White over Darks

●●●

1961

143,3 x 237 cm / 56.41 x 93.30 in.

Museum of Modern Art (MoMA), New York

Oil on canvas

Öl auf Leinwand

Olieverf op doek

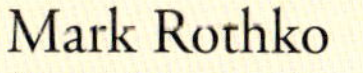

Mark Rothko

(Dvinsk 1903 - New York 1970)

Untitled

Ohne Titel

Zonder titel

●●●

1969

102,2 x 67,4 cm / 40.23 x 26.53 in.

Museum of Modern Art (MoMA), New York

Mixed technique

Mischtechnik

Verschillende technieken

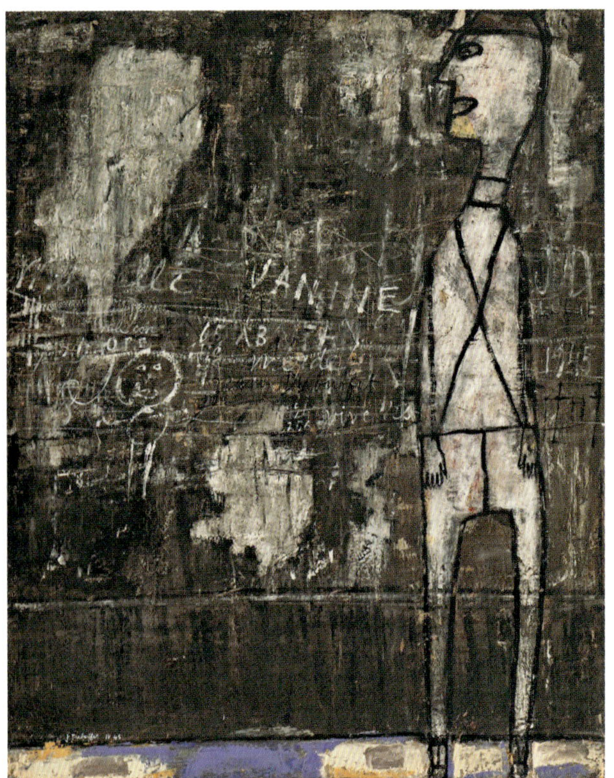

Jean Dubuffet
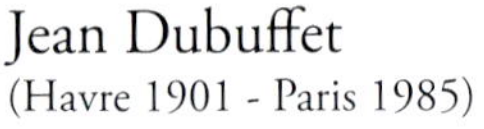
(Havre 1901 - Paris 1985)

Wall with Inscriptions
Wandinschrift
Muur met opschrift

●●

1945
99,7 x 81 cm / 39.25 x 31.88 in.
Museum of Modern Art (MoMA), New York

Oil on canvas
Öl auf Leinwand
Olieverf op doek

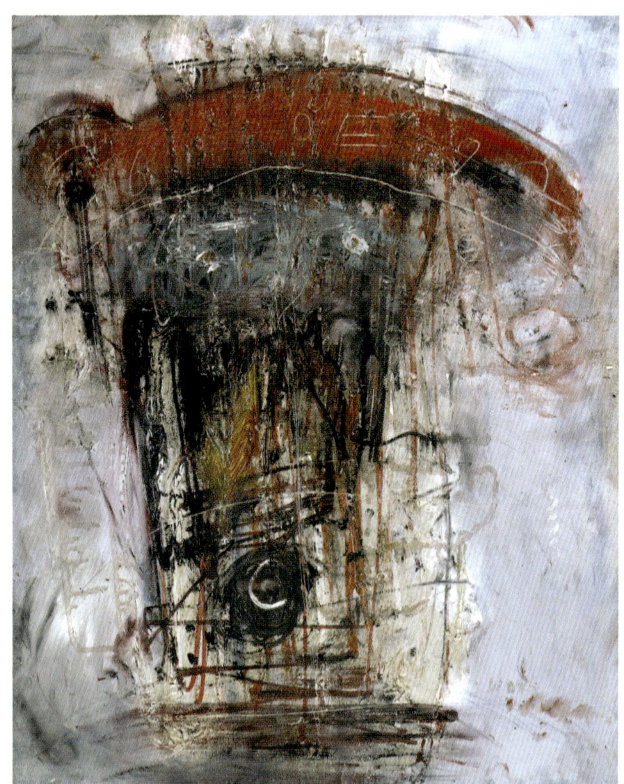

Wols
(Berlin 1913 - Paris 1951)

Composition
Komposition
Compositie

●

1947
81 x 64,7 cm / 31.88 x 25.47 in.
Hamburger Kunsthalle, Hamburg

Oil on canvas
Öl auf Leinwand
Olieverf op doek

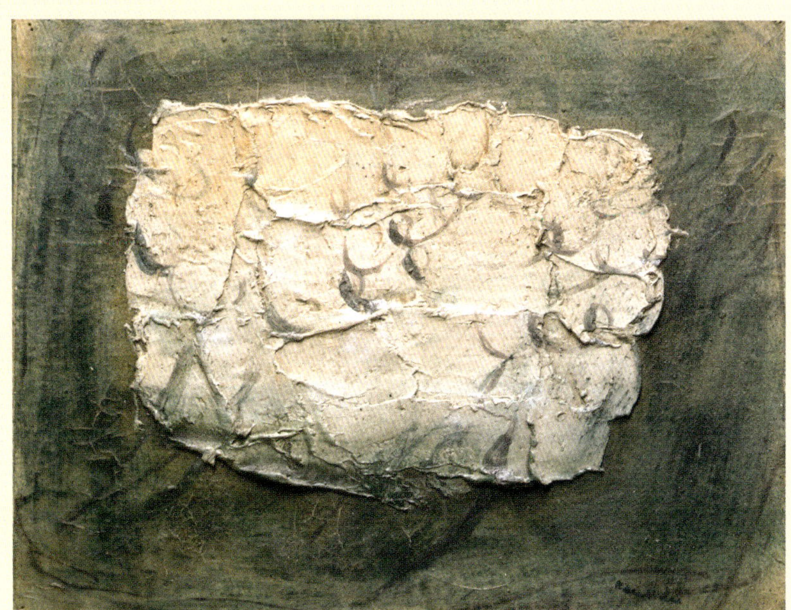

Jean Fautrier
(Paris 1898 - Châtenay-Malabry 1964)

Untitled
Ohne Titel
Zonder titel

●●

1943
27 x 35 cm / 10.62 x 13.77 in.
Artist's collection / Sammlung des Künstlers
Collectie van de kunstenaar

Mixed technique (oil, pastel, ink and paper marouflaged on cloth)
Mischtechnik (Öl, Pastell, Tinte, Papier, auf Leinwand übertragen)
Verschillende technieken (olieverf, pastel, inkt, maroufle)

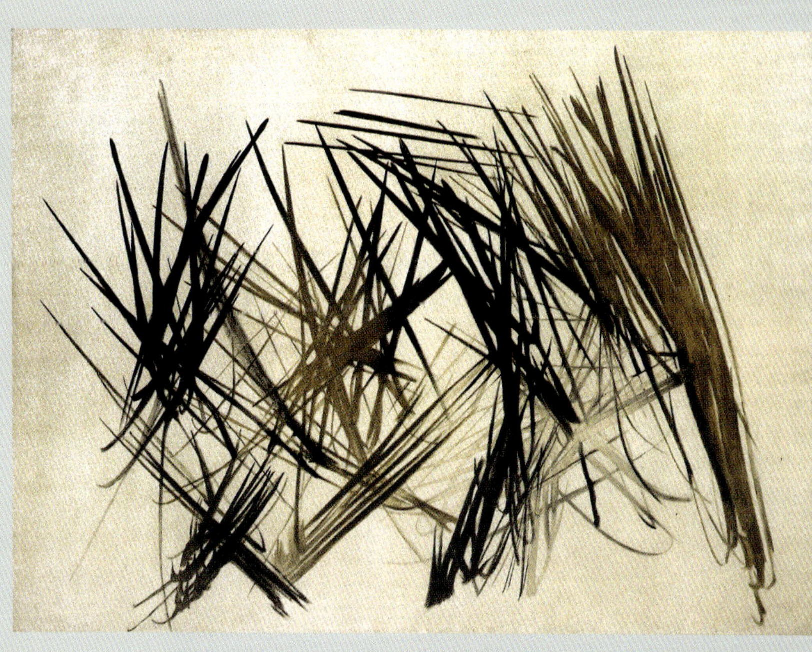

Hans Hartung
(Lcipzig 1904 - Antibes 1989)

T 1956 20

●●

1956
Fondation Hans Hartung et Anna Eva Bergman, Antibes

Oil on canvas
Öl auf Leinwand
Olieverf op doek

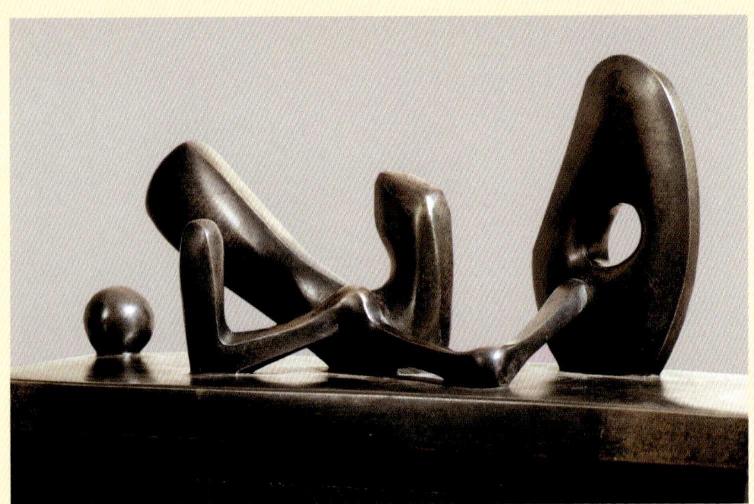

Henry Moore
(Castelford, Leeds 1898 - London 1986)

Composition
Komposition
Compositie

●●

1934
l. 42 cm / 16.5 in.
Smart Museum of Art, Chicago

Bronze / Brons

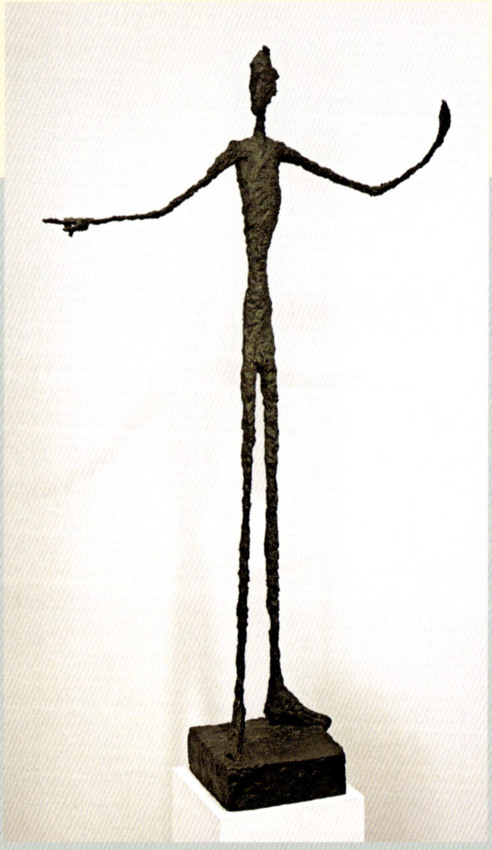

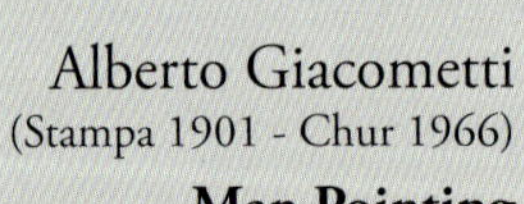

Alberto Giacometti
(Stampa 1901 - Chur 1966)

Man Pointing
Zeigender Mann
Wijzende man

●●●

1947
h. 179 cm / 70.47 in.
Museum of Modern Art (MoMA), New York

Bronze / Brons

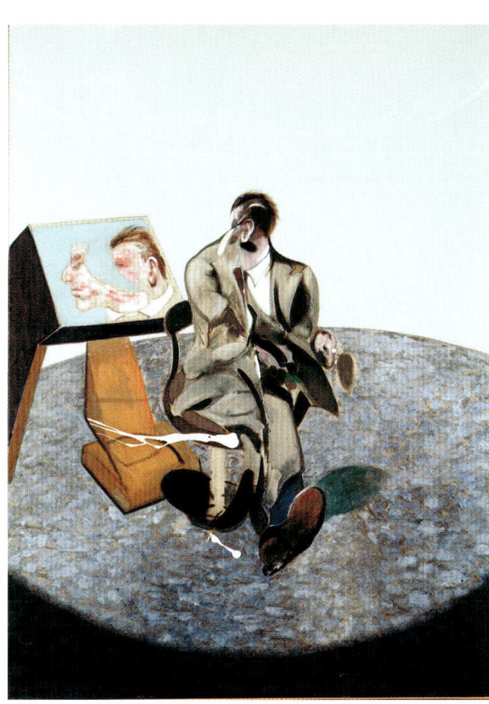

Francis Bacon
(Dublin 1909 - Madrid 1992)

Portrait of George Dyer in a Mirror
Portrait von George Dyer in einem Spiegel
Portret van George Dyer in een spiegel

●●●

1968
198 x 147 cm / 77.95 x 57.87 in.
Museo Thyssen-Bornemisza, Madrid

Oil on canvas / Öl auf Leinwand / Olieverf op doek

Francis Bacon
(Dublin 1909 - Madrid 1992)

Triptych
Triptychon
Triptiek

●●●

1991
Oil on linen, three panels / Öl auf Leinwand, drei Tafeln
Olieverf op linnen, drie panelen each panel / Jede davon / Ieder paneel 198.1 x 147.6 cm / 78 x 58.11 in.
Museum of Modern Art (MoMA), New York

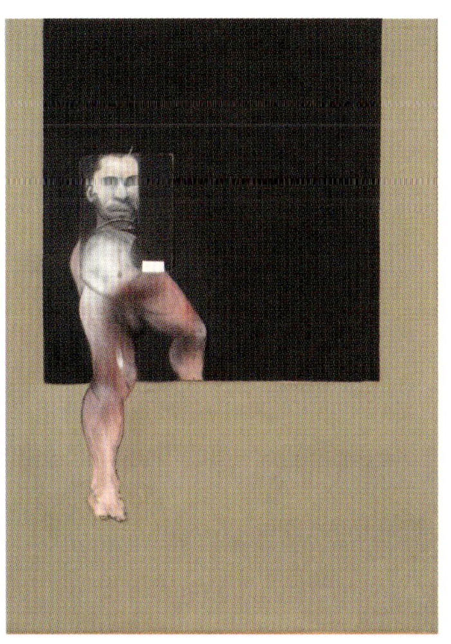

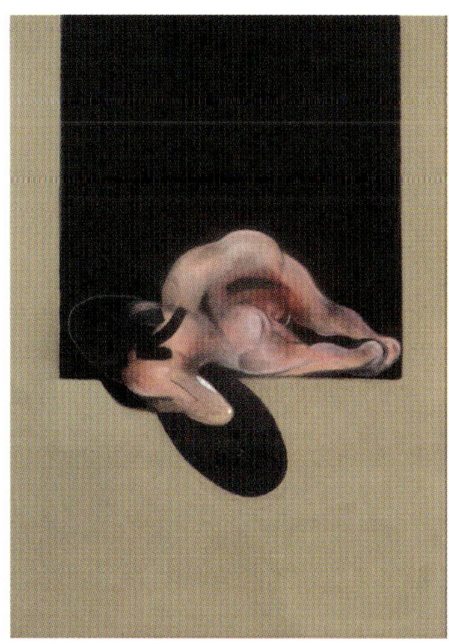

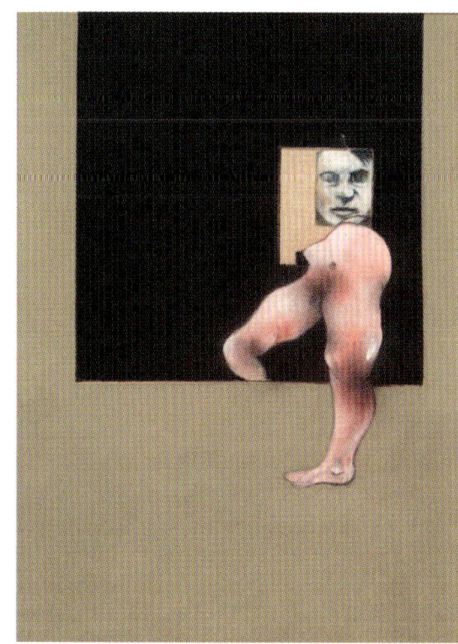

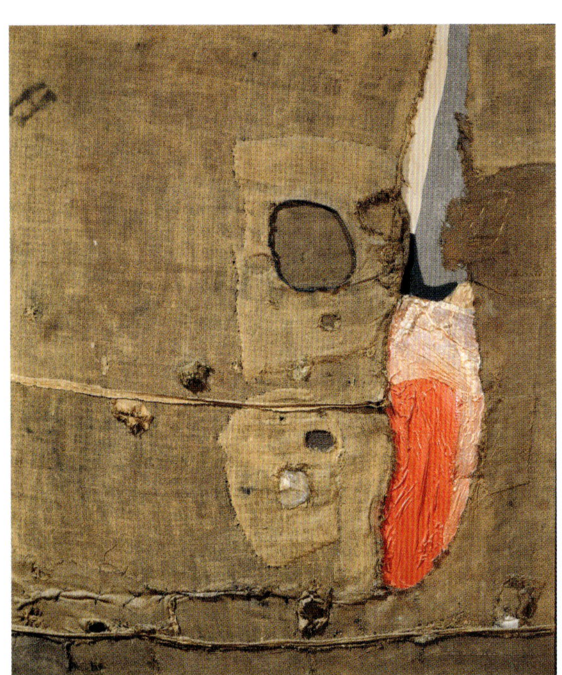

Alberto Burri
(Città di Castello 1915 - Nice 1995)

Sack 5P
Zak 5P

●●

1953
149 x 129, 5 cm / 58.67 x 60 in.
Fondazione Palazzo Albizzini - Collezione Burri,
Palazzo Albizzini, Città di Castello

Burlap, acrylic colours, white glue and fabric on canvas
Sack, Acryl, Vinavil, Stoff auf Leinwand
Zak, acrylverf, Vinavil, stof op doek

Alberto Burri
(Città di Castello 1915 - Nice 1995)

Voyage no. 4
Die Reise Nr. 4
Reis nr. 4

●

1979
Ex Seccatoi Tabacco - Collezione Burri,
Città di Castello

Acrylic vinyl colours on cellotex
Acrovinyl auf Cellotex
Acrovinilico op cellotex

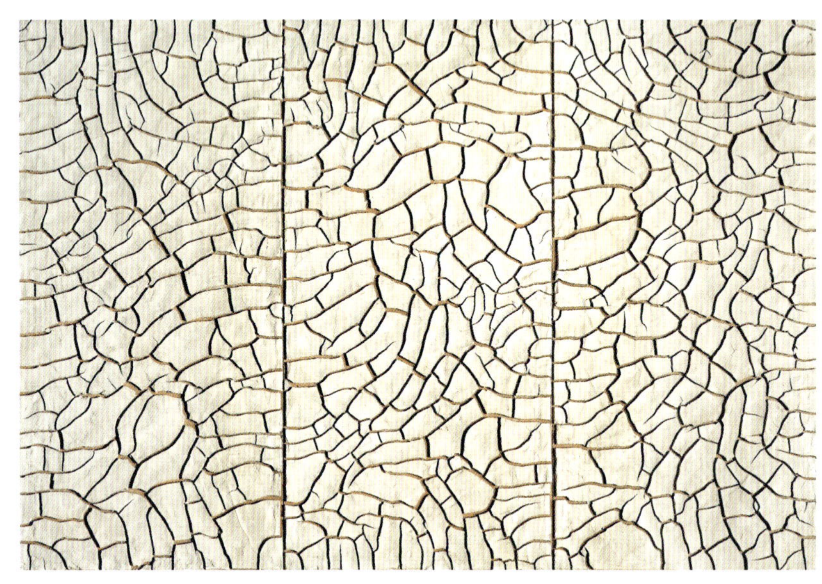

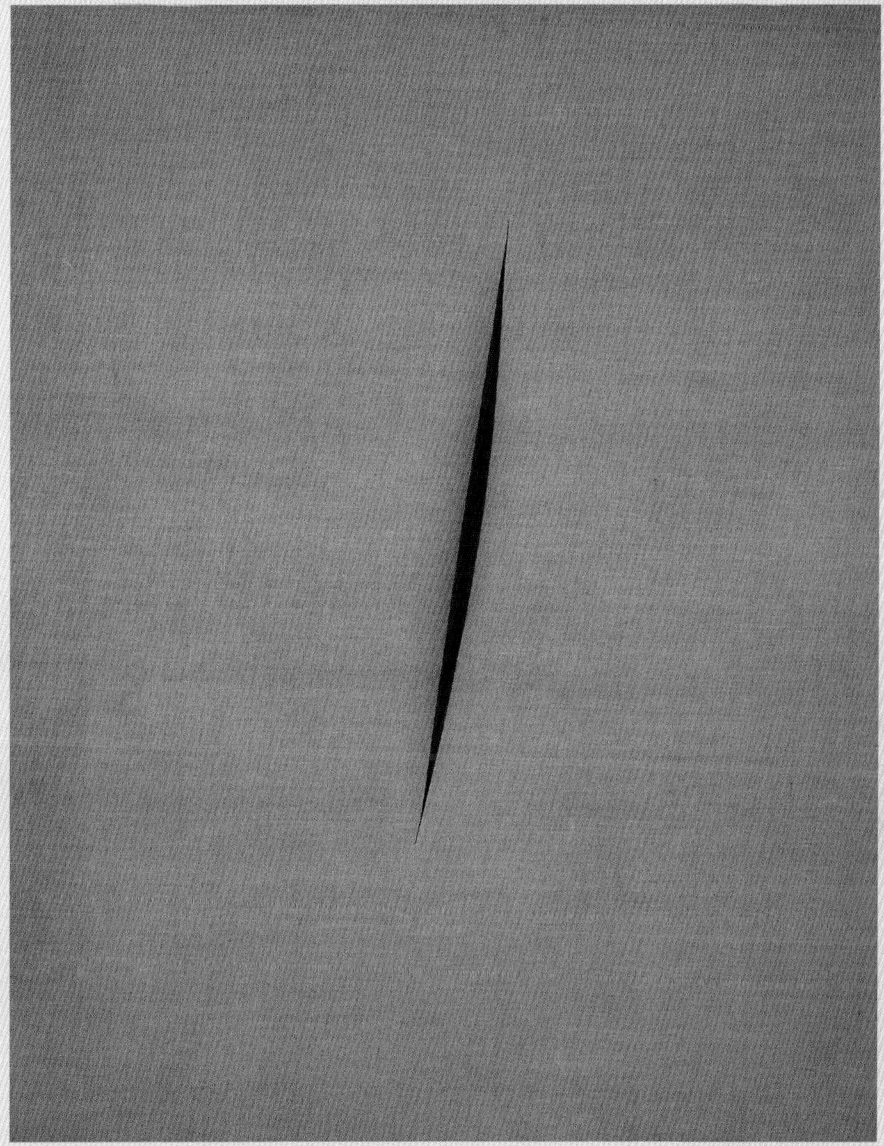

Lucio Fontana
(Rosario 1899 - Milano 1968)

Spatial Concept: Waiting
Raumkonzept, Warten
Ruimtelijk concept, Verwachtingen

●●●

1960
100,3 x 80,3 cm / 39.48 x 31.61 in.
Museum of Modern Art (MoMA), New York

Canvas and gauze
Leinwand und Garze
Doek en gaas

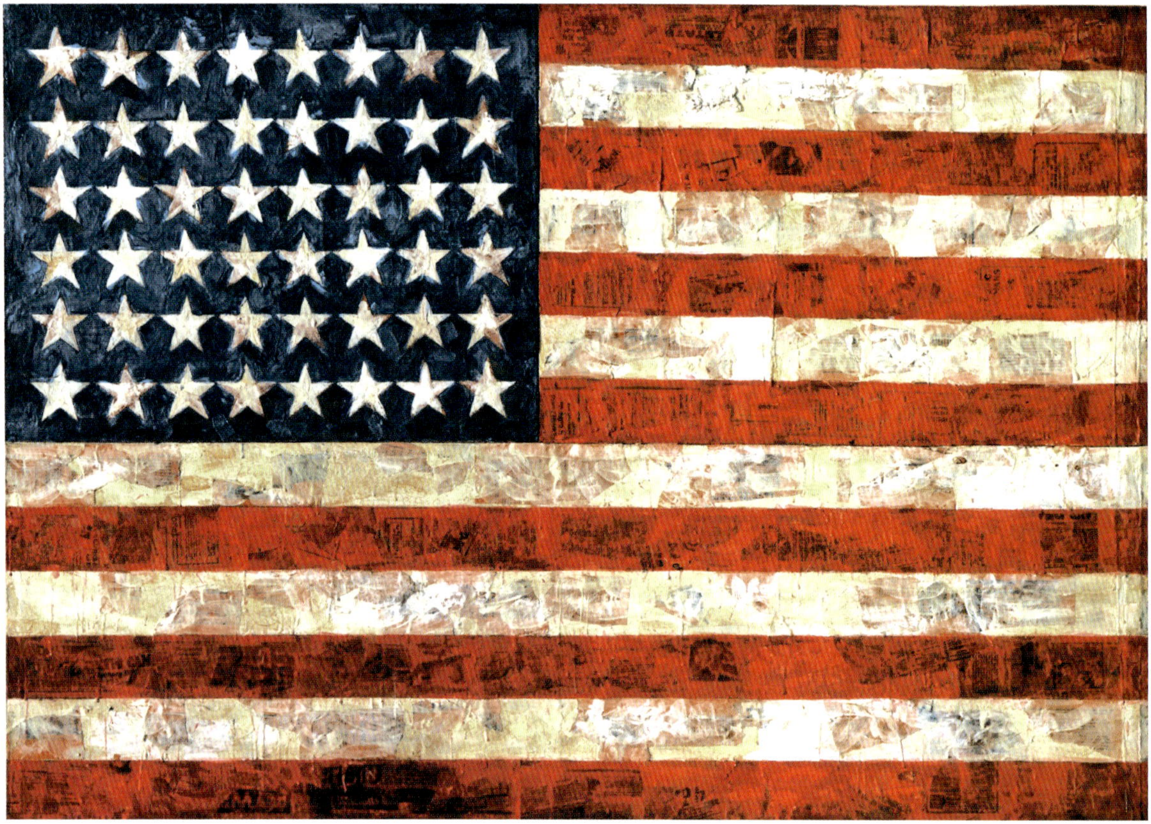

Jasper Johns
(Augusta 1930)

Flag
Fahne
Vlag

1954
107,3 x 153,8 cm / 42.24 x 60.55 in.
Museum of Modern Art (MoMA), New York

Encaustic on canvas
Wachsmalerei auf Leinwand
Encausto op doek

Figurative images drawn from the consumer society: Pop Art is America's apolitical answer to Dada.

Bildmotive der Konsumgesellschaft. Die Pop Art ist die amerikanische unpolitische Antwort auf Dada.

Beeldmotieven uit de consumptiemaatschappij. Pop Art is het niet-politieke Amerikaanse antwoord op Dada.

Robert Rauschenberg
(Port Arthur 1925 - Captiva 2008)

Summer
Sommer
Estate

●

1963
243,8 x 177,3 cm
95.98 x 69.80 in.
Philadelphia Museum of Art,
Philadelphia

Oil and ink on canvas
Öl und Tinte auf Leinwand
Olieverf en inkt op doek

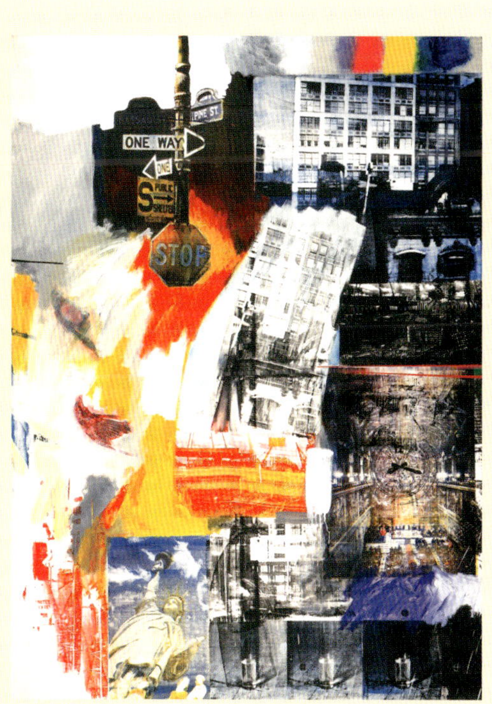

Robert Rauschenberg
(Port Arthur 1925 - Captiva 2008)

Bed
Bett

●●

1955
191.1 x 80 x 20.3 cm
75.23 x 31.49 x 7.99 in.
Museum of Modern Art (MoMA),
New York

Mixed technique
Mischtechnik
Verschillende technieken

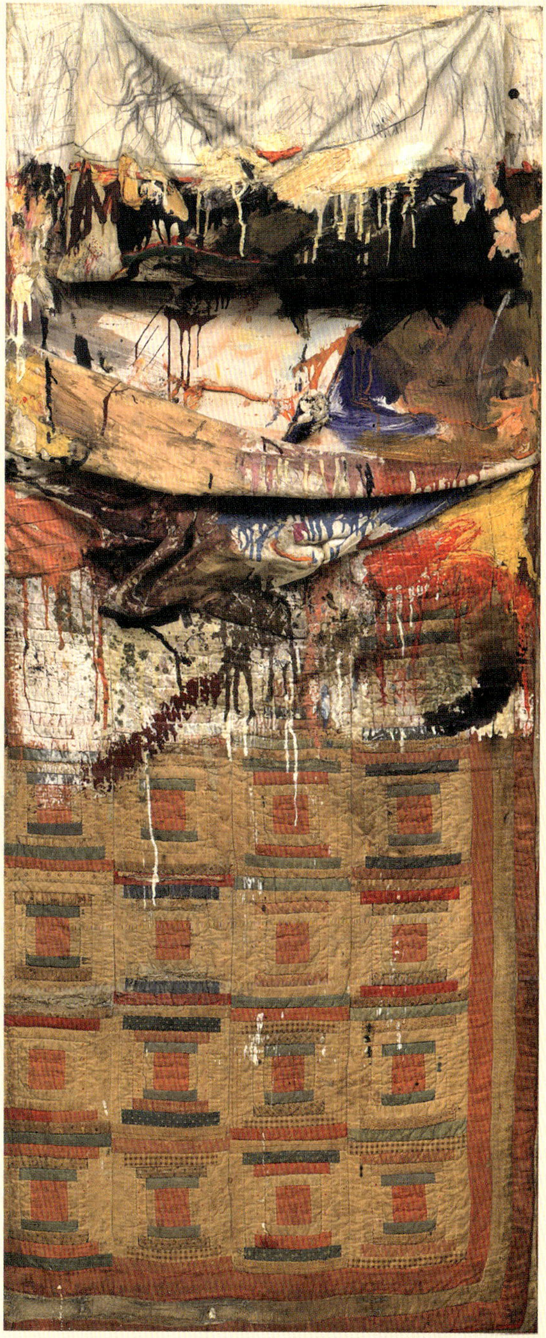

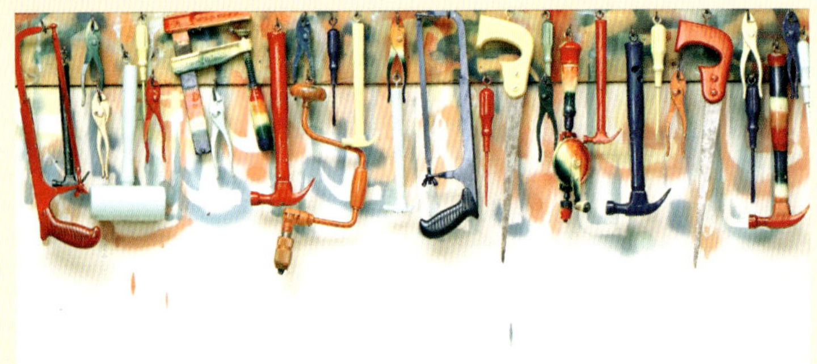

Jim Dine
(Cincinnati 1935)

Five Feet of Colorful Tools
Fünf Fuß farbenfrohes Werkzeug
Vijf feet van gekleurde gereedschappen

●

1962
141,2 x 152,9 x 11 cm / 55.59 x 60.19 x 4.33 in.
Museum of Modern Art (MoMA), New York

Oil on canvas and various materials
Öl auf Leinwand und verschiedene Materialien
Olieverf op doek en verschillende materialen

Claes Oldenburg
(Stockholm 1929)

Giant Piece of Cake
Überdimensionales Tortenstück
Gigantisch stuk taart

1962
148,2 x 290,2 x 148,2 cm
58.34 x 114.25 x 58.34 in.
Museum of Modern Art (MoMA), New York

Various materials
Verschiedene Materialien
Verschillende materialen

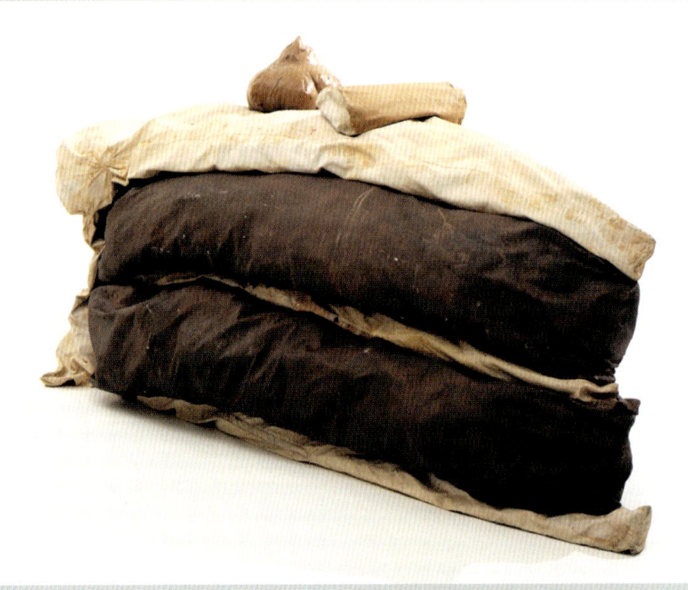

Roy Lichtenstein
(New York 1923 - 1997)

Drowning Girl
Ertrinkendes Mädchen
Verdrinkend meisje

●●●

1963
171,6 x 169,5 cm / 67.55 x 66.73 in.
Museum of Modern Art (MoMA),
New York

Oil and synthetic paint on canvas
Öl und synthetischer Lack auf Leinwand
Olieverf en synthetische verf op doek

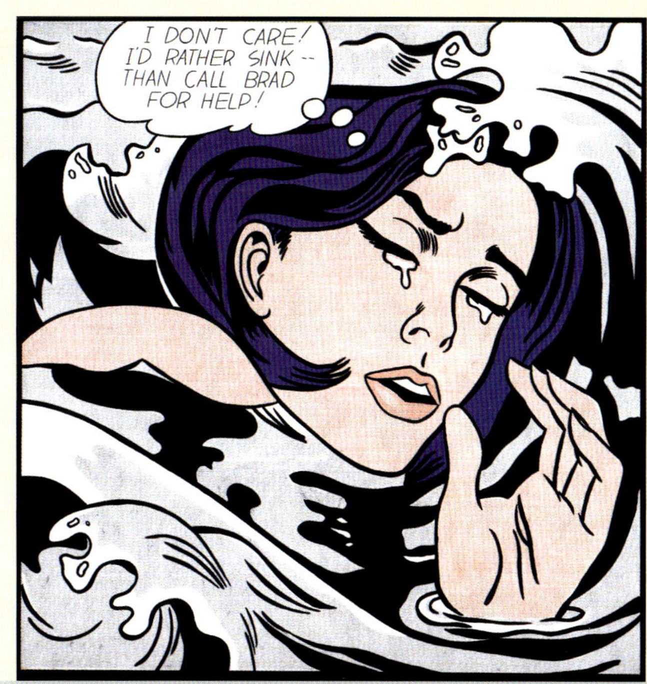

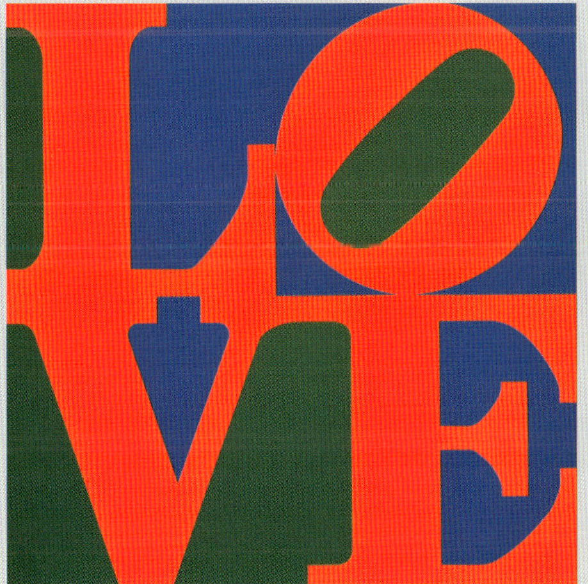

Robert Indiana
(New Castle 1928)

LOVE

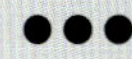

1967
86,3 x 86,3 cm / 33.97 x 33.97 in.
Museum of Modern Art (MoMA),
New York

Mixed technique
Mischtechnik
Verschillende technieken

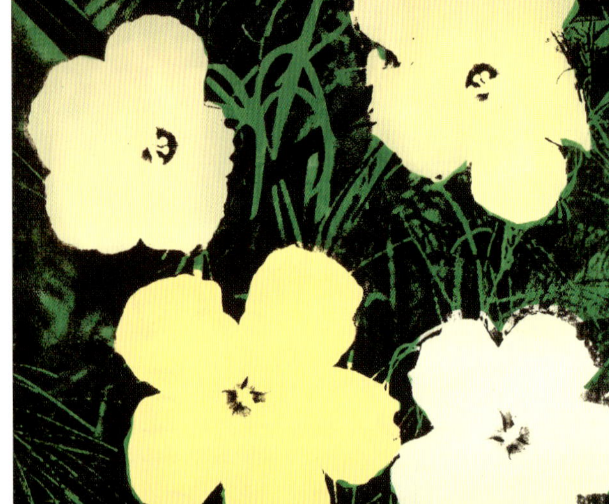

Andy Warhol
(PittsBurgh 1928 - New York 1987)

Flowers
Blumen
Bloemen

●●●

1964
119,7 x 117,2 cm / 47.12 x 46.14 in.
Yale University Art Gallery, New Haven

Screen-print / Serigraphie / Zeefdruk

Andy Warhol
(PittsBurgh 1928 - New York 1987)

Untitled from Marilyn Monroe (Marilyn)
Ohne Titel von Marilyn Monroe (Marilyn)
Zonder titel uit Marilyn Monroe (Marilyn)

●●●

1967
91,5 x 91,5 cm / 36.02 x 36.02 in.
Museum of Modern Art (MoMA), New York

Screen-print / Serigraphie / Zeefdruk

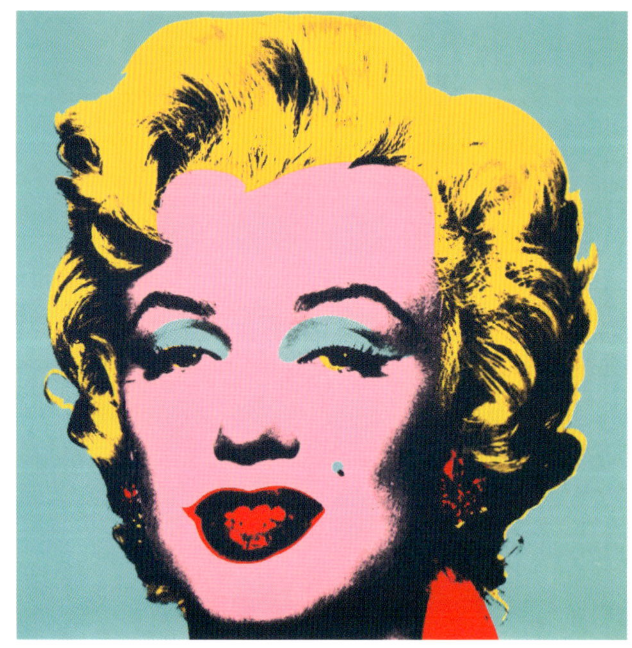

Art and marketing. Art is good only if it sells well: Andy Warhol.

Kunst und Kommerz. Kunst ist nur gute Kunst, wenn Sie sich gut verkaufen lässt: Andy Warhol.

Kunst en handel. Kunst is alleen goed als het goed verkoopt: Andy Warhol.

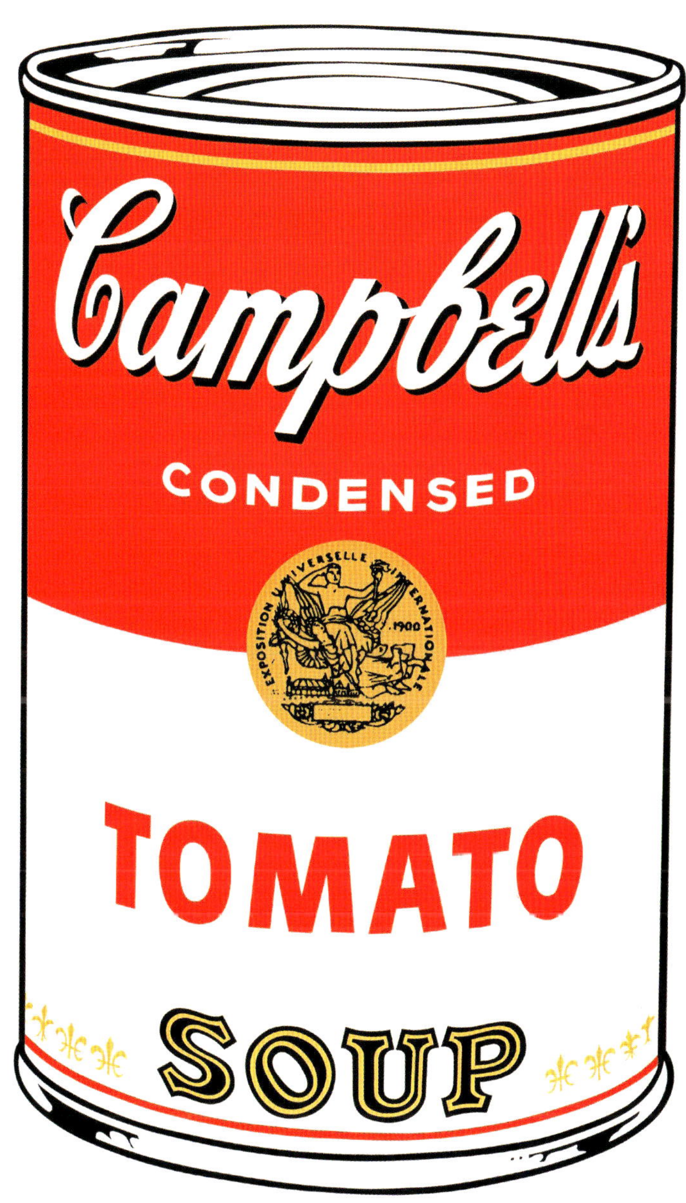

Andy Warhol
(PittsBurgh 1928 - New York 1987)

Untitled from Campbell's Soup I
Ohne Titel von Campbell's Soup I
Zonder titel uit Campbell's Soup I

●●●

1968
81 x 47,6 cm / 31.88 x 18.74 in.
Museum of Modern Art (MoMA), New York

Screen-print / Serigraphie / Zeefdruk

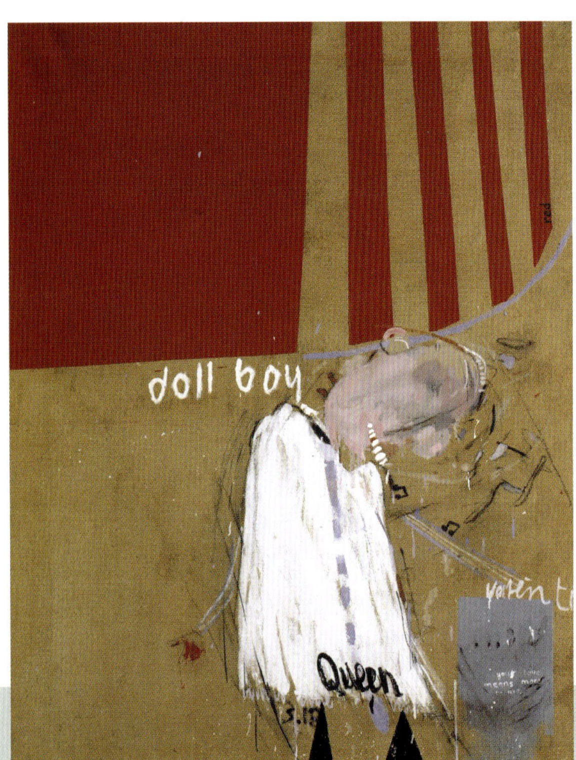

David Hockney
(Bradford 1937)

Doll boy

●

1960
122 x 99 cm / 48.03 x 38.97 in.
Hamburger Kunsthalle,
Hamburg

Oil on canvas
Öl auf Leinwand
Olieverf op doek

Pop Art reaches England.

Die Pop Art erreicht England.

De Pop Art bereikt Engeland.

Richard Hamilton
(London 1922)

Interior
Interieur

●●

1964
56 x 96.7 cm / 22.04 x 38.07 in.
Museum of Modern Art
(MoMA), New York

Screen-print
Serigraphie
Zeefdruk

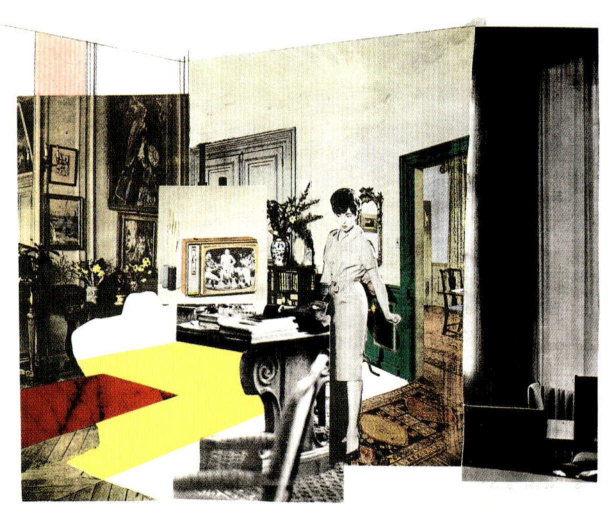

Eduardo Paolozzi
(Leith 1924 - London 2005)

Tortured Life (plate, folio 5)
Tortured Life (Tafel, Blatt 5)

●

1965
37 x 25 / 14.5 x 9.8 in.
Museum of Modern Art (MoMA),
New York

Screen-print
Serigraphie
Zeefdruk

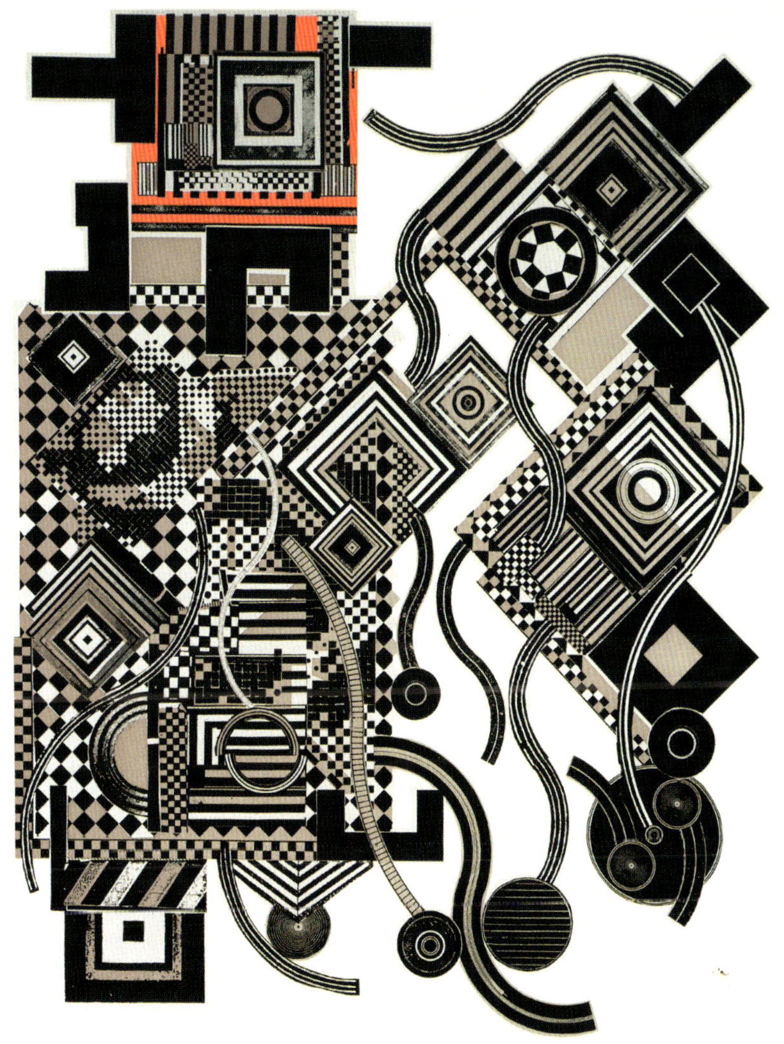

Yves Klein
(Nice 1928 - Paris 1962)

IKB Godet Untitled Blue Monochrome
IKB Godet Monochrome bleu sans titre

●●●

198 x 150 cm / 77.95 x 59.05 in.
Private Collection / Privatsammlung
Privécollectie

Mixed technique
Mischtechnik
Verschillende technieken

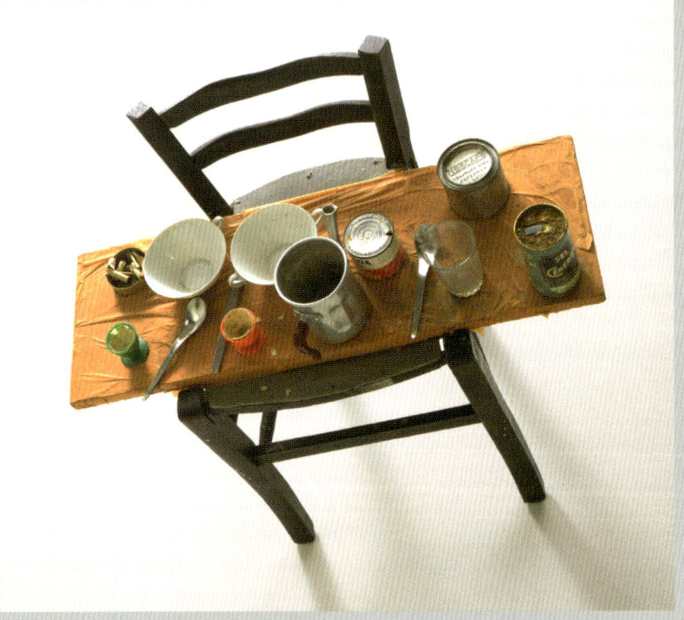

Nouveau Realisme: French Pop Art substitutes the intellect for marketing.

Nouveau Realisme, die französische Pop Art ersetzt Kommerz durch Intellekt.

Nouveau Realisme: de Franse Pop Art vervangt handel door intellect.

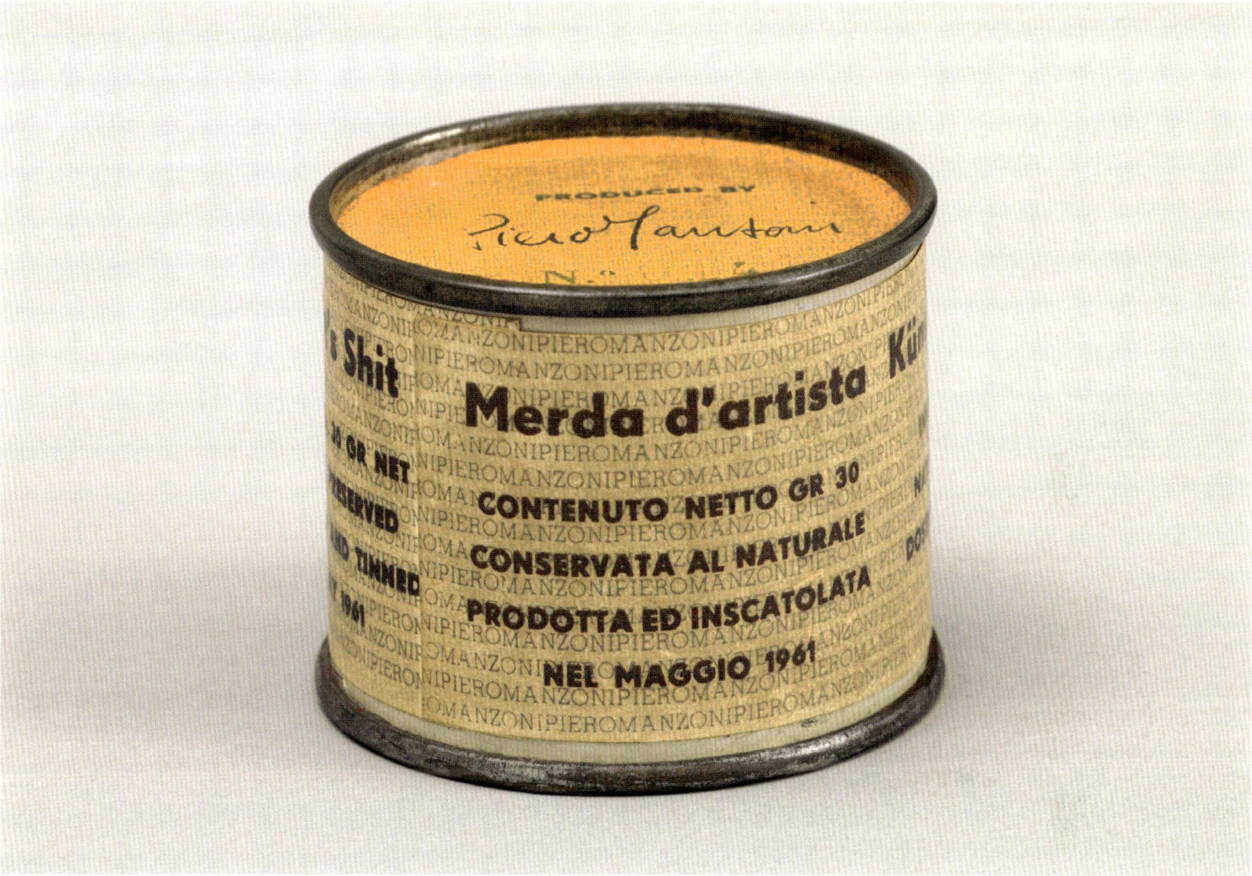

◂ Daniel Spoerri
(Galaţi 1930)

Kikchka's Breakfast I
Kichkas Frühstück I
Kikchka's onbijt I

●

1960
36,6 x 69,5 x 65,4 cm
14.40 x 27.36 x 25.74 in.
Museum of Modern Art (MoMA), New York

Assemblage / Assemblierte Gegenstände

Piero Manzoni
(Soncino 1933 - Milano 1963)

Artist's Shit
Künstlerscheiße
Stront van de kunstenaar

1961
h. 4,8 cm / 1.88 in.
Museum of Modern Art (MoMA), New York

Mixed technique
Mischtechnik
Verschillende technieken

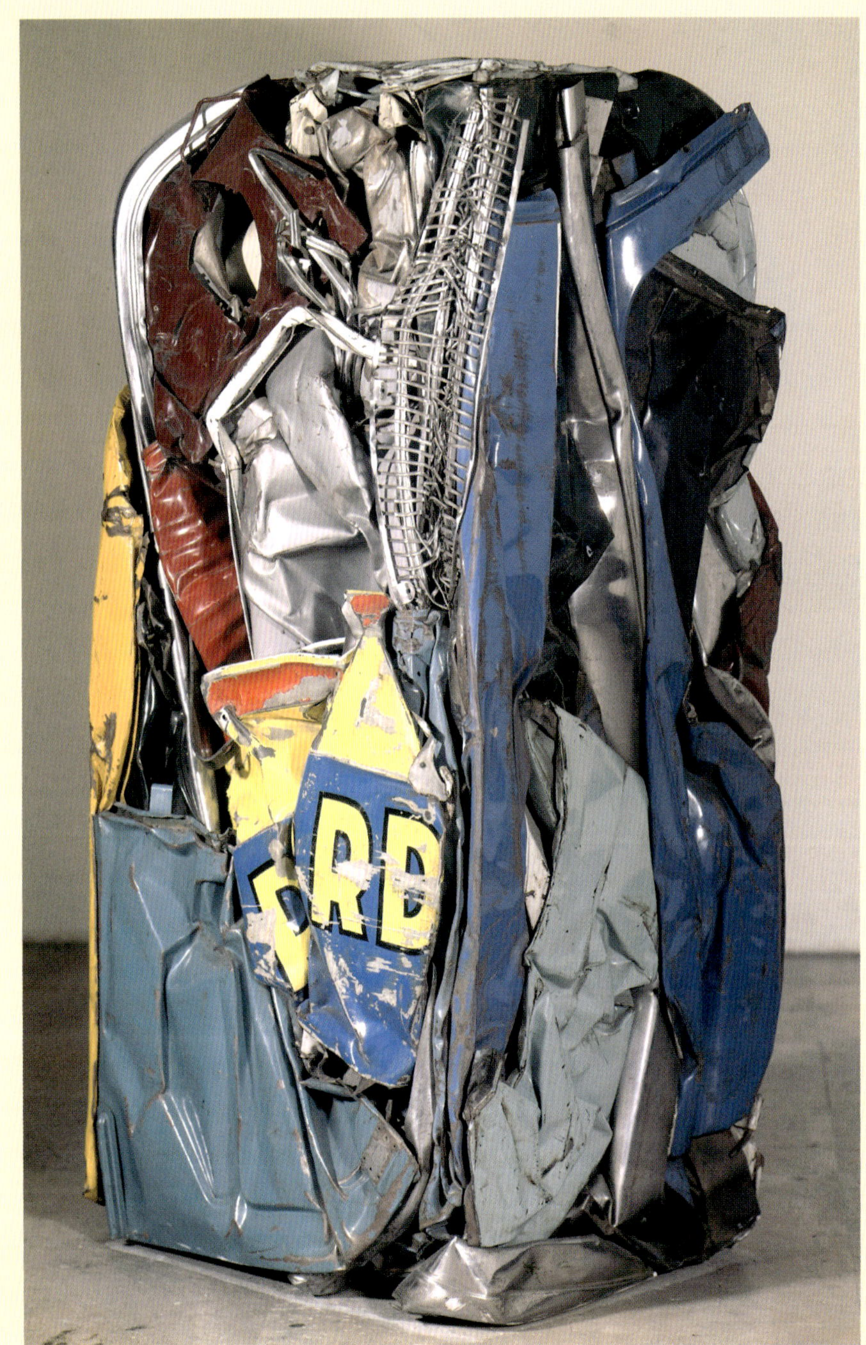

César
(Marseille 1921 - Paris 1998)

Compression
Kompression
Compressie

●

1962
Musée National d'Art Moderne - Centre Pompidou, Paris

Mixed technique
Mischtechnik
Verschillende technieken

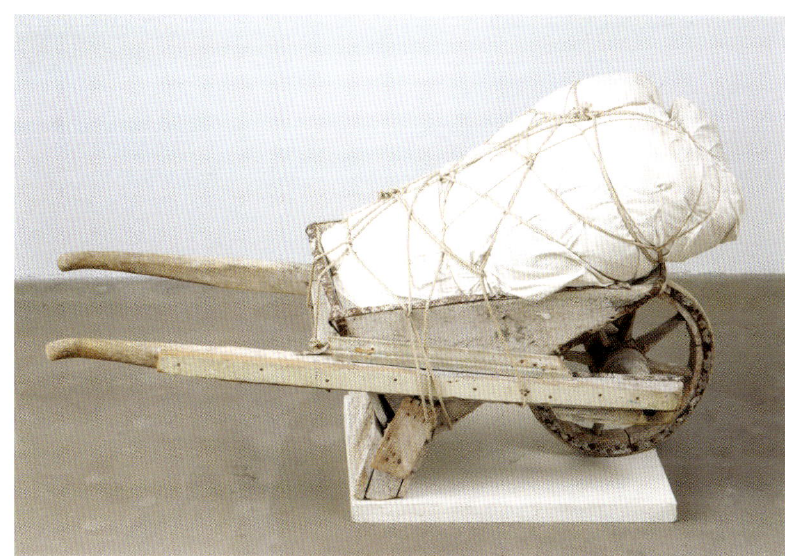

Christo
(Gabrovo 1935)

Package on Wheelbarrow
Paket auf einem Schubkarren
Kruiwagen met pakket

●●

1963
89,1 x 151 x 51,4 cm
35.07 x 59.44 x 20.23 in.
Museum of Modern Art (MoMA), New York

Mixed technique
Mischtechnik
Verschillende technieken

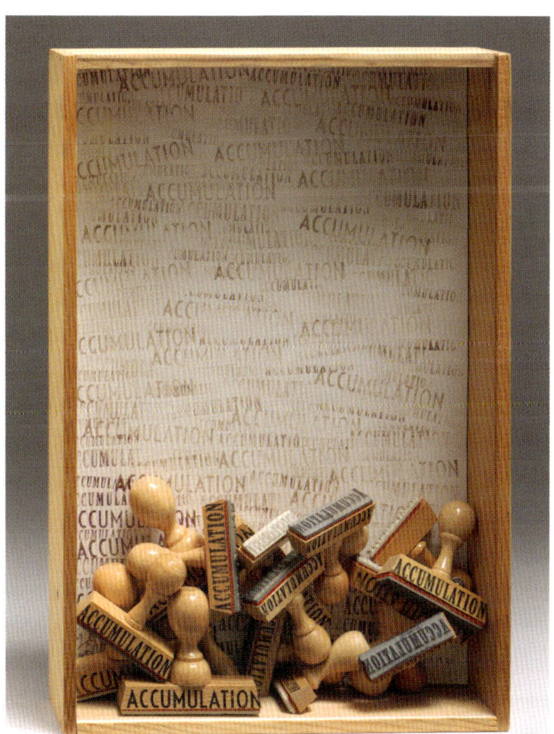

Arman
(Nice 1928 - New York 2005)

Accumulation
Anhäufung

1973
47 x 32 x 8,4 cm / 18.50 x 12.59 x 3.30 in.
Museum of Modern Art (MoMA), New York

Assemblage / Assemblierte Gegenstände

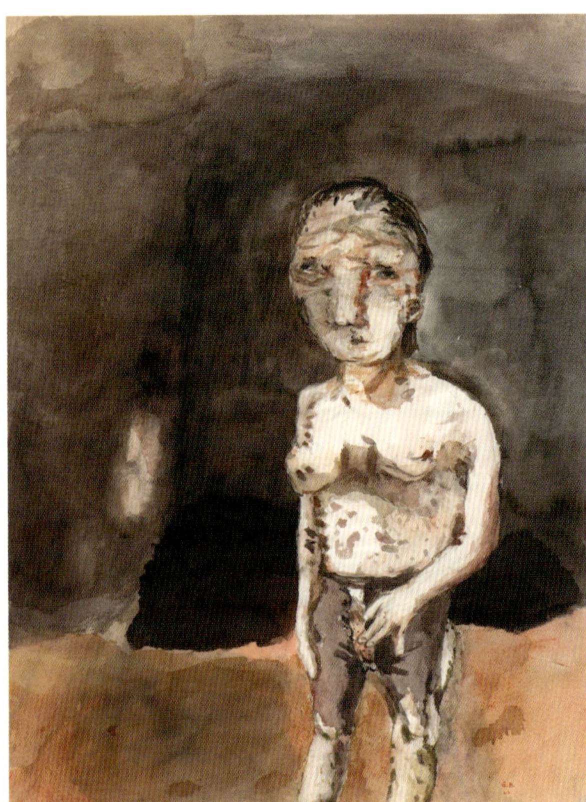

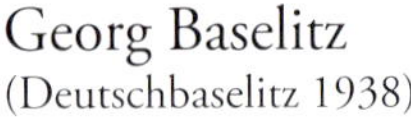

Georg Baselitz
(Deutschbaselitz 1938)

Big Night Down the Drain
Die große Nacht im Eimer
De grote nacht in de goot

●●

1963
62,9 x 48,3 cm / 24.76 x 19.01 in.
Museum of Modern Art (MoMA), New York

Mixed technique
Mischtechnik
Verschillende technieken

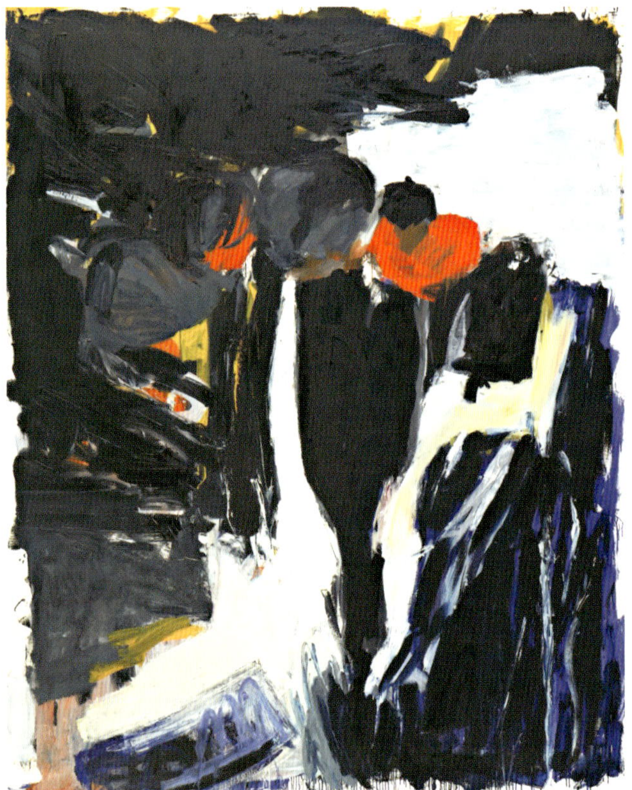

Georg Baselitz
(Deutschbaselitz 1938)

Still life
Stillleben
Stilleven

●●

c. 1976 - 1977
250,1 x 200,4 cm / 98.46 x 78.89 in.
Museum of Modern Art (MoMA), New York

Oil on canvas
Öl auf Leinwand
Olieverf op doek

A. R. Penck
(Dresden 1939)

Nightvision, from the portfolio First Concentration I
Nachtvision, aus Erste Konzentration I
Nightvision, from the portfolio First Concentration I

●●

1982
Museum of Modern Art (MoMA), New York

Woodcut, printed in black
Holzschnitt,schwarz gedruckt
Houtsnede, afgedrukt in zwart

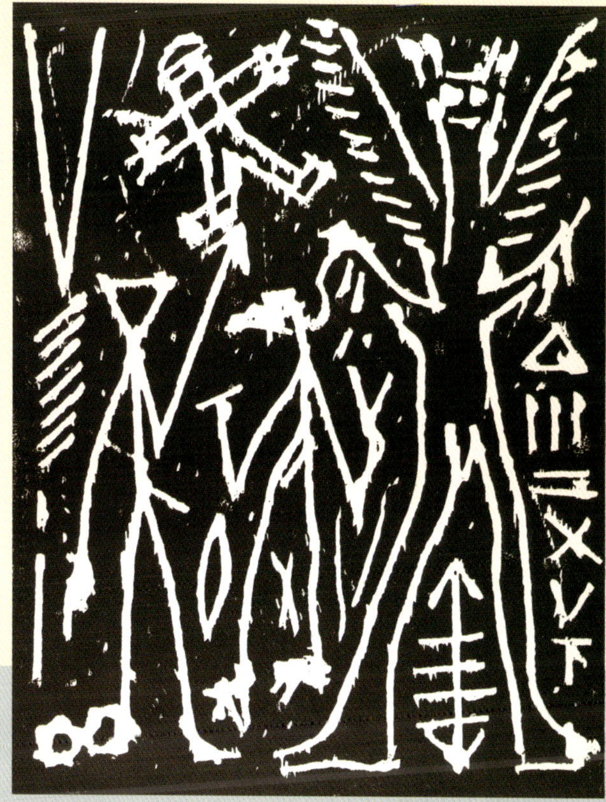

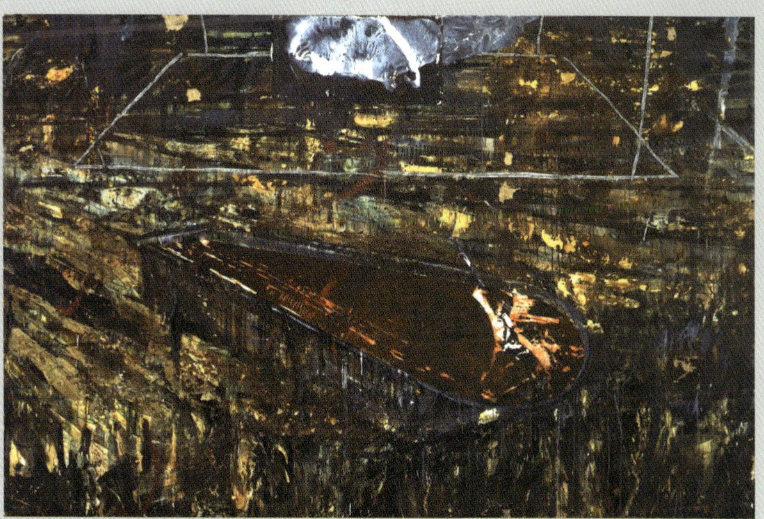

Anselm Kiefer
(Donaueschingen 1945)

The Red Sea
Das Rote Meer
De Rode Zee

●●

c. 1984-1985
278.8 x 425.1 cm / 109.76 x 167.36 in.
Museum of Modern Art (MoMA), New York

Oil on canvas
Öl auf Leinwand
Olieverf op doek

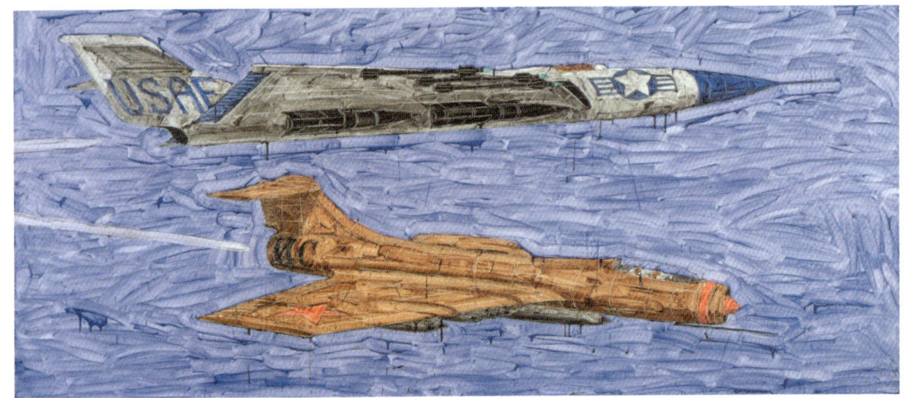

Neil Jenney
(Torrington 1945)

Them and Us
Sie und wir
Zij en wij

●●

1969
115 x 343 cm / 45.27 x 135.03 in.
Museum of Modern Art (MoMA), New York

Mixed technique
Mischtechnik
Verschillende technieken

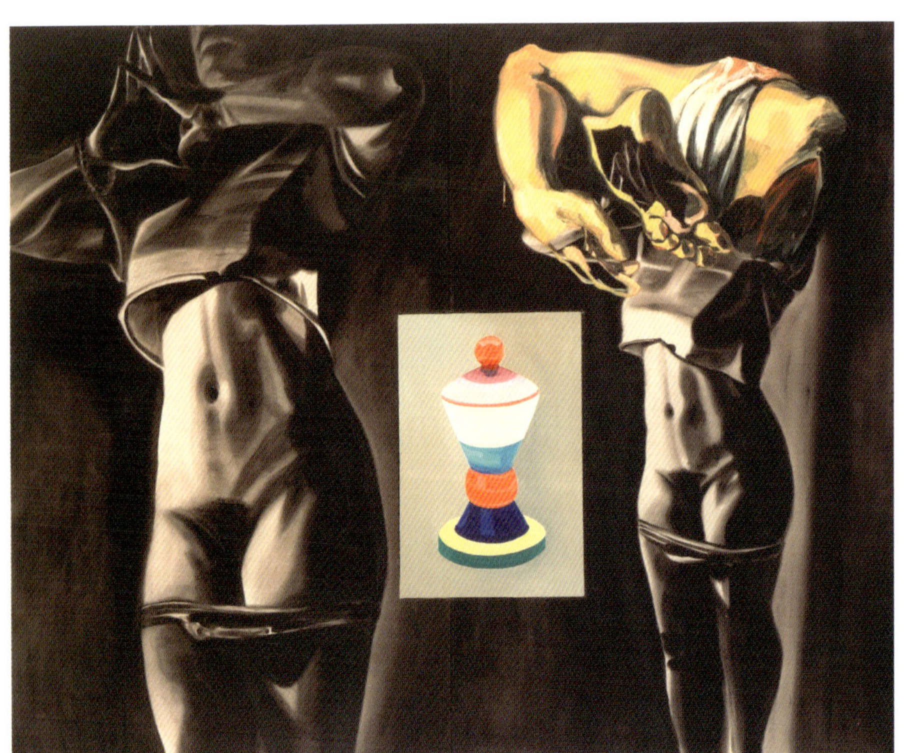

David Salle
(Norman 1952)

Gericault's Arm
De arm van Géricault

●●

1985
97,8 x 244,5 cm / 38.50 x 96.25 in.
Museum of Modern Art (MoMA), New York

Mixed technique
Mischtechnik
Verschillende technieken

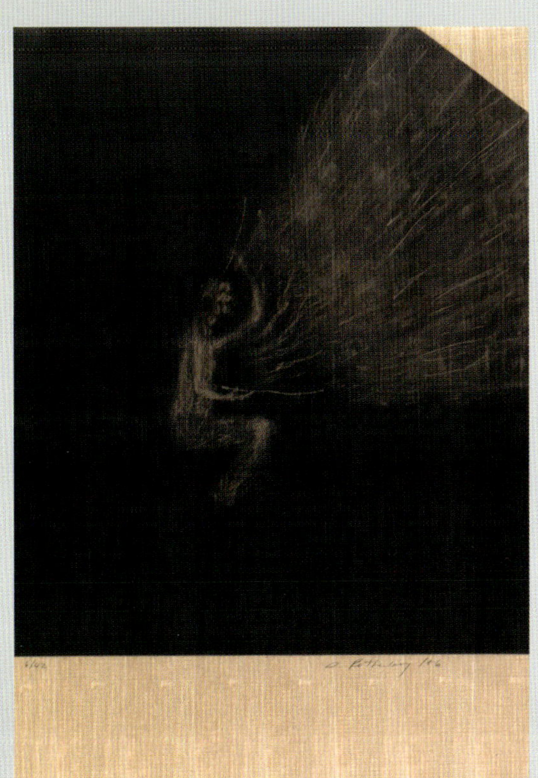

Susan Rothenberg
(Buffalo 1945)

Bone Man
Bone Man (Knochenmann)

●

1986
76,2 x 51,2 cm / 30 x 20.15 in.
Museum of Modern Art (MoMA), New York

Mezzotint on wood veneer paper
Mezzotinto auf Holzfurnier Papier
Mezzotint op houtfineer papier

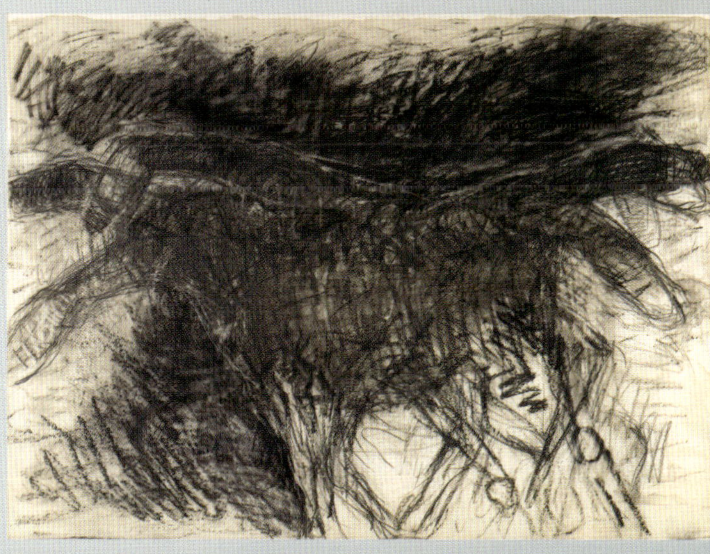

Susan Rothenberg
(Buffalo 1945)

Untitled
Ohne Titel
Zonder titel

●

1990
151,8 x 212,8 cm / 59.76 x 83.77 in.
Museum of Modern Art (MoMA), New York

Charcoal on paper
Kohle auf Papier
Houtskool op papier

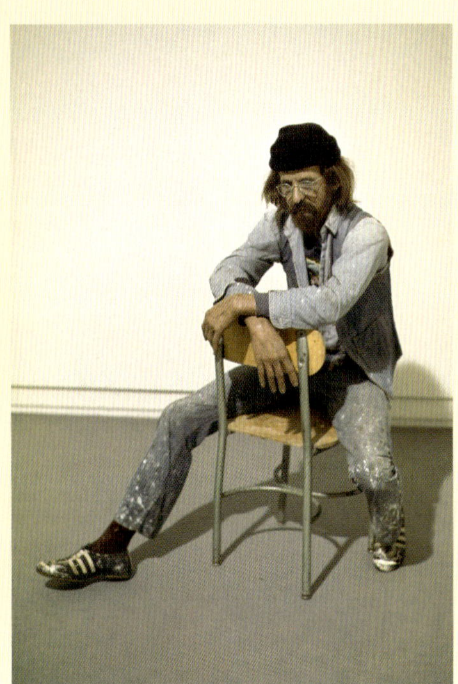

Duane Hanson

(Alexandria 1925 - Boca Raton 1996)

Seated Artist
Sitzender Künstler
Zittende kunstenaar

●

1971

Various materials
Verschiedene Materialien
Verschillende materialen

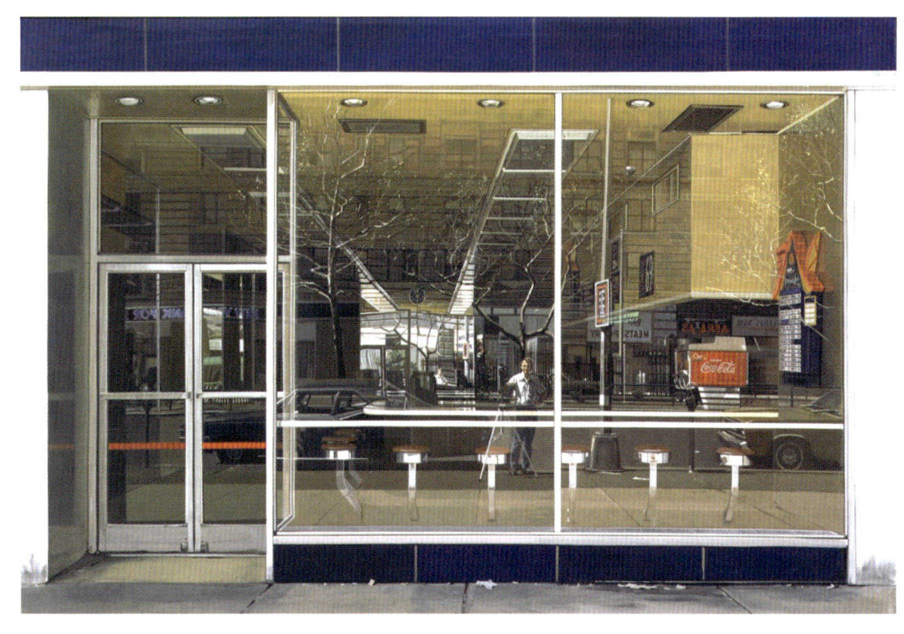

Richard Estes

(Kewanee 1932)

Double Self-Portrait
Doppeltes Selbstportrait
Dubbel zelfportret

●

1976
60,8 x 91,5 cm / 23.93 x 36.02 in.
Museum of Modern Art (MoMA),
New York

Oil on canvas
Öl auf Leinwand
Olieverf op doek

Chuck Close
(Monroe, Washington 1940)

Self-Portrait/Black Ink
Self-Portrait/Black Ink
Zelfportret/Zwarte inkt

●●

1977
138,43 x 103,5 cm / 54 x 40 in.
Yale University Art Gallery,
New Haven (CT)

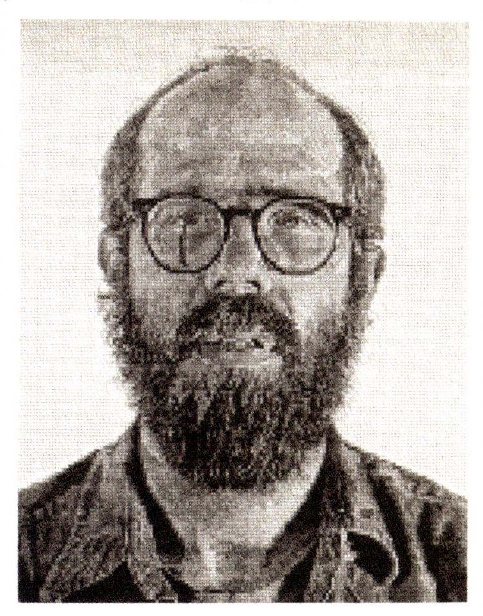

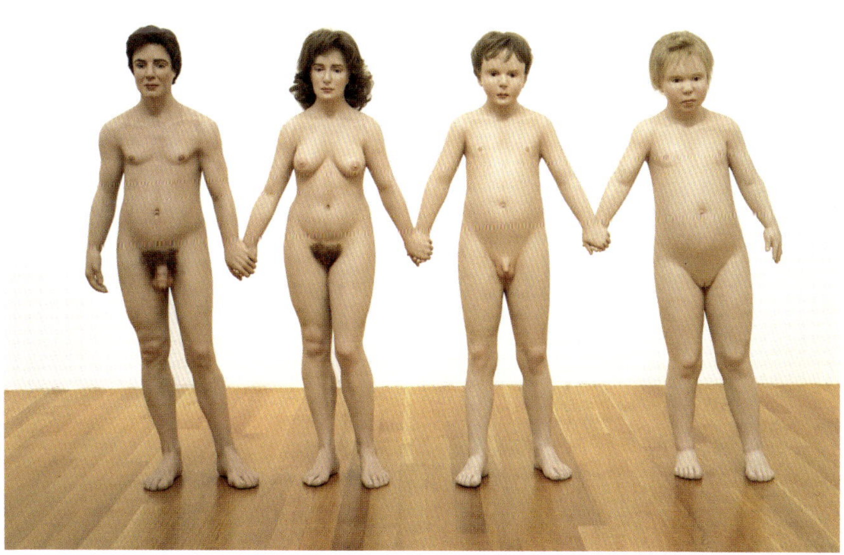

Ray Charlcs
(Chicago 1953)

Family Romance
Familie Romance

1993
134,6 x 215,9 x 27,9 cm
53 x 85 x 10.98 in.
Museum of Modern Art (MoMA),
New York

Various materials
Verschiedene Materialien
Verschillende materialen

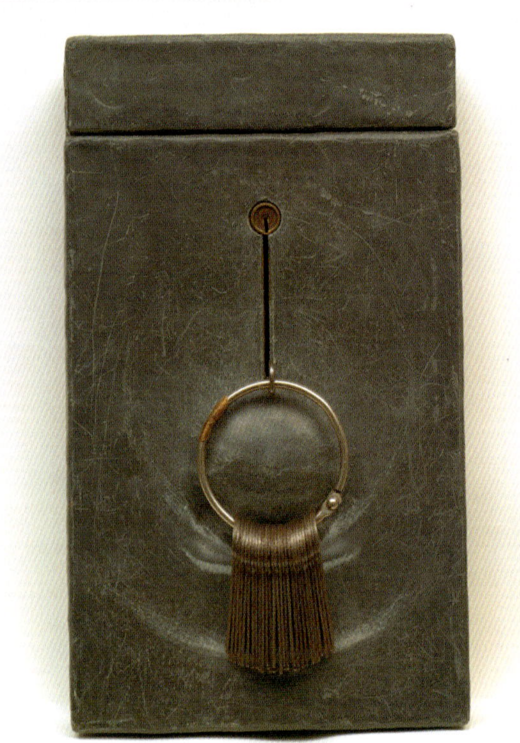

Robert Morris
(Kansas City 1931)

Litanies

●

1963
30.4 x 18 x 6.3 cm / 11.96 x 7.08 x 2.48 in.
Museum of Modern Art (MoMA), New York

Various materials
Verschiedene Materialien
Verschillende materialen

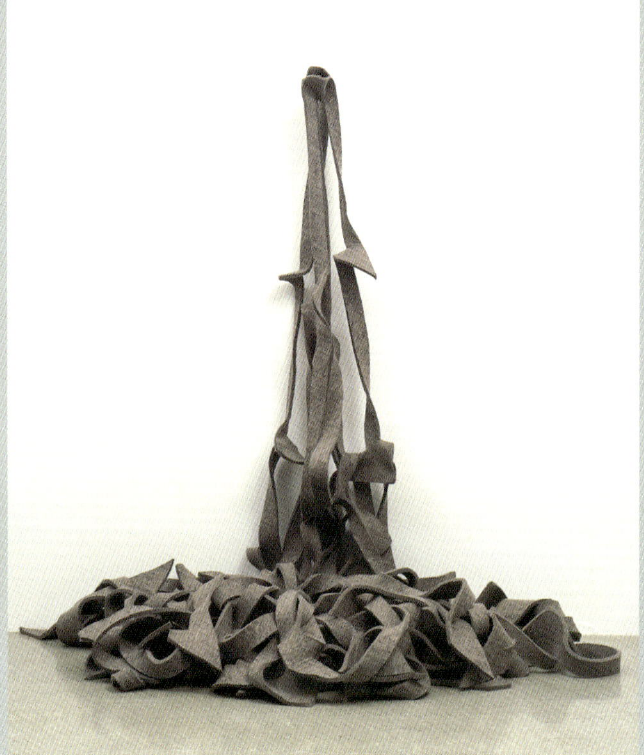

Robert Morris
(Kansas City 1931)

Untitled (Tangle)
Ohne Titel (Gewirr)
Zonder titel (Warboel)

●

1967
296,7 x 269,3 x 147,4 cm / 116.81 x 106.02 x 58.03 in.
Museum of Modern Art (MoMA), New York

Installation / Installatie

Richard Serra
(San Francisco 1939)

Untitled
Ohne Titel
Zonder titel

●

1967
244,5 x 186,7 x 17,2 cm /
96.25 x 73.50 x 6.77 in.
Museum of Modern Art (MoMA), New York

Installation / Installatie

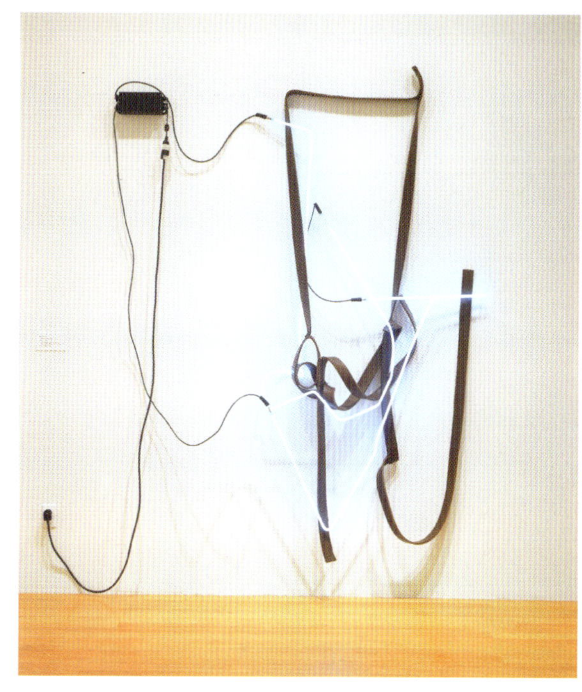

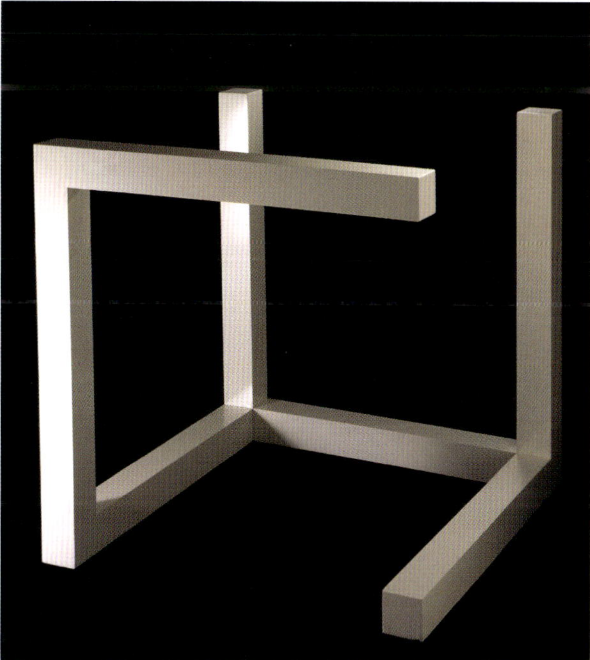

Sol LeWitt
(Hartford 1928 - New York 2007)

Open Cube
Offener Kubus
Open Kubus

1968
105 x 105 x 105 cm / 41.33 x 41.33 x 41.33 in.
Nationalgalerie, Staatliche Museen, Berlin

Aluminum / Aluminium

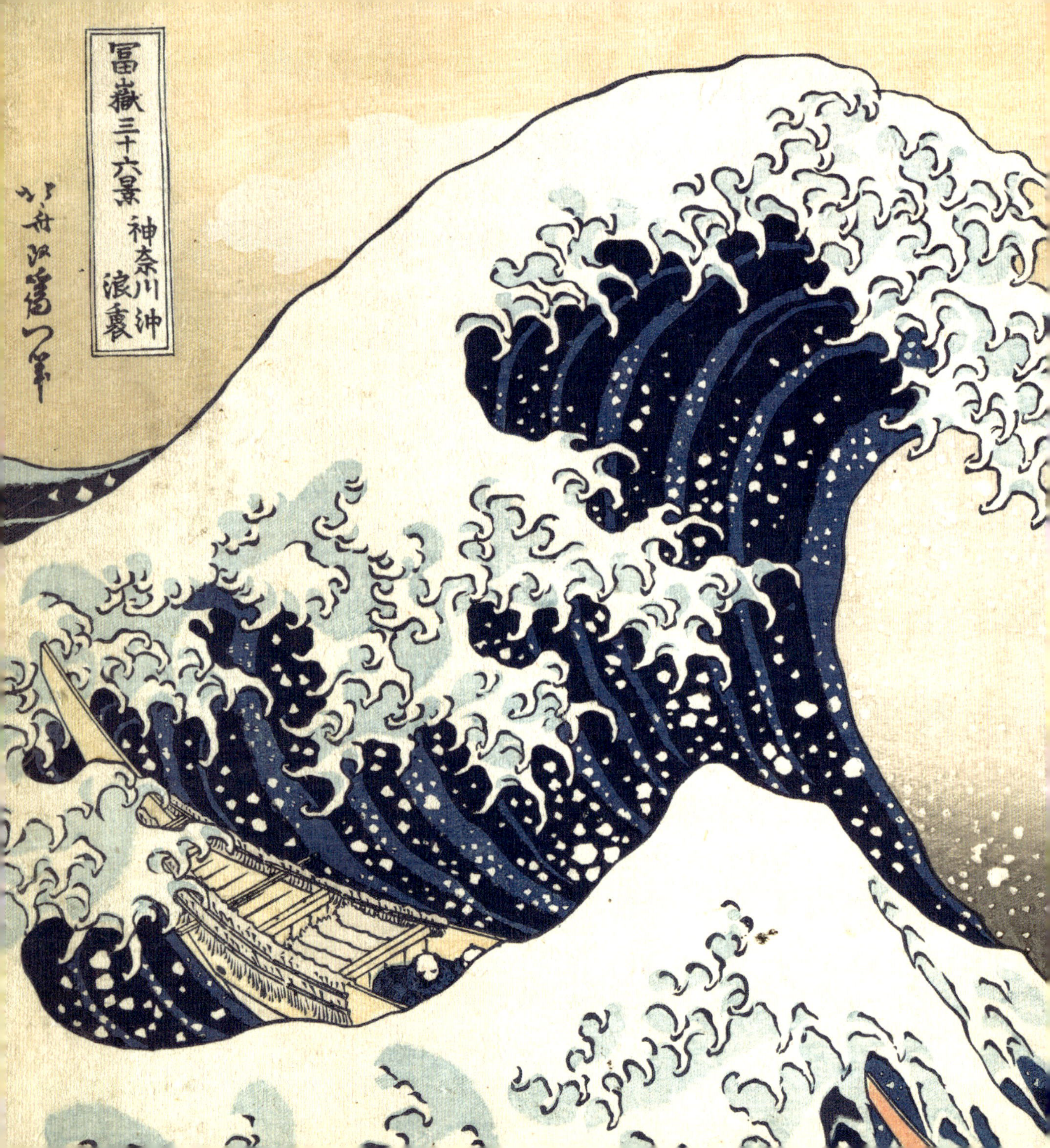
冨嶽三十六景
神奈川沖
浪裏

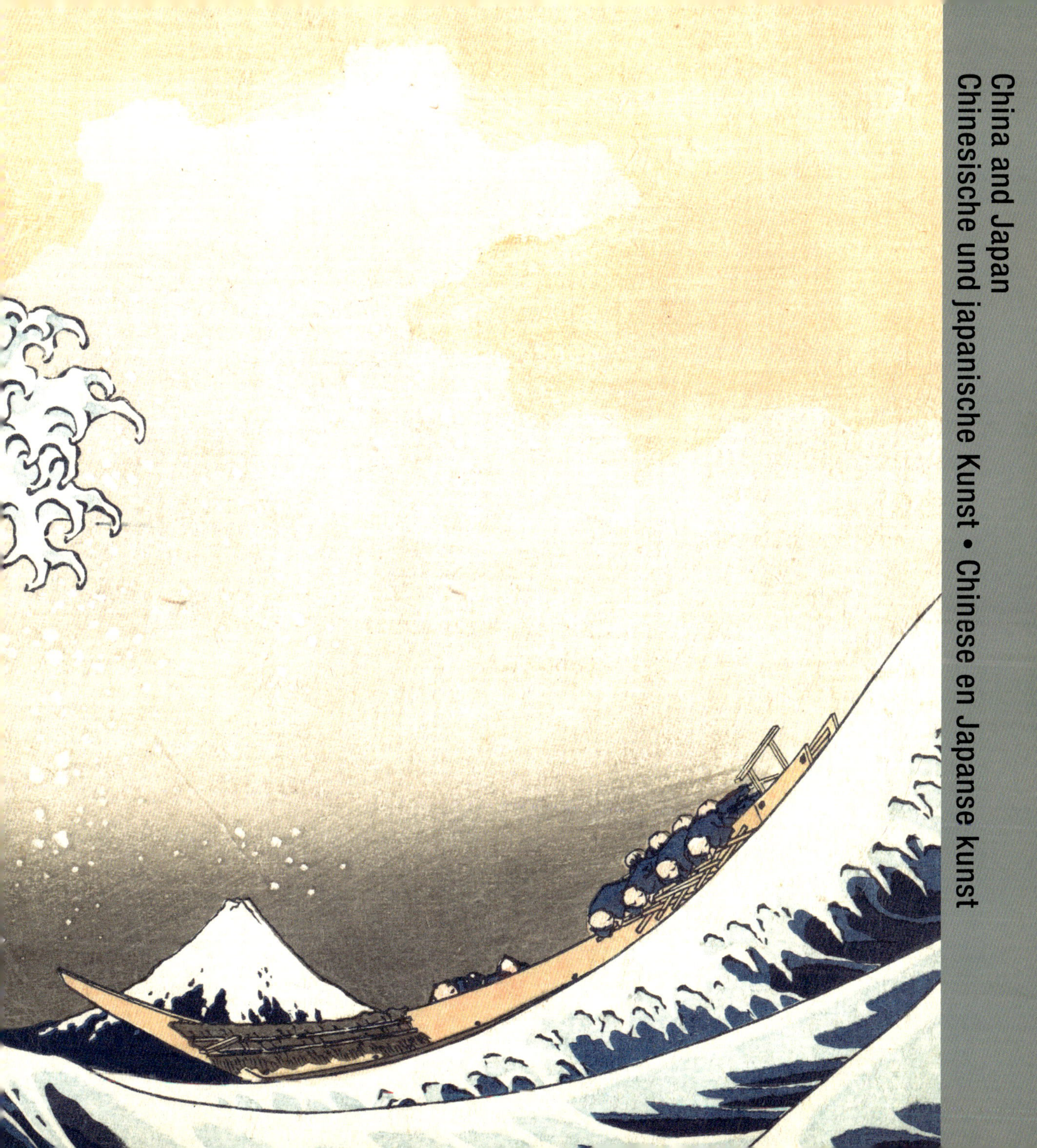
China and Japan
Chinesische und japanische Kunst • Chinese en Japanse kunst

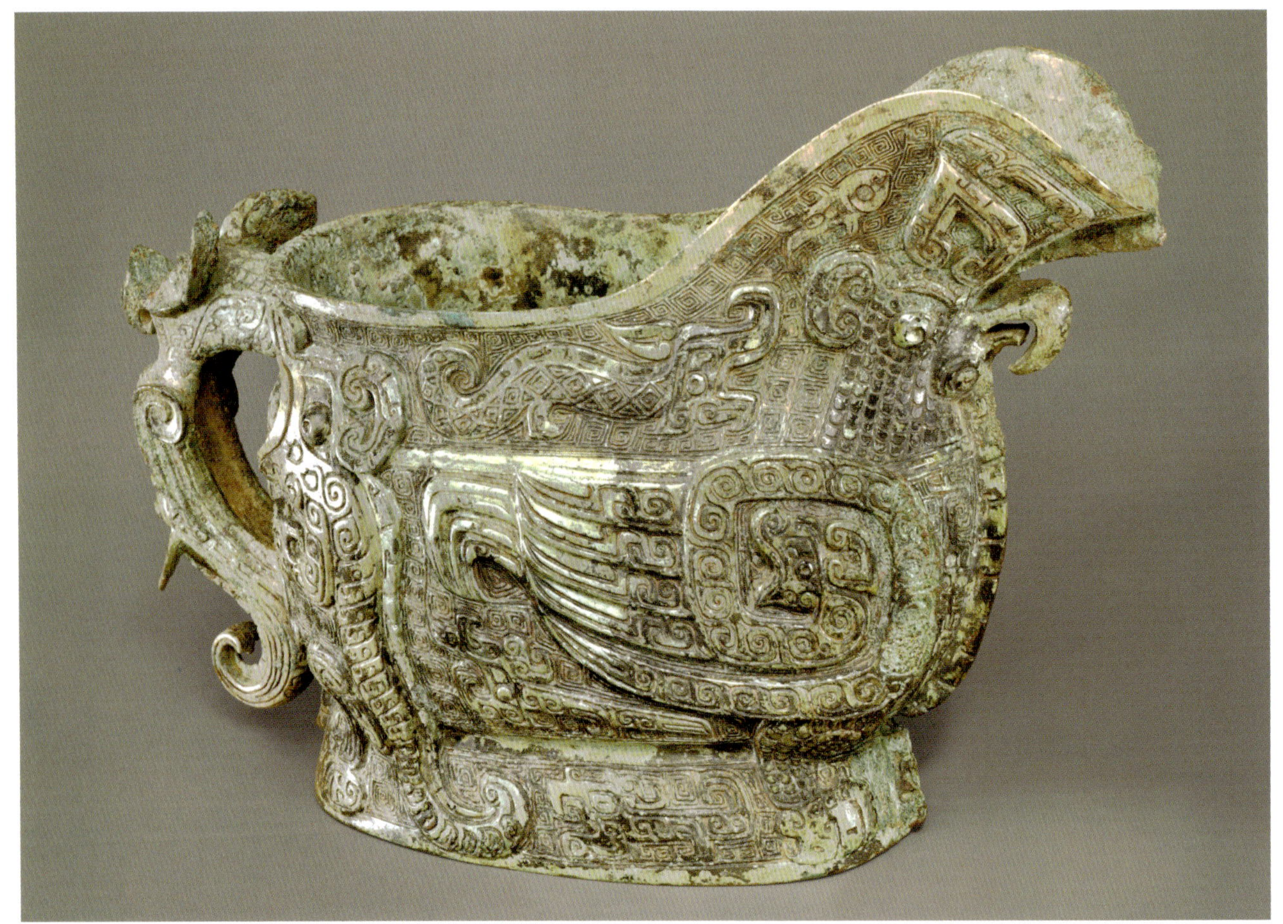

Spouted Ritual Wine Vessel (Guang)
Ritual-Krug für Wein (Guang)
Rituele vaas voor wijn (Guang)

●●

Shang Dynasty / Shang-Dynastie / Shang-dynastie
c. 1300 - 1050 BCE
h. 21,6 cm / 8.50 in.
Metropolitan Museum of Art, New York

Bronze / Brons

Bronze urns for the ancestor cult are the earliest evidence of Chinese culture.

Die frühesten Zeugnisse der chinesischen Hochkultur sind rituelle Bronzegefäße für den Ahnenkult.

Bronzen vazen voor de voorouderverering zijn de eerste getuigenissen van de Chinese beschaving.

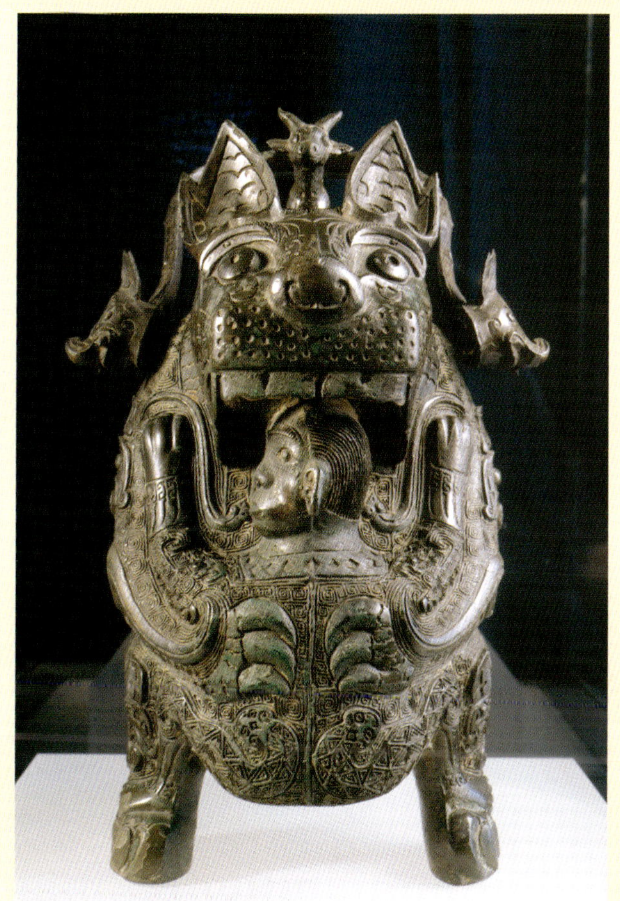

You Vase Known as "The Tiger"
Der Tiger, You Vase
De tijger, You vaas

●

c. 900 - 800 BCE
h. 35 cm / 31.77 in.
Musée Cernuschi, Paris

Bronze / Brons

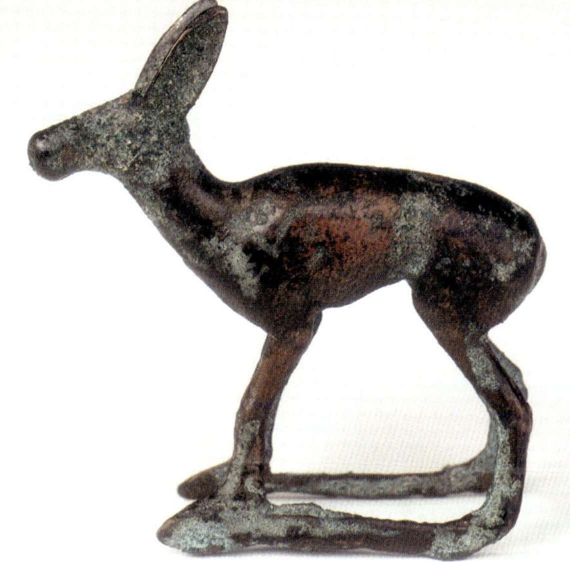

Standing Doe
Hirschkuh
Hinde

●

Eastern Zhou dynasty / Östliche Zhou-Dynastie
Oostelijke Zhou-dynastie
c. 590 - 410 BCE
Museum of East Asian Art, Bath

Bronze / Brons

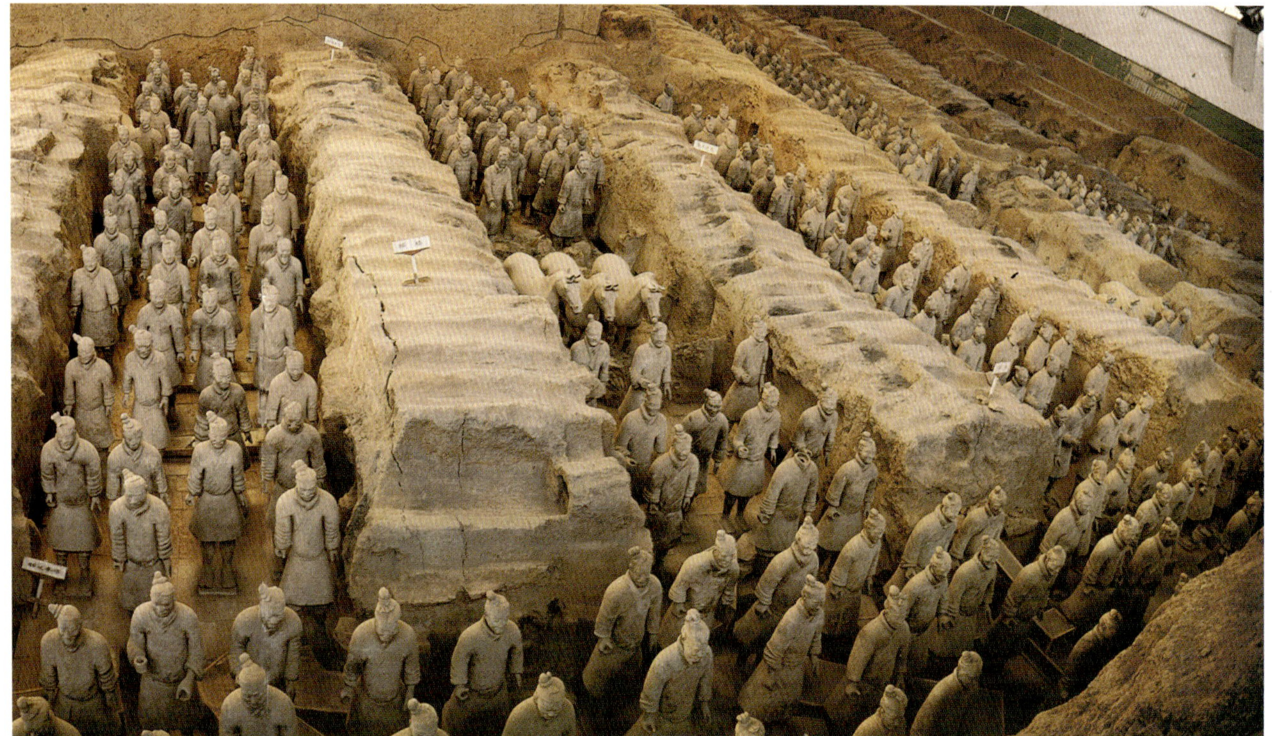

524

Terracotta Warriors
Krieger aus Terrakotta
Terracotta Krijgers

●●●

c. 300 - 200 BCE
Lintong, Xi'an

Terracotta / Terrakotta

March 1974, a sensational archaeological find: thousands of terracotta warriors, each portraying an individual, from the period of the first Chinese emperor.

Sensationeller archäologischer Fund im März 1974: Tausende Terrakottakrieger mit lebensechten Gesichtern aus der Zeit des "Ersten Kaisers von China".

In maart 1974 vindt er een sensationele archeologische vondst plaats: duizenden terracotta soldaten met levensechte gezichten uit de periode van de "Eerste keizer van China".

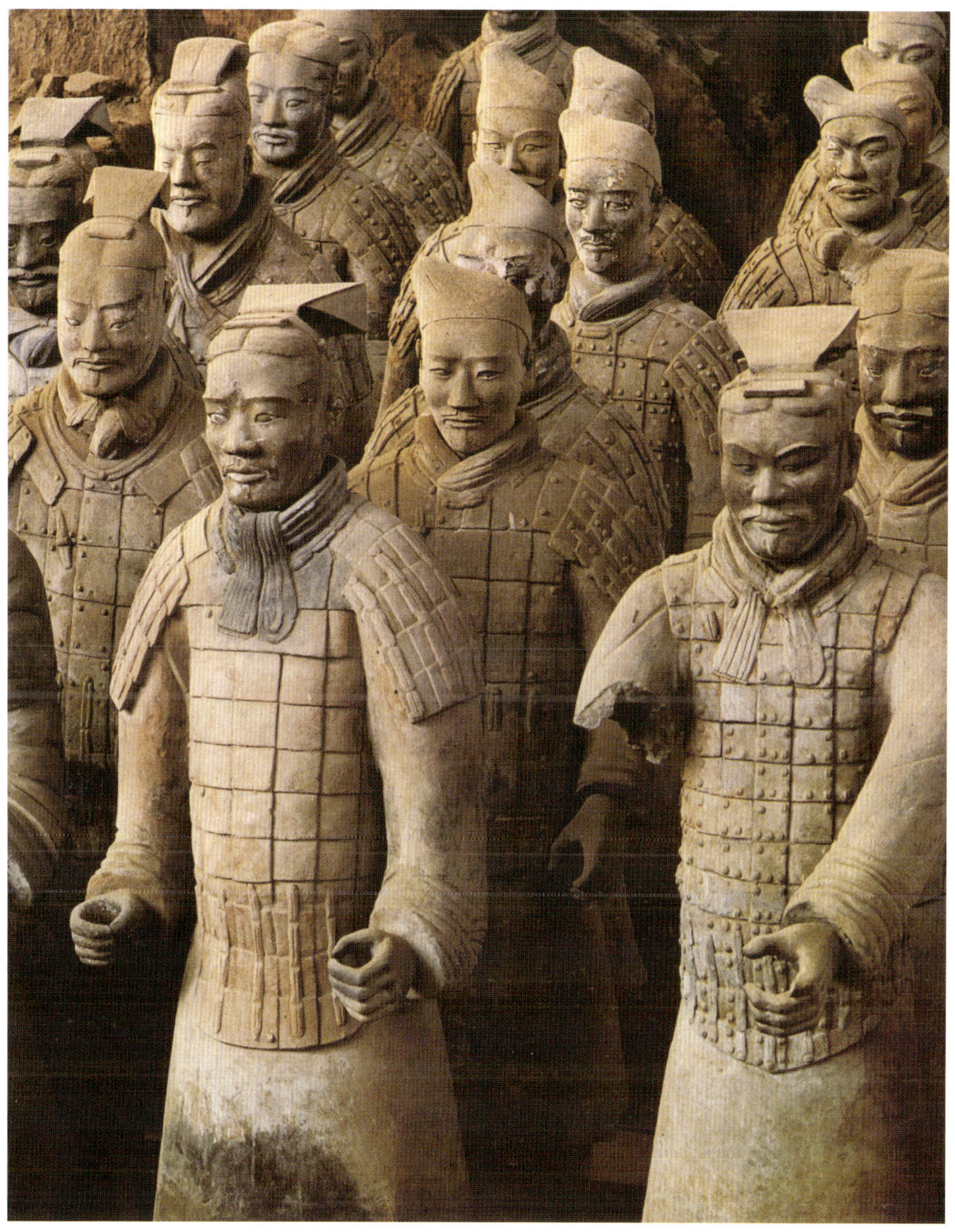

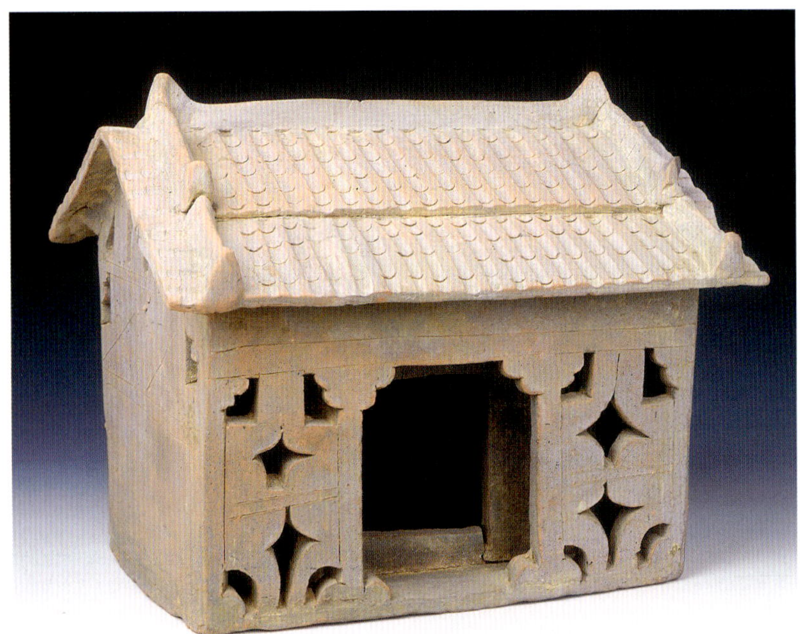

Model of a House
Modell eines Hauses
Model van een huis

●

Han Dynasty / Han-Dynastie / Han-dynastie
c. 200 - 250
Museum of East Asian Art, Bath

Ceramic / Keramik / Keramiek

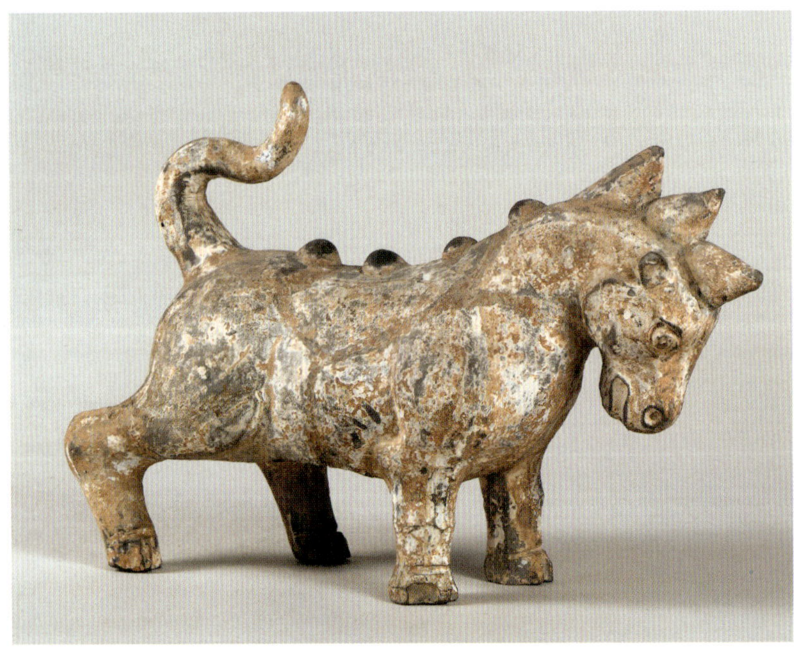

Funeral Statuette of a Horse
Grabstatuette eines Pferdes
Grafbeeldje dat een paard vertegenwoordigt

●

Han Dynasty / Han-Dynastie / Han-dynastie
206 BCE - 220 CE
Museo Nazionale d'Arte Orientale, Roma

Terracotta / Terrakotta

Figure of Woman
Frauenfigur
Vrouwenfiguurtje

●

Han Dynasty / Han-Dynastie
Han-dynastie
c. 206 BCE - 220 CE
Museum of Fine Arts, Boston

Terracotta / Terrakotta

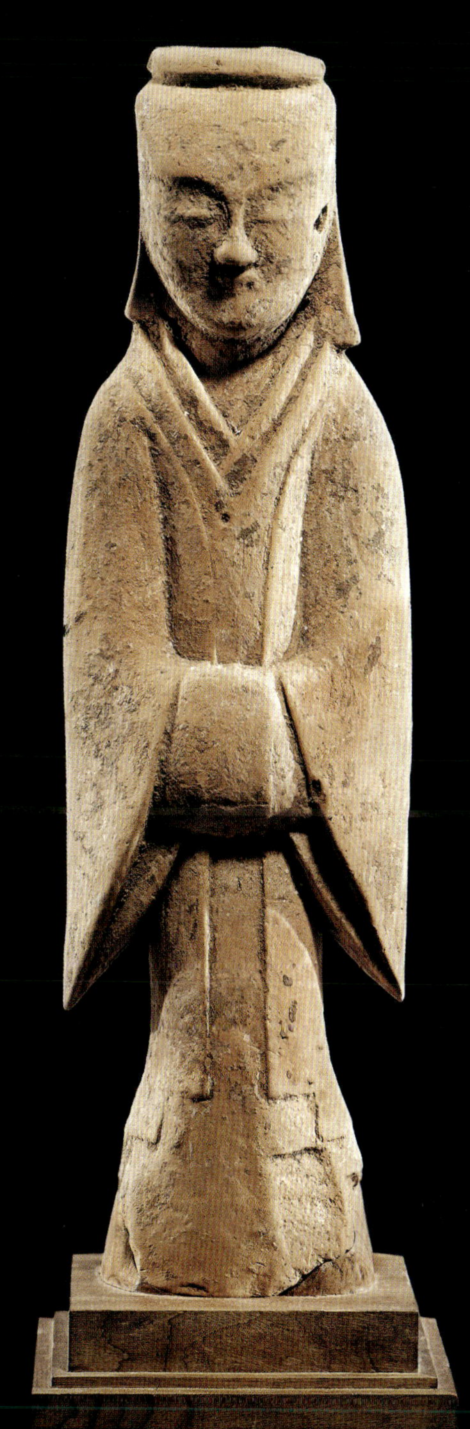

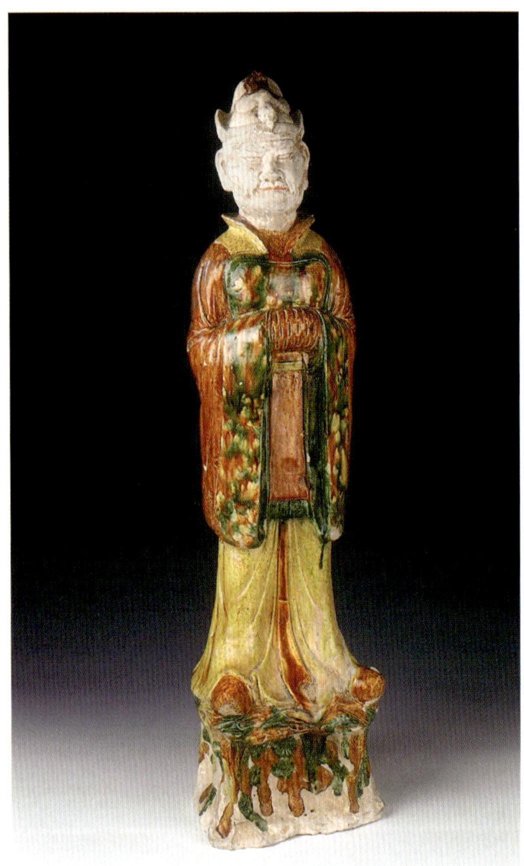

Khotanese official
Funktionär aus Khotan
Khotanese Functionaris

●●

Tang Dynasty / Tang-Dynastie / Tang-dynastie
c. 684-756
Museum of East Asian Art, Bath

Ceramic / Keramik / Keramiek

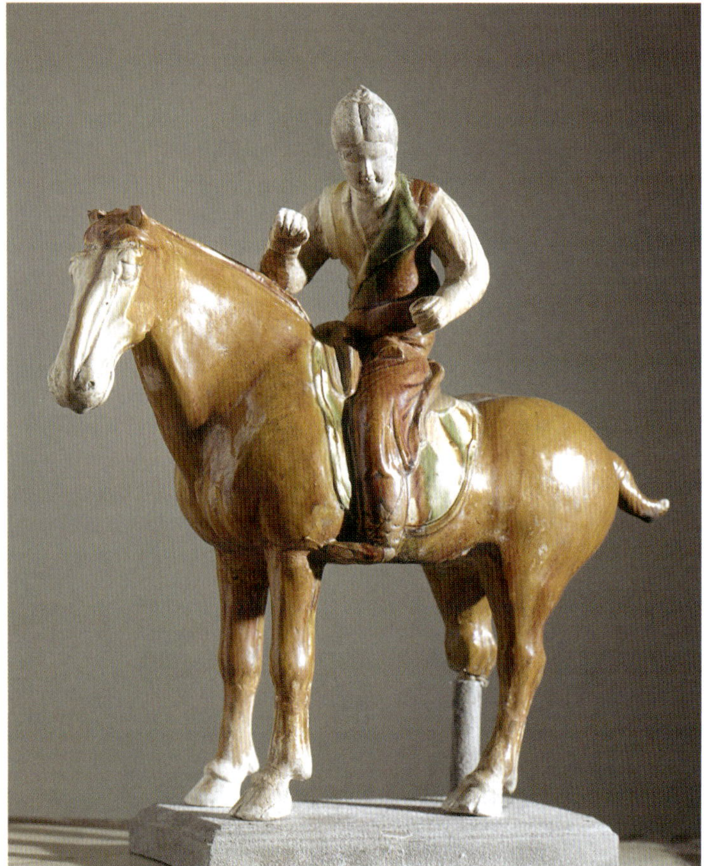

Polo Player
Polo-Spieler
Polospeler

Tang Dynasty / Tang-Dynastie / Tang-dynastie
c. 700-800
Musée Cernuschi, Paris

Ceramic / Keramik / Keramiek

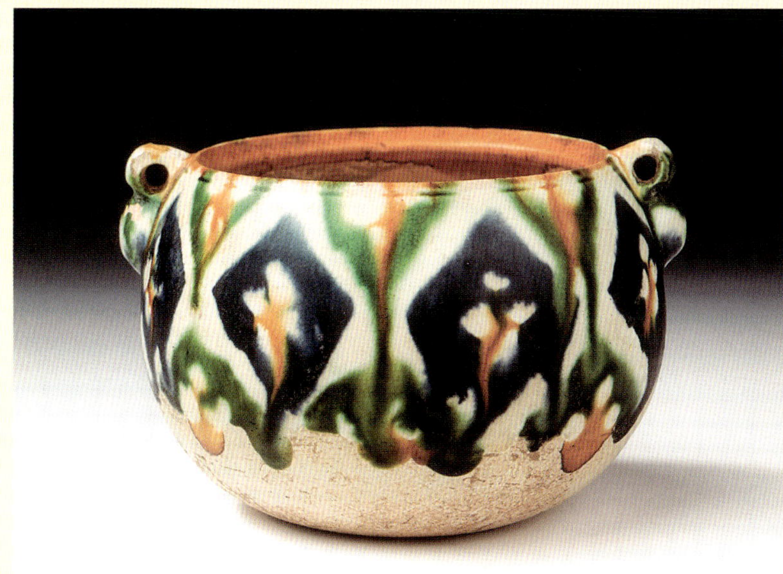

Jar
Krug
Aarden kruik

●●

Tang Dynasty / Tang-Dynastie / Tang-dynastie
c. 700-750
Museum of East Asian Art, Bath

Three-colour (sancai) ceramic
Sancai-Keramik
Sancai aardewerk

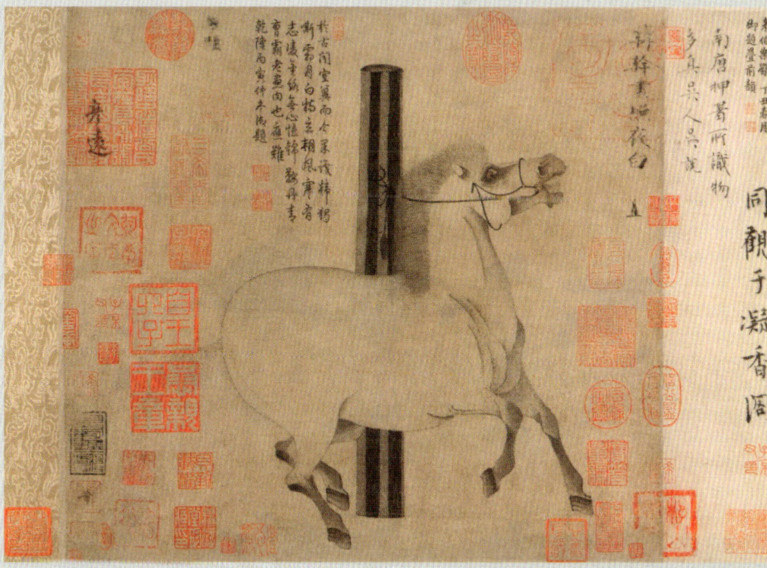

Han Gan
Night-Shining White
Weißes Pferd
Nacht- Schijnend Wit

●

Tang Dynasty / Tang-Dynastie / Tang-dynastie
c. 700-800
30,8 x 34 cm / 12.12 x 13.38 in.
Metropolitan Museum of Art, New York

Ink on paper / Tinte auf Papier / Inkt op papier

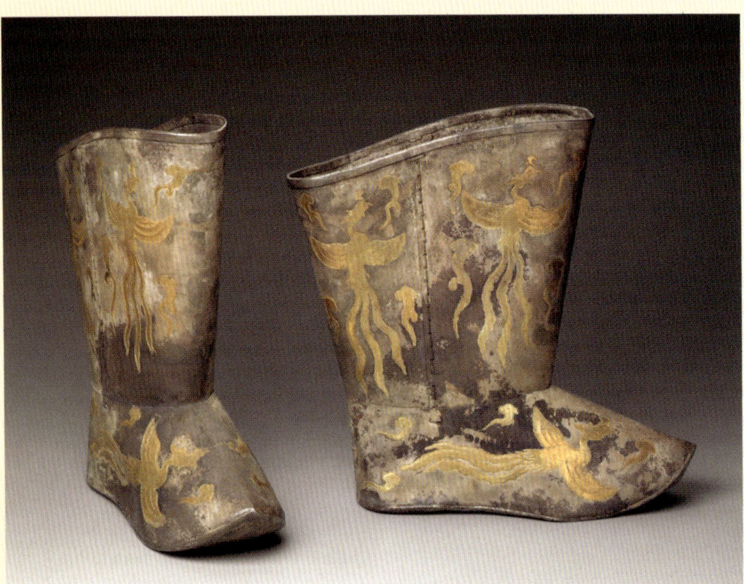

A pair of Boots
Stiefelpaar
Paar laarzen

●

Liao Dynasty / Liao-Dynastie / Liao-dynastie
c. 1000 - 1050
29,5 x 26 cm / 11.61 x 10.23 in.
Museum of Fine Arts, Boston

Gilded silver
Vergoldetes Silber
Verguld zilver

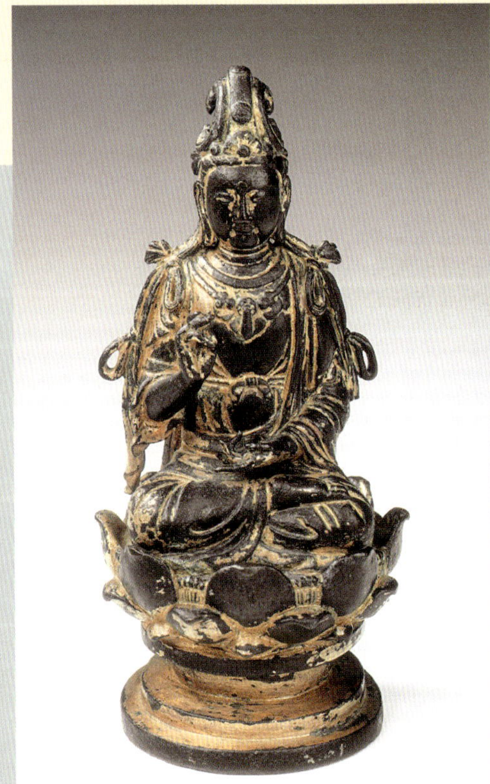

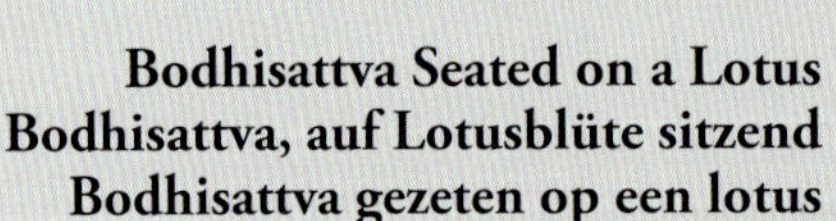

Bodhisattva Seated on a Lotus
Bodhisattva, auf Lotusblüte sitzend
Bodhisattva gezeten op een lotus

●

c. 1050
Museum of East Asian Art, Bath

Gilded bronze / Vergoldete Bronze / Verguld brons

Male Funerary Mask
Männliche Totenmaske
Dodenmasker van een man

●

Liao Dynasty / Liao-Dynastie
Liao-dynastie
c. 1100 - 1200
Musée Cernuschi, Paris

Gilded bronze and silver
Bronze und vergoldetes Silber
Brons en verguld zilver

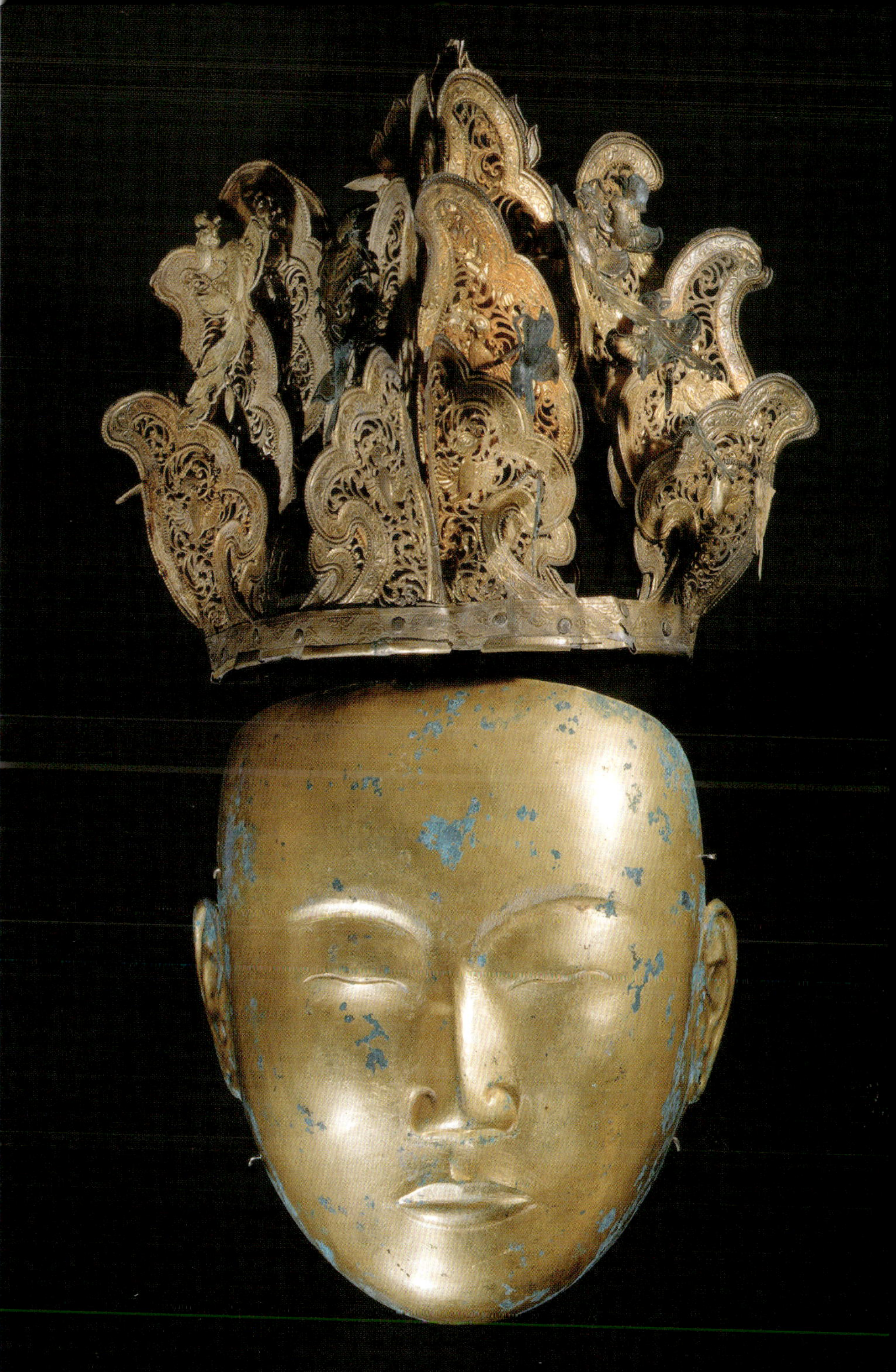

Simplicity and elegant design: the emperor-artist expects his court artists to provide realistic colours and forms in their representations.

Einfachheit und Noblesse der Linie. Der Künstlerkaiser fordert von seinen Hofkünstlern die wirklichkeitsnahe Wiedergabe in Farbe und Form.

Een eenvoudige en nobele lijnvoering. De keizer-kunstenaar eist van zijn hofkunstenaars een realistische weergave in kleur en vorm

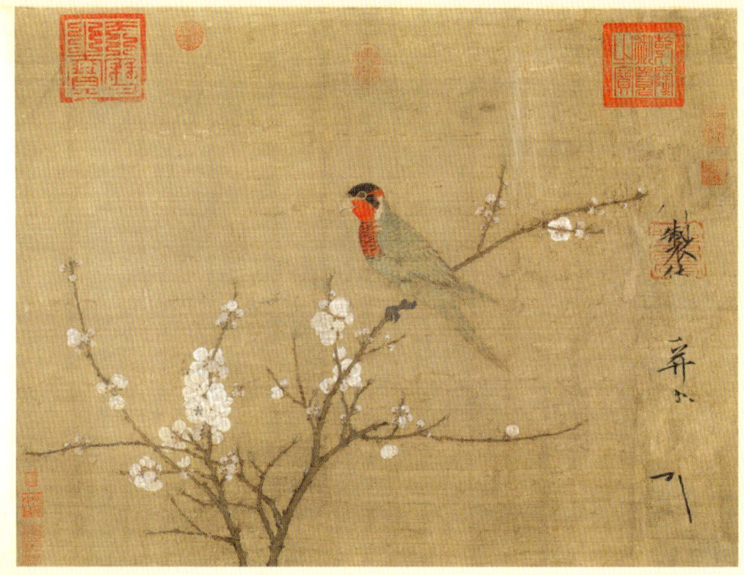

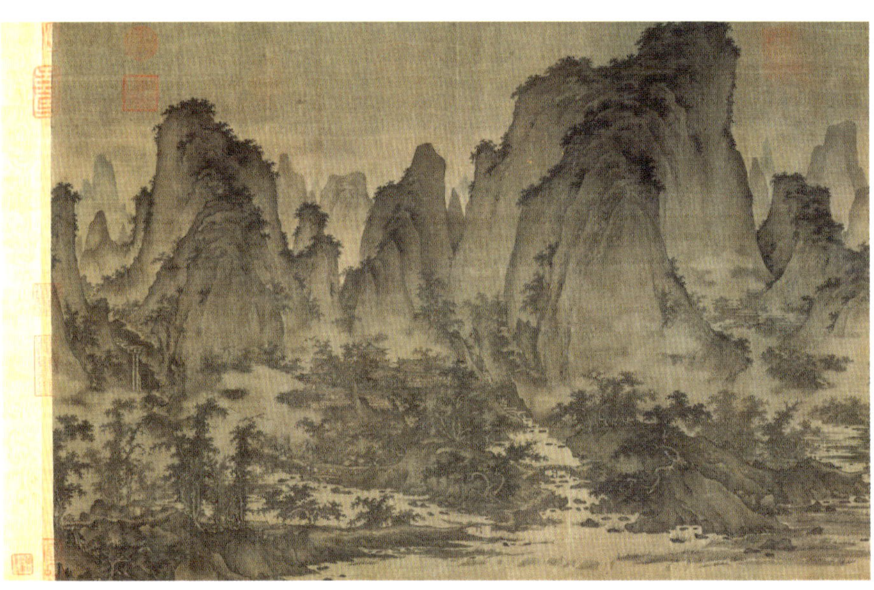

Qu Ding

Summer Mountains
Berge im Sommer
Zomer Bergen

●

Northern Song Dynasty
Nördliche Song-Dynastie
Noordelijke Song-dynastie
c. 1000 - 1100
44,1 x 116,8 cm / 17.36 x 45.98 in.
Metropolitan Museum of Art,
New York

Ink and colour on silk
Tinte und Farbe auf Seide
Inkten kleur opzijde

◂ Huizong

Parakeet on a Blossoming Apricot Tree
Sittich auf einem blühenden Aprikosenbaum
Parkiet in een bloeiende abrikozenboom

●

c. 1082-1135
53,3 x 125,1 cm / 20.98 x 49.25 in.
Museum of Fine Arts, Boston

Ink and colour on silk
Tinte und Farbe aud Seide
Inkt en kleur op zijde

Tortoise and Snake
Schildkröte und Schlange
Schildpad en slang

●

c. 1000 - 1100
Museum of East Asian Art, Bath

Ceramic / Keramik / Keramiek

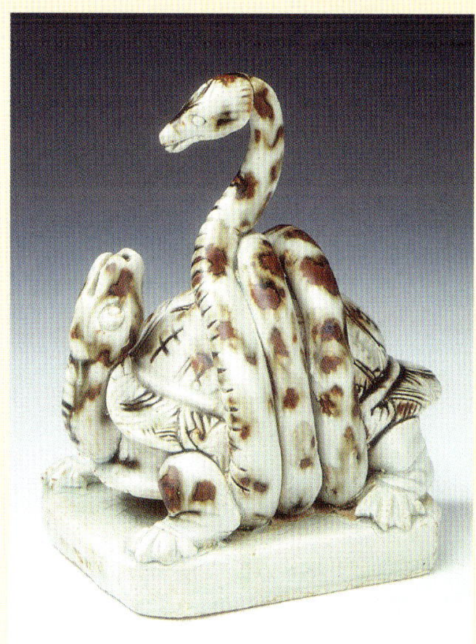

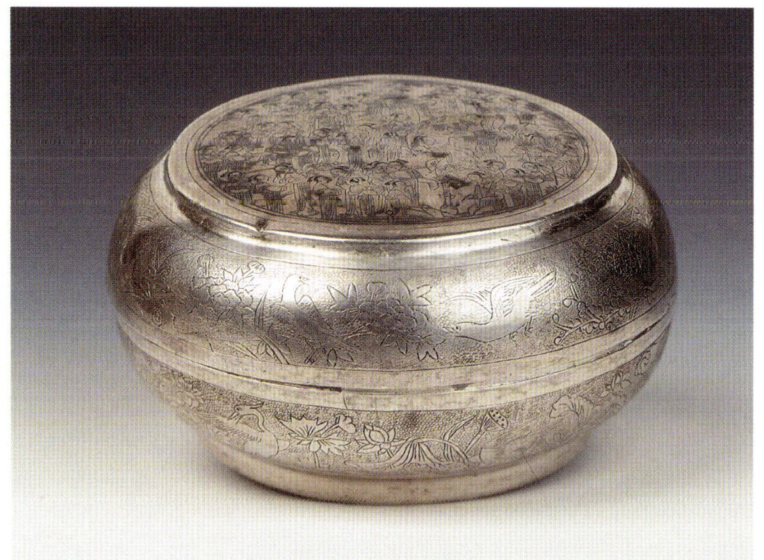

Box
Dose
Doosje

●

Southern Song-Yuan dynasty
Südliche Song-Yuan-Dynastie
Zuidelijke Song-dynastie
c. 1200 - 1300
Museum of East Asian Art, Bath

Chased silver
Ziseliertes Silber
Geciseleerd zilver

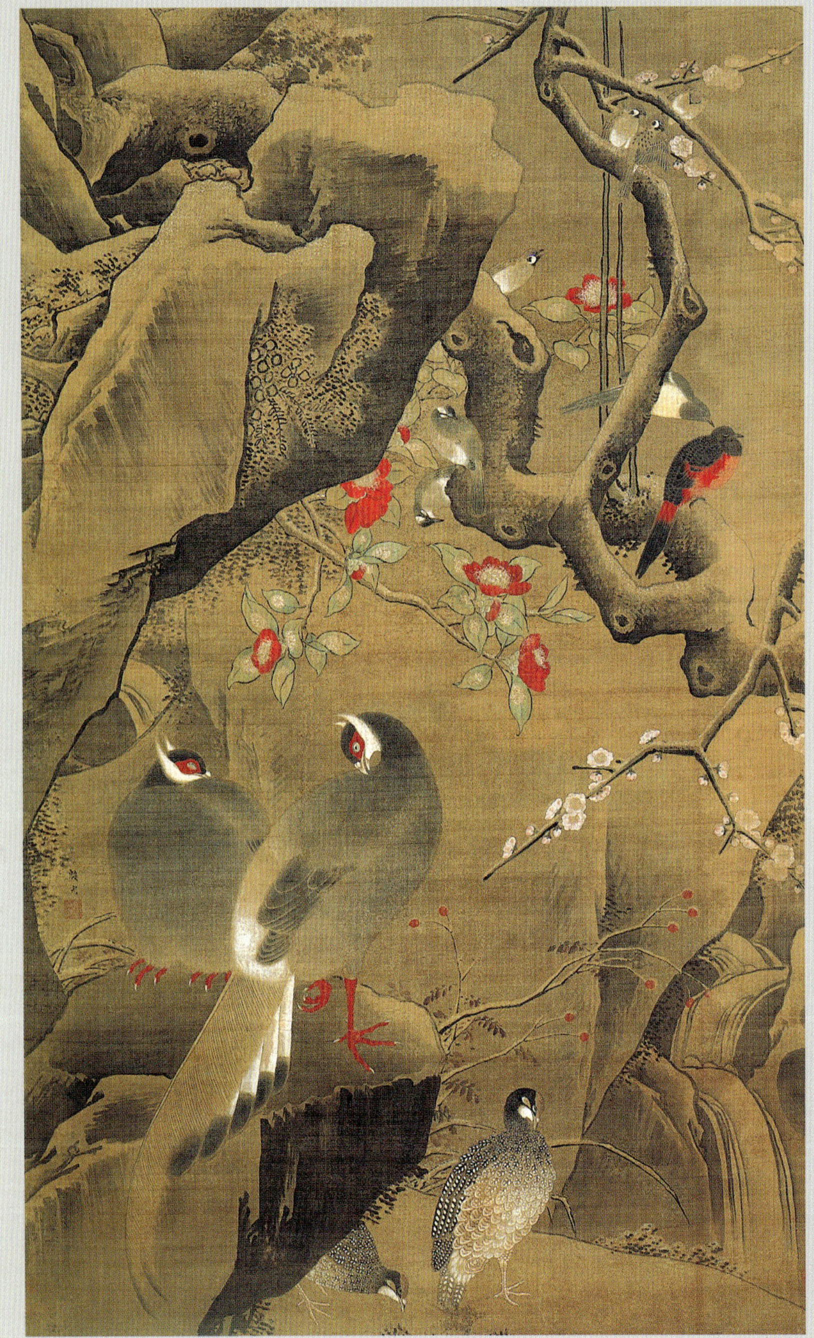

Yin Hong

Birds and Flowers of Early Spring
Vögel und Blumen zu Frühlingsbeginn
Vogels en bloemen in de vroege lente

●

Ming Dynasty / Ming-Dynastie / Ming-dynastie
c. 1500
168,7 x 102,7 cm / 66.41 x 40.43 in.
Kimbell Art Museum, Fort Worth

Ink on silk / Tinte auf Seide / Inkt op zijde

Ming ceramics are considered the epitome of excellence.

Die Erzeugnisse der Ming Dynasty gelten als absolute Spitzenleistungen der Keramik.

De voorwerpen van keramiek uit de Mingperiode worden als absolute meesterwerken beschouwd.

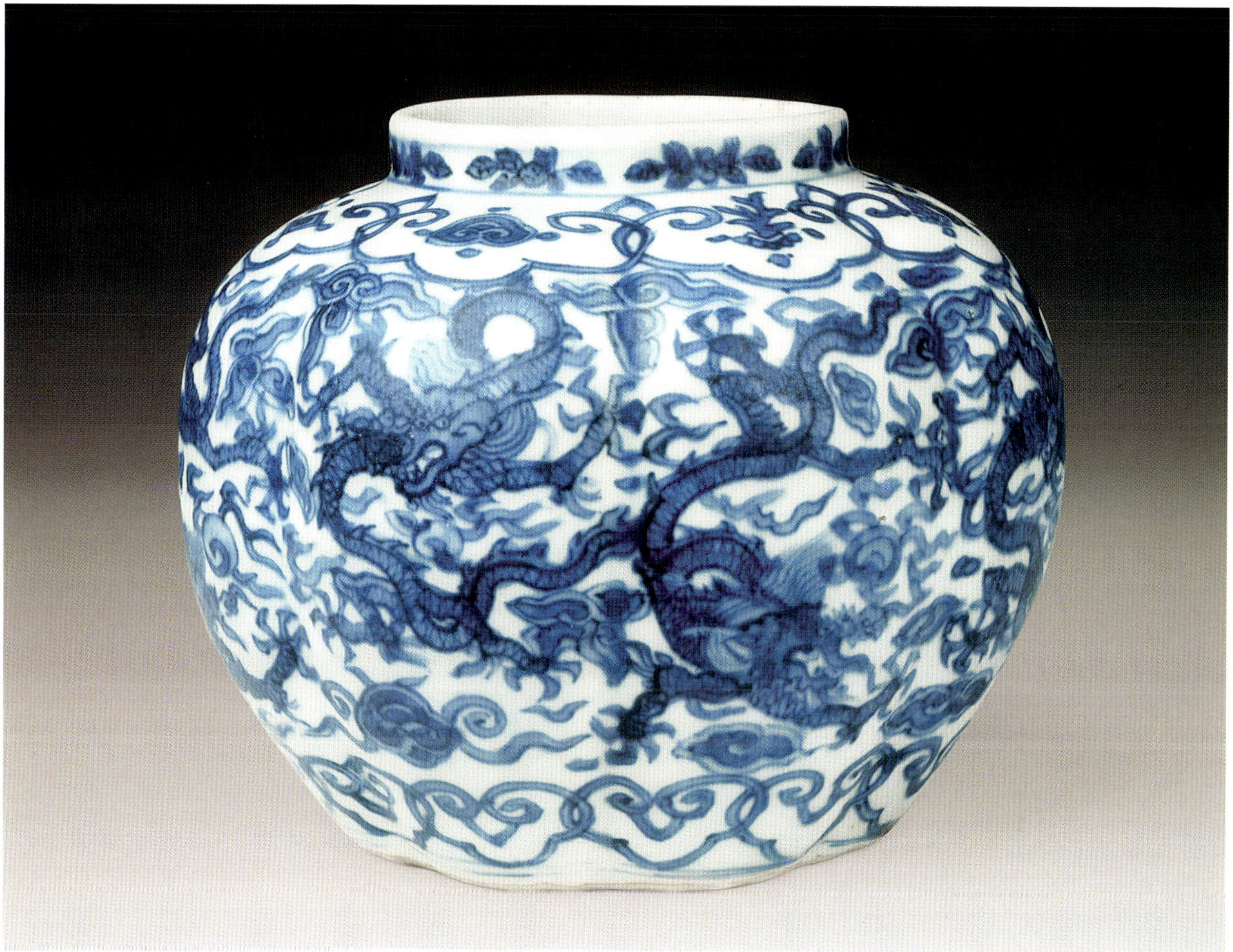

Lobed Vase with Dragons
Mehrlappige Vase mit Drachendekoration
Vaas veelpas, gedecoreerd met draken

Ming Dynasty / Ming-Dynastie / Ming-dynastie
c. 1572-1620
Museum of East Asian Art, Bath

Ceramic / Keramik / Keramiek

536

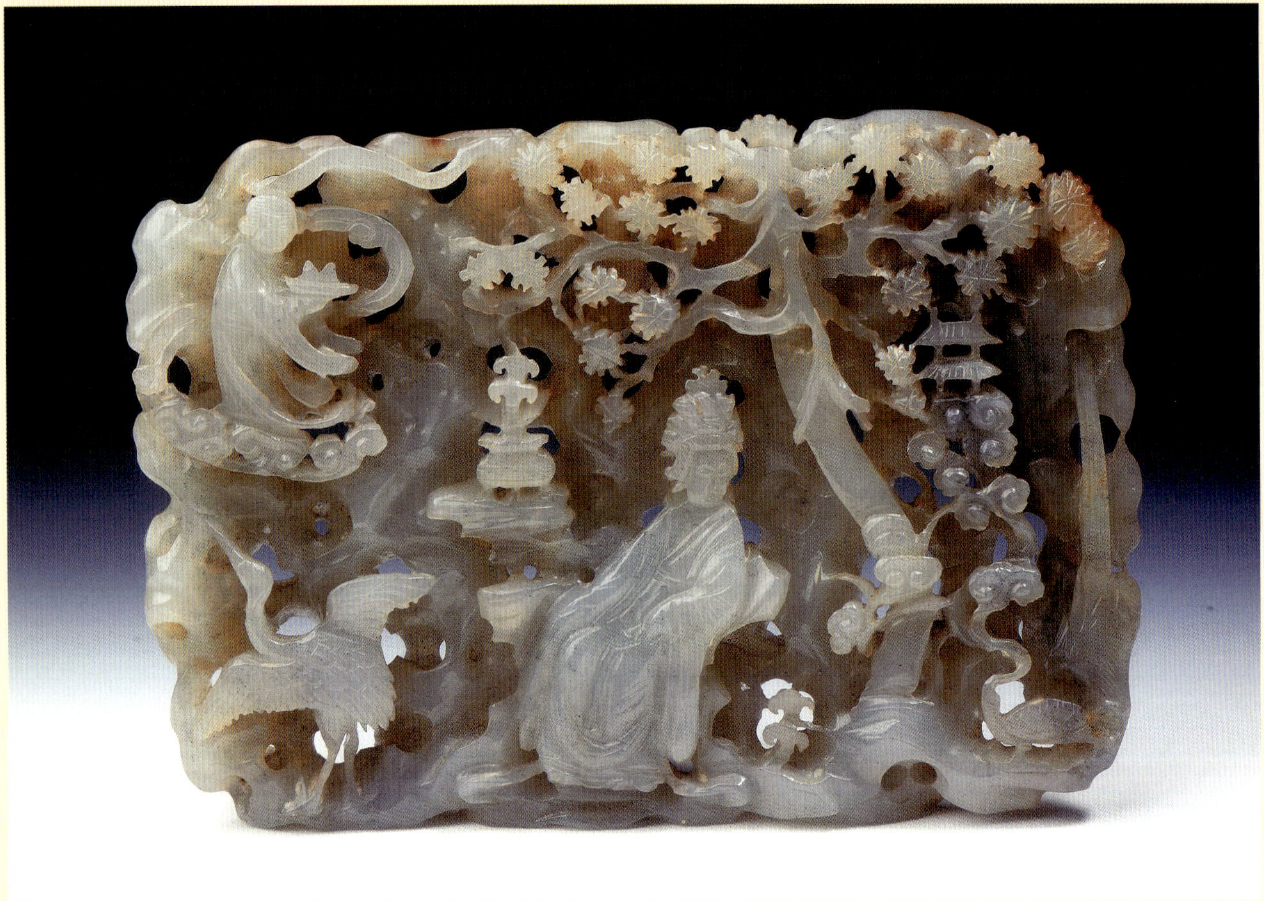

Daoist Paradise
Taoistisches Paradies
Taoïstisch Paradijs

●

Early Qing Dynasty
Erste Periode der Qing-Dynastie
Qing-dynastie eerste periode
c. 1600 - 1700
Museum of East Asian Art, Bath

Jade

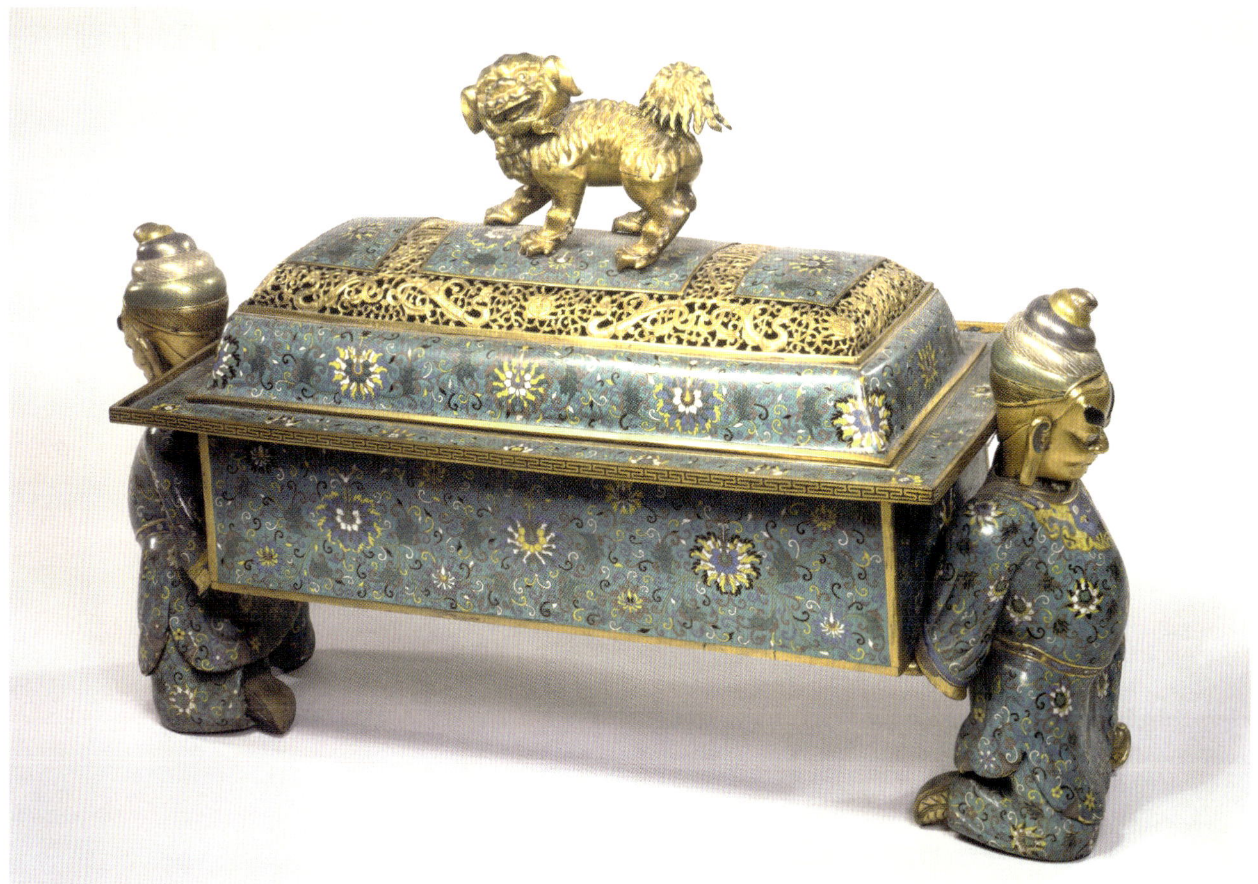

Ice Chest
Eisbehälter
Kist voor ijs

●

Qin Dynasty / Qing-Dynastie / Qing-dynastie
c. 1736-1795
Victoria & Albert Museum, London

Cloisonne enamel on copper with gilding
Cloisonné Emaille auf Kupfer mit Vergoldungen
Email cloisonné op koper met vergulding

The emperors of the last dynasty, the Qing, encourage all that is decorative.

Die Kaiser der letzten Dynastie, die Qing, fördern was immer dekorativ ist.

De keizers van de laatste dynastie, de Qing, vorderen alles wat gedecoreerd is.

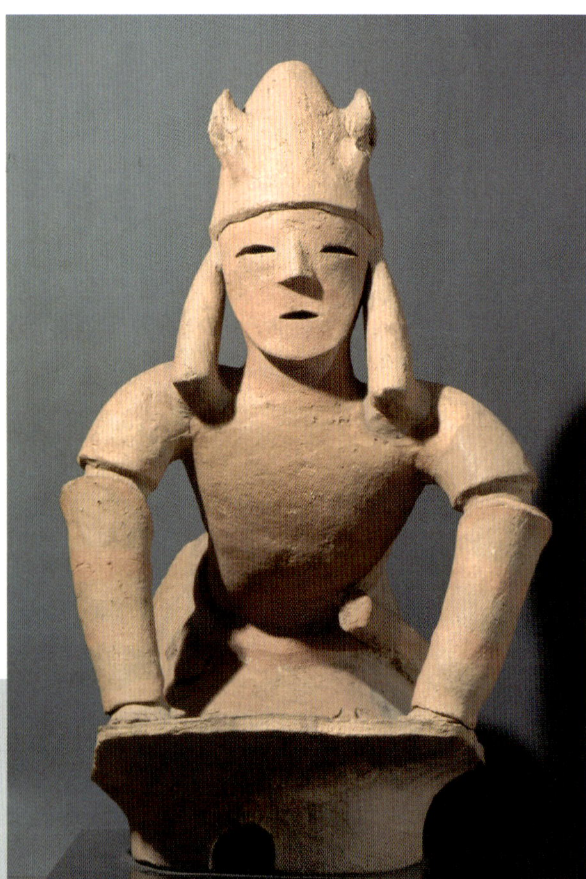

Haniwa, Figure of a Kneeling Man
Haniwa, Figur eines knienden Mannes
Haniwa, beeldje van een knielende man

●

Kofun period / Kofun-Zeit / Kofun-periode
c. 500-600
h. 55 cm
Ono Collection, Osaka

Terracotta / Terrakotta

Gigaku Mask
Maske für den Gigaku Tanz
Gigaku dansmasker

●●

Nara period / Nara-Zeit / Nara-periode
c. 700 - 800
h. 35,6 cm / 14.01 in.
Kimbell Art Museum, Fort Worth

Lacquer / Lackarbeit / Lak

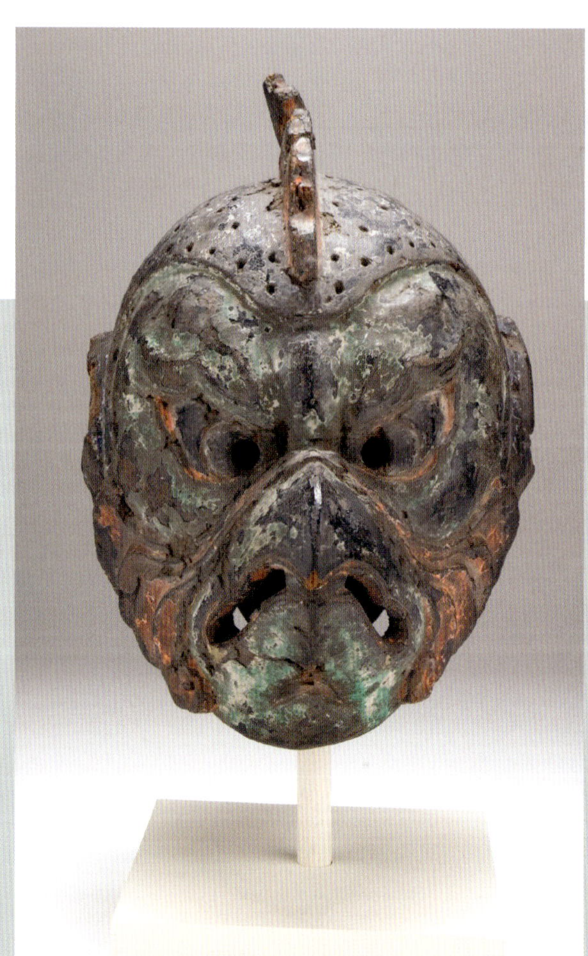

Zocho Ten, Protects the Region of the South
Zocho Ten, Schutzherr der südlichen Region
Zocho Ten, beschermer van de Zuidelijke Gewesten

●●

Heian period / Heian-Zeit / Heian-periode
c. 800-900
118 cm / 46.45 in.
Newark Museum, Newark

Wood / Holz / Hout

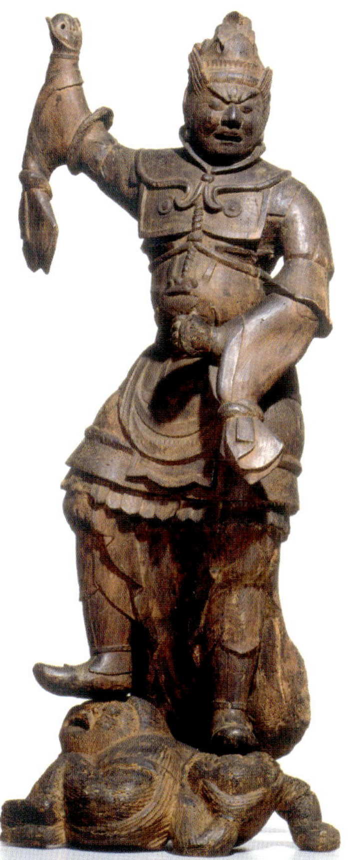

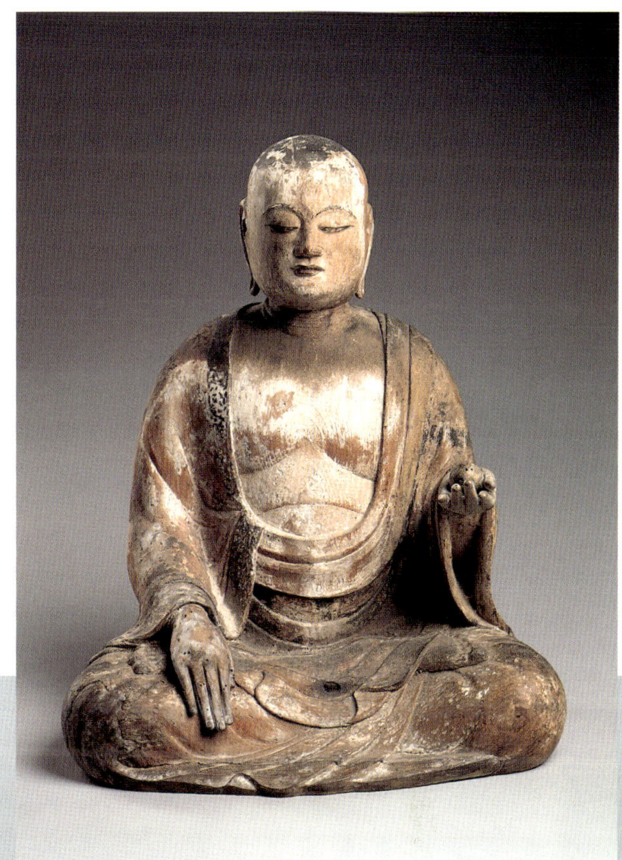

Hachiman in the guise of a Buddhist priest
Hachiman als Buddha-Priester
Hachiman als Boeddhistische monnik

●

Heian period / Heian-Zeit / Heian-periode
c. 1000 - 1100
h. 48,9 cm / 19.25 in.
Kimbell Art Museum, Forth Worth

Painted wood / Buntes Holz / Polychroom hout

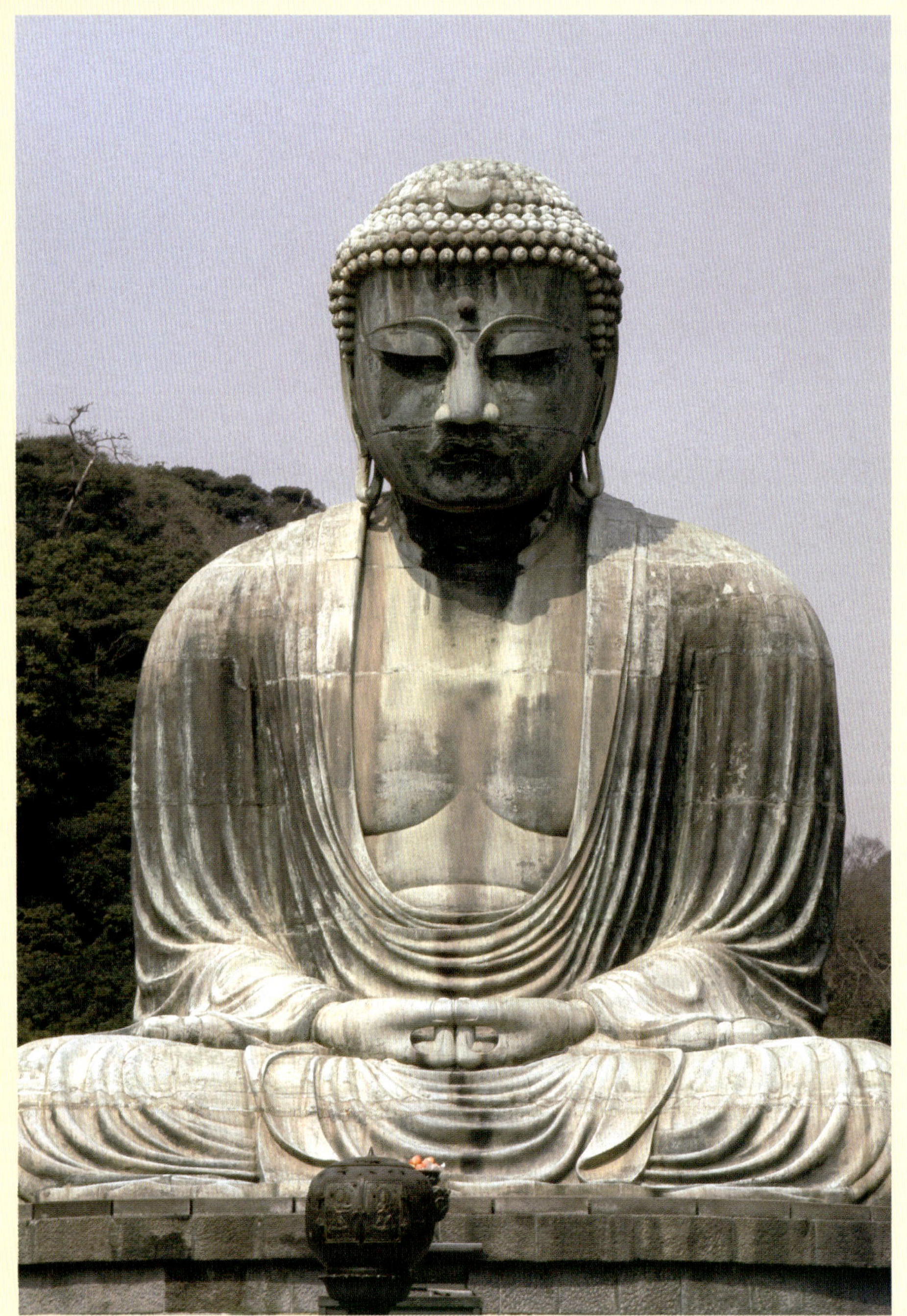

The Great Buddha
Der Große Buddha
De grote Boeddha

●●●

Kamakura period / Kamakura-Zeit
Kamakura-periode
1252
Kamakura

Bronze / Brons

The Great Buddha, the largest and most magnificent: 121 tonnes and 12 metres high, once fully gilded.

Souverän in Erhabenheit und Größe, 121 Tonnen schwer über 12 m hoch und früher vergoldet.

De Grote Boeddha, superieur in grootte en pracht: 121 ton zwaar en 12 meter hoog, was vroeger verguld.

Kaikei

Shaka Buddha
Shaka Boeddha

●

Kamakura period / Kamakura-Zeit
Kamakura-periode
c. 1210
Kimbell Art Museum, Fort Worth

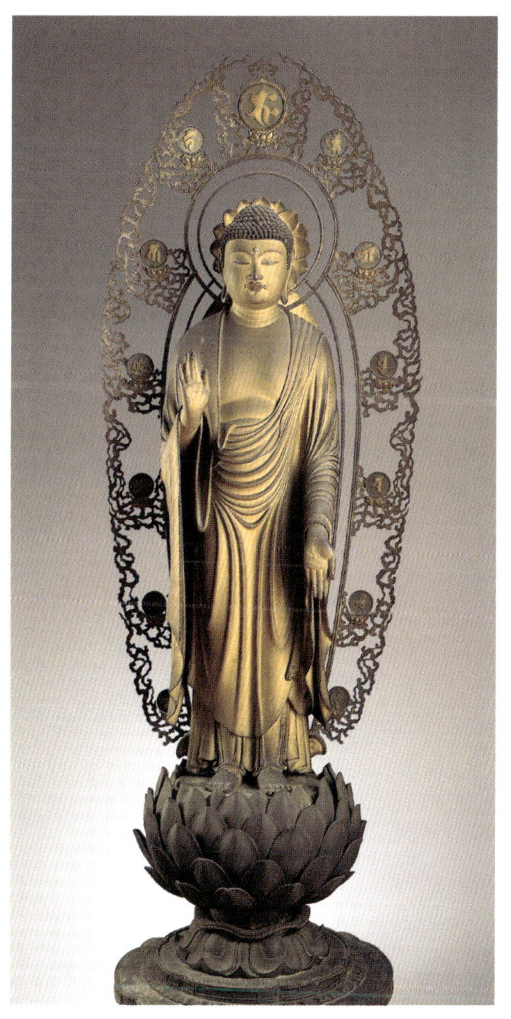

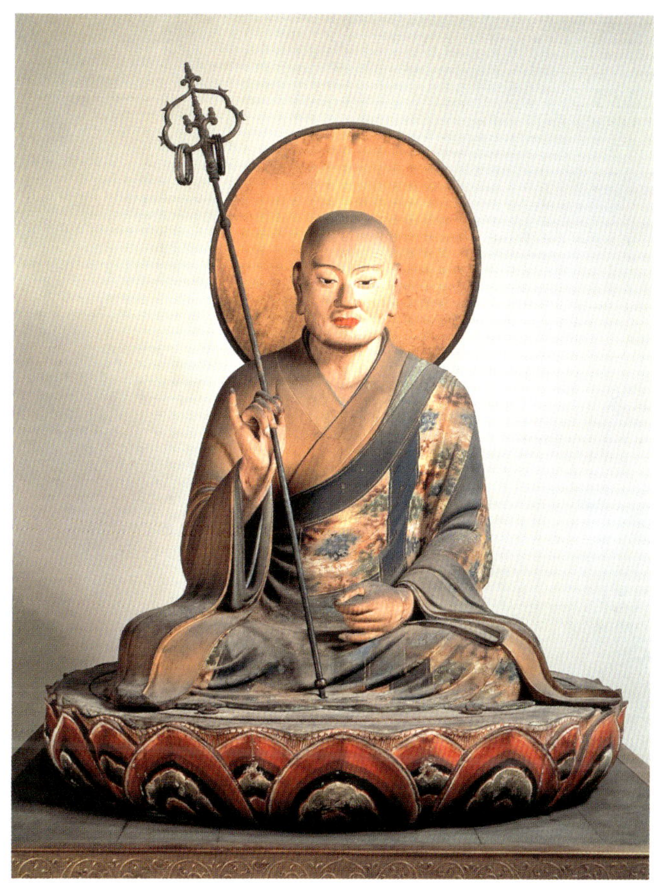

Hachiman (Shinto war god)
in the Guise of a Buddhist Monk
Hachiman, Shinto Kriegsgottheit
als Buddhistischer Mönch
Hachiman, Shinto oorlogsgod gekleed
als Boeddhistische monnik

●

Kamakura period / Kamakura-Zeit / Kamakura-periode
Todai Temple, Nara

Painted wood / Bemaltes Holz / Beschilderd hout

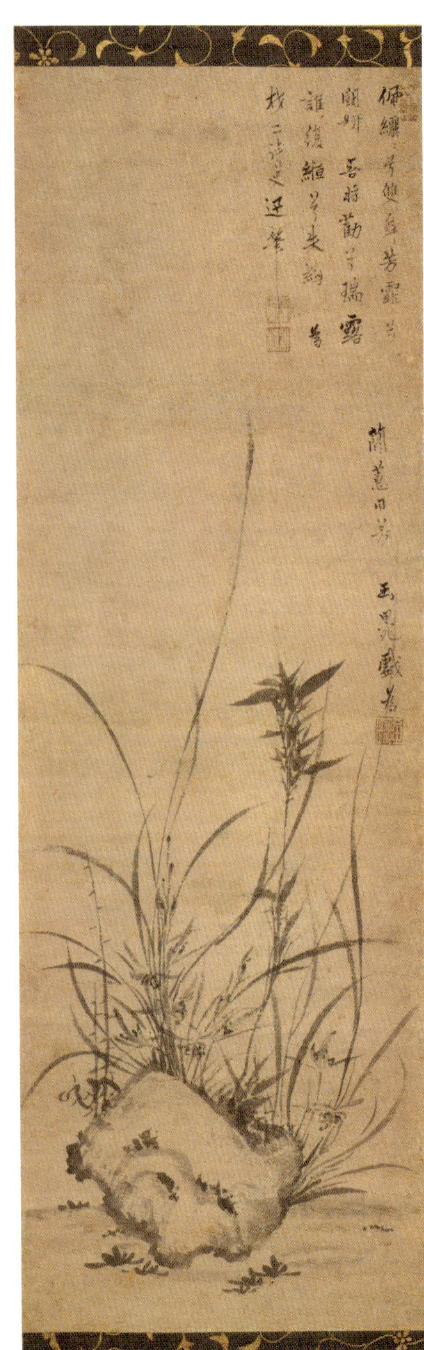

Gyokuen Bonpo

Orchids and Rock
Orchideen und Fels
Orchideeën en rots

●

Muromachi period
Muromachi-Zeit
Muromachi-periode
c. 1300 - 1500
Metropolitan Museum of Art, New York

Ink on paper
Tinte auf Papier
Inkt op papier

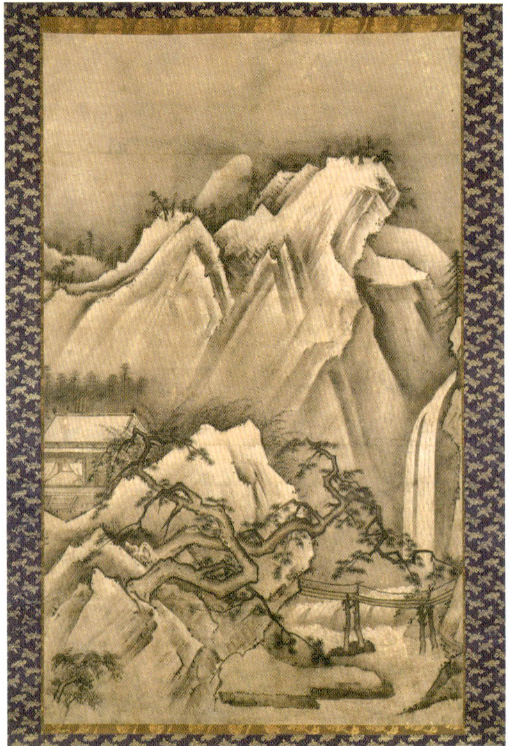

Pavilions in a Mountain Landscape
Pavillons in einer Berglandschaft
Paviljoenen in een berglandschap

●

Muromachi period / Muromachi-Zeit
Muromachi-periode
c. 1550
152,4 x 96,5 cm / 60 x 38 in.
Philadelphia Museum of Art, Philadelphia

Ink and colour on paper
Tinte und Farben auf Seide
Inkt en kleuren op papier

Kano school

Arrowroot Vines with six fan paintings of flowers and birds and six shikishi of calligraphy
Amaranth Kletterpflanze mit sechs Fächerbildern mit Blumen und Vögeln, sowie sechs Kalligraphie-Shikishis
Arrowroot ranken met zes waaierschilderingen met bloemen en vogels en zes shikishi kalligrafieën

●●

c. 1500 - 1600
154,2 x 353,4 cm / 60.70 x 99.76 in.
Metropolitan Museum of Art, New York

Ink and colour on paper
Tinte und Farben auf Seide
Inkt en kleuren op papier

When the Kano school is born, Chinese style painting (Kanga) is preferred and supported by the Shogunate.

Die Malerei im chinesischen Stil (Kanga) wird mit der Entstehung der Kano Schule zur vom Shogunat geförderten Kunst.

Met het ontstaan van de Kano school, wordt de schilderkunst in Chinese stijl (Kanga) de favoriete kunst van het Shogunaat

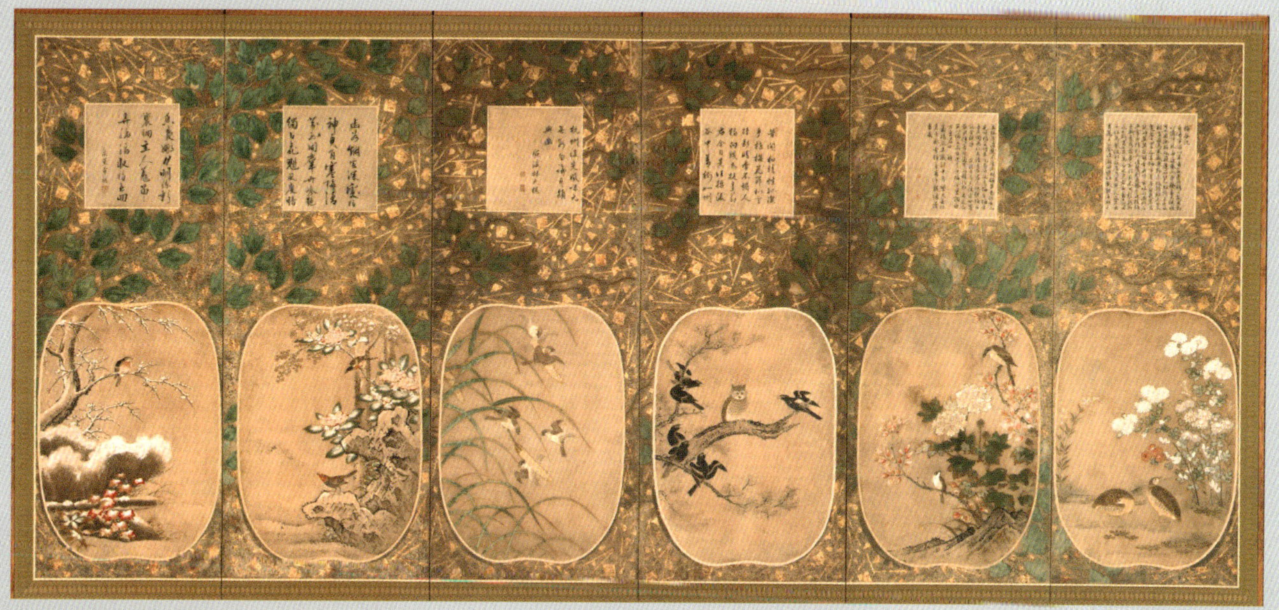

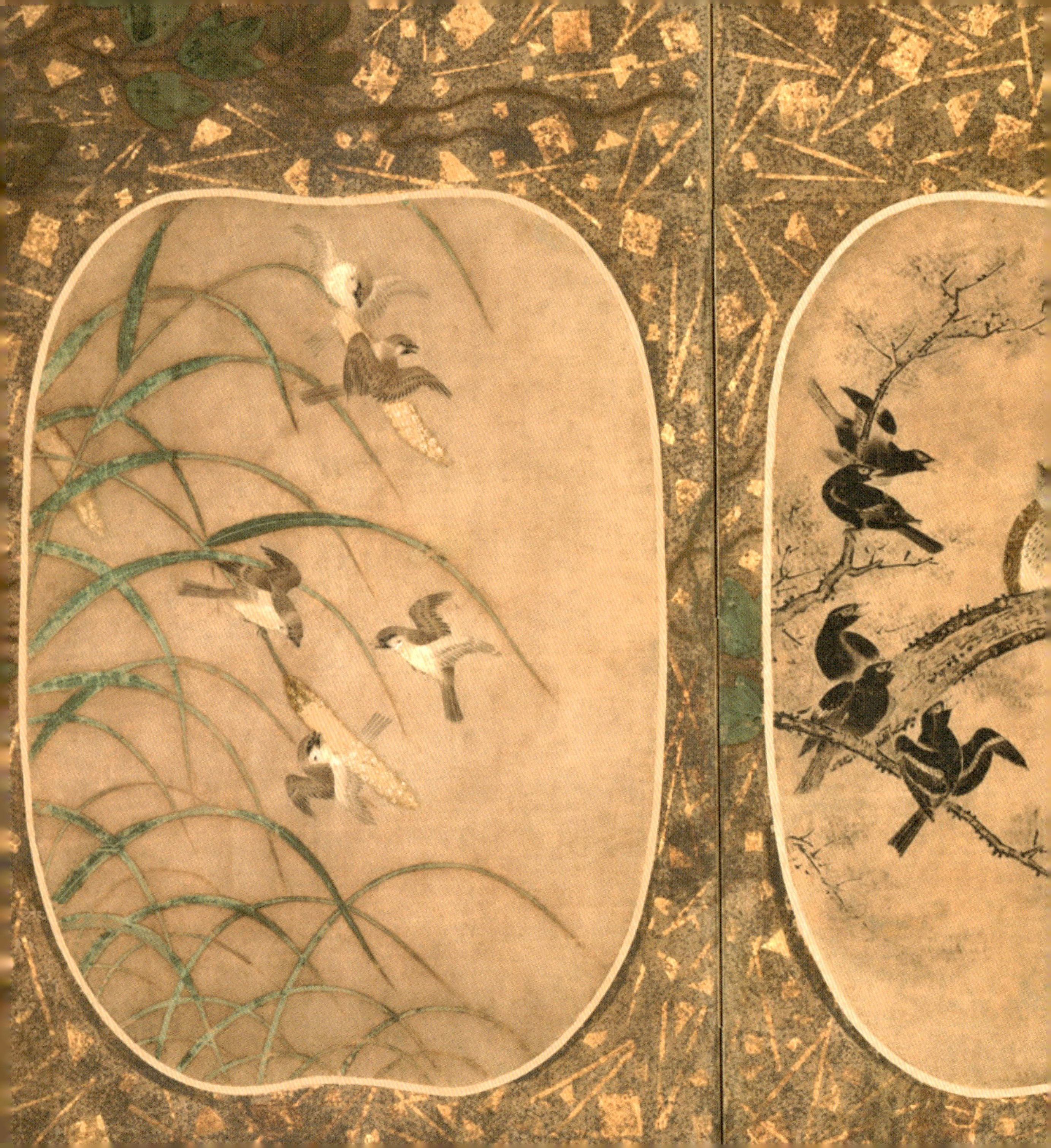

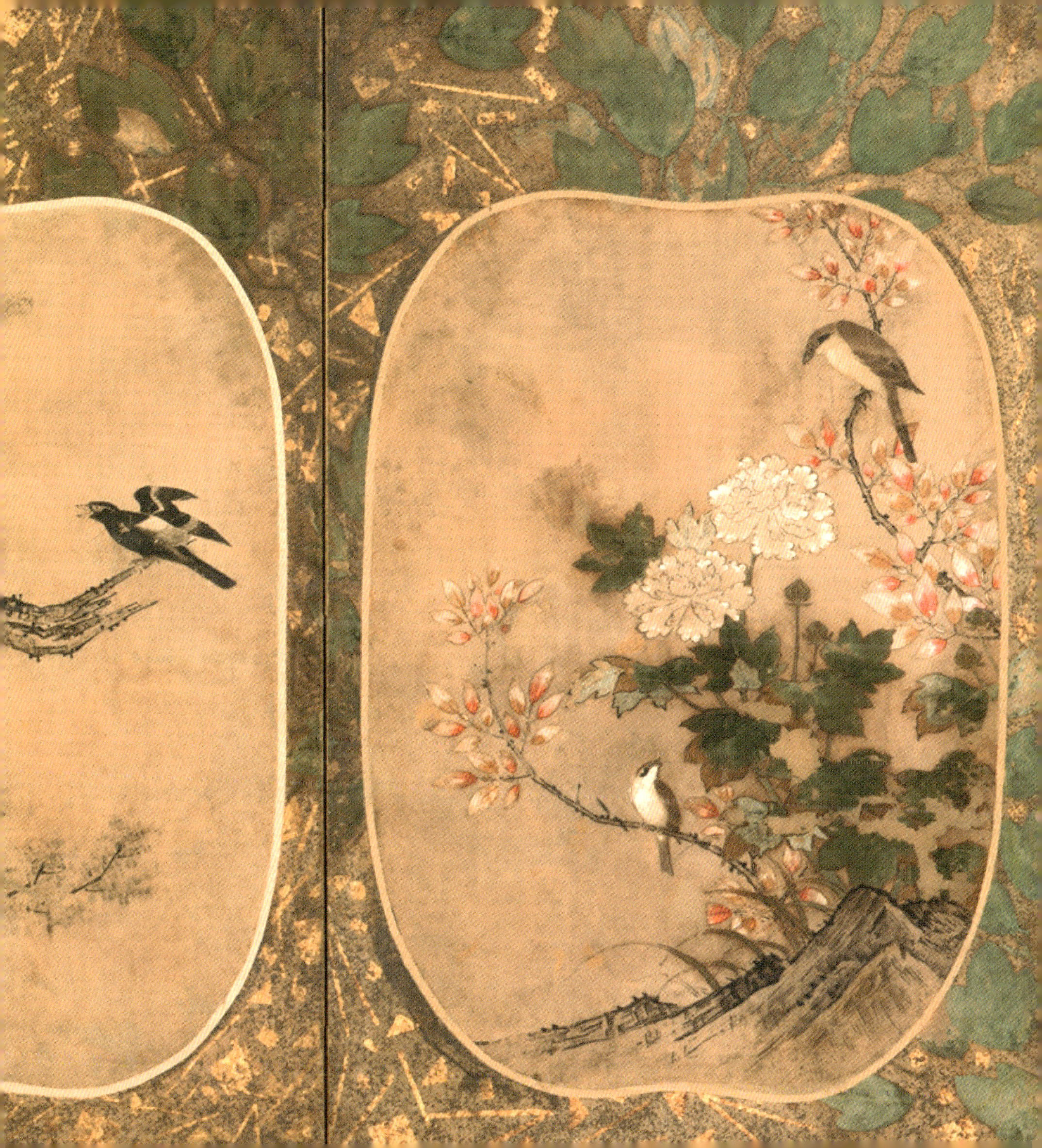

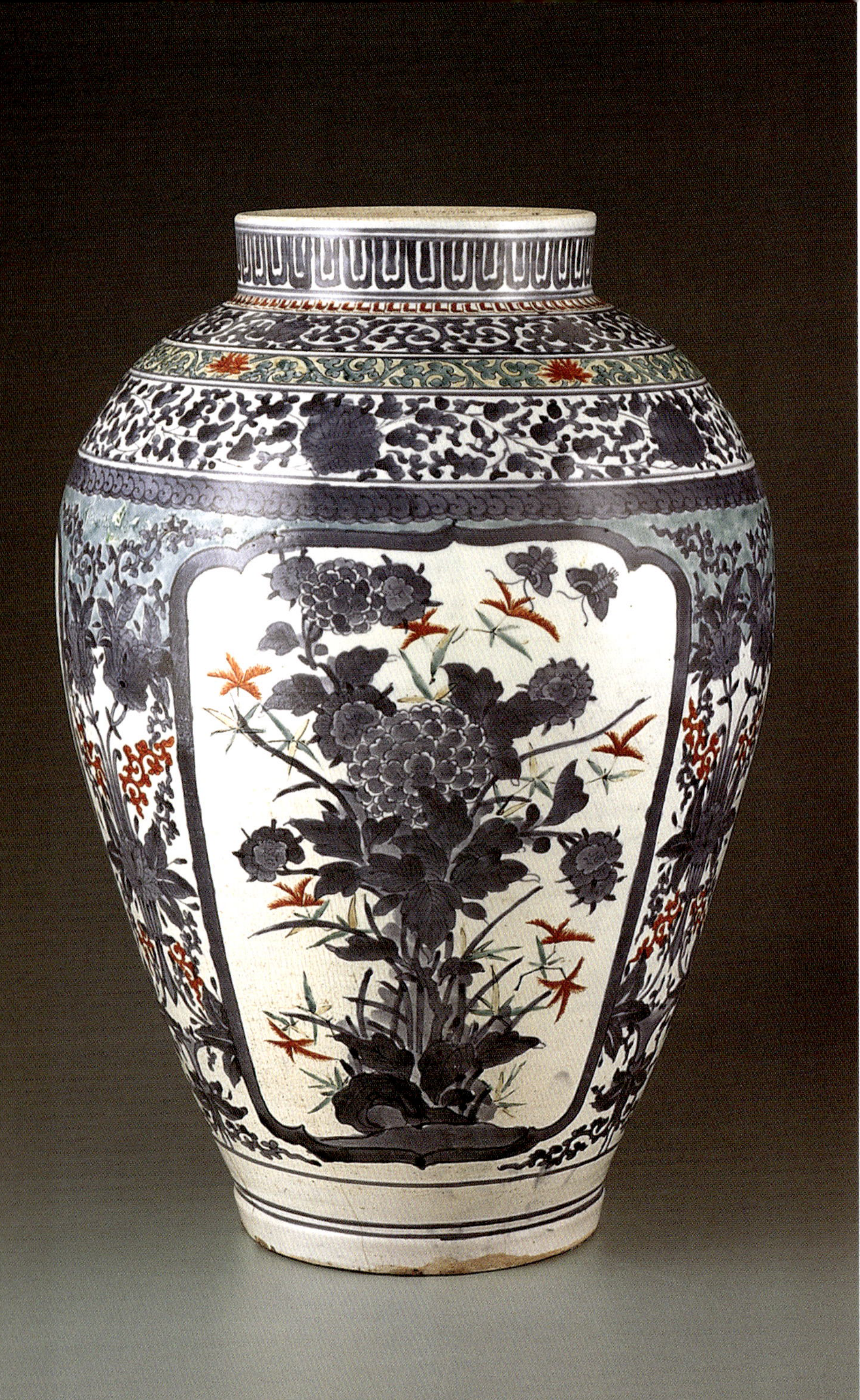

Jar with Floral Design
Gefäß mit Blumenmuster
Kruik met bloemmotief

●

Edo period / Edo-Zeit / Edo-periode
c. 1600 - 1700
h. 48,9 cm / 19.25 in.
Kimbell Art Museum, Forth Worth

Porcelain / Porzellan / Porselein

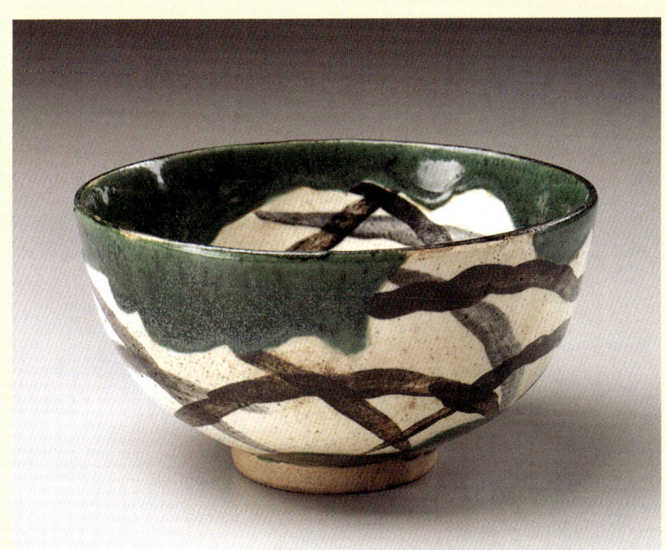

Kenzan Ogata

Bowl with Pampas Grass Design
Schale mit Pampasgras-Muster
Schaal met Pampasgras motief

●

Edo period / Edo-Zeit / Edo-periode
c. 1700 - 1750
8,5 x 10,2 cm / 3.34 x 4.01 in.
Kimbell Art Museum, Fort Worth

Ceramic / Keramik / Keramiek

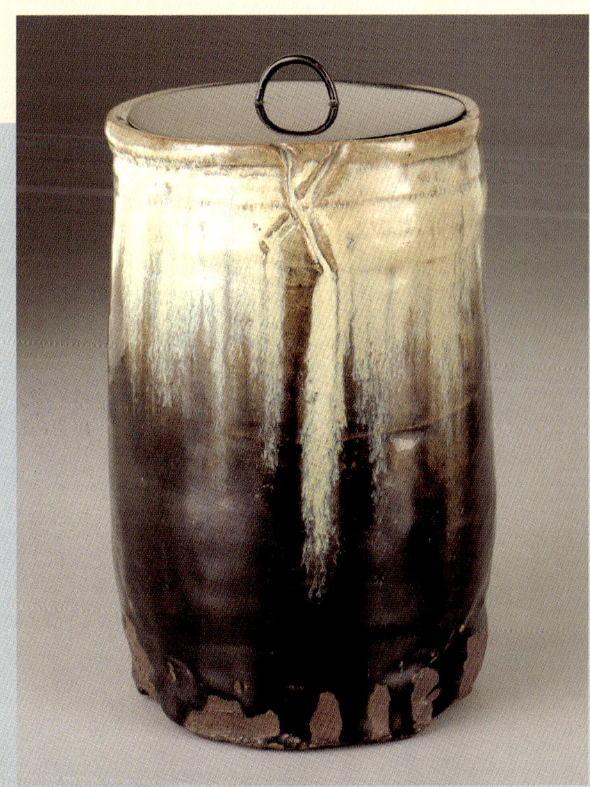

Water jar (mizusashi)
Mizusashi, Wassergefäß
Mizusashi, waterkan

●

Edo period / Edo-Zeit / Edo-periode
c. 1700 - 1800
h. 18,5 cm / 7.28 in.
Kimbell Art Museum, Forth Worth

Stoneware / Hartporzellan / Hard porselein

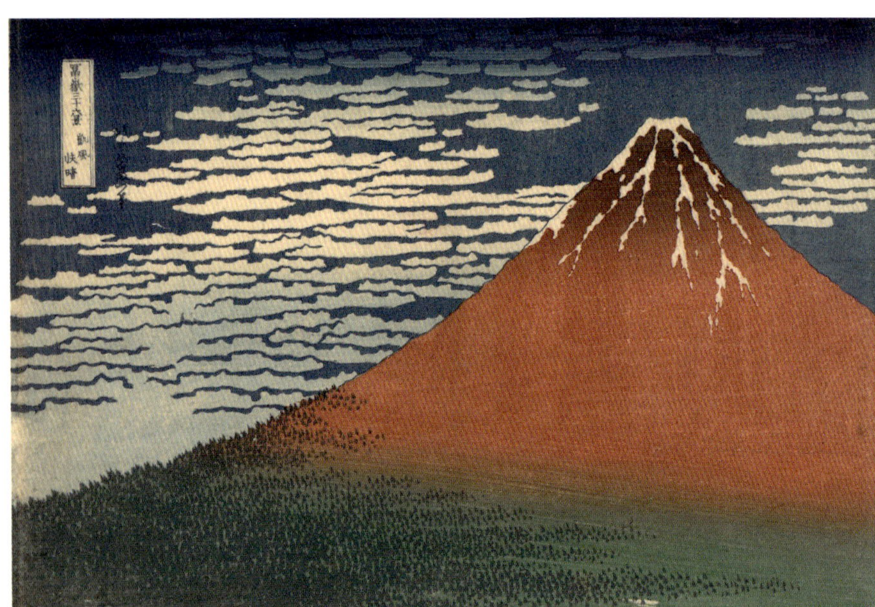

Katsushika Hokusai
(Edo 1760 - Tokyo 1849)

Red Fuji
Roter Fuji
Rode Fuji

●●●

c. 1826-1833
24,4 x 38,1 cm / 9.60 x 15 in.
Museum of Fine Arts, Boston

Colour wood-cut print on paper
Farbholzschnitt auf Papier
Kleurenhoutsnede op papier

Katsushika Hokusai
(Edo 1760 - Tokyo 1849)

Boatmen Crossing the Tamagawa River
Schiffer überqueren den Fluss Tamagawa
Schippers die de rivier Tamagawa oversteken

●●

c. 1826-1833
25,4 x 38,1 cm / 10 x 15 in.
The Newark Museum, Newark

Colour wood-cut print on paper
Farbholzschnitt auf Papier
Kleurenhoutsnede op papier

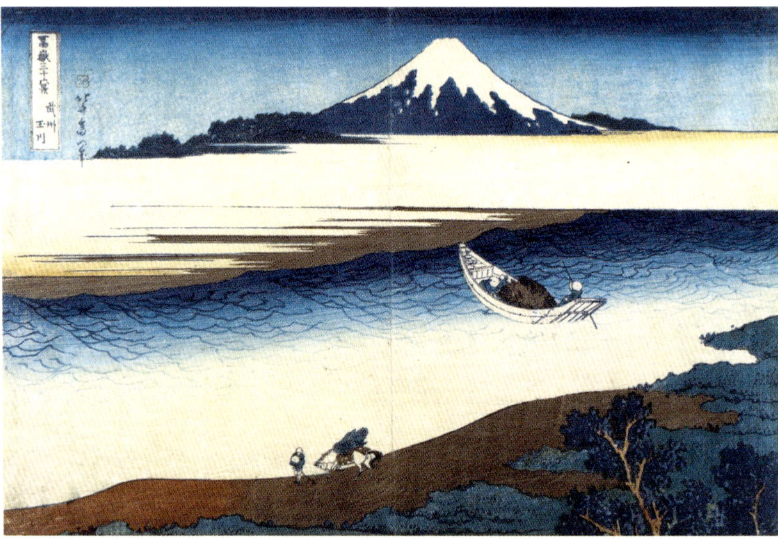

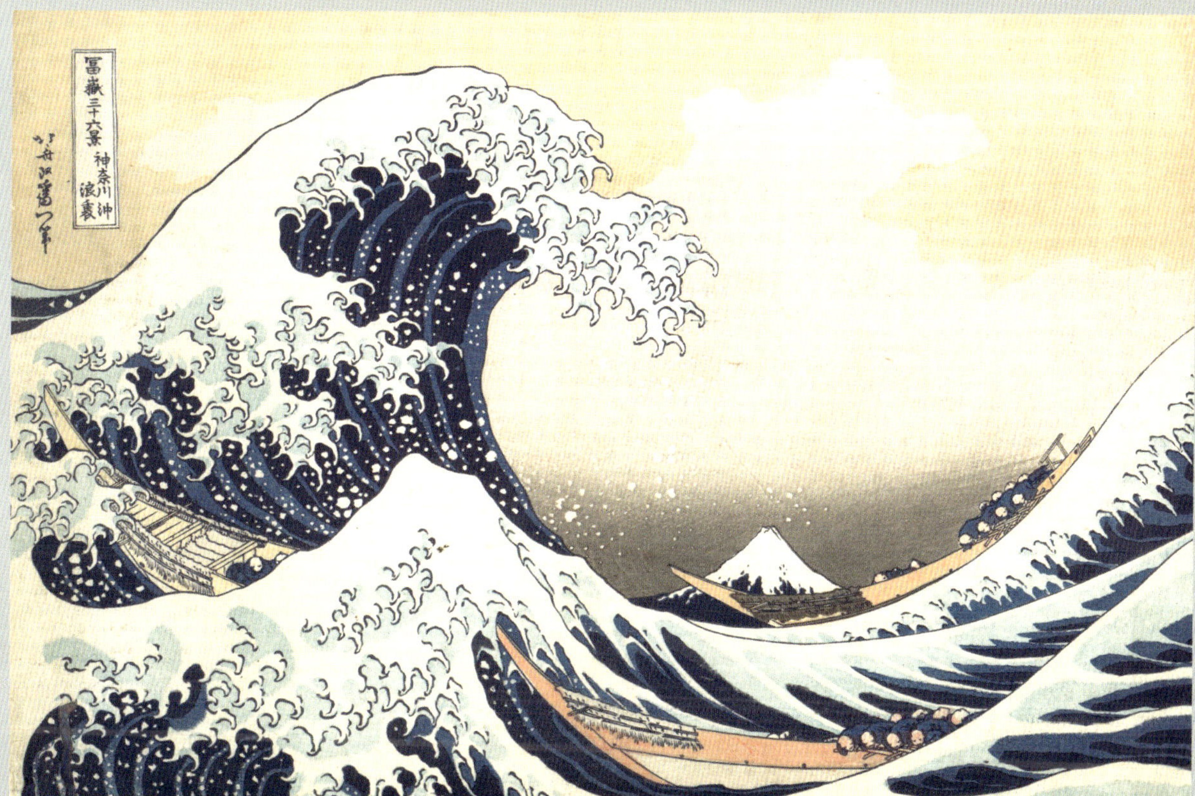

Katsushika Hokusai
(Edo 1760 - Tokyo 1849)

The Great Wave at Kanagawa
Die große Welle vor Kanagawa
De Grote Golf bij Kanagawa

●●●

c. 1830-1832
25,7 x 37,9 cm / 10.11 x 14.92 in.
Metropolitan Museum of Art, New York

Colour wood-cut print on paper
Farbholzschnitt auf Papier
Kleurenhoutsnede op papier

Katsushika Hokusai is the leading protagonist of the silkscreen colour woodblock printing process and the Ukiyo-e (floating world).

Katsushika Hokusai ist der wichtigste Vertreter der Ukiyo-e Technik(fließende vergängliche Welt).

Katsushika Hokusai is de belangrijkste vertegenwoordiger van de kleurenhoutsnede Ukiyo-e (vluchtige, vergankelijke wereld).

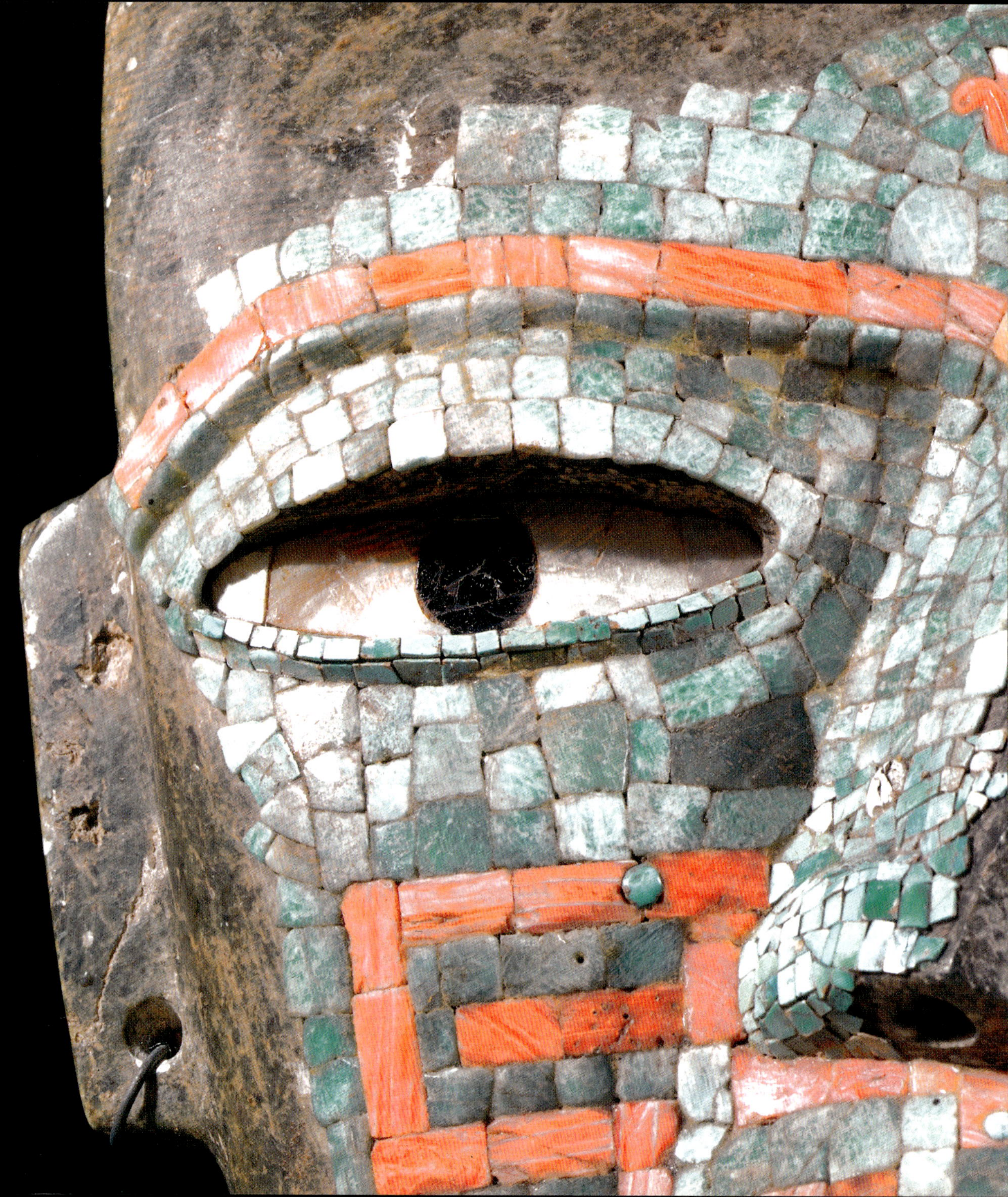

Ancient America
Altamerikanische Kunst • Precolumbiaanse kunst

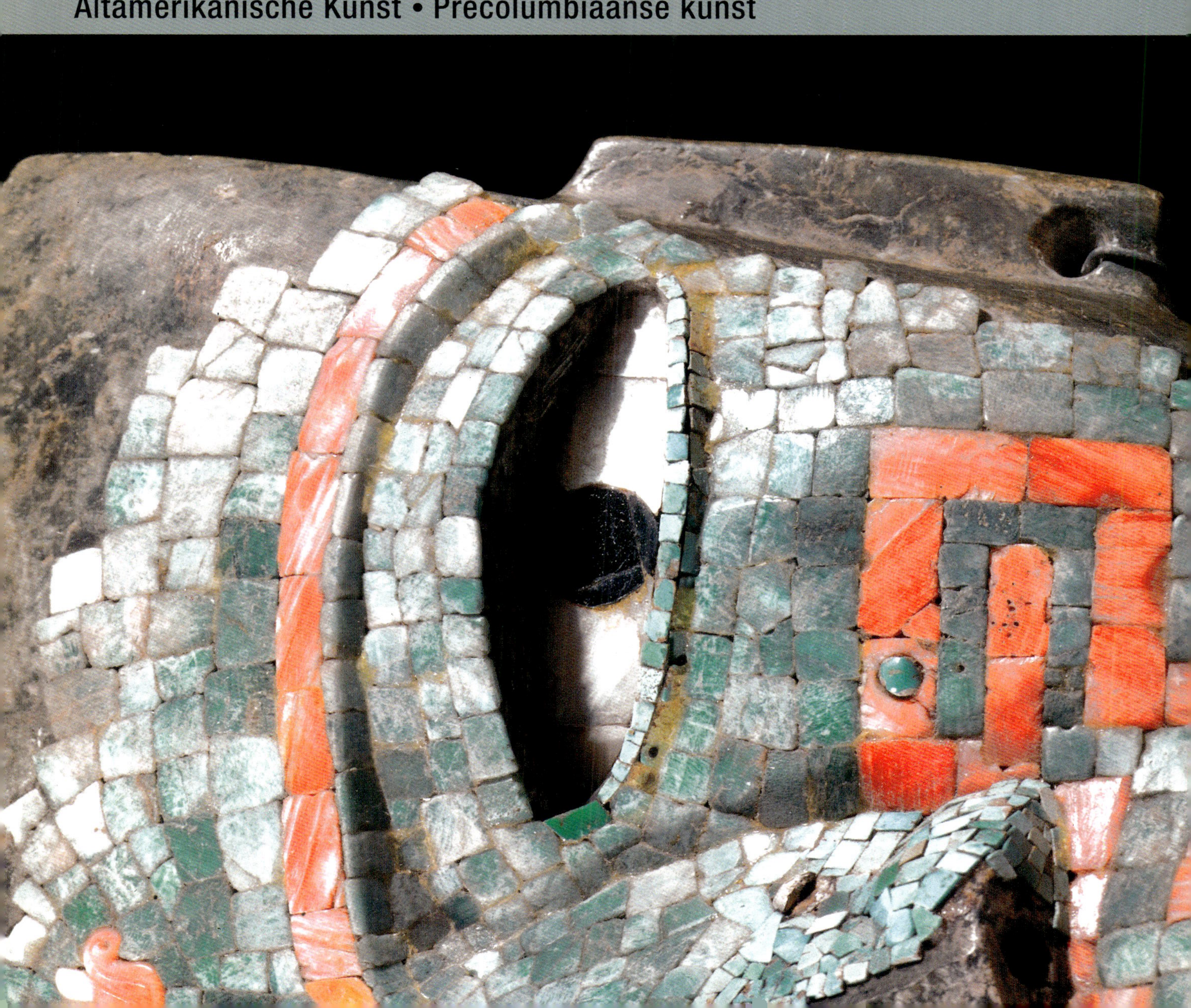

Hopewell culture, Ohio
Hopewell Kultur, Ohio
Hopewell kunst, Ohio

Effigy Platform Pipe with Bowl in the Form of a Toad
Flachpfeife mit einer krötenförmigen Tasse
Pijp effigie op platform met pijpkop in de vorm van een pad

●

1-400
Ohio Historical Society, Columbus, Ohio

Steatite / Steatit / Speksteen

Hopewell culture, Ohio
Hopewell Kultur, Ohio
Hopewell kunst, Ohio

Silhouette of a Hand
Silhouette einer Hand
Silhouet van een hand

●

1-400
Ohio Historical Society, Columbus, Ohio

Mica slab / Glimmerplatte / Micaplaat

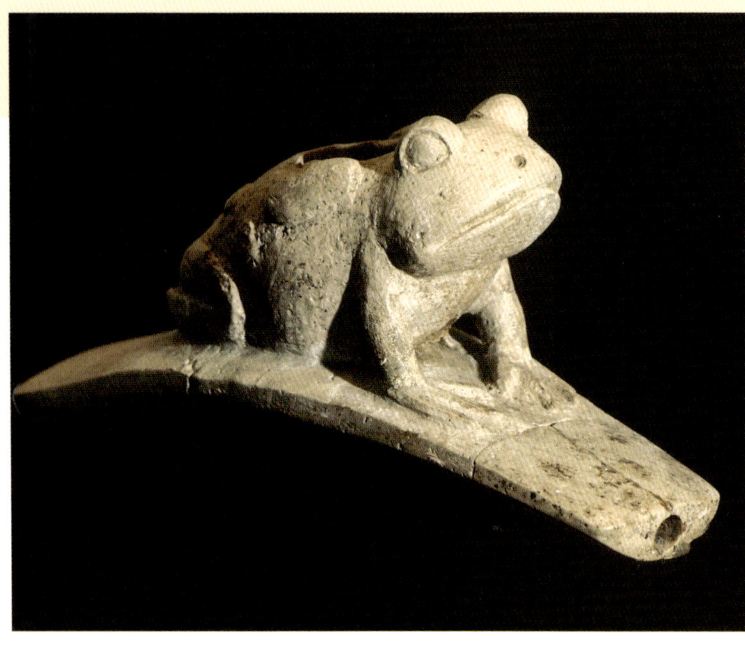

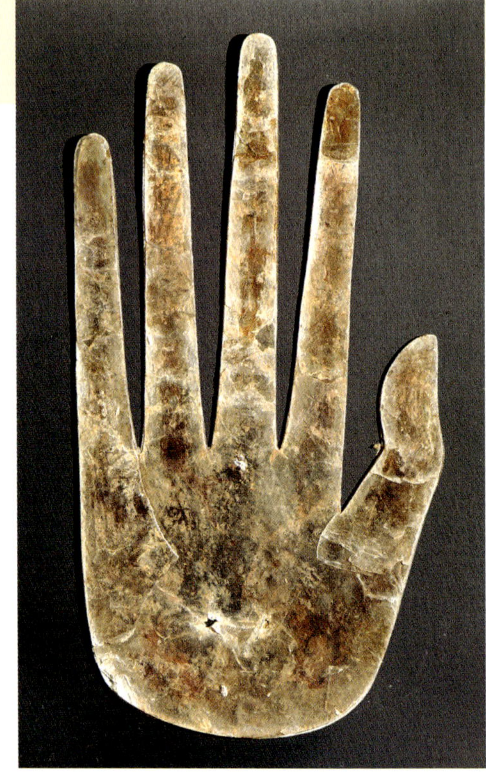

Mississippian culture, Tennessee
Kunst vom Mississippi, Tennessee
Mississippi kunst, Tennessee

Gorget with a Supernatural Warrior Holding a Mace in One Hand and a Skull in the Other
Ringkragen mit einem übernatürlichen Krieger, der eine Keule und ein Trophäen-Kopf festhält
Halsstuk met bovennatuurlijke krijger, die een knots en een trofeehoofd vastgrijpt

●

1250-1350
National Museum of the American Indian, Washington D.C.

Shell / Muschel / Schelp

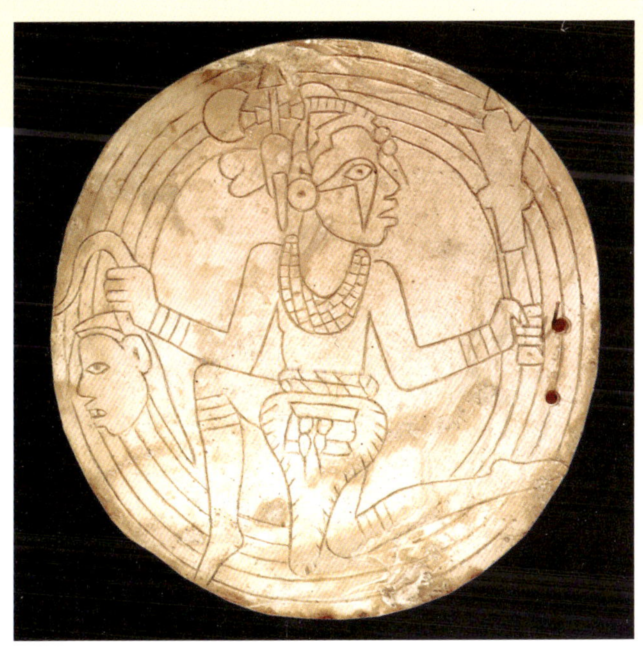

Mississippian culture, Arkansas
Kunst vom Mississippi, Arkansas
Mississippi kunst, Arkansas

Head Vase with Tattooed Face
Vasenbild mit tätowiertem menschlichen Gesicht
Vaas effigie met getatoeëerde mensengelaat

●

1300-1600
National Museum of the American Indian, Washington D.C.

Pottery / Keramik / Keramiek

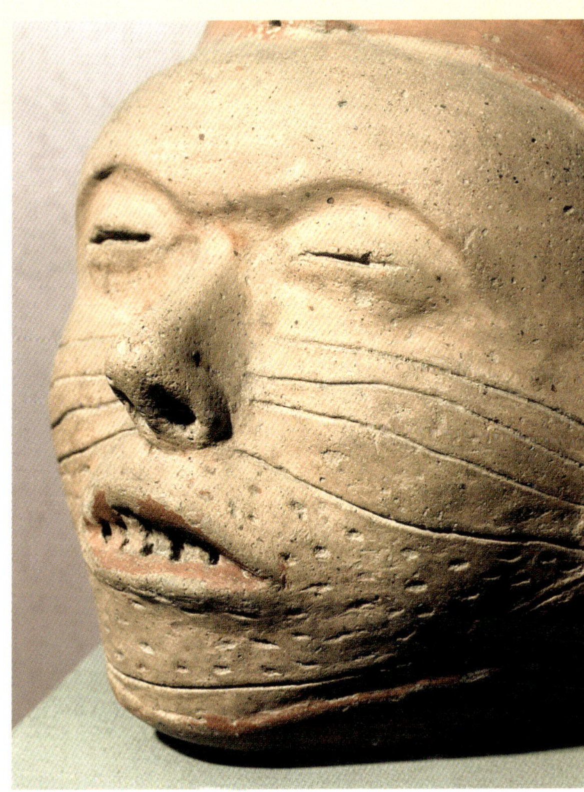

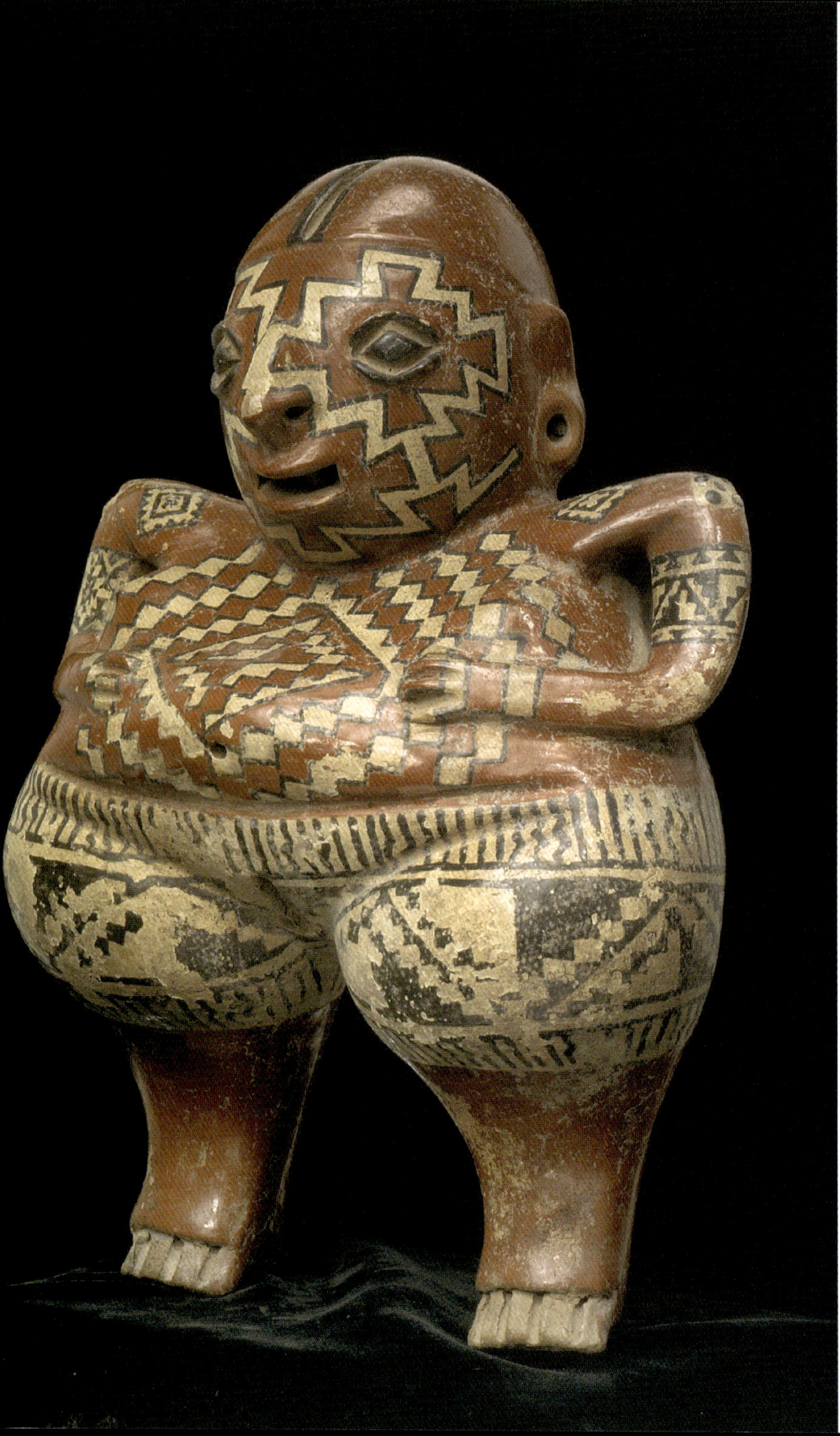

Chupícuaro culture
Chupícuaro Kunst

Female Statuette
Weibliche Figur
Vrouwenfiguur

600-200 BCE
Musée du quai Branly, Paris

Polychrome pottery (using clay slips)
Mehrfarbige Keramik mit Engobe
Polychroom keramiek met engobe

The Pre-Columbian cultures in Central America.

Die Zentren der altamerikanischen Hochkulturen liegen in Mittelamerika.

De Precolombiaanse culturen in Centraal-Amerika.

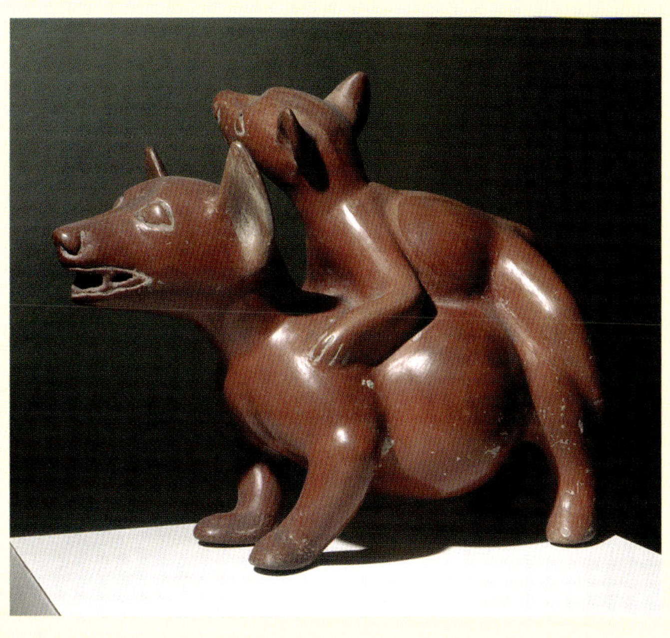

Shaft tomb culture, Colima style
Kultur der Brunnengräber, Comala-Stil
Schachttombecultuur, Comala stijl, Colima

Mating Dogs
Hundepaar
Hondenkoppel

●●

300 BCE-600 CE
Edward H. Merrin Gallery, New York

Pottery / Keramik / Keramiek

Guanajuato culture
Guanajuato Kunst
Guanajuato kunst

Vase in the form of a Pipe
Vase in Form einer Pfeife
Vaas in de vorm van een pijp

●

850-1150
Museo Nacional de Antropología e Historia,
Ciudad de México

Polychrome pottery
Bemalte Keramik
Polychroom keramiek

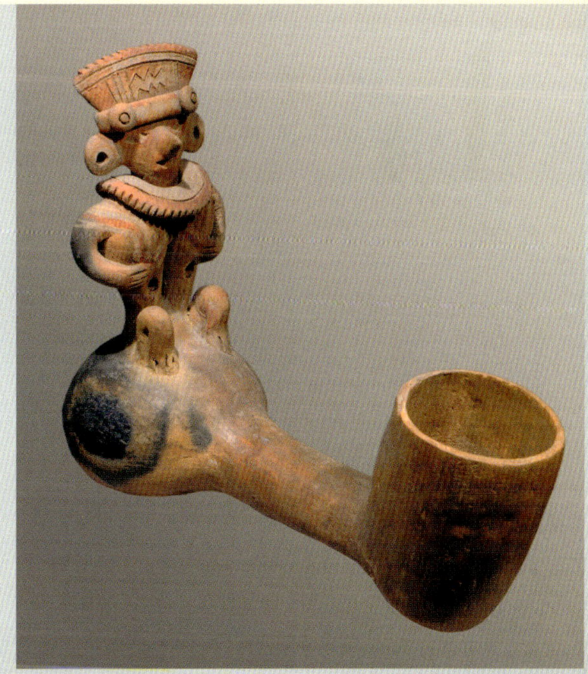

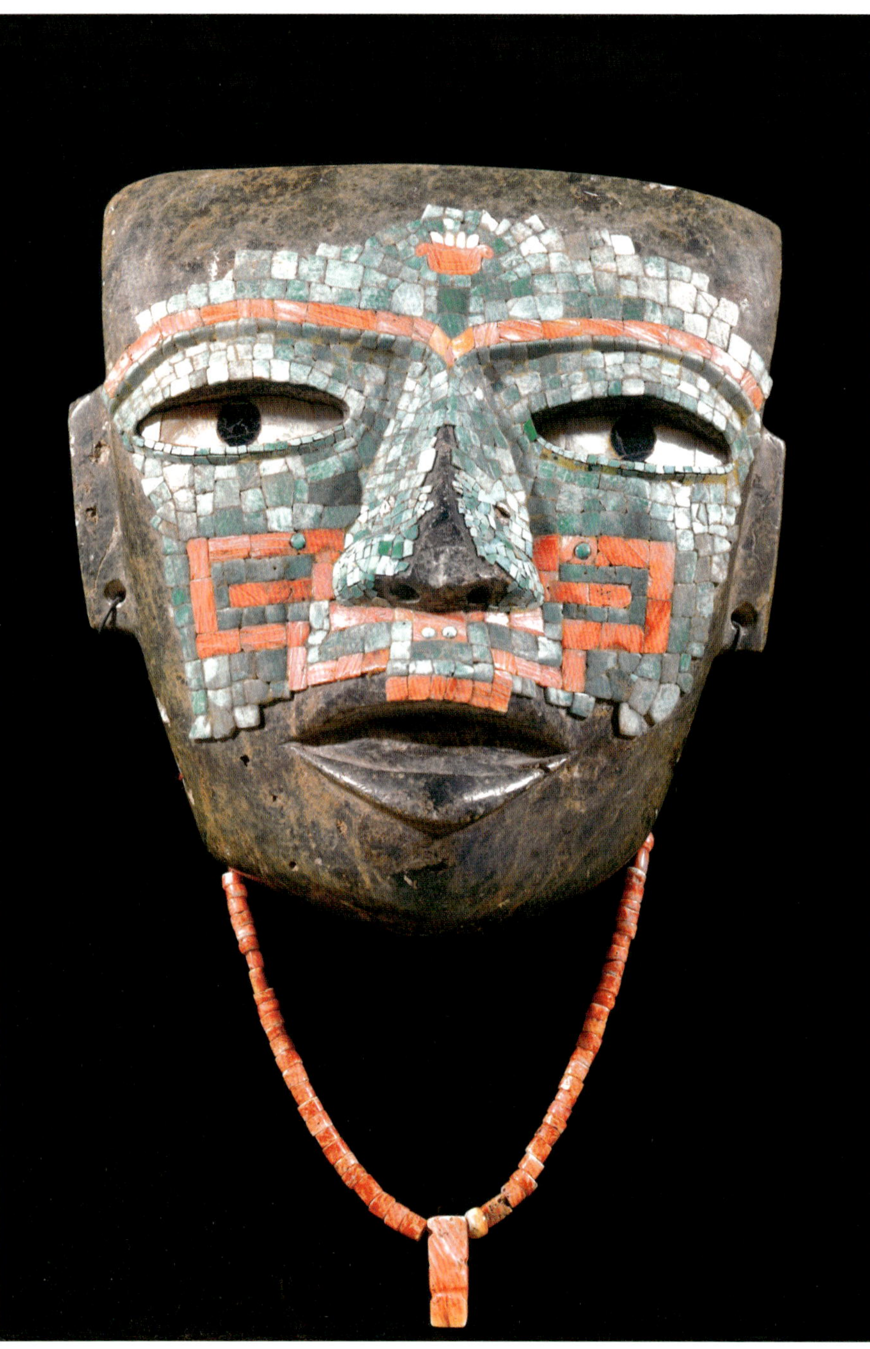

Teotihuacan culture
Teotihuacán Kunst
Teotihuacaanse kunst

Mask
Maske
Masker

●●

200-600
Museo Preistorico ed Etnografico
Pigorini, Roma

Stone with mosaic
of shell and turquoise
Stein und Mosaik
aus Muscheln und Türkisen
Steen en mozaïek
van schelp en turkoois

The wide flat faces of the masks and statues characterize the Teotihuacan style in Mexico.

Abgeflachte, in die Breite gezogene Gesichter der Masken und Statuen charakterisieren den Stil der Teotihuacan in Mexico.

De platte en verbrede gezichten van de maskers en beelden kenmerken de stijl van de Teotihuacan in Mexico.

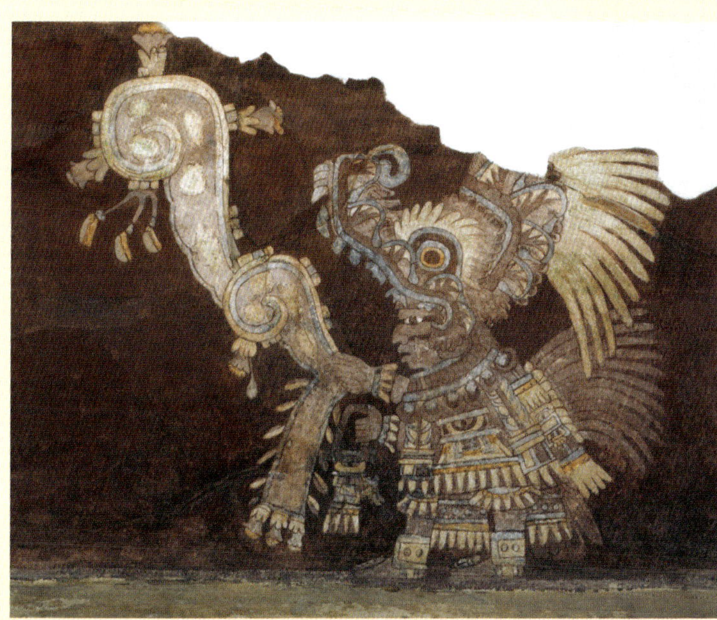

Teotihuacan culture
Teotihuacán Kunst
Teotihuacaanse kunst

Priest with Grain Sack
Priester mit Getreidesack
Priester met graanzak

●●

Fresco / Fresko

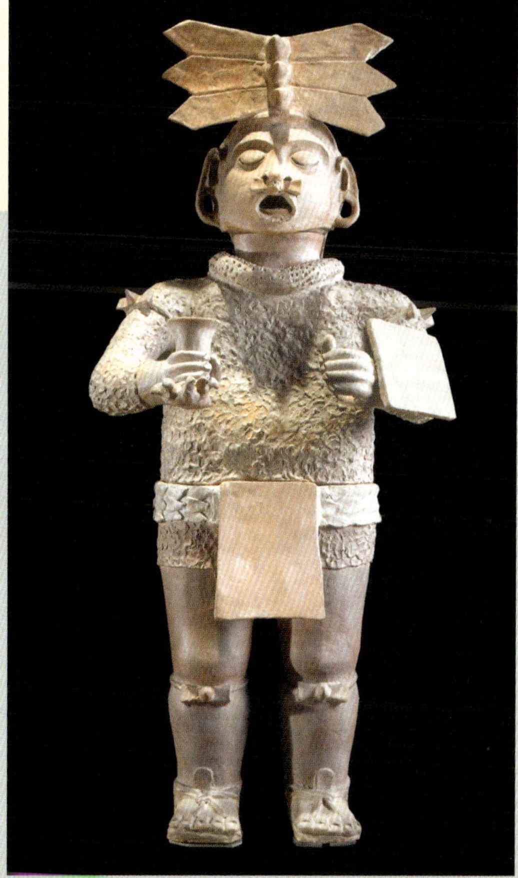

Teotihuacan culture
Teotihuacán Kunst
Teotihuacaanse kunst

Sculpture of Xipe Totec
Darstellung des Gottes Xipe Totec
Weergave van de god Xipe Totec

●●

650-900
Museo Nacional de Antropología e Historia, Ciudad de México

Ceramic / Keramik / Keramiek

558

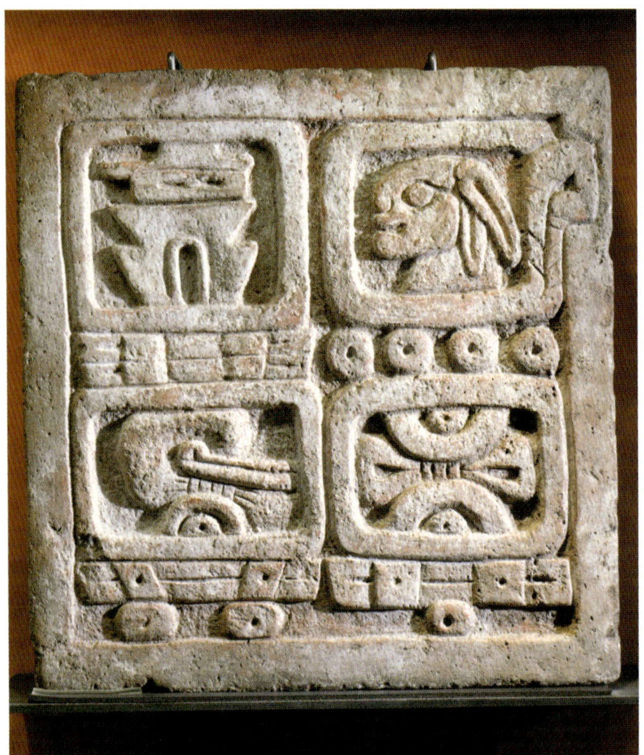

Xochicalco culture
Xochicalco-Kunst
Xochicalco kunst

Stone of the Four Glyphs
Gedenktafel mit vier Hieroglyphen
Steen met vier hiërogliefen

●

600/650-900
Museo Nacional de Antropología e Historia,
Ciudad de México

Stone / Stein / Steen

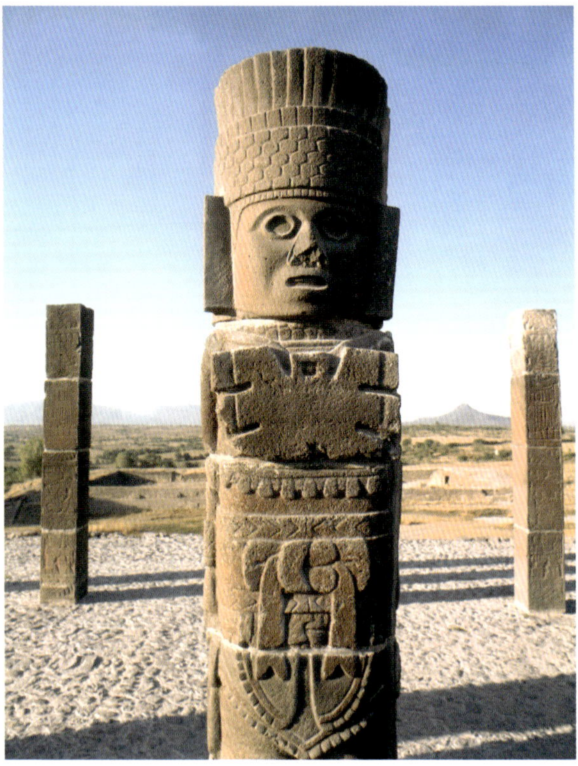

Toltec culture
Toltekische Kunst
Tolteekse kunst

The Atlantes
Blick auf die Atlanten
Aanzicht van de atlanten

●●

850-1150
Templo de Tlahuizcalpantecuhtli
Tula, México